Teacher's Wraparound Edition

GLENCOE

LITERATURE

The Reader's Choice

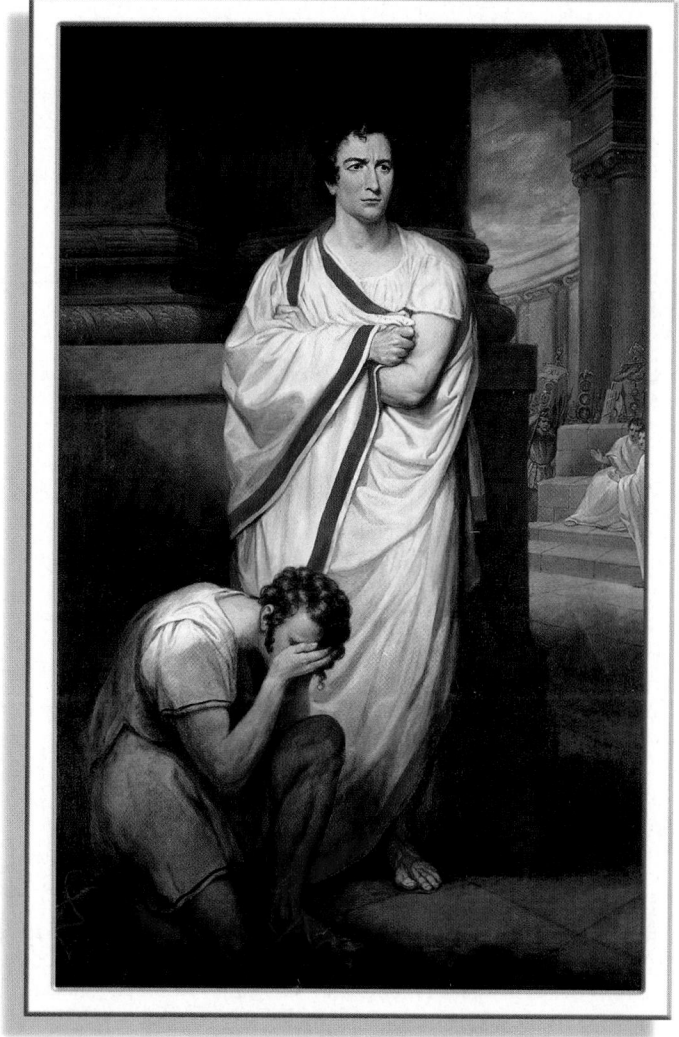

Program Consultants

Beverly Ann Chin

Denny Wolfe

Jeffrey Copeland

Mary Ann Dudzinski

William Ray

Jacqueline Jones Royster

Jeffrey Wilhelm

Course 5

 Glencoe McGraw-Hill

New York, New York   Columbus, Ohio   Woodland Hills, California   Peoria, Illinois

Acknowledgments

Grateful acknowledgment is given authors, publishers, photographers, museums, and agents for permission to reprint the following copyrighted material. Every effort has been made to determine copyright owners. In case of any omissions, the Publisher will be pleased to make suitable acknowledgments in future editions.

Acknowledgments continued on page R142.

The Standardized Test Practice pages in this book were written by The Princeton Review, the nation's leader in test preparation. Through its association with McGraw-Hill, The Princeton Review offers the best way to help students excel on standardized assessments.

The Princeton Review is not affiliated with Princeton University or Educational Testing Service.

Glencoe/McGraw-Hill

A Division of The McGraw-Hill Companies

Printed in the United States of America

Send all inquiries to:
Glencoe/McGraw-Hill
936 Eastwind Drive
Westerville, OH 43081

ISBN 0-02-635412-8
(Student Edition)

ISBN 0-02-635413-6
(Teacher's Wraparound Edition)

1 2 3 4 5 6 7 8 9 10 027/043 04 03 02 01 00 99

Book Overview

Table of Contents

Table of Contents T8

To the Teacher

Student Edition Overview T26
Teacher's Wraparound Edition Overview T36
Unit Planning Guide Overview T42
Program Resources T44
Scope and Sequence Overview T50
Program Philosophy T54
Professional Articles T56

Student Edition

UNIT ONE: The Short Story 1
UNIT TWO: Nonfiction 420
UNIT THREE: Poetry 576
UNIT FOUR: Drama 710
UNIT FIVE: Legends 910
UNIT SIX: Humor 998

Reference Section

Literary Terms Handbook R1
Language Handbook R14
Writing Handbook R58
Communications Skills Handbook R72
Reading Handbook R78
Glossary R108
Spanish Glossary R117
Index of Skills R126
Index of Authors and Titles R137
Index of Art and Artists R140
Acknowledgments R142

Senior Program Consultants

Beverly Ann Chin is Professor of English, Co-Director of the English Teaching Program, former Director of the Montana Writing Project, and former Director of Composition at the University of Montana in Missoula. In 1995–1996, Dr. Chin served as President of the National Council of Teachers of English. She currently serves as a Member of the Board of Directors of the National Board for Professional Teaching Standards. Dr. Chin is a nationally recognized leader in English language arts standards, curriculum, and assessment. Formerly a high school English teacher and adult education reading teacher, Dr. Chin has taught in English language arts education at several universities and has received awards for her teaching and service.

Denny Wolfe, a former high school English teacher and department chair, is Professor of English Education, Director of the Tidewater Virginia Writing Project, and Director of the Center for Urban Education at Old Dominion University in Norfolk, Virginia. For the National Council of Teachers of English, he has served as Chairperson of the Standing Committee on Teacher Preparation, President of the International Assembly, member of the Executive Committee of the Council on English Education, and editor of the SLATE Newsletter. Author of more than seventy-five articles and books on teaching English, Dr. Wolfe is a frequent consultant to schools and colleges on the teaching of English language arts.

Program Consultants

Jeffrey S. Copeland is Professor and Head of the Department of English Language and Literature at the University of Northern Iowa, where he teaches children's and young adult literature courses and a variety of courses in English education. A former public school teacher, he has published many articles in the professional journals in the language arts. The twelve books he has written or edited include *Speaking of Poets: Interviews with Poets Who Write for Children and Young Adults* and *Young Adult Literature: A Contemporary Reader.*

Mary Ann Dudzinski is a former high school English teacher and recipient of the Ross Perot Award for Teaching Excellence. She also has served as a member of the core faculty for the National Endowments for the Humanities Summer Institute for Teachers of Secondary School English and History at the University of North Texas. After fifteen years of classroom experience in grades 9–12, she currently is a language arts consultant.

William Ray has taught English in the Boston Public Schools; at Lowell University; University of Wroclaw, Poland; and, for the last fourteen years, at Lincoln-Sudbury Regional High School in Sudbury, Massachusetts. He specializes in world literature. He has worked on a variety of educational texts, as editor, consultant, and contributing writer.

Jacqueline Jones Royster is Associate Professor of English at The Ohio State University. She is also on the faculty of the Bread Loaf School of English at Middlebury College in Middlebury, Vermont. In addition to the teaching of writing, Dr. Royster's professional interests include the rhetorical history of African American women and the social and cultural implications of literate practices.

Jeffrey Wilhelm, a former English and reading teacher, is currently an assistant professor at the University of Maine where he teaches courses in middle and secondary level literacy. Author of several books and articles on the teaching of reading and the use of technology, he also works with local schools as part of the fledgling Adolescent Literacy Project and is the director of two annual summer institutes: the Maine Writing Project and Technology as a Learning Tool.

Teacher Reviewers

Rahn Anderson
Arapahoe High School
Littleton Public Schools
Littleton, Colorado

Linda Antonowich
West Chester Area School District
West Chester, Pennsylvania

Mike Bancroft
Rock Bridge High School
Columbia, Missouri

Luella Barber
Hays High School
Hays, Kansas

Lori Beard
Cypress Creek High School
Houston, Texas

Hugh Beattie
Bergenfield Public School District
Bergenfield, New Jersey

Patricia Blatt
Centerville High School
Centerville, Ohio

Edward Blotzer III
Wilkinsburg High School
Pittsburgh, Pennsylvania

Ruby Bowker
Mt. View High School
Mt. View, Wyoming

Darolyn Brown
Osborn High School
Detroit, Michigan

Rob Bruno
Atholton High School
Columbia, Maryland

Mary Beth Crotty
Bridgetown Junior High
Cincinnati, Ohio

Susan Dawson
Sam Barlow High School
Portland, Oregon

Thomas A. Della Salla
Schenectady City School District
Schenectady, New York

Sandra Denton
East High School
Columbus, Ohio

Charles Eisele
St. John Vianney High School
St. Louis, Missouri

Mel Farberman
Benjamin Cardozo High School
Bayside, New York

Caroline Ferdinandsen
San Joaquin Memorial High School
Fresno, California

Tye Ferdinandsen
San Joaquin Memorial High School
Fresno, California

Randle Frink
East Rowan High School
Salisbury, North Carolina

Pamela Fuller
Capital High School
Charleston, West Virginia

Tara Gallagher
River Hill High School
Columbia, Maryland

June Gatewood
Rio Americano
Sacramento, California

Ellen Geisler
Mentor High School
Mentor, Ohio

Leslie Gershon
Annapolis Senior High
Mitchellville, Maryland

Kim Hartman
Franklin Heights High School
Columbus, Ohio

Charlotte Heidel
Gaylord High School
Gaylord, Michigan

Keith Henricksen
Sutton Public Schools
Sutton, Nebraska

Patricia Herigan
Central Dauphin High School
Harrisburg, Pennsylvania

Azalie Hightower
Paul Junior High School
Washington, D.C.

Bobbi Ciriza Houtchens
San Bernadino High School
San Bernadino, California

Cheri Jefferson
Atholton High School
Columbia, Maryland

Marsha Jones
Seymour High School
Seymour, Indiana

Cheryl Keast
Glendale High School
Glendale, California

Glenda Kissell
Littleton High School
Littleton, Colorado

Jan Klein
Cypress Lake High School
Fort Myers, Florida

Beth Koehler
Nathan Hale High School
West Allis, Wisconsin

Sister Mary Kay Lampert
Central Catholic High School
Portland, Oregon

Elaine Loughlin
Palo Duro High
Amarillo, Texas

Tom Mann
Franklin Heights High School
Columbus, Ohio

Carolyn Sue Mash
Westerville North High School
Westerville, Ohio

Eileen Mattingly
McDonough High School
Pomfret, Maryland

Wanda McConnell
Statesville High School
Statesville, North Carolina

Victoria McCormick
John Jay High School
San Antonio, Texas

Sandra Sue McPherson
McKeesport Area High School
McKeesport, Pennsylvania

Jill Miller
Odessa High School
Odessa, Texas

Karmen Miller
Cypress Falls High School
Houston, Texas

Catherine Morse
Shelby High School
Shelby, Ohio

Tom Omli
Rogers High School
Puyallup, Washington

John O'Toole
Solon High School
Solon, Ohio

Helen Pappas
Bridgewater-Raritan High School
Bridgewater, New Jersey

Jill Railsback
Seymour High School
Seymour, Indiana

Doug Reed
Franklin Heights High School
Columbus, Ohio

Mary Jane Reed
Solon High School
Solon, Ohio

Dorlea Rikard
Bradshaw High School
Florence, Alabama

Diane Ritzdorf
Arapahoe High School
Littleton, Colorado

Leonor Rodriguez
Breckenridge High School
San Antonio, Texas

Susanne Rubenstein
Wachusett Regional High School
Holden, Massachusetts

Steve Slagle
San Gabriel High School
San Gabriel, California

Tammy Smiley
Littleton High School
Littleton, Colorado

Carol Smith
Moses Lake School District
Moses Lake, Washington

Helen Spaith
Franklin Heights High School
Columbus, Ohio

Marsha Spampinato
High School of Enterprise, Business,
and Technology
Smithtown, New York

Nora Stephens
Huntsville High School
Huntsville, Alabama

David Stocking
Wachusett Regional High School
Holden, Massachusetts

Mark Tavernier
Norfolk Public Schools
Norfolk, Virginia

Martin Tierney
Bishop Dwenger High School
Fort Wayne, Indiana

Elysa Toler-Robinson
Detroit Public Schools
Detroit, Michigan

Megan Trow
Sprague High School
Salem, Oregon

Joseph Velten Jr.
Archbishop Wood High School
Warminster, Pennsylvania

Margaret Wildermann
McDonough High School
Pomfret, Maryland

Kathy Young
Walnut Ridge High School
Columbus, Ohio

Mary Young
Greenville High School
Greenville, Illinois

Contents

UNIT ✦ ONE

UNIT ONE AT A GLANCE 1A–1D

The Short Story 1

	Genre Focus Short Stories	.2
	Active Reading Strategies The Short Story	.4
Alice Walker	**Active Reading Model: Everyday Use**	.7

Theme 1 | Transitions 21

	THEME 1 SKILLS SCOPE AND SEQUENCE 21A–21B	
	THEME 1 RESOURCE MANAGER 21C–21D	
Juanita Platero and Siyowin Miller	**Chee's Daughter**	.23
Chinua Achebe	🌐 **Civil Peace**	.39
Michael Henningsen	**Media Connection** **We, Too, Are One: Renowned Jazz Pianist Toshiko Akiyoshi Bridges the Gap** (Press release)	.47
Amy Tan	**Two Kinds**	.49
Judith Ortiz Cofer	**Catch the Moon**	.63
	Grammar Link Avoiding Sentence Fragments	.73

🌐 *indicates world literature*

CONTENTS

Paul Kvinta   **Media Connection**   **Where No One Has Gone Before?**
(Magazine article) 74

Doris Lessing   **Through the Tunnel** 76

Lame Deer   **The Vision Quest** 89

Comparing Selections: Through the Tunnel *and* The Vision Quest 93

Stephen Vincent Benét   **By the Waters of Babylon** 95

Reading & Thinking Skills Visualizing 107

Jamaica Kincaid   **What I Have Been Doing Lately** 109

Anne Tyler   **With All Flags Flying** 115

Listening, Speaking, and Viewing Debating 127

Amalia Rendic   **A Child, a Dog, the Night** 129

Writing Workshop Personal Writing: Reflective Essay 136

Theme 2	Making Choices

Making Choices 141

THEME 2 SKILLS SCOPE AND SEQUENCE 141A–141B
THEME 2 RESOURCE MANAGER 141C–141D

Sarah Orne Jewett   **A White Heron** 143

José Vasconcelos   **The Boar Hunt** 157

Alma Luz Villanueva   **Delicious Death** (Poem) .167

Comparing Selections: The Boar Hunt *and* Delicious Death 171

William Wymark Jacobs   **The Monkey's Paw** 173

Writing Skills Creating Emphasis 185

Technology Skills Multimedia: Creating Hyperfiction 186

Gabriel García Márquez   **Tuesday Siesta** 189

Thomas Bevier   **Media Connection**   **Holiday Traffic Brings Out Fear on
Suspension Bridge** (News article) 197

Jack Finney   **Contents of the Dead Man's Pocket** 199

Interdisciplinary Connection Sports and Fitness: Rock Climbing 215

Bill Amend   **Media Connection**   **Fox Trot** (Comic strip) 216

CONTENTS

Luisa Valenzuela ⬤⬤ **The Censors** 218

Reading & Thinking Skills Making Predictions .223

Isak Dinesen ⬤⬤ **The Ring** 225

Grammar Link Avoiding Run-on Sentences 233

Writing Workshop Persuasive Writing: Letter to the Editor 234

Theme 3 Twists

Twists 239

THEME 3 SKILLS SCOPE AND SEQUENCE 239A–239B
THEME 3 RESOURCE MANAGER 239C–239D

Italo Calvino ⬤⬤ **The Happy Man's Shirt** 241

Amanda Vogt **Media Connection** **What is the meaning of this? We ponder
happiness.** (Newspaper article) 245

Vocabulary Skills Context Clues 246

Mark Twain **The Californian's Tale** 248

Media Connection **This Week's Horoscope for Your Dog**
(Web site) 258

R. K. Narayan ⬤⬤ **An Astrologer's Day** 260

Listening, Speaking, and Viewing Storytelling 267

Saki (H. H. Munro) **The Interlopers** 269
Susan Beth Pfeffer **As It Is with Strangers** 279
Guy de Maupassant ⬤⬤ **The False Gems** 289
Colette ⬤⬤ **The Saleswoman** 299
Alice Childress **Mrs. James** 305

Comparing Selections: The Saleswoman *and* Mrs. James 307

Writing Workshop Narrative Writing: Short Story 308

Theme 4 Challenges and Consequences 313

THEME 4 SKILLS SCOPE AND SEQUENCE 313A–313B

THEME 4 RESOURCE MANAGER 313C–313D

Bill Watterson   **Media Connection** **Calvin and Hobbes** (Comic strip) 314

Ray Bradbury   **A Sound of Thunder** 316

Paul Zolbrod   **Media Connection** **Three Generations of Navajo Weavers**
(Magazine article) 328

Leslie Marmon Silko   **Lullaby** 330

Interdisciplinary Connection History: Navajo Code Talkers in World War II 341

Isabel Allende   **And of Clay Are We Created** 343

George Russell   **Colombia's Mortal Agony** (Nonfiction) 355

Comparing Selections: And of Clay Are We Created *and* Colombia's
Mortal Agony 360

Writing Skills Writing Dialogue 361

Kay Boyle   **Winter Night** 363

Vocabulary Skills Roots 375

Alberto Alvaro Ríos   **Waltz of the Fat Man** 377

Edgar Allan Poe   **The Masque of the Red Death** 389

Paule Marshall   **To Da-duh, in Memoriam** 399

Writing Workshop Expository Writing: Critical Response 412

Unit Wrap-Up 416

Standardized Test Practice 418

CONTENTS

UNIT ❧ TWO

UNIT TWO AT A GLANCE 419A–419D

Nonfiction 420

    Genre Focus Nonfiction 422

    Active Reading Strategies Nonfiction 424

John Steinbeck   **Active Reading Model:** *from* **Travels with Charley** 427

Theme 5 ## Remembering 431

    THEME 5 SKILLS SCOPE AND SEQUENCE 431A–431B
    THEME 5 RESOURCE MANAGER 431C–431D

Dylan Thomas   **A Child's Christmas in Wales** 433

    Media Connection **Destination Wales** (On-line travel guide) 443

Mark Mathabane   *from* **Kaffir Boy** 445

    Reading & Thinking Skills Identifying Cause and Effect 458

Jeanne Wakatsuki
Houston and
James D. Houston   *from* **Farewell to Manzanar** 460

Gerald Ford   **Media Connection** **Termination of Executive Order 9066: An
    American Promise** (Government document) 475

    Grammar Link Making Sure Subjects and Verbs Agree 476

    Vocabulary Skills Dictionary Skills: Pronunciation 477

Sea and Tidal River, 1916 (detail).

Santha Rama Rau   **By Any Other Name** 479
Maya Angelou   **Living Well. Living Good.** 489
Jewelle L. Gomez   **A Swimming Lesson** 495
    Comparing Selections: Living Well. Living Good. *and* A Swimming Lesson 499

    Writing Workshop Narrative Writing: Autobiographical Incident 500

Theme 6 · Quests and Encounters

Quests and Encounters 505

    THEME 6 SKILLS SCOPE AND SEQUENCE 505A–505B
    THEME 6 RESOURCE MANAGER 505C–505D

Slavenka Drakulić   **Pizza in Warsaw, Torte in Prague** 507

    Media Connection Dr. Martin Luther King's Early Days
       (Television transcript) 515

Martin Luther King Jr.   **I've Seen the Promised Land** 517

    Writing Skills Organizing Details 528

R. F. Scott   **Media Connection Return from First Summit Depot**
       (Journal entries) 529

Jane Ellen Stevens   **Exploring Antarctic Ice** 532

    Listening, Speaking, and Viewing Interviewing 541

    Interdisciplinary Connection Physical Science: Lightning 542

Gretel Ehrlich   *from* **A Match to the Heart** 544

    Technology Skills E-mail: Research Using E-mail 554

Loren Eiseley   **The Angry Winter** 557
Lewis Thomas   **The Tucson Zoo** 563
    Comparing Selections: The Angry Winter *and* The Tucson Zoo 567

    Writing Workshop Descriptive Writing: Observational Report 568
    Unit Wrap-Up 572
    Standardized Test Practice 574

CONTENTS

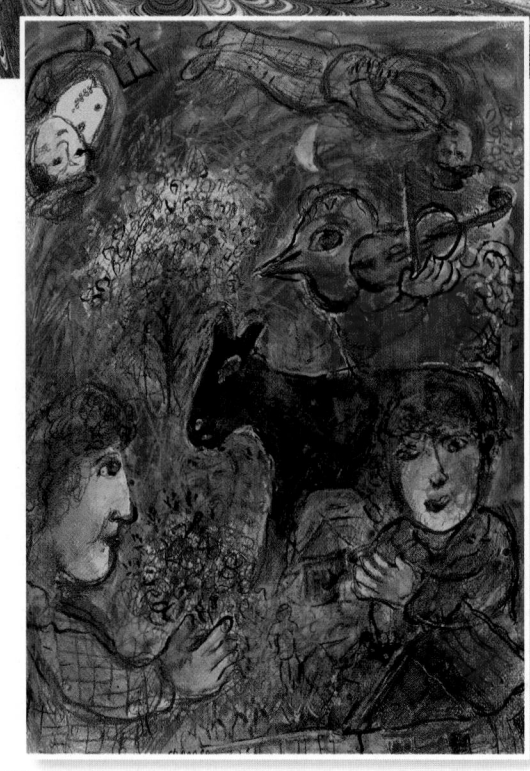

UNIT ❊ THREE

UNIT THREE AT A GLANCE 575A–575D

Poetry 576

  Genre Focus Poetry 578

  Active Reading Strategies Poetry 580

Edgar Allan Poe **Active Reading Model: Eldorado** 583

Theme 7 # Loves and Losses 585

  THEME 7 SKILLS SCOPE AND SEQUENCE 585A–585B
  THEME 7 RESOURCE MANAGER .585C–585D

Dorothy Parker **One Perfect Rose** 587
William Shakespeare **Shall I Compare Thee to a Summer's Day?** 587

C. Lewis and A. Wright **Media Connection When a Man Loves a Woman** (Song lyrics) 590

N. Scott Momaday **Simile** 592
Edna St. Vincent Millay **Well, I Have Lost You; and I Lost You Fairly** 592

  Grammar Link Making Sure Pronouns and Antecedents Agree 595

James Weldon Johnson **The Glory of the Day Was in Her Face** .597
Shu Ting 👓 **Missing You** 597

  Technology Skills Internet: Publishing Your Writing on the Web 600

Philip Booth **First Lesson** 603
Robert Hayden **Those Winter Sundays** 604

Vocabulary Skills Multiple-Meaning Words 607

Melanie L. Stephens   Media Connection **Halfway House for Horses** (Magazine article) 608

Gwendolyn Brooks   **Horses Graze** 611

James Wright   **A Blessing** 612

Reading & Thinking Skills Understanding Denotation and Connotation 615

Writing Workshop Business Writing: Interview 616

Theme 8 Issues of Identity 621

THEME 8 SKILLS SCOPE AND SEQUENCE 621A–621B

THEME 8 RESOURCE MANAGER 621C–621D

Langston Hughes   **Afro-American Fragment** 623

Cathy Song   **Heaven** 624

Robert Francis   **The Base Stealer** 629

Samuel Allen   **To Satch** 630

Listening, Speaking, and Viewing Oral Interpretation of a Poem 633

Tom Verducci   Media Connection **Making Hay** (Magazine article) 634

John Updike   **Ex-Basketball Player** 636

Lucille Clifton   **Miss Rosie** 638

Bill Moyers   Media Connection **Lucille Clifton** from *The Language of Life*
(Interview) 641

Robert Frost   **The Road Not Taken** 643

Pablo Neruda   **We Are Many** 644

Marilyn Chin   **The Floral Apron** 649

Teresa Palomo Acosta   **My Mother Pieced Quilts** 650

Margaret Atwood   **A Bus Along St. Clair: December** 655

Lorna Dee Cervantes   **Freeway 280** 656

Naomi Shihab Nye   **Making a Fist** 661

CONTENTS

Anita Endrezze   **What We Believe** 662

Rick Steves and
Bob Effertez with
John Gottberg   **Media Connection**   **The Culturally Sensitive Traveler** from *Asia Through the Back Door* (Travel guide) 665

Diana Chang   **Foreign Ways** 667
Linda Hogan   **Song for My Name** 668

Writing Workshop   Creative Writing: Poem 670

Theme 9   Observations and Expressions 675

THEME 9 SKILLS SCOPE AND SEQUENCE 675A–675B
THEME 9 RESOURCE MANAGER 675C–675D

Amy Lowell   **Night Clouds** 677
Laura Iwasaki   **Tiger Year** 678

Interdisciplinary Connection   Astronomy: Phases of the Moon 681

Al Young   **For Poets** 683
Jean Toomer   **Reapers** 683
Matsuo Bashō   **Three Haiku** 687
Lady Ise   **Two Tanka** 687

Media Connection   **U.S. Aerialists Are Golden**
(Press conference transcript) 689

Roberto Fernández
Retamar   **A Motto from Poets: Leave Stone** 691
Lawrence Ferlinghetti   **Constantly risking absurdity** .692

Writing Skills   Using Simile and Metaphor 695

Melita Marie Garza   **Media Connection**   **Hoops Picks Up a Jazz Beat** (Newspaper article) 696

Sandra María Esteves   **let my spirit fly in time** 698
Carl Sandburg   **Jazz Fantasia** 699

Writing Workshop   Descriptive Writing: Extended Metaphor 702
Unit Wrap-Up 706
Standardized Test Practice 708

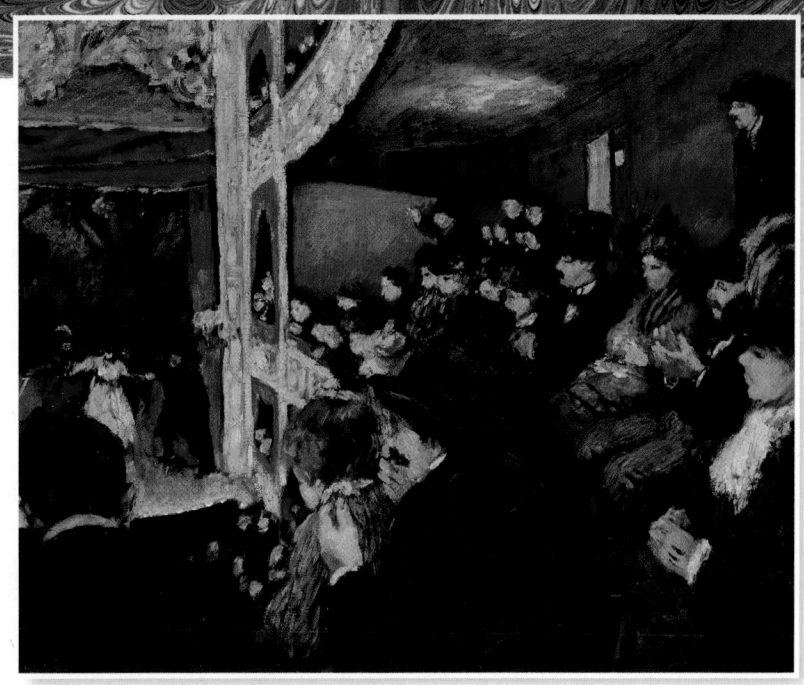

UNIT ✦ FOUR

UNIT FOUR AT A GLANCE 709A–709D

Drama 710

Genre Focus Drama 712

Active Reading Strategies Drama 714

William Hauptman **Active Reading Model:** *from* **Big River: The Adventures of Huckleberry Finn** 717

Theme 10 # Loyalty and Betrayal .721

THEME 10 SKILLS SCOPE AND SEQUENCE 721A–721B
THEME 10 RESOURCE MANAGER 721C–721D

Literature Focus Classical Greek Drama 722

Sophocles **Antigone** 727

Reading & Thinking Skills Monitoring Comprehension 771

Literature Focus Understanding Shakespeare and Elizabethan Drama 772

Lawrence Baines **Media Connection The Mark Antony Rap** (Rap) 776

William Shakespeare **Julius Caesar** 778

Writing Skills Effective Conclusions 799

Vocabulary Skills Homophones 819

Technology Skills Word Processing: Creating Academic Reports 874

Interdisciplinary Connection Language Arts: The Romance Languages 876

Ralph Cipriano **Media Connection The Ring Finders of Philly** (Magazine article) 877

Josephina Niggli   **The Ring of General Macías** 879

Carmen Tafolla   **Marked** (Poem) 897

Comparing Selections: The Ring of General Macías *and* Marked 899

Grammar Link Misplaced or Dangling Modifiers 900

Listening, Speaking, and Viewing Persuasive Speech 901

Writing Workshop Expository Writing: Compare-and-Contrast Essay 902

Unit Wrap-Up 906

Standardized Test Practice 908

UNIT ❦ FIVE

UNIT FIVE AT A GLANCE 909A–909D

Legends 910

Literature Focus Legends 912

Theme 11 # Heroism 913

THEME 11 SKILLS SCOPE AND SEQUENCE 913A–913B

THEME 11 RESOURCE MANAGER 913C–913D

Thomas Malory   *from* **Le Morte d'Arthur** 915

D. T. Niane   *from* **Sundiata** 935

Comparing Selections: *from* Le Morte d'Arthur *and from* Sundiata 941

Grammar Link Missing Commas with Nonessential Elements 942

Writing Skills Main Idea and Supporting Details 943

Alfred, Lord Tennyson   **The Passing of Arthur,** *from* **Idylls of the King** 945

Interdisciplinary Connection Geography: Arthurian Sites of England 959

Media Connection *from* **Monty Python and the Holy Grail**
(Screenplay) 960

T. H. White   **Arthur Becomes King,** *from* **The Once and Future King** 962

Vocabulary Skills Idioms 977

Technology Skills Citing Electronic Sources 978

Media Connection **Wonder Woman** (Theme song lyrics) 980

Joseph Bruchac and
Gayle Ross   **Where the Girl Rescued Her Brother** 983

Reading & Thinking Skills Identifying Sequence 989

Writing Workshop Expository Writing: Biographical Research Paper 990
Unit Wrap-Up 994
Standardized Test Practice 996

UNIT ❧ SIX

UNIT SIX AT A GLANCE 997A–997D

Humor 998

    Literature Focus Humor 1000

Theme 12 Comic Perspectives 1001

    THEME 12 SKILLS SCOPE AND SEQUENCE 1001A–1001B
    THEME 12 RESOURCE MANAGER 1001C–1001D

Nikki Giovanni   **Let's Sweat!** (Nonfiction) 1003

Jim Davis   **Media Connection Garfield** (Comic strip) 1008

Henry Beard   **From A Cat's Garden of Verses** (Poems) 1010

    Technology Skills Database: Critical Viewing Skills 1012

    Grammar Link Missing or Misplaced Possessive Apostrophes 1014

Robert H. Abel   **Appetizer** (Short story) 1016

Wen Smith   **Media Connection Too Much Spice** (Magazine article) 1028

Annie Dillard   *from* **An American Childhood** (Nonfiction) 1030

Dave Barry · **What Is and Ain't Grammatical** (Nonfiction) 1039

Comparing Selections: *from* An American Childhood *and* What Is and Ain't Grammatical 1043

James Thurber · **The Car We Had to Push** (Short story) 1045

Reading & Thinking Skills Synthesizing 1052

Interdisciplinary Connection Workplace Education: The Early Automobile 1053

Mary Helen Ponce · **How I Changed the War and Won the Game** (Nonfiction) 1055

Vocabulary Skills Analyzing Words 1059

Writing Skills Using Effective Language 1060

Anton Chekhov · **A Marriage Proposal** (Drama) 1062

Listening, Speaking, and Viewing Readers Theater 1077

Writing Workshop Expository Writing: Feature Article 1078

Unit Wrap-Up 1082

Standardized Test Practice 1084

Reference Section

Literary Terms Handbook R1

Language Handbook

Troubleshooter R14

Troublesome Words R29

Grammar Glossary R38

Mechanics R45

Spelling R54

Writing Handbook

The Writing Process R58

Writing Modes R62

Research Paper Writing R64

Business and Technical Writing R70

Communications Skills Handbook

Using Electronic Resources R72

Study and Test-Taking Skills R74

Reading Handbook R78

Glossary R108

Spanish Glossary R117

Index of Skills R126

Index of Authors and Titles R137

Index of Art and Artists R140

Acknowledgments R142

Features

MEDIA Connection

Press Release: We, Too, Are One: Renowned Jazz Pianist Toshiko Akiyoshi Bridges the Gap. 47

Magazine Article: Where No One Has Gone Before?. 74

News Article: Holiday Traffic Brings Out Fear on Suspension Bridge. 197

Comic Strip: Fox Trot 216

Newspaper Article: What is the meaning of this? We ponder happiness. 245

Web Site: This Week's Horoscope for Your Dog. 258

Comic Strip: Calvin and Hobbes. 314

Magazine Article: Three Generations of Navajo Weavers 328

On-line Travel Guide: Destination Wales. 443

Government Document: Termination of Executive Order 9066: An American Promise 475

Television Transcript: Dr. Martin Luther King's Early Days. 515

Journal Entries: Return from First Summit Depot 529

Song Lyrics: When a Man Loves a Woman 590

Magazine Article: Halfway House for Horses 608

Magazine Article: Making Hay 634

Interview: Lucille Clifton from *The Language of Life* 641

Travel Guide: The Culturally Sensitive Traveler from *Asia Through the Back Door* 665

Press Conference Transcript: U.S. Aerialists Are Golden 689

Newspaper Article: Hoops Picks Up a Jazz Beat. 696

Rap: The Mark Antony Rap 776

Magazine Article: The Ring Finders of Philly 877

Screenplay: *from* Monty Python and the Holy Grail. 960

Theme Song Lyrics: Wonder Woman. 980

Comic Strip: Garfield 1008

Magazine Article: Too Much Spice 1028

COMPARING selections

Through the Tunnel *and* The Vision Quest 93

The Boar Hunt *and* Delicious Death 171

The Saleswoman *and* Mrs. James 307

And of Clay Are We Created *and* Colombia's Mortal Agony 360

Living Well. Living Good. *and* A Swimming Lesson 499

The Angry Winter *and* The Tucson Zoo . . . 567

The Ring of General Macías *and* Marked. . . 899

from Le Morte d'Arthur *and* *from* Sundiata 941

from An American Childhood *and* What Is and Ain't Grammatical 1043

Interdisciplinary Connection

Sports and Fitness: Rock Climbing. 215

History: Navajo Code Talkers in World War II 341

Physical Science: Lightning. 542

Astronomy: Phases of the Moon 681

Language Arts: The Romance Languages. . . 876

Geography: Arthurian Sites of England. . . . 959

Workplace Education: The Early Automobile. 1053

Genre Focus

Short Stories 2

Nonfiction 422

Poetry 578

Drama 712

Literature FOCUS

The Short Story 4

Nonfiction 424

Poetry 580

Drama 714

Active Reading Strategies

Classical Greek Drama 722

Understanding Shakespeare and
    Elizabethan Drama 772

Legends 912

Humor 1000

Writing Workshop

Personal Writing: Reflective Essay 136

Persuasive Writing: Letter to the Editor 234

Narrative Writing: Short Story 308

Expository Writing: Critical Response 412

Narrative Writing: Autobiographical
    Incident 500

Descriptive Writing: Observational
    Report 568

Business Writing: Interview 616

Creative Writing: Poem 670

Descriptive Writing: Extended Metaphor . . . 702

Expository Writing: Compare and Contrast
    Essay 902

Expository Writing: Biographical Research
    Paper 990

Expository Writing: Feature Article 1078

Skills

Grammar Link

Avoiding Sentence Fragments 73

Avoiding Run-on Sentences 233

Making Sure Subjects and Verbs Agree 476

Making Sure Pronouns and Antecedents
    Agree 595

Misplaced or Dangling Modifiers 900

Missing Commas with Nonessential
    Elements 942

Missing or Misplaced Possessive
    Apostrophes 1014

Listening, Speaking, and Viewing

Debating 127

Storytelling 267

Interviewing 541

Oral Interpretation of a Poem 633

Persuasive Speech 901

Readers Theater 1077

Reading & Thinking Skills

Visualizing 107

Making Predictions 223

Identifying Cause and Effect 458

Understanding Denotation and
    Connotation 615

Monitoring Comprehension 771

Identifying Sequence 989

Synthesizing 1052

Features

Technology Skills

Technology Skills: Multimedia: Creating
Hyperfiction 186
Technology Skills: E-mail: Research
Using E-mail 554
Technology Skills: Internet: Publishing Your
Writing on the Web 600
Technology Skills: Word Processing:
Creating Academic Reports 874
Technology Skills: Citing Electronic
Sources 978
Technology Skills: Database: Critical
Viewing Skills 1012

Vocabulary Skills

Context Clues 246
Roots 375

Dictionary Skills: Pronunciation 477
Multiple-Meaning Words 607
Homophones 819
Idioms 977
Analyzing Words 1059

Writing Skills

Creating Emphasis 185
Writing Dialogue 361
Organizing Details 528
Using Simile and Metaphor 695
Effective Conclusions 799
Main Idea and Supporting Details 943
Using Effective Language 1060

Skill Minilessons

GRAMMAR AND LANGUAGE

Possessive Pronouns 20
Using Appositives 37
Using Descriptive Tag Lines 46
Participles and Participial Phrases 61
Understanding Connotations 72
Quotation Marks in Dialogue 126
Using Semicolons 155
Punctuating Dialogue 184
Introductory Phrases 214
Dashes 257
Concrete and Abstract Nouns 266
Sentence Variety 277
Vivid Verbs 287
Infinitives and Infinitive Phrases 297
Coordinate Adjectives 374
Denotations and Connotations 387
Subject Complements 397
Concrete and Abstract Nouns 411

Compound Adjectives 442
Intervening Prepositional Phrases 474
Parallelism 527
Capitalization 540
Abbreviations 553
Using the Dash 770
Active and Passive Voice 873
Subject-Verb Agreement 958
Sentence Fragments 976
Sentence Varieties 1076

READING AND THINKING

Chronological Order 20
Evaluating Generalizations 37
Analyzing Problems and Solutions 46
Summarizing 61
Recognizing Causes and Effects 72
Identifying Assumptions 126
Cause and Effect 155
Chronological Order 184

Problem Solving 214
Scanning 257
Making Inferences 266
Summarizing 277
Interpreting 287
Drawing Conclusions 297
Activating Prior Knowledge 374
Inferring Characters' Motivations 387
Visualizing 397
Activating Prior Knowledge 411
Clarifying 442
Summarizing 474
Recognizing Cause and Effect 540
Using Comparisons to Clarify 553
Identifying the Author's Purpose 770
Visualizing 873
Paraphrasing 958
Making Inferences 976
Responding 1076

VOCABULARY

Base Words 20
Synonyms—Shades of Meaning 37
Etymology 46
Analogies 61
Compound Words 72
Antonyms 87
The Prefix *Ante-* 106
Analogies 113
Prefixes Expressing Number 126
Analogies 135
Multiple-Meaning Words 155
Analogies 165
Unlocking Meaning 184
The Suffix *-ity* 196
Analogies 214
Usage 222

Antonyms 232
Analogies 244
The Prefix *Pre-* 257
Etymology 266
Analogies 277
Unlocking Meaning 287
Analogies 297
Borrowed Words 303
The Prefix *Com-* 327
The Latin Root *tort* 340
Analogies 353
Etymology 374
Analogies 387
Analogies 397
Synonyms: Shades of Meaning 411
Multiple-Meaning Words 430
Analogies 442
Analogies 457
Parts of Speech 474
Etymology 487
Analogies 493
Analogies 514
Analogies 540
Etymology 553
The Latin Root *vert* 561
Antonyms 770
Analogies 873
Connotation 895
Etymology 933
Semantic Mapping 958
Dictionary Skills: Definitions 976
The Latin Root *pend* 1007
Old Words 1027
The Latin Root *voc* 1037
The Latin Root *ject* 1051
Analogies 1058
Etymology 1076

Book Overview

THE LITERATURE UNITS

The literature that makes up the heart of the Student Edition is organized into six units. Each of the first five units focuses on a major genre (short story, nonfiction, poetry, drama, and legends). Unit Six: Humor includes a wide variety of genres.

The Persistent Sea, No. 2. O. Louis Guglielmi (1906–1956). Oil on canvas, 29¾ x 23¼ in. Private collection.

UNIT ONE

The Short Story

"[F]iction is like a spider's web, attached ever so lightly perhaps, but still attached to life at all four corners."

—Virginia Woolf

Theme 1
Transitions
pages 21–140

Theme 2
Making Choices
pages 141–238

Theme 3
Twists
pages 239–312

Theme 4
Challenges and Consequences
pages 313–415

Theme 1   Transitions

Transitions are changes—passages from one place to another, saying good-bye to the old and welcoming the new, growing into adulthood. The characters you will meet in this theme all face changes in their lives. How do you approach transitions in your life? Do you ease into new stages, or do you resist change and want things to stay the same?

THEME PROJECTS

Performing

Critic's Choice   You've probably seen a TV show in which two movie critics each give a thumbs-up or a thumbs-down review about a film. With a partner, create a similar show in which you review the stories in this theme.

1. Choose which elements of each story you will evaluate—for example, characters, plot, suspense, realism. Think about how well these elements work in the story.

2. Be prepared to defend your opinions if your partner challenges them. Use specific examples from the stories.

3. Consider having someone videotape your show so you can view it later.

Interdisciplinary Project

Art   Choose three characters in this theme whose transitions are most interesting to you, and represent their changes visually.

1. Think about how each moment of transition would look. What objects could symbolize the characters' past life or their new condition? What colors best represent the before and after stages of their change?

2. Make a painting, collage, or diorama representing each of your characters' transitions.

3. Show your work to your classmates; see if they can tell which characters you've chosen.

The Family, Diana Ong (b. 1940). Private collection.

THE SHORT STORY 21

Within each unit, selections are organized into one or more sections, each based on a universal theme.

REFERENCE SECTION

This comprehensive set of handbooks provides a valuable resource for students. References throughout the textbook direct students to specific handbook pages for additional information and support.

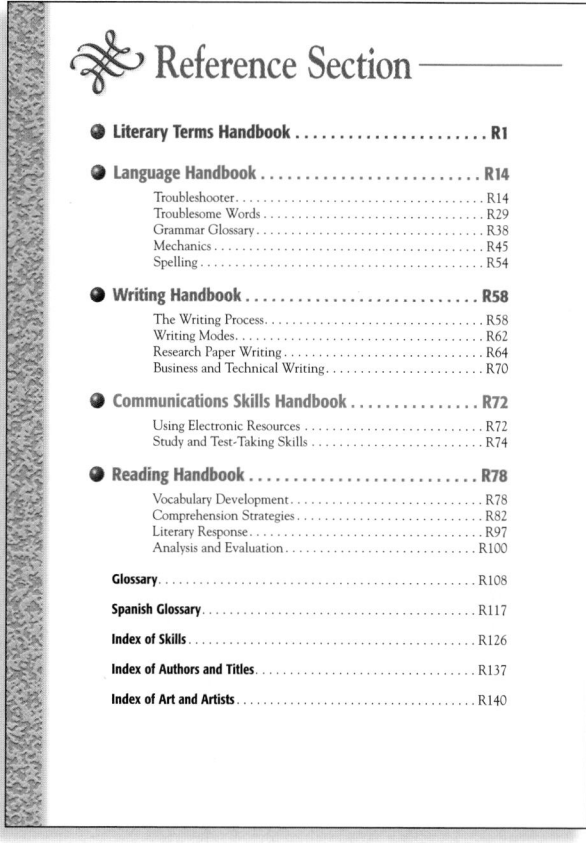

Reference Section

- **Literary Terms Handbook** **R1**

- **Language Handbook** **R14**
  - Troubleshooter. R14
  - Troublesome Words R29
  - Grammar Glossary R38
  - Mechanics R45
  - Spelling R54

- **Writing Handbook** **R58**
  - The Writing Process. R58
  - Writing Modes. R62
  - Research Paper Writing R64
  - Business and Technical Writing. R70

- **Communications Skills Handbook** **R72**
  - Using Electronic Resources R72
  - Study and Test-Taking Skills R74

- **Reading Handbook** **R78**
  - Vocabulary Development R78
  - Comprehension Strategies R82
  - Literary Response R97
  - Analysis and Evaluation R100

- **Glossary**. R108

- **Spanish Glossary**. R117

- **Index of Skills** R126

- **Index of Authors and Titles**. R137

- **Index of Art and Artists**. R140

Literary Terms Handbook provides a glossary of all the literary terms taught with the selections in the book.

Language Handbook supplies ready reference and instructional support for grammar, usage, mechanics, and spelling.

Writing Handbook includes an overview of the writing process and the major writing modes as well as support for research paper writing.

Communications Skills Handbook addresses the use of electronic resources as well as study and test-taking skills.

Reading Handbook provides instructional support and models for a comprehensive set of reading strategies and skills.

Selection Plan

Each selection in the program is presented in a three-part format:
(1) Before You Read, (2) the selection pages and (3) Responding to Literature.

BEFORE YOU READ

This section prepares students for reading by helping them draw upon their personal experience, build background knowledge, and set a purpose for reading.

Focus Activity creates a bridge into the selection by connecting the students' own experience to an important theme or aspect of the selection. Activities include quickwrites, journal entries, making graphic organizers, and group or whole class discussions.

Background presents nuggets of relevant background information to pique students' interest and enhance their understanding of the selection.

✎ —Before You Read—

Two Kinds

— FOCUS ACTIVITY —

Just for a moment imagine yourself as an acclaimed musician or artist, a champion athlete, a brilliant scientist, or an award-winning actor.

JOURNAL Write a description of yourself as a person who is at the top of his or her chosen field. Briefly tell what you have accomplished and what you enjoy most about your success.

SETTING A PURPOSE Read to discover two different viewpoints on successful living.

— BACKGROUND —

The Time and Place
The story takes place in Chinatown in San Francisco, probably during the early 1960s.

Did You Know?
Chinatown in downtown San Francisco is one of the largest Chinese communities outside of Asia. The neighborhood—with its fascinating mix of restaurants, shops, businesses, and religious and cultural institutions—is a crowded and bustling place. The area was settled by Chinese immigrants who arrived during the Gold Rush of 1849. Chinatown continues to grow, as immigrants arrive to begin a new life—just as the mother in "Two Kinds" had done in 1949.

— VOCABULARY PREVIEW —

prodigy (prod′ ə jē) *n.* an extraordinarily gifted or talented person, especially a child; p. 49
lament (lə ment′) *v.* to express sorrow or regret; p. 50
reproach (ri prōch′) *n.* blame; disgrace; discredit; p. 50
mesmerizing (mez′ mə rīz ing) *adj.* fascinating; p. 51
reverie (rev′ ər ē) *n.* fanciful thinking, daydream; p. 53
discordant (dis kôrd′ ənt) *adj.* not in agreement or harmony; p. 53
devastate (dev′ əs tāt) *v.* to destroy; overwhelm; p. 56
fiasco (fē as′ kō) *n.* a complete or humiliating failure; p. 56

48 ✿ UNIT 1

Meet Amy Tan

Amy Tan enjoys performing music much more than the girl in this story does. She sings in a rock band as a way to relax and to raise money for worthy causes.

Tan's first published writing was an article titled, "What the Library Means to Me," written when she was eight years old. Since then she has become an award-winning author. Her first novel, *The Joy Luck Club*, was made into a feature film of the same name. The book, which includes the selection you are about to read, tells about four women from China and their Chinese American daughters.

Amy Tan was born in Oakland, California, in 1952. This story was published in 1989.

Vocabulary Preview introduces key vocabulary that students will encounter in reading the selection. (Generally, these are words that appear often on the SAT and in students' everyday and academic reading.)

Meet the Author motivates students to read the selection by presenting high-interest author information and quotations in an inviting format.

SELECTION PAGES

The engaging design of the selection pages incorporates dynamic photography and fine art within a clean layout that promotes readability. A variety of carefully designed elements support and engage students as they read.

Did You Know? notes provide illustrated definitions to help students visualize unfamiliar settings or objects mentioned in the selection.

Vocabulary words are underscored at first use in the selection; a note at the bottom of the page provides the definition, pronunciation, and part of speech.

Viewing questions prompt students to connect the fine art and photographs to the selection.

Footnotes support comprehension by explaining unfamiliar references or clarifying difficult passages in the text. Footnotes also supply pronunciations for many names of people and places and for words from other languages.

Selection Plan

(Continued)

RESPONDING TO LITERATURE

This section provides a variety of ways for students to respond to the literature through listening, speaking, and writing activities. It also provides students with an opportunity to make connections to the theme.

Personal Response questions and activities allow all students to express an immediate response to the selection. The goal here is exploration not closure.

Analyzing Literature questions help guide students to a thorough understanding of the selection. Recall questions focus students' attention on significant details of the selection, which they will use in answering the Interpret questions. Evaluate and Connect questions often include a Theme Connection.

Responding to Literature

Personal Response

What was your opinion of Jing-mei's mother and the extremely ambitious goals she set for her daughter? Explain your answer.

— ANALYZING LITERATURE —

RECALL

1. What two faces does Jing-mei see when she looks in the mirror after another failed prodigy training session?
2. What makes Jing-mei's mother decide that her daughter will study the piano? How does Jing-mei react to this news?
3. At her recital, how does Jing-mei feel when it is her turn to perform? How well does she perform?
4. Explain what provokes the nasty argument between Jing-mei and her mother.
5. What reasons does Jing-mei's mother give for offering Jing-mei the piano for her thirtieth birthday? How does Jing-mei interpret her mother's offer?

INTERPRET

6. Why, do you think, does Jing-mei decide to stop trying to become a prodigy?
7. In your opinion, why does Jing-mei have such a lazy attitude toward her piano studies?
8. Why, do you think, do Jing-mei and her parents feel so humiliated by her performance at the recital?
9. What is so brutal about the dreadful thing Jing-mei says to her mother at the end of their argument?
10. Do you think that Jing-mei's mother finally forgives her daughter for the dreadful thing she said? Explain.

EVALUATE AND CONNECT

11. In your opinion, why does Jing-mei's mother long for her to be famous?
12. Jing-mei and her mother seem to be fighting about the piano. In your opinion, what are they really fighting about?
13. Do you think that well-meaning parents—such as Jing-mei's mother—sometimes set unrealistic goals for their children? Explain.
14. To what does the title of this story refer? Do you think it's a good title for the story? Give a reason for your answer.
15. What do you think Jing-Mei has learned by the end of the story?

THE SHORT STORY 59

Literary ELEMENTS

Conflict

Most stories are based on a problem, or conflict, that gets resolved over the course of the story. **External conflicts** exist when a character struggles with an outside force, such as another person, society, fate, or a force of nature. An **internal conflict** exists in a character's mind, when he or she is torn between different feelings or goals. Many stories have more than one conflict. Typically, the conflicts are related in some way.

1. What is the main external conflict in "Two Kinds"?
2. Identify another external conflict in the story. How does this conflict get resolved?
3. Describe an internal conflict that Jing-mei or her mother might have. How does it relate to the main conflict you identified in question 1 above?
● See **Literary Terms Handbook,** p. R3.

Literary Elements teach traditional literary skills and provide students with the tools necessary to analyze and interpret literature.

T30

Responding to Literature

LITERATURE AND WRITING

Writing About Literature
Evaluate a Character's Actions   Write a paragraph or two evaluating Jing-mei's actions. Do Jing-mei's actions seem appropriate for a girl her age and for her situation? What do you think of the way Jing-mei reacts to her mother? What does she think her mother wants? What does she want for herself? Support your opinions with details from the story.

Personal Writing
Side Effects of Success   Look back at the journal entry you made in the Focus Activity on page 48, in which you described yourself at the top of your chosen field. Now imagine some of the possible drawbacks of such success—for example, the pressure to achieve, the fear of failure, the loss of privacy, the time demands of your career. Write another journal entry in which you describe what you like least about your success.

EXTENDING YOUR RESPONSE

Literature Groups
Debating Issues   Should parents ever require their children to take music lessons, as Jing-mei's mother did, or to play a sport or participate in any particular activity? First, look back at "Two Kinds" and list the reasons why the mother's requirements of Jing-mei were good and why they were bad. Use specific examples from the story as you develop your list. Then add to your list other reasons for and against mandatory after-school activities for children. Compare your lists with those made by other groups, and debate whether it does more harm or more good to require a child to participate in an activity in which he or she has little or no interest.

Interdisciplinary Activity
History: Researching a Topic   Jing-mei's mother represents one of about 2 million Chinese citizens who fled their homeland at the end of the 1940s and into the next decade. Do some research on this wave of Chinese migrations. What were the political and economic conditions in China at that time? Find out why so many Chinese left their homeland. Create a pamphlet with charts and pictures that details the results of your research.

Performing
Presentation   Child prodigies—particularly in music—have been famous throughout history. Research a child prodigy and prepare a presentation about his or her work. For Mozart, for example, you might provide a brief biographical sketch and then play recordings of his music.

Leopold Mozart with Wolfgang and Nannerl, playing music, 1763 (detail). Louis Carrogis de Carmontelle. Watercolor, 33 x 20 cm. Musée Condé, Chantilly, France.

Reading Further
You might enjoy another work by Amy Tan:

Novel: *The Joy Luck Club* gives readers a moving look at the lives of four Chinese women in pre-1949 China and the lives of their American-born daughters.

Viewing: *The Joy Luck Club*

📖 **Save your work for your portfolio.**

60   UNIT 1

Literature and Writing provides options that all students can use to respond in writing to a selection. One option is always a Writing About Literature prompt; the other option is either a Creative Writing prompt or a Personal Writing prompt.

Extending Your Response includes diverse activities that appeal to different types of learners. This section always includes Literature Groups as well as other activities chosen from the following menu: Interdisciplinary Activity, Learning for Life, Internet Connection, Listening and Speaking, Performing, and Reading Further.

Skill Minilessons provide frequent opportunities for students to practice essential language arts skills in the context of the literature they are reading.

Grammar and Language minilessons focus on skills of grammar, usage, mechanics, and style to help students improve their own writing and better appreciate literature by making a link between literature and good writing.

Reading and Thinking minilessons teach reading and critical thinking skills that students can apply not just to literature but across the curriculum.

Vocabulary minilessons teach or reinforce important vocabulary skills. Many focus on the type of analogies used in the SAT.

Responding to Literature

Skill Minilessons

GRAMMAR AND LANGUAGE • Participles and Participial Phrases

Amy Tan uses **participles** (verb forms used as adjectives) and **participial phrases** to make her descriptions lively. For example:

I was a dainty ballerina girl standing by the curtains. (The participial phrase *standing by the curtains* describes *girl*.)

You can often improve your writing by using participles and participial phrases to combine short, choppy sentences. For example:

I dawdled over my piano piece. I daydreamed.
Daydreaming, I dawdled over my piano piece.

PRACTICE   Combine each pair of sentences into one sentence that includes a participle or participial phrase.

1. Auntie wanted to scold Waverly. She gave Waverly a look.
2. Jing-mei returned to her seat. She fought back tears.
3. My mother called me over with hurried hand gestures. She said, "Look here."
4. My mother looked at the story. She asked, "What's the capital of Finland?"

● For more about participles, see **Language Handbook,** p. R41.

READING AND THINKING • Summarizing

To increase your reading comprehension and to follow the sequence of events in a story, stop periodically and summarize what you have read. A **summary** is a brief statement of the main idea of a passage. Notice the breaks in the text of "Two Kinds." These breaks, which indicate a change in time or topic, are good places to stop and summarize. The first section of the story might be summarized this way: *The narrator's mother, who lost everything in China, looked upon America as a land of opportunity.*

PRACTICE   Review the remaining eight sections of the story. On your paper, write a one-sentence summary of each section.

APPLY   Now summarize your summaries! Write a title for each section, such as "From China to America" for the first one.

● For more about summarizing, see **Reading Handbook,** p. R91.

VOCABULARY • Analogies

An analogy is a type of comparison that is based on the relationships between things or ideas. Some analogies are based on antonyms.

conceal : uncover :: persevere : quit

The opposite of *conceal* is *uncover;* the opposite of *persevere* is *quit.*

To finish an analogy, decide what relationship exists between the first two things or ideas. Then apply that relationship to another pair of words and see if it is the same.

● For more about analogies, see **Communications Skills Handbook,** p. R77.

PRACTICE   Choose the word that best completes each analogy. Some of the analogies are based on antonyms.

1. lament : rejoice :: ignite :
   a. burn   b. cool   c. extinguish
2. harmonious : discordant :: mesmerizing :
   a. magical   b. boring   c. clashing
3. failure : fiasco :: meal :
   a. feast   b. snack   c. hunger
4. prodigy : talented :: giant :
   a. bold   b. tall   c. frightening
5. reproach : praise :: knowledge :
   a. learning   b. criticism   c. ignorance

THE SHORT STORY   61

Features

A variety of special features enhance students' learning through attention to active reading, language arts skills, and connections to other literature, to other disciplines, and to technology.

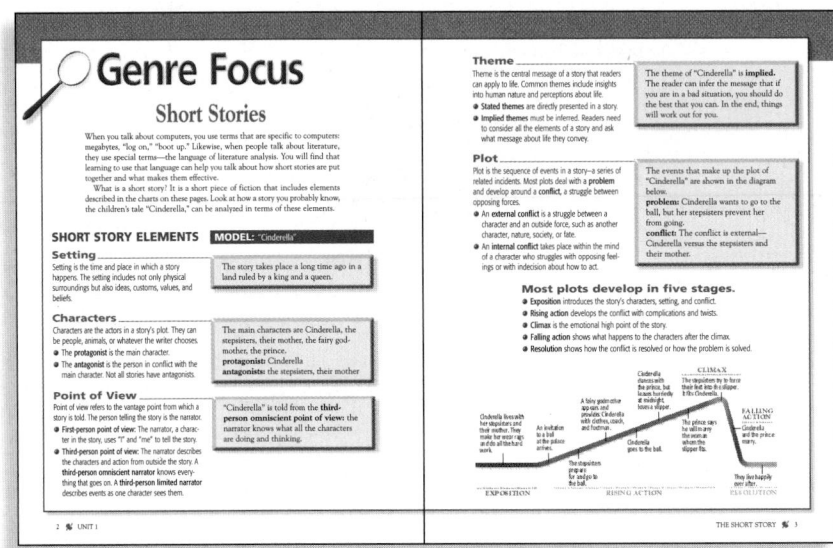

Genre Focus introduces students to the elements and characteristics of each of four major genres: short story, nonfiction, poetry, and drama. In addition, two Literature Focus features use a similar format to explore the epic and science fiction.

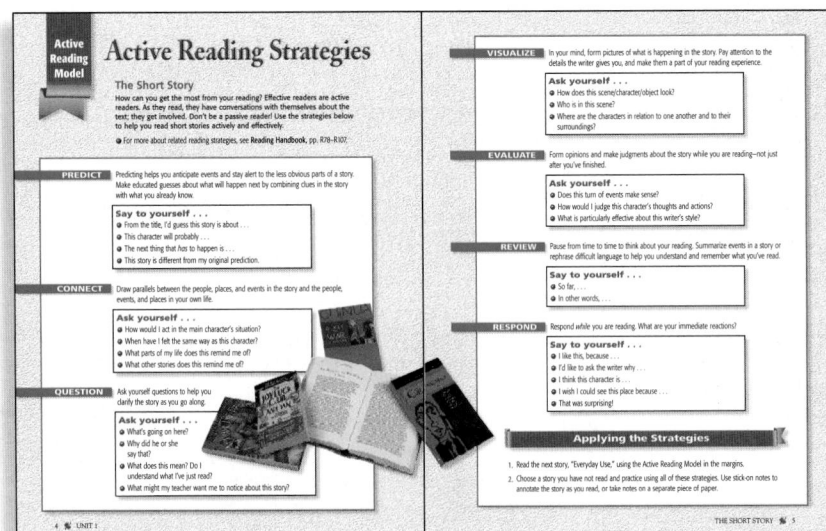

Active Reading Strategies models for students the kind of thinking and questioning that skillful readers do when reading a particular type of text.

Active Reading Model gives students the opportunity to apply active reading strategies as they read the first selection in the unit.

Media Connections provide engaging, contemporary connections to many selections through a variety of sources such as newspaper and magazine articles, Web sites, song lyrics, and screenplays.

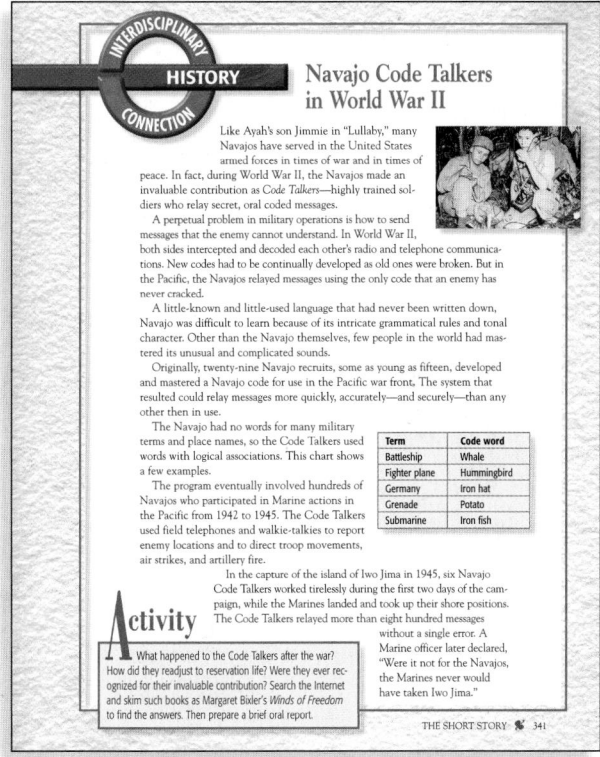

Interdisciplinary Connections connect selections to grade-level curricular goals in disciplines such as mathematics, science, history, and art.

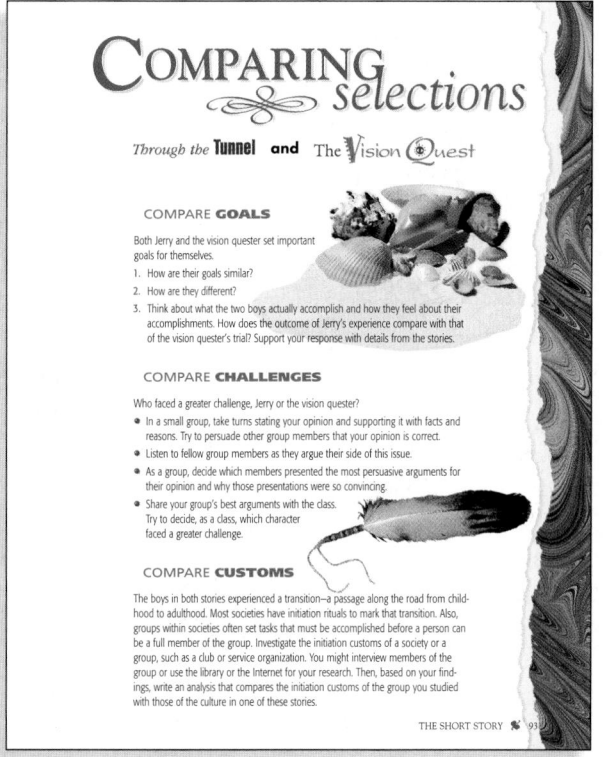

Comparing Selections Once in each theme, a Comparing Selections page presents options for comparing two selections through writing, discussions, and one of many other engaging activities.

Features

(Continued)

Skills Features offer students opportunities to develop key language arts skills in the context of the literature they are reading. Features include

- ❧ *Vocabulary Skills*
- ❧ *Listening, Speaking, and Viewing*
- ❧ *Reading & Thinking Skills*
- ❧ *Writing Skills*
- ❧ *Grammar Link*

Technology Skills features enrich students' experience of literature through specific applications such as word processing, multimedia, databases, E-mail, and the Internet. In Course 5, for example, students learn how to create hypertext documents and to use E-mail for research.

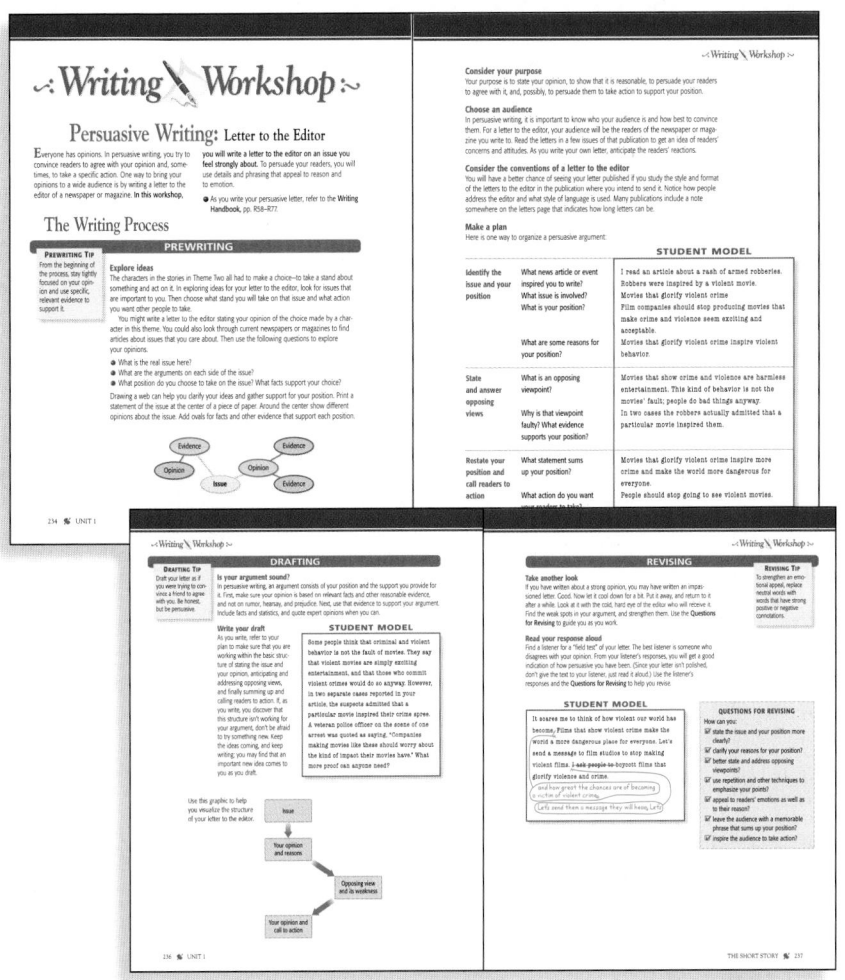

Writing Workshop at the end of each theme engages students in creating an extended piece of writing related to the theme or a specific selection within the theme. Models, strategies, and tips help students develop their writing through the stages of prewriting, drafting, revising, editing/proofreading, and publishing/presenting.

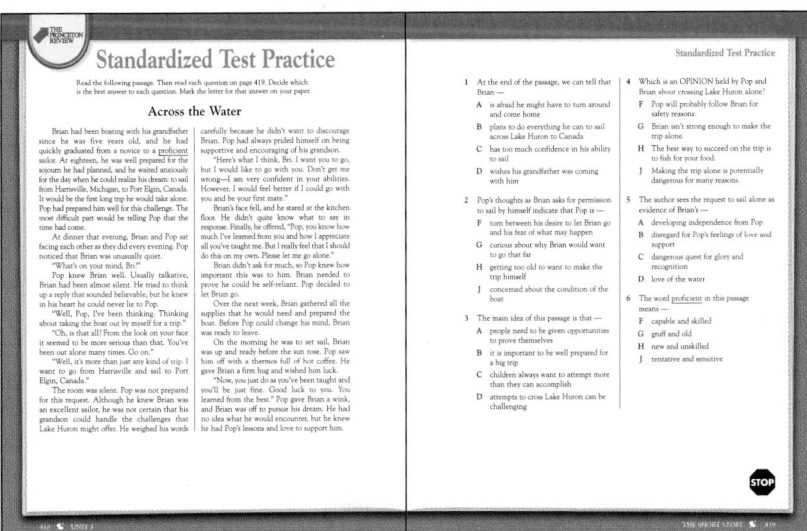

Standardized Test Practice at the end of each unit gives students practice with the types of reading and writing test formats used in many standardized tests.

Unit Support

UNIT AT A GLANCE

These four pages precede each unit of the Student Edition, providing a clear overview of the organization of the unit.

Unit One At a Glance
The Short Story

UNIT OPENING	Theme 1: MATTERS OF LIFE AND DEATH	Theme 2: FILLING A VOID	Theme 3: LOOKING BACK	UNIT WRAP-UP

UNIT OPENING
- Genre Focus: The Short Story (p. 2)
- Active Reading Strategies (p. 4)
- Active Reading Model: *The Gift of the Magi* (p. 6)

Theme 1: MATTERS OF LIFE AND DEATH

SELECTIONS
- The Open Window (p. 18)
- Before the End of Summer (p. 24)
- Media Connection: Editorials (p. 42)
- The Lady, or the Tiger? (p. 44)
- The Leap (p. 56)
- The Most Dangerous Game (p. 66)
- The Cask of Amontillado (p. 86)
- Media Connection: Magazine Articles (p. 96)
- Blues Ain't No Mockin Bird (p. 97)

SKILL FEATURES
- Writing Skills (p. 41)
- Interdisciplinary Connection (p. 54)
- Reading and Thinking Skills (p. 55)
- Comparing Selections (p. 94)
- Vocabulary Skills (p. 95)
- Grammar Link (p. 107)

WRITING WORKSHOP
- Personal Writing: Responding to a Short Story (p. 108)

Theme 2: FILLING A VOID

SELECTIONS
- Media Connection: Comic Strip (p. 114)
- The Secret Life of Walter Mitty (p. 115)
- Media Connection: Web Site (p. 125)
- Gaston (p. 126)
- And Sarah Laughed (p. 134)
- Elena (p. 150)
- American History (p. 155)
- The Necklace (p. 168)
- The Winner (p. 180)

SKILL FEATURES
- Grammar Link (p. 124)
- Comparing Selections (p. 153)
- Writing Skills (p. 154)
- Technology Skills (p. 166)
- Interdisciplinary Connection (p. 179)

WRITING WORKSHOP
- Descriptive Writing: Character Study (p. 192)

Theme 3: LOOKING BACK

SELECTIONS
- The Bass, the River, and Sheila Mant (p. 198)
- Media Connection: Magazine Article (p. 210)
- Sweet Potato Pie (p. 211)
- Rules of the Game (p. 224)
- The Child is the Master (p. 236)
- The Horned Toad (p. 244)
- Media Connection: Newspaper Column (p. 255)
- The Scarlet Ibis (p. 256)

SKILL FEATURES
- Vocabulary Skills (p. 209)
- Reading and Thinking Skills (p. 223)
- Comparing Selections (p. 242)
- Listening, Speaking, and Viewing (p. 243)

WRITING WORKSHOP
- Narrative Writing: Short Story (p. 270)

UNIT WRAP-UP
- Personal Response, Analyzing Literature, Evaluate and Set Goals (p. 274)
- Build Your Portfolio (p. 274)
- Reading on Your Own (p. 275)
  A Separate Peace by John Knowles
  Great Expectations by Charles Dickens
  Lord of the Flies by William Golding
  A Place Where the Sea Remembers by Sandra Benitez

KEYS TO LITERARY CONNECTIONS

World Literature
Glencoe Literature contains a variety of literature that represents cultures from around the world. World literature selections are highlighted with this symbol.

Comparing Selections
In each theme of Glencoe Literature, the Comparing Selections feature gives students an opportunity to compare two selections they have just read. Each Comparing Selections page provides a variety of options to address diverse aspects of the reading and literature curriculum.

KEYS TO TEACHING OPTIONS

Block Scheduling
Activities that are particularly suited to use within a block scheduling framework are identified throughout this unit by the following designation. For detailed suggestions on block scheduling, see the Block Scheduling Guide for this grade level.

Key to Ability Levels
The Teaching Options throughout this unit have been coded for students of various abilities.
L1 **BASIC** activities for all students
L2 **AVERAGE** activities for average to above-average students
L3 **CHALLENGING** activities for above-average students

1A UNIT 1

Unit One At a Glance
The Short Story

Reading Skills in this unit

Variety of Texts
In addition to numerous stories by authors from the United States and several other nations, this unit also includes the following text types:
- poetry
- editorial
- magazine article
- comic strip
- Web site
- newspaper column

Comprehension Skills
The following instructional support for comprehending skills appears in this unit of the Student Edition:
- Active Reading Strategies and Model (pp. 4–16)
- Making Inferences (p. 55)
- Comparing and Contrasting (p. 223)
- Reading and Thinking Minilessons (pp. 16, 40, 53, 106, 123, 149, 165, 178, 191, 208, 222, 254)

See also the Reading Minilessons throughout this unit in this Teacher's Wraparound Edition.

Reading Resources

Comprehension Skills Resources

Active Reading Guides
The Active Reading Guide provides graphic organizers and study guide questions to support students' reading of each selection. (Active Reading Guide, pp. 1–21)

Reading Workbook
The Reading Workbook (pp. 1–34) includes additional instruction and reinforcement of reading strategies and skills.

Audio Library
Available both on tape and on CD, the Audio Library provides valuable comprehension support.

Resources for Reading Widely

Glencoe Literature Library
Each title in the Glencoe Literature Library includes a full-length novel or play plus related readings. A separate Study Guide is available for each title.

Literature Classics CD-ROM
The 900 selections on this CD-ROM can be searched by author, theme, or genre.

inTIME
A coproduction of Glencoe and Time Inc., inTime includes a wealth of high-interest nonfiction related to the selections and themes in Unit One.

Writing Skills in this unit

Writing Skills
The Student Edition of Unit One offers strong instructional support for writing skills:

In Extending Your Response, which follows each selection:
- Writing About Literature
- Personal/Creative Writing

In Writing Skills Lessons:
- Main Idea and Supporting Details (p. 41)
- Using Elaboration (p. 154)

See also the Writing Minilessons throughout this unit in this Teacher's Wraparound Edition.

Writing Workshops
Each of the three themes in Unit One concludes with a Writing Workshop that guides students through the writing process.
- Personal Writing: Responding to a Short Story (pp. 108–112)
- Descriptive Writing: Character Study (pp. 192–196)
- Narrative Writing: Short Story (pp. 270–273)

Writing Resources

Writer's Assistant CD-ROM
Each Writing Workshop is supplemented by an interactive writing guide on the Writer's Assistant CD-ROM. This easy-to-use writing guide provides prompts, templates, and other tools that lead students through the writing process.

Writing and Proofreading Practice
Blackline masters present in-depth instruction and practice on a specific step in the writing process and proofreading. (pp. 1–27)

Writing and Proofreading Transparencies
Transparencies (1–12, 33–38) provide graphic organizers and proofreading exercises for whole class instruction.

Research and Report Writing Guide
This resource provides extensive tips and activities to guide students in their writing projects in the literature classroom as well as in classes across the curriculum.

Style and Documentation Sourcebook for Writers
This sourcebook is a combination reference and workbook, giving students the most up-to-date information and guidance regarding traditional as well as technological research strategies and documentation.

Grammar and Composition Handbook
The Grammar and Composition Handbook provides instruction that supplements activities in the student textbook.

Assessment in this unit

Assessment Options in the Student Edition
Glencoe Literature offers a number of diverse ways to evaluate student understanding and skill proficiency. In the Student Edition, use the following:
- **Responding to Literature**
Following each selection, students are asked to recall facts, interpret ideas, and evaluate concepts as they answer a variety of questions and complete activities to extend their understanding.
- **Unit Wrap-Up** (pp. 274–275)
Here students respond to the selections on personal and analytical levels. They also assume ownership of their learning by setting and evaluating goals and by selecting work for their portfolios.

See also the many Assessment Resources listed on the facing page.

THE PRINCETON REVIEW

Standardized Test Practice
The Princeton Review has developed the Standardized Test Practice pages found at the end of this unit (pp. 276–277). These pages contain practice test questions that help students remain familiar with standardized test formats and content.

Assessment Resources

Selection Quick Checks
For each selection, a Quick Check of three to five short-answer questions measures students' literal comprehension.

Selection and Theme Assessment
The Selection and Theme Assessment instrument tests students' abilities to recall, interpret, and evaluate what they've read. The tests consist of multiple-choice, short answer, and essay questions.

Performance Assessment
Alternative assessment instruments and rubrics for Unit One are found in the Performance Assessment ancillary.

Writing Assessment and Portfolio Management
These notes and strategies, student models, and assessment tools assist with the task of measuring students' progress as writers and as monitors of their own writing.

Testmaker
Teachers can customize selection, theme, and Unit One tests by accessing the Testmaker database.

MindJogger Videoquizzes
Using a popular game show format, MindJogger Videoquizzes enable teachers to evaluate students' understanding of Unit One in a quick and fun manner.

The second spread provides a detailed look at the reading skills, writing skills, and assessment options available.

Theme Support

THEME SKILLS SCOPE AND SEQUENCE

At the beginning of each new theme, this comprehensive chart shows a
selection-by-selection listing of the skill development and activities provided
in the Student Edition and Teacher's Wraparound Edition.

THEME RESOURCE MANAGER

The Theme Resource Manager simplifies classroom management and planning. A tremendous resource in itself, this chart makes it easy to see what print resources, transparencies, and technology resources are available for each selection in the theme. Planning was never so easy!

Selection Support

Comprehensive point-of-use notes and strategies provide effective, inclusive instructional support to help students get into, through, and beyond their reading of the literature.

BEFORE READING

Optional activities for motivating students and a list of all program resources get each lesson off to a solid start.

Objectives and Skills Teaching objectives and skill strands help you see at a glance the skills taught in the lesson.

Motivating Options Choose from a menu of options to engage your students' interest in the selection:

- ❧ **Literature Launchers** are short, high-interest video segments, available on videodisc or VHS.
- ❧ **Selection Focus Transparencies** pique students' interest and get them thinking about ideas such as the theme, the topic, or the setting of the selection.
- ❧ **Focus Activities** offer options to expand or extend the Focus Activity in the SE.

Resource Manager This handy chart gives a complete listing of teacher's classroom resources to use to teach, reinforce, extend, and assess the lesson. These print, transparency, and technology resources allow you to customize to accommodate your own classroom needs and teaching style.

READING THE SELECTION

Core notes and teaching options offer a wealth of interactive instructional support.

Summary This note provides a brief overview of each prose selection.

Core Notes Point-of-use notes and strategies in the side column provide instructional aid keyed to specific passages in the text. Core notes include
- *Active Reading*
- *Critical Thinking*
- *Literary Elements*
- *Author's Craft*

Reading the Selection

SUMMARY

Elena wants desperately to be friends with Eugene, who lives in the house next to her tenement building. Both teens are studious and outcast in their bleak public school. Though Eugene is friendly to Elena, his mother blocks them from studying together and makes it clear that race is the problem.

📖 *Spanish Summaries*, p. 13

Active Reading

CONNECT Have students recall times when they have been cold or uncomfortable or among unfriendly people. Students should be able to relate to Elena's misery in this physically and psychologically cold environment.

Additional Resources
- 📖 *Active Reading Guide*, p. 13
- 🎧 *Audio Library*
- 🎧 *Spanish Audio Library*

Teaching Options

American History

Judith Ortiz Cofer

I ONCE READ IN A *RIPLEY'S BELIEVE IT OR NOT* column that Paterson, New Jersey, is the place where the Straight and Narrow (streets) intersect. The Puerto Rican tenement known as El Building was one block up from Straight. It was, in fact, the corner of Straight and Market; not "at" the corner, but the corner.

At almost any hour of the day, El Building was like a monstrous jukebox, blasting out *salsas*[1] from open windows as the residents, mostly new immigrants just up from the island, tried to drown out whatever they were currently enduring with loud music. But the day President Kennedy was shot, there was a profound silence in El Building; even the abusive tongues of *viragoes*,[2] the cursing of the unemployed, and the screeching of small children had been somehow muted. President Kennedy was a saint to these people. In fact, soon his photograph would be hung alongside the Sacred Heart and over the spiritist altars that many women kept in their apartments. He would become part of the hierarchy of martyrs[3] they prayed to for favors that only one who had died for a cause could understand.

On the day that President Kennedy was shot, my ninth grade class had been out in the fenced playground of the Public School Number 13. We had been given "free" exercise time and had been ordered by our P.E. teacher, Mr. DePalma, to "keep moving." That meant that the girls should jump rope and the boys toss basketballs through a hoop at the far end of the yard. He in the meantime would "keep an eye" on us from just inside the building.

It was a cold gray day in Paterson. The kind that warns of early snow. I was miserable, since I had forgotten my gloves and my knuckles were turning red and raw from the jump rope. I was also taking a lot of abuse from the black girls for not turning the rope hard and fast enough for them.

"Hey, Skinny Bones, pump it, girl. Ain't you got no energy today?" Gail, the biggest of the black girls who had the other end of the rope yelled, "Didn't you eat your rice and beans and pork chops for breakfast today?"

---

1. *Salsas* are Latin American dance tunes.
2. *Viragoes* (vi rä′ gōz) are bad-tempered, scolding women who, here, use coarse or insulting *(abusive)* language.
3. The *hierarchy* (hī′ ə rär′ kē) of *martyrs* (mär′ tərz) is the ranking of those who have suffered or died for their religion.

Vocabulary
profound (prə found′) *adj.* significant; deep; intense

156 📖 UNIT 1

The other girls picked up the "pork chop" and made it into a refrain: "pork chop, pork chop, did you eat your pork chop?" They entered the double ropes in pairs and exited without tripping or missing a beat. I felt a burning on my cheeks, and then my glasses fogged up so that I could not manage to coordinate the jump rope with Gail. The chill was doing to me what it always did, entering my bones, making me cry, humiliating me. I hated the city, especially in winter. I hated Public School Number 13. I hated my skinny flat-chested body, and I envied the black girls who could jump rope so fast that their legs became a blur. They always seemed to be warm while I froze.

There was only one source of beauty and light for me that school year. The only thing I had anticipated at the start of the semester. That was seeing Eugene. In August, Eugene and his family had moved into the only house on the block with a yard and trees. I could see his place from my window in El Building. In fact, if I sat on the fire escape I was literally suspended above Eugene's backyard. It was my favorite spot to read my library books in the summer. Until that August the house had been occupied by an old Jewish couple. Over the years I had become part of their family, without their knowing it, of course. I had a view of their kitchen and their backyard, and though I could not hear what they said, I knew when they were arguing, when one of them was sick, and many other things. I knew all this by watching them at mealtimes. I could see their kitchen table, the sink and the stove. During good times, he sat at the table and read his newspapers while she fixed the meals. If they argued, he would leave and the old woman would sit and stare at nothing for a long time. When one of them was sick, the other would come and get things from the kitchen and carry them out on a tray. The old man had died in June. The last week of school I had not seen him at the table at all. Then one day I saw that there was a crowd in the kitchen. The old woman had finally emerged from the house on the arm of a stocky middle-aged woman whom I had seen there a few times before, maybe her daughter. Then a man had carried out suitcases. The house had stood empty for weeks. I had had to resist the temptation to climb down into the yard and water the flowers the old lady had taken such good care of.

THE SHORT STORY 📖 157

☐ Literary Elements
MAJOR CHARACTER Ask students to list physical and emotional character traits of Elena they learn in this paragraph. *(She wears glasses, and she is thinner and less developed than the other girls. She feels humiliated by them.)*

☐ Active Reading
VISUALIZE Have students sketch the tenement, fire escape, and Eugene's house and yard as they perceive them after reading the scene. Discuss how close the buildings must be and why they think Elena feels compelled to watch the neighbors.

☐ Literary Elements
MAJOR CHARACTER Ask students to summarize what they learn about Elena from this glimpse into her inner life. Why does she read and put herself into the lives of her neighbors? *(That is how she escapes from a reality that is too harsh.)*

Did You Know?
A fire escape is a fireproof stairway attached to an outside wall of a building.

CONNECTING TO OTHER SELECTIONS

The chart at the right shows three ways to connect "American History" to other selections in this book.

For specific teaching strategies, see the *Unit One Planning*.

Connection	Title
Life Skills: Planning and Designing	"A Christmas Memory," p. 405
Thematic: In the Face of Adversity	"Only Daughter," p. 314
Literary: Character	*The Miracle Worker*, p. 708

156 📖 UNIT 1

MEETING INDIVIDUAL NEEDS · ENGLISH LANGUAGE LEARNERS

Understanding Connotation Invite English language learners to discuss what they think Elena might be feeling. Why do students think Elena is nicknamed Skinny Bones? What does it mean? Do they think this is an insulting nickname or a kind one? Explain that this word has a *negative* connotation, a negative meaning that is implied. Other words may have *positive* connotations.

Activity As students continue to read, ask them to consider the connotation of expressions and of stylistic conventions such as the use of quotes around "a conference" on page 160. Invite pairs of students to identify other examples.

Additional Resources
📖 *English Language Learners Sourcebook*

THE SHORT STORY 📖 157

Teaching Options A wide range of teaching options in the bottom channel allow you to customize lessons to accommodate your students' individual needs and your own teaching preferences.

Connecting to Other Selections suggests three options for pairing the selection with another selection in the anthology.

Meeting Individual Needs These activities provide options to meet the needs of all your students, including
- English Language Learners
- Less-Proficient Readers
- Students with Special Needs

READING THE SELECTION (Continued)

Viewing Notes provide background information about the art or artist plus an answer to the student Viewing question.

Models that appear with many Critical Thinking and Active Reading notes serve as a tool for modeling thinking and reading strategies for students.

VIEWING THE ART

This earthenware was low-fired (at about 900°F instead of a more typical temperature of about 2,800°F), a process that produces a porous vessel. It was then burnished, or rubbed hard with an object such as a smooth stone or a spoon, to give it a finished look.

Viewing Response The building seems to burst off the confines of the vessel, giving the same crowded feeling as the tenement in the story.

Green Rooftscape Vessel, 1986. Lydia Buzio. Burnished earthenware, 19 × 12½ in. Collection of Glawn Bennett & Martin J. Davidson.

Viewing the art: How well does this artwork capture the setting of "American History"? Explain.

Literary Elements

MINOR CHARACTER Invite students to describe Eugene and explain how his appearance advances the plot. Students should note what he and Elena have in common, and how their habit of watching the life in the house progresses to a fantasy friendship with the boy.

Literary Elements

MAJOR AND MINOR CHARACTERS The initial meeting between Elena and Eugene helps flesh out his character and advance the plot. Have students describe him and explain what they think will happen between the two characters.

Critical Thinking

EVALUATING Help students evaluate what is revealed by Elena's continuing to watch Eugene at night. Use this model to illustrate evaluating.

Model: I know that Elena watched the old couple secretly and felt she was a part of their lives. I also know that Elena thinks of Eugene as being like her. Even though he has become a friend, she still depends on this "secret sharing." Why doesn't she tell Eugene? I think she must be unsure how real his friendship is. Because she fears rejection, she is unwilling to lose this fantasy that helps make her life more bearable.

Literary Elements

MINOR CHARACTER The mother's vigilance and criticism set her up as the antagonist of Elena and her "love." Have students draw the parallels between mother and daughter. *(They are both unhappy in Paterson and cling to dreams, which Elena ironically calls "fairy tales," never seeing her own infatuation as the same.)*

Active Reading

QUESTION Why does Elena like it that Eugene is also friendless and scorned? *(He will have time to spend with her, and it gives them a common bond.)*

Teaching Options

Writing *Minilesson*

Repetition for Effect Read aloud the passage on page 157 beginning "I felt a burning" and ending "while I froze." Then have students point out where repetition occurs. Ask them to explain the effect of repeating "I hated . . ." *(It emphasizes the strength of her emotion.)* Remind students that intentional repetition can build mood and underscore meaning. Unintentionally

overused, it makes writing weak and boring.

Activity Have students use one of the following writing prompts to write a paragraph using repetition for effect.
1. The lecture was boring.
2. My _____ defines the word cool.
3. The wind never seems to stop.

Suggest that students first brainstorm key phrases and words. Have them exchange their drafts with a partner and give feedback about where repetition is effective. Ask students to read their revised paragraphs aloud in class. **L3**

Additional Resources
Writer's Choice, Lesson 2.8

REAL-WORLD CONNECTION

Puerto Ricans Have students use a variety of sources to learn about Puerto Ricans and their contributions in the United States today. Some questions to guide research might include these: How many Puerto Ricans live in the 48 contiguous United States? Where do they live? What is their average level of earnings and education? Who are some Puerto Rican men and women who have become famous? **L2**

LITERATURE & HUMANITIES

Display *George Washington*, U.S. History and Art Transparency 8. Ask students why this unrealistic depiction of the first president of the U.S. might be fitting for this story.

THE SHORT STORY 159

Teaching Options

Reading *Minilesson*

Identifying Cause-and-Effect Relationships Explain that a cause is why something happened and an effect is what happened—the result. Point out that a cause can lead to an effect, which itself can then be the cause of another effect, and so on.

Activity Have small groups of students construct chains of causes and effects

using events from the story. Here are two possible starters:
1. Elena watches the new people in the little house.
2. Elena approaches Eugene directly.

Point out that students can build their chains by taking one of the sentences,

adding because to the beginning, naming an effect, then adding because to the beginning of the effect, and so on. **L2**

Additional Resources
Reading Workbook, p. 20

INCLUSION STRATEGIES

Less-Proficient Readers Page 161 contains many words about emotions. Students can relate to the climax of the story if they understand them in a familiar context.

Activity List the following words on the board and have students define each using a dictionary: elation, distraught, disbelief, hope, humiliation.

Have them recall specific incidents when they felt these emotions and then make up a sentence using each in a context that suggests this meaning. **L2**

Additional Resources
Inclusion Strategies

THE SHORT STORY 161

Minilessons provide regular opportunities for integrated language arts instruction in
- Writing
- Reading
- Grammar and Language
- Listening and Speaking

Connections activities relate the selection to another discipline or to the students' lives:
- Real-World Connections
- Interdisciplinary Connections
- Internet Connections
- Life Skills Connections

Literature & Humanities notes suggest activities using Glencoe humanities materials to enrich the study of the literature.

RESPONDING TO LITERATURE

Suggested answers and evaluation guidelines provide rubrics for thoughtful assessment of students' understanding of the selection.

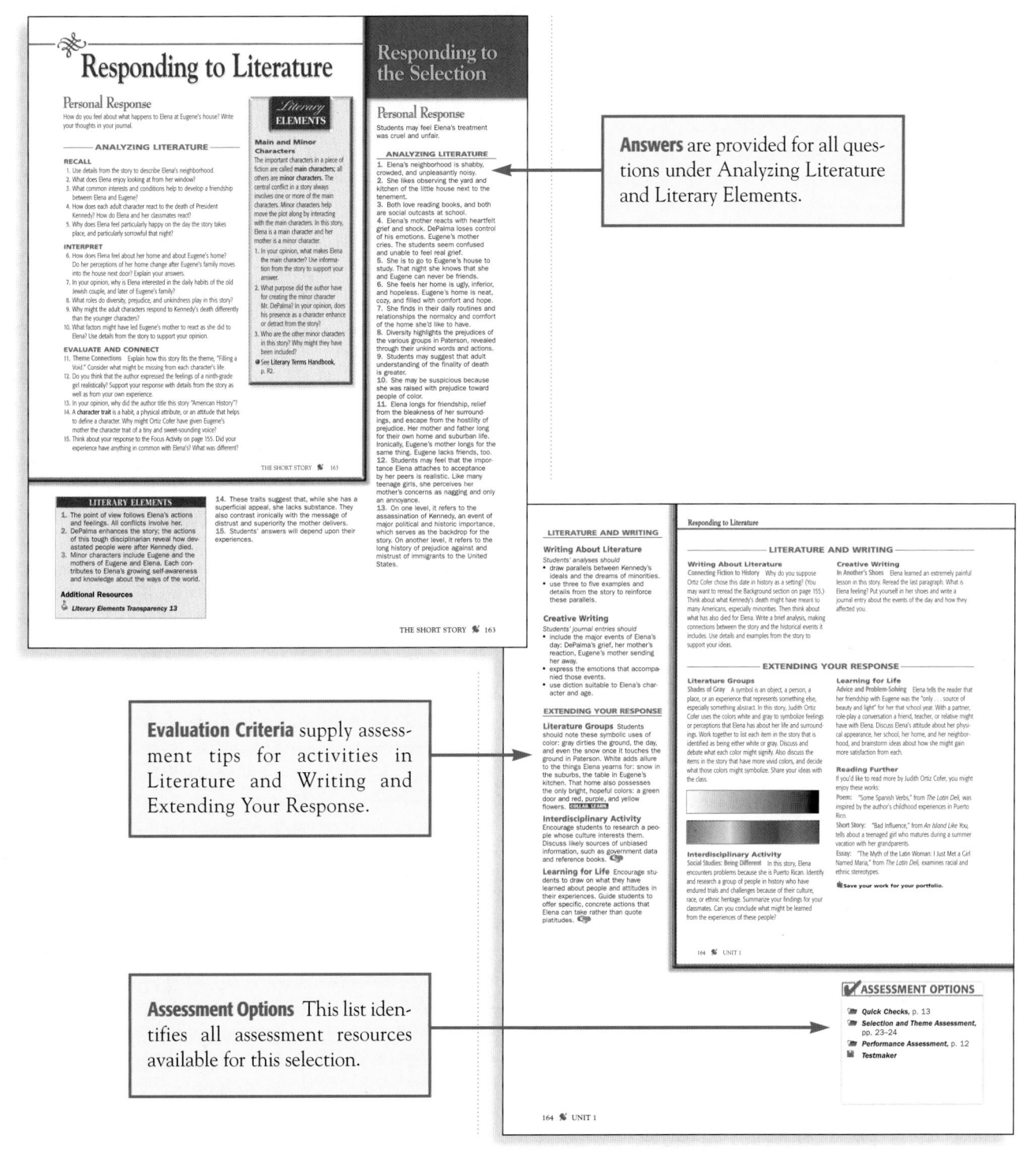

Answers are provided for all questions under Analyzing Literature and Literary Elements.

Evaluation Criteria supply assessment tips for activities in Literature and Writing and Extending Your Response.

Assessment Options This list identifies all assessment resources available for this selection.

Unit Planning Guide

The Unit Planning Guide is an invaluable companion to the Teacher's Wraparound Edition. This easy-to-use sourcebook provides

❧ *additional background and teaching tips*
❧ *detailed lesson plans*
❧ *at-a-glance access to all print and transparency resources*

UNIT OVERVIEW

This section offers additional background information and notes about the content and structure of the unit including

❧ information about the artist whose work is featured on the unit opener in the Student Edition
❧ suggestions for using the quote on the opener as a point of entry into discussion about the unit

Teacher's Wraparound Edition

Unit One Planning Guide

THEME INTRODUCTION

The theme introduction elaborates on the notes in the TWE, giving assessment rubrics for the theme projects as well as a suggested Extra Credit Project.

Theme Resources

Reproductions of print and transparency resources show at a glance what is available for use with this theme to make planning that much easier.

PROGRAM RESOURCES

LESSON PLAN

A detailed, reproducible lesson plan helps you organize and customize each lesson to your needs.

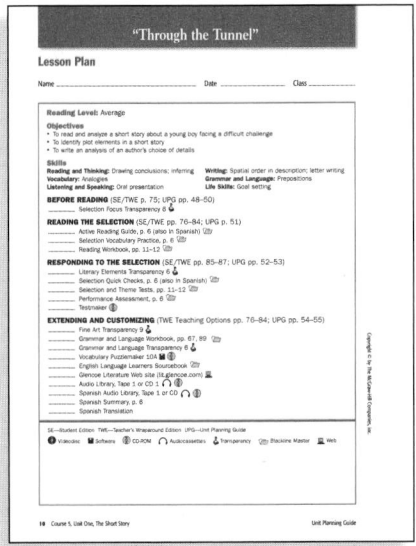

LESSON NOTES

These easy-to-use, yet comprehensive, strategies are organized to parallel the TWE plan of (1) Before Reading, (2) Reading the Selection, and (3) Responding to the Selection. Special features include

Motivating Options

These teaching tips support the use of each of the Motivating Options that appear on the Before Reading page of the TWE.

Connecting to Other Selections

Here you'll find a complete lesson plan for each of the connecting options listed in the TWE. You choose the approach—life skills, thematic, literary, or interdisciplinary.

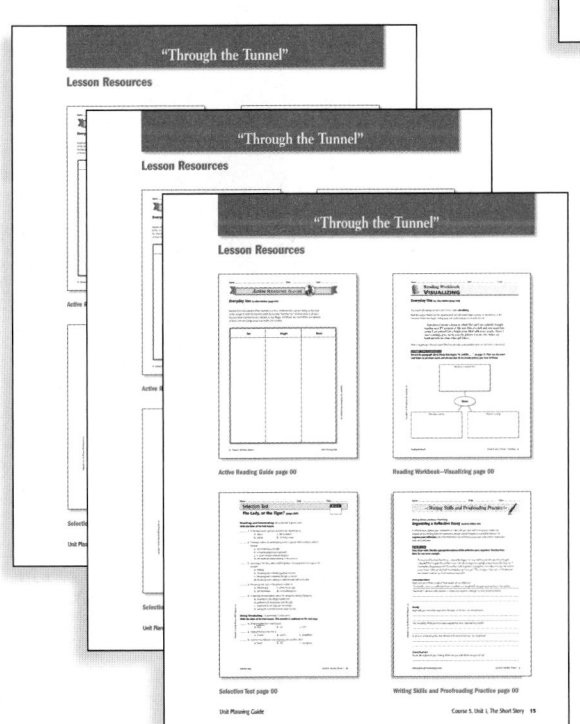

LESSON RESOURCES

Reproductions of lesson-specific print and transparency resources allow you to see quickly what is available, saving valuable planning time.

Glencoe Literature Library

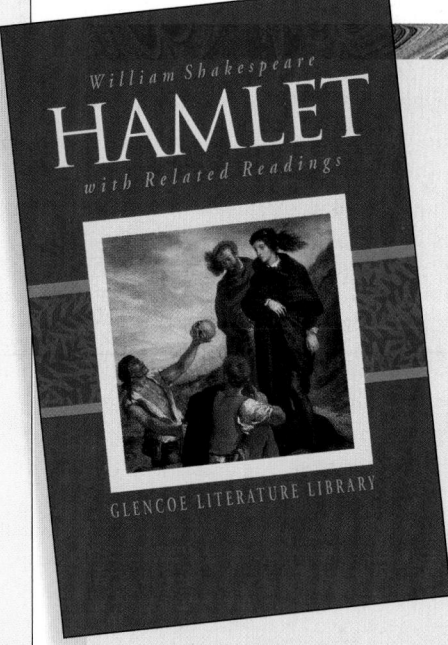

Novels and Plays~
with Related Readings

This collection of hardcover books allows you to extend the study of literature to your choice of full-length novels and plays. Each Literature Library book consists of a complete novel or play accompanied by several related readings, such as short stories, poems, essays, or informational articles.

Related Readings for *Hamlet*
- The Management of Grief • short story by Bharati Mukherjee
- Of Revenge • essay by Francis Bacon
- On the Meaning of *Hamlet* • essay by George Wilson Knight
- The Elizabethan Approach • essay by Martin Holmes
- To Be or Not To Be • parody by H. R. H. Charles, Prince of Wales
- The Character of Hamlet's Mother • essay by Caroline Heilbrun

The Adventures of Huckleberry Finn
BY MARK TWAIN

All Quiet on the Western Front
BY ERICH MARIA REMARQUE

And the Earth Did Not Devour Him
BY TOMÁS RIVERA

Annie John
BY JAMAICA KINCAID

Animal Farm
BY GEORGE ORWELL

The Autobiography of Benjamin Franklin
BY BENJAMIN FRANKLIN

The Autobiography of Miss Jane Pittman
BY ERNEST GAINES

The Brothers Karamazov
BY FYODOR DOSTOEVSKY

The Chosen
BY CHAIM POTOK

Cyrano de Bergerac
BY EDMOND ROSTAND

Frankenstein
BY MARY SHELLEY

Great Expectations
BY CHARLES DICKENS

Hamlet
BY WILLIAM SHAKESPEARE

A House for Mr. Biswas
BY V. S. NAIPAUL

Jane Eyre
BY CHARLOTTE BRONTË

The Metamorphosis
BY FRANZ KAFKA

A Midsummer Night's Dream
BY WILLIAM SHAKESPEARE

My Ántonia
BY WILLA CATHER

Study Guides ~

A separate Study Guide for each title in the Glencoe Literature Library provides teaching notes and reproducible activity pages for students.

Nectar in a Sieve
BY KAMALA MARKANDAYA

Night
BY ELIE WIESEL

One Day in the Life of Ivan Denisovich
BY ALEXANDER SOLZHENITSYN

Picture Bride
BY YOSHIKO UCHIDA

Pride and Prejudice
BY JANE AUSTEN

The Red Badge of Courage
BY STEPHEN CRANE

The Scarlet Letter
BY NATHANIEL HAWTHORNE

A Separate Peace
BY JOHN KNOWLES

The Strange Case of Dr. Jekyll and Mr. Hyde
BY ROBERT LOUIS STEVENSON

A Tale of Two Cities
BY CHARLES DICKENS

The Tempest
BY WILLIAM SHAKESPEARE

To Kill a Mockingbird
BY HARPER LEE

Wuthering Heights
BY EMILY BRONTË

The Yearling
BY MARJORIE KINNAN RAWLINGS

For the Teacher
❧ Synopsis
❧ Media links
❧ Teaching options
❧ Answer key

For the Student
❧ Background information
❧ Active reading guides
❧ Response activities
❧ Test

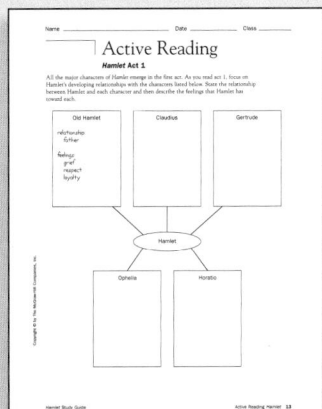

Active Reading pages include graphic organizers for students to complete as they read.

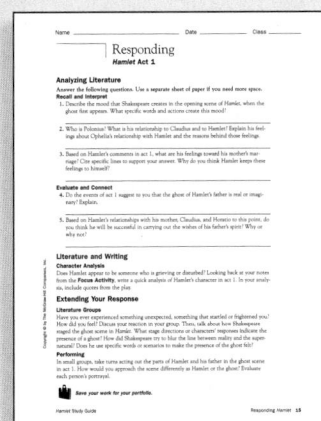

Responding pages include options for personal response, analyzing literature, and extending responses through writing and other activities.

Print Resources

Glencoe Literature has all the print resources you need to meet the needs of today's diverse classroom—and to save you valuable time.

Reading Resources
- Active Reading Guide
- inTime
- Literature Groups Sourcebook
- Media Connections Activities
- Reading Workbook

Language Arts Integration
- Critical Thinking Skills
- Grammar and Composition Handbook
- Grammar and Language Workbook
- Interdisciplinary Activities
- Language Arts Guide to the Internet and Other Electronic Resources
- Listening and Speaking Activities
- Research and Report Writing
- Selection Vocabulary Practice
- Spelling Power
- Style and Documentation Guide for Writers
- Viewing and Representing Activities
- Vocabulary Power
- Writing and Proofreading Practice

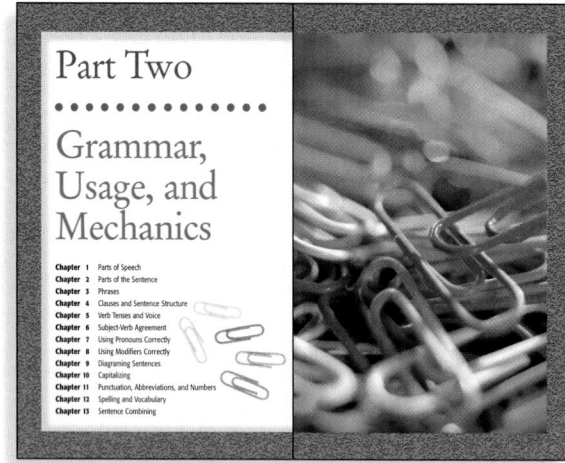

Grammar and Composition Handbook

Teacher Management
- Block Scheduling Guide
- Unit Planning Guide

Meeting Individual Needs
- English Language Learners Sourcebook
- Inclusion Strategies Sourcebook

Spanish Resources
- Spanish Summaries
- Spanish Translations
- Active Reading Guide in Spanish
- Selection Quick Checks in Spanish

Assessment Resources

- Selection and Theme Assessment
- Selection Quick Checks
- Performance Assessment
- Writing Assessment and Portfolio Management

THE PRINCETON REVIEW

The Princeton Review, the nation's leading test preparation firm, has developed the following assessment resources for *Glencoe Literature:*

- TerraNova Preparation and Practice
- SAT-9 Preparation and Practice
- ITBS Preparation and Practice

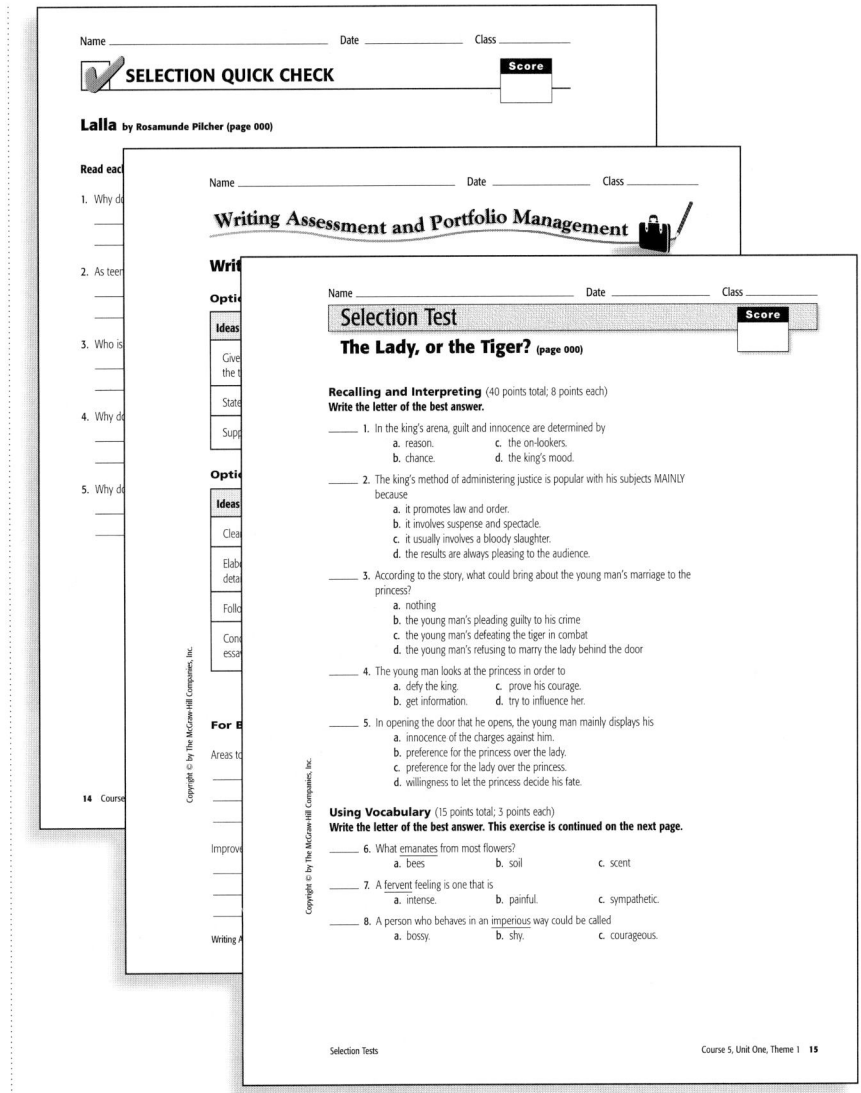

Name _____ Date _____ Class _____

SELECTION QUICK CHECK

Score

Lalla by Rosamunde Pilcher (page 000)

Read each...

1. Why do...

2. As teen...

3. Who is...

4. Why do...

5. Why do...

Name _____ Date _____ Class _____

Writing Assessment and Portfolio Management

Writ...

Option...

Ideas		
Give...		
State...		
Supp...		

Option...

Ideas		
Clea...		
Elabo... detai...		
Follo...		
Conc... essay...		

For E...

Areas to...

Improve...

Writing A...

14 Course...

Copyright © by The McGraw-Hill Companies, Inc.

Name _____ Date _____ Class _____

Selection Test

Score

The Lady, or the Tiger? (page 000)

Recalling and Interpreting (40 points total; 8 points each)
Write the letter of the best answer.

____ 1. In the king's arena, guilt and innocence are determined by
   a. reason.   c. the on-lookers.
   b. chance.   d. the king's mood.

____ 2. The king's method of administering justice is popular with his subjects MAINLY because
   a. it promotes law and order.
   b. it involves suspense and spectacle.
   c. it usually involves a bloody slaughter.
   d. the results are always pleasing to the audience.

____ 3. According to the story, what could bring about the young man's marriage to the princess?
   a. nothing
   b. the young man's pleading guilty to his crime
   c. the young man's defeating the tiger in combat
   d. the young man's refusing to marry the lady behind the door

____ 4. The young man looks at the princess in order to
   a. defy the king.   c. prove his courage.
   b. get information.   d. try to influence her.

____ 5. In opening the door that he opens, the young man mainly displays his
   a. innocence of the charges against him.
   b. preference for the princess over the lady.
   c. preference for the lady over the princess.
   d. willingness to let the princess decide his fate.

Using Vocabulary (15 points total; 3 points each)
Write the letter of the best answer. This exercise is continued on the next page.

____ 6. What emanates from most flowers?
   a. bees   b. soil   c. scent

____ 7. A fervent feeling is one that is
   a. intense.   b. painful.   c. sympathetic.

____ 8. A person who behaves in an imperious way could be called
   a. bossy.   b. shy.   c. courageous.

Selection Tests   Course 5, Unit One, Theme 1 15

Copyright © by The McGraw-Hill Companies, Inc.

FINE ART TRANSPARENCY 3

Personal Writing

Henry Ossawa Tanner, *The Ba...*

Context for Writing You have been invited to a f... the people attending are family members you know; o... you will meet for the very first time. You have been ask... ly member who helped to shape your life. This person... sonal attention and instruction, like the man in the pai... model. Your essay will be included in a book about the... future generations. Briefly describe a family member w... life or taught you something valuable. Then explain th... you learned.

Possible answers: Students will likely suggest the possibility of huge waves or tiredness overtaking swimmers, as well as menacing sea creatures.

LITERARY ELEMENTS TRANSPARENCY 12

The **plot,** or action of a story revolves around *conflict.*

- The **conflict** of the story is the problem that sets the plot in motion.
- The **climax,** or turning point, is the most exciting, interesting, or suspenseful moment in a story.
- The **resolution** of a story shows how the conflict is solved.

Analyze the plot of "Through the Tunnel."

Climax:

Jerry's conflicts:

Resolution:

Think of another selection you have read and identify the major conflict, the climax, and the resolution.

The Breakers, 19xx. Ken Danby. Oil on canvas, 000" x 000 The X Museum, Albany, N.Y.

...meone face swimming in these

Transparencies

Choose from a number of overhead transparencies to engage students and to reinforce and extend understanding.

- Selection Focus Transparencies
- Literary Elements Transparencies
- Grammar and Language Transparencies
- Writing and Proofreading Transparencies
- Fine Art Transparencies

Technology Resources

With *Glencoe Literature*, you can draw upon a wealth of audio, video, software, and Internet resources to help engage students' interest and enhance their experience of literature.

VIDEO RESOURCES

❧ **Literature Launchers** Short video segments that are motivating and engaging; available on videodisc or VHS tape

❧ **MindJogger Videoquizzes** One video quiz per unit, available on videodisc or VHS tape

❧ **Video Library** Collection of documentary and performance videos available on VHS tape

AUDIO RESOURCES

❧ **Audio Library** Literature selections available on audiotape or CD

❧ **Spanish Audio Library** Readings of many selections in Spanish available on audiotape or CD

Glencoe Literature Web Site lit.glencoe.com

On-line resources for you as well as for students and parents

Features include
❧ appropriate Web site links
❧ games and activities for lessons in the Student Edition
❧ state literary sites
❧ teacher-to-teacher exchange
❧ professional articles
❧ and much more!

Literature Classics CD-ROM

Title	Author	Year	Genre
Macbeth	William Hazlitt (1778-1830)	1817	Essay
from Macbeth, from On the Knocking at the Gate	Thomas De Quincey (1785-1859)	c. 1823	Essay
Madame Celestin's Divorce	Kate Chopin (1851-1904)	1894	Short Story
Madame, Withouten Many Words	Sir Thomas Wyatt (c. 1503-1542)	c. 1503-1542	Poetry
Maese Perez, the Organist	Gustavo Adolfo Becquer (1836-1870)	c. 1836-1870	Short Story
The Magna Carta	Anonymous	1215	Historical Document
from Magnalia Christi, Americana	Cotton Mather (1663-1728)	1702	Biography

Writer's Assistant

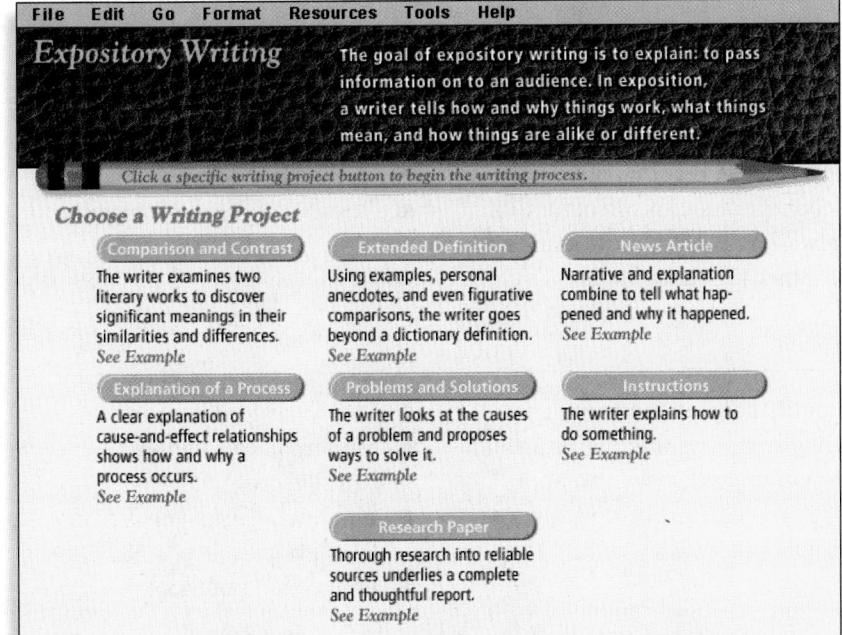

SOFTWARE

❧ **Literature Classics CD-ROM** More than 900 additional literature selections accessible by author, title, genre, theme, or date

❧ **Writer's Assistant** Easy-to-use, hands-on tools and templates to help students in all modes of writing

❧ **Presentation Plus** Dynamic multimedia PowerPoint® presentation tool

❧ **Testmaker** Editable electronic database of Selection and Theme Tests, with additional test items to customize your assessment to your needs

❧ **Vocabulary Puzzlemaker** Make vocabulary study fun with word searches based on selection vocabulary.

❧ **Language Arts Passkey™** Self-tutorial reading assistance for students

❧ **Electronic Teacher's Classroom Resources** All ancillary print resources available on CD-ROM

❧ **Interactive Grammar and Language Workbook**

Scope and Sequence Overview

Strand	Overview	Key Items for the Strand Student Edition
Literary Concepts and Techniques	Students develop knowledge of literary history and genres, analyze literary elements for their contribution to meaning in texts, and develop appreciation for aspects of writers' craft.	❧ Literary Elements ❧ Analyzing Literature ❧ Genre Focus ❧ Literature Focus ❧ Literary Terms Handbook
Reading and Thinking	Students develop proficiency with a full range of strategies and skills for comprehending a variety of texts and for thinking critically, creatively, and analytically.	❧ Active Reading Strategies ❧ Active Reading Models ❧ Reading and Thinking Skills ❧ Reading and Thinking Minilessons ❧ Reading Handbook
Writing	Students write in a variety of forms for various purposes and audiences, using a recursive writing process as appropriate. Students write to learn and to make personal connections to literature.	❧ Writing Workshops ❧ Writing Skills features ❧ Focus Activities ❧ Literature and Writing ❧ Extending Your Response ❧ Theme Projects ❧ Writing Handbook
Vocabulary and Spelling	Students build vocabulary through wide reading, attention to context clues and structural analysis, and use of dictionaries and other reference tools.	❧ Vocabulary Preview ❧ Vocabulary Minilessons ❧ Vocabulary Skills features
Grammar and Language	Students develop mastery of the conventions of grammar, usage, mechanics, and style, and apply these conventions in their own writing.	❧ Grammar Link features ❧ Grammar and Language Minilessons ❧ Grammar Hints (in Writing Workshops) ❧ Language Handbook

The charts on these and the following two pages provide an overview of the program scope and sequence for *Glencoe Literature*. For a detailed scope and sequence of skills for each Theme, see the Theme Skills Scope and Sequence chart that immediately follows each Theme Opener. See also the Index of Skills (pages R126–R136) for a comprehensive listing of all skills and concepts taught in this level of *Glencoe Literature*.

Key Items for the Strand **Teacher's Wraparound Edition**	Key Items for the Strand **Program Resources**
• Literary Elements sidenotes • Author's Craft sidenotes • Thematic Focus • Connecting to Other Selections	• Literary Elements Transparencies • Literature Classics CD-ROM • Literature Groups Sourcebook
• Active Reading sidenotes • Critical Thinking sidenotes • Reading Minilessons • Less Proficient Readers • English Language Learners	• Active Reading Guide • Reading Workbook • Critical Thinking Skills • Inclusion Strategies Sourcebook • English Language Learners Sourcebook • Language Arts Passkey
• Writing Minilessons • Meeting Individual Needs • Reading Journals	• Writing and Proofreading Activities • Writing and Proofreading Transparencies • Grammar and Composition Handbook • Writer's Assistant CD-ROM • Style and Documentation Sourcebook for Writers
• Vocabulary Skills sidenotes • English Language Learners	• Selection Vocabulary Practice • Vocabulary Power • Spelling Power • Vocabulary Puzzlemaker
• Grammar and Language Minilessons • Language Notes	• Grammar and Language Transparencies • Grammar and Language Workbook • Interactive Grammar and Language Workbook • Grammar and Composition Handbook

Continued on T52–T53

Scope and Sequence Overview

(Continued)

Strand	Overview	Key Items for the Strand Student Edition
Listening, Speaking, and Viewing	Students develop proficiency with skills of oral communication and visual literacy and apply them in a variety of contexts.	❧ Extending Your Response ❧ Theme Projects ❧ Focus Activities ❧ Literature Groups ❧ Image captions (for Viewing)
Life Skills	Within the context of literature study, students develop skills of problem solving, decision making, and collaboration. They also perform a variety of real-world reading and writing tasks.	❧ Learning for Life Activities (Extending Your Response) ❧ Theme Projects
Research and Study Skills	Students use reading and writing for inquiry and research and develop a variety of study and test-taking skills.	❧ Extending Your Response ❧ Reading Handbook ❧ Communications Skills Handbook ❧ Theme Projects ❧ Standardized Test Practice
Media and Technology	Students enhance their study of literature through the use of the Internet and other computer and media technologies.	❧ Internet Connections (Extending Your Response) ❧ Theme Projects ❧ Technology Skills
Interdisciplinary Studies	Students make frequent conceptual and thematic connections between literature and other fields of study.	❧ Interdisciplinary Connections ❧ Interdisciplinary Activities (Extending Your Response) ❧ Theme Projects

Key Items for the Strand **Teacher's Wraparound Edition**	Key Items for the Strand **Program Resources**
❧ Viewing the Painting sidenotes ❧ Listening and Speaking Minilessons	❧ Fine Art Transparencies ❧ Listening and Speaking Activities ❧ Viewing and Representing Activities ❧ Audio Library ❧ Video Library ❧ Literature Launchers
❧ Life Skills Connections ❧ Critical Thinking sidenotes ❧ Real-World Connections	❧ Critical Thinking Skills ❧ Unit Planning Guide (Life Skills Connections)
❧ Test-Taking Tips ❧ Multiple Learning Styles	❧ Research and Report Writing Guide ❧ Style and Documentation Sourcebook for Writers
❧ Technology Options ❧ Internet Connections ❧ Technology Tips	❧ Media Connections Activities ❧ Guide to Using the Internet and Other Electronic Resources ❧ Web Site (lit.glencoe.com) ❧ Writer's Assistant CD-ROM
❧ Interdisciplinary Connections ❧ Cultural Notes ❧ Historical Notes	❧ Interdisciplinary Activities ❧ Unit Planning Guide (Interdisciplinary Connections)

Program Philosophy

What are the goals of *Glencoe Literature*?

by Denny Wolfe

The impetus for *Glencoe Literature: The Reader's Choice* was the need for contemporary anthologies that would appeal to today's media-savvy students. A rich mix of classic and modern selections unites new and old voices chosen to represent our diverse communities. Each book's pages reflect a youthful energy, with color, images, media connections, interdisciplinary links, and quotations to enhance the featured literary works. The collection of poems and plays, stories and songs, letters and essays, myths and folklore enables teachers and students to explore together the literary legacies of many voices and many lands.

Glencoe Literature is particularly committed to supporting classroom teachers as they work
- to develop students' abilities as readers, writers, listeners, speakers, viewers, and critical and creative thinkers

- to guide students in developing interpretive skills that transcend specific literary voices, cultures, or times toward an understanding of the larger human experience
- to help students become life-long learners and responsible citizens for democracy in the twenty-first century

Through its varied and active instructional strategies, *Glencoe Literature* invites students to experience the entertaining and restorative powers of literature. Within this context students have frequent opportunities to
- engage in responsive reading, interpretation, and literary analysis through encounters with texts arranged by both theme and genre
- explore writing as a purposeful and flexible means of expression, reflection, and critical and creative thought
- use current and emerging technologies as tools for learning and extending the language arts
- participate in an approach to literacy development that integrates all the language arts
- experience multiple forms of assessment that are responsive to local, state, and national standards of achievement

Glencoe Literature prepares students for their literary encounters through prereading activities rooted in the experiences that students bring to texts. During and after the reading of a work, students respond personally to it; they share their responses with others; and they learn to probe ever more deeply into elements of the literary craft. This sequence enables students and teachers to create interpretive communities in their classrooms, to realize the highest standards of literary inquiry, and to participate vigorously in the cultural conversation of the twenty-first century.

How do we honor diverse voices in the classroom?

by William Ray

The classroom in which a diverse group of students meets a diverse curriculum is perhaps happiest of all, but all students need to be exposed to a culturally diverse literature program. Even in the most homogeneous school, hearing a rich mixture of literary voices is crucial not only to a democratic society, but also to a literary education. In the following statement, Sandra Cisneros describes her participation in a discussion of "the house of the imagination" at the University of Iowa; reading these words to students can be a lesson in both democracy and metaphor:

> Everyone seemed to have some communal knowledge which I did not have—and then I realized that the metaphor of house was totally wrong for me. Suddenly I was homeless. There were no attics and cellars and crannies. I had no such house in my memories. As a child I had read of such things in books, and my family had promised such a house, but the best they could do was offer the miserable bungalow I was embarrassed with all my life. This caused me to question myself, to become defensive. What did I, Sandra Cisneros, know? My classmates were from the best schools in the country. They had been bred as fine hothouse flowers. I was a yellow weed among the city's cracks.

Many of us are fortunate enough to teach students of diverse backgrounds and so have witnessed some of our students experiencing special moments of recognition when they see their culture reflected in a piece of literature. As a student of mine, some years ago, put it, "I like this book—it feels like home." For those who teach in more homogeneous classrooms, the importance of a multicultural curriculum is not diminished.

Using literature of many cultures not only can be a revelation for students who are not of the dominant culture, but also it can provide a jumping off point for students to share their experience. I recall one of my urban, African American students, during a discussion of Sandra Cisneros' *House on Mango Street,* educating her white, suburban classmates out of their stereotypical views of urban life. On another occasion a student of Nigerian descent explained to his classmates how Igbo customs have been maintained or changed since the time of Chinua Achebe's novel *Things Fall Apart.*

Democracy demands that the voices of everyone be heard. *Glencoe Literature,* then, includes representative voices from many corners of the world and from many cultures. For students to develop their own voices, views, and values—grounded in families and communities that schools serve—they must hear and consider the voices of others. Through their own responses and the responses of classmates to literature contained in these pages, students extend their own world views and take important steps toward becoming responsible thinkers and citizens. ❧

Reading

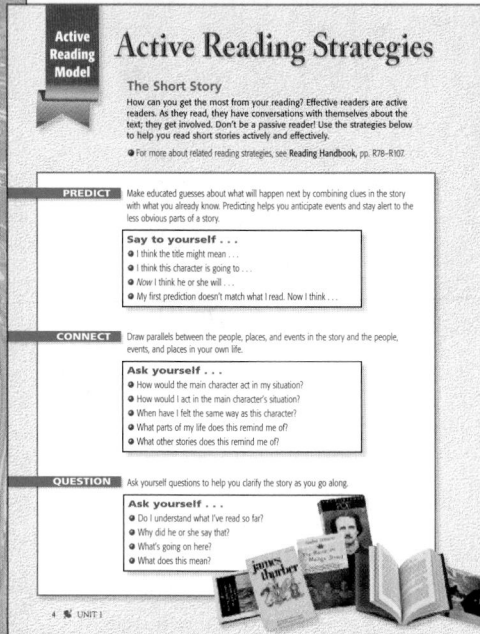

Active Reading Strategies and Models provide prompts to help readers engage in conversations with text.

Journals, drama, and art support students as engaged readers who relate to characters and other story elements.

How do we engage students through critical and creative reading?

by Jeffrey Wilhelm

Reading is a very complex act, and its complexity is largely invisible. When I studied the engagement or meaning-making strategies of young readers, I found that proficient readers regularly operated on ten different dimensions of response as they constructed meaning. Yet less proficient readers did not make any of the same response moves as their more capable peers—in fact, they did not understand that readers were supposed to "do" anything at all beyond decoding words. When I asked one student what he saw when he read, he replied, "Words, man. I see nothing but words!" Proficient readers, on the other hand, could richly describe characters, settings, and situations—often including details that went far beyond the implied meanings of the text.

Less proficient readers have an impoverished notion of reading, and they are usually not helped much by classroom materials that do not reflect a deep understanding of engagement. In *Glencoe Literature*, we base instructional activities on the notion that reading is "transactional"—that is, a conversation between a reader and a text that results in the creation of meaning. We also base our activities on knowledge of engagement—that is, that readers deploy a wide range of creative and critical strategies to evoke a "story world," to connect personally to it, and to critically reflect upon their reading experience.

A key research finding is that readers who do not first visualize a textual world and take on a relationship to characters or ideas will not do anything else. After all, they have nothing to connect to and reflect upon. So the first order of business in assisting reading performance is to support students in "seeing" and "relating" to characters, forces, and ideas. We use response journals, art, drama, and other creative activities to support this level of reading.

Once students have visualized and related, they can then begin to make inferences and elaborate on the story world. Far from being extras, inferencing and elaborating are essentials of reading. Roland Barthes writes that "elaboration is the surest sign of engagement in reading. . . The reader does not decode, he overcodes." This is why some students who can decode words still remain poor readers—they do not know how to use sophisticated creative strategies of engagement, of bringing their own prior experience to a text, and of creating and representing textual meaning. Many of the questions and activities in *Glencoe Literature* are designed to support students in personally connecting to their readings, and in making inferences and elaborations.

Finally, there is critical reading. Because students cannot reflect upon nor critique what they have not experienced, we introduce critical reading after a rich experiential reading has been supported. At this point students may consider how texts are constructed, the use of literary conventions, and an evaluation of their own reading experience.

Crucial to teaching readers is the notion of reading as a constructive act. In this series, students have many opportunities to practice and develop specific reading skills and strategies. They are also assisted to read in both creative and critical ways and through a variety of response dimensions. Our goal is to help them not only to develop a powerful repertoire of reading strategies, but also to reconceive of reading as a personally powerful and meaningful social pursuit. ✢

FOCUS ACTIVITY

Have you ever felt as if you were "caught between a rock and a hard place"—where you needed to make a choice between two courses of action, and neither option seemed quite right?

JOURNAL In your journal, write about this difficult situation. What were the advantages and disadvantages of each course of action? How do you know you made the right choice in the end?

SETTING A PURPOSE Read to learn about a difficult choice that's a matter of life and death.

Personal Response

What thoughts went through your mind as you finished reading this story? Describe them in your journal.

Focus Activities and Personal Response questions help students connect reading to their own experience.

ANALYZING LITERATURE

RECALL AND INTERPRET

1. How does Montresor get Fortunato to come with him to his vaults? What is Montresor's motive for leading Fortunato there?
2. What kind of relationship does Montresor have with the people who take care of his home? What does this reveal about him?
3. Describe the conversation between Montresor and Fortunato as they walk in the catacombs. What is *ironic* about Montresor's concern for Fortunato's health? (See Literary Terms Handbook, page R7.)
4. Describe Fortunato's state of mind as Montresor walls in the entrance to the niche. Include details from the story in your answer.
5. How does Montresor feel about what he has done? In your response, consider why he might be telling the story after so many years.

EVALUATE AND CONNECT

6. In your opinion, did Montresor commit the perfect crime? Explain.
7. Might the story be better or worse if you knew what Fortunato did or said to make Montresor take such terrible revenge? Explain.
8. Do you believe that Montresor resolves his conflict with Fortunato? Why

Analyzing Literature allows students to interpret and evaluate and to look critically at literary elements.

Reading & Thinking Skills

Making Inferences

Imagine that a new student has joined your class, and you notice a St. Louis Cardinals sticker on her folder. You conclude that she likes baseball, and you bring up the topic during your first conversation. You have made an **inference**, a conclusion based on what you know.

As a reader, you must also make inferences. You must look for clues in description and dialogue that can help you understand ideas that the author is implying, but not directly stating. Often you will also use information from your own experiences to help you make inferences and draw conclusions. For example, the narrator in "The Lady, or the Tiger?" says that the king "was a man of exuberant fancy, and, withal, of an authority so irresistible that, at his will, he turned his varied fancies into facts. He was greatly given to self-communing; and, when he and himself agreed upon any thing, the thing was done." From these statements,

Skills pages, minilessons, and a reading handbook are valuable tools for developing reading and thinking skills.

Writing

Personal Writing
Don't Forget   Look back at the writing you did for the Focus Activity on page 539. In your journal, make notes of any additional things that the poems of Harjo and Hove have convinced you are important to remember. Then write a letter to your imaginary grandchild, explaining what the child should not forget.

Focus Activities and Personal Writing activities help students make personal connections to literature.

Writing About Literature
Examining Setting   James Hurst once said that there were three characters in this story: the narrator, Doodle, and the setting. Why is the setting so important? Make a list of events that are influenced by different aspects of the setting–time, weather, vegetation, buildings. Then write several paragraphs explaining why the setting might be considered a "character" in the story.

Learning for Life
Memo to the Boss   Think about the story from Camera and Smilin's point of view. How did they first perceive the Cain family, and what did they think after they left the family's property, unable to complete the assignment? What will they tell their supervisor when they return to the office with the ruined film? Draft a memo Camera and Smilin might write to their boss explaining what happened and why. Include their recommendations for how the county should proceed with its plan to document the food stamps campaign.

Writing About Literature and Learning for Life activities let student writers try out many roles and points of view.

How does writing enhance the study of literature?
by Jacqueline Jones Royster

We think of the literature classroom as a language-rich environment, made all the richer by the collection of texts and activities in *Glencoe Literature*. As both art and artifact, writing is a flexible tool that can work dynamically with other elements of instruction as teachers help students to enhance both learning and performance. From this point of view, writing activities are generously incorporated throughout each unit for a variety of purposes.

Writing to understand and make personal connections with literature   Through reading response journals and other writing activities, students have a mechanism for noticing the details in a text and making sense of them. Writing can help students to
- make personal connections with ideas, images, and experiences;
- see ways to go beyond their own connections toward broader implications; and
- sometimes see critical distinctions between their own lives and experiences and what they are reading.

Writing to experiment as critical and creative thinkers   Through writing, students can assume many different roles and points of view as they think about what a text is saying, what it is doing, and whether it is successful. They can sort through ideas, weigh the impact and consequences of language choices, and use these assessments to make informed judgments about what works in written expression and why. They can write themselves into the text, take on characters in different times and places, or imagine on paper different scenarios as they think seriously about what it means to produce literature. As students respond to literature, writing enables them to stand back from a text to think about concepts such as "aesthetic value," "eloquence," or even "elegance"—in other words, to determine in more systematic ways what appeals to them as readers and how authors achieve those effects on readers.

Writing to discover one's own voice Teachers accomplish an important cultural task when we help students move from viewing themselves as just consumers of other people's writing to seeing themselves also as producers of writing. Literature as an expressive tradition is an ongoing enterprise, and the creative writing activities in *Glencoe Literature* encourage students to write in many genres, including fiction and nonfiction, and to compose and present their work through various media. In our view, the study of literature and the writing of literature go hand in hand as we help students to know both concretely and abstractly the power and joy of words.

Writing to understand form and function Through the Writing Workshops in *Glencoe Literature*, students can gain direct experiences with producing various forms and genres of writing. They learn to use genre options with a more creative and critical eye and to develop a more sophisticated vocabulary for talking about their writing choices. In this way the genre knowledge that they build as readers and writers helps them to see writing—like language use in general—as purposeful and capable of both consequence and reward.

Approaching writing in this way, as part and parcel of a language-rich environment, helps teachers extend students' definitions of writing to include

- writing to understand and connect with reading;
- writing to reflect on experiences (in the texts as well as in real life);
- writing to represent thoughts and ideas in multiple ways through various media for many purposes and audiences; and
- writing to display talent, ability, and understanding and thereby to demonstrate what they know and can do.

With such varied experience in using writing in the company of the other language arts, we believe that students will be well prepared to perform at high levels of quality and excellence.

Creative Writing

Reel It In   Write a new ending to this story in which the narrator chooses to reel in the fish. Consider the following questions before you write. How will the action play out? How will Sheila react? How will the narrator feel about his decision when he looks back on it many years later? Exchange your writing with a classmate, and discuss how your endings are alike or different.

Creative Writing activities encourage students to write in many genres and for various audiences.

Writing Skills

Using Transitions

Reading good writing is easy when the writer's ideas are logically linked from sentence to sentence and paragraph to paragraph. To ensure a clear, logical flow of ideas, writers use transitions—words and phrases that imply relationships between ideas. Notice how Linda Hogan uses transitions in the following paragraph from "Walking."

"I saw it first in early summer. It was a green and sleeping bud, raising itself toward the sun. Ants worked around the unopened bloom, gathering aphids and sap. A few days later, it was a tender young flower, soft and new, with a pale green center and a troop of silver-gray insects climbing up and down the stalk. Over the summer this sunflower grew into a plant of incredible beauty. . . ."

⚜ Writing ✕ Workshop ⚜

Narrative Writing: Short Story

If reading a short story can take you to another world, writing a short story makes you the captain of a globe-trotting vehicle. You can zoom into a character's mind, tour new kinds of conflicts and situations, or see how someone else would handle the problems you typically face. In the process, you may learn more about yourself and others. Explore the life of a fictional character by writing a short story, using this workshop as your guide.

- As you write your short story, refer to the **Writing Handbook**, pp. R58–R63.

The Writing Process

PREWRITING

PREWRITING TIP
Starting with your own experience is a good idea, but let your imagination take you beyond.

Explore ideas
The stories in this theme all involve looking back at events in a character's life. To find ideas for your story, look back at events in your life. If this search doesn't lead you to a story you want to tell, try using one of the following ideas as a starting point:

- characters in conflict, like the parent and child in Amy Tan's "Rules of the Game"
- a character your narrator admires, like Charley in Eugenia Collier's "Sweet Potato Pie"
- characters separated by generations or cultures, like the narrator and his great-grandmother in Gerald Haslam's "The Horned Toad"

Writing Workshops and Writing Skills pages help students become proficient with many forms of writing.

Technology & Media Literacy

How can we use technology to enhance the teaching of literature?

by Jeffrey Wilhelm

A technology can be defined as any tool that extends our human abilities—that helps us to do our work more easily. Literacy has always meant the ability to use the most powerful available tools to exchange information and to communicate, which humans do in a variety of deep and complex ways. Video and computer technologies, now melded through multimedia applications, currently constitute our culture's most sophisticated tools of communication. Technology offers us new and exciting ways to be literate, but of course there is also a downside. Neil Postman states that we must learn why and how to use technology for our higher human purposes or we will be doomed to be used by the technology. Many critics of computers in schools argue that this is exactly what happens: computers are often used as expensive ways to implement old and sometimes ineffective ways of teaching. Further, students often learn to use computers or particular applications in decontextualized situations—losing sight of the nature of technology as a tool, using it instead for its own sake.

However, there is an alternative, and this is the kind of technology use offered in *Glencoe Literature: The Reader's Choice*. We use technological applications in the context of sustained study to find information, organize data, and as a way to design and represent new understandings. The rewards of this kind of technological instruction are great. Students learn to use the Internet, hypermedia, and other applications in a meaningful context. They pool technological knowledge and information gleaned from electronic searches to form a community of use. Technology supports traditional ways of reading and composing as students use video and computers to construct knowledge documents that can be posted on the Internet and shared through other electronic means. Research shows that this kind of curriculum, called "learning by design," has many positive effects, particularly for students who are often considered to be reluctant or "at-risk."

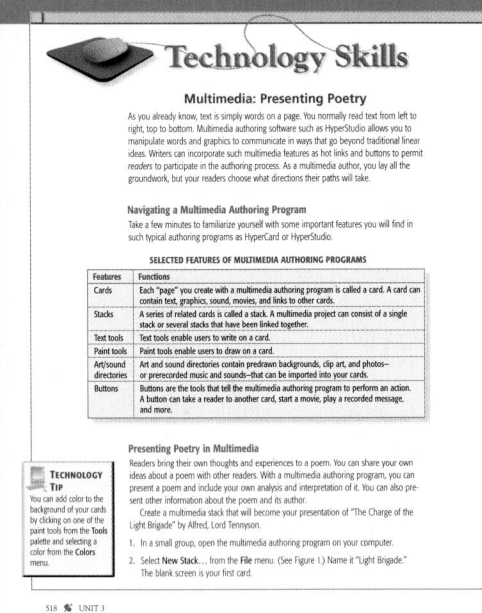

Technology Skills features provide opportunities for students to learn about and use a variety of technologies in the context of their study of literature.

Seymour Papert, one of the foremost authorities on computers and learning, writes that "the computer is the world's greatest construction kit." He concurs that literacy is intimately involved in technology and its critical use. Critical use, he tells us, can only occur if students find and design knowledge with technology. This kind of work is what Papert calls "hard fun," and it leads to powerful and exciting forms of learning. We have provided the context and support for this kind of learning in the text you hold in your hands. Buckle your seatbelts and get ready for some "hard fun" of your own.

How can we help students become media literate?

by Jeffrey Wilhelm

Media literacy is closely related to technology literacy, but it casts a wider net by considering how different technologies organize and represent information in different ways and with different effects. When my own students tell me that they "know" something because they read it on a Web site or saw it on MTV, I become very concerned that they have a critical understanding and standards for how knowledge is produced and represented. In response to these and similar needs, the National Communication Association created national standards for media literacy in 1996, and various states are now embedding similar standards into their curriculum and testing guidelines.

Because of the importance of media literacy, *Glencoe Literature* deals with media use and representation in a variety of ways. Students are asked to use and critique various media, often vis a vis literary texts so that they can compare the strengths and weaknesses of representing knowledge through different textual forms. Students are also asked to create media responses to literature they have read, and sometimes to create stories, arguments or presentations of their own using different media possibilities. Always, we have in mind to expand the notion of what it means to be literate to include an understanding of the nature of mass media, the techniques used by them, and the ability to both produce and critique meanings using various media. 🌿

Internet Connections **engage students in online research and in building databases of shared knowledge in the classroom.**

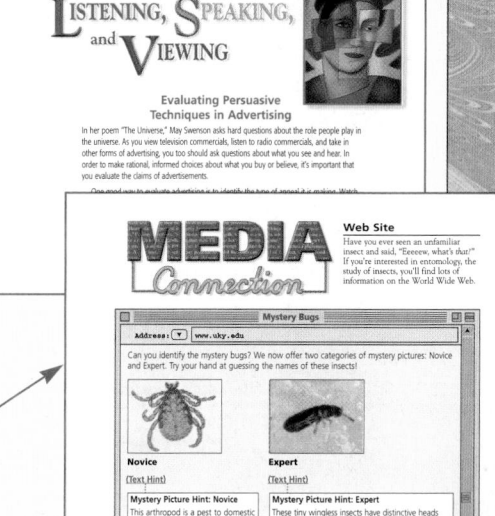

Media Connections **and** *Listening, Speaking, and Viewing* **features help students become critical readers and viewers of media.**

Integrated Language Arts

LISTENING, SPEAKING, and VIEWING

Oral Interpretation of a Poem

Have you noticed that two people's readings of the same poem can sound completely different? Since people's experiences are unique, they often have different interpretations of what they read. Oral interpretation of a poem gives readers a chance to share their impressions. It also offers listeners new insights on a poem's tone or meaning.

In preparing an oral interpretation of a poem, you might find these suggestions helpful:

● Read the poem silently to yourself and consider who the speaker might be. Do you "hear" the voice of the poet, of an unidentified person, or of a character? What is this person's

EXTENDING YOUR RESPONSE

Literature Groups
Do You Agree?   The narrator contradicts himself at the end of the story, saying first, "And here I have lamely related to you the uneventful chronicle of two foolish children in a flat who most unwisely sacrificed for each other the greatest treasures of their house." Then he says, "Let it be said that of all who give gifts these two were the wisest. Of all who give and receive gifts, such as they are wisest." With your group, discuss which of these statements is closer to your views about Della and Jim. Do you think there might be truth in both statements? Share your opinions with the rest of your classmates.

Reading Further
If you'd like to read more by O. Henry, you might enjoy these works:
Short Stories: "A Retrieved Reformation," which can be found in the collection 41 Stories, shows how love can reform a criminal.
"The Cop and the Anthem" and "The Last Leaf," from the collection The Best Short Stories of O. Henry, both feature beloved, simple characters and twisting plots.
Viewing: The Gift of Love is a film adaptation of "The Gift of the Magi."

Skill features help students develop key listening and speaking abilities, and Literature Groups activities provide opportunities for small group discussions with each selection.

Skill Minilessons
Responding to Literature

GRAMMAR AND LANGUAGE • Concrete and Abstract Nouns
A **concrete noun** names an object that occupies space or that can be recognized by any of the senses. Della as "car."
An **abstract noun** names an idea, a quality, or a charac-
teristic,
"The W
(somet
also con

"Arou
serve
since

PRACTICE   On your paper, identify the nouns in this passage. Label them abstract or concrete.
He saw at once that his shombo was well-nigh

READING AND THINKING • Making Inferences
When you make inferences as you read, you draw logical conclusions, combining clues from the text with what you already know from experience or other reading. For example, when you read this paragraph of Pius and Nantondo appears in the newspaper with the caption "Mr. Pius Ndawula and his happy wife," Pius is enraged and threatens to take legal action. From this you may infer that Pius is single—and he likes it that way!

PRACTICE   On your paper, make an inference on the basis of each of the following pieces of information about the characters and situations in "The Winner."

1. Pius's many relatives assured him that they knew the proper way for him to invest his winnings.
2. The first visitors to arrive at Pius's hut did not happily greet the arrival of additional visitors.
3. Musisi offers to read the telegram aloud.
4. Pius's visitors wreck his home and eat all his food.
5. At the end of the story, Salongo sends Pius home with bananas and a cabbage for Cousin Sarah.

● For more about reading strategies, see **Reading Handbook**, pp. R78–R107.

VOCABULARY • The Latin Root cred
The Latin root cred comes from the verb credere, which means "to trust or believe." Therefore, when you come across the word incredulity (which contains the negating prefix in-), you can guess that it has to do with not trusting or believing. Amazing events, extremely good news, and really bad excuses can all cause you to feel incredulity—an unwillingness or inability to believe. Similarly, a store owner will give you credit if he or she trusts you to pay for your goods later. Recognizing the cred root in an unfamiliar word can help you get at least a general sense of the word's meaning.

PRACTICE   Briefly state what you'd guess is the meaning of each underlined word.
1. It is easy to trick an innocent and credulous child.
2. I don't give much credence to the stories that appear in that tabloid paper!
3. If you place credit in what your doctor says, you are more likely to follow his or her advice.
4. "The Boy Who Cried Wolf" is about a child who loses his credibility by frequently lying.

Skill Minilessons provide frequent opportunities for students to develop reading and vocabulary skills in the context of their literature study.

How can we integrate the language arts through our teaching of literature?

by Beverly Ann Chin

Integrating the English language arts into our teaching of literature is an effective way to help students improve their communication and thinking skills. Today, the English language arts include speaking, listening, reading, writing, viewing, and visually representing. We can use each of the language arts to engage our students in the study and appreciation of literature.

Listening and Speaking We integrate listening and speaking skills whenever students participate in class discussions and literature groups. Students orally share their understandings of literature, and they listen to other people's ideas and opinions. We teach speaking and listening skills when our students work in cooperative learning groups and collaborate on literature projects. Speaking and listening skills are basic components in creative drama activities, such as role playing, readers theater, improvisation, and choral reading. As students interpret literature through creative drama and oral interpretation, they discover how language and nonverbal communication affect the audience's understanding of the story. Whether students are responding to literature through a small group conversation, listening to someone read a selection aloud, or participating in a dramatic performance, they are using and improving their speaking and listening abilities.

Reading When we teach literature, we help our students develop important reading strategies. For example, before students read a literature selection, we invite students to draw upon their prior knowledge and experiences to help them make connections with the literature. During the reading process, we encourage students to make inferences about the characters' motivations and to use context clues to determine the meaning of unfamiliar vocabulary. After reading the selection, students discuss their responses and extend their comprehension. By encouraging students to respond to and reflect on literature, we help students develop their critical and creative reading abilities.

Writing Writing enhances students' understanding and enjoyment of literature. We help students grow as writers when we invite them to write in their reading response journals, to create their own literary pieces, or to write expository essays. By keeping response journals, students record their questions, discover insights, and reflect on their meaning-making processes. When students write in the literary forms and styles they are reading, they share their understanding of literary genres. At the end of a unit, we often ask students to write an essay that shows their understanding of the theme, genre, or literary style. All of these writing activities also provide an authentic and meaningful context within which students can develop control of the conventions of grammar, usage and mechanics as well as of important elements of style. As we encourage students to use writing to learn about themselves and literature, we help students improve their abilities to write clearly, creatively, and effectively.

Viewing and Visually Representing The newest emphases in teaching English language arts are viewing and visually representing. We integrate viewing and representing in our literature curriculum when we help students see the similarities and differences between the stories they read and the films they view. For example, students can analyze how the narrator's point of view in a story is comparable to camera angles; how the story's tone and mood are conveyed through the sound-track, color, and lighting; and how a story's dialog and setting are interpreted by screen writers, location scouts, and film editors. By showing different film versions of the same work, we help students become aware of the parallel roles of authors and film directors.

We also help students become critical viewers when we encourage students to look at paintings and posters to discover how artists use color, texture, movement, shape, and form to create an effect on the audience. Many students convey their understanding and interpretation of literature by drawing character portraits, taking photographs of settings, creating story maps of the plot, illustrating book jackets, designing thematic collages, or creating multimedia projects. By encouraging students to visualize and graphically represent their ideas, we help them make connections between their lives and literature. ❧

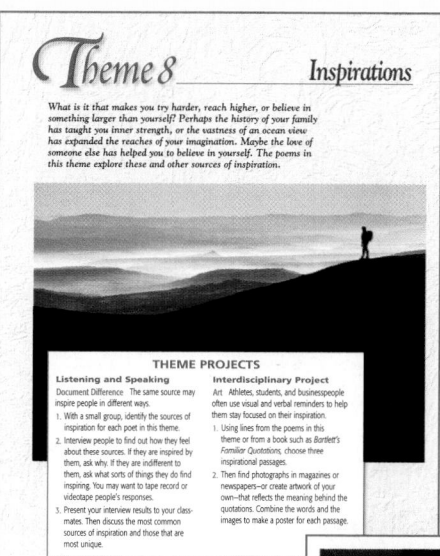

Minilessons and features help students develop proficiency with key elements of writing, including grammar and style.

Art projects and viewing questions assist students in becoming skilled producers and viewers of visual media.

Assessment

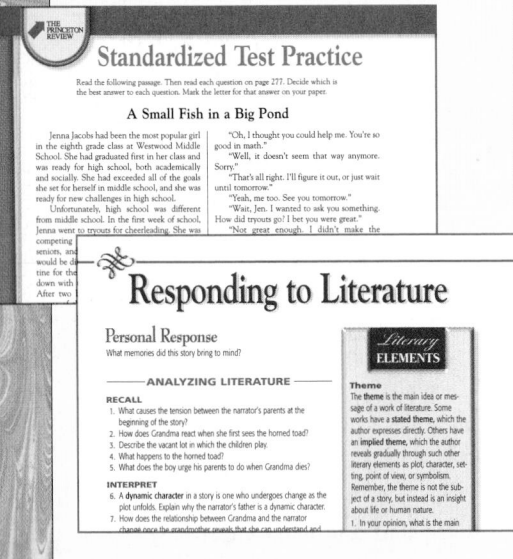

Options for formal assessment include Analyzing Literature and Standardized Test Practice as well as the Selection and Theme Assessment booklet.

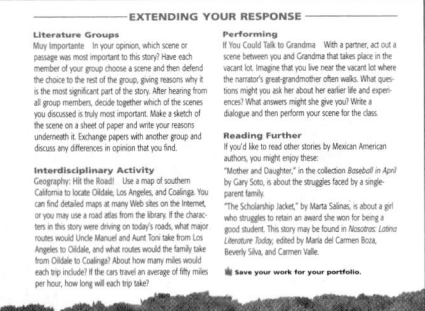

Extending Your Response activities can be used for performance assessment. In addition, the Performance Assessment booklet provides a performance task and rubric for each selection.

How can we use assessment and portfolios in our teaching of literature?

by Beverly Ann Chin

When we think about assessment in literature, we need to consider our purposes for teaching literature and our literature curriculum. Assessment in literature is authentic if it reflects what, how, and why we teach. For example, if we emphasize personal responses to literature, our assessment should evaluate students' ability to make connections with the texts and authors they read. If we emphasize critical analysis of literature, our assessment should evaluate students' ability to understand the elements of an author's craft and the structure of the text. If we emphasize the development of the full range of language arts skills through the study of literature, assessment should include activities that require students to demonstrate their understanding of literature through writing, speaking, and visual representation. If we want students to take more responsibility and ownership of their own learning, students should have regular opportunities to assess their own and their peers' accomplishments.

Formal Assessment Formal assessment focuses on measuring what students know. A variety of traditional paper-and-pencil test formats can be effective tools for assessing students' comprehension of selections and their ability to analyze and interpret what they have read. By incorporating experiences with standardized test formats into classroom assessment, teachers can also help prepare students for their participation in state and national assessments.

Performance Assessment Performance assessments in literature enable students to demonstrate their understandings of literature. For example, if your students keep reader response journals, you can ask students to select several entries and write a personal reflection paper that shows how their responses to the theme evolved during the literature unit. Creative drama activities can also serve as performance assessment; for example, students can identify and perform important events in a story to demonstrate their understanding of plot. Students can also demonstrate their interpretation of the theme by writing in a different genre or by creating interdisciplinary, multimedia projects that extend the theme.

Portfolios Portfolios can be a powerful assessment tool in the literature classroom. A portfolio is a purposeful collection of work that shows a student's accomplishments, growth, and learning processes. Many teachers who use portfolios in their literature classes encourage students to keep and review their work at the end of each unit. As teachers discuss with students the purposes of the literature portfolio, they help students develop criteria for selecting and organizing the works (entries) to be included in their portfolios.

To guide students in selecting items to include in the portfolio, teachers can ask questions such as

- Which works show your accomplishments in this course?
- Which works demonstrate your growth as a reader and writer?
- Which works reveal your abilities to think critically and creatively?
- Which works did you most enjoy?

Teachers also encourage students to reflect on each of their portfolio entries by considering these questions:

- What did you like best about this work?
- What did you learn from doing this work?
- What might you do differently if you were to do this work again?

Many students create portfolios that contain a table of contents, a preface to the portfolio, and an introduction (or reflection paragraph) for each selection. The process of creating and sharing portfolios provides students with ongoing opportunities to set goals and evaluate their own knowledge, skills, and attitudes.

Through portfolios and other forms of assessment, English language arts teachers gain important information about students' understanding and enjoyment of literature. By creating assessments that align with the literature curriculum and instruction, we enable our students to demonstrate their accomplishments, apply their knowledge, and reflect on their growth as learners. ❧

THE SHORT STORY

Unit Wrap-Up

PERSONAL RESPONSE

1. Which story in this unit did you find the most entertaining? Which story was the most thought-provoking? To which of the three narrators could you most strongly relate? Why?
2. As a result of the work you did in this unit, what new ideas do you have about the following:
   - how to read a short story
   - how to work with other students in pairs or in groups
   - how to connect literature to your own life and interests

ANALYZING LITERATURE

Creating Your Own Theme   The stories in this unit have been organized into three themes–"Matters of Life and Death," "Filling a Void," and "Looking Back." Choose at least five of the stories from this unit and organize them into a theme of your own choosing. Give a title to your theme, and then explain in writing how the selections you've chosen relate to your theme title and to each other.

EVALUATE AND SET GOALS

Evaluate
1. What was your strongest contribution to group work as you moved through this unit?
2. What was the most challenging task you faced in this unit?
   - How did you approach the task?
   - Were you satisfied with the results?
   - What did you learn from the challenge?
3. If you could give a grade to the overall work you did in this unit, what would it be? Give at least two reasons for your assessment.

Set Goals
1. Think about the activities in this unit in which you feel you did your weakest work. How could you improve?
2. Choose a goal to work toward in the next unit to improve your performance.
3. Meet with your teacher to discuss your goal and the steps you will take to achieve it.
4. Plan a way to evaluate whether you have reached your goal.

📖 BUILD YOUR PORTFOLIO

Select   Choose two pieces of work you did in this unit and include them in your portfolio. Use these questions to help you make your selection.
- Which are you most proud of?
- Which are the most creative?
- Which did you learn the most from?

Reflect   Write some notes to accompany the pieces you selected. Use these questions to guide you.
- What do you like best about these pieces?
- What sets these pieces apart from the rest?
- What did you learn while creating them?
- What might you change if given the chance to do them over again?

274 ❧ UNIT 1

Each Unit Wrap-Up supports students as they build their portfolios and assess their own performance. Portfolio resources for teachers appear in the Writing Assessment and Portfolio Management booklet.

Unit One — At a Glance
The Short Story

UNIT OPENING

- **Genre Focus: The Short Story** (p. 2)
- **Active Reading Strategies** (p. 4)
- **Active Reading Model:** *Everyday Use* (p. 6)

Theme 1: TRANSITIONS

SELECTIONS

Chee's Daughter (p. 22)

Civil Peace (p. 38)

Media Connection: Press Release (p. 47)

Two Kinds (p. 48)

Catch the Moon (p. 62)

Media Connection: Magazine Article (p. 74)

 Through the Tunnel (p. 75)

The Vision Quest (p. 88)

By the Waters of Babylon (p. 94)

What I Have Been Doing Lately (p. 108)

With All Flags Flying (p. 114)

A Child, a Dog, the Night (p. 128)

SKILL FEATURES

Grammar Link (p. 73)

Reading and Thinking Skills (p. 107)

Listening, Speaking, and Viewing (p. 127)

WRITING WORKSHOP

Personal Writing: Reflective Essay (p. 136)

Theme 2: MAKING CHOICES

SELECTIONS

The White Heron (p. 142)

 The Boar Hunt (p. 156)

Delicious Death (p. 166)

The Monkey's Paw (p. 172)

Tuesday Siesta (p. 188)

Media Connection: News Article (p. 197)

Contents of the Dead Man's Pocket (p. 198)

Media Connection: Comic Strip (p. 216)

The Censors (p. 217)

The Ring (p. 224)

SKILL FEATURES

Writing Skills (p. 185)

Technology Skills (p. 186)

Interdisciplinary Connection (p. 215)

Reading and Thinking Skills (p. 223)

Grammar Link (p. 233)

WRITING WORKSHOP

Persuasive Writing: Letter to the Editor (p. 234)

KEYS TO LITERARY CONNECTIONS

 World Literature

Glencoe Literature contains a variety of literature that represents cultures from around the world. World literature selections are highlighted with this symbol:

 Comparing Selections

In each theme of **Glencoe Literature**, the **Comparing Selections** feature gives students an opportunity to compare two selections they have just read. Each Comparing Selections page provides a variety of options to address diverse aspects of the reading and literature curriculum.

1A UNIT 1

Theme 3:
TWISTS

SELECTIONS

The Happy Man's Shirt (p. 240)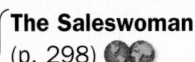

Media Connection: Newspaper Article (p. 245)

The Californian's Tale (p. 247)

Media Connection: Web Site (p. 258)

An Astrologer's Day (p. 259)

The Interlopers (p. 268)

As It Is with Strangers (p. 278)

The False Gems (p. 288)

The Saleswoman (p. 298)

Mrs. James (p. 304)

SKILL FEATURES

Vocabulary Skills (p. 246)

Listening, Speaking, and Viewing (p. 267)

WRITING WORKSHOP

Narrative Writing: Short Story (p. 308)

Theme 4:
CHALLENGES AND CONSEQUENCES

SELECTIONS

Media Connection: Comic Strip (p. 314)

A Sound of Thunder (p. 315)

Media Connection: Magazine Article (p. 328)

Lullaby (p. 329)

And of Clay Are We Created (p. 342)

Colombia's Mortal Agony (p. 354)

Winter Night (p. 362)

Waltz of the Fat Man (p. 376)

The Masque of the Red Death (p. 388)

To Da-duh, in Memoriam (p. 398)

SKILL FEATURES

Interdisciplinary Connection (p. 341)

Writing Skills (p. 361)

Vocabulary Skills (p. 375)

WRITING WORKSHOP

Expository Writing: Critical Response (p. 412)

UNIT WRAP-UP

- **Personal Response, Analyzing Literature, Evaluate and Set Goals** (p. 416)

- **Build Your Portfolio** (p. 416)

- **Reading on Your Own** (p. 417)
  Fahrenheit 451 by Ray Bradbury
  Of Mice and Men by John Steinbeck
  My Ántonia by Willa Cather
  Shabanu, Daughter of the Wind by Suzanne Fisher-Staples

- **Standardized Test Practice** (pp. 418–419)

KEYS TO TEACHING OPTIONS

Block Scheduling

Activities that are particularly suited to use within a block scheduling framework are identified throughout this unit by the following designation: For detailed suggestions on block scheduling, see the **Block Scheduling Guide** for this grade level.

Key to Ability Levels

The Teaching Options throughout this unit have been coded for students of various abilities.

L1 **BASIC** activities for all students

L2 **AVERAGE** activities for average to above-average students

L3 **CHALLENGING** activities for above-average students

Reading Skills in this unit

Variety of Texts

In addition to numerous stories by authors from the United States and several other nations, this unit also includes the following text types:

- poetry
- nonfiction
- press release
- magazine article
- news article
- Web site
- comic strip

Comprehension Skills

The following instructional support for comprehension skills appears in this unit of the Student Edition:

- **Active Reading Strategies and Model** (pp. 4–20)
- **Visualizing** (p. 107)
- **Making Predictions** (p. 223)
- **Reading and Thinking Minilessons** (pp. 37, 46, 61, 72, 126, 155, 184, 214, 257, 266, 277, 287, 297, 374, 387, 397, 411)

See also the **Reading Minilessons** throughout the unit in this Teacher's Wraparound Edition.

Reading Resources

Comprehension Skills Resources

📁 Active Reading Guides

The **Active Reading Guide** provides graphic organizers and study guide questions to support students' reading of each selection. (**Active Reading Guide**, pp. 1–35)

📁 Reading Workbook

The Reading Workbook (pp. 1–46) includes additional instruction and reinforcement of reading strategies and skills.

🎧 Audio Library

Available both on tape and on CD, the Audio Library provides valuable comprehension support.

Resources for Reading Widely

Glencoe Literature Library

Each title in the Glencoe Literature Library includes a full-length novel or play plus related readings. A separate Study Guide is available for each title.

💿 Literature Classics CD-ROM

The 900 selections on this CD-ROM can be searched by author, theme, or genre.

 inTIME

A coproduction of Glencoe and Time Inc., *inTime* includes a wealth of high-interest nonfiction related to the selections and themes in Unit One.

✓ Assessment in this unit

 GLENCOE'S ASSESSMENT ADVANTAGE

Assessment Options in the Student Edition

Glencoe Literature offers a number of diverse ways to evaluate student understanding and skill proficiency. In the Student Edition, use the following:

- **Responding to Literature**
  Following each selection, students are asked to recall facts, interpret ideas, and evaluate concepts as they answer a variety of questions and complete activities to extend their understanding.

- **Unit Wrap-Up (pp. 416–417)**
  Here students respond to the selections on personal and analytical levels. They also assume ownership of their learning by setting and evaluating goals and by selecting work for their portfolios.

See also the many **Assessment Resources** listed on the facing page.

 THE PRINCETON REVIEW

Standardized Test Practice

The Princeton Review has developed the Standardized Test Practice pages found at the end of this unit (pp. 418–419). These pages contain practice test questions that help students remain familiar with standardized test formats and content.

Writing Skills in this unit

Writing Skills

The Student Edition of Unit One offers strong instructional support for writing skills:

In **Extending Your Response**, which follows each selection:
- Writing About Literature
- Personal/Creative Writing

In **Writing Skills** Lessons:
- **Creating Emphasis** (p. 185)
- **Writing Dialogue** (p. 361)

See also the **Writing Minilessons** throughout the unit in this Teacher's Wraparound Edition.

Writing Workshops

Each of the four themes in Unit One concludes with a **Writing Workshop** that guides students through the writing process.
- **Personal Writing: Reflective Essay** (pp. 136–140)
- **Persuasive Writing: Letter to the Editor** (pp. 234–238)
- **Narrative Writing: Short Story** (pp. 308–312)
- **Expository Writing: Critical Response** (pp. 412–415)

Writing Resources

Writer's Assistant CD-ROM
Each Writing Workshop is supplemented by an interactive writing guide on the Writer's Assistant CD-ROM. This easy-to-use writing guide provides prompts, templates, and other tools that lead students through the writing process.

Writing and Proofreading Practice
Blackline masters present in-depth instruction and practice on a specific step in the writing process and proofreading. (pp. 1–36)

Writing and Proofreading Transparencies
Transparencies (1–14, 25–32) provide graphic organizers and proofreading exercises for whole class instruction.

Research and Report Writing Guide
This resource provides extensive tips and activities to guide students in their writing projects in the literature classroom as well as in classes across the curriculum.

Style and Documentation Sourcebook for Writers
This sourcebook is a combination reference and workbook, giving students the most up-to-date information and guidance regarding traditional as well as technological research strategies and documentation.

Grammar and Composition Handbook
The Grammar and Composition Handbook provides instruction that supplements activities in the student textbook.

Assessment Resources

Selection Quick Checks
For each selection, a Quick Check of three to five short-answer questions measures students' literal comprehension.

Selection and Theme Assessment
The Selection and Theme Assessment instrument tests students' abilities to recall, interpret, and evaluate what they've read. The tests consist of multiple-choice, short answer, and essay questions.

Performance Assessment
Alternative assessment instruments and rubrics for Unit One are found in the Performance Assessment ancillary.

Writing Assessment and Portfolio Management
These notes and strategies, student models, and assessment tools assist with the task of measuring students' progress as writers and as monitors of their own writing.

Testmaker
Teachers can customize selection, theme, and Unit One tests by accessing the Testmaker database.

MindJogger Videoquizzes
Using a popular game show format, MindJogger Videoquizzes enable teachers to evaluate students' understanding of Unit One in a quick and fun manner.

The Short Story

Unit Objectives

- To enjoy reading short stories
- To analyze the literary elements in short stories
- To apply strategies for reading short stories

VIEWING THE PAINTING

Much of the artwork of O. Louis Guglielmi was created during the 1930s as part of the Works Project Administration (WPA). The WPA was a government project designed to provide paying jobs for unemployed workers during the Great Depression. It also created jobs in the arts for writers, musicians, and artists.

Responding to the Art Discussion questions:

- What does the sea seem to be doing in the picture? (*gradually taking over the house*)
- What might the sea symbolize? (*the power of imagination or creativity; the effect of dreams or memories on reality or everyday life*)
- Why do you think the artist included an open door and a stairway in the painting? (*to show that people don't know what lies ahead; to show that people should be open to new ideas; to show the interplay between imagination and reality*)

The Persistent Sea, No. 2. O. Louis Guglielmi (1906–1956). Oil on canvas, 29⅞ x 23¼ in. Private collection.

TEACHER to TEACHER

Every student has a story to tell. To make it easier for students to talk about themselves, I tell them about my life. Next, I use a writing prompt and ask students to write a story. I may give a list of character descriptions and have students create sentences about characters. This preliminary exercise gives them a tool to fall back on when describing characters in their story. Using a list of writing tips I've put together, students correct their own papers and then break into peer groups to edit each other's work. The writing tips and corrections are progressive, so we edit only for those things we are working on that week or have worked on previously. In addition to writing their stories, students might write and perform rap songs about one of the short stories in the unit, or they might perform a skit based on one of the stories we have read.

JELANI KHALID

UNIT ✦ ONE

The Short Story

*"[F]iction is like a
spider's web, attached
ever so lightly perhaps,
but still attached to
life at all four
corners."*
—Virginia Woolf

Theme 1
Transitions
pages 21–140

Theme 2
Making Choices
pages 141–238

Theme 3
Twists
pages 239–312

Theme 4
Challenges and Consequences
pages 313–415

RESOURCE MANAGER

See the *Unit One Planning Guide*
(pp. vi–1) for additional teaching notes,
strategies, and resources for introducing
the short story unit.

Introducing the Unit

Have students read the quotation.
Then pose these questions for
discussion:
- What do you think Virginia Woolf
  means when she says that fiction
  is lightly but definitely attached
  to life?
- What does the comparison of
  fiction to a spider's web imply
  about fiction?

Theme 1: Transitions

The short stories in Theme 1 introduce students to characters facing
and trying to cope with changes in
their lives, such as the loss of a parent, moving from wartime into peace-
time, and planning for the final years
of life.

Theme 2: Making Choices

The choices made by the characters
in Theme 2 help define who they are
and the direction their lives will take.

Theme 3: Twists

Unexpected twists and turns of
events surprise both characters and
readers in Theme 3.

Theme 4: Challenges and
Consequences

Characters in Theme 4 face challenges from nature, prejudice, ignorance, or hate. Other characters
must deal with the consequences of
situations they caused or of events
beyond their control.

GLENCOE
TECHNOLOGY
LITERATURE CLASSICS
CD-ROM
Search for other short
stories by theme, author, or title.

Genre Focus

Objective

- To understand the elements of a short story

Teaching Strategies

Explain that most good stories become favorites because they have at least one outstanding element—setting, characters, point of view, theme, or plot. Ask students to name favorite short stories and give reasons why they are favorites.

Setting

Invite students to share examples of unusual or unfamiliar story settings from stories they have read.

Characters

Explain to students that the protagonist of a story is not necessarily a hero, and that the antagonist, if there is one, is not always a villain. Often they are ordinary people with both positive and negative qualities. Invite students to name stories with protagonists or antagonists who are ordinary, everyday people.

Point of View

Ask students to imagine that Cinderella is told by a narrator who describes events only as Cinderella sees them. Which details might the reader not learn if the story were told from this limited point of view?

Teaching Options

Genre Focus
Short Stories

When you talk about computers, you use terms that are specific to computers: megabytes, "log on," "boot up." Likewise, when people talk about literature, they use special terms—the language of literature analysis. You will find that learning to use that language can help you talk about how short stories are put together and what makes them effective.

What is a short story? It is a short piece of fiction that includes elements described in the charts on these pages. Look at how a story you probably know, the children's tale "Cinderella," can be analyzed in terms of these elements.

SHORT STORY ELEMENTS | MODEL: "Cinderella"

Setting

Setting is the time and place in which a story happens. The setting includes not only physical surroundings but also ideas, customs, values, and beliefs.

> The story takes place a long time ago in a land ruled by a king and a queen.

Characters

Characters are the actors in a story's plot. They can be people, animals, or whatever the writer chooses.

- The **protagonist** is the main character.
- The **antagonist** is the person in conflict with the main character. Not all stories have antagonists.

> The main characters are Cinderella, the stepsisters, their mother, the fairy godmother, the prince.
> **protagonist:** Cinderella
> **antagonists:** the stepsisters, their mother

Point of View

Point of view refers to the vantage point from which a story is told. The person telling the story is the narrator.

- **First-person point of view:** The narrator, a character in the story, uses "I" and "me" to tell the story.
- **Third-person point of view:** The narrator describes the characters and action from outside the story. A **third-person omniscient narrator** knows everything that goes on. A **third-person limited narrator** describes events as one character sees them.

> "Cinderella" is told from the **third-person omniscient point of view:** the narrator knows what all the characters are doing and thinking.

MEETING INDIVIDUAL NEEDS — ENGLISH LANGUAGE LEARNERS

Multicultural Stories Some English language learners will not be familiar with the story of Cinderella; others will know the story but not recognize the name of the story in English. Invite a volunteer—a more proficient English-speaking student—to give a brief summary of the story of Cinderella.

Activity As a whole group or in small groups, invite students to share (in English) summaries of similar stories, oral or written, from their native cultures. Then ask them to relate their stories to the elements of the short story.

Additional Resources
📁 *English Language Learners Sourcebook*

Theme

Theme is the central message of a story that readers can apply to life. Common themes include insights into human nature and perceptions about life.

- **Stated themes** are directly presented in a story.
- **Implied themes** must be inferred. Readers need to consider all the elements of a story and ask what message about life they convey.

> The theme of "Cinderella" is **implied.** The reader can infer the message that if you are in a bad situation, you should do the best that you can. In the end, things will work out for you.

Plot

Plot is the sequence of events in a story—a series of related incidents. Most plots deal with a **problem** and develop around a **conflict,** a struggle between opposing forces.

- An **external conflict** is a struggle between a character and an outside force, such as another character, nature, society, or fate.
- An **internal conflict** takes place within the mind of a character who struggles with opposing feelings or with indecision about how to act.

> The events that make up the plot of "Cinderella" are shown in the diagram below.
> **problem:** Cinderella wants to go to the ball, but her stepsisters prevent her from going.
> **conflict:** The conflict is external— Cinderella versus the stepsisters and their mother.

Theme

If students have difficulty determining the implied theme in a story, suggest that they first list major story events. Then they should ask themselves what lesson the story teaches, based on these events.

Plot

Students might better understand the concept of internal conflict if they apply it to their own lives. Ask them if they've ever had to decide how—or whether—to spend or save money, whether to take a part-time job, or which classes to sign up for.

Most plots develop in five stages.

- **Exposition** introduces the story's characters, setting, and conflict.
- **Rising action** develops the conflict with complications and twists.
- **Climax** is the emotional high point of the story.
- **Falling action** shows what happens to the characters after the climax.
- **Resolution** shows how the conflict is resolved or how the problem is solved.

CLIMAX
The stepsisters try to force their feet into the slipper. It fits Cinderella.

Cinderella dances with the prince, but leaves hurriedly at midnight, loses a slipper.

A fairy godmother appears and provides Cinderella with clothes, coach, and footman.

FALLING ACTION
Cinderella and the prince marry.

Cinderella lives with her stepsisters and their mother. They make her wear rags and do all the hard work.

An invitation to a ball at the palace arrives.

The prince says he will marry the woman whom the slipper fits.

Cinderella goes to the ball.

The stepsisters prepare for and go to the ball.

They live happily ever after.

EXPOSITION   **RISING ACTION**   **RESOLUTION**

Technology Option

Short Story Table

Students can use word processing software to create a table of short story elements as they read the stories in this unit. Have students open a new document and insert a six-column table with the following headings:

Story Title	Setting	Characters	Point of View	Theme	Plot

For each story, students can add a new row to the table and key in information about each of the five elements of that story. Students can use their completed tables as tools for study and review or as valuable sets of data for writing a comparison/contrast essay. **L2**

Active Reading Strategies

Objective

- To understand and apply strategies for reading and comprehending short stories

Teach the Strategies

Have students think of situations in life with predictable outcomes. Classmates can predict likely outcomes of those situations. Point out that making logical predictions is one of the strategies that good readers use.

Predict

Ask students how they can predict
- what a story will be about.
- what a character might do next.
- what event might occur later.

Point out to students that as they read further into a story, they may learn facts that may cause them to change a prediction.

Connect

Explain that connecting means to relate to a character or event in a story on a personal level. This strategy helps readers understand a character's motives and the causes and effects of events in a story.

Question

Point out that when good readers are confused about something in a story, they will reread that part, looking for details to clear up the confusion.

Active Reading Strategies

The Short Story

How can you get the most from your reading? Effective readers are active readers. As they read, they have conversations with themselves about the text; they get involved. Don't be a passive reader! Use the strategies below to help you read short stories actively and effectively.

● For more about related reading strategies, see **Reading Handbook,** pp. R78–R107.

PREDICT Predicting helps you anticipate events and stay alert to the less obvious parts of a story. Make educated guesses about what will happen next by combining clues in the story with what you already know.

> **Say to yourself . . .**
> ● From the title, I'd guess this story is about . . .
> ● This character will probably . . .
> ● The next thing that *has* to happen is . . .
> ● This story is different from my original prediction.

CONNECT Draw parallels between the people, places, and events in the story and the people, events, and places in your own life.

> **Ask yourself . . .**
> ● How would I act in the main character's situation?
> ● When have I felt the same way as this character?
> ● What parts of my life does this remind me of?
> ● What other stories does this remind me of?

QUESTION Ask yourself questions to help you clarify the story as you go along.

> **Ask yourself . . .**
> ● What's going on here?
> ● Why did he or she say that?
> ● What does this mean? Do I understand what I've just read?
> ● What might my teacher want me to notice about this story?

Teaching Options

Reading Journal

Contrasting Characters

Students can use their reading journals to record their thoughts and responses before, during, and after reading. Refer to pages T56–T57 in this Teacher's Wraparound Edition for more information about reading journals. In "Everyday Use," author Alice Walker draws sharp contrasts between the characters. Discuss ways in which authors create contrasts between characters. *(Sometimes one character is wise and one is foolish, or one is good while the other is evil, or one character may be serious and another playful.)*

Activity Have students divide two pages in their reading journal into two columns. As students read "Everyday Use," ask them to compare Mama and Dee on one page and Dee and Maggie on the other page. Suggest that students use both the author's words and their own words to describe each character. After students have read the story, ask volunteers to give an oral summary of each character.

VISUALIZE In your mind, form pictures of what is happening in the story. Pay attention to the details the writer gives you, and make them a part of your reading experience.

Ask yourself . . .
- How does this scene/character/object look?
- Who is in this scene?
- Where are the characters in relation to one another and to their surroundings?

EVALUATE Form opinions and make judgments about the story while you are reading—not just after you've finished.

Ask yourself . . .
- Does this turn of events make sense?
- How would I judge this character's thoughts and actions?
- What is particularly effective about this writer's style?

REVIEW Pause from time to time to think about your reading. Summarize events in a story or rephrase difficult language to help you understand and remember what you've read.

Say to yourself . . .
- So far, . . .
- In other words, . . .

RESPOND Respond *while* you are reading. What are your immediate reactions?

Say to yourself . . .
- I like this, because . . .
- I'd like to ask the writer why . . .
- I think this character is . . .
- I wish I could see this place because . . .
- That was surprising!

Applying the Strategies

1. Read the next story, "Everyday Use," using the Active Reading Model in the margins.

2. Choose a story you have not read and practice using all of these strategies. Use stick-on notes to annotate the story as you read, or take notes on a separate piece of paper.

Visualize
Suggest to students that if they have difficulty visualizing a scene, character, or event, they might find it helpful to draw a sketch using the details that the author provides.

Evaluate
Explain to students that as they read a story, they should evaluate not only the characters and events, but also the quality of the author's writing, such as the author's use of details, the ending of the story, and the author's choice of words.

Review
Acknowledge that it is not always easy to stop and summarize, but this strategy can significantly improve reading comprehension.

Respond
Make the analogy that just as people interact with each other, good readers interact with what they are reading. Emphasize that readers get as much out of a story as they put into it.

Objectives

- To read and analyze a short story about a family with conflicting values
- To identify point of view in a short story
- To compare and contrast two characters from the story

Skills

Reading/Thinking: Comparison and Contrast; Chronological Order

Writing: Character Description; Story Completion; Essay on Prized Possession

Vocabulary: Base Words

Grammar/Language: Usage: *Like* and *As*; Possessive Pronouns

Listening/Speaking: Storytelling; Interviewing

Life Skills: Interviewing

Collaboration: Storytelling; Literature Groups

Motivating
→OPTIONS

Selection Focus Transparency 1: Have students view and discuss *Bud Field's House*, a photograph by Walker Evans.

Focus Activity: Have each student choose one item from his or her list and write it on the board. Then ask students to describe why they think these items are prized.

 —Before You Read—
Everyday Use

FOCUS ACTIVITY

What objects have a special meaning for your family or for you?

QUICKWRITE List at least five objects that are prized by your family or by you. Briefly describe each one.

SETTING A PURPOSE Read to discover how the value of a prized possession can be seen in different ways.

BACKGROUND

The Time and Place

It is the 1970s somewhere in the South, deep in the country. The ancestors of the characters in "Everyday Use" probably were sharecroppers, like the author's parents. Sharecroppers rented land to farm, paid rent with a part of their crops, and sold the rest. In many cases, they worked brutally long hours and made just enough money to survive.

Did You Know?

Quilts developed as a way of making sure that nothing went to waste—even the scraps of fabric left over from making clothes. Women developed complicated patterns of arranging the scraps, and many quilts became works of art.

VOCABULARY PREVIEW

sidle (sīd′ əl) *v.* to move sideways, especially in a way that does not attract attention or cause disturbance; p. 8

furtive (fur′ tiv) *adj.* secret; shifty; sly; p. 11

oppress (ə pres′) *v.* to control or govern by the cruel and unjust use of force or authority; p. 12

doctrine (dok′ trin) *n.* a particular principle or position that is taught or supported, as of a religion; p. 13

priceless (prīs′ lis) *adj.* of greater value than can be measured; p. 16

Meet Alice Walker

If Alice Walker's brother had not accidentally shot her in the eye with a BB gun when she was eight, she might not have become a writer. The next year she had to go to a new school. The students made fun of her, and she became self-conscious and shy. Walker began spending her time alone, writing in her journal and reading. By the time she was fourteen and had eye surgery to improve her appearance, she was already hooked on writing and reading. Her most famous book is *The Color Purple*. It won a Pulitzer Prize and was made into a movie.

Alice Walker was born in 1944 in Georgia. She wrote this story in 1972.

RESOURCE MANAGER

Lesson Planning Resource

The *Unit One Planning Guide* (pp. 2–9) provides additional lesson notes and reduced versions of all print resources.

Other Print Resources

- Active Reading Guide, p. 1
- Vocabulary Practice, p. 1
- Reading Workbook, pp. 1–2
- Grammar and Language Workbook, pp. 225, 181

- Grammar and Composition Handbook, Lessons 1.6, 1.7, 1.2
- Quick Checks, p. 1
- Selection and Theme Assessment, pp. 1–2
- Performance Assessment, p. 1
- Spanish Summaries, p. 1
- Inclusion Strategies
- English Language Learners Sourcebook

 Transparencies

- Selection Focus 1
- Literary Elements 1
- Grammar and Language 1

Technology

- Audio Library
- Spanish Audio Library
- Glencoe Literature Web Site
- Testmaker

EVERYDAY Use

Alice Walker

I WILL WAIT FOR HER in the yard that Maggie and I made so clean and wavy yesterday afternoon. A yard like this is more comfortable than most people know. It is not just a yard. It is like an extended living room. When the hard clay is swept clean as a floor and the fine sand around the edges lined with tiny, irregular grooves, anyone can come and sit and look up into the elm tree and wait for the breezes that never come inside the house.

Maggie will be nervous until after her sister goes: she will stand hopelessly in corners, homely and ashamed of the burn scars down her arms and legs, eying her sister with a mixture of envy and awe. She thinks her sister has held life always in the palm of one hand, that "no" is a word the world never learned to say to her.

You've no doubt seen those TV shows where the child who has "made it" is confronted, as a surprise, by her own mother and father, tottering in weakly from backstage. (A pleasant surprise, of course: What would they do if parent and child came on the show only to curse out and insult each other?) On TV mother and child embrace and smile into each other's faces.

Active Reading Model

PREDICT

Based on the first paragraphs, what might this story be about?

Reading the Selection

SUMMARY

Mama and her stay-at-home daughter Maggie are awaiting the arrival of Dee, Maggie's older sister, who has broken away from rural poverty. Dee arrives with a boyfriend, with a wild Afro, and with a new name: Wangero. She is as condescending and assertive as Mama remembers her. After dinner Dee discovers two handmade quilts and demands to have them. For once Mama defies Dee and says that she has promised them to Maggie. She explains that the quilts are for everyday use and not to be hung on a wall. Dee leaves in a rage but Mama and Maggie enjoy the evening with a newfound respect for each other and their way of life.

📁 *Spanish Summaries,* p. 1

Active Reading Model

Predict

Students may say it will be about a family or about two sisters, one coming home for a visit.

Additional Resources
- 📁 *Active Reading Guide,* p. 1
- 🎧 *Audio Library*
- 🎧 *Spanish Audio Library*

Teaching Options

CONNECTING TO OTHER SELECTIONS

The chart on the right shows three ways to connect "Everyday Use" to selections in the book.

For specific teaching strategies, see the *Unit One Planning Guide,* pages 5–6.

Connection	Title
Life Skills: Problem Solving →	"Where the Girl Rescued Her Brother," p. 983
Thematic: Taking a Stand →	"I've Seen the Promised Land," p. 517
Literary: Characterization →	"To Da-duh, in Memoriam," p. 399

POINT OF VIEW Ask students how they know that this story is told in first-person point of view. *(The narrator uses* I, me, we, *and other first person pronouns to tell the story.)* **Who is the narrator in this story?** *(the mother of Dee and Maggie)*

Question

Some students will be confused by the introduction, which never explicitly states that the "sister" awaited in paragraph two is the same as Dee, Mama's glamorous daughter. Explain to students that their confusion is understandable but that there is enough evidence in the exposition to make an educated guess. If necessary, review the facts and ask students the question again.

Visualize

Students may get a clearer picture of Maggie if they try to visualize her apologetic body language. Invite students to visualize how Maggie would perform simple actions: opening a door, meeting a stranger, eating a meal. This activity will also help clarify the meaning of the word *sidle*.

Teaching Options

E**VERYDAY** *Use*

Active Reading Model

Sometimes the mother and father weep, the child wraps them in her arms and leans across the table to tell how she would not have made it without their help. I have seen these programs.

A Sometimes I dream a dream in which Dee and I are suddenly brought together on a TV program of this sort. Out of a dark and soft-seated limousine I am ushered into a bright room filled with many people. There I meet a smiling, gray, sporty man like Johnny Carson who shakes my hand and tells me what a fine girl I have. Then we are on the stage and Dee is embracing me with tears in her eyes. She pins on my dress a large orchid, even though she has told me once that she thinks orchids are tacky flowers.

Did You Know?
Johnny Carson hosted *The Tonight Show,* the popular late-night TV talk show, from 1962 to 1992.

In real life I am a large, big-boned woman with rough, man-working hands. In the winter I wear flannel nightgowns to bed and overalls during the day. I can kill and clean a hog as mercilessly as a man. My fat keeps me hot in zero weather. I can work outside all day, breaking ice to get water for washing; I can eat pork liver cooked over the open fire minutes after it comes steaming from the hog. One winter I knocked a bull calf straight in the brain between the eyes with a sledge hammer and had the meat hung up to chill before nightfall. But of course all this does not show on television. I am the way my daughter would want me to be: a hundred pounds lighter, my skin like an uncooked barley pancake. My hair glistens in the hot bright lights. Johnny Carson has much to do to keep up with my quick and witty tongue.

But that is a mistake. I know even before I wake up. Who ever knew a Johnson with a quick tongue? Who can even imagine me looking a strange white man in the eye? It seems to me I have talked to them always with one foot raised in flight, with my head turned in whichever way is farthest from them. Dee, though. She would always look anyone in the eye. Hesitation was no part of her nature.

QUESTION
Who is Dee?

H**ow do I look, Mama?"** Maggie says, showing just enough of her thin body enveloped in pink skirt and red blouse for me to know she's there, almost hidden by the door.

"Come out into the yard," I say.

VISUALIZE
How do you picture Maggie from these details?

Have you ever seen a lame animal, perhaps a dog run over by some careless person rich enough to own a car, <u>sidle</u> up to someone who is ignorant enough to be kind to him? That is the way my Maggie walks. She has been like this, chin on chest, eyes on ground, feet in shuffle, ever since the fire that burned the other house to the ground.

Vocabulary
sidle (sīd′ əl) *v.* to move sideways, especially in a way that does not attract attention or cause disturbance

---

As Others See Us English language learners may have difficulty understanding why Dee is so different from Mama and Maggie. Students should realize that the 1960s and 1970s were a time of significant social change in the United States, especially for the African American community. With the success of the Civil Rights movement, a more assertive and educated culture emerged.

Activity Have English language learners describe the extent to which they see themselves as typical or atypical representatives of their homelands or traditional cultures.

Additional Resources
📁 *English Language Learners Sourcebook*

Girl in a Green Dress, 1930. William H. Johnson. Oil on canvas, 24¼ x 19½ in. National Museum of American Art, Washington, DC.

Viewing the painting: Which of the two sisters might be more like the girl in this portrait? Explain.

VIEWING THE PAINTING

William H. Johnson (1901–1970) was an African American artist who captured the spirit of black America in his portrayals of ordinary people, from the southern farm to the streets of Harlem. Now recognized as one of America's major painters, he struggled to make a living by his art. In 1947 he was hospitalized for mental illness and never painted again.

Viewing Response *The wide-eyed, apprehensive expression of this girl will remind many readers of Maggie.*

At the **MOVIES**

Be sure to preview the following video for appropriateness for your class:

- **The Sum of Its Parts: Theme in Short Fiction*** (dramatization of "Everyday Use")

*Also available in the Glencoe Literature Video Library.

Writing Minilesson

Describing a Character The picture that emerges of Mama on page 8 is created not so much through her appearance as by a catalog of what she does (wears overalls, slaughters hogs, washes in ice water). Point out that character is only superficially defined by appearance.

Activity Have students write the following sentence: "_____ is the sort of person who . . ." Then ask them to think of someone they know well, fill in the blank, and complete the sentence several times with an action characteristic of that person. Finally, have them write a paragraph describing their subject. **L2**

Additional Resources

Writer's Choice, Lessons 3.3, 4.1

Maggie was badly burned on the arms and legs and emotionally traumatized by the fire. Dee was unhurt and pleased to see the old house destroyed.

Evaluate

The narrator is uncomfortable with Dee's aggressive and contemptuous manner. Her choice of words ("without pity," "forced us," "burned us," etc.) suggest that Maggie and she were almost under physical attack. Some students may interpret this to mean that Mama dislikes Dee, but Mama's feelings are not entirely spelled out: she is curiously objective, praising Dee where praise is due.

Connect

Remind students of Dee's complexity. It might be worth listing Dee's "good" traits versus her "bad" traits on the board in order to keep the complete character in sight.

Visualize

Have groups of three draw a picture of the house. Assign one "artist," one student to read aloud the description, and the third to check the details of the "drawing." Then have each group share their renderings with the class.

Teaching Options

EVERYDAY Use

Active Reading Model

QUESTION

What happened to the sisters in the fire?

EVALUATE

How would you judge the narrator's feelings about Dee's behavior?

CONNECT

Can you think of anyone you know who is like Dee?

VISUALIZE

Stop and form a detailed mental image of the house.

Dee is lighter than Maggie, with nicer hair and a fuller figure. She's a woman now, though sometimes I forget. How long ago was it that the other house burned? Ten, twelve years? Sometimes I can still hear the flames and feel Maggie's arms sticking to me, her hair smoking and her dress falling off her in little black papery flakes. Her eyes seemed stretched open, blazed open by the flames reflected in them. And Dee. I see her standing off under the sweet gum tree she used to dig gum out of; a look of concentration on her face as she watched the last dingy gray board of the house fall in toward the red-hot brick chimney. Why don't you do a dance around the ashes? I'd wanted to ask her. She had hated the house that much.

I used to think she hated Maggie, too. But that was before we raised the money, the church and me, to send her to Augusta[1] to school. She used to read to us without pity; forcing words, lies, other folks' habits, whole lives upon us two, sitting trapped and ignorant underneath her voice. She washed us in a river of make-believe, burned us with a lot of knowledge we didn't necessarily need to know. Pressed us to her with the serious way she read, to shove us away at just the moment, like dimwits, we seemed about to understand.

Dee wanted nice things. A yellow organdy[2] dress to wear to her graduation from high school; black pumps to match a green suit she'd made from an old suit somebody gave me. She was determined to stare down any disaster in her efforts. Her eyelids would not flicker for minutes at a time. Often I fought off the temptation to shake her. At sixteen she had a style of her own: and knew what style was.

I never had an education myself. After second grade the school was closed down. Don't ask me why: in 1927 colored asked fewer questions than they do now. Sometimes Maggie reads to me. She stumbles along good-naturedly but can't see well. She knows she is not bright. Like good looks and money, quickness passed her by. She will marry John Thomas (who has mossy teeth in an earnest face) and then I'll be free to sit here and I guess just sing church songs to myself. Although I never was a good singer. Never could carry a tune. I was always better at a man's job. I used to love to milk till I was hooked in the side in '49. Cows are soothing and slow and don't bother you, unless you try to milk them the wrong way.

I have deliberately turned my back on the house. It is three rooms, just like the one that burned, except the roof is tin; they don't make shingle roofs any more. There are no real windows, just some holes cut in the sides, like the portholes in a ship, but not round and not square, with rawhide holding the shutters up on the outside. This house is in a pasture, too, like the other one. No doubt when Dee sees it she will want to tear it down. She wrote me once that no matter where we "choose" to live, she will manage to come see us. But

---

1. *Augusta* is a city in Georgia.
2. *Organdy* is a lightweight fabric, usually made of cotton.

INCLUSION STRATEGIES
MEETING INDIVIDUAL NEEDS

Less-Proficient Readers The exposition of "Everyday Use" is long and fragmented, as Mama's narrative spans the decades with the speed of thought. It may be useful to review what the reader knows and does not know.

Activity Have students write three headings at the top of a sheet of paper: *What I Know, What I Think I Know,* and

What I Don't Get. Give them a few minutes to list as many items as they can under each of these headings. Then have them share information with a partner. Create a master list on the board. Point out that early in any story some confusion is common. **L1**

Additional Resources
📂 *Inclusion Strategies*

she will never bring her friends. Maggie and I thought about this and Maggie asked me, "Mama, when did Dee ever *have* any friends?"

She had a few. <u>Furtive</u> boys in pink shirts hanging about on washday after school. Nervous girls who never laughed. Impressed with her they worshiped the well-turned phrase, the cute shape, the scalding humor that erupted like bubbles in lye. She read to them.

When she was courting Jimmy T she didn't have much time to pay to us, but turned all her faultfinding power on him. He *flew* to marry a cheap city girl from a family of ignorant flashy people. She hardly had time to recompose herself.

When she comes I will meet—but there they are!

Maggie attempts to make a dash for the house, in her shuffling way, but I stay her with my hand. "Come back here," I say. And she stops and tries to dig a well in the sand with her toe.

It is hard to see them clearly through the strong sun. But even the first glimpse of leg out of the car tells me it is Dee. Her feet were always neat-looking, as if God himself had shaped them with a certain style. From the other side of the car comes a short, stocky man. Hair is all over his head a foot long and hanging from his chin like a kinky mule tail. I hear Maggie suck in her breath. "Uhnnnh," is what it sounds like. Like when you see the wriggling end of a snake just in front of your foot on the road. "Uhnnnh."

Dee next. A dress down to the ground, in this hot weather. A dress so loud it hurts my eyes. There are yellows and oranges enough to throw back the light of the sun. I feel my whole face warming from the heat waves it throws out. Earrings gold, too, and hanging down to her shoulders. Bracelets dangling and making noises when she moves her arm up to shake the folds of the dress out of her armpits. The dress is loose and flows, and as she walks closer, I like it. I hear Maggie go "Uhnnnh" again. It is her sister's hair. It stands straight up like the wool on a sheep. It is black as night and around the edges are two long pigtails that rope about like small lizards disappearing behind her ears.

"Wa-su-zo-Tean-o!" she says, coming on in that gliding way the dress makes her move. The short stocky fellow with the hair to his navel is all grinning and follows up with "Asalamalakim,[3] my mother and sister!" He moves to hug Maggie but she falls back, right up against the back of my chair. I feel her trembling there and when I look up I see the perspiration falling off her chin.

"Don't get up," says Dee. Since I am stout it takes something of a push. You can see me trying to move a second or two before I make it. She turns,

PREDICT

What do you think this family reunion will be like?

---

3. *Wa-su-zo-Tean-o!* (wä sōō′ zō tēn′ ō) and *Asalamalakim* (ä säl ä mä′ lä kēm) are greetings.

Vocabulary
furtive (fur′ tiv) *adj.* secret; shifty; sly

Active Reading Model

Predict

Have students close their books after reading, "but there they are!" Encourage students to review the differences between Dee and her family and discuss how these might affect their communication. Urge them to support their predictions with evidence from the text.

MEETING INDIVIDUAL NEEDS — GIFTED AND TALENTED

Changing Oneself Returning to one's family or hometown as a "new" person may be a common fantasy. Some individuals, like Dee, may actually do so.

Activity Challenge students to write a scenario in which they return to their hometown after an absence of ten years. For example, they might visualize themselves returning as a famous athlete or a celebrated author. Have students share their scenarios and discuss aspects which might suggest worthwhile goals and those which are merely superficial, such as a new style of dress.
L3 COLLAB. LEARN.

Evaluate

If students are aware of how different Dee's life is now from that of her upbringing, they will understand that she is like a tourist in a foreign country, taking snapshots of the strange world she is passing through. Dee may also have in mind amazing her new friends with images of primitive country life.

Question

Mama has not yet been introduced to Dee's companion. "Asalamalakim" is all she has heard him say. She also has a wry sense of humor, finding him a curious-looking man, who will doubtless have a curious name.

Review

Ask students what Dee means by "the people who oppress me." Point out that enslaved people generally took their names from white culture, a tradition that continued long after the Civil War. Make sure that students realize how Dee's rebellious assumption of an African name may at first have seemed unusual, even shocking, to many Americans in the 1960s and 1970s.

Teaching Options

E verYDAY *Use*

Active Reading Model

EVALUATE

Does it make sense for Dee to take pictures of a place she hates so much?

QUESTION

Why does the narrator keep calling him *Asalamalakim?*

REVIEW

Think about what you know about this family so far.

Did You Know?
The *Model A* was manufactured by the Ford Motor Company from 1927 to 1931.

showing white heels through her sandals, and goes back to the car. Out she peeks next with a Polaroid. She stoops down quickly and lines up picture after picture of me sitting there in front of the house with Maggie cowering behind me. She never takes a shot without making sure the house is included. When a cow comes nibbling around the edge of the yard she snaps it and me and Maggie *and* the house. Then she puts the Polaroid in the back seat of the car, and comes up and kisses me on the forehead.

Meanwhile Asalamalakim is going through motions with Maggie's hand. Maggie's hand is as limp as a fish, and probably as cold, despite the sweat, and she keeps trying to pull it back. It looks like Asalamalakim wants to shake hands but wants to do it fancy. Or maybe he don't know how people shake hands. Anyhow, he soon gives up on Maggie.

"Well," I say. "Dee."

"No, Mama," she says. "Not 'Dee,' Wangero Leewanika Kemanjo!"[4]

"What happened to 'Dee'?" I wanted to know.

"She's dead," Wangero said. "I couldn't bear it any longer, being named after the people who oppress me."

"You know as well as me you was named after your aunt Dicie," I said. Dicie is my sister. She named Dee. We called her "Big Dee" after Dee was born.

"But who was *she* named after?" asked Wangero.

"I guess after Grandma Dee," I said.

"And who was she named after?" asked Wangero.

"Her mother," I said, and saw Wangero was getting tired. "That's about as far back as I can trace it," I said. Though, in fact, I probably could have carried it back beyond the Civil War through the branches.

"Well," said Asalamalakim, "there you are."

"Uhnnnh," I heard Maggie say.

"There I was not," I said, "before 'Dicie' cropped up in our family, so why should I try to trace it that far back?"

He just stood there grinning, looking down on me like somebody inspecting a Model A car. Every once in a while he and Wangero sent eye signals over my head.

"How do you pronounce this name?" I asked.

"You don't have to call me by it if you don't want to," said Wangero.

"Why shouldn't I?" I asked. "If that's what you want us to call you, we'll call you."

"I know it might sound awkward at first," said Wangero.

---

4. *Wangero Leewanika Kemanjo* (wän gär′ ō lē wä′ nē kə   ke män′ ō)

Vocabulary
oppress (ə pres′) *v.* to control or govern by the cruel and unjust use of force or authority

REAL-WORLD CONNECTION

Changing One's Life Dee's way of life is a far cry from the rural poverty in which she was raised.

Activity Have students think of real-life examples of men or women whose present careers have little in common with their backgrounds—people who have risen to prominence from deprivation or from different cultures. Ask students to cut out newspaper or magazine articles about

their subjects and to share their findings with others in groups. Have them consider such questions as these: How did the person transform his or her life? Is he or she happier as a result? **L2** **COLLAB. LEARN.**

Active Reading Model

Question

It appears that Mama has been sharing a joke with the reader at "Asalamalakim's" expense. Ask students how intelligent they think Mama is. Point out that a lack of education does not mean that a person is dull or unobservant. Encourage students to find other examples of Mama's keen mind and wry humor.

"I'll get used to it," I said. "Ream it out again."

Well, soon we got the name out of the way. Asalamalakim had a name twice as long and three times as hard. After I tripped over it two or three times he told me to just call him Hakim-a-barber.[5] I wanted to ask him was he a barber, but I didn't really think he was, so I didn't ask.

"You must belong to those beef cattle peoples down the road," I said. They said "Asalamalakim" when they met you, too, but they didn't shake hands. Always too busy: feeding the cattle, fixing the fences, putting up salt-lick shelters, throwing down hay. When the white folks poisoned some of the herd the men stayed up all night with rifles in their hands. I walked a mile and a half just to see the sight.

Hakim-a-barber said, "I accept some of their doctrines, but farming and raising cattle is not my style." (They didn't tell me, and I didn't ask, whether Wangero (Dee) had really gone and married him.)

We sat down to eat and right away he said he didn't eat collards and pork was unclean. Wangero, though, went on through the chitlins and corn bread, the greens and everything else. She talked a blue streak over the sweet potatoes. Everything delighted her. Even the fact that we still used the benches her daddy made for the table when we couldn't afford to buy chairs.

"Oh, Mama!" she cried. Then turned to Hakim-a-barber. "I never knew how lovely these benches are. You can feel the rump prints," she said, running her hands underneath her and along the bench. Then she gave a sigh and her hand closed over Grandma Dee's butter dish. "That's it!" she said. "I knew

Active Reading Model

QUESTION

Do you think this means that Mama knew all along that *Asalamalakim* was a greeting?

---

5. *Hakim-a-barber* (hä kēm′ ä bär′ bər)

Vocabulary

doctrine (dok′ trin) *n.* a particular principle or position that is taught or supported, as of a religion

THE SHORT STORY 🐦 13

Traditional Food Mama and Maggie serve food traditional to the African American South. Point out to English language learners that food such as collard greens (plant in the mustard family), chitterlings or chitlins (the small intestines of pigs), and sweet potatoes became known as *soul food* by African Americans hungry to preserve their traditions. Discuss with students the importance of traditional food in their own lives.

Activity Have students think about foods traditional to their ethnic or family cultures. Ask them to list them under the following headings: *I Don't Like, I Like,* and *Everyone Would Like.*

Additional Resources

 English Language Learners Sourcebook

Like many black artists of his generation, William H. Johnson (1901–1970) had difficulty gaining acceptance in the United States. He married a Danish artist in 1930, living with her in Denmark and Norway until the threat of war drove the couple to New York City.

Viewing Response *Like Mama, Minnie in this painting appears to be a wise and humorous woman, whose spirit is in no way broken by a hard life.*

Minnie, 1930. William H. Johnson. Oil on canvas, 17½ x 12¼ in. National Museum of American Art, Washington, DC.

Viewing the painting: What qualities might this woman share with the narrator of the story?

Teaching Options

interNET CONNECTION

The largest collection of paintings by the African American artist William H. Johnson is in the National Museum of American Art in Washington, D.C. The museum's Web site offers an exploration of Johnson's life and work, designed especially for high school students. Have students visit the Web site and click on *education*. Ask students to read the material and complete one of the exercises. **L2**

LITERATURE & HUMANITIES

Display *A Day at the Fair*, Transparency 29 in *U.S. History and Art*. Have students note the girl's position, the window, and the title. Have them discuss how each of the story characters would perceive the girl in the painting.

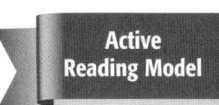

there was something I wanted to ask you if I could have." She jumped up from the table and went over in the corner where the churn stood, the milk in it clabber[6] by now. She looked at the churn and looked at it.

"This churn top is what I need," she said. "Didn't Uncle Buddy whittle it out of a tree you all used to have?"

"Yes," I said.

"Uh huh," she said happily. "And I want the dasher, too."

"Uncle Buddy whittle that, too?" asked the barber.

Dee (Wangero) looked up at me.

"Aunt Dee's first husband whittled the dash," said Maggie so low you almost couldn't hear her. "His name was Henry, but they called him Stash."

"Maggie's brain is like an elephant's," Wangero said, laughing. "I can use the churn top as a centerpiece for the alcove[7] table," she said, sliding a plate over the churn, "and I'll think of something artistic to do with the dasher."

When she finished wrapping the dasher the handle stuck out. I took it for a moment in my hands. You didn't even have to look close to see where hands pushing the dasher up and down to make butter had left a kind of sink in the wood. In fact, there were a lot of small sinks; you could see where thumbs and fingers had sunk into the wood. It was beautiful light yellow wood, from a tree that grew in the yard where Big Dee and Stash had lived.

After dinner Dee (Wangero) went to the trunk at the foot of my bed and started rifling through it. Maggie hung back in the kitchen over the dishpan. Out came Wangero with two quilts. They had been pieced by Grandma Dee and then Big Dee and me had hung them on the quilt frames on the front porch and quilted them. One was in the Lone Star pattern. The other was Walk Around the Mountain. In both of them were scraps of dresses Grandma Dee had worn fifty and more years ago. Bits and pieces of Grandpa Jarrell's Paisley shirts. And one teeny faded blue piece, about the size of a penny matchbox, that was from Great Grandpa Ezra's uniform that he wore in the Civil War.

"Mama," Wangero said sweet as a bird. "Can I have these old quilts?"

I heard something fall in the kitchen, and a minute later the kitchen door slammed.

"Why don't you take one or two of the others?" I asked. "These old things was just done by me and Big Dee from some tops your grandma pieced before she died."

"No," said Wangero. "I don't want those. They are stitched around the borders by machine."

Dasher/Plunger

Churn

Did You Know?
A *dasher* is the plunger of a churn, a device used to stir cream to make butter.

PREDICT

Do you think Dee will end up with the quilts? Why?

---

6. *Clabber* is the thick, clotted part of sour milk.
7. An *alcove* (al′ kōv) is a small room or recessed opening off of a larger room.

Active Reading Model

Predict

Encourage students to consider Dee's personality, Mama's attitude toward her, and the fate of the churn in making their predictions.

Reading *Minilesson*

Comparison and Contrast Conducting a detailed comparison of the two sisters in the story can help students draw conclusions about the story's theme and about the character of the narrator.

Activity Have students create a chart contrasting Maggie and Dee. Suggest that they begin with superficial traits such as physical appearance and style of dress,

progress to obvious traits such as speaking styles, and end with traits they infer from the characters' dialogue and actions, such as kindness and generosity. Have volunteers contribute items for a chart on the board. **L2**

Additional Resources
📁 ***Reading Workbook,*** pp. 1–2

Connect

Ask students what they notice about Dee's statement. Ask them whether the phrase *everyday use* has positive or negative connotations for them. How is Dee using the expression? Does Mama agree with her?

Question

Have students consider how perspectives change as one grows older. They might appreciate Dee's change of mind by thinking of objects or events in their own lives whose values have changed for them.

Connect

Remind students that there has already been a hint of how Maggie feels about the quilts (the noise in the kitchen). Ask students whether Maggie is being sincere when she offers to give up the quilts. If not, why would she make the offer?

Respond

Most students will feel happy that Mama has finally taken charge. Have them discuss why she has chosen to defy Dee at this moment.

B Literary Elements

POINT OF VIEW Ask students to consider what the story would be like if it had been told from Maggie's point of view. How would she tell about the scene in which Mama snatches the quilts from Dee and gives them to Maggie?

Teaching Options

EVERYDAY *Use*

Active Reading Model

CONNECT

How does this statement relate to the story's title?

QUESTION

Why does Dee want the quilts now, when she did not want to take one to college?

CONNECT

How would you feel if you were Maggie?

RESPOND

How do you feel about what Mama did?

"That'll make them last better," I said.

"That's not the point," said Wangero. "These are all pieces of dresses Grandma used to wear. She did all this stitching by hand. Imagine!" She held the quilts securely in her arms, stroking them.

"Some of the pieces, like those lavender ones, come from old clothes her mother handed down to her," I said, moving up to touch the quilts. Dee (Wangero) moved back just enough so that I couldn't reach the quilts. They already belonged to her.

"Imagine!" she breathed again, clutching them closely to her bosom.

"The truth is," I said, "I promised to give them quilts to Maggie, for when she marries John Thomas."

She gasped like a bee had stung her.

"Maggie can't appreciate these quilts!" she said. "She'd probably be backward enough to put them to everyday use."

"I reckon she would," I said. "God knows I been saving 'em for long enough with nobody using 'em. I hope she will!" I didn't want to bring up how I had offered Dee (Wangero) a quilt when she went away to college. Then she had told me they were old-fashioned, out of style.

"But they're *priceless!*" she was saying now, furiously; for she has a temper. "Maggie would put them on the bed and in five years they'd be in rags. Less than that!"

"She can always make some more," I said. "Maggie knows how to quilt."

Dee (Wangero) looked at me with hatred. "You just will not understand. The point is these quilts, *these* quilts!"

"Well," I said, stumped. "What would *you* do with them?"

"Hang them," she said. As if that was the only thing you *could* do with quilts.

Maggie by now was standing in the door. I could almost hear the sound her feet made as they scraped over each other.

"She can have them, Mama," she said, like somebody used to never winning anything, or having anything reserved for her. "I can 'member Grandma Dee without the quilts."

I looked at her hard. She had filled her bottom lip with checkerberry snuff and it gave her face a kind of dopey, hangdog look. It was Grandma Dee and Big Dee who taught her how to quilt herself. She stood there with her scarred hands hidden in the folds of her skirt. She looked at her sister with something like fear but she wasn't mad at her. This was Maggie's portion. This was the way she knew God to work.

When I looked at her like that something hit me in the top of my head and ran down to the soles of my feet. Just like when I'm in church and the spirit of God touches me and I get happy and shout. I did something I never

B

Vocabulary

priceless (prīs′ lis) *adj.* of greater value than can be measured

---

Grammar and Language *Minilesson*

Usage: Like and As Write the following sentences on the board:

She looked at her sister with something like fear.

She gasped like a bee had stung her.

In each sentence, underline *like*. Point out that in the first case the word is employed before a noun as a preposition, which is conventional Standard English. In the sec-

ond example, *like* is used as a conjunction, connecting two clauses. This usage is common in everyday speech, but in more formal, written English the word *as* or the phrase *as if* is preferred.

Activity Have students find other examples of the word *like* in this story, discuss their findings in small groups, and decide which of their examples represent Stan-

dard English and which represent more informal usage. **L2 COLLAB. LEARN.**

Additional Resources

Grammar and Language Transparency 1

Grammar and Language Workbook, p. 225

Grammar and Composition Handbook, Lessons 1.6–1.7

Writer's Choice

Quilts on the Line, 1994. Anna Belle Lee Washington. Oil on canvas, 20 x 30 in.
Viewing the painting: Compare and contrast the family and the setting of this painting with those in the story. What are the most striking differences? similarities?

had done before: hugged Maggie to me, then dragged her on into the room, snatched the quilts out of Miss Wangero's hands and dumped them into Maggie's lap. Maggie just sat there on my bed with her mouth open.

"Take one or two of the others," I said to Dee.

But she turned without a word and went out to Hakim-a-barber.

"You just don't understand," she said, as Maggie and I came out to the car.

"What don't I understand?" I wanted to know.

"Your heritage," she said. And then she turned to Maggie, kissed her, and said, "You ought to try to make something of yourself, too, Maggie. It's really a new day for us. But from the way you and Mama still live you'd never know it."

She put on some sunglasses that hid everything above the tip of her nose and her chin.

Maggie smiled; maybe at the sunglasses. But a real smile, not scared. After we watched the car dust settle I asked Maggie to bring me a dip of snuff. And then the two of us sat there just enjoying, until it was time to go in the house and go to bed.

Respond

Ask students why they think Mama and Maggie, with nothing but a quiet evening ahead of them, are happier than Dee, with her car, clothes, and modern ideas. Extend the discussion by inviting students to describe times when they *just enjoy.*

☑ **ASSESSMENT OPTIONS**

📁 *Quick Checks,* p. 1

RESPOND

"... the two of us sat there just enjoying ..." What do you think of this description of contentment?

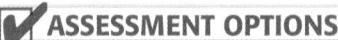

MULTIPLE LEARNING STYLES

MEETING INDIVIDUAL NEEDS

Linguistic Words are what makes Dee tick. In the old days, she would "force" words on Mama and Maggie, and at dinner in "Everyday Use," she talks "a blue streak." She will almost certainly talk about this day's events to her friends when she returns home.

Activity Ask students to imagine that they are Dee. Have them take notes on what they think is on Dee's mind as she returns to her new home. Have them pretend that Dee is talking to a friend about her visit to the country. Remind them that Dee is a fast talker, barely pausing to breathe. Let students practice telling their stories in groups. Invite volunteers to entertain the class with Dee's version of events.
L2 **COLLAB. LEARN.**

Responding to the Selection

Personal Response

If students are slow to respond to this prompt, write the names of the three women on the board and spend a few minutes listing their characteristics.

ACTIVE READING RESPONSE

Make sure that students choose one of the seven strategies listed on pages 4–5 and that they are using the strategy correctly in the three places in the story they choose.

ANALYZING LITERATURE

1. Mama says that Maggie is homely, envious, insecure, good-natured, "not bright," and short-sighted. Dee is bold, light-skinned, attractive, ambitious, determined, and aggressive.
2. Dee says she was tired of being named after whites, "the people who oppress me." Mama is willing to accept the change but has trouble understanding why it is necessary, since Dee was, in fact, named after relatives.
3. They had been pieced by Grandma Dee from scraps of old clothing and quilted by Mama and her sister.
4. Dee is outraged. Maggie tells Mama to let Dee have them.
5. Dee is angry that she did not get the quilts and is irritated by Mama and Maggie's conservative ways.
6. Mama is in awe of Dee's ambition and drive; she is affectionate toward Maggie but a little sorry for her.
7. Dee may well have wished to forget her humble upbringing. She may also want to keep up with a new fashion.
8. Maggie sees the quilts both as useful objects and as a way of remembering her grandmother; Dee is primarily interested in their aesthetic, commercial, and cultural value.
9. Dee is contemptuous and condescending toward Maggie. She refers to her in the third person, calling her "backward" and finally telling her she ought to "make something" out of herself.
10. Mama finally does understand. She realizes that Dee is largely selfish and superficial and that Maggie and she have more true care for their heritage than Dee ever will.
11. The author is establishing a contrast between Mama's homely surroundings and the world of cities and glamour that she knows only through television.

12. Setting is important here, emphasizing the revolution in a way of life among African Americans, from rural simplicity to urban stylishness. Similar stories can be told about cultural conflict in other settings, but the characters would probably be of different ethnic origins.
13. Although sensitive readers will probably find Maggie the nicer sister, some may think Dee is more exciting and attractive.
14. Some students may say that they "understand" but do not entirely appreciate their heritage; others may revere their backgrounds.
15. Encourage students to be specific in their advice (i.e., avoid "Grow up!").

Responding to Literature

Personal Response

The author has said that she thinks of Dee and Maggie and Mama as herself split into three parts. Which of the characters do you think is most like you? Explain in your journal.

Active Reading Response

Look back at the strategies described in the notes on pages 4 and 5. Which of these strategies do you use most often? Choose one and find three places in the story where you could apply it.

─── ANALYZING LITERATURE ───

RECALL

1. Tell what Mama says about each daughter before Dee's arrival.
2. What reason does Dee give for changing her name? What is Mama's opinion of Dee's reason?
3. What is special about the two quilts that Dee wants?
4. How does Dee react when she learns what Mama plans to do with the quilts? What does Maggie say that Mama should do with them?
5. Why does Dee leave the house so abruptly?

INTERPRET

6. What can you infer about Mama's feelings toward Maggie and Dee, based on the information she gives before Dee arrives?
7. Do you think the reason Dee gives for changing her name is her only reason? Explain your answer.
8. How does the origin of the quilts affect Maggie's feelings about them? How does it affect Dee?
9. How does Dee feel about Maggie? Support your answer with details from the story.
10. Dee says at the end, "You just don't understand." In your opinion, does Mama understand? Explain.

EVALUATE AND CONNECT

11. Why, do you think, does the author begin the story with a description of the yard and a daydream about being on a television show?
12. How important a role does the **setting** play? How might the story be different if the characters lived in another time and another place?
13. Which sister do you like better, Maggie or Dee? Give reasons.
14. Do you feel that you understand your own heritage? Explain.
15. What advice would you like to give to Maggie? To Dee? To Mama?

Literary ELEMENTS

Point of View

In **first-person point of view,** the story is told by one of the characters, a narrator who uses "I" and "me" to relate the story. This point of view is limited because the reader "sees" the story only through that character's eyes. In "Everyday Use," for example, the author uses the first-person point of view to tell the story through Mama's eyes. The reader learns what Mama sees, thinks, feels, and experiences as she tells the story in her own voice.

1. The author might have told this story from the point of view of Dee or of Maggie. Why, do you think, did she choose to give Mama's version of what happened?
2. A reader must decide whether to trust the accuracy of the information a narrator presents. Do you trust Mama's version of events? Why or why not?
3. Retell or rewrite a scene from the point of view of Maggie, then of Dee.

● See **Literary Terms Handbook,** p. R9.

LITERARY ELEMENTS

1. Mama is a relatively objective observer. Through her eyes the reader sees the virtues and flaws of Maggie and Dee.
2. Mama comes across as a wise woman who can distinguish between fantasy and reality. Most readers will trust her.
3. Students may find a few prompts useful: Dee arriving or discovering the quilts; Maggie preparing for Dee's arrival.

Additional Resources

✍ *Literary Elements Transparency 1*

— LITERATURE AND WRITING —

Writing About Literature

Comparing Characters In what ways are Dee and Maggie alike? In what ways are they different? Write several paragraphs in which you compare and contrast their personalities, values, attitudes toward life, and their development in the course of the story. Share your writing with one or two classmates. Are your views of the two sisters similar?

Creative Writing

Prized Possessions Look back at your response to the Focus Activity on page 6. Choose one of the listed prized objects that has special meaning for your family or for you. Describe the object carefully, and explain what makes it so special. Also tell whether you would want it to be put to everyday use.

— EXTENDING YOUR RESPONSE —

Literature Groups

Seeing Both Sides "Dee really deserved the quilts. She treasured them, not like Maggie. Besides, Dee knew how to take care of them. Maggie didn't even care about keeping them nice."

Do you agree with this statement? Did the right person get the quilts? First, make a list of reasons that Maggie should have gotten the quilts. Then do the same for Dee. Compare your reasons with those listed by other groups, and decide which reasons are the most convincing.

Interdisciplinary Activity

Social Studies: Creating an Heirloom Create a piece of woodworking, needlework, or some other object that can be given "everyday use." If you have begun such a project, take this opportunity to complete it. After displaying the object, put it to "everyday use."

Learning for Life

Interview Talk to older relatives or friends about their childhoods or about the way things used to be when they were young. Use questions like these to get started:

- When you think of your childhood, what memories stand out most clearly?
- Where did you live when you were growing up? Where did you go to school? Where did you "hang out"?
- What special objects do you remember from your past? Why were they important to you?
- What was the best thing about the "good old days"? What was the worst thing?

Tape-record your interviews or take notes. Share the information you have gathered with the rest of the class.

Reading Further

You might enjoy these poems by Alice Walker: "For My Sister Molly Who in the Fifties" and "Beyond What" from her collection *Revolutionary Petunias and Other Poems* present themes of family, transitions, and love.

📖 **Save your work for your portfolio.**

LITERATURE AND WRITING

Writing About Literature

Students' comparisons should
- offer clearly stated views concerning the two sisters.
- follow subject by subject or feature by feature organization.
- give specific examples from the story to support all opinions and generalizations.

Creative Writing

Students' descriptions should
- bring the object to "life" with well-chosen details.
- suggest the importance of the object by means of persuasive writing.
- include a convincing argument for putting the object to everyday use or not.

EXTENDING YOUR RESPONSE

Literature Groups Point out to students that they must be able to support any inferences they make about Maggie or Dee. **COLLAB. LEARN.**

Interdisciplinary Activity Explain to students that their "heirloom" does not have to be antique in design. Encourage them to be creative. 🖥️

Learning for Life Suggest to students that a good interviewer will abandon a written script if a subject of greater interest comes up. 🖥️

Skill Minilessons

GRAMMAR AND LANGUAGE
Possessive Pronouns

1. its
2. their
3. Your
4. hers

READING AND THINKING
Chronological Order

4. Mama quit school after second grade, when her school closed down.
3. Maggie was badly burned in the fire.
1. Dee told Mama that her new name was Wangero.
5. Mama snatched the quilts from Dee and gave them to Maggie.
2. Dee told Maggie that she ought to try to make something of herself.

VOCABULARY
Base Words

1. e   2. d   3. a
4. b   5. c

Additional Resources

- *Grammar and Composition Handbook,* Lesson 1.2
- *Grammar and Language Workbook,* p. 181
- *Writer's Choice,* Lesson 10.2
- *Reading Workbook,* pp. 1–2
- *Vocabulary Practice,* p. 1

Responding to Literature

Skill Minilessons

GRAMMAR AND LANGUAGE • Possessive Pronouns

Possessive pronouns are pronouns that show ownership:

Dee acted as if the quilts were already *hers.*

Dee said, "You don't understand *your* heritage."

Other common possessive pronouns include *my, mine, his, its, our,* and *their.* Remember that apostrophes are not used with possessive pronouns. Thus, always write *its* (not *it's*) and *your* (not *you're*) to show possession.

● For more about pronouns, see **Language Handbook,** p. R42.

PRACTICE On your paper, write the possessive pronoun that correctly completes each sentence.

1. Dee and Maggie both want a quilt with (its, it's) own special history.
2. Maggie and Dee have very different relationships with (they're, their) mother.
3. (Your, You're) grandmother and I made these quilts.
4. That blue one is (hers, her's).

READING AND THINKING • Chronological Order

Chronological order is the order, or sequence, in which events actually take place. In most short stories, the author relates the events of the story in chronological order. Sometimes, however, an author may describe events that occurred before or after the events of the story. In "Everyday Use," for example, as Mama sits in the yard waiting for Dee, she remembers an event from the past.

"How long ago was it that the other house burned? Ten, twelve years? Sometimes I can still hear the flames . . ."

As you read a short story, think about the order in which the events actually occur.

PRACTICE On your paper, arrange these events in chronological order.

1. Dee told Mama that her new name was Wangero.
2. Dee told Maggie that she ought to try to make something of herself.
3. Maggie was badly burned in the fire.
4. Mama quit school after second grade, when her school closed down.
5. Mama snatched the quilts from Dee and gave them to Maggie.

● For more about text structure, see **Reading Handbook,** pp. R86–R87.

VOCABULARY • Base Words

Sometimes prefixes or suffixes are added to whole words, called base words, which are often words you know. Although a final vowel may be dropped from a base word when a suffix is added, base words are usually easy to recognize. For example, now that you know the word *doctrine,* you can figure out that a doctrinaire approach would probably involve sticking to a principle or position. By knowing what *oppress* means, you can tell that an oppressive government would be one that controls by the cruel use of force.

PRACTICE Use the familiar base words contained in the words in the left column to match each word to its meaning, given in the right column.

1. inelegancies   a. friendly remarks
2. fatalities   b. to break up, as by spreading out
3. pleasantries   c. having to do with what is to come
4. decentralize   d. deaths
5. futuristic   e. crude behaviors

Theme 1 _____ Transitions

Transitions are changes—passages from one place to another, saying good-bye to the old and welcoming the new, growing into adulthood. The characters you will meet in this theme all face changes in their lives. How do you approach transitions in your life? Do you ease into new stages, or do you resist change and want things to stay the same?

THEME PROJECTS

Performing

Critic's Choice   You've probably seen a TV show in which two movie critics each give a thumbs-up or a thumbs-down review about a film. With a partner, create a similar show in which you review the stories in this theme.

1. Choose which elements of each story you will evaluate—for example, characters, plot, suspense, realism. Think about how well these elements work in the story.

2. Be prepared to defend your opinions if your partner challenges them. Use specific examples from the stories.

3. Consider having someone videotape your show so you can view it later.

Interdisciplinary Project

Art   Choose three characters in this theme whose transitions are most interesting to you, and represent their changes visually.

1. Think about how each moment of transition would look. What objects could symbolize the characters' past life or their new condition? What colors best represent the before and after stages of their change?

2. Make a painting, collage, or diorama representing each of your characters' transitions.

3. Show your work to your classmates; see if they can tell which characters you've chosen.

The Family, Diana Ong (b. 1940). Private collection.

THE SHORT STORY ❧ 21

LITERATURE & HUMANITIES

Have students view *Double Portrait of an Artist in Time*, Art Talk Transparency 3, and discuss how transitions are represented.

GLENCOE TECHNOLOGY

LITERATURE CLASSICS CD-ROM
Search for other selections related to the theme of transitions.

Teaching Strategies

The following suggestions may help your students plan and carry out their theme projects.

Performing

- Suggest that students create a checklist for each story, indicating which literary elements will receive a thumbs up or a thumbs down.

- Remind students that they must be able to defend their opinions. Therefore, if they have a strong opinion—either positive or negative—about a particular story, they might want to make some notes listing the reasons for their opinion.

- Let students discuss with a partner possible ways of presenting their opinions and what it would take to carry out each idea.

Interdisciplinary Project

- Allow students to work with a partner to identify the point of transition in each story.

- Discuss with the group the possible ways the transitions could be shown artistically. Students might mention drawings, paintings in various mediums, collages, masks, or dioramas.

- With the group decide on how best to present the finished products to the class and how best to exhibit them later.

Additional Resources

- 📁 *Interdisciplinary Activities,* pp. 2–3
- 📁 *Viewing and Representing Activities,* pp. 7–8
- 📁 *Listening and Speaking Activities,* pp. 1–2
- 📁 *Critical Thinking Skills,* pp. 2–4
- 📁 *Selection and Theme Assessment,* pp. 171–172
- 📁 *Performance Assessment,* p. 89

SELECTIONS	Literary Elements	Reading and Thinking	Writing	Vocabulary and Spelling
Chee's Daughter JUANITA PLATERO AND SIYOWIN MILLER	Theme, SE p. 35 *Theme, TWE pp. 24, 29, 34* *Plot, TWE pp. 26, 29* *Setting, TWE p. 30* *Personification, TWE p. 32*	Evaluating Generalizations, SE p. 37 *Logical Reasoning, TWE p. 31*	Setting Analysis, SE p. 36 Conversation, SE p. 36 *Character Description, TWE p. 33*	Synonyms—Shades of Meaning, SE p. 37 *Context Clues, TWE p. 27* *Word Forms, TWE p. 31*
Civil Peace CHINUA ACHEBE	Dialogue, SE p. 44 *Dialogue, TWE pp. 42, 43* *Character, TWE p. 40* *Irony, TWE p. 42*	Analyzing Problems and Solutions, SE p. 46 *Varying Reading Rate, TWE p. 43*	Character Sketch, SE p. 45 Interview, SE p. 45	Etymology, SE p. 46 *Onomatopoeia, TWE p. 43*
Two Kinds AMY TAN	Conflict, SE p. 59 *Tone, TWE p. 50* *Plot, TWE pp. 51, 52, 56, 57* *Irony, TWE p. 53*	Summarizing, SE p. 61 *Sequence of Events, TWE p. 47* *Judging the Credibility of a Source, TWE p. 52* *Generalizing, TWE p. 57*	Journal, SE pp. 48, 60 Character Evaluation, SE p. 60 *Self-Description, TWE p. 51*	Analogies, SE p. 61 *Eponyms, TWE p. 51* *Figurative Meanings, TWE p. 56*
Catch the Moon JUDITH ORTIZ COFER	Imagery, SE p. 70 *Imagery, TWE pp. 64, 65* *Plot: TWE p. 64* *Simile, TWE p. 67* *Symbol, TWE p. 68*	Recognizing Causes and Effects, SE p. 72 *Verifying Predictions, TWE p. 65* *Evaluating, TWE p. 67*	Character Analysis, SE p. 71 Poem, SE p. 71 *Fairy Tales, TWE p. 69* *Dialogue, TWE p. 73*	Compound Words, SE p. 72
Through the Tunnel DORIS LESSING	Plot, SE p. 86 *Plot, TWE pp. 82, 83, 84*	*Drawing Conclusions, TWE p. 78* *Inferring, TWE p. 85* *Identifying Cause-and-Effect Relationships, TWE p. 85*	Analysis, SE p. 87 Letter, SE p. 87 *Spatial Order in Descriptions, TWE p. 78*	Antonyms, SE p. 87 *Word Meanings, TWE p. 78* *Context Clues, TWE p. 84*
The Vision Quest LAME DEER AND RICHARD ERDOES	Legend, SE p. 92 *Legend, TWE p. 90* *Irony, TWE p. 91*	*Judging the Credibility of a Source, TWE p. 91*	Song or Poem, SE p. 92 Comparing Customs, SE p. 93	
By the Waters of Babylon STEPHEN VINCENT BENÉT	Moral, SE p. 105 *Character, TWE p. 96* *Metaphor, TWE p. 96* *Moral, TWE pp. 97, 98, 104* *Imagery, TWE p. 100*	Visualizing, SE p. 107 *Drawing Conclusions, TWE p. 100* *Comparing and Contrasting, TWE p. 102*	Literary Evaluation, SE p. 106 Dialogue, SE p. 106	The Prefix *Ante-*, SE p. 106
What I Have Been Doing Lately JAMAICA KINCAID	Description, SE p. 112 *Description, TWE pp. 110, 111* *Dialogue, TWE p. 110* *Mood, TWE p. 111*	*Drawing Conclusions, TWE p. 110*	Freewrite, SE p. 108 Analysis, SE p. 113 Dream Narrative, SE p. 113	Analogies, SE p. 113
With All Flags Flying ANNE TYLER	Characters, SE p. 124 *Imagery, TWE p. 118* *Symbol, TWE p. 122* *Setting, TWE p. 122*	*Monitoring Comprehension, TWE p. 121*	Analysis, SE p. 125 Obituary, SE p. 125	Prefixes Expressing Number, SE p. 126 *Synonyms, TWE p. 117* *Etymology, TWE p. 121*
A Child, a Dog, the Night AMALIA RENDIC	Narrator, SE p. 134 *Setting, TWE p. 130* *Narrator, TWE p. 131* *Imagery, TWE p.131* *Personification, TWE p. 132*	*Drawing Conclusions, TWE p. 133* *Paraphrasing and Summarizing, TWE p. 133*	Definition, SE p. 128 Review, SE p. 135 Definition, SE p. 135	Analogies, SE p. 135

Key: Student material is in roman. Teacher material is in italic. 🖳 Technology **COLLAB. LEARN.** Collaboration

Grammar and Language	Listening, Speaking, and Viewing	Life Skills	Study, Research, and Technology
Using Appositives, SE p. 37 *Present Participles as Adjectives, TWE p. 34*	**COLLAB. LEARN.** Literature Groups, SE p. 36 Storytelling, SE p. 36		Research, SE p. 36 *Research, TWE p. 27*
Using Descriptive Tag Lines, SE p. 46 *Personal Pronouns—Objective Case, TWE p. 42*	**COLLAB. LEARN.** Literature Groups, SE p. 45		🖥 Internet Connection, SE p. 45
Participles and Participial Phrases, SE p. 61 *Past Perfect Tense, TWE p. 58*	**COLLAB. LEARN.** Literature Groups, SE p. 60 Presentation, SE p. 60 *Recounting an Experience, TWE p. 55*		Research, SE p. 60
Understanding Connotations, SE p. 72 Avoiding Sentence Fragments, SE p. 73 *Adjective Clauses, TWE p. 68*	**COLLAB. LEARN.** Literature Groups, SE p. 71	Car Diagrams, SE p. 71	Research, SE p. 71
Prepositions, TWE p. 84	**COLLAB. LEARN.** Literature Groups, SE p. 87 **COLLAB. LEARN.** Dialogue, SE p. 87	*Goal Setting, TWE p. 81* *Achieving a Goal, TWE p. 82*	🖥 *Internet Connection, TWE p. 74* *Research, TWE p. 79* 🖥 *Internet Connection, TWE p. 82*
Infinitive and Prepositional Phrases, TWE p. 91	**COLLAB. LEARN.** Literature Groups, SE p. 92		
Capitalization of Proper Nouns, TWE p. 104	**COLLAB. LEARN.** Literature Groups, SE p. 106 Speech, SE p. 106		Research, SE p. 106 *Research, TWE p. 101* *Research, TWE p. 103*
Coordinating Conjunctions, TWE p. 111	**COLLAB. LEARN.** Literature Groups, SE p. 113	Researching Dreams, SE p. 113	Research, SE p. 113
Quotation Marks in Dialogue, SE p. 126 *Gerund Phrases, TWE p. 122*	**COLLAB. LEARN.** Literature Groups, SE p. 125 **COLLAB. LEARN.** Debating, SE p.127 *Interview, TWE p. 119*	Researching Community Resources, SE p. 125	Research, SE p. 125 *Research, TWE p. 117*
Using Apostrophes to Show Possession, TWE p. 132	**COLLAB. LEARN.** Literature Groups, SE p. 135 **COLLAB. LEARN.** Dialogue, SE p. 135	Letter of Inquiry, SE p. 135	

SELECTIONS	🗁 Print Resources		

Chee's Daughter
JUANITA PLATERO AND SIYOWIN MILLER
	Unit One Planning Guide, pp. 16–23
	* Active Reading Guide, p. 2
	Vocabulary Practice, p. 2
		Grammar & Comp. Handbook,
		  Lessons 1.4, 3.3, 3.2
		Grammar & Lang. Workbook, pp. 93,
		  141, 91
		Reading Workbook, pp. 3–4
			* Quick Checks, p. 2
			Sel. & Theme Assmt., pp. 3–4
			Performance Assessment, p. 2
			Spanish Summaries, p. 2

CivilPeace CHINUA ACHEBE	Unit One Planning Guide, pp. 24–31 * Active Reading Guide, p. 3 Vocabulary Practice, p. 3	Grammar & Comp. Handbook, Lessons 7.1–7.3, 11.6 Grammar & Lang. Workbook, pp. 181–185 Reading Workbook, pp. 5–6	* Quick Checks, p. 3 Sel. & Theme Assmt., pp. 5–6 Performance Assessment, p. 3 Spanish Summaries, p. 3 Spanish Translations
TwoKinds AMY TAN	Unit One Planning Guide, pp. 32–39 * Active Reading Guide, p. 4 Vocabulary Practice, p. 4	Grammar & Comp. Handbook, Lessons 5.4, 3.3 Grammar & Lang. Workbook, pp. 147, 93 Reading Workbook, pp. 7–8	* Quick Checks, p. 4 Sel. & Theme Assmt., pp. 7–8 Performance Assessment, p. 4 Spanish Summaries, p. 4
Catch the Moon JUDITH ORTIZ COFER	Unit One Planning Guide, pp. 40–47 * Active Reading Guide, p. 5 Vocabulary Practice, p. 5	Grammar & Comp. Handbook, Lesson 4.3 Grammar & Lang. Workbook, pp. 107–110 Reading Workbook, pp. 9–10	* Quick Checks, p. 5 Sel. & Theme Assmt., pp. 9–10 Performance Assessment, p. 5 Spanish Summaries, p. 5
Through the **Tunnel** DORIS LESSING	Unit One Planning Guide, pp. 48–55 * Active Reading Guide, p. 6 Vocabulary Practice, p. 6	Grammar & Comp. Handbook, Lessons 1.6, 3.1 Grammar & Lang. Workbook, pp. 67, 89 Reading Workbook, pp. 11–12	* Quick Checks, p. 6 Sel. & Theme Assmt., pp. 11–12 Performance Assessment, p. 6 Spanish Summaries, p. 6
The Vision Quest LAME DEER AND RICHARD ERDOES	Unit One Planning Guide, pp. 56–63 * Active Reading Guide, p. 7 Vocabulary Practice, p. 7	Grammar & Comp. Handbook, Lessons 3.1, 3.3 Grammar & Lang. Workbook, pp. 89, 97 Reading Workbook, pp. 11–12	* Quick Checks, p. 7 Sel. & Theme Assmt., pp. 13–14 Performance Assessment, p. 7 Spanish Summaries, p. 7
BY THE WATERS OF BABYLON STEPHEN VINCENT BENÉT	Unit One Planning Guide, pp. 64–71 * Active Reading Guide, p. 8 Vocabulary Practice, p. 8	Grammar & Comp. Handbook, Lessons 1.1, 10.3 Grammar & Lang. Workbook, pp. 49, 237 Reading Workbook, p. 13	* Quick Checks, p. 8 Sel. & Theme Assmt., pp. 15–16 Performance Assessment, p. 8 Spanish Summaries, p. 8
What I Have Been Doing Lately JAMAICA KINCAID	Unit One Planning Guide, pp. 72–79 * Active Reading Guide, p. 9 Vocabulary Practice, p. 9	Grammar & Comp. Handbook, Lesson 1.7 Grammar & Lang. Workbook, p. 69 Reading Workbook, p. 13	* Quick Checks, p. 9 Sel. & Theme Assmt., pp. 17–18 Performance Assessment, p. 9 Spanish Summaries, p. 9 Spanish Translations
With All Flags Flying ANNE TYLER	Unit One Planning Guide, pp. 80–87 * Active Reading Guide, p. 10 Vocabulary Practice, p. 10	Grammar & Comp. Handbook, Lessons 3.3, 11.9 Grammar & Lang. Workbook, pp. 95, 271 Reading Workbook, pp. 14	* Quick Checks, p. 10 Sel. & Theme Assmt., pp. 19–20 Performance Assessment, p. 10 Spanish Summaries, p. 10
A Child, a Dog, the Night AMALIA RENDIC	Unit One Planning Guide, pp. 88–95 * Active Reading Guide, p. 11 Vocabulary Practice, p. 11	Grammar & Comp. Handbook, Lesson 11.11 Grammar & Lang. Workbook, p. 277 Reading Workbook, p. 14	* Quick Checks, p. 11 Sel. & Theme Assmt., pp. 21–22 Performance Assessment, p. 11 Spanish Summaries, p. 11 Spanish Translations

*Also available in Spanish

Transparencies

Technology Resources

Selection Focus Transparency 2
Grammar and Language Transparency 2
Literary Elements Transparency 2
Fine Art Transparency 26

Literature Launchers Videodisc
Audio Library
Spanish Audio Library
Vocabulary Puzzlemaker
Web Site: lit.glencoe.com

Selection Focus Transparency 3
Grammar and Language Transparency 3
Literary Elements Transparency 3

Audio Library
Spanish Audio Library
Vocabulary Puzzlemaker
Web Site: lit.glencoe.com

Selection Focus Transparency 4
Grammar and Language Transparency 4
Literary Elements Transparency 4

Literature Launchers Videodisc
Audio Library/Spanish Audio Library
Vocabulary Puzzlemaker
Web Site: lit.glencoe.com

Selection Focus Transparency 5
Grammar and Language Transparency 5
Literary Elements Transparency 5

Audio Library
Spanish Audio Library
Vocabulary Puzzlemaker
Web Site: lit.glencoe.com

Selection Focus Transparency 6
Grammar and Language Transparency 6
Literary Elements Transparency 6
Fine Art Transparency 9

Audio Library
Spanish Audio Library
Vocabulary Puzzlemaker
Web Site: lit.glencoe.com

Selection Focus Transparency 7
Grammar and Language Transparency 7
Literary Elements Transparency 7

Audio Library
Spanish Audio Library
Vocabulary Puzzlemaker
Web Site: lit.glencoe.com

Selection Focus Transparency 8
Grammar and Language Transparency 8
Literary Elements Transparency 8

Audio Library
Spanish Audio Library
Vocabulary Puzzlemaker
Web Site: lit.glencoe.com

Selection Focus Transparency 9
Grammar and Language Transparency 9
Literary Elements Transparency 9
Fine Art Transparency 11

Literature Launchers Videodisc
Audio Library
Spanish Audio Library
Vocabulary Puzzlemaker
Web Site: lit.glencoe.com

Selection Focus Transparency 10
Grammar and Language Transparency 10
Literary Elements Transparency 10
Fine Art Transparency 14

Audio Library
Spanish Audio Library
Vocabulary Puzzlemaker
Web Site: lit.glencoe.com

Selection Focus Transparency 11
Grammar and Language Transparency 11
Literary Elements Transparency 11

Audio Library
Spanish Audio Library
Vocabulary Puzzlemaker
Web Site: lit.glencoe.com

📁 𝒯heme RESOURCES

- Listening and Speaking Activities (pp. 1–2)
- Viewing and Representing Activities (pp. 7–8)
- Critical Thinking Skills (pp. 2–4)
- Media Connections Activities (pp. 1–2)
- Interdisciplinary Activities (pp. 2–3)

See also these additional planning resources:
- English Language Learners Sourcebook
- Inclusion Strategies Sourcebook
- Literature Groups Sourcebook

PRESENTATION Plus!

Use Glencoe's *Presentation Plus!* This multimedia teaching tool lets you present dynamic lessons that will engage your students. Using Microsoft PowerPoint,® you can customize the presentations to create your own personalized lessons.

Objectives
- To read and analyze a short story about losing and winning back a precious person
- To identify theme
- To write an analysis of setting

Skills

Reading/Thinking: Inferring; Drawing Conclusions; Logical Reasoning; Evaluating Generalizations
Writing: Character Description; Conversation
Vocabulary: Context Clues; Word Forms; Synonyms
Grammar/Language: Present Participles as Adjectives; Using Appositives
Listening/Speaking: Debating; Storytelling
Life Skills: Decision Making
Collaboration: Literature Groups

Motivating
→OPTIONS

Literature Launchers:
"Navajo Traditions"

Videodisc
Side A, Segment 2

Also available in VHS.

Selection Focus Transparency 2: Have students discuss whether their choices are realistic or mutually exclusive.

Focus Activity: Encourage students who have lost something precious to describe their experiences.

Before You Read

Chee's Daughter

FOCUS ACTIVITY

What would you do if someone took away something that was especially precious to you? Would you plot revenge, give up and feel very sad about the loss, or would you try to find a way to get the item back?

CHART IT! Develop a flow chart like the one shown that details the steps you would take to get back something precious.

SETTING A PURPOSE Read to learn how one Navajo man reacts to the loss of something precious.

BACKGROUND

The Time and Place
During the mid-1900s, a young Navajo (also spelled Navaho) father in the southwestern United States honors the ancient traditions and way of life despite the growth of modern civilization.

Did You Know?
Traditional Navajo culture is matrilineal—that is, a family traces its ancestry back through the mother's line, and children belong to the mother's clan. Typically, several generations of a family live close together. For example, a married daughter, her husband, and their children, and perhaps even her sisters and their families, would all live with or near her parents. The oldest woman in the family, usually the grandmother, enjoys a place at the center of family life.

Meet Juanita Platero and Siyowin Miller

Juanita Platero, a Navajo writer, began working in collaboration with California writer Siyowin Miller in 1929. Most of the stories the two wrote together explore the intersection of the traditional ways of the Navajo and the modern ways of twentieth-century America. The stories explore how these ways come into conflict, both in personal and family relationships, and how the conflicts are resolved. Platero and Miller also wrote a novel, *The Winds Erase Your Footprints*.

VOCABULARY PREVIEW

gaudy (gô′ dē) *adj.* bright and showy to the point of being in bad taste; p. 26
indolence (ind′ əl əns) *n.* laziness; idleness; p. 27
acrid (ak′ rid) *adj.* irritating or upsetting; p. 30
banter (ban′ tər) *n.* good-natured, witty joking or teasing; p. 30

zealously (zel′ əs lē) *adv.* eagerly; enthusiastically; p. 31
flaunt (flônt) *v.* to display in a showy manner; p. 32
deference (def′ ər əns) *n.* courteous respect or regard for the judgment, opinions, or desires of another; p. 33
surmise (sər mīz′) *v.* to guess or conclude from little or no evidence; p. 33

RESOURCE MANAGER

Lesson Planning Resource
The *Unit One Planning Guide* (pp. 16–23) provides additional lesson notes and reduced versions of all print resources.

 Other Print Resources
- Active Reading Guide, p. 2
- Vocabulary Practice, p. 2
- Reading Workbook, pp. 3–4
- Grammar and Language Workbook, pp. 93, 141, 91

- Grammar and Composition Handbook, Lessons 1.4, 3.3, 3.2
- Quick Checks, p. 2
- Selection and Theme Assessment, pp. 3–4
- Performance Assessment, p. 2
- Spanish Summaries, p. 2
- Inclusion Strategies
- English Language Learners Sourcebook

 Transparencies
- Selection Focus 2
- Fine Art 26
- Literary Elements 2
- Grammar and Language 2

Technology
 Literature Launchers
 Audio Library
 Spanish Audio Library
 Glencoe Literature Web Site
 Testmaker

Chee's Daughter

Juanita Platero
and Siyowin Miller

A THE HAT TOLD THE STORY, the big, black, drooping Stetson. It was not at the proper angle, the proper rakish angle for so young a Navaho. There was no song, and that was not in keeping either.

There should have been at least a humming, a faint, all-to-himself "he he he heya," for it was a good horse he was riding, a slender-legged, high-stepping buckskin that would race the wind with light knee-urging. This was a day for singing, a warm winter day, when the touch of the sun upon the back belied the snow high on distant mountains.

Wind warmed by the sun touched his high-boned cheeks like flicker feathers, and still he rode on silently, deeper into Little Canyon, until the red rock walls rose straight upward from the stream bed and only a narrow piece of blue sky hung above. Abruptly the sky widened where the canyon walls were pushed back to make a wide place, as though in ancient times an angry stream had tried to go all ways at once.

This was home—this wide place in the canyon—levels of jagged rock and levels of rich red earth. This was home to Chee, the rider of the buckskin, as it had been to many generations before him.

He stopped his horse at the stream and sat looking across the narrow ribbon of water to the bare-branched peach trees. He was seeing them each springtime with their age-gnarled limbs transfigured beneath veils of blossom pink; he was seeing them in autumn laden with their yellow fruit, small and sweet. Then his eyes searched out the indistinct furrows of the fields beside the stream, where each year the corn and beans and squash drank thirstily of the overflow from summer rains. Chee was trying to out-weigh today's bitter betrayal of hope by gathering to himself these reminders of the integrity of the land. Land did not cheat! His mind lingered deliberately on all the days spent here in the sun caring for the young plants, his songs to the earth and to **B**

SUMMARY

Chee, a traditional Navajo farmer and herder, is mourning the death of his wife when he suffers a second loss: his daughter, the Little One, has been taken to live with his wife's parents in accordance with Navajo custom. Old Man Fat, Chee's father-in-law, makes his living off tourists and despises Chee's "primitive" way of life. Chee learns that a new cutoff road is about to put Old Man Fat out of business. He works to produce a bountiful harvest, then "buys" back his daughter from his impoverished in-laws. Chee returns home with the Little One, his faith in traditional ways renewed.

📁 *Spanish Summaries,* p. 2

A Active Reading

QUESTION Have students read the first paragraph of the story. Ask them what questions they might have based on this paragraph. *(Examples: What story is the hat telling? What angle should it be at? Who is the young Navajo?)*

Additional Resources
📁 *Active Reading Guide,* p. 2
🎧 *Audio Library*
🎧 *Spanish Audio Library*

Teaching Options

CONNECTING TO OTHER SELECTIONS

The chart on the right shows three ways to connect "Chee's Daughter" to selections in this book.

For specific teaching strategies, see the *Unit One Planning Guide,* pages 19–20.

Connection	Title
Life Skills: Planning and Designing	→ "Waltz of the Fat Man," p. 377
Thematic: Determination	→ from *A Match to the Heart,* p. 544
Literary: Setting	→ "The Masque of the Red Death," p. 389

B Literary Elements

THEME Discuss with students the relationship between Chee and the natural world. Ask what his singing to the corn suggests and why the words *integrity* and *cheat* are used in reference to the land. *(Chee sees spiritual qualities in all natural things. He believes he can communicate with his crops and that even the earth and rocks are part of the moral universe.)*

C Active Reading

QUESTION and PREDICT Some students will be puzzled by the story's opening. Point out that there is a mystery here and that it is perfectly natural to ask, "What's going on?" Elicit predictions based on evidence from the text: Chee's mood, the deserted compound, etc.

D Author's Craft

EXPOSITION By now most students will understand the cause of Chee's unhappiness. Point out that the authors never explicitly state, "Chee's wife has just died." Ask students how they learned this vital information. *(There are several significant clues, including Chee's reaction to his sister's grief, references to his wife's illness, and the Little One's inability to understand.)*

B the life springing from it—". . . In the middle of the wide field . . . Yellow Corn Boy . . . He has started both ways . . ." then the harvest and repayment in full measure. Here was the old feeling of wholeness and of oneness with the sun and earth and growing things.

Chee urged the buckskin toward the family compound where, secure in a recess of overhanging rock, was his mother's dome-shaped hogan, red rock and red adobe like the ground on which it nestled. Not far from the hogan was the half-circle of brush like a dark shadow against the canyon wall—corral for sheep and goats. Farther from the hogan, in full circle, stood the horse corral made of heavy cedar branches sternly interlocked. Chee's long thin lips curved into a smile as he passed his daughter's tiny hogan squatted like a round Pueblo oven beside the corral. He remembered the summer day when together they sat back on their heels and plastered wet adobe all about the circling wall of rock and the woven dome of piñon twigs. How his family laughed when the Little One herded the bewildered chickens into her tiny hogan as the first snow fell.

Did You Know?
Piñon (pin' yōn), is any of several small pine trees found in Mexico and the southwestern United States.

C Then the smile faded from Chee's lips and his eyes darkened as he tied his horse to a corral post and turned to the strangely empty compound. "Someone has told them," he thought, "and they are inside weeping." He passed his mother's deserted loom on the south side of the hogan and pulled the rude wooden door toward him, bowing his head, hunching his shoulders to get inside.

His mother sat sideways by the center fire, her feet drawn up under her full skirts. Her hands were busy kneading dough in the chipped white basin. With her head down, her voice was muffled when she said, "The meal will soon be ready, Son."

Chee passed his father sitting against the wall, hat over his eyes as though asleep. He passed his older sister, who sat turning mutton ribs on a crude wire grill over the coals, noticed tears dropping on her hands: "She cared more for my wife than I realized," he thought.

Then because something must be said sometime, he tossed the black Stetson upon a bulging sack of wool and said, "You have heard, then." He could not shut from his mind how confidently he had set the handsome new hat on his head that very morning, slanting the wide brim over one eye: he was going to see his wife, and today he would ask the doctors about bringing her home; last week she had looked so much better.

His sister nodded but did not speak. His mother sniffled and passed her velveteen sleeve beneath her nose. Chee sat down, leaning against the wall. "I suppose I was a fool for hoping all the time. I should have expected this. Few of our people get well from the coughing sickness.[1] But *she* seemed to be getting better."

His mother was crying aloud now and blowing her nose noisily on her skirt. His father sat up, speaking gently to her.

D Chee shifted his position and started a cigarette. His mind turned back to the Little One. At least she was too small to understand what had happened, the Little One who had been born three years before in the sanitarium where his wife was being treated for the coughing sickness, the Little One he had brought home to his mother's hogan to be nursed by his sister, whose baby was a few months older. As she

---

1. *Coughing sickness* is a common name for tuberculosis, an infectious disease that affects the lungs and other body tissues and is characterized by a persistent cough.

Teaching Options

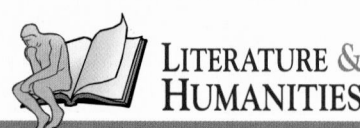

LITERATURE & HUMANITIES

Display "Quilled Buckskin Robe," Transparency 1 in *U.S. History and Art.* Have students examine the images and their positions and consider how these aspects of the robe celebrate nature.

MEETING INDIVIDUAL NEEDS — ENGLISH LANGUAGE LEARNERS

Culture Clash Some English language learners may not understand why Old Man Fat's way of life is distasteful to Chee. Point out how changes in technology and the economy have not always been welcomed by Native American cultures. Help students distinguish between traditional and nontraditional elements in the story.

Activity Ask students to list aspects of their own lives that they consider traditional, such as ceremonies or customs. Then have students create another list showing ways in which their lives are affected by modern society.

Additional Resources
📁 *English Language Learners Sourcebook*

Moonlight. Marvin Toddy (b. 1954). Oil on canvas, 16 x 20 in. La Fonda Indian Shop and Gallery, Santa Fe.

Viewing the painting: How well does this painting help you visualize the place where Chee lives?

FYI

Hogans Chee and his family live in a hogan, the traditional housing of the Navajo. A cone-shaped structure made of logs or strips of wood and covered with mud, the hogan consists of one circular room 20 to 30 feet across. The single entrance faces east to greet the rising sun; a hole in the roof lets the smoke escape. Chee and his daughter are putting the final touches on her little hogan when they plaster it with adobe.

---

grew fat-cheeked and sturdy-legged, she followed him about like a shadow; somehow her baby mind had grasped that of all those at the hogan who cared for her and played with her, he—Chee—belonged most to her. She sat cross-legged at his elbow when he worked silver at the forge; she rode before him in the saddle when he drove the horses to water; often she lay wakeful on her sheep pelts until he stretched out for the night in the darkened hogan and she could snuggle warm against him.

Chee blew smoke slowly, and some of the sadness left his dark eyes as he said, "It is not as bad as it might be. It is not as though we are left with nothing."

Chee's sister arose, sobs catching in her throat, and rushed past him out the doorway. Chee sat upright, a terrible fear possessing him. For a moment his mouth could make no sound. Then: "The Little One! Mother, where is she?"

His mother turned her stricken face to him. "Your wife's people came after her this morning. They heard yesterday of their daughter's death through the trader at Red Sands."

Chee started to protest, but his mother shook her head slowly. "I didn't expect they would want the Little One either. But there is nothing you can do. She is a girl child and belongs to her mother's people; it is custom."

E Critical Thinking

INFERRING Ask students what they can infer from Chee's oblique reference to hogan construction. Ask them why they think Chee says this. *(Alert readers will infer that a basic tenet of Navajo tradition must be to build hogans facing east. A person who does not observe this fundamental rule is clearly no respecter of "custom.")*

F Literary Elements

PLOT: Conflict Help students recognize the conflict of cultures that is evident even before they meet Old Man Fat. *(The reader is suddenly in the familiar world of cars, tourists, gas stations, sodas, and "Indian Curios." After the beauties of the rocky landscape, this strikes a jarring note for the reader as well as for Chee.)*

G Literary Elements

TONE The description of Old Man Fat's property includes several words that impel the reader to view the scene with Chee's disapproving eyes. In some cases—*garish, pseudo,* and *drab,* for example—the denotations are negative. Other words, such as *squatted, treeless,* and *smoke-smudged,* have connotations that contribute to the general effect. Ask students if they think Old Man Fat's compound is a pleasant place. Encourage them to find words that support their views.

Teaching Options

Frowning, Chee got to his feet, grinding his cigarette into the dirt floor. "Custom! When did my wife's parents begin thinking about custom? Why, the hogan where they live doesn't even face the east!" He started toward the door. "Perhaps I can overtake them. Perhaps they don't realize how much we want her here with us. I'll ask them to give my daughter back to me. Surely, they won't refuse."

His mother stopped him gently with her outstretched hand. "You couldn't overtake them now. They were in the trader's car. Eat and rest, and think more about this."

"Have you forgotten how things have always been between you and your wife's people?" his father said.

That night, Chee's thoughts were troubled—half-forgotten incidents became disturbingly vivid—but early the next morning he saddled the buckskin and set out for the settlement of Red Sands. Even though his father-in-law, Old Man Fat, might laugh, Chee knew that he must talk to him. There were some things to which Old Man Fat might listen.

Chee rode the first part of the fifteen miles to Red Sands expectantly. The sight of sandstone buttes near Cottonwood Spring reddening in the morning sun brought a song almost to his lips. He twirled his reins in salute to the small boy herding sheep toward many-colored Butterfly Mountain, watched with pleasure the feathers of smoke rising against tree-darkened western

Did You Know?
A *butte* (byūt) is an isolated, flat-topped land formation created by the erosion of all but a portion of a mesa or plateau. A *mesa* (mā′ sə) is a flat-topped hill or mountain with steep, rocky sides.

mesas from the hogans sheltered there. But as he approached the familiar settlement sprawled in mushroom growth along the highway, he began to feel as though a scene from a bad dream was becoming real.

Several cars were parked around the trading store, which was built like two log hogans side by side, with red gas pumps in front and a sign across the tar-paper roofs: *Red Sands Trading Post—Groceries   Gasoline   Cold Drinks   Sandwiches   Indian Curios.* Back of the trading post an unpainted frame house and outbuildings squatted on the drab, treeless land. Chee and the Little One's mother had lived there when they stayed with his wife's people. That was according to custom—living with one's wife's people—but Chee had never been convinced that it was custom alone which prompted Old Man Fat and his wife to insist that their daughter bring her husband to live at the trading post.

Beside the post was a large hogan of logs, with brightly painted pseudo-Navaho[2] designs on the roof—a hogan with smoke-smudged windows and a garish blue door which faced north to the highway. Old Man Fat had offered Chee a hogan like this one. The trader would build it if he and his wife would live there and Chee would work at his forge, making silver jewelry where tourists could watch him. But Chee had asked instead for a piece of land for a cornfield and help in building a hogan far back from the highway and a corral for the sheep he had brought to this marriage.

A cold wind blowing down from the mountains began to whistle about Chee's ears. It flapped the <u>gaudy</u> Navaho rugs which were hung in one long bright line to attract tourists. It swayed the sign *Navaho Weaver at*

---

2. The prefix *pseudo-* (sōō′ dō) means "false or imitation."

Vocabulary
gaudy (gô′ dē) *adj.* bright and showy to the point of being in bad taste

MEETING INDIVIDUAL NEEDS — MULTIPLE LEARNING STYLES

Spatial Keeping track of buildings and natural features described in a story is made easier for many students by the use of a plan. Drawn with careful reference to the text, a plan can enhance students' ability to visualize the "geography" of the story.

Activity Tell students to imagine that they are cartographers flying over

Chee's compound and then to the settlement where Old Man Fat lives. Their assignment is to draw a plan, or aerial map, of what they see. When they have finished a draft, ask them to team up with a partner in order to compare and revise their plans. Invite a few promising cartographers to share their plans with the rest of the class for critiquing.
L2 COLLAB. LEARN.

Juanita Platero and Siyowin Miller ✎

Work beside the loom where Old Man Fat's wife sat hunched in her striped blanket, patting the colored thread of a design into place with a wooden comb. Tourists stood watching the weaver. More tourists stood in a knot before the hogan where the sign said: *See Inside a Real Navaho Home 25¢.*

Then the knot seemed to unravel as a few people returned to their cars; some had cameras; and there against the blue door Chee saw the Little One standing uncertainly. The wind was plucking at her new purple blouse and wide green skirt; it freed truant strands of soft dark hair from the meager queue into which it had been tied with white yarn.

Did You Know?
Here, *queue* (kyū) refers to a braid of hair at the back of the head.

"Isn't she cunning!" one of the women tourists was saying as she turned away.

Chee's lips tightened as he began to look around for Old Man Fat. Finally he saw him passing among the tourists collecting coins.

Then the Little One saw Chee. The uncertainty left her face, and she darted through the crowd as her father swung down from his horse. Chee lifted her in his arms, hugging her tight. While he listened to her breathless chatter, he watched Old Man Fat bearing down on them, scowling.

As his father-in-law walked heavily across the graveled lot, Chee was reminded of a statement his mother sometimes made: "When you see a fat Navaho, you see one who hasn't worked for what he has."

Vocabulary
indolence (ind′ əl əns) *n.* laziness; idleness

Old Man Fat was fattest in the middle. There was <u>indolence</u> in his walk even though he seemed to hurry, indolence in his cheeks so plump they made his eyes squint, eyes now smoldering with anger.

Some of the tourists were getting into their cars and driving away. The old man said belligerently to Chee, "Why do you come here? To spoil our business? To drive people away?"

"I came to talk with you," Chee answered, trying to keep his voice steady as he faced the old man.

"We have nothing to talk about," Old Man Fat blustered and did not offer to touch Chee's extended hand.

"It's about the Little One." Chee settled his daughter more comfortably against his hip as he weighed carefully all the words he had planned to say. "We are going to miss her very much. It wouldn't be so bad if we knew that *part* of each year she could be with us. That might help you too. You and your wife are no longer young people and you have no young ones here to depend upon." Chee chose his next words remembering the thriftlessness of his wife's parents, and their greed. "Perhaps we could share the care of this little one. Things are good with us. So much snow this year will make lots of grass for the sheep. We have good land for corn and melons."

Chee's words did not have the expected effect. Old Man Fat was enraged. "Farmers, all of you! Long-haired farmers! Do you think everyone must bend his back over the short-handled hoe in order to have food to eat?" His tone changed as he began to brag a little. "We not only have all the things from cans at the trader's, but when the Pueblos come past here on their way to town, we buy their salty jerked mutton, young corn for roasting, dried sweet peaches."

INTERDISCIPLINARY CONNECTION

Art Although Chee may disapprove of the way Old Man Fat exploits his wife's skill, explain to students that Navajo weaving is one of the fine arts of this Native American group. Ironically, the Navajo did not take up weaving as a major occupation until they encountered Europeans, who introduced sheep to the Southwest; however, there is nothing European about the results. The geometric designs and subtle colors of traditional Navajo rugs have a unique place in the art of North America. The "gaudy" rugs hanging by the loom in this story are probably colored with chemical dyes, not the herbal dyes of tradition.

Activity Have students research Navajo weaving and share with the class some characteristic examples. Ask them to create their own designs for a rug, encouraging them to imitate the traditional colors. **L2**

Born in Philadelphia in 1866, Frank Reed Whiteside studied in both the United States and France. *The Canyon* is a landscape painting typical of the romantic era, the immensity of nature dwarfing a human onlooker.

Viewing Response *Some students may suggest that the man in the picture, like Chee, is struck by the beauty of his surroundings. Perhaps, like Chee, he gains spiritual strength from the natural world.*

FYI

The Navajo The largest Native American nation in the southwestern United States, the Navajo are relative newcomers to the area. Originally they were a nomadic, hunting people from Canada who settled in what is now Arizona and New Mexico between 900 and 1200. Learning from their Pueblo neighbors, the Navajo became farmers, growing corn as a staple crop. (One of their myths describes how human beings were fashioned out of ground corn.) The introduction of sheep and cattle by Europeans diversified their way of life. Although some Navajo still maintain the farming and herding traditions, many, like Chee's cousins, make their livings outside the reservations.

Teaching Options

The Canyon, 1919. Frank Reed Whiteside. Oil on canvas, 20 x 16 in. David David Gallery, Philadelphia.
Viewing the painting: How does this scene reflect what Chee might have been feeling as he rode back to Little Canyon?

28 ❧ UNIT 1

MEETING INDIVIDUAL NEEDS **GIFTED AND TALENTED**

Change Versus Tradition While the United States is often perceived as a country obsessed with material progress and economic growth, a strand of simplicity and asceticism runs through its history. "Chee's Daughter" takes a firm stand for the simple life.

Activity Frame a statement that will provide for a lively debate: "An obsession with materialism will ultimately undermine the values of this country" or "Traditional cultures and simple lifestyles are attractive only to those who do not have to live them." Ask students to discuss their ideas in groups before forming sides and debating the issue in class. **L3** **COLLAB. LEARN.**

Chee's dark eyes surveyed the land along the highway as the old man continued to brag about being "progressive." *He* no longer was tied to the land. He and his wife made money easily and could *buy* all the things they wanted. Chee realized too late that he had stumbled into the old argument between himself and his wife's parents. They had never understood his feeling about the land—that a man took care of his land and it in turn took care of him. Old Man Fat and his wife scoffed at him, called him a Pueblo farmer, all during that summer when he planted and weeded and harvested. Yet they ate the green corn in their mutton stews, and the chili paste from the fresh ripe chilis,[3] and the tortillas from the cornmeal his wife ground. None of this working and sweating in the sun for Old Man Fat, who talked proudly of his easy way of living—collecting money from the trader who rented this strip of land beside the highway, collecting money from the tourists.

Yet Chee had once won that argument. His wife had shared his belief in the integrity of the earth, that jobs and people might fail one, but the earth never would. After that first year she had turned from her own people and gone with Chee to Little Canyon.

Old Man Fat was reaching for the Little One. "Don't be coming here with plans for my daughter's daughter," he warned. "If you try to make trouble, I'll take the case to the government man in town."

The impulse was strong in Chee to turn and ride off while he still had the Little One in his arms. But he knew his time of victory would be short. His own family would uphold the old custom of children, especially girl children, belonging to the mother's people. He

---

3. People string together *chilis*, or hot peppers, and preserve them by hanging them up to dry. The chilis are then used in cooking.

would have to give his daughter up if the case were brought before the headman of Little Canyon, and certainly he would have no better chance before a strange white man in town.

He handed the bewildered Little One to her grandfather who stood watching every movement suspiciously. Chee asked, "If I brought you a few things for the Little One, would that be making trouble? Some velvet for a blouse, or some of the jerky she likes so well . . . this summer's melon?"

Old Man Fat backed away from him. "Well," he hesitated, as some of the anger disappeared from his face and beads of greed shone in his eyes. "Well," he repeated. Then as the Little One began to squirm in his arms and cry, he said, "No! No! Stay away from here, you and all your family."

The sense of his failure deepened as Chee rode back to Little Canyon. But it was not until he sat with his family that evening in the hogan, while the familiar bustle of meal preparing went on about him, that he began to doubt the wisdom of the things he'd always believed. He smelled the coffee boiling and the oily fragrance of chili powder dusted into the bubbling pot of stew; he watched his mother turning round crusty fried bread in the small black skillet. All around him was plenty—a half of mutton hanging near the door, bright strings of chili drying, corn hanging by the braided husks, cloth bags of dried peaches. Yet in his heart was nothing.

REAL-WORLD CONNECTION

Active Reading

EVALUATE Is Chee right to believe that an education might have helped him get the Little One back? *(Some students will point out that tribal law is against Chee: no argument will alter the fact that the Little One is a girl and belongs to her mother's family. Others may observe that informed people are frequently able to manipulate the system. Chee's poverty, ignorance, and lack of fluent English (see page 31) may well work against him.)*

Literary Elements

SETTING Point out to students that authors frequently use setting to reflect the mood of the protagonist. Ask what they notice about the setting in this passage. *(It is winter, a cold, lifeless time of year, corresponding to Chee's self-doubt and spiritual depression. Chee is alone in a harsh, rocky landscape that appears to offer no consolation.)*

FINE ART
TRANSPARENCY 26

You may want to show Fine Art Transparency 26 to students and compare the scene to events in the story.

Chee's Daughter

He heard the familiar sounds of the sheep outside the hogan, the splash of water as his father filled the long drinking trough from the water barrel. When his father came in, Chee could not bring himself to tell a second time of the day's happenings. He watched his wiry, soft-spoken father while his mother told the story, saw his father's queue of graying hair quiver as he nodded his head with sympathetic exclamations.

Chee's doubting, acrid thoughts kept forming: Was it wisdom his father had passed on to him, or was his inheritance only the stubbornness of a long-haired Navaho resisting change? Take care of the land and it will take care of you. True, the land had always given him food, but now food was not enough. Perhaps if he had gone to school, he would have learned a different kind of wisdom, something to help him now. A schoolboy might even be able to speak convincingly to this government man whom Old Man Fat threatened to call, instead of sitting here like a clod of earth itself—Pueblo farmer indeed. What had the land to give that would restore his daughter?

In the days that followed, Chee herded sheep. He got up in the half-light, drank the hot coffee his mother had ready, then started the flock moving. It was necessary to drive the sheep a long way from the hogan to find good winter forage. Sometimes Chee met friends or relatives who were on their way to town or to the road camp where they hoped to get work; then there was friendly banter and an exchange of news. But most of the days seemed endless; he could not walk far enough or fast enough from his memories of the Little One or from his bitter thoughts. Sometimes it seemed his daughter trudged beside him, so real he could almost hear her footsteps—the muffled pad-pad of little feet in deerhide. In the glare of a snowbank he would see her vivid face, brown eyes sparkling. Mingling with the tinkle of sheep bells he heard her laughter.

When, weary of following the small sharp hoof marks that crossed and recrossed in the snow, he sat down in the shelter of a rock, it was only to be reminded that in his thoughts he had forsaken his brotherhood with the earth and sun and growing things. If he remembered times when he had flung himself against the earth to rest, to lie there in the sun until he could no longer feel where he left off and the earth began, it was to remember also that now he sat like an alien against the same earth; the belonging together was gone. The earth was one thing and he was another.

It was during the days when he herded sheep that Chee decided he must leave Little Canyon. Perhaps he would take a job

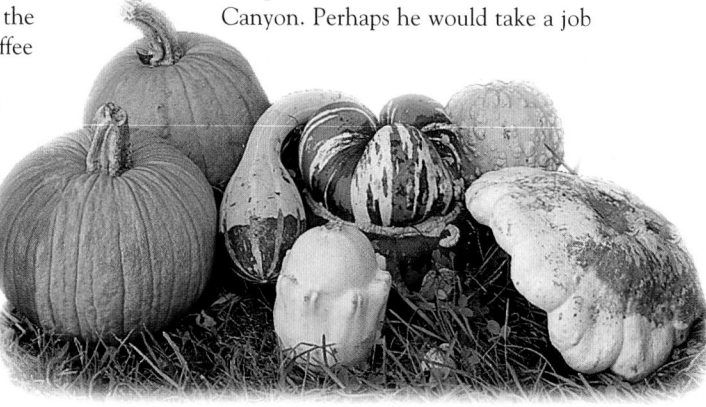

Vocabulary
acrid (ak′ rid) *adj.* irritating or upsetting
banter (ban′ tər) *n.* good-natured, witty joking or teasing

MULTIPLE LEARNING STYLES
MEETING INDIVIDUAL NEEDS

Musical Some learners associate different sounds and rhythms with the moods, characters, or settings of fiction. Just as music will enhance the emotional impact of a film, so matching sounds to verbal images will help some students engage more fully in the reading experience.

Activity Create with the class a list of the characters, settings, and key scenes from "Chee's Daughter." Ask students to choose two or three of these items and to compose or create sounds, songs, tunes, or rhythms that they feel correspond to their selection. Invite students to demonstrate their aural interpretations, and see if the class can accurately guess what aspects of the story are represented. **L3**

Juanita Platero and Siyowin Miller ∿

silversmithing for one of the traders in town. Perhaps, even though he spoke little English, he could get a job at the road camp with his cousins; he would ask them about it.

Springtime transformed the mesas. The peach trees in the canyon were shedding fragrance and pink blossoms on the gentled wind. The sheep no longer foraged for the yellow seeds of chamiso[4] but ranged near the hogan with the long-legged new lambs, eating tender young grass.

Chee was near the hogan on the day his cousins rode up with the message for which he waited. He had been watching with mixed emotions while his father and his sister's husband cleared the fields beside the stream.

"The boss at the camp says he needs an extra hand, but he wants to know if you'll be willing to go with the camp when they move it to the other side of the town?" The tall cousin shifted his weight in the saddle.

The other cousin took up the explanation. "The work near here will last only until the new cutoff beyond Red Sands is finished. After that, the work will be too far away for you to get back here often."

That was what Chee had wanted—to get away from Little Canyon—yet he found himself not so interested in the job beyond town as in this new cutoff which was almost finished. He pulled a blade of grass, split it thoughtfully down the center, as he asked questions of his cousins. Finally he said: "I need to think more about this. If I decide on this job, I'll ride over."

P Before his cousins were out of sight down the canyon, Chee was walking toward the fields, a bold plan shaping in his mind. As the plan began to flourish, wild and hardy as young tumbleweed, Chee added his own voice softly to the song his father was singing: ". . . In the middle of the wide field . . . Yellow Corn Boy . . . I wish to put in."

Chee walked slowly around the field, the rich red earth yielding to his footsteps. His plan depended upon this land and upon the things he remembered most about his wife's people.

Through planting time Chee worked zealously and tirelessly. He spoke little of the large new field he was planting, because he felt so strongly that just now this was something between himself and the land. The first days he was ever stooping, piercing the ground with the pointed stick, placing the corn kernels there, walking around the field and through it, singing, ". . . His track leads into the ground . . . Yellow Corn Boy . . . his track leads into the ground." After that, each day Chee walked through his field watching for the tips of green to break through; first a few spikes in the center and then more and more, until the corn in all parts of the field was above ground. Surely, Chee thought, if he sang the proper songs, if he cared for this land faithfully, it would not forsake him now, even though through the lonely days of winter he had betrayed the goodness of the earth in his thoughts. **Q**

Through the summer Chee worked long days, the sun hot upon his back, pulling weeds from around young corn plants; he planted squash and pumpkin; he terraced a

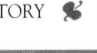

Did You Know?
Tumbleweed is any of several kinds of bushy prairie plants that break off from their roots and get blown around by the wind.

---

4. *Chamiso* (chä mē′ sō), from the Spanish, is an evergreen shrub found in the western United States.

Vocabulary
zealously (zel′ əs lē) *adv.* eagerly; enthusiastically

P **Author's Craft**

PLOT: *Rising Action* Point out to students that until this moment the reader has been kept informed of everything Chee thinks or feels. Suddenly, the authors are concealing information: Chee's "bold plan." Invite students to speculate as to why there has been a change in technique. Many will correctly observe that a mystery always creates reader interest and helps promote rising action.

Vo•cab•u•lar•y Skills

Word Forms Ask students if they notice anything unusual about the word *gentled*. Some will recognize that *gentle* would be the more conventional form of adjective. In fact, *gentled* is here the past participle of a verb not commonly encountered: "to gentle." Extend this discussion by eliciting a list of adjectives that can also be used as verbs. There is little apparent logic in the results: *yellow* can be a verb, but not *blue*, etc.

Q **Active Reading**

PREDICT What is Chee's plan? How can the land help him win back his daughter? *(Many students will realize that Chee's extra work will result in extra produce, but why would Old Man Fat want Chee's crops when he has money to purchase all his needs? Astute readers will realize that the new cutoff road plays a part in his decision, though the connection may not be obvious enough for an accurate prediction.)*

Reading *Minilesson*

Logical Reasoning Explain to students that decision making should involve logical reasoning. Chee has made an important decision. He has refused his cousins' offer of work at the road camp in spite of the job's reliable income.

Activity As they read, have students chart the factors involved in Chee's decision. Encourage students to share their charts with the class. Then have them discuss whether Chee's reasoning is logical and valid and whether it leads to the decision that is best for him. **L2**

Additional Resources
📁 *Reading Workbook*, pp. 3–4

Literary Elements

R **PERSONIFICATION** Ask students what they notice about the description of corn in this passage. If no one identifies personification, draw students' attention to how the plants "waved green arms and bent to embrace each other." Find other examples of personification in the passage. Point out that personification is a particularly relevant literary technique in this story, as it corresponds closely with Chee's own corn songs and his reverence for the natural world.

S Critical Thinking

INFERRING What game is Chee playing? Why does he not appear curious about the Little One? *(Chee knows from experience that Old Man Fat will exploit any position of power. If Chee still appears eager to have the Little One back, his father-in-law doubtless will revert to his wily, selfish ways.)*

T Active Reading

EVALUATE Old Man Fat's transformation may not be easy for some students to accept. Would this old bully really expect to get anything out of Chee, especially after his contemptuous behavior at their last meeting? Encourage students to speculate on the likelihood of this bold piece of characterization.

Teaching Options

small piece of land near his mother's hogan and planted carrots and onions and the moisture-loving chili. He was increasingly restless. Finally he told his family what he hoped the harvest from this land would bring him. Then the whole family waited with him, watching the corn: the slender graceful plants that waved green arms and bent to embrace each other as young winds wandered through the field, the maturing plants flaunting their pollen-laden tassels in the sun, the tall and sturdy parent corn with new-formed ears and a froth of purple, red, and yellow corn beards against the dusty emerald of broad leaves.

Summer was almost over when Chee slung the bulging packs across two pack ponies. His mother helped him tie the heavy rolled pack behind the saddle of the buckskin. Chee knotted the new yellow kerchief about his neck a little tighter, gave the broad black hat brim an extra tug, but these were only gestures of assurance and he knew it. The land had not failed him. That part was done. But this he was riding into? Who could tell?

When Chee arrived at Red Sands, it was as he had expected to find it—no cars on the highway. His cousins had told him that even the Pueblo farmers were using the new cutoff to town. The barren gravel around the Red Sands Trading Post was deserted. A sign banged against the dismantled gas pumps: *Closed until further notice.*

Old Man Fat came from the crude summer shelter built beside the log hogan from a few branches of scrub cedar and the sides of wooden crates. He seemed almost friendly when he saw Chee.

"Get down, my son," he said, eyeing the bulging packs. There was no bluster in his voice today, and his face sagged, looking somewhat saddened, perhaps because his cheeks were no longer quite full enough to push his eyes upward at the corners. "You are going on a journey?"

Chee shook his head. "Our fields gave us so much this year, I thought to sell or trade this to the trader. I didn't know he was no longer here."

Old Man Fat sighed, his voice dropping to an injured tone. "He says he and his wife are going to rest this winter; then after that he'll build a place up on the new highway."

Chee moved as though to be traveling on, then jerked his head toward the pack ponies. "Anything you need?"

"I'll ask my wife," Old Man Fat said as he led the way to the shelter. "Maybe she has a little money. Things have not been too good with us since the trader closed. Only a few tourists come this way." He shrugged his shoulders. "And with the trader gone—no credit."

Chee was not deceived by his father-in-law's unexpected confidences. He recognized them as a hopeful bid for sympathy and, if possible, something for nothing. Chee made no answer. He was thinking that so far he had been right about his wife's parents: their thriftlessness had left them with no resources to last until Old Man Fat found another easy way of making a living.

Old Man Fat's wife was in the shelter working at her loom. She turned rather wearily when her husband asked with noticeable

---

Vocabulary
flaunt (flônt) *v.* to display in a showy manner

MEETING INDIVIDUAL NEEDS — MULTIPLE LEARNING STYLES

Logical-Mathematical Time plays an important role in "Chee's Daughter"; the units of measurement are the seasons. Students may have a clearer understanding of the story if they connect graphically the sequence of events with the succession of the seasons.

Activity Have students construct a time line under which they write *winter,* *spring,* and *summer.* These can be further subdivided into three-month periods from December to August. Then ask students to write above the lines the major events of the story in chronological order, starting with Chee's unhappy arrival at Little Canyon and ending with his triumphant return. Have students share their time lines with a partner. **L2**

Friends in the Dark. Don Clark (b. 1955). Pastel, 30 x 20 in. Collection of the artist.
Viewing the painting: If this girl were Little One, would this picture be more typical of her life with Chee or with Old Man Fat? Explain.

deference if she would give him money to buy supplies. Chee surmised that the only income here was from his mother-in-law's weaving.

She peered around the corner of the shelter at the laden ponies, and then she looked at Chee. "What do you have there, my son?"

Chee smiled to himself as he turned to pull the pack from one of the ponies, dragged

it to the shelter where he untied the ropes. Pumpkins and hard-shelled squash tumbled out, and the ears of corn—pale yellow husks fitting firmly over plump ripe kernels, blue corn, red corn, yellow corn, many-colored corn, ears and ears of it—tumbled into every corner of the shelter.

"Yooooh," Old Man Fat's wife exclaimed as she took some of the ears in her hands. Then she glanced up at her son-in-law. "But we have no money for all this. We have sold almost everything we own—even the brass bed that stood in the hogan."

Old Man Fat's brass bed. Chee concealed his amusement as he started back for another pack. That must have been a hard parting. Then he stopped, for, coming from the cool darkness of the hogan was the Little One, rubbing her eyes as though she had been asleep. She stood for a moment in the doorway, and Chee saw that she was dirty, barefoot, her hair uncombed, her little blouse shorn of all its silver buttons. Then she ran toward Chee, her arms outstretched. Heedless of Old Man Fat and his wife, her father caught her in his arms, her hair falling in a dark cloud across his face, the sweetness of her laughter warm against his shoulder.

It was the haste within him to get this slow waiting game played through to the finish that made Chee speak unwisely. It

---

Vocabulary
deference (def′ ər ans) *n.* courteous respect or regard for the judgment, opinions, or desires of another
surmise (sər mīz′) *v.* to guess or conclude from little or no evidence

---

Author's Craft

PLOT A plot may have a last-minute complication. Point out how Chee's plan nearly backfires just at the moment when the reader believes that the story is over.

Active Reading

EVALUATE Is Chee being sincere or manipulative in this sudden act of generosity? *(Some students may believe that Chee would do anything to improve his daughter's welfare. Others may feel that Chee is playing a psychological game with his in-laws: by seeming to have given up hope, he will deny Old Man Fat the satisfaction of hurting him and will be more likely to regain the Little One.)*

Literary Elements

THEME Point out to students how fitting it is that Chee's last words are sung to the natural world that has given him strength.

Thematic Focus

Transitions Ask students what Chee has learned during the course of the story. Is he a different person when he rides home with the Little One at the end?

✔ ASSESSMENT OPTIONS

📁 **Quick Checks**, p. 2

Teaching Options

---

was the desire to swing her before him in the saddle and ride fast to Little Canyon that prompted his words. "The money doesn't matter. You still have something. . . ."

Chee knew immediately that he had overspoken. The old woman looked from him to the corn spread before her. Unfriendliness began to harden in his father-in-law's face. All the old arguments between himself and his wife's people came pushing and crowding in between them now.

Old Man Fat began kicking the ears of corn back onto the canvas as he eyed Chee angrily. "And you rode all the way over here thinking that for a little food we would give up our daughter's daughter?"

Chee did not wait for the old man to reach for the Little One. He walked dazedly to the shelter, rubbing his cheek against her soft dark hair, and put her gently into her grandmother's lap. Then he turned back to the horses. He had failed. By his own haste he had failed. He swung into the saddle, his hand touching the roll behind it. Should he ride on into town?

Then he dismounted, scarcely glancing at Old Man Fat, who stood uncertainly at the corner of the shelter, listening to his wife. "Give me a hand with this other pack of corn, Grandfather," Chee said, carefully keeping the small bit of hope from his voice.

Puzzled, but willing, Old Man Fat helped carry the other pack to the shelter, opening it to find more corn as well as carrots and round, pale yellow onions. Chee went back for the roll behind the buckskin's saddle and carried it to the entrance of the shelter, where he cut the ropes and gave the canvas a nudge with his toe. Tins of coffee rolled out, small plump cloth bags; jerked meat from several butcherings spilled from a flour sack; and bright red chilis splashed like flames against the dust.

"I will leave all this anyhow," Chee told them. "I would not want my daughter nor even you old people to go hungry."

Old Man Fat picked up a shiny tin of coffee, then put it down. With trembling hands he began to untie one of the cloth bags—dried sweet peaches.

The Little One had wriggled from her grandmother's lap, unheeded, and was on her knees, digging her hands into the jerked meat.

"There is almost enough food here to last all winter." Old Man Fat's wife sought the eyes of her husband.

Chee said, "I meant it to be enough. But that was when I thought you might send the Little One back with me." He looked down at his daughter noisily sucking jerky. Her mouth, both fists, were full of it. "I am sorry that you feel you cannot bear to part with her."

Old Man Fat's wife brushed a straggly wisp of gray hair from her forehead as she turned to look at the Little One. Old Man Fat was looking too. And it was not a thing to see. For in that moment the Little One ceased to be their daughter's daughter and became just another mouth to feed.

"And why not?" the old woman asked wearily.

Chee was settled in the saddle, the barefooted Little One before him. He urged the buckskin faster, and his daughter clutched his shirtfront. The purpling mesas flung back the echo: ". . . My corn embrace each other. In the middle of the wide field . . . Yellow Corn Boy embrace each other."

Grammar and Language *Minilesson*

Present Participles as Adjectives
Write this sentence on the board:
> With <u>trembling</u> hands he began to untie one of the cloth bags.

Explain that a present participle is a verb in its *-ing* form that often acts as an adjective.

Activity Ask students to find three examples of present participles used as adjectives in this story. **L3** **COLLAB. LEARN.**

Additional Resources

🖋 *Grammar and Language Transparency 2*

📕 *Grammar and Language Workbook,* pp. 93, 141

📕 *Grammar and Composition Handbook,* Lessons 1.4, 3.3

📘 *Writer's Choice,* Lessons 10.4, 12.3

Responding to Literature

Personal Response

What was your response when Chee's plan to deal with Old Man Fat seemed to be falling apart?

——— ANALYZING LITERATURE ———

RECALL

1. What is the way of life that Chee and his family live? How do Old Man Fat and his wife live?
2. Why does Little One go to live with Old Man Fat and his wife?
3. What does the building of the cutoff mean to Chee and his friends?
4. Why does Chee begin to doubt his way of life on the land?
5. What is finally decided by Chee and Old Man Fat about Little One?

INTERPRET

6. What do the differences in the two men's ways of life tell you about their attitudes toward their Navajo heritage?
7. Who do you think could provide Little One with the better life, Chee or Old Man Fat? Why?
8. In your opinion, was the new cutoff a positive or a negative addition to the area? Explain your opinion using details from the selection.
9. What might have happened if Chee had made a different decision about trusting the land?
10. How does Old Man Fat's attitude toward Chee change at the end of the story? What do you think accounts for this change?

EVALUATE AND CONNECT

11. **Irony** exists when a character's actions are the opposite of what people might expect. What is ironic about Old Man Fat and his wife taking Little One to live with them after her mother dies?
12. Look back at the flow chart you created for the Focus Activity on page 22. How does Chee's response to losing Little One compare to your predicted response if someone took something you valued?
13. Chee plans very carefully how he is going to get what he wants. In your opinion, was his planning worthwhile? Why or why not?
14. In your opinion, does Old Man Fat act true to character at the end of the story? Explain your answer.
15. **Theme Connections**   Do you think traditional ways have value in a world of fast-paced changes? Support your response with examples from the selection and from your own experience.

Literary ELEMENTS

Theme

The **theme** is the central message of a story that readers can apply to life. For example, the theme of many stories and movies is that goodness and courage will be rewarded. In some stories the theme is stated directly, but more often the theme is implied. To discover an implied theme, the reader might look at the experiences of the main characters and ask what message about life the story communicates.

1. Ideas about Navajo heritage are an important element in "Chee's Daughter." How do their attitudes toward their heritage affect the lives of Chee and Old Man Fat?
2. The writers could have chosen to state the theme of this selection directly. What might Chee have said that would summarize the story's message about heritage and tradition?
3. Explain how the theme of this story might apply to other life situations.

● See **Literary Terms Handbook**, p. R13.

THE SHORT STORY 35

Personal Response

Chee's near failure to bring home his daughter is calculated to create a feeling of anguish and defeat.

ANALYZING LITERATURE

1. Chee and his family are traditional farmers and shepherds; Old Man Fat and his wife make their living off tourists and by renting their property.
2. Navajo daughters traditionally belong to their mothers' families.
3. The cutoff reroutes the tourist traffic from Old Man Fat's property, effectively removing his source of income. Chee's cousins, who work on the road, have to move camp as construction proceeds.
4. Chee feels powerless after his first confrontation with Old Man Fat. The traditional ways seem to offer him no hope of retrieving his daughter.
5. Chee returns home with the Little One. Old Man Fat and his wife cannot feed another person.
6. Old Man Fat lives near the highway in a frame house surrounded by imitation Indian artifacts. Depending on outsiders for his livelihood, he has rejected the traditional Navajo ways. Chee lives far from the road, still following the farming and herding ways of his ancestors, whose faith ultimately gives him strength to prevail.
7. Chee would provide the Little One with a better life. He will give her love, food, and an extended family, and will teach her to respect the land.
8. The new cutoff has removed a source of income from Old Man Fat and others like him, who exploit their traditions for material ends. No cars use the old highway, and the trading post has gone out of business. Some students will say that this will encourage a return to the earth; others may argue that depression and suffering are the result.
9. Chee might have become a road worker like his cousins. He probably could have bought his daughter back from Old Man Fat, but his spiritual strength, which derived from the land, would have been compromised.
10. Old Man Fat is "almost friendly"; he has lost his "bluster." His near civility seems to result from desire for what Chee may offer.
11. Old Man Fat and his wife have rejected the Navajo way of life, yet they insist on their traditional right to their daughter's daughter.

LITERARY ELEMENTS

1. Chee wins back his daughter as a direct result of his traditional life. Old Man Fat, who has rejected his heritage, is left poor and helpless when the tourists depart.
2. "Faith in the land and in the ways of our people will give us strength."
3. Students may explain how their religious beliefs or cultural traditions have sustained them in times of difficulty.

Additional Resources

🖋 *Literary Elements Transparency 2*

---

12. Chee's response to loss is determination and thoughtful planning.
13. Most students will agree that Chee's planning was worthwhile. He attained his goal, but without the extra work to provide the abundance of produce he might have failed. Some may argue that the plan was too risky.
14. Old Man Fat is essentially selfish and gives up the Little One for his own well-being.
15. Traditional ways are shown to have value in this selection. Chee's faith in hard work and the earth brings him back his daughter.

LITERATURE AND WRITING

Writing About Literature

Students' analyses should
- indicate a careful reading of the selection in the choice of relevant details.
- reflect an understanding of the theme and show how setting strengthens the authors' purpose.

Creative Writing

Students' conversations should
- pose a specific problem for Chee to answer.
- suggest a solution that reveals Chee's steadfast personality and attachment to tradition.
- indicate an ability to transpose character traits from one setting to another.

EXTENDING YOUR RESPONSE

Literature Groups Make clear to students that the power of their responses will depend greatly upon supporting evidence from the story.
`COLLAB. LEARN.`

Performing Point out to students that the art of storytelling can be much more than a mere recital of details. Encourage them to include expressive language, dialogue, and even physical movement in their renditions. 📦

Interdisciplinary Activity Students who express an interest in a particular aspect of Navajo culture should be encouraged to explore that area in greater depth. 📦

LITERATURE AND WRITING

Writing About Literature

The Importance of Place How important is the **setting** in this story? Write an analysis of the role the physical surroundings play in Chee's life and in his struggles with Old Man Fat. You might consider the natural landscape, the farmland and grazing lands, and the town where Old Man Fat lives and has his business. What attitudes and experiences do the authors associate with each part of the setting?

Creative Writing

Conversations with Chee Imagine that Chee and you are discussing a problem you have, and you have asked him for advice. For example, you might ask his advice on career planning or on what classes to sign up for next year. Or, you might wonder how to best get along with a classmate with whom you have very little in common. How would you describe your problem to Chee? How do you think he would respond? Record your conversation in writing.

EXTENDING YOUR RESPONSE

Literature Groups

Life in Transition During the course of this story, Chee experiences several transitions, many of which involve permanent or temporary loss. In your group, identify as many of these transitions as you can. Then choose two or three and discuss how they affect Chee's life and the decisions he makes. Do you agree with the way he handles these transitions? Find examples from the selection to support your responses. Compare your ideas with those of other groups in the class.

Performing

Tell a Story In many Native American cultures, the storyteller is an important figure. Storytellers pass on through generations the stories important to the people. Imagine that you are a storyteller who feels that "Chee's Daughter" is an important story to preserve. Choose the most important elements of this story and turn them into an oral story. Share the story with a friend.

Interdisciplinary Activity

History: Navajo Heritage Find out more about traditional Navajo culture.
- Research the history of the people, as well as the customs, way of life, arts, and beliefs that contribute to Navajo heritage.
- Display your findings on a series of posters and share them with the class.

Reading Further

If you'd like to read more works about contemporary Native American life, you might enjoy these works:

Novels: *Tracks,* by Louise Erdrich, follows a group of Chippewa as they cling to their lands in North Dakota.

Go-Ahead Rider, by Robert J. Conley, is a story in which a mystery confronts a young Cherokee deputy.

Nonfiction: *Mad Bear—Spirit, Healing, and the Sacred in the Life of a Native American Medicine Man,* by Doug Boyd, recreates Mad Bear's tales of magic, his healing powers as a medicine man, and Native American legends.

📖 **Save your work for your portfolio.**

✔ ASSESSMENT OPTIONS

- 📁 *Quick Checks,* p. 2
- 📁 *Selection and Theme Assessment,* pp. 3–4
- 📁 *Performance Assessment,* p. 2
- 💾 *Testmaker*

Skill Minilessons

GRAMMAR AND LANGUAGE • Using Appositives

An appositive is a noun or pronoun placed next to another noun to identify or give more information about it. An appositive phrase is an appositive plus any words that modify it.

His father-in-law, Old Man Fat, might laugh. (*Old Man Fat* is an appositive identifying *father-in-law*.)

Chee was riding a good horse, a high-stepping buckskin. (The appositive phrase a *high-stepping buckskin* identifies the *horse*.)

Appositives are set off by commas unless they are essential to the meaning of the sentence.

PRACTICE On your paper write the appositive or appositive phrase in each of these sentences.

1. Chee rode toward his mother's home, a dome-shaped hogan.

2. Chee wanted to help his daughter, Little One.

3. He wanted to bring a gift, some velvet for a dress perhaps.

4. The family had only one source of income, his mother-in-law's weaving.

● For more about appositives, see **Language Handbook,** p. R27.

READING AND THINKING • Evaluating Generalizations

A generalization is a statement in which a collection of facts from specific situations is applied to more general circumstances. In "Chee's Daughter," Chee recalls the statement:

"Take care of the land and it will take care of you."

For Chee, this is a valid generalization because the land he has cared for has always provided him with food. If he had toiled in the fields and had gone hungry, then the generalization would have been invalid, or false.

PRACTICE Look back at the story to see the statement Chee's mother makes about "a fat Navajo." On a sheet of paper, explain the generalization she is making. Then write whether or not you think this is a valid generalization. Base your response on the facts in the story.

APPLY Use the facts in this story, or in another story you have read, to make another generalization. Share your generalization with a partner and discuss why you believe it is valid.

● For more on related reading skills, see **Reading Handbook,** pp. R78–R107.

VOCABULARY • Synonyms—Shades of Meaning

Synonyms are words that have the same or nearly the same meaning. For example, although *exhibit* and *flaunt* are synonyms, they do not mean exactly the same thing. To *exhibit* a talent is not obnoxious; to *flaunt* one is.

You will better understand what you read, and you will communicate more precisely when you write, if you pay attention to shades of meaning–those small but important differences that exist among many synonyms.

PRACTICE For each numbered word, choose the synonym that best matches the precise meaning.

1. acrid	a. bitter	b. tangy	c. penetrating
2. banter	a. heckling	b. talking	c. joking
3. deference	a. adoration	b. esteem	c. affection
4. zealously	a. spiritedly	b. insanely	c. carefully
5. indolence	a. laziness	b. inactivity	c. passivity

Skill Minilessons

GRAMMAR AND LANGUAGE
Using Appositives

1. a dome-shaped hogan
2. Little One
3. some velvet for a dress perhaps
4. his mother-in-law's weaving

READING AND THINKING
Evaluating Generalizations

Practice

The generalization referred to is on page 27: "'When you see a fat Navajo, you see one who hasn't worked for what he has.'" It suggests that honest work keeps people fit, physically and spiritually.

VOCABULARY
Synonyms—Shades of Meaning

1. a   2. c   3. b
4. a   5. a

Additional Practice

📖 *Grammar and Composition Handbook,* Lesson 3.2

📖 *Grammar and Language Workbook,* p. 91

📖 *Writer's Choice,* Lesson 12.2

📂 *Reading Workbook,* pp. 3–4

📂 *Vocabulary Practice,* p. 2

Objectives

- To read and analyze a short story about a man who retains his optimistic philosophy in a challenging situation
- To analyze the use of dialogue in a short story
- To write a character sketch

Skills

Reading/Thinking: Identifying Assumptions; Inferring; Varying Reading Rate; Analyzing Problems and Solutions
Writing: Interview
Vocabulary: Onomatopoeia; Etymology
Grammar/Language: Personal Pronouns; Using Descriptive Tag Lines
Listening/Speaking: Reporting Findings; Discussing Ideas
Collaboration: Literature Groups

Motivating

→ OPTIONS

Selection Focus Transparency 3: Have students view and discuss *Sarajevo*, a photograph by Martin A. Sugarman.

Focus Activity: Have students compare their spider maps in groups and come up with a list of "essentials" that they have in common.

Before You Read

Civil Peace

FOCUS ACTIVITY

Imagine surviving a war or a natural disaster, such as a hurricane or flood. What would be absolutely essential to ensure your happy survival after such a catastrophic experience?

MAP IT! Complete a spider map like the one at the right with words that identify the people and things in your life that you consider essential to your happiness.

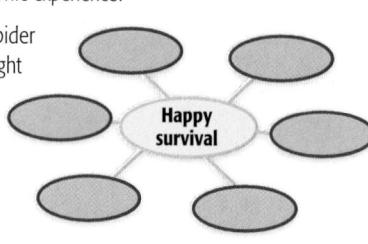

Happy survival

SETTING A PURPOSE Read to learn the part that attitude plays in one man's happy survival.

BACKGROUND

The Time and Place

This story takes place in Nigeria, probably in 1970, shortly after the end of the Nigerian Civil War.

Did You Know?

Nigeria, located on the western coast of Africa, is the most densely populated country on the continent. Once a British colony, it became an independent nation in 1960. The Nigerian Civil War began in 1967 when the Ibo—one of Nigeria's largest ethnic groups—tried to separate from Nigeria to form the independent Republic of Biafra. After enduring years of bloody battles, the Ibo were forced to surrender in 1970, ending the war. In connection with the war, Biafrans suffered a severe famine, in which nearly a million people died of starvation.

VOCABULARY PREVIEW

commandeer (kom′ ən dēr′) *v.* to seize for use by the military or government; p. 39
amenable (ə mē′ nə bəl) *adj.* responsive; able to be controlled; p. 40
retail (rē′ tāl) *v.* to sell directly to the consumer; p. 40
fortnight (fôrt′ nīt′) *n.* two weeks; p. 40
edifice (ed′ ə fis) *n.* a building, especially a large, important-looking one; p. 40

Meet Chinua Achebe

"It doesn't matter what language you write in, as long as what you write is good."

These words of Chinua Achebe (ə chā′ bā) refer to his use of English, rather than his native Ibo tongue, to write short stories and novels about Nigeria. In these works, he has tried to give English-speaking readers a deeper and more realistic view of African culture. Achebe's novel *Things Fall Apart* is recognized as a masterpiece of modern African literature.

Chinua Achebe was born in 1930 in Ogidi, Nigeria. This story was first published in 1971.

RESOURCE MANAGER

Lesson Planning Resource
The *Unit One Planning Guide* (pp. 24–31) provides additional lesson notes and reduced versions of all print resources.

Other Print Resources
- Active Reading Guide, p. 3
- Vocabulary Practice, p. 3
- Reading Workbook, pp. 5–6
- Grammar and Language Workbook, pp. 181–185

- Grammar and Composition Handbook, Lessons 7.1–7.3, 11.6
- Quick Checks, p. 3
- Selection and Theme Assessment, pp. 5–6
- Performance Assessment, p. 3
- Spanish Summaries, p. 3
- Spanish Translations
- Inclusion Strategies
- English Language Learners Sourcebook

 Transparencies
- Selection Focus 3
- Literary Elements 3
- Grammar and Language 3

Technology
 Audio Library
  Spanish Audio Library
  Glencoe Literature Web Site
  Testmaker

Civil Peace

Chinua Achebe

Jonathan Iwegbu counted himself extraordinarily lucky. "Happy survival!" meant so much more to him than just a current fashion of greeting old friends in the first hazy days of peace. It went deep to his heart. He had come out of the war with five inestimable blessings—his head, his wife Maria's head and the heads of three out of their four children. As a bonus he also had his old bicycle—a miracle too but naturally not to be compared to the safety of five human heads.

The bicycle had a little history of its own. One day at the height of the war it was commandeered "for urgent military action." Hard as its loss would have been to him he would still have let it go without a thought had he not had some doubts about the genuineness of the officer. It wasn't his disreputable rags, nor the toes peeping out of one blue and one brown canvas shoes, nor yet the two stars of his rank done obviously in a hurry in biro,[1] that troubled Jonathan; many good and heroic soldiers looked the same or

_____
1. The stars signifying the officer's rank had been hand-drawn in ink. *Biro* (bi′ rō) is a British term for a ballpoint pen.

Vocabulary
commandeer (kom′ ən dēr′) v. to seize for use by the military or government

Reading the Selection

A **Active Reading**

QUESTION Write *Civil War* on the board. Have students contrast this phrase with the title "Civil Peace." What might be the differences between the two? How might they be similar? Remind students to alter their thinking as they read the selection and gain new information.

Additional Resources
📁 *Active Reading Guide,* p. 3
🎧 *Audio Library*
🎧 *Spanish Audio Library*

Teaching Options

CONNECTING TO OTHER SELECTIONS

The chart on the right shows three ways to connect "Civil Peace" to selections in this book.

For specific teaching strategies, see the *Unit One Planning Guide,* pages 27–28.

Connection	Title
Life Skills: Leading and Organizing	→ "And of Clay Are We Created," p. 343
Thematic: Determination	→ "A Swimming Lesson," p. 495
Literary: Tone	→ "The Happy Man's Shirt," p. 241

Literary Elements

CHARACTER Discuss what the episode with the bicycle reveals about Jonathan's character. *(Jonathan is perceptive, quick thinking, pragmatic, and resourceful.)*

Author's Craft

WORD CHOICE Ask students why they suppose Achebe has used the phrase "of course" to begin the second sentence describing Jonathan's house. *(These two words suggest the terrible damage brought about by the war. If Jonathan is lucky to have a house without doors and windows, what must the city look like?)*

FYI

How Much Is That?
Nigerian currency at the time of this story was based upon the British system of pounds, shillings, and pence. Twelve pennies made up a shilling and twenty shillings a pound. Point out to students that at the exchange rate cited here, one Nigerian pound equaled 200 Biafran pounds.

Teaching Options

CivilPeace

Did You Know?
A *raffia bag* is one woven from the fibers of the raffia palm tree.

worse. It was rather a certain lack of grip and firmness in his manner. So Jonathan, suspecting he might be <u>amenable</u> to influence, rummaged in his raffia bag and produced the two pounds with which he had been going to buy firewood which his wife, Maria, <u>retailed</u> to camp officials for extra stock-fish and corn meal, and got his bicycle back. That night he buried it in the little clearing in the bush where the dead of the camp, including his own youngest son, were buried. When he dug it up again a year later after the surrender all it needed was a little palm-oil greasing. "Nothing puzzles God," he said in wonder.

He put it to immediate use as a taxi and accumulated a small pile of Biafran money ferrying camp officials and their families across the four-mile stretch to the nearest tarred road. His standard charge per trip was six pounds and those who had the money were only glad to be rid of some of it in this way. At the end of a <u>fortnight</u> he had made a small fortune of one hundred and fifteen pounds.

Then he made the journey to Enugu[2] and found another miracle waiting for him. It was unbelievable. He rubbed his eyes and looked again and it was still standing there before him. But, needless to say, even that

monumental blessing must be accounted also totally inferior to the five heads in the family. This newest miracle was his little house in Ogui Overside. Indeed nothing puzzles God! Only two houses away a huge concrete <u>edifice</u> some wealthy contractor had put up just before the war was a mountain of rubble. And here was Jonathan's little zinc house[3] of no regrets built with mud blocks quite intact! Of course the doors and windows were missing and five sheets off the roof. But what was that? And anyhow he had returned to Enugu early enough to pick up bits of old zinc and wood and soggy sheets of cardboard lying around the neighborhood before thousands more came out of their forest holes looking for the same things. He got a destitute carpenter with one old hammer, a blunt plane and a few bent and rusty nails in his tool bag to turn this assortment of wood, paper and metal into door and window shutters for five Nigerian shillings or fifty Biafran pounds. He paid the pounds, and moved in with his overjoyed family carrying five heads on their shoulders.

His children picked mangoes near the military cemetery and sold them to soldiers' wives for a few pennies—real pennies this time—and his wife started making breakfast akara balls[4] for neighbors in a hurry to start life again. With his family earnings he took his bicycle to the villages around and bought fresh palm wine which he mixed generously in his rooms with the water which had recently started running again in the public

---

2. *Enugu* (ā nōō′ gōō) is a city in southeastern Nigeria.

3. A *zinc house* is one with a zinc-coated metal roof.
4. *Akara balls* are ball-shaped bean cakes.

Vocabulary
amenable (ə mē′ nə bəl) *adj.* responsive; able to be controlled
retail (rē′ tāl) *v.* to sell directly to the consumer
fortnight (fôrt′ nīt′) *n.* two weeks
edifice (ed′ ə fis) *n.* a building, especially a large, important-looking one

---

MEETING INDIVIDUAL NEEDS — ENGLISH LANGUAGE LEARNERS

Dialect Nearly half of "Civil Peace" consists of an exchange between Jonathan and the leader of a gang of thieves, both of whom speak in a regional dialect. Students can understand the gist of the "tief-man's" language with a little effort.

Activity Write the following words on the board: *tief-man, hopen, de,* and *frien.* Ask students to find these words on page 42 and to deduce their meanings. Then have students make a list of four more dialect words they can identify and one that puzzles them. Discuss the words with the entire class.

Additional Resources
📁 *English Language Learners Sourcebook*

tap down the road, and opened up a bar for soldiers and other lucky people with good money.

At first he went daily, then every other day and finally once a week, to the offices of the Coal Corporation where he used to be a miner, to find out what was what. The only thing he did find out in the end was that that little house of his was even a greater blessing than he had thought. Some of his fellow ex-miners who had nowhere to return at the end of the day's waiting just slept outside the doors of the offices and cooked what meal they could scrounge together in Bournvita tins. As the weeks lengthened and still nobody could say what was what Jonathan discontinued his weekly visits altogether and faced his palm wine bar.

But nothing puzzles God. Came the day of the windfall when after five days of endless scuffles in queues and counter queues in the

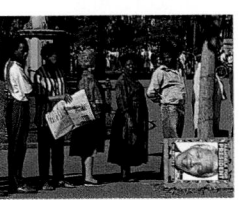

Did You Know?
Here a *queue* (kyū) means a line of people.

sun outside the Treasury he had twenty pounds counted into his palms as ex gratia[5] award for the rebel money he had turned in. It was like Christmas for him and for many others like him when the payments began. They called it (since few could manage its proper official name) *egg rasher.*

As soon as the pound notes were placed in his palm Jonathan simply closed it tight over them and buried fist and money inside his trouser pocket. He had to be extra careful

5. Something that is awarded *ex gratia* (eks gräsh′ ē ə) is given as a favor rather than as a legal right. The Latin word *gratia* means "kindness."

because he had seen a man a couple of days earlier collapse into near madness in an instant before that oceanic crowd because no sooner had he got his twenty pounds than some heartless ruffian picked it off him. Though it was not right that a man in such an extremity of agony should be blamed yet many in the queues that day were able to remark quietly on the victim's carelessness, especially after he pulled out the innards of his pocket and revealed a hole in it big enough to pass a thief's head. But of course he had insisted that the money had been in the other pocket, pulling it out too to show its comparative wholeness. So one had to be careful.

Jonathan soon transferred the money to his left hand and pocket so as to leave his right free for shaking hands should the need arise, though by fixing his gaze at such an elevation as to miss all approaching human faces he made sure that the need did not arise, until he got home.

He was normally a heavy sleeper but that night he heard all the neighborhood noises die down one after another. Even the night watchman who knocked the hour on some metal somewhere in the distance had fallen silent after knocking one o'clock. That must have been the last thought in Jonathan's mind before he was finally carried away himself. He couldn't have been gone for long, though, when he was violently awakened again.

"Who is knocking?" whispered his wife lying beside him on the floor.

"I don't know," he whispered back breathlessly.

The second time the knocking came it was so loud and imperious that the rickety old door could have fallen down.

"Who is knocking?" he asked then, his voice parched and trembling.

D Critical Thinking
IDENTIFYING ASSUMPTIONS What assumption does the crowd make about people who lose their money? What does this suggest about Biafra's postwar society? *(It is assumed that the unfortunate person has been careless. This suggests that the public has adopted an every-man-for-himself philosophy. People are fearful and suspicious. One's own survival is the principal objective.)*

E Active Reading
PREDICT Have students predict who might be at the door. Point out that there has been enough evidence in this story to make a reasonably accurate prediction. *(Achebe has concentrated on Jonathan's acquisition of wealth and on the danger of loss. The importance of the twenty pounds will be enough to persuade some students that he is bound to lose it.)*

INCLUSION STRATEGIES

Special Needs An African country in the aftermath of a brutal war is a setting far removed from the experiences of most students. Some students may not understand the situation and its impact on people. Help bridge the gap by discussing what human beings, whatever their circumstances, have in common. Point out that physical differences are often superficial.

Activity Have pairs or small groups of students write the headings *What Is Different?* and *What Is the Same?* Ask them to list aspects of Jonathan's life that are like and unlike aspects of their lives. **L1 COLLAB. LEARN.**

Additional Resources
📁 *Inclusion Strategies*

F **Literary Elements**

DIALOGUE Ask students what begins at this point in the story that has not previously appeared in the story. *(dialogue, or conversation between characters)*

G **Literary Elements**

IRONY Ask students what they find unusual about this situation. Point out that thieves calling for the police is a perfect example of irony of situation. Ask for their opinions of the leader of the gang. Suggest that irony is often a key ingredient of the cool, confident hero, or villain.

H **Critical Thinking**

INFERRING Why does no one respond? *(An obvious answer is that everyone is too frightened. The police may well be outgunned and outnumbered by this gang. Alert readers may infer that these thieves are so confident about calling the soldiers because they are the soldiers.)*

Children Dancing, c. 1948. Robert Gwathmey. Oil on canvas, 30 x 40 in. The Butler Institute of American Art, Youngstown, OH.

Viewing the painting: How does the atmosphere these parents are creating for their children reflect the way Jonathan cares for his family?

F "Na tief-man and him people," came the cool reply. "Make you hopen de door." This was followed by the heaviest knocking of all.

Maria was the first to raise the alarm, then he followed and all their children.

"Police-o! Thieves-o! Neighbors-o! Police-o! We are lost! We are dead! Neighbors, are you asleep? Wake up! Police-o!"

This went on for a long time and then stopped suddenly. Perhaps they had scared the thief away. There was total silence. But only for a short while.

G "You done finish?" asked the voice outside. "Make we help you small. Oya, everybody!"

"Police-o! Tief-man-o! Neighbors-o! we done loss-o! Police-o! . . ."

There were at least five other voices besides the leader's.

Jonathan and his family were now completely paralyzed by terror. Maria and the children sobbed inaudibly like lost souls. Jonathan groaned continuously.

The silence that followed the thieves' alarm vibrated horribly. Jonathan all but begged their leader to speak again and be done with it.

"My frien," said he at long last, "we don try our best for call dem but I tink say dem all done sleep-o . . . So wetin we go do now? Sometaim you wan call soja? Or you wan make we call dem for you? Soja better pass police. No be so?"

"Na so!" replied his men. Jonathan thought he heard even more voices now than before and groaned heavily. His legs were sagging under him and his throat felt like sandpaper.

"My frien, why you no de talk again. I de ask you say you wan make we call soja?"

"No."

"Awrighto. Now make we talk business. We no be bad tief. We no like for make trouble.

H

42 UNIT 1

Teaching Options

Grammar and Language *Minilesson*

Personal Pronouns • Objective Case
Write the following sentence on the board:
  I tink say <u>dem</u> all done sleep-o.

Underline *dem* and point out that *dem* is the subject of a clause. It would be *they* in Standard English. (Translated, the sentence reads, *I would say they are all asleep.*) Now write the objective case pronouns on the board: *me, you, her, him,* and

it; us, you, and *them.* Point out that these are used as direct objects, indirect objects, or objects of a preposition.

Activity Have students pair up and compose four sentences using the following phrases: *Jonathan and her; the thieves and them; you and me; us and them.*

L1 **COLLAB. LEARN.**

Additional Resources

🖨 *Grammar and Language Transparency 3*

📕 *Grammar and Language Workbook,* pp. 181–185

📗 *Grammar and Composition Handbook,* Lesson 7.1–7.3

📘 *Writer's Choice,* Lesson 17.1–17.3

Trouble done finish. War done finish and all the katakata[6] wey de for inside. No Civil War again. This time na Civil Peace. No be so?"

"Na so!" answered the horrible chorus.

"What do you want from me? I am a poor man. Everything I had went with this war. Why do you come to me? You know people who have money. We . . ."

"Awright! We know say you no get plenty money. But we sef no get even anini.[7] So derefore make you open dis window and give us one hundred pound and we go commot. Orderwise we de come for inside now to show you guitar-boy like dis . . ."

A volley of automatic fire rang through the sky. Maria and the children began to weep aloud again.

"Ah, missisi de cry again. No need for dat. We done talk say we na good tief. We just take our small money and go nwayorly. No molest. Abi we de molest?"

"At all!" sang the chorus.

"My friends," began Jonathan hoarsely. "I hear what you say and I thank you. If I had one hundred pounds . . ."

"Lookia my frien, no be play we come play for your house. If we make mistake and step for inside you no go like am-o. So derefore . . ."

"To God who made me; if you come inside and find one hundred pounds, take it and shoot me and shoot my wife and children. I swear to God. The only money I have in this life is this twenty-pounds *egg rasher* they gave me today . . ."

6. The word *katakata* may be meant to imitate the sound of gunfire. The rest of the phrase is Nigerian dialect for "that went with it."
7. An *anini* (ä nē′ nē) is a small coin of Nigeria worth less than one cent.

"OK. Time de go. Make you open dis window and bring the twenty pound. We go manage am like dat."

There were now loud murmurs of dissent among the chorus: "Na lie de man de lie; e get plenty money . . . Make we go inside and search properly well . . . Wetin be twenty pound? . . ."

"Shurrup!" rang the leader's voice like a lone shot in the sky and silenced the murmuring at once. "Are you dere? Bring the money quick!"

"I am coming," said Jonathan fumbling in the darkness with the key of the small wooden box he kept by his side on the mat.

At the first sign of light as neighbors and others assembled to commiserate with him he was already strapping his five-gallon demijohn to his bicycle carrier and his wife, sweating in the open fire, was turning over akara balls in a wide clay bowl of boiling oil. In the corner his eldest son was rinsing out dregs of yesterday's palm wine from old beer bottles.

Did You Know?
A *demijohn* is a large earthenware or glass bottle, encased in wicker.

"I count it as nothing," he told his sympathizers, his eyes on the rope he was tying. "What is *egg rasher*? Did I depend on it last week? Or is it greater than other things that went with the war? I say, let *egg rasher* perish in the flames! Let it go where everything else has gone. Nothing puzzles God."

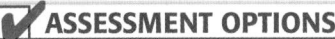

Reading *Minilesson*

Varying Reading Rate Point out that readers naturally read certain kinds of text more slowly than others. Have students list reasons for slowing down one's reading rate (to comprehend text with many facts; to understand difficult words or sentence structure; to appreciate text with interesting literary effects.)

Activity Have students work in pairs.

Explain that students will time one another's reading of two paragraphs. Instruct them to read paragraph 10 on page 42 and then to read paragraph 10 on page 43 while they are timed. Discuss why the paragraph written in dialect takes longer to read and understand. **L1 COLLAB. LEARN.**

Additional Resources
📁 *Reading Workbook*, pp. 5–6

Responding to Literature

Personal Response

Students' responses will vary as a result of their initial choices and the extent to which they were able to empathize with Jonathan's predicament.

Personal Response

Do you share Jonathan Iwegbu's values? Look again at the "Happy Survival" map you made in the Focus Activity on page 38. Having read this story, what changes would you make to your map?

ANALYZING LITERATURE

RECALL

1. What does Jonathan consider to be his greatest blessing?
2. Where are Jonathan and his family at the beginning of the story? Where is the rest of the story set?
3. What job did Jonathan have before the war? How do he and his family earn money after the war?
4. What are the official and unofficial names of the award Jonathan gets? Why does he receive the award?
5. Summarize what happens after Jonathan and his family are awakened by loud knocking at their door.

INTERPRET

6. What profound loss has Jonathan suffered? In your opinion, why does Jonathan dwell on his blessings and not on his losses?
7. How important is the story **setting**? Could this story have happened in another time or another place? Give reasons for your answer.
8. Theme Connections   How does Jonathan seem to feel about the changes inflicted on him and his family by the war? Explain.
9. Do you think Jonathan would have collapsed "into near madness" if he had been robbed when he left the Treasury? Why or why not?
10. In your opinion, why is Jonathan able to deal with his latest loss so philosophically? Do you think his reaction is predictable? Explain.

EVALUATE AND CONNECT

11. Do you think Jonathan is a good role model for his children? Would he be a good role model for young people today? Explain.
12. In your opinion, should Jonathan have told the thieves about the *egg rasher?* What would you have done?
13. What do you think Jonathan means by "Nothing puzzles God"?
14. How does the author use **local color** (see page R7) to evoke the region he's writing about? Cite specific details from the story.
15. The author has said that "any good story . . . should have a message, . . . a purpose." In your opinion, what is the message of this story?

Literary ELEMENTS

Dialogue

Dialogue is conversation between characters in a literary work. Good dialogue sounds natural and flows smoothly. Used effectively, dialogue helps reveal a character's personality and can help readers understand the events of a story and predict what might happen next. Dialogue also can add drama and suspense to a story.

1. The only dialogue in this story is the conversation during the robbery. Why, do you think, did the author use dialogue in this scene? Why didn't the author just describe the robbery, as he did the other events in the story? Explain your response.
2. Why do you think the author has the thieves speak in a regional dialect, while Jonathan uses standard English?

● See **Literary Terms Handbook,** p. R3.

ANALYZING LITERATURE

1. Jonathan considers the safety of his family to be his greatest blessing.
2. At the beginning, the family is in a refugee camp. The rest of the story is set in the city of Enugu.
3. Before the war, Jonathan was a miner. Afterwards, he runs a palm wine bar, his wife sells akara balls, and his children sell mangoes.
4. Jonathan receives an *ex gratia* payment in Nigerian pounds for handing in his Biafran money. The unofficial name for his award is *egg rasher.*
5. A gang of thieves demands money. Jonathan and his family call for help, but neither neighbors nor police will stir. To make matters worse, the thieves assist them in their cries. Threatened with execution, Jonathan hands his 20 pounds through the window. The next morning he sets out to collect palm wine and start all over again.
6. Jonathan has suffered the death of his youngest son. Many students will realize that he is an optimist with a capacity to accept life's ups and downs.
7. While the details of the setting are specifically Nigerian, this story could have taken place in any lawless, war-torn society. Where people are desperately poor and there is no effective police force, might will be right.
8. Jonathan not only accepts the misfortunes of war but considers himself blessed to have so much to call his own.
9. Many students will realize that Jonathan's buoyant spirit enables him to survive almost any misfortune.
10. Students who have understood that Jonathan is able to make the most of any small mercy will not be surprised by his reaction. He will probably rejoice at not being killed.
11. Many students will understand that Jonathan values a happy life above possessions and see this as a useful antidote to today's material culture.
12. Some students will advocate deception or resistance; some will say the thieves already knew about the money and were overwhelmingly powerful.

13. "Nothing puzzles God" can be translated as "Life is full of surprises, but they all have their reasons." It is Iwegbu's way of acknowledging that some situations are beyond human explanation. In an upside-down world, he is not trying to explain things.
14. Instances of local color abound: the officer with the biro stars; the rickety bicycle used to carry passengers; selling mangoes, palm wine, and akara balls; the thieves' dialect, etc.
15. One possibility: in an unpredictable world, work hard and make the best of what you have.

LITERARY ELEMENTS

1. The robbery scene is the heart of this story. Dialogue slows down the narrative pace, conveying to the reader the lawlessness and violence of post-war society. Dialogue also creates the scene's grim humor.
2. Regional dialect may suggest the thieves' lack of education. It shows that they are different and potentially an enemy.

Additional Resources

Literary Elements Transparency 3

LITERATURE AND WRITING

Writing About Literature

Character Sketch   Make a five-column chart with these headings: *Actions, Words, Thoughts, Appearance,* and *Reactions of others.* Go through the story, looking for details that reveal Jonathan's character and record each detail in the appropriate column. Then use the information in your chart as you write a character sketch of Jonathan. Compare your sketch with those of other students.

Creative Writing

Just the Facts   Imagine that a police officer has come to Jonathan's house to interview him about the robbery. List questions that the police officer might ask. For each question, write the type of reply you would expect Jonathan to make.

EXTENDING YOUR RESPONSE

Literature Groups

To See or Not to See   A character in an Achebe novel entitled *Anthills of the Savannah* says: "It is the story that outlives the sound of war-drums and the exploits of brave fighters. . . . The story is our escort; without it, we are blind." Discuss how "Civil Peace" might help the reader "see" life in Nigeria after the Civil War more clearly. Have one group member jot down the group's ideas about this topic. Share your ideas with the class.

Interdisciplinary Activity

Art: Nigerian Style   The painting at the right is a celebration of the Nigerian tradition by an African American artist. Use library resources or the Internet to research Nigerian art. Then design your own cover for a collection of stories by Chinua Achebe, incorporating a piece of Nigerian art or a traditional Nigerian pattern.

Internet Connection

Web Insight   Several universities have created Web sites dedicated to Chinua Achebe; some have links to sites related to the languages, customs, traditions, and people of Nigeria. Use these sites to explore a topic that you find particularly interesting. Be sure to narrow your topic to a manageable size. Report your findings to the class.

Save your work for your portfolio.

Reading Further

You might enjoy these other works by Chinua Achebe:

Novel: *Things Fall Apart,* set in an Ibo village in Nigeria, is a powerful and moving account of a "strong" man whose life is dominated by fear and anger.

Short Story Collection: *Girls at War and Other Stories* includes several stories that are rich in the folklore and traditions of Nigeria's Ibo culture.

Magic of Nigeria, 1971. Loïs Mailou Jones. Watercolor, 34 x 22 in. Collection of Dr. Tritobia Hayes Benjamin.

LITERATURE AND WRITING

Writing About Literature

Students' character sketches should
- refer specifically to details from the story.
- create generalizations about Jonathan's character from the details selected.

Creative Writing

Students' interviews should
- simulate a real-life police investigation.
- include specific details from the story.
- create a recognizable portrait of Jonathan.

EXTENDING YOUR RESPONSE

Literature Groups   Suggest to students that they ask themselves the question, "What is important about this story?" **COLLAB. LEARN.**

Interdisciplinary Activity
Remind students who discover regional differences in Nigerian art that Achebe is an Ibo, from the eastern part of the country.

Internet Connection   Familiarize students with the location and other key facts about Nigeria before they begin their research.

✔ ASSESSMENT OPTIONS

- *Quick Checks,* p. 3
- *Selection and Theme Assessment,* pp. 5–6
- *Performance Assessment,* p. 3
- *Testmaker*

Skill Minilessons

GRAMMAR AND LANGUAGE
Using Descriptive Tag Lines

Practice

Typical tag lines include
- Page 42: "'Na tief-man and him people,' *came the cool reply*." (confidence)
- Page 43: "'My friends,' *began Jonathan hoarsely*." (fear)
- Page 43: "'Shurrup!' *rang the leader's voice like a lone shot. . . .*" (command)

READING AND THINKING
Analyzing Problems and Solutions

Practice

Two other problems Jonathan faces are his joblessness and the attack by the thieves. He solves the first by establishing a palm wine bar, knowing that some people had money and would want a drink. He gives the thieves all his money when he realizes that they mean business. He understands that life is more valuable than possessions.

VOCABULARY
Etymology

- *amenable*: originally from the Latin verb *minare*, meaning to drive cattle. An amenable person, like a domestic animal, is responsive to persuasion.
- *retail*: from the French verb *retaillier* meaning to cut up. Retail items are sold in small quantities, cut from larger, wholesale, quantities.

Additional Practice

📕 *Grammar and Composition Handbook*

📕 *Grammar and Language Workbook*

📕 *Writer's Choice* Lesson 4.4

📂 *Reading Workbook,* pp. 5–6

📂 *Vocabulary Practice,* p. 3

Responding to Literature

Skill Minilessons

GRAMMAR AND LANGUAGE • Using Descriptive Tag Lines

When the characters in "Civil Peace" speak, you know what they are feeling because Achebe has used descriptive tag lines to convey the tone of voice and emotional state of each speaker. For example, when Jonathan says "Nothing puzzles God," the tag line, "he said in wonder" conveys his awe and reverence of a higher power. Later, you know that Jonathan feels threatened and scared when he asks, "Who is knocking?" because "his voice is parched and trembling."

PRACTICE Review "Civil Peace," looking for tag lines with descriptive language. Pay particular attention to the tag lines used with the dialogue of the thieves. On your paper, write the tag lines and explain what they show about the emotions of the speaker or speakers.

APPLY Review a piece of your own writing that includes dialogue. Revise or add tag lines to convey the tone of voice and emotions of each speaker.

● For more about dialogue, see **Language Handbook,** p. R48.

READING AND THINKING • Analyzing Problems and Solutions

Often characters in stories come up against problems they need to solve. For example, at the beginning of "Civil Peace," Jonathan is confronted by an officer who wants his treasured old bicycle "for urgent military action." Jonathan would have given up the bike if he truly believed he had no other option. He accurately and cleverly suspects, however, that the officer will settle for a bribe. Jonathan keeps his bike and makes the officer happy at the same time.

PRACTICE Identify two other problems that Jonathan faces in "Civil Peace." On your paper, state each problem, describe how Jonathan solves it, and explain the thinking that leads to his solution.

APPLY Look at another story in this text that you have read. Explain how the main character in that story solves a problem.

● For more about comprehension strategies, see **Reading Handbook,** pp. R82–R94.

VOCABULARY • Etymology

English words come from many languages—Latin, Greek, French, Old English, Dutch, and others. Etymology is the study of the history of a word, from its origin to its current meaning. For example, *edifice* comes from the Latin word *aedificium* meaning "a building."

If you trace the history of *commandeer,* you will find the Afrikaans *kommandeer,* then the French *commander,* and eventually you will get to the Latin *com-* ("very much") and *mando* ("hand" plus "to give"). So, if you emphatically tell someone "Take care of this; it's in your hands now!" you've given a command. When you commandeer someone's property, you command them to turn it over to you.

Some word etymologies are easier to follow. *Fortnight,* for example, makes sense when you find out that it's an Old English word that means "fourteen nights."

PRACTICE Use a dictionary to look up the etymologies of *amenable* and *retail.* (A word's etymology is usually shown in brackets right after the abbreviation for the part of speech or at the end of the entry.) Then, for each word, briefly describe something that the etymology helps you to understand about the word.

MEDIA Connection

Press Release

Have you read about or do you know anyone who has followed her heart and realized her dreams? Toshiko Akiyoshi has worked her way to the top of the American jazz scene, despite certain obstacles.

We, Too, Are One:
Renowned Jazz Pianist Toshiko Akiyoshi Bridges the Gap

by Michael Henningsen

There was a time early in Toshiko Akiyoshi's career when she was convinced that she had no place in jazz. The musical culture from which Akiyoshi came was quite different from that which created the bulk of be-bop, swing, and big band jazz some 50 years ago. But it wasn't long before the gifted pianist realized that she could, indeed, contribute to jazz history while delicately infusing her music with her own rich Asian heritage. And since the mid-1970s, Toshiko Akiyoshi and her orchestra have done just that—and to much critical and audience acclaim.

Born in Manchuria, China, Akiyoshi was studying classical piano by the age of six. Upon her family's return to their native Japan, she considered a career in medicine before stumbling upon a "Pianist Wanted" sign posted outside one of the many dance halls that dotted the streets of the then

still occupied country. She was hired on the spot. Her family insisted that she quit when school started. But, she says, "March came and went and no one noticed. I just kept on playing." She moved to Tokyo in the early 1950s and found herself quickly at the top of the city's burgeoning jazz scene, where she often played with touring American jazz artists. It was Oscar Petersen's rhythm section, in fact, who joined Akiyoshi on her first recording after Petersen hailed her the best female jazz pianist he'd ever heard.

Shortly thereafter, Akiyoshi moved to the United States to attend the Berklee College of Music and, in 1973, formed what would later become her 17-piece jazz orchestra. And in the 25 years that have followed, Akiyoshi has continued to define and redefine jazz with her unique melding of cultures and heritage. "I read a history book," she remembers, "that said the Israelis came through China to Japan, so I thought, we are all connected, hand in hand." And if music is indeed the international language, then Akiyoshi is truly fluent.

Respond

1. Explain how much of Akiyoshi's success you think is due to fate and how much is due to hard work.

2. Why do you think her family never pressed her to go into medicine as she had originally planned?

MEDIA Connection

Objective

- To read and understand a press release

Literature LINK

Two Kinds Akiyoshi's biography is a mirror-image of the story told by the narrator of "Two Kinds" (pp. 49–58). While the young Japanese pianist was determined to become a performing artist, the Chinese American heroine of Amy Tan's short story practiced reluctantly and performed disastrously.

Respond

1. Fate may have steered Akiyoshi past the "Pianist Wanted" sign and brought her into the path of Oscar Peterson. Hard work developed her natural abilities, without which her success would have been impossible.

2. Her family may have understood that a musical talent like hers was not to be suppressed. Akiyoshi may also have been extremely determined to pursue her career.

Additional Resources
📁 *Media Connections Activities,* p. 1

Teaching Options

Reading *Minilesson*

Sequence of Events Press releases often summarize the events of the subject's life. To illustrate this technique, have a few volunteers choose five events each that tell a brief story of their lives. Emphasize that the events must be told in chronological order; for example, birth date, family moved to the city, new sister was born, starred in the school play, started banjo lessons.

Activity Have students scan the article and list the major sequence of events in Akiyoshi's life. Direct students to number each event and to be sure to keep them in order. Have students share their lists in groups and check to see if anyone missed any event.

Additional Resources
📁 *Reading Workbook*

Objectives

- To read and analyze a short story about a girl whose mother wants her to become a prodigy
- To identify types of conflict in a short story
- To write a character evaluation

Skills

Reading/Thinking: Judging the Credibility of a Source; Drawing Conclusions; Evaluating; Generalizing; Summarizing

Writing: Self-Description; Journal Entry

Vocabulary: Eponyms; Figurative Meanings; Analogies

Grammar/Language: Past Perfect Tense; Participles and Participial Phrases

Listening/Speaking: Storytelling; Prodigy Presentation

Collaboration: Literature Groups

Motivating

→ OPTIONS

Literature Launchers: "Introducing Amy Tan"

Videodisc
Side A, Segment 1

Also available in VHS.

Selection Focus Transparency 4: Have students view and discuss *The Piano Recital*, a photograph by Yale Joel.

Focus Activity: Invite students to tell of their accomplishments.

Before You Read

Two Kinds

FOCUS ACTIVITY

Just for a moment imagine yourself as an acclaimed musician or artist, a champion athlete, a brilliant scientist, or an award-winning actor.

JOURNAL Write a description of yourself as a person who is at the top of his or her chosen field. Briefly tell what you have accomplished and what you enjoy most about your success.

SETTING A PURPOSE Read to discover two different viewpoints on successful living.

BACKGROUND

The Time and Place
The story takes place in Chinatown in San Francisco, probably during the early 1960s.

Did You Know?
Chinatown in downtown San Francisco is one of the largest Chinese communities outside of Asia. The neighborhood—with its fascinating mix of restaurants, shops, businesses, and religious and cultural institutions—is a crowded and bustling place. The area was settled by Chinese immigrants who arrived during the Gold Rush of 1849. Chinatown continues to grow, as immigrants arrive to begin a new life—just as the mother in "Two Kinds" had done in 1949.

VOCABULARY PREVIEW

prodigy (prod′ ə jē) *n.* an extraordinarily gifted or talented person, especially a child; p. 49
lament (lə ment′) *v.* to express sorrow or regret; p. 50
reproach (ri prōch′) *n.* blame; disgrace; discredit; p. 50
mesmerizing (mez′ mə rīz ing) *adj.* fascinating; p. 51
reverie (rev′ ər ē) *n.* fanciful thinking, daydream; p. 53
discordant (dis kôrd′ ənt) *adj.* not in agreement or harmony; p. 53
devastate (dev′ əs tāt) *v.* to destroy; overwhelm; p. 56
fiasco (fē as′ kō) *n.* a complete or humiliating failure; p. 56

48   UNIT 1

Meet Amy Tan

Amy Tan enjoys performing music much more than the girl in this story does. She sings in a rock band as a way to relax and to raise money for worthy causes.

Tan's first published writing was an article titled, "What the Library Means to Me," written when she was eight years old. Since then she has become an award-winning author. Her first novel, *The Joy Luck Club*, was made into a feature film of the same name. The book, which includes the selection you are about to read, tells about four women from China and their Chinese American daughters.

Amy Tan was born in Oakland, California, in 1952. This story was published in 1989.

RESOURCE MANAGER

Lesson Planning Resource
The *Unit One Planning Guide* (pp. 32–39) provides additional lesson notes and reduced versions of all print resources.

Other Print Resources
- Active Reading Guide, p. 4
- Vocabulary Practice, p. 4
- Reading Workbook, pp. 7–8
- Grammar and Language Workbook, pp. 147, 93
- Grammar and Composition Handbook, Lessons 5.4, 3.3

- Quick Checks, p. 4
- Selection and Theme Assessment, pp. 7–8
- Performance Assessment, p. 4
- Spanish Summaries, p. 4
- Inclusion Strategies
- English Language Learners Sourcebook

 Transparencies
- Selection Focus 4
- Literary Elements 4
- Grammar and Language 4

Technology
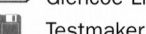
- Literature Launchers
- Audio Library
- Spanish Audio Library
- Glencoe Literature Web Site
- Testmaker

TWO Kinds

Amy Tan

MY MOTHER BELIEVED YOU could be anything you wanted to be in America. You could open a restaurant. You could work for the government and get good retirement. You could buy a house with almost no money down. You could become rich. You could become instantly famous.

"Of course, you can be <u>prodigy</u>, too," my mother told me when I was nine. "You can be best anything. What does Auntie Lindo know? Her daughter, she is only best tricky."

America was where all my mother's hopes lay. She had come to San Francisco in 1949 after losing everything in China: her mother and father, her family home, her first husband, and two daughters, twin baby girls. But she never looked back with regret. Things could get better in so many ways.

We didn't immediately pick the right kind of prodigy. At first my mother thought I could be a Chinese Shirley Temple.[1] We'd watch Shirley's old movies on TV as though they were training films. My mother would poke my arm and say, "*Ni kan.* You watch." And I would see Shirley tapping her feet, or singing a sailor song, or pursing her lips into a very round O while saying "Oh, my goodness."

"*Ni kan,*" my mother said, as Shirley's eyes flooded with tears. "You already know how. Don't need talent for crying!"

Soon after my mother got this idea about Shirley Temple, she took me to the beauty training school in the Mission District[2] and put me in the hands of a student who could barely hold the scissors without shaking. Instead of getting big fat curls, I emerged with an uneven mass of crinkly black fuzz. My

---

1. *Shirley Temple* was a popular child movie star of the 1930s.
2. The *Mission District* is a residential neighborhood in San Francisco.

Vocabulary
prodigy (prod′ ə jē) *n.* an extraordinarily gifted or talented person, especially a child

THE SHORT STORY 🦋 49

Two *Kinds*

mother dragged me off to the bathroom and tried to wet down my hair.

"You look like Negro Chinese," she lamented, as if I had done this on purpose.

The instructor of the beauty training school had to lop off these soggy clumps to make my hair even again. "Peter Pan is very popular these days," the instructor assured my mother. I now had hair the length of a boy's, with curly bangs that hung at a slant two inches above my eyebrows. I liked the haircut, and it made me actually look forward to my future fame.

In fact, in the beginning I was just as excited as my mother, maybe even more so. I pictured this prodigy part of me as many different images, and I tried each one on for size. I was a dainty ballerina girl standing by the curtain, waiting to hear the music that would send me floating on my tiptoes. I was like the Christ child lifted out of the straw manger, crying with holy indignity. I was Cinderella stepping from her pumpkin carriage with sparkly cartoon music filling the air.

In all of my imaginings I was filled with a sense that I would soon become perfect. My mother and father would adore me. I would be beyond reproach. I would never feel the need to sulk, or to clamor for anything.

But sometimes the prodigy in me became impatient. "If you don't hurry up and get me out of here, I'm disappearing for good," it warned. "And then you'll always be nothing."

Every night after dinner my mother and I would sit at the Formica-topped[3] kitchen table. She would present new tests, taking her examples from stories of amazing children that she had read in *Ripley's Believe It or Not* or *Good Housekeeping*, *Reader's Digest*, or any of a dozen other magazines she kept in a pile in our bathroom. My mother got these magazines from people whose houses she cleaned. And since she cleaned many houses each week, we had a great assortment. She would look through them all, searching for stories about remarkable children.

The first night she brought out a story about a three-year-old boy who knew the capitals of all the states and even of most of the European countries. A teacher was quoted as saying that the little boy could also pronounce the names of the foreign cities correctly. "What's the capital of Finland?" my mother asked me, looking at the story.

All I knew was the capital of California, because Sacramento was the name of the street we lived on in Chinatown. "Nairobi!"[4] I guessed, saying the most foreign word I could think of. She checked to see if that might be one way to pronounce *Helsinki* before showing me the answer.

The tests got harder—multiplying numbers in my head, finding the queen of hearts in a deck of cards, trying to stand on my head without using my hands, predicting the daily temperatures in Los Angeles, New York, and London. One night I had to look at a page from the Bible for three minutes and then report everything I could remember. "Now Jehoshaphat[5] had riches and honor in abundance and . . . that's all I remember, Ma," I said.

---

3. *Formica* (fôr mī′ kə) is a plastic substance used to cover kitchen and bathroom surfaces because it is resistant to heat and water.

4. *Nairobi* (nī rō′ bē) is the capital of Kenya in east central Africa.
5. *Jehoshaphat* (ji hosh′ ə fat′) was a king of Judah in the ninth century B.C.

Vocabulary
lament (lə ment′) *v.* to express sorrow or regret
reproach (ri prōch′) *n.* blame; disgrace; discredit

And after seeing, once again, my mother's disappointed face, something inside me began to die. I hated the tests, the raised hopes and failed expectations. Before going to bed that night I looked in the mirror above the bathroom sink, and when I saw only my face staring back—and understood that it would always be this ordinary face—I began to cry. Such a sad, ugly girl! I made high-pitched noises like a crazed animal, trying to scratch out the face in the mirror.

And then I saw what seemed to be the prodigy side of me—a face I had never seen before. I looked at my reflection, blinking so that I could see more clearly. The girl staring back at me was angry, powerful. She and I were the same. I had new thoughts, willful thoughts—or, rather, thoughts filled with lots of won'ts. I won't let her change me, I promised myself. I won't be what I'm not.

So now when my mother presented her tests, I performed listlessly, my head propped on one arm. I pretended to be bored. And I was. I got so bored that I started counting the bellows of the foghorns out on the bay while my mother drilled me in other areas. The sound was comforting and reminded me of the cow jumping over the moon. And the next day I played a game with myself, seeing if my mother would give up on me before eight bellows. After a while I usually counted only one bellow, maybe two at most. At last she was beginning to give up hope.

Two or three months went by without any mention of my being a prodigy. And then one day my mother was watching the *Ed Sullivan Show*[6] on TV. The TV was old and the sound kept shorting out. Every time my mother got halfway up from the sofa to adjust the set, the sound would come back on and Sullivan would be talking. As soon as she sat down, Sullivan would go silent again. She got up—the TV broke into loud piano music. She sat down—silence. Up and down, back and forth, quiet and loud. It was like a stiff, embraceless dance between her and the TV set. Finally, she stood by the set with her hand on the sound dial.

She seemed entranced by the music, a frenzied little piano piece with a <u>mesmerizing</u> quality, which alternated between quick, playful passages and teasing, lilting[7] ones.

"*Ni kan,*" my mother said, calling me over with hurried hand gestures. "Look here."

I could see why my mother was fascinated by the music. It was being pounded out by a little Chinese girl, about nine years old, with a Peter Pan haircut. The girl had the sauciness[8] of a Shirley Temple. She was proudly modest, like a proper Chinese child. And she also did a fancy sweep of a curtsy, so that the fluffy skirt of her white dress cascaded to the floor like the petals of a large carnation.

In spite of these warning signs, I wasn't worried. Our family had no piano and we couldn't afford to buy one, let alone reams of sheet music and piano lessons. So I could be generous in my comments when my mother bad-mouthed the little girl on TV.

"Play note right, but doesn't sound good!" my mother complained. "No singing sound." "What are you picking on her for?" I said carelessly. "She's pretty good. Maybe she's not the best, but she's trying hard."

---

6. The *Ed Sullivan Show* was a popular weekly variety show on TV in the 1950s and 1960s.

7. *Lilting* means "light and lively."

8. *Sauciness* means "boldness that is playful and lighthearted."

Vocabulary
mesmerizing (mez′ mə rīz ing) *adj.* fascinating

Writing Minilesson

Two Kinds

F

I knew almost immediately that I would be sorry I had said that.

"Just like you," she said. "Not the best. Because you not trying." She gave a little huff as she let go of the sound dial and sat down on the sofa.

The little Chinese girl sat down also, to play an encore of "Anitra's Tanz," by Grieg. I remember the song, because later on I had to learn how to play it.

Did You Know?
Edvard *Grieg* (grĕg), 1843–1907, was a Norwegian composer.

Three days after watching the *Ed Sullivan Show* my mother told me what my schedule would be for piano lessons and piano practice. She had talked to Mr. Chong, who lived on the first floor of our apartment building. Mr. Chong was a retired piano teacher, and my mother had traded housecleaning services for weekly lessons and a piano for me to practice on every day, two hours a day, from four until six.

When my mother told me this, I felt as though I had been sent to hell. I whined, and then kicked my foot a little when I couldn't stand it anymore.

G

"Why don't you like me the way I am?" I cried, "I'm *not* a genius! I can't play the piano. And even if I could, I wouldn't go on TV if you paid me a million dollars!"

H

My mother slapped me. "Who ask you to be genius?" she shouted. "Only ask you be your best. For you sake. You think I want you to be genius! Hnnh! What for! Who ask you!"

"So ungrateful," I heard her mutter in Chinese. "If she had as much talent as she has temper, she'd be famous now."

Mr. Chong, whom I secretly nicknamed Old Chong, was very strange, always tapping his fingers to the silent music of an invisible orchestra. He looked ancient in my eyes. He had lost most of the hair on the top of his head, and he wore thick glasses and had eyes that always looked tired. But he must have been younger than I thought, since he lived with his mother and was not yet married.

I

I met Old Lady Chong once, and that was enough. She had a peculiar smell, like a baby that had done something in its pants, and her fingers felt like a dead person's, like an old peach I once found in the back of the refrigerator; its skin just slid off the flesh when I picked it up.

Did You Know?
Ludwig van *Beethoven* (bā' tō vən), 1770–1827, was a German composer.

I soon found out why Old Chong had retired from teaching piano. He was deaf. "Like Beethoven!" he shouted to me. "We're both listening only in our head!" And he would start to conduct his frantic silent sonatas.[9]

Our lessons went like this. He would open the book and point to different things, explaining their purpose: "Key! Treble! Bass! No sharps or flats! So this is C major! Listen now and play after me!"

And then he would play the C scale a few times, a simple chord, and then, as if inspired by an old unreachable itch, he would gradually add more notes and running trills and a pounding bass until the music was really something quite grand.

---

9. *Sonatas* are instrumental compositions, commonly written for piano.

Amy Tan

I would play after him, the simple scale, the simple chord, and then just play some nonsense that sounded like a cat running up and down on top of garbage cans. Old Chong would smile and applaud and say, "Very good! But now you must learn to keep time!"

So that's how I discovered that Old Chong's eyes were too slow to keep up with the wrong notes I was playing. He went through the motions in half time. To help me keep rhythm, he stood behind me and pushed down on my right shoulder for every beat. He balanced pennies on top of my wrists so that I would keep them still as I slowly played scales and arpeggios.[10] He had me curve my hand around an apple and keep that shape when playing chords. He marched stiffly to show me how to make each finger dance up and down, staccato,[11] like an obedient little soldier.

He taught me all these things, and that was how I also learned I could be lazy and get away with mistakes, lots of mistakes. If I hit the wrong notes because I hadn't practiced enough, I never corrected myself. I just kept playing in rhythm. And Old Chong kept conducting his own private reverie.

So maybe I never really gave myself a fair chance. I did pick up the basics pretty quickly, and I might have become a good pianist at that young age. But I was so determined not to try, not to be anybody different, that I learned to play only the most ear-splitting preludes, the most discordant hymns.

Over the next year I practiced like this, dutifully in my own way. And then one day I heard my mother and her friend Lindo Jong both talking in a loud, bragging tone of voice so that others could hear. It was after church, and I was leaning against a brick wall, wearing a dress with stiff white petticoats. Auntie Lindo's daughter, Waverly, who was my age, was standing farther down the wall, about five feet away. We had grown up together and shared all the closeness of two sisters, squabbling over crayons and dolls. In other words, for the most part, we hated each other. I thought she was snotty. Waverly Jong had gained a certain amount of fame as "Chinatown's Littlest Chinese Chess Champion."

"She bring home too many trophy," Auntie Lindo lamented that Sunday. "All day she play chess. All day I have no time do nothing but dust off her winnings." She threw a scolding look at Waverly, who pretended not to see her.

"You lucky you don't have this problem," Auntie Lindo said with a sigh to my mother.

And my mother squared her shoulders and bragged: "Our problem worser than yours. If we ask Jing-mei[12] wash dish, she hear nothing but music. It's like you can't stop this natural talent."

And right then I was determined to put a stop to her foolish pride.

 few weeks later Old Chong and my mother conspired to have me play in a talent show that was to be held in the church hall. By then my parents had saved up enough to

---

10. Arpeggios (är pej′ ē ōz) are chords in which the notes are played in succession instead of all at the same time.
11. To play music *staccato* (stə kä′ tō) is to produce sharp, distinct breaks between successive tones.

12. *Jing-mei* (jing′ mā)

Vocabulary
reverie (rev′ ər ē) *n.* fanciful thinking; daydream
discordant (dis kôrd′ ənt) *adj.* not in agreement or harmony

INTERDISCIPLINARY CONNECTION

Music The piano recital, an occasion of triumph or tragedy for middle-class American children of previous generations, is a less familiar event for many students today. Typically, pieces chosen for performance are short, simple classics of no more than five minutes in length. A well-planned recital introduces pupils to a wide range of entertaining works.

Activity Have students bring to class a tape or CD of a short work for piano. Suggest that they consult musical friends or the reference librarian for suitable pieces. These may range in style from Bach to Scott Joplin. Encourage musical students to record their own performances. Ask each student to prepare a brief spoken introduction for his or her selection. Perform them consecutively for an in-class "recital." **L3**

Robert Schumann
Symphonist, songwriter, and critic, Robert Schumann (1810–56) was also one of the great composers for piano of the 19th century. Apart from his virtuoso keyboard compositions (many composed for his remarkable wife, the pianist Clara Schumann), he wrote a number of beautiful and delightfully simple pieces for beginning students, including such recital staples as *Spinning Song* and *The Happy Farmer*.

VIEWING THE PAINTING

Unlike oil paints, watercolor is a transparent medium: the effect of light is created not by paint but by the paper itself. Successful watercolorists often use the paint sparingly, creating a sense of space and airiness.

Viewing Response *The girl in the painting seems more focused and hardworking than Jing-mei.*

The Piano Lesson, 1994. Diana Ong. Watercolor. Private collection.

Viewing the painting: Compare how the girl in the painting approaches her piano practice with how Jing-mei approaches her practice.

54 🦢 UNIT 1

Teaching Options

REAL-WORLD CONNECTION

Feature Stories on Musicians The arts pages of magazines and daily newspapers frequently carry stories about musicians who are performing in upcoming concerts. These are not reviews, which may be outspokenly critical, but feature stories and interviews, which serve to publicize the performer's accomplishments.

Activity Have students bring to class feature stories on musicians. Let them read and discuss these in groups. Have them ask such questions as *Is this a well-rounded picture of the artist? Is the author telling me what to think? Does the article persuade me that the artist is worth hearing?* Choose a few of these issues to discuss with the class. **L3 COLLAB. LEARN.**

Amy Tan

Did You Know?
A *spinet* (spin' it) is a small, upright piano.

buy me a second-hand piano, a black Wurlitzer spinet with a scarred bench. It was the showpiece of our living room.

For the talent show I was to play a piece called "Pleading Child," from Schumann's[13] *Scenes From Childhood*. It was a simple, moody piece that sounded more difficult than it was. I was supposed to memorize the whole thing. But I dawdled over it, playing a few bars and then cheating, looking up to see what notes followed. I never really listened to what I was playing. I daydreamed about being somewhere else, about being someone else.

The part I liked to practice best was the fancy curtsy: right foot out, touch the rose on the carpet with a pointed foot, sweep to the side, bend left leg, look up, and smile.

My parents invited all the couples from their social club to witness my debut. Auntie Lindo and Uncle Tin were there. Waverly and her two older brothers had also come. The first two rows were filled with children either younger or older than I was. The littlest ones got to go first. They recited simple nursery rhymes, squawked out tunes on miniature violins, and twirled hula hoops in pink ballet tutus, and when they bowed or curtsied, the audience would sigh in unison, "*Awww*," and then clap enthusiastically.

M When my turn came, I was very confident. I remember my childish excitement. It was as if I knew, without a doubt, that the prodigy side of me really did exist. I had no fear whatsoever, no nervousness. I remember

13. Robert *Schumann* (shoo' män), 1810–1856, was a German composer.

thinking, This is it! This is it! I looked out over the audience, at my mother's blank face, my father's yawn, Auntie Lindo's stiff-lipped smile, Waverly's sulky expression. I had on a white dress, layered with sheets of lace, and a pink bow in my Peter Pan haircut. As I sat down, I envisioned people jumping to their feet and Ed Sullivan rushing up to introduce me to everyone on TV. **N**

And I started to play. Everything was so beautiful. I was so caught up in how lovely I looked that I wasn't worried about how I would sound. So I was surprised when I hit the first wrong note. And then I hit another, and another. A chill started at the top of my head and began to trickle down. Yet I couldn't stop playing, as though my hands were bewitched. I kept thinking my fingers would adjust themselves back, like a train switching to the right track. I played this strange jumble through to the end, the sour notes staying with me all the way.

When I stood up, I discovered my legs were shaking. Maybe I had just been nervous, and the audience, like Old Chong, had seen me go through the right motions and had not heard anything wrong at all. I swept my right foot out, went down on my knee, looked up, and smiled. The room was quiet, except for Old Chong, who was beaming and shouting, "Bravo! Bravo! Well done!" But then I saw my mother's face, her stricken face. The audience clapped weakly, and as I walked back to my chair, with my whole face quivering as I tried not to cry, I heard a little boy whisper loudly to his mother, "That was awful," and the mother whispered back, "Well, she certainly tried." **O**

And now I realized how many people were in the audience—the whole world, it seemed. I was aware of eyes burning into my back. I felt the shame of my mother and father as they sat stiffly through the rest of the show.

THE SHORT STORY 🎵 55

Listening and Speaking *Minilesson*

I Saw Something Funny Many students will have been asked at some point to write about an embarrassing experience. It is hard to understand that one's personal disaster may be amusing to an onlooker. Suggest to students that a good storyteller will be able to find a comic side to almost any situation.

Activity Have students recall an embarrassing situation and write notes about it. Urge them to choose either an incident that occurred a while ago, or one that happened to someone else. Then ask them to imagine that a person who was present is describing the situation to a friend. Have them tell the story as the *onlooker* saw it, speaking of themselves in the third person. Have students practice their stories in groups. **L2**

Vo•cab•u•lar•y Skills

Figurative Meanings Ask students what they would usually associate with the word *anchor*. Point out that here it is used figuratively, instead of literally: the parents are not ships and there is no heavy weight restraining them. Encourage students to think of other verbs that can be used figuratively, such as *leap*, *poison*, *strike*, *wound*, and *run*.

P Active Reading

RESPOND Have students respond to the father and the minimal role he is playing in this family drama. What sort of person is he? Might he have eased the tension by acting earlier?

Q Literary Elements

PLOT: *Internal Conflict* If Jing-mei's plan was "to put a stop to [her mother's] foolish pride," she would seem to have succeeded. So why is she devastated by her mother's expression after the recital? *(Jing-mei is torn between her desire to please her mother and her desire to be herself and do as she wishes.)*

R Critical Thinking

EVALUATING Why does Jing-mei want to "shout back and cry"? Is this a psychologically believable desire? *(Many students will understand that in being a dutiful daughter, Jing-mei has suppressed her need to be herself. The pressure has been building up. She is looking for an opportunity to "explode.")*

Teaching Options

We could have escaped during intermission. Pride and some strange sense of honor must have anchored my parents to their chairs. And so we watched it all: The eighteen-year-old boy with a fake moustache who did a magic show and juggled flaming hoops while riding a unicycle. The breasted girl with white makeup who sang an aria[14] from *Madame Butterfly* and got an honorable mention. And the eleven-year-old boy who won first prize playing a tricky violin song that sounded like a busy bee.

Did You Know?
Madame Butterfly is a famous opera by Italian composer Giacomo Puccini.

After the show the Hsus, the Jongs, and the St. Clairs, from the Joy Luck Club, came up to my mother and father.

"Lots of talented kids," Auntie Lindo said vaguely, smiling broadly.

"That was somethin' else," my father said, and I wondered if he was referring to me in a humorous way, or whether he even remembered what I had done.

Waverly looked at me and shrugged her shoulders. "You aren't a genius like me," she said matter-of-factly. And if I hadn't felt so bad, I would have pulled her braids and punched her stomach.

But my mother's expression was what devastated me: a quiet, blank look that said she had lost everything. I felt the same way, and everybody seemed now to be coming up, like gawkers at the scene of an accident, to see what parts were actually missing.

When we got on the bus to go home, my father was humming the busy-bee tune and my mother was silent. I kept thinking she wanted to wait until we got home before shouting at me. But when my father unlocked the door to our apartment, my mother walked in and went straight to the back, into the bedroom. No accusations. No blame. And in a way, I felt disappointed. I had been waiting for her to start shouting, so that I could shout back and cry and blame her for all my misery.

I had assumed that my talent-show fiasco meant that I would never have to play the piano again. But two days later, after school, my mother came out of the kitchen and saw me watching TV.

"Four clock," she reminded me, as if it were any other day. I was stunned, as though she were asking me to go through the talent-show torture again. I planted myself more squarely in front of the TV.

"Turn off TV," she called from the kitchen five minutes later.

I didn't budge. And then I decided. I didn't have to do what my mother said anymore. I wasn't her slave. This wasn't China. I had listened to her before, and look what happened. She was the stupid one.

She came out from the kitchen and stood in the arched entryway of the living room. "Four clock," she said once again, louder.

"I'm not going to play anymore," I said nonchalantly. "Why should I? I'm not a genius."

She stood in front of the TV. I saw that her chest was heaving up and down in an angry way.

---

14. An *aria* (är′ ē ə) is an elaborate composition for solo voice.

Vocabulary
devastate (dev′ əs tāt) *v.* to destroy; overwhelm
fiasco (fē as′ kō) *n.* a complete or humiliating failure

MEETING INDIVIDUAL NEEDS   MULTIPLE LEARNING STYLES

Spatial Jing-mei feels as though she is literally two people: the obedient daughter and the rebel trying to burst free. Some students will find this internal conflict easier to understand if they visualize Jing-mei's opposing personas.

Activity Have students find or create visual symbols for the two sides of Jing-mei's personality. These could be sketches of her two "faces," abstract designs, or symbolic objects. Ask them to present their representations to the class with a brief explanation of their significance. **L1**

"No!" I said, and I now felt stronger, as if my true self had finally emerged. So this was what had been inside me all along.

"No! I won't!" I screamed.

She snapped off the TV, yanked me by the arm and pulled me off the floor. She was frighteningly strong, half pulling, half carrying me toward the piano as I kicked the throw rugs under my feet. She lifted me up and onto the hard bench. I was sobbing by now, looking at her bitterly. Her chest was heaving even more and her mouth was open, smiling crazily as if she were pleased that I was crying.

"You want me to be someone that I'm not!" I sobbed. "I'll never be the kind of daughter you want me to be!"

"Only two kinds of daughters," she shouted in Chinese. "Those who are obedient and those who follow their own mind! Only one kind of daughter can live in this house. Obedient daughter!"

"Then I wish I weren't your daughter. I wish you weren't my mother," I shouted. As I said these things I got scared. It felt like worms and toads and slimy things crawling out of my chest, but it also felt good, that this awful side of me had surfaced, at last.

"Too late change this," my mother said shrilly.

And I could sense her anger rising to its breaking point. I wanted to see it spill over. And that's when I remembered the babies she had lost in China, the ones we never talked about. "Then I wish I'd never been born!" I shouted. "I wish I were dead! Like them."

It was as if I had said magic words. Alakazam!—her face went blank, her mouth closed, her arms went slack, and she backed out of the room, stunned, as if she were blowing away like a small brown leaf, thin, brittle, lifeless.

Portrait, c. 1950. Lawrence Chinn. Oil on canvas, 15 x 11 in. Collection of Frances Chinn.

Viewing the painting: Does the woman in this portrait fit your image of Jing-mei's mother? Why or why not?

It was not the only disappointment my mother felt in me. In the years that followed, I failed her many times, each time asserting my will, my right to fall short of expectations. I didn't get straight As. I didn't become class president. I didn't get into Stanford. I dropped out of college.

Unlike my mother, I did not believe I could be anything I wanted to be. I could only be me.

And for all those years we never talked about the disaster at the recital or my terrible declarations afterward at the piano bench. Neither of us talked about it again, as if it

REVIEW Where has Jing-mei's "true self" appeared before? *(Point out the face she sees staring back at her from the mirror on page 51.)*

T **Literary Elements**

EVALUATING GENERALIZATIONS Is the mother's generalization about daughters valid? Ask students what they think of her outburst. *(Many will feel that the mother is exercising irrational power in trying to impose her will upon Jing-mei. A few may believe that a parent's authority is central to family unity. Some may note a cultural clash. The Chinese value filial duty; Americans believe in obedience but also believe children have a right to live their own lives.)*

VIEWING THE PAINTING

Portrait artists often attempt to depict a subject's character as well as his or her appearance.

Viewing Response *The woman in the painting has a strong, confident face. Some students may have difficulty attributing the mother's domineering temperament to this smiling woman.*

U **Literary Elements**

PLOT: *Climax* Students may assume that the story's climax is the talent show. Point out that the main conflict is between mother and daughter. It reaches its climax in this scene.

Reading *Minilesson*

Generalizing Point out that reading about fictional characters often enables readers to understand the behavior of people in general. For example, analyzing the characters in "Two Kinds" can lead to generalizations about relationships between parents and children.

Activity Have each student formulate a generalization about parents and children

and their relationships based on the mother and daughter in "Two Kinds." Then have students state their generalization and the facts upon which it is based. Have the class decide whether each generalization is valid. **L2**

Additional Resources
📁 *Reading Workbook,* pp. 7–8

Active Reading

EVALUATE Is Jing-mei justified in feeling forgiven? Her mother still seems to think that she could have been a genius. *(The fact that the piano has even been mentioned is enough to relieve Jing-mei. Her mother has clearly not forgotten, but she seems to have gotten beyond her anger.)*

Thematic Focus

Transitions Ask students if they can describe how Jing-mei is a different person at the end of the story from the confused little girl at the beginning. Point out that learning to accept all aspects of one's personality is one indication of maturity.

✔ ASSESSMENT OPTIONS

📁 *Quick Checks,* p. 4

Two Kinds

were a betrayal that was now unspeakable. So I never found a way to ask her why she had hoped for something so large that failure was inevitable.

And even worse, I never asked her about what frightened me the most: Why had she given up hope? For after our struggle at the piano, she never mentioned my playing again. The lessons stopped. The lid to the piano was closed, shutting out the dust, my misery, and her dreams.

So she surprised me. A few years ago she offered to give me the piano, for my thirtieth birthday. I had not played in all those years. I saw the offer as a sign of forgiveness, a tremendous burden removed.

"Are you sure?" I asked shyly. "I mean, won't you and Dad miss it?"

"No, this your piano," she said firmly. "Always your piano. You only one can play."

"Well, I probably can't play anymore," I said. "It's been years."

"You pick up fast," my mother said, as if she knew this was certain. "You have natural talent. You could be genius if you want to."

"No, I couldn't."

"You just not trying," my mother said. And she was neither angry nor sad. She said it as if announcing a fact that could never be disproved. "Take it," she said.

But I didn't, at first. It was enough that she had offered it to me. And after that, every time I saw it in my parents' living room, standing in front of the bay window, it made me feel proud, as if it were a shiny trophy that I had won back.

Last week I sent a tuner over to my parents' apartment and had the piano reconditioned, for purely sentimental reasons. My mother had died a few months before, and I had been getting things in order for my father, a little bit at a time. I put the jewelry in special silk pouches. The sweaters she had knitted in yellow, pink, bright orange—all the colors I hated—I put in mothproof boxes. I found some old Chinese silk dresses, the kind with little slits up the sides. I rubbed the old silk against my skin, and then wrapped them in tissue and decided to take them home with me.

After I had the piano tuned, I opened the lid and touched the keys. It sounded even richer than I remembered. Really, it was a very good piano. Inside the bench were the same exercise notes with handwritten scales, the same secondhand music books with their covers held together with yellow tape.

I opened up the Schumann book to the dark little piece I had played at the recital. It was on the left-hand page, "Pleading Child." It looked more difficult than I remembered. I played a few bars, surprised at how easily the notes came back to me.

And for the first time, or so it seemed, I noticed the piece on the right-hand side. It was called "Perfectly Contented." I tried to play this one as well. It had a lighter melody but with the same flowing rhythm and turned out to be quite easy. "Pleading Child" was shorter but slower; "Perfectly Contented" was longer but faster. And after I had played them both a few times, I realized they were two halves of the same song.

Teaching Options

Grammar and Language *Minilesson*

Past Perfect Tense Write on the board: I opened the book to the piece I <u>had played</u> at the recital. Point out that this is an example of the past perfect tense. It refers to actions begun and ended before another past action begins.

Activity Have students use the past past perfect tense of the verbs *die, knit,* and *offer* in sentences of their own. **L2**

Additional Resources

🎙 *Grammar and Language Transparency 4*

📕 *Grammar and Language Workbook,* p. 147

📕 *Grammar and Composition Handbook,* Lesson 5.4

📗 *Writer's Choice,* Lesson 15.4

Responding to Literature

Personal Response

What was your opinion of Jing-mei's mother and the extremely ambitious goals she set for her daughter? Explain your answer.

ANALYZING LITERATURE

RECALL

1. What two faces does Jing-mei see when she looks in the mirror after another failed prodigy training session?
2. What makes Jing-mei's mother decide that her daughter will study the piano? How does Jing-mei react to this news?
3. At her recital, how does Jing-mei feel when it is her turn to perform? How well does she perform?
4. Explain what provokes the nasty argument between Jing-mei and her mother.
5. What reasons does Jing-mei's mother give for offering Jing-mei the piano for her thirtieth birthday? How does Jing-mei interpret her mother's offer?

INTERPRET

6. Why, do you think, does Jing-mei decide to stop trying to become a prodigy?
7. In your opinion, why does Jing-mei have such a lazy attitude toward her piano studies?
8. Why, do you think, do Jing-mei and her parents feel so humiliated by her performance at the recital?
9. What is so brutal about the dreadful thing Jing-mei says to her mother at the end of their argument?
10. Do you think that Jing-mei's mother finally forgives her daughter for the dreadful thing she said? Explain.

EVALUATE AND CONNECT

11. In your opinion, why does Jing-mei's mother long for her to be famous?
12. Jing-mei and her mother seem to be fighting about the piano. In your opinion, what are they really fighting about?
13. Do you think that well-meaning parents—such as Jing-mei's mother— sometimes set unrealistic goals for their children? Explain.
14. To what does the title of this story refer? Do you think it's a good title for the story? Give a reason for your answer.
15. What do you think Jing-Mei has learned by the end of the story?

Literary ELEMENTS

Conflict

Most stories are based on a problem, or conflict, that gets resolved over the course of the story. **External conflicts** exist when a character struggles with an outside force, such as another person, society, fate, or a force of nature. An **internal conflict** exists in a character's mind, when he or she is torn between different feelings or goals. Many stories have more than one conflict. Typically, the conflicts are related in some way.

1. What is the main external conflict in "Two Kinds"?
2. Identify another external conflict in the story. How does this conflict get resolved?
3. Describe an internal conflict that Jing-mei or her mother might have. How does it relate to the main conflict you identified in question 1 above?

● See **Literary Terms Handbook**, p. R3.

THE SHORT STORY 59

LITERARY ELEMENTS

1. The main external conflict is between Jing-mei and her mother over Jing-mei's refusal to study the piano seriously.
2. Another external conflict is between Jing-mei and her talented cousin Waverly. This ends with Jing-mei's complete humiliation.
3. Jing-mei wants to please her mother but also wants to think for herself. This conflict is inseparable from the external one.

Additional Resources

🖎 *Literary Elements Transparency 4*

---

13. Depending largely on their own experiences with parents and the other adults in their lives, students may or may not feel that parents set unrealistic goals for their children.
14. The mother says that there are two kinds of daughters: the obedient and the disobedient. Many students will understand that Jing-mei exemplifies both of these types.
15. By the end of the story, Jing-mei has learned to accept the ambivalence within her own personality.

Personal Response

Some students may be intolerant of the mother's obsessive demands. Recent immigrants, or those from more traditional homes, may recognize the pressure she puts on Jing-mei as an expression of her love and concern.

ANALYZING LITERATURE

1. She sees her ordinary face and her "angry, powerful" prodigy face.
2. Her mother is inspired upon seeing a young Chinese girl performing on the *Ed Sullivan Show*. Jing-mei feels she has been "sent to hell."
3. Jing-mei feels confident and excited. She performs terribly.
4. The two have a nasty argument when Jing-mei discovers that her mother intends her to keep playing the piano.
5. Jing-mei's mother says that the piano belongs to Jing-mei, who is the only one able to play. Jing-mei interprets the offer as "a sign of forgiveness."
6. Jing-mei discovers that becoming a prodigy involves a lot of hard work and a dedication that she does not possess.
7. Jing-mei has already decided that she is not going to be a prodigy. Old Chong's deafness gives her an easy way out. If she had been given a choice in the matter, she might have relented on her own.
8. Jing-mei feels humiliated because she had not realized the importance of the occasion or how poorly she actually played the piano. Her parents are humiliated to have their daughter, about whom they have boasted, disgrace herself in front of their friends.
9. In attempting to hurt her mother, Jing-mei brings up the taboo subject of the dead twin daughters. The effect is to make her mother feel a worthless failure.
10. Some students may feel that the offer of the piano is a genuine indication of forgiveness; others may feel that the hurt is too deep to be completely forgiven.
11. Perhaps the mother wants Jing-mei to have the success and glamour that she herself never could achieve.
12. Many students will recognize a generational conflict, heightened by the very different cultures in which mother and daughter have been brought up.

LITERATURE AND WRITING

Writing About Literature

Students' evaluations should
- reflect an understanding of Jing-mei's thoughts and responses.
- support all speculations with details from the story.

Personal Writing

Students' journal entries should
- persuade the reader that the writer's imagined situation is real.
- reflect thoughtfully on the problems of success.
- describe precisely how success has its drawbacks.

EXTENDING YOUR RESPONSE

Literature Groups Remind students that they may have a natural bias to support Jing-mei's position. Encourage them to be particularly fair-minded in assessing the mother's side of the story. **COLLAB. LEARN.**

Interdisciplinary Activity
Suggest to students who enjoy creative writing that they compose a journal to accompany their pamphlets, recounting their imaginary experiences as immigrants to the United States.

Performing Encourage students to look for information about the parents' role in the prodigy's success. Is there always a driving force like Jing-mei's mother?

— LITERATURE AND WRITING —

Writing About Literature

Evaluate a Character's Actions Write a paragraph or two evaluating Jing-mei's actions. Do Jing-mei's actions seem appropriate for a girl her age and for her situation? What do you think of the way Jing-mei reacts to her mother? What does she think her mother wants? What does she want for herself? Support your opinions with details from the story.

Personal Writing

Side Effects of Success Look back at the journal entry you made in the Focus Activity on page 48, in which you described yourself at the top of your chosen field. Now imagine some of the possible drawbacks of such success—for example, the pressure to achieve, the fear of failure, the loss of privacy, the time demands of your career. Write another journal entry in which you describe what you like least about your success.

— EXTENDING YOUR RESPONSE —

Literature Groups

Debating Issues Should parents ever require their children to take music lessons, as Jing-mei's mother did, or to play a sport or participate in any particular activity? First, look back at "Two Kinds" and list the reasons why the mother's requirements of Jing-mei were good and why they were bad. Use specific examples from the story as you develop your list. Then add to your list other reasons for and against mandatory after-school activities for children. Compare your lists with those made by other groups, and debate whether it does more harm or more good to require a child to participate in an activity in which he or she has little or no interest.

Interdisciplinary Activity

History: Researching a Topic Jing-mei's mother represents one of about 2 million Chinese citizens who fled their homeland at the end of the 1940s and into the next decade. Do some research on this wave of Chinese migrations. What were the political and economic conditions in China at that time? Find out why so many Chinese left their homeland. Create a pamphlet with charts and pictures that details the results of your research.

Performing

Presentation Child prodigies—particularly in music—have been famous throughout history. Research a child prodigy and prepare a presentation about his or her work. For Mozart, for example, you might provide a brief biographical sketch and then play recordings of his music.

Leopold Mozart with Wolfgang and Nannerl, playing music, 1763 (detail). Louis Carrogis de Carmontelle. Watercolor, 33 x 20 cm. Musée Condé, Chantilly, France.

Reading Further

You might enjoy another work by Amy Tan:

Novel: *The Joy Luck Club* gives readers a moving look at the lives of four Chinese women in pre-1949 China and the lives of their American-born daughters.

Viewing: *The Joy Luck Club*

📖 **Save your work for your portfolio.**

✔ ASSESSMENT OPTIONS

📁 *Quick Checks,* p. 4
📁 *Selection and Theme Assessment,* pp. 7–8
📁 *Performance Assessment,* p. 4
💾 *Testmaker*

Skill Minilessons

GRAMMAR AND LANGUAGE • Participles and Participial Phrases

Amy Tan uses **participles** (verb forms used as adjectives) and **participial phrases** to make her descriptions lively. For example:

I was a dainty ballerina girl standing by the curtains. (The participial phrase *standing by the curtains* describes *girl*.)

You can often improve your writing by using participles and participial phrases to combine short, choppy sentences. For example:

I dawdled over my piano piece. I daydreamed.
Daydreaming, I dawdled over my piano piece.

PRACTICE Combine each pair of sentences into one sentence that includes a participle or participial phrase.

1. Auntie wanted to scold Waverly. She gave Waverly a look.
2. Jing-mei returned to her seat. She fought back tears.
3. My mother called me over with hurried hand gestures. She said, "Look here."
4. My mother looked at the story. She asked, "What's the capital of Finland?"

● For more about participles, see **Language Handbook**, p. R41.

READING AND THINKING • Summarizing

To increase your reading comprehension and to follow the sequence of events in a story, stop periodically and summarize what you have read. A **summary** is a brief statement of the main idea of a passage. Notice the breaks in the text of "Two Kinds." These breaks, which indicate a change in time or topic, are good places to stop and summarize. The first section of the story might be summarized this way: *The narrator's mother, who lost everything in China, looked upon America as a land of opportunity.*

PRACTICE Review the remaining eight sections of the story. On your paper, write a one-sentence summary of each section.

APPLY Now summarize your summaries! Write a title for each section, such as "From China to America" for the first one.

● For more about summarizing, see **Reading Handbook**, p. R91.

VOCABULARY • Analogies

An analogy is a type of comparison that is based on the relationships between things or ideas. Some analogies are based on antonyms.

conceal : uncover :: persevere : quit

The opposite of *conceal* is *uncover;* the opposite of *persevere* is *quit.*

To finish an analogy, decide what relationship exists between the first two things or ideas. Then apply that relationship to another pair of words and see if it is the same.

● For more about analogies, see **Communications Skills Handbook**, p. R77.

PRACTICE Choose the word that best completes each analogy. Some of the analogies are based on antonyms.

1. lament : rejoice :: ignite :
   a. burn   b. cool   c. extinguish
2. harmonious : discordant :: mesmerizing :
   a. magical   b. boring   c. clashing
3. failure : fiasco :: meal :
   a. feast   b. snack   c. hunger
4. prodigy : talented :: giant :
   a. bold   b. tall   c. frightening
5. reproach : praise :: knowledge :
   a. learning   b. criticism   c. ignorance

THE SHORT STORY 61

Skill Minilessons

GRAMMAR AND LANGUAGE
Participles and Participial Phrases

1. Wanting to scold Waverly, Auntie gave her a look.
2. Fighting back tears, Jing-mei returned to her seat.
3. "Look here," my mother said, calling me over with hurried hand gestures.
4. "What's the capital of Finland?" asked my mother, looking at the story.

READING AND THINKING
Summarizing

Practice
Students should write summaries similar to the following, for the second section:
● Jing-mei's mother was determined that her daughter would become a prodigy.

VOCABULARY
Analogies
1. c   2. b   3. a
4. b   5. c

Additional Practice
📖 *Grammar and Composition Handbook,* Lesson 3.3
📖 *Grammar and Language Workbook,* p. 93
📖 *Writer's Choice,* Lesson 12.3
📁 *Reading Workbook,* pp. 7–8
📁 *Vocabulary Practice,* p. 4

Before Reading

Objectives
- To read and analyze a short story about a young man who learns the value of giving selflessly
- To understand the role of imagery in a short story
- To write a character analysis

Skills
Reading/Thinking: Verifying Predictions; Inferring; Evaluating; Recognizing Causes and Effects
Writing: Fairy Tale; Poem
Vocabulary: Compound Words
Grammar/Language: Adjective Clauses; Understanding Connotations
Listening/Speaking: Oral Presentations
Life Skills: Planning and Presenting
Collaboration: Literature Groups

Motivating →OPTIONS

Selection Focus Transparency 5: Have students discuss things they have both learned from and taught to other members of their family.

Focus Activity: Have students write about an occasion when someone did them a good deed.

Before You Read

Catch the Moon

FOCUS ACTIVITY

When was the last time you gave someone a special gift or did something really nice for another person?

LIST IDEAS Think of your experience and other stories you know about people doing good deeds. List several possible reasons why someone might do something special for another person.

SETTING A PURPOSE Read to discover how a teenager's gift-giving brings rewards to him in return.

BACKGROUND

The Time and Place
It is toward the end of the 1900s in the *barrio* of a city in the northern United States. A *barrio* is an urban neighborhood in which most of the people are of Hispanic heritage. People in a *barrio* may have been born in the United States or come from Spanish-speaking countries, such as Mexico, Puerto Rico, the Dominican Republic, and Cuba.

Did You Know?
Hubcaps, or wheel covers, come in thousands of different styles. While they are mostly for show, hubcaps do keep dirt and moisture away from the wheel nuts and bearings in a car's wheel assembly. The flashiest hubcaps were made during the 1950s and 1960s. Some antique hubcaps have become collectors' items. People have even been known to "play" hubcaps as if they were cymbals.

VOCABULARY PREVIEW

harass (hə ras′, har′ əs) *v.* to bother or annoy repeatedly; p. 63
makeshift (māk′ shift′) *adj.* suitable as a temporary substitute for the proper or desired thing; p. 64
vintage (vin′ tij) *adj.* characterized by enduring appeal; classic; p. 64
decapitate (di kap′ ə tāt′) *v.* to cut off the head of; p. 66
relic (rel′ ik) *n.* an object that has survived decay, destruction, or the passage of time and is valued for its historic interest; p. 67

Meet Judith Ortiz Cofer
"Latina wherever I am," is the way Judith Ortiz Cofer sees herself. When she was a child, her family moved from Puerto Rico to Paterson, New Jersey. However, they made frequent visits back to Puerto Rico, so the writer has always felt close to her cultural roots. Vivid memories of her childhood in both countries, combined with a passion for reading literature, gave rise to Ortiz Cofer's dedication to her own writing, which includes poetry and fiction. Ortiz Cofer teaches creative writing at the University of Georgia, and has won many prizes for her own writing.

Ortiz Cofer was born in 1952 in Puerto Rico. This story was published in 1995.

RESOURCE MANAGER

Lesson Planning Resource
The *Unit One Planning Guide* (pp. 40–47) provides additional lesson notes and reduced versions of all print resources.

📁 **Other Print Resources**
- Active Reading Guide, p. 5
- Vocabulary Practice, p. 5
- Reading Workbook, pp. 9–10
- Grammar and Language Workbook, pp. 107–110
- Grammar and Composition Handbook, Lesson 4.3

- Quick Checks, p. 5
- Selection and Theme Assessment, pp. 9–10
- Performance Assessment, p. 5
- Spanish Summaries, p. 5
- Inclusion Strategies
- English Language Learners Sourcebook

✍ **Transparencies**
- Selection Focus 5
- Literary Elements 5
- Grammar and Language 5

Technology
🎧 Audio Library
🎧 Spanish Audio Library
💻 Glencoe Literature Web Site
💾 Testmaker

Catch the Moon

Judith Ortiz Cofer

LUIS CINTRÓN SITS ON TOP OF A SIX-FOOT PILE OF HUBCAPS and watches his father walk away into the steel jungle of his car junkyard. Released into his old man's custody after six months in juvenile hall—for breaking and entering—and he didn't even take anything. He did it on a dare.

But the old lady with the million cats was a light sleeper, and good with her aluminum cane. He has a scar on his head to prove it.

Now Luis is wondering whether he should have stayed in and done his full time. Jorge Cintrón of Jorge Cintrón & Son, Auto Parts and Salvage, has decided that Luis should wash and polish every hubcap in the yard. The hill he is sitting on is only the latest couple of hundred wheel covers that have come in. Luis grunts and stands up on top of his silver mountain. He yells at no one, "Someday, son, all this will be yours," and sweeps his arms like the Pope blessing a crowd over the piles of car sandwiches and mounds of metal parts that cover this acre of land outside the city. He is the "Son" of Jorge Cintrón & Son, and so far his father has had more than one reason to wish it was plain Jorge Cintrón on the sign.

Luis has been getting in trouble since he started high school two years ago, mainly because of the "social group" he organized— a bunch of guys who were into harassing the local authorities. Their thing was taking something to the limit on a dare or, better still, doing something dangerous, like breaking into a house, not to steal, just to prove that they could do it. That was Luis's specialty, coming up with very complicated plans, like military strategies, and assigning the "jobs" to guys who wanted to join the Tiburones.[1]

Tiburón means "shark," and Luis had gotten the name from watching an old movie[2] about a Puerto Rican gang called the Sharks with his father. Luis thought it was one of the dumbest films he had ever seen. Everybody sang their lines, and the guys all pointed their toes and leaped in the air when they were supposed to be slaughtering each other. But he liked their name, the Sharks, so he made it Spanish and had it air-painted on his

---

1. *Tiburones* (tē′ boo rō′ nās)
2. *[old movie . . .]* The narrator is describing the feature film *West Side Story,* a 1961 musical based on Shakespeare's play *Romeo and Juliet* and set in the youth gang atmosphere of New York City in the late 1950s.

Vocabulary
harass (hə ras′, har′ əs) *v.* to bother or annoy repeatedly

SUMMARY

Luis Cintrón has been released from juvenile detention on the condition that he work in his father's junkyard for six months. Gloomy at his prospects and still depressed by his mother's death three years earlier, Luis encounters a young woman who comes to the yard looking for a hubcap. Her beauty and gentleness release in Luis a flood of emotions that allow him to grieve, love, and learn the self-respect that comes from hard work.

📁 *Spanish Summaries,* p. 5

A **Active Reading**

PREDICT Have students read the title and the first paragraph. Let volunteers tell what information they know about the main character at this point. Then focus on the title. Invite speculation as to what "catch the moon" might mean and who might "catch the moon."

Additional Resources
📁 *Active Reading Guide,* p. 5
🎧 *Audio Library*
🎧 *Spanish Audio Library*

Teaching Options

CONNECTING TO OTHER SELECTIONS

The chart on the right shows three ways to connect "Catch the Moon" to selections in this book.

For specific teaching strategies, see the *Unit One Planning Guide,* pages 43–44.

Connection	Title
Life Skills: Problem Solving	→ "A White Heron," p. 143
Thematic: Changes	→ "Waltz of the Fat Man," p. 377
Literary: Theme	→ "The Angry Winter," p. 557

Teaching Options

B | Author's Craft

EXPOSITION Ask students how the shift in tense affects this story. Where does the tense shift permanently to the past? *(Present tense gives the opening an informal tone, almost as if Luis is the narrator. By the fourth paragraph the author has settled into the more conventional past.)*

C | Literary Elements

IMAGERY What does the image of Luis standing on top of his "silver mountain" tell you about him? *(He may be unhappy about working in the junkyard, but he has not lost his sense of humor.)*

D | Active Reading

CONNECT Can students imagine someone like Luis at their school? What do they think of his bad behavior? Is he fun or merely a troublemaker?

E | Literary Elements

PLOT: Exposition/Rising Action See if students can identify where the exposition ends and the action of this story begins. *(When Luis slides down the pile of hubcaps and the car pulls in, the story has started.)*

---

black T-shirt with a killer shark under it, jaws opened wide and dripping with blood. It didn't take long for other guys in the barrio to ask about it.

Man, had they had a good time. The girls were interested too. Luis outsmarted everybody by calling his organization a social club and registering it at Central High. That meant they were legal, even let out of last-period class on Fridays for their "club" meetings. It was just this year, after a couple of botched³ jobs, that the teachers had started getting suspicious. The first one to go wrong was when he sent Kenny Matoa to *borrow* some "souvenirs" out of Anita Robles's locker. He got caught. It seems that Matoa had been reading Anita's diary and didn't hear her coming down the hall. Anita was supposed to be in the gym at that time but had copped out with the usual female excuse of cramps. You could hear her screams all the way to Market Street.

She told the principal all she knew about the Tiburones, and Luis had to talk fast to convince old Mr. Williams that the club did put on cultural activities such as the Save the Animals talent show. What Mr. Williams didn't know was that the animal that was being "saved" with the ticket sales was Luis's pet boa, which needed quite a few live mice to stay healthy and happy. They kept E.S. (which stood for "Endangered Species") in Luis's room, but she belonged to the club and it was the members' responsibility to raise the money to feed their mascot. So last year they had sponsored their first annual Save the Animals talent show, and it had been a great success. The Tiburones had come dressed as Latino Elvises and did a grand finale to "All

Shook Up" that made the audience go wild. Mr. Williams had smiled while Luis talked, maybe remembering how the math teacher, Mrs. Laguna, had dragged him out in the aisle to rock-and-roll with her. Luis had gotten out of that one, but barely.

His father was a problem too. He objected to the T-shirt logo, calling it disgusting and vulgar. Mr. Cintrón prided himself on his own neat, elegant style of dressing after work, and on his manners and large vocabulary, which he picked up by taking correspondence courses in just about everything. Luis thought that it was just his way of staying busy since Luis's mother had died, almost three years ago, of cancer. He had never gotten over it.

All this was going through Luis's head as he slid down the hill of hubcaps. The tub full of soapy water, the can of polish, and the bag of rags had been neatly placed in front of a makeshift table made from two car seats and a piece of plywood. Luis heard a car drive up and someone honk their horn. His father emerged from inside a new red Mustang that had been totaled. He usually dismantled every small feature by hand before sending the vehicle into the *cementerio,*⁴ as he called the lot. Luis watched as the most beautiful girl he had ever seen climbed out of a vintage white Volkswagen Bug. She stood in the sunlight in her white sundress waiting for

Did You Know?
Many people consider the *Volkswagen Beetle*, also nicknamed "VW" or "Bug," to be a classic car. Compact, durable, and affordable, the Bug was extremely popular in the 1960s and early 1970s.

---

3. *Botched* means "badly or clumsily done."

4. *Cementerio* (se men te′ rē ō) is Spanish for "cemetery."

Vocabulary
makeshift (māk′ shift′) *adj.* suitable as a temporary substitute for the proper or desired thing
vintage (vin′ tij) *adj.* characterized by enduring appeal; classic

MEETING INDIVIDUAL NEEDS — ENGLISH LANGUAGE LEARNERS

Showing Emotions Point out the scene in which Luis bursts into tears at the memory of his mother. Point out to English language learners that we all react emotionally on occasion; every culture has conventions about the appropriateness of expressing feelings.

Activity Ask students to identify themselves as male or female, instead of by their names, on a piece of paper. Then have them write *It is OK to cry when . . .* and list several situations. Collect the papers and write a sample on the board. Discuss different ideas about expressing emotion.

Additional Resources
📁 *English Language Learners Sourcebook*

his father, while Luis stared. She was like a smooth wood carving. Her skin was mahogany, almost black, and her arms and legs were long and thin, but curved in places so that she did not look bony and hard—more like a ballerina. And her ebony hair was braided close to her head. Luis let his breath out, feeling a little dizzy. He had forgotten to breathe. Both the girl and his father heard him. Mr. Cintrón waved him over.

"Luis, the señorita here has lost a wheel cover. Her car is twenty-five years old, so it will not be an easy match. Come look on this side."

Luis tossed a wrench he'd been holding into a toolbox like he was annoyed, just to make a point about slave labor. Then he followed his father, who knelt on the gravel and began to point out every detail of the hubcap. Luis was hardly listening. He watched the girl take a piece of paper from her handbag.

"Señor Cintrón, I have drawn the hubcap for you, since I will have to leave soon. My home address and telephone number are here, and also my parents' office number." She handed the paper to Mr. Cintrón, who nodded.

"Sí, señorita, very good. This will help my son look for it. Perhaps there is one in that stack there." He pointed to the pile of caps that Luis was supposed to wash and polish. "Yes, I'm almost certain that there is a match there. Of course, I do not know if it's near the top or the bottom. You will give us a few days, yes?"

Luis just stared at his father like he was crazy. But he didn't say anything because the girl was smiling

at him with a funny expression on her face. Maybe she thought he had X-ray eyes like Superman, or maybe she was mocking him.

"Please call me Naomi, Señor Cintrón. You know my mother. She is the director of the funeral home. . . ." Mr. Cintrón seemed surprised at first; he prided himself on having a great memory. Then his friendly expression changed to one of sadness as he recalled the

IMAGERY Ask students to point out the details that make a vivid picture of Naomi not only for Luis but for the reader. *("white sundress"; "like a smooth wood carving"; mahogany skin; long, thin arms and legs "curved in places"; "like a ballerina"; "ebony hair . . . braided close to her head.")*

G **Active Reading**

QUESTION Ask students why the girl might be looking at Luis like this. Does she find him funny or attractive? Does she recognize him? Is she merely friendly?

Reading Minilesson

Verifying Predictions Point out that readers make predictions about what will happen in a story based on information from the author, their own experiences, and understanding people's behavior.

Activity After students have read the story through page 64, have them write a sentence predicting what will happen to Luis next: for example, he may get into

trouble again. After students have read page 65, have them predict the role that Naomi will play in the story. When students have finished reading the story, have them meet with a partner and discuss the accuracy of their predictions. **L2**

Additional Resources
📁 *Reading Workbook,* pp. 9–10

66   UNIT 1

Teaching Options

H   **Active Reading**

EVALUATE Ask students to explain how Luis's reaction to his mother's death is true to life.

I   **Literary Elements**

CHARACTERS Suggest to students that this paragraph is packed with implied information about Luis and his father. Ask what they learn from it. *(Luis is capable of hard work; he is playful; he laughs at his father but also cares for him. His father is ironic and long-suffering; he wants to better himself.)*

J   **Critical Thinking**

INFERRING Why does Luis notice at this moment that his father is "an old man"? You can guide students in making inferences by encouraging them to base their conclusions on the clues the author has given them about the relationship between Luis and his father. You may wish to share the following model to illustrate the thinking process involved in making inferences.

Model: I think his father's bruised head may be part of it. When you're really little, you don't believe your parents can get hurt. His father also talks about his "dream" of having a well-organized yard with Luis's help. Maybe Luis is beginning to see his dad as an equal, not as a superior. And that's probably why the author mentions at this point that Luis and his father are the same height and build.

Catch the Moon

day of his wife's burial. Naomi did not finish her sentence. She reached over and placed her hand on Mr. Cintrón's arm for a moment. Then she said "Adiós" softly, and got in her shiny white car. She waved to them as she left, and her gold bracelets flashing in the sun nearly blinded Luis.

Mr. Cintrón shook his head. "How about that," he said as if to himself. "They are the Dominican owners of Ramirez Funeral Home." And, with a sigh, "She seems like such a nice young woman. Reminds me of your mother when she was her age."

Hearing the funeral parlor's name, Luis remembered too. The day his mother died, he had been in her room at the hospital while his father had gone for coffee. The alarm had gone off on her monitor and nurses had come running in, pushing him outside. After that, all he recalled was the anger that had made him punch a hole in his bedroom wall. And afterward he had refused to talk to anyone at the funeral. Strange, he did see a black girl there who didn't try like the others to talk to him, but actually ignored him as she escorted family members to the viewing room and brought flowers in. Could it be that the skinny girl in a frilly white dress had been Naomi? She didn't act like she had recognized him today, though. Or maybe she thought that he was a jerk.

Luis grabbed the drawing from his father. The old man looked like he wanted to walk down memory lane. But Luis was in no mood to listen to the old stories about his falling in love on a tropical island. The world they'd lived in before he was born wasn't his world. No beaches and palm trees here. Only junk as far as he could see. He climbed back up his hill and studied Naomi's sketch. It had obviously been done very

carefully. It was signed "Naomi Ramirez" in the lower right-hand corner. He memorized the telephone number.

Luis washed hubcaps all day until his hands were red and raw, but he did not come across the small silver bowl that would fit the VW. After work he took a few practice Frisbee shots across the yard before showing his father what he had accomplished: rows and rows of shiny rings drying in the sun. His father nodded and showed him the bump on his temple where one of Luis's flying saucers had gotten him. "Practice makes perfect, you know. Next time you'll probably <u>decapitate</u> me." Luis heard him struggle with the word *decapitate*, which Mr. Cintrón pronounced in syllables. Showing off his big vocabulary again, Luis thought. He looked closely at the bump, though. He felt bad about it.

"They look good, hijo."[5] Mr. Cintrón made a sweeping gesture with his arms over the yard. "You know, all this will have to be classified. My dream is to have all the parts divided by year, make of car, and condition. Maybe now that you are here to help me, this will happen."

"Pop . . ." Luis put his hand on his father's shoulder. They were the same height and build, about five foot six and muscular. "The judge said six months of free labor for you, not life, okay?" Mr. Cintrón nodded, looking distracted. It was then that Luis suddenly noticed how gray his hair had turned—it used to be shiny black like his own—and that there were deep lines in his face. His father had turned into an old man and he hadn't even noticed.

"Son, you must follow the judge's instructions. Like she said, next time you get in

---

5. *Hijo* (ē′ hō) is Spanish for "son."

Vocabulary
decapitate (di kap′ ə tāt′) *v.* to cut off the head of

REAL-WORLD CONNECTION

Latinos' Accomplishments Jorge Cintrón, a hard-working Puerto Rican immigrant, will never be featured in the national press, but many of his compatriots and fellow Latinos have achieved stardom in their adopted country.

Activity Have students locate magazine or newspaper articles celebrating the accomplishments of Latino Americans. Ask them to tell the class about their subjects in brief oral reports. **L2**

trouble, she's going to treat you like an adult, and I think you know what that means. Hard time, no breaks."

"Yeah, yeah. That's what I'm doing, right? Working my hands to the bone instead of enjoying my summer. But listen, she didn't put me under house arrest, right? I'm going out tonight."

"Home by ten. She did say something about a curfew, Luis." Mr. Cintrón had stopped smiling and was looking upset. It had always been hard for them to talk more than a minute or two before his father got offended at something Luis said, or at his sarcastic tone. He was always doing something wrong.

Luis threw the rag down on the table and went to sit in his father's ancient Buick, which was in mint condition. They drove home in silence.

After sitting down at the kitchen table with his father to eat a pizza they had picked up on the way home, Luis asked to borrow the car. He didn't get an answer then, just a look that meant "Don't bother me right now."

Before bringing up the subject again, Luis put some ice cubes in a Baggie and handed it to Mr. Cintrón, who had made the little bump on his head worse by rubbing it. It had GUILTY written on it, Luis thought.

"Gracias, hijo." His father placed the bag on the bump and made a face as the ice touched his skin.

They ate in silence for a few minutes more; then Luis decided to ask about the car again.

"I really need some fresh air, Pop. Can I borrow the car for a couple of hours?"

"You don't get enough fresh air at the yard? We're lucky that we don't have to sit in a smelly old factory all day. You know that?"

"Yeah, Pop. We're real lucky." Luis always felt irritated that his father was so grateful to own a junkyard, but he held his anger back and just waited to see if he'd get the keys without having to get in an argument.

"Where are you going?"

"For a ride. Not going anywhere. Just out for a while. Is that okay?"

His father didn't answer, just handed him a set of keys, as shiny as the day they were manufactured. His father polished everything that could be polished: doorknobs, coins, keys, spoons, knives, and forks, like he was King Midas counting his silver and gold. Luis thought his father must be really lonely to polish utensils only he used anymore. They had been picked out by his wife, though, so they were like <u>relics</u>. Nothing she had ever owned could be thrown away. Only now the dishes, forks, and spoons were not used to eat the yellow rice and red beans, the fried chicken, or the mouth-watering sweet plantains that his mother had cooked for them. They were just kept in the cabinets that his father had turned into a museum for her. Mr. Cintrón

Did You Know?
A *plantain* (plant′ an) is a tropical fruit similar to a banana, which must be cooked before eating.

could cook as well as his wife, but he didn't have the heart to do it anymore. Luis thought that maybe if they ate together once in a while things might get better between them, but he always had something to do around dinnertime and ended up at a hamburger joint. Tonight was the first time in months they had sat down at the table together.

Vocabulary
relic (rel′ ik) *n.* an object that has survived decay, destruction, or the passage of time and is valued for its historic interest

Language Note
The word *curfew* refers to a regulation requiring certain people to be off the streets by a certain hour. *Curfew* comes from an Old French term that meant "cover the fire." In medieval times, curfew was a regulation that required people to put out their fires in the evening.

K Critical Thinking
EVALUATING Is Luis being manipulative in giving his father an ice pack when he wants to borrow the car? *(Some students will believe the two events are coincidental. Others may feel that Luis understands the importance of timing in asking for a favor.)*

L Literary Elements
SIMILE Remind students that King Midas was a miser from Greek mythology. Ask them if they think this simile is a fair one.

INCLUSION STRATEGIES

Less-Proficient Readers Like many fathers and sons, Jorge and Luis Cintrón have a complex relationship. Make sure students are aware of their conflicting feelings for each other.

Activity Have students write *My son . . .* at the top of a sheet of paper. Ask them to think of and write three or more ways that Jorge might complete this sentence. *(. . . is too much of a wise guy; . . . still misses his mother; etc.)* Then have them write *My father . . .* and complete that sentence several times from Luis's perspective. Let them compare their best ideas with the rest of the class. **L1**

Additional Resources
Inclusion Strategies

Literary Elements

SIMILE What does the phrase "like a skeleton" tell the reader about the oak tree's appearance and the season? *(The tree was all branches with no leaves; it must have been late fall or winter when his mother died.)* Based on what the tree looks like now, what season is it? *(The tree is "green with leaves," so it must be late spring or summer.)*

Active Reading

EVALUATE How does Naomi "tell" Luis with her eyes to come closer? And is it likely that she would have been drawing his picture at precisely that moment? Ask students what they think of this scene.

Author's Craft

TONE The author draws the reader's attention to the magical tone of this passage by a reference to Naomi as a "princess." Ask if students can find any other similarities to fairy tales in the story. Hint: Think of "Rapunzel" and "Cinderella."

Literary Elements

SYMBOL Ask students what the hubcap hanging in the tree represents. *(Most students will associate it with the moon, based on the story's title and references to the moon. Some will realize that the moon symbolizes beauty and purity, to which Luis now aspires. In finding the hubcap, Luis has found a new, radiant life.)*

Catch the Moon

Luis took the keys. "Thanks," he said, walking out to take his shower. His father kept looking at him with those sad, patient eyes. "Okay. I'll be back by ten, and keep the ice on that egg," Luis said without looking back.

He had just meant to ride around his old barrio, see if any of the Tiburones were hanging out at El Building, where most of them lived. It wasn't far from the single-family home his father had bought when the business started paying off: a house that his mother lived in for three months before she took up residence at St. Joseph's Hospital. She never came home again. These days Luis wished he still lived in that tiny apartment where there was always something to do, somebody to talk to.

Instead Luis found himself parked in front of the last place his mother had gone to: Ramirez Funeral Home. In the front yard was a huge oak tree that Luis remembered having climbed during the funeral to get away from people. The tree looked different now, not like a skeleton, as it had then, but green with leaves. The branches reached to the second floor of the house, where the family lived.

For a while Luis sat in the car allowing the memories to flood back into his brain. He remembered his mother before the illness changed her. She had not been beautiful, as his father told everyone; she had been a sweet lady, not pretty but not ugly. To him, she had been the person who always told him that she was proud of him and loved him. She did that every night when she came to his bedroom door to say good-night. As a joke he would sometimes ask her, "Proud of what? I haven't done anything." And she'd always say, "I'm just proud that you are my son." She wasn't perfect or anything. She had bad days when nothing he did could make her smile, especially after she got sick. But he never heard her say anything negative about anyone. She

always blamed *el destino*, fate, for what went wrong. He missed her. He missed her so much. Suddenly a flood of tears that had been building up for almost three years started pouring from his eyes. Luis sat in his father's car, with his head on the steering wheel, and cried, "Mami, I miss you."

When he finally looked up, he saw that he was being watched. Sitting at a large window with a pad and a pencil on her lap was Naomi. At first Luis felt angry and embarrassed, but she wasn't laughing at him. Then she told him with her dark eyes that it was okay to come closer. He walked to the window, and she held up the sketch pad on which she had drawn him, not crying like a baby, but sitting on top of a mountain of silver disks, holding one up over his head. He had to smile.

The plate-glass window was locked. It had a security bolt on it. An alarm system, he figured, so nobody would steal the princess. He asked her if he could come in. It was soundproof too. He mouthed the words slowly for her to read his lips. She wrote on the pad, "I can't let you in. My mother is not home tonight." So they looked at each other and talked through the window for a little while. Then Luis got an idea. He signed to her that he'd be back, and drove to the junkyard.

Luis climbed up on his mountain of hubcaps. For hours he sorted the wheel covers by make, size, and condition, stopping only to call his father and tell him where he was and what he was doing. The old man did not ask him for explanations, and Luis was grateful for that. By lamppost light, Luis worked and worked, beginning to understand a little why his father kept busy all the time. Doing something that had a beginning, a middle, and an end did something to your head. It was like the satisfaction Luis got out of planning "adventures" for his Tiburones, but there was

Teaching Options

Grammar and Language *Minilesson*

Adjective Clauses Write the following sentence on the board:

In the front yard was an oak tree <u>that Luis remembered having climbed.</u>

Underline the sentence from the word *that* to the end. Ask students what role these five words play. *(They modify the noun oak.)* Point out that clauses beginning with *that, which, who, whom, whose, where,* and *when* often act as adjectives, modify-

ing the nouns or pronouns they follow.

Activity Have students locate four adjective clauses in the second paragraph of this page and identify the noun that each clause modifies. *(where most of them lived, El Building; [that] his father had bought, home; that his mother lived in, house; where there was always something to do, apartment.)* **L2**

Additional Resources

- *Grammar and Language Transparency 5*
- *Grammar and Language Workbook,* pp. 107–110
- *Grammar and Composition Handbook,* Lesson 4.3
- *Writer's Choice,* Lesson 13.3

September 16, c. 1955. René Magritte. Oil on canvas, 14 x 10⅞ in. The Minneapolis Institute of Arts.

Viewing the painting: In what ways does this painting express the title and the mood of the story?

another element involved here that had nothing to do with showing off for others. This was a treasure hunt. And he knew what he was looking for.

Finally, when it seemed that it was a hopeless search, when it was almost midnight and Luis's hands were cut and bruised from

his work, he found it. It was the perfect match for Naomi's drawing, the moon-shaped wheel cover for her car, Cinderella's shoe. Luis jumped off the small mound of disks left under him and shouted, "Yes!" He looked around and saw neat stacks of hubcaps that he would wash the next day. He would build a display wall for his father. People would be able to come into the yard and point to whatever they wanted.

Luis washed the VW hubcap and polished it until he could see himself in it. He used it as a mirror as he washed his face and combed his hair. Then he drove to the Ramirez Funeral Home. It was almost pitch-black, since it was a moonless night. As quietly as possible, Luis put some gravel in his pocket and climbed the oak tree to the second floor. He knew he was in front of Naomi's window—he could see her shadow through the curtains. She was at a table, apparently writing or drawing, maybe waiting for him. Luis hung the silver disk carefully on a branch near the window, then threw the gravel at the glass. Naomi ran to the window and drew the curtains aside while Luis held on to the thick branch and waited to give her the first good thing he had given anyone in a long time.

Cultural Note

If any students are unfamiliar with the story of Cinderella, give a brief synopsis of the plot. Luis uses Naomi's drawing to find the right hubcap as the prince in "Cinderella" uses Cinderella's shoe to find the right woman.

Thematic Focus

Transitions Many people go through periods when they resolve to reform their lives. Ask students whether they believe Luis's transformation will be permanent.

✓ ASSESSMENT OPTIONS

📁 *Quick Checks,* p. 5

Writing *Minilesson*

Modern Fairy Tales Although "Catch the Moon" has a gritty, urban setting, its happy conclusion is like those in fairy tales. Discuss other elements of this story with a fairy-tale quality: a captive "princess," a noble young man in disguise, a quest (for a hubcap).

Activity Have students create their own nontraditional "fairy tales." Suggest that

they begin with a classic plot that they know well, such as "Cinderella." Have them transpose their plots to a modern setting and write summaries of the updated versions. Students may expand their summaries to short-story length. **L2**

Additional Resources

📓 *Writer's Choice,* Lessons 4.2–4.4

Responding to Literature

Personal Response

Some students may feel that Luis went to a lot of trouble for a girl with whom he had never had a real conversation. Others will argue that, to Luis, Naomi represents far more than a pretty face.

ANALYZING LITERATURE

1. Luis has been released from a juvenile detention center on the condition that he work at his father's junkyard for six months.
2. As the leader of a gang, or "social group," Luis has dedicated himself to devising pranks intended to "harass the authorities." He was arrested for breaking and entering.
3. Naomi comes to the junkyard for a VW hubcap. Luis is stunned by her beauty.
4. Luis and his father have trouble communicating, but there is a mutual respect. The father is concerned for his son; Luis understands that his father has had a hard time without his wife.
5. Luis leaves a hubcap in the tree.
6. Luis is frustrated and angry at having to work in the junkyard. He thinks of it as "slave labor," complains that he is working his hands to the bone, and shouts ironically, "Someday, son, all this will be yours."
7. His mother's death has made Luis reckless and defiant. His "social group" is a reflection of this.
8. Naomi is "a sweet lady" like Luis's mother. She releases a flood of memories for Luis, which permits him finally to show his emotions. In finding the hubcap for her, he does something about which he feels proud.
9. The relationship between Luis and his father will improve. Luis telephones to say he will be late. More importantly, he has finally learned to take pride in a job well done.
10. Luis discovers that giving is more rewarding than having fun and that he can get satisfaction from hard work.
11. Students may say love for Naomi, a desire to please his mother, or the need to feel good about himself.
12. Luis seems to remember most fondly his mother's uncritical pride in him.
13. Luis is learning to become a proud, uncomplaining worker who has ideas of his own about how to organize the junkyard.

Personal Response

Were you surprised by Luis's actions at the end of the story? Why or why not?

——— ANALYZING LITERATURE ———

RECALL

1. Why does Luis work at his father's car junkyard?
2. In what ways has Luis gotten into trouble?
3. Why does Naomi come to the junkyard? How does Luis react to seeing her?
4. Describe the relationship between Luis and his father.
5. What does Luis leave in the tree for Naomi?

INTERPRET

6. What do you think Luis's feelings are about his job at the junkyard? Cite details from the story to support your response.
7. How might the death of Luis's mother have affected his behavior? Explain.
8. How do Luis's feelings for Naomi help him deal with the loss of his mother?
9. Do you think there is a chance for Luis and his father to build a good relationship? Support your response with details from the story.
10. What do you think Luis discovers about himself as he searches for his gift to Naomi?

EVALUATE AND CONNECT

11. What do you think Luis's reasons were for giving the gift to Naomi? Think back to the Focus Activity on page 62 in which you listed reasons why a person might give a gift or do a good deed for someone. How do Luis's reasons compare with the reasons you listed?
12. Read Luis's description of his mother. In your opinion, what did Luis love most about her? Explain.
13. In addition to the gift he gives Naomi, Luis also will give something to his father. What will Luis give him?
14. In your opinion, what does Luis find so attractive about Naomi besides her good looks? Be specific and give examples to back up your opinion.
15. What does the title suggest about the **tone** of this story? Do you think it's a good title choice? Why or why not?

Literary ELEMENTS

Imagery

Writers make their work come alive by choosing words and phrases that appeal to readers' senses of sight, touch, taste, smell, and hearing. The use of these sensory details is called **imagery**.

1. What visual image is reflected in the title of the story? How does it show the tie between Luis and his father? Between Luis and Naomi?
2. What effect do the images of food on page 67 have on your reading of that part of the story?
3. How does the image of the oak tree outside Naomi's window help convey Luis's feelings at the times he saw the tree?

● See **Literary Terms Handbook,** p. R6.

---

14. Naomi reminds Luis of his mother's unjudgmental attitude. She smiles at him in the junkyard; she draws a picture of him sitting on the hubcaps; she does not laugh when he cries.
15. "Catch the Moon" suggests hopefulness and optimism, also magic and romance. It is a good title for a story that has elements of a fairy tale in it.

LITERARY ELEMENTS

1. The moon relates to Luis's father in the moonlike hubcaps; it relates to Naomi in her serene beauty.
2. Delicious home cooking has been replaced by soulless fast food, reflecting the loss of love in the family.
3. When his mother died, the tree was "a skeleton." As he becomes interested in Naomi, the tree is "green with leaves."

Additional Resources

📖 *Literary Elements Transparency 5*

LITERATURE AND WRITING

Writing About Literature
Character   Luis is the central character in this story. Analyze and describe him. Be sure to include the following in your analysis:
- a description of Luis's key personality traits
- a recap of what has happened to Luis and how he has responded to each event
- an explanation of how and why Luis changes

Creative Writing
On Love   Write a poem that Luis might have written about his memories of his mother and his relationship with her; about his growing feelings for Naomi; or about his relationship with his father. Try including visual and other sensory images that help express his memories and his feelings about the person.

EXTENDING YOUR RESPONSE

Literature Groups
Do the Tiburones Spell Trouble?   Does the author suggest that Luis's association with the Tiburones is good or bad for him? Divide into two opposing groups to debate the question. Use evidence from the story as well as your own understanding of Luis and life to present your group's side. Then listen to the opposing group. When your debate is finished, vote on which side was more convincing, then share your results with the rest of the class.

Learning for Life
Car Talk   Hubcaps aren't the only car part that Señor Cintrón sells at his salvage shop. He sells parts for all of the automotive systems that help a car run smoothly and safely. Find out about the various systems of a car. Then draw a diagram or build a simple model of one system and, using your diagram or model as a visual aid, explain to the class how that system works.

Interdisciplinary Activity
Art: Luis and His Logo   Three works of art are described in this story: the Tiburones' logo, Naomi's drawing of the hubcap, and the drawing she made of Luis. Draw or paint one of these images as you imagine it. Share your work and any explanation of it with the class.

Reading Further
If you'd like to read more by Judith Ortiz Cofer, you might enjoy these stories:

Collection: *An Island Like You—Stories of the Barrio* is a set of twelve funny, poignant short stories about what it's like to be a Puerto Rican teenager growing up in the United States.

 Save your work for your portfolio.

LITERATURE AND WRITING

Writing About Literature
Students' analyses should
- support all descriptions and generalizations with evidence from the story.
- show a clear understanding of Luis's character.
- indicate thoughtful organization.

Creative Writing
Students' poems should
- reveal an understanding of Luis's thoughts and emotions.
- include concise images drawn from the story or the poet's imagination.

EXTENDING YOUR RESPONSE

Literature Groups Suggest to students that their own experiences in dealing with problems will be of value in this debate. **COLLAB. LEARN.**

Learning for Life Point out to student presenters that some of their classmates will know nothing about cars. Remind them to keep their visual aids and explanations clear and simple.

Interdisciplinary Activity Remind students to think about how Naomi and Luis would have drawn their pictures. The character of the artist is often revealed in his or her work.

✔ ASSESSMENT OPTIONS

- *Quick Checks,* p. 5
- *Selection and Theme Assessment,* pp. 9–10
- *Performance Assessment,* p. 5
- *Testmaker*

Skill Minilessons

Skill Minilessons

GRAMMAR AND LANGUAGE
Understanding Connotations

1. Both words mean not ordinary; *peculiar* suggests something suspect.
2. Both words mean quick-witted, but *tricky* suggests deviousness.
3. Both words imply inexperience; *immature* implies childishness.
4. Both words indicate a strong will; *stubborn* suggests inflexibility.
5. Both words indicate physical courage, but *reckless* suggests negligence.

READING AND THINKING
Recognizing Causes and Effects

Practice

1. They need money to feed the pet boa.
2. He is lonely since his wife's death.
3. She needs a replacement hubcap.
4. He misses his mother.
5. He is looking for a hubcap for Naomi.

Apply
Possible effects:
1. Mr. Williams lets the club continue.
2. He has a large vocabulary.
3. Luis has a turning point in his life.
4. He feels angry and embarrassed.
5. He finds a hubcap for Naomi.

VOCABULARY
Compound Words

1. c   2. e   3. d
4. a   5. b

Additional Practice

- *Grammar and Composition Handbook*
- *Grammar and Language Workbook*
- *Writer's Choice,* p. 294
- *Reading Workbook,* pp. 9–10
- *Vocabulary Practice,* p. 5

GRAMMAR AND LANGUAGE • Understanding Connotations

Connotations are the positive or negative feelings that most people associate with a word. These associations go beyond the **denotation,** or the literal dictionary definition of the word. Skilled writers choose their words with careful attention to connotations to evoke specific feelings or responses in readers. For example, when the narrator says that Luis "was released into his old man's custody," the term *old man* has a connotation of disrespect that is missing from the neutral word *father.*

PRACTICE   On your paper, write an explanation of the differences in connotations between the two words in the following pairs.

1. unusual, peculiar
2. clever, tricky
3. youthful, immature
4. persistent, stubborn
5. adventurous, reckless

● For more about word choice, see **Reading Handbook,** p. R81.

READING AND THINKING • Recognizing Causes and Effects

A cause is the reason something happens; an effect is what happens as a result of the cause. For example, in "Catch the Moon," Luis is polishing hubcaps (effect) because a judge has sentenced him to work for his father for six months (cause).

PRACTICE   On your paper, identify the cause of each of these events from the story.

1. Luis and his friends put on the Save the Animals talent show.
2. Luis's father takes several correspondence courses.
3. Naomi comes to the Auto Parts and Salvage yard.
4. Luis sits in his car outside the Ramirez Funeral Home and cries "like a baby."
5. Luis sorts through and organizes a mountain of wheel covers.

APPLY   Return to the story. Find at least one effect for each of the events listed above. Write them on your paper.

● For more about text structure, see **Reading Handbook,** pp. R86–R87.

VOCABULARY • Compound Words

When two words are joined to form one, the result is a compound word. You can often figure out the meaning of an unfamiliar compound by thinking about the complete words that form it. For example, an outpouring of praise is a steadily flowing amount of praise. Some unfamiliar compounds are more difficult to figure out. *Makeshift* makes sense only if you know that *shift* can mean "a trick or scheme for use in an emergency."

● For more about compound words, see **Language Handbook,** p. R56.

PRACTICE   Use your knowledge of the words that form the compounds in the left column to match each with its definition on the right.

1. underlying   a. achieved dishonestly
2. quitclaim   b. an uncredited author
3. soul-searching   c. basic and fundamental
4. ill-gotten   d. an honest look at one's true feelings
5. ghostwriter   e. the giving up of a right or the title to property

72 ❧ UNIT 1

Grammar Link

Avoiding Sentence Fragments

A fragment is an incomplete part of something. You might whistle a fragment of a song or sweep up the fragments of a china plate. A **sentence fragment** is a word or group of words that is only part of a sentence.

Problem 1 Some sentence fragments lack either a subject or a verb (or both).
Stands on a pile of hubcaps. [lacks a subject]
Hundreds of hubcaps in the pile. [lacks a verb]

Solution Add the missing subject and/or verb.
Luis stands on a pile of hubcaps.
Hundreds of hubcaps are rusting in the pile.

Problem 2 Some sentence fragments are really subordinate clauses that have been mistaken for a complete sentence. Although they have a subject and a verb, subordinate clauses do not express a complete thought and cannot stand alone as a sentence.
Because he broke into someone's house.

Solution A Join the subordinate clause to a main clause.
Luis was in juvenile hall because he broke into someone's house.

Solution B Remove the subordinating conjunction at the beginning of the clause.
He broke into someone's house.

People often use sentence fragments in conversation. The fragment "Got to run" lacks a subject. It could mean that the speaker has to go or that the listener should hurry, but it is unlikely to be misunderstood because the listener understands the context. In writing, however, a fragment that leaves out important information can be confusing.

● For more about sentence fragments, see **Language Handbook,** pp. R14–R15.

ACTIVITIES

1. **Proofreading:** Use the strategies shown above to correct the sentence fragments in this paragraph.

   Naomi came to Mr. Cintrón's junkyard. Because she had lost a hubcap off her Volkswagon. She hoped they could find a replacement for it. Luis stared at her. The most beautiful girl in the world. Worked hard to find a match for her hubcap. Later that night, at Naomi's house. When she looked out the window and saw the gift Luis had brought her.

2. Revise a piece of your own writing using these strategies to eliminate sentence fragments.

Grammar Link

Objective

- To recognize and correct sentence fragments

Teaching Strategies

Point out that another way to correct a sentence fragment is to combine it with the sentence that precedes or follows it. Luis found the perfect hubcap. Under an old rusty one. *(Luis found the perfect hubcap under an old rusty one.)*

1. *One solution:* Naomi came to Mr. Cintrón's junkyard because she had lost a hubcap off her Volkswagen. She hoped to find a replacement for it. Luis stared at her, thinking she was the most beautiful girl in the world. He worked hard to find a match for her hubcap. Later that night, Naomi looked out the window of her house and saw the gift Luis had brought her.

Additional Resources

Grammar and Language Workbook, pp. 22–23, 121

Grammar and Composition Handbook, Lesson 4.9

Writer's Choice, Lesson 13.9

Teaching Options

Writing *Minilesson*

Writing Dialogue Ask volunteers to read aloud the conversation between Luis and his father on page 67 of "Catch the Moon." Then ask students if the characters' use of fragments interfered with their understanding of the conversation. Remind students that sentence fragments are acceptable in dialogue because they reflect the way that people naturally speak. Point out that even in dialogue, a fragment must be understandable.

Activity Have students write a short dialogue between two characters in "Catch the Moon," including several sentence fragments. Suggest that they present their completed dialogues with a partner. **L2**

Additional Resources

Writer's Choice, Lesson 4.4

Objective

- To read and understand a magazine article

Literature ▬▬ LINK

Through the Tunnel Point out to students that Heaney-Grier, the subject of this article, wants to break the women's free-diving record. The young male character in "Through the Tunnel" (pp. 76–85) also sets a goal for himself—to execute a daring breath-hold dive in order to swim through an underwater tunnel.

Respond

1. Some students may say the joy of the sport is the most important aspect. Others may say it is the challenge of breaking the free-diving record.
2. Responses may include winning a game, getting good grades, and learning a new sport or hobby.

Additional Resources
📁 *Media Connections Activities,* p. 2

Magazine Article

What lures people into the water and causes them to test their bodies against the challenges of the deep? For young diver Mehgan Heaney-Grier, it's the chance to set an underwater world record.

Where No One Has Gone Before?

by Paul Kvinta—*Outside* magazine, July 1997

The most peaceful part of Mehgan Heaney-Grier's life begins at 40 feet below sea level. This is the 19-year-old's "buoyancy point," the depth beyond which she can stop kicking her three-foot fins, straighten her long, slender frame, close her eyes, and fall headfirst like an anvil toward the bottom of the ocean. "Once I break 40 feet, I don't move a muscle," she explains. "I just put myself in God's hands, and he takes care of it."

. . . Heaney-Grier will take one deep breath and then attempt to propel herself past ten safety divers off Looe Key, Florida, snatch a tag at 210 feet, and swim back to the surface, delivering a new women's world record in the sport of free diving. Few observers doubt Heaney-Grier will break the current 204-foot mark held by Cuban Deborah Andollo—after all, some even think Heaney-Grier might be the finest free-diving prospect ever, male or female. . . .

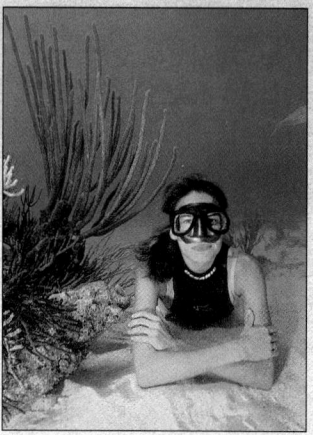

In free diving, practitioners must master but two things: equalizing their air passages rapidly as pressure builds during descent, and slowing their metabolism to conserve what precious little oxygen they have. Thus any discussion of Heaney-Grier's prowess inevitably focuses on her ears and her gender. "Mehgan has a very special pair of ears," her coach explains. "She can equalize at any depth. And she is a woman, which is good, because women have a much lower metabolic rate

than men. I'll make her into a diving machine."

Not that she wasn't headed that direction anyway. In 1995, when Heaney-Grier attempted her first free dive, she reached a phenomenal 87 feet. A year later, while setting her personal best and the American record of 155 feet, she surpassed her previous mark by a full 15 percent. Still, she remains a long way off from the men's record of 236 feet—and at least one observer doubts that she can ever get there. "I've heard she's very good, but I don't think she can make it," says Pipin Ferreras [champion Cuban free diver]. "Two hundred forty feet is very deep."

Respond

1. What do you think is the most important aspect of free diving for Mehgan Heaney-Grier?
2. What kinds of challenges do you set for yourself?

Teaching Options

Free Diving Have students use a search engine to look for additional information about free diving. Suggest that they try entering keywords such as *free diving, free-diving world records,* or *Heaney-Grier.*

Reading *Minilesson*

Identifying Author's Purpose Point out to students that the magazine article on this page is a nonfiction piece of writing. The author's purpose for writing it was to share factual information about a real person, Mehgan Heaney-Grier.

Activity Have partners interview each other about a self-imposed challenge. Then have students tell what they would include in the introduction and body of a magazine article about their subject.
L2 **COLLAB. LEARN.**

Additional Resources
📁 *Reading Workbook*

Before You Read

Through the Tunnel

FOCUS ACTIVITY

Think of times when you watched someone your age do something difficult or challenging. Perhaps you asked yourself, "Could I do that?"

CHART IT! Make a chart like this one, and fill it in.

The Challenge	Did I try it?	What happened?
	yes no	
	yes no	

SETTING A PURPOSE Read to see how one young boy faces a difficult challenge.

BACKGROUND

The Time and Place
This story takes place at a seashore, perhaps on the Mediterranean coast of France. The time is most likely the 1940s or 1950s.

Did You Know?

Underwater diving with no equipment other than goggles is called breath-hold diving. This type of diving can be very dangerous due to the great force of water pressure: water is more than a thousand times as dense as air. Most breath-hold divers can remain submerged for less than one minute, although with training, some divers can stay underwater for two minutes.

VOCABULARY PREVIEW

conscientiously (kon′ shē en′ shəs lē) *adv.* thoughtfully and carefully; p. 76

contrition (kən trish′ ən) *n.* sorrow for one's sin or wrongdoing; repentance; p. 76

supplication (səp′ lə kā′ shən) *n.* an earnest and humble request; p. 78

beseeching (bi sēch′ ing) *adj.* begging; asking earnestly; p. 81

myriad (mir′ ē əd) *n.* great or countless numbers; p. 81

incredulous (in krej′ ə ləs) *adj.* unwilling or unable to believe; p. 83

convulsive (kən vul′ siv) *adj.* sudden and violent; p. 84

Meet Doris Lessing

"It's a good thing for kids to be alone: you get a sense of yourself and ideas of your own. . . ." Solitude and independence have both been important to Lessing since she was very young. She grew up on an isolated farm with little supervision and spent much of her time roaming on her own.

Like the boy in this story, Lessing also has pushed herself to extremes in order to find out something about herself.

Doris Lessing was born in 1919 and lived in southern Africa until 1949, when she moved to England. This story was published in 1957.

THE SHORT STORY 🦋 75

Before Reading

Objectives
- To read and analyze a short story about a young boy facing a difficult challenge
- To identify plot elements in a short story
- To write an analysis of an author's choice of details

Skills
Reading/Thinking: Drawing Conclusions; Inferring; Identifying Cause-and-Effect Relationships
Writing: Spatial Order in Description; Letter
Vocabulary: Word Meanings; Context Clues; Antonyms
Grammar/Language: Prepositions
Listening/Speaking: Performing a Dialogue
Life Skills: Goal Setting
Collaboration: Literature Groups

Motivating → OPTIONS

 Selection Focus Transparency 6: Have students view and discuss *The Breakers*, a painting by Ken Danby.

 Focus Activity: Have pairs of students share their challenges and how those experiences changed them.

RESOURCE MANAGER

Lesson Planning Resource
The *Unit One Planning Guide* (pp. 48–55) provides additional lesson notes and reduced versions of all print resources.

📁 **Other Print Resources**
- Active Reading Guide, p. 6
- Vocabulary Practice, p. 6
- Reading Workbook, pp. 11–12
- Grammar and Language Workbook, pp. 67, 89
- Grammar and Composition Handbook, Lessons 1.6, 3.1

- Quick Checks, p. 6
- Selection and Theme Assessment, pp. 11–12
- Performance Assessment, p. 6
- Spanish Summaries, p. 6
- Inclusion Strategies
- English Language Learners Sourcebook

📖 **Transparencies**
- Selection Focus 6
- Fine Art 9
- Literary Elements 6

- Grammar and Language 6

Technology
🎧 Audio Library
🎧 Spanish Audio Library
💻 Glencoe Literature Web Site
💾 Testmaker

SUMMARY

Jerry, a young English boy on vacation at a beach resort, is amazed as he watches a group of local boys perform daring breath-holding dives from high rocks. When the boys reject him, apparently because he cannot duplicate their feat, he challenges himself to swim the tunnel and prove himself to the boys. His plan for accomplishing this goal includes learning to hold his breath for longer and longer periods of time. Finally, he successfully swims the tunnel and, in the process, makes an important discovery about himself.

📁 *Spanish Summaries,* p. 6

A **Active Reading**

PREDICT Ask students to use the title and text clues from the first paragraphs to predict what they think the conflict in the story may be. Suggest that students periodically revisit their prediction as they read to verify or revise it.

Additional Resources

📁 *Active Reading Guide,* p. 6
🎧 *Audio Library*
🎧 *Spanish Audio Library*

Teaching Options

Through the Tunnel

Doris Lessing ∾

GOING TO THE SHORE ON THE FIRST MORNING OF THE VACATION, the young English boy stopped at a turning of the path and looked down at a wild and rocky bay, and then over to the crowded beach he knew so well from other years. His mother walked on in front of him, carrying a bright striped bag in one hand.

Her other arm, swinging loose, was very white in the sun. The boy watched that white, naked arm, and turned his eyes, which had a frown behind them, toward the bay and back again to his mother. When she felt he was not with her, she swung around. "Oh, there you are, Jerry!" she said. She looked impatient, then smiled. "Why, darling, would you rather not come with me? Would you rather—" She frowned, conscientiously worrying over what amusements he might secretly be longing for, which she had been too busy or too careless to imagine. He was very familiar with that anxious, apologetic smile. Contrition sent him running after her. And yet, as he ran, he looked back over his shoulder at the wild bay; and all morning, as he played on the safe beach, he was thinking of it.

Next morning, when it was time for the routine of swimming and sunbathing, his mother said, "Are you tired of the usual beach, Jerry? Would you like to go somewhere else?"

"Oh, no!" he said quickly, smiling at her out of that unfailing impulse of contrition—a sort of chivalry.[1] Yet, walking down the path with her, he blurted out, "I'd like to go and have a look at those rocks down there."

She gave the idea her attention. It was a wild looking place, and there was no one there; but she said, "Of course, Jerry. When you've had enough, come to the big beach. Or just go straight back to the villa,[2] if you like." She walked away, that bare arm, now slightly reddened from yesterday's sun, swinging. And he almost ran after her again, feeling it unbearable that she should go by herself, but he did not.

---

1. Here, *chivalry* (shiv′ əl rē) means "an act of courtesy or politeness."
2. *Villa,* from the Italian, means "house," usually one in the country or at the seashore.

Vocabulary
conscientiously (kon′ shē en′ shəs lē) *adv.* thoughtfully and carefully
contrition (kən trish′ ən) *n.* sorrow for one's sin or wrongdoing; repentance

---

CONNECTING TO OTHER SELECTIONS

COMPARING selections

This selection is paired with "The Vision Quest" on pages 89–91. A lesson for teaching a comparison of the two selections appears on page 93.

The chart at the right shows three other ways to connect "Through the Tunnel" to selections in this book.

For specific teaching strategies, see the *Unit One Planning Guide,* pages 51–52.

Connection	Title
Life Skills: Making Decisions	➡ "The Road Not Taken," p. 643
Thematic: Rites of Passage	➡ "By the Waters of Babylon," p. 95
Literary: Character Traits	➡ *Antigone,* p. 727

She was thinking, Of course he's old enough to be safe without me. Have I been keeping him too close? He mustn't feel he ought to be with me. I must be careful.

He was an only child, eleven years old. She was a widow. She was determined to be neither possessive nor lacking in devotion. She went worrying off to her beach.

As for Jerry, once he saw that his mother had gained her beach, he began the steep descent to the bay. From where he was, high up among red-brown rocks, it was a scoop of moving bluish green fringed with white. As he went lower, he saw that it spread among small promontories and inlets of rough, sharp rock, and the crisping, lapping surface showed stains of purple and darker blue. Finally, as he ran sliding and scraping down the last few yards, he saw an edge of white surf and the shallow, luminous movement of water over white sand, and, beyond that, a solid, heavy blue.

Did You Know?
Promontories are high points of land or rock overlooking the water.

Crowded Day at the Beach, 1922. Martha Walter. Oil on board, 16 x 20 in. David David Gallery, Philadelphia.
Viewing the painting: Why might Jerry not want to go to a beach like this one with his mother?

DRAWING CONCLUSIONS What might the boys conclude after Jerry yells out his warning? *(Jerry is unaware of the passage through the tunnel and/or cannot perform breath-hold dives.)*

Vo•cab•u•lar•y Skills

Word Meanings Making a connection to the concrete noun *buoy* can help students grasp the literal meaning of *buoyant.* You may wish to have them extend their word knowledge by considering the metaphorical meaning of *buoyant* in contexts such as "buoyant feelings" or "a buoyant economy."

FINE ART
TRANSPARENCY 9

You might want to show Fine Art Transparency 9 and discuss how Jerry might approach the teenagers playing handball. Have students support their opinions with details from the story.

Teaching Options

Through the **Tunnel**

He ran straight into the water and began swimming. He was a good swimmer. He went out fast over the gleaming sand, over a middle region where rocks lay like discolored monsters under the surface, and then he was in the real sea—a warm sea where irregular cold currents from the deep water shocked his limbs.

When he was so far out that he could look back not only on the little bay but past the promontory that was between it and the big beach, he floated on the buoyant surface and looked for his mother. There she was, a speck of yellow under an umbrella that looked like a slice of orange peel. He swam back to shore, relieved at being sure she was there, but all at once very lonely.

On the edge of a small cape that marked the side of the bay away from the promontory was a loose scatter of rocks. Above them, some boys were stripping off their clothes. They came running, naked, down to the rocks. The English boy swam toward them, but kept his distance at a stone's throw. They were of that coast; all of them were burned smooth dark brown and speaking a language he did not understand. To be with them, of them, was a craving that filled his whole body. He swam a little closer; they turned and watched him with narrowed, alert dark eyes. Then one smiled and waved. It was enough. In a minute, he had swum in and was on the rocks beside them, smiling with a desperate, nervous supplication. They shouted cheerful greetings at him; and then, as he preserved his nervous, uncomprehending smile, they understood that he was a foreigner strayed from his own beach, and they proceeded to forget him. But he was happy. He was with them.

They began diving again and again from a high point into a well of blue sea between

Photograph by Douglass Faulkner.

Viewing the photograph: In what direction was the photographer shooting? How does this perspective reflect the feeling Jerry has about the diving boys?

rough, pointed rocks. After they had dived and come up, they swam around, hauled themselves up, and waited their turn to dive again. They were big boys—men, to Jerry. He dived, and they watched him; and when he swam around to take his place, they made way for him. He felt he was accepted, and he dived again, carefully, proud of himself.

Soon the biggest of the boys poised himself, shot down into the water, and did not come up. The others stood about, watching. Jerry, after waiting for the sleek brown head to appear, let out a yell of warning; they looked at him idly and turned their eyes back toward the water. After a long time, the boy came up on the other side of a big dark rock, letting the air out of his lungs in a sputtering gasp and a shout of triumph. Immediately the rest of them dived in. One moment, the morning seemed full of chattering boys; the next, the air and the surface of the water were empty. But through the heavy blue, dark shapes could be seen moving and groping.

Jerry dived, shot past the school of underwater swimmers, saw a black wall of rock looming at him, touched it, and bobbed up at once to the surface, where the wall was a low barrier he could see across. There was no one visible; under him, in the water, the dim shapes of the swimmers had disappeared. Then one, and then another of the boys came up on the far side of the barrier of rock, and he understood that they had swum through some gap or hole in it. He plunged down again. He could see nothing through the stinging salt water but the blank rock. When

Vocabulary
supplication (sap′ la kā′ shan) *n.* an earnest and humble request

---

Writing *Minilesson*

Writing Descriptions with Spatial Order Writers can organize details of a setting in spatial order, presenting details from left to right, far to near, top to bottom, or clockwise. Read aloud the description of the setting beginning in the third paragraph on page 77. Have students determine the kind of spatial order Lessing uses (top to bottom). Ask them to note phrases used to present that order,

such as *to the bay* and *over white sand.*

Activity Have students write a short descriptive paragraph about a favorite scene or setting. Suggest that they use phrases that convey spatial order to place the details in their settings. **L2**

Additional Resources

Writer's Choice, Lessons 2.7, 3.1

VIEWING THE PHOTOGRAPH

His work as a marine photographer has taken Douglass Faulkner (1938–) to exotic places all over the globe. Of his work, Faulkner once said, "I want to take photographs that somehow sing. If it doesn't sing, it's a bad photo."

Viewing Response *The photographer is looking up toward the surface of the water and swimmers as he shoots. Some viewers may suggest that because the boys have superior diving skills, Jerry feels outside of the group, or even "beneath" them.*

FYI

Where Are They?
Although Lessing does not state the exact location of this short story, indications are that it is near a beach resort along the Mediterranean Sea, where bays, capes, and peninsulas punctuate the coastline. A mild year-round climate and tropical waters make swimming and diving natural pastimes.

INTERDISCIPLINARY CONNECTION

Science Explain that digital cameras transmit images directly onto computer disks instead of using film. These cameras are used primarily by newspapers and magazines. Since the images they render can be sent directly over phone lines, pictures may be transmitted anywhere in the world within seconds. Thus, a photo like the one on this page could be shot, transmitted, and ready to print just as a paper or magazine is going to press.

Activity Have students research additional information about digital cameras. Areas to investigate might include the size and cost of such cameras, advantages and disadvantages of their use, and their availability to the public. **L3**

Literary Elements

E **Literary Elements**

CHARACTER Discuss what Jerry's clowning reveals about the way he responds to failure. *(He tries to cover up his failure by poking fun at himself and purposely pretending to fail.)*

F **Active Reading**

EVALUATE Ask students to suggest words that describe Jerry. *(immature, silly, insecure)*

E he came up the boys were all on the diving rock, preparing to attempt the feat again. And now, in a panic of failure, he yelled up, in English, "Look at me! Look!" and he began splashing and kicking in the water like a foolish dog.

F They looked down gravely, frowning. He knew the frown. At moments of failure, when he clowned to claim his mother's attention, it was with just this grave, embarrassed inspection that she rewarded him. Through his hot shame, feeling the pleading grin on his face like a scar that he could never remove, he looked up at the group of big brown boys on the rock and shouted, *"Bonjour! Merci! Au revoir! Monsieur, monsieur!"*[3] while he hooked his fingers round his ears and waggled them.

Water surged into his mouth; he choked, sank, came up. The rock, lately weighted with boys, seemed to rear up out of the water as their weight was removed. They were flying down past him, now, into the water; the air was full of falling bodies. Then the rock was empty in the hot sunlight. He counted one, two, three. . . .

At fifty, he was terrified. They must all be drowning beneath him, in the watery caves of the rock! At a hundred, he stared around him at the empty hillside, wondering if he should yell for help. He counted faster, faster, to hurry them up, to bring them to the surface quickly, to drown them quickly —anything rather than the terror of counting on and on

into the blue emptiness of the morning. And then, at a hundred and sixty, the water beyond the rock was full of boys blowing like brown whales. They swam back to the shore without a look at him.

He climbed back to the diving rock and sat down, feeling the hot roughness of it under his thighs. The boys were gathering up their bits of clothing and running off along

3. [*"Bonjour! . . . monsieur!"*] These words are French for "Hello! Thanks! Good-bye! Sir, sir!"

Teaching Options

Less-Proficient Readers Research shows that to comprehend and appreciate a story, readers must imaginatively enter the world of the story and relate to the characters—both difficult tasks for many less-proficient readers. A simple drama strategy called *tableau* or *frozen pictures* can help these readers connect with characters.

Activity Have students act out a scene from the story, such as Jerry's clowning at the top of page 80, freezing the action at its climax. Then tap students in the frozen picture to come to life and talk about the character's feelings or motivations. **L2**

Additional Resources
📁 *Inclusion Strategies*

the shore to another promontory. They were leaving to get away from him. He cried openly, fists in his eyes. There was no one to see him, and he cried himself out.

It seemed to him that a long time had passed, and he swam out to where he could see his mother. Yes, she was still there, a yellow spot under an orange umbrella. He swam back to the big rock, climbed up, and dived into the blue pool among the fanged and angry boulders. Down he went, until he touched the wall of rock again. But the salt was so painful in his eyes that he could not see.

He came to the surface, swam to shore, and went back to the villa to wait for his mother. Soon she walked slowly up the path, swinging her striped bag, the flushed, naked arm dangling beside her. "I want some swimming goggles," he panted, defiant and beseeching.

She gave him a patient, inquisitive look as she said casually, "Well, of course, darling."

But now, now, now! He must have them this minute, and no other time. He nagged and pestered until she went with him to a shop. As soon as she had bought the goggles, he grabbed them from her hand as if she were going to claim them for herself, and was off, running down the steep path to the bay.

Jerry swam out to the big barrier rock, adjusted the goggles, and dived. The impact of the water broke the rubber-enclosed vacuum, and the goggles came loose. He understood that he must swim down to the base of the rock from the surface of the water. He fixed the goggles tight and firm, filled his lungs, and floated, face down, on the water. Now, he could see. It was as if he had eyes of a different kind—fish eyes that showed everything clear and delicate and wavering in the bright water.

Under him, six or seven feet down, was a floor of perfectly clean, shining white sand, rippled firm and hard by the tides. Two grayish shapes steered there, like long, rounded pieces of wood or slate. They were fish. He saw them nose toward each other, poise motionless, make a dart forward, swerve off, and come around again. It was like a water dance. A few inches above them the water sparkled as if sequins were dropping through it. Fish again—myriads of minute fish, the length of his fingernail, were drifting through the water, and in a moment he could feel the innumerable tiny touches of them against his limbs. It was like swimming in flaked silver. The great rock the big boys had swum through rose sheer out of the white sand—black, tufted lightly with greenish weed. He could see no gap in it. He swam down to its base.

Again and again he rose, took a big chestful of air, and went down. Again and again he groped over the surface of the rock, feeling it, almost hugging it in the desperate need to find the entrance. And then, once, while he was clinging to the black wall, his knees came up, and he shot his feet out forward and they met no obstacle. He had found the hole.

He gained the surface, clambered about the stones that littered the barrier rock until he found a big one, and, with this in his arms, let himself down over the side of the rock. He dropped, with the weight, straight to the sandy floor.

Clinging tight to the anchor of stone, he lay on his side and looked in under the dark shelf at the place where his feet had gone. He could see the hole. It was an irregular, dark gap; but he could not see deep into it. He let go of his anchor, clung with his hands to the edges of the hole, and tried to push himself in.

Vocabulary

beseeching (bi sēch′ ing) *adj.* begging; asking earnestly
myriad (mir′ ē əd) *n.* great or countless numbers

Literary Elements

PLOT: *External Conflict* Students should note the conflict between Jerry and nature described by the words "he must find his way through that cave, or hole, or tunnel, and out the other side."

VIEWING THE PAINTING

Edward Hopper (1882–1967) painted this picture early in his career. It suggests the simple, realistic style reflected in his later urban paintings.

Viewing Response *The painting emphasizes the desolation of the beach, underscoring the possible dangers of Jerry's undertaking.*

He got his head in, found his shoulders jammed, moved them in sidewise, and was inside as far as his waist. He could see nothing ahead. Something soft and clammy touched his mouth; he saw a dark frond[4] moving against the grayish rock, and panic filled him. He thought of octopuses, of clinging weed. He pushed himself out backward and caught a glimpse, as he retreated, of a harmless tentacle[5] of seaweed drifting in the mouth

---

4. A *frond* is a large leaf with many divisions, or a leaflike part of a plant such as seaweed.
5. A *tentacle* is a long, flexible limb that could belong to a plant or to a creature such as an octopus.

of the tunnel. But it was enough. He reached the sunlight, swam to shore, and lay on the diving rock. He looked down into the blue well of water. He knew he must find his way through that cave, or hole, or tunnel, and out the other side.

First, he thought, he must learn to control his breathing. He let himself down into the water with another big stone in his arms, so that he could lie effortlessly on the bottom of the sea. He counted. One, two, three. He counted steadily. He could hear the movement of blood in his chest. Fifty-one, fifty-two. . . . His chest was hurting. He let go of

(Rocky Sea Shore), 1916–1919. Edward Hopper. Oil on canvas panel, 9½ x 12¹⁵⁄₁₆ in. Collection of Whitney Museum of American Art, New York. Josephine N. Hopper Bequest. 70.166.

Viewing the painting: How does the scene portrayed here affect your understanding of the beach that Jerry goes to?

82 UNIT 1

Teaching Options

REAL-WORLD CONNECTION

Achieving a Goal Have students locate a magazine or newspaper article that deals with a person's desire to achieve a goal. That goal can be a physical one, such as a sports achievement, or an academic or humanitarian goal.

Activity Have the class break into groups and discuss their articles. Students should answer such questions as these: Who is the subject of the article? What was the person's goal? Did the person achieve it? What challenges did the person face? **L1 COLLAB. LEARN.**

the rock and went up into the air. He saw that the sun was low. He rushed to the villa and found his mother at her supper. She said only, "Did you enjoy yourself?" and he said, "Yes."

All night the boy dreamed of the water-filled cave in the rock, and as soon as breakfast was over he went to the bay.

That night, his nose bled badly. For hours he had been underwater, learning to hold his breath, and now he felt weak and dizzy. His mother said, "I shouldn't overdo things, darling, if I were you."

That day and the next, Jerry exercised his lungs as if everything, the whole of his life, all that he would become, depended upon it. Again his nose bled at night, and his mother insisted on his coming with her the next day. It was a torment to him to waste a day of his careful self training, but he stayed with her on that other beach, which now seemed a place for small children, a place where his mother might lie safe in the sun. It was not his beach.

He did not ask for permission, on the following day, to go to his beach. He went, before his mother could consider the complicated rights and wrongs of the matter. A day's rest, he discovered, had improved his count by ten. The big boys had made the passage while he counted a hundred and sixty. He had been counting fast, in his fright. Probably now, if he tried, he could get through that long tunnel, but he was not going to try yet. A curious, most unchildlike persistence, a controlled impatience, made him wait. In the meantime, he lay underwater on the white sand, littered now by stones he had brought down from the upper air, and studied the entrance to the tunnel. He knew every jut and corner of it, as far as it was possible to see. It was as if he already felt its sharpness about his shoulders.

He sat by the clock in the villa, when his mother was not near, and checked his time. He was incredulous and then proud to find he could hold his breath without strain for two minutes. The words "two minutes," authorized by the clock, brought close the adventure that was so necessary to him.

In another four days, his mother said casually one morning, they must go home. On the day before they left, he would do it. He would do it if it killed him, he said defiantly to himself. But two days before they were to leave—a day of triumph when he increased his count by fifteen—his nose bled so badly that he turned dizzy and had to lie limply over the big rock like a bit of seaweed, watching the thick red blood flow on to the rock and trickle slowly down to the sea. He was frightened. Supposing he turned dizzy in the tunnel? Supposing he died there, trapped? Supposing—his head went around, in the hot sun, and he almost gave up. He thought he would return to the house and lie down, and next summer, perhaps, when he had another year's growth in him—*then* he would go through the hole.

But even after he had made the decision, or thought he had, he found himself sitting up on the rock and looking down into the water; and he knew that now, this moment, when his nose had only just stopped bleeding, when his head was still sore and throbbing—this was the moment when he would try. If he did not do it now, he never would. He was trembling with fear that he would not go; and he was trembling with horror at that long, long tunnel under the rock, under the sea. Even in the open sunlight, the barrier rock seemed very wide and very heavy; tons of rock pressed down on where he would go. If he died there, he would lie until

---

Vocabulary
incredulous (in krej′ ə ləs) *adj.* unwilling or unable to believe

---

J Literary Elements

CHARACTER The phrase "controlled impatience" reveals how Jerry has changed from his earlier pleading for goggles. By exhibiting patience, Jerry shows a growing maturity. He knows he will do better if he sticks to his plan of practice and preparation.

K Active Reading

REVIEW Have students recap the goal, or challenge, Jerry has set for himself, along with his plan of preparation to accomplish it. *(Jerry's goal is to swim the tunnel. His preparation has included getting the swimming goggles, locating the tunnel, exploring the tunnel's opening, and learning to hold his breath for extended periods.)*

L Literary Elements

PLOT: *Internal Conflict* Discuss the concerns Jerry has as he ponders the dangers of the deep waters and underground tunnel. *(Jerry is afraid he will die in the tunnel and that he won't ever attempt his goal if he doesn't swim the tunnel now.)*

Nosebleeds are often caused by changes in air pressure. In practicing, Jerry subjects himself to the pressure of the water for long periods of time. This greater pressure makes his heart beat faster. Then, when he makes an abrupt return to the lesser pressure of the air, blood vessels close to the surface of the nasal membrane rupture and cause bleeding.

MULTIPLE LEARNING STYLES

Spatial Students with strong spatial abilities may respond to their reading more readily through visual images than through words. These students can use sketching to help themselves and other students visualize settings, characters, and key story events.

Activity As students read the story, have them stop whenever they form a strong visual impression and make a quick sketch of that impression. They may also choose to add captions or labels to their sketches. Spatial learners may find these sketches very useful references as they respond to questions or complete activities in Responding to Literature (pp. 86–87). **L1**

PLOT: *Rising Action* You may wish to ask students to detail what Jerry sees, feels, and encounters as he begins and then continues his swim. Discuss how each mounting threat or danger helps build suspense. Students may better be able to respond if first you read aloud the passage beginning with "He put on his goggles" and ending with ". . . and his feet, kicking back, propelled him out into the open sea" on page 84.

N **Literary Elements**

PLOT: *Climax* Students should note what Jerry realizes when he first sees the crack in the rock and then only darkness ahead. *(Jerry realizes that he is not out of the tunnel yet and that he must keep going or he will drown.)*

Vo•cab•u•lar•y Skills

Context Clues Suggest that students think of other actions that might be described as *convulsive*. Have them define *convulsive* in these contexts: *convulsive* laughter; *convulsive* sobs.

Teaching Options

Through the **Tunnel**

one day—perhaps not before next year—those big boys would swim into it and find it blocked.

He put on his goggles, fitted them tight, tested the vacuum. His hands were shaking. Then he chose the biggest stone he could carry and slipped over the edge of the rock until half of him was in the cool, enclosing water and half in the hot sun. He looked up once at the empty sky, filled his lungs once, twice, and then sank fast to the bottom with the stone. He let it go and began to count. He took the edges of the hole in his hands and drew himself into it, wriggling his shoulders in sidewise as he remembered he must, kicking himself along with his feet.

Soon he was clear inside. He was in a small rock-bound hole filled with yellowish-gray water. The water was pushing him up against the roof. The roof was sharp and pained his back. He pulled himself along with his hands—fast, fast—and used his legs as levers. His head knocked against something; a sharp pain dizzied him. Fifty, fifty-one, fifty-two. . . . He was without light, and the water seemed to press upon him with the weight of rock. Seventy-one, seventy-two. . . . There was no strain on his lungs. He felt like an inflated balloon, his lungs were so light and easy, but his head was pulsing.

He was being continually pressed against the sharp roof, which felt slimy as well as sharp. Again he thought of octopuses, and wondered if the tunnel might be filled with weed that could tangle him. He gave himself a panicky, <u>convulsive</u> kick forward, ducked his head, and swam. His feet and hands moved freely, as if in open water. The hole must have widened out. He thought he must be swimming fast, and he was frightened of banging his head if the tunnel narrowed.

A hundred, a hundred and one. . . . The water paled. Victory filled him. His lungs were beginning to hurt. A few more strokes and he would be out. He was counting wildly; he said a hundred and fifteen, and then, a long time later, a hundred and fifteen again. The water was a clear jewel-green all around him. Then he saw, above his head, a crack running up through the rock. Sunlight was falling through it, showing the clean, dark rock of the tunnel, a single mussel shell, and darkness ahead.

He was at the end of what he could do. He looked up at the crack as if it were filled with air and not water, as if he could put his mouth to it to draw in air. A hundred and fifteen, he heard himself say inside his head—but he had said that long ago. He must go on into the blackness ahead, or he would drown. His head was swelling, his lungs cracking. A hundred and fifteen, a hundred and fifteen pounded through his head, and he feebly clutched at rocks in the dark, pulling himself forward, leaving the brief space of sunlit water behind. He felt he was dying. He was no longer quite conscious. He struggled on in the darkness between lapses into unconsciousness. An immense, swelling pain filled his head, and then the darkness cracked with an explosion of green light. His hands, groping forward, met nothing; and his feet, kicking back, propelled him out into the open sea.

He drifted to the surface, his face turned up to the air. He was gasping like a fish. He felt he would sink now and drown; he could

Did You Know?
A *mussel* is a kind of shellfish. Mussels are in the same scientific classification as clams, oysters, and scallops.

Vocabulary
convulsive (kən vul′ siv) *adj.* sudden and violent

Grammar and Language *Minilesson*

Prepositions Point out that a *preposition* is a word that shows the relationship of a noun or pronoun to some other word in a sentence. A *prepositional phrase* includes a preposition, a noun or pronoun that is the object of the preposition, and any modifiers. Write the following example on the board:
   Jerry ran <u>into the water</u>.
Explain that *into* is a preposition. Ask students: Into what? *(water)* List other prepositions, such as *with, to, at, about, for*.

Activity Have students underline the prepositional phrases and circle the prepositions in the following sentences.
1. She looked at him closely.
2. They must all be drowning beneath him, in the watery caves of the rock.
3. He dropped, with the weight, straight to the sandy floor. **L2**

Additional Resources

📠 *Grammar and Language Transparency 6*

📕 *Grammar and Language Workbook,* pp. 67, 89

📘 *Grammar and Composition Handbook,* Lessons 1.6, 3.1

📙 *Writer's Choice,* Lessons 10.6, 12.1

not swim the few feet back to the rock. Then he was clutching it and pulling himself up on to it. He lay face down, gasping. He could see nothing but a red-veined, clotted dark. His eyes must have burst, he thought; they were full of blood. He tore off his goggles and a gout[6] of blood went into the sea. His nose was bleeding, and the blood had filled the goggles.

He scooped up handfuls of water from the cool, salty sea, to splash on his face, and did not know whether it was blood or salt water he tasted. After a time, his heart quieted, his eyes cleared, and he sat up. He could see the local boys diving and playing half a mile away. He did not want them. He wanted nothing but to get back home and lie down.

In a short while, Jerry swam to shore and climbed slowly up the path to the villa. He flung himself on his bed and slept, waking at the sound of feet on the path outside. His mother was coming back. He rushed to the bathroom, thinking she must not see his face

---

6. Here, *gout* refers to a mass of fluid that gushes or bursts forth.

with bloodstains, or tearstains, on it. He came out of the bathroom and met her as she walked into the villa, smiling, her eyes lighting up.

"Have a nice morning?" she asked, laying her hand on his warm brown shoulder a moment.

"Oh, yes, thank you," he said.

"You look a bit pale." And then, sharp and anxious, "How did you bang your head?"

"Oh, just banged it," he told her.

She looked at him closely. He was strained; his eyes were glazed-looking. She was worried. And then she said to herself, Oh, don't fuss! Nothing can happen. He can swim like a fish.

They sat down to lunch together.

"Mummy," he said, "I can stay under water for two minutes—three minutes, at least." It came bursting out of him.

"Can you, darling?" she said. "Well, I shouldn't overdo it. I don't think you ought to swim any more today."

She was ready for a battle of wills, but he gave in at once. It was no longer of the least importance to go to the bay.

⓿ Critical Thinking

INFERRING Be sure that students understand why Jerry is no longer interested in the local boys. *(He has learned that preparing for and accomplishing a goal is more important than impressing a group of boys.)*

Thematic Focus

Transitions Have students compare Jerry with themselves and other young people they know. Are Jerry's thoughts, feelings, words, and actions during his transition typical of young people his age? Ask students for examples to support their answers.

☑ ASSESSMENT OPTIONS

📁 *Quick Checks,* p. 6

Reading *Minilesson*

Identifying Cause-and-Effect Relationships Point out that when a reader asks "why," he or she is analyzing cause and effect. Explain that there is often more than one cause for an effect or more than one effect of a cause.

Activity Have students create a cluster map showing the causes of Jerry's dive through the tunnel. Suggest that they write the effect—"Jerry's Dive"—in the center and connect each cause to it with a line. Encourage students to look beyond the obvious cause—Jerry's admiration for the older boys—to subtle causes such as his loneliness or desire for challenge. **L2**

Additional Resources
📁 *Reading Workbook,* pp. 11–12

Responding to the Selection

Personal Response

There is no one correct response to a challenge like the one Jerry experienced. His response was based on who he was and what his experiences had been up to that time.

ANALYZING LITERATURE

1. Jerry's beach is the rocky shore that leads him to the tunnel. His mother prefers the usual, calmer beach; she is concerned about the "wild looking" bay.
2. The boys are "burned smooth dark brown," and they "speak a language he did not understand." They are initially very friendly, smiling and waving; after he clowns around, they frown and leave.
3. He dives, looking for the cave. After finding it, he uses a large rock as a weight and lowers himself to the entrance. He explores the first few feet of the cave.
4. Jerry does not stay underwater for the full length of time; he is never in any real danger while practicing.
5. He sleeps. His mother does not want him to swim any more that day.
6. He wants the freedom from his mother's watchful care; he wants a more exciting beach.
7. He wants to make friends but cannot speak the boys' language; he is embarrassed that he cannot dive as they can.
8. Jerry wants to prove that he is as good as the other boys; he wants to prove that he is mature.
9. The most dramatic moment occurs when Jerry realizes that he is not at the end of the tunnel and must go beyond his best practice time if he is to escape drowning.
10. Jerry proves his skills to himself, and that is all that matters.
11. Some students may see his decision as foolish; others as brave.
12. Students may point out that Jerry's mother is protective but allows him some freedom; Jerry obeys his mother in most situations.
13. Jerry has learned that he can meet even the most extreme challenge.
14. The tunnel might symbolize a journey, rebirth, a test, passage to adulthood or maturity.
15. Students may suggest that the chief lesson is to not run away from new experiences or to persevere when challenged.

Responding to Literature

Personal Response

If you had been in Jerry's place, do you think you would have tested yourself the way he did? If so, do you think you would have succeeded? Give reasons for your answers.

——— ANALYZING LITERATURE ———

RECALL

1. How is Jerry's beach different from his mother's?
2. Describe the boys Jerry encounters, and trace the change in their attitude toward him.
3. Summarize what Jerry does when he goes to his beach the second time.
4. How is Jerry's preparation unlike the real test?
5. What happens after Jerry returns to the villa?

INTERPRET

6. In your opinion, why is Jerry first drawn to his beach?
7. Jerry begins clowning in the water while the boys are on the diving rock. In your opinion, why does Jerry do this?
8. Why, do you think, does Jerry decide that he must do what the other boys have done?
9. In your opinion, what is the most dramatic moment of Jerry's actual test? Explain your answer.
10. Why, do you think, doesn't Jerry feel a need to show his new ability to the other boys?

EVALUATE AND CONNECT

11. Was Jerry's decision to test himself a good one, or did he risk too much? Give reasons for your answer.
12. In your opinion, is Jerry a good son? Is his mother a good mother? Support your opinions with evidence from the story.
13. Theme Connections   What do you think Jerry has learned about himself by the end of the story?
14. Stories sometimes contain a **symbol**—an object that stands for something else, often an idea or a concept. What do you think the tunnel in this story might symbolize?
15. Look back at the chart you made in the Focus Activity on page 75. How does Jerry's experience compare with the way you have handled difficulties or challenges in your own life?

Literary ELEMENTS

Plot

As the problem, or **conflict**, in a story is explored, the story often becomes more suspenseful. A story's **climax** is its turning point, the moment of greatest emotional intensity, interest, or suspense. Usually the climax is found at the point in a story where the conflict begins to be resolved. For instance, in a story about a race, the climax probably would occur as the main character or other characters approach the finish line.

1. What is the major conflict in this story? What other conflicts are present?
2. What is the climax of this story? Explain why you think this event is the story's turning point.
3. What conflict or conflicts are resolved by the end of the story? Explain your answer.

● See **Literary Terms Handbook**, p. R9.

LITERARY ELEMENTS

1. **Major conflict:** Jerry against the tunnel (or Jerry against his physical limitations).
   Minor conflicts: Jerry and his mother, Jerry and the boys.
2. The climax occurs when Jerry realizes that he will drown if he doesn't continue.
3. The major conflict of Jerry against the tunnel or against his limitations is resolved.

Additional Resources

Literary Elements Transparency 6

LITERATURE AND WRITING

Writing About Literature
Author's Choice of Details   The author gives vivid descriptions of the physical effects that Jerry suffers during and after his breath-hold dives. Find at least five examples of such descriptions. Explain how each one helps the reader better understand the danger and the discomfort that Jerry faces as he struggles to meet the challenge he has set for himself.

Creative Writing
Dear Jerry   Was Jerry brave or foolish? Write a letter to him expressing your opinion about his decision to try to swim through the tunnel. Support your opinion with reasons. Base your reasons on details from the story or on personal experience.

EXTENDING YOUR RESPONSE

Literature Groups
Reading the Author's Mind   Does the author believe it's a good idea to push oneself beyond one's limits? Debate this question in your group. Each group member should use evidence from the story to support his or her opinion. Tally your group's responses and share the results with the rest of the class.

Interdisciplinary Activity
Art: Illustrating a Scene   Illustrate one of the underwater scenes that is described in a passage in this story. Reread the passage before you begin your illustration, so that you remember to include all of the details described in the scene.

Performing
You Can't Be Serious   Imagine that you are Jerry's mother or another of his family members, and that he has told you he is planning to swim through the tunnel. What would you say to him? Work with a partner as you prepare a dialogue. One partner should take Jerry's role, and the other partner should take the family member's role. Perform your dialogue for the class.

📖 **Save your work for your portfolio.**

Skill Minilesson

VOCABULARY • Antonyms

Not all words have perfect antonyms. *Huge* has one (*tiny*), but no word means the opposite of *sigh* or *apple.* Then there are such words as *supplication.* What would be the opposite of an earnest and humble request? If you are asked to come up with an antonym for a word like this, think about the primary meaning of the word, in this case "a request." Thinking about *supplication* this way allows you to choose a word such as *requirement* or *order* as an antonym.

PRACTICE   Use your knowledge of the words in the left column to match each one to its antonym in the right column. If a word is unfamiliar, use a dictionary to find out its meaning.

1. conscientiously   a. calm
2. convulsive   b. few
3. beseeching   c. gullible
4. myriads   d. carelessly
5. incredulous   e. demanding

LITERATURE AND WRITING

Writing About Literature
Students' explanations should
- give appropriate examples of Lessing's descriptive details.
- explain clearly how each detail contributes to understanding the danger.

Creative Writing
Students' letters should
- express a clear opinion regarding Jerry's behavior.
- support the opinion with specific reasons in a logical sequence.
- follow the format and tone of a friendly letter.

EXTENDING YOUR RESPONSE

Literature Groups Point out to students that they are to determine and then debate the author's opinion, not their own. **COLLAB. LEARN.**

Interdisciplinary Activity Students could use colored pencils for clear details, and pastels for overall effects. 🖍️

Performing Encourage students to spend time planning and rehearsing their dialogues. If possible, videotape each group's performance and make tapes available. 📼

Skill Minilesson

VOCABULARY • Antonyms
1. d   2. a   3. e
4. b   5. c

Additional Resources
📁 *Vocabulary Practice,* p. 6

✔ ASSESSMENT OPTIONS

📁 *Quick Checks,* p. 6
📁 *Selection and Theme Assessment,* pp. 11–12
📁 *Performance Assessment,* p. 6
💾 *Testmaker*

88 ❧ UNIT 1

Objectives

- To read and analyze a short story about a young man who learns through failure
- To understand the role of legends in literature
- To write a poem or song summarizing the short story

Skills

Reading/Thinking: Judging the Credibility of a Source
Writing: Poem or Song
Grammar/Language: Infinitive and Prepositional Phrases
Listening/Speaking: Debating; Storytelling
Collaboration: Literature Groups

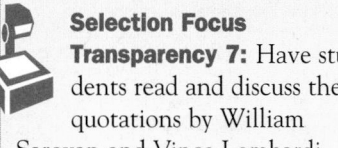

Motivating
→ OPTIONS

Selection Focus Transparency 7: Have students read and discuss the quotations by William Saroyan and Vince Lombardi.

Focus Activity: Have students write about an experience in which they did not achieve their goals.

Before You Read
The Vision Quest

FOCUS ACTIVITY

How important are goals? Can an experience be useful even if you fail to reach the goal you set?

LIST IDEAS List some benefits a person might get from an experience even if the original goal is not reached.

SETTING A PURPOSE Read to discover what one young Sioux learns from striving to reach a goal.

BACKGROUND

The Time and Place
The events of "The Vision Quest" take place somewhere in or around South Dakota. The time is not specified, nor is it important, since the tale is timeless.

Did You Know?
Visions have always been an important part of Native American culture. Among some peoples, the quest for a vision is an initiation into adulthood, and the vision helps shape the young person's goals. However, individuals who face major life challenges or who feel the need for spiritual guidance might also seek a vision. Some vision quests involve fasting and solitude; others require physical suffering. The search for visions is still an important ritual in Native American culture.

VOCABULARY PREVIEW

brash (brash) *adj.* boldly disrespectful; p. 90
obliterate (ə blit′ ə rāt′) *v.* to destroy completely; p. 91
gaunt (gônt) *adj.* extremely thin and hollow-eyed, as from hunger or illness; looking like skin and bones; p. 91
humility (hū mil′ ə tē) *n.* the quality of being humble or modest; p. 91

Meet Lame Deer and Richard Erdoes

Recalling his own vision quest, Lame Deer said,

"I thought of my forefathers who had crouched here before me . . . I felt their presence."

Lame Deer is a spiritual name that has been handed down from father to son in one Sioux family. The Lame Deer who told the story "Vision Quest" is also called John Fire.

Richard Erdoes was born in the early 1900s in what is now Austria. He came to New York in the 1940s. As an artist and writer on assignment in the United States, Erdoes met many Native Americans and became involved in their civil rights struggle.

John Fire Lame Deer was born in the late 1800s. He told this story to Richard Erdoes in 1967.

RESOURCE MANAGER

Lesson Planning Resource
The *Unit One Planning Guide* (pp. 56–63) provides additional lesson notes and reduced versions of all print resources.

📁 **Other Print Resources**
- Active Reading Guide, p. 7
- Vocabulary Practice, p. 7
- Reading Workbook, pp. 11–12
- Grammar and Language Workbook, pp. 89, 97
- Grammar and Composition Handbook, Lessons 3.1, 3.3

- Quick Checks, p. 7
- Selection and Theme Assessment, pp. 13–14
- Performance Assessment, p. 7
- Spanish Summaries, p. 7
- Inclusion Strategies
- English Language Learners Sourcebook

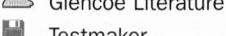 **Transparencies**
- Selection Focus 7
- Literary Elements 7
- Grammar and Language 7

Technology
🎧 Audio Library
🎧 Spanish Audio Library
💻 Glencoe Literature Web Site
💾 Testmaker

The Vision Quest

Told by Lame Deer ∿
Recorded by Richard Erdoes

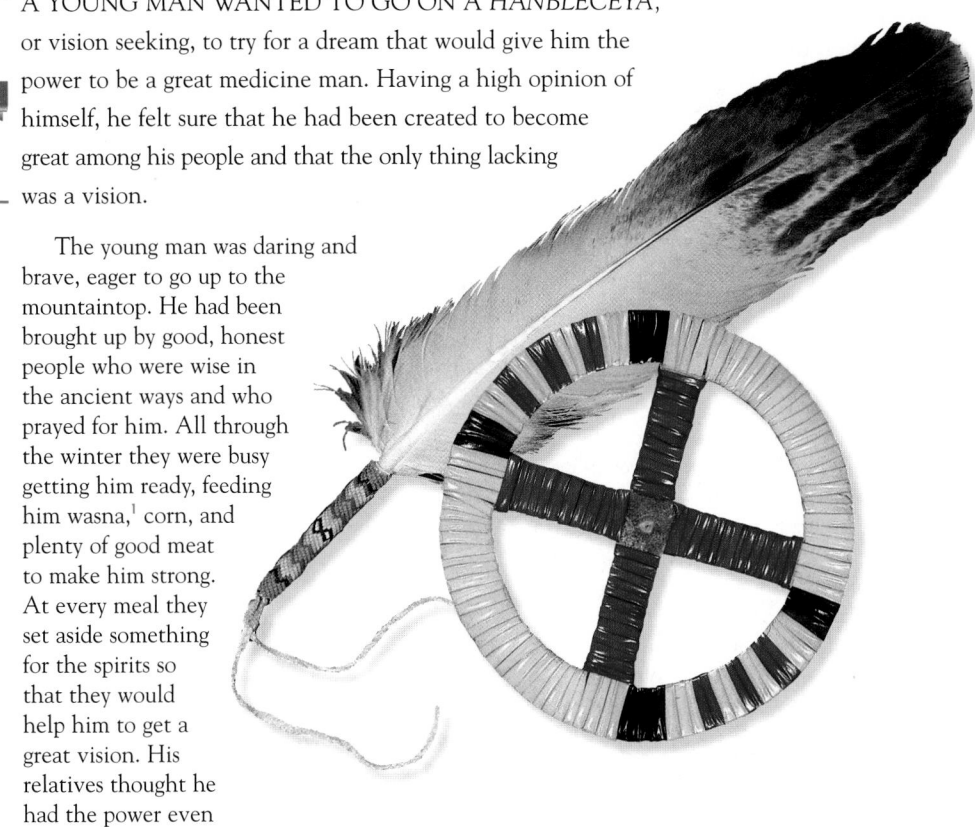

A YOUNG MAN WANTED TO GO ON A *HANBLECEYA*,
or vision seeking, to try for a dream that would give him the
power to be a great medicine man. Having a high opinion of
himself, he felt sure that he had been created to become
great among his people and that the only thing lacking
was a vision.

A

The young man was daring and
brave, eager to go up to the
mountaintop. He had been
brought up by good, honest
people who were wise in
the ancient ways and who
prayed for him. All through
the winter they were busy
getting him ready, feeding
him wasna,[1] corn, and
plenty of good meat
to make him strong.
At every meal they
set aside something
for the spirits so
that they would
help him to get a
great vision. His
relatives thought he
had the power even

---

1. *Wasna* is a high-energy food made of meat, fat, and berries
   pounded together.

B Literary Elements

LEGEND After students read the phrase "as this is an Indian legend," ask them to tell what they know about legends. Did they recognize that this story was a legend? If so, how?

C Active Reading

PREDICT What do students believe will happen? Point out that there have been a few helpful clues. *(The young man's vanity and the confidence with which he prepares for his ordeal will suggest to some students that he will learn a bitter lesson.)*

D Active Reading

RESPOND Ask students what they think of the young man. Is he a fool, a hero, or a little of both?

Did You Know?
A *travois* (trə voi′) is a V-shaped sled made of hide or netting supported by two long poles that are harnessed to a horse or dog.

before he went up, but that was putting the cart before the horse, or rather the travois before the horse, as this is an Indian legend.

When at last he started on his quest, it was a beautiful morning in late spring. The grass was up, the leaves were out, nature was at its best. Two medicine men accompanied him. They put up a sweat lodge[2] to purify him in the hot, white breath of the sacred steam. They sanctified him with the incense of sweet grass, rubbing his body with sage, fanning it with an eagle's wing. They went to the hilltop with him to prepare the vision pit and make an offering of tobacco bundles. Then they told the young man to cry, to humble himself, to ask for holiness, to cry for power, for a sign from the Great Spirit, for a gift which would make him into a medicine man. After they had done all they could, they left him there.

He spent the first night in the hole the medicine men had dug for him, trembling and crying out loudly. Fear kept him awake, yet he was cocky, ready to wrestle with the spirits for the vision, the power he wanted. But no dreams came to ease his mind. Toward morning before the sun came up, he heard a voice in the swirling white mists of dawn. Speaking from no particular direction, as if it came from different places, it said: "See here, young

man, there are other spots you could have picked; there are other hills around here. Why don't you go there to cry for a dream? You disturbed us all night, all us creatures and birds; you even kept the trees awake. We couldn't sleep. Why should you cry here? You're a brash young man, not yet ready or worthy to receive a vision."

But the young man clenched his teeth, determined to stick it out, resolved to force that vision to come. He spent another day in the pit, begging for enlightenment which would not come, and then another night of fear and cold and hunger.

When dawn arrived once more, he heard the voice again: "Stop disturbing us; go away!" The same thing happened the third morning. By this time he was faint with hunger, thirst, and anxiety. Even the air seemed to oppress him, to fight him. He was panting. His stomach felt shriveled up, shrunk tight against his backbone. But he was determined to endure one more night, the fourth and last. Surely the vision would come. But again he cried for it out of the dark and loneliness until he was hoarse, and still he had no dream.

Just before daybreak he heard the same voice again, very angry: "Why are you still here?" He knew then that he had suffered in vain; now he would have to go back to his people and confess that he had gained no knowledge and no power. The only thing he could tell them was that he got bawled out every morning. Sad and cross, he replied, "I can't help myself; this is my last day, and I'm crying my eyes out. I know you told me to go home, but who are you to give me orders? I don't know you. I'm going to stay until my uncles come to fetch me, whether you like it or not."

---

2. A *sweat lodge* is a hut made of branches bent and tied to form a framework, which is covered by hides or blankets. Inside, steam is produced by pouring or sprinkling water over red-hot rocks contained in a central pit.

Vocabulary
brash (brash) *adj.* boldly disrespectful

MEETING INDIVIDUAL NEEDS — ENGLISH LANGUAGE LEARNERS

The Oral Tradition "The Vision Quest" has some qualities of a legend (see page 92). Although now in written form, it likely originated as an oral story, passed down through the generations. Remind students that people still love to hear stories. English language learners may have stories to share that they have never seen in writing.

Activity Have students think of some stories that they could tell aloud. Then have students pair up and each tell one story to his or her partner. Invite students to recite their partner's story to the class.

Additional Resources
📁 *English Language Learners Sourcebook*

All at once there was a rumble from a larger mountain that stood behind the hill. It became a mighty roar, and the whole hill trembled. The wind started to blow. The young man looked up and saw a boulder poised on the mountain's summit. He saw lightning hit it, saw it sway. Slowly the boulder moved. Slowly at first, then faster and faster, it came tumbling down the mountainside, churning up earth, snapping huge trees as if they were little twigs. And the boulder was coming right down on him!

The young man cried out in terror. He was paralyzed with fear, unable to move. The boulder dwarfed everything in view; it towered over the vision pit. But just as it was an arm's length away and about to crush him, it stopped. Then, as the young man stared open-mouthed, his hair standing up, his eyes starting out of his head, the boulder *rolled up the mountain*, all the way to the top. He could hardly believe what he saw. He was still cowering motionless when he heard the roar and rumble again and saw that immense boulder coming down at him once more. This time he managed to jump out of his vision pit at the last moment. The boulder crushed it, obliterated it, grinding the young man's pipe and gourd rattle into dust.

Again the boulder rolled up the mountain, and again it came down. "I'm leaving, I'm leaving!" hollered the young man.

Regaining his power of motion, he scrambled down the hill as fast as he could. This time the boulder actually leap-frogged over him, bouncing down the slope, crushing and pulverizing everything in its way. He ran unseeingly, stumbling, falling, getting up again. He did not even notice the boulder rolling up once more and coming down for the fourth time. On this last and most fearful descent, it flew through the air in a giant leap, landing right in front of him and embedding itself so deeply in the earth that only its top was visible. The ground shook itself like a wet dog coming out of a stream and flung the young man this way and that.

Gaunt, bruised, and shaken, he stumbled back to his village. To the medicine men he said: "I have received no vision and gained no knowledge. I have made the spirits angry. It was all for nothing." **E**

"Well, you did find out one thing," said the older of the two, who was his uncle. "You went after your vision like a hunter after buffalo, or a warrior after scalps. You were fighting the spirits. You thought they owed you a vision. Suffering alone brings no vision nor does courage, nor does sheer will power. A vision comes as a gift born of humility, of wisdom, and of patience. If from your vision quest you have learned nothing but this, then you have already learned much. Think about it." **F**

Vocabulary
obliterate (ə blit′ ə rāt′) *v.* to destroy completely
gaunt (gônt) *adj.* extremely thin and hollow-eyed, as from hunger or illness; "looking like skin and bones"
humility (hū mil′ ə tē) *n.* the quality of being humble or modest

THE SHORT STORY ✒ 91

E Critical Thinking

JUDGING THE CREDIBILITY OF A SOURCE Did the young man really fail to have a vision? *(Some students may argue that the menacing boulder itself was a vision, although not what the protagonist had been anticipating.)*

F Literary Elements

IRONY How can a failure also be a success? Ask students how the ending of this story is ironic. *(The young man's expectations are shattered, but he learns an important lesson, which is what he had hoped for in the first place.)*

Thematic Focus

Transitions Will the young man act more humbly as a result of this experience? Will he go on another vision quest with greater success? Ask students whether they believe he has truly undergone a change in attitude.

☑ ASSESSMENT OPTIONS

📁 *Quick Checks,* p. 7

® *The following videotape program is available from Glencoe. Be sure to preview the video for appropriateness for your class.*

• **The Real West: Sitting Bull and the Great Sioux Nation***

Grammar and Language *Minilesson*

Infinitive and Prepositional Phrases
Write the following sentences on the board, underlining the phrases beginning with the word *to* in each:

He managed <u>to jump out</u> of his vision pit.
He stumbled back <u>to his village</u>.

Point out that the word *to* is used to introduce both infinitive and prepositional phrases. In the first case *to* is followed by

a verb and in the second by a noun or pronoun.

Activity Ask students to read the first page of the story again, locating all the phrases beginning with the word *to*. Have them identify the phrases as infinitive or prepositional. *(The word* to *is used eight times on page 89, only once as a preposition:* to the mountaintop.) **L2**

Additional Resources

📖 *Grammar and Language Transparency 7*

📑 *Grammar and Language Workbook,* pp. 89, 97

📑 *Grammar and Composition Handbook,* Lessons 3.1, 3.3

📑 *Writer's Choice,* Lessons 12.1, 12.3

91

Responding to
the Selection

Personal Response

Encourage students to explain *why* they were struck or surprised by the aspects of the story they have chosen.

ANALYZING LITERATURE

1. The young man is expecting a vision that will enable him to become a great medicine man. He is vain and overconfident.
2. The voice complains about the noise the young man makes, asks him why he chose that spot, and finally orders him away. The youth is defiant, determined to experience a vision.
3. The quest ends in a failure to achieve a vision. He believes he has wasted his time.
4. The quester's uncle suggests that the value of humility is an important lesson to learn. Students may or may not think the response is appropriate.
5. The central conflict is between the young man and the spirit world.
6. Students may say that the humor and modern language added to the story. Examples of modern language include the dialogue between the young man and the spirit. There is humor in the threatening rock and in the young man's terrified response.
7. Students may say that the experience helped them learn humility or patience.
8. The young man experiences failure. If he listens to his uncle, he will behave more humbly in the future and treat the spirits with respect.

EXTENDING YOUR RESPONSE

Literature Groups Suggest to students that the young man's future behavior may depend upon how he responded to his uncle at the end of the story. **COLLAB. LEARN.**

Creative Writing Point out to students that a rap version of this story would also be in the spirit of the Native American custom of oral transmission.

Responding to Literature

Personal Response

What aspect of this story struck you most forcefully? Did anything surprise or impress you? Share your reactions with your classmates.

ANALYZING LITERATURE

RECALL AND INTERPRET

1. What kind of vision is the young man expecting? What does his expectation tell you about him?
2. What are some of the things the voice in the mountains says? How would you describe the vision quester's reaction to the voice?
3. How does the young man's vision quest end? Based on what he reports to the medicine men, what do you think his attitude is about his quest?
4. What response does the vision quester's uncle give him? In your opinion, is the response appropriate?

EVALUATE AND CONNECT

5. What is the central **conflict** in this story?
6. Do you think that the humor and modern language in the story added to or took away from its effectiveness for you? Use examples from the story to explain your answer.
7. Look over your response to the Focus Activity on page 88 and think of a time when you failed to reach a goal you had set for yourself. What did you learn from the experience?
8. Theme Connections   In what way was this experience a transition for the young man? How was he different afterwards?

EXTENDING YOUR RESPONSE

Literature Groups
Debate the Question   Do you think the young man would ever undertake another vision quest? Form two groups, one that will support a *yes* answer, and one supporting *no*. Hold a debate, with each group giving details from the story to back up its position.

Creative Writing
Summary in Verse   Write a song, poem, or limerick that summarizes the main points of "The Vision Quest." First, decide which elements of the story should be included. Then, include those elements in either a serious or humorous poem or song.

📖 **Save your work for your portfolio.**

Literary ELEMENTS

Legend
A **legend** is a traditional narrative, such as a story or poem, that has been handed down from one generation to the next. It is presented as a type of history, even though it may not be factually accurate. Most legends help convey a culture's learning, knowledge, and values.

1. What Native American custom is central to this story?
2. Which parts of the story might be true and which parts could not be proven true?
3. What are some of the values that this story transmits?

● See **Literary Terms Handbook,** p. R7.

LITERARY ELEMENTS

1. The custom of seeking a vision is central to the story.
2. The four nights in a sweat lodge are likely based on Native American custom. The spirit voices and the threatening boulder could not be proven true.
3. The story teaches the importance of humility, also of respect for one's elders and the natural world.

Additional Resources
🖊 *Literary Elements Transparency 7*

✅ ASSESSMENT OPTIONS

📁 *Quick Checks,* p. 7
📁 *Selection and Theme Assessment,* pp. 13–14
📁 *Performance Assessment,* p. 7
💾 *Testmaker*

COMPARING *selections*

Through the **Tunnel** and The **V**ision **Q**uest

COMPARE **GOALS**

Both Jerry and the vision quester set important goals for themselves.

1. How are their goals similar?
2. How are they different?
3. Think about what the two boys actually accomplish and how they feel about their accomplishments. How does the outcome of Jerry's experience compare with that of the vision quester's trial? Support your response with details from the stories.

COMPARE **CHALLENGES**

Who faced a greater challenge, Jerry or the vision quester?

- In a small group, take turns stating your opinion and supporting it with facts and reasons. Try to persuade other group members that your opinion is correct.
- Listen to fellow group members as they argue their side of this issue.
- As a group, decide which members presented the most persuasive arguments for their opinion and why those presentations were so convincing.
- Share your group's best arguments with the class. Try to decide, as a class, which character faced a greater challenge.

COMPARE **CUSTOMS**

The boys in both stories experienced a transition—a passage along the road from childhood to adulthood. Most societies have initiation rituals to mark that transition. Also, groups within societies often set tasks that must be accomplished before a person can be a full member of the group. Investigate the initiation customs of a society or a group, such as a club or service organization. You might interview members of the group or use the library or the Internet for your research. Then, based on your findings, write an analysis that compares the initiation customs of the group you studied with those of the culture in one of these stories.

THE SHORT STORY ✿ 93

COMPARING *selections*

Objective

- To compare two short stories that deal with the theme of transition

COMPARE **GOALS**

1. Both goals are opportunities for the boys to mature. Both goals become learning experiences.
2. One quest is a personal goal; the vision quest is a community ritual. One goal requires physical action while the other requires a more subtle approach.
3. Jerry accomplishes his goal and makes the transition from childhood to adulthood. While the vision quester does not receive a vision, he learns that as he grows in humility, the vision will come.

COMPARE **CHALLENGES**

Groups' persuasive arguments should
- include opinions and reasons with well-chosen facts and details.
- be chosen on the basis of group discussion and evaluation.
  COLLAB. LEARN.

Additional Resources
📁 *Literature Groups Sourcebook*

COMPARE **CUSTOMS**

Students' analyses should
- compare the initiation event in one of the stories with the initiation customs of a group they have researched.

Teaching Options

PORTFOLIO OPTIONS

Select and Reflect Have students reflect on their analyses for the activity above by asking themselves these questions:
- Does my analysis include background information about each custom?
- In what ways does my analysis detail the steps involved in each custom?

Students should clip their reflections to their analyses and place them in their portfolios. At a later time, they might consider using the comments to revise their analyses as portfolio showcase pieces. **L2**

Additional Resources
📁 *Writing Assessment and Portfolio Management,* pp. 20–22

THE SHORT STORY ✿ 93

Objectives

- To read and analyze a short story about the remarkable way in which one boy experiences the passage from adolescence to adulthood
- To identify a moral in a short story
- To write an evaluation of a literary technique

Skills

Reading/Thinking: Inferring; Drawing Conclusions; Comparing and Contrasting
Writing: Dialogue
Vocabulary: The Prefix *Ante-*
Grammar/Language: Capitalization of Proper Nouns
Listening/Speaking: Speech
Collaboration: Literature Groups

Motivating

→ OPTIONS

Selection Focus Transparency 8: Have students view and discuss *The Shelton with Sunspots*, a painting by Georgia O'Keeffe.

Focus Activity: Have students discuss with their partners why the activities they have listed are usually done by adults.

Before You Read

By the Waters of Babylon

FOCUS ACTIVITY

Have you ever accomplished—or wanted to accomplish—a task that is usually thought of as an adult responsibility?

SHARING IDEAS List things that you have done, or would like to do, that are usually considered adult responsibilities. Share your list with a partner.

SETTING A PURPOSE Read to discover the remarkable way in which one boy experiences the passage from adolescence to adulthood.

BACKGROUND

The Time and Place
The events of this story unfold in a strange and forbidding landscape, at an unspecified time.

Did You Know?
The title "By the Waters of Babylon" alludes to Psalm 137, from the Bible, which begins:

"By the rivers of Babylon, there we sat down, yea, we wept, when we remembered Zion."

The psalm describes the Israelites' intense grief over the destruction of their sacred temple, their separation from their homeland Jerusalem (referred to here as Zion), and their enforced captivity at the hands of the Babylonians.

VOCABULARY PREVIEW

bade (bād) *v.* past tense of *bid,* to command, order, or ask; p. 96
anteroom (an′ tē rōōm′) *n.* a small room serving as a waiting area or entrance to a larger, main room; p. 101
perplexed (pər plekst′) *adj.* troubled with doubt or uncertainty; puzzled; p. 103

Meet Stephen Vincent Benét

Stephen Vincent Benét (bə nā′) was fascinated and inspired by the American past. Historical themes and the American landscape dominate his work, which includes novels, poetry, plays, radio scripts, and short stories. Benét is most celebrated for his poetry, for which he was awarded two Pulitzer Prizes—the first, in 1929, for his epic poem *John Brown's Body*, and the second, in 1944, for another long poem entitled *Western Star.*

Stephen Vincent Benét was born in Bethlehem, Pennsylvania, in 1898; he died in New York City in 1943. This story was first published in 1937.

RESOURCE MANAGER

Lesson Planning Resource
The *Unit One Planning Guide* (pp. 64–71) provides additional lesson notes and reduced versions of all print resources.

📁 **Other Print Resources**
- Active Reading Guide, p. 8
- Vocabulary Practice, p. 8
- Reading Workbook, p. 13
- Grammar and Language Workbook, pp. 49, 237
- Grammar and Composition Handbook, Lessons 1.1, 10.3

- Quick Checks, p. 8
- Selection and Theme Assessment, pp. 15–16
- Performance Assessment, p. 8
- Spanish Summaries, p. 8
- Inclusion Strategies
- English Language Learners Sourcebook

 Transparencies
- Selection Focus 8
- Literary Elements 8
- Grammar and Language 8

Technology
🎧 Audio Library
🎧 Spanish Audio Library
💻 Glencoe Literature Web Site
💾 Testmaker

BY THE WATERS OF BABYLON

The north and the west and the south are good hunting ground, but it is forbidden to go east. It is forbidden to go to any of the Dead Places except to search for metal and then he who touches the metal must be a priest or the son of a priest. Afterwards, both the man and the metal must be purified. These are the rules and the laws; they are well made. It is forbidden to cross the great river and look upon the place that was the Place of the Gods—this is most strictly forbidden. We do not even say its name though we know its name. It is there that spirits live, and demons—it is there that there are the ashes of the Great Burning. These things are forbidden—they have been forbidden since the beginning of time.

My father is a priest; I am the son of a priest. I have been in the Dead Places near us, with my father—at first, I was afraid. When my father went into the house to search for the metal, I stood by the door and my heart felt small and weak. It was a dead man's house, a spirit house. It did not have the smell of man, though there were old bones in a corner. But it is not fitting that a priest's son should show fear. I looked at the bones in the shadow and kept my voice still.

Then my father came out with the metal—a good, strong piece. He looked at me with both eyes but I had not run away. He gave me the metal to hold—I took it and did not die. So he knew that I was truly his son and would be a priest in my time. That was when I was very young—nevertheless, my brothers would not have done it, though they are good hunters. After that,

Stephen Vincent Benét

SUMMARY

The narrator is John, the son of a priest in an unspecified time and culture. To become a priest, John sets off on a journey alone. Although it is forbidden, he goes to the Place of the Gods, where he finds marks from the Great Burning. He finds broken towers, furniture, and paintings, but no people. In a vision he sees the Place of the Gods first with lights, roads, and people, then destroyed by fire and poison mist. On waking, John finds the body of a preserved "god" and realizes that he was a man. At home John's father will not let him tell of his discovery. But John plans to rebuild the civilization of "newyork" when he becomes chief priest.

📁 *Spanish Summaries,* p. 8

A **Active Reading**

QUESTION Have students read the first paragraph and summarize the setting. Why might the author purposely make the setting vague?

Additional Resources
📁 *Active Reading Guide*
🎧 *Audio Library*
🎧 *Spanish Audio Library*

Teaching Options

CONNECTING TO OTHER SELECTIONS

The chart at the right shows three ways to connect "By the Waters of Babylon" to selections in this book.

For specific teaching strategies, see the *Unit One Planning Guide,* pages 67–68.

Connection	Title
Life Skills: Life-long Learning	→ "Through the Tunnel," p. 76
Thematic: Discoveries	→ "Pizza in Warsaw, Torte in Prague," p. 507
Literary: Conflict	→ *Julius Caesar,* p. 778

B Literary Elements

CHARACTER Ask students to characterize the narrator. *(He is brave, intelligent, hungry for knowledge, and mature beyond his years.)*

Cultural Note

The narrator indicates that his people are more advanced than the Forest People because "our women spin wool on the wheel." Spinning is the process by which wool or other fibers are twisted together to make yarn or thread, which can then be woven into cloth. Most ancient peoples knew how to spin and weave some kind of cloth. Prior to that, people wore the skins of the animals they hunted and killed to eat. Probably the Forest People wear animal skins since they do not know how to spin.

C Literary Elements

FIGURES OF SPEECH: *Metaphor*
Remind students that a metaphor is a comparison between two unlike things that does not use the word *like* or *as*. Have them explain what the narrator means by the metaphor "my spirit was a cool stone." *(His state of mind is solid, calm, and peaceful.)*

Teaching Options

---

they gave me the good piece of meat and the warm corner by the fire. My father watched over me—he was glad that I should be a priest. But when I boasted or wept without a reason, he punished me more strictly than my brothers. That was right.

After a time, I myself was allowed to go into the dead houses and search for metal. So I learned the ways of those houses—and if I saw bones, I was no longer afraid. The bones are light and old—sometimes they will fall into dust if you touch them. But that is a great sin.

I was taught the chants and the spells— I was taught how to stop the running of blood from a wound and many secrets. A priest must know many secrets—that was what my father said. If the hunters think we do all things by chants and spells, they may believe so—it does not hurt them. I was taught how to read in the old books and how to make the old writings—that was hard and took a long time. My knowledge made me happy—it was like a fire in my heart. Most of all, I liked to hear of the Old Days and the stories of the gods. I asked myself many questions that I could not answer, but it was good to ask them. At night, I would lie awake and listen to the wind—it seemed to me that it was the voice of the gods as they flew through the air.

Did You Know?
A *grub* is the soft, wormlike larva of an insect, especially of a beetle.

We are not ignorant like the Forest People— our women spin wool on the wheel, our priests wear a white robe. We do not eat grubs from the tree, we have not forgotten the old writings, although they are hard to understand. Nevertheless, my knowledge and my lack of knowledge burned in me—I wished to know more. When I was a man at last, I came to my father and said, "It is time for me to go on my journey. Give me your leave."

He looked at me for a long time, stroking his beard, then he said at last, "Yes. It is time." That night, in the house of the priesthood, I asked for and received purification. My body hurt but my spirit was a cool stone. — C It was my father himself who questioned me about my dreams.

He bade me look into the smoke of the fire and see—I saw and told what I saw. It was what I have always seen—a river, and, beyond it, a great Dead Place and in it the gods walking. I have always thought about that. His eyes were stern when I told him— he was no longer my father but a priest. He said, "This is a strong dream."

"It is mine," I said, while the smoke waved and my head felt light. They were singing the Star song in the outer chamber and it was like the buzzing of bees in my head.

He asked me how the gods were dressed and I told him how they were dressed. We know how they were dressed from the book, but I saw them as if they were before me. When I had finished, he threw the sticks three times and studied them as they fell.

"This is a very strong dream," he said. "It may eat you up."

"I am not afraid," I said and looked at him with both eyes. My voice sounded thin in my ears but that was because of the smoke.

He touched me on the breast and the forehead. He gave me the bow and the three arrows.

"Take them," he said. "It is forbidden to travel east. It is forbidden to cross the river. It is forbidden to go to the Place of the Gods. All these things are forbidden."

Vocabulary
bade (băd) *v.* past tense of *bid*, to command, order, or ask

---

MEETING INDIVIDUAL NEEDS ENGLISH LANGUAGE LEARNERS

Homographs Explain that some sets of words may be spelled the same but have different meanings. On page 96, *leave* does not mean "to go away" but "permission." Encourage English language learners to check a dictionary if the meaning of a word they know does not fit the context of a sentence.

Activity Have students look up each word below in a dictionary and write a sentence using the word's most common meaning and then one using the word as it is used in the story. *fast (fasting)* (p. 97), *wind* (p. 97), *bow* (p. 97), *current* (p. 99), *banks* (p. 99), *close* (p. 102)

Additional Resources
English Language Learners Sourcebook

D "All these things are forbidden," I said, but it was my voice that spoke and not my spirit. He looked at me again.

E "My son," he said. "Once I had young dreams. If your dreams do not eat you up, you may be a great priest. If they eat you, you are still my son. Now go on your journey."

D I went fasting, as is the law. My body hurt but not my heart. When the dawn came, I was out of sight of the village. I prayed and purified myself, waiting for a sign. The sign was an eagle. It flew east.

Sometimes signs are sent by bad spirits. I waited again on the flat rock, fasting, taking no food. I was very still—I could feel the sky above me and the earth beneath. I waited till the sun was beginning to sink. Then three deer passed in the valley, going east—they did not wind me or see me. There was a white fawn with them—a very great sign.

I followed them, at a distance, waiting for what would happen. My heart was troubled about going east, yet I knew that I must go. My head hummed with my fasting—I did not even see the panther spring upon the white fawn. But, before I knew it, the bow was in my hand. I shouted and the panther lifted his head from the fawn. It is not easy to kill a panther with one arrow but the arrow went through his eye and into his brain. He died as he tried to spring—he rolled over, tearing at the ground. Then I knew I was meant to go east—I knew that was my journey. When the night came, I made my fire and roasted meat.

Soleil Couchant. Eugene Boudin (1824–1898). Pastel on paper, 6⅛ x 8¼ in. Private collection.
Viewing the painting: How does this painting reflect the mood of John's dreams?

D Literary Elements

MORAL Call attention to the author's use of phrases such as "my voice... spoke and not my spirit," "my body hurt but not my heart," "my body hurt but my spirit was a cool stone." Have students discuss these contrasts and consider how they might contribute to a moral of the story. *(The author is emphasizing that people have an inner life consisting of conscience, inner strength, and a moral sense. This "spirit" is separate from physical facts such as pain or hunger.)*

E Critical Thinking

INFERRING Discuss John's father's remark that he too once had "young dreams." Ask students to infer what John's dreams are. *(He wants to cross the river and explore the Place of the Gods.)*

VIEWING THE PAINTING

The French title of the painting translates as "Sunset." Boudin was a friend of Claude Monet's and introduced Monet to landscape painting.

Viewing Response *The painting reflects the somber, apocalyptic mood of John's dream.*

MEETING INDIVIDUAL NEEDS

INCLUSION STRATEGIES

Learning Disabled Some students may be confused by the unrealistic setting of the story. Point out that some stories, like "Through the Tunnel," describe characters and situations similar to those in real life. Other stories have elements that are not part of realistic experience.

Activity Have students make a chart with two columns headed *Real Life* and *Imaginary*. Have them write details from the story in each column. For example, searching for pieces of metal is an imaginary detail not done in any real culture. Have students compare and discuss the charts in small groups. **L1**

Additional Resources
📁 *Inclusion Strategies*

Teaching Options

F Active Reading

EVALUATE Have students decide whether John has done the right thing in going east in defiance of his father's warnings. How does he rationalize his action to himself? *(He has good luck in finding a knife, finding game, and avoiding discovery by the Forest People, so he thinks some force is telling him he did the right thing.)*

G Literary Elements

MORAL What character traits does John demonstrate when he says, "It is better to lose one's life than one's spirit"? How does the statement relate to a possible moral of the story? *(The statement shows wisdom, curiosity, courage, and idealism. It states a moral of the story.)*

H Author's Craft

FIGURES OF SPEECH Have students explain how the author uses simile and metaphor to reiterate his idea of the human spirit. *(He uses similes to describe how his fear affects him physically and a metaphor to describe the uneasiness of his mind. He emphasizes the separation of body and spirit when he describes his physical condition as "cold" and his mental as "burning.")*

It is eight suns' journey to the east and a man passes by many Dead Places. The Forest People are afraid of them but I am not. Once I made my fire on the edge of a Dead Place at night and, next morning, in the dead house, I found a good knife, little rusted. That was small to what came afterward but it made my heart feel big. Always when I looked for game, it was in front of my arrow, and twice I passed hunting parties of the Forest People without their knowing. So I knew my magic was strong and my journey clean, in spite of the law.

Toward the setting of the eighth sun, I came to the banks of the great river. It was half-a-day's journey after I had left the god-road—we do not use the god-roads now for they are falling apart into great blocks of stone, and the forest is safer going. A long way off, I had seen the water through trees but the trees were thick. At last, I came out upon an open place at the top of a cliff. There was the great river below, like a giant in the sun. It is very long, very wide. It could eat all the streams we know and still be thirsty. Its name is Ou-dis-sun, the Sacred, the Long. No man of my tribe had seen it, not even my father, the priest. It was magic and I prayed.

Then I raised my eyes and looked south. It was there, the Place of the Gods.

How can I tell what it was like—you do not know. It was there, in the red light, and they were too big to be houses. It was there with the red light upon it, mighty and ruined. I knew that in another moment the gods would see me. I covered my eyes with my hands and crept back into the forest.

Surely, that was enough to do, and live. Surely it was enough to spend the night upon the cliff. The Forest People themselves do not come near. Yet, all through the night, I knew that I should have to cross the river and walk in the places of the gods, although

the gods ate me up. My magic did not help me at all and yet there was a fire in my bowels, a fire in my mind. When the sun rose, I thought, "My journey has been clean. Now I will go home from my journey." But, even as I thought so, I knew I could not. If I went to the Place of the Gods, I would surely die, but, if I did not go, I could never be at peace with my spirit again. It is better to lose one's life than one's spirit, if one is a priest and the son of a priest.

Nevertheless, as I made the raft, the tears ran out of my eyes. The Forest People could have killed me without fight, if they had come upon me then, but they did not come. When the raft was made, I said the sayings for the dead and painted myself for death. My heart was cold as a frog and my knees like water, but the burning in my mind would not let me have peace. As I pushed the raft from the shore, I began my death song—I had the right. It was a fine song.

"I am John, son of John," I sang. "My people are the Hill People. They are the men.
I go into the Dead Places but I am not slain.
I take the metal from the Dead Places but I am not blasted.
I travel upon the god-roads and am not afraid. E-yah! I have killed the panther, I have killed the fawn!
E-yah! I have come to the great river. No man has come there before.
It is forbidden to go east, but I have gone, forbidden to go on the great river, but I am there.
Open your hearts, you spirits, and hear my song.
Now I go to the Place of the Gods, I shall not return.
My body is painted for death and my limbs weak, but my heart is big as I go to the Place of the Gods!"

Musical Musically talented students can add to their classmates' enjoyment of the story.

Activity Challenge students to present John's song in a variety of forms such as a church chant, a rap song, an American Indian chant, and a folk song. They may work individually, with a partner, or with a group and use any musical instruments they wish. After the performances, have the class discuss the style to which the song best lends itself. **L1 COLLAB. LEARN.**

Stephen Vincent Benét ∿

All the same, when I came to the Place of the Gods, I was afraid, afraid. The current of the great river is very strong—it gripped my raft with its hands. That was magic, for the river itself is wide and calm. I could feel evil spirits about me, in the bright morning; I could feel their breath on my neck as I was swept down the stream. Never have I been so much alone—I tried to think of my knowledge, but it was a squirrel's heap of winter nuts. There was no strength in my knowledge any more and I felt small and naked as a new-hatched bird—alone upon the great river, the servant of the gods.

Yet, after a while, my eyes were opened and I saw. I saw both banks of the river—I saw that once there had been god-roads across it, though now they were broken and fallen like broken vines. Very great they were, and wonderful and broken—broken in the time of the Great Burning when the fire fell out of the sky. And always the current took me nearer to the Place of the Gods, and the huge ruins rose before my eyes.

I do not know the customs of rivers—we are the People of the Hills. I tried to guide my raft with the pole but it spun around. I thought the river meant to take me past the Place of the Gods and out into the Bitter Water of the legends. I grew angry then—my heart felt strong. I said aloud, "I am a priest and the son of a priest!" The gods heard me—they showed me how to paddle with the pole on one side of the raft. The current changed itself—I drew near to the Place of the Gods.

When I was very near, my raft struck and turned over. I can swim in our lakes—I swam to the shore. There was a great spike of rusted metal sticking out into the river—I hauled myself up upon it and sat there, panting. I had saved my bow and two arrows and the knife I found in the Dead Place but that was all. My raft went whirling downstream toward the Bitter Water. I looked after it, and thought if it had trod me under, at least I would be safely dead. Nevertheless, when I had dried my bowstring and restrung it, I walked forward to the Place of the Gods.

It felt like ground underfoot; it did not burn me. It is not true what some of the tales say, that the ground there burns forever, for I have been there. Here and there were the marks and stains of the Great Burning, on the ruins, that is true. But they were old marks and old stains. It is not true either, what some of our priests say, that it is an island covered with fogs and enchantments. It is not. It is a great Dead Place—greater than any Dead Place we know. Everywhere in it there are god-roads, though most are cracked and broken. Everywhere there are the ruins of the high towers of the gods.

How shall I tell what I saw? I went carefully, my strung bow in my hand, my skin ready for danger. There should have been the wailings of spirits and the shrieks of demons, but there were not. It was very silent and sunny where I had landed—the wind and the rain and the birds that drop seeds had done their work—the grass grew in the cracks of the broken stone. It is a fair island—no wonder the gods built there. If I had come there, a god, I also would have built.

How shall I tell what I saw? The towers are not all broken—here and there one still stands, like a great tree in a forest, and the birds nest high. But the towers themselves look blind, for the gods are gone. I saw a fish hawk, catching fish in the river. I saw a little dance of white butterflies over a great heap of broken stones and columns. I went there and looked about me—there was a carved stone with cut-letters, broken in half. I can read letters but I could not understand these. They said UBTREAS. There was also the shattered

---

I Literary Elements

FIGURES OF SPEECH: *Metaphor* Ask students to explain how John's knowledge is "a squirrel's heap of winter nuts." *(It is stored in his mind somewhere, but he cannot use it at the moment. Also, it seems small and useless in his current situation.)*

J Critical Thinking

INFERRING How has the Dead Place been described to John? Why has it been characterized in this way? *(He has been told that the ground there burns forever, that the wailings and shrieks of demons can be heard, and that it is covered with fogs and enchantments. These things were probably true to some extent in the past. Because of the frightening aspects of the place, additional legends have developed surrounding it; these legends are used to keep young people from exploring the place.)*

K Active Reading

VISUALIZE Encourage students to visualize John and the landscape in which he finds himself. What kind of expression might John's face have? *(He would probably have a wide-eyed, open look of wonder and curiosity.)*

MULTIPLE LEARNING STYLES

MEETING INDIVIDUAL NEEDS

Spatial The author's description of a deserted, fallen city being gradually taken over by nature lends itself to artistic interpretation.

Activity Have students assemble drawing paper and pencil, charcoal, or crayons. Explain that you will read the description of the Dead Place (the last three paragraphs of page 99) aloud. As you do so, students should sketch the landscape. **L2**

The Father of Our Country Two prominent statues of George Washington stand in New York City in Washington Square in Greenwich Village. They are called *Washington at War* and *Washington at Peace*.

L Critical Thinking

DRAWING CONCLUSIONS Use the following model to help students draw conclusions about the Dead Place.

Model: The author has said that the Dead Place is surrounded by many broken-down roads. It has tall towers, many also broken, and broken stones with parts of words that might be English. There are many pigeons. Food and drink are stored in bottles and jars. All of these details make me think that the place could be the ruins of a 20th-century American city.

M Literary Elements

IMAGERY Remind students that images are descriptions that appeal to one or more of the five senses. Help students identify the vivid imagery used to describe the animals in the Dead Place. To which senses do the images appeal? *(The images of the green-eyed cats wailing appeal to the senses of sight and sound; the image of the squeaking rats appeals to the sense of sound; the image of the laughing dog appeals to the sense of sight.)*

Teaching Options

---

image of a man or a god. It had been made of white stone and he wore his hair tied back like a woman's. His name was ASHING, as I read on the cracked half of a stone. I thought it wise to pray to ASHING, though I do not know that god.

How shall I tell what I saw? There was no smell of man left, on stone or metal. Nor were there many trees in that wilderness of stone. There are many pigeons, nesting and dropping in the towers—the gods must have loved them, or, perhaps, they used them for sacrifices. There are wild cats that roam the god-roads, green-eyed, unafraid of man. At night they wail like demons but they are not demons. The wild dogs are more dangerous, for they hunt in a pack, but them I did not meet till later. Everywhere there are the carved stones, carved with magical numbers or words.

I went north—I did not try to hide myself. When a god or a demon saw me, then I would die, but meanwhile I was no longer afraid. My hunger for knowledge burned in me—there was so much that I could not understand. After a while, I knew that my belly was hungry. I could have hunted for my meat, but I did not hunt. It is known that the gods did not hunt as we do—they got their food from enchanted boxes and jars. Sometimes these are still found in the Dead Places—once, when I was a child and foolish, I opened such a jar and tasted it and found the food sweet. But my father found out and punished me for it strictly, for, often, that food is death. Now, though, I had long gone past what was forbidden, and I entered the likeliest towers, looking for the food of the gods.

I found it at last in the ruins of a great temple in the mid-city. A mighty temple it must have been, for the roof was painted like the sky at night with its stars—that much

I could see, though the colors were faint and dim. It went down into great caves and tunnels—perhaps they kept their slaves there. But when I started to climb down, I heard the squeaking of rats, so I did not go—rats are unclean, and there must have been many tribes of them, from the squeaking. But near there, I found food, in the heart of a ruin, behind a door that still opened. I ate only the fruits from the jars—they had a very sweet taste. There was drink, too, in bottles of glass—the drink of the gods was strong and made my head swim. After I had eaten and drunk, I slept on the top of a stone, my bow at my side.

When I woke, the sun was low. Looking down from where I lay, I saw a dog sitting on his haunches. His tongue was hanging out of his mouth; he looked as if he were laughing. He was a big dog, with a gray-brown coat, as big as a wolf. I sprang up and shouted at him but he did not move—he just sat there as if he were laughing. I did not like that. When I reached for a stone to throw, he moved swiftly out of the way of the stone. He was not afraid of me; he looked at me as if I were meat. No doubt I could have killed him with an arrow, but I did not know if there were others. Moreover, night was falling.

I looked about me—not far away there was a great, broken god-road, leading north. The towers were high enough, but not so high, and while many of the dead-houses were wrecked, there were some that stood. I went toward this god-road, keeping to the heights of the ruins, while the dog followed. When I had reached the god-road, I saw that there were others behind him. If I had slept later, they would have come upon me asleep and torn out my throat. As it was, they were sure enough of me; they did not hurry. When I went into the dead-house, they kept watch at the entrance—doubtless they thought they

---

MEETING INDIVIDUAL NEEDS **GIFTED AND TALENTED**

Exploration Discuss John's courage in continuing to explore the Dead Place: he "had long gone past what was forbidden," but his "hunger for knowledge burned" in him.

Activity Encourage students to discuss people in real life who have gone to forbidden places in pursuit of knowledge, such as 15th- and 16th-century explorers, explorers of the Arctic and Antarctica, mountain climbers, oceanographers, and astronauts. Have small groups of students research one of these explorers and report their findings to the class. **L3 COLLAB. LEARN.**

Abismo. David Alfaro Siqueiros (1896–1974). Piroxyline on Masonite, 23⅝ x 27½ in.

Viewing the painting: What elements in this painting remind you of the setting of the story?

VIEWING THE PAINTNG

The Spanish title of the painting translates as "abyss." Siqueiros, a Mexican painter, started a mural renaissance. He was known for his innovations in tools and materials.

Viewing Response *The brightness and colors are like the painting of the sky in the "mighty temple"; the spreading shape is like the fire in the sky during the "Great Burning."*

N Author's Craft

THEME The author contrasts John's primitive superstitions with his intelligence and ability to reason. Have students point out details that show his superstition and those that show his rationality. *(He superstitiously thinks a magic word could open the door and speaks to the spirits as he enters the "god's" anteroom; yet he escapes the dogs by knowing they cannot open a door and uses his knowledge that the gods lived on high.)*

Cultural Note

Students may see a similarity between this story and *The Planet of the Apes* movies. The theme of both the story and the movies are similar. Both involve people from the future discovering the ruins of a United States of the past. Invite students familiar with the movies to share the plots with classmates.

would have a fine hunt. But a dog cannot open a door and I knew, from the books, that the gods did not like to live on the ground but on high.

I had just found a door I could open when the dogs decided to rush. Ha! They were surprised when I shut the door in their faces—it was a good door, of strong metal. I could hear their foolish baying beyond it but I did not stop to answer them. I was in darkness—I found stairs and climbed. There were many stairs, turning around till my head was dizzy. At the top was another door—I found the knob and opened it. I was in a long small chamber—on one side of it was a bronze door that could not be opened, for it had no handle. Perhaps there was a magic word to open

it but I did not have the word. I turned to the door in the opposite side of the wall. The lock of it was broken and I opened it and went in.

Within, there was a place of great riches. The god who lived there must have been a powerful god. The first room was a small anteroom—I waited there for some time, telling the spirits of the place that I came in peace and not as a robber. When it seemed to me that they had had time to hear me, I went on. Ah, what riches! Few, even, of the windows had been broken—it was all as it had been. The great windows that looked over the city had not been broken at all though they were dusty and streaked with many years. There were coverings on the floors, the colors

---

Vocabulary

anteroom (an′ tē room′) *n.* a small room serving as a waiting area or entrance to a larger, main room

---

REAL-WORLD CONNECTION

Protesting Atomic Weapons On page 103, John has a vision of the Great Burning and the Destruction that destroyed the great city.

Activity After students have completed the story, have them use an on-line periodical index to find articles on atomic weapons and warfare and people and organizations that fight against them. Have them report their findings and then lead a discussion on what can be done to prevent the kind of destruction described in the story. **L2**

Critical Thinking

○ Critical Thinking

DRAWING CONCLUSIONS The narrator says his heart feels strange when he looks at the painting. Have students conclude what specific type of painting the author is describing and explain the narrator's reaction to it. *(The painting seems to be by an Impressionist such as Monet; the author indicates that great art naturally causes a profound reaction.)*

Ⓟ Critical Thinking

DRAWING CONCLUSIONS Ask students to name each item John describes. *(a sink, a stove, an oven, and lamps)*

Ⓠ Active Reading

EVALUATE Have students summarize the explanations the author gives for John's vision. Are they convincing? *(John thinks it is magic; he says that some people will think he was asleep and dreaming; he thinks that the spirits from the Dead Place wish to speak after many long years. The author's previous emphasis of the separation of the body and the spirit helps make this spiritual vision convincing.)*

---

not greatly faded, and the chairs were soft and deep. There were pictures upon the walls, very strange, very wonderful—I remember one of a bunch of flowers in a jar—if you came close to it, you could see nothing but bits of color, but if you stood away from it, the flowers might have been picked yesterday. It made my heart feel strange to look at this picture—and to look at the figure of a bird, in some hard clay, on a table and see it so like our birds. Everywhere there were books and writings, many in tongues that I could not read. The god who lived there must have been a wise god and full of knowledge. I felt I had right there, as I sought knowledge also.

Nevertheless, it was strange. There was a washing-place but no water—perhaps the gods washed in air. There was a cooking-place but no wood, and though there was a machine to cook food, there was no place to put fire in it. Nor were there candles or lamps—there were things that looked like lamps but they had neither oil nor wick. All these things were magic, but I touched them and lived—the magic had gone out of them. Let me tell one thing to show. In the washing-place, a thing said "Hot" but it was not hot to the touch—another thing said "Cold" but it was not cold. This must have been a strong magic but the magic was gone. I do not understand—they had ways—I wish that I knew.

It was close and dry and dusty in their house of the gods. I have said the magic was gone but that is not true—it had gone from the magic things but it had not gone from the place. I felt the spirits about me, weighing upon me. Nor had I ever slept in a Dead Place before—and yet, tonight, I must sleep there. When I thought of it, my tongue felt dry in my throat, in spite of my wish for knowledge. Almost I would have gone down again and faced the dogs, but I did not.

I had not gone through all the rooms when the darkness fell. When it fell, I went back to the big room looking over the city and made fire. There was a place to make fire and a box with wood in it, though I do not think they cooked there. I wrapped myself in a floor-covering and slept in front of the fire—I was very tired.

Now I tell what is very strong magic. I woke in the midst of the night. When I woke, the fire had gone out and I was cold. It seemed to me that all around me there were whisperings and voices. I closed my eyes to shut them out. Some will say that I slept again, but I do not think that I slept. I could feel the spirits drawing my spirit out of my body as a fish is drawn on a line.

Why should I lie about it? I am a priest and the son of a priest. If there are spirits, as they say, in the small Dead Places near us, what spirits must there not be in that great Place of the Gods? And would not they wish to speak? After such long years? I know that I felt myself drawn as a fish is drawn on a line. I had stepped out of my body—I could see my body asleep in front of the cold fire, but it was not I. I was drawn to look out upon the city of the gods.

It should have been dark, for it was night, but it was not dark. Everywhere there were lights—lines of light—circles and blurs of light—ten thousand torches would not have been the same. The sky itself was alight—you could barely see the stars for the glow in the sky. I thought to myself "This is strong magic" and trembled. There was a roaring in my ears like the rushing of rivers. Then my eyes grew used to the light and my ears to the sound. I knew that I was seeing the city as it had been when the gods were alive.

That was a sight indeed—yes, that was a sight: I could not have seen it in the body— my body would have died. Everywhere went the gods, on foot and in chariots—there were

---

Teaching Options

Reading *Minilesson*

Comparing and Contrasting The author describes the city in its broken-down, deserted state. Then he describes the city as it was before its destruction. Encourage students to visualize the similarities and differences in the city in its two states as they read the descriptions.

Activity Have students make a chart with two columns labeled *Before* and

After. Have them list details that describe the city in each state. For example, under *Before* they might write "light" and "filled with chariots"; under *After,* "dark" and "broken-down roads." Have volunteers write their details on a chart on the board. **L1**

Additional Resources
📁 *Reading Workbook,* p. 13

gods beyond number and counting and their chariots blocked the streets. They had turned night to day for their pleasure—they did not sleep with the sun. The noise of their coming and going was the noise of many waters. It was magic what they could do—it was magic what they did.

I looked out of another window—the great vines of their bridges were mended and the god-roads went east and west. Restless, restless, were the gods and always in motion! They burrowed tunnels under rivers—they flew in the air. With unbelievable tools they did giant works—no part of the earth was safe from them, for, if they wished for a thing, they summoned it from the other side of the world. And always, as they labored and rested, as they feasted and made love, there was a drum in their ears—the pulse of the giant city, beating and beating like a man's heart.

Were they happy? What is happiness to the gods? They were great, they were mighty, they were wonderful and terrible. As I looked upon them and their magic, I felt like a child—but a little more, it seemed to me, and they would pull down the moon from the sky. I saw them with wisdom beyond wisdom and knowledge beyond knowledge. And yet not all they did was well done—even I could see that—and yet their wisdom could not but grow until all was peace.

Then I saw their fate come upon them and that was terrible past speech. It came

August, 1982. Avigdor Arikha. Oil on canvas, 31¾ x 39¼ in.
Viewing the painting: Compare the view in this picture with what John imagined he saw when he looked out the window.

© Avigdor Arikha/Licensed by VAGA, New York, NY/ Marlborough Gallery, NY.

upon them as they walked the streets of their city. I have been in the fights with the Forest People—I have seen men die. But this was not like that. When gods war with gods, they use weapons we do not know. It was fire falling out of the sky and a mist that poisoned. It was the time of the Great Burning and the Destruction. They ran about like ants in the streets of their city—poor gods, poor gods! Then the towers began to fall. A few escaped—yes, a few. The legends tell it. But, even after the city had become a Dead Place, for many years the poison was still in the ground. I saw it happen, I saw the last of them die. It was darkness over the broken city and I wept.

All this, I saw. I saw it as I have told it, though not in the body. When I woke in the morning, I was hungry, but I did not think first of my hunger for my heart was perplexed and confused. I knew the reason

Vocabulary
perplexed (pər plekst´) *adj.* troubled with doubt or uncertainty; puzzled

THE SHORT STORY 103

VIEWING THE PAINTING

Avigdor Arikha was born in 1929 in Bukovina, then part of the USSR. After spending his youth in a kibbutz near Jerusalem, he studied fine art and philosophy. Arikha's paintings, drawings, and etchings are displayed in museums in Paris; London; Madrid; Washington, D.C.; New York; and San Francisco. A world-renowned artist, Arikha currently lives and works in Paris and Jerusalem.

Viewing Response *The view from the window in the story would show the ruins of a great city.*

R **Active Reading**

REVIEW Encourage students to review John's vision by listing or paraphrasing what he saw in the city before its destruction.

S **Active Reading**

QUESTION According to John, what characteristics did the people who used to live in the city have? *(They were restless, inventive, hard-working, and creative.)*

T **Critical Thinking**

DRAWING CONCLUSIONS Ask students to explain what happened to the city and its people. *(It was destroyed by some sort of atomic weapon, which killed almost everyone and poisoned the earth.)*

INTERDISCIPLINARY CONNECTION

History The story's description of the destruction of the city is similar to the reports of the bombing of Hiroshima, Japan, during World War II.

Activity Assign small groups of students one of the following specific topics involving the bombing of Hiroshima. Have the groups research their topics and report their findings to the class.
- reasons for the bombing
- the bombing: who, what, when, where
- results in lives lost and property damage
- eyewitness reports
- long-term effects

L2 **COLLAB. LEARN.**

Literary Elements

MORAL How does John's characterization of the man he finds help make the story's moral clear? *(John sees wisdom and sadness in the man's face and concludes that he had watched the death of his city. He identifies with the man and repeats his earlier statement: "it is better to lose one's life than one's spirit." He brings out the moral that men's bodies are capable of causing destruction; their spirits are capable of wisdom and good.)*

Active Reading

EVALUATE Have students discuss whether they agree with John and his father's opinion that too much knowledge gained too quickly is dangerous.

Thematic Focus

Transitions Have students discuss the effects on John of his new knowledge. Does his knowledge make him less curious? unhappy? disillusioned?

✔ ASSESSMENT OPTIONS

📁 *Quick Checks,* p. 8

Teaching Options

for the Dead Places but I did not see why it had happened. It seemed to me it should not have happened, with all the magic they had. I went through the house looking for an answer. There was so much in the house I could not understand—and yet I am a priest and the son of a priest. It was like being on one side of the great river, at night, with no light to show the way.

Then I saw the dead god. He was sitting in his chair, by the window, in a room I had not entered before and, for the first moment, I thought that he was alive. Then I saw the skin on the back of his hand—it was like dry leather. The room was shut, hot and dry—no doubt that had kept him as he was. At first I was afraid to approach him—then the fear left me. He was sitting looking out over the city—he was dressed in the clothes of the gods. His age was neither young nor old— I could not tell his age. But there was wisdom in his face and great sadness. You could see that he would have not run away. He had sat at his window, watching his city die—then he himself had died. But it is better to lose one's life than one's spirit—and you could see from the face that his spirit had not been lost. I knew, that, if I touched him, he would fall into dust—and yet, there was something unconquered in the face.

That is all of my story, for then I knew he was a man—I knew then that they had been men, neither gods nor demons. It is a great knowledge, hard to tell and believe. They were men—they went a dark road, but they were men. I had no fear after that— I had no fear going home, though twice I fought off the dogs and once I was hunted for two days by the Forest People. When I saw my father again, I prayed and was purified. He touched my lips and my breast, he said, "You went away a boy. You come back a man and a priest." I said, "Father, they were men! I have been in the Place of the Gods and seen it! Now slay me, if it is the law—but still I know they were men."

He looked at me out of both eyes. He said, "The law is not always the same shape—you have done what you have done. I could not have done it in my time, but you come after me. Tell!"

I told and he listened. After that, I wished to tell all the people but he showed me otherwise. He said, "Truth is a hard deer to hunt. If you eat too much truth at once, you may die of the truth. It was not idly that our fathers forbade the Dead Places." He was right—it is better the truth should come little by little. I have learned that, being a priest. Perhaps, in the old days, they ate knowledge too fast.

Nevertheless, we make a beginning. It is not for the metal alone we go to the Dead Places now—there are the books and the writings. They are hard to learn. And the magic tools are broken —but we can look at them and wonder. At least, we make a beginning. And, when I am chief priest we shall go beyond the great river. We shall go to the Place of the Gods—the place newyork—not one man but a company. We shall look for the images of the gods and find the god ASHING and the others—the gods Lincoln and Biltmore[1] and Moses.[2] But they were men who built the city, not gods or demons. They were men. I remember the dead man's face. They were men who were here before us. We must build again.

---

1. The *Biltmore* is a famous hotel in New York City.
2. Robert *Moses* (1888–1981) was a New York state public official whose name appears on many bridges and other structures built during his administration.

Grammar and Language *Minilesson*

Capitalization of Proper Nouns Write the words *Ann, Colorado River,* and *Aztecs* on the board. Remind students that names of specific people, places, historical events, and nationalities are capitalized. The author of the selection uses several imaginary proper nouns.

Activity Have students find and write six proper nouns from the selection. **L1**

Additional Resources

🖌 ***Grammar and Language Transparency 8***

📕 ***Grammar and Language Workbook,*** pp. 49, 237

📕 ***Grammar and Composition Handbook,*** Lessons 1.1, 10.3

📕 ***Writer's Choice,*** Lesson 20.3

Responding to Literature

Personal Response

Which line or passage in the story had the greatest impact on you? Why?

ANALYZING LITERATURE

RECALL

1. Which event determines that John will one day be a priest? How does John's life change after this event?
2. In which direction does John decide to travel? Why?
3. Describe John's journey down the great river.
4. What does John find to be untrue about the Place of the Gods? What is his greatest discovery?
5. When John returns home, he wants to share his knowledge with all of the Hill People. What does his father tell him to do? Why?

INTERPRET

6. In your opinion, does John consider his priestly calling a privilege or a burden? Support your answer with evidence from the story.
7. What internal conflict must John overcome before choosing a direction for his journey? How does he know he has made the right choice?
8. What does John believe will happen to him when he reaches the Place of the Gods? In your opinion, what does John's decision to continue on his journey reveal about his character?
9. Name four objects or places that John sees in the Place of the Gods, and explain what you think they actually are.
10. Theme Connections   How does John's journey change him? In your opinion, what long-term impact will his journey have on his people?

EVALUATE AND CONNECT

11. Do you believe that John is being disrespectful by ignoring his father's advice and the law? Explain your answer.
12. Compare the civilization of the Hill People with that of the people who once lived in the Place of the Gods.
13. In your opinion, is our society in danger of being destroyed in the same way as the Place of the Gods? Explain your answer.
14. John believes that "it is better to lose one's life than one's spirit." Do you agree? Why or why not?
15. How does knowing the source of the biblical **allusion** in the title of this story enrich your understanding of the story? (See page R1.)

Literary ELEMENTS

Moral

A **moral** is a practical lesson about right and wrong conduct. Do you recall Aesop's fable about the shepherd boy who, as a joke, kept shouting "Wolf!"? When a wolf really did come, no one answered the boy's cry. The moral is given at the end of the fable: *Even when liars tell the truth, they are seldom believed.* In most stories, however, the moral is not stated directly. The reader must infer the moral by thinking about the events of the story and by examining what the characters do, say, and think.

1. What do you think the moral of this story is? What details helped you determine the moral?
2. In your opinion, what does the story reveal about the author's convictions about right and wrong and about his views of the conflicts between good and evil in the world?

● See **Literary Terms Handbook**, p. R8.

LITERARY ELEMENTS

1. Possible morals are that knowledge does not necessarily bring wisdom and that if our civilization is not careful, we could destroy ourselves. They are implied in the description of the Hill People and in John's ideas about the human spirit.
2. The author reveals his conviction that people must strive to preserve good in our society or the society will be destroyed.

Additional Resources

Literary Elements Transparency 8

who lived in the Place of the Gods had sophisticated technology, buildings, and art.
13. Students may say our society is in danger of being destroyed because many countries possess the technology to make atomic bombs, and there may be unwise people who would use them.
14. Students may agree because no person is fully alive without his or her spirit, or they may disagree because without life there is nothing.
15. Understanding the allusion enriches the story because the Place of the Gods is comparable to Zion; readers should also weep as they see the possible end of our civilization.

Personal Response

Choices may include a philosophical statement such as "It is better to lose one's life than one's spirit."

ANALYZING LITERATURE

1. When John holds a piece of metal and does not die, it is clear he will become a priest. After that, he gets the best food and the best seat but is also punished more severely for wrongdoings.
2. John decides to travel east because he sees certain signs that he should do so.
3. John builds a raft, and the river's current carries him toward the Place of the Gods. The raft spins until, according to him, the gods show him how to paddle on one side of the raft. When he nears land, his raft turns over and he swims to shore.
4. John finds that the ground is not burning, there are no fogs and enchantments, and there are no wails of demons in the Place of the Gods. His greatest discovery is of a dead man.
5. John's father tells him not to tell all at once because too much knowledge gained too quickly is dangerous.
6. John considers his calling a privilege; he says the knowledge he gets makes him happy. He continues his quest despite physical discomfort.
7. John must overcome the conflict of knowing that his journey east is forbidden by his father. He knows he has made the right choice when he easily finds game to hunt and luckily avoids enemies.
8. John believes he will be struck dead when he reaches the Place of the Gods. His decision to continue reveals that he is courageous and values knowledge above his safety.
9. The shattered image of a god or a man is a statue of George Washington; the fallen towers are skyscrapers; the washing-place is a sink; the cooking-place is a stove.
10. John becomes a man. He becomes wise, calm, and fearless. His knowledge will lead his people to advance their civilization.
11. Some students may see John as disrespectful while others may see him as having the courage to act according to his convictions.
12. The Hill People have a much less advanced civilization. They are hunters; they do not have technology and must find any metal they use. The people

LITERATURE AND WRITING

Writing About Literature

Students' evaluations should
- state an opinion about the author's use of clues to increase suspense.
- use specific details from the story to support the opinion.

Personal Writing

Students' dialogues should
- refer to specific events in John's story.
- express their ideas about adult responsibilities.
- be written in standard dialogue form.

EXTENDING YOUR RESPONSE

Literature Groups Encourage students to carefully consider the consequences of each course of action as they discuss the wisdom of each. **COLLAB. LEARN.**

Interdisciplinary Activity You may wish to have students work in groups and assign one of the civilizations mentioned to each group.

Listening and Speaking Encourage students to discuss the meaning of Huxley's statement before preparing their speeches.

Skill Minilesson

LITERATURE AND WRITING

Writing About Literature

Evaluate a Literary Technique Benét expects the reader to use clues to infer key aspects of the story. Evaluate the effectiveness of this technique. Does gradually revealing the truth about the Place of the Gods add suspense and interest to the story? Use details from the selection to support your ideas. Share your evaluation with others.

Personal Writing

Rites of Passage Compare the adult responsibilities John took on as part of his passage to adulthood with those that you and a partner discussed in the Focus Activity on page 94. Write a dialogue between you and John in which you share your thoughts and feelings about the passage from adolescence to adulthood.

EXTENDING YOUR RESPONSE

Literature Groups

Full Disclosure? At the end of the story, John's father tells him: "Truth is a hard deer to hunt. If you eat too much truth at once, you may die of the truth." John then realizes that "the truth should come little by little." Do you agree with John and his father? Or do you think that John should immediately share all his knowledge with his people? Debate these issues in your group. Share your ideas with the class.

Interdisciplinary Activity

History: Lost Worlds Although this story is fantasy, history has shown that the knowledge and advancements of great civilizations—such as those of the ancient Maya, Egyptians, Greeks, and Romans—can be lost to subsequent generations. Investigate a lost civilization that was later rediscovered. Look for parallels between that civilization and the culture of the former dwellers of the Place of the Gods. Share your findings with the class.

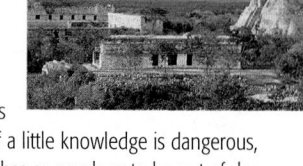

Listening and Speaking

Rebuttal In 1877 British biologist Thomas Henry Huxley wrote: "If a little knowledge is dangerous, where is the man who has so much as to be out of danger?" Prepare a speech that John might give in response to this quote. Use the dialogue in the story to model John's speech patterns and manner of expressing himself. Then rehearse and perform the speech for the class.

💼 **Save your work for your portfolio.**

Skill Minilesson

VOCABULARY • The Prefix *Ante-*

The prefix *ante-* means "before, in space or time"; therefore, a room that comes before a main room is called an *anteroom*. There are only three words in which *ante-* is joined to an English base word: *anteroom*, its synonym, *antechamber*, and *antedate*. All other words with the prefix *ante-* have Latin roots.

PRACTICE Read the definitions of the three words to the right. Then write a sentence for each word, using it correctly in a meaningful context.

antebellum: *adj.* before the war, usually used to describe the period before the American Civil War

antediluvian: *adj.* before the flood (the one in the biblical story about Noah's ark); usually used to refer to something extremely old or someone extremely old-fashioned

antecedent: *n.* a noun that is referred to by a pronoun (The noun usually comes before the pronoun.)

Reading & Thinking Skills

Visualizing

Imagine that your friend has just come back from visiting her relatives in another state. As she talks about that state's scenery—the overcast skies and the foothills covered with red-leaved maple trees—you can picture the scene even though you've never been there. That's because you're **visualizing** what your friend saw, or using her words to form a mental picture of what she's describing.

Good readers also visualize. Turning an author's verbal descriptions into mental images can help you enter into a story's world and better understand the action. In order to visualize, pay careful attention to the descriptive words the author uses. Read the passage slowly, then close your eyes and let the words form a picture.

If the passage describes movement, pay attention to the nouns and verbs the author uses to convey action and then turn the picture into a movie in your mind. For example, the narrator in "By the Waters of Babylon" says "I saw a little dance of white butterflies over a great heap of stone." This sentence provides information about the color of the butterflies, the size of the stone pile, and where the butterflies are in relation to the stones. Close your eyes and picture the butterflies dancing over the stones.

● For more reading strategies, see **Reading Handbook,** pp. R78–R107.

ACTIVITY

Before filmmakers start shooting a movie, they make a storyboard, or a series of sketches that show the scenes in order of sequence. Read the following paragraph from "By the Waters of Babylon." Then make a storyboard that shows what you visualize when you read this passage.

> "I looked around me—not far away there was a great, broken god-road, leading north. The towers were high enough, but not so high, and while many of the dead-houses were wrecked, there were some that stood. I went toward this god-road, keeping to the heights of the ruins, while the dog followed. When I had reached the god-road, I saw that there were others behind him. If I had slept later, they would have come upon me asleep and torn out my throat. As it was, they were sure enough of me; they did not hurry. When I went into the dead-house, they kept watch at the entrance—doubtless they thought they would have a fine hunt. But a dog cannot open a door and I knew, from the books, that the gods did not like to live on the ground but on high."

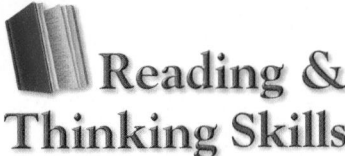

Objective

• To utilize visualizing to improve reading skills

Teaching Strategies

After students read the first part of page 107, ask them to recall passages of the selection that they visualized as they read them. Have volunteers summarize those passages and describe how they visualized them.

Activity

Students' storyboards should
• contain several sketches that illustrate specific scenes.
• place events in chronological order.
• show an understanding of the story's characters and events.

Additional Resources
📁 *Reading Workbook*

Teaching Options

 INCLUSION STRATEGIES

Less-Proficient Readers Provide additional practice visualizing with the selection "By the Waters of Babylon."

Activity Tell students to visualize three separate descriptive passages as you read them aloud. Then identify one of the passages and have students make an illustration of it. Passages to read include paragraph 4, page 99; paragraph 2, page 102; and paragraph 2, page 104. After students complete their drawings, have them reread the paragraph to check for details they missed. **L1**

Additional Resources
📁 *Inclusion Strategies*

Objectives

- To read and analyze a short story to experience the sights and sounds of a dream world
- To identify description in a short story
- To write an analysis contrasting events in a short story

Skills

Reading/Thinking: Drawing Conclusions
Writing: Dream Narrative; Song Lyrics
Vocabulary: Analogies
Grammar/Language: Coordinating Conjunctions
Listening/Speaking: Calypso Music
Life Skills: Dream Research
Collaboration: Literature Groups

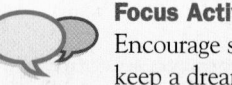

OPTIONS

Selection Focus Transparency 9: After discussing the painting, ask students what music might further enhance the mood the artist was trying to create.

Focus Activity: Encourage students to keep a dream journal, describing their dreams over the course of several days.

Before You Read

What I Have Been Doing Lately

FOCUS ACTIVITY

Have you ever dreamed that you were someplace that seemed familiar in certain ways, but was strange or even bizarre in other ways?

FREEWRITE Try to recall the most fantastic dream you've ever had. Jot down as many descriptive details as you can remember.

SETTING A PURPOSE Read to experience the sights and sounds of a dream world.

BACKGROUND

The Time and Place
"What I Have Been Doing Lately" is set in the recent past, probably on a tropical island in the Caribbean. The climate and landscape of this island, with its cloudless skies, monkeys, and flowering trees, seem similar to the island of Antigua, where the author grew up.

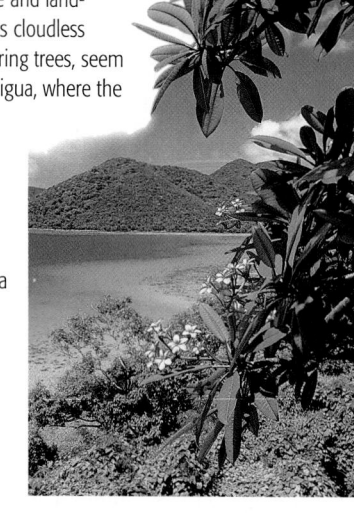

Did You Know?
Stream of consciousness is a literary technique that combines a series of thoughts and images into a flowing narrative. Feelings, impressions, and ideas—both rational and irrational—unfold in the same pattern and at the same speed that they occur in a character's mind.

VOCABULARY

verandah (və ran′də) *n.* a long porch, usually with a roof, that extends along one or more sides of a house; p. 110
interlaced (in′ tər lāst′) *adj.* connected by or as if by being woven together; interwoven; p. 111
psalm (sälm) *n.* a sacred poem, song, or hymn; p. 111

Meet Jamaica Kincaid

❝I read *Jane Eyre* as a child, and I totally loved it and totally identified with it. I did not think about the race difference at all, and I think that's very natural.❞

Growing up in Antigua under the oppression of racism, Jamaica Kincaid found that books were a great equalizer. At sixteen, Kincaid moved to New York City, where her passion for books led her to a successful career in writing. Kincaid's writing focuses on the Caribbean and often deals with the relationship between mothers and daughters.

Jamaica Kincaid was born in 1949 in St. John's, Antigua. This story first appeared in The Paris Review.

RESOURCE MANAGER

Lesson Planning Resource
The *Unit One Planning Guide* (pp. 72–79) provides additional lesson notes and reduced versions of all print resources.

📁 **Other Print Resources**
- Active Reading Guide, p. 9
- Vocabulary Practice, p. 9
- Reading Workbook, p. 13
- Grammar and Language Workbook, p. 69
- Grammar and Composition Handbook, Lesson 1.7

- Quick Checks, p. 9
- Selection and Theme Assessment, pp. 17–18
- Performance Assessment, p. 9
- Spanish Summaries, p. 9
- Spanish Translations
- Inclusion Strategies
- English Language Learners Sourcebook

🔊 **Transparencies**
- Selection Focus 9
- Fine Art 11

- Literary Elements 9
- Grammar and Language 9

Technology
🎧 Audio Library
🎧 Spanish Audio Library
💻 Glencoe Literature Web Site
💾 Testmaker

Eight Huts in Haiti. D. Roosevelt (b. 1952.) Oil on canvas. Private collection.

What I Have Been Doing Lately

Jamaica Kincaid ✺

SUMMARY

The narrator describes a dreamlike sequence of events that begin when she gets out of bed to answer the doorbell. She walks outside and sees a monkey and a body of water. She sees a dog, a boy playing ball, hills, and trees. She falls into a hole and comes out of the hole. A woman asks her what she has been doing. She recites the first part of her narrative with added details. She says she saw shiny black people having a picnic who turned to mud. She says she kept walking and looked forward to getting home or going to church. She says she began to feel sad. The story ends where it began: she is lying in bed just before the doorbell rings.

📁 *Spanish Summaries,* p. 9

🅰 Active Reading

PREDICT Ask students to make predictions about the setting. Where might the story take place? What might someone do there? What clues do the picture and caption give them?

Additional Resources

📁 *Active Reading Guide,* p. 9
🎧 *Audio Library*
🎧 *Spanish Audio Library*

Teaching Options

CONNECTING TO OTHER SELECTIONS

The chart at the right shows three ways to connect "What I Have Been Doing Lately" to selections in this book.

For specific teaching strategies, see the *Unit One Planning Guide,* pages 75–76.

Connection	Title
Life Skills: Creating and Producing	→ "A Sound of Thunder," p. 316
Thematic: Dreams	→ "Catch the Moon," p. 63
Literary: Setting	→ "Exploring Antarctic Ice," p. 532

DESCRIPTION To help readers experience what the narrator is experiencing, the author uses sensory details. Point out that the details in the sentence that begins "Either it was drizzling or . . ." appeal to the senses of sight and touch. Ask students to note other sensory details as they read the selection.

C Critical Thinking

DRAWING CONCLUSIONS The following model can help students determine that the story narrates a dream.

Model: The story does not have the elements usually found in a short story: a clear conflict and events that are arranged in a plot. Instead, it tells of a series of events that are seemingly unrelated. Time passes inconsistently and unrealistic things happen. I have experienced dreams that have the same characteristics. I think the story relates the fantastic details of a vivid dream.

D Literary Elements

DIALOGUE Point out that the story contains little dialogue. Have students analyze the passages of dialogue. In what ways are they consistent or inconsistent with the dreamlike tone of the rest of the story? *(The narrator's remarks are dreamlike; some are nonsense and some are non sequiturs. The woman's remarks might be spoken in reality; this combination of realistic and unrealistic elements is characteristic of dreams.)*

Teaching Options

What I Have Been Doing Lately

What I have been doing lately: I was lying in bed and the doorbell rang. I ran downstairs. Quick. I opened the door. There was no one there. I stepped outside. Either it was drizzling or there was a lot of dust in the air and the dust was damp. I stuck out my tongue and the drizzle or the damp dust tasted like government school ink. I looked north. I looked south. I decided to start walking north. While walking north, I noticed that I was barefoot. While walking north, I looked up and saw the planet Venus. I said, "It must be almost morning." I saw a monkey in a tree. The tree had no leaves. I said, "Ah, a monkey. Just look at that. A monkey." I walked for I don't know how long before I came up to a big body of water. I wanted to get across it but I couldn't swim. I wanted to get across it but it would take me years to build a boat. I wanted to get across it but it would take me I didn't know how long to build a bridge. Years passed and then one day, feeling like it, I got into my boat and rowed across. When I got to the other side, it was noon and my shadow was small and fell beneath me. I set out on a path that stretched out straight ahead. I passed a house, and a dog was sitting on the <u>verandah</u> but it looked the other way when it saw me coming. I passed a boy tossing a ball in the air but the boy looked the other way when he saw me coming. I walked and I walked but I couldn't tell if I walked a long time because my feet didn't feel as if they would drop off. I turned around to see what I had left behind me but nothing was familiar. Instead of the straight path, I saw hills. Instead of the boy with his ball, I saw tall flowering trees. I looked up and the sky was without clouds and seemed near, as if it were the ceiling in my house and, if I stood on a chair, I could touch it with the tips of my fingers. I turned around and looked ahead of me again. A deep hole had opened up before me. I looked in. The hole was deep and dark and I couldn't see the bottom. I thought, What's down there?, so on purpose I fell in. I fell and I fell, over and over, as if I were an old suitcase. On the sides of the deep hole I could see things written, but perhaps it was in a foreign language because I couldn't read them. Still I fell, for I don't know how long. As I fell I began to see that I didn't like the way falling made me feel. Falling made me feel sick and I missed all the people I had loved. I said, I don't want to fall anymore, and I reversed myself. I was standing again on the edge of the deep hole. I looked at the deep hole and I said, You can close up now, and it did. I walked some more without knowing distance. I only knew that I passed through days and nights, I only knew that I passed through rain and shine, light and darkness. I was never thirsty and I felt no pain. Looking at the horizon, I made a joke for myself: I said, "The earth has thin lips," and I laughed.

Looking at the horizon again, I saw a lone figure coming toward me, but I wasn't frightened because I was sure it was my mother. As I got closer to the figure, I could see that it wasn't my mother, but still I wasn't frightened because I could see that it was a woman.

When this woman got closer to me, she looked at me hard and then she threw up her hands. She must have seen me somewhere before because she said, "It's you. Just look at that. It's you. And just what have you been doing lately?"

I could have said, "I have been praying not to grow any taller."

I could have said, "I have been listening carefully to my mother's words, so as to make a good imitation of a dutiful daughter."

Vocabulary

verandah (və ran′ də) *n.* a long porch, usually with a roof, that extends along one or more sides of a house

110   UNIT 1

Nonstandard Sentence Structure
On the board, write the following sentence from the first paragraph of the story: "I wanted to get across it but it would take me I didn't know how long to build a bridge." Circle the clause "I didn't know how long." Explain that the author uses unusual sentence structure to imitate the way a person's mind works during a dream. The clause is an informal way of saying "a very long time."

Activity Have English language learners find two more uses of the clause "I didn't know how long" in the story. Have them rewrite them using a paraphrase for the clause.

Additional Resources
📁 *English Language Learners Sourcebook*

I could have said, "A pack of dogs, tired from chasing each other all over town, slept in the moonlight."

Instead, I said, What I have been doing lately: I was lying in bed on my back, my hands drawn up, my fingers interlaced lightly at the nape of my neck.[1] Someone rang the doorbell. I went downstairs and opened the door but there was no one there. I stepped outside. Either it was drizzling or there was a lot of dust in the air and the dust was damp. I stuck out my tongue and the drizzle or the damp dust tasted like government school ink. I looked north and I looked south. I started walking north. While walking north, I wanted to move fast, so I removed the shoes from my feet. While walking north, I looked up and saw the planet Venus and I said, "If the sun went out, it would be eight minutes before I would know it." I saw a monkey sitting in a tree that had no leaves and I said, "A monkey. Just look at that. A monkey." I picked up a stone and I threw it at the monkey. The monkey, seeing the stone, quickly moved out of its way. Three times I threw a stone at the monkey and three times it moved away. The fourth time I threw the stone, the monkey caught it and threw it back at me. The stone struck me on my forehead over my right eye, making a deep gash. The gash healed immediately but now the skin on my forehead felt false to me. I walked for I don't know how long before I came to a big body of water. I wanted to get across, so when the boat came I paid my fare. When I got to

the other side, I saw a lot of people sitting on the beach and they were having a picnic. They were the most beautiful people I had ever seen. Everything about them was black and shiny. Their skin was black and shiny. Their shoes were black and shiny. Their hair was black and shiny. The clothes they wore were black and shiny. I could hear them laughing and chatting and I said, I would like to be with these people, so I started to walk toward them, but when I got up close to them I saw that they weren't at a picnic and they weren't beautiful and they weren't chatting and laughing. All around me was black mud and the people all looked as if they had been made up out of the black mud. I looked up and saw that the sky seemed far away and nothing I could stand on would make me able to touch it with my fingertips. I thought, If only I could get out of this, so I started to walk. I must have walked for a long time because my feet hurt and felt as if they would drop off. I thought, If only just around the bend I would see my house and inside my house I would find my bed, freshly made at that, and in the kitchen I would find my mother or anyone else that I loved making me a custard. I thought, If only it was a Sunday and I was sitting in a church and I had just heard someone sing a psalm. I felt very sad so I sat down. I felt so sad that I rested my head on my own knees and smoothed my own head. I felt so sad I couldn't imagine feeling any other way again. I said, I don't like this. I don't want to do this anymore. And I went back to lying in bed, just before the doorbell rang.

⚜

1. The *nape of my neck* refers to the back of the neck.

Vocabulary
interlaced (in′ tər lāst′) *adj.* connected by or as if by being woven together; interwoven
psalm (säm) *n.* a sacred poem, song, or hymn

Grammar and Language *Minilesson*

Coordinating Conjunctions Write this sentence from the story on the board:

I could hear them laughing and chatting and I said, I would like to be with these people, so I started to walk toward them, but when I got up close to them I saw that they weren't at a picnic and they weren't beautiful and they weren't chatting and laughing.

Remind students that the coordinating conjunctions *and, but, or, nor, yet, so,* and *for* connect words, phrases, or clauses. Have students circle each coordinating conjunction in the sentence.

Activity Have students write two sentences from the story that contain two or more coordinating conjunctions and circle the coordinating conjunctions. **L1**

Additional Resources

✎ *Grammar and Language Transparency 9*

📕 *Grammar and Language Workbook,* p. 69

📕 *Grammar and Composition Handbook,* Lesson 1.7

📗 *Writer's Choice,* Lesson 10.7

Personal Response

Students may say they would feel relieved, disoriented, upset, curious, or frightened.

ANALYZING LITERATURE

1. The narrator is a young woman.
2. At the beginning and end of the story, the narrator is in bed.
3. In the first part of the narrative, the narrator faces a big body of water and a deep hole.
4. In the picnic scene, the narrator sees beautiful, "black, shiny" people having a good time at a picnic. When she gets close to them, she sees they are not having a picnic and are not happy and they seem to turn into mud.
5. The narrator goes back to lying in bed because she gets sad and doesn't want to continue what she is doing.
6. The narrator may be a teenager who has a difficult relationship with her mother because she refers to not wanting to grow taller and to trying to pretend to be a dutiful daughter for her mother.
7. The events in the story did not really happen. They are unrelated and unrealistic; things happen magically, as when the narrator suddenly has a boat to row across the water; and time passes unrealistically ("Years passed").
8. The body of water might symbolize a huge hurdle that the narrator is having trouble getting over, such as growing up. The hole might symbolize depression or death.
9. The change in the picnic scene makes the narrator feel sad and upset. The way she views the sky changes, and she suddenly wants to go home or to church.
10. The narrator's sadness and anxiety might be caused by the difficulties of growing up, such as wanting independence but also being fearful of it, or by a difficult relationship with her mother.
11. Students may say the narrator's hopes and fears are typical of people their age because she is concerned about growing too tall and about getting along with her mother.
12. The use of repetition helps create the eerie effect of a dream world.
13. The author is saying that the transition from childhood to adulthood is a difficult one and that the anxiety caused by it may show up in dreams.

Responding to Literature

Personal Response

How might you feel if you awoke from the dream described by the narrator?

——— ANALYZING LITERATURE ———

RECALL

1. Who is the narrator of this story?
2. Where is the narrator at the beginning of the story? At the end?
3. The account the narrator gives is divided into two parts. What obstacles does the narrator face in the first part?
4. Describe the picnic scene in the second part of the story. What happens when the narrator gets close to the people?
5. Why does the narrator go back to lying in bed?

INTERPRET

6. What can you infer about the narrator's age and family relationships? Support your inferences with details from the story.
7. Do you think that the events in this story really happened? Give reasons for your answer.
8. Consider the obstacles faced by the narrator in the first part of the description. What might these obstacles **symbolize**? (See page R13.)
9. How does the change in the picnic scene affect the narrator? Explain your answer.
10. In your opinion, what might be causing the narrator's sadness and anxiety?

EVALUATE AND CONNECT

11. Some experts say that dreams are the result of subconscious hopes and fears. Do you think the narrator's hopes and fears are typical of people your age? Explain your answer.
12. How does the author's use of **repetition** affect your appreciation and understanding of the story?
13. Theme Connections   What do you think the author is saying about transition and change?
14. Which images linger in your mind after reading the story?
15. Why, do you think, did the author choose to write this story in the first person, using the **stream-of-consciousness** technique? (See page R12.)

Literary ELEMENTS

Description

A **description** is a carefully detailed portrayal of a person, place, thing, or event. Writers often use **sensory details** in their descriptions to help readers understand what story characters see, hear, touch, taste, or smell. Notice the sensory details in the following description from this story: "I stuck out my tongue and the drizzle or the damp dust tasted like government school ink." These details help you "see" and "taste" what is being described.

1. Read the first paragraph of the story. Identify five sensory details that describe what the narrator experiences during her journey. Tell whether each detail appeals to the sense of sight, hearing, touch, taste, or smell.
2. After meeting the woman, the narrator retells the first part of the story. Write a brief comparison of the two descriptions. Which details in the two versions are alike? Which details are different?

● See **Literary Terms Handbook**, p. R3.

---

14. Students may mention images such as the narrator throwing a stone at the monkey or the people at the picnic turning to mud.
15. First-person narration is crucial to the telling of a dream because it is something that happens in the mind of one person. The stream-of-consciousness technique effectively recreates the random, jumbled sequence of events and feelings of a dream.

LITERARY ELEMENTS

1. Sensory details include the damp dust—touch and taste; the planet Venus—sight; a monkey in a tree—sight; tall flowering trees—sight and smell; a deep hole—sight and touch.
2. A comparison might include the repetition of the detail of the damp dust and the addition of the detail of taking off her shoes.

Additional Resources

  Literary Elements Transparency 9

LITERATURE AND WRITING

Writing About Literature

Analyze Events   Choose one particular event from the first part of the story that is repeated in the second part. Write a two- or three-paragraph analysis comparing and contrasting the two versions. You might use a Venn diagram to organize your thoughts.

Personal Writing

You Must Be Dreaming   Look back at the dream details you jotted down in the Focus Activity on page 108. Re-tell your dream in the first person, using the **stream-of-consciousness** technique employed in this story. Be sure to include sensory details.

EXTENDING YOUR RESPONSE

Literature Groups

Responding to Imagery   Some book reviewers find the imaginative images in Kincaid's stories difficult to understand and confusing; others like their poetic, musical quality and their ability to appeal to all kinds of people. Discuss with your group which reviews reflect your response to Kincaid's imagery.

Interdisciplinary Activity

Music: Compose a Calypso Song   Listen to calypso—a type of folk music that originated in Trinidad and spread throughout the Caribbean region. With a partner, compose a calypso song using the story title "What I Have Been Doing Lately" as a refrain. Try to incorporate images from the story into your lyrics. Perform the song for the class.

Learning for Life

Dreaming Themes   Researchers have identified several common dream themes. Often, dreams with these themes occur during times of stress or transition in people's lives. Investigate to learn what these common dream themes are, what researchers believe they mean, and when people are most likely to have such dreams. Try using an on-line periodical index, such as InfoTrack, to find magazine articles about recent dream research. Share your findings with the class.

 Save your work for your portfolio.

Skill Minilesson

VOCABULARY • *Analogies*

An analogy is a type of comparison that is based on the relationships between things or ideas. Some analogies are based on a relationship that could be called "class and member."

   book : novel :: doctor : pediatrician

One type of *book* is a *novel;* one type of *doctor* is a *pediatrician.*

   To finish an analogy, decide what relationship exists between the first two things or ideas. Then apply that relationship to another pair of words.

● For more about analogies, see **Communications Skills Handbook,** p. R77.

PRACTICE   Choose the pair that best completes each analogy.

1. porch : verandah ::
   a. truck : car
   b. house : mansion
   c. painter : sculptor
   d. church : steeple
   e. playground : swing

2. poem : psalm ::
   a. island : peninsula
   b. ocean : lake
   c. mammal : reptile
   d. symphony : conductor
   e. institution : hospital

LITERATURE AND WRITING

Writing About Literature

Students' analyses should
- focus on specific details from each part of the story.
- discuss similarities and differences in the details.

Personal Writing

Students' dream narratives should
- use first person and stream-of-consciousness.
- include several sensory details.

EXTENDING YOUR RESPONSE

Literature Groups Encourage students to base their evaluations on specific features of Kincaid's writing. **COLLAB. LEARN.**

Interdisciplinary Activity You may wish to pair musical learners with other students who may be adept at writing lyrics for the song.

Learning for Life Encourage students to share their experiences in using an on-line index.

Skill Minilesson

VOCABULARY • Analogies
   1. b   2. e

Additional Resources
   Vocabulary Practice, p. 9

✔ ASSESSMENT OPTIONS

📁 *Quick Checks,* p. 9
📁 *Selection and Theme Assessment,* pp. 17–18
📁 *Performance Assessment,* p. 9
💾 *Testmaker*

Objectives

- To read and analyze a short story about one elderly man's choice
- To identify types of characters
- To write an analysis of an author's attitude

Skills

Reading/Thinking: Inferring; Monitoring Comprehension; Identifying Assumptions
Writing: Script; Obituary
Vocabulary: Synonyms; Etymology; Prefixes Expressing Number
Grammar/Language: Gerund Phrases; Quotation Marks
Listening/Speaking: Performing Scripts; Discussing Issues; Performing Dialogue

→OPTIONS

Selection Focus Transparency 10: Have students discuss their ideas of when "old age" begins and list advantages and disadvantages of aging in America.

Focus Activity: Have students write a short character sketch of the elderly person.

Before You Read

With All Flags Flying

FOCUS ACTIVITY

Do you know an elderly person who is no longer able to live on his or her own? Does that person live with family members, in a nursing home, or in another kind of situation?

THINK/PAIR/SHARE Think about the advantages and disadvantages of that elderly person's living arrangements. Jot down your reactions and then share them with a partner.

SETTING A PURPOSE Read to learn about a choice one elderly man makes between self-reliance and loneliness.

BACKGROUND

The Time and Place
This story takes place in and around Baltimore, Maryland, the area where Anne Tyler has lived and worked since 1976. Baltimore is a large industrial and port city on Chesapeake Bay, approximately forty miles northeast of Washington, D.C. The story probably takes place in the 1960s.

Did You Know?
Throughout history, ships' captains have used flags to communicate with each other at sea. During the era of great naval battles, a defeated captain could signal surrender by "striking his colors," or lowering the flag of his ship. If a captain meant never to surrender, he'd hoist all flags on board as a promise to fight on to victory or to go down "with all flags flying."

VOCABULARY PREVIEW

appurtenance (ə purt′ ən əns) *n.* an optional article or piece of equipment that adds to one's convenience or comfort; accessory; p. 117
wince (wins) *v.* to draw back slightly, as in pain; flinch; p. 119
subtle (sut′ əl) *adj.* not open or direct; not obvious; p. 121
doddering (dod′ ər ing) *adj.* trembling or shaking, as from age; p. 121
monosyllabic (mon′ ə si lab′ ik) *adj.* having only one syllable; p. 121
chronic (kron′ ik) *adj.* lasting a long time or returning repeatedly; p. 121
cavernous (kav′ ər nəs) *adj.* large and spacious, like a cavern; p. 122

Meet Anne Tyler

"I had never used a telephone and could strike a match on the soles of my bare feet."

Anne Tyler has used these words to describe herself at age eleven when her family moved to Raleigh, North Carolina. Tyler grew up in rural North Carolina, where, with her Quaker parents, she lived in utopian communes and followed the simple ideals of her family's religion. From this country life came many ideas that Tyler later developed in her writing. Her novels include *The Accidental Tourist* and the Pulitzer Prize–winning *Breathing Lessons*.

Anne Tyler was born in Minneapolis, Minnesota, in 1941. This story was published in 1971.

RESOURCE MANAGER

Lesson Planning Resource
The *Unit One Planning Guide* (pp. 80–87) provides additional lesson notes and reduced versions of all print resources.

📁 **Other Print Resources**
- Active Reading Guide, p. 10
- Vocabulary Practice, p. 10
- Reading Workbook, p. 14
- Grammar and Language Workbook, pp. 95, 271
- Grammar and Composition Handbook, Lessons 3.3, 11.9

- Quick Checks, p. 10
- Selection and Theme Assessment, pp. 19–20
- Performance Assessment, p. 10
- Spanish Summaries, p. 10
- Inclusion Strategies
- English Language Learners Sourcebook

🖥 **Transparencies**
- Selection Focus 10
- Fine Art 14
- Literary Elements 10

- Grammar and Language 10

Technology
 🎧 Audio Library
🎧 Spanish Audio Library
 🖥 Glencoe Literature Web Site
💾 Testmaker

With All Flags Flying

Anne Tyler ⁓

Weakness was what got him in the end. He had been expecting something more definite—chest pains, a stroke, arthritis—but it was only weakness that put a finish to his living alone. A numbness in his head, an airy feeling when he walked. A wateriness in his bones that made it an effort to pick up his coffee cup in the morning. He waited some days for it to go away, but it never did. And meanwhile the dust piled up in corners; the refrigerator wheezed and creaked for want of defrosting. Weeds grew around his rosebushes.

A

THE SHORT STORY 🦢 115

Reading the Selection

SUMMARY

Mr. Carpenter is an elderly man who lives alone. He decides he can no longer live on his own and sets out for Baltimore to visit his daughter. She and her family beg him to move in with them, but he has decided to move into an old folks' home. He enjoys talking with his 13-year-old granddaughter, Francie. Mr. Carpenter is taken to the home by his daughter and Francie, who are sad to leave him there. He lies down on his new bed, thinking about dying and hoping that he continues to have the will to fight it.

📁 *Spanish Summaries,* p. 10

A **Active Reading**

PREDICT Have students read the title and the first page. Help them identify the story's narrative point of view and predict what will happen in the story based on the information they now have. *(The third-person limited-omniscient narrator can describe the thoughts and feelings of the main character.)*

Additional Resources
📁 *Active Reading Guide,* p. 10
🎧 *Audio Library*
🎧 *Spanish Audio Library*

Teaching Options

CONNECTING TO OTHER SELECTIONS

The chart at the right shows three ways to connect "With All Flags Flying" to selections in this book.

For specific teaching strategies, see the *Unit One Planning Guide,* pages 83–84.

Connection	Title
Life Skills: Decision Making	→ "Living Well. Living Good." p. 489
Thematic: Choices	→ "To Da-duh, in Memoriam," p. 399
Literary: Characterization	→ "Mrs. James," p. 305

DESCRIPTION Have students tell what they learn about Mr. Carpenter from the clothes he is wearing. *(He is frugal, practical, and a bit eccentric.)*

VIEWING THE PAINTING

Charles Burchfield was an Ohio landscape artist. He based many of his paintings on his memories from his childhood in Ohio. He often pictured nature with certain distortions.

Viewing Response *The mood is one of loneliness and desolation, like that of the old man at this point.*

FINE ART
TRANSPARENCY 14

You may want to show Fine Art Transparency 14 and have students discuss the character of the old man in the story.

Teaching Options

With All Flags Flying

He was awake and dressed at six o'clock on a Saturday morning, with the patchwork quilt pulled up neatly over the mattress. From the kitchen cabinet he took a hunk of bread and two Fig Newtons, which he dropped into a paper bag. He was wearing a brown suit that he had bought on sale in 1944, a white T-shirt and copper-toed work boots. These and his other set of underwear, which he put in the paper bag along with a razor, were all the clothes he took with him. Then he rolled down the top of the bag and stuck it under his arm, and stood in the middle of the kitchen staring around him for a moment.

Country Road in July, 1937. Charles Burchfield. Watercolor on paper, 26½ x 26½ in. Collection of Washington State University Museum of Art, Pullman, WA. Gift of Charles and Virginia Orton.

Viewing the painting: How does the mood of this painting reflect the emotions of the old man at this point in the story?

MEETING INDIVIDUAL NEEDS ENGLISH LANGUAGE LEARNERS

The Elderly in Society English language learners may be unfamiliar with the lifestyles of older people in American society. Explain that many older people live independently, but grandparents often play a big role in young people's lives. If older people cannot care for themselves, they may move in with their children's families or into a group home often called a retirement home.

Activity Have students describe the lifestyles of older people in cultures with which they are familiar. How are the lives of older people in these cultures similar to and different from those in the United States?

Additional Resources
📁 *English Language Learners Sourcebook*

The house had only two rooms, but he owned it—the last scrap of the farm that he had sold off years ago. It stood in a hollow of dying trees beside a superhighway in Baltimore County. All it held was a few sticks of furniture, a change of clothes, a skillet and a set of dishes. Also odds and ends, which disturbed him. If his inventory were complete, he would have to include six clothespins, a salt and a pepper shaker, a broken-toothed comb, a cheap ballpoint pen—oh, on and on, past logical numbers. Why should he be so cluttered? He was eighty-two years old. He had grown from an infant owning nothing to a family man with a wife, five children, everyday and Sunday china and a thousand <u>appurtenances</u>, down at last to solitary old age and the bare essentials again, but not bare enough to suit him. Only what he needed surrounded him. Was it possible he needed so much?

Now he had the brown paper bag; that was all. It was the one satisfaction in a day he had been dreading for years.

He left the house without another glance, heading up the steep bank toward the superhighway. The bank was covered with small, crawling weeds planted especially by young men with scientific training in how to prevent soil erosion. Twice his knees buckled. He had to sit and rest, bracing himself against the slope of the bank. The scientific weeds, seen from close up, looked straggly and gnarled. He sifted dry earth through his fingers without thinking, concentrating only on steadying his breath and calming the twitching muscles in his legs.

Once on the superhighway, which was fairly level, he could walk for longer stretches of time. He kept his head down and his fingers clenched tight upon the paper bag,

which was growing limp and damp now. Sweat rolled down the back of his neck, fell in drops from his temples. When he had been walking maybe half an hour he had to sit down again for a rest. A black motorcycle buzzed up from behind and stopped a few feet away from him. The driver was young and shabby, with hair so long that it drizzled out beneath the back of his helmet.

"Give you a lift, if you like," he said. "You going somewhere?"

"Just into Baltimore."

"Hop on."

He shifted the paper bag to the space beneath his arm, put on the white helmet he was handed and climbed on behind the driver. For safety he took a clutch of the boy's shirt, tightly at first and then more loosely when he saw there was no danger. Except for the helmet, he was perfectly comfortable. He felt his face cooling and stiffening in the wind, his body learning to lean gracefully with the tilt of the motorcycle as it swooped from lane to lane. It was a fine way to spend his last free day.

Half an hour later they were on the outskirts of Baltimore, stopped at the first traffic light. The boy turned his head and shouted, "Whereabouts did you plan on going?"

"I'm visiting my daughter, on Belvedere near Charles Street."

"I'll drop you off, then," the boy said. "I'm passing right by there."

The light changed, the motor roared. Now that they were in traffic, he felt more conspicuous, but not in a bad way. People in their automobiles seemed sealed in, overprotected; men in large trucks must envy the way the motorcycle

---

Vocabulary

appurtenance (ə purt′ ən əns) *n.* an optional article or piece of equipment that adds to one's convenience or comfort; accessory

---

Vo•cab•u•lar•y Skills

Synonyms Explain that often different terms are used in different regions to describe the same objects. Point out the words *hollow* and *skillet* and ask students what these things are and what names they use for these things. *(valley or basin; frying pan)*

C Active Reading

EVALUATE Have students discuss Mr. Carpenter's attitude toward material possessions. Ask if they can identify with his dislike of things and whether they have ever felt the urge to get rid of material possessions.

D Literary Elements

CHARACTERS Authors create characters with many techniques, including showing what they say and what they do. What does Mr. Carpenter's accepting a motorcycle ride and his reaction to it show about his character? *(He is open to new things; he enjoys simple pleasures in life; he is not fearful.)*

E Critical Thinking

INFERRING What can students infer about Mr. Carpenter and his life from the narrator's statement that it was "his last free day"? *(He defines independence as living completely on his own, and independence is very important to him. He is not happy about becoming less independent.)*

REAL-WORLD CONNECTION

Publications for Senior Citizens Have groups of students use on-line resources to locate newspapers and magazines that appeal to senior citizens.

Activity Have each group report on one publication. Groups should describe the types of articles in the publication and the nature of its advertisements. Then they should summarize or quote from one article, discuss the tone and mood of the publication, and evaluate it.
L1 COLLAB. LEARN.

F Literary Elements

IMAGERY To what sense does the image appeal? How does it help characterize Mr. Carpenter? *(The image appeals to the sense of hearing. Since the limited-omniscient narrator is reporting the main character's thoughts and feelings, the positive image helps show Mr. Carpenter's pleasure in the motorcycle ride.)*

G Literary Elements

CHARACTERS Have students characterize Mr. Carpenter's daughter Clara. According to the definitions on page 124, is she a flat character or a round one? *(Clara is down-to-earth, good-natured, and loving. Most students will agree that although she is an interesting character, she is a flat character because the main trait she reveals is that she is a caring daughter.)*

FINE ART
TRANSPARENCY 14

You may want to show Fine Art Transparency 14 and have students discuss the character of the old man in the story.

Teaching Options

looped in and out, hornet-like, stripped to the bare essentials of a motor and two wheels. By tugs at the boy's shirt and single words shouted into the wind he directed him to his daughter's house, but he was sorry to have the ride over so quickly.

His daughter had married a salesman and lived in a plain, square stone house that the old man approved of. There were sneakers and a football in the front yard, signs of a large, happy family. A bicycle lay in the driveway. The motorcycle stopped just inches from it. "Here we are," the boy said.

"Well, I surely do thank you."

He climbed off, fearing for one second that his legs would give way beneath him and spoil everything that had gone before. But no, they held steady. He took off the helmet and handed it to the boy, who waved and roared off. It was a really magnificent roar, ear-dazzling. He turned toward the house, beaming in spite of himself, with his head feeling cool and light now that the helmet was gone. And there was his daughter on the front porch, laughing. "Daddy, what on *earth?*" she said. "Have you turned into a teeny-bopper?"[1] Whatever that was. She came rushing down the steps to hug him— a plump, happy-looking woman in an apron. She was getting on toward fifty now. Her hands were like her mother's, swollen and veined. Gray had started dusting her hair.

"You never *told* us," she said. "Did you ride all this way on a motorcycle? Oh, why didn't you find a telephone and call? I would have come. How long can you stay for?"

"Now . . ." he said, starting toward the house. He was thinking of the best way to put it. "I came to a decision. I won't be living

---

1. *Teeny-bopper* is a slang word, commonly used in the 1960s and 1970s, that refers to a young teenager who follows the latest fad or craze, as in music or dress.

alone any more. I want to go to an old folks' home. That's what I *want,*" he said, stopping on the grass so she would be sure to get it clear. "I don't want to live with you—I want an old folks' home." Then he was afraid he had worded it too strongly. "It's nice *visiting* you, of course," he said.

"Why, Daddy, you know we always asked you to come and live with us."

"I know that, but I decided on an old folks' home."

"We couldn't do that. We won't even talk about it."

"Clara, my mind is made up."

Then in the doorway a new thought hit her, and she suddenly turned around. "Are you sick?" she said. "You always said you would live alone as long as health allowed."

"I'm not up to that any more," he said.

"What is it? Are you having some kind of pain?"

"I just decided, that's all," he said. "What I *will* rely on you for is the arrangements with the home. I know it's a trouble."

"We'll talk about that later," Clara said. And she firmed the corners of her mouth exactly the way her mother used to do when she hadn't won an argument but wasn't planning to lose it yet either.

In the kitchen he had a glass of milk, good and cold, and the hunk of bread and the two Fig Newtons from his paper bag. Clara wanted to make him a big breakfast, but there was no sense wasting what he had brought. He munched on the dry bread and washed it down with milk, meanwhile staring at the Fig Newtons, which lay on the smoothed-out bag. They were the worse for their ride—squashed and pathetic-looking, the edges worn down and crumbling. They seemed to have come from somewhere long ago and far away. "Here, now, we've got cookies I baked

---

MULTIPLE LEARNING STYLES

Bodily-Kinesthetic Students may have difficulty identifying with an old person. Writing and acting out scripts can help them better understand people who they think are much different from themselves.

Activity Have students work in pairs or groups to write a short script involving one or more older people. Suggest that students begin by thinking of a conflict that an older person might face. Remind them that the conflict must be resolved through dialogue with one or more other people. You might pair bodily-kinesthetic learners with linguistic learners. After the script is written, the students can present their plays to the class. **L1** **COLLAB. LEARN.**

only yesterday," Clara said; but he said, "No, no," and ate the Fig Newtons, whose warmth on his tongue filled him with a vague, sad feeling deeper than homesickness. "In my house," he said, "I left things a little messy. I hate to ask it of you, but I didn't manage to straighten up any."

"Don't even think about it," Clara said. "I'll take out a suitcase tomorrow and clean everything up. I'll bring it all back."

"I don't want it. Take it to the colored people."

"Don't want any of it? But, Daddy—"

He didn't try explaining it to her. He finished his lunch in silence and then let her lead him upstairs to the guest room.

Clara had five boys and a girl, the oldest twenty. During the morning as they passed one by one through the house on their way to other places, they heard of his arrival and trooped up to see him. They were fine children, all of them, but it was the girl he enjoyed the most. Francie. She was only thirteen, too young yet to know how to hide what she felt. And what she felt was always about love, it seemed: whom she just loved, who she hoped loved her back. Who was just a darling. Had thirteen-year-olds been so aware of love in the old days? He didn't know and didn't care; all he had to do with Francie was sit smiling in an armchair and listen. There was a new boy in the neighborhood who walked his English sheepdog past her yard every morning, looking toward her house. Was it because of her, or did the dog just like to go that way? When he telephoned her brother Donnie, was he hoping for her to answer? And when she did answer, did he want her to talk a minute or to hand the receiver straight to Donnie? But what would she say to him, anyway? Oh, all her questions had to do with where she might find love, and

everything she said made the old man <u>wince</u> and love her more. She left in the middle of a sentence, knocking against a doorknob as she flew from the room, an unlovable-looking tangle of blond hair and braces and scrapes and Band-Aids. After she was gone the room seemed too empty, as if she had accidentally torn part of it away in her flight.

Getting into an old folks' home was hard. Not only because of lack of good homes, high expenses, waiting lists; it was harder yet to talk his family into letting him go. His son-in-law argued with him every evening, his round, kind face anxious and questioning across the supper table. "Is it that you think you're not welcome here? You are, you know. You were one of the reasons we bought this big house." His grandchildren when they talked to him had a kind of urgency in their voices, as if they were trying to impress him with their acceptance of him. His other daughters called long distance from all across the country and begged him to come to them if he wouldn't stay with Clara. They had room, or they would make room; he had no idea what homes for the aged were like these days. To all of them he gave the same answer: "I've made my decision." He was proud of them for asking, though. All his children had turned out so well, every last one of them. They were good, strong women with happy families, and they had never given him a moment's worry. He was luckier than he had a right to be. He had felt lucky all his life, dangerously lucky, cursed by luck; it had seemed some disaster must be waiting to even things up. But the luck had held. When his wife died it was at a late age, sparing her the pain she would have had to face, and his life had continued in its steady, reasonable pattern with no more sorrow than any other

Vocabulary

wince (wins) v. to draw back slightly, as in pain; flinch

H **Literary Elements**

CHARACTERS Explain that a foil is a character who has certain traits that contrast with the main character. Through the contrast, the traits of the main character are made clearer. Ask students to explain how Francie is a foil to Mr. Carpenter. (*Francie is young and emotional and likes to talk about her feelings. These traits emphasize Mr. Carpenter's hiding his feelings and his not liking to talk about them.*)

I **Active Reading**

CONNECT Encourage students to put themselves in Mr. Carpenter's place. How would they feel if their children and grandchildren clearly wanted them to live with them? What might change their minds about moving to a retirement home?

GIFTED AND TALENTED

Interviewing Older People Review interview techniques. Challenge students to find out more about the lives of elderly people by conducting personal interviews.

Activity Have each student think of an elderly relative, friend, or neighbor they might interview. Encourage students to work together to compile lists

of questions to ask. For example, they may wish to focus on historical events such as World War II, changes in the world, or the positive and negative aspects of growing old. Instruct students to take notes as they conduct their interviews and to write up a transcript of the interview. Students can share their interviews in discussion or in a class notebook. **L3**

J Literary Elements

CHARACTERS What do the elements of Mr. Carpenter's daily life demonstrate about his character? *(He is stubborn in his refusal to give in to his physical weakness and proud in his insistence on helping around the house and not allowing his family to see that his body is failing.)*

VIEWING THE PAINTING

Alice Neel was an American painter known for her portraits of friends and neighbors. She often emphasized and even exaggerated the facial features of her subjects and left other parts of her canvas very simple or blank.

Viewing Response *The man looks dignified, serious, and independent, much like the main character in the story.*

man's. His final lot was to weaken, to crumble and to die—only a secret disaster, not the one he had been expecting.

He walked two blocks daily, fighting off the weakness. He shelled peas for Clara and mended little household articles, which gave him an excuse to sit. Nobody noticed how he arranged to climb the stairs only once a day, at bedtime. When he had empty time he chose a chair without rockers, one that would not be a symbol of age and weariness and lack of work. He rose every morning at six and

stayed in his room a full hour, giving his legs enough warning to face the day ahead. Never once did he disgrace himself by falling down in front of people. He dropped nothing more important than a spoon or a fork.

Meanwhile the wheels were turning; his name was on a waiting list. Not that that meant anything, Clara said. "When it comes right down to driving you out there, I just won't let you go," she told him. "But I'm hoping you won't

Virgil Thompson, 1971. Alice Neel. Oil on canvas, 48 x 37 in. National Portrait Gallery, Washington, DC.

Viewing the painting: How would you describe the personality of this man? How is he similar to or different from the man in the story?

Teaching Options

MEETING INDIVIDUAL NEEDS INCLUSION STRATEGIES

Special Needs Some students may have difficulty connecting with the story's main character or sustaining interest in this story about an older man.

Activity Have pairs of students do role-plays. Partners choose one of these characters—the young man on the motorcycle, Clara, or Francie—and review the scenes with that character.

Then one student in each pair acts the part of Mr. Carpenter and the other plays the second character. Explain that students should take the relationship as it stands in the story and use it to expand on a conversation that the two characters might have. **L1 COLLAB. LEARN.**

Additional Resources
📁 *Inclusion Strategies*

carry things that far. Daddy, won't you put a stop to this foolishness?"

He hardly listened. He had chosen long ago what kind of old age he would have; everyone does. Most, he thought, were weak, and chose to be loved at any cost. He had seen women turn soft and sad, anxious to please, and had watched with pity and impatience their losing battles. And he had once known a schoolteacher, no weakling at all, who said straight out that when she grew old she would finally eat all she wanted and grow fat without worry. He admired that—a simple plan, dependent upon no one. "I'll sit in an armchair," she had said, "with a lady's magazine in my lap and a box of homemade fudge on the lampstand. I'll get as fat as I like and nobody will give a hang." The schoolteacher was thin and pale, with a kind of stooped, sloping figure that was popular at the time. He had lost track of her long ago, but he liked to think that she had kept her word. He imagined her fifty years later, cozy and fat in a puffy chair, with one hand moving constantly between her mouth and the candy plate. If she had died young or changed her mind or put off her eating till another decade, he didn't want to hear about it.

He had chosen independence. Nothing else had even occurred to him. He had lived to himself, existed on less money than his family would ever guess, raised his own vegetables and refused all gifts but an occasional tin of coffee. And now he would sign himself into the old folks' home and enter on his own two feet, relying only on the impersonal care of nurses and cleaning women. He could have chosen to

die alone of neglect, but for his daughters that would have been a burden too—a different kind of burden, much worse. He was sensible enough to see that.

Meanwhile, all he had to do was to look as busy as possible in a chair without rockers and hold fast against his family. Oh, they gave him no peace. Some of their attacks were obvious— the arguments with his son-in-law over the supper table—and some were subtle; you had to be on your guard every minute for those. Francie, for instance, asking him questions about what she called the "olden days." Inviting him to sink unnoticing into doddering reminiscence. "Did I see Granny ever? I don't remember her. Did she like me? What kind of person was she?" He stood his ground, gave monosyllabic answers. It was easier than he had expected. For him, middle age tempted up more memories. Nowadays events had telescoped. The separate agonies and worries—the long, hard births of each of his children, the youngest daughter's chronic childhood earaches, his wife's last illness—were smoothed now into a single, summing-up sentence: He was a widowed farmer with five daughters, all married, twenty grandchildren and three great-grandchildren. "Your grandmother was a fine woman," he told Francie; "just fine." Then he shut up.

Francie, not knowing that she had been spared, sulked and peeled a strip of sunburned skin from her nose.

Clara cried all the way to the home. She was the one who was driving; it made him nervous. One of her hands on the steering wheel held a balled-up tissue, which she had stopped using. She let

---

Vocabulary

subtle (sut′ əl) *adj.* not open or direct; not obvious
doddering (dod′ ər ing) *adj.* trembling or shaking, as from age
monosyllabic (mon′ ə si lab′ ik) *adj.* having only one syllable
chronic (kron′ ik) *adj.* lasting a long time or returning repeatedly

---

K Literary Elements

CHARACTERS What does the story about the woman whom Mr. Carpenter once knew say about his character? *(He admired her independence and her asking for very little from life; he also has these qualities.)*

L Active Reading

RESPOND The following model can help students analyze and respond to the ways in which Mr. Carpenter refuses to give in to stereotypes about old age.

Model: Mr. Carpenter refuses to show his physical weakness, sit in a rocking chair, let his family take care of him, or reminisce about the old days. His refusal may show wisdom: by rejecting the stereotypes of old age, he is rejecting death and disability. However, if he were not so afraid to show weakness, he might share his transition to old age with his family. He might find that there are positive aspects to being old, such as getting to know the younger family members.

Vo•cab•u•lar•y Skills

Etymology The word *reminiscence* may give students difficulty in spelling, pronunciation, or meaning. Explain that it comes from the Latin *reminisci* meaning "to remember." The base word *mens* means "mind," as in *mental*.

Reading Minilesson

Monitoring Comprehension Point out that formulating questions about a story or other text often helps a reader comprehend and remember it better. While reading fiction, readers often make up questions mentally as they read the story. For nonfiction pieces, it is often helpful to write a list of questions and answer them.

Activity Have students write a list of five questions about the selection that leads to a greater understanding of the story. For example, the question "Why does Mr. Carpenter refuse to live with his daughter and her family?" is crucial to the theme of the story. Have students exchange questions and discuss the answers. **L2**

Additional Resources
📁 *Reading Workbook,* p. 14

M Literary Elements

SYMBOL Remind students that a symbol is a concrete object that can suggest various abstract meanings. What might the motorcycle symbolize to Mr. Carpenter? *(freedom, youth, pleasure, independence, defiance)*

Language Note

A ramrod is a thin, metal stick used to push the powder or other charge down into a cannon or rifle that is loaded through its muzzle. *Ramrod-straight* implies a very straight, even stiff, posture.

N Literary Elements

SETTING Have students review the author's description of the old folks' home. Which images present the setting in a positive light? Which present it in a negative light? What is the overall mood of the setting? *(Positive words and phrases include "cavernous," "old-fashioned parlors," "plush couches," and "green room flooded with sunlight." Negative ones include "creaking elevator" and "a long, dark corridor deadened by carpeting." The overall mood is somewhat impersonal and institutional.)*

---

tears run unchecked down her face and drove jerkily with a great deal of brake-slamming and gear-gnashing.

"Clara, I wish you wouldn't take on so," he told her. "There's no need to be sad over *me*."

"I'm not sad so much as mad," Clara said. "I feel like this is something you're doing *to* me, just throwing away what I give. Oh, why do you have to be so stubborn? It's still not too late to change your mind."

The old man kept silent. On his right sat Francie, chewing a thumbnail and scowling out the window, her usual self except for the unexplainable presence of her other hand in his, tight as wire. Periodically she muttered a number; she was counting red convertibles, and had been for days. When she reached a hundred, the next boy she saw would be her true love.

He figured that was probably the reason she had come on this trip—a greater exposure to red convertibles.

Whatever happened to DeSotos? Didn't there used to be a car called a roadster?

They parked in the U-shaped driveway in front of the home, under the

Did You Know?
The *DeSoto*, manufactured by Chrysler from 1928 to 1961, was so popular that it was called "America's family car." It was named after Spanish explorer Hernando de Soto.

shade of a poplar tree. If he had had his way, he would have arrived by motorcycle, but he made the best of it—picked up his underwear sack from between his feet, climbed the front steps ramrod-straight. They were met by a smiling woman in blue who had to check his name on a file and ask more questions. He made sure to give all the answers himself, overriding Clara when necessary. Meanwhile Francie spun on one squeaky sneaker heel

and examined the hall, a cavernous, polished square with old-fashioned parlors on either side of it. A few old people were on the plush[2] couches, and a nurse sat idle beside a lady in a wheel chair.

They went up a creaking elevator to the second floor and down a long, dark corridor deadened by carpeting. The lady in blue, still carrying a sheaf of files, knocked at number 213. Then she flung the door open on a narrow green room flooded with sunlight.

"Mr. Pond," she said, "this is Mr. Carpenter. I hope you'll get on well together."

Mr. Pond was one of those men who run to fat and baldness in old age. He sat in a rocking chair with a gilt-edged Bible on his knees.

"How-do," he said. "Mighty nice to meet you."

They shook hands cautiously, with the women ringing them like mothers asking their children to play nicely with each other. "Ordinarily I sleep in the bed by the window," said Mr. Pond, "but I don't hold it in much importance. You can take your pick."

"Anything will do," the old man said.

Clara was dry-eyed now. She looked frightened.

"You'd best be getting on back now," he told her. "Don't you worry about me. I'll let you know," he said, suddenly generous now that he had won, "if there is anything I need."

Clara nodded and kissed his cheek. Francie kept her face turned away, but she hugged him tightly, and then she looked up at him as she stepped back. Her eyebrows were tilted as if she were about to ask him one of

---

2. *Plush* is a fabric (similar to velvet) that is used in furniture upholstery.

Vocabulary
cavernous (kav′ ər nəs) *adj.* large and spacious, like a cavern

---

Teaching Options

Grammar and Language *Minilesson*

Gerund Phrases Explain that a gerund is the *-ing* form of a verb used as a noun. It may be used as a subject, direct object, object of a preposition, predicate nominative, or appositive. A gerund phrase consists of a gerund and its modifiers. Write this sentence on the board:

Getting into an old folks' home was hard.

Have students identify the gerund phrase *("Getting into an old folks' home")* and tell

how it is used in the sentence *(subject)*.

Activity Write the following sentences from the story. Have students identify each gerund phrase and its function in the sentence.

- "He didn't try explaining it to her." *("explaining it to her"—direct object)*
- "He was proud of them for asking, though." *("asking"—object of preposition)*

L3

Additional Resources

Grammar and Language Transparency 10

Grammar and Language Workbook, p. 95

Grammar and Composition Handbook, Lesson 3.3

Writer's Choice, Lesson 12.3

her questions. Was it her the boy with the sheepdog came for? Did he care when she answered the telephone?

They left, shutting the door with a gentle click. The old man made a great business out of settling his underwear and razor in a bureau drawer, smoothing out the paper bag and folding it, placing it in the next drawer down.

"Didn't bring much," said Mr. Pond, one thumb marking his page in the Bible.

"I don't need much."

"Go on—take the bed by the window. You'll feel better after awhile."

"I *wanted* to come," the old man said.

"That there window is a front one. If you look out, you can see your folks leave."

He slid between the bed and the window and looked out. No reason not to. Clara and Francie were just climbing into the car, the sun lacquering the tops of their heads. Clara was blowing her nose with a dot of tissue.

"*Now* they cry," said Mr. Pond, although he had not risen to look out himself. "Later they'll buy themselves a milk shake to celebrate."

"I wanted to come. I made them bring me."

"And so they did. *I* didn't want to come. My son wanted to put me here—his wife was expecting. And so he did. It all works out the same in the end."

"Well, I could have stayed with one of my daughters," the old man said. "But I'm not like some I have known. Hanging around making burdens of themselves, hoping to be loved. Not me."

"If you don't care about being loved," said Mr. Pond, "how come it would bother you to be a burden?"

Then he opened the Bible again, at the place where his thumb had been all the time and went back to reading.

The old man sat on the edge of the bed, watching the tail of Clara's car flash as sharp and hard as a jewel around the bend of the road. Then, with nobody to watch that mattered, he let his shoulders slump and eased himself out of his suit coat, which he folded over the foot of the bed. He slid his suspenders down and let them dangle at his waist. He took off his copper-toed work boots and set them on the floor neatly side by side. And although it was only noon, he lay down full-length on top of the bedspread. Whiskery lines ran across the plaster of the ceiling high above him. There was a cracking sound in the mattress when he moved; it must be covered with something waterproof.

The tiredness in his head was as vague and restless as anger; the weakness in his knees made him feel as if he had just finished some exhausting exercise. He lay watching the plaster cracks settle themselves into pictures, listening to the silent, neuter voice in his mind form the words he had grown accustomed to hearing now: Let me not give in at the end. Let me continue gracefully till the moment of my defeat. Let Lollie Simpson be alive somewhere even as I lie on my bed; let her be eating homemade fudge in an overstuffed armchair and growing fatter and fatter and fatter.

Literary Elements

O

CHARACTERS What details indicate Mr. Carpenter's mood as he settles in at his new home? *(His slumping shoulders; his taking off his suit coat, suspenders, and boots; and his lying down all indicate that he is sad, depressed, and tired.)*

Literary Elements

P

SYMBOL The author makes the minor character Lollie Simpson, Mr. Carpenter's friend from long ago, important by ending the story with Mr. Carpenter's thoughts of her. What does Lollie Simpson seem to symbolize to Mr. Carpenter? *(She seems to symbolize the will to live as one likes instead of living to please other people.)*

Thematic Focus

Transitions Despite his idea that he is simplifying his life, Mr. Carpenter seems to find the transition into old age very difficult. Have students discuss ways in which he might have made this change easier.

✔ ASSESSMENT OPTIONS

📁 *Quick Checks*, p. 10

MEETING INDIVIDUAL NEEDS — MULTIPLE LEARNING STYLES

Spatial The story includes several scenes in which a specific mood is vividly depicted. Point out that mood is often communicated in visual art.

Activity Have students choose a scene from the story with a mood that they find interesting. Have them illustrate the scene, communicating its mood with form, style, and color.

Scenes they may wish to choose include Mr. Carpenter riding on the back of a motorcycle to his daughter's house, Mr. Carpenter living with his daughter, Mr. Carpenter being driven to the home, or Mr. Carpenter resting on his bed at the end of the story. Have students display their pictures. Encourage the class to identify the moods expressed. **L2**

Responding to Literature

Personal Response

Personal Response

Students may admire Mr. Carpenter
for his independence or feel frustrated
at his pushing away the people who
love him.

What are your feelings about Mr. Carpenter? Do you admire him, pity him,
or find him frustrating? Explain in your journal.

ANALYZING LITERATURE

ANALYZING LITERATURE

1. Mr. Carpenter takes a paper bag
containing a hunk of bread, two Fig
Newtons, underwear, and a razor with
him when he leaves his house.

2. Mr. Carpenter has decided to spend
his old age in an old folks' home
because he is feeling too physically
weak to live alone, and he says he
does not want to impose on his daughters by living with them.

3. Mr. Carpenter's family members
want him to live with them.

4. When Mr. Carpenter arrives at the
old folks' home, he meets his room-
mate, Mr. Pond, and he puts his
belongings away.

5. After Clara and Francie leave, Mr.
Pond says that Mr. Carpenter's family
is glad to leave him at the home. Mr.
Carpenter watches Clara and Francie
drive away. Then he lies down on his
bed and hopes that he can continue to
live gracefully until he dies.

6. The bag might symbolize the completion of a satisfactory life cycle. He
came into the world with nothing, and
he believes it fitting to leave the world
with nothing.

7. Mr. Carpenter's choice suggests
that he values independence above all
else. He does not want others to have
to take responsibility for him.

8. Mr. Carpenter seems to reject his
family's love because he does not
want to be a burden to them and
because he wants to preserve his
independence. In reality, he is too
proud to allow his children to see his
creeping frailty.

9. Mr. Pond believes that Mr.
Carpenter's family asked him to move
to the old folks' home and that he
does not really want to be there. This
was Mr. Pond's own experience.

10. Mr. Carpenter was probably thinking he had done the right thing
although he felt sad and lonely. He is
no less determined to preserve his dignity and independence.

11. Mr. Carpenter does not talk about
love with his family because he does
not want it to be a determining factor
in how he lives the rest of his life. He
enjoys hearing Francie talk about love
because he has blocked this emotion

RECALL

1. What does Mr. Carpenter take with him when he leaves his house?
2. What choice has Mr. Carpenter made about how he will spend his old
   age? Summarize his reasons for making that choice.
3. What do the members of Mr. Carpenter's family want him to do?
4. What happens when Mr. Carpenter arrives at the old folks' home?
5. What does Mr. Carpenter do after Clara and Francie leave?

INTERPRET

6. Why, do you think, does the paper bag give Mr. Carpenter such satisfaction? Might the bag be a **symbol** for something else? Explain.
7. What does Mr. Carpenter's choice suggest about what he values above
   all else? Explain your answer.
8. Why, do you think, does Mr. Carpenter seem to reject the love his
   family offers him?
9. Does Mr. Pond seem to believe that Mr. Carpenter really wants to be
   at the old folks' home? Explain your answer.
10. What do you think Mr. Carpenter was thinking as he stretched out on
    the bed at the old folks' home? Do you think he is any less deter-
    mined to maintain his dignity and independence? Explain.

EVALUATE AND CONNECT

11. In your opinion, why does Mr. Carpenter never discuss love with his
    family? Why, do you think, does hearing Francie talk about love give
    him so much pleasure?
12. What choice do you think you would have made in Mr. Carpenter's
    situation? How does that choice fit in with your response to the Focus
    Activity on page 114?
13. Mr. Carpenter seems to feel that only the weak depend on loved ones.
    Do you agree with him? Explain.
14. To what does the title of this story refer? What does it suggest about
    how Mr. Carpenter will face death?
15. Do you think this story presents a realistic view of the dilemmas faced
    by older people and their families? Explain.

out of his own life.

12. Some students may say they would have
moved in with their family. Others may say they
would have maintained their independence like
Mr. Carpenter.

13. Most students will say that strong people
also depend on loved ones because it takes
strength to trust enough to love and be loved.

14. The title refers to Mr. Carpenter. It suggests
that he will die still fighting to maintain his dignity and independence.

15. Some students may find the view realistic
while others will feel that many older people are
not as fortunate as Mr. Carpenter to have a loving family begging him to come live with them.

Literary ELEMENTS

Characters
A short story may have one or many
characters who take part in the story's
action. The **main characters** are the
most important to the story. Most stories also have **minor characters** who
interact with the main characters, but
who may not be especially important
to the plot. Characters who reveal only
one personality trait are called **flat
characters**. Those who show varied
traits, which may even seem contradictory, are called **round characters**.

1. Who are the main characters in
   "With All Flags Flying"? Who is the
   central character of the story?

2. In your opinion, is Mr. Pond a main
   character or a minor one? Support
   your response with examples from
   the story.

3. Do you think Mr. Carpenter is a
   round, fully developed character or
   a flat character showing only one or
   two traits? Give specific examples
   from the story to support your
   claim.

● See **Literary Terms Handbook**,
p. R2.

LITERARY ELEMENTS

1. The main characters are Clara, Francie,
   and Mr. Carpenter. Mr. Carpenter is the
   central character.
2. Mr. Pond is a minor character. His interaction with Mr. Carpenter is important, but
   he is not important in himself.
3. Mr. Carpenter is a round character. He
   exhibits various traits, such as independence, stubbornness, and pride.

Additional Resources
Literary Elements Transparency 10

LITERATURE AND WRITING

Writing About Literature
The Author's Voice Write an analysis of the author's attitude toward Mr. Carpenter, his behavior, and his plans for his future. Does she agree with his decisions? Or is she trying to show that Mr. Carpenter is misguided in his plan? Use specific examples from the story to illustrate the author's feelings about the main character and the choices he makes for himself.

Creative Writing
Obituary Imagine that Mr. Carpenter has died after living at the old folks' home for several years. Write his obituary for the local newspaper. Feel free to make up details about his life, but make sure that they are consistent with what you know about Mr. Carpenter from the story. For models, refer to some of the obituaries in your local newspaper.

EXTENDING YOUR RESPONSE

Literature Groups
Discussing Issues Mr. Carpenter tries to pare down his life before he goes to the old folks' home, to get rid of anything he doesn't need. He seems to think that love is not one of the essentials of life. What do you think? Is love essential to life, or can people get by without it? Can love be put away like an extra suit of clothes? Discuss the question in your group. Support your opinions with examples from the story and from your own experience. Finally, share the results of your discussion with the class.

Learning for Life
Elder Care Working with a partner, find out what resources exist in your community for older people who can no longer live without assistance. These may include traditional "old folks' homes," also called nursing homes; "meals-on-wheels" programs; visiting nurse or housekeeping services; and retirement communities. Call or write to one of the resources to learn about the services offered. Share your findings with the class.

Performing
Dialogue With a partner, practice the dialogue between Mr. Pond and Mr. Carpenter. Add an answer that Mr. Carpenter might have given to Mr. Pond's final question: "If you don't care about being loved, how come it would bother you to be a burden?" Perform your dialogue for the class.

Reading Further
Anne Tyler has written a number of books. Here is one you might enjoy:

Novel: *The Accidental Tourist,* in which the main character hates to travel, but makes his living as the anonymous author of travel guidebooks.

Viewing: *The Accidental Tourist*

📖 **Save your work for your portfolio.**

THE SHORT STORY 🐾 125

LITERATURE AND WRITING

Writing About Literature
Students' analyses should
- specifically state the author's attitude toward Mr. Carpenter.
- use specific examples to illustrate the author's attitude.

Creative Writing
Students' obituaries should
- include details about Mr. Carpenter that are consistent with the story.
- be written in the style of newspaper obituaries.

EXTENDING YOUR RESPONSE

Literature Groups Suggest that students use Mr. Carpenter as an example and consider his attitude at the end of the story. How has his philosophy affected his own life? **COLLAB. LEARN.**

Learning for Life Encourage students who have visited relatives in a nursing home or retirement community to share their personal observations and experiences.

Performing Suggest that students discuss Mr. Carpenter's and Mr. Pond's feelings and attitudes before practicing their dialogues.

✓ ASSESSMENT OPTIONS

📁 *Quick Checks,* p. 10
📁 *Selection and Theme Assessment,* pp. 19–20
📁 *Performance Assessment,* p. 10
💾 *Testmaker*

GRAMMAR AND LANGUAGE
Quotation Marks in Dialogue

Have students discuss whether there is more than one way in which some dialogues may be written.

READING AND THINKING
Identifying Assumptions

1. The assumption is incorrect. Although many older people do develop definite health problems that change their ways of life, others like Mr. Carpenter himself simply become less able to take care of themselves.
2. The assumption appears to be correct. His family is hurt and does not understand why he won't live with them, but they accept his decision.
3. The assumption is incorrect. Love among older people and family members causes them to depend on one another; love is not a sign of weakness.
4. The assumption is incorrect. Her father has misguided ideas about dignity and independence, which cause him to refuse to live with the family.
5. The assumption is correct. However, Mr. Carpenter did choose on his own to live in the old folks' home.

VOCABULARY
Prefixes Expressing Number

1. trilingual
2. a government led by two kings or queens
3. Humans are bipeds. Dogs are quadrupeds.
4. two hands

Additional Resources

Grammar and Composition Handbook, Lesson 11.9

Grammar and Language Workbook, p. 271

Writer's Choice, Lesson 21.9

Reading Workbook, p. 14

Vocabulary Practice, p. 10

GRAMMAR AND LANGUAGE • Quotation Marks in Dialogue

Dialogue is the conversation between characters in a literary work. Quotation marks are used to enclose the exact words spoken by a character. Each time the speaker changes, a new paragraph begins and a new set of quotation marks is used. Here's an example of dialogue from "With All Flags Flying."

> "Give you a lift, if you like," he said. "You going somewhere?"
>
> "Just into Baltimore."
>
> "Hop on."

PRACTICE Copy several examples of dialogue from the story, omitting the quotation marks and the paragraph breaks. Exchange papers with a classmate. Rewrite each dialogue, adding quotation marks and paragraph breaks as needed. Check your work by comparing it with the dialogues in the story.

● For more about punctuating dialogue, see **Language Handbook,** p. R49.

READING AND THINKING • Identifying Assumptions

An assumption is something that is taken for granted without proof. In fiction, characters often base their actions on assumptions they make. For example, in "With All Flags Flying," Mr. Carpenter assumes that Clara will try to convince him to make his home with her. This assumption turns out to be correct. Mr. Carpenter also assumes that he would be a burden to Clara and her family. This assumption appears to be incorrect. Clara and her family try hard to convince Mr. Carpenter to live with them; it's unlikely that they would consider him a burden.

● For information on related comprehension skills, see **Reading Handbook,** pp. R78–R107.

PRACTICE Indicate whether you think each assumption below is correct or incorrect. Support your answers with information from the story or from your own experience.

1. Mr. Carpenter assumes that something definite, like a stroke or arthritis, will put an end to his living alone.
2. Mr. Carpenter assumes that his family will finally accept his decision to live in an old folks' home.
3. Mr. Carpenter assumes that older people who depend on their families are weak.
4. Clara assumes that her father is rejecting *her* when he refuses to live with her and her family.
5. Mr. Pond assumes that Mr. Carpenter is not as happy about being in the old folks' home as he pretends to be.

VOCABULARY • Prefixes Expressing Number

One of the vocabulary words for "With All Flags Flying" is *monosyllabic,* which means "having only one syllable." Like *uni-, mono-* is a prefix that means "one." If you speak in a monotone, you use only one tone. A monochromatic picture uses one color; a monologue is one person speaking.

Many prefixes and combining forms express number. *Bi-* (or *bin-*), *di-*, and *du-* mean "two"; *tri-* means three; *tetra-* and *quadri-* (or *quadru-*) mean four.

PRACTICE Use your knowledge of familiar words and prefixes to answer the following questions.

1. What word describes someone who can speak three languages? (Hint: Think about *bilingual.*)
2. What is a diarchy? (Hint: Think about *monarchy.*)
3. Name one animal that's a biped and one that's a quadruped. (Hint: Think about *pedal.*)
4. What is required to do a *bimanual* task? (Hint: Think about *manual labor.*)

LISTENING, SPEAKING, and VIEWING

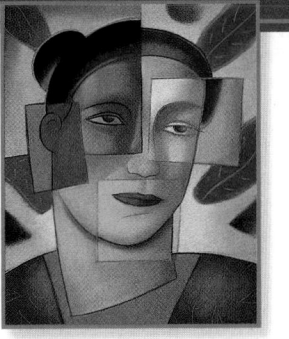

Debating

The story "With All Flags Flying" pits the wishes of an aging father against those of his daughter. The two characters could have held a debate to settle their differences. A debate is a contest between two people or teams who argue for or against an idea. In a debate, two sides take turns presenting their cases. Then, each side has a chance to refute the other's arguments. Finally, a panel of judges selects the winning side. The checklists below can help you plan and present a debate.

Gathering Information

- Choose a statement or question that has two clear sides.
- Take a position and back it up with facts, statistics, and examples.
- Make sure that each point you make includes accurate and relevant facts. Avoid information that can be interpreted in more than one way.
- Consider the knowledge and sympathies of the judges or your audience. Present your case in a way that will be understandable and convincing to them.
- Anticipate and address the arguments of your opponent.
- Write key ideas and facts on note cards that you can refer to when presenting the debate.

Presenting a Debate

- Speak clearly and loudly enough for everyone to hear. Put some enthusiasm in your voice.
- Stand straight, but be natural. Use hand gestures to emphasize important points. Vary your gaze to include every person in the room.

ACTIVITIES

1. Television news programs such as *Crossfire* and *NewsHour with Jim Lehrer* regularly invite guests to discuss their opposing views on current events. Watch one of these broadcasts and take notes on what the speakers say and how they say it. Then use the checklists above to evaluate which speaker was most convincing. Share your results with the class.

2. Brainstorm a list of debate topics with your class. Find a partner who will debate the opposite side of a topic you feel strongly about. Research the topic and prepare a short (five-minute) presentation of your case. With your partner, take turns giving your presentation. Then, as a class, discuss the ideas that each side should include when refuting the other's argument.

LISTENING, SPEAKING, and VIEWING

Objective

- To understand and use the techniques for debating

Teaching Strategies

Have students name several controversial topics currently in the news. Choose one and have students give facts and examples to back each side. Chart the supporting points on the board under the headings *Pro* and *Con*. Explain that in preparing a debate, participants would find facts and statistics to support each point.

Activities

1. If possible, show a videotape of one of these programs to the class. Have the class discuss speakers' tactics such as tone of voice, gestures, and facial expression, evaluating those that are effective and those that are not.
2. Discuss constructive ways to critique a speaker or debater. Have the class give constructive criticism to two or three pairs who present their debates.

Teaching Options

MEETING INDIVIDUAL NEEDS — ENGLISH LANGUAGE LEARNERS

Taking Sides English language learners may be unfamiliar with the art of debate. Explain that debaters do not engage in an emotional argument. They research their topic and present facts to support each side of the argument.

Activity Have pairs of students list facts to support two sides of the following or similar statements, using facts they know. Have each pair present their facts.

1. High school classes should not start early in the morning.
2. The legal driving age should be raised to eighteen.

Additional Resources

📁 *English Language Learners Sourcebook*

Objectives

- To read and analyze a short story about what a young boy learns about the power of friendship
- To learn about the purpose of a narrator in a short story
- To write a review of a story

Skills

Reading/Thinking: Inferring; Drawing Conclusions; Paraphrasing and Summarizing
Writing: Personal Writing
Vocabulary: Analogies
Grammar/Language: Using Apostrophes to Show Possession
Listening/Speaking: Role-Playing Dialogue
Life Skills: Letter of Inquiry

Motivating
→OPTIONS

Selection Focus Transparency 11: Have students discuss the benefits and disadvantages of pet ownership.

Focus Activity: Have students discuss whether relationships with animals might be included in their definitions of true friendship.

Before You Read

A Child, a Dog, the Night

FOCUS ACTIVITY

How would you define true friendship?

SHARING IDEAS Write a definition of true friendship. Meet with a small group of classmates to compare and discuss your definitions.

SETTING A PURPOSE Read to discover what a young boy learns about the power of friendship.

BACKGROUND

The Time and Place
The time of this story is the not-too-distant past. The place is the rugged landscape of northern Chile—a country on the west coast of South America—in and around the town of Chuquicamata, site of the world's largest open-pit copper mines.

Did You Know?
The places mentioned in this story—Chuquicamata, Calama, and Antofagasta—are located in the Northern Desert region of Chile. The Atacama Desert, one of the driest places in the world, covers the northern half of this region. Chuquicamata, in the Atacama Desert, is known for its enormous copper mine, where one of the main characters in this story works. Exports of copper and other valuable minerals support Chile's economy.

Meet Amalia Rendic

In her native Chile, Amalia Rendic was a renowned author of literature for young people. She also was a teacher of Castilian Spanish, one of the more common forms of the language spoken in Spain. In addition, Rendic was a contributor to two Latin American newspapers, *El Mercurio*, of Santiago, Chile, and *La Nación*, published in Costa Rica.

Amalia Rendic was born in Chile in 1928; she died in 1988. This story appears in Landscapes of a New Land, *a collection of short stories by Latin American women.*

VOCABULARY PREVIEW

disperse (dis purs′) v. to go off in different directions; scatter; p. 129
intrigue (in trēg′) v. to excite the curiosity or interest of; fascinate; p. 130
monologue (mon′ ə lôg′) n. a long speech made by one person; p. 131
residue (rez′ ə dōō′) n. what remains after part is removed; p. 131

contemplate (kon′ təm plāt′) v. to give intense attention to; consider carefully; p. 132
plaintive (plān′ tiv) adj. expressing sorrow; mournful; sad; p. 133
reciprocal (ri sip′ rə kəl) adj. given, felt, or shown in return; p. 133

128   UNIT 1

RESOURCE MANAGER

Lesson Planning Resource
The *Unit One Planning Guide* (pp. 88–95) provides additional lesson notes and reduced versions of all print resources.

Other Print Resources
- Active Reading Guide, p. 11
- Vocabulary Practice, p. 11
- Reading Workbook, p. 14
- Grammar and Language Workbook, p. 277
- Grammar and Composition Handbook, Lesson 11.11

- Quick Checks, p. 11
- Selection and Theme Assessment, pp. 21–22
- Performance Assessment, p. 11
- Spanish Summaries, p. 11
- Inclusion Strategies
- English Language Learners Sourcebook

Transparencies
- Selection Focus 11
- Literary Elements 11
- Grammar and Language 11

Technology
 Audio Library
 Spanish Audio Library
 Glencoe Literature Web Site
 Testmaker

A Child, a Dog, the Night

Amalia Rendic ∾

Translated by Miriam Ben-Ur

THE SUN FADED SHORTLY IN GOLDEN RAYS. The faint light of the street-lamps could scarcely hold back the darkness and fog that invaded the entire mining camp. A large group of men handling the pile drivers, machinists, ore workers, and miners were going home. The return journey was slow and silent because of the breathing difficulty caused by the thin air. The Chuquicamata[1] mine is situated at over two thousand eight hundred meters above sea level.

As the group arrived at the Binkeroft neighborhood, it began to disperse toward different streets of the workers camp. Household lights could be seen through half-open windows and doors. The worker, Juan Labra,[2] a strong machinist and loyal friend, continued walking on one of the many narrow streets, still sighing because of the shrill whistles and sirens of the work areas. The wrinkles quickly vanished from his young face, which was already furrowed with deep wrinkles like veins of ore, and a burst of tenderness filled his eyes. He readily accepted his young family's loving welcome. Little Juan was waiting at the door of the house as he did every afternoon. He was a small nine-year-old boy, with lively, curious eyes, quite strong for his age and with feet that loved to walk. For him, the mine had no secrets. He knew every inch of the mine and all of its mysteries. He was a talkative child whose constant chatter could be interrupted only by smiles. With his face pressed against the

---

1. *Chuquicamata* (chōō kwē′ kə mä′ tə)
2. *Juan Labra* (wän lä′ brə)

Vocabulary
disperse (dis purs′) *v.* to go off in different directions; scatter

---

SUMMARY

Juan Labra, a copper mine worker, is asked by Mr. Davies, one of his company's owners, to take care of his dog Black for a few days. Little Juan, Labra's nine-year-old son, and the dog become fast friends. Little Juan becomes anxious about Black's master taking his dog back. He asks his father to buy the dog, but the dog is too expensive. Mr. Davies returns and takes Black away. During the night, Little Juan begins to cry and the dog begins to howl. Mr. Davies realizes that the dog loves another human. Labra, upset by his son's sadness, goes to see Mr. Davies. Mr. Davies tells Labra that the dog no longer belongs to him. Labra takes the dog home to his son.

📁 *Spanish Summaries,* p. 11

A Active Reading

PREDICT Invite predictions as to what the story is about. Challenge students to imagine the connections between the three key elements: a child, a dog, and the night.

Additional Resources
📁 *Active Reading Guide,* p. 11
🎧 *Audio Library*
🎧 *Spanish Audio Library*

Teaching Options

CONNECTING TO OTHER SELECTIONS

The chart at the right shows three ways to connect "A Child, a Dog, the Night" to selections in this book.

For specific teaching strategies, see the **Unit One Planning Guide,** pages 91–92.

Connection	Title
Life Skills: Decision Making	→ "Two Kinds," p. 49
Thematic: Companions	→ "The Angry Winter," p. 557
Literary: Point of View	→ from *Farewell to Manzanar,* p. 460

Copper Country Much of the world's copper is found in North and South America, in the mountain ranges extending from Alaska to the tip of South America. Chile is the top copper-mining country in the world.

B Literary Elements

SETTING The author uses several sensory images to describe the story's setting. Have students point out these images and tell to which sense each one appeals. *(the sun fading in golden rays—sight; breathing difficulty caused by the thin air—touch; whistles and sirens—sound)*

C Critical Thinking

INFERRING What can students infer about the relationship between the North American owners of the copper mine and their South American employees? *(The owners keep a distance; the two groups do not socialize.)*

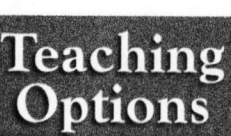

VIEWING THE ART

Antonio Berni was an Argentinian artist known for his portraits of poor workers, with whom he lived for a time.

Viewing Response *The boy's expression is sensitive and observant, like Little Juan.*

Teaching Options

El Chico de la Gorra Verde (Juanito Laguna), c. 1954. Antonio Berni. Gouache, charcoal, and wax crayon on board, 28½ x 20½ in. Private collection.
Viewing the art: How would you describe the expression on this boy's face? Does he fit your image of Little Juan? Why or why not?

iron garden gate, he curiously watched a very tall North American who was walking behind his father.

"Dad, a gringo[3] is following you, he is coming to our house!" he whispered, frightened, to his father. The street was deserted.

Little Juan was <u>intrigued</u> by the presence of Black, the huge shepherd dog that followed Mr. Davies, his master. Black was one of the few beings that had managed to enter Davies' affections. A solitary companion in his lonely existence in a foreign land.

"Please come in, Mr. Davies. What can we do for you?" said the miner Juan Labra, respectfully taking off his metal hat and opening the small door of the gate. He could barely hide his astonishment at seeing one of the company's owners at his door.

"I'll be brief, Mr. Labra. I need a big favor from you. I soon must leave for Antofagasta[4] and want to leave in your custody for a few days my good friend, Black. You'll be kind. In Calama[5] you organized a society for the protection of animals. Everybody knows this," said Mr. Davies, looking at his dog.

"That's fine, Mr. Davies, thank you for your trust. He will be happy here. We will make sure the dog doesn't suffer. My son, Little Juan, will take care of him in my absence," promised Labra, adjusting his jacket and feeling strangely satisfied inside.

"I leave him in your hands and thank you very much. See you later, Mr. Labra. I'll return very soon, Black . . . Ah, I forgot! Here I'll leave his provisions of canned meat. It is his favorite food."

The master and his dog seemed sad. Black tugged at his master's pants, Davies

---

3. In Latin American countries, *gringo* refers to a foreigner, especially a non-Hispanic North American.

4. *Antofagasta* (än′ tō fə gäs′ tə)

5. *Calama* (kə lä′ mə)

Vocabulary
intrigue (in trēg′) *v.* to excite the curiosity or interest of; fascinate

MEETING INDIVIDUAL NEEDS

ENGLISH LANGUAGE LEARNERS

Pet Stories Explain that stories about children and their dogs or other pets are very popular in American culture and in other cultures as well. For example, the story of the collie Lassie has been the basis for popular American television shows and movies.

Activity Lead a discussion about pet stories that English language learners know from their own cultures. What do the stories have in common? Why do these stories continue to be popular in many cultures? You may wish to have each student write a paragraph summarizing a pet story he or she knows.

Additional Resources
📁 *English Language Learners Sourcebook*

Amalia Rendic ❧

bent over to pet the dog's head, with its pointed snout, and left. The animal started to follow, but Little Juan's arms held him back like chains. Black barked falteringly, sniffing the air. His red, wet tongue was hanging out of his mouth. He panted anxiously. The boy closed the gate. Black stood erect, looking lonesome. His shining fur, his slenderness, his dignified bearing, were indications of his pedigree. He was an expensive dog and had won many dog shows because of his pedigree.

The boy began talking to the dog as if it were a younger brother. For a long time they watched each other without even blinking. The dog's gaze was steady, and the boy's face was reflected in his eyes like tiny bright points. He shyly petted the back of the dog, who was sniffing the air and later responded with a reluctant movement of his tail.

Little Juan continued his strange monologue with Black. They started to become fond of each other. Across the dark, foggy hours of the night the dawn arrived. Then the day broke, as always, in the middle of the two huge mounds that formed the San Pedro and San Pablo volcanoes. Everything seemed to be a wet blue color.

Black awoke with the first sirens on the patio of the workers' house and watched the procession of miners; it was almost as if a great thing had awakened in his heart, too. He responded to these new impressions with barks that sounded like explosions. First thing in the morning, Little Juan, in a fantasy

The dog's gaze was steady, and the boy's face was reflected in his eyes like tiny bright points.

world, went out to see his new friend, and during the next few days they went everywhere together.

Challenging the wind, they ran along the winding ribbon that was the road to Calama. They tirelessly penetrated the immense vastness of the thin air.

They played together, diving into the gray residues of the copper mine pit, that shapeless, majestic mass of metallic land. They tried to collect the shining blue-green and yellow reflections that make bright colors in the sunlight.

They passed the hours this way until the nights came, the ties of the friendship that bound Little Juan and Black becoming stronger and stronger. A growing anxiety clouded the boy's short-lived happiness. He was dreading the day that their time together would end. It was certain that Mr. Davies would return.

"Papa, can't you ask the mister to give us Black? Why can't you buy him?"

"No, Little Juan, he will never be ours. He is very elegant, and worth his weight in gold. He is a rich man's dog. The gringos like to take walks with dogs like this one and present them in shows," answered the worker with a bitter smile.

"When I grow up I will buy him," responded little Juan decisively. "I don't want them to take him away! He's my friend!" he shouted at his father.

One day, as they returned from their walk on the banks of the Loa River, a nasty mountain wind began to blow. They were wet from

Vocabulary
monologue (mon′ ə lôg′) *n.* a long speech made by one person
residue (rez′ ə do͞o′) *n.* what remains after part is removed

THE SHORT STORY 🐾 131

D **Literary Elements**

NARRATOR Have students discuss the effect of having an omniscient narrator in describing the meeting of the boy and the dog. *(The reader gets a touching picture of the interaction between the two and infers their feelings for himself or herself.)*

Language Note

A dog's pedigree is its family tree, a record listing all its ancestors, which is used to show that the dog is descended only from dogs of the same breed. The word *pedigree* comes from the French *pie de grue*, or crane's foot. The shape made by the branches in a family tree resembles a crane's foot.

E **Literary Elements**

IMAGERY The author emphasizes color in her descriptions of the setting. Have students point out each example of a color image on the page and discuss its effects. *(The volcanoes are a "wet blue color"; the copper mine residues are gray; reflections in the mine are blue-green and yellow. The color imagery makes the setting vivid and emphasizes the liveliness of Juan and Black.)*

MEETING INDIVIDUAL NEEDS **MULTIPLE LEARNING STYLES**

Spatial Drawing maps of the story's setting can help make the story more concrete for spatial learners.

Activity Ask students to locate a detailed map of Chile. Have them draw maps that show Chile's location in South America and the locations of Chuquicamata, Calama, Antofagasta, the Atacama Desert, the San Pedro and San Pablo volcanoes, and the Loa River.
L1

PLOT: *Conflict* Remind students that most stories are based on a conflict that the main character experiences. Have them define the story's conflict. Tell whether the protagonist has an internal conflict or a conflict against an antagonist, nature, society, or a supernatural force. *(Little Juan's conflict is that he loves Black but knows he must give him up when his master, Mr. Davies, returns. It is against an antagonist, Mr. Davies.)*

G **Literary Elements**

PERSONIFICATION What human trait does the author give to the dog in this figure of speech? *(the ability to speak)*

H **Critical Thinking**

INFERRING What is the author saying about how people are affected by the night? *(People reach their lowest emotional points at night; they become introspective and feel lonely and hopeless.)*

VIEWING THE PAINTING

The title, *Amanecer,* is Spanish for "sunrise."

Viewing Response *The darkness and empty, bleak landscape create a sense of the loneliness and sadness that Little Juan felt.*

Amanecer, c. 1917–1918. Dr. Atl. Oil on burlap, 15¾ x 24 in. Private collection.
Viewing the painting: What elements of this painting reflect Little Juan's mood when he returned Black to his owner?

the silky mist of Camanchaca.[6] When they came to the door, they stopped as if in fear and dread.

"Mr. Davies!" He had returned. The little boy tried to explain what the dog meant to him, but the words welled up in his heart and stayed in his parched throat. It was a sad moment.

"Good-bye, little friend, and good luck," he stammered, weeping and wringing his hands nervously.

Mr. Davies thanked him sincerely. Like a little gentleman, the child refused to accept any payment.

_____

6. *Camanchaca* (kə´ män chä´ kə)

Black reluctantly started to walk behind his former owner, and eagerly examining the corners of the road, said good-bye to the workers' neighborhoods on the road toward the American camp. Now that Little Juan's first encounter with despair was over, he pondered the fact that he could never have an elegant dog. Black continued his walk. The harmony settled in both of them.

But the loneliness of night came, when souls <u>contemplate</u> themselves to the last fragment of life itself and then everything was useless. Little Juan's defenses collapsed and he began to cry. Something provoked a flow of communication between the boy and the animal across the space and at that very moment,

Vocabulary
contemplate (kon´ təm plāt´) *v.* to give intense attention to; consider carefully

Teaching Options

Grammar and Language *Minilesson*

Using Apostrophes to Show Possession On the board, write the phrase "the dog's head" and discuss its meaning. Review rules for using an apostrophe to show possession.
• To form the possessive of a singular noun or of a plural noun that does not end in -s, add an apostrophe and -s.
• To form the possessive of a plural noun ending in -s, add only an apostrophe.

Activity Read the following sentences aloud. Have students write each sentence, using apostrophes correctly.
1. The dog's gaze was steady, and the boy's face was reflected in his eyes like tiny bright points.
2. Black said good-bye to the workers' neighborhoods on the road toward the American camp. (Point out that *workers* is plural.) **L1**

Additional Resources
Grammar and Language Transparency 11
Grammar and Language Workbook, p. 277
Grammar and Composition Handbook, Lesson 11.11
Writer's Choice, Lesson 21.11

the dog began to howl in the American camp. Memories of Black were flashing through the boy's mind, and as if driven by a secret force, the dog barked furiously, asking the wind to transmit his message. It began as a <u>plaintive</u> concert, and then it became deafening.

Little Juan cried the whole night in a beseeching moan that became a strange concert that whipped through the still streets of the mining town.

Mr. Davies was bewildered by Black's behavior. What could a man do when faced with a crying dog? A new truth took possession of the gringo's mind. Black didn't belong to him anymore; he had lost his love.

Labra could not comfort his tearful and feverish little boy. For what could a man do when faced with a crying child? Labra wanted to see his son's quick, confident smile once again. He felt obliged to win back Little Juan's smile. Poverty had stung him many times, but he could not stand this. Something extraordinary would have to happen in the mining town on this uneasy night. As if the time had come for all men to be brothers, Labra threw his poncho on his shoulders, took the flashlight, and set off for the high neighborhood to see if a miracle could become reality. Yes, he must be courageous and daring. He, a simple laborer, always shy and silent, would ask for the elegant, beautiful, prize-winning Black from one of the company bosses. He inhaled the cold night air deeply and shuddered to

think of his own boldness. He climbed up toward the American camp.

Suddenly, a pair of brown, phosphorescent[7] eyes were glowing in the light of the lantern. Labra was startled. The smell of a pipe and fine tobacco, and a familiar bark stopped him . . .

Mr. Davies had gone out to see him at that very moment and had been coming toward the workers' housing area!

Something touched the hearts of the two men. Words were not necessary.

"He doesn't belong to me anymore," stammered Mr. Davies, depositing Black's heavy metal leash in the worker's hands.

Labra took the animal in his trembling hands and a melancholy[8] happiness warmed his smile. There were no elaborate thanks, only a silent and <u>reciprocal</u> understanding. Black, tugging, forced him to continue following his tracks toward Little Juan's neighborhood.

In that miraculous moment, a new warmth tempered the night of Chuqui.

---

7. Here, *phosphorescent* (fos′fə res′ənt) means "glowing."
8. Here, *melancholy* (mel′ ən kol′ ē) means "thoughtful and serious."

Vocabulary
plaintive (plān′ tiv) *adj.* expressing sorrow; mournful; sad
reciprocal (ri sip′ rə kəl) *adj.* given, felt, or shown in return

THE SHORT STORY ✿ 133

❶ Critical Thinking

DRAWING CONCLUSIONS How are Mr. Davies and Juan Labra alike? Help students understand one of the author's themes by using the following model to draw conclusions.

Model: Mr. Davies and Juan Labra have very different positions in society. Mr. Davies is a wealthy owner of a company while Juan is a poor employee of the company. At the end of the story, the author says about Mr. Davies, "What could a man do when faced with a crying dog?" She says about Juan, "For what could a man do when faced with a crying child?" I think the author uses this repetition to show that despite superficial differences, Mr. Davies and Juan share human emotions. They have been brought closer together by the love of the boy and the dog.

❶ Active Reading

QUESTION The author says that "Something touched the hearts of the two men." What is that "something"? *(sympathy, understanding)*

Thematic Focus

Transitions Have students discuss whether the changes experienced by the story's characters are permanent or temporary. Is it unrealistic that social gaps can be bridged because of the love between a boy and a dog?

✓ ASSESSMENT OPTIONS

📁 *Quick Checks,* p. 11

Reading *Minilesson*

Paraphrasing and Summarizing Point out the differences between paraphrasing and summarizing. In paraphrasing, a short passage, such as a paragraph, is translated into one's own words, keeping the original details. In summarizing, a reader extracts the basic meaning of a longer passage by condensing the ideas.

Activity Have students practice paraphrasing and summarizing. First, have them write a summary of the story. Then, have them write a paraphrase of the story's second-to-last paragraph. Have volunteers read their summaries and paraphrases aloud. **L1**

Additional Resources
📁 *Reading Workbook,* p. 14

Responding to the Selection

Personal Response

Students may describe reactions such as warmth, pleasure, or happiness.

ANALYZING LITERATURE

1. The characters are Juan Labra and his son and Mr. Davies and his dog Black. Juan is an employee of Mr. Davies.
2. Mr. Davies chooses Juan to take care of the dog because he knows that Juan has previously organized a society to protect animals.
3. Little Juan first talks to the dog and gently pets it. As he continues talking to it, he and the dog begin to like one another. They begin playing together for hours each day and soon they have a strong affection for each other.
4. Little Juan begins crying during the night and Black begins howling. Labra decides to go to Mr. Davies and ask him for Black.
5. The story ends with Mr. Davies handing Black over to Labra, and Labra heading home with the dog.
6. At the beginning of the story, there is distance between the Labras and Mr. Davies. This is conveyed by Little Juan's fear and excitement at seeing Mr. Davies in his neighborhood and in Labra's surprise and his polite, respectful behavior.
7. Labra is proud to be asked to take care of Black. This is shown by his thanking Mr. Davies and his feeling "strangely satisfied."
8. Labra probably feels sad and frustrated because he knows how much his son loves the dog, but he is too poor to buy the dog for him.
9. The climax of the story is when Mr. Davies gives the dog to Labra. This is the point at which the conflict is resolved; the characters undergo a change.
10. The warmth is the sympathy, understanding, and friendship experienced by Labra and Mr. Davies.
11. Students may say that Labra is the hero of the story because his actions lead to the story's climax; he changes as a result of the story's events.
12. Students may say that female characters might have shown their emotions more obviously. A girl might have cried when the dog was taken away or told the owner of her love for the animal. A mother might have immediately asked the owner for the dog.
13. Little Juan will not accept the

money because he is proud and feels that he has cared for the dog out of love and friendship and not as a job. Some students may say they would have done the same thing while others may say they would have taken the money because they did perform a valuable service.
14. Juan Labra and Mr. Davies feel like equals because they realize they share many human emotions such as love and sympathy.
15. Students may say that dogs might become devoted to a new master as quickly as Black if the new master were particularly loving and suited to the dog's temperament as Little Juan is.

Responding to Literature

Personal Response

How did the ending of the story make you feel? Describe your reactions in your journal.

ANALYZING LITERATURE

RECALL

1. Who are the characters in this story? What is their relationship to one another?
2. Why does Mr. Davies choose Juan Labra to take care of Black?
3. Use details from the story to describe how the relationship between Little Juan and Black develops.
4. Describe how Little Juan and Black react to being separated after Mr. Davies returns. What does Labra decide to do?
5. How does the story end?

INTERPRET

6. Explain the characters' attitudes toward each other at the beginning of the story. How does the author convey these attitudes?
7. How does Labra feel about being asked to take care of Black? Cite evidence from the story to support your answer.
8. How do you think Labra feels when Little Juan asks him to buy Black from Mr. Davies? Explain your answer.
9. What is the **climax** of the story? Explain why you think this is the turning point in the story.
10. What is your interpretation of the last line of the story?

EVALUATE AND CONNECT

11. In your opinion, who is the **hero** of this story? Give reasons for your answer. (See Literary Terms Handbook, page R6.)
12. All of the characters in this story are male. In your opinion, might female characters, in the same situation, express their feelings differently? Explain.
13. Juan Labra and his family probably need the money Mr. Davies offers to Little Juan. Why do you think Little Juan will not accept the money? What would you have done?
14. **Theme Connections** How are the characters in this story transformed by the events that occur?
15. Do you think most dogs would become devoted to a new master as quickly and completely as Black did? Explain your answer.

Narrator
The **narrator**, or storyteller, lets the reader know what is going on in a story. A fiction writer chooses the narrator's point of view that will tell a story in the most appealing way. The author of "A Child, a Dog, the Night," for example, uses an **omniscient**, or "all knowing," narrator who stands outside the story and knows the thoughts and feelings of every character. As a result, the reader knows more than any one character does.

1. Why might Rendic have chosen to tell readers the thoughts and observations of all the main characters?
2. Choose one of the characters in the story: Juan Labra, Little Juan, Mr. Davies, or Black. In your opinion, would the story be as interesting if the point of view were limited to that one character's point of view? Explain.

● See **Literary Terms Handbook**, p. R8.

LITERARY ELEMENTS

1. Rendic may have chosen to tell readers the thoughts of all the characters because they all contribute to the story's theme.
2. Had the reader known only Juan Labra's point of view, he or she would not understand the intense love between Little Juan and Black.

Additional Resources

📖 *Literary Elements Transparency 11*

LITERATURE AND WRITING

Writing About Literature
Literary Review   Write a review of this story for the literary section of your school newspaper. Briefly describe the setting and the main characters. Then identify the central conflict of the story, but do not reveal how it is resolved. Tell what you think is the most important idea or issue explored in the story. You may want to discuss how effectively the author deals with that issue.

Personal Writing
Friends for Life   Look back at the definition of true friendship that you wrote in the Focus Activity on page 128. After reading this story, is there anything you would change or add to your definition? Once you are satisfied with your definition, identify what you feel is the ultimate act of true friendship in this story. In a paragraph, tell what that act is and why you think it deserves that description.

EXTENDING YOUR RESPONSE

Literature Groups
Look into the Future   Imagine that on a trip to Chile, you encounter Little Juan, who is now thirty years old. After spending some time with him, you return home. Form a small group and share what you have learned about what has happened to "Little" Juan and his family. Compare your group's scenarios with those imagined by other groups.

Learning for Life
Letter of Inquiry   Before this story began, Juan Labra had organized a society for the protection of animals. Write a letter to a local animal protection agency, requesting information about the history, goals, and accomplishments of the group. Share the information with the class.

Listening and Speaking
Create a Different Ending   What might have happened if Labra had not met Mr. Davies on the road? What if he had continued on to the mine owner's home and confronted him there? Discuss what the two might have said to each other. Then take turns role-playing the dialogue between the two men. Present your dialogue to the class.

 Save your work for your portfolio.

VOCABULARY • Analogies

An analogy is a type of comparison that is based on the relationships between things or ideas. Some analogies are based on a relationship that could be called "degree of intensity."

dislike : hate :: irritate : enrage

To intensely *dislike* is to *hate;* to intensely *irritate* is to *enrage.*

To finish an analogy, decide what relationship exists between the first two things or ideas. Then apply that relationship to another pair of words.

● For more about analogies, see **Communications Skills Handbook,** p. R77.

PRACTICE   Choose the pair that best completes each analogy.

1. think : contemplate ::
   a. look : inspect
   b. question : answer
   c. debate : discuss
   d. remember : recall
   e. surrender : escape

2. interest : intrigue ::
   a. awaken : doze
   b. perplex : mystify
   c. encourage : support
   d. criticize : correct
   e. instruct : demonstrate

LITERATURE AND WRITING

Writing About Literature
Students' reviews should
- briefly describe the story's setting, characters, and conflict.
- identify the story's most important idea.
- evaluate the author's treatment of the main idea.

Personal Writing
Students' paragraphs should
- offer a definition of friendship.
- identify and describe the ultimate act of friendship in the story.

EXTENDING YOUR RESPONSE

Literature Groups Encourage students to consider Little Juan's character in the story and possible educational and career opportunities for a boy with his qualities. **COLLAB. LEARN.**

Learning for Life Encourage students also to find out about volunteer opportunities at the agencies they contact.

Listening and Speaking If possible, use audiotape or videotape to record students' dialogues.

VOCABULARY • Analogies
1. a   2. b

Additional Resources
📁 *Vocabulary Practice,* p. 11

Writing Workshop

Objectives

- To create a personal response to literature
- To plan, draft, revise, edit, and present a reflective essay
- To reflect on and assess the essay

GLENCOE
T E C H N O L O G Y

WRITER'S ASSISTANT
CD-ROM
Students can use Glencoe's templates and guidelines software for expository writing to aid them in working through the steps in the writing process in this lesson.

Teaching Strategies

PREWRITING

Explore ideas Have students pair off and interview each other. Suggest that they take notes.

Choose an audience If the audience is not familiar with the story, students must provide a brief summary of the characters and events.

Consider your purpose Students might take notes in a three-column chart headed *First Impressions, Later Impressions,* and *Reason for Change.* They can refer to their notes when writing.

Teaching Options

Personal Writing: Reflective Essay

First impressions are often wrong, and they're always incomplete—whether they're first impressions of people or of short stories. Upon reflection, you often discover more than you noticed at first. **In this workshop you will write a reflective essay that explores your impressions of a** story you have read. A reflective essay shows the progress of your thinking: from first impressions, through second thoughts, to a considered opinion.

- As you write your reflective essay, refer to the **Writing Handbook,** pp. R59–R71.

The Writing Process

PREWRITING

> **PREWRITING TIP**
> Use freewriting to begin reflecting on your responses to a work of literature. Let your ideas flow and jot them down as they come to you.

Explore ideas

Think about the short stories you've read so far in this unit. You'll base your essay on your reflections about a particular aspect of one of those stories. Begin exploring ideas for your reflective essay with questions such as the following:

- Which story made the strongest impression on you?
- What were your first impressions of this story?
- Upon further reflection, what other ideas occurred to you? What questions did the story raise in your mind?
- What experiences of your own came to mind as a result of reading the story?
- What new ideas about life's transitional moments did the story suggest to you?
- Which aspect of the story intrigued you the most, or made the strongest impression on you?

Choose an audience

Do you want to write for people who have read the story, or for people who have *not* read it? Remember to summarize the plot for those who aren't familiar with it.

Consider your purpose

The stories in this theme are about moving from one phase of life to another; your essay will move from first impressions to later ideas. You will take your reader through each step.

MEETING INDIVIDUAL NEEDS
ENGLISH LANGUAGE LEARNERS

Speaking Before Writing Before English language learners begin to write their reflective essays, have them form small groups with other students, including more proficient English speakers, who have chosen to write about the same story. Have groups first discuss the plot of the story. Then have members describe their reactions to the story. Suggest that students describe their first impressions, second thoughts, and considered opinions. Encourage members to ask each other for clarification or elaboration of any of their thoughts or ideas.

Additional Resources
📁 *English Language Learners Sourcebook*

Make a plan

You'll be asking your audience to follow your thoughts over the course of your essay. In order to organize your reflections into a form that others can understand, jot down notes for the three parts of your essay.

STUDENT MODEL

Introduction	What is the story and what is it about? What aspect of the story will you reflect on? Where will your reflections lead?	"Two Kinds" is about a conflict between a mother and daughter. I changed my mind about the mother.
Body	Begin with your first impressions: What was your immediate response to the aspect of the story you're reflecting on?	Hooray for Jing-mei! She won!
	Then reconsider: What other responses are possible?	What puzzled me: Why Jing-mei had the piano tuned.
	Arrive at a considered opinion: Upon reflection, what interpretation seems truest to the story and to your own experience?	Maybe the mother wasn't totally wrong in having high expectations for Jing-mei.
Conclusion	Review the progress of your thinking: Where did you start? Where did you end up?	Started by disagreeing with the mother. The mature Jing-mei came to understand her mother's viewpoint. I did, too.

Introduction

An invitation to follow your thoughts about "Two Kinds."

Body

First impressions → passages that shaped your first impressions

Second thoughts → passages that made you reconsider

Considered opinion → passages that support your new opinion

Conclusion

Review and sum up.

Make a plan Have students make a chart similar to the one described. Then have them answer the questions in the model. They may find it helpful to refer to their notes from their Explore ideas interview. Remind students that they need only jot down notes at this point.

As students make their plans, they should review the selection to find evidence to support their second thoughts and considered opinions. Suggest that they use self-stick notes to mark relevant passages.

Additional Resources

📁 ***Writing and Proofreading Practice,*** pp. 1–7, 8–13

🖌 ***Writing and Proofreading Transparencies,*** pp. 1–6, 7–8, 25–26

📕 ***Writer's Choice,*** Lessons 1.1–1.2, 1.5

MEETING INDIVIDUAL NEEDS — MULTIPLE LEARNING STYLES

Bodily-Kinesthetic Students who process knowledge through bodily sensations may have a difficult time organizing their ideas about the selection. Suggest that they spend extra time planning their essays before they begin the writing process. An activity like the one below may help these students organize their ideas for writing.

Activity Have students write notes about the story on index cards and then arrange the notes as a way to physically organize their ideas. Students can then number the index cards and use them as a reference as they write their outlines. **L2**

Write your draft Have students begin their draft by freewriting for about 20 minutes. Ask them to use their graphics as a guide but to feel free to add other ideas as they come to mind. Tell students that they need to keep their audience in mind as they write. For example, if they are writing for someone who hasn't read the story, they should include a short summary of the plot as part of the introduction.

Teaching Options

~: *Writing* \ *Workshop* :~

DRAFTING

TECHNOLOGY TIP
If you're working on a computer, save your notes under a new file name. Presto! You've started your draft. Now expand it.

Think on paper

Drafting a reflective essay should be like thinking on paper—or, if you're using a computer, thinking on the screen. Refer to the notes you made when you planned your essay. Then go ahead and "think."

Let one idea suggest another. This is a time to write too much rather than too little. Think, question, respond, react, meditate, and reflect. Put it all down without trying to measure one idea against another. If your ideas lead you in surprising directions, that's great! It means your thoughts are making new thoughts—you're reflecting.

Write your draft

Concentrate on getting your ideas down, not on phrasing everything perfectly. You can always change your draft later. As you write, refer to your plan to make sure you include each part of your introduction, body, and conclusion.

STUDENT MODEL

At first, I felt glad for Jing-mei. Every girl has to separate from her mother if she's ever going to become herself. When Jing-mei said to her mother, "Why don't you like me the way I am?" that really hit home. I think all kids ask that question.

But after thinking about the story for a while, something began to puzzle me. After her mother had died, Jing-mei had the piano tuned. Why? This piano made her miserable. It was the battleground where she and her mother fought their battle of wills. Why did she have it tuned? Was it just sentimentality? Was it guilt? Or was it regret? Maybe Jing-mei regretted that she didn't even try to live up to her mother's expectations.

REVISING

Read your essay aloud As students read aloud, partners should jot down any clarity issues or any specific ideas they have for revisions.

Take another look

After you finish your draft, you may be tempted to begin revising it right away. Resist the temptation! Instead, set your draft aside for a while. Then return to it with a fresh eye, and read it through without making any changes at all. Next, revise it, using the **Questions for Revising** as a guide. You may want to repeat this process two or three times, constantly trying to convey your ideas more clearly to your audience.

> **REVISING TIP**
>
> Be sure to use transitions that help your audience follow your thinking.

Read your essay aloud

Read your work aloud to someone else to hear how it sounds. (Keep the written copy to yourself, since it hasn't been edited.) Ask your listener if he or she had any difficulty following the progress of your thinking. Go through the **Questions for Revising** with him or her, but don't feel that you have to make every change your listener suggests. It's your essay, and it reports *your* reflections.

STUDENT MODEL

Amy Tan's story "Two Kinds" ~~tells the story of~~ a [describes]
conflict between a mother and daughter over the
question of who the daughter is. It's a classic
confrontation. ~~It's a~~ mother's hopes and dreams [between]
for her ~~daughter v. a daughter's~~ hopes and dreams. [child and the child's own]
~~I started out on the daughter's side, but as she~~ [At the beginning of the story, I sided with the]
~~grow up she saw her mother's side of the issue,~~ [daughter. By the end, though, the daughter had]
~~and I did, too.~~ [begun to see her mother's side, and so did I.]

> **QUESTIONS FOR REVISING**
>
> In the introduction, how can you:
> - ☑ write a more concise statement telling what the story is about?
> - ☑ more clearly state what you will reflect on and where your reflections will lead?
>
> In the body, how can you:
> - ☑ tighten your focus so that you devote one paragraph each to your first impressions, second thoughts, and considered opinion?
> - ☑ provide better transitions between the stages in your thinking?
> - ☑ improve or expand your use of quoted passages?
>
> In the conclusion, how can you:
> - ☑ briefly review and sum up the content of your essay?
> - ☑ leave the audience with something that they will remember?
>
> In general, how can you:
> - ☑ clear up confusing parts?
> - ☑ improve any parts that are dull, bland, or uninteresting?
> - ☑ add some "sparkle" to your essay by using vivid words and images?

TECHNOLOGY TIP

Using a word processor allows students to revise their work by moving text. Encourage them to manipulate text and to experiment with different organizations. Remind them, however, to reread their work to make sure that the text flows and makes sense.

Writing *Minilesson*

Precise Words As students revise their work, have them focus on their word choices, avoiding vague words or phrases. As an example of using precise words for clarity, read the sentence *The <u>girl</u> was unhappy with her <u>parent.</u>* Discuss how the meaning of the sentence can be made clearer by changing the underlined words. For instance, *the girl* might be changed to *Jing-mei,* and *parent* might be changed to *mother*.

Activity Have students pair up and help each other find vague words and phrases in each other's writing that could be replaced with more precise terminology.
 L2 **COLLAB. LEARN.**

Additional Resources

📗 ***Writer's Choice,*** Lessons 10.1, 12.1–12.3

Have students use the *Proofreading Checklist* on the inside back cover of their textbook.

Comment that some writers prefer to read their essays aloud to find errors in grammar, while others prefer to read silently. Encourage students to try different techniques until they find the one that suits them. Suggest that they read their essays one time to focus on one type of error, a second time to focus on a second type of error, and so on.

PUBLISHING/PRESENTING

Students who opt to post their essays on the Internet may want to include an introductory note asking for comments from other students who have read the same selection.

Reflecting

Portfolio Encourage students to ask themselves these questions as they review their writing.

Does my reflective essay
- clearly state my first impressions?
- logically explain to my audience why my first impressions changed?
- represent work I am proud of?

Suggest that if students answer "yes" to more than one of these questions they consider including their reflective essay in their portfolio.

Teaching Options

~: *Writing Workshop* :~

EDITING/PROOFREADING

PROOFREADING TIP
Use the **Proofreading Checklist** on the inside back cover of this book to help you catch mistakes.

Are you satisfied with the content of your reflective essay? If so, then it's time to edit and proofread your essay carefully for errors in grammar, usage, mechanics, and spelling.

Grammar Hint

Do not shift, or change, verb tenses when you describe two or more events that occur at the same time.

INCORRECT: *In the story, the mother wants Jing-mei to be a prodigy, but Jing-mei had other ideas.*

CORRECT: *In the story, the mother wants Jing-mei to be a prodigy, but Jing-mei has other ideas.*

● For more about verb tenses, see **Language Handbook,** pp. R23–R24.

STUDENT MODEL

I realized that it wasn't just exces̆sive pride that made Jing-mei's mother demand so much of her, her mother loved her and really believed that Jing-mei was talented.

PUBLISHING/PRESENTING

PRESENTING TIP
Ask the members of your audience to read the story before you present your essay.

How you choose to present your essay depends on your audience. If you've written for family members, you might read your essay to them. To reach a wider audience, you could post your essay in an Internet forum devoted to the author of the story you reflected upon.

Reflecting

The great French writer Marcel Proust wrote that "great works of art do not begin by giving us all their best." In mediocre work, the obvious is all there is; in great work, the best is usually found only upon reflection. How does this idea relate to what you just wrote?

Read your essay one last time, reflecting upon its strengths and weaknesses. Plan to build on the strengths in your next piece of writing.

 Save your work for your portfolio.

✔ ASSESSMENT OPTIONS

📁 ***Writing Assessment and Portfolio Management***
- Writing Assessment, pp. 2–19, 23–24
- Portfolio Management, pp. 20–22

Theme 2 — Making Choices

Thinking things over and deciding for oneself are freedoms that people value. Yet making choices can also be one of the most difficult aspects of life. Many of the characters you will meet in this theme are making choices that will forever define who they are. What are the major choices you can expect to face in your lifetime?

THEME PROJECTS

Journalism

Choose the Way Out Imagine that several characters from this theme are stranded in the African savanna. Their challenge is to get back to civilization and safety.

1. Working in a group, have each member pretend to be a character from a story in this theme. All the characters must act as a group to plan an escape from the savanna.

2. Stay in character as you argue for the choices you think will best help the group. Each character may choose one object from his or her story to help in the escape.

3. Afterward, write a press release for the newspaper stating how you made the decisions that brought you home safely.

Interdisciplinary Project

Geography From the sports you play to the food you eat, your surroundings influence everything in your life. The same is true for characters in fiction.

1. On a large sheet of paper, draw a world map. Identify the setting for each story in this theme and mark it on your map.

2. For each story, locate the place farthest away from its original setting and imagine that the story took place there.

3. On a note card, describe how the new setting might affect the story. Attach the note card to your map.

Theme 2

Teaching Strategies

The following suggestions may help your students plan and carry out their theme projects.

Journalism

- Let students first discuss ways that they could portray the different characters, such as using an accent or choosing an item of clothing to wear.
- Before presenting their arguments, students should list two or more objects that would be of use in the escape. Then have them narrow the choice to the object they think would work best.
- Before writing the press release, the group could make a list of the decisions that got them home.

Interdisciplinary Project

- Refer students to classroom maps and atlases for help in drawing the map and locating each setting.
- Students may find it useful to consult encyclopedias or the Internet for information about each setting.
- The comments that students write should be short. Remind them to write their comments in a summary.

Additional Resources

📁 *Interdisciplinary Activities,* pp. 4–5
📁 *Viewing and Representing Activities,* pp. 9–10
📁 *Listening and Speaking Activities,* p. 3–4
📁 *Critical Thinking Skills,* pp. 5–7
📁 *Selection and Theme Assessment,* pp. 173–174
📁 *Performance Assessment,* p. 90

FINE ART
TRANSPARENCY 4

You may wish to use Fine Art Transparency 4 to discuss making choices.

GLENCOE
TECHNOLOGY
LITERATURE CLASSICS
CD-ROM
Search for other selections related to making choices.

SELECTIONS	Literary Elements	Reading and Thinking	Writing	Vocabulary and Spelling	
A White Heron SARAH ORNE JEWETT	Setting, SE p. 153 *Setting, TWE pp. 145, 147, 151* *Simile, TWE p. 145* *Plot: Internal Conflict, TWE p. 148* *Plot: Rising Action, TWE p. 152* *Plot: Resolution, TWE p. 152*	Cause and Effect, SE p. 155 *Synthesizing, TWE p. 144* *Identifying Assumptions, TWE p. 145* *Analyzing Arguments, TWE p. 150*	Literary Analysis, SE p. 154 Nature Journal Entry, SE p. 154 *Exploring Point of View, TWE p. 151*	Multiple Meaning Words, SE p. 155 *Word Meanings, TWE p. 146*	
The **Boar Hunt** JOSÉ VASCONCELOS	Point of View, SE p. 164 *Point of View, TWE pp. 158, 159, 163* *Plot: Internal and External Conflict, TWE p. 161*	*Sequence of Events, TWE p. 159*	Journal Entry, SE p. 156 Literary Analysis, SE p. 165 Talk-Show Script, SE p. 165	Analogies, SE p. 165	
Delicious **Death** ALMA LUZ VILLANUEVA	Colloquial Language, SE p. 170 *Colloquial Language, TWE pp. 167, 169* *Tone, TWE p. 168*	*Inferring, TWE p. 168*			
The Monkey's Paw W. W. JACOBS	Suspense, SE p. 182 *Suspense, TWE pp. 175, 176, 178, 181* *Theme, TWE p. 175* *Plot: Internal Conflict, TWE p. 177*	Chronological Order, SE p. 184 *Identifying Cause-Effect Relationships, TWE p. 178* *Verifying Predictions, TWE p. 179*	Humor Analysis, SE p. 183 Letter, SE p. 183 Creating Emphasis, SE p. 185	Unlocking Meaning, SE p. 184	
Tuesday Siesta GABRIEL GARCÍA MÁRQUEZ	Tone, SE p. 195 *Character, TWE p. 190* *Tone, TWE pp. 190, 191*	*Predicting, TWE p. 191* *Verifying Predictions, TWE p. 192*	Character Sketch, SE p. 196 Letter, SE p. 196	The Suffix -ity, SE p. 196	
Contents of the Dead Man's Pocket JACK FINNEY	Point of View, SE p. 212 *Point of View, TWE pp. 200, 205, 207, 209* *Irony, TWE p. 204* *Metaphor, TWE p. 204* *Character, TWE p. 205* *Theme, TWE p. 211*	Problem Solving, SE p. 214 *Analyzing Arguments, TWE p. 201* *Logical Reasoning, TWE p. 201* *Inferring, TWE p. 202*	Setting Analysis, SE p. 213 Story Ending, SE p. 213 *Creating Suspense with Chronological Order, TWE p. 211*	Analogies, SE p. 214 *Synonyms, TWE p. 206*	
THE CENSORS LUISA VALENZUELA	Satire, SE p. 221 *Tone, TWE p. 219* *Satire, TWE pp. 219, 220*	Making Predictions, SE p. 223 *Author's Purpose, TWE p. 216* *Drawing Conclusions, TWE p. 220*	Character Analysis, SE p. 222 Ballad, SE p. 222	Usage, SE p. 222	
The **Ring** ISAK DINESEN	Characterization, SE p. 231 *Character, TWE pp. 226, 228,* *Plot: Internal Conflict, TWE p. 226* *Plot: External Conflict, TWE p. 229*	*Inferring, TWE p. 227* *Identifying Spatial Relationships, TWE p. 229*	Character Comparison, SE p. 232 Story Sequel, SE p. 232	Antonyms, SE p. 232 *Multiple-Meaning Words, TWE p. 228*	

Key: Student material is in roman. Teacher material is in italic.   🖥 Technology   Collaboration

Grammar and Language	Listening, Speaking, and Viewing	Life Skills	Study, Research, and Technology
Using Semicolons, SE p. 155 *Subject-Verb Agreement: Collective Nouns, TWE p. 152*	**COLLAB. LEARN.** Literature Groups, SE p. 154	*Making Difficult Choices, TWE p. 149*	Research, SE p. 154 🖥 Internet Connection, SE p. 154 🖥 *Internet Connection, TWE p. 148* *Research, TWE p. 148*
Compound Sentences, TWE p. 162	**COLLAB. LEARN.** Literature Groups, SE p. 165	🖥 Using the Internet, SE p. 165	🖥 Internet Connection, SE p. 165
Using Dashes, TWE p. 169	Oral Presentation, SE p. 171		Research, SE p. 170
Punctuating Dialogue, SE p. 184 *Four Kinds of Sentences, TWE p. 180* *Subordinate Clauses, TWE p. 185*	**COLLAB. LEARN.** Literature Groups, SE p. 183 Performing a Play, SE p. 183 **COLLAB. LEARN.** *Discussing Opinions, TWE p. 175*	Learning for Life: Interviews, SE p. 183	
Quotation Marks, TWE p. 194	**COLLAB. LEARN.** Literature Groups, SE p. 196 **COLLAB. LEARN.** *Discussion, TWE p. 193*	🖥 Using the Internet, SE p. 196	🖥 Internet Connection, SE p. 196
Introductory Phrases, SE p. 214 *Compatibility of Tenses, TWE p. 210*	**COLLAB. LEARN.** Literature Groups, SE p. 213 Delivering a Monologue, SE p. 213	*Setting Goals, TWE p. 202*	🖥 *Internet Connection, TWE p. 197*
Intervening Prepositional Phrases, TWE p. 220	**COLLAB. LEARN.** Literature Groups, SE p. 222	Using Satire to Effect Change, SE p. 222	🖥 Internet Connection, SE p. 222 🖥 *Internet Connection, TWE p. 216*
Avoiding Run-on Sentences, SE p. 233 *Perfect Tense, TWE p. 230*	**COLLAB. LEARN.** Literature Groups, SE p. 232 Dialogue, SE p. 232	🖥 Using the Internet, SE p. 232	🖥 Internet Connection, SE p. 232

SELECTIONS	📁 Print Resources		

A White Heron
SARAH ORNE JEWETT
	Unit One Planning Guide, pp. 102–109
	* Active Reading Guide, p. 12
	Vocabulary Practice, p. 12
		Grammar & Comp. Handbook,
		  Lessons 6.4, 11.5
		Grammar and Language Workbook,
		  pp. 169, 249
		Reading Workbook, pp. 15–16
			* Quick Checks, p. 12
			Selection Assessment, pp. 23–24
			Performance Assessment, p. 12
			Spanish Summaries, p. 12
			Spanish Translations

The Boar Hunt
JOSÉ VASCONCELOS
	Unit One Planning Guide, pp. 110–117
	* Active Reading Guide, p. 13
	Vocabulary Practice, p. 13
		Grammar & Comp. Handbook,
		  Lessons 2.3, 4.7
		Grammar and Language Workbook,
		  p. 103
		Reading Workbook, pp. 17–18
			* Quick Checks, p. 13
			Selection Assessment, pp. 25–26
			Performance Assessment, p. 13
			Spanish Summaries, p. 13
			Spanish Translations

Delicious Death
ALMA LUZ VILLANUEVA
	Unit One Planning Guide,
	  pp. 118–123
	* Active Reading Guide, p. 14
		Grammar & Comp. Handbook,
		  Lesson 11.7
		Grammar and Language Workbook,
		  p. 267
		Reading Workbook, pp. 17–18
			* Quick Checks, p. 14
			Selection Assessment, pp. 27–28
			Performance Assessment, p. 14
			Spanish Summaries, p. 14
			Spanish Translations

The Monkey's Paw
W. W. JACOBS
	Unit One Planning Guide,
	  pp. 124–131
	* Active Reading Guide, p. 15
	Vocabulary Practice, p. 14
		Grammar & Comp. Handbook,
		  Lessons 4.6, 11.9
		Grammar and Language Workbook,
		  pp. 119, 271
		Reading Workbook, p. 19
			* Quick Checks, p. 15
			Selection Assessment, pp. 29–30
			Performance Assessment, p. 15
			Spanish Summaries, p. 15

Tuesday Siesta
GABRIEL GARCÍA MÁRQUEZ
	Unit One Planning Guide,
	  pp. 132–139
	* Active Reading Guide, p. 16
	Vocabulary Practice, p. 15
		Grammar & Comp. Handbook,
		  Lesson 11.9
		Grammar and Language Workbook,
		  p. 271
		Reading Workbook, p. 20
			* Quick Checks, p. 16
			Selection Assessment, pp. 31–32
			Performance Assessment, p. 16
			Spanish Summaries, p. 16
			Spanish Translations

Contents of the Dead Man's Pocket
JACK FINNEY
	Unit One Planning Guide,
	  pp. 140–147
	* Active Reading Guide, p. 17
	Vocabulary Practice, p. 16
		Grammar & Comp. Handbook,
		  Lesson 5.6
		Grammar and Language Workbook,
		  p. 153
		Reading Workbook, p. 21
			* Quick Checks, p. 17
			Selection Assessment, pp. 33–34
			Performance Assessment, p. 17
			Spanish Summaries, p. 17

THE CENSORS
LUISA VALENZUELA
	Unit One Planning Guide,
	  pp. 148–155
	* Active Reading Guide, p. 18
	Vocabulary Practice, p. 17
		Grammar & Comp. Handbook,
		  Lesson 6.2
		Grammar and Language Workbook,
		  p. 163
		Reading Workbook, p. 20
			* Quick Checks, p. 18
			Selection Assessment, pp. 35–36
			Performance Assessment, p. 18
			Spanish Summaries, p. 18
			Spanish Translations

The Ring
ISAK DINESEN
	Unit One Planning Guide,
	  pp. 156–163
	* Active Reading Guide, p. 19
	Vocabulary Practice, p. 18
		Grammar & Comp. Handbook,
		  Lesson 5.4
		Grammar and Language Workbook,
		  p. 147
		Reading Workbook, p. 22
			* Quick Checks, p. 19
			Selection Assessment, pp. 37–38
			Performance Assessment, p. 19
			Spanish Summaries, p. 19

*Also available in Spanish

Transparencies	Technology Resources
Selection Focus Transparency 12 Grammar and Language Transparency 12 Literary Elements Transparency 12	Literature Launchers Videodisc Audio Library Spanish Audio Library Vocabulary Puzzlemaker Web Site: lit.glencoe.com
Selection Focus Transparency 13 Grammar and Language Transparency 13 Literary Elements Transparency 13 Fine Art Transparency 13	Audio Library Spanish Audio Library Vocabulary Puzzlemaker Web Site: lit.glencoe.com
Selection Focus Transparency 14 Grammar and Language Transparency 14 Literary Elements Transparency 14	Audio Library Spanish Audio Library Vocabulary Puzzlemaker Web Site: lit.glencoe.com
Selection Focus Transparency 15 Grammar and Language Transparencies 15, 16 Literary Elements Transparency 15	Audio Library Spanish Audio Library Vocabulary Puzzlemaker Web Site: lit.glencoe.com
Selection Focus Transparency 16 Grammar and Language Transparency 17 Literary Elements Transparency 16 Fine Art Transparency 12	Literature Launchers Videodisc Audio Library Spanish Audio Library Vocabulary Puzzlemaker Web Site: lit.glencoe.com
Selection Focus Transparency 17 Grammar and Language Transparency 18 Literary Elements Transparency 17 Fine Art Transparency 15	Audio Library Spanish Audio Library Vocabulary Puzzlemaker Web Site: lit.glencoe.com
Selection Focus Transparency 18 Grammar and Language Transparency 19 Literary Elements Transparency 18	Audio Library Spanish Audio Library Vocabulary Puzzlemaker Web Site: lit.glencoe.com
Selection Focus Transparency 19 Grammar and Language Transparency 20 Literary Elements Transparency 19	Audio Library Spanish Audio Library Vocabulary Puzzlemaker Web Site: lit.glencoe.com

Theme RESOURCES

- Listening and Speaking Activities (pp. 3–4)
- Viewing and Representing Activities (pp. 9–10)
- Critical Thinking Skills (pp. 5–7)
- Media Connections Activities (pp. 3–4)
- Interdisciplinary Activities (pp. 4–5)

See also these additional planning resources:
- English Language Learners Sourcebook
- Inclusion Strategies Sourcebook
- Literature Groups Sourcebook

Use Glencoe's *Presentation Plus!* This multimedia teaching tool lets you present dynamic lessons that will engage your students. Using Microsoft PowerPoint,® you can customize the presentations to create your own personalized lessons.

Objectives

- To read and analyze a short story about a young girl who chooses to keep a secret
- To identify the setting in a story
- To write about the allegorical elements in a story

Skills

Reading/Thinking: Inferring; Identifying Assumptions; Analyzing Arguments; Cause and Effect
Writing: Exploring Point of View; Nature Journal
Vocabulary: Word Meanings; Multiple-Meaning Words
Grammar/Language: Subject-Verb Agreement; Using Semicolons
Collaboration: Literature Groups

Motivating

→OPTIONS

Literature Launchers:
"Protecting Endangered Birds"

Videodisc
Side A, Segment 3

Also available in VHS.

Selection Focus Transparency 12: Point out that birds play a vital role in keeping the balance of nature. Ask students what other purposes birds serve.

Focus Activity: Have pairs of students share and discuss their charts.

Before You Read

A White Heron

FOCUS ACTIVITY

Have you ever been tempted to reveal a secret? Can you recall why you did or did not reveal a particular secret?

CHART IT! A secret may be told to you by another person, or you may discover a secret on your own. Think about secrets you have known. Then fill in a chart like this one.

The secret	Did you keep this secret?	Why or why not?

SETTING A PURPOSE Read to discover how difficult the decision to keep or reveal a secret can be.

BACKGROUND

The Time and Place

"A White Heron" is set in the early summer, probably in the late 1800s. The place is somewhere in rural New England, not far from the ocean.

Did You Know?

The heron in this story is most likely the *great egret*—a tall, white heron with a long, thin, yellow bill and black legs. In the late 1800s, some species of egrets were brought to the point of near extinction by hunters who killed the birds to obtain their showy feathers, used to decorate ladies' hats. Killing egrets is now illegal.

VOCABULARY PREVIEW
---

wary (wār′ ē) *adj.* cautious; on the alert; p. 144
discreetly (dis krēt′ lē) *adv.* in a manner showing good judgment; cautiously; p. 145
squalor (skwol′ ər) *n.* wretchedness; misery and filth; p. 146
wane (wān) *v.* to decrease gradually; p. 148
giddy (gid′ ē) *adj.* causing dizziness or lightheadedness; p. 151
vexed (vekst) *adj.* impatient or angry; annoyed; p. 151
perilous (per′ ə ləs) *adj.* dangerous; risky; p. 151
rebuke (ri būk′) *v.* to scold sharply; p. 152

Meet Sarah Orne Jewett

As a child, Sarah Orne Jewett loved to read. Fortunately for her—and for readers who have benefited from her exposure to fine literature—the Jewett home was filled with so many books that stacks of them had to be removed from chairs before guests could sit down. Jewett also spent time with her father, a country doctor, who took her along on visits to patients. On these outdoor rides, the author developed her keen perception of nature and her great love for the natural world.

Sarah Orne Jewett was born in South Berwick, Maine, in 1849, and died there in 1909. This story was published in 1886.

RESOURCE MANAGER

Lesson Planning Resource
The *Unit One Planning Guide* (pp. 102–109) provides additional lesson notes and reduced versions of all print resources.

📁 Other Print Resources

- Active Reading Guide, p. 12
- Vocabulary Practice, p. 12
- Reading Workbook, pp. 15–16
- Grammar and Language Workbook, pp. 169, 249
- Grammar and Composition Handbook, Lessons 6.4, 11.5

- Quick Checks, p. 12
- Selection and Theme Assessment, pp. 23–24
- Performance Assessment, p. 12
- Spanish Summaries, p. 12
- Spanish Translations
- Inclusion Strategies
- English Language Learners Sourcebook

📑 Transparencies
- Selection Focus 12
- Literary Elements 12

- Grammar and Language 12

Technology
 Literature Launchers
 Audio Library
 Spanish Audio Library
 Glencoe Literature Web Site
Testmaker

A White Heron

Sarah Orne Jewett

THE WOODS WERE ALREADY FILLED WITH SHADOWS one June evening, just before eight o'clock, though a bright sunset still glimmered faintly among the trunks of the trees. A little girl was driving home her cow, a plodding, dilatory,[1] provoking creature in her behavior, but a valued companion for all that.

1. *Dilatory* (dil′ ə tôr′ ē) means "causing delay; slow."

Taking a Walk, 1886. George Inness. Oil on canvas, 36 x 50 in. David David Gallery, Philadelphia.

SUMMARY

One evening Sylvia, a quiet young girl who lives with her grandmother in rural New England, encounters a charming hunter while driving her cow home through the woods. His desire to capture a rare white heron forces Sylvia to question for the first time her loyalty to the animals with whom she shares a secret bond.

📁 *Spanish Summaries,* p. 12

A Active Reading

QUESTION After students read the first page, ask questions such as these: Where is the girl now? *(a woods)* Where must she be going with a cow? *(to a farm)* What is the mood of the story? *(peaceful)* What clue do you have about the girl's attitude toward animals? *(She values their companionship.)* Have students suggest questions they would like to have answered as the story is read. List them on the board and have them answered later.

Additional Resources
📁 *Active Reading Guide,* p. 12
🎧 *Audio Library*
🎧 *Spanish Audio Library*

Teaching Options

CONNECTING TO OTHER SELECTIONS

The chart at the right shows three ways to connect "A White Heron" to selections in this book.

For specific teaching strategies, see the *Unit One Planning Guide,* pp. 4–5.

Connection	Title
Life Skills: Decision Making	→ "By Any Other Name," p. 479
Thematic: Valuing All Life	→ "Travels with Charley," p. 427
Literary: Characterization	→ "Catch the Moon," p. 63

B Author's Craft

WORD CHOICE Why does the author write that the cow turned in the right direction "for once"? *(This phrase supports the narrator's earlier statement that the cow is a "dilatory, provoking" animal. Usually she doesn't go where she is supposed to go.)*

C Critical Thinking

INFERRING How does Sylvia feel about the geranium in town? *(She identifies with the poor plant because it is a wild thing out of place in the urban environment; she feels sorry for it and perhaps wishes it could be in the country too.)*

D Critical Thinking

INFERRING Ask students to use the information given to figure out the relationship between Sylvia and Mrs. Tilley. *(Mrs. Tilley is Sylvia's grandmother.)*

Teaching Options

A White Heron

They were going away from whatever light there was, and striking deep into the woods, but their feet were familiar with the path, and it was no matter whether their eyes could see it or not.

There was hardly a night the summer through when the old cow could be found waiting at the pasture bars; on the contrary, it was her greatest pleasure to hide herself away among the huckleberry bushes, and though she wore a loud bell she had made the discovery that if one stood perfectly still it would not ring. So Sylvia had to hunt for her until she found her, and call Co'! Co'! with never an answering Moo, until her childish patience was quite spent. If the creature had not given good milk and plenty of it, the case would have seemed very different to her owners. Besides, Sylvia had all the time there was, and very little use to make of it. Sometimes in pleasant weather it was a consolation to look upon the cow's pranks as an intelligent attempt to play hide and seek, and as the child had no playmates she lent herself to this amusement with a good deal of zest. Though this chase had been so long that the wary animal herself had given an unusual signal of her whereabouts, Sylvia had only laughed when she came upon Mistress Moolly at the swamp-side, and urged her affectionately homeward with a twig of birch leaves. The old cow was not inclined to wander farther; she even turned in the right direction for once as they left the pasture and stepped along the road at a good pace. She was quite ready to be milked now, and seldom stopped to browse. Sylvia wondered what her grandmother would say because they were so late. It was a great while since she had left home at half past five o'clock, but everybody knew the difficulty of making this errand a short one. Mrs. Tilley had chased the hornéd torment too many summer evenings herself to blame any one else for lingering, and was only thankful as she waited that she had Sylvia, nowadays, to give such valuable assistance. The good woman suspected that Sylvia loitered occasionally on her own account; there never was such a child for straying about out-of-doors since the world was made! Everybody said that it was a good change for a little maid who had tried to grow for eight years in a crowded manufacturing town, but, as for Sylvia herself, it seemed as if she never had been alive at all before she came to live at the farm. She thought often with wistful compassion of a wretched geranium that belonged to a town neighbor.

"'Afraid of folks,'" old Mrs. Tilley said to herself, with a smile, after she had made the unlikely choice of Sylvia from her daughter's houseful of children, and was returning to the farm. "'Afraid of folks,' they said! I guess she won't be troubled no great with 'em up to the old place!" When they reached the door of the lonely house and stopped to unlock it, and the cat came to purr loudly and rub against them, a deserted pussy, indeed, but fat with young robins, Sylvia whispered that this was a beautiful place to live in, and she never should wish to go home.

The companions followed the shady wood-road, the cow taking slow steps and the child very fast ones. The cow stopped long at the brook to drink, as if the pasture were not half a swamp, and Sylvia stood still and waited, letting her bare

Vocabulary
wary (wār' ē) *adj.* cautious; on the alert

MEETING INDIVIDUAL NEEDS — ENGLISH LANGUAGE LEARNERS

Multiple-Meaning Words Write these words on the board: *maid* (p. 144), *leaves* (p. 145), *rushes* (p. 147). Point out that in English, words may have multiple meanings; the first meaning that comes to mind is not always the correct one for the context. Have students look up the words in an English dictionary. Then refer them to each word in the story and have volunteers identify which definition is the most appropriate based on the context.

Activity As students read the selection, discuss other multiple-meaning words, such as *fare* (p. 146), *bough* (p. 148), *wayfarer* and *hermitage* (p. 146).

Additional Resources
📁 *English Language Learners Sourcebook*

feet cool themselves in the shoal[2] water, while the great twilight moths struck softly against her. She waded on through the brook as the cow moved away, and listened to the thrushes with a heart that beat fast with pleasure. There was a stirring in the great boughs overhead. They were full of little birds and beasts that seemed to be wide awake, and going about their world, or else saying good night to each other in sleepy twitters. Sylvia herself felt sleepy as she walked along. However, it was not much farther to the house, and the air was soft and sweet. She was not often in the woods so late as this, and it made her feel as if she were a part of the gray shadows and the moving leaves. She was just thinking how long it seemed since she first came to the farm a year ago, and wondering if everything went on in the noisy town just the same as when she was there; the thought of the great red-faced boy who used to chase and frighten her made her hurry along the path to escape from the shadow of the trees.

_____
2. *Shoal* means "shallow."

Suddenly this little woods-girl is horror-stricken to hear a clear whistle not very far away. Not a bird's whistle, which would have a sort of friendliness, but a boy's whistle, determined, and somewhat aggressive. Sylvia left the cow to whatever sad fate might await her, and stepped discreetly aside into the bushes, but she was just too late. The enemy had discovered her, and called out in a very cheerful and persuasive tone, "Halloa, little girl, how far is it to the road?" and trembling Sylvia answered almost inaudibly, "A good ways."

She did not dare to look boldly at the tall young man, who carried a gun over his shoulder, but she came out of her bush and again followed the cow, while he walked alongside.

"I have been hunting for some birds," the stranger said kindly, "and I have lost my way, and need a friend very much. Don't be afraid," he added gallantly. "Speak up and tell me what your name is, and whether you think I can spend the night at your house, and go out gunning early in the morning."

Sylvia was more alarmed than before. Would not her grandmother consider her much to blame? But who could have foreseen such an accident as this? It did not seem to be her fault, and she hung her head as if the stem of it were broken, but managed to answer "Sylvy," with much effort when her companion again asked her name.

Vocabulary
discreetly (dis krēt′ lē) *adv.* in a manner showing good judgment; cautiously

THE SHORT STORY 🐦 145

E Literary Elements

SETTING Ask students to pay particular attention to details of setting before having a volunteer reread the paragraph. Challenge students to identify a detail that appeals to each of their senses. *(sight: shady wood-road; touch: twilight moths strike against her; hearing: sound of thrushes; taste/smell: sweet air)*

F Literary Elements

FORESHADOWING What foreshadows the sound of the young man's whistle and his appearance on the road? *(Sylvia's thoughts about a boy in town who used to chase and frighten her)*

G Critical Thinking

IDENTIFYING ASSUMPTIONS What does Sylvia assume will be her grandmother's response to the stranger? *(Her grandmother is going to be angry with her for running into this stranger and bringing him home with her.)*

H Literary Elements

FIGURATIVE LANGUAGE: *Simile* What does the author compare Sylvia to in this sentence? *(a flower with a broken stem)* What does this comparison tell the reader about Sylvia at this moment? *(She is so shy and frightened that she cannot hold her head up to look at the young man. The comparison emphasizes her delicate nature contrasted with the boldness of the young man.)*

MULTIPLE LEARNING STYLES

Bodily-Kinesthetic Students who are comfortable with physical expression may respond strongly to Sylvia's experiences. These students can help others impersonate Sylvia's actions.

Activity Write the following sentences on note cards and then distribute the cards to groups of students.

- Sylvia felt sleepy.
- Trembling, she answered almost inaudibly.
- Sylvia was alarmed.
- She hung her head as if the stem of it were broken.

Each group enacts the sentence on its card. The rest of the class scans the page and guesses which sentence is being performed. **L1** **COLLAB. LEARN.**

Mrs. Tilley was standing in the doorway when the trio came into view. The cow gave a loud moo by way of explanation.

"Yes, you'd better speak up for yourself, you old trial! Where'd she tucked herself this time, Sylvy?" But Sylvia kept an awed silence; she knew by instinct that her grandmother did not comprehend the gravity of the situation. She must be mistaking the stranger for one of the farmer lads of the region.

The young man stood his gun beside the door, and dropped a lumpy game bag beside it; then he bade[3] Mrs. Tilley good evening, and repeated his wayfarer's story, and asked if he could have a night's lodging.

"Put me anywhere you like," he said. "I must be off early in the morning, before day; but I am very hungry, indeed. You can give me some milk at any rate, that's plain."

"Dear sakes, yes," responded the hostess, whose long slumbering hospitality seemed to be easily awakened. "You might fare better if you went out to the main road a mile or so, but you're welcome to what we've got. I'll milk right off, and you make yourself at home. You can sleep on husks or feathers," she proffered[4] graciously. "I raised them all myself. There's good pasturing for geese just below here towards the ma'sh.[5] Now step

> It was a surprise to find so clean and comfortable a little dwelling in this New England wilderness.

round and set a plate for the gentleman, Sylvy!" And Sylvia promptly stepped. She was glad to have something to do, and she was hungry herself.

It was a surprise to find so clean and comfortable a little dwelling in this New England wilderness. The young man had known the horrors of its most primitive housekeeping, and the dreary squalor of that level of society which does not rebel at the companionship of hens. This was the best thrift of an old-fashioned farmstead, though on such a small scale that it seemed like a hermitage. He listened eagerly to the old woman's quaint talk, he watched Sylvia's pale face and shining gray eyes with ever growing enthusiasm, and insisted that this was the best supper he had eaten for a month, and afterward the new-made friends sat down in the doorway together while the moon came up.

Soon it would be berry-time, and Sylvia was a great help at picking. The cow was a good milker, though a plaguy[6] thing to keep track of, the hostess gossiped frankly, adding presently that she had buried four children, so Sylvia's mother, and a son (who might be dead) in California were all the children she had left. "Dan, my boy, was a great hand to go gunning," she explained sadly. "I never wanted for pa'tridges or gray squer'ls while he was to home. He's been a great wand'rer,

---

3. *Bade* is the past tense of *bid* and, here, means "said in greeting."
4. *Proffered* rhymes with, and means the same as, *offered.*
5. In the grandmother's New England dialect, *ma'sh* is *marsh,* a low-lying wetland.
6. Something that is *plaguy* (plä′ gē) is troublesome or annoying.

Vocabulary
squalor (skwol′ ər) *n.* wretchedness; misery and filth

I expect, and he's no hand to write letters. There, I don't blame him, I'd ha' seen the world myself if it had been so I could."

"Sylvy takes after him," the grandmother continued affectionately, after a minute's pause. "There ain't a foot o' ground she don't know her way over, and the wild creaturs counts her one o' themselves. Squer'ls she'll tame to come an' feed right out o' her hands, and all sorts o' birds. Last winter she got the jaybirds to bangeing[7] here, and I believe she'd 'a' scanted herself of her own meals to have plenty to throw out amongst 'em, if I hadn't kep' watch. Anything but crows, I tell her, I'm willin' to help support—though Dan he had a tamed one o' them that did seem to have reason same as folks. It was round here a good spell after he went away. Dan an' his father they didn't hitch,[8]—but he never held up his head ag'in after Dan had dared him an' gone off."

The guest did not notice this hint of family sorrows in his eager interest in something else.

"So Sylvy knows all about birds, does she?" he exclaimed, as he looked round at the little girl who sat, very demure but increasingly sleepy, in the moonlight. "I am making a collection of birds myself. I have been at it ever since I was a boy." (Mrs. Tilley smiled.) "There are two or three very rare ones I have been hunting for these five years. I mean to get them on my own ground if they can be found."

"Do you cage 'em up?" asked Mrs. Tilley doubtfully, in response to this enthusiastic announcement.

"Oh no, they're stuffed and preserved, dozens and dozens of them," said the

7. *Bangeing* (bān′ jing) is a New England expression meaning "gathering or lounging around in groups."
8. *Didn't hitch,* another New England expression, means "didn't get along."

ornithologist,[9] "and I have shot or snared every one myself. I caught a glimpse of a white heron a few miles from here on Saturday, and I have followed it in this direction. They have never been found in this district at all. The little white heron, it is," and he turned again to look at Sylvia with the hope of discovering that the rare bird was one of her acquaintances.

But Sylvia was watching a hop-toad in the narrow footpath.

"You would know the heron if you saw it," the stranger continued eagerly. "A queer tall white bird with soft feathers and long thin legs. And it would have a nest perhaps in the top of a high tree, made of sticks, something like a hawk's nest."

Sylvia's heart gave a wild beat; she knew that strange white bird, and had once stolen softly near where it stood in some bright green swamp grass, away over at the other side of the woods. There was an open place where the sunshine always seemed strangely yellow and hot, where tall, nodding rushes grew, and her grandmother had warned her that she might sink in the soft black mud underneath and never be heard of more. Not far beyond were the salt marshes just this side the sea itself, which Sylvia wondered and dreamed much about, but never had seen, whose great voice could sometimes be heard above the noise of the woods on stormy nights.

"I can't think of anything I should like so much as to find that heron's nest," the handsome stranger was saying. "I would give ten dollars to anybody who could show it to me," he added desperately, "and I mean to spend my whole vacation hunting for it if need be. Perhaps it was only migrating, or had been chased out of its own region by some bird of prey."

9. An *ornithologist* is someone who studies, or is an expert on, birds.

THE SHORT STORY ❧ 147

K **Critical Thinking**

INFERRING Mrs. Tilley says that she would have seen the world if she could have. Why couldn't she do so? What might have prevented her? *(In the 1800s, most women would not have had the option of "seeing the world." They were expected to stay home and care for their parents or for their husband and children.)*

L **Author's Craft**

DIALECT Writers sometimes have characters speak in dialect, modifying the spellings of words and deviating from standard sentence structure in order to capture the sound of characters' speech. Have students look at abbreviated words and tell what standard word each one represents.

M **Active Reading**

EVALUATE What does this paragraph imply about the young man? *(He has a selfish interest in what his hosts can offer him and has little real interest in them.)*

N **Literary Elements**

SETTING Have students close their eyes before you reread the description of the place where Sylvia saw the white heron. What do the details tell them about the different habitats near Sylvia's home? *(Beyond the woods, there is a swamp; beyond that, there are marshes; and beyond that, there is the sea.)*

MEETING INDIVIDUAL NEEDS — GIFTED AND TALENTED

Dialect Remind students that dialect is a way of speaking developed by the people in a certain region or group. Point out examples of Mrs. Tilley's dialect and invite a student to read her words aloud as he or she imagines Mrs. Tilley would say them.

Activity Invite students to consider other dialects they have heard. Ask small groups of students to choose a passage of dialogue and summarize what is being said. They may experiment verbally until they figure out the best words to use. Then they should rewrite the dialogue in standard English. Groups can select a spokesperson to present the rewritten dialogue to the class. **L2** **COLLAB. LEARN.**

Mrs. Tilley gave amazed attention to all this, but Sylvia still watched the toad, not divining,[10] as she might have done at some calmer time, that the creature wished to get to its hole under the doorstep and was much hindered by the unusual spectators at that hour of the evening. No amount of thought, that night, could decide how many wished-for treasures the ten dollars, so lightly spoken of, would buy.

The next day the young sportsman hovered about the woods, and Sylvia kept him company, having lost her first fear of the friendly lad, who proved to be most kind and sympathetic. He told her many things about the birds and what they knew and where they lived and what they did with themselves. And he gave her a jackknife, which she thought as great a treasure as if she were a desert islander. All day long he did not once make her troubled or afraid except when he brought down some unsuspecting singing creature from its bough. Sylvia would have liked him vastly better without his gun; she could not understand why he killed the very birds he seemed to like so much. But as the day waned, Sylvia still watched the young man with loving admiration. She had never seen anybody so charming and delightful; the woman's heart, asleep in the child, was vaguely thrilled by a dream of love. Some premonition of that great power stirred and swayed these young creatures who traversed[11] the solemn woodlands with soft-footed silent care. They stopped to listen to a bird's song; they pressed forward again eagerly, parting the branches— speaking to each other rarely and in whispers; the young man going first and Sylvia following, fascinated, a few steps behind, with her gray eyes dark with excitement.

She grieved because the longed-for white heron was elusive,[12] but she did not lead the guest, she only followed, and there was no such thing as speaking first. The sound of her own unquestioned voice would have terrified her—it was hard enough to answer yes or no when there was need of that. At last evening began to fall, and they drove the cow home together, and Sylvia smiled with pleasure when they came to the place where she heard the whistle and was afraid only the night before.

Half a mile from home, at the farther edge of the woods, where the land was highest, a great pine tree stood, the last of its generation. Whether it was left for a boundary mark, or for what reason, no one could say; the wood choppers who had felled its mates were dead and gone long ago, and a whole forest of sturdy trees, pines and oaks and maples, had grown again. But the stately head of this old pine towered above them all and made a landmark for sea and shore miles and miles away. Sylvia knew it well. She had always believed that whoever climbed to the top of it could see the ocean; and the little girl had often laid her hand on the great rough trunk and looked up wistfully at those dark boughs that the wind always stirred, no matter how hot and still the air might be below. Now she thought of the tree with a new excitement, for why, if one climbed it at break of day could not one see all the world, and easily discover from whence the white heron flew, and mark the place, and find the hidden nest?

---

10. Here, *divining* means "guessing."
11. To *traverse* is to pass across or through.

12. If a thing is *elusive* (i lōō' siv), it is difficult to discover or catch.

Vocabulary
wane (wān) *v.* to decrease gradually

Forest in the Dew. Wolfgang Muller (b. 1877).

Viewing the painting: Imagine you are Sylvy, perched on the highest tree in the forest. What emotions do you feel as you look upon this vista?

REAL-WORLD CONNECTION

Making Difficult Choices Have students locate a magazine article that tells about a person who makes a difficult choice between two things she or he wants. Students can form small discussion groups and share their articles, explaining what conflict the person faced, what decision that person made, and how he or she made the decision. Group members should take notes about each article and hand them in at the end of class.

Their notes should indicate the title and source of each article, the subject, the major conflict, and the final decision. **L2** **COLLAB. LEARN.**

Model: I think the young man has brought about a big change in Sylvia. Before she met him, she was in tune with nature and content to be that way. The young man plants the seeds of desire and greed in her. She wants to please him. She wants to make ten dollars. She will risk climbing the tall pine not to see the ocean as she once dreamed but to sight the heron's nest so that she might thrill and impress the young man.

S **Author's Craft**

FIGURATIVE LANGUAGE: *Simile* What two things does the author compare in the simile? *(Sylvia's feet and fingers to bird's claws)* Why is this an ironic comparison? *(Sylvia is being compared to the animal that she is in the process of betraying.)*

T **Author's Craft**

PERSONIFICATION Explain that in personification, a writer gives human characteristics to something that is not human. What human feelings and actions does the author give to the tree? *(it reaches, it is amazed, it feels, it loves, it frowns)*

A White Heron

What a spirit of adventure, what wild ambition! What fancied triumph and delight and glory for the later morning when she could make known the secret! It was almost too real and too great for the childish heart to bear.

All night the door of the little house stood open and the whippoorwills came and sang upon the very step. The young sportsman and his old hostess were sound asleep, but Sylvia's great design kept her broad awake and watching. She forgot to think of sleep. The short summer night seemed as long as the winter darkness, and at last when the whippoorwills ceased, and she was afraid the morning would after all come too soon, she stole out of the house and followed the pasture path through the woods, hastening toward the open ground beyond, listening with a sense of comfort and companionship to the drowsy twitter of a half-awakened bird, whose perch she had jarred in passing. Alas, if the great wave of human interest which flooded for the first time this dull little life should sweep away the satisfactions of an existence heart to heart with nature and the dumb life of the forest!

There was the huge tree asleep yet in the paling moonlight, and small and silly Sylvia began with utmost bravery to mount to the top of it, with tingling, eager blood coursing the channels of her whole frame, with her bare feet and fingers, that pinched and held like bird's claws to the monstrous ladder reaching up, up, almost to the sky itself. First she must mount the white oak tree that grew alongside, where she was almost lost among the dark branches and the green leaves heavy and wet with dew; a bird fluttered off its nest, and a red squirrel ran to and fro and scolded pettishly[13] at the harmless housebreaker. Sylvia felt her way easily. She had often climbed there, and knew that higher still one of the oak's upper branches chafed against the pine trunk, just where its lower boughs were set close together. There, when she made the dangerous pass from one tree to the other, the great enterprise would really begin.

She crept out along the swaying oak limb at last, and took the daring step across into the old pine tree. The way was harder than she thought; she must reach far and hold fast, the sharp dry twigs caught and held her and scratched her like angry talons, the pitch made her thin little fingers clumsy and stiff as she went round and round the tree's great stem, higher and higher upward. The sparrows and robins in the woods below were beginning to wake and twitter to the dawn, yet it seemed much lighter there aloft in the pine tree, and the child knew she must hurry if her project were to be of any use.

The tree seemed to lengthen itself out as she went up, and to reach farther and farther upward. It was like a great mainmast to the voyaging earth; it must truly have been amazed that morning through all its ponderous frame as it felt this determined spark of human spirit wending its way from higher branch to branch. Who knows how steadily the least twigs held themselves to advantage this light, weak creature on her way! The old pine

> **She crept out along the swaying oak limb at last, and took the daring step across into the old pine tree.**

---

13. *Pettishly* means "crossly or irritably."

Teaching Options

Reading *Minilesson*

Analyzing Arguments Sylvia has decided she will tell the young man where to find the heron. But has she really considered the pros and cons of the situation? Students can help Sylvia weigh both sides of the argument in an organized, logical way.

Activity Have students make a chart like the one shown and list the pros and cons

of revealing the secret. Their suggestions may come from the story or from their own thoughts and ideas. After the chart is completed, have the class vote on whether the pros or the cons win this argument. **L2**

Additional Resources
📁 *Reading Workbook,* pp. 15–16

Should Sylvia Reveal the Secret of the Heron?	
Pros	Cons

must have loved his new dependent. More than all the hawks, and bats, and moths, and even the sweet voiced thrushes, was the brave, beating heart of the solitary gray-eyed child. And the tree stood still and frowned away the winds that June morning while the dawn grew bright in the east.

Sylvia's face was like a pale star, if one had seen it from the ground, when the last thorny bough was past, and she stood trembling and tired but wholly triumphant, high in the tree-top. Yes, there was the sea with the dawning sun making a golden dazzle over it, and toward that glorious east flew two hawks with slow-moving pinions.[14] How low they looked in the air from that height when one had only seen them before far up, and dark against the blue sky. Their gray feathers were as soft as moths; they seemed only a little way from the tree, and Sylvia felt as if she too could go flying away among the clouds. Westward, the woodlands and farms reached miles and miles into the distance; here and there were church steeples, and white villages; truly it was a vast and awesome world!

The birds sang louder and louder. At last the sun came up bewilderingly bright. Sylvia could see the white sails of ships out at sea, and the clouds that were purple and rose-colored and yellow at first began to fade away. Where was the white heron's nest in the sea of green branches, and was this wonderful sight and pageant of the world the only reward for having climbed to such a giddy height? Now look down again, Sylvia, where the green marsh is set among the

shining birches and dark hemlocks; there where you saw the white heron once you will see him again; look, look! a white spot of him like a single floating feather comes up from the dead hemlock and grows larger, and rises, and comes close at last, and goes by the landmark pine with steady sweep of wing and outstretched slender neck and crested head. And wait! wait! do not move a foot or a finger, little girl, do not send an arrow of light and consciousness from your two eager eyes, for the heron has perched on a pine bough not far beyond yours, and cries back to his mate on the nest and plumes his feathers for the new day!

The child gives a long sigh a minute later when a company of shouting catbirds comes also to the tree, and vexed by their fluttering and lawlessness the solemn heron goes away. She knows his secret now, the wild, light, slender bird that floats and wavers, and goes back like an arrow presently to his home in the green world beneath. Then Sylvia, well satisfied, makes her perilous way down again, not daring to look far below the branch she stands on, ready to cry sometimes because her fingers ache and her lamed feet slip. Wondering over and over again what the stranger would say to her, and what he would think when she told him how to find his way straight to the heron's nest.

Did You Know?
When a heron *plumes its feathers*, it cleans and smooths them with its bill.

---

14. Here, the bird's *pinions* are its wings. The word may also be used to refer to a bird's feathers.

Vocabulary
giddy (gid′ ē) *adj.* causing dizziness or lightheadedness
vexed (vekst) *adj.* impatient or angry; annoyed
perilous (per′ ə ləs) *adj.* dangerous; risky

Literary Elements

U **Literary Elements**

SETTING Discuss how the details that the author gives help the reader imagine what it would be like to be at the top of the tall pine. Encourage students to offer specific details by asking these questions: *What does the landscape look like? What animals does Sylvia see? How do they look? How do the sea and the sky look?*

V **Literary Elements**

POINT OF VIEW Until now the story is told by a third person omniscient narrator who stands outside the action of the story and relates the thoughts, feelings, words, and actions of all the characters. In this paragraph, a different voice speaks. Why might the author have shifted the point of view? *(At this point, Sylvia is closer to nature than she has ever been and the voice of nature speaks directly to her. This shift helps readers feel the power of this experience.)*

Writing *Minilesson*

Exploring Point of View Review with students the key elements of the three basic points of view that they can use to tell a story: first person, third person limited, and third person omniscient.

Activity Have pairs of students think of a significant or entertaining event that happened recently and write (using the first person point of view) a brief anecdote based on the incident. Then have them rewrite the anecdote using the third person limited and then the third person omniscient point of view. Invite students to read their anecdotes aloud and discuss how the point of view affects the anecdote. **L2** **COLLAB. LEARN.**

Additional Resources

📙 *Writer's Choice,* Lesson 2.11

Literary Elements

PLOT: *Rising Action* Sylvia has scaled the tree and knows the heron's secret, which marks a turning point for her. Then the story's action builds toward the climax—her decision not to reveal the secret.

Literary Elements

PLOT: *Resolution* The resolution shows how the main conflict is worked out. What is the resolution here? *(Sylvia decides to keep the heron's secret rather than tell the young man where it is, thus saving the bird's life but disappointing the man.)*

Thematic Focus

Making Choices Have students compare Sylvia with themselves or someone they know. Do her challenges reflect any they have experienced? Invite students to share and explain their answers.

☑ ASSESSMENT OPTIONS

📁 *Quick Checks,* p. 12

Teaching Options

A White Heron

"Sylvy, Sylvy!" called the busy old grandmother again and again, but nobody answered, and the small husk bed was empty and Sylvia had disappeared.

The guest waked from a dream, and remembering his day's pleasure hurried to dress himself that might it sooner begin. He was sure from the way the shy little girl looked once or twice yesterday that she had at least seen the white heron, and now she must really be made to tell. Here she comes now, paler than ever, and her worn old frock is torn and tattered, and smeared with pine pitch. The grandmother and the sportsman stand in the door together and question her, and the splendid moment has come to speak of the dead hemlock tree by the green marsh.

But Sylvia does not speak after all, though the old grandmother fretfully <u>rebukes</u> her, and the young man's kind, appealing eyes are looking straight in her own. He can make them rich with money; he has promised it, and they are poor now. He is so well worth making happy, and he waits to hear the story she can tell.

No, she must keep silence! What is it that suddenly forbids her and makes her dumb? Has she been nine years growing and now, when the great world for the first time puts out a hand to her, must she thrust it aside for a bird's sake? The murmur of the pine's green branches is in her ears, she remembers how the white heron came flying through the golden air and how they watched the sea and the morning together, and Sylvia cannot speak; she cannot tell the heron's secret and give its life away.

Dear loyalty, that suffered a sharp pang as the guest went away disappointed later in the day, that could have served and followed him and loved him as a dog loves! Many a night Sylvia heard the echo of his whistle haunting the pasture path as she came home with the loitering cow. She forgot even her sorrow at the sharp report[15] of his gun and the sight of thrushes and sparrows dropping silent to the ground, their songs hushed and their pretty feathers stained and wet with blood. Were the birds better friends than their hunter might have been,—who can tell? Whatever treasures were lost to her, woodlands and summertime, remember! Bring your gifts and graces and tell your secrets to this lonely country child!

---

15. A gun's *report* is the explosive noise of its being fired.

Vocabulary
rebuke (ri būk′) *v.* to scold sharply

Grammar and Language *Minilesson*

Subject-Verb Agreement: Collective Nouns A collective noun (*family, team*) is singular when it refers to a group as a whole and plural when it refers to the individual members of the group.

Activity Have students use each noun as the subject of a sentence, once as a plural noun and once as a singular noun: press, student council, herd. **L1**

Additional Resources

🖌 *Grammar and Language Transparency 12*

📘 *Grammar and Language Workbook,* p. 169

📘 *Grammar and Composition Handbook,* Lesson 6.4

📘 *Writer's Choice,* Lesson 16.4

Responding to Literature

Personal Response

Were you surprised by the decision Sylvia makes at the end of the story? Why or why not?

ANALYZING LITERATURE

RECALL

1. Summarize the information the author gives about Sylvia during the first part of the story, before she meets the young man.
2. What is Sylvia's initial reaction to the young man? How do her feelings toward him change as the story progresses?
3. What is the stranger looking for? What does he plan to do if he finds it?
4. Describe how Sylvia finds what the stranger is looking for.
5. At the end of the story, what does the stranger expect Sylvia to do? What course of action does Sylvia follow?

INTERPRET

6. What conclusions can you draw about Sylvia's **character,** based on what you learn about her before she meets the young man?
7. Why do Sylvia's feelings toward the young man change?
8. What reasons does Sylvia have for wanting to help the stranger find what he is looking for? In your opinion, what reason matters the most to her?
9. What emotions do you think Sylvia experiences during her climb? How does she feel when she finally reaches the top?
10. **Theme Connections**   What does the choice made by Sylvia reveal about her character and her values?

EVALUATE AND CONNECT

11. When Sylvia is high up in the pine tree, the narrator addresses her directly instead of speaking to the reader. How does this change in point of view affect your reading of the story?
12. What is your opinion of the young man? Would you have wanted to help him? Explain why or why not.
13. If you had been in Sylvia's situation, what choice do you think you would have made? Give reasons for your answer.
14. How does the author's use of **local color** (see page R7) affect your appreciation and enjoyment of the story? Give specific examples.
15. What environmental issues are raised in this story? Are these issues still relevant today? Explain your answer.

Literary ELEMENTS

Setting

Setting is the time and place in which the events of a story occur. "A White Heron" takes place in a rural area of New England, near the sea, probably in the late 1800s. The setting of a story often helps to create a particular atmosphere, or mood. For example, some reviewers have characterized the setting of this story as "benevolent and kind."

1. Do you agree that the setting of this story is "benevolent and kind"? Why or why not? What other words might you use to characterize the setting? Support your ideas with evidence from the story.
2. In your opinion, is the setting of this story essential to the plot? In other words, could this story occur in a different place? In a different time? Explain.

● See **Literary Terms Handbook,** p. R11.

Responding to the Selection

Personal Response

Students who were surprised may explain that they thought Sylvia was prepared to help the young man. Students who were not surprised may explain that they felt Sylvia's ties to nature were too strong to be broken.

ANALYZING LITERATURE

1. Sylvia is a lonely girl who has experienced pain and suffering. She is scared of people, which is why she takes comfort in her quiet rural life.
2. She fears him at first. But then she feels attracted to him, takes a liking to him, and wants to please him.
3. He is looking for a white heron to shoot, stuff, and add to his collection.
4. She climbs to the top of the tallest tree in the woods; from there she spots the heron's nest.
5. He expects her to reveal the location of the heron's nest. But her loyalty to animals and nature holds fast and she decides to keep the secret.
6. Her longing for friendship combined with her inability to relate to people lead her to form extraordinarily close ties to animals and nature. Although she is sensitive and wary, she would probably warm to any human who reached out to her.
7. She is impressed by his knowledge of birds and also is flattered by the interest he takes in her.
8. She wants to help because she is attracted to him and wants to please him and because he offers money. Some students may say that the money is the more important reason because ten dollars represents a lot to this poor family. Others may say that pleasing him is the more important reason because she wants him to like her.
9. She feels fear, elation, triumph, and in the end, awe and amazement.
10. The choice she makes involves great sacrifice and reveals the depth of her loyalty, her compassion for wild creatures, and her lack of greed.
11. It seems as if a higher power is speaking, and it makes her decision to keep the heron's secret seem inevitable.
12. Students may say that he is crafty and selfish because he tries to take advantage of Sylvia's vulnerability and use her to further his own plans; therefore, they would not have helped him.

LITERARY ELEMENTS

1. The setting seems benevolent, kind, and reverent as well. The tone reveals respect, awe, and deep appreciation.
2. The *natural* setting is essential. But the story could take place in *another* natural setting. The time is less crucial. It could take place at another time.

Additional Resources

✍ *Literary Elements Transparency 12*

---

13. Students may say that in Sylvia's situation they would have made the same choice because they could not bring themselves to help destroy the heron. Others may say that they would have helped the young man because the family really needed the money.
14. Students may say they liked the grandmother's dialect because it revealed something about her and the region and it was entertaining.
15. Hunting and logging are addressed in the story; both are still hotly debated issues in contemporary society.

LITERATURE AND WRITING

Writing About Literature

Students' paragraphs should

- name a few characters and events that have meaning beyond their literal meaning.
- explain what those meanings are.
- give reasons for their choices of characters and events and meanings.

Creative Writing

Students' nature journal entries should

- be written from Sylvia's point of view.
- describe at least two of her observations of the natural world.
- use details from the story.
- describe sensory perceptions and emotions.

EXTENDING YOUR RESPONSE

Literature Groups Students should take turns sharing their opinions. Remind them to save their questions and comments until the speaker has finished speaking. **COLLAB. LEARN.**

Interdisciplinary Activity While on-line research is convenient, remind students that encyclopedias would be an excellent resource for information on this topic. 🖳

Internet Connection Suggest that students list the kinds of information they want to include about the birds. This will help them find the needed information more quickly. 🖳

— LITERATURE AND WRITING —

Writing About Literature

Is It an Allegory? "A White Heron" can be read as an **allegory** in which the characters and events represent ideas and concepts that go beyond the literal meaning of the story. Write a paragraph about what you think the characters and events in this story might represent and why you think as you do. Compare your ideas with those of several classmates.

Creative Writing

Nature Journal As a nature lover, Sylvia may have kept a journal to record her observations of the natural world. Imagine that you are Sylvia. Write one or two entries in your nature journal using sensory details from the story. Describe not only what you perceive through your five senses, but also the emotions that you experience.

— EXTENDING YOUR RESPONSE —

Literature Groups

Debating a Character's Choice Do you think Sylvia made the right choice? Debate this issue with your group. Justify your opinion with evidence from the story or from your own experience. Feel free to ask fellow group members to do the same. Then tally the opinions of your group. Share the results with the class.

Interdisciplinary Activity

History Research the attitudes of Americans toward nature and the environment in the late 1800s and early 1900s. Find out what conservation laws were enacted during this era. Share what you learn with the class.

Internet Connection

Birds of a Feather Check out Web sites of the National Audubon Society or of a large university in your area to find out what birds are indigenous to your region. With a partner, make a poster with drawings or photographs of at least several of these birds. List information related to their nesting habits, diet, migratory patterns, and so on. Display the poster in the classroom.

Reading Further

If you would like to read more by Sarah Orne Jewett, you might enjoy these works:

Short Story Collection: *The King of Folly Island, and Other Pieces* contains stories that depict women as the guardians of community.

Novels: *The Country of the Pointed Firs* features a Maine village and its people.

A Country Doctor relates the conflicts of a woman physician.

🏛 **Save your work for your portfolio.**

Skill Minilessons

GRAMMAR AND LANGUAGE • Using Semicolons

Good writers vary the length and structure of their sentences. One way to do this is to use a semicolon to join two shorter, related sentences to make a longer one. See how the author combined these two short sentences with a semicolon in "A White Heron."

The good woman suspected that Sylvia loitered occasionally on her own account; there never was such a child for straying about out-of-doors since the world was made!

She could have written this as two sentences.

The good woman suspected that Sylvia loitered occasionally on her own account.

There never was such a child for straying about out-of-doors since the world was made!

PRACTICE Review a piece of your own writing. Find passages where the flow of the writing could be improved by combining short sentences with related ideas. Then, using a semicolon to join those sentences, rewrite the passages.

● For more about semicolons, see **Language Handbook**, p. R47.

READING AND THINKING • Cause and Effect

Events in a story sometimes have a cause-and-effect relationship—that is, one event may be the **cause** of a second event, the **effect**. In "A White Heron," Sylvia's cow hides from her when it is time to go home (cause). As a result, Sylvia spends a lot of time hunting for the cow (effect). Sometimes an effect may be the cause of yet another event. Because Sylvia spends so much time looking for her cow (cause), she arrives home late (effect).

PRACTICE On your paper, write the effect of each cause or the cause of each effect listed.

1. **Cause:** The stranger sees a white heron near Mrs. Tilley's farm.
2. **Effect:** Sylvia leaves the house before daybreak.
3. **Cause:** Sylvia climbs to the top of the old pine tree.
4. **Effect:** The stranger goes away.

● For more about cause and effect, see **Reading Handbook**, pp. R78–R107.

VOCABULARY • Multiple-Meaning Words

Many words have more than one meaning. Some, such as *gravity,* have meanings so different from each other that they're unlikely to be confusing. Other words have several meanings that are extremely similar. For example, *rebuke* can be a verb or a noun; *vexed* can be a verb or an adjective, but in either case, the meanings are similar. Then there are words like *giddy,* for which you need to consider the context to determine the meaning.

In "A White Heron," *giddy* means "causing dizziness," but *giddy* can also mean "dizzy" or "lightheartedly silly." If the reference is to "a giddy height," you know *giddy* must mean "causing dizziness." A giddy smile, on the other hand, might mean that the smiler is dizzy, or that the smile itself is silly. You would need to keep reading and hope for enough context clues to make the meaning clear.

PRACTICE Each pair of phrases below uses the same word, once with a meaning that is probably familiar to you and once with a meaning that may not be familiar. For each pair, write two sentences using the underlined word, one with each meaning.

1. a. <u>entertain</u> a child   b. <u>entertain</u> a thought
2. a. <u>offensive</u> remark   b. on the <u>offensive</u>
3. a. a bad <u>temper</u>   b. <u>temper</u> the criticism

Skill Minilessons

GRAMMAR AND LANGUAGE
Using Semicolons

Students should revise a paragraph using semicolons to vary the length and structure of their sentences. Make sure they use semicolons to combine related complete sentences.

READING AND THINKING
Cause and Effect

1. Effect: He stays near the farm for a few days in hopes of capturing the bird.
2. Cause: She wants to climb the tall pine tree and find the heron's nest.
3. Effect: She sees the heron's nest.
4. Cause: Sylvia doesn't tell where the bird lives.

VOCABULARY
Multiple-Meaning Words

Possible sentences:
1. a. Anton and Dave always entertain us with their jokes.
   b. For a moment, she did entertain the idea of accepting his offer.
2. a. Spoiled milk has an offensive smell.
   b. Sandra takes the offensive whenever she talks to her mother.
3. a. Her temper flares up over the slightest delay.
   b. I must temper my response so that I don't hurt his feelings.

Additional Resources

📗 *Grammar and Composition Handbook,* Lesson 11.5

📗 *Grammar and Language Workbook,* p. 249

📘 **Writer's Choice,** Lesson 21.5

📁 *Vocabulary Practice,* p. 12

📁 *Reading Workshop,* p. 15–16

The Boar Hunt

Objectives

- To read and analyze a short story about a nightmarish hunt that changes a man's life
- To analyze the story's point of view
- To write about the narrator's change in attitude

Skills

Reading/Thinking: Drawing Conclusions; Sequence of Events
Writing: Talk-Show Script
Vocabulary: Analogies
Grammar/Language: Compound Sentences
Collaboration: Literature Groups

Motivating
→OPTIONS

Selection Focus Transparency 13: Explain to students that endangered animals face the most serious threat of extinction. Encourage students to brainstorm ideas for providing direct protection for endangered species.

Focus Activity: Invite students to share their journal entries.

FOCUS ACTIVITY

Have you ever had an experience that completely changed your attitude toward something? Perhaps you were injured while playing a dangerous sport, and you vowed never to play that sport again.

JOURNAL Write about an experience that completely changed your attitude toward something. Explain how your outlook changed.

SETTING A PURPOSE Read to learn what changes a hunter's attitude toward his sport.

BACKGROUND

The Time and Place
"The Boar Hunt" takes place in the not-too-distant past, in a remote, unexplored jungle in Peru.

Did You Know?
Wild boars are wild hogs with razor-sharp tusks, pointy ears, straight tails, and a hard, thick hide covering their chests. They weigh an average of 200 pounds, although some may weigh as much as 500 pounds. Wild boars run much faster than domestic hogs and are naturally aggressive toward other creatures, including humans. The prospect of bagging a wild boar—despite the danger, or perhaps because of it—has challenged hunters since ancient times.

VOCABULARY PREVIEW

rejuvenate (ri jōō′ və nāt′) v. to make fresh or young again; p. 158
lethargy (leth′ ər jē) n. sluggish inactivity or drowsiness; p. 159
impotent (im′ pət ənt) adj. ineffective, powerless, or helpless; p. 160
horde (hôrd) n. a large group; multitude; p. 160
tenaciously (ti nā′ shəs lē) adv. stubbornly; persistently; p. 160
sporadic (spə rad′ ik) adj. irregular; occasional; p. 160
atonement (ə tōn′ mənt) n. something done to make up for a sin, injury, or loss; p. 163
implicit (im plis′ it) adj. suggested but not directly stated; p. 163
infamy (in′ fə mē) n. extreme wickedness or shameful evil; p. 163

Meet José Vasconcelos

In 1908, a year after he had graduated from law school, José Vasconcelos (hō sā′ väs cōn sā′ lōs) joined the revolutionary movement that led to the eventual resignation of Mexican dictator Porfirio Díaz. A prolific writer, philosopher, politician, educational reformer, and university president, Vasconcelos helped Mexicans discover a cultural identity that stressed the dignity and nobility of their Indian heritage. His belief in the superiority of Mexican culture helped to awaken a spirit of national pride.

José Vasconcelos was born in Oaxaca, Mexico, in 1882. He died in 1959. A Mexican Ulysses is an abridged translation of Vasconcelos's autobiography.

RESOURCE MANAGER

Lesson Planning Resource
The *Unit One Planning Guide* (pp. 110–117) provides additional lesson notes and reduced versions of all print resources.

📁 **Other Print Resources**
- Active Reading Guide, p. 13
- Vocabulary Practice, p. 13
- Reading Workbook, pp. 17–18
- Grammar and Language Workbook, p. 103
- Grammar and Composition Handbook, Lessons 2.3, 4.7

- Quick Checks, p. 13
- Selection and Theme Assessment, pp. 25–26
- Performance Assessment, p. 13
- Spanish Summaries, p. 13
- Spanish Translations
- Inclusion Strategies
- English Language Learners Sourcebook

📖 **Transparencies**
- Selection Focus 13
- Fine Art 12

- Literary Elements 13
- Grammar and Language 13

Technology
🎧 Audio Library
🎧 Spanish Audio Library
💻 Glencoe Literature Web Site
💾 Testmaker

The Boar Hunt

José Vasconcelos
Translated by Paul Waldorf

WE WERE FOUR COMPANIONS, and we went by the names of our respective nationalities: the Colombian, the Peruvian, the Mexican; the fourth, a native of Ecuador, was called Quito[1] for short. Unforeseen chance had joined us together a few years ago on a large sugar plantation on the Peruvian coast.

We worked at different occupations during the day and met during the evening in our off time. Not being Englishmen, we did not play cards. Instead, our constant discussions led to disputes. These didn't stop us from wanting to see each other the next night, however, to continue the interrupted debates and support them with new arguments. Nor did the rough sentences of the preceding wrangles indicate a lessening of our affection, of which we assured ourselves reciprocally with the clasping of hands and a look. On Sundays we used to go on hunting parties. We roamed the fertile glens, stalking, generally with poor results, the game of the warm region around the coast, or we entertained ourselves killing birds that flew in the sunlight during the siesta hour.

1. Perhaps he was called this because *Quito* (kē′ tō) is the capital of Ecuador.

SUMMARY

Four men venture across the Andean slopes to hunt wild boars. Their initial surprise at the ease with which they are able to slaughter dozens of the aggressive creatures turns to terror as they discover themselves no match against a herd of thousands of enraged and crafty boars. Tragedy ensues, but the narrator escapes and is ever more a changed man.

📁 **Spanish Summaries,** p. 13

A Active Reading

PREDICT Have students read the first page. Ask questions such as these to help students begin predicting: What does the group like to do? *(hunt)* Why might they go somewhere else to hunt? *(The hunting in the area is not very good.)* What might they hunt? How do you know? *(boar; The title is "The Boar Hunt.")*

Additional Resources
📁 *Active Reading Guide,* p. 13
🎧 *Audio Library*
🎧 *Spanish Audio Library*

Teaching Options

CONNECTING TO OTHER SELECTIONS

COMPARING selections

This selection is paired with "Delicious Death" on pages 167–169. A lesson for teaching a comparison of the two selections appears on page 171.

The chart at the right shows three other ways to connect "The Boar Hunt" to selections in this book.

For specific teaching strategies, see the *Unit One Planning Guide,* pp. 113–114. 📁

Connection	Title
Life Skills: Collaborating	→ "And of Clay Are We Created," p. 343
Thematic: Gaining Wisdom	→ "The Vision Quest," p. 89
Literary: Point of View	→ "The Masque of the Red Death," p. 389

POINT OF VIEW What point of view is the story told from? *(first person point of view)* Ask students how they can tell what the point of view of the story is. *(The narrator says "we," so the point of view is first person. The narrator identifies the "we" as a Colombian, a Peruvian, a Mexican, and Quito, but he does not say which man is the narrator. If necessary, explain that "we" is first person plural. The narrator is talking about the group.)*

C **Critical Thinking**

DRAWING CONCLUSIONS Why do the men want to go across the Andes to the jungles? *(They want to hunt in unexplored regions. They feel that wild nature is calling to them and that this contact will invigorate them.)*

D **Active Reading**

EVALUATE Ask students what they think the author means by this statement: "Ultimately nature and events are largely what our imaginations make them out to be." Is this an optimistic or a pessimistic viewpoint? *(The author seems to be saying that things are whatever we imagine them to be; that is, reality does not actually exist independently of our conception of it. The statement may be judged optimistic or pessimistic, depending on the reader's reaction to this definition of reality.)*

The Boar Hunt

We came to be tireless wanderers and excellent marksmen. Whenever we climbed a hill and gazed at the imposing range of mountains in the interior, its attractiveness stirred us and we wanted to climb it. What attracted us more was the trans-Andean[2] region: fertile plateaus extending on the other side of the range in the direction of the Atlantic toward the immense land of Brazil. It was as if primitive nature called us to her breast. The vigor of the fertile, untouched jungles promised to rejuvenate our minds, the same vigor which rejuvenates the strength and the thickness of the trees each year. At times we devised crazy plans. As with all things that are given a lot of thought, these schemes generally materialized. Ultimately nature and events are largely what our imaginations make them out to be. And so we went ahead planning and acting. At the end of the year, with arranged vacations, accumulated money, good rifles, abundant munitions, stone- and mudproof boots, four hammocks, and a half dozen faithful Indians, our caravan descended the Andean slopes, leading to the endless green ocean.

At last we came upon a village at the edge of the Marañón River. Here we changed our safari. The region we were going to penetrate had no roads. It was unexplored underbrush into which we could enter only by going down the river in a canoe. In time we came to the area where we proposed to carry out the purpose of our journey, the hunting of wild boars.

We had been informed that boars travel in herds of several thousands, occupying a region, eating grass and staying together, exploiting the grazing areas, organized just like an army. They are very easy to kill if one attacks them when they are scattered out satisfying their appetites—an army given over to the delights of victory. When they march about hungry, on the other hand, they are usually vicious. In our search we glided down river between imposing jungles with our provisions and the company of three faithful Indian oarsmen.

One morning we stopped at some huts near the river. Thanks to the information gathered there, we decided to disembark a little farther on in order to spend the night on land and continue the hunt for the boars in the thicket the following day.

Sheltered in a backwater, we came ashore, and after a short exploration found a clearing in which to make camp. We unloaded the provisions and the rifles, tied the boat securely, then with the help of the Indians set up our camp one half kilometer from the river bank. In marking the path to the landing, we were careful not to lose ourselves in the thicket. The Indians withdrew toward their huts, promising to return two days later. At dawn we would set out in search of the prey.

Though night had scarcely come and the heat was great, we gathered at the fire to see each other's faces, to look instinctively for protection. We talked a little, smoked, confessed to being tired, and decided to go to bed. Each hammock had been tied by one end to a single tree, firm though not very thick in the trunk. Stretching out from this

Did You Know?
The *Marañón* (mä′ rə nyōn′) *River* runs through northeast Peru and flows into the Amazon.

---

2. The prefix *trans-* means "across, through, or over." Here, *trans-Andean* refers to the Andes Mountains.

Vocabulary
rejuvenate (ri jōō′ və nāt′) *v.* to make fresh or young again

MEETING INDIVIDUAL NEEDS **ENGLISH LANGUAGE LEARNERS**

Where Are You From? The United States is a nation of immigrants. Most residents can trace their heritage to another country. These diverse cultural influences make the United States an interesting place to live.

Activity The characters in the story good-naturedly refer to one another by their nationalities. Use the characters'

nicknames as a springboard to discuss ethnic heritage. Invite students to share information about where they, their parents, their grandparents, or other ancestors were born and what they know about those cultures.

Additional Resources
📁 *English Language Learners Sourcebook*

E **Author's Craft**

CHARACTER The hunters don't want to dwell on their fear, but certain details reveal their true feelings. Challenge students to point out those details. *(They gather around the fire to make eye contact with each other; they tie their hammocks to the same tree; they sleep with their rifles; they try to laugh and talk to distract themselves.)*

Selva, 1981. Luis Monje. Oil on canvas, 51⅛ x 67 in. Private collection.
Viewing the painting: What elements of this painting reflect the sense of foreboding in the story?

VIEWING THE PAINTING

Explain to students that a landscape is a work of art that depicts a scene in nature. Point out that *selva* is the Spanish word for forest, woods, or jungle.

Viewing Response *The colors are dark and the landscape is filled with shadows. The vegetation is so dense that little sunlight comes through and only a patch of sky is visible. Everything seems thick and slow-moving.*

E axis in different directions, the hammocks were supported by the other end on other trunks. Each of us carried his rifle, cartridges, and some provisions which couldn't remain exposed on the ground. The sight of the weapons made us consider the place where we were, surrounded by the unknown. A slight feeling of terror made us laugh, cough, and talk. But fatigue overcame us, that heavy fatigue which compels the soldier to scorn danger, to put down his rifle, and to fall asleep though the most persistent enemy pursues him. We scarcely noticed the supreme grandeur of that remote tropical night.

I don't know whether it was the light of the magnificent dawn or the strange noises which awakened me and made me sit up in my hammock and look carefully at my surroundings. I saw nothing but the awakening of that life which at night falls into the lethargy of the jungle. I called my sleeping companions and, alert and seated in our hanging beds, we

F **Literary Elements**

POINT OF VIEW Point out that for the first time in the story the narrator refers to himself alone: "I don't know. . . ." Before, he has always said *we.* Does this mean that the point of view has changed? *(No, the point of view is still first person. But the narrator does step forward now as an individual.)* Ask students to note throughout the rest of the story when the narrator says *we* and when he says *I.*

Vocabulary
lethargy (leth′ ər jē) *n.* sluggish inactivity or drowsiness

Reading *Minilesson*

Sequence of Events What series of events led the men to where they are now? Tracing the sequence of events— what happened first, second, and so on— helps students make sense of the story and remember the events and their order.

Activity Have small groups of students make a story map. This can be a series of circles connected by arrows. Let the groups decide what events to put in the circles. Discuss what events they chose and why. Later, they can add events to complete their story maps. **L2**
COLLAB. LEARN.

Additional Resources
📁 *Reading Workbook,* pp. 17–18

G Author's Craft

FORESHADOWING The distant rustling hints at danger to come and increases the tension in the plot. Even the hunters, while loathe to admit their fears, sense a threat that makes them take refuge in their hammocks.

H Active Reading

EVALUATE When he refers to the men's shooting of the boars, the narrator uses the words *destruction* and *slaughter*. What kind of connotation do these words have? What do these words imply about the narrator's attitude toward hunting? You may wish to share the following model to illustrate evaluating word choice.

Model: Even though he says they enjoyed their "good fortune," the narrator also uses the words destruction and slaughter, which have negative connotations. I think this shows that he feels shooting the boars is bad. If he felt hunting were good, he might have written "the magnitude of our success" and "The shooting spree lasted for hours." However, I can't tell if his attitude at the time was negative. He may be letting his current attitude affect the way he views the past.

FINE ART
TRANSPARENCY 3

You may wish to use Fine Art Transparency 3 to discuss choices the main character faces.

Teaching Options

---

dressed ourselves. We were preparing to jump to the ground when we clearly heard a somewhat distant, sudden sound of rustling branches. Since it did not continue, however, we descended confidently, washed our faces with water from our canteens, and slowly prepared and enjoyed breakfast. By about 11:00 in the morning we were armed and bold and preparing to make our way through the jungle.

But then the sound again. Its persistence and proximity in the thicket made us change our minds. An instinct made us take refuge in our hammocks. We cautiously moved our cartridges and rifles into them again, and without consulting each other we agreed on the idea of putting our provisions safely away. We passed them up into the hammocks, and we ourselves finally climbed in. Stretched out face down, comfortably suspended with rifles in hand, we did not have to wait long. Black, agile boars quickly appeared from all directions. We welcomed them with shouts of joy and well-aimed shots. Some fell immediately, giving comical snorts, but many more came out of the jungle. We shot again, spending all the cartridges in the magazine.[3] Then we stopped to reload. Finding ourselves safe in the height of our hammocks, we continued after a pause.

We counted dozens of them. At a glance we made rapid calculations of the magnitude of the destruction, while the boars continued to come out of the jungle in uncountable numbers. Instead of going on their way or fleeing, they seemed confused. All of them emerged from the jungle where it was easy for us to shoot them. Occasionally we had to stop firing because the frequent shooting heated the barrels of our rifles. While they were cooling we smoked and were able to joke, celebrating our good fortune. The impotent anger of the boars amazed us. They raised their tusks in our direction, uselessly threatening us. We laughed at their snorts, quietly aimed at those who were near, and Bang! a dead boar. We carefully studied the angle of the shoulder blade so that the bullet would cross the heart. The slaughter lasted for hours.

At 4:00 P.M. we noticed an alarming shortage of our ammunition. We had been well supplied and had shot at will. Though the slaughter was gratifying, the boars must have numbered, as we had been informed previously, several thousands, because their hordes didn't diminish. On the contrary, they gathered directly beneath our hammocks in increasing groups. They slashed furiously at the trunk of the tree which held the four points of the hammocks. The marks of the tusks remained on the hard bark. Not without a certain fear we watched them gather compactly, tenaciously, in tight masses against the resisting trunk. We wondered what would happen to a man who fell within their reach. Our shots were now sporadic, well aimed, carefully husbanded.[4] They did not drive away the aggressive beasts, but only redoubled their fury. One of us ironically noted that from being the attackers we had gone on the defensive. We did not laugh very long at the joke. Now we hardly shot at all. We needed to save our cartridges.

---

3. A *magazine* is the supply chamber from which cartridges are fed into the firing chamber.

4. To *husband* something is to manage it in a careful, economic way.

Vocabulary
impotent (im′ pət ənt) *adj.* ineffective, powerless, or helpless
horde (hôrd) *n.* a large group; multitude
tenaciously (ti nā′ shəs lē) *adv.* stubbornly; persistently
sporadic (spə rad′ ik) *adj.* irregular; occasional

160 ✹ UNIT 1

MEETING
INDIVIDUAL
NEEDS
MULTIPLE LEARNING STYLES

Spatial Students with strong spatial abilities may respond more readily to descriptive passages by creating drawings. They can make sketches to help themselves and other students visualize how the hunters set up their camp.

Activity Have students review passages in which the narrator describes how the hunters set up their hammocks (final paragraph, page 160; final paragraph, page 158). Invite them to sketch the setup as if they were viewing it from above. They might also include images to represent the hunters, their rifles, and their provisions. Remind them to use captions and labels to help other viewers understand the sketch. **L2**

I The afternoon waned and evening came upon us. After consulting each other, we decided to eat in our hammocks. We applauded ourselves for taking the food up—meat, bread, and bottles of water. Stretching ourselves on our hammocks, we passed things to each other, sharing what we needed. The boars deafened us with their angry snorts.

J After eating, we began to feel calm. We lit cigars. Surely the boars would go. Their numbers were great, but they would finally leave peacefully. As we said so, however, we looked with greedy eyes at the few unused cartridges that remained. Our enemies, like enormous angry ants, stirred beneath us, encouraged by the ceasing of our fire. From time to time we carefully aimed and killed one or two of them, driving off the huge group of uselessly enraged boars at the base of the trunk which served as a prop for our hammocks.

K Night enveloped us almost without our noticing the change from twilight. Anxiety also overtook us. When would the cursed boars leave? Already there were enough dead to serve as trophies to several dozen hunters. Our feat would be talked about; we had to show ourselves worthy of such fame. Since there was nothing else to do, it was necessary to sleep. Even if we had had enough bullets it would have been impossible to continue the fight in the darkness. It occurred to us to start a fire to drive the herd off with flames, but apart from the fact that we couldn't leave the place in which we were suspended, there were no dry branches in the lush forest. Finally, we slept.

We woke up a little after midnight. The darkness was profound, but the well-known noise made us aware that our enemies were still there.

We imagined they must be the last ones which were leaving, however. If a good army needs several hours to break camp and march off, what can be expected of a vile army of boars but disorder and delay? The following morning we would fire upon the stragglers, but this painful thought bothered us: they were in large and apparently active numbers. What were they up to? Why didn't they leave? We thus spent long hours of worry. Dawn finally came, splendid in the sky but noisy in the jungle still enveloped inwardly in shadows. We eagerly waited for the sun to penetrate the foliage in order to survey the appearance of the field of battle of the day before. **L**

What we finally saw made us gasp. It terrified us. The boars were painstakingly continuing the work which they had engaged in throughout the entire night. Guided by some extraordinary instinct, with their tusks they were digging out the ground underneath the tree from which our hammocks hung; they gnawed the roots and continued to undermine

THE SHORT STORY 🐾 161

CONNECT Some students may think that the hunters were foolish to use up their last shots. Others may feel that they had nothing to lose. What would students have done in the same situation?

VIEWING THE PAINTING

In contrast to the cold reception he received in New York in the 1960s, Armando Morales now holds a position of status in Paris and the United States. He has been included in significant shows of Latin American art throughout the world.

Viewing Response *The painting may convey the bleak feelings of shock and terror in the end of the story.*

FYI

Fight or Flight "Fight or flight" is human instinct. When people are faced with danger, an endocrine organ called the adrenal gland sends out a biochemical stimulus in the form of adrenaline. This stimulant prepares them to either fight the threat or flee from it.

The Boar Hunt

them like large, industrious rats. Presently the tree was bound to fall and we with it, among the beasts. From that moment we neither thought nor talked. In desperation we used up our last shots, killing more ferocious beasts.

Still the rest renewed their activity. They seemed to be endowed with intelligence. However much we concentrated our fire against them, they did not stop their attack against the tree.

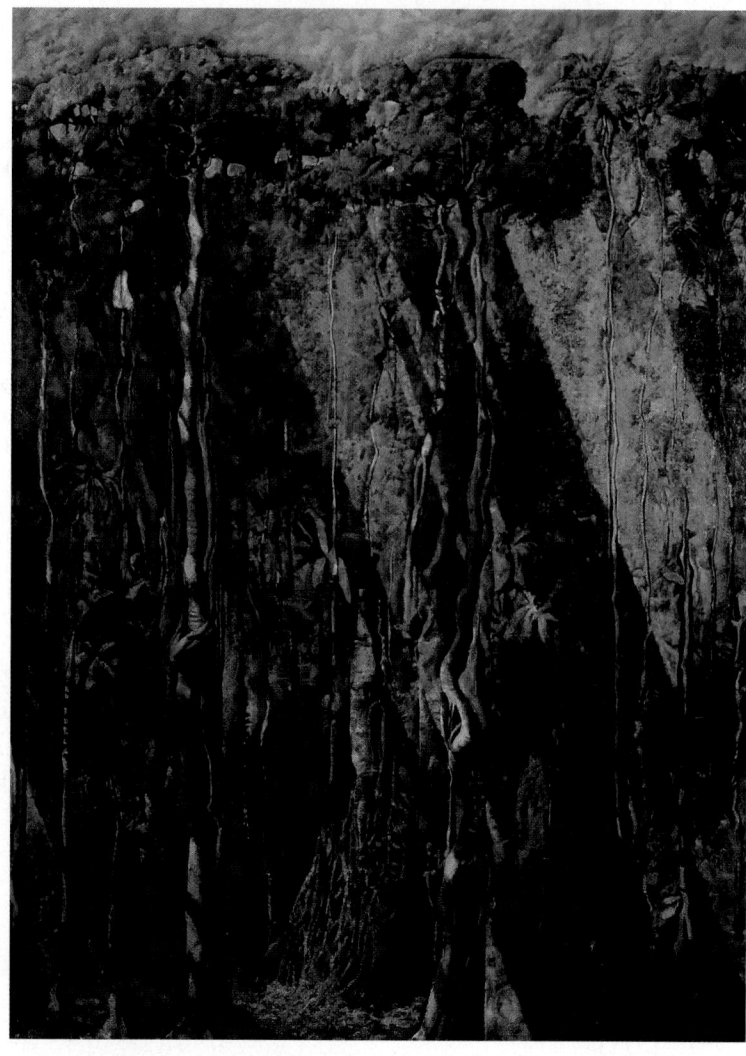

Foresta Tropical 1 (Jungla), 1985. Armando Morales. Oil on canvas, 64 x 51 in. Private collection.

Viewing the painting: What emotions does the scene in this painting convey to you? How are they similar to the emotions depicted in the end of the story?

Teaching Options

Grammar and Language *Minilesson*

Compound Sentences A compound sentence has two or more main clauses. Each main clause has its own subject and predicate. The main clauses of a compound sentence are joined by a comma and a coordinating conjunction (*and, but, or, nor, yet, so,* or *for*) or by a semicolon.

Activity Have students make the sentences into a compound sentence.
1. We killed many. We were still surrounded by an ocean of the beasts. (*many, but we*)
2. I looked nervously at my bullets. I had few left. (*bullets; I*)
3. I had to escape. I couldn't see a way out. (*escape, but I*) **L2**

Additional Resources

Grammar and Language Transparency 13

Grammar and Language Workbook, p. 103

Grammar and Composition Handbook, Lesson 2.3, 4.7

Writer's Choice, Lesson 13.7

José Vasconcelos ⁓

Soon our shots stopped. We emptied our pistols, and then silently listened to the tusks gnawing beneath the soft, wet, pleasant-smelling earth. From time to time the boars pressed against the tree, pushing it and making it creak, eager to smash it quickly. We looked on hypnotized by their devilish activity. It was impossible to flee because the black monsters covered every inch in sight. It seemed to us that, by a sudden inspiration, they were preparing to take revenge on us for the ruthless nature of man, the unpunished destroyer of animals since the beginning of time. Our imagination, distorted by fear, showed us our fate as an atonement for the unpardonable crimes implicit in the struggle of biological selection. Before my eyes passed the vision of sacred India, where the believer refuses to eat meat in order to prevent the methodical killing of beasts and in order to atone for man's evil, bloody, treacherous slaughter, such as ours, for mere vicious pleasure. I felt that the multitude of boars was raising its accusing voice against me. I now understood the infamy of the hunter, but what was repentance worth if I was going to die with my companions, hopelessly devoured by that horde of brutes with demonlike eyes?

 N

Stirred by terror and without realizing what I was doing, I hung from the upper end of my hammock, I balanced myself in the air, I swung in a long leap, I grasped a branch of a tree facing the one on which the boars were digging. From there I leaped to other branches and to others, reviving in myself habits which the species had forgotten.

The next moment a terrifying sound and unforgettable cries told me of the fall of the tree and the end of my companions. I clung to a trunk, trembling and listening to the chattering of my jaws. Later, the desire to flee gave me back my strength. Leaning out over the foliage, I looked for a path, and I saw the boars in the distance, marching in compressed ranks and holding their insolent snouts in the air. I knew that they were now withdrawing, and I got down from the tree. Horror overwhelmed me as I approached the site of our encampment, but some idea of duty made me return there. Perhaps one of my friends had managed to save himself. I approached hesitantly. Each dead boar made me tremble with fear.

But what I saw next was so frightful that I could not fix it clearly in my mind: remains of clothing—and footwear. There was no doubt; the boars had devoured them. Then I ran toward the river, following the tracks we had made two days before. I fled with great haste, limbs stiff from panic.

Running with long strides, I came upon the boat. With a great effort, I managed to row to the huts. There I went to bed with a high fever which lasted many days.

I will participate in no more hunts. I will contribute, if I have to, to the extermination of harmful beasts. But I will not kill for pleasure. I will not amuse myself with the ignoble[5] pleasure of the hunt.

---

5. *Ignoble* means "without honor or worth" or, since *ig-* is a negative prefix, "not noble."

⁓

Vocabulary
atonement (ə tōn′ mənt) *n.* something done to make up for a sin, injury, or loss
implicit (im plis′ it) *adj.* suggested but not directly stated
infamy (in′ fə mē) *n.* extreme wickedness or shameful evil

REAL-WORLD CONNECTION

Personal Response

Many students may have felt both the thrill of the hunt and the ensuing terror. Some may have felt revulsion at the slaughter of the boars and sadness at the deaths of the hunters.

ANALYZING LITERATURE

1. Four men from Mexico, Peru, Colombia, and Ecuador work together on a Peruvian sugar plantation.
2. They save money; arrange vacations; acquire rifles, ammunition, boots, and hammocks; and hire Indian guides. Their purpose is to explore and to hunt wild boars.
3. The camp is a half kilometer from the riverbank in the thick of the jungle. They fasten their hammocks to a central tree in a pattern resembling spokes fanning out from a hub.
4. Taking refuge in their hammocks, they kill dozens and dozens of boars after the animals invade their camp. No matter how many they kill, the boars refuse to go away. The men lie awake most of the night, worrying. In the daylight, they see the boars have attacked the tree that supports the hammocks.
5. They realize that they are doomed when they see the boars uprooting the hammock tree. The narrator swings from his hammock to another tree and escapes the fate of his companions who fall to the ground and are devoured.
6. They are four close friends who enjoy spending their free time engaging in lively conversation and debate.
7. Hiring the Indian guides was excellent. The amount of ammunition they brought was poor. Their estimation of the challenges awaiting them was very poor.
8. The way they set up camp shows that they were aware of certain dangers. Nevertheless, they had an unfounded sense of superiority over nature.
9. The boars become the hunters and the men the hunted as the men run out of ammunition and realize they are trapped in their hammocks.
10. Now that the tables are turned, he sees how wicked it is to brutalize other living creatures.
11. He foreshadows things that are about to happen. For example, he mentions rustling branches twice before the boars actually appear.

Responding to Literature

Personal Response

What emotions did you experience as you read this story? Did any of your reactions surprise you? Explain in your journal.

──── ANALYZING LITERATURE ────

RECALL

1. Who are the main characters in this story? What has brought them together?
2. What preparations do the men make for their journey? What is the purpose of their journey?
3. Describe the location and layout of the camp that the men and their helpers set up.
4. Summarize what happens during the men's first full day in the camp.
5. At what point in the story do the men realize their fate? How do the narrator's actions determine his particular fate?

INTERPRET

6. What conclusions can you draw about the main characters based on the way they spend their free time? Use evidence from the story to support your answer.
7. Rate the preparations the men make for their journey—*Excellent, Good, Fair,* or *Poor*—in terms of usefulness. Explain your rating.
8. In camp the first evening, what do the men's actions and thoughts seem to indicate about their attitude toward their surroundings?
9. How do the roles played by the men and the boars change as the story progresses? What causes these changes?
10. The narrator says, "I now understood the infamy of the hunter." What do you think he means?

EVALUATE AND CONNECT

11. What techniques does the author use to build suspense? Give specific examples from the story.
12. Explain how the **mood** of the story changes as the plot develops. (See Literary Terms Handbook, page R8.)
13. Explain how the terms "self-preservation" and "survival of the fittest" might be applied to this story.
14. How do you feel about what happened to the men? Do you think justice was served? Why or why not?
15. In your opinion, what is the moral, or lesson, that this story teaches?

Literary ELEMENTS

Point of View

Point of view is the relationship of the narrator, or storyteller, to the story. In "The Boar Hunt," the author uses first-person point of view—that is, the story is told by one of the characters, referred to as "I." The reader sees everything through the eyes of this character, who is a participant in the hunt.

1. How does the narrator's eyewitness description of events affect your emotional reaction to the story?
2. Imagine that a different character in the story had been the narrator. Explain how the story might be different when told from that narrator's point of view. For example, in what ways might the descriptions of the characters and events change?

● See **Literary Terms Handbook,** p. R9.

12. First, the mood is cheerful and upbeat. Then it becomes more and more tense until it finally becomes terrifying.
13. When faced with life or death, the narrator saves his own life. It could be argued that he was more fit to survive—quicker, stronger, smarter—than the others.
14. Students may say their deaths are sad, but since the men were out to kill the boars and did, in fact, kill many, many of them, it does seem fitting that the boars repaid them in kind.
15. The moral seems to be "Do not kill any animal except in self-defense."

LITERARY ELEMENTS

1. It draws the reader into the action and makes it seem more real and terrifying.
2. A different character might have expressed more fear or been less sensitive to the surroundings and the escalating tension.

Additional Resources

📖 *Literary Elements Transparency 13*

LITERATURE AND WRITING

Writing About Literature

Cause and Effect   Write a paragraph in which you trace the narrator's change in attitude toward hunting. Identify specific events from the story that cause this change. In a second paragraph, compare the narrator's experience with the one you described in the Focus Activity on page 156.

Creative Writing

Eyewitness Account   Television talk shows often invite survivors of terrible ordeals to tell their stories. The host usually prepares questions that will lead the guest to tell his or her story. With a partner, write a script for a talk show starring the survivor of "The Boar Hunt."

EXTENDING YOUR RESPONSE

Literature Groups

Coping with Life   An important aspect of Mexican philosophical thought is the idea that human beings are destined to lead tragic lives dominated by conflicts that can never be totally resolved. An individual must learn to cope with conflicts that arise from chance and circumstance, as well as conflicts created by personal desires. In your group, discuss how these ideas might be applied to the characters in "The Boar Hunt."

Internet Connection

Know the Law   In the United States, the hunting of wild game has caused the extinction or near extinction of several species of wild animals and birds, including the bison, passenger pigeon, and whooping crane. As a result, laws

have been enacted in many states to limit the hunting of wild animals. Use the Web to research hunting laws in your region. Share your findings with the class.

Interdisciplinary Activity

Art: Create a Mural   José Vasconcelos was part of a cultural movement in Mexico that supported muralists. How do you think a muralist might depict "The Boar Hunt"? Draw a sketch of your ideas. Meet with a small group of classmates to compare and discuss your sketches. Then work together to create a mural, using a large piece of art paper, or pieces of poster board taped together. Display your mural in the classroom.

 Save your work for your portfolio.

Skill Minilesson

VOCABULARY • Analogies

An analogy is a type of comparison that is based on the relationships between things or ideas. Some analogies are based on synonyms.

   sluggish : slow :: lucky : fortunate

Sluggish is a synonym for *slow; lucky* is a synonym for *fortunate*.

   To finish an analogy, decide what relationship exists between the first two things or ideas. Then apply that relationship to the second pair of words.

● For more about analogies, see **Communications Skills Handbook,** p. R77.

PRACTICE   Choose the word that best completes each analogy.

1. horde : mob :: farming :
   a. farmer   b. agriculture   c. land
2. rejuvenate : renew :: annoy :
   a. irritate   b. avoid   c. torture
3. mischief : infamy :: drizzle :
   a. sprinkle   b. moisture   c. downpour
4. exact : precise :: implicit :
   a. stated   b. understood   c. picky

LITERATURE AND WRITING

Writing About Literature

Students' paragraphs should
- explore cause and effect by tracing the narrator's change in attitude.
- identify events from the story that cause the change.
- compare the narrator's experience to the experience they described in the Focus Activity on page 156.

Creative Writing

Students' scripts should
- contain questions that would lead the narrator of the story to describe specific events.
- try to elicit vivid and exciting responses.
- maintain a sensitivity to the trauma the narrator experienced and not focus on the gory details.

EXTENDING YOUR RESPONSE

Literature Groups Ask students these questions: What conflicts arose from chance and circumstance in the story? What conflicts were created by personal desires?
COLLAB. LEARN.

Internet Connection As a class, students can use their research to help them contribute to a list of animals that can not be legally hunted in the state where you live.

Interdisciplinary Activity Suggest that students research examples of murals painted by Mexican muralists such as Diego Rivera.

Skill Minilesson

VOCABULARY • Analogies
1. b   2. a
3. c   4. b

Additional Resources
📁 *Vocabulary Practice,* p. 13

✔ ASSESSMENT OPTIONS

📁 **Quick Checks,** p. 13
📁 **Selection and Theme Assessment,** pp. 25–26
📁 **Performance Assessment,** p. 13
💾 **Testmaker**

Delicious Death

Objectives

- To read a poem about a mother's response to her son's first hunting experience
- To recognize the use of colloquial language in a poem
- To write a dialogue between the speaker's son and a friend

Skills

Reading/Thinking: Inferring
Writing: Dialogue
Grammar/Language: Using Dashes
Collaboration: Making Posters

Motivating

→ OPTIONS

Selection Focus Transparency 14: Encourage students to discuss their feelings about peer pressure in light of Eliot's quotation.

Focus Activity: Discuss tactics that can be used for effective persuasion.

FOCUS ACTIVITY

Have you ever tried to convince a parent or someone else in authority that you were mature enough to participate in a particular activity? Perhaps you wanted to attend a concert with a friend, camp in the wilderness, or get a job.

DISCUSS Identify the activity in which you wanted to participate, and list the arguments you used. As a group, discuss which argument seems the most convincing. Then tell whether your arguments were successful—did you get permission to do what you wanted to do?

SETTING A PURPOSE Read to discover how a mother responds to her son's hunting experience.

BACKGROUND

The Time and Place

The speaker of this poem is recalling a time in the recent past when she and her son lived in a mountainous region of the country.

Did You Know?

A traditional belief common to Native American cultures is that all things on earth—humans, animals, plants, even rocks—are endowed with a living spirit. Although humans are given the privilege of hunting

and using animals for food, shelter, and clothing, they must hunt only what they need for survival, as game animals are considered kindred spirits and a revered gift. Thus, in traditional Native American cultures, hunting is not a sport engaged in for amusement or to prove one's skill but rather a necessary and often dangerous occupation.

Meet
Alma Luz Villanueva

In response to a thank-you letter from one of her readers, Alma Luz Villanueva said that it forced her to "acknowledge the paradox, the mystery of writing: that when we touch the most personal, the most hidden within ourselves, we touch the universal."

Villanueva grew up in San Francisco's Mission District where she was raised by her grandmother, a Yaqui Indian from Mexico. Her work shows influences of her combined Native American and Mexican heritage. Villanueva's books of poetry include *Bloodroot* and *The Ultraviolet Sky*, for which she won the American Book Award in 1989.

Alma Luz Villanueva was born in 1944 in Santa Barbara, California.

RESOURCE MANAGER

Lesson Planning Resource
The *Unit One Planning Guide* (pp. 118–123) provides additional lesson notes and reduced versions of all print resources.

📁 **Other Print Resources**
- Active Reading Guide, p. 14
- Reading Workbook, pp. 17–18
- Grammar and Language Workbook, p.267
- Grammar and Composition Handbook, Lesson 11.7
- Quick Checks, p. 14

- Selection and Theme Assessment, pp. 27–28
- Performance Assessment, p. 14
- Spanish Summaries, p. 14
- Spanish Translations
- Inclusion Strategies
- English Language Learners Sourcebook

✋ **Transparencies**
- Selection Focus 14
- Literary Elements 14
- Grammar and Language 14

Technology
- 🎧 Audio Library
- 🎧 Spanish Audio Library
- 💻 Glencoe Literature Web Site
- 💾 Testmaker

Delicious Death

Alma Luz Villanueva

to my son, Marc

Memory: You were fifteen in the mountains,
your friends were going hunting,
you wanted to go.

Cold, autumn day-sky of steel
5   and rifles, the shade of bullets. We
fought. I didn't want to let you go.

And you stood up to me, "My friends are
going, their parents let them hunt, like
am I some kind of wimp or what, Mom . . ."

10 We walked into Thrifty's to buy the bullets,
you would use one of their rifles—I imagined
you being shot or shooting another eager boy/man.

COMPARING *selections*

This selection is paired with "The Boar Hunt" on pages 157–163. A lesson for teaching a comparison of the two selections appears on page 171.

CONNECTING TO OTHER SELECTIONS

For a teaching strategy that connects this selection to "The Vision Quest," turn to page 59 in the *Unit One Planning Guide*.

Reading the Selection

A Active Reading

QUESTION Focus on the title. Ask students what questions come to mind that they want answered as they read. *(Students might ask these questions: How can death be delicious? What does the title mean?)* Remind students to look for answers to their questions as they read.

Additional Resources
📁 *Active Reading Guide,* p. 14
🎧 *Audio Library*
🎧 *Spanish Audio Library*

B Literary Elements

COLLOQUIAL LANGUAGE Point out that the speaker's son uses colloquial, or informal, language when he speaks: "like am I some kind of wimp or what." Encourage students to look for other examples of colloquial language in the poem.

C Active Reading

CLARIFY The speaker calls her son an "eager boy/man." What does she mean by that? *(She recognizes that although he is still a boy, he is yearning to grow up and be a man.)*

Teaching Options

D Active Reading

IMAGINE Ask students to visualize how the speaker stared each word into the boy's eyes. Why would she do that? *(She wants to impress each word on him and show him that she really means what she says.)*

E Critical Thinking

INFERRING How can the boy always be alive in the man? *(by maintaining boyish qualities such as curiosity, enthusiasm, open-mindedness, and sensitivity)*

F Literary Elements

TONE What tone do the speaker's words convey? *(The tone is reverent, thankful, and honest. She enjoys the meal but understands and appreciates the sacrifice the quail made.)*

G Active Reading

INTERPRET Ask students what point they think the speaker is making about humans' relationship to the animals they hunt. *(Humans hunt [kill] in order to eat. For the speaker, this is a fact of life, not an issue to feel guilty about, but one to accept and honor respectfully.)*

Teaching Options

D

"What you kill you eat, do you understand?"
I stared each word into your eyes. As you
15 walked away, I said to the Spirits, "Guard

this human who goes
in search of
lives."

* * * * *

You brought home four small quail.
20 I took them saying, "Dinner." I stuffed
them with rice, apples, baked them in garlic,
onions, wine. "Tonight, Mom?" "Yes, tonight."
I plucked the softest tail feathers and as you
showered, I placed them in your pillow case:

25 "May the thunder and
the prey be
one.

May the hunter eat
and be eaten in
30 time.

May the boy always
be alive in the
man."

* * * * *

We ate, mostly, in silence—
35 I felt you thinking, I just
killed this, what I'm chewing . . .

On the highest peaks the first
powder shines like the moon—
winter comes so quickly.

40 On your face soft, blonde hair (yes, this
son is a gringo) shines like manhood—
childhood leaves so quickly.

MEETING INDIVIDUAL NEEDS

ENGLISH LANGUAGE LEARNERS

Informal vs. Formal Language Point out that people express themselves differently depending whom they're talking with, as when the son in the poem says "like am I a wimp or what" to his mom.

Activity Write statements such as the following on the board.
• I want to express my thanks to you for inviting me.

• This is the best-tasting meal I have ever had.

Have groups choose one of the following characters: senator, tenth grader, preschooler. Ask students how they would say each statement to their character.

Additional Resources
📁 *English Language Learners Sourcebook*

The wonder of the hunt is on my tongue,
I taste it—wild, tangy, reluctant—
45 this flesh feeds me well.

I light the candles and thank the quail
in a clear voice—I thank them for their
small bodies, their immense, winged souls.

"God, Mom, you're making me feel like a
50 killer." "Well, you are and so am I."
Swallowing, swallowing this delicious death.

H Literary Elements

COLLOQUIAL LANGUAGE Ask students to identify the colloquial language found in the final stanza. ("God, Mom, you're making me feel like a killer.")

VIEWING THE PAINTING

Carlos Vierra, born in California in 1876, was one of the first artists to settle in Santa Fe, New Mexico. He developed an interest in local Mission and Indian architecture and helped it gain the appreciation of the general public. Vierra died in 1937.

Viewing Response *The colors suggest conflicting elements existing in harmony, which creates a balanced mood. This mood is similar to the mood of the poem in which the speaker and her son feel conflict but resolve it and find a sense of peace.*

New Mexico in Winter, 1922. Carlos Vierra. Oil on canvas, 28 x 38 in. Courtesy of the Gerald Peters Gallery, Sante Fe.
Viewing the painting: What sort of mood does the mixture of pastels and rich greys in this painting create? Does the mood of the painting fit the mood of the poem?

Thematic Focus

Making Choices What choices did the speaker and the son make? Ask students to whether they agree with those choices.

☑ ASSESSMENT OPTIONS

📁 *Quick Checks,* p. 14

THE SHORT STORY 🦋 169

Grammar and Language *Minilesson*

Using Dashes The poet often uses dashes. A dash can indicate an abrupt break or change in thought within a sentence: "We ate, mostly, in silence—/I felt you thinking, I just/killed this, what I'm chewing . . ." A dash also can set off and emphasize supplemental information: "I taste it—wild, tangy, reluctant—/this flesh feeds me well."

Activity Have students rewrite the sentences, setting off the appropriate phrases with dashes.

1. Chris do you know him? often sends me e-mail. *(Chris—do you know him?—often sends me e-mail.)*

2. I didn't lock the door behind me my first mistake. *(I didn't lock the door behind me—my first mistake.)* **L2**

Additional Resources

✍ *Grammar and Language Transparency 14*

📖 *Grammar and Language Workbook,* p. 267

📖 *Grammar and Composition Handbook,* Lesson 11.7

📖 *Writer's Choice,* Lesson 21.7

Responding to the Selection

Personal Response

Encourage students to consider the question from an adult's perspective.

ANALYZING LITERATURE

1. He says that all his friends are going hunting. However, she probably is not convinced by that so much as by her knowledge that children need to learn their own lessons.
2. She tells him he has to eat whatever he kills. She says this to reinforce her personal views on the issue and to get his agreement beforehand.
3. She puts feathers in her son's pillow case and says a prayer. It affirms the kinship between the hunter and the hunted.
4. He is revolted and feels guilty. She says what is traditionally said in her culture, but she knows that it will have a profound effect on her son. She wants him to realize and respect what it really means to be a hunter.
5. She now sees him as a young man rather than as a boy.
6. She contrasts the first winter snows on a mountain and the first hairs on her son's face. The first represents her growing old; the second her son becoming an adult.
7. She feels reverent and thankful. He feels pensive, considering his first kill.
8. Students may say that the dialogue sounds real because it contains expressions from everyday speech.

EXTENDING YOUR RESPONSE

Creative Writing

Students' dialogues should
- identify who is speaking each time the speaker changes.
- use colloquial language for both speakers.

Interdisciplinary Activity

Suggest that students conduct research in one or more of the following sources: encyclopedias, National Audubon Society publications, the Internet (keyword: "quail").

COLLAB. LEARN.

Responding to Literature

Personal Response

Do you think the mother should have allowed her son to go hunting? Why or why not?

— ANALYZING LITERATURE —

RECALL AND INTERPRET

1. What argument does the son use in trying to persuade his mother to let him go hunting? Compare his argument with those you listed in the Focus Activity on page 166. What do you think is the real reason for the mother's decision?
2. What does the mother say to her son right before he walks away? Why do you think she says this?
3. Describe the ritual that the mother performs using the quail feathers. What is your interpretation of her prayer or chant?
4. How does the boy react to what his mother says and does at dinner? Do you think that she wanted him to react this way? Explain.

EVALUATE AND CONNECT

5. **Theme Connections** How does the mother's decision seem to change the way she looks at her son? Explain your answer.
6. What two **images** does the speaker create in lines 37–42? In your opinion, what do these images seem to suggest? (See Literary Terms Handbook, page R6.)
7. How does the mother feel as she eats her dinner? How do you think the boy feels? Do you think you would have had the same feelings if you had been in their place? Explain.
8. This poem includes some dialogue between the mother and son. In your opinion, does this dialogue sound real? Why or why not?

Literary ELEMENTS

Colloquial Language

Colloquial language is a type of language used in everyday speech but not used in formal speech or formal writing. Colloquial language sometimes differs from formal language in grammar, vocabulary, or pronunciation. The expressions "That's cool" and "I'm out of here" are examples of colloquial language. Writers use colloquial language to create an informal, conversational tone. Colloquial expressions are not considered slang, although they may contain slang words.

1. What examples of colloquial language can you find in "Delicious Death"?
2. How does the use of colloquial language affect your appreciation of the poem? Explain.

● See **Literary Terms Handbook,** p. R2.

— EXTENDING YOUR RESPONSE —

Creative Writing

Guess What Happened at Dinner? Imagine a conversation the son might have with one of his friends the day after the quail dinner. Write a dialogue in which the son describes the events of the previous evening, as well as his feelings about those events. Include the comments and questions of the son's friend.

Interdisciplinary Activity

Biology: On the Quail Trail About twenty species of quail live in North America. Gather information about one species. In a small group, create a poster-sized chart displaying the facts your group has gathered about different species of quail. Illustrate your chart.

■ **Save your work for your portfolio.**

LITERARY ELEMENTS

1. "like am I some kind of wimp or what, Mom"; "God, Mom"
2. Students may say that the colloquial language helps them connect with the poem and get a clearer picture of the boy.

Additional Resources

📖 *Literary Elements Transparency 14*

✓ ASSESSMENT OPTIONS

📁 *Quick Checks,* p. 14
📁 *Selection and Theme Assessment,* pp. 27–28
📁 *Performance Assessment,* p. 14
💾 *Testmaker*

COMPARING selections

The Boar Hunt and Delicious Death

COMPARE **PURPOSES**

Both Vasconcelos and Villanueva use literature to make a statement about choices and consequences.

- What is similar about the authors' messages?
- How are the messages different?
- In your opinion, which message is stronger? Why?

COMPARE **ATTITUDES**

How do your attitudes about hunting compare with the attitudes of the characters in the two selections?

- In a small group, list five to ten survey questions about hunting animals in the wild. For example: *Should hunters be allowed to kill wild animals for sport?*
- Discuss how you think the narrator of "The Boar Hunt," as well as the mother and son in "Delicious Death," would answer the survey questions. Record the answers you think these characters would give.
- Have group members write down their own answers to the survey questions. Compile your survey results and share them with the class, comparing your groups' attitudes with those of the characters in the two selections.

COMPARE **MEDIA USE**

Gather copies of a variety of articles, photographs, paintings, posters, and advertisements about hunting, as well as tapes of TV and radio programs about this topic, if possible. Label the items and display them in a central location. Then, give a brief oral presentation to the class telling which items you find most effective for conveying information about the topic. Include your reasons for your choices.

COMPARING selections

Objective

- To compare a short story and a poem that deal with the theme of making choices

COMPARE **PURPOSES**

- Both authors convey a message about hunting.
- Vasconcelos's message is that animals should be killed only in self-defense. Villanueva suggests that animals should be hunted only when one needs to eat them for survival.
- The horror of the hunt is more immediate in "The Boar Hunt." The moral reflection is well-articulated in the poem.

COMPARE **ATTITUDES**

Student groups should

- assign a chairperson to maintain order and elicit the participation of each member.
- assign a recorder to write the survey questions and, later, compile students' and characters' answers.
- discuss their answers to the survey questions before writing them.

 Literature Groups Sourcebook

COMPARE **MEDIA USE**

You may wish to divide the tasks among several small groups. Each group could look for information about hunting in one type of media.

Teaching Options

 PORTFOLIO OPTIONS _____

Select and Reflect Have students reflect on their survey questions by asking the following questions.

- Were my questions relevant, and did they target key issues relating to the topic?
- Did my answers accurately reflect opinions the characters might have voiced?

Students should save their survey questions and answers in their portfolios. Later,

they might rethink their responses to the survey questions. **L2**

Additional Resources

 Writing Assessment and Portfolio Management, pp. 20–22

Objectives

- To read and analyze a suspenseful story about how a family's lives change when their wish is granted
- To identify suspense
- To write an analysis of the use of humor and adventure

Skills

Reading/Thinking: Drawing Conclusions; Inferring; Identifying Cause-Effect Relationships; Verifying Predictions; Chronological Order

Writing: Letter

Vocabulary: Unlocking Meaning

Grammar/Language: Four Kinds of Sentences; Punctuating Dialogue

Listening/Speaking: Discussing Opposing Opinions; Performing a Play

Life Skills: Reviewing Stories

Collaboration: Literature Groups

Motivating
OPTIONS

 Selection Focus Transparency 15: Discuss wish-making folklore.

 Focus Activity: Invite students to explain the possible consequences of their top three wishes.

Before You Read

The Monkey's Paw

FOCUS ACTIVITY

What would you wish for if you could have three wishes granted? How might the granting of these wishes change your life and the lives of others around you? Would all the changes be positive?

FREEWRITE Make a list of wishes. Study the list and consider the possible consequences of each wish. Circle your top three wishes.

SETTING A PURPOSE Read to learn how lives change when wishes are granted.

BACKGROUND

The Time and Place

"The Monkey's Paw" takes place in Laburnam Villa, the cozy home of an elderly English couple and their grown son. It is probably sometime in the late 1800s.

Did You Know?

As this story opens, Mr. White and his son, Herbert, are playing chess, a board game between two players. Each player has sixteen pieces—a king, a queen, two rooks, two bishops, two knights, and eight pawns—to move strategically around the board. The game is won when one player attacks and then captures the opponent's king. A player usually announces the attack by saying "Check" and the final victory with the word "Checkmate."

VOCABULARY PREVIEW

amiably (ā′ mē ə blē) *adv.* in a friendly, good-natured way; p. 173

grimace (grim′ is) *n.* a twisting of the face; p. 175

presumptuous (pri zump′ chōō əs) *adj.* too forward; bold; p. 175

doggedly (dô′ gid lē) *adv.* stubbornly; firmly; p. 175

enthralled (en thrôld′) *adj.* fascinated; charmed; p. 176

credulity (kri dōō′ li tē) *n.* a tendency to believe too readily; p. 176

prosaic (prō zā′ ik) *adj.* ordinary; commonplace; p. 177

avaricious (av′ ə rish′ əs) *adj.* greedy; p. 177

sinister (sin′ is tər) *adj.* threatening or suggesting evil; p. 178

oppressive (ə pres′ iv) *adj.* hard to bear; distressing; p. 181

Meet William Wymark Jacobs

William Wymark Jacobs, the son of an English wharf supervisor, was a bank employee and postal worker before he turned his writing hobby into a profession. Childhood memories of sailors and dock workers inspired the sea stories for which Jacobs became famous. He also wrote humorous stories and horror tales. "The Monkey's Paw"—the selection you are about to read—is the author's best-known story.

William Wymark Jacobs was born in London in 1863; he died in 1943. This story appeared in the collection The Lady of the Barge, *published in 1902.*

RESOURCE MANAGER

Lesson Planning Resource
The *Unit One Planning Guide* (pp. 124–131) provides additional lesson notes and reduced versions of all print resources.

📁 Other Print Resources
- Active Reading Guide, p. 15
- Vocabulary Practice, p. 14
- Reading Workbook, p. 19
- Grammar and Language Workbook, pp. 119, 271
- Grammar and Composition Handbook, Lessons 4.6, 11.9

- Quick Checks, p. 15
- Selection and Theme Assessment, pp. 29–30
- Performance Assessment, p. 15
- Spanish Summaries, p. 15
- Spanish Translations
- Inclusion Strategies
- English Language Learners Sourcebook

📖 Transparencies
- Selection Focus 15
- Literary Elements 15

- Grammar and Language 15, 16

Technology
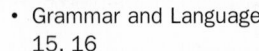
- 🎧 Audio Library
- 🎧 Spanish Audio Library
- 💻 Glencoe Literature Web Site
- 💾 Testmaker

The Monkey's Paw

W. W. Jacobs

I

WITHOUT, THE NIGHT WAS COLD and wet, but in the small parlor of Laburnam Villa the blinds were drawn and the fire burned brightly. Father and son were at chess, the former, who possessed ideas about the game involving radical changes, putting his king into such sharp and unnecessary perils that it even provoked comment from the white-haired old lady knitting placidly[1] by the fire.

"Hark at the wind," said Mr. White, who, having seen a fatal mistake after it was too late, was amiably desirous of preventing his son from seeing it.

"I'm listening," said the latter, grimly surveying the board as he stretched out his hand. "Check."

"I should hardly think that he'd come tonight," said his father, with his hand poised over the board.

"Mate," replied the son.

"That's the worst of living so far out," bawled Mr. White, with sudden and unlooked-for violence; "of all the beastly, slushy, out-of-the-way places to live in, this is the worst. Pathway's a bog, and the road's a torrent. I don't know what people are thinking about. I suppose because only two houses on

---

1. *Placidly* (plas' id lē) means calmly; peacefully.

Vocabulary
amiably (ā' mē ə blē) *adv.* in a friendly, good-natured way

SUMMARY

One evening an old soldier visits Mr. and Mrs. White and their son Herbert and tells them a tale about a withered monkey's paw. Long ago, an Indian fakir put a spell on the paw so that three men could each have three wishes from it. The soldier warns of awful consequences, but Mr. White, eager to give the paw a try, wishes for two hundred pounds. Shortly thereafter, he gets the money but loses something priceless instead. Too late the Whites learn the folly of interfering with fate.

📁 *Spanish Summaries,* p. 15

A **Active Reading**

EVALUATE Have students read the first five paragraphs. Discuss what they know about the father's personality and how that might play a role in the story. *(The father seems to make rash decisions. This may cause problems.)*

Additional Resources
📁 *Active Reading Guide,* p. 15
🎧 *Audio Library*
🎧 *Spanish Audio Library*

Teaching Options

CONNECTING TO OTHER SELECTIONS

The chart at the right shows three ways to connect "The Monkey's Paw" to selections in this book.

For specific teaching strategies, see the *Unit One Planning Guide,* pp. 127–128.

Connection	Title
Life Skills: Decision Making	→ "By the Waters of Babylon," p. 95
Thematic: Lessons Learned	→ "A Sound of Thunder," p. 316
Literary: Mood	→ "Winter Night," p. 363

CHARACTER What does this scene tell the reader about the characters? *(The details of the game and Mrs. White's reaction to her husband tell the reader that the three form a close-knit and loving family.)*

B

Cultural Note

In 1858, the British government took direct control of many Indian territories. Other parts of India, through treaties with local princes, came under Britain's indirect control. A British viceroy answerable to Parliament was appointed and governors, always Britons, ruled local provinces.

VIEWING THE PAINTING

Thomas Eakins is often called the greatest American artist. His are masterpieces of nineteenth-century psychological realism. In his art the human figure is central, owing to his mastery of perspective, anatomy, and the mechanics of human motion.

Viewing Response *His upright posture suggests confidence and dignity, while his crossed legs suggest that he is relaxed. He resembles Morris by the fire.*

the road are let, they think it doesn't matter."

"Never mind, dear," said his wife soothingly; "perhaps you'll win the next one."

Mr. White looked up sharply, just in time to intercept a knowing glance between mother and son. The words died away on his lips, and he hid a guilty grin in his thin gray beard.

"There he is," said Herbert White, as the gate banged to loudly and heavy footsteps came toward the door.

The old man rose with hospitable haste, and, opening the door, was heard condoling with the new arrival. The new arrival also condoled[2] with himself, so that Mrs. White said, "Tut, tut!" and coughed gently as her husband entered the room, followed by a tall burly man, beady of eye and rubicund of visage.[3]

"Sergeant Major Morris," he said, introducing him.

The sergeant major shook hands, and, taking the proffered seat by the fire, watched contentedly while his host got out whiskey and tumblers and stood a small copper kettle on the fire.

At the third glass his eyes got brighter, and he began to talk, the little family circle regarding with eager interest this visitor from distant parts, as he squared his broad shoulders in the chair and spoke of strange scenes and doughty[4] deeds, of wars and plagues and strange peoples.

"Twenty-one years of it," said Mr. White, nodding at his wife and son. "When he went

Frank John St. Jay, 1900. Thomas Eakins. Oil on canvas, 23⅞ x 19⅞ in. Fine Arts Museums of San Francisco. Gift of Mr. and Mrs. John D. Rockefeller, 3rd. 1979.7.7.

Viewing the painting: What does the posture of the man in the painting reveal about his character? How is this man similar to Sergeant Major Morris?

away he was a slip of a youth in the warehouse. Now look at him."

"He don't look to have taken much harm," said Mrs. White politely.

"I'd like to go to India myself," said the old man, "just to look around a bit, you know."

"Better where you are," said the sergeant major, shaking his head. He put down the empty glass and, sighing softly, shook it again.

"I should like to see those old temples and fakirs[5] and jugglers," said the old man. "What was that you started telling me the other day about the monkey's paw or something, Morris?"

---

2. To *condole* is to express sympathy.
3. *Rubicund of visage* means reddish or rosy in the face.
4. A *doughty* (dou′ tē) deed is a brave or valiant one.

5. A *fakir* (fə kēr′) is a member of a Muslim or Hindu sect who takes a vow of poverty and lives by begging. Fakirs sometimes do extraordinary and dangerous tricks.

Teaching Options

MEETING INDIVIDUAL NEEDS — ENGLISH LANGUAGE LEARNERS

Sharing Stories Just as the Whites are eager to hear Morris tell of his adventures, English language learners will enjoy hearing stories from cultures, societies, or communities with which they are not familiar.

Activity Have students form small groups. Invite students to tell a brief story to their group about an experience of their own or of others from their culture. Stories might pertain to mealtime rituals, etiquette, family traditions or relationships, celebrations, national heroes, superstitions, myths, or beliefs.

Additional Resources
📁 *English Language Learners Sourcebook*

"Nothing," said the soldier hastily. "Leastways, nothing worth hearing."

"Monkey's paw?" said Mrs. White curiously.

"Well, it's just a bit of what you might call magic, perhaps," said the sergeant major offhandedly.

His three listeners leaned forward eagerly. The visitor absent-mindedly put his empty glass to his lips and then set it down again. His host filled it for him.

"To look at," said the sergeant major, fumbling in his pocket, "it's just an ordinary little paw, dried to a mummy."

He took something out of his pocket and proffered it. Mrs. White drew back with a grimace, but her son, taking it, examined it curiously.

"And what is there special about it?" inquired Mr. White as he took it from his son and, having examined it, placed it upon the table.

"It had a spell put on it by an old fakir," said the sergeant major, "a very holy man. He wanted to show that fate ruled people's lives, and that those who interfered with it did so to their sorrow. He put a spell on it so that three separate men could each have three wishes from it."

His manner was so impressive that his hearers were conscious that their light laughter jarred somewhat.

"Well, why don't you have three, sir?" said Herbert White cleverly.

The soldier regarded him in the way that middle age is wont[6] to regard presumptuous

youth. "I have," he said quietly, and his blotchy face whitened.

"And did you really have the three wishes granted?" asked Mrs. White.

"I did," said the sergeant major, and his glass tapped against his strong teeth.

"And has anybody else wished?" inquired the old lady.

"The first man had his three wishes, yes," was the reply. "I don't know what the first two were, but the third was for death. That's how I got the paw."

His tones were so grave that a hush fell upon the group.

"If you've had your three wishes, it's no good to you now, then, Morris," said the old man at last. "What do you keep it for?"

The soldier shook his head. "Fancy, I suppose," he said slowly. "I did have some idea of selling it, but I don't think I will. It has caused enough mischief already. Besides, people won't buy. They think it's a fairy tale, some of them, and those who do think anything of it want to try it first and pay me afterward."

"If you could have another three wishes," said the old man, eyeing him keenly, "would you have them?"

"I don't know," said the other. "I don't know."

He took the paw, and dangling it between his front finger and thumb, suddenly threw it upon the fire. White, with a slight cry, stooped down and snatched it off.

"Better let it burn," said the soldier solemnly.

"If you don't want it, Morris," said the old man, "give it to me."

"I won't," said his friend doggedly. "I threw it on the fire. If you keep it, don't

---

6. *Wont* means accustomed; used. Different people (and dictionaries) are wont to pronounce it with a long *o*, a short *o*, or a short *u*.

Vocabulary
grimace (grim′ is) *n.* a twisting of the face
presumptuous (pri zump′ choo əs) *adj.* too forward; excessively bold
doggedly (dô′ gid lē) *adv.* stubbornly; firmly

Sidebar

C Literary Elements

SUSPENSE Here is the first hint that all will not continue to be cozy. How do Morris's first two comments about the monkey's paw create suspense? *(He is reluctant to talk about it; then he tries to be offhanded.)*

D Literary Elements

THEME Call attention to the fakir's message—that interfering with fate will bring great sorrow—and encourage students to keep it in mind as they read on. They will discover that it is the story's central theme.

Language Note

Fate refers to the supposed power that determines the outcome of events before they occur. It implies an inevitable, often adverse outcome. In Greek mythology, three goddesses, the Fates, were believed to rule the destinies of both gods and people. They spun a web made of the threads of people's lives; they could cut the threads whenever they pleased.

E Literary Elements

SUSPENSE The suspense heightens with each of Morris's replies. First his face pales; then his teeth rattle against his glass. What does his reply about the first man's wishes imply? *(The man's third wish was for death. This implies that something so bad happened to him that he wanted to die—a sobering thought.)*

Listening and Speaking *Minilesson*

Discuss Opposing Opinions The narrator of "The Boar Hunt" said, "Ultimately nature and events are largely what our imaginations make them out to be." In this story, Morris says that the Indian fakir "wanted to show that fate ruled people's lives." Have students think about the two men's ideas.

Activity Ask the class to discuss which view makes more sense to them based on their personal experiences. Remind students to listen respectfully to one another. Because they will express different views, help them keep the discussion focused on ideas, not individuals. Have a few students record their classmates' comments on the chalkboard. **L3**

F Active Reading

QUESTION If Sergeant Major Morris is sincere in all his warnings and doesn't want Mr. White or anyone else to have and use the monkey's paw, then why does he tell Mr. White how to use it? *(Perhaps he thinks he can't stop Mr. White from using the paw if he really wants to. Perhaps he thinks others will have to find out as he and the first man did.)*

FYI

The Arabian Nights

You might bring in a copy of *The Arabian Nights*. This suspenseful book comprises stories that are supposedly told night after night. The stories could be categorized as fables, fairy tales, romances, and historical anecdotes. The tales are of various origins (Indian, Persian, and Arabic); however, through time they have come to reflect Arab society and customs.

G Literary Elements

SUSPENSE Ask students how they felt when they read Mr. White's claim that the monkey's paw moved when he wished on it. What do they think this might mean?

Teaching Options

---

blame me for what happens. Pitch it on the fire again, like a sensible man."

The other shook his head and examined his new possession closely. "How do you do it?" he inquired.

"Hold it up in your right hand and wish aloud," said the sergeant major, "but I warn you of the consequences."

"Sounds like the *Arabian Nights*," said Mrs. White, as she rose and began to set the supper. "Don't you think you might wish for four pairs of hands for me?"

Her husband drew the talisman[7] from his pocket and then all three burst into laughter as the sergeant major, with a look of alarm on his face, caught him by the arm. "If you must wish," he said gruffly, "wish for something sensible."

Mr. White dropped it back into his pocket, and placing chairs, motioned his friend to the table. In the business of supper the talisman was partly forgotten, and afterward the three sat listening in an <u>enthralled</u> fashion to a second installment of the soldier's adventures in India.

"If the tale about the monkey paw is not more truthful than those he has been telling us," said Herbert, as the door closed behind their guest, just in time for him to catch the last train, "we shan't make much out of it."

"Did you give him anything for it, Father?" inquired Mrs. White, regarding her husband closely.

"A trifle," said he, coloring slightly. "He didn't want it, but I made him take it. And he pressed me again to throw it away."

"Likely," said Herbert, with pretended horror. "Why, we're going to be rich, and

famous, and happy. Wish to be an emperor, Father, to begin with: then you can't be bossed around."

He darted round the table, pursued by the maligned[8] Mrs. White armed with an antimacassar.

Did You Know?
An *antimacassar* (an' ti mə kas' ər) is a small, decorative covering put over the back and arms of a chair or sofa to prevent soiling.

Mr. White took the paw from his pocket and eyed it dubiously. "I don't know what to wish for, and that's a fact," he said slowly. "It seems to me I've got all I want."

"If you only cleared the house, you'd be quite happy, wouldn't you?" said Herbert, with his hand on his shoulder. "Well, wish for two hundred pounds, then; that'll just do it."

His father, smiling shamefacedly at his own <u>credulity</u>, held up the talisman, as his son, with a solemn face somewhat marred by a wink at his mother, sat down at the piano and struck a few impressive chords.

"I wish for two hundred pounds," said the old man distinctly.

A fine crash from the piano greeted the words, interrupted by a shuddering cry from the old man. His wife and son ran toward him.

"It moved," he cried, with a glance of disgust at the object as it lay on the floor. "As I wished it twisted in my hands like a snake."

"Well, I don't see the money," said his son, as he picked it up and placed it on the table, "and I bet I never shall."

"It must have been your fancy, Father," said his wife, regarding him anxiously.

---

7. A *talisman* is a charm believed to have magical powers.

8. If you are *maligned,* someone has spoken ill of you or told harmful untruths about you.

Vocabulary
enthralled (en thrôld') *adj.* fascinated; charmed
credulity (kri dōō' li tē) *n.* a tendency to believe too readily

---

MEETING INDIVIDUAL NEEDS — GIFTED AND TALENTED

Explaining an Expression High-ability students may enjoy discussing the following expression: It is often said to overly inquisitive people that "curiosity killed the cat." Ask a student who has heard the expression to describe the situation in which he or she heard it used.

Activity Have students review the story and note examples of Mr. White's students exhibiting curiosity that could kill the cat, so to speak. Did Mrs. White ever display such curiosity? Did Herbert? Have students write a paragraph explaining how the expression pertains to the tragedy that befell the White family. **L3**

W. W. Jacobs

He shook his head. "Never mind, though; there's no harm done, but it gave me a shock all the same."

They sat down by the fire again while the two men finished their pipes. Outside, the wind was higher than ever, and the old man started nervously at the sound of a door banging upstairs. A silence unusual and depressing settled upon all three, which lasted until the old couple rose to retire for the night.

"I expect you'll find the cash tied up in a big bag in the middle of your bed," said Herbert, as he bade them good night, "and something horrible squatting up on top of the wardrobe watching you as you pocket your ill-gotten gains."

He sat alone in the darkness, gazing at the dying fire, and seeing faces in it. The last face was so horrible and so simian[9] that he gazed at it in amazement. It got so vivid that, with a little uneasy laugh, he felt on the table for a glass containing a little water to throw over it. His hand grasped the monkey's paw, and with a little shiver he wiped his hand on his coat and went up to bed.

II

In the brightness of the wintry sun next morning as it streamed over the breakfast table Herbert laughed at his fears. There was an air of prosaic wholesomeness about the room which it had lacked on the previous night, and the dirty, shriveled little paw was pitched on

His hand grasped the monkey's paw, and with a little shiver he wiped his hand on his coat and went up to bed.

the sideboard with a carelessness which betokened[10] no great belief in its virtues.

"I suppose all old soldiers are the same," said Mrs. White. "The idea of our listening to such nonsense! How could wishes be granted in these days? And if they could, how could two hundred pounds hurt you, Father?"

"Might drop on his head from the sky," said the frivolous Herbert.

"Morris said the things happened so naturally," said his father, "that you might if you so wished attribute it to coincidence."

"Well, don't break into the money before I come back," said Herbert, as he rose from the table. "I'm afraid it'll turn you into a mean, avaricious man, and we shall have to disown you."

His mother laughed, and following him to the door, watched him down the road, and, returning to the breakfast table, was very happy at the expense of her husband's credulity. All of which did not prevent her from scurrying to the door at the postman's knock, nor prevent her from referring somewhat shortly to retired sergeant majors of bibulous[11] habits when she found that the post brought a tailor's bill.

"Herbert will have some more of his funny remarks, I expect, when he comes home," she said, as they sat at dinner.

---

9. To be *simian* is to resemble a monkey.

10. *Betokened* means "indicated."
11. A sergeant major or anyone else of *bibulous* (bib′ yə ləs) habits is fond of alcoholic beverages and drinks them regularly.

Vocabulary
prosaic (prō zā′ ik) *adj.* ordinary; commonplace
avaricious (av′ ə rish′ əs) *adj.* greedy

THE SHORT STORY 177

H Literary Elements

PLOT: *Internal Conflict* Herbert's joking suggests that he has little faith in the powers of the paw; however, his reaction to the apelike face he sees in the fire reveals that he may believe in the paw more than he cares to admit.

I Active Reading

RESPOND Mrs. White won't admit it, but she does seem to be expecting the 200 pounds to arrive. The idea of having a wish granted is very enticing. Encourage students to explore why they too might feel expectant at this point in the story. Share the following model to illustrate the thought processes involved in responding to a story.

Model: If I were one of the characters, the suspense would be killing me. What's going to happen? Will the wish come true or not? If it does, how will it come true? As a reader, the sense of anticipation really draws me into the story. I feel as jumpy and excited as the Whites must feel.

J Active Reading

PREDICT As they read about this strange visitor, students' minds may race with possibilities. Encourage them to predict who he is and what his purpose is. Can they explain his bizarre behavior?

K Critical Thinking

DRAWING CONCLUSIONS Who is the visitor, and what is his connection with the Whites? *(He is the spokesperson for a company, Maw and Meggins, where Herbert White apparently works.)*

L Critical Thinking

INFERRING What does Mrs. White realize that the visitor means when he says Herbert is badly hurt but not in any pain? Why are her fears confirmed when the man won't look at her? *(She realizes that Herbert can't be badly hurt and not also be in pain, so he must be dead. The visitor can't look at her because he is uncomfortable with the news he brings. This action tells her that what she fears is indeed true.)*

M Literary Elements

SUSPENSE Point out that "a long silence" is a classic way of building suspense in oral communication. The characters and the readers are all waiting to hear what comes next.

"I dare say," said Mr. White, pouring himself out some beer; "but for all that, the thing moved in my hand; that I'll swear to."

"You thought it did," said the old lady soothingly.

"I say it did," replied the other. "There was no thought about it. I had just—What's the matter?"

His wife made no reply. She was watching the mysterious movements of a man outside, who, peering in an undecided fashion at the house, appeared to be trying to make up his mind to enter. In mental connection with the two hundred pounds, she noticed that the stranger was well dressed and wore a silk hat of glossy newness. Three times he paused at the gate, and then walked on again. The fourth time he stood with his hand upon it, and then with sudden resolution flung it open and walked up the path. Mrs. White at the same moment placed her hands behind her, and hurriedly unfastening the strings of her apron, put that useful article of apparel beneath the cushion of her chair.

She brought the stranger, who seemed ill at ease, into the room. He gazed furtively at Mrs. White, and listened in a preoccupied fashion as the old lady apologized for the appearance of the room, and her husband's coat, a garment which he usually reserved for the garden. She then waited patiently for him to broach[12] his business, but he was at first strangely silent.

"I—was asked to call," he said at last, and stooped and picked a piece of cotton from his trousers. "I came from Maw and Meggins."

The old lady started. "Is anything the matter?" she asked breathlessly. "Has anything happened to Herbert? What is it? What is it?"

Her husband interposed. "There, there, Mother," he said hastily. "Sit down and don't jump to conclusions. You've not brought bad news, I'm sure, sir," and he eyed the other wistfully.

"I'm sorry—" began the visitor.

"Is he hurt?" demanded the mother wildly.

The visitor bowed in assent. "Badly hurt," he said quietly, "but he is not in any pain."

"Oh, thank God!" said the old woman, clasping her hands. "Thank God for that! Thank—"

She broke off suddenly as the sinister meaning of the assurance dawned upon her and she saw the awful confirmation of her fears in the other's averted face. She caught her breath, and turning to her husband, laid her trembling old hand upon his. There was a long silence.

"He was caught in the machinery," said the visitor at length, in a low voice.

"Caught in the machinery," repeated Mr. White, in a dazed fashion, "yes."

He sat staring blankly out at the window, and taking his wife's hand between his own, pressed it as he had been wont to do in their old courting days nearly forty years before.

"He was the only one left to us," he said, turning gently to the visitor. "It is hard."

The other coughed, and, rising, walked slowly to the window. "The firm wished me to convey their sincere sympathy with you in your great loss," he said, without looking around. "I beg that you will understand I am only their servant and merely obeying orders."

There was no reply; the old woman's face was white, her eyes staring, and her breath inaudible; on the husband's face was a look such as his friend the sergeant might have carried into his first action.

"I was to say that Maw and Meggins disclaim all responsibility," continued the other.

---

12. To *broach* a subject is to mention it for the first time.

Vocabulary
sinister (sin′ is tər) *adj.* threatening or suggesting evil

178 UNIT 1

Teaching Options

Reading *Minilesson*

Identifying Cause-Effect Relationships
Explain that in a cause-and-effect relationship, something that makes something else happen is the cause, and the something that happens is the effect. Mr. and Mrs. White believe that wishing on the monkey's paw causes Herbert's death. In other words, the cause is wishing on the monkey's paw; the effect is Herbert's death.

Activity Have students identify the cause and the effect in each pair of sentences. (Hint: Try connecting the sentences with *because*.)

1. a. It rained all night. *(Cause)*
   b. The road flooded. *(Effect)*
2. a. Mr. White opened the door. *(Effect)*
   b. There was a knock on the door. *(Cause)*
3. a. Mrs. White chased Herbert around

the table. *(Effect)*
   b. Herbert teased his mother. *(Cause)*
4. a. Mr. White felt the monkey's paw move. *(Cause)*
   b. Mr. White dropped the monkey's paw. *(Effect)* **L2**

Additional Resources
Reading Workbook, p. 19

"They admit no liability at all, but in consideration of your son's services they wish to present you with a certain sum as compensation."

Mr. White dropped his wife's hand, and rising to his feet, gazed with a look of horror at his visitor. His dry lips shaped the words, "How much?"

"Two hundred pounds," was the answer.

Unconscious of his wife's shriek, the old man smiled faintly, put out his hands like a sightless man, and dropped, a senseless heap, to the floor.

III

In the huge new cemetery, some two miles distant, the old people buried their dead, and came back to a house steeped in shadow and silence. It was all over so quickly that at first they could hardly realize it, and remained in a state of expectation as though of something else to happen— something else which was to lighten this load, too heavy for old hearts to bear.

But the days passed, and expectations gave place to resignation—the hopeless resignation of the old, sometimes miscalled apathy. Sometimes they hardly exchanged a word, for now they had nothing to talk about, and their days were long to weariness.

It was about a week after that the old man, waking suddenly in the night, stretched out his hand and found himself alone. The room was in darkness, and the sound of subdued weeping came from the window. He raised himself in bed and listened.

The Old Version, 1881. Thomas Hovenden. Oil on canvas, 24 x 19 in. Fine Arts Museums of San Francisco. Gift of Mr. and Mrs. John D. Rockefeller, 3rd. 1993.35.17.

Viewing the painting: At what point in the story might Mr. and Mrs. White have resembled the couple in the painting? Explain.

"Come back," he said tenderly. "You will be cold."

"It is colder for my son," said the old woman, and wept afresh.

The sound of her sobs died away on his ears. The bed was warm, and his eyes heavy with sleep. He dozed fitfully, and then slept until a sudden wild cry from his wife awoke him with a start.

"The paw!" she cried wildly. "The monkey's paw!"

REAL-WORLD CONNECTION

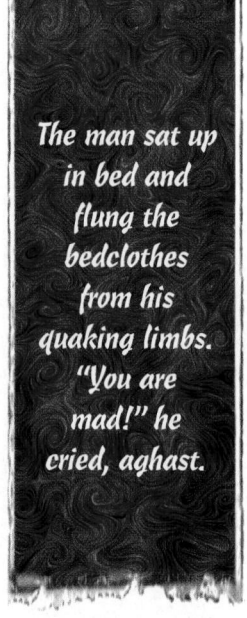

Active Reading

EVALUATE Ask students to explain why Mr. White calls his wife mad for wanting to wish Herbert alive again. *(They were warned to make only sensible wishes; that is not a sensible wish. Mr. White thinks immediately of how long Herbert has been dead and what he looked like after the accident. He can't believe his wife would wish to see their son like that.)*

Critical Thinking

INFERRING Why does Mr. White do as his wife demands? *(She is so insistent that he is pushed along against his will. He fears her because she seems possessed by her desperation and will not listen to reason.)*

The Monkey's Paw

He started up in alarm. "Where? Where is it? What's the matter?"

She came stumbling across the room toward him. "I want it," she said quietly. "You've not destroyed it?"

"It's in the parlor, on the bracket," he replied, marveling. "Why?"

She cried and laughed together, and bending over, kissed his cheek.

"I only just thought of it," she said hysterically. "Why didn't I think of it before? Why didn't *you* think of it?"

"Think of what?" he questioned.

"The other two wishes," she replied rapidly. "We've only had one."

"Was not that enough?" he demanded fiercely.

"No," she cried triumphantly; "we'll have one more. Go down and get it quickly, and wish our boy alive again."

The man sat up in bed and flung the bedclothes from his quaking limbs. "You are mad!" he cried, aghast.

"Get it," she panted; "get it quickly, and wish— Oh, my boy, my boy!"

Her husband struck a match and lit the candle. "Get back to bed," he said unsteadily. "You don't know what you are saying."

"We had the first wish granted," said the old woman feverishly; "why not the second?"

"A coincidence," stammered the old man.

"Go and get it and wish," cried his wife, quivering with excitement.

The old man turned and regarded her, and his voice shook. "He has been dead ten days, and besides he—I would not tell you else, but—I could only recognize him by his

> The man sat up in bed and flung the bedclothes from his quaking limbs. "You are mad!" he cried, aghast.

clothing. If he was too terrible for you to see then, how now?"

"Bring him back," cried the old woman, and dragged him toward the door. "Do you think I fear the child I have nursed?"

He went down in the darkness, and felt his way to the parlor, and then to the mantelpiece. The talisman was in its place, and a horrible fear that the unspoken wish might bring his mutilated son before him ere he could escape from the room seized upon him, and he caught his breath as he found that he had lost the direction of the door. His brow cold with sweat, he felt his way round the table, and groped along the wall until he found himself in the small passage with the unwholesome thing in his hand.

Even his wife's face seemed changed as he entered the room. It was white and expectant, and to his fears seemed to have an unnatural look upon it. He was afraid of her.

"*Wish!*" she cried, in a strong voice.

"It is foolish and wicked," he faltered.

"*Wish!*" repeated his wife.

He raised his hand. "I wish my son alive again."

The talisman fell to the floor, and he regarded it shudderingly. Then he sank trembling into a chair as the old woman, with burning eyes, walked to the window and raised the blind.

He sat until he was chilled with the cold, glancing occasionally at the figure of the old woman peering through the window. The candle end, which had burned below the rim of the china candlestick, was throwing pulsating shadows on the ceiling and walls, until, with a flicker larger than the rest, it expired. The old man, with an unspeakable sense of relief at the

Teaching Options

Grammar and Language *Minilesson*

Four Kinds of Sentences Remind students of the four kinds of sentences.
- A declarative sentence makes a statement and ends with a period.
- An imperative sentence commands or makes a request and ends with a period.
- An interrogative sentence asks a question and ends with a question mark.
- An exclamatory sentence expresses emotion and ends with an exclamation point.

Activity Have students copy each sentence, add the correct end mark, and write what kind of sentence it is.
1. You're a fool *(! exclamatory)*
2. Let me make the wish then *(. imperative)*
3. You can't do it *(! exclamatory)*
4. Why can't I *(? interrogative)*
5. I am that person *(. declarative)* **L1**

Additional Resources

Grammar and Language Transparency 15

Grammar and Language Workbook, Lesson 4.6

Grammar and Composition Handbook, p. 119

Writer's Choice, Lesson 13.6

failure of the talisman, crept back to his bed, and a minute or two afterward the old woman came silently and apathetically beside him.

Neither spoke, but both lay silently listening to the ticking of the clock. A stair creaked, and a squeaky mouse scurried noisily through the wall. The darkness was oppressive, and after lying for some time screwing up his courage, he took the box of matches, and striking one, went downstairs for a candle.

At the foot of the stairs the match went out, and he paused to strike another, and at the same moment a knock, so quiet and stealthy as to be scarcely audible, sounded on the front door.

The matches fell from his hand and spilled in the passage. He stood motionless, his breath suspended until the knock was repeated. Then he turned and fled swiftly back to his room, and closed the door behind him. A third knock sounded through the house.

"What's that?" cried the old woman, starting up.

"A rat," said the old man, in shaking tones—"a rat. It passed me on the stairs."

His wife sat up in bed listening. A loud knock resounded through the house.

"It's Herbert!" she screamed. "It's Herbert!"

She ran to the door, but her husband was before her, and catching her by the arm, held her tightly.

"What are you going to do?" he whispered hoarsely.

"It's my boy; it's Herbert!" she cried, struggling mechanically. "I forgot it was two miles away. What are you holding me for? Let's go. I must open the door."

"Don't let it in," cried the old man, trembling.

"You're afraid of your own son," she cried, struggling. "Let me go. I'm coming, Herbert; I'm coming."

There was another knock, and another. The old woman with a sudden wrench broke free and ran from the room. Her husband followed to the landing, and called after her appealingly as she hurried downstairs. He heard the chain rattle back and the bottom bolt drawn slowly and stiffly from the socket. Then the old woman's voice, strained and panting.

"The bolt," she cried loudly. "Come down. I can't reach it."

But her husband was on his hands and knees groping wildly on the floor in search of the paw. If he could only find it before the thing outside got in. A perfect fusillade[13] of knocks reverberated through the house, and he heard the scraping of a chair as his wife put it down in the passage against the door. He heard the creaking of the bolt as it came slowly back, and at the same moment he found the monkey's paw, and frantically breathed his third and last wish.

The knocking ceased suddenly, although the echoes of it were still in the house. He heard the chair drawn back and the door opened. A cold wind rushed up the staircase, and a long loud wail of disappointment and misery from his wife gave him courage to run down to her side, and then to the gate beyond. The street lamp flickering opposite shone on a quiet and deserted road.

---

13. A *fusillade* (fyū′ sə läd′) is the firing of many guns in rapid succession or anything that resembles such a sound, as the knocks do here.

Vocabulary

oppressive (ə pres′ iv) *adj.* hard to bear; distressing

Responding to
the Selection

Personal Response

Students who say they would have done the same thing as Mr. White may explain that because the wishes always come with a consequence, he was smart to wish the dead man away.

ANALYZING LITERATURE

1. The story begins at night. Inside the house is cozy; outside it is raining.
2. The paw has a spell on it. The Whites are curious but doubtful.
3. Morris throws it in the fire. Mr. White grabs it out of the fire.
4. White wishes for 200 pounds. He gets the money, but only because his son dies. His second wish is to bring his son back from the dead.
5. The Whites hear someone knocking on the door. The wife thinks it is Herbert and wants to let him in. The husband finds the paw and makes the last wish. The knocking stops.
6. The mood is mysterious and ominous, created by these details: cold, wet night; a house in an out-of-the-way place; a visitor tells of faraway places and strange events.
7. Morris thinks the paw is dangerous. At first, he doesn't even want to talk about it; then he turns pale and shakes when he does speak of it. Finally, he throws it into the fire.
8. He probably regrets it because he knows that it is inevitable they will use it and suffer.
9. He gets the money but loses something far more valuable, his son.
10. He believes that the rotting corpse of his son is outside the door. With his third wish he asks to send his son back to the grave.
11. His wish seemed sensible enough, but perhaps he should have stated it in more specific terms; for example, "I wish to receive 200 pounds without harm to my family, my property, or myself." Students' wishes may be more or less sensible than White's.
12. Since Mr. White has everything he wants, he should have resisted the temptation to wish for more.
13. Examples of foreshadowing: Morris says the paw has a spell on it; Morris presses White to throw the paw away; Herbert sees a vision in the fire and feels a shiver when he grasps the paw.
14. Students might describe a wish gone bad such as getting a date with the guy or girl of their dreams only to find out he or she is a bore, earning lots of money only to find people con-

stantly asking for a loan, or getting a car only to have it break down or be too expensive to maintain.
15. Students may say that Mrs. White's behavior at the end of the story is unsettling because she seems insane with grief. She saw that with a wish comes sorrow and yet she wants to make another wish, regardless of the consequences, because she is so desperate to get her son back.

Responding to Literature

Personal Response

Consider Mr. White's actions at the end of the story. In his place, what would you have done? Give a reason for your answer.

——— ANALYZING LITERATURE ———

RECALL

1. At what time of day does the story begin? Compare the weather outside with the atmosphere inside the parlor.
2. What is special about the monkey's paw that Sergeant Major Morris shows to the Whites? How do the Whites react to it?
3. What does Morris do with the paw after telling about its background? What does Mr. White immediately do?
4. What is Mr. White's first wish? What happens after he makes it? What is his second wish?
5. Summarize what happens after Mr. White makes the second wish.

INTERPRET

6. What is the **mood** at the beginning of the story? What details help to create this mood?
7. How does Morris feel about the paw? How do you know?
8. Do you think Morris regrets showing the monkey's paw to the Whites? Why or why not?
9. A situation is said to be **ironic** when what happens is the opposite of what is expected. What is ironic about Mr. White's first wish?
10. Why doesn't Mr. White want his wife to open the door? What do you think Mr. White's third wish is?

EVALUATE AND CONNECT

11. Theme Connections   Do you think Mr. White's first wish was a sensible choice? Why or why not? Evaluate your wish list from the Focus Activity on page 172. Are your wishes sensible? Explain.
12. Before making his first wish, Mr. White says, "It seems to me I've got all I want." In your opinion, what point is the author making?
13. How does the author use **foreshadowing** to prepare the reader for the events to come (see page R5)? Give three examples.
14. Have you ever gotten something you wished for and then regretted that your wish was granted? Describe your experience.
15. In your opinion, what is the most unsettling aspect of this story? Explain your answer.

Suspense
Suspense is a feeling of uncertainty, a sense that something disastrous is about to happen. Authors can build suspense through the characters' actions and words. For example, an ominous feeling is created when Morris throws the monkey's paw on the fire and Mr. White snatches it up. Suspense builds when Morris tells Mr. White, "If you keep [the paw], don't blame me for what happens." A description of the setting also can create suspense.

1. Look for examples of how the author creates suspense by telling what characters do or say. Find two examples of each.
2. In your opinion, what is the most suspenseful moment in the story? Explain your choice.

● See **Literary Terms Handbook,** p. R13.

LITERARY ELEMENTS

1. Characters' actions: Morris throws the paw into the fire; Herbert feels a shiver. Characters' statements: Morris says, "If you keep it, don't blame me for what happens." Mr. White cries, "It moved."
2. Possible answer: when the knocking on the door grows louder.

Additional Resources

Literary Elements Transparency 15

LITERATURE AND WRITING

Writing About Literature

Analyze Literary Techniques   W. W. Jacobs was known for his ability to combine humor and a sense of adventure in his stories. Write a paragraph or two explaining how the author uses the elements of humor and adventure in "The Monkey's Paw." Describe how the use of these elements affects your appreciation and enjoyment of the story. Share and discuss your ideas in a small group.

Creative Writing

My Dear Friend   Have you ever heard this old saying? "Be careful what you wish for, because you just might get your wish." Imagine that you are Mrs. White. Write a letter to a close friend, explaining the sad truth of this saying.

EXTENDING YOUR RESPONSE

Literature Groups

Wasted Wishes?   Mrs. White convinces her husband to make a horrifying second wish, which Mr. White then cancels out with the third wish. Do you think the Whites wasted their last two wishes? Why or why not? Is there something they could have wished for that might have eased the pain of their great loss? Or do you think the monkey's paw is such an evil thing that nothing but sorrow can come from it? Debate these questions in your group, supporting your ideas with evidence from the story. Share your opinions with the class.

Learning for Life

Horror Reviews   Interview friends or family members about their favorite horror stories. Have them rate the "scariness level" of each story, using a rating scale you have created. For example: 1 = "Mildly scary—won't keep you up past your bedtime"; 5 = "Horrific—do not read at night or on a camping trip." Then make a pamphlet that includes the story titles, their ratings, and a brief review of each story. (Remember: Don't spoil the stories by giving away their endings!) Share the pamphlet with your classmates and then ask your school librarian to add it to the library's pamphlet file.

Performing

Drama   "The Monkey's Paw" is often performed as a one-act play. If possible, obtain a script of the play version of this story or write a script of your own based on the text. Perform the play for other students, faculty, and family members.

Reading Further

If you would like to read other stories by William Wymark Jacobs, you might check out these books:

Short Story Collections: *Many Cargoes, The Skipper's Wooing, Sea Urchins,* and *Snug Harbour* contain stories about sailing and life at sea.

   You also might enjoy reading stories by other suspense authors, such as Edgar Allan Poe and Nathaniel Hawthorne.

 Save your work for your portfolio.

Skill Minilessons

GRAMMAR AND LANGUAGE
Punctuating Dialogue

Students' dialogues should
- follow the rules for punctuating dialogue given in the text.
- include tag lines.

READING AND THINKING
Chronological Order

I. A rainy night at Laburnum Villa
 1. Mr. White loses at chess.
 2. Sergeant Major Morris comes to the house.
 3. Morris tells the story of the monkey's paw.
 4. Morris throws the paw in the fire, but White insists on keeping it.
 5. White wishes for 200 pounds, at Herbert's urging.

II. The next day
 1. Herbert leaves for work in the morning, joking about the wish.
 2. A man comes to the house with bad news: Herbert was killed at work.
 3. The man gives Mr. White 200 pounds compensation.

III. One night, ten days after Herbert's accident
 1. Mrs. White, overcome with grief, insists that her husband use the monkey's paw to wish Herbert back to life.
 2. Reluctantly, Mr. White makes the wish.
 3. Someone begins knocking on the door.
 4. Mrs. White races to open the door but can't reach the bolt.
 5. Mr. White, terrified about what he might have called from the grave, makes a third wish.

VOCABULARY
Unlocking Meaning

1. believable
2. belief
3. statement of beliefs
4. disbelieving
5. unbelievable

Skill Minilessons

GRAMMAR AND LANGUAGE • Punctuating Dialogue

Read this dialogue between two characters from "The Monkey's Paw." Notice that the actual words spoken by the characters are enclosed in quotation marks and that the appropriate commas and end marks appear *inside* the closing quotation mark.

> "I'd like to go to India myself," said the old man, "just to look round a bit, you know."
>
> "Better where you are," said the sergeant major.
>
> Did you notice that the tag lines, which identify the speakers, are set off by a comma or commas? Also, when a sentence within a quotation is interrupted by a tag line,

the second part of the quoted sentence does not begin with a capital letter. When you write dialogue, remember to begin a new paragraph and use a new set of quotation marks each time the speaker changes.

PRACTICE Write a dialogue between Mr. White and Sergeant Major Morris in which the two men discuss Mr. White's three wishes. Be sure to punctuate your dialogue correctly.

● For more about punctuating dialogue, see **Language Handbook**, p. R48.

READING AND THINKING • Chronological Order

"The Monkey's Paw," like most short stories, is told in chronological, or actual time, order. The story is divided into three numbered parts, each of which corresponds to the two nights and one day on which the major events of the story take place.

● For more about related comprehension skills, see **Reading Handbook**, pp. R78–R107.

PRACTICE Copy the three headings listed below. Under each heading, list in chronological order the major events that occur in that part of "The Monkey's Paw."

 I. A rainy night at Laburnum Villa
 II. The next day
 III. One night, ten days after Herbert's accident

VOCABULARY • Unlocking Meaning

When you learn a new word, your vocabulary rarely increases by only that one word. Many words share roots with other words. For example, knowing *credulity* gives you a good shot at understanding *incredulity, credible, incredulous, credibility, credence,* and *credo,* all of which have to do with beliefs or believability. The context in which each word appears will help you narrow down its possible meaning. (This isn't a foolproof system. If you put down a credenza, you're lowering a piece of furniture, not insulting a belief.)

PRACTICE Briefly state what you'd guess is the meaning of each underlined word.

1. Her calm and thoroughness made her a credible witness.
2. I wouldn't give too much credence to gossip if I were you.
3. All members of the group stood to recite its credo.
4. When I announced I'd received straight A's, Dad gave me an incredulous look.
5. The man's story was so bizarre that I found it incredible.

Additional Resources

📒 ***Grammar and Composition Handbook,*** Lesson 11.9

📒 ***Grammar and Language Workbook,*** p. 271

📓 ***Writer's Choice,*** Lesson 21.9

📁 ***Vocabulary Practice,*** p. 14

📁 ***Reading Workbook,*** p. 19

✔ ASSESSMENT OPTIONS

📂 ***Quick Checks,*** p. 15

📂 ***Selection and Theme Assessment,*** pp. 29–30

📂 ***Performance Assessment,*** p. 15

💾 ***Testmaker***

Writing Skills

Creating Emphasis

To write persuasively, you must **emphasize**, or draw attention to, your most important ideas. Read the letter to the editor below to see how one writer makes a strong point about the factory mentioned in "The Monkey's Paw." Notice how the writer uses repetition and asks questions to create emphasis.

> Dear Editor,
> In your article about the work-related accident of a Maw and Meggins employee, the firm was applauded for offering money to the victim's family.
>
> I am writing to say that Maw and Meggins should not be applauded for its actions in this matter. Instead, the firm should be forced to take responsibility for what went wrong with its machinery. Factories must be held accountable for the condition of their equipment. Factories must be held accountable for the safety of their workers. How else can job-related accidents be prevented? Money can not replace someone's life.

The writer draws attention to the issue of responsibility by repeating the phrase *Factories must be held accountable* in two sentences. By asking the question *How else can job-related accidents be prevented?* the writer involves the reader in the argument by requiring an answer.

You might also try some of these other strategies for creating emphasis:

- Use short, simple, direct sentences.
- Use alliteration—that is, draw attention to important ideas by using words that begin with the same consonant sound.
- Use parallel construction, so that phrases or sentences with similar functions also have similar construction.
- Use inverted sentence order, placing the verb before the subject.

You don't need to use all of these strategies in one piece of writing. Choose the strategies that work best for your particular purpose and audience.

EXERCISES

1. Identify an issue that you believe in strongly. Then write an introductory paragraph for a letter to the editor about this topic. Ask a partner to read your paragraph and tell you which of your ideas come across most strongly. If these ideas aren't the ones that are most important to you, rewrite the paragraph.

2. Look through the letters to the editor sections of newspapers and magazines and notice when your attention is drawn to certain ideas. Make a list of at least four ways the letter writers have created emphasis. In your list, include examples from the letters.

Writing Skills

Objective

- To recognize how to create emphasis in persuasive writing

Teaching Strategies

Share these additional strategies for creating emphasis:
- Include a testimonial: a quotation from a real person.
- Use emotional language to reach people, but don't overdo it.

Exercises

1. *One acceptable solution:*
   Dear Editor:
   Your article about the mayor's reluctance to create bike paths overlooked a few key points. When people ride bicycles instead of drive cars, our society and our planet benefit in many ways.
2. Students should refer to the techniques listed on this page.

Additional Resources

- *Writing and Proofreading Practice,* pp. 9–10
- *Writing and Proofreading Transparencies 27–28*
- *Writer's Choice,* Lessons 6.1–6.3

Teaching Options

Grammar and Language *Minilesson*

Subordinate Clauses A subordinate clause has a subject and a predicate but cannot stand alone as a sentence.

Activity Ask volunteers to underline the subordinate clause in each sentence.
1. Unless certain animals are protected from hunters, they will become extinct.
2. Taxes can be lowered when government spends less. **L1**

Additional Resources

- *Grammar and Language Transparency 16*
- *Grammar and Language Workbook,* p. 101
- *Grammar and Composition Handbook,* Lesson 4.2
- *Writer's Choice,* Lesson 13.2

Technology Skills

Objectives

- To use a computer and hypertext software to create a hyperfiction story
- To explore the changes in traditional fiction structure allowed by hypertext
- To learn techniques for including other media in hypertext

Teaching Strategies

Assess students' familiarity with manipulating hypertext online. If possible, have student volunteers demonstrate working through a series of linked files, explaining how such links are shown onscreen.

TechnoTalk

Hypertext The *OED Additions Series* defines *hypertext* as "text which does not form a single sequence and which may be read in various orders; . . . interconnected in such a way that a reader . . . can discontinue reading one document at certain points in order to consult other related matter."

Hypertext and the Elements of a Short Story

Have students respond to the diagram. Review plot structure if necessary. Then discuss reasons hypertext is well-suited to the presentation of multiple plot lines and resolutions.

Teaching Options

Technology Skills

Multimedia: Creating Hyperfiction

Hyperfiction is a fairly new kind of fiction made possible by the computer and hypertext software. Hyperfiction makes use of **hypertext** links—words, phrases, or buttons a reader can click on to display other documents. In hyperfiction, these hyperlinks lead to other parts of a story.

Hypertext and the Elements of a Short Story

Most short stories follow a pattern that can be diagrammed something like this:

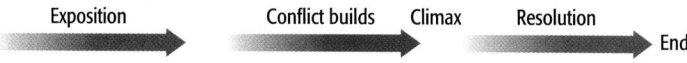

Hypertext allows you to write a story that looks more like this:

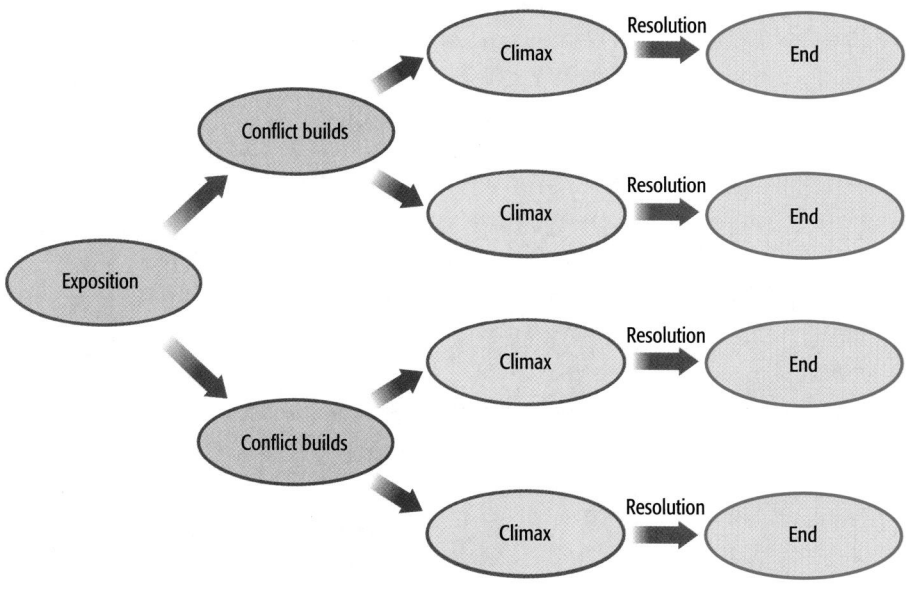

In the hypertext example above, the plot soon splits into two possible paths. As the conflict builds, each plot line splits again, leading to four different plot lines. The reader can follow any path he or she chooses to read one of four possible versions of the story.

MEETING INDIVIDUAL NEEDS — INCLUSION STRATEGIES

Special Needs Creating different scenarios for the same characters and setting is a task that offers high-interest variety. A plan for the hyperfiction can also be made visual through a diagram like the one on page 186.

Activity Have small groups of students create different fictional scenarios for the same character and setting based on students' ideas about how alternate decisions change the course of the day. As each group explains/acts out its scenario, add it to a diagram on the board. Have each group add its conflict and resolution to the hypertext story. **L1** **COLLAB. LEARN.**

Additional Resources
📂 *Inclusion Strategies*

This diagram is an extremely simple example of hyperfiction. There can be many more alternate paths, and paths can even lead back into one another. In addition, authors can include hyperlinks to flashbacks of earlier events, further descriptions of characters or scenes, changes in point of view, or any other variations. In really complex hyperfiction, it's possible that no two readers will ever read the exact same story.

Before You Get Started . . .

Think about what you did to get ready for school this morning. For each action, consider what you might have done differently and what effect each change could have had on your day. For instance, what if you hadn't eaten breakfast? Would you have stopped at a snack machine? If you had done so, might you have met someone there? How might that meeting have affected what you did next? Would that meeting have happened if you had eaten breakfast?

In your journal, write down possible scenarios for your day, including the results for all the alternate decisions that might have changed the course of your day. With a partner, share the scenarios you explored in your journals. Discuss how each decision might have led to a different unfolding of events.

ACTIVITIES

1. Work with a partner to create your own hyperfiction story.

   a. Together, decide on a title for an original short story.

   b. Create a plot line leading to four different conflicts, each one involving a personal decision. You may find it helpful to sketch out a diagram similar to the hypertext diagram on page 186 to show how the parts of your story will fit together.

   c. Using HyperCard, HyperStudio, or another hypertext program, create a card stack that takes readers on an interactive journey through your short story. Start with a title card and one or more cards that set the scene for the story. At the conclusion of your scene setting, include four buttons, each one leading the reader to a different conflict. Each conflict should lead to a climax, and so on.

   d. When you finish, ask another pair of students to read through your story and suggest ways the cards may be improved. Make changes as appropriate.

2. To further develop your hypertext skills, do one or more of the following:

   a. Write your own hypertext short story for inclusion in your electronic portfolio.

   b. Ask your teacher if you can complete your next creative assignment using a hypertext program.

   c. If you are comfortable with your hypertext program, explore other objects you can include in your card stack, such as movie clips, sound clips, pop-up objects, or animation.

> **TECHNOLOGY TIP**
> When you've completed your short-story project, save it on a disk or on the shared drive of your local area network. (Ask your lab instructor for directions on saving your work.)

After students read pages 186–187, discuss the hypertext software they will use to create their stories. HyperCard is an Apple product; America On Line has information and an introduction to this program on its Webopaedia. HyperStudio works for either Mac or IBM platforms and is available through its home page on the Web.

TechnoTalk

Terms to Know A *card stack* in HyperCard and HyperStudio is a collection of cards, or documents, capable of doing many things. A *card* is the rectangular area containing buttons, text, fields, and sometimes graphics. A *field* is a specialized container for text. A *button* is the mouse-activated shape that is used to initiate an action.

Activities

1. *Students' stories should*
   - develop at least four separate plot lines with distinct conflicts.
   - lead readers via links through each plot.
   - demonstrate appropriate control of story structure and English conventions.
2. *Students' other uses of hypertext to create genre pieces should*
   - use a hypertext software program successfully to organize the piece.
   - include multimedia elements such as sound or animation in addition to text.
   - demonstrate understanding of the genre and its structure.

LIFE SKILLS CONNECTION

Data Gathering Suggest that students use formal data-gathering tools to help test thier hypertext project and to analyze the response to the finished product. For example, they may use group discussions to collect peer suggestions for revision and questionnaires or feedback forms to gather data about audience response to their finished product. L2

 inter NET CONNECTION

Hyperfiction After students write their stories, or as an alternative assignment, have students find and read hyperfiction stories and novels online. Several students may want to give "book reports" about their reading. Encourage them to describe differences between hyperfiction and fiction.

Objectives

- To read and analyze a short story about a journey to a small town on a hot afternoon
- To identify tone in a short story
- To write a character sketch

Skills

Reading/Thinking: Predicting; Verifying Predictions; Inferring
Writing: Letter
Vocabulary: The Suffix *-ity*
Grammar/Language: Quotation Marks
Listening/Speaking: Proverbs
Collaboration: Literature Groups

Motivating
→OPTIONS

Literature Launchers:
"Gabriel García Márquez and Magical Realism"

Videodisc
Side A, Segment 4

Also available in VHS.

Selection Focus Transparency 16: Invite students to list appropriate activities for the hottest time of the day.

Focus Activity: Have pairs of students share their maps and compare the words and phrases they chose.

Before You Read

Tuesday Siesta

——— FOCUS ACTIVITY ———

Have you ever experienced oppressively hot weather or become overheated while exercising or spending time in a hot, stuffy room?

MAP IT! Create a spider map to explore how oppressive heat made you feel. Surround the word HEAT with words and phrases that express your feelings. Continue branching out with additional details.

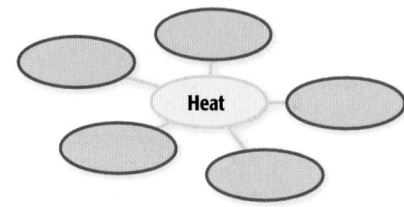

Heat

SETTING A PURPOSE Read to learn the importance of time of day to the action in this story.

——— BACKGROUND ———

The Time and Place
"Tuesday Siesta" takes place in a Latin American country, probably in the 1930s or 1940s.

Did You Know?
During the hottest part of the day in tropical or Mediterranean climates, people avoid heatstroke and sunstroke by taking a siesta. Siesta time usually begins around noon. Schools and shops close, and people enjoy a meal followed by several hours of resting. Later in the day, when the sun is not so hot, activities resume.

——— VOCABULARY PREVIEW ———

interminable (in tur′ mi nə bəl) *adj.* lasting, or seeming to last, forever; endless; p. 189
stifling (stī′ fling) *adj.* smothering; suffocating; p. 189
serenity (sə ren′ ə tē) *n.* calmness; peacefulness; p. 190
permeated (pur′ mē ā′ təd) *adj.* filled with; p. 191
scrutinize (skrōōt′ ən īz) *v.* to look at closely; inspect carefully; p. 192
inscrutable (in skrōō′ tə bəl) *adj.* mysterious; p. 193
skeptical (skep′ ti kəl) *adj.* having or showing doubt or suspicion; questioning; disbelieving; p. 193

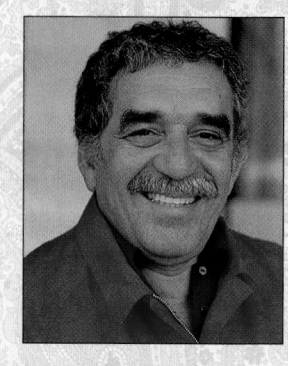

Meet Gabriel García Márquez

"I had a fabulous childhood," García Márquez has said of his youth. He was raised by his grandparents, who "had an enormous house, full of ghosts. They were very superstitious. . . . It was a world of fantastic terrors." For García Márquez, the process of writing involves recovering experiences that are buried and then re-creating them in realistic and magical detail. He won the Nobel Prize for literature in 1982.

Gabriel García Márquez was born in Aracata, Colombia, in 1928 and has lived most of his life in Mexico City. This story was written in 1948.

RESOURCE MANAGER

Lesson Planning Resource
The *Unit One Planning Guide* (pp. 132–139) provides additional lesson notes and reduced versions of all print resources.

📁 **Other Print Resources**
- Active Reading Guide, p. 16
- Vocabulary Practice, p. 15
- Reading Workbook, p. 20
- Grammar and Language Workbook, p. 271
- Grammar and Composition Handbook, Lesson 11.9

- Quick Checks, p. 16
- Selection and Theme Assessment, pp. 31–32
- Performance Assessment, p. 16
- Spanish Summaries, p. 16
- Spanish Translations
- Inclusion Strategies
- English Language Learners Sourcebook

Transparencies
- Selection Focus 16
- Fine Art 12

- Literary Elements 16
- Grammar and Language 17

Technology
 Literature Launchers
 Audio Library
 Spanish Audio Library
 Glencoe Literature Web Site
 Testmaker

Tuesday Siesta

Gabriel García Márquez
Translated by J. S. Bernstein

THE TRAIN EMERGED FROM THE QUIVERING tunnel of sandy rocks, began to cross the symmetrical, <u>interminable</u> banana plantations, and the air became humid and they couldn't feel the sea breeze any more.

A <u>stifling</u> blast of smoke came in the car window. On the narrow road parallel to the railway there were oxcarts loaded with green bunches of bananas. Beyond the road, in uncultivated spaces set at odd intervals there were offices with electric fans, red-brick buildings, and residences with chairs and little white tables on the terraces among dusty palm trees and rosebushes. It was eleven in the morning, and the heat had not yet begun.

"You'd better close the window," the woman said. "Your hair will get full of soot."

The girl tried to, but the shade wouldn't move because of the rust.

They were the only passengers in the lone third-class car. Since the smoke of the locomotive kept coming through the window, the girl left her seat and put down the only things they had with them: a plastic sack with some things to eat and a bouquet of flowers wrapped in newspaper. She sat on the opposite seat, away from the window, facing her mother. They were both in severe and poor mourning clothes.

The girl was twelve years old, and it was the first time she'd ever been on a train. The woman seemed too old to be her mother, because of the blue veins on her eyelids and

A

B

Vocabulary

interminable (in tur′ mi nə bəl) *adj.* lasting, or seeming to last, forever; endless
stifling (stī′ fling) *adj.* smothering; suffocating

SUMMARY

A girl and her mother ride a train through choking heat to a distant village, arriving at siesta time. The mother leads her daughter to the parish house and insists on seeing the priest. She needs the keys to the cemetery. When the priest discovers why she wants to visit the cemetery, he is shocked, but the woman maintains her dignity. When she returns to the street a curious crowd has gathered to see her.

📁 *Spanish Summaries,* p. 16

A **Active Reading**

PREDICT Ask students to read the title and the first page. Have them make predictions about what they think will happen in the story. Remind them to revise their predictions as they read on.

Additional Resources
📁 *Active Reading Guide,* p. 16
🎧 *Audio Library*
🎧 *Spanish Audio Library*

Teaching Options

CONNECTING TO OTHER SELECTIONS

The chart at the right shows three ways to connect "Tuesday Siesta" to selections in this book.

For specific teaching strategies, see the *Unit One Planning Guide,* pp. 135–136.

Connection	Title
Life Skills: Planning and Designing	→ "Through the Tunnel," p. 76
Thematic: Dignity	→ "Lullaby," p. 330
Literary: Setting	→ "The Masque of the Red Death," p. 389

B Literary Elements

CHARACTER Ask students how the details in this paragraph help them visualize the two characters. What else does the paragraph tell them about the characters? *(that they are used to being poor and it hasn't defeated them yet)*

C Author's Craft

IMAGERY Discuss how the phrase "the shadows seemed clean" stands in stark contrast to the sweaty, filthy interior of the train.

D Literary Elements

TONE What details create a mournful, weary tone as the train enters the town? *(drying the sweat, wiping the oil, "sadder than the earlier ones")*

E Author's Craft

FIGURATIVE LANGUAGE What does the author mean when he says, "The town was floating in the heat"? *(Waves of heat shimmering above the ground can create mirages. In the extreme heat, the town looks like a mirage. It shimmers or appears to float above the ground.)*

Teaching Options

B

Did You Know?
A *cassock* is the black, ankle-length garment traditionally worn by a Roman Catholic priest.

her small, soft, and shapeless body, in a dress cut like a cassock. She was riding with her spinal column braced firmly against the back of the seat, and held a peeling patent-leather handbag in her lap with both hands. She bore the conscientious <u>serenity</u> of someone accustomed to poverty.

By twelve the heat had begun. The train stopped for ten minutes to take on water at a station where there was no town. Outside, in the mysterious silence of the plantations, the shadows seemed clean. But the still air inside the car smelled like untanned leather. The train did not pick up speed. It stopped at two identical towns with wooden houses painted bright colors. The woman's head nodded and she sank into sleep. The girl took off her shoes. Then she went to the washroom to put the bouquet of flowers in some water.

When she came back to her seat, her mother was waiting to eat. She gave her a piece of cheese, half a corn-meal pancake, and a cookie, and took an equal portion out of the plastic sack for herself. While they ate, the train crossed an iron bridge very slowly and passed a town just like the ones before, except that in this one there was a crowd in the plaza. A band was playing a lively tune under the oppressive sun. At the other side of town the plantations ended in a plain which was cracked from the drought.

The woman stopped eating.

"Put on your shoes," she said.

The girl looked outside. She saw nothing but the deserted plain, where the train began

to pick up speed again, but she put the last piece of cookie into the sack and quickly put on her shoes. The woman gave her a comb.

"Comb your hair," she said.

The train whistle began to blow while the girl was combing her hair. The woman dried the sweat from her neck and wiped the oil from her face with her fingers. When the girl stopped combing, the train was passing the outlying houses of a town larger but sadder than the earlier ones.

"If you feel like doing anything, do it now," said the woman. "Later, don't take a drink anywhere even if you're dying of thirst. Above all, no crying."

The girl nodded her head. A dry, burning wind came in the window, together with the locomotive's whistle and the clatter of the old cars. The woman folded the plastic bag with the rest of the food and put it in the handbag. For a moment a complete picture of the town, on that bright August Tuesday, shone in the window. The girl wrapped the flowers in the soaking-wet newspapers, moved a little farther away from the window, and stared at her mother. She received a pleasant expression in return. The train began to whistle and slowed down. A moment later it stopped.

There was no one at the station. On the other side of the street, on the sidewalk shaded by the almond trees, only the pool hall was open. The town was floating in the heat. The woman and the girl got off the train and crossed the abandoned station—the tiles split apart by the grass growing up between—and over to the shady side of the street.

It was almost two. At that hour, weighted down by drowsiness, the town was taking a siesta. The stores, the town offices, the public school were closed at eleven, and didn't reopen until a little before four, when the train went

D

E

Vocabulary
serenity (sə ren′ ə tē) *n.* calmness; peacefulness

MEETING INDIVIDUAL NEEDS — ENGLISH LANGUAGE LEARNERS

Oral Storytelling English language learners may not be able to fully appreciate the tone of a story. When they listen to a story told aloud, however, they can easily recognize its tone.

Activity First, play the recording of the selection from the *Audio Library* as student pairs read along in their books. Then form small groups made up of

both English language learners and more proficient English speakers. Starting from the beginning of the story, students should take turns reading a few paragraphs aloud, doing their best to convey the author's tone.

Additional Resources
📁 *English Language Learners Sourcebook*

back. Only the hotel across from the station, with its bar and pool hall, and the telegraph office at one side of the plaza stayed open. The houses, most of them built on the banana company's model, had their doors locked from inside and their blinds drawn. In some of them it was so hot that the residents ate lunch in the patio. Others leaned a chair against the wall, in the shade of the almond trees, and took their siesta right out in the street.

Keeping to the protective shade of the almond trees, the woman and the girl entered the town without disturbing the siesta. They went directly to the parish house.[1] The woman scratched the metal grating on the door with her fingernail, waited a moment,

───────────────

1. A *parish house* is the home of the priest of a local church district.

Vocabulary
permeated (pur′ mē ā′ təd) *adj.* filled with

and scratched again. An electric fan was humming inside. They did not hear the steps. They hardly heard the slight creaking of a door, and immediately a cautious voice, right next to the metal grating: "Who is it?" The woman tried to see through the grating.

"I need the priest," she said.

"He's sleeping now."

"It's an emergency," the woman insisted. Her voice showed a calm determination.

The door was opened a little way, noiselessly, and a plump, older woman appeared, with very pale skin and hair the color of iron. Her eyes seemed too small behind her thick eyeglasses.

"Come in," she said, and opened the door all the way.

They entered a room permeated with an old smell of flowers. The woman of the

Campanario, c. 1947.
Joaquin Torres-Garcia.
Oil on board laid down
on panel, 13¼ x 16½ in.
Private collection.

Viewing the painting:
How does this scene help
you envision the town
during siesta?

F Active Reading

QUESTION Some students may notice something secretive about the woman and the girl's behavior. Could there be a reason for their quiet arrival? Might they have planned to arrive at siesta time?

G Literary Elements

TONE Discuss how the tone here becomes mysterious and suspenseful. Details that create the tone include the humming fan and the creaking door. Ask a student to point out additional details. *(the cautious voice behind the metal grating, the fact that the woman can't see the person behind the door)*

VIEWING THE PAINTING

Joaquin Torres-García's ambitious work was shown widely in the United States during the 1930s, 40s, and 50s. He strove to temper instinct with reason, creating an intellectual framework for his art. Reason and symbols form the basis of his expression.

Viewing Response *The scene depicts the silence and emptiness of the town during siesta.*

Reading *Minilesson*

Predicting Now is a good time to make predictions in this story. Readers know that the woman and the girl have a purpose for coming to this town at this time, but they do not yet know what that purpose is.

Activity Ask students to predict what they think will happen in the story. Suggest that they look for hints that the

author has given them *(mourning clothes, flowers, no drinking, no crying, going to the priest)*. Then encourage them to write their predictions. Have them check their predictions after they finish reading the story.
L2

Additional Resources
📁 *Reading Workbook,* p. 20

Active Reading

QUESTION Ask students to consider why the parish woman now smiles. *(Something in the mourning woman's undertones conveyed a message that the parish woman understood. Now she warms to the woman and shows her some kindness.)*

Literary Elements

CHARACTER Note that the woman's statement is brief and to the point. Here she does not even use a complete sentence to make a request of the priest. Why does she speak that way? *(She is determined, self-assured, and quite dedicated to her project. She does not have time to waste on unnecessary words. Also, she has no intention of being overly friendly to anyone in this town.)*

Critical Thinking

VERIFYING PREDICTIONS Now that the woman has revealed the reason for their visit, were students surprised to discover this information or had they expected it? Have them check their lists of predictions.

---

house led them to a wooden bench and signaled them to sit down. The girl did so, but her mother remained standing, absent-mindedly, with both hands clutching the handbag. No noise could be heard above the electric fan.

The woman of the house reappeared at the door at the far end of the room. "He says you should come back after three," she said in a very low voice. "He just lay down five minutes ago."

"The train leaves at three-thirty," said the woman.

It was a brief and self-assured reply, but her voice remained pleasant, full of undertones.[2] The woman of the house smiled for the first time.

"All right," she said.

When the far door closed again, the woman sat down next to her daughter. The narrow waiting room was poor, neat, and clean. On the other side of the wooden railing which divided the room, there was a worktable, a plain one with an oilcloth cover, and on top of the table a primitive typewriter next to a vase of flowers. The parish records were beyond. You could see that it was an office kept in order by a spinster.[3]

The far door opened and this time the priest appeared, cleaning his glasses with a handkerchief. Only when he put them on was it evident that he was the brother of the woman who had opened the door.

"How can I help you?" he asked.

"The keys to the cemetery," said the woman.

The girl was seated with the flowers in her lap and her feet crossed under the bench. The

priest looked at her, then looked at the woman, and then through the wire mesh of the window at the bright, cloudless sky.

"In this heat," he said. "You could have waited until the sun went down."

The woman moved her head silently. The priest crossed to the other side of the railing, took out of the cabinet a notebook covered in oilcloth, a wooden penholder, and an inkwell, and sat down at the table. There was more than enough hair on his hands to account for what was missing on his head.

"Which grave are you going to visit?" he asked.

"Carlos Centeno's," said the woman.

"Who?"

"Carlos Centeno," the woman repeated.

The priest still did not understand.

"He's the thief who was killed here last week," said the woman in the same tone of voice. "I am his mother."

The priest <u>scrutinized</u> her. She stared at him with quiet self-control, and the Father blushed. He lowered his head and began to write. As he filled the page, he asked the woman to identify herself, and she replied unhesitatingly, with precise details, as if she were reading them. The Father began to sweat. The girl unhooked the buckle of her left shoe, slipped her heel out of it, and rested it on the bench rail. She did the same with the right one.

It had all started the Monday of the previous week, at three in the morning, a few blocks from there. Rebecca, a lonely widow who lived in a house full of odds and ends, heard above the sound of the drizzling rain someone trying to force the front door from outside. She got up, rummaged around in her closet for an ancient revolver that no one had fired since the

---

2. *Undertones* are underlying or implied meanings.
3. *Spinster* usually refers to an older woman who has never been married.

Vocabulary
scrutinize (skrōōt′ ən īz) *v.* to look at closely; inspect carefully

192   UNIT 1

Teaching Options

LITERATURE & HUMANITIES

Display the painting *The Waiting* from *Art Talk*, page 308. Have students discuss what elements might make this an appropriate illustration for the story.

MEETING INDIVIDUAL NEEDS   **MULTIPLE LEARNING STYLES**

Logical-Mathematical Logical learners excel at exploring relationships. They may enjoy looking for examples of cause-and-effect relationships in the story and then sharing their findings with their classmates.

Activity Have small groups of students complete and compare diagrams like these. **L3** **COLLAB. LEARN.**

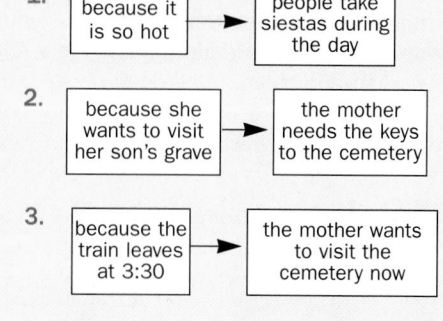

1. because it is so hot → people take siestas during the day
2. because she wants to visit her son's grave → the mother needs the keys to the cemetery
3. because the train leaves at 3:30 → the mother wants to visit the cemetery now

days of Colonel Aureliano Buendía,[4] and went into the living room without turning on the lights. Orienting herself not so much by the noise at the lock as by a terror developed in her by twenty-eight years of loneliness, she fixed in her imagination not only the spot where the door was but also the exact height of the lock. She clutched the weapon with both hands, closed her eyes, and squeezed the trigger. It was the first time in her life that she had fired a gun. Immediately after the explosion, she could hear nothing except the murmur of the drizzle on the galvanized roof. Then she heard a little metallic bump on the cement porch, and a very low voice, pleasant but terribly exhausted: "Ah, Mother." The man they found dead in front of the house in the morning, his nose blown to bits, wore a flannel shirt with colored stripes, everyday pants with a rope for a belt, and was barefoot. No one in town knew him.

"So his name was Carlos Centeno," murmured the Father when he finished writing.

"Centeno Ayala,"[5] said the woman. "He was my only boy."

The priest went back to the cabinet. Two big rusty keys hung on the inside of the door; the girl imagined, as her mother had when she was a girl and as the priest himself must have imagined at some time, that they were Saint Peter's keys.[6] He took them down, put them on the open notebook on the railing, and pointed with his forefinger to a place on the page he had just written, looking at the woman.

"Sign here."

The woman scribbled her name, holding the handbag under her arm. The girl picked up the flowers, came to the railing shuffling her feet, and watched her mother attentively.

The priest sighed.

"Didn't you ever try to get him on the right track?"

The woman answered when she finished signing.

"He was a very good man."

The priest looked first at the woman and then at the girl, and realized with a kind of pious[7] amazement that they were not about to cry. The woman continued in the same tone:

"I told him never to steal anything that anyone needed to eat, and he minded me. On the other hand, before, when he used to box, he used to spend three days in bed, exhausted from being punched."

"All his teeth had to be pulled out," interrupted the girl.

"That's right," the woman agreed. "Every mouthful I ate those days tasted of the beatings my son got on Saturday nights."

"God's will is inscrutable," said the Father.

But he said it without much conviction, partly because experience had made him a little skeptical and partly because of the heat. He suggested that they cover their heads to guard against sunstroke. Yawning, and now almost completely asleep, he gave them instructions about how to find Carlos Centeno's grave. When they came back, they didn't have to knock. They should put the key under the door; and in the same place, if they could, they should put an offering for the Church.

---

4. *Aureliano Buendía* (ou´ rā lyä´ nō   bwän dē´ ä)
5. *[Ayala]* The young man's full name was Carlos *Centeno Ayala* (sen tä´ nō   ä yä´ lä). In Spanish-speaking countries, one's first name and surname are, by custom, followed by the mother's maiden name.
6. *Saint Peter's keys* refers to the traditional belief of some Christians that Saint Peter is in charge of the keys to the gates of heaven.

7. The word *pious* (pī´ əs) may mean *either* having genuine reverence for God *or* having a false or hypocritical religious devotion.

Vocabulary
inscrutable (in skrōō´ tə bəl) *adj.* mysterious
skeptical (skep´ ti kəl) *adj.* having or showing doubt or suspicion; questioning; disbelieving

K Active Reading

CONNECT Point out the connection between the girl, the mother, and the priest. Share the following model to illustrate the thought processes involved in connecting.

Model: Circumstances may create divisions among people, but here the author points out something that bonds the characters—a shared childhood fantasy. No matter what we are as adults, childhood links us to other people. We all were children once, and then, as children, our differences were relatively few.

FINE ART
TRANSPARENCY 12

You may wish to use Fine Art Transparency 12 to compare and contrast with characters in the selection.

Listening and Speaking *Minilesson*

Proverbs Write this proverb on the board: "Never judge a person until you have walked a mile in his or her shoes." Discuss basic rules for effective group work: allow members to speak without interruption, stay on the subject, respond politely and constructively.

Activity Suggest that small groups discuss how the proverb applies to what they read in the story. Groups should choose a chairperson to keep the discussion focused, a recorder to write down all ideas and read ideas to be reviewed, and an observer to keep track of how well the group functions. After 15 minutes of discussion, students should evaluate their group interaction. **L2 COLLAB. LEARN.**

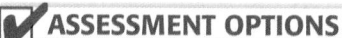

VIEWING THE PAINTING

Modern artists such as Vargas championed invention and innovation, using strong lines, shapes, colors, forms, and patterns in their work.

Viewing Response *The people in the painting seem to be mother and daughter. As in the story, they seem to be lonely figures of modest means.*

L **Critical Thinking**

INFERRING The interaction between the woman and the priest is cool. Discuss reasons that this unstated attitude, each toward the other, may exist. *(She is critical of his pious loftiness, and he has judged her unworthy of his time and a poor mother.)*

Thematic Focus

Making Choices Have students consider the woman's choice to walk past the people in the streets. What would they have done?

✓ ASSESSMENT OPTIONS

📁 *Quick Checks,* p. 16

Landscape with Figures (Paisaje con Figura). Arturo Gordon Vargas (1853–1933). Oil on canvas, 43 x 54 cm.

Viewing the painting: In your opinion, how are the characters in the painting similar to the woman and the girl in the story?

The woman listened to his directions with great attention, but thanked him without smiling.

The Father had noticed that there was someone looking inside, his nose pressed against the metal grating, even before he opened the door to the street. Outside was a group of children. When the door was opened wide, the children scattered. Ordinarily, at that hour there was no one in the street. Now there were not only children. There were groups of people under the almond trees. The Father scanned the street swimming in the heat and then he understood. Softly, he closed the door again.

"Wait a moment," he said without looking at the woman.

His sister appeared at the far door with a black jacket over her nightshirt and her hair down over her shoulders. She looked silently at the Father.

"What was it?" he asked.

"The people have noticed," murmured his sister.

"You'd better go out by the door to the patio," said the Father.

"It's the same there," said his sister. "Everybody is at the windows."

The woman seemed not to have understood until then. She tried to look into the street through the metal grating. Then she took the bouquet of flowers from the girl and began to move toward the door. The girl followed her.

"Wait until the sun goes down," said the Father.

"You'll melt," said his sister, motionless at the back of the room. "Wait and I'll lend you a parasol."

"Thank you," replied the woman. "We're all right this way."

She took the girl by the hand and went into the street.

Teaching Options

Grammar and Language *Minilesson*

Quotation Marks Explain that quotation marks are placed around the words a person speaks. Tag lines are separated from the quotation with a comma unless the quotation ends with a question mark or an exclamation point. In dialogue, a new paragraph and new quotation marks are used every time the speaker changes.

Activity Have students write these sen-tences, adding quotation marks and paragraphing.

Wait, Mama. Please! pleaded the girl. Come now. Hurry. Look at no one, said the woman. But, Mama, . . . said the girl.

("Wait, Mama. Please!" pleaded the girl as her mother moved away.

"Come now. Hurry. Look at no one," said the woman.

"But, Mama, . . ." said the girl. **L2**

Additional Resources

📖 ***Grammar and Language Transparency 17***

📕 ***Grammar and Language Workbook,*** p. 271

📕 ***Grammar and Composition Handbook,*** Lesson 11.9

📕 ***Writer's Choice,*** Lesson 21.9

Responding to Literature

Personal Response

Do you approve of the way the woman and the girl leave the parish house at the end of the story? Why or why not?

——— ANALYZING LITERATURE ———

RECALL

1. How do the woman and the girl act on the train?
2. Describe what the woman and the girl see as they walk from the train station to the parish house.
3. Why do the girl and the woman go to the parish house?
4. What happened to Carlos Centeno?
5. What happens outside the parish house while the woman is inside?

INTERPRET

6. From the way the woman and the girl act, what can you infer about their relationship and about their journey?
7. Why might the woman have decided to arrive in town during the afternoon siesta?
8. How would you characterize the way the woman behaves when telling the priest who she is and why she is there? Do you find anything unusual about her behavior in those circumstances? Explain.
9. Carlos's mother refers to him as a thief but also tells the priest: "He was a very good man." What do you think she means by this? What details from the story support your opinion?
10. In your opinion, why do the woman and the girl leave the parish house right away, rather than waiting until later? What might happen to them after they leave?

EVALUATE AND CONNECT

11. Think about your response to the Focus Activity on page 186. Why do you think the author might have chosen such an oppressively hot day for the **setting** of the story?
12. How would you describe the relationship between Carlos, his mother, and his sister?
13. Do you have more sympathy for Carlos or Rebecca? Why?
14. Describe the moral code that Carlos's mother has taught him. Do you think her attitude is common in society today? Explain.
15. In your opinion, why might people hide their true feelings? Do you think any of those reasons apply to the woman in this story? Explain.

Literary ELEMENTS

Tone

The **tone** of a story is the attitude the writer takes toward the story's subject. A writer selects language and details to create a desired tone. For example, a writer might describe a desert as "sunny, hot, filled with unexpected flowers," or as "scorching, arid, dangerous." In the first description, the tone is cheerful and appreciative; in the second, the tone is fearful.

1. Read the first four paragraphs that describe the initial setting of "Tuesday Siesta." Identify the tone and cite two or three phrases that seem to convey that tone.
2. List two phrases that introduce the woman and girl. Explain how these descriptions support or alter the tone of the story.
3. Examine the description on pages 192–193 of the night Carlos was killed. What details help convey the tone of this passage? Using specific details from the story, compare and contrast the tone of this passage with that of the rest of the story.

● See **Literary Terms Handbook,** p. R13.

Responding to the Selection

Personal Response

Students may say that they admire the woman's determination to visit her son's grave, even if it means having to walk past staring people on her way to the cemetery.

ANALYZING LITERATURE

1. They are quiet, purposeful, and self-contained. They sit in their seats, doze, eat, and look at the scenery.
2. They see a hot, empty town in which the offices, stores, and homes are all closed for the siesta. Only a few places are open.
3. They want to visit the cemetery.
4. He was shot dead while attempting to break into a house.
5. A crowd gathers.
6. The girl is used to obeying her mother. The mother is determined to make this trip.
7. Perhaps she wants to arrive at a time when few people would see her.
8. She shows no shame, which is surprising because her mission is difficult. Most people would find the situation awkward and embarrassing.
9. She thinks he was good because he risked his life to feed his poor family, because he committed crimes only out of necessity, and because he minded his mother.
10. If they wait, an even larger crowd might gather. The train they want to take home leaves at 3:30, so they do not have time to wait. They might be hounded by the people.
11. The oppressive heat increases the oppressive atmosphere of the story. People are more likely to behave uncharacteristically in such heat.
12. They seem to take care of one another and share everything.
13. Students may sympathize with the fear that led Rebecca to shoot at the intruder. Others may sympathize with Carlos and the poverty that led him to steal.
14. She taught that if you truly are in need, then it is okay to take things from others, but only take those things they do not need. Stealing in general is frowned upon in society today.

LITERARY ELEMENTS

1. The tone is oppressive and miserable: "interminable banana plantations," "stifling blast of smoke."
2. "Only passengers in the lone third-class car," "severe and poor mourning clothes"; add sadness and a sense of hopelessness.
3. The author mentions Rebecca's terror and loneliness. He creates an unsympathetic image of Carlos with his nose blown off.

Additional Resources

✍ *Literary Elements Transparency 16*

15. People may hide their feelings to save face or because they don't want to confront those feelings personally. The woman probably was trying to preserve her pride and rise above the ridicule and scorn she might receive because of her son's fate.

LITERATURE AND WRITING

Writing About Literature

Students' character sketches should
- note several traits that the mother exhibits.
- clearly explain how details from the story illustrate each trait.
- demonstrate an organizational strategy to ensure coherence.

Creative Writing

Students' letters should
- develop a tone that expresses the priest's reaction to the encounter.
- summarize the story events accurately.
- follow the tone and format of a friendly letter.

EXTENDING YOUR RESPONSE

Literature Groups Remind students that before they share their opinions they should be prepared to give evidence from the story to support those opinions. **COLLAB. LEARN.**

Interdisciplinary Activity
Students may refer to the story to refresh their mental pictures of the story and to find details to include in their sketches.

Internet Connection Have students work in pairs and set a time limit of 15 minutes per pair. Prevent inefficient, aimless net surfing by suggesting key words.

Skill Minilesson

VOCABULARY • The Suffix -ity

1. The acidity of the tomatoes added a sharp taste to the sauce.
2. With the antique came a certificate of authenticity.
3. I worry about the durability of those cheap shoes.
4. Funerals require expressions of proper solemnity.
5. The film's continuity was disrupted by unnecessary musical interludes.

Additional Resources
📁 *Vocabulary Practice,* p. 15

———— LITERATURE AND WRITING ————

Writing About Literature
Character Sketch Brainstorm a list of character traits that the mother in "Tuesday Siesta" exhibits. Next to each item, note a detail or incident from the story that illustrates this character trait. Use your notes to write a brief character sketch of the mother. Compare your sketch with those made by other students.

Creative Writing
Dear Father Imagine that you are the priest in this story. Write a letter to a fellow member of the clergy, describing the visit made by the mother and daughter. Be sure to describe not only what happened but also your reaction to the encounter.

———— EXTENDING YOUR RESPONSE ————

Literature Groups
Evaluating a Character's Actions In your opinion, was it more honorable for Carlos to try to support his family by boxing or by stealing? Let each member of your group give an opinion about this question, and feel free to challenge your fellow group members to support their opinions with evidence from the story. Finally, tally up the group's responses and share the results with the class.

Interdisciplinary Activity
Art: Making an Illustration Imagine that you are riding the same train as the mother and daughter in this story. Illustrate something that you see as you look out of the window, or sketch a character or scene aboard the train.

Internet Connection
Location, Location, Location
Use the Internet to find which countries might be settings for this story. Find locations in Central or South America that have hot, dry climates and that supported a flourishing banana industry in the first half of the 1900s. Use other clues from the story to help focus your search.

📖 **Save your work for your portfolio.**

Skill Minilesson

VOCABULARY • The Suffix -ity

Knowing how to use a single suffix can increase a person's vocabulary by a hundred words or so, all at once. For example, the suffix -ity means "state or condition." It turns adjectives into nouns.

The mother in "Tuesday Siesta" has *serenity*; therefore, she is *serene*. The weather is humid (an adjective); therefore, people feel the humidity (a noun). Just as with *-ing* endings, a final *e* drops off when *-ity* is added.

PRACTICE For each word shown below, write a sentence that uses the word correctly.

1. acidity
2. authenticity
3. durability
4. solemnity
5. continuity

● For more about adding suffixes, see **Language Handbook,** Spelling, p. R55.

✓ ASSESSMENT OPTIONS

📁 *Quick Checks,* p. 16
📁 *Selection and Theme Assessment,* pp. 31–32
📁 *Performance Assessment,* p. 16
💾 *Testmaker*

MEDIA Connection

News Article

For some drivers, crossing a long bridge can be terrifying. In Michigan, acrophobic drivers have a helping hand.

Holiday Traffic Brings Out Fear on Suspension Bridge

by Thomas Bevier—*Gannett News Service*, May 28, 1994

DETROIT—Even an Upper Peninsula engineering professor can't look down when he drives above northern Michigan's Straits of Mackinac on the world's largest suspension bridge.

"I dread it," said Edward Fisher of Michigan Technological University in Houghton. "My feet tingle just thinking about it."

Panic attacks on the five-mile Mackinac Bridge can bring the truly frightened to a halt. Many people with acrophobia—fear of heights—can't drive from one Michigan peninsula to the other.

That's when a professional bridge-crosser slips behind the wheel. The Mackinac Bridge Authority provides free escort drivers.

"For some people, it's terrifying," said Operations Manager William Frazier. "Some of them put their heads between their legs and cry all the way across. Some try to grab you."

The span's peak season started this weekend, and even Frazier will take his turn helping dizzy drivers who request the service five to ten time a day.

"They keep us busy," he said. "We put on extra help in the summer."

Anyone needing a designated driver can call the Bridge Authority at or before driving onto the approach ramps. Patrol cars are on standby for dispatch to Mackinaw City or St. Ignace on the northern side. An employee will drive timid travelers across the span, which has a roadway rising nearly 200 feet above water.

Occasionally, motorists freeze and stop on the bridge—waiting until an escort arrives.

There is no stereotypical acrophobia victim.

"We get young people and old people," Frazier said. "Motorcyclists need help and so do even a few over-the-road truck drivers."

Dr. James R. Creps, a psychiatrist at the anxiety disorder center at Henry Ford Medical Center in Detroit, said the bridge is the toughest test for skittish sightseers.

Those who point at passing freighters as they drive across can't understand why anyone sees the trip as an ordeal, Creps said. But he stressed that the panic is vivid and real.

"They are overcome with fear of suffocation and of dying. They have troubling breathing. Something as awesome as the Mackinac Bridge can be overwhelming," Creps said.

"They may even realize that their fear is unreasonable, but they still can't control it."

Respond

1. What do you think it might be like to work as an escort driver on the Mackinac Bridge?

2. When faced with fear, how do you deal with it?

Objective

- To read and understand a news article

Literature LINK

Contents of the Dead Man's Pocket The news article tells about people who are afraid to drive over the Mackinac Bridge. The narrator of "Contents of the Dead Man's Pocket" (pp. 199–211) finds out about acrophobia after he recklessly climbs out on an eleventh-story window ledge.

Respond

1. Students may say that it would be boring to make the same drive back and forth all the time, but that the behavior of the passengers might make the drive interesting.

2. Students may say that they confront their fears head on or deal with their fears a step at a time.

Additional Resources

📁 *Media Connections Activities,* p. 6

Teaching Options

interNET CONNECTION

Phobias Have students use a search engine to look for additional information on phobias. Suggest that they try entering keywords such as *phobias, phobic disorders, anxiety disorders,* or *psychopathology.* They might choose to focus on one of the following phobias: *acrophobia, agoraphobia, arachnophobia, claustrophobia, hydrophobia, hypnophobia, xenophobia, zoophobia.*

Objectives

- To read and analyze a short story about a man who, facing death, discovers what is most important in his life
- To explore what point of view contributes to a story
- To write an analysis of the setting

Skills

Reading/Thinking: Analyzing Arguments; Logical Reasoning; Inferring; Drawing Conclusions; Problem Solving
Writing: Creating Suspense with Chronological Order; New Ending
Vocabulary: Synonyms; Analogies
Grammar/Language: Compatibility of Tenses; Introductory Phrases
Listening/Speaking: Performing a Monologue
Life Skills: Setting Goals
Collaboration: Literature Groups

Motivating
→OPTIONS

Selection Focus Transparency 17: Ask students to think about a possession they treasure and discuss what they would do to protect or save that possession.

Focus Activity: Ask students if they think they are making the most of their time.

Before You Read

Contents of the Dead Man's Pocket

FOCUS ACTIVITY

What activity in your life gets your greatest effort, attention, and time? Is this activity also what matters most to you?

CHART IT! Estimate how you spend your time over the course of an average day. Chart the time you spend on each activity. Which activity takes up the most time? Is this activity of great value to you?

SETTING A PURPOSE Read to learn how the narrator discovers what is most important in his life.

BACKGROUND

The Time and Place
"Contents of the Dead Man's Pocket" takes place in New York City, probably sometime during the 1950s.

Did You Know?
At the time the story takes place, copies of documents typically were made by hand or with layers of carbon paper inserted between sheets of paper. Developments in copying and printing technology during the 1950s and 1960s led to photocopying as we now know it.

VOCABULARY PREVIEW

convoluted (kon′ və loo′ təd) *adj.* turned in or wound up upon itself; coiled; twisted; p. 201
improvised (im′ prə vīzd′) *adj.* invented, composed, or done without preparing beforehand; p. 201
taut (tôt) *adj.* tense; tight; p. 204
spasmodic (spaz mod′ ik) *adj.* sudden, violent, and temporary; p. 204
deftness (deft′ nəs) *n.* the quality of being skillful and nimble; p. 205
pent-up (pent′ up) *adj.* not expressed or released; held in; p. 206
reveling (rev′ əl ing) *adj.* taking great pleasure; p. 207
unimpeded (un′ im pē′ dəd) *adj.* not obstructed; unblocked; p. 211

Meet Jack Finney

Although several of Finney's works have been made into movies, Finney himself shunned the limelight. Born in Milwaukee, Wisconsin, Walter Braden (Jack) Finney grew up in the Midwest. He did not begin writing fiction until he was thirty-five.

Although one of his best-known works is *Invasion of the Body Snatchers*, Finney did not consider himself a science fiction writer but rather a writer of fantasy who was most interested in ordinary people's responses to extraordinary situations. He developed this interest in the story you are about to read.

Jack Finney was born in 1911 and died in 1995. This story, from a collection called The Third Level, *was published in 1957.*

RESOURCE MANAGER

Lesson Planning Resource
The *Unit One Planning Guide* (pp. 140–147) provides additional lesson notes and reduced versions of all print resources.

📁 **Other Print Resources**
- Active Reading Guide, p. 17
- Vocabulary Practice, p. 16
- Reading Workbook, p. 21
- Grammar and Language Workbook, p. 153
- Grammar and Composition Handbook, Lesson 5.6

- Quick Checks, p. 17
- Selection and Theme Assessment, pp. 33–34
- Performance Assessment, p. 17
- Spanish Summaries, p. 17
- Spanish Translations
- Inclusion Strategies
- English Language Learners Sourcebook

📇 **Transparencies**
- Selection Focus 17
- Fine Art 15

- Literary Elements 17
- Grammar and Language 18

Technology
 Audio Library
 Spanish Audio Library
💻 Glencoe Literature Web Site
💾 Testmaker

Room in New York, 1932. Edward Hopper. Oil on canvas, 29 x 36 in. Sheldon Memorial Art Gallery, University of Nebraska–Lincoln, F. M. Hall Collection. 1936.H-166.

Contents of the Dead Man's Pocket

Jack Finney ∾

A At the little living-room desk Tom Benecke rolled two sheets of flimsy and a heavier top sheet, carbon paper sandwiched between them, into his portable.[1] *Inter-office Memo,* the top sheet was headed, and he typed tomorrow's date just below this; then he glanced at a creased yellow sheet, covered **B** with his own handwriting, beside the typewriter. "Hot in here," he muttered to himself. Then, from the short hallway at his back, he heard the muffled clang of wire coat hangers in the bedroom closet, and at this reminder of what his wife was doing he thought: Hot, hell—guilty conscience.

He got up, shoving his hands into the back pockets of his gray wash slacks,[2] stepped to the living-room window beside the desk and stood breathing on the glass, watching the expanding circlet of mist, staring down through the autumn night at Lexington Avenue, eleven stories below. He was a tall, lean, dark-haired young man in a pullover sweater, who looked as though he had played not football, probably, but basketball in college. Now he placed

A **B**

---

1. Before the laptop computer, one might type on a compact, fairly lightweight typewriter called a *portable.*

2. *Wash slacks* are pants that, because they are cotton, can be washed instead of dry-cleaned.

Reading the Selection

SUMMARY

Tom, an ambitious young professional, plans to work while his wife goes off alone to the movies. A gust of air snatches up his only copy of his notes and whisks it out the window. The paper settles on a ledge about 15 feet from the window of Tom's eleventh-floor apartment. Weeks of research—gone. Not willing to let go so easily, Tom goes out on the ledge to get the sheet of paper. The events that follow change his life.

📁 **Spanish Summaries,** p. 17

A **Active Reading**

PREDICT Have students read the first paragraph. Ask them to make predictions about what will happen in the story. Remind them to revise their predictions as they read.

Additional Resources

📁 **Active Reading Guide,** p. 17
🎧 **Audio Library**
🎧 **Spanish Audio Library**

Teaching Options

CONNECTING TO OTHER SELECTIONS

The chart at the right shows three ways to connect "Contents of the Dead Man's Pocket" to selections in this book.

For specific teaching strategies, see the **Unit One Planning Guide,** pp. 143–144.

Connection	Title
Life Skills: Problem Solving	→ "With All Flags Flying," p. 115
Thematic: Life-Changing Events	→ from *Farewell to Manzanar,* p. 46
Literary: Conflict	→ *The Ring of General Macías,* p. 877

B Literary Elements

POINT OF VIEW Ask students who is telling the story. *(The story is being told from Tom's perspective but not by him.)* Explain that the author is using the limited third-person point of view. Ask volunteers to explain what that means. *(The narrator stands outside the story and reveals the thoughts and feelings of only one character.)*

Language Note

Although "Tom lighted a cigarette" may sound awkward, explain that in American English *lighted* is an acceptable past tense form of the verb *light*. More common, however, is *lit* as in "Tom lit a cigarette."

C Literary Elements

PLOT: *Internal Conflict* Help students recognize the conflicting feelings pulling at Tom as he kisses his wife good-bye. *(He is tempted to accompany her, but he also wants to work on his special project.)*

D Author's Craft

FORESHADOWING Here the author uses foreshadowing: A breeze rushing through an open door is a seemingly insignificant event, yet the author describes it in detail. Readers naturally begin wondering how it will affect subsequent events.

Teaching Options

---

the heels of his hands against the top edge of the lower window frame and shoved upward. But as usual the window didn't budge, and he had to lower his hands and then shoot them hard upward to jolt the window open a few inches. He dusted his hands, muttering.

But still he didn't begin his work. He crossed the room to the hallway entrance and, leaning against the doorjamb, hands shoved into his back pockets again, he called, "Clare?" When his wife answered, he said, "Sure you don't mind going alone?"

"No." Her voice was muffled, and he knew her head and shoulders were in the bedroom closet. Then the tap of her high heels sounded on the wood floor and she appeared at the end of the little hallway, wearing a slip, both hands raised to one ear, clipping on an earring. She smiled at him—a slender, very pretty girl with light brown, almost blonde, hair—her prettiness emphasized by the pleasant nature that showed in her face. "It's just that I hate you to miss this movie; you wanted to see it too."

"Yeah, I know." He ran his fingers through his hair. "Got to get this done though."

She nodded, accepting this. Then, glancing at the desk across the living room, she said, "You work too much, though, Tom—and too hard."

He smiled. "You won't mind though, will you, when the money comes rolling in and I'm known as the Boy Wizard of Wholesale Groceries?"

"I guess not." She smiled and turned back toward the bedroom.

At his desk again, Tom lighted a cigarette; then a few moments later as Clare appeared, dressed and ready to leave, he set it on the rim of the ash tray. "Just after seven," she said. "I can make the beginning of the first feature."

He walked to the front-door closet to help her on with her coat. He kissed her then and, for an instant, holding her close, smelling the perfume she had used, he was tempted to go with her; it was not actually true that he had to work tonight, though he very much wanted to. This was his own project, unannounced as yet in his office, and it could be postponed. But then they won't see it till Monday, he thought once again, and if I give it to the boss tomorrow he might read it over the weekend . . . "Have a good time," he said aloud. He gave his wife a little swat and opened the door for her, feeling the air from the building hallway, smelling faintly of floor wax, stream gently past his face.

He watched her walk down the hall, flicked a hand in response as she waved, and then he started to close the door, but it resisted for a moment. As the door opening narrowed, the current of warm air from the hallway, channeled through this smaller opening now, suddenly rushed past him with accelerated force. Behind him he heard the slap of the window curtains against the wall and the sound of paper fluttering from his desk, and he had to push to close the door.

Turning, he saw a sheet of white paper drifting to the floor in a series of arcs, and another sheet, yellow, moving toward the window, caught in the dying current flowing through the narrow opening. As he watched, the paper struck the bottom edge of the window and hung there for an instant, plastered against the glass and wood. Then as the moving air stilled completely the curtains swinging back from the wall to hang free again, he saw the yellow sheet drop to the window ledge and slide over out of sight.

He ran across the room, grasped the bottom edge of the window and tugged, staring through the glass. He saw the yellow sheet, dimly now in the darkness outside, lying on the ornamental ledge a yard below the window. Even as he watched, it was moving,

---

MEETING INDIVIDUAL NEEDS — ENGLISH LANGUAGE LEARNERS

Vivid Verbs Help English language learners understand how Tom moves on the ledge. Write these phrases on the board: *(p. 204) he <u>shuffled</u> along crabwise (crabs move sideways), he began to <u>tremble</u>, his body <u>swayed</u> outward; (p. 205) he <u>slid</u> his left foot; (p. 207) he saw himself <u>striding</u>, he <u>staggered</u> sideways; he <u>stumbled</u>; (p. 210) his body began <u>teetering</u> backward*

Activity Call on a student to read aloud the sentence in which one of the vivid verbs appears. Invite another student to act out the verb. Continue this activity for each phrase.

Additional Resources
📁 *English Language Learners Sourcebook*

Jack Finney

scraping slowly along the ledge, pushed by the breeze that pressed steadily against the building wall. He heaved on the window with all his strength and it shot open with a bang, the window weight rattling in the casing. But the paper was past his reach and, leaning out into the night, he watched it scud[3] steadily along the ledge to the south, half plastered against the building wall. Above the muffled sound of the street traffic far below, he could hear the dry scrape of its movement, like a leaf on the pavement.

The living room of the next apartment to the south projected a yard or more farther out toward the street than this one; because of this the Beneckes paid seven and a half dollars less rent than their neighbors. And now the yellow sheet, sliding along the stone ledge, nearly invisible in the night, was stopped by the projecting blank wall of the next apartment. It lay motionless, then, in the corner formed by the two walls—a good five yards away, pressed firmly against the ornate corner ornament of the ledge, by the breeze that moved past Tom Benecke's face.

He knelt at the window and stared at the yellow paper for a full minute or more, waiting for it to move, to slide off the ledge and fall, hoping he could follow its course to the street, and then hurry down in the elevator and retrieve it. But it didn't move, and then he saw that the paper was caught firmly between a projection of the <u>convoluted</u> corner ornament and the ledge. He thought about the poker from the fireplace, then the broom, then the mop—discarding each thought as it occurred to him. There was nothing in the apartment long enough to reach that paper.

It was hard for him to understand that he actually had to abandon it—it was ridiculous—and he began to curse. Of all the papers on his desk, why did it have to be this one in particular! On four long Saturday afternoons he had stood in supermarkets counting the people who passed certain displays, and the results were scribbled on that yellow sheet. From stacks of trade publications, gone over page by page in snatched half hours at work and during evenings at home, he had copied facts, quotations and figures onto that sheet. And he had carried it with him to the Public Library on Fifth Avenue, where he'd spent a dozen lunch hours and early evenings adding more. All were needed to support and lend authority to his idea for a new grocery-store display method; without them his idea was a mere opinion. And there they all lay, in his own <u>improvised</u> shorthand—countless hours of work—out there on the ledge.

For many seconds he believed he was going to abandon the yellow sheet, that there was nothing else to do. The work could be duplicated. But it would take two months, and the time to present this idea, damn it, was *now*, for use in the spring displays. He struck his fist on the window ledge. Then he shrugged. Even though his plan were adopted, he told himself, it wouldn't bring him a raise in pay—not immediately, anyway, or as a direct result. It won't bring me a promotion either, he argued—not of itself.

But just the same, and he couldn't escape the thought, this and other independent projects, some already done and others planned for the future, would gradually mark him out from the score of other young men in

---

3. To *scud* is to run or move swiftly.

Vocabulary

convoluted (kon′ və lo͞o′ təd) *adj.* turned in or wound up upon itself; coiled; twisted
improvised (im′ prə vīzd′) *adj.* invented, composed, or done without preparing beforehand

THE SHORT STORY 🐸 201

Reading *Minilesson*

Logical Reasoning Tom has two choices: duplicate two months of work, or get the paper. His career ambitions spur him to go after the paper, but has he considered his choices logically?

Activity Have small groups of students make a chart in which they compare the advantages of each option with the possible consequences. As a class, discuss this question: Did Tom make a logical choice? What choice would students make? **L2** COLLAB. LEARN.

Additional Resources
📁 *Reading Workbook,* p. 21

Active Reading

QUESTION Ask students what other options Tom might have considered. *(He could have called the fire department; they might have been willing to help him. He could have waited and discussed the situation with his wife.)*

Critical Thinking

INFERRING Why does Tom act "on a sudden impulse"? Why does he not want to think too much? *(If he thinks, he may not do it. Students might recall a time when they did something risky on impulse. Often that is the only way to do such things.)*

Literary Elements

SETTING Have students stop at this point and visualize the setting based on what they have read about the building, the apartment, the time of day, and the ledge so far.

Contents of the
Dead Man's Pocket

his company. They were the way to change from a name on the payroll to a name in the minds of the company officials. They were the beginning of the long, long climb to where he was determined to be, at the very top. And he knew he was going out there in the darkness, after the yellow sheet fifteen feet beyond his reach.

By a kind of instinct, he instantly began making his intention acceptable to himself by laughing at it. The mental picture of himself sidling along the ledge outside was absurd—it was actually comical—and he smiled. He imagined himself describing it; it would make a good story at the office and, it occurred to him, would add a special interest and importance to his memorandum, which would do it no harm at all.

To simply go out and get his paper was an easy task—he could be back here with it in less than two minutes—and he knew he wasn't deceiving himself. The ledge, he saw, measuring it with his eye, was about as wide as the length of his shoe, and perfectly flat. And every fifth row of brick in the face of the building, he remembered—leaning out, he verified this—was indented half an inch, enough for the tips of his fingers, enough to maintain balance easily. It occurred to him that if this ledge and wall were only a yard aboveground—as he knelt at the window staring out, this thought was the final confirmation of his intention—he could move along the ledge indefinitely.

On a sudden impulse, he got to his feet, walked to the front closet and took out an old tweed jacket, it would be cold outside. He put it on and buttoned it as he crossed the room rapidly toward the open window. In the back of his mind he knew he'd better hurry and get this over with before he thought too much, and at the window he didn't allow himself to hesitate.

He swung a leg over the sill, then felt for and found the ledge a yard below the window with his foot. Gripping the bottom of the window frame very tightly and carefully, he slowly ducked his head under it, feeling on his face the sudden change from the warm air of the room to the chill outside. With infinite care he brought out his other leg, his mind concentrating on what he was doing. Then he slowly stood erect. Most of the putty, dried out and brittle, had dropped off the bottom edging of the window frame, he found, and the flat wooden edging provided a good gripping surface, a half inch or more deep, for the tips of his fingers.

Now, balanced easily and firmly, he stood on the ledge outside in the slight, chill breeze, eleven stories above the street, staring into his own lighted apartment, odd and different-seeming now.

First his right hand, then his left, he carefully shifted his finger-tip grip from the puttyless window edging to an indented row of bricks directly to his right. It was hard to take the first shuffling sideways step then—to make himself move—and the fear stirred in his stomach, but he did it, again by not allowing himself time to think. And now—with his chest, stomach, and the left side of his face pressed against the rough cold brick—his lighted apartment was suddenly gone, and it was much darker out here than he had thought.

Without pause he continued—right foot, left foot, right foot, left—his shoe soles shuffling and scraping along the rough stone, never lifting from it, fingers sliding along the exposed edging of brick. He moved on the balls of his feet, heels lifted slightly; the ledge was not quite as wide as he'd expected. But leaning slightly inward toward the face of the building and pressed against it, he could feel his balance firm and secure, and moving

LIFE SKILLS CONNECTION

Setting Goals Tom has a long-term goal: to work his way to the top of his company. He intends to (1) show initiative, (2) work long hours, (3) conduct independent research, and (4) present independent projects. He believes that eventually his efforts will be noticed and rewarded.

Activity Have students think about setting a long-term goal for themselves. The goal could be academic, work-related, career, or personal. They should write the goal at the end of a flowchart. Along the flowchart they can note actions they plan to take in the weeks, months, and years to come. When finished, students may present their charts and explain how committing to a long-term plan will help them finally arrive at their goal. **L3**

William Street at Night, 1981. Richard Haas. Watercolor, 33¼ x 23 in.

Viewing the painting: How does this painting affect your reaction to Tom's climbing out of his window? Explain.

VIEWING THE PAINTING

Richard Haas is well known for his 1970s trompe l'oeil paintings on a monumental scale. He painted illusionist architectural facades on the flat exteriors of buildings.

Viewing Response *Students may say the painting emphasizes the danger of Tom's undertaking, causing a fearful reaction.*

MEETING INDIVIDUAL NEEDS — INCLUSION STRATEGIES

Learning Disabled To monitor students' comprehension, review key events every few pages. Write events, including but not limited to the following events, on a set of note cards:

• Tom's wife leaves for the movie.
• The paper blows out the window.
• Tom steps onto the window ledge.
• At the corner, Tom bends down to grasp the paper.
• Terror overcomes him when he sees the avenue far below.

Activity Review the story by choosing cards naming only events that students have already read about. Shuffle the cards and have students arrange them in chronological order. **L1**

Additional Resources
📁 *Inclusion Strategies*

Language Note

Show students a picture of a crab and explain that crabs move sideways, not forward or backward. So when Tom moves *crabwise*, he moves sideways.

K Literary Elements

IRONY Point out this example of irony: one expects the moment when Tom actually gets the yellow paper to be a moment of triumph, but it is also the moment when he gets his first look at Lexington Avenue *far* below. So instead of triumph, he feels only terror.

L Literary Elements

FIGURES OF SPEECH: *Metaphor* How does the language that the author uses help the reader imagine Tom's terror? *(The image of a violent explosion coupled with the word* roared *conveys the suddenness and power of Tom's fear.)*

along the ledge was quite as easy as he had thought it would be. He could hear the buttons of his jacket scraping steadily along the rough bricks and feel them catch momentarily, tugging a little, at each mortared crack. He simply did not permit himself to look down, though the compulsion to do so never left him; nor did he allow himself actually to think. Mechanically—right foot, left foot, over and again—he shuffled along crabwise, watching the projecting wall ahead loom steadily closer. . . .

Then he reached it and, at the corner—he'd decided how he was going to pick up the paper—he lifted his right foot and placed it carefully on the ledge that ran along the projecting wall at a right angle to the ledge on which his other foot rested. And now, facing the building, he stood in the corner formed by the two walls, one foot on the ledging of each, a hand on the shoulder-high indentation of each wall. His forehead was pressed directly into the corner against the cold bricks, and now he carefully lowered first one hand, then the other, perhaps a foot farther down, to the next indentation in the rows of bricks.

Very slowly, sliding his forehead down the trough of the brick corner and bending his knees, he lowered his body toward the paper lying between his outstretched feet. Again he lowered his fingerholds another foot and bent his knees still more, thigh muscles taut, his forehead sliding and bumping down the brick V. Half squatting now, he dropped his left hand to the next indentation and then slowly reached with his right hand toward the paper between his feet.

He couldn't quite touch it, and his knees now were pressed against the wall; he could bend them no farther. But by ducking his head another inch lower, the top of his head now pressed against the bricks, he lowered his right shoulder and his fingers had the paper by a corner, pulling it loose. At the same instant he saw, between his legs and far below, Lexington Avenue stretched out for miles ahead.

He saw, in that instant, the Loew's theater sign, blocks ahead past Fiftieth Street; the miles of traffic signals, all green now; the lights of cars and street lamps; countless neon signs; and the moving black dots of people. And a violent instantaneous explosion of absolute terror roared through him. For a motionless instant he saw himself externally—bent practically double, balanced on this narrow ledge, nearly half his body projecting out above the street far below—and he began to tremble violently, panic flaring through his mind and muscles, and he felt the blood rush from the surface of his skin.

In the fractional moment before horror paralyzed him, as he stared between his legs at that terrible length of street far beneath him, a fragment of his mind raised his body in a spasmodic jerk to an upright position again, but so violently that his head scraped hard against the wall, bouncing off it, and his body swayed outward to the knife edge of balance, and he very nearly plunged backward and fell. Then he was leaning far into the corner again, squeezing and pushing into it, not only his face but his chest and stomach, his back arching; and his fingertips clung with all the pressure of his pulling arms to the shoulder-high half-inch indentation in the bricks.

He was more than trembling now; his whole body was racked with a violent

---

Vocabulary
taut (tôt) *adj.* tense; tight
spasmodic (spaz mod' ik) *adj.* sudden, violent, and temporary

Teaching Options

A&E HOME VIDEO ® *The following videotape program is available from Glencoe. Be sure to preview the video for appropriateness for your class.*

- **Time Machine: Heroes Hispanos**

  Also available in the Glencoe Literature Video Library

MEETING INDIVIDUAL NEEDS — MULTIPLE LEARNING STYLES

Spatial Students with strong spatial abilities may create detailed mental images when they read visual descriptions. They can use sketching to record their mental pictures. In addition, their sketches can help other students visualize key story events.

Activity Because this story is filled with visual descriptions, students may have too many visual impressions. Encourage them to quickly sketch these images in a notebook. However, remind them not to take too much time on each sketch. Instead suggest they jot down a quick sketch and note the page number and paragraph from which the image came. Later, they can return to the sketches and work up their favorites into finished drawings to share with the class. **L2**

shuddering beyond control, his eyes squeezed so tightly shut it was painful, though he was past awareness of that. His teeth were exposed in a frozen grimace, the strength draining like water from his knees and calves. It was extremely likely, he knew, that he would faint, to slump down along the wall, his face scraping, and then drop backward, a limp weight, out into nothing. And to save his life he concentrated on holding onto consciousness, drawing deliberate deep breaths of cold air into his lungs, fighting to keep his senses aware.

Then he knew that he would not faint, but he could not stop shaking nor open his eyes. He stood where he was, breathing deeply, trying to hold back the terror of the glimpse he had of what lay below him; and he knew he had made a mistake in not making himself stare down at the street, getting used to it and accepting it, when he had first stepped out onto the ledge.

It was impossible to walk back. He simply could not do it. He couldn't bring himself to make the slightest movement. The strength was gone from his legs; his shivering hands— numb, cold and desperately rigid—had lost all deftness; his easy ability to move and balance was gone. Within a step or two, if he tried to move, he knew that he would stumble clumsily and fall.

Seconds passed, with the chill faint wind pressing the side of his face, and he could hear the toned-down volume of the street traffic far beneath him. Again and again he slowed and then stopped, almost to silence; then presently, even this high, he would hear the click of the traffic signals and the subdued roar of the cars starting up again. During a lull in the street sounds, he called out. Then he was shouting "Help!" so loudly it rasped

his throat. But he felt the steady pressure of the wind, moving between his face and the blank wall, snatch up his cries as he uttered them, and he knew they must sound directionless and distant. And he remembered how habitually, here in New York, he himself heard and ignored shouts in the night. If anyone heard him, there was no sign of it, and presently Tom Benecke knew he had to try moving; there was nothing else he could do.

Eyes squeezed shut, he watched scenes in his mind like scraps of motion-picture film— he could not stop them. He saw himself stumbling suddenly sideways as he crept along the ledge and saw his upper body arc outward, arms flailing. He saw a dangling shoestring caught between the ledge and the sole of his other shoe, saw a foot start to move, to be stopped with a jerk, and felt his balance leaving him. He saw himself falling with a terrible speed as his body revolved in the air, knees clutched tight to his chest, eyes squeezed shut, moaning softly.

Out of utter necessity, knowing that any of these thoughts might be reality in the very next seconds, he was slowly able to shut his mind against every thought but what he now began to do. With fear-soaked slowness, he slid his left foot an inch or two toward his own impossibly distant window. Then he slid the fingers of his shivering left hand a corresponding distance. For a moment he could not bring himself to lift his right foot from one ledge to the other; then he did it, and became aware of the harsh exhalation of air from his throat and realized that he was panting. As his right hand, then, began to slide along the brick edging, he was astonished to feel the yellow paper pressed to the bricks underneath his stiff fingers, and he uttered a terrible, abrupt bark that might have been a laugh or a moan.

Vocabulary
deftness (deft′ nəs) *n.* the state or quality of being skillful and nimble

---

VIEWING THE PAINTING

Yvonne Jacquette was among a group of American painters who questioned the role of realism in the modern world and struggled to find worthwhile content. John L. Ward explains in his book *American Realist Painting 1945–1980* that Jacquette, in the late 1960s, chose objects for their formal possibilities and painted them in a neutral style. The interaction of large shapes and movements was stressed.

Viewing Response *Students may find the perspective a little dizzying or frightening if they imagine looking down from a ledge on a tall building. Had Tom gotten used to seeing the world from this perspective, he might have found it less terrifying when he moved along the ledge, or he might have realized how far up eleven stories really is and not gone on.*

Vo•cab•u•lar•y Skills

Synonyms *Pent-up* refers to something—usually an emotion—that is kept inside, hidden. Similar expressions include *bottled up, corked up, shut up, held in, sealed off, held back, restrained, curbed, bridled, repressed,* and *suppressed.*

Flatiron Intersection, 1975. Yvonne Jacquette. Oil on canvas, 60 x 80 in. Courtesy DC Moore Gallery, New York.

Viewing the painting: What sensations does this painting portray? How might they be similar to Tom's feelings as he stepped along the ledge?

He opened his mouth and took the paper in his teeth, pulling it out from under his fingers.

By a kind of trick—by concentrating his entire mind on first his left foot, then his left hand, then the other foot, then the other hand—he was able to move, almost imperceptibly, trembling steadily, very nearly without thought. But he could feel the terrible strength of the <u>pent-up</u> horror on just the other side of the flimsy barrier he had erected in his mind; and he knew that if it broke through he would lose this thin artificial control of his body.

During one slow step he tried keeping his eyes closed; it made him feel safer, shutting him off a little from the fearful reality of where he was. Then a sudden rush of giddiness swept over him and he had to open his eyes wide, staring sideways at the cold rough brick and angled lines of mortar, his cheek tight against the building. He kept his eyes open then, knowing that if he once let them flick outward, to stare for an instant at the lighted windows across the street, he would be past help.

He didn't know how many dozens of tiny sidling steps he had taken, his chest, belly

Vocabulary
pent-up (pent' up) *adj.* not expressed or released; held in

MEETING INDIVIDUAL NEEDS — MULTIPLE LEARNING STYLES

Logical-Mathematical Students with strong logical-mathematical skills excel at exploring patterns and relationships and learn well when given opportunities to categorize and classify.

Activity Divide the class into groups (with at least one logical learner per group). Have groups choose one of the following main ideas:

- Tom made an intelligent choice.
- Tom made a foolish choice.

Then have them come up with a graphic organizer in which to list supporting details. They may include supporting details from the text or use their own ideas as long as they are well thought out. Remind students to divide the work among themselves and to elicit each member's participation. **L1** and face pressed to the wall; but he knew the slender hold he was keeping on his mind and body was going to break. He had a sudden mental picture of his apartment on just the other side of this wall—warm, cheerful, incredibly spacious. And he saw himself striding through it, lying down on the floor on his back, arms spread wide, reveling in its unbelievable security. The impossible remoteness of this utter safety, the contrast between it and where he now stood, was more than he could bear. And the barrier broke then, and the fear of the awful height he stood on coursed through his nerves and muscles.

A fraction of his mind knew he was going to fall, and he began taking rapid blind steps with no feeling of what he was doing, sidling with a clumsy desperate swiftness, fingers scrabbling along the brick, almost hopelessly resigned to the sudden backward pull and swift motion outward and down. Then his moving left hand slid onto not brick but sheer emptiness, an impossible gap in the face of the wall, and he stumbled.

His right foot smashed into his left anklebone; he staggered sideways, began falling, and the claw of his hand cracked against glass and wood, slid down it, and his finger tips were pressed hard on the puttyless edging of his window. His right hand smacked gropingly beside it as he fell to his knees; and, under the full weight and direct downward pull of his sagging body, the open window dropped shudderingly in its frame till it closed and his wrists struck the sill and were jarred off.

For a single moment he knelt, knee bones against stone on the very edge of the ledge, body swaying and touching nowhere else, fighting for balance. Then he lost it, his shoulders plunging backward, and he flung his arms forward, his hands smashing against the window casing on either side; and—his body moving backward—his fingers clutched the narrow wood stripping of the upper pane.

For an instant he hung suspended between balance and falling, his finger tips pressed onto the quarter-inch wood strips. Then, with utmost delicacy, with a focused concentration of all his senses, he increased even further the strain on his finger tips hooked to these slim edgings of wood. Elbows slowly bending, he began to draw the full weight of his upper body forward, knowing that the instant his fingers slipped off these quarter-inch strips he'd plunge backward and be falling. Elbows imperceptibly bending, body shaking with the strain, the sweat starting from his forehead in great sudden drops, he pulled, his entire being and thought concentrated in his finger tips. Then suddenly, the strain slackened and ended, his chest touching the window sill, and he was kneeling on the ledge, his forehead pressed to the glass of the closed window.

Dropping his palms to the sill, he stared into his living room—at the red-brown davenport across the room, and a magazine he had left there; at the pictures on the walls and the gray rug; the entrance to the hallway; and at his papers, typewriter and desk, not two feet from his nose. A movement from his desk caught his eye and he saw that it was a thin curl of blue smoke; his cigarette, the ash long, was still burning in the ash tray where he'd left it—this was past all belief—only a few minutes before.

His head moved, and in faint reflection from the glass before him he saw the yellow paper clenched in his front teeth. Lifting a hand from the sill he took it from his mouth; the moistened corner parted from the paper, and he spat it out.

Vocabulary
reveling (rev′al ing) *adj.* taking great pleasure

P Literary Elements

POINT OF VIEW Read aloud this passage. Then ask students how they felt. Discuss how the suspense is related to the point of view from which the story is told. *(Because the events are told from the point of view of a narrator who knows all Tom's thoughts and feelings, readers exist in the moment with Tom, not knowing what is going to happen until it actually does. When Tom teeters off balance, readers teeter with him; is he going to make it? Will they make it?)*

MEETING INDIVIDUAL NEEDS — INCLUSION STRATEGIES

Special Needs Students with special needs must have opportunities to exercise the conventions of conversational exchange. Engage them in one-on-one or small-group activities with peers who can model conversational skills.

Activity Choose a discussion topic related to this story: for example, "the scariest thing that ever happened to me." Stress these practical skills: vocal quality (pitch, loudness, stress); eye contact; facial expressions; and interactive features (not interrupting, turn taking, staying on topic, and giving feedback) **L1**

Additional Resources
📁 *Inclusion Strategies*

CHARACTER Even though his attempt to break the glass failed, Tom maintains that "it was not possible that there wasn't a way past it." What does this tell the reader about him? *(Despite the trauma he has been through, he remains determined and resourceful. He is not the type who gives up. If there's a problem, he tries to solve it.)*

R **Active Reading**

CONNECT Elicit students' responses to Tom's behavior here. Have they ever stepped outside themselves in a serious situation and found the whole thing humorous?

Teaching Options

Contents of the
Dead Man's Pocket

For a moment, in the light from the living room, he stared wonderingly at the yellow sheet in his hand and then crushed it into the side pocket of his jacket.

He couldn't open the window. It had been pulled not completely closed, but its lower edge was below the level of the outside sill; there was no room to get his fingers underneath it. Between the upper sash and the lower was a gap not wide enough—reaching up, he tried—to get his fingers into; he couldn't push it open. The upper window panel, he knew from long experience, was impossible to move, frozen tight with dried paint.

Very carefully observing his balance, the finger tips of his left hand again hooked to the narrow stripping of the window casing, he drew back his right hand, palm facing the glass, and then struck the glass with the heel of his hand.

His arm rebounded from the pane, his body tottering, and he knew he didn't dare strike a harder blow.

But in the security and relief of his new position, he simply smiled; with only a sheet of glass between him and the room just before him, it was not possible that there wasn't a way past it. Eyes narrowing, he thought for a few moments about what to do. Then his eyes widened, for nothing occurred to him. But still he felt calm: the trembling, he realized, had stopped. At the back of his mind there still lay the thought that once he was again in his home, he could give release to his feelings. He actually *would* lie on the floor, rolling, clenching tufts of the rug in his hands. He would literally run across the room, free to move as he liked, jumping on the floor, testing and reveling in its absolute security, letting the relief flood through him, draining the fear from his mind and body. His yearning for this was astonishingly intense, and somehow he understood that he had better keep this feeling at bay.

He took a half dollar from his pocket and struck it against the pane, but without any hope that the glass would break and with very little disappointment when it did not. After a few moments of thought he drew his leg up onto the ledge and picked loose the knot of his shoelace. He slipped off the shoe and, holding it across the instep, drew back his arm as far as he dared and struck the leather heel against the glass. The pane rattled, but he knew he'd been a long way from breaking it. His foot was cold and he slipped the shoe back on. He shouted again, experimentally, and then once more, but there was no answer.

The realization suddenly struck him that he might have to wait here till Clare came home, and for a moment the thought was funny. He could see Clare opening the front door, withdrawing her key from the lock, closing the door behind her and then glancing up to see him crouched on the other side of the window. He could see her rush across the room, face astounded and frightened, and hear himself shouting instructions: "Never mind how I got here! Just open the wind—" She couldn't open it, he remembered, she'd never been able to; she'd always had to call him. She'd have to get the building superintendent or a neighbor, and he pictured himself smiling and answering their questions as he climbed in. "I just wanted to get a breath of fresh air, so—"

He couldn't possibly wait here till Clare came home. It was the second feature she'd wanted to see, and she'd left in time to see the first. She'd be another three hours or—He glanced at his watch; Clare had been gone eight minutes. It wasn't possible, but only eight minutes ago he

INTERDISCIPLINARY CONNECTION

Art This story comprises many scenes in which readers see Tom act out the story events. The strong visual elements in the scenes lend themselves to illustrations. In fact, students may enjoy creating an illustrated version of this story, modeled on high-quality comic books. If you can find a few samples of good comic books that convey classic stories, bring them in for students to view.

Activity Have the whole class work

together to create images for a comic version of "Contents of the Dead Man's Pocket." Assign each student a dramatic scene to illustrate in one or two frames. Students may add dialogue or use a narrator's voice to set the scene. Point out that comic book writers use some conversation or thought balloons in almost every frame. Students may team up and divide the tasks of drawing, inking (coloring in the outlines), and writing. **L2** had kissed his wife good-by. She wasn't even at the theater yet!

It would be four hours before she could possibly be home, and he tried to picture himself kneeling out here, finger tips hooked to these narrow strippings, while first one movie, preceded by a slow listing of credits, began, developed, reached its climax and then finally ended. There'd be a newsreel next, maybe, and then an animated cartoon, and then interminable scenes from coming pictures. And then, once more, the beginning of a full-length picture—while all the time he hung out here in the night.

He might possibly get to his feet, but he was afraid to try. Already his legs were cramped, his thigh muscles tired; his knees hurt, his feet felt numb and his hands were stiff. He couldn't possibly stay out here for four hours, or anywhere near it. Long before that his legs and arms would give out; he would be forced to try changing his position often—stiffly, clumsily, his co-ordination and strength gone—and he would fall. Quite realistically, he knew that he would fall; no one could stay out here on this ledge for four hours.

A dozen windows in the apartment building across the street were lighted. Looking over his shoulder, he could see the top of a man's head behind the newspaper he was reading; in another window he saw the blue-gray flicker of a television screen. No more than twenty-odd yards from his back were scores of people, and if just one of them would walk idly to his window and glance out. . . . For some moments he stared over his shoulder at the lighted rectangles, waiting. But no one appeared. The man reading his paper turned a page and then continued his reading. A figure passed another of the windows and was immediately gone.

In the inside pocket of his jacket he found a little sheaf of papers, and he pulled one out and looked at it in the light from the living room. It was an old letter, an advertisement of some sort; his name and address, in purple ink, were on a label pasted to the envelope. Gripping one end of the envelope in his teeth, he twisted it into a tight curl. From his shirt pocket he brought out a book of matches. He didn't dare let go the casing with both hands but, with the twist of paper in his teeth, he opened the matchbook with his free hand; then he bent one of the matches in two without tearing it from the folder, its red-tipped end now touching the striking surface. With his thumb, he rubbed the red tip across the striking area.

He did it again, then again, and still again, pressing harder each time, and the match suddenly flared, burning his thumb. But he kept it alight, cupping the matchbook in his hand and shielding it with his body. He held the flame to the paper in his mouth till it caught. Then he snuffed out the match flame with his thumb and forefinger, careless of the burn, and replaced the book in his pocket. Taking the paper twist in his hand, he held it flame down, watching the flame crawl up the paper, till it flared bright. Then he held it behind him over the street, moving it from side to side, watching it over his shoulder, the flame flickering and guttering in the wind.

There were three letters in his pocket and he lighted each of them, holding each till the flame touched his hand and then dropping it to the street below. At one point, watching over his shoulder while the last of the letters burned, he saw the man across the street put down his paper and stand—even seeming, to Tom, to glance toward his window. But when he moved, it was only to walk across the room and disappear from sight.

Contents of the Dead Man's Pocket

There were a dozen coins in Tom Benecke's pocket and he dropped them, three or four at a time. But if they struck anyone, or if anyone noticed their falling, no one connected them with their source, and no one glanced upward.

His arms had begun to tremble from the steady strain of clinging to this narrow perch, and he did not know what to do now and was terribly frightened. Clinging to the window stripping with one hand, he again searched his pockets. But now—he had left his wallet on his dresser when he'd changed clothes—there was nothing left but the yellow sheet. It occurred to him irrelevantly that his death on the sidewalk below would be an eternal mystery; the window closed—why, how, and from where could he have fallen? No one would be able to identify his body for a time, either—the thought was somehow unbearable and increased his fear. All they'd find in his pockets would be the yellow sheet. *Contents of the dead man's pockets,* he thought, *one sheet of paper bearing penciled notations—incomprehensible.*

He understood fully that he might actually be going to die; his arms, maintaining his balance on the ledge, were trembling steadily now. And it occurred to him then with all the force of a revelation that, if he fell, all he was ever going to have out of life he would then, abruptly, have had. Nothing, then, could ever be changed; and nothing more—no least experience or pleasure—could ever be added to his life. He wished, then, that he had not allowed his wife to go off by herself tonight—and on similar nights. He thought of all the evenings he had spent away from her, working; and he regretted them. He thought wonderingly of his fierce ambition and of the direction his life had taken; he thought of the hours he'd spent by himself, filling the yellow sheet that had brought him out here. *Contents of the dead*

man's pockets, he thought with sudden fierce anger, *a wasted life.*

He was simply not going to cling here till he slipped and fell; he told himself that now. There was one last thing he could try; he had been aware of it for some moments, refusing to think about it, but now he faced it. Kneeling here on the ledge, the finger tips of one hand pressed to the narrow strip of wood, he could, he knew, draw his other hand back a yard perhaps, fist clenched tight, doing it very slowly till he sensed the outer limit of balance, then, as hard as he was able from the distance, he could drive his fist forward against the glass. If it broke, his fist smashing through, he was safe; he might cut himself badly, and probably would, but with his arm inside the room, he would be secure. But if the glass did not break, the rebound, flinging his arm back, would topple him off the ledge. He was certain of that.

He tested his plan. The fingers of his left hand clawlike on the little stripping, he drew back his other fist until his body began teetering backward. But he had no leverage now—he could feel that there would be no force to his swing—and he moved his fist slowly forward till he rocked forward on his knees again and could sense that his swing would carry its greatest force. Glancing down, however, measuring the distance from his fist to the glass, he saw that it was less than two feet.

It occurred to him that he could raise his arm over his head, to bring it down against the glass. But, experimenting in slow motion, he knew it would be an awkward girl-like blow without the force of a driving punch, and not nearly enough to break the glass.

Facing the window, he had to drive a blow from the shoulder, he knew now, at a distance of less than two feet; and he did not know whether it would break through the heavy glass. It might; he could picture it

---

Grammar and Language *Minilesson*

Compatibility of Tenses A writer may have to occasionally shift tenses to show that one event precedes or follows another. Point out the first paragraph in the second column on page 201. When Tom thinks back to his earlier activities, the author shifts from the past tense to the past perfect tense, indicating that those events occurred at an earlier time than the events in the story.

Activity Have students write sentences using compatible tenses of the verbs.
1. called, had heard *(I called to warn them, but they had already heard the rumor.)*
2. thawed, had frozen *(Although the ice had frozen around the ship, it thawed quickly once the sun came out.)* **L3**

Additional Resources

 Grammar and Language Transparency 18

 Grammar and Language Workbook, p. 153

 Grammar and Composition Handbook, Lesson 5.6

Writer's Choice, Lesson 15.6

happening, he could feel it in the nerves of his arm. And it might not; he could feel that too—feel his fist striking this glass and being instantaneously flung back by the unbreaking pane, feel the fingers of his other hand breaking loose, nails scraping along the casing as he fell.

He waited, arm drawn back, fist balled, but in no hurry to strike; this pause, he knew, might be an extension of his life. And to live even a few seconds longer, he felt, even out here on this ledge in the night, was infinitely better than to die a moment earlier than he had to. His arm grew tired, and he brought it down and rested it.

Then he knew that it was time to make the attempt. He could not kneel here hesitating indefinitely till he lost all courage to act, waiting till he slipped off the ledge. Again he drew back his arm, knowing this time that he would not bring it down till he struck. His elbow protruding over Lexington Avenue far below, the fingers of his other hand pressed down bloodlessly tight against the narrow stripping, he waited, feeling the sick tenseness and terrible excitement building. It grew and swelled toward the moment of action, his nerves tautening. He thought of Clare—just a wordless, yearning thought—and then drew his arm back just a bit more, fist so tight his fingers pained him, and knowing he was going to do it. Then with full power, with every last scrap of strength he could bring to bear, he shot his arm forward toward the glass, and he said, *"Clare!"*

He heard the sound, felt the blow, felt himself falling forward, and his hand closed on the living-room curtains, the shards and fragments of glass showering onto the floor. And then, kneeling there on the ledge, an arm thrust into the room up to the shoulder, he began picking away the protruding slivers and great wedges of glass from the window frame, tossing them in onto the rug. And, as he grasped the edges of the empty window frame and climbed into his home, he was grinning in triumph.

He did not lie down on the floor or run through the apartment, as he had promised himself; even in the first few moments it seemed to him natural and normal that he should be where he was. He simply turned to his desk, pulled the crumpled yellow sheet from his pocket and laid it down where it had been, smoothing it out; then he absently laid a pencil across it to weight it down. He shook his head wonderingly, and turned to walk toward the closet.

There he got out his topcoat and hat and, without waiting to put them on, opened the front door and stepped out, to go find his wife. He turned to pull the door closed and warm air from the hall rushed through the narrow opening again. As he saw the yellow paper, the pencil flying, scooped off the desk and, unimpeded by the glassless window, sail out into the night and out of his life, Tom Benecke burst into laughter and then closed the door behind him.

❧

Vocabulary
unimpeded (un´ im pē´ dəd) *adj.* not obstructed; unblocked

THE SHORT STORY 🐾 211

Y **Literary Elements**

THEME The author states a theme in this paragraph. Ask students to summarize the message. *(Living under any circumstances is better than dying earlier than one has to.)*

Z **Literary Elements**

PLOT: *Climax* You may wish to ask students to detail what Tom sees, thinks, and feels in the moments before he strikes the windowpane. Why does he cry, "Clare"? *(He calls her name for inspiration, as if he can draw strength from the very thought of her.)*

AA **Active Reading**

EVALUATE After going to such lengths to retrieve his paper, would Tom have so carelessly parted with it? Students may question Tom's action. Help them recognize that the author is setting up a final plot twist. What do they predict might happen next? *(The paper will blow away again.)*

Thematic Focus

Making Choices Point out that Tom laughs when the paper once again blows out the window. What does this reaction seem to indicate about the choice he has made? Make sure they support their opinions with evidence from the story.

☑ **ASSESSMENT OPTIONS**

📁 *Quick Checks*, p. 17

Writing *Minilesson*

Creating Suspense with Chronological Order Jack Finney used chronological, or time, order in this story. Time order helps the reader sort out what happened when. It's also an excellent way to create suspense.

[Activity] Have students choose a topic that contains an element of suspense and write a few paragraphs describing the sequence of events. Suggest that they use phrases that denote time order, such as *before, then, next, after, meanwhile, yesterday, later, now,* and *soon.* **L1**

Additional Resources

📓 *Writer's Choice,* Lesson 4.3

Responding to the Selection

Personal Response

Students may say they reacted most strongly to Tom's initial terror on the ledge or the moment when the window slammed shut.

ANALYZING LITERATURE

1. He wants to work on his project.
2. It blows out the window. Tom decides to go out and get it because it represents two months of work.
3. When he first looks down, sees the street far below, and panics, the adventure becomes terrifying.
4. He realizes that he has devoted his life to the wrong things and that his wife is more important to him than his work.
5. It blows out the window again. Tom laughs.
6. He is ambitious and determined to rise in his company.
7. Besides representing a lot of hard work, it also represents the future he wants in his company. Because it is important to him, he decides to go out after it.
8. He sees the danger in which he has placed himself. Before, he thought of the situation as risky but doable. He was confident he could succeed. After, he is so frightened, he has a hard time thinking at all.
9. He feels he has spent too much time working and not enough time with Clare, which he now sees as a waste.
10. The paper symbolizes his old set of values. Now he is starting a new life and doesn't care that the paper and all it represents have blown away.
11. Thinking about those words causes Tom to have a revelation that changes his priorities in life.
12. Successful people are sometimes ambitious risk takers who sacrifice personal relationships to single-mindedly pursue their careers.
13. The author is saying that people should put their loved ones before their ambitions. Students should offer reasons for their opinions.
14. Students may have noticed the following examples of foreshadowing as they read: page 200, as Tom closes the door; page 201, as Tom looks helplessly at the paper caught on the ledge; page 211, when Tom sets his paper on the desk again.
15. Finney builds suspense by taking us through Tom's every step and decision and letting us experience his full range of emotions.

212 UNIT 1

Responding to Literature

Personal Response

Which part of the story did you react to most strongly? Discuss your reaction with a partner.

ANALYZING LITERATURE

RECALL

1. Why does Tom decide not to go to the movies with Clare?
2. What happens to the yellow sheet of paper? What does Tom plan to do about it? Why?
3. At what moment does Tom's adventure change from risky to terrifying?
4. What is the revelation Tom has when looking into his living room?
5. What happens to the yellow sheet of paper at the end of the story? What is Tom's reaction then?

INTERPRET

6. What do you learn about Tom from his decision not to go with Clare?
7. What does the yellow paper represent to Tom? How might his feelings about the paper have influenced his decision to retrieve it?
8. In your opinion, why does terror suddenly seize Tom when he had been fairly calm up until that moment? What kinds of thoughts might he have had before and after he became terrified?
9. Before his revelation, Tom thinks, "Contents of the dead man's pockets, . . . one sheet of paper bearing penciled notations—incomprehensible." After the revelation, he thinks, "Contents of the dead man's pockets, . . . a wasted life." Why might he feel this way?
10. Why do you think Tom reacts as he does when he sees the yellow sheet of paper at the end of the story?

EVALUATE AND CONNECT

11. What is the significance of the title of the story?
12. Think about successful businesspeople and famous musicians, athletes, dancers, or artists; what might they have in common with Tom? Explain.
13. What is the author saying about priorities in life? Do you agree?
14. What examples of **foreshadowing** do you find in the story? (See page R5.) Did you notice the foreshadowing as you read, or did you recognize it after you had finished the story? Explain.
15. Tom was on the ledge for eight minutes, yet to the reader it seems much longer. How does Finney build suspense and hold our attention?

212 UNIT 1

See **Literary Terms Handbook**, p. R9.

Literary ELEMENTS

Point of View

The **point of view** a fiction writer uses depends on which approach would tell the story in the most interesting and appealing way. The writer of "Contents of the Dead Man's Pocket" uses **limited third-person** point of view, in which the narrator stands outside the story and reveals the thoughts and feelings of only one character. The narrator refers to that character as "he" or "she."

1. Why might Finney have chosen to limit the reader's information to Tom's thoughts and observations?
2. In your opinion, would the story be stronger or more interesting if the narrator also included Clare's thoughts and feelings? Explain.
3. Imagine a third character in the story—perhaps a neighbor across the street who watches the action from a window. Retell one scene from that neighbor's point of view. How does the change in point of view change the story?

LITERARY ELEMENTS

1. Since Tom experiences the central situation of the story, readers need to know what he thinks and feels.
2. Possible answer: It is better that readers focus all their attention on Tom, as the story does.
3. Readers would no longer experience what Tom is feeling and thinking.

Additional Resources

Literary Elements Transparency 17

LITERATURE AND WRITING

Writing About Literature

Setting   Write an analysis of the way Jack Finney uses the setting to help create suspense in this story. Consider not only the place where the action occurs but also the time of day, the weather conditions, and the contrast between where Tom is and where he wants to be.

Creative Writing

A Different Twist   How might this story have ended if it were a comedy, a tragedy, a mystery, or a science fiction piece? Choose one of these types of fiction and rewrite the ending of the story to make it fit that type. Use your imagination, but try to keep your ending consistent with the first part of the story.

EXTENDING YOUR RESPONSE

Literature Groups

Relating to the Character   Discuss Tom Benecke's discovery about the way he spends his time. How does Tom's revelation compare with what you discovered when you created the chart for the Focus Activity on page 198? Compile the results of the Focus Activity from members in the group and develop some generalizations about how people your age spend their time. Do you come to the same conclusion Tom did? Share your findings with the class.

7–7:30	get ready for school
7:30–7:45	travel to school
7:45–8	talk to friends at school

Interdisciplinary Activity

Art: Illustrate the Highlights   Choose a significant part of the story and retell it in a drawing. Use whatever style you like—cartoon, abstract, with captions or without—and present your drawing to the class. Explain why you chose the scene you did.

Performing

A Monologue   Finney writes what Tom is thinking as he gropes his way along the ledge, but if this were a play, Tom would speak what he thinks. Write a first-person monologue for Tom based on part of the story. Deliver it to the class as if you were standing on a ledge!

Reading Further

If you would like to read more by Jack Finney, you might enjoy these works:

Novels: In *Time and Again* and its sequel, *From Time to Time,* the hero travels back in time to New York City of the 1800s and finds romance and mystery.

Invasion of the Body Snatchers is a science fiction thriller.

Short Story Collections: *Forgotten News: The Crime of the Century and Other Lost Stories*

About Time: Twelve Stories

Viewing: *Time and Again* has gained a loyal following of fans. Other popular films based on Finney's work include *Invasion of the Body Snatchers* and *Good Neighbor Sam.*

 Save your work for your portfolio.

LITERATURE AND WRITING

Writing About Literature

Students' setting analyses should
- discuss the place, the time, the weather, and other external conditions.
- give examples of setting and explain how each adds to the suspense.
- demonstrate an organizational strategy that ensures coherence.

Creative Writing

Students' story endings should
- fit the requirements of a specific genre: comedy, tragedy, mystery, or science fiction.
- follow logically from the first part of the story.
- let readers know this is the end of the story.

EXTENDING YOUR RESPONSE

Literature Groups   Allow students to quietly consider their activities and priorities in relation to Tom's. Then students may come together with their groups to compare ideas. **COLLAB. LEARN.**

Interdisciplinary Activity
Students may use any medium with which they are comfortable working. Suggest to students who do not enjoy drawing that they try making a collage that retells their favorite part of the story.

Performing   If possible, videotape each student's monologue and make the tapes available for viewing.

 ASSESSMENT OPTIONS

📁 *Quick Checks,* p. 17
📁 *Selection and Theme Assessment,* pp. 33–34
📁 *Performance Assessment,* p. 17
💾 *Testmaker*

Skill Minilessons

Skill Minilessons

GRAMMAR AND LANGUAGE
Introductory Phrases

Possible answers:
1. Wishing he could go with her, Tom waved to Clare.
2. With his heart in his mouth, Tom sidled across the ledge.
3. Fearing he would faint, Tom took deep breaths.
4. Pressing his face to the wall, Tom felt the rough bricks.
5. In a nearby apartment, a man was reading.

READING AND THINKING
Problem Solving

An example chart:
Problem: Is the ledge wide enough? What will he hold on to?
Steps Taken to Solve the Problem: He measures the ledge with his eye. It is as wide as his foot is long. It is flat. There are indentations in the brick wall. He leans out and verifies this.
The Outcome: He can walk on the ledge and grip the bricks.

VOCABULARY
Analogies

1. b   2. c   3. b
4. a   5. a

Additional Resources

📔 *Grammar and Composition Handbook*

📔 *Grammar and Language Workbook*

📔 *Writer's Choice,* Lesson 8.2

📁 *Reading Workbook,* p. 21

📁 *Vocabulary Practice,* p. 16

GRAMMAR AND LANGUAGE • Introductory Phrases

Jack Finney uses many introductory prepositional and participial phrases to describe Tom's actions and emotions. For example:

Introductory Prepositional Phrase: *During a lull in the street sounds,* he called out.

Introductory Participial Phrases: *Glancing down,* however, *measuring the distance from his fist to the glass,* he saw that it was less than two feet.

PRACTICE   On your paper, combine each pair of sentences by changing one of the sentences into an introductory prepositional or participial phrase.

1. Tom waved to Clare. He wished he could go with her.
2. Tom sidled across the ledge. His heart was in his mouth.
3. Tom took deep breaths. He was afraid he would faint.
4. Tom felt the rough bricks. He pressed his face to the wall.
5. A man was reading. He was in a nearby apartment.

APPLY   Revise a response you wrote for "Contents of the Dead Man's Pocket" to include an introductory phrase.

● For more about phrases, see **Language Handbook,** p. R41.

READING AND THINKING • Problem Solving

Tom Benecke had a problem—an important paper blew out the window of his eleventh-story apartment. This was his first attempt to solve the problem: "He thought about the poker from the fireplace, then the broom, then the mop—discarding each thought as it occurred to him. There was nothing in the apartment long enough to reach that paper."

PRACTICE   Make a chart like the one shown to list the steps that Tom eventually follows to solve his problem.

Problem:	An important paper blew out a window.
Steps Taken to Solve the Problem:	Tom thinks about tools to use to retrieve the paper.
The Outcome:	That solution is unsuccessful; the tools are all too short.

● For more about problem solving, see **Reading Handbook,** pp. R78–R107.

VOCABULARY • Analogies

An analogy is a type of comparison that is based on the relationships between things or ideas. Some analogies are of a type that could be called "defining characteristic." The characteristic given need not be the most important or most distinguishing trait, but it is part of what makes the person, object, idea, or animal what it is.

    rabbit : furry :: bird : feathered

    A rabbit is furry; a bird is feathered.

    To finish an analogy, decide what relationship exists between the first two things or ideas. Then apply that relationship to another pair of words and see if it is the same.

● For more about analogies, see **Communications Skills Handbook,** p. R77.

PRACTICE   Choose the word that best completes each analogy.

1. knot : convoluted :: noose :
   a. tight   b. looped   c. stretched
2. tightrope : taut :: net :
   a. safe   b. delicate   c. meshed
3. improvised : rehearsed :: temporary :
   a. skit   b. permanent   c. brief
4. sneeze : spasmodic :: waltz :
   a. rhythmic   b. irregular   c. natural
5. deftness : clumsiness :: honesty :
   a. deceit   b. skill   c. truth

Rock Climbing

SPORTS AND FITNESS

INTERDISCIPLINARY CONNECTION

For Tom Benecke, the main character of "Contents of the Dead Man's Pocket," climbing along a building ledge was a terrifying experience, yet many men and women enthusiastically scale vertical surfaces to dizzying heights. They wedge their fingers and toes into cracks that may be no wider than a fingernail. Then they pull themselves up boulders, walls, and sheer mountain cliffs one step at a time.

While many people get dizzy looking down from high places, climbers actively seek out climbs that take them to new heights with vast, impressive views. Sometimes the final destinations are so high that after a full day of climbing, climbers must spend the night on a rock wall. They sleep on a narrow ledge or in a portable hammock-type device attached to a cliff, and at dawn they continue their ascent.

In addition to being physically fit and carefully trained, good climbers use special equipment designed to increase their climbing ability and protect them from accidents.

The Equipment

Perhaps the most important piece of rock climbing equipment is a strong, stretchable rope. The rope attaches to a harness the climber wears, which has a padded waistband and leg loops. Climbers either affix the rope to a fixture at their destination at the top before they begin their ascent—this is called top-roping, or they climb in groups or pairs with the rope attached to one another—which is called lead climbing. Sometimes, climbers rely on their ropes only for protection in case of a fall. Other times, they use the ropes to scale a cliff face or wall. In either case, they maintain their equipment carefully. A faulty harness or frayed rope could send the wearer crashing down to his or her death.

Climbers wear special shoes to enhance their ability. Much smaller, slimmer, and tighter than ordinary sneakers, they allow a climber greater control and balance. These shoes have sticky rubber soles to grip onto surfaces and tapered toes so that the wearer can jam them into cracks or crevices to get a toehold.

Rock climbers also give their hands special attention. Climbers sometimes coat their palms and fingers with powdered chalk to improve their grip and keep them from slipping. They may also wrap tape around their hands to prevent rocks from cutting or scraping their skin.

Activity

Find the rock climbing locations nearest you. Read nature guides, search the Internet, or conduct telephone research to locate one indoor and one outdoor location. Note the kind of surface on which the climbing is done and each location's levels of difficulty.

Objective

- To understand the skills and equipment needed to engage in the sport of rock climbing

Teaching Strategies

Stress that rock climbing is a serious, potentially dangerous endeavor that should be attempted only under the supervision of qualified professionals.

Activity

Students should name one indoor and one outdoor rock climbing facility or location and note the kind of surface and level of difficulty at each. They can organize this information in chart form for easier reading.

Teaching Options

MEETING INDIVIDUAL NEEDS — MULTIPLE LEARNING STYLES

Intrapersonal and Interpersonal
Intrapersonal learners prefer to work alone on an individual project. Interpersonal learners like to work in groups because they want to share and mediate. The following activity can be adapted for both groups.

Activity Ask students to imagine that they are one of a small group of rock climbers who plan to climb a smooth, sheer rock face. Have them write either a journal entry or a short story in which the group spends a day together climbing this rock formation. Students may focus on their own thoughts and contributions during the climb (intrapersonal), or create a set of well-defined characters (including themselves) and focus on their actions and motivations (interpersonal). **L2**

MEDIA Connection

Objective

- To read and understand a comic strip

Respond

1. Some students may say that he is disappointed that his creative efforts were wasted. Others may say that he is disappointed to find censorship in the school paper.
2. Responses may include frustrated, angry, confused, determined to take action, defeated, and disappointed.

Additional Resources

- **Media Connection Activities,** p. 7

Teaching Options

MEDIA Connection

Comic Strip

How important is it to be able to express thoughts freely—without fear of censorship—even if other people don't like what they hear? Jason Fox, of the *Fox Trot* comic strip, believes it is a right that should not be squished or squashed.

Respond

1. What do you think was most disappointing to Jason about having his comic strip rejected by the school paper?

2. How might you react if your freedom of expression was being squashed?

Reading Minilesson

Author's Purpose As stated earlier, comic strips share certain literary elements with short stories. But comic strips aim mainly to entertain. Even comic strips that take on serious topics such as politics maintain a touch of levity.

Activity Bring in comic strips for students to read. Have student pairs read five different strips. On five note cards, students write the title of each comic and answer the questions: *What is the topic of the comic strip? What is funny about the comic strip? What is the author's purpose in writing this comic strip?* **L2**
COLLAB. LEARN.

Additional Resources

- **Reading Workbook**

Before You Read

The Censors

FOCUS ACTIVITY

Have you ever heard the expression, "If you can't lick 'em, join 'em"? It refers to a strategy for dealing with strong opponents when other attempts at besting them have failed. Can you imagine a situation in which you might use this strategy?

LIST IDEAS List the advantages and disadvantages of the strategy of joining up with opponents.

SETTING A PURPOSE Read to learn how a careful strategy backfires.

BACKGROUND

The Time and Place
Luisa Valenzuela doesn't name a specific city, country, or time in which "The Censors" takes place. The events most likely occur in Latin America during the middle of the 1900s. However, a story of censors and censorship could take place almost anywhere at any time.

Did You Know?
The job of a censor is to limit the kinds of information people have access to. Censors examine print materials or other media, such as films, and either remove objectionable parts or completely reject the material. For example, a censor might remove a book with crude language from a school library. A censor in the military might examine personal mail and delete information that would threaten national secu-

rity. Some authoritarian governments control the news media, dictating what kinds of news can be reported.

People disagree over the issue of censorship. Some think there should be no censorship at all. Others believe that it is desirable to control the spread of information that might harm people. Still others use censorship as a form of power, to control people by controlling what they hear or read.

Meet Luisa Valenzuela

Luisa Valenzuela wrote her first short story, "City of the Unknown," when she was seventeen, claiming that she "slipped into mother's footsteps." (Her mother is also a writer.) Valenzuela writes about Argentinean politics as well as the fate of women in repressive societies. Many of her works combine the real and the fantastic, a Latin American style called "magical realism."

Luisa Valenzuela was born in 1938 in Buenos Aires, Argentina. "The Censors" was first published in 1976.

VOCABULARY PREVIEW

irreproachable (ir′ i prō′ chə bəl) *adj.* free from blame or criticism; faultless; p. 218

albeit (ôl bē′ it) *conj.* although; even if; p. 219

ulterior (ul tēr′ ē ər) *adj.* intentionally withheld or concealed; p. 219

staidness (stād′ nəs) *n.* the state or quality of being serious, steady, or conservative in character; p. 219

subversive (sub vur′ siv) *adj.* seeking to weaken, destroy, or overthrow; p. 220

Before Reading

Objectives
- To read and analyze a short story about a man who is a victim of his own careful strategy
- To identify satire in the story
- To write a character analysis

Skills
Reading/Thinking: Drawing Conclusions
Writing: Ballad
Vocabulary: Usage
Grammar/Language: Intervening Prepositional Phrases
Life Skills: Writing Satire
Collaboration: Literature Groups

Motivating → OPTIONS

Selection Focus Transparency 18: Discuss ways that governments and social groups use both formal and informal methods of censorship to control what people say, hear, write, read, see, or do.

Focus Activity: Have the class compile a master list of advantages and disadvantages.

RESOURCE MANAGER

Lesson Planning Resource
The *Unit One Planning Guide* (pp. 148–155) provides additional lesson notes and reduced versions of all print resources.

📁 **Other Print Resources**
- Active Reading Guide, p. 18
- Vocabulary Practice, p. 17
- Reading Workbook, p. 20
- Grammar and Language Workbook, p. 163
- Grammar and Composition Handbook, Lesson 6.2

- Quick Checks, p. 18
- Selection and Theme Assessment, pp. 35–36
- Performance Assessment, p. 18
- Spanish Summaries, p. 18
- Spanish Translations
- Inclusion Strategies
- English Language Learners Sourcebook

📖 **Transparencies**
- Selection Focus 18
- Literary Elements 18

- Grammar and Language 19

Technology
- 🎧 Audio Library
- 🎧 Spanish Audio Library
- 💻 Glencoe Literature Web Site
- 💾 Testmaker

THE CENSORS

Luisa Valenzuela

SUMMARY

Juan thinks he is outsmarting the system by taking a government job as a censor. He applies himself so diligently to his work, no one would ever guess he is merely biding his time—waiting weeks, months, years even, if that's how long it takes, to intercept a letter he himself wrote. But his life takes an unexpected twist. Zeal and duty win out over his original mission, and Juan, the perfect censor, seals his own fate.

📁 *Spanish Summaries,* p. 18

A Active Reading

PREDICT Have students read the title and first paragraph. Ask them why Juan is so worried simply because of writing a letter. Ask them to predict what he might do. Remind students that good readers revise their predictions as they read.

Additional Resources

📁 *Active Reading Guide,* p. 18
🎧 *Audio Library*
🎧 *Spanish Audio Library*

Teaching Options

POOR JUAN! One day they caught him with his guard down before he could even realize that what he had taken as a stroke of luck was really one of fate's dirty tricks. These things happen the minute you're careless, as one often is. Juancito[1] let happiness—a feeling you can't trust—get the better of him when he received from a confidential source Mariana's new address in Paris and knew that she hadn't forgotten him. Without thinking twice, he sat down at his table and wrote her a letter. *The* letter that now keeps his mind off his job during the day and won't let him sleep at night (what had he scrawled, what had he put on that sheet of paper he sent to Mariana?).

Juan knows there won't be a problem with the letter's contents, that it's <u>irreproachable</u>, harmless. But what about the rest? He knows that they examine, sniff, feel, and read between the lines of each and every letter, and check its tiniest comma and most accidental stain. He knows that all letters pass from hand to hand and go through all sorts of tests in the huge censorship offices and that, in the end, very few continue on their way. Usually it takes months, even years, if there aren't any snags; all this time the freedom, maybe even the life, of both sender and receiver is in jeopardy. And that's why Juan's so troubled: thinking that something might happen to Mariana because of his letters. Of all people, Mariana, who must finally feel safe there where she always dreamt she'd live. But he knows that the *Censor's Secret Command* operates all over the world and cashes in on the discount in air fares; there's nothing to stop them from going as far as that hidden Paris neighborhood, kidnapping Mariana, and returning to their cozy homes, certain of having fulfilled their noble mission.

Well, you've got to beat them to the punch, do what everyone tries to do: sabotage the machinery, throw sand in its gears, get to the bottom of the problem so as to stop it.

This was Juan's sound plan when he, like many others, applied for a censor's job—not because he had a calling or needed a job: no,

---

1. *Juancito* (wän sē′ tō)

Vocabulary
irreproachable (ir′ i prō′ chə bəl) *adj.* free from blame or criticism; faultless

CONNECTING TO OTHER SELECTIONS

The chart at the right shows three ways to connect "The Censors" to selections in this book.

For specific teaching strategies, see the *Unit One Planning Guide,* pp. 151–152.

Connection	Title
Life Skills: Implementing and Performing	→ "Through the Tunnel," p. 76
Thematic: Devotion to Duty	→ "With All Flags Flying," p. 115
Literary: Irony	→ "Winter Night," p. 363

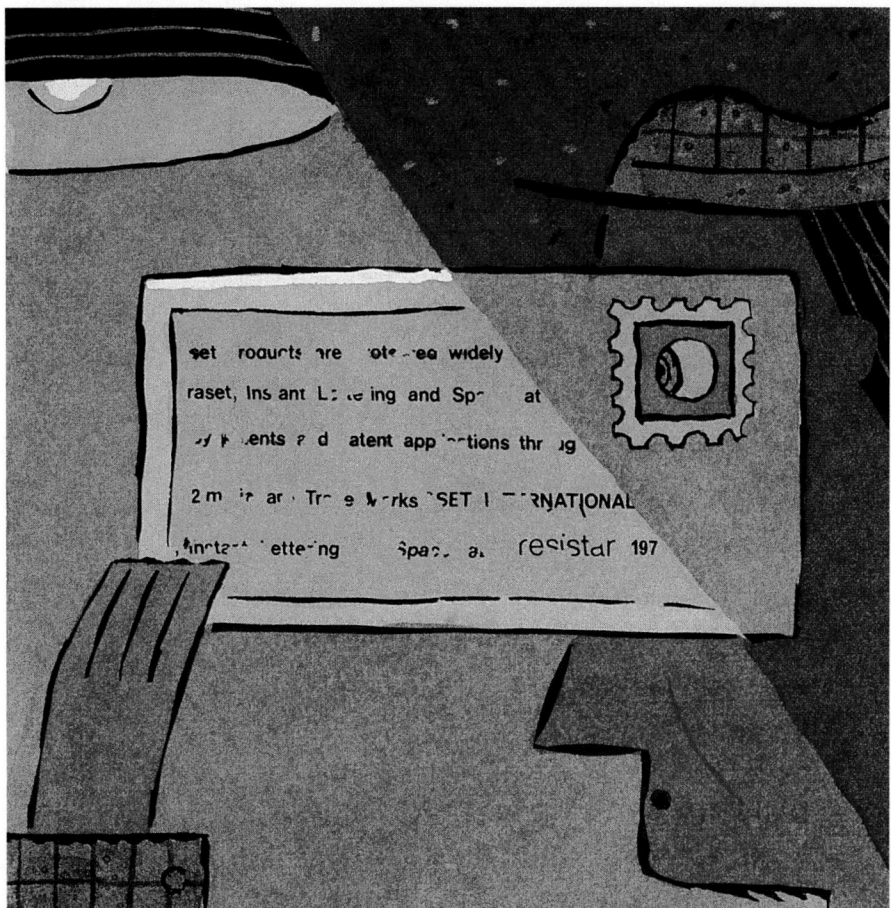

he applied simply to intercept his own letter, a consoling <u>albeit</u> unoriginal idea. He was hired immediately, for each day more and more censors are needed and no one would bother to check on his references.

Ulterior motives couldn't be overlooked by the *Censorship Division*, but they needn't be too strict with those who applied. They knew how hard it would be for the poor guys to find the

letter they wanted and even if they did, what's a letter or two when the new censor would snap up so many others? That's how Juan managed to join the *Post Office's Censorship Division*, with a certain goal in mind.

The building had a festive air on the outside that contrasted with its inner <u>staidness</u>. Little by little, Juan was absorbed by his job, and he felt at peace since he was doing

---

Vocabulary
albeit (ôl bē′ it) *conj.* although; even if
ulterior (ul tēr′ ē ər) *adj.* intentionally withheld or concealed; hidden
staidness (stād′ nəs) *n.* the state or quality of being serious, steady, or conservative in character

B **Literary Elements**

TONE Ask students to point out phrases that create an ominous tone. *("they caught him with his guard down"; "one of fate's dirty tricks"; "a feeling you can't trust"; "without thinking twice")*

C **Literary Elements**

SATIRE Explain that satire is the use of humor or wit to ridicule institutions or humanity with the goal of changing things. Point out humorous details in the author's satire of the censors' work. *(cashing in on discount airfares, kidnapping, returning to cozy homes, feeling that they fulfill a noble mission)*

D **Active Reading**

PREDICT What does the ease with which Juan is hired suggest about his situation? Use the following model to show students how to predict.

Model: If Juan's scheme is unoriginal, then the government must know he is up to something. Many people have probably done the same thing. That he is hired without a hitch should make him suspect a setup. The government might be manipulating him into a position in which he will have to incriminate Mariana or himself.

MEETING INDIVIDUAL NEEDS — ENGLISH LANGUAGE LEARNERS

Discussing Civil Rights Some English language learners may come from cultures in which government censorship is common. Set aside time for students to explain how life in such a society differs from life in the United States.

Activity Bring in newspaper and magazine articles that deal with censorship issues in students' native countries or

other countries. Use the articles to illustrate that censorship is a reality in many parts of the world today. Encourage students who have firsthand experience with censorship to share what they know.

Additional Resources
📁 *English Language Learners Sourcebook*

E Critical Thinking

DRAWING CONCLUSIONS What was Juan's "noble mission"? What is happening to him? *(He wanted to retrieve his letter. But in his eagerness to move up and into sections where he might find the letter, he begins to forget why he became a censor and to take his work very seriously.)*

F Literary Elements

SATIRE Juan has now decided that his mission all along was to become the perfect censor. How does this transformation become the punch line of the satire? *(Juan becomes such a perfect censor that he censors his own letter. Because of that, he ends up "censoring" his entire existence: the government executes him.)*

Thematic Focus

Making Choices Ask students whether they think what happened to Juan happens to most people who join an enemy in order to try to defeat the enemy from within.

✓ ASSESSMENT OPTIONS

📁 *Quick Checks,* p. 18

THE CENSORS

everything he could to get his letter for Mariana. He didn't even worry when, in his first month, he was sent to *Section K* where envelopes are very carefully screened for explosives.

It's true that on the third day, a fellow worker had his right hand blown off by a letter, but the division chief claimed it was sheer negligence on the victim's part. Juan and the other employees were allowed to go back to their work, though feeling less secure. After work, one of them tried to organize a strike to demand higher wages for unhealthy work, but Juan didn't join in; after thinking it over, he reported the man to his superiors and thus got promoted.

You don't form a habit by doing something once, he told himself as he left his boss's office. And when he was transferred to *Section J,* where letters are carefully checked for poison dust, he felt he had climbed a rung in the ladder.

By working hard, he quickly reached *Section E* where the job became more interesting, for he could now read and analyze the letters' contents. Here he could even hope to get hold of his letter, which, judging by the time that had elapsed, had gone through the other sections and was probably floating around in this one.

E Soon his work became so absorbing that his noble mission blurred in his mind. Day after day he crossed out whole paragraphs in red ink, pitilessly chucking many letters into the censored basket. These were horrible days when he was shocked by the subtle and conniving ways employed by people to pass on <u>subversive</u> messages; his instincts were so

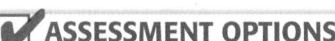

sharp that he found behind a simple "the weather's unsettled" or "prices continue to soar" the wavering hand of someone secretly scheming to overthrow the Government.

His zeal brought him swift promotion. We don't know if this made him happy. Very few letters reached him in *Section B*—only a handful passed the other hurdles—so he read them over and over again, passed them under a magnifying glass, searched for microprint with an electronic microscope, and tuned his sense of smell so that he was beat by the time he made it home. He'd barely manage to warm up his soup, eat some fruit, and fall into bed, satisfied with having done his duty. Only his darling mother worried, but she couldn't get him back on the right track. She'd say, though it wasn't always true: Lola called, she's at the bar with the girls, they miss you, they're waiting for you. Or else she'd leave a bottle of red wine on the table. But Juan wouldn't overdo it: any distraction could make him lose his edge and the perfect censor had to be alert, keen, attentive, and sharp to nab cheats. He had a truly patriotic task, both self-denying and uplifting.

His basket for censored letters became the best fed as well as the most cunning basket in the whole *Censorship Division.* He was about to congratulate himself for having finally discovered his true mission, when his letter to Mariana reached his hands. Naturally, he censored it without regret. And just as naturally, he couldn't stop them from executing him the following morning, another victim of his devotion to his work. **F**

Vocabulary
subversive (sub vur′ siv) *adj.* seeking to weaken, destroy, or overthrow

220 ❦ UNIT 1

Teaching Options

Grammar and Language *Minilesson*

Intervening Prepositional Phrases A verb must agree with its subject in number and person. Students may mistakenly match the verb with the object of a preposition that comes between the subject and the predicate. Suggest that they delete the prepositional phrase so that the actual subject is placed next to the verb.

Activity Have students rewrite each sentence, underlining the simple subject and the verb and enclosing the intervening prepositional phrase in parentheses.
1. Juan's passion for censoring letters takes over his life. *(Juan's <u>passion</u> (for censoring letters) <u>takes</u> over his life.)*
2. His mission during the early weeks is to help Mariana. *(His <u>mission</u> (during the early weeks) <u>is</u> to help Mariana.)* **L2**

Additional Resources

🖌 *Grammar and Language Transparency 19*

📗 *Grammar and Language Workbook,* p. 163

📘 *Grammar and Composition Handbook,* Lesson 6.2

📘 *Writer's Choice,* Lesson 16.2

220

Responding to Literature

Personal Response

What feelings did you have about Juan at the end of the story? Did your feelings about him change during the course of the story? Explain.

───── ANALYZING LITERATURE ─────

RECALL

1. What does Juan do as soon as he gets Mariana's address? How does he feel?
2. What was Juan's plan in applying for a censor's job?
3. What accounts for Juan's promotion from *Section K*?
4. Briefly describe Juan's way of life by the time he's promoted to *Section B*.
5. What happens to Juan as a "natural" result of his censoring skills?

INTERPRET

6. Why, do you think, does Juan feel so strongly about what he has done?
7. At the beginning of the story, how does Juan feel about the *Censor's Secret Command* and the government of his country in general?
8. "'You don't form a habit by doing something once,' he told himself as he left his boss's office." What, do you think, is the "something," and what has it got to do with Juan's transfer from *Section K* to *Section J*?
9. In your opinion, what are the advantages and disadvantages of Juan's new way of life?
10. Valenzuela says of Juan, "naturally he couldn't stop them . . . ," but she doesn't say why. In your opinion, why can't Juan stop them?

EVALUATE AND CONNECT

11. Think back to the list you made for the Focus Activity on page 217. After reading this story, what other advantages and disadvantages would you add to your list?
12. What do you think accounts for the change in Juan over the course of the story?
13. What parts of this story seem logical and believable to you? Are there any parts that are unbelievable? Use details from the story to explain.
14. In your opinion, what does Valenzuela achieve by keeping the **tone** of the story so light and "natural"? (See page R13.)
15. Is there anything in this story that frightens you? Explain your answer.

Literary ELEMENTS

Satire

Satire is writing that uses humor or wit to ridicule institutions or humanity for the purpose of effecting change or improvement. There are two kinds of satire: one that uses gentle, accepting humor, and one that attacks with bitter and angry humor. Many satiric works fall into one of these categories.

1. How does Valenzuela signal the reader in paragraph one that this story may be a satire?
2. Identify the subtle humor in the way Valenzuela describes the method the *Censor's Secret Command* uses for retrieving criminals.
3. What do you think the object of Valenzuela's satire is in this story? What is she trying to correct by using satire?

● See **Literary Terms Handbook**, p. R11.

Personal Response

Some students may have thought he lost his mind; others may have felt sorry for him. At first, students may have thought him clever and later thought him cold-hearted.

ANALYZING LITERATURE

1. He writes her a letter because he is so happy to know where she is and that she is thinking of him. Then he worries about writing the letter.
2. He planned to intercept the letter he wrote Mariana.
3. He reports a fellow employee who tries to organize a strike.
4. He is obsessed with his job, caring for little else but censorship. He barely eats and sleeps and has no social life.
5. He gets promoted to the top, censors his own letter, and is executed.
6. He fears for Mariana's safety.
7. He realizes they are powerful but disagrees with what they do.
8. Turning in a fellow employee is the "something" Juan did, and it was the reason he was promoted to *Section J*.
9. Students may say that the advantages are that he has the power to intercept letters or to let information slip through the system, and the disadvantages are that he works too hard and he has lost his sense of values.
10. Some students may say that since he judged his own letter subversive, he knows he must pay the same penalty as others have whose letters he judged subversive.
11. Possible advantages: gain power, get an insider's perspective on the problem. Possible disadvantages: you get swayed to the other side, you never get the chance to "beat 'em."
12. He becomes obsessed with power; the job gives him an outlet for his zeal and devotion; he loses sight of his original goal.
13. Government censorship, people's fear of censorship, and execution for crimes, all seem believable. Students may say that it seems unbelievable that Juan would think he could retrieve one letter; that his letter would come

---

LITERARY ELEMENTS

1. She uses humor to describe Juan's predicament with regard to the letter.
2. She pokes fun by claiming they use discount airfares.
3. She is speaking out against government censorship. She uses satire to show that censorship does not cure problems.

Additional Resources

📖 *Literary Elements Transparency 18*

---

to him; and that Juan would change so much.

14. Students may say that the light, natural tone keeps the story from being too somber and depressing and is in keeping with the author's wish to criticize the system by poking fun at it.

15. Students may find the change that overcame Juan frightening.

LITERATURE AND WRITING

Writing About Literature

Students' character analyses should
- tell what Juan is like at the beginning of the story.
- tell what Juan is like at the end of the story.
- compare and contrast these two sets of traits.
- give reasons for the changes.

Creative Writing

Students' ballads should
- follow the tone and format of ballads or folk songs.
- characterize Juan as either hero or victim.
- convey a message about his actions, particularly in the refrain.

EXTENDING YOUR RESPONSE

Literature Groups Students may wish to refer back to what they discovered about censorship and personal freedom in the Media Connection Internet activity on page 216.
COLLAB. LEARN.

Learning for Life Students could also submit their satires to the school or community newspaper.

Internet Connection As an extension, students might want to bring in examples of political cartoons by prizewinning cartoonists.

Skill Minilesson

VOCABULARY • Usage

1. I wonder what ulterior plans he has.
2. Some people find her ideas alarming, but really they are irreproachable.
3. There is nothing at all subversive about her message.

Additional Resources
📁 *Vocabulary Practice,* p. 17

LITERATURE AND WRITING

Writing About Literature

Character Analysis Juan undergoes many changes during his attempt to intercept his letter to Mariana. Write a character analysis of Juan comparing the traits he exhibits at the beginning of the story with those he exhibits as the story unfolds. Discuss the reasons for the changes in his character.

Creative Writing

Juan, Juan, Juan A **ballad** is a narrative poem or song often about a folk hero. Write a ballad about Juan. For models, listen to folk songs of the 1960s and 1970s. Before writing your ballad, decide if Juan was a victim or a hero. Then decide on the message you want to deliver. Use the refrain, or repeated chorus, to stress your point.

EXTENDING YOUR RESPONSE

Literature Groups

Uncensored Thoughts Imagine that you live in a country like Juan's where the government denies freedom to the citizens. How might government officials react to "The Censors"? How might you, the people, react to the story if you were allowed to read it? In your group, discuss whether Valenzuela's satire could be an effective tool for changing people's opinion. Share your groups' thoughts with the class.

Learning for Life

A Gentle Satire Think of something that you feel should be changed: bus routes in your town, the length of lunch break in your school, the voting age. Address the issue by writing a gentle satire for your school's literary magazine. Use humor and wit to make your point.

Internet Connection

Prize-Winning Cartoons Creators of political cartoons for newspapers and newsmagazines often use satire to express their views. Political cartoons are so important that the Pulitzer Prize committee awards a prize each year in the category of Editorial Cartoons. Search the Internet for winners from the past five years.

📖 **Save your work for your portfolio.**

Skill Minilesson

VOCABULARY • Usage

Dictionaries rarely provide enough information about how words are used. Although one meaning for *ulterior* is "intentionally withheld or concealed; hidden," a person concealed in the closet during Hide and Seek is not ulterior. In "The Censors," *ulterior* is used to modify *motive,* or intentions, and this is its most common use.

A word used to describe one thing may not be appropriate to describe something else. For example, a painter's work habits may be irreproachable; a perfectly painted wall is not. Reading and listening are the best ways to discover how words are actually used.

PRACTICE Review how each of the following words is used in "The Censors." Then write your own sentence for each, using it in a similar way.

1. ulterior
2. irreproachable
3. subversive

✔ ASSESSMENT OPTIONS

📁 *Quick Checks,* p. 18
📁 *Selection and Theme Assessment,* pp. 35–36
📁 *Performance Assessment,* p. 18
💾 *Testmaker*

Reading & Thinking Skills

Making Predictions

As you read "The Censors," did you suspect that Juan might be in danger? If so, you were **predicting**, or making an educated guess about what would happen next. Make predictions and check them as you read to add to your involvement in the story.

As you're making predictions, notice the author's use of foreshadowing, or signs about what's going to happen next. Small details, or even the author's expressions and tone, can signal big events or deeper meaning. In "The Censors," for example, the narrator says:

> Little by little, Juan was absorbed by his job, and he felt at peace since he was doing everything he could to get his letter for Mariana. He didn't even worry when, in his first month, he was sent to *Section K* where envelopes are very carefully screened for explosives.

The narrator's tone implies that perhaps Juan *should* have been worried and suggests that Juan really might be in danger. As you gather more information in the course of your reading, you may find that you want to change your predictions.

● For more about related reading strategies, see **Reading Handbook**, pp. R78–R107.

ACTIVITY

The following paragraphs are from "The False Gems," by Maupassant, a story that appears later in this unit. The passage describes a young middle-class couple in Paris in the 1800s. Read the passage, then, on a separate piece of paper, do the exercise that follows.

> He found fault with only two of [his wife's] tastes: Her love for the theatre, and her taste for imitation jewelry. . . . Around her neck she wore strings of false pearls, and on her arms bracelets of imitation gold. . . .
>   Sometimes, . . . she would . . . examine the false gems with a passionate attention, as though they imparted some deep and secret joy; and she often persisted in passing a necklace around her husband's neck, and, laughing heartily, would exclaim: "How droll you look!" Then she would throw herself into his arms, and kiss him affectionately.

● Predict two possible conflicts that might be central to "The False Gems." Then predict the outcome of each conflict. Note the information that helped you make your predictions.

Reading & Thinking Skills

Objective

● To recognize details that help readers make predictions as they read

Teaching Strategies

For additional tips on making predictions, refer students back to the Active Reading Strategies on pages 14–15 of this book.

Activity

Students may predict that the husband and wife have a conflict when the wife wants to spend money on luxuries beyond their means, such as attending the theater or buying jewelry. The outcome might be that she drives him to financial ruin with her overspending. They may also predict that the couple will have a conflict about the costume jewelry she loves to wear but he dislikes. The outcome might be that she is very hurt and he buys her real jewelry to make her feel better.

Additional Resources
📁 *Reading Workbook*

MEETING INDIVIDUAL NEEDS — INCLUSION STRATEGIES

Less-Proficient Readers Most students enjoy making predictions about the final outcome of a story. Encourage students to always make predictions about content before reading a selection. After reading, have them defend or reject their predictions.

Activity Brainstorming with a small group of classmates might help students make predictions about the conflicts the young couple might face. Encourage students to read each sentence carefully and to list as many possibilities as they can before narrowing their choices to two. **L1**

Additional Resources
📁 *Inclusion Strategies*

Objectives

- To read and analyze a short story about how a wife's choice affects her marriage
- To identify how the author develops characters in the story
- To compare and contrast two characters

Skills

Reading/Thinking: Inferring; Identifying Spatial Relationships
Writing: Sequel
Vocabulary: Antonyms
Grammar/Language: Perfect Tenses
Listening/Speaking: Performing a Dialogue
Collaboration: Literature Groups

Motivating
→OPTIONS

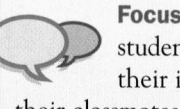

Selection Focus Transparency 19: Encourage students to discuss what body language reveals about relationships between people.

Focus Activity: Have student pairs compare their ideas with those of their classmates.

Before You Read
The Ring

──── FOCUS ACTIVITY ────

Do you know anyone who has been happily married for a long time? In your opinion, what character traits are necessary for a long and successful marriage?

SHARING IDEAS Discuss with a partner the character traits you would most value in a spouse. What traits might make a marriage difficult?

SETTING A PURPOSE Read to learn how the choice a wife makes affects her relationship with her husband.

──── BACKGROUND ────

The Time and Place
"The Ring" takes place in the Danish countryside, around 1800. At that time, most people in Denmark lived on farms.

Did You Know?
Gentle and submissive by nature, sheep make ideal farm animals. Domestic sheep provide a variety of valuable products, including meat, wool, pelts, and milk. Sheep live in flocks

and are known as followers. When out grazing, they may separate slightly, but as soon as one sheep begins to move to a new location, the rest will follow, often in a single file. Domestic sheep are quite timid and virtually defenseless when attacked by predators. Thus, they must depend on humans to protect and care for them.

──── VOCABULARY PREVIEW ────

rustic (rus′ tik) *adj.* of, or relating to, the country; p. 226
void (void) *n.* an empty space; vacuum; p. 228
apparition (ap′ ə rish′ ən) *n.* something strange or unexpected that comes suddenly into view, as a ghost; p. 229
definitive (di fin′ ə tiv) *adj.* conclusive; final; decisive; p. 230
unconditional (un′ kən dish′ ən əl) *adj.* absolute; complete; p. 230
conceive (kən sēv′) *v.* to form a mental image or idea of; imagine; p. 230

Meet Isak Dinesen

Isak Dinesen (ē′ säk di′ nə sən) is the pen name of the Danish writer Karen Blixen, who spent seventeen years managing a coffee plantation in eastern Africa. Dinesen recorded the triumphs and sorrows of those years in her memoir *Out of Africa*, from which the Oscar-winning film of the same name was made in 1985. Dinesen returned to the family estate at Rungstedlund in 1931 and devoted herself to her writing. "As for me I have one ambition only: to invent stories, very beautiful stories," she said. Her short story collections include *Seven Gothic Tales* and *Winter's Tales*.

Isak Dinesen was born in 1885 in Rungsted, Denmark. She died there in 1962. This story was first published in 1953.

RESOURCE MANAGER

Lesson Planning Resource
The *Unit One Planning Guide* (pp. 156–163) provides additional lesson notes and reduced versions of all print resources.

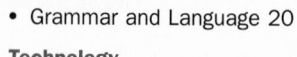 **Other Print Resources**
- Active Reading Guide, p. 19
- Vocabulary Practice, p. 18
- Reading Workbook, p. 22
- Grammar and Language Workbook, p. 147
- Grammar and Composition Handbook, Lesson 5.4

- Quick Checks, p. 19
- Selection and Theme Assessment, pp. 37–38
- Performance Assessment, p. 19
- Spanish Summaries, p. 19
- Spanish Translations
- Inclusion Strategies
- English Language Learners Sourcebook

 Transparencies
- Selection Focus 19
- Literary Elements 19

- Grammar and Language 20

Technology

 Audio Library
 Spanish Audio Library
Glencoe Literature Web Site
 Testmaker

The Ring

Isak Dinesen :~

ON A SUMMER MORNING a hundred and fifty years ago a young Danish squire and his wife went out for a walk on their land. They had been married a week. It had not been easy for them to get married, for the wife's family was higher in rank and wealthier than the husband's. But the two young people, now twenty-four and nineteen years old, had been set on their purpose for ten years; and in the end her haughty parents had had to give in to them.

Summer Day near Thordager, Arrhus. Pauline Thomsen (1858–1931). Oil on canvas, 36½ x 50 in. Private collection.

SUMMARY

In Denmark around 1800, newlyweds Sigismund and Lise stroll blissfully across their sheep fields. Their pleasure is interrupted when they learn that a thief has been terrorizing neighboring sheepfolds and has killed a shepherd. While Sigismund looks after two sick lambs, Lise walks on. Feeling spurned, she decides to hide from Sigismund. As she enters a hidden grove, she finds herself face to face with the sheep thief. The ensuing events change Lise—and her marriage.

📁 *Spanish Summaries,* p. 19

🅐 Active Reading

CONNECT Help students make connections between what they read and their personal experiences. Ask questions such as these: What do you think the title refers to? When do couples give each other rings? Why might a ring be important in this story?

Additional Resources

📁 *Active Reading Guide,* p. 19
🎧 *Audio Library*
🎧 *Spanish Audio Library*

Teaching Options

CONNECTING TO OTHER SELECTIONS

The chart at the right shows three ways to connect "The Ring" to selections in this book.

For specific teaching strategies, see the *Unit One Planning Guide,* pp. 159–160.

Connection	Title
Life Skills: Life-long Learning	→ "A Swimming Lesson," p. 495
Thematic: Responsibilities	→ "A White Heron," p. 143
Literary: Theme	→ "To Da-duh, in Memoriam," p. 399

B Author's Craft

FORESHADOWING What foreshadowing, or hints of things to come, does the author offer in the thoughts of the young husband and wife? *(Sigismund wants to remove all stones and shadows from his wife's path. There will probably be stones and shadows for her. Lise believes she can never have any secret from her husband. She will probably keep a secret from him.)*

C Literary Elements

CHARACTER What do these details tell the reader about Lise? *(That she compares marriage to playing with dolls would seem to say that she is very young and very ignorant about marriage.)*

D Literary Elements

PLOT: *Internal Conflict* How does Lise's internal monologue reveal conflicting feelings about her husband? Are these feelings a good sign for the marriage? *(On the one hand, she thinks he is clever; on the other, she thinks he is a baby. Such conflicting feelings may be another sign of her immaturity, which will not help the marriage.)*

E Literary Elements

CHARACTER How do Lise's thoughts further reveal her childish nature? *(She compares the sheep thief to a fairy tale character, Red Riding Hood's wolf. She feels a thrill at the thought of the thief-wolf.)*

Teaching Options

They were wonderfully happy. The stolen meetings and secret, tearful love letters were now things of the past. To God and man they were one; they could walk arm in arm in broad daylight and drive in the same carriage, and they would walk and drive so till the end of their days. Their distant paradise had descended to earth and had proved, surprisingly, to be filled with the things of everyday life: with jesting and railleries,[1] with breakfasts and suppers, with dogs, haymaking and sheep. Sigismund, the young husband, had promised himself that from now there should be no stone in his bride's path, nor should any shadow fall across it. Lovisa, the wife, felt that now, every day and for the first time in her young life, she moved and breathed in perfect freedom because she could never have any secret from her husband.

To Lovisa—whom her husband called Lise—the <u>rustic</u> atmosphere of her new life was a matter of wonder and delight. Her husband's fear that the existence he could offer her might not be good enough for her filled her heart with laughter. It was not a long time since she had played with dolls; as now she dressed her own hair, looked over her linen press and arranged her flowers she again lived through an enchanting and cherished experience: one was doing everything gravely and solicitously, and all the time one knew one was playing.

It was a lovely July morning. Little woolly clouds drifted high up in the sky, the air was full of sweet scents. Lise had on a white muslin frock and a large Italian straw hat. She and her husband took a path through the park; it wound on across the meadows, between small groves and groups of trees, to the sheep field. Sigismund was going to show his wife his sheep. For this reason she had not brought her small white dog, Bijou, with her, for he would yap at the lambs and frighten them, or he would annoy the sheep dogs. Sigismund prided himself on his sheep; he had studied sheep-breeding in Mecklenburg[2] and England, and had brought back with him Cotswold rams by which to improve his Danish stock. While they walked he explained to Lise the great possibilities and difficulties of the plan.

Did You Know?
Cotswold is a breed of sheep with long, coarse hair, originally bred in the Cotswold Hills of southwestern England.

She thought: "How clever he is, what a lot of things he knows!" and at the same time: "What an absurd person he is, with his sheep! What a baby he is! I am a hundred years older than he."

But when they arrived at the sheepfold the old sheepmaster Mathias met them with the sad news that one of the English lambs was dead and two were sick. Lise saw that her husband was grieved by the tidings; while he questioned Mathias on the matter she kept silent and only gently pressed his arm. A couple of boys were sent off to fetch the sick lambs, while the master and servant went into the details of the case. It took some time.

Lise began to gaze about her and to think of other things. Twice her own thoughts made her blush deeply and happily, like a red rose, then slowly her blush died away, and the two men were still talking about sheep. A little while after their conversation caught her attention. It had turned to a sheep thief.

---

1. *Railleries* are instances of good-natured ridicule or teasing.

2. *Mecklenburg* is a farming region in northeastern Germany.

Vocabulary
rustic (rus' tik) *adj.* of, or relating to, the country

ENGLISH LANGUAGE LEARNERS

Marriage Marital traditions have many variations. Invite English language learners to discuss marital and wedding traditions in their cultures.

Activity Ask students questions such as these: What is a typical wedding like? What do brides wear? Do people always dance at weddings? Do people always choose who they will marry?

What kinds of gifts are given to newlyweds? Who is invited to a wedding? At what age should a person usually marry? Students might interview older relatives about their weddings and report back to the class.

Additional Resources
📁 *English Language Learners Sourcebook*

This thief during the last months had broken into the sheepfolds of the neighborhood like a wolf, had killed and dragged away his prey like a wolf and like a wolf had left no trace after him. Three nights ago the shepherd and his son on an estate ten miles away had caught him in the act. The thief had killed the man and knocked the boy senseless, and had managed to escape. There were men sent out to all sides to catch him, but nobody had seen him.

Lise wanted to hear more about the horrible event, and for her benefit old Mathias went through it once more. There had been a long fight in the sheep house, in many places the earthen floor was soaked with blood. In the fight the thief's left arm was broken; all the same, he had climbed a tall fence with a lamb on his back. Mathias added that he would like to string up the murderer with these two hands of his, and Lise nodded her head at him gravely in approval. She remembered Red Ridinghood's wolf, and felt a pleasant little thrill running down her spine.

Sigismund had his own lambs in his mind, but he was too happy in himself to wish anything in the universe ill. After a minute he said: "Poor devil."

Lise said: "How can you pity such a terrible man? Indeed Grandmamma was right when she said that you were a revolutionary and a danger to society!" The thought of Grandmamma, and of the tears of past days, again turned her mind away from the gruesome tale she had just heard.

The boys brought the sick lambs and the men began to examine them carefully, lifting them up and trying to set them on their legs; they squeezed them here and there and made the little creatures whimper. Lise shrank from the show and her husband noticed her distress. "You go home, my darling," he said, "this will take some time. But just walk ahead slowly, and I shall catch up with you."

So she was turned away by an impatient husband to whom his sheep meant more than his wife. If any experience could be sweeter than to be dragged out by him to look at those same sheep, it would be this. She dropped her large summer hat with its blue ribbons on the grass and told him to carry it back for her, for she wanted to feel the summer air on her forehead and in her hair. She walked on very slowly, as he had told her to do, for she wished to obey him in everything. As she walked she felt a great new happiness in being altogether alone, even without Bijou. She could not remember that she had ever before in all her life been altogether alone. The landscape around her was still, as if full of promise, and it was hers. Even the swallows cruising in the air were hers, for they belonged to him, and he was hers.

She followed the curving edge of the grove and after a minute or two found that she was out of sight to the men by the sheep house. What could now, she wondered, be sweeter than to walk along the path in the long flowering meadow grass, slowly, slowly, and to let her husband overtake her there? It would be sweeter still, she reflected, to steal into the grove and to be gone, to have vanished from the surface of the earth from him when, tired of the sheep and longing for her company, he should turn the bend of the path to catch up with her.

An idea struck her; she stood still to think it over.

A few days ago her husband had gone for a ride and she had not wanted to go with him, but had strolled about with Bijou in order to explore her domain. Bijou then, gamboling, had led her straight into the grove. As she had followed him, gently forcing her way into the shrubbery, she had suddenly come upon a glade in the midst of it, a narrow space like a small alcove with hangings of thick green and

---

F Critical Thinking

INFERRING Ask students why they think Lise responds to Sigismund's comment, "Poor devil," the way she does. *(Perhaps she is teasing him. They do indulge in jesting and railleries. Perhaps she is trying to start a fight. She is bored with all the talk about sheep. Perhaps she is shocked by his comment and wonders if her family's complaints might be true.)*

G Active Reading

QUESTION Was Sigismund impatient? Did he turn her away? What is wrong with Lise's interpretation? *(She is overreacting to her husband's suggestion.)*

H Active Reading

EVALUATE Lise thinks she was "dragged out" by Sigismund to look at his sheep, and yet she can't imagine a sweeter experience. What does she mean? Share the following model to illustrate the thinking process involved in evaluating a character.

Model: From what I have read about her, I think Lise craves emotional rushes. Perhaps she loved fighting for Sigismund more than she loves him; she relished secret meetings, love letters, crying, and arguing with her family. Now she seems to be looking for a new conflict to fill her with emotion.

MEETING INDIVIDUAL NEEDS — INCLUSION STRATEGIES

Less-Proficient Readers Foster active reading. Help students create a cluster diagram as they read. By adding information to the diagram, students document their progress through the story, which will motivate their continued reading.

Activity Draw a cluster diagram on the board. Students can copy the diagram onto paper. As they read, they can add to the diagram details that describe Lise. Encourage students to note as many details as they can find about her thoughts, feelings, attitudes, personality, and appearance. **L1**

Additional Resources
📁 *Inclusion Strategies*

Le Chemineau (The Hobo). Gustave Courbet (1819–1877). Municipal Museum, Dole, France.

Viewing the painting: What characteristics do you see in this man that the thief might share?

golden brocade, big enough to hold two or three people in it. She had felt at that moment that she had come into the very heart of her new home. If today she could find the spot again she would stand perfectly still there, hidden from all the world. Sigismund would look for her in all directions; he would be unable to understand what had become of her and for a minute, for a short minute—or, perhaps, if she

was firm and cruel enough, for five—he would realize what a void, what an unendurably sad and horrible place the universe would be when she was no longer in it. She gravely scrutinized the grove to find the right entrance to her hiding-place, then went in.

She took great care to make no noise at all, therefore advanced exceedingly slowly. When a twig caught the flounces of her ample skirt she loosened it softly from the muslin, so as not to crack it. Once a branch took hold of one of her long golden curls; she stood still, with her arms lifted, to free it. A little way into the grove the soil became moist; her light steps no longer made any sound upon it. With one hand she held her small handkerchief to her lips, as if to emphasize the secretness of her course. She found the spot she sought and bent down to divide the foliage and make a door to her sylvan[3] closet. At this the hem of her dress caught her foot and she stopped to loosen it. As she rose she looked into the face of a man who was already in the shelter.

He stood up erect, two steps off. He must have watched her as she made her way straight toward him.

She took him in in one single glance. His face was bruised and scratched, his hands and wrists stained with dark filth. He was dressed in rags, barefooted, with tatters wound round his naked ankles. His arms hung down to his sides, his right hand clasped the hilt of a knife. He was about her own age. The man and the woman looked at each other.

---

3. *Sylvan* means "in or among woods, or formed by trees."

Vocabulary
void (void) *n.* an empty space; vacuum

228 UNIT 1

This meeting in the wood from beginning to end passed without a word; what happened could only be rendered by pantomime. To the two actors in the pantomime it was timeless; according to a clock it lasted four minutes.

She had never in her life been exposed to danger. It did not occur to her to sum up her position, or to work out the length of time it would take to call her husband or Mathias, whom at this moment she could hear shouting to his dogs. She beheld the man before her as she would have beheld a forest ghost: the apparition itself, not the sequels[4] of it, changes the world to the human who faces it.

Although she did not take her eyes off the face before her she sensed that the alcove had been turned into a covert.[5] On the ground a couple of sacks formed a couch; there were some gnawed bones by it. A fire must have been made here in the night, for there were cinders strewn on the forest floor.

After a while she realized that he was observing her just as she was observing him. He was no longer just run to earth and crouching for a spring, but he was wondering, trying to know. At that she seemed to see herself with the eyes of the wild animal at bay[6] in his dark hiding-place; her silently approaching white figure, which might mean death.

He moved his right arm till it hung down straight before him between his legs. Without lifting the hand he bent the wrist and slowly raised the point of the knife till it pointed at her throat. The gesture was mad, unbelievable.

He did not smile as he made it, but his nostrils distended,[7] the corners of his mouth quivered a little. Then slowly he put the knife back in the sheath by his belt.

She had no object of value about her, only the wedding ring which her husband had set on her finger in church, a week ago. She drew it off, and in this movement dropped her handkerchief. She reached out her hand with the ring toward him. She did not bargain for her life. She was fearless by nature, and the horror with which he inspired her was not fear of what he might do to her. She commanded him, she besought[8] him to vanish as he had come, to take a dreadful figure out of her life, so that it should never have been there. In the dumb[9] movement her young form had the grave authoritativeness[10] of a priestess conjuring down some monstrous being by a sacred sign.

He slowly reached out his hand to hers, his finger touched hers, and her hand was steady at the touch. But he did not take the ring. As she let it go it dropped to the ground as her handkerchief had done.

For a second the eyes of both followed it. It rolled a few inches toward him and stopped before his bare foot. In a hardly perceivable movement he kicked it away and again looked into her face. They remained like that, she knew not how long, but she felt that during that time something happened, things were changed.

He bent down and picked up her handkerchief. All the time gazing at her, he again drew his knife and wrapped the tiny bit of

---

4. Here, *sequels* refers to results or consequences.
5. As a noun, *covert* means "a hiding place." More often, you'll see the word used as an adjective to mean "secret, hidden, or concealed."
6. *At bay* refers to the position of a cornered animal that is forced to turn and confront its pursuers.

7. *Distended* means "enlarged or expanded."
8. *Besought* is the past tense of *beseech* and means "begged or asked earnestly."
9. Here, dumb means "silent; without words."
10. *Authoritativeness* is the quality of having and using the power to act or command.

Vocabulary
apparition (ap´ ə rish′ ən) *n.* something strange or unexpected that comes suddenly into view, as a ghost

---

K

J Author's Craft

MOOD Invite students to discuss how the author creates the mood in this paragraph. *(She describes Lise's progress in a slow, detailed fashion, taking the same kind of care that Lise does as she moves into the grove. The emphasis on quietness creates a mysterious mood edged with suspense.)*

K Author's Craft

PLOT Ask students why, at this crucial point in the plot, the narrator steps in to say something about the meeting. *(Perhaps she wants to decrease the suspense by breaking into it. Perhaps she wants to increase the suspense by making readers wait. Perhaps she really wants to emphasize the silence and the shortness of the meeting before readers find out what happens.)*

L Literary Elements

PLOT: External Conflict Students may note that Lise offers her ring after the thief points his knife at her. Even so, she is not motivated by fear: "the horror with which he inspired her was not fear of what he might do to her." So what is it then? *(Perhaps it is horror at his existence in her world. She wants him to go away.)*

M Critical Thinking

INFERRING Ask students to describe what happened and how "things were changed." *(She offers her ring. The thief kicks it away. Who is the superior one now? Perhaps what has changed are her sense of self and her ideas about the world.)*

Reading *Minilesson*

Identifying Spatial Relationships To understand "The Ring," readers must be able to visualize the two settings (the meadow, the woods) and the three characters (Sigismund, Lise, the thief) and follow the changing spatial relationships among the settings and characters.

Activity Ask students to draw or sketch pictures of the meadow, the woods,

Sigismund, Lise, and the thief based on details from the story. They might draw individual pictures of the five and arrange them in a collage, or they might draw one picture of a scene involving all five. Their drawings should answer questions such as these: *What do the settings look like? Where are the meadow and the woods in relation to each other? What do the characters look like? When Sigismund is in the*

meadow, where is Lise? Where is the thief in relation to Lise? Students who prefer not to draw can cut out magazine pictures that remind them of the characters and settings. **L2**

Additional Resources
📁 *Reading Workbook,* p. 22

Active Reading

EVALUATE In other words, Lise has finally snapped out of her childish, romantic, fairy-tale mentality. The true meaning of marital commitment dawns on her.

Literary Elements

CHARACTER What is significant about Lise's statement "No, I have no idea"? *(She is lying to Sigismund because she does know where her wedding ring is. More than that, she has gone against her belief that she would never have any secret from her husband.)*

Thematic Focus

Making Choices Lise has chosen to keep a secret from her husband. Have students explore what they think this means for Sigismund and Lise's future together.

✓ ASSESSMENT OPTIONS

📁 *Quick Checks,* p. 19

Teaching Options

---

cambric[11] round the blade. This was difficult for him to do because his left arm was broken. While he did it his face under the dirt and sun-tan slowly grew whiter till it was almost phosphorescent.[12] Fumbling with both hands, he once more stuck the knife into the sheath. Either the sheath was too big and had never fitted the knife, or the blade was much worn—it went in. For two or three more seconds his gaze rested on her face; then he lifted his own face a little, the strange radiance still upon it, and closed his eyes.

The movement was <u>definitive</u> and <u>unconditional</u>. In this one motion he did what she had begged him to do: he vanished and was gone. She was free.

She took a step backward, the immovable, blind face before her, then bent as she had done to enter the hiding-place, and glided away as noiselessly as she had come. Once outside the grove she stood still and looked round for the meadow path, found it, and began to walk home.

Her husband had not yet rounded the edge of the grove. Now he saw her and helloed to her gaily; he came up quickly and joined her.

The path here was so narrow that he kept half behind her and did not touch her. He began to explain to her what had been the matter with the lambs. She walked a step before him and thought: All is over.

After a while he noticed her silence, came up beside her to look at her face and asked, "What is the matter?"

She searched her mind for something to say, and at last said: "I have lost my ring."

"What ring?" he asked her.

She answered, "My wedding ring."

As she heard her own voice pronounce the words she <u>conceived</u> their meaning.

Her wedding ring. "With this ring"—dropped by one and kicked away by another—"with this ring I thee wed." With this lost ring she had wedded herself to something. To what? To poverty, persecution, total loneliness. To the sorrows and the sinfulness of this earth. "And what therefore God has joined together let man not put asunder."[13]

"I will find you another ring," her husband said. "You and I are the same as we were on our wedding day; it will do as well. We are husband and wife today too, as much as yesterday, I suppose."

Her face was so still that he did not know if she had heard what he said. It touched him that she should take the loss of his ring so to heart. He took her hand and kissed it. It was cold, not quite the same hand as he had last kissed. He stopped to make her stop with him.

"Do you remember where you had the ring on last?" he asked.

"No," she answered.

"Have you any idea," he asked, "where you may have lost it?"

"No," she answered. "I have no idea at all."

---

11. *Cambric* is the soft, lightweight linen of which Lise's handkerchief is made.
12. Here, *phosphorescent* (fos′ fə res′ ənt) means "glowing."

13. *Asunder* (ə sun′ dər) means "in separate parts." These words of Jesus (Matthew 19:6) are often repeated at the end of a traditional Christian marriage ceremony.

Vocabulary
definitive (di fin′ ə tiv) *adj.* conclusive; final; decisive
unconditional (un′ kən dish′ ən əl) *adj.* absolute; complete
conceive (kən sēv′) *v.* to form a mental image or idea of; imagine

---

Grammar and Language *Minilesson*

Perfect Tenses Discuss perfect tenses. *Present Perfect:* expresses an action that occurred at an *indefinite* time in the past. *Past Perfect:* indicates one past action began and ended before another past action began.

Activity Have students write the present perfect and past perfect tenses of the verbs *be* and *win* and use each in a sentence. **L2**

Additional Resources

📖 *Grammar and Language Transparency 20*

📕 *Grammar and Language Workbook,* p. 147

📕 *Grammar and Composition Handbook,* Lesson 5.4

📕 *Writer's Choice,* Lesson 15.4

Responding to Literature

Personal Response

By the end of the story, Lise's feelings toward her husband have changed dramatically. How did this change make you feel? If you had been in Lise's situation, how might you have felt and acted?

——— ANALYZING LITERATURE ———

RECALL

1. Summarize the information the author gives about Lise and Sigismund in the first three paragraphs of the story.
2. Describe the **setting** of the story, particularly the July morning on which the story takes place.
3. What idea strikes Lise as she walks home alone? What does she hope to accomplish with her plan?
4. Summarize what happens in the alcove.
5. How does Lise act when Sigismund rejoins her for the walk home? How does Sigismund interpret his wife's behavior?

INTERPRET

6. After reading the first three paragraphs of the story, what conclusions can you draw about the relationship between Lise and Sigismund?
7. What elements of the setting contrast with each other? What do you think the author's purpose might be in setting up these contrasts?
8. Consider the plan that Lise makes during her walk home. In your opinion, what does this plan reveal about her?
9. How does Lise feel when the thief closes his eyes? Explain.
10. After her encounter with the thief, Lise thinks, "All is over." In your opinion, what does Lise mean by this?

EVALUATE AND CONNECT

11. What do you think the author's attitude is toward Lise? How does the author reveal that attitude?
12. In your opinion, what is the importance of the sheep in this story? What might they **symbolize** (see page R13)?
13. Which of the characters most arouses your sympathy? Why?
14. **Theme Connections** Why, do you think, does Lise not tell Sigismund about the thief? Would you have made the same choice? Explain.
15. Think about the change in Lise's feelings toward her husband. Have you ever experienced such a dramatic change in your feelings toward another person? If so, what caused this change?

Literary ELEMENTS

Characterization

Authors use a variety of methods to reveal what their characters are like. They may describe their characters' appearance, as well as their actions, thoughts, feelings, and conversations. These methods are called **characterization**. In this story, for example, the author writes: "Lise wanted to hear more about the horrible event." This lets the reader know that Lise has an immature curiosity about such morbid things as the gruesome fight in the sheep house.

1. Choose Sigismund, Lise, or the thief. Go through the story and identify passages that help reveal what that character is like. Tell what you think each passage reveals about the character.
2. In your opinion, does Sigismund change over the course of the story? Explain your answers.

● See **Literary Terms Handbook**, p. R2.

Personal Response

Some students may feel amazed at the quickness of the change. Others may question the strength of Lise's feelings in the beginning. They may say that, as Lise, they would have screamed and run from the thief.

ANALYZING LITERATURE

1. They are very young and have been married a week. After 10 years of courtship, they finally convinced Lise's family to allow them to marry despite her family's higher social status. He wants to make everything perfect for her. She wants to have no secrets from him. To her, marriage is an enchanting experience, much like playing with dolls.
2. The story is set around 1800 on a farm in Denmark. It is a bright July morning filled with sweet scents from the meadows and trees.
3. She decides to hide from Sigismund to make him realize how empty his life would be without her.
4. She meets the sheep thief; wordlessly they make a connection; the experience changes her life.
5. She is unresponsive. He misinterprets her distance as sadness about her lost wedding ring.
6. Opposition may have strengthened it. Their notions about marriage are based more in fantasy than in reality.
7. The wide meadows beneath the bright sky contrast with the close, shadowy woodlands. Compared to the open meadows, the woods seem mysterious and foreboding.
8. Her plan is childish and suggests she likes to play games with people's feelings.
9. She feels powerful when he does what she mentally commanded him to do; at the same time, she is grateful and relieved.
10. Students may think Lise's comment refers to her marriage or to her run-in with the thief or both.
11. The author often mentions Lise's age and her childish ideas and fantasies; this reveals that she thinks Lise is immature, spoiled, and silly.
12. Sigismund's vocation turns his attention from romance to the here-and-now. They represent humdrum, everyday existence.
13. Students may sympathize with any one of the characters, with Lise because she has to spend the rest of her life unhappily married, or with

---

LITERARY ELEMENTS

1. Sigismund: "no stone in his bride's path" (protective). Lise: "never have any secret from her husband" (romantic). Thief: "had killed the man" (dangerous).
2. Sigismund's character is consistent. He acts as caregiver and protector of his wife and flocks. His devotion to both continues.

Additional Resources
📖 *Literary Elements Transparency 19*

Sigismund because his wife no longer loves him.
14. Students may say that she wants to keep the experience to herself, thus breaking her vow to have no secrets from her husband, or that she doesn't want any harm to come to the thief. Students should explain why they do or do not agree with Lise's action.
15. Students should support their responses with anecdotal information from their lives.

LITERATURE AND WRITING

Writing About Literature

Students' comparisons should

- explain differences between Lise and the thief in one paragraph.
- tell how they are alike in a second paragraph.
- compare and contrast their appearance, actions, attitudes, and beliefs.

Personal Writing

Students' sequels should

- follow the tone and format of "The Ring."
- extend logically and naturally from the events in "The Ring."
- explore what Lise does in the future.

EXTENDING YOUR RESPONSE

Literature Groups Suggest that students elect a group chairperson to lead the discussion, a recorder to create a tally sheet, and a spokesperson to present findings to the class.
COLLAB. LEARN.

Internet Connection As an extension, students may want to compare information found on the Internet to information from a good encyclopedia.

Performing Suggest that students write scripts and rehearse their dialogue. Encourage them to base their interpretations of the characters on information from the story.

Skill Minilesson

VOCABULARY • Antonyms

1. b   2. a   3. b
4. a   5. c

Additional Resources
📁 *Vocabulary Practice,* p. 18

LITERATURE AND WRITING

Writing About Literature
Comparing Characters   How are Lise and the thief alike? How are they different? Jot down notes about their appearance, behavior, values, and outlook on life. Use your notes to write two paragraphs about Lise and the thief. In the first paragraph, explain how they are different; in the second one, tell how they are alike.

Personal Writing
The Sequel   What do you think might happen after this story ends? Will Lise tell anyone where the thief is hiding? Will the thief just go away, or will he kill again? Will Lise leave her husband? Write a sequel to "The Ring." Compare your sequel with those written by other students.

EXTENDING YOUR RESPONSE

Literature Groups
Will This Marriage Last?   Think back to your responses to the Focus Activity on page 224. In your group, share your ideas about the character traits you would value in a spouse. Then discuss whether you think the character traits shown by Sigismund and Lise will enable them to have a successful marriage. Let each group member give his or her opinion on this topic. Tally your group's responses and share the results with the rest of the class.

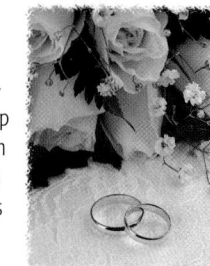

Internet Connection
Virtual Experience   Even if you never get the chance to travel to Denmark to visit the Karen Blixen (Isak Dinesen) Museum, you can learn more about the author on the Internet. Share the information you find with the rest of the group. You may want to print out some of this information and post it on a bulletin board.

Performing
Dialogue   Imagine that Lise is asking her parents' permission to marry Sigismund. With two partners, prepare a dialogue between Lise and her parents. Perform your dialogue for the class.

📑 **Save your work for your portfolio.**

Skill Minilesson

VOCABULARY • Antonyms

You already know that antonyms are words with opposite meanings and that many words don't have antonyms. Several of the vocabulary words in "The Ring" do not have antonyms. (What word could be the opposite of *apparition* or *conceive?*) Other words have many possible antonyms; therefore, you have to think carefully about what a word actually means to identify the word that best represents its opposite.

PRACTICE   For each numbered word write the letter of the answer choice that is an antonym.

1. solicitously
   a. hesitantly   b. heartlessly   c. impatiently
2. unendurably
   a. pleasantly   b. temporarily   c. cruelly
3. rustic
   a. luxurious   b. urban   c. cheerful
4. unconditional
   a. limited   b. lasting   c. neutral
5. definitive
   a. unknown   b. meaningful   c. hesitant

✓ ASSESSMENT OPTIONS

📁 *Quick Checks,* p. 19
📁 *Selection and Theme Assessment,* pp. 37–38
📁 *Performance Assessment,* p. 19
💾 *Testmaker*

Grammar Link

Avoiding Run-on Sentences

A clause is a group of words with a subject and a verb. If a clause can stand alone as a sentence, it is called a main, or independent, clause. Main clauses must be separated from each other by end punctuation, by a comma plus a conjunction, or by a semicolon. A **run-on sentence** is one that fails to obey this rule.

Problem 1 Some run-on sentences contain two main clauses with only a comma between them—an error called a comma splice. (To splice is to join together.)
Lise and Sigismund were happy, they had just been married.

Solution A Separate the main clauses into two sentences.
Lise and Sigismund were happy. They had just been married.

Solution B Add a conjunction with the comma.
Lise and Sigismund were happy, for they had just been married.

Solution C Replace the comma with a semicolon.
Lise and Sigismund were happy; they had just been married.
Beware! Use a semicolon only when the clauses are closely related.

Problem 2 Some run-on sentences contain two main clauses with only a conjunction between them. To hold two main clauses together in one sentence, both a comma and a conjunction are needed.
The couple walked through the meadow and her dog followed them.

Solution A Separate the main clauses into two sentences.
The couple walked through the meadow. Her dog followed them.

Solution B Add a comma before the conjunction.
The couple walked through the meadow, and her dog followed them.

Solution C Replace the conjunction with a semicolon.
The couple walked through the meadow; her dog followed them.

● For more about run-on sentences, see **Language Handbook,** p. R15.

EXERCISES

If the sentence is correct, write an *S* on your paper. If it is a run-on sentence, write *R* and rewrite the sentence to correct it.

1. Lise's little dog is named Bijou, it follows her everywhere.

2. Since childhood, Lise has loved Sigismund and Sigismund has loved Lise.

3. Lise did not take Bijou to the field, because the dog would have frightened the sheep.

4. Lise and her husband meet up on the path, they begin to walk home.

5. Will Lise and Sigismund stay together or will their marriage fail?

Grammar Link

Objective

• To recognize and correct run-on sentences

Teaching Strategies

A third type of run-on sentence is one which has two main clauses with no punctuation between them. This problem can be solved in the same three ways as those presented on page 233.

Exercises

1. R; Lise's little dog is named Bijou. It follows her everywhere.
2. R; Since childhood, Lise has loved Sigismund, and Sigismund has loved Lise.
3. S
4. R; Lise and her husband meet up on the path, and they begin to walk home.
5. R; Will Lise and Sigismund stay together, or will their marriage fail?

Additional Resources

📖 *Grammar and Language Workbook,* p. 123

📖 *Grammar and Composition Handbook,* Lesson 4.10

📖 *Writer's Choice,* Lesson 13.10

Teaching Options

Writing *Minilesson*

Varying Sentence Length When all the sentences in a paragraph are the same length, the rhythm is monotonous and boring. More interesting are paragraphs composed of sentences of varying lengths.

Activity Have students write a short narrative paragraph about something interesting that happened to them recently. Remind them to avoid run-on sentences by using the solutions on page 233. Encourage them to employ all three solutions so as to achieve a variety of sentence lengths in their paragraphs. **L1**

Additional Resources

📖 *Writer's Choice,* Lessons 13.3–13.4

Writing Workshop

Objectives

- To create a persuasive letter
- To plan, draft, revise, edit, and publish a persuasive letter
- To reflect on and assess one's letter

Teaching Strategies

PREWRITING

Explore ideas Help students understand that evidence must be relevant, reliable, and verifiable. Encourage them to include a variety of evidence in their persuasive letter. More kinds of evidence make for a stronger argument. On the other hand, inaccurate evidence greatly weakens an argument. Direct students to resources that will help them assess the accuracy of their evidence.

Remind students that while their response to an issue may be strongly emotional, their argument must be clearly rational.

Teaching Options

~: Writing Workshop :~

Persuasive Writing: Letter to the Editor

Everyone has opinions. In persuasive writing, you try to convince readers to agree with your opinion and, sometimes, to take a specific action. One way to bring your opinions to a wide audience is by writing a letter to the editor of a newspaper or magazine. **In this workshop, you will write a letter to the editor on an issue you feel strongly about.** To persuade your readers, you will use details and phrasing that appeal to reason and to emotion.

- As you write your persuasive letter, refer to the **Writing Handbook,** pp. R58–R77.

The Writing Process

PREWRITING

PREWRITING TIP
From the beginning of the process, stay tightly focused on your opinion and use specific, relevant evidence to support it.

Explore ideas
The characters in the stories in Theme Two all had to make a choice—to take a stand about something and act on it. In exploring ideas for your letter to the editor, look for issues that are important to you. Then choose what stand you will take on that issue and what action you want other people to take.

You might write a letter to the editor stating your opinion of the choice made by a character in this theme. You could also look through current newspapers or magazines to find articles about issues that you care about. Then use the following questions to explore your opinions.

- What is the real issue here?
- What are the arguments on each side of the issue?
- What position do you choose to take on the issue? What facts support your choice?

Drawing a web can help you clarify your ideas and gather support for your position. Print a statement of the issue at the center of a piece of paper. Around the center show different opinions about the issue. Add ovals for facts and other evidence that support each position.

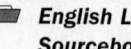

ENGLISH LANGUAGE LEARNERS

MEETING INDIVIDUAL NEEDS

Building Vocabulary Before students begin writing their persuasive letters, have a more proficient English speaker help them list words related to their issue of choice. For example, if the topic is part-time jobs, students need to have a working knowledge of words such as *salary, shift, minimum wage, responsibility, free-time, interfere, exhaustion, opportunity,* and *discipline.* Give students time to generate good-sized word lists and to find definitions for all the words on their lists.

Additional Resources
📁 *English Language Learners Sourcebook*

Consider your purpose
Your purpose is to state your opinion, to show that it is reasonable, to persuade your readers to agree with it, and, possibly, to persuade them to take action to support your position.

Choose an audience
In persuasive writing, it is important to know who your audience is and how best to convince them. For a letter to the editor, your audience will be the readers of the newspaper or magazine you write to. Read the letters in a few issues of that publication to get an idea of readers' concerns and attitudes. As you write your own letter, anticipate the readers' reactions.

Consider the conventions of a letter to the editor
You will have a better chance of seeing your letter published if you study the style and format of the letters to the editor in the publication where you intend to send it. Notice how people address the editor and what style of language is used. Many publications include a note somewhere on the letters page that indicates how long letters can be.

Make a plan
Here is one way to organize a persuasive argument:

STUDENT MODEL

Identify the issue and your position	What news article or event inspired you to write? What issue is involved? What is your position? What are some reasons for your position?	I read an article about a rash of armed robberies. Robbers were inspired by a violent movie. Movies that glorify violent crime Film companies should stop producing movies that make crime and violence seem exciting and acceptable. Movies that glorify violent crime inspire violent behavior.
State and answer opposing views	What is an opposing viewpoint? Why is that viewpoint faulty? What evidence supports your position?	Movies that show crime and violence are harmless entertainment. This kind of behavior is not the movies' fault; people do bad things anyway. In two cases the robbers actually admitted that a particular movie inspired them.
Restate your position and call readers to action	What statement sums up your position? What action do you want your readers to take?	Movies that glorify violent crime inspire more crime and make the world more dangerous for everyone. People should stop going to see violent movies.

Consider your purpose Students might create a small flow chart outlining the purpose. They can draw four boxes with arrows leading from one box to the next. Each box represents a key element of their purpose: statement of opinion, giving evidence, persuading readers to agree, persuading readers to act. Remind students to make the boxes large enough so that they have space for listing evidence, opinions, and reasons.

Choose an audience Students should think about the readership of various local papers, including the school papers and decide which audience would be most sympathetic to their cause.

Consider the conventions of a letter to the editor Explain that submitting a handwritten letter is really not acceptable. Urge students to type or word process their letters.

Make a plan Have students make a chart like the one shown on page 235 and answer the questions in the model. They may find it helpful to refer to the notes from the Explore Ideas activities.

Additional Resources
- *Writing and Proofreading Practice,* pp. 9–10
- *Writing and Proofreading Transparencies 1–6, 9–10, 27–28*
- *Writer's Choice,* Lesson 6.3; 6.6

MEETING INDIVIDUAL NEEDS — INCLUSION STRATEGIES

Special Needs Have students discuss in small groups the issue they plan to write about, the position they plan to take, and the supporting evidence they plan to use. Encourage them to help one another by suggesting sources of evidence and ways of gaining access to them.

Activity Provide groups with magazines and newspapers. Students can page through the periodicals and point out photographs of experts such as scientists and business leaders. Students should then discuss referring to such experts in their persuasive letters. **L1 COLLAB. LEARN.**

Additional Resources
- *Inclusion Strategies*

Is your argument sound? Explain that the purpose of the argument is to persuade readers to accept the opinion that students present. Help students construct logical arguments that take readers through the evidence step by step.

Write your draft Although students should use an organizational plan to structure their writing, at the outset they can benefit by freewriting for 15–20 minutes. When students are inspired to write and are brimming with ideas, it is important to get those thoughts down on paper. Afterwards they can refocus their efforts on organizing what they have written.

Teaching Options

∽: Writing ＼ Workshop :∽

DRAFTING

Is your argument sound?

In persuasive writing, an argument consists of your position and the support you provide for it. First, make sure your opinion is based on relevant facts and other reasonable evidence, and not on rumor, hearsay, and prejudice. Next, use that evidence to support your argument. Include facts and statistics, and quote expert opinions when you can.

Write your draft

As you write, refer to your plan to make sure that you are working within the basic structure of stating the issue and your opinion, anticipating and addressing opposing views, and finally summing up and calling readers to action. If, as you write, you discover that this structure isn't working for your argument, don't be afraid to try something new. Keep the ideas coming, and keep writing; you may find that an important new idea comes to you as you draft.

STUDENT MODEL

> Some people think that criminal and violent behavior is not the fault of movies. They say that violent movies are simply exciting entertainment, and that those who commit violent crimes would do so anyway. However, in two separate cases reported in your article, the suspects admitted that a particular movie inspired their crime spree. A veteran police officer on the scene of one arrest was quoted as saying, "Companies making movies like these should worry about the kind of impact their movies have." What more proof can anyone need?

Use this graphic to help you visualize the structure of your letter to the editor.

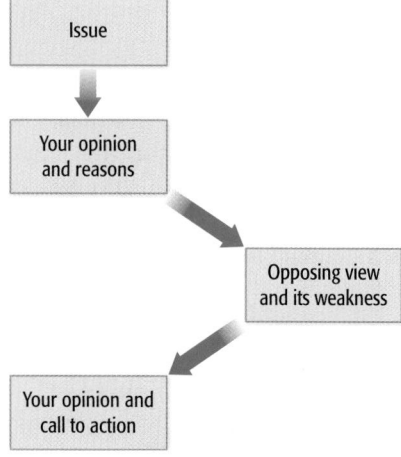

REVISING

Take another look

If you have written about a strong opinion, you may have written an impassioned letter. Good. Now let it cool down for a bit. Put it away, and return to it after a while. Look at it with the cold, hard eye of the editor who will receive it. Find the weak spots in your argument, and strengthen them. Use the **Questions for Revising** to guide you as you work.

Read your response aloud

Find a listener for a "field test" of your letter. The best listener is someone who disagrees with your opinion. From your listener's responses, you will get a good indication of how persuasive you have been. (Since your letter isn't polished, don't give the text to your listener, just read it aloud.) Use the listener's responses and the **Questions for Revising** to help you revise.

REVISING TIP

To strengthen an emotional appeal, replace neutral words with words that have strong positive or negative connotations.

STUDENT MODEL

It scares me to think of how violent our world has become. Films that show violent crime make the world a more dangerous place for everyone. Let's send a message to film studios to stop making violent films. I ask people to boycott films that glorify violence and crime.

and how great the chances are of becoming a victim of violent crime.

Let's send them a message they will hear. Let's

QUESTIONS FOR REVISING

How can you:

☑ state the issue and your position more clearly?

☑ clarify your reasons for your position?

☑ better state and address opposing viewpoints?

☑ use repetition and other techniques to emphasize your points?

☑ appeal to readers' emotions as well as to their reason?

☑ leave the audience with a memorable phrase that sums up your position?

☑ inspire the audience to take action?

Take another look Remind students that setting work aside and coming back later can help them spot weaknesses in their arguments or recognize ideas that are overly emotional.

Read your response aloud Remind listeners to refrain from making comments until the writer has read the entire letter. Listeners should jot down specific notes, comments, criticism, responses, and praise. Then they should go through the notes point by point with the writer.

TECHNOLOGY TIP

Encourage students to work on a word processor if possible. Using a word processor makes the revision process much easier. Students can cut and paste, create several versions, and manipulate text—in other words, experiment until they find the best organization for their letter. The spell-check feature is a bonus.

Writing *Minilesson*

Limiting Words Explain that readers are not easily fooled. They may discredit a writer who states, for example, that "Children love scary TV shows." It is better to say "some children" and earn the trust of an audience. Limiting words can help avoid generalization, oversimplification, overstatement, or exaggeration.

Activity Have students revise the statements by using limiting words such as *some, many, few, sometimes, often, almost always, frequently, occasionally,* and *in general.*

1. Parents never listen to their teenage children. *(Some parents never listen to their teenage children.)*

2. Children who watch television are inactive. *(Some children who watch televi-*

sion are inactive and overweight.)

3. No one recycles in this town! *(Few people recycle in this town!)* **L2**

Additional Resources

 Writer's Choice, Lesson 6.5

Have students use the Proofreading Checklist on the inside back cover of their books.

In the earlier stages, students focused mainly on content. Now they should edit to make their writing smoother. Suggest that students look for rough spots by reading their revised drafts silently and then aloud. If when reading aloud they falter at certain points, that could signal a problem with the writing. Students should examine their word choice, sentence construction, and use of transitions.

PUBLISHING/PRESENTING

Help students find the names of the editors to whom they should direct their letters. You might also want to discuss the benefits of including a cover letter and return postage along with the submission.

Reflecting

Portfolio Encourage students to ask themselves these questions as they review their letter.

Does my letter
- clearly state the issue and my opinion?
- include good, convincing evidence to support my opinion?
- reflect thinking and writing I'm proud of?

If students answer yes to more than one question, have them consider adding the letter to their portfolio.

Teaching Options

~ Writing Workshop ~

EDITING/PROOFREADING

EDITING TIP
Read your letter again. Have you varied the types of sentence structure?

Revise your letter until it says what you want it to say and does not include irrelevant information or unnecessary words. Then edit your letter to correct any errors. Make three editorial passes: one for grammar, one for spelling, and one for punctuation. Use the **Proofreading Checklist** on the inside back cover of this book.

Grammar Hint

Make sure that you have not tried to join independent clauses with a comma alone. Make each independent clause a separate sentence, join the clauses with a semicolon, or add a conjunction with the comma.

Violent movies teach acceptance of violence; they make us believe that violence is just a part of everyday human life.

STUDENT MODEL

I read about these crimes in your newspaper, ^{and} I was angry to see that a movie inspired them.

PUBLISHING/PRESENTING

PRESENTING TIP
Neatness counts. Newspaper and magazine editors don't have time to decipher poorly written letters.

You will start by sending your letter to your target publication—the newspaper or magazine that you've had in mind all along as the ideal place for your letter to appear. However, you should make a list of back-ups, publications that might be almost as good. If your letter doesn't appear in your first choice after a reasonable time, send it to the next one on your list. You can also post it on an Internet bulletin board devoted to the topic or a related topic.

Reflecting

Think about the process you went through to develop your opinion and find the best evidence to support it. Did your evidence provide strong, relevant support for your argument? Were you able to appeal to your readers' emotions as well as to their intellect?

 Save your work for your portfolio.

✓ ASSESSMENT OPTIONS

📁 ***Writing Assessment and Portfolio Management***
- Writing Assessment, pp. 2–19, 25–26
- Portfolio Management, pp. 20–22

Theme 3 _____ *Twists*

The journey of life is marked with unexpected twists and turns that surprise us and keep life interesting. The plots of the stories you will read in this theme all have twists that will intrigue and surprise you—and in some cases, even shock you.

THEME PROJECTS

Listening and Speaking

Where Are They Now?   Imagine that you are a reporter interviewing characters from two or three of the stories in this theme, years after the events described in their stories.

1. Consider the twist or surprise that confronts each of the characters you have chosen.

2. Create a list of questions to ask the characters, along with responses they might give.

3. Prepare a report for the "Where Are They Now?" segment of a television newsmagazine, explaining what has happened to the characters since their stories were in the news. Present your report to the class.

Interdisciplinary Project

Art: Design Video Cases   Working in a small group, design a video case for a movie version of one of the short stories in this theme.

1. Illustrate a scene from the story for the front cover of the case.

2. Decide how you will show the movie's title and the names of the actors. Experiment with different sizes and styles of type.

3. Create a design for the back cover of the case, as well as the spine. Display your finished video case for the class.

LITERATURE & HUMANITIES

To introduce the theme of "twists," have students examine *A Good Pool, Saguaney River (Art Talk,* Transparency 23) and discuss the "twist" at the end of this narrative.

GLENCOE
TECHNOLOGY

LITERATURE CLASSICS
CD-ROM
   Search for other sections related to the theme of "twists."

Teaching Strategies

The following suggestions may help your students plan and carry out their theme projects.

Listening and Speaking

- Students might want to make a list of the plot twists and put a check by the two or three they find most appealing and want to write about.

- Remind students that a good reporter seeks to answer questions such as Who? What? When? Where? and Why?

- Let students work in small groups to discuss possible ways the reports could be presented. Some students who have chosen the same character may be able to work out a joint presentation.

Interdisciplinary Project

- Suggest that students begin by doing a quick sketch for each of the selections. The preliminary results of the activity may help students choose the story that they want to illustrate.

- Encourage students to use a computer to experiment with type sizes and fonts.

- Remind students that sometimes the spine is the first thing a person choosing a video sees. Let pairs of students discuss the information needed for the spine and attention-getting ideas for the design.

Additional Resources

- 📁 *Interdisciplinary Activities,* pp. 6–7
- 📁 *Viewing and Representing Activities,* pp. 11–12
- 📁 *Listening and Speaking Activities,* pp. 5–6
- 📁 *Selection and Theme Assessment,* pp. 175–176
- 📁 *Critical Thinking,* pp. 8–9
- 📁 *Performance Assessment,* p. 91

SELECTIONS	Literary Elements	Reading and Thinking	Writing	Vocabulary and Spelling
The Happy Man's Shirt ITALO CALVINO	Symbol, SE p. 243 *Symbol, TWE p. 242*	*Generalizing, TWE p. 242* *Comparing and Contrasting, TWE p. 242*	Evaluation, SE p. 244 Personal Writing, SE p. 244	Analogies, SE p. 244 Context Clues, SE p. 246
The Californian's Tale MARK TWAIN	Style, SE p. 255 *Style, TWE pp. 249, 254* *Oxymoron, TWE p. 249* *Setting, TWE p. 250* *Characterization, TWE p. 252*	Scanning, SE p. 257 *Identifying Spatial Relationships, TWE p. 250* *Inferring, TWE p. 251*	Literary Analysis, SE p. 256 Story Ending, SE p. 256	The Prefix *-Pre*, SE p. 257
An Astrologer's Day R. K. NARAYAN	Description, SE p. 264 *Description, TWE pp. 261, 262* *Character, TWE p. 261*	Making Inferences, SE p. 266 *Skimming, TWE p. 258* *Drawing Conclusions, TWE p. 262*	Character Analysis, SE p. 265 Story, SE p. 265	Etymology, SE p. 266
The Interlopers SAKI	Conflict, SE p. 275 *Conflict, TWE pp. 270, 271, 274* *Point of View, TWE p. 270* *Mood, TWE p. 270* *Character, TWE p. 272* *Foreshadowing, TWE p. 273*	Summarizing, SE p. 277 *Paraphrasing, TWE p. 271* *Drawing Conclusions, TWE p. 273*	Quickwrite, SE p. 268 Description, SE p. 276 Story Sequel, SE p. 276	Analogies, SE p. 277 *Multiple-Meaning Words, TWE p. 273*
As It Is with Strangers SUSAN BETH PFEFFER	Understatement, SE p. 285 *Understatement, TWE p. 280* *Conflict, TWE p. 280* *Dialogue, TWE p. 281* *Metaphor, TWE p. 281*	Interpreting, SE p. 287 *Identifying Cause-and-Effect Relationships, TWE p. 282* *Drawing Conclusions, TWE p. 284*	Literary Analysis, SE p. 286 Letter, SE p. 286	Unlocking Meaning, SE p. 287
The False Gems GUY DE MAUPASSANT	Point of View, SE p. 295 *Point of View, TWE p. 290* *Style, TWE p. 291* *Conflict, TWE p. 292* *Theme, TWE p. 293* *Character, TWE p. 294*	Drawing Conclusions, SE p. 297 *Inferring, TWE p. 292* *Evaluating, TWE p. 292*	Quickwrite, SE p. 288 Character Sketch, SE p. 296 Personal Response, SE p. 296 *Using Details in Description, TWE p. 291*	Analogies, SE p. 297
THE SALESWOMAN COLETTE	Dialogue, SE p. 302 *Point of View, TWE p. 300* *Dialogue, TWE p. 301*	*Drawing Conclusions, TWE p. 300*	Literary Analysis, SE p. 303 Monologue, SE p. 303	Borrowed Words, SE p. 303
Mrs. James ALICE CHILDRESS	Tone, SE p. 306 *Tone, TWE p. 305*		Letter, SE p. 306	

Key: Student material is in roman. Teacher material is in italic.   Technology   **COLLAB. LEARN.** Collaboration

Grammar and Language	Listening, Speaking, and Viewing	Life Skills	Study, Research, and Technology
	COLLAB. LEARN. Literature Groups, SE p. 244 Performing a Story Ending, SE p. 244		🖥 Using Desktop Publishing, SE p. 244
Dashes, SE p. 257 *Semicolons, TWE p. 254*	**COLLAB. LEARN.** Literature Groups, SE p. 256 **COLLAB. LEARN.** *Dialogue, TWE p. 253*	Learning for Life: Community Support, SE p. 256 🖥 *Using the Internet, TWE p. 252*	Research, SE p. 256 🖥 *Internet Connection, TWE p. 252* *Research, TWE p. 252*
Concrete and Abstract Nouns, SE p. 266 *Colons, TWE p. 262*	**COLLAB. LEARN.** Literature Groups, SE p. 265 **COLLAB. LEARN.** Dialogue, SE p. 265 Storytelling, SE p. 267		🖥 *Internet Connection, TWE p. 258*
Sentence Variety, SE p. 277 *Adverbs, TWE p. 274*	**COLLAB. LEARN.** Literature Groups, SE p. 276 **COLLAB. LEARN.** Dialogue, SE p. 276		Research, SE p. 276
Vivid Verbs, SE p. 287 *Sentence Fragments, TWE p. 284*	**COLLAB. LEARN.** Literature Groups, SE p. 286 **COLLAB. LEARN.** Role Play, SE p. 286	🖥 Using the Internet, SE p. 286 **COLLAB. LEARN.** *Problem Solving, TWE p. 281*	🖥 Internet Connection, SE p. 286
Infinitives and Infinitive Phrases, SE p. 297 *Interjections, TWE p. 294*	**COLLAB. LEARN.** Literature Groups, SE p. 296 Monologue, SE p. 296		Research, SE, p. 296
Run-on Sentences, TWE p. 301	**COLLAB. LEARN.** Literature Groups, SE p. 303 Interview, SE p. 303	Learning for Life: Resume, SE p. 303	🖥 Using the Internet, SE p. 303
	COLLAB. LEARN. Literature Groups, SE p. 306		

SELECTIONS	🗁 Print Resources		
The Happy Man's Shirt ITALO CALVINO	Unit One Planning Guide, pp. 170-176 * Active Reading Guide, p. 20 Vocabulary Practice, p. 19	Reading Workbook, pp. 23-24	* Quick Checks, p. 20 Selection Assessment, pp. 39-40 Performance Assessment, p. 20 Spanish Summaries, p. 20 Spanish Translations
The Californian's Tale MARK TWAIN	Unit One Planning Guide, pp. 177-184 * Active Reading Guide, p. 21 Vocabulary Practice, p. 20	Grammar & Comp Handbook, Lessons 11.5, 11.7 Grammar and Language Workbook, pp. 123, 267 Reading Workbook, pp. 23-24	* Quick Checks, p. 21 Selection Assessment, pp. 41-42 Performance Assessment, p. 21 Spanish Summaries, p. 21
An Astrologer's Day R.K. NARAYAN	Unit One Planning Guide, pp. 185-192 * Active Reading Guide, p. 22 Vocabulary Practice, p. 21	Grammar & Comp Handbook, Lessons 11.4, 1.1 Grammar and Language Workbook, pp. 247, 48 Reading Workbook, pp. 25-26	* Quick Checks, p. 22 Selection Assessment, pp. 43-44 Performance Assessment, p. 22 Spanish Summaries, p. 22
The Interlopers SAKI	Unit One Planning Guide, pp. 193-200 * Active Reading Guide, p. 23 Vocabulary Practice, p. 22	Grammar & Comp Handbook, Lessons 1.5, 12.1-12.5 Grammar and Language Workbook, pp. 63, 323-325 Reading Workbook, pp. 25-26	* Quick Checks, p. 23 Selection Assessment, pp. 45-46 Performance Assessment, p. 23 Spanish Summaries, p. 23
As It Is with Strangers SUSAN BETH PFEFFER	Unit One Planning Guide, pp. 201-208 * Active Reading Guide, p. 24 Vocabulary Practice, p. 23	Grammar & Comp Handbook, Lessons 4.9, 1.5 Grammar and Language Workbook, pp. 121, 259 Reading Workbook, pp. 27-28	* Quick Checks, p. 24 Selection Assessment, pp. 47-48 Performance Assessment, p. 24 Spanish Summaries, p. 24
The False Gems GUY DE MAUPASSANT	Unit One Planning Guide, pp. 209-216 * Active Reading Guide, p. 25 Vocabulary Practice, p. 24	Grammar & Comp Handbook, Lessons 1.8, 3.3 Grammar and Language Workbook, pp. 257, 97 Reading Workbook, pp. 29-30	* Quick Checks, p. 25 Selection Assessment, pp. 49-50 Performance Assessment, p. 25 Spanish Summaries, p. 25
THE SALESWOMAN COLETTE	Unit One Planning Guide, pp. 217-224 * Active Reading Guide, p. 26 Vocabulary Practice, p. 25	Grammar & Comp Handbook, Lesson 4.10 Grammar and Language Workbook, p. 123 Reading Workbook, pp. 29-30	* Quick Checks, p. 26 Selection Assessment, pp. 51-52 Performance Assessment, p. 26 Spanish Summaries, p. 26
Mrs. James ALICE CHILDRESS	Unit One Planning Guide, pp. 225-231 * Active Reading Guide, p. 27 Vocabulary Practice, p. 26	Reading Workbook, pp. 29-30	* Quick Checks, p. 27 Selection Assessment, pp. 51-52 Performance Assessment, p. 26 Spanish Summaries, p. 27

*Also available in Spanish

📖 **Transparencies**	**Technology Resources**
Selection Focus Transparency 20 Literary Elements Transparency 20	🎧 💿 Audio Library 🎧 💿 Spanish Audio Library 💾 💿 Vocabulary Puzzlemaker 💻 Web Site: lit.glencoe.com
Selection Focus Transparency 21 Grammar and Language Transparency 21 Literary Elements Transparency 21	💿 Literature Launchers Videodisc 🎧 💿 Audio Library 🎧 💿 Spanish Audio Library 💾 💿 Vocabulary Puzzlemaker 💻 Web Site: lit.glencoe.com
Selection Focus Transparency 22 Grammar and Language Transparency 22 Literary Elements Transparency 22	💿 Literature Launchers Videodisc 🎧 💿 Audio Library 🎧 💿 Spanish Audio Library 💾 💿 Vocabulary Puzzlemaker 💻 Web Site: lit.glencoe.com
Selection Focus Transparency 23 Grammar and Language Transparency 23 Literary Elements Transparency 23	🎧 💿 Audio Library 🎧 💿 Spanish Audio Library 💾 💿 Vocabulary Puzzlemaker 💻 Web Site: lit.glencoe.com
Selection Focus Transparency 24 Grammar and Language Transparency 24 Literary Elements Transparency 24	🎧 💿 Audio Library 🎧 💿 Spanish Audio Library 💾 💿 Vocabulary Puzzlemaker 💻 Web Site: lit.glencoe.com
Selection Focus Transparency 25 Grammar and Language Transparency 25 Literary Elements Transparency 25 Fine Art Transparency 25	🎧 💿 Audio Library 🎧 💿 Spanish Audio Library 💾 💿 Vocabulary Puzzlemaker 💻 Web Site: lit.glencoe.com
Selection Focus Transparency 26 Grammar and Language Transparency 26 Literary Elements Transparency 26	🎧 💿 Audio Library 🎧 💿 Spanish Audio Library 💾 💿 Vocabulary Puzzlemaker 💻 Web Site: lit.glencoe.com
Selection Focus Transparency 27 Literary Elements Transparency 27	🎧 💿 Audio Library 🎧 💿 Spanish Audio Library 💾 💿 Vocabulary Puzzlemaker 💻 Web Site: lit.glencoe.com

📁 𝒯heme RESOURCES

- Listening and Speaking Activities (pp. 5–6)
- Viewing and Representing Activities (pp. 11–12)
- Critical Thinking Skills (pp. 8–9)
- Media Connections Activities (pp. 5–6)
- Interdisciplinary Activities (pp. 6–7)

See also these additional planning resources:
- English Language Learners Sourcebook
- Inclusion Strategies Sourcebook
- Literature Groups Sourcebook

Use Glencoe's *Presentation Plus!* This multimedia teaching tool lets you present dynamic lessons that will engage your students. Using Microsoft PowerPoint,® you can customize the presentations to create your own personalized lessons.

Objectives

- To read and analyze a short story about what might interfere with happiness
- To identify symbols in a short story
- To write an evaluation of a wise man's advice in the story

Skills

Reading/Thinking: Comparing and Contrasting
Writing: Personal Writing
Vocabulary: Analogies
Listening/Speaking: Telling a New Ending
Collaboration: Literature Groups

Motivating
→OPTIONS

Selection Focus Transparency 20: Have students discuss the meanings of metaphors that involve articles of clothing. Ask them to think of other metaphors that fit in this category.

Focus Activity: Have students write their own one-sentence statements defining happiness.

Before You Read

The Happy Man's Shirt

FOCUS ACTIVITY

Very little is needed to make a happy life.
—*Marcus Aurelius*

The two foes of human happiness are pain and boredom.
—*Arthur Schopenhauer*

To fill the hour—that is happiness.
—*Ralph Waldo Emerson*

SMALL GROUPS Which quote best describes your group's view of happiness? Explain your choice.

SETTING A PURPOSE Read to learn what might interfere with happiness.

BACKGROUND

The Time and Place

"The Happy Man's Shirt" takes place in Italy, in a time long ago.

Did You Know?

What is happiness? How can a person find happiness? People have been pondering these questions for thousands of years. The great

Greek philosopher Aristotle (384–322 B.C.) thought that happiness came through the search for the good life, a life made up of virtuous actions. During the Enlightenment, the French philosopher Jean-Jacques Rousseau (1712–1778) believed that people could find happiness and fulfillment with other people in situations free of the falseness of society. Today, many people seem to think that fame or material wealth will lead to happiness.

VOCABULARY PREVIEW

hue (hū) *n.* a color; shade or tint; p. 241
decree (di krē´) *n.* an order or decision made by a judge, monarch, or other official; p. 241
slew (slōō) *n.* a large number or group; p. 242
refrain (ri frān´) *n.* in a song or poem, a phrase or verse that is repeated regularly, especially at the end of each stanza; p. 242
retinue (ret´ ən ōō´) *n.* the group of attendants or servants accompanying a person of rank or authority; p. 242

240   UNIT 1

Meet Italo Calvino

Italo Calvino (ē´ tä lō   käl vē´ nō) began writing when he was a teenager in Italy, during the reign of dictator Benito Mussolini. Much of Calvino's early writings—which resemble fables or myths—were influenced by the oppressive political conditions of Mussolini's fascist regime. "When a man cannot give clear form to his thinking, he expresses it in fables." The spare, haunting quality of Calvino's work stems from this early period and continues into his later work. Calvino, who received many important literary awards, wrote novels, stories, essays, and translations.

Italo Calvino was born in Cuba in 1923. He died in 1985. The English translation of the collection in which this story appears was published in 1980.

RESOURCE MANAGER

Lesson Planning Resource
The *Unit One Planning Guide* (pp. 170–177) provides additional lesson notes and reduced versions of all print resources.

📁 **Other Print Resources**
- Active Reading Guide, p. 20
- Vocabulary Practice, p. 19
- Reading Workbook, pp. 23–24
- Quick Checks, p. 20
- Selection and Theme Assessment, pp. 39–40

- Performance Assessment, p. 20
- Spanish Summaries, p. 20
- Spanish Translations
- Inclusion Strategies
- English Language Learners Sourcebook

🖊 **Transparencies**
- Selection Focus 20
- Literary Elements 20

Technology
- 🎧 Audio Library
- 🎧 Spanish Audio Library
- 💻 Glencoe Literature Web Site
- 💾 Testmaker

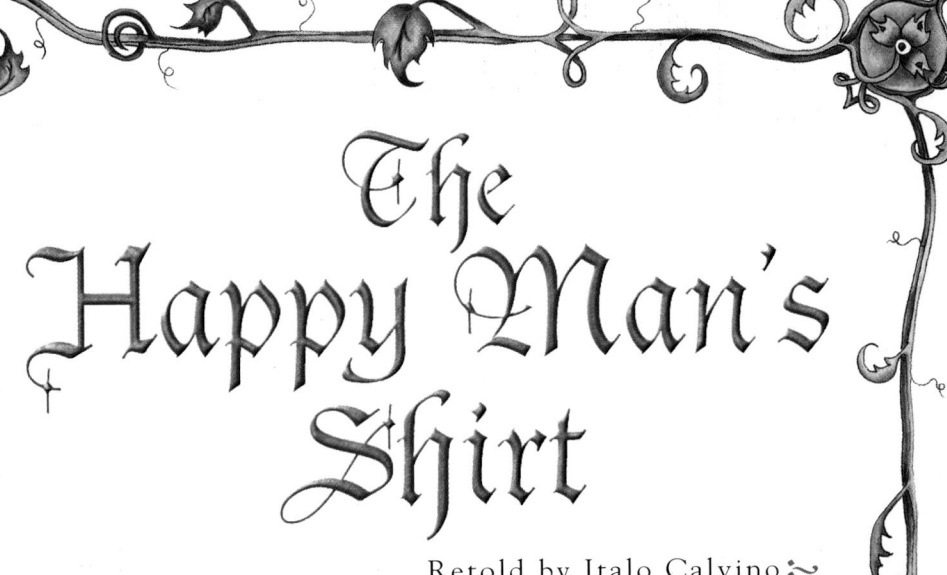

The Happy Man's Shirt

Retold by Italo Calvino
Translated by George Martin

A A king had an only son that he thought the world of. But this prince was always unhappy. He would spend days on end at his window staring into space.

"What on earth do you lack?" asked the king. "What's wrong with you?"

"I don't even know myself, Father."

"Are you in love? If there's a particular girl you fancy, tell me, and I'll arrange for you to marry her, no matter whether she's the daughter of the most powerful king on earth or the poorest peasant girl alive!"

B "No, Father, I'm not in love."

The king tried in every way imaginable to cheer him up, but theaters, balls, concerts, and singing were all useless, and day by day the rosy <u>hue</u> drained from the prince's face.

The king issued a <u>decree</u>, and from every corner of the earth came the most learned philosophers, doctors, and professors. The king showed them the prince and asked for their advice. The wise men withdrew to think, then returned to the king. "Majesty, we have given the matter close thought and we have studied the stars. Here's what you must do. Look for a happy man, a man who's happy through and through, and exchange your son's shirt for his." **C**

That same day the king sent ambassadors to all parts of the world in search of the happy man.

A priest was taken to the king. "Are you happy?" asked the king.

Vocabulary

hue (hū) *n.* a color; shade or tint
decree (di krē′) *n.* an order or decision made by a judge, monarch, or other official

---

SUMMARY

A king's only son is very unhappy, but he cannot explain why. Wise men advise the king to find the happiest man possible and exchange his son's shirt for that man's. The king searches the world for a genuinely happy man but finds that most men are only partly happy. Finally, the king finds a young man who is perfectly happy. However, when the king tries to exchange his son's shirt for that of the young man, he discovers that the happy man wears no shirt.

📁 *Spanish Summaries,* p. 20

A Active Reading

CONNECT Have students read the first paragraph. Ask them to tell what kind of story this reminds them of. *(a folk tale)* Let students tell stories they know that begin in a similar way, with a character being unhappy about something.

Additional Resources
📁 *Active Reading Guide,* p. 20
🎧 *Audio Library*
🎧 *Spanish Audio Library*

Teaching Options

CONNECTING TO OTHER SELECTIONS

The chart at the right shows three ways to connect "The Happy Man's Shirt" to selections in this book.

For specific teaching strategies, see the *Unit One Planning Guide,* pp. 173–174.

Connection	Title
Life Skills: Life-long Learning	→ "Civil Peace," p. 39
Thematic: Happiness	→ "A Child's Christmas in Wales," p. 433
Literary: Theme	→ "Living Well. Living Good." p. 489

B Critical Thinking

GENERALIZING After students read page 241, ask them to make a generalization about the aspects of life that make many people happy. Use the following model to show them how to generalize.

Model: The king's goal is to make his son happy. He thinks of specific ways to achieve this. I think the author is saying that many people find happiness in love and marriage, in entertainment, in socializing, and in art forms such as drama and music.

C Literary Elements

SYMBOL Have students speculate about what the shirt may symbolize. *(happiness, life, wealth)*

D Critical Thinking

GENERALIZING After reading the neighboring king's response, have students generalize about what may make otherwise happy people unhappy. *(the fact that they must eventually die)*

Thematic Focus

Twists What point about life does the author make with the unexpected twist at the end of the story? *(One cannot adopt another person's happiness.)*

☑ ASSESSMENT OPTIONS

📁 *Quick Checks,* p. 20

"Yes, indeed, Majesty."

"Fine. How would you like to be my bishop?"

"Oh, Majesty, if only it were so!"

"Away with you! Get out of my sight! I'm seeking a man who's happy just as he is, not one who's trying to better his lot."

Thus the search resumed, and before long the king was told about a neighboring king, who everybody said was a truly happy man. He had a wife as good as she was beautiful and a whole <u>slew</u> of children. He had conquered all his enemies, and his country was at peace. Again hopeful, the king immediately sent ambassadors to him to ask for his shirt.

The neighboring king received the ambassadors and said, "Yes, indeed, I have everything anybody could possibly want. But at the same time I worry because I'll have to die one day and leave it all. I can't sleep at night for worrying about that!" The ambassadors thought it wiser to go home without this man's shirt.

At his wit's end, the king went hunting. He fired at a hare but only wounded it, and the hare scampered away on three legs. The king pursued it, leaving the hunting party far behind him. Out in the open field he heard a man singing a <u>refrain</u>. The king stopped in his tracks. "Whoever sings like that is bound to be happy!" The song led him into a vineyard, where he found a young man singing and pruning the vines.

"Good day, Majesty," said the youth. "So early and already out in the country?"

"Bless you! Would you like me to take you to the capital? You will be my friend."

"Much obliged, Majesty, but I wouldn't even consider it. I wouldn't even change places with the Pope."

"Why not? Such a fine young man like you . . ."

"No, no, I tell you. I'm content with just what I have and want nothing more."

"A happy man at last!" thought the king. "Listen, young man. Do me a favor."

"With all my heart, Majesty, if I can."

"Wait just a minute," said the king, who, unable to contain his joy any longer, ran to get his <u>retinue</u>. "Come with me! My son is saved! My son is saved!" And he took them to the young man. "My dear lad," he began, "I'll give you whatever you want! But give me . . . give me . . ."

"What, Majesty?"

"My son is dying! Only you can save him. Come here!"

The king grabbed him and started unbuttoning the youth's jacket. All of a sudden he stopped, and his arms fell to his sides.

The happy man wore no shirt.

Vocabulary

slew (slōō) *n.* a large number or group
refrain (ri frān′) *n.* in a song or poem, a phrase or verse that is repeated regularly, especially at the end of each stanza
retinue (ret′ ən ōō′) *n.* the group of attendants or servants accompanying a person of rank or authority

Teaching Options

Reading *Minilesson*

Comparing and Contrasting Explain that the story is told in the form of a folk tale. On the board, create a cluster map for *folk tale*. Note these characteristics: brief, vague setting, stock characters and little character development, tells a general truth about life, may exist in different versions. Point out that fairy tales and fables are similar to folk tales.

Activity Have students take turns telling a folk tale, fairy tale, or fable. Discuss differences and similarities among the stories using the cluster map on the board as a guide. **L2**

Additional Resources
📁 *Reading Workbook,* pp. 23–24

Responding to Literature

Personal Response

How did you feel when you read the last line of the story? How do you think you would have reacted if you had been in the king's place?

ANALYZING LITERATURE

RECALL

1. What is wrong with the king's son?
2. What does the king do to try to cure his son? What do the wise men recommend?
3. What does the king eventually discover about the priest and the neighboring king?
4. How does the king discover the happy man? Who is this man?
5. Is the happy man able to do the favor the king requests? Why or why not?

INTERPRET

6. What might be the real reason the prince is unhappy?
7. Why do you think the wise men make the suggestion they do? How might a shirt help the prince?
8. Do you think the neighboring king would have given his shirt to the ambassadors, had they asked for it? Explain.
9. What makes the king believe that the young man he has found is truly happy?
10. How do you think the king feels when he unbuttons the young man's jacket? Why might the young man be dressed as he is?

EVALUATE AND CONNECT

11. Do you think it is possible to have everything one might wish for and still be unhappy, like the prince in this story? Explain.
12. Do you think the king is a good father to his son? Why or why not?
13. In your opinion, does a person like the happy man really exist? Do you think anyone is truly satisfied with what he or she has? Explain your answer.
14. In your opinion, what is the lesson, or **moral,** of this story?
15. Theme Connections   What makes the ending of this story so surprising? How is the surprise ending related to the moral of the story?

Literary ELEMENTS

Symbol

A **symbol** is a person, an object, or an act that means more than what it is. The symbol refers to or stands for someone or something else. Parables, fables, and folktales, such as "The Happy Man's Shirt," often contain symbols to help get the author's meaning across.

1. What kinds of people do the king and the son in "The Happy Man's Shirt" symbolize?
2. What does the king want for his son? What is the symbol for that quality?
3. What characteristics or qualities might the priest and the other king symbolize?

● See **Literary Terms Handbook,** p. R13.

Personal Response

Students may say they were surprised. They may say they would have felt surprised, disappointed, and frustrated in the king's place.

ANALYZING LITERATURE

1. The king's son is unhappy.
2. The king suggests marriage and tries many forms of entertainment such as balls and concerts. The wise men recommend exchanging the prince's shirt for that of a happy man.
3. He discovers that the priest is ambitious and that the neighboring king worries about dying.
4. The king goes hunting and overhears the happy man singing as he works in a vineyard.
5. The happy man is unable to do the favor because he does not have a shirt to give to the king.
6. Students may say the prince might be unhappy because his father has always given him everything he wanted. He has never had to work to achieve a goal.
7. The wise men may make the suggestion because by finding a truly happy man, the king and the prince might learn the nature of happiness. Wearing the clothes of the happy man may help the prince identify with his way of life.
8. Students may say the neighboring king would have given his shirt because he was happy and secure and would not mind helping someone else.
9. The king associates music with happiness; he hears happiness in the singer's voice.
10. The king probably feels disappointed and frustrated. The young man might be poor and unable to afford a shirt.
11. Students may say it is possible to have many material possessions and still be unhappy because happiness is brought on by personal relationships, spirituality, work, or appreciation of art and not by material wealth.
12. Some students may say the king is a good father because he does his best to make his son happy. Others may say he is not a good father because he makes himself responsible for his son's happiness instead of making his son take the responsibility.
13. Some students may say that if people accept their role in life, they can be truly happy. Others may say that life can never be perfect and that

LITERARY ELEMENTS

1. They symbolize wealthy people who have the leisure time to worry about their happiness.
2. He wants happiness for his son, symbolized by a shirt.
3. The priest might symbolize ambition. The other king might symbolize fear of death.

Additional Resources

 Literary Elements Transparency 20

everyone has some problem that makes true happiness impossible.
14. Students may say that true happiness is impossible to achieve, that a person cannot change places with another person to achieve happiness, or that material possessions do not make a person happy.
15. The ending is surprising because the difficult challenge is to find a truly happy man; finding that man and then discovering he has no shirt is ironic. The ending makes the point that one cannot "borrow" happiness.

LITERATURE AND WRITING

Writing About Literature

Students' evaluations should
- express why and how the wise men's advice could be improved.
- show creativity in generating alternative advice.

Personal Writing

Students' personal writing should
- describe realistic ideas of happiness.
- interpret and discuss a quote about happiness.

EXTENDING YOUR RESPONSE

Literature Groups Encourage students to consider the king's character and his demeanor at the end of the story as they brainstorm scenarios.
`COLLAB. LEARN.`

Performing Encourage students to use dialogue and read it as the characters would as they perform their endings.

Interdisciplinary Activity Point out that students will need to summarize the story and decide how many pages it will take before completing the other activities.

Skill Minilesson

VOCABULARY • Analogies

1. b	2. c	3. a
4. a	5. c	

Additional Resources

📁 *Vocabulary Practice,* p. 19

———— LITERATURE AND WRITING ————

Writing About Literature

Performance Review Imagine that you are one of the "wise men" in this story. Write a paragraph in which you evaluate the advice you gave to the king. Explain how you might advise him differently on the matter of his son's unhappiness, should he ever consult you again.

Personal Writing

Happiness Is . . . Record your own thoughts about what happiness is. Consider questions like these: What does a person need in order to be truly happy? Can happiness be bought? Read the quotes in the Focus Activity on page 240. Which quote expresses your ideas about happiness?

———— EXTENDING YOUR RESPONSE ————

Literature Groups

Brainstorming When this story ends, the king seems to have failed in his quest to find happiness for his son. Brainstorm ideas about what the king might do next. Will he give up, continue his quest, or ask his advisors for another plan of action? Share your ideas with another group, and discuss which scenarios are the most likely.

Performing

New Endings What might have happened if the happy man had been wearing a shirt? Work with a partner to create a new ending for the story based on this assumption. Share your ending with the rest of the class.

Interdisciplinary Activity

Art: A Picture Book With other students, create a picture-book retelling of this story. Look at several picture books for younger readers for models of how text and illustration interact to tell the story. You will need writers to retell the story, editors to read the story and suggest changes, illustrators to create the artwork, and designers to lay out the text and illustrations on the pages of the book. If you have access to desktop publishing software, it can help guide you through the process. Don't forget to create a cover for your book.

💼 **Save your work for your portfolio.**

Skill Minilesson

VOCABULARY • Analogies

An analogy is a type of comparison based on relationships between things or ideas. Some analogies are based on *part-to-whole* relationships.

  horse : herd :: book : library

There are many horses in a herd; there are many books in a library.

  To finish an analogy, decide what relationship exists between the first two things or ideas. Then apply that relationship to another pair of words.

PRACTICE Choose the word that best completes each analogy.

1. bee : swarm :: hue :
   a. color   b. rainbow   c. design

2. individual : slew :: tree :
   a. plant   b. root   c. forest

3. attendant : retinue :: bird :
   a. flock   b. nest   c. wing

4. hymn : refrain :: drama :
   a. scene   b. audience   c. playwright

5. decree : order :: verdict :
   a. court   b. jury   c. decision

● For more about analogies, see **Communications Skills Handbook,** p. R77.

✔ ASSESSMENT OPTIONS

📁 *Quick Checks,* p. 20

📁 *Selection and Theme Assessment,* pp. 39–40

📁 *Performance Assessment,* p. 20

💾 *Testmaker*

Newspaper Article

Have you ever gotten something that you wanted—a new game, a new pair of shoes, a sum of money—and found that you weren't happy after all? What is happiness, anyway? Read on for advice on how to find it.

What is the meaning of this? We ponder happiness.

by Amanda Vogt—*Chicago Tribune*, August 4, 1998

Happiness is so important to Americans that the right to pursue it is guaranteed in our Declaration of Independence.

Today, happiness often is more closely linked to fame and fortune than freedom. But many people who gain these things still don't find happiness. Think Kurt Cobain or Princess Diana. (It's kind of ironic that their freedom was actually limited by their fame and fortune.) So what is this happiness thing, anyway?

Happiness is a bit of a riddle. It's not a person, place or thing. You can't put a price tag on it.

OK, that tells us what happiness isn't. But what is it?

"Happiness has to do with things that can't be touched or measured," says Geri Piorkowski, director of the counseling center at University of Illinois at Chicago.

Like friendship? Absolutely, says Jeri B., 14, of Chicago, who says happiness

is "friends who love you enough [to] stay and comfort you" when you're down. How about achieving shared goals?

You bet, says Lawrence J., 15, of Wheaton. "Happiness is doing something you love, like building a treehouse or playing baseball, with a bunch of people who love to do it too."

In 1996, a study of more than 1,000 12- to 15-year-olds was conducted by Teenage Research Unlimited (TRU), a market research firm in Northbrook. [Illinois]. The study found that 93 percent of kids in this age group see themselves

as happy some or most of the time.

But TRU researchers found that as kids approach adulthood and start to worry about grades, appearance, dating and jobs, they report fewer happy times.

So must the happy times dwindle as we get bogged down in the weighty responsibilities of adulthood?

Of course not, counseling director Piorkowski says. "The people who are the most successful at finding happiness tend to be those who keep their lives simple."

So how do you do that? Figure out what you want out of life and go for it, she says. If you know what you want, someone else's ideas about success, happiness or popularity won't matter.

If you're true to yourself, chances are you'll discover a happiness that works for you.

Respond

1. Does the author think fame, fortune, or freedom is most likely to lead to happiness? Do you think the people she interviewed would agree with her opinion?

2. Which of the above definitions of happiness are most close to your own? What did the advice for finding happiness tell you that you didn't already know?

MEDIA Connection

Objective

- To read and understand a newspaper article

Literature LINK

The Happy Man's Shirt This newspaper article and the preceding selection "The Happy Man's Shirt" (pp. 241–242) seek to answer the same questions—what is happiness and how does a person find it?

Respond

1. The author states that many people who have fame and fortune but limited freedom are not happy, so that implies that she thinks freedom is essential to happiness. Her interviewees would probably agree with her, since without freedom many people may not be able to pursue the activities that would make them happy.

2. Guide students to scan the article before they speak.

Additional Resources

 Media Connection Activities, p. 8

Teaching Options

Reading *Minilesson*

Distinguishing Fact and Opinion Look at the statements the author presents. Is the information fact or opinion? Can the statements made by those she interviewed be supported by facts?

Activity Have students create a chart listing statements about happiness found in the article, who said them, if the statements are fact or opinion, and how they can tell. **L2**

Additional Resources

 Reading Workbook

Vo·cab·u·lar·y Skills

Objective

• To use context clues to derive the meanings of unfamiliar words

Teaching Strategies

For an additional example, point out the word *retinue* on page 242. Explain that the king's call to the retinue to "Come with me!" indicates that a retinue is one or more people. Remind students to recall prior knowledge—in this case, that a king generally has several attendants—as they use context clues.

Exercise

1. depression
2. apprehension
3. scholarly
4. difficult
5. persistently

Additional Resources

📁 *Vocabulary Power:* **Weekly Lessons and Activities**

Vo·cab·u·lar·y Skills

Context Clues

When you come across an unfamiliar word, it's a good idea to check its meaning in a dictionary. But face it, you won't always have a dictionary handy. Besides, stopping to look up every unfamiliar word can really slow down your reading. That's why **context clues** can be so valuable.

The **context** of a word is the sentence or group of sentences in which the word appears. Luckily, the context often provides clues that can help you figure out what an unfamiliar word means. For example, "The Happy Man's Shirt" provides details to explain a happy king's happiness. One detail is that he has "a whole slew of children." The context helps you figure out that *slew* means a large number of something—in this case, children.

There are many different kinds of context clues. Here are some other examples.

Contrast: Grandma was a laconic woman. Grandpa, on the other hand, never stopped talking. (The clue phrase *on the other hand* helps you figure out that *laconic* means the opposite of "never stopped talking.")

Definition: The prince's countenance, or facial expression, was always sad. (The clue word *or* lets you know that *countenance* means "facial expression.")

As you read, look for context clues that can help you figure out the meanings of unfamiliar words. It's easier than lugging a dictionary with you wherever you go!

▸ EXERCISE ◂

Use context clues to figure out what the underlined words mean. On your paper, write a synonym or a short definition for each one.

1. Day by day, the prince's malaise became more serious, and it seemed as though nothing could lift his spirits.

2. What feelings of dread and foreboding must have tortured the king as he thought about the future!

3. The men who came to advise the king were erudite—that is, they were very learned and intelligent men.

4. It seemed like it would be a simple matter to follow the wise men's advice; instead, it turned out to be an arduous task.

5. The king kept trying and trying and trying to help his son—as assiduously as any loving parent would.

Teaching Options

MEETING INDIVIDUAL NEEDS — ENGLISH LANGUAGE LEARNERS

Context Clues On the board, write the following example from the story.

> He had conquered all his enemies, and his country was at peace.

Help students determine the meaning of *conquered* by pointing out context clues. Point out that the country is peaceful; therefore, the enemies must have been gotten rid of.

Activity Have English language learners work in pairs and discuss context clues and meanings for each of the following words from the story: *peasant* (p. 241), *resumed* (p. 242), *vineyard* (p. 242), *pruning* (p. 242).

Additional Resources
📁 *English Language Learners Sourcebook*

Before You Read

The Californian's Tale

FOCUS ACTIVITY

Imagine that you are going on a mission to a distant planet. You will be gone for twenty years and will have little, if any, contact with home.

QUICKWRITE List the items you would take with you as reminders of the life you are leaving behind.

SETTING A PURPOSE Read to learn how furnishings from "home" affect a group of aging forty-niners.

BACKGROUND

The Time and Place
This story takes place in California, probably during the 1860s or 1870s. What was once a bustling gold-mining area is now overrun with weeds, inhabited only by a few remaining pioneers who could not or would not leave.

Did You Know?
In the ten years following the discovery of gold at Sutter's Mill in 1848, nearly 400,000 people—mostly men—journeyed to California to prospect for gold. During the gold rush many of the forty-niners, as the gold seekers were called, were young. However, hardship, hard work, and poor diet caused them to age quickly. Some did strike it rich, but many more returned east or were forced to take low-paying jobs.

VOCABULARY PREVIEW

predecessor (pred′ ə ses′ ər) *n.* one who comes, or has come, before another in time; p. 249

sever (sev′ ər) *v.* to break off; p. 249

materialistic (mə tēr′ ē ə lis′ tik) *adj.* overly concerned with material matters and worldly possessions; p. 250

solace (sol′ is) *n.* relief from sorrow or disappointment; comfort; p. 250

sedate (si dāt′) *adj.* quiet and restrained in style or manner; calm; p. 252

imploring (im plôr′ ing) *adj.* asking earnestly; begging; p. 253

boding (bōd′ ing) *n.* a warning or indication, especially of evil; p. 253

apprehension (ap′ ri hen′ shən) *n.* fear of what may happen; anxiety; p. 253

Meet Mark Twain

Printer, riverboat pilot, miner, journalist, author, lecturer—Mark Twain worked at all of these jobs at various times in his life. Born Samuel Langhorne Clemens, he took the pen name Mark Twain, a nautical term meaning "two fathoms deep," when he wrote humorous pieces for a Nevada newspaper. As a writer, humorist, and lecturer, Twain became a popular American favorite. His most famous works are *The Adventures of Tom Sawyer* and *The Adventures of Huckleberry Finn*. The story you are about to read draws on Twain's experience in prospecting for gold and silver in the West.

Mark Twain was born in 1835 in Missouri and died in 1910.

THE SHORT STORY 🐿 247

The Californian's Tale

Mark Twain ⁓

SUMMARY

In an area of California that used to be populated by gold miners, the narrator meets a man, Henry, who urges him to stay and meet his wife. Henry's miner friends visit and discuss the wife's homecoming. When Henry becomes increasingly agitated about his wife's return, his friends give him a specially made drink. After he falls asleep, the friends explain to the narrator that the wife died nineteen years ago and Henry has been insane with grief ever since. They conduct the annual charade on the anniversary of her death.

📁 **Spanish Summaries,** p. 21

🅰 Active Reading

RESPOND After the first paragraph has been read, ask students to respond to the description by identifying the contrasts the author makes. Help them see that while the area is beautiful, it is also somewhat desolate.

Additional Resources
📁 **Active Reading Guide,** p. 21
🎧 **Audio Library**
🎧 **Spanish Audio Library**

Teaching Options

Old House with Tree Shadows, 1916. Grant Wood. Oil on composition board, 13 x 15 in. Cedar Rapids Museum of Art, IA. Gift of Happy Young and John B. Turner II.

248 🐾 UNIT 1

CONNECTING TO OTHER SELECTIONS

The chart at the right shows three ways to connect "The Californian's Tale" to selections in this book.

For specific teaching strategies, see the *Unit One Planning Guide*, pp. 180–181.

Connection	Title
Life Skills: Collaborating	→ from *Farewell to Manzanar,* p. 460
Thematic: Ghosts of the Past	→ "Lullaby," p. 330
Literary: Foreshadowing	→ "Winter Night," p. 363

THIRTY-FIVE YEARS AGO I was out prospecting on the Stanislaus, tramping all day long with pick and pan and horn, and washing a hatful of dirt here and there, always expecting to make a rich strike, and never doing it. It was a lovely region, woodsy, balmy, delicious, and had once been populous, long years before, but now the people had vanished and the charming paradise was a solitude.[1]

They went away when the surface diggings gave out. In one place, where a busy little city with banks and newspapers and fire companies and a mayor and aldermen had been, was nothing but a wide expanse of emerald turf, with not even the faintest sign that human life had ever been present there. This was down toward Tuttletown.[2] In the country neighborhood thereabouts, along the dusty roads, one found at intervals the prettiest little cottage homes, snug and cozy, and so cobwebbed with vines snowed thick with roses that the doors and windows were wholly hidden from sight—sign that these were deserted homes, forsaken years ago by defeated and disappointed families who could neither sell them nor give them away. Now and then, half an hour apart, one came across solitary log cabins of the earliest mining days, built by the first gold-miners, the predecessors of the cottage-builders. In some few cases these cabins were still occupied; and when this was so, you could depend upon it that the occupant was the very pioneer who had built the cabin; and you could depend on another thing, too—that he was there because he had once had his opportunity to go home to the States rich, and had not done it; had rather lost his wealth, and had then in his humiliation resolved to sever all communication with his home relatives and friends, and be to them thenceforth as one dead. Round about California in that day were scattered a host of these living dead men—pride-smitten[3] poor fellows, grizzled[4] and old at forty, whose secret thoughts were made all of regrets and longings—regrets for their wasted lives, and longings to be out of the struggle and done with it all.

It was a lonesome land! Not a sound in all those peaceful expanses of grass and woods but the drowsy hum of insects; no glimpse of man or beast; nothing to keep up your spirits and make you glad to be alive. And so, at last, in the early part of the afternoon, when I caught sight of a human creature, I felt a most grateful uplift. This person was a man about forty-five years old, and he was standing at the gate of one of those cozy little rose-clad cottages of the sort already referred to. However, this one hadn't a deserted look; it had the look of being lived in and petted and cared for and looked after; and so had its front yard, which was a garden of flowers, abundant, gay, and flourishing. I was invited in, of course, and required to make myself at home—it was the custom of the country.

It was delightful to be in such a place, after long weeks of daily and nightly familiarity with miners' cabins—with all which this implies of dirt floor, never-made beds, tin plates and cups, bacon and beans and black coffee, and nothing of ornament but war pictures from the Eastern

---

1. The narrator was exploring for gold (prospecting) along the Stanislaus River in central California. Here, *solitude* refers to a lonely, isolated place.
2. *Tuttletown* was a mining town near the Stanislaus.

3. Someone who is *smitten* is strongly affected by some powerful feeling.
4. *Grizzled* means "gray or mixed with gray."

Vocabulary
predecessor (pred′ ə ses′ ər) *n.* one who comes, or has come, before another in time
sever (sev′ ər) *v.* to break off

B **Literary Elements**

STYLE The author contrasts the lush natural beauty of the countryside with its air of desertion by people. Have students list the words that connote natural lushness and those that connote human desertion. *(The countryside is "lovely," "woodsy," "balmy," "delicious." The once-populous area now has "dusty roads," "deserted homes," "forsaken . . . by defeated and disappointed families.")*

C **Literary Elements**

FIGURES OF SPEECH: *Oxymoron*
Explain that a paradox is a statement that seems to make no sense but on closer inspection states a truth. An oxymoron is a kind of paradox in which two contradictory words are used together. Point out the oxymoron "living dead men" and have students explain how it is true. *(They are literally alive, but their hopes and dreams have died.)*

D **Critical Thinking**

INFERRING How does the deserted region make the narrator feel?
(depressed, lonely, melancholy)

MEETING INDIVIDUAL NEEDS

ENGLISH LANGUAGE LEARNERS

California History Help English language learners picture California in the 1860s. Explain that until the 1800s California was populated mainly by Indians and by the Spanish. With the discovery of gold in 1848, California's population grew enormously.

Activity Display a map of the United States. Have students point out the Stanislaus River and San Francisco and then infer how immigrants came from China and South America to California. *(by ship on the Pacific Ocean)*

Additional Resources
📁 *English Language Learners Sourcebook*

Literary Elements

E

SETTING Have students list some adjectives they would use to describe the interior of the cottage. *(cozy, warm, homey, pretty)*

Literary Elements

F

FIGURES OF SPEECH: *Oxymoron* Have students identify the figure of speech "careful negligence" and explain its meaning. *(An oxymoron, it means that the woman has taken much trouble to make the house look casual and "undecorated.")*

Critical Thinking

G

INFERRING Ask students what they can infer about who decorated the cottage and the man's feelings for her. *(The man's wife was the decorator. He is proud of her, feels she is wise and talented, and loves her very much.)*

illustrated papers tacked to the log walls. That was all hard, cheerless, <u>materialistic</u> desolation, but here was a nest which had aspects to rest the tired eye and refresh that something in one's nature which, after long fasting, recognizes, when confronted by the belongings of art, howsoever cheap and modest they may be, that it has unconsciously been famishing and now has found nourishment. I could not have believed that a rag carpet could feast me so, and so content me; or that there could be such <u>solace</u> to the soul in wall-paper and framed lithographs,[5] and bright-colored tidies[6] and lamp-mats, and Windsor chairs, and varnished what-nots,[7] with sea-shells and books and china vases on them, and the score of little unclassifiable tricks and touches that a woman's hand distributes about a home, which one sees without knowing he sees them, yet would miss in a moment if they were taken away. The delight that was in my heart showed in my face, and the man saw it and was pleased; saw it so plainly that he answered it as if it had been spoken.

E **Did You Know?**
A *Windsor chair* has a high, spoked back, slanting legs, and a slightly curving seat. It is named for the city in England where this style of chair was first designed and built.

"All her work," he said, caressingly; "she did it all herself—every bit," and he took the room in with a glance which was full of affectionate worship. One of those soft Japanese

fabrics with which women drape with careful negligence the upper part of a picture-frame was out of adjustment. He noticed it, and rearranged it with cautious pains, stepping back several times to gauge the effect before he got it to suit him. Then he gave it a light finishing pat or two with his hand, and said: "She always does that. You can't tell just what it lacks, but it does lack something until you've done that—you can see it yourself after it's done, but that is all you know; you can't find out the law of it. It's like the finishing pats a mother gives the child's hair after she's got it combed and brushed, I reckon. I've seen her fix all these things so much that I can do them all just her way, though I don't know the law of any of them. But she knows the law. She knows the why and the how both; but I don't know the why; I only know the how."

F

He took me into a bedroom so that I might wash my hands; such a bedroom as I had not seen for years: white counterpane,[8] white pillows, carpeted floor, papered walls, pictures, dressing-table, with mirror and pin-cushion and dainty toilet things; and in the corner a washstand, with real chinaware bowl and pitcher, and with soap in a china dish, and on a rack more than a dozen towels—towels too clean and white for one out of practice to use without some vague sense of profanation.[9] So my face spoke again, and he answered with gratified words:

G

"All her work; she did it all herself—every bit. Nothing here that hasn't felt the touch of her hand. Now you would think— But I mustn't talk so much."

---

5. *Lithographs* are pictures printed by a process in which a flat surface is treated either to retain or to repel ink.
6. *Tidies* are small, decorative coverings placed over the back or arms of a chair or sofa to keep them from being soiled or worn.
7. *What-nots* are open shelves for displaying objects.

8. A *counterpane* is a quilt or bedspread.
9. *Profanation* is the act of making something impure through unworthy use.

Vocabulary
materialistic (mə tēr′ ē ə lis′ tik) *adj.* overly concerned with material matters and worldly possessions
solace (sol′ is) *n.* relief from sorrow or disappointment; comfort

Teaching Options

Reading *Minilesson*

Identifying Spatial Relationships
Being able to follow and visualize what an author is describing is an important reading skill. Mark Twain provides many details as the two men in the story move from room to room in the cottage.

Activity Have students work in a group or in pairs to create a poster montage illustrating the interior design of the cot-

tage based on story details. Point out that the interior Twain describes is of the typical Victorian style, a style that would have been popular in England and the United States in the mid-1800s. Students may want to go to the library and locate books that illustrate the houses and furniture of this period. Then suggest that students look through decorating magazines and cut out pictures of furniture and accessories

similar to those described in the story. Finally, have them create a poster montage, using the pictures. **L2** **COLLAB. LEARN.**

Additional Resources
📁 *Reading Workbook,* pp. 23–24

Mark Twain ∽

By this time I was wiping my hands and glancing from detail to detail of the room's belongings, as one is apt to do when he is in a new place, where everything he sees is a comfort to his eye and his spirit; and I became conscious, in one of those unaccountable ways, you know, that there was something there somewhere that the man wanted me to discover for myself. I knew it perfectly, and I knew he was trying to help me by furtive indications with his eye, so I tried hard to get on the right track, being eager to gratify him. I failed several times, as I could see out of the corner of my eye without being told; but at last I knew I must be looking straight at the thing—knew it from the pleasure issuing in invisible waves from him. He broke into a happy laugh, and rubbed his hands together, and cried out:

"That's it! You've found it. I knew you would. It's her picture."

I went to the little black-walnut bracket on the farther wall, and did find there

Did You Know?
Here, *bracket* refers to a small shelf hung on the wall and supported by brackets.

what I had not yet noticed—a daguerreotype-case.[10] It contained the sweetest girlish face, and the most beautiful, as it seemed to me, that I had ever seen.

The man drank the admiration from my face, and was fully satisfied.

H "Nineteen her last birthday," he said, as he put the picture back; "and that was the

---

10. A *daguerreotype* (də gerʹ ə tīpʹ) is a photograph produced by exposing light to a silver-coated copper plate, a process invented by Louis Daguerre in France in the mid-1800s.

That second glimpse broke down my good resolution.

day we were married. When you see her—ah, just wait till you see her!"

"Where is she? When will she be in?"

"Oh, she's away now. She's gone to see her people. They live forty or fifty miles from here. She's been gone two weeks today."

H "When do you expect her back?"

"This is Wednesday. She'll be back Saturday, in the evening—about nine o'clock, likely."

I felt a sharp sense of disappointment.

"I'm sorry, because I'll be gone then," I said, regretfully.

"Gone? No—why should you go? Don't go. She'll be so disappointed."

She would be disappointed—that beautiful creature! If she had said the words herself they could hardly have blessed me more. I was feeling a deep, strong longing to see her—a longing so supplicating, so insistent, that it made me afraid. I said to myself: "I will go straight away from this place, for my peace of mind's sake." **I**

"You see, she likes to have people come and stop with us—people who know things, and can talk—people like you. She delights in it; for she knows—oh, she knows nearly everything herself, and can talk, oh, like a bird—and the books she reads, why, you would be astonished. Don't go; it's only a little while, you know, and she'll be so disappointed."

I heard the words, but hardly noticed them, I was so deep in my thinkings and strugglings. He left me, but I didn't know. Presently he was back, with the picture-case in his hand, and he held it open before me and said:

"There, now, tell her to her face you could have stayed to see her, and you wouldn't."

That second glimpse broke down my good resolution. I would stay and take the risk. **I**

Portrait of Martha Pickman Rogers in Her Wedding Gown. Albert Sands Southworth (1811–1894) and Josiah Johnson Hawes (1801–1901). Daguerreotype. Courtesy, Museum of Fine Arts, Boston. Bequest of Maxim Karolik.

That night we smoked the tranquil pipe, and talked till late about various things, but mainly about her; and certainly I had had no such pleasant and restful time for many a day. The Thursday followed and slipped comfortably away. Toward twilight a big miner from three miles away came—one of the grizzled, stranded pioneers—and gave us warm salutation, clothed in grave and sober speech. Then he said:

"I only just dropped over to ask about the little madam, and when is she coming home. Any news from her?"

"Oh yes, a letter. Would you like to hear it, Tom?"

"Well, I should think I would, if you don't mind, Henry!"

Henry got the letter out of his wallet, and said he would skip some of the private phrases, if we were willing; then he went on and read the bulk of it—a loving, <u>sedate</u>, and altogether charming and gracious piece of handiwork, with a postscript full of affectionate regards and messages to Tom, and Joe, and Charley, and other close friends and neighbors.

As the reader finished, he glanced at Tom, and cried out:

"Oho, you're at it again! Take your hands away, and let me see your eyes. You always do that when I read a letter from her. I will write and tell her."

"Oh no, you mustn't, Henry. I'm getting old, you know, and any little disappointment makes me want to cry. I thought she'd be here herself, and now you've got only a letter."

"Well, now, what put that in your head? I thought everybody knew she wasn't coming till Saturday."

"Saturday! Why, come to think, I did know it. I wonder what's the matter with me lately? Certainly I knew it. Ain't we all getting ready for her? Well, I must be going now. But I'll be on hand when she comes, old man!"

Late Friday afternoon another gray veteran tramped over from his cabin a mile or so away, and said the boys wanted to have a little

Vocabulary
sedate (si dāt´) *adj.* quiet and restrained in style or manner; calm

252 UNIT 1

gaiety and a good time Saturday night, if Henry thought she wouldn't be too tired after her journey to be kept up.

"Tired? She tired! Oh, hear the man! Joe, *you* know she'd sit up six weeks to please any one of you!"

When Joe heard that there was a letter, he asked to have it read, and the loving messages in it for him broke the old fellow all up; but he said he was such an old wreck that *that* would happen to him if she only just mentioned his name. "Lord, we miss her so!" he said.

Saturday afternoon I found I was taking out my watch pretty often. Henry noticed it, and said, with a startled look:

"You don't think she ought to be here so soon, do you?"

I felt caught, and a little embarrassed; but I laughed, and said it was a habit of mine when I was in a state of expectancy. But he didn't seem quite satisfied; and from that time on he began to show uneasiness. Four times he walked me up the road to a point whence we could see a long distance; and there he would stand, shading his eyes with his hand, and looking. Several times he said:

"I'm getting worried, I'm getting right down worried. I know she's not due till about nine o'clock, and yet something seems to be trying to warn me that something's happened. You don't think anything has happened, do you?"

I began to get pretty thoroughly ashamed of him for his childishness; and at last, when he repeated that <u>imploring</u> question still another time, I lost my patience for the moment, and spoke pretty brutally to him. It seemed to shrivel him up and cow[11] him; and he looked so wounded and so humble after that, that I detested myself for having done the cruel and unnecessary thing. And so I was glad when Charley, another veteran, arrived toward the edge of the evening, and nestled up to Henry to hear the letter read, and talked over the preparations for the welcome. Charley fetched out one hearty speech after another, and did his best to drive away his friend's <u>bodings</u> and <u>apprehensions</u>.

"Anything *happened* to her? Henry, that's pure nonsense. There isn't anything going to happen to her; just make your mind easy as to that. What did the letter say? Said she was well, didn't it? And said she'd be here by nine o'clock, didn't it? Did you ever know her to fail of her word? Why, you know you never did. Well, then, don't you fret; she'll *be* here, and that's absolutely certain, and as sure as you are born. Come, now, let's get to decorating—not much time left."

Anything *happened* to her? Henry, that's pure nonsense.

Pretty soon Tom and Joe arrived, and then all hands set about adorning the house with flowers. Toward nine the three miners said that as they had brought their instruments they might as well tune up, for the boys and girls would soon be arriving now, and hungry for a good, old-fashioned breakdown.[12] A fiddle, a banjo, and a clarinet—these were the

---

11. To *cow* is to frighten with threats.
12. Here, *breakdown* refers to a fast, lively country dance.

Vocabulary
imploring (im plôr′ ing) *adj.* asking earnestly; begging
boding (bōd′ ing) *n.* a warning or indication, especially of evil
apprehension (ap′ ri hen′ shan) *n.* fear of what may happen; anxiety

L Active Reading

CONNECT The narrator grows impatient with Henry's worrying and speaks "pretty brutally to him." Have students think of times when they lacked sensitivity and expressed annoyance with a friend or relative. How did they feel afterwards?

M Literary Elements

CHARACTER Have students discuss the miners who are Henry's friends. How do they differ from what readers might expect? *(The miners live a rough life with few amenities. Yet they are sensitive and caring, comforting Henry and helping him decorate the house with flowers.)*

N Active Reading

VISUALIZE Encourage students to visualize the scene at Henry's house, with the miners decorating with flowers, setting up their instruments, and playing music for the homecoming.

Listening and Speaking *Minilesson*

Dialogue Review ways to communicate meaning while performing a dialogue: speakers can vary the tone, volume, and emphasis of their voices. Point out that facial expression is also an effective means of communication, especially in responding to a partner's speech.

Activity Have students work in pairs and read the dialogue on page 254 start-ing with the narrator's plea for the miners not to leave him alone. Encourage students to use facial expressions to express the narrator's feelings as he listens to Joe's story. **L1 COLLAB. LEARN.**

Author's Craft

FORESHADOWING Encourage students to review the story and find details the author planted to foreshadow the surprise ending. *(Henry's saying that his wife was nineteen while he was much older, about forty-five; the miners' crying as they talked about Henry's wife; Henry's panicking when his wife was a little late; the miners' preparing for the wife's homecoming; and Joe's telling the narrator not to take the drink meant for Henry)*

Literary Elements

STYLE Ask students how the author's choice of words here adds to the casual style of the story. *(Here, as in dialogue throughout the story, the author includes colloquial words phrases, and run-on sentences. Elsewhere, he uses incomplete sentences, short sentences, and contractions.)*

Thematic Focus

Twists How does the author use characterization to increase the effect of the story's surprise twist? *(Part of the surprise is at the sensitivity of the miners; they have taken care of Henry with an elaborate ruse for nineteen years.)*

✔ ASSESSMENT OPTIONS

📁 *Quick Checks,* p. 21

Teaching Options

The Californian's Tale

instruments. The trio took their places side by side, and began to play some rattling dance-music, and beat time with their big boots.

It was getting very close to nine. Henry was standing in the door with his eyes directed up the road, his body swaying to the torture of his mental distress. He had been made to drink his wife's health and safety several times, and now Tom shouted:

"All hands stand by! One more drink, and she's here!"

Joe brought the glasses on a waiter,[13] and served the party. I reached for one of the two remaining glasses, but Joe growled, under his breath:

"Drop that! Take the other."

Which I did. Henry was served last. He had hardly swallowed his drink when the clock began to strike. He listened till it finished, his face growing pale and paler; then he said:

"Boys, I'm sick with fear. Help me—I want to lie down!"

They helped him to the sofa. He began to nestle and drowse, but presently spoke like one talking in his sleep, and said: "Did I hear horses' feet? Have they come?"

One of the veterans answered, close to his ear: "It was Jimmy Parrish come to say the party got delayed, but they're right up the road a piece, and coming along. Her horse is lame, but she'll be here in half an hour."

"Oh, I'm *so* thankful nothing has happened!"

---

13. The *waiter,* in this case, is a small tray.

He was asleep almost before the words were out of his mouth. In a moment those handy men had his clothes off, and had tucked him into his bed in the chamber where I had washed my hands. They closed the door and came back. Then they seemed preparing to leave; but I said: "Please don't go, gentlemen. She won't know me; I am a stranger."

They glanced at each other. Then Joe said:

"She? Poor thing, she's been dead nineteen years!"

"Dead?"

"That or worse. She went to see her folks half a year after she was married, and on her way back, on a Saturday evening, the Indians captured her within five miles of this place, and she's never been heard of since."

"And he lost his mind in consequence?"

"Never has been sane an hour since. But he only gets bad when that time of the year comes round. Then we begin to drop in here, three days before she's due, to encourage him up, and ask if he's heard from her, and Saturday we all come and fix up the house with flowers, and get everything ready for a dance. We've done it every year for nineteen years. The first Saturday there was twenty-seven of us, without counting the girls; there's only three of us now, and the girls are all gone. We drug him to sleep, or he would go wild; then he's all right for another year—thinks she's with him till the last three or four days come round; then he begins to look for her, and gets out his poor old letter, and we come and ask him to read it to us. Lord, she was a darling!"

Grammar and Language *Minilesson*

Semicolons Call students' attention to the paragraph beginning "I felt caught" on page 253. Point out that three of the sentences contain semicolons. Explain that a semicolon can be used to join the independent clauses of a compound sentence.

Activity Have students write each of the three sentences joined with semicolons as two separate sentences. **L3**

Additional Resources

📖 *Grammar and Language Transparency 21*

📕 *Grammar and Language Workbook,* p. 123

📕 *Grammar and Composition Handbook,* Lesson 11.5

📗 *Writer's Choice,* Lesson 21.5

Responding to Literature

Personal Response

Did the ending of the story surprise you? Explain why or why not.

──── ANALYZING LITERATURE ────

RECALL

1. Describe the **setting** of the story. How does the narrator describe the men who still live in the log cabins?
2. How is the interior of the cottage different from the miners' cabins in which the narrator has been staying?
3. How does the narrator react to the woman's picture?
4. Summarize what happens at the cottage on Saturday evening before Henry falls asleep.
5. Summarize what the narrator learns about the woman from Henry's friend.

INTERPRET

6. What is the narrator's attitude toward the men who live in the log cabins? Support your answer with evidence from the story.
7. In your opinion, what do the furnishings, pictures, and other objects in the cottage **symbolize** for the narrator? Look at the list of items you made in the Focus Activity on page 247. What do these items symbolize for you?
8. In your opinion, how does the narrator feel about meeting the woman?
9. In your opinion, why do the miners encourage Henry in his delusion? Why don't they help him face the truth?
10. Why do Henry's friends wait so long to reveal the truth to the narrator?

EVALUATE AND CONNECT

11. Suggest possible reasons the author might have for not revealing the woman's name.
12. Identify three ways in which the author builds **suspense.**
13. Just as we celebrate happy anniversaries, we also commemorate sad ones. Give at least one example of a somber national event and describe how people choose to recognize it.
14. If a friend of yours were in a situation similar to Henry's, how would you handle the dilemma? Give reasons for your choice.
15. Theme Connections   In what ways does the twist in the plot change the way you think about the characters?

Literary ELEMENTS

Style

Style is the author's choice and arrangement of words in a piece of writing. In "The Californian's Tale," Mark Twain uses an intimate, conversational style that helps draw the reader into the story.

1. Find at least two passages in the story that express the narrator's personal reactions and opinions.
2. How does the use of dialogue help prepare the reader for the surprise ending?
3. Twain uses specific details to re-create the geography, customs, and speech of the region in which the story takes place. Give at least two examples of such details.

● See **Literary Terms Handbook,** p. R12.

LITERARY ELEMENTS

1. He is lonely and depressed (p. 249); he longs to see Henry's wife (p. 251).
2. Henry shows he is overly anxious and worried; his friends' reassurances seem exaggerated.
3. Details include Twain's descriptions of the cottages and dialogue such as "just make your mind easy as to that" (p. 253).

Additional Resources

📖 *Literary Elements Transparency 21*

Personal Response

Some students may say the ending was not a surprise because Twain gave subtle hints that the situation was not as it appeared.

ANALYZING LITERATURE

1. The setting is a rural area in California formerly populated by miners. The narrator characterizes the men still living in the log cabins as "living dead men" who lost their money and were too ashamed to go home.
2. It is cozy, pretty, and well cared for, unlike the others, which were dirty and undecorated.
3. The narrator admires the woman in the picture and becomes overwhelmed with a desire to meet her.
4. Henry begins worrying that something has happened to his wife. Three friends arrive and reassure him. They decorate the house with flowers and begin playing music. They give Henry a special drink and he falls asleep.
5. Joe explains that Henry's wife is dead.
6. The narrator feels sorry for the men in log cabins.
7. The objects symbolize beauty, warmth, love, and comfort to the narrator. Encourage students to see beyond the literal function of the objects.
8. He may be afraid to meet her because her beauty and charm may make him regret what he is missing in his own life.
9. The men may have wanted to pretend that Henry's wife is alive because she added a beauty and happiness to their lives.
10. They may think that the narrator will upset Henry with the truth.
11. She may serve as a symbol for all women, who add love, warmth, and beauty to men's lives.
12. The author builds suspense by having the narrator see the woman's picture, hear her letter, and hear her described without meeting her.
13. Students may say that events such as the assassinations of John F. Kennedy, Robert Kennedy, and Martin Luther King Jr. are often commemorated with articles, programs, and recollections by people who knew them.
14. Encourage students to consider actions that reflect the *friend's* best interests.
15. Students may say that the twist shows the men to be even kinder and more sensitive than they first seem.

LITERATURE AND WRITING

Writing About Literature

Students' analyses should
- describe specific ways in which Twain characterizes Henry's wife.
- explain how each way creates a clear image of the character.

Creative Writing

Students' endings should
- follow naturally from events that have gone before.
- add characters and/or details that will surprise readers.

EXTENDING YOUR RESPONSE

Literature Groups Encourage students to consider how each alternative will hurt or help Henry.
COLLAB. LEARN.

Interdisciplinary Activity You may also wish to have students find out about the forms in which gold is currently found.

Learning for Life Suggest specific kinds of services for students to research such as grief counseling and counseling for groups such as senior citizens, adolescents, and the homeless.

LITERATURE AND WRITING

Writing About Literature

Analyze a Literary Technique Although Henry's wife is absent from the story, a detailed image of her emerges. Analyze in two or three paragraphs how Twain is able to create such a clear image of a character who never appears in the story. Share your analysis with others in a small group.

Creative Writing

Double Twist Surprise readers one more time. Add a new twist to the ending, developing additional characters and details, as necessary.

EXTENDING YOUR RESPONSE

Literature Groups

To Tell the Truth? Were Henry's friends right not to make him face the truth nineteen years ago? How might Henry's life have been different had he faced the truth? Debate these questions in your group, then share your ideas with the class.

Interdisciplinary Activity

Earth Science: Gold Fever Find out about the gold deposits that lured forty-niners to California in the mid-1800s. You might focus on what geological forces created such gold deposits or on how miners extracted the gold from the land. Make a model or a drawing to illustrate your findings and share it with the class.

Learning for Life

Community Support The characters in this story find ways to cope with isolation, tragedy, and disappointment. When people in your own community find themselves in similar circumstances, where can they turn for help? Research the community resources that are available. List several resources and the services that each one offers.

Reading Further

You might enjoy these works by and about Mark Twain:

Novel: *Roughing It*, a semiautobiographical novel, includes Twain's humorous description of his own stagecoach journey through the American West.

Short Story: "The Celebrated Jumping Frog of Calaveras County," published in 1865, made Twain an "overnight sensation."

Viewing: *The Incredible Rocky Mountain Race* tells the epic story of a cross-country race between Mark Twain and legendary character Mike Fink.

📖 **Save your work for your portfolio.**

✔ **ASSESSMENT OPTIONS**

📁 *Quick Checks,* p. 21
📁 *Selection and Theme Assessment,* pp. 41–42
📁 *Performance Assessment,* p. 21
💾 *Testmaker*

Skill Minilessons

GRAMMAR AND LANGUAGE • Dashes

Dashes are used to indicate an abrupt break or change in thought within a sentence or to set off and emphasize supplemental information:

"Now you would think–But I mustn't talk so much."

"All her work; she did it all herself–every bit."

PRACTICE Rewrite the following sentences, adding dashes where needed.

1. The narrator is a miner but that's irrelevant to the plot.

2. Henry's wife was charming so charming that all of Henry's miner friends loved her.

3. Henry's home showed a woman's touch lovely linens, wallpaper, framed artwork, and a variety of decorative objects.

4. Gold fever spread like wildfire everyone wanted to strike it rich.

● For more about using dashes, see **Language Handbook,** p. R49.

READING AND THINKING • Scanning

Scanning is glancing over a piece of writing in search of specific information, such as the answer to a question, a detail to support a fact or opinion, or a quote from a character in a story. For example, you might have scanned "The Californian's Tale" after you had read it to find clues you missed about Henry's problem. To scan a story, quickly glance over the text, looking for key words or phrases that will help you find the information you need. Don't waste time reading every word.

● For more about related reading strategies, see **Reading Handbook,** pp. R78–R107.

PRACTICE Use scanning to find the answers to these questions about "The Californian's Tale."

1. Who are the people that the narrator refers to as "living dead men"?

2. Where had Henry's wife gone?

3. How does Tom react when Henry reads aloud the letter from his wife?

4. What is "the cruel and unnecessary thing" that the narrator does?

5. What does Joe say when the narrator reaches for the wrong glass?

VOCABULARY • The Prefix *Pre-*

The English prefix *pre-* always means either "before" (prehistoric) or "leading up to" (preschool). However, *pre-* is also a Latin prefix (spelled *prae*) that was attached to many Latin words before they became part of the English language. For example, *preface* comes from the Latin *prae* plus *fari* ("to speak"), not from the English *pre-* plus *face*.

PRACTICE For each of the following words, write *English* if you think the prefix *pre-* is attached to an English base word. Write *Latin* if you think it is attached to a Latin root. Then use a dictionary to check your work.

1. preheat
2. predict
3. predecessor
4. premature
5. preview
6. presume
7. pretense
8. preliminary
9. predetermined
10. present

Skill Minilessons

GRAMMAR AND LANGUAGE
Dashes

1. The narrator is a miner—but that's irrelevant to the plot.
2. Henry's wife was charming—so charming that all of Henry's miner friends loved her.
3. Henry's home showed a woman's touch—lovely linens, wallpaper, framed artwork, and a variety of decorative objects.
4. Gold fever spread like wildfire—everyone wanted to strike it rich.

READING AND THINKING
Scanning

1. The "living dead men" were gold miners who had lost their wealth and were too ashamed to return home.
2. Henry's wife had gone about fifty miles away to visit her parents.
3. Tom cries when Henry reads the letter.
4. The narrator loses his patience at Henry's worrying and expresses his annoyance.
5. Joe says, "Drop that! Take the other."

VOCABULARY
The Prefix *Pre-*

1. English
2. Latin
3. Latin
4. Latin
5. English
6. Latin
7. Latin
8. Latin
9. Latin
10. Latin

Additional Resources

📕 *Grammar and Composition Handbook,* Lesson 11.7

📕 *Grammar and Language Workbook,* p. 267

📕 *Writer's Choice,* Lesson 21.7

📁 *Reading Workbook,* pp. 23–24

📁 *Vocabulary Practice,* p. 20

MEDIA Connection

Objective

- To read and understand a Web site

Literature LINK

An Astrologer's Day This Web site connects to "An Astrologer's Day" (pp. 260–263). It satirizes the art of the astrologer, who claims to be able to predict a person's future based on his or her birth date. The protagonist of "An Astrologer's Day" earns a living as an astrologer.

Respond

1. Students should make a choice based on their own idea of fun and their knowledge of animals.
2. Students' responses should show careful reading and a use of prior knowledge of pets.

Additional Resources

📁 *Media Connection Activities,* p. 9

Teaching Options

MEDIA Connection

Web Site

Do you have a dog—or know a dog—who might like to know what the future holds? Here's what a dog's horoscope might look like.

This Week's Horoscope for Your Dog

Address: ▼ www.purina.com

Aquarius Dog *(Jan. 20–Feb. 18)* Break your routine. Head to an out-of-the-way park for new trees and scents.

Pisces Dog *(Feb. 19–Mar. 20)* Shine as a leader. Start the nightly neighborhood bark-a-thon. Stop the minute it starts so you don't get blamed.

Aries Dog *(Mar. 21–Apr. 19)* Keep alert and you'll enjoy the unexpected. An extra treat tossed your way for no reason. The long-lost ball that appears out of nowhere.

Taurus Dog *(Apr. 20–May 20)* Focus on the written word. Get out and fetch a newspaper. Chew on a magazine left carelessly within reach. It's a good way to digest the news.

Gemini Dog *(May 21–June 21)* Attention revolves around you. Soak it up. You won't have to look far for a hand to pet you, a lap to cuddle in, or a scratch behind the ears.

Cancer Dog *(June 22–July 22)* Decisions, decisions. Chew the rubber toy or the rawhide? Doze on the couch or in the sunbeam? Fetch or roll over? It's a week of tough choices.

Leo Dog *(July 23–Aug. 22)* You were just trying to help, but Mom and Dad didn't see it that way, and now you're in the doghouse (or basement, or garage). Oh, well. Time for a nap.

Virgo Dog *(Aug. 23–Sept. 22)* Communication is essential this week. Rev up those vocal chords with a few good growls and wait for the moon to make its debut. When it does, howl away.

Libra Dog *(Sept. 23–Oct. 23)* Teamwork is in the offing. Joining forces with the Lab next door may help you scare off that pesky little squirrel in the far oak. Pairing up with the kids gets you in the pool on a hot afternoon.

Scorpio Dog *(Oct. 24–Nov. 22)* Investigation is needed this week. Tune up the ol' sniffer and head out into the yard. Track that smell to the back fence, then around to the hose and over to the edge of the patio. Track the scent again and again; it'll be dinnertime soon.

Sagittarius Dog *(Nov. 23–Dec. 21)* Security is the watchword of the day. Pay close attention to the front and back doors. Prick up your ears and keep that tail up; the integrity of the perimeter depends on you.

Capricorn Dog *(Dec. 22–Jan. 19)* Tend to financial matters. You need to tally your assets, so head to the yard and start digging. There's satisfaction in seeing your wealth piled in front of you. Now re-bury and invest for the future.

258 🐾 UNIT 1

Respond

1. In your opinion, which dogs had the most fun this week?
2. Which horoscope reminds you of a pet you have known or read about? Explain.

Reading *Minilesson*

Skimming Point out that in order to quickly find useful information on Web sites, students should glance at headings, highlighted words, graphics, and sections of text.

Activity Have students skim for key words to quickly locate the following

1. If a dog was born on May 31, what would its horoscope sign be? *(Gemini Dog)*
2. Which dog should use teamwork? *(Libra Dog)*
3. Which dog might accumulate wealth? *(Capricorn Dog)*

Additional Resources

📁 *Reading Workbook*

Before You Read

An Astrologer's Day

FOCUS ACTIVITY

What would it be like to look into your future and learn what will happen in your life?

LIST IT! List three questions that you would like to have answered about your future.

SETTING A PURPOSE Read to learn what is revealed when a man asks about his future.

BACKGROUND

The Time and Place
"An Astrologer's Day" takes place in Malgudi, an imaginary town in southern India, probably in the 1940s.

Did You Know?
Some astrologers claim the ability to foretell an individual's future by drawing and studying a chart called a *horoscope*. A horoscope shows the configuration of the planets and stars at the moment of an individual's birth; this configuration supposedly influences that person's life. Those who believe in astrology may rely on their astrologers to counsel them on major decisions. Astronomers and other scientists, however, maintain that the configuration of heavenly bodies has nothing whatever to do with human destiny.

VOCABULARY PREVIEW

enhance (en hans´) *v.* to make greater, as in beauty or value; p. 260
dally (dal´ ē) *v.* to linger; delay; waste time; p. 260
impetuous (im pech´ ōo əs) *adj.* rushing headlong into things; rash; p. 262
paraphernalia (par´ ə fər nāl´ yə) *n.* things used in a particular activity; equipment; p. 262
piqued (pēkt) *adj.* aroused to anger or resentment; offended; p. 262
incantation (in´ kan tā´ shən) *n.* words spoken in casting a spell; p. 262

Meet
R. K. Narayan

After realizing that he did not want to be a teacher, civil servant, or journalist, R. K. Narayan (nä rä´ yan) turned to fiction writing as a career. His first novel, *Swami and Friends*, was published in 1935. Narayan has written ten novels and numerous short stories; he also has published nonfiction works. His tales of the fictional Indian village of Malgudi—the setting for the story you are about to read—have had a wide appeal. In fact, Narayan is probably best known as the creator of Malgudi, a place that has been called a "zany, eccentric and, at the same time, true-to-life world."

Rasipuram Krishnaswami Narayan was born in 1906 in Madras, India. "An Astrologer's Day" was published in 1947.

Objectives
- To read and analyze a short story about an astrologer's secret
- To analyze description
- To write about first and later impressions of a character

Skills

Reading/Thinking: Drawing Conclusions; Making Inferences
Writing: Story Retelling
Vocabulary: Etymology
Grammar/Language: Colons; Concrete and Abstract Nouns
Listening/Speaking: Dialogue
Collaboration: Literature Groups

Motivating
→OPTIONS

Literature Launchers: "Life in India"

Videodisc
Side A, Segment 6

Also available in VHS.

Selection Focus Transparency 22: Have students name and discuss unusual jobs.

Focus Activity: Tally the number of class members who wrote common questions, such as "What will I do for a living?"

RESOURCE MANAGER

Lesson Planning Resource
The *Unit One Planning Guide* (pp. 185–192) provides additional lesson notes and reduced versions of all print resources.

📁 **Other Print Resources**
- Active Reading Guide, p. 22
- Vocabulary Practice, p. 21
- Reading Workbook, pp. 25–26
- Grammar and Language Workbook, pp. 247, 48
- Grammar and Composition Handbook, Lessons 11.4, 1.1

- Quick Checks, p. 22
- Selection and Theme Assessment, pp. 43–44
- Performance Assessment, p. 22
- Spanish Summaries, p. 22
- Spanish Translations
- Inclusion Strategies
- English Language Learners Sourcebook

📑 **Transparencies**
- Selection Focus 22
- Literary Elements 22

- Grammar and Language 22

Technology
- 💿 Literature Launchers
- 🎧 Audio Library
- 🎧 Spanish Audio Library
- 💻 Glencoe Literature Web Site
- 📖 Testmaker

SUMMARY

One evening a man appears and agrees to give an astrologer more than his usual rate if he gives him satisfactory information. The astrologer correctly tells the customer that he was left for dead after being stabbed and pushed into a well, that he will not find the culprit because he is dead, and that he should go home immediately and never leave again. Later, the astrologer tells his wife that he has found that a man he thought he had killed in his village is still alive.

📁 *Spanish Summaries,* p. 22

A Active Reading

VISUALIZE Encourage students to visualize the street scene that the author describes. Have them relate the description to descriptions they have read and pictures they have seen of cities in India.

Additional Resources
📁 *Active Reading Guide,* p. 22
🎧 *Audio Library*
🎧 *Spanish Audio Library*

Teaching Options

An Astrologer's

R. K. Narayan ❧

PUNCTUALLY AT MIDDAY he opened his bag and spread out his professional equipment, which consisted of a dozen cowrie[1] shells, a square piece of cloth with obscure mystic charts on it, a notebook and a bundle of palmyra writing. His forehead was resplendent with sacred ash and vermilion,[2] and his eyes sparkled with a sharp abnormal gleam which was really an outcome of a continual searching look for customers, but which his simple clients took to be a prophetic light and felt comforted. The power of his eyes was considerably <u>enhanced</u> by their position—placed as they were between the painted forehead and the dark whiskers which streamed down his cheeks: even a half-wit's eyes would sparkle in such a setting. To crown the effect he wound a saffron-colored[3] turban around his head. This color scheme never failed. People were attracted to him as bees are attracted to cosmos or dahlia stalks. He sat under the boughs of a spreading tamarind tree which flanked a path running through the Town Hall Park. It was a remarkable place in many ways: a surging crowd was always moving up and down this narrow road morning till night. A variety of trades and occupations was represented all along its way: medicine-sellers, sellers of stolen hardware and junk, magicians and, above all, an auctioneer of cheap cloth, who created enough din all day to attract the whole town. Next to him in vociferousness[4] came a vendor of fried groundnuts, who gave his ware a fancy name each day, calling it Bombay Ice-Cream one day, and on the next Delhi Almond, and on the third Raja's Delicacy, and so on and so forth, and people flocked to him. A considerable portion of this crowd <u>dallied</u> before the astrologer too. The astrologer transacted his business by the light of a flare which crackled and smoked up above the groundnut heap nearby. Half the enchantment of the place was due to the fact that it did not have the benefit of municipal lighting. The place was lit up by shop lights. One or two had hissing gaslights, some had

---

1. The *cowrie* (kau′rē) is a small snail commonly found in warm, shallow waters of the Pacific and Indian Oceans.
2. Here, *obscure* means "difficult to understand" and *mystic* means "having hidden or secret meanings." *Palmyra* (pal mī′ ra) refers to paper made from the leaves of the palmyra tree. The man's forehead is full of splendor (*resplendent*) in that it is painted with dark ash and a red pigment called *vermilion*.
3. *Saffron* is an orange-yellow color.

4. *Vociferousness* (vō sif′ ər əs nəs) means "noisy outcrying."

Vocabulary
enhance (en hans′) *v.* to make greater, as in beauty or value
dally (dal′ ē) *v.* to linger; delay; waste time

CONNECTING TO OTHER SELECTIONS

The chart at the right shows three ways to connect "An Astrologer's Day" to selections in this book.

For specific teaching strategies, see the *Unit One Planning Guide,* pages 188–189.

Connection	Title
Life Skills: Problem Solving	→ *Antigone,* p. 727
Thematic: Making Amends	→ "A Child, a Dog, the Night," p. 129
Literary: Point of View	→ "What I Have Been Doing Lately," p. 109

Day

By permission of the British Library.

B naked flares stuck on poles, some were lit up by old cycle lamps and one or two, like the astrologer's, managed without lights of their own. It was a bewildering criss-cross of light rays and moving shadows. This suited the astrologer very well, for the simple reason that he had not in the least intended to be an astrologer when he began life; and he knew no more of what was going to happen to others than he knew what was going to happen to himself next minute. He was as much a stranger to the stars as were his innocent customers.

C Yet he said things which pleased and astonished everyone: that was more a matter of study, practice and shrewd guesswork. All the same, it was as much an honest man's labor as any other, and he deserved the wages he carried home at the end of a day.

He had left his village without any previous thought or plan. If he had continued there he would have carried on the work of his forefathers—namely, tilling the land, living, marrying and ripening in his cornfield and ancestral home. But that was not to be. He had to leave home without telling anyone, and he could not rest till he left it behind a couple of hundred miles. To a villager it is a great deal, as if an ocean flowed between.

He had a working analysis of mankind's troubles: marriage, money and the tangles of human ties. Long practice had sharpened his perception. Within five minutes he understood what was wrong. He charged three pice[5] per question and never opened his mouth till the other had spoken for at least ten minutes, which provided him enough stuff for a dozen answers and advices. When he told the person before him, gazing at his palm, "In many ways you are not getting the fullest results for your efforts," nine out of ten were disposed to agree with him. Or he questioned: "Is there any woman in your family, maybe even a distant relative, who is not well disposed[6] towards you?" Or he gave an analysis of character: **D**

---

5. A *pice* is a coin of India of very small value.
6. In this paragraph, *disposed* is used twice with slightly different meanings. The first time, you might substitute *likely* or *inclined*. The second time, substitute *favorable* for the phrase "well disposed."

FYI

Astrology Astrology is a form of fortune telling. It originated in ancient Babylonia and was practiced in ancient Egypt, Greece, India, and China. The earliest known horoscope dates to 409 B.C.

B Literary Elements

DESCRIPTION Have students compare the description of the lights to that of the astrologer's eyes ("his eyes sparkled with a sharp abnormal gleam") and to the "little shaft of green light" on page 262. How does the author use the various lights to create plot, setting, and character? *(The light in the astrologer's eyes is him searching for customers, but people think it is a "prophetic light." The streetlights help create the exotic scene. The dim green light keeps the customer from knowing the identity of the astrologer.)*

C Active Reading

EVALUATE Ask students whether they think the astrologer is cheating his customers or whether he deserves the money he makes for what he tells them.

D Literary Elements

CHARACTER Why do the astrologer's usual comments generally make people happy? *(He tells them what he knows they want to hear.)*

E Literary Elements

CHARACTER Ask students how the astrologer's client differs from most of the people he advises. *(He is impatient with the astrologer's standard comments; he knows they are worthless.)*

F Literary Elements

DESCRIPTION Have students identify the sound imagery and the vivid verbs used to describe the street scene in the midst of the dialogue between the astrologer and his client. *(Sound images include cars hooting, drivers swearing, and the crowd babbling. Vivid verbs include "hooted," "swore," and "agitated.")*

G Critical Thinking

DRAWING CONCLUSIONS Ask students if they think the astrologer may have recognized the identity of his client. You may wish to provide the following model to show how to draw conclusions from the text.

Model: The astrologer is very interested in having the man as a client and bargains eagerly with him. After the astrologer sees the man's face as he is lighting a match, the astrologer's attitude changes abruptly. He feels uncomfortable. He tries to give the man his money back and says it's late and come back tomorrow. I think the astrologer recognizes the man and is afraid to spend any more time with him.

"Most of your troubles are due to your nature. How can you be otherwise with Saturn where he is? You have an impetuous nature and a rough exterior." This endeared him to their hearts immediately, for even the mildest of us loves to think that he has a forbidding exterior.

The nuts-vendor blew out his flare and rose to go home. This was a signal for the astrologer to bundle up too, since it left him in darkness except for a little shaft of green light which strayed in from somewhere and touched the ground before him. He picked up his cowrie shells and paraphernalia and was putting them back into his bag when the green shaft of light was blotted out; he looked up and saw a man standing before him. He sensed a possible client and said: "You look so careworn. It will do you good to sit down for a while and chat with me." The other grumbled some vague reply. The astrologer pressed his invitation; whereupon the other thrust his palm under his nose, saying: "You call yourself an astrologer?" The astrologer felt challenged and said, tilting the other's palm towards the green shaft of light: "Yours is a nature . . ." "Oh, stop that," the other said. "Tell me something worthwhile. . . ."

Our friend felt piqued. "I charge only three pice per question, and what you get ought to be good enough for your money. . . ." At this the other withdrew his arm, took out an anna and flung it out to him, saying, "I have some questions to ask. If I prove you are bluffing, you must return that anna to me with interest."

"If you find my answers satisfactory, will you give me five rupees?"[7]

"No."

"Or will you give me eight annas?"

"All right, provided you give me twice as much if you are wrong," said the stranger. This pact was accepted after a little further argument. The astrologer sent up a prayer to heaven as the other lit a cheroot.[8] The astrologer caught a glimpse of his face by the matchlight. There was a pause as cars hooted on the road, jutka[9] drivers swore at their horses and the babble of the crowd agitated the semidarkness of the park. The other sat down, sucking his cheroot, puffing out, sat there ruthlessly. The astrologer felt very uncomfortable. "Here, take your anna back. I am not used to such challenges. It is late for me today. . . ." He made preparations to bundle up. The other held his wrist and said, "You can't get out of it now. You dragged me in while I was passing." The astrologer shivered in his grip; and his voice shook and became faint. "Leave me today. I will speak to you tomorrow." The other thrust his palm in his face and said, "Challenge is challenge. Go on." The astrologer proceeded with his throat drying up. "There is a woman . . ."

"Stop," said the other. "I don't want all that. Shall I succeed in my present search or not? Answer this and go. Otherwise I will not let you go till you disgorge[10] all your coins." The astrologer muttered a few incantations and replied, "All right. I will speak. But will you give me a rupee if what I say is convincing? Otherwise I will not open my mouth, and you may do what you like." After a

---

7. The *anna* is a former coin of India that was equal to four pice. The *rupee* is a coin of India (and other countries) equal to sixteen annas.

8. A *cheroot* (shə rōōt′) is a cigar cut square at both ends.
9. A *jutka* (jōōt′ kə) is a two-wheeled, horse-drawn vehicle.
10. Here, *disgorge* means "to give up or hand over."

Vocabulary

impetuous (im pech′ ōō əs) *adj.* rushing headlong into things; rash
paraphernalia (par′ ə fər nāl′ yə) *n.* things used in a particular activity; equipment
piqued (pēkt) *adj.* aroused to anger or resentment; offended
incantation (in′ kan tā′ shən) *n.* words spoken in casting a spell

---

Teaching Options

Grammar and Language *Minilesson*

Colons Explain that a colon is used to introduce a list of items or to separate two independent clauses when the second clause is an explanation of the first. Point out the four sentences using colons on page 261 and have students tell which use each sentence shows. *(The first, third, and fourth separate an independent clause from a second clause that explains it; the second introduces a list.)*

Activity Have students write two sentences for each use of a colon. Have volunteers write their sentences on the board. **L2**

Additional Resources

📖 *Grammar and Language Transparency 22*

📕 *Grammar and Language Workbook,* p. 247

📗 *Grammar and Composition Handbook,* Lesson 11.4

📘 *Writer's Choice,* Lesson 21.4

262

R. K. Narayan

good deal of haggling the other agreed. The astrologer said, "You were left for dead. Am I right?"

"Ah, tell me more."

"A knife has passed through you once?" said the astrologer.

"Good fellow!" He bared his chest to show the scar. "What else?"

"And then you were pushed into a well nearby in the field. You were left for dead."

"I should have been dead if some passerby had not chanced to peep into the well," exclaimed the other, overwhelmed by enthusiasm. "When shall I get at him?" he asked, clenching his fist.

"In the next world," answered the astrologer. "He died four months ago in a far-off town. You will never see any more of him." The other groaned on hearing it. The astrologer proceeded.

"Guru Nayak—"

"You know my name!" the other said, taken aback.[11]

"As I know all other things. Guru Nayak, listen carefully to what I have to say. Your village is two days' journey due north of this town. Take the next train and be gone. I see once again great danger to your life if you go from home." He took out a pinch of sacred ash and held it out to him. "Rub it on your forehead and go home. Never travel southward again, and you will live to be a hundred."

"Why should I leave home again?" the other said reflectively.[12] "I was only going away now and then to look for him and to choke out his life if I met him." He shook his head regretfully.

---

11. The expression *taken aback* means "suddenly surprised or startled."
12. Here, *reflectively* (ri flek′ tiv lē) means "in a way that shows serious and careful consideration."

"He has escaped my hands. I hope at least he died as he deserved." "Yes," said the astrologer. "He was crushed under a lorry."[13] The other looked gratified to hear it.

The place was deserted by the time the astrologer picked up his articles and put them into his bag. The green shaft was also gone, leaving the place in darkness and silence. The stranger had gone off into the night, after giving the astrologer a handful of coins.

It was nearly midnight when the astrologer reached home. His wife was waiting for him at the door and demanded an explanation. He flung the coins at her and said, "Count them. One man gave all that."

"Twelve and a half annas," she said, counting. She was overjoyed. "I can buy some *jaggery*[14] and coconut tomorrow. The child has been asking for sweets for so many days now. I will prepare some nice stuff for her."

"The swine has cheated me! He promised me a rupee," said the astrologer. She looked up at him. "You look worried. What is wrong?"

"Nothing."

After dinner, sitting on the *pyol*,[15] he told her, "Do you know a great load is gone from me today? I thought I had the blood of a man on my hands all these years. That was the reason why I ran away from home, settled here and married you. He is alive."

She gasped, "You tried to kill!"

"Yes, in our village, when I was a silly youngster. We drank, gambled and quarreled badly one day—why think of it now? Time to sleep," he said, yawning, and stretched himself on the *pyol*.

---

13. Here, the *lorry* is a long, flat, horse-drawn wagon.
14. *Jaggery* is unrefined sugar made from palm tree sap.
15. A *pyol* (pī′ ôl) is a low bench.

H **Literary Elements**

CHARACTER Ask students how their previous knowledge of the astrologer affects their interpretation of his comments to the client. *(The astrologer clearly does not have any supernatural powers. Therefore, when he tells details about the client's life, he must have known the client previously.)*

Historical Note

In 1947, India became an independent country after more than two centuries of British rule. However, this momentous event was marred by religious strife: parts of India became the separate Islamic country of Pakistan, and millions of Hindus and Muslims were displaced by the split.

Thematic Focus

Twists Discuss what the twist demonstrates about the astrologer's character. *(He is an opportunist. He has little sense of right and wrong or of personal responsibility.)*

✔ ASSESSMENT OPTIONS

📁 *Quick Checks*, p. 22

REAL-WORLD CONNECTION

Reunions Have students look for newspaper articles in which people are reunited with friends or family members after many years of being separated. When articles have been located, let students meet in small groups and discuss the information in their articles. Encourage students to make comparisons between their articles and the meeting that occurred in "An Astrologer's Day." In what ways were the story and article alike? In what ways were they different? **L1** COLLAB. LEARN.

Personal Response

Students may express surprise because the astrologer kept a secret from his wife for many years or because he expresses no remorse for what he did.

ANALYZING LITERATURE

1. He has a brightly painted face, wears a bright yellow turban, and has a gleam in his eye.
2. He spreads a cloth under a tree near a busy path in a park. He is near several other men who sell things.
3. The stranger will give the astrologer eight annas if he is satisfied. The astrologer will give the stranger twice as much if his answers are wrong. The astrologer tries to return the money and forget the deal.
4. The astrologer tells the stranger that he has been left for dead: stabbed and pushed into a well. He advises him to go home immediately.
5. He ran away from home many years earlier because he had quarreled with a man and thought he had killed him.
6. Students may say that the astrologer helps his customers by listening to them.
7. He expected to get married in his home village, farm, and stay there his entire life. He ended up moving far away and becoming an astrologer.
8. The astrologer is uncomfortable and tries to back out of the deal. He may fear the stranger will recognize him.
9. The astrologer is the one who attacked him and left him for dead years before. He tells the stranger to leave and never come back, so they will never meet again.
10. The astrologer may not feel remorseful because he says a great load has been lifted from him; he puts the incident out of his mind and goes to sleep.
11. Remind students that the astrologer is very clever.
12. Nayak, looking for revenge, unknowingly runs into his would-be killer and is deceived by him.
13. Guide students to note how the change of light through the day might affect the outcome.
14. The saying applies to the astrologer, who has run away from his past. The saying might apply to real-life situations in which people try to run away from problems.

Responding to Literature

Personal Response

Were you surprised by the outcome of the story, particularly the astrologer's conversation with his wife? Explain why or why not.

ANALYZING LITERATURE

RECALL

1. According to the narrator, how does the astrologer's appearance help him attract customers?
2. Describe the astrologer's place of business.
3. Summarize the agreement the astrologer and the stranger make. What does the astrologer try to do after making the agreement?
4. What does the astrologer tell the stranger about his past? What advice does he give him about his future?
5. What does the astrologer finally reveal to his wife about his past?

INTERPRET

6. In your opinion, what service does the astrologer actually perform for his customers?
7. Compare the life the astrologer expected to live with the one he is actually living.
8. What details indicate that the astrologer is afraid of the stranger? What causes this fear, in your opinion?
9. Why does the astrologer know so much about the stranger's past? Why does he give him this particular advice about his future?
10. Do you think the astrologer feels remorseful about the incident he reveals to his wife? Support your answer with details from the story.

EVALUATE AND CONNECT

11. Look back at the questions you listed in the Focus Activity on page 259. How do you think the astrologer might answer your questions?
12. In your opinion, what is **ironic** about Guru Nayak's meeting with the astrologer? (See Literary Terms Handbook, page R6.)
13. What do you think might have happened if the stranger had arrived earlier in the day? Explain your answer.
14. You may have heard the expression, "The past has a way of coming back to haunt you." How does that expression apply to this story? To what real-life experiences might the expression be applied?
15. In your opinion, why do people seek advice about the future? From whom do people today seek such advice?

Literary ELEMENTS

Description

Description is writing that helps readers imagine what characters see, hear, feel, taste, or touch. Notice the vivid description in this passage from "An Astrologer's Day": "The astrologer caught a glimpse of [the stranger's] face by the matchlight. There was a pause as cars hooted on the road, *jutka* drivers swore at their horses and the babble of the crowd agitated the semidarkness of the park." Descriptive language can help bring a character to life. Description also can help build suspense or provide clues about what might happen next.

1. List descriptive details that help you imagine the marketplace in which the astrologer conducts his business.
2. What details and techniques does Narayan use to describe the astrologer?

● See **Literary Terms Handbook,** p. R3.

15. Students may say that people seek such advice because they want to know what is going to happen. Some people may look to astrologers while others may consult psychologists.

LITERARY ELEMENTS

1. Details include descriptions of the other vendors, the vendors' lights, and the noises of the traffic and people.
2. He tells what he looks like, explains his techniques, and shows his words and his actions.

Additional Resources

Literary Elements Transparency 22

LITERATURE AND WRITING

Writing About Literature
Changing Impressions   The characters who live in or pass through the fictional town of Malgudi are not always what they first appear to be. In a paragraph, describe your first impression of either the astrologer or the stranger. Then write a second paragraph explaining how your impression may have changed as the story progressed. Support your first and later impressions with details from the story. Share your writing with others in a small group.

Creative Writing
Guru Nayak's Story   Retell all or part of this story from the first-person point of view, with the stranger as the narrator. You may wish to begin the story at an earlier time, perhaps the day on which the stranger quarreled with the man who later became an astrologer. Feel free to invent details or conversations, as necessary.

EXTENDING YOUR RESPONSE

Literature Groups
You Be the Judge   Does the astrologer deserve to be punished for what he did to Guru Nayak? Does his apparent lack of remorse make his crime seem even worse? Do you think it's unfair that he seems to have gotten away with his crime? Does the fact that he was a "silly youngster" when he committed the crime make him any less responsible for his actions? Debate these issues in your group. Share your ideas with the class.

Interdisciplinary Activity
Art: An Astrologer's Portrait   Create a portrait of the astrologer. Before you begin, carefully reread the description of the astrologer in the first paragraph of the story. Compare your portrait with those created by your classmates.

Performing
Dialogue   With a partner, practice performing all or part of the dialogue between the astrologer and the stranger. Do your best to duplicate the actions and gestures described in the story. Simulate these actions when necessary—for example, the student portraying the stranger should pretend to light a cigar. Perform your dialogue for the class.

Reading Further
You might also enjoy these short stories by R. K. Narayan:
"Uncle" from A Horse and Two Goats tells how a young boy grows up under the guidance of his uncle.
"A Career" from Under the Banyan Tree recounts how a young man seems perfect in every way, except for one major flaw.

📖 **Save your work for your portfolio.**

THE SHORT STORY 🐿 265

LITERATURE AND WRITING

Writing About Literature
Students' paragraphs should
- clearly describe a first impression of a character.
- clearly describe how the first impression changed.
- support the impressions with details from the story.

Creative Writing
Students' stories should
- use a first-person point of view.
- use the characters and plot from "An Astrologer's Day."
- demonstrate creativity in the use of setting or plot.

EXTENDING YOUR RESPONSE

Literature Groups   Suggest that students compare the issues in the astrologer's case with real-life incidents they have read about.
COLLAB. LEARN.

Interdisciplinary Activity
Encourage students to use any style they wish in their portraits and to discuss the style when the portraits are completed. 📦

Performing   Point out particularly appropriate vocal techniques, facial expressions, and gestures when students perform their dialogues. 📦

✔ ASSESSMENT OPTIONS

📁 *Quick Checks,* p. 22
📁 *Selection and Theme Assessment,* pp. 43–44
📁 *Performance Assessment,* p. 22
📁 *Testmaker*

Skill Minilessons

GRAMMAR AND LANGUAGE
Concrete and Abstract Nouns

Concrete Nouns
astrologer, turban, flare, money, palm, coins, coconut, blood
Abstract Nouns
thought, incantations, babble, enthusiasm, silence, challenge, perception

READING AND THINKING
Making Inferences

Practice

The astrologer's wife is strong-willed, a caring mother, sensitive, and morally upright.

Apply

Guru Nayak seems reasonably well off: he has the money to pay the astrologer and enough to afford cigars and train fare.

VOCABULARY
Etymology

1. *Impetuous* comes from a Latin word meaning "attack." *Petulant* comes from a Latin word meaning "pert" or "saucy." Both refer to kinds of behavior.
2. Both are from a French word meaning "to prick." *Pique* means "to arouse anger" and *piquant* "to stimulate the taste buds."
3. Both are from Latin words meaning "high." *Enhance* means "to increase or improve in value" and *haughty* "disdainfully proud."

Additional Resources

- *Grammar and Composition Handbook,* Lesson 11.1
- *Grammar and Language Workbook,* p. 48
- *Writer's Choice,* Lesson 10.1
- *Reading Workbook,* pp. 25–26
- *Vocabulary Practice,* p. 21

Skill Minilessons

GRAMMAR AND LANGUAGE • Concrete and Abstract Nouns

A **noun** is a word that names a person, place, thing, or idea. A **concrete noun** names something that occupies space, or that you can see, hear, taste, smell, or feel. "An Astrologer's Day" includes such concrete nouns as *magicians, shadows, din,* and *groundnuts.* An **abstract noun** names an idea, a quality, or a characteristic. Abstract nouns from the story include such words as *enchantment, danger,* and *guesswork.*

PRACTICE On your paper, make two columns. Label one column *Concrete Nouns* and the other *Abstract Nouns.* Write each of the following words in the correct column. Then write three or four sentences in which you use as many of the nouns as possible.

> astrologer, turban, flare, thought, money, palm, incantations, babble, enthusiasm, coins, coconut, silence, blood, challenge, perception

APPLY Review one or two pieces of your writing. List at least ten concrete nouns and five abstract nouns from your work.

● For more about nouns, see **Language Handbook,** pp. R40–R41.

READING AND THINKING • Making Inferences

The narrator of "An Astrologer's Day" reveals a great deal of information about the characters, especially the astrologer. Still, the reader must make **inferences—** reasonable judgments based on information in the story— in order to fully understand the characters and the plot. For example, the narrator doesn't directly state the astrologer's economic status. What can you infer about it from this passage describing the marketplace?

> The place was lit up by shop lights. One or two had hissing gaslights, some had naked flares stuck on poles, some were lit up by old cycle lamps and one or two, like the astrologer's, managed without lights of their own.

It would be reasonable to infer that the astrologer is poor, since he apparently cannot afford lighting for his place of business.

PRACTICE Reread the last seven paragraphs of the story. On your paper, list inferences you might make about the astrologer's wife, based on her words and actions.

APPLY What inference might you make about Guru Nayak's economic situation? List the information on which your inference is based.

● For more about inferences, see **Reading Handbook,** pp. R78–R107.

VOCABULARY • Etymology

Sometimes it is hard to recognize that two words are related in meaning because the spelling of one word has changed over time. For example, *incantation,* which means "words spoken in casting a spell," comes from the same root as *chant* and *enchant.* That connection would be clearer if the *h* hadn't been dropped. Still, learning the etymology, or history, of the word *incantation* makes the relationship clear and can help you remember what the word means.

PRACTICE Use a dictionary to look up the etymologies of each pair of words. (A word's etymology is usually given in brackets along with its definition.) Then briefly explain what their etymologies reveal about how the two words are related.

1. *impetuous* and *petulant*
2. *pique* and *piquant*
3. *enhance* and *haughty*

LISTENING, SPEAKING, and VIEWING

Storytelling

In "An Astrologer's Day," the astrologer is such a convincing storyteller that he makes the "stranger" believe a lie. Oral storytellers have played an important role in cultures around the world, from ancient times to the present day. Their stories have served not only to entertain people but also to pass on a culture's history, values, traditions, and customs from one generation to another. A storyteller brings a tale to life by making the telling of a story into a performance. The storyteller speaks dramatically, uses gestures, and sometimes includes sound effects and music. How would you like to step into the shoes of a storyteller? These guidelines can help you prepare and tell a story.

Practicing a Story

- Become familiar enough with your story that you remember all the important details in the correct order. Remember, you won't *read* the story, you'll *tell* it. So don't memorize the story word for word; just memorize what happens.
- Practice telling your story in front of a mirror. Speak clearly and distinctly. Vary the pitch and tone of your voice to convey excitement, surprise, and other emotions.
- If you wish, add sound effects or music to your performance. You can make your own sound effects using your voice, your hands, or simple tools.
- Use gestures and facial expressions to emphasize exciting parts of your story.
- Ask a friend or family members to watch your performance and give you tips on ways to make it more effective. You might even have someone videotape your performance so that you can critique it yourself.

Telling the Story

- Before you begin, take a deep breath and relax.
- Prepare your audience to listen to your story. If necessary, set the scene by telling where and when the story takes place, and what it is about.
- Enjoy your performance! Your listeners are likely to share your level of enthusiasm.

ACTIVITIES

1. Find and view a videotape of a master storyteller. Take notes on how the storyteller uses tone of voice, gestures, expressions, and sound effects to create a mood and "paint pictures" for the audience. Share your observations with the class.

2. Search through books of folktales and myths to find one you would like to tell, or choose one of the short stories in this book. Use the suggestions given in this lesson to prepare your performance. Then make your debut as a storyteller before the class.

LISTENING, SPEAKING, and VIEWING

Objective

- To learn and tell a story to an audience

Teaching Strategies

Have a volunteer tell a fable or a short folk tale. Suggest that students focus on the volunteer's delivery. Then discuss techniques the student used to bring the story and story characters to life. Let students suggest other ways for orally making a story come alive.

Activities

1. Garrison Keillor is one popular storyteller on videotape. Students can locate others at the library.
2. Suggest that students consider these points:
   Point of View: Telling a story from the first person point of view is similar to a monologue, while a third person narrator may take on several different characters.
   Tone: Students should consider whether they would like to tell a serious, funny, or sad story.
   Story Elements: Some students may want to tell a story with strong characters, while others prefer a story with a surprising plot twist or a colorful setting.

MEETING INDIVIDUAL NEEDS — ENGLISH LANGUAGE LEARNERS

Storytelling Have English language learners tell stories from their cultures in their native languages. Point out that basic vocal techniques, gestures, and facial expressions are common to storytelling in all languages.

Activity Encourage students to choose a folk tale or myth that they know in their native language and prepare to tell it in English. Encourage them to give any interesting information about the story's background before telling the story.

Additional Resources
📁 *English Language Learners Sourcebook*

Objectives

- To read and analyze a short story about two men trapped in an old feud
- To identify conflict and resolution
- To write a description of a story's setting

Skills

Reading/Thinking: Evaluating; Paraphrasing; Drawing Conclusions; Summarizing
Writing: Story Sequel
Vocabulary: Multiple Meaning Words; Analogies
Grammar/Language: Adverbs; Sentence Variety
Listening/Speaking: Dialogue
Collaboration: Literature Groups

Motivating
→OPTIONS

Selection Focus Transparency 23: Help students understand the meaning of the Prologue to *Romeo and Juliet*. Then ask them to name and discuss any examples of longtime feuds or rivalries they are familiar with.

Focus Activity: Have students offer ways in which longtime enemies or friends can change their relationship.

Before You Read
The Interlopers

── FOCUS ACTIVITY ──

Have you ever had an enemy you no longer disliked or a friend you no longer liked, and yet felt bound to maintain the relationship—just the way it was?

QUICKWRITE List reasons you might be unwilling or unable to break off with a friend, or to reconcile with a former enemy. Why is it sometimes so difficult to change an existing relationship with another person?

SETTING A PURPOSE Read to learn about two men who are caught in an old relationship.

── BACKGROUND ──

Black Sea

The Time and Place

"The Interlopers" takes place in the Carpathian Mountains in southeast Europe, probably in the early 1900s.

Did You Know?

Poaching—trespassing on another person's land to hunt or fish—has been a crime, sometimes punishable by death, for hundreds of years. In some parts of the world today, poachers illegally capture or kill wild animals to sell to collectors, or they kill the animals and then sell their skins or other body parts.

── VOCABULARY PREVIEW ──

acquiesce (ak′ wē es′) *v.* to consent or agree to without protest; p. 270
wont (wōnt) *adj.* accustomed; used; p. 270
pious (pī′ əs) *adj.* having either genuine or pretended religious devotion; p. 272
endeavor (en dev′ ər) *n.* a serious or strenuous attempt to accomplish something; p. 272
languor (lang′ gər) *n.* weakness; fatigue; p. 273
reconciliation (rek′ ən sil′ ē ā′ shən) *n.* a settlement of a controversy or disagreement; p. 274
succor (suk′ ər) *n.* help; assistance; relief; p. 274
pestilential (pes′ tə len′ shəl) *adj.* harmful; destructive; p. 274

268   UNIT 1

Meet H. H. Munro (Saki)

After his mother's early death, H. H. Munro, who was born in Burma (now Myanmar) to Scottish parents, was sent to England to live with relatives. As a young man, Munro had the opportunity to travel widely. Eventually he turned to journalism and short-story writing, using the name *Saki* (sä′ kē)— which he took from a twelfth-century Persian poem—as a pseudonym. During World War I, when he was forty-four, Munro felt compelled to enlist in the British army. Two years later he died on a battlefield in France.

Hector Hugh Munro was born in 1870 and died in 1916.

RESOURCE MANAGER

Lesson Planning Resource
The *Unit One Planning Guide* (pp. 193–200) provides additional lesson notes and reduced versions of all print resources.

📁 Other Print Resources
- Active Reading Guide, p. 23
- Vocabulary Practice, p. 22
- Reading Workbook, pp. 25–26
- Grammar and Language Workbook, pp. 63, 323–325
- Grammar and Composition Handbook, Lessons 1.5,

12.1–12.5
- Quick Checks, p. 23
- Selection and Theme Assessment, pp. 45–46
- Performance Assessment, p. 23
- Spanish Summaries, p. 23
- Spanish Translations
- Inclusion Strategies
- English Language Learners Sourcebook

Transparencies
- Selection Focus 23

- Literary Elements 23
- Grammar and Language 23

Technology
- 🎧 Audio Library
- 🎧 Spanish Audio Library
- 💻 Glencoe Literature Web Site
- 💾 Testmaker

Poacher, 1894. Bruno Liljefors. Oil on canvas, 41 x 61 cm.
Statens Konstmuseer, Stockholm.

IN A FOREST of mixed growth somewhere on the eastern spurs of the Carpathians,[1] a man stood one winter night watching and listening, as though he waited for some beast of the woods to come within the range of his vision, and, later, of his rifle. But the game for whose presence he kept so keen an outlook was none that figured in the sportsman's calendar as lawful and proper for the chase; Ulrich von Gradwitz[2] patrolled the dark forest in quest of a human enemy.

1. The *Carpathians* are a mountain range in southeast Europe, and their *spurs* are ridges of mountains that extend from the main range.
2. *Ulrich von Gradwitz* (ōōl′ rik   fōn   gräd′ vitz)

The Interlopers

Saki

269

SUMMARY

Ulrich von Gradwitz is searching for a poacher, Georg Znaeym, whose family has been feuding with Ulrich's family over land rights for three generations. When they come face to face, a huge tree falls, trapping them both. The men continue feuding. Then Ulrich says he has decided to drop the feud. Znaeym agrees to drop the feud and become friends. The two men begin yelling for help and soon they see figures running toward them. The men think they are saved until Ulrich sees what the approaching figures really are.

📁 *Spanish Summaries,* p. 23

A Active Reading

PREDICT Have students read the first page and make predictions about the selection. Ask questions such as these: Why is the man hunting at night? Why might the man be after the other person?

Additional Resources

📁 *Active Reading Guide,* p.23
🎧 *Audio Library*
🎧 *Spanish Audio Library*

Teaching Options

CONNECTING TO OTHER SELECTIONS

The chart at the right shows three ways to connect "The Interlopers" to selections in this book.

For specific teaching strategies, see the *Unit One Planning Guide,* pp. 196–197.

Connection	Title
Life Skills: Planning and Designing	→ "Tuesday Siesta," p. 189
Thematic: Righting Wrongs	→ "Chee's Daughter," p. 23
Literary: Mood	→ "The Masque of the Red Death," p. 389

B **Literary Elements**

CONFLICT What is the basic conflict that sets the plot in motion? *(The protagonist, Ulrich, wants to catch the antagonist, Znaeym.)*

C **Literary Elements**

POINT OF VIEW Have students identify the story's narrative point of view and explain its features. *(The point of view is third person limited. An outside narrator tells the story but is only able to tell what the protagonist, Ulrich, is thinking and feeling.)*

D **Literary Elements**

MOOD Ask students to describe the mood of the story and give examples of the images and diction that help create the mood. *(The author creates a dark, foreboding mood by describing the visual image of the restless creatures in the forest and the sound images of the wind blowing and the branches beating. The dark mood is also heightened by the fact that the story takes place at night. Words such as* prowling, unrest, disturbing, *and* restless *increase the mood.)*

The Interlopers

The forest lands of Gradwitz were of wide extent and well stocked with game; the narrow strip of precipitous woodland that lay on its outskirt was not remarkable for the game it harbored or the shooting it afforded, but it was the most jealously guarded of all its owner's territorial possessions. A famous lawsuit, in the days of his grandfather, had wrested it from the illegal possession of a neighboring family of petty landowners; the dispossessed party had never acquiesced in the judgment of the Courts, and a long series of poaching affrays[3] and similar scandals had embittered the relationships between the families for three generations. The neighbor feud had grown into a personal one since Ulrich had come to be head of his family; if there was a man in the world whom he detested and wished ill to it was Georg Znaeym,[4] the inheritor of the quarrel and the tireless game-snatcher and raider of the disputed border-forest. The feud might, perhaps, have died down or been compromised if the personal ill-will of the two men had not stood in the way; as boys they had thirsted for one another's blood, as men each prayed that misfortune might fall on the other, and this wind-scourged[5] winter night Ulrich had banded together his foresters to watch the dark forest, not in quest of four-footed quarry,[6] but to keep a look-out for the prowling

thieves whom he suspected of being afoot from across the land boundary. The roebuck, which usually kept in the sheltered hollows during a storm-wind, were running like driven things tonight, and there was movement and unrest among the creatures that were wont to sleep through the dark hours. Assuredly there was a disturbing element in the forest, and Ulrich could guess the quarter from whence it came.

Did You Know?
A *roebuck* is the male of the roe deer, which reaches a height of about thirty inches at the shoulder.

He strayed away by himself from the watchers whom he had placed in ambush on the crest of the hill, and wandered far down the steep slopes amid the wild tangle of undergrowth, peering through the tree-trunks and listening through the whistling and skirling[7] of the wind and the restless beating of the branches for sight or sound of the marauders. If only on this wild night, in this dark, lone spot, he might come across Georg Znaeym, man to man, with none to witness— that was the wish that was uppermost in his thoughts. And as he stepped round the trunk of a huge beech he came face to face with the man he sought.

The two enemies stood glaring at one another for a long silent moment. Each had a rifle in his hand, each had hate in his heart and murder uppermost in his mind. The chance had come to give full play to the

---

3. The woods are on a very steep *(precipitous)* hillside. The court took the land, as if by force *(wrested* it), and returned it to Gradwitz's family. However, the two families continued their dispute with noisy public quarrels *(affrays)* in which each side accused the other of hunting illegally *(poaching)* on its land.
4. *Georg Znaeym* (gā′ ôrg   znē′ əm)
5. *Wind-scourged* means "wind-whipped."
6. *Quarry* (kwôr′ ē) refers to an animal—or anything—that is being hunted or pursued.

7. *Skirling* is any long, shrill sound, but the word originally referred to the sound of a bagpipe.

Vocabulary
acquiesce (ak′ wē es′) *v.* to consent or agree to without protest
wont (wōnt) *adj.* accustomed; used

MEETING INDIVIDUAL NEEDS **ENGLISH LANGUAGE LEARNERS**

Idioms Point out the idioms "thirsted for one another's blood" (p. 270) and "in cold blood" (p. 271). Explain that both phrases are meant figuratively, not literally. *Bloodthirsty* means "eager for violence or killing." "In cold blood" means to commit an act without guilt.

Activity Point out other idioms using the word *blood* in these sentences: *The*

love of the sea was in the sailor's blood. Many Americans have some Indian blood. Have English language learners determine the meaning of each idiom through context.

Additional Resources
📁 *English Language Learners Sourcebook*

The Wood at Dusk. William Fraser Garden (1856–1921). Watercolor. Private collection.
Viewing the painting: How does this scene help you picture the setting of the story?

VIEWING THE PAINTING

Because watercolor dries rapidly, painters can create interesting effects by painting one stroke over another. Artists often use watercolors for outdoor sketching.

Viewing Response *The scene shows a dark, forbidding forest, much like the one in the story's setting.*

E **Literary Elements**

CONFLICT What inner conflict do both men have? *(Although each man has been wanting to kill the other and has the opportunity to do so, the men are civilized and feel the constraints against killing except in self-defense or defense of one's family.)*

F **Critical Thinking**

EVALUATING Ask students to decide whether the sudden crisis of the tree falling is believable or is an unrealistic plot device. Have them explain their answers. *(Students may say it is believable because it is in keeping with the forest setting. Also, the author has described the storm's heavy winds; the tree's falling is a realistic event.)*

E passions of a lifetime. But a man who has been brought up under the code of a restraining civilization cannot easily nerve himself to shoot down his neighbor in cold blood and without word spoken, except for an offense against his hearth[8] and honor. And before the moment of hesitation had given way to

F action a deed of Nature's own violence overwhelmed them both. A fierce shriek of the storm had been answered by a splitting crash over their heads, and ere[9] they could leap aside a mass of falling beech tree had

8. Here, *hearth* is used figuratively to mean "home and family."
9. *Ere* (ār) is an old word for *before.*

thundered down on them. Ulrich von Gradwitz found himself stretched on the ground, one arm numb beneath him and the other held almost as helplessly in a tight tangle of forked branches, while both legs were pinned beneath the fallen mass. His heavy shooting-boots had saved his feet from being crushed to pieces, but if his fractures were not as serious as they might have been, at least it was evident that he could not move from his present position till some one came to release him. The descending twigs had slashed the skin of his face, and he had to wink away some drops of blood from his eyelashes before he could take in a general view

Reading *Minilesson*

Paraphrasing Paraphrasing is a way of putting into one's own words a sentence, paragraph, or longer passage. When a selection has long sentences, paraphrasing is a quick way of checking comprehension. Use the first paragraph on page 270 and footnote 3 as an example of how to paraphrase sentences.

Activity After they have finished reading the story, have small groups of students go back to the beginning and take turns reading and paraphrasing several paragraphs at a time. Group members can offer help on more difficult passages.
L3 **COLLAB. LEARN.**

Additional Resources
📁 *Reading Workbook,* pp. 25–26

Literary Elements

CHARACTER Have students list words that describe the mood and emotions of the two men as shown in their dialogue. Then have them list the words that make the men's feelings clear. *(They are angry, frustrated, bitter, and sarcastic. The author uses words such as mockingly, savagely, fiercely, snarled, and bitterness to express Ulrich's and Georg's feelings.)*

Active Reading

CONNECT Encourage students to imagine they are in Ulrich and Georg's position. What feelings might they have? Would they be likely to focus on their feelings toward their enemy? *(Students may say they would focus on fear, panic, frustration, or hopefulness that someone would come help them instead of on their hatred of the enemy.)*

At the MOVIES

Be sure to preview the following video for appropriateness for your class:

- **The Interlopers***

 *Also available in the Glencoe Literature *Video Library.*

Teaching Options

---

of the disaster. At his side, so near that under ordinary circumstances he could almost have touched him, lay Georg Znaeym, alive and struggling, but obviously as helplessly pinioned[10] down as himself. All round them lay a thick-strewn wreckage of splintered branches and broken twigs.

Relief at being alive and exasperation at his captive plight brought a strange medley of pious thank-offerings and sharp curses to Ulrich's lips. Georg, who was nearly blinded with the blood which trickled across his eyes, stopped his struggling for a moment to listen, and then gave a short, snarling laugh.

"So you're not killed, as you ought to be, but you're caught, anyway," he cried; "caught fast. Ho, what a jest, Ulrich von Gradwitz snared in his stolen forest. There's real justice for you!"

And he laughed again, mockingly and savagely.

"I'm caught in my own forest-land," retorted Ulrich. "When my men come to release us you will wish, perhaps, that you were in a better plight than caught poaching on a neighbor's land, shame on you."

Georg was silent for a moment; then he answered quietly:

"Are you sure that your men will find much to release? I have men, too, in the forest tonight, close behind me, and *they* will be here first and do the releasing. When

they drag me out from under these damned branches it won't need much clumsiness on their part to roll this mass of trunk right over on the top of you. Your men will find you dead under a fallen beech tree. For form's sake I shall send my condolences to your family."

"It is a useful hint," said Ulrich fiercely. "My men had orders to follow in ten minutes' time, seven of which must have gone by already, and when they get me out—I will remember the hint. Only as you will have met your death poaching on my lands I don't think I can decently send any message of condolence to your family."

"Good," snarled Georg, "good. We fight this quarrel out to the death, you and I and our foresters, with no cursed interlopers[11] to come between us. Death and damnation to you, Ulrich von Gradwitz."

"The same to you, Georg Znaeym, forest-thief, game-snatcher."

Both men spoke with the bitterness of possible defeat before them, for each knew that it might be long before his men would seek him out or find him; it was a bare matter of chance which party would arrive first on the scene.

Both had now given up the useless struggle to free themselves from the mass of wood that held them down; Ulrich limited his endeavors to an effort to bring his one

> *Both men spoke with the bitterness of possible defeat before them.*

---

10. To be *pinioned* is to be disabled by the binding of one's arms.

11. *Interlopers* are people who violate or interfere with the rights of another, such as by trespassing.

Vocabulary
pious (pī′ əs) *adj.* having either genuine or pretended religious devotion
endeavor (en dev′ ər) *n.* a serious or strenuous attempt to accomplish something

---

MEETING INDIVIDUAL NEEDS — INCLUSION STRATEGIES

Less-Proficient Readers Creating a graphic aid can help students understand and remember the plot of a story.

Activity Have students make a time-line that shows each important event of the story. Explain that they should summarize each event as briefly as possible. As an example of the first event, write the sentence "Ulrich prepares to find Georg in the forest" on the board. **L1**

Additional Resources
📁 *Inclusion Strategies*

partially free arm near enough to his outer coat-pocket to draw out his wine-flask. Even when he had accomplished that operation it was long before he could manage the unscrewing of the stopper or get any of the liquid down his throat. But what a Heaven-sent draught[12] it seemed! It was an open winter, and little snow had fallen as yet, hence the captives suffered less from the cold than might have been the case at that season of the year; nevertheless, the wine was warming and reviving to the wounded man, and he looked across with something like a throb of pity to where his enemy lay, just keeping the groans of pain and weariness from crossing his lips.

"Could you reach this flask if I threw it over to you?" asked Ulrich suddenly; "there is good wine in it, and one may as well be as comfortable as one can. Let us drink, even if tonight one of us dies."

"No, I can scarcely see anything; there is so much blood caked round my eyes," said Georg, "and in any case I don't drink wine with an enemy."

Ulrich was silent for a few minutes, and lay listening to the weary screeching of the wind. An idea was slowly forming and growing in his brain, an idea that gained strength every time that he looked across at the man who was fighting so grimly against pain and exhaustion. In the pain and languor that Ulrich himself was feeling the old fierce hatred seemed to be dying down.

"Neighbor," he said presently, "do as you please if your men come first. It was a fair compact. But as for me, I've changed my mind. If my men are the first to come you

shall be the first to be helped, as though you were my guest. We have quarrelled like devils all our lives over this stupid strip of forest, where the trees can't even stand upright in a breath of wind. Lying here tonight, thinking, I've come to think we've been rather fools; there are better things in life than getting the better of a boundary dispute. Neighbor, if you will help me to bury the old quarrel I—I will ask you to be my friend."

Georg Znaeym was silent for so long that Ulrich thought, perhaps, he had fainted with the pain of his injuries. Then he spoke slowly and in jerks.

"How the whole region would stare and gabble[13] if we rode into the market-square together. No one living can remember seeing a Znaeym and a von Gradwitz talking to one another in friendship. And what peace there would be among the forester folk if we ended our feud tonight. And if we choose to make peace among our people there is none other to interfere, no interlopers from outside. . . . You would come and keep the Sylvester night beneath my roof, and I would come and feast on some high day[14] at your castle. . . . I would never fire a shot on your land, save when you invited me as a guest; and you should come and shoot with me down in the marshes where the wildfowl are. In all the countryside there are none that could hinder if we willed to make peace. I never thought to have wanted to do other than hate you all my life, but I think I have changed my mind about things too, this last half-hour. And you

---

12. *Draught* is the amount taken in one drink. The word is pronounced the same as, and is often spelled, *draft*.

13. *Gabble* means "to talk rapidly and foolishly; jabber."
14. *Sylvester night* refers to New Year's Eve festivities honoring Saint Sylvester who, according to legend, converted Constantine the Great to Christianity after curing him of leprosy. A *high day* is any holy day (or *holiday*) in the church calendar.

Vocabulary
languor (lang′ gər) *n.* weakness; fatigue

I Critical Thinking

DRAWING CONCLUSIONS Why does Ulrich decide to make friends with his lifelong enemy now? Provide the following model to help students see how to draw a conclusion from the text.

Model: The sip of wine that Ulrich takes refreshes him and makes him pause for a moment. Sharing the plight of lying trapped and injured with his enemy makes Ulrich put the feud into perspective. He realizes that his feud with Georg is a foolish habit. I think that all these elements combine to make him want to put the feud aside and become friends.

J Literary Elements

FORESHADOWING Point out the word *interlopers*, which echoes the story's title and Znaeym's previous use of the word on page 272. Have students predict how Znaeym's statement that no interlopers will prevent the two men from becoming friends may foreshadow coming events.

Vo•cab•u•lar•y Skills

Multiple-Meaning Words Here, the word *compact* is used to mean "an agreement between two or more parties." In this case, the compact is the lawsuit won by Ulrich's grandfather. But *compact* has many other meanings, as a noun, a verb, and an adjective. Have students look up the word and make a list of its meanings.

REAL-WORLD CONNECTION

Contemporary Feuds An important part of the story is the feud that exists between the two families. Be sure students know what a feud is. Discuss the concept with them, asking how feuds sometimes get started and why they continue.

Activity The story takes place in the past, and students may think that feuds are a thing of the past and no longer exist. Together discuss modern-day feuds and groups that nurse grudges and are willing to fight. Students might mention neighbors, families, and gangs. **L1**

Additional Resources
📁 *Inclusion Strategies*

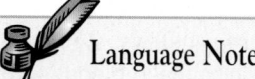

Language Note

The hunting call *halloo* is also spelled *hallo, hollo, holloa,* and *holla.* The word's exact origin is unknown, but since the 14th century it has been used to attract the attention of other hunters when, for example, a fox is spotted during a fox hunt.

K **Literary Elements**

CONFLICT and RESOLUTION Remind students that the climax of a plot occurs at the point at which the conflict is resolved. Ask them to describe what happens at the climax. *(Ulrich says only the word "wolves," meaning that the men are about to be found not by people who will save them but by wild animals who will probably kill them.)*

Thematic Focus

Twists Have students discuss the ironic twist at the end of the story. *(It is ironic that they will lose their lives at a point when they are expressing forgiveness and hope for the future, and as a direct result of their previous feud.)*

☑ **ASSESSMENT OPTIONS**

📁 *Quick Checks,* p. 23

Teaching Options

The Interlopers

offered me your wine-flask. . . . Ulrich von Gradwitz, I will be your friend."

For a space both men were silent, turning over in their minds the wonderful changes that this dramatic reconciliation would bring about. In the cold, gloomy forest, with the wind tearing in fitful gusts through the naked branches and whistling round the tree-trunks, they lay and waited for the help that would now bring release and succor to both parties. And each prayed a private prayer that his men might be the first to arrive, so that he might be the first to show honorable attention to the enemy that had become a friend.

Presently, as the wind dropped for a moment, Ulrich broke silence.

"Let's shout for help," he said; "in this lull our voices may carry a little way."

"They won't carry far through the trees and undergrowth," said Georg, "but we can try. Together, then."

The two raised their voices in a prolonged hunting call.

"Together again," said Ulrich a few minutes later, after listening in vain for an answering halloo.

"I heard something that time, I think," said Ulrich.

The two raised their voices in a prolonged hunting call.

"I heard nothing but the pestilential wind," said Georg hoarsely.

There was silence again for some minutes, and then Ulrich gave a joyful cry.

"I can see figures coming through the wood. They are following in the way I came down the hillside."

Both men raised their voices in as loud a shout as they could muster.

"They hear us! They've stopped. Now they see us. They're running down the hill towards us," cried Ulrich.

"How many of them are there?" asked Georg.

"I can't see distinctly," said Ulrich; "nine or ten."

"Then they are yours," said Georg; "I had only seven out with me."

"They are making all the speed they can, brave lads," said Ulrich gladly.

"Are they your men?" asked Georg. "Are they your men?" he repeated impatiently as Ulrich did not answer.

"No," said Ulrich with a laugh, the idiotic chattering laugh of a man unstrung with hideous fear.

"Who are they?" asked Georg quickly, straining his eyes to see what the other would gladly not have seen.

"*Wolves.*"

K

Vocabulary
reconciliation (rek´ ən sil´ ē ā´ shən) *n.* a settlement of a controversy or disagreement
succor (suk´ ər) *n.* help; assistance; relief
pestilential (pes´ tə len´ shəl) *adj.* harmful; destructive

274 🌾 UNIT 1

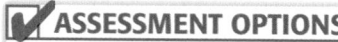

Grammar and Language *Minilesson*

Adverbs Remind students that adverbs are words that modify verbs, adjectives, or other adverbs by answering the questions how, when, where, why, or to what extent. Adverbs sometimes have the ending *-ly.*

Activity Have students write three story adverbs ending in *-ly,* the word that each adverb modifies, and a sentence using each adverb. **L1**

Additional Resources

📋 *Grammar and Language Transparency 23*

📗 *Grammar and Language Workbook,* p. 63

📗 *Grammar and Composition Handbook,* Lesson 1.5

📗 *Writer's Choice,* Lesson 10.5

Responding to Literature

Personal Response

Were you surprised by the way the story ended? What thoughts went through your mind at the end of the story? Describe your reactions in your journal.

— ANALYZING LITERATURE —

RECALL

1. What started the feud between Ulrich von Gradwitz and Georg Znaeym? What caused the feud to become personal?
2. Why are Ulrich and Georg out on such a "wind-scourged" night?
3. Describe what happens to Ulrich and Georg as a result of "a deed of Nature's own violence." How does the men's relationship gradually change after this event?
4. What events does Georg envision as coming from his new relationship with Ulrich?
5. Who are the figures that Ulrich sees coming through the forest?

INTERPRET

6. In your opinion, why do Ulrich and Georg hate each other so much?
7. Do Ulrich and Georg seem to meet by chance or by design? Explain your answer.
8. In your opinion, what causes the change in the men's relationship? Support your answer with evidence from the story.
9. Why do you think the feud between Ulrich and Georg has gone on for such a long time? As you consider this question, refer to the reasons you listed in the Focus Activity on page 268.
10. What is **ironic** about the way the story ends? (See page R6.)

EVALUATE AND CONNECT

11. Would you continue a family feud, as Ulrich and Georg have done? Give reasons for your answer.
12. Describe the **mood** of this story. How does the mood change as the story progresses?
13. To whom or what might the title of this story refer?
14. Theme Connections   "The Interlopers," like many of Saki's stories, has a "trick ending." Why might Saki have chosen to end the story in this manner? What message might the author wish to convey?
15. Do you agree with Ulrich when he says that "there are better things in life than getting the better of a boundary dispute"? Explain your answer.

Literary ELEMENTS

Conflict

The two main characters in "The Interlopers" confront both **internal** and **external conflicts**. For example, when Ulrich and Georg come face to face in the forest, each struggles with an internal conflict–the desire to shoot down the other in cold blood. Before either man can resolve this internal conflict, a falling tree creates an external conflict that both men must confront.

1. Briefly describe another internal conflict faced by either or both of the main characters in this story. How is this conflict resolved?
2. Consider the bitter family feud that Ulrich and Georg have inherited. In your opinion, is this feud an internal or external conflict? Explain your answer.
3. What external conflict do both men face at the end of the story? How do you think this conflict is resolved? In your opinion, why doesn't the author describe the resolution of this conflict?

● See **Literary Terms Handbook,** p. R3.

Responding to the Selection

Personal Response

Students may say they were surprised because the conflict between the two characters ended ironically. They may also say they were chilled, shocked, or frightened by the conclusion.

ANALYZING LITERATURE

1. Many years earlier, the Znaeyms had claimed ownership of the Gradwitz family's forestlands. Disagreeing with a judge's ruling that it belonged to the Gradwitz family, Znaeym's family had continued hunting game on it. Ulrich has regarded Georg Znaeym as a personal enemy since the two were boys.
2. Ulrich is out to catch Georg hunting on his land.
3. A huge tree falls on Ulrich and Georg. As they lie trapped and injured beneath the tree, they decide to put their feud aside and become friends.
4. Georg envisions the two men riding into town, celebrating holidays, and hunting together.
5. The figures Ulrich sees are wolves.
6. Students may say that the two men's hatred is a result of long habit and of family custom instead of anything that either man did personally.
7. Students may say that the two men meet by design in that each man is really only hunting for the other.
8. Students may say that being in a life-and-death situation makes the men put their feud into perspective.
9. Students should consider facts about human nature such as the power of habit and custom to control a person's behavior and the effect of family prejudices on people.
10. The ending is ironic because after finally becoming friends and making plans for the future, the men are about to be killed as a result of their previous feud.
11. Students may say they would not continue a family feud because it would be foolish and destructive. Some students may say they would continue because custom and family pressure would be hard to fight.
12. The mood of the story is scary and foreboding. As the story progresses, a sense of hope and optimism enters in, only to be replaced by foreboding once again at the end.
13. The title refers to Georg and his family, who trespassed on the Gradwitz land, to people referred to by Ulrich and Georg who might interfere in both the enmity and the friendship of the

---

LITERARY ELEMENTS

1. Both men decide on their own to dissolve the feud.
2. Both families have the internal conflict of whether to continue the external conflict.
3. They face wolves and will likely be killed. The ultimate conflict is not described because it is more shocking to imagine it.

Additional Resources

📖 *Literary Elements Transparency 23*

two men, and finally to the wolves.
14. The author might have used a "trick" ending to communicate a message to readers about the harm that can be done by continuing foolish feuds and waiting too late to resolve issues.
15. Students may say that Ulrich states an obvious truth; however, like him, people often lose perspective when under the influence of goals and prejudices that have become second nature.

LITERATURE AND WRITING

Writing About Literature
Students' descriptions should
- use details that appeal to the senses to describe the story's setting.
- discuss the mood of the story's setting.

Creative Writing
Students' sequels should
- describe subsequent events that are reasonable based on the story's plot and characters.

EXTENDING YOUR RESPONSE

Literature Groups Encourage students to compare the tree falling to accidents and natural disasters they have heard about. How have they affected everyday life? **COLLAB. LEARN.**

Interdisciplinary Activity Point out that students may share their findings as written reports, oral presentations, or artwork.

Performing Encourage students to keep in mind that the two men are pinned beneath a tree and can move very little. Point out that tone of voice and facial expression are very important in communicating the two men's emotions.

LITERATURE AND WRITING

Writing About Literature
Setting Saki uses many sensory details in describing the setting of "The Interlopers." Write a one-paragraph description of the story's setting, incorporating as many sensory details as possible. In a second paragraph, discuss how the setting of the story contributes to its mood, or atmosphere. Share your writing with others in a small group.

Creative Writing
The Sequel What happens after "The Interlopers" ends? Write a sequel to the story, in which you narrate the events that occur after Ulrich identifies the figures that are running toward him and Georg.

EXTENDING YOUR RESPONSE

Literature Groups
In Cold Blood? What might have happened if the tree had not fallen on Ulrich and Georg? At the time of the accident, each man "had a rifle in his hand, each had hate in his heart and murder uppermost in his mind." In your group, discuss what you think might have happened, had not "a deed of Nature's own violence overwhelmed them both." Support your opinion with evidence from the story or from your own experience. Share your ideas with the class.

Interdisciplinary Activity
History: Famous Feuds A feud between two families plays an important role in "The Interlopers." Throughout history there have been many famous feuds. For example, in the 1860s, a feud began between two Appalachian families, the Hatfields and the McCoys. This feud lasted about thirty years and left at least twenty people dead. One of the

most famous feuds in literature is the one between the Montagues and the Capulets in Shakespeare's *Romeo and Juliet.* Research a famous feud in history or in literature. Share your findings with the class.

Performing
Dialogue With a partner, practice all or part of the dialogue that Georg and Ulrich have while they are pinned under the fallen tree. Think about the emotions that each character is experiencing, and do your best to convey those emotions as you speak. Perform the dialogue for the class.

Reading Further
If you want to read more of Saki's short stories, you might consult these collections:

Surprising Stories by Saki: Twenty-Two Tales with Twists, a collection of fascinating stories, includes "Tobermory," a story about an unusual cat.

The Chronicles of Clovis includes "Sredni Vashtar," a story whose main character depicts Saki's Aunt Augusta.

Save your work for your portfolio.

✔ ASSESSMENT OPTIONS

- 📁 *Quick Checks,* p. 23
- 📁 *Selection and Theme Assessment,* pp. 45–46
- 📁 *Performance Assessment,* p. 23
- 💾 *Testmaker*

Skill Minilessons

GRAMMAR AND LANGUAGE • Sentence Variety

Varying the length of sentences is one way to make a piece of writing more interesting. For example, in the third paragraph of "The Interlopers," Saki uses three sentences. The first sentence is quite long; the second sentence is about half as long as the first; and the third sentence is shorter still. By varying the length of his sentences, Saki holds the reader's attention. He avoids the monotony of too many long sentences in a row, as well as the choppy sound of too many short sentences.

● For more about sentences, see **Language Handbook,** p. R43.

PRACTICE Rewrite the following passage so that it has sentences of varying lengths. Feel free to rearrange ideas and add words or phrases.

> Ulrich lay pinned under the tree. He was suffering great pain. He looked over at Georg. His enemy was in the same predicament. Ulrich's great hatred for Georg began to melt away. He realized how stupid their quarrel really was. Ulrich decided to ask Georg to be his friend.

APPLY Review a piece of your writing. Revise your sentences as needed to vary their length.

READING AND THINKING • Summarizing

When you summarize events in a short story, you briefly describe the main events, leaving out most of the details. For example, the following paragraph summarizes the first part of "The Interlopers."

> On a cold winter night, Ulrich von Gradwitz patrols a forest on the border of his property. He hopes to catch his neighbor, Georg Znaeym, in the act of trespassing. The two neighbors have inherited a bitter family feud over ownership of this forest. Soon Ulrich

gets his wish: he and his enemy come face to face. But before either man can act, a falling tree pins both of them to the ground.

PRACTICE Write a summary of the events that occur from the moment Ulrich and Georg find themselves pinned under the tree, to the end of "The Interlopers."

● For more about summarizing, see **Reading Handbook,** pp. R78–R107.

VOCABULARY • Analogies

An analogy is a type of comparison based on the relationships between things or ideas. (See pages 000 and 000). Some analogies are based on a relationship that can be called "an action and its significance."

hug : affection :: wince : pain

A hug is a sign of affection; a wince is a sign of pain.

To finish an analogy, decide what relationship exists between the first two things or ideas. Then apply that relationship to another pair of words.

● For more about analogies, see **Communications Skills Handbook,** p. R77.

PRACTICE Choose the word that best completes each analogy. Some of the analogies are based on a relationship of action and its significance.

1. nurse : succor :: teacher :
   a. education   b. school   c. homework
2. nod : acquiesce :: frown :
   a. agree   b. disapprove   c. displease
3. pestilential : beneficial :: studious :
   a. lazy   b. diligent   c. wealthy
4. handshake : reconciliation :: applause :
   a. explanation   b. truce   c. approval

Skill Minilessons

GRAMMAR AND LANGUAGE
Sentence Variety

One possible revision: Ulrich lay pinned under the tree, suffering great pain. He looked over at Georg, who was in the same predicament. Ulrich's great hatred for Georg began to melt away. Realizing how stupid their quarrel really was, Ulrich decided to ask Georg to be his friend.

READING AND THINKING
Summarizing

One possible summary: The men continue feuding, and each one threatens to kill the other when his own men come to help. Then Ulrich offers to share his wine with Georg. Pausing for a moment, he decides to drop the feud. Georg agrees to do the same, and the two men make plans for the future as friends. Ulrich sees figures in the distance, and each man thinks his assistants have come to the rescue. Then Ulrich sees that the approaching figures are, in fact, wolves.

VOCABULARY
Analogies

1. a
2. b
3. a
4. c

Additional Resources

📕 *Grammar and Composition Handbook,* Lessons 12.1–12.5

📕 *Grammar and Language Workbook,* pp. 323–326

📗 *Writer's Choice,* Lesson 7.3

📂 *Reading Workbook,* pp. 25–26

📂 *Vocabulary Practice,* p. 22

Objectives

- To read and analyze a short story about how a surprise visit affects a girl and her mother
- To identify understatement
- To write an analysis of a title

Skills

Reading/Thinking: Inferring; Identifying Cause-and-Effect Relationships; Drawing Conclusions; Interpreting
Writing: Thank-you Letter
Vocabulary: Unlocking Meaning
Grammar/Language: Sentence Fragments; Vivid Verbs
Listening/Speaking: Role Play
Life Skills: Problem Solving
Collaboration: Literature Groups

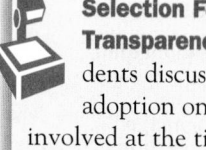

Motivating
→OPTIONS

Selection Focus Transparency 24: Have students discuss the effects of adoption on all the people involved at the time of adoption and twenty years later.

Focus Activity: Have pairs of students share the criteria they added to the continuum. Then have class members suggest other social situations that might be measured on the continuum.

—Before You Read—

As It Is with Strangers

FOCUS ACTIVITY

What might it be like to meet a relative you didn't know existed?

DRAW THE LINE! With a partner, brainstorm a list of feelings you might experience upon meeting a long-lost relative. Draw a line to show a continuum of feelings. Write "extremely uncomfortable" at one end of the line and "totally at ease" at the other. List a variety of feelings that might fall between the two extremes.

Extremely ——————————————————— Totally
uncomfortable   at ease

SETTING A PURPOSE Read to learn how a surprise relative affects the narrator's relationship with her mother.

BACKGROUND

The Time and Place

This story takes place in the recent past, in an unnamed city or town in the United States.

Did You Know?

The practice of adoption dates back to the time of ancient Greece and Rome. Today, the main purpose of adoption is to improve the lives of adoptive children. While adoption can be a joyful experience for adop-

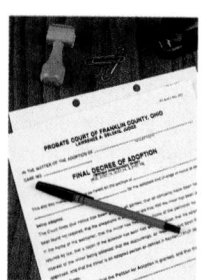

tive parents, it is often difficult for birth parents to give up a child. Also, problems can arise when adopted children want information about their birth parents, or when birth parents want to find a child they have given up for adoption. Many agencies refuse to provide access to adoption records. One approach to solving this problem has been to establish registries that help adopted children and birth parents make contact.

VOCABULARY PREVIEW

presumably (pri zōō′ mə blē) *adv.* supposedly; probably; p. 279
prodigal (prod′ i gəl) *adj.* recklessly wasteful; p. 280
sanctity (sangk′ tə tē) *n.* the quality of deserving solemn respect as something not to be violated; p. 281

278   UNIT 1

Meet
Susan Beth Pfeffer

When she was six, Susan Pfeffer's father, a lawyer, published a book and dedicated it to her. She loved seeing her name in print and decided then and there to become a writer. Earlier, she had planned to become either a cowgirl or the Queen of England. Pfeffer wrote often throughout school and was a professional writer by the time she was twenty-one. She hasn't forgotten her childhood fantasies, however. ". . . Queen of England is a job I could handle . . . (I look wonderful in crowns)," she has written.

Susan Beth Pfeffer was born in 1948 in New York City. This story was first published in 1989.

RESOURCE MANAGER

Lesson Planning Resource
The *Unit One Planning Guide* (pp. 201–208) provides additional lesson notes and reduced versions of all print resources.

📁 **Other Print Resources**
- Active Reading Guide, p. 24
- Vocabulary Practice, p. 23
- Reading Workbook, pp. 27–28
- Grammar and Language Workbook, pp. 121, 259
- Grammar and Composition Handbook, Lessons 4.9, 1.5

- Quick Checks, p. 24
- Selection and Theme Assessment, pp. 47–48
- Performance Assessment, p. 24
- Spanish Summaries, p. 24
- Spanish Translations
- Inclusion Strategies
- English Language Learners Sourcebook

✋ **Transparencies**
- Selection Focus 24

- Literary Elements 24
- Grammar and Language 24

Technology

🎧 Audio Library
🎧 Spanish Audio Library
💻 Glencoe Literature Web Site
💾 Testmaker

As It Is with Strangers

Susan Beth Pfeffer

IT WASN'T UNTIL right before I went to bed on Thursday that Mom bothered to tell me the son she'd given up for adoption twenty years earlier was coming over for supper the next day.

"What son?" I asked.

"I'm sure I've told you about him," Mom said. "You must have forgotten."

I figured I probably had. I'm always forgetting little things like my homework assignments and being elected President of the United States. Having an older brother must have just slipped my mind. "How'd you two find each other?" I asked. Presumably Mom had never told me that.

"I registered with an agency," she said. "Put my name and address in a book, so if he ever wanted to find me, he could. I guess he did. Don't be late for supper tomorrow."

"I won't be," I promised. This was one reunion I had no intention of missing.

School the next day really dragged on. School never goes fast on Fridays, but when your mind is on some newly acquired half brother, it's real hard to care about Julius Caesar.[1] I didn't tell anybody, though. It seemed to me it was Mom's story, not mine, and besides, my friends all think she's crazy anyway. Probably from things I've said over the years.

I went straight home from school, and was surprised, first to find the place spotless, and then to see Mom in the kitchen cooking away.

"I took a sick day," she informed me. "So I could prepare better."

---

1. In referring to *Julius Caesar,* the narrator probably means the title character in the play by William Shakespeare. (This play begins on page 778 of this anthology.)

Vocabulary
presumably (pri zoo′ ma blē) *adv.* supposedly; probably

SUMMARY

Fifteen-year-old Tiffany is surprised to learn that her mother had a child whom she gave up for adoption twenty years earlier. Her son, Jack, has located her through an agency and she has invited him to dinner. After Jack is gone, her mother tells Tiffany never to give up anything that she really loves. Tiffany later hears her mother crying in her bedroom. She reveals that she does not comfort her mother this time because it is impossible to comfort strangers.

📁 *Spanish Summaries,* p. 24

🅐 Active Reading

CONNECT After students have read the first four paragraphs, help them make connections between the narrator and someone they know who may be like her. What qualities do both share? Then ask students how they would react if they found out they had a brother or sister they knew nothing about.

Additional Resources
📁 *Active Reading Guide,* p. 24
🎧 *Audio Library*
🎧 *Spanish Audio Library*

Teaching Options

CONNECTING TO OTHER SELECTIONS

The chart at the right shows three ways to connect "As It Is with Strangers" to selections in this book.

For specific teaching strategies, see the *Unit One Planning Guide,* pp. 204–205.

Connection	Title
Life Skills: Supporting and Contributing	→ "Catch the Moon," p. 63
Thematic: Surprises	→ "The Angry Winter," p. 557
Literary: Characterization	→ "Waltz of the Fat Man," p. 377

Teaching Options

As It Is with Strangers

"Everything looks great," I told her. It was true. I hadn't seen the place look so good since Great-Aunt Trudy came with the goat, but that's another story. "You look very pretty too."

"I got my nails done," Mom said, showing them off for me. They were coral colored. "And my hair."

I nodded. Mom had taught me that nothing was unbearable if your hair looked nice.

"Is that what you're planning to wear tonight?" she asked.

"I thought I'd shower and change into my dress," I said. I own a grand total of one dress, but this seemed to be the right kind of occasion for it.

Mom gave me a smile like I'd just been canonized.[2] "Thank you," she said. "Tonight's kind of important for me."

I nodded. I wasn't sure just what to say anymore. Mom and I have been alone for eight years, and you'd figure by now I'd know how to handle her under any circumstances, but this one had me stumped. "What's for supper?" I finally asked.

"Southern fried chicken," Mom said. "At first I thought I'd make a roast, but then what if he doesn't like his meat rare? And turkey seemed too Thanksgivingish, if you know what I mean. Everybody likes fried chicken. And I made mashed potatoes and biscuits and a spinach salad."

"Spinach salad?" I asked. I could picture Mom pouring the spinach out of a can and dousing it with Wishbone.[3]

"From scratch," Mom informed me. "Everything's from scratch. And I baked an

apple pie too. The ice cream is store bought, but I got one of those expensive brands. What do you think?"

I thought that there obviously was something to that Prodigal Son[4] story, since Mom never made anything more elaborate for me than scrambled eggs. "It smells great," I said. It did, too, the way you picture a house in a commercial smelling, all homey and warm. "I'm sure everything will go fine."

"I want it to," Mom said, as though I'd suggested that maybe she didn't.

There were a few things I knew I'd better clear up before Big Brother showed up. "What's his name?" I asked, for starters.

"Jack," Mom said. "That's not what I would have named him. I would have named him Ronald."

"You would have?" I asked. I personally am named Tiffany, and Ronald would not have been my first guess.

"That was my boyfriend's name," Mom said. "Ronny."

"Your boyfriend," I said. "You mean his father?"

Mom nodded. "You think of them as boyfriends, not fathers, when you're sixteen," she said.

Well that answered question number two. It had seemed unlikely to me that my father was responsible, but who knew? I wasn't there. Maybe he and Mom had decided they wanted a girl, and chucked out any boys that came along first.

Speaking of which. "There aren't any other brothers I've forgotten about?" I asked. "Is this going to be the first of many such dinners?"

---

2. In some Christian religions, to be *canonized* is to be declared a saint. Here, of course, the narrator is making a joke.
3. *Wishbone* is the brand name of a line of salad dressings.

4. In the *Prodigal Son* story from the Christian Bible, an older son is bitter when his younger brother, who had left home and wasted his inheritance, is warmly welcomed home by their father.

Vocabulary
prodigal (prod′ i gəl) *adj.* recklessly wasteful

ENGLISH LANGUAGE LEARNERS

MEETING INDIVIDUAL NEEDS

Tone English language learners may need help understanding the narrator's tone and her use of humor.

Activity Read these sentences aloud: "There aren't any other brothers I've forgotten about?" I asked. "Is this going to be the first of many such dinners?" Have students explain the narrator's attitude that the questions show toward

her mother's keeping her son a secret. *(She is surprised and somewhat resentful.)* Have students find other examples of the narrator's jokes and sarcasm and discuss their meanings.

Additional Resources
📁 *English Language Learners Sourcebook*

"Jack's the only one," Mom replied. "I wanted to keep him, but Ronny wasn't about to get married, and Dad said if I gave him up for adoption then I could still go to college. I did the right thing, for him and for me. And I would have gone to college if I hadn't met your father. I don't know. Maybe because I gave up the baby, I was too eager to get married. I never really thought about it."

"Did Dad know?" I asked.

"I told him," Mom said. "He said it didn't matter to him. And it didn't. What- ever else was wrong in our marriage, he never threw the baby in my face."

Katie, 1964. Fairfield Porter. Oil on canvas, 15 x 14½ in. Permanent collection of the Art Students League of New York.

Viewing the painting: Does the girl in this painting fit your image of Tiffany? Explain.

I found myself pictur- ing a baby being thrown in Mom's face, and decided I should take my shower fast. So I sniffed the kitchen appreciatively and scurried out. In the shower I tried to imagine what this Jack would look like, but he kept resem- bling Dad's high-school graduation picture, which made no sense biologically at all. So I stopped imagining.

When I went to my bedroom to change, though, I was really shocked. Mom had extended her cleaning ways to include my room. All my carefully laid out messes were gone. It would probably take me months to reassemble things. I considered screaming at Mom about the sanctity of one's bedroom, but I decided against it. Mom obviously wanted this guy to think she and I were the

perfect American family, and if that meant even my room had to be clean, then nothing was going to stop her. I could live with it, at least for the evening.

Mom and I set the table three times before the doorbell finally rang. When it did, neither one of us knew who should answer it, but Mom finally opened the door.

"Hello," this guy said. "I'm Jack."

"I'm Linda," Mom replied. "Come on in. It's nice to . . . well, it's good seeing you."

"Good to see you too," Jack said. He didn't look anything like my father.

"This is Tiffany," Mom said. "She, uh . . ."

"Her daughter," I said. "Your sister." I mean, those words were going to be used at some point during the evening. We might as well get them out of the way fast. Then when we got around to the big tricky words like *mother* and *son,* at least some groundwork would have been laid.

"It's nice to meet you," Jack said, and he gave me his hand to shake, so I shook it. They say you can tell a lot about a man from his handshake, but not when he's your long- lost brother. "I hope my coming like this isn't any kind of a brother. I mean bother."

"Not at all," Mom said. "I'm going to check on dinner. Tiffany, why don't you show Jack the living room? I'll join you in a moment."

Vocabulary
sanctity (sangk′ tə tē) *n.* the quality of deserving solemn respect as something not to be violated

E **Literary Elements**

DIALOGUE How does the dialogue show the narrator's feelings about having a half-brother? *(Although she uses jokes and sarcasm to under- state her concern, her questions to her mother show that she takes the issue seriously and wants to under- stand it.)*

F **Literary Elements**

FIGURES OF SPEECH: *Metaphor* Point out the humorous effect the narrator achieves by taking her mother's metaphor literally. Have students explain the figurative meaning of "throwing something in one's face." *(It means to remind someone of a past deed or mistake.)*

VIEWING THE PAINTING

American artist Fairfield Porter (1907–1975) was known for his portraits.

Viewing Response *Some students may say the girl fits the image of Tiffany because she looks intelligent and observant. Others may say she looks more serious than Tiffany.*

LIFE SKILLS CONNECTION

Problem Solving Point out that it is often hard to make conversation with new acquaintances. Tiffany is in an espe- cially difficult situation because her new acquaintance is a half-brother whom she just found out about. People usually feel shy and uncomfortable in these situations and look for ways to get over the discomfort.

Activity Have students think of new acquaintances whom they have had to talk with recently, such as parents'

friends, new neighbors, doctors, or den- tists. Have pairs of students describe what happened, how they felt, and how they got through the situation. If some pairs desire, they could role-play the situa- tion. Later, the entire class could offer advice about things that can be done to feel less uncomfortable when meeting new people. **L2** **COLLAB. LEARN.**

INFERRING Have students discuss Tiffany's comment that "there was a lot I wanted to say, but I didn't say any of it." Why doesn't Tiffany say these things? *(She has only known Jack for a little while; she has mixed emotions about her mother's having another child and about sharing her with Jack; her use of humor and sarcasm show she is not the kind of person who talks about deep feelings with people she does not know well.)*

H **Active Reading**

CONNECT Have students note Jack's response to Tiffany's humorous characterization of her mother. Ask them to think of times when their attempts at humor were misunderstood or when they used humor at inappropriate moments. Have them discuss why people might make jokes when they feel tense or uncomfortable.

I **Literary Elements**

DIALOGUE Have a volunteer read Tiffany's questions to Jack. Ask students to describe Tiffany's tone of voice and explain what the questions reveal about Tiffany's character. *(She sounds nervous and eager to please, contrasting with her normally casual, sarcastic manner.)*

Teaching Options

As It Is with Strangers

"This is the living room," I said, which was pretty easy to show Jack, since we were already standing in it. "Want to sit down?"

"Yeah, sure," Jack said. "Have you lived here long?"

"Since the divorce," I said. "Eight years ago."

"That long," Jack said. "Where's your father?"

"He lives in Oak Ridge," I said. "That's a couple of hundred miles from here. I see him sometimes."

"Is he . . ." Jack began. "I mean, I don't suppose you'd know . . ."

"Is he your father too?" I said. "No. I kind of asked. Your father's name is Ronny. My father's name is Mike. I don't know much else about your father except he didn't want to marry Mom. They were both teenagers, I guess. Do you want to meet him too?"

"Sometime," Jack said. "Not tonight."

I could sure understand that one. "I've always wanted to have a big brother," I told him. "I always had crushes on my friends' big brothers. Did you want that—to have a kid sister, I mean?"

"I have one," Jack said. "No, I guess now I have two. I have a sister back home. Her name is Leigh Ann. She's adopted too. She's Korean."

"Oh," I said. "That's nice. I guess there isn't much of a family resemblance, then."

"Not much," Jack said, but he smiled. "She's twelve. How old are you?"

"Fifteen," I said. "Do you go to college?"

Jack nodded. "I'm a sophomore at Bucknell," he said. "Do you think you'll go to college?"

"I'd like to," I said. "I don't know if we'll have the money, though."

"It's rough," Jack said. "College costs a lot these days. My father's always griping about it. He owns a car dealership. New and used. I work there summers. My mom's a housewife."

I wanted to tell him how hard Mom had worked on supper, how messy the apartment usually was, how I never wore a dress, and

Mom's nails were always a deep sinful scarlet. I wanted to tell him that maybe someday I'd be jealous that he'd been given away to a family that could afford to send him to college, but that it was too soon for me to feel much of anything about him. There was a lot I wanted to say, but I didn't say any of it.

"What's she like?" Jack asked me, and he gestured toward the kitchen, as though I might not otherwise know who he was talking about.

"Mom?" I said. "She's terrible. She drinks and she gambles and she beats me black and blue if I even think something wrong."

Jack looked horrified. I realized he had definitely not inherited Mom's sense of humor.

"I'm only kidding," I said. "I haven't even been spanked since I was five. She's fine. She's a good mother. It must have really hurt her to give you away like that."

"Have you known long?" Jack asked. "About me?"

"Not until recently," I said. It didn't seem right to tell him I'd learned less than twenty-four hours before. "I guess Mom was waiting until I was old enough to understand."

"I always knew I was adopted," Jack said. "And for years I've wanted to meet my biological parents. To see what they looked like. I love Mom and Dad, you understand. But I felt this need."

"I can imagine," I said, and I could too. I was starting to develop a real need to see what Jack's parents looked like, and we weren't even related.

"Tiffany, could you come in here for a minute?" Mom called from the kitchen.

"Coming, Mom," I said, and left the living room fast. It takes a lot out of you making small talk with a brother.

"What do you think?" Mom whispered as soon as she saw me. "Does he look like me?"

"He has your eyes," I said. "And I think he has your old hair color."

Reading *Minilesson*

Identifying Cause-and-Effect Relationships Explain that a cause is why something happened and an effect is what happened as a result. Point out that a cause can lead to an effect, which itself can then be the cause of another effect, and so on. Use this example:

The salad has bacon on it. *(cause)*

Jack, a vegetarian, will not eat the salad. *(effect and cause)*

Tiffany offers to wash the bacon off the salad. *(effect)*

Activity Have small groups of students construct chains of causes and effects. Here are two possible starters:

1. The son Tiffany's mother had given up for adoption is coming for a visit.
2. Jack and his mother want to be alone and talk.

Point out that students can build their chains by taking one of the sentences, adding *because* to the beginning, naming an effect, then adding *because* to the beginning of the effect, and so on.

L2 COLLAB. LEARN.

Additional Resources

📁 *Reading Workbook*, pp. 27–28

"I know," Mom said, patting her bottle red hair. "I almost asked them to dye me back to my original shade, but I wasn't sure I could remember it anymore. Do you like him? Does he seem nice?"

"Very nice," I said. "Very good manners."

"He sure didn't inherit those from Ronny," Mom declared. "Come on, let's start taking the food out."

So we did. We carried out platters of chicken and mashed potatoes and biscuits and salad. Jack came to the table as soon as he saw what we were doing.

"Oh, no," he said. "I mean, I'm sorry. I should have told you. I'm a vegetarian."

"You are?" Mom said. She looked as shocked as if he'd told her he was a vampire. Meat is very important to Mom. "You're not sick or anything, are you?"

"No, it's for moral reasons," Jack said. "It drives my mom, my mother, her name's Cathy, it drives Cathy crazy."

"Your mom," my mom said. "It would drive me crazy, too, if Tiffany stopped eating meat just for moral reasons."

"Don't worry about it," I told her. "I'll never be that moral."

"There's plenty for me to eat," Jack said. "Potatoes and biscuits and salad."

"The salad has bacon in it," Mom said. "I crumbled bacon in it."

"We can wash the bacon off, can't we Jack?" I said. "You'll eat it if we wash the bacon off, won't you?"

Jerry, 1964. Fairfield Porter. Oil on canvas, 14½ x 14½ in. Portland Art Museum, Oregon Art Institute. Gift of Mrs. Fairfield Porter.

Viewing the painting: What personal qualities or characteristics does this young man seem to possess? Which of these qualities might Jack have also?

I thought he hesitated for a moment, but then he said, "Of course I can," and for the first time since we'd met, I kind of liked him. I took the salad into the kitchen and washed it all. The salad dressing went the way of the bacon, but we weren't about to complain. At least there'd be something green on Jack's plate. All his other food was gray-white.

Mom hardly ate her chicken, which I figured was out of deference to the vegetarian, but I had two and a half pieces, figuring it might be years before Mom made it again. Jack ate more potatoes than I'd ever seen another human being eat. No gravy, but lots of potatoes. We talked polite stuff during dinner, what he was studying in college, where Mom worked, the adjustments Leigh Ann had had to make. The real things could only be discussed one on one, so after the pie and ice cream, I excused myself and went to Mom's room to watch TV. Only I couldn't make my eyes focus, so I crossed the hall to my room, and recreated my messes. Once I had everything in proper order, though, I put things back the way Mom had had them. I could hear them talking while I moved piles around, and then I turned on my radio, so I couldn't even hear the occasional stray word, like *father* and *high school* and *lawyer.* That was a trick I'd learned years ago, when Mom and Dad were in their fighting stage. The radio played a lot of old songs that night. It made me feel like I was seven all over again.

VIEWING THE PAINTING

Fairfield Porter (1907–1975) often experimented with nonrealistic styles in his landscapes and portraits.

Viewing Response *The young man seems to have intelligence and sensitivity, traits that Jack also has.*

J **Literary Elements**

PLOT: *Conflict* How might the food served highlight the conflict? *(The fried-chicken is meant to express Linda's love for her son. However, it adds to the conflict because Jack is a vegetarian.)* How does Tiffany try to bring the two together? *(She offers to wash the salad.)* How does Jack react to the suggestion? *(After some hesitation, Jack agrees. Tiffany decides that she likes him.)*

MEETING INDIVIDUAL NEEDS **INCLUSION STRATEGIES**

Special Needs Students may need extra help understanding the emotions experienced by the characters in the story, each of whom looks at the issue of adoption from a different perspective.

Activity Have small groups of students discuss the issues and emotions of the various characters in the story—a mother who gave her child up for adoption, a young man who was given up for adoption, and a daughter whose mother gave up a child for adoption. Have students create a dialogue in which all three discuss their feelings. Let groups who wish to present their dialogues to the class. **L2** **COLLAB. LEARN.**

Additional Resources
📁 *Inclusion Strategies*

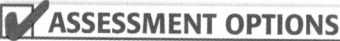

VIEWING THE PAINTING

Nell Blaine (1922–) is known for the brilliant colors in her still-lifes and interiors.

Viewing Response *The dinner scene looks attractive and carefully planned. The dinner scene in the story was also carefully planned and could be described as hearty fare, lovingly prepared.*

K **Critical Thinking**

DRAWING CONCLUSIONS Why doesn't Tiffany comfort her mother as she had done before? Offer the following model to help students draw conclusions about Tiffany's behavior.

Model: Tiffany's usual tone is sarcastic, especially with her mother. I think she is frightened of deep emotions, both her mother's and her own. She is too immature to deal with her mother's sadness, and that is why she does not comfort her.

Thematic Focus

Twists Have students discuss why the story's ending is a surprise. *(Tiffany clearly loves her mother, and it seems cruel to ignore her mother's sadness, but that night she sees her mother as a stranger and therefore cannot offer comfort.)*

✓ ASSESSMENT OPTIONS

📁 *Quick Checks,* p. 24

After a while Mom knocked on my door and said Jack was leaving, so I went to the living room and shook hands with him again. I still couldn't tell anything about his personality from his handshake, but he did have good manners, and he gave me a little pecking kiss on my cheek, which I thought was sweet of him. Mom kept the door open, and watched as he walked the length of the corridor to the stairs. She didn't close the door until he'd gotten into a car, his I assumed. Maybe it was a loaner from his father.

"You give away a baby," Mom said, "and twenty years later he turns up on your doorstep a vegetarian."

"He turns up a turnip," I said.

But Mom wasn't in the mood for those kinds of jokes. "Don't you ever make that mistake," she said.

"What mistake?" I asked, afraid she meant making jokes. If I couldn't make jokes with Mom, I wouldn't know how to talk with her.

"Don't you ever give up something so important to you that it breathes when you do," Mom said. "It doesn't have to be a kid. It can be a dream, an ambition, or a marriage, or a house. It can be anything you care about as deeply as you care about your own life. Don't ever just give it away, because you'll spend the rest of your life wondering about it, or pretending you don't wonder, which is the same thing, and you'll wake up one morning and realize it truly is gone and a big part of you is gone with it. Do you hear me, Tiffany?"

Big Table with Pomegranates, 1978. Nell Blaine. Oil on canvas, 22 x 26 in. Metropolitan Museum of Art. Gift of Arthur W. Cohen, 1985. 1985.36.1.

Viewing the painting: What adjectives might you use to describe the dinner scene pictured here? What adjectives could also be applied to the dinner scene in the story?

"I hear you," I said. I'd never seen Mom so intense, and I didn't like being around her. "I'm kind of tired now, Mom. Would you mind if I went to bed early?"

"I'll clean up tomorrow," Mom said. "You can go to bed."

So I did. I left her sitting in the living room and went to my bedroom and closed my door. But this time I didn't turn the radio on, and later, when I'd been lying on my bed for hours, not able to sleep, I could hear her in her room crying. I'd heard her cry in her room a hundred times before, and a hundred times before I'd gotten up and comforted her, and I knew she'd cry a hundred times again, and I'd comfort her then, too, but that night I just stayed in my room, on my bed, staring at the ceiling and listening to her cry. I think I did the right thing, not going in there. That's how it is with strangers. You can never really comfort them.

K

Teaching Options

Grammar and Language *Minilesson*

Sentence Fragments Remind students that a sentence fragment is a group of words that is punctuated as a complete sentence but is missing a subject, a verb, or both. Explain that writers sometimes use fragments for effect, especially in dialogue. Write the following sentence fragments from the story on the board and have students tell what is missing in these sentence fragments:

- No gravy, but lots of potatoes. *(subject and verb)*
- And my hair. *(subject and verb)*
- Put my name and address in a book, so if he ever wanted to find me, he could. *(subject)*

Activity Have students add the necessary elements and rewrite each fragment above as a sentence. **L1**

Additional Resources

🎙 *Grammar and Language Transparency 24*

📖 *Grammar and Language Workbook,* p. 121

📖 *Grammar and Composition Handbook,* Lesson 4.9

📖 *Writer's Choice,* Lesson 13.9

Responding to Literature

Personal Response

What are your thoughts about the relationship between Tiffany and her mother? Is it a "typical" mother-daughter relationship? Why or why not? Record your thoughts in your journal.

——— ANALYZING LITERATURE ———

RECALL

1. How does Tiffany describe her mother to the reader? To Jack?
2. What does Tiffany's mother, Linda, do to prepare for Jack's visit?
3. What is Linda's explanation for why she gave up Jack for adoption? What did Linda do after the adoption?
4. What does Jack tell Tiffany and Linda about himself and his adopted family?
5. Describe how Tiffany behaves after dinner and then after Jack leaves.

INTERPRET

6. Based on Tiffany's descriptions of her mother, what can you infer about Tiffany's personality? About her feelings toward her mother?
7. What might Linda's feelings be about this reunion with her son? What kind of impression does she seem to want to create?
8. Consider the choices Linda made after giving up her son for adoption. In your opinion, what are some possible reasons for her choices?
9. What conclusions might you draw about Jack's situation in life?
10. How would you explain Tiffany's behavior after dinner and after Jack's departure? Give reasons for your answers.

EVALUATE AND CONNECT

11. Susan Pfeffer has chosen to tell this story from Tiffany's **point of view**. How do you think the story might be different if it were told from Jack's point of view? From Linda's point of view?
12. Consider the alternatives Linda had as an unwed, pregnant teenager. In your opinion, did she make a good decision by giving up her son for adoption? Why or why not?
13. Do you think this story is humorous or serious—or is it both? Explain.
14. Look back at the continuum of feelings you made in the Focus Activity on page 278. Where might you place Tiffany, Jack, and Linda along that line? Explain your decisions.
15. **Theme Connections** What do you think the theme of this story is? Explain how the story theme relates to the subunit theme of Twists.

Literary ELEMENTS

Understatement

When a writer intentionally represents something as less than it is, that writer is using **understatement**. Understatement may be used to insert humor into a story or to focus the reader's attention on something the author wants to emphasize. For example, in "As It Is with Strangers," Tiffany explains that "when your mind is on some newly acquired half brother, it's real hard to care about Julius Caesar." Her understatement creates humor, while also emphasizing the uncertainty she feels about meeting her "new" brother, Jack.

1. Find two examples in which Tiffany uses understatement while talking to Jack.
2. Do you think Tiffany's understatements are anything other than attempts at humor? Explain your answer.

⬤ See **Literary Terms Handbook,** p. R13.

THE SHORT STORY 285

Personal Response

Students may say that the relationship is not "typical" because in some ways Tiffany takes care of her mother and acts more adult than she does.

ANALYZING LITERATURE

1. To the reader, Tiffany describes her mother as funny, flighty, and a little crazy. She describes her to Jack as a good mother.
2. She cleans and cooks a meal.
3. Her father told her that if she put the baby up for adoption, he would pay for her college education. She got married to a man who was not the baby's father, and she did not go to college.
4. He is a sophomore in college; his father is a car salesman; his mother is a housewife; and he has an adopted sister who is Korean.
5. After dinner, Tiffany goes to her room, rearranges it, and listens to loud music. After Jack leaves, she talks to her mother and goes to bed.
6. Tiffany seems caring and witty. She loves her mother but perhaps wishes she were more "typical."
7. Linda is feeling excited but nervous. She wants to show that she is an organized, efficient, caring mother.
8. Linda may have gotten married and had another child soon after giving her son up for adoption because she felt sad or guilty about giving up her child.
9. His family has been able to provide more material things than Linda could have.
10. Tiffany wants to give them some time alone but feels a little left out.
11. Jack's story would probably have been more serious. Linda's story would have reflected sorrow, regret, and nervousness.
12. Encourage students to weigh the best interests of Linda, Jack, and the adoptive parents.
13. The story is serious but provides humor through comic relief.
14. Students might place them on two lines, one to show their feelings before they meet, and one after.

LITERARY ELEMENTS

1. "Being elected President" (p. 279) "I guess there isn't much of a family resemblance" (p. 282)
2. Tiffany's understatements are also a way of expressing her surprise and uncertainty at learning that she has a half-brother.

Additional Resources

✎ *Literary Elements Transparency 24*

15. Students may say the theme of the story is that we never really know everything about somebody else, or that people must live the rest of their lives with choices they make as young people. The theme relates to "Twists" because Tiffany realizes that although she is close to her mother, in some ways they are strangers.

LITERATURE AND WRITING

Writing About Literature

Students' analyses should

- state specific ways in which Tiffany and her mother are strangers.
- discuss ways in which Jack is a stranger.
- use details from the story to analyze the title.

Creative Writing

Students' letters should

- express thoughts and feelings based on a knowledge of the story's characters.
- use knowledge of the story's characters to state specific future plans.
- incorporate a tone that reflects the level of their relationship.

EXTENDING YOUR RESPONSE

Literature Groups

Suggest that students consider whether Tiffany's behavior at the end of the story reflects her feelings toward her mother's keeping her son a secret.
COLLAB. LEARN.

Internet Connection

Have students share keywords and other useful methods to help others locate the information.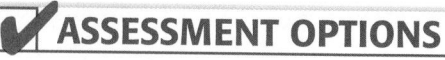

Performing

Encourage students to discuss, before creating their role-play, what Jack's parents might be like based on Jack's behavior at dinner.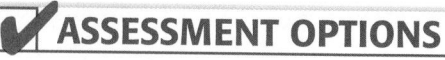

LITERATURE AND WRITING

Writing About Literature

Analyze the Story's Title Think about why the author may have chosen the title "As It Is with Strangers" for this story. Reread the last paragraph of the story, in which Tiffany refers to her mother as a stranger. In what ways might Tiffany and her mother be considered strangers? Which other character in the story might be considered a stranger? Use details from the selection to support your analysis of the story's title. Share your ideas with others in a small group.

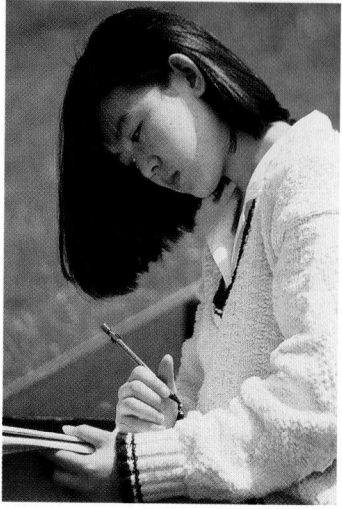

Creative Writing

Yours Truly Imagine that you are Jack. Write a thank-you letter to Linda and Tiffany. Besides the dinner, what else might you be grateful for? What thoughts or feelings might you want to convey to your birth mother? What might you want to say to your newly discovered half sister? What are your hopes or plans for a future relationship with Linda and Tiffany? You may want to compare your letter with those written by several classmates.

EXTENDING YOUR RESPONSE

Literature Groups

Too Late in the Game? Tiffany learns about Jack's existence less than twenty-four hours before she meets him. In your opinion, should Linda have told Tiffany about Jack long before she did? Was it right for Linda to conceal Jack's existence from Tiffany until Jack actually appeared in their lives? How do you think Tiffany feels about her mother's failure to tell her the truth much sooner? Debate these issues in your group. Share your ideas with the class.

Internet Connection

Where Are They Now? In this story, Jack was able to find his birth mother because Linda had registered with an agency that helped adopted children and their birth parents locate each other. Look for online resources that provide a similar service. Share with the class what you learn about these resources.

Performing

Role Play Working with two other students, role play a conversation that Jack and his adoptive parents might have after his visit with Linda and Tiffany. What might Jack say about his birth mother and half sister? What information or impressions might he choose *not* to convey? What questions might Jack's adoptive parents ask, or what concerns might they raise?

Reading Further

If you enjoyed reading this story, you might also enjoy these stories about teens and their families in Cynthia Rylant's collection, *Every Living Thing*:

"Shells" is a story about a boy and his aunt who are learning to live together after the death of the boy's parents.

"Stray" tells how a family adopts an abandoned puppy.

📖 **Save your work for your portfolio.**

✔ ASSESSMENT OPTIONS

- 📁 *Quick Checks,* p. 24
- 📁 *Selection and Theme Assessment,* pp. 47–48
- 📁 *Performance Assessment,* p. 24
- 💾 *Testmaker*

Skill Minilessons

GRAMMAR AND LANGUAGE • Vivid Verbs

"I could picture Mom pouring the spinach out of a can and *dousing* it with Wishbone."

Vivid verbs make an impact on readers. *Dousing* provides a mental picture of Linda *generously pouring* salad dressing on the spinach. In this example, one vivid verb conveys the same information that a verb and an adverb do.

PRACTICE Replace the underlined verb-adverb combination in each sentence with one vivid verb. Use a thesaurus for help.

1. Tiffany <u>nervously moved around</u> in her chair.
2. Jack <u>ate</u> the potatoes <u>quickly.</u>
3. Linda <u>cried softly.</u>
4. Tiffany <u>quickly walked</u> out of the kitchen.
5. Linda <u>finally told</u> her secret to Tiffany.

APPLY Review a piece of your writing. Try to improve it by adding a few vivid verbs. Consult a thesaurus, if necessary.

● For more about verbs, see **Language Handbook,** p. R44.

READING AND THINKING • Interpreting

In "As It Is with Strangers," Tiffany's words often do not mean what they literally say. As you read, you have to interpret what she really means in order to understand the story. Tiffany jokes around a lot; she creates humor using understatement, exaggeration, and sarcasm. For example, Tiffany is being sarcastic when she asks Linda, "Is this going to be the first of many such dinners?" Tiffany is really asking her mother if she has any other secrets to tell her—anything as important as the existence of a half brother.

PRACTICE Interpret each of these comments made by Tiffany. Explain what you think Tiffany really means.

1. "I'm always forgetting little things like my homework assignments and being elected President of the United States. Having an older brother must have just slipped my mind."
2. "There aren't any other brothers I've forgotten about?"
3. "Mom? She's terrible. She drinks and she gambles and she beats me black and blue if I even think something wrong."
4. "Don't worry about it. I'll never be that moral."
5. "He turns up a turnip."

● For more about related reading strategies, see **Reading Handbook,** pp. R78–R107.

VOCABULARY • Unlocking Meaning

Tiffany believes that the sanctity of her bedroom was violated. *Sanctity* comes from the Latin word *sanctus,* which means "holy." Although all words formed from *sanctus* originally had to do with holiness, they may or may not carry that specific meaning today. For example, in this story, Tiffany uses a broader meaning for *sanctity:* here, it means the quality of being regarded with respect.

Another useful word is *sanction.* Its most common meaning is "approval by a recognized authority." Originally, that authority was the Roman Catholic Church.

PRACTICE Briefly state what you'd guess is the meaning of each underlined word.

1. In some religions, it is a terrible fate to be buried in <u>unsanctified</u> ground.
2. The hunted fox searched desperately for a <u>sanctuary.</u>
3. There was a ceremony to <u>sanctify</u> the new altar.
4. Do not disturb me in my study, which I consider my <u>sanctum.</u>

GRAMMAR AND LANGUAGE
Vivid Verbs

Possible verbs include
1. fidgeted
2. gobbled
3. whimpered
4. scurried
5. disclosed

READING AND THINKING
Interpreting

1. Being told that she has a brother she did not know about is an important, shocking discovery.
2. She is telling her mother she resents not being told about her brother sooner.
3. Her mother is a good, loving mother.
4. Her behavior will never be perfect.
5. She doesn't want to talk seriously about her mother's son.

VOCABULARY
Unlocking Meaning

1. not made holy by a priest
2. safe place
3. make holy
4. private place

Additional Practice

📕 *Grammar and Composition Handbook,* Lesson 1.5

📕 *Grammar and Language Workbook,* p. 259

📕 *Writer's Choice* Lesson 10.5

📁 *Reading Workbook,* pp. 27–28

📁 *Vocabulary Practice,* p. 23

Objectives

- To read and analyze a short story about what becomes of a young wife's false gems
- To identify point of view
- To write a character sketch

Skills

Reading/Thinking: Inferring; Evaluating; Drawing Conclusions
Writing: Using Details in a Description; Personal Response
Vocabulary: Analogies
Grammar/Language: Interjections; Infinitives and Infinitive Phrases
Listening/Speaking: Monologue
Collaboration: Literature Groups

Motivating → OPTIONS

Selection Focus Transparency 25: Have students discuss their reactions to some famous jewels.

Focus Activity: Have students share their experiences with false first impressions in small groups.

Before You Read

The False Gems

FOCUS ACTIVITY

In what situations have you noticed that people and things are not what they seem?

QUICKWRITE Spend five minutes writing about people or things that turned out to be completely different from the way you first perceived them to be.

SETTING A PURPOSE Read to learn what happens to one man who discovers that things are not as they seem.

BACKGROUND

The Time and Place
"The False Gems" takes place in Paris, sometime in the 1870s or early 1880s.

Did You Know?
It's almost impossible to distinguish some false gems from real ones. Even the British Crown Jewels contain false gems, such as the Black Prince's Ruby and the Timur Ruby, which, despite their names, are not rubies at all. Synthetic gemstones made from the compound cubic zirconia can easily pass for diamonds in brilliance and color. To the naked eye, cultured pearls are virtually indistinguishable from natural ones.

VOCABULARY PREVIEW

remonstrate (ri mon′ strāt) *v.* to say or plead in protest; argue; p. 290
impart (im pärt′) *v.* to give or share; p. 290
droll (drōl) *adj.* amusingly odd or fanciful; p. 291
assuage (ə swāj′) *v.* to lessen in intensity; diminish; p. 291
incur (in kur′) *v.* to acquire (something undesirable); bring upon oneself; p. 291
rancor (rang′ kər) *n.* ill will; resentment; p. 291
perceive (pər sēv′) *v.* to be or become aware through the senses; p. 293
disdain (dis dān′) *n.* a feeling of contempt for something or someone; scorn; p. 294

Meet Guy de Maupassant

Few writers have achieved more than Guy de Maupassant (gē də mō pä san′), who died when he was only forty-two. Maupassant published more than three hundred short stories, each so finely crafted that he is renowned as one of the finest short-story writers in any language. An athletic and energetic person, the author loved the sport of rowing. Maupassant also had an active social life in Paris, where he worked as a government clerk as well as a writer. His stories reflect his views about the world. In fact, one French critic has claimed that it is "impossible to fully comprehend the France of 1850–90 without these stories."

Guy de Maupassant was born in 1850 in France and died in 1893. This story was first published in 1883.

RESOURCE MANAGER

Lesson Planning Resource
The *Unit One Planning Guide* (pp. 209–216) provides additional lesson notes and reduced versions of all print resources.

📁 **Other Print Resources**
- Active Reading Guide, p. 25
- Vocabulary Practice, p. 24
- Reading Workbook, pp. 29–30
- Grammar and Language Workbook, pp. 257, 97
- Grammar and Composition Handbook, Lessons 1.8, 3.3

- Quick Checks, p. 25
- Selection and Theme Assessment, pp. 49–50
- Performance Assessment, p. 25
- Spanish Summaries, p. 25
- Spanish Translations
- Inclusion Strategies
- English Language Learners Sourcebook

📖 **Transparencies**
- Selection Focus 25
- Fine Art 25

- Literary Elements 25
- Grammar and Language 25

Technology
🎧 Audio Library
🎧 Spanish Audio Library
💻 Glencoe Literature Web Site
💾 Testmaker

MONSIEUR LANTIN[1] had met the young girl at a reception at the house of the second head of his department, and had fallen head over heels in love with her.

She was the daughter of a provincial tax collector, who had been dead several years. She and her mother came to live in Paris, where the latter, who made the acquaintance of some of the families in her neighborhood, hoped to find a husband for her daughter.

They had very moderate means, and were honorable, gentle, and quiet.

The young girl was a perfect type of the virtuous woman in whose hands every sensible young man dreams of one day intrusting his happiness. Her simple beauty had the charm of angelic modesty, and the imperceptible smile which constantly hovered about the lips seemed to be the reflection of a pure and lovely soul.

1. *Monsieur Lantin* (mə syœ′ län taɴ′)

Woman with a Pearl Necklace in a Loge, 1897. Mary Cassatt. Oil on canvas, 32 x 23½ in. Philadelphia Museum of Art. Bequest of Charlotte Dorrance Wright.

The False Gems

Guy de Maupassant

THE SHORT STORY 289

Reading the Selection

SUMMARY

Monsieur Lantin, a government clerk, meets and marries a young woman. They are very happy except that she likes theater-going and wearing artificial jewels. Madame Lantin dies suddenly, and Monsieur Lantin decides to sell his wife's fake jewels. To his surprise, he finds that the jewels are real. He realizes that someone else gave his wife the jewelry and that she was living a lie during their marriage. He sells the jewels, becoming a very wealthy man and quitting his job.

📁 *Spanish Summaries,* p. 25

A Active Reading

EVALUATE Ask a volunteer to read aloud the first page. Have other volunteers suggest words to describe the woman. Based on twists in other stories in this theme, what do students think will happen? Will the woman turn out to be as she seems?

Additional Resources
📁 *Active Reading Guide,* p. 25
🎧 *Audio Library*
🎧 *Spanish Audio Library*

Teaching Options

CONNECTING TO OTHER SELECTIONS

The chart at the right shows three ways to connect "The False Gems" to selections in this book.

For specific teaching strategies, see the *Unit One Planning Guide,* pp. 212–213.

Connection	Title
Life Skills: Problem Solving	→ "By Any Other Name," p. 479
Thematic: Trust and Betrayal	→ "Chee's Daughter," p. 23
Literary: Setting	→ "The Boar Hunt," p. 157

B Literary Elements

POINT OF VIEW Have students identify the narrative point of view. How does the point of view affect our knowledge of the characters? *(The point of view is third person limited. The characters do not tell their own story, and there is no all-knowing narrator who tells the thoughts and feelings of all the characters. However, the narrator does tell the thoughts and feelings of the main character, Monsieur Lantin.)*

C Active Reading

EVALUATE Encourage students to evaluate Monsieur Lantin's behavior toward his wife. What would they like and/or dislike about having a spouse like him? *(Some students may say that if Lantin really loved his wife, he would share her interest in theater. Others would say that independent interests are healthy for married couples. Some students may think Lantin's disapproval of his wife's jewelry is petty and uncalled for.)*

D Active Reading

QUESTION Ask students whether they agree that Madame Lantin's love of jewelry is a "weakness" and explain their answers. *(Some students may say that it is an innocent love of beautiful objects that does not harm anyone, while others may think she places too much emphasis on material possessions.)*

Her praises resounded on every side. People never tired of repeating: "Happy the man who wins her love! He could not find a better wife."

Monsieur Lantin, then chief clerk in the Department of the Interior, enjoyed a snug little salary of three thousand five hundred francs, and he proposed to this model young girl, and was accepted.

He was unspeakably happy with her. She governed his household with such clever economy that they seemed to live in luxury. She lavished the most delicate attentions on her husband, coaxed and fondled him; and so great was her charm that six years after their marriage, Monsieur Lantin discovered that he loved his wife even more than during the first days of their honeymoon.

He found fault with only two of her tastes: Her love for the theatre, and her taste for imitation jewelry. Her friends (the wives of some petty officials) frequently procured[2] for her a box at the theatre, often for the first representations of the new plays; and her husband was obliged to accompany her, whether he wished it or not, to these entertainments which bored him excessively after his day's work at the office.

After a time, Monsieur Lantin begged his wife to request some lady of her acquaintance to accompany her, and to bring her home after the theatre. She opposed this arrangement, at first; but, after much persuasion, finally consented, to the infinite delight of her husband.

Now, with her love for the theatre, came also the desire for ornaments. Her costumes remained as before, simple, in good taste, and always modest; but she soon began to adorn

---

2. The tickets were acquired or obtained *(procured)* for her.

her ears with huge rhinestones, which glittered and sparkled like real diamonds. Around her neck she wore strings of false pearls, on her arms bracelets of imitation gold, and combs set with glass jewels.

Her husband frequently <u>remonstrated</u> with her, saying:

"My dear, as you cannot afford to buy real jewelry, you ought to appear adorned with your beauty and modesty alone, which are the rarest ornaments of your sex."

But she would smile sweetly, and say:

"What can I do? I am so fond of jewelry. It is my only weakness. We cannot change our nature."

Then she would wind the pearl necklace round her fingers, make the facets of the crystal gems sparkle, and say:

"Look! are they not lovely? One would swear they were real."

Monsieur Lantin would then answer, smilingly:

"You have bohemian[3] tastes, my dear."

Sometimes, of an evening, when they were enjoying a *tête-à-tête*[4] by the fireside, she would place on the tea table the morocco leather box containing the "trash," as Monsieur Lantin called it. She would examine the false gems with a passionate attention, as though they <u>imparted</u> some deep and secret

Did You Know?
Facets are the small, polished, plane surfaces of a cut gem.

---

3. *Bohemian* suggests following one's own sense of style rather than what is generally accepted as fashionable and proper.

4. A *tête-à-tête* (tet' ə tet') is a private or intimate conversation between two people. Directly translated from French, the phrase means "head to head."

Vocabulary

remonstrate (ri mon' strāt) *v.* to say or plead in protest; argue

impart (im pärt') *v.* to give or share

Teaching Options

LITERATURE & HUMANITIES

Display the painting *At the Moulin Rouge, Art Talk* Transparency 26. Have students compare and contrast the artist's garish portrayal of late nineteenth-century Parisians to the characters in the story.

ENGLISH LANGUAGE LEARNERS
MEETING INDIVIDUAL NEEDS

Formal Language Explain that the story, first published in 1883, has a more formal sentence structure and word choice than most modern writing.

Activity Have English language learners write a paraphrase for each of the following sentences, defining unfamiliar words using a dictionary or context.

She governed his household with such clever economy that they seemed to live in luxury.

Her husband was obliged to accompany her, whether he wished it or not, to these entertainments which bored him excessively.

Additional Resources

📁 *English Language Learners Sourcebook*

joy; and she often persisted in passing a necklace around her husband's neck, and, laughing heartily, would exclaim: "How droll you look!" Then she would throw herself into his arms, and kiss him affectionately.

One evening, in winter, she had been to the opera, and returned home chilled through and through. The next morning she coughed, and eight days later she died of inflammation of the lungs.

Monsieur Lantin's despair was so great that his hair became white in one month. He wept unceasingly; his heart was broken as he remembered her smile, her voice, every charm of his dead wife.

Time did not assuage his grief. Often, during office hours, while his colleagues were discussing the topics of the day, his eyes would suddenly fill with tears, and he would give vent to his grief in heart-rending sobs. Everything in his wife's room remained as it was during her lifetime; all her furniture, even her clothing, being left as it was on the day of her death. Here he was wont to seclude himself daily and think of her who had been his treasure—the joy of his existence.

But life soon became a struggle. His income, which, in the hands of his wife, covered all household expenses, was now no longer sufficient for his own immediate wants; and he wondered how she could have managed to buy such excellent wine and the rare delicacies which he could no longer procure with his modest resources.

He incurred some debts, and was soon reduced to absolute poverty. One morning, finding himself without a cent in his pocket, he resolved to sell something, and immediately the thought occurred to him of disposing of his wife's paste jewels,[5] for he cherished in his heart a sort of rancor against these "deceptions," which had always irritated him in the past. The very sight of them spoiled, somewhat, the memory of his lost darling.

To the last days of her life she had continued to make purchases, bringing home new gems almost every evening, and he turned them over some time before finally deciding to sell the heavy necklace, which she seemed to prefer, and which, he thought, ought to be worth about six or seven francs; for it was of very fine workmanship, though only imitation.

He put it in his pocket, and started out in search of what seemed a reliable jeweler's shop. At length he found one, and went in, feeling a little ashamed to expose his misery, and also to offer such a worthless article for sale.

"Sir," said he to the merchant, "I would like to know what this is worth."

The man took the necklace, examined it, called his clerk, and made some remarks in an undertone; he then put the ornament back on the counter, and looked at it from a distance to judge of the effect.

Monsieur Lantin, annoyed at all these ceremonies, was on the point of saying: "Oh! I know well enough it is not worth anything," when the jeweler said: "Sir, that necklace is worth from twelve to fifteen thousand francs; but I could not buy it, unless you can tell me exactly where it came from."

---

5. **Paste jewels** are artificial or imitation gems made of a hard, glasslike material.

Vocabulary
droll (drōl) *adj.* amusingly odd or fanciful
assuage (ə swāj′) *v.* to lessen in intensity; diminish
incur (in kur′) *v.* to acquire (something undesirable); bring upon oneself
rancor (rang′ kər) *n.* ill will; resentment

STYLE Point out the use of the word *unceasingly*. Have students compare it to the words *unspeakably* and *excessively* on the previous page. What generalization can they make about the author's style? How does it fit the story's main character? *(He uses somewhat exaggerated language, which is fitting for the overly passionate and emotional Monsieur Lantin.)*

F Active Reading

QUESTION Encourage students to question why Monsieur Lantin has much less money to spend after his wife's death. *(They may speculate that it was not only her good managing but another source of income that allowed her to buy luxuries.)*

FYI

What's It Worth? In today's currency, $1.00 is equivalent to approximately 6 francs. Monsieur Lantin thought the necklace was worth, in dollars, about $1.00. The jeweler, however, indicated that it was worth, in dollars, about $2,000 to $2,500. No wonder Monsieur Lantin was shocked. His annual salary was 3,500 francs. The necklace was worth 12,000 to 15,000 francs, roughly three to four times his yearly salary.

Writing *Minilesson*

Using Details in a Description Ask students to imagine that a friend has asked them how Monsieur Lantin is doing during his grieving period. They should give as many details as possible so that the friend can visualize exactly how Monsieur Lantin is behaving.

Activity Explain that psychologists offer advice on effective ways to deal with the death of a loved one. Have students research the steps in the grieving process and the best ways to handle grief. Ask them to write a description that would be useful for others who do not know about this topic. **L2**

Additional Resources

📗 *Writer's Choice,* Lesson 3.1

G Critical Thinking

INFERRING Ask students why Monsieur Lantin is so upset when he realizes that his wife must have received her jewels as presents. Provide the following model to show how to make an inference from the text.

Model: I know that someone else bought the jewels for his wife. Who would be likely to do that? If it were a relative or a mutual friend, Monsieur Lantin would know the person. Since he does not know the person, it must be a secret friend. Why would the friend be secret? Because it is most likely a male friend, a lover. I think Monsieur Lantin is upset because he assumes that his wife was unfaithful and that her lover gave her the jewels.

H Literary Elements

CONFLICT What is the conflict of the story? How does Monsieur Lantin's knowledge that the jewels are real complicate his conflict? *(Monsieur Lantin is struggling with an internal conflict about how to go on, both economically and emotionally, after his wife's death. Now he must struggle with his memory of her as he realizes he may not have seen his wife as she really was.)*

FINE ART
TRANSPARENCY 25

You may wish to use Fine Art Transparency 25 to discuss setting.

The widower opened his eyes wide and remained gaping, not comprehending the merchant's meaning. Finally he stammered: "You say—are you sure?" The other replied, drily: "You can try elsewhere, and see if any one will offer you more. I consider it worth fifteen thousand at the most. Come back here, if you cannot do better."

Monsieur Lantin, beside himself with astonishment, took up the necklace and left the store. He wished time for reflection.

Once outside, he felt inclined to laugh, and said to himself: "The fool! Oh, the fool! Had I only taken him at his word! That jeweler cannot distinguish real diamonds from the imitation article."

A few minutes after, he entered another store, in the Rue de la Paix.[6] As soon as the proprietor glanced at the necklace, he cried out:

"Ah, *parbleu!*[7] I know it well; it was bought here."

Monsieur Lantin, greatly disturbed, asked: "How much is it worth?"

"Well, I sold it for twenty thousand francs. I am willing to take it back for eighteen thousand, when you inform me, according to our legal formality, how it came to be in your possession."

This time, Monsieur Lantin was dumbfounded. He replied:

"But—but—examine it well. Until this moment I was under the impression that it was imitation."

The jeweler asked:

"What is your name, sir?"

"Lantin—I am in the employ of the Minister of the Interior. I live at number sixteen Rue des Martyrs."[8]

The merchant looked through his books, found the entry, and said: "That necklace was sent to Madame Lantin's address, sixteen Rue des Martyrs, July 20, 1876."

The two men looked into each other's eyes—the widower speechless with astonishment; the jeweler scenting a thief. The latter broke the silence.

"Will you leave this necklace here for twenty-four hours?" said he; "I will give you a receipt."

Monsieur Lantin answered hastily: "Yes, certainly." Then, putting the ticket in his pocket, he left the store.

He wandered aimlessly through the streets, his mind in a state of dreadful confusion. He tried to reason, to understand. His wife could not afford to purchase such a costly ornament. Certainly not. But, then, it must have been a present!—a present!—a present, from whom? Why was it given her?

He stopped, and remained standing in the middle of the street. A horrible doubt entered his mind—She? Then, all the other jewels must have been presents, too! The earth seemed to tremble beneath him—the tree before him to be falling; he threw up his arms, and fell to the ground, unconscious. He recovered his senses in a pharmacy, into which the passers-by had borne him. He asked to be taken home, and, when he reached the house, he shut himself up in his room, and wept until nightfall. Finally, overcome with fatigue, he went to bed and fell into a heavy sleep.

The sun awoke him next morning, and he began to dress slowly to go to the office. It

---

6. *Rue de la Paix* (ru̇ də lä pā′) translates as "Street of Peace."
7. *[parbleu]* (pär blœ′) In France in the 1200s, King Louis IX hated swear words, especially *pardieu* ("by God!"), *cordieu* ("God's heart!"), and *têtedieu* ("God's head!"). He punished swearers by branding their tongues with hot irons. Luckily, Louis had a pet dog named Bleu, and people began to substitute the dog's name for God's—*parbleu, corbleu, sacre bleu,* and so on.

8. *Rue des Martyrs* (ru̇ dā mär tēr′) translates as "Street of Martyrs." A martyr is one who dies or suffers greatly for a belief or cause.

292 **❧** UNIT 1

Teaching Options

Reading *Minilesson*

Evaluating Explain that an evaluation is a judgment. Readers make evaluations. Characters make evaluations, too. In "The False Gems," both the reader and the husband have opinions of the wife at the beginning of the story. By the end of the story, their opinions—their evaluations—of her have changed.

Activity Ask students to identify their reactions or feelings toward Madame Lantin at the beginning of the story. Then have them compare their evaluation of Madame Lantin with Monsieur Lantin's evaluation of her. Remind students that often something happens in a story to change characters' (and readers') opinions

of a character. Ask students to evaluate their feelings toward Madame Lantin at the end of the story. Did their feelings change? Why? How do their feelings about the wife compare to the husband's feelings about her? **L2**

Additional Resources
📁 *Reading Workbook,* pp. 29–30

Portrait of Zacharie Astruc, 1863. Eduoard Manet. Oil on canvas, 35½ x 45¾ in. Kunsthalle, Bremen, Germany.
Viewing the painting: Which characteristics of Monsieur Lantin do you think are reflected in this painting?

I Active Reading

REVIEW The story takes place in Paris, and certain elements of the setting play a role in the story. Ask students to look through the selection for information about Paris that was important to the story. Have volunteers characterize the city based on the information. *(Students will probably indicate that Paris is a thriving, sophisticated city. They may point to details such as the theatre, receptions for government workers, and many jewelers.)*

J Literary Elements

THEME Point out that many writers have developed the theme of the effects of wealth on human happiness. Have a student read Monsieur Lantin's comments on wealth aloud. Then encourage the class to discuss whether they agree or disagree.

VIEWING THE PAINTING

Edouard Manet (1832–1883) depicts a friend and supporter in this portrait. The books in the foreground indicate Astruc's occupation, writing. Have students note the contrast between the man's well-formed, detailed face and his sketchily painted hand, a discrepancy typical of Manet's style.

Viewing Response *The man in the painting seems serious, even a little stuffy, just like Monsieur Lantin.*

was hard to work after such shocks. He sent a letter to his employer, requesting to be excused. Then he remembered that he had to return to the jeweler's. He did not like the idea; but he could not leave the necklace with that man. He dressed and went out.

It was a lovely day; a clear, blue sky smiled on the busy city below. Men of leisure were strolling about with their hands in their pockets.

Monsieur Lantin, observing them, said to himself: "The rich, indeed, are happy. With money it is possible to forget even the deepest sorrow. One can go where one pleases, and in travel find that distraction which is the surest cure for grief. Oh! if I were only rich!"

He perceived that he was hungry, but his pocket was empty. He again remembered the necklace. Eighteen thousand francs! Eighteen thousand francs! What a sum!

He soon arrived in the Rue de la Paix, opposite the jeweler's. Eighteen thousand francs! Twenty times he resolved to go in, but shame kept him back. He was hungry, however—very hungry—and not a cent in his pocket. He decided quickly, ran across the street, in order not to have time for reflection, and rushed into the store.

The proprietor immediately came forward, and politely offered him a chair; the clerks glanced at him knowingly.

Vocabulary
perceive (pər sēv′) v. to be or become aware through the senses

Linguistic and Bodily-Kinesthetic
Point out that a monologue communicates the thoughts and feelings of a character through words, tone of voice, facial expression, and gestures.

Activity Have pairs of students write a monologue to show Monsieur Lantin's thoughts and feelings when he finds out that the valuable necklace was sent to his wife (p. 292). Then have students take turns performing the monologue, using voice, facial expression, and gestures to show Monsieur Lantin's emotions. **L1** **COLLAB. LEARN.**

The False Gems

Active Reading

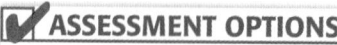

REVIEW Ask students to reread the scene on pages 290–291 in which the wife is examining her jewels. Invite them to tell, in the light of their disclosed value, what she may have been thinking. *(She may have been thinking about their true value and the fact that her husband does not know the jewels are real. She may have been thinking about the person who gave her the jewels and the fact that her husband does not know about that either.)*

Literary Elements

CHARACTER Ask students to describe how Lantin changes after becoming wealthy. *(He eats at expensive restaurants; he looks at the possessions of other wealthy people with disdain; he exaggerates the amount of money he has and says he inherited it; he enjoys leisure activities that he has never enjoyed before.)* Do students still sympathize with him? *(They may say that they do not since he now shows a less appealing side to his character.)*

Thematic Focus

Twists Does the ironic ending make any statements about the relationship between wealth and happiness? Have students discuss this question. Also discuss who the real "false gem" was—Madame Lantin.

☑ ASSESSMENT OPTIONS

📁 *Quick Checks,* p. 25

Teaching Options

"I have made inquiries, Monsieur Lantin," said the jeweler, "and if you are still resolved to dispose of the gems, I am ready to pay you the price I offered."

"Certainly, sir," stammered Monsieur Lantin.

Whereupon the proprietor took from a drawer eighteen large bills, counted, and handed them to Monsieur Lantin, who signed a receipt; and, with trembling hand, put the money into his pocket.

As he was about to leave the store, he turned toward the merchant, who still wore the same knowing smile, and lowering his eyes, said:

"I have—I have other gems, which came from the same source. Will you buy them, also?"

The merchant bowed: "Certainly, sir."

Monsieur Lantin said gravely, "I will bring them to you." An hour later, he returned with the gems.

Did You Know?
A *solitaire pendant* is a single gem suspended from a chain and worn as a necklace or bracelet.

The large diamond earrings were worth twenty thousand francs; the bracelets, thirty-five thousand; the rings, sixteen thousand; a set of emeralds and sapphires, fourteen thousand; a gold chain with solitaire pendant, forty thousand—making the sum of one hundred and forty-three thousand francs.

The jeweler remarked, jokingly:

"There was a person who invested all her savings in precious stones."

Monsieur Lantin replied, seriously:

"It is only another way of investing one's money."

That day he lunched at Voisin's, and drank wine worth twenty francs a bottle. Then he hired a carriage and made a tour of the Bois.[9] He gazed at the various turnouts[10] with a kind of <u>disdain</u>, and could hardly refrain from crying out to the occupants:

"I, too, am rich!—I am worth two hundred thousand francs."

Suddenly he thought of his employer. He drove up to the bureau, and entered gaily, saying:

"Sir, I have come to resign my position. I have just inherited three hundred thousand francs."

He shook hands with his former colleagues, and confided to them some of his projects for the future; he then went off to dine at the Café Anglais.

He seated himself beside a gentleman of aristocratic bearing; and, during the meal, informed the latter confidentially that he had just inherited a fortune of four hundred thousand francs.

For the first time in his life, he was not bored at the theatre, and spent the remainder of the night in a gay frolic.

Six months afterward, he married again. His second wife was a very virtuous woman; but had a violent temper. She caused him much sorrow.

---

9. *The Bois* (bwä) refers to Bois de Boulogne, a forested park in Paris.

10. A *turnout* is a carriage complete with attendants, horses, and rigging.

Vocabulary
disdain (dis dān′) *n.* a feeling of contempt for something or someone; scorn

294 ❧ UNIT 1

Grammar and Language *Minilesson*

Interjections Write the following sentences on the board:

> *Look! are they not lovely?*
> *Oh! if I were only rich!*

Explain that the words *look* and *oh* are interjections: words used to express surprise or other emotions. Explain that an interjection is followed by a comma or an exclamation point.

Activity Have students find and write two more uses of interjections in the story and write the sentences. Then have them write two sentences of their own using interjections. **L2**

Additional Resources

✒ *Grammar and Language Transparency 25*

📖 *Grammar and Language Workbook,* p. 257

📖 *Grammar and Composition Handbook,* Lesson 1.8

📖 *Writer's Choice,* Lesson 10.8

Responding to Literature

Personal Response

What aspect of the story surprised you the most? Explain your answer.

ANALYZING LITERATURE

RECALL

1. What admirable qualities does Monsieur Lantin's wife seem to possess?
2. According to Monsieur Lantin, what are his wife's only two flaws?
3. Why does Monsieur Lantin assume that the gems are false?
4. What does Monsieur Lantin do with his wife's jewelry? Why?
5. In what way does Monsieur Lantin's life change after his final visit to the jeweler?

INTERPRET

6. Which clues early in the story **foreshadow** the unexpected twist in the plot? Explain what each clue seems to suggest.
7. In your opinion, how are Madame Lantin's two "flaws" related to each other? Explain.
8. To what, besides Madame Lantin's jewels, might the title of this story refer? Explain.
9. What do you think accounts for Monsieur Lantin's financial difficulties?
10. Does Monsieur Lantin's attitude toward himself and others seem to change as a result of the new circumstances of his life? Explain your answer.

EVALUATE AND CONNECT

11. In your opinion, does Madame Lantin's fondness for the gems have anything to do with their source? Explain.
12. In your opinion, what lessons for husbands and wives might this story contain?
13. If you had been in Monsieur Lantin's situation, what do you think you would have done with the jewels? Give reasons for your answer.
14. Reread the story's last paragraph. What is **ironic** about the situation in which Monsieur Lantin finds himself? (See Literary Terms Handbook, page R6.)
15. How do you feel about the two main characters in this story? With whom do you sympathize more? Explain your thinking.

Literary ELEMENTS

Point of View

Point of view is the relationship of the narrator, or storyteller, to the story. When a story is told from a **first-person point of view**, the narrator is a character in the story, who refers to himself or herself as "I." In general, the reader sees everything through that character's eyes. In a story told from a **limited third-person point of view**, the narrator reveals the thoughts of only one character, through whose eyes the reader sees the story. The narrator refers to that character as "he" or "she." In a story with an **omniscient point of view**, the narrator—who is not a character in the story—reveals the thoughts of several characters.

1. What point of view does Maupassant use in "The False Gems"? How do you know?
2. Why do you think Maupassant chose to tell the story from this point of view?
3. How might the story be different if it were told from a different point of view? Give specific examples.

● See **Literary Terms Handbook**, p. R9.

LITERATURE AND WRITING

Writing About Literature
Students' character sketches should
- give a detailed description of Madame Lantin.
- use details from the story to support the description.

Personal Writing
Students' responses should
- relate the story to their own past experiences.
- use evidence from the story to explain Monsieur Lantin's behavior.

EXTENDING YOUR RESPONSE

Literature Groups
Encourage students to consider Monsieur Lantin's later life as they debate the issue. **COLLAB. LEARN.**

Interdisciplinary Activity
Encourage students to consider a variety of media for their illustrations such as pencil, watercolor, crayon, and pastel.

Performing
You may wish to have students work in pairs or in groups and divide the writing and acting roles.

LITERATURE AND WRITING

Writing About Literature
Character Sketch   Maupassant develops the character of Madame Lantin in a number of ways. He describes her appearance and family background. He also tells what she says and does, and shows how others react to her. Write a character sketch of Madame Lantin, using details from the story to support your description. Share your sketch with a group of your classmates.

Personal Writing
Clueless?   Monsieur Lantin lived with his wife for at least six years. How could he be so naive about her character? How could he not know they were living beyond their means? Think back to the Focus Activity on page 288. Then write a response to these questions: When our perceptions of people or things turn out to be wrong, is it because sometimes we allow ourselves to be fooled? Do you think this was the case with Monsieur Lantin? Explain.

EXTENDING YOUR RESPONSE

Literature Groups
Debate the Issue   What do you think Monsieur Lantin would have preferred: false gems and a true wife, or real gems and a false wife? Debate this question in your group. Support your ideas with evidence from the story and your knowledge of human nature. Share your opinions with the class.

Interdisciplinary Activity
Art: The Passing Scene
The scenes that Monsieur Lantin saw from the window of his hired carriage were those of a vibrant and colorful capital city. Do research to discover some of the scenes he might have viewed in late nineteenth-century Paris. Illustrate a scene as Monsieur Lantin might have viewed it from the carriage window.

Performing
Another View   Imagine that Madame Lantin had a close friend, Madame LeClair, to whom she confided everything. Now that her friend is dead, Madame LeClair wants to tell what she knows about the young woman's secret life. Write a monologue for Madame LeClair in which she explains Madame Lantin's behavior and the source of the jewels. Add details that are consistent with the information given in the story. Practice the monologue and perform it for your classmates.

Reading Further
If you enjoyed this story by Guy de Maupassant, you might also enjoy the following stories from *Fifteen by Maupassant*:

"Simon's Papa" tells of a discouraged boy who faces life without a father.

"My Uncle Jule" describes a working-class family who never seems to get ahead.

"On the River" is narrated by a boatman who expresses his fears of the river environment at night.

📖 **Save your work for your portfolio.**

✔ ASSESSMENT OPTIONS

- 📁 *Quick Checks,* p. 25
- 📁 *Selection and Theme Assessment,* pp. 49–50
- 📁 *Performance Assessment,* p. 25
- 💾 *Testmaker*

Skill Minilessons

GRAMMAR AND LANGUAGE • Infinitives and Infinitive Phrases

An **infinitive** is a verb form that usually is preceded by the word *to*. An infinitive may have complements and modifiers, forming an **infinitive phrase**. Sometimes an infinitive or an infinitive phrase is used as a noun in a sentence.

Monsieur Lantin fell in love and decided to marry. (infinitive used as a noun)

Madame Lantin's goal was to deceive her husband. (infinitive phrase used as a noun)

PRACTICE In "The False Gems," find three examples of sentences containing an infinitive or infinitive phrase used as a noun. Copy the sentences and underline the infinitive or infinitive phrase in each one.

● For more about infinitives, see **Language Handbook**, p. R40.

READING AND THINKING • Drawing Conclusions

When people draw conclusions, they come up with logical explanations for events, using reasons and details from the information they have available to them at the time. For example, after the first jeweler appraised the necklace, Monsieur Lantin drew this conclusion: "That jeweler cannot distinguish real diamonds from the imitation article." Lantin based his conclusion on these facts: his wife could not afford to buy real gems, she had told him the jewels were imitation, and he had no reason to doubt her. It was a reasonable conclusion, although it turned out to be incorrect.

PRACTICE At the end of the story, what can you conclude about Madame Lantin's character? State your conclusion on your paper. List the facts from the text on which you base your conclusion.

● For more about related comprehension skills, see **Reading Handbook**, pp. R78–R107.

VOCABULARY • Analogies

An analogy is a type of comparison that is based on the relationships between things or ideas. Some analogies are based on a relationship that could be called "an action and its significance."

blush : embarrassment :: laugh : amusement

A blush is a sign of embarrassment; a laugh is a sign of amusement. Instead of saying "is a sign of," you could substitute the word "indicates" or "signifies."

To finish an analogy, decide what relationship exists between the first two things or ideas. Then apply that relationship to another pair of words and see if it is the same.

● For more about analogies, see **Communications Skills Handbook**, p. R77.

PRACTICE Choose the word pair that best completes each analogy.

1. sneer : disdain ::
   a. bow : respect
   b. crown : royalty
   c. smile : face
   d. introduction : stranger
   e. hug : squeeze

2. snarl : hostility ::
   a. dog : danger
   b. snap : bite
   c. purr : contentment
   d. warning : siren
   e. yawn : bed

Skill Minilessons

GRAMMAR AND LANGUAGE
Infinitives and Infinitive Phrases

Possible choices:
His wife could not afford <u>to purchase such a costly ornament.</u> (p. 292)
The sun awoke him next morning, and he began <u>to dress slowly to go to the office.</u> (p. 292)
Twenty times he resolved <u>to go in,</u> but shame kept him back. (p. 293)

READING AND THINKING
Drawing Conclusions

Students may say that Madame Lantin is dishonest based on her telling her husband the jewels are fake; deceitful based on her having a source of income and a secret life that she does not tell her husband about; and shallow based on putting her love for jewels above faithfulness to her husband.

VOCABULARY
Analogies

1. a
2. c

Additional Practice

📙 *Grammar and Composition Handbook*, Lesson 3.3

📙 *Grammar and Language Workbook*, p. 97

📙 *Writer's Choice* Lesson 12.3

📁 *Reading Workbook*, pp. 29–30

📁 *Vocabulary Practice*, p. 24

Objectives

- To read and analyze a story about a saleswoman's technique
- To analyze dialogue
- To write about double meanings

Skills

Reading/Thinking: Drawing Conclusions
Writing: Monologue
Vocabulary: Borrowed Words
Grammar/Language: Run-on Sentences
Listening/Speaking: Interview
Life Skills: Résumés
Collaboration: Literature Groups

Motivating
→ OPTIONS

Selection Focus Transparency 26: Have students read and discuss the advertisements.

Focus Activity: Have groups of students compare their character maps.

Before You Read

The Saleswoman

FOCUS ACTIVITY

In your opinion, what qualities make a salesperson good at his or her job?

MAP IT! Create a character map by surrounding the word *salesperson* with words and phrases that describe the qualities of a successful salesperson.

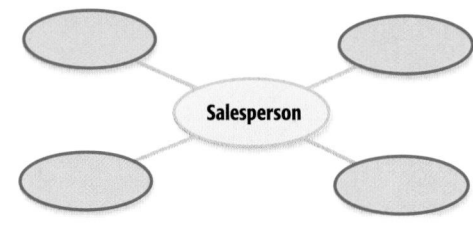

SETTING A PURPOSE Read to assess the saleswoman's technique.

BACKGROUND

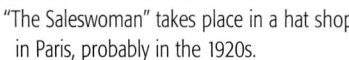

The Time and Place

"The Saleswoman" takes place in a hat shop in Paris, probably in the 1920s.

Did You Know?

The French *cloche*, a popular hat style of the 1920s, was a tight-fitting, bell-shaped hat that concealed most or all of a woman's hair and part of her face. Along with raised hemlines and short hairstyles, the *cloche* became a fashion symbol of the 1920s.

VOCABULARY PREVIEW

indulge (in dulj´) *v.* to yield to a desire (by doing something); take pleasure (in); p. 299
chic (shēk) *adj.* attractive, tasteful, and fashionable in style; p. 301
mortify (môr´ tə fī´) *v.* to shame, humiliate, or embarrass; p. 301
clientele (klī´ ən tel´) *n.* clients or customers considered as a group; p. 301

Meet Colette

The French author Colette once said of her writing that her "great landscape was always the human face." She was well known for her sensitive observations of human character—particularly of women. Like many of her female characters, Colette was a dynamic, independent, intelligent woman. She wrote numerous novels and short stories, performed in French cabarets as an actress and a dancer, and even introduced her own line of cosmetics. Her novel *Gigi* was also made into a movie, which won an Academy Award in 1958.

Colette, whose full name was Sidonie-Gabrielle Colette, was born in the Burgundy region of France in 1873. She died in 1954.

RESOURCE MANAGER

Lesson Planning Resource
The *Unit One Planning Guide* (pp. 217–224) provides additional lesson notes and reduced versions of all print resources.

📁 **Other Print Resources**
- Active Reading Guide, p. 26
- Vocabulary Practice, p. 25
- Reading Workbook, pp. 29–30
- Grammar and Language Workbook, p. 123
- Grammar and Composition Handbook, Lesson 4.10

- Quick Checks, p. 26
- Selection and Theme Assessment, pp. 51–52
- Performance Assessment, p. 26
- Spanish Summaries, p. 26
- Spanish Translations
- Inclusion Strategies
- English Language Learners Sourcebook

🖳 **Transparencies**
- Selection Focus 26
- Literary Elements 26

- Grammar and Language 26

Technology
🎧 Audio Library
🎧 Spanish Audio Library
🖥 Glencoe Literature Web Site
💾 Testmaker

The SALESWOMAN

Colette

AT THE HAT SHOP. With the arrival of a client, the saleswoman rushes up: twenty-five years old, with the eyes of a young tyrant, a tower of blond hair on the top of her head. Her hands, her figure, her mouth, her feet, all are thin to excess, witty, and aggressive.

"Ah, Madame! At last; you've come back to us! I had almost given up hope. I was saying to myself, 'That's it! She must have gone to Harry's to have some Berlin-style hats made for herself!' But . . . what is that you have on your head?"

". . . ?"

"Yes, that thing with the blue wing on the side and the velour[1] all around it?"

". . . ?"

"What, you made it yourself? All by yourself. Why, that's incredible, it's miraculous! If I may <u>indulge</u> in a little joke, you have a future in fashion. Would you do our *maison*[2] the honor of entering it as trimmer?"

". . . ?"

"The trimmer? She's . . . well, heavens, she's the one who puts the linings inside the hats, who . . . well . . . who does a lot of little things. Give me your lovely little 'creation'; oh, I'll give it back to you! Here, I'll give it back . . . let's see . . . tomorrow. Yes, tomorrow. Exactly, the car is making a delivery tomorrow in your suburb."

". . . ?"

"Yes, well, in your neighborhood, I meant. It's so far! I'm just a poor little Parisian girl who never has time to leave her post, you understand. The boulevard shop in winter, Deauville in the summer, the Biarritz shop in September, Monte Carlo in January . . . Oh, not everybody can live in Auteuil.[3] Quick, come with me, I have a nice corner in the little fitting room facing the street. It's poorly lit? You don't like being with your back to the light? But it's the best place for trying on hats! Your silhouette is projected on the window, and with hats, it's primarily a question of silhouette, this season; one disregards the details. And, you see, you're between Mademoiselle X, the 'little diva,'[4] who's trying on hats for her tour right now, and Princess Z, who's just back from the south."

---

1. *Velour* (vi loor´) is a soft, thick, velvety fabric.
2. The French word *maison* (mã zõn´) can mean a house, one's family, or a business. Here, the saleswoman is referring to the hat shop.
3. *[Deauville, Biarritz, Monte Carlo, Auteuil]* These are all high-class resort areas.
4. *Diva* (dē´ və), from the Italian, means "a famous female opera singer."

Vocabulary

indulge (in dulj´) *v.* to yield to a desire (by doing something); take pleasure (in)

Reading the Selection

SUMMARY

A young saleswoman is trying to sell hats to a regular customer whom she has not seen for a while. In the course of her sales pitch, the saleswoman reveals herself to be tactless and overbearing. She subtly insults the customer's hat, her hair color, her looks, her fashion sense, even her car. She gossips about her other customers. She ends by saying that she enjoys seeing this customer so much because she is tired of her American clients, to whom she feels like telling only disagreeable things.

📁 *Spanish Summaries,* p. 26

A **Active Reading**

RESPOND Have students read the first two paragraphs. Ask volunteers what their first reaction is to the saleswoman. Invite predictions about how they will feel about the character at the end of the story. What would have to happen to make them change their opinion?

Additional Resources

📁 *Active Reading Guide,* p. 26
🎧 *Audio Library*
🎧 *Spanish Audio Library*

Teaching Options

CONNECTING TO OTHER SELECTIONS

COMPARING *selections*

This selection is paired with "Mrs. James" on page 305. A lesson for teaching a comparison of the two selections appears on page 307.

The chart at the right shows three other ways to connect "The Saleswoman" to selections in this book.

For specific teaching strategies, see the **Unit One Planning Guide,** pp. 220–221. 📁

Connection	Title
Life Skills: Life-long Learning	→ "The Vision Quest," p. 89
Thematic: Selling Ourselves	→ "Waltz of the Fat Man," p. 377
Literary: Characterization	→ *Julius Caesar,* p. 778

POINT OF VIEW Ask students to identify the story's point of view and describe its features. *(The story has a third-person objective narrator. For the most part, the narrator merely reports what the saleswoman says.)*

C **Critical Thinking**

DRAWING CONCLUSIONS Help students conclude that the customer is answering the saleswoman based on the saleswoman's response. Ask students to explain the effect of indicating the customer's comments with punctuation instead of words. *(It puts the focus on the saleswoman; emphasizes the fact that she is pushy and talks too much; increases the humor by making the reader infer the customer's comments.)*

D **Active Reading**

PREDICT Ask students what they think the saleswoman will do when she is waiting on her next customer. Provide a model for predicting.

Model: The saleswoman has said unflattering things about other customers. She has also said some rude things to her present customer. I think she will make similar remarks about her current customer to her next customer. It's just the way she acts.

Extrèmement chic

"..?"

"Yes, that one, the fat old lady. In the shop, we call her the 'Pink Pompon.'"

"..?"

"Because whenever she doesn't like a hat, she always says, 'I think it's missing something, here, in the hollow . . . a little nothing, a little flower . . . a bouquet of pompon roses!' Mademoiselle X, that one there, to your left, she's not what you'd normally call pretty, but she has such a good heart!"

"..?"

"Oh, a heart of gold. Look, the lady who's with her, yes, that sort of little shark in black, is a poor friend she's taken in.

She takes her with her everywhere, to her couturier's,[5] to her jeweler's; she stays here for hours trying on twenty-five different hats under her poor friend's nose—to distract her.

"Let's see now, how about if we talk a little more seriously now? I've gotten it into my head that I could really do a job on you today. It's days like this when my mind is set on business. Okay, for starters, pull this little cloche down over your beautiful hair for me! . . . You haven't changed color?"

"..."

"Excuse me, it's a reflection from the outside light. I was saying to myself: it has more gold in it than usual. You might have gotten the urge to change, just for a change. And then there are some people who go gray very early. On the side, on the side, completely covering one ear! There! . . . What do you think of it?"

"...!"

"I can see it's not a hit. Besides, you're right, it's not your style. On you, it looks a little . . . a little too ladylike. It's funny, I just sold the same hat to Mrs. W. She is ravishing in it, Mrs. W, with her long neck, and especially here, you see, her chin, her cheeks, so fresh and the ear . . . Let's say good-bye to this style here for a minute; one lost, ten found. Look at that, what was I telling you! This is what we're after. Way down, all right?"

"..."

5. A *couturier* (kōō tōōr′ē ā′) is a dressmaker or designer who makes and sells highly fashionable, usually custom-made clothing for women.

300 ❦ UNIT 1

Teaching Options

MEETING INDIVIDUAL NEEDS **ENGLISH LANGUAGE LEARNERS**

Building Background Help familiarize English language learners with the kind of fashionable stores that the story depicts. Point out that the shop's customers are wealthy; they have the money and leisure to be concerned with buying the newest, most fashionable hats. Explain that in the time period in which the story is set, women always wore hats as part of their outfits.

Activity Have students find and bring in advertisements for expensive, fashionable stores in newspapers or magazines. Discuss the kinds of merchandise the stores sell and the kinds of customers they are aimed at.

Additional Resources
📁 *English Language Learners Sourcebook*

"More than that, more than that! I can still see the hair on your temple, and on the back of your neck! I believe you're familiar with the 'great hat principle of the season,' as the owner herself says?"

"...?"

"The great hat principle is that when you meet a woman on the street and her hat allows you to see whether she's a brunette, a blond, or a redhead, the woman in question is not wearing a chic hat. There! ... Notice I'm not saying anything, I'll let you make up your own mind. Well?"

"..."

"You prefer the navy-blue one? That one there, on the mushroom?[6] Yes? ... Well, really!"

"..."

"No, no, it's not sold."

"...?"

"Why no, Madame, I don't want to keep you from buying it! I wasn't suggesting it to you because I didn't think I was talented enough to sell hats like that one. But it's true, it does seem to go with your face. Ah, you really know what it is you want! Like I always say: there are only two categories of clients whose minds can't be changed: artists and lower-middle-class women."

"..."

"You're not an artist, but you still have a very independent sense of judgment. Try on this one here, just for me. It's not at all excessive, but I think it's both rich and discreet, because of this polished cotton fantasia which

gives it all its cachet[7] ... No? Ah, I'm not having any luck at all, you're just trying to mortify me. If your two sons have your personality, they'll be terrible men! Are those two big boys doing all right?"

"..."

"Already? How time flies, my Lord! And still good-looking, I'm sure. Well, there's nothing surprising about that."

"...!"

"No, Madame, there's no flattery intended at all; anyway, everybody in the shop agrees with me, it's just what everybody says about the presence, the charm, the intelligence of your husband ... and everyone knows that your two gorgeous children also inherited your beautiful health! What a shame they're not daughters! I'd already be fitting them for hats, and spoiling them as much as you. So, nothing more today, except the little blue hat? Shall I have it sent down to you in your car?"

"..."

"Yes, yes, don't worry, I give the description of the car to the messenger boy myself. You think I don't know the brown sedan you've had for six years? Good-bye, Madame, and thank you for your lovely visit, don't go so long without coming to see your faithful saleswoman; I enjoy seeing you so much ... it gives me a rest from our American clientele: all I feel like telling those women are disagreeable things."

---

6. Here, the *mushroom* is a mushroom-shaped stand used to display a hat.

7. A *fantasia* is a fanciful musical composition. Here, the saleswoman uses the word figuratively to describe the hat's adornment of fancifully constructed, shiny cotton ribbon. And this adornment, she says, gives the hat its special distinction or individuality—its *cachet* (ka shā').

Vocabulary
chic (shēk) *adj.* attractive, tasteful, and fashionable in style
mortify (môr′ tə fī′) *v.* to shame, humiliate, or embarrass
clientele (klī′ ən tel′) *n.* clients or customers considered as a group

Cultural Note

The art of millinery, which had long been a home craft, became a business in the late 1700s. Milliners made hats to order and sold them in shops. A woman did not consider herself properly dressed unless she wore a hat. But by the 1960s, hats were no longer a required fashion item.

E **Literary Elements**

DIALOGUE Have students list techniques that make the dialogue realistic. *(The author uses ellipses to indicate pauses and abrupt changes of subject; repetition and interjections like "well"; and many exclamation points.)*

F **Active Reading**

REVIEW Ask students to list the insults that the saleswoman makes. *(The saleswoman implies that the customer has chosen an awful hat; that she is a lower-middle-class woman; and that her car is old and unfashionable.)*

Thematic Focus

Twists Discuss the irony of the saleswoman's final remark.

✔ **ASSESSMENT OPTIONS**

📁 *Quick Checks*, p. 26

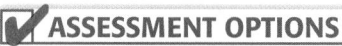

Grammar and Language *Minilesson*

Run-on Sentences Explain that a run-on sentence is one in which two or more independent clauses are punctuated as one sentence. A comma may be incorrectly used to separate the two clauses. To correct a run-on, make the clauses into separate sentences, separate them with a semicolon, or make one into a dependent clause by adding a subordinating conjunction such as *since* or *although*.

Activity Have students find two run-on sentences in the story and correct them. Possible choices:

"It's funny, I just sold the same hat to Mrs. W." (p. 300) *("It's funny. I just sold the same hat to Mrs. W.")*

"Look at that, what was I telling you!" (p. 300) *("Look at that! What was I telling you?")* **L2**

Additional Resources

🖋 *Grammar and Language Transparency 26*

📘 *Grammar and Language Workbook,* p. 123

📘 *Grammar and Composition Handbook,* Lesson 4.10

📘 *Writer's Choice,* Lesson 13.10

Personal Response

Students may say they feel the sales-woman is pushy, tactless, and insulting and that they probably would not seek her out.

ANALYZING LITERATURE

1. The words and phrases "a young tyrant," "thin to excess," "witty," and "aggressive" provide clues.
2. Princess Z is a fat old lady who often suggests putting an extra decoration on the hats she buys; Mademoiselle X is an opera singer who is not attractive but who has a good heart; her friend is "a little shark" who is supported by Mademoiselle X because she feels sorry for her.
3. Ellipses, question marks, and exclamation points mark the customer's words.
4. A woman's hair should be entirely covered by her hat.
5. No, she buys a simple navy blue hat instead of one of the stylish ones the saleswoman is pushing.
6. The client might say the sales-woman is pushy, insulting, and annoying.
7. They would have been offended and perhaps not have returned.
8. The saleswoman restates or implies the client's remark, as when she says, "What, you made it your-self?"; "Yes, that one, the fat old lady"; and "You prefer the navy-blue one?"
9. The saleswoman wants the client to feel obliged to be in style so she will have to buy one or more new hats.
10. The saleswoman tells the client she has "a very independent sense of judgment" and that her sons are good-looking. Students may say the flattery does not influence the client's pur-chase because she has a mind of her own.
11. In the first paragraph, the third-person narrator tells what the charac-ter of the saleswoman is like. In the rest of the story, the narrator merely reports what the saleswoman says, allowing her to characterize herself.
12. The author focuses attention on the saleswoman and emphasizes her character traits.
13. She compares her client to another customer, Mrs. W., saying that she looked better in a particular hat than the client does; she tells her what the latest fashion is. Allow time

Responding to Literature

Personal Response

How do you feel about the saleswoman? If she worked at your favorite store, would you seek her out? Explain in your journal.

——— ANALYZING LITERATURE ———

RECALL

1. In the first paragraph, which words and phrases provide clues about the saleswoman's personality?
2. Summarize the comments the saleswoman makes about Princess Z, Mademoiselle X, and her friend.
3. What punctuation marks are used to indicate that the customer is responding to the saleswoman's comments?
4. What is the "great hat principle of the season"?
5. In choosing which hat to buy, does the client follow the salesperson's advice? Explain your answer.

INTERPRET

6. What words do you think the client might use to describe the saleswoman?
7. If the saleswoman's customers had overheard her descriptions of them, how might they have reacted?
8. How do the saleswoman's remarks help you infer what the client is saying? Give three examples.
9. In your opinion, what is the saleswoman's motive for mentioning the "great hat principle of the season"?
10. Identify two instances of the saleswoman's flattery. In your opinion, how does the flattery influence the client's purchase?

EVALUATE AND CONNECT

11. Compare and contrast the opening paragraph with the rest of the story.
12. What do you think the author's purpose is in revealing only the sales-woman's words?
13. Identify at least two sales techniques that the saleswoman uses on her client. How would you respond to similar techniques?
14. Many of the saleswoman's "compliments" are actually disguised insults. How might you respond to backhanded compliments?
15. Use the character map you made in the Focus Activity on page 298 to evaluate the saleswoman. Would you consider her a successful salesperson?

Literary ELEMENTS

Dialogue

A **dialogue** is a conversation carried on between two people. Writers use dialogue to reveal their characters' traits and motivations. They also use it to convey information about other charac-ters or events in the story. In "The Saleswoman," readers only see the title character's side of a conversation.

1. Select two examples of dialogue that, in your opinion, help reveal the saleswoman's true character. Explain what each example reveals.
2. Even though the client's part of the dialogue does not appear in the story, the saleswoman's remarks reveal many facts about her client. Give three examples of such facts.
3. Select one or two paragraphs from the story. Complete the dialogue by supplying the words that the sales-woman's client might have spoken.

● See **Literary Terms Handbook**, p. R3.

for students to share some shopping experi-ences.
14. Some students may say they would ignore backhanded compliments. Others may say they would offer their own insults in return.
15. Most students will say that the saleswoman does not meet the criteria for a successful salesperson.

LITERARY ELEMENTS

1. One example: She compliments the looks of the client's husband; she feels competitive and jealous.
2. One fact: She is an independent thinker.
3. Students' dialogues should indicate that the client sees through the sales-woman's act.

Additional Resources

 Literary Elements Transparency 26

LITERATURE AND WRITING

Writing About Literature

Analyze Double Meanings Although the saleswoman seems to flatter her client, her compliments often are disguised insults. For example, she compliments the "beautiful health" that the client's children have inherited from her, while implying that they got their good looks from their father. In the story, find two other disguised insults and write an explanation of the double meaning of each one.

Creative Writing

The Beat Goes On Imagine that the client has left the shop after buying the blue hat, and the saleswoman begins telling a new client how glad she is to see her after the disagreeable experience she's just had with her last client. Write a paragraph or two of monologue for the saleswoman in which she describes what it was like to wait on her previous client.

EXTENDING YOUR RESPONSE

Literature Groups

Examining an Author's Attitude What does this story suggest about the author's attitude toward salespeople? Is the author suggesting that salespeople are insincere and motivated only by the final sale? Or is she suggesting that good salespeople must know their customers and their tastes? Discuss these ideas in your group, and then share your ideas with the class.

Listening and Speaking

Interview Talk to several salespeople in your community to find out what they regard as the most rewarding and most difficult aspects of their jobs. Ask them to describe the sales techniques they use and to evaluate the effectiveness of each one. Report your findings to the class.

Learning for Life

Send a Résumé, Please Prepare a résumé that the saleswoman might write. Use your imagination to fill in the details not supplied by the story. To find a suitable résumé style, consult library or Internet resources.

Reading Further

You might also enjoy these works by Colette:

Autobiography: "Laughter" from *My Mother's House and Sido* features Colette's memories of how her mother found joy even during the worst situations.

Viewing: *Gigi,* the movie of Colette's novel, won an Academy Award for Best Picture in 1958.

📖 **Save your work for your portfolio.**

 Skill Minilesson

VOCABULARY • Borrowed Words

English words came from many languages. Most often, the English word developed from a root taken from another language. Words adopted into our language with no change whatsoever are called "borrowed words." *Chic* and *clientele,* for example, are French words that mean exactly the same thing in English as they do in French.

Borrowed English words can be hard to spell because they follow the spelling rules of the language from which they were borrowed.

PRACTICE The following words were "borrowed" from the French language without any spelling changes. Think about how you might pronounce each word in English, then look up the word in the dictionary to find the correct pronunciation and the definition. Write sentences or a paragraph that correctly uses all the words.

1. cliché   4. boutique
2. croquet   5. champagne
3. fiancée

✔ ASSESSMENT OPTIONS

📁 *Quick Checks,* p. 26

📁 *Selection and Theme Assessment,* pp. 51–52

📁 *Performance Assessment,* p. 26

💾 *Testmaker*

LITERATURE AND WRITING

Writing About Literature

Students' analyses should
- describe at least two specific insults from the story.
- explain the double meaning of each insult.

Creative Writing

Students' monologues should
- show understanding of the saleswoman's character.
- show knowledge of specific exchanges between the saleswoman and the client in the story.

EXTENDING YOUR RESPONSE

Literature Groups Point out that students' discussions should center around determining the author's theme as communicated by her specific character. **COLLAB. LEARN.**

Listening and Speaking You might wish to have students volunteer to interview one salesperson they know and share their findings with the class.

Learning for Life Have students compare their résumés in small groups and decide on the style that is most effective.

 Skill Minilesson

VOCABULARY • Borrowed Words

1. cliché (klē shāʹ) a trite expression.
2. croquet (krō kāʹ) a game in which mallets are used to knock wooden balls through wickets.
3. fiancee (fē än sāʹ) a woman engaged to be married.
4. boutique (bü tēkʹ) a small fashionable specialty shop.
5. champagne (sham pānʹ) a white sparkling wine made in the province of Champagne, France.

Students' sentences should demonstrate an understanding of each word.

Additional Resources
📁 *Vocabulary Practice,* p. 25

Objectives

- To read and analyze a short story about the effect of an employer's peculiar habit
- To identify the tone of a short story
- To write a business letter

Skills

Writing: Letter
Collaboration: Literature Groups

Motivating
→ OPTIONS

Selection Focus Transparency 27: Have students discuss the employment want ads. What can they deduce about the jobs?

Focus Activity: Write on the board a list of the jobs held by students in the class.

LITERATURE & HUMANITIES

Show students *American Gothic* by Grant Wood (*American Art History and Culture*, p. 442). Ask students what values Wood's painting represents.

❧ —Before You Read—

Mrs. James

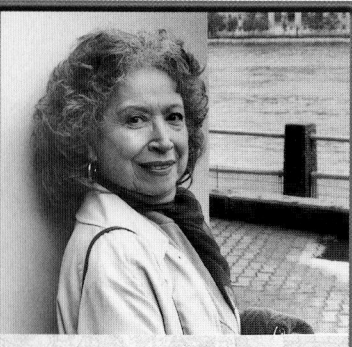

Meet Alice Childress

When Alice Childress was a girl, she lived with her grandmother in the Harlem section of New York City. Her grandmother encouraged Childress to believe that her ideas were valuable, and she urged her granddaughter to write them down. The young girl embraced this concept and dedicated herself to becoming a writer. She also became an accomplished actress and playwright, and was the first African American woman to have a play produced on Broadway.

Alice Childress was born in Charleston, South Carolina, in 1920. She lived in Manhattan at the time of her death in 1994. This story appears in the short story collection Like One of the Family: Conversations from a Domestic's Life.

FOCUS ACTIVITY

Have you ever had any kind of job? Perhaps you've worked as a baby-sitter, lifeguard, clerk, cashier, landscaper, or delivery person.

SHARING IDEAS In a small group, briefly describe any kind of job you've had. Tell what type of relationship you had with the person for whom you worked. Were you treated with respect? How did you resolve any conflicts that arose?

SETTING A PURPOSE Read to learn about the relationship between a woman and her employer.

BACKGROUND

The Time and Place
This story takes place in New York City, probably sometime in the late 1940s or early 1950s, when the Great Depression, a period of great economic hardship for most Americans, was still a vivid memory.

Did You Know?
In the first half of the twentieth century, African American women had few employment opportunities. The majority of those who found

work—like the character Mildred in this story, as well as the author herself—were employed as domestics. Domestics worked as maids, housekeepers, cooks, and nannies in the homes of families who could afford paid household help. At the time, most of these families were white.

VOCABULARY PREVIEW

pantry (pan′ trē) *n.* room or closet in which food and articles for preparing and serving food are kept; p. 305
sashay (sa shā′) *v.* to walk or move in a way that shows indifference or a lack of interest; p. 305

RESOURCE MANAGER

Lesson Planning Resource
The *Unit One Planning Guide* (pp. 225–231) provides additional lesson notes and reduced versions of all print resources.

📁 Other Print Resources
- Active Reading Guide, p. 27
- Reading Workbook, p. 29-30
- Quick Checks, p. 27
- Selection and Theme Assessment, pp. 51–52

- Performance Assessment, p. 26
- Spanish Summaries, p. 27
- Spanish Translations
- Inclusion Strategies
- English Language Learners Sourcebook

Transparencies
- Selection Focus 27
- Literary Elements 27

Technology
- 🎧 Audio Library
- 🎧 Spanish Audio Library
- 💻 Glencoe Literature Web Site
- 💾 Testmaker

Mrs. James

Alice Childress

WELL MARGE, YOU HAVEN'T HEARD anything! You should hear the woman I work for . . . she's really something. Calls herself "Mrs. James!" All the time she says "Mrs. James."

The first day I was there she come into the kitchen and says, "Mildred, Mrs. James would like you to clean the <u>pantry</u>." Well I looked 'round to see if she meant her mother-in-law or somebody and then she adds, "If anyone calls, Mrs. James is out shopping." And with that she <u>sashays</u> out the door.

Now she keeps on talking that way all the time, the whole time I'm there. That woman wouldn't say "I" or "me" for nothing in the world. The way I look at it . . . I guess she thought it would be too personal.

Now Marge, you know I don't work Saturdays for nobody! Well sir! Last Friday she breezed in the kitchen and fussed around a little . . . movin' first the salt and then the pepper, I could feel something brewin' in the air. Next thing you know she speaks up. "Mildred," she says, "Mrs. James will need you this Saturday." I was polishin' silver at the time but I turned around and looked her dead in the eye and said, "Mildred does not work on Saturdays."

Well, for the rest of the day things went along kind of quiet-like but just before time for me to go home she drifted by the linen closet to check the ruffle on a guest towel and threw in her two cents more. "Mildred," she says, "a depression might do this country some good, then some people might work eight days a week and be glad for the chance to do it."

I didn't bat an eyelash, but about 15 minutes later when I was headin' for home, I stopped off at the living room and called to her, "That's very true, but on the other hand some folks might be doin' their own house-work . . . don'tcha know." With that and a cool "goodnight" I gently went out the front door. . . .

Oh, but we get along fine now. . . . Just fine!

Vocabulary

pantry (pan' trē) *n.* room or closet in which food and articles for preparing and serving food are kept

sashay (sa shā') *v.* to walk or move in a way that shows indifference or a lack of interest

---

Reading the Selection

SUMMARY

Mildred, a housekeeper, tells about a confrontation with her employer, Mrs. James.

📁 *Spanish Summaries,* p. 27

A Active Reading

PREDICT Read aloud the first three paragraphs and invite predictions.

Additional Resources
📁 *Active Reading Guide,* p. 27
🎧 *Audio Library*
🎧 *Spanish Audio Library*

B Literary Elements

TONE How does the author feel about Mrs. James? *(She seems amazed, irritated, and a little angry.)*

Thematic Focus

Twists Discuss why Mildred's response is an example of a twist.

✔ ASSESSMENT OPTIONS
📁 *Quick Checks,* p. 27

Teaching Options

CONNECTING TO OTHER SELECTIONS

This selection is paired with "The Saleswoman" on pages 299–301. A lesson for teaching a comparison of the two selections appears on page 307.

The chart at the right shows three other ways to connect "Mrs. James" to selections in this book.

For specific teaching strategies, see the *Unit One Planning Guide,* pp. 228–229. 📁

Connection	Title
Life Skills: Decision Making	→ "The Road Not Taken," p. 643
Thematic: Unforgettable People	→ "The Ring," p. 225
Literary: Diction	→ "To Da-duh, in Memoriam," p. 399

Personal Response

Students may be largely unaware of conversational conventions for housekeepers and employers. Guide students to explore this relationship in their journals.

ANALYZING LITERATURE

1. She has the habit of referring to herself in the third person. It annoys and offends Mildred. Students may find it annoying, offensive, or amusing.
2. Mrs. James hangs around the kitchen and states that she will need Mildred to work on Saturday. Mrs. James seems a little nervous; she is "fussing" and moving things around. Mildred is suspicious; she can "feel something brewin'."
3. Mrs. James tells Mildred that if the country had an economic crisis, people would appreciate having to work long hours. Her remark shows that she feels that Mildred is ungrateful and implies that she feels superior to Mildred.
4. Mildred tells Mrs. James that if there were a depression, certain people might have to clean their own houses. Mrs. James was likely taken aback by the remark; it perhaps made her think about her assumptions of superiority.
5. She has already made her point with words. Most students will say they would have acted as Mildred did.
6. The employer's "checking the ruffle on a guest towel" shows the author's familiarity with being a domestic worker.
7. It might be more painful for Mrs. James because her lifestyle might change more dramatically. Mildred could probably continue to find work.
8. Students may be just beginning their work lives. Guide them to consider manners in the workplace.

Responding to Literature

Personal Response

Were you surprised by the way Mrs. James spoke to Mildred? By the way Mildred spoke to Mrs. James? Explain in your journal.

ANALYZING LITERATURE

RECALL AND INTERPRET

1. What peculiar habit does Mrs. James have? What impression does this habit seem to make on Mildred? What impression does it make on you?
2. Describe the scene in which Mrs. James tells Mildred that she is needed on Saturday. What feelings do the two characters seem to have during this scene? Use details from the story to support your answer.
3. Summarize what happens by the linen closet. In your opinion, what does Mrs. James's remark reveal about her attitude toward Mildred?
4. In your own words, explain what Mildred says to Mrs. James as she departs. How do you think Mrs. James might have reacted? Explain.

EVALUATE AND CONNECT

5. Rather than slamming the front door, Mildred leaves "gently." Why do you think she does this? What would you have done?
6. Early in her career, the author worked as a domestic. What specific details in the story reveal this firsthand experience?
7. Do you think an economic depression would be more painful for Mildred or for Mrs. James? Give reasons for your answer.
8. Look back at the Focus Activity on page 304. How does the relationship between Mildred and Mrs. James compare with your own relationship with a current or past employer? Be as specific as possible.

Literary ELEMENTS

Tone

Tone is the attitude of the author toward the subject of a work. The author's choice of details and language creates a particular tone. In "Mrs. James," Mildred explains that Mrs. James "drifted by the linen closet . . . and threw in her two cents more." Here, the narrator's tone is mocking and sarcastic. Note that a single piece of writing can convey more than one attitude, or tone.

1. What words would you use to describe Mildred's attitude toward Mrs. James? What specific details help to create this attitude, or tone?
2. Find two passages in the story that convey a particular tone, or attitude. Identify the tone of each passage.

● See **Literary Terms Handbook,** p. R13.

EXTENDING YOUR RESPONSE

Literature Groups
Survival and Dignity   Alice Childress once said that she focused on "portraying have-nots in a *have* society, those seldom singled out by the mass media, except as source material for derogatory humor. . . ." Compare the author's depiction of Mildred to ways that the "have-nots" in our society today are depicted in the mass media. Share your ideas with the class.

Creative Writing
Dear Mrs. James   Write a letter to Mrs. James, giving her advice about how to treat household employees. You may wish to organize your advice into two lists, one titled *Do* and the other titled *Don't.* For example: *Don't refer to yourself as "Mrs. James." It sounds silly and pretentious.*

📖 **Save your work for your portfolio.**

LITERARY ELEMENTS

1. Mildred is annoyed and insulted; she describes her as *sashaying, drifting,* and "throwing in two cents more."
2. "You should hear the woman I work for . . ." conveys a tone of disbelief. "With that and a cool 'goodnight' I gently went out the front door . . . ." conveys satisfaction.

Additional Resources

✎ *Literary Elements Transparency 27*

✔ ASSESSMENT OPTIONS

📁 *Quick Checks,* p.27
📁 *Selection and Theme Assessment,* pp. 51–52
📁 *Performance Assessment,* p. 26
💾 *Testmaker*

COMPARING selections

THE SALESWOMAN and Mrs. James

COMPARE **CHALLENGES**

DISCUSS   The main characters in "The Saleswoman" and "Mrs. James" are working women whose occupations present very different challenges.

1. What must the saleswoman do to succeed at her job? What challenge does Mildred face in dealing with Mrs. James?

2. Compare the different ways in which the women deal with the challenges of their jobs.

3. In your opinion, which character is more successful in her job? Give reasons for your answer.

COMPARE **DRAMATIC EVENTS**

DRAMATIZE   Both Colette and Alice Childress were playwrights, which perhaps explains why they told these stories through monologue—a dramatic technique in which a single character speaks.

● In a group, compare the two stories; decide which would make a better stage production.

● Develop a play script for "The Saleswoman" or "Mrs. James." Use the monologue from the story as the basis for your script. Include a set description and stage directions.

● Perform your play for the class.

COMPARE **RESPONSES**

GIVE ADVICE   Imagine that the saleswoman and Mildred have a newspaper column called "Work It Out," in which they give advice to working people. Write a response from each character to the following letter, and then compare your responses to those written by several classmates.

Dear Work It Out,
I am a sales clerk in a jewelry store that caters to the wealthy. I like my job, but my supervisor is very demanding and does not think I have a life outside the store. Also, some of my customers treat me like a servant. How can I keep my job and my dignity at the same time?

Objective

• To compare two short stories that deal with the theme of twists

COMPARE **CHALLENGES**

1. The saleswoman must talk women into buying hats. Mildred must show respect for an arrogant employer.

2. The saleswoman tries to flatter her customers. Mildred stands up to Mrs. James.

3. Students may say that Mildred is more successful because she makes a valid point and keeps her job.

COMPARE **DRAMATIC EVENTS**

Groups' scripts should

• be based on one of the monologues but use original words.

• include set descriptions and stage directions.

• reflect the participation of all members of the group.
COLLAB. LEARN.

Additional Resources
📁 *Literature Groups Sourcebook*

COMPARE **RESPONSES**

Students' responses should

• reflect the characters of the saleswoman and Mildred.

• answer the question in the letter.

💼 **PORTFOLIO OPTIONS**

Select and Reflect   Have students ask themselves the following questions as they reflect on their responses:

• Does the content of each letter reflect the different ways in which each character meets challenges?

• Does the style of each letter reflect the different personality of each character?

Have students attach their reflections to their letters and place them in their portfolios. Encourage them to review the letters at a later time for consideration as showcase pieces. **L2**

Additional Resources
📁 *Writing Assessment and Portfolio Management,* pp. 20–22

Writing Workshop

Objectives

- To create a short story
- To plan, draft, revise, edit, and present a short story
- To reflect on and assess one's story

GLENCOE
TECHNOLOGY

WRITER'S ASSISTANT CD-ROM

Students can use Glencoe's templates and guidelines software for narrative writing to aid them in working through the steps in the writing process in this lesson.

Teaching Strategies

PREWRITING

Explore ideas Have students share other sources of story ideas, such as daydreams, overheard conversations, a fascinating setting, or an unusual natural event such as an earthquake or a hurricane.

Consider your audience and purpose Have students make a note of their intended audience. Point out that they would tell a story much differently if it were intended for young children than if it were intended for their peers.

Teaching Options

~: Writing Workshop :~

Narrative Writing: Short Story

Would you like to resolve an old conflict with a friend in a different way, journey to an exotic world, or get inside the mind of a person who's very different from you? **You can venture anywhere you wish by writing your own short story, using this workshop as a guide.** You may want to write a realistic story, a fantasy, science fiction, a fable, or a mystery—the choice is yours. Don't be afraid to unleash your imagination. You may surprise yourself!

● As you write your narrative, refer to the **Writing Handbook**, pp. R58–R77.

The Writing Process

PREWRITING

PREWRITING TIP

Remember that a short story typically focuses on a single incident and has a limited number of characters.

Explore ideas

Story ideas can be based on your own experiences and relationships, as well as those you have observed or read about. Your imagination is another rich source of story ideas. As you read the following questions and suggestions, jot down any story ideas that come to you.

● What **characters** would you like to write about? You can create characters based on people you've known or other characters you've read about, such as Monsieur Lantin in "The False Gems" or Mildred in "Mrs. James." Or you might combine traits of different people to create a character.

● Think about the **conflicts**—both internal and external—that confronted the characters in the stories in this theme. Could you write a story about a similar type of conflict? Another approach is to recall conflicts you've experienced, observed, dreamed about, or imagined. Remember that everyday life is full of conflict!

Consider your audience and purpose

● Whom do you want to read your story? You might submit your story to a magazine or enter it in a contest. You might share it with your classmates or circulate it among friends and family.

● Why do you or your characters want to tell a particular story? Perhaps your purpose is to explore one of life's big questions, as Italo Calvino does in "The Happy Man's Shirt." If you're writing a humorous story, you might simply want to make your readers laugh. Think about your purpose before you begin your story, but don't be afraid to let your purpose change as your story develops.

MEETING INDIVIDUAL NEEDS ENGLISH LANGUAGE LEARNERS

Finding a Topic Point out that English language learners may have many rich sources for story ideas in addition to those listed above.

Activity Encourage students to set a story in another country that they know well or to look at the United States through the eyes of someone who comes from another country. They may also recall people, stories, and conflicts from another culture. Suggest that they first try telling their idea in oral story form to a partner to see if their idea will make a good story that appeals to an audience.

Additional Resources

📁 *English Language Learners Sourcebook*

Choose and develop an idea

Once you have a story idea you like, play around with it. Whether you start with a character, a conflict, or even a setting, start freewriting about your idea and see where it leads you. Or if you prefer, go ahead and work out the entire plot in your head before you write a single word. As you develop your idea, ask yourself questions about the basic elements of a short story. Jot down your answers.

STUDENT MODEL

Characters	Who are the characters? What are they like? Which ones do you really need? (Too many characters in a short story can cause confusion.)	Danielle: athletic teenager. Works as softball umpire one summer. Lisa and Gary: each manages a softball team in the same league. Lisa values good sportsmanship. Gary only pretends to.
Plot	What happens in the story? What is the main problem, or conflict? How do events build to a climax, or high point? How is the conflict resolved?	Gary's team plays against Lisa's. Danielle is the umpire. At critical point in game, Danielle makes bad call, causing Lisa's team to lose. Danielle feels bad. Lisa helps her put situation into perspective.
Setting	When and where does the story take place? What details will make the setting seem real to your readers and help them visualize it?	Time: A hot summer afternoon in the present. Place: a softball field in a small city park. Use details about the heat, the lack of shade, the dust, the playing field.
Point of view	Will you tell the story from the **first-person point of view,** using one of the story's characters as the narrator? Perhaps you will write from the **third-person point of view,** using a narrator from outside the story.	I'll use the third-person limited point of view. Narrator is not a character in the story but describes events as Danielle sees them. (If that point of view doesn't work, I might switch to first person.)
Theme	What message do you want your story to convey? (Your theme may change as you write your story.)	Something about winning, losing, and sportsmanship.

THE SHORT STORY ❧ 309

Characters Point out that students should identify their protagonist, the main character who will undergo a conflict. Then they can decide whether there will also be an antagonist. If not, what supporting characters will participate in the main character's conflict?

Plot Remind students that several events can lead to the climax of the story, the point at which the conflict is resolved. They may find a timeline of their proposed plot events useful. They may also want to make a cause-and-effect chain as a way of outlining their plot and determining the sequence of events.

Setting Suggest that students use their imaginations to see, feel, hear, taste, and smell the story setting and then make notes about their sensory images.

Point of view Encourage students to ask themselves whether it is important for the protagonist to report his or her thoughts and feelings. If so, a first-person point of view might work best. If more objectivity is required, a third-person point of view might be best.

Theme Point out that students may not have a strong idea of their theme until they have written a draft.

Additional Resources

📁 ***Writing and Proofreading Practice,*** pp. 1–7, 21–29

🖌 ***Writing and Proofreading Transparencies,*** pp. 1–6, 11–12, 29–30

📓 ***Writer's Choice,*** Lesson 4.2

MULTIPLE LEARNING STYLES

Spatial Some students may generate stories in visual terms and may wish to create storyboards as a prewriting step. These can be used to picture a setting, characters, and events visually before describing them with words.

Activity Have students create a multiple-frame drawing, picturing each event that happens in their story. Encourage them to use the storyboard as they draft their story but to feel free to make any changes they wish as they write. **L1**

Begin with the action List some possible choices for opening a short story, such as a description of a setting or character or a piece of dialogue.

Write your draft Remind students that some stories begin with an event in the middle of the story and have one or more flashbacks to an earlier time period. Students may want to use this method, especially if they wish to start with the most exciting or attention-getting event.

Teaching Options

~: *Writing* \ *Workshop* :~

DRAFTING

DRAFTING TIP
Skim your notes and your freewriting, and underline or highlight a few phrases or sentences to use as you start drafting your story.

Begin with the action
For many short-story writers, the hardest part is getting the story opening just right—so don't start with the opening unless you really want to do so. Just plunge right into the action of your story. Later, you can go back and write the opening.

Write your draft
Refer to your freewriting and your notes as you write, but let your ideas flow freely. If new ideas take your story in a different direction, go ahead and change the plot or other elements of the story. Rather than *telling* your readers what's happening, use details, description, and dialogue to help them *experience* your story. Don't forget that events should build to a climax and then end with a resolution. At some point, you'll need to write an opening that grabs readers' attention and draws them into your story.

Use this graphic to help shape your story.

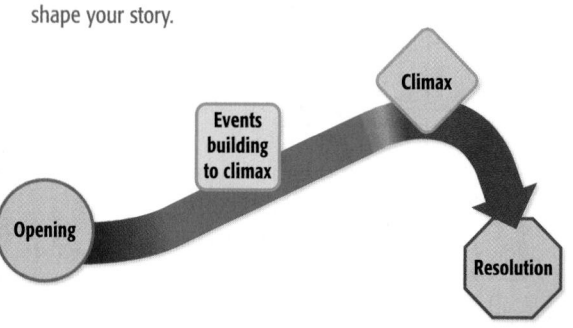

STUDENT MODEL

Danielle plopped down to sit under the shade of a large oak tree until it was time for the game to begin. Gary's team was on the field warming up. Lisa was talking to her players as they sat under a nearby tree. Danielle couldn't help overhearing.

"I was really upset after Wednesday's game," said Lisa. "A parent told me that some of you spit into your hands before shaking hands with the other team after the game. I couldn't believe it! We talked about sportsmanship before <u>every</u> practice this year. I mean it when I say that sportsmanship is <u>the</u> most important thing you will learn from playing a sport. We're bound to lose sometimes. Losing can be a worthwhile experience if you use it to learn something—such as the fact that your sense of self-worth doesn't depend on always winning. . . ."

The lecture went on. Danielle was amazed. What kind of coach told a team that losing was worthwhile? Danielle loved softball, and she always played to win. But she liked the idea that your self-worth doesn't depend on winning.

MEETING INDIVIDUAL NEEDS

GIFTED AND TALENTED

Genres Explain that different kinds of literature are called genres. A genre is characterized by a particular style, form, or content. Ask students to name as many genres as they can think of.

Activity Encourage students to create a story in a genre that they especially like and often read, such as mystery, horror, or science fiction. Have them first list some of the characteristics of the genre. For example, the plot of a mystery often includes a murder or another serious crime, a professional or amateur detective, and suspenseful events and language. You might have students work in groups with other students interested in the same genre.

L3 COLLAB. LEARN.

REVISING

Evaluate your work

Let your draft sit for a few hours or days before you come back to it. Then imagine that you are reading it for the first time. Using the **Questions for Revising** to guide you, mark the places where you could make improvements. Then revise your draft.

Have a writing conference

Read your story aloud to a friend. Ask your friend the **Questions for Revising**, and jot down the responses. Consider all responses, but make only the changes you feel are needed.

> **REVISING TIP**
> Read your story aloud to yourself. Put a check mark by any passages that sound confusing or awkward. Go back and rework those parts until they flow smoothly.

QUESTIONS FOR REVISING

How can I:

☑ make the opening more interesting or more powerful?

☑ add details to bring the characters, setting, and conflict to life?

☑ clarify confusing parts of the plot?

☑ keep the point of view consistent?

☑ make the dialogue reflect the age, background, and personality of each character?

☑ bring the conflict to a satisfying resolution?

STUDENT MODEL

It was so hot that Danielle was sure she could fry an egg on home plate.
~~Danielle couldn't believe how hot it was.~~ Her umpire's mask made her feel even hotter, and she could feel beads of sweat trickling down her face. She thrived on close games like this when she was playing. *but* It was a different story when she was umping. Gary's team was just one run ahead, and Lisa's team was batting in the bottom of the seventh *—and final—* inning.

There were two outs, and a runner was on third base. The batter hit a slow roller to the shortstop. The shortstop charged the ball and fired it to first. *This will be a close play, thought Danielle.* The ball reached the bag just an instant after the runner.

But before Danielle could make the call, Gary was screaming, "Out, she's OUT!"
Danielle lifted her right arm and her right thumb shot up. *almost automatically* "Out," she ~~said, almost like a robot.~~ *repeated.*

Gary's team erupted in ~~screams~~ *squeals* of celebration. Lisa's team seemed stunned.

So was Danielle. Why did she do that? What was she thinking? Why did she let ~~him~~ *Gary* influence her? *She didn't even like him.* But she couldn't change a call once it was made.

REVISING

Evaluate your work Encourage students to be alert for elements they may want to emphasize as they revise. For example, on reading their first drafts, they may find a theme that surprises them or a minor character whom they would like to get to know better. Encourage students to feel free to follow up on promising elements as they revise.

Have a writing conference Students might also wish to ask their partners to name the part of the story they liked best and the part that seemed most confusing.

Writing *Minilesson*

Transitions Point out that when narrating a story, writers should use transitions to help the reader follow the sequence of events. On the board, write a list of transitions such as *later, the next day, at the same time, then,* and *soon.*

Activity Have students consider adding one or more transitions to make time sequences clearer as they revise their stories. They might ask a partner to read their story and comment on any difficulties he or she had following the sequence of events. **L1 COLLAB. LEARN.**

Additional Resources

📖 ***Writer's Choice,*** Lesson 2.7

EDITING/PROOFREADING

Have students use the Proofreading Checklist on the inside back cover of their textbook.

In addition to quotation marks in dialogue, students may want to focus on verb tenses as they proofread their stories. Point out that most stories are told in past tense, although present tense may also be used if it is consistent. Have students check each verb to ensure they have used past or present tense consistently.

PUBLISHING/PRESENTING

Students may wish to illustrate their stories and compile them in a class journal.

Reflecting

Portfolio Encourage students to ask themselves these questions as they review their writing.

Does my short story
- have appeal and interest?
- include characters or plot ideas I'd like to use again?
- have natural-sounding dialogue?
- represent some of my best work?

If students answer yes to more than one of these questions, suggest that they include their short stories in their portfolio.

~ Writing Workshop ~

PROOFREADING TIP
Look for misspelled words by reading your story word by word. Or, if you're using a computer, use a spelling checker to help you find spelling errors.

EDITING/PROOFREADING

When you are satisfied with your story's content, proofread it carefully for errors in grammar, usage, mechanics, and spelling. Use the **Proofreading Checklist** on the inside back cover of this book as a guide.

> ## Grammar Hint
>
> Use punctuation marks to separate each part of a direct quotation from an explanatory phrase, such as *he said.* Begin a new paragraph and use a new set of quotation marks each time the speaker changes.
>
> *"Gary," Lisa said angrily, "you pull this same stunt in every game we play."*
>
> *"Don't be such a sore loser," replied Gary.*

STUDENT MODEL

> "That's okay" Lisa replied "it was a close play, a tough one to call."
>
> "But I was wrong," Danielle insisted.

TECHNOLOGY TIP
If you're using a computer, choose a typeface and layout that suit your story.

PUBLISHING/PRESENTING

Decide how you'll share your story with others. You might read it aloud to friends and classmates, or make copies for them to read. If you're submitting the story to a magazine, follow the submission guidelines. If you're entering a contest, follow the contest rules precisely.

Reflecting

Think about your story-writing experience. Do you like the result? Consider adding the piece to your portfolio. In your journal, comment on the most difficult part of the experience, the most enjoyable part, and what you learned as a writer. Set goals for your next adventure in story writing. What might you do differently the next time you write a short story?

 Save your work for your portfolio.

Teaching Options

✔ ASSESSMENT OPTIONS

📁 **Writing Assessment and Portfolio Management**
- Writing Assessment, pp. 2–19, 27–28
- Portfolio Management, pp. 20–22

Theme 4 — Challenges and Consequences

How do you face challenges in your life? Do you consider all of the possible consequences of your actions, or do you rush headlong into situations? In every story in this theme, one or more characters face challenges. Not all of them are prepared for the consequences, which will alter the course of their lives and, in some cases, seal their fate.

THEME PROJECTS

Creative Writing

Epigraphs An epigraph is a quotation used at the beginning of a story to suggest its overall theme.

1. As you read the stories in this theme, write down what you believe is the overall meaning of each story.

2. With a partner, select a meaningful quote that would be an appropriate epigraph for each story. Look in *Bartlett's Familiar Quotations* or in other favorite literary works. Share the epigraphs with your class and be prepared to explain why you chose each quote.

Interdisciplinary Project

Science: Expert Advice Several of the characters in these stories might have benefited from scientific knowledge related to the challenges and conflicts they faced.

1. Imagine that you are a scientist and that one or two characters from stories in this theme have come to you for advice.

2. Look up your topic in your biology or life science textbook, speak to a science teacher, or consult appropriate reference works. Then write a brief explanation of the advice you would give to each character.

Teaching Strategies

The following suggestions may help your students plan and carry out their theme projects.

Creative Writing

- To reinforce the idea of what an epigraph is, ask students to suggest possible quotations for some of the stories they have read.
- Students might want to set aside a page in their reading journal to write down the theme of each story as they read.
- Remind students that in using a reference book, such as *Bartlett's Familiar Quotations,* they will need to have some key words to use to look up quotations.

Interdisciplinary Project

- Have students choose several characters and make a list of questions they might ask.
- Suggest that students narrow their list of potential questions to those that are of most interest to them. Have them research the answers.
- Some students may want to present their answers orally. All written results could be put into a notebook for interested students to read.

Additional Resources

- 📁 *Interdisciplinary Activities,* pp. 8–9
- 📁 *Viewing and Representing Activities,* pp. 13–14
- 📁 *Listening and Speaking Activities,* pp. 7–8
- 📁 *Critical Thinking Skills,* pp. 10–12
- 📁 *Selection and Theme Assessment,* pp. 177–178
- 📁 *Performance Assesment,* p. 92

THE SHORT STORY 🕊 313

LITERATURE & HUMANITIES

After showing students *Woman Geeting Death* (*Art in Focus,* p. 537), ask them what they think is the woman's attitude toward death.

GLENCOE TECHNOLOGY

LITERATURE CLASSICS CD-ROM
Search for other selections related to the theme of challenges and consequences.

SELECTIONS	Literary Elements	Reading and Thinking	Writing	Vocabulary and Spelling	
A Sound of Thunder RAY BRADBURY	Foreshadowing, SE p. 326 *Foreshadowing, TWE p. 317 318, 324, 325* *Characters, TWE p. 319* *Simile and Metaphor, TWE p. 321* *Dialogue, TWE p. 322*	*Synthesizing, TWE p. 317* *Logical Reasoning, TWE p. 320* *Monitoring Comprehension, TWE p. 321* *Making Critical Judgments, TWE p. 325*	Evaluation, SE p. 327 Adventure, SE p. 327 *Vivid Adjectives, TWE p. 323*	The Prefix com-, SE p. 327 *Meanings from Latin, TWE p. 318*	
Lullaby LESLIE SILKO	Flashback, SE p. 339 *Flashback, TWE pp. 332, 335*	*Inferring, TWE p. 331* *Drawing Conclusions, TWE p. 332* *Evaluating, TWE p. 337*	Analysis, SE p. 340 Lyrics, SE p. 340	The Latin Root tort, SE p. 340	
And of Clay Are We Created ISABEL ALLENDE	Mood, SE p. 352 *Point of View, TWE p. 344* *Character, TWE p. 346* *Mood, TWE p. 347* *Personification, TWE p. 348* *Plot: Internal Conflict, TWE p. 350*	*Evaluating, TWE p. 345* *Cause/Effect, TWE p. 348* *Elaborating, TWE p. 350*	Character Analysis, SE p. 353 Letter, SE p. 353	Analogies, SE p. 353	
COLOMBIA'S MORTAL AGONY GEORGE RUSSELL	Description, SE p. 359 *Description, TWE p. 356* *Dialogue, TWE p. 356* *Simile, TWE p. 357*	*Distinguishing Fact and Opinion, TWE p. 357* *Making Critical Judgments, TWE p. 358*	Memorial Plaque, SE p. 359 Dialogue, SE p. 360 Writing Dialogue, SE p. 361		
WINTER NIGHT KAY BOYLE	Irony, SE p. 372 *Abstract v. Concrete Language, TWE p. 364* *Character, TWE p. 366* *Irony, TWE pp. 368, 369, 370*	Activating Prior Knowledge, SE p. 374 *Inferring, TWE p. 364* *Logical Reasoning, TWE p. 370* *Comparing and Contrasting, TWE p. 371*	Character Analysis, SE p. 373 Story Continuation, SE p. 373	Etymology, SE p. 374 Roots, SE p. 375	
Waltz of the Fat Man ALBERTO ALVARO RÍOS	Magical Realism, SE p. 385 *Plot: Internal Conflict, TWE p. 378* *Personification, TWE p. 378* *Symbolism, TWE p. 379* *Magical Realism, TWE pp. 380, 382*	Inferring Characters' Motivations, SE p. 387 *Drawing Conclusions, TWE p. 378* *Making Critical Judgments, TWE p. 380* *Generalizing, TWE p. 383* *Problem/Solution, TWE p. 383*	Analysis, SE p. 386 Case Study, SE p. 386	Analogies, SE p. 387	
The Masque of the Red Death EDGAR ALLEN POE	Setting and Mood, SE p. 395 *Character, TWE p. 390* *Setting and Mood, TWE p. 391* *Foreshadowing, TWE p. 393*	Visualizing, SE p. 397 *Comparing and Contrasting, TWE p. 393* *Varying Reading Rate, TWE p. 393*	Analysis, SE p. 396 R.S.V.P., SE p. 396	Analogies, SE p. 397 *Word Meanings, TWE p. 392*	
To Da-duh, in Memoriam PAULE MARSHALL	Local Color, SE p. 409 *Local Color, TWE pp. 400, 404* *Foreshadowing, TWE p. 401* *Symbol, TWE p. 406* *Point of View, TWE p. 407*	Activating Prior Knowledge, SE p. 411 *Cause and Effect, TWE p. 405* *Sequence, TWE p. 406*	Character Analysis, SE p. 410 Storybook, SE p. 410	Synonyms: Shades of Meaning, SE p. 411	

Key: Student material is in roman. Teacher material is in italic.   Technology   **COLLAB. LEARN.** Collaboration

Grammar and Language	Listening, Speaking, and Viewing	Life Skills	Study, Research, and Technology
Action Verbs, TWE p. 324	**COLLAB. LEARN.** Literature Groups, SE, p. 327 **COLLAB. LEARN.** Oral Defense, TWE p. 322	Learning for Life: Magazine Ad, SE p. 327 *Problem Solving, TWE p. 318*	Research, TWE p. 368
Clear Pronoun References, TWE p. 338	**COLLAB. LEARN.** Literature Groups, SE p. 340 **COLLAB. LEARN.** Dialogue, TWE p. 336	Learning for Life: Letter of Inquiry, SE p. 340 *Decision Making, TWE p. 334*	**COLLAB. LEARN.** Research, TWE p. 333
Compound Subjects, TWE p. 350	**COLLAB. LEARN.** Literature Groups, SE p. 353 **COLLAB. LEARN.** Dramatization, TWE p. 349	Learning for Life: Public Service Announcement, SE p. 353 🖥 *Using the Internet, TWE p. 346*	🖥 *Internet Connection, TWE p. 346*
Punctuating Dialogue, SE p. 361 Adjectives, TWE p. 358	**COLLAB. LEARN.** Literature Groups, SE p. 359		
Coordinate Adjectives, SE p. 374 *Irregular Verbs, TWE p. 370*	**COLLAB. LEARN.** Literature Groups, SE p. 373 Interviewing, SE p. 373 **COLLAB. LEARN.** *Dialogue, TWE p. 369*	🖥 Using the Internet, SE p. 373 *Problem Solving, TWE p. 367*	🖥 Internet Connection, SE p. 373 *Research, TWE p. 368*
Denotations and Connotations, SE p. 387 *Compound Sentences, TWE p. 384*	**COLLAB. LEARN.** Literature Groups, SE p. 386 Dramatic Presentation, SE p. 386 **COLLAB. LEARN.** *Oral Group Presentation, TWE p. 382*		Research, SE p. 386
Subject Complements, SE p. 397 *Demonstrative Pronouns, TWE p. 394*	**COLLAB. LEARN.** Literature Groups, SE p. 396 **COLLAB. LEARN.** Interview, SE p. 396 **COLLAB. LEARN.** *Creating Dialogue, TWE p. 392*		
Concrete and Abstract Nouns, SE p. 411 Apostrophes, TWE p. 408	**COLLAB. LEARN.** Literature Groups, SE p. 410 **COLLAB. LEARN.** *Persuasive Conversation, TWE p. 407*	🖥 Using the Internet, SE p. 410	🖥 Internet Connection, SE p. 410 *Research, TWE p. 403*

SELECTIONS	📁 Print Resources		

A Sound of Thunder
RAY BRADBURY
	Unit One Planning Guide,
	  pp. 238–245
	* Active Reading Guide, p. 28
	Vocabulary Practice, p. 27
		Grammar & Comp Handbook,
		  Lesson 4.4
		Grammar and Language Workbook,
		  p. 55
		Reading Workbook, pp. 31–32
			* Quick Checks, p. 28
			Selection and Theme Assessment,
			  pp. 53–54
			Performance Assessment, p. 27
			Spanish Summaries, p. 28

Lullaby
LESLIE SILKO
	Unit One Planning Guide,
	  pp. 246–253
	* Active Reading Guide, p. 29
	Vocabulary Practice, p. 28
		Grammar & Comp Handbook,
		  Lesson 7.7
		Grammar and Language Workbook,
		  p. 193
		Reading Workbook, pp. 33–34
			* Quick Checks, p. 29
			Selection and Theme Assessment,
			  pp. 55–56
			Performance Assessment, p. 28
			Spanish Summaries, p. 29

And of Clay Are We Created
ISABEL ALLENDE
	Unit One Planning Guide,
	* pp. 254–261
	Active Reading Guide, p. 30
	Vocabulary Practice, p. 29
		Grammar & Comp Handbook,
		  Lesson 2.3
		Grammar and Language Workbook,
		  p. 171
		Reading Workbook, pp. 35–36
			* Quick Checks, p. 30
			Selection and Theme Assessment,
			  pp. 57–58
			Performance Assessment, p. 29
			Spanish Summaries, p. 30
			Spanish Translations

COLOMBIA'S MORTAL AGONY
GEORGE RUSSELL
	Unit One Planning Guide,
	  pp. 262–269
	* Active Reading Guide, p. 31
	Vocabulary Practice, p. 30
		Grammar & Comp Handbook,
		  Lessons 1.4, 11.9
		Grammar and Language Workbook,
		  pp. 61, 271
		Reading Workbook, pp. 37–38
			* Quick Checks, p. 31
			Selection and Theme Assessment,
			  pp. 59–60
			Performance Assessment, p. 30
			Spanish Summaries, p. 31
			Spanish Translations

WINTER NIGHT
KAY BOYLE
	Unit One Planning Guide,
	  pp. 270–277
	* Active Reading Guide, p. 32
	Vocabulary Practice, p. 31
		Grammar & Comp Handbook,
		  Lessons 5.2, 11.6
		Grammar and Language Workbook,
		  pp. 143, 253
		Reading Workbook, pp. 39–40
			* Quick Checks, p. 32
			Selection and Theme Assessment,
			  pp. 61–62
			Performance Assessment, p. 31
			Spanish Summaries, p. 32

Waltz of the Fat Man
ALBERTO ALVARO RÍOS
	Unit One Planning Guide,
	  pp. 278–285
	* Active Reading Guide, p. 33
	Vocabulary Practice, p. 32
		Grammar & Comp Handbook,
		  Lesson 4.7
		Grammar and Language Workbook,
		  p. 103
		Reading Workbook, p. 41–42
			* Quick Checks, p. 33
			Selection and Theme Assessment,
			  pp. 63–64
			Performance Assessment, p. 32
			Spanish Summaries, p. 33
			Spanish Translations

The Masque of the Red Death
EDGAR ALLAN POE
	Unit One Planning Guide,
	  pp. 286–293
	* Active Reading Guide, p. 34
	Vocabulary Practice, p. 33
		Grammar & Comp Handbook,
		  Lessons 1.2, 2.5
		Grammar and Language Workbook,
		  pp. 54, 85
		Reading Workbook, pp. 43–44
			* Quick Checks, p. 34
			Selection and Theme Assessment,
			  pp. 65–66
			Performance Assessment, p. 33
			Spanish Summaries, p. 34
			Spanish Translations

To Da-duh, in Memoriam
PAULE MARSHALL
	Unit One Planning Guide,
	  pp. 294–301
	* Active Reading Guide, p. 35
	Vocabulary Practice, p. 34
		Grammar & Comp Handbook,
		  Lessons 11.11, 1.1
		Grammar and Language Workbook,
		  pp. 277, 48
		Reading Workbook, pp. 45–46
			* Quick Checks, p. 35
			Selection and Theme Assessment,
			  pp. 67–68
			Performance Assessment, p. 34
			Spanish Summaries, p. 35
			Spanish Translations

*Also available in Spanish

Transparencies	Technology Resources
Selection Focus Transparency 28 Grammar and Language Transparency 27 Literary Elements Transparency 28 Fine Art Transparency 13	Literature Launchers Videodisc Audio Library Spanish Audio Library Vocabulary Puzzlemaker Web Site: lit.glencoe.com
Selection Focus Transparency 29 Grammar and Language Transparency 28 Literary Elements Transparency 29	Audio Library Spanish Audio Library Vocabulary Puzzlemaker Web Site: lit.glencoe.com
Selection Focus Transparency 30 Grammar and Language Transparency 29 Literary Elements Transparency 30	Audio Library Spanish Audio Library Vocabulary Puzzlemaker Web Site: lit.glencoe.com
Selection Focus Transparency 31 Grammar and Language Transparencies 30, 31 Literary Elements Transparency 31	Audio Library Spanish Audio Library Vocabulary Puzzlemaker Web Site: lit.glencoe.com
Selection Focus Transparency 32 Grammar and Language Transparency 32 Literary Elements Transparency 32	Audio Library Spanish Audio Library Vocabulary Puzzlemaker Web Site: lit.glencoe.com
Selection Focus Transparency 33 Grammar and Language Transparencies 33, 34 Literary Elements Transparency 33	Audio Library Spanish Audio Library Vocabulary Puzzlemaker Web Site: lit.glencoe.com
Selection Focus Transparency 34 Grammar and Language Transparency 34 Literary Elements Transparency 34 Fine Art Transparency 10	Audio Library Spanish Audio Library Vocabulary Puzzlemaker Web Site: lit.glencoe.com
Selection Focus Transparency 35 Grammar and Language Transparency 35 Literary Elements Transparency 35	Literature Launchers Videodisc Audio Library Spanish Audio Library Vocabulary Puzzlemaker Web Site: lit.glencoe.com

Theme RESOURCES

- Listening and Speaking Activities (pp. 7–8)
- Viewing and Representing Activities (pp. 13–14)
- Critical Thinking Skills (pp. 10–12)
- Media Connections Activities (pp. 7–8)
- Interdisciplinary Activities (pp. 8–9)

See also these additional planning resources:
- English Language Learners Sourcebook
- Inclusion Strategies Sourcebook
- Literature Groups Sourcebook

PRESENTATION Plus!

Use Glencoe's *Presentation Plus!* This multimedia teaching tool lets you present dynamic lessons that will engage your students. Using Microsoft PowerPoint,® you can customize the presentations to create your own personalized lessons.

MEDIA
Connection

Objective

- To read and understand a comic strip

A Sound of Thunder This comic strip connects to the story "A Sound of Thunder" (pp. 316–325). Point out that the main character in the story goes back in time to the Cretaceous period and encounters a hungry *Tyrannosaurus rex*, just as Calvin in the comic strip imagines he does.

Respond

1. Students should identify a child or themselves as being similar to Calvin in the comic strip. They might explain how they or the child is a messy eater, how they like to imagine themselves as something else, or how they like to pretend to be in another time or place.
2. Students might suggest the words *self-conscious, embarrassed, sheepish,* or *humble.*

Additional Resources
📁 *Media Connections Activities,* p. 7

Teaching Options

MEDIA
Connection

Comic Strip

Have you ever wondered what it might have been like to live in the time of the dinosaurs? For Calvin, the dinosaur era doesn't seem any farther away than the dinner table.

Calvin and Hobbes

by Bill Watterson

Respond

1. Do the drawings of Calvin at the dinner table make you think of a child you know—or worse yet, of yourself as a child? Explain.
2. What words might you use to describe the scene shown in the last frame of the cartoon?

Reading *Minilesson*

Meaning Clues in Comic Strips
Discuss with students how a comic strip is like a short story and how it is different. *(Both have a setting, plot, characters, and a theme or main idea. A short story paints word pictures, while a comic strip uses drawings to tell part of the story.)* Explain that, as an author does in stories, a cartoonist may also provide clues to the meanings of words.

Activity Have students copy unfamiliar words from the comic strip and describe the context clues. Then have them discuss whose job is more difficult—a writer who uses only words or a cartoonist who uses mostly pictures and few words.

Additional Resources
📁 *Reading Workbook*

Before You Read

A Sound of Thunder

FOCUS ACTIVITY

What happens if you line up a set of dominoes on end, one in front of the other, and knock down the first one?

SHARING IDEAS The term "domino effect" is used to describe a series of events set into motion by a single event or cause. Discuss ways you may have seen a "domino effect" at work in the world around you.

SETTING A PURPOSE Read to discover how one small action causes a complex chain of events.

BACKGROUND

The Time and Place
This story begins in an unnamed part of the United States in A.D. 2055.

Did You Know?
Although the term *science fiction* was not used until about 1930, science fiction tales have been told since before the invention of writing. One of the earliest science fiction writers was Lucian of Samosata who, around A.D. 100, wrote a fantasy about a journey to the moon. Modern science fiction began to take shape in the 1800s. Landmarks of this period include Mary Shelley's *Frankenstein* (1818) and H. G. Wells's *The Time Machine* (1895).

VOCABULARY PREVIEW

expendable (iks pen′ də bəl) *adj.* not strictly necessary; capable of being sacrificed without negative effect; p. 319

correlate (kôr′ ə lāt′) *v.* to bring (one thing) into relation (with another thing); calculate; p. 320

paradox (par′ ə doks′) *n.* something that seems illogical, contradictory, or absurd, but that in fact may be true; p. 320

resilient (ri zil′ yənt) *adj.* capable of springing back into shape or position after being bent, stretched, or compressed; p. 321

primeval (prī mē′ vəl) *adj.* of or having to do with the first or earliest age; primitive; p. 324

Meet Ray Bradbury

❝You have to know fear and apprehension in some form before you can write about it thoroughly.❞

Bradbury experienced fear and apprehension early in life. "Some of my first memories," he says, "concern going upstairs at night and finding an unpleasant beast waiting at the next to the last step." An early love of reading led Bradbury quite naturally to a love of writing. At the age of twelve, using a toy typewriter, he wrote a story about Martians. A master of science fiction, he has published more than five hundred works since the 1940s.

Ray Bradbury was born in Waukegan, Illinois, in 1920. This story was first published in 1952.

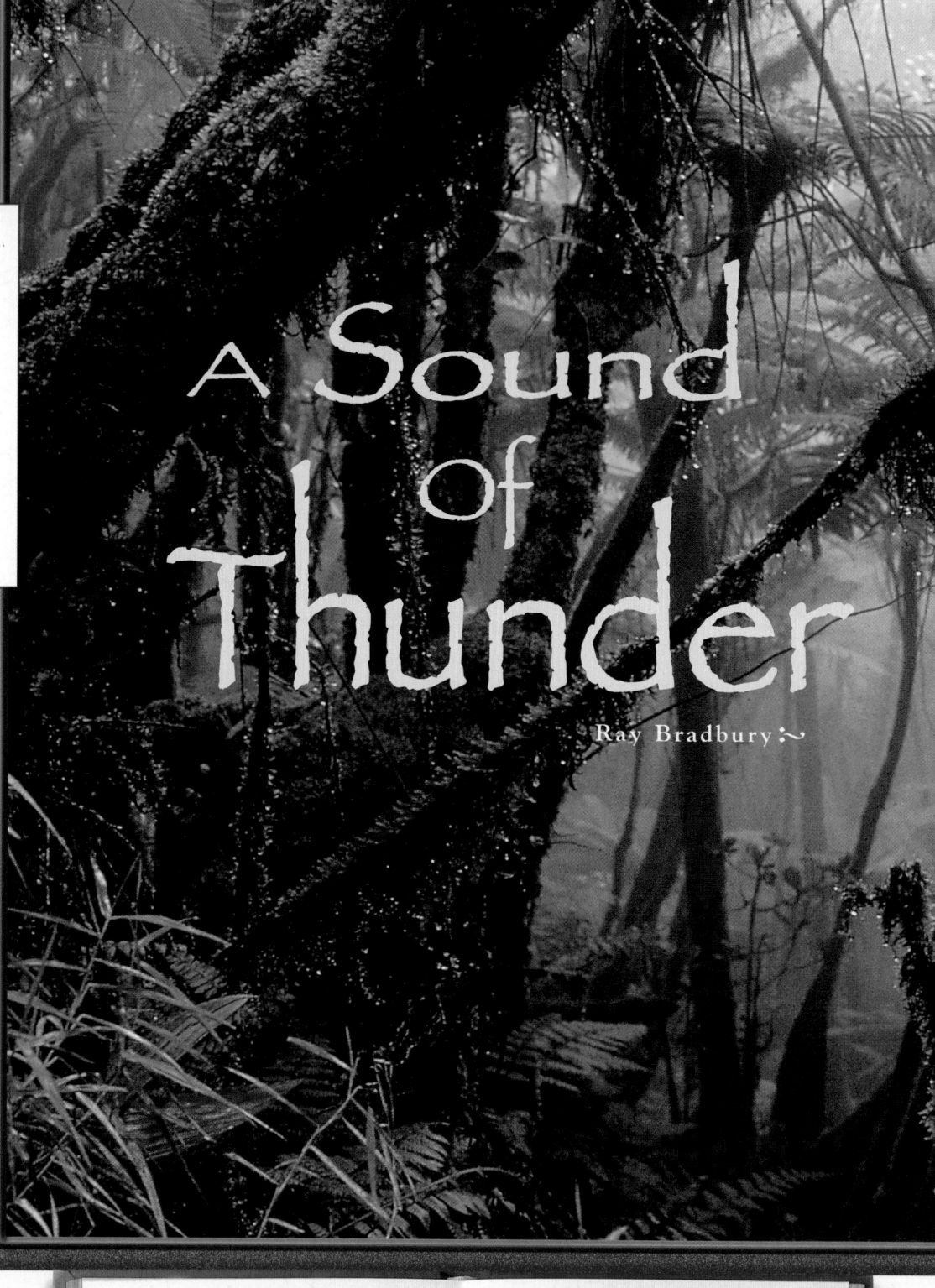

Reading the Selection

SUMMARY

Eckels and two other hunters travel to the past to hunt a *Tyrannosaurus rex*. Travis, the guide, warns them to stay on a special metal path because any environmental disturbance might change the future. When the dinosaur approaches, Eckels runs off the path. When he returns to the present, he discovers a crushed butterfly on the bottom of his shoe—and a present time that has been altered.

📁 *Spanish Summaries,* p. 28

A Active Reading

PREDICT How is the main character, Eckels, feeling as he prepares for his time safari? Have students read the first three paragraphs, suggest words to describe his feelings, and make a prediction about the outcome of the story. *(Nervous, uncertain, fearful; there seem to be clues that the outcome of the story will not be a good one.)*

Additional Resources
📁 *Active Reading Guide,* p. 28
🎧 *Audio Library*
🎧 *Spanish Audio Library*

Teaching Options

A Sound of Thunder

Ray Bradbury

CONNECTING TO OTHER SELECTIONS

The chart at the right shows three ways to connect "A Sound of Thunder" to selections in this book.

For specific teaching strategies, see the *Unit One Planning Guide,* pp. 241–242.

Connection	Title
Life Skills: Problem Solving	→ *Antigone,* p. 727
Thematic: Transitions	→ "The Vision Quest," p. 89
Literary: Description	→ "A White Heron," p. 143

THE SIGN ON THE WALL seemed to quaver under a film of sliding warm water. Eckels felt his eyelids blink over his stare, and the sign burned in this momentary darkness:

> TIME SAFARI, INC.
> SAFARIS TO ANY YEAR IN THE PAST.
> YOU NAME THE ANIMAL.
> WE TAKE YOU THERE.
> YOU SHOOT IT.

A warm phlegm gathered in Eckels' throat; he swallowed and pushed it down. The muscles around his mouth formed a smile as he put his hand slowly out upon the air, and in that hand waved a check for ten thousand dollars to the man behind the desk.

"Does this safari guarantee I come back alive?"

"We guarantee nothing," said the official, "except the dinosaurs." He turned. "This is Mr. Travis, your Safari Guide in the Past. He'll tell you what and where to shoot. If he says no shooting, no shooting. If you disobey instructions, there's a stiff penalty of another ten thousand dollars, plus possible government action, on your return."

Eckels glanced across the vast office at a mass and tangle, a snaking and humming of wires and steel boxes, at an aurora[1] that flickered now orange, now silver, now blue. There was a sound like a gigantic bonfire burning all of Time, all the years and all the parchment calendars, all the hours piled high and set aflame.

A touch of the hand and this burning would, on the instant, beautifully reverse itself. Eckels remembered the wording in the advertisements to the letter. Out of chars and ashes, out of dust and coals, like golden salamanders, the old years, the green years, might leap; roses sweeten the air, white hair turn Irish-black, wrinkles vanish; all, everything fly back to seed, flee death, rush down to their beginnings, suns rise in western skies and set in glorious easts, moons eat themselves opposite to the custom, all and everything cupping one in another like Chinese boxes, rabbits into hats, all and everything returning to the fresh death, the seed death, the green death, to the time before the beginning. A touch of a hand might do it, the merest touch of a hand.

---

1. Here, *aurora* refers to the shimmering lights that come off of the time machine.

D Literary Elements

FORESHADOWING Have students consider why the author would include a reference to an election and who won it in a story about hunting dinosaurs. *(The reference is an example of foreshadowing. The election information will probably play a role later in the story.)*

E Active Reading

RESPOND When the Time Machine stops in the past, the guide lists some events that have not happened yet. What other historical or cultural events worldwide would not have happened yet? *(Any historical or cultural event or person from any region of the world could be mentioned.)*

Vo•cab•u•lar•y Skills

Meanings from Latin In the story, the *Tyrannosaurus rex* is referred to as the Thunder Lizard, a common title given the dinosaur. However, the actual meaning of its name is based on Latin and means "tyrant lizard." Help students see the connection between *Tyranno* and *tyrant* and *saurus* and *lizard*. Discuss the meaning of *tyrant* ("a brutal absolute ruler") and how that relates to the dinosaur. Then ask for names of other dinosaurs. Discuss what the Latin word parts in their names mean.

Teaching Options

"Hell and damn," Eckels breathed, the light of the Machine on his thin face. "A real Time Machine." He shook his head. "Makes you think. If the election had gone badly yesterday, I might be here now running away from the results. Thank God Keith won. He'll make a fine President of the United States."

"Yes," said the man behind the desk. "We're lucky. If Deutscher had gotten in, we'd have the worst kind of dictatorship. There's an anti-everything man for you, a militarist, anti-Christ, anti-human, anti-intellectual. People called us up, you know, joking but not joking. Said if Deutscher became President they wanted to go live in 1492. Of course it's not our business to conduct Escapes, but to form Safaris. Anyway, Keith's President now. All you got to worry about is—"

"Shooting my dinosaur," Eckels finished it for him.

"A *Tyrannosaurus rex*. The Thunder Lizard, the damnedest monster in history. Sign this release. Anything happens to you, we're not responsible. Those dinosaurs are hungry."

Eckels flushed angrily. "Trying to scare me!"

"Frankly, yes. We don't want anyone going who'll panic at the first shot. Six Safari leaders were killed last year, and a dozen hunters. We're here to give you the damnedest thrill a *real* hunter ever asked for. Traveling you back sixty million years to bag the biggest damned game in all Time. Your personal check's still there. Tear it up."

Mr. Eckels looked at the check for a long time. His fingers twitched.

"Good luck," said the man behind the desk. "Mr. Travis, he's all yours."

They moved silently across the room, taking their guns with them, toward the Machine, toward the silver metal and the roaring light.

First a day and then a night and then a day and then a night, then it was day-night-day-night-day. A week, a month, a year, a decade! A.D. 2055. A.D. 2019. 1999! 1957! Gone! The Machine roared.

They put on their oxygen helmets and tested the intercoms.

Eckels swayed on the padded seat, his face pale, his jaw stiff. He felt the trembling in his arms and he looked down and found his hands tight on the new rifle. There were four other men in the Machine. Travis, the Safari Leader, his assistant, Lesperance, and two other hunters, Billings and Kramer. They sat looking at each other, and the years blazed around them.

"Can these guns get a dinosaur cold?" Eckels felt his mouth saying.

"If you hit them right," said Travis on the helmet radio. "Some dinosaurs have two brains, one in the head, another far down the spinal column. We stay away from those. That's stretching luck. Put your first two shots into the eyes, if you can, blind them, and go back into the brain."

The Machine howled. Time was a film run backward. Suns fled and ten million moons fled after them. "Good God," said Eckels. "Every hunter that ever lived would envy us today. This makes Africa seem like Illinois."

The Machine slowed; its scream fell to a murmur. The Machine stopped.

The sun stopped in the sky.

The fog that had enveloped the Machine blew away and they were in an old time, a very old time indeed, three hunters and two Safari Heads with their blue metal guns across their knees.

"Christ isn't born yet," said Travis. "Moses has not gone to the mountain to talk with God. The Pyramids are still in the earth, waiting to be cut out and put up. *Remember* that. Alexander, Caesar, Napoleon, Hitler—none of them exists."

LIFE SKILLS CONNECTION

Problem Solving In the story, some people wanted to go back in the past if Deutscher was elected president. Fleeing is one way of trying to solve a problem but not a very effective one. Discuss with students a process for solving problems. Write these steps on the board and discuss them, using the story example of people unhappy about an election:

1. Identify the problem.
2. List possible solutions.
3. Evaluate the choices.
4. Make a decision.
5. Take action.

Activity Let students work in groups to select a problem related to the school or community or a problem of their choice. Have them work through the problem-solving steps to identify the best possible action to take. **L2** **COLLAB. LEARN.**

Ray Bradbury ~

The men nodded.

"That"—Mr. Travis pointed—"is the jungle of sixty million two thousand and fifty-five years before President Keith."

He indicated a metal path that struck off into green wilderness, over steaming swamp, among giant ferns and palms.

"And that," he said, "is the Path, laid by Time Safari for your use. It floats six inches above the earth. Doesn't touch so much as one grass blade, flower, or tree. It's an anti-gravity metal. Its purpose is to keep you from touching this world of the past in any way. Stay on the Path. Don't go off it. I repeat. *Don't go off*. For *any* reason! If you fall off, there's a penalty. And don't shoot any animal we don't okay."

"Why?" asked Eckels.

They sat in the ancient wilderness. Far birds' cries blew on a wind, and the smell of tar and an old salt sea, moist grasses, and flowers the color of blood.

"We don't want to change the Future. We don't belong here in the Past. The government doesn't *like* us here. We have to pay big graft to keep our franchise.[2] A Time Machine is damn finicky business. Not knowing it, we might kill an important animal, a small bird, a roach, a flower even, thus destroying an important link in a growing species."

"That's not clear," said Eckels.

"All right," Travis continued, "say we accidentally kill one mouse here. That means all the future families of this one particular mouse are destroyed, right?"

"Right."

"And all the families of the families of the families of that one mouse! With a stamp of your foot, you annihilate first one, then a dozen, then a thousand, a million, a *billion* possible mice!"

"So they're dead," said Eckels. "So what?"

"So what?" Travis snorted quietly. "Well, what about the foxes that'll need those mice to survive? For want of ten mice, a fox dies. For want of ten foxes, a lion starves. For want of a lion, all manner of insects, vultures, infinite billions of life forms are thrown into chaos and destruction. Eventually it all boils down to this: fifty-nine million years later, a cave man, one of a dozen on the *entire world*, goes hunting wild boar or saber-tooth tiger for food. But you, friend, have *stepped* on all the tigers in that region. By stepping on one single mouse. So the cave man starves. And the cave man, please note, is not just any expendable man, no! He is an *entire future nation*. From his loins would have sprung ten sons. From *their* loins one hundred sons, and thus onward to a civilization. Destroy this one man, and you destroy a race, a people, an entire history of life. It is comparable to slaying some of Adam's grandchildren. The stomp of your foot, on one mouse, could start an earthquake, the effects of which could shake our earth and destinies down through Time, to their very foundations. With the death of that one cave man, a billion others yet unborn are throttled in the womb. Perhaps Rome never rises on its seven hills. Perhaps Europe is forever a dark forest, and only Asia waxes healthy and teeming. Step on a mouse and you crush the Pyramids. Step on a mouse and you leave your print, like a Grand Canyon, across Eternity. Queen

2. [*graft to keep our franchise*] Time Safari, Inc., pays money as bribes to government officials in return for continued permission to run its business.

Vocabulary
expendable (iks pen′ də bəl) *adj.* not strictly necessary; capable of being sacrificed without negative effect

---

H Author's Craft

DIALOGUE The author has Eckels ask questions. Discuss the author's purpose for this type of dialogue. *(Eckels's questions are the questions the reader probably has. By having Eckels ask questions, the author can provide information the reader needs to know.)*

FYI

La Brea Tar Pits The author mentions an animal drowning in a tar pit. Some of the most famous tar pits are found in Los Angeles, California, and are known as the La Brea tar pits. Skeletons of prehistoric Ice Age saber-toothed tigers, bears, llamas, camels, wolves, sloths, and other animals have been found. They became trapped when they came to drink water that covered the sticky goo.

I Critical Thinking

LOGICAL REASONING When Eckels realizes someone has already been back to where they are going, he wants to know what happened. Why would knowing the outcome be both good and bad? *(If he knew ahead of time that things turned out badly, he might be able to change events for the better, or he might be even more afraid and make things worse.)*

Teaching Options

Elizabeth might never be born. Washington might not cross the Delaware, there might never be a United States at all. So be careful. Stay on the Path. *Never* step off!"

"I see," said Eckels. "Then it wouldn't pay for us even to touch the grass?"

"Correct. Crushing certain plants could add up infinitesimally.[3] A little error here would multiply in sixty million years, all out of proportion. Of course maybe our theory is wrong. Maybe Time *can't* be changed by us. Or maybe it can be changed only in little subtle ways. A dead mouse here makes an insect imbalance there, a population disproportion later, a bad harvest further on, a depression, mass starvation, and, finally, a change in *social* temperament in far-flung countries. Something much more subtle, like that. Perhaps only a soft breath, a whisper, a hair, pollen on the air, such a slight, slight change that unless you looked close you wouldn't see it. Who knows? Who really can say he knows? We don't know. We're guessing. But until we do know for certain whether our messing around in Time *can* make a big roar or a little rustle in history, we're being damned careful. This Machine, this Path, your clothing and bodies, were sterilized, as you know, before the journey. We wear these oxygen helmets so we can't introduce our bacteria into an ancient atmosphere."

"How do we know which animals to shoot?"

"They're marked with red paint," said Travis. "Today, before our journey, we sent

---

3. *Infinitesimally* (in' fi nə tes' ə məl lē) describes something being done "in a way that is too small to be measured."

Lesperance here back with the Machine. He came to this particular era and followed certain animals."

"Studying them?"

"Right," said Lesperance. "I track them through their entire existence, noting which of them lives longest. Very few. How many times they mate. Not often. Life's short. When I find one that's going to die when a tree falls on him, or one that drowns in a tar pit, I note the exact hour, minute, and second. I shoot a paint bomb. It leaves a red patch on his hide. We can't miss it. Then I <u>correlate</u> our arrival in the Past so that we meet the Monster not more than two minutes before he would have died anyway. This way, we kill only animals with no future, that are never going to mate again. You see how *careful* we are?"

"But if you came back this morning in Time," said Eckels eagerly, "you must've bumped into *us*, our Safari! How did it turn out? Was it successful? Did all of us get through—alive?"

Travis and Lesperance gave each other a look.

"That'd be a <u>paradox</u>," said the latter. "Time doesn't permit that sort of mess—a man meeting himself. When such occasions threaten, Time steps aside. Like an airplane hitting an air pocket. You felt the Machine jump just before we stopped? That was us passing ourselves on the way back to the Future. We saw nothing. There's no way of telling *if* this expedition was a success, *if* we got our monster, or whether all of us— meaning *you*, Mr. Eckels—got out alive."

Eckels smiled palely.

"Cut that," said Travis sharply. "Everyone on his feet!"

They were ready to leave the Machine.

Vocabulary
correlate (kôr' ə lāt') *v.* to bring (one thing) into relation (with another thing); calculate
paradox (par' ə doks') *n.* something that seems illogical, contradictory, or absurd, but that in fact may be true

---

MEETING INDIVIDUAL NEEDS **ENGLISH LANGUAGE LEARNERS**

Understanding Print Draw English language learners' attention to Bradbury's use of capital letters and of italics. Discuss why Bradbury chose to emphasize some words by using capital letters. Also point out and explain the use of italics for emphasis and of italics and capital letters with the names of dinosaur species.

Activity Have pairs of students look for examples of Bradbury's use of capital letters and italics. Partners can discuss the significance of the examples they find.

Additional Resources
📁 *English Language Learners Sourcebook*

Did You Know?
Pterodactyls (ter′ ə dak′ tilz) are extinct flying reptiles with wingspans of up to forty feet.

Ray Bradbury ~

The jungle was high and the jungle was broad and the jungle was the entire world forever and forever. Sounds like music and sounds like flying tents filled the sky, and those were pterodactyls soaring with cavernous gray wings, gigantic bats out of a delirium and a night fever. Eckels, balanced on the narrow Path, aimed his rifle playfully.

"Stop that!" said Travis. "Don't even aim for fun, damn it! If your gun should go off—"

Eckels flushed. "Where's our *Tyrannosaurus?*"

Lesperance checked his wrist watch. "Up ahead. We'll bisect his trail in sixty seconds. Look for the red paint, for Christ's sake. Don't shoot till we give the word. Stay on the Path. *Stay on the Path!*"

They moved forward in the wind of morning.

"Strange," murmured Eckels. "Up ahead, sixty million years, Election Day over. Keith made President. Everyone celebrating. And here we are, a million years lost, and they don't exist. The things we worried about for months, a lifetime, not even born or thought about yet."

"Safety catches off, everyone!" ordered Travis. "You, first shot, Eckels. Second, Billings. Third, Kramer."

"I've hunted tiger, wild boar, buffalo, elephant, but Jesus, this is *it*," said Eckels. "I'm shaking like a kid."

"Ah," said Travis.

Everyone stopped.

Travis raised his hand. "Ahead," he whispered. "In the mist. There he is. There's His Royal Majesty now."

The jungle was wide and full of twitterings, rustlings, murmurs, and sighs.

Suddenly it all ceased, as if someone had shut a door.

Silence.

A sound of thunder.

Out of the mist, one hundred yards away, came *Tyrannosaurus rex.*

"Jesus God," whispered Eckels.

"Sh!"

It came on great oiled, resilient, striding legs. It towered thirty feet above half of the trees, a great evil god, folding its delicate watchmaker's claws close to its oily reptilian[4] chest. Each lower leg was a piston, a thousand pounds of white bone, sunk in thick ropes of muscle, sheathed over in a gleam of pebbled skin like the mail of a terrible warrior. Each thigh was a ton of meat, ivory, and steel mesh. And from the great breathing cage of the upper body those two delicate arms dangled out front, arms with hands which might pick up and examine men like toys, while the snake neck coiled. And the head itself, a ton of sculptured stone, lifted easily upon the sky. Its mouth gaped, exposing a fence of teeth like daggers. Its eyes rolled, ostrich eggs, empty of all expression save hunger. It closed its mouth in a death grin. It ran, its pelvic bones crushing aside trees and bushes, its taloned feet clawing damp earth, leaving prints six inches deep wherever it settled its weight. It ran with a gliding ballet

Did You Know?
Mail is a flexible body armor made of small, overlapping or interlinked metal plates or rings.

4. *Reptilian* (rep til′ ē ən) means "of or like a reptile."

Vocabulary
resilient (ri zil′ yənt) *adj.* capable of springing back into shape or position after being bent, stretched, or compressed

---

J Active Reading

PREDICT When Eckels jokingly aims his gun at a pterodactyl, Travis says "If your gun should go off—" but does not finish the sentence. What would the ending of the sentence have been? (*. . .the future would be changed.*)

Pop Culture

Dinosaur exhibits at museums draw huge crowds; Barney, the purple dinosaur, gets huge ratings; vitamins and diapers with dinosaurs get huge sales; and dinosaur movies, such as *Jurassic Park*, get huge box office returns. Young and old alike seem to enjoy dinosaurs.

K Literary Elements

FIGURES OF SPEECH: *Simile and Metaphor* Remind students that a simile is a comparison between two unlike things, using *like* or *as*. A metaphor is an implied comparison in which one thing is said to be another. Ask students to locate examples of each in the description of the dinosaur. (*Similes: pebbled skin like the mail of a terrible warrior, a fence of teeth like daggers; Metaphors: a great evil god; each lower leg was a piston; each thigh was a ton of meat, ivory, and steel mesh; its head was sculptured stone; its eyes were ostrich eggs*)

Reading *Minilesson*

Monitoring Comprehension

Comprehending long sentences can be difficult even for proficient readers. Suggest that students pay close attention to punctuation. What does punctuation, such as commas and semicolons, indicate? (*pauses—breaks in thought*)

Activity Have students use their index finger to block off separate parts of a long sentence to isolate each clause and phrase. Suggest that they read each blocked-off section separately. Point out that this blocking-off technique will help them break down a long sentence into manageable parts that make it easier to understand. **L1**

Additional Resources

📁 *Reading Workbook,* pp. 31–32

Literary Elements

DIALOGUE The author uses dialogue to create tension and fear. Have students examine how the dialogue is written. What technique does the author use? *(short phrases and sentences)*

Active Reading

REVIEW The author continues the description of the dinosaur, giving new information about the skin. Ask students to summarize the previous description of the dinosaur's skin and compare it with this new one.
(The skin was described as pebbled like the mail of a warrior. Here the skin is described as glittering like green coins. The image of the skin being like armor is continued. In the first example, mail was used, which is armor. In this example, the skin is called armor.)

FINE ART
TRANSPARENCY 13

You may wish to use Fine Art Tranparency 13 to discuss means of transportation.

Teaching Options

step, far too poised and balanced for its ten tons. It moved into a sunlit arena warily, its beautifully reptile hands feeling the air.

"My God!" Eckels twitched his mouth. "It could reach up and grab the moon."

"Sh!" Travis jerked angrily. "He hasn't seen us yet."

"It can't be killed." Eckels pronounced this verdict quietly, as if there could be no argument. He had weighed the evidence and this was his considered opinion. The rifle in his hands seemed a cap gun. "We were fools to come. This is impossible."

"Shut up!" hissed Travis.

"Nightmare."

"Turn around," commanded Travis. "Walk quietly to the Machine. We'll remit one half your fee."

"I didn't realize it would be this *big*," said Eckels. "I miscalculated, that's all. And now I want out."

"It *sees* us!"

"There's the red paint on its chest!"

The Thunder Lizard raised itself. Its armored flesh glittered like a thousand green coins. The coins, crusted with slime, steamed. In the slime, tiny insects wriggled, so that the entire body seemed to twitch and undulate,[5] even while the monster itself did not move. It exhaled. The stink of raw flesh blew down the wilderness.

"Get me out of here," said Eckels. "It was never like this before. I was always sure I'd come through alive. I had good guides, good safaris, and safety. This time, I figured wrong. I've met my match and admit it. This is too much for me to get hold of."

"Don't run," said Lesperance. "Turn around. Hide in the Machine."

---

5. *Undulate* (un′ jə lāt′) means "to move like a wave."

"Yes." Eckels seemed to be numb. He looked at his feet as if trying to make them move. He gave a grunt of helplessness.

"Eckels!"

He took a few steps, blinking, shuffling.

"Not *that* way!"

The Monster, at the first motion, lunged forward with a terrible scream. It covered one hundred yards in four seconds. The rifles jerked up and blazed fire. A windstorm from the beast's mouth engulfed them in the stench of slime and old blood. The Monster roared, teeth glittering with sun.

Eckels, not looking back, walked blindly to the edge of the Path, his gun limp in his

---

Listening and Speaking *Minilesson*

Oral Defense Sometimes it is necessary to make an oral defense of one's actions. With students, prepare a list of issues that might be covered when making such a defense. Guidelines might look something like this:
- What happened?
- Why did it happen?
- What was done or will be done to resolve the problem?

Activity Ask students to imagine Travis has been called before a supervisor to explain what happened. Let pairs of students work together—one as Travis and one as the supervisor. The supervisor could ask questions, and Travis could defend himself. Provide time for pairs to present their role-playing to the class.

L2 **COLLAB. LEARN.**

arms, stepped off the Path, and walked, not knowing it, in the jungle. His feet sank into green moss. His legs moved him, and he felt alone and remote from the events behind.

The rifles cracked again. Their sound was lost in shriek and lizard thunder. The great lever of the reptile's tail swung up, lashed sideways. Trees exploded in clouds of leaf and branch. The Monster twitched its jeweler's hands down to fondle at the men, to twist them in half, to crush them like berries, to cram them into its teeth and its screaming throat. Its boulder-stone eyes leveled with the men. They saw themselves mirrored. They fired at the metallic eyelids and the blazing black iris.

N

Like a stone idol, like a mountain avalanche, *Tyrannosaurus* fell. Thundering, it clutched trees, pulled them with it. It wrenched and tore the metal Path. The men flung themselves back and away. The body hit, ten tons of cold flesh and stone. The guns fired. The Monster lashed its armored tail, twitched its snake jaws, and lay still. A fount of blood spurted from its throat. Somewhere inside, a sac of fluids burst. Sickening gushes drenched the hunters. They stood, red and glistening.

O

The thunder faded.

The jungle was silent. After the avalanche, a green peace. After the nightmare, morning.

Billings and Kramer sat on the pathway and threw up. Travis and Lesperance stood with smoking rifles, cursing steadily.

In the Time Machine, on his face, Eckels lay shivering. He had found his way back to the Path, climbed into the Machine.

Travis came walking, glanced at Eckels, took cotton gauze from a metal box, and returned to the others, who were sitting on the Path.

"Clean up."

They wiped the blood from their helmets. They began to curse too. The Monster lay, a hill of solid flesh. Within, you could hear the sighs and murmurs as the furthest chambers of it died, the organs malfunctioning, liquids running a final instant from pocket to sac to spleen, everything shutting off, closing up forever. It was like standing by a wrecked locomotive or a steam shovel at quitting time, all valves being released or levered tight. Bones cracked; the tonnage of its own flesh, off balance, dead weight, snapped the delicate forearms, caught underneath. The meat settled, quivering.

Another cracking sound. Overhead, a gigantic tree branch broke from its heavy mooring, fell. It crashed upon the dead beast with finality.

"There." Lesperance checked his watch. "Right on time. That's the giant tree that was scheduled to fall and kill this animal originally." He glanced at the two hunters. "You want the trophy picture?"

"What?"

"We can't take a trophy back to the Future. The body has to stay right here where it would have died originally, so the insects, birds, and bacteria can get at it, as they were intended to. Everything in balance. The body stays. But we *can* take a picture of you standing near it."

The two men tried to think, but gave up, shaking their heads.

They let themselves be led along the metal Path. They sank wearily into the Machine cushions. They gazed back at the ruined Monster, the stagnating mound, where already strange reptilian birds and golden insects were busy at the steaming armor.

A sound on the floor of the Time Machine stiffened them. Eckels sat there, shivering.

"I'm sorry," he said at last.

"Get up!" cried Travis.

Eckels got up.

"Go out on that Path alone," said Travis.

O

P

N **Active Reading**

CONNECT The author talks about the eyes of the dinosaur and writes, "They saw themselves mirrored." Ask how the men saw themselves mirrored. This might be a good opportunity to model how to make a connection with this image.

Model: The dinosaur has fallen to the ground. The author describes how the dinosaur's eyes are now level with the men. From personal experience, I know it is possible to see objects mirrored in someone's eyes. The men saw themselves mirrored in the dinosaur's eyes.

O **Literary Elements**

FIGURES OF SPEECH: *Simile* Page 323 contains a number of similes. Challenge students to find them. *(The dinosaur's fall is compared to that of a stone idol and a mountain avalanche. The sounds from the dying dinosaur are compared to a wrecked locomotive and a steam shovel.)*

P **Literary Elements**

CHARACTERS Instead of being happy after the kill, the other hunters on the safari feel quite different. Discuss some of the emotions the hunters felt throughout the story. *(At first, they felt excited because they were going on an incredible hunt. When the dinosaur appeared, they were afraid. Then they felt relieved because they had survived. They felt sickened as they watched the animal die but also by what they had done. Finally, they felt weary and exhausted.)*

Writing *Minilesson*

Vivid Adjectives The description of the dinosaur and its death contains vivid adjectives. As a group, list some of these adjectives. *(Possible answers: oiled, resilient, striding, evil, delicate, oily, reptilian, thick, pebbled, taloned, boulder-stone, metallic)*

Activity Have students use the words they listed to write a descriptive paragraph about another kind of dinosaur. When the writing is completed, ask students to read their descriptions to a classmate. **L2**

Additional Resources

Writer's Choice, Lesson 3.3

Active Reading

QUESTION Travis had a number of reasons for telling Eckels he could not come back. Why did Travis want to leave him? Could Eckels really be left in the past? *(Eckels nearly got the others killed. He ran off the path, which meant losing money and having to report to the government. The company's license might get revoked. Eckels may have affected the past and the future. Leaving Eckels in the past would have definitely changed the past and, therefore, the present.)*

Historical Note

As the hunters are returning, three dates are mentioned. Students will probably recognize the dates and be able to identify their significance.

1492 Columbus lands on San Salvador in the Americas.

1776 Independence is declared in the American colonies. The Declaration of Independence is adopted.

1812 The War of 1812 begins between the United States and Great Britain.

Literary Elements

FORESHADOWING What clue is given about what will ultimately happen to Eckels? *(Travis says his gun is ready and that he may kill Eckels.)*

He had his rifle pointed. "You're not coming back in the Machine. We're leaving you here!"

Lesperance seized Travis' arm. "Wait—"

"Stay out of this!" Travis shook his hand away. "This son of a bitch nearly killed us. But it isn't *that* so much. Hell, no. It's his *shoes!* Look at them! He ran off the Path! My God, that *ruins* us! Christ knows how much we'll forfeit! Tens of thousands of dollars of insurance! We guarantee no one leaves the Path. He left it. Oh, the damn fool! I'll have to report to the government. They might revoke[6] our license to travel. God knows *what* he's done to Time, to History!"

"Take it easy, all he did was kick up some dirt."

"How do we *know?*" cried Travis. "We don't know anything! It's all a damn mystery! Get out there, Eckels!"

Eckels fumbled his shirt. "I'll pay anything. A hundred thousand dollars!"

Travis glared at Eckels' checkbook and spat. "Go out there. The Monster's next to the Path. Stick your arms up to your elbows in his mouth. Then you can come back with us."

"That's unreasonable!"

"The Monster's dead, you yellow bastard. The bullets! The bullets can't be left behind. They don't belong in the Past; they might change something. Here's my knife. Dig them out!"

The jungle was alive again, full of the old tremorings and bird cries. Eckels turned slowly to regard that primeval garbage dump, that hill of nightmares and terror. After a long time, like a sleepwalker, he shuffled out along the Path.

He returned, shuddering, five minutes later, his arms soaked and red to the elbows. He held out his hands. Each held a number of steel bullets. Then he fell. He lay where he fell, not moving.

"You didn't have to make him do that," said Lesperance.

"Didn't I? It's too early to tell." Travis nudged the still body. "He'll live. Next time he won't go hunting game like this. Okay." He jerked his thumb wearily at Lesperance. "Switch on. Let's go home."

1492. 1776. 1812.

They cleaned their hands and faces. They changed their caking shirts and pants. Eckels was up and around again, not speaking. Travis glared at him for a full ten minutes.

"Don't look at me," cried Eckels. "I haven't done anything."

"Who can tell?"

"Just ran off the Path, that's all, a little mud on my shoes—what do you want me to do—get down and pray?"

"We might need it. I'm warning you, Eckels, I might kill you yet. I've got my gun ready."

"I'm innocent. I've done nothing."

1999. 2000. 2055.

The Machine stopped.

"Get out," said Travis.

The room was there as they had left it. But not the same as they had left it. The same man sat behind the same desk. But the same man did not quite sit behind the same desk.

Travis looked around swiftly. "Everything okay here?" he snapped.

"Fine. Welcome home!"

Travis did not relax. He seemed to be looking at the very atoms of the air itself, at the way the sun poured through the one high window.

"Okay, Eckels, get out. Don't ever come back."

Eckels could not move.

---

6. *Revoke* means "to cancel or withdraw."

Vocabulary
primeval (prī mē′ vəl) *adj.* of or having to do with the first or earliest age; primitive

---

Teaching Options

Grammar and Language *Minilesson*

Action Verbs Ask students to look for some action verbs in the story. If necessary, remind them what an action verb is. List the verbs on the board as students identify them. *(Possible action verbs: cracked, howled, ceased, crashed, revoke, fumbled, glared, dig, turned, shuffled, soaked, nudged, twitched, screamed, whirled, trembled, pleaded)*

Activity Write the verbs below on the board. Ask students to replace the given verb with one that shows more action. Finally, have students write sentences using verbs listed on the board.

1. yelled   (screamed)
2. shook   (trembled)
3. stared   (glared)
4. wet   (soaked)
5. stopped   (ceased) **L1**

Additional Resources

Grammar and Language Transparency 27

Grammar and Language Workbook, p. 55

Grammar and Composition Handbook, Lesson 1.4

Writer's Choice, Lesson 3.3

Ray Bradbury

"You heard me," said Travis. "What're you *staring* at?"

Eckels stood smelling of the air, and there was a thing to the air, a chemical taint[7] so subtle, so slight, that only a faint cry of his subliminal[8] senses warned him it was there. The colors, white, gray, blue, orange, in the wall, in the furniture, in the sky beyond the window, were . . . were . . . And there was a *feel*. His flesh twitched. His hands twitched. He stood drinking the oddness with the pores of his body. Somewhere, someone must have been screaming one of those whistles that only a dog can hear. His body screamed silence in return. Beyond this room, beyond this wall, beyond this man who was not quite the same man seated at this desk that was not quite the same desk . . . lay an entire world of streets and people. What sort of world it was now, there was no telling. He could feel them moving there, beyond the walls, almost, like so many chess pieces blown in a dry wind. . . .

But the immediate thing was the sign painted on the office wall, the same sign he had read earlier today on first entering.

Somehow, the sign had changed:

> TYME SEFARI INC.
> SEFARIS TU ANY YEER EN THE PAST.
> YU NAIM THE ANIMALL.
> WEE TAEK YU THAIR.
> YU SHOOT ITT.

---

7. A *taint* is a trace of something that harms or spoils.
8. *Subliminal* (sub lim′ ən əl) means "existing below the limits of sensation or consciousness; subconscious."

Eckels felt himself fall into a chair. He fumbled crazily at the thick slime on his boots. He held up a clod of dirt, trembling. "No, it *can't* be. Not a *little* thing like that. No!"

Embedded in the mud, glistening green and gold and black, was a butterfly, very beautiful, and very dead.

"Not a little thing like *that*! Not a butterfly!" cried Eckels.

It fell to the floor, an exquisite thing, a small thing that could upset balances and knock down a line of small dominoes and then big dominoes and then gigantic dominoes, all down the years across Time. Eckels' mind whirled. It *couldn't* change things. Killing one butterfly couldn't be *that* important! Could it?

His face was cold. His mouth trembled, asking: "Who—who won the presidential election yesterday?"

The man behind the desk laughed. "You joking? You know damn well. Deutscher, of course! Who else? Not that damn weakling Keith. We got an iron man now, a man with guts, by God!" The official stopped. "What's wrong?"

Eckels moaned. He dropped to his knees. He scrabbled at the golden butterfly with shaking fingers. "Can't we," he pleaded to the world, to himself, to the officials, to the Machine, "can't we take it *back*, can't we *make* it alive again? Can't we start over? Can't we—"

He did not move. Eyes shut, he waited, shivering. He heard Travis breathe loud in the room; he heard Travis shift his rifle, click the safety catch, and raise the weapon.

There was a sound of thunder.

S **Critical Thinking**

MAKING CRITICAL JUDGMENTS Could the death of a butterfly really affect the future? Some people argue that what we are now doing to the environment will affect the future. Do students agree or disagree?

T **Literary Elements**

FORESHADOWING Ask students why Bradbury literally explains what will happen to Eckels (on page 324), but when it finally does happen, the reader is left to infer it. *(The author doesn't need to say it again. It was foreshadowed.)*

U **Active Reading**

REVIEW Have students find similes and metaphors in the story that use thunder. Then have them discuss the meaning of the title. The title of the story is "A Sound of Thunder." What were some of the sounds of thunder? *(The dinosaur is the Thunder Lizard and made a sound of thunder. The author calls the sound the animal makes in anger and pain "lizard thunder." It fell to the ground with a thundering sound. The title might symbolize the coming political change.)*

Thematic Focus

Challenges and Consequences
Discuss how Eckels faced his challenge and its consequence. Discuss the kinds of challenges the average person typically faces.

✔ ASSESSMENT OPTIONS

📁 *Quick Checks,* p. 28

THE SHORT STORY 🐾 325

REAL-WORLD CONNECTION

Facing Challenges Ask students to use newspapers and books to locate comic strips in which the characters face a challenge. Suggest that students make a copy of each comic strip, mount it on paper, and write a brief paragraph under it describing what the challenge is and what the possible consequences (which may also be shown in the comic strip) are. **L2**

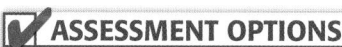

THE SHORT STORY 🐾 325

Responding to the Selection

Personal Response

Students will probably have varying opinions. Some may say Eckels should not have been shot because there may be a way to restore things. Other students may say it was a fitting end to a coward who had changed the future.

ANALYZING LITERATURE

1. Eckels has come to the office because he is going on a time safari. He wants to hunt a *Tyrannosaurus rex*.
2. Natural events occur in reverse as the group goes back in time.
3. The hunters must stay on the path. They must kill only the animals they are told they can kill. The future could be changed if the rules are not followed.
4. Eckels is terrified. He runs away off the path. The other men fire their guns at the dinosaur.
5. The future has been changed.
6. People who are curious about the past can go back in time and actually experience it.
7. He is awed by the power of such an invention.
8. Travis describes what could happen if anything changes in the past. His explanation is, in fact, an example of a domino effect.
9. The men are not fully prepared for just how huge and ferocious the dinosaur is.
10. The future has not changed for the better. The changes in the sign indicate a whole different evolution of thought among humanity. The kind of president elected indicates that society in general is crueler.
11. Events do occur in logical ways. That is part of what makes the story believable. The preliminary events in the office and the signing of the waiver are all predictable. The instructions about what to do after getting out of the machine are what one would expect to happen.
12. The company might say its services are educational. Pure greed may be another reason. There are always bored, wealthy people who like high stakes games.
13. The author says the dinosaur is a great god; that each leg is a piston; that each thigh is meat, ivory, and steel mesh; that its head is a ton of sculptured stone; that its eyes are ostrich eggs. These comparisons create clear word pictures of how the dinosaur looks by relating the body parts to things with which the reader is familiar.

Responding to Literature

Personal Response

What was your reaction to the outcome of the story? Explain.

——— ANALYZING LITERATURE ———

RECALL

1. Why has Eckels come to the Time Safari office? What does he plan to do?
2. Describe what happens after the party enters the Machine.
3. Summarize the rules the hunters are told to follow and the reasons Travis gives for those rules.
4. How does Eckels react when the *Tyrannosaurus rex* appears? Briefly describe what he and the other men do.
5. What do the men discover when they return from their trip?

INTERPRET

6. What do you think might be so appealing about the service Time Safari offers?
7. What feelings does Eckels experience during his first journey in the Machine? Use evidence from the story to support your answer.
8. Think back to the Focus Activity on page 315. How might the term "domino effect" be applied to Travis's explanation for Time Safari's rules?
9. In your opinion, why do Eckels and the other men react the way they do when the *Tyrannosaurus rex* appears?
10. Why do you think Eckels and Travis are so dismayed by the changes they find on their return? Explain your answer.

EVALUATE AND CONNECT

11. Within the fictional world that Bradbury has created, do events seem to occur in a logical, predictable way? Support your answer with specific examples from the story.
12. Considering how risky the activities of Time Safari are, what reasons might the company have for staying in business?
13. Identify at least three **metaphors** the author uses to describe the *Tyrannosaurus rex*. What two things are being compared in each metaphor? How do these metaphors help you visualize the Monster? (See Literary Terms Handbook, page R7.)
14. If it were possible to travel to the past in order to change the future, what might you want to change? Why?
15. **Theme Connections** In your opinion, which character in the story faced the greatest challenge? Explain your answer.

Literary ELEMENTS

Foreshadowing

Writers often give clues to prepare readers for events that will happen as a story develops. The use of such clues, called **foreshadowing**, also helps build suspense in a story. For example, when the official at the Time Safari office tells Eckels that the company doesn't guarantee his safe return, this creates suspense and helps prepare readers for the challenges the hunters will encounter.

1. What clues help prepare you for the way Eckels behaves in a crisis?
2. Reread the last section of the story, beginning with the words "1492. 1776. 1812." Identify two clues that foreshadow the outcome of the story.

● See **Literary Terms Handbook,** p. R5.

---

14. Students might mention historical events in which many people lost their lives, such as the Civil War or the Holocaust. Be sure students support their opinions with reasons.
15. Most students will say Eckels faced the greatest challenge because his fear changed the future. Some might argue Travis had the greater challenge because he had to decide what to do about what had happened.

LITERARY ELEMENTS

1. From the very beginning, there are clues that Eckels is nervous about the safari. He seeks reassurance that things will go well right up to the time the dinosaur appears.
2. The change in the sign and the dead butterfly are clues that foreshadow the final outcome.

Additional Resources

 Literary Elements Transparency 28

LITERATURE AND WRITING

Writing About Literature
Evaluate Imagery   The world that Bradbury has created in this story comes alive through the use of sensory images. Find a passage in the story that contains vivid imagery. In a paragraph, explain how each image helps you to imagine what it's like to see, hear, smell, taste, or touch the thing that's being described. Share your paragraph with several classmates.

Creative Writing
Time Travel   Imagine that, like the characters in this story, you can travel back to any year in the past. What year would you choose? What place on Earth would you want to visit at that time in history? Write your own time travel adventure. Add illustrations, if you wish.

EXTENDING YOUR RESPONSE

Literature Groups
Size Up a Character   What kind of man is Eckels? Is he a clumsy, cowardly person who simply makes a mistake, or is he an arrogant, thoughtless, self-centered man who deserves his fate? Or is he something else? Debate these questions in your group, using information from the story to support your opinions. Compare your group's responses with those of other groups.

Interdisciplinary Activity
Science: End of an Era   *Tyrannosaurus rex,* along with all the other remaining dinosaurs, became extinct at the end of the Cretaceous period 65 million years ago. There are numerous theories about what happened and why

dinosaurs did not survive into the modern world. Use the Internet or other resources to explore some of these theories. Discuss your findings with a group of classmates.

Learning for Life
Magazine Ad   Work with a partner to create a magazine advertisement for Time Safari, Inc. Discuss these points: Who are your prospective clients? What hook, or main idea, will you use to sell your service? What techniques—such as slogans, headlines, and testimonials from customers—will you use? How will you illustrate your ad? Now create your ad. You might use a computer to design and produce it.

📖 **Save your work for your portfolio.**

Skill Minilesson

┌───

VOCABULARY • The Prefix *com-*

If you look up the prefix *cor-* in the dictionary, the entry will probably read: "See **com-**." The basic prefix *com-* changes its spelling to *cor-* in front of *r.* It is spelled *col-, con-,* or *co-* in front of other letters. These prefixes mean "together" or "very much." To *cooperate* is to operate (work) together; to *correlate* is to relate together or to bring one thing into relation with another.

PRACTICE   Match each numbered word in the list with its Latin root (labeled with an uppercase letter) and its definition (labeled with a lowercase letter). Use the "together" meaning of the prefix *com-*.

1. colloquial   3. conjunction   5. constrict
2. concoct   4. compensate

A. *stringere* (to draw tight)
B. *loqui* (to speak)
C. *coquo* (to cook)
D. *jungere* (to join)
E. *pensare* (to weigh)

a. a union or combination
b. to hold in; limit; restrict
c. having to do with conversational speech
d. to make by combining ingredients
e. to balance in force or effect; make up for

LITERATURE AND WRITING

Writing About Literature
Students' paragraphs should
- quote a specific passage that contains vivid images.
- explain how the images help the reader visualize what is being described.
- tell whether each image appeals to the sense of sight, hearing, smell, taste, or touch.

Creative Writing
Students' adventures should
- identify a specific time and place in history.
- create an adventure appropriate to the setting.
- tell the adventure as a story with a beginning, middle, and end.

EXTENDING YOUR RESPONSE

Literature Groups   Remind students that not only must they identify the kind of man they think Eckels is, they must also support their opinions with proof from the story. **COLLAB. LEARN.**

Interdisciplinary Activity
Suggest that students begin by writing a list of research questions. Encourage them to research and summarize at least two theories that explain the dinosaurs' extinction.

Learning for Life   Suggest that students look for effective ads in magazines, identifying what techniques they think make the ads effective.

Skill Minilesson

VOCABULARY • Antonyms
1. B, c   2. C, d   3. D, a
4. E, e   5. A, b

Additional Resources
📁 *Vocabulary Practice,* p. 27

Objective

- To read and understand a magazine article

Respond

1. They learned by watching their mother weave and by listening to her explain what she was doing. Students may say they learned a skill such as cooking, carpentry, or sewing by watching and listening to parents or other family members.

2. Probably they would not have learned how to weave, and consequently they might not feel as strongly about carrying on Navajo traditions.

Additional Resources

📁 *Media Connections Activities,* p. 8

Teaching Options

MEDIA
Connection

Magazine Article

What traditions does your family have? How are they passed on? In the Navajo culture, girls learn about traditional ways of doing things by watching and talking to their female relatives.

Three Generations of Navajo Weavers

by Paul Zolbrod—*Indian Artist,* Fall 1997

"When my arm gets tired, she takes over," laughs Rondelle Benally, 18, motioning to Roxanne, who is two years younger. "And when hers does, it's my turn again." Once they get into the design, however, the two sisters weave together side by side. Their eyes sparkle with teenage enthusiasm while discussing this distinctive Navajo art with their mother, Bonnie, 41, and their grandmother Loretta, now in her late 70s, near their home in Crownpoint, New Mexico.

The two Benally sisters started learning the traditional way of weaving while they were still preschoolers. Much the way their grandmother had, they looked on as their mother wove. "We'd sit and watch her, and she'd tell us what she was doing and why she did it," Rondelle recalls.

Inevitable contrasts mark the experiences of the three generations of weavers. Loretta tells of growing up in a hogan with no electricity, traveling back and forth by horse, and never going to school. She remembers the shift from a pastoral way of life to a labor-based cash economy. Bonnie passed her childhood in a "square house," enjoyed the benefits of motor vehicles, and went to high school. Rondelle and Roxanne, of course, grew up with television and shopping malls and anticipate going to college.

Strong similarities underlie the differences, however. All four believe that the tradition of weaving must be maintained. All exhibit a deep love for sheep and the feel of raw wool. For them, the standing loom promises to perpetuate an art whose distinctiveness seems obvious and yet inexplicable.

"At first, I just wanted to learn because my grandmother knew and my mother knew," says Rondelle. "Now I realize that my pride as a weaver comes from the tradition I'm learning about."

Respond

1. How did Rondelle and Roxanne learn to weave? What skills have you learned in a similar manner?

2. If they had not grown up near their mother and grandmother, how might the lives of the Benally sisters be different today?

Reading *Minilesson*

Comparing and Contrasting The article's author compares and contrasts to help readers understand the people he is writing about.

Activity Have students draw and fill in a comparison-and-contrast chart with names across the top and categories such as *Age, Education, Childhood Home,* and *Attitudes Toward Weaving* down the side.

Then have them complete each column for Loretta, Bonnie, and Rondelle and Roxanne. Finally ask students to discuss what knowing the similarities and differences between the women adds to their understanding of the article. **L2**

Additional Resources

📁 *Reading Workbook*

Before You Read
Lullaby

─FOCUS ACTIVITY─

When you're feeling troubled or discouraged, do you ever think back to a happier time in the past? How can memories lift your spirits?

QUICKWRITE Take five minutes to write about a memory that has helped lift your spirits in some way.

SETTING A PURPOSE Read to share the painful and tender memories of one mother.

─BACKGROUND─

The Time and Place

This story takes place in west central New Mexico, near the Cañoncito (Navajo) Reservation; parts of the story may actually take place on the reservation. The time of the story is probably the late 1960s or the 1970s.

Did You Know?

Pulmonary tuberculosis, also known as TB, is a contagious lung disease that can lead to death if left untreated. The first antibiotic treatment for TB was not discovered until 1943. By the mid-1950s, chest X rays were used to test millions of Americans for TB; infected people were then treated for the disease. But large numbers of infected people remained

undiagnosed and thus continued to infect others. Included in this group were thousands of Navajo Indians, many of whom mistrusted white doctors. In the 1950s, U.S. government health agencies began testing Navajos for TB. Infected people were sent away—sometimes against their will—to special hospitals, called sanatoriums, for long-term care.

─VOCABULARY PREVIEW─

arroyo (ə roi′ ō) *n.* a dry gully or stream bed; p. 331

crevice (krev′ is) *n.* a narrow crack into or through something; p. 335

sparse (spärs) *adj.* thinly spread or distributed; p. 337

distortion (dis tôr′ shən) *n.* an appearance of being twisted or bent out of shape; p. 338

Meet Leslie Marmon Silko

"I suppose at the core of my writing is the attempt to identify what it is to be a half-breed, or mixed-blooded person; what it is to grow up neither white nor fully traditional Indian," Leslie Marmon Silko has written. Silko grew up in Laguna, New Mexico, where she spent much of her time with her great-grandmother, a Laguna Indian who had married a white man. From her great-grandmother, Silko heard stories about what life was like long ago. In her writing, Silko doesn't claim to represent Native Americans in general. "I am only one human being, one Laguna woman," she has written.

Leslie Marmon Silko was born in 1948 in Albuquerque, New Mexico. This story appears in Storyteller, *published in 1981.*

THE SHORT STORY 🦜 329

Objectives

- To read and analyze a short story in which an elderly Navajo woman remembers her past
- To identify examples of flashback
- To write an analysis of how the setting helps create the mood of the story

Skills

Reading/Thinking: Inferring; Evaluating; Drawing Conclusions
Writing: Song
Vocabulary: The Latin Root *tort*
Grammar/Language: Clear Pronoun References
Listening/Speaking: Dialogue
Life Skills: Decision Making; Letter of Inquiry
Collaboration: Literature Groups

Motivating
→OPTIONS

Selection Focus Transparency 29: Discuss with students words that describe vivid memories.

Focus Activity: Discuss ways an older person's memories might differ from memories students have at this point in their lives.

RESOURCE MANAGER

Lesson Planning Resource
The *Unit One Planning Guide* (pp. 246–253) provides additional lesson notes and reduced versions of all print resources.

📁 **Other Print Resources**
- Active Reading Guide, p. 29
- Vocabulary Practice, p. 28
- Reading Workbook, pp. 33–34
- Grammar and Language Workbook, p. 193
- Grammar and Composition Handbook, Lesson 7.7

- Quick Checks, p. 29
- Selection and Theme Assessment, pp. 55–56
- Performance Assessment, p. 28
- Spanish Summaries, p. 29
- Spanish Translations
- Inclusion Strategies
- English Language Learners Sourcebook

📖 **Transparencies**
- Selection Focus 29

- Literary Elements 29
- Grammar and Language 28

Technology
🎧 Audio Library
🎧 Spanish Audio Library
💻 Glencoe Literature Web Site
💾 Testmaker

SUMMARY

An elderly Navajo woman sits in the snow remembering her past life. She thinks of her happy childhood. She remembers the loss of her children to war and poverty. She remembers the time two of her children were taken because they had tuberculosis. She thinks about the difficulties of her present life. When her husband dies on that snowy night, she sings a song for all her losses—a lullaby that has been passed down through the generations.

📁 *Spanish Summaries,* p. 29

🅰 Active Reading

QUESTION Ask students to read the first twelve lines of the story. Point out that the woman is sitting outside at night while it is snowing. Ask students why they think she is there. *(There is no reason given at this point, but clearly the woman is in a reflective mood. She may have gone out to get away from something or someone.)*

Additional Resources
📁 *Active Reading Guide,* p. 29
🎧 *Audio Library*
🎧 *Spanish Audio Library*

Teaching Options

Lullaby

Leslie Marmon Silko

Navajo Zoned Blanket Design, c. 1870s. Wool, 72 x 51 in. The Lowe Art Museum, The University of Miami, Miami, FL.

CONNECTING TO OTHER SELECTIONS

The chart at the right shows three ways to connect "Lullaby" to selections in this book.

For specific teaching strategies, see the *Unit One Planning Guide,* pp. 249–250.

Connection		Title
Life Skills: Life-long Learning	→	"The Happy Man's Shirt," p. 241
Thematic: Remembering	→	"A Child's Christmas in Wales," p. 433
Literary: Internal Conflict	→	"With All Flags Flying," p. 115

THE SUN HAD GONE DOWN but the snow in the wind gave off its own light. It came in thick tufts like new wool—washed before the weaver spins it. Ayah[1] reached out for it like her own babies had, and she smiled when she remembered how she had laughed at them. She was an old woman now, and her life had become memories. She sat down with her back against the wide cottonwood tree, feeling the rough bark on her back bones; she faced east and listened to the wind and snow sing a high-pitched Yeibechei[2] song. Out of the wind she felt warmer, and she could watch the wide fluffy snow fill in her tracks, steadily, until the direction she had come from was gone. By the light of the snow she could see the dark outline of the big arroyo a few feet away. She was sitting on the edge of Cebolleta[3] Creek, where in the springtime the thin cows would graze on grass already chewed flat to the ground. In the wide deep creek bed where only a trickle of water flowed in the summer, the skinny cows would wander, looking for new grass along winding paths splashed with manure.

Ayah pulled the old Army blanket over her head like a shawl. Jimmie's blanket—the one he had sent to her. That was a long time ago and the green wool was faded, and it was unraveling on the edges. She did not want to think about Jimmie. So she thought about the weaving and the way her mother had done it. On the tall wooden loom set into the sand under a tamarack[4] tree for shade. She could

see it clearly. She had been only a little girl when her grandma gave her the wooden combs to pull the twigs and burrs from the raw, freshly washed wool. And while she combed the wool, her grandma sat beside her, spinning a silvery strand of yarn around the smooth cedar spindle. Her mother worked at the loom with yarns dyed bright yellow and red and gold. She watched them dye the yarn in boiling black pots full of beeweed petals, juniper berries, and sage. The blankets her mother made were soft and woven so tight that rain rolled off them like birds' feathers. Ayah remembered sleeping warm on cold windy nights, wrapped in her mother's blankets on the hogan's[5] sandy floor.

The snow drifted now, with the northwest wind hurling it in gusts. It drifted up around her black overshoes—old ones with little metal buckles. She smiled at the snow which was trying to cover her little by little. She could remember when they had no black rubber overshoes; only the high buckskin leggings that they wrapped over their elkhide moccasins. If the snow was dry or frozen, a person could walk all day and not get wet; and in the evenings the beams of the ceiling would hang with lengths of pale buckskin leggings, drying out slowly.

She felt peaceful remembering. She didn't feel cold any more. Jimmie's blanket seemed warmer than it had ever been. And she could

Did You Know?
In yarn-making, the *spindle* is a round, tapered stick that is turned by hand to twist wool fibers into a thread of yarn.

---

1. *Ayah* (ä′ yə)
2. The *Yeibechei* (yā′ bə chā) are masked Navajo dancers who sing in high-pitched voices.
3. *Cebolleta* (se′ bō yā′ tä) is also the name of a town in the story.
4. *Tamarack* is another name for the larch, a tree in the pine family.

5. Traditionally, a *hogan* is a Navajo dwelling made of wood and covered with earth.

Vocabulary
arroyo (ə roi′ ō) *n.* a dry gully or stream bed

FLASHBACK Review with students that a flashback is a shift back in time to a memory of an event or events from the past. It interrupts the time, or chronological, sequence of a story. Ask students to identify where the flashback begins. *(It begins with Ayah remembering the birth of Jimmie.)*

E **Critical Thinking**

INFERRING Ask students why Ayah does not want to remember Jimmie and then remembers him. *(His birth is a happy memory; so are the births of her other children. This leads her to be able to remember what did happen to him.)*

F **Critical Thinking**

DRAWING CONCLUSIONS Two things worked against Ayah that resulted, in part, in her losing her children. Discuss what these two factors were and why having Navajo women as interpreters would have helped. Conclude by asking students if Ayah would have signed the papers if she had known what they were. *(Ayah could not speak English, but she could sign her name. The Navajo women interpreters could have told her what was wrong with the children and why the doctors wanted to take them away. Ayah would probably not have signed.)*

Teaching Options

remember the morning he was born. She could remember whispering to her mother, who was sleeping on the other side of the hogan, to tell her it was time now. She did not want to wake the others. The second time she called to her, her mother stood up and pulled on her shoes; she knew. They walked to the old stone hogan together, Ayah walking a step behind her mother. She waited alone, learning the rhythms of the pains while her mother went to call the old woman to help them. The morning was already warm even before dawn and Ayah smelled the bee flowers blooming and the young willow growing at the springs. She could remember that so clearly, but his birth merged into the births of the other children and to her it became all the same birth. They named him for the summer morning and in English they called him Jimmie.

It wasn't like Jimmie died. He just never came back, and one day a dark blue sedan with white writing on its doors pulled up in front of the boxcar shack where the rancher let the Indians live. A man in a khaki uniform trimmed in gold gave them a yellow piece of paper and told them that Jimmie was dead. He said the Army would try to get the body back and then it would be shipped to them; but it wasn't likely because the helicopter had burned after it crashed. All of this was told to Chato[6] because he could understand English. She stood inside the doorway holding the baby while Chato listened. Chato spoke English like a white man and he spoke Spanish too. He was taller than the white man and he stood straighter too. Chato didn't explain why; he just told the military man they could keep the body if they found it. The white man looked bewildered; he nodded his head and he left. Then Chato looked at her and shook his head, and then he told her, "Jimmie isn't coming

home anymore," and when he spoke, he used the words to speak of the dead. She didn't cry then, but she hurt inside with anger. And she mourned him as the years passed, when a horse fell with Chato and broke his leg, and the white rancher told them he wouldn't pay Chato until he could work again. She mourned Jimmie because he would have worked for his father then; he would have saddled the big bay[7] horse and ridden the fence lines each day, with wire cutters and heavy gloves, fixing the breaks in the barbed wire and putting the stray cattle back inside again.

She mourned him after the white doctors came to take Danny and Ella away. She was at the shack alone that day they came. It was back in the days before they hired Navajo women to go with them as interpreters. She recognized one of the doctors. She had seen him at the children's clinic at Cañoncito[8] about a month ago. They were wearing khaki uniforms and they waved papers at her and a black ball-point pen, trying to make her understand their English words. She was frightened by the way they looked at the children, like the lizard watches the fly. Danny was swinging on the tire swing on the elm tree behind the rancher's house, and Ella was toddling around the front door, dragging the broomstick horse Chato made for her. Ayah could see they wanted her to sign the papers, and Chato had taught her to sign her name. It was something she was proud of. She only wanted them to go, and to take their eyes away from her children.

She took the pen from the man without looking at his face and she signed the papers in three different places he pointed to. She stared at the ground by their feet and waited for them to leave. But they stood there and began to point and gesture at the children.

---

6. *Chato* (chä′ tō)

7. Here, *bay* is the horse's color—a reddish brown.
8. *Cañoncito* (kän′ yən sē′ tō) is the name of the Navajo reservation located in west central New Mexico.

MEETING INDIVIDUAL NEEDS: INCLUSION STRATEGIES

Less-Proficient Readers Students may need help with the special vocabulary related to the Navajo culture and to the geographic location.

Activity Write words from the story that might cause problems for students. Invite students to keep a vocabulary journal. Have them jot down confusing words in their journals as they read. As clues in the text help them figure out the words, have them jot down their "best-guess" definitions. Let them use a dictionary for any words they were unable to figure out. **L1**

Additional Resources
📁 *Inclusion Strategies*

Danny stopped swinging. Ayah could see his fear. She moved suddenly and grabbed Ella into her arms; the child squirmed, trying to get back to her toys. Ayah ran with the baby toward Danny; she screamed for him to run and then she grabbed him around his chest and carried him too. She ran south into the foothills of juniper trees and black lava rock. Behind her she heard the doctors running, but they had been taken by surprise, and as the hills became steeper and the cholla cactus were thicker, they stopped. When she reached the top of the hill, she stopped to listen in case they were circling around her. But in a few

Did You Know?
A *cholla* (choi′ ə) is a spiny, shrubby, or treelike cactus.

G minutes she heard a car engine start and they drove away. The children had been too surprised to cry while she ran with them. Danny was shaking and Ella's little fingers were gripping Ayah's blouse.

She stayed up in the hills for the rest of the day, sitting on a black lava boulder in the sunshine where she could see for miles all around her. The sky was light blue and cloudless, and it was warm for late April. The sun warmth relaxed her and took the fear and anger away. She lay back on the rock and watched the sky. It seemed to her that she could walk into the sky, stepping through clouds endlessly. Danny played with little pebbles and stones, pretending they were birds' eggs and then little rabbits. Ella sat at her feet and dropped fistfuls of dirt into the breeze, watching the dust and particles of sand intently. Ayah watched a hawk soar high above them, dark wings gliding; hunting or only watching, she did not know. The hawk

was patient and he circled all afternoon before he disappeared around the high volcanic peak the Mexicans called Guadalupe.[9]

Late in the afternoon, Ayah looked down at the gray boxcar shack with the paint all peeled from the wood; the stove pipe on the roof was rusted and crooked. The fire she had built that morning in the oil drum stove had burned out. Ella was asleep in her lap now and Danny sat close to her, complaining that he was hungry; he asked when they would go to the house. "We will stay up here until your father comes," she told him, "because those white men were chasing us." The boy remembered then and he nodded at her silently.

If Jimmie had been there he could have read those papers and explained to her what they said. Ayah would have known then, never to sign them. The doctors came back the next day and they brought a BIA[10] policeman with them. They told Chato they had her signature and that was all they needed. Except for the kids. She listened to Chato sullenly; she hated him when he told her it was the old woman who died in the winter, spitting blood; it was her old grandma who had given the children this disease. "They don't spit blood," she said coldly. "The whites lie." She held Ella and Danny close to her, ready to run to the hills again. "I want a medicine man first," she said to Chato, not looking at him. He shook his head. "It's too late now. The policeman is with them. You signed the paper." His voice was gentle.

It was worse than if they had died: to lose the children and to know that somewhere, in a place called Colorado, in a place full of sick

9. *Guadalupe* (gwä′ də lōō′ pä)
10. The Bureau of Indian Affairs, or *BIA*, is the federal agency in charge of administering government policies toward Native Americans.

In Grandma's Care. Johnson J. Yazzi (b. 1957). Pastel, 22 x 18 in. Jesse Monongye Studios, Scottsdale, AZ.

Viewing the painting: How might the relationship of these two people compare with the relationship of Ayah and her children?

Teaching Options

LIFE SKILLS CONNECTION

Decision Making At several points in the story, the woman and her husband were involved in situations with white people in which the couple had to make a decision. In each instance, the outcome was negative for both sides. There was a clear lack of communication and cultural understanding. Point out that students will find themselves in decision-making situations throughout their lives. Planning and preparation are important.

Activity Ask students to suggest a time when they will face an important decision. As a class, list several steps to follow in deciding what decision to make. *(Students might suggest these steps: identify the problem or issue, list possible decisions, weigh the pros and cons, make a choice, and implement it.)* **L2**

and dying strangers, her children were without her. There had been babies that died soon after they were born, and one that died before he could walk. She had carried them herself, up to the boulders and great pieces of the cliff that long ago crashed down from Long Mesa; she laid them in the crevices of sandstone and buried them in fine brown sand with round quartz pebbles that washed down the hills in the rain. She had endured it because they had been with her. But she could not bear this pain. She did not sleep for a long time after they took her children. She stayed on the hill where they had fled the first time, and she slept rolled up in the blanket Jimmie had sent her. She carried the pain in her belly and it was fed by everything she saw: the blue sky of their last day together and the dust and pebbles they played with; the swing in the elm tree and broomstick horse choked life from her. The pain filled her stomach and there was no room for food or for her lungs to fill with air. The air and the food would have been theirs.

She hated Chato, not because he let the policeman and doctors put the screaming children in the government car, but because he had taught her to sign her name. Because it was like the old ones always told her about learning their language or any of their ways: it endangered you. She slept alone on the hill until the middle of November when the first snows came. Then she made a bed for herself where the children had slept. She did not lie down beside Chato again until many years later, when he was sick and shivering and only her body could keep him warm. The illness came after the white rancher told Chato he was too old to work for him anymore, and Chato and his old woman should be out of the shack by the next afternoon because the rancher had hired new people to work there. That had satisfied her. To

see how the white man repaid Chato's years of loyalty and work. All of Chato's fine-sounding English talk didn't change things.

It snowed steadily and the luminous light from the snow gradually diminished into the darkness. Somewhere in Cebolleta a dog barked and other village dogs joined with it. Ayah looked in the direction she had come, from the bar where Chato was buying the wine. Sometimes he told her to go on ahead and wait; and then he never came. And when she finally went back looking for him, she would find him passed out at the bottom of the wooden steps to Azzie's Bar. All the wine would be gone and most of the money too, from the pale blue check that came to them once a month in a government envelope. It was then that she would look at his face and his hands, scarred by ropes and the barbed wire of all those years, and she would think, this man is a stranger; for forty years she had smiled at him and cooked his food, but he remained a stranger. She stood up again, with the snow almost to her knees, and she walked back to find Chato.

It was hard to walk in the deep snow and she felt the air burn in her lungs. She stopped a short distance from the bar to rest and re-adjust the blanket. But this time he wasn't waiting for her on the bottom step with his old Stetson hat pulled down and his shoulders hunched up in his long wool overcoat.

She was careful not to slip on the wooden steps. When she pushed the door open, warm air and cigarette smoke hit her face. She looked around slowly and deliberately, in every corner, in every dark place that the old man might find to sleep. The bar owner didn't like Indians in there, especially Navajos, but he let Chato come in because he could talk Spanish like he was one of them. The men at the bar

Vocabulary

crevice (krev′ is) *n.* a narrow crack into or through something

❶ Critical Thinking

DRAWING CONCLUSIONS Discuss how Ayah feels about the children who had died. Then discuss the difference between the feelings Ayah has about the children taken from her by death and those taken by the white people. *(She loves her children. The way she carefully buried them indicates this. Ayah is able to bear the deaths because those children had been with her and were still with her. Her other children were taken away, and this she could not endure. She is deeply angered.)*

❻ Active Reading

EVALUATE Having their children taken is not the only unfair thing that happened to the couple. Ask students to identify other such events. *(When Chato got too old to work, the rancher gave the couple a day to get out of the shack that had been their home. Earlier, when the horse fell on Chato and his leg was hurt, he did not get paid.)*

❼ Literary Elements

FLASHBACK Be sure students can identify where the flashback ends. *(at the top of column two, after the break)*

MEETING INDIVIDUAL NEEDS — MULTIPLE LEARNING STYLES

Musical Some students have a special ability to create or perform music. They can help other students in creating musical presentations.

Activity At the end of the story, Ayah sings a lullaby. The reader knows the words, but not the tune. Invite students to create a melody to go with the words of the lullaby. Remind students that the melody will need to fit the rhythm of the words. Students might present the song by singing it or by accompanying the singing with a piano, guitar, violin, or other instrument. As another presentation alternative, students might play the tune as the words are recited. **L2**

Critical Thinking

INFERRING The last time the children come to visit, Ayah walks away and does not say good-bye. What does she realize about the children? How does she know this? *(She knows the children are no longer hers. They have grown accustomed to their new culture. The girl did not know who she was. The boy could not remember the Navajo language.)*

M Author's Craft

CHARACTER Ayah is satisfied that the men in the bar feared her. What does the author want the reader to understand about the kind of person Ayah is? *(that she is proud, endures, and perseveres)*

N Active Reading

RESPOND Ask students to review how the couple is now living. What is their life like? Ask students what their feelings are toward the couple. *(The couple is surviving on monthly checks from the government. They seem to be going through the motions of living. Students will probably say they feel sorry for the couple or are sad for them.)*

stared at her, and the bartender saw that she left the door open wide. Snowflakes were flying inside like moths and melting into a puddle on the oiled wood floor. He motioned to her to close the door, but she did not see him. She held herself straight and walked across the room slowly, searching the room with every step. The snow in her hair melted and she could feel it on her forehead. At the far corner of the room, she saw red flames at the mica window of the old stove door; she looked behind the stove just to make sure. The bar got quiet except for the Spanish polka music playing on the jukebox. She stood by the stove and shook the snow from her blanket and held it near the stove to dry. The wet wool smell reminded her of new-born goats in early March, brought inside to warm near the fire. She felt calm.

Did You Know?
Mica is a mineral (abundant in New Mexico) that can be split into thin, strong, flexible sheets. A sheet of colorless mica makes a decent, inexpensive substitute for glass.

In past years they would have told her to get out. But her hair was white now and her face was wrinkled. They looked at her like she was a spider crawling slowly across the room. They were afraid; she could feel the fear. She looked at their faces steadily. They reminded her of the first time the white people brought her children back to her that winter. Danny had been shy and hid behind the thin white woman who brought them. And the baby had not known her until Ayah took her into her arms, and then Ella had nuzzled close to her as she had when she was nursing. The blonde woman was nervous and kept looking at a dainty gold watch on her wrist. She sat on the bench near the small window and watched the dark snow clouds gather around the mountains; she was worrying about the unpaved road. She was frightened

by what she saw inside too: the strips of venison drying on a rope across the ceiling and the children jabbering excitedly in a language she did not know. So they stayed for only a few hours. Ayah watched the government car disappear down the road and she knew they were already being weaned from these lava hills and from this sky. The last time they came was in early June, and Ella stared at her the way the men in the bar were now staring. Ayah did not try to pick her up; she smiled at her instead and spoke cheerfully to Danny. When he tried to answer her, he could not seem to remember and he spoke English words with the Navajo. But he gave her a scrap of paper that he had found somewhere and carried in his pocket; it was folded in half, and he shyly looked up at her and said it was a bird. She asked Chato if they were home for good this time. He spoke to the white woman and she shook her head. "How much longer?" he asked, and she said she didn't know; but Chato saw how she stared at the boxcar shack. Ayah turned away then. She did not say good-bye.

She felt satisfied that the men in the bar feared her. Maybe it was her face and the way she held her mouth with teeth clenched tight, like there was nothing anyone could do to her now. She walked north down the road, searching for the old man. She did this because she had the blanket, and there would be no place for him except with her and the blanket in the old adobe barn near the arroyo. They always slept there when they came to Cebolleta. If the money and the wine were gone, she would be relieved because then they could go home again: back to the old hogan with a dirt roof and rock walls where she herself had been born. And the next day the old man could go back to the few sheep they still had, to follow along behind them, guiding them, into dry

Teaching Options

Listening and Speaking *Minilesson*

Dialogue An author uses dialogue in a number of ways—to tell about what has happened or what is happening, to let the reader know what the character is like or what the character is thinking. In this story, the author uses little dialogue. Discuss reasons why the author chose this approach. *(Most of the story takes place in Ayah's memory.)*

Activity Suggest that small groups of students select a scene from the story, such as when the couple is told about Jimmie's death or when the children come for a visit. Ask the groups to write dialogue, indicating what might have been said at the time. Remind students to use correct paragraphing, punctuation, and capitalization when writing their dialogues. Allow time for the groups to practice their

dialogues and then to present them. After each presentation, have students decide whether or not they think the story would be better with dialogue. **L2 COLLAB. LEARN.**

sandy arroyos where <u>sparse</u> grass grew. She knew he did not like walking behind old ewes when for so many years he rode big quarter horses and worked with cattle. But she wasn't sorry for him; he should have known all along what would happen.

There had not been enough rain for their garden in five years; and that was when Chato finally hitched a ride into the town and brought back brown boxes of rice and sugar and big tin cans of welfare[11] peaches. After that, at the first of the month they went to Cebolleta to ask the postmaster for the check; and then Chato would go to the bar and cash it. They did this as they planted the garden every May, not because anything would survive the summer dust, but because it was time to do this. The journey passed the days that smelled silent and dry like the caves above the canyon with yellow painted buffaloes on their walls.

He was walking along the pavement when she found him. He did not stop or turn around when he heard her behind her. She walked beside him and she noticed how slowly he moved now. He smelled strong of woodsmoke and urine. Lately he had been forgetting. Sometimes he called her by his sister's name and she had been gone for a long time. Once she had found him wandering on the road to the white man's ranch, and she asked him why he was going that way; he laughed at her and said, "You know they can't run that ranch

Her Precious Time, c. 1987. Redwing T. Nez. Mixed media, 29½ x 22½ in. Museum of Northern Arizona, Flagstaff, AZ.

Viewing the painting: What personal qualities do you see in this woman that might be shared by Ayah? Explain.

without me," and he walked on determined, limping on the leg that had been crushed many years before. Now he looked at her curiously, as if for the first time, but he kept shuffling along, moving slowly along the side of the highway. His gray hair had grown long and spread out on the shoulders of the long overcoat. He wore the old felt hat pulled down over his ears. His boots were worn out at the toes and he had stuffed pieces of an old red shirt in the holes. The rags

---

11. The canned peaches came from a government *welfare* program to help needy people.

Vocabulary
sparse (spärs) *adj.* thinly spread or distributed

Cave Paintings The cave paintings referred to were made by an ancient people known as the Anasazi. They lived about 2,000 years ago in the Four Corners region—where present-day Utah, Colorado, New Mexico, and Arizona meet. No one knows where they went, but they left behind petroglyphs—carvings in rock—and decorative murals. Some pictures are of bighorn sheep, buffalo, rabbits, and people.

VIEWING THE PAINTING

Redwing T. Nez (1960–) is both an artist and an author. Nez has written a fiction book for children called *Forbidden Talent*. In it a young Navajo boy is in conflict with his grandfather over the style of his painting. The grandfather does not think the grandson's painting follows the Navajo way.

Viewing Response *Like Ayah, the woman seems strong, determined, sad, and careworn. Perhaps, like Ayah, she has had a hard life.*

Reading *Minilesson*

Evaluating Throughout a selection, readers make evaluations about many things—the characters and the plot, for example. In "Lullaby," the reader forms opinions or judgments about Ayah. Sometimes those opinions or judgments will change.

Activity Ask students how they felt about Ayah at the beginning of the story.

Have them compare their evaluation of the woman with those of the white people she encountered throughout her life. Ask students if their opinions about Ayah changed by the end of the story and if so, how and why. **L2**

Additional Resources
📁 *Reading Workbook,* pp. 33–34

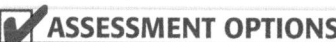

Active Reading

EVALUATE What part of the lullaby might Ayah find most comforting? Why? *(the last five lines; They seem to be saying the family will always be together and always have been.)*

Thematic Focus

Challenges and Consequences
Discuss with students some of the challenges Ayah faced and what the consequences of each was. Ask students which, if any, of the challenges are similar to ones they or their families face or have faced.

ASSESSMENT OPTIONS

📁 *Quick Checks,* p. 29

At the MOVIES

Be sure to preview the following video for appropiateness for your class:

• **Leslie M. Silko***

📼 *Also available in the Glencoe Literature *Video Library**

Teaching Options

---

made his feet look like little animals up to their ears in snow. She laughed at his feet; the snow muffled the sound of her laugh. He stopped and looked at her again. The wind had quit blowing and the snow was falling straight down; the southeast sky was beginning to clear and Ayah could see a star.

"Let's rest awhile," she said to him. They walked away from the road and up the slope to the giant boulders that had tumbled down from the red sandrock mesa throughout the centuries of rainstorms and earth tremors. In a place where the boulders shut out the wind, they sat down with their backs against the rock. She offered half of the blanket to him and they sat wrapped together.

The storm passed swiftly. The clouds moved east. They were massive and full, crowding together across the sky. She watched them with the feeling of horses—steely blue-gray horses startled across the sky. The powerful haunches pushed into the distances and the tail hairs streamed white mist behind them. The sky cleared. Ayah saw that there was nothing between her and the stars. The light was crystalline.[12] There was no shimmer, no <u>distortion</u> through earth haze. She breathed the clarity of the night sky; she smelled the purity of the half moon and the stars. He was lying on his side with his knees pulled up near his belly for warmth. His eyes were closed now, and in the light from the stars and the moon, he looked young again.

She could see it descend out of the night sky: an icy stillness from the edge of the thin moon. She recognized the freezing. It came

---

12. Here, *crystalline* means "clear and pure as a crystal."

gradually, sinking snowflake by snowflake until the crust was heavy and deep. It had the strength of the stars in Orion, and its journey was endless. Ayah knew that with the wine he would sleep. He would not feel it. She tucked the blanket around him, remembering how it was when Ella had been with her; and she felt the rush so big inside her heart for the babies. And she sang the only song she knew to sing for babies. She could not remember if she had ever sung it to her children, but she knew that her grandmother had sung it and her mother had sung it:

Did You Know?
The constellation *Orion* contains two of the brightest stars in the sky. In Greek mythology, Orion is traditionally depicted as a hunter wearing a belt with a sword at his side.

> The earth is your mother,
>   she holds you.
> The sky is your father,
>   he protects you.
> Sleep,
> sleep.
> Rainbow is your sister,
>   she loves you.
> The winds are your brothers,
>   they sing to you.
> Sleep,
> sleep.
> We are together always
> We are together always
> There never was a time
> when this
> was not so.

Vocabulary
distortion (dis tôr′ shən) *n.* an appearance of being twisted or bent out of shape

338 ❧ UNIT 1

Grammar and Language *Minilesson*

Clear Pronoun References The antecedent of a pronoun must be clearly stated so that the pronoun refers to only one antecedent.

Activity Revise this sentence to make the references clear: Ella stared at Ayah because she did not recognize her. *(Ella stared at Ayah because she did not recognize Ayah.)* **L2**

Additional Resources

📜 *Grammar and Language Transparency 28*

📗 *Grammar and Language Workbook,* p. 193

📗 *Grammar and Composition Handbook,* Lesson 7.7

📘 *Writer's Choice,* Lesson 17.7

Responding to Literature

Personal Response

For which character did you have more sympathy, Ayah or Chato? For whom did you have more respect or admiration? Give reasons.

——— ANALYZING LITERATURE ———

RECALL

1. In the first three paragraphs of the story, what things around Ayah remind her of events in the past? What are those events?
2. What happened to Jimmie, to Danny and Ella, and to Ayah's other children?
3. Describe the type of life Ayah and Chato are living at the present time. Why have they come to Cebolleta?
4. How does Chato look and act when Ayah finally finds him?
5. Describe Ayah's thoughts and actions after she and Chato find shelter among the boulders.

INTERPRET

6. Why might Ayah's thoughts turn so often to the past?
7. How did Ayah react to what happened to Jimmie? To Danny and Ella? To her other children? Explain why you think Ayah reacted the way she did. Use details from the story to support your answers.
8. Why have Ayah's and Chato's lives changed so much now that they are older? Compare and contrast their ways of coping.
9. In your opinion, how does Ayah feel about her husband? Use evidence from the story to support your ideas.
10. What is the **mood** at the end the story, when Ayah and Chato are resting? What details help to create that mood? (See page R8.)

EVALUATE AND CONNECT

11. What do you think happens to Chato at the end of the story? Give reasons for your answer.
12. In your opinion, is "Lullaby" an appropriate title for this story? Explain.
13. Compare the ways Ayah and Chato reacted when the doctors came to take the children. What do you think you would have done?
14. Look back at your response to the Focus Activity on page 329. How do you think Ayah's response might compare to yours? Explain.
15. Theme Connections   Think about the obstacles that Ayah and Chato have faced, as well as the tragedies they have endured. In your opinion, have they triumphed over adversity, or has it defeated them? Explain.

THE SHORT STORY 🦢 339

Literary ELEMENTS

Flashback

A **flashback** is a memory or account of an event that took place at an earlier time. Although a flashback interrupts the chronological sequence of story events, it usually reveals important information. In "Lullaby," for example, the narrator includes a flashback to the day Ayah and Chato found out that Jimmie had died. This flashback reveals not only a tragic event in the characters' lives, but also their reactions to that event. This information gives the reader a better context for understanding the story's events and the characters who experience those events.

1. Describe two other flashbacks from the story. Explain how they help you better understand the story's characters and events.
2. In your opinion, are flashbacks an effective means of presenting information about Ayah and Chato's past experiences? Explain.

● See **Literary Terms Handbook,** p. R5.

Responding to the Selection

Personal Response

Most students will probably pick Ayah as the person for whom they have the most sympathy and respect since the story is written from her perspective.

ANALYZING LITERATURE

1. The snow reminds her of her children as babies; the blanket reminds her of Jimmie; the blanket reminds her of the weaving her mother and grandmother did and of the blankets they made; the black overshoes reminds her of the buckskin leggings she used to wear.
2. Jimmie died in the war. Danny and Ella were taken away to be cured of TB and were never returned. The other children died.
3. Chato and Ayah are barely existing. They live on a government check and seem to have little happiness in their lives. They have come for the monthly check and then for Chato's visit to the bar.
4. He looks puzzled by her, not quite knowing who she is. He keeps walking, not seeming to care who she is or if she comes along.
5. Ayah watches the sky as the storm clears. Noticing that Chato is dying, she wraps the blanket around him. She thinks of her children and sings a lullaby.
6. She has nothing in the present to be happy about and has no prospects for the future. She is at the end of her life.
7. She felt angry. When Jimmie died, she mourned as the years passed, especially when Chato got hurt because Jimmie wasn't there to help him. When Danny and Ella were taken, she blamed Chato and stayed away from home until winter. The other children were mourned when they were lovingly buried.
8. Chato can no longer work, so they have to depend on government checks for support. They both go through the motions of living. Chato drinks. Ayah relies on her memories.
9. She both loves and hates him. She cares for him lovingly but blames him for many of the things that happened. She is bitter about his language and writing skills and feels that they got him nowhere and that they caused her to lose her children.
10. The mood is one of peace and sadness. A crystal-clear night sky is described.
11. Chato dies. "The freezing" is a symbol for the onset of death.

LITERARY ELEMENTS

1. The flashback of the day people came and took her children explains why they were taken. The flashback of the second time the children visited explains why they never came back.
2. Flashbacks are an effective way of presenting information. Without them, key information would be missing.

Additional Resources

 Literary Elements Transparency 29

---

12. The title is appropriate because a lullaby is a song of comfort, just as Ayah's memories are her source of comfort. A lullaby sings one to sleep and Chato goes to "sleep" just as Ayah's children "sleep."
13. Ayah grabbed the children and ran away. Chato gave in, saying there was nothing that could be done. Students will probably say they would try to protect the children.
14. Most students will probably say that their response and Ayah's are similar—memories can sometimes lift the spirits.
15. They have endured the adversity and, therefore, triumphed over it.

LITERATURE AND WRITING

Writing About Literature

Students' analyses should
- clearly identify the setting and use of quotes to describe it.
- identify the atmosphere, or mood, created.
- explain how the setting helps create the atmosphere.

Creative Writing

Students' lyrics should
- reflect the personal character of Ayah.
- use some figurative language.

EXTENDING YOUR RESPONSE

Literature Groups Point out that the answers will not be clear-cut. There will be reasons to support both sides of each question. Opinions should be supported with reasons. Encourage students to express respect for other cultures. **COLLAB. LEARN.**

Learning for Life Review the parts of a business letter. Then suggest that students make a list of key questions to be asked in the letter.

Skill Minilesson

VOCABULARY • The Latin Root *tort*

1. twisted, winding
2. person able to bend or twist out of shape
3. twisting, turning

Additional Resources
📁 *Vocabulary Practice,* p. 28

LITERATURE AND WRITING

Writing About Literature

Analyze Setting and Mood The narrator of "Lullaby" describes a variety of settings in which present and past events take place. Choose one of those settings and identify details the narrator uses to describe the setting. Then write an analysis of how the setting helps to create a particular atmosphere, or mood, in that part of the story. Meet with a small group of classmates to share your analysis.

Creative Writing

Ayah's Song The song Ayah sings at the end of the story is a lullaby. Write the lyrics of a song for Ayah. It can be a lullaby, like the one in the story; a ballad that tells the story of Ayah's life; a rap, whose lyrics will be spoken or chanted; or any other type of song you choose to write. Share your song lyrics with the class. Set your lyrics to music, if you wish.

EXTENDING YOUR RESPONSE

Literature Groups

The Power of Language Ayah has never learned to speak or read English, following the advice of older Navajos who "told her about learning [the white people's] language or any of their ways: it endangered you." Evaluate this advice in light of events that occur in "Lullaby." Discuss and debate such questions as: How did the white doctors get Ayah's permission to take Danny and Ella? How might this situation have been avoided? Was it a mistake for Chato to teach Ayah to sign her name? Why or why not? How did Chato benefit from knowing how to speak English? Did Chato's knowledge of English help him when he was unable to work? Why or why not? Share your ideas with the class.

Learning for Life

Letter of Inquiry Imagine that you are Ayah's friend and she has come to you, confused and frightened about what the doctors want and what they intend to do. Write a letter of inquiry, asking the doctors to explain the situation. Be polite and businesslike in your approach. Use the proper form for a business letter.

Reading Further

You might also enjoy these essays by Leslie Marmon Silko: "The People and the Land are Inseparable" and "Fifth World: The Return of Ma ah shra true ee, the Giant Serpent" are from *Yellow Woman and a Beauty of the Spirit,* a partially autobiographical collection of essays about Native American experiences.

📕 **Save your work for your portfolio.**

Skill Minilesson

VOCABULARY • The Latin Root *tort*

The word *distortion* comes from the Latin prefix *dis-,* meaning (in this case) "thoroughly," and the root *tort,* which comes from *torquere,* meaning "to twist." A *retort* is a response of the same kind originally spoken. It is, in a sense, a remark that is twisted back upon the original speaker. To *extort* is to get money or goods by "twisting" them out of someone. *Torture* involves twisting a victim—physically, mentally, or emotionally.

Recognizing the root *tort* when you see it in an unfamiliar word can help you get at least a general sense of the word's meaning.

PRACTICE Briefly state what you think might be the meaning of each underlined word.

1. We followed a <u>tortuous</u> path down the mountain.
2. To do that exercise, you'd have to be a <u>contortionist</u>!
3. <u>Torsion</u> in the rope of a tire swing will cause it to spin.

 ASSESSMENT OPTIONS

📁 *Quick Checks,* p. 29
📁 *Selection and Theme Assessment,* pp. 55–56
📁 *Performance Assessment,* p. 28
💾 *Testmaker*

Navajo Code Talkers in World War II

Like Ayah's son Jimmie in "Lullaby," many Navajos have served in the United States armed forces in times of war and in times of peace. In fact, during World War II, the Navajos made an invaluable contribution as *Code Talkers*—highly trained soldiers who relay secret, oral coded messages.

A perpetual problem in military operations is how to send messages that the enemy cannot understand. In World War II, both sides intercepted and decoded each other's radio and telephone communications. New codes had to be continually developed as old ones were broken. But in the Pacific, the Navajos relayed messages using the only code that an enemy has never cracked.

A little-known and little-used language that had never been written down, Navajo was difficult to learn because of its intricate grammatical rules and tonal character. Other than the Navajo themselves, few people in the world had mastered its unusual and complicated sounds.

Originally, twenty-nine Navajo recruits, some as young as fifteen, developed and mastered a Navajo code for use in the Pacific war front. The system that resulted could relay messages more quickly, accurately—and securely—than any other then in use.

The Navajo had no words for many military terms and place names, so the Code Talkers used words with logical associations. This chart shows a few examples.

The program eventually involved hundreds of Navajos who participated in Marine actions in the Pacific from 1942 to 1945. The Code Talkers used field telephones and walkie-talkies to report enemy locations and to direct troop movements, air strikes, and artillery fire.

Term	Code word
Battleship	Whale
Fighter plane	Hummingbird
Germany	Iron hat
Grenade	Potato
Submarine	Iron fish

In the capture of the island of Iwo Jima in 1945, six Navajo Code Talkers worked tirelessly during the first two days of the campaign, while the Marines landed and took up their shore positions. The Code Talkers relayed more than eight hundred messages without a single error. A Marine officer later declared, "Were it not for the Navajos, the Marines never would have taken Iwo Jima."

Activity

What happened to the Code Talkers after the war? How did they readjust to reservation life? Were they ever recognized for their invaluable contribution? Search the Internet and skim such books as Margaret Bixler's *Winds of Freedom* to find the answers. Then prepare a brief oral report.

THE SHORT STORY 🌾 341

Objective

- To understand the contributions of the Navajo Code Talkers during World War II

Teaching Strategies

Ask students why the Navajo language might never have been written down. *(Perhaps there was no need for a written language or the language was too difficult to put in written form.)* Discuss why this factor may have made cracking a military code based on the Navajo language difficult. *(Only the Navajo could understand the spoken words, and there would be no way to write what was said down on paper. In this way, written messages could not be stolen, and oral messages could not be understood.)*

Activity

Most Code Talkers returned to the reservation. They had difficulty adjusting to reservation life. Little was done to honor them. However, in 1982, President Reagan declared August 14 National Navajo Code Talkers Day.

Teaching Options

MEETING INDIVIDUAL NEEDS

MULTIPLE LEARNING STYLES

Linguistic Students with strong linguistic skills can help classmates brainstorm code words similar to those used by the Navajo Code Talkers.

Activity Discuss the code words shown on the chart for common military terms. Have volunteers explain the associations that might have led to two or three of the code words. Then have small groups led by strong linguistic learners brainstorm a code word for each of the following additional terms: fighter pilot, aircraft carrier, bomb, prison camp, military base, and air raid. Have each group make up two or three sentences including their new code words. Then they can read them aloud and challenge other groups to guess their meaning. **L2**

Objectives

- To read and analyze a short story in which a reporter tries to rescue a young girl trapped by a mudslide
- To identify ways the author creates mood in a story
- To write an explanation of the author's characterization

Skills

Reading/Thinking: Evaluating; Inferring; Problem and Solution; Elaborating
Writing: Letter
Vocabulary: Analogies
Grammar/Language: Compound Subjects
Listening/Speaking: Dramatization
Life Skills: Public Service Announcement
Collaboration: Literature Groups

Motivating
→OPTIONS

Selection Focus Transparency 30: Discuss stories students may have heard or read about volcanoes.

Focus Activity: Discuss times students might have been involved in rescuing a person or an animal.

Before You Read

And of Clay Are We Created

FOCUS ACTIVITY

Would most people try to save the life of a total stranger? Would they do so even if it meant putting their own safety at risk?

SHARING IDEAS Firefighters and police officers put their lives on the line for strangers all the time. To what extent are ordinary people obligated to help another person in a life-threatening situation? Discuss these issues in a small group.

SETTING A PURPOSE Read to learn how one person responds to another's terrible situations.

BACKGROUND

The Time and Place
This story is based on actual events that took place in November 1985, in the town of Armero, Colombia, not far from the capital city of Bogotá.

Did You Know?
According to geologists, the greatest danger at many volcanic sites comes not from lava, but from sudden, massive mud flows called *lahars.* When the previously dormant volcano Nevado del Ruiz erupted on November 13, 1985, a monstrous mudslide cascaded from the volcano's icy peak and crashed into the town of Armero, Colombia. Although the eruption was relatively small, the lahar that the eruption produced smothered more than 20,000 people under its blanket of mud and debris.

VOCABULARY PREVIEW

cataclysm (kat' ə kliz' əm) *n.* a disaster, usually one that causes sudden and violent change; p. 344

presentiment (pri zen' tə mənt) *n.* a feeling that something is about to happen; p. 344

equanimity (ek' wə nim' ə tē) *n.* the ability to remain calm and assured; p. 345

fortitude (fôr' tə tōōd') *n.* firm courage or strength of mind in the face of pain or danger; p. 345

pandemonium (pan' də mō' nē əm) *n.* wild disorder and uproar; p. 347

tribulation (trib' yə lā' shən) *n.* great misery or distress; suffering; p. 350

Meet
Isabel Allende

"I write to preserve memory. I write what should not be forgotten."

With these words, Chilean author Isabel Allende (ēs' ä bel ä yen' dā) defines her purpose for writing, a purpose she believes she shares with all writers. Allende grew up in her grandparents' home in Santiago, Chile, where she learned to read and love books at an early age. After living in Bolivia, Europe, and the Middle East, Allende returned to Chile as a journalist. She was forced to flee the country in 1973 when her uncle, President Salvador Allende, was killed in a bloody government coup.

Allende was born in Lima, Peru, in 1942. This story appears in The Stories of Eva Luna, *which was published in 1991.*

RESOURCE MANAGER

Lesson Planning Resource
The *Unit One Planning Guide* (pp. 254–261) provides additional lesson notes and reduced versions of all print resources.

📁 **Other Print Resources**
- Active Reading Guide, p. 30
- Vocabulary Practice, p. 28
- Reading Workbook, pp. 35–36
- Grammar and Language Workbook, p. 171
- Grammar and Composition Handbook, Lesson 2.3

- Quick Checks, p. 30
- Selection and Theme Assessment, pp. 57–58
- Performance Assessment, p. 29
- Spanish Summaries, p. 30
- Spanish Translations
- Inclusion Strategies
- English Language Learners Sourcebook

🔖 **Transparencies**
- Selection Focus 30

- Literary Elements 30
- Grammar and Language 29

Technology
🎧 Audio Library
🎧 Spanish Audio Library
💻 Glencoe Literature Web Site
💾 Testmaker

And of Clay Are We Created

They discovered the girl's head protruding from the mudpit, eyes wide open, calling soundlessly. She had a First Communion name, Azucena.[1] Lily. In that vast cemetery where the odor of death was already attracting vultures from far away, and where the weeping of orphans and wails of the injured filled the air, the little girl obstinately clinging to life became the symbol of the tragedy.

A

1. *Azucena* (ä zoo kē′ nä)

Isabel Allende ∼
Translated by Margaret Sayers Peden

THE SHORT STORY 343

SUMMARY

After a volcanic eruption, a mudslide engulfs the surrounding countryside, killing many people. Television crews are dispatched to the scene. Shortly after arriving, a reporter films a group of volunteers who have discovered a young girl alive but trapped. During the next three days, the reporter struggles to free the girl. In the process, he is forced to face his own past.

📁 *Spanish Summaries,* p. 30

A **Active Reading**

PREDICT Have students read the first page and the first paragraph of the second page. Point out that the author gives a clue that one of the characters will find something from his past that was lost 30 years before. Ask what might have been lost and why. Remind students to revise their predictions as they read.

Additional Resources
📁 *Active Reading Guide,* p. 30
🎧 *Audio Library*
🎧 *Spanish Audio Library*

Teaching Options

CONNECTING TO OTHER SELECTIONS

COMPARING selections

This selection is paired with "Colombia's Mortal Agony" on pages 355–358. A lesson for teaching a comparison of the two selections appears on page 360.

The chart at the right shows three other ways to connect "And of Clay Are We Created" to selections in this book.

For specific teaching strategies, see the *Unit One Planning Guide,* pages 257–258.

Connection	Title
Life Skills: Problem Solving	→ "An Astrologer's Day," p. 260
Thematic: Risking It All	→ "Eldorado," p. 583
Literary: Setting	→ "The Interlopers," p. 269

B **Literary Elements**

POINT OF VIEW Who is telling the story? Why might the author have chosen this point of view? *(The narrator is a woman who is close to the main character. Using this point of view is almost like watching the events unfold on television—which is an important part of the story.)*

Teaching Options

And of Clay Are We Created

A

The television cameras transmitted so often the unbearable image of the head budding like a black squash from the clay that there was no one who did not recognize her and know her name. And every time we saw her on the screen, right behind her was Rolf Carlé,[2] who had gone there on assignment, never suspecting that he would find a fragment of his past, lost thirty years before.

First a subterranean[3] sob rocked the cotton fields, curling them like waves of foam. Geologists had set up their seismographs[4] weeks before and knew that the mountain had awakened again. For some time they had predicted that the heat of the eruption could detach the eternal ice from the slopes of the volcano, but no one heeded their warnings; they sounded like the tales of frightened old women. The towns in the valley went about their daily life, deaf to the moaning of the earth, until that fateful Wednesday night in November when a prolonged roar announced the end of the world, and walls of snow broke loose, rolling in an avalanche of clay, stones, and water that descended on the villages and buried them beneath unfathomable[5] meters of telluric[6] vomit. As soon as the survivors emerged from the paralysis of that first awful terror, they could see that houses, plazas, churches, white cotton plantations, dark coffee forests, cattle pastures—all had disappeared. Much later, after soldiers and volunteers had arrived to rescue the living and try to assess

the magnitude of the cataclysm, it was calculated that beneath the mud lay more than twenty thousand human beings and an indefinite number of animals putrefying in a viscous soup. Forests and rivers had also been swept away, and there was nothing to be seen but an immense desert of mire.[7]

When the station called before dawn, Rolf Carlé and I were together. I crawled out of bed, dazed with sleep, and went to prepare coffee while he hurriedly dressed. He stuffed his gear in the green canvas backpack he always carried, and we said goodbye, as we had so many times before. I had no presentiments. I sat in the kitchen, sipping my coffee and planning the long hours without him, sure that he would be back the next day.

B

He was one of the first to reach the scene, because while other reporters were fighting their way to the edges of that morass[8] in jeeps, bicycles, or on foot, each getting there however he could, Rolf Carlé had the advantage of the television helicopter, which flew him over the avalanche. We watched on our screens the footage captured by his assistant's camera, in which he was up to his knees in muck, a microphone in his hand, in the midst of a bedlam[9] of lost children, wounded survivors, corpses, and devastation. The story came to us in his calm voice. For years he had been a familiar figure in newscasts, reporting live at the scene of battles and catastrophes with awesome

---

2. *Rolf Carlé* (rälf   cär lā´)
3. Something *subterranean* is beneath the earth's surface.
4. *Seismographs* are scientific instruments that record the intensity and duration of earthquakes.
5. Here, *unfathomable* (un fath´ əm ə bəl) means "immeasurable."
6. *Telluric* (te loor´ ik) means "coming or rising from the earth."

7. The decaying (*putrefying*) corpses are buried in the muddy slime, a thick, syrupy (*viscous*) soup; the landscape has become a wasteland of mud (*mire*).
8. A *morass* (mə ras´) is any difficult, confused, or entangling condition or situation.
9. Here, *bedlam* refers to the noisy uproar and confusion of the situation.

Vocabulary
cataclysm (kat´ ə kliz´ əm) *n.* a disaster, usually one that causes sudden and violent change
presentiment (pri zen´ tə mənt) *n.* a feeling that something is about to happen

344 UNIT 1

Offering Comfort In the story, government officials, the armed forces, the media, and religious leaders come together to offer aid, provide information, and look for solutions. Each group, in its own way, offers aid and comfort to the victims. For example, a priest hangs a medal of Mary around the trapped girl as a way of comforting her and giving her hope.

Activity Ask English language learners to discuss what kinds of aid and comfort would be offered and by whom if a disaster similar to that in the story happened in their native country.

Additional Resources
📁 *English Language Learners Sourcebook*

Tepetl, 1991. Baruj Salinas. Acrylic on canvas, 54 x 54 in. Private collection.
Viewing the painting: How well does this painting capture the mood of the story? Explain.

VIEWING THE PAINTING

Baruj Salinas was born in Havana, Cuba, in 1935. He is a painter and print maker. He works in a variety of mediums including acrylics and watercolors.

Viewing Response *The painting fits the story's mood very well. The mountains are covered with clouds, and there is a sense of mystery and foreboding.*

C **Critical Thinking**

EVALUATING The narrator says that Rolf is able to watch events without actually participating in them. Is this a good or a bad quality? Help guide students with the following model for evaluating.

Model: I am asked to make an evaluation—to say why something may be good and bad. Rolf can watch events without participating in them. He is a reporter. This is a good characteristic because he needs to stay objective and not get emotionally involved. On the other hand, this is bad. It must be difficult not to feel emotion in certain situations. In fact, to be an effective reporter, it may be necessary to get emotionally involved in order to express in words what people experiencing or watching the event are feeling.

tenacity. Nothing could stop him, and I was always amazed at his equanimity in the face of danger and suffering; it seemed as if nothing could shake his fortitude or deter his curiosity. Fear seemed never to touch him, although he had confessed to me that he was not a courageous man, far from it. I believe that the lens of the camera had a strange effect on him; it was as if it transported him to a different time from which he could watch events without actually participating in them. When I knew him better, I came to realize that this fictive distance seemed to protect him from his own emotions.

Vocabulary
equanimity (ēk′ wə nim′ ə tē) *n.* the ability to remain calm and assured
fortitude (fôr′ tə tōōd′) *n.* firm courage or strength of mind in the face of pain or danger

 MULTIPLE LEARNING STYLES

Interpersonal Interpersonal learners are sensitive to and supportive of other people. The narrator knows Rolf, loves him, and understands him better as the story progresses. She admires some things about him. She knows he has problems, but she is nonjudgmental about them.

Activity Draw a pyramid of boxes on the board and write the title *Showing Support for Others.* Ask students to list ways one person can show support for another person. *(Possible answers: praising them, encouraging them, being nonjudgmental, defending them, and listening to them.)* **L1**

D **Active Reading**

QUESTION The narrator describes what is going on, yet she is not there on the scene. How is she able to do this? *(She is watching the scene on television. Rolf's assistant is probably holding the microphone and television camera.)*

E **Literary Elements**

CHARACTER Rolf's behavior of wading into the mud, which was dangerous, to try to help the girl is unusual for him. Why? *(The narrator has just said that he does not get emotionally involved—that he puts up barriers between himself and his subjects.)*

F **Critical Thinking**

INFERRING At this point in the story, how do you think the reporter feels about his chances of saving the girl? *(He feels confident and determined. He believes he can save the girl.)*

And of Clay Are We Created

Rolf Carlé was in on the story of Azucena from the beginning. He filmed the volunteers who discovered her, and the first persons who tried to reach her; his camera zoomed in on the girl, her dark face, her large desolate eyes, the plastered-down tangle of her hair. The mud was like quicksand around her, and anyone attempting to reach her was in danger of sinking. They threw a rope to her that she made no effort to grasp until they shouted to her to catch it; then she pulled a hand from the mire and tried to move, but immediately sank a little deeper. Rolf threw down his knapsack and the rest of his equipment and waded into the quagmire, commenting for his assistant's microphone that it was cold and that one could begin to smell the stench of corpses.

"What's your name?" he asked the girl, and she told him her flower name. "Don't move, Azucena," Rolf Carlé directed, and kept talking to her, without a thought for what he was saying, just to distract her, while slowly he worked his way forward in mud up to his waist. The air around him seemed as murky as the mud.

It was impossible to reach her from the approach he was attempting, so he retreated and circled around where there seemed to be firmer footing. When finally he was close enough, he took the rope and tied it beneath her arms, so they could pull her out. He smiled at her with that smile that crinkles his eyes and makes him look like a little boy; he told her that everything was fine, that he was here with her now, that soon they would have her out. He signaled the others to pull, but as soon as the cord tensed, the girl screamed. They tried again, and her shoulders and arms appeared, but they could move her no farther; she was trapped. Someone suggested that her legs might be caught in the collapsed walls of her house, but she said it was not just rubble, that she was also held by the bodies of her brothers and sisters clinging to her legs.

"Don't worry, we'll get you out of here," Rolf promised. Despite the quality of the transmission, I could hear his voice break, and I loved him more than ever. Azucena looked at him, but said nothing.

During those first hours Rolf Carlé exhausted all the resources of his ingenuity to rescue her. He struggled with poles and ropes, but every tug was an intolerable torture for the imprisoned girl. It occurred to him to use one of the poles as a lever but got no result and had to abandon the idea. He talked a couple of soldiers into working with him for a while, but they had to leave because so many other victims were calling for help. The girl could not move, she barely could breathe, but she did not seem desperate, as if an ancestral resignation allowed her to accept her fate. The reporter, on the other hand, was determined to snatch her from death. Someone brought him a tire, which he placed beneath her arms like a life buoy, and then laid a plank near the hole to hold his weight and allow him to stay closer to her. As it was impossible to remove the rubble blindly, he tried once or twice to dive toward her feet, but emerged frustrated, covered with mud, and spitting gravel. He concluded that he would have to have a pump to drain the water, and radioed a request for one, but received in return a message that

> The girl could not move, she barely could breathe, but she did not seem desperate . . .

Teaching Options

CONNECTION

Volcanoes Suggest that students locate additional information about volcanoes and the aftermath of their eruptions by using the Internet. Students might begin by entering keywords such as *volcano, Nevado del Ruiz, Pompeii, Mt. Pinatubo,* or *Mount St. Helens.*

MEETING INDIVIDUAL NEEDS — ENGLISH LANGUAGE LEARNERS

Contrasting Conjunctions Ask a volunteer to locate a sentence on page 346 with the conjunction *and* and one with the conjunction *but.* Have students describe what the difference is in meaning between *and* and *but.* Provide or have students provide several example sentences with each word. Discuss the added sense of hopelessness and failure that Allende's repeated choice of *but* rather than *and* conveys.

Activity Have students locate additional examples of *but* in the story. Ask them to consider how the impact of the sentence would change if they substituted *and.*

Additional Resources
📁 *English Language Learners Sourcebook*

there was no available transport and it could not be sent until the next morning.

"We can't wait that long!" Rolf Carlé shouted, but in the pandemonium no one stopped to commiserate.[10] Many more hours would go by before he accepted that time had stagnated and reality had been irreparably distorted.

A military doctor came to examine the girl, and observed that her heart was functioning well and that if she did not get too cold she could survive the night.

"Hang on, Azucena, we'll have the pump tomorrow," Rolf Carlé tried to console her.

"Don't leave me alone," she begged.

"No, of course I won't leave you."

Someone brought him coffee, and he helped the girl drink it, sip by sip. The warm liquid revived her and she began telling him about her small life, about her family and her school, about how things were in that little bit of world before the volcano had erupted. She was thirteen, and she had never been outside her village. Rolf Carlé, buoyed by a premature optimism, was convinced that everything would end well: the pump would arrive, they would drain the water, move the rubble, and Azucena would be transported by helicopter to a hospital where she would recover rapidly and where he could visit her and bring her gifts. He thought, She's already too old for dolls, and I don't know what would please her; maybe a dress. I don't know much about women, he concluded, amused, reflecting that although he had known many women in his lifetime, none had taught him these details. To pass the hours he began to tell Azucena about his travels and adventures as

a newshound, and when he exhausted his memory, he called upon imagination, inventing things he thought might entertain her. From time to time she dozed, but he kept talking in the darkness, to assure her that he was still there and to overcome the menace of uncertainty.

That was a long night.

Many miles away, I watched Rolf Carlé and the girl on a television screen. I could not bear the wait at home, so I went to National Television, where I often spent entire nights with Rolf editing programs. There, I was near his world, and I could at least get a feeling of what he lived through during those three decisive days. I called all the important people in the city, senators, commanders of the armed forces, the North American ambassador, and the president of National Petroleum, begging them for a pump to remove the silt, but obtained only vague promises. I began to ask for urgent help on radio and television, to see if there wasn't *someone* who could help us. Between calls I would run to the newsroom to monitor the satellite transmissions that periodically brought new details of the catastrophe. While reporters selected scenes with most impact for the news report, I searched for footage that featured Azucena's mudpit. The screen reduced the disaster to a single plane and accentuated the tremendous distance that separated me from Rolf Carlé; nonetheless, I was there with him. The child's every suffering hurt me as it did him; I felt his frustration, his impotence. Faced with the impossibility of communicating with him, the fantastic idea came to me that if I tried, I could reach him by force of mind and in that

---

10. No one stopped to show or express sympathy—to *commiserate* (kə miz′ ə rāt′).

Vocabulary
pandemonium (pan′ də mō′ nē əm) *n.* wild disorder and uproar

---

Author's Craft

J

CHARACTER What evidence is there that Rolf is beginning to change? *(The narrator says that Rolf can no longer look at the girl through the lens. He can no longer distance himself from his subject. He sees her as more than someone to shoot with a television camera.)*

K Literary Elements

MOOD What details does the author use to show that there is a change in mood? *(Things start going badly. The reporter cannot get to the girl after more tries at digging her out. She threw up when fed some food. She had a fever, but there was no medicine for her. It began to rain. She began to cry.)*

L Literary Elements

FIGURES OF SPEECH: *Personification*

Ask students to identify the example of personification. Have them explain what is being given human characteristics. *(Azucena says that the sky is weeping. The sky is being personified.)*

---

way give him encouragement. I concentrated until I was dizzy—a frenzied and futile activity. At times I would be overcome with compassion and burst out crying; at other times, I was so drained I felt as if I were staring through a telescope at the light of a star dead for a million years.

I watched that hell on the first morning broadcast, cadavers of people and animals awash in the current of new rivers formed overnight from the melted snow. Above the mud rose the tops of trees and the bell towers of a church where several people had taken refuge and were patiently awaiting rescue teams. Hundreds of soldiers and volunteers from the Civil Defense were clawing through rubble searching for survivors, while long rows of ragged specters awaited their turn for a cup of hot broth. Radio networks announced that their phones were jammed with calls from families offering shelter to orphaned children. Drinking water was in scarce supply, along with gasoline and food. Doctors, resigned to amputating arms and legs without anesthesia, pled that at least they be sent serum and painkillers and antibiotics; most of the roads, however, were impassable, and worse were the bureaucratic obstacles that stood in the way. To top it all, the clay contaminated by decomposing bodies threatened the living with an outbreak of epidemics.

Azucena was shivering inside the tire that held her above the surface. Immobility and tension had greatly weakened her, but she was conscious and could still be heard when a microphone was held out to her. Her tone was humble, as if apologizing for all the fuss. Rolf

> "The sky is weeping," Azucena murmured . . .

Carlé had a growth of beard, and dark circles beneath his eyes; he looked near exhaustion. Even from that enormous distance I could sense the quality of his weariness, so different from the fatigue of other adventures. He had completely forgotten the camera; he could not look at the girl through a lens any longer. The pictures we were receiving were not his assistant's but those of other reporters who had appropriated Azucena, bestowing on her the pathetic responsibility of embodying the horror[11] of what had happened in that place. With the first light Rolf tried again to dislodge the obstacles that held the girl in her tomb, but he had only his hands to work with; he did not dare use a tool for fear of injuring her. He fed Azucena a cup of the cornmeal mush and bananas the Army was distributing, but she immediately vomited it up. A doctor stated that she had a fever, but added that there was little he could do: antibiotics were being reserved for cases of gangrene. A priest also passed by and blessed her, hanging a medal of the Virgin around her neck. By evening a gentle, persistent drizzle began to fall.

"The sky is weeping," Azucena murmured, and she, too, began to cry.

"Don't be afraid," Rolf begged. "You have to keep your strength up and be calm. Everything will be fine. I'm with you, and I'll get you out somehow."

Reporters returned to photograph Azucena and ask her the same questions, which she no

---

11. *[appropriated . . . horror]* In other words, the reporters have begun to use TV images of Azucena's situation, making her a living symbol of the tragedy.

Teaching Options

Reading *Minilesson*

Cause and Effect Most students will be able to identify and understand one of the story problems—the external conflict—the struggle to free the girl. They may need some help, however, in identifying the other story problem—the internal conflict.

Activity Write these headings on the board:

External Conflict	Internal Conflict
Challenge	Challenge
Consequence	Consequence

Discuss the challenge and consequence faced by Rolf in each kind of problem or conflict. Help students understand that the external conflict is about freeing a

trapped girl. The consequence of failing is death for the girl. The internal conflict is about freeing a man trapped by his memories. His challenge is to face his past and himself. The consequence is not liking what he sees. **L2**

Additional Resources

📁 *Reading Workbook,* pp. 35–36

longer tried to answer. In the meanwhile, more television and movie teams arrived with spools of cable, tapes, film, videos, precision lenses, recorders, sound consoles, lights, reflecting screens, auxiliary motors, cartons of supplies, electricians, sound technicians, and cameramen: Azucena's face was beamed to millions of screens around the world. And all the while Rolf Carlé kept pleading for a pump. The improved technical facilities bore results, and National Television began receiving sharper pictures and clearer sound; the distance seemed suddenly compressed, and I had the horrible sensation that Azucena and Rolf were by my side, separated from me by impenetrable glass. I was able to follow events hour by hour; I knew everything my love did to wrest the girl from her prison and help her endure her suffering; I overheard fragments of what they said to one another and could guess the rest; I was present when she taught Rolf to pray, and when he distracted her with the stories I had told him in a thousand and one nights beneath the white mosquito netting of our bed.

When darkness came on the second day, Rolf tried to sing Azucena to sleep with old Austrian folk songs he had learned from his mother, but she was far beyond sleep. They spent most of the night talking, each in a stupor of exhaustion and hunger, and shaking with cold. That night, imperceptibly, the unyielding floodgates that had contained Rolf Carlé's past for so many years began to open, and the torrent of all that had lain hidden in the deepest and most secret layers of memory poured out, leveling before it the obstacles that had blocked his consciousness for so long. He could not tell it all to Azucena; she perhaps did not know there was a world beyond the sea or time previous to her own; she was not capable of imagining Europe in the years of the war. So he could not tell her of defeat, nor of the afternoon the Russians

had led them to the concentration camp to bury prisoners dead from starvation. Why should he describe to her how the naked bodies piled like a mountain of firewood resembled fragile china? How could he tell this dying child about ovens and gallows? Nor did he mention the night that he had seen his mother naked, shod in stiletto-heeled red boots, sobbing with humiliation. There was much he did not tell, but in those hours he relived for the first time all the things his mind had tried to erase. Azucena had surrendered her fear to him and so, without wishing it, had obliged Rolf to confront his own. There, beside that hellhole of mud, it was impossible for Rolf to flee from himself any longer, and the visceral[12] terror he had lived as a boy suddenly invaded him. He reverted to the years when he was the age of Azucena, and younger, and, like her, found himself trapped in a pit without escape, buried in life, his head barely above ground; he saw before his eyes the boots and legs of his father, who had removed his belt and was whipping it in the air with the never-forgotten hiss of a viper coiled to strike. Sorrow flooded through him, intact and precise, as if it had lain always in his mind, waiting. He was once again in the armoire where his father locked him to punish him for imagined misbehavior, there where for eternal hours he had crouched with his eyes closed, not to see the darkness, with his hands over his ears, to shut out the beating of his

Did You Know?
An *armoire* (ärm wär′) is a large, moveable cupboard or wardrobe.

---

12. Here, *visceral* means "emotional or instinctive rather than intellectual."

M Critical Thinking

INFERRING Be sure students understand what is meant when Rolf remembers ovens and gallows. *(Ovens and gallows refer to things found in the concentration camps. The ovens were used to burn live prisoners as well as bodies of prisoners who had died or were killed. Gallows were used to hang people.)*

N Literary Elements

CHARACTERIZATION Have students focus on the revealed events of Rolf's childhood and infer how these events influenced his current actions. *(He was beaten as a child. He seems now to feel a need to comfort Azucena, as he was never comforted.)*

O Active Reading

CONNECT With what story might this one be compared? How are they alike? *(This story and "Lullaby" are similar. In both stories, a person remembers past events in his or her life, many of which are painful.)*

Listening and Speaking *Minilesson*

Dramatization Discuss tips and suggestions for presenting a dramatization of a story event. Possible tips and suggestions might include these:

- Decide how many people will speak.
- Write dialogue for them or choose dialogue from the story to read.
- Practice reading the dialogue as the characters would say it.
- Decide what props, if any, are needed.

Activity Ask students to work in groups to dramatize a scene from the story. Provide time for students to prepare and practice their scenes. Then ask them to present their dramatizations to the class.
L2 **COLLAB. LEARN.**

P Critical Thinking

ELABORATING Rolf remembers and weeps for his sister. He feels guilty about abandoning her. How might he have abandoned her? *(He might have left her with an abusive father and not kept in touch.)*

Q Literary Elements

PLOT: *Internal Conflict* What monsters were tormenting Rolf? What does he realize? *(The monsters are his past memories. He realizes that he can no longer run from the past.)*

---

heart, trembling, huddled like a cornered animal. Wandering in the mist of his memories he found his sister Katherina, a sweet, retarded child who spent her life hiding, with the hope that her father would forget the disgrace of her having been born. With Katherina, Rolf crawled beneath the dining room table, and with her hid there under the long white tablecloth, two children forever embraced, alert to footsteps and voices. Katherina's scent melded with his own sweat, with aromas of cooking, garlic, soup, freshly baked bread, and the unexpected odor of putrescent clay. His sister's hand in his, her frightened breathing, her silk hair against his cheek, the candid gaze of her eyes. Katherina . . . Katherina materialized before him, floating on the air like a flag, clothed in the white tablecloth, now a winding sheet, and at last he could weep for her death and for the guilt of having abandoned her. He understood then that all his exploits as a reporter, the feats that had won him such recognition and fame, were merely an attempt to keep his most ancient fears at bay, a stratagem[13] for taking refuge behind a lens to test whether reality was more tolerable from that perspective. He took excessive risks as an exercise of courage, training by day to conquer the monsters that tormented him by night. But he had come face to face with the moment of truth; he could not continue to escape his past. He *was* Azucena; he was buried in the clayey mud; his terror was not the distant emotion of an almost forgotten childhood, it was a claw sunk in his throat. In the flush of his tears he saw his mother, dressed in black and clutching her imitation-crocodile pocketbook to her

bosom, just as he had last seen her on the dock when she had come to put him on the boat to South America. She had not come to dry his tears, but to tell him to pick up a shovel: the war was over and now they must bury the dead.

"Don't cry. I don't hurt anymore. I'm fine," Azucena said when dawn came.

"I'm not crying for you," Rolf Carlé smiled. "I'm crying for myself. I hurt all over."

The third day in the valley of the cataclysm began with a pale light filtering through storm clouds. The President of the Republic visited the area in his tailored safari jacket to confirm that this was the worst catastrophe of the century; the country was in mourning; sister nations had offered aid; he had ordered a state of siege; the Armed Forces would be merciless, anyone caught stealing or committing other offenses would be shot on sight. He added that it was impossible to remove all the corpses or count the thousands who had disappeared; the entire valley would be declared holy ground, and bishops would come to celebrate a solemn mass for the souls of the victims. He went to the Army field tents to offer relief in the form of vague promises to crowds of the rescued, then to the improvised hospital to offer a word of encouragement to doctors and nurses worn down from so many hours of <u>tribulations</u>. Then he asked to be taken to see Azucena, the little girl the whole world had seen. He waved to her with a limp statesman's hand, and microphones recorded his emotional voice and paternal[14] tone as he told her that her courage

---

13. A *stratagem* is a trick or scheme for achieving some purpose.

14. Here, *paternal* means "fatherly."

Vocabulary
tribulation (trib′ yə lā′ shən) *n.* great misery or distress; suffering

350   UNIT 1

Teaching Options

Grammar and Language *Minilesson*

Compound Subjects Write this sentence on the board, underlining the words shown: *Immobility and tension had taken their toll on the girl.* Explain that the underlined words are an example of a compound subject. A compound subject is two or more simple subjects joined with a conjunction. The compound subjects share the same verb.

Activity Write each sentence on the board. Ask students to expand each sentence by using a compound subject. Possible answers are shown.
1. Water raced into the valley. *(and clay)*
2. Medicines were needed. *(and food)*
3. Azucena endured the chilly night. *(and Rolf)*
4. Ropes were used to try to free the girl. *(and poles)* **L1**

Additional Resources

Grammar and Language Transparency 29

Grammar and Language Workbook, p. 171

Grammar and Composition Handbook, Lesson 2.3

Writer's Choice, Lesson 11.3

had served as an example to the nation. Rolf Carlé interrupted to ask for a pump, and the President assured him that he personally would attend to the matter. I caught a glimpse of Rolf for a few seconds kneeling beside the mudpit. On the evening news broadcast, he was still in the same position; and I, glued to the screen like a fortuneteller to her crystal ball, could tell that something fundamental had changed in him. I knew somehow that during the night his defenses had crumbled and he had given in to grief; finally he was vulnerable. The girl had touched a part of him that he himself had no access to, a part he had never shared with me. Rolf had wanted to console her, but it was Azucena who had given him consolation.

I recognized the precise moment at which Rolf gave up the fight and surrendered to the torture of watching the girl die. I was with them, three days and two nights, spying on them from the other side of life. I was there when she told him that in all her thirteen years no boy had ever loved her and that it was a pity to leave this world without knowing love. Rolf assured her that he loved her more than he could ever love anyone, more than he loved his mother, more than his sister, more than all the women who had slept in his arms, more than he loved me, his life companion, who would have given anything to be trapped in that well in her place, who would have exchanged her life for Azucena's, and I watched as he leaned down to kiss her poor forehead, consumed by a sweet, sad emotion he could not name. I felt how in that instant both were saved from despair, how they were freed from

the clay, how they rose above the vultures and helicopters, how together they flew above the vast swamp of corruption and laments. How, finally, they were able to accept death. Rolf Carlé prayed in silence that she would die quickly, because such pain cannot be borne.

By then I had obtained a pump and was in touch with a general who had agreed to ship it the next morning on a military cargo plane. But on the night of that third day, beneath the unblinking focus of quartz lamps and the lens of a hundred cameras, Azucena gave up, her eyes locked with those of the friend who had sustained her to the end. Rolf Carlé removed the life buoy, closed her eyelids, held her to his chest for a few moments, and then let her go. She sank slowly, a flower in the mud.

You are back with me, but you are not the same man. I often accompany you to the station and we watch the videos of Azucena again; you study them intently, looking for something you could have done to save her, something you did not think of in time. Or maybe you study them to see yourself as if in a mirror, naked. Your cameras lie forgotten in a closet; you do not write or sing; you sit long hours before the window, staring at the mountains. Beside you, I wait for you to complete the voyage into yourself, for the old wounds to heal. I know that when you return from your nightmares, we shall again walk hand in hand, as before.

THE SHORT STORY ᭙ 351

Cultural Note

Explain that in some creation stories, the first human is made from the dust of the ground. Point out the title of the story and relate it to the words sometimes used in Christian funeral services—"Ashes to ashes. Dust to dust." Ask students what the expression means. Help them see that it means we all die and ultimately return to the earth, usually by being buried. Also help students see that the title emphasizes our shared humanity.

R Literary Elements

FIGURES OF SPEECH: *Metaphor* The author calls Azucena a flower in the mud. Discuss the various meanings of the phrase. *(She was a flower in the sense that she was a beautiful, courageous person. Her name meant "lily," which is the name of a flower. A flower can't survive in difficult circumstances but requires careful tending.)*

Thematic Focus

Challenges and Consequences Discuss with students the consequences Rolf ultimately faced as a result of the challenge of trying to rescue Azucena.

ASSESSMENT OPTIONS
Quick Checks, p. 30

REAL-WORLD CONNECTION

Media Coverage: When Is It Too Much? Reporters swarmed around Azucena, asking her the same questions over and over and shooting endless pictures of her for the television audience. Does this sound familiar? Much discussion has been held about the excesses of the media. Trials and scandals are covered endlessly. A war begins, and television cameras are on the beach waiting for the soldiers to land. Famines, floods, hur-ricanes, and tornadoes are pictured. Discuss with students their views about whether they feel the media "goes overboard" sometimes. What are some examples? Then ask them to discuss times when they were glad television was there to cover an event. **L1**

Personal Response

Either Azucena or Rolf can be cited as the person most admired.

ANALYZING LITERATURE

1. A volcano erupts. Water and clay flood the valley. Azucena is trapped in the mud.
2. Rolf is a television reporter.
3. He tries to pull her out with a rope. He tries to pry her out with ropes and poles. He tries to rig up a lever. He begs for a pump. He tries to dig her out with his hands.
4. He remembers the aftermath of the war and having to help bury the dead in the concentration camp. He remembers his mentally retarded sister and how the two of them hid together from a father who beat them.
5. Azucena dies. Rolf watches tapes of the event trying to see what he might have done and trying to heal old wounds.
6. She is a sympathetic character. She is young and struggling to live.
7. He is able to separate himself from his subjects. He is willing to take excessive risks. His willingness to take risks helps him in the rescue attempt. His desire to separate himself from his subject fails, but this failure ultimately makes him a better person.
8. Rolf cares about another human being, and he is fighting for his own survival in dealing with his past.
9. She encourages him and comforts him when he is in the midst of facing his past, although she does not realize it. Her courageous struggle is a model for him.
10. Azucena's death freed her from further fear and pain. Rolf was saved from the despair of his past and the grip it had on him.
11. He sees her as a victim, then as a young woman, and finally as a friend.
12. Most students will say he did have an obligation because she is a fellow human being. If there is a way to rescue a person, it should be done even if there is a risk.
13. The media does exploit people. Sometimes they are more interested in the story and ratings than in people and what the media attention might do to them.
14. The narrator sees the president as worthless. He offers little in the way of help and ultimately becomes a sightseer, visiting Azucena and offering lame platitudes about courage. The

tone is one of disdain and disapproval.
15. The title means that we all die and return to the earth. It is an appropriate title because the word *clay* has several meanings—the clay in which the girl is trapped, the "clay" of the past in which Rolf is trapped, and the "clay" or earth to which we all return.

Responding to Literature

Personal Response

Which character in the story do you admire the most? Why?

──── ANALYZING LITERATURE ────

RECALL

1. Describe the catastrophic event that occurs before the story begins. What is Azucena's predicament as a result of this event?
2. Why is Rolf Carlé sent to the disaster site?
3. Summarize the efforts Rolf makes to save Azucena.
4. What hidden memories flood into Rolf's mind during the second night he spends with Azucena?
5. What happens to Azucena at the end of the story? How does Rolf spend his time after this event?

INTERPRET

6. In your opinion, why does Azucena quickly become the **symbol** of the tragedy?
7. According to the narrator, what qualities does Rolf exhibit while doing his job? In your opinion, do these qualities help him? Explain.
8. Theme Connections   Why do you think Rolf tries so hard to save Azucena?
9. In your opinion, how does Azucena help Rolf? Use evidence from the story to support your answer.
10. What do you think the narrator means when she says that both Rolf and Azucena "were saved from despair" and "were freed from the clay"?

EVALUATE AND CONNECT

11. How does Rolf's attitude toward Azucena change as the story progresses? Support your answer with evidence from the story.
12. Look back at the issues raised in the Focus Activity on page 342. Do you think Rolf was obligated to help Azucena, even though it meant putting his own safety at risk? Give reasons for your answer.
13. In your opinion, do the news media sometimes exploit people, such as Azucena, who are the victims of tragedies? Explain your answer.
14. What conclusions can you draw about the narrator's opinion of the President of the Republic? How would you describe the **tone** of her description? (See Literary Terms Handbook, page R13.)
15. What do you think the title of this story means? In your opinion, is it an appropriate title? Why or why not?

Literary ELEMENTS

Mood

Mood is the emotional quality, or atmosphere, that a writer creates in a story. The writer's language and choice of details contribute to a story's mood. Allende immediately establishes the somber, tragic mood of "And of Clay Are We Created" with the horrific image of "the girl's head protruding from the mudpit, eyes wide open, calling soundlessly."

1. How does the author's description of the setting contribute to the mood of the story? Support your ideas with specific details from the selection.
2. Find two examples of events that help to create the tragic mood of the story. Identify words or images that the author uses to convey the horror of the situation.
3. Besides *somber* and *tragic*, what other words would you choose to describe the mood of this story? Explain your choices.

● See **Literary Terms Handbook**, p. R8.

LITERARY ELEMENTS

1. The setting of the eruption, its resulting devastation, and the trapped girl establish a mood of horror.
2. One example: When the girl dies, the author uses the image of a flower in the mud.
3. *Hopeful* could be used because Rolf is healing.

Additional Resources

Literary Elements Transparency 30

LITERATURE AND WRITING

Writing About Literature

Examine Characterization   Reflecting on the actual televised images of Azucena, Allende has said: "I see the girl again . . . talking to me about patience, about endurance, about courage." Write several paragraphs explaining how Allende shows that Azucena possesses these character traits. Share your ideas with a classmate.

Personal Writing

My Dearest   For some people, such as author Isabel Allende, writing letters is similar to keeping a diary. Imagine that you are Rolf. Write a letter to the narrator, giving your own account of some or all of the events described in the story.

EXTENDING YOUR RESPONSE

Literature Groups

More than Meets the Eye   A **symbol** is any object, person, place, or experience that means more than it is. Writers often use symbols to convey ideas and attitudes to the reader. In "And of Clay Are We Created," for example, the narrator says that Azucena became "the symbol of the tragedy" after the eruption. In your group, identify symbols that you think Allende uses in the story. Discuss and debate their possible meanings. Share your ideas with the class.

Learning for Life

Public Service Announcement   Prepare a public service announcement to be broadcast on radio or television

stations serving the areas near the disaster site described in this story. Include a brief update on conditions at the disaster site, as well as information about how volunteers can donate money, supplies, or services. Read your announcement to the class.

Reading Further

You might also enjoy this short story by Isabel Allende: "Phantom Palace" from *Eva Luna* tells how a foreign diplomat's wife becomes entangled in mystery.

✋ **Save your work for your portfolio.**

VOCABULARY • Analogies

An analogy is a type of comparison based on the relationships between things or ideas. One type of analogy deals with pairs of words that represent different degrees of intensity.

stunned : surprised :: exhausted : tired

Someone who is *stunned* is *extremely surprised;* someone who is *exhausted* is *extremely tired.*

To finish an analogy, decide what relationship exists between the first two things or ideas. Then apply that relationship to another pair of words and see if it is the same.

● For more about analogies, see **Communications Skills Handbook,** p. R77.

PRACTICE   Choose the word that best completes each analogy.

1. ecstasy : happiness :: tribulation :
   a. discomfort   b. faith   c. risk
2. hostility : unfriendliness :: pandemonium :
   a. peace   b. insecurity   c. confusion
3. cruel : kind :: candid :
   a. sneaky   b. planned   c. sympathetic
4. equanimity : calmness :: presentiment :
   a. insensitivity   b. uneasiness   c. anger
5. hurricane : wind :: cataclysm :
   a. effort   b. misfortune   c. luck

LITERATURE AND WRITING

Writing About Literature

Students' paragraphs should
- explain how Azucena possesses patience, endurance, and courage.
- give specific examples from the story.
- use quotes to support the examples.

Personal Writing

Students' letters should
- give a personal account of some or all of the events.
- describe the feelings associated with the events.
- be written in a conversational tone.

EXTENDING YOUR RESPONSE

Literature Groups   Several symbols should be identified. Be sure students identify what each symbol means. Remind them that several explanations may be possible.
COLLAB. LEARN.

Learning for Life   Students might want to videotape their announcements to make them seem more real. 📼

VOCABULARY • Analogies
1. a   2. c   3. a
4. b   5. b

Additional Resources

📁 *Vocabulary Practice,* p. 29

☑ ASSESSMENT OPTIONS

📁 *Quick Checks,* p. 30

📁 *Selection and Theme Assessment,* pp. 57–58

📁 *Performance Assessment,* p. 29

💾 *Testmaker*

Objectives

- To read and analyze a magazine article about the volcanic eruption that inspired the story "And of Clay Are We Created"
- To identify ways the author uses description
- To write a memorial plaque for the victims of a volcanic eruption

Skills

Reading/Thinking: Drawing Conclusions; Distinguishing Fact and Opinion; Making Critical Judgments
Writing: Memorial Plaque
Grammar/Language: Adjectives
Collaboration: Literature Groups

Motivating

→OPTIONS

Selection Focus Transparency 31: Work with students to identify questions to ask and people to interview during a natural disaster.

Focus Activity: Discuss the kinds of information the victims of a natural disaster might provide to a reporter compared with the kinds of information a rescue worker on the scene might provide.

Before You Read

Colombia's Mortal Agony

FOCUS ACTIVITY

Why are most people interested in catastrophic events, even ones that have absolutely no effect on their own lives?

DISCUSS Think about a recent disaster or tragedy in the news. How did you respond? How did people around you and around the world respond? Discuss different ways people react when disaster strikes.

SETTING A PURPOSE Read to appreciate the heroic efforts made in response to a natural disaster.

BACKGROUND

The Time and Place
The events described in this selection took place in November 1985, near Bogotá, Colombia.

Did You Know?
Have you ever heard of the ancient Italian city of Pompeii? This city was totally destroyed in A.D. 79 when Mount Vesuvius erupted. Two thousand people lost their lives in the catastrophe. Ironically, the wet volcanic ash and cinders that buried Pompeii also preserved many of the city's dwellings and public buildings, along with invaluable artifacts from this ancient Italian culture. Excavations of the ruins of Pompeii have revealed a picture of city life for first-century Italians.

VOCABULARY PREVIEW

phenomena (fə nom′ ə nə′) *n.* facts, events, or conditions that can be known through the senses; p. 355
pall (pôl) *n.* a covering that darkens or conceals; atmosphere of gloom; p. 355
ferocity (fə ros′ ə tē) *n.* great fierceness; extreme intensity; p. 357
tentative (ten′ tə tiv) *adj.* not fully worked out; uncertain; p. 357
spawn (spôn) *v.* to bring forth; give birth; p. 358

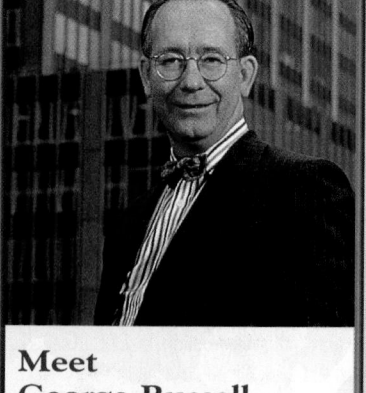

Meet George Russell

George Russell was hired by *Time* magazine in 1974 as a staff writer for its Canadian edition. Working his way through the ranks as writer, associate editor, and South American bureau chief, Russell became senior editor for Time International in 1987. Since 1992 he has been chiefly responsible for *Time*'s Canadian, Asian, and Latin American editions.

George Russell was born and educated in Calgary, Alberta, Canada. He is co-author of the book Eyewitness: 150 Years of Photojournalism, *published in 1990, and cowinner of the 1988 Hancock Award for business journalism.*

RESOURCE MANAGER

Lesson Planning Resource
The *Unit One Planning Guide* (pp. 262–269) provides additional lesson notes and reduced versions of all print resources.

📁 **Other Print Resources**
- Active Reading Guide, p. 31
- Vocabulary Practice, p. 29
- Reading Workbook, pp. 37–38
- Grammar and Language Workbook, pp. 61, 271
- Grammar and Composition Handbook, Lessons 1.4, 11.9

- Quick Checks, p. 31
- Selection and Theme Assessment, pp. 59–60
- Performance Assessment, p. 30
- Spanish Summaries, p. 31
- Spanish Translations
- Inclusion Strategies
- English Language Learners Sourcebook

🎞 **Transparencies**
- Selection Focus 31

- Literary Elements 31
- Grammar and Language 30, 31

Technology
🎧 Audio Library
🎧 Spanish Audio Library
💻 Glencoe Literature Web Site
💾 Testmaker

COLOMBIA'S MORTAL AGONY

George Russell

IT WAS SHORTLY AFTER 9 P.M. Wednesday, and Pilot Manuel Cervero was nearly home. Cervero was flying a DC-8 cargo jet from Miami to the Colombian capital, Bogotá, a sprawling city of 5 million in the Andes. The plane was cruising at 24,000 ft., 110 miles or ten minutes from El Dorado International Airport. Then, without warning, Cervero and his aircraft ran afoul of one of nature's most destructive phenomena.

"First came a reddish illumination that shot up to about 26,000 ft.," the pilot recalled. "Then came a shower of ash that covered us and left me without visibility. The cockpit filled with smoke and heat and the smell of sulfur."[1] The blast charred the nose of the DC-8 and turned the aircraft's windows white. Flying only on instruments, Cervero

---

1. *Sulfur* is an abundant element that, by itself, has no taste or odor. As sulfur burns (in a volcano, for instance), it combines with oxygen to form *sulfur dioxide,* a colorless, poisonous gas that does have a sharp odor.

diverted the plane to the city of Cali, 20 minutes from Bogotá. Making his final approach, the pilot said, he had to push open one of the cockpit's side windows in order to catch a glimpse of the airport's runway lights. He landed safely.

Cervero did not at first know that he had been flying 7,000 ft. above a 17,716-ft.-high, long-dormant volcano known as Nevado del Ruiz at the exact moment when it came thunderously alive. Within hours, that rebirth had left upwards of 20,000 people dead or missing in a steaming, mile-wide avalanche of gray ash and mud. Thousands more were injured, orphaned and homeless. The Colombian town of Armero (pop. about 22,500) had virtually disappeared. At week's end a huge cloud of ash, rising as high as 45,000 ft., hung dramatically over the area. The pall obscured the sun and caused the normal afternoon temperature of 77°F to drop to about 55°F. As rescuers hunted

Vocabulary
phenomena (fə nom′ ə nə′) *n.* facts, events, or conditions that can be known through the senses
pall (pôl) *n.* a covering that darkens or conceals; atmosphere of gloom

THE SHORT STORY ❧ 355

B Literary Elements

DESCRIPTION The author uses
descriptive language throughout the
selection to make the eruption of the
volcano and its aftermath come
alive. Ask students to identify words
or phrases that the author uses to
make the volcano seem like a bomb
that had exploded. *(blast, detonation,
terrorist bombing)*

C Literary Elements

DIALOGUE The author uses quotations from people on the scene.
Discuss reasons why this was done.
*(Quotations from eyewitnesses and
victims are an effective way to help
the reader understand what the people actually experienced. For a news
piece, reporting an eyewitness's own
words is the ideal.)*

Teaching
Options

COLOMBIA'S MORTAL AGONY

Did You Know?
Mount Vesuvius (vi soo′ vē as)
is a still-active volcano in
southern Italy.

frantically amid the
soupy devastation for
mud-covered survivors,
it was soon clear that
Nevado del Ruiz would
rate as one of the dead-
liest volcanic eruptions
in all of recorded history,
roughly equivalent to
the A.D. 79 explosion
of Mount Vesuvius, which destroyed the
cities of Pompeii and Herculaneum. . . .

The explosion in the snowy, rugged
Andean peak came from a buildup of molten
rock and trapped gases that was ultimately
caused by the movement of two of the earth's
huge tectonic plates.[2] Similar forces were
responsible for the Mexico City earthquake
(September 19, 1985), as well as the tremors
that perennially shake California. But the
eruption also bore an eerie similarity to the
1980 detonation[3] of Washington State's
Mount St. Helens, which left an estimated 65
people dead and missing. The initial Nevado
del Ruiz blast sent steam and millions of tons
of ash into the Andean air, but the debris was
followed by almost no lava. About 90 minutes
after the initial detonation, there was a second. It was so forceful that it shook the air in
Cali, 150 miles to the southwest. Said a civil
defense worker in that city: "At first I
thought it might be a terrorist bombing in
our neighborhood."

The double eruption produced none of the
spectacular lava displays that characterize
such perennially active volcanoes as Hawaii's
Kilauea. Instead, the superheated magma[4]
within Nevado del Ruiz began to melt the

thick blanket of snow
and ice that caps the
top 2,000 ft. of the
peak. Filthy water
started to flow down
the sides of the moun-
tain. The trickle swiftly
turned into a torrent of
viscous mud, stones,
ashes and debris with a
crest of 15 ft. to 50 ft.
The liquid avalanche,
known as a lahar, was
soon hurtling down
the steep slopes at
speeds of up to 30
m.p.h. With irresistible
force, it roared down
the flanks of Nevado
del Ruiz in the most
natural of channels: the
beds of the Guali, Azufrado and Lagunilla
rivers, which flow east and south from the
base of the volcano.

Some 30 miles from Nevado del Ruiz, in
the Lagunilla River canyon, lay Armero. A
thriving agricultural center of whitewashed,
tile-roofed homes and pastel colonial
churches, the town had taken little part in the
more turbulent eras of modern Colombian history. The region's wealth is based on cotton
and rice farming. The surrounding Lagunilla
River canyon contains some of the country's
finest agricultural land. . . .

The region's good life disappeared in a few
minutes on Wednesday night. . . . "First there
were earth tremors," remembered Rosa Maria
Henao, 39, the mother of two, as she lay in
the 30-bed hospital of Mariquita, a small
town about 15 miles north of Armero. "The
air suddenly seemed heavy. It smelled of sulfur. Then there was a horrible rumbling that
seemed to come from deep inside the earth."

---

2. The earth's crust is composed of about a dozen gigantic slabs
   called *tectonic plates.* Volcanoes commonly develop where
   these plates meet.
3. A *detonation* is a loud explosion.
4. The hot, melted rock deep inside the earth is called *magma.*

ENGLISH LANGUAGE LEARNERS

Volcano Vocabulary English language learners may need help understanding some of the descriptive
language in the story. Ask them to
give phrases in their native language
that describe an erupting volcano.

Activity Write these phrases on the
board: *molten rock, soupy devastation,
Andean peak, liquid avalanche, irre-*

sistible force. Discuss the meaning of
each phrase. Ask students to describe
each meaning in concrete terms. Here
is an example: **molten rock** *Molten*
means "liquid." The rock is so hot it
becomes liquid.

Additional Resources
📁 *English Language Learners
Sourcebook*

George Russell

As the avalanche poured down on Armero, it gained additional ferocity from several sources. Three days of torrential rains had greatly swollen the Lagunilla River, which was already choked with mudslides from the volcano's tentative stirrings in September. At that time geologists from the surrounding federal department[5] of Tolima had expressed concern about the dangers from the dammed-up river. At first the departmental governor, Eduardo Alzate García, said that "there are no immediate risks." Two days later he changed his mind. The geologists declared the region at the base of the volcano a local emergency area, and Alzate planned to have the water buildup drained through an escape canal. Work on that project had not begun when death thundered down the mountainside.

The first word to the outside world came from Armero's mayor, Ramón Antonio Rodríguez, 34. A ham[6] operator, he was on the radio to a fellow ham in Ibagué, 60 miles to the south, when Nevado del Ruiz erupted, scattering rock and ashes across the Lagunilla Canyon. The mayor was calmly describing the event when suddenly he shouted, "Wait a minute. I think the town is getting flooded." Those words were his last.

The mudslide that entombed Rodríguez cut through Armero like a liquid scythe. Henao later recollected that the wave "rolled into town with a moaning sound, like some sort of monster." Luckily, her home was on a hill. "Houses below us started cracking under the advance of the river of mud," she recalled. She grabbed her children and climbed to the roof of her home. As they watched, more than 80% of the roughly 4,200 buildings in Armero simply vanished into the torrents of slime. Said she: "It seemed like the end of the world."

Those with the opportunity and the presence of mind, like Henao, rushed desperately

---

5. Colombia is divided into twenty-three *departments,* nine territories, and the Special District of Bogotá. Each department has an elected legislature.

6. Amateur, or *ham,* radio is a hobby in which an individual (also called a *ham*) operates his or her own radio station, sending messages by voice or Morse code.

Vocabulary
ferocity (fə ros′ ə tē) *n.* great fierceness; extreme intensity
tentative (ten′ tə tiv) *adj.* not fully worked out; uncertain

---

D Critical Thinking

DRAWING CONCLUSIONS How does the author let readers know the people had little time and few ways to escape? *(He uses direct quotes and eyewitness accounts from the mayor and a survivor. One minute the mayor was speaking on the radio, and the next minute he was dead. People who lived on a hill had a little more time and climbed on roofs. People in the village had nowhere to go.)*

E Literary Elements

FIGURES OF SPEECH: *Simile* Ask students to identify the two things being compared in the two similes on the page. Remind students that a simile is a comparison of two unlike things, using *like* or *as. (In the first simile, the mudslide is compared to a scythe. In the second simile, the wave is compared to a monster.)*

Language Note

A scythe is a tool with a sharp, curved, cutting blade, a shaft, and one or two handles for holding the tool. With a sweeping motion, farmers would use the scythe to cut grain or hay. The scythe could level most things in its path. The figure of Death is sometimes shown carrying a scythe.

Reading *Minilesson*

Distinguishing Fact and Opinion
Newspaper and magazine articles may contain statements of both fact and opinion. Ask students to tell the difference between the two. *(A fact is something that can be proved. An opinion is what someone thinks.)*

Activity Ask students to look through the article for examples of facts and opinions. Let volunteers read their examples aloud, stating whether they are reading a statement of fact or opinion. In general, the information the author provides about the eruption is factual, while the comments by the eyewitnesses are opinions.
L2

Additional Resources
📁 *Reading Workbook,* pp. 37–38

⒡ Critical Thinking

MAKING CRITICAL JUDGMENTS Guide students in making judgments by asking them how the title of the selection relates to the final sentence. Use the model as a guide.

Model: I know from the title that there was great suffering. The details in the article support that. The last sentence indicates that the rescue squads were so busy they had no time to grieve. The words *mortal agony* in the title take on new meanings. The Colombians experience a mortal agony both literally and figuratively—as in a crushing agony. The title sums up the key point the author uses to end the article.

Thematic Focus

Challenges and Consequences
Discuss the challenges and consequences the author faced as he wrote this article.

☑ **ASSESSMENT OPTIONS**

📁 *Quick Checks,* p. 31

Teaching Options

COLOMBIA'S MORTAL AGONY

onto rooftops, or clambered into the branches of nearby trees. Some ran for the city's highest ground, its hilltop cemetery, or found other spots above the flood crest. Survivors later testified that the first wave of mud to hit the town was ice cold, like the mountain snows that spawned it. As it rolled onward, the mud carried along more and more of the inner fire of Nevado del Ruiz, until finally the cascade was smoking hot. . . .

The tidal wave rolled on, submerging the neighboring village of Santuario (pop. about 1,400) and two other small communities. To the west, on the opposite slope of Nevado del Ruiz, a second avalanche broke loose and headed for Chinchiná, a city of about 34,000. Some 200 families fled the area. Chinchiná, six miles from the base of the volcano, escaped major damage, but civil authorities estimate that 1,090 people died in the immediate area.

What was left behind in Armero, in Henao's words, was "one big beach of mud." A viscous gray layer, between 7 ft. and 15 ft. thick, covered most of the town. Thousands of bodies were buried in the sludge, their location sometimes marked by pools of blood on the surface. Other corpses lay half visible in miniature bogs that were as treacherous as quicksand. Some exhausted survivors lay on the surface of the mud in shallows, or staggered along in shock on drier ground. Many of the living were naked or only partly clothed; their garments had been torn from them by the swift-moving lahar. All were

"It seemed like the end of the world."

encrusted with ash-colored goo that quickly hardened under the next morning's sun into a gritty carapace.[7] Many of the survivors had suffered serious injuries. A sepulchral[8] silence reigned over the devastated town.

Most horrifying of all was the plight of those who were trapped, still living, in the mud. Many were buried up to their necks; some had their mouths stopped with filth, so they could not cry for help. Sometimes the buried survivors were still locked in gruesome embrace with the dead. One was Omaira Sanchez, 13, who remained up to her neck in ooze two days following the disaster. When the mudslide struck, Omaira was washed up against her aunt, who grabbed hold of her. The aunt died, but kept her grip, even after rigor mortis[9] had set in. Finally, after rescuers worked fruitlessly for 60 hours, Omaira died of a heart attack. In the days after the disaster, one doctor estimated that there were at least 1,000 living victims still trapped in the morass. . . .

At week's end the rescue squads working heroically in the shadow of the volcano were giving fear little thought. All their efforts were bent on saving the living. Only now and then did they have time to think of the thousands of dead who lay beneath their feet. Giving in fully to the release of grief was a luxury that Colombia could not yet afford.

⒡

---

7. A *carapace* (kar´ ə pās´) is a case or shell, such as a turtle's.
8. A *sepulchral* (si pul´ krəl) silence is deep and gloomy, like that at a burial.
9. *Rigor mortis* is the name for the stiffening of the muscles in the body after death.

Vocabulary
spawn (spôn) *v.* to bring forth; give birth

Grammar and Language *Minilesson*

Adjectives Ask students to identify the adjective in each phrase: <u>miniature</u> bogs, <u>drier</u> ground, <u>sepulchral</u> silence.

Activity Have students add one or more adjectives to complete each phrase.
1. _____ rains *(torrential)*
2. most _____ volcano *(destructive)*
3. produced a _____ display of lava *(stunning)* **L2**

Additional Resources

🖉 *Grammar and Language Transparency 30*

📘 *Grammar and Language Workbook,* p. 61

📘 *Grammar and Composition Handbook,* Lesson 1.4

📗 *Writer's Choice,* Lesson 10.4

Responding to Literature

Personal Response

What fact or image disturbed you the most as you read this selection? Explain in your journal.

——— ANALYZING LITERATURE ———

RECALL AND INTERPRET

1. What does pilot Manuel Cervero experience as he flies over Nevado del Ruiz? What is **ironic** about the author's reference to the "rebirth" of the volcano? Use specific details to support your answer. (See page R6.)

2. Describe the initial and secondary eruptions of Nevado del Ruiz. How do they compare with the other historic disasters mentioned?

3. Summarize what happens after the double eruption. What does the author seem to suggest about the government officials' response?

4. Describe what Armero looks like after the mudslide. In your opinion, are the dead better off than some of the survivors? Give reasons for your answer.

EVALUATE AND CONNECT

5. Look back at the Focus Activity on page 354. As you read this selection, how did you respond to the tragedy the author describes? To the fact that the rescue workers risked their own lives to save others? Explain.

6. How does the writer's use of specific measurements (for example, "a 17,716-ft.-high . . . volcano") affect your understanding of what the disaster was like?

7. Why, do you think, did the author choose Omaira Sanchez to illustrate the plight of the trapped survivors?

8. Do you think that the title of this selection is appropriate? Explain.

Literary ELEMENTS

Description

To enliven an expository essay such as "Colombia's Mortal Agony," a writer may use vivid descriptions of an event. For example, George Russell begins his account of a disastrous volcanic eruption by describing what Manuel Cervero sees, smells, and feels as he pilots an airplane seven thousand feet above the exploding volcano.

1. Why do you think Russell describes the pilot's experiences rather than stating that Nevado del Ruiz has erupted? What effect does this have on the reader?

2. Identify at least two other vivid descriptions that add interest to the essay. How does Russell make these descriptions come alive?

● See **Literary Terms Handbook,** p. R4.

——— EXTENDING YOUR RESPONSE ———

Literature Groups

Who's to Blame? Do you think that government officials could have done more to protect the people living near Nevado del Ruiz? What warnings did these officials have that a dangerous situation existed? How did they respond to these warnings? Do you think that the people living near the volcano should have been more aware of the dangers they faced? Discuss and debate these issues in your group. Share your ideas with the class.

Creative Writing

In Memoriam Imagine that a memorial is being built to commemorate the victims of the Nevado del Ruiz eruption. Write the text for a plaque that will be displayed at the memorial. Include the date of the disaster, the number of people killed, and the names of the towns where they lived. Add any additional information that you consider interesting and important.

💾 **Save your work for your portfolio.**

THE SHORT STORY 🦋 359

Responding to the Selection

Personal Response

A written response is asked for here. You may or may not want to have journal entries discussed, depending on your policy about the privacy of journals. You could ask for oral comments from volunteers, however.

——— ANALYZING LITERATURE ———

1. The pilot experiences the actual eruption of the volcano. Ironically, with the rebirth of the volcano comes the death of over 20,000 people. The entire town of Armero disappeared; the ash obscured the sun; the temperature dropped 22°—all signs of death.

2. The first eruption was a reddish illumination, a fiery blast, followed by a shower of ash. The eruptions would rate as some of the deadliest, on a par with some of the more destructive natural disasters in recent history.

3. An avalanche of ash and mud covers several towns and kills over 20,000 people. The author suggests that officials knew there was danger but did little.

4. The town has vanished. It is "one big beach of mud." Students will have varying opinions about whether the dead or the survivors were better off. They might note the suffering the survivors endured before either dying or being rescued.

5. Reactions of the students will vary. Most will indicate that they were horrified and felt grief and sympathy for the people. Most will say they think the rescue workers were extraordinary heroes.

6. The specific details help the reader understand and visualize just how devastating the destruction was.

7. Sanchez was the most famous of the people trapped. Her plight received the most attention. She was a young girl with her whole life ahead of her. People could identify with her and want her to be rescued.

8. The title is appropriate. The number of people killed and the amount of destruction were cause for great grief and agony.

✔ ASSESSMENT OPTIONS

📁 *Quick Checks,* p. 31

📁 *Selection and Theme Assessment,* pp. 59–60

📁 *Performance Assessment,* p. 30

💾 *Testmaker*

LITERARY ELEMENTS

1. It makes the beginning more interesting and exciting and helps the reader experience the eruption.

2. Students might choose the descriptions of the mud covering the village and the people trapped in the mud. Russell uses precise, vivid words.

Additional Resources

✏ *Literary Elements Transparency 31*

COMPARING
selections

Objective
- To compare a short story and a magazine article that deal with the theme of challenges and consequences

COMPARE DESCRIPTIONS

1. Both focus on the destruction caused by the mudslide. Allende uses more figurative language. Russell uses more specific details.
2. Encourage students to consider the differences between a narrative and a news article in making their decision.

COMPARE VIEWPOINTS

Students' dialogues should
- describe specific events.
- sound like a natural conversation.

COMPARE FACT AND FICTION

Ask students why they think the author changed the details. They will probably conclude that the changes helped her tell the story more dramatically. She wanted readers to be able to see the events through the eyes of a victim and a rescuer. **COLLAB. LEARN.**

Additional Resources
📁 *Literature Groups Sourcebook*

Teaching Options

COMPARING
selections

And of Clay Are We Created

and   COLOMBIA'S MORTAL AGONY

COMPARE **DESCRIPTIONS**

Both Allende and Russell describe the actual eruption of the volcano and the massive mudslide that followed.

1. How are these descriptions alike? How do the two descriptions differ?
2. In your opinion, which selection more effectively conveys the horror and terrible suffering caused by the volcano's eruption? Give reasons for your answer.

COMPARE **VIEWPOINTS**

Imagine that Rolf Carlé, Allende's fictional reporter, and Rosa Maria Henao, the survivor quoted by Russell, meet a week after the eruption.

- Write a dialogue in which Carlé and Henao compare their experiences and share their feelings about the catastrophe.
- Practice the dialogue with a classmate. Then present it to the class.

COMPARE **FACT AND FICTION**

Both selections are about the tragic plight of Omaira Sanchez.

- With a partner, reread Russell's account of what happens to Omaira Sanchez. Record the details in a chart like the one shown.
- Complete the chart by filling in the appropriate details from Allende's story.
- Compare the details in the Fact and Fiction columns of the chart. Discuss why you think Allende chose to change certain details.

	Fact: Russell	Fiction: Allende
Girl's name	Omaira Sanchez	Azucena
Age		
Predicament		
Attempted solution(s)		
Resolution		

💼 **PORTFOLIO OPTIONS** _____

Effective Dialogue Ask students to look at the dialogues they wrote and answer these questions:
- What did I do to vary characters' dialogue so that their speech expressed their individuality?
- Do their words accurately match their emotions?

Suggest that students staple their analyses to their dialogues and put the materials in their portfolios. At a later time, they might review their comments. **L2**

Additional Resources
📁 *Writing Assessment and Portfolio Management,* pp. 20–22

Writing Skills

Writing Dialogue

Dialogue—conversation between characters in a literary work—can serve many purposes in a short story. Writers may use dialogue to move the plot along, to show characters' personalities or relationships, to provide a sense of time and place, or to foreshadow certain events. Dialogue also can be used to draw attention to important moments in a story. Notice how Isabel Allende uses dialogue in this passage from "And of Clay Are We Created."

> A military doctor came to examine the girl, and observed that her heart was functioning well and that if she did not get too cold she could survive the night.
> "Hang on, Azucena, we'll have the pump tomorrow," Rolf Carlé tried to console her.
> "Don't leave me alone," she begged.
> "No, of course I won't leave you."

Allende quotes the doctor indirectly; she tells the reader what he says but does not repeat his exact words. Then she uses dialogue to draw attention to Rolf and Azucena. These direct quotations provide information about the characters' relationship. They show that Rolf is doing his best to help Azucena survive and that she desperately wants him to stay with her.

The words used to identify each speaker are called **tag lines.** In the dialogue above, the tag line *she begged* not only tells the reader who said the words *"Don't leave me alone,"* it also gives information about Azucena's emotional state. Adding such information can make a scene more vivid. Sometimes, however, if the identity of the speaker is obvious, the tag line can be omitted.

Follow these guidelines when you write dialogue:

- Make sure your dialogue has a purpose.
- Make your dialogue sound natural. Have your characters use words and phrases that they'd be likely to use if they were real people.
- Make your dialogue sound like real conversation by including interruptions and pauses where they might naturally occur.
- Make your dialogue easy to follow by using correct paragraphing and punctuation.

EXERCISE

Write a dialogue between two characters who are unlike each other. For example, your characters might be an assertive girl and a timid one. Use the dialogue to reveal each character's personality.

Writing Skills

Objective

- To write a dialogue that reveals characters' personalities

Teaching Strategies

Point out that for dialogue to be effective, it must be true to character; that is, it must sound and read like something a character might actually say. You might want to have students transcribe a portion of dialogue they heard recently in a setting such as on the school bus or in the cafeteria. Have students briefly evaluate why the dialogue sounds natural.

Exercise

Students' dialogues should
- reveal an identifiable personality for each character.
- sound natural.
- use correct paragraphing and punctuation.

Additional Resources

📁 ***Writing and Proofreading Practice,*** pp. 1–6, 13–14

🖋 ***Writing and Proofreading Transparency*** *1–6, 13–14, 31–32*

📓 ***Writer's Choice,*** Lesson 21.9

Grammar and Language *Minilesson*

Punctuating Dialogue Point out how the quotation on page 355 is punctuated.

Activity Write this dialogue without punctuation or paragraphing and ask students to supply both:
"Do not worry," the reporter said./"I am not worried," answered the child. "You are with me."/"If you have hope," he said, "it will help." **L2**

Additional Resources

🖋 ***Grammar and Language Transparency 31***

📓 ***Grammar and Language Workbook,*** p. 271

📓 ***Grammar and Composition Handbook,*** Lesson 11.9

📓 ***Writer's Choice,*** Lesson 21.9

Objectives

- To read and analyze a short story in which a woman confronts her past
- To identify examples of irony
- To write a paragraph describing a foil in the story

Skills

Reading/Thinking: Inferring; Drawing Conclusions; Logical Reasoning; Comparing and Contrasting; Activating Prior Knowledge
Writing: Continuation
Vocabulary: Etymology
Grammar/Language: Irregular Verbs; Coordinate Adjectives
Listening/Speaking: Dialogue; Interview
Life Skills: Problem Solving
Collaboration: Literature Groups

Motivating
→OPTIONS

Selection Focus Transparency 32: Discuss with students what the quotations say about the importance of the past in shaping the future.

Focus Activity: Discuss what things a former prisoner in a camp might value that the average person might not.

⚹ —Before You Read—
Winter Night

FOCUS ACTIVITY

Think back to late winter afternoons when you were a child. How did you feel at the early approach of darkness? Fearful? Apprehensive? Calm?

SKETCH IT! Using any colors you choose, try to re-create your childhood impressions in an abstract or realistic drawing. Somewhere on your drawing, write several words that describe your memories.

SETTING A PURPOSE Read to see what one child experiences on a winter evening.

BACKGROUND

The Time and Place
This story takes place in New York City, probably around the mid-1940s near the end of World War II (1939–1945).

Did You Know?

- During World War II, American women played a key role in the war effort by working in defense plants and in other businesses, replacing the millions of men who had gone off to war.

- Near the end of the war, the horrors of Nazi concentration camps began to come to light. In these camps, Nazi dictator Adolf Hitler carried out his plan to "purify" Europe by killing millions of Jews, Gypsies, and members of other ethnic groups.

VOCABULARY PREVIEW

abeyance (ə bā′ əns) *n.* a state of temporary inactivity; p. 363
reprieve (ri prēv′) *v.* to give temporary relief, as from something unpleasant or difficult; p. 363
obscurity (əb skyoor′ ə tē) *n.* darkness; dimness; p. 364
derision (di rizh′ ən) *n.* mockery; ridicule; p. 364
singular (sing′ gyə lər) *adj.* unusual or remarkable; p. 366

Meet Kay Boyle

By the age of seventeen, Kay Boyle had already written a novel, short stories, and a great deal of poetry. Boyle, who lived in Europe during much of her childhood, returned there with her French husband in the early 1920s and stayed for almost twenty years. During the late 1930s, she and her family moved from one European country to another as they fled from the threat of Nazism. In keeping with her belief that writers should "write of their times and of the issues of their times," Boyle often portrayed people looking for love in a chaotic world.

Kay Boyle was born in St. Paul, Minnesota, in 1902 and died in 1992. This story was first published in The New Yorker *magazine in 1946.*

RESOURCE MANAGER

Lesson Planning Resource
The *Unit One Planning Guide* (pp. 270–277) provides additional lesson notes and reduced versions of all print resources.

📁 **Other Print Resources**
- Active Reading Guide, p. 32
- Vocabulary Practice, p. 31
- Reading Workbook, p. 39–40
- Grammar and Language Workbook, pp. 143, 253
- Grammar and Composition Handbook, Lesson 5.2, 11.6

- Quick Checks, p. 32
- Selection and Theme Assessment, pp. 61–62
- Performance Assessment, p. 31
- Spanish Summaries, p. 32
- Spanish Translations
- Inclusion Strategies
- English Language Learners Sourcebook

 Transparencies
- Selection Focus 32

- Literary Elements 32
- Grammar and Language 32

Technology

🎧 Audio Library
🎧 Spanish Audio Library
💻 Glencoe Literature Web Site
💾 Testmaker

WINTER NIGHT

Kay Boyle ॰

THERE IS A TIME OF APPREHENSION which begins with the beginning of darkness, and to which only the speech of love can lend security. It is there, in abeyance, at the end of every day, not urgent enough to be given the name of fear but rather of concern for how the hours are to be reprieved from fear, and those who have forgotten how it was when they were children can remember nothing of this. It may begin around five o'clock on a winter afternoon when the light outside is dying in the windows. At that hour the New York apartment in which Felicia lived was filled with shadows, and the little girl would wait alone in the living room, looking out at the winter-stripped trees that stood black in the park against the isolated ovals of unclean snow. Now it was January, and the day had been a cold one; the water of the artificial lake was frozen fast, but because of the cold and the coming darkness, the skaters had ceased to move across its surface. The street that lay between the park and the apartment house was wide, and the two-way streams of cars and busses, some with their headlamps already shining, advanced and halted, halted and poured swiftly on to the tempo of the traffic signals' altering lights. The time of apprehension had set in, and Felicia, who was seven, stood at the window in the evening and waited before she asked the question. When the signals below would change from red to green again,

Vocabulary

abeyance (ə bā′ əns) *n.* a state of temporary inactivity
reprieve (ri prēv′) *v.* to give temporary relief, as from something unpleasant or difficult

THE SHORT STORY ❧ 363

SUMMARY

Night falls and a young girl waits for her mother to come home. As in many nights past, the child is left in the care of a baby-sitter. Unlike other sitters, this woman has a special interest and affection for the child, for the child reminds her of another little girl she cared for in a Nazi prison camp. Throughout the evening, she and the child bond as the woman tells her the story of the little girl and pours out the love she felt for the lost child to the one now in her care.

📁 *Spanish Summaries,* p. 32

A Active Reading

QUESTION Ask students to read the first eighteen lines. Let them formulate a list of questions they may have, based on the title and the opening lines. List the questions on the board. After the story is read, refer to them and have them answered.

Additional Resources

📁 *Active Reading Guide,* p. 32
🎧 *Audio Library*
🎧 *Spanish Audio Library*

Teaching Options

CONNECTING TO OTHER SELECTIONS

The chart at the right shows three ways to connect "Winter Night" to selections in this book.

For specific teaching strategies, see the *Unit One Planning Guide,* pages 273–274.

Connection	Title
Life Skills: Teaching and Mentoring	→ "Catch the Moon," p. 63
Thematic: Remembering	→ from *Farewell to Manzanar,* p. 460
Literary: Tone	→ "Tuesday Siesta," p. 189

ABSTRACT V. CONCRETE LANGUAGE
On page 363, the author refers to "the speech of love." Ask students what the speech of love might be. *(The speech of love might literally mean words such as "I love you" or it might be hugs or gestures, such as listening.)*

C Critical Thinking

INFERRING Discuss why Felicia is apprehensive and what she is reluctant to ask (p. 363). What does Felicia really want? *(Young children often feel anxious when it is dark and their parents are not home. The question Felicia seems reluctant to ask is, "When is my mother coming home?" The one thing she wants is her mother.)*

D Active Reading

QUESTION The housekeeper's comment about "buying your own freedom" should give students a clue about the mother. Ask what the phrase means. Use the model to demonstrate how to question.

Model: The idea of buying one's freedom seems to indicate that both women are slaves to something and want to get away. The housekeeper seems to be saying that getting paid for work gives her and the mother a way to buy freedom—a way to get away from their troubles. I think to get freedom, they have to work hard. I think they may be trading one form of "slavery" for another.

Teaching Options

WINTER NIGHT

Did You Know?
A *double-decker bus* has two decks, or floors, each containing passenger seats. Often, the upper deck is roofless and has low walls.

or when the double-decker bus would turn the corner below, she would ask it. The words of it were already there, tentative in her mouth, when the answer came from the far end of the hall.

"Your mother," said the voice among the sound of kitchen things, "she telephoned up before you came in from nursery school. She won't be back in time for supper. I was to tell you a sitter was coming in from the sitting parents' place."[1]

Felicia turned back from the window into the <u>obscurity</u> of the living room, and she looked toward the open door, and into the hall beyond it where the light from the kitchen fell in a clear yellow angle across the wall and onto the strip of carpet. Her hands were cold, and she put them in her jacket pockets as she walked carefully across the living-room rug and stopped at the edge of light.

"Will she be home late?" she said.

For a moment there was the sound of water running in the kitchen, a long way away, and then the sound of the water ceased, and the high, Southern voice went on:

"She'll come home when she gets ready to come home. That's all I have to say. If she wants to spend two dollars and fifty cents and ten cents' carfare on top of that three or four nights out of the week for a sitting parent to come in here and sit, it's her own business. It certainly ain't nothing to do with you or me."

---

1. Today, a *sitting parents' place* would be called a "baby-sitters' agency" or "child-care agency."

She makes her money, just like the rest of us does. She works all day down there in the office, or whatever it is, just like the rest of us works, and she's entitled to spend her money like she wants to spend it. There's no law in the world against buying your own freedom. Your mother and me, we're just buying our own freedom, that's all we're doing. And we're not doing nobody no harm."

"Do you know who she's having supper with?" said Felicia from the edge of dark. There was one more step to take, and then she would be standing in the light that fell on the strip of carpet, but she did not take the step.

"Do I know who she's having supper with?" the voice cried out in what might have been <u>derision</u>, and there was the sound of dishes striking the metal ribs of the drainboard by the sink. "Maybe it's Mr. Van Johnson, or Mr. Frank Sinatra,[2] or maybe it's just the Duke of Wincers[3] for the evening. All I know is you're having soft-boiled egg and spinach and applesauce for supper, and you're going to have it quick now because the time is getting away."

The voice from the kitchen had no name. It was as variable as the faces and figures of the women who came and sat in the evenings. Month by month the voice in the kitchen altered to another voice, and the sitting parents were no more than lonely aunts of an evening or two who sometimes returned and sometimes did not to this apartment in which they had sat before. Nobody stayed

---

2. *Van Johnson* and *Frank Sinatra* were popular movie stars in the 1940s.
3. *Wincers* is the character's pronunciation of "Windsor." In 1936, King Edward VIII gave up the British throne to marry an American divorcee. He was then given the title Duke of Windsor.

Vocabulary
obscurity (əb skyoor′ ə tē) *n.* darkness; dimness
derision (di rizh′ ən) *n.* mockery; ridicule

MEETING INDIVIDUAL NEEDS — ENGLISH LANGUAGE LEARNERS

Historical Context The baby-sitter is referring to the Nazi concentration camps of World War II. Work with the class to generate a list of questions about the camps such as these: *Why were people sent there? How were they sent?*

Activity Have English language learners discuss the questions in small groups that include students proficient in English. Encourage group members to share what they know or have read or heard about such camps. Be sensitive to the fact that some students or their families may have experienced these or similar kinds of camps.

Additional Resources
📁 *English Language Learners Sourcebook*

anywhere very long any more, Felicia's mother told her. It was part of the time in which you lived, and part of the life of the city, but when the fathers came back, all this would be miraculously changed. Perhaps you would live in a house again, a small one, with fir trees on either side of the short brick walk, and Father would drive up every night from the station just after darkness set in. When Felicia thought of this, she stepped quickly into the clear angle of light, and she left the dark of the living room behind her and ran softly down the hall.

The drop-leaf table[4] stood in the kitchen between the refrigerator and the sink, and Felicia sat down at the place that was set. The voice at the sink was speaking still, and while Felicia ate it did not cease to speak until the bell of the front door rang abruptly. The girl walked around the table and went down the hall, wiping her dark palms in her apron, and, from the drop-leaf table, Felicia watched her step from the angle of light into darkness and open the door.

"You put in an early appearance," the girl said, and the woman who had rung the bell came into the hall. The door closed behind her, and the girl showed her into the living room, and lit the lamp on the bookcase, and the shadows were suddenly bleached away. But when the girl turned, the woman turned from the living room too and followed her, humbly and in silence, to the threshold of the kitchen. "Sometimes they keep me standing around waiting after it's time for me to be getting on

Purple Wind, 1995. Alex Katz. Oil on canvas, 90 x 66 in. Courtesy, Marlborough Gallery, New York.

Viewing the painting: Do you think the mood of this scene reflects the mood of the story? Why or why not?

home, the sitting parents do," the girl said, and she picked up the last two dishes from the table and put them in the sink. The woman who stood in the doorway was a small woman, and when she undid the white silk scarf from around her head, Felicia saw that her hair was black. She wore it parted in the middle, and it had not been cut, but was drawn back loosely into a knot behind her head. She had very clean white gloves on, and her face was pale, and there was a look of sorrow in her soft black eyes. "Sometimes I have to stand out there in the hall with my hat and coat on, waiting for the sitting parents to turn up," the girl said, and, as she turned on the water in the sink, the contempt

---

4. A *drop-leaf table* has hinged sections that can be folded down when not in use.

THE SHORT STORY 🐾 365

E **Critical Thinking**

INFERRING Ask students to suggest words that describe how Felicia feels and what she wishes. *(lonely, wistful, sad; She wants an ideal home where her dad would come home every night, and everyone would be happy.)*

VIEWING THE PAINTING

Alex Katz (1927–) is an American artist who uses a simplified style of painting. The objects in his works are usually large in scale, and, as a result, seem to leap off the canvas at the viewer.

Viewing Response *The dark night creates a mood of apprehension, just like Felicia might be feeling because she doesn't know who her "sitting parent" will be. The painting also conveys a mood of warmth and comfort in the lighted windows, like the cozy indoors of Felicia's apartment.*

F **Author's Craft**

CHARACTER DESCRIPTION The appearance of the baby-sitter is described in detail, especially seemingly unimportant things like the way her hair is parted. Discuss why the author chose to do this. *(Such a description clues the reader that this person is going to be important to the story and that you, as a reader, will want to know about her. She will not be one of the "variable" ones.)*

MEETING INDIVIDUAL NEEDS

MULTIPLE LEARNING STYLES

Spatial Spatial learners sometimes find it helpful to literally draw a picture of what they are reading. The text on page 363 contains descriptions that offer an opportunity for spatial learners to draw and, in the process, help fellow classmates picture the text.

Activity Suggest that students choose the description of the table and kitchen arrangement or of the baby-sitter to draw. The kitchen scene could be done as a floor plan, while the baby-sitter might be shown as a portrait. Students can choose other descriptions in the story if they prefer. When the drawings are completed, have each student show his or her drawing to the class while a classmate reads the description on which it was based. **L1**

G Literary Elements

CHARACTER Discuss how the reader knows that the baby-sitter has had some kind of great sadness involving a child. *(The baby-sitter does not want to hurry the child through her milk, indicating she wants to linger with the child. She offers to wash the glass and clean the table—something she is not required to do. The woman's attention is clearly focused on the child. The author describes the unspoken grief in the woman's eyes.)*

H Active Reading

PREDICT The author explains what the normal bedtime routine is and then indicates that this time things are different. Invite students to predict what they think will happen. *(Accept all reasonable answers. Sample: The woman will explain why she is sad and how a child figures into that.)*

VIEWING THE PAINTING

Alicia Carletti uses a realistic style in this painting to depict the child and a fanciful style to illustrate the background. The title of the painting could also be "Once upon a time."

Viewing Response *The girl looks unhappy, which is how Felicia feels about the sitting parents.*

Teaching Options

---

she had for them hung on the kitchen air. "But you're ahead of time," she said, and she held the dishes, first one and then the other, under the flow of steaming water.

The woman in the doorway wore a neat black coat, not a new-looking coat, and it had no fur on it, but it had a smooth velvet collar and velvet lapels. She did not move, or smile, and she gave no sign that she had heard the girl speaking above the sound of water at the sink. She simply stood looking at Felicia, who sat at the table with the milk in her glass not finished yet.

"Are you the child?" she said at last, and her voice was low, and the pronunciation of the words a little strange.

"Yes, this here's Felicia," the girl said, and the dark hands dried the dishes and put them away. "You drink up your milk quick now, Felicia, so's I can rinse your glass."

"I will wash the glass," said the woman. "I would like to wash the glass for her," and Felicia sat looking across the table at the face in the doorway that was filled with such unspoken grief. "I will wash the glass for her and clean off the table," the woman was saying quietly. "When the child is finished, she will show me where her night things are."

A Long Time Ago (Hace Mucho Tiempo), 1995. Alicia Carletti. Oil on canvas, 100 x 80 cm. Zurbaran Galeria, Buenos Aires.
Viewing the painting: How does the girl's expression reflect how Felicia felt when the sitting parents come?

"The others, they wouldn't do anything like that," the girl said, and she hung the dish-cloth over the rack. "They wouldn't put their hand to housework, the sitting parents. That's where they got the name for them," she said.

Whenever the front door closed behind the girl in the evening, it would usually be that the sitting parent who was there would take up a book of fairy stories and read aloud for a while to Felicia; or else would settle herself in the big chair in the living room and begin to tell the words of a story in drowsiness to her, while Felicia took off her clothes in the bedroom, and folded them, and put her pajamas on, and brushed her teeth, and did her hair. But this time, that was not the way it happened. Instead, the woman sat down on the other chair at the kitchen table, and she began at once to speak, not of good fairies or bad, or of animals endowed with human speech, but to speak quietly, in spite of the eagerness behind her words, of a thing that seemed of <u>singular</u> importance to her.

"It is strange that I should have been sent here tonight," she said, her eyes moving slowly from feature to feature of Felicia's face,

---

Vocabulary
singular (sing′ gyə lər) *adj.* unusual or remarkable

MEETING INDIVIDUAL NEEDS INCLUSION STRATEGIES

Less-Proficient Readers Point out that an author sets the stage for what is going to happen next by providing certain clues. In the story, the author contrasts the ordinary events of a typical evening with clues and hints that things will not be the same. If necessary, explain that a contrast is a way of showing how two things or events are different.

Activity Let students work in groups of three. Have groups discuss the differences in the nightly routine. You might wish to invite groups to present a dramatization of the two bedtime routines to the class. **L1 COLLAB. LEARN.**

Additional Resources
📁 *Inclusion Strategies*

"for you look like a child that I knew once, and this is the anniversary of that child."

"Did she have hair like mine?" Felicia asked quickly, and she did not keep her eyes fixed on the unfinished glass of milk in shyness any more.

"Yes, she did. She had hair like yours," said the woman, and her glance paused for a moment on the locks which fell straight and thick on the shoulders of Felicia's dress. It may have been that she thought to stretch out her hand and touch the ends of Felicia's hair, for her fingers stirred as they lay clasped together on the table, and then they relapsed into passivity again. "But it is not the hair alone, it is the delicacy of your face, too, and your eyes the same, filled with the same spring lilac color," the woman said, pronouncing the words carefully. "She had little coats of golden fur on her arms and legs," she said, "and when we were closed up there, the lot of us in the cold, I used to make her laugh when I told her that the fur that was so pretty, like a little fawn's skin on her arms, would always help to keep her warm."

"And did it keep her warm?" asked Felicia, and she gave a little jerk of laughter as she looked down at her own legs hanging under the table, with the bare calves thin and covered with a down of hair.

"It did not keep her warm enough," the woman said, and now the mask of grief had come back upon her face. "So we used to take everything we could spare from ourselves, and we would sew them into cloaks and other kinds of garments for her and for the other children. . . ."

"Was it a school?" said Felicia when the woman's voice had ceased to speak.

"No," said the woman softly, "it was not a school, but still there were a lot of children there. It was a camp—that was the name the place had; it was a camp. It was a place where they put people until they could decide what was to be done with them." She sat with her hands clasped, silent a moment, looking at Felicia. "That little dress you have on," she said, not saying the words to anybody, scarcely saying them aloud. "Oh, she would have liked that little dress, the little buttons shaped like hearts, and the white collar—"

"I have four school dresses," Felicia said. "I'll show them to you. How many dresses did she have?"

"Well, there, you see, there in the camp," said the woman, "she did not have any dresses except the little skirt and the pullover. That was all she had. She had brought just a handkerchief of her belongings with her, like everybody else—just enough for three days away from home was what they told us, so she did not have enough to last the winter. But she had her ballet slippers," the woman said, and her clasped fingers did not move. "She had brought them because she thought during her three days away from home she would have the time to practice her ballet."

"I've been to the ballet," Felicia said suddenly, and she said it so eagerly that she stuttered a little as the words came out of her mouth. She slipped quickly down from the chair and went around the table to where the woman sat. Then she took one of the woman's hands away from the other that held it fast, and she pulled her toward the door. "Come into the living room and I'll do a pirouette[5] for you," she said, and then she

---

5. A *pirouette* (pir´ o͞o et´) is a rapid full turn done while standing on the toes of one foot.

Critical Thinking

DRAWING CONCLUSIONS The reader knows that the woman, the mothers, and the children were in a camp. Discuss possible reasons why they were there. *(The people were probably Jewish. Jewish people were those most frequently put into camps and put to death.)*

Active Reading

EVALUATE Under the circumstances, why doesn't the woman simply tell the little girl what happened to the other girl's mother? *(The woman may realize that the child is too young to hear such things, or she may realize that the child may fear that her own mother will never come back.)*

Literary Elements

IRONY The woman tells Felicia that the little girl's mother and other mothers went away. Felicia does not completely understand. Ask students to discuss what "went away" actually means and how they know Felicia does not understand the meaning. Also discuss why this is an example of irony. *(In this case, "went away" means the women were taken away and put to death. Felicia can only understand a mother going away in terms of what she knows. As a result, she asks if the mothers went out to supper, if the girl's mother came back late, and if she took a taxi. The dramatic irony exists because the reader knows what actually happened to the mothers, while this child's idea of a mother going away is so different.)*

Teaching Options

stopped speaking, her eyes halted on the woman's face. "Did she—did the little girl—could she do a pirouette very well?" she said.

"Yes, she could. At first she could," said the woman, and Felicia felt uneasy now at the sound of sorrow in her words. "But after that she was hungry. She was hungry all winter," she said in a low voice. "We were all hungry, but the children were the hungriest. Even now," she said, and her voice went suddenly savage, "when I see milk like that, clean, fresh milk standing in a glass, I want to cry out loud, I want to beat my hands on the table, because it did not have to be . . ." She had drawn her fingers abruptly away from Felicia now, and Felicia stood before her, cast off, forlorn, alone again in the time of apprehension. "That was three years ago," the woman was saying, and one hand was lifted, as in weariness, to shade her face. "It was somewhere else, it was in another country," she said, and behind her hand her eyes were turned upon the substance of a world in which Felicia had played no part.

"Did—did the little girl cry when she was hungry?" Felicia asked, and the woman shook her head.

"Sometimes she cried," she said, "but not very much. She was very quiet. One night when she heard the other children crying, she said to me, 'You know, they are not crying because they want something to eat. They are crying because their mothers have gone away.'"

"Did the mothers have to go out to supper?" Felicia asked, and she watched the woman's face for the answer.

"No," said the woman. She stood up from her chair, and now that she put her hand on the little girl's shoulder, Felicia was taken into the sphere of love and intimacy again. "Shall we go into the other room, and you will do your pirouette for me?" the woman said, and they went from the kitchen and down the strip

of carpet on which the clear light fell. In the front room, they paused hand in hand in the glow of the shaded lamp, and the woman looked about her, at the books, the low tables with the magazines and ash trays on them, the vase of roses on the piano, looking with dark, scarcely seeing eyes at these things that had no reality at all. It was only when she saw the little white clock on the mantelpiece that she gave any sign, and then she said quickly: "What time does your mother put you to bed?"

Felicia waited a moment, and in the interval of waiting the woman lifted one hand and, as if in reverence, touched Felicia's hair.

"What time did the little girl you knew in the other place go to bed?" Felicia asked.

"Ah, God, I do not know, I do not remember," the woman said.

"Was she your little girl?" said Felicia softly, stubbornly.

"No," said the woman. "She was not mine. At least, at first she was not mine. She had a mother, a real mother, but the mother had to go away."

"Did she come back late?" asked Felicia.

"No, ah, no, she could not come back, she never came back," the woman said, and now she turned, her arm around Felicia's shoulders, and she sat down in the low soft chair. "Why am I saying all this to you, why am I doing it?" she cried out in grief, and she held Felicia close against her. "I had thought to speak of the anniversary to you, and that was all, and now I am saying these other things to you. Three years ago today, exactly, the little girl became my little girl because her mother went away. That is all there is to it. There is nothing more."

Felicia waited another moment, held close against the woman, and listening to the swift, strong heartbeats in the woman's breast.

"But the mother," she said then in a small, persistent voice, "did she take a taxi when she went?"

INTERDISCIPLINARY CONNECTION

History Students may be surprised to learn that during World War II, the United States also had camps. These camps—called internment camps—were set up to hold Asian Americans, primarily of Japanese descent. It was believed the people were a threat to the security of the United States, particularly the West Coast.

Activity Ask students to research these camps and find out where they were and what the conditions there were like. Also have them find out what has been done by the United States government in recent years to try to make up for these past events. Have students write their findings in a report. **L3**

Kay Boyle ∽

"This is the way it used to happen," said the woman, speaking in hopelessness and bitterness in the softly lighted room. "Every week they used to come into the place where we were and they would read a list of names out. Sometimes it would be the names of children they would read out, and then a little later they would have to go away. And sometimes it would be the grown people's names, the names of the mothers or big sisters, or other women's names. The men were not with us. The fathers were somewhere else, in another place."

"Yes," Felicia said. "I know."

"We had been there only a little while, maybe ten days or maybe not so long," the woman went on, holding Felicia against her still, "when they read the name of the little girl's mother out, and that afternoon they took her away."

"What did the little girl do?" Felicia said.

"She wanted to think up the best way of getting out so that she could go find her mother," said the woman, "but she could not think of anything good enough until the third or fourth day. And then she tied her ballet slippers up in the handkerchief again, and she went up to the guard standing at the door." The woman's voice was gentle, controlled

Lamplight with Dora, c. 1973. John Koch. Oil on Masonite, 7⅞ x 10 in. Private collection.

Viewing the painting: In your opinion, does the setting of this painting capture the setting of the story? Why or why not?

Literary Elements

IRONY When the woman says that the men were not with the women and children, Felicia indicates that she knows. Discuss how this is an example of irony. *(Felicia's dad seems to be off fighting the war. The men that the woman was referring to were prisoners in a camp.)*

Critical Thinking

INFERRING The other little girl wanted to think of a way to get out. Why did she want to get out? How is the girl like Felicia as it relates to the fate of her mother? *(The girl wants to be with her mother, so she wants to get out. Like Felicia, she does not realize what has happened to her mother.)*

VIEWING THE PAINTING

The works of American artist John Koch (1909–) often include realistic scenes of people in their homes. While the scenes portrayed show great detail, the people in the scenes often show little emotion. The effect is a mood of a sweet but sad sentimental reverie.

Viewing Response *The painting does resemble the setting, as described by the author—glow of shaded lamp, low table, nice furnishings.*

Listening and Speaking *Minilesson*

Dialogue The author uses dialogue to tell the reader what is being said. With students, generate a list of suggestions for how dialogue in a story can be read aloud to reflect the characters and the mood of the story. Lists might include these points:

• Use the tone and quality of the voice to differentiate between characters.

• Vary the speed and emphasis of the words to express the emotion of the moment.

• Use facial expressions and gestures to help get across the meaning.

Activity Have pairs of students prepare to read a dialogue between the two main characters in the story. Allow time for them to present their dialogues to the class. **L1** **COLLAB. LEARN.**

Active Reading

QUESTION Why has the author included the description of the girl talking to the guard about her ballet lesson? *(Revealing more of the girl's simpleness adds to the poignancy of the story. This is the girl's strategy— her solution to the problem of how to get out of the camp. In her mind, missing a ballet lesson and having to pay for it anyway is a perfectly good reason for being let out.)*

Critical Thinking

LOGICAL REASONING The woman told the child stories of the ballet. What does this tell the reader about the woman? *(It lets the reader know that the woman was probably educated and sophisticated. Few people would actually know the stories of the ballet unless they had taken ballet or been to the ballet.)*

Literary Elements

IRONY When the woman explains that the child could not wash or brush her teeth, Felicia wants to do the same. Discuss why this is an example of irony. Also, discuss why the woman said Felicia did not have to wash and brush her teeth. *(The child did not wash or brush her teeth because she could not. Felicia does not want to because she has to. Perhaps the woman says Felicia does not have to wash and brush her teeth because the woman is wise enough to know what is important and what is not in a given situation. Insisting on the washing and brushing teeth would probably have broken the mood.)*

---

now. "She asked the guard please to open the door so that she could go out. 'This is Thursday,' she said, 'and every Tuesday and Thursday I have my ballet lessons. If I miss a ballet lesson, they do not count the money off, so my mother would be just paying for nothing, and she cannot afford to pay for nothing. I missed my ballet lesson on Tuesday,' she said to the guard, 'and I must not miss it again today.'"

Felicia lifted her head from the woman's shoulder, and she shook her hair back and looked in question and wonder at the woman's face.

"And did the man let her go?" she said.

"No, he did not. He could not do that," said the woman. "He was a soldier and he had to do what he was told. So every evening after her mother went, I used to brush the little girl's hair for her," the woman went on saying. "And while I brushed it, I used to tell her the stories of the ballets. Sometimes I would begin with *Narcissus*,"[6] the woman said, and she parted Felicia's locks with her fingers, "so if you will go and get your brush now, I will tell it while I brush your hair."

"Oh, yes," said Felicia, and she made two whirls as she went quickly to the bedroom. On the way back, she stopped and held on to the piano with the fingers of one hand while she went up on her toes. "Did you see me? Did you see me standing on my toes?" she called

---

6. *Narcissus* is a ballet based on the Greek myth of Narcissus, who scorns all women, believing he is more beautiful than they. The goddess of love punishes him by making him fall in love with his own reflection in a pool.

---

to the woman, and the woman sat smiling in love and contentment at her.

"Yes, wonderful, really wonderful," she said. "I am sure I have never seen anyone do it so well." Felicia came spinning toward her, whirling in pirouette after pirouette, and she flung herself down in the chair close to her, with her thin bones pressed against the woman's soft, wide hip. The woman took the silver-backed, monogrammed brush and the tortoise-shell comb in her hands, and now she began to brush Felicia's hair. "We did not have any soap at all and not very much water to wash in, so I never could fix her as nicely and prettily as I wanted to," she said, and the brush stroked regularly, carefully down, caressing the shape of Felicia's head.

"If there wasn't very much water, then how did she do her teeth?" Felicia said.

"She did not do her teeth," said the woman, and she drew the comb through Felicia's hair. "There were not any toothbrushes or tooth paste, or anything like that."

Felicia waited a moment, constructing the unfamiliar scene of it in silence, and then she asked the tentative question.

"Do I have to do my teeth tonight?" she said.

"No," said the woman, and she was thinking of something else, "you do not have to do your teeth."

"If I am your little girl tonight, can I pretend there isn't enough water to wash?" said Felicia.

"Yes," said the woman, "you can pretend that if you like. You do not have to wash," she said, and the comb passed lightly through Felicia's hair.

"Will you tell me the story of the ballet?"

Felicia came spinning toward her, whirling in pirouette after pirouette.

Teaching Options

Grammar and Language *Minilesson*

Irregular Verbs Write these headings on the board: *Base Form, Past Form, Past Participle.* Write these verbs under the heading *Base Form: be, do, eat, find, get, hold, say, speak, take, write.* Explain that each word is an irregular verb. Remind students that irregular verbs have special ways of forming their past and participial forms. Let volunteers fill in the correct forms for each verb.

Activity Write the sentences on the board. Have students write the correct past tense forms of each verb in parentheses.
1. The people on the trains (find) pieces of paper and sent notes. *(found)*
2. The mother (write) a special note. *(wrote)*
3. The note (say) good-by to the girl. *(said)*
L1

Additional Resources

📖 *Grammar and Language Transparency 32*

📖 *Grammar and Language Workbook,* p. 143

📖 *Grammar and Composition Handbook,* Lesson 5.2

📖 *Writer's Choice,* Lesson 15.2

said Felicia, and the rhythm of the brushing was like the soft, slow rocking of sleep.

"Yes," said the woman. "In the first one, the place is a forest glade with little pale birches growing in it, and they have green veils over their faces and green veils drifting from their fingers, because it is the spring-time. There is the music of a flute," said the woman's voice softly, softly, "and creatures of the wood are dancing—"

"But the mother," Felicia said as suddenly as if she had been awaked from sleep. "What did the little girl's mother say when she didn't do her teeth and didn't wash at night?"

"The mother was not there, you remember," said the woman, and the brush moved steadily in her hand. "But she did send one little letter back. Sometimes the people who went away were able to do that. The mother wrote it in a train, standing up in a car that had no seats," she said, and she might have been telling the story of the ballet still, for her voice was gentle and the brush did not falter on Felicia's hair. "There were perhaps a great many other people standing up in the train with her, perhaps all trying to write their little letters on the bits of paper they had managed to hide on them, or that they had found in forgotten corners as they traveled. When they had written their letters, then they must try to slip them out through the boards of the car in which they journeyed, standing up," said the woman, "and these letters fell down on the tracks under the train, or they were blown into the fields or onto the country roads, and if it was a kind person who picked them up, he would seal them in envelopes and send them to where they were addressed to go. So a letter came back like this from the little girl's mother,"

the woman said, and the brush followed the comb, the comb the brush in steady pursuit through Felicia's hair. "It said good-by to the little girl, and it said please to take care of her. It said: 'Whoever reads this letter in the camp, please take good care of my little girl for me, and please have her tonsils looked at by a doctor if this is possible to do.'"

"And then," said Felicia softly, persis-tently, "what happened to the little girl?"

"I do not know. I cannot say," the woman said. But now the brush and comb had ceased to move, and in the silence Felicia turned her thin, small body on the chair, and she and the woman suddenly put their arms around each other. "They must all be asleep now, all of them," the woman said, and in the silence that fell on them again, they held each other closer. "They must be quietly asleep somewhere, and not crying all night because they are hungry and because they are cold. For three years I have been saying 'They must all be asleep, and the cold and the hunger and the seasons or night or day or nothing matters to them—'"

It was after midnight when Felicia's mother put her key in the lock of the front door, and pushed it open, and stepped into the hallway. She walked quickly to the living room, and just across the threshold she slipped the three blue foxskins from her shoulders and dropped them, with her little velvet bag, upon the chair. The room was quiet, so quiet that she could hear the sound of breathing in it, and no one spoke to her in greeting as she crossed toward the bedroom door. And then, as startling as a slap across her delicately tinted face, she saw the woman lying sleeping on the divan, and Felicia, in her school dress still, asleep within the woman's arms.

QUESTION The woman says she does not know what happened to the little girl in spite of the fact that she cared for her on a daily basis. How could this be so? *(Either the woman or the girl might have been taken from the camp to some other location.)*

T **Critical Thinking**

DRAWING CONCLUSIONS The woman tells Felicia that the children are asleep. What does she mean? Why does she use the term *asleep*? *(She means they are dead. Words like* asleep *and* rest *are euphemisms for death.)*

Thematic Focus

Challenges and Consequences Ask students to choose any one of the characters in the story and to iden-tify the challenges that person faced and the consequences, or results, of those challenges.

✓ASSESSMENT OPTIONS

📂 *Quick Checks,* p. 32

Reading *Minilesson*

Comparing and Contrasting Point out that students have learned a number of things about the baby-sitter. The girl is intrigued by the woman because she is different from other sitters she has had. The reader also realizes that the baby-sitter is different from the mother.

Activity Have students list the charac-teristics and actions of the baby-sitter in one column on a sheet of paper. What do they know about her? What do they think of her? Then have them make a similar list for the mother. As a class, compare and contrast the two characters and in particular their influence on the girl and on the reader. **L1**

Additional Resources
📂 *Reading Workbook,* pp. 39–40

Personal Response

Students will need to defend their answers. Most will say they do not approve, but some may point out that there may be some extenuating circumstances that we do not know about.

ANALYZING LITERATURE

1. Felicia sees things typical of a city in winter—bare trees, a park, a frozen lake, and a busy street.
2. Her mother works and then seems to enjoy going out. While she is gone, a series of housekeepers and baby-sitters care for Felicia.
3. The woman has dark hair and eyes and a coat that is not new. Her eyes are sad. This woman is different because she seems to take a genuine interest in the child.
4. She tells Felicia that there was little food or clothing, so they were often hungry and cold. The other women tried to care for the children. Mothers were often taken away. The little girl liked ballet and looked a little like Felicia. Her mother had been taken away.
5. The woman tells Felicia she does not know what happened to her, but that she thinks the girl and the other children are all asleep.
6. Felicia is wondering if her mother will come home.
7. Felicia wishes her mother would come home. She has fantasies about a perfect home. She hesitates to ask if her mother will be coming home.
8. Felicia likes the woman. She may react as she does because this is the first person who has paid any real attention to her in a long time.
9. The two girls are about the same age. They both miss their mothers. They both like ballet. They both have the woman taking care of them. Felicia is well-off and safe. The other girl is a prisoner. Felicia has plenty to eat and wear. The other child does not.
10. They died or were killed. Many people in the camps died of starvation, overwork, or disease. Others were simply killed.
11. Students will likely say their feelings and Felicia's are similar.
12. Felicia is growing up without a mother, whom she desperately needs and wants. As a result, Felicia is fearful when her mother does not come home and is perhaps resentful of her absence.
13. In this story, love fails, in the form of the mother and the housekeeper,

Responding to Literature

Personal Response

Do you approve of the way Felicia's mother is raising her daughter? Why or why not?

——— ANALYZING LITERATURE ———

RECALL

1. Describe what Felicia sees as she looks out of the living room window.
2. Why is Felicia's mother gone so much of the time? Who takes care of Felicia when her mother is away?
3. Describe the woman who comes to take care of Felicia for the evening. How is she different from the other sitting parents?
4. Summarize what the woman tells Felicia about the camp and the little girl she met there.
5. How does the woman answer when Felicia asks what happened to the little girl?

INTERPRET

6. Why do you think Felicia feels so apprehensive as she stands at the window every evening?
7. How does Felicia seem to feel about her mother's frequent absences? Support your answer with evidence from the story.
8. How does Felicia react to the woman who has come to care for her? In your opinion, why does Felicia react this way?
9. Compare and contrast Felicia and the little girl in the camp. How are they alike? How are they different?
10. What do you think really happened to the little girl and to most of the others in the camp? Explain.

EVALUATE AND CONNECT

11. Look again at your response to the Focus Activity on page 362. Compare your feelings with the ones Felicia experiences at the start of the story.
12. **Theme Connections** What are some consequences of the ways in which Felicia's mother responds to the challenges of her time?
13. It has been said that Kay Boyle's stories provide a catalog of the ways in which love can fail. Do you think this story demonstrates the failure of love? Explain your answer.
14. Reread the Did You Know? section on page 362. How does this information help you better understand this story?
15. What advice would you like to give to Felicia's mother?

Literary ELEMENTS

Irony

Irony is a contrast between reality and what seems to be real. There are several types of irony. **Verbal irony** exists when a person says one thing and means another. Calling a very slow person a "speed demon" is an example of verbal irony. **Dramatic irony** occurs when the reader has important information that characters in a literary work do not have. For example, Felicia knows nothing about the type of camp the woman is describing, but the author assumes that the reader knows the woman is talking about a Nazi concentration camp.

1. Find two examples of dramatic irony in the conversation Felicia has with her baby-sitter. How does the author's use of irony affect your reaction to the story?

2. "Your mother and me, we're just buying our own freedom, that's all we're doing. And we're not doing nobody no harm." Explain the irony in this statement made by the housekeeper.

● See **Literary Terms Handbook**, p. R6.

---

but love succeeds in the form of the baby-sitter. Also, love fails when the woman cannot continue to take care of the little girl in the camp.
14. The information gives a possible explanation of what Felicia's mother and father are doing. It also provides background information about the camps.
15. Students will probably tell her to stop going out and start paying more attention to her child.

LITERARY ELEMENTS

1. Felicia asks if the little girl's mother came home in a taxi. Felicia is told she and the other children are asleep. The reader knows the truth and reacts with compassion and sympathy.
2. By working so hard to earn money, they have enslaved themselves to work.

Additional Resources

✎ *Literary Elements Transparency 32*

LITERATURE AND WRITING

Writing About Literature

Identifying a Foil   A **foil** is a character who is used as a contrast to another character. For example, a handsome but dull character might be a foil for one who is unattractive but dynamic. Authors sometimes use a foil to underscore the distinctive qualities of a character. Find a character in "Winter Night" who functions as a foil to another character. In a paragraph, explain your choice, identifying the distinctive qualities of each character.

Creative Writing

I Can Explain, Mother   What do you think happens when Felicia's mother wakes up her daughter and the baby-sitter? How do Felicia and the woman explain the situation? How does the mother react? Write a continuation to "Winter Night," in which you tell what happens next. Include a dialogue that the three characters might have.

EXTENDING YOUR RESPONSE

Literature Groups

Lasting Impressions   On the front of an index card, copy a brief passage from "Winter Night" that impressed you—for example, a passage that surprised you, made you angry, touched your heart, or caused you to think. On the back of the card, explain why you chose this passage. In your group, take turns reading your passages and discussing their meanings. After each passage has been discussed, the person who chose it should read the reason he or she wrote on the back of the card. Share your cards with another group in your class.

Internet Connection

Recalling the Horror   Like the baby-sitter in "Winter Night," many survivors of Nazi concentration camps have told about their experiences in these camps. Search the Internet to find one or two such accounts to share with the class.

Listening and Speaking

Interviewing   Interview someone who served in the armed forces during World War II, or someone who was left behind when a family member or close friend went off to war. Find out what life was like on the war front or on the home front. Tape-record your interview and select highlights to play for the class.

Reading Further

You might also enjoy these works by Kay Boyle:

Short Story Collections: *Fifty Stories* is set in Europe and the United States between 1927 and 1966.

Life Being the Best and Other Stories, thirteen of Boyle's earliest stories, was written in Paris in the 1920s.

Autobiography: *Being Geniuses Together* is a collaborative work by Kay Boyle and Robert McAlmon about their lives in the 1920s.

📖 **Save your work for your portfolio.**

LITERATURE AND WRITING

Writing About Literature

Students' paragraphs should
- identify two story characters.
- display an understanding that the foil is the more minor character.
- explain how the character is a foil by comparing the distinctive qualities of both characters.

Creative Writing

Students' story continuations should
- include dialogue for each of the three characters.
- be consistent with the characterizations already established in the story.
- use correct paragraphing and punctuation for a dialogue.

EXTENDING YOUR RESPONSE

Literature Groups   Be sure students realize that the reasons classmates give are their own and that there is no wrong answer.
COLLAB. LEARN.

Internet Connection   Encourage students to look for accounts made by actual victims. Provide time for students to share the accounts they found.

Listening and Speaking
Remind students to make a list of questions to use during the interview.

✔ ASSESSMENT OPTIONS

📁 *Quick Checks,* p. 32
📁 *Selection and Theme Assessment,* pp. 61–62
📁 *Performance Assessment,* p. 31
💾 *Testmaker*

Skill Minilessons

GRAMMAR AND LANGUAGE
Coordinate Adjectives

1. Felicia looks out of the window on a dark, cold evening and sees black, winter-stripped trees.
2. The housekeeper prepares a quick, unappetizing supper.
3. The baby-sitter is a pale, dark-haired woman.
4. No change.
5. No change.

READING AND THINKING
Activating Prior Knowledge

1. Students should point to experiences of childhood.
2. Some students may have experienced parents going off to the service or on business trips.
3. Students would need prior knowledge about what happened in the camps.
4. Students who have had a loved one die or move away will point to this kind of loss.
5. Students must know what happened in the camps and that death is sometimes referred to as sleep.

VOCABULARY
Etymology

Reprieve comes from Middle English *repreven*, form of *reproven* meaning "to reprove"; literally meaning "to test again."

Obscurity comes from Latin *ob-* meaning "over" and *scurus* meaning "covered." Thus, *obscure* means "covered over" or "not clear."

Singular comes from Latin *singularis*, meaning "separate" or "extraordinary."

Additional Resources

- **Grammar and Composition Handbook,** Lesson 11.6
- **Grammar and Language Workbook,** p. 253
- **Writer's Choice,** Lesson 21.6
- **Reading Workbook,** pp. 39–40
- **Vocabulary Practice,** p. 31

Responding to Literature

Skill Minilessons

GRAMMAR AND LANGUAGE • Coordinate Adjectives

Coordinate adjectives modify the same noun to an equal degree. If a sentence sounds correct when you reverse the adjectives or put *and* between them, the adjectives are coordinate. Place a comma between coordinate adjectives that precede a noun, as in this example: "The woman took the *silver-backed, monogrammed* brush. . . ."

PRACTICE Rewrite the sentences that have coordinate adjectives, adding a comma between coordinate adjectives that precede a noun.

1. Felicia looks out of the window on a dark cold evening and sees black winter-stripped trees.

2. The housekeeper prepares a quick unappetizing supper.

3. The baby-sitter is a pale dark-haired woman.

4. The girl's eyes were a beautiful lilac color.

5. Felicia's mother wears three blue foxskins.

APPLY Review a piece of your writing, adding coordinate adjectives where appropriate.

● For more about adjectives, see **Language Handbook,** p. R38.

READING AND THINKING • Activating Prior Knowledge

Reading is an interactive process between a reader and a piece of writing. When you read, you bring your prior knowledge and past experiences to the task. You derive meaning by combining what you already know with the words on the page. For example, to fully understand "Winter Night," you must use your prior knowledge about conditions in the United States and in Europe during World War II. You must also draw on your personal experiences to understand Felicia's relationships with her mother and with others.

PRACTICE On your paper, list the prior knowledge or personal experiences that help you understand each event or statement.

1. Felicia feels lonely and apprehensive each evening as darkness begins to fall.

2. Felicia's father is away from home, but she expects him to return one day.

3. The baby-sitter spent time in a camp where people were kept until a decision could be made about what to do with them.

4. The little girl's mother was taken away. She never came back.

5. The baby-sitter says the little girl and all the others must be "asleep" and are no longer hungry or cold.

● For more about related comprehension skills, see **Reading Handbook,** p. R83.

VOCABULARY • Etymology

Studying the etymology, or history, of a word can help you better understand its meaning. For example, *derision* is a noun formed from the verb *deride*, which comes from the Latin words *de-*, meaning "down," and *ridere*, meaning "to laugh." Thus, if you put someone down by laughing at him or her, you *deride* that person. The noun *derision*, which comes from *deride*, means "mockery" or "ridicule."

PRACTICE Use a dictionary to look up the etymologies of *reprieve, obscurity,* and *singular.* Explain the connection between the origin of each word and its current meaning.

Vo·cab·u·lar·y Skills

Roots

The **root** of a word can be a whole word, such as *self*. Word parts can be attached to the root to form new words, such as *unselfish* and *selfless*. A root that is a whole word is called a **base word**. Some words, such as *self-help*, are formed by combining two base words.

Most words, however, are formed from roots that are not whole words. These roots come from many languages; thus, their meanings may not be obvious at first glance. For example, the root of *magnify* is *magni*. It comes from a Latin word that means "great." From the same root grew such words as *magnificent, magnitude,* and *magnification.*

Because a number of words may come from the same root, recognizing commonplace roots can help you to unlock the meanings of many words. Here are a few roots.

Root	Meaning	Examples
anim	life; spirit	animal
cogn	know	recognize
miss	send	dismiss
mut	change	mutation, commute
sect	cut	section
sens	feel	sensation
ver	truth	verify, verdict
vol	wish; will	volunteer

You may not know what a new word means, even if you recognize its root. However, looking at its root is often a good place to start when trying to figure out its meaning.

EXERCISE

Use the list of roots above to decide which word is the best substitute for the underlined word in each sentence.

1. Felicia is not <u>cognizant</u> of the tragedy behind the baby-sitter's story.
   a. aware   b. part   c. doubtful

2. The past, as the baby-sitter knows too well, is <u>immutable</u>.
   a. horrifying   b. senseless   c. unchangeable

3. Felicia's mother, unlike the mother in the camp, is absent of her own <u>volition</u>.
   a. choice   b. selfishness   c. insensitivity

4. Although Felicia does not really understand the story she is told, she does not doubt its <u>veracity</u>.
   a. motivation   b. truthfulness   c. sadness

5. Felicia becomes quite <u>animated</u> when she learns that the little girl studied ballet.
   a. noticeable   b. lively   c. graceful

THE SHORT STORY 375

Vo·cab·u·lar·y Skills

Objective

- To use roots to help decide on the meaning of a word

Teaching Strategies

Remind students that locating roots is a starting place. Other things to look for when decoding words and determining their meanings are prefixes and suffixes as well as context clues. Challenge students to locate words in the story that have a root, a prefix, or a suffix and to explain how they would go about taking each word apart and determining its meaning.

Exercise

1. a
2. c
3. a
4. b
5. b

Additional Resources

📁 *Vocabulary Power: Weekly Lessons and Activities*

ENGLISH LANGUAGE LEARNERS

Root Words Many root words common to English have their basis in Latin, a language that is also the origin of many other languages, including Spanish. Refer to the list of roots on the page and ask English language learners to tell about words in their native language that may contain the same root. Also, have students give the meaning of each word they suggest.

Activity Have students compile a list of words using roots from the list. The words may be in their native language, in English, or in both. Remind students to include the meaning with each word.

Additional Resources

📁 *English Language Learners Sourcebook*

THE SHORT STORY 375

Objectives

- To read and analyze a short story in which a man must face his loneliness
- To identify examples of magical realism
- To write an analysis of the author's use of personification

Skills

Reading/Thinking: Drawing Conclusions; Making Critical Judgments; Generalizing; Problem and Solution; Inferring Characters' Motivations
Writing: Case Study
Vocabulary: Analogies
Grammar/Language: Compound Sentences; Denotation/Connotation
Listening/Speaking: Oral Group Presentation; Dramatic Presentation
Collaboration: Literature Groups

Motivating

→OPTIONS

Selection Focus Transparency 33: Have students identify and list ways a person who is lonely and feels isolated could solve the problem.

Focus Activity: Discuss with students how people feel and what they do when they are left out.

Before You Read

Waltz of the Fat Man

FOCUS ACTIVITY

Think about a situation in which you felt like an outsider.

QUICKWRITE Jot down a brief description of a situation in which you felt like an outsider. How did you deal with the situation? What emotions did you experience?

SETTING A PURPOSE Read to see how the main character in this story deals with feelings of being an outsider.

BACKGROUND

The Time and Place
The setting of "Waltz of the Fat Man" is not clearly identified, but details in the story suggest that it takes place in a small village in northern Mexico in the early 1900s.

Did You Know?
In traditional Mexican culture, the belief in ghosts, magic, and superstition can be very strong. For example, the Mexican celebration *El Día de los Muertos* (the Day of the Dead) recognizes the return of the spirits of the dead to visit the living. Such traditions and celebrations reflect an acceptance of the idea that fantastic or magical events are a natural part of life.

VOCABULARY PREVIEW

patronize (pā' trə nīz) v. to be a customer of (a business), especially on a regular basis; p. 378
consequent (kon' sə kwent') adj. following as a result or effect; p. 378
manifest (man' ə fest') v. to make obvious or clear; show plainly; p. 378
bereaved (bi rēvd') adj. sad and forlorn due to a loss, such as the death of a loved one; p. 379
propriety (prə prī' ə tē) n. the quality of being proper or appropriate; suitability; p. 379
theorize (thē' ə rīz') v. to form an idea that explains a group of facts; p. 380
gingerly (jin' jər lē) adv. with extreme caution; carefully; p. 383
intricacy (in' tri kə sē) n. something that is complicated, involved, or confusing; p. 383

376   UNIT 1

Meet Alberto Alvaro Ríos

"In working with poems and stories I have in the past found myself either filling out a poem to make a story, or paring down a story to find a poem," says poet and short story writer Alberto Alvaro Ríos. Of his work, Ríos also explains that "obsessions, characters, and places reappear from time to time. . . ."

Ríos was born in Nogales, Arizona, a town located on the Mexican border. His mother was born in England and his father in Mexico. He speaks Spanish fluently but chooses to write in English.

Alberto Alvaro Ríos was born in 1952. This story was first published in 1991.

RESOURCE MANAGER

Lesson Planning Resource
The *Unit One Planning Guide* (pp. 278–285) provides additional lesson notes and reduced versions of all print resources.

📁 Other Print Resources
- Active Reading Guide, p. 33
- Vocabulary Practice, p. 32
- Reading Workbook, pp. 41–42
- Grammar and Language Workbook, p. 103
- Grammar and Composition Handbook, Lesson 4.7

- Quick Checks, p. 33
- Selection and Theme Assessment, pp. 63–64
- Performance Assessment, p. 32
- Spanish Summaries, p. 33
- Spanish Translations
- Inclusion Strategies
- English Language Learners Sourcebook

 Transparencies
- Selection Focus 33

- Literary Elements 33
- Grammar and Language 33, 34

Technology
- 🎧 Audio Library
- 🎧 Spanish Audio Library
- 💻 Glencoe Literature Web Site
- 💾 Testmaker

Waltz of the Fat Man

Alberto Alvaro Ríos

Dancers, 1980. Fernando Botero. Watercolor. Courtesy, Marlborough Gallery, New York.

Noé's house trim was painted blue, good blue, deep and neat, with particular attention to the front door, that it should stand against spirits. He kept the house in repair, and hired a gardener in the three seasons, spring and summer, a little in autumn. In this place it was a gray wind after that, a time for planting things in the ground to save them, or to hide them.

SUMMARY

Noé is lonely. He wants friends. He tries a variety of strategies, none of which works. The people of his town reject him, possibly because he is fat. When he is humiliated by some soldiers, he leaves town. He finds the companionship he wants in the circus.

📁 *Spanish Summaries,* p. 33

Ⓐ Active Reading

QUESTION Have students read the first two paragraphs. Point out that the author describes in detail Noé's house and appearance. Why does the author do this? *(He wants to show there is nothing in either that should cause people to reject Noé. The common association of "fat" with "slovenly" does not apply to Noé.)* Suggest that as students read they look for other ways in which Noé tries to connect with people.

Additional Resources

📁 *Active Reading Guide,* p. 33
🎧 *Audio Library*
🎧 *Spanish Audio Library*

Teaching Options

CONNECTING TO OTHER SELECTIONS

The chart at the right shows three ways to connect "Waltz of the Fat Man" to selections in this book.

For specific teaching strategies, see the *Unit One Planning Guide,* pp. 281–282.

Connection	Title
Life Skills: Planning and Designing	→ "Through the Tunnel," p. 76
Thematic: Loneliness	→ "Chee's Daughter," p. 23
Literary: Point of View	→ "Pizza in Warsaw, Torte in Prague," p. 507

B Literary Elements

PLOT: *Internal Conflict* Although Noé is fat, he says his heaviness is inside. What is the heaviness inside? *(loneliness; a feeling of rejection)*

C Literary Elements

FIGURES OF SPEECH: *Personification* Remind students that personification is giving human characteristics to nonhuman objects. Discuss with students what things are personified and what personal qualities the author gives them. *(The wind and the black walnut trees are portrayed as women. Their branches become arms. Noé dances with them. The weeds are described as having tongues that spoke about him.)*

D Critical Thinking

DRAWING CONCLUSIONS Noé speaks about the "thin girl" inside him. What does the noise of the thin girl represent? You may wish to use the following model to illustrate the process of drawing a conclusion.

Model: I know that Noé is lonely. He says that he is fat because he is holding in the noise of his thin girl. This sounds to me like how I might look if I held my breath—puffed up. The noise of the thin girl is his need to talk to other people. He has to hold this back, like holding his breath, because no one wants to be his friend.

Waltz of the Fat Man

A His personal appearance suffered nothing from the attentions to his house, as Noé kept on himself a trim mustache and a clean face, neat clothes for which he thanked Mrs. Martínez, <u>patronizing</u> her for a quarter of a century. From ironing his clothing, she knew the shape of his body more than he did, and for her <u>consequent</u> attention to detail in that regard he was appreciative—just the right fold in the collars, a crease moving a little to the left along his right leg, the minor irregularities and embarrassments. And he was doubly thankful as she never said a word to him about it.

His was a body full of slow bones, after all, and Noé moved as if long fish swam in a small place.

B He did not think himself fat, but he felt himself heavy, in a manner he could not explain to anyone. His body to be sure was overweight, but he did not feel it to be something of the stomach or thighs; rather, it was a heaviness that came from the inside out, <u>manifesting</u> itself to the world as the body of a fat man.

On his best days, Noé could make that weight look like muscles. On his best days he could make his stomach go into his chest and his shoulders, and people would believe anything he had to say.

Noé had a business as a butcher, but it was too much for him, a sadness cutting the meats. He had become a butcher, after all, purely for social reasons. It was a civic service, and he wanted to do good things. But it was not a good choice, given what he desired, which was simply to be part of the town.

To be sure, people patronized his shop, and took him up on his offer of extra services and niceties, but they did not finally stay very long to talk, not in the way they stayed for coffee and to warm themselves at the baker's. He could see them in there, with their mouths open and their eyes rolling along a line of laughter.

He could not say why the townspeople were like this, exactly. Perhaps it was his full size, or something about his looks, or about being the butcher in a town and being too good at his trade. But, the whole of his life was that no one cared much for him, or even spoke to him very much, and when he attended wakes,[1] which he did because he was a courteous man, he left indentations in the kitchen linoleum, which would not go away.

Noé knew that, though he tried not to be, in the people's minds he was simply an irritation.

In whatever part of the town he walked, people spoke behind their hands, and pointed when they didn't think Noé could see them. But his eyes were fat as well, and because of that he could see more.

C When Noé danced, he wore a blue suit, and was always alone, always at the same place outside of town, by the river reeds.

He danced with the wind, which was also cruel like the women of the town, but the wind at least did not have a face. He locked the trunks of his arms with the branch arms of the black walnut trees, which also like the women of the town did not bend around to hold him, did not invite him to another, softer room.

But neither could these arms of a tree leave Noé so easily. They could not so quickly

---

1. A *wake* is a gathering of people to watch over the body of a dead person before burial.

Vocabulary
patronize (pā′ trə nīz′) *v.* to be a customer of (a business), especially on a regular basis
consequent (kon′ sə kwent′) *adj.* following as a result or effect
manifest (man′ ə fest′) *v.* to make obvious or clear; show plainly

---

Teaching Options

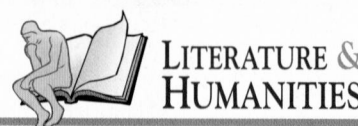

LITERATURE & HUMANITIES

Before students read the selection, have them listen to "The Monongohela Waltz" (Track 13, CD1, Glencoe's *World of Music*) and record in their journals the images and emotions they associate with the music.

MEETING INDIVIDUAL NEEDS — ENGLISH LANGUAGE LEARNERS

Colors Point out that in the story, blue is used on Noé's house, his suit is blue, and his favorite clock is blue. Noé sees blue as a welcoming color. Remind English language learners that in most cultures, colors have meanings. For example, in the American culture, red, white, and blue are patriotic colors.

Activity Draw a pie graph and label sections with color names, letting students choose some of the colors. Have them name a color and tell its significance in their native culture. Write the meaning in the appropriate color section of the wheel.

Additional Resources
📁 *English Language Learners Sourcebook*

C give him over cruelly to the half-hot tongues of the weeds so that they might talk about him, and make their disapproving sounds.

When he danced this dance he let out with a small noise his thin girl, which he kept inside himself. This is what had made him look fat, the holding in, the keeping in of the **D** noise inside himself, his desire to freely speak his needs as a human being in the company of other human beings. This was his thin girl.

And Noé would let her out and they would dance the dance of weddings into the night.

Noé took to wearing his blue suit to the shop, because he thought he looked better. He did this in case someone would look at him, and think the better of him, think him something of a fine man after all.

Then his plan of the blue suit grew into a great deal more, taking as he did the wearing of his suit as some small license. It was the license, he thought, of a regular man. And he tried what he imagined to be the secret work of a regular man in the company of a regular woman.

When he shook the hands of women, he did so vigorously, hoping to see movement on their bodies, some small adventure to take his breath, some nodding yes, some quiet dance of the upper body. This first adventure of a man.

His was a modest plan, and worked a little. The shaking of the hands was, however, the most Noé did. It gave to him so much, and he thought the intimate movements of a woman to be so loud, there in front of everybody, that he could go no further.

But it is why Noé attended wakes so faithfully as well, sometimes as if they were the whole of his social life: how in comforting a bereaved wife he could—properly and in front of everyone so that there was no question of propriety—kiss her on the cheek.

Even then, after the hour of praying for the deceased and thinking about what he would do, by the time his moment was at hand, his attempt at kissing was a dizzied missing of the mark. His lips to the cheek were so clumsy and so fast that the kiss was more of something else, something not quite anything, something in keeping with his life after all.

The butcher shop through the slow years began to change, as did Noé himself. He had taken up in his house the collection and caring of clocks, because, he said to himself, they had hands, and in so many clocks was a kind of heaven, a dream of sounds to make the hours pass in a manner that would allow him to open up shop again the next day.

His nighttime dream became a daytime dream as well. He did not keep them, could not keep the clocks, finally, only at home. Along with Noé in his blue suit, the shop also began to find itself dressed differently, hung with clocks, first one, a plain dark wood, and then two, and then a hundred. Each of them with two hands for him.

There was a blue clock. Cuckoos and 28-day, anniversary clocks to the side of the scale, large-faced numbers where once there had been letters in the sections of an illustrated cow.

What Noé knew and did not say was that here was the anniversary Mariquita, the schoolhouse Mariette, Marina the singular blue, Caras with her bird tongue. Armida had hands that sometimes rose outstretched to the two and ten like the blessing arms of Christ, and sometimes lowered to the five and seven of desire, one hand shorter, in the act of

E **Literary Elements**

SYMBOLISM Noé begins collecting clocks and even hangs them in the butcher shop. Discuss what the clocks represent to him. *(The clocks become a substitute for human companionship. Their sounds help pass the quiet hours. He treats them as an alternative to people, even to the point of giving them names and personalities. He can love them and lavish attention on them, and they cannot reject him.)*

Anniversary Clocks
These special kinds of clocks are sometimes called 400-day clocks. They run for a full year and are wound only once annually. They are sometimes given as wedding gifts with the idea that the couple would wind the clock each year on their anniversary.

Vocabulary
bereaved (bi rēvd′) *adj.* sad and forlorn due to a loss, such as the death of a loved one
propriety (prə prī′ ə tē) *n.* the quality of being proper or appropriate; suitability

THE SHORT STORY ❧ 379

INCLUSION STRATEGIES

Special Needs Noé uses a variety of strategies to get people to like him. Write the heading *Looking for Solutions* on the board. Ask students to look through the story and identify ideas Noé tries. List them as they are named. Discuss which did and did not work. Students might mention shaking hands and going to wakes.

Activity Point out that making friends, especially in a new situation, is never easy. Invite students to identify ideas from Noé's list that might help them in a similar situation and to add other ideas to the list. **L1**

Additional Resources
📁 *Inclusion Strategies*

F Active Reading

EVALUATE Have students ask themselves why the townspeople dislike the clocks and are so intolerant of them. *(The people seem to dislike Noé, so anything he does is subject to criticism. There seems to be no legitimate reason for them reacting as they do. It is simply another sign of their intolerance of him.)*

G Literary Elements

MAGICAL REALISM Discuss what real events occur as Noé is closing up the shop and what magical elements are added. *(Noé is closing the shop. He hears that one of his clocks is not ticking correctly. He examines the clock, wraps it up, and leaves with it. These are realistic events. When he applies human qualities to the clock, magical elements enter the scene. The ticking becomes a heartbeat. It seems to call to him. He sees the clock as a wife in pain.)*

H Critical Thinking

MAKING CRITICAL JUDGMENTS One of the townspeople says of Noé's misfortune, "You get back what you give." Ask students if they agree with this statement in general and if they agree with this statement in Noé's case. *(The statement is generally true. You do seem to get back what you give. However, in Noé's case, this is not true. He did a lot of giving and got nothing in return.)*

Waltz of the Fat Man

beckoning him, a come here, Noé. A come here, I've got something to tell you, Noé, come on, don't be afraid.

This was no butcher shop, the townspeople would say to themselves, not with clocks. One or two clocks maybe, but not so many as this. It would not have been so bad, except that he was the only butcher in town, and people had to make use of his services. An unofficial inquiry was opened as to whether or not there was perhaps a law, some ordinance, prohibiting such abuses of the known world, but no one could find any reference that applied to the walls of a butcher shop, other than cleanliness. And of that, there could be no discussion. Noé did not neglect the clocks, and therefore did not neglect the white-sheeted bed of his walls.

One evening in winter as Noé was closing up his shop, having wound the clocks for the night and having left just enough heat in the stove that they would not suffer, he heard the blue clock falter. So much like a heartbeat had the sounds of the clocks come to be for him, that he was alarmed and stumbled in his quickness to reach the clock, though it could not move and was not falling. It called to him nonetheless as a wife in pain might call to her husband: honey, it said, please.

He reached it too late, he thought, though it was simply a clock, and he laughed at himself.

He tried winding the clock again, thinking the unthinkable, that perhaps he had missed its turn in his haste to leave. But that was not it: the spring was taut, and there was no play.

He took it down from its nail, and looked at it from different angles in his hands, but he could see nothing extraordinary. There was no obvious damage, no one had dropped it

without telling him and rehung it, no insect had been boring into its side. Its blue was still blue, without blemish.

He took it to the counter and measured out some butcher's paper in which to wrap it, deciding that he would take it home to see to its difficulty. He put string around it and made a good blanket of the paper, which should comfort, he always said, what was inside. As he picked it up he could hear the workings move, and he resolved to be wary of its delicacy.

He need not have done it, but he warned himself, as if he were his own mother. He put the clock in the crook of his arm, closed and locked his door, took a deep breath in the cold air, hunched his shoulders and began his walk toward home.

He had errands, but they could wait. And he was, in any event, the last of the merchants to close for the evening, so he would have been out of luck anyway. Save for the clock, this was how his evenings most often came to an end, the closing of the door and the walk toward home.

An occasional voice greeted him, and he returned the hello, but it was the conversation of single words, friendly enough, and that was all.

Some theorized later it was the soldiers who were common in those days and who hung around with nothing better to do, that it was they who had been paid, because they never did anything for nothing, but would do anything for something, those soldiers from that kind of army.

There was nothing tragic, of course, nothing for which any charges could be drawn, in much the same manner that nothing could be legally said about what Noé had done to his butcher's shop. You get back what you give, — H

Vocabulary

theorize (thē′ ə rīz′) *v.* to form an idea that explains a group of facts

Linguistic In the story, the author refers to "the conversation of single words" as Noé passes people on the street. Linguistic learners have strong verbal skills. Ask them to suggest single-word or short-phrase conversations people might have as they pass on the street.

Activity Invite students to work in small groups to create single-word or short-phrase conversations for the people in the street scene on page 381. When the conversations are completed, allow time for the groups to perform a Readers Theater with their scenes.
L2 COLLAB. LEARN.

The Street, 1988. Fernando Botero. Oil on canvas, 74 x 52 in. Courtesy, Marlborough Gallery, New York.
Viewing the painting: In what ways does this scene compare with the atmosphere of Noé's town?

 MEETING INDIVIDUAL NEEDS

INCLUSION STRATEGIES

Less-Proficient Readers On pages 382 and 383, the author uses italics. Call attention to the italics and ask why they are being used. Students should note that the author is using italics instead of quotation marks to indicate what is being said. The italics stand for dialogue.

Activity Let students work in pairs with a more proficient reader. Ask them to practice reading the paragraphs that contain italics. Then let pairs take turns reading the passages to the class.
L2 COLLAB. LEARN.

Additional Resources
📁 *Inclusion Strategies*

Author's Craft

SPECIAL CLUES An author often pro-vides special clues that help the reader understand certain story events. What clues does the author provide that things had not been going well for Noé and that the sol-diers knew a lot about his secret behavior with the clocks? *(The author mentions broken windows and the fact that the soldiers had been watch-ing him. They probably knew, then, about his fantasy life with the clocks.)*

On The Lighter Side

Private Talks

People often talk to themselves. There is a humorous expression that says it's all right to talk to yourself, but you better watch out if you start answering back.

Literary Elements

MAGICAL REALISM Why is Noé so willing to believe that the clock is calling his name? *(He already views the clocks as human. The author injects this kind of magical realism into the story to emphasize Noé's loneliness.)*

Teaching Options

---

someone was later reported as having said, someone but not anyone in particular. That's how it was told to the captain of the police.

Noé was walking home with his package, which no one could have known was the blue clock. No one but perhaps the soldiers, and only then if they had been nosy enough to have been watching through his window, which had been recently broken and was full of cardboard patches, easy enough to hide behind.

The package's aspect was of a ham or a roast of some sort, a good rabbit, something simple and natural in the arm of a big man walking home to dinner.

Darkness had set and the moon was new. He cast no shadow and made his way quickly as he left the last of the downtown buildings. The ground was neither muddy nor dry, resembling something closer to a woody mulch,[2] and through him passed a moment of gardens from sometime in his life, gardens he had passed through, or that his mother had kept. It was a simple feeling, and brought a prickling to his skin.

Did You Know?
Oleander is a poisonous ever-green shrub that has fragrant white, pink, or purple flowers.

He next passed by the stand of walnut trees and wild oleander which was white-flowered in the summer.

The oleander called to him, *Noé.*

At first it was so quiet he said to himself he did not hear it, *Noé.*

Noé, the oleanders said, louder this time, and he stopped to look. Though it was dark and the moon was hidden, he was not afraid.

His size was such that he had never been made to be afraid, not at a moment like this.

---

2. *Mulch* is straw, wood chips, or other similar material that is spread around plants to protect them from cold, to hold in moisture, and to prevent weed growth.

It was, if one could read his face, a curiosity, this sound which was reminiscent of his name. It was like the mulch and his mother's garden, and it gave him a prickling of the skin once more.

Noé. He heard it again, and stopped, and turned to it, saying who was there, what did they want, that perhaps he could be of some service.

No one answered, so he reached his free hand into the leaves and moved them around. He heard the sound and then saw what seemed like, in the dimness, a rabbit, running into the underbrush.

Ha, he said, and let it go. He turned again to walk, pulling his coat back up onto his neck.

Noé. It was a whisper, this time he was sure. Not a voice, but more of a breath. A half-breath, but unmistakable in its enunciation.[3]

As a child, Noé might have crossed him-self, and as he was sometimes his own mother, he had the impulse, but he just stood there, once more.

He put down the clock in order to enter the oleander more fully, and see what was what, but he found nothing, only branches and the small noises of startled birds and lizards.

When he came out he could not find his package, though he concentrated with his eyes and with his hands. It was not there.

A voice whispered once more, *Noé. You know me,* it said, *you know who I am.*

Noé no longer moved around. He lis-tened, and he waited.

Noé. He did know the whisper. He had in fact heard it many times. He knew the whis-per more than the voice of his neighbor, whom he had seen a thousand times.

He would not have believed any of it had this not been the blue clock. Marina his blue, who had made so many places for herself in

---

3. Here, *enunciation* refers to the whispered pronunciation of the name *Noé*.

Listening and Speaking *Minilesson*

Oral Group Presentation Have students prepare oral group presentations, which can be in any form a group chooses: news conference, interview, discussion group, etc. First, make a list of goals for working in groups. Lists might look like this:

1. Be sure everyone participates in the planning and in the presentation.
2. Respect others' views and talents.
3. Look for ways to make the presenta-tion interesting to the listeners.

Activity The townspeople never got to know Noé, and he never got to know them. Ask small groups of students to present a discussion of this topic: A person is a terrible thing to waste.
L2 **COLLAB. LEARN.**

his life. Not big places, but so many, her hair color on the trim of his house, the color of her eyes in his suit, and so on. She was the blueness inside him, the color of his appetite, the color both of what filled him and what he needed more of.

J

Marina, he said.

Noé.

He stood there and waited.

Do you love me?

Noé did not answer.

You can love me if you love me like a horse, said the whisper. *Can you be a horse, Noé? Can you show me how you are a horse?*

Noé stood there, quietly.

He stamped his foot, <u>gingerly</u> at first, unsure and sure at the same time.

Is that it, Noé, is that all the horse you are?

Noé stamped his foot harder, and made a noise with his nose, and partway through his mouth.

Yes, Noé. And are you more of a horse still?

If this were anything but his blue clock, Marina, he would have gone, and given the moment up as the ghosts of this place. Or children, or who knew what. But he could not.

K

And then he heard the laughter of the soldiers as they could no longer contain themselves camouflaged so well otherwise in the oleanders. He heard the laughter, but did not bother with it. He turned and went home, without the clock.

He had gone away from home once before, from his family. He had to. One thing and another, right or wrong, these things didn't matter. It was simply too much to stay.

He had in some manner become an exponent to a regular number. He was ordinary times ten or times twenty, always too much.

And his desire carried an exponent as well. He wanted everything to be nice, to be only the Golden Rule,[4] but times ten, and that is too much. He had no sense of himself, and yet he was everything. In that sea of mathematics he had drowned a sailor's death.

And now he had to go away again. The tide had come up, and caught him once more. He sold what was left of his business at a loss finally to Mr. Molina, who had a scarred face and who wanted to do the work. There was an art in the cutting, and it took Noé, because he was a courteous man, the afternoon to teach the profession's immediate <u>intricacies</u> to Mr. Molina, who had no idea there was so much.

And that same night Noé bought a brown horse and rode it as far into the following days and weeks, as far into the future as he could because he could not wait to see what was there. He arrived at the circus, and in it he made his life again.

But he almost did not make it. A man and a sparrow—each puts a shoulder to the wind, each to his own intention: a sparrow to fly, a man to run. Noé on this night was in between, and even with his weight he felt himself lifted, as if he were in league with angels at the edge of heaven, not quite deserving, but sneaking in with some help through a back door, hoping to go unnoticed again, as he had felt when he had come to this town. But it was not heaven, these places.

L

He stopped because the circus people were the first to wave him down, all of them standing near the road, as if this were the place, and they knew him, and they had

---

4. The *Golden Rule* is the rule of conduct that one should treat others as one wishes to be treated.

Vocabulary

gingerly (jin' jər lē) *adv.* with extreme caution; carefully
intricacy (in' tri kə sē) *n.* something that is complicated, involved, or confusing

K **Active Reading**

RESPOND Have students ask themselves if they were Noé how they would feel after the soldiers started laughing. *(Students will probably indicate that they would feel humiliated and embarrassed.)*

L **Critical Thinking**

GENERALIZING Noé is anxious to ride into the future but has mixed feelings about what the future might hold. What is he concerned about? *(He thinks maybe he does not deserve happiness and that he will end up, not happier in a new place, but simply in the same situation in a different location.)*

Reading *Minilesson*

Problem and Solution Explain that one strategy for reading stories is to think of them as made up of problems and solutions. A character has a problem and tries different solutions to the problem, which may or may not be solved. Discuss this example:

Problem: Noé wants friends.

First Solution: He makes his house look attractive and inviting.

Second Solution: He keeps himself well-groomed.

Third Solution: He offers his customers extra services.

Activity Have students identify other ways Noé tries to solve his problem and write them in the above format. Have students take turns offering their solutions.

Compile them into a master list following the sequence of events in the story. **L2**

Additional Resources
📁 *Reading Workbook,* pp. 41–42

Ⓜ Critical Thinking

GENERALIZING Noé is disliked by the townspeople because he is fat. Discuss other reasons why individuals are rejected by people. What does this story teach about this practice? *(race, religion, sex, national origins, physical appearance, mental health, and sexual orientation; you may miss out on getting to know an interesting person.)*

Thematic Focus

Challenges and Consequences
Ask students to identify the challenge Noé faced.

Man on a Horse, 1981. Fernando Botero. Watercolor, 22 x 37.5 cm. Courtesy, Marlborough Gallery, New York.

Viewing the painting: How does this painting reflect the changes in Noé at the end of the story? Explain.

been waiting, and what took him so long, had he not heard them calling into the night for him.

But they had called him without telegraph or telephone. Something stronger.

His mustache curled up from the wind and his body, which had sometimes seemed fat, was hardened, tense in that moment from the cold which had made him hold his breath and flex his muscles for the whole distance of the ride.

He arrived as a beast, almost, something crazed and unshaven, out of breath.

Or as a beast on top of a man, as if the horse itself was more human, and asking for help.

His was a body full of slow bones still, but if it had taken his lifetime up to now to be slow, now the other foot was coming down, and it was fast.

It was the other half of himself now, for the rest of his years.

This was, after all, the place. And in that moment of dust kicked up and of noise, he began his real career, this life with a whole company of half-size men, two-bodied women, and all the rest of the animals who danced. Ⓜ

384 ❧ UNIT 1

384

Responding to Literature

Personal Response

Which images from the story have lingered in your mind? In your journal, describe these images and any thoughts and feelings they bring to mind.

--- **ANALYZING LITERATURE** ---

RECALL

1. Describe Noé's appearance and his business. Why did he choose this line of work?
2. How do the townspeople treat Noé? How does Noé account for their behavior toward him?
3. Who is Noé's "thin girl"? What does she represent?
4. Describe how Noé treats his clocks.
5. Summarize the incident with the blue clock. What changes does Noé make in his life after this incident?

INTERPRET

6. What do you think the narrator means when he says that Noé felt "a heaviness that came from the inside out"? What do you think this "heaviness" represents?
7. In your opinion, why might the townspeople treat Noé as they do?
8. Compare Noé's relationship with his "thin girl" to his relationships with women in general.
9. In your opinion, why are the clocks so important to Noé? What role do they seem to play in his life?
10. What does the last line of the story suggest to you about Noé's new life? Do you think he will find happiness in this new life? Why or why not?

EVALUATE AND CONNECT

11. Reread the description you wrote in the Focus Activity on page 376. Does your experience help you understand Noé's situation? Explain.
12. In your opinion, what lesson or lessons about human nature might this story suggest?
13. Suppose that you met a person like Noé. How might you respond to him or her? Why?
14. Do you think a person like Noé would find greater acceptance in your community than he found in his own? Why or why not?
15. In your opinion, is "Waltz of the Fat Man" a good title for this story? Explain your answer.

Literary ELEMENTS

Magical Realism

Magical realism is a style of writing in which realistic details, events, settings, characters, and dialogue are interwoven with elements of the magical, supernatural, fantastic, or bizarre. For example, Noé's occupation as a shop owner in a small town is realistic, but his relationship with his clocks is fantastic and bizarre. When the blue clock malfunctions, the narrator says the clock called to Noé "as a wife in pain might call to her husband: honey, it said, please." Clearly, the author is describing events that could happen only in the realm of the imagination.

1. Find one or two passages in the story in which realistic elements are interwoven with elements that are magical, fantastic, or bizarre.
2. What effect does the use of magical realism have on your experience of the story or your reaction to it? Support your answer using specific details from the story.

 See **Literary Terms Handbook,** p. R7.

Personal Response

Students may write about the trick the soldiers play on Noé or how he danced with the wind and the trees.

ANALYZING LITERATURE

1. Noé is overweight but neat in appearance. He is a butcher. He chose this profession so that he could have contact with people.
2. They are polite but remote. Noé does not understand why they treat him as they do. He thinks perhaps it is because he is fat.
3. She is the desire inside him for human interaction.
4. Noé treats his clocks as if they are human. They have names, and he views them as having personalities.
5. The soldiers call to him from the bushes. Pretending they are the blue clock talking, they have him act like a horse. He sells his business and leaves the town.
6. When there are strong emotions, a person sometimes can feel a tightness, or weight, inside the body. The heaviness is his loneliness and desire for love and friendship.
7. Noé seems to lack social skills and is a bit awkward, but he keeps trying. The title of the story suggests that his weight is noticeably out of the ordinary and thus may be a reason people avoid him.
8. Noé is familiar with and completely understands the "thin girl." With real women, he is awkward and uncertain.
9. The clocks literally help him pass the time. They take the place of people in his life.
10. The line suggests that Noé has found a place to be happy. Students will probably indicate that yes, Noé will now be happy because he is with people who accept him as he is.
11. Students will probably say that their own experiences helped them understand Noé's plight.
12. In general, people tend to react negatively toward people who are different.

LITERARY ELEMENTS

1. Noé's dance with the wind and the trees is magical, as is his relationship with the clocks.
2. It helps the reader enter the fantasy world Noé had created for himself.

Additional Resources

Literary Elements Transparency 33

---

13. Students may indicate they would try to get to know him. Most people are worth the effort.
14. Noé's lack of acceptance in his community was extreme. In most communities, Noé would not be rejected by everyone.
15. Most students will feel that the title is a good one. If the waltz is viewed as a symbol for our search for happiness in our lives, then it fits the story well.

LITERATURE AND WRITING

Writing About Literature

Students' analyses should
- identify three examples of personification.
- explain what is personified in each example.
- explain how personification contributes to the atmosphere of the story and the readers' opinion of Noé.

Creative Writing

Students' case studies should
- identify Noé's problem.
- state the cause or causes of his problem.
- suggest possible solutions.

EXTENDING YOUR RESPONSE

Literature Groups Some groups may not be able to come up with conclusive answers to certain passages. Allow time for these passages to be discussed by the entire class. **COLLAB. LEARN.**

Interdisciplinary Activity

Encourage students to bring pictures of art pieces done by their artist of choice to help them in their presentation.

Performing Be sure students have time to practice. Also, you may want to videotape the presentations and share them with another class.

LITERATURE AND WRITING

Writing About Literature

Analyzing Personification In "Waltz of the Fat Man" Alberto Alvaro Ríos uses personification—the giving of human form or characteristics to an animal, object, or idea. For example, the author portrays the wind as Noé's dancing partner and describes the wind as, "cruel like the women of the town." This conveys to readers a sense of Noé's loneliness and isolation from other people. List three other examples of personification in the story. Then write an analysis of how the author's use of this technique contributes to the atmosphere of the story and your impressions of Noé.

Creative Writing

In the Psychologist's Chair Why do you think Noé is the way he is? What lies at the root of his unhappiness? Look for clues in the story. Then, imagine that you are a psychologist analyzing Noé's mental state. Write a brief case study of Noé in which you describe his problem and analyze its cause or causes.

EXTENDING YOUR RESPONSE

Literature Groups

Puzzling Passages What lingering questions do you have about this story? What passages do you find confusing? Skim the story and use stick-on notes to mark one or two passages that you find puzzling. In your group, discuss possible interpretations of these passages. Then share your ideas with the class.

Interdisciplinary Activity

Art History: Mexican Muralists Working in a small group, do library or Internet research to find out about a Mexican muralist, such as José Orozco or Diego Rivera, or another Mexican artist. Find examples of your artist's work, then refer to these examples to suggest how he or she might have depicted a scene from "Waltz of the Fat Man." Prepare an oral presentation about your artist for the class and conclude with a description of the work he or she might have painted for this story.

Performing

Dramatic Presentation The language of "Waltz of the Fat Man" is rhythmic and musical. In a group, prepare a dramatic reading of a scene from the story. If you wish, you might also act out the scene. For example, you might perform Noé's dance with the wind and trees or his impression of a horse. After rehearsing, give your performance for the class.

Reading Further

If you enjoyed "Waltz of the Fat Man," you might also like these other works by Alberto Alvaro Ríos:

Short Story Collection: *Pig Cookies and Other Stories,* continues the tradition of magical realism in Ríos's work.

Poetry: *Whispering to Fool the Wind,* won the Walt Whitman Prize of the Poetry Society of America.

📖 Save your work for your portfolio.

Skill Minilessons

GRAMMAR AND LANGUAGE • Denotations and Connotations

A word's **denotations** are its definitions; its **connotations** are the feelings and values usually associated with the word. Although words may have similar denotations, their connotations may be quite different. For example, consider this description of Noé: "He did not think himself fat, but he felt himself heavy. . . . His body to be sure was overweight. . . ." *Fat, heavy,* and *overweight* all have similar definitions, or denotations; however, their connotations differ. Most people with a weight problem would prefer to be called *heavy* or *overweight* rather than *fat,* because of the negative connotations associated with the word *fat.*

PRACTICE For each word below that Noé might use to describe himself, write a word with a similar denotation, but a different connotation, that the townspeople might use to describe him.

1. confused
2. ingratiating
3. lonely
4. awkward
5. trusting

● For more about denotation and connotation, see **Literary Terms Handbook,** p. R3.

READING AND THINKING • Inferring Characters' Motivations

When you make inferences, you make reasonable judgments based on the information available to you. In "Waltz of the Fat Man," you can use details from the story, as well as your own knowledge of human nature, to make inferences about why the characters do certain things. For example, when the narrator says that people lingered to socialize at the baker's but never stayed long at Noé's shop, you might infer that people don't particularly like Noé.

PRACTICE Use details from the story, as well as your own knowledge and experience, to infer why the characters do each thing listed below.

1. Noé dances with the wind and the black walnut trees.
2. The townspeople investigate whether it's legal to hang a hundred clocks on the walls of a butcher shop.
3. Noé leaves town.
4. The circus people call out to Noé.

● For more about inference, see **Reading Handbook,** p. R92.

VOCABULARY • Analogies

An analogy is a type of comparison based on the relationships between things or ideas. Some analogies are based on antonyms, as in this example.

  enormous : diminutive :: thoroughly : partially

Enormous and *diminutive* have opposite meanings; *thoroughly* is an antonym of *partially.*

  To complete an analogy, determine what relationship exists between the first two things or ideas. Then apply the same relationship to another pair of words.

● For more about analogies, see **Communications Skills Handbook,** p. R77.

PRACTICE Choose the word that best completes each analogy.

1. elevate : lower :: patronize :
   a. lift   b. boycott   c. select
2. gloom : radiance :: intricacy :
   a. variety   b. confusion   c. simplicity
3. steady : wavering :: bereaved :
   a. unlucky   b. joyous   c. prompt
4. professionally : amateurishly :: gingerly :
   a. carelessly   b. angrily   c. properly

THE SHORT STORY 387

Skill Minilessons

GRAMMAR AND LANGUAGE
Denotations and Connotations

Possible answers:
1. puzzled (*flustered*)
2. polite (*fawning*)
3. friendless (*reclusive*)
4. unrefined (*crude*)
5. unsuspicious (*naive*)

READING AND THINKING
Inferring Characters' Motivations

1. Noé has no one else to dance with.
2. The people think what he has done is strange. Hanging so many clocks is unusual.
3. Noé wants to find a place where people will accept him. He has had enough of his present town.
4. The circus people recognize a person of their own kind. The circus people are friendly.

VOCABULARY
Analogies

1. b   2. c   3. b
4. a

Additional Resources

▮ *Grammar and Composition Handbook*

▮ *Grammar and Language Workbook*

▮ *Writer's Choice,* Lesson 6.4

🗀 *Reading Workbook,* p. 41–42

🗀 *Vocabulary Practice,* p. 32

Objectives

- To read and analyze a short story in which in a proud prince challenges death and loses
- To identify the setting and mood
- To analyze allegorical symbols

Skills

Reading/Thinking: Drawing Conclusions; Comparing and Contrasting; Varying Reading Rate; Inferring; Visualizing
Writing: R.S.V.P.
Vocabulary: Analogies
Grammar/Language: Demonstrative Pronouns; Subject Complements
Listening/Speaking: Creating Dialogue; Interview
Collaboration: Literature Groups

Selection Focus Transparency 34: Discuss the general atmosphere and purpose of a costume party.

Focus Activity: Discuss ways people act when they think they are better than someone else.

Before You Read

The Masque of the Red Death

───── FOCUS ACTIVITY ─────

How much control do you think you have over the events in your life?

DISCUSS In a small group, discuss these questions: What events in your life do you feel you can control? What events do you feel are beyond your control? Share your ideas with the members of another group.

SETTING A PURPOSE Read to learn about events that are beyond the control of some party goers.

───── BACKGROUND ─────

The Time and Place
"The Masque of the Red Death" takes place long ago, in an unnamed kingdom somewhere in Europe.

Did You Know?
A *pestilence*, also called an epidemic, is any contagious disease that spreads quickly and has a high death rate. An epidemic of a disease called plague caused an estimated twenty-five million deaths when it swept across Europe in the 1300s; at that time, the disease was called the Black Death. Between 1664 and 1665, an outbreak of plague in London killed more than 70,000 people. In modern times, improved sanitation and advances in medical science have all but eliminated many deadly diseases.

───── VOCABULARY PREVIEW ─────

profuse (prə fūs′) *adj.* great in amount; plentiful; p. 389
dauntless (dônt′ lis) *adj.* fearless; courageous; daring; p. 390
sagacious (sə gā′ shəs) *adj.* having or showing wisdom and good judgment; p. 390
countenance (koun′ tə nəns) *n.* the face; p. 391
wanton (wont′ ən) *adj.* shamelessly unrestrained; immoral; p. 392
appal (ə pôl′) *v.* to fill with horror or dismay; shock; p. 393
spectral (spek′ trəl) *adj.* ghostlike; p. 393
blasphemous (blas′ fə məs) *adj.* showing disrespect or scorn for God or anything sacred; p. 394

388   UNIT 1

Meet Edgar Allan Poe

❝I asked myself—'Of all melancholy topics, what, according to the universal understanding of mankind, is the most melancholy?' Death— was the obvious reply.❞

The melancholy associated with death was well known to Poe, who lost both his parents at an early age and watched his cherished young wife succumb to tuberculosis. But despite personal tragedies and frustrations, Poe was able to create some of the most astonishing and terrifying work of his age. Poe is credited with writing the world's first detective story, "The Murders in the Rue Morgue."

Poe was born in Boston, Massachusetts, in 1809 and died in 1849. This story was first published in 1842.

RESOURCE MANAGER

Lesson Planning Resource
The *Unit One Planning Guide* (pp. 286–293) provides additional lesson notes and reduced versions of all print resources.

📁 **Other Print Resources**
- Active Reading Guide, p. 34
- Vocabulary Practice, p. 33
- Reading Workbook, pp. 43–44
- Grammar and Language Workbook, pp. 54, 85
- Grammar and Composition Handbook, Lessons 1.2, 2.5

- Quick Checks, p. 34
- Selection and Theme Assessment, pp. 65–66
- Performance Assessment, p. 33
- Spanish Summaries, p. 34
- Spanish Translations
- Inclusion Strategies
- English Language Learners Sourcebook

 Transparencies
- Selection Focus 34
- Fine Art 10

- Literary Elements 34
- Grammar and Language 34

Technology
 Audio Library
🎧 Spanish Audio Library
💻 Glencoe Literature Web Site
💾 Testmaker

The Masque of the Red Death

Edgar Allan Poe

SUMMARY

The "Red Death" is raging. People are dying. Prince Prospero invites 1,000 friends into his abbey and locks out the world. There he and his friends live, believing themselves safe from the fate that has come to so many. One night the prince holds a special masked ball. The costumed revellers party until the stroke of midnight. As the clock chimes, an unusual guest appears dressed in red. The guest frightens and enrages the prince, who pursues the guest through the chambers of his home until at last he comes face to face with—the "Red Death."

📁 *Spanish Summaries,* p. 34

THE "RED DEATH" had long devastated the country. No pestilence had ever been so fatal, or so hideous. Blood was its Avatar[1] and its seal—the redness and the horror of blood. There were sharp pains, and sudden dizziness, and then profuse bleeding at the pores, with dissolution.[2] The scarlet stains upon the body and especially upon the face of the victim, were the pest ban[3] which shut him out from the aid and from the sympathy of his fellow-men. And the whole seizure, progress, and termination of the disease, were the incidents of half an hour.

A Active Reading

QUESTION Have students read the first page. Ask them why the "Red Death" is such a terrible and feared disease and how people might deal with such a pestilence.

Additional Resources

📁 *Active Reading Guide,* p. 34
🎧 *Audio Library*
🎧 *Spanish Audio Library*

---

1. In Hinduism, an *Avatar* is a god that takes on human form. Here, the word means a visible form, or embodiment, of the disease.
2. Here, *dissolution* is death.
3. A *pest ban* is an official declaration that a person has been stricken with plague. Here, the blood stains on the victim's body became their own pest ban.

Vocabulary
profuse (prə fūs′) *adj.* great in amount; plentiful

THE SHORT STORY 389

CONNECTING TO OTHER SELECTIONS

The chart at the right shows three ways to connect "The Masque of the Red Death" to selections in this book.

For specific teaching strategies, see the *Unit One Planning Guide,* pp. 289–290.

Connection	Title
Life Skills: Implementing and Performing	→ "A Swimming Lesson," p. 495
Thematic: The Unexpected	→ "The Interlopers," p. 269
Literary: Symbolism	→ "The Ring," p. 225

B Literary Elements

CHARACTER Help students recognize what kind of leader Prince Prospero is by asking them what the prince does after half of his people have died. *(He locks himself and his friends into his abbey in the belief the disease cannot reach them. He cares little for his people and their suffering.)*

FYI

The Plague The plague was caused by bacteria that live in rats and other rodents. The disease is usually spread by fleas from the infected rats. The outbreak of a disease that occurs over a wide geographic area and affects a high portion of the population is known as a pandemic.

But the Prince Prospero was happy and <u>dauntless</u> and <u>sagacious</u>. When his dominions[4] were half depopulated, he summoned to his presence a thousand hale and light-hearted friends from among the knights and dames of his court, and with these retired to the deep seclusion of one of his castellated abbeys.[5] This was an extensive and magnificent structure, the creation of the prince's own eccentric yet august taste. A strong and lofty wall girdled it in. This wall had gates of iron. The courtiers, having entered, brought furnaces and massy hammers and welded the bolts. They resolved to leave means neither of ingress nor egress[6] to the sudden impulses of despair or of frenzy from within. The abbey was amply provisioned. With such precautions the courtiers might bid defiance to contagion. The external world could take care of itself. In the meantime it was folly to grieve, or to think. The prince had provided all the appliances of pleasure. There were buffoons, there were improvisatori,[7] there were balletdancers, there were musicians, there was Beauty, there was wine. All these and security were within. Without was the "Red Death."

It was toward the close of the fifth or sixth month of his seclusion, and while the pestilence raged most furiously abroad, that the Prince Prospero entertained his thousand friends at a masked ball of the most unusual magnificence.

It was a voluptuous[8] scene, that masquerade. But first let me tell of the rooms in which it was held. There were seven—an imperial suite. In many palaces, however, such suites form a long and straight vista, while the folding doors slide back nearly to the walls on either hand, so that the view of the whole extent is scarcely impeded. Here the case was very different; as might have been expected from the duke's love of the *bizarre*. The apartments were so irregularly disposed[9] that the vision embraced but little more than one at a time. There was a sharp turn at every twenty or thirty yards, and at each turn a novel effect. To the right and left, in the middle of each wall, a tall and narrow Gothic window looked out upon a closed corridor which pursued the windings of the suite. These windows were of stained glass whose color varied in accordance with the prevailing hue of the decorations of the chamber into which it opened. That at the eastern extremity was hung, for example, in blue—and vividly blue were its windows. The second chamber was purple in its ornaments and tapestries, and

Did You Know?
Gothic architecture developed in Europe between the twelfth and sixteenth centuries. A Gothic window has a pointed arch and many small panes of stained or clear glass.

---

4. The prince's *dominions* are the territories he rules.
5. A *castellated abbey* is a fortified structure originally built as a monastery or intended, as the prince's was, to resemble one.
6. With *means neither of ingress nor egress*, there's no way in and no way out.
7. *Buffoons* are clowns or comedians, and *improvisatori* (im prov′ ə zə tôr′ ē) are poets who improvise, or make up, verses as they perform.

8. Here, *voluptuous* (və lup′ chōo əs) means "giving great pleasure to the senses."
9. *Bizarre* means "that which is extremely strange or odd." A bizarre feature of Prospero's abbey is the way the rooms *(apartments)* are arranged *(disposed)* so that only one is visible at a time.

Vocabulary
dauntless (dônt′ lis) *adj.* fearless; courageous; daring
sagacious (sə gā′ shəs) *adj.* having or showing wisdom and good judgment

---

Teaching Options

ENGLISH LANGUAGE LEARNERS

Costume Parties To help English language learners understand the setting and the kind of party that was being held, invite them to discuss questions similar to these: *Have you ever been to or seen movies of a costume party? What do people wear? What is a castle?*

Activity Invite students to draw a picture of a costume ball in a castle.

Challenge them to put labels on characters or furnishings that appear in the picture. Encourage students to use labels in their native language if they feel more comfortable doing so.

Additional Resources
📁 *English Language Learners Sourcebook*

here the panes were purple. The third was green throughout, and so were the casements.[10] The fourth was furnished and lighted with orange—the fifth with white—the sixth with violet. The seventh apartment was closely shrouded in black velvet tapestries that hung all over the ceiling and down the walls, falling in heavy folds upon a carpet of the same material and hue. But in this chamber only, the color of the windows failed to correspond with the decorations. The panes here were scarlet—a deep blood color. Now in no one of the seven apartments was there any lamp or candelabrum, amid the profusion of golden ornaments that lay scattered to and fro or depended from the roof. There was no light of any kind emanating from lamp or candle within the suite of chambers. But in the corridors that followed the suite, there stood, opposite to each window, a heavy tripod, bearing a brazier[11] of fire, that projected its rays through the tinted glass and so glaringly illumined the room. And thus were produced a multitude of gaudy and fantastic appearances. But in the western or black chamber the effect of the fire-light that streamed upon the dark hangings through the blood-tinted panes was ghastly in the extreme, and produced so wild a look upon the countenances of those who entered, that there were few of the company bold enough to set foot within its precincts at all.

It was in this apartment, also, that there stood against the western wall, a gigantic clock of ebony. Its pendulum swung to and fro with a dull, heavy, monotonous clang; and

Costume Ball in the Tuileries: Napoleon III and the Countess Castiglione, 1867. Jean Baptiste Carpeaux. Oil on canvas. Musee d'Orsay, Paris.

Viewing the painting: In what ways does this painting reflect the ball of the story?

---

10. *Casements* are windows.
11. A *brazier* (brā′ zhər) is a metal pan used to hold burning coal or charcoal, as a source of heat and light.

Vocabulary
countenance (koun′ tə nəns) *n.* the face

C **Literary Elements**

SETTING and MOOD What is special about the rooms in which the party is held? How do the rooms add to the mood of the story? *(Instead of being laid out in a straight line, they are irregularly arranged. To move from one room to the next, a person has to make twists and turns. In addition, each room is only one color and a different color from the others. The strange arrangement and bizarre color scheme of the rooms adds to the strange and disturbing mood.)*

VIEWING THE PAINTING

Jean Baptiste Carpeaux (1827–1875) was a French sculptor and painter. The Tuileries mentioned in the title of the painting was a royal palace in Paris, France. Napoleon III, shown in the painting, ruled France from 1852 to 1870. He was the nephew of Napoleon I (Napoleon Bonaparte).

Viewing Response *Like the ball in the story, this painting depicts a costume ball in grand surroundings, possibly a castle or an abbey.*

D **Critical Thinking**

DRAWING CONCLUSIONS Why is no one willing to go into the seventh room? How does it look? What does it probably remind people of? *(The room is scary. Everything is black except the red stained glass window. The room probably reminds people of death and the "Red Death.")*

Vo•cab•u•lar•y Skills

Word Meanings The word *masque* has a number of meanings: "a form of entertainment popular in the sixteenth and seventeenth centuries, often using masks and based on allegory," "a masquerade," and "a mask." Ask students to explain how Poe uses all three meanings. (*The party was a masque, or a masquerade, during which the people wore masks.*)

E Active Reading

QUESTION Guide students in a questioning technique to help them understand the significance of the clock. Use the following model:

Model: The clock seems important. How do people react to the chimes? (*They feel uneasy.*) What is special about the sound? (*The chimes are musical but peculiar.*) What happens when the clock chimes? (*Everything stops.*) What happens when the chimes stop? (*People give a little laugh and things continue.*) I think the chiming means that death is near. Life is passing.

F Literary Elements

CHARACTER Some people think the prince is mad, but his friends say he is not. Elicit students' opinions. (*There seems to be strong evidence in everything he does that his behavior and tastes go beyond the eccentric and into madness.*)

Teaching Options

---

when the minute-hand made the circuit of the face, and the hour was to be stricken, there came from the brazen[12] lungs of the clock a sound which was clear and loud and deep and exceedingly musical, but of so peculiar a note and emphasis that, at each lapse of an hour, the musicians of the orchestra were constrained to pause, momentarily, in their performance, to hearken to the sound; and thus the waltzers perforce ceased their evolutions; and there was a brief disconcert[13] of the whole gay company; and, while the chimes of the clock yet rang, it was observed that the giddiest grew pale, and the more aged and sedate passed their hands over their brows as if in confused revery or meditation. But when the echoes had fully ceased, a light laughter at once pervaded the assembly; the musicians looked at each other and smiled as if at their own nervousness and folly, and made whispering vows, each to the other, that the next chiming of the clock should produce in them no similar emotion; and then, after the lapse of sixty minutes (which embrace three thousand and six hundred seconds of the Time that flies), there came yet another chiming of the clock, and then were the same disconcert and tremulousness and meditation as before.

But, in spite of these things, it was a gay and magnificent revel. The tastes of the duke were peculiar. He had a fine eye for colors and effects. He disregarded the *decora* of mere fashion. His plans were bold and fiery, and his conceptions glowed with barbaric lustre. There are some who would have thought him

mad. His followers felt that he was not. It was necessary to hear and see and touch him to be *sure* that he was not.

He had directed, in great part, the movable embellishments of the seven chambers, upon occasion of this great *fête*;[14] and it was his own guiding taste which had given character to the masqueraders. Be sure they were grotesque. There were much glare and glitter and piquancy and phantasm—much of what has been since seen in "Hernani."[15] There were arabesque figures with unsuited limbs and appointments. There were delirious fancies such as the madman fashions. There were much of the beautiful, much of the wanton, much of the *bizarre*, something of the terrible, and not a little of that which might have excited disgust. To and fro in the seven chambers there stalked, in fact, a multitude of dreams. And these—the dreams—writhed in and about, taking hue from the rooms, and causing the wild music of the orchestra to seem as the echo of their steps. And, anon, there strikes the ebony clock which stands in the hall of the velvet. And then, for a moment, all is still, and all is silent save the voice of the clock. The dreams are stiff-frozen as they stand. But the echoes of the chime die away—they have endured but an instant—and a light, half-subdued laughter floats after them as they depart. And now again the music swells, and the dreams live, and writhe to and fro more merrily than ever, taking hue from the many-tinted windows through which stream the rays from the tripods. But

---

12. The clock's outer parts are *ebony*, a black wood; its inner workings are brass *(brazen)*.
13. The musicians feel obliged *(constrained)* to stop playing, the waltzers halt their complex patterns of movement *(evolutions)*, and everyone experiences temporary confusion and disorder *(disconcert)*.

14. A *fête* (fāt) is a large, elaborate party.
15. Here, *piquancy* (pē′ kən sē) refers to what is charming, and *phantasm* to what is fantastic and unreal. *"Hernani,"* an 1830 drama and, especially, an opera based on the drama, is notable for the use of colorful, imaginative spectacle.

Vocabulary
wanton (wont′ ən) *adj.* shamelessly unrestrained; immoral

Listening and Speaking *Minilesson*

Creating Dialogue There is little dialogue in the story. With students, list some guidelines a writer could use to add dialogue. Here are some guidelines students might suggest:

- Use language and vocabulary appropriate to the character and time of the setting.
- Provide information about what is happening, words that indicate reactions to

what is happening, or questions about what is happening.
- Use voice inflections appropriate to the mood and tone.

Activity Have small groups of students write a dialogue to go with the scene when the clock strikes midnight and the new figure appears. (If students prefer, they may choose another scene to perform.)

Suggest that they write the dialogue and then practice it before presenting it to the class. **L2** **COLLAB. LEARN.**

to the chamber which lies most westwardly of the seven there are now none of the maskers who venture; for the night is waning away; and there flows a ruddier light through the blood-colored panes; and the blackness of the sable drapery appals; and to him whose foot falls upon the sable carpet, there comes from the near clock of ebony a muffled peal more solemnly emphatic than any which reaches *their* ears who indulge in the more remote gaieties of the other apartments.

But these other apartments were densely crowded, and in them beat feverishly the heart of life. And the revel went whirlingly on, until at length there commenced the sounding of midnight upon the clock. And then the music ceased, as I have told; and the evolutions of the waltzers were quieted; and there was an uneasy cessation of all things as before. But now there were twelve strokes to be sounded by the bell of the clock; and thus it happened, perhaps that more of thought crept, with more of time, into the meditations of the thoughtful among those who revelled. And thus too, it happened, perhaps, that before the last echoes of the last chime had utterly sunk into silence, there were many individuals in the crowd who had found leisure to become aware of the presence of a masked figure which had arrested the attention of no single individual before. And the rumor of this new presence having spread itself whisperingly around, there arose at length from the whole company a buzz, or murmur, expressive of disapprobation[16] and surprise—then, finally, of terror, of horror, and of disgust.

In an assembly of phantasms such as I have painted, it may well be supposed that no ordinary appearance could have excited such sensation. In truth the masquerade license of the night was nearly unlimited; but the figure in question had out-Heroded Herod,[17] and gone beyond the bounds of even the prince's indefinite decorum. There are chords in the hearts of the most reckless which cannot be touched without emotion. Even with the utterly lost, to whom life and death are equally jests, there are matters of which no jest can be made. The whole company, indeed, seemed now deeply to feel that in the costume and bearing of the stranger neither wit nor propriety existed. The figure was tall and gaunt, and shrouded from head to foot in the habiliments[18] of the grave. The mask which concealed the visage was made so nearly to resemble the countenance of a stiffened corpse that the closest scrutiny must have had difficulty in detecting the cheat. And yet all this might have been endured, if not approved, by the mad revellers around. But the mummer had gone so far as to assume the type of the Red Death. His vesture[19] was dabbled in *blood*—and his broad brow, with all the features of the face, was besprinkled with the scarlet horror.

When the eyes of Prince Prospero fell upon this spectral image (which, with a slow and solemn movement, as if more fully to sustain its *rôle*, stalked to and fro among the waltzers) he was seen to be convulsed, in the first moment with a strong shudder either of

---

16. *Disapprobation* means "disapproval."

17. To have *out-Heroded Herod*, the mysterious figure has done something even more outrageous than Herod the Great, the tyrant who, in an effort to kill the baby Jesus, ordered the murder of all male infants in Bethlehem.
18. *Habiliments* are clothes.
19. A *mummer* is a person dressed in a mask and costume for a party or play, and *vesture* is clothing.

Vocabulary
appal (ə pôl′) *v.* to fill with horror or dismay; shock
spectral (spek′ trəl) *adj.* ghostlike

G Literary Elements

FORESHADOWING What clues does the author give that something is about to happen? *(The author seems to be indicating that someone or something is now in the seventh room—the room where no one goes.)*

H Critical Thinking

COMPARING AND CONTRASTING A waltz and clocks are important to another story. What is the story? Does the waltz mean the same thing in both stories? Do the clocks? Are the reactions to the clocks the same or different? *(Clocks and a waltz are part of "Waltz of the Fat Man." The waltz has similar meanings in both stories, signifying life. The clocks do not. In this story, the clock is a symbol of approaching death and is dreaded. In "Waltz of the Fat Man," the clocks are substitutes for people and are loved.)*

I Critical Thinking

DRAWING CONCLUSIONS In a room full of bizarrely costumed people, a new figure catches the attention of the revellers. Ask why the figure stands out and why he causes such a stir. *(He causes a stir because his costume not only draws attention to itself but is deemed inappropriate by the other guests. He is dressed as the "Red Death," something no one finds funny.)*

Reading Minilesson

Varying Reading Rate Good readers adjust the speed of their reading depending on their purpose or the difficulty of the text. Students will need to adjust their reading rate throughout this story because Poe's writing style is difficult to read and comprehend.

Activity Invite students to skim through the story to find places where they slowed down to read in order to understand better what they were reading. Then have them locate places where they were able to read faster because the text was easier to understand. **L2**

Additional Resources
📁 *Reading Workbook,* pp. 43–44

J Critical Thinking

INFERRING Have students explain how the prince reacts to the new figure and why the figure is able to walk from room to room without anyone stopping him. *(The prince is angry. He wants the man seized, unmasked, and hung at sunrise. No one touches the figure, even though he walks very close to the prince. Everyone is afraid and repulsed. He reminds them of something they do not want to think about.)*

Thematic Focus

Challenges and Consequences
Discuss with students how the prince chose to face his challenge and what the consequence was. Invite opinions as to whether the fate of the prince and his friends would have been different if he had chosen an alternative way of facing the challenge.

ASSESSMENT OPTIONS

📁 *Quick Checks*, p. 34

FINE ART
TRANSPARENCY 10

You may wish to use Fine Art Transparency 10 to discuss similarities of characters, settings and time to those in the story.

Teaching Options

terror or distaste; but, in the next, his brow reddened with rage.

"Who dares"—he demanded hoarsely of the courtiers who stood near him—"who dares insult us with this blasphemous mockery? Seize him and unmask him—that we may know whom we have to hang, at sunrise, from the battlements!"

It was in the eastern or blue chamber in which stood the Prince Prospero as he uttered these words. They rang throughout the seven rooms loudly and clearly, for the prince was a bold and robust man, and the music had become hushed at the waving of his hand.

It was in the blue room where stood the prince, with a group of pale courtiers by his side. At first, as he spoke, there was a slight rushing movement of this group in the direction of the intruder, who, at the moment was also near at hand, and now, with deliberate and stately step, made closer approach to the speaker. But from a certain nameless awe with which the mad assumptions of the mummer had inspired the whole party, there were found none who put forth hand to seize him; so that, unimpeded, he passed within a yard of the prince's person; and, while the vast assembly, as if with one impulse, shrank from the centres of the rooms to the walls, he made his way uninterruptedly, but with the same solemn and measured step which had distinguished him from the first, through the blue chamber to the purple—through the purple to the green—through the green to the orange—through this again to the white—and even thence to the violet, ere a decided movement had been made to arrest

him. It was then, however, that the Prince Prospero, maddening with rage and the shame of his own momentary cowardice, rushed hurriedly through the six chambers, while none followed him on account of a deadly terror that had seized upon all. He bore aloft a drawn dagger, and had approached, in rapid impetuosity, to within three or four feet of the retreating figure, when the latter, having attained the extremity of the velvet apartment, turned suddenly and confronted his pursuer. There was a sharp cry—and the dagger dropped gleaming upon the sable carpet, upon which, instantly afterward, fell prostrate in death the Prince Prospero. Then, summoning the wild courage of despair, a throng of the revellers at once threw themselves into the black apartment, and, seizing the mummer, whose tall figure stood erect and motionless within the shadow of the ebony clock, gasped in unutterable horror at finding the grave cerements[20] and corpse-like mask, which they handled with so violent a rudeness, untenanted[21] by any tangible form.

And now was acknowledged the presence of the Red Death. He had come like a thief in the night. And one by one dropped the revellers in the blood-bedewed halls of their revel, and died each in the despairing posture of his fall. And the life of the ebony clock went out with that of the last of the gay. And the flames of the tripods expired. And Darkness and Decay and the Red Death held illimitable dominion over all.

---

20. *Cerements* are strips of cloth used to wrap a dead body.
21. *Untenanted* means "unoccupied or uninhabited."

Vocabulary
blasphemous (blas′ fə məs) *adj.* showing disrespect or scorn for God or anything sacred

Grammar and Language *Minilesson*

Demonstrative Pronouns Write *this, these, that,* and *those* on the board. These demonstrative pronouns point out specific people or things.

Activity Ask students to identify the demonstrative pronoun and its referent.
1. That is a scary room. *(That; room)*
2. These were not people the prince invited to his abbey. *(These; people)* **L1**

Additional Resources

✒️ *Grammar and Language Transparency 34*

📘 *Grammar and Language Workbook,* p. 54

📘 *Grammar and Composition Handbook,* Lesson 1.2

📘 *Writer's Choice,* Lesson 10.2

Responding to Literature

Personal Response

If you had been a guest at the ball, what do you think you would have done when you saw the masked stranger? Why?

───── ANALYZING LITERATURE ─────

RECALL

1. What is the "Red Death"? Explain how it affects its victims.
2. Briefly describe the seven rooms in which the masked ball is held.
3. Describe the clock that stands in the seventh room. What happens each time the clock chimes?
4. How are the guests dressed for the ball? What are some words Poe uses to describe their appearance?
5. How does Prince Prospero react to the midnight guest? What happens to the prince? To his guests?

INTERPRET

6. In your opinion, what does Prince Prospero's response to the "Red Death" reveal about his character?
7. Why do you think Prospero decorated the rooms the way he did?
8. What do you think the clock **symbolizes?**
9. How is the appearance of the "midnight guest" similar to that of the other guests? How is it different?
10. At the end of the story, Poe alludes to a biblical prophecy that the day of judgment will come "as a thief in the night." Why do you think Poe makes this **allusion?**

EVALUATE AND CONNECT

11. Do you think Poe is using **irony** when he says that Prince Prospero is brave and wise? Explain your answer.
12. In your opinion, what is the **moral,** or lesson, of this story? Explain.
13. How might people react today if their political leaders responded to a crisis as Prince Prospero did? Explain.
14. Think back to the discussion you had in response to the Focus Activity on page 388. Has this story changed your ideas about the level of control you feel you have over events in your life? Explain.
15. Theme Connections   Consider Prince Prospero's response to the challenge he faces at the beginning of the story. If his response had been different, do you think it might have altered his fate? Explain.

Literary ELEMENTS

Setting and Mood

Setting refers to the time and place in which a story occurs. A writer's use of sensory details can make the setting come alive for readers and can affect the **mood,** or atmosphere, of the story. In a horror story, the setting often helps create a growing sense of terror. For example, Poe sets "The Masque of the Red Death" in Prince Prospero's extensive and magnificent abbey. The people within believe that nothing and no one can penetrate its gates of iron.

1. Contrast the mood outside the prince's abbey to that within. What details does Poe use at the beginning of the story to create these contrasting moods?
2. What sensory details used to describe the setting help to create a mood of horror? Find two examples each of details that appeal to the senses of sight, hearing, and touch. Explain how each detail contributes to the mood of horror.

⬤ See **Literary Terms Handbook,** p. R8.

Responding to the Selection

Personal Response

Reactions will vary, but most students will probably indicate they would try to flee from the masked stranger because they would be afraid.

ANALYZING LITERATURE

1. The "Red Death" is a contagious disease. People feel pains and dizziness. Then they start bleeding from the pores until they die.
2. Each room is a different color and has stained glass windows. The seventh room is black with red windows. It has a clock that chimes.
3. The clock is large, is made of ebony, and has a pendulum. When the clock chimes, everyone stops to listen and feels apprehensive.
4. The guests are dressed in bizarre costumes. Poe uses words like *barbaric lustre, grotesque, much glare, glitter, piquancy, phantasm, wanton,* and *bizarre.*
5. The prince is angry and is then the first to die. Shortly thereafter, everyone dies.
6. The Prince's response indicates he cares little for his people. He is selfish and self-centered, caring only about himself and his friends. He seems to think he is beyond the reach of death.
7. Perhaps he decorated as he did because he likes unusual things, or perhaps he did it because he is mad.
8. The clock seems to symbolize the passing of life and the approach of death.
9. The "midnight guest" is dressed in a grotesque costume. It is more outrageous and frightening than all the others.
10. He may have made the allusion to warn us to be prepared for death and not to act like we will live forever.
11. Most students will say that Poe is using irony. Perhaps his friends think the prince is brave and wise, but his actions indicate otherwise.
12. The moral might be that you cannot tempt fate. You cannot run away or avoid the inevitable. No one is beyond death. Death is the great leveler of the classes.
13. People would probably remove the

LITERARY ELEMENTS

1. Outside: disease and death; *devastated, pestilence,* and *hideous.* Inside: happiness and plenty; *light-hearted, amply provisioned,* and *appliances of pleasure.*
2. Allow students to suggest a variety of choices for each of the sensory details.

Additional Resources
📁 *Literary Elements Transparency 34*

leader from office. They expect leaders to look out for them and to work for their best interests.
14. Many students will probably admit that there are some things in life over which no one has control.
15. Some students might say that he could alter his fate by acting in positive, helpful ways. Others will probably say he would have died no matter what.

LITERATURE AND WRITING

Writing About Literature

Students' analyses should
- identify several allegorical symbols.
- explain what each symbol means or stands for.
- tell how the symbols are connected.
- explain how the symbols connect to the moral of the story.

Personal Writing

Students' R.S.V.P.'s should
- state whether the student is coming or not.
- give a reason for the decision.
- use a formal tone.

EXTENDING YOUR RESPONSE

Literature Groups Suggest that each group appoint a spokesperson to report the conclusions the group reached. **COLLAB. LEARN.**

Interdisciplinary Activity After the rooms have been drawn, you might appoint a group to make a display of the drawings, putting the rooms in the proper color sequence.

Listening and Speaking Remind students to prepare a list of questions to ask before attempting the interview. Also, remind them that the questions and answers should reflect the times and the setting.

At the MOVIES

Be sure to preview the following video for appropriateness for your class:

- **Masque of the Red Death**

———— LITERATURE AND WRITING ————

Writing About Literature

Analyze Allegorical Symbols In an **allegory**—a literary work whose underlying meaning differs from the literal meaning—the writer often uses characters, objects, or events as symbols. In this story, for example, Prince Prospero might represent selfishness. Identify other allegorical symbols in the story. Explain what you think each symbol represents, how the symbols are connected, and how they contribute to the lesson, or moral, of the story. Share your ideas with a small group of classmates.

Personal Writing

R.S.V.P. Imagine that you have received an invitation from Prince Prospero to be sealed up in the abbey with the one thousand knights and ladies. Write a note responding to the invitation. Explain why you will or will not come.

———— EXTENDING YOUR RESPONSE ————

Literature Groups

What Makes a Good Horror Story? Create a horror story web using words and phrases that, in your opinion, describe essential elements of a good horror story. Use "The Masque of the Red Death" and other horror stories you know as a guide. Refer to your web as you debate this question in your group: *What are the essential elements of a good horror story?* Share your ideas with the class.

Interdisciplinary Activity

Art: Party Decor Poe gives a detailed description of how Prince Prospero decorated the seven rooms in which the masked ball was held. Reread the description, and then draw a picture of one or more of the rooms. You may wish to include in your drawing the corridors that stand outside each room.

Listening and Speaking

Interview With a partner, prepare questions for an interview with a servant who survived Prince Prospero's masked ball. Conduct the interview, with one person playing the role of the servant and the other the role of the interviewer. Tape-record the interview and play it for the class, or do a live performance.

Reading Further

Edgar Allan Poe's best-known stories can be found in this collection:

Short Story Collection: *The Essential Poe Tales of Mystery and Horror* presents twenty-six thrilling tales including "The Tell-Tale Heart" and "The Murder in the Rue Morgue."

Viewing: *Masque of the Red Death,* stars Vincent Price as Prince Prospero.

📖 **Save your work for your portfolio.**

✓ ASSESSMENT OPTIONS

- 📁 *Quick Checks,* p. 34
- 📁 *Selection and Theme Assessment,* pp. 65–66
- 📁 *Performance Assessment,* p. 33
- 💾 *Testmaker*

Skill Minilessons

Skill Minilessons

GRAMMAR AND LANGUAGE • Subject Complements

The two kinds of **subject complements** are predicate nominatives and predicate adjectives. A **predicate nominative** is a noun or pronoun that follows a linking verb and points back to the subject to identify or rename it.

Prospero is a *prince* who tries to escape the Red Death.

A **predicate adjective** follows a linking verb and points back to the subject to further describe it.

The disease is *hideous* and *fatal.*

PRACTICE   Complete each sentence by adding one or more nouns, pronouns, or adjectives. (You may also add other words.) Write *PN* or *PA* to identify each predicate nominative or predicate adjective.

1. Prince Prospero seems _____ .
2. The prince's abbey is _____ .
3. The guests at the abbey are _____ .
4. In the black room, people's faces look _____ .
5. The mysterious guest is_____ .

● For more about complements, see **Language Handbook,** p. R39.

READING AND THINKING • Visualizing

Using story details, you can create a mental picture of the setting, characters, and events. Reread Poe's description of the "Red Death" at the beginning of the story. Feel the horror as you visualize its victims racked with dizziness, sharp pains, and bleeding at the pores.

PRACTICE   Find a passage in the story that helps you visualize a particular character, event, or element of the setting. Explain to a classmate the mental picture that you

"see" after reading this passage. Discuss how visualizing the passage adds to your understanding of the story.

APPLY   Visualize the final events of the story, starting with the moment when Prince Prospero first notices the ghastly guest. Then draw a picture that you think captures the horror of the final moments of the masked ball.

● For more about reading strategies, see **Reading Handbook,** p. R84.

VOCABULARY • Analogies

An analogy is a type of comparison that is based on the relationships between things or ideas. This relationship can be expressed in a statement:

owl : sagacious :: lion : dauntless

The **owl** often represents the quality of being **sagacious.** Replacing the boldface words with the second pair of words in the analogy results in another statement: *The lion often represents the quality of being* **dauntless.**

To finish an analogy, decide what relationship exists between the first two things or ideas. Then apply that relationship to another pair of words and see if it is the same.

● For more about analogies, see **Communications Skills Handbook,** p. R77.

PRACTICE   Choose the word that best completes each analogy.

1. nose : countenance :: finger :
   a. thumb   b. knuckle   c. hand
2. please : delight :: appal :
   a. interest   b. horrify   c. bore
3. spectral : tangible :: sagacious :
   a. wise   b. practical   c. ignorant
4. generous : stingy :: profuse :
   a. sufficient   b. meager   c. abundant
5. blasphemous : reverence :: wanton :
   a. evil   b. restraint   c. desire

THE SHORT STORY 🐾 397

GRAMMAR AND LANGUAGE
Subject Complements

Typical answers are given.
1. selfish; PA
2. castellated; PA
3. friends; PN
4. fearful; PA
5. death; PN

READING AND THINKING
Visualizing

Practice

Classmates can provide feedback after a description by telling the other person if they too were able to see the picture that was painted for them.

VOCABULARY
Analogies

1. c   2. b   3. c
4. b   5. b

Additional Resources

📗 *Grammar and Composition Handbook,* Lesson 2.5

📗 *Grammar and Language Workbook,* p. 85

📗 *Writer's Choice,* Lesson 11.5

📁 *Reading Workbook,* pp. 43–44

📁 *Vocabulary Practice,* p. 33

Before Reading

Objectives

- To read and analyze a short story about a girl, her grandmother, and clashing cultures
- To identify examples of local color
- To write a paragraph about a dynamic character

Skills

Reading/Thinking: Inferring; Cause and Effect; Sequence; Activating Prior Knowledge
Writing: Picture Storybook
Vocabulary: Synonyms
Grammar/Language: Apostrophes; Concrete and Abstract Nouns
Listening/Speaking: Persuasive Conversation
Collaboration: Literature Groups

Before You Read

To Da-duh, in Memoriam

FOCUS ACTIVITY

Have you ever heard the following sayings?
Opposites attract.
Birds of a feather flock together.

JOURNAL Think about the two sayings in terms of your own relationships with family members. With whom do you get along the best—relatives whose personalities are similar to yours, or those with personalities that are different from your own? Record your thoughts in your journal.

SETTING A PURPOSE Read to find out about the relationship between a child from the city and her Barbadian grandmother.

BACKGROUND

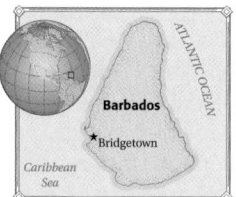

The Time and Place
"To Da-duh, in Memoriam" takes place in Barbados, in the 1930s.

Did You Know?
Barbados is a tiny Caribbean island, with mostly flat terrain. Its highest point, Mount Hillaby, is shorter than New York City's Empire State Building. The island became an independent state in 1966, after being under British colonial rule for more than three centuries. Although the people of Barbados speak English, the folk culture is of African origin. From 1937 to 1938, the island experienced violent unrest as a result of economic depression and other stresses.

VOCABULARY PREVIEW

formidable (fôr′ mi də bəl) *adj.* causing fear, dread, or awe by reason of size, strength, or power; p. 400

decrepit (di krep′ it) *adj.* broken down by long use or old age; p. 401

hurtle (hurt′ əl) *v.* to move rapidly, especially with much force or noise; p. 403

arrogant (ar′ ə gənt) *adj.* full of self-importance; haughty; p. 403

malicious (mə lish′ əs) *adj.* having or showing a desire to harm another; p. 407

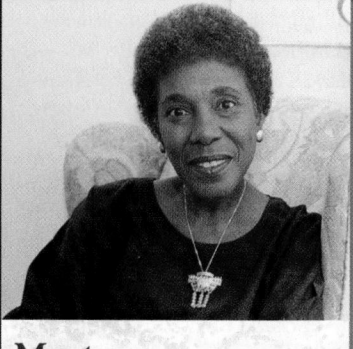

Meet Paule Marshall

Paule Marshall grew up in a Barbadian community in New York City, where, she says, she learned all about writing in her mother's kitchen. In this "word-shop," her mother and her mother's friends passed on to her "the rich legacy of language and culture" that they shared after their workdays of "scrubbing floor." Marshall went on to write many award-winning novels, short stories, and articles, including her most famous work, *Praisesong for the Widow.*

The story you are about to read is "the most autobiographical of the stories."

Paule Marshall was born in Brooklyn, New York, in 1929. This story was first published in 1967 in New World *Magazine.*

RESOURCE MANAGER

To Da-duh, in Memoriam

Paule Marshall

"... Oh Nana! all of you
is not involved in this evil
business Death,
Nor all of us in life."

—*from* "At My
Grandmother's Grave,"
by Lebert Bethune

Peaceful Day, 1994. Shakito. 18 x 24 in.
Private collection.

THE SHORT STORY 399

Reading the Selection

SUMMARY

A young girl from New York visits her grandmother in Barbados. The woman shows her favorite places to the child, and the child tells about New York. Each tries to top the other. Finally, the grandmother shows the child a high hill. The child counters with a description of the Empire State Building. The grandmother has been "topped" and loses interest in life. Soon after the child's return to New York, the grandmother dies. Throughout her life, the child remembers and feels guilty.

📁 *Spanish Summaries,* p. 35

A Active Reading

RESPOND Have students read the first paragraph on page 400. Discuss what the girl's first reaction to Barbados was and ask students what their reaction was. Ask students in what ways the setting might become important to the story.

Additional Resources
📁 *Active Reading Guide,* p. 35
🎧 *Audio Library*
🎧 *Spanish Audio Library*

Teaching Options

CONNECTING TO OTHER SELECTIONS

The chart at the right shows three ways to connect "To Da-duh, in Memoriam" to selections in this book.

For specific teaching strategies, see the **Unit One Planning Guide,** pages 297–298.

Connection	Title
Life Skills: Decision Making	→ "The Road Not Taken," p. 643
Thematic: Family Relationships	→ *Antigone,* p. 727
Literary: Setting	→ "By the Waters of Babylon," p. 95

B Literary Elements

LOCAL COLOR Ask students to identify some examples of local color included in the first paragraph. *(Students might mention the sheen of the tropical sunlight, the bay, the boat, and the ship.)*

C Active Reading

PREDICT Guide students to predict the kind of person Da-duh is. Remind them that in predicting they use clues from the text, personal experience, and things they know about stories. The following model could be used to illustrate the process.

Model: What kind of person is Da-duh? The author spends time describing how the woman will not give in to her bending back but instead is determined to stand tall. This information is meant to tell me something. When she steps forward and walks toward the group, she obviously does so as one who is used to being in charge of things. I predict the grandmother will be a strong, determined character, one who takes charge of everyone and everything.

D Literary Elements

FIGURES OF SPEECH: *Simile* Remind students that a simile is a comparison of two unlike things, using the word *like* or *as*. Ask students to identify what is being compared to the light that seems to flick out of the grandmother's eyes. *(a lizard's tongue)*

Teaching Options

400 🦋 UNIT 1

I did not see her at first I remember. For not only was it dark inside the crowded disembarkation[1] shed in spite of the daylight flooding in from outside, but standing there waiting for her with my mother and sister I was still somewhat blinded from the sheen of tropical sunlight on the water of the bay which we had just crossed in the landing boat, leaving behind us the ship that had brought us from New York lying in the offing.[2] Besides, being only nine years of age at the time and knowing nothing of islands I was busy attending to the alien sights and sounds of Barbados, the unfamiliar smells.

I did not see her, but I was alerted to her approach by my mother's hand which suddenly tightened around mine, and looking up I traced her gaze through the gloom in the shed until I finally made out the small, purposeful, painfully erect figure of the old woman headed our way.

Her face was drowned in the shadow of an ugly rolled-brim brown felt hat, but the details of her slight body and of the struggle taking place within it were clear enough—an intense, unrelenting[3] struggle between her back which was beginning to bend ever so slightly under the weight of her eighty-odd years and the rest of her which sought to deny those years and hold that back straight, keep it in line. Moving swiftly toward us (so swiftly it seemed she did not intend stopping when she reached us but would sweep past us out the doorway which opened onto the sea and like Christ walk upon the water!), she was caught between the

sunlight at her end of the building and the darkness inside—and for a moment she appeared to contain them both: the light in the long severe old-fashioned white dress she wore which brought the sense of a past that was still alive into our bustling present and in the snatch of white at her eye; the darkness in her black high-top shoes and in her face which was visible now that she was closer.

It was as stark and fleshless as a death mask, that face. The maggots might have already done their work, leaving only the framework of bone beneath the ruined skin and deep wells at the temple and jaw. But her eyes were alive, unnervingly so for one so old, with a sharp light that flicked out of the dim clouded depths like a lizard's tongue to snap up all in her view. Those eyes betrayed a child's curiosity about the world, and I wondered vaguely seeing them, and seeing the way the bodice of her ancient dress had collapsed in on her flat chest (what had happened to her breasts?), whether she might not be some kind of child at the same time that she was a woman, with fourteen children, my mother included, to prove it. Perhaps she was both, both child and woman, darkness and light, past and present, life and death—all the opposites contained and reconciled in her.

"My Da-duh," my mother said formally and stepped forward. The name sounded like thunder fading softly in the distance.

"Child," Da-duh said, and her tone, her quick scrutiny of my mother, the brief embrace in which they appeared to shy from each other rather than touch, wiped out the fifteen years my mother had been away and restored the old relationship. My mother, who was such a <u>formidable</u> figure in my eyes, had suddenly with a word been reduced to my status.

---

1. To *disembark* is to get off a ship or plane.
2. In this context, *in the offing* means "just in view from the shore."
3. An *unrelenting* (un′ ri len′ ting) struggle is one that does not ease or lessen in intensity.

Vocabulary
formidable (fôr′ mi də bəl) *adj.* causing fear, dread, or awe by reason of size, strength, or power

400 🦋 UNIT 1

ENGLISH LANGUAGE LEARNERS

Comparing Settings The author describes Barbados, a tropical island in the Caribbean. Have English language learners identify words and phrases they associate with a tropical island. They might mention *sunny, hot, palm trees, sandy beaches,* and *ocean.*

Activity Invite students to compare the story setting with the country they

came from or the place where they now live. Ask questions such as these: *What is the climate like? What kinds of trees and plants grow there?* Ask students to note similar details about the story setting.

Additional Resources
📁 *English Language Learners Sourcebook*

"Yes, God is good," Da-duh said with a nod that was like a tic.[4] "He has spared me to see my child again."

We were led forward then, apologetically because not only did Da-duh prefer boys but she also liked her grandchildren to be "white," that is, fair-skinned; and we had, I was to discover, a number of cousins, the outside children of white estate managers and the like, who qualified. We, though, were as black as she.

My sister being the oldest was presented first. "This one takes after the father," my mother said and waited to be reproved.

Frowning, Da-duh tilted my sister's face toward the light. But her frown soon gave way to a grudging smile, for my sister with her large mild eyes and little broad winged nose, with our father's high-cheeked Barbadian cast to her face, was pretty.

"She's goin' be lucky," Da-duh said and patted her once on the cheek. "Any girl child that takes after the father does be lucky."

She turned then to me. But oddly enough she did not touch me. Instead leaning close, she peered hard at me, and then quickly drew back. I thought I saw her hand start up as though to shield her eyes. It was almost as if she saw not only me, a thin truculent[5] child who it was said took after no one but myself, but something in me which for some reason she found disturbing, even threatening. We looked silently at each other for a long time there in the noisy shed, our gaze locked. She was the first to look away.

"But Adry," she said to my mother and her laugh was cracked, thin, apprehensive. "Where did you get this one here with this fierce look?"

"We don't know where she came out of, my Da-duh," my mother said, laughing also. Even I smiled to myself. After all I had won the encounter. Da-duh had recognized my small strength—and this was all I ever asked of the adults in my life then.

"Come, soul," Da-duh said and took my hand. "You must be one of those New York terrors you hear so much about."

She led us, me at her side and my sister and mother behind, out of the shed into the sunlight that was like a bright driving summer rain and over to a group of people clustered beside a decrepit lorry. They were our relatives, most of them from St. Andrews although Da-duh herself lived in St. Thomas, the women wearing bright print dresses, the colors vivid against their darkness, the men rusty black suits that encased them like strait-jackets. Da-duh, holding fast to my hand, became my anchor as they circled round us like a nervous sea, exclaiming, touching us with their calloused hands, embracing us shyly. They laughed in awed bursts: "But look Adry got big-big children!" / "And see the nice things they wearing, wristwatch and all!" / "I tell you, Adry has done all right for sheself in New York. . . ."

Da-duh, ashamed at their wonder, embarrassed for them, admonished them the while. . . . "Why you all got to get on like you never saw people from 'Away' before? You would think New York is the only place in the world to hear wunna.[6] That's why I don't like

Did You Know?
Lorry is what the British call a truck.

---

4. Here, a *tic* is an involuntary twitching.
5. To be *truculent* is to be fierce and ready to fight.

6. *To hear wunna* may be Da-duh's way of saying "to have wonders."

Vocabulary
decrepit (di krep′ it) *adj.* broken down by long use or old age

---

E Critical Thinking

INFERRING Be sure students understand what the girl means when she says her mother had been reduced to her status in a single word. *(The grandmother used the word* child. *With the word* child, *the mother became the grandmother's child—the same status as the girl.)*

F Literary Elements

FORESHADOWING What happens between the girl and her grandmother? How does the child feel afterwards? Why? What might this event foreshadow? *(She and the grandmother have a staring contest. The child feels happy, triumphant; she has won a small contest over a formidable opponent. This event might foreshadow other such contests.)*

G Active Reading

QUESTION Discuss what students think the grandmother sees when she looks at the child. *(herself; someone as stubborn and determined as she is)*

H Active Reading

REVIEW Students should note the developing bond between the grandmother and the child. At this point in the story, how does the grandmother feel about the child? How does the child feel about the grandmother? *(The grandmother likes the child. She takes her hand and leads her to the other relatives ahead of her mother and sister, thus giving the child a special status. The child likes the grandmother and sees her as an anchor in an unfamiliar place.)*

VIEWING THE PAINTING

The style and content of this painting reflect the mood and setting of the story.

Viewing Response *The house looks like Da-duh's small "weathered board and shingle" house. It is surrounded by tropical trees and other vegetation just as Da-duh's house is.*

ⓘ Literary Elements

FIGURES OF SPEECH: *Personification*
The trip through the town is called a "funereal procession." Discuss ways the author compares it to such a procession. Then have students identify the thing being personified. *(The trip is slow-moving with many vehicles in the procession. Slow-moving people also walk along, and dissonant voices are heard. The shops and offices are personified. They are said to march at a mournful pace.)*

Cultural Note

Each culture and place has its own funeral rituals. In New Orleans, a small band sometimes walks in the procession to the cemetery, playing sad music. On the trip back, however, the band plays lively tunes, such as "When the Saints Go Marchin' In."

Teaching Options

Good Old Days, 1993. Shakito. Private collection.

Viewing the painting:
How is this house similar to Da-duh's? How do the grounds reflect the island in the story?

to go anyplace with you St. Andrews people, you know. You all ain't been colonized."

We were in the back of the lorry finally, packed in among the barrels of ham, flour, cornmeal and rice and the trunks of clothes that my mother had brought as gifts. We made our way slowly through Bridgetown's clogged streets, part of a funereal[7] procession of cars and open-sided buses, bicycles and donkey carts. The dim little limestone shops and offices along the way marched with us, at the same mournful pace, toward the same grave ceremony—as did the people, the women balancing huge baskets on top their heads as if they were no more than hats they wore to shade them from the sun. Looking over the edge of the lorry I watched as their feet slurred the dust. I listened, and their voices, raw and loud and dissonant in the

heat, seemed to be grappling with each other high overhead.

Da-duh sat on a trunk in our midst, a monarch amid her court. She still held my hand, but it was different now. I had suddenly become her anchor, for I felt her fear of the lorry with its asthmatic motor (a fear and distrust, I later learned, she held of all machines) beating like a pulse in her rough palm.

As soon as we left Bridgetown behind though, she relaxed, and while the others around us talked she gazed at the canes standing tall on either side of the winding marl[8] road. "C'dear," she said softly to herself after a time. "The canes this side are pretty enough."

They were too much for me. I thought of them as giant weeds that had overrun the

---

7. *Funereal* means "like, or suitable to, a funeral."

8. A *marl* road is paved with a crumbly clay of the sort used to make cement.

402 UNIT 1

MEETING INDIVIDUAL NEEDS — INCLUSION STRATEGIES

Less-Proficient Readers Dialect can be difficult to comprehend, even by proficient readers. It often consists of abbreviated forms of words as in *goin'* or *din'*; words or phrases that have special meanings, such as *to hear wunna;* and special uses of grammar as in *Adry has done all right for sheself* and *Who tell you I need bush tea?*

Activity Have students use stick-on tabs to mark dialect in the story they have trouble understanding. Read the passages for them and as a group discuss the meanings. **L1**

Additional Resources
📁 *Inclusion Strategies*

island, leaving scarcely any room for the small tottering houses of sunbleached pine we passed or the people, dark streaks as our lorry hurtled by. I suddenly feared that we were journeying, unaware that we were, toward some dangerous place where the canes, grown as high and thick as a forest, would close in on us and run us through with their stiletto blades. I longed then for the familiar: for the street in Brooklyn[9] where I lived, for my father who had refused to accompany us ("Blowing out good money on foolishness," he had said of the trip), for a game of tag with my friends under the chestnut tree outside our aging brownstone house.

"Yes, but wait till you see St. Thomas canes," Da-duh was saying to me. "They's canes father, bo," she gave a proud arrogant nod. "Tomorrow, God willing, I goin' take you out in the ground and show them to you."

True to her word Da-duh took me with her the following day out into the ground. It was a fairly large plot adjoining her weathered board and shingle house and consisting of a small orchard, a good-sized canepiece and behind the canes, where the land sloped abruptly down, a gully. She had purchased it with Panama money sent her by her eldest son, my uncle Joseph, who had died working on the canal. We entered the ground along a trail no wider than her body and as devious and complex as her reasons for showing me her land. Da-duh strode briskly ahead, her slight form filled out this morning by the layers of sacking petticoats she wore under her working dress to protect her against the damp. A fresh white cloth, elaborately arranged around her head, added to her height, and lent her a vain, almost roguish air.

Her pace slowed once we reached the orchard, and glancing back at me occasionally over her shoulder, she pointed out the various trees.

"This here is a breadfruit," she said. "That one yonder is a papaw. Here's a guava. This is a mango. I know you don't have anything like these in New York. Here's a sugar apple." (The fruit looked more like artichokes than apples to me.) "This one bears limes. . . ." She went on for some time, intoning the names of the trees as though they were those of her gods. Finally, turning to me, she said, "I know you don't have anything this nice where you come from." Then, as I hesitated: "I said I know you don't have anything this nice where you come from. . . ."

"No," I said and my world did seem suddenly lacking.

Da-duh nodded and passed on. The orchard ended and we were on the narrow cart road that led through the canepiece, the canes clashing like swords above my cowering head. Again she turned and her thin muscular arms spread wide, her dim gaze embracing the small field of canes, she said—and her voice almost broke under the weight of her pride, "Tell me, have you got anything like these in that place where you were born?"

"No."

"I din' think so. I bet you don't even know that these canes here and the sugar you eat is one and the same thing. That they does throw the canes into some damn machine at the factory and squeeze out all the little life in them to make sugar for you all so in New York to eat. I bet you don't know that."

"I've got two cavities and I'm not allowed to eat a lot of sugar."

---

9. *Brooklyn* is one of New York City's five boroughs, or districts.

Vocabulary
hurtle (hurt′ əl) *v.* to move rapidly, especially with much force or noise
arrogant (ar′ ə gənt) *adj.* full of self-importance; haughty

---

J **Author's Craft**

CONTRASTS Throughout the story, the author creates contrasts between the girl and her grandmother and between the grandmother's home and the child's. The child's thoughts about the cane and the grandmother's comments are an example. Ask students to explain this contrast. *(The grandmother sees the canes as pretty and is proud to say that the ones where she lives are even bigger. She is eager to show her canes to the child. The girl dislikes the canes, seeing them as weeds overrunning the place and closing in on her.)*

FYI

Sugar Cane The cane the grandmother is showing the child is sugar cane. The stalks can grow from 7 to 30 feet high and to a diameter of 2 inches.

K **Active Reading**

QUESTION Students should stop and ask themselves what is happening here. *(The grandmother seems very proud of her orchard and cane. She seems to want the girl to like it, too. She does this by challenging the girl, asking her if New York has anything like this. Since the city does not, the girl seems defensive. This may be the beginning of a conflict.)*

GIFTED AND TALENTED

Panama Canal The narrator mentions Panama money that the grandmother got when her oldest son died working on the Panama Canal.

Activity Invite small groups of students to do research on the canal and to write a report about it. They might investigate how disease problems were eliminated and by whom, how the locks are arranged and how they work, and what the political issues regarding the canal—both past and present—have been. When the reports have been completed, ask each group to present its report to the class. **L3** **COLLAB. LEARN.**

L Literary Elements

LOCAL COLOR Have students discuss some of the details the author included here that reflect local color. *(On this page, the author describes the cane and banana plants, a gully, a small tropical wood, and the perennial summer of the place. The grandmother also speaks in dialect.)*

M Critical Thinking

INFERRING Why does the grandmother show the girl all these wonderful places? *(The grandmother loves these places and is fiercely proud of them. Because they mean so much to her, the grandmother wants her granddaughter to see them. These places are the grandmother's life. They are what matter to her.)*

N Critical Thinking

INFERRING What does the child's answer to the grandmother's question about snow tell you about the child? *(Her exaggerated description of snow tells the reader that she is feeling defensive. However, she is also pleased that an adult is actually interested in what she has to say.)*

But Da-duh didn't hear me. She had turned with an inexplicably angry motion and was making her way rapidly out of the canes and down the slope at the edge of the field which led to the gully below. Following her apprehensively down the incline amid a stand of banana plants whose leaves flapped like elephants' ears in the wind, I found myself in the middle of a small tropical wood—a place dense and damp and gloomy and tremulous with the fitful play of light and shadow as the leaves high above moved against the sun that was almost hidden from view. It was a violent place, the tangled foliage fighting each other for a chance at the sunlight, the branches of the trees locked in what seemed an immemorial[10] struggle, one both necessary and inevitable. But despite the violence, it was pleasant, almost peaceful in the gully, and beneath the thick undergrowth the earth smelled like spring.

This time Da-duh didn't even bother to ask her usual question, but simply turned and waited for me to speak.

"No," I said, my head bowed. "We don't have anything like this in New York."

"Ah," she cried, her triumph complete. "I din' think so. Why, I've heard that's a place where you can walk till you near drop and never see a tree."

"We've got a chestnut tree in front of our house," I said.

"Does it bear?" She waited. "I ask you, does it bear?"

It was a violent place, the tangled foliage fighting each other for a chance at the sunlight . . .

"Not anymore," I muttered. "It used to, but not anymore."

She gave the nod that was like a nervous twitch. "You see," she said. "Nothing can bear there." Then, secure behind her scorn, she added, "But tell me, what's this snow like that you hear so much about?"

Looking up, I studied her closely, sensing my chance, and then I told her, describing at length and with as much drama as I could summon not only what snow in the city was like, but what it would be like here, in her perennial summer kingdom.

". . . And you see all these trees you got here," I said. "Well, they'd be bare. No leaves, no fruit, nothing. They'd be covered in snow. You see your canes. They'd be buried under tons of snow. The snow would be higher than your head, higher than your house, and you wouldn't be able to come down into this here gully because it would be snowed under. . . ."

She searched my face for the lie, still scornful but intrigued. "What a thing, huh?" she said finally, whispering it softly to herself.

"And when it snows you couldn't dress like you are now," I said. "Oh no, you'd freeze to death. You'd have to wear a hat and gloves and galoshes and ear muffs so your ears wouldn't freeze and drop off, and a heavy coat. I've got a Shirley Temple[11] coat with fur on the collar. I can dance. You wanna see?"

Before she could answer I began, with a dance called the Truck which was popular back then in the 1930s. My right forefinger waving, I trucked around the nearby trees and

---

10. An *immemorial* struggle would be one that extended back beyond memory or record.

11. *Shirley Temple* was a popular child movie star of the 1930s.

LITERATURE & HUMANITIES

Show students *Papiamento* (*Art Talk*, p. 8) and ask them how the artist represents the woman's relationship to the earth and how this relationship compares to that of the grandmother and her home in the story.

MEETING INDIVIDUAL NEEDS — ENGLISH LANGUAGE LEARNERS

A Strange New World The grandmother asks the child to tell her about New York—a place strange and foreign to an eighty-year-old woman who has lived all her life in Barbados.

Activity Ask English language learners to imagine that they must describe the place where they now live to a person from their native culture who has never been to the United States. What things would the person need to know? Ask each student to create a list.

Additional Resources
📁 *English Language Learners Sourcebook*

around Da-duh's awed and rigid form. After the Truck I did the Suzy-Q, my lean hips swishing, my sneakers sidling zigzag over the ground. "I can sing," I said and did so, starting with "I'm Gonna Sit Right Down and Write Myself a Letter," then without pausing, "Tea For Two," and ending with "I Found a Million Dollar Baby in a Five and Ten Cent Store."

For long moments afterwards Da-duh stared at me as if I were a creature from Mars, an emissary from some world she did not know but which intrigued her and whose power she both felt and feared. Yet something about my performance must have pleased her, because bending down she slowly lifted her long skirt and then, one by one, the layers of petticoats until she came to a drawstring purse dangling at the end of a long strip of cloth tied round her waist. Opening the purse she handed me a penny. "Here," she said half-smiling against her will. "Take this to buy yourself a sweet at the shop up the road. There's nothing to be done with you, soul."

From then on, whenever I wasn't taken to visit relatives, I accompanied Da-duh out into the ground, and alone with her amid the canes or down in the gully I told her about New York. It always began with some slighting remark on her part: "I know they don't have anything this nice where you come from," or "Tell me, I hear those foolish people in New York does do such and such. . . ." But as I answered, recreating my towering world of steel and concrete and machines for her, building the city out of words, I would feel her give way. I came to know the signs of her surrender: the total stillness that would come over the little hard dry form, the probing gaze that like a surgeon's knife sought to cut through my skull to get at the images there, to see if I were lying; above all, her fear, a fear nameless and profound, the same

one I had felt beating in the palm of her hand that day in the lorry.

Over the weeks I told her about refrigerators, radios, gas stoves, elevators, trolley cars, wringer washing machines, movies, airplanes, the cyclone at Coney Island,[12] subways, toasters, electric lights: "At night, see, all you have to do is flip this little switch on the wall and all the lights in the house go on. Just like that. Like magic. It's like turning on the sun at night."

"But tell me," she said to me once with a faint mocking smile, "do the white people have all these things too or it's only the people looking like us?"

I laughed. "What d'ya mean," I said. "The white people have even better." Then: "I beat up a white girl in my class last term."

"Beating up white people!" Her tone was incredulous.

"How you mean!" I said, using an expression of hers. "She called me a name."

For some reason Da-duh could not quite get over this and repeated in the same hushed, shocked voice, "Beating up white people now! Oh, the lord, the world's changing up so I can scarce recognize it anymore."

One morning toward the end of our stay, Da-duh led me into a part of the gully that we had never visited before, an area darker and more thickly overgrown than the rest, almost impenetrable. There in a small clearing amid the dense bush, she stopped before an incredibly tall royal palm which rose cleanly out of the ground, and drawing the eye up with it, soared high above the trees around it into the sky. It appeared to be touching the blue dome of sky, to be flaunting its dark crown of fronds right in the blinding white face of the late morning sun.

---

12. *Coney Island* is an amusement park and beach in Brooklyn, and the *cyclone* was a popular thrill ride.

Critical Thinking

CAUSE and EFFECT The grandmother gives the girl a penny. What causes her to do this? What is an effect? *(The girl describes the snow, then dances and sings for the grandmother. After that, the grandmother takes the girl among the canes and to the gully and asks her questions about New York.)*

Active Reading

QUESTION At this point in the story, students might be asking themselves questions such as these: Why does the woman want to know these things? Why doesn't she ask her daughter? How does she react to the things she hears? *(The woman is curious. She wants to know but may be embarrassed to ask the daughter. The child is a safe choice. The grandmother finds the information incredible. Some things she has a hard time believing.)*

Active Reading

PREDICT The grandmother is proud of her special places. The granddaughter has told the grandmother all about the wonders of New York. Ask students what they think might happen. *(Students may indicate that they will both enjoy and respect each other's place, or, as is more typical in a story, there will be some kind of conflict or problem resulting from these discussions.)*

MULTIPLE LEARNING STYLES

Bodily-Kinesthetic Students who have good bodily-kinesthetic skills can often express ideas through physical movement. Point out that the girl dances the Truck and the Suzy-Q, both dances popular in the 1930s. Students with this special learning style could help the class visualize this part of the story.

Activity Ask volunteers to work in small groups to prepare their version of one of the dances. Encourage students to find music from the past or present that might fit with the dance. Allow time for groups to present their dances. Let classmates guess which one is being performed, based on the clues from the story. **L2 COLLAB. LEARN.**

VIEWING THE PAINTING

Charles Sheeler (1883–1965), an American painter and photographer, is known for his painting of architectural forms. His style of painting combines realism with the geometric forms associated with cubism.

Viewing Response *One painting shows a tropical setting, the other a city scene. The grandmother and her world are the natural setting. The granddaughter and her world are the city setting. Each person values her place and is proud of it.*

R Active Reading

RESPOND The grandmother shows the girl a soaring palm tree and asks if there is anything that tall in New York. Why does the girl choose to answer as she does? What would you have done? *(She knows that her grandmother wants her to say no, as before, but the girl wants to "win" the contest. She tells the truth. Students will probably say they would say no in order to spare the grandmother's feelings.)*

S Literary Elements

SYMBOL Discuss what students think the palm tree symbolizes and why the grandmother shows it to the girl. *(The palm tree seems to symbolize the best of the grandmother's world. After hearing all about the wonders of the child's world, the grandmother wants to prove hers is better.)*

Teaching Options

Skyscrapers (Offices), 1922. Charles Sheeler. Oil on canvas, 20 x 13 in. The Phillips Collection, Washington, DC.

Viewing the painting: Contrast the setting in this painting with *Peaceful Day* on page 399. How does this contrast relate to a conflict in the story?

406 🐌 UNIT 1

Reading *Minilesson*

Sequence Sequence refers to the order of the events in a story. Often the author presents the events in chronological or time order—in the order in which the events happened.

Activity Point out that in this story, the author presents the events in time order. However, at two points in the story, time passes between events. Draw a time line on the board. Have students identify the story events in sequence. Let volunteers write a short statement on the time line, identifying the event. At the two places in the story when time passes, erase part of the line to indicate a break. **L3**

Additional Resources

📁 *Reading Workbook,* pp. 45–46

Da-duh watched me a long time before she spoke, and then she said, very quietly, "All right, now, tell me if you've got anything this tall in that place you're from."

I almost wished, seeing her face, that I could have said no. "Yes," I said. "We've got buildings hundreds of times this tall in New York. There's one called the Empire State Building that's the tallest in the world. My class visited it last year and I went all the way to the top. It's got over a hundred floors. I can't describe how tall it is. Wait a minute. What's the name of that hill I went to visit the other day, where they have the police station?"

"You mean Bissex?"

"Yes, Bissex. Well, the Empire State Building is way taller than that."

"You're lying now!" she shouted, trembling with rage. Her hand lifted to strike me.

"No, I'm not," I said. "It really is, if you don't believe me I'll send you a picture post-card of it soon as I get back home so you can see for yourself. But it's way taller than Bissex."

All the fight went out of her at that. The hand poised to strike me fell limp to her side, and as she stared at me, seeing not me but the building that was taller than the highest hill she knew, the small stubborn light in her eyes (it was the same amber as the flame in the kerosene lamp she lit at dusk) began to fail. Finally, with a vague gesture that even in the midst of her defeat still tried to dismiss me and my world, she turned and started back through the gully, walking slowly, her steps groping and uncertain, as if she were suddenly no longer sure of the way, while I followed triumphant yet strangely saddened behind.

The next morning I found her dressed for our morning walk but stretched out on the Berbice chair in the tiny drawing room where she sometimes napped during the afternoon

heat, her face turned to the window beside her. She appeared thinner and suddenly indescribably old.

"My Da-duh," I said.

"Yes, nuh," she said. Her voice was listless and the face she slowly turned my way was, now that I think back on it, like a Benin mask, the features drawn and almost distorted by an ancient abstract sorrow.

"Don't you feel well?" I asked.

"Girl, I don't know."

"My Da-duh, I goin' boil you some bush tea," my aunt, Da-duh's youngest child, who lived with her, called from the shed roof kitchen.

"Who tell you I need bush tea?" she cried, her voice assuming for a moment its old authority. "You can't even rest nowadays without some malicious person looking for you to be dead. Come girl," she motioned me to a place beside her on the old-fashioned lounge chair, "give us a tune."

I sang for her until breakfast at eleven, all my brash irreverent Tin Pan Alley[13] songs, and then just before noon we went out into the ground. But it was a short, dispirited walk. Da-duh didn't even notice that the mangoes were beginning to ripen and would have to be picked before the village boys got to them. And when she paused occasionally and looked out across the canes or up at her trees it wasn't as if she were seeing them but something else. Some huge, monolithic[14] shape had imposed itself, it seemed, between her and the land, obstructing her vision.

---

13. *Tin Pan Alley* was a district in New York City associated with composers and publishers of popular music. These pop songs were bright and lively, often treating their subjects with rude and disrespectful (*brash, irreverent*) mockery.
14. A *monolithic* shape would resemble a monument or other structure formed from a single, giant block of stone.

Vocabulary
malicious (mə lish′ əs) *adj.* having or showing a desire to harm another

T Author's Craft

CONTRAST After the girl "tops" her grandmother, the two walk home. The author lets the reader know how they are feeling. Ask students to discuss the contrast between the two. *(The grandmother tries to be her authoritative self, but fails and walks home slowly and uncertainly. The girl follows with a triumphant step but feels sad.)*

U Literary Elements

POINT OF VIEW Be sure students understand from what point of view the story is told and when it is being told. *(The story is told from a first-person point of view. The narrator is a character in the story. However, the narrator is recalling this event, it is a memory. The story happened in the past.)*

V Active Reading

CONNECT Ask students to identify some of the elements in this story that connect with other stories in this theme. *(The narrator is recalling memories from her past, which is what Ayah does in "Lullaby." The girl dances for her grandmother; Felicia in "Winter Night" dances for the baby-sitter; Noé dances for himself; and a dance is held at Prince Prospero's. Something the girl does changes the future for her grandmother and herself. Eckels in "A Sound of Thunder" also changes the future. The grandmother has lost a child just as Ayah in "Lullaby" has lost several children.)*

Listening and Speaking *Minilesson*

Persuasive Conversation Explain that from time to time a person needs to conduct a persuasive conversation. Ask students to suggest times when they do this. *(Students will probably suggest times when they are asking their parents for permission to do or buy something.)* Have students develop a list of suggestions to use when trying to persuade someone. Possible suggestions might include these:

- Explain what you want.
- Give good reasons.
- Be prepared to answer any objections with reason, not emotion.

Activity Have students imagine that the girl can see the effect her answer has on her grandmother. She wants her grandmother to feel better about things. What could the girl say? Suggest that students

work in pairs to come up with a short, persuasive conversation they might have with the grandmother. Let each pair role-play the conversation. **L2 COLLAB. LEARN.**

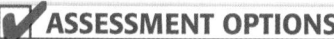

CONNECT Ask students what the words *in memoriam* mean and where the words are usually seen. Then have students refer to the title and discuss its meaning. *(In memoriam means "in memory of" or "in remembrance of" and is often used in obituaries and on plaques or other objects honoring a person who has died. The title means that the grandmother is not completely dead because she is remembered.)*

X **Critical Thinking**

INFERRING The narrator says she lives within the shadow of her grandmother's death. What does this mean? *(The girl is feeling guilty, as if she is responsible for causing her grandmother's death.)*

Thematic Focus

Challenges and Consequences
Discuss with students the challenges the grandmother and the girl faced and what the consequences of their actions were.

ASSESSMENT OPTIONS

📁 *Quick Checks,* p. 35

FINE ART
TRANSPARENCY 16

You may wish to use Fine Art Transparency 16 to discuss the idea of community.

Teaching Options

To Da-duh, in Memoriam

Returning to the house she slept the entire afternoon on the Berbice chair.

She remained like this until we left, languishing away the mornings on the chair at the window gazing out at the land as if it were already doomed; then, at noon, taking the brief stroll with me through the ground during which she seldom spoke, and afterwards returning home to sleep till almost dusk sometimes.

On the day of our departure she put on the austere, ankle length white dress, the black shoes and brown felt hat (her town clothes she called them), but she did not go with us to town. She saw us off on the road outside her house and in the midst of my mother's tearful protracted[15] farewell, she leaned down and whispered in my ear, "Girl, you're not to forget now to send me the picture of that building, you hear."

By the time I mailed her the large colored picture postcard of the Empire State Building she was dead. She died during the famous '37 strike which began shortly after we left. On the day of her death England sent planes flying low over the island in a show of force—so low, according to my aunt's letter, that the downdraft from them shook the ripened mangoes from the trees in Da-duh's orchard. Frightened, everyone in the village fled into the canes. Except Da-duh. She remained in the house at the window so my aunt said,

watching as the planes came swooping and screaming like monstrous birds down over the village, over her house, rattling her trees and flattening the young canes in her field. It must have seemed to her lying there that they did not intend pulling out of their dive, but like the hardback beetles which hurled themselves with suicidal force against the walls of the house at night, those menacing silver shapes would hurl themselves in an ecstasy of self-immolation[16] onto the land, destroying it utterly.

When the planes finally left and the villagers returned they found her dead on the Berbice chair at the window.

She died and I lived, but always, to this day even, within the shadow of her death. For a brief period after I was grown I went to live alone, like one doing penance,[17] in a loft above a noisy factory in downtown New York and there painted seas of sugarcane and huge swirling Van Gogh[18] suns and palm trees striding like brightly-plumed Tutsi[19] warriors across a tropical landscape, while the thunderous tread of the machines downstairs jarred the floor beneath my easel, mocking my efforts.

---

15. A *protracted* (prō trak′ təd) farewell would be one that takes a lot of time.

16. *Self-immolation* is the act of setting oneself on fire.
17. *Penance* (pen′ əns) is a punishment one undergoes, usually voluntarily, to show sorrow for having committed a sin or offense.
18. *Van Gogh* was a nineteenth-century Dutch painter famous for his swirling brush strokes and for the dramatic effects they produced.
19. The *Tutsi* are a people in central Africa.

Grammar and Language *Minilesson*

Apostrophes Apostrophes are used to show possession (*grandmother's orchard*) and to show that letters or numbers have been omitted (*don't, '37*).

Activity Ask students to find words with apostrophes in the selection and tell how the apostrophe is used in each word. **L2**

Additional Resources

📜 *Grammar and Language Transparency 35*

📙 *Grammar and Language Workbook,* p. 277

📘 *Grammar and Composition Handbook,* Lesson 11.11

📕 *Writer's Choice,* Lesson 21.11

Responding to Literature

Personal Response

Do you approve of the way the narrator treated Da-duh? Explain.

ANALYZING LITERATURE

RECALL

1. Describe the narrator's initial impression of Da-duh.
2. Summarize what happens the first time Da-duh takes her granddaughter "out into the ground."
3. Describe how the girl re-creates New York for her grandmother.
4. At what point in the story do Da-duh's appearance and behavior abruptly change? Describe this change.
5. What happens to Da-duh shortly after the narrator leaves? Under what circumstances does this event occur?

INTERPRET

6. Why do you think the narrator tries to "win" the initial encounter between Da-duh and herself?
7. In your opinion, why does Da-duh compare Barbados with New York?
8. What conclusions can you draw about Da-duh, based on her reactions to the girl's descriptions of New York?
9. In your opinion, what causes the abrupt change in the way Da-duh looks and acts? Explain.
10. In what **setting** does the narrator later live and paint? How does this setting reflect the **conflict** between Da-duh and the narrator? (See Literary Terms Handbook, page R11.)

EVALUATE AND CONNECT

11. Da-duh and her granddaughter seem to be playing a game that might be called, "Can You Top This?" Describe a time when you played a game of one-upmanship. Did you win or lose?
12. In your opinion, what does the Empire State Building **symbolize** in this story?
13. Look back at the Focus Activity on page 398. Which saying, do you think, describes the relationship between the narrator and Da-duh? Explain.
14. Theme Connections   In your opinion, what are the consequences of the narrator's triumph over the challenges she faces?
15. The narrator finds herself in unfamiliar surroundings. Describe a similar experience you have had. How did you cope with it?

Literary ELEMENTS

Local Color

Local color is a technique of writing that uses specific details to evoke a particular region. In "To Da-duh, in Memoriam," Paule Marshall re-creates Barbados in the 1930s by describing the characters' habits and customs, their clothing, and the land they inhabit. For example, Marshall writes about "the women balancing huge baskets on top their heads" and "the small tottering houses of sunbleached pine." The characters use distinctively Barbadian expressions and dialect, such as, "I tell you, Adry has done all right for sheself in New York." All of these details help to re-create the region in which the story takes place.

1. Find five details the author uses to evoke the landscape of Barbados.

2. Give three examples of Barbadian expressions or dialect used in the story. What other words might the narrator use to express the same ideas?

3. What are three other examples of specific details that evoke the region in which this story takes place?

● See **Literary Terms Handbook,** p. R7.

Responding to the Selection

Personal Response

Most students will probably wish the narrator had acted differently out of respect for the grandmother and her way of life. Students should recognize, though, that the narrator was a child at the time and did not realize fully the hurt she was causing.

ANALYZING LITERATURE

1. The narrator sees the grandmother as a formidable and interesting person.
2. The grandmother shows off her favorite places, asking the granddaughter if she has anything like it where she lives. The granddaughter tells about snow and sings and dances.
3. She tells her grandmother about everyday things from toasters to electric lights, ordinary things to the girl, but amazing things to the grandmother.
4. After the granddaughter says New York has something bigger than the palm tree and the hill, the grandmother's health begins to fail. She seems tired and sickly. She changes from a determined, authoritative woman to a person seemingly overcome by the world.
5. The grandmother dies. Her death occurs after airplanes fly low over her house and the village in a British show of force.
6. Trying to win small battles is the narrator's way of asserting herself, of having some control over her life.
7. Da-duh thinks Barbados is better but is curious about New York.
8. Da-duh seems to have experienced little of the modern world of her time, out of fear or poverty or both.
9. The change comes after the girl wins the final game of "Can You Top This?" Probably a series of events caused the change, most likely the daily recounting of modern-day mysteries the grandmother knew nothing about and realized that she did not.
10. The narrator went to live in a loft above a noisy factory. The girl tries to re-create the natural beauty of her grandmother's home by painting pictures of it, but the machines keep reminding her of progress and the world in which she really lives.
11. Most students will be able to provide an example of this game and when they played it as well as their success or failure at it.
12. The Empire State Building symbolizes the modern, urban world.

LITERARY ELEMENTS

1. Any details that correctly evoke the landscape are acceptable.
2. One example: *has done all right for sheself* (has done all right for herself)
3. Examples: reference to the water of the bay and the ship, use of the word *lorry,* the British planes.

Additional Resources

📖 *Literary Elements Transparency 35*

---

13. "Birds of a Feather Flock Together" is probably the better choice. Although they were from different worlds, their personalities were similar. They were both fiercely proud.
14. The narrator contributed to the death of her grandmother and lives with the guilt.
15. Students should describe the unfamiliar surroundings they experienced and explain how they coped.

LITERATURE AND WRITING

Writing About Literature

Students' paragraphs should
- identify the change the narrator goes through.
- include specific details of what the change was.
- explain why the change happened.

Creative Writing

Students' storybooks should
- contain illustrations or photographs that reflect the setting and characters of the story.
- tell a recognizable story.
- be age appropriate.

EXTENDING YOUR RESPONSE

Literature Groups Remind students that their opinions should be supported by details from the story. **COLLAB. LEARN.**

Internet Connection Remind students that a travel brochure needs to be written to convince people that this is a place they want to go. Suggest that they look at magazine ads for the kind of persuasive language used. Students might also want to visit a travel agency and get some actual brochures.

Interdisciplinary Activity Allow students to work together. Those who play a musical instrument might be able to provide an accompaniment if sheet music is found. Also, some parents and grandparents may know the tunes and words to the songs mentioned in the story. They might be another source to consult.

LITERATURE AND WRITING

Writing About Literature

Explore Character Development A character who grows or changes during a story is called a **dynamic character**. Write a paragraph in which you explain how the narrator of "To Da-duh, in Memoriam" grows and changes as a result of her visit to Barbados. Use specific details from the story to support your ideas. Share your writing with others in a small group.

Creative Writing

What's It Like, Da-duh? Use the characters of Da-duh and the narrator to create a picture storybook for young children, in which an old woman named Da-duh tells her American granddaughter about Barbados. Illustrate your story with your own drawings, with photocopies of pictures from books or magazines, or with images you have downloaded from the Internet. Display your book in the classroom.

EXTENDING YOUR RESPONSE

Literature Groups

Two Worlds Colliding Paule Marshall has said that she wanted this story to tell more than just the story of a grandmother and granddaughter. She also wanted it to be about the "relationship of Western civilization and the Third World." Find examples from the story that explore the relationship of western civilization—represented by the United States, a highly developed and industrialized nation—and the Third World, represented by Barbados, which in the 1930s was still under British colonial rule. Do you think Marshall achieved the goal stated above? Compare your group's findings and opinions with those of other groups.

Internet Connection

Fun-in-the-Sun Brochure Work with a partner to create a tourist brochure about Barbados. Use the Internet to locate information about the sights, sounds, and tastes of this West Indian island. Create a brochure that lists key attractions, gives up-to-date travel information, and offers brief advice on what to do, where to eat, and where to stay. Illustrate your brochure, if you wish.

Interdisciplinary Activity

Music: Pop Songs from the Past Find sheet music or a recording of one of the songs the narrator sings in this story. Then look for an example of a Caribbean song—if possible, a song that was popular around the time of the story (the 1930s). Play a recording of each song, or sing it to the class. Discuss the similarities and differences between the two songs. Which one do you prefer? Explain your preference.

Reading Further

If you'd like to read more of Paule Marshall's writing, you might enjoy this short story:

"The Valley Between" from *Reena and Other Stories* tells about a young woman who juggles the roles of wife and mother while striving to reach her educational goals.

📖 Save your work for your portfolio.

410 🐾 UNIT 1

✔ ASSESSMENT OPTIONS

- 📁 *Quick Checks,* p. 35
- 📁 *Selection and Theme Assessment,* pp. 67–68
- 📁 *Performance Assessment,* p. 34
- 💾 *Testmaker*

Skill Minilessons

GRAMMAR AND LANGUAGE • Concrete and Abstract Nouns

A **concrete noun,** such as the word *ship,* names an object that occupies space or that can be recognized by any of the senses. An **abstract noun,** such as the word *foolishness,* names an idea, a quality, or a characteristic. Notice how the narrator uses a string of concrete nouns as she tries to re-create her world for Da-duh: ". . . I told her about refrigerators, radios, gas stoves, elevators, trolley cars, wringer washing machines, movies, airplanes, the cyclone at Coney Island, subways, toasters, electric lights. . . ." In the same paragraph, she uses an abstract noun–*magic*–to help Da-duh understand how wonderful electric lights really are.

PRACTICE Find a passage in the story that includes both concrete and abstract nouns. Copy the passage and label each noun as *concrete* or *abstract.* Then explain how the use of both types of nouns helps the author convey her intended meaning.

APPLY Review your use of concrete and abstract nouns in a piece of your writing. Have you used both types of nouns effectively in order to convey your intended meaning? Make any necessary revisions to your work.

● For more about nouns, see **Language Handbook,** p. R40.

READING AND THINKING • Activating Prior Knowledge

Prior knowledge–what you already know from your own experience–often helps you better understand a piece of writing. For example, have you ever felt almost blinded by the reflection of bright sunlight on a body of water? If so, you understand what the narrator means when she says that she "was still somewhat blinded from the sheen of tropical sunlight on the water." Have you ever won an argument with someone but felt bad about it? This prior knowledge helps you understand how the narrator could

feel "triumphant yet strangely saddened" after telling Da-duh about the Empire State Building.

PRACTICE On your paper, create a chart listing three story events or details and explain how your prior knowledge adds to your understanding of each one.

● For more about reading strategies, see **Reading Handbook,** p. R82.

VOCABULARY • Synonyms: Shades of Meaning

A thesaurus (a book of words and their synonyms) is a very useful tool for writers, but every thesaurus should begin with the warning, "Use with caution!" If you aren't completely sure what a listed synonym means and you plug it into your essay or report anyway, you may say something you didn't mean to say at all and may look quite foolish while doing so. Even if that doesn't happen, you may fail to communicate precisely what you mean.

Good speakers and good writers choose words carefully. When they want to emphasize the feeling of awe (perhaps tinged with some fear) that a particular person

inspires, they might choose *formidable* to describe that person, not just *impressive,* even though *impressive* is a synonym for *formidable.*

PRACTICE Each word on the left is a vocabulary word from "To Da-duh, in Memoriam." Briefly explain how each word differs in meaning from the synonym that follows it.

1. *malicious*	synonym: *unkind*
2. *decrepit*	synonym: *weak*
3. *arrogant*	synonym: *proud*
4. *hurtle*	synonym: *hurry*

THE SHORT STORY ❦ 411

Skill Minilessons

GRAMMAR AND LANGUAGE
Concrete and Abstract Nouns

PRACTICE

Any passage that contains both types of nouns is acceptable. The last paragraph on page 400 and the first paragraph on page 404 provide examples. In general, concrete nouns help a reader visualize the setting and characters, while abstract nouns help convey feelings and ideas.

READING AND THINKING
Activating Prior Knowledge

The events or details each student lists will vary, but students should be able to explain how particular personal experiences helped them understand the story.

VOCABULARY
Synonyms: Shades of Meaning

1. Malicious has a much stronger meaning of evil intent than does unkind.
2. Decrepit generates a visual image of something that is completely falling apart while weak carries a visual image of something not strong.
3. Arrogant carries with it a nega-tive feeling of smugness, while proud car-ries with it a positive feeling of happi-ness.
4. Hurtle has a connotation of some-thing being thrown forcefully forward while hurry indicates extra speed.

Additional Resources

 Grammar and Composition Handbook, Lesson 1.1

 Grammar and Language Workbook, p. 48

Writer's Choice, Lesson 10.1

 Reading Workbook, pp. 45–46

 Vocabulary Practice, p. 33

Writing Workshop

Objectives

- To create a critical response to a short story
- To plan, draft, revise, edit, proofread, and present a critical response
- To reflect on one's critical response

Teaching Strategies

PREWRITING

Explore ideas Tell students that as they skim the Contents, they should write the titles of those stories that immediately bring about a reaction. Suggest that as students begin to narrow their choices, they start with the first title on their list and answer the questions in the activity to themselves. If they find they are unable to come up with a good answer to some or most of the questions, they might want to cross the story off the list.

Teaching Options

~: Writing ✕ Workshop :~

Expository Writing: Critical Response

When you look at a full moon on a clear night, what do you see? A white circle with a few dark splotches on it? If you examine the moon carefully through a telescope, you'll see much more. A short story is much the same: the closer you look, the more you'll see—deeper meanings, additional ideas, details that show the author's craftsmanship, maybe even some flaws. Writing a critical response is a good way to closely inspect and evaluate a literary work. **Write a critical response to a short story, using this workshop as a guide.**

- As you write your critical response, refer to **Writing Handbook**, pp. R58–R71.

The Writing Process

PREWRITING

PREWRITING TIP
Choose a story that made a strong impression on you—even if it was a negative one. When you have definite opinions and strong feelings about something, it's usually easier to write about it.

Explore ideas

Skim the Table of Contents to recall the titles of all the short stories you've read in this unit. Choose a story that particularly impressed or intrigued you. As you reread the story, jot down notes on the elements that made the strongest impression on you.

- Is the plot clever? Believable? Suspenseful? Explain in your notes.
- How are the characters developed? Do they seem true to life? Why or why not?
- How does the author establish the story's setting?
- How does the setting contribute to the story's mood?
- How does the point of view affect your understanding of the plot or the characters?
- What is the theme of the story, and how is it conveyed? What is your reaction to the theme?

Consider your purpose and audience

Your purpose is to evaluate some element of a short story and to explain and support your evaluation. Who will read your critical response? Will other students read it, as well as your teacher? Will you submit it to a student literary journal or post it on the Internet? Identify your readers and keep their understanding of the subject in mind as you prepare your critical response.

412 ✄ UNIT 1

ENGLISH LANGUAGE LEARNERS
MEETING INDIVIDUAL NEEDS

Getting Down to Details English language learners may benefit from group prewriting activities.

Activity Let students who have selected the same story work together. Have each group member describe what element he or she plans to focus on. Other students can offer suggestions about details and examples they recall from the story that might illustrate that element. Then the group can search for the specific passages in which those details and examples appear.

Additional Resources
📁 *English Language Learners Sourcebook*

Make a plan

Review your prewriting notes, and circle the element of the story that most intrigues you. Develop a **thesis**—a one- or two-sentence statement that sums up your opinion on this element. Then plan your critical response using the basic essay structure of **introduction, body,** and **conclusion.** Write notes on how you will develop each section.

STUDENT MODEL

Introduction	Set the stage for your readers: What is the title of the story, who is the author, and what is the story about? On what element of the story are you focusing? What is your evaluation of this element? (Your evaluation is your **thesis statement.**)	"Winter Night" by Kay Boyle. About Felicia, lonely seven-year-old girl living in New York City during World War II. Baby-sitter tells Felicia about young girl she knew in concentration camp. Focus on dramatic irony. **Thesis statement:** Boyle uses dramatic irony to point out both the horror of the concentration camps and the sadness of Felicia's situation.
Body	Elaborate on your thesis: Define or explain the element you're focusing on. How is this element developed in the story? Use passages from the story as examples. Evaluate the author's effectiveness in handling this element of the story.	**Dramatic irony:** Reader has information that character doesn't have. Reader knows baby-sitter is talking about Nazi concentration camp. Felicia doesn't. Felicia tries to relate baby-sitter's story to her own experience. Comparison emphasizes tragedy of both situations.
Conclusion	Restate your thesis and leave the reader with a final thought or two.	Using dramatic irony, Boyle compares a mother who is forcibly separated from her child, to another mother who willingly gives up the care of her child. Both "abandoned" children suffer.

THE SHORT STORY 413

Consider your purpose and audience
Write these questions on the board as students consider their purpose and audience: Do you want to get people to read the story because you think the author did a fantastic job? Do you want to provide an in-depth analysis for people who have read the story and can appreciate your insights? Remind students that if they are writing for people who have not read the story, they should provide a summary.

Make a plan Suggest that students use three sheets of paper, one for each section—introduction, body, conclusion. Point out the way the student model follows closely the questions or suggestions in each part of the three sections.

Remind students that they will need to find examples in the story that support their thesis. Stress that if there are not many examples to support their thesis, they may have to consider a different thesis or revise the one they have written.

Additional Resources

📁 ***Writing and Proofreading Practice,*** p. 1–7, 13–14

🖨 ***Writing and Proofreading Transparencies 1–6, 13–14, 31–32***

📔 ***Writer's Choice,*** Lesson 6.3

MEETING INDIVIDUAL NEEDS — MULTIPLE LEARNING STYLES

Spatial Students who learn best through visual images may want to create a graphic organizer to help them sort, evaluate, and order the examples they will find and use.

Activity Suggest that students write in their graphic organizers all the examples they find. Then they will be able to easily identify the best examples to use. Those to be eliminated could be crossed out. The remaining ones could be numbered to show the order in which they will appear. **L2**

DRAFTING

Begin at the beginning Remind students that if their audience is made up of people who have read the story, the story summary can be very brief. However, if their audience is people who have never read the story, their summary will be longer. The model shows a longer version of the summary. Stress that the summary is there only to set the stage. It is not the main purpose of the piece.

Write your draft If students have set aside three sheets of paper (one each for introduction, body, and conclusion), have them begin freewriting on one of the pages. Suggest that they move from page to page as they have ideas. Stress that the key here is getting the ideas in writing, not having perfect writing.

DRAFTING TIP

If you get stuck while drafting, turn to the story and copy a passage that you want to use as an example. Explain how this passage illustrates the element of the story you're focusing on.

Begin at the beginning

In your introductory paragraph, briefly tell what the story is about. Identify the element of the story that will be your focus. End with your thesis statement.

Write your draft

Refer to your plan as you write. Don't worry too much about form. Just get your ideas down.

STUDENT MODEL

Kay Boyle's short story "Winter Night" focuses on seven-year-old Felicia, who lives with her mother in New York City during World War II. Felicia's mother works during the day and spends many evenings out. A new baby-sitter tells her about a young girl in a place called a "camp." Although Felicia doesn't know what kind of camp this was, the reader knows that it was a Nazi concentration camp. The author effectively uses dramatic irony to point out both the horror of the concentration camps and the sadness of Felicia's situation.

REVISING

Take another look If students have additional ideas or a fresh insight, be sure they know it is all right to include the new material as well as to revise the material already there.

Read your work aloud Before beginning this activity, each pair of students should establish a set of guidelines about how they will proceed. Will the reader read the entire piece while the listener jots down notes? Will the listener interrupt whenever questions arise? Be sure students discuss this issue before they begin so that the process can move ahead smoothly and be beneficial to both students.

REVISING TIP

As you revise, cross out phrases like "I think that," "It seems to me that," or "It appears to be true that." Your readers know that you're sharing your opinions, so just go ahead and state them.

Take another look

Set your work aside for a few hours or days so you can shift gears from writing to rewriting. Then look at your essay with a fresh eye.

Read your work aloud

Invite a friend to listen as you read your critical response aloud. Ask for feedback, using the **Questions for Revising** to stimulate discussion.

QUESTIONS FOR REVISING

How can I:

☑ make my story summary clear and concise?

☑ strengthen my thesis statement?

☑ make sure each body paragraph supports my thesis?

☑ make my main points easier to understand?

☑ clearly restate my thesis in the conclusion?

☑ clear up any confusing parts of my essay?

STUDENT MODEL

The dramatic irony ~~is presented through~~ the [occurs in] dialogue between the baby-sitter and Felicia. For example, when the baby-sitter describes the children in the camp crying[at night] because their mothers [had gone] ~~went~~ away, Felicia asks, "Did the mothers have to go out to supper?" ~~This is her~~ [Felicia's question reflects her own] experience of why mothers go [are] away[at night ☉]

Teaching Options

Writing Minilesson

Precise Action Verbs One change that can improve the flow and tone of a piece is the use of precise action verbs. Compositions with sentences that use general verbs or passive forms of verbs can be improved simply by changing the verbs. For example, changing the general verb *flew* to *soared* improves this sentence:

The bird flew.
The bird soared.

Activity Suggest that students use a highlighter pen and mark each verb in their writing. Have them consider changing general verbs or passive forms to precise action verbs. Stress, however, that it is not possible or desirable to change every verb

to an action verb. Part of the revising process is making decisions about word choices. **L2**

Additional Resources

📖 *Writer's Choice,* Lesson 3.3

EDITING/PROOFREADING

Once you're satisfied with the content of your critical response, edit and proofread it to correct errors in grammar, usage, mechanics, and spelling. Use the **Proofreading Checklist** on the inside back cover of this book as a guide. When necessary, consult a dictionary and the Language Handbook.

> **PROOFREADING TIP**
> What types of mistakes do you make most often in your writing? Keep this "hit list" in mind as you proofread your critical response.

Grammar Hint

A verb must agree with its subject. Be careful not to mistake words in a prepositional phrase for the subject of a sentence. The subject of the following sentence is *fate*; it takes a singular verb. *The tragic fate of the little girl and the other children haunts the baby-sitter.*

● For more about subject-verb agreement, see **Language Handbook**, p. R17.

STUDENT MODEL

What a striking way to point out the thoughtlessness of a Mother who puts her own amusement above the care of her child. By using dramatic irony to compare Felicias situation with the trajic plight of the girl in a concentration camp Kay Boyle shows that their are diffrent ways of being abandoned.

PUBLISHING/PRESENTING

If you're submitting your critical response to a student literary journal, make sure you have met all the journal's requirements. If your classmates are your audience, you might distribute copies of your essay or post one copy on a bulletin board in your classroom.

> **PRESENTING TIP**
> Are you planning to read your critical response aloud in class? If so, you might want to begin with a dramatic reading of an excerpt from the story.

Reflecting

How did writing this critical response affect your appreciation of the short story you chose? Jot down your response in your journal. Then evaluate your own writing.

📑 **Save your work for your portfolio.**

THE SHORT STORY ❧ 415

EDITING/PROOFREADING

Suggest that students use the Proofreading Checklist on the inside back cover of their textbook.

A spell-checker can be a useful tool, but students should be reminded that it can check spelling but not meaning. For example, if the wrong homonym is used, *there* for *their*, the spell-checker will not catch the mistake. Before making a final copy, a final proofreading of the piece should be done. Sometimes it helps to have the final proofreading done by someone who has never read the paper before. New readers often see things writers cannot see because writers are so close to the work.

PUBLISHING/PRESENTING

There are many ways students could present their writing. Ask the group to brainstorm a list of possibilities. Try to come up with at least ten choices. Suggest that students copy the list and keep it handy for future projects.

Reflecting

📑 **Portfolio** Ask students to make one final personal evaluation of their work using the questions that follow.

Does my critical response
• evaluate one particular element of a story?
• clearly express my opinion?
• represent my best effort?

Suggest that students consider their responses as they decide whether to put their work in their portfolio.

✔ ASSESSMENT OPTIONS

📁 **Writing Assessment and Portfolio Management**
• Writing Assessment, pp. 2–19, 23–24
• Portfolio Management, pp. 20–22

Unit Wrap-Up

Objectives

- To give a personal response about the stories, discussions, and activities in this unit
- To write a comparison of two stories
- To complete a self-evaluation, set a goal, and devise a plan for achieving the goal

PERSONAL RESPONSE

1. Students should provide valid reasons and logical explanations for their recommendations.
2. Accept all reasonable responses.

ANALYZING LITERATURE

Students' writing should
- have an introductory paragraph that identifies the stories and the elements being compared.
- include details from the stories to support their conclusions.

EVALUATE AND SET GOALS

Evaluate

Have students list the projects and assignments they completed in the unit. Suggest that they add other contributions they made as well, such as showing others how to navigate the Internet.

To help students formulate various reasons for their ratings, you might suggest they develop a class rubric.

Set Goals

In a chart, have students jot down their goals, the steps they will take for achieving them, and checkpoints they can use to track their progress. Then discuss students' plans in individual conferences.

Unit Wrap-Up

PERSONAL RESPONSE

1. Which of the stories in this unit would you recommend to a friend? Explain your reasons.
2. How did your work in this unit enhance your skills in these areas?
   - reading for enjoyment and enrichment
   - discussing short stories in ways that lead to a deeper understanding of their meanings
   - understanding various literary techniques
   - working cooperatively with your classmates

ANALYZING LITERATURE

Comparing Two Elements   Choose two stories from this unit and compare them, using the short story elements you have studied. (See the Genre Focus on short stories on pages 2 and 3.) Avoid choosing elements of stories that were already compared in the unit. You might, for example, choose to compare and contrast the character traits of Eckels in "A Sound of Thunder" and Prince Prospero in "The Masque of the Red Death," explaining how the traits of these two characters influence the final outcome of their stories.

EVALUATE AND SET GOALS

Evaluate

1. What was your most valuable contribution to the class as you worked through this unit?
2. What assigned task in this unit did you find most challenging?
   - How did you approach this task?
   - What was the outcome?
3. How would you assess your work in this unit, using the following scale? Give at least two reasons for your assessment.
   4 = outstanding   **3** = good   **2** = fair   **1** = weak

Set Goals

1. Choose a goal to work toward in Unit 2. Concentrate on any skill you wish to improve, such as reading, writing, speaking, or working in a group.
2. Discuss your goal with your teacher.
3. Write down three steps you will take to help you achieve your goal.
4. Plan checkpoints at specific intervals in the unit to assess your progress toward your goal.
5. Include a self-evaluation plan to determine whether you have reached your goal.

BUILD YOUR PORTFOLIO _____

Select   Choose two pieces of writing you did in this unit and include them in your portfolio. Use these questions to help you make your selection.
- Which pieces represent your best work?
- Which challenged you the most?
- Which pieces expanded your mind in unexpected ways?
- Which gave you the greatest sense of accomplishment?

Reflect   Write some notes to accompany the pieces you selected. Use these questions to guide you.
- What do you like best about the piece?
- How did you grow as a writer because of the work you did on it?
- How else might you have approached this piece?

 ## ASSESSMENT OPTIONS

📁 ***Writing Assessment and Portfolio Management***
- Writing Assessment, pp. 2–19
- Portfolio Management, pp. 20–22

Reading on Your Own

You might also be interested in the following books.

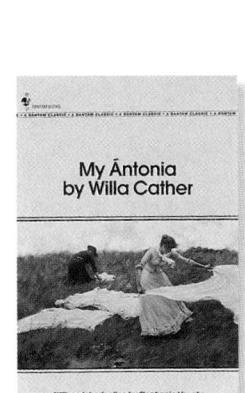

Fahrenheit 451
by Ray Bradbury Can you envision a future in which all books are not only banned, but burned? Firefighter Guy Montag goes about his job of burning books until he encounters a young woman who introduces him to the adventure that books can offer. Guy makes a decision that sets him on the adventure of his life.

Of Mice and Men
by John Steinbeck Their dreams of someday owning a small farm are all that sustain ranch hands George and Lennie as they go from one difficult job and disheartening experience to the next. When Lennie inadvertently causes a tragedy, George must make a painful decision about how best to help his friend.

My Antonia
by Willa Cather The courage, joys, and suffering of immigrant farmers who settled the Nebraska frontier are realistically portrayed in this classic novel. Narrator Jim Burden remembers his innocent childhood on the prairie and recounts the triumphs of his strong and capable lifelong friend Antonia.

Shabanu, Daughter of the Wind
by Suzanne Fisher-Staples Shabanu is a Pakistani girl with a fierce sense of self. She loves her family and their life as camel herders in the desert, but her world is shattered when her parents arrange for her to marry a wealthy older man. Shabanu is torn between accepting the marriage or suffering the consequences of going against tradition.

THE SHORT STORY 417

Reading on Your Own

Glencoe Literature Library

My Ántonia by Willa Cather is available in the *Glencoe Literature Library*. For a complete listing, see p. T44 in this book.

The *Glencoe Literature Library: Study Guides* provide instructional support and student activities for works in the *Glencoe Literature Library*.

At the MOVIES

Be sure to preview the following video for appropriateness for your class:

- **Of Mice and Men**

MEETING INDIVIDUAL NEEDS — INCLUSION STRATEGIES

Less-Proficient Readers You may wish to recommend *Shabanu, Daughter of the Wind* by Suzanne Fisher-Staples to your less-proficient readers. The accessible subject matter and writing style make this book particularly appropriate for these students. **L1**

These books may be recommended to more proficient readers
- *Fahrenheit 451* by Ray Bradbury **L2**
- *Of Mice and Men* by John Steinbeck **L2**
- *My Ántonia* by Willa Cather **L3**

Additional Resources
📁 *Inclusion Strategies*

Standardized Test Practice

Answers and Analyses

1. **B** Students should reread the final lines of the passage to establish Brian's attitude toward his trip. It is said that Brian *had no idea what he would encounter, but he knew he had Pop's lessons and love to support him.* While Brian is a bit apprehensive, he feels prepared to go ahead with his journey. The most reasonable answer is therefore B.

 THE PRINCETON REVIEW

Standardized Test Practice

Read the following passage. Then read each question on page 419. Decide which is the best answer to each question. Mark the letter for that answer on your paper.

Across the Water

Brian had been boating with his grandfather since he was five years old, and he had quickly graduated from a novice to a <u>proficient</u> sailor. At eighteen, he was well prepared for the sojourn he had planned, and he waited anxiously for the day when he could realize his dream: to sail from Harrisville, Michigan, to Port Elgin, Canada. It would be the first long trip he would take alone. Pop had prepared him well for this challenge. The most difficult part would be telling Pop that the time had come.

At dinner that evening, Brian and Pop sat facing each other as they did every evening. Pop noticed that Brian was unusually quiet.

"What's on your mind, Bri?"

Pop knew Brian well. Usually talkative, Brian had been almost silent. He tried to think up a reply that sounded believable, but he knew in his heart he could never lie to Pop.

"Well, Pop, I've been thinking. Thinking about taking the boat out by myself for a trip."

"Oh, is that all? From the look on your face it seemed to be more serious than that. You've been out alone many times. Go on."

"Well, it's more than just any kind of trip. I want to go from Harrisville and sail to Port Elgin, Canada."

The room was silent. Pop was not prepared for this request. Although he knew Brian was an excellent sailor, he was not certain that his grandson could handle the challenges that Lake Huron might offer. He weighed his words

carefully because he didn't want to discourage Brian. Pop had always prided himself on being supportive and encouraging of his grandson.

"Here's what I think, Bri. I want you to go, but I would like to go with you. Don't get me wrong—I am very confident in your abilities. However, I would feel better if I could go with you and be your first mate."

Brian's face fell, and he stared at the kitchen floor. He didn't quite know what to say in response. Finally, he offered, "Pop, you know how much I've learned from you and how I appreciate all you've taught me. But I really feel that I should do this on my own. Please let me go alone."

Brian didn't ask for much, so Pop knew how important this was to him. Brian needed to prove he could be self-reliant. Pop decided to let Brian go.

Over the next week, Brian gathered all the supplies that he would need and prepared the boat. Before Pop could change his mind, Brian was ready to leave.

On the morning he was to set sail, Brian was up and ready before the sun rose. Pop saw him off with a thermos full of hot coffee. He gave Brian a firm hug and wished him luck.

"Now, you just do as you've been taught and you'll be just fine. Good luck to you. You learned from the best." Pop gave Brian a wink, and Brian was off to pursue his dream. He had no idea what he would encounter, but he knew he had Pop's lessons and love to support him.

1 At the end of the passage, we can tell that Brian —

    A is afraid he might have to turn around and come home

    B plans to do everything he can to sail across Lake Huron to Canada

    C has too much confidence in his ability to sail

    D wishes his grandfather was coming with him

2 Pop's thoughts as Brian asks for permission to sail by himself indicate that Pop is —

    F torn between his desire to let Brian go and his fear of what may happen

    G curious about why Brian would want to go that far

    H getting too old to want to make the trip himself

    J concerned about the condition of the boat

3 The main idea of this passage is that —

    A people need to be given opportunities to prove themselves

    B it is important to be well prepared for a big trip

    C children always want to attempt more than they can accomplish

    D attempts to cross Lake Huron can be challenging

4 Which is an OPINION held by Pop and Brian about crossing Lake Huron alone?

    F Pop will probably follow Brian for safety reasons.

    G Brian isn't strong enough to make the trip alone.

    H The best way to succeed on the trip is to fish for your food.

    J Making the trip alone is potentially dangerous for many reasons.

5 The author sees the request to sail alone as evidence of Brian's —

    A developing independence from Pop

    B disregard for Pop's feelings of love and support

    C dangerous quest for glory and recognition

    D love of the water

6 The word <u>proficient</u> in this passage means —

    F capable and skilled

    G gruff and old

    H new and unskilled

    J tentative and sensitive

Answers and Analyses

2. **F** Students should look back to the point in the passage where Pop's feelings are described. *Although he knew Brian was an excellent sailor, he was not certain that his grandson could handle the challenges* of the trip he had proposed.

3. **A** Choices B and D may be true, but they are too precise to be the main idea. Choice C implies that Brian will fail, which is not supported by the passage. We don't know if he will succeed or fail. The passage begins with Brian's wish to sail alone; the middle of the text describes Brian's attempt to explain to Pop why he wishes to go alone; and the end of the text shows Brian's resoluteness to try the difficult trip by himself. The most reasonable answer is therefore A.

4. **J** This is a good chance to teach students to solve problems by process of elimination. Nothing is said in the passage that would imply that Brian believes choices F or H. While Pop probably believes choice G, Brian does not. Choice J remains, and it is the most reasonable answer.

5. **A** Students should reread the passage and look for a statement which expresses the author's point of view. After Brian's discussion with Pop, the author states *Brian needed to prove he could be self-reliant.*

6. **F** Students should reread the sentence containing the word *proficient,* and use context clues to help establish its meaning. Since the word is used in contrast to a novice, the word must mean someone experienced or able. The most reasonable choice is therefore F.

Tested Objectives

Questions	Reading Objective
1, 2, 5	Analyze information to make inferences and generalizations
3	Summarize a variety of written texts
4	Recognize points of view, propaganda, and/or statements of fact and opinion
6	Determine the meaning of words

MORE PRACTICE

For additional practice, assign pages from one of the following standardized test resources available as part of Glencoe Literature.

Additional Resources
ITBS Preparation and Practice
SAT-9 Preparation and Practice
TerraNova Preparation and Practice

UNIT OPENING

- **Genre Focus: Nonfiction** (p. 422)
- **Active Reading Strategies** (p. 424)
- **Active Reading Model:** from *Travels with Charley* (p. 426)

KEYS TO LITERARY CONNECTIONS

 World Literature

Glencoe Literature contains a variety of literature that represents cultures from around the world. World literature selections are highlighted with this symbol:

 Comparing Selections

In each theme of **Glencoe Literature**, the **Comparing Selections** feature gives students an opportunity to compare two selections they have just read. Each Comparing Selections page provides a variety of options to address diverse aspects of the reading and literature curriculum.

Theme 5: REMEMBERING

SELECTIONS

A Child's Christmas in Wales (p. 432)

Media Connection: On-line Travel Guide (p. 443)

from **Kaffir Boy** (p. 444)

from **Farewell to Manzanar** (p. 459)

Media Connection: Government Document (p. 475)

By Any Other Name (p. 478)

Living Well. Living Good. (p. 488)

A Swimming Lesson (p. 494)

SKILL FEATURES

Reading and Thinking Skills (p. 458)

Grammar Link (p. 476)

Vocabulary Skills (p. 477)

WRITING WORKSHOP

Narrative Writing: Autobiographical Incident (p. 500)

Theme 6: QUESTS AND ENCOUNTERS

SELECTIONS

Pizza in Warsaw, Torte in Prague (p. 506)

Media Connection: Television Transcript (p. 515)

I've Seen the Promised Land (p. 516)

Media Connection: Journal Entries (p. 529)

Exploring Antarctic Ice (p. 531)

from **A Match to the Heart** (p. 543)

The Angry Winter (p. 556)

The Tucson Zoo (p. 562)

SKILL FEATURES

Writing Skills (p. 528)

Listening, Speaking, and Viewing (p. 541)

Interdisciplinary Connection (p. 542)

Technology Skills (p. 554)

WRITING WORKSHOP

Descriptive Writing: Observational Report (p. 568)

UNIT WRAP-UP

- **Personal Response, Analyzing Literature, Evaluate and Set Goals** (p. 572)
- **Build Your Portfolio** (p. 572)
- **Reading on Your Own** (p. 573)
  Night by Elie Wiesel
  Baseball: An Illustrated History by Geoffrey C. Ward and Ken Burns
  The Edge of the Sea by Rachel Carson
  A Separate Battle: Women and the Civil War by Ina Chang
- **Standardized Test Practice** (pp. 574–575)

KEYS TO TEACHING OPTIONS

 Block Scheduling

Activities that are particularly suited to use within a block scheduling framework are identified throughout this unit by the following designation: For detailed suggestions on block scheduling, see the **Block Scheduling Guide** for this grade level.

Key to Ability Levels

The Teaching Options throughout this unit have been coded for students of various abilities.

L1 BASIC activities for all students

L2 AVERAGE activities for average to above-average students

L3 CHALLENGING activities for above-average students

Reading Skills in this unit

Variety of Texts

In addition to essays by authors from the United States and several other nations, this unit also includes the following text types:

- memoir
- autobiography
- speech
- on-line travel guide
- government document
- television transcript
- journal entries

Comprehension Skills

The following instructional support for comprehension skills appears in this unit of the Student Edition:

- **Active Reading Strategies and Model** (pp. 424–430)
- **Identifying Cause and Effect** (p. 458)
- **Reading and Thinking Minilessons** (pp. 442, 474, 540, 553)

See also the **Reading Minilessons** throughout the unit in this Teacher's Wraparound Edition.

Reading Resources

Comprehension Skills Resources

📁 **Active Reading Guides**

The **Active Reading Guide** provides graphic organizers and study guide questions to support students' reading of each selection. (**Active Reading Guide**, pp. 36–48)

📁 **Reading Workbook**

The Reading Workbook (pp. 47–60) includes additional instruction and reinforcement of reading strategies and skills.

🎧 **Audio Library**

Available both on tape and on CD, the Audio Library provides valuable comprehension support.

Resources for Reading Widely

🦉 **Glencoe Literature Library**

Each title in the Glencoe Literature Library includes a full-length novel or play plus related readings. A separate Study Guide is available for each title.

💿 **Literature Classics CD-ROM**

The 900 selections on this CD-ROM can be searched by author, theme, or genre.

 inTIME

A coproduction of Glencoe and Time Inc., *inTime* includes a wealth of high-interest nonfiction related to the selections and themes in Unit Two.

✔ Assessment in this unit

 GLENCOE'S ASSESSMENT ADVANTAGE

Assessment Options in the Student Edition

Glencoe Literature offers a number of diverse ways to evaluate student understanding and skill proficiency. In the Student Edition, use the following:

- **Responding to Literature**

  Following each selection, students are asked to recall facts, interpret ideas, and evaluate concepts as they answer a variety of questions and complete activities to extend their understanding.

- **Unit Wrap-Up** (pp. 572–573)

  Here students respond to the selections on personal and analytical levels. They also assume ownership of their learning by setting and evaluating goals and by selecting work for their portfolios.

See also the many **Assessment Resources** listed on the facing page.

 THE PRINCETON REVIEW

Standardized Test Practice

The Princeton Review has developed the Standardized Test Practice pages found at the end of this unit (pp. 574–575). These pages contain practice test questions that help students remain familiar with standardized test formats and content.

Writing Skills in this unit

Writing Skills

The Student Edition of Unit Two offers strong instructional support for writing skills:

In **Extending Your Response**, which follows each selection:
- **Writing About Literature**
- **Personal/Creative Writing**

In **Writing Skills** Lessons:
- **Organizing Details** (p. 528)

   See also the **Writing Minilessons** throughout the unit in this Teacher's Wraparound Edition.

Writing Workshops

Each of two themes in Unit Two concludes with a **Writing Workshop** that guides students through the writing process.
- **Narrative Writing: Autobiographical Incident** (pp. 500–501)
- **Descriptive Writing: Observational Report** (pp. 568–569)

Writing Resources

🔵 Writer's Assistant CD-ROM

Each Writing Workshop is supplemented by an interactive writing guide on the Writer's Assistant CD-ROM. This easy-to-use writing guide provides prompts, templates, and other tools that lead students through the writing process.

📁 Writing and Proofreading Practice

Blackline masters present in-depth instruction and practice on a specific step in the writing process and proofreading. (pp. 1–7, 37–52)

✒ Writing and Proofreading Transparencies

Transparencies (1–6, 15–18, 33–36) provide graphic organizers and proofreading exercises for whole class instruction.

📁 Research and Report Writing Guide

This resource provides extensive tips and activities to guide students in their writing projects in the literature classroom as well as in classes across the curriculum.

📘 Style and Documentation Sourcebook for Writers

This sourcebook is a combination reference and workbook, giving students the most up-to-date information and guidance regarding traditional as well as technological research strategies and documentation.

📘 Grammar and Composition Handbook

The Grammar and Composition Handbook provides instruction that supplements activities in the student textbook.

Assessment Resources

📁 Selection Quick Checks

For each selection, a Quick Check of three to five short-answer questions measures students' literal comprehension.

📁 Selection and Theme Assessment

The Selection and Theme Assessment instrument tests students' abilities to recall, interpret, and evaluate what they've read. The tests consist of multiple-choice, short answer, and essay questions.

📁 Performance Assessment

Alternative assessment instruments and rubrics for Unit Two are found in the Performance Assessment ancillary.

📁 Writing Assessment and Portfolio Management

These notes and strategies, student models, and assessment tools assist with the task of measuring students' progress as writers and as monitors of their own writing.

💾 Testmaker

Teachers can customize selection, theme, and Unit Two tests by accessing the Testmaker database.

📼 🔵 MindJogger Videoquizzes

Using a popular game show format, MindJogger Videoquizzes enable teachers to evaluate students' understanding of Unit Two in a quick and fun manner.

Nonfiction

Unit Objectives

- To enjoy reading nonfiction
- To analyze the literary elements in nonfiction
- To apply strategies for reading nonfiction

VIEWING THE PAINTING

Dona Nelson is an American contemporary artist who was born in Grand Island, Nebraska, in 1947. Nelson's work, which can be seen in both private galleries and major museums throughout the country, is mainly in acrylic and cloth collage.

Responding to the Art Discussion questions:

- What is the most prominent object in the painting? Why? *(the newspaper on the table; its black and white stands out in contrast to the colors in the rest of the painting)*
- What else do you see in the painting? *(cat, table, typewriter, saw, hammer, iron, teapot, plate, chair, coat)* What do you think these things represent? *(They are just ordinary things that might be seen in any household.)*
- What is unusual about the perspective of the painting? *(The table and the things on it are painted vertically, not in their proper perspective to the wall and window behind them. Perhaps the artist wants to make sure the items can be seen.)*

420

TEACHER to TEACHER

CLAY COUNTY HIGH SCHOOL • CLAY, WEST VIRGINIA

I introduce my students to nonfiction by having them write essays and create graphics focusing on our community with the goal of learning more about our heritage and the art forms of the Appalachian Mountains. After I introduced this activity, the students decided to publish their work in a book. The first one—a 100-page paperback—came out in 1976. Every year since then students have chosen to put together a new book. In its thirtieth volume, the book is now hardcover edition and includes photos students have taken and their stories and essays about our people and their art. Since we are one of the poorest counties in the nation, students publish this book without school funds; it's all done with hard work and a few donations. I believe that this activity helps teach students that the classroom is an open window to the nature of human accomplishments, thoughts, beliefs, and values.

JERRY D. STOVER

UNIT ❦ TWO

Nonfiction

"When you write, you lay out a line of words. The line of words is a miner's pick, a woodcarver's gouge, a surgeon's probe. You wield it, and it digs a path you follow."

—*Annie Dillard*

Theme 5
Remembering
pages 431–504

Theme 6
Quests and Encounters
pages 505–571

Daily News, 1983. Dona Nelson. 84 x 60 in. Metropolitan Museum of Art, New York. Museum purchase, Emman P. Ziprik Memorial Fund Gift, in memory of Fred and Emma P. Ziprik, 1984.

Introducing the Unit

Have students read the quotation. Then pose these questions for discussion:
- What types of writing are considered nonfiction?
- What are some differences between nonfiction and fiction?
- In what ways do nonfiction writers lay out and follow "paths" of words?

Theme 5: Remembering

Theme 5 features nonfiction essays based on authors' memories, ranging from a recollection of a childhood Christmas in Wales in the early 1900s to a frightening personal account of internment in a Japanese American camp in California during World War II.

Theme 6: Quests and Encounters

The nonfiction selections in Theme 6 explore significant journeys and experiences in the lives of the authors, including a trek across Antarctica and the experience of being struck by lightning.

GLENCOE
TECHNOLOGY
**LITERATURE CLASSICS
CD-ROM**
Search for other nonfiction works by theme, author, or title.

RESOURCE MANAGER

See the *Unit Two Planning Guide* (pp. vi–1) for additional teaching notes, strategies, and resources for introducing the nonfiction unit.

Genre Focus

Nonfiction

Objective
- To understand the elements of nonfiction

Teaching Strategies

Challenge students to think of as many kinds of nonfiction as they can, beyond the examples given in the text. Ask them to give examples of nonfiction they have read and identify what types they were. Encourage them to describe each piece of writing and to discuss their opinion of it.

Narrative Nonfiction

Point out that *narrative* means *story*; thus, narrative nonfiction tells a story based on real life. Review some of the elements of stories, such as characters, plot, setting, and theme. Then explain that narrative nonfiction has these elements, too, and their presence helps a reader identify the writing as this genre.

Informative Nonfiction

Invite students to tell about different kinds of nonfiction they have written. Ask them to give their opinion about what type of nonfiction writing—narrative or informative—is most difficult to write and why. Point out that although many essays follow the lead-body-conclusion format, essays can be written using any format that effectively conveys the writer's ideas.

Nonfiction—writing about real people, events, and ideas—is the broadest category of literature. Under this huge umbrella come autobiographies, biographies, memoirs, diaries, letters, essays, speeches, travelogues, news articles, and many more types of writing. Like works of fiction, all these types of writing can be inventive and creative, even though they deal with real, rather than imaginary, subjects.

Narrative Nonfiction

Some works of nonfiction tell a story, just as works of fiction do. Autobiographies, memoirs, biographies, and narrative essays are types of narrative nonfiction.

- An **autobiography** presents the story of a person's life written by that person. Most autobiographies are told from the first-person point of view, using the pronoun *I*. Writers of autobiographies typically focus on themselves and events in their own lives.
- A **memoir** is also a first-person account of events in the author's life. Memoirs, however, tend to emphasize subjects outside the writer's personal life, such as significant historical events the writer has been a part of or has witnessed, or other people the writer has known.
- A **biography** is an account of a person's life written by someone else. It is presented from the third-person point of view.
- A **narrative essay** is a short composition that relates a true story from either the first- or the third-person point of view.

Because they tell stories, autobiographies, memoirs, biographies, and narrative essays share many characteristics of fiction. Like fictional stories, they may include such elements as setting, characters, theme, plot, and conflict. They also are organized like fictional stories. A writer might choose to present events in **chronological order,** or the order in which they occurred. Or the writer might use a **flashback,** going back in time to present incidents that happened before the beginning of the story.

Informative Nonfiction

While narrative nonfiction tells a story, informative nonfiction explains a topic or promotes an opinion. Examples of informative nonfiction include essays, speeches, letters, and news articles. The differences between narrative and informative nonfiction are not always clear, however, because writers of informative works sometimes weave stories into their writing, and writers of narratives sometimes explain topics and promote opinions.

Teaching Options

MEETING INDIVIDUAL NEEDS — ENGLISH LANGUAGE LEARNERS

Identifying Types of Nonfiction Pair English language learners with more proficient English speakers. Ask the partners to tell each other about different types of nonfiction they have read. Have students also identify whether the examples they think of are narrative or informative nonfiction. Encourage partners to give each other feedback and, if needed, assistance on their English usage.

Activity Have students write down the name and definition of each type of nonfiction they have learned about, along with examples of each. Have students save their notes to refer to as they read the nonfiction selections in this unit.

Additional Resources
📁 *English Language Learners Sourcebook*

Essays are one of the most common types of literary nonfiction. An essay is a short piece of writing devoted to a single topic. Two main kinds of informative essays are expository and persuasive.

- **Expository essays** offer information about a topic, from explaining how a process works, to analyzing or commenting on a political or historical event, to reviewing a theatrical production.
- **Persuasive essays** promote an opinion or position. Commonly, persuasive essays describe a situation and then offer reasons that the reader should believe or act in a certain way regarding the issue.

Many expository and persuasive essays follow a general structure of lead, body, and conclusion. This diagram shows the structure of a typical informative essay.

- The **lead,** or introduction, serves to pique the reader's interest. It also often includes the **thesis,** or main idea, of the essay. Sometimes, though, a writer saves the thesis statement for the end of the work.
- The **body** develops or attempts to prove the thesis with **supporting details,** such as facts, reasons, statistics, sensory details, examples, observations, and personal experiences. This part of the work might also include quotations from expert sources and graphics, such as diagrams, graphs, and illustrations.
- The **conclusion** typically restates the thesis and provides the reader with a final or summarizing thought. It might also call on readers to accept a new idea or to take a specific action.

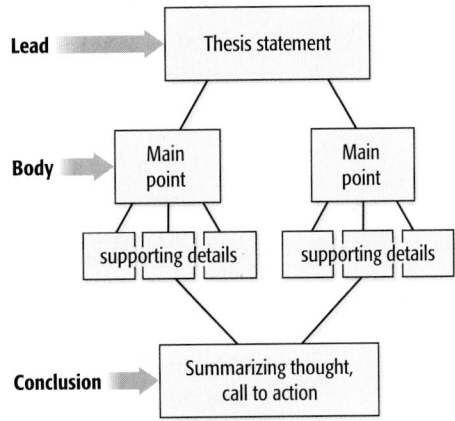

Analyzing Nonfiction

The first step in analyzing nonfiction is to identify the type of work you are reading. By looking at the title and skimming the first few paragraphs, you can usually tell whether the work is an autobiography or a memoir, a biography, an essay, or another type of nonfiction.

As you read, you might further classify the type of work by identifying the **author's purpose,** or reason for writing. Ask yourself what the writer is trying to achieve. Is the writer's purpose to entertain, to inform, or to persuade the reader? The answer to that question will help you classify the work you are reading.

Once you know the type of work you are reading, you will know what to look for, such as elements of fiction, a thesis and supporting details, or persuasive techniques. Be aware, however, that writers may combine various elements, and purposes, in a single work. For example, you might read a persuasive essay that is not only entertaining but also tells a story. Perhaps the best approach is to think of each work of nonfiction as a unique combination of familiar elements.

Analyzing Nonfiction

Explain that the line between fiction and nonfiction can be blurry, since nonfiction frequently stretches the truth, and fiction is often loosely based on real life. Classifying types of nonfiction can be difficult, too, since writers combine literary elements in many different ways. Nevertheless, identifying types of literature is helpful as a way to understand a writer's intentions and to compare pieces of writing.

Technology Option

Nonfiction Chart

Students can use word processing software to create a chart in which they compare examples of narrative and informative nonfiction. Have them open a new document and insert a chart with the title *Nonfiction* and two columns with the headings *Narrative* and *Informative.* Students should decide whether each work they read is primarily narrative or informative nonfiction and then key in information about the work in the appropriate column. At the end of the unit, they can use the chart to help them review the differences between narrative and informative nonfiction. **L2**

NONFICTION	
Narrative	**Informative**

Active Reading Strategies

Objective

- To understand and apply strategies for reading and comprehending nonfiction

Teach the Strategies

The Modernist poet Muriel Rukeyser called reading an exchange between the writer and reader. Ask students to offer their opinions about what this means. Discuss the idea that reading is an active, not a passive, experience.

Predict

Ask students to identify clues in nonfiction that might help them predict what the work will be about and what the writer's main ideas will be.

Explain that good readers revise their predictions as they read and learn new information.

Connect

Invite students to name examples of nonfiction with which they have felt a personal connection and to tell how that affected their appreciation.

Question

Emphasize that active reading includes questioning a writer's ideas, intentions, and language.

Teaching Options

Active Reading Strategies

Nonfiction

To get the most from reading nonfiction, active readers use strategies similar to those used in reading short stories. As an active reader, however, you will need to adapt the strategies to the particular type of nonfiction you are reading.

● For more about related reading strategies, see **Reading Handbook**, pp. R78–R107.

PREDICT   Make educated guesses about what you are reading. Preview the work by looking at the title, skimming the text, and examining photographs, illustrations, charts, and other graphics. Make predictions before beginning to read and also as you read.

Ask yourself . . .
- What will this work be about?
- What might the writer's main idea about this topic be?
- What supporting evidence might the writer use?
- What point will the writer make next?

CONNECT   Make connections with what you already know and with your own life.

Ask yourself . . .
- What people, events, and experiences in my own life are similar to those written about here?
- What have I heard or read about the subject?
- How does this subject relate to other subjects I know about?

QUESTION   Question anything you do not understand. Reread any part that confuses you, and then read on to see if your questions are answered.

Ask yourself . . .
- What is the writer really saying here?
- Why is the writer giving me these facts?
- What does this concept have to do with what I just read?

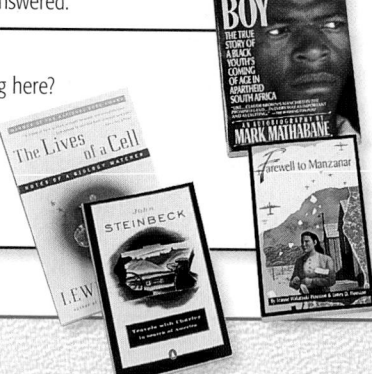

Reading Journal

Listing Information

A nonfiction selection often provides the reader with information about a particular topic. In the excerpt from *Travels with Charley,* as John Steinbeck describes his unexpected encounter with the coyotes, he provides the reader with a picture of the Mojave Desert and information about coyotes. He also gives the reader some insight into himself.

Activity Ask students to begin a set of lists in their reading journals. Three possible lists are "Things I Learned About the Mojave Desert," "Things I Learned About Coyotes," and "Things I Learned About the Author." Students might wish to add other lists of their own choosing. After they have read the selection, let students work in small groups to share the entries they

made in their lists. They may wish to add or revise their lists based on what they learn in the groups.

VISUALIZE Use details the writer gives you to form mental pictures of people, places, and objects, and to see the steps in a process or how something works.

Ask yourself . . .
- What does this person look like?
- How does this scene or object look?
- Where does this part fit with the others?
- How does this step relate to the next one? the one before?

EVALUATE Make judgments about what you read.

Ask yourself . . .
- Is this statement a fact or an opinion?
- Does this information really support the thesis?
- Do I agree with the writer's opinions and interpretations?
- What does this action reveal about this person?

REVIEW Pause often to think about what you have read.

Say to yourself . . .
- The main idea is . . .
- Details supporting this thesis include . . .
- The steps in this process are . . .
- The writer's purpose is to . . .

RESPOND React to what you are reading. Identify and consider your spontaneous thoughts about what the writer is saying. Decide what you like or dislike about the work.

Say to yourself . . .
- I'd like to ask the writer why . . .
- I think this thesis is . . .
- That's pretty interesting. I'd like to know more about . . .
- Who else might benefit from learning this information?

Applying the Strategies

Read the next selection from *Travels with Charley* by John Steinbeck using the Active Reading Model in the margins. Then practice the strategies as you read another work of nonfiction.

NONFICTION 425

Visualize

Explain that visualizing is a good way to understand and remember what is being read. Suggest to students that if they have trouble "seeing" what they are reading, they should try to visualize something or someone similar with which they are familiar.

Evaluate

Point out that writers are not always right and that all writing is, to some extent, subjective; therefore, it is important that students evaluate everything they read. Explain that as they evaluate a piece of nonfiction, they should consider both style and substance. Encourage them to ask themselves questions such as the following:
- Did the piece hold my attention?
- Was the writing clear?
- Was the language interesting, and did it flow well?

Review

Point out that reviewing during and after reading is especially helpful for understanding longer or more complicated kinds of nonfiction.

Respond

Remind students that reading is an exchange. Point out that responding is a way of "giving back" to the writer and deepening their own understanding and appreciation of what they have read. Point out that responding to reading can also include talking to others, writing, drawing, singing, and so on. Encourage students to share responses to things they have read both in and outside the class.

Objectives

- To read and analyze a narrative essay about an internal conflict the author experienced
- To explore external and internal conflict in narrative nonfiction
- To write an analysis of the author's use of double meanings

Skills

Writing: Humorous Monologue
Vocabulary: Multiple-Meaning Words
Grammar/Language: Adjectives
Listening/Speaking: Persuasive Speech
Collaboration: Literature Groups

Motivating
→OPTIONS

Selection Focus
Transparency 36: After identifying descriptive words for the coyote, take an opinion poll to see how many students think that coyotes are simply nuisance animals or that they have a purpose and belong in the wild.

Focus Activity: Invite students to tell about the conflict they faced and how they resolved it.

Before You Read

from *Travels with Charley*

FOCUS ACTIVITY

When you make important decisions, does your intellect sometimes tell you to do one thing, while your emotions urge you to do something different?

JOURNAL Write about a time when your head told you to do one thing, and your heart told you to do the opposite.

SETTING A PURPOSE Read to learn how the author resolved a conflict between his head and his heart.

BACKGROUND

The Time and Place
In the early 1960s, author John Steinbeck traveled across the United States with his dog, Charley, in a truck outfitted as a camper. This selection recounts an encounter they had as they crossed the Mojave Desert in southeastern California.

Did You Know?
Coyotes are members of the wild dog family and are related to foxes, wolves, and jackals. Intelligent and extremely adaptable, they live almost everywhere in the United States, including deserts, farmland, and even cities and suburbs. Because many people consider them nuisances and blame them for killing farm animals, about 100,000 coyotes are hunted and killed each year. Recent studies, however, show that coyotes account for only a fraction of the deaths of domestic animals.

VOCABULARY PREVIEW

constancy (kon′ stən sē) *n.* the quality of being unchanging; faithfulness; loyalty; p. 427
loll (lol) *v.* to hang down loosely; droop; p. 427
temper (tem′ pər) *v.* to moderate by mingling with another thing; p. 427
vermin (vur′ min) *n.* any animals that are harmful, destructive, or troublesome; p. 428
token (tō′ kən) *adj.* symbolic; p. 428

Meet John Steinbeck

John Steinbeck is best known for his sympathetic portrayals of people living on the fringes of society: the poor, the socially outcast, the dispossessed. In *The Grapes of Wrath*, Steinbeck's most famous novel, the author chronicled the struggles of an Oklahoma farm family who lost their land during the Great Depression. Although much of Steinbeck's work is serious, even grim, the author also wrote a number of humorous works and often showed a sense of humor in dealing with critics' reactions to his work. Steinbeck was awarded the Nobel Prize for Literature in 1962.

John Steinbeck was born in 1902 in Salinas, California, and died in 1968. Travels with Charley was published in 1962.

RESOURCE MANAGER

Lesson Planning Resource
The *Unit Two Planning Guide* (pp. 2–9) provides additional lesson notes and reduced versions of all print resources.

 Other Print Resources
- Active Reading Guide, p. 36
- Vocabulary Practice, p. 35
- Grammar and Language Workbook, p. 61
- Grammar and Composition Handbook, Lesson 1.4
- Quick Checks, p. 36

- Selection and Theme Assessment, pp. 69–70
- Performance Assessment, p. 35
- Spanish Summaries, p. 36
- Spanish Translations
- Inclusion Strategies

 Transparencies
- Selection Focus 36
- Literary Elements 36
- Grammar and Language 36

Technology
- Audio Library
- Spanish Audio Library
- Glencoe Literature Web Site
- Testmaker

from Travels with Charley

John Steinbeck ∾

THE MOJAVE IS A BIG DESERT AND A FRIGHTENING ONE. It's as though nature tested a man for endurance and <u>constancy</u> to prove whether he was good enough to get to California. The shimmering dry heat made visions of water on the flat plain. And even when you drive at high speed, the hills that mark the boundaries recede before you. Charley, always a dog for water, panted asthmatically, jarring his whole body with the effort, and a good eight inches of his tongue hung out flat as a leaf and dripping. I pulled off the road into a small gulley to give him water from my thirty-gallon tank. But before I let him drink I poured water all over him and on my hair and shoulders and shirt. The air is so dry that evaporation makes you feel suddenly cold.

I opened a can of beer from my refrigerator and sat well inside the shade of Rocinante,[1] looking out at the sunpounded plain, dotted here and there with clumps of sagebrush.

About fifty yards away two coyotes stood watching me, their tawny coats blending with sand and sun. I knew that with any quick or suspicious movement of mine they could drift into invisibility. With the most casual slowness I reached down my new rifle from its sling over my bed—the .222 with its bitter little high-speed, long-range stings. Very slowly I brought the rifle up. Perhaps in the shade of my house I was half hidden by the blinding light outside. The little rifle has a beautiful telescope sight with a wide field. The coyotes had not moved.

I got both of them in the field of my telescope, and the glass brought them very close. Their tongues <u>lolled</u> out so that they seemed to smile mockingly. They were favored animals, not starved, but well furred, the golden hair <u>tempered</u> with black guard hairs.[2] Their little lemon-yellow eyes were plainly visible in the glass. I moved the cross hairs to the breast of the right-hand animal, and pushed the safety. My elbows on the table steadied the gun. The cross hairs lay unmoving on

---

1. Steinbeck named his truck *Rocinante* (rō′ sə nän′ tā) in honor of the broken-down old horse that carries a broken-down old knight into his romantic and crazy adventures in *Don Quixote,* a novel by Miguel de Cervantes.
2. A coyote's *guard hairs* are the long, coarse outer hairs that protect its soft undercoat.

Vocabulary
constancy (kon′ stən sē) *n.* the quality of being unchanging; faithfulness; loyalty
loll (lol) *v.* to hang down loosely; droop
temper (tem′ pər) *v.* to moderate by mingling with another thing

---

Reading the Selection

SUMMARY

In this excerpt from *Travels with Charley*, John Steinbeck recalls stopping briefly in the Mojave Desert and spotting two coyotes. He aims his rifle at them, feeling that coyotes are "vermin" that should be shot. Then he hesitates, identifying with their doglike qualities and their struggle to survive in the desert. The author spares the coyotes and leaves behind an offering of dog food.

📁 *Spanish Summaries,* p. 36

Active Reading Model

Predict
Based on the title and the first paragraph, what type of nonfiction is this?

QUESTION
Why is Steinbeck getting his rifle?

VISUALIZE
Picture the view of the two coyotes through the telescope sight.

Active Reading Model

Predict
The use of the first person and the personal details indicate an autobiographical narrative.

Question
Steinbeck intends to shoot the coyotes.

Visualize
Have students sketch the coyotes.

Additional Resources
📁 *Active Reading Guide,* p. 36
🎧 *Audio Library*
🎧 *Spanish Audio Library*

Teaching Options

CONNECTING TO OTHER SELECTIONS

The chart at the right shows three ways to connect the excerpt from *Travels with Charley* to selections in this book.

For specific teaching strategies, see the **Unit Two Planning Guide,** pages 5–6.

Connection	Title
Life Skills: Decision Making	→ "Chee's Daughter," p. 23
Thematic: Choices	→ "With All Flags Flying," p. 115
Literary: Mood	→ "The Interlopers," p. 269

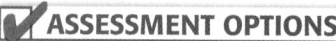

A Literary Elements

PLOT: Conflict Ask students to identify the conflict that Steinbeck faces. *(He feels that he should shoot the coyotes because he has been taught to think of them as vermin, yet he is reluctant to kill them.* Is Steinbeck's conflict internal or external? *(It is internal.)*

Connect

Some students may say they would not feel obligated to kill the coyotes in the first place. Others may appreciate his conflicting feelings.

Respond

Students may admire Steinbeck's thoughtfulness and respect for life.

Evaluate

Many students will feel Steinbeck made the right decision, since the coyotes were posing no threat.

Review

Ask students to analyze the last two paragraphs and identify the realization the author has.

✔ ASSESSMENT OPTIONS

📁 *Quick Checks,* p. 36

Teaching Options

---

from Travels with Charley

Active Reading Model

CONNECT

How would you react in this situation?

RESPOND

Do you like Steinbeck's character as it is portrayed here?

EVALUATE

Do you think Steinbeck made the right decision? Why or why not?

REVIEW

What is Steinbeck's purpose and thesis?

the brisket.[3] And then the coyote sat down like a dog and its right rear paw came up to scratch the right shoulder.

My finger was reluctant to touch the trigger. I must be getting very old and my ancient conditioning worn thin. Coyotes are <u>vermin</u>. They steal chickens. They thin the ranks of quail and all other game <u>birds</u>. They must be killed. They are the enemy. My first shot would drop the sitting beast, and the other would whirl to fade away. I might very well pull him down with a running shot because I am a good rifleman.

And I did not fire. My training said, "Shoot!" and my age replied, "There isn't a chicken within thirty miles, and if there are any they aren't my chickens. And this waterless place is not quail country. No, these boys are keeping their figures with kangaroo rats and jackrabbits, and that's vermin eat vermin. Why should I interfere?"

"Kill them," my training said. "Everyone kills them. It's a public service." My finger moved to the trigger. The cross was steady on the breast just below the panting tongue. I could imagine the splash and jar of angry steel, the leap and struggle until the torn heart failed, and then, not too long later, the shadow of a buzzard, and another. By that time I would be long gone—out of the desert and across the Colorado River. And beside the sagebush there would be a naked, eyeless skull, a few picked bones, a spot of black dried blood and a few rags of golden fur.

I guess I'm too old and too lazy to be a good citizen. The second coyote stood sidewise to my rifle. I moved the cross hairs to his shoulder and held steady. There was no question of missing with that rifle at that range. I owned both animals. Their lives were mine. I put the safety on and laid the rifle on the table. Without the telescope they were not so intimately close. The hot blast of light tousled the air to shimmering.

Then I remembered something I heard long ago that I hope is true. It was unwritten law in China, so my informant told me, that when one man saved another's life he became responsible for that life to the end of its existence. For, having interfered with a course of events, the savior could not escape his responsibility. And that has always made good sense to me.

Now I had a <u>token</u> responsibility for two live and healthy coyotes. In the delicate world of relationships, we are tied together for all time. I opened two cans of dog food and left them as a votive.[4]

---

3. The coyote's *brisket* is its chest or breast.
4. In this context, *votive* means "an offering."

Vocabulary
vermin (vur′ min) *n.* any animals that are harmful, destructive, or troublesome
token (tō′ kən) *adj.* symbolic

Grammar and Language *Minilesson*

Adjectives Remind students that adjectives are words that describe, or modify, nouns. They tell what kind, which one, how many, or how much.

Activity Have students list 15 particularly colorful or useful adjectives from the selection. Ask them to identify the noun each adjective modifies and the question the adjective answers about the noun. **L2**

Additional Resources

📠 *Grammar and Language Transparency 36*

📗 *Grammar and Language Workbook,* p. 61

📗 *Grammar and Composition Handbook,* Lesson 1.4

📓 *Writer's Choice,* Lesson 10.4

Responding to Literature

Personal Response

Did the outcome of this selection surprise you? Why or why not?

Active Reading Response

Review the Active Reading Strategies described on pages 424–425. Which of these strategies did you use when reading this selection? Which other strategies might you apply to it? Give two specific examples.

— ANALYZING LITERATURE —

RECALL

1. Summarize Steinbeck's description of the Mojave in the first two paragraphs.
2. Describe the appearance and actions of the coyotes.
3. Summarize the thoughts that go through Steinbeck's mind as he watches the coyotes.
4. What "unwritten law" does Steinbeck remember?
5. What does Steinbeck do at the end of the selection?

INTERPRET

6. What might you infer about Steinbeck's attitude toward the Mojave, based on the way he describes it in the first two paragraphs?
7. How might the coyotes' appearance and actions influence Steinbeck's behavior? Explain.
8. What do Steinbeck's thoughts and actions seem to suggest about his character? Support your answer with evidence from the selection.
9. Why do you think Steinbeck feels that the "unwritten law" applies to him?
10. Do you think this experience has changed Steinbeck in any way? Use evidence from the selection to support your answer.

EVALUATE AND CONNECT

11. Do you think owning pets makes people more responsive to animals in the wild? Give reasons for your answer.
12. Review your response to the Focus Activity on page 426. Compare and contrast your experience with the one Steinbeck describes.
13. Steinbeck says, "I guess I'm too old and too lazy to be a good citizen." Is being old and lazy the real reason he acts as he does? Explain.
14. Identify at least two **sensory details** (see page R11) from the selection. Explain how each one helps you understand what is being described.
15. According to Steinbeck, "In the delicate world of relationships, we are tied together for all time." Do you agree? Why or why not?

Literary ELEMENTS

Conflict

Conflict is a struggle between two opposing forces. An **external conflict** exists when a character struggles against an outside force, such as another person, nature, or society. In this excerpt from *Travels with Charley*, Steinbeck's dog "panted asthmatically, jarring his whole body with the effort," as he struggles against the searing heat of the desert. Steinbeck also suffers from the intense heat of the "sun-pounded plain." In addition, he faces an **internal conflict**—a struggle that takes place within the mind of a character. Usually, the character is torn between two opposing feelings or courses of action. In this selection, Steinbeck wrestles with a decision he has to make about the coyotes.

1. What external conflicts do the coyotes face in their daily lives in the desert? What new conflict might develop for them when Steinbeck stops his truck?
2. What internal conflict does Steinbeck face in this selection? How does he resolve this conflict? What details make the outcome uncertain?

● See **Literary Terms Handbook**, p. R3.

NONFICTION 🐾 429

Responding to the Selection

Personal Response

Some students may be surprised that Steinbeck did not shoot the coyotes since that was his first inclination. Others may not be surprised because he showed reluctance to do so.

Active Reading Response

Have students explain how the active reading strategies helped their reading comprehension and enjoyment. If they did not find particular strategies useful, discuss possible ways of modifying them.

ANALYZING LITERATURE

1. The Mojave is a "big" and "frightening" place that tests a person's endurance, a place that is dangerously hot, dry, and seemingly endless.
2. The coyotes blend in with their environment. Like dogs, they pant, and one casually sits down to scratch its shoulder. They are sleek and well fed, not overly concerned with Steinbeck's presence.
3. Steinbeck feels obligated to kill the coyotes because he has been taught to think of them as "the enemy," but he also questions killing animals that aren't posing any threat.
4. The "unwritten law" dictates that when a person saves another's life, that person becomes forever responsible for that life.
5. He leaves two open cans of dog food for the coyotes.
6. He seems to have a healthy fear of and respect for the desert.
7. The coyotes' doglike appearance and behavior probably makes him sympathetic.
8. His first instinct to shoot the coyotes shows that he identifies with ranchers and hunters, who view all predators as the enemy; yet his decision not to kill the animals reveals his commitment to a moral code that tells him not to kill without reasonable justification. His sense of responsibility toward the coyotes reflects his feeling of connection with living things.
9. Steinbeck appears to accept the unwritten Chinese law as universally sensible.
10. Steinbeck appears to have a realization about his own connectedness with all living things.
11. Students may say having relationships with pets makes people more responsive to all animals.

LITERARY ELEMENTS

1. The coyotes face the daily conflict of finding sufficient food and water. They might face being shot by Steinbeck.
2. Steinbeck is torn between his training to kill "vermin" and his feeling that doing so would be wrong under the circumstances. He decides that killing the coyotes is not justified. The outcome is uncertain as Steinbeck aims his gun at the coyotes.

Additional Resources

 Literary Elements Transparency 36

12. Students' experiences should involve a moral dilemma based on conflicting impulses.
13. Students should recognize that Steinbeck chooses not to shoot the coyotes out of a sense of morality and not because he is lazy.
14. "Charley, always a dog for water, panted asthmatically" conveys a feeling of extreme dryness and thirst. "The hot blast of light tousled the air to shimmering" conveys the intensity of the desert sunlight.
15. Many students may agree with Steinbeck, especially given the current emphasis on the interrelatedness of Earth's life forms.

LITERATURE AND WRITING

Writing About Literature

Students' explanations should

- explain the first meaning: Steinbeck knew he could kill the coyotes.
- explain the second meaning: Steinbeck felt that by not killing the coyotes he became responsible for them.

Creative Writing

Students' monologues should

- express a version of the events as a dog might view them.
- offer dialogue that is humorous.

EXTENDING YOUR RESPONSE

Literature Groups Remind students to set aside their own biases and analyze what Steinbeck says in the essay. **COLLAB. LEARN.**

Interdisciplinary Activity Encourage students to use drawings, cartoons, charts, graphs, or photographs from magazines.

Listening and Speaking Encourage students to consider the environmental and moral implications of controlling or not controlling animal populations.

Skill Minilesson

VOCABULARY • Multiple-Meaning Words

1. Trevor will sing the tenor part. She enjoyed the even tenor of her school days.
2. We planted gardens in the vacant lot. It was her lot to be everyone's counselor.
3. Plucking the turkey was slow, messy work. Jan showed pluck in rescuing the child.

Additional Resources

Vocabulary Practice, p. 35

LITERATURE AND WRITING

Writing About Literature

Explore Double Meanings When Steinbeck is looking at the coyotes through his telescope sight, he says, "I owned both animals. Their lives were mine." This statement has two different meanings: one in the context of the paragraph in which it appears, and another in the context of the two paragraphs that follow. In two or three paragraphs, analyze the two meanings of the statement. Share your analysis with a classmate.

Creative Writing

It's a Dog's Life Try to imagine how Charley might have viewed the encounter described in the selection. What thoughts might have gone through his mind as he watched his master aiming the rifle at the coyotes, or opening the cans of dog food and leaving them in the desert? Imagine that after Charley returns home, he tells the dog next door about this incident. Write a brief, humorous monologue giving Charley's view of the encounter.

EXTENDING YOUR RESPONSE

Literature Groups

What If? Steinbeck finds the coyotes in a desert, where "There isn't a chicken within thirty miles. . . . And this waterless place is not quail country." What if he had found the coyotes in a farming area or in a place where quail do live? Would he have made the same decision? Debate this question in your group. Use evidence from the story to support your opinion. Share your ideas with the class.

Interdisciplinary Activity

Biology: Desert Animals Steinbeck mentions four animals that live in the Mojave Desert: the coyote, kangaroo rat, jackrabbit, and buzzard. Generate research questions about how these and other animals survive in an inhospitable environment. Then, research the answers and create a poster summarizing your conclusions from information gathered.

Listening and Speaking

Where Do You Stand? Consider whether humans ever have the right to control animal populations. If so, under what circumstances should this right be exercised? Decide where you stand on this issue. Then research and write a speech aimed at persuading your classmates to accept your point of view. Practice your speech with a friend or family member. Then present your speech to the class.

Reading Further

You may enjoy these other works by John Steinbeck:

Novel: *The Pearl,* about a fisherman who finds a valuable pearl but discovers that it does not bring him happiness.

Short Story: "The Red Pony," a coming-of-age story about a boy living on a California ranch.

📖 **Save your work for your portfolio.**

Skill Minilesson

VOCABULARY • Multiple-Meaning Words

Most words have more than one meaning. *Temper* is an example. When a coyote's golden coat is *tempered* with black, the basic color is moderated and made less intense. Steel, on the other hand, is *tempered* to make it harder and stronger. And when you lose your *temper,* you get angry.

PRACTICE For each pair, write two sentences, one with each meaning. Use a dictionary as needed.

1. a. a **tenor** voice   b. the **tenor** of the times
2. a. to build on a **lot**   b. her **lot** in life
3. a. to **pluck** a chicken b. to demonstrate **pluck**

✔ ASSESSMENT OPTIONS

- 📁 *Quick Checks,* p. 36
- 📁 *Selection and Theme Assessment,* pp. 69–70
- 📁 *Performance Assessment,* p. 35
- 💾 *Testmaker*

Theme 5 _____ Remembering

Memories are one of the treasures of life. They help define who we are and who we might become. Memories link us to loved ones and help shape the way we look at our lives. Each author in this theme shares the memory of a unique experience that left an impression for a lifetime. How do your own memories enrich your understanding of the past and present?

THEME PROJECTS

Learning for Life

Journeys Unlimited   Work with a partner to create a travel brochure for one of the places you "visit" in this theme.

1. Make a list of the settings in this theme. Choose one for your brochure.

2. Using the Internet, library resources, and materials from a travel agency, write and research a list of questions about the land, climate, people, customs, language, and foods of the place you have chosen.

3. With your partner, design and write a travel brochure that summarizes your findings and presents this place in an interesting way. Illustrate your brochure with photographs, maps, or drawings. Think of a captivating title for your brochure.

Interdisciplinary Project

Music: A Medley of Memories   Create an audiotape of musical pieces that convey the subjects or moods of selections in this theme.

1. Investigate music from the various cultures represented in this theme. For three or four selections, choose music that fits the subject or mood of the selection.

2. Prepare a brief introduction that gives information about each piece. Tell which selection the music goes with and why you chose it.

3. Make an audiotape of the selections and introductions. Play the tape for your classmates, and discuss their reactions.

NONFICTION 🖎 431

LITERATURE & HUMANITIES

Display the photograph of the sculpture *Family Group* from *Art Talk*, page 20. Discuss how a family group from a selection in Theme 5 compares to this image.

GLENCOE
TECHNOLOGY

LITERATURE CLASSICS
CD-ROM
Search for other selections related to the theme of remembering.

Theme 5 _____

Teaching Strategies

The following suggestions may help your students plan and carry out their theme projects.

Learning for Life

- Suggest that students start by selecting two or three possible places and then make a list of the pros and cons for each one.
- Remind students to look for specific information about tourist attractions and special events.
- Tell students to develop ideas as to how they can make someone want to read the brochure. What can be used to grab a reader's attention? 🖎

Interdisciplinary Project

- List with students places they can find music for the project, including the library and personal music collections of friends.
- Discuss ways they can find out information they want to include about each piece. For example, the composer and performers are usually included on notes included with cassettes and CD's. What other information may be useful?
- Talk with students about ways of getting the audiotape made. Students with special skills in this area may be willing to volunteer their help. 🖎

Additional Resources
- 📁 *Interdisciplinary Activities,* pp. 10–11
- 📁 *Viewing and Representing Activities,* pp. 15–16
- 📁 *Listening and Speaking Activities,* pp. 9–10
- 📁 *Critical Thinking Skills,* pp. 13–15
- 📁 *Selection and Theme Assessment,* pp. 179–180
- 📁 *Performance Assessment,* p. 93

SELECTIONS	Literary Elements	Reading and Thinking	Writing	Vocabulary and Spelling	
A Child's Christmas in Wales DYLAN THOMAS	Memoir, SE p. 440 *Memoir, TWE pp. 434, 438* *Character, TWE p. 436*	Clarifying, SE p. 442 *Sequence of Events, TWE p. 439* *Identifying Author's Purpose, TWE p. 443*	Sensory Description, SE p. 441	Analogies, SE p. 442	
from Kaffir Boy MARK MATHABANE	Monologue, SE p. 456 *Character, TWE pp. 447, 453* *Setting, TWE p. 448* *Paradox, TWE p. 450* *Monologue, TWE p. 455*	Identifying Cause and Effect, SE p. 458 *Problem and Solution, TWE p. 455*	Paragraphs about Freedom, SE p. 457 *Expository Writing, TWE p. 453*	Analogies, SE p. 457	
from Farewell to Manzanar JEANNE WAKATSUKI HOUSTON AND JAMES D. HOUSTON	Autobiography, SE p. 472 *Autobiography, TWE pp. 461, 465* *Dialogue, TWE p. 469* *Narrative Details, TWE p. 469* *Sensory Imagery, TWE p. 470*	Summarizing, SE p. 474 *Identifying Spatial Relationships, TWE p. 471* *Summarizing, TWE p. 475*	Letter of Protest, SE p. 473 Song Lyrics, SE p. 473 *Sentence Combining, TWE p. 476* *Personal Writing, TWE p. 463*	Parts of Speech, SE p. 474 Dictionary Skills: Pronunciation, SE p. 477	
By Any Other Name SANTHA RAMA RAU	Atmosphere, SE p. 486 *Atmosphere, TWE pp. 481, 483* *Details, TWE p. 482*	*Inferring, TWE p. 484* *Comparing and Contrasting, TWE p. 485*	Diary Entries, SE p. 487	Etymology, SE p. 487 *Root Words, TWE p. 480*	
Living Well. Living Good. MAYA ANGELOU	Using Character to Understand Theme, SE p. 492 *Theme, TWE p. 491* *Character, TWE p. 491*	*Inferring, TWE p. 490* *Drawing Conclusions, TWE p. 491*	Description of a Person, SE p. 493	Analogies, SE p. 493	
A Swimming Lesson JEWELLE L. GOMEZ	Motif, SE p. 498 *Setting, TWE p. 496* *Motif, TWE p. 496*	*Drawing Conclusions, TWE p. 497*	Thank-you Letter, SE p. 498		

Key: Student material is in roman. Teacher material is in italic.   Technology   **COLLAB. LEARN.** Collaboration

Grammar and Language	Listening, Speaking, and Viewing	Life Skills	Study, Research, and Technology
Compound Adjectives, SE p. 442 *Capitalization of Proper Nouns, TWE p. 438*	**COLLAB. LEARN.** Literature Groups, SE p. 441 Listening to Recordings, SE p. 441		*Research, TWE p. 437*
Quotation Marks, TWE p. 454	**COLLAB. LEARN.** Literature Groups, SE p. 457 Reenactment, SE p. 457		*Research, TWE pp. 448, 450, 452*
Intervening Prepositional Phrases, SE p. 474 Making Sure Subjects and Verbs Agree, SE p. 476 *Dashes, TWE p. 470*	**COLLAB. LEARN.** Literature Groups, SE p. 473 Performing Songs, SE p. 473 *Interviewing, TWE p. 464*	*Map Reading, TWE p. 468*	🖳 Internet Connection, SE p. 473 *Research, TWE p. 466, 469*
Parts of Speech, TWE p. 484	**COLLAB. LEARN.** Literature Groups, SE p. 487 Dramatizing, SE p. 487		Research, SE p. 487 *Research, TWE p. 483*
	COLLAB. LEARN. Literature Groups, SE p. 493	Wisdom in Bumper Stickers, SE p. 493	
Main and Subordinate Clauses, TWE p. 497			

SELECTIONS	📁 Print Resources		

A Child's Christmas in Wales
DYLAN THOMAS
	Unit Two Planning Guide, pp. 16–23
	* Active Reading Guide, p. 37
	Vocabulary Practice, p. 36
		Grammar & Comp Handbook,
		  Lessons 10.3, 11.12
		Grammar and Language Workbook,
		  pp. 237, 279
		Reading Workbook, pp. 47–48
			* Quick Checks, p. 37
			Selection and Theme Assessment,
			  pp. 71–72
			Performance Assessment, p. 36
			Spanish Summaries, p. 37

from **Kaffir Boy**
MARK MATHABANE
	Unit Two Planning Guide, pp. 24–31
	* Active Reading Guide, p. 38
	Vocabulary Practice, p. 37
		Grammar & Comp Handbook,
		  Lesson 11.9
		Grammar and Language Workbook,
		  pp. 235, 271, 273
		Reading Workbook, p. 49
			* Quick Checks, p. 38
			Selection and Theme Assessment,
			  pp. 73–74
			Performance Assessment, p. 37
			Spanish Summaries, p. 38
			Spanish Translations

from **Farewell to Manzanar**
JEANNE WAKATSUKI HOUSTON
AND JAMES D. HOUSTON
	Unit Two Planning Guide, pp. 32–39
	* Active Reading Guide, p. 39
	Vocabulary Practice, p. 38
		Grammar & Comp Handbook,
		  Lessons 11.7, 6.2, 6.1
		Grammar and Language Workbook,
		  pp. 267, 163, 161
		Reading Workbook, p. 50
			* Quick Checks, p. 39
			Selection and Theme Assessment,
			  pp. 75–76
			Performance Assessment, p. 38
			Spanish Summaries, p. 39

By Any Other Name
SANTHA RAMA RAU
	Unit Two Planning Guide, pp. 40–47
	* Active Reading Guide, p. 40
	Vocabulary Practice, p. 39
		Grammar & Comp Handbook,
		  Lessons 1.1–1.8
		Grammar and Language Workbook,
		  pp. 47–72
		Reading Workbook, pp. 51–52
			* Quick Checks, p. 40
			Selection and Theme Assessment,
			  pp. 77–78
			Performance Assessment, p. 39
			Spanish Summaries, p. 40

Living Well. Living Good.
MAYA ANGELOU
	Unit Two Planning Guide, pp. 48–55
	* Active Reading Guide, p. 41
	Vocabulary Practice, p. 40
		Grammar & Comp Handbook,
		  Lesson 3.3
		Grammar and Language Workbook,
		  p. 97
		Reading Workbook, pp. 51–52
			* Quick Checks, p. 41
			Selection and Theme Assessment,
			  pp. 79–80
			Performance Assessment, p. 40
			Spanish Summaries, p. 41

A Swimming Lesson
JEWELLE L. GOMEZ
	Unit Two Planning Guide, pp. 56–63
	* Active Reading Guide, p. 42
	Vocabulary Practice, p. 41
		Grammar & Comp Handbook,
		  Lessons 4.1, 4.2
		Grammar and Language Workbook,
		  p. 105
		Reading Workbook, pp. 51–52
			* Quick Checks, p. 42
			Selection and Theme Assessment,
			  pp. 81–82
			Performance Assessment, p. 41
			Spanish Summaries, p. 42
			Spanish Translations

*Also available in Spanish

🖥 **Transparencies**	**Technology Resources**
Selection Focus Transparency 37 Grammar and Language Transparency 37 Literary Elements Transparency 37	💿 Literature Launchers Videodisc 🎧 💿 Audio Library 🎧 💿 Spanish Audio Library 💾 💿 Vocabulary Puzzlemaker 💻 Web Site: lit.glencoe.com
Selection Focus Transparency 38 Grammar and Language Transparency 38 Literary Elements Transparency 38	💿 Literature Launchers Videodisc 🎧 💿 Audio Library 🎧 💿 Spanish Audio Library 💾 💿 Vocabulary Puzzlemaker 💻 Web Site: lit.glencoe.com
Selection Focus Transparency 39 Grammar and Language Transparency 39 Literary Elements Transparency 39 Fine Art Transparency 19	🎧 💿 Audio Library 🎧 💿 Spanish Audio Library 💾 💿 Vocabulary Puzzlemaker 💻 Web Site: lit.glencoe.com
Selection Focus Transparency 40 Grammar and Language Transparency 40 Literary Elements Transparency 40 Fine Art Transparency 7	🎧 💿 Audio Library 🎧 💿 Spanish Audio Library 💾 💿 Vocabulary Puzzlemaker 💻 Web Site: lit.glencoe.com
Selection Focus Transparency 41 Literary Elements Transparency 41	🎧 💿 Audio Library 🎧 💿 Spanish Audio Library 💾 💿 Vocabulary Puzzlemaker 💻 Web Site: lit.glencoe.com
Selection Focus Transparency 42 Grammar and Language Transparency 41 Literary Elements Transparency 42	🎧 💿 Audio Library 🎧 💿 Spanish Audio Library 💾 💿 Vocabulary Puzzlemaker 💻 Web Site: lit.glencoe.com

📁 *Theme* **RESOURCES**

- Listening and Speaking Activities (pp. 9–10)
- Viewing and Representing Activities (pp. 15–16)
- Critical Thinking Skills (pp. 13–15)
- Media Connections Activities (pp. 9–10)
- Interdisciplinary Activities (pp. 10–11)

See also these additional planning resources:
- English Language Learners Sourcebook
- Inclusion Strategies Sourcebook
- Literature Groups Sourcebook

Use Glencoe's *Presentation Plus!* This multimedia teaching tool lets you present dynamic lessons that will engage your students. Using Microsoft PowerPoint,® you can customize the presentations to create your own personalized lessons.

Objectives

- To read and analyze a memoir about the author's childhood Christmas experiences in Wales
- To analyze memoir narrative techniques and their effects
- To evaluate an author's strategy

Skills

Reading/Thinking: Drawing Conclusions; Inferring; Logical Reasoning; Sequence of Events; Clarifying
Writing: Sensory Description
Vocabulary: Analogies
Grammar/Language: Capitalization of Proper Nouns; Compound Adjectives
Listening/Speaking: Listening to Recordings
Collaboration: Literature Groups

Motivating

→ OPTIONS

Literature Launchers:
"Welsh Memories"

Videodisc
Side A, Segment 10

Also available in VHS.

Selection Focus Transparency 37: Discuss with students the memories that the painting brings to mind.

Focus Activity: Invite students to offer examples of sensory details.

Before You Read

A Child's Christmas in Wales

FOCUS ACTIVITY

What are your strongest holiday memories from your childhood?

WEB IT! Recall a holiday from your childhood. Try to remember what you saw, heard, smelled, tasted, and touched. Record your sensory memories in a web like this one.

Touch · Taste · Holiday · Sight · Smell · Sound

SETTING A PURPOSE Read to share the author's childhood Christmas memories.

BACKGROUND

The Time and Place
The events described in this selection take place in Swansea, Wales, in the early 1900s.

Did You Know?
Although Wales has been part of Great Britain for four hundred years, the Welsh have maintained their own traditions, literature, and language. The people of Wales primarily speak English, although about one-fifth of them speak Welsh, an ancient Celtic language. The Welsh people have always loved poetry and music, and each year they hold a national singing and poetry competition, the Royal National Eisteddfod. This celebration dates back to the 1700s.

VOCABULARY PREVIEW

daft (daft) *adj.* without sense or reason; crazy; silly; p. 435
judiciously (jōō dish′ əs lē) *adv.* in a way that shows good judgment; sensibly; p. 437
hale (hāl) *adj.* in good physical condition; healthy; p. 437
stridently (strīd′ ənt lē) *adv.* in a loud, harsh manner; shrilly; p. 437
loom (lōōm) *v.* to appear to the mind as large; to stand out prominently; p. 438
lurk (lurk) *v.* to stay hidden, ready to attack; p. 438

432   UNIT 2

Meet Dylan Thomas

From the time he first listened to childhood nursery rhymes, Dylan Thomas loved language. "What the words stood for, symbolized, or meant was of very secondary importance," he said. "What mattered was the *sound* of them." Thomas published his first poem when he was seventeen and his first volume of poetry, *18 Poems*, when he was twenty. He achieved fame not only for his poetry and other writing but also for his personal charm and passionate poetry readings. Thomas made three poetry-reading tours of the United States; he died in New York during the last tour, at the age of thirty-nine.

Dylan Thomas was born in 1914 and died in 1953. "A Child's Christmas in Wales" was first published in 1955.

RESOURCE MANAGER

Lesson Planning Resource
The *Unit Two Planning Guide* (pp. 16–23) provides additional lesson notes and reduced versions of all print resources.

📁 **Other Print Resources**
- Active Reading Guide, p. 37
- Vocabulary Practice, p. 36
- Reading Workbook, pp. 47–48
- Grammar and Language Workbook, pp. 237, 279

- Grammar and Composition Handbook, Lessons 10.3, 11.12
- Quick Checks, p. 37
- Selection and Theme Assessment, pp. 71–72
- Performance Assessment, p. 36
- Spanish Summaries, p. 37
- Spanish Translations
- Inclusion Strategies
- English Language Learners Sourcebook

 Transparencies
- Selection Focus 37
- Literary Elements 37
- Grammar and Language 37

Technology
 Literature Launchers
🎧 Audio Library
🎧 Spanish Audio Library
💻 Glencoe Literature Web Site
💾 Testmaker

A Child's Christmas in Wales

Dylan Thomas

Winter in Wales, c. 1954. Fred Uhlman. Oil on canvas, 46 x 61 cm. Private collection.

One Christmas was so much like another, in those years around the sea-town corner[1] now and out of all sound except the distant speaking of the voices I sometimes hear a moment before sleep, that I can never remember whether it snowed for six days and six nights when I was twelve or whether it snowed for twelve days and twelve nights when I was six.

All the Christmases roll down toward the two-tongued sea, like a cold and headlong moon bundling down the sky that was our street; and they stop at the rim of the ice-edged, fish-freezing waves, and I plunge my hands in the snow and bring out whatever I can find. In goes my hand into that wool-white bell-tongued ball of holidays resting at the rim of the carol-singing sea, and out come Mrs. Prothero and the firemen.

It was on the afternoon of the day of Christmas Eve, and I was in Mrs. Prothero's

---

1. The expression *around the sea-town corner* means "out of sight" or "long gone."

SUMMARY

In "A Child's Christmas in Wales," Thomas recalls his boyhood memories of Christmases spent at home in Wales, dreamily shifting from past to present and from real details to mythical, imagined events. Beginning with a humorous description of a small fire in a neighbor's house, Thomas's narrative is interrupted by a boy who is apparently listening to his stories. The boy asks Thomas questions about his past, and Thomas tells him what the snow was like, what kinds of presents he received, and what various relatives did. Thomas then shifts to recollections of adventures with friends and conversations they had, finally ending back at home, where he falls asleep.

📁 *Spanish Summaries,* p. 37

A Active Reading

CONNECT After the title and first paragraph are read, discuss with students similar remembrances they have of special holidays or family gatherings.

Additional Resources
📁 *Active Reading Guide,* p. 37
🎧 *Audio Library*
🎧 *Spanish Audio Library*

Teaching Options

CONNECTING TO OTHER SELECTIONS

The chart at the right shows three ways to connect "A Child's Christmas in Wales" to selections in this book.

For specific teaching strategies, see the *Unit Two Planning Guide,* pp. 19–20.

Connection	Title
Life Skills: Teaching and Mentoring	→ "To Da-duh, in Memoriam," p. 399
Thematic: Times Past	→ "Those Winter Sundays," p. 604
Literary: Style	→ "Pizza in Warsaw, Torte in Prague," p. 507

MEMOIR Ask students to identify what type of nonfiction "A Child's Christmas in Wales" is. *(narrative nonfiction, specifically, a memoir)* Prompt them by asking what point of view Thomas writes in *(first person I)* and what content he focuses on *(childhood Christmas memories).*

VIEWING THE PAINTING

Dame Laura Knight (1877–1970) was a successful twentieth-century English artist. She often depicted scenes from the ballet, theater, circus, and sports.

Viewing Response *There is a body of water, it's snowy, and people are throwing snowballs.*

C **Active Reading**

QUESTION Ask students why Thomas calls Mrs. Prothero's house an "igloo." *(Thomas has just been telling about how he and his friend were pretending to be Eskimo hunters in the Arctic. So an igloo rather than a house fits in their fantasy.)*

D **Author's Craft**

HYPERBOLE Point out that Thomas is using hyperbole, or exaggeration, by comparing Mrs. Prothero's cries to those of a town crier in Pompeii during the eruption of a nearby volcano. Explain that writers often use hyperbole for comic effect.

Teaching Options

Snowballing, c. 1917. Dame Laura Knight. Watercolor heightened with bodycolor over pencil, 52 x 75 cm. Private collection.

Viewing the painting: What similarities do you find between the scene in this painting and the winter memories that Thomas describes?

garden, waiting for cats, with her son Jim. It was snowing. It was always snowing at Christmas. December, in my memory, is white as Lapland, though there were no reindeers. But there were cats. Patient, cold, and callous, our hands wrapped in socks, we waited to snowball the cats. Sleek and long as jaguars and horrible-whiskered, spitting and snarling, they would slink and sidle over the white back-garden walls, and the lynx-eyed[2] hunters, Jim and I, fur-capped and moccasined trappers from Hudson Bay, off Mumbles Road, would hurl our deadly snowballs at the green of their eyes.

The wise cats never appeared. We were so still, Eskimo-footed arctic marksmen in the muffling silence of the eternal snows—eternal, ever since Wednesday—that we never heard Mrs. Prothero's first cry from her igloo at the bottom of the garden. Or, if we heard it at all, it was, to us, like the far-off challenge of our enemy and prey, the neighbour's polar cat. But soon the voice grew louder. "Fire!" cried Mrs. Prothero, and she beat the dinner-gong.

And we ran down the garden, with the snowballs in our arms, toward the house; and smoke, indeed, was pouring out of the

dining-room, and the gong was bombilating, and Mrs. Prothero was announcing ruin like a town crier in Pompeii.[3] This was better than all the cats in Wales standing on the wall in a row. We bounded into the house, laden with snowballs, and stopped at the open door of the smoke-filled room.

Something was burning all right; perhaps it was Mr. Prothero, who always slept there after midday dinner with a newspaper over his face. But he was standing in the middle of the room, saying, "A fine Christmas!" and smacking at the smoke with a slipper. "Call the fire brigade," cried Mrs. Prothero as she beat the gong.

"They won't be there," said Mr. Prothero, "it's Christmas."

There was no fire to be seen, only clouds of smoke and Mr. Prothero standing in the middle of them, waving his slipper as though he were conducting.

"Do something," he said.

And we threw all our snowballs into the smoke—I think we missed Mr. Prothero—and ran out of the house to the telephone box.

"Let's call the police as well," Jim said.

"And the ambulance."

2. The *lynx-eyed* hunters have sharp vision like the lynx, a wildcat of Europe and Asia.

3. *Pompeii* (pom pā´) was a Roman city destroyed and buried by a volcanic eruption in A.D. 79.

Figurative Language Thomas uses vivid yet idiosyncratic imagery. English language learners may have difficulty with this unusual use of language, as in the first sentence in paragraph 2 on page 433. Write this passage on the board and discuss it. Have students look up words they do not know. Help them visualize each image, until they can accurately paraphrase the sentence.

Activity Have students select passages from the selection that they find difficult. Have them work in groups, looking up unfamiliar words, visualizing images, and writing paraphrases.

Additional Resources
📁 *English Language Learners Sourcebook*

"And Ernie Jenkins, he likes fires."

But we only called the fire brigade, and soon the fire engine came and three tall men in helmets brought a hose into the house and Mr. Prothero got out just in time before they turned it on. Nobody could have had a noisier Christmas Eve. And when the firemen turned off the hose and were standing in the wet, smoky room, Jim's aunt, Miss Prothero, came downstairs and peered in at them. Jim and I waited, very quietly, to hear what she would say to them. She said the right thing, always. She looked at the three tall firemen in their shining helmets, standing among the smoke and cinders and dissolving snowballs, and she said: "Would you like anything to read?"

Years and years and years ago, when I was a boy, when there were wolves in Wales, and birds the color of red-flannel petticoats whisked past the harp-shaped hills, when we sang and wallowed all night and day in caves that smelt like Sunday afternoons in damp front farmhouse parlors, and we chased, with the jawbones of deacons, the English and the bears, before the motor-car, before the wheel, before the duchess-faced horse, when we rode the daft and happy hills bareback, it snowed and it snowed. But here a small boy says: "It snowed last year, too. I made a snowman and my brother knocked it down and I knocked my brother down and then we had tea."

"But that was not the same snow," I say. "Our snow was not only shaken from white-wash buckets down the sky, it came shawling[4] out of the ground and swam and drifted out of the arms and hands and bodies of the trees; snow grew overnight on the roofs of the houses like a pure and grandfather moss, minutely

white-ivied the walls and settled on the post-man, opening the gate, like a dumb, numb thunderstorm of white, torn Christmas cards."

"Were there postmen then, too?"

"With sprinkling eyes and wind-cherried noses, on spread, frozen feet they crunched up to the doors and mittened on them manfully. But all that the children could hear was a ringing of bells."

"You mean that the postman went rat-a-tat-tat and the doors rang?"

"I mean that the bells that the children could hear were inside them."

"I only hear thunder sometimes, never bells."

"There were church bells, too."

"Inside them?"

"No, no, no, in the bat-black, snow-white belfries, tugged by bishops and storks. And they rang their tidings over the bandaged town, over the frozen foam of the powder and ice-cream hills, over the crackling sea. It seemed that all the churches boomed for joy under my window; and the weathercocks crew for Christmas, on our fence."

"Get back to the postmen."

"They were just ordinary postmen, fond of walking and dogs and Christmas and the snow. They knocked on the doors with blue knuckles. . . ."

"Ours has got a black knocker. . . ."

"And then they stood on the white Welcome mat in the little, drifted porches and huffed and puffed, making ghosts with their breath, and jogged from foot to foot like small boys wanting to go out."

"And then the Presents?"

"And then the Presents, after the Christmas box.[5] And the cold postman, with a rose on his

---

4. Snow that is *shawling* is rising up like a shawl that is pulled up over the shoulders.

5. A *Christmas box* is a present for the postman.

Vocabulary
daft (daft) *adj.* without sense or reason; crazy; silly

FYI

Deadly Eruption In A.D. 79, the Roman city of Pompeii was buried in lava and ash from the sudden eruption of nearby Mt. Vesuvius. Since 1748, archaeologists have uncovered the ruins, which were preserved in perfect condition. Archaeologists have found art, food, and household effects.

E **Active Reading**

QUESTION Students should notice this interruption in the narrative. Prompt them to stop, reread if necessary, and consider what is happening and who is speaking. (*Apparently, a young boy who has been listening to Thomas talk about his past is interrupting him to comment on what he is saying. They continue to talk back and forth for many paragraphs.*)

F **Critical Thinking**

DRAWING CONCLUSIONS Ask students what they think Thomas means when he says "the bells that the children could hear were inside them." (*He means that the children feel the excitement of Christmas ringing inside them like bells.*)

G **Critical Thinking**

INFERRING Ask students what they can infer from the fact that the postmen make "ghosts with their breath" and jog "from foot to foot like small boys wanting to go out." (*They are cold standing outside on the porch.*)

MEETING INDIVIDUAL NEEDS **INCLUSION STRATEGIES**

Less-Proficient Readers Throughout the selection, Thomas shifts between real and imaginary details. Sorting out the real from the imagined among Thomas's details can be difficult. For example, when Thomas says they chased bears, he doesn't mean they literally did this.

Activity Review the Active Reading Strategies at the beginning of Unit Two. Have students stop periodically to review what they have read to make sure they understand it. **L1**

Additional Resources
📁 *Inclusion Strategies*

A Child's Christmas in Wales

Did You Know?
Sloths are shaggy-haired, tree-dwelling mammals native to the tropical forests of Central and South America. They have long limbs with long, curved claws.

H

Did You Know?
A *tam-o'-shanter* is a round, flat hat that often has a pom-pom in the center.

button-nose, tingled down the tea-tray-slithered run of the chilly glinting hill. He went in his ice-bound boots like a man on fishmonger's slabs.[6] He wagged his bag like a frozen camel's hump, dizzily turned the corner on one foot, and, by God, he was gone."

"Get back to the Presents."

"There were the Useful Presents: engulfing mufflers of the old coach days, and mittens made for giant sloths; zebra scarfs of a substance like silky gum that could be tug-o'-warred down to the galoshes; blinding tam-o'-shanters like patchwork tea cosies and bunny-suited busbies and balaclavas[7] for victims of headshrinking tribes; from aunts who always wore wool next to the skin there were moustached and rasping vests that made you wonder why the aunts had any skin left at all; and once I had a little crocheted nose bag from an aunt now, alas, no longer whinnying with us. And pictureless books in which small boys, though warned with quotations not to, *would* skate on Farmer Giles' pond and did and drowned; and books that told me everything about the wasp, except why."

I

"Go on to the Useless Presents."

---

6. The blocks or trays of ice on which fish are displayed at a market are *fishmonger's slabs*.
7. *Busbies* and *balaclavas* are different types of hats made of wool or fur.

"Bags of moist and many-coloured jelly babies and a folded flag and a false nose and a tram[8] conductor's cap and a machine that punched tickets and rang a bell; never a catapult; once, by mistake that no one could explain, a little hatchet; and a celluloid[9] duck that made, when you pressed it, a most unducklike sound, a mewing moo that an ambitious cat might make who wished to be a cow; and a painting book in which I could make the grass, the trees, the sea and the animals any color I pleased, and still the dazzling sky-blue sheep are grazing in the red field under the rainbow-billed and pea-green birds.

Hardboileds, toffee, fudge and allsorts, crunches, cracknels, humbugs, glaciers, marzipan, and butterwelsh for the Welsh. And troops of bright tin soldiers who, if they could not fight, could always run. And Snakes-and-Families and Happy Ladders. And Easy Hobbi-Games for Little Engineers, complete with instructions.

Oh, easy for Leonardo! And a whistle to make the dogs bark to wake up the old man next door to make him beat on the wall with his stick to shake our picture off the wall.

And a packet of cigarettes: you put one in your mouth and you stood at the corner of the street and you waited for hours, in vain, for an old lady to scold you for smoking a cigarette, and then with a smirk you ate it. And then it was breakfast under the balloons."

J

"Were there Uncles, like in our house?"

"There are always Uncles at Christmas. The same Uncles. And on Christmas mornings, with dog-disturbing whistle and sugar fags[10] I would scour the swatched[11]

K

---

8. In Britain, a streetcar is called a *tram*.
9. *Celluloid* is a kind of plastic.
10. *Sugar fags* are candy cigarettes.
11. *Swatched* is a variation of the word *swathed* and means "bound" or "wrapped."

Dylan Thomas

town for the news of the little world, and find always a dead bird by the white Post Office or by the deserted swings; perhaps a robin, all but one of his fires out. Men and women wading or scooping back from chapel, with taproom noses and wind-bussed cheeks, all albinos, huddled their stiff black jarring feathers against the irreligious snow.

Did You Know?
Here, *crackers* are small, decorated tubes that hold candy or party favors and, when opened, make a popping sound.

Mistletoe hung from the gas brackets[12] in all the front parlours; there was sherry and walnuts and bottled beer and crackers by the dessertspoons; and cats in their fur-abouts watched the fires; and the high-heaped fire spat, all ready for the chestnuts and the mulling pokers.[13]

Some few large men sat in the front parlours, without their collars, Uncles almost certainly, trying their new cigars, holding them out judiciously at arms' length, returning them to their mouths, coughing, then holding them out again as though waiting for the explosion; and some few small Aunts, not wanted in the kitchen, nor anywhere else for that matter, sat on the very edges of their chairs, poised and brittle, afraid to break, like faded cups and saucers."

Not many those mornings trod the piling streets: an old man always, fawn-bowlered,[14]

yellow-gloved and, at this time of year, with spats[15] of snow, would take his constitutional to the white bowling green[16] and back, as he would take it wet or fine on Christmas Day or Doomsday; sometimes two hale young men, with big pipes blazing, no overcoats and wind-blown scarfs, would trudge, unspeaking, down to the forlorn sea, to work up an appetite, to blow away the fumes, who knows, to walk into the waves until nothing of them was left but the two curling smoke clouds of their inextinguishable briars. Then I would be slap-dashing home, the gravy smell of the dinners of others, the bird smell, the brandy, the pudding and mince, coiling up to my nostrils, when out of a snow-clogged side lane would come a boy the spit of myself, with a pink-tipped cigarette and the violet past of a black eye, cocky as a bullfinch, leering all to himself.

I hated him on sight and sound, and would be about to put my dog whistle to my lips and blow him off the face of Christmas when suddenly he, with a violet wink, put *his* whistle to *his* lips and blew so stridently, so high, so exquisitely loud, that gobbling faces, their cheeks bulged with goose, would press against their tinselled windows, the whole length of the white echoing street. For dinner we had turkey and blazing pudding,[17] and after dinner the Uncles sat in front of the fire, loosened all buttons, put

---

12. *Gas brackets* are wall-mounted gas lamps that are fed by gas piped through the walls.
13. *Mulling pokers* are fireplace pokers used to heat and stir *mull,* a hot, spiced wine.
14. The man who is *fawn-bowlered* is wearing a fawn-colored *bowler,* a round, narrow-brimmed hat.

15. *Spats* are short coverings made of cloth or leather, worn over the tops of the shoes and around the ankles.
16. The old man took his *constitutional,* or walk, every day, regardless of the weather. A *bowling green* is the lawn used in a bowling game.
17. *Blazing pudding* is a fancy pudding that's doused with brandy and served flaming.

Vocabulary
judiciously (joō dish′ əs lē) *adv.* in a way that shows good judgment; sensibly
hale (hāl) *adj.* in good physical condition; healthy
stridently (strīd′ ənt lē) *adv.* in a loud, harsh manner; shrilly

NONFICTION 437

L **Active Reading**

QUESTION Ask students what Thomas means when he says the men and women coming out of the chapel are "all albinos." *(Albinos have very pale or white skin and hair. The people are covered in snow.)*

M **Author's Craft**

SIMILE Point out that Thomas is a master at conveying lushly imaginative and surprising descriptions in the form of similes and metaphors. Read aloud the passage beginning "Some few large men . . . ." Ask students to identify the simile Thomas uses in the description. *(Aunts . . . sat on the very edges of their chairs, poised and brittle, afraid to break, like faded cups and saucers.)*

N **Critical Thinking**

DRAWING CONCLUSIONS Ask students to offer explanations of why Thomas hated the boy with the whistle. *(Apparently Thomas hated him because he was just like himself ["the spit of myself"] and he felt competitive with him.)*

REAL-WORLD CONNECTION

The Welsh and the English Remind students that Dylan Thomas grew up in Wales, a country that is part of Great Britain. In his memoir, Thomas mentions chasing "the English and the bears," reflecting long-standing resentment toward the English among non-English British citizens.

Activity Have students do some research at the library or on the Internet to find out about the political history of Wales and its relationship to England. Ask them to try to determine how Thomas and others in the early 1900s would have felt about the English, as well as how the Welsh feel about them today. **L3**

NONFICTION 437

Critical Thinking

LOGICAL REASONING Ask students about how old Thomas seems to be in this passage and have them explain their reasoning. Encourage them to consider Thomas's actions and dialogue. You may use the following model of logical reasoning.

Model: The fact that Thomas is playing far from home in the snow indicates that he is probably at least seven, while the conversation he has with his friends about hippos shows that he is probably not much older than ten. So, I think he is probably between seven and ten years old.

Literary Elements

MEMOIR Ask students whether they think a description such as the one about the boys' caroling at the spooky house would change if Thomas had written it not as part of his memoir but as part of a fictional story. *(The description may not change, since in his memoir Thomas uses the same kind of vivid descriptions and sensory details that make good fiction come alive.)*

Did You Know?
Tureens are deep dishes used for serving food at the table.

their large moist hands over their watch chains, groaned a little and slept. Mothers, aunts and sisters scuttled to and fro, bearing tureens. Auntie Bessie, who had already been frightened, twice, by a clock-work mouse, whimpered at the sideboard and had some elderberry wine. The dog was sick. Auntie Dosie had to have three aspirins, but Auntie Hannah, who liked port, stood in the middle of the snowbound backyard, singing like a big-bosomed thrush. I would blow up balloons to see how big they would blow up to; and, when they burst, which they all did, the Uncles jumped and rumbled. In the rich and heavy afternoon, the Uncles breathing like

Did You Know?
Festoons are decorations that hang in loops or curves.

dolphins and the snow descending, I would sit among festoons and Chinese lanterns and nibble dates and try to make a model man-o'-war, following the Instructions for Little Engineers, and produce what might be mistaken for a sea-going tramcar.

Or I would go out, my bright new boots squeaking, in to the white world, on to the seaward hill, to call on Jim and Dan and Jack and to pad through the still streets, leaving huge deep footprints on the hidden pavements.

"I bet people will think there's been hippos."

"What would you do if you saw a hippo coming down our street?"

"I'd go like this, bang! I'd throw him over the railings and roll him down the hill and

then I'd tickle him under the ear and he'd wag his tail."

"What would you do if you saw *two* hippos?"

Iron-flanked and bellowing he-hippos clanked and battered through the scudding snow toward us as we passed Mr. Daniel's house.

"Let's post Mr. Daniel a snowball through his letter box."

"Let's write things in the snow."

"Let's write, 'Mr. Daniel looks like a spaniel' all over his lawn."

Or we walked on the white shore.

"Can the fishes see it's snowing?"

The silent one-clouded heavens drifted on to the sea. Now we were snow-blind travellers lost on the north hills, and vast dewlapped[18] dogs, with flasks round their necks, ambled and shambled up to us, baying "Excelsior."[19] We returned home through the poor streets where only a few children fumbled with bare red fingers in the wheel-rutted snow and catcalled after us, their voices fading away, as we trudged uphill, into the cries of the dock birds and the hooting of ships out in the whirling bay. And then, at tea the recovered Uncles would be jolly; and the ice cake loomed in the center of the table like a marble grave. Auntie Hannah laced her tea with rum, because it was only once a year.

Bring out the tall tales now that we told by the fire as the gaslight bubbled like a diver. Ghosts whooed like owls in the long nights when I dared not look over my shoulder; animals lurked in the cubbyhole under the stairs where the gas meter ticked. And I remember that we went singing carols once, when there

---

18. *Dewlapped* dogs have a loose fold of skin under the throat.
19. *Baying* means "howling." *Excelsior* is a Latin word meaning "still higher; ever upward." It is often used as an inspirational motto.

Vocabulary
loom (lo͞om) *v.* to appear to the mind as large; to stand out prominently
lurk (lurk) *v.* to stay hidden, ready to attack

438   UNIT 2

Teaching Options

Grammar and Language *Minilesson*

Capitalization of Proper Nouns Explain to students that proper nouns are the names of particular persons, places, things, or ideas. Proper nouns always begin with capital letters, and they may consist of more than one word. Write these examples on the board:

    Dylan Thomas
    Atlantic Ocean
    Royal National Eisteddfod

Activity Have students rewrite the following phrases adding capital letters to any proper nouns.

1. day of christmas eve *(day of Christmas Eve)*
2. mrs. prothero and the firemen *(Mrs. Prothero and the firemen)*
3. wolves in wales *(wolves in Wales)*
4. from hudson bay, off mumbles road *(from Hudson Bay, off Mumbles Road)* **L2**

Additional Resources

Grammar and Language Transparency 37

Grammar and Language Workbook, p. 237

Grammar and Composition Handbook, Lesson 10.3

Writer's Choice, Lesson 20.3

wasn't the shaving of a moon to light the flying streets. At the end of a long road was a drive that led to a large house, and we stumbled up the darkness of the drive that night, each one of us afraid, each one holding a stone in his hand in case, and all of us too brave to say a word. The wind through the trees made noises as of old and unpleasant and maybe webfooted men wheezing in caves. We reached the black bulk of the house.

"What shall we give them? 'Hark the Herald'?"

"No," Jack said, " 'Good King Wenceslas.' I'll count three."

One, two, three, and we began to sing, our voices high and seemingly distant in the snow-felted darkness round the house that was occupied by nobody we knew. We stood close together, near the dark door.

Good King Wenceslas looked out
On the Feast of Stephen . . .

And then a small, dry voice, like the voice of someone who has not spoken for a long time, joined our singing: a small dry, eggshell voice from the other side of the door: a small dry voice through the keyhole. And when we stopped running we were outside *our* house; the front room was lovely; balloons floated under the hot-water-bottle-gulping gas; everything was good again and shone over the town.

"Perhaps it was a ghost," Jim said.

"Perhaps it was trolls," Dan said, who was always reading.

"Let's go in and see if there's any jelly left," Jack said. And we did that.

Always on Christmas night there was music. An uncle played the fiddle, a cousin sang "Cherry Ripe," and another uncle sang

Ennui, c. 1914. Walter Richard Sickert. Oil on canvas, 152.4 x 112.4 cm. Tate Gallery, London.
Viewing the painting: How might the mood of this painting reflect the after-dinner mood in the selection?

"Drake's Drum." It was very warm in the little house.

Auntie Hannah, who had got on to the parsnip wine, sang a song about Bleeding Hearts and Death, and then another in which she said her heart was like a Bird's Nest; and then everybody laughed again; and then I went to bed. Looking through my bedroom window, out into the moonlight and the unending smoke-coloured snow, I could see the lights in the windows of all the other houses on our hill and hear the music rising from them up the long, steadily falling night. I turned the gas down, I got into bed. I said some words to the close and holy darkness, and then I slept.

 Active Reading

EVALUATE Ask students whether they think Thomas has done a good job of relating his childhood Christmas memories. *(Possible answers: yes, his descriptions bring the memories alive.)*

 Active Reading

RESPOND Ask students to supply several words to describe their own response to the end of the memoir. *(Possible answers: warm, nostalgic, moved, happy)*

Thematic Focus

Remembering Ask students why they think Thomas wanted to write about his memories of childhood Christmases. Have them offer reasons for their opinions.

✓ ASSESSMENT OPTIONS

📁 *Quick Checks,* p. 37

Reading *Minilesson*

Sequence of Events Although the author merges several Christmases in his memoir, there is a sequence of events in the narrative ordered from Christmas Eve afternoon through Christmas night. Analyzing the sequence can help students understand the narrative.

Activity Have pairs of students make a time line indicating the main events of the narrative and when they occur. For example, on Christmas afternoon, the aunts do the dishes while the uncles smoke cigars. Point out that the time when an event occurs can be determined by its context. Encourage discussion as students come up with the most likely chronology. **L1** **COLLAB. LEARN.**

Additional Resources
📁 *Reading Workbook,* pp. 47–48

Personal Response

Students may mention the scene of the relatives after dinner and the boys' caroling at the old house as the images or events that made the strongest impression.

ANALYZING LITERATURE

1. Mrs. Prothero calls, "Fire!" Thomas and Jim find Mr. Prothero standing in his smoky dining room waving his slipper. The boys throw their snowballs at the fire and call the fire brigade, which arrives promptly and puts out the fire. Jim's aunt, Miss Prothero, asks the firemen if they want anything to read.
2. Useful Presents—mufflers, scarfs, balaclavas; Useless Presents—fudge, painting book, tin soldiers
3. He spends Christmas mornings wandering around the town.
4. The men nap, the women clean up, and the children play.
5. People sing and play music.
6. He is thrilled by the excitement of a fire ("This was better than all the cats in Wales standing on the wall in a row"), and he thinks Mrs. Prothero is hysterical ("announcing ruin like a town crier in Pompeii"), Mr. Prothero is silly ("waving his slipper as though he were conducting"), and Miss Prothero is amusing ("Jim and I waited, very quietly, to hear what she would say").
7. His family is comfortable but not rich; the children are provided treats and games along with practical necessities.
8. They tell us that his experiences were memorable, exciting, and joyful.
9. He describes the boys' conversation about hippos and then an imagined encounter with hippos; he shifts from walking in the snow to a fantasy of "snow-blind travelers."
10. He seems to associate Christmas with feelings of happiness and well-being.
11. He probably embellished his memoir in order to reflect the playful and imaginative nature of childhood.
12. Possible answers: The presence of relatives and holiday ritual suggests the importance of family. The fact that the women cooked and cleaned while the men relaxed suggests traditional gender roles. The fact that the children wandered and played outside on their own suggests that the town is safe.
13. Sample answers: "Our snow . . . drifted out of the arms and hands and bodies of the trees" does a good job of conveying the all-encompassing swirl

---

Responding to Literature

Personal Response

What images or events from the story made the strongest impression on you? Why? Share your reactions with your classmates.

——— ANALYZING LITERATURE ———

RECALL
1. Summarize what happens at the Prothero home.
2. What categories of presents does the narrator describe? Give at least three examples from each category.
3. How does the narrator spend Christmas morning?
4. What do the adults and children do after Christmas dinner?
5. How does Christmas day end?

INTERPRET
6. How does the narrator seem to feel about the incident at the Prothero home? Support your answer with evidence from the selection.
7. What might you infer about the narrator's childhood, based on the presents he describes?
8. What do the sights, sounds, smells, and feelings described by the narrator tell you about his experiences?
9. How does the narrator mix reality and fantasy in his description of the children's activities on Christmas afternoon? Give specific examples.
10. What do the last two sentences of the selection seem to suggest about the narrator's attitude toward Christmas?

EVALUATE AND CONNECT
11. Although this selection is nonfiction, Thomas embellished it with imaginary incidents. Why do you think he did this?
12. What conclusions might you draw about the culture in which Thomas grew up? Support your conclusions using evidence from the selection.
13. Find at least two examples of **imagery**. (See page R6.) Evaluate how effectively each image helps you imagine what it's like to see, hear, touch, smell, or taste what is being described.
14. Thomas relates only the pleasant memories from his childhood Christmases. Do you do the same thing when you recall your childhood holidays? Explain.
15. **Theme Connections** Why do you think people record their memories of past experiences? In your opinion, why do other people enjoy reading about such memories?

Memoir

A **memoir** is a personal account of events from the author's past. It is usually written from the first-person point of view, using the pronoun *I;* this point of view allows the reader to see events as the author did. While an autobiography usually tells the story of a person's entire life, a memoir—such as "A Child's Christmas in Wales"—typically focuses on a single incident or a particular period in a person's life. Unlike a historical account, which is objective and emphasizes facts, a memoir usually includes the author's personal observations and responses to people and events.

1. Choose a favorite passage from Thomas's memoir. Explain how the author's personal responses and observations add to your understanding and appreciation of the passage.
2. Imagine reading a historical account of Christmas in Wales in the early 1900s. How might such an account differ from Thomas's memoir? Cite specific details from the text to support your response.

● See **Literary Terms Handbook**, p. R7.

---

of white snow. "I could see the lights in the windows of all the other houses on our hill and hear the music rising from them up the long, steadily falling night" does a good job of conveying the warm, happy sights and sounds.

14. Some students may say that they remember only the happy parts of events and forget, possibly deliberately, the unpleasant parts.

15. People might record their memories to relive, gain distance from, or understand them. People read about others' memories to be reminded of or understand their own pasts or learn about others' experiences.

LITERARY ELEMENTS

1. Sample answer: Thomas's description of the boy in the street who blows his whistle before Thomas does conveys much about the young Thomas and the competitive, humorous nature of being a boy.
2. It would be more factual and objective. It would lack Thomas's vividness, as in his descriptions of the uncles and aunts before and after dinner.

Additional Resources

🖌 *Literary Elements Transparency 37*

LITERATURE AND WRITING

Writing About Literature
Evaluate the Author's Approach   In this memoir, Thomas merged his recollections of many Christmases. In a paragraph, evaluate this approach. Consider these questions: What are the advantages and disadvantages of such an approach? Why do you think Thomas chose this approach? Share your ideas with your classmates.

Personal Writing
Childhood Memory   Review your response to the Focus Activity on page 432. Try to add more **sensory details** to your web. Then write a description of this holiday from your childhood. Include **images** to help the reader imagine what you saw, heard, smelled, tasted, and touched.

EXTENDING YOUR RESPONSE

Literature Groups
Clarifying Meaning   What passages from the selection did group members find difficult or confusing? Write down each difficult passage on one side of a note card; then discuss each passage in your group, with the goal of better understanding and appreciating the passage. Finally, on the back of each card, paraphrase the passage according to the meaning the group develops. Share your insights with the members of another group.

Interdisciplinary Activity
Social Studies: Winter Holidays   Many cultures observe winter holidays, such as Chanukah, Christmas, Kwanzaa, and New Year's Day. Interview a friend, relative, or acquaintance who celebrates one of these holidays. Ask the person to describe the significance of the holiday and to recall his or her favorite childhood memories of it. In a small group, share the information you have gathered.

Listening and Speaking
Sound of Wales   In addition to being a writer, Dylan Thomas was a gifted and popular speaker who read from his works with a forceful, distinctive voice. Find and listen to a recording of Dylan Thomas reading his work. You can find recordings on the Internet as well as in many libraries. After listening, try reading some of Thomas's poetry or prose aloud, modeling his speaking style.

Reading Further
If you have enjoyed this memoir, you might also enjoy these works:

Poetry: *Collected Poems of Dylan Thomas 1934–1952* includes some of Thomas's most famous poems.

Memoirs: *An American Childhood,* by Annie Dillard, a best-selling collection of the author's experiences growing up in Pittsburgh in the 1950s.

Boy: Tales of Childhood, by Roald Dahl, includes stories about Dahl's childhood in Wales, England, and Norway.

Viewing: *A Child's Christmas in Wales* is a video adaptation of Thomas's memoir.

 Save your work for your portfolio.

Family celebrating Kwanzaa.

LITERATURE AND WRITING

Writing About Literature
Students' evaluations should
- identify the advantages and disadvantages of Thomas's narrative approach.
- explore possible reasons Thomas chose to merge memories from different Christmases.
- express an opinion about whether Thomas's narrative approach is successful and explain why or why not.

Personal Writing
Students' descriptions should
- focus on memories of a childhood holiday.
- include imagery that conveys details about all five senses.

EXTENDING YOUR RESPONSE

Literature Groups As students work together to clarify difficult passages, encourage them to look up unfamiliar or confusing words in a dictionary. **COLLAB. LEARN.**

Interdisciplinary Activity Invite students in the class who have lived or traveled in other countries to share their knowledge of winter holidays in other cultures.

Listening and Speaking Thomas's style of reading, while engaging, may sound overly dramatic to contemporary listeners. Point out to students that an effective oral reading strategy is to focus on the language and try to feel what you are reading as you read it.

✔ ASSESSMENT OPTIONS

📂 *Quick Checks,* p. 37

📂 *Selection and Theme Assessment,* pp. 71–72

📂 *Performance Assessment,* p. 36

💾 *Testmaker*

Skill Minilessons

Skill Minilessons

GRAMMAR AND LANGUAGE
Compound Adjectives

1. wheel-rutted snow
2. smoke-colored snow
3. snow-clogged lane
4. harp-shaped hills
5. wind-cherried noses

READING AND THINKING
Clarifying

Example: for the third paragraph, page 437—"The Uncles sat in the parlours smoking their new cigars and some of the Aunts who were not needed in the kitchen sat nervously on the edges of their chairs."

VOCABULARY
Analogies

1. a
2. d

Additional Resources

📙 **Grammar and Composition Handbook,** Lesson 11.12

📙 **Grammar and Language Workbook,** p. 279

📗 **Writer's Choice,** Lesson 21.12

📁 **Reading Workbook,** pp. 47–48

📁 **Vocabulary Practice,** p. 36

GRAMMAR AND LANGUAGE • Compound Adjectives

Dylan Thomas commonly creates evocative, condensed descriptions by using compound adjectives—two words connected by a hyphen and used as an adjective before a noun. For example, instead of "the sea that sounds like it's singing carols," Thomas says "the carol-singing sea." "Carol-singing" is a compound adjective.

● For more about adjectives, see **Language Handbook,** p. R38.

PRACTICE Rewrite the following phrases so they contain compound adjectives:
1. snow that has been rutted by wheels
2. snow that is colored by smoke
3. a lane clogged by snow
4. hills that are shaped like a harp
5. noses that were cherried by the wind

READING AND THINKING • Clarifying

One outstanding feature of "A Child's Christmas in Wales" is the long complicated sentences that Thomas sometimes includes. If such sentences confuse you as you read, you might find it helpful to stop from time to time and clarify, or check your understanding of the text. One way to work through a difficult sentence is to find the subject of the sentence, and then examine sentence parts set off by commas to see if they contain extra, nonessential information that you can overlook. Next, find the verb that goes with the subject, and see how the main parts of the sentence fit together. Finally, try restating the meaning of the sentence in your own words. For example, after working through the first sentence of this selection, you might say, "The Christmases were so much alike that I can't remember whether I was twelve or six when we got the big snow."

PRACTICE Review "A Child's Christmas in Wales," looking for three sentences that are complicated or confusing. Work through each sentence to clarify the meaning for yourself, then restate that meaning on your paper.

● For more about related comprehension skills, see **Reading Handbook,** pp. R82–R94.

VOCABULARY • Analogies

An **analogy** is a type of comparison that is based on the relationships between things or ideas. To complete an analogy, look for the relationship that exists between the first pair of ideas and describe it in a sentence. Then substitute the ideas in the second pair, and see if the same relationship exists. If more than one of the answer choices fits your sentence, construct a more specific sentence.

● For more about analogies, see **Communications Skills Handbook,** p. R77.

PRACTICE Choose the word pair that best completes each analogy.
1. screech : stridently ::
   a. murmur : quietly   c. scold : unfairly
   b. look : sneakily   d. giggle : uncontrollably
2. hale : disease ::
   a. tall : strength   c. jealous : love
   b. wise : mistake   d. fair : bias

MEDIA Connection

On-line Travel Guide

Did Dylan Thomas's lavish descriptions of his boyhood in Wales capture your imagination? If so, you might want to visit Wales one day. One of the highlights of your trip could be an excursion to a 700-year old castle.

Destination Wales

Address: ▼ http://www.lonelyplanet.com

Wales landscape

PEMBROKESHIRE COAST NATIONAL PARK
Most famous for the 167-mile Pembrokeshire Coast Path, the park runs along a coastline riddled with rugged cliffs, superb sandy beaches, rocky coves, and tiny fishing villages – there's some gorgeous scenery and spectacular coastal walks. Inland, the historic Preseli Hills hide ancient trade routes, hill forts, standing stones, and burial chambers. Offshore, the islands of Skomer, Skokholm, and Grassholm are inhabited by colonies of puffins, guillemots, razorbills, gannets, and grey seals. The area is an activity-lover's paradise, with a choice of hiking, pony trekking, surfing, windsurfing, kayaking, and fishing opportunities.

GOWER PENINSULA This area was the first part of Britain to be officially designated an Area of Outstanding Beauty—for good reason. A favorite haunt of Dylan Thomas, the predominantly National Trust–owned peninsula has superb sandy beaches, beautiful cliff scenery, smugglers' coves, and some great walks. Points of interest include Worm's Head and the village of Rhossili.

Caernarfon Castle

CASTLES Edward I's superb castles are one of Wales' biggest drawcards. His legacy includes the classically geometric Beaumaris, Caernarfon with its Prince of Wales affiliations, crenellated Conwy, and the sturdy ruins of Harlech. Wales' other castles include fairy-tale Caerphilly (9 miles (14 km) north of Cardiff), Victorian Gothic Cardiff, the rambling ruins of 12th-century Carew, the cliff-top drama of Chepstow, Swansea's Oystermouth, and tower-topped Pembroke.

Respond

1. Why, do you think, was the Gower Peninsula a "favorite haunt" of Dylan Thomas?

2. Which of these places would you enjoy visiting most? least? Give reasons for your answers.

Objectives

- To read and analyze part of Mark Mathabane's autobiographical book about growing up in South Africa under apartheid
- To identify the elements of a monologue
- To analyze in writing the selection's different moods

Skills

Reading/Thinking: Inferring; Drawing Conclusions; Logical Reasoning; Problem and Solution
Writing: Expository Essay; Paragraphs about Freedom
Vocabulary: Analogies
Grammar/Language: Quotation Marks
Collaboration: Literature Groups

Motivating
→OPTIONS

Literature Launchers:
"Discussing Apartheid"

Videodisc
Side A, Segment 9

Also available in VHS.

Selection Focus Transparency 38: Use the photograph to discuss the opportunities that an education presents.

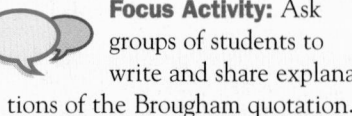
Focus Activity: Ask groups of students to write and share explanations of the Brougham quotation.

 # Before You Read
from *Kaffir Boy*

———FOCUS ACTIVITY———

Henry Peter Brougham said, "Education makes a people easy to lead, but difficult to drive; easy to govern but impossible to enslave."

DISCUSS Do you agree with the ideas expressed in this quote? Why or why not?

SETTING A PURPOSE Read about a boy who is forming his own ideas about education.

———BACKGROUND———

The Time and Place
The events described in this selection take place in Johannesburg, South Africa, in the 1960s.

Did You Know?
Apartheid, which means "separateness," was a policy of racial discrimination that was officially adopted in 1948 by South Africa's white government. Under apartheid, black South Africans, who made up more than seventy-five percent of the population, were forced to live and work under a system of strict racial segregation. The separate and unequal conditions under which blacks lived extended to every facet of life, including education.

Apartheid sparked strong opposition in South Africa and in many other parts of the world and came to a definitive end in 1994, with the electoral victory of Nelson Mandela's African National Congress. Mandela then became the first black president of South Africa.

———VOCABULARY PREVIEW———

coterie (kō′ tər ē) *n.* a small group of people who share a particular interest and often meet socially; p. 448
admonish (ad mon′ ish) *v.* to warn, as against a specific action; p. 448
peruse (pə rōōz′) *v.* to read through or examine carefully; p. 450
credence (krēd′ əns) *n.* belief, especially in the reports or statements of others; p. 451
tirade (tī rād′) *n.* a long, angry or scolding speech; p. 453
vehemently (vē′ ə mənt lē) *adv.* strongly; intensely; passionately; p. 454

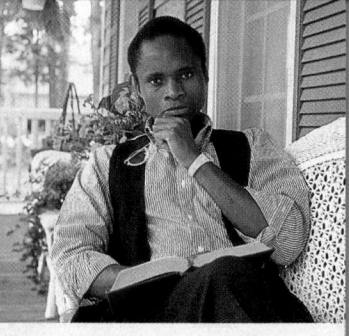

Meet
Mark Mathabane

What was it like to grow up in South Africa under the system of apartheid? For Mark Mathabane (mä tä bä′ ne) "it meant hate, bitterness, hunger, pain, terror, violence, fear, dashed hopes and dreams." Although illiterate, his mother understood the importance of education and insisted that her son attend school. Mathabane made up his mind to master English, which black South Africans were forbidden to learn. At the age of thirteen, he took up tennis and eventually won a tennis scholarship to an American college; he later called this scholarship "my passport to freedom."

Mark Mathabane was born in Johannesburg, South Africa, in 1960. Kaffir Boy was published in 1986.

RESOURCE MANAGER

Lesson Planning Resource
The *Unit Two Planning Guide* (pp. 24–31) provides additional lesson notes and reduced versions of all print resources.

 Other Print Resources
- Active Reading Guide, p. 38
- Vocabulary Practice, p. 37
- Reading Workbook, p. 49
- Grammar and Language Workbook, pp. 235, 271, 273
- Grammar and Composition Handbook, Lesson 11.9

- Quick Checks, p. 38
- Selection and Theme Assessment, pp. 73–74
- Performance Assessment, p. 37
- Spanish Summaries, p. 38
- Spanish Translations
- Inclusion Strategies
- English Language Learners Sourcebook

 Transparencies
- Selection Focus 38
- Literary Elements 38

- Grammar and Language 38

Technology
 Literature Launchers
 Audio Library
 Spanish Audio Library
 Glencoe Literature Web Site
 Testmaker

from Kaffir Boy

Mark Mathabane ∼

"EDUCATION WILL OPEN DOORS WHERE NONE SEEM TO EXIST."

When my mother began dropping hints that I would soon be going to school,
I vowed never to go because school was a waste of time. She laughed and said,
"We'll see. You don't know what you're talking about." My philosophy on
school was that of a gang of ten-, eleven-, and twelve-year-olds whom I
so revered that their every word seemed that of an oracle.[1]

---

1. In Greek mythology, the gods sometimes spoke through an *oracle*.

NONFICTION 🐾 445

SUMMARY

In this excerpt from *Kaffir Boy*, Mark
Mathabane recalls the events that propelled him into school at age seven. At
first, the young Mathabane agrees with
a gang of older street kids that school
is a waste of time. Early one morning,
Mama pulls him out of bed, bathes
him, and drags him to school against
his will. On the way, they meet a
woman who tells them about her oldest
son who refused to go to school, joined
a gang, and was stabbed to death.
When Mama is beaten up by his alcoholic father for putting him in school,
the boy begins to comprehend the
importance of an education.

📁 *Spanish Summaries,* p. 38

🅰 Active Reading

PREDICT Have a volunteer read the
text on page 445. Ask students to
predict whether and how the narrator's views will change. *(Many students will predict that he will come to
understand the value of education.)*

Additional Resources
📁 *Active Reading Guide,* p. 38
🎧 *Audio Library*
🎧 *Spanish Audio Library*

Teaching Options

CONNECTING TO OTHER SELECTIONS

The chart at the right
shows three ways to
connect the excerpt
from *Kaffir Boy* to
selections in this book.

For specific teaching
strategies, see the
*Unit Two Planning
Guide,* pp. 27–28.

Connection	Title
Life Skills: Life-long Learning	→ "The Tucson Zoo," p. 563
Thematic: Child-Parent Relationships	→ from *An American Childhood,* p. 1030
Literary: Thesis	→ "The Angry Winter," p. 557

Active Reading

EVALUATE Have students explain what this passage reveals about the South African "white world." *(It is a culture distant from the narrator's, where people play golf, typically a wealthy person's sport.)*

Critical Thinking

INFERRING Ask students what they can infer about the role of the police at this time in the lives of black South Africans like the Mathabanes. *(Since the Mathabanes believe they could be raided by the police in the middle of the night, this kind of harassment was probably a common occurrence.)*

Active Reading

PREDICT Invite students to predict what Mama is up to. *(Some students will have figured out that she is planning to take her son to school.)*

Teaching Options

These boys had long left their homes and were now living in various neighborhood junkyards, making it on their own. They slept in abandoned cars, smoked glue and benzene,[2] ate pilchards and brown bread, sneaked into the white world to caddy and, if unsuccessful, came back to the township to steal beer and soda bottles from shebeens,[3] or goods from the Indian traders on First Avenue. Their life style was exciting, adventurous, and full of surprises; and I was attracted to it. My mother told me that they were no-gooders, that they would amount to nothing, that I should not associate with them, but I paid no heed. What does she know? I used to tell myself. One thing she did not know was that the gang's way of life had captivated me wholly, particularly their philosophy on school: they hated it and considered an education a waste of time.

They, like myself, had grown up in an environment where the value of an education was never emphasized, where the first thing a child learned was not how to read and write and spell, but how to fight and steal and rebel; where the money to send children to school was grossly[4] lacking, for survival was first priority. I kept my membership in the gang, knowing that for as long as I was under its influence, I would never go to school.

One day my mother woke me up at four in the morning.

"Are they here? I didn't hear any noises," I asked in the usual way.

"No," my mother said. "I want you to get into that washtub over there."

"What!" I balked, upon hearing the word *washtub*. I feared taking baths like one feared the plague. Throughout seven years of hectic

living the number of baths I had taken could be counted on one hand with several fingers missing. I simply had no natural inclination for water; cleanliness was a trait I still had to acquire. Besides, we had only one bathtub in the house, and it constantly sprung a leak.

"I said get into that tub!" My mother shook a finger in my face.

Reluctantly, I obeyed, yet wondered why all of a sudden I had to take a bath. My mother, armed with a scrobbrush and a piece of Lifebuoy soap, purged[5] me of years and years of grime till I ached and bled. As I howled, feeling pain shoot through my limbs as the thistles of the brush encountered stubborn calluses, there was a loud knock at the door.

Instantly my mother leaped away from the tub and headed, on tiptoe, toward the bedroom. Fear seized me as I, too, thought of the police. I sat frozen in the bathtub, not knowing what to do.

"Open up, Mujaji [my mother's maiden name]," Granny's voice came shrilling through the door. "It's me."

My mother heaved a sigh of relief; her tense limbs relaxed. She turned and headed to the kitchen door, unlatched it, and in came Granny and Aunt Bushy.

"You scared me half to death," my mother said to Granny. "I had forgotten all about your coming."

"Are you ready?" Granny asked my mother.

"Yes—just about," my mother said, beckoning me to get out of the washtub.

She handed me a piece of cloth to dry myself. As I dried myself, questions raced through my mind: What's going on? What's Granny doing at our house this ungodly[6] hour of the morning? And why did she ask my

---

2. The boys are taking a risk with *benzene*, a poisonous liquid obtained from coal.
3. *Shebeens* are taverns operating without government license or approval.
4. Here, *grossly* means "totally; entirely."

5. To *purge* is to cleanse or get rid of whatever is unclean or undesirable.
6. In this context, *ungodly* means "outrageous; shocking."

MEETING INDIVIDUAL NEEDS — ENGLISH LANGUAGE LEARNERS

Sharing Prior Knowledge Having students from other cultures share what they know can help draw them out socially while benefiting others in the class by teaching them about cultural differences. Invite students who have lived or traveled in South Africa or other countries to share their knowledge about and experiences with the schools and/or the culture of that country.

Activity Have students who have lived or traveled in South Africa or in other countries bring in photographs, music, books, or clothing that reflect the culture. Invite them to share their objects with the class.

Additional Resources
📁 *English Language Learners Sourcebook*

mother, "Are you ready?" While I stood debating, my mother went into the bedroom and came out with a stained white shirt and a pair of faded black shorts.

"Here," she said, handing me the togs, "put these on."

"Why?" I asked.

"Put them on I said!"

I put the shirt on; it was grossly loose-fitting. It reached all the way down to my ankles. Then I saw the reason why: it was my father's shirt!

"But this is Papa's shirt," I complained. "It don't fit me."

"Put it on," my mother insisted. "I'll make it fit."

"The pants don't fit me either," I said. "Whose are they anyway?"

"Put them on," my mother said. "I'll make them fit."

Moments later I had the garments on; I looked ridiculous. My mother started working on the pants and shirt to make

Did You Know?
Sisal is a coarse, strong fiber obtained from the leaves of a tropical plant.

them fit. She folded the shirt in so many intricate ways and stashed it inside the pants, they too having been folded several times at the waist. She then choked the pants at the waist with a piece of sisal rope to hold them up. She then lavishly smeared my face, arms, and legs with a mixture of pig's fat and vaseline. "This will insulate you from the cold," she said. My skin gleamed like the morning star, and I felt as hot as the center of the sun, and I smelled God knows like what. After embalming me, she headed to the bedroom.

"Where are we going, Gran'ma?" I said, hoping that she would tell me what my mother refused to tell me. I still had no idea I was about to be taken to school.

"Didn't your mother tell you?" Granny said with a smile. "You're going to start school."

"What!" I gasped, leaping from the chair where I was sitting as if it were made of hot lead. "I am not going to school!" I blurted out and raced toward the kitchen door.

My mother had just reappeared from the bedroom and guessing what I was up to, she yelled, "Someone get the door!"

Aunt Bushy immediately barred the door. I turned and headed for the window. As I leaped for the windowsill, my mother lunged at me and brought me down. I tussled, "Let go of me! I don't want to go to school! Let me go!" but my mother held fast onto me.

"It's no use now," she said, grinning tri-umphantly as she pinned me down. Turning her head in Granny's direction, she shouted, "Granny! Get a rope quickly!"

Granny grabbed a piece of rope nearby and came to my mother's aid. I bit and clawed every hand that grabbed me, and howled protesta-tions against going to school; however, I was no match for the two determined matriarchs.[7] In a jiffy they had me bound, hands and feet.

"What's the matter with him?" Granny, bewildered, asked my mother. "Why did he suddenly turn into an imp[8] when I told him you're taking him to school?"

"You shouldn't have told him that he's being taken to school," my mother said. "He doesn't want to go there. That's why I requested you come today, to help me take him there. Those boys in the streets have been a bad influence on him."

---

7. *Matriarchs* (mā′ trē ärks′) are women who head families or who have great authority in other groups.
8. Here, *imp* means "a mischievous child."

VIEWING THE PHOTOGRAPH

Alexandra Township, with a population of around 50,000, is six miles northeast of Johannesburg, South Africa. It is in the midst of a gold mining area, and most of its residents work in the gold mines.

Viewing Response *The boys look watchful and wary. They might tell Mathabane not to trust adults about school or anything else.*

G Literary Elements

SETTING Ask students what details of setting are especially effective in conveying the poverty and struggle of life on the street. *(Students may mention the children looking for food and carrying babies.)*

H Active Reading

QUESTION Ask students to consider why the narrator and other children like him are so resistant to school. If necessary, students should reread the early passage in which Mathabane expresses his initial opinions about education. *(On page 446, Mathabane explains that education was not valued in his environment and most people he knew were busy struggling for basic survival. Also, he was very impressed with a gang of boys who had not gone to school and now lived by their wits.)*

Teaching Options

As the two matriarchs hauled me through the door, they told Aunt Bushy not to go to school but stay behind and mind the house and the children.

The sun was beginning to rise from beyond the veld[9] when Granny and my mother dragged me to school. The streets were beginning to fill with their everyday traffic: old men and women, wizened,[10] bent, and ragged, were beginning their rambling; workless men and women were beginning to assemble in their usual <u>coteries</u> and head for shebeens in the backyards where they discussed how they escaped the morning pass raids[11] and contemplated the conditions of life amidst intense beer drinking and vacant, uneasy laughter; young boys and girls, some as young as myself,

were beginning their aimless wanderings along the narrow, dusty streets in search of food, carrying bawling infants piggyback.

As we went along some of the streets, boys and girls who shared the same fears about school as I were making their feelings known in a variety of ways. They were howling their protests and trying to escape. A few managed to break loose and make a mad dash for freedom, only to be recaptured in no time, <u>admonished</u> or whipped, or both, and ordered to march again.

As we made a turn into Sixteenth Avenue, the street leading to the tribal school I was being taken to, a short, chubby black woman came along from the opposite direction. She had a scuttle[12] overflowing with coal on her *doek*-covered (cloth-covered) head. An infant, bawling deafeningly, was loosely swathed with a piece of sheepskin onto her back. Following closely behind the woman, and picking up

9. In South Africa, the *veld* (velt) is a rolling grassland with scattered trees or bushes.
10. When old people become *wizened* (wiz′ənd), they are shriveled or withered due to age.
11. *Pass raids* refers to the practice whereby police periodically stopped black South Africans to see that they had the proper papers authorizing them to be in specific areas.

12. Here, a *scuttle* is a coal container.

Vocabulary
coterie (kō′ tər ē) *n.* a small group of people who share a particular interest and often meet socially
admonish (ad mon′ ish) *v.* to warn, as against a specific action

448 UNIT 2

INTERDISCIPLINARY CONNECTION

Social Studies Apartheid, which means "apartness," a legalized system of racial segregation and oppression of blacks, was formally instituted in South Africa in 1948. Black Africans, who comprise nine major groups, were forced into nine separate "nations" and restricted to small rural areas of infertile land. Most of the country's land, including its cities and major mineral areas, was reserved for whites. Blacks were not allowed to travel freely or own land and were impoverished by lack of employment and education. Political changes, social resistance, and worldwide economic sanctions brought apartheid to an end in 1994.

Activity Have students find out more about apartheid. They might investigate the history of South Africa, including ethnic cultures and white colonization. Have them share their findings. **L3**

Mark Mathabane ⤳

pieces of coal as they fell from the scuttle and placing them in a small plastic bag, was a half-naked, potbellied, and thumb-sucking boy of about four. The woman stopped abreast.[13] For some reason we stopped too.

"I wish I had done the same to my oldest son," the strange woman said in a regretful voice, gazing at me. I was confounded[14] by her stopping and offering her unsolicited opinion.

"I wish I had done that to my oldest son," she repeated, and suddenly burst into tears; amidst sobs, she continued, "before . . . the street claimed him . . . and . . . turned him into a *tsotsi*."[15]

Granny and my mother offered consolatory remarks to the strange woman.

"But it's too late now," the strange woman continued, tears now streaming freely down her puffy cheeks. She made no attempt to dry them. "It's too late now," she said for the second time, "he's beyond any help. I can't help him even if I wanted to. *Uswile*[16] [He is dead]."

"How did he die?" my mother asked in a sympathetic voice.

"He shunned school and, instead, grew up to live by the knife. And the same knife he lived by ended his life. That's why whenever I see a boy-child refuse to go to school, I stop and tell the story of my dear little *mbitsini*[17] [heartbreak]."

Having said that, the strange woman left as mysteriously as she had arrived.

"Did you hear what that woman said!" my mother screamed into my ears. "Do you want the same to happen to you?"

I dropped my eyes. I was confused.

---

13. *Abreast* means "alongside the others."
14. To be *confounded* is to be confused or bewildered.
15. A *tsotsi* (tsot′ sē) is an armed street hoodlum or gangster.
16. *Uswile* (ōō swē′ lā)
17. *mbitsini* (əm bit sē′ nē)

"Poor woman," Granny said ruefully. "She must have truly loved her son."

Finally, we reached the school and I was ushered into the principal's office, a tiny cubicle facing a row of privies[18] and a patch of yellowed grass.

"So this is the rascal we'd been talking about," the principal, a tall, wiry man, foppishly[19] dressed in a black pin-striped suit, said to my mother as we entered. His austere,[20] shiny face, inscrutable and imposing, reminded me of my father. He was sitting behind a brown table upon which stood piles of dust and cobweb-covered books and papers. In one upper pocket of his jacket was arrayed a variety of pens and pencils; in the other nestled a lily-white handkerchief whose presence was more decorative than utilitarian.[21] Alongside him stood a disproportionately portly[22] black woman, fashionably dressed in a black skirt and a white blouse. She had but one pen, and this she held in her hand. The room was hot and stuffy and buzzing with flies.

"Yes, Principal," my mother answered, "this is he."

"I see he's living up to his notoriety," remarked the principal, noticing that I had been bound. "Did he give you too much trouble?"

"Trouble, Principal," my mother sighed. "He was like an imp."

"He's just like the rest of them, Principal," Granny sighed. "Once they get out into the streets, they become wild. They take to the many vices of the streets like an infant takes to its mother's milk. They begin to think that there's no other life but the one shown them

---

18. *Privies* (priv′ ēz) are outhouses, or toilets.
19. The man surely wouldn't think that he dressed *foppishly*—in the style of one who pays too much attention to his clothes.
20. *Austere* means "serious, strict, or severe."
21. Something that is *utilitarian* is functional or practical.
22. A *portly* person has a heavy or stout but dignified appearance.

NONFICTION 🐾 449

FYI

End of Apartheid In 1990, the newly elected South African leader F. W. De Klerk freed Nelson Mandela from 27 years of political imprisonment. With support from Mandela, President De Klerk dismantled apartheid, receiving the Nobel Peace Prize jointly with Mandela in 1993. Mandela was elected president of South Africa in 1994.

I **Active Reading**

QUESTIONS Ask students to explain what the principal means when he says the narrator is "living up to his notoriety." If necessary, have them look up *notoriety* in a dictionary. *(The narrator is acting in a way that confirms his reputation as a rebellious child.)*

J **Critical Thinking**

LOGICAL REASONING Ask students what they think Mama and Granny would think of the older boys in the narrator's gang. Would they consider them *tsotsis*? *(The women would disapprove of the boys in the gang. They are indeed* tsotsis.*)*

Active Reading

QUESTION Ask students why Mama and Granny smile in this scene. *(Students should realize that the women are glad to see that the young Mathabane is frightened of the canes because that will make him more likely to not run away and to stay in school.)*

Literary Elements

PARADOX Explain to students that Granny's comment is a paradox—a statement with two parts that are both true, yet seem to contradict each other. Ask students to explain how her comment is contradictory but also true. *(She understands about regulations but doesn't understand their justice or sense.)*

from **Kaffir Boy**

by the *tsotsis.* They come to hate school and forget about the future."

"Well," the principal said. "We'll soon remedy all that. Untie him."

"He'll run away," my mother cried.

"I don't think he's that foolish to attempt that with all of us here."

"He *is* that foolish, Principal," my mother said as she and Granny began untying me. "He's tried it before. Getting him here was an ordeal in itself."

The principal rose from his seat, took two steps to the door and closed it. As the door swung closed, I spotted a row of canes of different lengths and thicknesses hanging behind it. The principal, seeing me staring at the canes, grinned and said, in a manner suggesting that he had wanted me to see them, "As long as you behave, I won't have to use any of those on you."

Use those canes on me? I gasped. I stared at my mother—she smiled; at Granny—she smiled too. That made me abandon any inkling of escaping.

"So they finally gave you the birth certificate and the papers," the principal addressed my mother as he returned to his chair.

"Yes, Principal," my mother said, "they finally did. But what a battle it was. It took me nearly a year to get all them papers together." She took out of her handbag a neatly wrapped package and handed it to the principal. "They've been running us around for so long that there were times when I thought he would never attend school, Principal," she said.

"That's pretty much standard procedure, Mrs. Mathabane," the principal said, unwrapping the package. "But you now have the papers and that's what's important.

"As long as we have the papers," he continued, minutely <u>perusing</u> the contents of the

package, "we won't be breaking the law in admitting your son to this school, for we'll be in full compliance with the requirements set by the authorities in Pretoria."[23]

"Sometimes I don't understand the laws from Pitori,"[24] Granny said. "They did the same to me with my Piet and Bushy. Why, Principal, should our children not be allowed to learn because of some piece of paper?"

"The piece of paper you're referring to, Mrs. Mabaso [Granny's maiden name]," the principal said to Granny, "is as important to our children as a pass is to us adults. We all hate passes; therefore, it's only natural we should hate the regulations our children are subjected to. But as we have to live with passes, so our children have to live with the regulations, Mrs. Mabaso. I hope you understand, that is the law of the country. We would have admitted your grandson a long time ago, as you well know, had it not been for the papers. I hope you understand."

"I understand, Principal," Granny said, "but I don't understand," she added paradoxically.

One of the papers caught the principal's eye and he turned to my mother and asked, "Is your husband a Shangaan, Mrs. Mathabane?"

"No, he's not Principal," my mother said. "Is there anything wrong? He's Venda and I'm Shangaan."[25]

The principal reflected for a moment or so and then said, concernedly, "No, there's nothing seriously wrong. Nothing that we can't take care of. You see, Mrs. Mathabane, technically,

---

23. The rules come from South Africa's capital, *Pretoria.*
24. *Pitori* is Granny's pronunciation of "Pretoria."
25. The people of South Africa belong to many different ethnic groups, including *Venda* and *Shangaan,* each with its own language.

Vocabulary
peruse (pə rōōz′) *v.* to read through or examine carefully

LITERATURE & HUMANITIES

⊙ Display the photo *Witwatersrand Goldminer Watching Sunday Mime Dance* from the National Museum of Women in the Arts CD. Have students discuss the connection between the symbolism of the photo and the promise of education.

REAL-WORLD CONNECTION

South African Ethnic Groups Have students search the Internet to find out about South African ethnic groups and their languages, history, and customs. In particular, students should look for information about the two groups the narrator belongs to, Shangaan and Venda, as well as the others mentioned, Zulu and Sisotho. Students may also find information in an atlas that has a language map of South Africa's major ethnic group languages. **L2**

Mark Mathabane ∾

the fact that your child's father is a Venda makes him ineligible to attend this tribal school because it is only for children whose parents are of the Shangaan tribe. May I ask what language the children speak at home?"

"Both languages," my mother said worriedly, "Venda and Shangaan. Is there anything wrong?"

The principal coughed, clearing his throat, then said, "I mean which language do they speak more?"

"It depends, Principal," my mother said, swallowing hard. "When their father is around, he wants them to speak only Venda. And when he's not, they speak Shangaan. And when they are out at play, they speak Zulu and Sisotho."[26]

"Well," the principal said, heaving a sigh of relief. "In that case, I think an exception can be made. The reason for such an exception is that there's currently no school for Vendas in Alexandra. And should the authorities come asking why we took in your son, we can tell them that. Anyway, your child is half-half."

Everyone broke into a nervous laugh, except me. I was bewildered by the whole thing. I looked at my mother, and she seemed greatly relieved as she watched the principal register me; a broad smile broke

Man displaying passbook.

across her face. It was as if some enormously heavy burden had finally been lifted from her shoulders and her conscience.

"Bring him back two weeks from today," the principal said as he saw us to the door. "There're so many children registering today that classes won't begin until two weeks hence. Also, the school needs repair and cleaning up after the holidays. If he refuses to come, simply notify us, and we'll send a couple of big boys to come fetch him, and he'll be very sorry if it ever comes to that."

As we left the principal's office and headed home, my mind was still against going to school. I was thinking of running away from home and joining my friends in the junkyard.

I didn't want to go to school for three reasons: I was reluctant to surrender my freedom and independence over to what I heard every school-going child call "tyrannous discipline." I had heard many bad things about life in tribal school—from daily beatings by teachers and mistresses who worked you like a mule to long school hours— and the sight of those canes in the principal's office gave ample credence to rumors that school was nothing but a torture chamber. And there was my allegiance to the gang.

But the thought of the strange woman's lamentations over her dead son presented a

---

26. *Zulu* and *Sisotho* are ethnic groups as well as languages.

Vocabulary
credence (krēd′ əns) *n.* belief, especially in the reports or statements of others

---

M Literary Elements

CHARACTERIZATION Point out to students that writers create character by describing the character's actions, appearance, and speech, as well as how other characters interact with him or her. Ask students to briefly describe in their own words the character of the principal, based on his appearance, actions, words, and interactions with others. *(The principal is a serious, fastidious, and officious man who is aware that he must follow government policy but is also willing to bend rules slightly because he wants to help Mama and the narrator.)*

N Active Reading

EVALUATE Ask students if they think the rumors the narrator believes about school being "nothing but a torture chamber" are accurate. Encourage them to consider all the evidence they have read so far in the selection as they evaluate the validity of the rumors. Here is an example of the kind of thinking process students might use to evaluate this question.

Model: Since the principal has canes he uses on disobedient students, I know the school must be a strict place. However, the principal does not seem mean, since he wants to help Mama. And Mama seems to want the best for her son and probably would not put him in a bad place. The children on the street seem biased against school because of what the gangs say, so the rumors are probably not accurate.

MEETING INDIVIDUAL NEEDS — ENGLISH LANGUAGE LEARNERS

Multilingualism Point out that the narrator speaks four different languages, depending on who he is with and where he is. Explain that speaking more than one language is common in many parts of the world, and the fact that most Americans speak only one language is somewhat unusual. Discuss the advantages of being multilingual, such as being able to converse with people from other cultures.

Activity Invite students who speak more than one language to tell what languages they speak and in what situations they speak them. Invite them to say a few words or sentences in those languages.

Additional Resources
📁 *English Language Learners Sourcebook*

Children in Alexandra Township.

Viewing the photograph: What does the background in this photograph tell you about these children's daily lives? How might the older three react to being enrolled in school like the author?

Teaching Options

somewhat strong case for going to school: I didn't want to end up dead in the streets. A more compelling argument for going to school, however, was the vivid recollection of all that humiliation and pain my mother had gone through to get me the papers and the birth certificate so I could enroll in school. What should I do? I was torn between two worlds.

But later that evening something happened to force me to go to school.

I was returning home from playing soccer when a neighbor accosted[27] me by the gate and told me that there had been a bloody fight at my home.

"Your mother and father have been at it again," the neighbor, a woman, said.

"And your mother left."

I was stunned.

"Was she hurt badly?"

"A little bit," the woman said. "But she'll be all right. We took her to your grandma's place."

I became hot with anger.

"Is anyone in the house?" I stammered, trying to control my rage.

"Yes, your father is. But I don't think you should go near the house. He's raving mad. He's armed with a meat cleaver. He's chased out your brother and sisters, also. And some of the neighbors who tried to intervene he's threatened to carve them to pieces. I have never seen him this mad before."

I brushed aside the woman's warnings and went. Shattered windows convinced me that there had indeed been a skirmish of some sort. Several pieces of broken bricks, evidently broken after being thrown at the door, were lying about the door. I tried opening the door; it was locked from the inside. I knocked. No one answered. I knocked again. Still no one answered, until, as I turned to leave:

"Who's out there?" my father's voice came growling from inside.

"It's me, Johannes,"[28] I said.

---

27. In this case, to *accost* is to approach and speak to, often in a pushy way.

28. The author's name was *Johannes* (yō hä′ nis) before he changed it to Mark.

452 🦋 UNIT 2

Mark Mathabane ⤳

"Go away, . . . !" he bellowed. "I don't want you or that . . . mother of yours setting foot in this house. Go away before I come out there and kill you!"

"Let me in!" I cried. "Dammit, let me in! I want my things!"

"What things? Go away, you black swine!"

I went to the broken window and screamed obscenities at my father, daring him to come out, hoping that if he as much as ever stuck his black face out, I would pelt him with the half-a-loaf brick in my hand. He didn't come out. He continued launching a <u>tirade</u> of obscenities at my mother and her mother. . . . He was drunk, but I wondered where he had gotten the money to buy beer because it was still the middle of the week and he was dead broke. He had lost his entire wage for the past week in dice and had had to borrow bus fare.

"I'll kill you someday for all you're doing to my mother," I threatened him, overwhelmed with rage. Several nosey neighbors were beginning to congregate by open windows and doors. Not wanting to make a spectacle of myself, which was something many of our neighbors seemed to always expect from our family, I backtracked away from the door and vanished into the dark street. I ran, without stopping, all the way to the other end of the township where Granny lived. There I found my mother, her face swollen and bruised and her eyes puffed up to the point where she could scarcely see.

"What happened, Mama?" I asked, fighting to hold back the tears at the sight of her disfigured face.

"Nothing, child, nothing," she mumbled, almost apologetically, between swollen lips. "Your papa simply lost his temper, that's all."

"But why did he beat you up like this, Mama?" Tears came down my face. "He's never beaten you like this before."

My mother appeared reluctant to answer me. She looked searchingly at Granny, who was pounding millet with pestle and mortar and mixing it with sorghum[29] and nuts for an African delicacy. Granny said, "Tell him, child, tell him. He's got a right to know. Anyway, he's the cause of it all."

"Your father and I fought because I took you to school this morning," my mother began. "He had told me not to, and when I told him that I had, he became very upset. He was drunk. We started arguing, and one thing led to another."

"Why doesn't he want me to go to school?"

"He says he doesn't have money to waste paying for you to get what he calls a useless white man's education," my mother replied. "But I told him that if he won't pay for your schooling, I would try and look for a job and pay, but he didn't want to hear that, also. 'There are better things for you to work for,' he said. 'Besides, I don't want you to work. How would I look to other men if you, a woman I owned, were to start working?' When I asked him why shouldn't I take you to school, seeing that you were now of age, he replied that he doesn't believe in schools. I told him that school would keep you off the streets and out of trouble, but still he was belligerent."

"Is that why he beat you up?"

"Yes, he said I disobeyed his orders."

Did You Know?
The *pestle* is a blunt tool used to pound or grind substances in a mortar, a thick, hard bowl, often made of wood or stone.

---

29. *Millet* is a grain similar to wheat, and *sorghum* is a syrup made from a tropical grass.

Vocabulary
tirade (tī rād′) *n.* a long, angry or scolding speech

Language Note
Make sure students understand that "lost his entire wage . . . in dice" means that the narrator's father lost all his earnings playing and betting in dice games.

Q **Literary Elements**

CHARACTER The narrator's feelings for his mother are evident in this passage. Ask students to identify what specific actions and speech reveal his feelings. *(His intense anger at his father and his pain at seeing his mother's beaten face both reveal his love.)*

R **Critical Thinking**

INFERRING Encourage students to consider how the narrator's father's own experiences in life influence his opinion about his son going to school. Ask them to suggest possible reasons, besides those expressed, that the father feels the way he does about education. *(The father appears to be a bitter and broken man who feels powerless to help himself or his family. He may resent or fear the idea that his son will have more opportunity than he did.)*

Writing *Minilesson*

Expository Writing Remind students that one type of expository writing analyzes or comments on a significant social or political situation or event. Explain that a good way to begin writing is to make a list of main points and then fill in specific details that support those points. The thesis will often emerge naturally once these points are laid out. Refer students to the graphic of an expository essay on page 423.

Activity Have students write a couple of paragraphs analyzing some of the social and political conditions mentioned in the selection that are most likely to have caused the characters to have negative ideas about education. **L3**

Additional Resources

📖 *Writer's Choice,* Lesson 5.1

Active Reading

REVIEW Have students reread the conversation between Mama and Granny. Ask them to explain what Mama's father did and why she feels she cannot leave her husband.

(Mama's husband paid her parents money to marry their daughter, and then her father squandered it and left Granny penniless. Mama may feel obligated to stay with her husband because of the money he spent for her. If her father had not lost the lobola, she might have been able to return the money and get divorced, or at least move in with her mother and rely on her for financial help.)

Cultural Note

A *lobola*, or bride price, is a part of Zulu marriage arrangements. A price is determined to make up for the "loss" of a daughter. Ten head of cattle is usually the price paid by the future husband of the bride.

T **Critical Thinking**

DRAWING CONCLUSIONS This passage reveals a lot about Mama. Ask students to briefly describe what kind of person she is based on what they have learned so far. *(She is an independent-minded, strong-willed, intelligent woman who does not believe in the gender restrictions of her culture and wants more from life than most people in her community.)*

Teaching Options

from **Kaffir Boy**

"He's right, child," Granny interjected. "He paid *lobola* [bride price] for you. And your father ate it all up before he left me."

To which my mother replied, "But I desperately want to leave this beast of a man. But with his *lobola* gone I can't do it. That worthless thing you call your husband shouldn't have sold Jackson's scrawny cattle and left you penniless."

"Don't talk like that about your father, child," Granny said. "Despite all, he's still your father, you know. Anyway, he asked for *lobola* only because he had to get back what he spent raising you. And you know it would have been taboo for him to let you or any of your sisters go without asking for *lobola*."

"You and Papa seemed to forget that my sisters and I have minds of our own," my mother said. "We didn't need you to tell us whom to marry, and why, and how. If it hadn't been for your interference, I could have married that schoolteacher."

Granny did not reply; she knew well not to. When it came to the act of "selling" women as marriage partners, my mother was vehemently opposed to it. Not only was she opposed to this one aspect of tribal culture, but to others as well, particularly those involving relations between men and women and the upbringing of children. But my mother's sharply differing opinion was an exception rather than the rule among tribal women. Most times, many tribal women questioned her sanity in daring to question well-established mores.[30] But my mother did not seem to care; she would always scoff at her opponents and call them fools in letting their husbands enslave them completely.

Though I disliked school, largely because I knew nothing about what actually went on

there, and the little I knew had painted a dreadful picture, the fact that a father would not want his son to go to school, especially a father who didn't go to school, seemed hard to understand.

"Why do you want me to go to school, Mama?" I asked, hoping that she might, somehow, clear up some of the confusion that was building in my mind.

"I want you to have a future, child," my mother said. "And, contrary to what your father says, school is the only means to a future. I don't want you growing up to be like your father."

The latter statement hit me like a bolt of lightning. It just about shattered every defense mechanism[31] and every pretext[32] I had against going to school.

"Your father didn't go to school," she continued, dabbing her puffed eyes to reduce the swelling with a piece of cloth dipped in warm water, "that's why he's doing some of the bad things he's doing. Things like drinking, gambling, and neglecting his family. He didn't learn how to read and write; therefore, he can't find a decent job. Lack of any education has narrowly focused his life. He sees nothing beyond himself. He still thinks in the old, tribal way, and still believes that things should be as they were back in the old days when he was growing up as a tribal boy in Louis Trichardt. Though he's my husband, and your father, he doesn't see any of that."

"Why didn't he go to school, Mama?"

"He refused to go to school because his father led him to believe that an education was a tool through which white people were

---

30. The customs and moral standards followed by most people in a given society are called *mores* (môr′ āz).

31. A *defense mechanism* is an attitude or behavior a person unconsciously adopts to help block out painful or unpleasant feelings.

32. A *pretext* is a false reason or excuse one gives to hide a true reason or motive.

Vocabulary
vehemently (vē′ ə mənt lē) *adv.* strongly; intensely; passionately

Grammar and Language Minilesson

Quotation Marks Explain to students that quotation marks are used to enclose a direct quotation. Show students these rules for quotation marks:
Place quotation marks
- outside periods and commas.
- outside exclamation points and question marks when the quoted matter is an exclamation or question.
- inside exclamation points and question marks when the quoted matter is not an exclamation or question.

Activity Have students correct the punctuation in the following sentences as needed:
1. "Don't talk to me about your father, child," Granny said. *(correct)*
2. "Why do you want me to go to school, Mama"? *(correction: Mama?")*
3. "I said get into that tub"! *(correction: tub!")* **L2**

Additional Resources

 Grammar and Language Transparency 38

Grammar and Language Workbook, pp. 235, 271, 273

 Grammar and Composition Handbook, Lesson 11.9

Writer's Choice, Lesson 21.9

going to take things away from him, like they did black people in the old days. And that a white man's education was worthless insofar as black people were concerned because it prepared them for jobs they can't have. But I know it isn't totally so, child, because times have changed somewhat. Though our lot isn't any better today, an education will get you a decent job. If you can read or write you'll be better off than those of us who can't. Take my situation: I can't find a job because I don't have papers, and I can't get papers because white people mainly want to register people who can read and write. But I want things to be different for you, child. For you and your brother and sisters. I want you to go to school, because I believe that an education is the key you need to open up a new world and a new life for yourself, a world and life different from that of either your father's or mine. It is the only key that can do that, and only those who seek it earnestly and perseveringly will get anywhere in the white man's world. Education will open doors where none seem to exist. It'll make people talk to you, listen to you, and help you; people who otherwise wouldn't bother. It will make you soar, like a bird lifting up into the endless blue sky, and leave poverty, hunger, and suffering behind. It'll teach you to learn to embrace what's good and shun what's bad and evil. Above all, it'll make you a somebody in this world. It'll make you grow up to be a good and proud person. That's why I want you to go to school, child, so that education can do all that, and more, for you."

A long, awkward silence followed, during which I reflected upon the significance of my mother's lengthy speech. I looked at my mother; she looked at me.

Finally, I asked, "How come you know so much about school, Mama? You didn't go to school, did you?"

"No, child," my mother replied. "Just like your father, I never went to school." For the second time that evening, a mere statement of fact had a thunderous impact on me. All the confusion I had about school seemed to leave my mind, like darkness giving way to light. And what had previously been a dark, yawning void in my mind was suddenly transformed into a beacon of light that began to grow larger and larger, until it had swallowed up, blotted out, all the blackness. That beacon of light seemed to reveal things and facts, which, though they must have always existed in me, I hadn't been aware of up until now.

"But unlike your father," my mother went on, "I've always wanted to go to school, but couldn't because my father, under the sway of tribal traditions, thought it unnecessary to educate females. That's why I so much want you to go, child, for if you do, I know that someday I too would come to go, old as I would be then. Promise me, therefore, that no matter what, you'll go back to school. And I, in turn, promise that I'll do everything in my power to keep you there."

With tears streaming down my cheeks and falling upon my mother's bosom, I promised her that I would go to school "forever." That night, at seven and a half years of my life, the battlelines in the family were drawn. My mother on the one side, illiterate but determined to have me drink, for better or for worse, from the well of knowledge. On the other side, my father, he too illiterate, yet determined to have me drink from the well of ignorance. Scarcely aware of the magnitude of the decision I was making or, rather, the decision which was being emotionally thrust upon me, I chose to fight on my mother's side, and thus my destiny was forever altered.

Literary Elements

MONOLOGUE Ask students why Mama's monologue is a crucial part of this selection. *(It explains Mama's conviction to send her children to school, her husband's resistance to education, her troubled relationship with her husband, and the social conditions that make education so important for black Africans.)*

Critical Thinking

DRAWING CONCLUSIONS The narrator has sudden clarity after hearing his mother's speech. Ask students what they think he realizes and why. *(When he realizes why his mother thinks education is so important, he understands that he can have a brighter future if he takes the opportunity that was denied to her.)*

Active Reading

EVALUATE Ask students if they think the narrator made the right decision. *(Most students will agree that he was right to choose knowledge over ignorance, even if school presents certain problems.)*

Thematic Focus

Remembering Ask students why the episode Mathabane relates in this selection was crucial to his life. Did he know that it was important at the time, or is that something he realized only in retrospect?

✓ ASSESSMENT OPTIONS

📁 *Quick Checks,* p. 38

Reading *Minilesson*

Problem and Solution Point out that the selection deals with education as a solution to a major problem. It also illustrates the theme of education as a solution in the conflicts among the characters.

Activity Have students make a chart illustrating various problems and solutions in the story. At the top, they should write the headings *Problem* and *Solution*. Down the left side, they should write *Mathabane, Mathabane's Mother, Mathabane's Father,* and *Position of Blacks in South Africa.* After students have completed their charts, have them discuss the various problems and solutions. **L2**

Additional Resources
📁 *Reading Workbook,* p. 49

Responding to the Selection

Personal Response

Students may find the scene in which Mama and Granny tie up the narrator to get him to school or the scene in which Mama explains why an education is important as the most memorable.

ANALYZING LITERATURE

1. He thinks it is a waste of time. His goal is to live off the street like the members of the gang he admires.
2. The woman, seeing Mama hauling her son to school, stops to tell them about her own son who refused to go to school, got involved in street violence, and was murdered.
3. The narrator sees the principal's canes, and the principal explains that he will not be beaten if he behaves. Mama gives the principal the papers it has taken her months to get. The principal questions Mama about her son's ethnic heritage and decides to admit him to the school.
4. Mathabane's father becomes enraged and beats up his wife. Mama says that her husband's father taught him to believe that school was a white man's trick and useless to blacks.
5. She wants him to go to school because she was denied an education herself and does not want him to face the same limitations she faced. Initially, he resists this goal, but after her speech, he accepts the goal as his destiny.
6. He has been influenced by the prevailing disregard for education in his community.
7. Her story contradicts what he has believed about gang life on the street.
8. Mama's long struggle to get papers for her son to attend school and the principal's concerns about young Mathabane's ethnic heritage indicate that there are great restrictions on the lives of black South Africans, limiting their freedom and educational opportunities.
9. Their conflict reveals the father's hopelessness about his family's future and Mama's belief that her children can and should have better lives.
10. What Mathabane learns about his father and mother and about life for blacks makes him move from hating the idea of school and resisting his mother to embracing school as his life's goal.
11. It suggests that education is a form of power.
12. Most students will agree that education gives people a broader and

deeper understanding of the world and equips them to make sound decisions, get rewarding work, and enjoy a fuller life.
13. The tradition of arranged marriages in which the man pays for a wife and then owns her and the belief that women do not need to be educated both severely oppress women.
14. The setting is essential, since the specific oppressive conditions depicted are unique to blacks in South Africa in the mid-twentieth century.
15. Most students will recognize that Mathabane probably chose to write about these events because they fundamentally shaped his identity and future.

Responding to Literature

Personal Response

What scene from this selection lingers in your mind? Why?

ANALYZING LITERATURE

RECALL

1. As this account begins, what is Mathabane's opinion of school? What are his goals?
2. Describe the encounter with the woman on the street.
3. Summarize what happens in the principal's office.
4. How does Mathabane's father react to the day's events? According to his mother, what accounts for his father's behavior and outlook on life?
5. What goal does Mathabane's mother have for him? Why? How does he react to this goal?

INTERPRET

6. What do you think accounts for Mathabane's outlook on life at the beginning of the selection?
7. What might cause Mathabane to be confused after the encounter with the "strange woman"?
8. What conclusions can you draw about what life is like for blacks in South Africa, based on what happens in the principal's office?
9. How does the **conflict** between Mathabane's parents reflect their different outlooks on life?
10. Compare Mathabane's attitude toward school at the beginning of the selection with his attitude at the end. What factors account for this change?

EVALUATE AND CONNECT

11. Under apartheid, blacks in South Africa had limited access to education. What does this suggest about the relationship between education and power?
12. Do you agree that "Education will open doors where none seem to exist"? Explain.
13. In this account, what aspects of tribal culture serve to oppress women and limit their freedom?
14. Evaluate the importance of **setting** (see page R11) in this true story. How do the time and place influence the events that occur?
15. Why do you think Mathabane chose to write about this experience?

456 ❧ UNIT 2

Literary ELEMENTS

Monologue

A **monologue** is a long speech made by a character in a literary work. In this excerpt from *Kaffir Boy,* Mark Mathabane asks Mama why his father didn't go to school. Mama responds with a monologue. In this lengthy speech, Mathabane's mother not only answers her son's question but also gives him compelling information about her own life. In addition, she expresses her views about an important topic: education. Throughout the monologue, Mama's words reveal a great deal about her own character.

1. In this monologue, what do you learn about Mathabane's parents? about social and economic conditions for blacks in South Africa?
2. What views about education does Mama express in this monologue?
3. What does the monologue seem to suggest about Mama's character? Use specific details from the monologue to support your answer.

● See **Literary Terms Handbook**, p. R8.

LITERARY ELEMENTS

1. Mathabane's father did not go to school because his father thought it was worthless; his mother could not go because she is female. Whites control many aspects of black lives.
2. Mama believes education provides self-confidence and opportunity.
3. Mama's eloquent words on education indicate that she is hopeful, idealistic, strong, and brave.

Additional Resources

 Literary Elements Transparency 38

LITERATURE AND WRITING

Writing About Literature

Analyze Mood   **Mood** is the emotional quality, or atmosphere, of a literary work. Sometimes the mood of a piece changes as the setting shifts. In the selection, find several passages that have different moods. Write a paragraph about each passage, identifying the mood, as well as the specific details that help to create that mood. Share your analysis with a group of classmates.

Creative Writing

Double Trouble   Mathabane's mother must struggle not only against the racist policies of apartheid but against a tribal culture that treats women as their husband's "possessions." Imagine that Mama—who can neither read nor write—asks you to record her thoughts about her own desire for freedom. In a paragraph or two, write down the ideas you think Mama would express.

EXTENDING YOUR RESPONSE

Literature Groups

Compare Reactions   Think back to the discussion you had about the quote in the Focus Activity on page 444. In your group, discuss and compare possible responses that different characters in this selection might have.

Performing

Dramatic Presentation   With a small group, reenact the encounter that Mathabane, Mama, and Granny have with the "strange woman" on the street. Practice the scene and present it to the class. Justify your choice of performance techniques with details from the selection.

Internet Connection

South Africa Today   Use the Internet to learn about the political situation in South Africa today. Make a list of research questions such as the following: What form of government does South Africa have? Who is the head of state? What are the most pressing political and social issues? What is the state of racial relations in South Africa? What progress has been made in healing the wounds caused by decades of apartheid? Share your findings with the class.

📖 **Save your work for your portfolio.**

Skill Minilesson

VOCABULARY • Analogies

An analogy is a type of comparison that is based on the relationships between things or ideas. One type of analogy deals with pairs of words that represent different degrees of intensity.

  hilarious : amusing :: tragic : unfortunate

Something that is *hilarious* is extremely *amusing;* something that is *tragic* is extremely *unfortunate.*

  To complete an analogy, decide what relationship exists between the first two things or ideas. Then apply that relationship to another pair of words.

● For more about analogies, see **Communications Skills Handbook,** p. R77.

PRACTICE   Choose the word that best completes each analogy.

1. terror : fear :: tirade :
   a. apology   b. sensation   c. criticism
2. hate : dislike :: revere :
   a. admire   b. worship   c. ignore
3. vehemently : strongly :: amazingly :
   a. surprisingly   b. soothingly   c. generally
4. forbid : discourage :: captivate :
   a. coax   b. interest   c. chase

LITERATURE AND WRITING

Writing About Literature

Students' analyses should
• examine several passages from the selection with different moods.
• identify the mood in each passage.
• analyze what specific details create the mood in each passage.

Creative Writing

Students' paragraphs should
• express a plausible account of Mama's thoughts based on what is revealed about her in the selection.
• express Mama's opinions about her personal and political circumstances, including details about black social status as well as her marriage, parents, and lack of education.

EXTENDING YOUR RESPONSE

Literature Groups You may want to suggest that students begin their discussions by first deciding what they think the quote means.
COLLAB. LEARN.

Performing Students may justify an overwrought portrayal of the woman by noting that she "burst into tears" and had "tears . . . streaming from her face."

Internet Connection Suggest to students that they try using the following search words: *South Africa, apartheid, Nelson Mandela,* and *F. W. De Klerk.*

Skill Minilesson

VOCABULARY • Analogies
1. c   2. a   3. a
4. b

Additional Resources
📁 *Vocabulary Practice,* p. 37

☑ ASSESSMENT OPTIONS

📁 *Quick Checks,* p. 38
📁 *Selection and Theme Assessment,* pp. 73–74
📁 *Performance Assessment,* p. 37
💾 *Testmaker*

Objective

• To recognize cause-and-effect relationships

Teaching Strategies

After students read the text, ask them to think of their own examples of cause-and-effect relationships, identifying the cause and the effect in each instance. Encourage them to offer their examples as two sentences with no word clues as to which is the cause and which is the effect. Then have the rest of the class name the cause and the effect.

Activity

1. a. She cannot get a job.
   b. Most blacks cannot get registered.
2. He refused to go to school because his father taught him that education (1) prepared blacks for jobs they could not have and (2) was a means by which white men took things away from black people.

Additional Resources
📁 *Reading Workbook*

Identifying Cause and Effect

Suppose you go to an out-of-town hockey game on a school night. You get home very late. The next day you feel so tired that you doze off in English class. The hockey game is the **cause** of your not getting enough sleep. Your dozing off is an **effect** of getting home late. When one event causes another one to happen, a **cause-and-effect relationship** exists.

If you can answer *why* something happened, you know its cause. If you can answer *what happened as a result* of something, you know the effect. Words and phrases such as *because, as a result,* and *consequently* often signal cause-and-effect relationships.

In written accounts of events, just as in real life, a single cause may have several effects, and one effect may have multiple causes. In *Kaffir Boy,* for example, Mark Mathabane explains how he came to side with his mother in the battle over education: "I chose to fight on my mother's side, and thus my destiny was forever altered." His decision is an *effect.* It is also the *cause* of events in his future. Here are three causes of Mathabane's decision to go to school.

- He is moved by his mother's speech about education.
- He does not want to be like his father.
- He does not want to die in the streets, like the son of the "strange woman" he encounters on the way to school.

● For more about related comprehension skills, see **Reading Handbook,** pp. R82–R94.

ACTIVITY

Read the following excerpt from *Kaffir Boy.* Complete the exercises.

> "[Your father] refused to go to school because his father led him to believe that an education was a tool through which white people were going to take things away from him. . . . And that a white man's education was worthless insofar as black people were concerned because it prepared them for jobs they can't have. But I know it isn't totally so, child, because times have changed somewhat. . . . If you can read or write you'll be better off than those of us who can't. Take my situation: I can't find a job because I don't have papers, and I can't get papers because white people mainly want to register people who can read and write."

1. Identify an effect of each of the following causes:
   a. Mathabane's mother does not have papers.
   b. White people mainly want to register people who can read and write.

2. Identify two causes for this effect: Mathabane's father refused to go to school.

MEETING INDIVIDUAL NEEDS — INCLUSION STRATEGIES

Less-Proficient Readers Students who have trouble keeping track of cause-and-effect relationships may benefit from seeing a visual representation of these concepts.

Activity To convey the basic idea that a cause leads to an effect, show students the cause-and-effect graphic pictured here. Encourage them to use arrows to visually represent the cause-and-effect relationships in the Activity questions. **L1**

leads to

| Cause | ➡ | Effect |

Additional Resources
📁 *Inclusion Strategies*

Before You Read

from *Farewell to Manzanar*

FOCUS ACTIVITY

How might you react if you and your family were forced to pack up and move on very short notice?

FREEWRITE Imagine that you and your family have forty-eight hours to pack your belongings and move to a new and unfamiliar place. Spend five minutes writing about how you might feel and what you might do in such a situation.

SETTING A PURPOSE Read to find out what life was like for many Japanese Americans who were forced to move during World War II.

BACKGROUND

The Time and Place

The events described in this selection take place in California in 1941 and 1942, after Japan's surprise attack on the U.S. Pacific Fleet in Pearl Harbor, Hawaii, on December 7, 1941. After this attack, the United States entered World War II, declaring war on Japan on December 8, 1941.

Did You Know?

After the Japanese attack on Pearl Harbor, many Americans were suspicious of people of Japanese ancestry living in the United States. In February 1942, President Franklin D. Roosevelt issued Executive Order 9066, which essentially gave the U.S. War Department the authority to remove Japanese Americans from their homes on the West Coast and confine them to special camps for the duration of the war. Some 110,000 Japanese Americans, two-thirds of them U.S. citizens, were relocated by the military to ten remotely situated, prison-like camps.

VOCABULARY PREVIEW

exclusively (iks klōō′ siv lē) *adv.* only; excluding any other; p. 462

internment (in turn′ mənt) *n.* the act of restricting or being restricted to a particular place, especially during a war; p. 463

patriarch (pā′ trē ärk′) *n.* the male head of a family or group; p. 463

irrational (i rash′ ən əl) *adj.* contrary to reason; illogical; p. 464

designation (dez′ ig nā′ shən) *n.* a distinguishing name or mark; p. 464

alleviate (ə lē′ vē āt′) *v.* to make easier to bear; relieve; lessen; p. 467

whimsical (hwim′ zi kəl) *adj.* fanciful; curiously humorous; p. 467

subordinate (sə bôr′ də nāt′) *v.* to cause to be, or treat as, secondary, inferior, or less important; p. 471

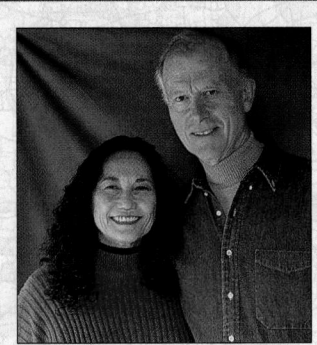

Meet Jeanne Wakatsuki Houston and James D. Houston

"Everybody knows an injustice was done," James Houston has said about the internment of Japanese Americans in relocation camps during World War II. Houston's wife, Jeanne Wakatsuki Houston, spent more than three years of her childhood at the Manzanar Relocation Center in California. The Houstons wrote about that experience in *Farewell to Manzanar*, a book that she refers to as "a true story, involving an extraordinary episode in American history."

Jeanne Wakatsuki Houston was born in 1934; James D. Houston was born in 1933. Both are natives of California. Farewell to Manzanar was first published in 1973.

Before Reading

Objectives

- To read and analyze an excerpt from an account of the author's childhood experience living in a Japanese American internment camp during World War II
- To learn about the elements of autobiography
- To write an analysis of different settings

Skills

Reading/Thinking: Inferring; Identifying Spatial Relationships; Summarizing
Writing: Personal Writing; Letter of Protest; Song Lyrics
Vocabulary: Parts of Speech
Grammar/Language: Dashes; Intervening Prepositional Phrases
Listening/Speaking: Interviewing; Songs
Collaboration: Literature Groups

Motivating
→OPTIONS

Selection Focus Transparency 39: Have students use the photograph to envision themselves living in small, close quarters.

Focus Activity: Ask students to think of possible scenarios in which ordinary citizens could be forced to leave their homes on short notice.

RESOURCE MANAGER

Lesson Two Planning Resource
The *Unit Two Planning Guide* (pp. 32–39) provides additional lesson notes and reduced versions of all print resources.

📁 **Other Print Resources**
- Active Reading Guide, p. 39
- Vocabulary Practice, p. 38
- Reading Workbook, p. 50
- Grammar and Language Workbook, pp. 267, 163, 161

- Grammar and Composition Handbook, Lessons 11.7, 6.2, 6.1
- Quick Checks, p. 39
- Selection and Theme Assessment, pp. 75–76
- Performance Assessment, p. 38
- Spanish Summaries, p. 39
- Spanish Translations
- Inclusion Strategies
- English Language Learners Sourcebook

Transparencies
- Selection Focus 39
- Fine Art 19
- Literary Elements 39
- Grammar and Language 39

Technology
- Audio Library
- Spanish Audio Library
- Glencoe Literature Web Site
- Testmaker

Reading the Selection

SUMMARY

In this excerpt from *Farewell to Manzanar,* Jeanne Wakatsuki Houston remembers her experience as a child during World War II. After the narrator's father is arrested by the U. S. government, her mother moves her children to two different Japanese American ghettos. Then they are forced to relocate to Manzanar, a Japanese American internment camp in California, where the family endure inadequate living conditions, including cramped quarters, latrines with no privacy, and poor food.

📁 *Spanish Summaries,* p. 39

A Active Reading

CONNECT Have students read the first two paragraphs of the selection. Remind them that in December 1941 the Japanese bombed the American naval base at Pearl Harbor. Then ask them to use what they know about this time period to figure out why Mama would feel safer in an area where there were other Japanese people.

Additional Resources
📁 *Active Reading Guide,* p. 39
🎧 *Audio Library*
🎧 *Spanish Audio Library*

Teaching Options

---

from Farewell to Manzanar

Jeanne Wakatsuki Houston and James D. Houston

IN DECEMBER OF 1941 Papa's disappearance didn't bother me nearly so much as the world I soon found myself in.

He had been a jack-of-all-trades. When I was born he was farming near Inglewood. Later, when he started fishing, we moved to Ocean Park, near Santa Monica, and until they picked him up, that's where we lived, in a big frame house with a brick fireplace, a block back from the beach. We were the only Japanese family in the neighborhood. Papa liked it that way. He didn't want to be labeled or grouped by anyone. But with him gone and no way of knowing what to expect, my mother moved all of us down to Terminal Island.[1]

Woody already lived there, and one of my older sisters had married a Terminal Island boy. Mama's first concern now was to keep the family together; and once the war began, she felt safer there than isolated racially in Ocean Park. But for me, at age seven, the island was a country as foreign as India or Arabia would have been. It was the first time I had lived among other Japanese, or gone to school with them, and I was terrified all the time.

This was partly Papa's fault. One of his threats to keep us younger kids in line was "I'm going to sell you to the Chinaman." When I had entered kindergarten two years earlier, I was the only Oriental in the class. They sat me next to a Caucasian girl who happened to have very slanted eyes. I looked at her and began to scream, certain Papa had sold me out at last. My fear of her ran so deep I could not speak of

1. *Terminal Island,* part of the Port of Los Angeles, is at the city's southern tip.

CONNECTING TO OTHER SELECTIONS

The chart at the right shows three ways to connect the excerpt from *Farewell to Manzanar* to selections in this book.

For specific teaching strategies, see the ***Unit Two Planning Guide,*** pp. 35–36.

Connection		Title
Life Skills: Supporting and Contributing	→	"And of Clay Are We Created," p. 343
Thematic: Coping	→	"Winter Night," p. 363
Literary: Setting	→	"Exploring Antarctic Ice," p. 532

B **Literary Elements**

AUTOBIOGRAPHY Ask students how they can tell that this excerpt is from an autobiography. *(It is written in the first person by a person who is recounting events from her childhood.)*

Language Note

Explain to students that people of the narrator's generation commonly used the term *Oriental* to refer to Asian people, because parts of Asia are known as the Orient. The term *Oriental* has taken on negative connotations in recent decades and has been replaced with *Asian.*

C **Active Reading**

EVALUATE Ask students what the family's move to Terminal Island is probably like for the narrator's mother. Have them consider what they know about the Wakatsuki family's former lifestyle and what life is like on Terminal Island. You may want to share the following model.

Model: I know the family moved from a big frame house in a neighborhood near Santa Monica. On Terminal Island, the narrator's mother has to manage the family without her husband and work odd hours in a canning factory. Their house is a shack, and the people are rough. The conditions of her life on Terminal Island must be difficult and stressful.

it, even to Mama, couldn't explain why I was screaming. For two weeks I had nightmares about this girl, until the teachers finally moved me to the other side of the room. And it was still with me, this fear of Oriental faces, when we moved to Terminal Island.

In those days it was a company town, a ghetto owned and controlled by the canneries. The men went after fish, and whenever the boats came back—day or night—the women would be called to process the catch while it

was fresh. One in the afternoon or four in the morning, it made no difference. My mother had to go to work right after we moved there. I can still hear the whistle—two toots for French's, three for Van Camp's—and she and Chizu would be out of bed in the middle of the night, heading for the cannery.

The house we lived in was nothing more than a shack, a barracks with single plank walls and rough wooden floors, like the cheapest kind of migrant workers' housing. The people around

Student Histories English language learners may have endured displacement and hardship similar to that recounted in this selection. They may be refugees who experienced religious or political persecution, loss of family members, injury, poverty, and/or evacuation from homes. Even those who have not experienced such hardships may relate to the feelings of cultural alien-

ation expressed by the narrator.

Activity Invite volunteers to compare and contrast their experiences with the author's. Encourage them to express whatever thoughts and feelings the selection elicits.

Additional Resources
English Language Learners Sourcebook

Teaching Options

---

from Farewell to Manzanar

us were hardworking, boisterous, a little proud of their nickname, *yo-go-re,* which meant literally *uncouth one,* or roughneck, or dead-end kid. They not only spoke Japanese <u>exclusively,</u> they spoke a dialect peculiar to Kyushu,[2] where their families had come from in Japan, a rough, fisherman's language, full of oaths and insults. Instead of saying *ba-ka-ta-re,* a common insult meaning *stupid,* Terminal Islanders would say *ba-ka-ya-ro,* a coarser and exclusively masculine use of the word, which implies gross stupidity. They would swagger and pick on outsiders and persecute anyone who didn't speak as they did. That was what made my own time there so hateful. I had never spoken anything but English, and the other kids in the second grade despised me for it. They were tough and mean, like ghetto kids anywhere. Each day after school I dreaded their ambush. My brother Kiyo, three years older, would wait for me at the door, where we would decide whether to run straight home together, or split up, or try a new and unexpected route.

None of these kids ever actually attacked. It was the threat that frightened us, their fearful looks, and the noises they would make, like miniature Samurai, in a language we couldn't understand.

At the time it seemed we had been living under this reign of fear for years. In fact, we lived there about two months. Late in February the navy decided to clear Terminal Island completely.

Did You Know?
For centuries, the *Samurai* (sam′ oo rī′) were a class of fearsome warriors. Japan abolished its class system in the 1860s.

Even though most of us were American-born, it was dangerous having that many Orientals so close to the Long Beach Naval Station, on the opposite end of the island. We had known something like this was coming. But, like Papa's arrest, not much could be done ahead of time. There were four of us kids still young enough to be living with Mama, plus Granny, her mother, sixty-five then, speaking no English, and nearly blind. Mama didn't know where else she could get work, and we had nowhere else to move *to.* On February 25 the choice was made for us. We were given forty-eight hours to clear out.

The secondhand dealers had been prowling around for weeks, like wolves, offering humiliating prices for goods and furniture they knew many of us would have to sell sooner or later. Mama had left all but her most valuable possessions in Ocean Park, simply because she had nowhere to put them. She had brought along her pottery, her silver, heirlooms like the kimonos Granny had brought from Japan, tea sets, lacquered tables, and one fine old set of china, blue and white porcelain, almost translucent.[3] On the day we were leaving, Woody's car was so crammed with boxes and luggage and kids we had just run out of room. Mama had to sell this china.

Did You Know?
A *kimono* (ki mō′ na) is a loose robe or gown tied with a sash, traditionally worn as an outer garment by Japanese men and women.

---

3. A material that is *translucent,* such as frosted glass, allows light to pass through but doesn't permit objects on the other side to be clearly distinguished.

---

2. *Kyushu* is the southernmost of Japan's four main islands.

Vocabulary
exclusively (iks kloo′siv lē) *adv.* only; excluding any other

---

Jeanne Wakatsuki Houston and James D. Houston ∿

One of the dealers offered her fifteen dollars for it. She said it was a full setting for twelve and worth at least two hundred. He said fifteen was his top price. Mama started to quiver. Her eyes blazed up at him. She had been packing all night and trying to calm down Granny, who didn't understand why we were moving again and what all the rush was about. Mama's nerves were shot, and now navy jeeps were patrolling the streets. She didn't say another word. She just glared at this man, all the rage and frustration channeled at him through her eyes.

He watched her for a moment and said he was sure he couldn't pay more than seventeen fifty for that china. She reached into the red velvet case, took out a dinner plate and hurled it at the floor right in front of his feet.

The man leaped back shouting, "Hey! Hey, don't do that! Those are valuable dishes!"

Mama took out another dinner plate and hurled it at the floor, then another and another, never moving, never opening her mouth, just quivering and glaring at the retreating dealer, with tears streaming down her cheeks. He finally turned and scuttled out the door, heading for the next house. When he was gone she stood there smashing cups and bowls and platters until the whole set lay in scattered blue and white fragments across the wooden floor.

The American Friends Service[4] helped us find a small house in Boyle Heights, another minority ghetto, in downtown Los Angeles, now inhabited briefly by a few hundred Terminal Island refugees. Executive Order 9066 had been signed by President Roosevelt, giving the War Department authority to define military areas in the western states and to exclude from them anyone who might threaten the war effort. There was a lot of talk about internment, or moving inland, or something like that in store for all Japanese Americans. I remember my brothers sitting around the table talking very intently about what we were going to do, how we would keep the family together. They had seen how quickly Papa was removed, and they knew now that he would not be back for quite a while. Just before leaving Terminal Island Mama had received her first letter, from Bismarck, North Dakota. He had been imprisoned at Fort Lincoln, in an all-male camp for enemy aliens.

Papa had been the patriarch. He had always decided everything in the family. With him gone, my brothers, like councilors in the absence of a chief, worried about what should be done. The ironic thing is, there wasn't much left to decide. These were mainly days of quiet, desperate waiting for what seemed at the time to be inevitable. There is a phrase the Japanese use in such situations, when something difficult must be endured. You would hear the older heads, the Issei,[5] telling others very quietly, "*Shikata ga nai*" (It cannot be helped). "*Shikata ga nai*" (It must be done).

Mama and Woody went to work packing celery for a Japanese produce dealer. Kiyo and my sister May and I enrolled in the local school, and what sticks in my memory from those few weeks is the teacher—not her

---

4. The *American Friends Service* is a Quaker charity that provides assistance to political and religious refugees and other displaced persons.

5. *Issei* (ēs′ sā′) literally means "first generation" and refers to Japanese natives who immigrated to the United States.

Vocabulary
internment (in turn′ mənt) *n.* the act of restricting or being restricted to a particular place, especially during a war
patriarch (pā′ trē ärk′) *n.* the male head of a family or group

NONFICTION 🐾 463

F **Literary Elements**

CHARACTER Ask students what this scene reveals about the character of Mama. Why does she break the china rather than take the dealer's offer? *(Destroying the china rather than allowing the dealer to take advantage of her shows she is a very proud person and extremely angry about her circumstances.)*

G **Critical Thinking**

INFERRING Ask students to consider how the narrator's older siblings probably feel about the situation they are in. How do their ages make the experience different for them? *(They are probably more aware of what is likely to happen, more worried about their father, and more frustrated about their inability to control the situation than the younger siblings are.)*

FINE ART
TRANSPARENCY 19

You may want to use Fine Art Transparency 19 to discuss what items the internees might have taken with them.

Writing *Minilesson*

Personal Writing Remind students that connecting what they read to thoughts, feelings, and experiences in their own lives is one of the most rewarding parts of reading. Making personal connections to literature can help them understand themselves, as well as the literature.

Activity Write the Japanese quotation on the board with its English translation:

"*Shikata ga nai*" (It cannot be helped; it must be done). Have students recall a saying their family uses and explore in writing what it reflects about their family's or culture's attitudes or beliefs. Invite students to share their writing. **L2**

Additional Resources

📗 *Writer's Choice,* Lesson 1.1

NONFICTION 🐾 463

NARRATIVE DETAILS Point out that although the author was too young to understand the political climate in the United States during the war, she recalls specific details from her own experience that convey the anti-Japanese feelings common at the time. Ask students to identify those details. *(She recalls the coldness of her school teacher and the bus driver who took her family to Manzanar.)*

FYI

Internment After the bombing of Pearl Harbor, anti-Japanese sentiment was high in the United States. Although Japanese Americans had shown no disloyalty, many people feared their presence on the West Coast. However, other reasons influenced the decision to intern Japanese Americans. Politicians attempted to garner popular support by appealing to pre-existing racial prejudice against Asians, and farmers and businesspeople hoped to benefit from removing Japanese American competitors.

from Farewell to Manzanar

looks, her remoteness. In Ocean Park my teacher had been a kind, grandmotherly woman who used to sail with us in Papa's boat from time to time and who wept the day we had to leave. In Boyle Heights the teacher felt cold and distant. I was confused by all the moving and was having trouble with the classwork, but she would never help me out. She would have nothing to do with me.

This was the first time I had felt outright hostility from a Caucasian. Looking back, it is easy enough to explain. Public attitudes toward the Japanese in California were shifting rapidly. In the first few months of the Pacific war, America was on the run. Tolerance had turned to distrust and <u>irrational</u> fear. The hundred-year-old tradition of anti-Orientalism on the west coast soon resurfaced, more vicious than ever. Its result became clear about a month later, when we were told to make our third and final move.

The name Manzanar meant nothing to us when we left Boyle Heights. We didn't know where it was or what it was. We went because the government ordered us to. And, in the case of my older brothers and sisters, we went with a certain amount of relief. They had all heard stories of Japanese homes being attacked, of beatings in the streets of California towns. They were as frightened of the Caucasians as Caucasians were of us. Moving, under what appeared to be government protection, to an area less directly threatened by the war seemed not such a bad idea at all. For some it actually sounded like a fine adventure.

Our pickup point was a Buddhist church in Los Angeles. It was very early, and misty, when we got there with our luggage. Mama had bought heavy coats for all of us. She

grew up in eastern Washington and knew that anywhere inland in early April would be cold. I was proud of my new coat, and I remember sitting on a duffel bag trying to be friendly with the Greyhound driver. I smiled at him. He didn't smile back. He was befriending no one. Someone tied a numbered tag to my collar and to the duffel bag (each family was given a number, and that became our official <u>designation</u> until the camps were closed), someone else passed out box lunches for the trip, and we climbed aboard.

I had never been outside Los Angeles County, never traveled more than ten miles from the coast, had never even ridden on a bus. I was full of excitement, the way any kid would be, and wanted to look out the window. But for the first few hours the shades were drawn. Around me other people played cards, read magazines, dozed, waiting. I settled back, waiting too, and finally fell asleep. The bus felt very secure to me. Almost half its passengers were immediate relatives. Mama and my older brothers had succeeded in keeping most of us together, on the same bus, headed for the same camp. I didn't realize until much later what a job that was. The strategy had been, first, to have everyone living in the same district when the evacuation began, and then to get all of us included under the same family number, even though names had been changed by marriage. Many families weren't as lucky as ours and suffered months of anguish while trying to arrange transfers from one camp to another.

We rode all day. By the time we reached our destination, the shades were up. It was late afternoon. The first thing I saw was a

H

Vocabulary
irrational (i rash′ ən əl) *adj.* contrary to reason; illogical
designation (dez′ ig nā′ shən) *n.* a distinguishing name or mark

Teaching Options

Listening and Speaking *Minilesson*

Interviewing Review with students these basics of interviewing:
- Contact the person you want to interview and explain your purpose and the types of questions you plan to ask.
- Give your full attention to the person you are interviewing.
- Be respectful and polite. If the person does not wish to discuss a particular question, move on to the next one.

- Be prepared to add new questions as you go along.
- Thank the person at the end of the interview.

Activity Most students will have older relatives, such as grandparents, who can remember World War II. Have students choose a person to interview about the war and prepare a list of questions in

advance. Encourage them to ask about the bombing of Pearl Harbor, Americans' feelings about Japan, and the internment of Japanese Americans. Students may tape record, videotape, or keep a written record of their interviews. Invite them to share their interview highlights with the class. **L2**

Jeanne Wakatsuki Houston
and James D. Houston ∾

yellow swirl across a blurred, reddish setting sun. The bus was being pelted by what sounded like splattering rain. It wasn't rain. This was my first look at something I would soon know very well, a billowing flurry of dust and sand churned up by the wind through Owens Valley.[6]

We drove past a barbed-wire fence, through a gate, and into an open space where trunks and sacks and packages had been dumped from the baggage trucks that drove out ahead of us. I could see a few tents set up, the first rows of black barracks, and beyond them, blurred by sand, rows of barracks that seemed to spread for miles across this plain. People were sitting on cartons or milling around, with their backs to the wind, waiting to see which friends or relatives might be on this bus. As we approached, they turned or stood up, and some moved toward us expectantly. But inside the bus no one stirred. No one waved or spoke. They just stared out the windows, ominously silent. I didn't understand this. Hadn't we finally arrived, our whole family intact? I opened a window, leaned out, and yelled happily. "Hey! This whole bus is full of Wakatsukis!"

Outside, the greeters smiled. Inside there was an explosion of laughter, hysterical, tension-breaking laughter that left my brothers choking and whacking each other across the shoulders.

We had pulled up just in time for dinner. The mess halls[7] weren't completed yet. An outdoor chow line snaked around a half-finished building that broke a good part of the wind. They issued us

army mess kits, the round metal kind that fold over, and plopped in scoops of canned Vienna sausage, canned string beans, steamed rice that had been cooked too long, and on top of the rice a serving of canned apricots. The Caucasian servers were thinking that the fruit poured over rice would make a good dessert. Among the Japanese, of course, rice is never eaten with sweet foods, only with salty or savory foods. Few of us could eat such a mixture. But at this point no one dared protest. It would have been impolite. I was horrified when I saw the apricot syrup seeping through my little mound of rice. I opened my mouth to complain. My mother jabbed me in the back to keep quiet. We moved on through the line and joined the others squatting in the lee[8] of half-raised walls, dabbing courteously at what was, for almost everyone there, an inedible concoction.

After dinner we were taken to Block 16, a cluster of fifteen barracks that had just been finished a day or so earlier—although finished was hardly the word for it. The shacks were built of one thickness of pine planking covered with tarpaper. They sat on concrete footings, with about two feet of open space between the floorboards and the ground. Gaps showed between the planks, and as the weeks passed and the green wood dried out, the gaps widened. Knotholes gaped in the uncovered floor.

Each barracks was divided into six units, sixteen by twenty feet, about the size of a living room, with one bare bulb hanging from

Did You Know?
A soldier in the field eats from a *mess kit*, which is a metal container that holds eating utensils and opens into a plate with two compartments.

---

6. Manzanar was built in *Owens Valley*, near Death Valley, about two hundred miles north of Los Angeles.

7. In the army, a *mess hall* is the place where meals are eaten.

8. *Lee* is shelter or protection, especially on the side of something facing away from the wind.

I Active Reading

QUESTION Ask students why the people in the bus suddenly burst into uncontrollable laughter. *(The passengers were relieved to have the journey's tense silence broken by the narrator's innocent enthusiasm.)*

J Active Reading

CONNECT Ask students to think of similar examples of food dishes in American or other cultures that would be considered inappropriate or unappetizing.

K Literary Elements

AUTOBIOGRAPHY Reread the description of the barracks and their rooms. Then ask students how this description would be different if it had been written for an encyclopedia article about the camps instead for an autobiography. *(The article would include details about number and size and perhaps about building materials, but it would probably not give information about the poor construction, the barren appearance, or people's reaction to the barracks.)*

MEETING INDIVIDUAL NEEDS — MULTIPLE LEARNING STYLES

Logical-Mathematical Logical-mathematically oriented students can connect to the story with an activity that involves facts and numbers.

Activity Have students use an atlas and almanac or the Internet to research the geographical features and climate of Owens Valley, California, where Manzanar was built. Have them find out the altitude and typical weather patterns in each season to determine what conditions were like for the narrator and other internees at Manzanar. Ask them to compare these to conditions in L.A. Encourage students to present their findings graphically and display them for the class. Then ask them how this new information affects their understanding of the selection. **L3**

Teaching Options

Japanese Americans en route to internment camp. Library of Congress.

Viewing the photograph: What atmosphere does the photograph convey? What word would you use to describe these children's and adults' reactions upon arriving at the camp?

---

the ceiling and an oil stove for heat. We were assigned two of these for the twelve people in our family group; and our official family "number" was enlarged by three digits—16 plus the number of this barracks. We were issued steel army cots, two brown army blankets each, and some mattress covers, which my brothers stuffed with straw.

The first task was to divide up what space we had for sleeping. Bill and Woody contributed a blanket each and partitioned off the first room: one side for Bill and Tomi, one side for Woody and Chizu and their baby girl. Woody also got the stove, for heating formulas.

The people who had it hardest during the first few months were young couples like these, many of whom had married just before the evacuation began, in order not to be separated and sent to different camps. Our two rooms

were crowded, but at least it was all in the family. My oldest sister and her husband were shoved into one of those sixteen-by-twenty-foot compartments with six people they had never seen before—two other couples, one recently married like themselves, the other with two teenage boys. Partitioning off a room like that wasn't easy. It was bitter cold when we arrived, and the wind did not abate.[9] All they had to use for room dividers were those army blankets, two of which were barely enough to keep one person warm. They argued over whose blanket should be sacrificed and later argued about noise at night—the parents wanted their boys asleep by 9:00 P.M.—and they continued arguing over matters like that

---

9. The fact that the wind did not *abate* means that it did not lessen in force or intensity.

466 ❦ UNIT 2

for six months, until my sister and her husband left to harvest sugar beets in Idaho. It was grueling[10] work up there, and wages were pitiful, but when the call came through camp for workers to alleviate the wartime labor shortage, it sounded better than their life at Manzanar. They knew they'd have, if nothing else, a room, perhaps a cabin of their own.

That first night in Block 16, the rest of us squeezed into the second room—Granny, Lillian, age fourteen, Ray, thirteen, May, eleven, Kiyo, ten, Mama, and me. I didn't mind this at all at the time. Being youngest meant I got to sleep with Mama. And before we went to bed I had a great time jumping up and down on the mattress. The boys had stuffed so much straw into hers, we had to flatten it some so we wouldn't slide off. I slept with her every night after that until Papa came back.

We woke early, shivering and coated with dust that had blown up through the knotholes and in through the slits around the doorway. During the night Mama had unpacked all our clothes and heaped them on our beds for warmth. Now our cubicle looked as if a great laundry bag had exploded and then been sprayed with fine dust. A skin of sand covered the floor. I looked over Mama's shoulder at Kiyo, on top of his fat mattress, buried under jeans and overcoats and sweaters. His eyebrows were gray, and he was starting to giggle. He was looking at me, at my gray eyebrows and coated hair, and pretty soon we were both giggling. I looked at Mama's face to see if she thought Kiyo was funny. She lay very still next to me on our mattress, her eyes scanning everything—

___

10. *Grueling* work is very difficult, exhausting work.

bare rafters, walls, dusty kids—scanning slowly, and I think the mask of her face would have cracked had not Woody's voice just then come at us through the wall. He was rapping on the planks as if testing to see if they were hollow.

"Hey!" he yelled. "You guys fall into the same flour barrel as us?"

"No," Kiyo yelled back. "Ours is full of Japs."

All of us laughed at this.

"Well, tell 'em it's time to get up," Woody said. "If we're gonna live in this place, we better get to work."

He gave us ten minutes to dress, then he came in carrying a broom, a hammer, and a sack full of tin can lids he had scrounged somewhere. Woody would be our leader for a while now, short, stocky, grinning behind his mustache. He had just turned twenty-four. In later years he would tour the country with Mr. Moto, the Japanese tag-team wrestler, as his sinister assistant Suki—karate chops through the ropes from outside the ring, a chunky leg reaching from under his kimono to trip up Mr. Moto's foe. In the ring Woody's smile looked sly and crafty; he hammed it up. Offstage it was whimsical, as if some joke were bursting to be told.

"Hey, brother Ray, Kiyo," he said. "You see these tin can lids?"

"Yeah, yeah," the boys said drowsily, as if going back to sleep. They were both young versions of Woody.

"You see all them knotholes in the floor and in the walls?"

They looked around. You could see about a dozen.

Woody said, "You get those covered up before breakfast time. Any more sand comes in here through one of them knotholes, you have to eat it off the floor with ketchup."

Vocabulary

alleviate (ə lē′ vē āt′) *v.* to make easier to bear; relieve; lessen
whimsical (hwim′ zi kəl) *adj.* fanciful; curiously humorous

NONFICTION 🐚 467

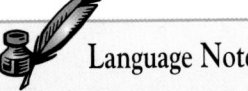

VIEWING THE PHOTOGRAPH

The composition, or arrangement, of a photograph, draws the viewer into the picture. In this photograph, strong vertical and horizontal lines highlight the starkness of the room.

Viewing Response *Students may say that life in the camps was crowded and spartan.*

from Farewell to Manzanar

"What about sand that comes in through the cracks?" Kiyo said.

Woody stood up very straight, which in itself was funny, since he was only about five-foot-six.

"Don't worry about the cracks," he said. "Different kind of sand comes in through the cracks."

He put his hands on his hips and gave Kiyo a sternly comic look, squinting at him through one eye the way Papa would when he was asserting his authority. Woody mimicked Papa's voice: "And I can tell the difference. So be careful."

The boys laughed and went to work nailing down lids. May started sweeping out the sand. I was helping Mama fold the

clothes we'd used for cover, when Woody came over and put his arm around her shoulder. He was short; she was even shorter, under five feet.

He said softly, "You okay, Mama?"

She didn't look at him, she just kept folding clothes and said, "Can we get the cracks covered too, Woody?"

Outside the sky was clear, but icy gusts of wind were buffeting our barracks every few minutes, sending fresh dust puffs up through the floorboards. May's broom could barely keep up with it, and our oil heater could scarcely hold its own against the drafts.

"We'll get this whole place as tight as a barrel, Mama. I already met a guy who told me where they pile all the scrap lumber."

Viewing the photograph: What does this photograph say about life in the internment camp?

Teaching Options

INTERDISCIPLINARY CONNECTION

Geography The narrator tells about several places she and her family lived, all within California. Conduct the following activity to help orient students to places named in the selection and give them practice reading maps.

Activity Divide the class into small groups, giving each group a map of California (use photocopies from an atlas). Have students work together to list all the places the narrator mentions

throughout the selection, starting with Inglewood and ending with Owens Valley, the location of Manzanar. Then have them find and mark each location on the map, drawing an arrow to show the progression of moves. Have groups check each other's maps for accuracy. **L1 COLLAB. LEARN.**

Jeanne Wakatsuki Houston and James D. Houston ∾

"Scrap?"

"That's all they got. I mean, they're still building the camp, you know. Sixteen blocks left to go. After that, they say maybe we'll get some stuff to fix the insides a little bit."

Her eyes blazed then, her voice quietly furious. "Woody, we can't live like this. Animals live like this."

It was hard to get Woody down. He'd keep smiling when everybody else was ready to explode. Grief flickered in his eyes. He blinked it away and hugged her tighter. "We'll make it better, Mama. You watch."

We could hear voices in other cubicles now. Beyond the wall Woody's baby girl started to cry.

"I have to go over to the kitchen," he said, "see if those guys got a pot for heating bottles. That oil stove takes too long—something wrong with the fuel line. I'll find out what they're giving us for breakfast."

"Probably hotcakes with soy sauce," Kiyo said, on his hands and knees between the bunks.

"No." Woody grinned, heading out the door. "Rice. With Log Cabin Syrup and melted butter."

I don't remember what we ate that first morning. I know we stood for half an hour in cutting wind waiting to get our food. Then we took it back to the cubicle and ate huddled around the stove. Inside, it was warmer than when we left, because Woody was already making good his promise to Mama, tacking up some ends of lath[11] he'd found, stuffing rolled paper around the door frame.

Trouble was, he had almost nothing to work with. Beyond this temporary weather stripping, there was little else he could do.

---

11. In construction, *lath* is any of the thin, narrow strips of wood used as a foundation for plaster or tiles.

Months went by, in fact, before our "home" changed much at all from what it was the day we moved in—bare floors, blanket partitions, one bulb in each compartment dangling from a roof beam, and open ceilings overhead so that mischievous boys like Ray and Kiyo could climb up into the rafters and peek into anyone's life.

The simple truth is the camp was no more ready for us when we got there than we were ready for it. We had only the dimmest ideas of what to expect. Most of the families, like us, had moved out from southern California with as much luggage as each person could carry. Some old men left Los Angeles wearing Hawaiian shirts and Panama hats and stepped off the bus at an altitude of 4000 feet, with nothing available but sagebrush and tarpaper to stop the April winds pouring down off the back side of the Sierras.[12]

The War Department was in charge of all the camps at this point. They began to issue military surplus from the First World War—olive-drab knit caps, earmuffs, peacoats, canvas leggings. Later on, sewing machines were shipped in, and one barracks was turned into a clothing factory. An old seamstress took a peacoat of mine, tore the lining out, opened and flattened the sleeves, added a collar, put arm holes in and handed me back a beautiful cape. By fall dozens of seamstresses were working full-time transforming thousands of these old army clothes into capes, slacks and

Did You Know?
A *peacoat* is a double-breasted jacket of thick woolen cloth, worn especially by sailors.

---

12. The *Sierras,* or Sierra Nevada Mountains, run through eastern California. Manzanar was between these mountains and Death Valley.

O Literary Elements

DIALOGUE The conversation between Woody and Mama should give students some insight into their relationship. *(Mama depends on Woody to take responsibility and reassure her, and he fulfills that role by taking charge and staying positive.)*

P Critical Thinking

INFERRING Ask students what particular worries Woody is facing. *(In addition to helping his mother and siblings, he and his wife have to keep their baby warm and fed.)*

Q Literary Elements

NARRATIVE DETAILS The narrator says, "The camp was no more ready for us when we got there than we were ready for it." Ask students to identify narrative details that support this statement. *(The barracks were uninsulated and underfurnished. There were not enough of them. The internees came from warm climates wearing light clothing and bringing only what they could carry. Not much suitable clothing was available at the camps.)*

MEETING INDIVIDUAL NEEDS — GIFTED AND TALENTED

Life in the Camps Explain to students that all ten of the internment camps were built like Manzanar and located in unpopulated areas in climates that could be quite extreme, some harsher than Manzanar's. Yet, despite their living conditions, many of the people in these camps found creative ways to keep their lives active and meaningful, such as starting schools and publishing newspapers.

Activity Have students research to learn more about the resourceful ways that interned Japanese Americans created culture and meaning in their lives despite their circumstances. Have them share their findings with the class. **L3**

R Literary Elements

SENSORY IMAGERY The narrator describes herself and others in the camp as "a band of Charlie Chaplins" because of the oversized clothes they wore. This conjures a humorous, clownish visual image.

Language Note

Make sure students understand that the shots the narrator received were immunizations. Explain that an immunization shot exposes recipients to a small dose of the disease so that they develop antibodies to fight the disease, or antigen, if they come into contact with it again. In this case, the shots contained overly high dosages of the disease, making people sick.

S Active Reading

RESPOND Ask students what part of life in Manzanar they think they would have found most difficult and why. *(Some students may say the lack of privacy; others may say the spoiled food and constant illness.)*

---

from *Farewell to Manzanar*

stylish coats. But until that factory got going and packages from friends outside began to fill out our wardrobes, warmth was more important than style. I couldn't help laughing at Mama walking around in army earmuffs and a pair of wide-cuffed, khaki-colored wool trousers several sizes too big for her. Japanese are generally smaller than Caucasians, and almost all these clothes were oversize. They flopped, they dangled, they hung.

R

Did You Know?
The great actor and director *Charlie Chaplin* gained fame for his role as a tramp in baggy pants in a series of movies in the 1920s.

It seems comical, looking back; we were a band of Charlie Chaplins marooned in the California desert. But at the time, it was pure chaos. That's the only way to describe it. The evacuation had been so hurriedly planned, the camps so hastily thrown together, nothing was completed when we got there, and almost nothing worked.

S I was sick continually, with stomach cramps and diarrhea. At first it was from the shots they gave us for typhoid, in very heavy doses and in assembly-line fashion: swab, jab, swab, *Move along now*, swab, jab, swab, *Keep it moving.* That knocked all of us younger kids down at once, with fevers and vomiting. Later, it was the food that made us sick, young and old alike. The kitchens were too small and badly ventilated. Food would spoil from being left out too long. That summer, when the heat got fierce, it would spoil faster. The refrigeration kept breaking down. The cooks, in many cases, had never cooked before. Each block had to provide its own volunteers. Some were lucky and had a professional or two in their midst. But the first chef in our block had been a gardener all his

life and suddenly found himself preparing three meals a day for 250 people.

"The Manzanar runs" became a condition of life, and you only hoped that when you rushed to the latrine, one would be in working order.

That first morning, on our way to the chow line, Mama and I tried to use the women's latrine in our block. The smell of it spoiled what little appetite we had. Outside, men were working in an open trench, up to their knees in muck—a common sight in the months to come. Inside, the floor was covered with excrement, and all twelve bowls were erupting like a row of tiny volcanoes.

Mama stopped a kimono-wrapped woman stepping past us with her sleeve pushed up against her nose and asked, "What do you do?"

"Try Block Twelve," the woman said, grimacing. "They have just finished repairing the pipes."

It was about two city blocks away. We followed her over there and found a line of women waiting in the wind outside the latrine. We had no choice but to join the line and wait with them.

Inside it was like all the other latrines. Each block was built to the same design, just as each of the ten camps, from California to Arkansas, was built to a common master plan. It was an open room, over a concrete slab. The sink was a long metal trough against one wall, with a row of spigots for hot and cold water. Down the center of the room twelve toilet bowls were arranged in six pairs, back to back, with no partitions. My mother was a very modest person, and this was going to be agony for her, sitting down in public, among strangers.

One old woman had already solved the problem for herself by dragging in a large cardboard carton. She set it up around one of the bowls, like a three-sided screen. OXYDOL was

S

Grammar and Language *Minilesson*

Dashes Write this sentence on the board: *We were up to our knees in muck—a common sight.* Point out the dash and ask what it is called. Explain that a dash is used in two different ways and that students will work together to determine what those two ways are.

Activity Have pairs of students find examples of dashes in the selection and

tell what purpose each dash serves. Discuss students' conclusions. On the board, write these two rules for using dashes.

1. Use a dash to indicate an abrupt change in a sentence.
2. Use a dash to set off explanatory matter.

Let the student pairs compare their results with these rules. **L3** **COLLAB. LEARN.**

Additional Resources

📖 *Grammar and Language Transparency 39*

📕 *Grammar and Language Workbook,* p. 267

📕 *Grammar and Composition Handbook,* Lesson 11.7

📕 *Writer's Choice,* Lesson 21.7

Jeanne Wakatsuki Houston and James D. Houston ➷

printed in large black letters down the front. I remember this well, because that was the soap we were issued for laundry; later on, the smell of it would permeate these rooms. The upended carton was about four feet high. The old woman behind it wasn't much taller. When she stood, only her head showed over the top.

 She was about Granny's age. With great effort she was trying to fold the sides of the screen together. Mama happened to be at the head of the line now. As she approached the vacant bowl, she and the old woman bowed to each other from the waist. Mama then moved to help her with the carton, and the old woman said very graciously, in Japanese, "Would you like to use it?"

Happily, gratefully, Mama bowed again and said, "*Arigato*" (Thank you). "*Arigato gozaimas*" (Thank you very much). "I will return it to your barracks."

"Oh, no. It is not necessary. I will be glad to wait."

The old woman unfolded one side of the cardboard, while Mama opened the other; then she bowed again and scurried out the door.

Those big cartons were a common sight in the spring of 1942. Eventually sturdier partitions appeared, one or two at a time. The first were built of scrap lumber. Word would get around that Block such and such

shikata ga nai, this cannot be helped

had partitions now, and Mama and my older sisters would walk halfway across the camp to use them. Even after every latrine in camp was screened, this quest for privacy continued. Many would wait until late at night. Ironically, because of this, midnight was often the most crowded time of all.

Like so many of the women there, Mama never did get used to the latrines. It was a humiliation she just learned to endure: *shikata ga nai*, this cannot be helped. She would quickly subordinate her own desires to those of the family or the community, because she knew cooperation was the only way to survive. At the same time she placed a high premium on personal privacy, respected it in others and insisted upon it for herself. Almost everyone at Manzanar had inherited this pair of traits from the generations before them who had learned to live in a small, crowded country like Japan. Because of the first they were able to take a desolate stretch of wasteland and gradually make it livable. But the entire situation there, especially in the beginning—the packed sleeping quarters, the communal mess halls, the open toilets—all this was an open insult to that other, private self, a slap in the face you were powerless to challenge.

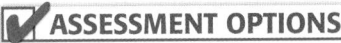

Vocabulary
subordinate (sə bôr′də nāt′) *v.* to cause to be, or treat as, secondary, inferior, or less important

---

Reading *Minilesson*

Identifying Spatial Relationships

Explain that readers often need to analyze the relative positions of people, places, and things in a story. On pages 465–466, the narrator describes the size of the internment camp's living areas and the number of residents in them.

Activity Encourage students to visualize a 16-by-20-foot space. Have them name spaces of a similar size such as a living room. Have them measure and mark off a 16-by-20-foot space in the classroom. Place desks in the space to stand as seven beds, and have seven students occupy the space. Discuss what life must have felt like in such close quarters. **L2**

Additional Resources
📁 *Reading Workbook,* p. 50

Responding to Literature

Personal Response

ANALYZING LITERATURE

1. They live in a shack, Mama works odd hours in a canning factory, and the narrator and her brother are bullied by local children.
2. Anti-Japanese sentiment becomes common. The family is taken to Manzanar, an internment camp in California.
3. The mess halls are under construction, the food is poor, and the barracks are drafty, cold, and mostly unfurnished.
4. They partition parts of rooms and seal up holes in the barracks' walls and floors for warmth and cleanliness.
5. Privacy is highly valued in Japanese culture as a way to help people live together in a small, crowded country.
6. The Terminal Islanders live in a ghetto and identify strongly with their Japanese ancestry. They probably feel excluded from American culture and have little tolerance for people unlike themselves.
7. She is excited to be traveling on a bus for the first time. Unlike the adults, she does not understand the implications of what is happening.
8. The small and poorly furnished living quarters, inadequate heat, and poor food indicate that the people in charge do not understand or care much about even the basic needs of the internees.
9. Humor helps relieve tension and keeps people positive. Woody's jokes about the sand reassure his family that they can handle their situation.
10. It symbolizes personal dignity, as she endeavors to reclaim her privacy. It also symbolizes adjustment, as she finds a way to cope with her situation.
11. Writing about her traumatic experience has helped her come to terms with it. People reading her story are likely to help prevent a similar violation of civil rights from happening again.
12. Some students may say they admire Woody because he takes charge and remains positive; others may admire Mama for holding her family together throughout all their moves

Personal Response

Did this account of the treatment of Japanese Americans during World War II shock or surprise you? Share your reactions with your classmates.

ANALYZING LITERATURE

RECALL

1. Describe what life on Terminal Island is like for the narrator and her family.
2. How do public attitudes toward the Japanese change during the family's stay in Boyle Heights? Where does the family go next? Why?
3. Describe the living conditions the Wakatsukis encounter when they first arrive at the camp.
4. How do the people interned at Manzanar make it more livable?
5. According to the narrator, why is privacy so important to the people living at the camp?

INTERPRET

6. Why do you think the Terminal Islanders treat "outsiders" as they do?
7. How does the narrator's attitude during the bus trip differ from that of her adult relatives? What do you think accounts for this difference?
8. What do the living conditions at the camp seem to suggest about the attitudes of the people who are in charge of the facility? Explain.
9. How does humor help the Wakatsukis cope with their situation? Give specific examples.
10. What might the old woman's cardboard carton **symbolize**, or stand for? Explain your response.

EVALUATE AND CONNECT

11. **Theme Connections** Reread the biography of the Houstons on page 459. How has remembering Manzanar helped Jeanne Wakatsuki Houston? How might others benefit from sharing her memories?
12. Which character in the selection do you admire the most? the least? Give reasons for your answer.
13. *Shikata ga nai* means "It cannot be helped. It must be done." To what situations in your own life might this expression apply? Explain.
14. What lesson or lessons about prejudice do you think this selection teaches? Explain.
15. The U.S. government has acknowledged that the internment of Japanese Americans was a mistake. Do you think this kind of mistake could happen again? Why or why not?

Literary ELEMENTS

Autobiography

An **autobiography** is a person's account of his or her own life. In most autobiographies, the writer tells the story from the first-person point of view, using the pronoun *I*. The use of this point of view makes most autobiographies very personal and subjective. In *Farewell to Manzanar,* for example, Jeanne Wakatsuki Houston gives a personal account of her experiences at an internment camp. She describes not only the events that occurred, but also her reactions to those events. For example, she describes the apricot and rice dessert served at the camp as "an inedible concoction." This description helps the reader understand the cultural gap that seems to exist between the Caucasians running the camp and the Japanese Americans who are interned there.

1. List some details from the selection that you would not find in a more objective source, such as an encyclopedia. How do these details help you better understand this episode in U.S. history?
2. How might this account be different if it were written from the point of view of one of the Caucasians working at the camp? Explain.

● See **Literary Terms Handbook,** p. R2.

and struggles; still others may admire the narrator for having the courage to tell her story. Students may dislike the dealer who tried to take advantage of Mama's need for money, or the teacher in Boyle Heights who wanted nothing to do with the author.
13. Students should describe the situation and explain how the expression applies to it.
14. It demonstrates the injustice, cruelty, and destructiveness of prejudice.
15. Students should realize that anywhere there is prejudice and intolerance there can be injustice and loss of civil rights for a group of people.

LITERARY ELEMENTS

1. Personal details, such as Mama breaking her valuable china and the children waking up in the barracks with dust on their eyebrows, help readers understand in a direct way what the experience was like.
2. The account might lack an intimate understanding of and empathy for the losses and humiliations that the Japanese Americans endured.

Additional Resources

 Literary Elements Transparency 39

LITERATURE AND WRITING

Writing About Literature

Analyze Setting In *Farewell to Manzanar,* the narrator describes the different settings in which the events of the selection occur. Briefly describe each setting, and then compare and contrast the different places in which the narrator's family lived in 1941 and 1942. Which place does the narrator seem to like best? least? Why? Share your analysis with several classmates.

Creative Writing

It's Not Fair! Reread your response to the Focus Activity on page 459. Now imagine that you and your family, like the Wakatsukis, are being forced to move because of your ethnic background. Write a letter to your congressional representative in which you protest the injustice of this situation. Explain your position clearly, but avoid abusive language. Be sure to use the proper form for a business letter.

EXTENDING YOUR RESPONSE

Literature Groups

Compare Passages Identify a passage in the selection that you found particularly powerful or moving. Share the passage with your group, as well as your reasons for choosing it. Discuss how each passage chosen helps to illuminate what Jeanne Wakatsuki Houston has called "an extraordinary episode in American history." Compare your group's choices with those of another group.

Interdisciplinary Activity

Music: Song Lyrics Protest songs are a traditional vehicle for responding to injustice. Write the lyrics of a song protesting the unjust treatment of Japanese Americans during World War II. Set your lyrics to music, if you wish, and perform your song for the class.

Internet Connection

Manzanar Today Manzanar is now a National Historic Site under the administration of the National Park Service. Create a list of questions about Manzanar. For example, you might ask what is being done to preserve this camp and to honor the people once interned there? Use the Internet to find answers to these questions. Then, with a group, create a multimedia display that presents what you have discovered.

Reading Further

If you'd like to read more about Japanese Americans during World War II, you might enjoy these works:

Nonfiction: *Behind Barbed Wire: The Imprisonment of Japanese Americans During World War II,* by Daniel S. Davis, looks at the factors that led to the internment of Japanese Americans.

Interviews: *And Justice for All,* by John Tateishi, contains Japanese Americans' accounts of their experiences in relocation camps.

 Save your work for your portfolio.

Memorial at the Manzanar National Historic Site.

LITERATURE AND WRITING

Writing About Literature

Students' analyses should
- describe each setting of the selection.
- compare and contrast the different places that the narrator's family lived.
- analyze which places the narrator liked best and least and why.

Creative Writing

Students' letters should
- clearly state the causes of the protest.
- support the protest by citing violations of law, policy, or custom.
- use civil and coherent language.

EXTENDING YOUR RESPONSE

Literature Groups After students share their chosen passages, encourage groups to decide if they think Houston's story is "an extraordinary episode in American history." Have them share their conclusions with the class. **COLLAB. LEARN.**

Interdisciplinary Activity You may want to bring in examples of protest songs, such as antiwar folk songs of the 1960s, to share with the class. 📦

Internet Connection You might suggest that students include articles, photographs, quotations, dioramas, drawings, statistics, personal responses, and music in their multimedia displays. 📦

✔ ASSESSMENT OPTIONS

📁 *Quick Checks,* p. 39

📁 *Selection and Theme Assessment,* pp. 75–76

📁 *Performance Assessment,* p. 38

💾 *Testmaker*

GRAMMAR AND LANGUAGE
Intervening Prepositional Phrases

Practice

1. The plates in the velvet-lined box are valuable.
2. The aroma from the many foods on the table makes my mouth water.
3. OK
4. The noises in our barrack sound strange to us.
5. The people from that bus live in this barrack.

READING AND THINKING
Summarizing

When Mama and the narrator try to use the latrine in their block, it is out of order. A woman tells them the latrine in Block Twelve is working, so they go there. They wait in a long line and find that the latrine has no partitions for privacy. One woman uses a large carton for privacy, and she lets Mama use it. Soon many women use similar cartons, until privacy screens are provided for all the latrines. Mama never gets used to the lack of privacy in the camp.

VOCABULARY
Parts of Speech

Possible answers:
1. restrictive or snobbish
2. relief from
3. fanciful notions
4. male-headed group
5. restrict
6. repression

Additional Practice

📕 *Grammar and Composition Handbook,* Lesson 6.2

📕 *Grammar and Language Workbook,* p. 163

📕 *Writer's Choice,* Lesson 16.2

📂 *Reading Workbook,* p. 50

📂 *Vocabulary Practice,* p. 38

Responding to Literature

GRAMMAR AND LANGUAGE • Intervening Prepositional Phrases

A verb must agree with its subject in person and number. Sometimes, however, prepositional phrases intervene between the subject and verb. Make sure you don't mistake a word in the prepositional phrase for the subject. The object of a preposition is never the subject of a sentence.

Look at these examples. The subjects and verbs have been underlined.

The <u>food</u> from the kitchens <u>makes</u> the children sick.

<u>Knotholes</u> in the wall <u>let</u> the wind blow through the cabin.

● For information about similar usage problems, see **Language Handbook,** pp. R17–R19.

PRACTICE Some of the following sentences lack subject-verb agreement. Rewrite those sentences correctly on your paper. Write *OK* if a sentence is correct.

1. The plates in the velvet-lined box is valuable.
2. The aroma from the many foods on the table make my mouth water.
3. Only one of the spigots works.
4. The noises in our barrack sounds strange to us.
5. The people from that bus lives in this barrack.

APPLY Review a piece of your recent writing, looking for a lack of subject-verb agreement. Revise if necessary.

READING AND THINKING • Summarizing

You can track the plot and understand how events in a story relate to each other by stopping every so often and **summarizing**. When you summarize, you briefly state in your own words the important points of what you've read. For example, the following sentences summarize the first part of the excerpt from *Farewell to Manzanar.*

When Papa disappeared in December of 1941, Mama moved the family from Ocean Park to Terminal Island, a company town where everyone worked for the canneries. Their house was a shack in a ghetto. Every day the speaker and her brother lived in fear of encounters with the mean, threatening kids who lived there.

PRACTICE Write a summary of the events that occur from that first morning when Mama and the speaker try to use the women's latrine in their block to the end of the excerpt from *Farewell to Manzanar.* Ask yourself who, what, where, why, and when questions to come up with a good summary.

● For more about related comprehension skills, see **Reading Handbook,** pp. R82–R84.

VOCABULARY • Parts of Speech

When one word is modified to serve as a different part of speech, it still carries the central part of its meaning with it. So, when you learn one new word, you usually have a significant head start on understanding all the other forms of that word. For example, as a modified version of the word *patriarch,* the adjective *patriarchal* has much the same meaning.

PRACTICE Use your knowledge of the vocabulary words in *Farewell to Manzanar* to figure out the meanings of the underlined words below. For each, write either a synonym or a brief explanation of what the word means.

1. an <u>exclusive</u> club
2. <u>alleviation</u> of pain
3. a dislike of <u>whimsy</u>
4. organized as a <u>patriarchy</u>
5. to <u>intern</u> during wartime
6. her <u>subordination</u> of her own wishes

MEDIA Connection

Government Document

In 1976 President Gerald Ford officially terminated Executive Order 9066, which had permitted the U.S. government to force more than one hundred thousand Japanese Americans to live in internment camps during World War II.

Termination of Executive Order 9066
An American Promise

In this Bicentennial Year, we are commemorating the anniversary dates of many of the great events in American history. An honest reckoning, however, must include a recognition of our national mistakes as well as our national achievements. Learning from our mistakes is not pleasant, but as a great philosopher once admonished, we must do so if we want to avoid repeating them.

February 19th is the anniversary of a sad day in American history. It was on that date in 1942, in the midst of the response to the hostilities that began on December 7, 1941, that Executive Order No. 9066 was issued, subsequently enforced by the criminal penalties of a statute enacted March 21, 1942, resulting in the uprooting of loyal Americans. Over one hundred thousand persons of Japanese ancestry were removed from their homes, detained in special camps, and eventually relocated. . . .

We now know what we should have known then—not only was that evacuation wrong, but Japanese Americans were and are loyal Americans. . . . The Executive Order that was issued on February 19, 1942, was for the sole purpose of prosecuting the war with the Axis Powers, and ceased to be effective with the end of those hostilities. Because there was no formal statement of its termination, however, there is concern among many Japanese Americans that there may yet be some life in that obsolete document. I think it appropriate, in this our Bicentennial Year, to remove all doubt on that matter, and to make clear our commitment in the future.

Now, therefore, I, Gerald R. Ford, President of the United States of America, do hereby proclaim that all the authority conferred by Executive Order No. 9066 terminated upon the issuance of Proclamation No. 2714, which formally proclaimed cessation of the hostilities of World War II on December 31, 1946.

I call upon the American people to affirm with me this American Promise—that we have learned from the tragedy of that long-ago experience forever to treasure liberty and justice for each individual American, and resolve that this kind of action shall never again be repeated.

Gerald R. Ford
The White House, 1976

Respond

1. What is the "American Promise" that President Ford made?

2. If you had spent time in an internment camp for Japanese Americans, how do you think you might react to this document?

MEDIA Connection

Objective

- To understand a government document

Literature LINK

Farewell to Manzanar The government document issued by President Ford terminated Executive Order 9066, which made it legal to evacuate and intern Japanese Americans, such as the Wakatsuki family in the autobiography *Farewell to Manzanar* (pages 460–471). For 30 years after the war, the executive order was still legally binding and could have been enforced again.

Respond

1. The promise is to never repeat the kind of violation of civil rights that occurred as a result of Executive Order 9066.

2. Some students may say they would feel relieved or vindicated. Others may say that the document would not mean much to them because it could not make up for what was done to them.

Additional Resources

📁 *Media Connection Activities,* p. 10

Teaching Options

Reading *Minilesson*

Summarizing Summarizing can be especially useful in understanding less accessible forms of nonfiction, such as government documents, which are often written in a technical or formal style.

Activity Have pairs of students write a short summary of each paragraph of President Ford's "Termination of Executive Order 9066: An American Promise."

Explain that they should briefly identify the main idea of each paragraph. You may want to pair more-advanced readers with less-proficient readers. **L1 COLLAB. LEARN.**

Additional Resources

📁 *Reading Workbook*

Grammar Link

Objective

- To recognize and use appropriate subject-verb agreement in sentences

Teaching Strategies

In order for students to understand subject-verb agreement, they must be able to identify subjects and verbs in sentences. You may want to begin this lesson by briefly reviewing these terms. Write some simple sentences, perhaps from a selection students have read recently, on the board and have them identify the subject(s) and verb(s) in each sentence. The other important element in subject-verb agreement is recognizing whether the subject is singular or plural. Have students look at each of the subjects they identified in the simple sentences and tell whether it is singular or plural.

Activity

1. fill
2. settles
3. know
4. make

Additional Resources

- *Grammar and Language Workbook,* p. 161
- *Grammar and Composition Handbook,* Lesson 16.1
- *Writer's Choice,* Lesson 16.1

Teaching Options

Grammar Link

Making Sure Subjects and Verbs Agree

In every sentence, the subject and verb must agree; that is, if the subject—the who or what that is doing something—is singular, so is the verb. If the subject is plural, so is the verb. No matter how many words there are in a sentence, a verb agrees *only* with its subject.

Problem 1 A compound subject that is joined by *and*
Rice and canned apricots is not an agreeable dish.
The weather and the food are unfamiliar.

Solution If the parts of the compound subject belong to one unit, or if both parts refer to the same person or thing, use a singular verb. For example, *rice and canned apricots* belong to one unit: the dinner that was served. If the parts of the compound subject do not belong to one unit, use a plural verb. In this sentence *weather* and *food* refer to different things.

Problem 2 A compound subject that is joined by *or* or *nor*
Neither the living conditions nor the lack of privacy is acceptable to Mama.
Either chilling cold, blazing sun, or dusty winds keep us inside.

Solution Make the verb agree with the subject that is closest to it.

Problem 3 A collective noun as the subject
The number of Japanese Americans sent to camps is horrifying.
A number of the residents find ways to deal with various problems.

Solution If the collective noun refers to a group as a whole *(the number)*, use a singular verb. If the collective noun refers to individuals *(a number)*, use a plural verb.

Problem 4 A predicate nominative that differs in number from the subject
The floor is slats of scrap lumber.
Army blankets become a room divider.

Solution If the subject is singular, use a singular verb, even if the predicate nominative is plural. If the subject is plural, but the predicate nominative is singular, use a plural verb.

● For more about subject-verb agreement, see **Language Handbook,** pp. R17–R19.

ACTIVITY

For each sentence, write the correct form of the verb.

1. Boxes and luggage (fills, fill) the car.

2. At Manzanar the family (settles, settle) into two different shacks.

3. Neither Jeanne Wakatsuki nor her brothers (knows, know) what to expect.

4. Clear writing and a child's viewpoint (makes, make) *Farewell to Manzanar* interesting.

Writing *Minilesson*

Sentence Combining Point out that students can add interest to their writing by combining sentences for variety. For example:
We used blankets for warmth. We also used blankets as room dividers.
Could be combined as
We used blankets for warmth and as room dividers.

Activity Have students write five pairs of short, related sentences. Then have students exchange papers with a partner and combine each pair to make one sentence. Remind students to make sure subjects and verbs agree in their new sentences. **L1 COLLAB. LEARN.**

Additional Resources

- *Writer's Choice,* Lesson 8.2

Vo·cab·u·lar·y Skills

Dictionary Skills: Pronunciation

All vowels and some consonants can be pronounced in different ways. Dictionaries get around this problem by "respelling" words. For example, *gigantic* would appear like this: jī gan′tik. The first *g* has the "soft" *g* sound, the same sound that *j* has, so it is respelled as *j*. The second one has the "hard" *g* sound, which is represented by *g*.

Another consonant that can be pronounced two ways is *c*. Since both pronunciations can be represented by other letters, *c* never appears in a dictionary respelling. Instead, *s* or *k* is used, depending on which sound *c* has. Therefore, *circuit* is shown as: sur′kit.

In a dictionary pronunciation guide, a vowel without any symbol represents the normal "short" sound, like the vowels in *sat, set, sit, cot,* and *cut.* Other vowel sounds are shown by symbols, such as a straight line above the vowel to show that it is "long." (Long vowels "say their own names.")

Symbol	Pronunciation
ä	the **ah** sound in **father**
ô	the **aw** sound in **coffee**
oo	the vowel sound in **wood**
o͞o	the vowel sound in **fool**
oi	the vowel sound in **toy**
ou	the **ow** sound in **out**
ə	the vowel sound in the second syllable of **pencil** and **lemon**
hw	**wh** as in **white**
th	**th** as in **thin**
t͟h	**th** as in **this**
zh	the sound made by the **s** in **treasure**

EXERCISE

The words shown below are vocabulary words you have recently studied. Use the pronunciation given for each word to answer the question that follows it.

1. *loll* (lol)   Does this word rhyme with *bowl* or *parasol?*

2. *token* (tō′kən)   Does this word rhyme with *broken, soaking,* or *rockin'?*

3. *prodigious* (prə dij′əs)   Does the second syllable of this word rhyme with *ridge* or *big?*

4. *crucial* (kro͞o′shəl)   Is the first syllable of this word pronounced like *crook, crush,* or *crew?*

5. *judiciously* (jo͞o dish′əs lē)   Does the second syllable of this word rhyme with *sick, wish,* or *bike?*

Objective

- To learn how to use a dictionary pronunciation guide

Teaching Strategies

Encourage students to skim several pages of a dictionary looking at words they already know how to pronounce and noting how the dictionary shows the pronunciations of the words using symbols. This will help them become more familiar with pronunciation symbols and letter patterns.

Exercise

1. parasol
2. broken
3. ridge
4. crew
5. wish

Additional Resources

📁 *Vocabulary Power: Weekly Lessons and Activities*

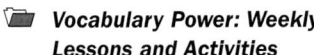

ENGLISH LANGUAGE LEARNERS

English Pronunciation Review the pronunciation symbol chart with English language learners, making sure they understand what the symbols stand for and how each sound is pronounced. Then have students copy each symbol from the pronunciation chart onto an index card and write examples of corresponding words they know how to pronounce on the other side of the card.

Activity Have partners use their index cards to quiz each other. Afterward, ask them which sounds they find easiest and most difficult to pronounce. As students read the selections in this unit, have them add new words they encounter.

Additional Resources

📁 *English Language Learners Sourcebook*

Objectives

- To read and analyze a short auto-biographical essay about the author's experiences at an English school during her childhood in India
- To analyze different atmospheres in the essay
- To write an evaluation of an author's attitude

Skills

Reading/Thinking: Drawing Conclusions; Inferring; Comparing and Contrasting
Writing: Diary Entries
Vocabulary: Etymology
Grammar/Language: Parts of Speech
Listening/Speaking: Dramatizing
Collaboration: Literature Groups

Motivating
→OPTIONS

Selection Focus Transparency 40: Have students view and discuss the flowers and their names. Encourage students to offer other flower names whose histories they know.

Focus Activity: Ask students to think of someone or something they have named or nicknamed. Invite them to tell their reasons for choosing the name/nickname.

Before You Read

By Any Other Name

FOCUS ACTIVITY

In *Romeo and Juliet,* William Shakespeare wrote, "What's in a name? that which we call a rose / By any other name would smell as sweet."

DISCUSS Do you agree with Shakespeare? Is your name just a name and nothing more? Discuss these questions in a small group.

SETTING A PURPOSE Read to find out what's in a name for Santha Rama Rau.

BACKGROUND

The Time and Place
The events described in this selection occur in the late 1920s, in Zorinabad, India, near the city of Allahabad in north central India.

Did You Know?
Between 1858 and 1947, India was a colony of Great Britain. During this time, British culture exerted a strong influence on Indian life. Some Indians adapted to British customs; others struggled to maintain their own traditions and cultural identity.

In 1920 Mohandas Gandhi organized a nonviolent resistance movement aimed at winning India's independence. As a result, tensions between India and Britain were high during the 1920s, when the events in this selection take place. Resistance continued until 1947, when Great Britain granted India independence.

VOCABULARY PREVIEW

intimidate (in tim′ə dāt′) *v.* to make timid or fearful; bully; p. 480
insular (in′ sə lər) *adj.* showing a limited point of view; p. 481
valid (val′ id) *adj.* acceptable; legitimate; p. 481
detached (di tacht′) *adj.* not involved emotionally; neutral; p. 481
palpitating (pal′ pə tāt′ ing) *adj.* quivering; trembling; vibrating; p. 482
incomprehensible (in′ kom pri hen′ sə bəl) *adj.* not understandable; p. 482
tepid (tep′ id) *adj.* moderately or slightly warm; lukewarm; p. 483

Meet Santha Rama Rau

Santha Rama Rau (sän′ tä rä′ mä rou) was raised in a traditional Indian family that she once referred to as an "unshakable little universe." She attended college in the United States and has lived in other parts of the world as well. Through all her journeys, however, Rama Rau has clung to her family and to her sense of national identity. In the 1940s, Rama Rau described herself as "a part of the great Indian struggle for independence." Her novels and nonfiction reflect her deep-seated love for her native land.

Santha Rama Rau was born in Madras, India, in 1923. This piece first appeared in the New Yorker *magazine and is included in the author's autobiography,* Gifts of Passage, *published in 1961.*

RESOURCE MANAGER

Lesson Planning Resource
The *Unit Two Planning Guide* (pp. 40–47) provides additional lesson notes and reduced versions of all print resources.

Other Print Resources
- Active Reading Guide, p. 40
- Vocabulary Practice, p. 39
- Reading Workbook, pp. 51–52
- Grammar and Language Workbook, pp. 47–72
- Grammar and Composition Handbook, Lessons 1.1–1.8

- Quick Checks, p. 40
- Selection and Theme Assessment, pp. 77–78
- Performance Assessment, p. 39
- Spanish Summaries, p. 40
- Spanish Translations
- Inclusion Strategies
- English Language Learners Sourcebook

Transparencies
- Selection Focus 40
- Fine Art 7

- Literary Elements 40
- Grammar and Language 40

Technology
- Audio Library
- Spanish Audio Library
- Glencoe Literature Web Site
- Testmaker

By Any Other Name

Santha Rama Rau

SUMMARY

In this autobiographical essay, Santha Rama Rau recalls attending, at age five, a British-run school in India. The English headmistress gives Santha and her older sister Premila English names, claiming she cannot pronounce Indian ones. Santha sits in the back of the class with the other Indian students. After a week of trying to fit in, Premila enters Santha's classroom and takes her home, explaining to their mother that they should not return to the school because her teacher had said Indian children cheat on tests.

📁 *Spanish Summaries,* p. 40

A **Active Reading**

PREDICT Have students use clues from the first three paragraphs to predict how Santha and Premila will be treated at the school. *(The students will be treated unfairly since Indian culture is not valued.)*

Additional Resources
📁 *Active Reading Guide,* p. 40
🎧 *Audio Library*
🎧 *Spanish Audio Library*

Teaching Options

CONNECTING TO OTHER SELECTIONS

The chart at the right shows three ways to connect "By Any Other Name" to selections in this book.

For specific teaching strategies, see the *Unit Two Planning Guide,* pp. 43–44.

Connection	Title
Life Skills: Problem Solving	→ "Through the Tunnel," p. 76
Thematic: Personal Identity	→ "Song for My Name," p. 668
Literary: Point of View	→ "Everyday Use," p. 7

At the Anglo-Indian[1] day school in Zorinabad to which my sister and I were sent when she was eight and I was five and a half, they changed our names. On the first day of school, a hot, windless morning of a north Indian September, we stood in the headmistress's study and she said, "Now you're the new girls. What are your names?"

My sister answered for us. "I am Premila, and she"—nodding in my direction—"is Santha."[2]

The headmistress had been in India, I suppose, fifteen years or so, but she still smiled her helpless inability to cope with Indian names. Her rimless half-glasses glittered, and the precarious[3] bun on the top of her head trembled as she shook her head. "Oh, my dears, those are much too hard for me. Suppose we give you pretty English names. Wouldn't that be more jolly? Let's see, now—Pamela for you, I think." She shrugged in a baffled way at my sister. "That's as close as I can get. And for you," she said to me, "how about Cynthia? Isn't that nice?"

My sister was always less easily <u>intimidated</u> than I was, and while she kept a stubborn silence, I said, "Thank you," in a very tiny voice.

We had been sent to that school because my father, among his responsibilities as an officer of the civil service, had a tour of duty to perform in the villages around that steamy little provincial town, where he had his

---

1. *Anglo-* is a combining form that means "English" or "English and." Here, the Anglo-Indian school belongs to British colonists in India but accepts both English and Indian students.
2. *Premila* (prem′ il ə), *Santha* (san′ thä)
3. Here, a *precarious* bun is one that seems in danger of coming loose if the headmistress moves her head too vigorously.

Vocabulary
intimidate (in tim′ə dāt′) *v.* to make timid or fearful; bully

---

Teaching Options

MEETING INDIVIDUAL NEEDS — ENGLISH LANGUAGE LEARNERS

Sensitivity Training It is likely that English language learners have had school experiences similar to some of those depicted in this selection.

Activity Have English language learners meet to discuss their experiences attending school in a different culture, speaking a second language. Then ask groups to set up guidelines for teachers and students about how they can help nonnative students feel comfortable and adapt successfully to their new school environment. Invite them to decide how they wish to share the guidelines with the rest of the class.

Additional Resources
📁 *English Language Learners Sourcebook*

headquarters at that time. He used to make his shorter inspection tours on horseback, and a week before, in the stale heat of a typically postmonsoon[4] day, we had waved good-bye to him and a little procession—an assistant, a secretary, two bearers, and the man to look after the bedding rolls and luggage. They rode away through our large garden, still bright green from the rains, and we turned back into the twilight of the house and the sound of fans whispering in every room.

Up to then, my mother had refused to send Premila to school in the British-run establishments of that time, because, she used to say, "you can bury a dog's tail for seven years and it still comes out curly, and you can take a Britisher away from his home for a lifetime and he still remains insular." The examinations and degrees from entirely Indian schools were not, in those days, considered valid. In my case, the question had never come up, and probably never would have come up if Mother's extraordinary good health had not broken down. For the first time in my life, she was not able to continue the lessons she had been giving us every morning. So our Hindi books were put away, the stories of the Lord Krishna[5] as a little boy were left in midair, and we were sent to the Anglo-Indian school.

That first day at school is still, when I think of it, a remarkable one. At that age, if one's name is changed, one develops a

---

4. In southern Asia, the *monsoon* is a seasonal wind that brings heavy rains from the Indian Ocean in the summer. Here, *postmonsoon* refers to the time following the rainy season.
5. India's official language is Hindustani, also called *Hindi*. Most Indians practice Hinduism, a religion in which *Lord Krishna* is one of the most important gods.

curious form of dual personality. I remember having a certain detached and disbelieving concern in the actions of "Cynthia," but certainly no responsibility. Accordingly, I followed the thin, erect back of the head-mistress down the veranda to my classroom feeling, at most, a passing interest in what was going to happen to me in this strange, new atmosphere of School.

The building was Indian in design, with wide verandas opening onto a central courtyard, but Indian verandas are usually white-washed, with stone floors. These, in the tradition of British schools, were painted dark brown and had matting on the floors. It gave a feeling of extra intensity to the heat.

I suppose there were about a dozen Indian children in the school—which contained perhaps forty children in all—and four of them were in my class. They were all sitting at the back of the room, and I went to join them. I sat next to a small, solemn girl who didn't smile at me. She had long, glossy-black braids and wore a cotton dress, but she still kept on her Indian jewelry— a gold chain around her neck, thin gold bracelets, and tiny ruby studs in her ears. Like most Indian children, she had a rim of black kohl around her eyes. The cotton dress should have looked strange, but all I could think of was that I should ask my mother

Did You Know?
Kohl is a powder used to darken the eyelids and eyelashes.

if I couldn't wear a dress to school, too, instead of my Indian clothes.

Vocabulary
insular (in′ sə lər) *adj.* showing a limited point of view
valid (val′ id) *adj.* acceptable; legitimate
detached (di tacht′) *adj.* not involved emotionally; neutral

---

B **Critical Thinking**

DRAWING CONCLUSIONS Ask students to draw conclusions about why the author's mother had not wanted to send Premila to British-run schools. *(Apparently she was trying to protect her from British cultural ignorance and racism.)*

C **Critical Thinking**

INFERRING Have students give reasons why Santha's first day at the school is an especially "remarkable one." *(It is remarkable because she has never been to any school before, she has probably never been around so many children at one time, and she has been given a different name.)*

D **Active Reading**

RESPOND Ask students how they imagine they would have felt in the narrator's situation. *(Some students may say they would have felt detached like Santha; others may say they would have been confused or frightened.)*

E **Literary Elements**

ATMOSPHERE Ask students how the details in this paragraph contribute to the atmosphere, or mood, at the school. *(The dark brown walls and floor matting add to the school's repressive atmosphere. Also, the mixture of Indian [verandahs and courtyard] and English [brown walls and floor mats] underscores the confusion that Santha feels in this new place.)*

INCLUSION STRATEGIES
MEETING INDIVIDUAL NEEDS

Special Needs Students with physical injuries or disabilities may experience separation from other people. They can benefit from opportunities to express their reactions to their circumstances.

Activity Invite students with special needs to write about their experiences of feeling separated from others, the way Santha feels in the British school. **L2**

Additional Resources
📁 *Inclusion Strategies*

F Active Reading

EVALUATE Students may judge Santha's response to be appropriate in light of the situation, or they may think she should have immediately given her real name.

G Critical Thinking

INFERRING Ask students why the girl with the braids touches the narrator. *(She seems to be letting Santha know that she cares and understands how she feels.)*

H Literary Elements

DETAILS Have students identify specific details in the selection that help explain the differences between an afternoon at home and an afternoon at school. Then ask what impressions they get of the two places from these details. *(At home Santha and her family nap after lunch during the hottest part of the day and then have tea. At school the children rest a little and then play games, first inside and then outside.)*

Language Note

Explain that *siesta* is Spanish for an afternoon nap.

FINE ART
TRANSPARENCY 7

You may want to use Fine Art Transparency 7 for discussion with this selection.

Teaching Options

I can't remember too much about the proceedings in class that day, except for the beginning. The teacher pointed to me and asked me to stand up. "Now, dear, tell the class your name."

I said nothing.

"Come along," she said, frowning slightly. "What's your name, dear?"

"I don't know," I said, finally.

The English children in the front of the class—there were about eight or ten of them—giggled and twisted around in their chairs to look at me. I sat down quickly and opened my eyes very wide, hoping in that way to dry them off. The little girl with the braids put out her hand and very lightly touched my arm. She still didn't smile.

> "Come along," she said, frowning slightly. "What's your name, dear?"
>
> "I don't know," I said, finally.

Most of that morning I was rather bored. I looked briefly at the children's drawings pinned to the wall, and then concentrated on a lizard clinging to the ledge of the high, barred window behind the teacher's head. Occasionally it would shoot out its long yellow tongue for a fly, and then it would rest, with its eyes closed and its belly <u>palpitating</u>, as though it were swallowing several times quickly. The lessons were mostly concerned with reading and writing and simple numbers—things that my mother had already taught me—and I paid very little attention. The teacher wrote on the easel blackboard words like "bat" and "cat,"

which seemed babyish to me; only "apple" was new and <u>incomprehensible</u>.

When it was time for the lunch recess, I followed the girl with braids out onto the veranda. There the children from the other classes were assembled. I saw Premila at once and ran over to her, as she had charge of our lunchbox. The children were all opening packages and sitting down to eat sandwiches. Premila and I were the only ones who had Indian food—thin wheat chapatties, some vegetable curry,[6] and a bottle of buttermilk. Premila thrust half of it into my hand and whispered fiercely that I should go and sit with my class, because that was what the others seemed to be doing.

The enormous black eyes of the little Indian girl from my class looked at my food longingly, so I offered her some. But she only shook her head and plowed her way solemnly through her sandwiches.

I was very sleepy after lunch, because at home we always took a siesta. It was usually a pleasant time of day, with the bedroom darkened against the harsh afternoon sun, the drifting off into sleep with the sound of Mother's voice reading a story in one's mind, and, finally, the shrill, fussy voice of the ayah[7] waking one for tea.

At school, we rested for a short time on low, folding cots on the veranda, and then we were expected to play games. During the hot part of the afternoon we played indoors, and after the shadows had begun to lengthen and the slight breeze of the evening had come up we moved outside to the wide courtyard.

---

6. *Chapatties* (chə pä′ tēz) are small, flat, disk-shaped loaves of bread, and *curry* is a stew seasoned with a combination of dried spices.

7. In India, an *ayah* (ä′ yə) is a governess or nursemaid.

Vocabulary
palpitating (pal′ pə tāt′ ing) *adj.* quivering; trembling; vibrating
incomprehensible (in′ kom pri hen′ sə bəl) *adj.* not understandable

---

MULTIPLE LEARNING STYLES
MEETING INDIVIDUAL NEEDS

Intrapersonal Students with an intrapersonal learning style often learn best through independent, self-reflective activities that encourage them to make personal connections to subject matter.

Activity Ask students to list all of the names they have been given in their lives and consider the origin and meaning of each one. Then have them write a

short creative piece in which they explore how those names have shaped their sense of identity. Invite students to share their pieces with the class if they wish. Remind them to add their pieces to their portfolios. **L2**

I had never really grasped the system of competitive games. At home, whenever we played tag or guessing games, I was always allowed to "win"—"because," Mother used to tell Premila, "she is the youngest, and we have to allow for that." I had often heard her say it, and it seemed quite reasonable to me, but the result was that I had no clear idea of what "winning" meant.

When we played twos-and-threes that afternoon at school, in accordance with my training, I let one of the small English boys catch me, but was naturally rather puzzled when the other children did not return the courtesy. I ran about for what seemed like hours without ever catching anyone, until it was time for school to close. Much later I learned that my attitude was called "not being a good sport," and I stopped allowing myself to be caught, but it was not for years that I really learned the spirit of the thing.

When I saw our car come up to the school gate, I broke away from my classmates and rushed toward it yelling, "Ayah! Ayah!" It seemed like an eternity since I had seen her that morning— a wizened,[8] affectionate figure in her white cotton sari, giving me dozens of urgent and useless instructions on how to be a good girl at school. Premila followed more sedately, and she told me on the way home

Did You Know?
The *sari* (sär´ē) is an outer garment worn chiefly by women of India and Pakistan.

never to do that again in front of the other children.

When we got home we went straight to Mother's high, white room to have tea with her, and I immediately climbed onto the bed and bounced gently up and down on the springs. Mother asked how we had liked our first day in school. I was so pleased to be home and to have left that peculiar Cynthia behind that I had nothing whatever to say about school, except to ask what "apple" meant. But Premila told Mother about the classes, and added that in her class they had weekly tests to see if they had learned their lessons well.

I asked, "What's a test?"

Premila said, "You're too small to have them. You won't have them in your class for donkey's years."[9] She had learned the expression that day and was using it for the first time. We all laughed enormously at her wit. She also told Mother, in an aside,[10] that we should take sandwiches to school the next day. Not, she said, that *she* minded. But they would be simpler for me to handle.

That whole lovely evening I didn't think about school at all. I sprinted barefoot across the lawns with my favorite playmate, the cook's son, to the stream at the end of the garden. We quarreled in our usual way, waded in the tepid water under the lime trees, and waited for the night to bring out the smell of the jasmine. I listened with

Did You Know?
The *jasmine* (jaz´ min) is a sweet-smelling flower of a plant in the olive family.

---

8. The ayah is *wizened* (wiz´ ənd), which means she is shriveled and withered, probably from old age.

9. The expression *donkey's years* means "an indefinitely long time."

10. A remark not meant to be heard by everyone is an *aside*.

Vocabulary
tepid (tep´ id) *adj.* moderately or slightly warm; lukewarm

NONFICTION ❧ 483

## Sidebar Annotations

I Critical Thinking

INFERRING Ask students why Premila does not want Santha to run to the ayah in front of the other children. *(She is concerned with what the other children think. She may be embarrassed by her sister's open display of feeling and worried that it will make Santha vulnerable to the other children.)*

J Author's Craft

SETTING Point out that the author uses setting to reflect her characters' feelings. Ask students to compare and contrast the setting of the school with the setting of the mother's bedroom and explain how each setting reveals the young Santha's feelings. *(The school is portrayed as dark and hot, suggesting Santha's discomfort there. The mother's bedroom is described as a "high, white room" where Santha has tea and sits on a comfortable bed, reflecting her happiness and ease there.)*

K Active Reading

EVALUATE Have students evaluate Premila's reason for suggesting that she and Santha bring sandwiches to school. *(The reason she gives is probably a false one. More likely, she feels uncomfortable eating different food from the others and wants to fit in.)*

L Literary Elements

ATMOSPHERE Reread the description of Santha's evening at home. Ask students what kind of atmosphere the author creates with the details she chooses. *(The atmosphere is one of freedom and happiness.)*

REAL-WORLD CONNECTION

India's Government Remind students that the selection takes place during the 1920s, when India was a colony of Great Britain, under British governmental control and cultural influence. Have students research to find out what type of government exists in India now, over 50 years after it gained independence from Great Britain. They might also investigate what British influences still exist in India today. **L2**

Interior of an Indic house. Anil A. Dave, photographer.

Viewing the photograph: Compare and contrast the mood of this photograph with Santha's thoughts and feelings after she comes home with Premila.

fascination to his stories of ghosts and demons, until I was too frightened to cross the garden alone in the semidarkness. The ayah found me, shouted at the cook's son, scolded me, hurried me in to supper—it was an entirely usual, wonderful evening.

It was a week later, the day of Premila's first test, that our lives changed rather abruptly. I was sitting at the back of my class, in my usual inattentive[11] way, only half listening to the teacher. I had started a rather guarded friendship with the girl with the braids, whose name turned out to be Nalini (Nancy, in school). The three other Indian children were already fast friends. Even at that age it was apparent to all of us that friendship with the English or Anglo-Indian children was out of the question.

Occasionally, during the class, my new friend and I would draw pictures and show them to each other secretly.

The door opened sharply and Premila marched in. At first, the teacher smiled at her in a kindly and encouraging way and said, "Now, you're little Cynthia's sister?"

Premila didn't even look at her. She stood with her feet planted firmly apart and her shoulders rigid, and addressed herself directly to me. "Get up," she said. "We're going home."

I didn't know what had happened, but I was aware that it was a crisis of some sort. I rose obediently and started to walk toward my sister.

"Bring your pencils and your notebook," she said.

I went back for them, and together we left the room. The teacher started to say something just as Premila closed the door, but we didn't wait to hear what it was.

---

11. To be *inattentive* is to be unmindful or neglectful.

Grammar and Language *Minilesson*

Parts of Speech Review the parts of speech with students:
- A **noun** is the name of a person, place, thing, or idea.
- A **pronoun** can take the place of a noun.
- A **verb** expresses action or state of being.
- An **adjective** describes nouns.
- An **adverb** describes verbs, adjectives, and other adverbs.
- A **conjunction** joins words, phrases, or clauses.
- A **preposition** shows the relationship between a noun or pronoun and another word.
- An **interjection** shows emotion.

Activity On the board, write some sentences from the selection and have students identify the different parts of speech in them. **L2**

Additional Resources

 Grammar and Language Transparency 40

 Grammar and Language Workbook, pp. 47–72

Grammar and Composition Handbook, Lessons 1.1–1.8

 Writer's Choice, Lessons 10.1–10.8

In complete silence we left the school grounds and started to walk home. Then I asked Premila what the matter was. All she would say was "We're going home for good."

It was a very tiring walk for a child of five and a half, and I dragged along behind Premila with my pencils growing sticky in my hand. I can still remember looking at the dusty hedges, and the tangles of thorns in the ditches by the side of the road, smelling the faint fragrance from the eucalyptus trees and wondering whether we would ever reach home. Occasionally a horse-drawn tonga[12] passed us, and the women, in their pink or green silks, stared at Premila and me trudging along on the side of the road. A few coolies[13] and a line of women carrying baskets of vegetables on their heads smiled at us. But it was nearing the hottest time of day, and the road was almost deserted. I walked more and more slowly, and shouted to Premila, from time to time, "Wait for me!" with increasing peevishness. She spoke to me only once, and that was to tell me to carry my notebook on my head, because of the sun.

When we got to our house the ayah was just taking a tray of lunch into Mother's room. She immediately started a long, worried questioning about what are you children doing back here at this hour of the day.

Mother looked very startled and very concerned, and asked Premila what had happened.

---

12. In India, a *tonga* is a small, two-wheeled carriage.
13. *Coolies* are unskilled, poorly paid laborers who often do hard work that no one else is willing to do.

Premila said, "We had our test today, and she made me and the other Indians sit at the back of the room, with a desk between each one."

Mother said, "Why was that, darling?"

"She said it was because Indians cheat," Premila added. "So I don't think we should go back to that school."

Mother looked very distant, and was silent a long time. At last she said, "Of course not, darling." She sounded displeased.

We all shared the curry she was having for lunch, and afterward I was sent off to the beautifully familiar bedroom for my siesta. I could hear Mother and Premila talking through the open door.

Mother said, "Do you suppose she understood all that?"

Premila said, "I shouldn't think so. She's a baby."

Mother said, "Well, I hope it won't bother her."

Of course, they were both wrong. I understood it perfectly, and I remember it all very clearly. But I put it happily away, because it had all happened to a girl called Cynthia, and I never was really particularly interested in her.

Active Reading

PREDICT Have students predict why Premila decides to take her sister out of school for good. (*Some students may predict that Premila's teacher or peers did something to offend or anger her.*)

Author's Craft

DESCRIPTIVE DETAILS Ask students to choose a descriptive detail from this passage and explain why they think the author included it.

Thematic Focus

Remembering Santha Rama Rau says she remembers the incident at the school "very clearly." Why do you think the events impressed themselves on her memory? How does the author create a picture of her home and family as an "unshakable little universe"?

✓ ASSESSMENT OPTIONS

📁 *Quick Checks,* p. 40

Reading *Minilesson*

Comparing and Contrasting Point out that students may be able to better understand Santha's unhappiness at school if they compare and contrast her life at home with her life at school.

Activity Have students create a chart to describe Santha's home life and school life. Suggest that they consider such items as her name, her lunch, her siesta, and her surroundings. Have volunteers discuss some of the contrasts on their charts. **L1**

Additional Resources
📁 *Reading Workbook,* pp. 51–52

Responding to
the Selection

Personal Response

Students may be upset or angered by
the unjust way in which the Indian children were treated.

ANALYZING LITERATURE

1. The headmistress gives the girls
English names because she says
their Indian names are too hard to
pronounce.
2. After being renamed "Cynthia,"
Santha goes to class, where she sits
in the back with the other Indian
children. When her teacher asks her
name, she is unsure how to answer,
and her classmates laugh at her.
Later, she plays confusing games.
3. After her teacher seats the Indian
students apart during the test because
she says they cheat, Premila leaves
the school with Santha and tells their
mother they should not return.
4. She puts it "happily away."
5. She believed that British people
were narrow-minded, perhaps racist.
6. Premila's "stubborn silence" suggests her dislike for the headmistress,
and Santha's polite but scared response
shows she is intimidated by her.
7. At home, Santha is nurtured, comfortable, and stimulated. She enjoys
learning. At school, she is mistreated,
confused, and bored.
8. Premila has a strong sense of pride
and justice and the confidence to act
on her convictions.
9. Although the experience was difficult
for Santha, she seems to have overcome the trauma of racial prejudice.
10. The mother's belief is confirmed
by the fact that the teachers make
Indian students answer to English
names, sit in the back of the class,
and sit apart during tests.
11. The background information
explains the British presence in India
and the resentment that the mother
seems to feel toward the British.
12. The author may have wanted to
expose the racism that she and
others experienced during Britain's colonization of India.
13. Students may say they would have
been angry but too intimidated to leave
the school.
14. The author's story effectively
shows that names define people insofar as they show where we come from;
yet they do not always reflect who we
are.

Responding to Literature

Personal Response

What is your reaction to the way in which the Indian children were treated
at the school? Explain in your journal.

ANALYZING LITERATURE

RECALL

1. Describe what happens in the headmistress's study.
2. Summarize the events and activities of Santha's first day at school.
3. What happens on the day of Premila's test?
4. How does Santha react to the incident that occurs on the day of
Premila's test?
5. Why had the girls' mother been reluctant to send her daughters to a
British-run school?

INTERPRET

6. How do Premila and Santha seem to feel about the headmistress?
Support your answer with evidence from the selection.
7. For Santha, how does learning at school differ from learning at home?
Compare and contrast the two environments.
8. In your opinion, what do Premila's actions on the day of the test reveal
about her character?
9. Do you think Santha's self-esteem has been damaged by her school
experience? Explain.
10. Do the actions of the headmistress and teachers seem to confirm or
contradict the mother's opinion of British-run schools? Explain.

EVALUATE AND CONNECT

11. How does the information in the Did You Know? section on page 478
help you to better understand this selection?
12. Theme Connections   Why do you think the author chose to write
about this particular incident from her childhood?
13. If you had been in Premila's situation, how do you think you might
have responded? Explain.
14. Look back at the questions you discussed in the Focus Activity on
page 478. Evaluate how well the author addresses those questions in
this selection.
15. Which character did you admire most? least? Give reasons for your
choices.

486 🦥 UNIT 2

Literary ELEMENTS

Atmosphere
Atmosphere is the emotional quality,
or mood, of a piece of writing. For
example, a piece may have a romantic, light mood; an atmosphere of
doom; or one of confusion and discomfort. The use of descriptive details
is one way writers create a particular
atmosphere. A writer's description of
characters' words and actions also
helps to convey the atmosphere. In
"By Any Other Name," Santha Rama
Rau re-creates two distinct atmospheres—one at her home and one at
the Anglo-Indian school.

1. Describe the atmosphere at
the school. How does the writer
re-create this atmosphere? Use
examples from the selection to
support your answer.
2. Describe the atmosphere at the
author's home. How does Rama
Rau convey the special mood of
this place? Give specific examples
from the selection.
3. Based on the atmospheres in these
two settings, what can you tell
about the author's feelings about
the events in this selection?

● See **Literary Terms Handbook**,
p. R1.

15. Students may say they admire Premila for
being brave and strong enough to leave the
school when she disliked the way she was being
treated. Students may say they least admire the
headmistress and teachers for their narrow-
mindedness and insensitivity to Indian students.

LITERARY ELEMENTS

1. School is dark, hot, and uncomfortable:
"[the verandahs] were painted dark brown
and had matting on the floors."
2. Home is fun and pleasant, with tea, stories, and "the sound of fans whispering in
every room."
3. The contrasting atmospheres convey her
discomfort at school and her happiness
at home.

Additional Resources

 Literary Elements Transparency 40

LITERATURE AND WRITING

Writing About Literature
Evaluate the Author's Attitude   In a biography of Santha Rama Rau, S. K. Desai writes that in "By Any Other Name," Rama Rau shows "a remarkable power of observation and an equally remarkable attitude of detachment." Do you agree? Write a paragraph or two in which you respond to this question. Support your opinion with evidence from the selection. Meet with a small group of classmates to share your evaluation.

Creative Writing
Dear Diary   Imagine that both Premila and Santha kept diaries. Write brief entries for both girls in which they record their feelings about the events that occur on the first day of school and on the day of Premila's test. As you write your diary entries, keep in mind the different ages and personalities of the two sisters.

EXTENDING YOUR RESPONSE

Literature Groups
Actions and Reactions   Do you think Premila was right to pull Santha out of class and take her home on the day of the test? Why or why not? Do you think their mother made a good decision in allowing them to stop attending school? What if the girls had stayed? Discuss these issues in your group. Share your ideas with the class.

Performing
Dramatize   Imagine that Santha, Premila, and the headmistress have been invited to appear on a talk show to discuss the treatment of Indian students in the Anglo-Indian school. Work with a group to plan the interview.

Do research as necessary to learn more about Anglo-Indian relations in the 1920s. Then assign roles, rehearse the interview, and perform it for the class.

Interdisciplinary Activity
Social Studies: What's in Your Name?   Work with a small group to research the first names of group members. Explore the history of the names, including their origin, meaning, and changes in spelling. Decide as a group how you will present the information you have gathered. For example, you might display it in a chart or on a bulletin board, or you might want to create your own booklet.

📖 **Save your work for your portfolio.**

 Skill Minilesson

VOCABULARY • Etymology

The etymology, or history, of *intimidate* isn't very surprising, especially if you noticed the word *timid* in it. *Intimidate* is made up of the Latin prefix *in-,* meaning "in," plus *timidus,* "to be afraid." The history of *tepid* is even more straightforward. It comes from *tepere,* which means "to be slightly warm."

PRACTICE   Use the information provided about each word's etymology to answer these questions.

1. *Palpitating* comes from the Latin *palpare,* "to feel." What does a doctor do when he or she palpates a patient's spine?
2. *Incomprehensible* combines the English prefix *in-* ("not") with *comprehensible,* which comes from the Latin *comprehendere* ("to seize or grasp mentally"). What is an incomprehensible idea?
3. *Valid* comes from the Latin *validus* ("strong"). What does this tell you about a person who is described as an invalid?

LITERATURE AND WRITING

Writing About Literature
Students' evaluations should
- explain whether they agree or disagree with the quotation and tell why.
- include specific supportive details from the selection.

Creative Writing
Students' diary entries should
- present each girl's point of view plausibly, taking into account the difference between the characters.
- reflect an understanding of the characters' probable feelings based on their personalities and the events in the selection.

EXTENDING YOUR RESPONSE

Literature Groups Encourage students to weigh the advantages and disadvantages of the girls continuing school and quitting school.
COLLAB. LEARN.

Performing Point out to students that the headmistress's attitude toward the Indian students was common at the time and that she probably was unaware of her own bigotry.

Interdisciplinary Activity You might suggest to students that they check the Oxford English dictionary for information on name meanings and origins.

Skill Minilesson

VOCABULARY • Etymology
Possible answers:
1. examines by touch
2. impossible to understand
3. someone who is not strong

Additional Resources
📁 *Vocabulary Practice,* p. 39

 ASSESSMENT OPTIONS

📁 *Quick Checks,* p. 40
📁 *Selection and Theme Assessment,* pp. 77–78
📁 *Performance Assessment,* p. 39
💾 *Testmaker*

Objectives

- To read and analyze an essay in which the author describes her aunt who knew how to live well
- To analyze how the author uses characters to reveal her theme
- To write a critique of a selection

Skills

Reading/Thinking: Inferring; Drawing Conclusions
Writing: Description of a Person
Vocabulary: Analogies
Listening/Speaking: Debating Issues
Life Skills: Wisdom in Bumper Stickers
Collaboration: Literature Groups

Motivating

→OPTIONS

Selection Focus Transparency 41: Have students view and discuss the quotations about money. Then take an opinion poll to see how many students agree with each quotation.

Focus Activity: Have students share and compare their ideas with a partner.

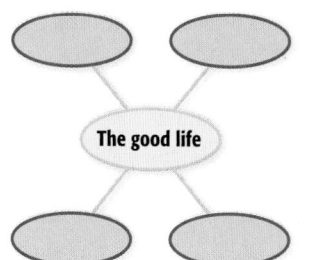

Before You Read

Living Well. Living Good.

FOCUS ACTIVITY

What do you need in order to live well and be happy?

The good life

EXPLORE IT! Explore your ideas about living well. Make a web like the one shown, and write in words and phrases that describe your concept of "the good life."

SETTING A PURPOSE Read to learn some important lessons about the art of living.

BACKGROUND

The Time and Place

The events described in this selection take place in Bel Air, California, in the mid-1900s, not long after World War II.

Did You Know?

In this selection, Maya Angelou's aunt recalls the pigs' feet, greens, fried chicken, and other foods that she and her friends shared on Saturday evenings. These dishes are part of the traditional African American cuisine that today is called soul food. Soul food has its roots in Southern cooking. On plantations of the Deep South before the Civil War, the enslaved people ate mainly cornmeal, which was most often eaten as mush, and poorer cuts of pork, such as chitlins (pig intestines). Occasionally, this diet was supplemented with hominy (made from corn), sweet potatoes, vegetables, and wild game and fish.

VOCABULARY PREVIEW

meticulous (mi tik′ yə ləs) *adj.* characterized by great or excessive concern about details; p. 490

commodious (kə mō′ dē əs) *adj.* having or containing ample room; spacious; p. 490

convivial (kən viv′ ē əl) *adj.* fond of merriment and parties with good company; sociable; p. 491

scenario (si nār′ ē ō′) *n.* an outline or model of an expected or imagined series of events; p. 491

inhibit (in hib′ it) *v.* to hold back one's natural impulses; restrain; p. 491

488 ❦ UNIT 2

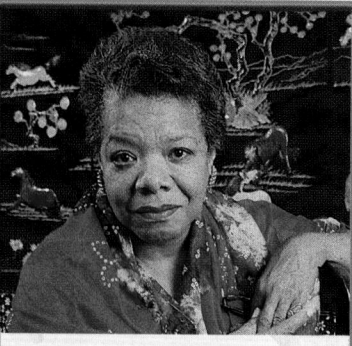

Meet Maya Angelou

"Somehow, we have come to the erroneous belief that we are all but flesh, blood, and bones, and that's all. . . . There is something more—the spirit, or the soul. I think that that quality encourages our courtesy and care and our minds."

With these words, author, poet, playwright, and songwriter Maya Angelou (mī′ yə   an′ jəl ō) identifies the source of the optimism that infuses this selection and her work as a whole. Angelou gained national prominence with the publication in 1969 of her autobiography *I Know Why the Caged Bird Sings.*

Maya Angelou was born in St. Louis in 1928. This selection appears in Wouldn't Take Nothing for My Journey Now, *published in 1993.*

RESOURCE MANAGER

Lesson Planning Resource
The *Unit Two Planning Guide* (pp. 48–55) provides additional lesson notes and reduced versions of all print resources.

📁 **Other Print Resources**
- Active Reading Guide, p. 41
- Vocabulary Practice, p. 40
- Reading Workbook, pp. 51–52
- Quick Checks, p. 41
- Selection and Theme Assessment, pp. 79–80

- Performance Assessment, p. 40
- Spanish Summaries, p. 41
- Spanish Translations
- Inclusion Strategies
- English Language Learners Sourcebook

 Transparencies
- Selection Focus 41
- Literary Elements 41

Technology
🎧 Audio Library
🎧 Spanish Audio Library
💻 Glencoe Literature Web Site
💾 Testmaker

Living Well. Living Good.

Maya Angelou ∾

Victorian Parlor II, 1945. Horace Pippin. Oil on canvas, 25¼ x 30 in. Metropolitan Museum of Art, New York. Arthur Hoppock Hearn Fund, 1958.

NONFICTION 🖊 489

SUMMARY

In this selection, Maya Angelou tells about her Aunt Tee, who worked for years as a live-in housekeeper. Angelou recounts a story of Aunt Tee's, about a wealthy couple she worked for who hosted elaborate dinner parties. As the couple got older, they stopped socializing and grew thin and sad. Aunt Tee grew more social, having friends over on Saturdays to play cards and dance. One day, the old wealthy couple approached Aunt Tee, asking if they might watch her and her friends having fun. Angelou concludes that living well is an art.

 Spanish Summaries, p. 41

A **Active Reading**

EVALUATE Have students discuss how well the first two paragraphs capture readers' attention. *(Students may say the vivid description of Aunt Tee is an effective way of hooking a reader.)*

Additional Resources
 Active Reading Guide, p. 41
🎧 *Audio Library*
🎧 *Spanish Audio Library*

Teaching Options

CONNECTING TO OTHER SELECTIONS

COMPARING *selections*

This selection is compared with "A Swimming Lesson" on pages 495–497. A lesson for teaching a comparison of the two selections appears on page 499.

The chart at the right shows three ways to connect "Living Well, Living Good" to other selections in this book.

For specific teaching strategies, see the *Unit Two Planning Guide*, pp. 51–52.

Connection	Title
Life Skills: Leading and Organizing	→ "Civil Peace," p. 39
Thematic: Satisfaction	→ "Chee's Daughter," p. 23
Literary: Characterization	→ *Antigone,* p. 727

CHARACTERIZATION Point out that Angelou uses the first two paragraphs to describe Aunt Tee and her apartment. Ask students what the effect is of such a detailed description. *(Describing her appearance and home creates a vivid image that helps bring Aunt Tee to life and reveals her strength of character.)*

C **Critical Thinking**

INFERRING Ask students why Aunt Tee sees her employers growing old but does not see herself aging at all. *(People grow old differently. Aunt Tee's socializing keeps her active and involved. Her employers have lost their ability to connect with others and with life.)*

D **Active Reading**

RESPOND Ask students how they would respond to the employers' request. *(Some students might say they would refuse them because they would feel uncomfortable knowing the employers were in the hall; others might say they would agree or even invite the couple to join them.)*

Living Well. Living Good.

AUNT TEE was a Los Angeles member of our extended family.[1] She was seventy-nine when I met her, sinewy,[2] strong, and the color of old lemons. She wore her coarse, straight hair, which was slightly streaked with gray, in a long braided rope across the top of her head. With her high cheekbones, old gold skin, and almond eyes, she looked more like an Indian chief than an old black woman. (Aunt Tee described herself and any favored member of her race as Negroes. *Black* was saved for those who had incurred her disapproval.)

She had retired and lived alone in a dead, neat ground-floor apartment. Wax flowers and china figurines sat on elaborately embroidered and heavily starched doilies. Sofas and chairs were tautly upholstered. The only thing at ease in Aunt Tee's apartment was Aunt Tee.

I used to visit her often and perch on her uncomfortable sofa just to hear her stories. She was proud that after working thirty years as a maid, she spent the next thirty years as a live-in housekeeper, carrying the keys to rich houses and keeping <u>meticulous</u> accounts.

"Living in lets the white folks know Negroes are as neat and clean as they are, sometimes more so. And it gives the Negro maid a chance to see white folks ain't no smarter than Negroes. Just luckier. Sometimes."

Aunt Tee told me that once she was housekeeper for a couple in Bel Air,[3] California, lived with them in a fourteen-room ranch house. There was a day maid who cleaned, and a gardener who daily tended the lush gardens.

Aunt Tee oversaw the workers. When she had begun the job, she had cooked and served a light breakfast, a good lunch, and a full three- or four-course dinner to her employers and their guests. Aunt Tee said she watched them grow older and leaner. After a few years they stopped entertaining and ate dinner hardly seeing each other at the table. Finally, they sat in a dry silence as they ate evening meals of soft scrambled eggs, melba toast, and weak tea. Aunt Tee said she saw them growing old but didn't see herself aging at all.

She became the social maven.[4] She started "keeping company" (her phrase) with a chauffeur down the street. Her best friend and her friend's husband worked in service[5] only a few blocks away.

On Saturdays Aunt Tee would cook a pot of pigs' feet, a pot of greens, fry chicken, make potato salad, and bake a banana pudding. Then, that evening, her friends—the chauffeur, the other housekeeper, and her husband—would come to Aunt Tee's <u>commodious</u> live-in quarters. There the four would eat and drink, play records and dance. As the evening wore on, they would settle down to a serious game of bid whist.[6]

Naturally, during this revelry jokes were told, fingers snapped, feet were patted, and there was a great deal of laughter.

Aunt Tee said that what occurred during every Saturday party startled her and her friends the first time it happened. They had been playing cards, and Aunt Tee, who had just

---

1. Parents and their children make up what is called the nuclear family. One's *extended family* includes other relatives who are related by blood or marriage.
2. Here, *sinewy* (sin′ ū ē) could mean "tough and stringy," "physically powerful," or "vigorously healthy."
3. *Bel Air* is one of the wealthiest, most fashionable communities in Los Angeles.

4. A *maven* is one whose special knowledge or experience makes him or her an expert in a given field.
5. Aunt Tee's two friends *in service* were servants in another household.
6. *Bid whist* is a card game, somewhat like bridge, for two players or two teams of two players.

Vocabulary
meticulous (mi tik′ yə ləs) *adj.* characterized by great or excessive concern about details
commodious (kə mō′ dē əs) *adj.* having or containing ample room; spacious

---

Teaching Options

LITERATURE & HUMANITIES

Play "Harlem Air Shaft" from *World of Music*, CD 1, Track 34. Have students consider how Duke Ellington's music of the Harlem Renaissance might have bridged the gap between whites and blacks.

MEETING INDIVIDUAL NEEDS

ENGLISH LANGUAGE LEARNERS

Historical Perspective Without knowing the history of American slavery, racial prejudice, and limited opportunities for African Americans, English language learners may not understand Aunt Tee and her circumstances as a maid and housekeeper for wealthy white people.

Activity Discuss briefly the situation of African Americans in the 19th and 20th centuries. Invite knowledgeable students to tell what they know about slavery, abolition, and the Civil Rights movement.

Additional Resources
📁 *English Language Learners Sourcebook*

won the bid, held a handful of trumps. She felt a cool breeze on her back and sat upright and turned around. Her employers had cracked her door open and beckoned to her. Aunt Tee, a little peeved, laid down her cards and went to the door. The couple backed away and asked her to come into the hall, and there they both spoke and won Aunt Tee's sympathy forever.

"Theresa, we don't mean to disturb you . . ." the man whispered, "but you all seem to be having such a good time . . ."

The woman added, "We hear you and your friends laughing every Saturday night, and we'd just like to watch you. We don't want to bother you. We'll be quiet and just watch."

The man said, "If you'll just leave your door ajar, your friends don't need to know. We'll never make a sound." Aunt Tee said she saw no harm in agreeing, and she talked it over with her company. They said it was OK with them, but it was sad that the employers owned the gracious house, the swimming pool, three cars, and numberless palm trees, but had no joy. Aunt Tee told me that laughter and relaxation had left the house; she agreed it was sad.

That story has stayed with me for nearly thirty years, and when a tale remains fresh in my mind, it almost always contains a lesson which will benefit me.

My dears, I draw the picture of the wealthy couple standing in a darkened hallway, peering into a lighted room where black servants were lifting their voices in merriment and comradery, and I realize that living well is an art which can be developed. Of course, you will need the basic talents to build upon: They are a love of life and ability to take great pleasure from small

offerings, an assurance that the world owes you nothing and that every gift is exactly that, a gift. That people who may differ from you in political stance, sexual persuasion, and racial inheritance can be founts of fun, and if you are lucky, they can become even <u>convivial</u> comrades.

Living life as art requires a readiness to forgive. I do not mean that you should suffer fools gladly, but rather remember your own shortcomings, and when you encounter another with flaws, don't be eager to righteously seal yourself away from the offender forever. Take a few breaths and imagine yourself having just committed the action which has set you at odds.

Because of the routines we follow, we often forget that life is an ongoing adventure. We leave our homes for work, acting and even believing that we will reach our destinations with no unusual event startling us out of our set expectations. The truth is we know nothing, not where our cars will fail or when our buses will stall, whether our places of employment will be there when we arrive, or whether, in fact, we ourselves will arrive whole and alive at the end of our journeys. Life is pure adventure, and the sooner we realize that, the quicker we will be able to treat life as art: to bring all our energies to each encounter, to remain flexible enough to notice and admit when what we expected to happen did not happen. We need to remember that we are created creative and can invent new <u>scenarios</u> as frequently as they are needed.

Life seems to love the liver of it. Money and power can liberate only if they are used to do so. They can imprison and <u>inhibit</u> more finally than barred windows and iron chains.

Vocabulary
convivial (kən viv′ē əl) *adj.* fond of merriment and parties with good company; sociable
scenario (si när′ē ō′) *n.* an outline or model of an expected or imagined series of events
inhibit (in hib′ it) *v.* to hold back one's natural impulses; restrain

---

E Literary Elements

THEME and CHARACTER Here Angelou reveals the theme of her essay and shows how the characters are connected to that theme. Ask students to explain both the theme and the connections. *(The theme is that living life well is an art and is more important than money or power. To illustrate her theme, Angelou uses the contrast between the servants who have little money but lots of friendship and fun and the employers who have money but no joy.)*

F Active Reading

CONNECT Ask students to tell about an occasion when they were startled out of their "set expectations." How did they react to the situation? Did they react as Angelou would want them to?

Thematic Focus

Remembering Have students discuss why the story might have stayed with Angelou for nearly thirty years. Do they agree with the conclusions Angelou draws from the story?

✔ ASSESSMENT OPTIONS

📁 *Quick Checks,* p. 41

Reading *Minilesson*

Drawing Conclusions Point out that the structure of the selection by Angelou is a narrative followed by the conclusions that the narrator draws from it. Discuss the fact that often readers must draw their own conclusions about the themes or morals found in a narrative.

Activity Have students write an anecdote about an experience of their own or a lesson they learned. Then have students exchange anecdotes with a partner and write a brief essay drawing conclusions about the lesson communicated in the anecdote. **L3 COLLAB. LEARN.**

Additional Resources
📁 *Reading Workbook,* pp. 51–52

Personal Response

Students may or may not know someone like Aunt Tee. They may be interested in meeting someone like her because she would have interesting stories to tell.

ANALYZING LITERATURE

1. Aunt Tee is an old woman "sinewy, strong, and the color of old lemons" who has compassion and pride, works hard, and knows how to have fun.
2. She thinks it teaches whites to respect African Americans more and shows African Americans that whites are not any better than they are.
3. She and her friends eat soul food, dance, and play cards. Her employers ask to watch them have fun.
4. She says a person needs "a love of life and ability to take great pleasure from small offerings, an assurance that the world owes you nothing and that every gift is exactly that, a gift."
5. She advises forgiving people, being aware of one's own limitations, assuming nothing, and bringing all one's energy to each experience.
6. Some students may say the neatness of her apartment reflects her proud and hardworking nature; others may say her neatness seems incongruous with her easygoing nature.
7. She seems to take pride in having been good at her jobs.
8. They feel sympathy for the old couple because they are lonely and unhappy; however, they do not see them as friends and do not ask them to join in.
9. Most students will agree that Aunt Tee loves life, appreciates "small offerings" such as good food and friends, and does not take anything in life for granted.
10. They seem to have let money "imprison and inhibit" them, which Angelou warns against. They also seem to have cut themselves off from others.
11. Most students will want to agree that it is possible, if difficult.
12. Aunt Tee's story creates pathos by revealing the emptiness and loneliness of the old couple's life.
13. Students may have read stories or encountered situations that have taught them lessons.
14. Aunt Tee lived life with appreciation and enthusiasm and was happy, whereas her employers lived ostentatiously and ended up unhappy.
15. Some students may rethink their emphasis on money or material objects.

Responding to Literature

Personal Response

Does Aunt Tee remind you of someone you know or have known? If not, do you think you would enjoy meeting someone like her? Explain.

——— ANALYZING LITERATURE ———

RECALL

1. Describe Aunt Tee's appearance and personality.
2. According to Aunt Tee, what benefits come from Negroes "living in"?
3. Describe a typical Saturday evening for Aunt Tee and her friends. What request do Aunt Tee's employers make one Saturday?
4. According to Angelou, what are the "basic talents" that one needs in order to live well?
5. What advice about the art of living does Angelou offer?

INTERPRET

6. Does Aunt Tee's apartment seem to match her personality? Explain.
7. In your opinion, does Aunt Tee resent having worked as a maid and housekeeper? Give reasons for your response.
8. Why do you think Aunt Tee and her friends respond as they do to the employers' request?
9. Do you think Aunt Tee has the "basic talents" that Angelou says are required for living well? Explain.
10. Do Aunt Tee's employers seem to understand the art of living, as described by Angelou? Explain.

EVALUATE AND CONNECT

11. Do you think it is possible to live life as art in the way that Angelou describes? Why or why not?
12. In literature, **pathos** is an element that evokes compassion or pity. How does Angelou create pathos in this selection?
13. Theme Connections   Angelou says that "when a tale remains fresh in my mind, it almost always contains a lesson which will benefit me." What kinds of stories remain fresh in your mind? Why?
14. In the final paragraph, Angelou writes: "Life seems to love the liver of it." How might Aunt Tee's story be used to illustrate this statement?
15. After reading this selection, what changes or additions would you make to the web you created in the Focus Activity on page 488?

Literary ELEMENTS

Using Character to Understand Theme

The **theme** of a literary work is the main idea, or message, that the writer wishes to convey. Writers sometimes reveal the theme of a work through the experiences of one or more characters. In "Living Well. Living Good." Maya Angelou uses the character of Aunt Tee to help convey the theme of the selection. The other characters in Aunt Tee's story—her employers and her friends—also help to reveal the theme.

1. When Aunt Tee begins working for the couple in Bel Air, who seems to have a better life, Aunt Tee or her employers? Explain.
2. How does Aunt Tee's view of her employers change over time? What causes this change?
3. What message, or theme, does Angelou convey through the experiences of Aunt Tee, her friends, and her employers?

● See **Literary Terms Handbook**, p. R13.

LITERARY ELEMENTS

1. Initially, the employers seem to have a better life because they have money, a big house, and parties.
2. She comes to feel sorry for them because they grow old, lonely, and unhappy.
3. She shows the importance of treating life as an adventure to be savored and of putting friendship and fun ahead of money and power.

Additional Resources

 Literary Elements Transparency 41

LITERATURE AND WRITING

Writing About Literature
Critique the Selection   After telling Aunt Tee's story, Angelou concludes the selection with an "essay" about how to live life as art. What is your opinion of this "essay"? Does it add to your understanding and appreciation of the selection, or does it simply repeat the ideas expressed in Aunt Tee's story? Write a critique in which you answer these questions. Support your ideas using specific details from the selection.

Personal Writing
Reflections   Choose someone you admire. Then close your eyes and reflect on the qualities that make that individual unique and admirable. Write a description of the person, modeling the style that Angelou uses to describe Aunt Tee in "Living Well. Living Good."

EXTENDING YOUR RESPONSE

Literature Groups
Stepping Over the Line?   Do you think Aunt Tee's employers invaded her privacy? Did they have a right to ask if they could watch her and her friends? Did Aunt Tee have a choice in her response? How might an employee react to such a request today? Debate these issues in your group. Share your ideas with the class.

Learning for Life
Bumper Sticker Wisdom   Bumper stickers sometimes offer bits of wisdom drawn from everyday experiences. With a partner, create several bumper stickers that express kernels of wisdom drawn from this selection—for example,

"Life loves those who love life." Write your sayings on poster board cut to the size of bumper stickers. Work with other pairs of students to create a bumper sticker display in the classroom.

Reading Further
You might also enjoy reading the following poems on the theme of remembering by Maya Angelou:

"In a Time" from *Just Give Me a Cool Drink of Water 'fore I Diiie*, "In Retrospect" from *And Still I Rise*, and "Caged Bird" from *Shaker, Why Don't You Sing?*

📖 **Save your work for your portfolio.**

 Skill Minilesson

VOCABULARY • **Analogies**

An analogy is a type of comparison that is based on the relationships between things or ideas. In one type of relationship called "synonym variant," the paired words would be synonyms if they were the same part of speech.

> spent : exhaustion :: shy : bashfulness

One who is *spent* feels *exhaustion;* one who is *shy* feels *bashfulness*. Once you have determined a relationship between the first two things or ideas, apply that relationship to the second pair of words.

PRACTICE   Choose the word pair that best completes each analogy.

1. meticulous : perfectionist ::
   a. tidy : housekeeper   c. irritable : grouch
   b. strong : athletic   d. demanding : boss

2. commodious : space
   a. large : gigantic   c. luxurious : comfort
   b. cramped : crowd   d. picturesque : view

● For more information on analogies, see
Communications Skills Handbook, p. R77.

LITERATURE AND WRITING

Writing About Literature
Students' critiques should
- offer their opinion of the "essay."
- evaluate whether the "essay" enhances the selection or merely repeats Aunt's Tee's story.
- include specific supportive details from the selection.

Personal Writing
Students' descriptions should
- describe a person they admire and explain what makes him or her admirable.
- model the style that Angelou uses in "Living Well. Living Good."

EXTENDING YOUR RESPONSE

Literature Groups   Point out to students that at the time when Aunt Tee was working, it would have been more difficult for her to refuse her employer because there were fewer laws protecting employees' rights then.
COLLAB. LEARN.

Learning for Life   You might wish to obtain blank bumper stickers so that students can create real bumper stickers. If you do, make sure students create mockups of their sayings before they write them on the stickers.

 Skill Minilesson

VOCABULARY • Analogies
1. c
2. c

Additional Resources
📁 *Vocabulary Practice,* p. 40

 ASSESSMENT OPTIONS

📁 *Quick Checks,* p. 41
📁 *Selection and Theme Assessment,* pp. 79–80
📁 *Performance Assessment,* p. 40
💾 *Testmaker*

Objectives

- To read and analyze an essay in which the author learns much from her grandmother
- To identify motifs in the essay
- To write an analysis of the author's reason for including the selection in her book of autobiographical essays

Skills

Reading/Thinking: Drawing Conclusions
Writing: Thank-You Letter
Grammar/Language: Main and Subordinate Clauses

Motivating
→OPTIONS

Selection Focus Transparency 42: Have students view the picture and discuss the question.

Focus Activity: Have students discuss what skills they still need to learn and why.

Before You Read

A Swimming Lesson

FOCUS ACTIVITY

Do you recall when you first learned to swim, skate, ride a bike, read, or do any activity you still enjoy today?

FREEWRITE Spend five minutes writing about a significant learning experience in your life. Think about questions like these as you write: Who taught you the skill? What teaching methods were used? How did you feel when you began to master the skill? How has this skill affected your life?

SETTING A PURPOSE Read to share an important learning experience with the author.

BACKGROUND

The Time and Place

This story takes place in the summer of 1957, at Revere Beach in Revere, Massachusetts, five miles north of Boston.

Did You Know?

Revere Beach, America's first public beach, was established in 1896. Revere is a city beach that is accessible by public transportation, which places it within reach of people from the entire Boston metropolitan area. Until the late 1980s, the sandy, crescent-shaped beach was flanked by amusement rides, restaurants and food stands, dance pavilions, and arcades. Today, only a few eating establishments remain.

VOCABULARY PREVIEW

torturous (tôr′ chər əs) *adj.* causing pain or suffering; p. 496
benevolence (bə nev′ ə ləns) *n.* kindness; generosity; p. 496
vulnerable (vul′ nər ə bəl) *adj.* easily damaged or hurt; p. 496
mainstream (mān′ strēm′) *adj.* representing the most widespread attitudes and values of a society or group; p. 496
superfluous (soo pur′ floo əs) *adj.* not needed; unnecessary; p. 496
invaluable (in val′ ū ə bəl) *adj.* very great in value; p. 497

Meet Jewelle L. Gomez

"What do I hope to achieve by writing? Changing the world!"
Award-winning writer and social activist Jewelle Gomez attributes much of her success to her great-grandmother. "My great-grandmother, with whom I lived until I was twenty-two years old, was born on an Indian reservation in Iowa and had been a widow for fifty years. She maintained an intellectual curiosity and graciousness that no amount of education could have created. She formed the basis of much of my intellectual yearnings." Gomez has written poetry, essays, and award-winning fiction.

Jewelle L. Gomez was born in Boston in 1948. "A Swimming Lesson" appears in Forty-three Septembers, *a collection of essays published in 1993.*

Lesson Planning Resource
The *Unit Two Planning Guide* (pp. 56–63) provides additional lesson notes and reduced versions of all print resources.

📁 Other Print Resources
- Active Reading Guide, p. 42
- Vocabulary Practice, p. 41
- Grammar and Language Workbook, p. 105
- Grammar and Composition Handbook, Lessons 4.1, 4.2
- Quick Checks, p. 42

- Selection and Theme Assessment, pp. 81–82
- Performance Assessment, p. 41
- Spanish Summaries, p. 42
- Spanish Translations
- Inclusion Strategies
- English Language Learners Sourcebook

✍ Transparencies
- Selection Focus 42
- Literary Elements 42
- Grammar and Language 41

Technology
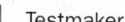
🎧 Audio Library
🎧 Spanish Audio Library
💻 Glencoe Literature Web Site
💾 Testmaker

A Swimming Lesson

Jewelle L. Gomez

At nine years old I didn't realize my grandmother, Lydia, and I were doing an extraordinary thing by packing a picnic lunch and riding the elevated train from Roxbury[1] to Revere Beach. It seemed part of the natural rhythm of summer to me. I didn't notice how the subway cars slowly emptied of most of their Black passengers as the train left Boston's urban center and made its way into the Italian and Irish suburban neighborhoods to the north. It didn't seem odd that all of the Black families stayed in one section of the beach and never ventured onto the boardwalk to the concession stands or the rides except in groups.

---

1. Boston's *Roxbury* neighborhood is southwest of downtown.

Sea and Tidal River, 1916. Alice Schille. Watercolor, gouache, and conte crayon on paper, 11½ x 13⅝ in. Columbus Museum of Art, Columbus, OH. Gift of Ferdinand Howald.

NONFICTION ❦ 495

Reading the Selection

SUMMARY

Jewelle L. Gomez recounts her childhood trips in the late 1950s with her grandmother, Lydia, to a mostly white beach in Revere, Massachusetts. Ignoring the racial tension at the beach, Lydia teaches her granddaughter to swim, modeling self-confidence, athleticism, and a fearless love of the sea. Later, Gomez discovers that her grandmother could not swim very well, but by teaching her granddaughter to swim, she also taught her to be proud of her accomplishments, her appearance, and her heritage.

📁 *Spanish Summaries,* p. 42

A Active Reading

PREDICT Have students read the first page. Ask them what they know about the narrator and what they can predict about the events in the selection from the opening paragraph.

Additional Resources
📁 *Active Reading Guide,* p. 42
🎧 *Audio Library*
🎧 *Spanish Audio Library*

Teaching Options

CONNECTING TO OTHER SELECTIONS

This selection is compared with "Living Well. Living Good" on pages 489–491. A lesson for teaching a comparison of the two selections appears on page 499.

The chart at the right shows three other ways to connect "A Swimming Lesson" to selections in this book.

For specific teaching strategies, see the *Unit Two Planning Guide*, pp. 59–60.

Connection	Title
Life Skills: Teaching and Mentoring	→ from *Kaffir Boy,* p. 445
Thematic: Prejudice	→ "By Any Other Name," p. 479
Literary: Conflict	→ *Julius Caesar,* p. 778

495

Literary Elements

SETTING Remind students that the setting of a literary work includes details about time and place. Have students summarize the setting of Gomez's essay. *(The time is during the summer when Gomez is nine; the place is a beach in a white community north of Boston.)*

C Author's Craft

CHARACTERIZATION Students may recognize that one way Gomez conveys what her grandmother is like is by comparing her to other African American women on the beach. Have students explain how Lydia is different from these women. *(She is confident and unself-conscious; they are cautious and vain.)*

D Literary Elements

MOTIF A motif is a repeated word, image, idea, or description. Ask students how Gomez's descriptions of her grandmother can be considered a motif. *(In every description, Gomez emphasizes her grandmother's size and strength.)*

E Active Reading

EVALUATE Ask students how accurately the narrator describes "the expectations for women's bodies." *(Students may say that "narrow hips, straight hair, flat stomachs, small feet" are indeed seen as ideal traits.)*

Teaching Options

I do remember Black women perched cautiously on their blankets, tugging desperately at bathing suits rising too high in the rear and complaining about their hair "going back." Not my grandmother, though. She glowed with unashamed athleticism as she waded out, just inside the reach of the waves, and moved along the riptide[2] parallel to the shore. Once submerged, she would load me onto her back and begin her long, tireless strokes. With the waves partially covering us, I followed her rhythm with my short, chubby arms, taking my cues from the powerful movement of her back muscles. We did this again and again until I'd fall off, and she'd catch me and set me upright in the strong New England surf. I was thrilled by the wildness of the ocean and my grandmother's fearless relationship to it. I loved the way she never consulted her mirror after her swim, but always looked as if she had been born to the sea, a kind of aquatic heiress.

None of the social issues of 1957 had a chance of catching my attention that year. All that existed for me was my grandmother, rising from the surf like a Dahomean[3] queen,

Sea and Tidal River, 1916 (detail).

shaking her head free of her torturous rubber cap, beaming down at me when I finally took the first strokes on my own. She towered above me in the sun with a benevolence that made simply dwelling in her presence a reward in itself. Under her gaze I felt part of a long line of royalty. I was certain that everyone around us—Black and white—saw and respected her magnificence.

Although I sensed her power, I didn't know the real significance of our summers together as Black females in a white part of town. Unlike winter, when we were protected by the cover of coats, boots and hats, summer left us vulnerable and at odds with the expectations for women's bodies—the narrow hips, straight hair, flat stomachs, small feet—handed down from the mainstream culture and media. But Lydia never noticed. Her long chorus-girl legs ended in size-nine shoes, and she dared to make herself even bigger as she stretched her broad back and became a woman with a purpose: teaching her granddaughter to swim.

My swimming may have seemed a superfluous skill to those who watched our lessons. After all, it was obvious that I wouldn't be doing the backstroke on the Riviera[4] or in

---

2. The *riptide* is the strong surface current that flows rapidly away from shore, returning the water carried landward by waves.

3. *Dahomean* (də hō′ mā ən) refers to Dahomey, a country in western Africa now called Benin (ben in′). Several kingdoms flourished in this region from the 1300s to the 1600s.

4. A popular resort area, the *Riviera* lies along the Mediterranean coasts of Italy and France.

Vocabulary
torturous (tôr′ chər əs) *adj.* causing pain or suffering
benevolence (bə nev′ ə ləns) *n.* kindness; generosity
vulnerable (vul′ nər ə bəl) *adj.* easily damaged or hurt
mainstream (mān′ strēm′) *adj.* representing the most widespread attitudes and values of a society or group
superfluous (soo pur′ floo əs) *adj.* not needed; unnecessary

---

MEETING INDIVIDUAL NEEDS **ENGLISH LANGUAGE LEARNERS**

Pronunciation English language learners may have difficulty pronouncing the numerous long, multisyllabic words in this selection. Write challenging words such as *concession, athleticism, aquatic, Dahomean, torturous, benevolence, vulnerable, superfluous, invaluable, comprehension,* and *tenement* on the board and review their correct pronunciations with students.

Activity Have students write each challenging word on a flash card and its definition on the back. They can work in pairs to practice pronouncing and defining the words.

Additional Resources
📁 *English Language Learners Sourcebook*

the pool of a penthouse spa. Certainly nothing in the popular media at that time made the "great outdoors" seem a hospitable place for Black people. It was a place in which we were meant to feel comfortable at best and hunted at worst. But my prospects for utilizing my skill were irrelevant to me, and when I finally got it right I felt as if I had learned some <u>invaluable</u> life secret.

When I reached college and learned the specifics of slavery and the Middle Passage,[5] the magnitude of that "peculiar institution"[6] was almost beyond my comprehension; it was like nothing I'd learned before about the history of my people. It was difficult making a connection with those Africans who had been set adrift from their own land. My initial reaction was "Why didn't the slaves simply jump from the ships while they were still close to shore, and swim home?" The child in me who had learned to survive in water was crushed to find that my ancestors had not necessarily shared this skill. Years later when I visited West Africa and learned of the poisonous, spiny fish that inhabit most of the coastal waters, I understood why swimming was not the local sport there that it was in New England. And now when I take to the surf, I think of those ancestors and of Lydia.

The sea has been a fearful place for us. It swallowed us whole when there was no escape from the holds of slave ships. For me, to whom the dark fathoms of a tenement hall-way were the most unknowable thing so far encountered in my nine years, the ocean was a mystery of terrifying proportions. In teaching me to swim, my grandmother took away my fear. I began to understand something outside myself—the sea—and consequently something about myself as well. I was no longer simply a fat little girl: My body had become a sea vessel—sturdy, enduring, graceful. I had the means to be safe.

Before she died last summer I learned that Lydia herself couldn't really swim that well. As I was splashing, desperately trying to learn the right rhythm—face down, eyes closed, air out, reach, face up, eyes open, air in, reach—Lydia was brushing the ocean's floor with her feet, keeping us both afloat. When she told me, I was stunned. I reached into my memory trying to combine this new information with the Olympic vision I'd always kept of her. At first I'd felt disappointed, tricked, the way I used to feel when I'd learn that a favorite movie star was only five feet tall. But then I quickly realized what an incredible act of bravery it was for her to pass on to me a skill she herself had not quite mastered—a skill that she knew would always bring me a sense of accomplishment. And it was more than just the swimming. It was the ability to stand on any beach anywhere and be proud of my large body, my African hair. It was *not* fearing the strong muscles in my own back; it was gaining control over my own life.

---

5. The *Middle Passage* was the route followed by slave traders from Africa to the Americas. Through the months-long voyage, slaves suffered filth, disease, abuse, and death.
6. Prior to the Civil War, Southerners referred to slavery as their *peculiar institution,* meaning that they considered it to be vital to their economy and way of life.

Vocabulary
invaluable (in val′ ū ə bəl) *adj.* very great in value

DRAWING CONCLUSIONS Ask students why learning to swim probably seemed "superfluous" to those watching on the beach but was an "invaluable life secret" to the author. *(Most people at the time would not think that an African American girl would have any reason to learn to swim, but for the author it was very empowering because it gave her confidence about her body and connected her to the natural world.)*

G Active Reading

CONNECT Ask students if they have been to the sea and, if so, what their first encounter with it was like.

H Active Reading

EVALUATE Students may agree that the grandmother is to be commended for her bravery.

Thematic Focus

Remembering The author says that learning to swim in the sea taught her something about herself. Encourage students to discuss why learning new skills is often memorable.

☑ ASSESSMENT OPTIONS

📁 *Quick Checks,* p. 42

Grammar and Language *Minilesson*

Main and Subordinate Clauses Explain to students that a clause is a group of words with a subject and a predicate. A **main clause** can stand alone as a complete sentence. A **subordinate clause** cannot stand alone as a sentence; it only makes sense when attached to a main clause.

Activity Write these sentences on the board and underline the main clause in each sentence:
1. <u>I glowed with pride</u> as my grandmother waded out into the sea.
2. When I took my first strokes alone, <u>my grandmother smiled at me.</u>
3. <u>I learned about the Africans</u> who had been captured and sold as slaves.
4. Before she died last summer, <u>Lydia told me a secret.</u> **L2**

Additional Resources

✒ *Grammar and Language Transparency 41*

📖 *Grammar and Language Workbook,* p. 105

📖 *Grammar and Composition Handbook,* Lessons 4.1, 4.2

📗 *Writer's Choice,* Lessons 13.1, 13.2

Responding to the Selection

Personal Response

Students may or may not wish to have a relative with Lydia's courage, determination, and boldness.

ANALYZING LITERATURE

1. Lydia likes the sea and is unself-conscious about her body. Gomez admires her fearlessness and confidence.
2. They might have thought that an African American would not have a lifestyle that would include swimming pools or outdoor activities. Gomez herself probably didn't see her circumstances as limited.
3. Learning that poisonous fish inhabit the coastal waters of West Africa explained why her African ancestors had not been swimmers. For Gomez swimming is liberating; for them it was dangerous.
4. First she is disappointed, but later she admires her grandmother more for her courage. Gomez is proud of her heritage and appreciative of her grandmother.
5. Lydia is an important role model for Gomez, giving her confidence in herself as an African American woman. Most students will say that young people need role models to give them confidence and guidance.
6. The social forces are racism and sexism. The adult Gomez is aware of the radical nature of her trips to the white part of town and her swimming lessons, whereas the child was not.
7. Students may offer stories about overcoming fears of water, heights, roller coasters, insects, and so on.
8. Possible themes: the social forces against African Americans and women and the importance of role models.

Responding to Literature

Personal Response

What was your reaction to Lydia? Do you have—or would you like to have—a relative with a similar personality and outlook? Explain.

ANALYZING LITERATURE

RECALL AND INTERPRET

1. What is Lydia's attitude toward the sea and toward her own body? How does this attitude seem to affect the author's feelings for her grandmother?
2. According to Gomez, why might observers have considered her lessons a waste of time? Why do you think Gomez did not view them in this light?
3. What historical information has helped Gomez understand her ancestors' attitude toward the sea? Compare her own attitude with that of her ancestors.
4. How does Gomez react when she learns the truth about her swimming lessons? What might the author's reaction suggest about her character?

EVALUATE AND CONNECT

5. Evaluate Lydia as a role model for her granddaughter. In your opinion, are role models important to young people? Why or why not?
6. What "social issues of 1957" does Gomez refer to in this essay? How does her adult view of these issues differ from her childhood view of them?
7. Have you ever conquered a fear, as Gomez did with Lydia's help? Describe your experience.
8. In your opinion, what is the **theme,** or main idea, of this essay? Explain.

Literary ELEMENTS

Motif

A **motif** (mō tēf´) is a significant word, description, idea, or image that is repeated throughout a literary work and is related to its theme. "A Swimming Lesson" contains several motifs related to the theme of life lessons. For example, the author repeats the word *rhythm* as she describes the natural rhythm of summers with her grandmother, the rhythm she imitated while learning to swim, the rhythm her grandmother followed to become a woman with a purpose, and the rhythm required to gain control over her life.

1. Find other motifs in "A Swimming Lesson."
2. Choose one, and explain how it relates to the selection's theme.

● See **Literary Terms Handbook,** p. R8.

EXTENDING YOUR RESPONSE

Writing About Literature

Analyze the Author's Purpose   "A Swimming Lesson" appears in a collection of autobiographical essays written by Jewelle Gomez. Write a paragraph explaining why you think Gomez included this piece in the collection. Use evidence from the selection to support your ideas. Share your analysis with several classmates.

Creative Writing

Thanks a Million   Choose one of the skills you listed in the Focus Activity on page 494. Write a thank-you letter to the person or persons who helped you master this skill. Explain why learning the skill was important to you and why you still enjoy the activity today. Be sure to express your appreciation for the time and effort spent in teaching the skill to you.

📖 **Save your work for your portfolio.**

LITERARY ELEMENTS

1. Sea as place of pleasure and pain, things unknown (*I didn't realize, notice, know*) now known, pride in physical appearance and strength.
2. Pride in physical appearance and strength supports the theme of fighting social forces.

Additional Resources

📖 *Literary Elements Transparency 42*

✓ ASSESSMENT OPTIONS

📁 *Quick Checks,* p. 42
📁 *Selection and Theme Assessment,* pp. 81–82
📁 *Performance Assessment,* p. 41
💾 *Testmaker*

COMPARING selections

Living Well. Living Good. **and** A Swimming Lesson

COMPARE **LESSONS**

Both Aunt Tee and Lydia serve as teachers, not only for Angelou and Gomez, but also for other people.

- What life lessons do Aunt Tee and Lydia teach? Compare and contrast these lessons.
- Do you think Angelou and Gomez are changed by the lessons they learn from Aunt Tee and Lydia? Give reasons for your answer.

COMPARE **DESCRIPTIONS**

Maya Angelou creates a memorable description of Aunt Tee, who has taught the author an important lesson. Gomez does the same thing with Lydia.

- Identify passages that describe the physical characteristics of Aunt Tee and Lydia. Record the details in a chart like the one shown.
- Look for clues to each woman's personality and character. Record these details.
- Compare the details to determine what the two women have in common. Which traits and characteristics make these women so impressive and so influential?

	Aunt Tee	Lydia
Physical characteristics		
Character traits		

COMPARE **ATTITUDES**

Imagine that Aunt Tee and Lydia have been asked to speak about the positive influence that older people can have on the lives of young people.

- With a partner, discuss the ideas and attitudes that the two women would be likely to express—how they might agree and disagree with each other.
- One partner should prepare Aunt Tee's remarks; the other, Lydia's.
- Practice your dialogue and then present it to the class. Compare the attitudes and ideas expressed in each woman's comments.

NONFICTION 🐾 499

COMPARING selections

Objective

- To compare two autobiographical essays that deal with the theme of remembering

COMPARE **LESSONS**

- Both women model strength and self-confidence. Aunt Tee reflects an appreciation for living; Lydia reflects a connection with nature and ease with her own body.
- Aunt Tee reminds Angelou to appreciate life's simple pleasures and gifts. Lydia teaches Gomez to swim and to be proud of herself.

COMPARE **DESCRIPTIONS**

Students' charts and answers should

- list physical descriptions and character traits.

COMPARE **ATTITUDES**

Students' dialogues should

- address, from Aunt Tee's and Lydia's point of view, how older people can have a positive influence on young people.
- express attitudes each woman would have based on her personality and values. **COLLAB. LEARN.**

Additional Resources
📁 *Literature Groups Sourcebook*

Teaching Options

💼 **PORTFOLIO OPTIONS**

Select and Reflect Have students write a paragraph in which they evaluate the dialogue they created and presented with a partner. Have them consider these questions:

- Does my part of the dialogue convey the character's attitudes and personality?
- How well did I express the character's "voice" in my presentation?

After they have written their self-evaluations, have students clip their dialogues and self-evaluations together to add to their portfolios. **L2**

Additional Resources
📁 *Writing Assessment and Portfolio Management,* pp. 20–22

Writing Workshop

Objectives
- To write an autobiographical incident
- To plan, draft, revise, edit, and proofread an autobiographical essay
- To reflect on and assess one's autobiographical incident

Teaching Strategies

PREWRITING

Explore ideas You may want to provide students with large pieces of paper or have them tape paper together so they have plenty of room to create their time lines. One way to prompt students to remember past experiences is to have them think about their lives chronologically, starting with their earliest memories.

Teaching Options

∻ Writing Workshop ∾

Narrative Writing: Autobiographical Incident

When asked if he knew Mark Twain as a young boy, an elderly resident of Hannibal, Missouri, replied: "Sure, I knew him. And I know just as many stories as he did, too. Only difference is, he writ 'em down." *You* know many stories, too. Your life is full of stories—episodes and incidents that have influenced you and helped shape the person you are. **In this workshop, you will focus on one of the many stories of your life and write an autobiographical incident.**

● As you write your narrative, refer to the **Writing Handbook,** pp. R58–R77.

The Writing Process

PREWRITING

PREWRITING TIP
To jog your memory about significant incidents in your life, watch family videotapes and browse through photo albums, scrapbooks, and any diaries or journals you may have kept.

Explore ideas
Make a time line of significant incidents in your life. As a starting point, you can use your birth or the beginning of a new phase in your life, such as a move to a new house or city. Along your time line, note important incidents. For example, perhaps a grandparent died, you made a new friend, or you won a sports competition. List as many incidents as you can think of, even if your time line becomes cluttered and you have to continue it on another sheet of paper.

Age 9	Age 10	Age 10½	Age 12	Age 13	Age 14	Age 15½
Moved to new house on Center Street.	Met Jenna, became best friends.	Learned to fish and canoe at summer camp.	Won second place in citywide science fair.	Tree fell on our house. We were on TV news!	Played lead role in school musical.	Worked as counselor at summer camp.

Consider your audience and purpose
Before you choose an incident to write about, think about your audience and purpose. Perhaps you'll want to limit your audience to your teacher because you consider your story too personal to share with classmates or with strangers. Or perhaps you *do* want to reach a wider audience, and so you'll select an incident that you don't mind sharing.

What is your purpose in writing an autobiographical incident? You might want to make your readers laugh by telling a humorous story. Perhaps you want to share a lesson you've learned, or you want to figure out the meaning of an experience by writing about it. These, and other purposes, are all valid reasons for writing an autobiographical incident.

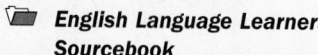

MEETING INDIVIDUAL NEEDS — ENGLISH LANGUAGE LEARNERS

Writing Autobiographically Because certain cultures discourage personal disclosure, some English language learners may feel uncomfortable writing about themselves. Point out that all writers write from their own experiences.

Activity To help students open up, have them work in pairs to discuss some of their memorable personal experiences and give each other feedback about what is interesting or amusing in their stories. Students can then use this feedback to determine the focus of their autobiographical incidents.

Additional Resources
📁 *English Language Learners Sourcebook*

Choose an incident

Look at the incidents on your time line and choose one to write about. Pick one that is particularly vivid or meaningful to you, perhaps because it strongly influenced you or caused you to grow or change. Such incidents often involve some type of conflict. You might choose to write about:

- a moral or ethical choice, such as the one John Steinbeck faces in the excerpt from *Travels with Charley*
- an encounter with prejudice, such as the one Santha Rama Rau describes in "By Any Other Name"
- an important life lesson that someone has taught you, such as the lesson that Jewelle L. Gomez learns in "A Swimming Lesson"
- a particular time and place that you want to bring to life for the reader, as Dylan Thomas does in "A Child's Christmas in Wales"

<u>Audience</u>: Family members and classmates

<u>Purpose</u>: To share an important life lesson

<u>Incident</u>: My dog, Duke, was hit by a car.

Identify basic story elements

A true story has many of the same elements as a fictional story—it occurs in a particular time and place, it usually involves people and sometimes animals, and it contains a sequence of events. You don't have to invent the elements of your story, but you do need to bring that story to life for your readers. So, to develop your idea, you'll have to identify the basic elements of your story. You might want to use a story map like this one.

Consider your audience and purpose

Point out to students that, although they should consider their purpose for writing, they do not necessarily need to decide what it is before they begin composing. Explain that many writers write without a specific purpose in mind, making discoveries along the way. Also explain that students may decide later whether they wish to share their pieces with the class.

Choose an incident To assist students in choosing a personal incident to write about, you may want to have them help you briefly review each of the selections in this theme. Encourage them to use one or more of the selections as a model for their own piece. Point out, however, that they need not be restricted to those models.

Identify basic story elements

Encourage students to use whatever form of outline they find most useful. Some may find a story map helpful; others may prefer to draw a cause-and-effect map with arrows or make lists or a chart with the following heads: *Characters, Setting, Events.* Of primary importance is that they identify the essential elements of their story.

Additional Resources

- **Writing and Proofreading Practice,** pp. 1–7, 37–45
- **Writing and Proofreading Transparencies,** 1–6, 15–16, 41–42
- **Writer's Choice,** Lessons 4.1–4.3

Intrapersonal Writing about personal experiences can be a powerful tool for intrapersonal learners. For them, reflecting on what they think and feel about a past event can bring self-understanding and insight into the present. Point out to students that many authors write to understand themselves and their experiences. Explain that writing can be a great way to learn about oneself and make sense of events in one's life.

Activity Encourage students to take time to reflect on how the event they have chosen to write about affected them personally. Suggest that they explore why they remember it, what impact it had on them at the time, how it changed them, and what it means to them now. Encourage them to include these insights in their final pieces. **L2**

Develop your autobiographical incident

Remind students that notes are meant to be short and that it is appropriate to write notes in phrases or incomplete sentences. Emphasize that at this point in the writing process the goal is to record ideas freely and not spend time worrying about correct grammar or punctuation. Explain that they will handle those details later.

DRAFTING

Set the stage Explain to students that in creating setting, authors often include sensory details to help readers imagine how things feel, look, sound, smell, and/or taste. Encourage students to include specific sensory details in their pieces.

Tell your story Point out that when authors write they often spend as much time sitting and thinking as they do actually putting words on paper. Invite students to take some time to meditate on the event they are writing about, feeling what it was like at the time and remembering as many details as they can.

Teaching Options

⌁ Writing ＼ Workshop ⌁

Develop your autobiographical incident

After you have identified the basic elements of your story, it's a good idea to make notes about those elements. You will use these notes later, as you draft your autobiographical incident. Here are the notes one student made.

> Characters
> Myself at age 12: Really into sports, especially basketball. Sometimes careless and irresponsible.
> Dad: A great guy. Jokes around a lot, but when I do something stupid, doesn't let me off the hook.
> Duke: Just a mutt, but a good dog. Likes to run away.
> Jason: My cousin who's the same age as I am. Like a brother to me.
> Setting
> Time: A Saturday afternoon in September, three years ago.
> Place: At my cousin's house, six blocks from my own house.
> Events
> Went to Jason's house to shoot baskets in his driveway. Took Duke with me, put him in Jason's fenced yard. Duke took off when ball bounced over fence and I went to get it. My fault—I left the gate open. Duke ran into street and got hit by car. Got banged up but recovered. Dad really upset—yelled at me for being so careless. I felt so bad and so guilty.

DRAFTING

DRAFTING TIP

As you draft your autobiographical incident, imagine that you are telling the story to a friend. Let the words flow. Write the way you would talk.

Set the stage

Begin by giving your readers any background information they need in order to understand your story. When and where did the incident happen? Who was involved? As you write, refer to your story map and to the prewriting notes you made.

Tell your story

After setting the stage, continue to refer to your story map and prewriting notes as you tell your story. During the drafting process, try to put yourself right back into the incident and lose yourself in the memory of events. Give yourself up to the rush of the experience. What do you see, hear, feel? Describe it all.

STUDENT MODEL

Jason and I shot baskets nonstop for almost an hour. The afternoon sun was really hot, and I was getting very tired. I let loose with a wild shot that bounced off the rim and sailed over the fence. I ran to get the ball, forgetting to close the gate behind me. Duke bolted out of the gate and raced toward the street. I screamed his name, but it was too late. I heard the sound of tires screeching, and then a sickening thud. Duke lay in the street, whimpering in pain.

Write your ending

At the end of your story, explain what the incident meant to you. Ask yourself: What is the point of my story? What did I learn, or how did I change as a result of what happened?

STUDENT MODEL

> Now that I'm older, I understand why Dad was so hard on me about what happened. My carelessness had resulted in an accident that could have been avoided. As Dad pointed out, Duke could easily have been killed.

REVISING

Take another look

Put your draft aside for a while so that you can come back to it with a reader's viewpoint. Then look at it with a fresh eye. Ask yourself: Have I made the incident come to life? Will the reader want to laugh, cry, or nod in understanding? Use the **Questions for Revising** to guide you in marking the places that need improvement. Then revise your draft.

Read your work aloud

Ask someone to listen to your autobiographical incident as you read it aloud. Ask your listener the **Questions for Revising**, and note the responses directly on your copy. If you agree with any of the comments, make additional changes.

REVISING TIP

As you revise your autobiographical incident, remember that your readers were not there when the incident occurred. Ask yourself: What do I need to add so that the experience will seem as real for them as it was for me?

STUDENT MODEL

> spoke to Dr. Song on the telephone,
> After he ~~got off the phone with the vet,~~ Dad told
> ⁋ had some injuries
> me that Duke ~~was pretty banged up but was going~~
> ⁋ "Whew," I said. "I was feeling so guilty."
> to be all right. ~~I was so relieved. Then Dad really~~
> ⁋ "You ought to feel guilty," said Dad.
> ~~chewed me out. He told me that~~ the whole thing
> you hadn't been
> could have been avoided if ~~I didn't act~~ so careless
> and absentminded. ~~I was feeling so guilty and so~~
> ⁋ I wondered   felt he had to
> ~~lousy already,~~ why did Dad ~~have to go and~~ make
> me feel worse? Wasn't I feeling bad enough already?

QUESTIONS FOR REVISING

How can I:
☑ improve the beginning so that it provides enough background information?
☑ describe the incident in clear, chronological order?
☑ add details and dialogue to bring the incident to life?
☑ better explain the significance of the incident?

Write your ending As they write their endings, encourage students to consider why they chose to write about the incident and how they feel about it now after describing it.

REVISING

Take another look Students should set aside their drafts at least overnight so that they can bring some perspective to the revision process. After time away, encourage them to read their pieces with a critical eye and make any obvious changes to it before discussing it with a classmate.

Read your work aloud Remind students that they should keep an open mind to peer feedback but also follow their own instincts if they do not agree with particular responses.

Writing *Minilesson*

Revision Strategies For most writers, revision is more important to the writing process than writing the first draft; yet among beginning writers, revision is typically the most neglected step. Emphasize the importance of revision, reminding students of Jewelle L. Gomez's advice to her writing students "to try to write down everything, then learn to throw half of it out."

Activity Write the following revision tips on the board and discuss them:
- Do not fall in love with your writing. Cut parts that do not serve a purpose even if you think they sound good.
- Avoid repeating words unless you are doing it for a specific effect.
- Write to be clear, never to hide or be mysterious.

- Search for the best, most precise word to describe what you want to say.

Invite students to add additional tips to the list and post the revision guidelines in the classroom. **L1**

Additional Resources

📖 ***Writer's Choice,*** pp. 161, 196

EDITING/PROOFREADING

Encourage students to read their pieces several times, each time focusing on a different aspect of editing, including grammar, spelling, and punctuation. Also suggest that they read their work aloud to themselves, since sometimes errors become obvious when a work is read orally. Emphasize to students that spell-check and other computer tools are not adequate substitutes for careful editing.

PUBLISHING/PRESENTING

Students who wish to share their autobiographical incident with the class may wish to present it as a dramatic enactment. If a piece contains dialogue, for example, they could recruit other students to take speaking roles in their enactment.

Reflecting

Portfolio Encourage students to ask themselves these questions as they review their writing.

Does my autobiographical essay
- focus on a significant incident in my life?
- clearly reveal what this incident means to me?
- describe an experience I would like to write about some more?

If students answer yes to more than one question, suggest that they include their essay in their portfolio.

Teaching Options

EDITING/PROOFREADING

PROOFREADING TIP

In real speech, people sometimes break the rules of grammar. You may do so in written dialogue to make it sound like real speech. In the rest of your writing, however, be sure to correct any grammatical errors.

Go over your writing again, checking for errors in grammar, usage, mechanics, and spelling. As a guide, use the **Proofreading Checklist** on the inside back cover.

Grammar Hint

A pronoun must agree with its antecedent in number (singular or plural) and gender (masculine, feminine, or neuter). Notice how the sentence below has been corrected so that the pronoun *they* agrees with its plural, neutral antecedent (*reactions*).

My reactions were a jumble; it was a mixture of shock, guilt, and pain. (they were)

● For more on pronoun agreement, see **Language Handbook,** pp. R19–R20.

STUDENT MODEL

Later, I learned that there was another reason Dad was so upset at me. The veterinarian's bill was more than ninety dollars. Wow! Luckily, Dad just paid Dr. Song's bill, along with the other bills, and didn't ask me to help pay them. (with / it)

PUBLISHING/PRESENTING

PRESENTING TIP

Include a photograph that relates to your autobiographical incident.

Share your autobiographical incident with your intended audience. As a class, you might consider compiling autobiographical incidents and creating an anthology with a title such as "Remembering" or "The Power of Memories."

Reflecting

Think about what you've learned about yourself from this writing experience. Jot down your thoughts in your journal. What did you find the hardest? What did you enjoy the most? What other incidents in your life would you like to write about?

 Save your work for your portfolio.

✔ ASSESSMENT OPTIONS

📁 ***Writing Assessment and Portfolio Management***
- Writing Assessment, pp. 2–19
- Portfolio Management, pp. 20–22

Theme 6 — Quests and Encounters

Think about a time when you worked hard to reach a goal or when an ordinary day turned extraordinary because of an unexpected event. Some of the people you will read about in this theme are on quests—seeking knowledge or striving for justice. Others have more chance encounters—with forces of nature or with themselves.

THEME PROJECTS

Listening, Speaking, and Viewing

Dog-Training Infomercial You and a few friends are opening a dog-training school. Prepare a ten-minute infomercial to advertise your school.

1. Choose three or four characters from this theme who are knowledgeable about animal behavior to be the experts in your infomercial.
2. Choose members of your group to be the host and the experts.
3. Prepare a list of research questions about dog behavior and the training of dogs. Then use the Internet or other resources to find information.
4. As a group, plan the interview between the host and the experts. Include topics such as the essentials of dog training and ownership, dog behavior, and the bond between dogs and humans.
5. Present your infomercial to your class.

Learning for Life

A Class Expedition Your school is planning two week-long excursions. One is a nature expedition to a wilderness area. The other is a cultural-exchange trip to a European city.

1. Decide which excursion you will join. Then, determine which characters from the selections you would like to have with you on the trip.
2. Write letters to the characters you have chosen. In each letter, explain the purpose of the trip and why you would like him or her to come along.

Jungfrau. John Cooke. Private collection.

Teaching Strategies

The following suggestions may help your students plan and carry out their theme projects.

Listening, Speaking, and Viewing

- Encourage students to make a list of people in the theme who have knowledge about animals and note the kinds of things the person knows about.
- Suggest that the group make a list of the cast of characters for the infomercial. They might want to have "try-outs" for the parts.
- Provide time for filming and help locate videotape equipment.

Learning for Life

- Encourage students to make a list of reasons why they might want to go on each excursion.
- Students will need a list of characters with expertise in each area.
- Remind students to use the correct form for a business letter.

Additional Resources

- 📁 *Interdisciplinary Activities,* pp. 12–13
- 📁 *Viewing and Representing Activities,* pp. 17–18
- 📁 *Listening and Speaking Activities,* pp. 11–12
- 📁 *Critical Thinking Skills,* pp. 17–19
- 📁 *Selection and Theme Assessment,* pp. 181–182
- 📁 *Performance Assessment,* p. 94

GLENCOE TECHNOLOGY

LITERATURE CLASSICS CD-ROM
Search for other selections related to the theme of quests and encounters.

Theme 6 SKILLS SCOPE AND SEQUENCE

SELECTIONS	Literary Elements	Reading and Thinking	Writing	Vocabulary and Spelling	
Pizza in Warsaw, Torte in Prague SLAVENKA DRAKULIC	Thesis, SE p. 513 *Paradox, TWE pp. 508, 510* *Thesis, TWE pp. 509, 511, 512* *Metaphor, TWE pp. 510, 512*	*Comparing and Contrasting, TWE p. 509*	Letter, SE p. 514	Analogies, SE p. 514	
I've Seen the Promised Land MARTIN LUTHER KING JR.	Allusion, SE p. 526 *Allusion, TWE pp. 518, 521, 523* *Thesis, TWE p. 519* *Metaphor, TWE p. 520* *Irony, TWE p. 524*	*Using Text Structures, TWE p. 515* *Activating Prior Knowledge, TWE p. 521*	Letter of Sympathy, SE p. 527 Organizing Details, SE p. 528 *Organizing a Persuasive Speech, TWE p. 520*		
Exploring Antarctic Ice JANE ELLEN STEVENS	Author's Purpose, SE p. 538 *Author's Purpose, TWE pp. 533, 537* *Irony, TWE p. 535*	Recognizing Cause and Effect, SE p. 540 *Previewing, TWE p. 529* *Summarizing, TWE p. 535*	Letter of Application, SE p. 539	Analogies, SE p. 540 *Homonyms and Puns, TWE p. 536*	
from **A Match to the Heart** GRETEL EHRLICH	Exposition, SE p. 551 *Exposition, TWE p. 545* *Simile/Metaphor, TWE p. 547* *Irony, TWE p. 549*	Using Comparisons to Clarify, SE p. 553 *Scanning, TWE p. 548*	Poem, SE p. 552	Etymology, SE p. 553	
The Angry Winter LOREN EISELEY	Creative Nonfiction, SE p. 560 *Creative Nonfiction, TWE p. 558*	*Cause-and-Effect Relationships, TWE p. 559*	Dialogue, SE p. 561	The Latin Root *vert*, SE p. 561	
The Tucson Zoo LEWIS THOMAS	Voice, SE p. 566 *Voice, TWE p. 564*	*Inferring, TWE p. 564*	*Report Writing, TWE p. 564*		

Key: Student material is in roman. Teacher material is in italic. Technology **COLLAB. LEARN.** Collaboration

Grammar and Language	Listening, Speaking, and Viewing	Life Skills	Study, Research, and Technology
Adverbs, TWE p. 512	**COLLAB. LEARN.** Literature Groups, SE p. 514	Organizing, SE p. 514	Research, SE p. 514 *Research, TWE p. 510*
Parallelism, SE p. 527 *Simple Subjects and Simple Predicates, TWE p. 524* *Irregular Comparisons, TWE p. 528*	**COLLAB. LEARN.** Literature Groups, SE p. 527 Listening to Recordings, SE p. 527	*Problem Solving, TWE p. 523*	*Research, TWE p. 519* 💻 Internet Connection, SE p. 527 💻 *Internet Connection, TWE p. 525*
Capitalization, SE p. 540 *Four Kinds of Sentences, TWE p. 536*	**COLLAB. LEARN.** Literature Groups, SE p. 539 Interviewing, SE p. 541	Planning, SE p. 539	💻 Internet Connection, SE p. 539 💻 *Internet Connection, TWE p. 530*
Abbreviations, SE p. 553 *Commas in a Series, TWE p. 550*	**COLLAB. LEARN.** Literature Groups, SE p. 552 *Internal Dialogue, TWE p. 546*	Learning about Lightning, SE p. 552	Research, SE p. 552 Technology Skills, SE p. 554 💻 *Internet Connection, TWE p. 549*
	COLLAB. LEARN. Literature Groups, SE p. 561		Research, SE p. 561 💻 Internet Connection, SE p. 561
Semicolons, TWE p. 565	**COLLAB. LEARN.** Literature Groups, SE p. 566 Performing Scenes, SE p. 566		

Theme 6 RESOURCE MANAGER

SELECTIONS	📁 Print Resources		

Pizza in Warsaw, Torte in Prague
 	
SLAVENKA DRAKULIC
	Unit Two Planning Guide, pp. 70–77
	* Active Reading Guide, p. 43
	Vocabulary Practice, p. 42
		Grammar & Comp. Handbook,
		  Lesson 1.5
		Grammar and Language Workbook,
		  p. 63
		Reading Workbook, pp. 53–54
			* Quick Checks, p. 43
			Selection and Theme Assessment,
			  pp. 83–84
			Performance Assessment, p. 42
			Spanish Summaries, p. 43

I've Seen the Promised Land
 	
MARTIN LUTHER KING JR.
	Unit Two Planning Guide, pp. 78–85
	* Active Reading Guide, p. 44
	Vocabulary Practice, p. 43
		Grammar & Comp. Handbook,
		  Lesson 2.1
		Grammar and Language Workbook,
		  p. 75
		Reading Workbook, pp. 55–56
			* Quick Checks, p. 44
			Selection and Theme Assessment,
			  pp. 85–86
			Performance Assessment, p. 43
			Spanish Summaries, p. 44
			Spanish Translations

Exploring Antarctic Ice
 	
JANE ELLEN STEVENS
	Unit Two Planning Guide, pp. 86–93
	* Active Reading Guide, p. 45
	Vocabulary Practice, p. 44
		Grammar & Comp. Handbook,
		  Lesson 4.6
		Grammar and Language Workbook,
		  p. 119
		Reading Workbook, pp. 57–58
			* Quick Checks, p. 45
			Selection and Theme Assessment,
			  pp. 87–88
			Performance Assessment, p. 44
			Spanish Summaries, p. 45
			Spanish Translations

from **A Match to the Heart**
 	
GRETEL EHRLICH
	Unit Two Planning Guide, pp. 94–101
	* Active Reading Guide, p. 46
	Vocabulary Practice, p. 45
		Grammar & Comp. Handbook,
		  Lesson 11.6
		Grammar and Language Workbook,
		  p. 253
		Reading Workbook, pp. 59–60
			* Quick Checks, p. 46
			Selection and Theme Assessment,
			  pp. 89–90
			Performance Assessment, p. 45
			Spanish Summaries, p. 46
			Spanish Translations

The Angry Winter
 	
LOREN EISELEY
	Unit Two Planning Guide,
	  pp. 102–108
	* Active Reading Guide, p. 47
	Vocabulary Practice, p. 46
		Reading Workbook, pp. 59–60	* Quick Checks, p. 47
			Selection and Theme Assessment,
			  pp. 91–92
			Performance Assessment, p. 46
			Spanish Summaries, p. 47

The Tucson Zoo
 	
LEWIS THOMAS
	Unit Two Planning Guide,
	  pp. 109–116
	* Active Reading Guide, p. 48
	Vocabulary Practice, p. 47
		Grammar & Comp. Handbook,
		  Lesson 11.5
		Grammar and Language Workbook,
		  p. 249
		Reading Workbook, pp. 59–60
			* Quick Checks, p. 48
			Selection and Theme Assessment,
			  p. 93
			Performance Assessment, p. 47
			Spanish Summaries, p. 48

*Also available in Spanish

Transparencies	Technology Resources
Selection Focus Transparency 43 Grammar and Language Transparency 42 Literary Elements Transparency 43	Literature Launchers Videodisc Audio Library Spanish Audio Library Vocabulary Puzzlemaker Web Site: lit.glencoe.com
Selection Focus Transparency 44 Grammar and Language Transparency 43 Literary Elements Transparency 44	Literature Launchers Videodisc Audio Library Spanish Audio Library Vocabulary Puzzlemaker Web Site: lit.glencoe.com
Selection Focus Transparency 45 Grammar and Language Transparency 45 Literary Elements Transparency 45	Audio Library Spanish Audio Library Vocabulary Puzzlemaker Web Site: lit.glencoe.com
Selection Focus Transparency 46 Grammar and Language Transparency 46 Literary Elements Transparency 46 Fine Art Transparency 1	Audio Library Spanish Audio Library Vocabulary Puzzlemaker Web Site: lit.glencoe.com
Selection Focus Transparency 47 Literary Elements Transparency 47 Fine Art Transparency 27	Audio Library Spanish Audio Library Vocabulary Puzzlemaker Web Site: lit.glencoe.com
Selection Focus Transparency 48 Grammar and Language Transparency 47 Literary Elements Transparency 48	Audio Library Spanish Audio Library Vocabulary Puzzlemaker Web Site: lit.glencoe.com

Theme RESOURCES

- Listening and Speaking Activities (pp. 11–12)
- Viewing and Representing Activities (pp. 17–18)
- Critical Thinking Skills (pp. 16–17)
- Media Connections Activities (pp. 11–12)
- Interdisciplinary Activities (pp. 12–13)

See also these additional planning resources:
- English Language Learners Sourcebook
- Inclusion Strategies Sourcebook
- Literature Groups Sourcebook

Use Glencoe's *Presentation Plus!* This multi-media teaching tool lets you present dynamic lessons that will engage your students. Using Microsoft PowerPoint,® you can customize the presentations to create your own personalized lessons.

Objectives

- To read and analyze an essay that describes food shortages in Eastern Europe
- To identify an author's thesis
- To write paragraphs drawing conclusions

Skills

Reading/Thinking: Evaluating; Implied Contrasts; Inferring
Writing: Letter
Vocabulary: Analogies
Grammar/Language: Adverbs
Life Skills: Organizing
Collaboration: Literature Groups

Motivating
→OPTIONS

Literature Launchers:
"The Taste of Freedom"

Videodisc
Side A, Segment 11

Also available in VHS.

**Selection Focus
Transparency 43:** Use the transparency to discuss reactions to the unavailability of foods.

Focus Activity: Discuss ways in which students' lives might be different from those of their counterparts in other countries.

Before You Read

Pizza in Warsaw, Torte in Prague

FOCUS ACTIVITY

Imagine that one day all the grocery stores in your neighborhood put up a sign reading: "No Milk, No Fresh Fruit or Vegetables, No Meat."

DISCUSS How might you react to the situation described above? What foods would you miss the most? Why?

SETTING A PURPOSE Read to find out how one writer learns about food shortages in Eastern Europe.

BACKGROUND

The Time and Place
The author describes her observations of daily life in Eastern Europe during a trip made in 1990.

Did You Know?
After World War II (1939–1945), the Soviet Union set up communist governments in nearly all the countries of Eastern Europe. Along with a loss of political freedom, most of the people of the region also endured such economic hardships as severe food and housing shortages. In 1989–1990, Soviet domination over Eastern Europe ended, and communist governments across the region crumbled. The Soviet Union collapsed in 1991.

VOCABULARY PREVIEW

impeccable (im pek′ ə bəl) *adj.* free from error; flawless; p. 507
affluent (af′ lōō ənt) *adj.* wealthy; prosperous; p. 509
totalitarian (tō tal′ ə tär′ ē ən) *adj.* characteristic of a government in which one political party has total control; p. 510
abstract (ab′ strakt) *adj.* thought of apart from any specific example or case; theoretical; p. 510
palpable (pal′ pə bəl) *adj.* capable of being touched or felt; p. 510
banality (bə nal′ ə tē) *n.* something that is trite; p. 511
ideology (ī′ dē ol′ə jē) *n.* the ideas on which a political, economic, or social system is based; p. 511

Meet Slavenka Drakulić

"Growing up in Eastern Europe you learn very young that politics is not an abstract concept, but a powerful force influencing people's everyday lives."

In early 1990, Croatian journalist Slavenka Drakulić (slä ven′ kä drä kū′ lich) traveled to five East European countries to learn how the collapse of communism affected women. "I sat in their kitchens—because that was always the warmest room in their poorly heated apartments—listening to their life stories."

Slavenka Drakulić was born in 1949 in Rijeka, Yugoslavia, now part of Croatia. This essay appears in How We Survived Communism and Even Laughed, *published in 1991.*

RESOURCE MANAGER

Lesson Planning Resource
The *Unit Two Planning Guide* (pp. 70–77) provides additional lesson notes and reduced versions of all print resources.

 Other Print Resources
- Active Reading Guide, p. 43
- Vocabulary Practice, p. 42
- Reading Workbook, pp. 53–54
- Grammar and Language Workbook, p. 63
- Grammar and Composition Handbook, Lesson 1.5

- Quick Checks, p. 43
- Selection and Theme Assessment, pp. 83–84
- Performance Assessment, p. 42
- Spanish Summaries, p. 43
- Spanish Translations
- Inclusion Strategies
- English Language Learners Sourcebook

 Transparencies
- Selection Focus 43
- Literary Elements 43

- Grammar and Language 42

Technology
 Literature Launchers
 Audio Library
 Spanish Audio Library
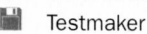 Glencoe Literature Web Site
Testmaker

Pizza in Warsaw, Torte in Prague

Slavenka Drakulić

WE WERE HUNGRY, so I said "Let's have a pizza!" in the way you would think of it in, say, New York, or any West European city—meaning, "Let's go to a fast-food place and grab something to eat." Jolanta,[1] a small, blond, Polish translator of English, looked at me thoughtfully, as if I were confronting her with quite a serious task. "There are only two such places," she said in an apologetic tone of voice. Instantly, I was overwhelmed by the guilt of taking pizza in Poland for granted. "Drop it," I said. But she insisted on this pizza place. "You must see it," she said. "It's so different from the other restaurants in Warsaw."

We were lucky because we were admitted without reservations. This is a privately owned restaurant, one of the very few. We were also lucky because we could afford a pizza and beer here, which cost as much as dinner in a fancy hotel. The restaurant was a small, cozy place, with just two wooden tables and a few high stools at the bar—you couldn't squeeze more than twenty people in, even if you wanted to.

It was raining outside, a cold winter afternoon in Warsaw. Once inside, everything was different: two waiters dressed in impeccable white shirts, with bow ties and red aprons, a bowl of fresh tropical fruit on the bar, linen napkins and the smell of pizza baked in a real charcoal-fired oven. Jolanta and I were listening to disco music, eating pizza, and drinking Tuborg beer from long, elegant glasses. Perhaps this is what you pay for, the feeling that you are somewhere else, in a different Warsaw, in a dreamland where there is everything—pizza, fruit juice, thick grilled steaks, salads—and the everyday life of shortages and poverty can't seep in, at least, for the moment.

---

1. *Jolanta* (yō län′ tə)

Vocabulary
impeccable (im pek′ ə bəl) *adj.* free from error; flawless

SUMMARY

We in America take food for granted. In an interesting look at everyday life in Eastern Europe, the author describes her experiences in trying to get such simple food items as pizza and torte. Her essay points out the failure of communist governments to provide for the basic needs of their people.

📁 *Spanish Summaries,* p. 43

A Active Reading

QUESTION Have the first paragraph read. Ask why the author feels guilty about asking for pizza. *(She realizes that she has taken food for granted and is in a country where food is difficult to come by.)* Further discuss why food might be difficult to come by and what students think they would like to find out as they read.

Additional Resources

📁 *Active Reading Guide,* p. 43
🎧 *Audio Library*
🎧 *Spanish Audio Library*

Teaching Options

CONNECTING TO OTHER SELECTIONS

The chart at the right shows three ways to connect "Pizza in Warsaw, Torte in Prague" to selections in this book.

For specific teaching strategies, see the *Unit Two Planning Guide,* pages 73–74.

Connection	Title
Life Skills: Collaborating	→ "Catch the Moon," p. 63
Thematic: Reflecting	→ "Lullaby," p. 330
Literary: Setting	→ "A White Heron," p. 143

PARADOX What paradox does the author describe when she tries to order juice in a restaurant? Of what is Coke a symbol? *(The soft drink, Coke, is everywhere, but in a country that grows fruit throughout, there is no fruit juice. Coke is a symbol of plenty.)*

C **Critical Thinking**

EVALUATING Why does the author say that *like* is not the best word to explain the food situation? *(People have to buy what is available, not necessarily what they like.)*

Cultural Note

Parents in the United States have sometimes urged children who are reluctant eaters to eat everything on their plates because children in other parts of the world were starving. Based on the essay, readers will note that parents were correct in their assessment of the food situation. Interestingly, children in some parts of the world where food is in short supply are given similar advice by parents.

Teaching Options

Pizza in Warsaw, Torte in Prague

Yet to understand just how different this place is, one has to see a "normal" coffee shop, such as the one in the modernistic building of concrete and glass that we visited the same day. Inside neon lights flicker, casting a ghostly light on the aluminum tables and chairs covered with plastic. This place looks more like a bus terminal than like a *kawiarnia*.[2] It's almost empty and the air is thick with cigarette smoke. A bleached blond waitress slowly approaches us with a very limited menu: tea, some alcoholic beverages, Coke, coffee. "With milk?" I ask.

"No milk," she shakes her head.

"Then, can I get a fruit juice perhaps?" I say, in the hopes of drinking just one in a Polish state-owned restaurant.

"No juice." She shakes her head impatiently (at this point, of course, there is no "sophisticated" question about the kind of juice one would perhaps prefer). I give up and get a cup of coffee. It's too sweet. Jolanta is drinking Coke, because there is Coke everywhere—in the middle of Warsaw as, I believe, in the middle of the desert. There may be neither milk nor water, but there is sure to be a bottle of Coke around. Nobody seems to mind the paradox that even though fruit grows throughout Poland, there is no fruit juice yet Coke is everywhere. But here Coke, like everything coming from America, is more of a symbol than a beverage.

To be reduced to having Coke and pizza offered not only as fancy food, but, what's more, as the idea of choice, strikes me as a form of imperialism, possible only where there is really very little choice. Just across the street from the private restaurant, where Jolanta parked her tiny Polski Fiat, is a grocery store. It is closed in the afternoon, so says a handwritten note on the door.

---

2. The Polish word *kawiarnia* (kä′ vē är′ nē ə) means "restaurant."

508 ❧ UNIT 2

Through the dusty shop window we can see the half-empty shelves, with a few cans of beans, pasta, rice, cabbage, vinegar. A friend, a Yugoslav living in Warsaw, told me that some years ago vinegar and mustard were almost all you could find in the stores. At another point, my friend noticed that shelves were stocked with prune compote. One might easily conclude that this is what Poles probably like the best or why else would it be in stores in such quantities? But the reason was just the opposite: Prune compote was what they had, not what they liked. However, the word "like" is not the best way to explain the food situation (or any situation) in Poland. Looking at a shop window where onions and garlic are two of the very few items on display, what meaning could the word "like" possibly have?

Slowly, one realizes that not only is this a different reality, but that words have a different meaning here, too. It makes you understand that the word "like" implies not only choice but refinement, even indulgence, *savoir-vivre*[3]—in fact, a whole different attitude toward food. It certainly doesn't imply that you stuff yourself with whatever you find at the farmer's market or in a grocery that day. Instead, it suggests a certain experience, a knowledge, a possibility of comparing quality and taste. Right after the overthrow of the Ceausescu government in Romania in December 1989, I read a report in

Did You Know?
Romania's dictator for thirty-four years, *Ceausescu* (chou shes′ kōō) was executed in 1989 for crimes against the state.

---

3. *Savoir-vivre* (sa′ vwär vēvr′) is a French term that refers to the ability to live elegantly, showing the tastes and social graces of fashionable society.

Food Supplies In the United States, a person can buy any kind of food desired in a supermarket, a luxury enjoyed in few other places in the world. English language learners from other cultures may know from personal experience what the author is describing.

Activity Let students who have lived in other countries explain how food was

obtained. Did their families raise food, buy it, or both? What kinds of stores sold food? Were there fast-food restaurants? What items were in short supply and in abundance?

Additional Resources
📁 *English Language Learners Sourcebook*

the newspaper about life in Bucharest.[4] There was a story about a man who ate the first banana in his life. He was an older man, a worker, and he said to a reporter shyly that he ate a whole banana, together with the skin, because he didn't know that he had to peel it. At first, I was moved by the isolation this man was forced to live in, by the fact that he never read or even heard what to do with a banana. But then something else caught my attention: "*It tasted good*," he said. I can imagine this man, holding a sweet-smelling, ripe banana in his hand, curious and excited by it, as by a forbidden fruit. He holds it for a moment, then bites. It tastes strange but "good." It must have been good, even together with a bitter, tough skin, because it was something unachievable, an object of desire. It was not a banana that he was eating, but the promise, the hope of the future. So, he liked it no matter what its taste.

One of the things one is constantly reminded of in these parts is not to be thoughtless with food. I remember my mother telling me that I had to eat everything in front of me, because to throw away food would be a sin. Perhaps she had God on her mind, perhaps not. She experienced World War II and ever since, like most of the people in Eastern Europe, she behaves as if it never ended. Maybe this is why they are never really surprised that even forty years afterwards there is a lack of sugar, oil, coffee, or flour. To be heedless—to behave as if you are somewhere else, where everything is easy to get—is a sin not against God, but against people. Here you have to think of food, because it has entirely diverse social meanings. To bring a cake for dessert when you are invited for a dinner—

a common gesture in another, more affluent country— means you invested a great deal of energy to find it if you didn't make it yourself. And even if you did, finding eggs, milk, sugar, and butter took time and energy. That makes it precious in a very different way from if you had bought it in the pastry shop next door.

When Jaroslav[5] picked me up at Prague airport, I wanted to buy a torte[6] before we went to his house for dinner. It was seven o'clock in the evening and shops were already closed. Czechs work until five or six, which doesn't leave much time to shop. "The old government didn't like people walking in the streets. It might cause them trouble," said Jaroslav, half joking. "Besides, there isn't much to buy anyway." My desire to buy a torte after six o'clock appeared to be quite an extravagance, and it was clear that one couldn't make a habit of bringing a cake for dessert. In the Slavia Café there were no pastries at all, not to mention a torte. The best confectioner[7] in Prague was closed, and in the Hotel Zlatá Husa[8] restaurant a waitress repeated "Torte?" after us as if we were in the wrong place. Then she shook her head. With every new place, my desire to buy a torte diminished. Perhaps it is not that there are no tortes—it's just hard to find them at that hour. At the end, we went to the only shop open until eight-thirty and bought ice cream. There were three kinds and Jaroslav picked vanilla, which is what his boys like the best.

---

5. *Jaroslav* (yär′ ə släv)
6. A *torte* (tôrt) is a rich cake.
7. A *confectioner* is a person who makes or sells candies and pastries.
8. *Zlatá Husa* (zlät′ yə   hoō′ zə)

---

4. *Bucharest* (boō′ kə rest′) is Romania's capital and largest city.

Vocabulary
affluent (af′ loō ənt) *adj.* wealthy; prosperous

D Active Reading

CONNECT The author tells about reading a newspaper story about an old man's experience eating a banana for the first time. Why would a newspaper run a story about this? You might use the example that follows to model how to make connections.

Model: I've just read how difficult it is to get food in certain countries. The man was old. Obviously, he had never eaten a banana in his life. This is strange to most of us. Even babies eat bananas in the United States. The newspaper may have run the story for several reasons. The story is amusing; the newspaper might have been making a point about food shortages; or the newspaper may have been, indirectly, explaining how a banana is eaten.

E Literary Elements

THESIS The author says that the man was not eating a banana but the promise of the future, so he liked it. How might this statement be considered a detail that supports the author's thesis? *(The author is writing about food shortages brought on by poor government. The man has eaten something new. This represents hope for a better economy and a better life. Anything would seem to be better than the past.)*

Reading *Minilesson*

Cultural Contrasts Students may need help with the implied cultural contrasts made throughout the selection. For example, the author describes a "pizza place" in Warsaw and expects the reader to understand how different the Polish pizzeria is from a typical pizza place in the United States. Explain that students should identify the part of the contrast that the author does not describe and

make a mental picture of it. Have students describe their mental picture of an American pizza place and tell how it is different from the one in Warsaw.

Activity Ask pairs of students to select a description, such as the pizza place, the coffee shop, the grocery store, or the dinner party, and devise a way to express the contrast. For example, they might draw pic-

tures or read the description from the text and then describe a typical scene in the United States. Have each pair present their contrasts to another pair of students. **L2 COLLAB. LEARN.**

Additional Resources
📁 *Reading Workbook,* pp. 53–54

Pizza in Warsaw, Torte in Prague

On another occasion, in the Bulgarian capital Sofia, Evelina is preparing a party. I am helping her in the small kitchen of the decaying apartment that she shares with a student friend, because as an assistant professor at the university, she cannot afford to rent an apartment alone. I peel potatoes, perhaps six pounds of them. She will make a potato salad with onions. Then she will bake the rest of them in the oven and serve them with . . . actually nothing. She calls it "a hundred-ways potato party"—sometimes humor is the only way to overcome depression. There are also four eggs for an omelet and two cans of sardines (imported from Yugoslavia), plus vodka and wine, and that's it, for the eight people she has invited.

We sit around her table: a Bulgarian theater director who lives in exile in Germany, three of Evelina's colleagues from the university, a historian friend and her husband, and the two of us. We eat potatoes with potatoes, drink vodka, discuss the first issue of the opposition paper *Demokratia*, the round-table talks between the Union of Democratic Forces and the communist government, and calculate how many votes the opposition will get in the forthcoming free elections—the first. Nobody seems to mind that there is no more food on the table—at least not as long as a passionate political discussion is going on. "*This* is our food," says Evelina. "We are used to swallowing politics with our meals. For breakfast you eat elections, a parliament discussion comes for lunch, and at dinner you laugh at the evening news or get mad at the lies that the Communist Party is trying to sell, in spite of everything." Perhaps these

people can live almost without food—either because it's too expensive or because there is nothing to buy, or both—without books and information, but not without politics.

One might think that this is happening only now, when they have the first real chance to change something. Not so. This intimacy with political issues was a part of everyday life whether on the level of hatred, or mistrust, or gossip, or just plain resignation during Todor Živkov's communist government. In a totalitarian society, one *has* to relate to the power directly; there is no escape. Therefore, politics never becomes abstract. It remains a palpable, brutal force directing every aspect of our lives, from what we eat to how we live and where we work. Like a disease, a plague, an epidemic, it doesn't spare anybody. Paradoxically, this is precisely how a totalitarian state produces its enemies: politicized citizens. The "velvet revolution"[9] is the product not only of high politics, but of the consciousness of ordinary citizens, infected by politics.

Before you get here, you tend to forget newspaper pictures of people standing in line in front of shops. You think they serve as proof in the ideological battle, the proof that

Did You Know?
Todor Živkov (tō' dôr ziv' köv) was Bulgaria's head of state from 1962 until his forced resignation in 1989, after the people held mass demonstrations to demand democracy and greater freedom.

---

9. In 1989 communist rule in Czechoslovakia was replaced by a new, noncommunist government in a process so smooth it became known as the *velvet revolution.*

Vocabulary
totalitarian (tō tal′ ə tār′ ē ən) *adj.* characteristic of a government in which one political party has total control
abstract (ab′ strakt) *adj.* thought of apart from any specific example or case; theoretical
palpable (pal′ pə bəl) *adj.* capable of being touched or felt

INTERDISCIPLINARY CONNECTION

History Many changes have occurred in Europe since the collapse of the Soviet Union. New countries came into being. Old countries came back into being. Communist leaders were ousted and new governments were formed.

Activity Have small groups of students investigate some of the changes that have taken place since the collapse of the Soviet Union. Some groups, for example, might want to choose a specific country

and write a brief report telling what has happened in that country and how the people are doing. You might want to mention that not all the changes have come about peacefully or have been positive. Ask groups to share their final reports with the class. **L3 COLLAB. LEARN.**

Slavenka Drakulić

People queuing for bread, Prague. Geoff Johnson, photographer.

Viewing the photograph: What would it be like to stand in a line this long every time you needed groceries?

communism is failing. Or you take them as mere pictures, not reality. But once here, you cannot escape the *feeling* of shortages, even if you are not standing in line, even if you don't see them. In Prague, where people line up only for fruit, there was enough of all necessities, except for oranges or lemons, which were considered a "luxury." It is hard to predict what will be considered a luxury item because this depends on planning, production, and shortages. One time it might be fruit, as in Prague, or milk, as in Sofia. People get used to less and less of everything. In Albania, the monthly ration for a whole family is two pounds of meat, two pounds of cheese, ten pounds of flour, less than half a pound each of coffee and butter. Everywhere, the bottom line is bread. It means safety—because the lack of bread is where real fear begins. Whenever I read a headline "No Bread" in the newspaper, I see a small, dark, almost empty bakery on Vladimir Zaimov Boulevard in Sofia, and I myself, even without

reason, experience a genuine fear. It makes my bread unreal, too, and I feel as if I should grab it and eat it while it lasts.

Every mother in Bulgaria can point to where communism failed, from the failures of the planned economy (and the consequent lack of food, milk), to the lack of apartments, child-care facilities, clothes, disposable diapers, or toilet paper. The banality of everyday life is where it has really failed, rather than on the level of ideology. In another kitchen in Sofia, Ana, Katarine and I sit. Her one-year-old daughter is trying to grab our cups from the table. She looks healthy. "She is fine now," says Ana, "but you should have seen her six months ago. There was no formula to buy and normal milk you hardly get as it is. At one point our shops started to sell Humana, imported powdered milk from the dollar shops, because its shelf life was over. I didn't have a choice. I had to feed my baby with that milk, and she got very, very sick. By allowing this milk to be sold, our own government poisoned

Vocabulary

banality (bə nal′ ə tē) *n.* something that is trite
ideology (ī′ dē ol′ ə jē) *n.* the ideas on which a political, economic, or social system is based

---

VIEWING THE PHOTOGRAPH
The word *queuing* is commonly used in other English-speaking countries when referring to standing in line.

Viewing Response *Most students will probably say that standing in line for groceries would be annoying or upsetting as well as extremely time-consuming.*

1 Active Reading

REVIEW The author describes food shortages, but there is one food that represents safety or fear. What is the food and why is it so symbolic? *(The food is bread. Bread is the most basic of all foods. As long as there is bread, the people feel a certain degree of reassurance. However, no bread indicates that things are extremely serious.)*

J Literary Elements

THESIS An author's thesis is the point that he or she is trying to make. What is the author's thesis? *(Communism failed the people because of its inability to meet the people's daily needs.)*

MEETING INDIVIDUAL NEEDS **INCLUSION STRATEGIES**

Less-Proficient Readers Encourage less-proficient readers to use audio and video resources to learn more about the changes in Eastern Europe.

Activity Ask students to create a sound and picture report about a specific change in Eastern Europe, an influential person, or an event that took place during the collapse of communism. Suggest that students use videotapes and Internet web sites. Provide these questions as a starting point: *What was the Berlin Wall and why was it erected? Why did the U.S. send troops to Bosnia?* **L2**

Additional Resources
 Inclusion Strategies

FIGURES OF SPEECH: *Metaphor* When the author brings strawberries, the friend and her mother each take one and save the rest for the friend's child. What metaphor does the author use to describe why they did this? *(Food is love.)*

L **Literary Elements**

THESIS At the very end of the selection, the author says she knows the answer to the woman's question "Why?" Ask students what they think it is. *(The answer is simply because it is possible. The answer doesn't help because growing up without any choices makes it nearly impossible to begin to know how to choose.)*

Thematic Focus

Quests and Encounters Discuss some of the encounters the author had and what her goal was in writing the essay.

✔ASSESSMENT OPTIONS

📁 *Quick Checks,* p. 43

Teaching Options

Pizza in Warsaw, Torte in Prague

babies. It was even on TV; they had to put it on because so many babies in Sofia got sick. We are the Third World[10] here."

If communism didn't fail on bread or milk, it certainly failed on strawberries. When I flew to Warsaw from West Berlin, I bought cosmetics, oranges, chocolates, Nescafé, as a present for my friend Zofia—as if I were going home. I also bought a small basket of strawberries. I knew that by now she could buy oranges or even Nescafé from street vendors at a good price—but not strawberries. I bought them also because I remembered when we were together in New York for the first time, back in the eighties, and we went shopping. In a downtown Manhattan supermarket, we stood in front of a fruit counter and just stared. It was full of fruits we didn't know the names of—or if we did, like the man with the banana in Bucharest, we didn't know how they would taste. But this sight was not a miracle; we somehow expected it. What came as a real surprise was fresh strawberries, even though it was December and decorated Christmas trees were in the windows already. In Poland or Yugoslavia, you could see strawberries only in spring. We would buy them for children or when we were visiting a sick relative, so expensive were they. And here, all of a sudden— strawberries. At that moment, they represented all the difference between the world we lived in and this one, so strange and uncomfortably rich. It was not so much that you could see them in the middle of winter, but because you could afford them. When I handed her the strawberries in Warsaw, Zofia said: "How wonderful! I'll save them for my son." The fact that she used the word "save" told me everything: that almost ten years after we saw each other in New York,

---

10. *Third World* generally refers to underdeveloped countries, mainly in Latin America, Africa, and Asia.

---

after the victory of Solidarity,[11] and private initiatives in the economy, there are still no strawberries and perhaps there won't be for another ten years. She was closer to me then, that evening, in the apartment where she lives with her sick, elderly, mother (because there is nobody else to take care of her and to put your parent in a state-run institution would be more than cruelty, it would be a crime). Both of them took just one strawberry each, then put the rest in the refrigerator "for Grzegorz."[12] This is how we tell our kids we love them, because food is love, if you don't have it, or if you have to wait in lines, get what you can, and then prepare a decent meal. Maybe this is why the chicken soup, cabbage stew, and mashed potatoes that evening tasted so good. K

All this stays with me forever. When I come to New York and go shopping at Grace Balducci's Marketplace on Third Avenue and 71st Street, I think of Zofia, my mother, my friend Jasmina[13] who loves Swiss chocolates, my daughter's desire for Brooklyn chewing gum, and my own hungry self, still confused by the thirty kinds of cheese displayed in front of me. In an article in *Literaturnaya Gazeta* May 1989 the Soviet poet Yevgenii Yevtushenko tells of a *kolkhoz*[14] woman who fainted in an East Berlin shop, just because she saw twenty kinds of sausages. When she came back to her senses, she repeated in despair: "Why, but why?" How well I understand her question— but knowing the answer doesn't really help. L

---

11. In the 1980s, *Solidarity,* an organization of trade unions, pushed for changes in the Polish economy and government. In 1990 Poland's Communist Party was dissolved, and Solidarity's leader was elected president.
12. *Grzegorz* (grzhe′ gôrzh)
13. *Jasmina* (yäz mē′ nə)
14. In the Soviet Union, a *kolkhoz* (kôl kôz′) was a collective farm, on which a group of laborers under state supervision shared the work and the management decisions.

Grammar and Language *Minilesson*

Adverbs Remind students that an adverb is a word that modifies a verb, an adjective, or another adverb.

Activity Have students underline each adverb and show the word it modifies.
1. It was a privately owned restaurant. *(privately; owned)*
2. The room was quite busy. *(quite; busy)*
L2

Additional Resources

🖋 *Grammar and Language Transparency 42*

📓 *Grammar and Language Workbook,* p. 63

📓 *Grammar and Composition Handbook,* Lesson 1.5

📓 *Writer's Choice,* Lesson 10.5

Responding to Literature

Personal Response

How did reading this essay change your attitude about the things available to you in your own life? Give reasons for your answer.

ANALYZING LITERATURE

RECALL

1. Describe Drakulić's visits to the pizza restaurant, the coffee shop, and the grocery store.
2. According to the author, how do most Eastern Europeans regard food? Why?
3. Summarize what happens during Drakulić's visit to Evelina's apartment.
4. What story does Ana relate to the author?
5. Why does Drakulić bring strawberries to Zofia? How does the author explain the way Zofia and her mother react to the gift?

INTERPRET

6. What can you infer about the food situation in Warsaw, based on Drakulić's visits to the two restaurants and the grocery store? Explain.
7. What do you think the author means when she says that in Eastern Europe, food has "entirely diverse social meanings"? Support your answer using details from the essay.
8. What do you think is **paradoxical**, or contradictory, about "politicized citizens" in a totalitarian state?
9. What do you think Drakulić means when she says, "The banality of everyday life is where [communism] has really failed"? Explain.
10. How do Drakulić's background and experiences seem to affect her own attitudes toward food?

EVALUATE AND CONNECT

11. Look back at the Focus Activity on page 506. Compare the way Eastern Europeans seem to react to shortages with the way you might react.
12. Theme Connections   How do Drakulić's encounters help you better understand people's quest for freedom and self-determination?
13. In your opinion, do many Americans take prosperity for granted? Explain your answer.
14. If communist governments in Eastern Europe had met people's basic needs, do you think they would have survived? Why or why not?
15. Imagine living in Eastern Europe before the fall of communism. What aspects of daily life do you think you would dislike the most? Why?

Literary ELEMENTS

Thesis

A **thesis** is the main idea of a work of nonfiction. Sometimes, the thesis is implied rather than stated. In such cases, you have to use details from the selection to figure out the point you think the writer is trying to make. In other cases, the writer states the thesis directly. For example, in "Pizza in Warsaw, Torte in Prague," Slavenka Drakulić states her thesis in this passage: "Every mother in Bulgaria can point to where communism failed, from the failures of the planned economy (and the consequent lack of food, milk), to the lack of apartments, child-care facilities, clothes, disposable diapers, or toilet paper. The banality of everyday life is where it has really failed, rather than on the level of ideology."

1. Briefly restate the thesis of this essay in your own words.
2. Choose two of the following anec- dotes, and explain how Drakulić uses them to develop her thesis: going out for pizza in Warsaw, try- ing to buy torte in Prague, Evelina's dinner party, Ana's milk story, a gift of strawberries for Zofia.

● See **Literary Terms Handbook,** p. R13.

Responding to the Selection

Personal Response

Students may say that the essay made them better appreciate the things they have.

ANALYZING LITERATURE

1. The pizza restaurant is small and cozy and has expensive but good food. The coffee shop is sterile and has lim- ited drink choices. The grocery store has half-empty shelves that contain only basic foods.
2. Food is precious. It represents life and love. Eastern Europeans feel this way because food is so scarce.
3. They make one dish using potatoes, and they bake the rest. There is little food for the crowd that comes. The people discuss politics and one person describes politics as their food.
4. Her child got sick drinking the pow- dered milk that was sold even though its shelf life was over because there was no other way to get milk.
5. Zofia likes strawberries, and they are impossible to buy out of season. The author says that adults save food for their children because giving them food is a way of showing them love.
6. There is little food, except in some exclusive places. The food choices are limited.
7. The lack of food demonstrates the government's inability to provide for the most basic needs of its people. Food means love. Parents save food to give to their children. Food means wealth. People with money can go to special places where the food is abundant.
8. Citizens who become "politicized" are aware of the political situation in their country and may want to change it, something not allowed in a totalitar- ian state.
9. The things most people should be able to take for granted—the banal— such as food, clothing, and shelter— become the burdens of daily existence when a government fails its citizens.
10. The author appreciates food and stops to remind herself of how lucky she is when she realizes she is taking food for granted.
11. Eastern Europeans would accept the sign indicating there was no food as typical. A person in the United States would find it inconvenient at first and then a sign that something is seriously wrong.
12. The author's encounters show that although people are living with hard- ship, they look for ways to maintain

---

LITERARY ELEMENTS

1. The author's thesis is that communism failed because of its inability to meet the basic needs of the people.
2. Asking for pizza requires going to a special place and paying a lot. Torte is impossible to find because basic ingredients are not available. At the dinner party, the meal offers little variety. The government cannot provide all the milk that is needed.

Additional Resources

 Literary Elements Transparency 43

their dignity, share love, and find ways to improve the overall situation.
13. Many students will say that Americans do take prosperity for granted. Many Americans cannot imagine not having abundant food.
14. Some students may argue that satisfaction of basic needs would have made people content with communism. Others may argue that once basic needs were satisfied, people would have the time and energy to think about other desires, such as freedom of speech and the press.
15. Many students will say that they would miss- not having enough food or dislike having to wait in line.

LITERATURE AND WRITING

Writing About Literature

Students' paragraphs should
- clearly state the conclusions they have drawn.
- identify details that support those conclusions.

Creative Writing

Students' letters should
- explain the food shortages in the country.
- tell what special food the friend is to bring.
- give reasons why that particular food is wanted.
- use the correct format for a friendly letter.

EXTENDING YOUR RESPONSE

Literature Groups Be sure students discuss how the attitudes differ. Point out that while there may be differences, there may also be some areas in which attitudes are similar. Remind students to support their opinions about the author's intent with reasons.
COLLAB. LEARN.

Interdisciplinary Activity Once posters have been prepared, have students present their information to the class. Later, let volunteers create a display, using the posters.

Learning for Life Be sure students get an accurate list of the kinds of food the food bank needs. Remind them to determine during the planning stage how and when the food will be delivered, especially if they expect that a large amount of food will be collected.

Skill Minilesson

VOCABULARY • Analogies

1. c   2. a   3. b

Additional Resources
📁 *Vocabulary Practice,* p. 42

LITERATURE AND WRITING

Writing About Literature
Drawing Conclusions   List details from Drakulić's essay that show how communism affected the daily lives of Eastern Europeans. What conclusions can you draw about communism's effect on people's hopes, dreams, and expectations? State your conclusions in one or two paragraphs, using details from the essay to support your ideas.

Creative Writing
Dear American Friend   Put yourself in the place of one of the people Drakulić mentions in her essay. Write a letter to a friend in the United States explaining the food shortages in your country. What special food would you like your friend to bring on his or her upcoming visit? Explain why you would like to have this particular food.

EXTENDING YOUR RESPONSE

Literature Groups
Count Your Blessings   Discuss Eastern European attitudes toward food, family, and politics, as described in this essay. How do these attitudes compare with your own? Do you think the author is implying that most Americans take the ease of their daily lives for granted? Do you think they do? Discuss and debate these questions in your group. Share your ideas with the class.

Interdisciplinary Activity
Social Studies: Before and After   Find maps that show Eastern Europe before and after the collapse of the Soviet Union. Select a country that did not exist as an independent nation in 1988. Using the Internet and other sources, find out what system of government the country has, what

daily life is like there, as well as what major problems the country has. Prepare a poster display listing the information you have found. Add copies of maps and photographs, if you wish.

Learning for Life
Organize a Food Drive   Drakulić says that "the lack of bread is where real fear begins." Unfortunately, many people in our own prosperous country do not have enough bread and other food to eat. Contact a local food bank to learn about its work and its current needs. Organize a food drive in your classroom and donate the food you collect to the food bank.

📕 **Save your work for your portfolio.**

Skill Minilesson

VOCABULARY • Analogies

An analogy is a type of comparison that is based on the relationships between things or ideas. To complete an analogy, you must figure out the relationship represented by the first pair of words. Then apply that relationship to another pair of words and see if it is the same.

● For more about analogies, see **Communications Skills Handbook,** p. R77.

PRACTICE   Choose the word that best completes each analogy.

1. affluent : money :: brilliant :
   a. wealth   b. luck   c. intelligence
2. banality : original :: cruelty :
   a. merciful   b. weak   c. unfortunate
3. dictator : totalitarian :: president :
   a. powerful   b. republican   c. governmental

☑ ASSESSMENT OPTIONS

📁 *Quick Checks,* p. 43
📁 *Selection and Theme Assessment,* pp. 83–84
📁 *Performance Assessment,* p. 42
💾 *Testmaker*

Television Transcript

What qualities do employers look for in their job applicants? Dr. Martin Luther King once applied to another church before coming to the Dexter Avenue Baptist Church in Montgomery, Alabama.

Dr. Martin Luther King's Early Days

CBS Saturday Morning, January 17, 1998

RUSS MITCHELL, co-host
The official holiday is Monday, but this week marked the 69th anniversary of the birth of the Reverend Martin Luther King Jr. Langston University historian Currie Ballard has been studying Dr. King for some 20 years and came across an early chapter in the life of the civil rights leader. It happened in 1954 when the young King passed through Oklahoma City.
[*film clip*]

DR. MARTIN LUTHER KING JR.
I accept this prize on behalf of all men who love peace and brotherhood.

MR. CURRIE BALLARD, Langston University Historian
Before Dr. King won the Nobel Peace Prize, before he led the march to Montgomery, and even before the Montgomery bus boycott, he applied for the pastor's position here at Calvary Baptist Church in Oklahoma City. The real story is that he was turned down.

DR. A. L. DOWELL, member, Calvary Baptist Church
When he came to Calvary, he preached, and some members liked him and others didn't. The membership was looking for a man who was older. They thought that Dr. King was too young. They were looking for someone who would

preach somewhat on an emotional scale. In black churches they call that gravy. And they said that Dr. King didn't have enough gravy.

MR. BALLARD
What was a missed opportunity by Calvary Baptist Church and the people of Oklahoma City turned out to be a golden opportunity for Dexter Avenue Baptist Church and the people of Montgomery. Dr. King went on to lead the Montgomery bus boycott after the arrest of Mrs. Rosa Parks.

DR. A. L. DOWELL
This is what God had a calling for him to do. Come here and be denied and be accepted to go down there to help Miss Rosa Parks in Montgomery, Alabama. And that's the way God works.

MITCHELL
A fascinating story. Ballard says Dr. King did return to Calvary Baptist Church in 1960. He was the keynote speaker at a freedom rally there. And Dr. Dowell got to shake his hand. Hmm.

Respond
What do you find most ironic about the membership's first impression of Dr. King? Why?

Objectives

- To read and analyze a speech by Martin Luther King Jr.
- To identify examples of allusion
- To write a character sketch

Skills

Reading/Thinking: Inferring; Drawing Conclusions; Activating Prior Knowledge
Writing: Organizing a Persuasive Speech; Letter
Grammar/Language: Simple Subject and Simple Predicate; Parallelism
Listening/Speaking: Speech Delivery Techniques
Life Skills: Problem Solving
Collaboration: Literature Groups

Motivating
→OPTIONS

Literature Launchers:
"Martin Luther King Jr."

Videodisc
Side A, Segment 12

Also available in VHS.

Selection Focus Transparency 44: Use the transparency to discuss with students events from King's life as depicted in the quilt pieces.

Focus Activity: Discuss individuals and groups that still face discrimination in the United States today. Then ask students what causes they would support and why.

Before You Read
I've Seen the Promised Land

FOCUS ACTIVITY

Would you be willing to dedicate your life to a cause in which you believed strongly? Why or why not?

JOURNAL Record your responses to these questions in your journal. Consider what personal sacrifices you might be willing to make to further a cause you believed in.

SETTING A PURPOSE Read to learn the views of a man who dedicated his life to a cause.

BACKGROUND

The Time and Place
Martin Luther King Jr. delivered this speech at the Mason Temple in Memphis, Tennessee, on April 3, 1968.

Did You Know?
In April 1968, Martin Luther King Jr. traveled to Memphis, Tennessee, to lend his support to black sanitation workers who were on strike against the city. Memphis Mayor Henry Loeb had refused to recognize and negotiate with the nearly all-black union organization that had called the strike. King had led one march and planned to lead another to dramatize the workers' plight. On the evening of April 3, he spoke to a crowd of about 2,000; the speech he gave is the one you are about to read. The next evening, King was assassinated as he stood on the balcony outside his motel room.

VOCABULARY PREVIEW

grapple (grap' əl) *v.* to attempt to deal with; struggle; p. 519
articulate (är tik' yə lāt) *v.* to put into words; express clearly and effectively; p. 521
relevant (rel' ə vənt) *adj.* connected with the matter at hand; pertinent; meaningful; p. 521
agenda (ə jen' də) *n.* a program or schedule of things to be done; p. 522
compassionate (kəm pash' ə nit) *adj.* having or showing sympathy for another's suffering or misfortune, combined with a desire to help; p. 522
speculate (spek' yə lāt') *v.* to guess; p. 523

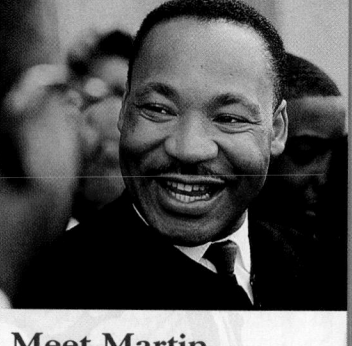

Meet Martin Luther King Jr.

"**I have a dream my four little children will one day live in a nation where they will not be judged by the color of their skin but by the content of their character. I have a dream today!**"

With his famous "I Have a Dream" speech, Martin Luther King Jr. set the moral tone for the civil rights movement during his historic March on Washington in 1963. In 1964 he was awarded the Nobel Peace Prize, for leading nonviolent demonstrations to help black Americans gain their civil rights.

Martin Luther King Jr. was born in 1929 in Atlanta, Georgia. He died in 1968, at the age of thirty-nine.

RESOURCE MANAGER

Lesson Planning Resource
The *Unit Two Planning Guide* (pp. 78–85) provides additional lesson notes and reduced versions of all print resources.

 Other Print Resources
- Active Reading Guide, p. 44
- Vocabulary Practice, p. 43
- Reading Workbook, pp. 55–56
- Grammar and Language Workbook, p. 75
- Grammar and Composition Handbook, Lesson 2.1

- Quick Checks, p. 44
- Selection and Theme Assessment, pp. 85–86
- Performance Assessment, p. 43
- Spanish Summaries, p. 44
- Spanish Translations
- Inclusion Strategies
- English Language Learners Sourcebook

 Transparencies
- Selection Focus 44
- Literary Elements 44

- Grammar and Language 43

Technology
 Literature Launchers
 Audio Library
Spanish Audio Library
Glencoe Literature Web Site
Testmaker

I've Seen the Promised Land

Martin Luther King Jr.

Portrait of Martin Luther King Jr.
Flip Schulke, photographer.

THANK YOU VERY KINDLY, MY FRIENDS. As I listened to Ralph Abernathy[1] in his eloquent and generous introduction and then thought about myself, I wondered who he was talking about. It's always good to have your closest friend and associate say something good about you. And Ralph is the best friend that I have in the world.

---

1. With King and other black ministers, *Ralph Abernathy* founded the Southern Christian Leadership Conference (SCLC), an organization devoted to the nonviolent struggle against racism and discrimination.

NONFICTION 517

Literary Elements

ALLUSION Be sure students understand the biblical allusion used in the title by asking questions such as these: Who was promised a land? By whom? *(In the Bible, God promised the Israelites a land of their own. This land is referred to as the promised land.)*

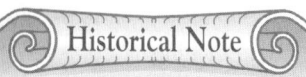
Historical Note

The Emancipation Proclamation was issued by Lincoln on January 1, 1863, during the Civil War. It declared all slaves in the areas of the Confederacy still in rebellion against the Union as free. Although the proclamation did not actually free any slaves, it did lead to the Thirteenth Amendment to the Constitution, which abolished slavery in the United States.

C **Active Reading**

QUESTION King says that if the Almighty asked him in what age he would like to live, King would answer the present time. Why does King say he would choose this time? *(He believes something important is happening in the world, namely, the struggle for freedom.)*

I've Seen the Promised Land

I'm delighted to see each of you here tonight in spite of a storm warning. You reveal that you are determined to go on anyhow. Something is happening in Memphis, something is happening in our world.

As you know, if I were standing at the beginning of time, with the possibility of general and panoramic view of the whole human history up to now, and the Almighty said to me, "Martin Luther King, which age would you like to live in?"—I would take my mental flight by Egypt through, or rather across the Red Sea, through the wilderness on toward the promised land. And in spite of its magnificence, I wouldn't stop there. I would move on by Greece, and take my mind to Mount Olympus. And I would see Plato, Aristotle, Socrates, Euripides and Aristophanes[2] assembled around the Parthenon as they discussed the great and eternal issues of reality.

Did You Know?
The *Parthenon,* a temple built in the fifth century B.C., still stands in Athens, Greece.

But I wouldn't stop there. I would go on, even to the great heyday of the Roman Empire. And I would see developments around there, through various emperors and leaders. But I wouldn't stop there. I would even come up to the day of the Renaissance, and get a quick picture of all that the Renaissance did for the cultural and esthetic life of man. But I wouldn't stop there. I would even go by the way that the man for whom I'm named had his habitat. And I would watch Martin Luther as he tacked his ninety-five theses[3] on the door at the church in Wittenberg.

But I wouldn't stop there. I would come on up even to 1863, and watch a vacillating president by the name of Abraham Lincoln finally come to the conclusion that he had to sign the Emancipation Proclamation. But I wouldn't stop there. I would even come up to the early thirties, and see a man grappling with the problems of the bankruptcy of his nation. And come with an eloquent cry that we have nothing to fear but fear itself.[4]

But I wouldn't stop there. Strangely enough, I would turn to the Almighty, and say, "If you allow me to live just a few years in the second half of the twentieth century, I will be happy." Now that's a strange statement to make, because the world is all messed up. The nation is sick. Trouble is in the land. Confusion all around. That's a strange statement. But I know, somehow, that only when it is dark enough, can you see the stars. And I see God working in this period of the twentieth century in a way that men, in some strange way, are responding—something is happening in our world. The masses of people are rising up. And wherever they are assembled today, whether they are in Johannesburg, South Africa; Nairobi, Kenya; Accra, Ghana; New York City; Atlanta, Georgia; Jackson, Mississippi;

Did You Know?
Martin Luther (1483–1546) was a German theologian whose arguments challenging certain teachings of the Roman Catholic Church led to the Protestant Reformation.

C

---

2. The lives of these five Greek teachers and writers spanned a 160-year period ending with Aristotle's death in 322 B.C. Their ideas greatly influenced modern Western civilization.

3. Here, *theses* means "arguments."
4. In these two sentences, King is referring to President Franklin D. Roosevelt, who led the United States during the Great Depression of the 1930s.

Teaching Options

LITERATURE & HUMANITIES

🎧 Have students listen to "We Shall Overcome," (Track 23, CD 1, Glencoe's *The World of Music*), which became synonymous with the Civil Rights movement, and discuss the role of such music in sustaining the movement.

ENGLISH LANGUAGE LEARNERS

MEETING INDIVIDUAL NEEDS

Great Leaders Individuals throughout history and in all parts of the world have led struggles for freedom and equality.

Activity Certain words and expressions are associated with the Civil Rights movement, such as *boycott, I have a dream,* and *free at last.* Let English language learners from other cultures make a list of words and expressions that are associated with great leaders and great movements in those cultures. Have students share their lists with the class.

Additional Resources
📁 *English Language Learners Sourcebook*

Martin Luther King Jr.

or Memphis, Tennessee—the cry is always the same—"We want to be free."

And another reason that I'm happy to live in this period is that we have been forced to a point where we're going to have to grapple with the problems that men have been trying to grapple with through history, but the demands didn't force them to do it. Survival demands that we grapple with them. Men, for years now, have been talking about war and peace. But now, no longer can they just talk about it. It is no longer a choice between violence and nonviolence in this world; it's nonviolence or nonexistence.

D That is where we are today. And also in the human rights revolution, if something isn't done, and in a hurry, to bring the colored peoples of the world out of their long years of poverty, their long years of hurt and neglect, the whole world is doomed. Now, I'm just happy that God has allowed me to live in this period, to see what is unfolding. And I'm happy that he's allowed me to be in Memphis.

I can remember, I can remember when Negroes were just going around as Ralph has said, so often, scratching where they didn't itch, and laughing when they were not tickled. But that day is all over. We mean business now, and we are determined to gain our rightful place in God's world.

And that's all this whole thing is about. We aren't engaged in any negative protest and in any negative arguments with anybody. We are saying that we are determined to be men. We are determined to be people. We are saying that we are God's children. And that we don't have to live like we are forced to live.

Now, what does all of this mean in this great period of history? It means that we've **E** got to stay together. We've got to stay together and maintain unity. You know,

whenever Pharaoh[5] wanted to prolong the period of slavery in Egypt, he had a favorite, favorite formula for doing it. What was that? He kept the slaves fighting among themselves. But whenever the slaves get together, something happens in Pharaoh's court, and he cannot hold the slaves in slavery. When the slaves get together, that's the beginning of getting out of slavery. Now let us maintain unity. **E**

Secondly, let us keep the issues where they are. The issue is injustice. The issue is the refusal of Memphis to be fair and honest in its dealings with its public servants, who happen to be sanitation workers. Now, we've got to keep attention on that. That's always the **F** problem with a little violence. You know what happened the other day, and the press dealt only with the window-breaking. I read the articles. They very seldom got around to mentioning the fact that one thousand, three hundred sanitation workers were on strike, and that Memphis is not being fair to them, and that Mayor Loeb is in dire[6] need of a doctor. They didn't get around to that.

Now we're going to march again, and we've got to march again, in order to put the issue where it is supposed to be. And force everybody to see that there are thirteen hundred of God's children here suffering, sometimes going hungry, going through dark and dreary nights wondering how this thing is going to come out. That's the issue. And we've got to say to the nation: we know it's coming out. For when people get caught up with that which is right and they are willing to sacrifice for it, there is no stopping point short of victory.

---

5. In the Bible, the *Pharaoh* (ruler) of ancient Egypt enslaved the Israelites until Moses led them out of Egypt and into Canaan, which they called the "promised land."
6. *Dire* means "dreadful" or "terrible."

Vocabulary
grapple (grap´ əl) *v.* to attempt to deal with; struggle

D Critical Thinking

INFERRING What, for King, would be the goal of a human rights revolution? *(to bring the people of color throughout the world out of poverty, hurt, and neglect)*

E Literary Elements

THESIS King tells his listeners what must be done to succeed. What two things does he believe must be done? *(The people have to stay together and maintain unity, and they have to stay focused on the issues of injustice.)*

F Active Reading

REVIEW In stressing the need to stay focused on the issues, King says, "That's always the problem with a little violence." Discuss what King meant and how his point connects to his overall approach to confronting society with the need for freedom and equality for African Americans. *(Violence, even a small incident, distracts people from the real issues. King believes that a nonviolent approach is needed. Nonviolence will force people to focus on issues, not on incidents of little importance.)*

GIFTED AND TALENTED

Greek Philosophers In his speech, King mentions a number of Greek philosophers and writers from the ancient world. These philosophers contributed some key ideas about government that Americans consider important.

Activity Ask students to choose one of the philosophers or writers and to research that person's ideas. Have

them look especially for any connections between the person's ideas and American concepts of government, equality, and democracy. Ask students to write a brief report about their findings. Allow them to read their reports to small groups of classmates. **L3**

I've Seen the Promised Land

We aren't going to let any mace stop us. We are masters in our nonviolent movement in disarming police forces; they don't know what to do. I've seen them so often. I remember in Birmingham, Alabama, when we were in that majestic struggle there we would move out of the 16th Street Baptist Church day after day; by the hundreds we would move out. And Bull Connor[7] would tell them to send the dogs forth and they did come; but we just went before the dogs singing, "Ain't gonna let nobody turn me round." Bull Connor next would say, "Turn the fire hoses on." And as I said to you the other night, Bull Connor didn't know history. He knew a kind of physics that somehow didn't relate to the transphysics[8] that we knew about.

And that was the fact that there was a certain kind of fire that no water could put out. And we went before the fire hoses; we had known water. If we were Baptist or some other denomination, we had been immersed. If we were Methodist, and some others, we had been sprinkled, but we knew water.[9]

That couldn't stop us. And we just went on before the dogs and we would look at them; and we'd go on before the water hoses and we would look at it, and we'd just go on singing "Over my head I see freedom in the air." And then we would be thrown in the paddy wagons, and sometimes we were stacked in there like sardines in a can. And they would throw us in, and old Bull would say, "Take them off," and they did; and we would just go in the paddy wagon singing, "We Shall Overcome." And every now and

---

7. *Bull Connor,* whose given name was Eugene, was Birmingham's Commissioner of Public Safety and a candidate for mayor in the 1964 election.
8. *Physics* is the study of the physical properties of light, heat, electricity, magnetism, and so on. With the invented word *transphysics,* King refers to things that transcend, or go beyond, the physical, such as morality and philosophy.
9. King is referring to the Christian ritual of baptism, which may involve immersion in water or the sprinkling or pouring of water over a person's head.

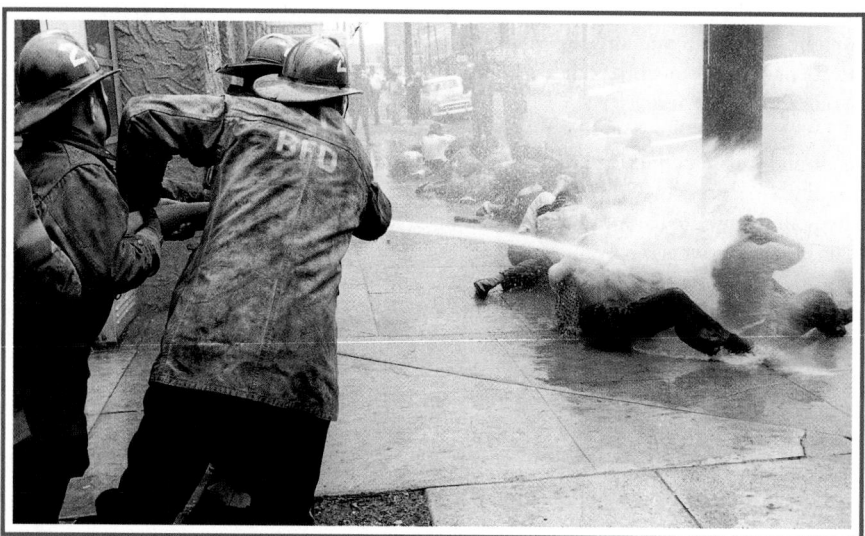

Corner of 5th Avenue North and 17th Street, May 3, 1963. Charles Moore, photographer.
Viewing the photograph: This photograph was taken in Birmingham, Alabama. Describe what is happening.

520 🦫 UNIT 2

---

then we'd get in the jail, and we'd see the jailers looking through the windows being moved by our prayers, and being moved by our words and our songs. And there was a power there which Bull Connor couldn't adjust to; and so we ended up transforming Bull into a steer, and we won our struggle in Birmingham.

Now we've got to go on to Memphis just like that. I call upon you to be with us Monday. Now about injunctions: We have an injunction[10] and we're going into court tomorrow morning to fight this illegal, unconstitutional injunction. All we say to America is, "Be true to what you said on paper." If I lived in China or even Russia, or any totalitarian country, maybe I could understand the denial of certain basic First Amendment privileges, because they hadn't committed themselves to that over there. But somewhere I read of the freedom of assembly. Somewhere I read of the freedom of speech. Somewhere I read of the freedom of the press. Somewhere I read that the greatness of America is the right to protest for right. And so just as I say, we aren't going to let any injunction turn us around. We are going on.

We need all of you. And you know what's beautiful to me, is to see all of these ministers of the Gospel. It's a marvelous picture. Who is it that is supposed to articulate the longings and aspirations of the people more than the preacher? Somehow the preacher must be an Amos,[11] and say, "Let justice roll down like waters and righteousness like a mighty stream." Somehow, the preacher must say

with Jesus, "The spirit of the Lord is upon me, because he hath anointed me to deal with the problems of the poor."[12]

And I want to commend the preachers, under the leadership of these noble men: James Lawson, one who has been in this struggle for many years; he's been to jail for struggling; but he's still going on, fighting for the rights of his people. Rev. Ralph Jackson, Billy Kiles; I could just go right on down the list, but time will not permit. But I want to thank them all. And I want you to thank them, because so often, preachers aren't concerned about anything but themselves. And I'm always happy to see a relevant ministry.

It's alright to talk about "long white robes over yonder," in all of its symbolism. But ultimately people want some suits and dresses and shoes to wear down here. It's alright to talk about "streets flowing with milk and honey," but God has commanded us to be concerned about the slums down here, and his children who can't eat three square meals a day. It's alright to talk about the new Jerusalem, but one day, God's preacher must talk about the New York, the new Atlanta, the new Philadelphia, the new Los Angeles, the new Memphis, Tennessee. This is what we have to do.

Now the other thing we'll have to do is this: Always anchor our external direct action with the power of economic withdrawal. Now, we are poor people, individually, we are poor when you compare us with white society in America. We are poor. Never stop and forget that collectively, that means all of us together, collectively we are richer than all the nations in the world, with the exception of nine. Did

10. An *injunction* is a court order barring a specific action, such as a march, demonstration, or strike.
11. The Hebrew prophet *Amos* lived in the eighth century B.C.

12. Here, King has freely paraphrased the words that Jesus was reading from the prophet Isaiah.

Vocabulary
articulate (är tik′ yə lāt) *v.* to put into words; express clearly and effectively
relevant (rel′ ə vənt) *adj.* connected with the matter at hand; pertinent; meaningful

NONFICTION 521

K **Active Reading**

REVIEW What is another suggestion King has for supporting the strikers? *(King suggests withdrawing economic support—not buying certain products from companies that do not support fair treatment for African Americans.)*

L **Active Reading**

EVALUATE In attempting to persuade the listeners of the importance of joining the march, King says they must "develop a kind of dangerous unselfishness." Discuss why unselfishness could be dangerous. *(An unselfish person is willing to do just about anything for others, even risk danger.)*

FYI

That Question King refers to "that question" and then tells the parable of the good Samaritan. In the Christian Bible, the question King refers to comes immediately before Jesus tells the parable. In Luke 10, a man asks Jesus what he must do to inherit eternal life. The answer is to love God and to love our neighbor as ourselves. The man, trying to justify the fact that there were some people he did not love, asks the question King refers to: "Who is my neighbor?"

Teaching Options

I've Seen the Promised Land

you ever think about that? After you leave[13] the United States, Soviet Russia, Great Britain, West Germany, France, and I could name the others, the Negro collectively is richer than most nations of the world. We have an annual income of more than thirty billion dollars a year, which is more than all of the exports of the United States, and more than the national budget of Canada. Did you know that? That's power right there, if we know how to pool it.

We don't have to argue with anybody. We don't have to curse and go around acting bad with our words. We don't need any bricks and bottles, we don't need any Molotov cocktails, we just need to go around to these stores, and to these massive industries in our country, and say, "God sent us by here, to say to you that you're not treating his children right. And we've come by here to ask you to make the first item on your agenda—fair treatment, where God's children are concerned. Now, if you are not prepared to do that, we do have an agenda that we must follow. And our agenda calls for withdrawing economic support from you . . ."

But not only that, we've got to strengthen black institutions. I call upon you to take your money out of the banks downtown and deposit your money in Tri-State Bank—we want a "bank-in" movement in Memphis. So go by the savings and loan association. I'm not asking you something that we don't do ourselves at SCLC. Judge Hooks and others will tell you that we have an account here in the savings and loan association from the Southern Christian Leadership Conference. We're just telling you to follow what we're doing. Put your money there. You have six

or seven black insurance companies in Memphis. Take out your insurance there. We want to have an "insurance-in."

Now these are some practical things we can do. We begin the process of building a greater economic base. And at the same time, we are putting pressure where it really hurts. I ask you to follow through here.

Now, let me say as I move to my conclusion that we've got to give ourselves to this struggle until the end. Nothing would be more tragic than to stop at this point, in Memphis. We've got to see it through. And when we have our march, you need to be there. Be concerned about your brother. You may not be on strike. But either we go up together, or we go down together.

Let us develop a kind of dangerous unselfishness. One day a man came to Jesus; and he wanted to raise some questions about some vital matters in life. At points, he wanted to trick Jesus, and show him that he knew a little more than Jesus knew, and through this, throw him off base. Now that question could have easily ended up in a philosophical and theological debate. But Jesus immediately pulled that question from mid-air, and placed it on a dangerous curve between Jerusalem and Jericho. And he talked about a certain man, who fell among thieves. You remember that a Levite and a priest passed by on the other side. They didn't stop to help him. And finally a man of another race came by. He got down from his beast, decided not to be compassionate by proxy.[14] But

___

13. Here, the expression *after you leave* means "not counting" or "apart from."

14. In ancient Israel, men of the *Levite* tribe were temple priests or assistants. One might expect the two religious men to help, especially since the victim is also Jewish. Instead, it is *a man of another race* who decides not to leave it to someone else—a *proxy,* or substitute—to help.

Vocabulary
agenda (ə jen′ də) *n.* a program or schedule of things to be done
compassionate (kəm pash′ ə nit) *adj.* having or showing sympathy for another's suffering or misfortune, combined with a desire to help

MEETING INDIVIDUAL NEEDS

MULTIPLE LEARNING STYLES

Intrapersonal King's words are powerful and persuasive. However, in the final analysis, each person had to make his or her own decision about what to do—to join the march or not. Intrapersonal learners are introspective and may be able to shed special insights into the reasoning that takes place within a person when making such a decision.

Activity Invite students to choose an issue on which people have been asked to take a stand. Ask them to write a dialogue-journal entry based on the topic. **L2**

"I AM A MAN" march in Memphis, TN. United Press International.

Viewing the photograph: This photograph was taken in Memphis, Tennessee, the day after Martin Luther King Jr. led a march. Describe the action and mood that is depicted. What stands out the most?

On March 28, King led a march in support of the striking garbage workers. The march ended in violence. The National Guard was called in. The next day, the strikers continued with their protest. The photograph shows the march that took place. The speech King is making took place several days later in Memphis.

Viewing Response *The protesters are walking down the street between soldiers with fixed bayonets on one side and tanks on the other. The mood is one of tension and determination. The words on the signs stand out most.*

with him, administered first aid, and helped the man in need. Jesus ended up saying, this was the good man, this was the great man, because he had the capacity to project the "I" into the "thou," and to be concerned about his brother. Now you know, we use our imagination a great deal to try to determine why the priest and the Levite didn't stop. At times we say they were busy going to church meetings—an ecclesiastical gathering—and they had to get on down to Jerusalem so they wouldn't be late for their meeting. At other times we would speculate that there was a religious law that "One who was engaged in religious ceremonials was not to touch a human body twenty-four hours before the ceremony." And every now and then we begin to wonder whether maybe they were not going down to Jerusalem, or down to Jericho, rather to organize a "Jericho Road

Improvement Association." That's a possibility. Maybe they felt that it was better to deal with the problem from the causal root, rather than to get bogged down with an individual effort.

But I'm going to tell you what my imagination tells me. It's possible that these men were afraid. You see, the Jericho road is a dangerous road. I remember when Mrs. King and I were first in Jerusalem. We rented a car and drove from Jerusalem down to Jericho. And as soon as we got on that road, I said to my wife, "I can see why Jesus used this as a setting for his parable."[15] It's a winding, meandering road. It's really conducive for ambushing. You start out in Jerusalem, which is about 1200 miles, or rather 1200 feet above sea level.

---

15. A *parable* is a brief story intended to illustrate some truth or moral lesson.

Vocabulary
speculate (spek′ yə lāt′) *v.* to guess

M **Literary Elements**

ALLUSION King uses a parable to stress the need to aid others in their struggles. Ask students who recognize the parable to identify it and tell the story. *(The parable, "The Good Samaritan," tells of a Jewish traveler who is robbed and beaten. A priest and a Levite, both religious men, pass by. A Samaritan, an enemy of the Jews, stops to help.)*

N **Active Reading**

REVIEW What does King ultimately conclude was the reason the priest and Levite did not stop? Why is this a good reason to use with his listeners? *(He says they were afraid. No doubt many listeners are also afraid to join King in a march.)*

LIFE SKILLS CONNECTION

Problem Solving King had the continuing problem of motivating and mobilizing people. Speeches and marches were methods he used. When looking for solutions, options need to be considered and possible consequences evaluated. For example, King's earlier garbage strike march resulted in violence.

Activity As a class, identify a local or national problem of interest to students. List possible solutions and consequences

using an "If—Then" chart like the one shown. **L2**

Problem

If		Then
	⟶	
	⟶	
	⟶	
	⟶	
	⟶	

RESPOND Ask students what they might have decided if they had been in the meeting. *(Answers will vary. Students may say they would be willing to march with King, or they may indicate they would have been afraid.)*

P **Literary Elements**

IRONY King tells about being stabbed and almost dying. Ask students what is ironic about the attack. *(It was committed by an African American woman.)*

I've Seen the Promised Land

And by the time you get down to Jericho, fifteen or twenty minutes later, you're about 2200 feet below sea level. That's a dangerous road. In the days of Jesus it came to be known as the "Bloody Pass." And you know, it's possible that the priest and the Levite looked over that man on the ground and wondered if the robbers were still around. Or it's possible that they felt that the man on the ground was merely faking. And he was acting like he had been robbed and hurt, in order to seize them over there, lure them there for quick and easy seizure. And so the first question that the Levite asked was, "If I stop to help this man, what will happen to me?" But then the Good Samaritan came by. And he reversed the question: "If I do not stop to help this man, what will happen to him?"

That's the question before you tonight. Not, "If I stop to help the sanitation workers, what will happen to all of the hours that I usually spend in my office every day and

Dr. Martin Luther King Jr. hugs his wife Coretta after learning he had been awarded the Nobel Prize for Peace. United Press International.

524 🌊 UNIT 2

every week as a pastor?" The question is not, "If I stop to help this man in need, what will happen to me?" "If I do not stop to help the sanitation workers, what will happen to them?" That's the question.

Let us rise up tonight with a greater readiness. Let us stand with a greater determination. And let us move on in these powerful days, these days of challenge to make America what it ought to be. We have an opportunity to make America a better nation. And I want to thank God, once more, for allowing me to be here with you.

You know, several years ago, I was in New York City autographing the first book that I had written. And while sitting there autographing books, a demented[16] black woman came up. The only question I heard from her was, "Are you Martin Luther King?"

And I was looking down writing, and I said yes. And the next minute I felt something beating on my chest. Before I knew it I had been stabbed by this demented woman. I was rushed to Harlem Hospital. It was a dark Saturday afternoon. And that blade had gone through, and the X rays revealed that the tip of the blade was on the edge of my aorta, the main artery. And once that's punctured, you drown in your own blood— that's the end of you.

It came out in the *New York Times* the next morning, that if I had sneezed, I would have died. Well, about four days later, they allowed me, after the operation, after my chest had been opened, and the blade had been taken out, to move around in the wheel chair in the hospital. They allowed me to read some of the mail that came in, and from all over the states, and the world, kind letters came in. I read a few, but one of them I will never forget. I had received one from the President and the Vice-President. I've forgotten what those telegrams

---

16. *Demented* means "insane."

Grammar and Language *Minilesson*

Simple Subjects and Simple Predicates Write these sentences on the board:

> The issue is injustice. *(issue; is)*
> The priest was going to Jericho. *(priest; was going)*

Ask students to identify the simple subject and the simple predicate in each sentence.

Activity Ask students to underline the simple subject and circle the simple predicate in the following sentences.

1. Now these are some practical things. *(these; are)*
2. You can develop a kind of dangerous unselfishness. *(You; can develop)*
3. Ordinary everyday people can deposit money in African American-owned banks. *(people; can deposit)* **L1**

Additional Resources

📘 *Grammar and Language Transparency 43*

📕 *Grammar and Language Workbook,* p. 75

📕 *Grammar and Composition Handbook,* Lesson 2.1

📕 *Writer's Choice,* Lesson 11.1

said. I'd received a visit and a letter from the Governor of New York, but I've forgotten what the letter said. But there was another letter that came from a little girl, a young girl who was a student at the White Plains High School. And I looked at that letter, and I'll never forget it. It said simply, "Dear Dr. King: I am a ninth-grade student at the White Plains High School." She said, "While it should not matter, I would like to mention that I am a white girl. I read in the paper of your misfortune, and of your suffering. And I read that if you had sneezed, you would have died. And I'm simply writing you to say that I'm so happy that you didn't sneeze."

And I want to say tonight, I want to say that I am happy that I didn't sneeze. Because if I had sneezed, I wouldn't have been around here in 1960, when students all over the South started sitting in at lunch counters. And I knew that as they were sitting in, they were really standing up for the best in the American dream. And taking the whole nation back to those great walls of democracy which were dug deep by the Founding Fathers in the Declaration of Independence and the Constitution. If I had sneezed, I wouldn't have been around in 1962, when Negroes in Albany, Georgia,[17] decided to straighten their backs up. And whenever men and women straighten their backs up, they are going somewhere, because a man can't ride your back unless it is bent. If I had sneezed, I wouldn't have been here in 1963, when the black people of Birmingham, Alabama, aroused the conscience of this nation, and brought into being the Civil Rights Bill. If I had sneezed, I wouldn't have had a chance later that year, in August, to try to tell

---

17. In 1962 King took part in demonstrations in *Albany, Georgia,* protesting the segregation of public facilities.

America about a dream that I had had. If I had sneezed, I wouldn't have been down in Selma, Alabama,[18] to see the great movement there. If I had sneezed, I wouldn't have been in Memphis to see a community rally around those brothers and sisters who are suffering. I'm so happy that I didn't sneeze.

And they were telling me, now it doesn't matter now. It really doesn't matter what happens now. I left Atlanta this morning, and as we got started on the plane, there were six of us, the pilot said over the public address system, "We are sorry for the delay, but we have Dr. Martin Luther King on the plane. And to be sure that all of the bags were checked, and to be sure that nothing would be wrong with the plane, we had to check out everything carefully. And we've had the plane protected and guarded all night."

And then I got into Memphis. And some began to say the threats, or talk about the threats that were out. What would happen to me from some of our sick white brothers?

Well, I don't know what will happen now. We've got some difficult days ahead. But it doesn't matter with me now. Because I've been to the mountaintop. And I don't mind. Like anybody, I would like to live a long life. Longevity has its place. But I'm not concerned about that now. I just want to do God's will. And He's allowed me to go up to the mountain. And I've looked over. And I've seen the promised land. I may not get there with you. But I want you to know tonight, that we, as a people will get to the promised land. And I'm happy, tonight. I'm not worried about anything. I'm not fearing any man. Mine eyes have seen the glory of the coming of the Lord.

---

18. In *Selma, Alabama,* in 1965, King led a march to protest restrictions on black voting rights. Soon afterward, the Voting Rights Act of 1965 was passed.

Personal Response

Some students may cite the final paragraph and say that it impressed them because King spoke as if he knew he was going to die soon.

ANALYZING LITERATURE

1. King begins in ancient Egypt and moves on to Greece, the Roman Empire, the Renaissance, the Protestant Reformation, the Civil War, the Depression, and finally the present. He wants to live in the present because humanity is finally being forced to deal with the issue of equality.
2. The general goals are to bring African Americans out of poverty, hurt, and neglect. In Memphis the specific issue is a strike by the sanitation workers.
3. King says that they have to stay united, stay focused on the issue, not become violent, and march for their brothers.
4. If he had sneezed, he would not have seen the lunch-counter sit-ins or how people in Atlanta, Montgomery, Selma, and Memphis stood up for their rights. He would not have been able to give his famous speech about his dream.
5. He says he is happy and not worried. He says he feels this way because he knows things are going to turn out right. He has seen the future, and it is a good one.
6. A person could infer that King is the kind of person who believes he can do something useful and important in his own life and time.
7. King is referring to the rights guaranteed in the Constitution. He goes on to cite the freedoms of assembly, speech, and the press and says that the greatness of America is the right to protest for right.
8. His purpose is to get people to support the strikers and to march on their behalf. He expects people will do this.
9. The message he wants to convey is that together they have already accomplished a great deal.
10. The promised land is freedom and equality.
11. King uses repetition not only to emphasize important ideas but also to cause an emotional reaction that will motivate his listeners. Students may mention the use of the term *collectively* as King stresses the economic power of African Americans. Students

Responding to Literature

Personal Response

Which sentence or passage made the greatest impression on you? Why?

——— ANALYZING LITERATURE ———

RECALL

1. Summarize King's mental journey through history. In which age does he want to live? Why?
2. According to King, what general goal are African Americans striving for? What specific issue faces them in Memphis?
3. What plan of action does King outline for black people in Memphis?
4. What reasons does King give for being happy he didn't sneeze after he was stabbed?
5. What feelings does King express about the dangers he faces? What reasons does he give for his feelings?

INTERPRET

6. What might you infer about King's character and beliefs, based on his mental journey through history?
7. What do you think King means when he tells Americans to "be true to what you said on paper"? Support your answer using details from the speech.
8. What is the purpose of King's plan of action? What results do you think he expects?
9. What message do you think King wants to convey by telling why he is glad he didn't sneeze?
10. At the end of his speech, King refers to the "promised land." What do you think this is?

EVALUATE AND CONNECT

11. How does King use **repetition** to emphasize important ideas? Find two examples, and explain what ideas King is emphasizing in each example.
12. What is your opinion of King's nonviolent approach to instituting political and social change? Give reasons for your opinion.
13. If King were alive today, what issues do you think he might be addressing? Why?
14. How did the prophetic aspects of this speech affect your reaction to it? Explain.
15. **Theme Connections**   Look back at the Focus Activity on page 516. Evaluate the level of dedication that King brought to his quest for justice and equality. What sacrifices did he make?

Literary ELEMENTS

Allusion

An **allusion** is a reference to a well-known character, place, or situation from history or from a work of literature, music, or art. In this speech, King uses both historical and biblical allusions. For example, King says, "I would take my mental flight by Egypt through, or rather across the Red Sea, through the wilderness on toward the promised land." He is alluding to the biblical story in which Moses leads the Israelites out of slavery in Egypt to the promised land of Canaan. An example of a historical allusion is King's reference to President Franklin D. Roosevelt's struggles during the Great Depression: "I would even come up to the early thirties, and see a man grappling with the problems of the bankruptcy of his nation."

1. Why do you think King alludes to the Israelites' flight from Egypt? To what might this journey be compared?
2. Locate two more examples of historical allusions, and explain why you think King included them.

● See **Literary Terms Handbook**, p. R1.

---

might also mention the repetition of *mountain, mountaintop,* and *promised land* in the final paragraph.
12. Most students may agree that King's nonviolent approach was successful. Social and political changes did result.
13. Issues that students might mention include the need for more jobs, better housing, equal opportunities for all, drugs, and the breakup of the family.
14. Students will probably indicate that they were amazed by just how prophetic his words were.
15. King sacrificed his time and, ultimately, his life, for the cause.

LITERARY ELEMENTS

1. The struggle of the Israelites, who had also been slaves, might be compared to the African American journey toward equality.
2. Students may mention the allusion to Lincoln's signing of the Emancipation Proclamation or to Martin Luther and the Protestant Reformation. King uses them to compare the current struggle for equality to these momentous events.

Additional Resources

📖 *Literary Elements Transparency 44*

LITERATURE AND WRITING

Writing About Literature

Character Sketch Think about what this speech reveals about King's character, beliefs, personality, and outlook on life. Go back to page 516 and reread the Did You Know? section and the author biography. Then write a character sketch of Martin Luther King Jr., using details from the speech and from page 516 to support your ideas. Share your character sketch in a small group.

Creative Writing

With Deepest Sympathy Imagine that you were in the audience the night King delivered this speech. The next evening, you turn on the television and learn that King has been assassinated. Write a letter of sympathy to King's widow and children in which you reflect on how you felt as you listened to his speech, and how you feel now in light of King's violent and untimely death.

EXTENDING YOUR RESPONSE

Literature Groups

Define a Term King challenges his audience by saying, "Let us develop a kind of dangerous unselfishness." He uses the biblical story of the Good Samaritan to illustrate the concept of "dangerous unselfishness." Discuss what you think King means by that term. As a group, write a definition of dangerous unselfishness. Compare your definition with those written by other groups.

Listening and Speaking

The Spoken Word With a partner, listen to recordings of this speech and others given by King. (King's speeches are available on video and audiocassettes, and you can find excerpts on the Internet.) Listen carefully to the cadence, or rhythmic flow, of King's delivery. Notice how King raises and lowers his voice to emphasize an idea.

Make notes on how King's delivery affects his message. Share your ideas with the class.

Internet Connection

Notable People Use the Internet to gather information about another important figure in the civil rights movement, such as Ralph Abernathy, Rosa Parks, A. Philip Randolph, or Roy Wilkins. Share your findings with the class.

Rosa Parks

 Save your work for your portfolio.

Skill Minilesson

GRAMMAR AND LANGUAGE • Parallelism

The use of a series of words, phrases, clauses, or sentences that have a similar grammatical structure is called **parallelism.** Skillful speakers and writers often use parallelism to emphasize an idea and to create a rhythmic flow to the language. King's speech "I've Seen the Promised Land" includes many examples of parallelism, such as this one: "But either we go up together, or we go down together." The two clauses repeat the pattern of subject *(we),* verb *(go),* and two adverbs *(up/down, together).* Because of the repetition of specific words, the emphasis falls on the two adverbs *up* and *down.*

PRACTICE On your paper, write two more examples of parallelism you find in "I've Seen the Promised Land." Explain what grammatical elements are parallel, and describe the effect of this parallelism.

● For more about parallelism, see **Literary Terms Handbook,** p. R9.

LITERATURE AND WRITING

Writing About Literature

Students' character sketches should
- describe specific character traits, beliefs, personality traits, and outlook.
- identify examples of how these traits, beliefs, and outlook were revealed.

Creative Writing

Students' letters should
- express their sympathy.
- tell how they felt the night of the speech and why.
- use the format for a friendly letter.

EXTENDING YOUR RESPONSE

Literature Groups Remind students that their final product should be in the form of a definition and that it should be short and to the point. **COLLAB. LEARN.**

Listening and Speaking Suggest that students listen for specific places where King raises or lowers his voice and explain why. Ask them also to listen for the musical quality of his voice—when and why he gradually gets louder and louder.

Internet Connection Remind students that they may write about the individuals listed or others. They might start by simply entering *civil rights movement* as a source for names.

Skill Minilesson

GRAMMAR AND LANGUAGE • Parallelism

p. 518: "But I wouldn't stop there." Entire sentence repeated several times; to emphasize his desire to live in the time that he lives in.
p. 521: "It's alright to talk about . . ." Phrase repeated as beginning of series of sentences; to emphasize the list of biblical allusions made by preachers.

Additional Resources

 Grammar and Composition Handbook

 Grammar and Language Workbook, p. 323

✔ ASSESSMENT OPTIONS

📁 *Quick Checks,* p. 44

📁 *Selection and Theme Assessment,* pp. 85–86

📁 *Performance Assessment,* p. 43

💾 *Testmaker*

Writing Skills

Writing Skills

Teaching Strategies

Before presenting the skills lesson, you might want to ask students to select several pieces of writing from their portfolios. After you and the students have read and discussed the lesson, suggest that they analyze the pieces they selected. Let volunteers tell which method of organization they used for a particular piece and why.

Exercise

Students' paragraphs should show an identifiable pattern of organization and that pattern should work together with the details to effectively describe the place, routine, or holiday celebration that was chosen.

Additional Resources

📁 **Writing and Proofreading Practice,** pp. 1–7

✍ **Writing and Proofreading Transparencies 1–6**

📕 **Writer's Choice,** Lesson 3.1

Teaching Options

Organizing Details

Good descriptive writing must contain vivid details. It must also organize those details into meaningful patterns. There are several ways to organize details in your writing.

- **Chronological order** presents events in the order in which they occur.
- **Spatial order** presents details according to their physical placement. For example, details might be described from left to right, from front to back, from top to bottom, clockwise or counterclockwise, or from near to far.
- **Order of importance** presents the least important details first and builds to the most important ones.

Since each of these strategies creates a different effect, your purpose for writing will help you determine which to use. For example, if you want to create a vivid image of your best friend's bedroom, you'll probably want to describe the details in spatial order. If you want to emphasize an important idea, you'll probably want to describe details in the order of their importance. Sometimes, you may combine strategies. For example, you might describe your friend's bedroom from right to left because the most important detail—a six-foot-tall terrarium—is on the left side of the room.

Notice the way Martin Luther King Jr. organizes details in this excerpt from "I've Seen the Promised Land":

> I remember in Birmingham, Alabama, when we were in that majestic struggle there we would move out of the 16th Street Baptist Church day after day; by the hundreds we would move out. And Bull Connor would tell them to send the dogs forth and they did come; but we just went before the dogs singing, "Ain't gonna let nobody turn me round." Bull Connor next would say, "Turn the fire hoses on."

King presents the details of this scene in **chronological order.** He provides a detail about what happened first: the marchers moved out from the church. Then Bull Connor called on the dogs, and the dogs came, but the people "just went before the dogs singing," and so forth. King uses transitional words, such as *and, but,* and *next,* to show sequence in time. By organizing the details about this incident in chronological order, King can describe the event as it unfolded.

EXERCISE

Using concrete, vivid details, write a paragraph describing one of your favorite places, a daily routine, or a holiday celebration you enjoy. Organize your details in the way that will most effectively convey what you are trying to describe.

Grammar and Language *Minilesson*

Irregular Comparisons In choosing vivid details for descriptive writing, comparisons and comparative forms are needed.

Activity Write the following words on the board and ask volunteers to write the comparative and superlative forms: *good, well, bad, far, many, much.* **L2**

Additional Resources

✍ **Grammar and Language Transparency 44**

📕 **Grammar and Language Workbook,** p. 201

📕 **Grammar and Composition Handbook,** Lesson 8.2

📕 **Writer's Choice,** Lesson 18.2

Journal Entries

What draws explorers to the icy wilderness landscape of Antarctica? British naval officer R. F. Scott bravely undertook the Antarctic Expedition in 1910 mainly to achieve scientific results, but Scott and his crew died from exposure to the bitter cold.

Return from First Summit Depot

by R. F. Scott—Scott's Last Expedition

Thursday, February 8.

R. 22. Height 6260. Start Temp. −11°. . . . Had a beastly morning. Wind very strong and cold. Steered in for Mt. Darwin to visit rock. Sent Bowers on, on ski, as Wilson can't wear his at present. He obtained several specimens, all of much the same type, a close-grained granite rock which weathers red. Hence the pink limestone. After he rejoined we skidded downhill pretty fast, leaders on ski, Oates and Wilson on foot alongside sledge—Evans detached. We lunched at 2 well down towards Mt. Buckley, the wind half a gale and everybody very cold and cheerless. However better things were to follow. . . . We found ourselves under perpendicular cliffs of Beacon sandstone, weathering rapidly and carrying veritable coal seams. From the last Wilson, with his sharp eyes, has picked several plant impressions, the last a piece of coal with beautifully traced leaves in layers. . . . Altogether we have had a most interesting afternoon, and the relief of being out of the wind and in a warmer temperature is inexpressible. . . . A lot could be written on the delight of setting foot on rock after 14 weeks of snow and ice and nearly 7 out of sight of aught else. It is like going ashore after a sea voyage. We deserve a little good bright weather after all our trials. . . .

Friday, February 9.

R. 23. Height 5210 ft. Lunch Temp. +10°. . . . Kept along the edge of moraine to the end of Mt. Buckley. Stopped and geologized. Wilson got great find of vegetable impression in piece of limestone. Too tired to write geological notes. We all felt very slack this morning, partly rise of temperature, partly reaction, no doubt. . . . Did pretty well in the afternoon, marching 3¾ hours; the sledgemeter is

Objective

- To read and understand journal entries

Literature — LINK

Exploring Antarctic Ice Point out that Scott was an Antarctic explorer in the early 1900s and that the next selection, "Exploring Antarctic Ice" (pp. 532–537), is about modern-day Antarctic scientists.

Reading *Minilesson*

Previewing Tell students that a good technique to use before reading a selection is to preview it. Previewing is simply looking through the selection, studying the pictures, reading captions, reading any headings, and noting how the selection is organized. By doing these things, a reader gets clues about the selection.

Activity As a class, preview the journal entries. Ask students to name some of the features the selection has. Have them tell some of the information they learned simply by looking at the pictures and reading the first line of each entry. **L1**

Respond

1. Some students may mention Scott's finding interesting things, such as coal seams and vegetable impressions in limestone. These are remarkable because the Antarctic must have been a different place at some earlier time.

2. Scott seems to be a brave, determined, and insightful person. Even in the face of death, he seems able to keep a very matter-of-fact, almost scientific approach to the situation. He is heroic.

Additional Resources

📁 *Media Connections Activities,* p. 12

---

unshipped, so cannot tell distance traversed. Very warm on march and we are all pretty tired. Tonight it is wonderfully calm and warm, though it has been overcast all the afternoon. It is remarkable to be able to stand outside the tent and sun oneself. Our food satisfies now, but we must march to keep on the full ration, and we want rest, yet we shall pull through all right, D.V. We are by no means worn out.

Monday, March 19.

Lunch. . . . Sledge dreadfully heavy. We are 15½ miles from the depot and ought to get there in three days. What progress! We have two days' food but barely a day's fuel. All our feet are getting bad—Wilson's best, my right foot worst, left all right. There is no chance to nurse one's feet till we can get hot food into us. Amputation is the least I can hope for now, but will the trouble spread? That is the serious question. The weather doesn't give us a chance— the wind from N. to N.W. and −40° temp. today. . . .

Thursday, March 22 and 23.

Blizzard bad as ever—Wilson and Bowers unable to start—tomorrow last chance—no fuel and only one or two of food left—must be near the end. . . .

Thursday, March 29.

Since the 21st we have had a continuous gale from W.S.W. and S.W. We had fuel to make two cups of tea apiece and bare food for two days on the 20th. Every day we have been ready to start for our depot 11 miles away, but outside the door of the tent it remains a scene of whirling drift. I do not think we can hope for any better things now. We shall stick it out to the end, but we are getting weaker, of course, and the end cannot be far.

It seems a pity, but I do not think I can write more.

Interior view of living quarters.

Respond

1. What do you find most remarkable about the experiences that Scott recorded here in his journal? Why?

2. What does his account tell you about him as a person? Explain.

Antarctica For students who want to find out more about Antarctica via the Internet, suggest that they use a search engine and enter keywords such as *Antarctica, ozone hole, Antarctic Treaty,* and *Ross Ice Shelf.*

Before You Read

Exploring Antarctic Ice

FOCUS ACTIVITY

What might it be like to visit Antarctica?

QUICKWRITE Imagine that you have been invited to participate in a scientific expedition to Antarctica. Spend five minutes writing about what you think the trip might be like. What might you and your fellow scientists explore and study? What dangers or discomforts might you face? What wonders might you observe?

SETTING A PURPOSE Read to learn about one author's experiences during a scientific expedition to Antarctica.

BACKGROUND

The Time and Place
The events described in this selection take place in August and September 1995, on the winter sea ice surrounding Antarctica.

Did You Know?
Under extremely cold conditions, ice forms on the surface of the sea. Sea ice exists year-round on the waters surrounding Antarctica; during winter, the ice expands to cover an area that is almost twice as big as the United States. Scientists believe they can learn much about global warming and climate change by studying Antarctic ice, the sea beneath it, and the living things that inhabit this environment.

VOCABULARY PREVIEW

ephemeral (i fem′ ər əl) *adj.* short-lived; temporary; p. 534

ecosystem (e′ kō sis′ təm) *n.* a community of organisms together with their environment, functioning as a unit; p. 534

proliferation (prō lif′ ə rā′ shən) *n.* growth by rapidly producing new cells or offspring; p. 534

tedious (tē′ dē əs) *adj.* boring; tiresome; p. 534

disconcerting (dis′ kən surt′ ing) *adj.* disturbing, confusing, or frustrating; p. 536

devoid (di void′) *adj.* not possessing; lacking (with *of*); p. 536

transient (tran′ shənt) *adj.* of temporary or brief duration; not lasting; p. 537

Meet Jane Ellen Stevens

❝I was always very curious about how the world worked, how people designed ways to solve problems.❞

When Jane Stevens was asked what she likes best about her work as a science and technology writer, she replied, "Asking people about what they do and how they think and discover, learning incredible things about this world, traveling to fascinating places." Indeed, Stevens is no armchair adventurer: she has traveled the world researching science, technology, and medical topics for newspaper and magazine articles.

Jane E. Stevens was born in 1948 in East Orange, New Jersey. This article first appeared in the May 1996 issue of National Geographic.

NONFICTION 531

NONFICTION 531

SUMMARY

Ice is ice. Right? Not so, as the author of this article explains. She spends 50 days on an international scientific expedition to investigate Antarctica's ice. As she points out, there is much to be learned. The ultimate importance of Antarctica's ice on currents and climate, especially if warming or cooling should occur, is part of why Antarctica's ice needs to be studied.

📁 *Spanish Summaries,* p. 45

A Active Reading

QUESTION Have the first three paragraphs read. Ask students what the purpose of the expedition was. Suggest that the class make a list of questions they would like to find out about Antarctic ice as they read. List the questions and refer to them after the reading of the selection.

Additional Resources

📁 *Active Reading Guide,* p. 45
🎧 *Audio Library*
🎧 *Spanish Audio Library*

Teaching Options

The temperature is 1°F, not very cold for this part of the world, and a moderate breeze ruffles the fur around the hoods of our regulation-issue bloodred parkas. It's our first day out on the ice, and with a dozen other people I am shoveling snow from a frozen ocean that stretches to the horizon like a white desert.

A

I hear a radio crackle with the voice of second officer Michael Watson. Like a plantation manager supervising his field hands, Watson eyes us through binoculars from the bridge of the *Nathaniel B. Palmer.* "Greg, be advised that there's a crack from the bow that's crossing the end of your line." Watson refers to the marker line along which we are digging holes to measure the snow and ice thickness.

B

"Roger that," says Greg Packard, the marine projects coordinator. "We'll keep an eye on it."

The skies, which dawned a clear, blazing blue, have grayed. Watson's disembodied voice emerges again from Packard's radio: "Greg, be advised, a section of ice under the ship's starboard wing just buckled and it's filling with water."

Exploring Antarctic Ice

Jane Ellen Stevens

CONNECTING TO OTHER SELECTIONS

The chart at the right shows three ways to connect "Exploring Antarctic Ice" to selections in this book.

For specific teaching strategies, see the *Unit Two Planning Guide,* pages 86–93.

Connection	Title
Life Skills: Implementing and Performing	→ "Chee's Daughter," p. 23
Thematic: Nature at Work	→ "Colombia's Mortal Agony," p. 355
Literary: Setting	→ "A Sound of Thunder," p. 316

"Roger that."

As I push the shovel into the snow, a hairline crack streaks from the ship's bow a hundred yards away right past the tips of my boots. I point it out to Martin Jeffries, our chief scientist. Jeffries, a 37-year-old glaciologist[1] from the Geophysical Institute of the University of Alaska Fairbanks, has 14 years' experience with Arctic and Antarctic sea ice.

"Watch it," he advises.

The icy landscape looks solid enough, but just two feet below my white rubber boots lies 12,000 feet of frigid water. Padded with 20 pounds of clothes, I might survive in the water a few minutes—if I had the presence of mind to inflate my life vest.

Suddenly Packard shouts a warning. The crack at the end of the line is widening. We stop digging and, in the silence, hear Watson's calm voice: "Greg, the pool under the wing is getting deeper."

Jeffries doesn't hesitate. "Get back to the ship!" he yells.

---

1. A scientist who studies glaciers is a *glaciologist*.

We seize shovels, tape measures, ice corers, and sledges and shuffle across the floe as fast as we can. The buckled section of ice is now a large pond from which seawater pours onto the rest of the floe like a mountain stream. As we gather inside the ship, the flat ice we stood on with all the confidence of explorers on newly conquered land begins disintegrating.

"Rats!" Jeffries says. Then relief swells his voice: "Thanks to all for coming in alive."

We're at day seven of a fifty-day international scientific expedition that will take us 8,400 miles through the winter sea ice encircling Antarctica. It is early August, and a little more than a month from now the ice will reach its greatest expanse—twice the area of the entire United States. The ice appears and disappears every year. Beginning in March, the Antarctic autumn, it grows rapidly—at a rate of 22 square miles a minute—to an

Did You Know?
A *floe* is a large sheet of floating ice.

NONFICTION 533

B Literary Elements

AUTHOR'S PURPOSE What is the author's purpose in including the radio transmissions from the ship to the group on the ice? *(The author is introducing people on the team, but she is also building a mood of tension in order to heighten the awareness that what they are doing is dangerous.)*

C Critical Thinking

INFERRING Ask students to suggest words to describe the events that take place in the opening of the article. *(dangerous, serious, exciting, professional)*

FYI

Who Owns Antarctica?
In the past, various countries have claimed parts of Antarctica. However, from July 1957 through December 1958, a group of nations worked together doing scientific research in Antarctica. This time period was called the International Geophysical Year. One of the great achievements of the research effort was not scientific but political. The countries cooperated so well that they decided to continue working together. A treaty, called the Antarctic Treaty, was signed. In it, treaty countries agreed to put aside their territorial claims indefinitely. So, who owns Antarctica? No one.

MEETING INDIVIDUAL NEEDS

ENGLISH LANGUAGE LEARNERS

Differing Climates English language learners who live in or come from a climate that is warm most of the time may need background on life in cold climates. Ask students to discuss the climate in the area in which they live or the country from which they came, using these questions: *How would you describe the climate? What is special about the climate? How is it different* *from a place that is cold most of the time? How is it alike?*

Activity Draw a chart on the board. Let students make a comparison by describing features of their climate and Antarctica's climate.

Additional Resources
📁 *English Language Learners Sourcebook*

D Active Reading

REVIEW Have students review the significance of the name of the ship, *Palmer*. (*It was named for one of the first people to see Antarctica.*)

E Active Reading

QUESTION What is an unexpected discovery made by the German researchers? (*They discover that there are lots of animals in Antarctica during the winter and that they are fatter than those observed during the summer.*)

F Active Reading

REVIEW Discuss some of the questions that scientists are trying to answer by expeditions such as the one the author is on. (*They want to find out why the thickness of the ice varies and how this affects ocean currents, how algae survive in the ice during winter, and what the winter lives of penguins are like.*)

Cultural Note

The ancient Greeks gave Antarctica its name. They believed there had to be a large landmass in the southern hemisphere. A constellation in the northern sky was called Arktos, the bear, from which the word *Arctic* is derived. The Greeks named the southern landmass Antarktikos, meaning "opposite the bear" or "anti-Arctic."

Teaching Options

Exploring Antarctic Ice

average thickness of three feet. By October, the middle of spring, it is melting twice as fast.

With me on the *Palmer*, a privately owned research icebreaker under contract to the National Science Foundation (NSF), are 35 men and 7 other women. It's my second voyage on the ship; this year, as a science journalist with an NSF fellowship,[2] I've signed on as a working member of Jeffries's group of ten researchers. We're as zealous as Nathaniel B. Palmer himself, the American seal hunter who in 1820 was one of the first people to see Antarctica. . . .

Martin Jeffries and his fellow scientists call this <u>ephemeral</u> frontier the "Antarctic winter sea-ice <u>ecosystem</u>" —a dull name that doesn't even hint at the dangers and mysteries that kept all but a handful of humans away until a decade ago. Science began nibbling at the winter sea ice in 1974, but it was not until 1986 that the first research ship, the German icebreaker *Polarstern*, ventured deep into it. People criticized that expedition as foolhardy[3] and unnecessary: The ice had trapped or crushed every ship that had gone in, and everyone assumed the place was a wasteland.

Yet the researchers on the *Polarstern* found life in abundance. Penguins, seals, and seabirds appeared out of nowhere on their way to no known place. They were fatter than those observed in summer. Even the sea ice itself seemed to breathe, opening into

---

2. A *fellowship* is a sum of money granted to allow work or advanced study in one's chosen field.
3. *Foolhardy* means "bold or daring in a foolish or unthinking way."

Vocabulary

ephemeral (i fem′ ər əl) *adj.* short-lived; temporary
ecosystem (e′ kō sis′ təm) *n.* a community of organisms together with their environment, functioning as a unit
proliferation (prō lif′ ə rā′ shən) *n.* growth by rapidly producing new cells or offspring
tedious (tē′ dē əs) *adj.* boring; tiresome

what looked like rivers meandering through a snowy prairie and then, without warning, closing again.

Since that pioneering voyage, only ten other scientific expeditions have explored the winter sea ice, seven of them on the *Nathaniel B. Palmer*. The information collected so far shows that the ice is vital for the <u>proliferation</u> of life throughout the southern oceans. In winter, algae living in the ice provide a rich pasture for krill, tiny shrimp-like creatures that are a staple food of larger animals such as whales. Dust particles blown in from distant landmasses are trapped in the ice. In spring when the ice melts, algae—perhaps fertilized by iron in the dust—bloom in the meltwater.

Did You Know?
Krill are tiny marine animals belonging to the same family as lobsters, crabs, and shrimp.

But we don't yet know, for instance, why the sea ice varies in thickness, structure, and distribution from one area to another or how changes in its mass affect ocean currents and climate. We don't know exactly how algae in the ice survive the winter, and we know hardly anything about the winter lives of the millions of Adélie and emperor penguins, Antarctic and snow petrels, and Weddell, crabeater, and leopard seals.

Solving these "whys" requires hours of <u>tedious</u> work, observing and measuring to first sort out the "whats" and "hows." How thick is the sea ice? How much snow covers it? How much of the ice is flooded with seawater? What is the temperature of the snow and ice?

MEETING INDIVIDUAL NEEDS — INCLUSION STRATEGIES

Learning Disabled Creating a graphic organizer can help students keep track of such things as the sequence of events or the relationships between individual pieces of information. In the essay, the author explains why the ice is important and then goes on to describe a food chain. Remind students that in a food chain a group of organisms lives in a special balance in which each member of the community feeds on the member below it.

Activity Ask pairs of students to use a graphic organizer to diagram the food chain described on page 534. **L2**

Additional Resources
📁 *Inclusion Strategies*

What kinds of crystals are present? Our expedition will help answer these questions.

After the ominous[4] incident our first day on the ice, we push south in the Ross Sea along longitude 180°, the date line,[5] meandering between yesterday and today through a world that will disappear two months from now. The *Palmer* makes 60 nautical miles—one degree of latitude—every 24 hours, and four days later, on Julian day 220,[6] we reach 69° south. At 9:30 A.M., as a neon orange rim appears along the horizon, we make a stop to collect atmospheric and oceanographic data. . . .

G I consider myself lucky to be part of the snow and ice thickness team: Our time is vigorously spent. With shovels, four of us begin digging holes a yard apart along the 164-yard (150-meter) line. Even though the snow is fluffy and only about a foot deep, I soon work up a sweat. Five emperor penguins slide toward us on their white-pillowed bellies, push themselves up with their beaks, and spend the rest of the afternoon studying us.

The next job is to drill small holes through the ice itself. Each time I haul out the gas-powered drill, seawater spouts through the hole like a geyser. (We employ gas-powered machinery as little as possible to keep pollution to a minimum.) We then use a measuring stick to record the depth of the snow and tailor's tape attached to a weighted piece of string to measure the thickness of the ice. There's an irony in sailing to the Antarctic in a ship that costs more than $25,000 a day to run so we can work with a wooden stick and a piece of string.

H At 3 P.M., three hours after we began shoveling, we trudge back to our warm metal

---
4. Here, *ominous* means "unfavorable" or "threatening."
5. The *date line* is the imaginary north-south line on the earth that marks the time boundary between one day and the next.
6. *Julian day 220* is August 8. The Julian calendar numbers the days of the year from 1 to 365 (or 366 in a leap year).

G **Critical Thinking**

DRAWING CONCLUSIONS The author says she is lucky she is on the snow and ice thickness team. Why does she feel this way? You might use this question to model the thinking process used in drawing conclusions.

Model: The author says that the time she spends on the team is vigorously spent. She has already described some of the physical labor and danger involved with the experiments. Being on the team, therefore, means she is kept busy physically. She also gets to go out and help conduct the experiments, experience the danger of the work, see firsthand what the ice is like, and work side by side with scientists. I think if she had to remain on the ship, she would probably have less interesting duties like keeping records or simply observing from a distance.

H **Literary Elements**

IRONY Ask students to explain the irony the author identifies and to tell why they think such simple equipment is used. *(The author finds it ironic that it costs a lot of money for a highly technical ship so that scientists can conduct experiments using basic, simple tools. The equipment has no mechanical parts to freeze up or malfunction in the cold. The simple equipment can be used easily and data recorded accurately by just about anyone. The equipment is inexpensive and can easily be replaced if lost or broken.)*

Reading *Minilesson*

Summarizing One way of comprehending and remembering information found in scientific or technical writing is to summarize the information. Use the third and fourth paragraphs on page 535 to model the process. Have students read the paragraphs. Then ask volunteers to summarize them. A typical summary might go something like this: The author is describing what they do when they measure the snow and ice. First, they dig a hole through the snow. Next, they drill a hole through the ice. Then they measure.

Activity Have pairs of students select several passages from the essay and write summaries of them. **L3**

Additional Resources

📁 *Reading Workbook,* pp. 57–58

Active Reading

I **Active Reading**

INTERPRET When the author says she is disconcerted about the thinness of the skin between herself and eternity, what does she mean? *(The skin is the ice. She does not know how thick it is or when the floe might break apart or sink. She could end up in the icy water of the ocean and drown.)*

J **Active Reading**

REVIEW Why are the whales making holes in the ice? How are the other animals taking advantage of the holes? What are the other animals eating? *(The whales need the holes to breathe. The other animals use the holes as places to find food. They are eating things that live in the sea, such as fish, squid, and krill.)*

Vo•cab•u•lar•y Skills

Homonyms and Puns In using the idiomatic expression "go with the flow," the speaker is saying he has to accept the way things are. In using the word *flow*, the speaker has created a play on words, known as a pun, in which special or double meanings apply. You may want to point out the word *floe* and its picture and word clue on page 533. Help students recognize that the expression "go with the flow" could just as easily have been written "go with the floe." Point out that the pun is formed because *flow* and *floe* are homonyms—words that sound alike but are spelled differently—and that each sentence has an almost identical meaning.

Exploring Antarctic Ice

cocoon—a daily routine that hardly ever varies. This evening, though, I pause at the gangway. The sun, huge and vermilion[7] as it drops toward the western horizon, is framed by sun dogs, rainbows of brilliant color that appear when ice crystals are thick in the sunlit air. In the east a stark white moon rises against a cerulean[8] sky. The penguins, their white necks streaked with the colors of the sun, are standing on their heels, the tops of their feet tucked under their bellies for warmth.

If day 220 was tolerably comfortable, there are times on the ice when the windchill drops to minus 50°F, and the wind, blinding us with snow that turns the *Palmer* into a dim ghost ship, sucks the life heat from our fingers and toes so they ache and grow numb. Sometimes the floes are partly submerged under a burden of several feet of snow, and I find myself sloshing ankle-deep in water—a <u>disconcerting</u> reminder of the thinness of the skin between me and eternity. . . .

The ship rams the ice, stops, slides back, and rams again. Back and ram. Back and ram. It's day 224, and for the past three days we've been stopped at 70° south. Jeffries faces a dilemma. If he pushes on toward the Ross Ice Shelf as he had planned, he risks wasting fuel and precious time. However long it takes to get in, it will take that long to get out. The ice here is four to five feet thick, with ridges of nine feet, and the weather changes so quickly we also risk being trapped without warning. Jeffries decides to change course. You can't fight Antarctic sea ice, he says. "You've got to go with the flow." We will retrace the

---

7. *Vermilion* is a bright red color.
8. *Cerulean* (sə rōō′ lē ən) is a bright blue color, often described as sky-blue.

route he took the year before, northeast through the frozen Amundsen and Bellingshausen Seas.

Minke[9] whales off the bow! The word goes out at dawn on day 227, a morning so gray no horizon divides sky from ice. I run to the bridge and see two minkes, gray-black and about 30 feet long, break a hole in the thin, frozen sheet, then submerge. Out of the mist a dozen or so Adélie penguins scuttle single file across the ice to the hole and, like kids at a swimming hole, mill around before jumping in. They pop back out and spy another hole made by the minkes farther on. Again they rush over, inspect the hole, and plunge in.

Most likely the whales are feeding on krill, and the Adélies are probably tagging along to exploit the ready-made fishing holes. Penguins, seals, and birds such as snow petrels also use natural cracks in the ice to feed and, in the case of minke whales, to breathe.

That the great, shifting expanses of ice around us, utterly <u>devoid</u> of soil and rooted plants, support any life at all—let alone in such profusion—seems impossible. André Belém, a

---

9. *Minke* (ming′ kē)

Did You Know?
In 1911 Roald *Amundsen,* a Norwegian, became the first person to reach the South Pole. The Amundsen Sea is named after him.

Did You Know?
From 1819 to 1821, Fabian *Bellingshausen,* a Russian, led an expedition that sailed completely around Antarctica. The Bellingshausen Sea is named after him.

J

Vocabulary
disconcerting (dis′ kən surt′ ing) *adj.* disturbing, confusing, or frustrating
devoid (di void′) *adj.* not possessing; lacking (with *of*)

536 🐚 UNIT 2

Teaching Options

Grammar and Language *Minilesson*

Four Kinds of Sentences Review the four kinds of sentences.
- A declarative sentence makes a statement.
- An imperative sentence gives a command or makes a request.
- An interrogative sentence asks a question.
- An exclamatory sentence expresses strong emotion.

Activity Ask students to identify the kind of each sentence and to write the punctuation mark needed.
1. What would happen if the ice were to shrink *(interrogative; ?)*
2. The ship rammed the ice forcefully *(declarative; .)*
3. Watch out *(imperative; !)*
4. Rats *(exclamatory; !)* **L1**

Additional Resources
- *Grammar and Language Transparency 45*
- *Grammar and Language Workbook,* p. 119
- *Grammar and Composition Handbook,* Lesson 4.6
- *Writer's Choice,* Lesson 13.6

graduate student from the University of Rio Grande in Brazil, offers me a dramatic insight when he shows me a test tube in which he has melted a small chunk of sea ice. "Look," he says in amazement. A thick yellowish sludge of algae floats in the bottom. "There's more life in there than in the water of an estuary."[10]

Indeed algal concentrations in the sea ice are among the highest ever recorded in any ocean. As the ice grows, the crystals snag algae. Channels winding among the crystals bring seawater—and nutrients—to the algae, which lure krill and krill larvae to the bottom of the ice floes, where they graze like tiny cows.

One day during our last week I climb with Jim Cooper, the electronics technician, to the top of the science mast, 130 feet above the ice. As he rubs the frost off the satellite receivers and meteorological sensors, I look down at a quilt of ice floes spreading to the horizon under the clear blue sky. Smoky wisps curl up around the ship like genies—ice crystals forming as water vapor from the lead we're gliding through encounters the colder air.

This transfer of heat from water to air is expressive of a much grander redistribution triggered by the sea ice: the streaming of cold water from the Antarctic toward the Equator. As seawater around Antarctica freezes, it squeezes out cold, dense brine,[11] some of which

---

10. An *estuary* is the wide mouth of a river where the ocean's tide meets the river's current. Estuaries are very fertile ecosystems that are believed to account for more than half of the life in all oceans.

11. Here, the *brine* is water that has a much higher salt content than ordinary sea water, which is also sometimes called brine.

---

sinks to deeper water then moves north. It eventually mixes with warmer water, rises, and begins flowing back toward Antarctica.

One place where this warmer water comes to the surface is the Weddell Sea. On a *Palmer* expedition there two years ago, scientists measured the heat flow from a 38,000-square-mile area at 20 watts per square yard—enough energy during the austral[12] winter to power every U.S. household more than 20 times over.

What disruptions would occur if a warming or cooling trend were to shrink or expand the winter sea ice? Presumably ocean currents would shift, perhaps causing drastic shifts in climate. The *Palmer's* next two winter voyages will look into such questions.

Our last working day, Julian day 254—Monday, September 11—is typically dreary and windy. After watching the crew hoist the gangway for the last time, I stroll to the stern deck and stare at the ice around me as the *Palmer's* engines rumble to life.

I have grown to love this cold, strange place with an intensity that I could never have anticipated. Such a reaction may seem odd to those who have never heard the sigh of ice floes jostling on the swells or watched the vapors curling up out of a lead or felt the knife blade of an Antarctic gale. Alighting here briefly, like a bird of passage, I have come to see this <u>transient</u> frontier not as a harsh place but as a living creature that nurtures a multitude of other lives. Yet no humans can ever live here. We can't conquer it, settle it, even own it. The winter ice belongs only to itself.

---

12. *Austral* means "southern." It comes from the same Latin word that gives Australia its name.

Vocabulary
transient (tran′ shənt) *adj.* of temporary or brief duration; not lasting

---

K **Literary Elements**

AUTHOR'S PURPOSE What is the author's purpose in mentioning warming or cooling and their possible result? *(This is a scientific article. She may have included this to provide information about future research and to remind the reader of the important role the ice may play with currents and climate.)*

Thematic Focus

Quests and Encounters Ask students to discuss what they think the author's quest may have been. Then have them give some examples of encounters the author had with the ice and the animals and what reactions she had to these encounters.

☑ **ASSESSMENT OPTIONS**

📁 *Quick Checks,* p. 45

® *The following videotape program is available from Glencoe. Be sure to preview the video for appropriateness for your class.*

• **Pole to Pole**

REAL-WORLD CONNECTION

In the Form of a Journal Throughout the selection, the author uses time clues to tell the reader when certain events are taking place. As a result, the selection could easily be labeled as a journal, with a date preceding each section that describes events that occurred during a certain time period. Remind students how Scott did this in his journal on pages 529 and 530. Suggest that they date each part of the essay. You might also want to suggest that students use the library card catalog to find other examples of journals that they might like to read. **L2**

Responding to the Selection

Personal Response

Some students may mention the scientists' abrupt departure from the dissolving ice floe or the view of the ice floes from atop the science mast as the most striking visual image.

ANALYZING LITERATURE

1. The ice begins to break apart, and there is a danger that they might fall into the water or that they might not be able to get back to the ship.
2. Early scientists had discovered that there were many animals there and that they were fatter in winter than in summer.
3. She drills holes in the ice and measures the thickness of the snow and ice.
4. The whales and penguins eat krill, which feed on algae, which live in the winter sea ice.
5. She loves and respects it.
6. The work is dangerous, strenuous, and challenging.
7. The research of earlier expeditions proved that there was a lot going on with both the living creatures and the natural wonders of the Antarctic. As a result, other groups have come to study the place.
8. The author feels awe and wonder at the beauty of Antarctica.
9. The animals are dependent on the ice. The ice is able to support life.
10. The more one learns about something, the more appreciative one becomes. She knows what an awesome world the winter sea ice is because she has seen it and studied it closely.
11. Students may say that their response focused on the coldness of the place while Stevens's description focused on its awesomeness.
12. Students may say that the information learned is worth the danger and expense. The information may become vital to the well-being of the planet.
13. Three possible examples are "frozen ocean . . . like a white desert" (page 532), "seawater pours . . . like a mountain stream" (page 533), and "seawater . . . spouts like a geyser" (page 535). In each simile, the unfamiliar qualities of Antarctica are described using images the reader can relate to.

Responding to Literature

Personal Response

What visual image was most striking to you as you read the selection? What made it so striking?

ANALYZING LITERATURE

RECALL

1. Describe what happens during the researchers' first day out on the ice.
2. Summarize what scientists on previous expeditions had learned about the Antarctic winter sea-ice ecosystem.
3. How does Stevens spend Julian day 220?
4. Describe the relationship among the whales, penguins, krill, algae, and winter sea ice.
5. In the article's last paragraph, how does Stevens describe her attitude toward the winter sea ice?

INTERPRET

6. What can you infer about the work that the researchers are doing, based on the author's description of their first day on the ice?
7. How did previous expeditions change scientists' attitudes about studying the winter sea-ice ecosystem in Antarctica? Explain.
8. What feelings do you think Stevens might experience as she views the scene from the gangway on day 220?
9. What conclusions might you draw from Stevens's description of the relationship among the animals and the winter sea ice?
10. What do you think accounts for Stevens's attitude toward the winter sea ice in Antarctica?

EVALUATE AND CONNECT

11. Look back at your response to the Focus Activity on page 531. Compare your response with what Stevens actually experiences on this expedition.
12. Do you think the benefits of expeditions like this one outweigh the risks and expense? Explain.
13. Find three examples of **figurative language** in the selection. Explain how each example helps you better understand or appreciate what is being described. (See Literary Terms Handbook, page R5.)
14. How does this selection help you better understand the "balance of nature"? Explain.
15. Would you like to participate in a research expedition like this one? Why or why not?

Literary ELEMENTS

Author's Purpose

When you read a piece of nonfiction, think about the **author's purpose**, or reason, for writing. For example, the author may want to inform, entertain, tell a story, or persuade the reader. Keep in mind that in any work of nonfiction, the author may have more than one purpose. For example, in a piece of narrative nonfiction, the author may want to not only tell a story, but also persuade the reader to agree with a particular point of view. In informative nonfiction, the author may want to entertain the reader while providing information about a particular topic. In "Exploring Antarctic Ice," Jane Ellen Stevens uses elements of both narrative and informative nonfiction to achieve several purposes.

1. Do you think Stevens wrote this article to inform, to entertain, to tell a story, or to persuade the reader? Give reasons for your answers.
2. Evaluate how well you think Stevens achieved each of her purposes in writing this article.
3. Which purpose do you think was most important to Stevens? Explain.

● See **Literary Terms Handbook**, p. R1.

---

14. In simple terms that are easy to understand, the author shows how the creatures in the Antarctic are dependent on one another. To disrupt one part of the system disrupts the entire system.
15. Students may answer that they would like to go to Antarctica to learn things or for the adventure of it.

LITERARY ELEMENTS

1. The author wrote for all the reasons given. The story is entertaining, and the information persuades us that the ice and the study of ecosystems are important.
2. She achieved all of her purposes. Her article is informative, entertaining, and persuasive.
3. Possibly her need to inform will be mentioned as most important.

Additional Resources

✍ *Literary Elements Transparency 45*

LITERATURE AND WRITING

Writing About Literature

Evaluate a Concluding Statement   Jane Stevens concludes her article with this statement: "The winter ice belongs only to itself." In a paragraph, explain what you think the author means by this statement, using details from the article to support your explanation. Then write another paragraph in which you tell whether you agree or disagree with this statement. Support your position using evidence from the article or from your own knowledge or experience. Compare your ideas with those of other students.

Creative Writing

Expedition Application   Imagine that you are a science writer and want to join a research expedition to gain first-hand field experience. You have learned of an expedition to the region of the world that interests you the most. Write a letter of application to the expedition leader, explaining why you are interested in the research and what qualifications you would bring to the team.

EXTENDING YOUR RESPONSE

Literature Groups

Intriguing Information   Write the answer to this question on a note card: What fact about the Antarctic exploration intrigued you the most? On the back of the card, describe why this fact made such an impression on you. Then take turns in your group reading your answer to the question. After everyone has read his or her response, go around the group again, taking turns explaining why you chose the fact you did. Using specific details from the selection, try to convince other group members that your fact is much more intriguing than theirs are.

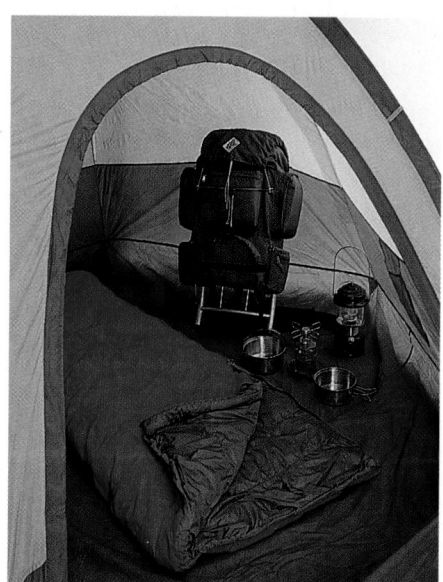

Learning for Life

Pack Your Bags   Imagine that you have been invited to join a scientific expedition to a remote region of the world. Research the location, as well as the scientific field in which you'll be working. Then make a list of equipment and personal belongings that you and your team members will need for your expedition.

Internet Connection

Cold Enough for You?   If you had been in the Antarctic on July 21, 1983, you could have experienced the coldest temperature on record: $-128.6°F$ ($-89.2°C$). Generate a list of research questions about extremes in weather or climate. Then use the Internet to discover the answers to your questions. Summarize the information using a graphic such as a chart, graph, or map.

Reading Further

You may enjoy reading more articles about the Antarctic:

"Journey Into the Cold Unknown," by Jane E. Stevens (*International Wildlife,* January 1996).

"The Antarctic Pack-ice Ecosystem," by Jane E. Stevens (*BioScience,* March 1995).

"Lessons on the Ice," by Robert Lee Hotz (*Technology Review,* October 1996).

📖 **Save your work for your portfolio.**

LITERATURE AND WRITING

Writing About Literature

Students' paragraphs should
- explain the statement, using details from the article.
- express an opinion as to whether they agree or disagree with the statement and why.

Creative Writing

Students' letters should
- explain why they want to go on the expedition.
- include a list of their qualifications.
- use the format for a business letter.
- incorporate enthusiasm for the work, expressed appropriately for the tone of a business letter.

EXTENDING YOUR RESPONSE

Literature Groups Remind students that this is to be a friendly debate. As a result, they should try to convince classmates by using positive statements and facts. **COLLAB. LEARN.**

Learning for Life Remind students that not only should they identify the region but they should also identify the purpose of the scientific expedition. This will help them be more specific in the things they list. 📋

Internet Connection Suggest that students list possible topics to investigate before they begin. For example, they might ask themselves what kinds of extremes occur in nature. They might begin by looking up such extremes as temperature, rainfall, snow, or wind. 📋

Skill Minilessons

GRAMMAR AND LANGUAGE
Capitalization

Journalist Jane Stevens participated in two expeditions to Antarctica aboard the *Nathaniel B. Palmer*. They were sponsored by the National Science Foundation. In an article that Stevens wrote for *International Wildlife*, she stated, "This is a coveted scientific odyssey."

READING AND THINKING
Recognizing Cause and Effect

Other cause-and-effect relationships would include these: Because dust is in the ice, it fertilizes the algae. Because the algae grow, the krill have something to eat. Because the krill can live and grow, the whales have something to eat.

VOCABULARY
Analogies

1. a   2. e

Additional Resources

- *Grammar and Composition Handbook,* Lessons 10.1, 10.3
- *Grammar and Language Workbook,* pp. 235–238
- *Writer's Choice,* Lessons 20.1, 20.3
- *Reading Workbook,* pp. 57–58
- *Vocabulary Practice,* p. 44

Skill Minilessons

GRAMMAR AND LANGUAGE • Capitalization

Capitalize the first word of every sentence, the first word of a direct quotation that is a complete sentence, and all proper nouns. Note the capitalization in these sentences from the article.

André Belém, a graduate student from the University of Rio Grande in Brazil, offers me a dramatic insight when he shows me a test tube. . . . "There's more life in there than in the water of an estuary."

PRACTICE On your paper, rewrite the following paragraph. Correct any mistakes in capitalization that you find.

journalist jane stevens participated in two expeditions to antarctica aboard the *nathaniel b. palmer.* they were sponsored by the national science foundation. in an article that stevens wrote for *International Wildlife,* she stated, "this is a coveted scientific odyssey."

● For more on capitalization, see **Language Handbook,** p. R45.

READING AND THINKING • Recognizing Cause and Effect

Science writers, such as Stevens, use cause-and-effect relationships to explain the connection between a specific event (the cause) and the results of that event (effects). The cause is what makes something happen. The effect is what happens. Sometimes, one event begins a chain reaction of causes and effects. For example, Stevens points out that when wind blows dust particles from distant land-masses (cause), the particles become trapped in the winter sea ice (effect). This cause-and-effect relationship is the first in a chain of events that have a major effect on the Antarctic ecosystem.

PRACTICE Reread the part of the selection that discusses dust particles in the sea ice, and list other cause-and-effect relationships that result from the trapping of the particles in the ice.

● For more on text structures, see **Reading Handbook,** pp. R86–R87.

VOCABULARY • Analogies

An analogy is a type of comparison that is based on the relationships between things or ideas. To complete an analogy, decide what relationship exists between the first two things or ideas. Then apply that relationship to another pair of words and see if it is the same. Many analogies are based on description. In this type of analogy, one word in a pair could be used as part of an accurate description of the other:

skywriting : ephemeral :: engraving : lasting

Skywriting is a method of writing that is *ephemeral; engraving* is a method of writing that is *lasting.* In identifying the relationship illustrated by the first pair of words, it is important to be as specific as possible.

PRACTICE Choose the word pair that best completes each analogy.

1. daredevil : foolhardy ::
   a. tattletale : disloyal   d. neighbor : nearby
   b. cousin : related   e. soldier : drafted
   c. athlete : muscular
2. tourist : transient ::
   a. traveler : tired   d. souvenir : memorable
   b. hotel : urban   e. resident : permanent
   c. host : gracious

● For more on analogies, see **Communications Skills Handbook,** p. R77.

✔ ASSESSMENT OPTIONS

- *Quick Checks,* p. 45
- *Selection and Theme Assessment,* pp. 87–88
- *Performance Assessment,* p. 44
- *Testmaker*

LISTENING, SPEAKING, and VIEWING

Interviewing

When the journalist Slavenka Drakulić, author of "Pizza in Warsaw, Torte in Prague," wanted to find out how the collapse of communism was affecting the everyday lives of women in Eastern Europe, she interviewed a number of women there. Interviewing is a skill that all good journalists must master, but even if you're not a journalist, you'll find that your interviewing skills will come in handy in many situations, both inside and outside of school. For example, if you want to learn about a particular career, you might interview someone who's pursuing that career. If a class assignment requires you to find out about community resources for homeless people, you might interview the director of a local shelter for the homeless.

Preparing for an Interview
- Request an interview, explain your purpose, and make an appointment. If you have a tape recorder, ask permission to tape the interview.
- Research the background of the person and the topic.
- Write interview questions that are clear and tightly focused.

Conducting an Interview
- Arrive on time. Be polite, friendly, and businesslike.
- Ask a question, and listen to the answer. Don't interrupt. Ask follow-up questions.
- If you're taking notes rather than taping the interview, summarize the main points. Write down, word for word, any quotations you want to use.

Writing Up an Interview
Decide how you will present the information you have gathered—a script, a report, or another piece of writing.

ACTIVITIES

1. Learn from the experts by reading interviews in newspapers and magazines and on the Internet or by watching or listening to interviews on television and radio. Evaluate the techniques used by each interviewer. Share your observations with the class.

2. Polish your own skills by conducting an interview. You might interview someone to fulfill a class assignment, or simply to learn about a topic that interests you. Follow the steps described in this lesson as you prepare, conduct, and write up your interview. Then share the interview with your classmates.

Objective
- To learn techniques for conducting an interview

Teaching Strategies
After reading and discussing the sections related to preparing for and conducting an interview, discuss with students possible people they might interview and why. Remind them that they must be prepared to ask questions from their list. However, often during an interview, the person may provide new information that leads to a new and interesting topic. Be sure to discuss ways of organizing and writing the interview, as described in the final section. Let students offer additional suggestions.

Activities
1. Students should name several techniques they used and tell why they think the techniques were or were not effective.
2. *Students' interviews should*
   - be organized in an identifiable way.
   - have a clearly identified purpose.
   - contain information that stays on the point.
   - be interesting and informative.
   - include a substantial number of direct quotations.

MEETING INDIVIDUAL NEEDS — ENGLISH LANGUAGE LEARNERS

Interviewing English language learners may have language or cultural difficulties when conducting an interview. Discuss ways these special situations can be addressed. Students might mention getting help writing questions, taking someone with them to help with language problems, or practicing the interview with a friend.

Activity Have students prepare interview questions and practice them with a person who speaks their first language. Later, students can conduct the interview in English or in another language.

Additional Resources
 English Language Learners Sourcebook

Objective

- To understand the causes and types of lightning

Teaching Strategies

You may want to deal with the selection paragraph by paragraph. As each section is read, ask students to summarize the information. Write, or have a volunteer write, the summary on the board to create a brief outline of lightning facts.

Activity

Students' pamphlets should
- contain interesting facts about lightning.
- indicate the sources of the facts.
- be written in pamphlet format.

Teaching Options

INTERDISCIPLINARY

PHYSICAL SCIENCE

CONNECTION

Lightning

Where there's smoke, there's fire—and where there's thunder, there's lightning, as Gretel Ehrlich's experience shows. But what about rain? Ehrlich was hit by lightning during what she describes as "a dry storm with only sputtering rain." Not only are there such things as dry thunderstorms, there are also many forms of lightning.

Thunderstorms develop within high, puffy clouds that can reach more than 75,000 feet in altitude. Within the clouds, air currents move rapidly up and down, producing electrical charges. A single flash of lightning may transmit from 100 million to a billion volts of electricity. In comparison, the typical current in a household electrical outlet, which is enough to kill a person, is 110 volts.

Common Forms of Lightning	
Streak	A single, jagged flash
Forked	A flash with multiple branches
Ribbon	Separate, side-by-side flashes of light
Bead or chain	A flash that fades into a dotted line

Lightning greatly heats up the air along its path—to more than 50,000°F—and causes the air to expand explosively. The hot, expanding air generates shock waves, which become sound waves—or thunder. Thus, lightning causes thunder. Because sound travels more slowly than light, you hear thunder a number of seconds after you see the flash of lightning.

Lightning is not always visible, and it's not always accompanied by heavy rain. *Invisible lightning* occurs when an electric current continues to flow along the path set up by a visible strike. *Dry thunderstorms*, which bring lightning without rain, are common in arid regions of the western United States. In those areas, low humidity often causes the rain to evaporate before it ever hits the ground. Such conditions may have prevailed when lightning struck Gretel Ehrlich as she was walking with her dogs.

Other unusual and interesting forms of lightning exist, such as *ball lightning*, which consists of a glowing red, yellow, or orange ball seen for a few seconds after ordinary lightning. People have reported seeing these grapefruit-size balls floating along the ground and in houses, barns, and even airplanes. Other forms, called *red sprites*, *blue jets*, and *green elves* are colored lights flashing in the upper atmosphere above a thunderstorm. Like other aspects of thunderstorms, these lights have proven difficult for scientists to explain.

Activity

The Internet has a host of facts and figures about thunderstorms and lightning. Collect information that you find interesting and use it to create a pamphlet of thunderstorm facts. For example, you might discover which state has the most thunderstorms and which has hardly any. (And see if you can find out more about red sprites, blue jets, and green elves!)

MEETING INDIVIDUAL NEEDS

MULTIPLE LEARNING STYLES

Logical-Mathematical Logical-mathematical learners think conceptually. They can reason in a highly abstract and logical way. These learners often excel in subjects such as science and math, which require abstract or logical thinking. Students with this learning style may be able to help explain scientific concepts to their classmates.

Activity How is lightning created? What is thunder? These are questions answered by the material on this page. Ask students to create diagrams and explanations of lightning and thunder based on the information provided here. Allow time for students to present their displays and information to the class. **L3**

Before You Read

from *A Match to the Heart*

FOCUS ACTIVITY

What have been your experiences with electrical storms? How do these storms make you feel?

LIST IDEAS List words and phrases that describe what you experienced during a specific electrical storm. Include your emotional responses, your sensory responses (sight, sound, touch, smell), the time, and the place.

SETTING A PURPOSE Read to learn about one person's experience with lightning.

BACKGROUND

The Time and Place
This story takes place in Wyoming in 1991 on the ranch where the author was living and in nearby towns.

Did You Know?
Lightning occurs when the rising and falling air currents in a cloud cause positive and negative electrical charges in the air to separate. When accumulated positive and negative charges recombine, intense energy is released as lightning.

The lightning can occur within a cloud or between the air and the ground. Lightning that strikes the earth begins as an invisible channel of electrically charged air reaching toward the ground. When it nears the earth, an opposite charge of electricity surges upward toward the cloud, producing the visible bolt of lightning.

VOCABULARY PREVIEW

muse (mūz) *v.* to think or reflect, especially in an idle manner; p. 546
expend (iks pend′) *v.* to use up; consume; spend; p. 546
inert (i nurt′) *adj.* without power to move or act; lifeless; p. 546
incoherently (in′ kō hēr′ ənt lē) *adv.* in a confused, disconnected manner; unintelligibly; p. 547
abyss (ə bis′) *n.* an immeasurably deep hole; vast emptiness; nothingness; p. 547
fortuitous (fôr tōō′ ə təs) *adj.* fortunate; lucky; p. 549
equilibrium (ēk′ wə lib′ rē əm) *n.* mental, emotional, or physical balance; p. 550

Meet Gretel Ehrlich

"Physical work has a spiritual equivalent: the ax cuts away self-delusion and the hoe turns mental compost into insight and understanding."

Gretel Ehrlich (ār′ liкн) is a novelist and essayist who has honed her writing skills while living and working on ranches in California and Wyoming. She has "built and maintained fence, irrigated alfalfa, worked livestock, run a baler, stacked hay, pulled calves." She sees the writing and the ranch work as complementary endeavors that help her achieve mental and spiritual balance. "Whole books," she says, "came into my mind as I shoveled out ditches. . . ."

Gretel Ehrlich was born in Santa Barbara, California, in 1946. A Match to the Heart *was published in 1994.*

Objectives

- To read and analyze an informational article in which an author describes her experiences after being struck by lightning
- To learn what an exposition provides
- To develop a chart evaluating how minor characters relate to the main character

Skills

Reading/Thinking: Inferring; Skimming; Generalizing; Using Comparisons
Writing: Poem
Vocabulary: Etymology
Grammar/Language: Commas in a Series; Abbreviations
Listening/Speaking: Internal Dialogue; Oral Report
Collaboration: Literature Groups

Motivating → OPTIONS

Selection Focus Transparency 46: Use the photograph and the poem to discuss with students the beauty and the danger of lightning.

Focus Activity: Let students share their experiences with electrical storms, using the lists they generated in the Focus Activity.

RESOURCE MANAGER

Lesson Planning Resource
The *Unit Two Planning Guide* (pp. 94–101) provides additional lesson notes and reduced versions of all print resources.

📁 **Other Print Resources**
- Active Reading Guide, p. 46
- Vocabulary Practice, p. 45
- Reading Workbook, pp. 59–60
- Grammar and Language Workbook, p. 253
- Grammar and Composition Handbook, Lesson 11.6

- Quick Checks, p. 46
- Selection and Theme Assessment, pp. 89–90
- Performance Assessment, p. 45
- Spanish Summaries, p. 46
- Spanish Translations
- Inclusion Strategies
- English Language Learners Sourcebook

Transparencies
- Selection Focus 46
- Fine Art 1

- Literary Elements 46
- Grammar and Language 46

Technology
🎧 Audio Library
🎧 Spanish Audio Library
💻 Glencoe Literature Web Site
💾 Testmaker

SUMMARY

The author is out walking her dogs on her Wyoming ranch. Suddenly, she is struck by lightning. The tale that follows describes her efforts to get back to the house, summon help, and get medical attention. One would think that once the author called for help, her problems would be over. Unfortunately, this was not the case, as both doctors and nurses were unfamiliar with victims of lightning strikes and unable to offer much help. The author's bravery and humor shine through in this amazing narrative.

📁 *Spanish Summaries*, p. 46

 Active Reading

PREDICT After the first paragraph has been read, ask students what happened to the narrator. *(She was struck by lightning.)* Have students make predictions about what experiences they think the person will have and what the final outcome will be.

Additional Resources
📁 *Active Reading Guide*, p. 46
🎧 *Audio Library*
🎧 *Spanish Audio Library*

Teaching Options

from

A Match to the Heart

Gretel Ehrlich ∾

544

CONNECTING TO OTHER SELECTIONS

The chart at the right shows three ways to connect the excerpt from *A Match to the Heart* to selections in this book.

For specific teaching strategies, see the *Unit Two Planning Guide*, pages 97–98.

Connection	Title
Life Skills: Problem Solving	→ "An Astrologer's Day," p. 260
Thematic: Courage	→ "And of Clay Are We Created," p. 343
Literary: Characters	→ from *Kaffir Boy,* p. 445

Before electricity carved its blue path toward me, before the negative charge shot down from cloud to ground, before "streamers" jumped the positive charge back up from ground to cloud, before air expanded and contracted producing loud pressure pulses I could not hear because I was already dead, I had been walking.

When I started out on foot that August afternoon, the thunderstorm was blowing in fast. On the face of the mountain, a mile ahead, hard westerly gusts and sudden updrafts collided, pulling black clouds apart. Yet the storm looked harmless. When a distant thunderclap scared the dogs, I called them to my side and rubbed their ears: "Don't worry, you're okay as long as you're with me."

I woke in a pool of blood, lying on my stomach some distance from where I should have been, flung at an odd angle to one side of the dirt path. The whole sky had grown dark. Was it evening, and if so, which one? How many minutes or hours had elapsed since I lost consciousness, and where were the dogs? I tried to call out to them but my voice didn't work. The muscles in my throat were paralyzed and I couldn't swallow. Were the dogs dead? Everything was terribly wrong: I had trouble seeing, talking, breathing, and I couldn't move my legs or right arm. Nothing remained in my memory—no sounds, flashes, smells, no warnings of any kind. Had I been shot in the back? Had I suffered a stroke or heart attack? These thoughts were dark pools in sand.

The sky was black. Was this a storm in the middle of the day or was it night with a storm traveling through? When thunder exploded over me, I knew I had been hit by lightning.

The pain in my chest intensified and every muscle in my body ached. I was quite sure I was dying. What was it one should do or think or know? I tried to recall the Buddhist instruction regarding dying—which position to lie in, which direction to face. Did the "Lion's position" taken by the Buddha mean lying on the left or the right? And which sutra to sing? Oh yes, the Heart Sutra . . . gaté, gaté, paragaté . . .[1] form and formlessness. Paradox and cosmic jokes. Surviving after trying to die "properly" would be truly funny, but the chances of that seemed slim.

---

1. A *sutra* (sōō′ trə) is a passage from Buddha's writings, and the words *gaté, gaté, paragaté* (pär′ ə gä′ tä) are part of a meditative chant recited at the end of the passage known as the *Heart Sutra*.

B Literary Elements

EXPOSITION Explain that exposition is the part of a plot that gives necessary background information. Have students tell what information the narrator gives in the first two paragraphs that explain her physical condition: "I could not hear because I was already dead." *(She is outside when a thunderstorm occurs and she is struck by lightning.)*

C Active Reading

EVALUATE Discuss with students the various medical problems the author has after being struck by lightning. What does the author think her prognosis is? Under the circumstances, what do you think the author can or should do? *(She is bleeding; her throat is paralyzed and she can neither speak nor swallow. She has trouble seeing, talking, and breathing. She cannot move her legs or her right arm. She can remember nothing. She has a pain in her chest. She believes she is dying. Students' answers will vary. Some might say she should crawl back to her home.)*

D Author's Craft

HUMOR The author has been hit by lightning and is badly hurt, yet there is a clue that this selection is not going to be entirely serious. What clue does the author give? *(She makes a joke about not dying. She tries to think of the right way to die. Then she jokes about surviving after trying to die properly.)*

Other words drifted in: how the "gateless barrier" was the gate through which one passes to reach enlightenment. Yet if there was no gate, how did one pass through? Above me, high on the hill, was the gate on the ranch that lead nowhere, a gate I had <u>mused</u> about often. Now its presence made me smile. Even when I thought I had no aspirations for enlightenment, too much effort in that direction was being <u>expended</u>. How could I learn to slide, yet remain aware?

To be struck by lightning: what a way to get enlightened. That would be the joke if I survived. It seemed important to remember jokes. My thinking did not seem connected to the <u>inert</u> body that was in such terrible pain. Sweep the mind of weeds, I kept telling myself—that's what years of Buddhist practice had taught me. . . . But where were the dogs, the two precious ones I had watched being born and had raised in such intimacy and trust? I wanted them with me. I wanted them to save me again.

It started to rain. Every time a drop hit bare skin there was an explosion of pain. Blood crusted my left eye. I touched my good hand to my heart, which was beating wildly, erratically. My chest was numb, as if it had been sprayed with novocaine. No feeling of peace filled me. Death was a bleakness,[2] a grayness about which it was impossible to be

E

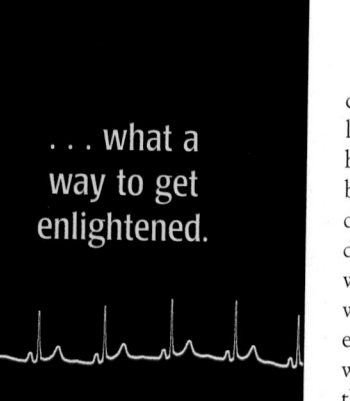

> . . . what a way to get enlightened.

curious or relieved. I loved those dogs and hoped they weren't badly hurt. If I didn't die soon, how many days would pass before we were found, and when would the scavengers come? The sky was dark, or was that the way life flew out of the body, in a long tube with no light at the end? I lay on the cold ground waiting. The mountain was purple, and sage stirred against my face. I knew I had to give up all this, then my own body and all my thinking. Once more I lifted my head to look for the dogs but, unable to see them, I twisted myself until I faced east and tried to let go of all desire.

E

When my eyes opened again I knew I wasn't dead. Images from World War II movies filled my head: of wounded soldiers dragging themselves across a field, and if I could have laughed—that is, made my face work into a smile and get sounds to discharge from my throat—I would have. It would have been good to laugh. Instead, I considered my options: either lie there and wait for someone to find me—how many days or weeks would that take?—or somehow get back to the house. I calmly assessed what might be wrong with me—stroke, cerebral hemorrhage, gunshot wound—but it was bigger than I could understand. The instinct to survive does not rise from particulars; a deep but general misery rollercoasted me into

F

---

2. **Bleakness** is a condition of cold and dreary gloom.

Vocabulary
muse (mūz) *v.* to think or reflect, especially in an idle manner
expend (iks pend´) *v.* to use up; consume; spend
inert (i nurt´) *adj.* without power to move or act; lifeless

---

Listening and Speaking *Minilesson*

Internal Dialogue Throughout the article, the reader is able to "listen in" on the author's internal dialogue—the things Ehrlich is saying to herself. Discuss with students typical things a person might say in such a situation. Comments such as *What should I do now? This really hurts. I wonder if anyone is coming to help me?* might be suggested.

Activity Let students prepare an internal dialogue that might take place during an emergency situation. Suggest that they tape-record their internal dialogue and play the tape for the class. **L2**

action. I tried to propel myself on my elbows but my right arm didn't work. The wind had swung around and was blowing in from the east. It was still a dry storm with only sputtering rain, but when I raised myself up, lightning fingered the entire sky.

It is not true that lightning never strikes the same place twice. I had entered a shower of sparks and furious brightness and, worried that I might be struck again, watched as lightning touched down all around me. Years before, in the high country, I'd been hit by lightning: an electrical charge had rolled down an open meadow during a fearsome thunderstorm, surged up the legs of my horse, coursed through me, and bounced a big spark off the top of my head. To be struck again—and this time it was a direct hit—what did it mean?

The feeling had begun to come back into my legs and after many awkward attempts, I stood. To walk meant lifting each leg up by the thigh, moving it forward with my hands, setting it down. The earth felt like a peach that had split open in the middle; one side moved up while the other side moved down and my legs were out of rhythm. The ground rolled the way it does during an earthquake and the sky was tattered book pages waving in different directions. Was the ground liquifying under me, or had the molecular composition of my body deliquesced?[3] I struggled to piece together fragments. Then it occurred to me that my brain was torn and that's where the blood had come from.

I walked. Sometimes my limbs held me, sometimes they didn't. I don't know how many times I fell but it didn't matter because I was making slow progress toward home.

Home—the ranch house—was about a quarter of a mile away. I don't remember much about getting there. My concentration went into making my legs work. The storm was strong. All the way across the basin, lightning lifted parts of mountains and sky into yellow refulgence[4] and dropped them again, only to lift others. The inside of my eyelids turned gold and I could see the dark outlines of things through them. At the bottom of the hill I opened the door to my pickup and blew the horn with the idea that someone might hear me. No one came. My head had swollen to an indelicate shape. I tried to swallow—I was so thirsty—but the muscles in my throat were still paralyzed and I wondered when I would no longer be able to breathe.

Inside the house, sounds began to come out of me. I was doing crazy things, ripping my hiking boots off because the bottoms of my feet were burning, picking up the phone when I was finally able to scream. One of those times, someone happened to be on the line. I was screaming incoherently for help. My last conscious act was to dial 911.

Dark again. Pressing against sore ribs, my dogs pulled me out of the abyss, pulled and pulled. I smelled straw. My face was on tatami.[5] I opened my eyes, looked up, and saw neighbors. Had they come for my funeral? The phone rang and I heard someone give directions to the ambulance driver, who was lost. . . .

---

3. *Deliquesced* means to have dissolved and become liquid.

4. *Refulgence* means "brightness; radiance."
5. The *tatami* (tä tä′ mē) is a mat woven from rice straw or a similar material.

Vocabulary
incoherently (in′ kō hēr′ ənt lē) *adv.* in a confused, disconnected manner; unintelligibly
abyss (ə bis′) *n.* an immeasurably deep hole; vast emptiness; nothingness

G **Literary Elements**

FIGURES OF SPEECH: *Simile and Metaphor* Remind students that a simile is a comparison between two unlike things using the word *like* or *as* and that a metaphor is a comparison in which one thing is said to be another. Have students identify the simile used to describe the earth and the metaphor used to describe the sky. What things are being compared? *(In the simile, the author compares the earth to a peach. In the metaphor, she says the sky is tattered book pages.)*

H **Literary Elements**

SEQUENCE There is a lapse of time between the author's dialing of 911 and her next memory. Discuss what happened during this time interval. *(Some of her neighbors had arrived. Help was on the way.)*

I **Active Reading**

PREDICT What clue does the author give that her ordeal may not yet be over even though help has arrived? *(The ambulance driver is lost.)*

MEETING INDIVIDUAL NEEDS INCLUSION STRATEGIES

Special Needs Discuss with students how the author is able to get herself home and why it is a challenge. Let students with special needs discuss ways they adapt to the physical challenges they face.

Activity Remind students that at times the author could not speak or see. Suggest that pairs of students investigate ways people who cannot see or hear or speak communicate. Have students research either the Braille alphabet or American Sign Language. Ask them to write a report or prepare a demonstration to share with another pair. **L1**

Additional Resources
📁 *Inclusion Strategies*

Author's Craft

VOICE The author uses a contrast when she indicates that the arrival at the hospital was both a portent of disaster and an occasion for comedy. Point out that this contrast tells the reader something about the author's personality. Ask students what they would say they know from her contrast. *(that she has a sense of humor)*

Active Reading

EVALUATE What things happen at the hospital that are both a disaster and a comedy? *(Nothing in the hospital works. The EKG machine does not work, the doctor has not arrived, no IV has been started. When the doctor arrives, he is apparently not a good one because he has been barred from ER and ICU work at hospitals elsewhere.)*

Critical Thinking

INFERRING What does the author mean by her answer that she is too short to be struck by lightning? *(Lightning usually hits the tallest thing around, such as a tree or a building. The author makes a joke but is indicating she is finding it hard to believe that she was the tallest thing around.)*

I slipped back into unconsciousness and when I woke again two EMTs[6] were listening to my heart. I asked them to look for my dogs but they wouldn't leave me. Someone else in the room went outside and found Sam and Yaki curled up on the porch, frightened but alive. Now I could rest. I felt the medics jabbing needles into the top of my hands, trying unsuccessfully to get IVs[7] started, then strapping me onto a backboard and carrying me out the front door of the house, down steps, into lightning and rain, into what was now a full-blown storm.

The ambulance rocked and slid, slamming my bruised body against the metal rails of the gurney. Every muscle was in violent spasm and there was a place on my back near the heart that burned. I heard myself yell in pain. Finally the EMTs rolled up towels and blankets and wedged them against my arms, shoulders, hips, and knees so the jolting of the vehicle wouldn't dislodge me. The ambulance slid down into ditches, struggled out, bumped from one deep rut to another. I asked to be taken to the hospital in Cody, but they said they were afraid my heart might stop again. As it was, the local hospital was thirty-five miles away, ten of them dirt, and the trip took more than an hour.

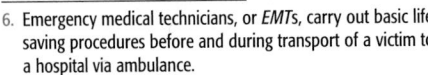

Did You Know?
An electrocardiograph, or *EKG machine*, is used to detect heart problems.

Our arrival seemed a portent[8] of disaster—and an occasion for comedy. I had been struck by lightning around five in the afternoon. It was now 9:00 P.M. Nothing at the hospital worked. Their one EKG machine was nonfunctional,

---

6. Emergency medical technicians, or *EMTs*, carry out basic life-saving procedures before and during transport of a victim to a hospital via ambulance.
7. The *IVs* are medical equipment that allow drugs and fluids to be injected intravenously, or directly into a vein.
8. A *portent* is a warning or indication of something significant or disastrous that is about to happen.

---

and jokingly the nurses blamed it on me. "Honey, you've got too much electricity in your body," one of them told me. Needles were jammed into my hand—no one had gotten an IV going yet—and the doctor on call hadn't arrived, though half an hour had elapsed. The EMTs kept assuring me: "Don't worry, we won't leave you here." When another nurse, who was filling out an admission form, asked me how tall I was, I answered: "Too short to be struck by lightning."

"Electrical injury often results in ventricular fibrillation[9] and injury to the medullary centers of the brain. Immediately after electric shock patients are usually comatose, apneic, and in circulatory collapse. . . ."

When the doctor on call—the only doctor in town, waddled into what they called the emergency room, my aura,[10] he said, was yellow and gray—a soul in transition. I knew that he had gone to medical school but had never completed a residency and had been barred from ER or ICU[11] work in the hospitals of Florida, where he had lived previously. Yet I was lucky. Florida has many lightning victims, and unlike the doctors I would see later, he at least recognized the symptoms of a lightning strike. The tally sheet read this way: I had suffered a hit by lightning which caused ventricular

---

9. This is the first of three paragraphs that describe the diagnosis and treatment of electrical injuries such as lightning strikes. *Ventricular fibrillation* is a series of rapid, irregular heart contractions. The last three terms in the paragraph refer to unconsciousness, a temporary suspension of breathing, and a rapid drop in blood pressure.
10. Here, the *aura* is a halo or glow said to surround the body, reflecting one's personal qualities and emotional, spiritual, and physical state. This concept is not endorsed by most traditional physicians.
11. A *residency* is a period during which a physician receives specialized training in, for example, the emergency room (*ER*) or intensive care unit (*ICU*).

Reading *Minilesson*

Scanning Explain that scanning is the process of looking through written material quickly to find a specific piece of information. Point out that the reader does not read every word but looks for key words, headings, abbreviations, or even pictures as guides to specific information.

Activity Ask the questions that follow, having students scan the selection to find the answers.

1. What religious leader does Ehrlich cite? *(Buddha, page 545)*
2. What are her dogs' names? *(Sam and Yaki, page 549)*
3. Who cleaned the cuts on her head while the author was in the hospital? *(Laura, page 549)*
4. To what city did Ehrlich want to be taken for treatment in the hospital? *(Cody, page 548)*
5. When would her husband be back? *(in a month, page 550)*

Let students suggest additional questions.
L2

Additional Resources
📁 *Reading Workbook,* pp. 59–60

fibrillation—cardiac arrest—though luckily my heart started beating again. Violent contractions of muscles when one is hit often causes the body to fly through the air: I was flung far and hit hard on my left side, which may have caused my heart to start again, but along with that fortuitous side effect, I sustained a concussion, broken ribs, a possible broken jaw, and lacerations above the eye. The paralysis below my waist and up through the chest and throat—called kerauno-paralysis—is common in lightning strikes and almost always temporary, but my right arm continued to be almost useless. Fernlike burns—arborescent erythema—covered my entire body. These occur when the electrical charge follows tracings of moisture on the skin—rain or sweat—thus the spidery red lines.

. . . lightning inlaid the walls with cool gold.

"Rapid institution of fluid and electrolyte therapy is essential with guidelines being the patient's urine output, hematocrit, osmolality, central venous pressure, and arterial blood gases. . . ."[12]

The nurses loaded me onto a gurney. As they wheeled me down the hall to my room, a front wheel fell off and I was slammed into the wall. Once I was in bed, the deep muscle aches continued, as did the chest pains. Later, friends came to visit. Neither doctor nor nurse had cleaned the cuts on my head,

---

12. [*Rapid institution . . . blood gases*] This paragraph suggests administering fluids (by IV), based on urine output and various blood tests.

so Laura, who had herded sheep and cowboyed on all the ranches where I had lived and whose wounds I had cleaned when my saddle horse dragged her across a high mountain pasture, wiped blood and dirt from my face, arms, and hands with a cool towel and spooned yogurt into my mouth.

I was the only patient in the hospital. During the night, sheet lightning inlaid the walls with cool gold. I felt like an ancient, mummified child who had been found on a rock ledge near our ranch: bound tightly, unable to move, my dead face tipped backwards toward the moon.

In the morning, my regular doctor, Ben, called from Massachusetts, where he was vacationing, with this advice: "Get yourself out of that hospital and go somewhere else, anywhere." I was too weak to sign myself out, but Julie, the young woman who had a summer job on our ranch, retrieved me in the afternoon. She helped me get dressed in the cutoffs and torn T-shirt I had been wearing, but there were no shoes, so, barefoot, I staggered into Ben's office, where a physician's assistant kindly cleansed the gashes in my head. Then I was taken home.

Another thunderstorm slammed against the mountains as I limped up the path to the house. Sam and Yaki took one look at me and ran. These dogs lived with me, slept with me, understood every word I said, and I was too sick to find them, console them—even if they would have let me.

Vocabulary
fortuitous (fôr tŏo′ ə təs) *adj.* fortunate; lucky

Critical Thinking

GENERALIZING There is an expression sometimes used when people are in difficult situations: You either laugh or you cry. What does the author choose to do? Why would she have had reason to do the opposite? *(She chooses to laugh, at least in hindsight. The doctors do not know how to treat her. She fails all the tests, yet she is released. Her husband leaves to buy cattle, and a rattlesnake is in the house.)*

Critical Thinking

SEQUENCE OF EVENTS At the end of the account, the author lies in bed with her dogs nearby. Have students take turns listing the events in the account in order beginning with "The author is out walking with her dogs" and concluding with the above event.

Active Reading

EVALUATE What words describe the author? *(brave, persistent, strong)*

Thematic Focus

Quests and Encounters The author does not set out on a quest to get hit by lightning, but she has the quest of surviving. Have students discuss how she is able to survive and whether the encounters she has are positive, negative, or both.

ASSESSMENT OPTIONS

📁 *Quick Checks*, p. 46

Teaching Options

The next day my husband, who had just come down from the mountains where he worked in the summer, took me to another hospital. I passed out in the admissions office,

Did You Know?
A *CAT scan* is a sort of three-dimensional X ray. (*CAT* stands for "computerized axial tomography.")

was loaded onto a gurney, and taken for a CAT scan. No one bothered to find out why I had lost consciousness. Later, in the emergency unit, the doctor argued that I might not have been struck by lightning at all, as if I had imagined the incident. "Maybe a meteor hit me," I said, a suggestion he pondered seriously. After a blood panel and a brief neurological exam,[13] which I failed—I couldn't follow his finger with my eyes or walk a straight line—he promptly released me.

"Patients should be monitored electrocardiographically for at least 24 hours for significant arrhythmias which often have delayed onset. . . ."[14]

 It was difficult to know what was worse: being in a hospital where nothing worked and nobody cared, or being alone on an

---

13. A *blood panel* is a series of blood tests, and a *neurological exam* checks the nervous system.
14. *[Patients should . . . delayed onset]* In other words, an EKG machine should be used to watch for the possible development of irregularities in the heartbeat.

---

isolated ranch hundreds of miles from decent medical care.

In the morning I staggered into the kitchen. My husband, from whom I had been separated for three months, had left at 4:00 A.M. to buy cattle in another part of the state and would not be back for a month. Alone again, it was impossible to do much for myself. In the past I'd been bucked off, stiff and sore plenty of times but this felt different: I had no sense of equilibrium. My head hurt, every muscle in my body ached as if I had a triple dose of the flu, and my left eye was swollen shut and turning black and blue. Something moved in the middle of the kitchen floor. I was having difficulty seeing, but then I did see: a rattlesnake lay coiled in front of the stove. I reeled around and dove back into bed. Enough tests of character. I closed my eyes and half-slept. Later, when Julie came to the house, she found the snake and cut off its head with a shovel.

My only consolation was that the dogs came back. I had chest pains and all day Sam lay with his head against my heart. I cleaned a deep cut over Yaki's eye. It was half an inch deep but already healing. I couldn't tell if the dogs were sick or well, I was too miserable to know anything except that Death resided in the room: not as a human figure but as a dark fog rolling in, threatening to cover me; but the dogs stayed close and while my promise to keep them safe during a thunderstorm had proven fraudulent, their promise to keep me alive held good.

Vocabulary
equilibrium (ēk′ wə lib′ rē əm) *n.* mental, emotional, or physical balance

---

Grammar and Language *Minilesson*

Commas in a Series Write this sentence on the board: *I opened my eyes, looked up, and saw neighbors.*

Explain that commas are used to separate three or more words, phrases, or clauses in a sentence.

Activity Write these sentences on the board, omitting the commas. Ask students to add commas where needed.

1. Lightning flashed, thunder rumbled, and gusts of wind swirled the dust as the storm moved in.
2. I had trouble seeing, talking, breathing, and moving my legs.
3. To walk I had to lift each leg by the thigh, move it forward with my hands, and set it down.
4. I sustained a concussion, broken ribs, a possible broken jaw, and lacerations above the eye. **L2**

Additional Resources

🔖 *Grammar and Language Transparency 46*
📙 *Grammar and Language Workbook*, p. 253
📙 *Grammar and Composition Handbook*, Lesson 11.6
📙 *Writer's Choice*, Lesson 21.6

Responding to Literature

Personal Response

What is your strongest or most immediate reaction to this selection? What is the basis for your response?

ANALYZING LITERATURE

RECALL

1. Why does Ehrlich tell her dogs: "Don't worry, you're okay as long as you're with me"?
2. Describe Ehrlich's physical condition and state of mind immediately following the accident.
3. What does Ehrlich do to help herself?
4. Briefly summarize the medical treatment Ehrlich receives.
5. What happens that provokes Ehrlich to say that she has had enough "tests of character"?

INTERPRET

6. What is **ironic** about the comment Ehrlich makes to her dogs that they will be safe with her?
7. What do you think might account for the kinds of thoughts that come to Ehrlich right after the accident?
8. Why do you think Ehrlich's attitude changes when she awakens the second time?
9. How might Ehrlich describe her opinion of the medical care she received?
10. At the end of the selection, what does the incident in the kitchen reveal about Ehrlich's character?

EVALUATE AND CONNECT

11. Analyze the author's use of **humor** in the narrative. In your opinion, why does she use humor and what does it add to this account?
12. How important are the medical facts Ehrlich provides? Why do you think Ehrlich includes so many medical facts in her narrative? In what ways are they important to the selection?
13. Considering Ehrlich's experience, how would you respond to a person who belittles someone else's fear of lightning?
14. Has your attitude toward lightning changed as a result of reading this selection? Explain.
15. A Buddhist monk told Ehrlich, "You know how to be strong; now you must learn how to be weak." Do you think Ehrlich has learned this lesson? Explain.

Literary ELEMENTS

Exposition

The **exposition** provides important background information about the plot, the characters, and the setting in a literary work. The details a writer chooses to include in the exposition set the tone for the rest of the work. In the excerpt from *A Match to the Heart,* the exposition appears in the first two paragraphs. Ehrlich's first sentence, "before electricity carved its blue path toward me . . . ," immediately draws readers into the plot.

1. What do you learn about the plot, the setting, and the narrator in the first two paragraphs of the excerpt?
2. What tone does the exposition set for the rest of the story?

 See **Literary Terms Handbook,** p. R4.

Personal Response

Students may indicate that they are amazed that the author survived and give examples of all of her injuries as the reasons for their answer.

ANALYZING LITERATURE

1. She wants to reassure them and herself.
2. Ehrlich is seriously injured. She believes she is dying and is preparing herself to do so.
3. When she can move, she makes herself walk back to the house. She honks the horn. She calls 911.
4. At the first hospital, she is examined and put to bed. No equipment works and no one cleans her wounds. At the second hospital, she is given tests but not helped after she fails them. At the doctor's office, her wounds are cleaned.
5. The author sees a rattlesnake in her house and decides not to deal with it.
6. She cannot protect either the dogs or herself from lightning.
7. Ehrlich is seriously injured. She is confused about what has happened. She knows it will be difficult to get help. She thinks she will probably die, and so she prepares for it.
8. She knows she has to act. Her instincts seem to tell her to do so.
9. Ehrlich might say that it was terrible, unprofessional, or irresponsible.
10. The incident with the rattlesnake reveals that she is courageous. Not many people could go back to bed after seeing a rattlesnake in the house.
11. Ehrlich may have used humor to express her personality or to make the selection more enjoyable. The use of humor helped "lighten up" what could have been an upsetting piece.
12. The medical facts are important, helping the reader understand how serious her condition is at each stage of her ordeal. The medical facts also provide a contrast to the story's humor.
13. A healthy fear and respect of lightning are wise. Lightning is a dangerous force of nature.

LITERARY ELEMENTS

1. The first two paragraphs indicate that the plot involves being struck by lightning; the setting is near a mountain; the narrator is calm and rational.
2. The exposition sets a suspenseful tone.

Additional Resources

 Literary Elements Transparency 46

---

14. Students may say that they have changed their opinion, have a greater respect for the power of lightning and a better understanding of why they should be careful during a storm.
15. Yes, she learned the lesson. Ehrlich seemed to be a self-reliant person, but she learned to be weak—afraid—when facing pain and death.

LITERATURE AND WRITING

Writing About Literature

Students' charts should
- consist of three completed columns.
- identify minor characters in the narrative, the role they played, and the writer's reaction to how each person treated Ehrlich.

Creative Writing

Students' poems should
- describe a thunderstorm, using sensory images.
- use descriptive language.
- create visual images for the reader.

EXTENDING YOUR RESPONSE

Literature Groups Students from different cultures will have varying views on dying. Be sure groups provide these varied views in the summary of their discussion. **COLLAB. LEARN.**

Learning for Life Before students begin, suggest that they choose an age group for which they are preparing their report. Very young children will need simpler explanations and more graphics than older children.

Interdisciplinary Activity Remind students that when technical information is being presented, visual aids can be extremely important in helping the listener understand what is being said. Students might try reading a rough draft of their report to a classmate in order to get some feedback on where visual aids might be useful.

LITERATURE AND WRITING

Writing About Literature

Analyzing Supporting Characters Several people have an opportunity to help Gretel Ehrlich through her ordeal. Some do; others don't. Create a three-column chart to examine these people and your reaction to them. In the first column, list the people referred to in the narrative. In the second column, describe the role these people play. In the last column, write your reaction to how these people treat Ehrlich. Compare your chart to classmates' charts.

Creative Writing

Lightning Verse Skim the selection for the words and phrases Ehrlich uses to describe lightning and thunderstorms. Then review the list you prepared for the Focus Activity on page 543. Draw upon these ideas to write a poem about a thunderstorm you've witnessed. Illustrate your poem if you wish.

EXTENDING YOUR RESPONSE

Literature Groups

Identifying with a Character After being struck by lightning, Gretel Ehrlich is convinced she is going to die. How does she try to prepare herself for death? What observation does she make about death? Do you think that she is afraid of dying? Would you have been? What images and thoughts might flash through your mind in similar circumstances? In your group, discuss these questions and jot down the group's responses. Then compare your responses with those of other groups.

Learning for Life

Learning About Lightning Work with a partner to prepare a lesson about lightning for younger students. Include a description of lightning, its causes, the risks to humans and property, and safety precautions. Include statistics and graphics appropriate to the age of your audience. The Internet is an excellent source of information.

Interdisciplinary Activity

Biology: The Brain Gretel Ehrlich suffered a serious brain injury when she was struck by lightning. Do research to learn how electrical impulses in the brain work; how electrical shock injures the brain; and what the typical after-effects of electrical shock are. Summarize your findings in an oral report to the class. Include diagrams and illustrations to help your audience understand your presentation.

Reading Further

You might enjoy this essay by Gretel Ehrlich:

"The Smooth Skull of Winter" from *The Solace of Open Spaces* presents Ehrlich's winter experiences in Wyoming.

📖 **Save your work for your portfolio.**

MRI of the human brain.

552 ❧ UNIT 2

Skill Minilessons

GRAMMAR AND LANGUAGE • Abbreviations

Abbreviations are shortened forms of words or groups of words. Writers use abbreviations to save space and avoid wordiness. Abbreviations for proper nouns and for those related to dates and time are capitalized and usually followed by periods. *(Dr., U.S., P.M.)* Many abbreviations that stand for the names of organizations and agencies, as well as those used in medical and scientific writing, are written without periods. Ehrlich uses several medical abbreviations in her narrative, including *EMT* for "emergency medical technician" and *ICU* for "intensive care unit."

PRACTICE Write the abbreviation for each of the following terms. If in doubt about the correct form of an abbreviation, check a dictionary.

> National Transportation Safety Board
> Central Intelligence Agency
> Veterans of Foreign Wars
> National Aeronautics and Space Administration

● For more on abbreviations, see **Language Handbook,** p. R52.

READING AND THINKING • Using Comparisons to Clarify

Writers use comparisons to help readers understand concepts and images that may be unclear to them. Comparisons can also serve to make the images and concepts more emphatic. For example, to explain the numbness in her chest, Ehrlich says it was "as if it had been sprayed with novocaine." Anyone who has been given novocaine at a doctor's or dentist's office can understand the feeling Ehrlich had in her chest.

PRACTICE Review Ehrlich's narrative and identify three comparisons. On your paper, explain what is being compared and how the comparison helps you better understand the concept or image.

● For more on comprehension skills, see **Reading Handbook,** pp. R82–R94.

VOCABULARY • Etymology

A muse is a spirit that inspires an artist or writer. So what does the verb *muse* have to do with thinking in an idle manner? That question is just one of many that can be answered by etymology. By checking a dictionary, you'll learn that the noun *muse* comes from the Greek word for the nine goddesses of art and literature. The verb *muse* is not related; it comes from a French word that means "to loiter."

The *aura* that surrounds the narrator in the selection comes from a Greek word meaning "air." An *aural* signal, however, is one you can hear; *aural* comes from a Latin

word meaning "ear." Most words that seem to be connected actually are related; however, some are not. Check a dictionary if you are not sure.

PRACTICE Use a dictionary to look up the etymologies of *incoherently, abyss,* and *equilibrium.* (A word's etymology is usually given with its definition.) For each, explain the connection between the origin of the word and its current meaning.

Skill Minilessons

GRAMMAR AND LANGUAGE
Abbreviations

NTSB, CIA, VFW, NASA

READING AND THINKING
Using Comparisons to Clarify

Possible comparisons include these: The earth and a peach are compared to help the reader know how difficult it was to walk. The ground rolling is compared to an earthquake to indicate her unsteadiness. The sky is compared to book pages waving to show that she is dizzy when she looks up.

VOCABULARY
Etymology

Incoherently comes from a Latin word meaning "to stick together," a Latin prefix meaning "not," and an Old English suffix. The meaning of *incoherently* is roughly the same as the original Latin—"not holding together or being logically connected."

Abyss comes from a Latin word that means "bottomless pit," still the current meaning of abyss.

Equilibrium comes from a Latin word meaning "level position" or "equal balance," which is what the word still means today.

Additional Resources

📙 *Grammar and Composition Handbook, Lesson 11.3*
📙 *Grammar and Language Workbook,* p. 281
📕 *Writer's Choice, Lesson 21.3*
📁 *Reading Workbook,* pp. 59–60
📁 *Vocabulary Practice,* p. 45

✔ ASSESSMENT OPTIONS

📁 *Quick Checks,* p. 46
📁 *Selection and Theme Assessment,* pp. 89–90
📁 *Performance Assessment,* p. 45
💾 *Testmaker*

Technology Skills

Objectives

- To subscribe to mailing lists through E-mail
- To identify mailing lists that will help with current topics of study
- To create links to mailing lists for a school Web site

Teaching Strategies

Be sure students understand the difference between information on Internet pages and that received via E-mail. The former is posted at large and publicly available over an extended period at a site; it is located through a Web address or by entering keywords into a search engine. The latter is direct, personal correspondence with an individual about specific topics.

Research Through E-mail

Discuss the value of E-mail correspondence with an expert in a field of research. Students should readily see certain advantages:

- Very specific questions can be asked and answers tailor-made to specific subjects.
- Information will likely be the most up-to-date available and can inform about very recent events and discoveries.
- Suggestions by an expert in the field might change the course of the research and improve the product (paper, report, presentation).

Teaching Options

Technology Skills

E-mail: Research Using E-mail

Much research is done through the World Wide Web. However, you can also conduct a scholarly investigation via E-mail. With a group, brainstorm ways in which you might use E-mail to research a topic.

Research Through E-mail

Your E-mail inbox can be similar to your mailbox. Companies that discover your E-mail address can fill your electronic mailboxes with ads, leaving you to sift through subject lines looking for legitimate messages. In addition, you can't see who's sending you E-mail. Just because someone says she or he is an expert doesn't make it so. When doing research, you must determine the accuracy of your E-mail information.

Getting Started

1. To begin, conduct a keyword search on the Net for electronic mailing lists that pertain to your research topic. Just add *+mailing list* following your topic keyword on the search engine.

2. Subscribing to a mailing list involves sending an E-mail to the electronic administrator of the list. When you find a list that interests you, click on "Subscribe" and follow the on-screen instructions. Generally, you will be asked to send the message "subscribe [list name] [your name]" to the list administrator.

3. The next time you log in to check your mail, you should receive a welcome message in your E-mail box. Be sure to save this message! It includes instructions for posting to the list and for unsubscribing.

4. After you've subscribed to the list, you can post questions that relate to your research. Other subscribers may answer your questions or point you to WWW sites that can help.

5. When you participate on a mailing list, it is considered polite to respond to E-mail directly rather than posting a response to the list. Be sure to always respond quickly when someone has taken the time to help you with your research.

6. One way to determine the accuracy of the information you've gathered through E-mail is to do what good journalists do: get confirmation. In other words, never trust what you get from only one source. Locate other experts who can confirm the information.

> **TECHNOLOGY TIP**
>
> The short code following a period in an E-mail address (and in a home page address as well) tells you the domain's type of organization. *Com* (the "dot com" you often hear when someone gives a Net address in a TV ad) indicates a commercial organization. Some other codes are:
> - **edu** educational institution
> - **gov** nonmilitary government organization
> - **net** network (usually an internet service provider)
> - **org** nonprofit organization

MEETING INDIVIDUAL NEEDS — MULTIPLE LEARNING STYLES

Interpersonal/Logical-Mathematical Students who work well alone and think conceptually will excel at this sort of assignment and may be able to help others learn.

Activity Ask students to keep a journal describing techniques and sites they find particularly helpful and to list these sites and describe them briefly in their electronic file. Their notes can be adapted for a "Techno-Success Tips" column and shared with classmates who are having difficulty linking with sites they need. **L2**

E-mail and List Server Citations

When you turn your research into a written presentation, be sure to always cite the sources of your information. To find guidelines for documenting electronic sources, type "MLA guidelines + electronic" into your search engine. (See also the Writing Handbook, pp. R72–R73.) Here's a model for an E-mail or mailing list citation:

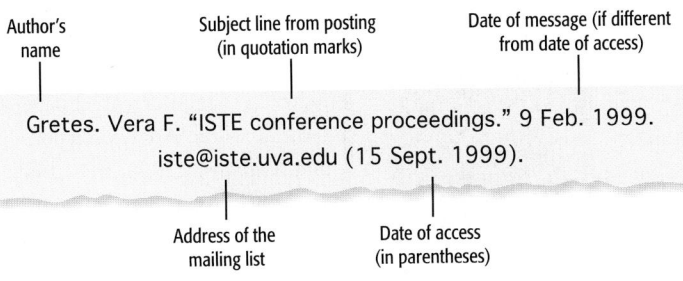

Author's name • Subject line from posting (in quotation marks) • Date of message (if different from date of access)

Gretes. Vera F. "ISTE conference proceedings." 9 Feb. 1999. iste@iste.uva.edu (15 Sept. 1999).

Address of the mailing list • Date of access (in parentheses)

ACTIVITIES

1. Search for a "list of lists" on the Web. These sites include directories of mailing lists divided by subject. Subscribe to one or two that can help you with your schoolwork. Save any messages you exchange on a mailing list in your electronic portfolio.

2. Look for lists that are applicable to topics you are studying in other classes. Ask your teachers if active participation on these lists can count toward fulfilling a technology requirement.

3. On your school's Web site, create a page of links to mailing lists that would be of interest to the school community.

Getting Started

Be sure students can identify the E-mail address of their correspondent on the Internet page and understand that they should use this address to respond directly to the expert.

Who's Who

Point out to students that the portion of the E-mail address that identifies the site comes between the @ symbol and the "dot" (.).

E-mail and List Server Citations

Review bibliography style. Point out that the author is listed last name first for insertion into an alphabetical listing. The subject or title in quotation marks corresponds to a book or article title in a print citation.

Activities

1. *Students' mailing list subscriptions and messages should*
   - relate to a topic to be researched.
   - show how to subscribe to the list.
2. Same as 1.
3. *Students' links should*
   - include mailing lists useful to specific subject areas.
   - include lists useful to extracurricular areas.

REAL-WORLD CONNECTION

Confirming the Accuracy of Information
Suggest to students that the ability to evaluate the accuracy of information is a skill required in work and personal decision making. Discuss situations in which we count on the correctness of data. (Some examples include inventory records, statistics on a car or other major purchase, and medical diagnoses.)

Activity Have students check the credentials of an expert they used as an online resource and confirm the information they received in at least one other source. Ask students to list the steps in their checking process and comment about the results in a class discussion. **L2**

Objectives

- To read and analyze an essay in which a man and a dog experience an encounter that seems full of instincts from the ancestral past
- To identify examples of creative nonfiction
- To write an analysis of a character from the essay

Skills

Reading/Thinking: Comparing; Cause-and-Effect Relationships
Writing: Dialogue
Vocabulary: The Latin Root *vert*
Collaboration: Literature Groups

Motivating
→OPTIONS

Selection Focus Transparency 47: Use the drawing of the dog and the labels to discuss ways in which a dog and a wolf are alike and different.

Focus Activity: Ask students to select an item from the chart they made and tell how it might affect them in the future.

Before You Read

The Angry Winter

FOCUS ACTIVITY

Are you affected today by what happened in the past? How might past events—either from the recent past or long ago—influence your behavior in the present?

CHART IT! In a chart like the one shown, list events from the past, either from history or from your own life, and note their influence in the present.

Past Events	Influence in the Present

SETTING A PURPOSE Read to discover how two characters are influenced by the past.

BACKGROUND

The Time and Place

The events in this essay take place on a snowy winter night at an unspecified time and place.

Did You Know?

Dogs belong to the animal family known as *Canidae,* along with wolves, coyotes, jackals, and foxes. Scientists think that canines have been a part of people's lives for thousands of years. Anthropologists have discovered the fossilized bones of wolves with human bones at sites dating back 400,000 years. Scientists speculate that some wolves may have ventured into campsites looking for food scraps. When humans realized that the wolves could be useful in warning of approaching danger, they accepted the wolves into their communities. Domesticated dogs, the descendants of those wolves, were first kept as pets about 14,000 years ago.

VOCABULARY PREVIEW

divert (di vurt′) *v.* to draw attention away; distract; p. 558
indifferently (in dif′ ər ənt lē) *adv.* in a way that shows a lack of feeling, concern, or care; p. 558
augment (ôg ment′) *v.* to make greater; increase; p. 559

556 ❧ UNIT 2

Meet Loren Eiseley

Loren Eiseley once compared the brain of a writer to an attic in which pictures of the past are collected. The writer draws upon these pictures, expanding and reducing them, to create a pattern, he wrote. An avid reader and naturalist, Eiseley filled his "attic" with pictures from books, from the Nebraska prairie land of his youth, from his observations of nature, and from his work with fossils. In his lifetime he pursued many careers: anthropologist, university professor, philosopher, essayist, and poet.

Loren Eiseley was born in Nebraska in 1907 and died in 1977. "The Angry Winter" appears in The Unexpected Universe, *a collection of Eiseley's essays published in 1969.*

RESOURCE MANAGER

Lesson Planning Resource
The *Unit Two Planning Guide* (pp. 102–108) provides additional lesson notes and reduced versions of all print resources.

📁 **Other Print Resources**
- Active Reading Guide, p. 47
- Vocabulary Practice, p. 46
- Reading Workbook
- Quick Checks, p. 47
- Selection and Theme Assessment, pp. 91–92

- Performance Assessment, p. 46
- Spanish Summaries, p. 47
- Spanish Translations
- Inclusion Strategies
- English Language Learners Sourcebook

📖 **Transparencies**
- Selection Focus 47
- Fine Art 27
- Literary Elements 47

Technology
🎧 Audio Library
🎧 Spanish Audio Library
💻 Glencoe Literature Web Site
💾 Testmaker

Hearth, 1957. Loren McIver. Oil on plaster on Masonite, 49⅝ x 34⅝ in. Metropolitan Museum of Art, New York. Museum purchase, Marie-Gaetana Matisse Gift, 1993. 1993.280.

The Angry Winter

Loren Eiseley

SUMMARY

One winter night, the narrator is working with artifacts from the Ice Age—lance points and a fossilized bison bone. He lays the bone on the floor. Suddenly, the narrator's dog begins to growl. A memory of food and survival from the remote past causes the dog to warn the man to stay away from the bone. The man, too, seems to feel the tug of the past as he has a sudden urge to fight for the bone. Later, as the two walk in the woods, the narrator reflects on what happened and how these vestiges of the past are still present in both human and dog.

📁 **Spanish Summaries,** p. 47

🅰 Active Reading

QUESTION Have the first paragraph read. Ask students to identify some creatures whose paths may have crossed in the remote past. What greater winter is the author referring to? *(an Ice Age)*

Additional Resources

📁 *Active Reading Guide,* p. 47
🎧 *Audio Library*
🎧 *Spanish Audio Library*

Teaching Options

CONNECTING TO OTHER SELECTIONS

COMPARING *selections*

This selection is paired with "The Tucson Zoo" on pages 563–565. A lesson for teaching a comparison of the two selections appears on page 567.

The chart at the right shows three other ways to connect "The Angry Winter" to selections in this book.

For specific teaching strategies, see the *Unit Two Planning Guide,* pages 105–106.

Connection	Title
Life Skills: Decision Making	→ "Waltz of the Fat Man," p. 377
Thematic: Instincts	→ *Travels with Charley,* p. 427
Literary: Suspense	→ "The Monkey's Paw," p. 173

QUESTION Why is Wolf's reaction to the bone so astonishing? *(There is no meat on the bone, and it is so mineralized it rings. The dog cannot have smelled meat or tasted bone.)*

C **Critical Thinking**

COMPARING Discuss what happens to the dog and compare this to what happens to the man. What words might describe what they experience? *(The dog remembers the remote past when animals fought for or hunted for food. The man remembers a similar experience and has an urge to lunge for the bone as if it were meat. The words "instinct" and "reverting" might be used.)*

D **Literary Elements**

CREATIVE NONFICTION Explain that a nonfiction author sometimes adds creatively to the details to help make a point. Have students suggest ways the author may have creatively enhanced the details. *(The actual event may not have taken place in winter, but setting the story in winter helps make the point. The dog's name may not have been Wolf, but the name helps make the point.)*

FINE ART
TRANSPARENCY 27

You may want to use Fine Art Transparency 27 to discuss instinctive animal reaction.

Teaching Options

The Angry Winter

A time comes when creatures whose destinies have crossed somewhere in the remote past are forced to appraise each other as though they were total strangers. I had been huddled beside the fire one winter night, with the wind prowling outside and shaking the windows. The big shepherd dog on the hearth before me occasionally glanced up affectionately, sighed, and slept. I was working, actually, amidst the debris of a far greater winter. On my desk lay the lance points of ice age hunters and the heavy leg bone of a fossil bison. No remnants of flesh attached to these relics. The deed lay more than ten thousand years remote. It was represented here by naked flint and by bone so mineralized it rang when struck. As I worked on in my little circle of light, I absently laid the bone beside me on the floor. The hour had crept toward midnight. A grating noise, a heavy rasping of big teeth diverted me. I looked down.

The dog had risen. That rock-hard fragment of a vanished beast was in his jaws and he was mouthing it with a fierce intensity I had never seen exhibited by him before.

"Wolf," I exclaimed, and stretched out my hand. The dog backed up but did not yield. A low and steady rumbling began to rise in his chest, something out of a long-gone midnight. There was nothing in that bone to taste, but ancient shapes were moving in his mind and determining his utterance. Only fools gave up bones. He was warning me.

"Wolf," I chided again.

As I advanced, his teeth showed and his mouth wrinkled to strike. The rumbling rose to a direct snarl. His flat head swayed low and wickedly as a reptile's above the floor. I was the most loved object in his universe, but the past was fully alive in him now. Its shadows were

whispering in his mind. I knew he was not bluffing. If I made another step he would strike.

Yet his eyes were strained and desperate. "Do not," something pleaded in the back of them, some affectionate thing that had followed at my heel all the days of his mortal life, "do not force me. I am what I am and cannot be otherwise because of the shadows. Do not reach out. You are a man, and my very god. I love you, but do not put out your hand. It is midnight. We are in another time, in the snow."

"The *other* time," the steady rumbling continued while I paused, "the other time in the snow, the big, the final, the terrible snow, when the shape of this thing I hold spelled life. I will not give it up. I cannot. The shadows will not permit me. Do not put out your hand."

I stood silent, looking into his eyes, and heard his whisper through. Slowly I drew back in understanding. The snarl diminished, ceased. As I retreated, the bone slumped to the floor. He placed a paw upon it, warningly.

And were there no shadows in my own mind, I wondered. Had I not for a moment, in the grip of that savage utterance, been about to respond, to hurl myself upon him over an invisible haunch ten thousand years removed? Even to me the shadows had whispered—to me, the scholar in his study.

"Wolf," I said, but this time, holding a familiar leash, I spoke from the door indifferently. "A walk in the snow." Instantly from his eyes that other visitant[1] receded. The bone was left lying. He came eagerly to my side, accepting the leash and taking it in his mouth as always.

---

1. A *visitant* is a visitor, especially one that seems to be supernatural.

Vocabulary
divert (di vurt′) *v.* to draw attention away; distract
indifferently (in dif′ ər ənt lē) *adv.* in a way that shows a lack of feeling, concern, or care

---

MEETING INDIVIDUAL NEEDS — ENGLISH LANGUAGE LEARNERS

Animals in a Culture Dogs and cats are common family pets in American culture. The eagle is a symbol of the United States. Discuss with English language learners animals that are important to their native cultures. Ask questions such as these: *What animals are important in your culture? Why? Are there any animals that are symbols for something else? Are any animals sacred or special?*

Activity Many cultures have stories that involve animals. Often they teach lessons. Have groups of students tell a story from their cultural heritage that is about an animal. Ask the group to discuss what lesson the story teaches.

Additional Resources
📁 *English Language Learners Sourcebook*

Portrait of Donald Schrader,
1962. Fairfield Porter. Oil on
canvas, 30 x 28 in. Metropolitan
Museum of Art. Bequest of Arthur
M. Bullowa, 1993. 1993.406.12.
**Viewing the painting: What
mood do this man's expression
and posture convey? How
might that mood apply to
the narrator?**

E **Active Reading**

CONNECT What is the narrator thinking about as he talks about "moving
from midnight to midnight"? In what
other story does something similar
happen? You might use these questions to model for students how to
make connections.

Model: The author, when talking
about moving from midnight to midnight, seems to be thinking back in
time. He goes on to mention more
remote and vaster snows. Previously,
the narrator was working with artifacts from the Ice Age. He seems to
be thinking back in time to that
period. In the story "A Sound of
Thunder," the hunters travel back in
time and a similar "ticking away of
the centuries" happens.

Thematic Focus

Quests and Encounters Both the
dog and the narrator have an unexpected encounter. Discuss what
each encounters. How are the
encounters similar and different?

ASSESSMENT OPTIONS

 Quick Checks, p. 47

A blizzard was raging when we went out,
but he paid no heed. On his thick fur the
driving snow was soon clinging heavily. He
frolicked a little—though usually he was a
grave dog—making up to me for something
still receding in his mind. I felt the snowflakes
fall upon my face, and stood thinking of
another time, and another time still, until I
was moving from midnight to midnight under
ever more remote and vaster snows. Wolf
came to my side with a little whimper. It was
he who was civilized now. "Come back to the
fire," he nudged gently, "or you will be lost."
Automatically I took the leash he offered. He
led me safely home and into the house.

"We have been very far away," I told him
solemnly. "I think there is something in us that
we had both better try to forget." Sprawled on
the rug, Wolf made no response except to
thump his tail feebly out of courtesy. Already he
was mostly asleep and dreaming. By the movement of his feet I could see he was running far
upon some errand in which I played no part.

Softly I picked up his bone—our bone,
rather—and replaced it high on a shelf in my
cabinet. As I snapped off the light the white
glow from the window seemed to <u>augment</u>
itself and shine with a deep, glacial blue. As
far as I could see, nothing moved in the long
aisles of my neighbor's woods. There was no
visible track, and certainly no sound from the
living. The snow continued to fall steadily,
but the wind, and the shadows it had
brought, had vanished.

Vocabulary
augment (ôg ment′) *v.* to make greater; increase

Reading *Minilesson*

Cause-and-Effect Relationships The
plot of a story, or in this case the main
idea, or thesis, of an essay, is sometimes
advanced by a series of cause-and-effect
relationships. In the opening of the essay,
the narrator is working with a fossilized
bison bone. Because he puts the bone on
the floor, the dog is able to grab it.

Activity Ask students to create a cause-
and-effect chain based on this selection.
Have them begin statements with a
Because clause, followed by an arrow, followed by an effect clause. Later, students
could share their chains with a classmate.
L3

Additional Resources
 Reading Workbook

**LITERATURE &
HUMANITIES**

Have students examine *Monolith, the
Face of Halfe Dome, Yosemite National
Park, 1927 (American Art, History, and
Culture,* p. 481) and discuss how nature is
characterized in the photograph.

Responding to the Selection

Personal Response

Students may say that their reaction was one of surprise, curiosity, or disbelief.

ANALYZING LITERATURE

1. The narrator and the dog are beside the fire one winter night. The narrator is examining Ice Age artifacts, and the dog is sleeping.
2. A grating sound, a rasping of teeth, distracts the narrator. The dog is making the sound.
3. The dog sees the bone and claims it as his own. He is ready to fight for it.
4. The narrator knows the dog is telling him to stay away from the bone, yet he has a strange urge to grab for it, as if fighting over food.
5. The dog becomes himself again, while the narrator thinks back to the distant past. The dog brings him out of this reverie.
6. The wind is compared to an animal prowler or intruder. The comparison is apt because each character's experience is like an intruder from the past. They each behave primitively.
7. Eiseley means that some instinct or ancient memory is being stirred in the dog.
8. The shadows may represent past memories or ancient experiences that are present in the unconscious mind.
9. The narrator had a similar desire to fight for the bone caused by a distant unconscious memory from a time when fighting for food meant survival.
10. They have been remembering the past. The narrator makes a number of references to the cold and snows of past Ice Ages.
11. The mood is suspenseful and eerie. The author uses the coldness of winter, the wind rattling the windows, and the firelight to set the mood.
12. Students who disagree may say that the bone looked like a bone and that is why the dog wanted it. The dog's reaction had nothing to do with unconscious memories of the past.
13. Students may indicate that Eiseley is an effective writer and is able to make scientific topics interesting.
14. Students may indicate that they did not go back in the past. Most students will be able to identify some talent, physical characteristic, or personality trait inherited from a relative or other person from their past.

Responding to Literature

Personal Response

How did you react to the confrontation between Wolf and the narrator?

ANALYZING LITERATURE

RECALL

1. Describe where the narrator and Wolf are and what they are doing as the essay begins.
2. What sound distracts the narrator? What is making this sound?
3. Recount the confrontation between Wolf and the narrator.
4. How did the narrator momentarily want to respond to Wolf during the confrontation?
5. Summarize what happens between the narrator and Wolf on their walk.

INTERPRET

6. In the opening paragraph, Eiseley describes "the wind prowling outside and shaking the windows." What is the **metaphor** in this description? Why is it an apt one? (See Literary Terms Handbook, page R7.)
7. When Wolf growls, Eiseley says, "Ancient shapes were moving in his mind and determining his utterance." What does Eiseley mean?
8. Eiseley uses the word *shadows* several times in explaining Wolf's behavior. What might the shadows represent?
9. In reflecting on the confrontation, what similarity does the narrator see between himself and Wolf?
10. The narrator says to Wolf, "We have been very far away." Where do you think Eiseley is suggesting they've been? What details help you draw this conclusion?

EVALUATE AND CONNECT

11. Describe the **mood**, or atmosphere, of this essay. What details help establish this mood? Explain.
12. Do you agree with Eiseley's explanation for Wolf's behavior? Why or why not? If not, what explanation would you give?
13. Based on this essay, what are your impressions of Loren Eiseley?
14. Look at the chart you completed for the Focus Activity on page 556. After reading this essay, have your thoughts about links to the past changed? Identify behaviors or reactions you may have inherited from people in your distant past.
15. This essay also appeared in *Reader's Digest* under the title, "The Night the Shadows Whispered." Suggest another title for the essay.

15. Students may suggest titles such as "Voices from the Past" or "Remnants of Past Memories."

Literary ELEMENTS

Creative Nonfiction

"The Angry Winter" belongs to a literary genre known as creative nonfiction. In **creative nonfiction**, writers apply their own point of view to factual details about real people, settings, or events. The facts, however, aren't as important as the writer's larger ideas about real issues. Creative nonfiction writers typically start with an actual event or character and then creatively expand or dress up the details to make their overall message more engaging and lively. For example, Loren Eiseley never had a German shepherd named Wolf. He probably based Wolf's character on two actual dogs that he had known. Wolf was a literary vehicle that Eiseley used to help convey his message.

1. What, do you think, is the main idea of Eiseley's essay? Summarize it in a few sentences.
2. What references and details does Eiseley use to convey this idea? Cite specific examples from the selection.

● See **Literary Terms Handbook**, p. R3.

LITERARY ELEMENTS

1. Each of us has in our unconscious mind memories from the ancient past that aided survival. In certain instances, traces of this unconscious memory come out.
2. The narrator mentions destinies that have crossed somewhere in the distant past. He refers to ancient shapes moving in the dog's mind, and he mentions wanting to respond as someone long ago may have.

Additional Resources

Literary Elements Transparency 47

LITERATURE AND WRITING

Writing About Literature

Analyze Characterization Eiseley portrays two sides of Wolf's personality. What labels would you apply to each? In a two-column chart, list the details that Eiseley provides to reveal these two sides of Wolf's personality. Then use the details to write a one-paragraph analysis of Eiseley's portrayal of Wolf.

Creative Writing

If Dogs Could Talk Imagine that Wolf could verbalize his thoughts and feelings. How might his glances and growls be interpreted? What might he be thinking when the narrator tries to get the bone? Write a dialogue that might take place between Wolf and the narrator during the confrontation. Share your dialogue with the class.

EXTENDING YOUR RESPONSE

Literature Groups

The Marriage of Literature and Science Loren Eiseley believed that the literary and the scientific acts of creation had much in common because both were products of the human imagination. Do you think that science and the arts differ greatly, or do you agree with Eiseley that they have many similarities? In this essay, what evidence do you see of both scientific imagination and literary creativity? Share your ideas in your group.

Interdisciplinary Activity

Anthropology: Ice-Age Hunters and Beasts Investigate what anthropologists have pieced together about the lives of Ice Age people. Where and how did they live? What did they wear? What did they eat? What kinds of plants and animals shared their world? Use your findings to create a diorama of life in the Ice Age.

Internet Connection

Nature's Voices Use the Internet to find out more about Loren Eiseley and other naturalist writers, such as Rachel Carson, Gretel Ehrlich, Annie Dillard, Aldo Leopold, and John Muir. Create a bibliography of recommended books or essays about the natural world.

 Save your work for your portfolio.

Skill Minilesson

VOCABULARY • **The Latin Root** *vert*

The word *divert* comes from the Latin root *vert,* which means "to turn," and the Latin prefix *dis-,* meaning "away." If you *divert* someone, you turn his or her attention away from something. You could *divert* a stream by digging a channel to carry the water in a different direction.

PRACTICE Use your knowledge of the root *vert* to help you answer the following questions.

1. Does a *versatile* person turn easily from one task to another, or is he or she limited to one skill?
2. Is *vertigo* a feeling of itchiness or dizziness?
3. If a four-year-old's behavior *reverts,* does the child begin acting like a younger child or continue to act normally?
4. Is a *convert* a person who sticks to one belief or one who changes to another belief?
5. If you *avert* your eyes, do you look away or stare?

NONFICTION 🐾 561

LITERATURE AND WRITING

Writing About Literature

Students' character analyses should
- be based on a two-column chart detailing the two sides of Wolf's personality.
- consist of a paragraph describing Wolf, using information from the chart.

Creative Writing

Students' dialogues should
- include comments that would be appropriate to a dog if it could speak.
- include comments that fit the personality of the narrator.

EXTENDING YOUR RESPONSE

Literature Groups Students should present instances of how both science and literature involve creativity. They might use an event such as Ben Franklin's kite flying as an example of creative scientific thinking. **COLLAB. LEARN.**

Interdisciplinary Activity Before students begin the activity, work together to list possible sources for the research. You might also review what a diorama is. If the diorama is to be made during class time, work with students to collect materials to use.

Internet Connection Before students begin, have them create two or three researchable questions. Then review with them the style to use when creating a bibliography. You might want to show them examples of entries for books, reference books, and magazines.

Skill Minilesson

VOCABULARY • **The Latin Root** *vert*

1. A versatile person turns easily from one task to another.
2. Vertigo is a feeling of dizziness.
3. A four-year-old who reverts begins acting like a younger child.
4. A convert changes to another belief.
5. When you avert your eyes, you look away.

Additional Resources
📁 *Vocabulary Practice,* p. 46

✔️ **ASSESSMENT OPTIONS**

📁 *Quick Checks,* p. 47
📁 *Selection and Theme Assessment,* pp. 91–92
📁 *Performance Assessment,* p. 46
💾 *Testmaker*

Objectives

- To read and analyze an essay in which the author discusses the desire of humans and animals to be part of a group
- To identify examples of voice

Skills

Reading/Thinking: Inferring
Grammar/Language: Semicolons
Listening/Speaking: Performing a Scene
Collaboration: Literature Groups

Motivating
→ OPTIONS

Selection Focus Transparency 48: Use the photograph and the quotation to discuss how ants and altruism relate to human relationships.

Focus Activity: Have students summarize the results of the freewriting activity in a word or phrase. Make a list on the board and tally the responses to see how many people had similar kinds of reactions.

Before You Read

The Tucson Zoo

FOCUS ACTIVITY

How do you respond to new people or situations? Do you react instinctively? Or do you stand back, analyze the situation, and then make a decision about what to do?

FREEWRITE In your journal, describe your typical response to new people or situations.

SETTING A PURPOSE Read to find out how the author responds to a new experience and what he discovers about himself.

BACKGROUND

The Time and Place
The author reflects upon an experience he had at the Tucson Zoo in Arizona.

Did You Know?
The cortex of the brain has two cerebral hemispheres, or sides. The left side is analytical; it allows you to recognize the parts, or details, of a whole; it cannot, however, combine the parts to let you see the whole. The right hemisphere is creative. It allows you to see the whole of something from its parts. The right side also allows you to be in a good mood while the left side controls your darker moods. The *corpus callosum*, which Lewis Thomas refers to in this essay, is an arch of nervous tissue that bridges the two hemispheres and allows them to communicate with each other.

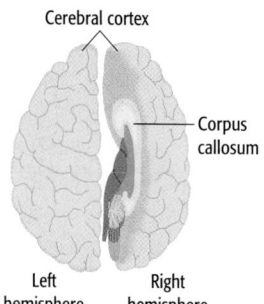

Cerebral cortex

Corpus callosum

Left hemisphere   Right hemisphere

VOCABULARY PREVIEW

elation (i lā′ shən) *n.* a feeling of great joy; ecstasy; p. 564
intact (in takt′) *adj.* entire; untouched, uninjured, and having all parts; p. 564
exultation (eg′ zul tā′ shən) *n.* joy; jubilation; p. 564
debasement (di bās′ mənt) *n.* the state of being lowered in quality, value, or character; degradation; p. 565
attribute (at′ rə būt) *n.* a quality or characteristic of a person or thing; p. 565

562 ❦ UNIT 2

Meet Lewis Thomas

❝There is a tendency for living things to join up, establish linkages, . . . get along whenever possible. This is the way of the world.❞

Award-winning author Lewis Thomas was a renowned physician and research biologist who taught at some of the top medical schools in the United States. With the publication of his first book, *The Lives of a Cell*, Thomas established a reputation as a master writer of the short essay. In his inquisitive musings on nature, science, technology, and other subjects, he celebrated the mystery and marvel of life.

Lewis Thomas was born in 1913 in Flushing, New York. He died in 1993. This essay appeared in The Medusa and the Snail *in 1979.*

RESOURCE MANAGER

Lesson Planning Resource
The *Unit Two Planning Guide* (pp. 109–116) provides additional lesson notes and reduced versions of all print resources.

📁 **Other Print Resources**
- Active Reading Guide, p. 48
- Vocabulary Practice, p. 47
- Reading Workbook, pp. 59–60
- Grammar and Language Workbook, p. 249
- Grammar and Composition Handbook, Lesson 11.5

- Quick Checks, p. 48
- Selection and Theme Assessment, p. 93
- Performance Assessment, p. 47
- Spanish Summaries, p. 48
- Spanish Translations
- Inclusion Strategies
- English Language Learners Sourcebook

 Transparencies
- Selection Focus 48
- Literary Elements 48

- Grammar and Language 47

Technology
🎧 Audio Library
🎧 Spanish Audio Library
💻 Glencoe Literature Web Site
💾 Testmaker

The Tucson Zoo

Lewis Thomas

SCIENCE GETS MOST of its information by the process of reductionism,[1] exploring the details, then the details of the details, until all the smallest bits of the structure, or the smallest parts of the mechanism, are laid out for counting and scrutiny. Only when this is done can the investigation be extended to encompass the whole organism or the entire system. So we say.

---

1. *Reductionism* is a method of explaining complex processes or structures by reducing them to more basic principles or units.

Sometimes it seems that we take a loss, working this way. Much of today's public anxiety about science is the apprehension that we may forever be overlooking the whole by an endless, obsessive preoccupation with the parts. I had a brief, personal experience of this misgiving one afternoon in Tucson, where I had time on my hands and visited the zoo, just outside the city. The designers there have cut a deep pathway between two small artificial ponds, walled by clear glass, so when you stand in the center of the path you can

NONFICTION 563

SUMMARY

On a visit to the Tucson Zoo, the narrator views a tank of otters and beavers from an underwater perspective. He is fascinated and realizes that some kind of positive response mechanism has been triggered in his brain. In analyzing the experience, the narrator concludes that "we hanker for friends" and that usefulness may be more important to civilization than individuality and solitary selfishness.

📁 *Spanish Summaries,* p. 48

A Active Reading

PREDICT After students read the first paragraph, ask them what they think the author's opinion about reductionism seems to be. Then ask if they think the article will support or refute the idea of reductionism and why. Suggest that students revise their predictions as needed.

Additional Resources
📁 *Active Reading Guide,* p. 48
🎧 *Audio Library*
🎧 *Spanish Audio Library*

Teaching Options

CONNECTING TO OTHER SELECTIONS

This selection is paired with "The Angry Winter" on pages 557–559. A lesson for teaching a comparison of the two selections appears on page 567.

The chart at the right shows three other ways to connect "The Tucson Zoo" to selections in this book.

For specific teaching strategies, see the *Unit Two Planning Guide,* pages 112–113.

Connection	Title
Life Skills: Life-long Learning	→ "To Da-duh, in Memoriam," p. 399
Thematic: Amazed	→ "The Californian's Tale," p. 248
Literary: Irony	→ "The Interlopers," p. 269

INFERRING What is the narrator's first reaction to the animals? What happens to change his thinking? *(At first, he is amazed and elated. When the scientist part of his brain takes over, he loses the wonder.)*

C Literary Elements

VOICE Explain that *voice* in writing is the way the author uses language to let his or her personality shine through. Have students suggest words to describe the author's voice and some examples of the language he uses that are clues. *(Words to describe voice might be "humorous" or "excited." He uses expressions such as "I could hear shouts across my corpus callosum.")*

D Active Reading

RESPOND Discuss words that describe the narrator's reaction to the otters and beavers. Ask students to describe a time when they felt a similar way. *(Words for the narrator's feeling might include "amazed," "excited," "fascinated," and "amused.")*

A&E HOME VIDEO. ® *The following videotape program is available from Glencoe. Be sure to preview the video for appropriateness for your class.*

- Quest for the Lost Tribes

Teaching Options

The Tucson Zoo

look into the depths of each pool, and at the same time you can regard the surface. In one pool, on the right side of the path, is a family of otters; on the other side, a family of beavers. Within just a few feet from your face, on either side, beavers and otters are at play, underwater and on the surface, swimming toward your face and then away, more filled with life than any creatures I have ever seen before, in all my days. Except for the glass, you could reach across and touch them.

I was transfixed. As I now recall it, there was only one sensation in my head: pure elation mixed with amazement at such perfection. Swept off my feet, I floated from one side to the other, swiveling my brain, staring astounded at the beavers, then at the otters. I could hear shouts across my corpus callosum, from one hemisphere to the other. I remember thinking, with what was left in charge of my consciousness, that I wanted no part of the science of beavers and otters; I wanted never to know how they performed their marvels; I wished for no news about the physiology[2] of their breathing, the coordination of their muscles, their vision, their endocrine systems,[3] their digestive tracts. I hoped never to have to think of them as collections of cells. All I asked for was the full hairy complexity, then in front of my eyes, of whole, intact beavers and otters in motion.

It lasted, I regret to say, for only a few minutes, and then I was back in the late twentieth century, reductionist as ever, wondering about

the details by force of habit, but not, this time, the details of otters and beavers. Instead, me. Something worth remembering had happened in my mind, I was certain of that; I would have put it somewhere in the brain stem; maybe this was my limbic system[4] at work. I became a behavioral scientist, an experimental psychologist, an ethologist, and in the instant I lost all the wonder and the sense of being overwhelmed. I was flattened.

But I came away from the zoo with something, a piece of news about myself: I am coded, somehow, for otters and beavers. I exhibit instinctive behavior in their presence, when they are displayed close at hand behind glass, simultaneously below water and at the surface. I have receptors for this display. Beavers and otters possess a "releaser" for me, in the terminology of ethology,[5] and the releasing was my experience. What was released? Behavior. What behavior? Standing, swiveling flabbergasted, feeling exultation and a rush of friendship. I could not, as the result of the transaction, tell you anything more about beavers and otters than you already know. I learned nothing new about them. Only about me, and I suspect also about you, maybe about human beings at large: we are endowed with genes which code out our reaction to beavers and otters, maybe our reaction to each other as well. We are stamped with stereotyped, unalterable patterns of response, ready to be released. And the behavior

---

2. *Physiology* is the branch of biology that studies the functions of living organisms and their parts.
3. The *endocrine system* consists of glands that secrete hormones into the bloodstream, affecting such bodily processes as growth and sexual development.

4. The *limbic system* is a region of the brain involved in the control of emotions and some types of behavior.
5. *Receptor* refers to a sensory nerve cell that responds to a stimulus in the environment and sends a message to the brain. *Ethology* (eth ol′ ə jē) is the study of animal behavior, including instinctive, or inherited, behavior.

Vocabulary
elation (i lā′ shən) *n.* a feeling of great joy; ecstasy
intact (in takt′) *adj.* entire; untouched, uninjured, and having all parts
exultation (eg′ zul tā′ shən) *n.* joy; jubilation

MEETING INDIVIDUAL NEEDS — ENGLISH LANGUAGE LEARNERS

Individuals or Groups Discuss with English language learners how their native cultures view the role of the individual. What happens if a person acts in a way different from what the culture expects? Sometimes change comes when an individual or a group decides to act in ways different from what is expected and encourages others to do

the same. Ask groups of students to discuss what happens as a result.

Activity Have each group write a report about a country where individuals or groups brought about change.

Additional Resources
📁 *English Language Learners Sourcebook*

released in us, by such confrontations, is, essentially, a surprised affection. It is compulsory behavior and we can avoid it only by straining with the full power of our conscious minds, making up conscious excuses all the way. Left to ourselves, mechanistic and autonomic,[6] we hanker for friends.

Everyone says, stay away from ants. They have no lessons for us; they are crazy little instruments, inhuman, incapable of controlling themselves, lacking manners, lacking souls. When they are massed together, all touching, exchanging bits of information held in their jaws like memoranda, they become a single animal. Look out for that. It is a _debasement_, a loss of individuality, a violation of human nature, an unnatural act.

Sometimes people argue this point of view seriously and with deep thought. Be individuals, solitary and selfish, is the message. Altruism,[7] a jargon word for what used to be called love, is worse than weakness, it is sin, a violation of nature. Be separate. Do not be a social animal. But this is a hard argument to make convincingly when you have to depend on language to make it. You have to print up leaflets or publish books and get them bought and sent around, you have to turn up on television and catch the attention of millions of other human beings all at once, and then you have to say to all of them, all at once, all collected and paying attention: be solitary; do not depend on each other. You can't do this and keep a straight face.

Maybe altruism is our most primitive _attribute_, out of reach, beyond our control. Or perhaps it is immediately at hand, waiting to be released, disguised now, in our kind of civilization, as affection or friendship or attachment. I don't see why it should be unreasonable for all human beings to have strands of DNA coiled up in chromosomes, coding out instincts for usefulness and helpfulness. Usefulness may turn out to be the hardest test of fitness for survival, more important than aggression, more effective, in the long run, than grabbiness. If this is the sort of information biological science holds for the future, applying to us as well as to ants, then I am all for science.

Did You Know?
 Chromosomes are strands of DNA and proteins in the nucleus of cells. DNA carries the genes that pass on hereditary information from parent to child.

One thing I'd like to know most of all: when those ants have made the Hill, and are all there, touching and exchanging, and the whole mass begins to behave like a single huge creature, and _thinks_, what on earth is that thought? And while you're at it, I'd like to know a second thing: when it happens, does any single ant know about it? Does his hair stand on end?

---

6. In psychology, _compulsory_ means "arising from an irresistible, illogical urge." Here, _mechanistic_ means physically or biologically determined, and _autonomic_ means involuntary and spontaneous.

7. In ethology, _altruism_ is an animal's self-sacrificing behavior that benefits another animal or group of animals. Similarly, in humans, the term means "unselfish concern for others."

Vocabulary
debasement (di bās′ mənt) _n._ the state of being lowered in quality, value, or character; degradation
attribute (at′ rə būt) _n._ a quality or characteristic of a person or thing

---

Active Reading

EVALUATE The author says that usefulness may turn out to be the hardest test of fitness for survival. Is this a reasonable possibility? You might use this question to model how to evaluate an author's statement.

Model: I am familiar with the expression "survival of the fittest," and I know it means only the best of a group survive. Usually I think of superior strength and intelligence as the attributes that help one be "the fittest." Usefulness is a new concept. However, if I accept the argument that the need to be part of a group is our most primitive instinct and has helped us survive to this point, then usefulness could help an individual survive. If that individual provided an indispensable service, his or her strength or intelligence might be irrelevant. Proving one's usefulness might be very difficult—much harder than proving how strong or how smart one is. So the author's statement seems valid.

Thematic Focus

Quests and Encounters The narrator has an encounter with beavers and otters. Discuss with students what he learns as a result. Ask how the encounter is similar to the one the narrator in "An Angry Winter" experiences.

✔ASSESSMENT OPTIONS

📁 _Quick Checks,_ p. 48

Grammar and Language _Minilesson_

Semicolons Write this sentence on the board:

Something worth remembering had happened in my mind, I was certain of that; I would have put it somewhere in the brain stem; maybe this was my limbic system at work.

Circle the semicolons and ask volunteers why semicolons are used to punctuate the sentence. Point out that a semicolon is used to join main clauses that are not joined by a coordinating conjunction.

Activity Ask students to rewrite the following pair of sentences using semicolons:

On the other side of the glass were beavers and otters at play. These animals dove beneath the surface, played underwater, and swam toward us. **L2**

Additional Resources

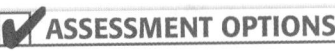
📖 _Grammar and Language Transparency 47_

📒 _Grammar and Language Workbook_, p. 249

📒 _Grammar and Composition Handbook,_ Lesson 11.5

📒 _Writer's Choice,_ Lesson 21.5

Personal Response

Students' questions may include *How do you think people can be useful? What do you think the ants might think?*

ANALYZING LITERATURE

1. An entire organism can be investigated only after its parts have been studied down to the smallest detail. The drawback is that science may overlook the whole.
2. Thomas is elated. He says he has receptors coded for otters and beavers. He concludes that we long for and need friends.
3. Some people say there is nothing to be learned from ants. They are social animals. Some people believe that ants represent a debasement of individuality. Thomas does not agree.
4. Thomas suggests that altruism may be our most primitive instinct. He says that usefulness may be one of the most important characteristics a member of a group can possess. In the conclusion, he wonders if any of the individual ants is aware of what is happening and if that ant gets excited about what it has realized.
5. Thomas seems to be saying that being a useful member of a group and showing others love and friendship are valuable assets. Students might point to the comments about ants and the comments about getting everyone in front of a television set as examples.
6. Most students will agree. Most people have at one time or another felt the need for friendship and love, emotions that seem instinctive.
7. Many students will note that they get excited about new encounters and learn from them just as Thomas did.
8. Students may argue both ways on this issue. Thomas concludes that the whole is most important. Yet, to reach his conclusion, he studies the parts of his reaction and still points to the role and reaction of the individual.

Responding to Literature

Personal Response
What questions would you like to ask the author of this essay?

─── **ANALYZING LITERATURE** ───

RECALL AND INTERPRET

1. According to the process of reductionism, when can an entire organism be investigated? What does Thomas say is a drawback of reductionism?
2. Theme Connections   What reaction does Thomas have to his encounter with the beavers and otters? What scientific explanation does he give for his reaction? What conclusions about himself and other people does he draw from his encounter?
3. According to Thomas, why does everyone say to "stay away from ants"? What is the message some people learn from ants? Does Thomas agree with this point of view?
4. What ideas does Thomas present about altruism? What do you think Thomas means in his final reference to ants?

EVALUATE AND CONNECT

5. In your opinion, what was Thomas's purpose in writing this essay? Support your answer with details from the selection.
6. Do you agree with the conclusions that Thomas draws about instinctive behavior in people? Why or why not?
7. Look at the freewriting you did for the Focus Activity on page 562. How does your typical response to new encounters compare with Thomas's response to the beavers and otters?
8. In your opinion, is Thomas a reductionist? Explain and support your answer.

─── **EXTENDING YOUR RESPONSE** ───

Literature Groups
Analyzing Meaning   Thomas once explained a state of mind in which the mind empties itself of all acquired knowledge and shuts itself off from interior and exterior messages. This state, called "no-knowledge," provides a different or enlightened look at the world. With your group, discuss whether or not you think Thomas realizes this state of mind in "The Tucson Zoo." Compare your findings with other groups' results.

Interdisciplinary Activity
Performing: Lowly Creatures Speak Out   At the end of the essay, Thomas expresses a desire to know what the ants who have made the Hill think and know. In a small group, brainstorm and then write a scene in which ants discuss their thoughts and feelings. Try to incorporate some of the ideas about ants that Thomas includes in the essay. Perform the scene for the class.

👆 **Save your work for your portfolio.**

Literary ELEMENTS

Voice
Voice is a writer's particular use of language to convey the writer's or the narrator's personality to the reader. Various elements of style determine a writer's voice. These elements include sentence structure, word choice, and tone. For example, when Thomas uses such words as "I am," "only about me," and "you," he shows a friendly voice.

1. Find other examples of Thomas's sentence structure, word choice, and tone that contribute to his voice.
2. What does Thomas's writing voice tell you about his personality, attitudes, and emotions? In what ways does his voice affect your appreciation of the subject of his essay?

● See **Literary Terms Handbook,** p. R13.

LITERARY ELEMENTS

1. Among the examples students may choose are these: "I was flattened"; "we hanker for friends"; "You can't do this and keep a straight face."
2. The voice of the piece tells readers that he has a sense of humor, likes people, and enjoys new experiences. Students will probably say the voice used helped them enjoy the piece.

Additional Resources
📖 *Literary Elements Transparency 48*

✔ ASSESSMENT OPTIONS

📁 *Quick Checks,* p. 48
📁 *Selection and Theme Assessment,* p. 93
📁 *Performance Assessment,* p. 48
💾 *Testmaker*

COMPARING *selections*

The Angry Winter **and** The Tucson Zoo

COMPARE **EXPERIENCES**

In both "The Angry Winter" and "The Tucson Zoo," ordinary events become extraordinary when the author-narrator of each essay experiences startling and unexpected insights.

- How are the experiences similar? How do they differ?
- Which author's experiences and comments, do you think, provide a more positive view of the human condition? Use evidence from the essays to support your opinion.

COMPARE **SCIENTIFIC FIELDS**

Loren Eiseley was an anthropologist. Lewis Thomas was a biologist. Their different scientific fields led them to explore different issues and concepts. Create a chart like that shown to compare anthropology and biology. In the third column, show how the characteristics and goals of each author's particular field are illustrated in the essay.

Field	Definition	Characteristics/Goals
Anthropology		
Biology		

COMPARE **VIEWPOINTS**

These two essays present opposing viewpoints on instincts and survival. Eiseley writes, ". . . ancient shapes were moving in his mind and determining his utterance. Only fools gave up bones." But Thomas says, "Maybe altruism is our most primitive attribute. . . . Usefulness may turn out to be the hardest test of fitness for survival, more important than aggression, more effective, in the long run, than grabbiness."

- With a partner, list examples and evidence to support each viewpoint.
- Role-play a debate between Eiseley and Thomas, arguing each viewpoint and providing evidence to support your argument.

Objective

- To compare two essays that deal with the theme of quests and encounters

COMPARE **EXPERIENCES**

- Both author-narrators have an unexpected experience. Eiseley has an encounter with his dog; Thomas has an encounter with otters and beavers. Eiseley concludes that each living thing fights for its own survival. Thomas concludes that we need each other.
- Thomas's view is more positive. He points out that usefulness to the group may be the most important survival technique. Eiseley indicates that both he and the dog were ready to fight for the bone.

COMPARE **SCIENTIFIC FIELDS**

Students' charts should

- include a definition of anthropology and a definition of biology.
- include at least one example of how characteristics and goals of each field are shown in the essay.

COMPARE **VIEWPOINTS**

- Students may want to have one partner find evidence for Eiseley's point of view and the other for Thomas's point of view.
- Discuss ground-rules for debates.

Additional Resources

 Literature Groups Sourcebook

Teaching Options

 PORTFOLIO OPTIONS

Effective Comparisons An effective comparison shows how two things are alike. Have students use these questions to evaluate the comparisons in their charts.

- Is it clear that the authors work in related fields?
- Do the examples give evidence that each author reflected the characteristics and goals of his particular field?

Have students staple their analyses to their charts and place them in their portfolios. At a later time, they might want to do further research and add to the examples on their chart.

Additional Resources

Writing Assessment and Portfolio Management, pp. 20–22

Writing Workshop

Objectives

- To create an observational report
- To plan, draft, revise, edit, proofread, and present an observational report
- To reflect on one's observational report

Teaching Strategies

PREWRITING

Explore ideas Encourage students to list at least ten possible topics. Explain that this will help them stretch their imaginations and may lead them in new directions toward ideas they may not have considered at first.

Teaching Options

~: Writing Workshop :~

Descriptive Writing: Observational Report

Pick up any newspaper or magazine and you'll probably find a nonfiction article that is an observational report. An observational report is just what it sounds like—a report that describes a person, a place, a thing, an event, or a process that the writer has observed. Have you closely observed birds in the wild or aquatic life in creeks? Could you describe a pitcher's throwing technique? Do you pay special attention to changes in car styles, hair styles, slang, or musical groups? **In this workshop, you will write an observational report that describes something you have observed.**

● As you write your observational report, refer to the **Writing Handbook,** pp. R58–R77.

The Writing Process

PREWRITING

PREWRITING TIP

If your memories are vivid, you can base your report on something that you have observed in the past. If not, choose a subject that you can make fresh observations of.

Explore ideas

With a partner or a small group, brainstorm for a list of subjects that you could observe and write about. Think about your everyday life, interests, activities, and travels. Almost anything and everything around you could be a possible topic. Like Slavenka Drakulić in "Pizza in Warsaw, Torte in Prague," you might focus on an aspect of everyday life in a city. Or, like Jane Ellen Stevens in "Exploring Antarctic Ice," you might make scientific observations, perhaps of the plant life in a vacant lot or of the wildlife in your backyard.

Consider your purpose and audience

Your main purpose in writing an observational report is to inform your readers about a subject you have observed and reflected upon. Decide whom you want to read your report. Then think about what your readers already know about your subject and be prepared to provide any background information they need to understand it.

Observe and take notes

Set aside time to make your observations. As you watch, use all your senses to observe your subject. Use an idea web like the one shown and jot down specific details that strike you. Be as specific and thorough as possible when you record what you observe.

MEETING INDIVIDUAL NEEDS — ENGLISH LANGUAGE LEARNERS

Focus on the Senses This assignment is an excellent opportunity for English language learners to report on people, places, or things that may be familiar and comfortable to them but unknown to other classmates.

Activity To help students identify sensory words, work together as a class. Name the topics listed below and have students suggest words and phrases that appeal to the senses. Here are some possible topics: backstage at a concert, changing a flat tire, making a pizza, mall activities.

Additional Resources

📁 *English Language Learners Sourcebook*

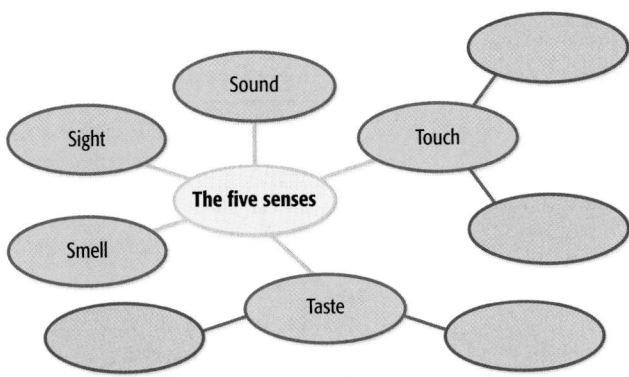

Make a plan

Review your notes and circle those that are necessary to give a complete picture of what you have observed. Think about the conclusions you can draw from these observations. To what main point do your observations lead? For example, in "Exploring Antarctic Ice," the author comes to the conclusion that the winter sea ice encircling Antarctica is an untamed, beautiful world teeming with life.

Once you know your main point, use the basic essay structure of **introduction, body,** and **conclusion** to plan your report.

STUDENT MODEL

Introduction	Tell what your subject is and provide any background information your readers need to understand your subject.	In winter, bald eagles gather along the Mississippi River north of St. Louis. The turbulence in the water near the locks and dams there breaks up the ice and stuns the fish in the river. The eagles can easily catch the fish.
Body	Present your observations.	I'll describe where I saw the eagles, how many there were, what they looked like perched in trees, and how they fish on the river.
Conclusion	State the conclusions you draw from your observations.	Bald eagles are magnificent birds that deserve our protection in the wild.

NONFICTION 569

Consider your purpose and audience Stress with students that part of their responsibility as a writer is to be sure the reader can understand the information in the report. If, for example, they are reporting on a certain pitcher's pitching style, they must decide whether their audience is a sports fan or someone who does not follow sports. Some content will be determined by the intended audience.

Observe and take notes Explain that the observation itself and reflecting on the experience are the heart of the assignment. Point out the experiences of Eiseley and Thomas as examples. They observed something and had a deep reaction to it. Later, they reflected on the experience and wrote about it.

Make a plan In planning their report, students might want to begin at the end. Point out that some authors in this theme came to important conclusions about their experiences. Suggest that students begin by identifying their own conclusions based on their observations. Point out the basic three-part structure of an essay. Explain that students may want to start at the conclusion and work their way up through the body and finally to the introduction.

Additional Resources

📁 **Writing and Proofreading Practice,** pp. 1–7, 46–52

✍ **Writing and Proofreading Transparencies 1–6, 17–18, 35–36**

📕 **Writer's Choice,** Lessons 3.1, 3.2

MULTIPLE LEARNING STYLES

Bodily-Kinesthetic For students who learn best through being active, you might suggest that they try to act out their observations, especially if they are writing about an activity. Acting out the observation may help them develop words and phrases that will help them express verbally what they have experienced physically.

Activity Ask students to suggest an activity that might serve as a topic for an observation. Let volunteers pantomime some of the actions or activities associated with the observation. Have classmates suggest sensory words or phrases to describe what they observe. **L1**

Suggest that students who are having trouble getting started draw a picture of something they observed. Then have them verbally describe or label what is in the picture. Finally, tell them to write one or two sensory words or phrases to describe what is happening in the picture.

REVISING

Evaluate your work Reading a piece of writing aloud is one way that awkward sentences or problems with the flow of the text can be detected.

Have a writing conference After the student has read his or her draft to a classmate and before they discuss the "Questions for Revising," suggest that the student who listened give a general reaction to the piece. Then the pair can get into more detail by using the questions.

TECHNOLOGY TIP

If students are working on a computer, they might use boldface type to highlight words, phrases, or sentences that they feel need further improvement. They can then make a hard copy of the report and focus specifically on improving the boldfaced sections.

Teaching Options

~: Writing Workshop :~

DRAFTING

DRAFTING TIP
Think about your subject as if you were painting a picture of it for your readers.

Refer to your notes and your plan as you draft your report. If you have trouble getting started, just copy one of your notes and begin with your observations. You can go back and write your introduction later.

STUDENT MODEL

One eagle dove for a fish right in front of me. The most striking thing I noticed about the bird, aside from its size, was its yellow feet. Its sharp talons snatched a slippery silver fish from the water and held on tight as the bird soared away.

REVISING

REVISING TIP
Revise your draft sentence by sentence, making sure each sentence follows logically from the one before.

Evaluate your work
Wait a few hours or days before you begin revising. That way, you can approach your report with a clear mind. Use the **Questions for Revising** as a guide in making improvements in your draft.

Have a writing conference
Read your observational report aloud to a friend or classmate. Ask your listener the **Questions for Revising** and note the responses on your draft. Make any further changes you think are necessary.

STUDENT MODEL

Through the binoculars, I discovered a mature bald eagle with the characteristic white head, white tail, and dark brown body. ~~As I watched it,~~ the bird took off from its perch and flew directly over my head. Its outstretched wings ~~seemed~~ spanned more than two yards ~~huge~~. Its wing tips looked like the open fingers of a hand.

It appeared to be more than two feet tall. Suddenly

QUESTIONS FOR REVISING

How can I:
- ☑ make sure I've provided background information that the reader may need?
- ☑ add specific details to make my descriptions more vivid and precise?
- ☑ organize details to best communicate what I observe?
- ☑ introduce my subject in a clear, interesting way?
- ☑ make sure my conclusions follow from my observations?
- ☑ clear up any confusing parts of my report?

Writing Minilesson

Making Transitions Transitions are words or phrases that connect one sentence or idea to another to show the relationship between the two. Some transitional words and phrases show time, or chronological, order. Words such as *later, next, then, about the same time, during,* or *whenever* are examples of transitions indicating time. Other transitional words and phrases show spatial relation-

ships. Typical examples would include *between, around, in front of, next to, under,* or *against.*

Activity Let students work in pairs. Suggest that they look for places in each other's reports where transitional words and phrases might be used. Emphasize that the word chosen must accurately state the relationship between the ideas

in the sentence. Remind students to add such words and phrases only if they help make the report clearer and easier to read. **L2 COLLAB. LEARN.**

Additional Resources

📗 *Writer's Choice,* Lesson 2.7

EDITING/PROOFREADING

Edit and proofread your observational report to find and correct errors in grammar, usage, mechanics, and spelling. Use the **Proofreading Checklist** on the inside back cover as a guide.

PROOFREADING TIP
Look for errors by reading through your report word by word, using a pencil to point to each word and punctuation mark.

Grammar Hint

To avoid confusion, place modifying phrases and clauses as close as possible to the word they modify. In the sentence below, the modifying clause *as it swooped down* should be placed near *eagle*, the word it modifies.

The eagle extended its long, hooked talons and snatched up the fish as it swooped down.

● For more about modifiers, see **Language Handbook,** pp. R24–R25.

STUDENT MODEL

Seeing so many bald eagles fishing on the river and in the trees perching along the riverbank fill^ed me with a sense of hope. If the bald eagle could come back after years of being endanger^ed then perhaps other animals can two. could too

PUBLISHING/PRESENTING

Share your observational report with your chosen audience. Also, consider compiling your report with those of your classmates and making a magazine to share with the rest of the school.

PRESENTING TIP
If you prepared your report on a computer, you might style it to look like a feature article in a magazine and add photographs or illustrations.

Reflecting

How did observing your subject and writing this report enhance your appreciation or understanding of the subject? Note your response in your journal. Then evaluate the strengths and weaknesses of your writing.

📖 **Save your work for your portfolio.**

EDITING/PROOFREADING

Have students use the **Proofreading Checklist** on the inside back cover of their textbooks.

One way to proofread a piece of writing is to read it backward. Explain to students that this forces the reader to read what is actually written rather than what the reader thinks is there. Often small words that are missing, such as *the* or *a*, can be found. This technique is also useful for detecting spelling errors.

PUBLISHING/PRESENTING

Since the observational reports were modeled after newspaper and magazine articles, students might want to consider submitting their reports to the local newspaper for publication, especially if the report is about something that would be of interest to local readers.

Reflecting

Portfolio Before students set their reports aside, ask them to make one final personal evaluation of it using the questions that follow.
- What are the main strengths of my report?
- What are the weaknesses and how could I eliminate them in the future?
- What did I like most about writing my report? Why?

Suggest that, based on their answers, students may decide to include their report in their portfolio.

✔ ASSESSMENT OPTIONS

📁 ***Writing Assessment and Portfolio Management***
- Writing Assessment, pp. 2–19, 35–37
- Portfolio Management, pp. 20–22

Unit Wrap-Up

Objectives

- To give a personal response about the readings, discussions, and activities in this unit
- To write definitions for and a comparison of narrative nonfiction and informative nonfiction
- To complete a self-evaluation, set a goal, and devise a plan for achieving the goal

PERSONAL RESPONSE

1. Students should offer logical explanations for their choices. Students may wish to share examples from the readings that they found most exciting.
2. Ask students to support their choices with examples from the readings that were most memorable or poignant.
3. Students should mention specific ways to classify readings, understand author's purpose, and work collaboratively.

ANALYZING LITERATURE

Students' paragraphs should
- define the terms *narrative nonfiction* and *informative nonfiction.*
- accompany each definition with examples from the selections in this unit.
- discuss how the content, author's purpose, and writing style are different in each type of nonfiction.

EVALUATE AND SET GOALS

Evaluate

Suggest that students may want to review their work in this unit by scanning the selections in their books, looking at their writing in their portfolios, and talking with others they worked with on projects.

Set Goals

Have students construct a flowchart, a series of boxes connected by arrows. Point out that they should write their goal in the last box and the steps they plan to take to reach that goal in order in the other boxes.

NONFICTION

Unit Wrap-Up

PERSONAL RESPONSE

1. Which of the readings in this unit did you find the most exciting?
2. Which readings did you find the most moving or inspiring?
3. As a result of the work you have done in this unit, what new ideas do you have about the following?
   - how to classify the type of material you are reading
   - how to understand the author's purpose
   - how to work with other students in pairs or in groups

ANALYZING LITERATURE

Classifying Nonfiction   Write a few paragraphs defining the terms *narrative nonfiction* and *informative nonfiction.* Cite examples from the selections in this unit to support your definitions. (For help in identifying these types of nonfiction, see the Genre Focus on Nonfiction on pages 422–423.) Focus on the differences between these types of nonfiction by contrasting the content, author's purpose, and writing style of the selections you cite.

EVALUATE AND SET GOALS

Evaluate

1. What was your strongest contribution to group activities as you worked through this unit?
2. What was your most challenging task in this unit?
   - How did you approach this task?
   - What was the result?
3. How would you assess your work in this unit, using the following scale? Give at least two reasons for your assessment.
   4 = outstanding   **3** = good   **2** = fair   **1** = weak

Set Goals

1. Choose a goal to work toward in the next unit. It could involve reading, writing, speaking, researching, or working in a group.
2. Discuss your goal with your teacher.
3. Jot down three or four steps that you will take to achieve your goal.
4. Decide at which points in the next unit you will stop and assess your progress toward your goal.

BUILD YOUR PORTFOLIO

Select   Choose two pieces of writing that you did in this unit and include them in your portfolio. Use these questions to help you make your selection.
- Which piece are you most satisfied with?
- Which one did you find most challenging to write?
- Which piece are you most likely to share?
- Which one led you to new discoveries as you wrote?

Reflect   Write some notes to accompany the pieces you selected. Use these questions to guide you.
- What do you like best about each piece?
- What did you learn from the process of writing each one?
- What might you do or try if you were writing one or both of these pieces now?

 ASSESSMENT OPTIONS

📁 ***Writing Assessment and Portfolio Management***
- Writing Assessment, pp. 2–19
- Portfolio Management, pp. 20–22

 GLENCOE

T E C H N O L O G Y

💿 **MINDJOGGER VIDEOQUIZZES**
VIDEODISC

Use *MindJogger* to review the Unit 2 content.

‖‖‖‖‖‖‖‖‖‖   Unit 2
Side A

   Also available in VHS.

Reading on Your Own

You might also be interested in the following books.

Night
by Elie Wiesel During World War II, the Nazis sent sixteen-year-old Elie Wiesel and his family to concentration camps. This memoir presents an account of young Wiesel's experiences of the horrors of the death camp. Wiesel's memories of that nightmare world force him to confront harsh realities about human nature.

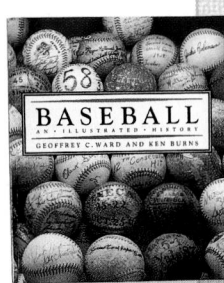

Baseball: An Illustrated History
by Geoffrey C. Ward and Ken Burns The authors use photographs and narrative to document baseball's evolution since the mid-nineteenth century and bring to life baseball's most memorable players, such as Ty Cobb, Satchel Paige, Babe Ruth, Jackie Robinson, and Joe DiMaggio. This book also shows baseball's connection to American history and its influence on our national life.

The Edge of the Sea
by Rachel Carson How do small sea creatures hold on to rocks while strong waves wash over them? How does the arctic jellyfish survive "being solidly frozen for hours"? Carson reveals the dramatic and varied communities of plant and animal life along the rocky shores, sandy beaches, and coral reefs of the Atlantic Ocean. Delicate drawings depict the rich variety of life forms.

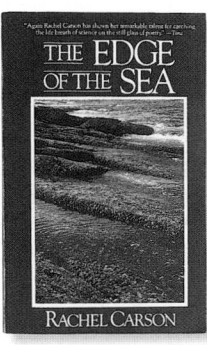

A Separate Battle: Women and the Civil War
by Ina Chang In both the North and South, women during the Civil War served vital roles. Some were doctors, nurses, and spies; others donned trousers and fought on the battlefront. This enlightening book reveals the wartime heroics of famous women like Louisa May Alcott and Harriet Beecher Stowe and of women such as Loreta Velazquez and Sarah Edmonds.

Glencoe Literature Library

Night by Elie Wiesel is one of the titles available in the *Glencoe Literature Library*. For a complete listing, see page T44 in this book.

The *Study Guides for Glencoe Literature* provide instructional support and student activities for works in the *Glencoe Literature Library*.

At the MOVIES

Be sure to preview the following video for appropriateness for your class:

  • **Call of the Wild**

MEETING INDIVIDUAL NEEDS

INCLUSION STRATEGIES

You may wish to recommend *A Separate Battle: Women and the Civil War* by Ina Chang to your less-proficient readers. The accessible subject matter and writing style make this book particularly appropriate for these students. **L1**
These books may be recommended to more proficient readers:

- *Night* by Elie Wiesel **L2**
- *Baseball: An Illustrated History* by Geoffrey C. Ward and Ken Burns **L2**
- *The Edge of the Sea* by Rachel Carson **L3**

Additional Resources
📁 *Inclusion Strategies*

Standardized Test Practice

Show students how the titles and headings in this passage can help them understand the main idea and the organization of the passage. The title of the whole passage and the headings of the individual sections contain a great deal of information about the point of the text. When students begin to answer the questions, show them how they can locate information in the text more rapidly by skimming the text for appropriate section headings.

Answers and Analyses

1. **B** While choices A and D are true, they are not the main point of the paragraph. This paragraph is about the conditions that Mexico placed on those who wanted to settle in Texas. The most reasonable answer is therefore B.

2. **G** At the end of the fourth paragraph, it is stated that *Austin was thrown in jail* for promoting the independence of Texas. There is no evidence to support the other three answer choices.

3. **A** Students should reread the sentence containing the word *exacerbated* and use context clues to help establish its meaning. Since the word is used to describe the increasing *tensions,* it must be a word that means something like *worsened.*

Standardized Test Practice

Read the following passage. Then read each question on page 575. Decide which is the best answer to each question. Mark the letter for that answer on your paper.

Why Is Texas the Lone Star State?

The United States flag received its twenty-eighth star in 1848, when Texas became a state. If Texas is one of so many states, why do we call it the Lone Star State?

Colonizing Texas

In the early 1800s, Texas was a Spanish colony. Only a handful of people from the United States lived in Texas at the time. Most residents were Tejanos, or Mexicans who claimed Texas as their home. The Spaniards were afraid of losing control of the area, so they offered large tracts of land to *empresarios* (people who promised to recruit settlers to the region), in the hope that the *empresario system* would help ensure loyalty.

After Mexico gained its independence from Spain in 1821, the Mexican government granted these tracts of land only under the conditions that the settlers become citizens of Mexico, obey Mexican law, and accept the Roman Catholic faith. Despite these efforts to limit land ownership, thousands came into Texas without Mexico's permission. These settlers never formally agreed to the Mexicans' conditions. By 1830 there were far more United States settlers than Tejanos living in Texas, and the Mexican government took note. They banned any further U.S. immigration and ordered the construction of five new army posts in Texas.

The Fight for Independence

In 1833 Stephen Austin traveled to Mexico City with a petition demanding that Mexico repeal the ban against immigration and create a separate Texas state. General Antonio López de Santa Anna, the head of the Mexican government, agreed to the first demand but insisted Texas remain a part of Mexico. In response,

Austin wrote a letter urging Texas to go ahead with plans for independence. When the letter fell into the Mexican government's hands, Austin was thrown in jail.

By the time Austin was released eight months later, Santa Anna had assumed the powers of a dictator. Many Texans believed that the time had finally come to break away from Mexican rule. On March 2, 1836, Texas announced its independence, creating an autonomous Republic of Texas and putting former Tennessee Governor Sam Houston in command of the army.

In April 1836, after several brutal skirmishes with the Mexican Army, Sam Houston decided to take the offensive. The perfect opportunity arose when he found the Mexican soldiers settled down near the San Jacinto River. The Texans launched a surprise attack, killing more than 600 Mexican soldiers and capturing hundreds more. This 18-minute Battle of San Jacinto ended the war.

On May 14, Santa Anna was forced to sign a peace treaty as well as a secret treaty endorsing Texan independence. Five months later, Sam Houston was elected president of the newly formed Republic of Texas. In 1839 the red, white, and blue Lone Star flag first flew over Texas.

From Sea to Shining Sea

The United States officially recognized Texas as an independent nation in 1837, but the peace between Texas and Mexico rested on shaky ground. Mexico never officially recognized Texas as independent, and twice in 1842 Mexican troops recaptured San Antonio. Tensions were only <u>exacerbated</u> when Texas passed a resolution claiming land reaching far west, to present-day California. Meanwhile, "manifest destiny," a theory arguing that America was meant to stretch across the continent, had caught on in the United States. For its own security, Texas sought admission to the United States, and in early 1845, Congress voted to annex Texas. By the end of the year, Texas became our twenty-eighth state.

---

1 What is the main idea of the third paragraph?

A The settlers had to accept the Roman Catholic faith.

B The Mexican government did not want settlers coming to Texas without their permission.

C The settlers did not like the Mexican form of government.

D The Mexican government built five new army posts in Texas.

2 Which is a FACT from the passage?

F Texas was a fertile place to farm.

G Stephen Austin was jailed for urging Texas to become independent.

H The settlers were looking for a new way of life.

J California became a state soon after Texas.

3 The word <u>exacerbated</u> means —

A worsened

B regulated

C eased

D reduced

4 Why did the Spaniards employ the *empresario* system?

F They wanted someone to farm their land.

G The Tejanos were threatening to go to war.

H They wanted to make sure settlers were loyal to their government.

J They wanted to improve relations with the United States government.

5 Which is the best summary of the passage?

A The Texans suffered greatly under the Mexican government.

B It was manifest destiny for the United States to annex Texas.

C Before 1845, Texas was an independent nation.

D There were many obstacles in the way of Texas becoming a state.

6 What conditions were set by the Mexican government to limit early land settlement?

F Settlers had to learn Spanish.

G Settlers had to obey Mexican law, become Mexican citizens, and accept the Roman Catholic faith.

H Settlers had to join the Mexican Army.

J Settlers had to accept their manifest destiny.

7 Why did Sam Houston decide to fight the Mexicans at San Jacinto?

A Because he was trapped

B Because the river was of tactical importance

C Because he wanted to capture General Santa Anna

D Because he had the element of surprise on his side

STOP

Answers and Analyses

4. H Students should scan the passage to find the term *empresario system*. The second paragraph states that the Spaniards *offered large tracts of land . . . in the hope that the empresario system would help ensure loyalty*.

5. D The text as a whole discusses the history of Texas and how it achieved statehood. The passage begins with the question *why do we call it the Lone Star State?* It goes on to describe Texas's struggle for independence from Mexico and admission to the United States. While there may be support for choices A, B, and C in the text, only choice D is broad enough to constitute a summary of the passage.

6. G Students should look back to the text and find the point at which the early policies of the Mexican government are discussed. In the third paragraph, the passage states that the Mexican government granted land *only under the conditions that the settlers become citizens of Mexico, obey Mexican law, and accept the Roman Catholic faith*.

7. D Students should find the place in the text where the attack at San Jacinto is discussed. There it is said that Houston fought at San Jacinto because it was the perfect opportunity for a surprise attack.

Tested Objectives

Questions	Reading Objective
1, 5	Summarize a variety of written texts
2	Recognize points of view, propaganda, and/or statements of fact and opinion
3	Determine the meaning of words
4, 7	Perceive relationships and recognize outcomes
6	Identify supporting ideas

MORE PRACTICE

For additional practice, assign pages from one of the following standardized test resources available as part of Glencoe Literature.

Additional Resources
ITBS Preparation and Practice
SAT-9 Preparation and Practice
TerraNova Preparation and Practice

Unit Three At a Glance
Poetry

UNIT OPENING

- Genre Focus: Poetry (p. 578)
- Active Reading Strategies (p. 580)
- Active Reading Model: *Eldorado* (p. 582)

Theme 7: LOVES AND LOSSES

SELECTIONS

One Perfect Rose and Shall I Compare Thee to a Summer's Day? (p. 586)

Media Connection: Song Lyrics (p. 590)

Simile and Well, I Have Lost You; and I Lost You Fairly (p. 591)

The Glory of the Day Was in Her Face and Missing You (p. 596)

First Lesson and Those Winter Sundays (p. 602)

Media Connection: Magazine Article (p. 608)

Horses Graze and A Blessing (p. 610)

SKILL FEATURES

Grammar Link (p. 595)

Technology Skills (p. 600)

Vocabulary Skills (p. 607)

Reading and Thinking (p. 615)

WRITING WORKSHOP

Business Writing: Interview (p. 616)

Theme 8: ISSUES OF IDENTITY

SELECTIONS

Afro-American Fragment and Heaven (p. 622)

The Base Stealer and To Satch (p. 628)

Media Connection: Magazine Article (p. 634)

Ex-Basketball Player and Miss Rosie (p. 635)

Media Connection: Interview (p. 641)

The Road Not Taken and We Are Many (p. 643)

The Floral Apron and My Mother Pieced Quilts (p. 648)

A Bus Along St. Clair: December and Freeway 280 (p. 654)

Making a Fist and What We Believe (p. 660)

Media Connection: Travel Guide (p. 665)

Foreign Ways and Song for My Name (p. 666)

SKILL FEATURES

Listening, Speaking, and Viewing (p. 633)

WRITING WORKSHOP

Creative Writing: Poem (p. 670)

KEYS TO LITERARY CONNECTIONS

 World Literature

Glencoe Literature contains a variety of literature that represents cultures from around the world. World literature selections are highlighted with this symbol:

Theme 9:
OBSERVATIONS AND EXPRESSIONS

SELECTIONS

Night Clouds and **Tiger Year** (p. 676)

For Poets and **Reapers** (p. 682)

Three Haiku and **Two Tanka** (p. 686)

Media Connection: Press Conference Transcript (p. 689)

A Motto from Poets: Leave Stone and **Constantly risking absurdity** (p. 690)

Media Connection: Newspaper Article (p. 696)

let my spirit fly in time and **Jazz Fantasia** (p. 697)

SKILL FEATURES

Interdisciplinary Connection (p. 681)

WRITING WORKSHOP

Descriptive Writing: Extended Metaphor (p. 702)

UNIT WRAP-UP

● **Personal Response, Analyzing Literature, Evaluate and Set Goals** (p. 706)

● **Build Your Portfolio** (p. 706)

● **Reading on Your Own** (p. 707)

The Joy Luck Club by Amy Tan

A Poetry Handbook by Mary Oliver

The Space Between Our Footsteps: Poems and Paintings from the Middle East selected by Naomi Shihab Nye

A Haiku Menagerie: Living Creatures in Poems and Prints by Stephen Addiss with Fumiko and Akira Yamamoto

● **Standardized Test Practice** (pp. 708–709)

KEYS TO TEACHING OPTIONS

Block Scheduling

Activities that are particularly suited to use within a block scheduling framework are identified throughout this unit by the following designation: For detailed suggestions on block scheduling, see the **Block Scheduling Guide** for this grade level.

Key to Ability Levels

The Teaching Options throughout this unit have been coded for students of various abilities.

L1 BASIC activities for all students

L2 AVERAGE activities for average to above-average students

L3 CHALLENGING activities for above-average students

Reading Skills in this unit

Variety of Texts

In addition to numerous poems by authors from the United States and several other nations, this unit also includes the following text types:

- song lyrics
- magazine articles
- interview
- travel guide
- press conference transcript
- newspaper article

Comprehension Skills

The following instructional support for comprehension skills appears in this unit of the Student Edition:

- **Active Reading Strategies and Model** (pp. 580–584)
- **Understanding Denotation and Connotation** (p. 615)

See also the **Reading Minilessons** throughout the unit in this Teacher's Wraparound Edition.

Reading Resources

Comprehension Skills Resources

📁 **Active Reading Guides**

The **Active Reading Guide** provides graphic organizers and study guide questions to support students' reading of each selection. (**Active Reading Guide**, pp. 49–67)

📁 **Reading Workbook**

The Reading Workbook (pp. 61–68) includes includes additional instruction and reinforcement of reading strategies and skills.

🎧 **Audio Library**

Available both on tape and on CD, the Audio Library provides valuable comprehension support.

Resources for Reading Widely

📚 **Glencoe Literature Library**

Each title in the Glencoe Literature Library includes a full-length novel or play plus related readings. A separate Study Guide is available for each title.

💿 **Literature Classics CD-ROM**

The 900 selections on this CD-ROM can be searched by author, theme, or genre.

 *in*TIME

A coproduction of Glencoe and Time Inc., *inTime* includes a wealth of high-interest nonfiction related to the selections and themes in Unit Three.

✓ Assessment in this unit

Assessment Options in the Student Edition

Glencoe Literature offers a number of diverse ways to evaluate student understanding and skill proficiency. In the Student Edition, use the following:

- **Responding to Literature**
  Following each selection, students are asked to recall facts, interpret ideas, and evaluate concepts as they answer a variety of questions and complete activities to extend their understanding.
- **Unit Wrap-Up (pp. 706–707)**
  Here students respond to the selections on personal and analytical levels. They also assume ownership of their learning by setting and evaluating goals and by selecting work for their portfolios.

See also the many **Assessment Resources** listed on the facing page.

 THE PRINCETON REVIEW

Standardized Test Practice

The Princeton Review has developed the Standardized Test Practice pages found at the end of this unit (pp. 708–709). These pages contain practice test questions that help students remain familiar with standardized test formats and content.

Writing Skills in this unit

Writing Skills

The Student Edition of Unit Three offers strong instructional support for writing skills:

In **Extending Your Response**, which follows each selection:
- **Writing About Literature**
- **Personal/Creative Writing**

In **Writing Skills** Lessons:
- **Using Simile and Metaphor** (p. 695)

See also the **Writing Minilessons** throughout the unit in this Teacher's Wraparound Edition.

Writing Workshops

Each of the three themes in Unit Three concludes with a **Writing Workshop** that guides students through the writing process.
- **Business Writing: Interview** (pp. 616–620)
- **Creative Writing: Poem** (pp. 670–674)
- **Descriptive Writing: Extended Metaphor** (pp. 702–705)

Writing Resources

Writer's Assistant CD-ROM

Each Writing Workshop is supplemented by an interactive writing guide on the Writer's Assistant CD-ROM. This easy-to-use writing guide provides prompts, templates, and other tools that lead students through the writing process.

Writing and Proofreading Practice

Blackline masters present in-depth instruction and practice on a specific step in the writing process and proofreading. (pp. 1–7, 53–72)

Writing and Proofreading Transparencies

Transparencies (1–6, 19–20, 37–42) provide graphic organizers and proofreading exercises for whole class instruction.

Research and Report Writing Guide

This resource provides extensive tips and activities to guide students in their writing projects in the literature classroom as well as in classes across the curriculum.

Style and Documentation Sourcebook for Writers

This sourcebook is a combination reference and workbook, giving students the most up-to-date information and guidance regarding traditional as well as technological research strategies and documentation.

Grammar and Composition Handbook

The Grammar and Composition Handbook provides instruction that supplements activities in the student textbook.

Assessment Resources

Selection Quick Checks

For each selection, a Quick Check of three to five short-answer questions measures students' literal comprehension.

Selection and Theme Assessment

The Selection and Theme Assessment instrument tests students' abilities to recall, interpret, and evaluate what they've read. The tests consist of multiple-choice, short answer, and essay questions.

Performance Assessment

Alternative assessment instruments and rubrics for Unit Three are found in the Performance Assessment ancillary.

Writing Assessment and Portfolio Management

These notes and strategies, student models, and assessment tools assist with the task of measuring students' progress as writers and as monitors of their own writing.

Testmaker

Teachers can customize selection, theme, and Unit Three tests by accessing the Testmaker database.

MindJogger Videoquizzes

Using a popular game show format, MindJogger Videoquizzes enable teachers to evaluate students' understanding of Unit Three in a quick and fun manner.

Unit Objectives

- To enjoy reading poems
- To analyze literary elements
- To apply strategies for reading poems

VIEWING THE PAINTING

Marc Chagall (1887–1985), a giant of the twentieth-century art world, was influenced by both Russian Expressionism and French Cubism. He infused his fanciful artworks with personal imagery—often representing people, animals, and themes from his native village in Russia. The "characters" in his paintings float and swirl with exuberant color and imagination, as in this painting, *Summer.*

Responding to the Art Discussion questions:

- What is unusual about the sizes and placement of people and animals in this painting? (*They float upside down; sizes are ignored.*)
- Knowing that *l'ete* means summer, why do you think Chagall chose these colors? (*The brilliant greens, blues, reds, and yellows express the vibrancy of the season and the artist's enjoyment of it.*)
- In what way is this painting similar to a poem in its expression? (*It transforms literal meanings, presents ideas with originality, and renders an experience imaginatively.*)

L'eté, 1964. Marc Chagall. Gouache, watercolor, pastel, and brush and black ink on paper, 27 x 19¾ in. Private collection.

576

TEACHER to TEACHER

GALLUP CATHOLIC HIGH SCHOOL • GALLUP, NEW MEXICO

My students are Zuni and Navaho, so I have their grandfathers and grandmothers come to class on separate days and tell stories of their traditions. Grandparents teach students how to fine-tune their listening skills using stories passed down through great oral storytelling traditions. Then when we begin the poetry unit, I first give students an overview of a poet, before reading his or her work aloud. Students are better prepared to listen to the images and sensory descriptions they hear in the poetry. Then I ask students to watch a sunrise or sunset. I remind them that this is the same sun that shone on their grandparents and that will shine on their children and their children's children. Students then write a poem about their experiences, and they write a reflection on their poems.

MELODIE GARCIA WICK

Poetry

"The poem on the page is only a shadow of
the poem in the mind. And the poem in the mind
is only a shadow of the poetry and the
mystery of the things of this world."

—Stanley Kunitz

Theme 7
Loves and Losses
pages 585–620

Theme 8
Issues of Identity
pages 621–674

Theme 9
Observations and Expressions
pages 675–705

Introducing the Unit

Have students read the quotation. Then pose these questions for discussion:

- Why do you think people write poetry?
- Why do you think people like to read poetry?
- What poems do you know? What do they mean to you?

Theme 7: Loves and Losses

The poems in Theme 7 explore the reasons people love, the emotions they experience—both positive and negative—and the lessons they learn when love is lost.

Theme 8: Issues of Identity

Poems in Theme 8 explore what makes us who we are and why we sometimes react as we do.

Theme 9: Observations and Expressions

Theme 9 poems look at the sky, the countryside, poets, and jazz, finding remarkable qualities in all.

GLENCOE
TECHNOLOGY

LITERATURE CLASSICS
CD-ROM
Search for other poems by theme, author, or title.

RESOURCE MANAGER

See the *Unit Three Planning Guide* (pp. vi–1) for additional teaching notes, strategies, and resources for introducing the poetry unit.

Genre Focus

Objective

- To understand the elements of a poem

Teaching Strategies

Explain that poetry's appeal is ancient and universal. From tribal chants to epics such as the *Odyssey*, poems gave our ancestors a way to express their ideas and emotions about life's experiences. Just as ancient poems were shared orally by a community, poetry is still meant to be heard so that its musical quality can be appreciated. Ask students to quote lines from poems that they remember and explain why they remember them.

Speaker

Select one brief, well-known poem (e.g., "Dream Deferred" by Langston Hughes, "My Last Duchess" by Robert Browning, "I'm Nobody" by Emily Dickinson) from an anthology and read the opening stanza aloud to the class. Ask students to listen and decide who is speaking to whom and explain how they know.

Lines and Stanzas

Have students scan the section and note different formats of poems. Invite them to compare and contrast the line and stanza arrangements of specific poems. Point out that stanzas and lines give form to a poem and can reinforce meaning.

Teaching Options

Genre Focus
Poetry

Mexican poet Octavio Paz believes that the purpose of poetry is "to create among people the possibility of wonder, admiration, enthusiasm, mystery, the sense that life is marvelous . . . to *make* life a marvel—that is the role of poetry." How does poetry give us a sense of the mystery and marvel of life? It does so through what African American poet Quincy Troupe calls "the music of language." Says Troupe, "I want the words to sing." Understanding the basic elements of poetry will help you hear the singing and sense the marvel in the poems you read and hear.

ELEMENTS OF POETRY

MODELS:

Speaker

The **speaker** is the voice that communicates with the reader of a poem. A poem's speaker can be the voice of a person, an animal, or even a thing.

> Lie back, daughter, let your head / be tipped back in the cup of my hand.
>
> *from "First Lesson" by Philip Booth*

speaker = a parent

Lines and Stanzas

A **line** is a horizontal row of words, which may or may not form a complete sentence. A **stanza** is a group of lines forming a unit. The stanzas in a poem are separated by a line of space.

> Drum on your drums,
>   batter on your banjoes,
> sob on the long cool
>   winding saxophones.
> Go to it, O jazzmen.
>
> *from "Jazz Fantasia" by Carl Sandburg*

line
stanza

Rhythm and Meter

Rhythm is the pattern of sound created by the arrangement of stressed and unstressed syllables in a line. Rhythm can be regular or irregular. **Meter** is a regular pattern of stressed and unstressed syllables that sets the overall rhythm of certain poems. The basic unit in measuring rhythm is the **foot**, which usually contains one stressed syllable marked with (′) and one or more unstressed syllables marked with (˘).

> If Í / had lovéd / you léss / or playéd / you slyly
> I míght / have héld / you fór / a súm / mer móre,
>
> *from "Well, I Have Lost You; and I Lost You Fairly" by Edna St. Vincent Millay*

MEETING INDIVIDUAL NEEDS — ENGLISH LANGUAGE LEARNERS

A Universal Language of Poetry
Rhythm, sound effects, and shape can be appreciated even when words are not understood. In fact, these elements can help English language learners learn English by making it memorable. In the same way, students can share their native languages through poems.

Activity Invite students to share a poem (or the words to a song) in their first languages. Then they can explain its meaning, in English, with assistance in translating by more proficient English speakers. Ask students to explain poetic elements in the poem.

Additional Resources
📁 *English Language Learners Sourcebook*

Rhyme

Rhyme is the repetition of the same stressed vowel sound and any succeeding sounds in two or more words. **Internal rhyme** occurs within lines of poetry. **End rhyme** occurs at the ends of lines. **Rhyme scheme,** the pattern of rhyme formed by the end rhyme, may be designated by assigning a different letter of the alphabet to each new rhyme.

> The glory of the day was in her face,   a
> The beauty of the night was in her eyes.   b
> And over all her loveliness, the grace   a
> Of Morning blushing in the early skies.   b
>
> *from "The Glory of the Day Was in Her Face"*
> *by James Weldon Johnson*

Other Sound Devices

- **Alliteration** is the repetition of consonant sounds at the beginnings of words.
- **Consonance** is the repetition of consonant sounds within words or at the ends of words.
- **Assonance** is the repetition of vowel sounds within non-rhyming words.
- **Onomatopoeia** is the use of a word or phrase, such as *swoosh* or *clank,* that imitates or suggests the sound of what it describes.

> a drum in the desert, harder
>   and harder to hear   — alliteration
> *from "Making a Fist" by Naomi Shihab Nye*

> harder and harder to hear   — consonance

> The setting sun is watching
>   from a distance.   — assonance
> *from "Missing You" by Shu Ting*

Imagery

Imagery is descriptive language used to represent objects, feelings, and thoughts. It often appeals to one or more of the five senses: sight, hearing, touch, taste, and smell.

> Black horses drive a mower
>   through the weeds,   appeals
> And there, a field rat, startled,   to senses
>   squealing bleeds.   of sight,
>   smell, and
> *from "Reapers" by Jean Toomer*   hearing

Figures of Speech

A **figure of speech** is a word or expression that is not meant to be taken literally.

- A **simile** uses the word *like* or *as* to compare two seemingly unlike things.
- A **metaphor** compares two or more different things by stating or implying that one thing *is* another.
- **Personification** involves giving human characteristics to an animal, object, or idea.

> the poet like an acrobat /
> climbs on rime   — simile
> *from "Constantly Risking Absurdity"*
> *by Lawrence Ferlinghetti*

> the spring rain / is a / thread
> of pearls   — metaphor
> *from a tanka by Lady Ise*

> Sometimes too hot the eye of
> heaven shines, / And often is   — personification
> his gold complexion dimmed;
> *from "Shall I Compare Thee to a Summer's Day?"*
> *by William Shakespeare*

Rhythm and Meter

Be sure students understand that every poem has rhythm but not necessarily the regular pattern called meter. Explain that rhythm adds to the mood and musicality of a poem.

Rhyme

Have students use nursery rhymes and familiar ballads or songs to illustrate internal rhyme and end rhyme. Review notation for showing rhyme scheme and have students write the rhyme scheme of their examples.

Other Sound Devices

Have students highlight repeated vowel and consonant sounds in lines like the following:
    may came home with a smooth
        round stone
    as small as a world and as large
        as alone.
Have students choose and use colors to mark *m* sounds, *s* sounds, long *a* sounds, and long *o* sounds.

Imagery

Images that appeal to sight and hearing are most common. Challenge students to recall lines from favorite poems that appeal to senses of smell, taste, or touch.

Figures of Speech

Explain that metaphors do not use the verb *is* but may be implied *("The white mares of the moon . . .")*.

Technology Option

Form for Line Analysis of Poems

Students can use word-processing software to create a page design for line-by-line analysis of poems. Have students open a new file for each poem and create two columns, one on the left for the lines of a poem and one on the right for noting poetic elements in the lines. Students can use this format to analyze poems of their choosing in the unit, until they have analyzed several examples of each poetic element. **L2**

Shall I compare thee to a summer's day?	**Speaker: man to his love**
Thou art more lovely and more temperate.	**Metaphor: woman/summer day; both give beauty,**
Rough winds do shake the darling buds of May,	**warmth, joy**
	Imagery: appeal to senses of touch and sight

Active Reading Strategies

Objective

- To understand and apply strategies for reading and comprehending poems

Teach the Strategies

Ask students to tell how their responses differ when they listen to a song being sung versus reading its lyrics on the page. Point out that poetry comes alive when read aloud because its sound effects and musical elements can be heard. Suggest to students that they slow down, reread, and read aloud the poems they will study in order to appreciate the many elements used to communicate their messages.

Listen

Have students listen as you read "Jabberwocky" (or any poem with strong sound effects) and then comment on how its sounds communicate, although the poem is composed mostly of nonsense words.

Imagine

Explain to students that one must involve oneself actively in the poem's images and actions in order to bring a poem to life and understand it. Recalling similar scenes or sensations allows a reader to relive the poet's experience.

Active Reading Strategies

Poetry

Use the following strategies to help you fully understand and appreciate each poem you read.

- For more about related reading strategies, see **Reading Handbook**, pp. R78–R107.

LISTEN   Read a poem aloud, listening to the way it sounds. Read without stopping until you come to a punctuation mark or a natural pause. Notice how the poem is formed and the lines are grouped. Are there sound patterns within these groups?

Ask yourself . . .
- What kind of rhythm does this poem have? Is it slow, fast, regular, irregular?
- Does the poem use rhyme? If so, what is the pattern of rhyme?
- What other sound devices does the poet use? How do these devices affect me? How do they affect the mood of the poem?

IMAGINE   Conjure up the sights, sounds, smells, tastes, and tactile sensations the poem describes or evokes.

Ask yourself . . .
- How does this scene or subject look?
- What details appeal to my different senses? How would they sound, smell, taste, or feel?
- What overall feeling does the poem convey?

RESPOND   Think about your spontaneous reaction to the poem.

Say to yourself . . .
- This poem makes me think . . .
- This poem reminds me of . . .
- That's pretty funny!
- What I really like about this poem is . . .
- I didn't expect that this poem would . . .

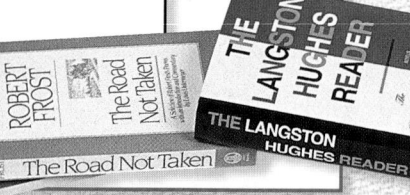

580   UNIT 3

Reading Journal

Telling the Story of a Poem

Explain that not only do poets use poems to create word pictures, they also use these word pictures to tell stories. In a few short lines, a poet can tell the life story of a character or tell about a lost friendship. Help students recall simple examples of story poems from their childhood, such as Mother Goose rhymes. In the process of painting the word picture and telling a story, the poet is often making a point, just as Edgar Allan Poe does in "Eldorado."

Activity Suggest that after students read "Eldorado" they write in their reading journals the story of the poem in the form of a short paragraph. Ask students to write below the paragraph a sentence that summarizes the point Poe was trying to make. Let students read their stories and conclusions about the meaning of the poem to a partner.

QUESTION Ask yourself questions to help you understand and interpret the poem. Write down or mentally note questions you can't answer.

Ask yourself . . .
- Do I understand what this poem is about?
- What does this image mean or represent? Why does the poet use figurative language in this way?
- What allusions or references does the poet use and how do they help me understand the poem's message?

CLARIFY Put the poem into your own words. Then summarize the poem, and think about what it might mean on a deeper level.

Say to yourself . . .
- These lines can be restated like this: . . .
- This stanza is about . . .
- This image brings to mind or symbolizes . . .
- Rereading this stanza helps me understand that . . .

INTERPRET Read the poem several times, focusing on interpreting its overall meaning.

Ask yourself . . .
- Does the title give a clue to the meaning of the poem?
- What main theme, or message, is the poet trying to convey?
- Does the poem have more than one meaning?
- How do the symbols and language support the meaning of this poem?

Applying the Strategies

1. Practice the strategies again as you read the poem "Eldorado" on page 583, using the Active Reading Model in the margins.

2. Choose another poem and practice using these strategies.

Respond
Point out to students that readers respond differently to poems based on their own experiences and emotions. Also suggest that any reader's response is valid, even if he or she does not have the same experiences or emotions as the poet or speaker.

Question
Invite students to recall poems that they could not understand on first reading. Explain that often poems express meanings through suggestion and comparison and word pictures rather than statements. Good readers remain alert and ask many questions that will help reveal meaning on a second or third reading.

Clarify
Acknowledge that this step takes time and effort, but it pays off. By rephrasing the poem's meaning in his or her own words, the reader focuses and interprets on a personal level. A poem digested in this way is not only understood better, it is remembered longer.

Interpret
You may want to suggest that students combine this step and the preceding one and write a journal entry for each poem in the unit summarizing the poem's subject and message.

Objectives

- To read and analyze a poem about a man who spends his life in a doomed quest for wealth
- To identify elements in a narrative poem
- To analyze the key idea in each stanza of a poem

Skills

Reading/Thinking: Using Active Reading Strategies
Writing: Analysis of Key Ideas

Motivating

→ **OPTIONS**

Selection Focus Transparency 49: Have students compare ways people might acquire wealth: earning it through hard work, inheriting it, winning it in a lottery or other contest or game, or getting it as returns on investments.

Focus Activity: Have students pair up to create a classified newspaper ad for a get-rich-quick scheme.

Before You Read

Eldorado

BACKGROUND

- The name *El Dorado*, meaning "the golden one," originally comes from a legendary region in northern South America where the ruler would cover his body with gold dust during festivals. At the end of the ceremonies, he would wash off the gold dust in a lake while his subjects threw jewels and golden objects into the water. In the early 1530s, explorers from Spain and Germany heard the tale and set off in search of the "gilded man." As the tale spread, the search for El Dorado came to mean the search for an entire region of gold, and explorers from around the world joined in the quest for the fabled golden city. El Dorado was never found (neither the man nor the place), but the name endured and is applied to any place of great wealth or to the dream of acquiring it.

Hernán Cortés

- Poe wrote the poem "Eldorado" in 1849, the year gold was discovered in California. That discovery brought many fortune seekers to the area in what later was called the "gold rush."

Meet Edgar Allan Poe

Edgar Allan Poe experienced loss at a young age, and throughout his lifetime he endured loneliness and suffering. Poe was orphaned before he was three and was then taken in by the Allans, a wealthy family in Richmond, Virginia. The Allans sent Poe to one of England's best boarding schools. There, when he was twelve years old, he wrote the poem "The Lake," which expressed his fears and his feelings of loss. While later poems such as "The Raven" and stories such as "The Gold-Bug" brought Poe admiration from critics, his writing never earned him much money, and he struggled with poverty until he died of unknown causes at forty.

Edgar Allan Poe was born in 1809 and died in 1849.

RESOURCE MANAGER

Lesson Planning Resource
The *Unit Three Planning Guide* (pp. 2–8) provides additional lesson notes and reduced versions of all print resources.

📁 **Other Print Resources**
- Active Reading Guide, p. 49
- Reading Workbook, pp. 61–62
- Quick Checks, p. 49
- Selection and Theme Assessment, p. 94
- Performance Assessment, p. 48
- Spanish Summaries, p. 49
- Inclusion Strategies

💾 **Transparencies**
- Selection Focus 49
- Literary Elements 49

Technology
🎧 Audio Library
🎧 Spanish Audio Library
💻 Glencoe Literature Web Site
💾 Testmaker

War memorial window. St. Mary's, Aldworth, Berkshire, UK.

Eldorado

Edgar Allan Poe

Gaily bedight,°
A gallant knight,
In sunshine and in shadow,
Had journeyed long,
5   Singing a song,
In search of Eldorado.

But he grew old—
This knight so bold—
And o'er his heart a shadow
10   Fell as he found
No spot of ground
That looked like Eldorado.

And, as his strength
Failed him at length,
15   He met a pilgrim shadow°—
"Shadow," said he,
"Where can it be—
This land of Eldorado?"

"Over the Mountains
20   Of the Moon,
Down the Valley of the Shadow,°
Ride, boldly ride,"
The shade° replied,—
"If you seek for Eldorado!"

A

Active Reading Model

IMAGINE
Picture a knight dressed in bright colors. Imagine his physical characteristics.

LISTEN
Hear how the rhythm of the first stanza is very regular, with a songlike quality.

QUESTION
Who is the pilgrim shadow?

INTERPRET
What do you think Poe is really saying about the search for wealth?

Reading the Selection

A **Literary Elements**

NARRATIVE POETRY Like a story, a narrative poem has characters, setting, plot, and point of view. Have students identify each element in this poem.

Additional Resources
📁 *Active Reading Guide,* p. 49
🎧 *Audio Library*
🎧 *Spanish Audio Library*

Active Reading Model

Imagine
Have students describe the knight as he appears in the mind's eye.

Listen
Have students tell how rhythm and rhyme add to the poem's interest.

Question
It is the ghost of someone who went on the same quest.

Interpret
One may find wealth in the afterlife but not on earth.

✔ **ASSESSMENT OPTIONS**
📁 *Quick Checks,* p. 49

Teaching Options

CONNECTING TO OTHER SELECTIONS

The chart at the right shows three ways to connect "Eldorado" to selections in this book.

For specific teaching strategies, see the *Unit Three Planning Guide,* pages 5–6.

Connection	Title
Life Skills: Life-long Learning	→ "The Tucson Zoo," p. 563
Thematic: Life Quests	→ "The Vision Quest," p. 89
Literary: Theme	→ "The Happy Man's Shirt," p. 241

Responding to the Selection

Personal Response

Students may find the energetic, confident young knight or the haunting "pilgrim shadow" the strongest image.

ACTIVE READING RESPONSE

No one strategy is most important.

ANALYZING LITERATURE

1. The knight seeks for his fortune, gradually growing old, discouraged, and pessimistic. The failure to find the fabled place depresses him.
2. He meets a wandering figure who represents all those who went in search of Eldorado before the knight.
3. He must "ride, boldly ride" to his death to gain his fortune. Eldorado does not exist—true wealth is enjoyed after death.
4. The third line of each stanza ends with *shadow*. Meanings for the word change from a focus on outer to inner reality and from ghost to death.
5. The knight might die or give up the quest. The fact that one like him is now a ghost argues for death.
6. Few explorers gained the wealth they set out to find. Christopher Columbus found lands but not gold. Hernando Cortes took huge quantities of gold from Mexican ruler Montezuma but lost most of his personal fortune. Both died with modest means and out of political favor.
7. Students may feel the speaker would discourage others from wasting their lives on a vain quest, as he did.
8. The poem may temper dreams of instant wealth with understanding that "wealth" eludes most, but human nature makes most of us dream of "striking it rich."

EXTENDING YOUR RESPONSE

Interdisciplinary Activity

Remind students to invent map features to show topography, political information, or "historic" facts about the region. Have students present an original "history" of the knight using their maps.

Writing About Literature

Students' analyses should
- express a main idea for each stanza.
- include details from the stanza to develop each main idea.
- use transitions to connect ideas.

584 UNIT 3

Responding to Literature

Personal Response

What images remain in your mind after reading the poem? List them.

ACTIVE READING RESPONSE

Look back at the strategies described in the Active Reading Model notes on pages 580–581. Which Active Reading Strategy was most helpful to you in understanding the poem?

ANALYZING LITERATURE

RECALL AND INTERPRET

1. What is the knight doing in the first two stanzas? How does the knight change in the second stanza? What might account for those changes?
2. Whom does the knight meet in the third stanza? Whom or what do you think this person represents?
3. What advice does the knight receive in the last stanza? What, in your opinion, does this advice mean?
4. How often does Poe use the word *shadow*? What do you think the word means in each case? Based on the meanings for *shadow*, what would you say is the main message of this poem?

EVALUATE AND CONNECT

5. What might have happened to the knight after his encounter? Explain and support your response with evidence from the poem.
6. Have you read or heard about other quests of explorers or knights? What was the outcome of those quests?
7. What advice might the speaker give to fortune seekers today? In your opinion, why would he give this advice?
8. Think about your response to the Focus Activity on page 582. What insights have you gained after reading this selection? Explain.

EXTENDING YOUR RESPONSE

Interdisciplinary Activity

Geography: Map a Story Elaborate and expand on the story presented in the poem. Place the characters in the poem in a particular time and place, and map the region where the knight travels. Put captions at each place the knight visits, and explain whom he met or what he did there.

Writing About Literature

Analyzing Stanzas Each stanza, or group of lines, in Poe's poem presents one main idea and helps move the story along. In a few paragraphs, tell the key idea each stanza expresses. Then explain how the stanzas combine to tell a story.

 Save your work for your portfolio.

Literary ELEMENTS

Narrative Poetry

Narrative poetry is poetry that tells a story. Narrative poetry has one or more characters and includes setting, plot, and point of view. In some narrative poems, such as "Eldorado," long periods of time may pass in a few lines. "Eldorado" tells the story of a knight's lifelong search in just four stanzas.

1. What events in the knight's life does the poem cover?
2. In your opinion, what does the brevity of the poem highlight?

● See **Literary Terms Handbook**, p. R8.

LITERARY ELEMENTS

1. It covers his youth and maturity in search of Eldorado, his aging disillusionment, and his meeting with a ghost, who foreshadows the knight's own death.
2. The brevity of the poem underscores the brevity of life.

Additional Resources

📖 *Literary Elements Transparency 49*

✓ ASSESSMENT OPTIONS

📁 *Quick Checks,* p. 49
📁 *Selection and Theme Assessment,* p. 94
📁 *Performance Assessment,* p. 48
💾 *Testmaker*

Theme 7

Loves and Losses

What role does love play in life? Because love is such an important part of human life, its loss can be a painful experience. In this theme you will find poems about the joys and insights love can bring as well as the emptiness and pain of its loss.

THEME PROJECTS

Performing

Coffeehouse Poetry Poetry comes alive when it is read aloud. With a small group, choose three or four poems from this theme to present at a "coffeehouse" poetry reading.

1. Look carefully at each poem and decide how you can best convey the speaker's message. Assign poems or parts of poems to different members of the group.

2. Decide on appropriate music to accompany your readings of the poems. Choose from recorded music or ask a group member who is also a musician to play or sing.

3. With other groups, create the coffeehouse atmosphere and take turns presenting your performance.

Multimedia Project

Picturing Poetry With a partner, choose words and images from three or four of the poems, and create a multimedia presentation.

1. Decide which words or images from the poem represent the speaker's main idea.

2. Use a still camera or a video camera to create slides or a videotape of these images.

3. Then, using a tape recorder or video camera, create a voiceover for your presentation.

4. Present your mixed-media show to the class.

In Our Nature, 1996. Daniel Nevins. Oil, acrylic, and collage on wood, 37 x 29 in. Private collection.

POETRY 585

LITERATURE & HUMANITIES

To provide a musical introduction appropriate to the theme of "Loves and Losses," use "Barbara Allen," CD 1, Track 20, from Glencoe's *World of Music.*

GLENCOE
TECHNOLOGY

 LITERATURE CLASSICS
CD-ROM
Search for other selections related to the theme of loves and losses.

Teaching Strategies

The following suggestions may help your students plan and carry out their theme projects.

Performing

- Point out that some poems may lend themselves better to oral presentations than others.
- If students are using recorded music for their presentations, they might want to tape record the chosen music so that it can easily be incorporated into the presentation.
- You might want to describe a coffeehouse setting by explaining that some coffeehouses are dark or dimly lit and have small tables with candles.

Multimedia Project

- Be sure students have access to the equipment and related supplies that they will need. Also be sure they know how to operate the equipment.
- Suggest that students make a list of the images that come to mind and how these images might be pictured. Point out that some concepts, such as love, will require creative thinking in how the concept or image is pictured.
- Partners may want to write a script in order to time the voiceover with the pictures.

Additional Resources

- *Interdisciplinary Activities*, pp. 14–15
- *Viewing and Representing Activities*, pp. 19–20
- *Listening and Speaking Activities*, pp. 13–14
- *Critical Thinking Skills*, pp. 18–20
- *Selection and Theme Assessment*, pp. 183–184
- *Performance Assessment*, p. 95

Theme 7   SKILLS SCOPE AND SEQUENCE

SELECTIONS	Literary Elements	Reading and Thinking	Writing	Vocabulary and Spelling
One Perfect Rose DOROTHY PARKER *Shall I Compare Thee to a Summer's Day?* WILLIAM SHAKESPEARE	Sonnet, SE p. 589 *Rhyme and Form, TWE p. 587*	*Questioning, TWE p. 587*	Word Web, SE p. 586 Comparing Poems, SE p. 589 Poem, SE p. 589	*Keywords, TWE p. 590*
Simile N. SCOTT MOMADAY Well, I Have Lost You; and I Lost You Fairly EDNA ST. VINCENT MILLAY	Simile, SE p. 594	*Clarify, TWE p. 592*	List, SE p. 591 Analyze Mood, SE p. 594 Advice Column, SE p. 594 *Explaining How To, TWE p. 595*	
The Glory of the Day Was in Her Face JAMES WELDON JOHNSON *Missing You* SHU TING	Metaphor, SE p. 599	*Questioning, TWE p. 597* *Paraphrasing, TWE p. 597*	Freewrite, SE p. 596 Letter, SE p. 599 Poem, SE p. 599 Report, SE p. 599 *Group Creative Writing, TWE p. 600*	
First Lesson PHILIP BOOTH Those Winter Sundays ROBERT HAYDEN	Alliteration, SE p. 606 *Assonance and Consonance, TWE p. 604*	Summarizing, SE p. 606 *Inferring, TWE p. 604*	Character Sketch, SE p. 606 Letter, SE p. 606	Multiple-Meaning Words, SE p. 607
Horses Graze GWENDOLYN BROOKS A Blessing JAMES WRIGHT	Personification, SE p. 614 *Repetition, TWE p. 611*	*Distinguishing Fact and Opinion, TWE p. 608* *Understanding Denotation and Connotation, TWE p. 615*	Analyze Mood, SE p. 614 Paragraph, SE p. 614 Report, SE p. 614	*Keywords, TWE p. 609* *Context Clues, TWE p. 612* *Analyze Connotation in Ads, TWE p. 615*

Key: Student material is in roman. Teacher material is in italic.   ⌨ Technology   Collaboration

Grammar and Language	Listening, Speaking, and Viewing	Life Skills	Study, Research, and Technology
Degrees of Comparison, TWE p. 587	**COLLAB. LEARN.** Literature Groups, SE p. 589 Share Findings, SE p. 589	Charting, SE p. 589	Researching Costs, SE p. 589 💻 *Internet Connection, TWE p. 590*
Pronoun and Antecedent Agreement, SE p. 595	**COLLAB. LEARN.** Literature Groups, SE p. 594 Dialogue, SE p. 594	*Decision Making, TWE p. 592*	💻 Using the Internet, SE p. 594 Researching Geography, SE p. 594
	COLLAB. LEARN. Literature Groups, SE p. 599 Share Research Findings, SE p. 599		💻 Internet Connection, SE p. 599 💻 Internet: Publishing Writing on the Web, SE p. 600 💻 *Create a Current Events Web Site, TWE p. 601*
	COLLAB. LEARN. Literature Groups, SE p. 606 Compare Oral Effects, SE p. 606 *Pantomime, TWE p. 603*	Learning for Life: Survival Floating, SE p. 606	Research Survival Floating, SE p. 606 *Using a Dictionary, TWE p. 607*
	COLLAB. LEARN. Literature Groups, SE p. 614 Interviews, SE p. 614 *Presenting a Poem, TWE p. 612*	Learning for Life: Log, SE p. 614	💻 *Internet Connection, TWE p. 609* *Scanning Magazine Articles, TWE p. 611*

SELECTIONS	📁 Print Resources		
One Perfect Rose DOROTHY PARKER Shall I Compare Thee to a Summer's Day? WILLIAM SHAKESPEARE	Unit Three Planning Guide, pp. 16–21 * Active Reading Guide, p. 50	Grammar & Comp Handbook, Lesson 8.1 Grammar and Language Workbook, p. 199	* Quick Checks, p. 50 Selection and Theme Assessment, pp. 95–96 Performance Assessment, p. 49 Spanish Summaries, p. 50
Simile N. SCOTT MOMADAY Well, I Have Lost You; and I Lost You Fairly EDNA ST. VINCENT MILLAY	Unit Three Planning Guide, pp. 22–26 * Active Reading Guide, p. 51		* Quick Checks, p. 51 Selection and Theme Assessment, pp. 97–98 Performance Assessment, p. 50 Spanish Summaries, p. 51
The Glory of the Day Was in Her Face JAMES WELDON JOHNSON Missing You SHU TING	Unit Three Planning Guide, pp. 27–31 * Active Reading Guide, p. 52		* Quick Checks, p. 52 Selection and Theme Assessment, pp. 99–100 Performance Assessment, p. 51 Spanish Summaries, p. 52
First Lesson PHILIP BOOTH Those Winter Sundays ROBERT HAYDEN	Unit Three Planning Guide, pp. 32–36 * Active Reading Guide, p. 53		* Quick Checks, p. 53 Selection and Theme Assessment, pp. 101–102 Performance Assessment, p. 52 Spanish Summaries, p. 53 Spanish Translations
Horses Graze GWENDOLYN BROOKS A Blessing JAMES WRIGHT	Unit Three Planning Guide, pp. 37–41 * Active Reading Guide, p. 54		* Quick Checks, p. 54 Selection and Theme Assessment, pp. 103–104 Performance Assessment, p. 53 Spanish Summaries, p. 54 Spanish Translations

*Also available in Spanish

⛉ **Transparencies**	**Technology Resources**
Selection Focus Transparency 50 Grammar and Language Transparency 48 Literary Elements Transparency 50 Fine Art Transparency 32	🎧 💿 Audio Library 🎧 💿 Spanish Audio Library 💾 💿 Vocabulary Puzzlemaker 💻 Web Site: lit.glencoe.com
Selection Focus Transparency 51 Literary Elements Transparency 51	💿 Literature Launchers Videodisc 🎧 💿 Audio Library 🎧 💿 Spanish Audio Library 💾 💿 Vocabulary Puzzlemaker 💻 Web Site: lit.glencoe.com
Selection Focus Transparency 52 Literary Elements Transparency 52	🎧 💿 Audio Library 🎧 💿 Spanish Audio Library 💾 💿 Vocabulary Puzzlemaker 💻 Web Site: lit.glencoe.com
Selection Focus Transparency 53 Literary Elements Transparency 53 Fine Art Transparency 2	💿 Literature Launchers Videodisc 🎧 💿 Audio Library 🎧 💿 Spanish Audio Library 💾 💿 Vocabulary Puzzlemaker 💻 Web Site: lit.glencoe.com
Selection Focus Transparency 54 Literary Elements Transparency 54	🎧 💿 Audio Library 🎧 💿 Spanish Audio Library 💾 💿 Vocabulary Puzzlemaker 💻 Web Site: lit.glencoe.com

📁 𝒯heme **RESOURCES**

- Listening and Speaking Activities (pp. 13–14)
- Viewing and Representing Activities (pp. 19–20)
- Critical Thinking Skills (pp. 18–20)
- Media Connections Activities (pp. 13–14)
- Interdisciplinary Activities (pp. 14–15)

See also these additional planning resources:
- English Language Learners Sourcebook
- Inclusion Strategies Sourcebook
- Literature Groups Sourcebook

Use Glencoe's *Presentation Plus!* This multimedia teaching tool lets you present dynamic lessons that will engage your students. Using Microsoft PowerPoint,® you can customize the presentations to create your own personalized lessons.

Objectives

- To read and analyze poems about love offerings
- To analyze meter and rhyme in a sonnet
- To write a comparison of tone in two poems

Skills

Writing: Poem
Grammar/Language: Degrees of Comparison
Collaboration: Literature Groups

Motivating
→ OPTIONS

Selection Focus Transparency 50: Explain to students that Cupid, the son of the goddess Venus, was the god of love in Roman mythology. According to myth, a person shot with one of Cupid's gold-tipped arrows fell in love.

Focus Activity: Have students share their reasons and give examples.

 —Before You Read—

One Perfect Rose and *Shall I Compare Thee . . .*

FOCUS ACTIVITY

Why do people write about love? What kinds of things do they say?

MAP IT! Create a word web to show some of the reasons people write about love. Write *love poem* in the middle of your map and connect it to at least four different reasons.

SETTING A PURPOSE Read to find out what the speakers of two poems say about love and why they say it.

BACKGROUND

- Throughout history, people in love have expressed their feelings by giving tokens of their affection, such as flowers, poems, candy, jewelry, locks of hair, and rings. Many of these items have symbolic meaning. A ring is a never-ending circle that represents endless love. A lock of hair may be a cherished reminder of a beloved person. Flowers often symbolize ardent love.

- Dorothy Parker had a reputation for being clever and amusing, but she was also sensitive to matters of the heart and suffered her share of disappointments in love. In difficult times her humor sustained her. Once, after the death of her husband, someone asked if there was anything she needed, and she replied, "Get me a new husband." When her remark was considered unfeeling, she said, "So sorry. Then run down to the corner and get me a ham and cheese on rye and tell them to hold the mayo."

- To make his sonnets believable to the reader, Shakespeare uses the voice of a speaker that, as critic Helen Vendler explains, is like "a 'real voice' coming from a 'real mind' like our own." In each sonnet the speaker presents his inner thoughts and feelings. Although each sonnet is a complete poem that stands on its own, all 154 of Shakespeare's sonnets together form a sonnet sequence—a series of sonnets on the same subject.

586 ❧ UNIT 3

Meet Dorothy Parker

Dorothy Parker wrote light verse for magazines such as the *Saturday Evening Post* and *Vogue*. Parker, one of the first writers to publish in the *New Yorker*, helped establish the style that became known as the *New Yorker* short story. Known for her biting wit, Parker said that genuine humor required courage and criticism, as well as "a disciplined eye and a wild mind."

Dorothy Parker was born in 1893 in West End, New Jersey. She died in 1967.

Meet William Shakespeare

English poet and playwright William Shakespeare wrote during the Elizabethan Age in England. Some historians believe that by the age of twenty, Shakespeare was known in London as a rising playwright. In addition to sonnets and numerous plays, Shakespeare wrote two long narrative poems.

William Shakespeare was born in 1564 in Stratford-upon-Avon, England, and died there in 1616.

RESOURCE MANAGER

Lesson Planning Resource
The *Unit Three Planning Guide* (pp. 16–21) provides additional lesson notes and reduced versions of all print resources.

 Other Print Resources
- Active Reading Guide, p. 50
- Grammar and Language Workbook, p. 199
- Grammar and Composition Handbook, Lesson 8.1
- Quick Checks, p. 50

- Selection and Theme Assessment, pp. 95–96
- Performance Assessment, p. 49
- Spanish Summaries, p. 50
- Inclusion Strategies

 Transparencies
- Selection Focus 50
- Fine Art 32
- Literary Elements 50
- Grammar and Language 48

Technology

- 🎧 Audio Library
- 🎧 Spanish Audio Library
- 💻 Glencoe Literature Web Site
- 💾 Testmaker

One Perfect Rose

Dorothy Parker ✌

A
A single flow'r he sent me, since we met.
    All tenderly his messenger he chose;
Deep-hearted, pure, with scented dew still wet—
    One perfect rose.

5 I knew the language of the floweret;
    "My fragile leaves," it said, "his heart enclose."
Love long has taken for his amulet°
    One perfect rose.

B
    Why is it no one ever sent me yet
10   One perfect limousine, do you suppose?
    Ah no, it's always just my luck to get
    One perfect rose.

---

7 An *amulet* (am′ yə lit) is an object thought to bring good
fortune or to protect against bad luck.

Shall I Compare Thee to a Summer's Day?

William Shakespeare ✌

Shall I compare thee to a summer's day?
Thou art more lovely and more temperate.°
Rough winds do shake the darling buds of May,
And summer's lease hath all too short a date.
5 Sometime too hot the eye of heaven shines,
And often is his gold complexion dimmed;
And every fair° from fair sometime declines,
By chance, or nature's changing course untrimmed:°
But thy eternal summer shall not fade
10 Nor lose possession of that fair thou ow'st,°
Nor shall Death brag thou wand'rest in his shade,
When in eternal lines to time thou grow'st.
    So long as men can breathe or eyes can see,
    So long lives this, and this gives life to thee. **C**

---

2 In terms of the weather, a *temperate* day is calm and free
from extremes of temperature.
7 *Fair,* in this context, is a synonym for *beauty.*
8 Here, *untrimmed* means "stripped of beauty."
10 *[thou ow'st]* Read this poetic phrase as "you own" or
"you possess."

POETRY ✿ 587

Reading the Selection

A **Literary Elements**

RHYME and FORM Ask why the poet
chose a formal and exact structure.
*(It is in the tradition of romantic,
courtly love; it is songlike. The rhyme
scheme is abab for all three stanzas.)*

Additional Resources

📁 *Active Reading Guide,* p. 50
🎧 *Audio Library*
🎧 *Spanish Audio Library*

B **Active Reading**

QUESTION Students should note the
abrupt change in tone. How does it
change their reading of the poem?

C **Literary Elements**

FORM: Sonnet Invite students to
describe the rhythm and use of
rhyme. How could lines be grouped
into units that belong together?
*(Lines 1–4, 5–8, 9–12, and 13–14;
three quatrains and a rhymed couplet)*

Thematic Focus

Loves and Losses Have students
compare flowers and love poems as
gifts to someone loved.

☑ **ASSESSMENT OPTIONS**

📁 *Quick Checks,* p. 50

Teaching Options

Grammar and Language *Minilesson*

Degrees of Comparison Write on the
board the headings *Positive, Comparative,*
and *Superlative.* Explain that these are the
degrees of modifiers, and add examples
*(quickly, more quickly, most quickly; hot,
hotter, hottest).* Point out that it is never
correct to use both an ending *(-er, -est)* and
the word *more* or *most.*

Activity Have students form the comparative and superlative forms for each modifier
and write sentences using them correctly.

1. temperate *(more temperate, most
   temperate)*
2. rough *(rougher, roughest)*
3. fair *(fairer, fairest)*
4. short *(shorter, shortest)* **L1**

Additional Resources

🖐 *Grammar and Language Transparency 48*

📙 *Grammar and Language Workbook,*
p. 199

📙 *Grammar and Composition Handbook,*
Lesson 8.1

📙 *Writer's Choice,* Lesson 18.1

Personal Response

Students may describe an attitude that is neither as cynical as Parker's nor as idealized as Shakespeare's.

ANALYZING LITERATURE

1. The man who loves her has sent one pure, dewy, and perfect rose.
2. It symbolizes the heart of the man, which he has given to her.
3. She regrets that he doesn't show his love with a more tangible, comfort-providing gesture, such as a limousine. Her tone suggests a worldly woman who knows one doesn't live on love.
4. She is not sentimental or easily swayed by traditional, romantic gestures. She likes luxuries.
5. The tone changes from tender romanticism to cynical humor, reminding the reader of economic reality, which is often ignored by romantics.
6. Students may or may not appreciate receiving such a token. Much would probably depend on who gave them the token.
7. Students may suggest disillusionment, a sardonic sense of humor, or a desire to dismiss romantic notions about love.
8. The speaker is a man who addresses a "lovely," "temperate" young woman in her prime ("summer").
9. The woman is like a summer's day, but better because her sweet nature is more dependable. Her beauty is more lasting, because it is immortalized in this poem.
10. With his words, he captures for all time her beauty and grace. Rather than fading, it will grow with time, as more and more people read the poem. His love has inspired him to give her the gift of immortality.
11. The sun ("eye of heaven" with a "gold complexion"), a summer's day, and death (a braggart) are personified. By making these larger-than-life things human, he magnifies the importance of his love and the woman he loves.
12. Summer is a time of growth, warmth, sun, and fruitfulness; all forms of life are at their best. This matches the time of life and stage of love he and the woman are experiencing.
13. The poem expresses a devoted, admiring love that recognizes the losses time will bring but has found a way to keep itself alive.

Responding to Literature

Personal Response

Which poem better reflects your own attitude toward love? Explain in your journal.

ANALYZING LITERATURE

One Perfect Rose

RECALL AND INTERPRET

1. What words does the speaker use to describe the gift she receives? Who do you think has sent the gift?
2. According to the speaker, what does the gift **symbolize**, or stand for? Use evidence from the poem to support your answer.
3. How does the speaker react to the gift? Why do you think she reacts in this manner?
4. After reading this poem, what might you infer about the speaker's personality and character?

EVALUATE AND CONNECT

5. How does the speaker's **tone**, or attitude toward her subject, change in the last stanza of the poem? What is the effect of this shift in tone?
6. How might you react if you received a token gift similar to the one the speaker receives? Give reasons for your answer.
7. Look again at the word web you made for the Focus Activity on page 586. In your opinion, why did Parker write this love poem? Add your suggested reason to the web, if it doesn't already appear there.

Shall I Compare Thee to a Summer's Day?

RECALL AND INTERPRET

8. Who might the speaker of this poem be? In your opinion, who is the speaker addressing? Use details from the poem to support your answers.
9. What two things is the speaker comparing? Which one does the speaker consider to be superior? Why? Support your answer with specific details from the poem.
10. According to the speaker, why will the subject of the poem have a summer that is eternal? What might this tell you about the poet's reason for writing the poem?

EVALUATE AND CONNECT

11. Find three examples of **personification** (see Literary Terms Handbook, page R9). Why might Shakespeare have chosen to give human characteristics to these things?
12. Think about the extended comparison Shakespeare uses in this poem. Why might he have chosen this particular comparison?
13. Theme Connections   How is this poem related to the theme of "Loves and Losses"? Explain.
14. Reread critic Helen Vendler's comment in the Background section on page 586. Do you agree with Vendler about the speaker in Shakespeare's sonnet? Why or why not?

588   UNIT 3

14. Many students will find Shakespeare's language a barrier to their acceptance of the speaker as "real." Guide them to look beyond this beginner's prejudice to the fervency of his expression.

FINE ART
TRANSPARENCY 32

You may want to use Fine Art Transparency 32 to discuss the role love plays in life and literature.

Literary ELEMENTS

Sonnet

Shakespeare used a poetic form known as a **sonnet**. Sonnets have fourteen lines that are almost always written in iambic pentameter—a meter in which the predominant foot, or unit of rhythm, is the *iamb*—that is, an unstressed syllable followed by a stressed syllable. There are five feet in each line of iambic pentameter. The Shakespearean sonnet contains three groups of four lines, called *quatrains*. Typically, the quatrains have a rhyme scheme of *abab cdcd efef*. A rhymed couplet ends the sonnet. The following lines from "Shall I Compare Thee . . ." are an example of iambic pentameter and the sonnet's *abab* rhyme scheme:

Shall Ī compāre thēe tō a sūmmer's dāy?   (a)
Thou art more lovely and more temperate.   (b)
Rough winds do shake the darling buds of May,   (a)
And summer's lease hath all too short a date.   (b)

1. Copy a different quatrain from the sonnet and mark the meter and rhyme scheme as modeled above.
2. The rhymed couplet of a sonnet often presents a conclusion to the issues or questions presented in the three quatrains. What is the effect of the couplet in the Shakespearean sonnet you have just read?

● See **Literary Terms Handbook**, p. R12.

LITERARY ELEMENTS

1. Sometime too hot the eye of
   heaven shines,   (a)
   And often is his gold complexion
   dimmed;   (b)
   And every fair from fair sometime declines,   (a)
   By chance, or nature's changing
   course untrimmed: (b)
2. The poet's final declaration summarizes his point: As long as people read them, his words will keep his love and her beauty alive.

Additional Resources

📖 *Literary Elements Transparency 50*

LITERATURE AND WRITING

Writing About Literature

Comparing the Poems   How does the **tone** in "Shall I Compare Thee . . ." compare to the tone in "One Perfect Rose"? What words or other techniques does each poet use to create the tone? In a two-column chart, jot down specific information from each poem that relates to its tone. Then write a few paragraphs comparing the tone in the two poems. Share your comparison with the class.

Creative Writing

Shall I Compare Thee . . . ?   Write a poem about a beloved friend or family member, in which you compare him or her to something else. You might start by listing some of the person's qualities and then identifying things that have similar qualities. For example, if your beloved is moody, you might compare him or her to unpredictable spring weather. Try writing your poem in sonnet form.

EXTENDING YOUR RESPONSE

Literature Groups

Designing a Visual Representation   Choose one or two pairs of lines that your group especially likes from the two poems. Then design a visual representation of the lines. You may want to use a cartoon approach or a more serious fine art style. Display your work in your classroom.

Interdisciplinary Activity

Mathematics: What's the Difference?   Should you send roses or a limousine? Research the cost of an individual rose, a dozen roses, and the price of a rented limousine per hour and day. How many roses could be sent for the price of a rented limousine? Present your findings in a chart. Share your discoveries with the class.

Reading Further

You might also enjoy the following collection:
Committed to Memory: 100 Best Poems to Memorize, edited by John Hollander. The work contains sonnets and songs by Shakespeare as well as other types of poems by many poets.

📖 **Save your work for your portfolio.**

LITERATURE AND WRITING

Writing About Literature

Students' comparisons should
- clearly state the tone of each poem.
- list details and quotes from each poem that help create the tone.

Creative Writing

Students' poems should
- establish a simile or metaphor.
- develop likenesses with details and images.
- imitate sonnet meter, rhyme scheme, and format.

EXTENDING YOUR RESPONSE

Literature Groups Suggest that groups first discuss materials they need, how large to make their visual, and what colors and textures to use.
COLLAB. LEARN.

Interdisciplinary Activity
Remind students to record their sources of information. Discuss other likely sources of information besides the Internet: greenhouses, florists, limousine services, and so on.

ASSESSMENT OPTIONS

📁 ***Quick Checks,*** p. 50
📁 ***Selection and Theme Assessment,*** pp. 95–96
📁 ***Performance Assessment,*** p. 49
💾 ***Testmaker***

MEDIA Connection

Objective

- To read and understand song lyrics

Literature — LINK

Simile and **Well, I Have Lost You; and I Lost You Fairly** The singer here expresses blind devotion to his love no matter how she deceives him. The speaker in "Simile" (p. 592) is wary of the hurt that loved ones can inflict on each other. The speaker in "Well, I Have Lost You; and I Lost You Fairly" (p. 592) expresses the pride and self-reliance of one who releases a lost love without petty games.

Respond

1. There are no incorrect responses. Some students may like the informal language of the lyrics. Others may not care for the portrayal of the man or the woman in the song.
2. Students may prefer love songs about satisfied or requited love, or those in which the singer pays tribute to the charm or faithfulness of the loved one.

Additional Resources

📁 *Media Connections Activities,* p. 13

Teaching Options

MEDIA Connection

Song Lyrics

Romantic love has inspired not only countless poems but also innumerable songs. Here's a version of one well-known love song from the 1960s performed by the soul singer Percy Sledge.

When a Man Loves a Woman
by C. Lewis and A. Wright

When a man loves a woman,
Can't keep his mind on nothin'
    else,
He'd trade the world
For the good thing he's found.
If she's bad, he can't see it,
She can do no wrong,
Turn his back on his best friend
If he put her down.

When a man loves a woman,
Spend his very last dime
Trying to hold on to what he
    needs.
He'd give up all his comforts
And sleep out in the rain,
If she said that's the way it
    ought to be.
Well, this man loves you,
    woman.
I gave you everything I had,
Trying to hold on to your
    precious love.
Baby, please don't treat me bad.

When a man loves a woman,
Down deep in his soul,
She can bring him such misery.
If she plays him for a fool,
He's the last one to know.
Loving eyes can never see.

When a man loves a woman,
He can do her no wrong.
He can never hold her love
    again.
Yes, when a man loves a
    woman,
I know exactly how he feels.
Oh, baby, baby, baby, I know
    so well.

When a man loves a woman,
I know exactly how he feels.
Oh, baby, baby, baby, I know
    so well.
When a man loves a woman …

590 🦋 UNIT 3

Respond

1. What do you like or dislike about these lyrics?
2. What is your favorite love song? How do its lyrics compare with these?

interNET CONNECTION

Soul Music Have students use a search engine to look for additional information about Percy Sledge and soul music. Suggest that they try entering keywords such as *Percy Sledge, soul,* and *rhythm and blues.*

Before You Read

Simile and Well, I Have Lost You; and I Lost You Fairly

FOCUS ACTIVITY

What happens when two people who were in love find out that their feelings have changed?

LIST IDEAS Think about the possible consequences of falling out of love. Do such couples always break up? Should they? Can they remain friends? List your ideas, and then share them with a partner.

SETTING A PURPOSE Read the poems to learn how falling out of love affects two speakers.

BACKGROUND

Kiowa woman in traditional dress.

- Much of N. Scott Momaday's writing reflects the Native American world view that there is, as he puts it, "harmony in the universe." Momaday has said, "I believe that the Indian has an understanding of the physical world and of the earth as a spiritual entity that is his, very much his own. The non-Indian can benefit a good deal by having that perception revealed to him."

- Edna St. Vincent Millay wrote "Well, I Have Lost You; and I Lost You Fairly" in the form of the **English sonnet.** The English sonnet is also called the **Shakespearean sonnet** because Shakespeare was the master of this sonnet form. English sonnets are divided into three quatrains, or groups of four lines, and one couplet, or group of two lines. The rhyme scheme is usually *abab cdcd efef gg.* The English sonnet form allows for the presentation and development of a problem or question in the three quatrains, and a solution in the couplet.

Meet N. Scott Momaday

N. Scott Momaday (mə mä′ dā) grew up on Southwestern reservations, where he was influenced by his Kiowa Indian heritage. When a small journal published one of Momaday's early poems, he wrote, "There was something about seeing my words in print that mattered to me greatly." His first novel, *House Made of Dawn,* won the Pulitzer Prize for Fiction in 1969.

N. Scott Momaday was born in 1934 in Lawton, Oklahoma.

Meet Edna St. Vincent Millay

Edna St. Vincent Millay wrote her first poem at age five, and in 1917 she published her first volume of poetry. Millay then moved to New York City's Greenwich Village, where she found the writers and artists to be "very, very poor and very, very merry." At age thirty-one, Millay won the Pulitzer Prize for Poetry.

Edna St. Vincent Millay was born in 1892 in Rockland, Maine, and died in 1950.

POETRY ❧ 591

Before Reading

Objectives

- To read and analyze poems about the loss of love
- To analyze the effectiveness of similes
- To write an analysis of the mood

Skills

Writing: Advice Column
Listening/Speaking: Dialogue
Life Skills: Decision Making
Collaboration: Literature Groups

Motivating →OPTIONS

 Literature Launchers: "Remembering Edna St. Vincent Millay"

Videodisc
Side B, Segment 13

Also available in VHS.

 Selection Focus Transparency 51: Encourage students to discuss their views on Samuel Butler's comment.

 Focus Activity: Have partners select one consequence of falling out of love, write a one-sentence prediction, and give a reason for this prediction.

RESOURCE MANAGER

Lesson Planning Resource
The *Unit Three Planning Guide* (pp. 22–26) provides additional lesson notes and reduced versions of all print resources.

Other Print Resources
- Active Reading Guide, p. 51
- Quick Checks, p. 51
- Selection and Theme Assessment, pp. 97–98
- Performance Assessment, p. 50
- Spanish Summaries, p. 51
- Inclusion Strategies

Transparencies
- Selection Focus 51
- Literary Elements 51

Technology
- Literature Launchers
- Audio Library
- Spanish Audio Library
- Glencoe Literature Web Site
- Testmaker

A **Literary Elements**

FIGURES OF SPEECH: *Simile* Have students read the poem to discover where the simile occurs. *(The entire poem uses an extended comparison between two people and deer.)*

Additional Resources

📁 *Active Reading Guide,* p. 51
🎧 *Audio Library*
🎧 *Spanish Audio Library*

B **Active Reading**

CLARIFY Have students paraphrase the rhymed couplet: (1) "Should . . . anguish" *(The hurt is deep.)* (2) "and men do" *(She knows healing will come eventually.)* (3) "I shall . . . you." *(She is not bitter.)*

Thematic Focus

Loves and Losses The speaker in "Simile" is wary of words that lovers use to wound. The speaker in "Well, I Have Lost You" is proud and practical in recovering from a lost love. Which voice do students find more realistic?

✓ ASSESSMENT OPTIONS

📁 *Quick Checks,* p. 57

A

Simile

N. Scott Momaday ~

What did we say to each other
that now we are as the deer
who walk in single file
with heads high
5 with ears forward
with eyes watchful
with hooves always placed on firm ground
in whose limbs there is latent° flight

---

8 Something that is *latent* (lā′ tənt) is unseen or undeveloped but capable of bursting into full activity under certain conditions.

Well, I Have Lost You; and I Lost You Fairly

Edna St. Vincent Millay ~

Well, I have lost you; and I lost you fairly;
In my own way, and with my full consent.
Say what you will, kings in a tumbrel° rarely
Went to their deaths more proud than this one went.
5 Some nights of apprehension and hot weeping
I will confess; but that's permitted me;
Day dried my eyes; I was not one for keeping
Rubbed in a cage a wing that would be free.
If I had loved you less or played you slyly
10 I might have held you for a summer more,
But at the cost of words I value highly,
And no such summer as the one before.
Should I outlive this anguish—and men do—
I shall have only good to say of you.

B

---

3 A *tumbrel* is a farmer's two-wheeled cart. During the French Revolution, such carts were used to carry condemned people—including King Louis XVI—to their execution.

Woman and the Sea, 1972. Will Barnet. Oil on canvas, 51¾ x 41 in. Private collection.

© Will Barnet/Licensed by VAGA, New York, NY.

Teaching Options

LITERATURE & HUMANITIES

Have students view the photograph of Edna St. Vincent Millay, available from the National Museum of Women in the Arts, to get a sense of Millay before reading.

LIFE SKILLS CONNECTION

Decision Making In "Well, I Have Lost You," the speaker reasons that her decision to end her relationship cleanly and quickly is best. Point out that responding to this poem requires more than simply taking the speaker's statements at face value. Analyzing the speaker's argument and decision making encourages students to understand nuances of meaning. Invite them to list criteria to analyze the validity of an argument and the decisions the speaker makes. *(Note reasons given; assess their logic; distinguish facts from opinions.)*

Activity As they read the poem, have students list reasons the speaker gives for believing it was best to end the relationship. Then pair students to discuss the logic of each reason and the persuasiveness of the argument. **L2**

Responding to Literature

Personal Response

Describe the mental image you formed after reading one of the poems.

ANALYZING LITERATURE

Simile

RECALL AND INTERPRET

1. Whom do you think the speaker is addressing? Give reasons for your answer.
2. Summarize in your own words the question the speaker is asking. What impression of the speaker does this question give you?
3. According to the speaker, how do deer behave? What might the comparison to deer suggest?
4. How would you describe the current relationship between the speaker and the person being addressed?

EVALUATE AND CONNECT

5. Do you think the comparison to deer is effective? Why or why not?
6. Theme Connections   Explain how this poem is related to the theme of "Loves and Losses."
7. Have you experienced or observed a situation like the one described in this poem? Explain.

Well, I Have
Lost You;
and I Lost
You Fairly

RECALL AND INTERPRET

8. Summarize the speaker's reaction and attitude toward the loss in lines 1–2. What does the speaker mean by losing "fairly" and "with my full consent"?
9. How does the speaker describe his or her reaction to the loss in lines 5–7? What does the tone of this description tell you about the speaker?
10. What **metaphor** does the speaker use in lines 7–8? What feeling does this comparison convey to you? (See Literary Terms Handbook, page R7.)
11. In your opinion, what does the speaker mean in lines 9–12? What does this tell you about the speaker's values?

EVALUATE AND CONNECT

12. Do you think the speaker will "outlive this anguish"? Give reasons for your answer.
13. Millay wrote this poem in the form of an English **sonnet** (see Literary Terms Handbook, page R12). Reread the background information on page 591 and explain how the content of the poem suits the English sonnet form.
14. Do you think the speaker acted wisely in the relationship described here? Would you have acted the same way? Why or why not?

Personal Response

Images formed from "Simile" may be of a white-tailed deer, common in North America. For "Well, I Have Lost You," students may picture a proud, independent, no-nonsense speaker.

ANALYZING LITERATURE

1. He speaks to someone he loves, with whom he has had a quarrel or conflict. References to their words, which have hurt and caused an instinctive flight response, reveal this.
2. He wonders what injuring words caused them to be ill at ease and ready to part on short notice. The speaker seems regretful and sad.
3. They are listening for the least hint of danger, at which they will run. It suggests the pair's relationship is now tenuous, and any small problem will cause them to "take flight."
4. It is wary and tentative; the speaker and loved one are like frightened deer.
5. Students may point to the vulnerability of deer, whose one defense is flight, as a sound comparison for someone who loves and makes himself or herself vulnerable to the loved one.
6. The poem highlights how easily a loved one can inflict pain and alter the balance of a relationship. Their words have made the relationship unstable and the possible loss of their love a tangible threat.
7. Students' responses will depend on their experiences and/or observations.
8. Her reaction is honest, proud, and independent. She has not tried to manipulate the loved one or the situation; her words suggest that they entered the relationship with no "strings," as equals.
9. Although the speaker is hurt and suffers, she does not let it stop her from functioning in the daily world; she shows resilience and self-reliance.
10. The lover who no longer loves is compared to a caged bird that wants its freedom. It suggests fear of entrapment.

---

13. The sonnet requires strict discipline and control of form, just as the speaker demands discipline of herself. Traditionally, the form has been used for serious poems on love.
14. The speaker's actions seem honorable, if stiff; they protect from self-hatred—worse than the anguish of losing love.

11. The speaker values honesty both from herself and in her dealings with others. She refuses to lie or manipulate to hold on to someone who no longer cares.
12. The speaker's tone and words suggest that she will survive, although the use of *should* makes her seem uncertain, conveying the depth of the hurt.

LITERARY ELEMENTS

1. Students may mention their grace, speed, and ability to sense danger. The lovers resemble deer in their vulnerability and sensitivity to that which means them harm.
2. The simile gives their situation immediacy and urgency; it reveals the pair's quiet and tension, and the instinctiveness of their reactions.

Additional Resources

📇 *Literary Elements Transparency 51*

LITERATURE AND WRITING

Writing About Literature

Students' analyses of mood should
- accurately state the mood in each poem.
- list details from the poem that support this mood.
- state the theme of each poem and relate mood to it.

Creative Writing

Students' advice column responses should
- state a relationship problem and the actions that each speaker has taken.
- point out and evaluate the effect that the action has had.
- list an alternative response and identify its probable effect.

EXTENDING YOUR RESPONSE

Literature Groups Have students assess whether their thinking has changed since they completed the Focus Activity and explain why or why not. `COLLAB. LEARN.`

Interdisciplinary Activity Point out to students that "place" includes population, livelihoods, weather, and cultural values as well as geography, plants, and animals.

Performing Suggest to students that they decide the setting, characters, and purpose of their dialogues before they begin writing.

Literary ELEMENTS

Simile

Poets often make comparisons in order to convey ideas and feelings. One kind of comparison is called a **simile**–a direct comparison that uses *like* or *as*. By comparing an experience, idea, or image to something that is familiar, a writer may reveal new insights about his or her subject. For example, in "Simile," Momaday reveals something about people in a relationship by comparing them to deer.

1. When you picture deer, what qualities do you think of that the poem does not specifically mention? Which of these qualities might also apply to the people?
2. What does this simile convey about the people that an ordinary description of them would not convey?

● See **Literary Terms Handbook,** p. R12.

LITERATURE AND WRITING

Writing About Literature

Analyze Mood   The emotional quality or atmosphere of a literary work is its **mood.** List words and phrases that describe the mood of each poem. Then write a paragraph about each poem, in which you describe its mood and explain how the mood reinforces the message each speaker is trying to convey. Share your analysis in a small group.

Creative Writing

Advice Column   Imagine that you are an advice columnist and the two speakers have submitted their poems to you and asked you to advise them about their romantic dilemmas. Write a response to the speakers in which you evaluate what they've already done and also give them advice for the future.

EXTENDING YOUR RESPONSE

Literature Groups

Breaking Up Is Hard to Do   Review the ideas you listed in response to the Focus Activity on page 591. Which speaker in the two poems do you think is better off? Why? Are there "good" or "bad" ways to end a relationship? Is it possible to remain friendly with someone after splitting up? Use details from the selections to support or refute your arguments. Share your ideas with another group.

Interdisciplinary Activity

Geography: The Influence of Place   Often physical environment influences a writer's work. Momaday grew up on Indian reservations in the southwestern United States, where he observed the natural world. Millay grew up in Maine and came to know its coast and countryside. Use the library or the Internet to research these places. How might the poets' different backgrounds have affected their poetry? Present your conclusions to the class.

Performing

Dialogue   Work with a partner to create a dialogue that the speaker of either poem might have with the person to whom the poem is addressed. The speaker's part of the dialogue may include lines from the poem; you will need to supply the other person's response. Practice your dialogue and then perform it for the class.

Reading Further

You might enjoy these poems by Momaday and Millay:

"Earth and I Gave You Turquoise" by N. Scott Momaday from *Harper's Anthology of 20th Century Native American Poetry.*

"Love is not blind. I see with single eye" from *Collected Poems* by Edna St. Vincent Millay.

📓 **Save your work for your portfolio.**

✔ ASSESSMENT OPTIONS

📁 *Quick Checks,* p. 51
📁 *Selection and Theme Assessment,* pp. 97–98
📁 *Performance Assessment,* p. 50
💾 *Testmaker*

Grammar Link

Making Sure Pronouns and Antecedents Agree

Using pronouns correctly is not difficult or complicated; it's quite logical. Still, using pronouns incorrectly is a common grammatical error.

Every **pronoun** gets its meaning from a noun or another pronoun, called its **antecedent.** This is the word to which the pronoun refers. In order for your writing to be clear, each pronoun must agree with its antecedent in number, gender, and person.

Problem 1 A singular antecedent that can be either male or female
A poet may express deep and personal feelings in their poetry. [*Their* is plural; its antecedent, *poet,* is singular.]

Solution A Change the pronoun to agree with its antecedent. Although the pronoun *his* is grammatically correct in this example, *his or her* is preferable.
A poet may express deep and personal feelings in his or her poetry.

Solution B Reword the sentence so that both the antecedent and pronoun are plural.
Poets may express deep and personal feelings in their poetry.

Problem 2 A singular indefinite pronoun as an antecedent
Neither poet used rhyme in their poems. [The pronoun *their* is plural; its antecedent, *neither,* is singular.]

Solution A Change the antecedent to agree with the pronoun.
These poets did not use rhyme in their poems.

Solution B Change the pronoun to agree with its antecedent.
Neither poet used rhyme in his or her poem.

Problem 3 A second-person pronoun that refers to a third-person antecedent
Jo is going to a workshop that teaches you how to write poetry.

Solution A Replace the second-person pronoun with a third-person pronoun.
Jo is going to a workshop that teaches her to write poetry.

Solution B Replace the pronoun with the appropriate noun.
Jo is going to a workshop that teaches students to write poetry.

● For more about pronouns and antecedents, see **Language Handbook,** p. R19.

EXERCISE

Revise the sentences to correct problems in pronoun use.

1. Jo and Amy like the bookstore that sells you snacks as well as books.

2. However, a poet may write such personal work that they do not want it published.

3. Each of the girls writes in their journal regularly.

4. Each poet who wrote about love dealt with romance in their own way.

Grammar Link

Objective

• To recognize and correct errors in pronoun-antecedent reference

Teaching Strategies

Before students read the lesson, review the meanings of *gender* (masculine, feminine, or neuter), *number* (singular or plural), and *person* (first, second, or third) as they refer to pronouns.

Exercise

Possible answers are shown.
1. Jo and Amy like the bookstore that sells snacks as well as books.
2. However, poets may write such personal work that they do not want it published.
3. Each of the girls writes in her journal regularly.
4. Each poet who wrote about love dealt with romance in his or her own way.

Additional Resources

▮ *Grammar and Language Workbook,* pp. 187–190

▮ *Grammar and Composition Handbook*, Lesson 7.6

▮ *Writer's Choice,* Lesson 17.6

Teaching Options

Writing *Minilesson*

Writing Directions Explain to students that written directions should list all steps in order; explain unfamiliar terms; use transitions such as *first, next,* and *finally;* and have pronoun-antecedent agreement.

Activity Have each student list the steps to a simple process, such as sending an E-mail message, and underline each pronoun. Then have them exchange papers with a partner and note on each other's papers places where steps seem out of order or missing and any unclear antecedents of the pronouns. Have partners exchange papers again and revise the steps. **L2** COLLAB. LEARN.

Additional Resources

▮ *Writer's Choice,* Lesson 2.7

Objectives

- To read and understand poems about reactions to the loss of a loved one
- To identify and analyze metaphors in poems
- To write a letter explaining the impact of a poem to its speaker

Skills

Reading/Thinking: Paraphrasing
Writing: Poem
Listening/Speaking: Science Report
Collaboration: Literature Groups

Motivating
→ OPTIONS

Selection Focus Transparency 52: After viewing the transparency, have students discuss how they might express their reactions.

Focus Activity: Encourage students to add comparisons to their freewriting about their losses. How might students compare their losses to an occurrence in the natural world? in the world of work? in their daily routine?

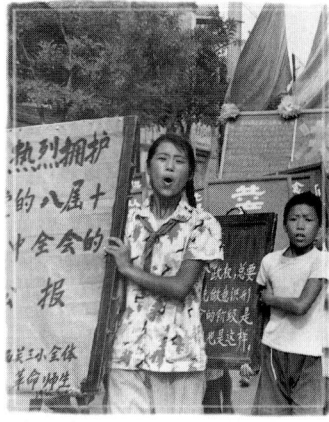

Before You Read

The Glory of the Day Was in Her Face *and* Missing You

FOCUS ACTIVITY

How might you react if you lost the friendship or affection of someone you care about deeply?

FREEWRITE Spend five minutes writing an answer to the question above. If you have actually experienced such a loss, you might want to write about it.

SETTING A PURPOSE Read the poems to learn how two speakers feel about losing love.

BACKGROUND

The Time and Place

- During the 1920s, a New York City neighborhood called Harlem became a gathering place for African American writers, musicians, and other artists. Harlem writers such as Langston Hughes, Zora Neale Hurston, and James Weldon Johnson emerged as strong voices against racism and helped shape the important intellectual and artistic movement that became known as the Harlem Renaissance.

- The work of Chinese writers has long been tightly controlled by the Chinese communist government. One of the worst times for Chinese writers was during the Cultural Revolution, from 1966 to 1976, when educated people in China were systematically persecuted under the brutal rule of Mao Tse-tung. Mao and his Red Guard drove hundreds of thousands of Chinese citizens out of cities and forced them to work in the countryside as farm and factory laborers.

Meet James Weldon Johnson

Raised in a home where education was highly prized, Johnson refused to allow racial discrimination to limit his aspirations. "I will not allow one prejudiced person or one million or one hundred million to blight my life," he wrote. Johnson's outlook empowered him to express his diverse talents in a variety of careers, including writer, teacher, lawyer, diplomat, and civil rights leader.

James Weldon Johnson was born in 1871 in Jacksonville, Florida, and died after a car accident in 1938.

Meet Shu Ting

As a teenager, Shu Ting was driven from her Beijing home during China's Cultural Revolution and was forced to work in a factory. She began reading Western poets and writing poetry, and during the 1980s, Shu Ting became one of the Misty Poets, known for their powerful imagery, emotional expression, and belief in individual experience.

Shu Ting was born in Fujian, China, in 1952.

RESOURCE MANAGER

Lesson Planning Resource
The *Unit Three Planning Guide* (pp. 27–31) provides additional lesson notes and reduced versions of all print resources.

📁 **Other Print Resources**
- Active Reading Guide, p. 52
- Reading Workbook
- Quick Checks, p. 52
- Selection and Theme Assessment, pp. 99–100

- Performance Assessment, p. 51
- Spanish Summaries, p. 52
- Inclusion Strategies

✎ **Transparencies**
- Selection Focus 52
- Literary Elements 52

Technology
- 🎧 Audio Library
- 🎧 Spanish Audio Library
- 💻 Glencoe Literature Web Site
- 💾 Testmaker

The Glory of the Day Was in Her Face

James Weldon Johnson

The glory of the day was in her face,
The beauty of the night was in her eyes.
And over all her loveliness, the grace
Of Morning blushing in the early skies.

5   And in her voice, the calling of the dove;
Like music of a sweet, melodious part.
And in her smile, the breaking light of love;
And all the gentle virtues° in her heart.

And now the glorious day, the beauteous night,
10   The birds that signal to their mates at dawn,
To my dull ears, to my tear-blinded sight
Are one with all the dead, since she is gone.

---

8 Her *virtues* are her good or admirable qualities.

Missing You

Shu Ting
Translated by
Carolyn Kizer

A multi-colored chart without a boundary;
An equation chalked on the board, with no solution;
A one-stringed lyre° that tells the beads of rain;
A pair of useless oars that never cross the water.

5   Waiting buds in suspended animation;°
The setting sun is watching from a distance.
Though in my mind there may be an enormous ocean,
What emerges is the sum: a pair of tears.

Yes, from these vistas,° from these depths,
10   Only this.

---

3 The harplike *lyre* normally has four to ten strings.
5 In a state of *suspended animation,* a living thing shows no
signs of life or appears to be frozen in time.
9 *Vista* can mean "a view of a landscape" or "an overall mental
view of something."

POETRY 597

Reading *Minilesson*

Paraphrasing Explain that paraphrasing—restating a poet's words in one's own—can help make a poem's meaning clear. Have students briefly practice paraphrasing. Provide these two common sayings and have students paraphrase them: *Birds of a feather flock together. A stitch in time saves nine.*

Activity Have students paraphrase a part of one of the poems that is unclear to them. Encourage students to listen to each other paraphrase and help each other fine tune their verbal expression until the poem's meaning is clear.

Additional Resources
📁 *Reading Workbook*

Reading the Selection

A Active Reading

QUESTION What qualities does the speaker want to make clear through the comparison in these lines? *(His love is not only beautiful but also has the grace and freshness of dawn.)*

Additional Resources
📁 *Active Reading Guide,* p. 52
🎧 *Audio Library*
🎧 *Spanish Audio Library*

B Literary Elements

FIGURES OF SPEECH: *Metaphor* Ask students to list adjectives that describe the things named in these lines. *(unfinished, neglected, ruined, useless)* What effect of the loss does this building up of comparisons suggest? *(It colors every part of life in a negative way.)*

Thematic Focus

Loves and Losses Have students describe how the absence of someone loved has affected the speakers in these poems. Do students think these altered perceptions of the world are typical when a loved one is lost?

☑️ **ASSESSMENT OPTIONS**
📁 *Quick Checks,* p. 52

Teaching Options

LITERATURE & HUMANITIES

🎧 Play the selection "April Is in My Mistress' Face," CD 3, Track 17, from Glencoe's *World of Music.* Ask volunteers to compare the descriptions found in "The Glory of the Day Was in Her Face," and in the song. Then discuss the impact love has on a person's perceptions of the world.

POETRY 597

Personal Response

Point out that all responses are valid. Some students may prefer the sharp contrast of ocean and tears; others may relate personally to an image such as birdsong or dawn.

ANALYZING LITERATURE

1. The speaker describes a beautiful, graceful woman he loved, comparing her to all that is lovely and graceful in the day and night.
2. Her voice is like a dove's call; her smile brought light and displayed her "gentle virtues." He adored her for physical, mental, and spiritual qualities that he found.
3. It changes from adoration to grief. That the woman is dead explains why he idealizes her so.
4. "The glory of the day," "the beauty of the night," and "morning blushing" are visual images; the "calling of the dove" appeals to the sense of sound. The images have the effect of conveying adoration, almost awe.
5. Students' responses will vary widely, although many will likely choose images from nature.
6. Someone has been separated from a loved one and feels that absence strongly.
7. They are all incomplete and unable to fulfill their purpose; the speaker feels this way, too.
8. Inside, the speaker's sadness and sense of loss are vast, yet only "a pair of tears" show outwardly.
9. The speaker finds the loss numbing and disabling. Students may express anger or confusion over loss.
10. She creates powerful, evocative images and focuses on her personal experience. While her poem never openly refers to the loss of love, her title clearly shows her subject matter; the poem is emotionally expressive.

Responding to Literature

Personal Response

Which line or lines from either poem affected you most strongly? Why?

--- **ANALYZING LITERATURE** ---

The Glory of the Day Was in Her Face

RECALL AND INTERPRET

1. Whom might the speaker be describing? In the first stanza, to what does the speaker compare this person?
2. What **images** does the speaker use to describe the person in the second stanza? What do these images and the ones in the first stanza suggest about his feelings for the person he is describing? (See Literary Terms Handbook, page R6.)
3. How does the speaker's **tone**, or attitude toward the subject, change in the third stanza? How does this shift in tone help you better understand the poem?

EVALUATE AND CONNECT

4. Identify an image from the poem that appeals to sight and one that appeals to sound. Evaluate the effect each image creates.
5. If you were writing a poem on a similar subject, what types of images might you use to describe the person? Give reasons for your choices.

Missing You

RECALL AND INTERPRET

6. What does the title suggest to you about the subject of this poem?
7. Explain what the images in lines 1–4 have in common. What do these images reveal about the speaker's feelings?
8. Explain the meaning of lines 7–10. What **irony** is the speaker pointing out? (See Literary Terms Handbook, page R6.)

EVALUATE AND CONNECT

9. Theme Connections   Review the freewriting you did for the Focus Activity on page 596. How does your response to loss compare with the speaker's response in "Missing You"?
10. Reread Shu Ting's biography on page 596. Based on this poem, evaluate whether you think she has been properly classified as a member of the group called the Misty Poets.

Literary ELEMENTS

Metaphor

A **metaphor** is a type of figurative, or nonliteral, language that compares two or more things that have something in common. Metaphors create fresh insights and provide new understandings of familiar things. For example, in "The Glory of the Day Was in Her Face," Johnson compares a woman's eyes to the night: both are dark, beautiful, and perhaps mysterious.

1. Identify another metaphor in each of the poems. What things are compared, and what do they have in common?
2. How does the use of metaphor enhance your understanding and appreciation of these poems? Give specific examples.

● See **Literary Terms Handbook,** p. R7.

LITERATURE AND WRITING

Writing About Literature

Message to the Speaker   Choose one of the poems, and write a two-paragraph letter to the speaker. Explain what you particularly like about the poem and what your favorite metaphor is. Tell the speaker what overall impact the poem had on you. Explain what you wish for the speaker in the future.

Creative Writing

Missing Someone   Think of a time when you were separated from a close friend or relative. Write a poem expressing your thoughts and feelings about missing that person. You may want to use sensory details in your poem, as well as figurative language (such as metaphors and symbols) in order to better convey your ideas and emotions.

EXTENDING YOUR RESPONSE

Literature Groups

Analyze Metaphors   As a group, choose three or four metaphors from the poems you have just read and analyze them in detail. What do you think each one represents? How effectively do the metaphors help convey the speaker's message? What fresh insights does each metaphor contribute to your reading of the poem? What would be lacking if more literal words were substituted? After discussing these questions with your group, compare your ideas with those of other groups.

Internet Connection

Social Context   Both James Weldon Johnson and Shu Ting were shaped by the social and political conditions of their time. Generate a list of research questions about the Harlem Renaissance or China's Cultural Revolution. Research them on the Internet and share your findings with the class.

Interdisciplinary Activity

Science: The Language of Loss   How is a person's body affected by sadness and grief? Are tears, sleeplessness, or a lack of appetite typical human reactions to the loss of a loved one? Research current scientific data on the ways a person's body can react to the loss of a loved one. Present your findings in a short report to your class. Consider including diagrams or other visual aids.

Reading Further

These works can help you understand Johnson and Shu Ting in historical context:

One More River to Cross, An African American Photograph Album documents the African American experience.

A Splintered Mirror, a collection of poetry from China's democracy movement.

📖 **Save your work for your portfolio.**

POETRY 🐾 599

Technology Skills

Objectives

- To prepare a piece of writing for publication on the World Wide Web
- To submit a piece of writing to an Internet site or publish it on the school's Web site

Teaching Strategies

To motivate students, have them spend time reading student work published on teen 'zine sites or print out several pieces for the class to share.

Before You Get Started. . .

Inform students that overly general keywords can result in hundreds of thousands of "hits" on the Internet—an impossible number to sift through in search of interesting sites. Generally, entering two or more related keywords connected by "and" helps narrow the search still more: *figure skating and World Cup competitions* will generate a more specific list than *figure skating* alone. The list will include a brief description of each site with its title.

Suggest that students double click on the titles of sites that seem interesting; they will then access the site and can browse to see if it is suitable before listing it in their journals.

Internet: Publishing Your Writing on the Web

Much of the writing done in school is written for one particular person: your teacher. The World Wide Web provides a place where you can share your creativity and opinions with the rest of the world. Sites that publish teen 'zines often accept submissions of student writing, as do many other sites. For example, if you have an interest in in-line skating, you may want to submit a poem on the joys of the sport to a site dedicated to in-line skating. Similarly, if there's a band or musical group you really like, you could write a tribute article for submission.

Before You Get Started . . .

What interests you? Do you like to watch TV? go to movies? play video games? feed on baseball statistics? Choose one topic, and use a search engine to look for sites on the World Wide Web that relate to your interest. Try to be as specific as possible in your quest. For example, don't do a keyword search for sports. Instead, key in *baseball, field hockey,* or *figure skating.* In your journal, write the topic you've chosen and list the URLs (Uniform Resource Locators, or Web addresses) of sites you find interesting and relevant.

But What Do I Write?

Often writers have plenty of good ideas about interesting subjects, but when it comes to putting everything down in writing, they freeze up. If you're having trouble thinking of a format to write in, glance through the list below. Perhaps it will spark some new ideas. Looking at what others have written and placed on a site might also suggest something.

song	letter	newspaper article
rap	preview	opinion column
joke	review	script
riddle	critique	play
top ten list	summary	poem
recipe	proposal	haiku
menu	reasons for	character sketch
description	reasons against	short story
application	endorsement	essay

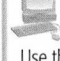 **TECHNOLOGY TIP**

Use the grammar-check that comes with your word processing program cautiously. Grammar-checks can't think; they just look for patterns. You must do the thinking. Consider each suggested change carefully before accepting or rejecting it.

1. Using one of the formats above, write about your chosen topic using the word processing software on your computer. Don't forget to save your work often.

2. When you finish, run the spell-check and, if you wish, the grammar-check. Then proofread it yourself.

Teaching Options

MEETING INDIVIDUAL NEEDS — MULTIPLE LEARNING STYLES

Interpersonal A group creative-writing project can help students overcome anxieties about writing and spark enthusiasm for the assignment. Students may collaborate, for example, on a movie review, story, or opinion column. Encourage groups to complement each other's strengths and experiment with forms.

Activity Form student groups based on a common interest in a subject or a common opinion about an issue. Have groups brainstorm ideas for their piece and discuss original ways of organizing it (perhaps combining several types of writing). Be sure students share tasks at every stage of the project.
L2 COLLAB. LEARN.

3. Share your writing with a classmate. Ask her or him to suggest ways your message can be made clearer.

4. Make the appropriate changes, and share your work with your teacher. (Ask whether to submit hard copy or a floppy disk.)

5. Once you've gotten approval from your teacher, submit your piece to one of the Web sites you listed in your journal. Be sure to read through the site's submission guidelines before sending in your work.

6. If you would like to include your writing on your school's Web site, convert your work to HyperText Markup Language (HTML) using HTML editing software. If you don't have access to HTML software, you may convert your document using some basic codes:

Style	Type as . . .
headline	\<H3> headline \</H3>
bold text	\<B> bold text \</B>
italicized text	\<I> italicized text \</I>
underlined text	\<U> underlined text \</U>
end paragraph	paragraph\<P>
link to another Web site	\<A HREF = "http://www.sitename.edu">Click here\</A>

For instance, the following piece can be converted just by adding a few codes.

Original Text:
It's Great to Skate
I **love** in-line skating. When I get my
   skates on,
I know I'm ready to *fly*.
I used to fall a lot,
   but now I know what I'm doing.

To find out more about in-line skating,
   Click Here!

HyperText Markup Language:
\<H3>It's Great to Skate\</H3>
I \<B>love\</B> in-line skating. When I get my
   skates on,
I know I'm ready to \<I>fly.\</I>
I used to fall \<U>a lot,\</U>
   but now I know what I'm doing.\<P>

To find out more about in-line skating, \<A HREF =
   "http://www.sitename.com">Click here!\</A>

EXERCISES

1. Look through your portfolio and choose a piece you would like to share on the World Wide Web. Convert it to HTML, and submit it to relevant sites. If your submission is turned down, ask the editors to offer feedback so you can make your work better.

2. Create a subdirectory for your class on your school's Web site. Ask the computer lab instructor to help you with the programming.

3. Once you've practiced with HTML editors, consider creating a Web site for your class, a school club, or yourself.

Teaching Options

But What Do I Write?

Claris Works is a program commonly used to convert MAC files to HTML. Working on an IBM platform, if students use Word 95 or later software, they will be able to convert to HTML using Internet Assistant. Internet Assistant is available free from Microsoft customer service or can be downloaded from various electronic bulletin boards.

Exercises

1. *Students' submissions should*
   - be edited and revised to acceptable standard for publication.
   - be converted to HTML without loss of appropriate formatting and other features important to the genre.
2. Your school Web site may not be accessible for students' subdirectories. Check with your district technology expert and school administrator before assigning this activity.
3. Invite students who have created Web pages to demonstrate the process. Internet servers offer instructions on how to create a Web page.

INTERDISCIPLINARY CONNECTION

Social Studies Some students may want to collaborate with social studies classmates and write articles, columns, political cartoons, and analyses relating to current events that interest them.

Activity Have the group of interested students meet with their social studies teacher and you to decide how and what to produce in a current events Web site for teens. They should outline
- features to be included
- procedures required to design and produce the Web site
- contributions each group member will make.

L3 **COLLAB. LEARN.**

Objectives

- To read and analyze poems about lessons passed from parent to child
- To identify and analyze the effects of alliteration
- To write a character sketch

Skills

Reading/Thinking: Inferring
Writing: Letter of Thanks
Listening/Speaking: Oral Reading
Life Skills: Survival Floating
Collaboration: Literature Groups

Motivating

→OPTIONS

Literature Launchers:
"Fatherhood"

Videodisc
Side B, Segment 14

Also available in VHS.

Selection Focus Transparency 53: Invite students to discuss different ways parents and other family members typically show love for their children.

Focus Activity: Have students use their journal entries to write an interest-grabbing opening for a short story about the lesson.

Before You Read

First Lesson and *Those Winter Sundays*

FOCUS ACTIVITY

What important lessons about life have you learned?

JOURNAL Think of an important life lesson that a parent or other family member has taught you. How have you benefited from this lesson? Describe your experience in your journal.

SETTING A PURPOSE Read poems that share life lessons taught and learned by others.

BACKGROUND

- Philip Booth sets many of his poems in New England, where he was born and has lived for most of his life. In particular, he focuses on the New England seacoast, incorporating the motions and rhythms of the tides into tight, spare poems about life, loss, love, and other affairs of the human heart. Booth explained that his love of words goes back to his parents. "If my father taught me respect for words, my mother's imagination intuitively made real to me the world that words reach for."

- Poet and teacher Robert Hayden dedicated his life to his craft and to working "closely with young people" in order "to encourage creative writing." Hayden researched and celebrated his heritage and wrote poetry that appealed to many audiences. Hayden said, "I believe in the essential oneness of all people," and his poems portray universal human concerns of loss and love. Hayden won many awards for his poetry and was the first African American to be named as the Library of Congress consultant in poetry, a position now called poet laureate.

602 ❦ UNIT 3

Meet Philip Booth

"Save for long Maine summers . . . where I hung around wharf-talk, . . . my boyhood was sheltered and lonely," says Philip Booth. He emerged from that boyhood to become a respected poet whose work reflects a strong identification with his native New England. More than a regional poet, Booth imparts in his poems truths relevant to all people.

Philip Booth was born in 1925 in Hanover, New Hampshire.

Meet Robert Hayden

Too nearsighted to play sports with his friends, Robert Hayden found companionship in books. After high school, Hayden read many contemporary poets, including those of the Harlem Renaissance, and won a scholarship to college. In graduate school he studied under the poet W. H. Auden, who greatly influenced him. Regarding civil rights, Hayden said, "I have the right to deal with these matters . . . as an artist."

Robert Hayden was born in 1913 in Detroit, Michigan, and died in 1980.

RESOURCE MANAGER

Lesson Planning Resource
The *Unit Three Planning Guide* (pp. 32–36) provides additional lesson notes and reduced versions of all print resources.

📁 **Other Print Resources**
- Active Reading Guide, p. 53
- Quick Checks, p. 53
- Selection and Theme Assessment, pp. 101–102
- Performance Assessment, p. 52

- Spanish Summaries, p. 53
- Spanish Translations
- Inclusion Strategies
- English Language Learners Sourcebook

✏️ **Transparencies**
- Selection Focus 53
- Fine Art 2
- Literary Elements 53

Technology
 Literature Launchers
 Audio Library
🎧 Spanish Audio Library
💻 Glencoe Literature Web Site
💾 Testmaker

First Lesson

Philip Booth ～

Lie back, daughter, let your head
be tipped back in the cup of my hand.
Gently, and I will hold you. Spread
your arms wide, lie out on the stream
5   and look high at the gulls. A dead-
man's-float is face down. You will dive
and swim soon enough where this tidewater
ebbs° to the sea. Daughter, believe
me, when you tire on the long thrash°
10 to your island, lie up, and survive.
As you float now, where I held you
and let go, remember when fear
cramps your heart what I told you:
lie gently and wide to the light-year
15 stars, lie back, and the sea will hold you.

---

8 When the tide flows out to sea, it *ebbs* and is called the
   "ebb tide."
9 In this context, *thrash* means "a swim," from the idea that a
   swimmer beats, or thrashes, the water with the arms.

Father and Kids, 1997. Patti Mollica. Oil on canvas,
10 x 7¾ in.
Viewing the painting: What images from
the poem does this painting reflect? Do you
find the tone of the painting similar to the
tone of the poem? Explain.

POETRY 🦢 603

A Active Reading

LISTEN Guide students to read from
sentence to sentence. How might
they describe the rhythm? *(It has a
conversational rhythm.)*

Additional Resources
📁 *Active Reading Guide,* p. 53
🎧 *Audio Library*
🎧 *Spanish Audio Library*

B Literary Elements

ALLITERATION Point out that Booth
has used alliteration to suggest the
sound of the tidewater. What initial
consonant sounds are repeated?
*(L sounds are liquid; h and s sounds
imitate those of waves.)*

VIEWING THE PAINTING

American Patti Mollica's paintings
are known for their bold use of color
and strong sense of light and shadow.

Viewing Response *The father's head,
bowed toward the children, suggests a
nurturing attitude similar to the father's
in "First Lesson."*

MEETING INDIVIDUAL NEEDS   GIFTED AND TALENTED

**Expressing Poems Through
Movement** Some students might enjoy
expressing their grasp of the poems
through movement. Encourage students
to point out words and phrases that
lend themselves to actions. Ask the students to express the poems' actions as
well as underlying circumstances and
feelings.

Activity Invite volunteers to act out
the parent's instructions and the child's
actions in "First Lesson" or the father's
actions and the child's actions in
"Those Winter Sundays." Have students
discuss the underlying emotions of the
speakers and of parents. **L3**

C Literary Elements

SOUND EFFECTS: *Assonance and Consonance* Have students look for repeated vowel and consonant sounds that reinforce the feeling of discomfort. *(K and long a sounds give a feeling of hardness and aching.)*

D Critical Thinking

INFERRING What state of mind is implied by the speaker's repetition here? *(He feels remorse for not recognizing his father's sacrifices and kindness or the love that inspired them.)*

Viewing the Painting

The first-name only title of the painting suggests perhaps a familiar relationship of the subject to the artist.

Viewing Response *The portrait's subject seems pensive and sorrowful, perhaps contemplating some regretful event, just as the speaker in "Those Winter Sundays."*

Thematic Focus

Loves and Losses Ask students to identify how a father expresses love in each of these poems. Invite them to give other examples of the words and acts that demonstrate love.

ASSESSMENT OPTIONS

📁 *Quick Checks,* p. 53

Teaching Options

Those Winter Sundays

Robert Hayden ∿

Sundays too my father got up early
and put his clothes on in the blueblack cold,
then with cracked hands that ached
from labor in the weekday weather made
5   banked fires° blaze. No one ever thanked him.

I'd wake and hear the cold splintering, breaking.
When the rooms were warm, he'd call,
and slowly I would rise and dress,
fearing the chronic angers of that house,

10 Speaking indifferently to him,
who had driven out the cold
and polished my good shoes as well.
What did I know, what did I know
of love's austere° and lonely offices?°

---

5 *Banked fires* are ones that have been covered with ashes to keep them burning at a very low level.

14 The word *austere* has a number of meanings: "severe; stern; strict; serious; simple." Similarly, *offices* can mean either "duties and responsibilities" or "favors and kindnesses."

Lynford, 1969. Karen Armitage. Oil on canvas. Private collection.

Viewing the painting: What words would you use to describe this man's expression and mood? Compare and contrast these traits to the personal qualities the speaker of the poem conveys to you.

604 UNIT 3

ENGLISH LANGUAGE LEARNERS

Cultural Aspects of Family Dynamics Some English language learners may come from cultures in which the father has absolute authority and never performs menial tasks. The actions of the boy and father in this poem may puzzle them. Ask students to discuss different expectations of behavior between fathers and children in their native cultures.

Activity Group students with more proficient English speakers to reread "Those Winter Sundays." Ask each group to discuss the reasons for the "chronic angers of that house" and for the father's actions.

Additional Resources
📁 *English Language Learners Sourcebook*

Responding to Literature

Personal Response

What people or events in your own life do either or both of these poems bring to mind? Explain in your journal.

ANALYZING LITERATURE

First Lesson

RECALL AND INTERPRET

1. Who might the speaker be? Who is the speaker addressing? What activity is the speaker describing?
2. Summarize the advice the speaker gives in lines 1–8. What can you infer about the speaker's feelings from these lines?
3. The speaker tells the daughter she will "tire on the long thrash to your island." What do you think the long thrash to the island might **symbolize** or represent?
4. What is the literal meaning of the advice the speaker gives in lines 11–15? What broader meaning do you think the speaker might wish to convey? Explain.

EVALUATE AND CONNECT

5. Evaluate how the speaker's **tone,** or attitude toward the subject, contributes to the meaning and overall effect of the poem.
6. Do you think "First Lesson" is a good title for this poem? Why or why not? What lesson do you think it refers to? Explain.
7. Theme Connections   How does this poem help you better understand the conflict that parents face between loving and protecting their children and helping them achieve independence?

Those Winter Sundays

RECALL AND INTERPRET

8. What did the speaker's father do on Sunday mornings in winter? As a child, did the speaker appreciate his father's efforts? How do you know?
9. Based on what the speaker says, what kind of life did the father live? What might you infer about the father's character, based on the information given?
10. What type of relationship did the speaker and his father seem to have? Support your response with details from the poem.
11. What does the speaker mean by "love's austere and lonely offices"? What has the speaker learned about his father since those winter Sundays?

EVALUATE AND CONNECT

12. Evaluate how the **mood,** or atmosphere, of the poem helps to reinforce its message.
13. Do you think that most people take for granted the many things that their parents or other family members do for them? Give specific examples to support your answer.
14. One critic said that this poem causes readers to "reevaluate their lives." Explain.

POETRY 605

---

14. The poem's regretful tone can give readers a new perspective on parents' words and actions; it might make them think of ways to show their appreciation and love for parents now, not later.

12. Students might feel a mood of longing from reading the poem. Such longing reinforces the poem's message that parents' love cannot be fully understood until one is also an adult.

13. Students might cite failure of children to appreciate food, clothing, shelter, extracurricular activities, special treats, and attendance at school and other special events that parents take time for. Some might note checking on homework and following up to see that responsibilities are carried out.

than soft words and indulgence. Now grown, the son realizes that responsibilities of parenthood require taking stands that children resent and misunderstand.

Responding to the Selection

Personal Response

Students might describe parents, grandparents, and learning skills such as how to ride a bike or hit a ball.

ANALYZING LITERATURE

1. A father speaks to his daughter; he describes how to float in the tidewater with his help.
2. He advises her to relax, spread her arms, and look up, not be impatient to "dive and swim." He feels protective of his daughter but wants to prepare her for independence when the time comes.
3. It symbolizes the struggle to establish an independent life, separate from family, and to survive difficult times.
4. The sea is buoyant and will not let her sink. If she is on her back and does not fight the water, she will be able to breathe. In a broader sense, he means that if she remembers his love and advice and opens herself to life's challenges, she will find the support she needs in life.
5. His tenderness, concern, and certainty show that he speaks from experience and out of love. His use of the word "remember" reveals the deeper life lesson he knows he is also teaching.
6. It is the first, most basic, lesson in learning to swim, as well as the primary, lesson for survival in life. The poem hints that the father learns a lesson in "letting go."
7. It makes one think about how a parent teaches children in order to prepare them for the future and recognize how difficult it is for parents to let go when they know the hardships life holds.
8. He rose early to build a fire and shine shoes. Only as an adult does the speaker recognize how ungrateful he was and wishes he could say thank you.
9. He worked long, hard hours out in all kinds of weather. The "chronic angers" of the house suggest frustration and exhaustion for what must have been poor wages, but his actions show his love, responsibility, and self-discipline.
10. The speaker feared his father's anger and spoke "indifferently" to him. The relationship was not demonstrative, but the father's actions showed his love.
11. The father's sternness and conflicts with his son grew out of the father's understanding that a child requires discipline and direction more

LITERARY ELEMENTS

1. The *l* sound is repeated in lines 14–15 of "First Lesson": "*l*ie gently . . . *l*ight-year/stars, *l*ie back . . . ." "Those Winter Sundays" features alliteration in "*w*eekday *w*eather" and "*b*anked fires *b*laze" and repeats the initial *k* sound in stanza two (*c*old, *c*all, *c*hronic) as well as using it within other words (wa*k*e, brea*k*ing).
2. Booth uses alliteration to build a mood of calm and knowing tenderness; Hayden uses it to make us feel the harshness and hurt of the father's world.

Additional Resources

📖 *Literary Elements Transparency 53*

LITERATURE AND WRITING

Writing About Literature

Students' character sketches should
- describe the father and analyze his actions.
- describe the son's reaction to the father.
- name specific traits of the father.
- explain the logic used to infer the traits from details in the poem.

Personal Writing

Students' letters should
- establish a grateful tone.
- summarize the lesson learned.
- list concrete ways the lesson has helped.

EXTENDING YOUR RESPONSE

Literature Groups Before groups begin their lists, review extended metaphor (a comparison that is sustained through an entire literary work). **COLLAB. LEARN.**

Learning for Life You may want to suggest that students seek information from instructors of local swimming programs such as the YMCA or park district. 📦

Listening and Speaking Encourage students to use tone, pace, and gestures to enhance the sound devices and themes of the poems. 📦

Literary ELEMENTS

Alliteration

Alliteration is the repetition of consonant sounds at the beginnings of words. In poetry, alliteration may be used to create a musical effect, to emphasize meaning, or to draw attention to particular words. Poets also use alliteration to help create a particular mood, or atmosphere, in a poem. Notice the alliteration in these lines from "First Lesson."

> *L*ie *b*ack, daughter, *l*et your *h*ead
> *b*e tipped *b*ack in the cup of my *h*and.

The repetition of the initial consonants *l*, *b*, and *h* produces a musical effect and helps create a mood of peace and tranquility. The alliteration also reinforces the speaker's meaning by drawing attention to the words the poet wants to emphasize. As you read poetry, pay attention to the way alliteration contributes to the overall meaning and effect of a particular poem.

1. Find several examples of alliteration in "First Lesson" and in "Those Winter Sundays." What words does the alliteration emphasize in each example?
2. What effects are created by each example of alliteration?

● See **Literary Terms Handbook**, p. R1.

LITERATURE AND WRITING

Writing About Literature

Character Sketch Use the information in "Those Winter Sundays" to write a character sketch of the speaker's father. As you write your sketch, think about what is directly stated in the poem, as well as what can be inferred. Compare your character sketch with those created by other students.

Personal Writing

I Just Wanted to Say . . . Reread the journal entry you wrote in response to the Focus Activity on page 602. Then write a letter of thanks to the person who taught you an important life lesson. Explain how you have benefited from learning this lesson.

EXTENDING YOUR RESPONSE

Literature Groups

Hidden Meaning A **metaphor** is a figure of speech that compares two things. Poets often use metaphors to help convey the poem's message. In your group, look for possible metaphors in "First Lesson" and "Those Winter Sundays." Create a list for each poem and jot down the group's ideas about what each metaphor is comparing. What impact do the metaphors have on the meaning of the poem? How do they affect your appreciation of the poem? Share your insights with the class.

Learning for Life

Survival Floating Imagine that you are reading "First Lesson" from a completely literal point of view, hoping to get advice on survival floating. Do research to find out what survival floating is, and when and how it should be done. Then evaluate the advice given in the poem. Create an illustrated poster that summarizes this information.

Listening and Speaking

Compare Oral Effects With a partner, take turns reading "First Lesson" and "Those Winter Sundays" out loud. Compare and contrast the **sound devices,** or techniques used to emphasize particular sounds in the poems. After hearing each other recite the poems, do you feel that you have a deeper understanding and appreciation of the poems and their meaning? Discuss these issues with your partner. Share and compare your conclusions with your classmates.

📁 **Save your work for your portfolio.**

606 　 UNIT 3

FINE ART
TRANSPARENCY 2

You may want to use Fine Art Transparency 2 to discuss how parents influence children.

✓ ASSESSMENT OPTIONS

📁 *Quick Checks,* p. 53

📁 *Selection and Theme Assessment,* pp. 101–102

📁 *Performance Assessment,* p. 52

💾 *Testmaker*

Vo·cab·u·lar·y Skills

Multiple-Meaning Words

Words with the same spelling but different meanings can sometimes be a source of confusion. Robert Hayden speaks of "love's austere and lonely *offices*," and the reader who thinks he means "places where work is done" will fail to understand what Hayden is saying.

Some words happen to have the same spelling but do not share a history. *Bank* as Hayden uses it in "*banked* fires" and *bank* in a phrase such as "*banked* earnings" are two different words with completely different meanings. Dictionaries provide separate entries for these two words.

Confusion is more likely to occur when a reader must deal with the multiple meanings of a single word. The varied meanings of a word can range from extremely to only slightly different. Both *bank* and *office* have several related but different meanings.

Here are typical dictionary definitions for the transitive verb form of *bank* and for *office*.

bank *v.t.* **1.** to form into a bank; pile up; heap up: *Bank soil around the roses before the first frost.* **2.** to cause to slope up from an inside edge: *Bank the race track's curves to help cars hold the road.* **3.** to tilt or cause to slope to one side, especially while making a turn: *The pilot banked the plane.* **4.** to pile ashes on [a fire] or lessen a draft to cause slower burning: *Bank the fire before turning in for the night.*

office *n.* **1.** something done for another; an act of kindness; service: *to obtain a job through the good offices of a friend.* **2.** the duty, function, or role of a particular position: *to act in the office of advisor to the king.* **3.** a position of duty, trust, or authority: *named to the office of treasurer.* **4.** a place where work is done or business is carried out: *Go to the doctor's office.* **5.** a room assigned to a specific person or group in an organization: *His secretary works right outside his office.* **6.** those who carry on work in an office: *Inform the office regarding absences.*

EXERCISE

Use context clues to decide which definition of *bank* or *office* is used in each sentence below and write the number of that definition on your paper.

1. Her sharp turn *banked* the bicycle, but speed kept it upright.

2. Just *bank* the laundry up against the washing machine.

3. Absence from his beloved only *banked* his passion; nothing could extinguish it.

4. Base runners *bank* their bodies as they pass first, trying to stretch a single into a double.

5. Nearly half of the *office* is out with the flu.

6. Please stop by our main *office* and pick up a brochure.

7. I have lost respect for the man but not for the *office* he holds.

8. Sergio will faithfully carry out the *office* of classroom monitor.

Vo·cab·u·lar·y Skills

Objective

- To use context clues and dictionary entries to determine which definition of a multiple-meaning word is intended

Teaching Strategies

As students analyze the dictionary entries, point out the examples that follow meanings. Suggest that they use these as a second source of context against which to compare the use in the selection they are reading. Explain that words that are spelled the same but have separate entries have different origins. The *bank* used in this lesson comes from Scandinavian languages; the entry for an institution for money comes from Old Italian *banca*, a table used by moneylenders.

Exercise

1. meaning 3
2. meaning 1
3. meaning 4
4. meaning 3
5. meaning 6
6. meaning 4
7. meaning 3
8. meaning 2

Additional Resources

📁 *Vocabulary Power: Weekly Lessons and Activities*

MEETING INDIVIDUAL NEEDS — ENGLISH LANGUAGE LEARNERS

Using a Dictionary Multiple-meaning words are doubly confusing for English language learners. Explain that it is important to know more than one meaning for a word.

Activity Guide students in using a dictionary to find meanings for a *foul* odor, *foul* weather, *foul* language, and a *foul* ball.

Have students analyze dictionary entries and note various meanings for the following words from the selection: *cup, stream, tire, rise, driven, polished.* Have students decide which sense is used in the poems.

Additional Resources

📁 *English Language Learners Sourcebook*

Objective

- To read and understand a magazine article

Literature — LINK

Horses Graze and **A Blessing**
This article looks compassionately at how mustangs have been harmed by people and may now be helped by them to survive. The following poems (pp. 611–612) praise horses for their gentleness and ability to "love the world" in the moment.

MEDIA
Connection

Magazine Article

Many people feel a special connection to horses. A few have given back to wild horses in the West something they had lost—the freedom to run.

Halfway House for Horses

by Melanie L. Stephens, *Time*, January 1, 1990

Their high-pitched whinnies roll across the plains like a tumbleweed-scattering wind. At dusk one of them rears and paws the air, casting a silhouette that is the very image of freedom. These are mustangs, the legendary wild horses of the American West. Two decades ago, mustangs were headed for extinction. Now, at Mustang Meadows Ranch, a 32,000-acre spread near St. Francis, S. Dak., 1,500 of them have found sanctuary and a managed independence that may help assure their survival.

Descended from horses that escaped from Spanish herds, millions of mustangs roamed the prairie at the start of the 19th century. But as the wildness went out of the West and more and more rangeland was plowed for crops or fenced off for cattle, the number of mustangs dwindled. By 1970 only 17,000 were left, despite the passage of federal laws that banned the use of airplanes and motor vehicles to round them up for slaughter. In 1971 Congress responded to a massive letter-writing campaign by enacting the Wild Free-Roaming Horses and Burros Act, which assigned the federal Bureau of Land

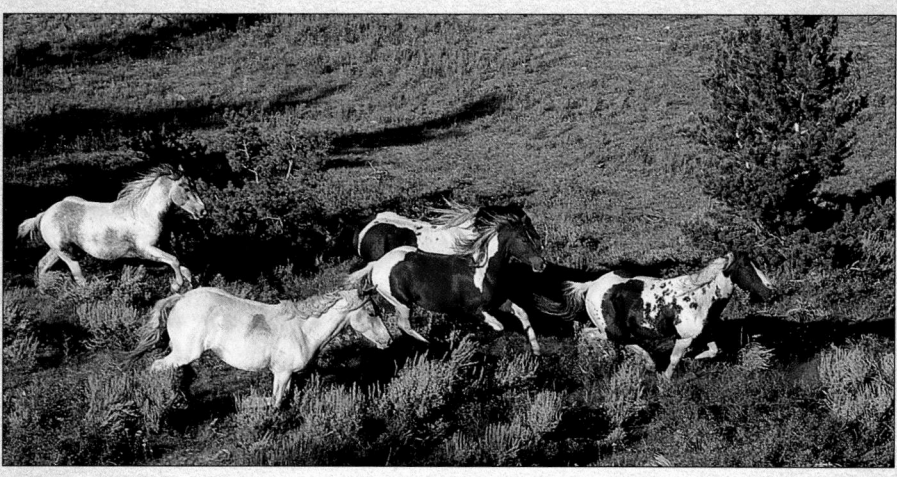

Teaching Options

Reading *Minilesson*

Distinguishing Fact and Opinion

Remind students that understanding and evaluating magazine articles depends upon the ability to differentiate between facts and opinions. *Facts* give information that can be proven true or false by personal experience or a reliable source; *opinions* express the author's beliefs. Suggest that students evaluate opinions they encounter in reading by asking: Is the opinion a reasonable conclusion supported by evidence? Have students identify the following sentences as fact or opinion and evaluate their content: *Millions of wild horses were killed directly or indirectly by western settlers. The mustang's greatest enemy is the human.*

Activity Have students work in groups to locate five facts and three opinions in "Halfway House for Horses." In discussion, members should decide how they would check the accuracy of facts and evaluate the reasonableness of opinions. **L2**

Additional Resources

📁 *Reading Workbook*

Management [BLM] the responsibility for protecting these "living symbols of the historic and pioneer spirit of the West."

Under BLM, the mustangs have recovered: 42,000 horses now run free on the range. But their numbers have greatly surpassed the ability of the land to support them. To ease the overpopulation, BLM in 1976 inaugurated a national Adopt-a-Horse program, under which 90,000 wild horses have been sold to private owners. But the mustangs taken off the range annually include many that are too old, crippled, ugly or mean to make good pets. Until two years ago, thousands of unadoptable mustangs were crowded into dusty feeding pens in Nebraska, Nevada and Texas at a cost to taxpayers of $13 million a year.

Enter Dayton Hyde, an Oregon rancher with a reputation for unorthodox management and a deep interest in conservation. "In my travels I kept going by feedlots, seeing these poor creatures cooped up," says Hyde, 64. "I thought, 'That's no way to treat a wild horse.'

My dream was to get these horses out of the feedlots and running free again."

In 1988 Hyde founded the nonprofit Institute for Range and the American Mustang [IRAM] in order to create sanctuaries—retirement homes of sorts—where unadoptable wild horses could once again roam freely. He convinced BLM that with foundation and public funds he could establish a self-sustaining sanctuary within three years. IRAM's first project was a 12,600-acre sanctuary in the Black Hills of South Dakota. . . . The project makes Hyde smile. "The horses are finally getting over their depression," he says. "They got so bored in the feedlots that they didn't know how to run anymore."

Hyde's ambition went beyond his successes at the Black Hills sanctuary. He next sought to establish a larger range that could accommodate thousands of horses. But since IRAM lacked both money and land, Hyde needed the help of a private investor. He turned out to be Alan Day, an owner of cattle ranches in Arizona

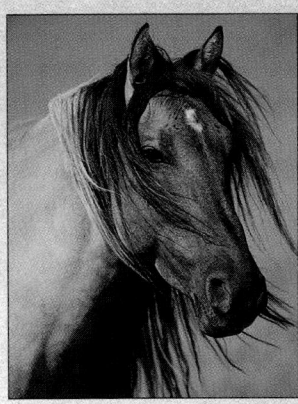

and Nebraska. Day, says Hyde, "knew how to manage grass and was not afraid of the immensity of my dream."

The first mustangs arrived in August 1988. After being cooped up in corrals anywhere from one month to several years, they needed to readjust psychologically to the comparative freedom of the ranch's open pastures. By gradually approaching the wary mustangs in corrals, Day and his wranglers taught them to become comfortable around people. "They have had so much negative training before they get here, they think they are going to suffer if they see a man on horseback," says Day. "We want to show them that we are not the enemy."

Respond

1. What do you think—are people the enemy of wild animals? Explain your answer.

2. What actions can you take in your everyday life to improve the lives of wild animals?

Wild Horses Have students use a search engine to look for additional information about the American mustang. Suggest that they try entering key words such as *wild horses, Dayton Hyde,* and *Wild Free-Roaming Horses and Burros Act.* Point out that *mustang* should be avoided because it calls up information about the Ford Mustang and numerous sports teams with that name.

Objectives

- To read and analyze poems about lessons in the love and acceptance offered by animals
- To identify and analyze the effect of personification
- To write an analysis comparing mood in two poems

Skills

Writing: Description of Relationship
Listening/Speaking: Interview
Life Skills: Observing and Reporting
Collaboration: Literature Groups

Motivating
→OPTIONS

Selection Focus Transparency 54: Have students discuss qualities that a horse possesses that make it a source of literary inspiration.

Focus Activity: Have students order themselves by the first letter of the animals' name and proceed alphabetically, giving a one-sentence summary of the lesson learned.

Before You Read

Horses Graze and A Blessing

── FOCUS ACTIVITY ──

Some people believe that animals have much to teach people if we pay attention. What have you learned from observing, interacting with, or hearing about an animal?

QUICKWRITE Spend five minutes writing about what you learned and what it meant to you.

SETTING A PURPOSE Read to see how two poets describe lessons that animals can teach.

── BACKGROUND ──

- Horses are hooved, herbivorous (plant-eating) mammals related to the zebra. They are herd animals well-adapted for living on the plains. Horses have wide, flat teeth designed for grinding grasses and other plants, and long foot bones designed for swift running. For centuries, people used horses extensively in warfare, agriculture, and transportation. Today, most horses are kept for sport and show.
- Horses have played an important role in literature and art. In cave paintings from the Ice Age, wild horses and cattle were the most prominent images. Because of their speed and vitality, horses in ancient Greek and Roman mythology, like the winged horse Pegasus, were associated with the sun and heavenly chariots. Today, the winged horse is a symbol for poetic inspiration.

Meet Gwendolyn Brooks

Gwendolyn Brooks recalls her youth as a "sparkly childhood, with two fine parents and one brother, in a plain but warmly enclosing two-story gray house." Her best times were at home with her family, where she wrote and read every day, dreaming of being a poet. Brooks's poetry, which she calls "wild, raw, ragged free verse," earned her the Pulitzer Prize in 1950.

Gwendolyn Brooks was born in Kansas in 1917 but has lived most of her life in Chicago, Illinois.

Meet James Wright

Referring to the small working-class town where he grew up, James Wright said, "I love the variety of Martins Ferry, a skinny place stretched out along the river between the railroad and the abrupt hills." Influenced by his childhood experiences, Wright wrote about poor people and social outcasts, and found dignity in the pain and sadness of living.

James Wright was born in Ohio in 1927 and died in 1980.

RESOURCE MANAGER

Lesson Planning Resource
The *Unit Three Planning Guide* (pp. 37–41) provides additional lesson notes and reduced versions of all print resources.

📁 **Other Print Resources**
- Active Reading Guide, p. 54
- Quick Checks, p. 54
- Selection and Theme Assessment, pp. 103–104
- Performance Assessment, p. 53
- Spanish Summaries, p. 54
- Spanish Translations
- Inclusion Strategies

🖨 **Transparencies**
- Selection Focus 54
- Literary Elements 54

Technology
- 🎧 Audio Library
- 🎧 Spanish Audio Library
- 💻 Glencoe Literature Web Site
- 💾 Testmaker

Horses Graze

Gwendolyn Brooks

A
Cows graze.
Horses graze.
They
eat
5 eat
eat.
Their graceful heads
are bowed
bowed
10 bowed
in majestic° oblivion.°

B
They are nobly oblivious
to your follies,°
your inflation,°
15 the knocks° and nettles° of administration.
They
eat
eat
eat.
20 And at the crest° of their brute satisfaction,
with wonderful gentleness, in affirmation,°
they lift their clean calm eyes and they lie down
and love the world.

C
They speak with their companions.
25 They do not wish that they were otherwhere.
Perhaps they know that creature feet may press
only a few earth inches at a time,
that earth is anywhere earth,
that an eye may see,
30 wherever it may be,
D
the Immediate arc, alone, of life, of love.
In Sweden,
China,
Afrika,
35 in India or Maine
the animals are sane;
they know and know and know
there's ground below
and sky
40 up high.

11 **majestic:** a quality of dignified greatness. **oblivion:** a lack of awareness or memory.
13 **folly:** a lack of good sense or a tragically foolish or wicked action.
14 **inflation:** an economic condition that occurs when consumer prices continuously rise or the purchasing power of money continuously declines; also, pomposity or empty pretentiousness.
15 **knock:** a sharp blow or hit. **nettle:** a weedy plant that releases a substance irritating to skin; metaphorically, nettle can be anything that irritates.
20 **crest:** a peak, high point, or climax.
21 **affirmation:** a positive judgment or an act or statement supporting the truth.

Earthenware Horse.
Tang dynasty, China.

A Literary Elements

REPETITION Ask students to read lines 1–11 silently and describe the effect of repeated words. *(She wants to stress the steady single-mindedness of the cows and horses.)*

Additional Resources
- *Active Reading Guide,* p. 54
- *Audio Library*
- *Spanish Audio Library*

B Literary Elements

SOUND EFFECTS Have students read aloud and identify repeated consonant and vowel sounds in these lines. *(F and n sounds as well as long o, short o, and long a sounds recur.)*

C Literary Elements

FIGURES OF SPEECH: *Personification*
What human quality is given to horses in line 24? *(speech)*

D Active Reading

INTERPRET Ask students to explain what they think the poet is saying in these lines. What is the "Immediate arc, alone, of life, of love"? *(The portion of the circle [arc] of earth where you are forms, at that moment, the only meaningful stage for life and love.)*

Teaching Options

REAL-WORLD CONNECTION

Animal Articles Ask students to look for one magazine article about horses or other domesticated animals of interest to them. Point out that it is a good idea to scan an article before reading it to decide if the article meets the student's needs.

Have students scan introductory sentences in paragraphs, captions, and subtitles to determine if the article is worth reading in full. Allow time for students to share their articles with small groups of classmates. **L2**

E **Literary Elements**

FIGURES OF SPEECH: *Personification*
Ask students what the poet highlights by describing the horses as
happy to see people. *(They are social
and feel a bond with these humans.
Ascribing human emotions to animals
is personification.)*

F **Literary Elements**

FIGURES OF SPEECH: *Personification*
Have students speculate why the
poet attributes human emotions of
love and loneliness to the horses.
*(He wants to express the closeness
he felt to them and they to him.)*

G **Active Reading**

INTERPRET Ask students to explain
what the speaker means here. What
has made this moment remarkable?
*(He is accepted by the horses and
feels kinship with them; the awareness of unity among life forms
makes him feel as though he could
be transformed.)*

Thematic Focus

Loves and Losses Have we lost
something valuable by moving away
from our natural instincts? Have the
class discuss this question based
on their reading of the poems.

☑ ASSESSMENT OPTIONS

📁 *Quick Checks,* p. 54

A Blessing

James Wright ∾

Just off the highway to Rochester, Minnesota,
Twilight bounds° softly forth on the grass.
And the eyes of those two Indian ponies
Darken with kindness.
5 They have come gladly out of the willows
To welcome my friend and me.
We step over the barbed wire into the pasture
Where they have been grazing all day, alone.
They ripple tensely, they can hardly contain their happiness
10 That we have come.
They bow shyly as wet swans. They love each other.
There is no loneliness like theirs.
At home once more,
They begin munching the young tufts of spring in the darkness.
15 I would like to hold the slenderer one in my arms,
For she has walked over to me
And nuzzled my left hand.
She is black and white,
Her mane falls wild on her forehead,
20 And the light breeze moves me to caress her long ear
That is delicate as the skin over a girl's wrist.
Suddenly I realize
That if I stepped out of my body I would break
Into blossom.

*Two Blue Horses (Zwei blaue
Pferde),* 1913. Franz Marc.
Watercolor and india ink on
paper, 7⅞ x 5¼ in.
Solomon R. Guggenheim
Museum, New York.

---

2 To *bound* is to move by leaping.

MEETING INDIVIDUAL NEEDS **INCLUSION STRATEGIES**

Learning Disabled Be sure students
are able to visualize and understand the
context for the phrases *Indian ponies* and
wet swans. Invite a volunteer to sketch or
describe these animals.

Activity Have students read the poem
aloud several times. Then have them
work in pairs to prepare a presentation
of the poem, including artwork and fur-

ther oral interpretation. After they have
practiced their presentations, ask partners to present them for the class.
L1 **COLLAB. LEARN.**

Additional Resources
📁 *Inclusion Strategies*

Responding to Literature

Personal Response

What images or descriptions in the poems did you find most striking?

ANALYZING LITERATURE

Horses Graze

RECALL AND INTERPRET

1. What animals does the speaker describe in this poem? To whom or what does the speaker compare them?
2. How does the speaker describe the animals in lines 7–11? Explain in your own words what the speaker means by "bowed in majestic oblivion."
3. How do the animals show their gentleness in lines 21–23? What might the animals be affirming?
4. According to the speaker, what do animals "know," and in what way are they "sane"? What might the poet be implying here about people?

EVALUATE AND CONNECT

5. Brooks uses only a few words to describe people. Why, in your view, might she have chosen the word *inflation?* Explain its meaning in the context of the poem.
6. What does the speaker think people could learn from animals? Review your response to the Focus Activity on page 610. How do the speaker's ideas compare to what you wrote?
7. How has this poem changed the way you see horses and cows? How has it changed the way you see people? Explain.

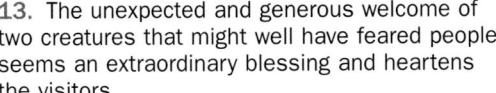

A Blessing

RECALL AND INTERPRET

8. What words does the speaker use in lines 1–10 to describe the ponies? What might this description convey about the speaker? Why?
9. According to the speaker, what feelings do the ponies express in lines 11–13? Why might they feel this way? Support your answer with evidence from the poem.
10. How does the speaker describe the slenderer animal? How do you think the speaker feels about that animal? Why?
11. Describe in your own words what the speaker experiences at the end of the poem. What message do you think the poet is communicating by describing this experience?

EVALUATE AND CONNECT

12. Which of Wright's **images** appeal to the sense of touch? Choose an image that you think is especially effective and explain why it is effective. (See page R6).
13. What, do you think, is the "blessing" referred to in the title of the poem?
14. What animals that you have known or read about seem similar to the animals described in the poem? Explain the similarities.

POETRY 🐾 613

---

13. The unexpected and generous welcome of two creatures that might well have feared people seems an extraordinary blessing and heartens the visitors.
14. Most students will have experienced similar welcoming by dogs and cats.

11. He feels a closeness to the horses and the natural world as well as a joy in the unexpected encounter that makes him feel a rebirth like the blossoming of spring.
12. Students may mention stepping over barbed wire, the ripple of tense muscles, the nuzzling of "the slenderer one," and the speaker's caress of a silky ear.

Responding to the Selection

Personal Response

Students might find the image of lifting "clean calm eyes" and lying down in "Horses Graze" compelling. In "A Blessing," the bowed necks of the horses or the nuzzling of the speaker's hand stand out.

ANALYZING LITERATURE

1. Horses and cows are compared to wise and noble humans.
2. Their grace and unconcern for the worries of the world are stressed. Bowing suggests humility and acceptance; the animals have dignity and greatness because they are centered in the here and now.
3. Their gentleness shows in their "clean calm eyes" and their lying down in ease. They seem to affirm the goodness of life and the bounty of earth.
4. Animals know that the place where they stand is real and sufficient, that earth will provide. The poet implies that humans have lost this intuition.
5. *Inflation* ties to the human tendency to pursue wealth and worry about finances; it also suggests the self-important attitude of many people.
6. Animals teach humility, dignity, gentleness, a centered perspective, and contentment.
7. Students might not have considered horses or cows capable of love or thought of human ambition as foolish.
8. They are kind, happy, and welcoming. He is observant and open and sees the harmony in the world around him.
9. They express shyness, love, and loneliness. Their isolation ("they have been grazing all day, alone") could explain their close interdependence and reactions to the visitors.
10. He describes her as gentle and delicate. He associates her with an affectionate and appealing young woman to whom he feels a physical connection and closeness because of her grace and giving attitude.

LITERARY ELEMENTS

1. When he speaks of the horses' love for each other and their loneliness, he is attributing human qualities to them in order to create an emotional world. In this world, readers can experience joy in a common bond with creatures.
2. The animals "love the world," "speak with their companions," and willfully avoid the trap of being discontented. By placing animals and people on the same level, the poet shows how unhappy and foolish humans are in comparison.

Additional Resources

 Literary Elements Transparency 54

LITERATURE AND WRITING

Writing About Literature

Students' analyses should
- clearly describe the mood of each poem.
- draw from details of the poems to show how mood is established.
- explain how mood helps communicate theme.

Personal Writing

Students' writing should
- describe the encounter using specific verbs and exact modifiers.
- use figures of speech to establish effective comparisons.
- end with a summarizing statement of the effect of the experience.

EXTENDING YOUR RESPONSE

Literature Groups You may want to suggest that groups first define the terms *sane* and *animal nature*, giving examples of behaviors that illustrate each concept. **COLLAB. LEARN.**

Listening and Speaking Have students create a list of leading and follow-up questions prior to conducting their interviews. If possible, have students use a tape recorder to record interview responses.

Literary ELEMENTS

Personification

Personification is a figure of speech that describes an animal as if it has human qualities, or an inanimate object, an idea, or force of nature as if it is alive or has human traits or feelings. Wright uses personification in "A Blessing" when he writes that the twilight "bounds." By personifying the twilight, Wright creates a strong visual image and communicates the sense that the natural world is alive. He also associates the twilight with the movement of the ponies, who actually do bound.

1. Give an example of the ponies being personified in "A Blessing" and tell what effect you think Wright was trying to achieve.
2. Give an example of the animals in "Horses Graze" being personified. What effect does this personification create?

● See **Literary Terms Handbook**, p. R9.

LITERATURE AND WRITING

Writing About Literature

Analyzing Mood The **mood** of a poem is its general feeling or atmosphere. In a few paragraphs, write about the mood of each poem. Using details from the poem, tell how the mood is conveyed, what its effects are, and how it relates to the poem's message. Support your interpretation with evidence from the poems.

Personal Writing

Animal Understanding Using your response to the Focus Activity on page 610 as a starting point, write about a memorable relationship or encounter you've had with an animal. What was the relationship or encounter like? How did it affect you and why? Share your writing with a classmate.

EXTENDING YOUR RESPONSE

Literature Groups

Animal Madness or Method? Both Wright and Brooks admire qualities they see in animals and seem to share a longing for the lost animal in themselves. Do you think people have lost their connection with animals and their own animal nature? Do you agree with Brooks' implication that animals are more "sane" than people? Debate these questions within your group and use details from each poem to support or refute each other's ideas. Share your conclusions with the class.

Listening and Speaking

Wild and Woolly Animal Stories Using a tape recorder or taking notes, interview several friends and/or relatives about enlightening or unusual experiences they've had with animals, including pets, domestic animals, and wildlife. Share your best stories with the class.

Learning for Life

Naturalist's Log Brooks and Wright paid close attention to the behavior and habits of the animals they wrote about. Making sure not to frighten or disturb it, observe a wild animal, a pet, or another domestic animal. Take notes about what it eats, when it is active and when it sleeps, what dangers it faces, and so on. Summarize your information in a report to share with the class.

Reading Further

You might enjoy these poems:
"The Bean Eaters" from *The Bean Eaters* and "Medgar Evers" from *After Mecca* by Gwendolyn Brooks. "Sitting in a Small Screenhouse on a Summer Morning" and "Autumnal" from *Above the River: The Complete Poems* by James Wright.

💾 **Save your work for your portfolio.**

Learning for Life You may want to have a biology teacher make suggestions about appropriate scientific method for observations.

✔ ASSESSMENT OPTIONS

 Quick Checks, p. 54

 Selection and Theme Assessment, pp. 103–104

 Performance Assessment, p. 53

💾 *Testmaker*

Reading & Thinking Skills

Understanding Denotation and Connotation

How would you react if someone called you "slender"? How might you react to being called "scrawny"? You would probably respond differently. *Slender* and *scrawny* have the same **denotation**, or explicit meaning. They both describe something that is lean or thin. However, the words have very different **connotations**, or meanings that go beyond the simple literal definition. Connotations are the feelings and values commonly associated with a word. The word *slender,* for example, has a positive connotation. It implies a pleasing slimness. The word *scrawny,* on the other hand, has a negative connotation. It suggests a malnourished appearance.

In his poem "A Blessing," James Wright uses the connotations of words to create a gentle, loving image of two horses. Words such as *nuzzled* and *delicate* suggest tenderness, gentleness, and gracefulness. Even the word *munching* has a connotation of gentleness. Imagine the difference in effect if the poet had used the word *chomping* instead.

In this poem, Wright also purposefully pairs words that have negative connotations with words that have positive ones. For example, at the end of the poem, the narrator says, "I would break / Into blossom." While the word *break* usually has a connotation of destruction, it is paired with *blossom,* which suggests springtime. The phrase thus brings to mind an image of joyous rebirth.

● For more about denotation and connotation, see **Reading Handbook,** p. R81.

EXERCISE

Read the following passage from Gwendolyn Brooks's poem "Horses Graze." Then answer the questions below.

> Their graceful heads
> are bowed
> bowed
> bowed
> in majestic oblivion.
> They are nobly oblivious
> to your follies,
> your inflation,
> the knocks and nettles of administration.

1. Which words have a positive connotation? Which words have a negative connotation?

2. How does Brooks use connotation in this passage to compare "you" to "them"?

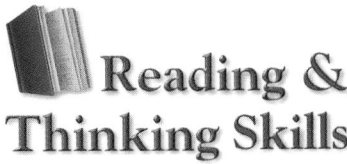

Reading & Thinking Skills

Objective

- To analyze the differences between the denotations and the connotations of words

Teaching Strategies

As part of a discussion of connotation, you might also discuss the fact that synonyms can have different connotations. Show how various dictionaries offer descriptions of differences in meaning and associations for synonyms of some words. Analyze such an entry with students. The following example is for *laugh.*

SYN.: laugh is the general word for the sounds or exhalation made in expressing mirth, amusement, etc.; **chuckle** implies soft laughter in low tones, expressive of <u>mild</u> amusement or <u>inward satisfaction</u>; . . . **snicker** is used of a <u>sly, half-suppressed</u> laugh, as <u>at another's discomfiture</u> or a <u>bawdy story</u>; **guffaw** refers to <u>loud, coarse</u> laughter.

Exercise

1. *Graceful, majestic,* and *nobly* are positive; *follies, inflation, knocks,* and *nettles* are negative.
2. The animals are given admirable qualities; humans, negative ones that point out how striving causes pain and disappointment.

Additional Resources
📁 *Reading Workbook*

MEETING INDIVIDUAL NEEDS — INCLUSION STRATEGIES

Less-Proficient Readers Explain that connotations, or associations and emotions, become attached to words through the way they are used and through experience. Have students verbalize their reactions to the following: Fred once again found himself *unemployed.* His wife explained that Fred was *between jobs.* His father-in-law complained about Fred's being a *free-loader.*

Activity Give groups of students a print advertisement and have them read it and analyze at least five words for positive or negative connotations. Encourage students to verbalize the connotations for each word. **L1**
COLLAB. LEARN.

Additional Resources
📁 *Inclusion Strategies*

Writing Workshop

Writing Workshop

Objectives

- To write an informational article based on an interview
- To plan, draft, revise, edit, and present or publish the interview or article
- To reflect on and assess one's informative writing

GLENCOE
TECHNOLOGY

WRITER'S ASSISTANT CD-ROM

You may want to have students use Glencoe's templates and guidelines software for expository writing to aid them in working through the steps in the writing process in this lesson.

Teaching Strategies

PREWRITING

Consider your purpose In order to set a purpose, students will first need to select the interview subject. Encourage them to select someone they admire and might learn from, but at the same time caution them to be realistic. The person must be accessible to them for the interview.

Teaching Options

Business Writing: Interview

An interview is a focused conversation in which an interviewer questions another person—the subject—on a topic. You will be interviewed when you apply for college or for a job, and you might interview potential employees or clients as part of your job. Interviewing is also a great way to get material for your writing. For example, direct comments from an interview can enliven nonfiction writing. **In this workshop, you will conduct an interview and write it so that it can stand on its own as an informative written piece.**

● As you write your interview, refer to the **Writing Handbook,** pp. R58–R69.

The Writing Process

PREWRITING

> **PREWRITING TIPS**
>
> "Do your homework." Good interviewers learn as much as they can about their subject before asking questions.
>
> When you request an interview, explain your purpose and make an appointment. Be polite, friendly, and businesslike.

Consider your purpose

The way you conduct and write your interview will depend on your purpose. If the interview is for business, you will ask questions designed to get specific information. For example, you might ask a potential employee about his or her work experience. If your interview is for a magazine article or to gain material for another piece of writing, you would probably ask other kinds of questions. For instance, you might want general information about the subject's life, or you might need to have a conversation focused on a more specific topic, such as your subject's views of love.

After the interview, your purpose will be to present that information to your readers. Your presentation will suffer if you don't get all the information you need from the interview, so be sure to ask the right questions.

Choose an audience

Before you start the interview, think about how much your audience knows about the topic you will explore with your subject. Try to put yourself into the minds of your readers and think of the questions they would want answered if they were interviewing your subject. You may need to ask some simple questions just to get background information that your audience will need.

Explore ideas

Your interview will be most productive if you focus your topic and plan your questions in advance. For example, in an interview on love and loss, you might explore topics that touch on

- the reasons for love lost, as in "Well, I Have Lost You; and I Lost You Fairly."
- the way love affects a lover's views, as in "Shall I Compare Thee to a Summer's Day?"
- a child's coming to understand a parent's love, as in "Those Winter Sundays."
- the distance that can come between friends, as in "Simile."
- the love of a pet or other animal, as in "A Blessing."

Clustering is a good way to focus your ideas for an interview. Start by writing down the general topic you want to cover. Circle it. Then surround that circle with related ideas. Connect each of those ideas with others, creating groups, or clusters, of ideas. For example, a student who wanted to write about a celebrity's views of love and loss began a cluster like this one.

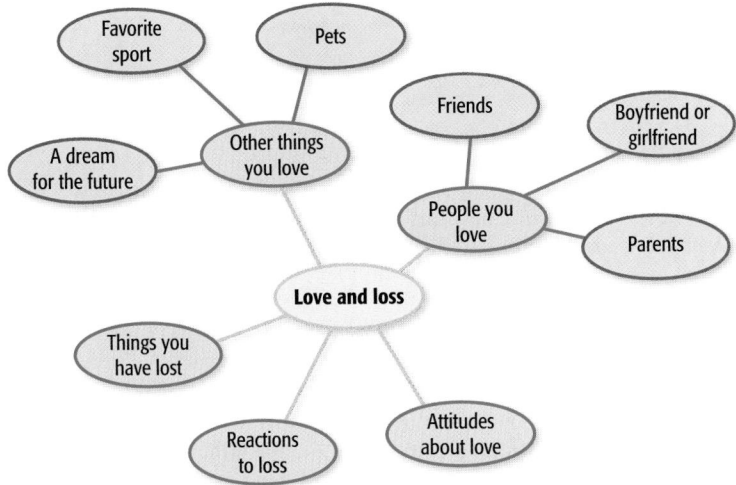

Prepare questions

Choose the ideas in the clusters that seem most appropriate for your purpose. Then compose questions around those ideas.

The success of an interview depends on asking good questions. Prepare questions that

- require more than yes or no answers.
- are clearly worded and easily understood.
- are related directly to your topic and purpose.

Choose an audience Discuss special expertise or knowledge of the interviewee. Students can assume they are writing for their peers. For example, assuming that a music teacher is interviewed by his or her pupil, what terms and concepts do the teacher and pupil take for granted that most readers will not know?

Explore ideas Explain that clustering enables free thinking and basic organization at the same time. Stress that most clusters will not look as neat as the one on page 617. The first goal is to capture many ideas; the second, to show how they are related.

Prepare questions Remind students to keep their purpose and topic in mind as they write questions and to frame questions that they think their audience wants answered.

Additional Resources

- 📁 *Writing and Proofreading Practice,* pp. 1–7, 53–59
- 🖨 *Writing and Proofreading Transparencies 1–6, 19–20, 37–38*
- 📕 *Writer's Choice,* Lessons 2.5, 5.1, 5.2, 5.8

MEETING INDIVIDUAL NEEDS — MULTIPLE LEARNING STYLES

Spatial Students who easily visualize ideas will find clustering most helpful if they use a blend of pictures, symbols, and phrases.

Activity Have students use illustrations as well as words to create their clusters. To organize their ideas into the general subtopics they will explore, first have students write each idea on a note card. They can then think of a symbol for each category and add the appropriate symbol in the upper left-hand corner of each card and separate the cards into subject piles. **L2**

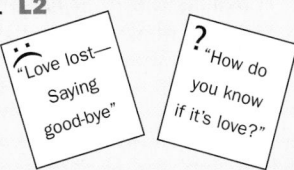

Ask on-the-spot questions You may wish to have students ask you hypothetical questions and respond as briefly and literally as possible to give them practice in framing questions that lead to in-depth answers.

During the interview: Take notes Insist that students tape record their interviews if at all possible, then listen to the recording to flesh out notes and check accuracy of impressions.

Make a plan Have students evaluate their information to note any background, facts, or responses readers must have first in order to understand other explanations or responses. Also suggest that students review their notes to delete information that lacks interest or relevance.

Writing Workshop

Ask on-the-spot questions

Be flexible during the interview. Listen closely to the subject's answers and be aware of opportunities to ask follow-up questions. This diagram shows how an insight would have been lost if the interviewer plowed ahead with a prepared question instead of considering a follow-up question.

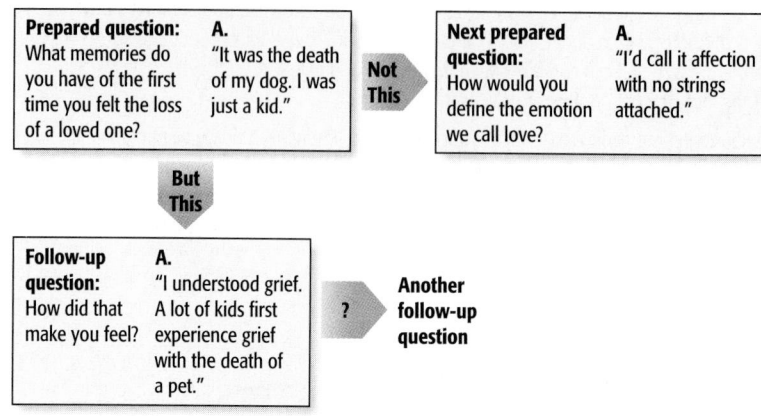

During the interview: Take notes

Even if you use a tape recorder, written notes will help you organize the information you get on tape. Listen carefully. Write words and phrases that summarize your subject's ideas. When a remark stands out, write the exact words and enclose them in quotation marks.

Make a plan

After the interview, plan to present the information you have gathered in a way that will make it understandable and interesting. You can use **chronological order** to present a narrative of the interview itself. However, many written interviews are more effective with the points arranged in **order of importance.** If you decide to use order of importance, take a tip from retailers. When they have a sale, they put the sale items at the back of the store, so that shoppers have to pass everything else to get to them. Put your most important or most interesting items at the end.

Use this order-of-importance organizer to help you put the sections of your interview into the most effective order.

If you haven't already done so, gather your questions into related groups. Choose the three most important groups. Give each one a title. Write the titles of the groups in the blocks in any order. Then jot the key questions and their answers in the block, too. Finally, number the blocks in the order you will write about them. Review the answers, and delete questions you decide not to use.

2	The experience of loss
1	What is love?
3	Why do we love?

Practice Questions and Interviews
English language learners have a disadvantage in interviewing, for they must speak and comprehend spoken English. They may need help in framing questions and anticipating probable responses.

Activity Have students work with a more proficient English speaker to be sure their questions ask what they intend. Have students practice the interview with their partner so they might anticipate unfamiliar terms and idioms that may arise in the actual interview.

Additional Resources
📁 *English Language Learners Sourcebook*

∽ Writing Workshop ∽

DRAFTING

Start by selecting from your notes. Just write down the best of what you have in your notepad or on tape.

Hooks and previews
To catch your readers' attention, use a hook. Pick something interesting that your subject said and use it in your introduction. To hold your readers' attention, use a preview. Tease readers in the introduction with an intriguing piece of information that will be developed later in the interview.

Write your draft
Check your notes and plan. Keep the writing flowing. Alter your plan if new ideas come.

STUDENT MODEL

HOOK	PREVIEW
"I thought I was an all-star at the game of love," said Lloyd Timmons, "until somebody struck me out." A major league center-fielder may not seem like the obvious choice to ask about love, but I had my reasons.	I learned quite a lot about Lloyd Timmons, not only what he thinks love is, but how that person who struck him out in the game of love is important in his life.

DRAFTING TIP
Adding details about the setting of the interview will make readers feel that they were there.

REVISING

Evaluate your work
Let your draft "rest." Then use the **Questions for Revising** to help you make revisions to your draft. Pay special attention to the use of order for emphasis and clarity.

Have a writing conference
Now read your written interview to a writing partner. Together, discuss the **Questions for Revising**.

REVISING TIP
Don't change your subject's words. Check your notes carefully.

STUDENT MODEL

> I ~~chose~~ Timmons because I had ~~seen~~ an article about the children he and his wife adopted.
> *asked ... to talk about love ... read ... seven disabled*

QUESTIONS FOR REVISING

How can you:
- ☑ make the opening more attention-getting?
- ☑ add details to bring the setting and subject to life?
- ☑ clarify confusing parts?
- ☑ add background information that readers may need?
- ☑ summarize the subject's main points in a conclusion?

POETRY 🐟 619

DRAFTING

Hooks and previews If students are writing magazine articles from their interview materials, they will find it helpful at this point to read example articles. Ask them to note how descriptive details, quotes, and interviewer impressions are interwoven to create interest and immediacy.

Write your draft Encourage students to write their drafts using a computer if possible. If they must write by hand, suggest that they leave space between subtopics or categories. They can add suitable transitions or additional information later.

REVISING

Have a writing conference As students read their interview papers aloud, partners should write down questions, comments, and suggestions for revision.

Writing *Minilesson*

Writing Headings Point out that the headings and captions in a magazine article highlight its important elements and grab the reader's interest. Make a transparency of a page of a magazine article and ask students to explain what topics and types of information they would expect to find discussed under each heading.

Activity Block out the headings of a brief newspaper article and copy it for small groups. Have students read it and write headings for it. Remind students that a heading can be a phrase that summarizes each section. **L2** **COLLAB. LEARN.**

Additional Resources

📗 ***Writer's Choice,*** Lesson 6.5

EDITING/PROOFREADING

Have students use the Proofreading Checklist on the inside back cover of their textbooks.

Suggest that students check their wordings and quotes against their notes or tape recordings of the interview to be sure they are accurate. Remind them that they can and should continue to change wording, order, and even content if the changes will improve clarity and add interest.

PUBLISHING/PRESENTING

Students who want to submit their articles for publication should write query letters to the editor of the periodical in which they want it to appear. The query letter should be persuasive and outline the story idea.

Reflecting

Portfolio Students should ask themselves the following questions as they review their work.

- How does the final presentation compare with others in the file?
- Is there some aspect of the final form that I would like to repeat the next time?
- Is this piece typical of my abilities, or does it represent a forward move in my understanding of the writing process?

Suggest that if students answer yes to two or more questions, they consider placing their article in their portfolios.

Teaching Options

~ *Writing Workshop* ~

EDITING/PROOFREADING

When your interview has the form and content you want, edit it carefully for errors in grammar, usage, mechanics, and spelling. Use the **Proofreading Checklist** on the inside back cover for help. Work through your manuscript several times, looking for only one kind of error at a time. Give your subject a copy of the interview to check and correct.

Grammar Hint

The possessive of *it* is *its*.

The contraction of *it is* is *it's*.

Do you think that the word love *has lost so much of it's meaning that its now equal to* like?

● For more about possessives, see **Language Handbook,** p. R25.

STUDENT MODEL

We sat at the kitchen table in Timmons's ~~comfterble~~ comfortable house. The house is modern ~~in style~~ and stylish, and it's filled with sunlight that ~~pores~~ pours through it's many windows.

PUBLISHING/PRESENTING

PRESENTING TIP
Photos of your subject are ideal illustrations. Portions of a taped interview can provide audio "illustrations" for a live presentation.

You might want to use your interview as a script for a mock interview to perform for the class. For a written presentation, you might submit the interview to a magazine that specializes in your subject's field of work. Interviews are often welcome as articles for school newspapers or magazines. Be sure that your work meets the requirements of the publication. Be sure to get your subject's approval of your plans before you go ahead with them.

Reflecting

Now that you've interviewed someone else, interview yourself. In your journal, conduct an interview about the interview experience. Be sure to ask yourself what you learned as a writer and how that will influence your goals for your next piece of writing.

 Save your work for your portfolio.

✔ ASSESSMENT OPTIONS

📁 ***Writing Assessment and Portfolio Management***
- Writing Assessment, pp. 2–19, 35–36
- Portfolio Management, pp. 20–22

Theme 8 — Issues of Identity

What determines who you really are? Is it your background and experiences? The way you think and respond? What other people say about you? The poems in this theme examine several aspects of identity.

THEME PROJECTS

Listening and Speaking

Casting Call Play the part of a casting agent.

1. With a group, choose at least three poems from this theme that you think could be turned into films.
2. Brainstorm a list of actors or other public figures who could portray the main characters of the poems.
3. Plan speeches that will convince the director to cast the actors you've chosen. Each member of the group should take a turn explaining to the class why your choices are best.

Performing

Each poem has a rhythm that affects the mood of the piece.

1. With a small group, choose three poems that have strong and different rhythms.
2. Think about how you could use performance to stress these poems' rhythms. For example, one person could read the poem while others play percussive instruments. Or you could do a choral reading, with members expressing rhythm by echoing, whispering, or shouting.
3. Perform your pieces live or record them ahead of time and play them for the class.

Electra #1, 1996. Diana Ong. Computer illustration.

POETRY 621

Teaching Strategies

The following suggestions may help your students plan and carry out their theme projects.

Listening and Speaking

- Let the groups refer to newspapers and magazines for names of recent films, actors, and public figures.
- Review persuasive techniques with students before they begin planning their speeches.
- Remind students to use pauses, gestures, eye contact, and varied tone and pitch when giving their speeches.

Performing

- Students may be able to borrow instruments from the school's music department.
- Encourage students with good technical skills to help the groups record their pieces.
- If the groups perform live, invite another class to listen to the performances.

Additional Resources

- 📁 *Interdisciplinary Activities,* pp. 16–17
- 📁 *Viewing and Representing Activities,* pp. 21–22
- 📁 *Listening and Speaking Activities,* pp. 15–16
- 📁 *Critical Thinking Skills,* pp. 21–33
- 📁 *Selection and Theme Assessment,* pp. 185–186
- 📁 *Performance Assessment,* p. 96

GLENCOE TECHNOLOGY

LITERATURE CLASSICS CD-ROM
Search for other selections related to the theme of issues of identity.

Theme 8 SKILLS SCOPE AND SEQUENCE

SELECTIONS	Literary Elements	Reading and Thinking	Writing	Vocabulary and Spelling	
Afro-American Fragment LANGSTON HUGHES *Heaven* CATHY SONG	Free Verse, SE p. 627 *Imagery and Tone, TWE p. 625*	*Inferring, TWE p. 623* *Activating Prior Knowledge, TWE p. 623*	List, SE p. 622 Analyze Diction, SE p. 627 Journal, SE p. 627	Analyze Word Choices, SE p. 627	
The Base Stealer ROBERT FRANCIS *To Satch* SAMUEL ALLEN	Hyperbole, SE p. 632 *Simile, TWE p. 629*	*Visualizing, TWE p. 629*	Evaluate Form, SE p. 632 Letter, SE p. 632	*Pronunciations and Meanings, TWE p. 633*	
Ex-Basketball Player JOHN UPDIKE *Miss Rosie* LUCILLE CLIFTON	Tone, SE p. 640 *Imagery, TWE p. 638*	*Main Idea and Supporting Details, TWE p. 634* *Making Comparisons, TWE p. 636* *Inferring, TWE p. 637* *Summarizing, TWE p. 641*	Charting Ideas, SE p. 635 Analyze Approaches, SE p. 640 Journal, SE p. 640	*Keywords, TWE pp. 634, 638*	
The Road Not Taken ROBERT FROST *We Are Many* PABLO NERUDA	Lyric Poem, SE p. 647 *Theme, TWE p. 645*	*Inferring, TWE p. 643*	Making Connections, SE p. 647 Paragraph or Poem, SE p. 647	*Antonyms, TWE p. 645*	
The Floral Apron MARILYN CHIN *My Mother Pieced Quilts* TERESA PALOMO ACOSTA	Imagery, SE p. 653 *Metaphor and Personification, TWE p. 650* *Symbol, TWE p. 651*	*Using Imagination, TWE p. 649*	Journal, SE p. 648 Character Sketch, SE p. 653 Letter, SE p. 653	*Etymology, TWE p. 649*	
A Bus Along St. Clair: December MARGARET ATWOOD Freeway 280 LORNA DEE CERVANTES	Speaker, SE p. 659 *Metaphor, TWE p.655*	*Identifying Author's Purpose, TWE p. 657*	Compare Themes, SE p. 659 Poem, Monologue, or Dialogue, SE p. 659 *Fairy Tale Framework, TWE p. 655*	*Words with Emotional Effects, TWE p. 656*	
MAKING A FIST NAOMI SHIHAB NYE WHAT WE BELIEVE ANITA ENDREZZE	Symbol, SE p. 664 *Metaphor, TWE p. 661*	*Interpreting Text, TWE p. 662*	Quickwrite, SE p. 660 Compare Observations, SE p. 664 Paragraphs, SE p. 664		
Foreign Ways DIANA CHANG *Song for My Name* LINDA HOGAN	Sensory Details, SE p. 669	Using Graphic Aids, SE p. 665 *Identifying Assumptions, TWE p. 667* *Drawing Conclusions, TWE p. 668*	List, SE p. 666	*Keywords, TWE p. 665*	

Key: Student material is in roman. Teacher material is in italic. 🖳 Technology   **Collaboration**

Grammar and Language	Listening, Speaking, and Viewing	Life Skills	Study, Research, and Technology
Four Kinds of Sentences, TWE p. 625	**COLLAB. LEARN.** Literature Groups, SE p. 627 Interview, SE p. 627	*Using a Map, TWE p. 624*	🖥 Internet Connection, SE p. 627
Verbals, TWE p. 629	**COLLAB. LEARN.** Literature Groups, SE p. 632 Oral Interpretation of a Poem, SE p. 633 *Sports Actions, TWE p. 630*	🖥 Using the Internet, SE, p. 632 Learning for Life: Sportscasting, SE p. 632	🖥 Research African American Athletes, SE p. 632
	COLLAB. LEARN. Literature Groups, SE p. 640 Monologue, SE p. 640 *Group Presentation, TWE p. 637*	*Using Magazine Articles, TWE p. 634*	Research Sports Statistics, SE p. 640 🖥 *Internet Connection, TWE pp. 634, 638* *Skimming, TWE p. 638*
Subject Complements, TWE p. 644	**COLLAB. LEARN.** Literature Groups, SE p. 647 Present Songs, SE p. 647	Learning for Life: Career Choices, SE p. 647 *Establishing Criteria, TWE p. 643*	*Research Songs, TWE p. 647*
Nouns Used as Adjectives, TWE p. 650	**COLLAB. LEARN.** Literature Groups, SE p. 653 Explain and Demonstrate a Home Art or Craft, SE p. 653	Learning for Life: Quilt, SE p. 653 *Decision Making, TWE p. 649*	*Using a Map, TWE p. 651* *Researching Migrant Workers, TWE p. 651*
	COLLAB. LEARN. Literature Groups, SE p. 659 Interviews, SE p. 659		Develop a Chart or Map, SE p. 659 🖥 *Using a Videotape, TWE p. 656*
Verb Tense, TWE p. 661	**COLLAB. LEARN.** Literature Groups, SE p. 664 Dramatic Reading or Enactment, SE p. 664 *Summarize Myths, TWE p. 662*	Using the Internet, SE p. 664	🖥 Internet Connection, SE p. 664 Researching Yaqui Culture, SE p. 664
	Perform Songs, TWE p. 668		🖥 *Internet Connection, TWE p. 665*

SELECTIONS	📁 Print Resources		
Afro-American Fragment — LANGSTON HUGHES *Heaven* — CATHY SONG	Unit Three Planning Guide, pp. 48–53 * Active Reading Guide, p. 55	Grammar & Comp. Handbook, Lesson 4.6 Grammar and Language Workbook, p. 119	* Quick Checks, p. 55 Selection and Theme Assessment, pp. 105–106 Performance Assessment, p. 54 Spanish Summaries, p. 55
The Base Stealer — ROBERT FRANCIS *To Satch* — SAMUEL ALLEN	Unit Three Planning Guide, pp. 54–59 * Active Reading Guide, p. 56	Grammar & Comp. Handbook, Lesson 3.3 Grammar and Language Workbook, pp. 93–98	* Quick Checks, p. 56 Selection and Theme Assessment, pp. 107–108 Performance Assessment, p. 55 Spanish Summaries, p. 56 Spanish Translations
Ex-Basketball Player — JOHN UPDIKE *Miss Rosie* — LUCILLE CLIFTON	Unit Three Planning Guide, pp. 60–65 * Active Reading Guide, p. 57	Reading Workbook, pp. 63–64	* Quick Checks, p. 57 Selection and Theme Assessment, pp. 109–110 Performance Assessment, p. 56 Spanish Summaries, p. 57
The Road Not Taken — ROBERT FROST *We Are Many* — PABLO NERUDA	Unit Three Planning Guide, pp. 66–71 * Active Reading Guide, p. 58	Grammar & Comp. Handbook, Lesson 2.5 Grammar and Language Workbook, p. 85 Reading Workbook, pp. 65–66	* Quick Checks, p. 58 Selection and Theme Assessment, pp. 111–112 Performance Assessment, p. 57 Spanish Summaries, p. 58 Spanish Translations
The Floral Apron — MARILYN CHIN *My Mother Pieced Quilts* — TERESA PALOMO ACOSTA	Unit Three Planning Guide, pp. 72–77 * Active Reading Guide, p. 59	Grammar & Comp. Handbook, Lesson 1.4 Grammar and Language Workbook, p. 61	* Quick Checks, p. 59 Selection and Theme Assessment, pp. 113–114 Performance Assessment, p. 58 Spanish Summaries, p. 59 Spanish Translations
A Bus Along St. Clair: December — MARGARET ATWOOD *Freeway 280* — LORNA DEE CERVANTES	Unit Three Planning Guide, pp. 78–82 * Active Reading Guide, p. 60		* Quick Checks, p. 60 Selection and Theme Assessment, pp. 115–116 Performance Assessment, p. 59 Spanish Summaries, p. 60 Spanish Translations
MAKING A FIST — NAOMI SHIHAB NYE *WHAT WE BELIEVE* — ANITA ENDREZZE	Unit Three Planning Guide, pp. 83–88 * Active Reading Guide, p. 61	Grammar & Comp. Handbook, Lessons 5.3–5.4 Grammar and Language Workbook, pp. 145–150	* Quick Checks, p. 61 Selection and Theme Assessment, pp. 117–118 Performance Assessment, p. 60 Spanish Summaries, p. 61
Foreign Ways — DIANA CHANG *Song for My Name* — LINDA HOGAN	Unit Three Planning Guide, pp. 89–93 * Active Reading Guide, p. 62		* Quick Checks, p. 62 Selection and Theme Assessment, pp. 119–120 Performance Assessment, p. 61 Spanish Summaries, p. 62

*Also available in Spanish

🖥 **Transparencies**	**Technology Resources**
Selection Focus Transparency 55 Grammar and Language Transparency 49 Literary Elements Transparency 55	🎧 💿 Audio Library 🎧 💿 Spanish Audio Library 💾 💿 Vocabulary Puzzlemaker 🖥 Web Site: lit.glencoe.com
Selection Focus Transparency 56 Grammar and Language Transparency 50 Literary Elements Transparency 56 Fine Art Transparency 21	🎧 💿 Audio Library 🎧 💿 Spanish Audio Library 💾 💿 Vocabulary Puzzlemaker 🖥 Web Site: lit.glencoe.com
Selection Focus Transparency 57 Literary Elements Transparency 57	🎧 💿 Audio Library 🎧 💿 Spanish Audio Library 💾 💿 Vocabulary Puzzlemaker 🖥 Web Site: lit.glencoe.com
Selection Focus Transparency 58 Grammar and Language Transparency 51 Literary Elements Transparency 58	💿 Literature Launchers Videodisc 🎧 💿 Audio Library 🎧 💿 Spanish Audio Library 💾 💿 Vocabulary Puzzlemaker 🖥 Web Site: lit.glencoe.com
Selection Focus Transparency 59 Grammar and Language Transparency 52 Literary Elements Transparency 59	🎧 💿 Audio Library 🎧 💿 Spanish Audio Library 💾 💿 Vocabulary Puzzlemaker 🖥 Web Site: lit.glencoe.com
Selection Focus Transparency 60 Literary Elements Transparency 60 Fine Art Transparency 29	💿 Literature Launchers Videodisc 🎧 💿 Audio Library 🎧 💿 Spanish Audio Library 💾 💿 Vocabulary Puzzlemaker 🖥 Web Site: lit.glencoe.com
Selection Focus Transparency 61 Grammar and Language Transparency 53 Literary Elements Transparency 61	🎧 💿 Audio Library 🎧 💿 Spanish Audio Library 💾 💿 Vocabulary Puzzlemaker 🖥 Web Site: lit.glencoe.com
Selection Focus Transparency 62 Literary Elements Transparency 62	🎧 💿 Audio Library 🎧 💿 Spanish Audio Library 💾 💿 Vocabulary Puzzlemaker 🖥 Web Site: lit.glencoe.com

📁 *Theme* **RESOURCES**

- Listening and Speaking Activities (pp. 15–16)
- Viewing and Representing Activities (pp. 21–22)
- Critical Thinking Skills (pp. 21–23)
- Media Connections Activities (pp. 15–17)
- Interdisciplinary Activities (pp. 16–17)

See also these additional planning resources:
- English Language Learners Sourcebook
- Inclusion Strategies Sourcebook
- Literature Groups Sourcebook

Use Glencoe's *Presentation Plus!* This multimedia teaching tool lets you present dynamic lessons that will engage your students. Using Microsoft PowerPoint,® you can customize the presentations to create your own personalized lessons.

Objectives

- To read and analyze poems about how identity is tied to a place of origin
- To identify and analyze elements of free verse
- To write an analysis of diction

Skills

Reading/Thinking: Inferring; Activating Prior Knowledge
Writing: Journal Entry
Grammar/Language: Four Kinds of Sentences
Listening/Speaking: Interview
Collaboration: Literature Groups

Motivating
→ OPTIONS

Selection Focus Transparency 55: Have students study the picture and discuss what they know about their ancestors.

Focus Activity: Have students list and compare the nationalities represented by their family trees.

Before You Read

Afro-American Fragment and Heaven

FOCUS ACTIVITY

Why do you think so many people are interested in their cultural heritage, or their family's history, customs, beliefs, and values?

LIST IDEAS Make a list of reasons you might have for studying your cultural heritage.

SETTING A PURPOSE Read to learn how the speakers are influenced by their cultural heritage.

BACKGROUND

Did You Know?

- After visiting Africa, Langston Hughes realized that his primary cultural influences were not African but African American: "I . . . loved the surface of Africa and the rhythms of Africa—but I was not Africa," said Hughes. "I was Chicago and Kansas City and Broadway and Harlem." Indeed, Hughes was an important figure in the Harlem Renaissance—the intellectual and artistic movement that African Americans created in the New York City neighborhood of Harlem during the 1920s.

- The discovery of gold in California in 1848 sparked a worldwide "gold rush" of fortune seekers. Driven by poverty at home, thousands of Chinese men migrated to California, hoping to return home rich. By the 1860s, however, much of California's gold was gone, and many immigrants turned to railroad work for money. Enduring arduous, sometimes deadly working conditions, at one point as many as 12,000 Chinese worked for the Central Pacific Railroad, helping to complete the first transcontinental railway.

Building the Union Pacific, Wyoming, 1868.

Meet Langston Hughes

Langston Hughes won "instant" fame in 1925 when poet Vachel Lindsay dined at the hotel where Hughes was working. Hughes left three of his poems next to Lindsay's plate; Lindsay liked the poems, and when Hughes arrived at work the next day, reporters were waiting to interview the "bus boy poet."

Langston Hughes was born in Joplin, Missouri, in 1902 and died in 1967.

Meet Cathy Song

Cathy Song prefers to be classified not as an Asian American writer, but as simply a writer. Song often writes about women's experiences and family relationships. One of her best-known poems, "Picture Bride," describes her Korean grandmother coming to the United States at twenty-three as a mail-order bride. Song now teaches writing and has published three books of poetry.

Cathy Song was born in 1955 in Honolulu, Hawaii.

RESOURCE MANAGER

Lesson Planning Resource
The *Unit Three Planning Guide* (pp. 48–53) provides additional lesson notes and reduced versions of all print resources.

📁 **Other Print Resources**
- Active Reading Guide, p. 55
- Reading Workbook
- Grammar and Language Workbook, p. 119
- Grammar and Composition Handbook, Lesson 4.6
- Quick Checks, p. 55

- Selection and Theme Assessment, pp. 105–106
- Performance Assessment, p. 54
- Spanish Summaries, p. 55
- Inclusion Strategies
- English Language Learners Sourcebook

 Transparencies
- Selection Focus 55
- Literary Elements 55
- Grammar and Language 49

Technology
🎧 Audio Library
🎧 Spanish Audio Library
💻 Glencoe Literature Web Site
💾 Testmaker

Afro-American Fragment

Langston Hughes

A
So long,
So far away
Is Africa.
Not even memories alive
5 Save those that history books create,
Save those that songs
Beat back into the blood—
B
Beat out of blood with words sad-sung
In strange un-Negro tongue—
10 So long,
So far away
Is Africa.

Subdued° and time-lost
Are the drums—and yet
15 Through some vast mist of race
There comes this song
I do not understand,
This song of atavistic° land,
Of bitter yearnings lost
20 Without a place—
So long,
So far away
Is Africa's
Dark face.

---

13 Here, *subdued* means "toned down; softened."
18 In this context, *atavistic* means "showing ancestral characteristics that have reappeared after being absent for many generations."

A Literary Elements

FORM: *Free Verse* Have students note the lines' lengths and read them silently. Remind them that free verse avoids set line lengths, stanzas, and meter. What effects does this form create? *(It frees readers from traditional expectations and helps them think like the speaker.)*

Additional Resources
📁 *Active Reading Guide*, p. 55
🎧 *Audio Library*
🎧 *Spanish Audio Library*

B Critical Thinking

INFERRING Help students infer the meaning behind the sad songs described in these lines using what they know about the speaker. The following model illustrates the thinking process involved in inferring.

Model: From the title, I know that the speaker is African American and descended from slaves. I know that slaves were forced to labor for foreign masters. They probably sang songs from their homeland as they worked. Their voices would express their sadness; over time, they would adapt the songs to their new language. The African words would seem strange.

Teaching Options

Reading *Minilesson*

Activating Prior Knowledge Give students the article title "Yellowstone Renewal" and the thesis statement "Ten years later, fire-ravaged forests of the park have come back, and the healing is dramatic." Discuss prior knowledge of the national park to demonstrate prereading processes that aid comprehension.

Activity Have students study the visual, title, and lines 1–3 on page 623 to decide the subject of the poem and then list what they already know about Africa, African American history, and slavery in the United States. Ask students what their knowledge leads them to expect or ask as they read the poem. **L2**

Additional Resources
📁 *Reading Workbook*

Heaven

Cathy Song ~

He thinks when we die we'll go to China.
Think of it—a Chinese heaven
where, except for his blond hair,
the part that belongs to his father,
5 everyone will look like him.
China, that blue flower on the map,
bluer than the sea
his hand must span like a bridge
to reach it.
10 An octave° away.

I've never seen it.
It's as if I can't sing that far.
But look—
on the map, this black dot.
15 Here is where we live,
on the pancake plains
just east of the Rockies,
on the other side of the clouds.
A mile above the sea,
20 the air is so thin, you can starve on it.
No bamboo trees
but the alpine equivalent,
reedy aspen with light, fluttering leaves.
Did a boy in Guangzhou° dream of this
25 as his last stop?

---

10 In music, an *octave* (ok' tiv) refers to eight notes in a scale. On a piano keyboard, an octave is any group of eight white keys in a row, a distance of seven to eight inches.
24 Formerly called Canton, *Guangzhou* (gwàng' jō') is a large city in southern China.

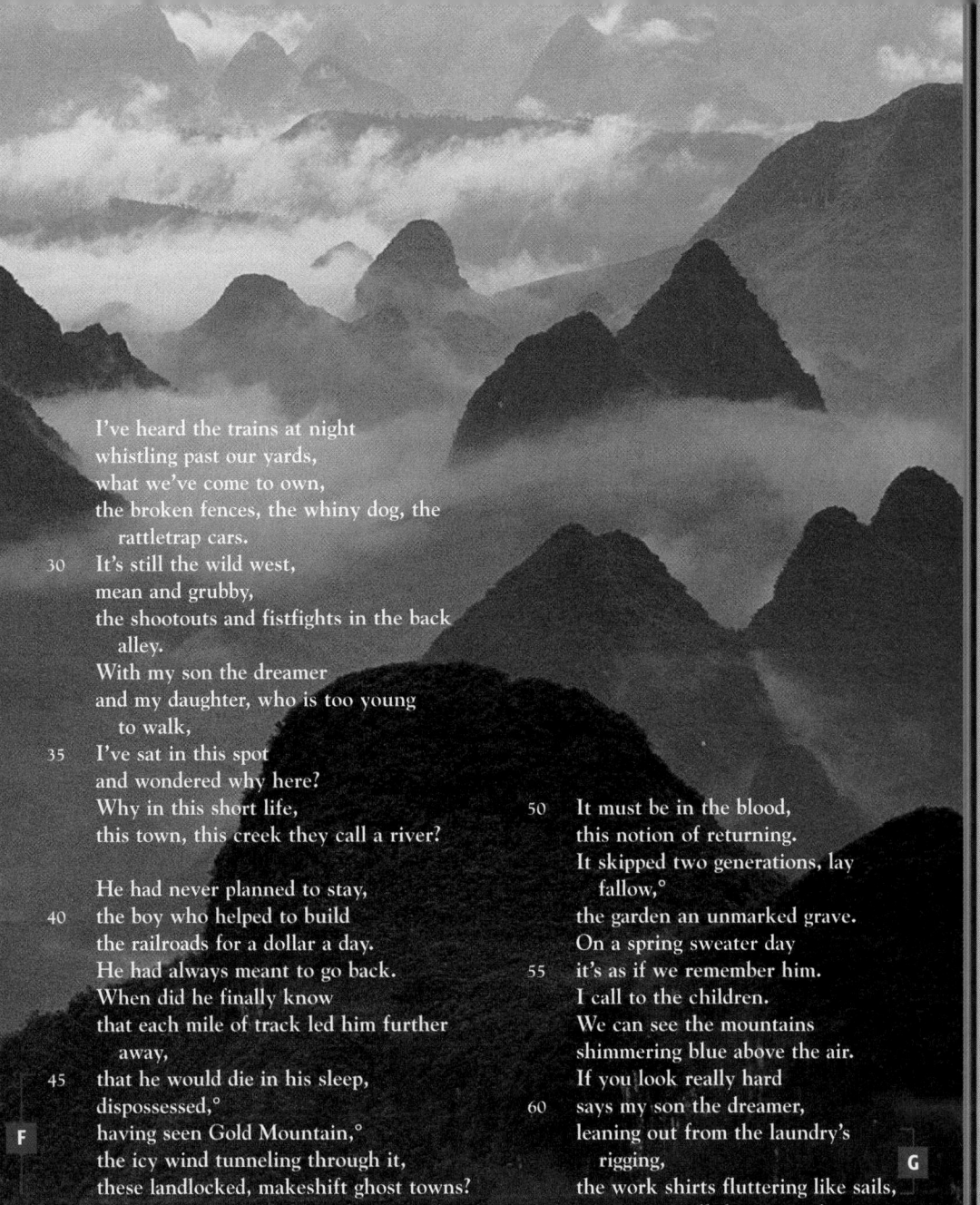

I've heard the trains at night
whistling past our yards,
what we've come to own,
the broken fences, the whiny dog, the
 rattletrap cars.
30 It's still the wild west,
mean and grubby,
the shootouts and fistfights in the back
 alley.
With my son the dreamer
and my daughter, who is too young
 to walk,
35 I've sat in this spot
and wondered why here?
Why in this short life,
this town, this creek they call a river?

He had never planned to stay,
40 the boy who helped to build
the railroads for a dollar a day.
He had always meant to go back.
When did he finally know
that each mile of track led him further
 away,
45 that he would die in his sleep,
dispossessed,°
having seen Gold Mountain,°
the icy wind tunneling through it,
these landlocked, makeshift ghost towns?

50 It must be in the blood,
this notion of returning.
It skipped two generations, lay
 fallow,°
the garden an unmarked grave.
On a spring sweater day
55 it's as if we remember him.
I call to the children.
We can see the mountains
shimmering blue above the air.
If you look really hard
60 says my son the dreamer,
leaning out from the laundry's
 rigging,
the work shirts fluttering like sails,
you can see all the way to heaven.

---
46 *Dispossessed* means "deprived of possessions or homes."
47 Enthralled by tales of California's gold, the Chinese began
 referring to California, and the United States more generally,
 as *Gam Saan*, or Gold Mountain.

---
52 *Fallow* land has been left unplanted or unfarmed for at least
 one growing season.

POETRY 💰 625

F Literary Elements

IMAGERY and TONE Point out details that create the desolate mood of someone who is *dispossessed*. Have students describe the feelings associated with "icy wind" and "landlocked, makeshift ghost towns."

G Literary Elements

FIGURES OF SPEECH: *Metaphor* Have students explain what is compared in lines 61–62 and why the comparison is effective. (*The laundry is like the sails of a ship; the boy is like a sailor looking for land. It suits his longing to go to China and recalls the ancestor who sailed to America.*)

Thematic Focus

Issues of Identity Discuss why the speaker in each poem lacks a firm sense of identity.

✓ ASSESSMENT OPTIONS

📁 *Quick Checks,* p. 55

Grammar and Language *Minilesson*

Four Kinds of Sentences Review the four kinds of sentences, using a table like the following:

Type	Job	End Mark
Declarative	makes statement	period (.)
Imperative	commands	period (.)
Interrogative	asks question	question mark (?)
Exclamatory	expresses emotion	exclamation point (!)

Have students locate examples of the first three of these kinds in "Heaven."

Activity Have pairs of students write two examples of each type of sentence in a dialogue between the mother and her son. (*Sentences and dialogues will vary.*) **L1**

Additional Resources

✍ *Grammar and Language Transparency 49*

📘 *Grammar and Language Workbook,* p. 119

📘 *Grammar and Composition Handbook,* Lesson 4.6

📘 *Writer's Choice,* Lesson 13.6

625

Personal Response

Students may wonder how knowing more about his African ancestry would alter his own identity. They might ask Song what details she recalls about the "boy in Guangzhou."

ANALYZING LITERATURE

1. His ancestors came from Africa. He feels only a slight connection and wishes it were stronger.
2. He is thinking of African songs his forbears sang, adapted by slaves to the rhythms of their work.
3. The song is the collective feeling of his people that binds them to Africa and symbolizes his blood connection to it.
4. "So long,/So far away/Is Africa" is repeated three times, emphasizing the physical and emotional distance of the speaker. Rhymes *(sung-tongue, race-place-face)* add a musical effect appropriate to the poem's "songs."
5. His identity is not whole because he lacks a strong bond to his homeland.
6. Some students may cite vacation places or relatives' homes.
7. Her son, who is part Chinese and part Caucasian, longs to go to China.
8. Home is just east of the Rocky Mountains in the Plains. She both loves and hates it, for it is where her family history lies yet is also the place that disappointed and rejected her people.
9. He is the speaker's ancestor, who emigrated from China to find gold but instead became a laborer for the railroad. She shows compassion for his suffering and disappointment.
10. The boy feels he will be accepted and belong in China. To him it is a perfect place, perhaps because of family stories and a tone of longing that have been passed down through generations. She identifies her son with the ancestor—both dreamers—and seems both proud and protective.
11. Students' answers will vary with their experiences. The places they mention may well be imaginary.
12. Students may point out how one can feel closer to someone who shares such intimacy by "just talking."

Responding to Literature

Personal Response

What questions would you like to ask each poet? Why?

ANALYZING LITERATURE

Afro-American Fragment

RECALL AND INTERPRET

1. What is the speaker's relationship to Africa? How do you think the speaker feels about that relationship? Cite details from the poem.
2. In the first stanza, to what songs do you think the speaker is referring? Explain what you think the speaker is talking about in lines 6–9.
3. What is the "song" the speaker refers to in the second stanza? What does this "song" seem to **symbolize**, or stand for? Explain.

EVALUATE AND CONNECT

4. Evaluate how **repetition** and **rhyme** help to convey the poem's meaning and message. (See Literary Terms Handbook, page R10.)
5. Theme Connections   What does the poem's title seem to imply about the speaker's sense of identity?
6. What place or places have helped shape your own sense of identity? Explain.

Heaven

RECALL AND INTERPRET

7. Who is the boy the speaker describes in the first stanza? What is his dream?
8. Where does the speaker live? What seems to be her attitude toward this place? Explain.
9. Who is the "boy" introduced in line 24? What did he do, and what happened to him? What does the speaker's description of him imply about her feelings toward him?
10. What does China seem to represent to the speaker's son? According to the speaker, why does her son have this attitude toward China? How do you think the speaker feels about his attitude?

EVALUATE AND CONNECT

11. What place do you think about or dream of visiting like the speaker's son thinks about China? Explain.
12. What is your reaction to the conversational tone of this poem? How does it affect your attitude toward the speaker and the message of the poem?

LITERATURE & HUMANITIES

Have students examine the picture *Singing Their Songs*, available from the National Museum of Women in the Arts.

Discuss how the picture suggests a relationship between Africans and African Americans. Then discuss the kinds of cross-cultural connections and influences Huges makes in his poem.

Literary ELEMENTS

Free Verse

Free verse is poetry that has no fixed meter—that is, it does not have a regular pattern of stressed and unstressed syllables. Most free verse has irregular line lengths and lacks a regular rhyme scheme. For example, these lines from "Heaven" are written in free verse: "It's still the wild west, / mean and grubby, / the shootouts and fistfights in the back alley." Many poets of the 1900s have chosen to explore the looser, more subtle effects of free verse.

1. Why might Song have chosen to write "Heaven" in free verse? Do you think it is an effective form for the ideas and emotions she expresses? Why or why not?
2. Is "Afro-American Fragment" written in free verse? How do you know? Do you think the chosen style matches the poem's subject matter? Explain.

● See **Literary Terms Handbook,** p. R5.

LITERARY ELEMENTS

1. She intends for it to imitate conversation between people who are close. Strict meter and rhyme would make the poem too formal.
2. Long and short lines of varying rhythm and intermittent use of rhyme reveal the free verse leanings of the poem. The form is suited to the subject (how the "song" of ancestry is fragmented).

Additional Resources

Literary Elements Transparency 55

LITERATURE AND WRITING

Writing About Literature

Analyze Diction   Because poetry is a concentrated form of writing, poets choose words carefully to get the most meaning from each word. Write two or three paragraphs analyzing the word choice, or **diction,** in "Afro-American Fragment" or "Heaven." What words and phrases are especially effective in conveying the poet's intended meaning? Explain how the poet's choice of words affects your understanding and appreciation of the poem.

Personal Writing

Home Sweet Home   What might it be like to live in a different country? What would you miss most about your current life? What would you miss least? What difficulties might you face in adjusting to life in another culture? As you record your ideas about this topic in your journal, consider how the culture in which you grew up has helped to shape your own identity.

EXTENDING YOUR RESPONSE

Literature Groups

Past and Present   In your group, identify the ways the speakers in each poem, as well as the son and grandfather in "Heaven," seem to feel about their family history and cultural heritage. Then, using information from your discussion and the ideas you listed for the Focus Activity on page 622, debate this question: Is it important for people to appreciate and preserve their cultural heritage? Why or why not? As a group, decide which side has the stronger argument, and then share your ideas with other groups.

Listening and Speaking

Cultural Traditions   Interview an older family member or a family friend to learn about cultural traditions that have been preserved over the years. Ask the person to explain the significance and importance of each tradition. Share what you have learned with the class.

Internet Connection

Virtual Visits   One way to learn about other cultures is to "visit" them on the Internet. Choose a culture that interests you and use a search engine to locate Web sites about it. Share your findings with the class.

📁 **Save your work for your portfolio.**

LITERATURE AND WRITING

Writing About Literature

Students' analyses of diction should
- describe the effects of specific words on meaning.
- consider connotations of words.
- summarize the overall diction of the poem and relate it to theme.

Personal Writing

Students' journal entries should
- convey personal reactions and feelings.
- list specific aspects of culture and evaluate them.

EXTENDING YOUR RESPONSE

Literature Groups   Suggest that groups list reasons cited by both sides of the debate side by side before deciding which argument is stronger.
COLLAB. LEARN.

Listening and Speaking   Have students write out five open-ended questions for their interviews.

Internet Connection   To find information about specific cultures, students might try key words such as, for example, *Ukrainian culture, Irish customs,* or *Cherokee history.*

✔ ASSESSMENT OPTIONS

📁 *Quick Checks,* p. 55
📁 *Selection and Theme Assessment,* pp. 105–106
📁 *Performance Assessment,* p. 54
💾 *Testmaker*

Objectives

- To read and analyze poems about skilled, confident baseball players
- To identify, analyze, and create hyperboles
- To write an analysis of stanzaic form in two poems

Skills

Writing: Letter
Grammar/Language: Verbals
Listening/Speaking: Sportscast
Life Skills: Planning and Designing
Collaboration: Literature Groups

Motivating
→OPTIONS

Selection Focus Transparency 56: After students view the photograph, lead them in a discussion of the personal and physical qualities of athletes.

Focus Activity: Have students tally and compare the areas (e.g., sports, speaking, singing) in which they have self-confidence.

Before You Read

The Base Stealer and To Satch

FOCUS ACTIVITY

Think about a time when you felt full of energy and confidence.

FREEWRITE Spend about three minutes freewriting about that time. What were the circumstances? What did you accomplish?

SETTING A PURPOSE Read to learn about two athletes who display great energy and confidence.

BACKGROUND

Did You Know?

- In baseball, base stealing is a battle of wits between pitcher and base runner. The base runner's goal is to advance to the next base or to so rattle the pitcher that he or she makes a mistake. The pitcher's goal is to stop the runner.

  The runner takes a leadoff, or stands a few feet from the base ready to steal. Timing and a quick eye are crucial. The pitcher might throw to the batter or to the base to "pick off" the runner. The runner is thus pulled in both directions— forward to the next base and back to the base he or she is straying from.

- Leroy "Satchel" Paige, also known as "Satch," was a Baseball Hall of Famer whose legendary pitching career lasted almost thirty years. Although Paige began pitching in the Negro leagues in the 1920s, his major-league career did not begin until 1948, a year after Jackie Robinson became the first African American player in modern major-league baseball. Paige, who stood over six feet three inches tall, had long, lean legs and was known for kicking out his left leg to an almost impossible height during his windup, a move he referred to as "blacking out the sky." The title of his autobiography, *Maybe I'll Pitch Forever,* refers to the extraordinary length of his career.

- Although Samuel Allen never got to see Paige pitch, he met him one day after a sporting event in Washington, D.C. Allen introduced himself and handed Paige his poem "To Satch." Paige read it and said, "I'm mighty glad you stopped me."

628 ❧ UNIT 3

Meet Robert Francis

Robert Francis had a love-hate relationship with poetry. "I do not like poetry. I dislike it. Much of it I detest," he wrote in his autobiography. Despite these sentiments, Francis devoted most of his life to writing poetry. He published more than a dozen books and taught at writing workshops across the country.

Robert Francis was born in Upland, Pennsylvania, in 1901 and died in 1987.

Meet Samuel Allen

Samuel Allen advises young writers to "find meaning in [your] surroundings and in the events that are part of [your] life." He adds, "No matter how humdrum one's life may be, there is meaning and poetry if one has the sight to see it." He still writes today, but laughingly confesses that "the muse doesn't visit as often as she used to."

Samuel Allen was born in Columbus, Ohio, in 1917.

RESOURCE MANAGER

Lesson Planning Resource
The *Unit Three Planning Guide* (pp. 54–59) provides additional lesson notes and reduced versions of all print resources.

📁 **Other Print Resources**
- Active Reading Guide, p. 56
- Grammar and Language Workbook, pp. 93–98
- Grammar and Composition Handbook, Lesson 3.3
- Quick Checks, p. 56
- Selection and Theme

Assessment, pp. 107–108
- Performance Assessment, p. 55
- Spanish Summaries, p. 56
- Spanish Translations
- Inclusion Strategies
- English Language Learners Sourcebook

 Transparencies
- Selection Focus 56
- Fine Art 21
- Literary Elements 56
- Grammar and Language 50

Technology
🎧 Audio Library
🎧 Spanish Audio Library
💻 Glencoe Literature Web Site
💾 Testmaker

The Base Stealer

Robert Francis

Poised between going on and back, pulled
Both ways taut like a tightrope-walker,
Fingertips pointing the opposites,
Now bouncing tiptoe like a dropped ball
5 Or a kid skipping rope, come on, come on,
Running a scattering of steps sidewise,
How he teeters, skitters, tingles, teases,
Taunts° them, hovers like an ecstatic bird,
He's only flirting, crowd him, crowd him,
10 Delicate, delicate, delicate, delicate—now!

---

8 To *taunt* is to challenge in a scornful, insulting way.

POETRY   629

Reading the Selection

A Literary Elements

FIGURES OF SPEECH: Simile Ask students to evaluate the effectiveness of the comparison. How are the ball player and the tightrope-walker alike? *(Both extend the arms for balance and remain alert and poised; the danger zone for both lies in the no-man's land between.)*

Additional Resources
- *Active Reading Guide,* p. 56
- *Audio Library*
- *Spanish Audio Library*

B Literary Elements

TONE Invite students to explain who they think is speaking and in what tone he or she says "come on, come on." *(The speaker could be an announcer or a fan fully engaged in the action; the tone would be urgent, like someone trying to advance the action with his voice.)*

C Active Reading

VISUALIZE Ask students to describe or demonstrate the action as these verbs make them see it. Point out the sound values of the words. What is their effect? *(The t and s sounds are intricate and abrupt like the movements they describe.)*

Teaching Options

Grammar and Language *Minilesson*

Verbals Explain that a verbal is a verb form that functions in a sentence as a noun or modifier. A verbal can be imbedded in a phrase that acts as one part of speech.

Write the following on the board:

Verbal	Acts as	Example
Participle	adj.	<u>Elated</u> fans cheered loudly.
Gerund	n.	<u>Playing</u> the game is fun.
Infinitive	n., adj., adv.	The object is <u>to win</u> fairly.

Have students explain the function of each underlined verbal.

Activity Have students locate verbals and verbal phrases in "The Base Stealer" and write sentences using each kind. **L2**

Additional Resources
- *Grammar and Language Transparency 50*
- *Grammar and Language Workbook,* pp. 93–98
- *Grammar and Composition Handbook,* Lesson 3.3
- *Writer's Choice,* Lesson 12.3

To Satch

Samuel Allen :~

D
Sometimes I feel like I will *never* stop
Just go on forever
Till one fine mornin
E I'm gonna reach up and grab me a handfulla stars
Swing out my long lean leg
And whip three hot strikes burnin down the heavens
And look over at God and say
How about that!

Responding to Literature

Personal Response

Which of the two players from the poems do you admire more? Why?

——— ANALYZING LITERATURE ———

The Base Stealer

RECALL AND INTERPRET

1. Identify several **similes** in the poem. (See Literary Terms Handbook, page R11.) What two things are being compared in each simile? What sense do these comparisons give you about the act of base stealing?
2. How would you explain the action described in lines 6–9 in your own words?
3. What do you think the speaker is describing in the last two lines of the poem? How do you know?

EVALUATE AND CONNECT

4. How does the use of **repetition** affect the **tone,** or atmosphere, of the poem? Give several examples.
5. Why do you think the poet chose not to reveal the outcome of the action?
6. Some people think base stealing is the most exciting part of a baseball game. What aspect of your favorite sport do you find most exciting? How does that compare with the description in this poem?

To Satch

RECALL AND INTERPRET

7. What do you think the speaker is referring to in lines 1–2? How would you describe the speaker based on these two lines?
8. What does the speaker plan to do "one fine mornin"? What might you infer about the speaker's outlook on life from this description?
9. What do you think the poet's attitude is toward the speaker? Explain.

EVALUATE AND CONNECT

10. How does the Background information on page 628 help you better understand this poem?
11. Evaluate how the use of **imagery** adds to your understanding and appreciation of the poem. (See Literary Terms Handbook, page R6.)
12. Many fans admired Satchel Paige. Think of an athlete whom you admire. What do you admire most about this person?

FINE ART
TRANSPARENCY 21

You may want to use Fine Art Transparency 21 to discuss aspects of baseball that connect to the poems.

12. Athletes named will vary. Students may admire both their talent and their attitudes or ethics.

Responding to the Selection

Personal Response

"To Satch" focuses on the hero and his great skill, and many students will like the humor and presence of Satch as speaker.

ANALYZING LITERATURE

1. The base stealer is compared to a tightrope walker, a dropped ball, a kid skipping rope, and a bird. These emphasize motion, balance, and energy.
2. Unsure which way he will go, the player runs sidewise, keeping an eye on the pitcher and the ball. He moves farther away from the base, changing the odds that the fielding team can get him out.
3. He advises the men on base to force the runner to commit to run by letting him get too far off his base to get back to it, then throwing the ball from base to base to get him out.
4. The repetition adds tension and excitement and suggests the timing and recurrence of the player's movements.
5. He focuses on the intricate dance and the tension it creates as a way of writing a more interesting poem.
6. Students' answers should describe the action briefly and explain how it is similar to or different from the poem's action.
7. He expresses delight in his work and his boundless energy. He takes great joy in baseball and is proud of his skill.
8. He will pitch stars through the heavens. Far from wanting to retire, he wants to continue even after death. Confident of afterlife, he looks at it as even better than his earthly career.
9. He seems to like and admire him. The speaker's entertaining, confident tone suggests that the poet is amused at and proud of the speaker's vitality.
10. It tells about Paige's amazing longevity in the sport and the racism he battled. Given this context, Paige's humor and positive attitude seem more admirable.
11. Images place Paige on stage in the vast reaches of the universe, which cannot dwarf his greatness.

LITERARY ELEMENTS

1. Hurling strikes "down the heavens" and saying to God "How about that!" are exaggerations that show Paige's confidence in his skill and in a God who shares his love for baseball. They suggest that Paige's talent gives him immortality.
2. The comparisons point out valid likenesses in movement and balance. Use of *like* also shows the poet wants readers to focus on the runner's real physical gifts. In this sense, there is no hyperbole in the poem.
3. Encourage students to imitate the exaggeration in tall tales they remember.

Additional Resources

Literary Elements Transparency 56

LITERATURE AND WRITING

Writing About Literature

Students' evaluations of form should
- describe the effect of a single-stanza format.
- discuss each poem's subject, tone, and/or theme as a reason for format.

Creative Writing

Students' letters should
- use correct format for a friendly letter.
- give accurate information about the recipient's accomplishments.
- establish an admiring tone.

EXTENDING YOUR RESPONSE

Literature Groups
Encourage groups to draft poems. You may want to suggest that they use one of the selection poems as a model.
COLLAB. LEARN.

Interdisciplinary Activity
Encourage students to research changes in American society that paralleled the achievements of these athletes.

Literary ELEMENTS

Hyperbole

Hyperbole is a figure of speech in which an obvious overstatement or exaggeration is made for either serious or comic effect. When the speaker in "To Satch" says, "I'm gonna reach up and grab me a handfulla stars," the reader knows he cannot really grab stars—yet the exaggeration conveys the speaker's high level of skill and exuberant love of pitching a baseball.

1. Find another example of hyperbole in Allen's poem, and describe its effect.
2. Is there hyperbole in "The Base Stealer"? Explain.
3. Write your own example of hyperbole in a line or two, and share it with a classmate.

⬤ See **Literary Terms Handbook**, p. R6.

LITERATURE AND WRITING

Writing About Literature

Evaluate Poetic Form Both poems were written as a single stanza. Why do you think the poets chose this form instead of breaking their poems into more than one stanza? What effect does the use of a single, uninterrupted stanza create in these poems? List your ideas, and then develop them in a paragraph or two.

Creative Writing

To ??? Review your answer to question 12 on page 631. Write a letter to this person or to someone else you admire, saying what you admire about him or her. In your letter, you might want to focus on the aspect of the person's accomplishments that you admire the most. If you wish, share your letter with the class.

EXTENDING YOUR RESPONSE

Literature Groups

Poetic Portrayal As a group, discuss the ways Francis and Allen portray the energy and confidence of the base stealer and Satch. Consider diction, punctuation, and such poetic devices as repetition, figurative language, and sound devices. Then look back at your responses to the Focus Activity on page 628, and choose one experience that most of the group can identify with. Discuss how you would create a poem similar to "The Base Stealer" or "To Satch" about that experience. Share either your ideas or your poem with the rest of the class.

Interdisciplinary Activity

Sports History: African American Athletes For many years, African American athletes such as Leroy "Satchel" Paige were excluded from participating at certain levels of professional sports. Use the library or the Internet to learn about the struggles and triumphs of such African

American athletes as boxer Joe Louis, track stars Jesse Owens and Wilma Rudolph, and baseball player Jackie Robinson. Share your findings.

Learning for Life

Sportscasting Imagine that you are a radio or television sportscaster covering the events described in the two poems. Write a brief description of each one for your sportscast and deliver it to the class.

Reading Further

You might also enjoy the poem "Touchdown" from *Every Round and Other Poems,* Allen's most recent volume of poetry, which also includes "To Satch."

📖 **Save your work for your portfolio.**

Learning for Life Have students discuss the jargon and style of sportscasters in groups before they begin writing.

✓ ASSESSMENT OPTIONS

- 📁 *Quick Checks,* p. 56
- 📁 *Selection and Theme Assessment,* pp. 107–108
- 📁 *Performance Assessment,* p. 55
- 💾 *Testmaker*

LISTENING, SPEAKING, and VIEWING

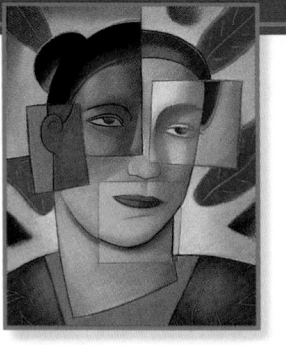

Oral Interpretation of a Poem

Have you ever heard poets recite their work, either in person or on recordings? If you have, you probably gained a deeper understanding and appreciation of the poems you heard. But anyone can prepare and deliver an oral presentation of a favorite poem, based on his or her own interpretation of the work.

Preparing Your Oral Interpretation

Follow these steps as you prepare your oral interpretation of a poem.

● As you read the poem silently, think about who the speaker might be. Whose "voice" do you hear? Does it belong to the poet, to an unidentified person, or to a character the poet has created? (In some poems, the speaker may be an animal or even a thing.) What is the speaker's tone, or attitude toward the subject of the poem? Think about how you might use your voice to convey that tone.

● Read through the poem again, this time focusing on your own reaction to it. What emotions do you experience as you read? What ideas and questions come to mind? Jot down your responses to the poem, and look up any unfamiliar words. Has the poet used imagery or figurative language? Make notes about how the poet's choice of language helps convey the intended meaning. Think about what words, phrases, or sentences you will emphasize in your oral interpretation.

● Notice how the poet has used rhyme, rhythm, and alliteration. How do these devices affect you? How do they affect the mood of the poem? Consider how you will emphasize sound devices as you recite or read the poem aloud.

● Remember to pause at the end of a line only if there is a punctuation mark or a natural pause there. Otherwise, read through the ends of lines, even rhyming lines, until you reach a proper place to pause.

● Practice reciting or reading the poem aloud. Experiment with your voice, using volume, speed, and other vocal devices to convey your own interpretation of the poem. Remember that your goal is to help the listener "hear" the poem as you do.

ACTIVITY

Prepare an oral interpretation of a poem that has captured your imagination. You might choose "The Base Stealer," "To Satch," or another poem you have read in this unit. Follow the suggestions given above as you practice reciting or reading the poem aloud. Then share your oral interpretation with a group. After everyone in your group has made his or her oral interpretation, discuss your understanding of each one.

POETRY ❧ 633

LISTENING, SPEAKING, and VIEWING

Objective

• To prepare and deliver an oral interpretation of a poem

Teaching Strategies

As students practice reading, have them use a tape recorder or camcorder to record their rehearsals. They can listen to the tape or watch the videotape to evaluate and adjust their interpretations. Depending upon the selection, students may wish to use a prop or elements of costume to add atmosphere.

Activity

Students' oral interpretations should

• use tone, rate, pauses, emphasis, and inflection effectively to create mood and communicate ideas.
• use posture, gesture, and eye contact effectively.
• reflect the character and attitude of the poem's speaker.

Teaching Options

Phrasing in Reciting a Poem The cadences of English may present problems for English language learners, whose native languages may have different rhythms and emphasis.

Activity Have students add unfamiliar words in the poem (with pronunciations and meanings) to their vocabulary notebooks. Then have them read the poem several times with a more proficient English speaker to (1) mark phrases to be spoken as a unit, (2) learn the meanings of the sense units and note their sound effects, and (3) practice oral presentation of each part.

Additional Resources

📁 *English Language Learners Sourcebook*

MEDIA Connection

Objective

- To read and understand a magazine article

Respond

1. He would probably say he is a family man and a hard worker who has been lucky enough to play a game he loves for money. Gossage is committed to family and ranch but feels his principal commitment now is to baseball.

2. Students' responses about future attitudes will depend on the level of commitment and the nature of the activity. Some, such as cheerleading or team sports, become irrelevant to most students after they finish school.

Additional Resources

📁 *Media Connections Activities,* p. 15

Teaching Options

MEDIA Connection

Magazine Article

Your current actions can affect your future life, but there will always be some things you can't control. In this article, an athlete contemplates the player strike that may end his long baseball career.

Making Hay

by Tom Verducci—*Sports Illustrated,* September 12, 1994

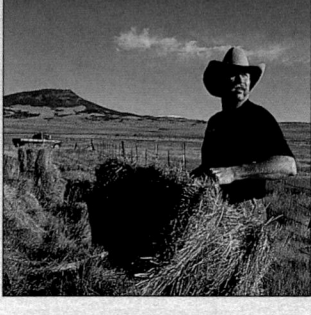

The bushes need trimming. The barn out back is in need of repair. The green '57 Chevy, the first car he ever called his own, stands like some beleaguered sentry over the backyard, awaiting a fresh coat of paint before it becomes his eldest son's car. The carpet must be cleaned (thanks to the puppy) and the hay over at the cattle ranch needs to be baled, and surely he cannot forget his promise to take the three boys fishing. There is much for Rich (Goose) Gossage to do, and goodness knows he has the time to get around to all of it.

There is no ball game tonight, and there might never be another one for Gossage, who, though seated on a chair in front of his Colorado Springs house, appears prepared should one, like a brushfire, break out.

"For me [playing baseball has] been like going to Disneyland and riding the best ride in the whole place and never getting off. That's what I wish people understood. We're players. There's nothing we'd rather be doing than playing baseball right now."

Gossage is housebound because of a player strike that is now in its fourth week, with no sign that it will end anytime soon.

Someday there will be baseball in major league cities again. There is no recovery, though, of a ballplayer's most precious commodity: time. It runs out especially quickly if you're a 43-year-old pitcher and four teams in the past five years have already decided you're finished.

Twenty-four years have passed since that day he ran home to the one-bedroom house on Beacon Street in Colorado Springs, flung open the door and announced, "Mom, I've got a job working as a counselor at the summer camp!" Mother Goose had replied, "Son, you've got another job. There's a man here from the Chicago White Sox, and he says they've drafted you in the ninth round." So overwhelmed was the boy that he ran off alone into the mountains and cried.

Gazing now upon the same range of mountains, he knows that it might all be over, this heart-racing ride of a major league career.

Respond

1. Based on this article, how do you think Gossage would describe himself? What appears to be the most important part of his life?

2. What interests are most important to you now? Do you think these interests will still be important to you in a few years? Why or why not?

Rich (Goose) Gossage Have students look for additional information about Gossage using keywords such as *Gossage, ESPN Sports Zone,* and *Yankees legends.*

Reading *Minilesson*

Identifying Main Ideas and Supporting Details Explain that, just as a poet uses figures of speech, sound devices, and images to reinforce meaning and enrich theme, the writer of an article uses details to support main ideas, enliven prose, and make subjects real. Anecdotes create empathy, quotes give play to the subject's voice, and vivid descriptions make main points memorable.

Activity Have students work in pairs to select a magazine article about a subject of interest. Have them locate and summarize the article's subject and topic, then identify examples of quotes, anecdotes, and descriptions. Ask pairs to explain the effect of these details. **L3**

Additional Resources

📁 *Reading Workbook*

Before You Read

Ex-Basketball Player and Miss Rosie

FOCUS ACTIVITY

Is it better to achieve greatness and then fall from glory, or never to be great at all?

CHART IT! List the pros and cons of both sides of this issue in a comparison chart like the one shown. Consider examples of once-great people you've known or heard about, such as actors, musicians, or athletes.

To achieve greatness, but fall from glory		To never be great at all	
Pros	Cons	Pros	Cons

SETTING A PURPOSE Read about two characters who have known glory.

BACKGROUND

Did You Know?

- In 1926 a premium brand of gasoline called Esso was first marketed in the United States. Today, Esso is known in the United States as Exxon; around the world, however, there are still Esso subsidiaries and service stations. At the time that Esso gasoline was common in the United States, packaged candies such as Necco Wafers, Nibs, and jujubes (jōō′ jōōbs′) (Juju Beads) were popular, and people drank *phosphates,* beverages made with carbonated water and fruit syrup, much like modern soft drinks.

- In addition to writing poetry, Lucille Clifton has written nearly twenty books for children: "Well, I had six kids in seven years, and when you have a lot of children, you tend to attract children, and you see so many kids, you get ideas from that. And I have such a good memory from my own childhood, my own time. I have great respect for young people; I like them enormously." Although Clifton often writes about the effects of poverty, unemployment, and lack of education in black communities, she says her books "celebrate life."

Meet John Updike

John Updike has been admired and criticized for writing about ordinary life and ordinary characters. He believes, however, ". . . either nobody is a hero or everyone is. I vote for everyone." Updike has written scores of novels, poems, short stories, and essays. Many of his novels have appeared on best-seller lists.

John Updike was born in Pennsylvania in 1932.

Meet Lucille Clifton

Lucille Clifton has said, "In the bigger scheme of things the universe is not asking us to *do* something, the universe is asking us to *be* something." True to her words, Clifton is many things: a writer, teacher, mother, and spokesperson for the African American family, especially young people and women.

Lucille Clifton was born in New York in 1936.

Before Reading

Objectives
- To read and analyze poems about people whose greatness is behind them
- To identify and analyze the tone of poems
- To write an analysis of the effects of the approaches the poets use in the poems

Skills
Reading/Thinking: Inferring
Writing: Journal Entry
Listening/Speaking: Monologue
Collaboration: Literature Groups

Motivating
→ OPTIONS

Selection Focus Transparency 57: Use the discussion of the futures of the subjects of the photographs as a way of encouraging students to speculate on their own futures.

Focus Activity: Have students use the data on their charts to write a paragraph supporting one side of the issue.

RESOURCE MANAGER

Lesson Planning Resource
The *Unit Three Planning Guide* (pp. 60–65) provides additional lesson notes and reduced versions of all print resources.

📁 **Other Print Resources**
- Active Reading Guide, p. 57
- Reading Workbook, pp. 63–64
- Quick Checks, p. 57
- Selection and Theme Assessment, pp. 109–110
- Performance Assessment, p. 56

- Spanish Summaries, p. 57
- Spanish Translations
- Inclusion Strategies
- English Language Learners Sourcebook

 Transparencies
- Selection Focus 57
- Literary Elements 57

Technology
🎧 Audio Library
🎧 Spanish Audio Library
💻 Glencoe Literature Web Site
💾 Testmaker

Ex-Basketball Player
John Updike ~

A Active Reading

QUESTION Why do students think the poet wants readers to picture Flick next to the pumps? What do Flick and the pumps have in common and how do they differ? *(The pumps' human qualities—mindless, out of shape—suggest the waste of Flick's life. Flick is numbed by the mindlessness and routine of his dead-end job but still towers over and seems out of place among the "football type" pumps.)*

Additional Resources

- *Active Reading Guide,* p. 57
- *Audio Library*
- *Spanish Audio Library*

B Active Reading

RESPOND Have students describe the crowd reactions for an exciting high school basketball game they have attended. What must the noise and energy level have been at one of Flick's games?

Ex-Basketball Player
John Updike ~

Pearl Avenue runs past the high-school lot,
Bends with the trolley tracks, and stops, cut off
Before it has a chance to go two blocks,
At Colonel McComsky Plaza. Berth's Garage
5   Is on the corner facing west, and there,
Most days, you'll find Flick Webb, who helps Berth out.

Flick stands tall among the idiot pumps—
Five on a side, the old bubble-head style,°
Their rubber elbows hanging loose and low.
10   One's nostrils are two S's, and his eyes
An E and O. And one is squat, without
A head at all—more of a football type.

Once Flick played for the high-school team, the Wizards.
He was good: in fact, the best. In '46
15   He bucketed° three hundred ninety points,
A county record still. The ball loved Flick.
I saw him rack up thirty-eight or forty
In one home game. His hands were like wild birds.

---

8 *Bubble-head style* refers to early gas station pumps that were sometimes topped with lighted glass globes.
15 Flick *bucketed,* or scored, 390 points playing basketball.

MEETING INDIVIDUAL NEEDS — INCLUSION STRATEGIES

Less-Proficient Readers The pathos of Flick Webb's situation arises from the contrasting descriptions of the boy basketball star and the man who pumps gas. Explain that a writer places descriptions of two very different things next to each other in order to intensify the differences and thus make a point.

Activity Have students list details about Flick in a chart:

Flick in high school	Flick as an adult

Ask students to tell how Flick is different as an adult. **L2**

Additional Resources
- *Inclusion Strategies*

Gas, 1940. Edward Hopper. Oil on canvas, 20¼ x 40¼ in. The Museum of Modern Art, New York. Mrs. Simon Guggenheim Fund.

C Critical Thinking

INFERRING Students should be able to infer from this detail that Flick is ill suited to his work. His movements show delicacy and physical intelligence that are not needed to work at a gas station.

D Active Reading

INTERPRET Why has Flick not "learned a trade"? Why is he stuck in this dead-end job? These lines show that he retreats from reality into daydreams of his former glory. Ask students to comment about the consequences of avoiding real problems by not facing them.

E Literary Elements

TONE Ask students to identify the tone in the poem and to note words and phrases the poet uses to convey that tone. *(Conversational, admiring, a little sad; "stands tall," "was good," "the best," hands like "wild birds," hands "fine and nervous")*

VIEWING THE ART
Edward Hopper's paintings convey an atmosphere of loneliness and anonymity within familiar surroundings.

He never learned a trade, he just sells gas,
20 Checks oil, and changes flats. Once in a while,
As a gag, he dribbles an inner tube,
But most of us remember anyway.
His hands are fine and nervous on the lug wrench.
It makes no difference to the lug wrench, though.

25 Off work, he hangs around Mae's Luncheonette.
Grease-gray and kind of coiled, he plays pinball,
Smokes those thin cigars, nurses lemon phosphates.
Flick seldom says a word to Mae, just nods
Beyond her face toward bright applauding tiers°
30 Of Necco Wafers, Nibs, and Juju Beads.

---

29 A sports stadium has *tiers,* or rows, of seats arranged one above another. Many restaurants have tiers of candies stacked near the cash register.

POETRY ❧ 637

MEETING INDIVIDUAL NEEDS

ENGLISH LANGUAGE LEARNERS

Sports Subculture Help students who were not born in the United States understand American attitudes toward sports heroes, even at the high school level. Have English-speaking volunteers describe action and crowd reaction in a basketball game and the special treatment given to specific sports figures.

Activity Have small groups of students discuss a sport and a sports hero popular in their native countries. Have the groups prepare a brief talk in English about one such heroic figure, describing how people treat him or her.

Additional Resources
📁 *English Language Learners Sourcebook*

F Literary Elements

IMAGERY Have students point out images in the opening lines that appeal to the senses of touch and smell. *("wrapped up . . . garbage," "too old potato peels")*

G Literary Elements

TONE What is the speaker's attitude toward Miss Rosie? *(She thinks of her fondly as she was; she is sad but honest about what Miss Rosie has become; she wants to protect her.)*

Thematic Focus

Issues of Identity The aura of greatness has faded from the characters described in these poems. Ask students why those once-great qualities still define Flick and Miss Rosie. How does the contrast affect students' perceptions of Flick and Miss Rosie?

☑ ASSESSMENT OPTIONS

📁 *Quick Checks,* p. 57

Teaching Options

Yellow Hat, 1936. Norman Lewis. Oil on burlap, 36½ x 26 in. Collection of Loide Lewis and the late Reginald Lewis.

Viewing the painting: How does the woman in the painting compare with your image of the speaker in the poem? with your image of the young Miss Rosie? Which characteristics are the same and which are different?

Miss Rosie

Lucille Clifton ∿

When I watch you
wrapped up like garbage
sitting, surrounded by the smell   **F**
of too old potato peels
5   or
when I watch you
in your old man's shoes
with the little toe cut out
sitting, waiting for your mind
10   like next week's grocery
I say
when I watch you
you wet brown bag of a woman
who used to be the best looking
   gal in Georgia
15   used to be called the Georgia Rose
I stand up   **G**
through your destruction
I stand up

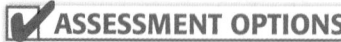

Sports and Sports Heroes Have students use a search engine to locate information about a favorite sports hero or about a favorite sport. Encourage them to look for facts that are out of the ordinary and might not be known by most people. Suggest that as key words they enter the name of their favorite sports hero or the name of their favorite sport.

REAL-WORLD CONNECTION

Heroes Ask students to locate two magazine articles about people they consider heroes: well-known personalities or ordinary people. Point out that in such articles, the subject is introduced early. To determine whether an article is one they want to consider, suggest that they skim the opening paragraph. Have students meet in small groups to discuss the heroes they chose. **L2**

Responding to Literature

Personal Response

If you could speak to the characters in the poems, what would you say to them?

ANALYZING LITERATURE

Ex-Basketball Player

RECALL AND INTERPRET

1. Who is Flick Webb? What does the speaker remember about him? How would you characterize the speaker's attitude toward Flick's high school accomplishments?
2. How has Flick's life changed since high school and why?
3. What qualities does the speaker notice in Flick that reveal his past glory? Provide details from the poem.
4. Explain what happens in the poem's last stanza. How do you think the speaker views Flick as an adult? Use details from the poem to support your response.

EVALUATE AND CONNECT

5. Look again at the description of the street in the first stanza. Evaluate the meaning and effect of this image.
6. Think about your response to the Focus Activity on page 635. Do you think Flick's talent changed his life for the better or worse? Explain.

Miss Rosie

RECALL AND INTERPRET

7. Who is the speaker describing in this poem? What is the subject's current state, and how is it different from what she once was?
8. What do lines 9–10 imply about Miss Rosie?
9. In your opinion, what does the speaker think about Miss Rosie? What effect does Miss Rosie's life have on the speaker's life?

EVALUATE AND CONNECT

10. Clifton uses details that appeal to the senses to describe Miss Rosie. Give an example of a **sensory detail** in the poem, explaining what sense it appeals to and its effect.
11. How might you react to seeing someone you know fall into a state similar to Miss Rosie's? Explain.
12. In your opinion, does this poem present a stronger picture of Miss Rosie or of the speaker? Support your response with details from the poem.

Personal Response

Students might ask about the most thrilling moment in their heydays or want to know how they lost everything.

ANALYZING LITERATURE

1. He is a gas station employee who was once a spectacular high school basketball player. The speaker admires Webb's old exploits.
2. Once adored and applauded for his talent, Flick has become a gray, shadowy man who does menial work and daydreams. He is hardly noticed.
3. His "fine and nervous" hands reveal his skill, he dribbles inner tubes, and he "stands tall among the idiot pumps." Qualities that caused him to excel in basketball are useless at the gas station.
4. Flick retreats to a high-school type hangout and relives his glory days in fantasy. That he drinks "lemon phosphates" and is surrounded by "tiers of Necco Wafers, Nibs, and Juju Beads" suggest his failure to grow up.
5. Like Flick, the street "runs past the high-school lot" and is "cut off," sharing his fate of remaining tied to the high school. Like Flick's basketball career, it goes nowhere.
6. Students may point out that Flick's early fame at least gives him something to look back on with pride; others may feel his experience gave him unrealistic expectations and prevents him from focusing and achieving in the present.
7. The speaker describes a bag lady, probably homeless, who has lost physical and mental soundness. She was once "the best looking gal in Georgia."
8. She has apparently lost touch with reality and is mentally ill.
9. Students may feel the speaker's primary response is compassion; however, admiration for Miss Rosie's tenacity and what she once was also color the poem. Miss Rosie shows that physical traits are not lasting but also moves the speaker to give a tribute.
10. A possible example is lines 2–4, which appeal to the senses of touch, smell, and sight to conjure distasteful sensations.

11. Most students will feel they would react with sympathy and act to help the unfortunate, but some may react angrily or fearfully.
12. The speaker's description of Miss Rosie is powerful, and it is she we picture "wrapped up like garbage" in "old man's shoes" and "waiting for [her] mind." The speaker is, like the reader, a watcher who remains anonymous.

LITERARY ELEMENTS

1. The tone is familiar and warm as the speaker talks to Miss Rosie. It is honest and hides nothing but also bestows respect.

2. The tone remains objective and informal. Whether he reports that Flick "helps Berth out," "bucketed three hundred ninety points," or "nods . . . toward bright applauding tiers" of candy, the speaker allows readers to decide for themselves how to feel about Flick and his failures.

Additional Resources

Literary Elements Transparency 57

LITERATURE AND WRITING

Writing About Literature

Students' essays should
- state opinions about the effectiveness of each poem's voice.
- list reasons for the opinions.
- explore differences in effect if voices were reversed.
- list reasons for those differences.

Creative Writing

Students' journal entries should
- use a diction consistent with the character chosen.
- include details that fit the spirit of the poems and the facts of the character's life.
- make statements and draw conclusions that could logically be expected, given the characters drawn in the poems.

EXTENDING YOUR RESPONSE

Literature Groups Before students begin their discussions, ask the class to develop a top five list of qualities and abilities that our society values most. **COLLAB. LEARN.**

Interdisciplinary Activity Interested students may wish to research records over a period of years and prepare a graph, showing where Flick falls on it.

Literary ELEMENTS

Tone

Tone is the reflection of a writer's or speaker's attitude toward the subject. In a poem, tone may be expressed through particular words, details, structure, and other poetic devices that convey certain emotions and that evoke an emotional response in the reader. For example, in "Ex-Basketball Player," the poet's use of basketball jargon helps create a familiar, conversational tone. To identify the tone of a poem, read the poem aloud and listen to how your voice sounds. The tone in your voice may reflect the tone of the poem.

1. How would you describe the tone of "Miss Rosie"? List the emotions that the tone conveys.
2. Does the tone of "Ex-Basketball Player" change in the poem, or does it stay the same? Support your response with details from the poem.

● See **Literary Terms Handbook**, p. R13.

LITERATURE AND WRITING

Writing About Literature

Analyzing Approaches   In "Ex-Basketball Player," the speaker tells readers about Flick Webb, the subject of the poem. In "Miss Rosie," the speaker addresses Miss Rosie directly. Write two or three paragraphs analyzing how effective each approach is at conveying a sense of the subject. Then examine how effective each poem might be if the approaches were switched—that is, what would "Ex-Basketball Player" be like if the speaker addressed Flick directly? How would the impact of Clifton's poem change if the speaker told readers about Miss Rosie? Discuss which approach seems more powerful to you and why.

Creative Writing

Speaking for Themselves   Write a journal entry from the point of view of either Flick Webb or Miss Rosie. What might they say about their past and present circumstances? You may make up details, as long as they are consistent with the poems' representations.

EXTENDING YOUR RESPONSE

Literature Groups

Value Statements   In your group, discuss what these poems suggest about the value of beauty and athletic ability in our society. As a group, develop a statement that you think reflects each poet's views on these social values. Use details from the poems and your own experiences in formulating your statements. Then be ready to support your group's statements as you compare them with those of other groups.

Interdisciplinary Activity

Sports: Stats   Just how great a player was young Flick Webb? Do some research to check out high school basketball records for 1946. Would scoring 390 points in a season have been outstanding then, or merely good? Would Flick have broken any records? If possible, look at your school's yearbook from 1946 or newspapers to get the hometown story. Share your discoveries with the class.

Performing

Different Perspectives   Prepare a monologue in which you tell about Flick from the point of view of the secondary characters Berth or Mae. You may invent details as long as they don't contradict those in the poem. Perform your piece for the class.

■ **Save your work for your portfolio.**

Performing Encourage students to build a character for their monologues and think through that character's relationship to Flick.

☑ ASSESSMENT OPTIONS

🗁 *Quick Checks,* p. 57

🗁 *Selection and Theme Assessment,* pp. 109–110

🗁 *Performance Assessment,* p. 56

💾 *Testmaker*

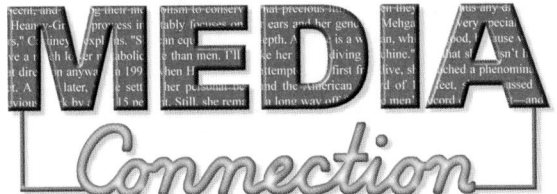
Interview

After hearing Lucille Clifton read her poetry, Bill Moyers interviewed her about her writing and her life. During the conversation, she discusses how she has managed to turn bad times into positive experiences.

Lucille Clifton
from *The Language of Life*

by Bill Moyers

MOYERS: The audience was really with you last night, riding every current of pleasure and surprise. I kept asking myself, should poetry *be* this much fun?

CLIFTON: I hope so. It *can* be fun, but that doesn't mean it's not serious. I'm very serious.

MOYERS: What happens to you when the audience comes back to you the way they did last night?

CLIFTON: Well, I sort of ride that energy. I often don't know what I'm going to read until I get in front of people, then I try to feel out where it seems to be going for them, and for me as well.

MOYERS: So, you're improvising—in a way.

CLIFTON: Well, I'm improvising what poems to read, yes. I often have a feeling for what I want to hear so I usually include a couple of those poems, but I also try to feel out what this particular group of people needs or wants or what poem should follow this one. It's like riding a wave, or what I like to think riding a wave must be like.

MOYERS: Listening to you recite your poems I imagined you having had a very hard life.

CLIFTON: I don't know if I think I've had a hard life, but I *have* had a challenging life. Everybody's life is more difficult than people think. . . . [P]oetry's probably saved my life. It has been *the* stable thing, something to love. . . . I think poetry has been the one faithful, good thing.

MOYERS: By doing *what* for you? Exactly what does it mean to sit and wrestle with those words until they line up on the page just the way you want them?

CLIFTON: I'm not sure that's how it happens exactly. I have a feeling that sometimes rather than wrestle and look for words, you have to be still and let them come. I was not trained as a poet, and I've never taken poetry lessons or had workshops. Nobody taught me anything much, really. So, I learned how to learn, and what I learned is that I could be still and allow the world and the impressions and the feelings—I'm very good with feelings—to come to me, and I could use our language to write them down.

MOYERS: You're good with feelings?

CLIFTON: I never learned to cut feelings off. I never learned that you were supposed to contain your feelings if you were an educated person, a sophisticated person. I did learn that I had to see things wholly and I learned to feel wholly as well, especially the complexities of what it means to be human and the complexities of what it means to be me.

Respond

1. Does Clifton think her life has been hard? Would she think your life is hard? What quality does she believe can help ease life's difficulties?
2. How do Clifton's strategies for coping with life compare with your own strategies?

Objective

- To read and understand an interview

Literature LINK

Miss Rosie Point out to students that Lucille Clifton, the poet interviewed in this piece, has struggled with the curves life throws and prevailed. In contrast, Miss Rosie, of the preceding poem (pp. 636–638), seems to have hit a wall of failure and disappointment.

Respond

1. Clifton recognizes that every life has challenges and rough spots. She says her sense of humor and her affinity for the "faithfulness" of poetry provided stability and helped her get through.
2. Clifton intuits, tries to see things "wholly," and never denies the complexity of being human. Students may not think of themselves as having strategies for coping, but many probably use humor, music, and networks of friends to help them work through problems.

Additional Resources
📁 *Media Connections Activities,* p. 16

Teaching Options

Reading *Minilesson*

Summarizing Discuss unique traits of the interview:

1. a live forum in which two people interact to get and give information
2. spontaneous, capable of changing direction quickly
3. a slice of living history colored by the rhythms of the participants

Point out how Clifton's poem uses structure, phrasing, and poetic devices to illuminate a meaningful experience.

Activity Have students select one of Clifton's answers that they find insightful and summarize it. Then have them write a paragraph explaining how this insight has added to their understanding of "Miss Rosie." **L2**

Additional Resources
📁 *Reading Workbook*

Objectives

- To analyze poems about choices and self-knowledge that define us and set our course for life
- To analyze lyric poems
- To write paragraphs explaining poets' connection to everyday life

Skills

Reading/Thinking: Inferring
Writing: Poem or Paragraphs
Grammar/Language: Subject Complements
Life Skills: Career Choices
Collaboration: Literature Groups; Interdisciplinary Activity

Motivating

→ OPTIONS

Literature Launchers: "Choosing a Different Path"

Videodisc Side B, Segment 15

Also available in VHS.

Selection Focus Transparency 58: Have students share their ideas about the nature of personal motivations and choices.

Focus Activity: Pair students to compare their choices. Discuss reasons why these choices are significant in life.

❧ ─ Before You Read ─

The Road Not Taken and We Are Many

─── **FOCUS ACTIVITY** ───

How would you visualize your life's journey? Can you picture it as a road?

ILLUSTRATE Draw a picture of a road that depicts your life's journey. Show where you have been and where you think you are going. Mark and label five spots along the road where you have made or expect to make significant choices.

SETTING A PURPOSE Read to see how the speakers in two poems reflect upon their life journeys.

─── **BACKGROUND** ───

Did You Know?

- Robert Frost found delight and inspiration in the commonplace tasks and diversions associated with working on his New England farm: mending a wall, taking a walk through the woods, picking apples, or meeting a couple of tramps. Frost's poems, which contain rustic images and are deceptively simple, often present a moral problem or a question about life that the reader is left to ponder.

- Pablo Neruda was influenced in his decision to be a writer by the renowned Chilean poet, Gabriela Mistral. Mistral taught Neruda at the Temuco school, where she was headmistress, in southern Chile. With Mistral's encouragement and support, Neruda, a railroad worker's son, was able to pursue his passion for poetry.

- Both Frost and Neruda had reservations about their chosen profession. Robert Frost once confided, "Sometimes I have my doubts about words altogether. . . . They are worse than nothing unless they do something, unless they amount to deeds." Pablo Neruda at times expressed envy of the craftsperson who shapes tangible materials into objects of art. The poet's hand, he said, "grasps nothing but paper and pen, and gropes for the words to accommodate thoughts and feelings."

Meet Robert Frost

Robert Frost once said "A poem should begin in delight and end in wisdom." Frost, who in his youth worked at odd jobs, was invited to read his poem "The Gift Outright" at John F. Kennedy's presidential inauguration ceremony in 1961. Frost is the only American poet to be awarded four Pulitzer Prizes.

Robert Frost was born in 1874 in San Francisco. He died in 1963.

Meet Pablo Neruda

"Anyone who hasn't been in the Chilean forest doesn't know this planet. I have come out of that landscape, . . . to go singing through the world." Neruda, a spokesman for the poor and working class, found inspiration in simple objects, and even fashioned a piece of driftwood into a work table at which he wrote many of his poems. Neruda received the Nobel Prize for Literature in 1971.

Pablo Neruda was born Neftalí Ricardo Reyes Basoalto in 1904. He died in 1973.

RESOURCE MANAGER

Lesson Planning Resource
The *Unit Three Planning Guide* (pp. 66–71) provides additional lesson notes and reduced versions of all print resources.

📁 **Other Print Resources**
- Active Reading Guide, p. 58
- Reading Workbook, pp. 65–66
- Grammar and Language Workbook, p. 85
- Grammar and Composition Handbook, Lesson 2.5
- Quick Checks, p. 58

- Selection and Theme Assessment, pp. 111–112
- Performance Assessment, p. 57
- Spanish Summaries, p. 58
- Spanish Translations
- Inclusion Strategies
- English Language Learners Sourcebook

🖋 **Transparencies**
- Selection Focus 58
- Literary Elements 58
- Grammar and Language 51

Technology
 Literature Launchers
🎧 Audio Library
🎧 Spanish Audio Library
💻 Glencoe Literature Web Site
💾 Testmaker

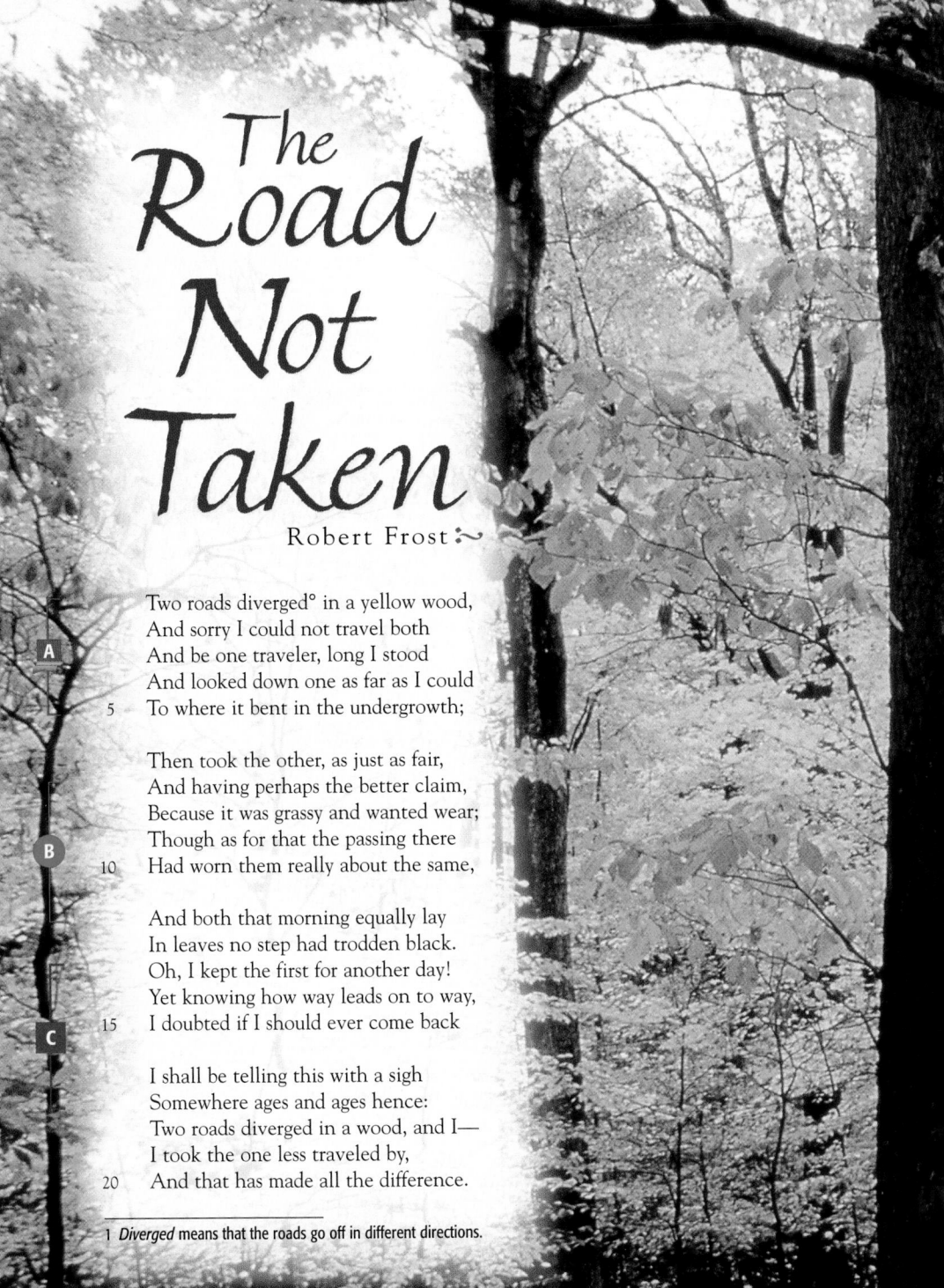

The Road Not Taken
Robert Frost

Two roads diverged° in a yellow wood,
And sorry I could not travel both
And be one traveler, long I stood
And looked down one as far as I could
5 To where it bent in the undergrowth;

Then took the other, as just as fair,
And having perhaps the better claim,
Because it was grassy and wanted wear;
Though as for that the passing there
10 Had worn them really about the same,

And both that morning equally lay
In leaves no step had trodden black.
Oh, I kept the first for another day!
Yet knowing how way leads on to way,
15 I doubted if I should ever come back

I shall be telling this with a sigh
Somewhere ages and ages hence:
Two roads diverged in a wood, and I—
I took the one less traveled by,
20 And that has made all the difference.

---

1 *Diverged* means that the roads go off in different directions.

Reading the Selection

A **Active Reading**

LISTEN: Have students take turns reading aloud the first stanza, listening for the musical qualities of rhyme and rhythm. Point out that the musical qualities indicate that this is a lyric poem.

Additional Resources
- *Active Reading Guide,* p. 58
- *Audio Library*
- *Spanish Audio Library*

B **Critical Thinking**

INFERRING What is implied about the speaker's values when he chooses the less-traveled road? *(He values nonconformity and wants life to be an adventure into the unknown.)*

C **Literary Elements**

FORM: *Lyric Poem* Ask students to describe the speaker's mood and attitude about his choice. *(He feels some sadness that life will limit him to his one path, but he accepts that this is the nature of life.)* Ask a volunteer to point out details and poetic devices that emphasize the speaker's emotions. *(exclamation point, words such as* doubted *and* sigh, *songlike rhythm and rhyme)*

Teaching Options

MEETING INDIVIDUAL NEEDS **GIFTED AND TALENTED**

Establishing Criteria In explaining a decision, a writer establishes criteria he or she used to make the decision. Explain that *criteria* are the standards or rules used to make a judgment. Discuss ways a reader can analyze criteria and decide whether they lead the writer to a valid decision.

Activity Have students work in pairs to discover the criteria the speaker used to choose a path. As a class, ask students to list the criteria, evaluate them, and offer other criteria that might have been used. *(To the speaker, the road should be little traveled, unworn, fair, not "blackened" by many feet. Other criteria might include direction, uphill or downhill slant, and variety of geographical terrain.)* **L3**

D **Active Reading**

CONNECT Ask students to recall incidents in which their words and actions made them look foolish instead of smart. Why might Neruda have chosen the word *concealed* in this context? *(Everyone speaks or behaves foolishly at times but prefers to keep this side of the self out of view.)*

E **Active Reading**

RESPOND What situation in their own lives does this stanza remind students of? Are there times when they have been afraid to speak up, to make their ideas known, because they are "in the midst of people of some distinction"?

F **Literary Elements**

FORM: *Lyric Poem* Point out this emotional outburst of the speaker, which reveals his distress at his divided, disappointing, and fragmentary self. Ask students to point out other places where emotion underscores this lyric. *(lines 12–14, 24, 26–27, 32–33)*

We Are Many

Pablo Neruda :~

Translated by Alastair Reid

Of the many men whom I am, whom we are,
I cannot settle on a single one.
They are lost to me under the cover of clothing.
They have departed for another city.

5   When everything seems to be set
to show me off as a man of intelligence,
the fool I keep concealed on my person
takes over my talk and occupies my mouth.   **D**

On other occasions, I am dozing in the midst
10 of people of some distinction,
and when I summon my courageous self,
a coward completely unknown to me
swaddles° my poor skeleton   **E**
in a thousand tiny reservations.°

15 When a stately home bursts into flames,
instead of the fireman I summon,
an arsonist° bursts on the scene,
and he is I. There is nothing I can do.
What must I do to distinguish myself?   **F**
20 How can I put myself together?

All the books I read
lionize° dazzling hero figures,
always brimming with self-assurance.
I die with envy of them;
25 and, in films where bullets fly on the wind,
I am left in envy of the cowboys,
left admiring even the horses.

---

13 To *swaddle* is to wrap or bind with cloth.
14 Here, *reservations* means "doubts" or "hesitations."
17 An *arsonist* is someone who intentionally sets fire to a building.
22 To look upon or to treat people as celebrities is to *lionize* them.

644 ❧ UNIT 3

Teaching Options

Grammar and Language *Minilesson*

Subject Complements Remind students that subject complements usually follow linking verbs and identify or describe the subject. Provide examples on the board:
    Most *people* are <u>disappointed</u> in themselves.
    The *self* is a <u>chameleon</u>.
After students identify each subject and linking verb, ask them to identify the underlined word as a *predicate nominative* (noun or pronoun renaming the subject) or *predicate adjective* (describing the subject).

Activity Have students work in groups to locate sentences with linking verbs and subject complements in "We Are Many." Ask that each group write four of these sentences and identify the subject, linking verb, and predicate nominative or adjective in each. **L2**

Additional Resources

📖 *Grammar and Language Transparency 51*

📖 *Grammar and Language Workbook,* p. 85

📖 *Grammar and Composition Handbook,* Lesson 2.5

📖 *Writer's Choice,* Lesson 11.5

644

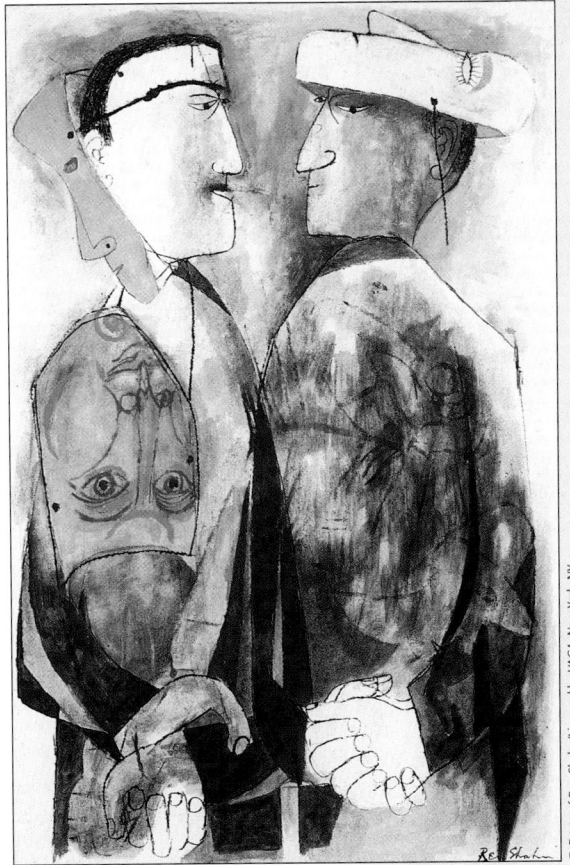

Viewing the Painting: What ideas
from "We Are Many" do you see
represented in this painting? Explain.

But when I call upon
   my dashing being,
out comes the same
   old lazy self,
30   and so I never know just who I am,
nor how many I am, nor who we will be being.
I would like to be able to touch a bell
and call up my real self, the truly me,
because if I really need my proper self,
35   I must not allow myself to disappear.

While I am writing, I am far away;
and when I come back, I have already left.
I should like to see if the same thing happens
to other people as it does to me,
40   to see if as many people are as I am,
and if they seem the same way to themselves.
When this problem has been thoroughly explored,
I am going to school myself so well in things
that, when I try to explain my problems,
45   I shall speak, not of self, but of geography.

VIEWING THE ART

Benjamin Shahn "Ben" Shahn was
born in Lithuania. His works often
deal with political or social issues.

Viewing Response *Many different
faces and masks hidden in the painting
reflect different sides to the personalities.*

G Literary Elements

THEME Ask students to paraphrase
the main idea the speaker expresses
here. *(It is vital to have a firm sense
of who you are and what you stand
for, even if you disappoint yourself.)*

H Active Reading

CLARIFY Challenge students to
explain the meaning of lines 36–37,
using their own words and examples. *(The speaker feels unable to
grasp his true nature or identity,
which seems to keep changing and
slipping away.)* Encourage them to
explain the speaker's concern about
other people in lines 38–41. *(If all
people have this problem, then it is a
universal concern and unites us.)*

Thematic Focus

Issues of Identity Are we the product of our choices? Which of our
traits defines us "truly"? Ask students to use details from these
poems to support their answers.

✔ ASSESSMENT OPTIONS

📁 *Quick Checks,* p. 58

MEETING INDIVIDUAL NEEDS — INCLUSION STRATEGIES

Learning Disabled Write these words
on the board: *intelligent, foolish.* Explain
that antonyms have opposite meanings.
Discuss this poem's pairing of opposites to illustrate the opposing fragments of a person's identity. Point out
that an intelligent person would speak
wisely and truly; a fool would say something stupid or laughable.

Activity Have students work in groups
to find three other sets of antonyms.
Ask groups to create a skit illustrating
these opposite qualities. *(Possible
answers: courageous self/coward, fire-
man/arsonist, dashing/lazy)* **L1**

Additional Resources
📁 *Inclusion Strategies*

Responding to the Selection

Personal Response

Some students will recognize themselves in the rueful decision maker, who wonders about the possibilities of the other road. Others will relate more strongly to the frustrated underachiever, who seems doomed to disappoint the "proper" self.

ANALYZING LITERATURE

1. Lines 6–10 explain the decision to take the path that seems less traveled. In fact, looking back, the speaker admits both were traveled about the same.

2. The roads are like mirror images; they Y off into the woods—both "fair," "grassy," and not "trodden black." They differ only in that one was chosen and one was not.

3. His is the road "less traveled by." They appear to represent decisions that lead to a definite life direction, such as career choices or selection of a spouse.

4. Students may describe a choice between obeying rules or not, pursuing music or sports, committing to working hard on studies or refusing to do one's best.

5. His concern is not that he has taken the wrong path but that he will never know what his life would have been had he taken the other. He acknowledges that they are "about the same" and admits he knew he would not get back to the other path. His backward look "with a sigh" may indicate regret at what he has missed.

6. His many traits are always shifting, so he cannot tell which self is "real"; often, he makes a poor showing when he would like to act with moral, physical, and mental courage. The poet illustrates this conflict by contrasting the wished-for sterling qualities with the unsavory ones too often exhibited.

7. Instead of intelligence, he exhibits foolishness; rather than courage, cowardice. He destroys where he intends to save, envies where he wants to be heroic, and dallies where he wishes to be dashing.

8. Students may cite lines 15–18, in which the speaker says he is an arsonist, or lines 36–37, in which the speaker is always far from himself. These uses of hyperbole emphasize the conflict between opposing traits in his identity.

Responding to Literature

Personal Response

Which speaker do you identify with more closely? Why?

— ANALYZING LITERATURE —

The Road Not Taken

RECALL AND INTERPRET

1. What lines explain the decision the speaker makes? On what does the speaker base his decision?

2. What **sensory details** does Frost use to help you visualize the two roads? How are the roads alike? How are they different? (See Literary Terms Handbook, page R11.)

3. What name does the speaker give to the road he has decided to take? What do you think the two roads **symbolize** or represent? Explain.

EVALUATE AND CONNECT

4. Theme Connections   Look at the illustration you created for the Focus Activity on page 642. Describe a time when you were faced with choices that affected your future. How does the poem reflect your own inner conflict over having to make two relatively equal choices?

5. Why do you think Frost entitled this poem "The Road Not Taken," rather than "The Road Taken"? Support your answer with details from the poem.

We Are Many

RECALL AND INTERPRET

6. What is the speaker's dilemma in "We Are Many"? How does the poet illustrate the speaker's problem?

7. What character traits does the speaker exhibit? Which traits would he like to exhibit?

EVALUATE AND CONNECT

8. **Hyperbole** is intentional exaggeration. This figure of speech may be used to achieve a humorous effect or to emphasize a serious situation. Identify one example of hyperbole in "We Are Many" and explain why the poet may have used it.

9. What is the predominant **mood**, or attitude, of the speaker in this poem? How does Neruda achieve this mood? How does the mood affect your own attitude toward the speaker's problem? (See Literary Terms Handbook, page R8.)

10. Do you think that the speaker's dilemma is realistic? Have you ever felt like the speaker does? Explain.

9. The speaker seems frustrated and distressed because his positive goals are defeated by human foibles. By presenting the failures in comic, everyday terms, Neruda makes readers smile and identify with the speaker.

10. The speaker exaggerates his failures, for they are blown out of proportion in his mind. Students may have doubted themselves when they failed to speak up out of fear, misspoke, failed to do something expected, or did something petty and hurtful out of spite.

Literary ELEMENTS

Lyric Poem

A **lyric poem** is a short poem in which a speaker expresses intense personal thoughts and feelings. Lyric poetry got its name from the *lyre,* a stringed instrument that was used to accompany the singer of a lyric poem in ancient Greece. A lyric poem is melodic in its pattern of rhythm and may have rhymed or unrhymed verse. While a lyric poem might be about an object, a person, or an event, the focus of the lyric poem is on an emotional experience of the speaker, which may

or may not be the poet. For example, the speaker in "The Road Not Taken" expresses his or her thoughts and feelings on the subject of making a decision about which path to follow.

1. Describe the emotions expressed by each poem's speaker toward the subject.
2. Which poem do you think is more melodic? Why?

● See Literary Terms Handbook, p. R7.

LITERATURE AND WRITING

Writing About Literature

Understanding Connections   Neruda and Frost wanted the general public to feel comfortable reading and listening to their poetry. Write one or two paragraphs explaining how you think the poets connect to ordinary people through the poems "The Road Not Taken" and "We Are Many." Use details from the poems to illustrate your ideas.

Personal Writing

Difficult Choices   Write about a time when you were in a situation like that of one of the speakers in "The Road Not Taken" or "We Are Many." In a few paragraphs, or in a poem modeled on one of the poems above, describe your dilemma, how you faced it, and how you resolved it.

EXTENDING YOUR RESPONSE

Literature Groups

Understanding Meaning   Frost suggested that "The Road Not Taken" was simply about a friend with whom he took frequent walks. After their walks, the friend usually regretted that they had not taken a different path. Do you think this is all Frost wanted readers to learn from this poem? What does this poem teach you about life? Working with your group, discuss these questions and share your findings with the class.

Interdisciplinary Activity

Music: Songs of Life   Find a piece of contemporary music related to the ideas explored in "The Road Not Taken" or "We Are Many." With your group, come to a consensus about how the song's message relates to one of the two poems. Then, play the song and present your ideas for the class.

Learning for Life

Career Choices   What path might you choose in life? Where would you look for information on career possibilities? Use the Internet and the library to put together a source list on a career or on how to choose a career. Present your findings in a chart or poster and share it with the class.

Reading Further

You might also enjoy these works:

Listening: "Birches" and "The Road Not Taken" are read by Robert Frost in Volume One of *In Their Own Voices: A Century of Recorded Poetry.*

Poem: "Quartz opens its eyes in the snow," from *Las piedras del cielo / Stones of the Sky* by Pablo Neruda.

📖 **Save your work for your portfolio.**

LITERARY ELEMENTS

1. In "The Road Not Taken," the speaker expresses regret that he will never know how his life would have differed if he had taken the other path. The speaker in "We Are Many" expresses frustration that he remains unsure of his essential self, since he cannot control the many conflicting aspects within himself.
2. Students will point to the pleasing, regular rhythm and rhyme scheme of Frost's poem, which enhance its songlike quality. However, point out that Neruda's poem is translated from Spanish; in its original language its melodious elements would be evident.

Additional Resources

Literary Elements Transparency 58

LITERATURE AND WRITING

Writing About Literature

Students' paragraphs should
- note word choices and sentence structures in the poems that copy ordinary speech.
- point out situations and emotions in the poems that are universal.
- analyze use of such traditional poetic features as rhythm and rhyme.

Personal Writing

Students' writings should
- describe the situation in which the conflict occurs.
- detail the emotions and actions involved in facing the dilemma.
- explain the results of the decision.

EXTENDING YOUR RESPONSE

Literature Groups Have students pick out details that suggest the deeper level of meaning in Frost's poem.

✔ ASSESSMENT OPTIONS

📁 *Quick Checks,* p. 58
📁 *Selection and Theme Assessment,* pp. 111–112
📁 *Performance Assessment,* p. 57
💾 *Testmaker*

Interdisciplinary Activity

Students may want to provide classmates with copies of the lyrics for the song they play. Suggest that they make a list of similarities in the poem and song.

Learning for Life Before students begin, you may wish to explore new career options and likely future trends in a class discussion. A guidance counselor may be able to provide useful information.

Objectives

- To read and analyze poems honoring culture and family
- To identify and describe the effect of imagery
- To write a character sketch

Skills

Writing: Letter
Vocabulary: Etymology
Grammar/Language: Nouns Used as Adjectives
Life Skills: Decision Making; Planning and Designing
Collaboration: Literature Groups

Motivating
→OPTIONS

Selection Focus Transparency 59: Have students look at the artifact, tell what they know about it, and respond to the questions.

Focus Activity: Ask students to write and share an explanation of why this object is cherished and what it symbolizes.

Before You Read

The Floral Apron and My Mother Pieced Quilts

FOCUS ACTIVITY

What things in your home have special value or significance to your family?

JOURNAL Think of a cherished item in your home, such as a photograph, piece of furniture, or holiday decoration. Describe the item, and tell why it is important to your family.

SETTING A PURPOSE Read about how two different household items take on great significance for the speakers.

BACKGROUND

Did You Know?

- A plentiful, inexpensive seafood in China, squid is often called a "poor man's lobster." Cleaning squid is not difficult, but it is time-consuming because squid are so small. The cook first removes the head and tentacles, peels back the purple skin, and slits the body to remove the cartilage and the jellylike inner material. A popular way to prepare squid is to roll it in batter and fry it in hot oil. Squid has a firm, chewy texture and a mild flavor.

- Cleavers are large knives with wide, heavy blades. Cleavers are important and common tools in Chinese food preparation. Complicated chopping techniques are such a distinctive feature of Chinese cuisine that dishes are sometimes named according to the shapes and sizes into which the ingredients are cut.

- Most quilts have three layers: a top layer of pieced-together patchwork or design units, a middle layer of filler or batting, and a bottom layer of cotton or muslin. The top layer takes the longest to sew and often consists of a complex, colorful design. Traditionally, pieces of fabric for the top layer are cut from the family's old, discarded clothing.

Meet Marilyn Chin

Born to Chinese parents, Marilyn Chin was raised in Portland, Oregon, by her mother and grandmother. She believes that people like herself, Americans from all over the world, have important stories to tell: "We're breaking new ground, and *this* is the voice of America. My voice is one of the *many* voices of America."

Marilyn Chin was born in 1955.

Meet Teresa Palomo Acosta

"The poem 'My Mother Pieced Quilts' came to me at an early age—as I literally passed my hands along them . . . when I awoke on cold winter mornings," says Teresa Palomo Acosta. Later, as an adult, she was able to write the poem "fairly quickly," after "carrying its images inside" for so long. Acosta, who grew up in a small town in Texas, says she writes about everyday life from her own point of view as a Chicana woman.

Teresa Palomo Acosta was born in 1949.

RESOURCE MANAGER

Lesson Planning Resource
The *Unit Three Planning Guide* (pp. 72–77) provides additional lesson notes and reduced versions of all print resources.

📁 **Other Print Resources**
- Active Reading Guide, p. 59
- Grammar and Language Workbook, p. 61
- Grammar and Composition Handbook, Lesson 1.4
- Quick Checks, p. 59
- Selection and Theme

Assessment, pp. 113–114
- Performance Assessment, p. 58
- Spanish Summaries, p. 59
- Spanish Translations
- Inclusion Strategies
- English Language Learners Sourcebook

✏ **Transparencies**
- Selection Focus 59
- Literary Elements 59
- Grammar and Language 52

Technology
🎧 Audio Library
🎧 Spanish Audio Library
💻 Glencoe Literature Web Site
💾 Testmaker

THE FLORAL APRON

Marilyn Chin ❦

The woman wore a floral apron around her neck,
that woman from my mother's village
with a sharp cleaver in her hand.
She said, "What shall we cook tonight?
5 Perhaps these six tiny squids
lined up so perfectly on the block?"

She wiped her hand on her apron,
pierced the blade into the first.
There was no resistance,
10 no blood, only cartilage
soft as a child's nose. A last
iota of ink° made us wince.

Suddenly, the aroma of ginger and scallion°
    fogged our senses,
and we absolved° her for that moment's
    barbarism.
15 Then, she, an elder of the tribe,
without formal headdress, without elegance,
deigned° to teach the younger
about the Asian plight.

And although we have traveled far
20 we would never forget that primal lesson—
on patience, courage, forbearance,°
on how to love squid despite squid,
how to honor the village, the tribe,
that floral apron.

Girl in Blue Sweater, 1991. Huang Jinsheng. Oil on canvas, 21⅝ x 17¾ in. Private collection.

---

12 The *iota* (ī ō′ tə) *of ink* is a very small quantity of the squid's ink.
13 Young green onions are called *scallions.*
14 In *absolving* the woman, they freed her of guilt or blame.
17 *Deigned* means "willing to do something beneath one's normal level of dignity."
21 To have *forbearance* is to show self-control and restraint, especially when provoked.

POETRY ❦ 649

My Mother Pieced Quilts

Teresa Palomo Acosta

B
they were just meant as covers
in winters
as weapons
against pounding january winds

C
5   but it was just that every morning I awoke to these
october ripened canvases
passed my hand across their cloth faces
and began to wonder how you pieced
all these together
10   these strips of gentle communion cotton and flannel nightgowns
wedding organdies
dime store velvets

D
how you shaped patterns square and oblong and round
positioned
15   balanced
then cemented them
with your thread
a steel needle
a thimble

650   UNIT 3

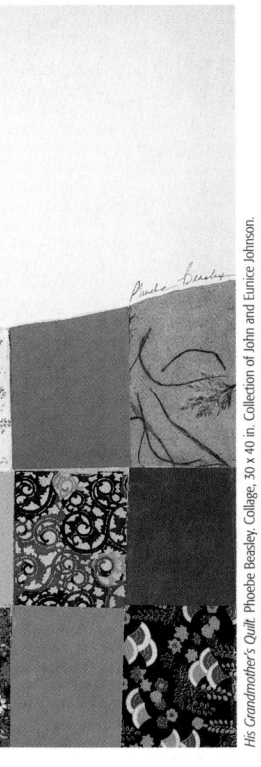

His Grandmother's Quilt. Phoebe Beasley. Collage, 30 x 40 in. Collection of John and Eunice Johnson.

20   how the thread darted in and out
      galloping along the frayed edges, tucking them in
      as you did us at night
      oh how you stretched and turned and re-arranged
      your michigan spring faded curtain pieces
25   my father's santa fe work shirt°
      the summer denims, the tweeds of fall

      in the evening you sat at your canvas
      —our cracked linoleum floor the drawing board
      me lounging on your arm
30   and you staking out the plan:
      whether to put the lilac purple of easter against the red plaid of
          winter-going-
      into-spring
      whether to mix a yellow with blue and white and paint the
      corpus christi° noon when my father held your hand
35   whether to shape a five-point star from the
      somber black silk you wore to grandmother's funeral

      you were the river current
      carrying the roaring notes
      forming them into pictures of a little boy reclining
40   a swallow flying
      you were the caravan master at the reins
      driving your threaded needle artillery across the mosaic° cloth
          bridges
      delivering yourself in separate testimonies.

      oh mother you plunged me sobbing and laughing
45   into our past
      into the river crossing at five
      into the spinach fields
      into the plainview cotton rows
      into tuberculosis wards
50   into braids and muslin dresses
      sewn hard and taut to withstand the thrashings of twenty-five years

      stretched out they lay
      armed/ready/shouting/celebrating

      knotted with love
55   the quilts sing on

---

25 A *Santa Fe work shirt* was named for the Santa Fe Railroad.
34 *Corpus Christi* (kôr′ pəs kris′ tē), Texas, is a port city on the Gulf of Mexico.
42 Here, *mosaic* refers to variously colored bits of materials.

F Literary Elements

IMAGERY and METAPHOR Invite students to describe the mother as these word pictures and comparisons make her appear. *(She is as powerful and constant a force as a river, a caravan master in control of strategy and attack in times of conflict.)* What is the effect of this language? *(It captures the mother's force of love and resolve to keep the family from harm.)*

G Literary Elements

SYMBOL What have the quilts come to represent? How has their personification been important to this symbolism? *(They are the carriers for the family's history and love. Giving them human traits brings the quilts to life and makes them characters that speak for the family.)*

Thematic Focus

Issues of Identity Ask students why preparing ethnic dishes and making quilts are important to a sense of cultural and family identity. What other activities do they think are important to a sense of identity?

✔ ASSESSMENT OPTIONS

📁 *Quick Checks,* p. 59

INTERDISCIPLINARY CONNECTION

Geography Some students may be unfamiliar with the locations of states and the life style of migrant workers in the United States. Have students locate New Mexico, Texas, and Michigan on a United States map. Explain that migrant workers move with the seasons to different places to pick crops for low wages. Many of these workers came to this country from Mexico.

Activity Have students work in pairs to research the history of migrant workers and learn about their life styles and economic, social, and educational difficulties. After they meet in groups to share facts, have students prepare a brief talk explaining what life was probably like for the speaker as a girl. **L2**

Personal Response

Students may gravitate to powerful images (such as the tribal elder wielding a cleaver), poetic devices (such as the armed and singing quilts), or language (such as "october ripened canvases").

ANALYZING LITERATURE

1. An elder from the village of the speaker's mother ritualistically cleans and prepares squid as a lesson in tribal culture for youngsters. The speaker is aghast at the woman's matter-of-fact dressing of the squid.

2. As the dish is prepared and delicious smells reach them, the children become pleased with the experience and anticipate a feast. They are grateful that the elder "deigns" to teach them.

3. The speaker mentions lessons in "patience, courage, forbearance" and honoring one's culture. "To love squid despite squid" is to accept the ugly, unpleasant aspects of life that make possible the beautiful, pleasing ones.

4. It represents the practical, beautiful, and protective aspects of the speaker's culture. It has become a concrete reminder of ancestry; its use to protect the elder from the dirt of her work as well as its natural, floral pattern give it further levels of meaning.

5. By demonstrating how the squid is prepared traditionally, the elder helped the speaker comprehend the life-sustaining nature of the culture's food, customs, and values.

6. Students may mention patience, a need to plan ahead, the enlivening nature of imagination, and the importance of balance, cleanliness, and order. Such lessons apply to life at other levels, as the poem's lessons do.

7. The speaker's mother made the quilts to keep her family warm.

8. They remind the speaker of childhood, studying the patterns of the quilts and watching the mother plan and create them. They have become works of art ("ripened canvases" with "cloth faces") that embody emotional family events ("armed . . . celebrating").

9. Like a river current, the mother sweeps them along on memories. Like a caravan master, she controls the story told on the "mosaic cloth" and wields her needle like artillery, battling to preserve in memory the good in their lives.

10. Students may mention that the quilts celebrate memories and emo-

tions of the family members' shared history. The quilts "sing" about the past; their colors, patterns, and the fabrics themselves create the rhythm, melody, and words of the songs.

11. The speaker admires and loves the mother for her skill ("positioned, balanced, cemented"), her art and architecture ("your canvas," "the plan"), and her lessons of the heart ("plunged me sobbing and laughing into our past").

12. Accept any answers that students can tie to sensory impressions, emotional associations, or events of lasting importance to the family.

Responding to Literature

Personal Response

What do you find most memorable, interesting, or powerful about these poems? Share your response with a classmate.

ANALYZING LITERATURE

The Floral Apron

RECALL AND INTERPRET

1. Who is wearing the floral apron? What is she doing in the first two stanzas? How does the speaker react to the woman's actions?
2. What happens in the third stanza? How does the attitude of the observers change? Why does it change?
3. What lesson does the speaker describe in stanza four? What do you think it means "to love squid despite squid"?
4. What does the floral apron seem to **symbolize**, or represent, to the speaker in the last line? Explain.

EVALUATE AND CONNECT

5. **Theme Connections** In your opinion, how did the speaker's experience affect his or her sense of identity?
6. What lessons about life have you learned in a kitchen? How do these lessons compare with the lesson the speaker learns?

My Mother Pieced Quilts

RECALL AND INTERPRET

7. Who made the quilts? What was the quilts' original purpose?
8. What childhood memories or associations do the quilts bring to the speaker's mind? What have the quilts come to **symbolize**, or represent, to the speaker? Give details from the poem to support your answer.
9. What two things does the speaker compare the mother to in lines 37–43? What is your interpretation of these comparisons? Explain.
10. In line 53, what do you think the speaker means by the statement that the quilts are "armed/ready/shouting/celebrating"? How do the quilts "sing on"?

EVALUATE AND CONNECT

11. What are the speaker's feelings toward his or her mother? What lines or details support your views?
12. What common household activities, such as gardening, carpentry, and cooking, are practiced in your household? Which of these, in your opinion, is most likely to leave a lasting impression in your life? Explain why.

LITERATURE & HUMANITIES

Display the picture *The Earth*, available from the National Museum of Women in the Arts. Point out that quilt making arose out of necessity, but became a way of communicating heritage. Using the picture and the poem "My Mother Pieced Quilts," discuss with students how quilts became a way for women to tell stories.

Literary ELEMENTS

Imagery

Imagery is descriptive language that represents a feeling, triggers a memory or idea, or evokes a sensory experience. For example, an effective image might help a reader visualize a baseball game, hear an old woman laugh, feel the texture of a stone, smell rotting potatoes, or taste a sweet melon. In addition to creating vivid pictures, images also convey ideas and feelings. Teresa Palomo Acosta creates a compelling image of her mother sewing when she says her mother's thread "darted in and out / galloping along the frayed edges, tucking them in / as you did us at night." These lines

show how skillful, confident, and loving the mother was, both in sewing and taking care of her children. In "The Floral Apron," Chin uses an image of a child's soft nose to convey the texture of the raw squid and to reveal the speaker's squeamishness.

1. Find two other examples of imagery in "My Mother Pieced Quilts." Explain their meaning and effect.
2. In your opinion, what is the most effective image in "The Floral Apron"? Why is it effective?

⦿ See **Literary Terms Handbook,** p. R6.

LITERATURE AND WRITING

Writing About Literature
Character Sketch Think about each speaker's personal observations about identity. What do they reveal about the speaker? Write a character sketch of one of the speakers based on what you know directly and what you can infer from the poem. Share and compare character sketches with a classmate.

Creative Writing
Prized Possession Reread the journal entry you wrote in response to the Focus Activity on page 648. Then write a letter to your family or to a specific family member telling your thoughts about the significant family item and what it means to you.

EXTENDING YOUR RESPONSE

Literature Groups
Women Teachers The woman at the heart of each of these poems possesses important qualities, skills, and knowledge. What does each woman know? What does each woman teach and to whom? Work with your group to create a chart comparing and contrasting these women according to as many criteria as you can identify in both poems. Share your chart with the class.

Interdisciplinary Activity
Family and Consumer Sciences: Presentation Prepare a brief presentation in which you explain and, if possible, demonstrate a home art or craft, such as cooking, sewing, woodworking, canning, soap-making, or gardening.

Learning for Life
Design a Quilt Create a quilt block (section of several individual pieces) or a visual representation of a quilt block in any medium of your choice. Like the quilts in the poem, your design should represent an image or images that are meaningful to you.

Reading Further
You might enjoy this book and video:

An interview with Marilyn Chin in Bill Moyer's video series and companion book *The Language of Life: A Festival of Poets*.

 Save your work for your portfolio.

POETRY 🎋 653

Objectives

- To read and analyze poems about the effects of industrialization on people's identity
- To analyze the tone and effect of speakers in poems
- To write an essay comparing themes

Skills

Reading/Thinking: Identifying Author's Purpose
Writing: Speaker's Remarks; Fairy Tales
Listening/Speaking: Interview
Collaboration: Literature Groups

Motivating

→OPTIONS

Literature Launchers: "Getting to Know Margaret Atwood"

Videodisc
Side B, Segment 16

Also available in VHS.

Selection Focus Transparency 60: Have students view the photograph and use the questions to discuss effects of people on nature and vice versa.

Focus Activity: Ask students to consider the effects of development on the place they discuss. One effect causes another, and so on. Discuss and diagram some of these interconnected effects on the board.

Before You Read

A Bus Along St. Clair: December and Freeway 280

What natural places have you seen or heard about that existed in the midst of an urban environment?

DISCUSS Think of such a place, and, with your group, discuss the following questions. How do people, animals, and nature adapt to urban environments? What do they lose? What do they gain?

SETTING A PURPOSE Read two poems that explore what happens when people build over natural places.

BACKGROUND

Did You Know?

- Margaret Atwood believes that "a voice is a gift; it should be cherished and used. . . . Powerlessness and silence go together." In her poetry, stories, and novels, Atwood speaks in her wry, intelligent voice and explores social concerns, such as isolation from nature and the destructiveness of gender roles.

- Although strongly influenced by her Spanish-speaking heritage, Lorna Dee Cervantes writes mainly in English because it is the language she spoke at home growing up: "I think to write poetry, you have to write in the language of your childhood, and the language you dream in." Spanish words, especially the names of trees and plants, often communicate meaning more precisely or poetically than English words. *Albaricoqueros* (äl bär′ ē kō kä′ rōs) are apricot trees; *cerezos* (ser ā′ zōs) are cherry trees; *nogales* (nō gä′ läs) are walnut trees. *Espinaca* (es′ pē nä′ kə) is spinach; *verdolagas* (ver′ dō lä′ gäs) is purslane; *yerbabuena* (yer′ bə bwä′ nə) is mint.

- The titles of both poems contain references to major cities. St. Clair is a densely urban, primarily commercial street in Toronto, Canada. Freeway 280 runs from San Jose, California, where Cervantes grew up, to San Francisco, California, where she was born.

Meet Margaret Atwood

As a child, Canadian poet and novelist Margaret Atwood spent summers in the woods, where her father, an entomologist, studied insects and her mother read to her. Often alone, Atwood spent much of her time reading: "I became a reading addict, and have remained so ever since." Today she is an internationally known and respected writer.

Margaret Atwood was born in 1939.

Meet Lorna Dee Cervantes

Mexican American Lorna Dee Cervantes clearly states who she is: "I'm a Chicana writer, I am a feminist writer, I am a political writer." Cervantes became a political activist in the feminist and Hispanic American cultural movements and she formed her own small press to publish the works of Hispanic American women writers. Today, Cervantes continues to run Mango Publications and to write poetry.

Lorna Dee Cervantes was born in 1954.

RESOURCE MANAGER

Lesson Planning Resource
The *Unit Three Planning Guide* (pp. 78–82) provides additional lesson notes and reduced versions of all print resources.

 Other Print Resources
- Active Reading Guide, p. 60
- Reading Workbook
- Quick Checks, p. 60
- Selection and Theme Assessment, pp. 115–116

- Performance Assessment, p. 59
- Spanish Summaries, p. 60
- Spanish Translations
- Inclusion Strategies

Transparencies
- Selection Focus 60
- Fine Art 29
- Literary Elements 60

Technology
 Literature Launchers
 Audio Library
Spanish Audio Library
 Glencoe Literature Web Site
Testmaker

A Bus Along St. Clair: December

Margaret Atwood

It would take more than that to banish
me: this is my kingdom still.

Turn, look up
through the gritty window: an unexplored
5   wilderness of wires

Though they buried me in monuments
of concrete slabs, of cables
though they mounded a pyramid
of cold light over my head
10 though they said, We will build
silver paradise with a bulldozer

it shows how little they know
about vanishing: I have
my ways of getting through.

15 Right now, the snow
is no more familiar
to you than it was to me:
this is my doing.
The gray air, the roar
20 going on behind it
are no more familiar.

I am the old woman
sitting across from you on the bus,
her shoulders drawn up like a shawl;
25 out of her eyes come secret
hatpins, destroying
the walls, the ceiling

Turn, look down:
there is no city;
30 this is the center of a forest

your place is empty

Reading the Selection

A Active Reading

IMAGINE Encourage students to imagine the position of the listener who is being told these details. *(The gritty window and "wilderness of wires" along with the title should help students imagine that the listener is a rider in the bus.)* Ask students to be on the watch for clues to the speaker's identity as they complete the poem.

Additional Resources
- 📁 *Active Reading Guide,* p. 60
- 🎧 *Audio Library*
- 🎧 *Spanish Audio Library*

B Literary Elements

FIGURES OF SPEECH: *Metaphor* What attitude toward the city is revealed through these metaphors? *(It is cold, hard, angular, and imprisoning.)*

C Literary Elements

SPEAKER Help students see that the speaker has not literally become an old woman. Rather, it associates itself with a vengeful human presence. This association suggests that humans are basically aligned with nature and destroy themselves when they destroy nature.

Teaching Options

Writing Minilesson

Fairy Tale Framework Atwood's poem depends upon readers' knowledge of fairy tales to build a polarized, magical atmosphere. Point out that, although the poem does not mention a specific fairy tale, it borrows the language and actions of the genre. Have a volunteer describe the typical plot and characters of a fairy tale. Ask students to summarize stories they know.

Activity Have students work in groups to identify fairy tale elements and phrases in the poem. Invite groups to extend this framework, add details and characters, and rewrite the poem as a fairy tale. **L3**
COLLAB. LEARN.

Additional Resources
- 📗 *Writer's Choice,* Lesson 3.5

A&E HOME VIDEO.® *The following videotape program is available from Glencoe. Be sure to preview the video for appropriateness for your class.*

- **Biography: Malcolm X—A Search for Identity**

VIEWING THE ART

Mary Lou Ferbert's painting juxtaposes different elements of a city—the harshness of its buildings and the soft beauty of its simple wayside plants.

Chicory and Flatiron Building, 1991. (detail). Mary Lou Ferbert. Transparent watercolor on d'Arches, 98 x 48 in. Collection of the artist.

Teaching Options

MEETING INDIVIDUAL NEEDS — INCLUSION STRATEGIES

Less-Proficient Readers Write the following on the board: *The freeway conceals it beneath a _____ scar.* Ask students to suggest different adjectives for the blank and explain how each changes the mood of the sentence. Point out Cervantes's choice ("raised scar").

Activity Have students locate five adjectives in "Freeway 280" that have an emotional effect and write the word pair. Have volunteers explain the effect of each adjective choice on meaning and mood. *(Possible phrases: raised scar, fake windsounds, rigid lanes, greasy summer air, loose seed)* **L1**

Additional Resources
📁 *Inclusion Strategies*

Freeway 280

Lorna Dee Cervantes

Las casitas° near the gray cannery,
nestled amid wild abrazos° of climbing roses
and man-high red geraniums
are gone now. The freeway conceals it

5   all beneath a raised scar.

But under the fake windsounds of the open lanes,
in the abandoned lots below, new grasses sprout,
wild mustard remembers, old gardens
come back stronger than they were,

10   trees have been left standing in their yards.
Albaricoqueros, cerezos, nogales . . .
Viejitas° come here with paper bags to gather greens.
Espinaca, verdolagas, yerbabuena . . .

I scramble over the wire fence

15   that would have kept me out.
Once, I wanted out, wanted the rigid lanes
to take me to a place without sun,
without the smell of tomatoes burning
on swing shift° in the greasy summer air.

20   Maybe it's here
en los campos extraños de esta ciudad°
where I'll find it, that part of me
mown under
like a corpse

25   or a loose seed.

---

1 *Las casitas* (läs cǝ sē′ tǝs) is Spanish for "little houses."
2 *Abrazos* (ǝ brä′ zōs) is Spanish for "embraces" or "hugs."
12 *Viejitas* (vē′ e hē′ tǝs) means "old women" in Spanish.
19 In factories, hospitals, and some businesses the *swing shift* is the work period
   from midafternoon to midnight, between the day and night shifts.
21 *en los campos extraños de esta ciudad* (en lōs cäm′ pōs eks′ trä nyōs′
   dā es′ tǝ sē′ oo däd′) In English, this is "in the strange fields of this city."

Reading *Minilesson*

Identifying Author's Purpose Explain that a writer has a purpose for including a specific content using specific word choices. For example, Atwood uses harsh and defiant language in "A Bus Along St. Clair: December" in order to make clear nature's anger at being covered over. Cervantes also has a purpose in mixing two languages in "Freeway 280."

Activity Have students work in pairs to analyze which parts of Cervantes's poem are in Spanish and to infer (1) why the poet uses two languages and (2) why Spanish is used in those specific places. Invite partners to share their analyses with the class. *(Cervantes highlights her dual heritage and echoes the mixing of cultures that causes her conflict. Most Spanish*

phrases denote pleasant sensory memories of the old neighborhood, where the language likely prevailed.) **L2**

Additional Resources
🗁 *Reading Workbook*

Personal Response

Any image derived from the poems is a legitimate response. Students' personalities and experiences will determine which images speak most powerfully to them.

ANALYZING LITERATURE

1. The poem is set in a dirty, grim-looking city filled with a "wilderness of wires," imposing "concrete slabs," and "cold" artificial lights. The atmosphere is cold and forbidding.
2. The speaker has been buried under the city's "silver paradise." It is the natural world, waiting and certain it will "get through" to topple the human structures.
3. The speaker says that nature, always indifferent to humans and their ambitions, will ultimately destroy the "silver paradise" and re-establish a forest where the city once stood.
4. The title points out the urban setting and the time of year as well as gives the vantage point from which we view the city (a city bus moving along its streets).
5. The city is empty in the sense that it lacks the richness, beauty, resilience, and unlimited power of nature. It will also be empty of people and all things human-made when nature reclaims the territory.
6. Students may relate most readily to the skyscrapers ("monuments of concrete slabs") that dominate urban landscapes, but the dirt ("gritty window"), "cold light," and hostile bus rider (old woman glaring "secret hatpins") may capture the imagination of some.
7. The homes and gardens of her old neighborhood have been destroyed to build the freeway. Where once people laughed, children played, and flowers and vegetables flourished, there is the ugly scar of the road.
8. The grasses, garden plants, and trees begin to grow and produce again, revealing the resilience of nature.
9. When she was young, she believed the freeway offered escape from the poor neighborhood and cannery. Now she wants to be a part of that neighborhood and to reclaim the part of herself "mown under," as she shows when she scrambles over the fence to get in.
10. Students may feel that revisiting the site of her former home, despite its changes, will make her feel connected to her culture and bloom like a "loose seed." Others may argue that

---

Responding to Literature

Personal Response

Describe an image that stays in your mind after reading the poems.

--- **ANALYZING LITERATURE** ---

A Bus Along St. Clair: December

RECALL AND INTERPRET

1. What is the **setting**, or place, at the beginning of this poem? What is the general atmosphere of this place? Support your answer with specific details from the poem.
2. According to the third stanza, what has happened to the speaker? Who might the speaker be in this poem? Explain and support your response.
3. In the last five stanzas, what does the speaker tell the person being addressed? What message do the speaker's words convey to you?

EVALUATE AND CONNECT

4. What does the title add to your understanding of the poem?
5. What do you think the speaker's last statement, "your place is empty" means? Do you agree with the speaker? Why or why not?
6. Which of the images in the poem best matches your own experiences of being in a dense urban area?

Freeway 280

RECALL AND INTERPRET

7. What does the speaker say that the freeway conceals? What might have gone on there in the past?
8. In stanza two, what remains despite the freeway? What does their presence tell you about them?
9. What did the speaker want from the freeway? How does she or he seem to feel about it now? Give details from the poem to support your answers.

EVALUATE AND CONNECT

10. Theme Connections   Do you think the speaker will find "that part of me" that he or she is hoping to find in line 22? Why or why not?
11. In your opinion, how do the Spanish words enhance Cervantes's poem? How would the poem be different without them?
12. Think about your response to the Focus Activity on page 654. How does your group's view of urban environments compare with the views expressed in this poem?

---

destruction makes it impossible for her to reanimate what was "mown under like a corpse."
11. The Spanish words make the poem resonate with the culture the speaker wants to reclaim. Without them, the poem would lack direct connection with that culture.
12. Students' responses will depend upon the magnitude and personal involvement of the losses and gains they reported in the Focus Activity.

Literary ELEMENTS

Speaker

Like the narrator in a work of prose, the **speaker** in a poem is the voice that communicates with the reader. The speaker may be a fictional person, an animal or thing, or even the voice of the poet. Often a poet invents a speaker with a particular identity in order to create a desired impact or impression. For example, the speaker in "Freeway 280" uses many Spanish words and expressions, indicating to the reader that the speaker could be Cervantes herself or someone with a similar background. The speaker's words also create a

particular tone. The speaker in "A Bus Along St. Clair: December" addresses the reader angrily and powerfully, expressing a tone of indignation and perhaps vengeance.

1. How effectively does the speaker in "A Bus Along St. Clair: December" convey the poem's message? Use evidence from the poem to support your answer.
2. Describe the speaker's tone in "Freeway 280."

● See **Literary Terms Handbook,** p. R12.

LITERATURE AND WRITING

Writing About Literature

Comparing Themes There are similarities between these poems, but how close are they in **theme,** or message? In a paragraph, state the main theme of each poem. Then write another paragraph or two discussing how the themes are alike and how they are different. Use specific details from the poems to elaborate on your thoughts.

Creative Writing

Along for the Ride Suppose the speaker in "A Bus Along St. Clair: December" shows up in your community on some form of public or private transportation. What might the speaker have to say? To whom might the speaker's words be addressed? Record the speaker's remarks as a poem, a monologue, or a dialogue.

EXTENDING YOUR RESPONSE

Literature Groups

A Dim View of Progress Both speakers present views of the industrialized world. How do they make their case? Work with your group to find details in each poem that suggest how construction and building affect the world. Then decide how convincing, as well as how realistic, each speaker's case is. Share your opinions and your reasons with other groups.

Listening and Speaking

Understanding the Past Interview older relatives, friends, or neighbors who lived in your community a long time ago. Ask them to show you old photographs and describe what their neighborhood was like, what changes they've seen, and what they think about the changes. Share your findings.

Interdisciplinary Activity

Science: Close to Home As land is developed for human use, animal populations may move, decline, or become extinct. Working with a partner, contact your state or local park district, or local chapters of environmental organizations, to find out the status of animal species in your area. Present your findings in a chart or map.

Reading Further

You might enjoy these poems:

"The Ottawa River by Night" and "Bored" from *morning in the burned house,* new poems by Margaret Atwood.

📖 **Save your work for your portfolio.**

Objectives

- To read and analyze poems in which families pass along insights about life
- To explain the meaning and effect of symbols in poems
- To write a comparison of the observations in two poems

Skills

Writing: Evaluating an Explanation
Grammar/Language: Verb Tense
Collaboration: Literature Groups

Motivating →OPTIONS

Selection Focus Transparency 61: Have students view the art, describe what they see, and discuss what it tells them about the culture from which it came.

Focus Activity: Give pairs of volunteers a concept and have them role-play parent and child, using the method of explanation they think is best. Limit role-plays to a minute.

Before You Read

Making a Fist and *What We Believe*

——— FOCUS ACTIVITY ———

How might a parent or other adult explain a difficult concept to a young child? What kinds of details should be told and what, if anything, should be left out?

QUICKWRITE Briefly write about which methods you think might work best in explaining things to young children. Give examples of when you think a factual approach is best and when you'd suggest a story or a fictional approach.

SETTING A PURPOSE Read to find out how two speakers talk about things that are difficult to explain.

——— BACKGROUND ———

Did You Know?

- To make a fist, the muscles in the hands have to contract. To contract, a muscle needs a signal from the brain, transmitted through the nervous system, as well as energy and oxygen, carried by the blood. When a person is dying, the heart stops pumping blood to the peripheral nervous system, which controls the hands and other extremities of the body. Therefore, making a fist becomes impossible.

- There are many Native American stories that explain the origin of horses. Apaches and Navajos were some of the first peoples to obtain horses. Their traditions suggest that horses were formed from colored clay. Similarly, a Skidi Pawnee story tells of a young boy who forms a pony out of mud and brings it to life.

Meet
Naomi Shihab Nye

"I believe poetry is as basic to our lives . . . and to education as anything else there could possibly be," says Naomi Shihab Nye (shiʹ häb nē). To promote her belief, Nye travels around the world, reading poetry and visiting schools. Growing up with a Palestinian father and an American mother, Nye lived in Missouri, the Middle East, and Texas. Nye sees poetry as a uniting force among people and cultures everywhere.

Naomi Shihab Nye was born in 1952.

Meet
Anita Endrezze

Half Yaqui Indian and half European, Anita Endrezze (enʹ drə zē) often writes about her Yaqui heritage, capturing the rhythms of the natural world and exploring relationships between humans and nature. Endrezze was raised in Hawaii and the western United States and attended college in Washington, where she later built a log cabin in a pine forest with her husband.

Anita Endrezze was born in 1952.

RESOURCE MANAGER

Lesson Planning Resource
The *Unit Three Planning Guide* (pp. 83–88) provides additional lesson notes and reduced versions of all print resources.

📁 **Other Print Resources**
- Active Reading Guide, p. 61
- Grammar and Language Workbook, pp. 145–150
- Grammar and Composition Handbook, Lessons 5.3–5.4
- Quick Checks, p. 61

- Selection and Theme Assessment, pp. 117–118
- Performance Assessment, p. 60
- Spanish Summaries, p. 61
- Inclusion Strategies
- English Language Learners Sourcebook

Transparencies
- Selection Focus 61
- Literary Elements 61

- Grammar and Language 53

Technology
- Audio Library
- Spanish Audio Library
- Glencoe Literature Web Site
- Testmaker

MAKING A FIST

Naomi Shihab Nye

For the first time, on the road north of
   Tampico,°
I felt the life sliding out of me,
a drum in the desert, harder and harder
   to hear.
5 I was seven, I lay in the car
watching palm trees swirl a sickening
   pattern past the glass.
My stomach was a melon split wide inside
   my skin.

"How do you know if you are going
   to die?"
I begged my mother.
We had been traveling for days.
10 With strange confidence she answered,
"When you can no longer make a fist."

Years later I smile to think of that journey,
the borders we must cross separately,
stamped with our unanswerable woes.
15 I who did not die, who am still living,
still lying in the backseat behind all my
   questions,
clenching and opening one small hand.

_____
1 *Tampico* (tam pē′ kō) is a port city on Mexico's east coast.

Fritzmobile, 1984. Frank Romero. Acrylic on canvas, 66 x 108 in. Private collection.

POETRY ❧ 661

SYMBOL Help students recognize the symbolic significance of the "grass-weaver." Who weaves "gentle blankets" out of grasses? *(A spirit that planned for the growth, death, and rebirth of the seasons.)*

E **Active Reading**

INTERPRET Students may need help with the meaning of these statements. Ask what the lines imply about time's passage and the identity of the tribe. *(The assertions extend to the past and the future and state that personal identity is interwoven with the earth, its animals, and stories about all three.)*

Thematic Focus

Issues of Identity In "Making a Fist," the sense of self grows out of a small, personal gesture. In "What We Believe," it comes from a feeling of oneness with others. With which outlook do most students identify?

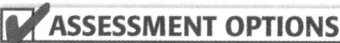

ASSESSMENT OPTIONS

📁 *Quick Checks,* p. 61

Teaching Options

Dakota Teaching, c. 1951. Oscar Howe. Watercolor, 13¾ x 21⅛. The Phillbrook Museum of Art. Museum Purchase 1951.8.

WHAT WE BELIEVE

Anita Endrezze ᵔ

We believe in a land where sweating horses
kick up the dust, forming clay ponies
that sigh with red and yellow breaths.

D 5   We believe in a grass-weaver,
whose fingers make gentle blankets,
trusting in green, yellow, and brown.

We believe the horses will wear our blankets,
will drift forever past our campfires,
listening to us telling stories of long ago.

E 10   We believe that long ago we were horses
and grass, that our stories are our children's
dreams. We are waiting for the sound of hoof-beats

to rise from our throats and for the tall grasses
to stamp and snort in the wind. What we believe
15   will always be—and always be true.

662 ❧ UNIT 3

MEETING INDIVIDUAL NEEDS **ENGLISH LANGUAGE LEARNERS**

Native American Culture English language learners may lack background knowledge about Native American outlooks. They need to understand that the poem is based on a world view that interweaves all things on earth harmoniously and sees a spirit in each.

Activity Have students locate myths of native peoples of the Southwest and Plains. Working in groups with more-proficient English speakers, students can read and discuss several myths. Encourage students to summarize the myths orally for the class in English and to compare them to myths of their native cultures.

Additional Resources
📁 *English Language Learners Sourcebook*

Responding to Literature

Personal Response

With which poem do you more closely identify? Why?

Personal Response

Probably more students will have had an experience like that in "Making a Fist."

ANALYZING LITERATURE

MAKING A FIST

RECALL AND INTERPRET

1. What does the speaker say he or she was feeling at the beginning of the poem? What do you think the third line is describing?

2. What does the speaker ask? Do you think the mother might have intended more than one meaning with her answer? Explain.

3. In your own words, state what the speaker is thinking and doing in the last stanza.

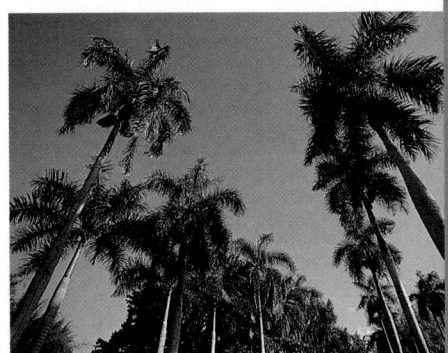

EVALUATE AND CONNECT

4. Why, do you think, is the speaker still carrying the memory of that road trip? Have you had a similarly memorable experience from your early childhood? Explain.

5. Do you agree with the speaker's comments and conclusion in the last stanza? Cite specific lines and give reasons.

6. Theme Connections   In your opinion, does this poem present positive or negative observations about life? Support your answer with lines from the poem.

WHAT WE BELIEVE

RECALL AND INTERPRET

7. What do the speakers in this poem believe? What do their beliefs tell you about them?

8. In what does the grass-weaver trust? What do you think this trust means?

9. What are the speakers waiting for? Why do they have to wait?

10. What is the speakers' concluding comment? What is the meaning of that comment?

EVALUATE AND CONNECT

11. How do lines 12–14 affect the rest of the poem? Explain.

12. After reading the poem, what do you think the speakers value? Do you share any of these values? Why or why not?

ANALYZING LITERATURE

1. She is carsick and believes she is dying; she is hearing her heartbeat grow fainter.
2. She asks her mother how to tell if she is going to die. Yes. Her mother offers a concrete gesture that comforts and gives self-reliance to battle fears.
3. She smiles as she compares her present state, in which she still has fears, questions, and confusions as she travels through life, to that literal trip.
4. It was a frightening, uncomfortable time and therefore memorable. Responses may include accidents, sicknesses, and near misses during trips.
5. Despite "unanswerable woes" and the need to travel "separately," the speaker finds comfort in the gesture of self- affirmation, making a fist. Those who agree will admire her for this.
6. The poem compares life to a journey in the backseat of a car, driven by other forces, enduring trouble alone; however, a positive tone emerges from the focus on survival and self-reliance.
7. They believe in their stories, which teach interdependence of all things on earth: horses made from clay, blankets woven from grass. They trust and love the natural world.
8. He or she trusts in "green, yellow, and brown" (colors of growing things through the year), i.e., in the ability of the earth to provide through the seasons.
9. They wait for their oneness with horses and grass to show itself. Perhaps they must wait for the proper attitude of humility and acceptance, or perhaps for a cycle of creation to renew itself.
10. Asserting that these beliefs are true and eternal, the speaker shows faithfulness and links the beliefs to the endless passage of seasons.

LITERARY ELEMENTS

1. It symbolizes her power to keep herself going. A fist connotes defiance and strength, both needed to beat back "unanswerable woes."
2. Red and yellow symbolize earth; green, yellow, and brown symbolize growing things in their life cycle. These symbols draw the earth and its life force into the belief system described and show their goodness (*sigh* and *gentle* imply this).

Additional Resources

Literary Elements Transparency 61

LITERATURE AND WRITING

Writing About Literature

Students' comparisons should
- summarize the observation about life in each poem.
- discuss the speaker's reaction to this observation in each poem.
- draw details of support from each poem.
- end with a summary of similarities and differences in the poems.

Personal Writing

Students' anecdotal descriptions should
- summarize the explanation and its circumstances.
- evaluate the explanation's impact.
- give logical reasons for this evaluation.

EXTENDING YOUR RESPONSE

Literature Groups Suggest that groups review their responses to questions 6, 10, and 12 on page 663 as a starting point for this discussion.
COLLAB. LEARN.

Internet Connection Encourage students to present what they learn about Yaqui language, songs, art, and beliefs orally. 🗨

Performing Have students review the lesson on oral interpretation on page 633. 🗨 **COLLAB. LEARN.**

Literary ELEMENTS

Symbol

A **symbol** is a sign that represents, or stands for, something else. In poetry and other forms of literature, a symbol is a word or phrase that conveys an idea or a range of ideas beyond its literal meaning. For example, in "Making a Fist," when the speaker refers to "that journey," she or he is talking about both a literal journey taken as a child and the larger journey of life. In "What We Believe," the blankets the grass-weaver makes for the horses might symbolize the care and respect the speakers feel toward the horses.

1. What does making a fist symbolize to the speaker in "Making a Fist"? Do you think this is an effective symbol? Why or why not?
2. What might the colors mentioned throughout "What We Believe" symbolize? How do these symbols affect the poem overall? Explain and support your answer.

● See **Literary Terms Handbook**, p. R13.

LITERATURE AND WRITING

Writing About Literature

Comparing Observations   In both poems, the speakers express strong observations about life. Briefly characterize the observations expressed in each poem. Then discuss similarities and differences between the two observations and how they affect the speakers' approach to life.

Personal Writing

Living Through It   Using your response to the Focus Activity on page 660 as a starting point, write a few paragraphs about a time when an adult explained a difficult concept to you. Did the explanation help you to understand? Was it a good or memorable explanation? How could the explanation be improved? If you wish, share your writing with a classmate.

EXTENDING YOUR RESPONSE

Literature Groups

Pass It Along   Which of these two poems would you be more likely to recommend to another reader? Within your group, share what you think are the main ideas expressed in the two poems. Discuss which ideas seem most important to you and which ones you think could really benefit someone else. Share your group's conclusions with the class.

Internet Connection

Yaqui Culture   Endrezze's poem reflects her Yaqui Indian heritage. Look on the Internet to find out more about Yaqui culture. Find out in what part of North America the Yaqui originally lived, what Yaqui art is like, and what life is like for Yaqui Indians today.

Performing

Performance Piece   Work with a partner or several other students to prepare a dramatic reading or enactment of one of the poems. Use voices, movements, music, and props to help convey the poem's words, actions, mood, and meaning. Share your performance with the class.

Reading Further

You might enjoy these works:

"Thank You in Arabic" from *Never in a Hurry,* a collection of Nye's essays.

"The Girl Who Loved the Sky," a poem by Anita Endrezze from *Harper's Anthology of 20th Century Native American Poetry.*

📖 **Save your work for your portfolio.**

✔ ASSESSMENT OPTIONS

📁 *Quick Checks,* p. 61
📁 *Selection and Theme Assessment,* pp. 117–118
📁 *Performance Assessment,* p. 60
💾 *Testmaker*

MEDIA Connection

Travel Guide

When two cultures collide, misunderstandings sometimes occur. The more you know about the foreign cultures you come into contact with, the easier it is to blend in with them.

The Culturally Sensitive Traveler

from *Asia Through the Back Door*

by Rick Steves and Bob Effertz with John Gottberg

You can be a "Beautiful American." Your fate as a tourist lies in your own hands.

Cultural No No's

Before you land, you should at least know a few things that would shock the locals. Then you can decide whether you want to do just that or to fit in. The following are some cultural faux pas [social blunders] that apply to most places in Asia.

Saving Face

You'll be taking giant steps backward if you get angry, if you raise your voice and shout when you're not getting the service you expect or are otherwise frustrated. Not only will you be causing the person on whom you vent your anger a loss of face [embarrassment] but you yourself will lose respect in their eyes, which you can't expect to regain.

Body Language

The following gestures are regarded as universally offensive or obscene throughout Asia: pointing with your forefinger (use your open hand); beckoning someone (including a taxi) with a crooked forefinger (use your whole hand, palm down, waving toward you); making a fist and hitting it against your open palm.

Many Asians feel the head is the home of the soul. Resist patting even small children on the beanie; it's disrespectful.

If someone laughs or smiles at a seemingly inappropriate moment, don't be surprised. Smiles and laughter are used to cover up embarrassment and shock as well as to show happiness. In many Asian cultures (as well as in America), strong feelings are not shown in public.

In general, dress conservatively. In temples and mosques, anticipate modesty dress codes: keep your upper arms and back covered, and don't wear shorts. You may need to take your shoes off before entering a religious place. If in doubt, watch what the locals are doing.

When visiting a private home, be observant. In many countries, you'll remove your shoes before you enter.

Respond

1. Which cultural taboo do you think the average American would have the most trouble avoiding during a visit to Asia? Why would avoiding the taboo be difficult?

2. If you were planning a visit to another country, what else could you do to help ensure that you would be a "culturally sensitive traveler"?

Reading *Minilesson*

Using Graphic Aids Point out that travel guides often feature maps of regions, cities, or even of famous buildings, designed to aid travelers to these sights. Such graphic aids or visuals can be a quick way to learn specific facts as well as spatial layout. Whether armchair traveling or planning a tour, one can gain a great deal if one knows how to "read" such maps.

Activity Have students work in pairs to analyze a map in a travel brochure or magazine article, noting each kind of information given and explaining symbols in legends. Ask students to use the map to create a brief travelogue for a tour based on the map's information. **L2**

Additional Resources
📁 *Reading Workbook*

MEDIA Connection

Objective

- To read and understand a travel guide

Literature — LINK

Foreign Ways and **Song for My Name** The article details ways to avoid conflict with a visited culture. The poems that follow (pp. 667–668) focus on cultural differences that set the speakers apart.

Respond

1. Students may think gestures, which are habitual and automatic, the most difficult to restrict.
2. Students may suggest researching the country's customs before traveling, carefully observing the behavior of people in that country, and asking questions if there is doubt about correct behavior.

Additional Resources
📁 *Media Connections Activities,* p. 17

Teaching Options

interNET CONNECTION

Traveling in Asia Have students use a search engine to look for further information about Asian cultural expectations.

Objectives

- To read and analyze poems about the uniqueness of cultural identity
- To identify and analyze the effects of sensory details in poems

Skills

Reading/Thinking: Identifying Assumptions; Drawing Conclusions
Listening/Speaking: Songs

Motivating
→ OPTIONS

Selection Focus Transparency 62: Have students use the photographs as a starting point for a discussion of cultural diversity.

Focus Activity: Have students make a master list of clues of national identity.

Before You Read

Foreign Ways and *Song for My Name*

FOCUS ACTIVITY

If you visited another country and spent some time with the people there, what things about yourself, besides your language, might reveal that you are an American?

LIST IDEAS Use your journal to list the clues that point to your national identity.

SETTING A PURPOSE Read to find out how two speakers reveal their cultural identities.

BACKGROUND

Did You Know?

- Chinese is different from most Western languages in that the words have only one syllable and do not in themselves contain varying stresses. Since many Chinese words sound alike, speakers convey different meanings by using tonal variations—words are said at high or low pitches, or at pitches that vary by rising or falling. Chinese consists of many different dialects, including Mandarin, which is China's official national language.

- Historically, the Chickasaw people are known for their tall, strong bodies and very dark eyes and hair, which the women typically wore in braids. The Chickasaw traditionally have lived in harmony with nature and used the cycles of the moon to measure time. During European colonization of North America, the Chickasaw and other Native American cultures had begun to decline. By the twentieth century, the Chickasaw people had been driven from their ancestral land, and centuries of Chickasaw tradition were lost. Major centers of the Chickasaw Nation exist today in Oklahoma.

Meet Diana Chang

The daughter of a Chinese father and a European-Asian mother, Diana Chang spent her childhood in China but moved to New York City when she was in high school. Although her works reveal her Chinese influences, she considers herself "an American writer whose background is Chinese."

Diana Chang was born in New York City in 1934.

Meet Linda Hogan

"If you believe that the earth, and all living things, and all the stones are sacred, your responsibility really is to protect those things," says Linda Hogan. Although Hogan belongs to the Chickasaw tribe, she grew up outside the Indian community. Today, Hogan expresses her commitment to Chickasaw values through her writings about relationships between humans and other species and as a volunteer for wildlife rehabilitation.

Linda Hogan was born in Denver, Colorado, in 1947.

RESOURCE MANAGER

Lesson Planning Resource
The *Unit Three Planning Guide* (pp. 89–93) provides additional lesson notes and reduced versions of all print resources.

Other Print Resources
- Active Reading Guide, p. 62
- Reading Workbook
- Quick Checks, p. 62
- Selection and Theme Assessment, pp. 119–120

- Performance Assessment, p. 61
- Spanish Summaries, p. 62
- Inclusion Strategies
- English Language Learners Sourcebook

Transparencies
- Selection Focus 62
- Literary Elements 62

Technology
- Audio Library
- Spanish Audio Library
- Glencoe Literature Web Site
- Testmaker

Foreign Ways

Diana Chang ∾

If I were in China this minute
and running after a friend
spied across from the hotel
I was staying at

5 waving to him, say
calling his name in Mandarin

Still they'd know me—
the body giving the person away
betrays a mind
10 of its own—

my voice from Duluth°
my lope with its prairie air

_____

11 *Duluth* is a port city on Lake Superior in
Minnesota; its citizens are mostly of northern
European descent.

Night Lights of Kowloon. Dong Kingman. Watercolor, 22 x 22 in. Private collection.

A Active Reading

VISUALIZE Ask students to imagine and describe the scene using sensory details. Encourage them to use the watercolor to help set the scene. How does the speaker sound and move within that scene?

Additional Resources
📁 *Active Reading Guide,* p. 62
🎧 *Audio Library*
🎧 *Spanish Audio Library*

B Active Reading

INTERPRET In what sense does the body have "a mind of its own"? *(It acts automatically, using the gestures, intonations, and ways of moving drawn from culture.)* Ask students to explain why the speaker considers this a betrayal. *(She wants to fit in, to belong in China, where her ancestors probably lived.)*

VIEWING THE ART

Dong Kingman's art is owned by over fifty museums, including the Metropolitan Museum of Art. In this painting, he conveys the active life of a foreign city.

Teaching Options

Reading *Minilesson*

Identifying Assumptions Remind students that to understand fully a writer's meaning, it may be necessary to dig for underlying assumptions that are not stated, but rather implied.

Activity Pair students to have them reread the poem and list two assumptions about the speaker's self-image and philosophy of identity. Ask pairs to present their answers. *(She feels she is American, not Chinese. The place where one is raised, not ancestry, gives more to one's identity.)* **L2**

Additional Resources
📁 *Reading Workbook*

Song for My Name

Linda Hogan

C

Before sunrise
think of brushing out an old woman's
dark braids.
Think of your hands,
5 fingertips on the soft hair.

D

If you have this name,
your grandfather's dark hands
lead horses toward the wagon
and a cloud of dust follows,
10 ghost of silence.

E

That name is full of women
with black hair
and men with eyes like night.
It means no money
15 tomorrow.

Such a name my mother loves
while she works gently
in the small house.
She is a white dove
20 and in her own land
the mornings are pale,
birds sing into the white curtains
and show off their soft breasts.

If you have a name like this,
25 there's never enough water.
There is too much heat.
When lightning strikes, rain
refuses to follow.
It's my name,
30 that of a woman living
between the white moon
and the red sun, waiting to leave.
It's the name that goes with me
back to earth
35 no one else can touch.

Seated Woman, 1990. Robert C. Gorman. Oil pastel drawing.

Viewing the painting: What specific images, words, or impressions from the poem do you think this painting reflects? Cite the line and explain the connection.

668 UNIT 3

Responding to Literature

Personal Response

Which lines from each of the two poems made the most impression on you? Why?

ANALYZING LITERATURE

Foreign Ways

RECALL AND INTERPRET

1. What does the speaker imagine doing in the first two stanzas? What does this reveal about him or her?
2. In the third stanza, who would know the speaker? Why?
3. Where is the speaker's home? What else do the last two lines reveal?

EVALUATE AND CONNECT

4. Think about your response to the Focus Activity on page 666. Which of the clues that reveal the speaker's identity are similar to those that might reveal your own?

Song for My Name

RECALL AND INTERPRET

5. What details about family members does the speaker present in the first three stanzas? What do these facts suggest about the speaker's life?
6. What information about her mother does the speaker give in the fourth stanza? Why, do you think, does her mother love her name?
7. What conditions does the speaker's name evoke in the last stanza? What might her references to the moon, the sun, and the earth mean? Explain.

EVALUATE AND CONNECT

8. What effect does Hogan create by the **repetition** of the word "name" throughout the poem? (See Literary Terms Handbook, page R10.) In what ways is this poem a "song" for her name?

Literary ELEMENTS

Sensory Details

Sensory details are words, phrases, or images that convey sensory experiences—seeing, hearing, tasting, touching, and smelling. "Song for My Name," for example, appeals to the sense of touch as the speaker says, "Think of your hands, / fingertips on the soft hair."

1. Find three other sensory details in "Song for My Name." Tell what sense(s) each appeals to, and what effect each creates.
2. To what senses does "Foreign Ways" appeal? Explain and give examples.

● See **Literary Terms Handbook,** p. R11.

POETRY 669

Responding to the Selection

Personal Response

Students may mention lines of vivid concrete imagery such as "my lope with its prairie air" from "Foreign Ways" and "It means no money tomorrow" from "Song for My Name."

ANALYZING LITERATURE

1. She imagines visiting China and calling to a friend in native Mandarin. She wants to belong there.
2. The Chinese who saw her and heard her would realize she is American because of her intonation and manner of moving.
3. She is from Duluth, Minnesota, and has grown up in the prairies of North America.
4. Students may mention accent, inflection, and speed of speaking, in addition to language itself. Other identifiers are clothing and, possibly, racial features.
5. She describes grandparents and ancestors, suggesting that she has spent much time with them, steeped in traditional ways.
6. The white mother has adopted Chickasaw ways most likely out of love for her family by marriage, although "her own land" is much softer and easier.
7. The name evokes drought and the violence of a storm without rain. Moon and sun may symbolize mother and father, white and Native American worlds, between which she is pulled. Together with earth, they suggest the strength of name, or identity, which goes with one throughout life and beyond.
8. The repetition of *name* intensifies the effect of the word and makes readers think of all that is "in a name"—cultural heritage, personal family inheritance, and so on.

LITERARY ELEMENTS

1. "Dark braids," "dark hands," "women with black hair" appeal to the sense of sight. "A cloud of dust" and the birds' "soft breasts" are both visual and tactile; the birdsong appeals to hearing.
2. Running and waving give a tactile sense to the poem. The voice calling a name in Mandarin draws on the sense of sound.

Additional Resources

✍ *Literary Elements Transparency 62*

Writing Workshop

Objectives

- To create a poem inspired by a character or a real person
- To plan, draft, revise, edit, and present a poem
- To reflect on and assess one's poem

Teaching Strategies

PREWRITING

Explore ideas After students have selected at least three possible subjects, have them pair off and describe the characters to each other. Listeners should ask questions and give feedback on the character who offers the most potential.

Teaching Options

~: Writing Workshop :~

Creative Writing: Poem

Many of the poems you have read in Theme 8 paint striking portraits of distinctive characters—a base runner poised to steal a base, an old woman who's lost her youthful beauty, a mother who stitched her family's history into her quilts. **In this workshop, you will write a poem** about a person—real or fictional—who has interested or inspired you.

- As you write your poem, refer to the **Writing Handbook**, pp. R58–R72.

The Writing Process

PREWRITING

PREWRITING TIP
Scan your journal, a scrapbook, or a photo album to find people you might write about.

Explore ideas
The following suggestions might help you find a subject for your poem.

- Skim the poems in Theme 8. Do any of the characters in these poems remind you of someone you want to write about?
- Think of people in occupations or situations that intrigue you. Could you write about a soccer player, a drummer, or a coach?
- Jot down names of people who have made strong impressions on you. Have you admired a friend? Envied a character from a book?

Consider your purpose
The type of poem you write will depend on what aspects of the character you want to describe. Use the following chart as a guide.

Use this type of poem . . .	Which is defined as a . . .	If you want to . . .
lyric poem	poem in which the speaker expresses personal thoughts and feelings	describe the character or your feelings about him or her
dramatic poem	poem that consists entirely of a dialogue or monologue	show how the character thinks or feels about something
narrative poem	poem that tells a story	show what a character does or how he or she behaves

---

MEETING INDIVIDUAL NEEDS
ENGLISH LANGUAGE LEARNERS

Means of Characterization English language learners may not immediately understand the associations of character traits that other Americans have for certain colors or animals. Explain, for example, that the dragon is a villain in Western thought, but in China it brings good luck.

Activity Ask students to explain the symbolism of different animals and colors in their cultures. Have them write several phrases describing their characters' most interesting and appealing traits.

Additional Resources
📁 *English Language Learners Sourcebook*

Choose your audience

Do your readers already know your character? If not, think about what background information you will need to convey for your poem to make sense.

Freewrite about your character

Most poems are concise—they are shorter than stories or essays. However, this doesn't mean that poets have little to say about their subject. To find the most precise, exciting words and phrases, poets usually draw from a large store of material. You can create a store of material for yourself by freewriting about your character. The springboards below can help get you started.

- What colors come to mind when you think of your character? What smells? What textures?
- If your character were an animal, which one would he or she be? Why do you think so?
- Describe your character in action as if you were watching him or her. Describe that same action from his or her point of view.

STUDENT MODEL

> I see the base stealer take off, leaving small clouds of dust hovering over third base as he flies home. He runs so fast he's a blur. Like a really fast bird? The pitcher pulls back his arm and shoots the ball like a rocket. The player is sliding in, becoming invisible in a big cloud of dust.

Review poetry elements

Poetic elements can help you convey sights, sounds, and emotions. For descriptions of these elements, turn to Genre Focus: Poetry on pages 578–579.

Consider using sound devices:

Sound Device	STUDENT MODEL
alliteration	Got to get
rhyme	roar/more
repetition	waiting, waiting, waiting—
onomatopoeia	thumping feet

POETRY 671

Consider your purpose Students may find it helpful to review examples of each type of poem and the way it presents a character. Poems by Frost, Kipling, Tennyson, and Browning provide outstanding examples of lyric, dramatic, and narrative poems. Point out that a dramatic poem would most probably feature the character as the speaker.

Choose your audience Have students list two or three details that readers will need to visualize or hear about in order to understand the character.

Freewrite about your character Encourage students to write out all the details and associations that come to mind, even though they may only use a small amount of the material. First notes sometimes just "grease the wheels" for the subconscious, but they are important preparation for meatier memories.

Review poetry elements You may want to have students create a chart for sound devices and types of figures of speech, then experiment with details from their notes to create examples.

Additional Resources

- *Writing and Proofreading Practice,* pp. 1–7, 60–65
- *Writing and Proofreading Transparencies 1–6, 39–40*
- *Writer's Choice,* Lesson 3.5

MEETING INDIVIDUAL NEEDS — MULTIPLE LEARNING STYLES

Logical-Mathematical Students with a gift for logic and working with patterns may have more success beginning their poems by considering the structure that will complement their character. Explain that structure includes the overall shape of a poem and the way lines and stanzas are shaped. Give an example of a concrete poem, in which much of meaning comes from the poem's shape.

Activity Have students sketch the shape or shapes within which their poem will lie and keep this paper in view as they freewrite. Encourage students to underline ideas and sound effects words they may want to repeat or give prominent placement to emphasize character traits within the structure they have chosen. **L3**

DRAFTING

Experiment Encourage students to rearrange, rewrite, and read aloud their first ideas. Encourage them to list various synonyms and related words down the margin of their notepaper and try several on for size to see what sound and connotations fit the context best.

Write your draft Assure students that even seasoned poets must go through this frustrating process of working and reworking, moving and trying. The process is intuitive and exhaustive but can pay off with a poem that seems right and "effortless."

Use imagery to heighten the effect Encourage students to write as many images as they can for each line of their poems. Then they can review their ideas and pick out the image that they feel adds the most to the line.

TECHNOLOGY TIP

Using a word processor in the drafting stage is invaluable to the writer of poems. It allows words, phrases, and lines to be moved easily or duplicated and tried in another location. It also allows alternative ideas and wordings to be placed in the margin or a second column so they won't be forgotten.

Teaching Options

~: Writing Workshop :~

DRAFTING

DRAFTING TIP
Finding the right word can be one of the most difficult aspects of writing poetry. Keep a thesaurus, a dictionary, and a rhyming dictionary handy as you draft and revise.

Experiment

Take a playful approach in drafting your poem. Experiment with words, phrases, and sound effects, and don't pressure yourself to create a perfect poem immediately. Let your intuition guide you. Try different rhyme schemes and different line and stanza lengths. Read your writing aloud to see if it has a rhythmic flow. The rhythm you create should suit your subject. It might be fast or slow, smooth or choppy.

STUDENT MODEL

> Now! No turning back, decision made
>   heart pounding, pulse pounding
> Got to, got to, got to get from here to there
>   white sliver of the plate
> Thumping feet, the muffled roar
>   rush of hot breath to my lungs
> The pounding effort of the run, the run
>   aching strain of every muscle
> And then the dream-slow slide
>   a thoughtless freedom like sleep
> The cloud of dust, the momentary mystery
>   limp, drained, done
> Waiting, waiting, waiting, waiting—safe!

Write your draft

Writing a poem is a little like solving a puzzle. If you fit the right words in the right places, the picture suddenly appears. However, you may spend a lot of time trying to fit the wrong words in the wrong places. Accept that possibility, and as you draft, feel free to change your plan, your images, and your ideas.

Use imagery to heighten the effect

Poetry relies on **imagery**. The images that a poet creates in words can arouse a feeling, trigger a memory, or evoke a response similar to a physical sensation. Read each of the lines of your poem and put yourself emotionally and imaginatively into the moment. Add a word or phrase that you associate with how you feel.

Writing Minilesson

Sharpening Images Explain that imagery allows sense experience within the imagination, so it is vital to bringing the poem to life. As students review their drafts, they should evaluate the imagery they have included. Are images specific and originally worded? Do they appeal vividly to more than one sense? (Smell and touch are usually neglected.) As an example, have students discuss how the following

image might be sharpened:

> My son ran excitedly through the flowers.

It could be rephrased as *My boy flew, white flower heads shooting like sparks where his knees pumped.*

Activity Have students work in pairs to sharpen these images with vivid sounds, smells, sights, and touches:
1. She could really dance up a storm.
2. He looked proud and confident.
3. The pianist's fingers flew over the keys.

L2 COLLAB. LEARN.

Additional Resources

 Writer's Choice, Lesson 3.5

REVISING

Take another look

As you revise, ask yourself where you can use poetic techniques such as figurative language and sound devices to enhance the reader's experience of the poem. Use the **Questions for Revising** to guide your work.

Have a writing conference

Read your poem aloud to a writing partner. Ask your listener to be aware of any places where you can improve your use of imagery and sound devices to make the poem more engaging. Then go through the **Questions for Revising** with your listener.

QUESTIONS FOR REVISING

How can I

- ☑ use sensory details to bring my character to life?
- ☑ use similes and metaphors to create images of my character?
- ☑ replace clichéd and vague expressions with precise and original ones?
- ☑ make better use of rhythm and other sound devices to match the subject of the poem?
- ☑ clarify any confusing lines or expressions?

STUDENT MODEL

Got to get from here to there,

Get to that white sliver, the plate,

Get these thumping feet from ~~here to there,~~ third safe

Got to get through the ~~crowd noise,~~ muffled roar

Got to draw one hot breath more,

Got to make the pounding effort,

Got to
~~I~~gnore the aching strain,

And slip into the dream-slow slide,

Into a thoughtless freedom like sleep,

Through the momentary ~~cloud~~ mystery of dust

And the limp, drained, done doubt

Of waiting, waiting, waiting, waiting—

Got to
~~I hope I'll~~ be safe!

Take another look You may want to suggest to students that they read their drafts aloud to hear rhythms. Have them ask themselves these questions:

- Do these rhythms suit the theme and subject of my poem?
- Do the sound values of words mesh with the mood I want to create?

Have a writing conference Remind partners to make notes about any comments or ideas for improvements as they listen, without interrupting the reader.

Have students use the Proofreading Checklist on the inside back cover of their textbooks.

Be sure students understand that poetry is not an excuse for ignoring rules of punctuation. While there is some flexibility to use mechanics to enhance meaning, their unintentional misuse will invariably confuse readers rather than clarify points.

PUBLISHING/PRESENTING

If possible, videotape students' performances for their evaluation. Students may enjoy publishing their work in a class magazine or school publication or on-line.

Reflecting

Portfolio Students may ask themselves these questions as they evaluate their poems.

Does my poem
- create a true impression of the character?
- use the most precise, vivid language possible to characterize?
- represent some of my best work?

If students answer yes to two or more of these questions, suggest they consider adding their poem to their portfolio.

Teaching Options

~ Writing Workshop ~

EDITING/PROOFREADING

PROOFREADING TIP
There are no ironclad rules for punctuation and capitalization in poetry. Follow the rules that make sense for your poem, keeping readability in mind.

Although poets sometimes depart from conventional rules of grammar for effect, unintentional mistakes are still distracting. The **Proofreading Checklist** on the inside back cover can help you catch errors in your poem.

Grammar Hint

Use punctuation to indicate the pauses that you want your readers to make in reading your poem. A period, an exclamation point, or a question mark calls for the longest pause. A comma calls for the shortest.

LONG PAUSES, SLOW PACE: *Should I go? Should I go? I go?*

SHORT PAUSES, QUICK PACE: *I've got to go, got to go, to go.*

● For more about punctuation, see **Language Handbook,** pp. R26–R28.

STUDENT MODEL

Go! Go now! Got to go now!

After should I go, should I go,

Hart pounding, pulse pumping,

Comes got to go, got to go, got to go—

PUBLISHING/PRESENTING

PRESENTING TIP
When reading your poem aloud, be sure your audience is able to absorb your words.

Consider holding a class poetry festival featuring readings of student poems. Each student might tell about the source of inspiration for his or her poem and describe how the poem developed.

Reflecting

What did you find most difficult about writing this poem? What was most gratifying? How has writing a poem changed your appreciation of the poems you have read? Answer these questions in your journal.

Save your work for your portfolio.

✔ ASSESSMENT OPTIONS

📁 ***Writing Assessment and Portfolio Management***
- Writing Assessment, pp. 2–19, 37–38
- Portfolio Management, pp. 20–22

Theme 9

Observations and Expressions

How observant are you? Do you notice small details or do you tend to take in the "big picture"? Do you find ways to share what you see? Poets—among the world's best observers—use language to express what they feel as well as what they witness. In this theme you'll encounter poetry that examines everything from minute details to cosmic events.

THEME PROJECTS

Learning for Life

Get Out the News Turn the language of poetry into the language of everyday life.

1. Choose two poems from this theme. How might the events they describe be recounted in a newspaper article?

2. Write a newspaper article about each poem's events. Be objective; focus on facts rather than opinions.

3. Read the news stories aloud to the class. Ask your classmates to identify the poems.

Internet Connection

Poetic Resource On-line poetic activity abounds.

1. Using a keyword such as "poetry" and a search engine such as Yahoo! or Excite, research Web

sites that may be of interest to poets, such as journals that allow poets to submit their work on-line, chat rooms for writers, sites that give bibliographic information on famous poets, and more.

2. Present your most interesting findings in a database or poster. Make sure you describe each site and list its address.

"There sleeps Titania sometime of the night lull'd in flowers . . . ," 1994. Carmen Garcia. Etching, 57 x 76 cm. Private collection.

POETRY 675

LITERATURE & HUMANITIES

 To set the mood for this poetry theme, play "Summertime," CD 1, Track 41, in Glencoe's *World of Music*.

GLENCOE
TECHNOLOGY
LITERATURE CLASSICS CD-ROM
Search for other selections related to the theme of observations and expressions.

Theme 9

Teaching Strategies

The following suggestions may help your students plan and carry out their theme projects.

Learning for Life

- Have students begin by listing possible news events that could be derived from the poems.
- Explain that the opening paragraph of a newspaper article often answers Who? What? When? Where? Why?
- Before presenting their articles to the class, students might want to watch newscasts to review how news anchors read the news.

Internet Connection

- If students need help using the Internet, arrange for student volunteers to help them.
- Remind students to include a detailed description of each Web site.
- Encourage students to use a logical plan of organization to present categories of information.

Additional Resources

📁 *Interdisciplinary Activities,* pp. 18–19
📁 *Viewing and Representing Activities,* pp. 23–24
📁 *Listening and Speaking Activities,* pp. 17–18
📁 *Critical Thinking Skills,* pp. 24–26
📁 *Selection and Theme Assessment,* pp. 187–188
📁 *Performance Assessment,* p. 78

FINE ART
TRANSPARENCY 8

You may want to use Fine Art Transparency 8 to compare and contrast how artists and poets observe the world and express ideas.

POETRY 675

Theme 9 SKILLS SCOPE AND SEQUENCE

SELECTIONS	Literary Elements	Reading and Thinking	Writing	Vocabulary and Spelling	
Night Clouds Amy Lowell **Tiger Year** Laura Iwasaki	Figurative Language, SE p. 680 *Alliteration, TWE p. 677*	*Drawing Conclusions, TWE p. 677*	Freewrite, SE p. 676 Comparing and Contrasting Poems, SE p. 680 Poem, SE p. 680	Explaining Scientific Terms, SE p. 680	
FOR POETS Al Young **REAPERS** Jean Toomer	Sound Devices, SE p. 685	*Identifying Assumptions, TWE p. 683*	Compare Tone, SE p. 685 Poem, SE p. 685		
Three Haiku Matsuo Bashō **Two Tanka** Lady Ise	*Imagery, TWE p. 687* *Haiku and Tanka, TWE p. 688*	*Visualizing, TWE p. 687* *Main Idea, TWE p. 687*	Quickwrite, SE p. 686 Haiku and Tanka, SE p. 688		
A Motto from Poets: Leave Stone Roberto Fernández Retamar **Constantly risking absurdity** Lawrence Ferlinghetti	Epic Simile, SE p. 694 *Extended Metaphor, TWE p.691*	*Questioning, TWE p. 691*	Cluster Map, SE p. 690 Paragraphs, SE p. 694 Personal Motto, SE p. 694 Using Simile and Metaphor, SE p. 695 *Article, TWE p. 691*	*Keywords, TWE p. 689*	
let my spirit fly in time Sandra María Esteves **Jazz Fantasia** CARL SANDBURG	Onomatopoeia, SE p. 701 *Diction, TWE p. 699*	Author's Purpose, SE p. 696 *Inferring, TWE p. 698*	Analyze Structure, SE p. 701 Musical Word Composition, SE p. 701 **COLLAB. LEARN.** *Summarizing, TWE p. 698*	*Keywords, TWE p. 696* *Onomatopoeic Words, TWE p. 699*	

Key: Student material is in roman. Teacher material is in italic.   Technology   **COLLAB. LEARN.** Collaboration

Grammar and Language	Listening, Speaking, and Viewing	Life Skills	Study, Research, and Technology
	COLLAB. LEARN. Literature Groups, SE p. 680 *Pantomime Moon and Planetary Movements, TWE p. 681*	Learning for Life: Comparison Chart, SE p. 680	**COLLAB. LEARN.** *Research Phases of the Moon, TWE p. 678* ⌨ *Using the Internet, TWE p. 680*
Subject-Verb Agreement, TWE p. 683	**COLLAB. LEARN.** Literature Groups, SE p. 685	⌨ Using the Internet, SE p. 685	Research: Reaping, SE p. 685 ⌨ Internet Connection, SE p. 685
	Elaboration, TWE p. 687		Research: Art, SE p. 688 ⌨ Using the Internet, SE p. 688
Concrete and Abstract Nouns, TWE p. 695	**COLLAB. LEARN.** Literature Groups, SE p. 694 Multimedia Presentation, SE p. 694 Poetry Reading, SE p. 694	⌨ *Using the Internet, TWE p. 694*	⌨ Internet Connection, SE p. 694 ⌨ *Internet Connection, TWE pp. 689, 691* ⌨ *Using a Film, TWE p. 692*
	COLLAB. LEARN. Literature Groups, SE p. 701 Acting Out a Poem, SE p. 701	Using an Encyclopedia, SE p. 701 Time Line, SE p. 701	**COLLAB. LEARN.** Using the Internet, SE p. 701 Time Line, SE p. 701 ⌨ *Internet Connection, TWE p. 696* ⌨ *Using an Audiotape, TWE p. 699*

SELECTIONS	Print Resources		
Night Clouds AMY LOWELL *Tiger Year* LAURA IWASAKI	Unit Three Planning Guide, pp. 100–104 * Active Reading Guide, p. 63		* Quick Checks, p. 63 Selection and Theme Assessment, pp. 121–122 Performance Assessment, p. 62 Spanish Summaries, p. 63
FOR POETS AL YOUNG REAPERS JEAN TOOMER	Unit Three Planning Guide, pp. 105–109 * Active Reading Guide, p. 64	Grammar & Comp Handbook, Lesson 6.2 Grammar and Language Workbook, p. 173	* Quick Checks, p. 64 Selection and Theme Assessment, pp. 123–124 Performance Assessment, p. 63 Spanish Summaries, p. 64
Three Haiku MATSUO BASHŌ *Two Tanka* LADY ISE	Unit Three Planning Guide, pp. 110–114 * Active Reading Guide, p. 65		* Quick Checks, p. 65 Selection and Theme Assessment, pp. 125–126 Performance Assessment, p. 64 Spanish Summaries, p. 65
A Motto from Poets: Leave Stone ROBERTO FERNÁNDEZ RETAMAR *Constantly risking absurdity* LAWRENCE FERLINGHETTI	Unit Three Planning Guide, pp. 115–120 *Active Reading Guide, p. 66	Grammar & Comp Handbook, Lesson 1.1 Grammar and Language Workbook, p. 48 Reading Workbook, pp. 67–68	* Quick Checks, p. 66 Selection and Theme Assessment, pp. 127–128 Performance Assessment, p. 65 Spanish Summaries, p. 66 Spanish Translations
let my spirit fly in time SANDRA MARÍA ESTEVES *Jazz Fantasia* CARL SANDBURG	Unit Three Planning Guide, pp. 121–125 * Active Reading Guide, p. 67		* Quick Checks, p. 67 Selection and Theme Assessment, pp. 129–130 Performance Assessment, p. 66 Spanish Summaries, p. 67 Spanish Translations

*Also available in Spanish

Transparencies	Technology Resources
Selection Focus Transparency 63 Literary Elements Transparency 63	🎧 💿 Audio Library 🎧 💿 Spanish Audio Library 💾 💿 Vocabulary Puzzlemaker 💻 Web Site: lit.glencoe.com
Selection Focus Transparency 64 Grammar and Language Transparency 54 Literary Elements Transparency 64	🎧 💿 Audio Library 🎧 💿 Spanish Audio Library 💾 💿 Vocabulary Puzzlemaker 💻 Web Site: lit.glencoe.com
Selection Focus Transparency 65 Literary Elements Transparency 65	🎧 💿 Audio Library 🎧 💿 Spanish Audio Library 💾 💿 Vocabulary Puzzlemaker 💻 Web Site: lit.glencoe.com
Selection Focus Transparency 66 Grammar and Language Transparency 55 Literary Elements Transparency 66 Fine Art Transparency 17	💿 Literature Launchers Videodisc 🎧 💿 Audio Library 🎧 💿 Spanish Audio Library 💾 💿 Vocabulary Puzzlemaker 💻 Web Site: lit.glencoe.com
Selection Focus Transparency 67 Literary Elements Transparency 67 Fine Art Transparency 31	💿 Literature Launchers Videodisc 🎧 💿 Audio Library 🎧 💿 Spanish Audio Library 💾 💿 Vocabulary Puzzlemaker 💻 Web Site: lit.glencoe.com

📁 Theme RESOURCES

- Listening and Speaking Activities (pp. 17–18)
- Viewing and Representing Activities (pp. 23–24)
- Critical Thinking Skills (pp. 24–26)
- Media Connections Activities (pp. 18–19)
- Interdisciplinary Activities (pp. 18–19)

See also these additional planning resources:
- English Language Learners Sourcebook
- Inclusion Strategies Sourcebook
- Literature Groups Sourcebook

PRESENTATION Plus!

Use Glencoe's *Presentation Plus!* This multi-media teaching tool lets you present dynamic lessons that will engage your students. Using Microsoft PowerPoint,® you can customize the presentations to create your own personalized lessons.

Objectives

- To read and analyze poems about the impact of the night sky
- To identify, classify, and analyze the effects of types of figures of speech
- To write a comparison of subject and structure for two poems

Skills

Reading/Thinking: Drawing Conclusions
Writing: Poem
Life Skills: Comparing Messages
Collaboration: Literature Groups

Before You Read

Night Clouds and *Tiger Year*

FOCUS ACTIVITY

Close your eyes and picture the night sky. What do you see?

FREEWRITE In your journal, freewrite about your impressions of the night sky; write for five minutes without stopping.

SETTING A PURPOSE Read to see how the night sky affects the speakers of two poems.

BACKGROUND

Did You Know?

- In the early 1900s, Amy Lowell was a leader of a poetic movement known as **Imagism.** Poets create an image when they describe or portray something, such as a feeling, an idea, or a sensory experience, in vivid language. Imagist poets believed that an image in a poem should be so precise, so concrete, that it immediately evokes in the reader all the emotion and meaning of the poem. The Imagists were inspired by the precision and simplicity of the Japanese haiku and believed that imagery was the essence of poetry. Lowell and other Imagist poets experimented with new verse forms, unusual rhythms, and surprising themes.

- The Chinese calendar is based on the cycles of the moon. A new year begins with the second new moon of the winter season. According to Chinese legend, a designated animal rules over each year within a twelve-year cycle. The twelve animals are, in order: rat, ox, tiger, hare, dragon, snake, horse, sheep, monkey, rooster, dog, and pig. Numerous cultures hold claim to the origins and sequence of the twelve-animal cycle. One legend says that Buddha invited all the animals to visit him before he departed Earth. Only these twelve animals showed up, arriving in this order. In Chinese tradition the animal ruling in the year a person is born influences that person's personality. The year in which Laura Iwasaki was born—1950—was the Year of the Tiger.

Meet Amy Lowell

"I do not suppose that anyone [who is] not a poet can realize the agony of creating a poem. Every nerve, even every muscle, seems strained to the breaking point." Despite her words about the writing process, Amy Lowell was known as a dedicated, versatile poet, who wrote more than 650 poems. Her first major collection, *A Dome of Many-Colored Glass*, was published in 1912. In 1926, a year after her death, Lowell was awarded the Pulitzer Prize.

Amy Lowell was born in Massachusetts in 1874 and died in 1925.

Meet Laura Iwasaki

Asian American poet Laura Iwasaki grew up in Los Angeles, California. She attended the University of Hawaii where she majored in pharmacology. After college, Iwasaki traveled throughout South America and then moved back to Los Angeles to live.

Laura Iwasaki was born in Hawaii in 1950.

Diamonds in the Sky. Eric Sloane (1905–1985). Oil on board, 50 x 52 in. Courtesy of the Estate of Eric Sloane and the Michael Wigley Galleries Ltd., Santa Fe.

Night Clouds

Amy Lowell

The white mares of the moon rush along the sky
Beating their golden hoofs upon the glass Heavens;
The white mares of the moon are all standing on their hind legs
Pawing at the green porcelain doors of the remote Heavens.
5   Fly, Mares!
Strain your utmost,
Scatter the milky dust of stars,
Or the tiger sun will leap upon you and destroy you
With one lick of his vermilion° tongue.

---

9 The color *vermilion* is vivid red to reddish orange.

POETRY 677

A Literary Elements

IMAGERY As students analyze the metaphor comparing clouds to mares, have them note the colors used and describe their effect. *(White mares appear ghostly; golden hooves add flash and excitement; green porcelain doors are exotic. Color is used in painterly fashion.)*

Additional Resources
📁 *Active Reading Guide,* p. 63
🎧 *Audio Library*
🎧 *Spanish Audio Library*

B Literary Elements

ALLITERATION Have students identify examples of alliteration. *(mares of the moon, golden . . . glass, hoofs . . . Heavens, pawing . . . porcelain)*

C Literary Elements

FIGURES OF SPEECH: *Metaphor and Mood* Invite students to tell why the poet compares the sun to a tiger. What mood does this metaphor create? *(The tiger's ferocity and murderous intent add the urgency of a life-and-death conflict, making the sky reflect the earth's dramas.)*

Teaching Options

Reading Minilesson

Drawing Conclusions Lowell's images and metaphors allow readers to draw conclusions about how the scene looks. Remind students that to draw conclusions, a reader must evaluate what is given and compare it to personal experience and observations.

Activity Ask students to write a description of this sky as a meteorologist would.

Then have them point out in the poem verbs that suggest movement in the sky, as well as images that suggest the appearance of the sky, clouds, and moon. Ask them what words refer to atmospheric conditions that match appearances. **L3**

Additional Resources
📁 *Reading Workbook*

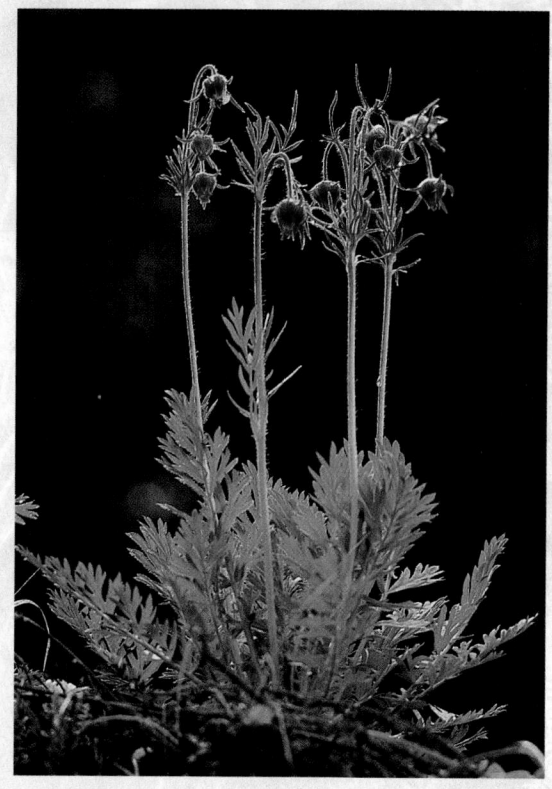

Tiger Year

Laura Iwasaki ⁓

new moon,
    you lie
in shadow—
traveling over the face
5 of silent water

as planets circle in the gathering dark
like pale insects
around the opened throats of flowers.

see how the stars are blossoming
10 one by one:
as if merely to breathe.

they blossom for you,
defining your way
through the clear night air
15 with hands as pure and bright as clouds.

will you hurry to my season?
it is time:
you bring the light.

INTERDISCIPLINARY CONNECTION

Responding to Literature

Personal Response

What images from these poems remain with you after reading?

ANALYZING LITERATURE

Night Clouds

RECALL AND INTERPRET

1. In your own words, tell what the speaker is describing in lines 1–4. What is the emotional impact of the speaker's description? Explain.
2. Summarize the advice that the speaker gives in lines 5–7. What does the speaker imply will happen in lines 8–9 if this advice is not followed?
3. What, do you think, is the overall **theme,** or message, of this poem? What words or lines from the poem imply this message?

EVALUATE AND CONNECT

4. Theme Connections   Recall how you pictured the night sky for the Focus Activity on page 676. How does Lowell's observation of the night sky compare with yours?
5. Which lines from the poem do you find the most creative or unusual? Why? Support your answer with specific details from the poem.

Tiger Year

RECALL AND INTERPRET

6. Whom or what does the speaker address? What is the speaker describing in the first two stanzas?
7. What image does the speaker present in lines 9–15? What does this suggest about the poet's view of the night sky?
8. What do you think the speaker means in the last stanza? Support your response with details from the poem.

EVALUATE AND CONNECT

9. How would you summarize the speaker's **tone** or attitude toward the subject of this poem? How does the tone affect your reading of the poem? Explain.
10. In what ways does this poem alter or add to your appreciation of the sky? Explain.

Responding to the Selection

Personal Response

Both poems are rich in vivid imagery; "white mares pawing at the green porcelain doors" and planets as "pale insects" circling "opened throats of flowers" are likely choices.

ANALYZING LITERATURE

1. Storm clouds—perhaps lit by lightning—are pushed rapidly across the vivid sky and past the moon, roiling up with unstable air currents. The images create a hurried, unpredictable atmosphere.
2. The mares should flee or the sun will destroy them.
3. The violence and destructiveness of nature and humankind are reflected (or duplicated) in the cyclical activities of the heavens.
4. Students' descriptions may have been quieter and calmer.
5. Images of clouds as white mares rearing at the green doors of heaven and of a leaping tiger sun with vermilion tongue are most unique. They defy the typical views of night sky as majestic or romantic.
6. The speaker addresses the moon, shrouded in darkness above a quiet body of water and surrounded by planets.
7. As stars appear, they are likened to blooms that anticipate the fullness of the moon and create a stage for its drama. For the poet, the sky is alive with beauty, mystery, and drama.
8. She too is anxious for the moon's full light, which is especially favorable (accompanied by blossoming, purity, and brightness) in her "season" (the year of the tiger).
9. Her voice has a hushed and devout tone that reveals both excitement and belief in the moon's power. Her quiet innocence adds mystery to the poem.
10. Some students may find their view of the sky less scientific and cold.

LITERARY ELEMENTS

1. Stars blossom, as though the sky is filled with living plants (metaphor, line 9), and have hands (personification, line 15), whose purpose is to usher in the moon. These elements make the heavens reflect earth's living system, where energies and movements are interdependent and purposeful.

2. Lowell's entire poem is an extended metaphor of a stampede of horses battering at the doors of heaven. The poem's color, energy, and excitement level derive wholly from this metaphor.

Additional Resources

Literary Elements Transparency 63

LITERATURE AND WRITING

Writing About Literature

Students' comparisons should
- use subject-by-subject or feature-by-feature organization to analyze the same elements in both poems.
- begin each paragraph with a clear topic sentence about an aspect of the poems.
- develop each topic sentence using details from the poems.

Creative Writing

Students' poems should
- contain two or more images.
- develop images fully and suggestively with descriptive details.

EXTENDING YOUR RESPONSE

Literature Groups You may want to make books on astronomy available to groups as they make their lists.
COLLAB. LEARN.

Interdisciplinary Activity Ask students to compare with a partner information they have located and to discuss how the information helps them understand the poem.

Literary ELEMENTS

Figurative Language

Figurative language conveys meaning beyond the literal definition of a word. In these two poems, Lowell and Iwasaki use three types of figurative language: **similes**, which compare two unlike things using *like* and *as*; **metaphors**, which compare two or more things that have something in common; and **personification**, the giving of human qualities to nonhuman things. For example, Iwasaki uses the simile "planets circle in the gathering dark / like pale insects / around the opened throats of flowers" to compare planets to insects. The simile suggests that the planets seem to be alive and appear to have a reason for their movements.

1. What other figurative language does Iwasaki use in "Tiger Year"? List at least one example of each type and explain its effect.
2. How do metaphor and personification make Lowell's poem "Night Clouds" lively and vivid?

● See **Literary Terms Handbook,** p. R5.

LITERATURE AND WRITING

Writing About Literature
Compare and Contrast Poetic Elements   In two or three paragraphs, compare and contrast "Night Clouds" and "Tiger Year," considering similarities and differences in language, subject matter, form and structure, imagery, and theme. Cite examples from the poems.

Creative Writing
Sky Poem   Choose an object in the sky–day or night, near or far. Think of at least two images that the object suggests. Then, using those images, write a short poem about the object you chose. Try to describe the images in a way that conveys your ideas about this object.

EXTENDING YOUR RESPONSE

Literature Groups
Strong Yet Fragile   In your group, discuss how "Night Clouds" conveys both the strength and fragility of the night sky. Use specific details from the poem to support your ideas. Then list other elements or events in the sky that might support this contrast. Share your list with the class.

Interdisciplinary Activity
Science: Explaining Terms   Choose a line from one of the poems that contains a reference to the sky, the stars, clouds, insects, or the planets. Use library resources or the Internet to find scientific information about the reference. Then write a few paragraphs in which you summarize the information and explain whether or not it helps your understanding or alters your appreciation of the poem.

Learning for Life
Comparison Report   Search the Internet or library references to identify a work of art that illustrates the imagery in one of the poems or that conveys a similar meaning or message. Prepare a brief report to explain your choice to the class. Create a comparison chart with pictures of the art work and your comments to illustrate your points.

Reading Further
You might enjoy the following poems by Amy Lowell and Laura Iwasaki.

"Music," from *The Complete Poetical Works of Amy Lowell,* illustrates how reality can be transformed by the imagination.

"Geography," by Laura Iwasaki, is filled with images of space and time. It appears in *Counterpoint, Perspectives on Asian America* by Emma Gee.

📖 **Save your work for your portfolio.**

Learning for Life If students are unable to locate a suitable artwork, you may want to suggest that they create their own.

✓ ASSESSMENT OPTIONS

📁 *Quick Checks,* p. 63
📁 *Selection and Theme Assessment,* pp. 121–122
📁 *Performance Assessment,* p. 62
💾 *Testmaker*

Phases of the Moon

As you read "Tiger Year," did you wonder how long it takes for a new moon to "bring the light"? It takes just a day. The night after a darkened new moon, a sliver of light appears in the sky.

Moonlight is actually reflected sunlight. As the moon revolves around the earth, varying amounts of its sunlit surface are visible. A new moon occurs when the moon is between the sun and the earth; the sun lights only the side facing away from the earth. A full moon occurs when the earth is between the moon and the sun, allowing sunlight to flood the entire surface of the moon facing the earth. The moon travels around the earth in about 29½ days, completing the cycle from new moon to full moon and back to new moon again.

Since ancient times, people have studied the phases of the moon and planned important activities, such as planting and harvesting, around the lunar cycle. Even today, some people use the lunar cycle to time fishing trips, haircuts, medical treatments, and many other ventures.

As the moon is "growing," or changing from a new moon to a full moon, it is called a **waxing moon.** As it is "shrinking," or changing from a full moon back to a new moon, it is called a **waning moon.** A **crescent moon** is banana-shaped; a **gibbous moon** is roughly oval.

Phases of the moon

Activity

Some people believe that human emotions and energy levels are influenced by the lunar cycle. Why not find out for yourself? Follow one lunar cycle and keep a record of the phases of the moon and how you felt and acted. Compare your record with those of your classmates and see what conclusions you can draw.

Objective

- To understand and explore the effects of changes in the moon

Teaching Strategies

Show students the movements that cause the moon to appear different; display a diagrammatic model of the relative positions of the sun, moon, and earth for each of the phases shown in the photographs. Prepare students for the Activity by inviting speculation about why the moon affects behavior.

Activity

Students' records should
- account for each day in the lunar cycle.
- attempt to control variables such as time of observations and types of behaviors noted.
- maintain reasonable objectivity.

Teaching Options

MEETING INDIVIDUAL NEEDS MULTIPLE LEARNING STYLES

Bodily-Kinesthetic Students who process knowledge through movement will benefit by demonstrating the movements and positions of the sun, moon, and earth at different phases of the moon.

Activity Have students use balls to model the earth and moon and a flashlight for the sun. Ask volunteers to stand in position and imitate the movement of each body relative to the others. As the positions change, ask students to explain why the moon appears to people on earth to grow or shrink. **L1**

Objectives

- To read and analyze poems that observe both treachery and exhilaration in a rural setting
- To identify examples of alliteration and assonance and their effect
- To write a comparison of tone

Skills

Reading/Thinking: Identifying Assumptions
Writing: Poem
Grammar/Language: Subject-Verb Agreement with Intervening Expressions
Collaboration: Literature Groups

Motivating
└──→OPTIONS

Selection Focus Transparency 64: After they view the transparency, have students discuss things in the scene that could serve as poetic inspiration.

Focus Activity: Have each student in turn name something pictured in his or her sketch, without repeating. Expand the list until all details have been named.

Before You Read

For Poets and Reapers

FOCUS ACTIVITY

In your mind's eye, picture an area of open land that has no buildings on it.

JOURNAL In your journal, describe the scene you are visualizing. Include everything you "see," such as plants, animals, rocks, and perhaps even people.

SETTING A PURPOSE Read to share the speakers' observations and images of people interacting with the natural world.

BACKGROUND

Did You Know?

- "The stuff of poetry is life itself," says African American poet Al Young. From childhood on, Young's life has included both urban and rural influences. Growing up in Detroit, he absorbed the city's working-class culture and Motown music. At his grandparents' home in rural Mississippi as a youth, Young came under the sway of "the mystery of natural things."

- A *scythe* is a tool with a long, curved blade attached to a long handle. It may be used for cutting tall grasses or for *reaping,* or harvesting, grain by hand. The movement of a reaper wielding a scythe is graceful and rhythmic. Holding the scythe in front of his or her body, the reaper moves it back and forth in wide, sweeping arcs. Like much other farm labor, the work of reaping by hand is exhausting: the same motion is repeated hundreds and thousands of times, and the work is performed in a stooped-over position.

Meet Al Young

Novelist, screenwriter, and poet, Al Young says that part of the American dream is the yearning to be somewhere else. Following that impulse, he moved to California and has made that state his home. Believing that poetry and music go together, Young sometimes bursts into song when giving poetry readings.

Al Young was born in 1939 in Ocean Springs, Mississippi.

Meet Jean Toomer

"Life is mystery in motion," said Jean Toomer, a poet, novelist, and philosopher who spent much of his own life seeking to understand the mysteries of human existence. This quest took Toomer to Georgia in 1921, where he found his ancestral roots in the richly textured culture of blacks living in the American South. Toomer celebrated this culture in *Cane*, a book of poetry and fiction.

Jean Toomer was born in 1894 in Washington, D.C., and died in 1967.

RESOURCE MANAGER

Lesson Planning Resource
The *Unit Three Planning Guide* (pp. 105–109) provides additional lesson notes and reduced versions of all print resources.

📁 **Other Print Resources**
- Active Reading Guide, p. 64
- Grammar and Language Workbook, p. 173
- Grammar and Composition Handbook, Lesson 6.2
- Quick Checks, p. 64

- Selection and Theme Assessment, pp. 123–124
- Performance Assessment, p. 63
- Spanish Summaries, p. 64
- Inclusion Strategies

🖉 **Transparencies**
- Selection Focus 64
- Literary Elements 64
- Grammar and Language 54

Technology
🎧 Audio Library
🎧 Spanish Audio Library
💻 Glencoe Literature Web Site
💾 Testmaker

FOR POETS

Al Young ～

A

Stay beautiful
but don't stay down underground too long
Don't turn into a mole
or a worm
5 or a root
or a stone

B

Come on out into the sunlight
Breathe in trees
Knock out mountains
10 Commune° with snakes
& be the very hero of birds

Don't forget to poke your head up
& blink
think
15 Walk all around
Swim upstream

Don't forget to fly

---

10 To *commune* means to exchange feelings
and ideas with someone else.

REAPERS

Jean Toomer ～

Black reapers with the sound of steel on stones
Are sharpening scythes. I see them place the hones°
In their hip-pockets as a thing that's done,
And start their silent swinging, one by one.
5 Black horses drive a mower through the weeds,
And there, a field rat, startled, squealing bleeds.
His belly close to ground. I see the blade,
Blood-stained, continue cutting weeds and shade.

C

---

2 The fine-grained stones used to sharpen any kind of blade are called *hones.*

A Critical Thinking

IDENTIFYING ASSUMPTIONS Help students verbalize the view of the underground poet. What danger does Young see in the isolation that poets may impose on themselves?

Additional Resources

📁 *Active Reading Guide,* p. 64
🎧 *Audio Library*
🎧 *Spanish Audio Library*

B Literary Elements

ASSONANCE Ask students to find examples of assonance in lines 8 and 9. (*Breathe in trees; Knock out mountains*)

C Literary Elements

SOUND EFFECTS Read the first two lines aloud while students listen for repeated sounds. (*Initial s sounds and long e sounds predominate.*)

Thematic Focus

Observations and Expressions
Have students contrast the two poets' observations of a rural setting. Which view do students identify with?

✓ **ASSESSMENT OPTIONS**

📁 *Quick Checks,* p. 64

Teaching Options

Grammar and Language *Minilesson*

Subject-Verb Agreement with Intervening Expressions
Remind students that the subject and verb of a sentence must agree in number and person, even if they are not side by side. Write this sentence on the board: *The turmoil of creatures living in the weeds does not trouble the reapers.* Have students identify the subject and verb (underlined) and confirm their agreement. Discuss the

confusion caused by words that come between the subject and verb.

Activity Have students find the subjects and verbs of the sentences in lines 1–2 and 6 of "Reapers" and identify the intervening words. Then have students write two sentences in which the subject and verb are separated and check for subject-verb agreement. **L2**

Additional Resources

🖨 *Grammar and Language Transparency 54*

📖 *Grammar and Language Workbook,* p. 173

📖 *Grammar and Composition Handbook,* Lesson 6.2

📖 *Writer's Choice,* Lesson 16.2

Responding to the Selection

Personal Response

"To Poets" makes open land exuberant; "Reapers" leaves the impression of a relentless, thoughtless relationship between man and nature.

ANALYZING LITERATURE

1. He warns poets against "staying underground"—an isolated mental existence in search of beauty that can lead to a warped perception of the life going on all around.
2. The emphasis on action ("breathe," "knock out," "commune") suggests delight in nature's vitality and a desire for intimate involvement with nature.
3. The speaker wants poets to immerse themselves in every aspect of life, including its difficulties ("swim upstream"). Only in this way can the poet "fly" (receive legitimate inspiration and write what relates to real life).
4. The tone is inviting and invigorating—suitable qualities for convincing someone of the value and sensual appeal of plunging into life.
5. Students may suggest becoming more observant, more willing to take on challenges, and more willing to take chances.
6. They sharpen blades and swing them to cut grass and weeds.
7. They move mechanically, silently, implying resignation, not satisfaction, in their work. An act completed only registers as "a thing that's done."
8. The blade of a mower pulled by horses hits a rat and continues with no pause. Like the reapers, the horses are on "automatic pilot."
9. The style is realistic and matter-of-fact, creating a feeling of detachment from the events. This feeling distances readers, making them realize that they are like the reapers.
10. He observes that the grind of repetitive work creates indifference to real pain and suffering.

Responding to Literature

Personal Response

What was your reaction to each poem? Share your reaction with your classmates.

ANALYZING LITERATURE

FOR POETS

RECALL AND INTERPRET

1. What advice does the speaker give in the first stanza? What do you think the speaker means by this advice?
2. What does the speaker tell poets in the second stanza? What do these lines suggest to you about the speaker's views of people and nature?
3. Express in your own words what the speaker says in the last two stanzas. In your opinion, why might the advice be important for poets? for non-poets?

EVALUATE AND CONNECT

4. What is the **tone** of this poem? (See Literary Terms Handbook, page R13.) How does the tone help convey the poet's message?
5. If you took the advice offered in this poem, how might your life change?

REAPERS

RECALL AND INTERPRET

6. Describe in your own words what the reapers do.
7. What attitude do the reapers seem to have toward their work? What words or phrases convey that attitude?
8. Summarize what happens in the last four lines of the poem. What connections do you see between the reapers and the horses? Explain.

EVALUATE AND CONNECT

9. How would you characterize the way in which the accident with the field rat is described? How does the **style** of the description affect your reaction to the event? (See Literary Terms Handbook, page R12.)
10. Theme Connections   What observations does the poet make in this poem? What message do you think he is conveying? Explain.

Literary ELEMENTS

Sound Devices

Poets use sound devices to help develop the mood or tone of a poem and to draw attention to particular words or ideas. One type of sound device is **alliteration,** the repetition of sounds, usually consonant sounds, at the beginning of words. As you read "Reapers" aloud, you can hear alliteration in the repetition of the *st* sound in the first line: "*st*eel on *st*one." Another type of sound device is **assonance,** the repetition of vowel sounds in a line of poetry. You can hear

assonance in the repetition of the long *e* sound in "a f*ie*ld rat, startled, squ*ea*ling bl*ee*ds."

1. Identify another example of alliteration and one of assonance in "Reapers." How do these examples affect your reading of the poem?
2. Find an example of assonance in "For Poets." What does it add to the poem?

● See **Literary Terms Handbook,** p. R12.

LITERATURE AND WRITING

Writing About Literature

Comparing Tone   The **tone** of a poem is the emotional attitude that the speaker takes toward the subject. In a paragraph, compare the tone of "Reapers" with that of "For Poets." Identify words and phrases that convey the tone in each poem.

Creative Writing

Poem   Use the description that you wrote for the Focus Activity on page 682 as the starting point for a one- or two-stanza poem about the object you described. Choose the most vivid words from your description, and add **sound devices** such as **alliteration** and **assonance.** Share your poem with the class.

EXTENDING YOUR RESPONSE

Literature Groups

Powerful Images   The power of these poems lies largely in their vivid imagery. In your group, choose the lines from each poem that you find most powerful or memorable. Discuss what makes these lines so compelling, then with your group, design an illustration for each poem based on the lines you choose. Make the lines of poetry part of your design.

Interdisciplinary Activity

History: Reaping   Research the history behind Jean Toomer's poem. What time period is he probably referring to? Who were the reapers? Where did they reap? What were their living and working conditions? Present your findings in a brief report to the class.

Internet Connection

Poet Profiles   Search the Internet for more information about Al Young and Jean Toomer. Use what you find to create a poster profile of one of the two poets, conveying what you find most interesting about him or his life.

Reading Further

You might also enjoy these works by Al Young and Jean Toomer:

Poems: "Sweet Sixteen Lines" and "Son" in *Heaven: Collected Poems 1958–1990,* by Al Young, capture some of the varied feelings of youth.

"November Cotton Flower" and "Storm Ending" in *Cane,* by Jean Toomer, offer other brief portraits of southern culture and landscape.

📖 **Save your work for your portfolio.**

✔ ASSESSMENT OPTIONS

📁 *Quick Checks,* p. 64
📁 *Selection and Theme Assessment,* pp. 123–124
📁 *Performance Assessment,* p. 63
💾 *Testmaker*

Objectives

- To read and analyze poems that suggest large ideas through precise, direct observations of nature
- To write haiku or tanka

Skills

Writing: Haiku or Tanka
Listening/Speaking: Elaboration; Sharing Poems

Motivating
→OPTIONS

Selection Focus Transparency 65: Have students study the photograph and discuss how cycles of nature parallel life in general.

Focus Activity: Invite students to share their descriptions. Note traits that these objects share.

LITERATURE & HUMANITIES

After students view *One Waterfall* (*World History and Art*, Transparency 35), have them examine how the images in the woodcut and in the poem suggest rather than represent nature.

Before You Read

Three Haiku and Two Tanka

FOCUS ACTIVITY

Do most beautiful things last for a long time? Or are most beautiful objects impermanent or temporary? Is something more beautiful if it lasts only a short while?

QUICKWRITE Briefly describe an object of beauty. It may be an item you possess or something in nature. As you describe the object, consider how its permanence or impermanence affects your appreciation of the object.

SETTING A PURPOSE Read to see how two Japanese poets use ancient literary forms to describe the beauty in nature.

BACKGROUND

Did You Know?

- **Haiku** is an unrhymed Japanese verse form consisting of seventeen syllables that are arranged in three lines. The first and third lines have five syllables each; the second line has seven syllables. Traditionally, the goal of haiku is to suggest large ideas, using the simplest and fewest words. Although they leave much to the reader's imagination, haiku poets use explicit and evocative words to lead readers in the right direction. Matsuo Bashō, perhaps the greatest haiku poet of all time, said that a good poem should "seem light as a shallow river flowing over its sandy bed."

- **Tanka** is an unrhymed Japanese verse form that consists of five lines. The first and third lines have five syllables each; the other lines have seven syllables each. Tanka is considered the basic form of Japanese poetry and is sometimes used as a synonym for *waka*. Most tanka focus on a single thought or idea related to love or to an appreciation of nature, a common theme in Japanese poetry. Because the poems are so short and simple, tanka poets, like haiku poets, must rely on precise, direct language to suggest ideas. A tanka can have different meanings for different readers, depending on the life experiences of the reader.

- Some translations of haiku and tanka may lose the poet's original syllable count when the poems are translated into English.

686 ❦ UNIT 3

Meet Matsuo Bashō

"Don't follow in the footsteps of the old poets, seek what they sought." Matsuo Bashō's words echo his approach to life. Using traditional Japanese verse forms of his time, Bashō began his writing career in his twenties. By his early thirties he was considered a *haiku* master. During the last ten years of his life, Bashō perfected the simple and direct haiku style.

Matsuo Bashō was born in 1644 in Iga-Uen, Japan. He died in 1694.

Meet Lady Ise

Considered one of the Thirty-six Poetic Geniuses of Japan, Lady Ise enjoyed the celebrity status and fame that accompanied literary accomplishment in ancient Japan. She served in Emperor Uda's court and was known there for her literary works. Much of her poetry is found in a collection of Japanese poetry known as the *Kokin Wakashū*, or *Kokinshū*, published around the year 905. It was the first in a series of imperially commissioned collections of Japanese poetry.

Lady Ise lived in Japan from approximately 875–938.

RESOURCE MANAGER

Lesson Planning Resource
The *Unit Three Planning Guide* (pp. 104–114) provides additional lesson notes and reduced versions of all print resources.

📁 **Other Print Resources**
- Active Reading Guide, p. 65
- Quick Checks, p. 65
- Selection and Theme Assessment, pp. 125–126
- Performance Assessment, p. 64
- Spanish Summaries, p. 65
- Spanish Translations
- Inclusion Strategies

Transparencies
- Selection Focus 65
- Literary Elements 65

Technology
 Audio Library
 Spanish Audio Library
🖥 Glencoe Literature Web Site
💾 Testmaker

Three Haiku

Matsuo Bashō
Translated by Robert Hass

It would melt
in my hand—
    the autumn frost.

    First day of spring—
I keep thinking about
    the end of autumn.

    Spring!
a nameless hill
in the haze.

Two Tanka

Lady Ise
Translated by Willis Barnstone

Hanging from the branches of a green
willow tree,
the spring rain
is a
thread of pearls.

Translated by Etsuko Terasaki
with Irma Brandeis

Lightly forsaking°
the Spring mist as it rises,
the wild geese are setting off.
Have they learned to live
in a flowerless country?

---

1 *Forsaking* means turning away
  from or abandoning.

Flowers and grasses of the seasons: Autumn, c. 1840s.
Seisei Kiitsu. Ink and colors on silk, approx. 1032 x 346 mm.
The British Museum, London.

Reading the Selection

A Literary Elements

IMAGERY To which sense does this image appeal? *(touch)* What is accomplished by touching the frost? *(Readers feel the strong contrast between the warmth of living tissue and the cold of a force that takes away life; the frost is melted.)*

Additional Resources
Active Reading Guide, p. 65
Audio Library
Spanish Audio Library

B Active Reading

VISUALIZE Have students describe or sketch the structure of willow branches. Why is this effect like a necklace? *(The downward curving branch and the drops of water clinging to it resemble the string and the pearls strung on it that make a necklace.)*

Thematic Focus

Observations and Expressions
Which observation by Bashō or Lady Ise expresses an insight or mood that students share?

✓ ASSESSMENT OPTIONS
Quick Checks, p. 65

Teaching Options

Listening and Speaking *Minilesson*

Elaboration Point out that reading haiku requires readers to recognize a main idea and elaborate from experience. Ask students to state the idea suggested by the image of the first haiku. *(the fragility of frost, despite its killing cold)* Then ask them to use elaboration to flesh out the idea in their own words. *(Elaboration might include a personal anecdote, sensory details, or a quotation.)*

Activity Have students state the idea suggested by another poem and elaborate by adding details orally. Suggest that students use sensory details, specific examples, facts and statistics, anecdotes, quotations, and/or opinions. Students may want to write out their elaborations before presenting them. **L3**

688 UNIT 3

Responding to the Selection

Personal Response

Familiarity of images depends upon students' personal experiences. Raindrops on branches seem most universal.

ANALYZING LITERATURE

1. The image suggests a delicate whorl of frost. It suggests that all living things retreat or die, while it muses on frost's fragility.
2. The poet's distraction from spring's renewal suggests awareness of how quickly seasons turn and new life grows old and dies.
3. Spring, the hill, and the haze suggest the difficulty in seeing as well as a world full of mysterious possibilities.
4. Students may choose the first, citing the expressive image of melting frost.
5. The brevity of natural beauty is one focus of the haiku, and its message inspires the haiku poet.
6. Raindrops on a willow branch are compared to a string of pearls. The metaphor deftly suggests the precious value of rain to nature and its role in bringing spring's adornments to life.
7. Wild geese begin their migration, flying up out of a mist; the reader senses the speaker's sense of loss at their going.
8. The geese leave despite spring's coming and will miss its flowering; the speaker wonders if their cycle of migration means they never experience this season.
9. Students' responses should take impressions of greening plants and spring rain and mist as a starting point.
10. All the poems provoke thoughts about nature and mortality.

EXTENDING YOUR RESPONSE

Writing About Literature

Students' haiku (tanka) should
- focus on a single natural phenomenon or object.
- conform to the line and syllabic requirements of the chosen form.
- create an image with larger suggestive possibilities.

Responding to Literature

Personal Response

Which of the images in these poems seems most familiar to you? Describe the image in your journal and explain why you think it seems familiar.

ANALYZING LITERATURE

Three Haiku

RECALL AND INTERPRET

1. What does the first haiku describe? What does this image make you think about autumn?
2. What is the second haiku about? What sentiment might the poet be trying to evoke?
3. What things does the speaker name in the third haiku? What might this combination of things suggest about daily life?

EVALUATE AND CONNECT

4. Theme Connections   Which haiku do you find most expressive? Support your choice with examples from the poems.
5. Refer to the description you wrote for the Focus Activity on page 686. How well do you think the speaker's descriptions and observations capture the beauty of nature? Do you think the impermanence of nature affects the message of the haiku?

Two Tanka

RECALL AND INTERPRET

6. What two things are compared in the first tanka? What insights about these things does the comparison bring to mind?
7. What natural events does the speaker present in the second tanka? How do these events contribute to the **mood**, or atmosphere, of the tanka?
8. What question does the speaker ask in the second tanka? What might be the meaning of this question?

EVALUATE AND CONNECT

9. In what ways do the images of spring in the two tanka reflect your own observations of spring? Explain.
10. In your opinion, which tanka offers more for you to think about? Why?

EXTENDING YOUR RESPONSE

Writing About Literature

Haiku and Tanka   Use the information provided in the Background section on page 686, as well as the form and content of the Bashō and Lady Ise poems you have read, to help you write three haiku or tanka of your own. Share your poems with other students.

Interdisciplinary Activity

Art: Visualizing Poetry   Search the Internet or library references for a work of art or create your own to reflect the theme in one of the Bashō or Lady Ise poems.

 Save your work for your portfolio.

688 UNIT 3

Interdisciplinary Activity Sumi inkwash painting complements haiku and tanka. Suggest that students search the Internet, entering keywords such as *Japanese art* and *World Art Gallery* to find examples.

LITERARY ELEMENTS

Haiku and Tanka

Additional Resources

Literary Elements Transparency 65

 ASSESSMENT OPTIONS

- *Quick Checks*, p. 65
- *Selection and Theme Assessment*, pp. 125–126
- *Performance Assessment*, p. 64
- *Testmaker*

Press Conference Transcript

Have you ever wanted to leave your mark by accomplishing something special that people would remember? Read the February 18, 1998, press conference with U.S. gold medalist Nikki Stone to hear her comments after winning the freestyle aerial in Nagano, Japan.

Objective

• To read and understand a press conference transcript

U.S. Aerialists Are Golden

I wore number four today, and February 4th was my birthday. Every time I've blown the candles out on my birthday cake my wish has come true. I wished I would make the team a few years ago, and I did. I wished I would win a World Championship, and I did. And I wished this year that I would win the Olympic gold, and now I did.

My first jump I felt really good. The weather was right, the wind was mellow, it felt good in the air and the landing was good. I tried to stay calm and tell myself "you have another jump to do." O[n] my second jump I did a wind check and I think I heard Wayne [Hilterbrand, U.S. ski aerialist head coach] yell louder than he ever had[:] "REACH for the landing."

Two years ago I was the most miserable person you've ever met. Things got turned around, though. But coming here to win a gold medal does make [life] that much sweeter. Every time I went out to the gym I just kept saying, "gold medal, gold medal, gold medal."

Last year at [the] Worlds [Championship] here I set my focus to show everyone that I wasn't 10th best.

I think the guys are just getting scared that the girls are catching up.

On my second jump my nerves were definitely stronger. My form wasn't as good and I just said, "hey, just land this thing."

We've got great coaches, great facilities and a great program in the United States. . . .

[return from back injury]

When I got back in the gym, I just kept telling myself "gold medal, gold medal, gold medal." I got myself to the Olympics and I got myself a gold medal.

[waiting for final scores]

I was nervous, I was definitely nervous. I was thinking gold or silver, but I wanted us to win as many gold medals as we can.

This was my goal in life. I don't know what I'm going to do now.

It feels good to prove a lot of people wrong.

Respond

1. Stone's persistence, work ethic, and positive attitude all seem to play a part in reaching her goals.
2. Students may describe recovery from injuries, setting a goal to win a title in a team sport, or other competitive goals they have achieved after great effort.

Additional Resources

📁 *Media Connections Activities,* p. 18

Respond

1. What personal qualities helped Stone to succeed?
2. Have you or someone you know attempted to reach a difficult goal? Explain.

Teaching Options

Objectives

- To read and analyze poems about the efforts and risks of poets
- To define and analyze an epic simile
- To write a description of the poet and poet's task

Skills

Writing: Personal Motto
Listening/Speaking: Giving a Multimedia Presentation; Poetry Reading
Collaboration: Literature Groups

Before You Read

A Motto from Poets: Leave Stone and
Constantly risking absurdity

FOCUS ACTIVITY

What ideas come to mind when you hear the word *poet*?

MAP IT! Create a cluster map. Surround the word *poet* with words and phrases that express your ideas about what poets are like and what they do.

SETTING A PURPOSE Read to discover how two speakers view the work of a poet.

BACKGROUND

Did You Know?

- While still a teenager, Roberto Fernández Retamar interviewed the renowned American author Ernest Hemingway, who was living near Havana, Cuba, at the time. This interview was Fernández Retamar's first published work, a piece that he later described as "unreadably adolescent." The young man declined Hemingway's offer to assist him in getting his poetry published; he says he felt too embarrassed to accept the famous author's help.

- Lawrence Ferlinghetti is perhaps best known for the role he played in promoting the Beat Movement of the 1950s. The Beats were a group of writers who wanted to take art away from academia and bring it to the people in the streets. Beatniks—as the followers of this movement were dubbed—wore shabby clothing and used the "hip" language of jazz musicians to show their unconventionality. The Beat poets, who included Ferlinghetti, Allen Ginsberg, and Gregory Corso, created poetry that was meaningful and powerful yet free of the rigidity of conventional poetry.

© Fred W. McDarrah

Meet Roberto Fernández Retamar

After Roberto Fernández Retamar graduated from high school at the top of his class, his parents rewarded him by sending him to New York City. "I had just turned seventeen," he said, "and although I had not yet published a single line, I felt certain . . . that I was a poet." Fernández Retamar has since become one of Cuba's most respected and influential writers.

Roberto Fernández Retamar was born in 1930 in Havana, Cuba.

Meet Lawrence Ferlinghetti

The early years of Lawrence Ferlinghetti's life were plagued by the loss of his parents and other family. However, a wealthy family let Ferlinghetti stay in their home and also financed his education. Ferlinghetti became associated with the Beat Movement and produced volumes of powerful poetry.

Lawrence Ferlinghetti was born in 1919 in Yonkers, New York.

A Motto from Poets: Leave Stone

Roberto Fernández Retamar ❧
Translated by Tim Reynolds

A motto° from poets: leave stone
alone, it won't grow; try
trees, working their way up
and up into air.
5   And there they inscribe their names magnificent
in the sun as banners
But its rock keeps when trees
are ash, or furniture; you eat, or sleep, or lie
dead among the painted detritus° of trees.
10   And all the time there's some stone
somewhere, planted, not
bigger, not
smaller, carrying still
across its livid° frontage some savage
15   scrawl, some few letters
of someone long gone who,
one afternoon, graved° them there,
laughing, dreaming, remembering.

---

1 A *motto* is a saying that expresses a guiding principle.
9 *Detritus* (di trī′ tas) is the accumulated remains of something destroyed, eroded, or discarded.
14 Here, *livid* means "pale or grayish-blue."
17 The person who *graved* the letters carved them into the stone.

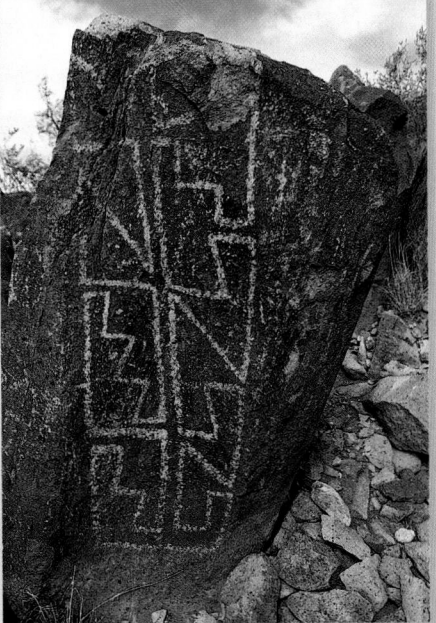

Petroglyphs on exposed stones, Arches National Park, UT. Gerry Ellis, photographer.

A Active Reading

CLARIFY Discuss with students what the poet is saying figuratively here. Why do they think a poet should model his or her efforts on those of a tree? *(Growth in understanding and skill determine the poet's abilities.)*

Additional Resources

📁 *Active Reading Guide,* p. 66
🎧 **Audio Library**
🎧 **Spanish Audio Library**

B Active Reading

QUESTION Students should ask themselves how the speaker's point of view changes here and why. *(The tree's "magnificent inscription" is temporary, like the poet's life. The speaker must look for some other way a poet can "last.")*

C Literary Elements

FIGURES OF SPEECH: *Extended Metaphor* Point out that stone and trees are used metaphorically throughout the poem. Ask students to explain in their own words what stone represents to the speaker.

Teaching Options

REAL-WORLD CONNECTION

Television Press Conferences Have students describe press conferences they have watched on television. Who was questioned and about what? Discuss how a press conference is different from an interview. Then ask students to watch examples of press conferences on television. Have them take notes as if they were a reporter present in the room. Later, ask students to write a brief article based on their notes. **L2**

interNET CONNECTION

Favorite Poets Ask students to use a search engine to locate information about one or more of their favorite poets. They might look up poets from this theme or poets who are personal favorites. Let students share their information with a classmate.

Teaching Options

Constantly risking absurdity

Lawrence Ferlinghetti ∾

      Constantly risking absurdity°
                and death
        whenever he performs
             above the heads
5   of his audience
  the poet like an acrobat
        climbs on rime°
           to a high wire of his own making
  and balancing on eyebeams°
10   above a sea of faces
      paces his way
         to the other side of day
    performing entrechats°
        and sleight-of-foot tricks
15   and other high theatrics
         and all without mistaking
     any thing
       for what it may not be

    For he's the super realist
20   who must perforce° perceive
   taut° truth
        before the taking of each stance or step
 in his supposed advance
        toward that still higher perch
25 where Beauty stands and waits
       with gravity
         to start her death-defying leap

    And he
     a little charleychaplin° man
30   who may or may not catch
   her fair eternal form
        spreadeagled° in the empty air
  of existence

1 absurdity: being ridiculously unreasonable or irrational.

7 rime: an old way of spelling **rhyme.**

9 eyebeams: a play on "I-beam," an iron or steel construction beam that looks like a capital *I,* and that construction workers sometimes walk across.

13 entrechat (ôn′ trə shä′): in ballet a jump during which the dancer crosses the legs a number of times, alternately back and forth.

20 perforce: by force of circumstances.
21 taut: orderly; neat and tidy.

29 charleychaplin man: Charlie Chaplin, a star of silent movies, most famous for his tragic-comic character known as "The Little Tramp."

32 spreadeagled: arms and legs spread wide, suggesting the appearance of an eagle with stretched out wings and legs.

692 ❦ UNIT 3

692 ❦ UNIT 3

Responding to Literature

Personal Response

Sketch the image from the poem that made the strongest impression on you.

ANALYZING LITERATURE
---

*A Motto
from Poets:
Leave Stone*

RECALL AND INTERPRET

1. What is the "motto from poets" that the speaker expresses in lines 1–4? What do you think this motto means?
2. How does Fernández Retamar use **personification** (see Literary Terms Handbook, page R9) in line 5? To whom might the speaker be comparing the personified object? Explain.
3. What characteristics does the speaker attribute to stone and to trees in lines 7–9? What do these lines convey about the speaker's attitude toward stone and trees?
4. Restate lines 10–18 in your own words. What ideas do you think the speaker is trying to convey in these lines? Explain.

EVALUATE AND CONNECT

5. How does the extended comparison between stone and trees help you understand the **theme**, or main idea, of this poem?
6. Do you think poets should adopt the motto expressed in this poem? Why or why not?
7. If you wanted to leave a message for future generations, what material or technique would you use to record your message? Explain your choice.

*Constantly
risking absurdity*

RECALL AND INTERPRET

8. In the extended comparison in this poem, to whom does the speaker compare the poet? How are the two alike, according to the speaker?
9. What occupations are suggested by the references to *eyebeams, entrechats,* and *sleight-of-foot tricks*? What might these occupations have in common with the job of poet?
10. Who is the "super realist" in line 19? What is his ultimate goal? What must he do to approach it, and how likely is he to attain it?

EVALUATE AND CONNECT

11. Evaluate the poet's choice of title. How does it help you better understand the poem's **theme**, or main idea? Explain.
12. Have you ever tried to do something that involved "risking absurdity"? Explain.
13. **Theme Connections** In your opinion, does the speaker accurately portray the poet's task? Give reasons for your answer.
14. Find examples of **sound devices** and evaluate how their use affects your understanding and appreciation of the poem. (See Literary Terms Handbook, page R12.)

POETRY 🐾 693

---

14. Students may point out the assonance created by the many long *i* sounds in lines 6–9, in which the assonance created by stretched sound imitates the climb and tension on the high wire; and by the long *a* sounds in lines 10–12, which communicate tension and quickness of motion. The alliterative phrases "perforce perceive" and "taut truth" in lines 20–21 emphasize the poet's responsibility.

essence of that truth). The perch is precarious; the task difficult.
11. The title reminds readers that the poet is exposed in public while attempting a demanding and difficult task. Any false step ("mistaking any thing for what it may not be") makes the whole performance a joke and a total loss (Beauty dies).
12. Students may mention performing in talent shows or recitals, giving speeches, or asking for a first date.
13. Students who agree may cite the need for a poet to balance literal and figurative meanings, to translate feeling into words, to make clear an elusive truth, and to make it all seem effortless.

Responding to the Selection

Personal Response

Students have many powerful images from which to choose. Encourage them to combine words and pictures if they feel unable to sketch the image they choose.

ANALYZING LITERATURE

1. "Leave stone alone, it won't grow." Focus on the dynamic, not the lifeless, to find inspiration and glory in life; make your vision and talent grow.
2. Trees are compared to writers making their mark ("inscribe their names magnificent in the sun"); fame is the reward for their stretching to the sun.
3. The speaker admires stone's lasting, unchanging qualities and realizes that a tree, despite its vigor, will be cut down by time or people and cease to be.
4. Because it lasts, stone keeps the living words of the writer and brings to life his or her thoughts, dreams, and emotions.
5. Like trees, the writer's consciousness must grow and strive throughout life; ambition and vitality may reward the writer with fame. To last, however, the writer's work must be inscribed on stone (symbolizing the printed page or expression of universal truths). Ironically, stone, which had never been alive, gives a kind of immortality to the writer's thoughts.
6. Some students will agree that it is futile to consciously try to assure one's place in history during life.
7. Students' choices should consider the durability of the medium.
8. The poet is an acrobat on the high wire. Both poet and acrobat must focus all their ability on staying balanced, making no mistakes, and judging perfectly how and when to catch "Beauty" when she leaps. One misstep (for the poet, failure to see truly) makes the artist ridiculous and means death to the "fair eternal form."
9. *Eyebeams* suggest construction work on skyscrapers, reminding readers of the care taken in structuring the poem. *Entrechats*, intricate ballet footwork, suggest the skillful use of poetic elements to move along the path of truth. *Sleight-of-foot tricks* suggest the poet's "magical" skill in making everyday words say extraordinary things.
10. The poet is the "super realist" who must balance and feel the way along "taut truth" to grasp Beauty (the

LITERARY ELEMENTS

1. He compares the task of a poet to the balancing act of an acrobat on a high wire, who is being watched by an audience, as he crosses from one side of the arena to the other. The risk the acrobat takes is similar to the risk the poet takes each time he writes a poem and then that poem is read by an audience.

2. Students may say that it helped them understand that writing poetry is as difficult, gut-wrenching, and courageous an act for a poet as walking a high wire is for an acrobat.

Additional Resources

Literary Elements Transparency 66

LITERATURE AND WRITING

Writing About Literature

Students' paragraphs should
- identify qualities required of a poet and/or summarize the poet's task.
- elaborate the concept(s) using explanations, examples, and details.

Personal Writing

Students' mottoes and explanations should
- state a principle for behavior in strong, plain, brief language.
- provide anecdotes and illustrations as supporting details.

EXTENDING YOUR RESPONSE

Literature Groups Groups may find their responses to questions 5, 11, and 13 (page 693) a good place to begin discussing secret meanings they feel the poets have revealed.

COLLAB. LEARN.

Internet Connection Before groups begin their search for materials, list equipment that might be used for their presentations and discuss its availability.

Performing If possible, allow students to practice reading with a partner before making their class presentation.

Literary ELEMENTS

Epic Simile

An **epic simile** is an extended simile that typically uses the words *like* or *as* to compare two things in an elaborate or detailed way. Epic similes usually compare a complex action, rather than a simple thing, with another complex action, and the comparison continues for several lines. For example, in "Constantly risking absurdity," Lawrence Ferlinghetti uses a variety of detailed images and actions to compare a poet to an acrobat.

1. What details for comparison does Ferlinghetti present in lines 9–12? In your opinion, what idea does the speaker express in these lines?
2. How does Ferlinghetti's epic simile, comparing the work of a poet to the risk-taking act of an acrobat, contribute to your understanding of the work of a poet?

● See **Literary Terms Handbook,** p. R12.

LITERATURE AND WRITING

Writing About Literature

Describe a Poet and the Poet's Task Use the ideas expressed in the two poems you have just read to expand and revise the cluster map you created in the Focus Activity on page 690. Then write a paragraph or two describing your concept of a poet and the poet's task.

Personal Writing

My Motto Write a personal motto—a saying that expresses a principle that guides your behavior and outlook on life. Explain how you arrived at your motto and why you think it is a good guiding principle. If you wish, explain your motto to your classmates.

EXTENDING YOUR RESPONSE

Literature Groups

Secret Meanings Lawrence Ferlinghetti once suggested that the poet's duty is "to uncover the secret meaning of things." Assuming that statement is valid, do you think Fernández Retamar and Ferlinghetti have fulfilled their duty in the poems you have just read? Use specific details from the poems as you discuss this question in your group. Share and compare your ideas with the members of another group.

Internet Connection

Multimedia Presentation Work with a small group of classmates to create a multimedia presentation about the Beat poets. Do research to get information about the authors. Find poems, articles, critical reviews, recordings, and other materials to use in your presentation. Plan and deliver your presentation for the class.

Performing

Beatnik Poetry Reading Research the Beat poets of the 1950s. Then prepare and perform a Beatnik poetry reading. Choose an unconventional poem of the Beatnik era that is meaningful to you, and read it aloud with expression for the class. If you wish, dress the part of a Beatnik poet.

Reading Further

You might also enjoy these poems:

Poems: "London, Rainy Day," from *Open Eye, Open Heart,* by Lawrence Ferlinghetti, describes life on a rainy morning in London.

"400-Meter Freestyle," from *Maxine Kumin, Selected Poems, 1960–1990,* reveals a swimmer's race to the finish.

"Fireworks," from *John Updike, Collected Poems, 1953–1993,* gives different perspectives about a fireworks display.

📖 **Save your work for your portfolio.**

FINE ART
TRANSPARENCY 17

You may want to use Fine Art Transparency 17 to discuss poets' methods and goals.

☑ ASSESSMENT OPTIONS

📁 *Quick Checks,* p. 66

📁 *Selection and Theme Assessment,* pp. 127–128

📁 *Performance Assessment,* p. 65

💾 *Testmaker*

Writing Skills

Using Simile and Metaphor

If you look up the word *love* in a dictionary, you may find that the definition doesn't do justice to that exalted emotion. Poets and other writers often express meaning beyond the literal definition by using **similes** and **metaphors**, figurative language that compares seemingly unlike things to reveal new truths about them. A **simile** uses *like* or *as* to compare the two things. A **metaphor** makes a comparison without using *like* or *as*. Notice how Lawrence Ferlinghetti uses simile and metaphor.

> the poet like an acrobat
> > climbs on rime
> > > to a high wire of his own making
> and balancing on eyebeams
> > > above a sea of faces
> > paces his way
> > > to the other side of day
> performing entrechats
> > > and sleight-of-foot tricks
> and other high theatrics
> > > and all without mistaking
> > any thing
> > > for what it may not be

The first line of this excerpt contains a simile. Ferlinghetti uses the word *like* to compare a poet to an acrobat. He then extends this simile throughout the poem by describing the poet's activities in terms of those of the acrobats. Ferlinghetti also uses metaphor. In the second line of this excerpt, the poet/acrobat is said to "climb on rime." Here, Ferlinghetti uses an **implied metaphor**, or a metaphor in which one of the things being compared is suggested rather than directly stated. The rime (rhyme) is being implicitly compared to the ladder an acrobat would use to ascend to the high wire. In other words, the rime is just a tool to get somewhere else; it is not an end in itself.

To arrive at effective comparisons in your writing, let your mind free-associate. Use simile and metaphor to startle a reader into a deeper understanding of the meaning you want to convey.

▬ EXERCISE ▬

Using at least one simile, one metaphor, and one implied metaphor, write sentences that describe each of the following things.

1. an emotion   2. a sound   3. an activity   4. a type of physical pain

---

Writing Skills

Objective

- To use similes, metaphors, and implied metaphors effectively in sentences

Teaching Strategies

Be sure students understand that similes and metaphors are not just the province of poetry; they are a vital part of English expression. Suggest that students take one day and tally the number of times they hear or read these figures of speech in conversation, in the media, and in reading material. Point out that similes and metaphors are widely used because they add imaginative pleasure and emotional intensity and make abstract meanings concrete.

Exercise

Students' similes and metaphors should

- compare two unlike things but show a true connection between the two things.
- suggest emotions as well as likenesses that can be perceived by the senses.

Additional Resources

📕 *Writer's Choice*, Lesson 3.5

Teaching Options

Grammar and Language *Minilesson*

Concrete and Abstract Nouns An abstract noun names an idea, quality, or characteristic; a concrete noun names an object recognized by the senses.

Activity Ask students to label each noun as abstract *(a)* or concrete *(c)*. "My love *(a)* is like a red, red rose *(c)*." "Poplars *(c)* are standing there still as death *(a)*." **L2**

Additional Resources

🖊 *Grammar and Language Transparency 55*

📕 *Grammar and Language Workbook,* p. 48

📕 *Grammar and Composition Handbook,* Lesson 1.1

📕 *Writer's Choice*, Lesson 10.1

Objective

- To read and understand a newspaper article

Respond

1. Students should see that Ewart created a collaborative environment in which students could feel and live the elements of jazz in something they loved. By helping them "own" jazz, he assured that they would understand it.
2. The basketball court is the most popular draw for kids; Ewart went where they were and adapted his form to their interests. He understands the similarities of the two forms.

Additional Resources

📁 *Media Connections Activities,* p. 19

Teaching Options

MEDIA
Connection

Newspaper Article

Jazz is an art form based on rhythm, teamwork, and improvisation. Because basketball relies on these three qualities as well, one jazz musician has been able to combine the music with the sport.

Hoops Picks Up a Jazz Beat

by Melita Marie Garza—*Chicago Tribune,* April 7, 1998

Douglas Ewart and Fred Hopkins swayed and paced under the basketball nets in the Washington Park gym while nine kids dribbled and shot to the duo's saxophone and acoustic bass.

"Get back in line; get back in line," admonished Ewart, as the kids started shooting randomly at the gym's six hoops. "Keep bouncing; keep bouncing. C'mon, man, let's keep to the same tempo."

Ewart, 51, is one of several prominent jazz artists who has taken up a challenge from the Chicago Park District and the Jazz Institute of Chicago to help bring jazz music to children.

"They told me they wanted to have concerts and get young people in the neighborhoods to attend," said Ewart, who quickly caught on that he would be competing for the kids' attention with the No. 1 pastime at the park—basketball.

Ewart has fashioned a musical score with the beat of children's basketballs and the tempo of jazz.

The piece is part of a Park District and Jazz Institute project called JazzCity.

Ewart, who stands 5 feet, 5 inches, doesn't even play basketball, and the kids, whose musical tastes run to rap and rhythm and blues, had rarely, if ever, heard improvisational jazz.

By the end of the second rehearsal, it was clear that the boys and girls in the gym would never hear a basketball bounce in the same way.

"It gave me a rhythm to dribble the ball," Eric Lewis, 12, a 5th grader at Carter School, said of his experience in going one-on-one with jazz and basketball. "The music gave me a happy feeling inside," Lewis said.

"There are many parallels between 'the game' and the music," said Ewart.

"Each form demonstrates individual and collective capacity, the combination of movement and sound. Players and musicians also have to combine discipline with spontaneity," he said.

Jazz artist Douglas Ewart plays one of his homemade instruments in the Washington Park gym.

The new experience was not lost on Max Costello, 12, 6th grader at Dulles School. "I thought it was really, really cool. It made basketball and music come together."

Respond

1. Do you think Ewart was playing music for the kids, or was he making music with them? Explain your answer.
2. Why did Ewart choose a basketball court as the place to introduce the kids to jazz? What skills of his make it possible for him to do this?

Before You Read

let my spirit fly in time and *Jazz Fantasia*

FOCUS ACTIVITY

If you could use only words to capture the mood or effects of a piece of music, how would you do it?

DISCUSS With a partner, identify a piece of instrumental music that you both enjoy. Discuss ways to express it in words.

SETTING A PURPOSE Read to learn how two poets use words to convey the spirit and rhythms of jazz.

BACKGROUND

Did You Know?
- *Jazz* is the name given to many styles of music that share certain characteristics, the most important of which is improvisation. In music, improvisation is the act of inventing a new version of a melody while playing it.
- Esteves's poem reflects the jazz of the 1950s and 1960s, when saxophonist John Coltrane and other musicians pioneered new sounds. Coltrane was known for his creative improvisations, which he played with great emotional power.
- When Sandburg published "Jazz Fantasia" in 1920, the jazz era was underway. Rooted in the musical traditions of African Americans, jazz evolved from ragtime and the blues into the New Orleans style: an upbeat, lively sound created by an ensemble of reed and brass instruments, plus drums. Experimental New Orleans musicians, such as jazz trumpeter and singer Louis Armstrong, moved to Chicago, where Sandburg lived, and influenced local jazz artists. One of Armstrong's most original types of improvisation was *scat singing:* using the voice, without words, to imitate the sounds of an instrument.

Louis Armstrong

Meet Sandra María Esteves

"I am two parts," says Sandra María Esteves (ā stā′ vās) in her poem "Here." Born in the Bronx in New York City, Esteves belongs to the "Nuyorican" group of poets, so called because they live in New York and have Puerto Rican heritage. Much of Esteves's early poetry explores her Afro-Caribbean roots; her later work includes the experiences of other ethnic groups.

Sandra María Esteves was born in 1948.

Meet Carl Sandburg

Nicknamed the "Poet of the People," Carl Sandburg was a distinguished poet, novelist, journalist, and historian. In exuberant free verse and song, he wrote about everyday life in America on subjects ranging from the prairie to steel factories. An accomplished guitarist, he also sang and studied regional music. Sandburg produced the most famous biography of Abraham Lincoln ever written.

Carl Sandburg was born in 1878 and died in 1967.

POETRY 697

A Active Reading

QUESTION Ask students to view the overall shape of these lines. Why might Esteves have used these line breaks? What does the shape suggest? *(A free form is in the spirit of jazz. The shape also suggests the movement of rivers described in the poem.)*

Additional Resources
📁 **Active Reading Guide,** p. 67
🎧 **Audio Library**
🎧 **Spanish Audio Library**

B Critical Thinking

INFERRING If the rivers and dark blooms represent Coltrane's notes, what can readers infer the sunrise represents? *(enlightenment, emotional or meditative fulfillment, the goal of the music)*

FYI

John Coltrane Coltrane wrote and played his groundbreaking music on tenor, alto, and soprano saxophone in the 1950s and 1960s. His wife Alice Coltrane has said his work drew from mathematics, elementals, rhythmic structure, and the power of repetition as well as from music.

let my spirit fly in time

Sandra María Esteves

let my spirit fly in time
        the outer world   spaceless
                no boundaries
      deep, black rhythms and John Coltrane
5   fast movin' notes flying into space
           the open eye
     and peace descends across the earth
   Sahara
black desert
    rivers moving in line towards the sunrise
 one
   rivers moving over mountains and highways
            going to the sunrise
     rivers flowing
    black flowers
      ebony flowers
   velvet
     magic rivers flowing closer and closer
        towards the sunrise
20   sun beating down
    deep base laying down step down
       base laying down life roots deep breaths
ancient stones glittering red ruby
      jewels running deep running deep
25 running deep rivers towards the sunrise

       lightening clouds
    thundering wars
        charcoal juju° heat soul
   flow thru rivers moving towards the sunrise

30   poetry and sun music

---

28 *Juju* (jü′ jü) is a type of Nigerian pop music that features singing, guitars, and traditional drums.

LITERATURE & HUMANITIES

🎧 As students listen to "'Round Midnight" (CD 1, Track 35, Glencoe's *The World of Music*), ask them to record the images they visualize and compare their words and imagery to Sandburg's.

MEETING INDIVIDUAL NEEDS

GIFTED AND TALENTED

Spatial Relationships A paragraph may use spatial order to describe a scene to a reader. Explain that these poems describe the emotional impact of jazz and movement in music. They use the spatial relationships between lines and between stanzas to move the reader from one emotion to the next.

Activity Have small groups of students analyze and explain the structure of lines in "let my spirit fly in time" and of blocks of words in "Jazz Fantasia." Ask them to summarize their findings for the class and to evaluate how well these structures go with imagery, mood, and theme. **L3 COLLAB. LEARN.**

Jazz Fantasia
Carl Sandburg

Drum on your drums, batter on your banjoes,
sob on the long cool winding saxophones.
Go to it, O jazzmen.

Sling your knuckles on the bottoms of the happy
5 tin pans, let your trombones ooze, and go husha-
husha-hush with the slippery sand-paper. **C**

Moan like an autumn wind high in the lonesome tree-
tops, moan soft like you wanted somebody terrible,
cry like a racing car slipping away from a motorcycle **D**
10 cop, bang-bang! you jazzmen, bang altogether drums,
traps, banjoes, horns, tin cans—make two people fight
on the top of a stairway and scratch each other's eyes
in a clinch tumbling down the stairs.

Can the rough stuff . . . now a Mississippi steamboat **E**
15 pushes up the night river with a hoo-hoo-hoo-oo . . .
and the green lanterns calling to the high soft stars
. . . a red moon rides on the humps of the low river
hills . . . go to it, O jazzmen.

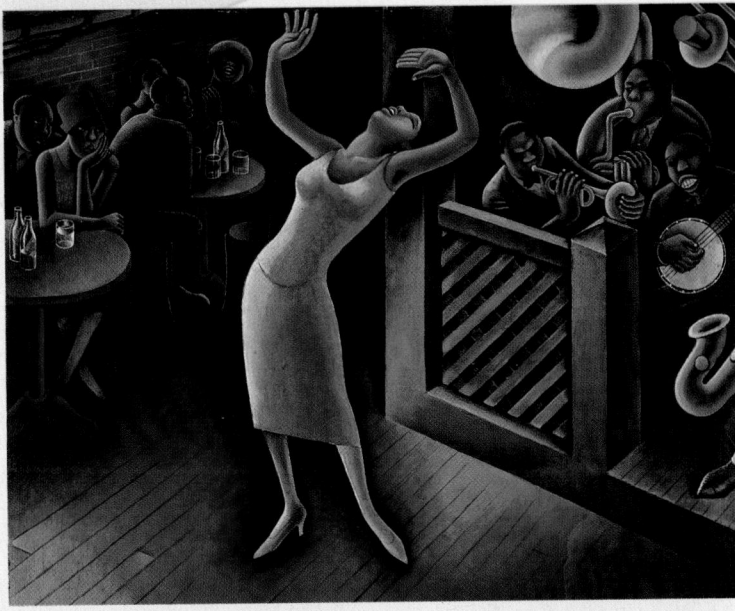

Rhapsody in Blue, c. 1925.
Miguel Covarrubias. Oil
on canvas, 25¼ x 31 in.
Private collection.

C Literary Elements

SOUND DEVICES: *Onomatopoeia* Have students identify words with strong sound effects as you read these lines aloud. *(sling, ooze, husha-husha-hush)* What effect does Sandburg achieve with them? *(imitates the sounds of instruments)*

D Active Reading

IMAGINE What do students imagine the music sounds like and the musicians look like? What feeling is established through tone? *(the sorrow and agony of unrequited passion; the raw fear of being pursued)*

E Literary Elements

DICTION Point out that the speaker talks directly to the musicians throughout the poem. What does this suggest about his involvement? *(He identifies with the jazzmen as well as their music and is fully engaged in their art form.)* Ask students to describe the effect of word choices like "Can the rough stuff." Who is the poet writing for? *(He speaks to and for everyday people.)*

Thematic Focus

Observations and Expressions
Ask students to summarize the way each speaker feels about jazz and then describe it for the class in their own words.

> ✓ **ASSESSMENT OPTIONS**
>
> 📁 *Quick Checks,* p. 67

INCLUSION STRATEGIES

MEETING INDIVIDUAL NEEDS

Less-Proficient Readers Explain that onomatopoeia is the use (or invention) of words that mimic the sounds they name. The desired effect is for sound to help carry meaning. Give examples such as *howl, cluck, hiss,* and *whir.*

Activity Have students listen to the tape of "Jazz Fantasia" and list onomatopoeic words they hear. Then have them write the words, their pronunciations, meanings, and sound effects in a special onomatopoeia page in their vocabulary notebooks. Let students work in groups to brainstorm other onomatopoeic words and make up sentences using them. **L1**

Additional Resources
📁 *Inclusion Strategies*

Responding to the Selection

Personal Response

Students may list words such as *excited, ecstatic, free, mysterious, earthy,* and *urgent.*

ANALYZING LITERATURE

1. The speaker is lost in the "deep, black rhythms" of Coltrane's music, described as liberation into space. The words "in time" and "fast movin' notes" are clues.
2. These lines focus on the melodic line of the saxophone Coltrane plays ("rivers" of sound), which gives a feeling of dark peace while it pushes toward a promised "sunrise" (perhaps representing spiritual revelation).
3. The deep music (base/bass) is like strong sunlight "laying down life" and illuminating ancient truths ("red ruby jewels"). Within this resonant, flashing context, the melody continues flowing toward "sunrise." The music is as profound as poetry and vibrant as sun.
4. The poem observes the jazz scene with vivid detail; it also expresses the speaker's emotional reaction to jazz.
5. The appeal is largely visual: readers see rivers flowing across the night desert, "over mountains and highways"; the glitter of red jewels; the coming of sunrise through "lightening clouds." One hearing impression is given in "thundering wars." As a result, a purely aural experience is translated into images and sensations related to various senses.
6. The words imitate certain rhythms and impressions of music phrases; the tone reflects the ecstatic pull of the music; and the words, like notes, are committed to paper. However, music has resonance, flexibility, and range that outstrip language.
7. The speaker is caught up in the intensity of jazz and encourages the jazzmen to express the extremes of their emotions and his own.
8. It begins with mournful sounds and moves into urgent, aggressive rhythms and notes. They change or evolve quickly from one kind of expression into another, just as improvisational jazz does.
9. The final stanza's images evoke loneliness and mysterious beauty, whereas earlier stanzas expressed sadness, anger, and passion of human interaction. Jazz runs the gamut of human emotions.

10. The poem's imagery and format do not conform to those usually expected in poetry. The stanzas vary in length. The lines are interrupted with dashes and ellipses. The words are as fanciful and fantastic as the music they describe.
11. Allow all choices that students can relate in some way to the emotional intensity or improvisational freedom of jazz.
12. Some jazz fans might appreciate the attempt to recreate in words the effects of this unique music. Others might relate much more strongly to music than to words and find language inadequate.

Responding to Literature

Personal Response

Make a list of words that show your reaction to one or both of these poems.

ANALYZING LITERATURE

let my spirit fly in time

RECALL AND INTERPRET

1. What is the speaker in this poem thinking about in the first five lines? What clues tell you this?
2. What is the poem describing in lines 6–19? What do you think these images might stand for?
3. What comparisons does the speaker make in lines 20–29? Explain the impact of line 30.

EVALUATE AND CONNECT

4. **Theme Connections**   Would you call this poem an observation, an expression, or both? Explain your answer.
5. In your opinion, does the poem as a whole appeal more to one of the five senses than to the others? What is the effect of the sensory appeal? Support your response with evidence from the poem.
6. In what ways is this poem like a piece of music? In what ways is it different from music?

Jazz Fantasia

RECALL AND INTERPRET

7. In the first two stanzas, what does the speaker want the jazzmen to do? What do these instructions tell you about the speaker?
8. How does the **tone** of the poem change from the beginning of the third stanza to the end of that stanza? How does this change reflect the sounds of jazz?
9. What differences do you see between the images in the last stanza and those in the rest of the poem? Based on all these images, how would you summarize Sandburg's message?

EVALUATE AND CONNECT

10. One definition of *fantasia* is "a fanciful musical composition not conforming to strict style or form." Why is "Jazz Fantasia" an appropriate title of this poem? Give evidence from the poem to support your answer.
11. In your opinion, which sensory images in this poem best convey a sense of lively, rhythmic music like jazz? Explain your choices.
12. Why might a jazz fan or any music fan like or dislike this poem? Explain.

FINE ART
TRANSPARENCY 31

You may want to use Fine Art Transparency 31 to discuss the emotional impact of music.

Literary ELEMENTS

Onomatopoeia

Onomatopoeia is the use of a word or phrase that imitates or describes the sound it names. When Carl Sandburg writes, "go husha- / husha-hush with the slippery sand-paper," he is actually imitating the sound of sandpaper as it is rubbed against a surface. By using onomatopoeia, poets call attention to sounds and draw readers into the mood or message of the poem through their sense of hearing. Onomatopoeia can make the sounds of the poem seem almost musical,

and it can stimulate images in readers' minds. The use of onomatopoeia may make a poem more lively and fun to read.

1. Identify two other examples of onomatopoeia in "Jazz Fantasia."
2. How does the use of onomatopoeia in this poem affect your reading of the poem?

● See **Literary Terms Handbook,** p. R9.

LITERATURE AND WRITING

Writing About Literature

Analyzing Structure   Both Esteves and Sandburg have used unusual structures in their poems. Look at how each poet has used punctuation, line breaks, stanzas, and placement of words on the page to express their thoughts and feelings about music. In two to four paragraphs, analyze the ways the structure of each poem helps convey the poet's message and contributes to your enjoyment of the poem.

Creative Writing

Musical "Composition"   Think about your response to the Focus Activity on page 697. Then develop a word composition that somehow "plays" or "sings" or depends on sound for its power and effect. If you wish, you can model your work on Sandburg's or Esteves's example or create a jingle, slogan, riddle, or newspaper headline.

EXTENDING YOUR RESPONSE

Literature Groups

Definitive Analysis   Following are a few of the many definitions Carl Sandburg wrote for *poetry:*

> "Poetry is an echo asking a shadow dancer to be a partner."

> "Poetry is a type-font design for an alphabet of fun, hate, love, death."

> "Poetry is the silence and speech between a wet struggling root of a flower and a sunlit blossom of that flower."

> "Poetry is the capture of a picture, a song, or a flair, in a deliberate prism of words."

In your group, discuss each of these definitions and decide which one best applies to these poems. Share your opinion and reasons with another group.

Performing

All That Jazz   Work with a partner or a small group to interpret and perform one of these poems. You may choose to bring the poem to life by setting it to music, dancing to it, creating a dramatic reading, or using sound, words, music, or movement together or separately, in another way.

Interdisciplinary Activity

Music History: Jazz Time   Work with a small group to create a time line showing the history of jazz. You might borrow informative headings from a comprehensive encyclopedia article to highlight events and dates. You might also download images from the Internet or photocopy illustrations to add interest to your jazz history.

 Save your work for your portfolio.

LITERARY ELEMENTS

1. "Sob" and "cool winding" imitate the sound of the saxophones, just as "ooze" mimics the trombone sound. Moaning sounds like the music it suggests, and "hoo-hoo-hoo-oo" is an invention recreating the music and the steamboat's horn it suggests.
2. It makes the words sound like parts of the jazz the speaker listens to. It creates immediacy and communicates the moods of the music.

Additional Resources

 Literary Elements Transparency **67**

LITERATURE AND WRITING

Writing About Literature

Students' analyses should
• describe the structure of each poem accurately.
• explain how each structure relates to the subject and theme of the poem.
• draw specific examples from the poems.

Creative Writing

Students' word "music compositions" should
• use sound devices and diction to imply qualities of music.
• suggest musical values or moods.

EXTENDING YOUR RESPONSE

Literature Groups   You may want to extend the activity by having students identify poems in the text that match each definition. **COLLAB. LEARN.**

Performing   You may want to play examples of New Orleans and improvisational jazz for students before they begin this assignment.

Interdisciplinary Activity   Encourage students to "jazz" up their histories and time lines (in poster or report form), improvising formats and including visual elements in unusual ways.

✔ ASSESSMENT OPTIONS

🗀 *Quick Checks,* p. 67
🗀 *Selection and Theme Assessment,* pp. 129–130
🗀 *Performance Assessment,* p. 66
💾 *Testmaker*

Writing Workshop

Objectives

- To develop an extended metaphor throughout a composition
- To plan, draft, revise, edit, and present an extended metaphor
- To reflect on and assess one's extended metaphor

GLENCOE
TECHNOLOGY

WRITER'S ASSISTANT
CD-ROM
You may want to have students use Glencoe's templates and guidelines software for descriptive writing to aid them in working through the steps in the writing process in this lesson.

Teaching Strategies

PREWRITING

Explore ideas Before students begin, you may wish to explore ideas for an extended metaphor with the whole class, writing students' observations on the board. Point out that in an extended metaphor the things compared must have many connections and be similar on many levels. Students should not be discouraged if it takes several attempts to find a pair with rich parallels.

Teaching Options

∽: Writing Workshop :∼

Descriptive Writing: Extended Metaphor

Have you ever explained one thing by comparing it to something else? Writers typically use comparisons to help a reader see things in a new light and to show their own attitude toward a subject. One type of comparison, a metaphor, speaks of a subject as though it were something else. When a metaphor continues throughout a paragraph, a stanza, or a selection, it is called an extended metaphor. **In this workshop, you will write an extended metaphor.**

● As you write your extended metaphor, refer to the **Writing Handbook,** pp. R58–R71.

The Writing Process

PREWRITING

> **PREWRITING TIP**
> Metaphors will be easier to create for a subject that has a strong personal meaning for you than for a subject that does not interest you.

Explore ideas
A metaphor compares two things by identifying one with the other. A simile directly states that one thing is *like* another, but a metaphor implies the comparison; it suggests a shared quality between two things. An *extended* metaphor goes even further. It continues the comparison throughout a paragraph, a stanza, or an entire work.

You might choose to write about an abstract subject, such as *loyalty* or *greed.* Or you might decide to write about an event, a person, a scene—even a relationship. To get yourself thinking about your subject metaphorically, try thinking of the topic as if it were

- an animal, like the cloud-mares in "Night Clouds."
- a person, like the poet-acrobat in "Constantly risking absurdity."
- a place, like the spring-hill in the third of Bashō's three haiku.
- a kind of weather, like the music-wind in "Jazz Fantasia."

Consider your purpose and audience
The purpose of your essay is to describe your subject. The purpose of the extended metaphor is to create connections and deeper meanings by comparing your subject to something else. Keep in mind, though, that your audience will probably not have made exactly the same observations about your subject that you have made. You will want to craft your metaphor to give your audience your perspective.

MEETING INDIVIDUAL NEEDS
ENGLISH LANGUAGE LEARNERS

Enriching a Vocabulary for Abstractions To write an extended metaphor requires a broad grasp of the vocabulary and concepts involved in the two elements compared. English language learners may lack this basis.

Activity After students have chosen their subjects and likely concrete objects for comparison, have them

share their brainstorming with a more proficient English-speaking partner. The pair can use reference books and conversation to add to these notes and pinpoint meanings of specific words.

Additional Resources
📁 *English Language Learners Sourcebook*

Make a plan

Once you've chosen a subject that you feel strongly about, think about the point you want to make. Consider the kind of emotional response you have for your subject and why. An idea web like the one shown can help you identify those feelings.

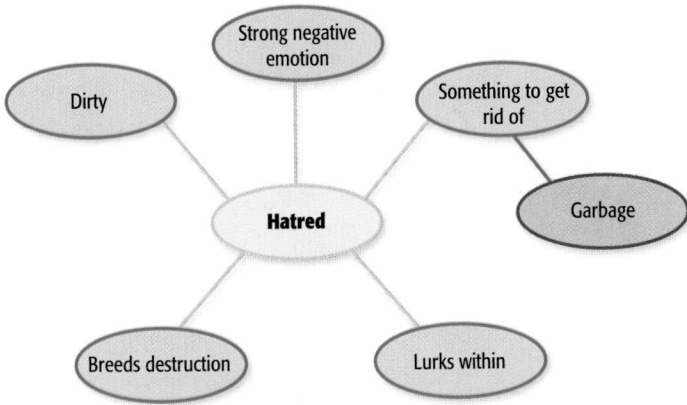

Reread your idea web, looking for any concrete things on which you can build your metaphor. Choose something that you have close, personal experience with, something that people can experience fully with their senses. Freewrite to develop ideas of how your subject is like that concrete thing. Then underline any words or phrases that are especially descriptive of your topic or your feelings about it. Use some or all of the underlined items in your poem. Perhaps one will lead you to your extended metaphor.

As you read the student model below, notice that the student chose "garbage" as the concrete thing on which to build the extended metaphor.

STUDENT MODEL

> GARBAGE: like the muck at the bottom of the city
> harbor, the sludge that settles there, the junk of
> society, trash, rotting, the runoff from the city's
> streets, settles to the bottom, hidden under the
> water, far below the shimmering surface, thick,
> stinking, sticky, hard to wash off once it's on you,
> leaves a stain, polluted, foul and dead, repulsive

Consider your purpose and audience
Remind students that clichéd comparisons (such as spring and youth or a dog and loyalty) will not yield effective metaphors. Point out that if the audience had heard of the metaphors, it is a good clue that they are clichés. Original thinking is required.

Make a plan Have students create a web on a sheet of paper and continue until the page is filled with ideas and concrete objects they associate with their subject. Encourage them to think and write about the impressions that involve their senses directly.

Additional Resources

📁 **Writing and Proofreading Practice,** pp. 1–7, 66–72

🖋 **Writing and Proofreading Transparencies 1–6, 41–42**

📕 **Writer's Choice,** Lesson 3.5

MULTIPLE LEARNING STYLES

Logical-Mathematical Logical-mathematical learners may have difficulty freewriting about the similarities between subjects and concrete objects. Suggest that they design a chart with two columns to compare these aspects.

Activity Have students write their subject and its concrete partner as column headings, then write details about the concrete item under that heading. Then they can fill in each blank under the subject heading.

Concrete object: Spring	Subject: Imagination
flows up from underground	flows from subconscious
refreshes itself perpetually	self-renewing; always fresh **L1**

DRAFTING

Write your draft If possible, have students draft their extended metaphors using a word processor. This gives them flexibility to shift from their plans, to move quickly back and forth between sections, to insert new material as it occurs to them, even to turn instantly to a new page if a new inspiration strikes.

REVISING

Evaluate your work Have students remain alert for mixed metaphors they may have introduced in their drafts. Remind them that an extended metaphor is a single framework, related to one large comparison. Combining several different metaphors confuses readers and undermines the effect of this powerful device.

Have a writing conference Instruct students to keep the Questions for Revising in mind as they listen and to write down comments and ideas for revising that come to mind. Also suggest that they offer ideas for improvement tactfully and look for at least one aspect to praise.

Teaching Options

~: *Writing* Workshop :~

DRAFTING

DRAFTING TIPS
Experiment. Try something new. Try something daring. You can always change or cut words or ideas in the revision.

Follow your plan, but don't feel that it has you on a leash. Shift from the plan if a good new idea comes along.

Write your draft
Jump right into your draft. Turn to a thesaurus for additional ideas and inspiration for the extended metaphor.

Stay flexible
When you draft the extended metaphor, let your writing and your thinking work with each other. If your writing suggests new ideas, let the new ideas change the direction of what you write. This back-and-forth exchange will help your ideas develop and help you focus on the point you're trying to make.

STUDENT MODEL

FIRST DRAFT

Hatred is like the muck at the bottom of the harbor, the sludge that settles there. It is the junk of society's emotions. It's trash, like rotting garbage. Like the runoff from the city's streets, it settles to the bottom.

SECOND DRAFT

Hatred is the muck at the bottom of the human heart, the sludge that settles there. It's the rotting garbage of emotions, thick, stinking, and sticky. It's hard to wash out of your heart once you've let it in.

REVISING

REVISING TIP
Make sure the images in your metaphor work together. For example, don't mix metaphors by calling something a spider at the beginning of a paragraph and then later including descriptions of a ship at sea.

Evaluate your work
Set your draft aside for a while. Then read it slowly, marking places that you think should be improved. Using the **Questions for Revising** to guide you, make revisions to your draft.

Have a writing conference
Read your extended metaphor aloud to a group of students. Then use the **Questions for Revising** to prompt constructive comments about your work. Discuss parts of the extended metaphor that don't seem clear. You may want to jot down a few notes so that you can consider the comments when you make changes.

QUESTIONS FOR REVISING

How can I:
- ☑ polish the topic sentence to express the point I want to make?
- ☑ provide more or better examples?
- ☑ improve the imagery in my metaphor?
- ☑ clarify anything confusing?
- ☑ improve my choice of adjectives and adverbs?
- ☑ conclude with a clear, final impression of my subject?

STUDENT MODEL

> Hatred is ~~the~~ ^{an} emotion that ~~most people want to~~ ^{we would like} ~~get rid of~~ _{discard}. It's the trash left ^{at the bottom of} ~~after the human~~ ~~human emotions~~ ^{the human heart} ~~party.~~

Writing *Minilesson*

Using Connotations to Evoke Mood
Students will have an emotional attitude toward their subject. Explain that they can convey this mood by choosing words with connotations, or emotional associations, that suit their attitude. Have students consider and comment on the effects of synonyms with different connotations, such as *bold/reckless, freakish/unique,* and *pale/sickly.*

Activity Have pairs of students read each other their drafts to note the connotations of their word choices and suggest synonyms with more suitable connotations. **L2**
COLLAB. LEARN.

Additional Resources
📖 *Writer's Choice,* Lesson 6.5

EDITING/PROOFREADING

Edit your essay carefully. Work your way through the entire essay several times, looking for one kind of error each time. Use the **Proofreading Checklist** on the inside back cover to help you find and correct errors in grammar, usage, mechanics, and spelling.

> **PROOFREADING TIP**
> Reading your essay backwards, one word at a time, will help you to look at each word and to spot spelling errors more easily.

Grammar Hint

Make sure that each pronoun's antecedent—the noun to which the pronoun refers—is clearly stated. Clarify the pronoun reference either by rewording the sentence or by eliminating the pronoun altogether.

UNCLEAR REFERENCE: *When hatred and bigotry are compared with other emotions, they seem mean.*

CLEAR: *When compared with other emotions, hatred and bigotry seem mean.*

● For more on pronouns, see **Language Handbook,** p. R20.

STUDENT MODEL

People group hatred with fear and anger, and we
turn our backs on them. We don't want to think
about it any more than we want to think about
garbage. But we found ways to recicle garbage, and
maybe we can find ways to recicle hatred.

PUBLISHING/PRESENTING

You might read your metaphor aloud for a class discussion. Or, with your classmates, make a booklet that contains each student's extended metaphor. Display the booklet in your classroom.

> **PRESENTING TIP**
> To illustrate your essay, draw a picture or cartoon that depicts the subject metaphorically.

Reflecting

When people share their feelings, they often are trying to help others see things from another point of view. What did you learn as you wrote your extended metaphor?

 Save your work for your portfolio.

EDITING/PROOFREADING

Have students use the Proofreading Checklist on the inside back cover of their textbooks.

Remind students that some common misunderstandings and confusions can be avoided by making sure modifiers (including adjective and adverb clauses) are placed correctly. Point out that creativity is not an excuse for sloppiness in grammatical expression.

PUBLISHING/PRESENTING

If students choose to broadcast their essays, be sure they practice reading them aloud with appropriate pacing and expression.

Reflecting

Portfolio Invite students to ask themselves these questions as they review their writing process.

In writing an extended metaphor,

- did I discover more connections and deeper meanings between the paired things?
- was I successful in affecting my classmates' attitudes toward this subject?
- did I use original, insightful images and express my ideas clearly?

If students answer yes to one or more of these questions, suggest they consider adding their extended metaphor to their portfolio.

✔ ASSESSMENT OPTIONS

📁 ***Writing Assessment and Portfolio Management***
- Writing Assessment, pp. 2–19, 39–40
- Portfolio Management, pp. 20–22

Unit Wrap-Up

Objectives

- To give a personal response about the poems, discussion, and activities in this unit
- To write a comparison of poetic elements in two poems
- To complete a self-evaluation, set a goal, and devise a plan for achieving the goal

PERSONAL RESPONSE

1. Students should explain elements that interested them.
2. Students should explain what about each poem moved or inspired them.
3. Accept all reasonable answers.

ANALYZING LITERATURE

Students' writing should

- have an introductory paragraph that identifies the two poems and the two elements being compared.
- summarize the effect of each element's use in each poem.
- include details from the two poems to support their conclusions.

EVALUATE AND SET GOALS

Evaluate

Have students list each project and assignment they completed in this unit on a separate card. Suggest that they order the cards to show degree of challenge and then reorder them to show value of their contribution.

Have a class discussion of the criteria that students think should be evaluated. Create column headings (4, 3, 2, 1) on the board. List qualities the majority of students think are necessary to earn each evaluation under the headings.

Set Goals

Have students design a flowchart showing the steps needed to achieve the goal, with checkpoints at each stage to be marked as they are completed. Discuss students' plans in individual conferences.

Unit Wrap-Up

PERSONAL RESPONSE

1. Which of the poems in this unit did you find the most interesting?
2. Which poems did you find the most moving or inspiring?
3. As a result of the work you have done in this unit, what new ideas do you have about the following?
   - what the elements of poetry are
   - how a poet combines elements to communicate a theme or main idea
   - how to work with other students in pairs or in groups

ANALYZING LITERATURE

Comparing Elements of Poetry Choose two poems from this unit and compare at least two basic elements, such as *speaker, lines and stanzas, rhythm and meter, rhyme, sound devices, imagery,* and *figures of speech.* For help in understanding the elements of poetry, see Genre Focus: Poetry on page 578. At the end of your comparison, explain how those elements work in each poem to make the words sing.

EVALUATE AND SET GOALS

Evaluate

1. What was your strongest contribution to group activities as you worked through this unit?
2. What was your most challenging task in this unit?
   - How did you approach this task?
   - What was the result?
3. How would you assess your work in this unit, using the following scale? Give at least two reasons for your assessment.
   4 = outstanding   3 = good   2 = fair   1 = weak

Set Goals

1. Choose a goal to work toward in Unit 4. It could involve reading, writing, speaking, researching, or working in a group.
2. Discuss your goal with your teacher.
3. Jot down three or four steps that you will take to achieve your goal.
4. Decide at which points in the next unit you will stop and assess your progress toward your goal.

BUILD YOUR PORTFOLIO

Select Choose two pieces of writing that you did in this unit and include them in your portfolio. Use these questions to help you make your selection.
- Which piece are you most satisfied with?
- Which one did you find most challenging to write?
- Which piece are you most likely to share?
- Which one led you to new discoveries as you wrote?

Reflect Write brief notes for the two pieces you selected. These questions can help you.
- What did this writing teach you?
- What changes would you make if you were just beginning the piece?

 ASSESSMENT OPTIONS

 Writing Assessment and Portfolio Management
- Writing Assessment, pp. 2–19
- Portfolio Management, pp. 20–22

GLENCOE

TECHNOLOGY

 MINDJOGGER VIDEOQUIZZES
VIDEODISC

Use *MindJogger* to review the Unit 3 content.

Unit 3
Side A

 Also available in VHS.

Reading on Your Own

You might also be interested in the following books.

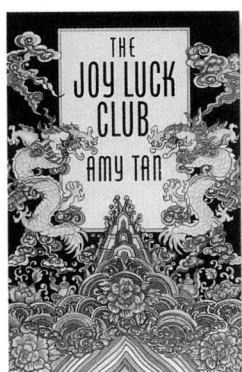

The Joy Luck Club
by Amy Tan For forty years, four Chinese mothers gather in San Francisco to socialize, talking about their lives and their Chinese American daughters. The daughters are establishing their own identities in a different culture from that of their mothers. A fierce love carries both generations to an understanding of each other's needs.

A Poetry Handbook
by Mary Oliver In this highly readable handbook, Oliver empowers the student of poetry and demonstrates that "out of writing, and the rewriting, beauty is born." Citing works from other poets, such as Elizabeth Bishop, T. S. Eliot, William Carlos Williams, and Lucille Clifton, Oliver demonstrates that writing good poetry is a craft.

The Space Between Our Footsteps: Poems and Paintings from the Middle East
selected by Naomi Shihab Nye This collection of the works of more than one hundred poets and artists from nineteen Middle Eastern countries explores themes that include exile, family, childhood, journeys, and joy. Award-winning poet and anthologist Naomi Shihab Nye pairs poems with full-color art from the countries represented.

A Haiku Menagerie: Living Creatures in Poems and Prints
by Stephen Addiss with Fumiko and Akira Yamamoto Showing how fascinating the smallest animal or insect can be, this collection of Japanese haiku features master poets' insights into the natural world. More than forty-eight woodblock prints illustrate the creatures described in the poems. The poems are presented both in English translation and the original Japanese.

Reading on Your Own

Glencoe Literature Library

For a complete listing of the titles available in the *Glencoe Library*, see page T44 in this book.

The *Study Guides for Glencoe Literature* provide instructional support and student activities for works in the *Glencoe Library*.

  ® *The following videotape program is available from Glencoe. Be sure to preview the video for appropriateness for your class.*

- **Carl Sandburg: Poet of the People***

  *Also available in the Glencoe Literature *Video Library*.

INCLUSION STRATEGIES
MEETING INDIVIDUAL NEEDS

You may wish to recommend *A Haiku Menagerie: Living Creatures in Poems and Prints* by Stephen Addiss to your less-proficient readers. The accessible subject matter and writing style make this book particularly appropriate. **L1**

These books may be recommended to more proficient readers:

- *The Joy Luck Club* by Amy Tan **L2**
- *A Poetry Handbook* by Mary Oliver **L3**
- *The Space Between Our Footsteps: Poems and Paintings from the Middle East* selected by Naomi Shihab Nye **L2**

Additional Resources
📁 *Inclusion Strategies*

Standardized Test Practice

Answers and Analyses

1. **B** Students should read the entire sentence and choose the verb in the infinitive.
2. **F** This question looks as if it's about verbs, but in fact it requires that students recognize and avoid double negatives. Remind them that *hardly* and *scarcely* are negative words.
3. **D** What does the missing modifier describe? (how the stones were *fitted*) The missing word modifies a verb, so it must be an adverb. *Tightly* is therefore the only possible answer.
4. **J** Students should go back to the beginning of the sentence to find the antecedent. The *it* found in the middle of the sentence is misleading. They should choose the pronoun that agrees with the antecedent, *stones,* in person and number, and is in the correct case.
5. **B** Again, students need to go back to the beginning of the sentence. *Chambers* is the subject, and students must choose a verb that agrees with a plural subject. *Treasure* is not the subject, even though it has been placed closer to the verb than *chambers*. The answer choices try to confuse students with tenses, but the only plural verb is choice B.
6. **H** Students will need to look at the verb *are considered*, which is plural, and then find the antecedent for the pronoun they are to select. It refers to the Great Pyramids of Egypt. *They,* the only plural pronoun listed, is the correct choice.

Standardized Test Practice

Read the passage and choose the word or group of words that belongs in each space. Mark the letter for your answer on your paper.

> If you get a chance __(1)__ a trip to Egypt, you must make time to see the Great Pyramids!
>
> No one knows how or when the pyramids were built. No ancient society __(2)__ the technology that would have been needed to produce them. Scientists are left to speculate as to how ancient architects could have designed such perfectly aligned structures. The stones in each pyramid are fitted so __(3)__ together that it's impossible to drive a knife blade between __(4)__, and no cement or mortar was used! The inside chambers, which used to be filled with treasure, __(5)__ masterfully constructed. There are air passages to allow excellent circulation and hallways to provide easy access to burial chambers.
>
> The Great Pyramids of Egypt are truly a wonderful sight to behold. It is no wonder that __(6)__ are considered part of the Seven Wonders of the World. Don't miss them!

1. **A** take
   B to take
   C taking
   D took

2. **F** should have had
   G shouldn't have had
   H should hardly have had
   J shouldn't never have had

3. **A** tightest
   B tighter
   C tight
   D tightly

4. **F** it
   G their
   H its
   J them

5. **A** is
   B are
   C is being
   D has been

6. **F** it
   G you
   H they
   J he

 TEST-TAKING TIP

Tell students that when taking an actual standardized test, it is best to fill in the answer oval for each question as they answer it. If students need to skip a question, they should be very careful to skip it on the answer sheet also. They should check periodically to be sure that they are on the same question in the test booklet and on the answer sheet.

Read the passage and decide which type of error, if any, appears in each underlined section. Mark the letter for your answer on your paper.

Ranada leaned into her swing <u>and felt the ball hit, the center of her racquet.</u> <u>Her shot</u>
                              (7)   (8)
flew strait as an arrow toward the net, brushing the top edge as it flew over. On the other

side of the court, Jessica looked startled as the ball rocketed toward her like a rifle shot.

   <u>The tennis ball hit Jessicas racquet so hard</u> she could feel the impact up to her shoul-
                        (9)
der. <u>The crowd on either side of the stadium let out a roar of suprise.</u>
                        (10)
   Ranada returned the volley, but Jessica's previous effort made her slow to react.

Ranada smiled slowly, as she realized <u>she had finally won the Pinefield high school</u>
                                                            (11)
<u>Tennis Championship.</u> She raised her racquet <u>and ran off the court to celabrate.</u>
                                                            (12)

7 A Spelling error
   B Capitalization error
   C Punctuation error
   D No error

8 F Spelling error
   G Capitalization error
   H Punctuation error
   J No error

9 A Spelling error
   B Capitalization error
   C Punctuation error
   D No error

10 F Spelling error
   G Capitalization error
   H Punctuation error
   J No error

11 A Spelling error
   B Capitalization error
   C Punctuation error
   D No error

12 F Spelling error
   G Capitalization error
   H Punctuation error
   J No error

Answers and Analyses

7. **C** A comma should not be placed between the verb, *hit,* and its direct object, *the center of her racquet.*
8. **F** The word *straight* is misspelled.
9. **C** Since *Jessica's* is possessive, it requires an apostrophe.
10. **F** The word *surprise* is misspelled.
11. **B** *Pinefield High School* is a proper name and should be capitalized.
12. **F** The word *celebrate* is misspelled.

 TEST-TAKING TIP

If possible, help students find out how their test is scored. If there is no penalty for random guessing, students should fill in an answer for every question. If there is a penalty, students should fill in an answer only if they have been able to eliminate at least one choice.

Tested Objectives

Questions	Reading Objective
1–6	Recognize appropriate English usage within the context of a written passage
7–12	Recognize appropriate spelling, capitalization, and punctuation within the context of a written passage

MORE PRACTICE

For additional practice, assign pages from one of the following standardized test resources available as part of Glencoe Literature.

Additional Resources
ITBS Preparation and Practice
SAT-9 Preparation and Practice
TerraNova Preparation and Practice

Unit Four — At a Glance

Drama

UNIT OPENING

- **Genre Focus: Drama** (p. 712)
- **Active Reading Strategies** (p. 714)
- **Active Reading Model:** from *Big River: The Adventures of Huckleberry Finn* (p. 716)

Theme 10: LOYALTY AND BETRAYAL

SELECTIONS

Literature Focus: Classical Greek Drama (p. 722)

Antigone (p. 726)

Literature Focus: Understanding Shakespeare and Elizabethan Drama (p. 772)

Media Connection: Rap (p. 776)

Julius Caesar (p. 777)

Media Connection: Magazine Article (p. 877)

The Ring of General Macías (p. 878)

Marked (p. 896)

SKILL FEATURES

Reading and Thinking Skills (p. 771)

Writing Skills (p. 799)

Vocabulary Skills (p. 819)

Technology Skills (p. 874)

Interdisciplinary Connection (p. 876)

Grammar Link (p. 900)

Listening, Speaking, and Viewing (p. 901)

WRITING WORKSHOP

Expository Writing: Compare-and-Contrast Essay (p. 902)

KEYS TO LITERARY CONNECTIONS

 World Literature

Glencoe Literature contains a variety of literature that represents cultures from around the world. World literature selections are highlighted with this symbol:

 Comparing Selections

In each theme of Glencoe Literature, the Comparing Selections feature gives students an opportunity to compare two selections they have just read. Each Comparing Selections page provides a variety of options to address diverse aspects of the reading and literature curriculum.

UNIT WRAP-UP

- **Personal Response, Analyzing Literature, Evaluate and Set Goals** (p. 906)
- **Build Your Portfolio** (p. 906)
- **Reading on Your Own** (p. 907)

  The Adventures of Huckleberry Finn by Mark Twain

  The Post Office by Rabindranath Tagore

  Seven Against Thebes by Aeschylus

  Shakespeare by F. E. Halliday

- **Standardized Test Practice** (pp. 908–909)

KEYS TO TEACHING OPTIONS

 Block Scheduling

Activities that are particularly suited to use within a block scheduling framework are identified throughout this unit by the following designation: For detailed suggestions on block scheduling, see the **Block Scheduling Guide** for this grade level.

Key to Ability Levels

The Teaching Options throughout this unit have been coded for students of various abilities.

L1 BASIC activities for all students

L2 AVERAGE activities for average to above-average students

L3 CHALLENGING activities for above-average students

Unit Four At a Glance
Drama

Reading Skills in this unit

Variety of Texts
In addition to plays by authors from the United States and other nations, this unit also includes the following text types:
- poetry
- rap
- magazine article

Comprehension Skills
The following instructional support for comprehension skills appears in this unit of the Student Edition:
- **Active Reading Strategies and Model** (pp. 714–720)
- **Monitoring Comprehension** (p. 771)
- **Reading and Thinking Minilessons** (pp. 770, 873)

See also the **Reading Minilessons** throughout the unit in this Teacher's Wraparound Edition.

Reading Resources

Comprehension Skills Resources

📁 **Active Reading Guides**
The **Active Reading Guide** provides graphic organizers and study guide questions to support students' reading of each selection. (**Active Reading Guide**, pp. 68–77)

📁 **Reading Workbook**
The Reading Workbook (pp. 69–76) includes additional instruction and reinforcement of reading strategies and skills.

🎧 **Audio Library**
Available both on tape and on CD, the Audio Library provides valuable comprehension support.

Resources for Reading Widely

📚 **Glencoe Literature Library**
Each title in the Glencoe Literature Library includes a full-length novel or play plus related readings. A separate Study Guide is available for each title.

💿 **Literature Classics CD-ROM**
The 900 selections on this CD-ROM can be searched by author, theme, or genre.

 inTIME
A coproduction of Glencoe and Time Inc., *inTime* includes a wealth of high-interest nonfiction related to the selections and themes in Unit Four.

✔ Assessment in this unit

Assessment Options in the Student Edition
Glencoe Literature offers a number of diverse ways to evaluate student understanding and skill proficiency. In the Student Edition, use the following:
- **Responding to Literature**
  Following each selection, students are asked to recall facts, interpret ideas, and evaluate concepts as they answer a variety of questions and complete activities to extend their understanding.
- **Unit Wrap-Up (pp. 906–907)**
  Here students respond to the selections on personal and analytical levels. They also assume ownership of their learning by setting and evaluating goals and by selecting work for their portfolios.

See also the many **Assessment Resources** listed on the facing page.

THE PRINCETON REVIEW

Standardized Test Practice
The Princeton Review has developed the Standardized Test Practice pages found at the end of this unit (pp. 908–909). These pages contain practice test questions that help students remain familiar with standardized test formats and content.

Writing Skills in this unit

Writing Skills

The Student Edition of Unit Four offers strong instructional support for writing skills:

In **Extending Your Response**, which follows each selection:
- **Writing About Literature**
- **Personal/Creative Writing**

In **Writing Skills** Lessons:
- **Effective Conclusions** (p. 799)

See also the **Writing Minilessons** throughout the unit in this Teacher's Wraparound Edition.

Writing Workshops

The theme in Unit Four concludes with a **Writing Workshop** that guides students through the writing process.
- **Expository Writing: Compare-and-Contrast Essay** (pp. 902–905)

Writing Resources

Writer's Assistant CD-ROM
Each Writing Workshop is supplemented by an interactive writing guide on the Writer's Assistant CD-ROM. This easy-to-use writing guide provides prompts, templates, and other tools that lead students through the writing process.

Writing and Proofreading Practice
Blackline masters present in-depth instruction and practice on a specific step in the writing process and proofreading. (pp. 1–7, 73–79)

Writing and Proofreading Transparencies
Transparencies (1–6, 43–44) provide graphic organizers and proofreading exercises for whole class instruction.

Research and Report Writing Guide
This resource provides extensive tips and activities to guide students in their writing projects in the literature classroom as well as in classes across the curriculum.

Style and Documentation Sourcebook for Writers
This sourcebook is a combination reference and workbook, giving students the most up-to-date information and guidance regarding traditional as well as technological research strategies and documentation.

Grammar and Composition Handbook
The Grammar and Composition Handbook provides instruction that supplements activities in the student textbook.

Assessment Resources

Selection Quick Checks
For each selection, a Quick Check of three to five short-answer questions measures students' literal comprehension.

Selection and Theme Assessment
The Selection and Theme Assessment instrument tests students' abilities to recall, interpret, and evaluate what they've read. The tests consist of multiple-choice, short answer, and essay questions.

Performance Assessment
Alternative assessment instruments and rubrics for Unit Four are found in the Performance Assessment ancillary.

Writing Assessment and Portfolio Management
These notes and strategies, student models, and assessment tools assist with the task of measuring students' progress as writers and as monitors of their own writing.

Testmaker
Teachers can customize selection, theme, and Unit Four tests by accessing the Testmaker database.

MindJogger Videoquizzes
Using a popular game show format, MindJogger Videoquizzes enable teachers to evaluate students' understanding of Unit Four in a quick and fun manner.

UNIT ✿ FOUR

Drama

Unit Objectives

- To enjoy reading drama
- To analyze the literary elements in drama
- To apply strategies for reading drama

Au Theatre. Albert Andre (1869–1954).

710

UNIT ✤ FOUR

Drama

"Drama . . . makes the point, ceaselessly, that our lives are now; there is no history that is not now."

—Joyce Carol Oates

Theme 10
Loyalty and Betrayal
pages 721–905

Introducing the Unit

Have students read the quotation. Then pose these questions for discussion:
- How does drama help focus on our lives now?
- What makes a good drama?
- Where have you seen dramas performed?

Theme 10: Loyalty and Betrayal

The plays in Theme 10 dramatize situations in which characters must make decisions that determine whether they remain loyal or betray their friends, leaders, and countries.

GLENCOE
TECHNOLOGY
LITERATURE CLASSICS
CD-ROM
Search for other plays by theme, author, or title.

RESOURCE MANAGER

See the *Unit Four Planning Guide* (pp. iv–1) for additional teaching notes, strategies, and resources for introducing the drama unit.

Genre Focus

Objective
- To understand the elements of drama

Teaching Strategies

Explain that most plays are written to be performed. Therefore, the act of reading a play is different from that of reading a short story or novel, which are written to be read by individual readers. Becoming familiar with techniques such as visualizing and with elements of drama such as dialogue can make reading plays an enjoyable literary experience. Have students describe plays they have seen performed on stage and ones they have read.

Characters

Point out that plays and playwrights often become well-known for their memorable characters. For example, Romeo and Juliet, characters in a drama by Shakespeare, are among the world's most famous fictional characters. Invite students to name other memorable characters from drama.

Setting

Point out that the setting in many plays, such as those by Sophocles and Shakespeare, is described only briefly and with little detail. More modern plays may have elaborate sets, and playwrights give detailed descriptions of them.

Teaching Options

Genre Focus

Drama

A play, or **drama,** is a story told mainly through the words and actions of characters and is intended to be performed by actors. Feature films can be dramas, as well as many television programs. Although drama shares certain elements with other kinds of narrative, it also has elements that are specifically characteristic of drama alone. Knowing about these elements can help you appreciate and discuss plays that you see and read.

When playwrights develop a script for a play, they include **stage directions** to help actors, directors, and readers visualize what is to be happening on stage. These directions are interspersed between the lines of dialogue, and are usually printed in italics and enclosed in parentheses or brackets. The directions explain how characters should look, speak, act, and move on the stage; they also specify details of the stage set, such as lighting, props, and sound effects.

This chart describes the key elements of drama with models from the play *The Ring of General Macías*, which appears on pages 879–893.

ELEMENTS OF DRAMA

MODEL: *The Ring of General Macías*

Characters

The cast of characters is listed at the beginning of a play and might include a short description of each character. The playwright may further describe a character when he or she first appears in the play. Audiences learn about characters through their actions and through the dialogue.

> **CHARACTERS**
> **MARICA:** the sister of General Macías
> **RAQUEL:** the wife of General Macías
> **ANDRÉS DE LA O:** a captain in the Revolutionary Army
> **CLETO:** a private in the Revolutionary Army
> **BASILIO FLORES:** a captain in the Federal Army

Setting

Typically, the setting is described at the beginning of a play. Additional details might appear throughout the play, such as at the beginning of acts and scenes, when the setting changes.

> **PLACE:** *Just outside Mexico City*
> **TIME:** *A night in April, 1912*

MEETING INDIVIDUAL NEEDS

ENGLISH LANGUAGE LEARNERS

Plays from Around the World
Explain that drama is one of the oldest literary forms, much older than the novel or the short story. Most countries have a dramatic tradition going back hundreds of years. For example, dramas have been written and produced in India since around 200 B.C. China's Peking opera and Japan's kabuki play have been important dramatic forms for hundreds of years.

Activity Have English language learners describe plays they are familiar with from their cultures. Encourage other students to research the history of drama in a country that interests them.

Additional Resources
English Language Learners Sourcebook

Plot

The plot of a drama, like the plots of other narratives, is the series of related events that revolve around a central conflict. The conflict may be a struggle between people, ideas, or other forces.

> *The Ring of General Macías* tells the story of a Mexican general's wife who is confronted with an opportunity to save her husband's life at the cost of betraying the government's side in the Mexican Revolution. She is torn between her love for her husband and her sense of honor and duty.

Dialogue

Most plays consist largely of dialogue, or conversation between the characters. The dialogue helps reveal the plot and characters of the play.

> **RAQUEL.**   Yes. Tell me, captain, do you think it possible to love a person too much?
>
> **ANDRÉS.**   Yes, señora. I do.
>
> **RAQUEL.**   So do I. Let us drink a toast, captain—to honor. To bright and shining honor.

Acts and Scenes

Many plays are divided into acts and scenes, which indicate a change in location or the passage of time. One-act plays take place in one location over a brief, continuous span of time.

> *The Ring of General Macías* is a one-act play.

Plot

Explain that the plot of a drama can be discussed in the same terms as that of fiction. Like the plot of a short story, a dramatic plot usually has a climax, the moment of highest interest at which the main conflict is resolved.

Dialogue

Have two students read aloud the sample dialogue. Point out that well-written dialogue helps the reader sense the tone and mood of a character's words.

Acts and Scenes

Point out that there is no set number of acts and scenes in a play. Many contemporary plays have two or three acts. Shakespeare's plays usually contain five acts. Each act may contain as few as one or as many as ten or more scenes.

Technology Option

Character Chart

Have students use word processing software to begin a chart on memorable dialogue and important characters in Unit Four.

Dialogue	Character	Play

Encourage them to make an entry on their chart each time they come across a piece of memorable dialogue in a play. The dialogue may strongly delineate a character or be crucial to a play's plot or theme. Encourage students to quote short passages and to copy them exactly as they appear in the play. The completed charts will provide examples for writing about plays or characters. **L2**

Active Reading Strategies

Objective

- To understand and apply strategies for reading and comprehending drama

Teach the Strategies

Encourage students to picture in their minds the production of a play they have seen. Have several students describe memorable aspects, such as sets, lighting, props, and acting, of the play. Explain that in reading a play, it may be helpful to visualize its staging. This is one way to understand a play.

Visualize

Encourage students to use any clues provided in a play about the set and the characters to help them visualize it. Encourage them to relate their visualizations to the appearances of other plays they have seen with similar sets or characters.

Listen

Point out that reading aloud a particularly interesting or important speech can help students understand the words and the character who speaks them.

Active Reading Model

Active Reading Strategies

Drama

To actively read a script, you use the stage directions and the dialogue to visualize and hear the play in your mind. When you interact with the words, you create the performance in your mind. Use these strategies when you read a play to help you understand and appreciate what you are reading.

● For more about reading strategies, see **Reading Handbook,** pp. R78–R107.

VISUALIZE As you read, picture in your mind all the elements described in the script.

Ask yourself . . .

- What does this scene look like? Is this like a place I've seen or been in before?
- What does this character look like?
- What does this gesture or movement look like? How would I interpret the gesture or movement?
- What might the character's facial expressions convey?

LISTEN Imagine how each character says his or her lines. Sometimes stage directions will give hints about how a line should be delivered. Other times, readers must infer how the line sounds from the words and the context of the play.

Ask yourself . . .

- What tone of voice would the character use here?
- Which words would the character emphasize?
- How loudly or quickly would the person speak this line?

QUESTION Note the questions you have as you read, and see if those questions are answered as you read on.

Ask yourself . . .

- Why does this action take place in this setting?
- What is really happening here? Do I understand the plot so far?
- Why did the character say or do this?
- Why are other characters reacting as they do?
- Will these props be important?

Teaching Options

Reading Journal

Students may think they have seen little drama if they think that drama is limited to school productions or plays seen at theaters. They may not realize that movies and television programs, including sit-coms and dramatic programs are, in fact, examples of drama.

Activity Have students keep a record of memorable drama they see. Encourage them to expand their definition of drama to include television programs and movies. Ask them to write a reaction to each program and why they find it memorable. Suggest that they describe memorable characters or quotations also.

CONNECT

Find connections between the characters and events in the play and the people and events in your own life.

Think to yourself . . .
- Whom does this character remind me of?
- When have I felt or acted like this?
- How would my friends and I react in a similar situation?
- This stage set reminds me of . . .

PREDICT

Use clues in the dialogue and stage directions to guess what will happen next.

Think to yourself . . .
- What is this character likely to do next?
- How might this conflict be resolved?
- What will the other characters do?

INTERPRET

Think about the characters, what they do, and what happens to them. Assess why the characters act as they do.

Say to yourself . . .
- What does this character's actions or words indicate about his or her personality and values?
- What effects do the characters' decisions have on their lives?
- What philosophy about life or people is the playwright conveying?

EVALUATE

Form opinions and make judgments about what you are reading.

Ask yourself . . .
- Are the characters, plot, and dialogue believable? clever? funny?
- Do the stage set and the actor's movements contribute to the play or distract from it?

Applying the Strategies

Read the next selection, an excerpt from the play *Big River,* using the Active Reading Model in the margins. Then choose another play and practice using all of these strategies.

Question

Remind students that a play's dialogue develops its plot and its characters. Constantly questioning how the dialogue relates to the plot and what it shows about its characters can help students understand the entire play.

Connect

Point out that students may not know people in the same circumstances as the characters in a play. Encourage them to look for emotions and behaviors in characters that they have experienced themselves or have seen in people they know.

Predict

Encourage students to keep the play's conflict in mind as they read and to question how the characters' dialogue and behavior is leading up to a resolution of that conflict.

Interpret

Emphasize that interpretations of literature are based on specific evidence in the work. In a play, the evidence consists mainly of dialogue.

Evaluate

Point out that in addition to evaluating the quality of a play, students may also evaluate the decisions and behavior of its characters.

Objectives

- To read and analyze part of a play about how the classic literary character Huck Finn responds to a friend in need
- To identify dialect in a play

Skills

Grammar/Language: Past Tense of Irregular Verbs
Collaboration: Literature Groups; Design a Set

Motivating
→OPTIONS

Selection Focus Transparency 68: Show the transparency and have students discuss special friendships.

Focus Activity: Have students meet in groups and discuss their journal entries. Students who wish may read their entries; others may discuss issues of loyalty to friends more generally.

FINE ART
TRANSPARENCY 18

You may want to use Fine Art Transparency 18 to compare and contrast the role of setting in the painting with the role of setting in the play.

Before You Read

from *Big River: The Adventures of Huckleberry Finn*

FOCUS ACTIVITY

How much would you risk to help a friend in need? Would you risk danger? punishment? your reputation?

JOURNAL Reflect on your sense of loyalty and commitment to friends. Then, in your journal, tell what you'd be willing to risk for a friend.

SETTING A PURPOSE Read to see how the classic literary character Huck Finn responds to a friend in need.

BACKGROUND

The Time and Place

The events in this play take place around the 1840s, before the Civil War (1861–1865), on an island in the Mississippi River between Missouri and Illinois.

Did You Know?

- Based on Mark Twain's classic novel *The Adventures of Huckleberry Finn,* the musical play *Big River* recounts the adventures of Huck, a teenaged boy who fakes his own death to escape from his drunken, abusive father, and Jim, a runaway from enslavement. In this scene from the play, Huck acknowledges that he will probably be called a "dirty abolitionist" for his decision. Abolitionists campaigned to end the practice of slavery, and some were despised in areas where slavery was viewed as an economic necessity.

- In the late 1700s, laws known as "fugitive slave laws" made it illegal to assist runaway enslaved people or to prevent those who owned them from recovering them. Anyone caught helping enslaved people escape faced severe punishment.

Elderly Ex-Slave, May 1941. Jack Delano. Black-and-white photography. Greene County, Georgia, U.S.A.

Meet
William Hauptman

"Writing is hard work," says one-time actor William Hauptman. Hauptman switched from acting to playwriting in graduate school. He traces his love of theater to his childhood days in the oil boomtown of Wichita Falls, Texas, where he saw plays, magic shows, and dramatic readings in the city auditorium. Although he has also written screenplays, television scripts, short stories, and a novel, Hauptman is best known as the author of the Tony Award-winning musical *Big River,* which first appeared on Broadway in 1985. His other writings include the short story collection *Good Rockin' Tonight* and the novel *The Storm Season.*

William Hauptman was born in 1942 in Wichita Falls, Texas.

RESOURCE MANAGER

Lesson Planning Resource
The *Unit Four Planning Guide* (pp. 2–9) provides additional lesson notes and reduced versions of all print resources.

📁 **Other Print Resources**
- Active Reading Guide, p. 68
- Reading Workbook, pp. 69–70
- Grammar and Language Workbook, p. 143
- Grammar and Composition Handbook, Lesson 5.2

- Quick Checks, p. 68
- Selection and Theme Assessment, pp. 131–132
- Performance Assessment, p. 67
- Spanish Summaries, p. 68
- Inclusion Strategies
- English Language Learners Sourcebook

 Transparencies
- Selection Focus 68
- Fine Art 18
- Literary Elements 68
- Grammar and Language 56

Technology
- 🎧 Audio Library
- 🎧 Spanish Audio Library
- 💻 Glencoe Literature Web Site
- 💾 Testmaker

from

BIG RIVER:

The Adventures of Huckleberry Finn

William Hauptman ⁓

SUMMARY

Runaways Huck Finn and Jim meet on an island in the Mississippi River. Huck faked his death when his father, drunk and hallucinating, tried to kill him. Jim has run away from his owner because he overheard her say that she intended to sell him in New Orleans. Huck promises not to tell anyone about Jim even though he might be in danger for aiding a runaway enslaved person. Jim intends to take a raft down the river and then float north on the Ohio River to the free states. Huck says he will go along with Jim and pretend to be his owner so Jim won't be harassed. Jim is moved by and thankful for Huck's offer.

📁 *Spanish Summaries,* p. 68

Additional Resources
📂 *Active Reading Guide,* p. 68
🎧 *Audio Library*
🎧 *Spanish Audio Library*

Active Reading Model

CHARACTERS

JIM (ADULT)   HUCK (13–14)

HUCK has just set off on his own when he comes face to face with JIM.

HUCK. Hello, Jim!

JIM. Get back in the river where you belong, and don't do nothing to ole Jim, who was always your friend!

DRAMA 🦋 717

Teaching Options

CONNECTING TO OTHER SELECTIONS

The chart shows three ways to connect this excerpt from *Big River: The Adventures of Huckleberry Finn* to selections in the book.

For specific teaching strategies, see the **Unit Four Planning Guide,** pp. 5–6.

Connection	Title
Life Skills: Problem Solving	→ "With All Flags Flying," p. 115
Thematic: Friendship	→ "The Californian's Tale," p. 248
Literary: Setting	→ "Exploring Antarctic Ice," p. 532

Listen

Most students will imagine Huck speaking with a happy, excited tone since he is glad to see Jim and anxious to explain his situation to him. Jim's tone is fearful until he realizes Huck is not a ghost.

Visualize

Point out the author's stage directions in brackets. Emphasize that these details can help readers clearly visualize the scene.

Question

Explain that, as in most plays, the necessary background information is provided through the characters' dialogue. In this case, Jim explains on pages 718–719 that he is running away from his owner because she needs money and has an opportunity to sell him.

A Literary Elements

DIALECT Explain that dialect is a variation of language spoken by a particular group of people. Ask students what words of Huck's are examples of his dialect. *(seegars for cigars; somewheres for somewhere)* Suggest that students look for other examples of dialect in the play.

Teaching Options

---

from **BIG RIVER**: The Adventures of Huckleberry Finn

> **Active Reading Model**

LISTEN

Notice the distinctive speech of Jim and Huck. What tone of voice do you imagine them using here?

VISUALIZE

Picture in your mind the makeshift camp that Jim has built on the river island.

QUESTION

Why has Jim run off?

HUCK. Jim, I'm not dead! I'm alive—and ever so glad to see you!

JIM. You ain't a ghost, is you?

HUCK. Touch me—I'm solid enough. I had to run away from Pap. He got the *delirium tremens*[1] and tried to stab me with his Barlow-Knife. So I faked the whole thing.

[*JIM just keeps staring. HUCK addresses the audience.*]

I talked along, but Jim just stood there. Finally he says—

JIM. See those birds flyin' low? That means rain. Let's go to my camp.

HUCK. I followed Jim to a lean-to he'd built on the Illinois side.

[*A flash of lightning and a roll of thunder. They cross to a lean-to. An enormous catfish hangs from a line. There is a trunk and a raft of logs nearby.*]

You got a great place here, Jim! That must be the biggest catfish ever pulled out of the Mississippi River!

JIM. [*Taking out knife and cutting down the fish.*] Found him on my trotline[2] this morning. I was just getting ready to clean him up.

HUCK. I never seen a bigger one . . . what's all this?

JIM. Trash come floating down on the high water.

A **HUCK.** [*Opening the trunk.*] Here's a calico gown . . . and some seegars . . .[3] there must be a flood somewheres upriver . . . and look at this raft!

JIM. That came floating down, too.

HUCK. Jim? What *are* you doing here?

JIM. You wouldn't tell on me if I was to tell you?

HUCK. Blamed if I would, Jim.

JIM. Huck—I run off.

HUCK. Jim!

JIM. You said you wouldn't tell.

HUCK. And I'll stick to it, Jim, honest Injun. People can call me a dirty abolitionist and despise me for it—that don't make no difference. I ain't a-going to tell and I ain't a-going back there anyways—so let's hear about it.

JIM. Miss Watson always say she won't sell me. But I notice lately there's been a slave trader around the place considerable. The night you was killed, I creep to the door, and I hear the missus telling the

---

1. *Delirium tremens* is a temporary form of mental disturbance usually caused by excessive drinking of alcohol. The condition is often accompanied by restlessness, violent shaking, and terrifying hallucinations.
2. Jim's *trotline* is a fishing line suspended across a stream with many baited hooks hung at intervals along it.
3. This is Huck's way of pronouncing *cigars*.

MEETING INDIVIDUAL NEEDS — ENGLISH LANGUAGE LEARNERS

Building Background English language learners may not know that parts of the United States allowed slavery while others outlawed it during the time in which *Big River: The Adventures of Huckleberry Finn* takes place.

Activity If possible, find a map in a history book that shows the division between slave states and free states before the Civil War. Point out the boundary between the slave states and the free states. Have students locate the Mississippi River. Explain that the river divides Missouri, a slave state, from Illinois, a free state.

Additional Resources
📁 *English Language Learners Sourcebook*

Widow Douglas[4] she's going to sell me down to New Orleans. She don't want to, but she can get eight hundred dollars for me, and it's such a big stack of money, she can't refuse. I never hear the rest. I light out.

[*He cuts open the belly of the catfish—bloodlessly—and several objects spill out.*]

Big fish like this eat all sorts of trash in his years.

HUCK. I'll say. Here's a spool.

JIM. And a horseshoe.

HUCK. [*Picks up a hard little sphere.*] What's this?

JIM. Must a been in there a long time to coat it over so.

[*JIM cuts open the sphere and hands HUCK a coin.*]

HUCK. It's gold.

JIM. What sort of writing is that on it?

HUCK. Spanish . . . I think. This is a Spanish d'bloon,[5] Jim, it's pirate gold! Why I reckon this fish could be a hundred years old. Do you reckon so, Jim?

JIM. [*Nodding.*] He go along on the bottom. Eat the little ones. Get older and older and bigger and bigger. He here before people come maybe. Before this was a country. When there was nothing here but that big river . . .

[*He grabs HUCK's arm.*]

I'm going down that river, Huck. To Cairo,[6] where the Mississippi joins the Ohio. Then I'm following the Ohio north, to the Free States. I'm going down on that raft, and I'm getting my freedom!

HUCK. I'm going with you, Jim!

JIM. You get in a powerful lot of trouble, helping Jim. You might find yourself hangin' from a cottonwood tree.

HUCK. You can't do it alone. But if I came along, I can tell people you belong to me, and they won't bother you.

JIM. [*Greatly moved.*] You'd do that for Jim? Then you a friend, Huck.

---

4. Jim had belonged to *Miss Watson*, an unpleasant woman whose sister is the good *Widow Douglas. The night you was killed* refers to the night Huck made it appear that he had been murdered so that he could run away without being pursued.
5. *D'bloon* refers to a doubloon, a gold coin used in Spain and by Spanish colonists in the Americas.
6. This *Cairo* is a river port at the southern tip of Illinois, where people pronounce it (kā′ rō).

Active Reading Model

Active Reading Model

Evaluate

Help students realize that a catfish swallowing a horseshoe is an unrealistic detail added for humor.

Connect

Remind students that Huck's situation is a dilemma because helping Jim is against the law, and Huck could be severely punished for it.

Interpret

Jim's definition of a friend is apparently someone who is loyal and prepared to make sacrifices for his or her friend. Most students will say that Huck is a true friend in his unquestioning willingness to break the law for Jim's sake.

B Literary Elements

DIALECT Have students choose several lines of dialogue and say them in standard English, pointing out examples of dialect as they do so.

ASSESSMENT OPTIONS

📁 *Quick Checks,* p. 68

EVALUATE

Is it realistic that a catfish could swallow a horseshoe? Why do you think the writer included this detail?

CONNECT

What would you do in Huck's situation?

INTERPRET

What is Jim's definition of *friend*? Do you agree that Huck really is a friend? Why or why not?

Grammar and Language Minilesson

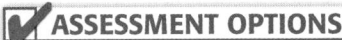

Past Tense of Irregular Verbs In writing dialect for his characters, the author includes what are considered grammatical errors in standard English. One of these is the incorrect past tense of irregular verbs, as when Jim says on page 718, "Huck—I run off." Point out that the past tense of *run* is *ran*.

Activity Have students correct the following additional sentences from the play in which the characters use the incorrect past tense of irregular verbs:

I never seen a bigger one . . . what's all this? *(saw)*

I never hear the rest. *(heard)*

I light out. *(lit)*

L1

Additional Resources

✍ *Grammar and Language Transparency 56*

📖 *Grammar and Language Workbook,* p. 143

📖 *Grammar and Composition Handbook,* Lesson 5.2

📕 *Writer's Choice,* Lesson 15.2

Responding to the Selection

Personal Response

Most readers will feel sympathy for Jim and his quest for freedom from the inhumane institution of slavery.

ANALYZING LITERATURE

1. Jim is frightened at first seeing Huck. He thinks he must be a ghost because Huck has faked his death.
2. Huck is on the island because he is running away from his father, who tried to kill him in a drunken fit. Jim is on the island because he ran away from his owner, who planned to sell him.
3. Jim's plan is to float the raft down the Mississippi to the Ohio River and then float north to a free state. Huck's response is to tell Jim he will go along and pretend he is Jim's owner so that Jim doesn't get caught as a runaway from slavery.
4. Jim is a good person who values freedom and friendship. This is shown by his refusal to be sold down the river to New Orleans and his appreciation of Huck's offer of help. Huck is a loyal friend, evidenced by his willingness to risk punishment to help Jim.
5. Jim and Huck are both running from injustices. They both value freedom, loyalty, and friendship.
6. The purpose of Huck's aside is to emphasize Jim's amazement at his friend's being alive.
7. Students' answers should reflect weighing personal loyalty against possible serious consequences.
8. Students should give specific reasons for identifying with Huck or with Jim.

EXTENDING YOUR RESPONSE

Interdisciplinary Activity
Encourage students who are particularly interested in theater set design to make three-dimensional models of their designs.

Literature Groups Also have students discuss whether Huck's other motives make his loyalty to Jim less valuable. **COLLAB. LEARN.**

Responding to Literature

Personal Response

What is your reaction to Jim and his quest for freedom?

Active Reading Response
Look back at the strategies described in the Active Reading Model on pages 717–719. Which Active Reading Strategy was most helpful to you in understanding this scene from the play?

ANALYZING LITERATURE

RECALL AND INTERPRET

1. How does Jim first react to seeing Huck? Why?
2. Why is Huck on the island? Why is Jim there?
3. What is Jim's plan? What is Huck's response to Jim's plan?
4. Based on his words and actions, how would you describe Jim? What does he value? What kind of person is Huck? Give evidence from the play to support your answers.

EVALUATE AND CONNECT

5. In what ways are Jim and Huck alike?
6. An **aside** is a comment made by a character who is heard by the audience but not by the other characters onstage. What is the purpose of Huck's aside in this scene? (See Literary Terms Handbook, page R1.)
7. Look back at the writing you did for the Focus Activity on page 716. Knowing the potential consequences of your actions, would you have made the same decision that Huck makes at the end of this scene? Why or why not?
8. Whom do you identify with most in this scene, Huck or Jim? Why?

Literary ELEMENTS

Dialect
Dialect is a variation of language spoken by a particular group, often within a particular region. Dialects differ in pronunciation, grammar, and vocabulary from the standard form of a language. Huck and Jim speak dialects of English common in the small river towns in northeastern Missouri in the mid-1800s. For example, Huck pronounces cigars, *seegars,* and says "there must be a flood *somewheres*" instead of *somewhere.*

1. Find three other examples of dialect in this scene. Rewrite the examples in standard English.
2. What does the use of dialect add to your reading of this scene?

● See **Literary Terms Handbook,** p. R3.

EXTENDING YOUR RESPONSE

Interdisciplinary Activity
Art and Drama: Set Designers Wanted   With a partner, consider the relevance of setting and time frame to this play's meaning. Then, design a set for this scene from *Big River.* Work to convey the essential elements of the setting in a clear and simple way. Then share your set design with your classmates.

Literature Groups
Analyzing Motivation   Does Huck act purely out of friendship for Jim? What other reasons might he have for wanting to go with Jim? Discuss these questions in your group and share your responses with your classmates. Be prepared to justify your responses.

📖 **Save your work for your portfolio.**

LITERARY ELEMENTS

1. Examples may include "You ain't a ghost, is you?"—"You aren't a ghost, are you?"; "I ain't a-going to tell and I ain't a-going back there, anyways"—"I'm not going to tell and I'm not going back there, anyway."
2. The use of dialect makes the characters and the setting realistic and believable.

Additional Resources
🖐 *Literary Elements Transparency 68*

✔ ASSESSMENT OPTIONS

📁 *Quick Checks,* p. 68
📁 *Selection and Theme Assessment,* pp. 131–132
📁 *Performance Assessment,* p. 67
💾 *Testmaker*

Theme 10 — Loyalty and Betrayal

Has a friend ever betrayed you? Have you, yourself, ever been the betrayer? Loyalty is a highly valued trait, but perhaps, sometimes, there are justifiable reasons to turn against someone. The plays in this theme will take you into a world where the line between loyalty and betrayal sometimes becomes blurred.

THEME PROJECTS

Performing

Time Travel Show how the themes in *Julius Caesar* can be applied to a different time.

1. Choose a monologue from *Julius Caesar* and show how it could relate to another time or historical event, for example, the American Revolution, the American Civil War, the 1960s, or the present.
2. Rewrite the monologue so that it is relevant to the period you have chosen.
3. Perform your revised monologue for the class.

Interdisciplinary Project

Art: Comic Strip With a partner, choose any scene from this theme and depict it as a comic strip.

1. Together, discuss what kind of illustrations and how much dialogue are necessary to re-create the drama of the scene.
2. Consider having one person act as a writer and create the script that will be used in the comic. The other person could act as the artist and draw the panels, including captions and word bubbles to fill with dialogue.
3. Share your comic strip with your classmates.

Othello, Desdemona and Emilia, 1867. Daniel Maclise. Oil on canvas, 130 x 87 cm. Johannesburg Art Gallery, South Africa.

Viewing the art: Do you think the characters portrayed in this scene from Shakespeare's tragedy *Othello* are the betrayers or the betrayed? Why?

DRAMA 721

Theme 10

Teaching Strategies

The following suggestions may help your students plan and carry out their theme projects.

Performing

- Encourage students to keep the monologue's original tone and meaning as much as possible.
- Encourage students to use language, voice, and gestures that fit the time period and event referred to in their monologues.

Interdisciplinary Project

- Emphasize that the comic strips do not need to be funny but should illustrate and summarize an interesting scene.
- Encourage students to focus on one specific piece of action.

Additional Resources

- 📁 *Interdisciplinary Activities,* pp. 20–21
- 📁 *Viewing and Representing Activities,* pp. 25–26
- 📁 *Listening and Speaking Activities,* pp. 19–20
- 📁 *Critical Thinking Skills,* pp. 27–29
- 📁 *Selection and Theme Assessment,* pp. 189–190
- 📁 *Performance Assessment,* p. 98

VIEWING THE PAINTING

Maclise uses Moorish architecture in the background. In the play, *Othello,* the main character, is a Moor.

Viewing Response *The people look like the betrayed because of their sad demeanors.*

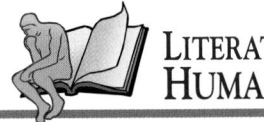

LITERATURE & HUMANITIES

Display *Judith and Maidservant with the Head of Holofernes,* page 436 in *Art in Focus.* Explain that this painting of a courageous woman was painted by Artemisia Gentileschi, one of the first women artists recognized as having a significant impact on the art of her time.

GLENCOE TECHNOLOGY

LITERATURE CLASSICS CD-ROM

Search for other selections related to the theme of loyalty and betrayal.

SELECTIONS	Literary Elements	Reading and Thinking	Writing	Vocabulary and Spelling
ANTIGONE SOPHOCLES	Protagonist and Antagonist, SE p. 746 Tragic Flaw, SE p. 769 *Protagonist and Antagonist, TWE pp. 728, 729, 731, 733, 741* *Dialogue, TWE pp. 734, 757, 762, 765, 767* *Stage Directions, TWE p. 736* *Tragic Flaw, TWE pp. 750, 751, 756, 759*	Identifying Author's Purpose, SE p. 770 Monitoring Comprehension, SE p. 771 *Drawing Conclusions TWE p. 730* *Identifying Author's Purpose, TWE p. 732* *Identifying Fallacies, TWE p. 737* *Evaluating, TWE p. 742* *Inferring, TWE pp. 745, 751* *Paraphrasing, TWE p. 745* *Identifying Bias, TWE p. 749* *Comparison and Contrast, TWE p. 764*	Compare Viewpoints, SE p. 747 Letter, SE p. 747 Analyzing Bias, SE p. 769 Explanation, SE p. 769 *Write and Evaluate Monologues, TWE p. 737* *Poem, TWE p. 738* *Using Alliteration, TWE p. 743* *Using Metaphors, TWE p. 765*	Keywords, SE p. 747 Antonyms, SE p. 770 *Word Meanings, TWE pp. 734, 740* *Words Related to Government, TWE p. 749* *Prefixes, TWE p. 751* *Paraphrasing Words Related to Death, TWE p. 755* *Use Context to Determine Meaning, TWE p. 758*
JULIUS CAESAR WILLIAM SHAKESPEARE	Blank Verse, SE p. 798 Soliloquies and Asides, SE p. 818 Prose, SE p. 841 Foreshadowing, SE p. 857 Tragedy and Tragic Hero, SE p. 871 *Setting, TWE p. 780* *Blank Verse, TWE pp. 782, 785, 789, 833* *Symbol, TWE p. 787* *Foreshadowing, TWE p. 788, 851, 852, 856* *Irony, TWE pp. 789, 838* *Soliloquy, TWE pp. 791, 800, 829* *Aside, TWE p. 815* *Prose, TWE pp. 830, 832* *Tone, TWE p. 830* *Tragic Hero, TWE pp. 864, 868*	Visualizing, SE p. 873 *Using Text Structure, TWE pp. 776, 861* *Inferring, TWE p. 780* *Drawing Conclusions, TWE pp. 785, 786, 790, 801* *Problem and Solution, TWE p. 797* *Comparing, TWE p. 810* *Analyzing Arguments, TWE pp. 814, 835* *Using Graphic Aids, TWE p. 814* *Identifying Author's Purpose, TWE p. 817* *Evaluating, TWE p. 822* *Cause-Effect Relationships, TWE, p. 839* *Summarizing, TWE p. 854* *Identifying Assumptions, TWE p. 863* *Generalizing, TWE p. 869*	Word Web, SE p. 777 Effective Conclusions, SE p. 799 Play Review, SE p. 872 Interview Questions and Answers, SE p. 872 *Paraphrase, TWE p. 784* *Extended Metaphor, TWE p. 785* 🖥 *Multimedia Report, TWE pp. 786, 850, 862, 867* *Rap Song, TWE p. 790* *Description, TWE p. 795* *List Figures of Speech, TWE p. 801* *Letter, TWE p. 809* *Comparisons, TWE p. 822* *Report on Roman Architecture, TWE p. 827* *Blank Verse, TWE p. 838* *Vivid Verbs, TWE p. 864*	Homophones, SE p. 819 Analogies, SE p. 873 *Shakespearean Word Meanings, TWE p. 791* *Suffix -ous, TWE p. 794* *Etymology, TWE pp. 795, 802* *Abstract and Concrete Words, TWE p. 803* *Practicing Homophones, TWE p. 819* *Synonyms, TWE pp. 824, 847* *Specialized Vocabulary, TWE pp. 859, 876*
The Ring of General Macías JOSEPHINA NIGGLI	Irony, SE p. 894 *Stage Directions, TWE p. 880* *Imagery, TWE p. 882* *Conflict, TWE pp. 883, 886* *Irony, TWE pp. 883, 888* *Symbol, TWE p. 887* *Dramatic Irony, TWE p. 889*	*Problem and Solution, TWE p. 877* *Inferring, TWE pp. 881, 882* *Comparing and Contrasting, TWE p. 889* *Drawing Conclusions, TWE p. 890*	Cluster Map, SE p. 878 Paragraphs, SE p. 895 New Scene, SE p. 895 *Report, TWE p. 882* *Using Adverbs, TWE p. 887* *Irony, TWE p. 891* *Paragraph, TWE p. 893*	Connotation, SE p. 895 *Words for Emotions and Behavior, TWE p. 880* *Denotation and Connotation, TWE, p. 881*
Marked CARMEN TAFOLLA	Free Verse, SE p. 898 *Free Verse, TWE p. 897*	*Drawing Conclusions, TWE p. 897*	List Ideas, SE p. 896 Using Participles to Modify, SE p. 900 *Outline a Persuasive Speech, TWE p. 901*	

Key: Student material is in roman. Teacher material is in italic.   🖥 Technology   **COLLAB. LEARN.** Collaboration

Grammar and Language	Listening, Speaking, and Viewing	Life Skills	Study, Research, and Technology
Using the Dash, SE p. 770 *Capitalizing and Punctuating in Poetry,* TWE p. 728 *Present Perfect Tense,* TWE p. 744 *End Punctuation,* TWE p. 766	**COLLAB. LEARN.** Literature Groups, SE pp. 747, 769 *Reading Aloud,* TWE p. 728 *Tone,* TWE p. 730 *Political Speeches,* TWE p. 733 *Monologue,* TWE pp. 737, 740 *Evaluating Dialogue,* TWE, p. 742 *Present a Dialogue,* TWE pp. 752, 763 *Perform a Dance,* TWE p. 753 *Recount a Fable,* TWE p. 757 *Chant the Paean,* TWE p. 761	Learning for Life: Incident Report, SE p. 747 Learning for Life: Genealogical Chart, SE p. 769 *Persuasive Techniques,* TWE p. 750	🖳 Using the Internet, SE p. 747 *Using a Map,* TWE p. 729 *Using an Encyclopedia,* TWE p. 729 *Research,* TWE pp. 734, 735, 751, 756 *Charting Differences,* TWE p. 741 🖳 *Internet Connection,* TWE p. 751
Active and Passive Voice, SE p. 873 *Commas with Introductory Words,* TWE p. 796 *Affect and Effect,* TWE p. 799 *Parallel Sentence Structure,* TWE p. 813 *Commas After Adverb Clauses,* TWE p. 816 *Word Order,* TWE p. 821 *Complete Subjects and Predicates,* TWE p. 840 *Commas in a Series,* TWE p. 855 *Superlative Degree,* TWE p. 870	*Paraphrase and Act Out Dialogue,* TWE pp. 787, 846 *Paraphrase Speeches,* TWE pp. 804, 805, 826 *Read a Speech Aloud,* TWE pp. 812, 833, 853, 868 *Perform Asides,* TWE p. 815 *Role-Play, Using Persuasive Techniques,* TWE p. 835 *Group Discussion,* TWE p. 837 *Act Out a Scene,* TWE p. 849 *Choreograph a Battle Scene,* TWE p. 866	Learning for Life: Radio News Report, SE p. 872 *Solving Problems,* TWE p. 809 *Techniques for Comprehending Abstract Dialogue,* TWE p. 843 *Collaborating,* TWE p. 844	Draw a Map, SE p. 872 Create a Time Line, SE p. 872 🖳 Using a CD-ROM, SE p. 872 🖳 Word Processing: Creating Academic Reports, SE p. 874 🖳 *Internet Connection,* TWE p. 776 *Using a Dictionary,* TWE p. 779, 859, 876 *Using Side Notes,* TWE p. 780 *Using a Map,* TWE p. 782 *Using an Encyclopedia,* TWE p. 782 *Research,* TWE pp. 788, 802, 807 *Using a Thesaurus,* TWE p. 824 🖳 *Using Recorded Music,* TWE pp. 828, 852 *Create a Diagram,* TWE p. 830 *Find Newspaper and Magazine Photographs,* TWE p. 831 *Research Political Speeches,* TWE p. 832 🖳 *Using a Videotape,* TWE p. 839, 862
Compound Sentences and Predicates, TWE p. 892	**COLLAB. LEARN.** Literature Groups, SE p. 895 Perform a Scene, SE p. 895 *Role-Playing,* TWE p. 881 *Reading a Monologue,* TWE p. 884 *Discuss Viewpoints,* TWE p. 890	Learning for Life: Incident Report, SE p. 895	🖳 *Internet Connection,* TWE p. 882 *Research,* TWE p. 882 *Using a Map,* TWE p. 885 *Using a Dictionary,* TWE p. 888
Misplaced or Dangling Modifiers, SE p. 900	Persuasive Speech, SE p. 901		

SELECTIONS	📁 Print Resources		

ANTIGONE
 	
SOPHOCLES
	Unit Four Planning Guide, pp. 16–24
	* Active Reading Guide, p. 69
	Vocabulary Practice, p. 48
		Grammar & Comp. Handbook, Lessons
		  5.4, 11.1–11.3, 11.7
		Grammar and Language Workbook,
		  pp. 147–150, 245, 267
		Reading Workbook, pp. 71–72
			* Quick Checks, p. 69
			  Selection and Theme Assessment, pp.
			  133–136
			  Performance Assessment, pp. 68–69
			  Spanish Summaries, p. 69
			  Spanish Translations, p. 69

JULIUS CAESAR
 	
WILLIAM SHAKESPEARE
	Unit Four Planning Guide, pp. 25–34
	* Active Reading Guide, p. 71
		Grammar & Comp. Handbook, Lessons
		  11.6, 2.2, 8.1–8.2, 5.7
		Grammar and Language Workbook, pp.
		  259, 219, 77, 253, 199–201, 155
		Reading Workbook, pp. 73–74
			* Quick Checks, p. 71
			  Selection and Theme Assessment, pp.
			  137–146
			  Performance Assessment, pp. 70–74
			  Spanish Summaries, p. 70

The Ring of General Macías
 	
JOSEPHINA NIGGLI
	Unit Four Planning Guide, pp. 39–46
	* Active Reading Guide, p. 76
	Vocabulary Practice, p. 49
		Grammar & Comp. Handbook,
		  Lessons 2.3, 4.7
		Grammar and Language Workbook,
		  pp. 79, 103
		Reading Workbook, pp. 75–76
			* Quick Checks, p. 76
			  Selection and Theme Assessment, pp.
			  147–148
			  Performance Assessment, p. 75
			  Spanish Summaries, p. 71

Marked
 	
CARMEN TAFOLLA
	Unit Four Planning Guide, pp. 47–51
	* Active Reading Guide, p. 77
			* Quick Checks, p. 77
			  Selection and Theme Assessment, pp.
			  147–148
			  Performance Assessment, p. 75
			  Spanish Summaries, p. 72

*Also available in Spanish

✍ **Transparencies**	**Technology Resources**
Selection Focus Transparency 69 Grammar and Language Transparencies 57, 58 Literary Elements Transparency 69	Literature Launchers Videodisc Audio Library Spanish Audio Library Vocabulary Puzzlemaker Web Site: lit.glencoe.com
Selection Focus Transparency 70 Grammar and Language Transparencies 59–64 Literary Elements Transparency 71	Literature Launchers Videodisc Audio Library Vocabulary Puzzlemaker Web Site: lit.glencoe.com
Selection Focus Transparency 71 Grammar and Language Transparency 65 Literary Elements Transparency 76	Audio Library Vocabulary Puzzlemaker Web Site: lit.glencoe.com
Selection Focus Transparency 72 Literary Elements Transparency 77	Audio Library Vocabulary Puzzlemaker Web Site: lit.glencoe.com

📁 *Theme* **RESOURCES**

- Listening and Speaking Activities (pp. 19–20)
- Viewing and Representing Activities (pp. 25–26)
- Critical Thinking Skills (pp. 27–29)
- Media Connections Activities (pp. 20–21)
- Interdisciplinary Activities (pp. 20–21)

See also these additional planning resources:
- English Language Learners Sourcebook
- Inclusion Strategies Sourcebook
- Literature Groups Sourcebook

PRESENTATION *Plus!*

Use Glencoe's *Presentation Plus!* This multimedia teaching tool lets you present dynamic lessons that will engage your students. Using Microsoft Powerpoint,® you can customize the presentations to create your own personalized lessons.

Objectives

- To read a descriptive history of the development of the theater in ancient Greece
- To recognize how ancient Greek drama has influenced modern drama

Teaching Strategies

After students have read the Literature Focus, have them think of modern analogies of some of the elements of Greek drama. Point out that a Greek theater was similar to an amphitheater where large outdoor concerts are held today. The Greek chorus was somewhat like the chorus of musicals such as *The Music Man* or *My Fair Lady* in which singing and dancing choruses represent townspeople. Theater and film festivals are still held today, although they are generally artistic, not religious or political.

Language Note

The word *thespian*, from the name of the Greek poet Thespis, is used today as a synonym for *actor*. Some students may be members of the International Thespian Society, an organization of high school student actors.

Teaching Options

Literature **FOCUS**

Classical Greek Drama

The sun has not yet risen over Athens, but the city's narrow streets are already alive with people. Chatting excitedly, family parties carry with them provisions for the long day ahead: baskets of food, cushions, blankets to ward off the chill March air. This happy crowd streams toward the Acropolis, the rocky hill that towers over the city. Those who look up can make out the snowy columns of the Parthenon silhouetted against the morning sky. But it is not for this elegant temple on the summit that the travelers are bound. Their journey stops on the lower slopes of the Acropolis, at the gates of the Theater of Dionysos. The crowd slows to a crawl, for it seems that the entire city is trying to squeeze through the entryways. Inside, however, there is room for everyone. Banked up the slopes of the hill are curving tiers of stone benches. The spectators check their admission tokens to find their designated sections. They spread out their cushions and watch the eastern sky. The sun is rising. The first play is about to begin.

Theater was far more than entertainment for the people of ancient Greece. It was part of their religion, a way of displaying loyalty to their city-state, and a method of honoring local heroes. It was also a major social event, a thrilling competition, and a place where important philosophical issues could be aired.

Origins

Like most great traditions, Greek drama began very simply. For centuries the people of Greece had loved to sing and dance as a way of worshiping their gods and celebrating important occasions. When work was done, a circular threshing floor, used for separating the grains of wheat from their inedible husks, made an ideal space for people to rejoice in the harvest with circle dances and songs that Greek people still enjoy. Over the centuries, these circle dances developed into the **dithyramb,** a religious ritual performed by a chorus of men wearing masks. Special arenas were established for these rituals at the base of hills, allowing spectators to sit on the slopes and watch the performance unobstructed. A theater was taking shape, with a circular stage and seating, but as yet there were no plays.

An Athenian poet called Thespis is traditionally credited with inventing what we now call drama. In 534 B.C. he discovered that a dithyramb could be creatively expanded by adding a character separate from the chorus of male singers. Thus the first actor appeared on the circular stage, and with him there emerged a whole new world of possibilities for writers. Now there could be dialogue, an exchange of ideas, even a lively argument. Clearly the spectators approved, because drama continued to develop and grow in popularity.

In the early fifth century B.C., the great dramatist Aeschylus (525–456 B.C.) added a second actor to the stage; within a few

Terra-cotta grinning mask. 6th century B.C., Motya.

Words Pertaining to Theater

Keeping a list of words that relate to drama may help English language learners understand the meanings of words they may not encounter in other contexts.

Activity Encourage students to start a list of words relating to drama as they read the Literature Focus. They may include the words *theater, spectator, arena, performance, chorus, tragedy, comedy,* and *costume.* Write a composite list on the board as volunteers contribute words. Have students define and give an example of each word.

Additional Resources

📁 *English Language Learners Sourcebook*

years, his rival Sophocles (496–406 B.C.) answered with a third. The chorus remained, but the audience's attention had shifted from the chants and dances of a group to the lives and struggles of individuals. European theater was born.

The Theaters

The theaters that graced Greek cities of the late fifth century were not buildings at all. Instead, architects had merely adapted the hillside and circle of the ancient dances. An early innovation was to add a few wooden benches curving around the lower slopes for the comfort of important spectators. Then the circular dancing area, known as the **orchestra,** might be paved with stones so that the chorus members would have a more formal place to perform. Another early addition was the **skene,** a rectangular building made of wood, which faced the audience from the opposite side of the orchestra and had several doors opening out toward the audience. This building provided changing rooms for actors and a place to store props.

Theater design naturally evolved from these early innovations. Wooden seats gave way to stone, not just for the privileged front-row customers, but for the entire audience. Benches of stone curved around the hillside with gangways radiating up from the orchestra, creating wedge-shaped seating areas. It was not long before the wooden skene was replaced by a permanent building of stone. This provided a formal backdrop to the action and served as a built-in piece of stage scenery, such as a palace or a temple, from which actors could make their entries. As the centuries progressed, theaters became more decorative and complex, but for more than a thousand years, they maintained their basic elements: a circle for the actors, a slope for the spectators, and the open air for a roof.

Chorus, Actors, and Stage Sets

What would you have seen from the benches of an ancient Greek theater? Dominating the area below the spectators, and partly surrounded by the curved seating, was the great circle of the orchestra. More than sixty-five feet in diameter, this was the domain of the **chorus,** which would enter at the beginning of the drama and remain throughout the performance. Only men were allowed to perform. As they had for centuries, choruses chanted and danced, though now they moved in lines rather than the traditional circle. Their role was to comment on the action of the play, reacting to the plot with expressive, stylized dances. A single musician, playing a type of pipe called the **aulos,** accompanied the chorus. The **choragos,** or leader of the chorus, sometimes participated in the dialogue and generally represented the

Two statuettes of elderly comic actors. c. 375–350 B.C., Attica.

Historical Note

The peak of ancient Greek drama occurred during the Golden Age of Greece, 477 B.C.–431 B.C. The Greek city-states had developed by the 700s B.C. These were cities such as Athens, Sparta, and Thebes and their surrounding villages and rural areas. Although the city-states had common language, culture, and religion, each was independent. Athens and Sparta, the strongest city-states, were constant rivals. The democratic government of Athens enabled its people to attain great prosperity. During the Golden Age, Athens was led by the great statesman Pericles. Aeschylus, Euripedes, and Sophocles wrote their great plays. Other arts, especially architecture, also flourished. The Golden Age ended in 431 B.C. when the Peloponnesian War, between Athens and Sparta, broke out. Athens eventually lost the war, and the highly civilized way of life in Greece continued to decline.

FYI

Masks Some historians believe that the mouthpieces of Greek actors' masks were shaped to serve as a megaphone to amplify the actors' voices in the huge theater.

Technology Option

Tragedy Chart

Suggest that students use word processing software to create a chart in which they list the tragic character, the fatal flaw, and the theme of a tragedy. Have them open a new document and insert a chart with the title *Tragedy* and three columns with the headings *Tragic Hero*, *Fatal Flaw*, and *Theme*. Have students identify examples as they read dramas or see them in the theater or on television. At the end of the unit students can share their information with a small group of classmates. **L2**

Tragedy

Tragic Hero	Fatal Flaw	Theme

typical responses of an ordinary citizen to the events of the play.

The enormous size of Greek theaters influenced the style of acting. Up to fifteen thousand spectators could watch performances in the Theater of Dionysos in Athens. Perched in the upper rows of seats, a spectator was more than fifty-five yards from the action below. The actors' gestures had to be exaggerated and dramatic, for no one in the back row could have interpreted slight movements.

All the participants, except the musician, wore masks. Made of wool, linen, wood, plaster or other perishable materials, none of these masks have survived, but enough paintings remain to give us an idea of what they were like. In the mid-fifth century, the time of Sophocles, masks were fairly realistic representations of human faces. In later centuries, masks grew in size and became less realistic, featuring deep eye sockets and wide, gaping mouths, making actors appear larger against the background skene. Typically, tragic actors wore striking, richly decorated robes that set them apart from the audience. Chorus members wore more conventional costumes, which identified the roles they were playing: soldiers, priests, mourners, or even—in the case of comedies—frogs, birds, or wasps.

Performances were full of color and movement but were lacking the scenery and technical magic that modern audiences would expect from a major production. The skene, directly behind the actors, served as a palace, temple, cave, or whatever other structure the spectators were asked to imagine. It is likely that painted panels were sometimes installed in front of the skene, but they could do little more than provide a decorative backdrop in such a huge space. Actors made their entrances and exits through doors of the skene, and probably remained at the far end of the orchestra, where a low wooden platform may have raised them a foot or two above the ground. In later centuries, this platform was built up to stand several feet above ground level—the forerunner of the modern theater stage.

The lighting, of course, was natural, and there were very few props. A hunter might carry a bow; an old man, a stick; a soldier, a sword and shield; but these props served more as symbols to identify the character's role in the play than to provide an imitation of life. The violence—murder, suicide, and battles—almost always occurred offstage. Typically, a messenger would appear after the event and describe in gory detail what had just happened.

The Plays

During the fifth century B.C., known as the golden age of Greek drama, four playwrights emerged as the greatest Greek dramatists: Aeschylus, Sophocles, Euripides (480–406 B.C.), and Aristophanes (448–385 B.C.). These masters—all from Athens—wrote plays in verse, based on themes familiar to their audiences. They retold myths, rewrote history, and ridiculed politicians. Aristophanes, the sole comic writer among the four Athenian masters, boldly and uproariously satirized society, politics, and even the gods, landing himself in legal trouble for doing so. However, his three great contemporaries were all tragic poets, whose plays capture humankind's timeless struggle to find the purpose of life and to achieve self-understanding.

Central to the **tragedy** is the fall of a great man (or woman, though her part would have been acted by a man)—the **tragic hero,** whose fate is brought about by a flaw within his or her own character. The aim of the tragic hero was to inspire audiences to examine their own lives, to define their beliefs, and to cleanse their emotions of pity and terror through compassion for the character.

Teaching Options

MEETING INDIVIDUAL NEEDS — GIFTED AND TALENTED

What Is Tragedy? One of the Greek philosopher Aristotle's greatest works was the *Poetics,* one of the world's most influential works of literary criticism. In the *Poetics,* written around 330 B.C., Aristotle described the nature of tragedy, based on his study of the tragedies of Sophocles and other Greek playwrights.

Activity Have students read the parts of the *Poetics* that deal with tragedy, such as sections 6 and 13–15. Have them report on Aristotle's ideas, answering the following questions:
- What is Aristotle's definition of tragedy?
- What kind of person is the ideal tragic hero? **L3**

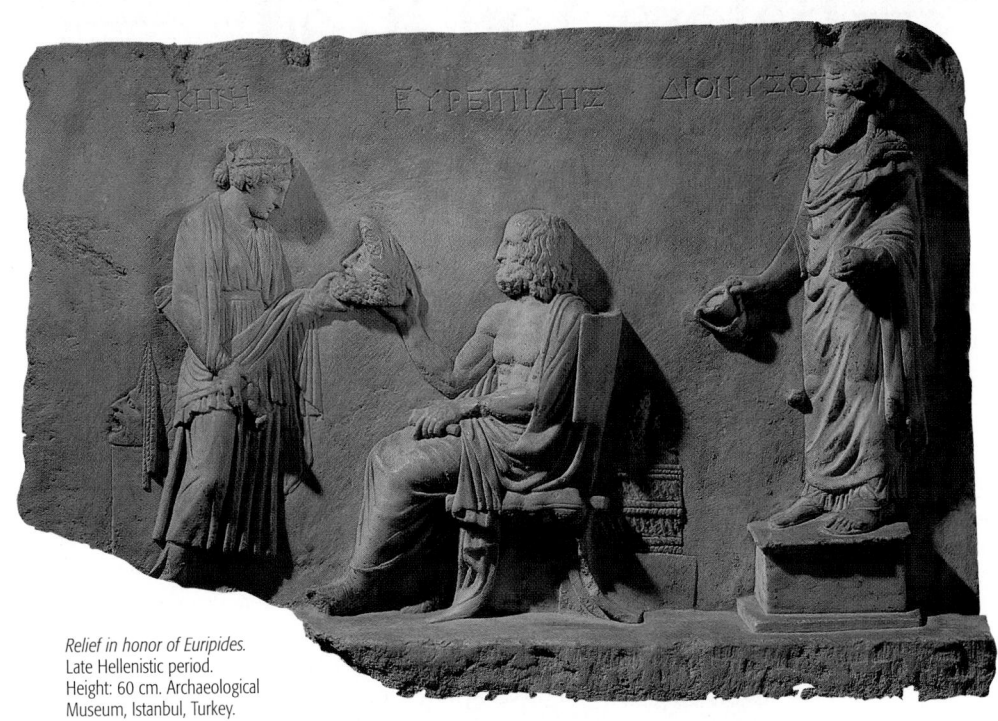

Relief in honor of Euripides. Late Hellenistic period. Height: 60 cm. Archaeological Museum, Istanbul, Turkey.

Theater as Festival

Plays in ancient Greece were never performed day after day for a "season" as they often are now. Instead, drama was the centerpiece of annual festivals that were partly religious and partly political. In one such festival, three tragic poets competed for first prize. Each author had to write and direct three tragedies and a farce; these four offerings would then be performed on a single day. Ten judges, chosen at random from among prominent citizens, were responsible for selecting a winner, but the crowd took an intense interest in the results, making their opinions loudly known and no doubt influencing the outcome with their emotional reactions. Sophocles came away with first prize at least eighteen times and never placed lower than second. There were also competitions for best comic poet, best tragic actor, and best comic actor.

Theater was far more than a popularity contest for the people of Athens, however. Audiences cared deeply for the content of the plays. People would memorize and quote their favorite passages, and there are many accounts of crowds being moved to tears by an emotional performance.

Nearly 2,500 years have passed since the golden age of Greek drama, but it is safe to say that any stage, television, or movie production we enjoy today owes its existence to that open theater, those pioneering actors, the dedicated poets, and the passionate audiences of ancient Greece.

REAL-WORLD CONNECTION

Greek Drama and Today's Theater
Have students discuss in small groups how Greek drama is similar to or different from today's theater and movies. Have them consider the physical construction of the theater, the function of drama in people's lives, and the following features of Greek drama:
- Violence always occurred offstage.
- Most plots were from old legends or history.

- The purpose of the protagonist's story was to inspire audiences and to cleanse their emotions through fear and pity.

L2 **COLLAB. LEARN.**

Objectives

- To read and analyze a play about a character who stands up for what she believes is right
- To identify the protagonist and antagonist of a play
- To identify the tragic flaw of a character in a tragedy
- To write a comparison of the viewpoints of a play's characters
- To write an analysis of bias

Skills

Reading/Thinking: Identifying the Author's Purpose; Identifying Fallacies; Paraphrasing
Writing: Adjectives in Poetry; Using Alliteration; Interpretive Account; Letter
Vocabulary: Antonyms
Grammar/Language: Present Perfect Tense; Dashes
Listening/Speaking: Listening to Tone of Voice; Political Speeches
Life Skills: Genealogical Chart
Collaboration: Literature Groups

Motivating

→OPTIONS

Literature Launchers: "An Ancient Greek Drama"

Videodisc Side B, Segment 19

Also available in VHS.

Selection Focus Transparency 69: Have students view and discuss the transparency.

Focus Activity: Have students discuss their examples, defining the decision each person had to make in order to act courageously.

Before You Read

Antigone

FOCUS ACTIVITY

Do you know of someone who had to act bravely in order to do what was right?

DISCUSS Think of an example of someone who, in your opinion, acted bravely. Share your story with the rest of the class.

SETTING A PURPOSE Read to learn about a character who courageously stands up for what she believes is right.

BACKGROUND

The Time and Place
This play takes place in ancient Greece, in the city of Thebes, which is about thirty miles northwest of Athens. At the time, Thebes was one of the greatest cities of Greece.

Did You Know?
The Greeks of Sophocles's day believed that if a corpse was not buried or cremated according to a strict ritual, his or her soul might not get to Hades, the underworld of the dead, but would wander the earth, bringing shame

upon its survivors and angering the gods. To leave a body unburied was a terrible insult to the family of the deceased.

VOCABULARY PREVIEW

repulse (ri puls′) *n.* an act of beating back or driving away, as with force; p. 728
arrogance (ar′ ə gəns) *n.* overbearing pride; p. 745
perverse (pər vurs′) *adj.* determined to go against what is reasonable, expected, or desired; contrary; p. 752
absolve (ab zolv′) *v.* to free from guilt or blame; p. 752
prevail (pri vāl′) *v.* to be superior in power or influence; succeed; p. 754
defile (di fīl′) *v.* to spoil the purity of; to make dirty or unclean; p. 758

Meet Sophocles

Sophocles, a handsome, athletic youth skilled in music, was only sixteen when he was chosen to lead a chorus in honor of Greece's victory at the Battle of Salamis. He studied music under Lamprus, the most acclaimed musician of his time, and tragedy, musical composition, and choreography under Aeschylus, the great writer of tragedy. During his ninety years, Sophocles wrote 123 dramas, winning 24 of 30 competitions. Other credits include inventing "scene paintings" and adding a third actor to dramas. He was also elected one of the ten military commanders of Athens and served on embassies to foreign states.

Sophocles was born about 496 B.C. at Colonus, a village near Athens. He died in Athens in 406 B.C.

RESOURCE MANAGER

Lesson Planning Resource
The *Unit Four Planning Guide* (pp. 16–24) provides additional lesson notes and reduced versions of all print resources.

Other Print Resources
- Active Reading Guide, p. 69
- Vocabulary Practice, p. 48
- Reading Workbook, pp. 71–72
- Grammar and Language Workbook, pp. 147–150, 245, 267

- Grammar and Composition Handbook, Lessons 5.4, 11.1–11.3, 11.7
- Quick Checks, p. 69
- Selection and Theme Assessment, pp. 133–136
- Performance Assessment, pp. 68–69
- Spanish Summaries, p. 69
- Spanish Translations
- Inclusion Strategies
- English Language Learners Sourcebook

 Transparencies
- Selection Focus 69
- Literary Elements 69
- Grammar and Language 57, 58

Technology
 Literature Launchers
 Audio Library
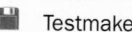 Spanish Audio Library
Glencoe Literature Web Site
Testmaker

ANTIGONE

Sophocles

Translated by Dudley Fitts and Robert Fitzgerald

Funerary Mask. c. 1600 B.C., Mycenaean.

Reading the Selection

SUMMARY, Scenes 1–2

Antigone is the daughter of Oedipus, former king of Thebes. Her uncle Creon is now King of Thebes. Her brothers, Eteocles and Polyneices, have been killed in a civil war. Antigone tells her sister Ismene of Creon's decree: Eteocles will be buried honorably, but Polyneices was a traitor and will not be buried. Anyone who tries to bury him will be put to death. Antigone asks Ismene to help her bury their brother, but Ismene refuses. Creon is told that someone has tried to bury Polyneices. When Antigone admits to burying her brother, Creon imprisons her and Ismene. He sentences Antigone, who is engaged to marry his son, to death.

📁 *Spanish Summaries,* p. 69

A Active Reading

PREDICT After students have read the title, the cast of characters, and the first page of the play, have them predict who the protagonist and the antagonist of the play are.

Additional Resources

📁 *Active Reading Guide,* p. 69
🎧 *Audio Library*
🎧 *Spanish Audio Library*

Teaching Options

CONNECTING TO OTHER SELECTIONS

The chart at the right shows three ways to connect *Antigone* to selections in this book.

For specific teaching strategies, see the *Unit Four Planning Guide,* pp. 20–21.

Connection	Title
Life Skills: Decision Making	→ "The Road Not Taken," p. 643
Thematic: Principles	→ "Tuesday Siesta," p. 189
Literary: Characters	→ "As It Is with Strangers," p. 279

PROTAGONIST/ANTAGONIST Point out that Sophocles gives very brief information about the characters in the list at the beginning of the play. Ask students to describe the nature of the information given. *(Sophocles specifies family relationships.)* Also ask how the cast of characters may help them predict who the protagonist and antagonist of the play will be. *(Antigone, the title character, is listed first and is probably the protagonist. Creon is the king and the play takes place in his palace; he may be the antagonist.)*

Argive Army The Argive army was the military force from Argos, a rival city state of Thebes.

At the MOVIES

Be sure to preview the following video for appropriateness for your class:

- Antigone*

* *Also available in the Glencoe Literature Video Library.*

Teaching Options

ANTIGONE

CHARACTERS

ANTIGONE: daughter of Oedipus

ISMENE: daughter of Oedipus

EURYDICE: wife of Creon

CREON: King of Thebes, uncle of Antigone and Ismene

HAIMON: son of Creon

TEIRESIAS: a blind prophet

A SENTRY

A MESSENGER

CHORUS: elders of Thebes

CHORAGOS: leader of the Chorus

SCENE: *Before the palace of* CREON, *King of Thebes. A central double door, and two lateral doors. A platform extends the length of the façade, and from this platform three steps lead down into the "orchestra," or chorus-ground.* **TIME:** *Dawn of the day after the repulse of the Argive army from the assault on Thebes.*

Vocabulary
repulse (ri puls´) *n.* an act of beating back or driving away, as with force

Theatre of Ancient Epidaurus. Mid-4th century B.C. to Hellenistic period. Palaia Epidaurus, Greece.

A

B

MEETING INDIVIDUAL NEEDS

ENGLISH LANGUAGE LEARNERS

Reading Verse Point out that *Antigone* is written in verse form and thus is divided into lines. Each line starts with a capital letter. Remind students that the capital letters at the beginning of lines do not necessarily indicate a new sentence. Explain that to understand the lines' meaning, readers should pay attention to the punctuation indicating the end of a sentence and read the play in sentence units.

Activity Have both English language learners and English speakers take turns reading the first speeches of Antigone and Ismene aloud. Remind students to read in sentence units.

Additional Resources
📁 *English Language Learners Sourcebook*

Prologue

[ANTIGONE and ISMENE enter from the central door of the Palace.]

ANTIGONE.° Ismene,° dear sister,
    You would think that we had already suffered enough
    For the curse on Oedipus:°
    I cannot imagine any grief
5   That you and I have not gone through. And now—
    Have they told you of the new decree of our King Creon?

ISMENE.   I have heard nothing: I know
    That two sisters lost two brothers, a double death
    In a single hour; and I know that the Argive army°
10   Fled in the night; but beyond this, nothing.

ANTIGONE.   I thought so. And that is why I wanted you
    To come out here with me. There is something we must do.

ISMENE.   Why do you speak so strangely?

ANTIGONE.   Listen, Ismene:
15   Creon buried our brother Eteocles
    With military honors, gave him a soldier's funeral,
    And it was right that he should; but Polyneices,
    Who fought as bravely and died as miserably,—
    They say that Creon has sworn
20   No one shall bury him, no one mourn for him,
    But his body must lie in the fields, a sweet treasure
    For carrion birds to find as they search for food.
    That is what they say, and our good Creon is coming here
    To announce it publicly; and the penalty—
25   Stoning to death in the public square!
                        There it is,
    And now you can prove what you are:
    A true sister, or a traitor to your family.

ISMENE.   Antigone, you are mad! What could I possibly do?

ANTIGONE.   You must decide whether you will help me or not.

30 ISMENE.   I do not understand you. Help you in what?

ANTIGONE.   Ismene, I am going to bury him. Will you come?

ISMENE.   Bury him! You have just said the new law forbids it.

ANTIGONE.   He is my brother. And he is your brother, too.

ISMENE.   But think of the danger! Think what Creon will do!

35 ANTIGONE   Creon is not strong enough to stand in my way.

ISMENE.   Ah sister!

---

1 **Antigone:** (an tig′ ə nē). **Ismene:** (is mē′ nē).

3 **Oedipus:** (ed′ ə pəs).

8–9 **two sisters . . . Argive army:** After the death of Oedipus, King of Thebes (thēbz), his sons, Eteocles (ē tē′ ə klēz′) and Polyneices (pä′ lə nī′ sēz), struggled to gain the throne. Argos, a rival city-state, sent its army in support of Polyneices. Before the Argive (ar′ jīv) army was driven back, both Eteocles and Polyneices were killed in battle. Creon (krē′ on), their uncle and Oedipus's brother-in-law, became king.

C Literary Elements

PLOT: Exposition Point out that background information in a play, like other elements, must be communicated through dialogue. Have students summarize the important background information they learn from Antigone and Ismene's conversation on the first page of the play. *(Antigone and Ismene belong to a family that has suffered much tragedy. Now they have lost their two brothers in a war; Creon had one brother buried but proclaimed the other a traitor. He said that anyone who tried to bury him would be put to death.)*

D Literary Elements

PROTAGONIST Have students summarize what they learn about Antigone from the first page of the play. *(She is strong, determined, decisive, and loyal to her family. She is active and not passive in her reactions to events.)* How do these qualities help her as a protagonist? *(She will stand and fight for what she believes in against whatever or whoever threatens those beliefs.)*

MEETING INDIVIDUAL NEEDS — MULTIPLE LEARNING STYLES

Spatial A map of ancient Greece will reinforce the location of Greece and help students recognize that the places mentioned in the play actually existed over 2,000 years ago.

Activity Have students find in an encyclopedia or other reference book a map of ancient Greece. Have them draw the map, including on it the cities of Thebes and Argos which are referred to in the play. Also have them include the two most powerful city-states, Athens and Sparta, and other places of interest such as Olympia, where the Olympic games were held. **L2**

ANTIGONE

Oedipus died, everyone hating him
For what his own search brought to light, his eyes
Ripped out by his own hand; and Jocasta died,
40   His mother and wife at once: she twisted the cords
That strangled her life;° and our two brothers died,
Each killed by the other's sword. And we are left:
But oh, Antigone,
Think how much more terrible than these
45   Our own death would be if we should go against Creon
And do what he has forbidden! We are only women,
We cannot fight with men, Antigone!
The law is strong, we must give in to the law
In this thing, and in worse. I beg the Dead
50   To forgive me, but I am helpless: I must yield
To those in authority. And I think it is dangerous business
To be always meddling.

ANTIGONE.   If that is what you think,
I should not want you, even if you asked to come.
You have made your choice, you can be what you want to be.
55   But I will bury him; and if I must die,
I say that this crime is holy: I shall lie down
With him in death, and I shall be as dear
To him as he to me.
                It is the dead,
Not the living, who make the longest demands:
60   We die for ever . . .
                You may do as you like,
Since apparently the laws of the gods mean nothing to you.

ISMENE. They mean a great deal to me; but I have no strength
To break laws that were made for the public good.

ANTIGONE. That must be your excuse, I suppose. But as for me,
65   I will bury the brother I love.

ISMENE.   Antigone,
I am so afraid for you!

ANTIGONE.   You need not be:
You have yourself to consider, after all.

ISMENE. But no one must hear of this, you must tell no one!
I will keep it a secret, I promise!

ANTIGONE.   Oh tell it! Tell everyone!
70   Think how they'll hate you when it all comes out
If they learn that you knew about it all the time!

37–41 Oedipus died . . . her life: Oedipus had killed Laïos (lī′ as), the king of Thebes at the time, and married the queen, Jocasta (jō kas′ tə). Together, they had four children—Antigone, Ismene, and two sons. When it was revealed that Oedipus had, without realizing it, killed his own father and married his own mother, he blinded himself, was banished from Thebes, and died, and Jocasta hanged herself.

ISMENE. So fiery! You should be cold with fear.

ANTIGONE. Perhaps. But I am only doing what I must.

ISMENE. But can you do it? I say that you cannot.

75 ANTIGONE Very well: when my strength gives out, I shall
do no more.

ISMENE. Impossible things should not be tried at all.

ANTIGONE. Go away, Ismene:
I shall be hating you soon, and the dead will too,
For your words are hateful. Leave me my foolish plan:
80 I am not afraid of the danger; if it means death,
It will not be the worst of deaths—death without honor.

ISMENE. Go then, if you feel that you must.
You are unwise,
But a loyal friend indeed to those who love you.

[*Exit into the Palace.* ANTIGONE *goes off,* L. *Enter the* CHORUS.]

Antigone. Marie Spartali Stillman (1844–1927). Simon Carter Gallery, Woodbridge, Suffolk, U.K.

Viewing the art: What characters are portrayed here? How does this image differ from the storyline that you've read so far?

H Literary Elements

PROTAGONIST/ANTAGONIST Have students identify the protagonist and the antagonist in the Prologue of the play. Encourage students to analyze each character's motives and make a generalization about the relationship between a dramatic protagonist and antagonist. *(In the Prologue, Antigone is the protagonist and Ismene is the antagonist. Although Antigone's motives are pure, she is not entirely admirable; she is willful and impatient. Although Ismene is in conflict with her, Ismene's motives are sincere. Students might generalize that a protagonist is not necessarily good and an antagonist necessarily evil. The antagonist is simply a person with whom the protagonist is in conflict.)*

VIEWING THE PAINTING

Marie Spartali Stillman was an English painter and model who associated with the Pre-Raphaelites, a group of artists whose romantic works were set in the distant past.

Viewing Response *Antigone and Ismene are shown burying Polyneices. The image differs from the play so far in that it shows Ismene accompanying her sister on her mission although she has said that she won't help her.*

MEETING INDIVIDUAL NEEDS GIFTED AND TALENTED

Two Views In refusing to help Antigone break the law, Ismene says, "Impossible things should not be tried at all." This illustrates the different temperaments and views of life of the two sisters.

Activity Have students discuss Ismene's statement and decide whether they agree or disagree with it. Have them give examples of people who have lived by this philosophy and those who have not. **L3**

PLOT: _Flashback_ Point out that the Parodos flashes back to the battle between Thebes and the Argives. Ask students how they can tell the action happened in the past. *(The Prologue made it clear that the war was over and Antigone's brothers were dead. The first stanza of the Parados begins in the present tense, but it mentions "the enemy." It then recounts the killing of the brothers in the past tense.)*

J **Literary Elements**

IMAGERY Have students name several sight images describing light in the Parodos. *("long blade of the sun," "unlidded eye of golden day," "marching light," "blaze of morning")*

K **Literary Elements**

FIGURES OF SPEECH: _Personification_ Point out that the description of the sun as "the unlidded/Eye of golden day" is an example of personification. Have students find another example of personification in the third stanza of the Parodos. *("The famished spears" likens the army's weapons to a hungry person.)*

L **Literary Elements**

IMAGERY Ask students to name sound images in the first six stanzas of the Parodos. *("Polyneices . . . roused them with windy phrases"; "He the wild eagle screaming insults"; "great Thebes . . . shouting war"; "the bray of bragging tongues"; "clanging arms")*

Teaching Options

ANTIGONE

Parodos°

CHORUS.   Now the long blade of the sun, lying
   Level east to west, touches with glory
   Thebes of the Seven Gates. Open, unlidded
   Eye of golden day! O marching light
5   Across the eddy and rush of Dirce's stream,°
   Striking the white shields of the enemy
   Thrown headlong backward from the blaze of morning!

CHORAGOS.   Polyneices their commander
   Roused them with windy phrases,
10   He the wild eagle screaming
   Insults above our land,
   His wings their shields of snow,
   His crest their marshalled helms.

CHORUS.   Against our seven gates in a yawning ring
15   The famished spears came onward in the night;
   But before his jaws were sated with our blood,
   Or pinefire took the garland of our towers,
   He was thrown back; and as he turned, great Thebes—
   No tender victim for his noisy power—
20   Rose like a dragon behind him, shouting war.

CHORAGOS.   For God° hates utterly
   The bray of bragging tongues;
   And when he beheld their smiling,
   Their swagger of golden helms,
25   The frown of his thunder blasted
   Their first man from our walls.

CHORUS.   We heard his shout of triumph high in the air
   Turn to a scream; far out in a flaming arc
   He fell with his windy torch, and the earth struck him.
30   And others storming in fury no less than his
   Found shock of death in the dusty joy of battle.

CHORAGOS.   Seven captains at seven gates
   Yielded their clanging arms to the god
   That bends the battle-line and breaks it.°
35   These two only, brothers in blood,
   Face to face in matchless rage,
   Mirroring each the other's death,
   Clashed in long combat.

CHORUS.   But now in the beautiful morning of victory
40   Let Thebes of the many chariots sing for joy!

732   UNIT 4: DRAMA

Parodos (păr′ ə dos): the first "song" of the Chorus.

5 Dirce's stream: This stream, which flows past Thebes, was named after a murdered queen.

21 God: Here, "God" refers to Zeus (zoōs), the king of the gods, who used thunderbolts to strike down the invading Argives.

32–34 Seven captains . . . breaks it: The Thebans offered the captains' armor (**arms**) as a sacrifice to Ares (ā′ rēz), the god of war.

Reading _Minilesson_

Identifying Author's Purpose In the Parodos, Sophocles shifts the style and tone he used in the Prologue. In vivid language, he describes events that happened before the dialogue between Antigone and Ismene in the Prologue.

Activity Have students identify and write a statement of the author's purpose in the Parodos. *(Possible answer: To pro-vide background information. First, the deaths of Eteocles and Polyneices, which are recounted, have a direct bearing on the action of the play. Second, Sophocles uses vivid language to help readers imagine the sights and sounds of war and remind them of its violence and destruction.)* **L2**

Additional Resources
📁 *Reading Workbook,* pp. 71–72

With hearts for dancing we'll take leave of war:
Our temples shall be sweet with hymns of praise,
And the long night shall echo with our chorus.

⁓ SCENE 1 ⁓

CHORAGOS. But now at last our new King is coming:
Creon of Thebes, Menoikeus'° son.
In this auspicious° dawn of his reign
What are the new complexities
5   That shifting Fate° has woven for him?
What is his counsel? Why has he summoned
The old men to hear him?

[Enter CREON *from the Palace, C. He addresses the* CHORUS *from the top step.]*

CREON. Gentlemen: I have the honor to inform you that our
Ship of State, which recent storms have threatened to
10   destroy, has come safely to harbor at last,° guided by the
merciful wisdom of Heaven. I have summoned you here this
morning because I know that I can depend upon you: your
devotion to King Laïos was absolute; you never hesitated in
your duty to our late ruler Oedipus; and when Oedipus died,
15   your loyalty was transferred to his children. Unfortunately,
as you know, his two sons, the princes Eteocles and Polyneices,
have killed each other in battle; and I, as the next in blood,
have succeeded to the full power of the throne.
I am aware, of course, that no Ruler can expect complete
20   loyalty from his subjects until he has been tested in office.
Nevertheless, I say to you at the very outset that I have
nothing but contempt for the kind of Governor who is
afraid, for whatever reason, to follow the course that he
knows is best for the State; and as for the man who sets
25   private friendship above the public welfare,—I have no use
for him, either. I call God to witness that if I saw my
country headed for ruin, I should not be afraid to speak out
plainly; and I need hardly remind you that I would never
have any dealings with an enemy of the people. No one
30   values friendship more highly than I; but we must remember
that friends made at the risk of wrecking our Ship are not real
friends at all.
These are my principles, at any rate, and that is why I have
made the following decision concerning the sons of Oedipus:

2 Menoikeus (me noi′ kē əs)

3 auspicious: favorable, indicating good fortune.

5 Fate: The ancient Greeks believed that three sisters, called the Fates, controlled human destiny. The first sister was said to spin the thread of human life, the second decided its length, and the third cut it.

8–10 Gentlemen . . . at last: The expression "Ship of State" likens a nation to a ship under sail. In reassuring the citizens of Thebes that the "storms" are over, Creon is referring to the Argive invasion and the many troubles in the house of Oedipus.

Sophocles ⁓

M Author's Craft

IMAGERY How does the imagery the author uses in the last stanza of the Parodos contrast with that he uses in the other stanzas? *(Images of peace and joy, such as "with hearts for dancing" and "Our temples shall be sweet with hymns of praise," contrast with the violent images of war.)*

N Active Reading

CONNECT In reading Creon's speech to the townspeople of Thebes, encourage students to recall speeches they have heard by other government leaders. How is Creon's speech similar to speeches they have heard? How does it differ? *(Like modern leaders, Creon begins on a positive note, reassuring the citizens about the strength of the country. He uses formal, serious language. He expresses his loyalty and patriotism to the country. Students may find that Creon is somewhat more outspoken than modern leaders might be in expressing the value of loyalty to the State over friendship or other values.)*

O Literary Elements

ANTAGONIST Ask students to list character traits apparent in Creon from his speech. *(He seems skilled in politics, strong-willed, religious, forthright, and patriotic. He seems to be a man of action.)* How do these qualities help him as an antagonist? *(He will willingly fight anyone who opposes him.)*

Listening and Speaking *Minilesson*

Political Speeches Creon's speech demonstrates the serious, formal style used by political leaders to speak to their citizens.

Activity Have students videotape a speech by the president, vice-president, a senator, representative, or state governor. Many speeches or portions of speeches are shown on C-SPAN and other cable news channels. Have students write a report that summarizes the speech and the speaker's style. Encourage them to consider questions such as:

• What is the speaker's overall tone: sincere, somber, concerned, sympathetic, or something else?
• What tone of voice, gestures, and facial expressions reinforce the speaker's overall tone?

• How appropriate is the speaker's tone to his or her message?
• What flaws in the speaker's delivery, if any, detract from his or her tone and message?
• What is your overall evaluation of the speaker's effectiveness?

L3

ANTIGONE

35 Eteocles, who died as a man should die, fighting for his
country, is to be buried with full military honors, with all
the ceremony that is usual when the greatest heroes die;
but his brother Polyneices, who broke his exile to come
back with fire and sword against his native city and the

40 shrines of his fathers' gods, whose one idea was to spill the
blood of his blood and sell his own people into slavery—
O Polyneices, I say, is to have no burial: no man is to touch
him or say the least prayer for him; he shall lie on the plain,
unburied; and the birds and the scavenging dogs can do

45 with him whatever they like.
This is my command, and you can see the wisdom behind
it. As long as I am King, no traitor is going to be honored
P with the loyal man. But whoever shows by word and deed
that he is on the side of the State,—he shall have my

50 respect while he is living, and my reverence when he is dead.

CHORAGOS.   If that is your will, Creon son of Menoikeus,
You have the right to enforce it: we are yours.

CREON.   That is my will. Take care that you do your part.

CHORAGOS.   We are old men: let the younger ones carry it out.

55 CREON.   I do not mean that: the sentries have been appointed.

CHORAGOS.   Then what is it that you would have us do?

CREON.   You will give no support to whoever breaks this law.

CHORAGOS.   Only a crazy man is in love with death!

Q CREON.   And death it is; yet money talks, and the wisest
60 Have sometimes been known to count a few coins too many.

[*Enter* SENTRY *from L.*]

SENTRY.   I'll not say that I'm out of breath from running, King,
because every time I stopped to think about what I have to
tell you, I felt like going back. And all the time a voice kept
saying, "You fool, don't you know you're walking straight

65 into trouble?"; and then another voice: "Yes, but if you let
somebody else get the news to Creon first, it will be even
worse than that for you!" But good sense won out, at least
I hope it was good sense, and here I am with a story that
makes no sense at all; but I'll tell it anyhow, because, as

70 they say, what's going to happen's going to happen, and—

CREON.   Come to the point. What have you to say?

SENTRY.   I did not do it. I did not see who did it. You must not
punish me for what someone else has done.

Marble gravestone of Sosinos from Gortyna, a bronze founder. Classical Greek, Attic period, last quarter of the 5th century B.C. Louvre Museum, Paris.

Viewing the art: What might Antigone and Ismene have wanted depicted on Polyneices's gravestone if they had been allowed to bury their brother properly?

Cultural Note

Classical Greek religion was based on the belief that people had to do certain things to please the gods, such as being hospitable to strangers and properly burying deceased family members. Greeks also honored the gods by creating sanctuaries devoted to specific gods, making sacrifices of domestic animals, and holding festivals. Greeks believed that if they fulfilled their duties, the gods would bring good fortune. If not, they would bring famine, epidemics, and natural disasters.

INTERDISCIPLINARY CONNECTION

Art The sculptures on the Parthenon in Athens, created around the same time Sophocles was writing his tragedies, are considered the highest achievement in Classical Greek art. The Parthenon was a temple in Athens dedicated to Athena, the city's patron goddess. In 1801, Lord Elgin, a British ambassador to Turkey, got permission from the Greek government to remove several Parthenon sculptures and ship them to England. They were put into the British Museum in 1816 and are known as the Elgin Marbles.

Activity Have students research the sculptures of the Parthenon. Ask them to find information including the following definitions: *caryatid* (a column carved in the shape of a woman); *frieze* (a band of relief sculpture around the top of the temple); *metopes* (square panels in the frieze); and *pediments* (triangular pieces from the temple's roof). **L2**

S Literary Elements

STAGE DIRECTIONS Call students' attention to the three stage directions, which specifically describe Creon's attitude as the sentry speaks. Remind students that these directions help actors portray a play's characters. Have one or two volunteers demonstrate how they would follow the directions in playing the role of Creon.

T Active Reading

VISUALIZE Remind students that in Greek drama, much action is described and not shown. Encourage students to visualize, as the original Greek audiences would have done, the scene of the sentries discovering the corpse of Polyneices partially covered with dirt. Have them name some particularly vivid images that help them see the scene, such as "new dust on the slimy flesh," and "not a wheeltrack in the dust."

ANTIGONE

CREON. A comprehensive defense! More effective, perhaps,
75   If I knew its purpose. Come: what is it?

SENTRY. A dreadful thing . . . I don't know how to put it—

CREON. Out with it!

SENTRY.   Well, then;
    The dead man—
                 Polyneices—

[Pause. The SENTRY is overcome, fumbles for words. CREON waits impassively.]

                      out there—
                           someone,—
    New dust on the slimy flesh!

S — *[Pause. No sign from CREON.]*

80   Someone has given it burial that way, and
    Gone . . .

S — *[Long pause. CREON finally speaks with deadly control.]*

CREON. And the man who dared do this?

SENTRY.   I swear I
    Do not know! You must believe me!
                      Listen:
    The ground was dry, not a sign of digging, no,
85   Not a wheeltrack in the dust, no trace of anyone.
    It was when they relieved us this morning: and one of them,
    The corporal, pointed to it.
                   There it was,
    The strangest—
            Look:
    The body, just mounded over with light dust: you see?
90   Not buried really, but as if they'd covered it
    Just enough for the ghost's peace. And no sign
    Of dogs or any wild animal that had been there.

    And then what a scene there was! Every man of us
    Accusing the other: we all proved the other man did it,
95   We all had proof that we could not have done it.
    We were ready to take hot iron in our hands,
    Walk through fire, swear by all the gods,
    It was not I!
    I do not know who it was, but it was not I!

736   🐦   UNIT 4: DRAMA

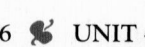

The Chorus of Elders.
Van Brantegham
Collection, Brussels.

Teaching Options

REAL-WORLD CONNECTION

Funeral Customs In the time when *Antigone* was written, a correct burial was extremely important for religious reasons. Have students discuss funeral customs in the United States and other cultures and religions with which they are familiar. What are the religious reasons for these customs? What other reasons exist for funeral customs? **L2**

[CREON's *rage has been mounting steadily, but the* SENTRY *is too intent upon his story to notice it.*]

100 And then, when this came to nothing, someone said
A thing that silenced us and made us stare
Down at the ground: you had to be told the news,
And one of us had to do it! We threw the dice,
And the bad luck fell to me.° So here I am,
105 No happier to be here than you are to have me:
Nobody likes the man who brings bad news.

CHORAGOS. I have been wondering, King: can it be that the gods have done this?

CREON. [*Furiously.*] Stop!
110 Must you doddering wrecks
Go out of your heads entirely? "The gods!"
Intolerable!
The gods favor this corpse? Why? How had he served them?
Tried to loot their temples, burn their images,
115 Yes, and the whole State, and its laws with it!
Is it your senile opinion that the gods love to honor bad men?
A pious thought!—
No, from the very beginning
There have been those who have whispered together,
Stiff-necked anarchists, putting their heads together,
120 Scheming against me in alleys.° These are the men,
And they have bribed my own guard to do this thing.
[*Sententiously.*] Money!
There's nothing in the world so demoralizing as money.
Down go your cities,
125 Homes gone, men gone, honest hearts corrupted,
Crookedness of all kinds, and all for money!
[*To* SENTRY.]   But you—!
I swear by God and by the throne of God,
The man who has done this thing shall pay for it!
Find that man, bring him here to me, or your death
130 Will be the least of your problems: I'll string you up
Alive, and there will be certain ways to make you
Discover your employer before you die;
And the process may teach you a lesson you seem to have missed:
The dearest profit is sometimes all too dear:
135 That depends on the source. Do you understand me?
A fortune won is often misfortune.

103–104 We threw . . . to me: Like tossing a coin, throwing dice is a way to determine something randomly. In this case, it is who must do what no one wants to do.

117–120 A pious . . . in alleys: Anarchy is a state of disorder and confusion or lawlessness, often due to the absence of governmental authority. Anarchists believe that all forms of government are unjust and should be resisted. Here, Creon calls those who oppose him anarchists.

U Critical Thinking

IDENTIFYING FALLACIES What assumptions does Creon make about the gods? Does his reasoning show clear logic or is it a fallacy? *(Creon assumes that "the gods" are on his side and that they share his value system and his judgment of who is right and wrong; he says, therefore, that the gods cannot be responsible for burying Polyneices. His assumption that the gods agree with his views is false; therefore, his reasoning is a fallacy.)*

V Literary Elements

IRONY Have students define *pious* in line 117 to explain why Creon's statement is said ironically. *(Pious means "showing reverence and devotion"; Creon is sneering at people who think that the gods are responsible for burying the man whom Creon considers a traitor.)*

W Literary Elements

STAGE DIRECTION Have students define *sententiously* in the stage direction in line 122. How is it appropriate in describing Creon's next speech? *(Sententious means "abounding in aphoristic expression or excessive moralizing." Creon's speech begins with a version of the aphorism "The love of money is the root of all evil"; he goes on to moralize about people who are willing to break the law for money.)*

ANTIGONE

> **SENTRY.** King, may I speak?
>
> **CREON.** Your very voice distresses me.
>
> **SENTRY.** Are you sure that it is my voice, and not your conscience?
>
> **CREON.** By God, he wants to analyze me now!
>
> 140 **SENTRY.** It is not what I say, but what has been done, that hurts you.
>
> **CREON.** You talk too much.
>
> **SENTRY.** Maybe; but I've done nothing.
>
> **CREON.** Sold your soul for some silver: that's all you've done.
>
> **SENTRY.** How dreadful it is when the right judge judges wrong!
>
> **CREON.** Your figures of speech
> 145 May entertain you now; but unless you bring me the man,
> You will get little profit from them in the end.
>
> [*Exit CREON into the Palace.*]
>
> **SENTRY.** "Bring me the man"—!
> I'd like nothing better than bringing him the man!
> But bring him or not, you have seen the last of me here.
> 150 At any rate, I am safe!
>
> [*Exit SENTRY.*]

ODE° 1

> **CHORUS.** Numberless are the world's wonders, but none
> More wonderful than man; the stormgray sea
> Yields to his prows,° the huge crests bear him high;
> Earth, holy and inexhaustible, is graven°
> 5 With shining furrows where his plows have gone
> Year after year, the timeless labor of stallions.
>
> The lightboned birds and beasts that cling to cover,
> The lithe° fish lighting their reaches of dim water,
> All are taken, tamed in the net of his mind;
> 10 The lion on the hill, the wild horse windy-maned,
> Resign to him; and his blunt yoke has broken
> The sultry shoulders of the mountain bull.
>
> Words also, and thought as rapid as air,
> He fashions to his good use; statecraft is his,
> 15 And his the skill that deflects the arrows of snow,

Ode: a song chanted by the Chorus.

3 prows: ships.

4 graven: formed or shaped with a chisel; sculpted.

8 lithe: easily bent; flexible.

Writing *Minilesson*

Adjectives in Poetry Sophocles's ode includes vivid adjectives used in unusual contexts. For example, he describes the "*shining* furrows" of the earth, "the *stormgray* sea," and "the *sultry* shoulders of the mountain bull."

Activity Challenge students to write a poem of at least four lines on any subject they wish. Encourage them to use inter-esting, unusual adjectives to make their images more compelling. Suggest that they get their ideas on paper first. During revision they can brainstorm for vivid descriptive words. Have students read their poems to the class. **L2**

Additional Resources

Writer's Choice, Lesson 3.5

Sophocles ∾

The spears of winter rain: from every wind
He has made himself secure—from all but one:
In the late wind of death he cannot stand.

20 O clear intelligence, force beyond all measure!
O fate of man, working both good and evil!
When the laws are kept, how proudly his city stands!
When the laws are broken, what of his city then?
Never may the anarchic man find rest at my hearth,
Never be it said that my thoughts are his thoughts.

⌐ SCENE 2 ⌐

[*Re-enter* SENTRY *leading* ANTIGONE.]

CHORAGOS.   What does this mean? Surely this captive woman
  Is the Princess, Antigone? Why should she be taken?

SENTRY.   Here is the one who did it! We caught her
  In the very act of burying him.—Where is Creon?

5 **CHORAGOS.**   Just coming from the house.

[*Enter* CREON, C.]

CREON.   What has happened?
  Why have you come back so soon?

SENTRY. [*Expansively.*]   O King,
  A man should never be too sure of anything:
  I would have sworn
  That you'd not see me here again: your anger
10 Frightened me so, and the things you threatened me with;
  But how could I tell then
  That I'd be able to solve the case so soon?

  No dice-throwing this time: I was only too glad to come!

  Here is this woman. She is the guilty one:
15 We found her trying to bury him.
  Take her, then; question her; judge her as you will.
  I am through with the whole thing now, and glad of it.

CREON.   But this is Antigone! Why have you brought her here?

SENTRY.   She was burying him, I tell you!

CREON. [*Severely.*]   Is this the truth?

20 **SENTRY.**   I saw her with my own eyes. Can I say more?

ANTIGONE, SCENE 2 ❧ 739

Active Reading

INTERPRET Remind students that the chorus chants the ode. With which character's value system does the chorus seem to agree? *(The chorus's views of the importance of obeying the law and the dangers of anarchy agree with those of Creon.)*

Active Reading

INTERPRET Why are the choragos and Creon surprised that Antigone has been arrested? *(She is the niece of Creon, who decreed that Polyneices should not be buried. In addition, she is a woman; men apparently did not expect women to show disrespect for men.)*

On The Lighter Side

Summarizing *Antigone*

In his poem "A Humorous Distillation of *Antigone*," Maurice Sagoff begins:

> Tyrant Creon's stern advice is
> "Do not bury Polyneices!
> Thebes' defenders had to
> squash him—
> Now we'll let the buzzards nosh him!"
> But Antigone, the brave,
> Dared to dig her brother's grave:
> "Man-made laws my soul defies—
> Live by laws divine!" she cries.

The poem appears in *Shrinklits: Seventy of the World's Towering Classics Cut Down to Size* (New York: New Chapter Press, 1980).

INCLUSION STRATEGIES
MEETING INDIVIDUAL NEEDS

Less-Proficient Readers Remind students that the chorus represents the townspeople of Thebes. The chorus does not further the play's plot. Instead, it comments on various elements of the play.

Activity On the board, keep a running list of the chorus's function in each part of the play in which it appears. Have students refer to the Parodos on page 732 and tell what its function is. *(It gives important background information.)* In the ode on pages 738–739, the chorus affirms Creon's value system and brings up some themes of the play. **L1**

Additional Resources
📁 *Inclusion Strategies*

DRAMA ❧ 739

ANTIGONE

CREON. The details: come, tell me quickly!

SENTRY. It was like this:
After those terrible threats of yours, King,
We went back and brushed the dust away from the body.
The flesh was soft by now, and stinking,
25 So we sat on a hill to windward and kept guard.
No napping this time! We kept each other awake.
But nothing happened until the white round sun
Whirled in the center of the round sky over us:
Then, suddenly,
30 A storm of dust roared up from the earth, and the sky
Went out, the plain vanished with all its trees
In the stinging dark. We closed our eyes and endured it.
The whirlwind lasted a long time, but it passed;
And then we looked, and there was Antigone!
35 I have seen
A mother bird come back to a stripped nest, heard
Her crying bitterly a broken note or two
For the young ones stolen. Just so, when this girl
Found the bare corpse, and all her love's work wasted,
40 She wept, and cried on heaven to damn the hands
That had done this thing.
And then she brought more dust
And sprinkled wine three times for her brother's ghost.

We ran and took her at once. She was not afraid,
Not even when we charged her with what she had done.
45 She denied nothing.
And this was a comfort to me,
And some uneasiness: for it is a good thing
To escape from death, but it is no great pleasure
To bring death to a friend.
Yet I always say
There is nothing so comfortable as your own safe skin!

50 **CREON.** [*Slowly, dangerously.*] And you, Antigone,
You with your head hanging,—do you confess this thing?

ANTIGONE. I do. I deny nothing.

CREON. [*To* SENTRY.] You may go.

[*Exit* SENTRY.]

[*To* ANTIGONE.] Tell me, tell me briefly:
Had you heard my proclamation touching this matter?

Peplos Kore from the Athenian Acropolis. c. 530 B.C., Greek. Three-quarters life-size. The Acropolis Museum, Athens.

Viewing the sculpture: How does the woman shown here compare with your image of Antigone? In what ways are they the same? In what ways are they different?

55 **ANTIGONE.** It was public. Could I help hearing it?

CREON. And yet you dared defy the law.

ANTIGONE. I dared.
It was not God's proclamation. That final Justice
That rules the world below makes no such laws.

Your edict,° King, was strong,
60 But all your strength is weakness itself against
The immortal unrecorded laws of God.
They are not merely now: they were, and shall be,
Operative for ever, beyond man utterly.

I knew I must die, even without your decree:
65 I am only mortal. And if I must die
Now, before it is my time to die,
Surely this is no hardship: can anyone
Living, as I live, with evil all about me,
Think Death less than a friend? This death of mine
70 Is of no importance; but if I had left my brother
Lying in death unburied, I should have suffered.
Now I do not.
                    You smile at me. Ah, Creon,
Think me a fool, if you like; but it may well be
That a fool convicts me of folly.

75 **CHORAGOS.** Like father, like daughter: both headstrong, deaf to
        reason!
She has never learned to yield.

CREON. She has much to learn.
The inflexible heart breaks first, the toughest iron
Cracks first, and the wildest horses bend their necks
At the pull of the smallest curb.
                                Pride? In a slave?
80 This girl is guilty of a double insolence,
Breaking the given laws and boasting of it.
Who is the man here,
She or I, if this crime goes unpunished?
Sister's child, or more than sister's child,
85 Or closer yet in blood—she and her sister
Win bitter death for this!
[*To* SERVANTS.]   Go, some of you,
Arrest Ismene. I accuse her equally.
Bring her: you will find her sniffling in the house there.

59 edict: an official order or decree issued by a person in authority.

EE Active Reading

INTERPRET Antigone's speech enumerates her reasons for disobeying Creon's law and burying her brother. Have students summarize them. *(She believes God's laws take priority over human laws; according to God's laws, her brother must be properly buried; life would not be worth living for her if she did not show respect for her brother and fight against the evil that she sees in Creon's law.)*

FF Active Reading

QUESTION What reason does the choragos offer for Antigone's actions? *(He says she has inherited stubbornness from her father.)*

GG Active Reading

INTERPRET Creon's speech begins with several images. Have students explain how they relate to the action of the play. *(Creon gives three examples illustrating the negative effects of stubbornness and inflexibility. He is stating that, similarly, Antigone's stubbornness will be destructive.)*

HH Literary Elements

PROTAGONIST/ANTAGONIST Point out that the main conflict of the play, between Antigone, the protagonist, and Creon, the antagonist, is clear at this point. In addition to the conflict between human law and God's law defined by Antigone in her speech, Creon points out another area of conflict. Have students define it. *(Creon describes a conflict between men and women. He believes that men have authority over women that women should not defy.)*

MEETING INDIVIDUAL NEEDS — INCLUSION STRATEGIES

Less-Proficient Readers A graphic aid can help students clearly visualize the areas of conflict between Antigone and Creon.

Activity Have students contribute ideas as you write a chart on the board similar to the one here.

Creon	Antigone
humanity	God
patriotism to State	loyalty to family

L2

Additional Resources
📁 *Inclusion Strategies*

Active Reading

INTERPRET Have students explain how Creon compares Ismene and Antigone in lines 89–92. (*He says that Ismene is behaving guiltily because a person's subconscious will betray him or her after wrongdoing. He compares what he sees as Ismene's guilty behavior to Antigone's bragging about breaking the law; he says the latter is worse.*)

Critical Thinking

EVALUATING Have students describe and evaluate Antigone's behavior toward Creon. (*Some students may describe Antigone's attitude as rebellious and rude and feel that she should show more respect for Creon, her uncle and the king. Others may admire Antigone for strongly standing up for what she believes in and expressing her opinions to Creon.*)

Active Reading

QUESTION In what way, according to Creon, is Antigone insulting the memory of her brother Eteocles? (*She is honoring Polyneices, who fought against their country, in the same way that she honors Eteocles, who fought for their country.*)

Teaching Options

ANTIGONE

Her mind's a traitor: crimes kept in the dark
90 Cry for light, and the guardian brain shudders;
But how much worse than this
Is brazen boasting of barefaced anarchy!

ANTIGONE. Creon, what more do you want than my death?

CREON.   Nothing.
That gives me everything.

ANTIGONE.   Then I beg you: kill me.
95 This talking is a great weariness: your words
Are distasteful to me, and I am sure that mine
Seem so to you. And yet they should not seem so:
I should have praise and honor for what I have done.
All these men here would praise me
100 Were their lips not frozen shut with fear of you.
[*Bitterly.*] Ah the good fortune of kings,
Licensed to say and do whatever they please!

CREON. You are alone here in that opinion.

ANTIGONE. No, they are with me. But they keep their tongues
in leash.

105 **CREON.** Maybe. But you are guilty, and they are not.

ANTIGONE. There is no guilt in reverence for the dead.

CREON. But Eteocles—was he not your brother too?

ANTIGONE. My brother too.

CREON.   And you insult his memory?

ANTIGONE. [*Softly.*] The dead man would not say that I insult it.

110 **CREON.** He would: for you honor a traitor as much as him.

ANTIGONE. His own brother, traitor or not, and equal in blood.

CREON. He made war on his country. Eteocles defended it.

ANTIGONE. Nevertheless, there are honors due all the dead.

CREON. But not the same for the wicked as for the just.

115 **ANTIGONE.** Ah Creon, Creon,
Which of us can say what the gods hold wicked?°

CREON. An enemy is an enemy, even dead.

ANTIGONE. It is my nature to join in love, not hate.

CREON. [*Finally, losing patience.*] Go join them, then; if you
must have your love,
120 Find it in hell!

742 🌀 UNIT 4: DRAMA

116 Which . . . wicked: Note Antigone's belief that people cannot understand the thinking of the gods.

MULTIPLE LEARNING STYLES

MEETING INDIVIDUAL NEEDS

Interpersonal Point out that individuals often have differences of opinion. Learning to express opposing points of view without becoming angry or violent is an important interpersonal skill. Have students discuss ways of doing this.

Activity Have students analyze the dialogue between Creon and Antigone. How does each character help or harm effective communication during their disagreement? For example, what is the effect of Antigone's comment, "Ah the good fortune of kings,/Licensed to say and do whatever they please!" or of Creon's angry comment in lines 118–120? Encourage students to think of ways in which Creon and Antigone might communicate more effectively. **L2**

CHORAGOS. But see, Ismene comes:

[*Enter* ISMENE, *guarded.*]

> Those tears are sisterly, the cloud
> That shadows her eyes rains down gentle sorrow.

CREON. You too, Ismene,
125   Snake in my ordered house, sucking my blood
> Stealthily—and all the time I never knew
> That these two sisters were aiming at my throne!
>   Ismene,
> Do you confess your share in this crime, or deny it?
> Answer me.

130 ISMENE. Yes, if she will let me say so. I am guilty.

ANTIGONE. [*Coldly.*] No, Ismene. You have no right to say so.
> You would not help me, and I will not have you help me.

ISMENE. But now I know what you meant; and I am here
> To join you, to take my share of punishment.

135 ANTIGONE. The dead man and the gods who rule the dead
> Know whose act this was. Words are not friends.

ISMENE. Do you refuse me, Antigone? I want to die with you:
> I too have a duty that I must discharge to the dead.

ANTIGONE. You shall not lessen my death by sharing it.

140 ISMENE. What do I care for life when you are dead?

ANTIGONE. Ask Creon. You're always hanging on his opinions.

ISMENE. You are laughing at me. Why, Antigone?

ANTIGONE. It's a joyless laughter, Ismene.

ISMENE.   But can I do nothing?

ANTIGONE. Yes. Save yourself. I shall not envy you.
145   There are those who will praise you; I shall have honor, too.

ISMENE. But we are equally guilty!

ANTIGONE.   No more, Ismene.
> You are alive, but I belong to Death.

CREON. [*To the* CHORUS.] Gentlemen, I beg you to observe
> these girls:
> One has just now lost her mind; the other,
150   It seems, has never had a mind at all.

ISMENE. Grief teaches the steadiest minds to waver, King.

CREON. Yours certainly did, when you assumed guilt with the
> guilty!

Literary Elements

FIGURES OF SPEECH: *Metaphor* To what does Creon compare Ismene in lines 124–126? How does he make the comparison particularly negative? *(Creon compares Ismene to a snake, an ugly, negative image. He makes the comparison more negative with the image "sucking my blood" and the adverb "stealthily.")*

Literary Elements

CHARACTERS Have students list the character traits they find in Antigone and in Ismene in the sisters' conversation. Does the conversation show each sister in a positive or a negative light? *(Ismene exhibits positive traits: she is courageous and unselfish. Antigone shows several negative traits: she is cold, sarcastic, and vengeful.)*

Writing *Minilesson*

Using Alliteration Point out Creon's use of alliteration (the repetition of initial consonant sounds) in line 92: "brazen boasting of barefaced anarchy." The repetition of the *b* sound emphasizes Creon's angry opinion of Antigone's behavior. Explain that alliteration can be effective in prose or poetry when used sparingly. If it is overused, it can have an unintentionally humorous effect.

Activity Have students write three sentences containing alliteration that describe any of the characters in *Antigone*. Point out that an alliterative phrase must repeat an initial consonant sound two or more times; the alliterative consonants do not have to be consecutive, but they are usually separated by one or two words at the most. **L2**

Additional Resources

📖 ***Writer's Choice,*** Lesson 3.5

NN **Active Reading**

EVALUATE Ask students if their opinion of Creon has changed since the beginning of the play. If so, how? *(Some students may say that at the end of this scene Creon seems more cruel and ruthless than he did earlier. His treatment of Antigone may strike readers as a fair though tragic application of the law; however, he seems to callously disregard his son's happiness here.)*

VIEWING THE ART

Knossos was a prosperous Greek city-state on the island of Crete. The Cretans were sailors and had come into contact with Egyptian painting, which was used to decorate tombs. The Cretans used painting to decorate not tombs but living areas.

00 **Literary Elements**

FIGURES OF SPEECH: *Simile* Point out the simile in lines 3–6. Have students identify the two things being compared. *(The tragedy that befalls the child of a family cursed by fate is like a storm at sea that causes destructive waves.)*

ISMENE. But how could I go on living without her?

CREON.   You are.
     She is already dead.

ISMENE.   But your own son's bride!

155 **CREON.** There are places enough for him to push his plow.
     I want no wicked women for my sons!°

ISMENE. O dearest Haimon, how your father wrongs you!

CREON. I've had enough of your childish talk of marriage!

CHORAGOS. Do you really intend to steal this girl from your son?

160 **CREON.** No; Death will do that for me.

CHORAGOS.   Then she must die?

CREON. [*Ironically.*] You dazzle me.
                          —But enough of this talk!

154–156 She is . . . sons: Here's a new complication: Antigone is engaged to marry Creon's son, Haimon. Thus, punishing her means punishing him, a fact that doesn't appear to bother Creon greatly.

Throne room, in the palace at Knossos.

744 🌀 UNIT 4: DRAMA

Teaching Options

Grammar and Language Minilesson

Present Perfect Tense Remind students that the present perfect verb tense is used to describe an action completed at some indefinite past time but which still affects the present, or to describe an action that started in the past and continues into the present. The present perfect is formed by using the auxiliary, or helping, verb *has* or *have* with the past participle of a verb. For example, on line 60 of page 734, Creon says,
". . . the wisest/Have sometimes been known to count a few coins too many."

Activity Have students find two additional examples of the present perfect verb tense on page 734. *(line 55: "the sentries have been appointed"; line 73: "for what someone else has done.")* **L1**

Additional Resources

📎 ***Grammar and Language Transparency 57***

📖 ***Grammar and Language Workbook,*** pp. 147–150

📖 ***Grammar and Composition Handbook,*** Lesson 5.4

📖 ***Writer's Choice,*** Lesson 15.4

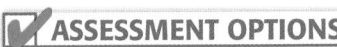

[*To* GUARDS.] You, there, take them away and guard them well:
For they are but women, and even brave men run
When they see Death coming.

[*Exit* ISMENE, ANTIGONE, *and* GUARDS.]

ODE 2

CHORUS.   Fortunate is the man who has never tasted God's
       vengeance!
  Where once the anger of heaven has struck, that house is
      shaken
  For ever: damnation rises behind each child
  Like a wave cresting out of the black northeast,
5 When the long darkness under sea roars up
  And bursts drumming death upon the windwhipped sand.
  I have seen this gathering sorrow from time long past
  Loom upon Oedipus' children: generation from generation
  Takes the compulsive rage of the enemy god.
10 So lately this last flower of Oedipus' line
  Drank the sunlight! but now a passionate word
  And a handful of dust have closed up all its beauty.

     What mortal <u>arrogance</u>
     Transcends° the wrath of Zeus?
15 Sleep cannot lull him, nor the effortless long months
  Of the timeless gods: but he is young for ever,
  And his house is the shining day of high Olympos.°
     All that is and shall be,
     And all the past, is his.
20 No pride on earth is free of the curse of heaven.

     The straying dreams of men
     May bring them ghosts of joy:
  But as they drowse, the waking embers burn them;
  Or they walk with fixed eyes, as blind men walk.
25 But the ancient wisdom speaks for our own time:
     Fate works most for woe
     With Folly's fairest show.
  Man's little pleasure is the spring of sorrow.

14 Transcends: is greater or better than.

17 Olympos: Zeus and the other gods and goddesses were believed to live on Mount Olympus.

Vocabulary
arrogance (ar′ə gəns) *n.* overbearing pride

PP Active Reading

INTERPRET On what does the chorus blame Antigone's tragedy? *(her father's sins and the tragedy visited on her entire family because of them)*

QQ Critical Thinking

INFERRING What can students infer about the nature of Zeus according to the ancient Greek religion? *(He is eternal, he never forgets sins of arrogance by humans, and he will eternally continue punishing those sins.)*

RR Active Reading

INTERPRET Have students explain the ancient Greek view of life as described in the last stanza of the ode. Is it an optimistic or pessimistic view? *(People may sometimes feel they are happy, but this is a fleeting illusion. Fate is bound to bring unhappiness; most unhappiness, however, is caused by people's own foolish actions. It is a fairly pessimistic view of life.)*

Thematic Focus

Loyalty and Betrayal In *Antigone*, who do students think is loyal, and to what? Who do they think betrays someone or something?

✔ ASSESSMENT OPTIONS

📁 *Quick Checks,* p. 69

Reading *Minilesson*

Paraphrasing Students may wish to paraphrase when they read relatively difficult parts of *Antigone* such as Ode 2. Remind them that when they paraphrase, they restate text in their own words without omitting any important details.

Activity Have pairs of students paraphrase the first stanza of the ode. The first line may be paraphrased "People who have never experienced God's vengeance are lucky." Tell students to change difficult words to simpler ones and adjust the sentence structure if necessary. Have volunteers read their paraphrases line by line.
L2 COLLAB. LEARN.

Additional Resources
📁 *Reading Workbook,* pp. 71–72

Personal Response

Students should consider the motivations and consequences of Antigone's decision in evaluating it.

ANALYZING SCENES 1 AND 2

1. Creon has enacted a law stating that Eteocles will be buried with full military honors and Polyneices will be left unburied. Antigone proposes to bury Polyneices anyway.

2. Creon announces that the state is secure, that Eteocles and Polyneices have been killed in battle, that Creon has succeeded to the throne, and that Eteocles will be buried and Polyneices will not.

3. The sentry brings news that someone has given Polyneices a ceremonial burial. Creon reacts angrily and demands that the sentry capture the person who committed the crime.

4. The sentry leads Antigone into Creon's presence because she was caught reburying Polyneices. She explains her actions by saying that following God's laws is more important than following human laws.

5. Ismene tries to share the guilt and punishment of burying Polyneices. Antigone angrily rejects her offer.

6. Antigone means that although burying Polyneices has been proclaimed illegal by Creon, the law of the gods requires that he must be buried.

7. Creon's speech shows that he values patriotism and loyalty to the king and the state over loyalty to the gods or to family.

8. Creon's reaction shows that he is arrogant, easily angered, and domineering.

9. Antigone values obedience to the gods and loyalty to family members. Creon values obedience to the law and patriotism to the state above all other values.

10. Ismene has become more courageous and willing to defy the law because she loves her sister and wants to help and support her.

11. Students should show an understanding of the nature of Antigone's courage in making their comparisons.

12. Students may say it is still possible for Creon and Antigone to resolve their differences because no irrevocable actions have been taken.

13. Students may say the chorus makes the play enjoyable by discussing the action and themes with vivid images. They may find that the chora-

---

Responding to Literature

Personal Response

How do you feel about Antigone's decision?

——— ANALYZING SCENES 1 AND 2 ———

RECALL

1. What new law has Creon just enacted? What does Antigone propose doing about it?
2. What does Creon announce from the palace steps?
3. What news does the sentry bring on his first visit to Creon? How does the king react?
4. Why does the sentry lead Antigone into Creon's presence on his second visit? How does she explain her actions?
5. What does Ismene try to share with Antigone? How does Antigone answer her?

INTERPRET

6. In explaining her plans to Ismene, Antigone says that "this crime is holy." What do you think she means?
7. What does Creon's speech suggest about his values? Explain.
8. What can you infer about Creon's personality from his reaction to the sentry's first report?
9. Compare and contrast what Antigone holds to be important with what Creon values.
10. How has Ismene changed since the beginning of the play? Why, do you think, has she done so?

EVALUATE AND CONNECT

11. How does Antigone's action compare with the one you described for the Focus Activity on page 726? Explain.
12. Do you think it would still be possible for Creon and Antigone to resolve their differences at the end of scene 1? Why or why not?
13. How do the choragos and chorus affect your understanding and enjoyment of the play?
14. What is your reaction to the sentry in scene 1? What purpose or purposes does he seem to serve in the play?
15. If you were in a similar situation, would you be more likely to respond as Antigone does or as Ismene does? Explain.

Literary ELEMENTS

Conflict: Protagonist and Antagonist

The **conflict** in a work of literature is a struggle between opposing forces. One force, the **protagonist**, is the central character and is often the character with whom the audience sympathizes or identifies. Any character or force that opposes the protagonist is called an **antagonist**. Sometimes the protagonist and antagonist are two characters who oppose each other, such as Antigone and Creon. However, a conflict could exist between a character and nature; between a character and society; or between ideas, values, or emotions within a character's own mind.

1. Review the prologue of *Antigone*, up to the *Parodos* on page 732. Identify two conflicts, citing the protagonist and antagonist in each. Which conflict do you think is more important? Explain.

2. In scene 1, line 138, the sentry asks Creon, "Are you sure that it is my voice, and not your conscience?" Do you think that he has hit upon the truth in identifying this conflict? Explain.

● See **Literary Terms Handbook**, p. R3.

---

gos provides a fairly objective viewpoint through which to see Creon and Antigone.

14. Students may find the sentry humorous in a bumbling way, providing a sort of comic relief.

15. Students should show understanding of the characters and actions of Antigone and Ismene in their answers.

LITERARY ELEMENTS

1. One conflict is between Antigone and Creon; the other is between Ismene and Antigone. Both are over burying Polyneices. The more important conflict is the one between Antigone and Creon: Creon can order Antigone's death.

2. The sentry refers to Creon's conflict. Creon may regret his decree but to protect the state's authority he cannot back down.

Additional Resources

🎵 *Literary Elements Transparency 69*

LITERATURE AND WRITING

Writing About Literature

Comparing Viewpoints Skim scenes 1 and 2 for a sentence or phrase spoken by Antigone that you feel best expresses her viewpoint. Copy the sentence and underneath it write a paragraph summarizing her side of the argument with Creon. On another sheet of paper, do the same for Creon, making his case against Antigone. Compare your summaries with those of other students in the class.

Creative Writing

I've Got a Problem Imagine that you are Ismene, desperately in need of advice about your sister Antigone. Write a letter to the "Personal Problem" page of the *Thebes Gazette*. Tell your story without giving away who you are or revealing the names and positions of the other characters.

EXTENDING YOUR RESPONSE

Literature Groups

Getting to Know Her Write at least two questions that you would like to ask Antigone. In your group, share your questions, and then discuss how you think Antigone might answer. Finally, select one person from your group to play the part of Antigone and to respond to questions from other groups. Be prepared to justify your responses based on scenes 1 and 2.

Interdisciplinary Activity

Art: Making Masks Greek drama was performed by actors wearing masks. Using cardboard, papier mâché, fabric, or other materials, make a mask that covers your entire face and expresses the dominant personality trait of one of the characters of *Antigone*. Use yarn for hair, and make sure to include eye holes and a substantial mouth opening.

Internet Connection

Surfing to Ancient Greece Generate several questions to research about ancient Greece. Then, search the Internet for answers. You might narrow your search by using keywords such as Thebes, Acropolis, Theatre of Dionysos. Prepare a report on any interesting findings and present it to the class.

Learning for Life

Incident Report Imagine that the sentry has to write a formal report for a superior officer about his discovery of Antigone's "crime." Describe the incident as accurately as possible in modern English. Make sure that you stick to the sentry's point of view. Invent details if necessary, but be careful not to contradict the text.

 Save your work for your portfolio.

Reconstruction of Greek theater masks.

ANTIGONE 747

LITERATURE AND WRITING

Writing About Literature

Students' summaries should
- begin with sentences or phrases spoken by Antigone and Creon.
- mention the main points of each character's viewpoint.

Creative Writing

Students' letters should
- clearly describe Antigone's motivations and behavior.
- show an understanding of the character of Ismene and her relationship with her sister.

EXTENDING YOUR RESPONSE

Literature Groups Encourage students to ask questions that require explanation and cannot be answered "yes" or "no." **COLLAB. LEARN.**

Interdisciplinary Activity Have volunteers wear their masks and act out part of a scene between the characters pictured.

Internet Connection Students may wish to post a list of interesting facts they discover on the Internet about ancient Greece and the theater on a school Web site.

Learning for Life Point out that the style of an incident report should be simple, clear, and factual.

✔ ASSESSMENT OPTIONS

- 📁 *Quick Checks,* p. 69
- 📁 *Selection and Theme Assessment,* pp. 133–134
- 📁 *Performance Assessment,* p. 68
- 💾 *Testmaker*

SUMMARY, Scenes 3–5

Haimon begs his father to save Antigone and threatens to kill himself if Antigone dies, but Creon will not change his mind. Teiresias tells Creon that Creon will suffer deeply if Antigone is not freed. Creon begins to doubt his decision and finally goes to the tomb to save Antigone. A messenger tells Eurydice what happened at the tomb: when Creon arrived, Antigone had hung herself. Haimon then killed himself. When Creon returns to the palace, he finds that Eurydice has killed herself in grief. Creon, a broken man, admits that he has brought about his own downfall through arrogance.

📁 **Spanish Summaries**, p. 69

A Active Reading

PREDICT How will Creon react to his son's appeals for Antigone?

Additional Resources

📁 *Active Reading Guide*, p. 70
🎧 *Audio Library*
🎧 *Spanish Audio Library*

B Active Reading

CONNECT Have students describe what makes a good son according to Creon and compare it with expectations of modern American parents. *(Creon says a son should show absolute obedience and put his father's desires first. Students may note that modern parents are more realistic.)*

Teaching Options

SCENE 3

CHORAGOS. But here is Haimon, King, the last of all your
    sons.
  Is it grief for Antigone that brings him here,
  And bitterness at being robbed of his bride?

[Enter HAIMON.]

CREON. We shall soon see, and no need of diviners.°
                  —Son,

5 You have heard my final judgment on that girl:
  Have you come here hating me, or have you come
  With deference° and with love, whatever I do?

HAIMON. I am your son, father. You are my guide.
  You make things clear for me, and I obey you.
10 No marriage means more to me than your continuing wisdom.

CREON. Good. That is the way to behave: subordinate
  Everything else, my son, to your father's will.
  This is what a man prays for, that he may get
  Sons attentive and dutiful in his house,
15 Each one hating his father's enemies,
  Honoring his father's friends. But if his sons
  Fail him, if they turn out unprofitably,
  What has he fathered but trouble for himself
  And amusement for the malicious?
                       So you are right
20 Not to lose your head over this woman.
  Your pleasure with her would soon grow cold, Haimon,
  And then you'd have a hellcat in bed and elsewhere.
  Let her find her husband in Hell!
  Of all the people in this city, only she
25 Has had contempt for my law and broken it.

  Do you want me to show myself weak before the people?
  Or to break my sworn word? No, and I will not.
  The woman dies.
  I suppose she'll plead "family ties." Well, let her.
30 If I permit my own family to rebel,
  How shall I earn the world's obedience?
  Show me the man who keeps his house in hand,
  He's fit for public authority.
                  I'll have no dealings
  With law-breakers, critics of the government:
35 Whoever is chosen to govern should be obeyed—

4 diviners: people who predict the future.

7 deference: respect and honor due to another.

Must be obeyed, in all things, great and small,
Just and unjust! O Haimon,

D

The man who knows how to obey, and that man only,
Knows how to give commands when the time comes.

40   You can depend on him, no matter how fast
The spears come: he's a good soldier, he'll stick it out.

Anarchy, anarchy! Show me a greater evil!
This is why cities tumble and the great houses rain down,
This is what scatters armies!

45   No, no: good lives are made so by discipline.
We keep the laws then, and the lawmakers,

E

And no woman shall seduce us. If we must lose,
Let's lose to a man, at least! Is a woman stronger than we?

CHORAGOS. Unless time has rusted my wits,
50   What you say, King, is said with point and dignity.

HAIMON. [*Boyishly earnest.*] Father:
Reason is God's crowning gift to man, and you are right
To warn me against losing mine. I cannot say—
I hope that I shall never want to say!—that you
55   Have reasoned badly. Yet there are other men
Who can reason, too; and their opinions might be helpful.
You are not in a position to know everything
That people say or do, or what they feel:
Your temper terrifies them—everyone
60   Will tell you only what you like to hear.
But I, at any rate, can listen; and I have heard them
Muttering and whispering in the dark about this girl.
They say no woman has ever, so unreasonably,

F

Died so shameful a death for a generous act:
65   "She covered her brother's body. Is this indecent?
She kept him from dogs and vultures. Is this a crime?
Death?—She should have all the honor that we can give her!"

This is the way they talk out there in the city.

You must believe me:
70   Nothing is closer to me than your happiness.
What could be closer? Must not any son
Value his father's fortune as his father does his?
I beg you, do not be unchangeable:

G

Do not believe that you alone can be right.

TRAGIC FLAW Explain that a tragic flaw is a character fault, such as jealousy, anger, or pride, that causes a person to come to grief. What character fault does Haimon seem to think his father has? *(inflexibility, an inability to admit that someone besides himself may be right)* How could this character fault prove to be a tragic flaw? *(It may cause Creon to cling to a bad decision even after he realizes it is wrong, despite the hardships it may cause.)*

The Armentum Rider. c. 550 B.C., Greek. Bronze, height: 23.6 cm. The British Museum, London.

75   The man who thinks that,
      The man who maintains that only he has the power
      To reason correctly, the gift to speak, the soul—
      A man like that, when you know him, turns out empty.

      It is not reason never to yield to reason!

G

80   In flood time you can see how some trees bend,
      And because they bend, even their twigs are safe,
      While stubborn trees are torn up, roots and all.
      And the same thing happens in sailing:
      Make your sheet fast, never slacken,—and over you go,
85   Head over heels and under: and there's your voyage.
      Forget you are angry! Let yourself be moved!
      I know I am young; but please let me say this:

750   🦢 UNIT 4: DRAMA

Teaching Options

LIFE SKILLS CONNECTION

Persuasive Techniques Discuss Haimon's techniques in trying to convince his father to change his mind. Point out that Haimon begins by being polite, respectful, calm, flattering, and reasonable. He tries to convince his father with facts: for example, he tells Creon that the people disapprove of Creon's treatment of Antigone. He uses analogies to illustrate the dangers of stubbornness. Only when Creon insults Haimon and refuses to listen to reason does Haimon get angry.

Activity Have students discuss situations in which they or others have tried to persuade parents, teachers, or friends to take a specific course of action. Which techniques are most and least effective? Point out that sometimes, as in Haimon's case, even the most tactful and skillful persuasive techniques may be ineffective.
L1

The ideal condition
Would be, I admit, that men should be right by instinct;
90   But since we are all too likely to go astray,
The reasonable thing is to learn from those who can teach.

CHORAGOS.   You will do well to listen to him, King,
If what he says is sensible. And you, Haimon,
Must listen to your father.—Both speak well.

95   CREON.   You consider it right for a man of my years and
experience
To go to school to a boy?

HAIMON.   It is not right
If I am wrong. But if I am young, and right,
What does my age matter?

CREON.   You think it right to stand up for an anarchist?

100   HAIMON.   Not at all. I pay no respect to criminals.

CREON.   Then she is not a criminal?

HAIMON.   The City would deny it, to a man.

CREON.   And the City proposes to teach me how to rule?

HAIMON.   Ah. Who is it that's talking like a boy now?

105   CREON.   My voice is the one voice giving orders in this City!

HAIMON.   It is no City if it takes orders from one voice.

CREON.   The State is the King!

HAIMON.   Yes, if the State is a desert.

[Pause.]

CREON.   This boy, it seems, has sold out to a woman.

HAIMON.   If you are a woman: my concern is only for you.

110   CREON.   So? Your "concern"! In a public brawl with your father!

HAIMON.   How about you, in a public brawl with justice?

CREON.   With justice, when all that I do is within my rights?

HAIMON.   You have no right to trample on God's right.

CREON.   [Completely out of control.] Fool, adolescent fool!
Taken in by a woman!

115   HAIMON.   You'll never see me taken in by anything vile.

CREON.   Every word you say is for her!

HAIMON.   [Quietly, darkly.]   And for you.
And for me. And for the gods under the earth.

H Critical Thinking

IDENTIFYING ASSUMPTIONS What assumption does Creon make? Is it a valid assumption? *(He assumes that the older a person is, the wiser he or she is, an invalid assumption.)*

Vo•cab•u•lar•y Skills

Prefixes The combining form *-archy*, "rule or government," comes from the Greek word *archein*, "to rule." Therefore, *anarchy*, with the prefix *an-*, "without," means "an absence of government." *Anarchist*, with the suffix *-ist*, "one that adheres to a doctrine," means "one who promotes anarchy." Have students give the definition of each prefix and each word with the combining form *-archy* that follows: *monarchy*, *squirearchy*, *oligarchy*.

I Critical Thinking

INFERRING What disagreement do Haimon and Creon have about governing the city-state? *(Creon believes one man should be all-powerful while Haimon believes all citizens should have a voice.)*

J Literary Elements

TRAGIC FLAW What character faults, besides inflexibility, does Creon exhibit in his dialogue with Haimon? *(pride, arrogance, stubbornness, and a bad temper)* Could any of these faults be a tragic flaw? *(Any or all of them could lead to his downfall.)*

REAL-WORLD CONNECTION

Dictatorships Have students research and discuss countries in the world today that are ruled by a dictatorship, a form of government in which one individual holds all the power. Some governments to suggest are those in Cuba, Iraq, and Libya. **L3**

interNET CONNECTION

Revolutions Ask students to use a search engine to find out about dictatorships or other oppressive forms of government that have been overthrown throughout history. Have students make a list of research questions and then research one revolution that is of interest to them. Students might enter keywords such as *revolutions, dictatorships, French Revolution, American Revolution,* or *Russian Revolution.*

K Literary Elements

CHARACTERS Based on what has been shown of Haimon's character, how believable is the threat he makes to kill himself if Antigone is killed? *(Because Haimon has behaved calmly and reasonably, it is easy to believe that he is serious about his threat and will follow through on it.)*

L Active Reading

CONNECT Suggest that students imagine they are psychologists asked to advise Creon on how to handle his conflict with his son. What advice might they offer? *(Students may suggest that Creon control his anger, take time to consider the points made by his son, and consult other trusted advisers about whether to change his mind.)*

M Author's Craft

TONE Remind students that the tone of a literary work is the author's or speaker's attitude toward the plot and characters, such as amused, sad, or angry. Have students identify the tone of the play and explain how it helps them predict how the conflict will be resolved. *(The tone is serious and tragic; this supports a prediction that Creon will have Antigone killed and Haimon will also die.)*

ANTIGONE

CREON. You'll never marry her while she lives.

K HAIMON. Then she must die.—But her death will cause another.

120 CREON. Another?
Have you lost your senses? Is this an open threat?

HAIMON. There is no threat in speaking to emptiness.

CREON. I swear you'll regret this superior tone of yours!
You are the empty one!

HAIMON.   If you were not my father,
125 I'd say you were <u>perverse</u>.

CREON. You girlstruck fool, don't play at words with me!

HAIMON. I am sorry. You prefer silence.

CREON.   Now, by God—!
I swear, by all the gods in heaven above us,
You'll watch it, I swear you shall!
[*To the* SERVANTS.]   Bring her out!
130 Bring the woman out! Let her die before his eyes!
Here, this instant, with her bridegroom beside her!

HAIMON. Not here, no; she will not die here, King.
And you will never see my face again.
Go on raving as long as you've a friend to endure you.

[*Exit* HAIMON.]

135 CHORAGOS. Gone, gone.
Creon, a young man in a rage is dangerous!

CREON. Let him do, or dream to do, more than a man can.
He shall not save these girls from death.

CHORAGOS.   These girls?
You have sentenced them both?

CREON.   No, you are right.
140 I will not kill the one whose hands are clean.

CHORAGOS. But Antigone?

CREON. [*Somberly.*]   I will carry her far away
Out there in the wilderness, and lock her
Living in a vault of stone. She shall have food,
As the custom is, to <u>absolve</u> the State of her death.

Vocabulary

perverse (pər vurs′) *adj.* determined to go against what is reasonable, expected, or desired; contrary
absolve (ab zolv′) *v.* to free from guilt or blame

MEETING INDIVIDUAL NEEDS — MULTIPLE LEARNING STYLES

Bodily-Kinesthetic Students who enjoy expressing themselves through acting may enjoy portraying two characters, Haimon and Creon, as their discussion disintegrates into angry threats and insults.

Activity Have volunteers work in pairs. Have one student in each pair portray Haimon and the other Creon.

Have them practice reading the dialogue on page 752, discussing techniques for showing anger. Point out that shouting may not be as effective as facial expression, posture, and gestures in communicating Haimon's cold anger and Creon's rage. Have the pairs perform their dialogue for the class. **L2**
COLLAB. LEARN.

145   And there let her pray to the gods of hell:
       They are her only gods:
       Perhaps they will show her an escape from death,
       Or she may learn,
                     though late,
       That piety shown the dead is pity in vain.

       [*Exit* CREON.]

ODE 3

        CHORUS. Love, unconquerable
                Waster of rich men, keeper
                Of warm lights and all-night vigil
                In the soft face of a girl:
5   Sea-wanderer, forest-visitor!
                Even the pure Immortals cannot escape you,
                And mortal man, in his one day's dusk,
                Trembles before your glory.

                Surely you swerve upon ruin
10   The just man's consenting heart,
                As here you have made bright anger
                Strike between father and son—
                And none has conquered but Love!
                A girl's glance working the will of heaven:
15   Pleasure to her alone who mocks us,
                Merciless Aphrodite.°

16 Aphrodite (af′ rə dī′ tē): the goddess of love and beauty.

◠ SCENE 4 ◠

        CHORAGOS. [*As* ANTIGONE *enters guarded.*] But I can no longer
                stand in awe of this,
                Nor, seeing what I see, keep back my tears.
                Here is Antigone, passing to that chamber
                Where all find sleep at last.

5   ANTIGONE. Look upon me, friends, and pity me
                Turning back at the night's edge to say
                Good-by to the sun that shines for me no longer;
                Now sleepy Death
                Summons me down to Acheron,° that cold shore:
10   There is no bridesong there, nor any music.

        CHORUS. Yet not unpraised, not without a kind of honor,
                You walk at last into the underworld;

9 Acheron (ak′ ə ron): The Greeks believed that the souls of the dead inhabited an underworld bordered by the river Acheron.

MEETING INDIVIDUAL NEEDS — MULTIPLE LEARNING STYLES

Bodily/Kinesthetic The chorus in a Greek tragedy not only chanted or sang their lines but danced. Portions of the chorus's lines were marked *strophe,* meaning that the actors danced from stage right to stage left while chanting them. Other parts were marked *antistrophe,* during which the actors danced in the opposite direction.

Activity Have musically talented students create a performance of Ode 3 on page 753. Explain that the first stanza is the strophe and the second stanza is the antistrophe. Encourage students to imagine how the chorus might have chanted and danced and to choreograph their performance accordingly. Have them perform the ode for the class. **L3** **COLLAB. LEARN.**

Teacher Sidebar

N **Literary Elements**

FIGURES OF SPEECH: *Metaphor* The chorus calls love "Sea-wanderer, forest visitor!" What idea does the metaphor express? *(Love is capable of affecting people everywhere, including on the sea and in the forest.)*

O **Active Reading**

INTERPRET Have students state the topic of Ode 3. What does the chorus say about the topic? *(The topic is the power of love. The chorus says love for a woman is capable of making men powerless. It is such a strong force that it even strikes the gods, so men are particularly susceptible to it. Love can bring even the best men close to ruin, as seen in Haimon and Creon's argument over Haimon's fiancee, Antigone.)*

P **Active Reading**

QUESTION What feelings does the choragos express as Antigone prepares to go to her death? *(The choragos expresses deep grief and sadness.)*

Q Literary Elements

CHARACTERS Have students describe Antigone's mood as she prepares for her death. *(She is depressed and sad; she seems to feel sorry for herself; she blames "the blasphemy" of her birth.)*

R Active Reading

CONNECT Have students paraphrase lines 45–46 and discuss whether people in the United States today live by these guidelines. *(The chorus says it is good to be religious and show reverence for God; however, in any conflict between religion and human law, human law must be obeyed. In our society, secular law also takes precedence in any conflict with religious law.)*

S Active Reading

EVALUATE Encourage students to discuss the way Creon is punishing Antigone. Do they agree with him that his "hands are clean"? *(Creon is rationalizing his punishment, which consists of locking Antigone in a stone vault with some food. Most readers will recognize that Creon knows that she will soon die and that he is responsible for her death.)*

ANTIGONE

    Untouched by sickness, broken by no sword.
    What woman has ever found your way to death?

15 **ANTIGONE.** How often I have heard the story of Niobe,
    Tantalos' wretched daughter, how the stone
    Clung fast about her, ivy-close: and they say
    The rain falls endlessly
20 And sifting soft snow; her tears are never done.
    I feel the loneliness of her death in mine.°

    CHORUS. But she was born of heaven, and you
    Are woman, woman-born. If her death is yours,
    A mortal woman's, is this not for you
    Glory in our world and in the world beyond?

25 **ANTIGONE.** You laugh at me. Ah, friends, friends,
    Can you not wait until I am dead? O Thebes,
    O men many-charioted, in love with Fortune,
    Dear springs of Dirce, sacred Theban grove,
    Be witnesses for me, denied all pity,
30 Unjustly judged! and think a word of love
    For her whose path turns
    Under dark earth, where there are no more tears.

    CHORUS. You have passed beyond human daring and come
      at last
    Into a place of stone where Justice sits.
35 I cannot tell
    What shape of your father's guilt appears in this.

    ANTIGONE. You have touched it at last: that bridal bed
    Unspeakable, horror of son and mother mingling:
    Their crime, infection of all our family!
40 O Oedipus, father and brother!
    Your marriage strikes from the grave to murder mine.
    I have been a stranger here in my own land:
    All my life
    The blasphemy of my birth has followed me.°

45 **CHORUS.** Reverence is a virtue, but strength
    Lives in established law: that must <u>prevail</u>.
    You have made your choice,
    Your death is the doing of your conscious hand.

    ANTIGONE. Then let me go, since all your words are bitter,
50 And the very light of the sun is cold to me.

15–20 How often . . . mine: Niobe (nī′ ō bē′), a former queen of Thebes, was punished by the gods for excessive pride. After all of her children were killed, she was turned to stone, but she continued to shed tears.

35–44 I cannot . . . followed me: Incest, or sexual relations between siblings or between parents and children, was a sin against the gods. Oedipus and Jocasta did not know, at the time, that they were committing incest, but their marriage was cursed nonetheless, and that curse now plagues their daughter, Antigone.

Vocabulary
prevail (pri vāl′) *v.* to be superior in power or influence; succeed

754   UNIT 4: DRAMA

MEETING INDIVIDUAL NEEDS   MULTIPLE LEARNING STYLES

Spatial Antigone's tragic fate is clear in this scene of the play. Artistic students may wish to create a visual interpretation of this character and her emotions.

Activity Have students make a drawing, painting, collage, or sculpture showing the character of Antigone and the emotions she feels as she awaits death. Have them display and discuss their artwork. **L3**

Sophocles ~

Lead me to my vigil, where I must have
Neither love nor lamentation;° no song, but silence.

[CREON interrupts impatiently.]

CREON. If dirges and planned lamentations could put off death,
Men would be singing for ever.
[To the SERVANTS.]   Take her, go!

55 You know your orders: take her to the vault
And leave her alone there. And if she lives or dies,
That's her affair, not ours: our hands are clean.

ANTIGONE. O tomb, vaulted bride-bed in eternal rock,
Soon I shall be with my own again

60 Where Persephone° welcomes the thin ghosts underground:
And I shall see my father again, and you, mother,
And dearest Polyneices—
                    dearest indeed
To me, since it was my hand
That washed him clean and poured the ritual wine:

65 And my reward is death before my time!

And yet, as men's hearts know, I have done no wrong,
I have not sinned before God. Or if I have,
I shall know the truth in death. But if the guilt

52 lamentation: mournful outcry of sorrow or grief.

60 Persephone (pər sef′ ə nē): Persephone is the queen of the underworld of the dead.

Black figure vase depicting soldiers armed with spears and decorated shields. c. 540–520 B.C. Greek. Fired clay, height: 46.5 cm. The British Museum, London.

ANTIGONE, SCENE 4 ❧ 755

Literary Elements

TRAGIC FLAW In Antigone's last speech before she is led to the vault, she says that she is being punished because she "would not transgress the laws of heaven." Have students discuss whether this is truly the case or whether there are character flaws or other reasons for Antigone's fate. *(Some students may think Antigone's tragic outcome is caused by her stubborn refusal to give in to Creon's authority or to apologize for her actions; another possibility is that her death is an inescapable fate decreed by the gods because of her father's sins.)*

Active Reading

QUESTION What do all the legends related by the chorus have in common? How do they relate to Antigone's situation? *(Each legend tells of someone who came to a tragic end because of Fate. Because the stories involve kings and gods, the outcomes are even more tragic. The chorus is comparing Antigone's tragic situation to those of the legends' protagonists.)*

Literary Elements

THEME Point out that the chorus is communicating a moral through the legends they tell in Ode 4. Have students discuss the moral or theme that emerges through these legends. *(No one "can prevail against untiring Destiny"; neither gods nor mortals, including Antigone, can avoid their fate once it has been decreed by the gods.)*

Teaching Options

ANTIGONE

70   Lies upon Creon who judged me, then, I pray,
     May his punishment equal my own.

CHORAGOS.   O passionate heart,
     Unyielding, tormented still by the same winds!

CREON.   Her guards shall have good cause to regret their
     delaying.

ANTIGONE.   Ah! That voice is like the voice of death!

CREON.   I can give you no reason to think you are mistaken.

75   **ANTIGONE.**   Thebes, and you my fathers' gods,
     And rulers of Thebes, you see me now, the last
     Unhappy daughter of a line of kings,
     Your kings, led away to death. You will remember
     What things I suffer, and at what men's hands,
80   Because I would not transgress° the laws of heaven.
     [*To the* GUARDS, *simply.*] Come: let us wait no longer.

[*Exit* ANTIGONE, *L., guarded.*]

80 **transgress:** break or violate.

ODE 4

CHORUS.   All Danäe's beauty was locked away
     In a brazen cell where the sunlight could not come:
     A small room, still as any grave, enclosed her.
     Yet she was a princess too,
5   And Zeus in a rain of gold poured love upon her.
     O child, child,
     No power in wealth or war
     Or tough sea-blackened ships
     Can prevail against untiring Destiny!°

10   And Dryas' son also, that furious king,
     Bore the god's prisoning anger for his pride:
     Sealed up by Dionysos in deaf stone,
     His madness died among echoes.
     So at the last he learned what dreadful power
15   His tongue had mocked:
     For he had profaned the revels,
     And fired the wrath of the nine
     Implacable Sisters that love the sound of the flute.°

     And old men tell a half-remembered tale
20   Of horror done where a dark ledge splits the sea
     And a double surf beats on the gray shores:

756 ❦ UNIT 4: DRAMA

1–9 All Danäe's . . . Destiny: The Chorus briefly relates three Greek legends. Danäe (dan′ ā ē′) was imprisoned by her father when it was foretold that she would bear a child who would kill him. After Zeus visited Danäe, she gave birth to Zeus's son, who did eventually kill his grandfather.

10–18 And Dryas' . . . flute: Dionysos (dī′ ə nī′ səs) is the god of wine and fertility, and the Implacable Sisters (also called the Muses) are the goddesses of the arts and sciences. After Dryas's son (King Lycurgus) objected to the worship of Dionysos, the Sisters imprisoned him and drove him mad.

MEETING INDIVIDUAL NEEDS   GIFTED AND TALENTED

Greek Mythology Some students may like to find out more about the Greek gods, goddesses, and mortal heroes and heroines mentioned in Ode 4.

Activity Suggest that students research the Muses, nine goddesses of the arts and sciences. They were the daughters of Zeus and Mnemosyne, the goddess of memory. The Muses, whom Greek writers and artists called upon for inspiration, were Calliope—epic poetry; Erato—love poetry; Euterpe—lyric poetry; Melpomene—tragedy; Thalia—comedy; Clio—history; Urania—astronomy; Polyhymnia—sacred music; and Terpsichore—dance. Have students present their findings in an oral or written report. **L3**

How a king's new woman, sick
With hatred for the queen he had imprisoned,
Ripped out his two sons' eyes with her bloody hands
25   While grinning Ares watched the shuttle plunge
Four times: four blind wounds crying for revenge,

Crying, tears and blood mingled.—Piteously born,
Those sons whose mother was of heavenly birth!
Her father was the god of the North Wind
30   And she was cradled by gales,
She raced with young colts on the glittering hills
And walked untrammeled in the open light:
But in her marriage deathless Fate found means
To build a tomb like yours for all her joy.°

⁓ SCENE 5 ⁓

[*Enter blind* TEIRESIAS, *led by a boy. The opening speeches of* TEIRESIAS *should be in singsong contrast to the realistic lines of* CREON.]

TEIRESIAS.   This is the way the blind man comes, Princes,
Princes, Lock-step, two heads lit by the eyes of one.

CREON.   What new thing have you to tell us, old Teiresias?

TEIRESIAS.   I have much to tell you: listen to the prophet, Creon.

5   **CREON.**   I am not aware that I have ever failed to listen.

TEIRESIAS.   Then you have done wisely, King, and ruled well.

CREON.   I admit my debt to you. But what have you to say?

TEIRESIAS.   This, Creon: you stand once more on the edge of fate.°

CREON.   What do you mean? Your words are a kind of dread.

10   **TEIRESIAS.**   Listen, Creon:
I was sitting in my chair of augury, at the place
Where birds gather about me. They were all a-chatter,
As is their habit, when suddenly I heard
A strange note in their jangling, a scream, a
15   Whirring fury; I knew that they were fighting,
Tearing each other, dying
In a whirlwind of wings clashing. And I was afraid.°
I began the rites of burnt-offering at the altar,
But Hephaistos failed me: instead of bright flame,
20   There was only the sputtering slime of the fat thighflesh
Melting: the entrails dissolved in gray smoke,
The bare bone burst from the welter. And no blaze!

19–34 And old men . . . all her joy: It was King Phineus who imprisoned his first wife (the queen) and allowed his jealous new wife to blind the queen's sons. This horrible act was done under the gleeful gaze of Ares, the war god.

1–8 This is . . . of fate: The blind prophet serves as the gods' agent, or go-between, in their dealings with people.

11–17 I was sitting . . . afraid: Teiresias sits in his chair of augury to listen to the birds, whose sounds he interprets as messages from the gods, allowing him to foretell, or augur, the future. The birds' fighting is a very bad sign.

ANTIGONE, SCENE 5   757

[X] Literary Elements

DIALOGUE Have students characterize Creon's treatment of Teiresias. *(He is somewhat more respectful to him than to others, but still abrupt and impatient.)*

[Y] Active Reading

VISUALIZE Ask a volunteer to read Teiresias's speech, lines 10–22. Encourage students to visualize the sights and imagine the sounds of Teiresias's experience. Have them name some words to describe the images in the speech. *(Students may find the imagery violent, exciting, spooky, disturbing, and somewhat repellent.)*

[Z] Literary Elements

ALLITERATION Have students identify the alliterative phrases (phrases with the repetition of initial consonant sounds) in the last three lines of Teiresias's speech and describe their effect. *(The alliteration in "sputtering slime," "fat thigh flesh," and "bare bone burst" emphasize the vividly physical, repellent nature of the signs Teiresias sees.)*

Listening and Speaking *Minilesson*

Recounting Fables In Ode 4, the chorus tells of three events to teach the lesson that a person cannot escape his or her fate.

Activity Have students create a fable that communicates a moral. Suggest that they think of a real situation in which they or someone else learned an important lesson or make up a story to illustrate an important lesson they have learned. You may also suggest that students find a fable such as one by Aesop and retell it. Have students tell their fables to the class. Suggest that they use an informal, conversational tone and end by stating the moral of their story. **L2**

Active Reading

EVALUATE Have a student read aloud the advice that Teiresias gives Creon in lines 33–35. Encourage students to evaluate the advice and give examples of people following or not following it.

Active Reading

QUESTION Of what does Creon accuse Teiresias? *(He accuses him of accepting money to try to convince Creon to bury Polyneices.)*

This was a sign from heaven. My boy described it,
Seeing for me as I see for others.

25 I tell you, Creon, you yourself have brought
This new calamity upon us. Our hearths and altars
Are stained with the corruption of dogs and carrion birds
That glut themselves on the corpse of Oedipus' son.
The gods are deaf when we pray to them, their fire
30 Recoils from our offering, their birds of omen
Have no cry of comfort, for they are gorged
With the thick blood of the dead.°

                    O my son,
These are no trifles! Think: all men make mistakes,
But a good man yields when he knows his course is wrong,
35 And repairs the evil. The only crime is pride.

Give in to the dead man, then: do not fight with a corpse—
What glory is it to kill a man who is dead?
Think, I beg you:
It is for your own good that I speak as I do.
40 You should be able to yield for your own good.

CREON. It seems that prophets have made me their especial
    province.
All my life long
I have been a kind of butt for the dull arrows
Of doddering fortune-tellers!
                    No, Teiresias:
45 If your birds—if the great eagles of God himself
Should carry him stinking bit by bit to heaven,
I would not yield. I am not afraid of pollution:
No man can <u>defile</u> the gods.
                 Do what you will,
Go into business, make money, speculate
50 In India gold or that synthetic gold from Sardis,°
Get rich otherwise than by my consent to bury him.
Teiresias, it is a sorry thing when a wise man
Sells his wisdom, lets out his words for hire!

TEIRESIAS. Ah Creon! Is there no man left in the world—

55 **CREON.** To do what?—Come, let's have the aphorism!°

Vocabulary
defile (di fīl′) *v.* to spoil the purity of; make dirty or unclean

18–32 I began . . . of the dead:
Another bad sign: Hephaistos
(hi fes′ tas), the god of fire, is withholding fire. Teiresias says that the gods are rejecting the Thebans' sacrificial offerings because the animals have fed on Polyneices's corpse.

50 synthetic gold from Sardis: The people of Sardis, the capital of ancient Lydia (in modern-day Turkey), invented metallic coinage, the "synthetic gold" that Creon speaks of.

55 aphorism: a concise statement of a general truth.

Teaching Options

INCLUSION STRATEGIES

Less-Proficient Readers Words in a text may have definitions students are not used to. For example, on page 758, the words *province* (line 41), *pollution* (line 47), and *speculate* (line 49) are used in unusual senses.

Activity Point out the words noted above and have students explain what they mean in context. Suggest that if students come across a word whose meaning they think they know but which does not make sense in the sentence, they should try to figure out the definition through context. If this does not work, suggest that they write it down and look it up at the end of a page. **L1**

Additional Resources
📁 *Inclusion Strategies*

TEIRESIAS. No man who knows that wisdom outweighs any
wealth?

CREON. As surely as bribes are baser than any baseness.

TEIRESIAS. You are sick, Creon! You are deathly sick!

CREON. As you say: it is not my place to challenge a prophet.

60 **TEIRESIAS.** Yet you have said my prophecy is for sale.

CREON. This generation of prophets has always loved gold.

TEIRESIAS. The generation of kings has always loved brass.

CREON. You forget yourself! You are speaking to your King.

TEIRESIAS. I know it. You are a king because of me.°

65 **CREON.** You have a certain skill; but you have sold out.

TEIRESIAS. King, you will drive me to words that—

CREON.   Say them, say them!
Only remember: I will not pay you for them.

TEIRESIAS. No, you will find them too costly.

CREON.   No doubt. Speak:
Whatever you say, you will not change my will.

70 **TEIRESIAS.** Then take this, and take it to heart!
The time is not far off when you shall pay back
Corpse for corpse, flesh of your own flesh.
You have thrust the child of this world into living night,
You have kept from the gods below the child that is theirs:
75 The one in a grave before her death, the other,
Dead, denied the grave. This is your crime:
And the Furies° and the dark gods of Hell
Are swift with terrible punishment for you.

Do you want to buy me now, Creon?

        Not many days,
80 And your house will be full of men and women weeping,
And curses will be hurled at you from far
Cities grieving for sons unburied, left to rot
Before the walls of Thebes.

These are my arrows, Creon: they are all for you.

85 [*To* BOY.] But come, child: lead me home.
Let him waste his fine anger upon younger men.

64 I know . . . me: It was Teiresias who revealed the truth of Oedipus's relationship to Jocasta and thus set off the chain of events that led to Creon's becoming king.

77 Furies: three goddesses who avenge crimes.

CC Literary Elements

TRAGIC FLAW Ask two students to read aloud the statements of Creon and Teiresias in lines 61–62. Have them name the character flaws Teiresias calls attention to when he says, "The generation of kings has always loved brass." If they are not sure of the meaning of *brass* in the sentence, have them look it up in a dictionary and determine its meaning in this context. (*Brass can mean brash self-assurance and impudence, character traits Creon displays in this scene.*)

DD Author's Craft

PARALLELISM Point out lines 72–76. Have students identify the stylistic devices Sophocles uses to emphasize Teiresias's summary of Creon's crime. (*Sophocles uses parallel sentence structure and contrast to describe the similarities and differences in what Creon has done to Antigone and to Polyneices.*)

EE Active Reading

CONNECT Have a volunteer read Teiresias's prophecy in lines 79–83. Ask students how they would respond to such a prophecy given by a figure like Teiresias. (*Many students will say that they would take such a prophecy seriously given the wisdom and reason of Teiresias.*)

MEETING INDIVIDUAL NEEDS — MULTIPLE LEARNING STYLES

Spatial Point out that the art of costuming is an important element of the theater. Even in ancient Greece, actors wore elaborate costumes to make their roles realistic and inspire the audience.

Activity Have students make an illustration for a costume design for one of the play's characters. Have them consider the character's position in society and his or her personality in creating appropriate clothing. Also emphasize that the costume should be visually appealing to the audience. Have students display their work. **L2**

EVALUATE Urge students to consider whether Creon's change of heart is in keeping with his character or whether it is too sudden to seem realistic.

GG **Literary Elements**

PLOT: *Climax* Remind students that as in fiction, a play's most suspenseful moment occurs just before the climax, when the conflict is finally resolved. Here the suspense is based on whether Creon will reach Antigone's tomb before it is too late. Have students predict the plot's outcome. *(Most students will realize that Creon finally bows to the "laws of the gods" but has changed his mind too late.)*

ANTIGONE

Maybe he will learn at last
To control a wiser tongue in a better head.

[*Exit* TEIRESIAS.]

90   **CHORAGOS.** The old man has gone, King, but his words
Remain to plague us. I am old, too,
But I cannot remember that he was ever false.

CREON. That is true. . . . It troubles me.
Oh it is hard to give in! but it is worse
To risk everything for stubborn pride.

95   **CHORAGOS.** Creon: take my advice.

CREON.   What shall I do?

CHORAGOS. Go quickly: free Antigone from her vault
And build a tomb for the body of Polyneices.

CREON. You would have me do this?

CHORAGOS.   Creon, yes!
And it must be done at once: God moves
100   Swiftly to cancel the folly of stubborn men.

FF   **CREON.** It is hard to deny the heart! But I
Will do it: I will not fight with destiny.

CHORAGOS. You must go yourself, you cannot leave
it to others.

CREON. I will go.
          —Bring axes, servants:
105   Come with me to the tomb. I buried her, I
Will set her free.
             Oh quickly!
GG   My mind misgives—
The laws of the gods are mighty, and a man
must serve them
To the last day of his life!

[*Exit* CREON.]

Paean°

CHORAGOS. God of many names

CHORUS.   O Iacchos°
                     son
of Kadmeian Semele
            O born of the Thunder!

Aphrodite. Greek, from eastern Turkey.

Paean (pē′ ən): a song of praise, joy, or thanksgiving. Here, the Chorus praises Dionysos.

3 **Iacchos** (yä′ kəs): considered Thebes's special protector because his mother had been a Theban princess. The Chorus begs Dionysos to come to Thebes and drive out evil.

Teaching Options

MEETING INDIVIDUAL NEEDS   GIFTED AND TALENTED

Another Antigone The French playwright Jean Anouilh wrote a modern version of *Antigone.* He wrote the play in 1942 when Paris was occupied by the Nazis. Many people thought that Antigone represented the French resistance movement and Creon German authority in Anouilh's play.

Activity Have students read Anouilh's play. Encourage them to discuss, orally or in an essay, whether the moral issues in Sophocles' play transfer effectively to the twentieth century. (The play has adult themes. You may wish to review the play before recommending it to students.) **L3**

> Guardian of the West
>   Regent
> of Eleusis' plain
>   O Prince of maenad Thebes
> 5 and the Dragon Field by rippling Ismenos:°
>
> **CHORAGOS.** God of many names
>
> **CHORUS.**   the flame of torches
> flares on our hills
>   the nymphs of Iacchos
> dance at the spring of Castalia:
>
> from the vine-close mountain
>   come ah come in ivy:°
> 10 *Evohé° evohé!* sings through the streets of Thebes
>
> **CHORAGOS.** God of many names
>
> **CHORUS.**   Iacchos of Thebes
> heavenly Child
>   of Semele bride of the Thunderer!
> The shadow of plague is upon us:
>   come
> with clement° feet
>   oh come from Parnasos
> 15 down the long slopes
>   across the lamenting water
>
> **CHORAGOS.** Io Fire! Chorister of the throbbing stars!
> O purest among the voices of the night!
> Thou son of God, blaze for us!
>
> **CHORUS.** Come with choric rapture of circling Maenads
> 20 Who cry *Io Iacche!*
>   *God of many names!*

Exodos°

[*Enter* MESSENGER, *L.*]

> **MESSENGER.** Men of the line of Kadmos, you who live
> Near Amphion's citadel:°
>   I cannot say
> Of any condition of human life "This is fixed,
> This is clearly good, or bad." Fate raises up,
> 5 And Fate casts down the happy and unhappy alike:
> No man can foretell his Fate.

1–5 God of . . . Ismenos: The names of Dionysos refer to people and places associated with him. His mother, **Kadmeian Semele** (sem´ ə lē), was the daughter of Kadmos, a king of Thebes. His father was Zeus, who controlled thunder. This plain was the site of religious ceremonies performed in honor of Dionysos, and the river **Ismenos** ran near Thebes. The **maenads** (mē´ nadz) were Dionysos's devoted priestesses.

7–9 the nymphs . . . come in ivy: Dionysos was raised by **nymphs,** long-lived women who were associated with trees and other parts of nature. The **spring of Castalia** is on Parnasos, a holy mountain. The grape **vine** and **ivy** were symbols of Dionysos.

10 *Evohé:* "Hallelujah."

14 clement: forgiving; merciful.

Exodos: the last part of the play.

2 Amphion's citadel: the wall around Thebes, which Amphion built by charming stones into place with music.

Active Reading

CONNECT Have students summarize the values evident in the messenger's dialogue in lines 6–22. Which elements of life are said to be important and unimportant? Have students discuss whether these values are held in our society today. *(The messenger says that power, success, and wealth are unimportant compared to the health and happiness of one's family. These are widely held values in today's society.)*

Literary Elements

DIALOGUE Remind students that much action, especially violence, in Greek drama, occurs offstage; one of the characters describes it. Have students discuss whether this method detracts from the play's drama and suspense or adds to it.

Cultural Note

Athena was the goddess of warfare and of wisdom and also the patroness of arts and crafts. A myth says that Athens was named for her after a contest between her and Poseidon. The town's citizens said they would name their city after the god or goddess who offered the most useful gift. Poseidon offered a horse and Athena offered an olive tree. The gods decided that Athena's gift was more valuable and the city was named in her honor.

Teaching Options

ANTIGONE

                                   Take the case of Creon:
        Creon was happy once, as I count happiness:
        Victorious in battle, sole governor of the land,
        Fortunate father of children nobly born.
10   And now it has all gone from him! Who can say
        That a man is still alive when his life's joy fails?
        He is a walking dead man. Grant him rich,
        Let him live like a king in his great house:
        If his pleasure is gone, I would not give
15   So much as the shadow of smoke for all he owns.

CHORAGOS.   Your words hint at sorrow: what is your news for us?

MESSENGER.   They are dead. The living are guilty of their death.

CHORAGOS.   Who is guilty? Who is dead? Speak!

MESSENGER.   Haimon.
        Haimon is dead; and the hand that killed him
20   Is his own hand.

CHORAGOS.   His father's? or his own?

MESSENGER.   His own, driven mad by the murder his father
        had done.

CHORAGOS.   Teiresias, Teiresias, how clearly you saw it all!

MESSENGER.   This is my news: you must draw what conclusions
        you can from it.

CHORAGOS.   But look: Eurydice, our Queen:
25   Has she overheard us?

[Enter EURYDICE from the Palace, C.]

EURYDICE.   I have heard something, friends:
        As I was unlocking the gate of Pallas'° shrine,
        For I needed her help today, I heard a voice
        Telling of some new sorrow. And I fainted
30   There at the temple with all my maidens about me.
        But speak again: whatever it is, I can bear it:
        Grief and I are no strangers.°

MESSENGER.   Dearest Lady,
        I will tell you plainly all that I have seen.
        I shall not try to comfort you: what is the use,
35   Since comfort could lie only in what is not true?
        The truth is always best.
                                    I went with Creon
        To the outer plain where Polyneices was lying,
        No friend to pity him, his body shredded by dogs.

27 Pallas: the goddess of wisdom; also known as Athena.

32 Grief and I . . . strangers: Eurydice (yoo rid′ i sē) is referring to the death of Megareus (me gàr′ ā ōōs), her older son, who died in the battle for Thebes.

REAL-WORLD CONNECTION

Modern Tragedies Have students discuss some modern tragedies that they have heard about through the news media. Ask them to consider whether any tragedies today compare with the family and state tragedy described in *Antigone*. Point out that the tragedy in *Antigone* is not brought about by an accident or a natural disaster but by deliberate actions of people who feel they are behaving morally. **L2**

REAL-WORLD CONNECTION

Comparing Reviews Have students attend a performance of Antigone or another play of your choice in your community. Suggest that they take along a small notebook to jot down their responses to aspects of the performance, including the staging, the sets, and the performances of individual actors. Afterwards have each student find and read one or more reviews of the play from local newspapers and then write a brief essay comparing his or her own responses with those of the reviewers. **L2**

We made our prayer in that place to Hecate°

40 And Pluto,° that they would be merciful. And we bathed
The corpse with holy water, and we brought
Fresh-broken branches to burn what was left of it,
And upon the urn we heaped up a towering barrow
Of the earth of his own land.

When we were done, we ran

45 To the vault where Antigone lay on her couch of stone.

39 Hecate (hek′ ə tē): another name for Persephone, the goddess of the underworld.

40 Pluto: another name for Hades, the god of the underworld.

Cult Statue of Aphrodite. 425–400 B.C., Greek. Limestone and marble, height: 7 ft. 6 in. The J. Paul Getty Museum, Los Angeles.

Viewing the sculpture: How does this sculpture reflect the mood of this scene? Explain.

LL Literary Elements

CHARACTERS Eurydice, the wife of Creon, does not appear until this late moment in the play. Have students discuss whether this is a flaw in the play and how it affects the drama. *(Some students may find it disconcerting that Eurydice has not played a more important role in the play. She adds to the effect of the tragedy in her role as the grief-stricken mother of Haimon.)*

MM Literary Elements

CHARACTERS Have students describe the minor character of the Messenger. In what ways are his character traits appropriate to his role in the play? *(The Messenger is honest, serious, and straightforward. He narrates the tragic events clearly; therefore, the events are clearly understood and the tragedy is not belittled.)*

VIEWING THE SCULPTURE

One of the main purposes of temples was to house cult statues like this one.

Viewing Response *The sculpture has a gravity that reflects the mood of the scene; even her robe is like a shroud.*

Listening and Speaking *Minilesson*

Performing Dialogue Choosing and performing a portion of the play's dialogue can help students better appreciate and understand the play.

Activity Have students work in pairs and choose a portion of dialogue that includes two or more characters in the play and that they feel is particularly important to the play's themes. Have them practice reading the dialogue, discussing the vocal tone, emphasis, facial expression, and gestures to best communicate the dialogue's meaning. Have each pair perform their dialogue for the class, explaining why they think it is especially meaningful. **L2 COLLAB. LEARN.**

Active Reading

VISUALIZE Encourage students to visualize the scene in the vault. Have them point out visual details that are particularly vivid, such as Haimon lying beside Antigone, who has hanged herself with her linen veil; or Haimon's red blood on Antigone's white skin after he kills himself.

Active Reading

PREDICT Have students predict whether the Messenger is right in his assumption that Eurydice has left the room to grieve privately.

LITERATURE & HUMANITIES

Display *The Burghers of Calais* on page 325 of *Art Talk*. Have students examine this memorial commemorating six leading citizens of Calais who gave their lives for their fellow citizens. Discuss the memorial's images. Then have students create their own memorials to honor Antigone.

Teaching Options

One of the servants had gone ahead,
And while he was yet far off he heard a voice
Grieving within the chamber, and he came back
And told Creon. And as the King went closer,
50   The air was full of wailing, the words lost,
And he begged us to make all haste. "Am I a prophet?"
He said, weeping, "And must I walk this road,
The saddest of all that I have gone before?
My son's voice calls me on. Oh quickly, quickly!
55   Look through the crevice there, and tell me
If it is Haimon, or some deception of the gods!"

We obeyed; and in the cavern's farthest corner
We saw her lying:
She had made a noose of her fine linen veil
60   And hanged herself. Haimon lay beside her,
His arms about her waist, lamenting her,
His love lost under ground, crying out
That his father had stolen her away from him.

When Creon saw him the tears rushed to his eyes
65   And he called to him: "What have you done, child? Speak
        to me.
What are you thinking that makes your eyes so strange?
O my son, my son, I come to you on my knees!"
But Haimon spat in his face. He said not a word,
Staring—
        And suddenly drew his sword
70   And lunged. Creon shrank back, the blade missed; and the boy,
Desperate against himself, drove it half its length
Into his own side, and fell. And as he died
He gathered Antigone close in his arms again,
Choking, his blood bright red on her white cheek.
75   And now he lies dead with the dead, and she is his
At last, his bride in the houses of the dead.

[*Exit* EURYDICE *into the Palace.*]

CHORAGOS.   She has left us without a word. What can this mean?

MESSENGER.   It troubles me, too; yet she knows what is best,
Her grief is too great for public lamentation,
80   And doubtless she has gone to her chamber to weep
For her dead son, leading her maidens in his dirge.

Reading *Minilesson*

Comparison and Contrast Many of the conflicts of *Antigone* exist in the form of opposite or contrasting values. Have students contribute as you write the following conflicts on the board:

   mortal vs. gods
   law vs. religion
   man vs. woman
   age vs. youth
   state vs. family

Activity Have students quote or summarize a portion of dialogue from *Antigone* that illustrates each set of contrasts. **L2**

Additional Resources
Reading Workbook

Sophocles ~

CHORAGOS. It may be so: but I fear this deep silence

[*Pause.*]

MESSENGER. I will see what she is doing. I will go in.

[*Exit* MESSENGER *into the Palace.*]

[*Enter* CREON *with attendants, bearing* HAIMON's *body.*]

CHORAGOS. But here is the King himself: oh look at him,
85   Bearing his own damnation in his arms.

CREON. Nothing you say can touch me any more.
    My own blind heart has brought me
    From darkness to final darkness. Here you see
    The father murdering, the murdered son—
90   And all my civic wisdom!

    Haimon my son, so young, so young to die,
    I was the fool, not you; and you died for me.

CHORAGOS. That is the truth; but you were late in learning it.

CREON. This truth is hard to bear. Surely a god
95   Has crushed me beneath the hugest weight of heaven,
    And driven me headlong a barbaric way
    To trample out the thing I held most dear.

    The pains that men will take to come to pain!

[*Enter* MESSENGER *from the Palace.*]

MESSENGER. The burden you carry in your hands is heavy,
100   But it is not all: you will find more in your house.

CREON. What burden worse than this shall I find there?

MESSENGER. The Queen is dead.

CREON. O port of death, deaf world,
    Is there no pity for me? And you, Angel of evil,
105   I was dead, and your words are death again.
    Is it true, boy? Can it be true?
    Is my wife dead? Has death bred death?

MESSENGER. You can see for yourself.

[*The doors are opened, and the body of* EURYDICE *is disclosed within.*]

CREON. Oh pity!
110   All true, all true, and more than I can bear!
    O my wife, my son!

ANTIGONE, EXODOS 765

Active Reading

VISUALIZE Have students visualize the scene described in the stage directions. Point out that although much of the action of the play has occurred offstage, this scene would be visually moving on stage.

QQ Literary Elements

FIGURES OF SPEECH: *Metaphor* Have students explain the metaphor of blindness in Creon's speech. What is being compared? *(Creon compares his inability to see right and wrong to an inability to see physically. He compares his emotional darkness to literal darkness.)*

RR Literary Elements

DIALOGUE Ask students to characterize the attitude of the choragos toward Creon at this point. Is his attitude surprising? *(Some students will find the bluntness of the choragos's remark that Creon has taken too long to learn his lesson surprising in light of Creon's grief. Others will see that the choragos is being honest and objective as he has throughout the play.)*

SS Active Reading

RESPOND Have students discuss their feelings toward Creon at this point in the play. *(Some students will pity him because of his great tragedy and his weakened state. Others will not feel pity because he has brought his tragedy on himself.)*

Writing Minilesson

Using Metaphors Sophocles uses many metaphors to make his characters and plot compelling. For example, on page 765 Creon says, "Surely a god has crushed me beneath the hugest weight of heaven." Point out that he is comparing his emotional burden to a physical one. The comparison is implied; it does not include the word *like* or *as*.

Activity Have students write three metaphors that describe an emotion experienced by themselves, someone else, or a fictional character. Suggest that students first think of something they want to compare the emotion to and then experiment with ways of suggesting the comparison without using the word *like* or *as*. Students may wish to refer to other

metaphors throughout the play, particularly in the choral odes. Have volunteers read their metaphors. **L2**

Additional Resources

Writer's Choice, Lesson 5.2

765

Statue of Chrysippus, the Greek philosopher. 3rd century B.C. Marble. Louvre Museum, Paris.

Viewing the sculpture: What emotions does this sculpture convey? How might these emotions compare with what Creon may be feeling at this point in the play?

Grammar and Language *Minilesson*

End Punctuation Review with students the three kinds of punctuation used to end sentences and when each is used.
Period—at the end of declarative sentences and most imperative sentences
Question mark—at the end of interrogative sentences
Exclamation point—at the end of exclamatory sentences, strong interjections, and imperative sentences that express strong emotion

Activity Have students find at least three examples of each use of end punctuation in sentences from the play. Ask them to write the sentences and a brief explanation of why each is an example of a particular usage. **L1**

Additional Resources

- *Grammar and Language Transparency 58*
- *Grammar and Language Workbook,* p. 245
- *Grammar and Composition Handbook,* Lessons 11.1–11.3
- *Writer's Choice,* Lessons 21.1–21.3

MESSENGER. She stood before the altar, and her heart
Welcomed the knife her own hand guided,
And a great cry burst from her lips for Megareus dead,
115 And for Haimon dead, her sons; and her last breath
Was a curse for their father, the murderer of her sons.°
And she fell, and the dark flowed in through her closing eyes.

CREON. O God, I am sick with fear.
Are there no swords here? Has no one a blow for me?

120 **MESSENGER.** Her curse is upon you for the deaths of both.

CREON. It is right that it should be. I alone am guilty.
I know it, and I say it. Lead me in,
Quickly, friends.
I have neither life nor substance. Lead me in.

125 **CHORAGOS.** You are right, if there can be right in so much wrong.
The briefest way is best in a world of sorrow.

CREON. Let it come,
Let death come quickly, and be kind to me.
I would not ever see the sun again.

130 **CHORAGOS.** All that will come when it will; but we, meanwhile,
Have much to do. Leave the future to itself.

CREON. All my heart was in that prayer!

CHORAGOS. Then do not pray any more: the sky is deaf.

CREON. Lead me away. I have been rash and foolish.
135 I have killed my son and my wife.
I look for comfort; my comfort lies here dead.
Whatever my hands have touched has come to nothing.
Fate has brought all my pride to a thought of dust.

[*As* CREON *is being led into the house, the* CHORAGOS *advances and speaks directly to the audience.*]

CHORAGOS. There is no happiness where there is no wisdom;
140 No wisdom but in submission to the gods.
Big words are always punished,
And proud men in old age learn to be wise.

116 **Was a curse . . . sons:** Note that even though Haimon stabbed himself and Megareus died in battle, Eurydice blames Creon for their deaths.

 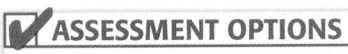

TT Literary Elements

CHARACTERS Have students characterize Creon's behavior in responding to the death of his son and his wife. How, if at all, does his response change students' view of his character? *(Creon is utterly grief-stricken and does not hesitate to admit that the deaths are ultimately his fault. His understanding of his foolish actions may increase readers' compassion for his tragedy.)*

UU Literary Elements

PLOT: Resolution Remind students that the resolution or denouement of the plot is the tying up of loose ends after the main conflict has been resolved. Ask students to summarize what happens in the denouement of *Antigone* and how it helps make the play's themes clear.

VV Literary Elements

DIALOGUE Have students discuss how the final speech of the choragos contributes to the play's themes. *(The choragos sums up the lessons that Creon has learned. He seems to lay the blame entirely on Creon and to agree with Antigone that the wishes of the gods should come first.)*

Thematic Focus

Loyalty and Betrayal Have students discuss the ways in which both Antigone and Creon demonstrated loyalty. What people or values did each betray, if any?

✔ ASSESSMENT OPTIONS

📁 *Quick Checks,* p. 70

REAL-WORLD CONNECTION

Catharsis Explain Aristotle's idea of *catharsis*: people enjoy watching tragedy on stage because it purges them of emotions such as sadness and grief. The idea of catharsis seeks to resolve the paradox of enjoying other people's tragic experiences. Have students think of movies they have seen that have evoked an emotional response. What was their overall emotion on leaving the theater? Did the filmed tragedy succeed in "purging" them of certain emotions? **L3**

 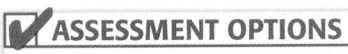

Responding to the Selection

Personal Response

Students' choices should show understanding of the events and the characters in the play.

ANALYZING SCENES 3 TO 5

1. Haimon is trying to convince his father to change his mind about having Antigone put to death. Creon says that obeying the law is the highest virtue, that Haimon should not let a woman run his life, and that he, Creon, is wiser than his son because he is older.
2. Creon sentences Antigone to be imprisoned in a vault with little food. Antigone responds sorrowfully, knowing she will not live to be married, but convinced that she is right. The chorus sadly says her death is her own fault for breaking the law and that she is paying for her father's sins.
3. Teiresias tells Creon that Creon is bringing a plague upon Thebes; if he doesn't let Antigone go, his family will suffer great tragedy. Creon accuses him of accepting a bribe.
4. Creon goes to release Antigone. He finds Antigone a victim of suicide and Haimon grieving beside her.
5. Creon's wife kills herself in grief over her son's death. Creon reacts by accepting blame for his actions.
6. Haimon's dialogue shows that he feels Antigone should be forgiven because her act was loving, though illegal. Creon's words show that he feels men should have authority over women.
7. The chorus and Antigone imply that her father's sins and the stubbornness she inherited from her father are responsible for her fate. This suggests that her fate was inevitable.
8. Some students may say that Creon changes his mind based on self-interest because he is frightened by Teiresias's prophecy of tragedy. Others may say he is finally convinced that he has wronged Antigone.
9. Students may say that Antigone and Haimon were motivated by a sense of hopelessness.
10. Students may say the message is that a person must listen to other people or that the gods' law should be obeyed over human law. Most students will say Creon learned that lesson.
11. Foreshadowing is found in Teiresias's prophecy and in Eurydice's exit after learning of her son's death. Most students will say this did not

detract from enjoyment of the play.
12. In answering, students should show an understanding of the threat of anarchy on the one hand and the dangers of obedience to a possibly corrupt leader on the other.
13. Students may find the dialogue between Creon and Haimon realistic in that issues of authority and generational differences made communication between father and son difficult.
14. Students may say that the more one knows about the characters and works referred to, the more allusions increase one's enjoyment.
15. Students should state a lesson that shows understanding of the play's themes, such as the inevitability of fate or the dangers of arrogance.

Responding to Literature

Personal Response

In your opinion, what is the most tragic event of the play? Why?

ANALYZING SCENES 3 TO 5

RECALL

1. Why has Haimon come to see his father? What does he try to persuade Creon to do? How does Creon respond?
2. To what punishment does Creon sentence Antigone? How does she respond? How does the chorus react to her?
3. What does Teiresias tell Creon? What does Creon accuse Teiresias of at first?
4. What does Creon set out to do after his conversation with Teiresias? What does he find?
5. What final events add to Creon's sorrow? How does he react?

INTERPRET

6. What does the discussion between Haimon and Creon reveal about their attitudes toward Antigone's actions? toward each other?
7. What reasons do the chorus and Antigone imply are responsible for her fate? What does this suggest about the inevitability of Antigone's fate?
8. In your opinion, what finally causes Creon to change his mind? Do you think he is motivated by compassion or by self-interest? Explain.
9. What do you think motivated Antigone and Haimon to act as they did?
10. What do you think is the main message, or lesson, of this play? Do you think Creon learned that message? Explain.

EVALUATE AND CONNECT

11. What examples of **foreshadowing** do you find in the play? Did they add to or detract from your enjoyment of the play? Why?
12. In scene 3, Creon says, "Whoever is chosen to govern should be obeyed— / Must be obeyed, in all things, great and small, / Just and unjust!" Do you agree with this statement? Explain your response.
13. How did you react to the dialogue between Creon and Haimon? Was it a realistic confrontation between a parent and child? Explain.
14. Audiences in ancient Greece would have understood the references to the house of Oedipus and to Greek mythology. How did these **allusions** affect your appreciation of the play?
15. What lesson do you take away from this play?

Literary ELEMENTS

Tragic Flaw

According to the Greek philosopher Aristotle (384–322 B.C.), the hero of a tragedy is a person of great ability who comes to grief because of a fault within his or her character: a **tragic flaw**. Pride, ambition, jealousy, self-doubt, and anger are among those human weaknesses that can defeat the tragic hero. Sometimes a tragic flaw can even be an excess of virtue, such as the love of honor or the pursuit of duty. *Antigone*, a play that Aristotle knew well, is one of the tragedies from which he derived his definition.

1. Reread Teiresias's warning to Creon (scene 5, lines 10–40). What flaw does he specifically identify in the king's character? Do you believe that this weakness is sufficient to cause the tragedy that results? Explain.
2. How would you describe Antigone's personality? Does she have a fault that might qualify as a tragic flaw? Is she, too, a tragic hero, or is she an innocent victim of Creon? Explain.

● See **Literary Terms Handbook**, p. R13.

LITERARY ELEMENTS

1. Teiresias says Creon has the flaw of pride, a weakness sufficient to cause the tragedy; it prevents Creon from accepting that he is wrong and others are right.
2. Although Antigone is admirable in performing her duty, she is also stubborn and uncompromising. Students may see this as a tragic flaw and see Antigone as a tragic hero who contributes to her own tragedy.

Additional Resources

 Literary Elements Transparency 70

LITERATURE AND WRITING

Writing About Literature

Analyzing Bias   Would Antigone's fate have been different if she had been a man? Review the play for statements that reveal Creon's and other characters' attitudes toward women and their role in Thebes society. Then write two or three paragraphs summarizing these attitudes and stating whether or not, in your opinion, bias against women affected Creon's judgment and Antigone's fate. Support your analysis with specific quotations and other details from the play.

Creative Writing

Here's What Happened   Imagine that you have witnessed the day's terrible events in front of Creon's palace. That evening, your sixteen-year-old son or daughter asks you to explain why such a tragedy has occurred. How would you interpret to him or her what has happened? Write your account in modern English.

EXTENDING YOUR RESPONSE

Literature Groups

Ranking Loyalty   Much of the struggle in *Antigone* revolves around the question of which power or authority most deserves people's loyalty. In your group, review the speeches made by Creon, Antigone, the chorus, the choragos, and other characters, to determine where they think a person's loyalty should ultimately rest. Use specific citations from the play to support your ideas. Then rank each character's position on a line like the one shown. Feel free to add other kinds of loyalties to the line as they are needed. Finally, decide as a group where you think Sophocles himself should be placed on the continuum. Share your group's results with the rest of the class, and discuss any differences you find.

Religious   King's
law   law

Learning for Life

Genealogical Chart   Skim scenes 3 and 4 for references to Antigone's ancestors. Then use resource materials on Greek drama, mythology, and legend to trace the genealogy, or family tree, of the House of Oedipus. Create a chart showing Antigone's ancestors, parents, and siblings and their relationships to one another. Indicate which relatives died untimely deaths—a possible result of the curse of Oedipus.

Interdisciplinary Activity

Drama: Stage Sets   With a partner, design a stage set for *Antigone,* and create a diorama to show your design. You might choose to create the set for a presentation of the play as it would have been staged in ancient Greece, or you could choose to design a set for a more modern, contemporary staging. Display your diorama in your classroom.

Reading Further

If you enjoyed *Antigone,* you might also enjoy these works by Sophocles:

Plays: *Oedipus Rex,* the powerful tragedy of Oedipus, king of Thebes and father of Antigone. In this play, the curse of Oedipus, mentioned in *Antigone,* is explained. *Oedipus at Colonus,* a sequel to *Oedipus Rex,* which recounts the final moments of the exiled king.

Save your work for your portfolio.

Family Tree of the Cornaro Family, 18th century. Italian school. Palazzo Corner Ca'Grande, Venice, Italy.

ANTIGONE   769

LITERATURE AND WRITING

Writing About Literature

Students' analyses should
- summarize the attitudes toward women of two or more characters.
- use quotations from the play to support ideas.

Creative Writing

Students' accounts should
- show understanding of the play's plot and issues.
- use style and language appropriate for the audience.

EXTENDING YOUR RESPONSE

Literature Groups   As students discuss their completed diagrams, encourage them to describe the character traits indicated by each character's position on the line. **COLLAB. LEARN.**

Learning for Life   Students may want to refer to books about genealogy in creating their charts.

Interdisciplinary Activity   Have students brainstorm possible methods and materials for their projects before working with their partners.

✔ ASSESSMENT OPTIONS

📂 *Quick Checks,* p. 70
📂 *Selection and Theme Assessment,* pp. 135–136
📂 *Performance Assessment,* p. 69
💾 *Testmaker*

GRAMMAR AND LANGUAGE
Using the Dash

Possible examples are Antigone's statement in the Prologue: "It will not be the worst of deaths—death without honor," in which the dash introduces an explanation; or Creon's remarks at the end of Scene 2: "You dazzle me.—But enough of this talk!" indicating a change in idea.

READING AND THINKING
Identifying the Author's Purpose

1. Students may agree: tragedies were a form of entertainment.
2. Students may agree: the play strongly presents some moral lessons.
3. Students may disagree: teaching history was not a primary purpose of the play.

VOCABULARY
Antonyms

Possible choices:
1. humility   2. restore
3. agreeable   4. fail
5. blame

Additional Resources

- **Grammar and Composition Handbook,** Lesson 11.7
- **Grammar and Language Workbook,** p. 267
- **Writer's Choice,** Lesson 21.7
- **Reading Workbook**
- **Vocabulary Practice,** p. 48

Teaching Options

Responding to Literature

Skill Minilessons

GRAMMAR AND LANGUAGE • Using the Dash

The dash is a form of punctuation that is often used where a comma is not quite strong enough. An author may use a dash to suggest hesitation in speech, to introduce an explanation, or to separate a phrase from the rest of a sentence, indicating a slight change of idea. For example, in scene 1 of *Antigone,* when the Sentry stammers, "The dead man—Polyneices—out there—someone,— / New dust on the slimy flesh!" the dashes show hesitation in his speech and also confusion in his thoughts.

PRACTICE   Copy several passages from *Antigone* that include dashes, and read them to a partner. Discuss what purpose you think the dash serves in each case.

● For more about dashes, see **Language Handbook,** p. R49.

READING AND THINKING • Identifying the Author's Purpose

Authors often write fiction or drama with a purpose: to entertain, to inform or teach a lesson, to tell a story, to try to persuade readers to accept an idea, or for a number of purposes. To identify an author's purpose, look carefully at the way a piece of literature is written, at your reactions to it, and at the message that seems to come across to you.

PRACTICE   Review the passages of the play that seem most important to you. Then, on your paper, copy each of the following statements and write a sentence saying why you agree or disagree with the statement.

1. Sophocles wrote *Antigone* to entertain his audiences at the Greek festivals.
2. Sophocles probably intended his audience to learn from the lessons Creon and other characters learn in the play.
3. *Antigone* was intended solely as a way of teaching the history of a famous family from Thebes.

● For more about inference, see **Reading Handbook,** p. R92.

VOCABULARY • Antonyms

Antonyms are words with opposite meanings. Identifying an antonym for a word helps you refine your understanding of that particular word. Also, because antonyms have opposite meanings, using them in your writing or speaking provides a good, clear way to present a contrast.

PRACTICE   Write down a word that could go in each blank. It should be the best antonym you can think of for the underlined word. Use a dictionary as needed.

1. I expected a man of great <u>arrogance</u>, but he surprised me with his _____ .

2. Before the conquerors were driven out, they had <u>defiled</u> the temple, and it was now the job of the faithful to _____ it.

3. Sisters, even twin sisters, are not always alike. One may be completely _____ and the other, totally <u>perverse</u>.

4. Preparation, courage, and effort will help you <u>prevail</u>, but lacking any one of these will guarantee that you _____ .

5. You may _____ me now, but the facts, when they are known, will <u>absolve</u> me.

Reading & Thinking Skills

Monitoring Comprehension

Have you ever read a paragraph without registering the meaning of the words? Because not understanding one passage can hinder your understanding of later sections, it's important to monitor your comprehension. Check your understanding as you read by using these techniques:

- Slow your reading rate. Reread to clarify.
- Ask yourself *who, what, where, when, why,* and *how* questions.
- Paraphrase—restate in your own words—difficult passages.

Try these techniques on the following lines from Sophocles's *Antigone:*

> Against our seven gates in a yawning ring
> The famished spears came onward in the night. . . .

As you read the passage slowly, ask yourself questions. For example, after reading the first line, you might ask, "Whose seven gates are these?" To answer this question, you need to understand previous passages. If you are unable to answer the question, look back through the selection to find that Thebes is referred to as "Thebes of the Seven Gates." Then, think about "famished spears" as "hungry weapons of war," moving forward, or attacking. To paraphrase this passage, you might simply state, "The enemy launched an attack at night on the walled city of Thebes."

- For more about related comprehension skills, see **Reading Handbook,** pp. R82–R85.

EXERCISE

Read the following words spoken by Cassius to Brutus in Shakespeare's play *Julius Caesar.* Then write and answer three questions that you could use to monitor your comprehension of this passage.

> Brutus and Caesar; what should be in that "Caesar"?
> Why should that name be sounded more than yours?
> Write them together, yours is as fair a name;
> Sound them, it doth become the mouth as well;
> Weigh them, it is as heavy; conjure with 'em,
> "Brutus" will start a spirit as soon as "Caesar."
> Now, in the names of all the gods at once,
> Upon what meat doth this our Caesar feed,
> That he is grown so great?

Reading & Thinking Skills

Objective

- To identify ways to monitor reading comprehension

Teaching Strategies

Have a volunteer choose another passage from the play that he or she found difficult to focus on or to understand. Go through each step described on page 771, having volunteers provide questions and paraphrases.

Exercise

Possible questions may include "Why is Cassius encouraging Brutus to consider himself equal to Caesar?" Answer: He seems to be trying to inflate Brutus's ego. He also seems to resent or dislike Caesar.

Additional Resources
📁 *Reading Workbook*

INCLUSION STRATEGIES

Less-Proficient Readers Practicing paraphrasing will help students improve their comprehension.

Activity Remind students that in paraphrasing for comprehension, they should replace difficult or unusual words with simple words and simplify sentence structure. Point out that in the excerpt from *Julius Caesar* in the exer- cise, they might replace the word *sound* with *pronounce,* the word *doth* with *does,* and the word *become* with *please.* Have students paraphrase line 3: "When you write the names together, yours is as attractive as his." **L1**

Additional Resources
📁 *Inclusion Strategies*

Literature F O C U S

Understanding Shakespeare and Elizabethan Drama

Objectives

- To understand the nature of the theater in Shakespeare's time
- To learn about Shakespeare's life and the historical events he described in Julius Caesar

Teaching Strategies

Have students read the Literature Focus and describe productions of plays they have seen. Ask them to compare modern theater with the English theater of the 1500s and 1600s. How do the theaters, audiences, and productions differ today?

Cultural Note

Present in Shakespeare's audiences were people from all walks of life. The desire to give everyone a character with whom to identify probably contributed to the wide variety of characters Shakespeare depicted. His plays include kings, queens, and the nobility; actors and craftsmen; and clowns, rustics, and fools.

Teaching Options

Literature F O C U S

Understanding Shakespeare and Elizabethan Drama

On a typical summer afternoon, Londoners from all levels of Elizabethan society could be found heading to the suburb of Southwark. They would walk over the London Bridge or ferry across the River Thames, then trudge through a muddy field in the direction of an open-air building—the Globe Theater, where William Shakespeare's newest plays were performed. As trumpets sounded, those who had paid for seats found their way to them, while "groundlings" paid less and stood in the open yard around three sides of the stage. Vendors wandered through the crowd, selling beer, water, hazelnuts, oranges, and other snacks. No lights dimmed and no curtain was raised. Instead, actors simply walked onto the nearly bare stage. With Shakespeare's language, these players could capture the attention of the thousands of people who had come to see them.

The Globe Theatre, 1616. Cornelius de Visscher. Engraving. British Library, London.

The Age of Shakespeare

William Shakespeare lived and wrote during what is known as the English Renaissance, which lasted from about 1485 through the 1660s. This period is also known as the Elizabethan Age, named after Queen Elizabeth I, who ruled England from 1558 to 1603. During Elizabeth's reign, society celebrated poets, such as Edmund Spenser, and politicians and courtiers who surrounded the queen. Elizabethans would have been surprised to learn that their age would become best known for its theater, as most considered drama a less distinguished form of literature than poetry.

Elizabeth was a clever and powerful queen. She deftly eased religious conflicts that had plagued England for years, and her skill at international diplomacy helped safeguard England from its enemies abroad. The British economy grew rapidly, and London, the center of English business and government, was becoming the largest city in Europe.

Despite England's flourishing society, life was not easy for everyone. Catholics experienced religious persecution. English women were subject to many restrictions. In addition, most English people endured crowded living conditions and an unsatisfactory diet. Rich and poor alike were defenseless against frequent outbreaks of bubonic plague. In 1564, the year Shakespeare was born, nearly one-third of the residents in his hometown died from the plague.

After Elizabeth died in 1603, her cousin, King James of Scotland, took over the English throne. James, like Elizabeth, was a great supporter of literature and the arts, and he eventually became the direct patron of Shakespeare's theater company.

MEETING INDIVIDUAL NEEDS — ENGLISH LANGUAGE LEARNERS

Introduction to Shakespeare

Students from other cultures may be unfamiliar with the importance of Shakespeare to English language literature. Begin by helping students locate London and the Thames River on a world map.

Activity Have students contribute ideas for a cluster map on the board. In the center write "William Shakespeare." Ask English language learners and others to contribute titles, characters, and ideas associated with him, such as Hamlet, *Romeo and Juliet,* tragedy, sonnets, Stratford, and *A Midsummer Night's Dream.*

Additional Resources

📁 *English Language Learners Sourcebook*

The Theater and the Stage

In the late 1500s, when Shakespeare began his career, English theater was going through major changes. For hundreds of years leading up to this time, professional actors, called "players," traveled the countryside, playing to audiences in towns and villages. They set up makeshift stages in public halls, marketplaces, and the courtyards of inns. Local officials, many of whom believed that "play-acting" violated biblical commandments, typically greeted acting companies with hostility.

Distrust of theater was so great that in 1574 the Common Council of London issued an order banishing players from London. To get around the order, actor James Burbage and his company of players built a playhouse in nearby Shorebridge. Completed in 1576, the building resembled the courtyard of an inn. Burbage's playhouse became the first public theater in England and was an immediate success, leading to the development of other public theaters over the next few years.

Shakespeare's company, the Lord Chamberlain's Men, performed at Burbage's theater until 1599, when they built their own playhouse, the Globe. Shakespeare referred to the Globe as "this wooden O," a term that led scholars to believe it was a circular building. The theater had three levels of galleries, covered by thatched roofs, overlooking an open courtyard. Projecting out into the yard was a platform stage about forty feet wide, with trapdoors for the entrance and exit of actors playing ghosts or other supernatural characters. At the back of the main stage was a small curtained inner stage used for indoor scenes. Above this stood a two-tiered gallery. The first tier was used to stage balcony and bedroom scenes; the second, to house musicians. Sound effects, such as the booming of thunder, were produced in a hut on top of the stage roof.

The Globe could hold about three thousand spectators. Members of the middle class and nobility typically sat in the galleries. Admission to the gallery benches was twopence. For sixpence (what a skilled laborer earned in a day), wealthier spectators could sit in a "lords' room" directly over the stage. Less well-to-do spectators, called "groundlings," could stand and watch from the courtyard for only a penny. Their close proximity to the stage created a noisy theatrical experience. Accounts of the time suggest that the groundlings did not hesitate to shout comments to the actors onstage. As theater became more profitable, its reputation improved. Eventually, Shakespeare's company received the support of Queen Elizabeth and, later, King James.

The Illusions of Theater

Because there was no artificial lighting, all performances at the Globe took place in the after-

The New Globe, interior.

Historical Note

The Puritans were partly responsible for the prohibitions on play production during Shakespeare's time. Led by John Calvin in the 1500s, the Puritans sought to reform the Church of England to emphasize preaching, Bible reading, and personal prayer. The Puritans had a reputation for having a strong work ethic. They wanted to prohibit theatrical productions not only because such productions were "immoral," but because they interrupted business. To free themselves from municipal and Puritanical restrictions, theaters moved outside the city limits in 1574.

FYI

The New Globe In 1987 ground was broken in London, on the approximate site of Shakespeare's original Globe Theater, for a reconstruction of the theater. During construction, two exciting discoveries were made: some re-mains of the Rose Theater, dating to 1587–88, and of the original Globe Theater of 1599. *The Two Gentlemen of Verona* was produced in the new Globe in August 1996. Organizers plan to duplicate the conditions of Shakespeare's era as much as possible, producing most plays during the day without an intermission in Elizabethan costumes.

Technology Option
Shakespeare's English Chart

Have students use word processing software to create a chart in which they list words from the play that may be unfamiliar to them and to give the meaning. Ask students to open a new document and insert a chart with the title *Shakespearean Vocabulary* and two columns with the headings *Word* and *Meaning*. Have students list words as they read. Then suggest that they look up the meanings or write what they think the words mean. **L2**

Shakespearean Vocabulary	
Word	**Meaning**

Women's Roles

Women actors appeared on stage in other European countries. The English belief that allowing women to act on stage was immoral was a limitation for English playwrights. It was especially difficult for young boys to convincingly act the part of a mature woman. As a consequence, Shakespeare created relatively few strong mature female characters. (Cleopatra and Lady Macbeth are notable exceptions.) This limitation also led Shakespeare to create female characters who disguised themselves as men, such as Viola in *Twelfth Night*.

A&E HOME VIDEO.® *The following videotape program is available from Glencoe. Be sure to preview the video for appropriateness for your class.*

- **William Shakespeare—A Life of Drama**

noon. There were few props and no movable scenery. Shakespeare made up for the lack of scenery by inviting audiences to visualize the scenes based on descriptive passages spoken by the characters. For example, a character's description of a storm would help Elizabethan audiences visualize raging weather.

What the Elizabethan stage lacked in scenery, it made up for in costumes and other spectacles. Elizabethan audiences considered clothing an important indication of rank, so they demanded realistic costumes. Audiences also thought it immoral for women to appear on stage, so boys performed the female roles.

Shakespeare's Life

Nearly four centuries after the death of William Shakespeare, his plays are still performed around the world. In fact, Shakespeare's writings are more widely read and more often quoted than any other literature, aside from the Bible. Unfortunately, there are no biographies of Shakespeare from his own time. Most of the information we have comes from public records and comments by contemporaries such as Ben Jonson, a friend and rival playwright, who readily recognized Shakespeare's genius.

Shakespeare was born in 1564 in Stratford-upon-Avon, a small market town about one hundred miles from London. His father, a tradesman and landowner, was elected bailiff (the equivalent of a mayor) in 1567, and his mother came from a prosperous farming family. William was the third of at least eight children born to this couple. He was their first boy and their first child to survive past childhood. Most likely, he attended the local grammar school, where he would have studied Latin and classical literature. At age eighteen, Shakespeare married twenty-six-year-old Anne Hathaway. The couple had three children: Susanna, born in 1583, and twins Judith and Hamnet, born two years later. Hamnet, their only son, died when he was eleven.

Shakespeare moved to London sometime between 1585 and the early 1590s and worked as an actor and playwright. He was soon known for his comedies and historical plays. By 1594 he had joined a company of players called the Lord Chamberlain's Men, with whom he spent the remainder of his career. Although Shakespeare maintained his family home in Stratford, he himself spent much of each year in London.

Shakespeare eventually retired in Stratford and died in 1616. Seven years later, a group of friends brought out a collected edition of his works known as the *First Folio*. The volume played a crucial role in preserving his plays for future generations.

Reading Shakespeare

Shakespeare was a prolific writer. In addition to thirty-seven plays, he wrote two narrative

Painted frieze from the Great Chamber, c. 1585. Gilling Castle, Yorkshire, England.

REAL-WORLD CONNECTION

Films Based on Shakespeare Point out that many of Shakespeare's plays have been made into popular films. Students may be familiar with *Romeo and Juliet*, featuring Leonardo DiCaprio and Claire Danes, produced in 1996. A popular version of *Romeo and Juliet* was also made in 1968. *West Side Story*, a musical adaptation of *Romeo and Juliet*, was also filmed. A popular version of *Hamlet* starring Mel Gibson was filmed in 1990. Have students view one of these films on home video. Then have students use the Internet or periodical indexes to find a professional review of the film. Finally, ask each student to prepare a written or oral report comparing his or her own responses with those of the reviewer. **L2**

poems, a series of sonnets, and other poetry. He excelled in all forms of drama. His tragic masterpieces include *Hamlet*, *Romeo and Juliet*, *Othello*, *Macbeth*, and *King Lear*. The beauty and richness of his language, as well as the universal issues his characters encounter, make his plays rewarding to read. However, some readers are intimidated by Shakespeare's use of language, which reflects English as it was spoken in Elizabethan times. The following suggestions may help you understand and enjoy his work:

- Some of the words in Shakespeare's plays are no longer used. Others have changed in meaning. Try to understand difficult words by looking at their context within a sentence or by consulting the side notes.
- Much of the dialogue in Shakespeare's plays is written as verse. These lines have a regular pattern of stressed and unstressed syllables. In order to follow such a pattern, Shakespeare often placed words in an unusual order within a sentence (for example, "Cassius from bondage will deliver Cassius"). If a sentence is confusing, try rearranging the words ("Cassius will deliver Cassius from bondage").
- Shakespeare's writing is full of imagery, figurative language, and wordplay. You might find a single metaphor or simile extended throughout an entire speech. Other speeches contain different metaphors and similes crowded together.

Shakespeare's *Julius Caesar*

Julius Caesar may be Shakespeare's most readable work. He probably wrote the play in 1599, the same year that the Globe Theater opened.

The Background *Julius Caesar* portrays a crucial period in history: Rome's transition from a republic to an empire. According to tradition, Rome became a republic about 509 B.C. and remained one for the next four and a half centuries. The Roman republic was governed by citizen assemblies: two elected consuls who could serve for just one year, and a powerful Senate, which proposed laws and oversaw officials.

The republic greatly expanded its territory and wealth through a series of foreign wars. However, as generals became more powerful from these wars, they began to ignore the Senate's authority. During its last fifty years, the republic was wracked by internal conflict.

In 60 B.C., Rome came under the control of a wealthy nobleman named Crassus and two generals, Pompey the Great and Julius Caesar. Crassus's death set off a power struggle between the generals. Caesar defeated Pompey in 48 B.C. To maintain order in Rome, Caesar seemed prepared to reestablish the monarchy.

Shakespeare's Retelling: Art and History Meet
While Shakespeare based his play on historical sources, he also imaginatively reshaped history. He left out many incidents, changed the timing of events, and fleshed out details to make the story more exciting and powerful.

Today, with its clear style and exciting plot, *Julius Caesar* still appeals to a wide audience. In the play, Shakespeare confronts some of the most difficult issues of his or any other time: What form of government is best? When does power become tyranny? How can one balance personal concerns with the public interest? These and other important themes are at the heart of Shakespeare's play.

FYI

Shakespeare's Plots
Students may be surprised to learn that Shakespeare borrowed nearly every one of his plots from other sources. Plays such as *Julius Caesar* and *Henry V* are rooted in history. *Romeo and Juliet* is based on a poem written in 1562 and *Othello* on a story written by an Italian writer in 1565.

Historical Note

Along with Crassus and Pompey, Julius Caesar formed Rome's First Triumvirate in 60 B.C. Pompey and his followers, alarmed by Caesar's power, ordered Caesar to give up his army in 49 B.C. Instead, Caesar crossed the Rubicon River into Italy, leading to a civil war. Caesar defeated Pompey and became Rome's sole ruler. "Crossing the Rubicon" now refers to any act in which a boundary is irrevocably crossed.

A&E HOME VIDEO. ® *The following videotape program is available from Glencoe. Be sure to preview the video for appropriateness for your class.*

- **Julius Caesar—Master of the Roman World**

MEETING INDIVIDUAL NEEDS — GIFTED AND TALENTED

The Glory of Ancient Rome *Julius Caesar* tells the story of one momentous event in ancient Roman history. From the founding of Rome in 753 B.C. to the overthrow of the last emperor of the West Roman Empire, Romulus Augustulus, in A.D. 476, ancient Rome was one of the greatest empires in history and had a huge impact on Western civilization.

Activity Have groups of students research one aspect or accomplishment of ancient Roman culture such as religion, architecture, engineering, art, literature, science, or political science. Have the groups report their findings, illustrated with maps, drawings, and photographs, to the class.
L2 COLLAB. LEARN.

Objective

- To read and understand a rap

Additional Resources

📁 *Media Connections Activities,* p. 20

Rap Music Have students use a search engine to find news on rap music. Have them share keywords and Web sites they locate.

Teaching Options

MEDIA
Connection

Rap

Shakespeare's "rhythm"—and Mark Antony's speech—takes on a whole new context in this student-written piece.

The Mark Antony Rap

by Beth—quoted in "The Shakespeare Frolic Project"
by Lawrence Baines, *The Clearing House,* March–April 1997

Hey everybody, listen up!
Caesar is gone, he's one dead pup.
His goodness is buried, but his evil lives on.
'Cause Brutus has you thinking that he done us wrong.
Brutus called him greedy, he called him bad,
But that way of thinking has got me mad.
Brutus is okay. He's a real cool dude,
But all this stuff he's saying is pretty rude.
Caesar was my friend, he was my bud,
But Brutus says he's greedy, so you think he's a dud.
What about the stuff that Caesar did?
He filled the treasure chest right up to its lid.
He brought lots of prisoners back to Rome
And we got lots of money 'fore we sent 'era home.
So was that greedy? Was it bad?
Brutus says it was and we know he's tad.
You all know that I told Caesar that he should
Make himself the only king of this hood.
Three times I told him, three times he refused.
If Brutus says that's greedy, I'd say he's confused.

Respond

1. What mood do you think is conveyed in this rap? What elements help create this mood?

2. How would you costume Mark Antony for this piece?

Reading *Minilesson*

Using Text Structures Explain that for a rap to work, it has to be written in very definite rhythm patterns. The pattern is indicated by the line lengths as well as punctuation and word choice.

Activity Help students find the rhythm of "The Mark Antony Rap." Have groups read the poem aloud either individually or chorally. When groups feel they have found the correct rhythm, invite them to read the rap chorally, adding any sound effects they choose. **L1 COLLAB. LEARN.**

Additional Resources

📁 *Reading Workbook*

Before You Read

The Tragedy of Julius Caesar

FOCUS ACTIVITY

Think of leaders of the country, of your state, of your community or school. What qualities do these leaders share?

MAP IT! Create a word web of qualities that you think are important for a leader. Share your ideas with the class.

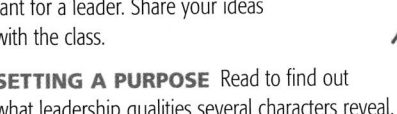

Leadership qualities

SETTING A PURPOSE Read to find out what leadership qualities several characters reveal.

BACKGROUND

The Time and Place

Shakespeare's *Julius Caesar* is set in ancient Rome between 44 and 42 B.C.

Did You Know?

- Julius Caesar was an immensely gifted military leader and politician. Born in 100 B.C., he belonged to a noble family, but he often looked for political support among Rome's lower classes. His daring military adventures made him famous and wealthy. After conquering Gaul in western Europe, he defeated his rival Pompey and became dictator of Rome in 48 B.C. Between military campaigns, he undertook popular reforms of Roman government and society.

Julius Caesar,
c. 60–44 B.C.
Capitoline Museums,
Rome.

- Caesar was a talented public speaker and writer whose war commentaries are considered literary classics. He introduced a new calendar, which is still used today in a slightly altered version. Although he could be charming, Caesar's arrogance and ambition created enemies in the Senate. A group of conspirators assassinated him in 44 B.C.

- Roman society was divided into several classes. Roman citizens, who had the right to vote, were either patricians (nobles) or plebeians (commoners). At first, only the noble landowners—the patricians—could hold office. But gradually the lower-class "commoners"—the plebeians—gained some political power and became represented in government by officials called tribunes.

- The Roman Senate watched over public officials and proposed new laws. Senators came from Rome's noble families. Popular assemblies enacted laws and elected public officials, including two powerful consuls responsible for the military. In times of emergency a dictator was appointed to replace the consuls for a brief period. Caesar acquired the title of dictator when he took control of Rome's government, although his powers exceeded those of a traditional dictator.

JULIUS CAESAR 🐾 777

SUMMARY, Act 1

Flavius and Murellus are angered by workers who are rejoicing over Caesar's triumph over Pompey. Caesar, celebrating a feast day, is warned to beware the ides of March by a sooth-sayer. Cassius flatters Brutus and asks him to participate in a plan to relieve Caesar of his power. Brutus confesses sympathy but won't commit himself. Casca returns from the festival and tells Brutus and Cassius that Mark Antony offered a crown to Caesar in front of the crowd, which he refused three times. Cassius plots to persuade Brutus to join his plan.

📁 *Spanish Summaries*, p. 70

🄰 Active Reading

CONNECT Invite students to discuss any travelling they may have done or would like to do to Rome. Have they seen any of the great ruins? What would they like to visit if they could?

Additional Resources
📁 *Active Reading Guide*, p. 71
🎧 *Audio Library*
🎧 *Spanish Audio Library*

Teaching Options

THE TRAGEDY OF
JULIUS CAESAR
William Shakespeare ❧

Tribute to Caesar. Andrea del Sarto (c. 1487–1530). Villa Medicea, Poggio a Caiano, Italy.

778 ❧ UNIT 4: DRAMA

CONNECTING TO OTHER SELECTIONS

The chart at the right shows three ways to connect *Julius Caesar* to selections in this book.

For specific teaching strategies, see the *Unit Four Planning Guide*, pages 32–33.

Connection	Title
Life Skills: Leading and Organizing	→ "And of Clay Are We Created," p. 343
Thematic: Ambition	→ "The False Gems," p. 289
Literary: Dialogue	→ "Catch the Moon," p. 63

CHARACTERS

JULIUS CAESAR: ambitious military leader and politician; the most powerful man in Rome

CALPHURNIA: wife of Caesar

MARCUS BRUTUS: friend of Caesar, appointed by him to high office in the Roman government; a believer in the republic and member of the conspiracy against Caesar

PORTIA: wife of Brutus and daughter of a Roman patriot

CAIUS CASSIUS: brother-in-law of Brutus and member of the conspiracy against Caesar

MARK ANTONY: friend of Caesar, senator, and eloquent orator; member of the triumvirate, the three-man governing body that ruled Rome after Caesar's death

OCTAVIUS CAESAR: Caesar's great-nephew and official heir; member of the triumvirate

M. AEMILIUS LEPIDUS: military leader and member of the triumvirate

Conspirators Against Caesar

CASCA	METELLUS CIMBER	TREBONIUS
CINNA	DECIUS BRUTUS	CAIUS LIGARIUS

Senators

CICERO	PUBLIUS	POPILIUS LENA

Tribunes *(Public Officials)*

FLAVIUS	MURELLUS

Officers in the Armies of Brutus and Cassius

LUCILIUS	MESSALA	VOLUMNIUS
TITINIUS	YOUNG CATO	FLAVIUS

Servants of Brutus

LUCIUS	CLITUS	STRATO
VARRUS	CLAUDIO	DARDANIUS

Others

A SOOTHSAYER (one who predicts the future)

ARTEMIDORUS OF CNIDOS: teacher of rhetoric

CINNA: a poet

PINDARUS: servant of Cassius

ANOTHER POET

SERVANTS TO CAESAR, ANTONY, AND OCTAVIUS; CITIZENS, GUARDS, SOLDIERS

B Active Reading

REVIEW Suggest that students read the cast of characters once and turn back and review it as necessary to identify a character who is speaking.

Shakespeare's Source

Four of Shakespeare's tragedies are set in ancient Rome: *Titus Andronicus, Antony and Cleopatra, Julius Caesar,* and *Coriolanus.* The background history for *Julius Caesar* came from essays on Brutus, Caesar, and Antony in *Lives of the Noble Grecians and Romans* by Plutarch (A.D. 46–A.D. 120), a Greek biographer. This book was translated into English by Thomas North in 1579.

MEETING INDIVIDUAL NEEDS — ENGLISH LANGUAGE LEARNERS

Shakespeare's Language English language learners may be intimidated by the language in Shakespeare. Point out that the use of unusual words and phrases, such as *art thou,* and the use of apostrophes to show omitted letters, as in *tow'rs,* are strange to proficient English speakers as well. Point out that the side notes explain words that had a different meaning from today or that are no longer used.

Activity Have a student read aloud the play's first speech. Point out that the small circles in lines 3 and 5 mean that side notes explain those lines. Explain that students may still need to look up some words, such as *beseech,* in a dictionary.

Additional Resources

📁 *English Language Learners Sourcebook*

ACT 1

C **SCENE 1. Rome. A street.**

[*Enter FLAVIUS, MURELLUS, and certain COMMONERS over the stage.*]

FLAVIUS. Hence! Home, you idle creatures, get you home!
Is this a holiday? What, know you not,
Being mechanical,° you ought not walk
Upon a laboring day without the sign

D 5 Of your profession? Speak, what trade art thou?°

CARPENTER. Why, sir, a carpenter.

MURELLUS. Where is thy leather apron and thy rule?
What dost thou with thy best apparel on?
You, sir, what trade are you?

10 **COBBLER.** Truly, sir, in respect of° a fine workman, I am but, as
you would say, a cobbler.°

MURELLUS. But what trade art thou? Answer me directly.

COBBLER. A trade, sir, that, I hope, I may use° with a safe
conscience, which is indeed, sir, a mender of bad soles.

15 **FLAVIUS.** What trade, thou knave? Thou naughty knave,
what trade?

COBBLER. Nay, I beseech you, sir, be not out° with me; yet, if
you be out,° sir, I can mend you.

MURELLUS. What mean'st thou by that? Mend me, thou saucy
fellow?

20 **COBBLER.** Why, sir, cobble you.

FLAVIUS. Thou art a cobbler, art thou?

COBBLER. Truly, sir, all that I live by is with the awl;° I meddle
with no tradesman's matters, nor women's matters; but
withal, I am indeed, sir, a surgeon to old shoes; when they

25 are in great danger, I recover them. As proper men as ever
trod upon neat's leather° have gone upon my handiwork.

FLAVIUS. But wherefore art not in thy shop today?
Why dost thou lead these men about the streets?

E 30 **COBBLER.** Truly, sir, to wear out their shoes, to get myself into
more work. But indeed, sir, we make holiday to see Caesar
and to rejoice in his triumph.°

780 ❧ UNIT 4: DRAMA

2–5 Is this a . . . art thou: Flavius and Murellus, public officials, remind the laborers that they should be dressed in their work outfits rather than their best clothes.

3 mechanical: manual laborers.

10 in respect of: in comparison with.

11 cobbler: "clumsy worker" or "shoe-maker." The Cobbler plays on the word's double meaning. Murellus and Flavius fail to understand his pun at first and keep pressing him to reveal a trade he has already identified.

13 use: practice.

16 out: angry.

16–17 if you be out: if your shoes are worn out.

22 awl: a tool for making holes in leather. The Cobbler puns on the words *all, awl,* and *withal,* which means "nevertheless."

26 neat's leather: cowhide. The Cobbler claims that his shoes have been worn by as fine men as ever walked in shoes.

31 triumph: triumphal celebration. (The triumph was held to celebrate Julius Caesar's defeat of two sons of Pompey the Great, his former rival. Caesar gained control over Rome when he defeated Pompey in 48 B.C.)

---

780 ❧ UNIT 4

A shoemaker with hammer. 1st–3rd century A.D., Gallo-Roman. Tombstone relief. Musée Rolin, Autun, France.

Viewing the art: Based on what you've read about the cobbler in this scene, what representative elements might you add to a tombstone relief for him? Why?

E **Literary Elements**

PLOT: *Exposition* What important background information do readers learn from the cobbler? *(Caesar has enjoyed a military victory and the people, who seem to revere him, are preparing to celebrate it.)*

VIEWING THE ART

The most common purpose of sculpture for private Roman citizens was for tombstone art.

Viewing Response *An awl and a shoe might be added to a tombstone for the cobbler.*

INTERDISCIPLINARY CONNECTION

Art Ancient Romans developed a unique style of creating realistic sculpture portraits of people. This realism often included showing wrinkles and skin defects. Other times, sculptors attempted to show a person's character. These sculptures were created both for funeral art and to honor important figures of the present and past.

Activity Have students find illustrations of ancient Roman sculptures of individuals. Ask them to find a photograph of a face that interests them and copy it in pencil or ink. **L2**

F Literary Elements

BLANK VERSE Have a volunteer read aloud the first four lines of Murellus's speech. Read line 35 and indicate on the board the pattern of stressed and unstressed syllables. Point out that the line is in perfect iambic pentameter: five metric feet, each with an unstressed syllable followed by a stressed syllable. Explain that the entire speech is written in blank verse—unrhymed iambic pentameter—and that Shakespeare uses blank verse for selected speeches. Have students finish reading the speech and characterize it. *(The speech is long, serious, and formal.)*

FYI

Blank Verse One reason for Shakespeare's use of blank verse was purely practical. Each actor in his company had to play several parts and learn many lines in a season. The regular rhythm of blank verse would have made the lines easier to memorize.

G Active Reading

INTERPRET Have students paraphrase Murellus's speech and describe his mood. *(He is angry: Rome's commoners are celebrating Caesar's victory, seeming to forget that the defeated Pompey was a hero whom the citizens loved and respected.)*

Teaching Options

MURELLUS. Wherefore rejoice? What conquest brings he home?
What tributaries° follow him to Rome,
To grace in captive bonds° his chariot wheels?
You blocks, you stones, you worse than senseless things!
O you hard hearts, you cruel men of Rome,
Knew you not Pompey? Many a time and oft
Have you climb'd up to walls and battlements,
To tow'rs and windows, yea, to chimney tops,
Your infants in your arms, and there have sate
The livelong day, with patient expectation,
To see great Pompey pass the streets of Rome;
And when you saw his chariot but° appear,
Have you not made an universal shout,
That Tiber° trembled underneath her banks
To hear the replication° of your sounds
Made in her concave shores?
And do you now put on your best attire?
And do you now cull out a holiday?°
And do you now strew flowers in his way,
That comes in triumph over Pompey's blood?°
Be gone!
Run to your houses, fall upon your knees,
Pray to the gods to intermit° the plague
That needs must light on this ingratitude.

FLAVIUS. Go, go, good countrymen, and, for this fault,
Assemble all the poor men of your sort;
Draw them to Tiber banks and weep your tears
Into the channel, till the lowest stream
Do kiss the most exalted shores of all.°

[*Exit all the* COMMONERS.]

See, whe'er their basest mettle be not mov'd;°
They vanish tongue-tied in their guiltiness.
Go you down that way towards the Capitol,
This way will I. Disrobe the images,
If you do find them deck'd with ceremonies.°

MURELLUS. May we do so?
You know it is the feast of Lupercal.°

FLAVIUS. It is no matter, let no images
Be hung with Caesar's trophies.° I'll about,
And drive away the vulgar° from the streets;
So do you too, where you perceive them thick.
These growing feathers pluck'd from Caesar's wing

Line numbers: 35, 40, 45, 50, 55, 60, 65, 70

33 tributaries: captured enemies who pay tribute, or ransom money, for their release.

34 captive bonds: the chains of prisoners.

43 but: only.

45 Tiber: a river running through Rome.

46 replication: echo.

49 cull out a holiday: pick out this day as a holiday.

51 Pompey's blood: Pompey's sons.

54 intermit: hold back.

58–60 Draw them to . . . of all: Flavius wants the commoners to weep into the Tiber until the river's lowest water reaches its highest banks.

61 whe'er . . . mov'd: whether their humble spirits have not been touched.

64–65 Disrobe the images . . . ceremonies: Flavius directs Murellus to remove any decorations from the statues.

67 feast of Lupercal: religious festival for a god worshiped by shepherds as a protector of flocks.

69 trophies: decorations honoring Caesar.

70 vulgar: common people.

MEETING INDIVIDUAL NEEDS — MULTIPLE LEARNING STYLES

Spatial The Tiber River, mentioned by Murellus, flowed along the western boundary of the ancient city of Rome.

Activity Have students locate a map of the ancient city of Rome in an encyclopedia or other reference book. Have them draw a copy of the map, including the Tiber River, the Appian Way, and the Forum. You might wish to make this an ongoing project. Have students add any other landmarks mentioned in Shakespeare's dialogue as they finish reading the play. **L2**

H Literary Elements

DIALOGUE What facts about Caesar are apparent in Flavius's speech? *(The officials have glimpsed a hunger for power in Caesar and want to keep him from finding out that the common people are prepared to glorify him.)*

H

Will make him fly an ordinary pitch,°
Who else would soar above the view of men
75   And keep us all in servile fearfulness.

[*They exit.*]

SCENE 2. Rome. A public place.

[*Enter* CAESAR, ANTONY *for the course,* CALPHURNIA,
PORTIA, DECIUS, CICERO, BRUTUS, CASSIUS, CASCA, CITIZENS,
and a SOOTHSAYER; *after them* MURELLUS *and* FLAVIUS.]

CAESAR.   Calphurnia!

CASCA.   Peace, ho, Caesar speaks.

[*All fall silent as* CAESAR *calls for his wife.*]

CAESAR.   Calphurnia!

CALPHURNIA.   Here, my lord.

CAESAR.   Stand you directly in Antonio's way
   When he doth run his course. Antonio!

5   **ANTONY.**   Caesar, my lord?

CAESAR.   Forget not in your speed, Antonio,
   To touch Calphurnia; for our elders say,
   The barren, touched in this holy chase,
   Shake off their sterile curse.°

ANTONY.   I shall remember;
10   When Caesar says, "Do this," it is perform'd.

CAESAR.   Set on, and leave no ceremony out.   [*Flourish.*]

SOOTHSAYER.   Caesar!

CAESAR.   Ha! Who calls?

CASCA.   Bid every noise be still; peace yet again!

15   **CAESAR.**   Who is it in the press° that calls on me?
   I hear a tongue shriller than all the music,
   Cry "Caesar!" Speak, Caesar is turn'd to hear.°

SOOTHSAYER.   Beware the ides of March.°

CAESAR.   What man is that?

BRUTUS.   A soothsayer bids you beware the ides of March.

20   **CAESAR.**   Set him before me, let me see his face.

CASSIUS.   Fellow, come from the throng, look upon Caesar.

CAESAR.   What say'st thou to me now? Speak once again.

SOOTHSAYER.   Beware the ides of March.

I

J

Bronze head of a woman, sometimes identified as Marciana. 1st quarter of the 2nd century A.D., Roman. Louvre Museum, Paris.
Viewing the sculpture: Describe the woman portrayed here. How might she reflect Calphurnia's feelings at this point in the drama?

72–73   These growing . . . pitch: Plucking feathers from a bird's wings prevents it from flying. Flavius uses this metaphor for his plan to keep Caesar's power at an ordinary **pitch**, or height.

6–9   Forget not . . . curse: Caesar, who has no children, refers to a traditional belief that barren women could become fertile if they were struck by leather thongs carried by runners who passed through Rome on the feast of Lupercal.

15   press: crowd.

17   turn'd to hear: Caesar turns his good ear to the Soothsayer (he was deaf in one ear).
18   ides of March: March 15. In the Roman calendar, a day in the middle of every month was called the ides.

Historical Note

Caesar is with his second wife, Calphurnia, whom he married in 59 B.C. With his first wife, Cornelia, who died in 68 B.C., Caesar had a daughter.

I Literary Elements

CHARACTERIZATION Have students characterize the relationship of Caesar and Antony. *(Caesar trusts Antony and expects him to follow his orders; Antony is respectful and willing to take orders.)*

J Author's Craft

PLOT: *Foreshadowing* Ask students how Shakespeare makes the foreshadowing here dramatic. *(Caesar and his friends are celebrating when the soothsayer dramatically interrupts with a cryptic message.)*

VIEWING THE SCULPTURE

Romans had developed methods of casting bronze to achieve realistic features in sculptures of people.

Viewing Response *Like the sculpture, Calphurnia is serious and meek.*

JULIUS CAESAR, ACT 1, SCENE 2   ❧   783

MEETING INDIVIDUAL NEEDS   **GIFTED AND TALENTED**

Roman Gods Like the Greeks, the ancient Romans worshipped gods related to the natural world. The feast of Lupercal, held on February 15, honored Lupercus, the god of flocks. Its purpose was to ensure fertility for people, crops, and animals.

Activity Have students research other gods, beliefs, and festivals of the ancient Romans. For example, they may research one or more of the following gods and goddesses: Vesta, the goddess of the hearth; Jupiter, god of the weather; Ceres, goddess of the harvest; and Janus, the god of doors and gates, who had two faces. Have students present their material as an oral or written report, an illustration, or a diorama. **L2**

JULIUS CAESAR

K — **CAESAR.** He is a dreamer, let us leave him. Pass.
[*They exit.* BRUTUS *and* CASSIUS *remain.*]

25 **CASSIUS.** Will you go see the order of the course?°

BRUTUS. Not I.

CASSIUS. I pray you do.

BRUTUS. I am not gamesome;° I do lack some part
Of that quick spirit that is in Antony.
30 Let me not hinder, Cassius, your desires;
I'll leave you.

CASSIUS. Brutus, I do observe you now of late;°
I have not from your eyes that gentleness
And show of love as I was wont to° have.
35 You bear too stubborn and too strange a hand
Over your friend that loves you.°

BRUTUS. Cassius,
Be not deceiv'd: if I have veil'd my look,
I turn the trouble of my countenance
Merely upon myself.° Vexed I am
40 Of late with passions of some difference,°
Conceptions only proper to myself,
Which give some soil, perhaps, to my behaviors;°
But let not therefore my good friends be griev'd
(Among which number, Cassius, be you one),
45 Nor construe any further° my neglect,
Than that poor Brutus, with himself at war,
Forgets the shows of love to other men.

CASSIUS. Then, Brutus, I have much mistook your passion,°
By means whereof this breast of mine hath buried
50 Thoughts of great value, worthy cogitations.°
Tell me, good Brutus, can you see your face?

BRUTUS. No, Cassius; for the eye sees not itself
But by reflection, by some other things.

CASSIUS. 'Tis just,
55 And it is very much lamented, Brutus,
That you have no such mirrors as will turn
Your hidden worthiness into your eye,
That you might see your shadow.° I have heard
Where many of the best respect in Rome
60 (Except immortal Caesar), speaking of Brutus
And groaning underneath this age's yoke,
Have wish'd that noble Brutus had his eyes.°

784 🪶 UNIT 4: DRAMA

25 **order ... course:** progress of the race.

28 **gamesome:** fond of games and sports.

32 **of late:** lately.

34 **was wont to:** used to.

35–36 **You bear ... loves you:** Cassius uses the metaphor of a rider holding a tight rein on an unfamiliar horse to suggest Brutus's unfriendly behavior toward him.

37–39 **Be not ... upon myself:** If I have seemed withdrawn, my displeased looks have been turned only on myself.
40 **passions of some difference:** conflicting emotions.
42 **Which give ... behaviors:** Which might blemish my conduct.

45 **Nor ... further:** Nor should you think any more of.

48 **mistook your passion:** misunderstood your feelings.

49–50 **By means ... cogitations:** Because of this I have kept important thoughts to myself.

58 **shadow:** reflection.

58–62 **I have heard ... eyes:** Cassius claims that many highly respected Roman citizens, groaning under the oppression of Caesar's rule, wished that Brutus would recognize his own worth.

BRUTUS. Into what dangers would you lead me, Cassius,
That you would have me seek into myself
65   For that which is not in me?

CASSIUS. Therefore, good Brutus, be prepar'd to hear;
And since you know you cannot see yourself
So well as by reflection, I, your glass
Will modestly discover to yourself
70   That of yourself which you yet know not of.°
And be not jealous on° me, gentle Brutus;
Were I a common laughter, or did use
To stale with ordinary oaths my love
To every new protester; if you know
75   That I do fawn on men and hug them hard,
And after scandal them; or if you know
That I profess myself in banqueting
To all the rout, then hold me dangerous.°

[*Flourish and shout.*]

BRUTUS. What means this shouting? I do fear the people
80   Choose Caesar for their king.

CASSIUS.   Ay, do you fear it?
Then must I think you would not have it so.

BRUTUS. I would not, Cassius, yet I love him well.
But wherefore° do you hold me here so long?
What is it that you would impart to me?
85   If it be aught toward the general good,
Set honor in one eye and death i' th' other,
And I will look on both indifferently;°
For let the gods so speed° me, as I love
The name of honor more than I fear death.

CASSIUS. I know that virtue to be in you, Brutus,
90   As well as I do know your outward favor.°
Well, honor is the subject of my story:
I cannot tell what you and other men
Think of this life; but for my single self,
I had as lief not be as live to be
95   In awe of such a thing as I myself.°
I was born free as Caesar; so were you;
We both have fed as well, and we can both
Endure the winter's cold as well as he;
For once, upon a raw and gusty day,
100   The troubled Tiber chafing with her shores,°

68–70 I, your . . . not of: I, your mirror, will reveal without exaggeration what you do not yet know about yourself.

71 jealous on: suspicious of.

72–78 Were I . . . dangerous: If I were a laughingstock or used to cheaply offering my affection to anyone, or if you know me to slander men after fawning on them, or if you know me to proclaim friendship to the common crowd while drinking, then consider me dangerous.

83 wherefore: why.

85–87 If it be aught . . . indifferently: If it is anything that concerns the public welfare, I will face honor and death impartially.

88 speed: favor.

91 favor: appearance.

94–96 for my single . . . myself: Personally, I would rather not live than live in awe of another human being.

101 chafing with her shores: dashing into the shores (as if angry with them for their restraint).

JULIUS CAESAR, ACT 1, SCENE 2   785

Writing *Minilesson*

CLARIFY Have students summarize the swimming anecdote about Caesar that Cassius relates. What point is Cassius making? *(He says that Caesar dared Cassius to a swimming competition and that Caesar tired and almost drowned; Cassius had to save him. His point is that Caesar is physically weak.)*

Q **Critical Thinking**

DRAWING CONCLUSIONS Cassius describes an epileptic seizure that Caesar had and compares Caesar to "a sick girl." What conclusion does he want Brutus to draw about Caesar? Is it a valid conclusion? *(He is implying that Caesar's physical weakness makes him an unfit leader. Many students will agree that this is an invalid conclusion.)*

R **Active Reading**

EVALUATE Have students summarize the philosophy of life that Cassius describes in lines 139–141 and discuss whether they agree or disagree. *(Cassius says that people control their own destinies; it is their fault if they are not leaders. Many students will agree with this philosophy to some extent.)*

Teaching Options

JULIUS CAESAR

Caesar said to me, "Dar'st thou,° Cassius, now
Leap in with me into this angry flood,
And swim to yonder point?" Upon the word,
105   Accoutred° as I was, I plunged in,
And bade him follow; so indeed he did.
The torrent roar'd, and we did buffet it
With lusty sinews,° throwing it aside
And stemming it with hearts of controversy;°
110   But ere we could arrive the point propos'd,
Caesar cried, "Help me, Cassius, or I sink!"
I, as Aeneas,° our great ancestor,
Did from the flames of Troy upon his shoulder
The old Anchises bear, so from the waves of Tiber
115   Did I the tired Caesar. And this man
Is now become a god, and Cassius is
A wretched creature, and must bend his body°
If Caesar carelessly but nod on him.
He had a fever when he was in Spain,
120   And when the fit was on him, I did mark
How he did shake—'tis true, this god did shake;
His coward lips did from their color fly,
And that same eye whose bend° doth awe the world
Did lose his° luster; I did hear him groan;
125   Ay, and that tongue of his that bade the Romans
Mark him, and write his speeches in their books,
Alas, it cried, "Give me some drink, Titinius,"
As a sick girl. Ye gods, it doth amaze me
A man of such a feeble temper should
130   So get the start of the majestic world,
And bear the palm alone.°

[*Shout. Flourish.*]

BRUTUS. Another general shout?
I do believe that these applauses are
For some new honors that are heap'd on Caesar.

135 **CASSIUS.** Why, man, he doth bestride the narrow world
Like a Colossus,° and we petty men
Walk under his huge legs, and peep about
To find ourselves dishonorable graves.
Men at some time are masters of their fates;
140   The fault, dear Brutus, is not in our stars,°
But in ourselves, that we are underlings.
Brutus and Caesar; what should be in that "Caesar"?

102 **Dar'st thou:** Do you dare?

105 **Accoutred:** dressed in armor.

108 **sinews:** muscles.
109 **stemming . . . controversy:** making headway against the river's flow in a spirit of rivalry.

112 **Aeneas** (i nē′ əs): The legendary founder of Rome, who carried his father Anchises on his back as he fled the burning city of Troy after it was conquered by the Greeks.

117 **bend his body:** bow.

123 **bend:** glance, look.
124 **his:** its.

130–131 **So get the . . . alone:** get ahead of all others and carry the victor's prize himself.

136 **Colossus:** The Colossus of Rhodes, a gigantic statue of the Greek god Apollo in the harbor of Rhodes, was said to be so tall that ships could sail through its legs.

140 **stars:** fate (believed to be determined by the position of the stars and planets at someone's birth).

MEETING INDIVIDUAL NEEDS | **GIFTED AND TALENTED**

The Aeneid *The Aeneid* is the Roman epic that tells the story of Aeneas, whose descendants founded Rome. It was written by Virgil, who lived from 70–19 B.C. In *Julius Caesar*, Cassius refers to a scene in which Aeneas leaves the burning city of Troy carrying his father on his shoulders and holding his son by the hand, symbolizing the continuity of the generations who would work for the glory of Rome.

Activity Have students locate a print or electronic edition of *The Aeneid* and read one book of the epic poem. Suggest that students prepare oral or multimedia reports in which they summarize an episode of the poem, and read a few lines. **L3**

145 Why should that name be sounded more than yours?
Write them together, yours is as fair a name;
Sound them,° it doth become the mouth as well;
Weigh them, it is as heavy; conjure° with 'em,
"Brutus" will start a spirit as soon as "Caesar."
Now, in the names of all the gods at once,
150 Upon what meat doth this our Caesar feed,
That he is grown so great? Age,° thou art sham'd!
Rome, thou hast lost the breed of noble bloods!
When went there by an age, since the great flood°
But it was fam'd with more than with one man?°
155 When could they say, till now, that talk'd of Rome,
That her wide walks encompass'd but one man?
Now is it Rome indeed and room enough,°
When there is in it but one only man.
O! you and I have heard our fathers say
160 There was a Brutus once that would have brook'd
Th' eternal devil to keep his state in Rome
As easily as a king.°

BRUTUS.   That you do love me, I am nothing jealous;°
What you would work me to, I have some aim.°
165 How I have thought of this, and of these times,
I shall recount hereafter. For this present,
I would not (so with love I might entreat you)
Be any further mov'd.° What you have said
I will consider; what you have to say
I will with patience hear, and find a time
170 Both meet° to hear and answer such high things.
Till then, my noble friend, chew° upon this;
Brutus had rather be a villager
Than to repute himself a son of Rome
Under these hard conditions as this time
175 Is like to lay upon us.

CASSIUS.   I am glad that my weak words
Have struck but thus much show of fire from Brutus.

[Enter CAESAR and his TRAIN.]

BRUTUS.   The games are done, and Caesar is returning.

CASSIUS.   As they pass by, pluck Casca by the sleeve,
180 And he will (after his sour fashion) tell you
What hath proceeded worthy note today.°

BRUTUS.   I will do so. But look you, Cassius,
The angry spot doth glow on Caesar's brow,

**Side notes:**
145 **Sound them:** say them.
146 **conjure:** call up spirits.
150 **Age:** the present era.
152 **great flood:** a time, according to Roman mythology, when a god let loose a flood that drowned all but two people.
153 **But it was . . . man:** That was not celebrated for more than one great man.
156 **Now is it . . . enough:** Cassius makes a pun on the words *Rome* and *room*, which were sometimes pronounced alike in Shakespeare's time.
159–161 **There was . . . king:** There once was a Brutus who would have accepted the devil ruling in Rome as easily as a king. (Cassius refers to Lucius Junius Brutus, who expelled the king and made Rome a republic in 509 B.C. Brutus claimed this hero as his ancestor.)
162 **am nothing jealous:** have no doubt.
163 **have some aim:** can guess.
167 **mov'd:** urged.
170 **meet:** suitable.
171 **chew:** ponder.
181 **What hath . . . today:** What noteworthy things have occurred today.

Literary Elements

FIGURES OF SPEECH: Symbol Cassius discusses Caesar's name at length and tells Brutus, "Yours is as fair a name." Have students explain what names symbolize in Cassius's speech. *(He uses a name to stand for the person and for accomplishments and abilities.)*

Active Reading

REVIEW Have students explain the grounds on which Cassius objects to Caesar. *(He believes there are many men besides Caesar who are fit to lead the republic; he objects to having a king or only one person in charge.)*

Active Reading

QUESTION How does Brutus respond to Cassius's implication that Caesar must be prevented from becoming king of Rome? *(He implies that he also does not want Caesar to become king but tells Cassius to be patient while Brutus considers what should be done.)*

MEETING INDIVIDUAL NEEDS — MULTIPLE LEARNING STYLES

Bodily-Kinesthetic Acting out scenes of the play by paraphrasing dialogue will help students understand both the dialogue and the characters' behavior and attitudes.

Activity Have pairs of students act out the discussion between Cassius and Brutus on pages 784–787 by paraphrasing each character's speeches. Suggest that students write brief summaries of each character's important speeches and discuss each one's motivation. Have volunteers act out their scenes. **L2 COLLAB. LEARN.**

Julius Caesar is offered the crown by Marcus Antonius, but he prudently refuses it.

Viewing the art: What qualities of Caesar's does this painting depict? Do you think they are accurate? Why or why not?

> And all the rest look like a chidden train;°
> 185 Calphurnia's cheek is pale, and Cicero°
> Looks with such ferret° and such fiery eyes
> As we have seen him in the Capitol,
> Being cross'd in conference by some senators.

CASSIUS. Casca will tell us what the matter is.

190 **CAESAR.** Antonio!

ANTONY. Caesar?

> **CAESAR.** Let me have men about me that are fat,
> Sleek-headed men, and such as sleep a-nights.
> Yond Cassius has a lean and hungry look,
> 195 He thinks too much; such men are dangerous.

> **ANTONY.** Fear him not, Caesar, he's not dangerous,
> He is a noble Roman, and well given.°

788 🌣 UNIT 4: DRAMA

184 chidden train: scolded band of followers.
185 Cicero: a Roman senator famous for his oratory.
186 ferret: a weasel-like animal with red eyes.

197 well given: favorably disposed (toward Caesar).

CAESAR. Would he were fatter! But I fear him not.
200   Yet if my name were liable to fear,°
  I do not know the man I should avoid
  So soon as that spare Cassius. He reads much,
  He is a great observer, and he looks
  Quite through the deeds of men.° He loves no plays,
205   As thou dost, Antony; he hears no music;
  Seldom he smiles, and smiles in such a sort
  As if he mock'd himself, and scorn'd his spirit
  That could be mov'd to smile at any thing.°
  Such men as he be never at heart's ease
  Whiles they behold a greater than themselves,
210   And therefore are they very dangerous.
  I rather tell thee what is to be fear'd
  Than what I fear; for always I am Caesar.
  Come on my right hand, for this ear is deaf,
  And tell me truly what thou think'st of him.

[CAESAR and his TRAIN exit. CASCA stays.]

215 **CASCA.** You pull'd me by the cloak, would you speak with me?

BRUTUS. Ay, Casca; tell us what hath chanc'd° today,
  That Caesar looks so sad.°

CASCA. Why, you were with him, were you not?

BRUTUS. I should not then ask Casca what had chanc'd.

220 **CASCA.** Why, there was a crown offer'd him; and being offer'd
  him, he put it by° with the back of his hand, thus, and then
  the people fell a-shouting.

BRUTUS. What was the second noise for?

CASCA. Why, for that too.

225 **CASSIUS.** They shouted thrice; what was the last cry for?

CASCA. Why, for that too.

BRUTUS. Was the crown offer'd him thrice?

CASCA. Ay, marry, was't,° and he put it by thrice, every time
  gentler than other; and at every putting-by mine honest
230   neighbors° shouted.

CASSIUS. Who offer'd him the crown?

CASCA. Why, Antony.

BRUTUS. Tell us the manner of it, gentle Casca.

CASCA. I can as well be hang'd as tell the manner of it; it was
235   mere foolery, I did not mark° it. I saw Mark Antony offer

199 **if my name . . . fear:** if it were possible for me to fear anyone.

202–203 **looks . . . of men:** sees people's true motives in their actions.

206–207 **scorn'd . . . any thing:** scorned anyone who ever smiles.

216 **chanc'd:** happened.
217 **sad:** serious.

221 **put it by:** pushed it aside.

228 **marry, was't:** indeed it was.

229–230 **mine honest neighbors:** Casca refers ironically to his "honest neighbors," for whom he has contempt.

235 **mark:** pay attention to.

W Active Reading
REVIEW Have students explain what kind of men Caesar wants and does not want around him. *(He likes men who are healthy and well-fed, implying that they are therefore satisfied with their position in life. He associates Cassius's lean look with a desire for power.)*

X Active Reading
REVIEW Have students summarize the reasons Caesar does not trust Cassius. *(He thinks Cassius is too serious: he likes to read and think, and does not enjoy plays and music. He says Cassius smiles scornfully and resents those who are greater than he.)*

Y Literary Elements
CHARACTERIZATION What does Caesar's comment in lines 211–214 indicate about his character? *(He is proud, refusing to admit he is afraid of anything or anyone. Also, he is deaf in one ear.)*

Z Literary Elements
BLANK VERSE Have students identify the form of Caesar's speech and compare it to that of Casca's speeches. *(Caesar uses blank verse; Casca speaks in prose.)*

MEETING INDIVIDUAL NEEDS — MULTIPLE LEARNING STYLES

Linguistic In reading *Julius Caesar*, students may find familiar quotations. For example, in line 194 Caesar says, "Yond Cassius has a lean and hungry look." Students may have heard "Beware the ides of March" and "he [Caesar] doth bestride the narrow world like a Colossus." Point out that people often use phrases and sentences first coined by Shakespeare in writing, in speeches, and in everyday conversations.

Activity Have students discuss reasons why the previous phrases have become part of our everyday language. Suggest that they start a notebook of quotes by Shakespeare as they complete the play, including phrases they have heard before and ones that strike them as particularly valid and original.

Literary Elements

AA

IRONY Remind students that in verbal irony, one thing is said and the opposite is true. Ask students to identify the irony in Casca's statement, "It was mere foolery, I did not mark it" (ll. 234–235). *(Casca says he hardly noticed the incident of Caesar's refusing the crown and then goes on to describe it in minute detail.)*

BB Critical Thinking

DRAWING CONCLUSIONS Have students interpret the reasons for Caesar's refusal of the crown. *(Students may conclude that his refusal is either genuine or done for political reasons. Because of Caesar's pride and many characters' suspicions of his hunger for power, students may conclude that he would like to accept the crown but puts on a show of modesty for the crowd.)*

CC Active Reading

INTERPRET Casca does not know what Cassius means when he says, "And honest Casca, we have the falling sickness." Have students explain the remark. *(Because of Caesar's increasing power, Cassius feels that he and Brutus and others will soon be reduced to being subjects of Caesar.)*

---

him a crown—yet 'twas not a crown neither, 'twas one of these coronets°—and as I told you, he put it by once; but for all that, to my thinking, he would fain° have had it. Then he offer'd it to him again; then he put it by again; but
240 to my thinking, he was very loath to lay his fingers off it. And then he offer'd it the third time; he put it the third time by; and still as he refus'd it, the rabblement hooted, and clapp'd their chopp'd° hands, and threw up their sweaty nightcaps, and utter'd such a deal of stinking breath be-
245 cause Caesar refus'd the crown, that it had, almost, chok'd Caesar; for he swounded,° and fell down at it; and for mine own part, I durst not laugh, for fear of opening my lips and receiving the bad air.

CASSIUS. But, soft,° I pray you; what, did Caesar swound?

250 **CASCA.** He fell down in the market place, and foam'd at mouth, and was speechless.

BRUTUS. 'Tis very like, he hath the falling sickness.°

CASSIUS. No, Caesar hath it not; but you, and I,
And honest Casca, we have the falling sickness.

255 **CASCA.** I know not what you mean by that, but I am sure Caesar fell down. If the tag-rag people° did not clap him and hiss him, according as he pleas'd and displeas'd them, as they use to do the players in the theater, I am no true man.

BRUTUS. What said he when he came unto himself?

260 **CASCA.** Marry, before he fell down, when he perceiv'd the common herd was glad he refus'd the crown, he pluck'd me ope his doublet,° and offer'd them his throat to cut. And I had been a man of any occupation,° if I would not have taken him at a word,° I would I might go to hell among the
265 rogues. And so he fell. When he came to himself again, he said, if he had done or said anything amiss, he desir'd their worships to think it was his infirmity. Three or four wenches, where I stood, cried, "Alas, good soul!" and forgave him will all their hearts. But there's no heed to be taken of
270 them; if Caesar had stabb'd their mothers, they would have done no less.

BRUTUS. And after that, he came thus sad away?

CASCA. Ay.

CASSIUS. Did Cicero say anything?

275 **CASCA.** Ay, he spoke Greek.

---

237 **coronets:** small crowns.
238 **fain:** rather.

243 **chopp'd:** chapped.

246 **swounded:** fainted.

249 **soft:** wait a minute.

252 **'Tis very . . . falling sickness:** It's very likely that he has epilepsy.

256 **tag-rag people:** ragged mob.

261–262 **pluck'd . . . doublet:** ripped open his short jacket.
262–263 **And I . . . occupation:** If I had been "a man of action" (or "a laborer").
264 **a word:** his word.

Teaching Options

REAL-WORLD CONNECTION

Political Leaders According to Casca, the Roman public adores Caesar. Have students discuss whether any political leaders or others are similarly idolized today; if so, who? Have pairs or small groups of students write a rap song about a political figure, movie star, athlete, or other celebrity who is revered by a large segment of the American public.
L2

CASSIUS. To what effect?

CASCA. Nay, and I tell you that, I'll ne'er look you i' th' face
again. But those that understood him smil'd at one another,
and shook their heads; but for mine own part, it was Greek
to me.° I could tell you more news too; Murellus and Flavius,
for pulling scarfs off Caesar's images, are put to silence.° Fare
you well. There was more foolery yet, if I could remember it.

CASSIUS. Will you sup with me tonight, Casca?

CASCA. No, I am promis'd forth.

285 CASSIUS. Will you dine with me tomorrow?

CASCA. Ay, if I be alive, and your mind hold,° and your dinner
worth the eating.

CASSIUS. Good, I will expect you.

CASCA. Do so. Farewell, both. [Exit.]

290 BRUTUS. What a blunt fellow is this grown to be!
He was quick mettle° when he went to school.

CASSIUS. So is he now in execution
Of any bold or noble enterprise,
However he puts on this tardy form.°
295 This rudeness is a sauce to his good wit,
Which gives men stomach to disgest° his words
With better appetite.

BRUTUS. And so it is. For this time I will leave you.
Tomorrow, if you please to speak with me,
300 I will come home to you, or, if you will,
Come home to me, and I will wait for you.

CASSIUS. I will do so. Till then, think of the world.°

[Exit BRUTUS.]

Well, Brutus, thou art noble; yet I see
Thy honorable mettle may be wrought
305 From that it is dispos'd;° therefore it is meet°
That noble minds keep ever with their likes;
For who so firm that cannot be seduc'd?
Caesar doth bear me hard,° but he loves Brutus.
If I were Brutus now and he were Cassius,
310 He should not humor° me. I will this night,
In several hands, in at his windows throw,
As if they came from several citizens,
Writings, all tending to the great opinion

279–280 it was Greek to me: I couldn't understand a word of it.

281 put to silence: barred from speaking in public (or perhaps exiled or executed).

286 your mind hold: you don't change your mind.

291 quick mettle: lively, clever.

294 However . . . form: Although he puts on this dull manner.

296 disgest: digest.

302 the world: the present state of affairs.

304–305 Thy honorable . . . dispos'd: Your honorable nature can be manipulated to go against its normal inclinations.
305 meet: appropriate.
308 doth bear me hard: dislikes me.

310 humor: influence.

FYI

"It Was Greek to Me"
Officials and members of the upper class in ancient Rome spoke Greek and Latin. That Casca does not speak Greek shows his lower social status.

DD Critical Thinking

INFERRING Ask students what the punishment of Murellus and Flavius indicates about Caesar's rule. *(He appears tyrannical in silencing men who disagree with him.)*

EE Literary Elements

FIGURES OF SPEECH: *Metaphor*
Have students explain the metaphor Cassius uses to describe Casca. *(Like a sauce that adds flavor to food, Casca's crudeness makes his sharp wit and intelligence more appealing to other people.)*

FF Literary Elements

SOLILOQUY Explain that a soliloquy is a convention of Shakespearean drama in which a character alone on stage delivers a speech explaining to the audience the character's feelings, plans, and motivations. Have students identify Cassius' soliloquy. *(ll. 303–317)*

MEETING INDIVIDUAL NEEDS

ENGLISH LANGUAGE LEARNERS

Shakespearean English English language learners may be confused by English words they know that have different meanings in Shakespeare's play.

Activity On the board, start a list of known words that Shakespeare uses in unusual ways. For example, *and* can mean *if*, as in lines 262 and 277. *Soft* in line 249 means "wait," and *meet* in line

305 means "appropriate." Explain that students may never encounter these words used like this except in Shakespeare. Have students contribute additional words to the word list to make a glossary.

Additional Resources
📁 *English Language Learners Sourcebook*

The Barber Shop of Licinius, 1881. Gustave Clarence Rodolphe Boulanger. Oil on canvas, 71.1 x 102.2 cm.
Viewing the painting: How does this portrayal of a Roman street scene enhance your understanding of the play's setting?

> That Rome holds of his name; wherein obscurely
> 315   Caesar's ambition shall be glanced at.°
> And after this, let Caesar seat him sure,°
> For we will shake him, or worse days endure. [*Exit.*]

SCENE 3. A Roman street. One month later.

[*Thunder and lightning. Enter (from opposite sides)* CASCA (*with his sword drawn*) *and* CICERO.]

    CICERO.   Good even,° Casca; brought you Caesar home?
       Why are you breathless? And why stare you so?

    CASCA.   Are not you mov'd, when all the sway° of earth
       Shakes like a thing unfirm? O Cicero,
5   I have seen tempests, when the scolding winds
       Have riv'd° the knotty oaks, and I have seen
       Th' ambitious ocean swell and rage and foam,
       To be exalted with° the threat'ning clouds;
       But never till tonight, never till now,
10   Did I go through a tempest dropping fire.
       Either there is a civil strife in heaven,
       Or else the world, too saucy° with the gods,
       Incenses them to send destruction.

310–315 I will . . . glanced at: Tonight I will throw letters in different handwriting, as if they came from several citizens, into Brutus's windows. The letters will relate that Brutus is highly regarded in Rome and will subtly hint at Caesar's ambition.

316 seat him sure: seat himself securely.

1 even: evening.

3 sway: realm.

6 riv'd: split.

8 exalted with: raised as high as.

12 saucy: insolent.

792   UNIT 4: DRAMA

CICERO. Why, saw you any thing more wonderful?

15 **CASCA.** A common slave—you know him well by sight—
Held up his left hand, which did flame and burn
Like twenty torches join'd; and yet his hand,
Not sensible of° fire, remain'd unscorch'd.
Besides—I ha' not since put up my sword—
20 Against the Capitol I met a lion,
Who glaz'd° upon me and went surly by,
Without annoying me. And there were drawn
Upon a heap° a hundred ghastly women,
Transformed with their fear, who swore they saw
25 Men, all in fire, walk up and down the streets.
And yesterday the bird of night° did sit
Even at noonday upon the marketplace,
Hooting and shrieking. When these prodigies°
Do so conjointly meet,° let not men say,
30 "These are their reasons, they are natural";
For I believe they are portentous things
Unto the climate that they point upon.°

CICERO. Indeed, it is a strange-disposed time;
But men may construe things after their fashion,
35 Clean from the purpose of the things themselves.°
Comes Caesar to the Capitol tomorrow?

CASCA. He doth; for he did bid Antonio
Send word to you he would be there tomorrow.

CICERO. Good night then, Casca; this disturbed sky
40 Is not to walk in.

CASCA.   Farewell, Cicero. [*Exit* CICERO.]

[*Enter* CASSIUS.]

CASSIUS. Who's there?

CASCA.   A Roman.

CASSIUS.   Casca, by your voice.

CASCA. Your ear is good. Cassius, what night is this!°

CASSIUS. A very pleasing night to honest men.

CASCA. Who ever knew the heavens menace so?

45 **CASSIUS.** Those that have known the earth so full of faults.
For my part, I have walk'd about the streets,
Submitting me° unto the perilous night;
And thus unbraced,° Casca, as you see,
Have bar'd my bosom to the thunder-stone;°

18 **sensible of:** sensitive to.

21 **glaz'd:** stared.

22–23 **drawn . . . heap:** huddled together.

26 **bird of night:** screech owl.

28 **prodigies:** bizarre events.
29 **conjointly meet:** coincide.

31–32 **portentous . . . point upon:** bad omens for the place where they occur.

34–35 **But men may . . . themselves:** But people may interpret things in their own way, regardless of the real meaning of the things.

42 **what night is this:** what a night this is!

47 **Submitting me:** exposing myself.
48 **unbraced:** with jacket open.
49 **thunder-stone:** thunderbolt.

FYI

Symbols The lion was the traditional symbol of Caesar. The screech owl was said to be a sign of bad luck.

▥ Active Reading

VISUALIZE Have students visualize and describe Casca's physical attitude during his speech in lines 15–32. Also have them imagine his tone of voice. *(Students should indicate that Casca's sense of wonder and fear would probably be apparent in his voice and body.)*

JJ Literary Elements

CHARACTER Ask students to compare and contrast the characters of Casca and Cicero as they appear in this scene. *(Casca is fearful and superstitious, seeing portents in a variety of phenomena. Cicero is down-to-earth and sensible, pointing out that people often project their own meanings onto objects and events.)*

Listening and Speaking *Minilesson*

Expressing Emotions Point out that Casca expresses fear and wonder in his speech on page 793. Similarly, Caesar expresses pride and suspicion in his speech on page 789.

Activity Have students choose a speech of eight lines or more in which a character clearly expresses a specific emotion. Have them define the emotion and prepare a reading of the speech in which the emotion is evident. Encourage students to use facial expression, vocal speed and tone, and gestures to communicate emotion. Have students present their readings in small groups. Other speeches students may want to consider are Murellus's speech on page 782, or one of Brutus's or Cassius's speeches on pages 784–787. **L3**

Critical Thinking

INFERRING Have students reread lines 72–84 and consider why Cassius does not want to name Caesar directly. Why does he speak in veiled terms? *(In fitting with the role of conspirator, Cassius' actions are secretive. He may be afraid of being overheard. He also wants others to come to their own conclusions about Ceasar, guided by his reasoning, but not forced into his conclusions. He is a manipulator.)*

Vo•cab•u•lar•y Skills

Suffix -ous Point out the words *perilous* (p. 793), *monstrous*, and *prodigious*. The suffix *-ous* means "full of" or "possessing the qualities of." Have students look up the root word *prodigy* and explain the meaning of *prodigious* in line 77. (*"portentous" or "exciting wonder"*)

50   And when the cross blue lightning seem'd to open
    The breast of heaven, I did present myself
    Even in the aim° and very flash of it.

  CASCA. But wherefore did you so much tempt the heavens?
    It is the part of men to fear and tremble
55   When the most mighty gods by tokens° send
    Such dreadful heralds to astonish° us.

  CASSIUS. You are dull,° Casca; and those sparks of life
    That should be in a Roman you do want,°
    Or else you use not. You look pale, and gaze,
60   And put on fear, and cast yourself in wonder,
    To see the strange impatience of the heavens;
    But if you would consider the true cause
    Why all these fires, why all these gliding ghosts,
    Why birds and beasts from quality and kind,°
65   Why old men, fools, and children calculate,°
    Why all these things change from their ordinance,
    Their natures and preformed faculties,
    To monstrous quality—why, you shall find
    That heaven hath infus'd them with these spirits,
70   To make them instruments of fear and warning
    Unto some monstrous state.°
    Now could I, Casca, name to thee a man
    Most like this dreadful night,
    That thunders, lightens, opens graves, and roars
75   As doth the lion in the Capitol—
    A man no mightier than thyself, or me,
    In personal action, yet prodigious grown
    And fearful,° as these strange eruptions are.

  CASCA. 'Tis Caesar that you mean; is it not, Cassius?

80 CASSIUS. Let it be who it is; for Romans now
    Have thews° and limbs like to their ancestors;
    But, woe the while,° our fathers' minds are dead,
    And we are govern'd with our mothers' spirits;
    Our yoke and sufferance° show us womanish.

85 CASCA. Indeed, they say, the senators tomorrow
    Mean to establish Caesar as a king;
    And he shall wear his crown by sea and land,
    In every place, save here in Italy.

  CASSIUS. I know where I will wear this dagger then;
90   Cassius from bondage will deliver Cassius.°
    Therein,° ye gods, you make the weak most strong;

52 in the aim: at the point where it was directed.

55 tokens: ominous signs.
56 astonish: stun with fear.
57 dull: stupid.
58 want: lack.

64 from quality and kind: act contrary to nature.
65 calculate: make prophecies.

66–71 Why all these . . . state: Cassius argues that things have changed from their normal behavior as a heavenly warning of some unnatural state of affairs.

77–78 yet prodigious . . . fearful: yet has become ominous and threatening.

81 thews: muscles.
82 woe the while: alas for these times.

84 yoke and sufferance: servitude and patient submission.

89–90 I know . . . deliver Cassius: Cassius says that he would rather kill himself than submit to Caesar.
91 Therein: in that way (referring to suicide).

794 ❧ UNIT 4: DRAMA

Teaching Options

Reading *Minilesson*

Paraphrasing Paraphrasing can be extremely useful to aid comprehension of Shakespeare. It requires a close reading and ensures that a passage's meaning will be understood.

Activity Have students paraphrase Cassius's speech in lines 80–84. Remind them to replace difficult or unusual words with simpler ones and to rearrange words and phrases to simplify sentence structure. (*"We are physically as strong as our fathers were, but unfortunately we are not as mentally strong as they. Instead, we are weak and submissive like our mothers."*) Suggest that students paraphrase any speeches they have difficulty comprehending. **L1**

Additional Resources
📁 *Reading Workbook,* pp. 73–74

William Shakespeare ∿

Therein, ye gods, you tyrants do defeat;
Nor stony tower, nor walls of beaten brass,
Nor airless dungeon, nor strong links of iron,
95   Can be retentive to the strength of spirit;
But life, being weary of these worldly bars,
Never lacks power to dismiss itself.
If I know this, know all the world besides,
That part of tyranny that I do bear
100   I can shake off at pleasure.

[*Thunder still.*]

   CASCA.   So can I;
So every bondman in his own hand bears
The power to cancel his captivity.

   CASSIUS.   And why should Caesar be a tyrant then?
Poor man, I know he would not be a wolf,
105   But that he sees the Romans are but sheep;

 LL

Augustus and lictors, detail from the south frieze of the Ara Pacis Augustae. 13–9 B.C., Roman. Museum of the Ara Pacis, Rome.
Viewing the art: One of the duties of Roman officers called *lictors* was to accompany officials like Caesar in public appearances. What does this image suggest to you about the government of Rome in Caesar's time?

Literary Elements

DICTION Have students give examples of the negative word choices Cassius uses to describe the Romans. How does his language help communicate his true motivation? *(Cassius uses several synonyms for "twigs" and "garbage" to describe the people. His description of the people as worthless and insignificant shows that he is motivated to get rid of Caesar not for the good of the people but because he hates Caesar.)*

Active Reading

QUESTION Cassius says to Casca, "There's a bargain made." What is the bargain? *(Casca has agreed to keep Cassius's hatred of Caesar secret and to help him in any plan to limit Caesar's power.)*

He were no lion, were not Romans hinds.°
Those that with haste will make a mighty fire
Begin it with weak straws. What trash° is Rome?
What rubbish and what offal?° when it serves
110 For the base matter° to illuminate
So vile a thing as Caesar! But, O grief,
Where hast thou led me? I, perhaps, speak this
Before a willing bondman; then I know
My answer must be made.° But I am arm'd,
115 And dangers are to me indifferent.

CASCA.   You speak to Casca, and to such a man
That is no fleering° tell-tale. Hold, my hand.
Be factious for redress of all these griefs,°
And I will set this foot of mine as far
120 As who goes farthest.

CASSIUS.   There's a bargain made.
Now know you, Casca, I have mov'd° already
Some certain of the noblest-minded Romans
To undergo with me an enterprise
Of honorable-dangerous consequence;
125 And I do know, by this they stay for me
In Pompey's Porch;° for now, this fearful night,
There is no stir or walking in the streets;
And the complexion of the element
[In] favor's like the work we have in hand,°
130 Most bloody, fiery, and most terrible.

[*Enter* CINNA.]

CASCA.   Stand close awhile, for here comes one in haste.

CASSIUS.   'Tis Cinna, I do know him by his gait,
He is a friend. Cinna, where haste you so?

CINNA.   To find out you. Who's that? Metellus Cimber?

135 CASSIUS.   No, it is Casca, one incorporate°
To our attempts. Am I not stay'd for, Cinna?

CINNA.   I am glad on't. What a fearful night is this!
There's two or three of us have seen strange sights.

CASSIUS.   Am I not stay'd for? tell me.

CINNA.   Yes, you are.
140 O Cassius, if you could
But win the noble Brutus to our party—

106 **hinds:** deer.

108 **trash:** "twigs" or "garbage."

109 **offal:** "chips of wood" or "garbage."

110 **base matter:** kindling.

112–114 **I, perhaps . . . be made:** Perhaps I am speaking to one who accepts his slavery; if so, I shall have to answer for my words (suggesting that Casca might inform on him).

117 **fleering:** sneering.

118 **Be factious . . . griefs:** Form a group to straighten out all these problems.

121 **mov'd:** persuaded.

125–126 **by this . . . Porch:** By this time they wait for me in the entrance to the theater built by Pompey.

128–129 **the complexion . . . in hand:** The condition of the sky appears similar to the work we have to do.

135 **incorporate:** joined.

Teaching Options

Grammar and Language *Minilesson*

Commas with Introductory Words

Remind students to use a comma after an introductory word, noun of direct address, or interjection at the beginning of a sentence. Point out line 135 on p. 796: "No, it is Casca . . ."

Activity Write the following sentences from the play on the board, omitting the comma after each introductory word. Have students come to the board and insert the commas.

- Why, saw you any thing more wonderful?
- Indeed, it is a strange-disposed time; . . .
- Ay, he spoke Greek.
- Caesar, my lord?
- O, he sits high in all the people's hearts; . . .

L1

Additional Resources

Grammar and Language Transparency 59

Grammar and Language Workbook, p. 259

Grammar and Composition Handbook, Lesson 11.6

Writer's Choice, Lesson 21.6

William Shakespeare

CASSIUS. Be you content. Good Cinna, take this paper,
And look you lay it in the praetor's chair,
Where Brutus may but find it; and throw this
145   In at his window; set this up with wax
Upon old Brutus' statue.° All this done,
Repair° to Pompey's Porch, where you shall find us.
Is Decius Brutus and Trebonius there?

CINNA. All but Metellus Cimber, and he's gone
150   To seek you at your house. Well, I will hie,°
And so bestow these papers as you bade me.

CASSIUS. That done, repair to Pompey's theater.

[*Exit CINNA.*]

Come, Casca, you and I will yet ere day
See Brutus at his house. Three parts of him
155   Is ours already, and the man entire
Upon the next encounter yields him ours.°

CASCA. O, he sits high in all the people's hearts;
And that which would appear offense in us,
His countenance, like richest alchemy,
160   Will change to virtue and to worthiness.°

CASSIUS. Him, and his worth, and our great need of him,
You have right well conceited.° Let us go,
For it is after midnight, and ere day
We will awake him and be sure of him.

[*They exit.*]

142–146 Good Cinna . . . statue:
Marcus Brutus held the office of praetor, a high-ranking judge who settled disputes brought before him. Cassius directs Cinna to leave one letter on Brutus's chair, throw a second into his window, and fasten a third onto the statue of the hero Lucius Junius Brutus.

147 Repair: go.

150 hie: hurry.

155–156 the man . . . ours: When we next meet him, he will be entirely in our hands.

159–160 His countenance . . . worthiness: Alchemy was the "science" of trying to turn base metals into gold. Casca says that Brutus's noble reputation will change the public's attitude toward their plot from condemnation to admiration.

162 conceited: understood.

Active Reading

QUESTION Why do Cassius, Cinna, and Casca want Brutus to go along with their conspiracy against Caesar? *(He is "noble"; the people respect him. If he is involved, Romans will believe that getting rid of Caesar is the right thing to do.)*

Thematic Focus

Loyalty and Betrayal Ask students to consider why Cassius wants to betray Caesar and why Brutus is reluctant to do so.

☑ ASSESSMENT OPTIONS

📁 *Quick Checks,* p. 71

Reading *Minilesson*

Problem and Solution It may be helpful for students to review act 1 in terms of problems and solutions.

Activity On the board, make a chart with the headings *Problem and Solution*. List the following problems and have students write the solutions seen so far: Cassius is jealous of Caesar's power; Roman citizens may object if Cassius and his friends kill Caesar. Brutus is a decent man and may not agree to killing Caesar. **L2**

Additional Resources
📁 *Reading Workbook,* pp. 73–74

Personal Response

Students should name a main character: Cassius, Brutus, or Caesar.

ANALYZING ACT 1

1. Flavius and Murellus get angry because in the past the Romans honored Pompey.

2. Cassius tells why Caesar is not a fit ruler and implies that he wants Brutus's help in getting rid of him. Brutus admits sympathy but does not commit to it. Cassius seems to be most concerned about Brutus's political talent being unfairly neglected.

3. Casca describes Mark Antony offering Caesar the crown three times, Caesar rejecting it, and Caesar having a seizure. Casca is scornful of Caesar.

4. Casca reacts with vague fear and superstition. Cassius asserts that the storm is the gods' message that Caesar has too much power. These reactions reveal that Casca is simple and naive and Cassius is crafty.

5. Cassius and Casca want to win over Brutus because they know the public trusts and respects him.

6. Students may find the portrayal realistic in the worker's annoying their social betters or unrealistic in their simplicity. Students should note the comedy in the wordplay.

7. Some students may find good reasons for the conspirator's reactions in Caesar's pride and enjoyment of his power or in his punishment of Murellus and Flavius.

8. The mood may be described as somber, dark, or angry based on Brutus's brooding, Cassius's plotting, and the thunderstorm.

9. Brutus cannot decide whether to support Cassius's conspiracy. His reluctance may inspire sympathy.

10. Students may see similarities in the public's respect of Caesar and Brutus or in the wisdom of Brutus and Cicero.

Responding to Literature

Personal Response

Which characters in act 1 made the strongest impression on you? Why?

ANALYZING ACT 1

RECALL AND INTERPRET

1. After seeing the public celebrating Caesar's triumph, what do Flavius and Murellus do? Why do they respond this way?

2. Summarize the conversation between Cassius and Brutus in scene 2. What does Cassius seem to be most concerned about?

3. What incident does Casca describe to Cassius and Brutus? What is Casca's attitude toward the incident?

4. Describe Cassius's and Casca's reactions to the storm. What do their reactions reveal about them?

5. Whom do Cassius and Casca want to win over to their plan? Why might they feel it is important for this person to join them?

EVALUATE AND CONNECT

6. Do you think Shakespeare's portrayal of the commoners in act 1 is realistic? How does their wordplay in scene 1 affect you?

7. Do you think that the conspirators have good reasons for their reactions to Caesar? Explain your answer.

8. How would you describe the overall **mood** of act 1? Use specific details from the act to support your description.

9. **Internal conflict** is a struggle that takes place within a character. Describe an internal conflict that occurs in act 1. What effect does this conflict have on your appreciation of that character?

10. What similarities in leadership qualities do you see between any of the characters in act 1? How do those qualities compare with the ones you listed for the Focus Activity on page 777?

Literary ELEMENTS

Blank Verse

Blank verse is lines of verse written in unrhymed iambic pentameter. Each line of iambic pentameter has five metrical feet, and each foot, or iamb, consists of an unstressed syllable followed by a stressed syllable. Because blank verse is intended to sound like spoken language, its meter is often not perfectly regular. These lines from *Julius Caesar* are examples of blank verse with perfect iambic pentameter:

Lĕt mé / hăve mén / ăbóut / mĕ thát / ăre fát,
Slĕek-héad / ĕd mén, / ănd súch / ăs sléep / ă-nights.

1. Find two other lines from act 1 written in blank verse with perfect iambic pentameter. Indicate the stressed and unstressed syllables.

2. Find two lines of blank verse with imperfect iambic pentameter. Show the stressed and unstressed syllables.

● See **Literary Terms Handbook,** p. R2.

EXTENDING YOUR RESPONSE

Literature Groups

Impressive Expressions With your group, identify three segments of dialogue or monologue from act 1 that seem particularly effective or descriptive. Discuss the elements that make each segment memorable. Compare your passages and analyses with those of other groups.

Creative Writing

In My Opinion Write a newspaper editorial about an event in act 1. Include details from the play and present your opinions in a clear and well-argued analysis.

📖 **Save your work for your portfolio.**

LITERARY ELEMENTS

1. "Whĕreforé/rĕjoíce?/Whăt cón/quĕst brings/hĕ hóme?" (scene 1, line 32)

2. "Éithĕr/thĕre ís/ă cív/ĭl strífe/ĭn heáv/ĕn" (scene 3, line 11); "Évĕn/ăt noón/dăy upón/thĕ márk/ĕt pláce" (scene 3, line 11); "Ănd dó/you nów/pŭt ón/yŏur bést/ăttíre?" (scene 1, line 48)

Additional Resources

✍ *Literary Elements Transparency 71*

✔ ASSESSMENT OPTIONS

📁 *Quick Checks,* p. 71

📁 *Selection and Theme Assessment,* pp. 137–138

📁 *Performance Assessment,* p. 70

💾 *Testmaker*

Writing Skills

Effective Conclusions

Even if you make many great points in the body of an essay, your reader may be left with an unsatisfactory feeling if you don't sum up your argument in a **conclusion**—the final paragraph that pulls the piece together and lets the reader know you are finishing your argument. Here are a few possible ways to conclude an essay.

Possible Conclusion	When to Use
sum up the main points and restate your thesis	if you've presented a great deal of information
make a recommendation	if you've described a problem
make a prediction	if you've described a current situation
ask a question	if you want your reader to continue thinking about the material presented
express your own thoughts and impressions	if you've discussed a personal experience

Read the paragraph below to see how one student concludes an essay that compares and contrasts *Antigone* and *Julius Caesar*. Note how she sums up her main points and, in the last two sentences, restates her thesis or main idea.

> Both *Antigone* and *Julius Caesar* deal with themes of loyalty and betrayal. However, in *Julius Caesar*, Cassius feels the need to convince Brutus to join him in betrayal, but Antigone does not feel the need to convince her sister Ismene. Cassius is looking for political power, while Antigone is trying to respect her brother and her gods. To me, these differences between main characters make *Antigone* a much more inspiring play. I learn more from reading about a selfless, brave person like Antigone than a selfish, power-hungry one like Cassius.

EXERCISE

On your paper, write the strategy that you might use to conclude essays on the following topics:

1. The first time you were separated from a parent

2. Destruction of the rain forest

3. Population growth in your community

4. Comparing and contrasting two films

Writing Skills

Objective

- To learn and apply strategies for concluding an essay

Teaching Strategies

After students have read the sample conclusion, point out that it reasserts and summarizes the comparison/contrast organization of the essay. Point out that a conclusion should follow through not only on the content but on the style and organization of an essay.

Exercise

1. express your own thoughts and impressions
2. make a recommendation
3. make a prediction
4. sum up the main points and restate your thesis

Additional Resources

Writer's Choice, Lesson 5.1

Teaching Options

Grammar and Language *Minilesson*

Affect and Effect Point out that *affect* is a verb meaning to "influence" or "impress." *Effect* is a noun meaning "the result of an action" or a verb meaning "to accomplish."

Activity Have students use the correct word in each of the following sentences. This movie will (affect, effect) your emotions. *(affect)* The ultimate (affect, effect) of the law will be positive. *(effect)* **L2**

Additional Resources

Grammar and Language Transparency 60

Grammar and Language Workbook, p. 219

Grammar and Composition Handbook

Writer's Choice

ACT 2

SCENE 1. BRUTUS's garden. The ides of March.

[*Enter BRUTUS in his orchard.*]

> **BRUTUS.** What, Lucius, ho!
> I cannot, by the progress° of the stars,
> Give guess how near to day. Lucius, I say!
> I would it were my fault° to sleep so soundly.
> 5   When, Lucius, when? Awake, I say! What, Lucius!

[*Enter LUCIUS.*]

> **LUCIUS.** Call'd you, my lord?
>
> **BRUTUS.** Get me a taper° in my study, Lucius.
> When it is lighted, come and call me here.
>
> **LUCIUS.** I will, my lord.

[*Exit LUCIUS.*]

> 10   **BRUTUS.** It must be by his death;° and for my part,
> I know no personal cause to spurn° at him,
> But for the general.° He would be crown'd:
> How that might change his nature, there's the question.
> It is the bright day that brings forth the adder,°
> 15   And that craves° wary walking. Crown him that,°
> And then I grant we put a sting in him
> That at his will he may do danger with.
> Th' abuse of greatness is when it disjoins
> Remorse from power;° and, to speak truth of Caesar,
> 20   I have not known when his affections° sway'd
> More than his reason. But 'tis a common proof°
> That lowliness° is young ambition's ladder,
> Whereto the climber-upward turns his face;
> But when he once attains the upmost round,°
> 25   He then unto the ladder turns his back,
> Looks in the clouds, scorning the base degrees
> By which he did ascend. So Caesar may;
> Then lest he may, prevent.° And since the quarrel
> Will bear no color for the thing he is,
> 30   Fashion it thus: that what he is, augmented,

2 progress: position.

4 I would . . . fault: I wish it were my weakness.

7 taper: candle.

10 his death: Caesar's death.
11 spurn: strike out.
12 the general: the public good.

14 adder: poisonous snake.
15 craves: demands. **Crown him that:** If we crown him.

18–19 Th' abuse . . . power: Greatness is misused when it separates mercy from power.
20 affections: feelings, desires.
21 a common proof: a common occurrence.
22 lowliness: humility.
24 upmost round: top rung.

28 Then lest . . . prevent: Let us act in advance to prevent it.

800 🦋 UNIT 4: DRAMA

Would run to these and these extremities;°
And therefore think him as a serpent's egg,
Which hatch'd, would as his kind grow mischievous,
And kill him in the shell.

[Enter LUCIUS.]

35 LUCIUS. The taper burneth in your closet,° sir.
Searching the window for a flint, I found
This paper thus seal'd up, and I am sure
It did not lie there when I went to bed.

[Gives him the letter.]

BRUTUS. Get you to bed again, it is not day.
40 Is not tomorrow, boy, the [ides] of March?

LUCIUS. I know not, sir.

BRUTUS. Look in the calendar, and bring me word.

LUCIUS. I will, sir. [Exit.]

BRUTUS. The exhalations° whizzing in the air
45 Give so much light that I may read by them.

[Opens the letter and reads.]

"Brutus, thou sleep'st; awake, and see thyself!
Shall Rome, etc. Speak, strike, redress!"°
"Brutus, thou sleep'st; awake."
Such instigations° have been often dropp'd
50 Where I have took them up.
"Shall Rome, etc." Thus must I piece it out:°
Shall Rome stand under one man's awe? What, Rome?
My ancestors did from the streets of Rome
The Tarquin° drive when he was call'd a king.
55 "Speak, strike, redress!" Am I entreated
To speak and strike? O Rome, I make thee promise,
If the redress will follow, thou receivest
Thy full petition at the hand of Brutus!°

[Enter LUCIUS.]

LUCIUS. Sir, March is wasted fifteen days.

[Knock within.]

60 BRUTUS. 'Tis good. Go to the gate, somebody knocks.

[Exit LUCIUS.]

Since Cassius first did whet° me against Caesar,
I have not slept.

28–31 since the quarrel . . . extremities: Since our complaints are not supported by Caesar's present behavior, we will have to put our case the following way: if given more power, Caesar's nature would lead him to such and such extremes.

35 closet: small private room.

44 exhalations: meteors.

47 redress: correct a wrong.

49 instigations: letters urging action.

51 piece it out: fill in the gaps in meaning.

54 Tarquin (tär′ kwin): the last king of Rome, driven out by Lucius Junius Brutus.

55–58 Speak, strike . . . Brutus: Brutus vows that Rome's petition for redress will be granted if it can be done through his words and actions.

61 whet: incite.

C Literary Elements

FIGURES OF SPEECH: *Metaphor* Point out the conclusion of Brutus's extended metaphor. Have students explain how Caesar is like a serpent's egg. *(Like an unhatched snake, he is not dangerous now but he will become dangerous.)*

Historical Note

The Romans borrowed and adapted the Greek calendar. The first Roman calendar, established in 738 B.C., had ten months and 304 days in a year. A later ruler added two months and 51 days to the year. However, by Julius Caesar's time the calendar was three months ahead of the seasons, so winter occurred in September. Caesar consulted an astronomer, Sosigenes. To make the seasons match the calendar, Caesar ordered that the year 46 B.C. have 445 days. Romans called this the "year of confusion." Julius Caesar's contribution to the calendar was honored by renaming a month July.

D Critical Thinking

DRAWING CONCLUSIONS Why are the appeals that Cassius makes in the letters to Brutus effective? *(Cassius plays on Brutus's sense of civic duty and his pride in his ancestors' accomplishments. He has effectively recognized Brutus's motivations.)*

ENGLISH LANGUAGE LEARNERS

Figurative Language English language learners may become confused by Shakespeare's frequent use of figurative language. Explain that Shakespeare uses two extended figures of speech at the beginning of act 2. Brutus compares Caesar to an adder (a poisonous snake) in the danger he may pose to Rome. He compares the rise of Caesar to a person climbing a ladder. These comparisons help readers picture the play's characters.

Activity Begin a list of figures of speech from the play on the board, using keywords such as *adder*. Have students suggest additional items for the list as they complete the play.

Additional Resources
📁 *English Language Learners Sourcebook*

E **Literary Elements**

CHARACTER What does Brutus's response to his decision indicate about his character? *(He takes his responsibility seriously; he is not coldhearted but emotional.)*

Vo•cab•u•lar•y Skills

Etymology The Latin word *phantasma*, usually written in English *phantasm*, can mean "an illusion" or "a ghost." It comes from the Greek word *phantazein*, "to present to the mind." Have students find other words with the same root, which include *fancy*, *fantasy*, *phantasmagoria*, and *phantom*.

F **Active Reading**

VISUALIZE Have students picture the scene described by Lucius. How would they describe the mood created by the image? *(frightening and mysterious)*

Teaching Options

Grave-relief of the corn-merchant Lucius Ampudius Philomusu, with his wife and daughter, c. 15 B.C.–A.D. 5 Marble, 0.63 x 1.63 m. The British Museum, London.

Viewing the art: Which characters at this point in the play might have facial expressions similar to those portrayed in the relief? Why?

> Between the acting of a dreadful thing
> And the first motion,° all the interim is
> 65 Like a phantasma,° or a hideous dream.
> The Genius and the mortal instruments°
> Are then in council, and the state of a man,
> Like to a little kingdom, suffers then
> The nature of an insurrection.°
>
> [*Enter* LUCIUS.]
>
> 70 LUCIUS. Sir, 'tis your brother° Cassius at the door,
>   Who doth desire to see you.
>
> BRUTUS.   Is he alone?
>
> LUCIUS. No, sir, there are moe° with him.
>
> BRUTUS.   Do you know them?
>
> LUCIUS. No, sir; their hats are pluck'd about their ears,
>   And half their faces buried in their cloaks,
> 75 That by no means I may discover° them
>   By any mark of favor.°
>
> BRUTUS.   Let 'em enter.
>
> [*Exit* LUCIUS.]
>
>   They are the faction. O Conspiracy,
>   Sham'st thou° to show thy dang'rous brow by night,

64 **motion:** prompting.

65 **phantasma:** nightmare.

66 **Genius . . . instruments:** the mental and physical powers that allow someone to take action.

67–69 **the state . . . insurrection:** Brutus compares his conflicted state of mind to a kingdom paralyzed by civil unrest.

70 **brother:** brother-in-law. (Cassius is married to Brutus's sister, Junia.)

72 **moe:** more.

75 **discover:** identify.

76 **favor:** appearance.

78 **Sham'st thou:** Are you ashamed?

802 🐚 UNIT 4: DRAMA

MEETING INDIVIDUAL NEEDS

MULTIPLE LEARNING STYLES

Spatial According to the stage direction at the beginning of scene 1, Brutus meets the conspirators in the garden of his house. The typical house of a wealthy Roman included a large walled garden in which fruits and vegetables were grown, thus the mention in the next stage direction of Brutus's "orchard."

Activity Have students research the design of a typical house of a well-to-do Roman. Have them draw a diagram or illustration of the house and display it. **L2**

When evils are most free? O then, by day
80   Where wilt thou find a cavern dark enough
To mask thy monstrous visage? Seek none, Conspiracy;
Hide it in smiles and affability;
For if thou path, thy native semblance° on,
Not Erebus° itself were dim enough
85   To hide thee from prevention.°

[Enter the CONSPIRATORS, CASSIUS, CASCA, DECIUS, CINNA, METELLUS, and TREBONIUS.]

CASSIUS.   I think we are too bold upon° your rest.
Good morrow,° Brutus, do we trouble you?

BRUTUS.   I have been up this hour, awake all night.
Know I these men that come along with you?

90   CASSIUS.   Yes, every man of them; and no man here
But honors you; and every one doth wish
You had but that opinion of yourself
Which every noble Roman bears of you.
This is Trebonius.

BRUTUS.   He is welcome hither.

95   CASSIUS.   This, Decius Brutus.

BRUTUS.   He is welcome too.

CASSIUS.   This, Casca; this, Cinna; and this, Metellus Cimber.

BRUTUS.   They are all welcome.
What watchful cares do interpose themselves
Betwixt your eyes and night?°

100   CASSIUS.   Shall I entreat a word?

[They whisper.]

DECIUS.   Here lies the east; doth not the day break here?

CASCA.   No.

CINNA.   O, pardon, sir, it doth; and yon gray lines
That fret° the clouds are messengers of day.

105   CASCA.   You shall confess that you are both deceiv'd.
Here, as I point my sword, the sun arises,
Which is a great way growing on the south,
Weighing the youthful season of the year.
Some two months hence, up higher toward the north
110   He first presents his fire, and the high east
Stands, as the Capitol, directly here.°

BRUTUS.   Give me your hands all over,° one by one.

---

83 path . . . semblance: go about undisguised.
84 Erebus (er′ ə bəs): in classical mythology, the dark place through which the dead pass on their way to Hades, the underworld.
85 prevention: discovery.
86 too bold upon: intruding upon.
87 morrow: morning.

98–99 What watchful . . . night: What cares keep you awake?

104 fret: interlace.

106–111 Here, as I . . . directly here: Casca insists that in the early spring the sun rises south of the spot pointed out by Decius and Cinna; it will rise farther north in about two months.
112 all over: all of you.

G Literary Elements

FIGURES OF SPEECH: *Personification*
Point out that Brutus personifies "Conspiracy." Have students describe the personification. *(He speaks to it and describes it as if it has a human face.)*

H Literary Elements

CHARACTERIZATION What does Brutus's personification of the conspiracy indicate about his attitude toward the undertaking? *(He despises its deceptive nature; he says it is too ugly to see the light of day and therefore must hide itself at night.)*

I Author's Craft

IMAGERY Have students consider why Shakespeare includes the discussion about the sun rising. *(He needed a way to indicate the time of day to the audience since the Elizabethans did not have the technology to present it onstage.)*

MEETING INDIVIDUAL NEEDS — ENGLISH LANGUAGE LEARNERS

Abstract Words Make sure English language learners understand the abstract terms *loyalty* and *betrayal*. If needed, have students look both words up in an English dictionary and say the words from their native languages that have the same meanings.

Activity Have both English language learners and English speakers give examples of ways in which people show loyalty to friends, family, and country. Then have them give examples of ways in which people betray friends, family, and country.

Additional Resources
📁 *English Language Learners Sourcebook*

JULIUS CAESAR

CASSIUS. And let us swear our resolution.

BRUTUS. No, not an oath. If not the face of men,
The sufferance of our souls, the time's abuse—
If these be motives weak, break off betimes,°   115
And every man hence to his idle bed.
So let high-sighted° tyranny range on
Till each man drop by lottery.° But if these
(As I am sure they do) bear fire° enough   120
To kindle cowards and to steel with valor
The melting spirits of women, then, countrymen,
What need we any spur but our own cause
To prick° us to redress? What other bond
Than secret Romans that have spoke the word   125
And will not palter?° and what other oath
Than honesty to honesty engag'd
That this shall be, or we will fall for it?°
Swear priests and cowards and men cautelous,°
Old feeble carrions,° and such suffering souls   130
That welcome wrongs; unto bad causes swear
Such creatures as men doubt; but do not stain
The even virtue of our enterprise,
Nor th' insuppressive mettle of our spirits,
To think that or our cause or our performance   135
Did need an oath;° when every drop of blood
That every Roman bears, and nobly bears,
Is guilty of a several bastardy,°
If he do break the smallest particle
Of any promise that hath pass'd from him.°   140

CASSIUS. But what of Cicero? Shall we sound him?°
I think he will stand very strong with us.

CASCA. Let us not leave him out.

CINNA.   No, by no means.

METELLUS. O, let us have him, for his silver hairs
Will purchase us a good opinion,   145
And buy men's voices to commend our deeds.
It shall be said his judgment rul'd our hands;
Our youths and wildness shall no whit° appear,
But all be buried in his gravity.°

BRUTUS. O, name him not! Let us not break with him,°   150
For he will never follow anything
That other men begin.

804 ❦ UNIT 4: DRAMA

114–116 If not . . . betimes: The sadness in people's faces, the suffering of our souls, the corruption of our age—if these are weak motives, let's give up at once.

118 high-sighted: arrogant.

119 drop by lottery: die by chance (at Caesar's whim).

120 bear fire: are spirited.

124 prick: spur.

126 palter: waver; deceive.

126–128 what other oath . . . for it: What other oath is needed than that of honest men who have pledged to each other that they will prevail or die trying?

129 cautelous: wary; crafty.

130 carrions: men no better than corpses.

132–136 do not stain . . . oath: Do not insult the steadfast virtue of our undertaking or the indomitable courage of our spirits to think that either our cause or our actions require an oath.

136–140 every drop . . . from him: Brutus claims that no one of true Roman blood would break a promise.

138 Is guilty . . . bastardy: is illegitimate.

141 sound him: find out his feelings.

148 no whit: not in the least.

149 gravity: dignity.

150 break with him: reveal our plot to him.

J Active Reading

REVIEW Have students summarize the point of Brutus's speech. *(He says that the idea of the conspirators' taking an oath of loyalty insults the conspirators' lofty motive: to do what is best for Rome.)*

K Active Reading

EVALUATE Have students discuss whether Brutus's speech is a convincing defense of the conspiracy or whether Brutus seems to be trying to rationalize a deed that he fears may be wrong. What effect does the parenthetical remark, "(As I am sure they do)," have on the way they view the speech?

L Active Reading

REVIEW Why does Metellus want to include Cicero in the conspiracy? *(People will trust his wisdom and good judgment because he is older.)*

Teaching Options

MEETING INDIVIDUAL NEEDS INCLUSION STRATEGIES

Less-Proficient Readers Explain that working with a group to paraphrase parts of Shakespeare's text can help comprehension. Explain that to paraphrase is to put something into your own words.

Activity Have groups of students work with lines 114–140. Direct them to paraphrase the speech orally, helping each other. Then have them settle on one interpretation and write down the group's paraphrase. Have a volunteer from each group read aloud their paragraphs. **L2**

Additional Resources
📁 *Inclusion Strategies*

804 ❦ UNIT 4

William Shakespeare ∾

CASSIUS.   Then leave him out.

CASCA. Indeed, he is not fit.

DECIUS. Shall no man else be touch'd but only Caesar?

155   CASSIUS. Decius, well urg'd. I think it is not meet
      Mark Antony, so well belov'd of Caesar,
      Should outlive Caesar; we shall find of him
      A shrewd contriver; and you know, his means,°
      If he improve them,° may well stretch so far
160   As to annoy us all; which to prevent,
      Let Antony and Caesar fall together.

  BRUTUS. Our course will seem too bloody, Caius Cassius,
      To cut the head off and then hack the limbs—
      Like wrath in death and envy afterwards;°
165   For Antony is but a limb of Caesar.
      Let's be sacrificers, but not butchers, Caius.
      We all stand up against the spirit of Caesar,°
      And in the spirit of men there is no blood.
      O that we then could come by° Caesar's spirit,
170   And not dismember Caesar! But, alas,
      Caesar must bleed for it. And, gentle friends,
      Let's kill him boldly, but not wrathfully;
      Let's carve him as a dish fit for the gods,
      Not hew him as a carcass fit for hounds;
175   And let our hearts, as subtle masters do,
      Stir up their servants° to an act of rage,
      And after seem to chide 'em. This shall make
      Our purpose necessary, and not envious;
      Which so appearing to the common eyes,
180   We shall be call'd purgers, not murderers.
      And for Mark Antony, think not of him;
      For he can do no more than Caesar's arm
      When Caesar's head is off.

  CASSIUS.   Yet I fear him,
      For in the ingrafted° love he bears to Caesar—

185   BRUTUS. Alas, good Cassius, do not think of him.
      If he love Caesar, all that he can do
      Is to himself—take thought and die° for Caesar.
      And that were much he should,° for he is given
      To sports, to wildness, and much company.

190   TREBONIUS. There is no fear in him;° let him not die,
      For he will live and laugh at this hereafter.

158 means: abilities.
159 improve them: uses them fully.

164 Like wrath . . . afterwards: as if the killings were motivated by anger and malice.

167 the spirit of Caesar: what Caesar represents.

169 come by: get possession of.

176 servants: hands.

184 ingrafted: deep-rooted.

187 take thought and die: die from grief.
188 that were much he should: It is unlikely that he would do such a thing.

190 no fear in him: nothing to fear from him.

M Active Reading

INTERPRET Ask students to explain the reasons Cassius gives for killing Mark Antony. *(He says Antony is close to Caesar, he is a clever politician, and he may use his intelligence to hurt the conspirators.)*

N Active Reading

EVALUATE Have students discuss Brutus's description of Caesar's murder. Is his description of killing "him boldly, but not wrathfully" convincing? What do students think of the distinction Brutus tries to make between "purgers" and "murderers"? *(Brutus once again seems to be rationalizing his decision to help murder Caesar. He says that if possible, they would kill not Caesar's body but only his spirit. Students may find Brutus's fine distinctions invalid: murder is murder.)*

O Active Reading

PREDICT Point out Brutus's statement, "We shall be call'd purgers, not murderers." Encourage students to predict whether this statement will come true.

P Author's Craft

CHARACTERIZATION Point out that one way Shakespeare exposes characters' natures is through others' descriptions of them. Have students summarize Brutus's description of Mark Antony. *(He is not serious but devotes himself to sports and socializing.)*

MULTIPLE LEARNING STYLES

Bodily-Kinesthetic Point out that each conspirator plays a different role in the meeting. While Cassius is the leader, he is willing to defer to Brutus, whose support is badly needed. Brutus acts as the conscience of the group, urging a civilized assassination. The other men are followers and change their opinions quickly if their leaders do so.

Activity Have groups of students act out the conspiracy scene by paraphrasing the speeches. Suggest that each student prepare his or her part by writing notes to help paraphrase the dialogue. Have the groups perform their scenes for the class. **L2 COLLAB. LEARN.**

Shakespeare's Anachronism

Shakespeare's detail of the clock striking is unrealistic since clocks were not invented until the late 1000s, by the Chinese. Clocks were not in common use until the late 1200s. Romans told time with sundials and hourglasses.

Q Active Reading

REVIEW Have students review and summarize the conspirators' plan. *(They will all go get Caesar and take him to the Capitol no later than eight o'clock.)*

R Active Reading

INTERPRET Have students describe and interpret Brutus's mood as he says good-bye to the men. *(He acts cheerful and optimistic, probably the opposite of his true feelings.)*

JULIUS CAESAR

[*Clock strikes.*]

BRUTUS. Peace, count the clock.

CASSIUS. The clock hath stricken three.

TREBONIUS. 'Tis time to part.

CASSIUS. But it is doubtful yet
195 Whether Caesar will come forth today or no;
For he is superstitious grown of late,
Quite from the main opinion° he held once
Of fantasy, of dreams, and ceremonies.°
It may be these apparent prodigies,
200 The unaccustom'd terror of this night,
And the persuasion of his augurers°
May hold him from the Capitol today.

DECIUS. Never fear that. If he be so resolv'd,
I can o'ersway him; for he loves to hear
That unicorns may be betray'd with trees,
205 And bears with glasses, elephants with holes,
Lions with toils, and men with flatterers;°
But when I tell him he hates flatterers
He says he does, being then most flattered.
Let me work;
210 For I can give his humor the true bent,°
And I will bring him to the Capitol.

CASSIUS. Nay, we will all of us be there to fetch him.

BRUTUS. By the eight hour; is that the uttermost?°

CINNA. Be that the uttermost, and fail not then.

215 **METELLUS.** Caius Ligarius doth bear Caesar hard,°
Who rated° him for speaking well of Pompey.
I wonder none of you have thought of him.

BRUTUS. Now, good Metellus, go along by him.
He loves me well, and I have given him reasons;
220 Send him but hither, and I'll fashion° him.

CASSIUS. The morning comes upon 's; we'll leave you, Brutus.
And, friends, disperse yourselves; but all remember
What you have said, and show yourselves true Romans.

BRUTUS. Good gentlemen, look fresh and merrily;
225 Let not our looks put on our purposes,
But bear it as our Roman actors do,
With untir'd spirits and formal constancy.°
And so good morrow to you every one.

806 🦢 UNIT 4: DRAMA

196 Quite from the main opinion: contrary to the strong opinion.
197 ceremonies: omens.

200 augurers: religious officials who interpreted omens to predict future events.

203–206 for he loves . . . flatterers: Decius refers to legends that the mythical unicorn could be tricked into charging a tree and getting its horn stuck, and that bears can be lured by mirrors. He also refers to trapping elephants in pits and using nets to catch lions, and tricking men with flattery.
210 give his . . . bent: put him in the right mood.
213 uttermost: latest.

215 bear Caesar hard: strongly resents Caesar.
216 rated: rebuked.

220 fashion: persuade.

224–227 look fresh . . . constancy: Brutus warns the others not to let their serious expressions show their intentions; they should carry out their plot appearing at ease and dignified.

Teaching Options

MEETING INDIVIDUAL NEEDS — GIFTED AND TALENTED

Political Assassinations Explain that the assassination of Julius Caesar is one of several well-known assassinations throughout history.

Activity Have students research and write a paper on other political assassinations, such as that of Archduke Ferdinand of Austria in 1914, which was a contributing factor to World War I.

They may also research the several attempts made to assassinate Adolf Hitler during World War II. Or they may choose to research one of the four American presidents who have been assassinated: Lincoln, Garfield, McKinley, and Kennedy. **L3**

William Shakespeare ∿

[*They exit.* BRUTUS *remains.*]

Boy! Lucius! Fast asleep? It is no matter,
230   Enjoy the honey-heavy dew of slumber.
Thou hast no figures nor no fantasies,
Which busy care draws in the brains of men;
Therefore thou sleep'st so sound.

[*Enter* PORTIA.]

PORTIA.   Brutus, my lord!

BRUTUS. Portia! what mean you? wherefore rise you now?
235   It is not for your health thus to commit
Your weak condition to the raw cold morning.

PORTIA. Nor for yours neither. Y'have ungently,° Brutus,
Stole from my bed; and yesternight at supper
You suddenly arose and walk'd about,
240   Musing and sighing, with your arms across;°

237 **ungently:** discourteously.

240 **across:** folded.

Portrait of Livia, from the Fayum. After 14 A.D., Roman. Ny Carlsberg Glyptotek, Copenhagen.

Viewing the sculpture: What words would you use to describe the person featured in this sculpture? Which character in the selection best fits your description? Why?

JULIUS CAESAR, ACT 2, SCENE 1 ✦ 807

S **Literary Elements**

CHARACTERIZATION What do students learn about Brutus from his speeches to Lucius and to Portia?

(He seems kind and gentle. His words to Lucius indicate his worried state while those to Portia are loving.)

VIEWING THE SCULPTURE

Livia was the wife of Augustus (Octavius).

Viewing Response *The bust conveys Livia's dignity and intelligence. Portia might also fit this description.*

INTERDISCIPLINARY CONNECTION

History Women had some rights in ancient Rome. Although they were forbidden to enter politics, matrons of leading Roman families sometimes wielded political influence. Women usually married at the age of 13 or 14, often to a boy chosen by their parents. Once married, their husbands were the head of the family. Although many girls were educated at home or in private schools, few were allowed to pursue higher education.

Activity Have students research the everyday lives of women in ancient Rome. You may wish to have some students focus on the lives of upper-class women and others on the enslaved population or on the lower classes. Encourage students to find out what rights women had and did not have. **L2**

Active Reading

VISUALIZE Portia gives a detailed description of Brutus's actions when he got out of bed earlier. Encourage students to visualize Brutus based on the description. What emotions do the gestures and expressions indicate? *(worry, stress, preoccupation, impatience)* One or two students may wish to demonstrate Brutus's behavior.

Critical Thinking

INFERRING What can students tell about Portia and her feelings for Brutus? Why is her statement "You have some sick offense within your mind" especially meaningful? *(She seems devoted to Brutus. She is intuitive in realizing something is bothering him and is worried about him; her description of his "offense" describes his situation accurately. She is stubborn and persistent in asking him to confide in her.)*

And when I ask'd you what the matter was,
You star'd upon me with ungentle looks.
I urg'd you further; then you scratch'd your head,
And too impatiently stamp'd with your foot.
245 Yet I insisted, yet you answer'd not,
But with an angry wafter° of your hand
Gave sign for me to leave you. So I did,
Fearing to strengthen that impatience
Which seem'd too much enkindled, and withal°
250 Hoping it was but an effect of humor,°
Which sometimes hath his° hour with every man.
It will not let you eat, nor talk, nor sleep,
And could it work so much upon your shape
As it hath much prevail'd on your condition,
255 I should not know you Brutus.° Dear my lord,
Make me acquainted with your cause of grief.

BRUTUS. I am not well in health, and that is all.

PORTIA. Brutus is wise and, were he not in health,
He would embrace the means to come by it.

260 **BRUTUS.** Why, so I do. Good Portia, go to bed.

PORTIA. Is Brutus sick, and is it physical°
To walk unbraced and suck up the humors
Of the dank morning?° What, is Brutus sick,
And will he steal out of his wholesome bed,
265 To dare the vile contagion of the night,
And tempt the rheumy and unpurged air°
To add unto his sickness? No, my Brutus;
You have some sick offense° within your mind,
Which by the right and virtue of my place,°
270 I ought to know of; and upon my knees
I charm you, by my once commended beauty,
By all your vows of love, and that great vow
Which did incorporate and make us one,
That you unfold to me, yourself, your half,
275 Why you are heavy, and what men tonight
Have had resort to you; for here have been
Some six or seven, who did hide their faces
Even from darkness.

BRUTUS.   Kneel not, gentle Portia.

PORTIA. I should not need, if you were gentle Brutus.
280 Within the bond of marriage, tell me, Brutus,
Is it excepted I should know no secrets

246 **wafter:** waving.

249 **withal:** also.
250 **but an . . . humor:** only a passing mood.
251 **his:** its.

253–255 **And could . . . Brutus:** And if it could change your appearance as much as it has changed your state of mind, I would not recognize you as Brutus.

261 **physical:** healthy.

262–263 **humors . . . morning:** damp morning mist.

266 **tempt the . . . air:** risk the damp and impure air. (It was believed that the night air was dangerous to breathe because it wasn't purified by the sun's rays.)
268 **sick offense:** harmful disorder.
269 **by the right . . . place:** as your wife.

808 🐿 UNIT 4: DRAMA

Teaching Options

INTERDISCIPLINARY CONNECTION

Science Portia tells Brutus that "were he not in health, he would embrace the means to come by it." One may infer that the ancient Romans had knowledge of health and medicine. The ancient Egyptians made great advances in medicine beginning around 2,500 B.C. In the 400s B.C., the Greek physician Hippocrates showed that diseases were not brought on by the gods but had natural causes. The Romans did not advance medical knowledge greatly but used the knowledge of the Egyptians and Greeks.

Activity Have students research medical science in ancient Rome, investigating the Romans' advancements in public health and the accomplishments of Galen, a Greek physician of the Roman Empire. Have students report their findings orally or in writing. **L2**

That appertain to you? Am I your self
But, as it were, in sort or limitation,°
To keep with you at meals, comfort your bed,
285 And talk to you sometimes? Dwell I but in the suburbs°
Of your good pleasure? If it be no more,
Portia is Brutus' harlot, not his wife.

  BRUTUS. You are my true and honorable wife,
    As dear to me as are the ruddy drops
290 That visit my sad heart.

  PORTIA. If this were true, then should I know this secret.
    I grant I am a woman; but withal
    A woman that Lord Brutus took to wife.
    I grant I am a woman; but withal
295 A woman well reputed, Cato's daughter.°
    Think you I am no stronger than my sex,
    Being so father'd and so husbanded?
    Tell me your counsels, I will not disclose 'em.
    I have made strong proof of my constancy,
300 Giving myself a voluntary wound
    Here, in the thigh;° can I bear that with patience,
    And not my husband's secrets?

  BRUTUS.   O ye gods!
    Render me worthy of this noble wife! [Knock.]
    Hark, hark, one knocks. Portia, go in a while,
305 And by and by thy bosom shall partake
    The secrets of my heart.
    All my engagements I will construe° to thee,
    All the charactery of my sad brows.°
    Leave me with haste.

  [Exit PORTIA.]

                Lucius, who's that knocks?
  [Enter LUCIUS and CAIUS LIGARIUS.]

310 LUCIUS. Here is a sick man that would speak with you.

  BRUTUS. Caius Ligarius, that Metellus spake of.
    Boy, stand aside. [Exit LUCIUS.] Caius Ligarius, how?°

  CAIUS. Vouchsafe° good morrow from a feeble tongue.

  BRUTUS. O, what a time have you chose out, brave Caius,
315 To wear a kerchief!° Would you were not sick!

  CAIUS. I am not sick, if Brutus have in hand
    Any exploit worthy the name of honor.

283 in sort or limitation: after a fashion or within limits.

285 suburbs: outskirts.

295 Cato's daughter: Portia's father, Marcus Porcius Cato, killed himself rather than submit to Caesar's rule after Pompey was defeated.

299–301 I have made . . . thigh: Portia reveals that she intentionally cut her thigh before approaching Brutus to show her strong determination.

307 construe: explain.
308 charactery of . . . brows: what is written in my sad brows (the reasons I am sad).

312 how: how are you?

313 Vouchsafe: Please accept.

315 kerchief: a scarf (wrapped around an ill person's head to protect against drafts).

Active Reading

CONNECT Have students discuss Portia's attitudes toward her husband. Are they similar or vastly different from those of wives of today? *(Portia is assertive and strong like many modern women, refusing to be excluded by her husband in an important matter. Although she respects her husband's wishes, she is not subservient.)*

Active Reading

INTERPRET How do Portia's pleas make Brutus feel? *(He feels guilty and undeserving of such a good and understanding wife.)*

Literary Elements

PLOT: Conflict Have students define Brutus's conflict at this point in the play. *(His conflict is whether or not to tell his wife of the assassination plot, but more deeply, his conflict is how to reconcile his decision to help assassinate Caesar with his guilt and misgivings about it.)*

LIFE SKILLS CONNECTION

Solving Problems Have students reread "The Mark Antony Rap" on page 776. Point out that Portia's feelings about her husband's excluding her from his problems are an interesting subject for a rap. Challenge students to create a rap for Portia that expresses her problems and her feelings about them. Alternatively, suggest that students write a letter to "Dear Abby" or create a monologue in contemporary language in which Portia tells a friend or counselor her problems. **L2**

Shakespeare in Music Ask students to use a search engine to locate music that might be based on the works of Shakespeare. Students might enter the key word *Shakespeare* in order to get a list of his works. Then they can try entering *Shakespeare—Music* or the titles of some of his works.

Literary Elements

CHARACTER Have students explain what Caius's behavior and dialogue tell them about Brutus. *(Brutus's trustworthy and respected character is stressed when Caius immediately "discards" his sickness on finding that Brutus needs his help; he agrees to help Brutus without knowing what he has in mind and says it is enough that Brutus leads him.)*

Critical Thinking

COMPARING Ask students whether Caesar demonstrates the same or different traits than he did in act 1. *(As in act 1, he expresses pride in the fact that he is frightened of nothing.)*

BRUTUS. Such an exploit have I in hand, Ligarius,
Had you a healthful ear to hear of it.

320 **CAIUS.** By all the gods that Romans bow before,
I here discard my sickness!
                              Soul of Rome!
Brave son, deriv'd from honorable loins!
Thou, like an exorcist,° hast conjur'd up
My mortified° spirit. Now bid me run,
325 And I will strive with things impossible,
Yea, get the better of them. What's to do?

BRUTUS. A piece of work that will make sick men whole.

CAIUS. But are not some whole that we must make sick?

BRUTUS. That must we also. What it is, my Caius,
330 I shall unfold to thee, as we are going
To whom it must be done.°

CAIUS.   Set on your foot.°
And with a heart new-fir'd I follow you,
To do I know not what; but it sufficeth
That Brutus leads me on.

[*Thunder.*]

BRUTUS.   Follow me, then. [*They exit.*]

SCENE 2. CAESAR's house. A few hours later.

[*Thunder and lightning. Enter* JULIUS CAESAR *in his nightgown.*]

CAESAR. Nor heaven nor° earth have been at peace tonight.
Thrice hath Calphurnia in her sleep cried out,
"Help, ho! they murther° Caesar!" Who's within?

[*Enter a* SERVANT.]

SERVANT. My lord?

5 **CAESAR.** Go bid the priests do present sacrifice,
And bring me their opinions of success.°

SERVANT. I will, my lord. [*Exit.*]

[*Enter* CALPHURNIA.]

CALPHURNIA. What mean you, Caesar? Think you to walk
forth?
You shall not stir out of your house today.

10 **CAESAR.** Caesar shall forth; the things that threaten'd me
Ne'er look'd but on my back; when they shall see
The face of Caesar, they are vanished.

810 ❧ UNIT 4: DRAMA

---

323 exorcist: one who summons up spirits.
324 mortified: deadened.

330–331 I shall . . . done: They are going to Caesar's house to escort him to the Capitol.
331 Set on your foot: Go ahead.

1 Nor . . . nor: neither . . . nor.

3 murther: murder.

5–6 Go bid . . . success: Tell the priests to make a sacrifice immediately, and bring me their interpretations of the results.

Teaching Options

MEETING INDIVIDUAL NEEDS — GIFTED AND TALENTED

Roman Religion Caesar sends his servant to "bid the priests do present sacrifice." In ancient Rome, priests were government officials whose job was to win the favor of the gods for the good of the country.

Activity Have students find out more about the religious practices of the ancient Romans such as the duties of the priests and priestesses and the role of sacrifices and other ceremonies. Have students present their findings orally to the class. **L2**

Portrait of a woman in encaustic on limewood with added gold leaf. c. A.D.160–170, Roman period, Egypt. 44.3 x 20.4 cm. The British Museum, London.

Viewing the art: What qualities do you think this woman possesses? Which of these qualities do you think Portia or Calphurnia shares? Explain.

Masks, busts, and elaborate public funerals were among the ways to honor the aristocratic deceased.

Viewing Response *The woman may possess seriousness and intelligence like Portia and Calphurnia.*

MEETING INDIVIDUAL NEEDS — MULTIPLE LEARNING STYLES

Spatial Many people are familiar with the simple styles of Roman clothing. Ancient Romans wore long wool or linen tunics. Men wore a toga over their tunics. Men wore white clothing and women wore clothing of various colors. Caesar is said to have been a vain man who added fringed sleeves to his tunic.

Activity Have students design a costume for one of the characters in *Julius Caesar*. Have them find pictures of Roman clothing for men and women. Students may draw their costume designs or make them and model them for the class. **L3**

CALPHURNIA. Caesar, I never stood on ceremonies,°
Yet now they fright me. There is one within,
15 Besides the things that we have heard and seen,
Recounts most horrid sights seen by the watch.°
A lioness hath whelped° in the streets,
And graves have yawn'd,° and yielded up their dead;
Fierce fiery warriors fight upon the clouds
20 In ranks and squadrons and right form of war,°
Which drizzled blood upon the Capitol;
The noise of battle hurtled in the air;

13 **stood on ceremonies:** believed in omens.

16 **watch:** night watchmen.

17 **whelped:** given birth.

18 **yawn'd:** opened.

20 **right form of war:** proper military formation.

The Ides of March. Sir Edward John Poynter (1836–1919). Manchester City Art Galleries, England.

Viewing the art: What is the mood of this piece? Does it support or contradict the mood created with each reference to the ides of March in the drama? Explain.

812 ❧ UNIT 4: DRAMA

Horses did neigh, and dying men did groan,
And ghosts did shriek and squeal about the streets.
25 O Caesar, these things are beyond all use,°
And I do fear them.

CAESAR.   What can be avoided
Whose end is purpos'd by the mighty gods?
Yet Caesar shall go forth; for these predictions
Are to the world in general as to Caesar.°

30 CALPHURNIA. When beggars die, there are no comets seen;
The heavens themselves blaze forth the death of princes.

CAESAR. Cowards die many times before their deaths,
The valiant never taste of death but once.
Of all the wonders that I yet have heard,
35 It seems to me most strange that men should fear,
Seeing that death, a necessary end,
Will come when it will come.

[Enter a SERVANT.]

                    What say the augurers?

SERVANT. They would not have you to stir forth today.
Plucking the entrails of an offering forth,
40 They could not find a heart within the beast.°

CAESAR. The gods do this in shame of° cowardice;
Caesar should be a beast without a heart
If he should stay at home today for fear.
No, Caesar shall not; Danger knows full well
45 That Caesar is more dangerous than he.
We [are] two lions litter'd in one day,°
And I the elder and more terrible;
And Caesar shall go forth.

CALPHURNIA.   Alas, my lord,
Your wisdom is consum'd in confidence.
50 Do not go forth today; call it my fear
That keeps you in the house and not your own.
We'll send Mark Antony to the Senate House,
And he shall say you are not well today.
Let me, upon my knee, prevail in this.

55 CAESAR. Mark Antony shall say I am not well,
And for thy humor,° I will stay at home.

[Enter DECIUS.]

Here's Decius Brutus, he shall tell them so.

25 use: normal experience.

29 Are to the . . . Caesar: apply to everyone as well as to me.

39–40 Plucking the . . . beast: Augurers would examine the inner organs of a sacrificed animal to predict the future. The absence of a heart would be a strange and unfavorable omen.
41 in shame of: to shame.

44–46 Danger knows . . . day: Caesar uses two figures of speech, first personifying danger and then using the metaphor that he and danger are lions born on the same day.

56 humor: whim.

CC Active Reading

EVALUATE Have a volunteer read aloud Caesar's speech, lines 32–37. Have them discuss how "cowards die many times before their deaths" and whether they agree with Caesar's view of death.

DD Active Reading

EVALUATE Ask students to reread lines 41–48. Is Caesar's attitude foolhardy or courageous? *(Caesar once again demonstrates his pride in his own fearlessness. Some students may admire the fact that he refuses to be intimidated by prophecies. Others may think he is foolish to tempt fate.)*

EE Literary Elements

PLOT: Conflict Have students define the main conflict at this point in the play. *(The conflict hinges on whether or not Caesar will go to the Capitol and whether the assassination plot will succeed.)*

Grammar and Language Minilesson

Parallel Sentence Structure Point out lines 172–174 in the speech by Brutus in scene 1. Point out Shakespeare's use of parallel sentence structure and have students describe its effect. *(It has a pleasing, balanced effect that adds weight to the speaker's words and makes his point easy to understand.)*

Activity Have students write their own sentences using lines 172–174 as a model. Instruct students to use subjects, verbs, and other sentence parts in the same positions as in the original. For example, a sentence modeled on lines 173–174 might read: We can shout it like a cheer created for a football game, not whisper it like a secret told to a friend. Have volunteers read their sentences. **L3**

Additional Resources

Writer's Choice, Lessons 15.6–15.7

Active Reading

VISUALIZE Caesar uses vivid imagery to describe Calphurnia's dream. Encourage students to visualize the dream. How does the vision change when Decius gives it a different meaning? *(The dream as Caesar describes it is morbid, frightening, and nightmarish. By twisting its meaning, Decius makes the same image less disturbing.)*

Critical Thinking

ANALYZING ARGUMENTS How does Decius convince Caesar to go to the Senate? Are his arguments valid? Use the following model to show how to analyze arguments.

Model: I think Decius is very clever. He reinterprets Calphurnia's dream, appeals to Caesar's egotistical wish to be crowned king, and says that Caesar will be laughed at if he does not go to the Senate. These are not necessarily valid arguments (in that they may not be proven true or false), but they are examples of effective persuasive techniques that take advantage of their target's weaknesses.

DECIUS. Caesar, all hail! good morrow, worthy Caesar,
I come to fetch you to the Senate House.

60 **CAESAR.** And you are come in very happy time°
To bear my greeting to the senators,
And tell them that I will not come today.
Cannot, is false; and that I dare not, falser;
I will not come today. Tell them so, Decius.

65 **CALPHURNIA.** Say he is sick.

CAESAR.   Shall Caesar send a lie?
Have I in conquest stretch'd mine arm so far
To be afeard to tell graybeards the truth?°
Decius, go tell them Caesar will not come.

DECIUS. Most mighty Caesar, let me know some cause,
70 Lest I be laugh'd at when I tell them so.

CAESAR. The cause is in my will, I will not come:
That is enough to satisfy the Senate.
But for your private satisfaction,
Because I love you, I will let you know.
75 Calphurnia here, my wife, stays° me at home:
She dreamt tonight° she saw my statue,
Which, like a fountain with an hundred spouts,
Did run pure blood, and many lusty Romans
Came smiling and did bathe their hands in it.
80 And these does she apply for° warnings and portents
And evils imminent, and on her knee
Hath begg'd that I will stay at home today.

DECIUS. This dream is all amiss interpreted,
It was a vision fair and fortunate.
85 Your statue spouting blood in many pipes,
In which so many smiling Romans bath'd,
Signifies that from you great Rome shall suck
Reviving blood, and that great men shall press
For tinctures, stains, relics, and cognizance.°
90 This by Calphurnia's dream is signified.

CAESAR. And this way have you well expounded it.

DECIUS. I have, when you have heard what I can say;
And know it now: the Senate have concluded
To give this day a crown to mighty Caesar.
95 If you shall send them word you will not come,
Their minds may change. Besides, it were a mock
Apt to be render'd,° for someone to say,

60 in very happy time: at the right moment.

66–67 Have I . . . truth: Have I made such conquests to be afraid to tell old men the truth?

75 stays: keeps.
76 tonight: last night.

80 apply for: interpret as.

85–89 Your statue . . . cognizance: **Tinctures** are features added to a coat of arms; **relics** are the remains of saints; **cognizance** is a mark identifying one as a lord's follower. Decius interprets Calphurnia's dream as a sign of Caesar's prestige, with great men coming to him to show their political loyalty and reverence.

96–97 it were a . . . render'd: it would be a joke likely to be made.

814 🐚 UNIT 4: DRAMA

Teaching Options

Reading *Minilesson*

Using Graphic Aids Students may better understand and remember the sequence of events in *Julius Caesar* if they record it graphically. One way to record the events of a plot is to make a time line.

Activity Have students make a time line showing the major events of *Julius Caesar* through the first two acts. Point out that the time line should show only the most important events, so students must first decide what those events are. For example, they will probably want to list "a soothsayer warns Caesar of the ides of March" and "Cassius enlists Brutus's aid in a plot against Caesar." They may not need to list "Casca speaks to Cicero on the street." When students have completed their graphics, have them contribute events to a class time line on the board. Encourage students to continue their time lines as they complete the play.
L2

Additional Resources
📁 *Reading Workbook*

"Break up the Senate till another time,
When Caesar's wife shall meet with better dreams."

GG

100   If Caesar hide himself, shall they not whisper,
"Lo, Caesar is afraid"?
Pardon me, Caesar, for my dear dear love
To your proceeding° bids me tell you this;
And reason to my love is liable.°

> 102–103   **my dear . . . proceeding:** my very deep desire for your advancement.
> 104   **liable:** subservient. Decius says that his love for Caesar forces him to say this, even though he may be overstepping himself.

105   **CAESAR.**   How foolish do your fears seem now, Calphurnia!
I am ashamed I did yield to them.
Give me my robe, for I will go.

[*Enter* BRUTUS, LIGARIUS, METELLUS CIMBER, CASCA, TREBONIUS, CINNA, *and* PUBLIUS.]

And look where Publius is come to fetch me.

PUBLIUS.   Good morrow, Caesar.

CAESAR.   Welcome, Publius.

HH

110   What, Brutus, are you stirr'd so early too?
Good morrow, Casca. Caius Ligarius,
Caesar was ne'er so much your enemy°
As that same ague° which hath made you lean.
What is't o'clock?

> 112   **your enemy:** Caesar had recently pardoned Ligarius for his support of Pompey during the civil war.
> 113   **ague:** sickness.

BRUTUS.   Caesar, 'tis strucken eight.

115   **CAESAR.**   I thank you for your pains and courtesy.

[*Enter* ANTONY.]

II

See, Antony, that revels long a-nights,°
Is notwithstanding up. Good morrow, Antony.

> 116   **that revels long a-nights:** who carouses late into the night.

ANTONY.   So to most noble Caesar.

CAESAR.   Bid them prepare within;
I am to blame to be thus waited for.

120   Now, Cinna; now, Metellus; what, Trebonius,
I have an hour's talk in store for you;
Remember that you call on me today;
Be near me, that I may remember you.

JJ 125   **TREBONIUS.**   Caesar, I will [*Aside.*] and so near will I be,
That your best friends shall wish I had been further.

CAESAR.   Good friends, go in, and taste some wine with me,
And we, like friends, will straightway go together.

JJ   **BRUTUS.**   [*Aside.*] That every like is not the same, O Caesar,
The heart of Brutus earns to think upon.°

> 128–129   **That every . . . upon:** Brutus grieves to think that not everyone who appears to be a friend is a real friend.

[*They exit.*]

HH Active Reading

RESPOND   Ask students how they feel about Caesar as he greets the men who have come to escort him to the Senate. *(Students may feel sympathy for Caesar because he greets the men sincerely; the reader knows that he is being tricked.)*

II Active Reading

QUESTION   How does Caesar's greeting to Antony relate to what the reader knows about Antony's character? *(Caesar refers to Antony's reputation for enjoying socializing.)*

JJ Literary Elements

ASIDE   Point out the asides of Trebonius and Brutus. Ask students to explain how the purposes of the two asides are similar and different. *(Both asides are meant to remind the reader of the conspirators' plot and move the audience to suspense and perhaps sympathy for Caesar. They differ in showing different motives: Trebonius is wholeheartedly involved in the plot while Brutus is still of two minds about the assassination.)*

Listening and Speaking *Minilesson*

Asides   Remind students that the aside is a convention of Elizabethan drama: an element that is not necessarily realistic but is accepted by the audience. Point out that an aside in everyday life may be rude since it involves talking to one person or oneself while ignoring others.

Activity   Have students work in pairs and perform the asides of Trebonius and Brutus. Discuss ways to dramatize an aside, such as by turning away from certain characters, putting a hand beside one's mouth, or using a stage whisper. Then have students invent their own dramatic situations that involve one or more asides. Have students perform their scenes. **L2** **COLLAB. LEARN.**

JULIUS CAESAR

SCENE 3. A street near the Capitol. Shortly afterward.

[Enter ARTEMIDORUS (reading a paper).]

ARTEMIDORUS. "Caesar, beware of Brutus; take heed of Cassius;
come not near Casca; have an eye to Cinna; trust not
Trebonius; mark well Metellus Cimber; Decius Brutus loves
thee not; thou hast wrong'd Caius Ligarius. There is but
5   one mind in all these men, and it is bent against Caesar. If
thou beest not immortal, look about you; security gives
way to conspiracy.° The mighty gods defend thee!
             Thy lover,° Artemidorus."
Here will I stand till Caesar pass along,
10   And as a suitor° will I give him this.
My heart laments that virtue cannot live
Out of the teeth of emulation.°
If thou read this, O Caesar, thou mayest live;
If not, the Fates with traitors do contrive.° *[Exit.]*

SCENE 4. Another Roman street. Immediately after.

[Enter PORTIA and LUCIUS.]

PORTIA. I prithee, boy, run to the Senate House;
Stay not to answer me, but get thee gone.
Why dost thou stay?

LUCIUS.   To know my errand, madam.

PORTIA. I would have had thee there and here again
5   Ere I can tell thee what thou shouldst do there°—
O constancy,° be strong upon my side;
Set a huge mountain 'tween my heart and tongue!
I have a man's mind, but a woman's might.
How hard it is for women to keep counsel!°—
10   Art thou here yet?

LUCIUS.   Madam, what should I do?
Run to the Capitol, and nothing else?
And so return to you, and nothing else?

PORTIA. Yes, bring me word, boy, if thy lord look well,
For he went sickly forth; and take good note
15   What Caesar doth, what suitors press to him.
Hark, boy, what noise is that?

LUCIUS. I hear none, madam.

PORTIA.   Prithee, listen well.
I heard a bustling rumor, like a fray,°
And the wind brings it from the Capitol.

816   UNIT 4: DRAMA

6–7 security gives . . . conspiracy: overconfidence opens the way for enemy plots.
8 lover: devoted friend.
10 suitor: person presenting a special request to a ruler.
12 Out of . . . emulation: beyond the reach of envy.
14 contrive: conspire.

4–5 I would . . . do there: You could go there and return here before I could explain what you should do there.
6 constancy: firmness.
9 counsel: a secret.

18 bustling . . . fray: noise of some activity such as a fight.

---

20   LUCIUS.   Sooth,° madam, I hear nothing.

[*Enter the* SOOTHSAYER.]

      PORTIA.   Come hither, fellow; which way hast thou been?

      SOOTHSAYER.   At mine own house, good lady.

      PORTIA.   What is't a'clock?

      SOOTHSAYER.   About the ninth hour, lady.

      PORTIA.   Is Caesar yet gone to the Capitol?

25   SOOTHSAYER.   Madam, not yet; I go to take my stand,
            To see him pass on to the Capitol.

      PORTIA.   Thou hast some suit to Caesar, hast thou not?

      SOOTHSAYER.   That I have, lady, if it will please Caesar
            To be so good to Caesar as to hear me:

30   I shall beseech him to befriend himself.

      PORTIA.   Why, know'st thou any harm's intended towards him?

      SOOTHSAYER.   None that I know will be, much that I fear
            may chance.
            Good morrow to you. Here the street is narrow;
            The throng that follows Caesar at the heels,

35   Of senators, of praetors, common suitors,
            Will crowd a feeble man almost to death.
            I'll get me to a place more void,° and there
            Speak to great Caesar as he comes along.

      [*Exit.*]

      PORTIA.   I must go in. Ay me! How weak a thing

40   The heart of woman is! O Brutus,
            The heavens speed thee in thine enterprise!
            Sure, the boy heard me—Brutus hath a suit
            That Caesar will not grant.°—O, I grow faint.—
            Run, Lucius, and commend me to my lord,°

45   Say I am merry. Come to me again,
            And bring me word what he doth say to thee.

      [*They exit separately.*]

**Side glosses (right column):**

20   **Sooth:** truly.

37   **void:** empty.

42–43   **Brutus hath . . . grant:** Portia makes up this excuse about Brutus's petition to explain her nervousness to Lucius.

44   **commend me to my lord:** send my regards to my husband.

FYI

Praetors Praetors were highly ranked judges, of which there were sixteen. Brutus was *praetor urbanus*, the chief justice. He was third in authority in the state below Caesar and Antony. Cassius, *praetor peregrinus*, ranked next below Brutus.

MM Literary Elements

PLOT: *Suspense* Have students describe Portia's mood and attitude and explain how they increase the play's suspense. *(She is so worried and upset that she is almost physically ill. Her worry puts a human face on the political situation, increasing the reader's suspense.)*

Thematic Focus

Loyalty and Betrayal Discuss with students why Brutus is now willing to betray Caesar.

✔ ASSESSMENT OPTIONS

📁 ***Quick Checks,*** p. 72

Reading *Minilesson*

Identifying Author's Purpose Explain that in writing a play, the author has a purpose for each scene, such as to give background information, show the nature of a character, further the plot, or increase suspense. Suggest that to aid understanding, students should define the author's purpose for each scene.

Activity Have students define the author's purpose in each scene below.

1. act 2, scene 1: Brutus and the conspirators in Brutus's garden *(to show character and advance plot)*
2. act 2, scene 1: Brutus and Portia *(to show character and increase the audience's emotional involvement)* **L2**

Additional Resources

📁 ***Reading Workbook***

Personal Response

ANALYZING ACT 2

1. Brutus believes if Caesar becomes king he will misuse his power and the citizens of Rome will suffer.
2. Brutus says they do not need an oath because their cause is noble; an oath would insult the virtue of their plan.
3. He does not want excessive violence; he says Antony will be powerless without his leader, Caesar. He thinks Antony is frivolous.
4. Calphurnia wants Caesar to stay home because a watchman has reported signs that bode ill. Caesar goes to the Capitol because Decius successfully appeals to his pride.
5. She wants to see how Brutus is feeling and what is happening to Caesar. Portia is strong and has a loving marriage. This is supported by her dismay at Brutus's inner conflict and Brutus's sorrow that he has upset his wife.
6. By doing what he decides is best for Rome, Brutus betrays his friend and leader, Caesar. Students may not accept Brutus's justification for killing Caesar because Caesar is not portrayed as tyrannical.
7. Students might agree with Brutus's recommendations because he seems wiser and more rational than Cassius.
8. Students may agree with Calphurnia since Shakespeare has revealed the truth of her omens.
9. Both women love and respect their husbands. Portia seems stronger and more independent than Calphurnia. Students may find Portia's strength similar to that of contemporary women.
10. Calphurnia's pleas to Caesar to stay home, Artemidorus's and the soothsayer's plans to find Caesar and warn him, and Portia's quest for information add suspense.

Responding to Literature

Personal Response

Which character are you most sympathetic toward? Why?

ANALYZING ACT 2

RECALL AND INTERPRET

1. According to Brutus, why must Caesar be killed?
2. According to Brutus, why don't the conspirators need to swear an oath? What can you infer about Cassius, Casca, and Brutus in scene 1 as these conspirators make their plans?
3. Why does Brutus want to spare Antony's life? What opinion does he seem to hold of Antony?
4. Why does Calphurnia want Caesar to remain at home? In your opinion, why does Caesar eventually decide to go to the Capitol?
5. Why does Portia send her servant to the Capitol? What impression do you have of Portia and her relationship with Brutus? Support your response with details from the selection.

EVALUATE AND CONNECT

6. Theme Connections   How do Brutus's intentions relate to the theme of loyalty and betrayal? Do you accept Brutus's justification for killing Caesar? Why or why not?
7. If you were one of the conspirators, would you agree with Brutus's recommendations or with Cassius's? Explain.
8. Calphurnia urges Caesar to act on her fears and remain at home. Do you agree with her reasoning? Why or why not?
9. Compare and contrast Portia and Calphurnia. How do they compare with women you know or with contemporary female characters?
10. What events or scenes in act 2 contribute to the **suspense?** Why?

Literary ELEMENTS

Soliloquies and Asides

Soliloquies are speeches delivered while a character is alone on stage. **Asides** are comments that a character makes to the audience that other characters on stage do not hear. Both of these theatrical devices are used frequently in Elizabethan drama to provide information to the audience and to reveal the characters' thoughts. For example, Cassius's soliloquy after his first meeting with Brutus (act 1, scene 2) reveals his plan to win over Brutus. It also influences the audience's opinion of Cassius.

1. What does Brutus reveal in his soliloquy at the beginning of act 2?
2. What does Trebonius mean in act 2, scene 2, lines 124–125? Why might Shakespeare have written these lines as an aside?

● See **Literary Terms Handbook,** pp. R12 and R1.

EXTENDING YOUR RESPONSE

Writing About Literature

Characterization   Shakespeare developed Caesar's character through his words and actions and through other characters' comments about him. Skim act 2 for examples of these three methods of characterization. In a paragraph explain whether Caesar's words and actions are consistent with what other characters say about him.

Performing

Act It Out!   In a small group, choose a scene or a portion of a scene to perform for the class. Discuss different ways of delivering the dialogue. For example, decide whether a line should be spoken softly or with great emphasis. Give reasons for your choices. Perform your scene for the class.

📖 **Save your work for your portfolio.**

LITERARY ELEMENTS

1. Brutus reveals that he has no reason to dislike Caesar and that Caesar has not done anything to deserve assassination; but he thinks that Caesar will eventually misuse his power.
2. He means that he will be close enough to Caesar to stab him. The aside emphasizes the irony of Caesar's closest colleagues turning on him.

Additional Resources

📖 **Literary Elements Transparency 72**

✔ ASSESSMENT OPTIONS

📁 *Quick Checks,* p. 72
📁 *Selection and Theme Assessment,* pp. 139–140
📁 *Performance Assessment,* p. 71
💾 *Testmaker*

Vo·cab·u·lar·y Skills

Homophones

The word **homophone** comes from the Greek *homo,* meaning "same," and *phone,* meaning "sound." Homophones are words that sound the same even though they are spelled differently and have different meanings.

When you are writing, using a homophone for the desired word can sometimes result in confusion. For example, you convey a totally different meaning if you write "a doctor who needs more *patience*" than if you wrote *patients.* Also, using homophones such as *marshal* instead of *martial,* or *profit* instead of *prophet,* can give the reader the impression that you are unaware of the difference in meaning or that you are careless.

If you use the wrong homophones in your writing, don't expect your computer to help you fix them. Computer programs that check spelling—and grammar—can be valuable. However, a computer probably won't tell you that you have used *rung* when you should have used *wrung,* because both of those are correctly spelled words.

Careful proofreading will help you eliminate any mistakes with homophones. Be especially careful with frequently overlooked homophones, such as *it's* and *its* or *who's* and *whose.* Thinking about the meaning of each homophone will help you use it correctly.

EXERCISE

List each underlined word on your paper. If the word is the correct one to use in the sentence, write *Correct.* If it is a homophone for the correct word, write the word that should have been used. Check definitions in a dictionary as needed.

> The incredible <u>feat</u> of creating *Julius Caesar* involved making a number of choices. That the <u>right</u> choices were made seems clear from the fact that the play has <u>born</u> the test of time.
>
> To <u>lesson</u> what would otherwise have been an impossibly long play, Shakespeare had to <u>altar</u> some historical facts. Certain events in *Julius Caesar* <u>very</u> from history, but this is mainly a matter of simplification. He also chose to center the play more on Brutus and his <u>dual</u> loyalties to Caesar and to Rome than on Caesar himself.
>
> Shakespeare chose his hero well, as Brutus is a <u>holy</u> fascinating character. Although Cassius hates Caesar the man, Brutus hates only the tyranny he fears will result from Caesar's <u>reign</u>. It is this fear that leads him to conclude that Caesar must <u>parish</u>.

JULIUS CAESAR ✤ 819

Vo·cab·u·lar·y Skills

Objective

- To recognize that homophones may sometimes be confused and to be aware of them when proofreading

Teaching Strategies

After students have read the first part of page 819, have them name several other homophones. Write them on the board.

Exercise

1. feat—Correct
2. right—Correct
3. born—borne
4. lesson—lessen
5. altar—alter
6. very—vary
7. dual—Correct
8. holy—wholly
9. reign—Correct
10. parish—perish

Additional Resources
📁 *Vocabulary Power: Weekly Lessons and Activities*

Teaching Options

MEETING INDIVIDUAL NEEDS — ENGLISH LANGUAGE LEARNERS

Practicing Homophones English language learners may find choosing the correct homophone difficult because experience in reading and writing English is the best way to distinguish homophones.

Activity Write the following pairs of homophones on the board: *bored, board; seam, seem; heard, herd; dear, deer; your, you're; peace, piece.* Discuss what the words mean and how they fit into a sentence.

Additional Resources
📁 *English Language Learners Sourcebook*

DRAMA ✤ 819

Teaching Options

ACT 3

SCENE 1. The Capitol in Rome. The ides of March. **A**

[*Flourish. Enter* CAESAR, BRUTUS, CASSIUS, CASCA, DECIUS, METELLUS, TREBONIUS, CINNA, ANTONY, PUBLIUS, POPILIUS, LEPIDUS, ARTEMIDORUS, *and the* SOOTHSAYER.]

    CAESAR. The ides of March are come.

    SOOTHSAYER. Ay, Caesar, but not gone.

    ARTEMIDORUS. Hail, Caesar! Read this schedule.°

    DECIUS. Trebonius doth desire you to o'er-read,
      (At your best leisure) this his humble suit.

5

    ARTEMIDORUS. O Caesar, read mine first; for mine's a suit
      That touches Caesar nearer. Read it, great Caesar.

    CAESAR. What touches us ourself shall be last serv'd. **C**

    ARTEMIDORUS. Delay not, Caesar, read it instantly.

10   **CAESAR.** What, is the fellow mad?

    PUBLIUS.   Sirrah,° give place.

    CASSIUS. What, urge you your petitions in the street?
      Come to the Capitol.

[CAESAR *enters the Capitol, the rest following.*]

    POPILIUS. I wish your enterprise today may thrive.

    CASSIUS. What enterprise, Popilius?

    POPILIUS.   Fare you well. [*Leaves him*
      and joins CAESAR.]

15   **BRUTUS.** What said Popilius Lena?

    CASSIUS. He wish'd today our enterprise might thrive.
      I fear our purpose is discovered.

    BRUTUS. Look how he makes° to Caesar; mark him.

    CASSIUS. Casca, be sudden, for we fear prevention.°
20   Brutus, what shall be done? If this be known,
    Cassius or Caesar never shall turn back,°
    For I will slay myself.

3 schedule: document.

10 Sirrah: an insulting form of address to an inferior.

18 makes: makes his way.

19 be sudden . . . prevention: be quick, for we fear that we will be stopped.

21 turn back: return alive.

BRUTUS.   Cassius, be constant;°
Popilius Lena speaks not of our purposes,
For look he smiles, and Caesar doth not change.

25   CASSIUS.   Trebonius knows his time; for look you, Brutus,
He draws Mark Antony out of the way.

[ANTONY and TREBONIUS exit.]

DECIUS.   Where is Metellus Cimber? Let him go
And presently prefer° his suit to Caesar.

BRUTUS.   He is address'd;° press near and second him.

30   CINNA.   Casca, you are the first that rears your hand.

CAESAR.   Are we all ready? What is now amiss
That Caesar and his Senate must redress?

METELLUS.   Most high, most mighty, and most puissant° Caesar,
Metellus Cimber throws before thy seat

35   An humble heart. [Kneeling.]

CAESAR.   I must prevent thee, Cimber.
These couchings and these lowly courtesies
Might fire the blood of ordinary men,
And turn preordinance and first decree
Into the [law] of children. Be not fond

40   To think that Caesar bears such rebel blood
That will be thaw'd from the true quality
With that which melteth fools—I mean sweet words,
Low-crooked curtsies, and base spaniel fawning.°
Thy brother by decree is banished;

45   If thou dost bend, and pray, and fawn for him,
I spurn thee like a cur° out of my way.
Know, Caesar doth not wrong, nor without cause
Will he be satisfied.°

METELLUS.   Is there no voice more worthy than my own,

50   To sound more sweetly in great Caesar's ear
For the repealing of my banish'd brother?

BRUTUS.   I kiss thy hand, but not in flattery, Caesar;
Desiring thee that Publius Cimber may
Have an immediate freedom of repeal.°

55   CAESAR.   What, Brutus?

CASSIUS.   Pardon, Caesar! Caesar,
pardon!
As low as to thy foot doth Cassius fall,
To beg enfranchisement° for Publius Cimber.

---

22   **constant**: calm.

28   **presently prefer**: immediately present.
29   **address'd**: ready.

33   **puissant**: powerful.

36–43   **These couchings . . . fawning:** This kneeling and humble behavior might influence ordinary men and turn laws and decisions that have been firmly established into the whims of children. But don't be foolish enough to think that Caesar's emotions are so out of control that he will be swayed from the proper course with compliments, bowing, and fawning like a dog.

46   **spurn thee . . . cur**: kick you like a dog.

47–48   **Know . . . satisfied**: Caesar is not unjust, nor will he grant a pardon without good reason.

54   **freedom of repeal**: permission to be recalled from exile.

57   **enfranchisement**: restoration of his rights as a citizen.

C   Literary Elements

CHARACTER How does Caesar's response to Artemidorus compare to his behavior in the previous acts? *(Caesar once again appears overly proud, as he has previously. He also shows a concern with the public perception of him.)*

D   Literary Elements

CHARACTER What does Cassius's reaction indicate about his personality? *(His panic seems to show that he is emotional instead of rational.)*

E   Active Reading

VISUALIZE Have students visualize the scene at the Capitol and describe it. What modern scene might it resemble? *(The scene is one of great activity and confusion, with Caesar at the center and many people trying to get his attention. It might be compared to a modern official being surrounded and questioned by members of the media.)*

F   Literary Elements

CHARACTER What traits does Caesar exhibit in his answer to Metellus's fawning attitude? *(He shows arrogance and pride in distinguishing himself from "ordinary men.")*

G   Active Reading

QUESTION Caesar refers to the request Metellus is making of him. Have students explain what it is. *(Caesar has banished Metellus's brother, and Metellus wants him recalled from exile.)*

MEETING INDIVIDUAL NEEDS — ENGLISH LANGUAGE LEARNERS

Elizabethan English Point out that one unusual feature of Shakespeare's English is word order. Although English language learners may not have difficulty understanding meaning in phrases with unusual word order, they should also recognize that Shakespeare's phrasing is not standard today.

Activity Have students revise the following sentences to reflect today's standard English. Point out that revision may require adding a helping verb such as *do*.
1. Delay not, Caesar, read it instantly.
2. What mean you, Caesar?

Additional Resources
📁 *English Language Learners Sourcebook*

FIGURES OF SPEECH: Simile Have students tell what Caesar compares himself to and what this shows about his character. *(He compares himself to the North Star, once again displaying his pride and arrogance. He also shows he is stubborn, unsympathetic, and unwilling to be moved by others.)*

I **Critical Thinking**

EVALUATING Have students discuss whether Shakespeare presents Caesar as an evil, ruthless tyrant who must be stopped at all costs, even assassination. Or does Shakespeare show Caesar as a flawed ruler who does not deserve the conspiracy against him? *(Many students will agree that the arrogance and strong will Caesar shows in the play do not seem to demand the conspirators' drastic measures.)*

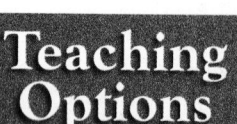

VIEWING THE PAINTING

Guillaume Lethière was a French painter who practiced the neoclassical style.

Viewing Response *The painting captures the panic and shock of the scene.*

Teaching Options

Death of Julius Caesar. Guillaume Lethière (1760–1832). Oil on paper, 47.5 x 71.5 cm. Private collection.

Viewing the painting: What emotions do you see expressed here? Do you think the same emotions are expressed in this scene? Explain.

	CAESAR. I could be well mov'd, if I were as you;
	If I could pray to move, prayers would move me;
60	But I am constant as the northern star,
	Of whose true-fix'd and resting quality
	There is no fellow in the firmament.°
	The skies are painted with unnumb'red sparks,
	They are all fire and every one doth shine;
65	But there's but one in all doth hold his place.
	So in the world: 'tis furnish'd well with men,
	And men are flesh and blood, and apprehensive;°
	Yet in the number I do know but one
	That unassailable holds on his rank,
70	Unshak'd of motion; and that I am he,
	Let me a little show it, even in this—
	That I was constant° Cimber should be banish'd,
	And constant do remain to keep him so.
	CINNA. O Caesar—
	CAESAR. Hence! Wilt thou lift up Olympus?°
75	**DECIUS.** Great Caesar—
	CAESAR. Doth not Brutus bootless° kneel?

62 no fellow in the firmament: no equal in the heavens. (Because the North Star appears directly above the North Pole, it seems to be stationary; the other stars seem to change position as the earth rotates.)

67 apprehensive: capable of reason.

72 constant: determined.

74 lift up Olympus: try to do the impossible. (Olympus is a mountain in Greece; in classical mythology, it was the home of the gods.)

75 bootless: in vain.

Writing *Minilesson*

Simile Julius Caesar says that he is as determined and unchanging as the North Star. Encourage students to think of people they know whom they might compare to an astronomical body.

Activity Have students write a paragraph or poem in which they compare themselves or someone they know to the sun, the moon, the earth or other planet, a star, a meteor, or any other heavenly body. Point out that they must make their comparisons as clear as Caesar does in his speech. **L2**

Additional Resources

▌ *Writer's Choice,* Lesson 5.2

CASCA. Speak hands for me!

[*They stab* CASEAR.]

CAESAR. *Et tu, Brute?°*—Then fall Caesar. [*Dies.*]

CINNA. Liberty! Freedom! Tyranny is dead!
Run hence, proclaim, cry it about the streets.

80 CASSIUS. Some to the common pulpits,° and cry out
"Liberty, freedom, and enfranchisement!"

BRUTUS. People, and senators, be not affrighted.
Fly not; stand still; ambition's debt is paid.°

CASCA. Go to the pulpit, Brutus.

DECIUS.   And Cassius too.

85 BRUTUS. Where's Publius?

CINNA. Here, quite confounded with this mutiny.°

METELLUS. Stand fast together, lest some friend of Caesar's
Should chance—

BRUTUS. Talk not of standing. Publius, good cheer,
90   There is no harm intended to your person,
Nor to no Roman else. So tell them, Publius.

CASSIUS. And leave us, Publius, lest that the people,
Rushing on us should do your age some mischief.

BRUTUS. Do so; and let no man abide° this deed,
95   But we the doers.

[*All but the* CONSPIRATORS *exit. Enter* TREBONIUS.]

CASSIUS. Where is Antony?

TREBONIUS.   Fled to his house amaz'd.°
Men, wives, and children stare, cry out and run,
As° it were doomsday.

BRUTUS.   Fates,° we will know your pleasures.
That we shall die, we know, 'tis but the time,
100   And drawing days out, that men stand upon.°

CASCA. Why, he that cuts off twenty years of life
Cuts off so many years of fearing death.

BRUTUS. Grant that, and then is death a benefit.
So are we Caesar's friends, that have abridg'd
105   His time of fearing death. Stoop, Romans, stoop,
And let us bathe our hands in Caesar's blood
Up to the elbows, and besmear our swords.
Then walk we forth, even to the marketplace,

JULIUS CAESAR, ACT 3, SCENE 1 ✦ 823

---

77 *Et tu, Brute?*: Latin for, "And you, Brutus?" (He is shocked that even Brutus would betray him.)

80 pulpits: platforms for public speaking.

83 ambition's debt is paid: Ambition received what was due to it.

86 confounded with this mutiny: confused by this uproar.

94 abide: pay the penalty for.

96 amaz'd: stunned.

98 As: as if.

98 Fates: in classical mythology, three goddesses who determined human destiny.

99–100 'tis but . . . upon: It is only the time of death and prolonging of life that men care about.

J Active Reading

RESPOND Have students describe their response to Caesar's dying words. *(Students may be moved by Caesar's shock and dismay that Brutus has betrayed him.)*

K Active Reading

REVIEW How do the conspirators differ in their immediate reactions to Caesar's murder? *(Cinna and Cassius feel triumphant and want to make their triumph public; Metellus is afraid a friend of Caesar's will seek revenge; Brutus's first impulse is to pacify the public and explain the deed.)*

L Active Reading

INTERPRET Ask students to interpret Brutus's remark, "So are we Caesar's friends, that have abridg'd his time of fearing death." Is his statement straightforward, ironic, or a rationalization? *(Students may argue that it is any of the above; judging by Brutus's desperate need to make his action seem righteous, a case could be made that he is rationalizing the murder.)*

REAL-WORLD CONNECTION

President Kennedy's Assassination
Trebonius says that in the aftermath of Caesar's assassination, "Men, wives, and children stare, cry out and run, as it were doomsday." Have students research the public reaction to the assassination of President Kennedy in 1963. Have them discuss similarities to the situation described by Trebonius. **L2**

M **Active Reading**

PREDICT Have students predict whether Cassius's prophecy of fame and glory for the conspirators will be true at the end of the play.

N **Literary Elements**

CHARACTER Mark Antony offers to follow Brutus if Brutus will explain why Caesar was killed. What character traits of Brutus prompt him to accept this offer? *(Brutus is trusting of Mark Antony and idealistic about his own motives for killing Caesar.)*

Vo•cab•u•lar•y Skills

Synonyms Mark Antony calls Brutus *valiant*. Brutus calls Antony *valiant* in return. The word *valiant* comes from the old French verb *valoir*, "to be of worth" and the Latin verb *valere*, "to be strong." Have students find at least three synonyms for *valiant*. *(courageous, brave, heroic, gallant, noble, chivalrous)*

JULIUS CAESAR

And waving our red weapons o'er our heads,
110　　Let's all cry "Peace, freedom, and liberty!"

CASSIUS. Stoop then, and wash. How many ages hence
　　Shall this our lofty scene be acted over
　　In states unborn and accents yet unknown!

BRUTUS. How many times shall Caesar bleed in sport,°
115　　That now on Pompey's basis° [lies] along
　　No worthier than the dust!

CASSIUS.　　　　　　　　So oft as that shall be,
　　So often shall the knot of us be call'd
　　The men that gave their country liberty.

DECIUS. What, shall we forth?

CASSIUS.　　　　　　　　Ay, every man away.
120　　Brutus shall lead, and we will grace his heels
　　With the most boldest and best hearts of Rome.

[Enter a SERVANT.]

BRUTUS. Soft, who comes here? A friend of Antony's.

SERVANT. Thus, Brutus, did my master bid me kneel;
　　Thus did Mark Antony bid me fall down;
125　　And, being prostrate, thus he bade me say;
　　Brutus is noble, wise, valiant, and honest;°
　　Caesar was mighty, bold, royal, and loving.
　　Say, I love Brutus, and I honor him;
　　Say, I fear'd Caesar, honor'd him, and lov'd him.
130　　If Brutus will vouchsafe° that Antony
　　May safely come to him, and be resolv'd°
　　How Caesar hath deserv'd to lie in death,
　　Mark Antony shall not love Caesar dead
　　So well as Brutus living; but will follow
135　　The fortunes and affairs of noble Brutus
　　Thorough the hazards of this untrod state°
　　With all true faith. So says my master Antony.

BRUTUS. Thy master is a wise and valiant Roman;
　　I never thought him worse.
140　　Tell him, so please him come unto this place,
　　He shall be satisfied and, by my honor,
　　Depart untouch'd.

SERVANT.　　　　　　I'll fetch him presently.° *[Exit SERVANT.]*

BRUTUS. I know that we shall have him well to friend.°

114 in sport: for entertainment. (These prophecies—of reenacting Caesar's assassination in countries not yet founded and in languages not yet known—are fulfilled by the performance of Shakespeare's play.)

115 Pompey's basis: the base of Pompey's statue.

126 honest: honorable.

130 vouchsafe: allow.

131 be resolv'd: receive a satisfactory explanation.

136 Thorough . . . state: through all the dangers of this new and uncertain state of affairs.

142 presently: immediately.

143 well to friend: as a good friend.

MEETING INDIVIDUAL NEEDS — INCLUSION STRATEGIES

Learning Disabled Have a volunteer read aloud lines 126–127 on page 824. Point out that although a list of words cannot truly characterize a person, the words have been chosen carefully to describe specific traits of each man.

Activity Have pairs of students choose four adjectives to describe another character in the play, such as Cassius, Mark Antony, or Portia. They may wish to consult a dictionary or thesaurus, but remind them that they need to double check words found in a thesaurus by looking their meanings up in a dictionary.

Additional Resources
📁 *Inclusion Strategies*

William Shakespeare ~

CASSIUS. I wish we may; but yet have I a mind
145   That fears him much; and my misgiving still
Falls shrewdly to the purpose.°

[Enter ANTONY.]

BRUTUS. But here comes Antony. Welcome, Mark Antony.

ANTONY. O mighty Caesar! dost thou lie so low?
Are all thy conquests, glories, triumphs, spoils,
150   Shrunk to this little measure? Fare thee well.
I know not, gentlemen, what you intend,
Who else must be let blood,° who else is rank.°
If I myself, there is no hour so fit
As Caesar's death's hour, nor no instrument
155   Of half that worth as those your swords, made rich
With the most noble blood of all this world.
I do beseech ye, if you bear me hard,°
Now, whilst your purpled° hands do reek and smoke,
Fulfill your pleasure. Live a thousand years,
160   I shall not find myself so apt° to die;
No place will please me so, no mean of death,°
As here by Caesar, and by you cut off,
The choice and master spirits of this age.

BRUTUS. O Antony! beg not your death of us.
165   Though now we must appear bloody and cruel,
As by our hands and this our present act
You see we do, yet see you but our hands
And this the bleeding business they have done.
Our hearts you see not, they are pitiful;°
170   And pity to the general wrong of Rome—
As fire drives out fire, so pity pity—
Hath done this deed on Caesar.° For your part,
To you our swords have leaden° points, Mark Antony;
Our arms in strength of malice,° and our hearts
175   Of brothers' temper, do receive you in
With all kind love, good thoughts, and reverence.

CASSIUS. Your voice shall be as strong as any man's
In the disposing of new dignities.°

BRUTUS. Only be patient till we have appeas'd
180   The multitude, beside themselves with fear,
And then we will deliver you the cause°
Why I, that did love Caesar when I struck him,
Have thus proceeded.

Side notes

145–146 **my misgiving . . . purpose:** My suspicions always turn out to be close to the truth.

152 **let blood:** killed. **rank:** swollen with disease. In Antony's metaphor, political corruption is like a disease that must be treated by drawing blood from the patient.

157 **bear me hard:** have a grudge against me.
158 **purpled:** blood-stained.

160 **apt:** ready.

161 **mean of death:** way of dying.

169 **pitiful:** full of pity.

170–172 **And pity . . . Caesar:** Brutus says that just as one fire can extinguish another, their pity for Rome overcame their pity for Caesar.
173 **leaden:** blunt.
174 **Our arms . . . malice:** our arms seemingly full of malice (because still blood-stained).
177–178 **Your voice . . . dignities:** You will have equal say in deciding who will hold political office.

181 **deliver you the cause:** explain.

Margin teacher notes

O Active Reading — PREDICT Brutus and Cassius disagree about whether or not Mark Antony is truly a friend. Have students predict which character is right about Antony.

P Literary Elements — CHARACTER Point out that this is the first long speech by Mark Antony. What do students learn about him from the style and content of the speech? *(He is loyal, loving, and emotional in his grief over Caesar. He also shows loyalty and grief, as well as courage, in his willingness to submit to death at the conspirators' hands.)*

Q Literary Elements — IMAGERY Have a volunteer read aloud line 158 of Antony's speech: "Now, whilst your purpled hands do reek and smoke." How do they help characterize the assassins' deed? *(The vivid adjective and verbs emphasize the ugly, shocking murder.)*

R Active Reading — INTERPRET Have students describe the feelings Brutus expresses toward Antony. Do the other conspirators share these feelings? *(Brutus is warm and friendly to Antony; he trusts that Antony will agree with the assassins' act when he understands the reasons for it. It is clear from the conspirators' meeting in act 2 and Cassius's comment in lines 144–146 in act 3 that others do not have the same feelings for Antony.)*

JULIUS CAESAR

ANTONY.   I doubt not of your wisdom.
      Let each man render me his bloody hand.
185   First, Marcus Brutus, will I shake with you;
      Next, Caius Cassius, do I take your hand;
      Now, Decius Brutus, yours; now yours, Metellus;
      Yours, Cinna; and, my valiant Casca, yours;
      Though last, not least in love, yours, good Trebonius.
190   Gentlemen all—alas, what shall I say?
      My credit° now stands on such slippery ground
      That one of two bad ways you must conceit° me,
      Either a coward or a flatterer.
      That I did love thee, Caesar, O, 'tis true;
195   If then thy spirit look upon us now,
      Shall it not grieve thee dearer than thy death,
      To see thy Antony making his peace,
      Shaking the bloody fingers of thy foes,
      Most noble, in the presence of thy corse?°
200   Had I as many eyes as thou hast wounds,
      Weeping as fast as they stream forth thy blood,
      It would become me better than to close°
      In terms of friendship with thine enemies.
      Pardon me, Julius! Here wast thou bay'd,° brave hart,°
205   Here didst thou fall, and here thy hunters stand,
      Sign'd in thy spoil,° and crimson'd in thy lethe.°
      O world! thou wast the forest to this hart,
      And this indeed, O world, the heart of thee.
      How like a deer, strooken by many princes,
210   Dost thou here lie!

CASSIUS. Mark Antony—

ANTONY.   Pardon me, Caius Cassius!
      The enemies of Caesar shall say this:
      Then, in a friend, it is cold modesty.°

CASSIUS. I blame you not for praising Caesar so,
215   But what compact mean you to have with us?
      Will you be prick'd° in number of our friends,
      Or shall we on,° and not depend on you?

ANTONY. Therefore I took your hands, but was indeed
      Sway'd from the point by looking down on Caesar.
220   Friends am I with you all, and love you all,
      Upon this hope, that you shall give me reasons
      Why, and wherein,° Caesar was dangerous.

191 credit: reputation (because he was Caesar's friend).
192 conceit: judge, consider.

199 corse: corpse.

202 close: come to an agreement.

204 bay'd: cornered like a hunted animal. **hart:** male deer. Antony plays on the words *hart* and *heart* later in this speech.
206 Sign'd in thy spoil: marked with your slaughter. **lethe:** bloodstream. (In classical mythology, Lethe was a river in Hades, the underworld.)

213 modesty: restraint.

216 prick'd: marked down; counted.
217 on: proceed.

222 wherein: in what way.

Bedroom from the villa of P. Fannius Sinistor (detail of west wall). 1st century B.C., Roman. Fresco on lime plaster, height: (average) 8 ft. The Metropolitan Museum of Art, New York. Rogers Fund, 1903. 03.14.13.

Viewing the art: Do the details in this fresco reinforce or alter the images you have developed of Brutus's and Caesar's homes? Explain.

Many wealthy Romans owned villas, fabulous country homes where they could retreat from city life.

Viewing Response *The details may reinforce impressions of wealth and splendor.*

INTERDISCIPLINARY CONNECTION

Art History The Romans borrowed many features of Greek architecture such as columns and the portico (a sort of covered porch or walkway). Their important architectural innovations were arches and concrete. These enabled the Romans to build huge buildings such as public baths and amphitheaters and other structures such as bridges.

Activity Have students research an ancient Roman architectural accomplishment such as the Coliseum, the Forum, the aqueduct system, or the Pantheon. Have them report on their topic orally or in a written report, including illustrations. **L2**

U Active Reading

INTERPRET Have students interpret Brutus's statement in line 223. *(He says that if there were not a good reason for murdering Caesar, the act would have to be considered savage. He is sure that there was a good reason, and he assumes that Antony will agree with him.)*

V Active Reading

QUESTION What is Cassius's objection to Antony's speaking at Caesar's funeral? *(He is afraid Antony will arouse emotion in the Roman citizens.)*

W Active Reading

REVIEW Brutus compromises between his belief that Antony will do no damage by speaking at Caesar's funeral and Cassius's belief that this is not a wise idea. Have students summarize his compromise. *(Brutus says he will speak first and explain the reasons why Caesar was killed, and he stipulates that Antony must not blame Brutus and the other conspirators in his speech.)*

X Author's Craft

DICTION Shakespeare has Antony use the word *butchers* in reference to the conspirators. Ask students to describe the effect of this word choice and to recall another significant use of the word in the play. *(The word has a negative connotation and emphasizes the brutal nature of the crime. It was previously used by Brutus in act 2, scene 1, line 166: "Let's be sacrificers, but not butchers, Caius.")*

U BRUTUS. Or else were this a savage spectacle.
Our reasons are so full of good regard°
225 That were you, Antony, the son of Caesar,
You should be satisfied.

ANTONY. That's all I seek;
And am moreover suitor° that I may
Produce° his body to the marketplace,
And in the pulpit, as becomes a friend,
230 Speak in the order° of his funeral.

BRUTUS. You shall, Mark Antony.

CASSIUS. Brutus, a word with you.
[*Aside to* BRUTUS.] You know not what you do. Do not consent
That Antony speak in his funeral.
Know you how much the people may be mov'd
235 By that which he will utter?

BRUTUS. By your pardon—
I will myself into the pulpit first,
And show the reason of our Caesar's death.
What Antony shall speak, I will protest°
He speaks by leave and by permission;
240 And that we are contented Caesar shall
Have all true rites and lawful ceremonies.
It shall advantage° more than do us wrong.

CASSIUS. I know not what may fall,° I like it not.

BRUTUS. Mark Antony, here, take you Caesar's body.
245 You shall not in your funeral speech blame us,
But speak all good you can devise of Caesar,
And say you do't by our permission;
Else shall you not have any hand at all
About his funeral. And you shall speak
250 In the same pulpit whereto I am going,
After my speech is ended.

ANTONY. Be it so;
I do desire no more.

BRUTUS. Prepare the body then, and follow us.
[*They exit.* ANTONY *remains.*]

ANTONY. O pardon me, thou bleeding piece of earth,
255 That I am meek and gentle with these butchers! **Y**
Thou art the ruins of the noblest man

224 **good regard:** sound considerations.

227 **am moreover suitor:** furthermore I ask.

228 **Produce:** bring forth.

230 **order:** ceremony.

238 **protest:** declare.

242 **advantage:** benefit.

243 **fall:** happen.

828 ❧ UNIT 4: DRAMA

Teaching Options

MEETING INDIVIDUAL NEEDS — MULTIPLE LEARNING STYLES

Musical Point out that music is often used on stage and on film to accompany dramatic productions. It can add to the mood and heighten the drama of a play.

Activity Challenge students to find recorded music to accompany an important scene of the play. Have students play the music in class as they read the scene. Then they may explain the reasoning behind their choice. **L2**

That ever lived in the tide of times.°
Woe to the hand that shed this costly blood!
Over thy wounds now do I prophesy

260 (Which like dumb mouths do ope their ruby lips
To beg the voice and utterance of my tongue)
A curse shall light° upon the limbs of men;
Domestic fury and fierce civil strife
Shall cumber° all the parts of Italy;

265 Blood and destruction shall be so in use,°
And dreadful objects so familiar,
That mothers shall but smile when they behold
Their infants quartered° with the hands of war;
All pity chok'd with custom of fell deeds;°

270 And Caesar's spirit, ranging° for revenge,
With Ate° by his side come hot from hell,
Shall in these confines with a monarch's voice
Cry "Havoc!"° and let slip the dogs of war,
That this foul deed shall smell above the earth

275 With carrion° men, groaning for burial.

[Enter Octavius's SERVANT.]

You serve Octavius Caesar, do you not?

SERVANT. I do, Mark Antony.

ANTONY. Caesar did write for him to come to Rome.

SERVANT. He did receive his letters and is coming,

280 And bid me say to you by word of mouth—
[Seeing the body.] O Caesar!—

ANTONY. Thy heart is big;° get thee apart and weep.
Passion, I see, is catching, [for] mine eyes,
Seeing those beads of sorrow stand in thine,

285 Began to water. Is thy master coming?

SERVANT. He lies tonight within seven leagues° of Rome.

ANTONY. Post° back with speed, and tell him what hath chanc'd.
Here is a mourning Rome, a dangerous Rome,
No Rome of safety for Octavius yet;

290 Hie hence,° and tell him so. Yet stay awhile,
Thou shalt not back till I have borne this corse
Into the marketplace. There shall I try,°
In my oration, how the people take
The cruel issue° of these bloody men,

295 According to the which thou shalt discourse

257 the tide of times: all of history.

262 light: fall.

264 cumber: burden; harass.
265 in use: common.

268 quartered: cut to pieces.
269 custom of fell deeds: familiarity with cruel deeds.
270 ranging: roving (like an animal in search of prey).
271 Ate: goddess of vengeance and strife.
273 Havoc: a battle cry to kill without mercy. (Only a king could give this order.)
275 carrion: dead and rotting.

282 big: swollen with grief.

286 seven leagues: twenty-one miles.

287 Post: Ride back quickly.

290 Hie hence: Go quickly from here.

292 try: test.

294 cruel issue: outcome of cruelty.

Y Literary Elements

SOLILOQUY Remind students that in a soliloquy a character appears on stage alone and expresses his or her true feelings. With the use of a soliloquy, Shakespeare is able for the first time to show Antony's true feelings about the conspirators and the murder they committed. Have students summarize them. *(He is furious and willing to make Rome and its citizens suffer to see that the conspirators are punished.)*

Z Author's Craft

DICTION and IMAGERY What is the effect of the words and images Shakespeare uses in Antony's speech? *(Words such as curse, fury, fierce, and hell communicate intense anger. The images of "infants quartered with hands of war" and "this foul deed . . . groaning for burial" are shocking and horrendous.)*

AA Active Reading

QUESTION Why does Antony want Octavius's servant to wait a while before returning to his master? *(He wants to take Caesar's corpse into the marketplace and see the people's response so that the servant can tell Octavius of it.)*

INTERDISCIPLINARY CONNECTION

Social Studies Octavius's servant has ridden "seven leagues," or 21 miles, to deliver Octavius's message to Antony. One great accomplishment of the ancient Romans was an excellent system of roads.

Activity Have students research the ancient Roman highway system. Have them find out how the roads were constructed, who built them, and where they were constructed. **L2**

To young Octavius of the state of things.
Lend me your hand.

[*They exit (with* CAESAR's *body*).]

SCENE 2. The Roman Forum, the city's great public square. A few days later.

[*Enter* BRUTUS *and* CASSIUS *with the* PLEBEIANS.]

 PLEBEIANS. We will be satisfied!° Let us be satisfied!

 BRUTUS. Then follow me, and give me audience, friends.
  Cassius, go you into the other street,
  And part the numbers.°
5 Those that will hear me speak, let 'em stay here;
  Those that will follow Cassius, go with him;
  And public reasons shall be rendered°
  Of Caesar's death.

 FIRST PLEBEIAN. I will hear Brutus speak.

 SECOND PLEBEIAN. I will hear Cassius, and compare
  their reasons,
10 When severally° we hear them rendered.

[*Exit* CASSIUS *with some of the* PLEBEIANS. BRUTUS *goes into the pulpit.*]

 THIRD PLEBEIAN. The noble Brutus is ascended; silence!

 BRUTUS. Be patient till the last.°
  Romans, countrymen, and lovers,° hear me for my cause,
  and be silent, that you may hear. Believe me for mine
15 honor, and have respect to mine honor,° that you may
  believe. Censure° me in your wisdom, and awake your
  senses,° that you may the better judge. If there be any in
  this assembly, any dear friend of Caesar's, to him I say, that
  Brutus' love to Caesar was no less than his. If then that
20 friend demand why Brutus rose against Caesar, this is my
  answer; Not that I lov'd Caesar less, but that I lov'd Rome
  more. Had you rather Caesar were living, and die all slaves,
  than that Caesar were dead, to live all free men? As Caesar
  lov'd me, I weep for him; as he was fortunate, I rejoice at it;
25 as he was valiant, I honor him; but, as he was ambitious, I
  slew him. There is tears for his love; joy for his fortune;
  honor for his valor; and death for his ambition. Who is
  here so base that would be a bondman?° If any, speak, for
  him have I offended. Who is here so rude,° that would not
30 be a Roman? If any, speak, for him have I offended. Who

**Side notes (right column):**

1 **satisfied:** The common people (plebeians) demand a full explanation of the assassination.

4 **part the numbers:** divide the crowd.

7 **rendered:** presented.

10 **severally:** separately.

12 **last:** end of the speech.
13 **lovers:** dear friends.

15 **have respect . . . honor:** remember that I am honorable.
16 **Censure:** judge.
17 **senses:** reason.

28 **bondman:** slave.
29 **rude:** uncivilized.

Language Note

Plebeian is a Latin word meaning "common people." Forms of it are used today in the word *plebe*, a freshman at a military or naval academy, and in the word *plebiscite*, a special vote by all the people of a country or district for a ruler or a proposal.

BB **Literary Elements**

PROSE Point out that Brutus's speech is written in prose. Have students explain how this form differs from blank verse. *(Prose is written in sentences and paragraphs with no regular rhythm. Blank verse is written with line divisions and in a pattern of stressed and unstressed syllables.)*

CC **Literary Elements**

TONE Ask students to identify the tone of Brutus's speech to the people. How would they respond to such a speech by a leader? *(The tone is reasonable and unemotional; once again Brutus seems to be rationalizing his decision to murder Caesar. Some students may say they would not be won over by such a speech; others, like the Romans who speak, would be impressed.)*

Teaching Options

MEETING INDIVIDUAL NEEDS **MULTIPLE LEARNING STYLES**

Spatial The Forum was the section of ancient Rome that served as its center of law and government. It included the Senate House, temples, and Hall of Records. The Forum existed in this form from the mid-100s B.C. until after the fall of Rome in A.D. 476. Today the ruins of the Forum's buildings still stand in Rome.

Activity Have students research the Forum and make a diagram or drawing indicating the locations and identities of its buildings. Other students may wish to research the excavation of the Forum in modern times and the building parts that were recovered. **L2**

Edmund Kean as Brutus, 1819. James Northcote. Oil on canvas, 236.5 x 145 cm.

Viewing the painting: What, do you think, is Brutus thinking about? Why do you think so?

EE Critical Thinking

DRAWING CONCLUSIONS At the end of his speech, Brutus asks, "Who is here so vile that will not love his country?" What is he implying? Is this a valid conclusion? *(He says that killing Caesar was a patriotic act; anyone who objects is unpatriotic. It is not a valid conclusion because the premise is not proven.)*

FF Active Reading

INTERPRET Have students describe how the people react to Brutus's speech and explain why they think they react in this way. *(The people are apparently satisfied with Brutus's explanation of Caesar's murder. They are emotionally moved by his speech and want to crown him in Caesar's place. Students may say they react in this way because Brutus speaks well and seems honest or because the people are impressionable and ready to follow anyone with leadership qualities.)*

GG Literary Elements

PROSE Brutus begins speaking to the people again, but what is different about his speech this time? *(This speech is in verse. His previous speech was in prose.)* Point out that all of Brutus's lines are in verse, except for his funeral speech. Have students consider why Shakespeare did that.

JULIUS CAESAR

is here so vile that will not love his country? If any, speak, **EE** for him have I offended. I pause for a reply.

ALL. None, Brutus, none.

35 **BRUTUS.** Then none have I offended. I have done no more to Caesar than you shall do to Brutus. The question of his death is enroll'd in the Capitol;° his glory not extenuated,° wherein he was worthy; nor his offenses enforc'd,° for which he suffer'd death.

CC [*Enter* MARK ANTONY (*and others*) *with* CAESAR'S *body.*]

40 Here comes his body, mourn'd by Mark Antony, who, though he had no hand in his death, shall receive the benefit of his dying, a place in the commonwealth,° as which of you shall not? With this I depart, that, as I slew my best lover for the good of Rome, I have the same dagger for myself, when it shall please my country to need my death.

45 **ALL.** Live, Brutus, live, live!

FIRST PLEBEIAN. Bring him with triumph home unto his house.

SECOND PLEBEIAN. Give him a statue with his ancestors.

THIRD PLEBEIAN. Let him be Caesar.

FOURTH PLEBEIAN.   Caesar's better parts°
Shall be crown'd in Brutus.

FIRST PLEBEIAN.   We'll bring him to his house
50 With shouts and clamors.

BRUTUS.   My countrymen—

SECOND PLEBEIAN. Peace, silence! Brutus speaks.

FIRST PLEBEIAN. Peace, ho!

BRUTUS. Good countrymen, let me depart alone,
And, for my sake, stay here with Antony.
55 Do grace to Caesar's corpse, and grace his speech
Tending to Caesar's glories,° which Mark Antony
(By our permission) is allow'd to make.
I do entreat you, not a man depart,
Save I alone, till Antony have spoke.

60 **FIRST PLEBEIAN.** Stay, ho, and let us hear Mark Antony.

THIRD PLEBEIAN. Let him go up into the public chair;°
We'll hear him. Noble Antony, go up.

ANTONY. For Brutus' sake, I am beholding° to you.

[*Goes into the pulpit.*]

35–36 The question . . . Capitol: The reasons for his death are recorded in the public archives of the Capitol.

37 extenuated: diminished.

38 enforc'd: exaggerated.

41 a place in the commonwealth: citizenship in a free republic.

48 parts: qualities.

55–56 Do grace . . . glories: Pay respect to Caesar's body and listen respectfully to Antony's speech dealing with Caesar's glories.

61 public chair: pulpit.

63 beholding: indebted.

Political Speeches In act 3, Brutus and Antony give important political speeches that evoke a strong response in their audience.

Activity Have students research a famous political speech or speaker. Speakers they may want to focus on include Abraham Lincoln, Franklin Roosevelt, Winston Churchill, Martin Luther King, Jr., and John F. Kennedy. Encourage students to find information on the speaker's style and content and the historical events for which they made their famous speeches. Also urge them to find excerpts or quotes from important speeches. **L2**

William Shakespeare

FOURTH PLEBEIAN.   What does he say of Brutus?

THIRD PLEBEIAN.   He says, for Brutus' sake,

65   He finds himself beholding to us all.

FOURTH PLEBEIAN.   'Twere best he speak no harm of Brutus
        here!

FIRST PLEBEIAN.   This Caesar was a tyrant.

THIRD PLEBEIAN.   Nay, that's certain.
        We are blest that Rome is rid of him.

SECOND PLEBEIAN.   Peace, let us hear what Antony can say.

70   **ANTONY.**   You gentle Romans—

[*The noise continues.*]

        ALL.   Peace, ho, let us hear him.

        ANTONY.   Friends, Romans, countrymen, lend me your ears!
            I come to bury Caesar, not to praise him.
            The evil that men do lives after them,
            The good is oft interred° with their bones;
75   So let it be with Caesar. The noble Brutus
            Hath told you Caesar was ambitious;
            If it were so, it was a grievous fault,
            And grievously hath Caesar answer'd° it.
            Here, under leave° of Brutus and the rest
80   (For Brutus is an honorable man,
            So are they all, all honorable men),
            Come I to speak in Caesar's funeral.
            He was my friend, faithful and just to me;
            But Brutus says he was ambitious,
85   And Brutus is an honorable man.
            He hath brought many captives home to Rome,
            Whose ransoms did the general coffers° fill;
            Did this in Caesar seem ambitious?
            When that the poor have cried, Caesar hath wept;
90   Ambition should be made of sterner stuff:
            Yet Brutus says he was ambitious;
            And Brutus is an honorable man.
            You all did see that on the Lupercal°
            I thrice presented him a kingly crown,
95   Which he did thrice refuse.° Was this ambition?
            Yet Brutus says he was ambitious;
            And sure he is an honorable man.
            I speak not to disprove what Brutus spoke,
            But here I am to speak what I do know.

74 interred: buried.

78 answer'd: paid the penalty for.
79 leave: permission.

87 general coffers: public treasury.

93 Lupercal: See act 1, scene 1, line 67.

95 Which he . . . refuse: the incident described by Casca in act 1, scene 2, lines 234–242.

Critical Thinking

INFERRING The following model can help students make inferences from the language used in Antony's speech.

Model: In his speech, Antony pretends to support Brutus while actually raising doubts about his character. Toward the end of the speech, Antony says that judgment has "fled to brutish beasts." The word *brutish* sounds a lot like Brutus. Listeners would probably make this connection consciously or subconsciously. I think Antony is using this negative word to purposely remind his audience of Brutus's participation in the murder of Caesar.

Author's Craft

CHARACTERIZATION What character traits are evident in the plebeians? *(Shakespeare characterizes them as emotional, sympathetic, and easily swayed.)*

---

100 You all did love him once, not without cause;
What cause withholds you then to mourn for him?
O judgment, thou art fled to brutish beasts,
And men have lost their reason. Bear with me,
My heart is in the coffin there with Caesar,
105 And I must pause till it come back to me.

FIRST PLEBEIAN. Methinks there is much reason in his sayings.

SECOND PLEBEIAN. If thou consider rightly of the matter,
Caesar has had great wrong.

THIRD PLEBEIAN. Has he, masters?
I fear there will a worse come in his place.

110 **FOURTH PLEBEIAN.** Mark'd ye° his words? He would not take the crown,
Therefore, 'tis certain he was not ambitious.

FIRST PLEBEIAN. If it be found so, some will dear abide it.°

SECOND PLEBEIAN. Poor soul, his eyes are red as fire with weeping.

THIRD PLEBEIAN. There's not a nobler man in Rome than Antony.

115 **FOURTH PLEBEIAN.** Now mark him, he begins again to speak.

ANTONY. But yesterday the word of Caesar might
Have stood against the world; now lies he there,
And none so poor to do him reverence.°
O masters! if I were dispos'd to stir
120 Your hearts and minds to mutiny and rage,
I should do Brutus wrong and Cassius wrong,
Who (you all know) are honorable men.
I will not do them wrong; I rather choose
To wrong the dead, to wrong myself and you,
125 Than I will wrong such honorable men.
But here's a parchment with the seal of Caesar;
I found it in his closet, 'tis his will.
Let but the commons° hear this testament—
Which, pardon me, I do not mean to read—
130 And they would go and kiss dead Caesar's wounds,
And dip their napkins° in his sacred blood;
Yea, beg a hair of him for memory,
And dying, mention it within their wills,
Bequeathing it as a rich legacy
135 Unto their issue.°

110 Mark'd ye: Did you listen to?

112 dear abide it: pay dearly for it.

118 none . . . reverence: No one is humble enough to honor him.

128 commons: common people.

131 napkins: handkerchiefs. (Antony refers to the custom of dipping cloths in the blood of martyrs.)

135 issue: children.

Teaching Options

MEETING INDIVIDUAL NEEDS

GIFTED AND TALENTED

The Art of Rhetoric The main subject of higher education in ancient Rome was *rhetoric*, the art of speaking and persuasion. Mark Antony proves to be skilled in both disciplines. Upper-class men studied rhetoric in order to enter law or politics.

Activity Have students research the history of rhetoric in ancient Greece and Rome. Have them find out about the people who influenced the art and the guidelines they created. Have them share their findings with the class in oral reports or in multimedia presentations. **L3**

FOURTH PLEBEIAN. We'll hear the will; read it, Mark Antony.

ALL. The will, the will! we will hear Caesar's will!

ANTONY. Have patience, gentle friends, I must not read it.
140   It is not meet° you know how Caesar lov'd you:
      You are not wood, you are not stones, but men;
      And being men, hearing the will of Caesar,
      It will inflame you, it will make you mad.
      'Tis good you know not that you are his heirs,
      For if you should, O, what would come of it?

145   **FOURTH PLEBEIAN.** Read the will, we'll hear it, Antony.
      You shall read us the will, Caesar's will.

ANTONY. Will you be patient? Will you stay awhile?
      I have o'ershot myself° to tell you of it.
      I fear I wrong the honorable men
150   Whose daggers have stabb'd Caesar; I do fear it.

FOURTH PLEBEIAN. They were traitors; honorable men!

ALL. The will! the testament!

SECOND PLEBEIAN. They were villains, murderers. The will,
      read the will!

ANTONY. You will compel me then to read the will?
155   Then make a ring about the corpse of Caesar,
      And let me show you him that made the will.
      Shall I descend? And will you give me leave?

ALL. Come down.

SECOND PLEBEIAN. Descend.

160   **THIRD PLEBEIAN.** You shall have leave.

[ANTONY *comes down from the pulpit.*]

FOURTH PLEBEIAN. A ring, stand round.

FIRST PLEBEIAN. Stand from the hearse, stand from the body.

SECOND PLEBEIAN. Room for Antony, most noble Antony.

ANTONY. Nay, press not so upon me; stand far° off.

165   **ALL.** Stand back; room, bear back.

ANTONY. If you have tears, prepare to shed them now.
      You all do know this mantle.° I remember
      The first time ever Caesar put it on;
      'Twas on a summer's evening, in his tent,
170   That day he overcame the Nervii.°
      Look, in this place ran Cassius' dagger through;

139 meet: proper.

148 o'ershot myself: gone further than I intended.

The Artemision with Artemis Ephesia. A.D. 117, Roman. Silver, diameter: 2.7 cm. Kunsthistorisches Museum, Muenzkabinett, Vienna, Austria.

164 far: farther.

167 mantle: cloak, toga.

170 Nervii: a fierce Gallic tribe defeated by Caesar in 57 B.C.

Active Reading

QUESTION How does Antony treat the common people? Is it effective? *(Antony treats the people respectfully and kindly and flatters them: "You are not wood, you are not stones, but men." Remember, Murellus called the people "You blocks, you stones, you worse than senseless things!" in act 1, scene 1. Antony's treatment is effective; the people are solidly on his side.)*

Critical Thinking

ANALYZING ARGUMENTS Have students describe the techniques Antony uses to gain the support of the people. *(He pretends that he does not want the people to know what was in Caesar's will; he predicts that they will be angered by what they hear; he plays on their emotions by having them look at Caesar's corpse; he points out each stab wound and tells which conspirator made it. His argument is based largely on emotional appeal.)*

MEETING INDIVIDUAL NEEDS — INCLUSION STRATEGIES

Less-Proficient Readers Role-plays may help students understand Antony's clever manipulation of the people.

Activity Have students work in pairs. Partners are to pretend that each must convince the other to help him or her spend the next Saturday volunteering to clean the school. Suggest that students try any of the following techniques:

1. flattery, 2. bandwagon, 3. authority, 4. sincerity, 5. trickery, 6. emotion

After students have taken turns using various persuasive techniques, have them discuss which were most and least effective. **L2** **COLLAB. LEARN.**

Additional Resources
📁 *Inclusion Strategies*

VIEWING THE ART

Knowing that his audience will react with shock and dismay, Mark Antony flings back Caesar's mantle to reveal his stabbed and bloody body. Two men react with shock and dismay.

Responding to the Art *The art may accurately depict Antony uncovering Caesar's mutilated body. He seems angry in the painting and the crowd seems appropriately shocked.*

Mark Antony's funeral oration over the corpse of Caesar.

Viewing the art: How does the scene depicted here differ from events in the play? How is it the same?

836 🐾 UNIT 4: DRAMA

Teaching Options

Reading *Minilesson*

Identifying Main Idea and Supporting Details Point out that in their respective funeral speeches, Brutus and Antony each have one or more main points to make about Caesar and his murder.

Activity Have students state one main idea of each speech. Then have them state the details that each man uses to support that idea. Point out that the main idea may not always be stated by the speaker. For example, one of Antony's points is that Caesar was a great leader, which he never explicitly states. You may wish to have half the students work on one speech and half on the other. Then volunteers can write their main ideas and supporting details on the board. **L2**

Additional Resources

📁 *Reading Workbook*

Literary Elements

FIGURES OF SPEECH: *Personification*
Have a volunteer reread lines 172–177 and identify the figure of speech used. *(personification)* Ask students what human qualities are attributed to the wound. *(It is treated as Brutus's neighbor who answered a knock at the door.)* Ask students what kind of neighbor Shakespeare calls Brutus. *(an unkind one)*

Active Reading

REVIEW According to Antony, why was Brutus's "the unkindest cut of all"? *(Antony says Caesar dearly loved Brutus, and his betrayal broke Caesar's heart.)*

175   See what a rent° the envious Casca made;
Through this the well-beloved Brutus stabb'd,
And as he pluck'd his cursed steel away,
Mark how the blood of Caesar followed it,
As rushing out of doors, to be resolv'd
If Brutus so unkindly knock'd or no;°
For Brutus, as you know, was Caesar's angel.°
Judge, O you gods, how dearly Caesar lov'd him!
180   This was the most unkindest cut of all;
For when the noble Caesar saw him stab,
Ingratitude, more strong than traitors' arms,
Quite vanquish'd him. Then burst his mighty heart,
And, in his mantle muffling up his face,
185   Even at the base of Pompey's statue
(Which all the while ran blood) great Caesar fell.
O, what a fall was there, my countrymen!
Then I, and you, and all of us fell down,
Whilst bloody treason flourish'd° over us.
190   O now you weep, and I perceive you feel
The dint° of pity. These are gracious drops.
Kind souls, what weep you when you but behold
Our Caesar's vesture wounded? Look you here, [*Lifting*
     CAESAR's *mantle*.]
Here is himself, marr'd as you see with traitors.°

195   **FIRST PLEBEIAN.** O piteous spectacle!

    SECOND PLEBEIAN. O noble Caesar!

    THIRD PLEBEIAN. O woeful day!

    FOURTH PLEBEIAN. O traitors, villains!

    FIRST PLEBEIAN. O most bloody sight!

200   **SECOND PLEBEIAN.** We will be reveng'd.

    ALL. Revenge! About! Seek! Burn! Fire! Kill! Slay!
Let not a traitor live!

    ANTONY. Stay, countrymen.

    FIRST PLEBEIAN. Peace there, hear the noble Antony.

205   **SECOND PLEBEIAN.** We'll hear him, we'll follow him, we'll die
with him.

    ANTONY. Good friends, sweet friends, let me not stir you up
To such a sudden flood of mutiny.
They that have done this deed are honorable.
What private griefs° they have, alas, I know not,

172 rent: rip.

176–177 As rushing . . . no: as if rushing outside to learn for certain whether or not Brutus so cruelly and unnaturally "knocked."
178 angel: favorite.

189 flourish'd: swaggered.

191 dint: force; blow.

192–194 Kind souls . . . traitors: In a dramatic gesture, Antony uncovers Caesar's mutilated body after remarking how much the commoners weep when they gaze merely upon Caesar's mutilated clothing.

209 private griefs: personal grievances. Antony suggests that the conspirators killed Caesar not for the public reasons Brutus has declared but rather for personal, and therefore less worthy, motives.

Listening and Speaking *Minilesson*

Discussing Antony's Ideas In Antony's funeral speech, lines 73–74, he says, "The evil that men do lives after them, the good is oft interred with their bones." Encourage students to consider this idea.

Activity Have students hold group discussions about Antony's statement, using examples of famous people from history to support their viewpoints. Have them think of people who are known for good and for evil. Encourage them to consider whether a person's evil deeds will overshadow his or her good ones and whether human nature makes people more likely to dwell on a person's evil than on his or her good. Is history always fair to the reputations of past leaders? **L2** **COLLAB. LEARN.**

Teaching Options

QQ Literary Elements

IRONY Remind students that ironic statements are ones that state the opposite of the truth. Have students discuss Antony's use of irony in his speech, lines 206–226. What is ironic about his statements, and for what purpose is he making these statements? (*Antony says he does not want to stir the people to mutiny or to affect them emotionally; he says he is not a talented speaker as Brutus is. The opposite of these statements is true. His irony is part of his manipulation of the people; he wants them to think he is a simple man with no hidden motives.*)

RR Author's Craft

ALLITERATION Have students read line 217 aloud and identify the sound device Shakespeare uses. (*alliteration*) Have them describe its effect in the speech. (*It calls attention to Antony's skill with words, which, ironically, he is denying.*)

SS Literary Elements

FIGURES OF SPEECH: *Metaphor* Have students identify the two things being compared in lines 221–222. (*Antony says Caesar's stab wounds are like mouths that can speak of the treachery of Brutus and the other conspirators.*)

210
That made them do it. They are wise and honorable,
And will, no doubt, with reasons answer you.
I come not, friends, to steal away your hearts.
I am no orator, as Brutus is;
But (as you know me all) a plain blunt man
215
That love my friend, and that they know full well
That gave me public leave to speak of him.
For I have neither wit, nor words, nor worth,
Action, nor utterance, nor the power of speech
To stir men's blood;° I only speak right on.
220
I tell you that which you yourselves do know,
Show you sweet Caesar's wounds, poor, poor, dumb mouths,
And bid them speak for me. But were I Brutus,
And Brutus Antony, there were an Antony
Would ruffle up° your spirits, and put a tongue
225
In every wound of Caesar, that should move
The stones of Rome to rise and mutiny.

ALL. We'll mutiny.

FIRST PLEBEIAN.   We'll burn the house of Brutus.

THIRD PLEBEIAN. Away then, come, seek the conspirators.

ANTONY. Yet hear me, countrymen, yet hear me speak.

230
ALL. Peace, ho, hear Antony, most noble Antony!

ANTONY. Why, friends, you go to do you know not what.
Wherein hath Caesar thus deserv'd your loves?
Alas, you know not! I must tell you then;
You have forgot the will I told you of.

235
ALL. Most true. The will! Let's stay and hear the will.

ANTONY. Here is the will, and under Caesar's seal:
To every Roman citizen he gives,
To every several° man, seventy-five drachmas.°

SECOND PLEBEIAN. Most noble Caesar! we'll revenge his death!

240
THIRD PLEBEIAN. O royal° Caesar!

ANTONY. Hear me with patience.

ALL. Peace, ho!

ANTONY. Moreover, he hath left you all his walks,
His private arbors and new-planted orchards,°
245
On this side Tiber; he hath left them you,
And to your heirs forever—common pleasures,°
To walk abroad and recreate yourselves.
Here was a Caesar! when comes such another?

217–219 For I have . . . blood: Antony claims that he doesn't have the cleverness (**wit**), fluency (**words**), high personal standing or reputation (**worth**), gestures (**action**), and manner of speaking (**utterance**) of a skilled orator.

224 ruffle up: enrage.

238 several: individual. **drachmas:** silver coins.

240 royal: most generous.

244 orchards: gardens.

246 common pleasures: public recreation areas.

Writing *Minilesson*

Writing Blank Verse The funeral speeches of Brutus and Antony differ in emotional impact. This is partly because Brutus's speech is written in prose while Antony's is in blank verse.

Activity Review iambic pentameter by writing the scansion of a line from Antony's speech on the board. Have students write a paragraph about an issue they feel strongly about. Then challenge them to write the same ideas in blank verse. Have them discuss their writing experiences: What was challenging and/or satisfying about writing blank verse? How well did it fit their ideas? **L3**

Additional Resources

Writer's Choice, Lessons 1.1–1.3

FIRST PLEBEIAN. Never, never! Come, away, away!
250   We'll burn his body in the holy place,°
  And with the brands° fire the traitors' houses.
  Take up the body.

SECOND PLEBEIAN. Go fetch fire.

THIRD PLEBEIAN. Pluck down benches.

255 FOURTH PLEBEIAN. Pluck down forms,° windows,° anything.

[*Exit* PLEBEIANS *with the body.*]

ANTONY. Now let it work. Mischief, thou art afoot,
  Take thou what course thou wilt!

[*Enter* SERVANT.]

               How now, fellow?

SERVANT. Sir, Octavius is already come to Rome.

ANTONY. Where is he?

260 SERVANT. He and Lepidus° are at Caesar's house.

ANTONY. And thither will I straight to visit him;°
  He comes upon a wish.° Fortune is merry,
  And in this mood will give us anything.

SERVANT. I heard him say, Brutus and Cassius
265   Are rid° like madmen through the gates of Rome.

ANTONY. Belike° they had some notice of the people,
  How I had mov'd them. Bring me to Octavius.

[*They exit.*]

SCENE 3. Shortly afterward. A street near the Forum.

[*Enter* CINNA *the poet, and after him the* PLEBEIANS.]

CINNA.° I dreamt tonight° that I did feast with Caesar,
  And things unluckily charge my fantasy.°
  I have no will to wander forth of doors,
  Yet something leads me forth.

5 FIRST PLEBEIAN. What is your name?

SECOND PLEBEIAN. Whither are you going?

THIRD PLEBEIAN. Where do you dwell?

FOURTH PLEBEIAN. Are you a married man or a bachelor?

SECOND PLEBEIAN. Answer every man directly.

10 FIRST PLEBEIAN. Ay, and briefly.

FOURTH PLEBEIAN. Ay, and wisely.

250 the holy place: the site of the most sacred Roman temples.
251 brands: pieces of burning wood.

255 forms: benches. **windows:** shutters.

260 Lepidus: one of Caesar's generals.
261 thither will . . . him: I will go there immediately to visit him.
262 upon a wish: just as I had wished.

265 Are rid: have ridden.
266 Belike: probably.

1 Cinna: a well-known poet, not the same Cinna who helped kill Caesar.
tonight: last night.
2 things . . . fantasy: my imagination is burdened with bad omens.

TT Active Reading

QUESTION What effect does Antony's reading of the will have on the people? *(It is the crowning touch to Antony's rousing them to hysteria. They begin planning violence.)*

UU Active Reading

RESPOND Have students describe their responses to the dialogue as the crowd plans their violent acts. *(Many students will find the scene loathsome and disturbing.)*

VV Literary Elements

CHARACTER Have a student read aloud lines 256–257. Have students discuss the character traits it shows. Ask them whether it affects their opinion of Antony's character. *(Antony's speech shows the purposeful nature of his manipulation of the crowd and his willingness to resort to violence to get revenge. Readers who were impressed by Antony's graceful funeral speech may be disappointed by his coldheartedness.)*

At the MOVIES

Be sure to preview the following video for appropriateness for your class:

• Julius Caesar*

 *Also available in the Glencoe Literature *Video Library.*

Reading *Minilesson*

Identifying Cause-Effect Relationships Identifying the causes of several events in *Julius Caesar* can help students understand and review the play.

[Activity] List the following events of the play on the board. Have students write one or more causes of each event.

1. Brutus's agreeing to join the conspirators

2. Caesar's agreeing to go to the Capitol on the ides of March
3. Caesar's assassination
4. Antony's anger at Brutus
5. the crowd rioting **L2**

Additional Resources
📁 *Reading Workbook*

Active Reading

RESPOND Have students describe their response to the plebeians' assault of Cinna. *(Many students will be horrified at Shakespeare's description of the rioting crowd attacking an innocent man.)*

Active Reading

CONNECT Encourage students to consider whether a scene similar to this riot could happen today. What events does it resemble? What truths about human nature does Shakespeare depict in the scene? *(Students may agree that the event could happen today. Riots resulting from protests against the government and racial issues have occurred in the United States in the past 30 years. Shakespeare depicts the mentality of an out-of-control crowd and the ability of a clever manipulator to provoke a crowd to violence.)*

Thematic Focus

Loyalty and Betrayal Who betrays Caesar? Who remains loyal to him? Discuss which characters have changed in their feelings in the play so far.

☑ ASSESSMENT OPTIONS

📁 **Quick Checks,** p. 73

JULIUS CAESAR

THIRD PLEBEIAN. Ay, and truly, you were best.°

CINNA. What is my name? Whither am I going? Where do I dwell? Am I a married man or a bachelor? Then, to answer
15 every man directly and briefly, wisely and truly: wisely I say, I am a bachelor.

SECOND PLEBEIAN. That's as much as to say, they are fools that marry. You'll bear me a bang° for that, I fear. Proceed directly.

20 **CINNA.** Directly, I am going to Caesar's funeral.

FIRST PLEBEIAN. As a friend or an enemy?

CINNA. As a friend.

SECOND PLEBEIAN. That matter is answer'd directly.

FOURTH PLEBEIAN. For your dwelling—briefly.

25 **CINNA.** Briefly, I dwell by the Capitol.

THIRD PLEBEIAN. Your name, sir, truly.

CINNA. Truly, my name is Cinna.

FIRST PLEBEIAN. Tear him to pieces, he's a conspirator.

CINNA. I am Cinna the poet, I am Cinna the poet.

30 **FOURTH PLEBEIAN.** Tear him for his bad verses, tear him for his bad verses.

CINNA. I am not Cinna the conspirator.

FOURTH PLEBEIAN. It is no matter, his name's Cinna. Pluck but his name out of his heart, and turn him going.

35 **THIRD PLEBEIAN.** Tear him, tear him!
Come, brands, ho, firebrands! To Brutus', to Cassius'; burn all! Some to Decius' house, and some to Casca's; some to Ligarius'. Away, go!

[All the PLEBEIANS exit (dragging off CINNA).]

12 you were best: you had better.

18 bear me a bang: get a blow from me.

840 ❦ UNIT 4: DRAMA

Teaching Options

Grammar and Language *Minilesson*

Complete Subjects and Predicates
Remind students that the complete subject of a sentence includes all the words that identify who or what the sentence is about. The complete predicate includes all the words that tell what the subject is or does or what happened to the subject. Write this example:

That matter is answer'd directly.

Point out that *That matter* is the complete subject of the sentence and *is answer'd directly* is the complete predicate.

Activity Have students write each complete subject and complete predicate.
1. I am going to Caesar's funeral.
2. Then I, and you, and all of us fell down.
L1

Additional Resources

📖 *Grammar and Language Transparency 62*

📙 *Grammar and Language Workbook,* p. 77

📙 *Grammar and Composition Handbook,* Lesson 2.2

📙 *Writer's Choice,* Lesson 11.2

840

Responding to Literature

Personal Response

What was your reaction to Caesar's murder?

— ANALYZING ACT 3 —

RECALL AND INTERPRET

1. What action does Caesar refuse to take just before he is murdered? How would you describe his behavior in refusing?
2. What most surprises Caesar when he is attacked? What might Caesar have been thinking as he died?
3. How does Antony respond to the conspirators immediately after Caesar's murder? In your opinion, why does he behave this way?
4. Summarize the crowd's reactions to Brutus's and Antony's funeral speeches. What can you infer about the crowd from their reactions?
5. What was the content of Caesar's will? Why might Antony have made a point of reading the will to the people?

EVALUATE AND CONNECT

6. How did Caesar's behavior outside the Capitol just before he died affect your reaction to his death?
7. Did Antony's **soliloquy** (see page R12) after his discussion with the conspirators surprise you? Explain.
8. What is your opinion of Brutus? Has it changed since act 1? Explain.
9. Why might Shakespeare have chosen to include the scene of the attack on Cinna the poet? Do you know of a similar incident of mob violence? If so, how do the incidents compare?
10. If you had been an eyewitness to Caesar's murder and the following speeches, whose funeral speech would have moved you more, Brutus's or Antony's? Why?

> ### *Literary* ELEMENTS
>
> #### Prose
>
> **Prose** is literature that is written in sentence and paragraph form. The dialogue in Shakespeare's plays is a mixture of verse and prose. Clowns, servants, and other lower-class characters usually speak in prose. Well-born characters often speak in verse, especially when making speeches.
>
> However, Shakespeare's use of prose varies from play to play and even within plays. For example, Antony's address to the crowd at Caesar's funeral is in blank verse. Brutus's speech is in prose.
>
> 1. Why, do you think, did Shakespeare have his lower-class characters speak in prose rather than verse?
> 2. Why might Shakespeare have chosen to write Brutus's funeral oration in prose rather than verse?
>
> ● See **Literary Terms Handbook**, p. R10.

— EXTENDING YOUR RESPONSE —

Literature Groups

The Art of Rhetoric   With your group, analyze the techniques that Antony uses in his funeral speech. Does he portray Caesar's murder fairly, or does he distort the event? How does he use repetition, irony, and other rhetorical or persuasive techniques to make his point? What else does he do to win over his audience? Present to the class a list of techniques that Antony uses.

Creative Writing

In Cassius's Words   Write a speech that Cassius might have delivered while Brutus gave his funeral speech. First consider Cassius's character and what he said earlier in the play about Caesar. Would Cassius make an emotional or a low-key speech? How might he justify his action?

📖 **Save your work for your portfolio.**

Responding to the Selection

Personal Response

Students may say they were shocked by the murder or satisfied that his assassination was for the best.

ANALYZING ACT 3

1. Caesar refuses to read the warning letter from Artemidorus. His behavior is arrogant and political.
2. Brutus's participation most surprises Caesar. He might have been experiencing shock at the betrayal of his friend as he died.
3. Antony acts conciliatory to the conspirators. He is hiding his true feelings until he can get public support for revenge.
4. The crowd agrees with Brutus and wants to crown him but is later swayed by Antony's rhetoric and joins him in seeking revenge. The crowd is emotional and easily persuaded.
5. Caesar's will specified that money, walks, and gardens be given to the Roman citizens. Antony made a point of reading the will to the people to prove that Caesar loved them, further inciting them to seek revenge.
6. Students may say Caesar's behavior made them feel less sorry for him.
7. Students may express surprise at Antony's true feelings because his conciliatory gestures with the conspirators were convincing.
8. Students may have less respect for Brutus because he seems to be rationalizing his part in the murder.
9. Shakespeare may have wanted to show the potential dangers when a crowd is incited to violence. Students may know of an incident of mob violence from recent American history.
10. Students may find Antony's speech more moving because blank verse makes it memorable; Antony's rhetoric is expert.

EXTENDING YOUR RESPONSE

Literature Groups Have groups make notes on the speech before discussion. **COLLAB. LEARN.**

✔ ASSESSMENT OPTIONS

📁 ***Quick Checks,*** p. 73

📁 ***Selection and Theme Assessment,*** pp. 141–142

📁 ***Performance Assessment,*** p. 72

💾 ***Testmaker***

LITERARY ELEMENTS

1. Students may say that prose is less elegant and graceful than blank verse; therefore, Shakespeare may have felt it more appropriate for his lower-class characters.
2. Brutus's prose matches his rational, unemotional nature. Mark Antony's verse reflects his need to stir the crowd's emotions.

Additional Resources

📠 *Literary Elements Transparency 73*

842 ❧ UNIT 4

ACT 4

SCENE 1. Antony's house in Rome. A year and a half after Caesar's death.

🅰

[*Enter ANTONY, OCTAVIUS, and LEPIDUS.*]

    ANTONY.   These many then shall die, their names are prick'd.°

    OCTAVIUS.   Your brother too must die, consent you, Lepidus?°

    LEPIDUS.   I do consent—

    OCTAVIUS.   Prick him down, Antony.

    LEPIDUS.   Upon condition Publius shall not live,
5   Who is your sister's son, Mark Antony.

1 **prick'd:** marked down on a list.

2 **Your brother . . . Lepidus:** Lepidus's brother was a prominent politician who sided with the conspirators after Caesar's assassination.

Interior of a Roman House/Home of Cornelius Rufus in Pompeii (Reconstruction). Artist unknown.

Viewing the art: What impressions of Roman life do you get from this scene? How do those impressions relate to the lives of the characters in the play?

William Shakespeare ∾

ANTONY. He shall not live; look, with a spot I damn him.
But, Lepidus, go you to Caesar's house;
Fetch the will hither, and we shall determine
How to cut off some charge in legacies.°

10 LEPIDUS. What? shall I find you here?

OCTAVIUS. Or here or at the Capitol.

[*Exit LEPIDUS.*]

ANTONY. This is a slight unmeritable man,
Meet° to be sent on errands; is it fit,
The threefold world° divided, he should stand
15 One of the three to share it?

OCTAVIUS.   So you thought him,
And took his voice who should be prick'd to die
In our black sentence and proscription.°

ANTONY. Octavius, I have seen more days than you,
And though we lay these honors on this man
20 To ease ourselves of divers sland'rous loads,°
He shall but bear them as the ass bears gold,
To groan and sweat under the business,
Either led or driven, as we point the way;
And having brought our treasure where we will,
25 Then take we down his load, and turn him off
(Like to the empty ass) to shake his ears
And graze in commons.°

OCTAVIUS.   You may do your will;
But he's a tried and valiant soldier.

ANTONY. So is my horse, Octavius, and for that
30 I do appoint him store of provender.°
It is a creature that I teach to fight,
To wind,° to stop, to run directly on,
His corporal° motion govern'd by my spirit;
And in some taste° is Lepidus but so.
35 He must be taught, and train'd, and bid go forth;
A barren-spirited fellow; one that feeds
On objects, arts, and imitations,
Which, out of use and stal'd by other men,
Begin his fashion.° Do not talk of him
40 But as a property.° And now, Octavius,
Listen great things. Brutus and Cassius
Are levying powers; we must straight make head;
Therefore let our alliance be combin'd,

9 cut off . . . legacies: reduce the amount of money left to the people in Caesar's will.

13 Meet: fit.

14 threefold world: three parts of the Roman world. (In the autumn of 43 B.C., Antony, Octavius Caesar, and Lepidus formed a triumvirate—a committee of three—to rule Rome. They divided up among themselves territory that the Romans had conquered.)

15–17 So you . . . proscription: Octavius wonders why Antony asked Lepidus to name people who should be sentenced to death if he had so poor an opinion of him.

20 divers sland'rous loads: the burden of accusations for our various actions.

24–27 And having . . . commons: When Lepidus has brought our treasure where we want it, we will send him off to shake his ears and graze on public land like an unburdened donkey.

30 appoint . . . provender: allot him a supply of food.

32 wind: turn.

33 corporal: bodily.

34 taste: degree.

36–39 A barren-spirited . . . fashion: a man with no originality, one who indulges in curiosities, tricks, and fashions, which he takes up only after they have become outmoded.

40 a property: a mere tool.

JULIUS CAESAR, ACT 4, SCENE 1 ∾ 843

B Literary Elements

DIALOGUE Have students describe the relationship between Antony and Octavius. How might their dialogue be portrayed on stage? *(The two leaders seem to have a fragile relationship. Their dialogue on stage might appear as petty bickering.)*

C Literary Elements

FIGURES OF SPEECH: *Simile* To what does Antony compare Lepidus? What do the comparisons show about Antony's feelings toward him? *(He compares Lepidus to a donkey and a horse; he does not respect his intellect.)*

D Literary Elements

CHARACTER What can students tell about Mark Antony? Have them give examples to support their responses. *(He is abrupt and cold-hearted, unflinchingly ordering his own nephew killed. He is critical and belittling toward Lepidus. He is arrogant, single-minded, and ruthless in his pursuit of power.)*

MEETING INDIVIDUAL NEEDS — ENGLISH LANGUAGE LEARNERS

Abstract Dialogue In act 4, English language learners may find the play more abstract and difficult to follow.

Activity Encourage students to slow down when they come to dialogue that they find difficult to understand. Have students look at Brutus's speech, scene 3, lines 203–212. Encourage them to use the following methods to comprehend the speech:

1. Paraphrase.
2. Look up abstract and unknown words.
3. Use any similes and other figures of speech in the dialogue to make the abstract ideas more concrete.

Additional Resources
📁 *English Language Learners Sourcebook*

DRAMA ∾ 843

Historical Note

Octavius was the nephew of Julius Caesar. After Caesar's death, in 44 B.C., Octavius, commanding Caesar's forces, defeated Antony's army. He forced Antony to accept him as a chief officer. Octavius, Antony, and Lepidus formed the Second Triumverate. This is the situation at the beginning of act 4. In 27 B.C., several years later, Octavius became the first Roman emperor and became known as Augustus.

FYI

Roman Sport Students may be shocked by the reference to bear-baiting, a cruel sport of the ancient Romans. Romans also enjoyed gladiator fights, in which trained warriors fought one another until one died. Audiences also watched criminals or other outcasts get thrown to lions or other vicious animals.

E Active Reading

REVIEW Have students paraphrase lines 18–24. Who is Brutus describing? *(Brutus says that Cassius's friendship is pulling away. He says that one can tell when friendships are dying by the forced civility between the parties.)*

Teaching Options

> Our best friends made, our means stretch'd;
> 45   And let us presently go sit in council,
> How covert matters may be best disclos'd,
> And open perils surest answered.°

> **OCTAVIUS.**   Let us do so; for we are at the stake,
> And bay'd about with many enemies,°
> 50   And some that smile have in their hearts, I fear,
> Millions of mischiefs. *[They exit.]*

SCENE 2. A military camp near Sardis in Asia Minor. Several months later.

[Drum. Enter BRUTUS, LUCILIUS, LUCIUS, and the army. TITINIUS and PINDARUS meet them.]

> **BRUTUS.**   Stand ho!

> **LUCILIUS.**   Give the word ho! and stand.°

> **BRUTUS.**   What now, Lucilius, is Cassius near?

> **LUCILIUS.**   He is at hand, and Pindarus is come
> 5   To do you salutation from his master.

> **BRUTUS.**   He greets me well. Your master, Pindarus,
> In his own change, or by ill officers,
> Hath given me some worthy cause to wish
> Things done undone,° but if he be at hand,
> 10   I shall be satisfied.°

> **PINDARUS.**   I do not doubt
> But that my noble master will appear
> Such as he is, full of regard and honor.

> **BRUTUS.**   He is not doubted. A word, Lucilius.
> How he receiv'd you; let me be resolv'd.°

> 15   **LUCILIUS.**   With courtesy and with respect enough,
> But not with such familiar instances,°
> Nor with such free and friendly conference,°
> As he hath us'd of old.

> **BRUTUS.**   Thou hast describ'd
> A hot friend cooling. Ever note, Lucilius,
> **E** 20   When love begins to sicken and decay
> It useth an enforced ceremony.°
> There are no tricks in plain and simple faith;
> But hollow men, like horses hot at hand,
> Make gallant show and promise of their mettle;

[Low march within.]

844   UNIT 4: DRAMA

41–47 Listen great . . . answered: Listen to important matters. Brutus and Cassius are raising armies; we must press forward immediately. Therefore let us become united, choose our allies, and make the most of our resources. And let us decide at once how hidden threats may be uncovered and open dangers most safely confronted.

48–49 we are . . . enemies: Octavius's metaphor refers to bear-baiting, a popular entertainment in which bears were tied to stakes and surrounded by vicious dogs.

2 Give the . . . stand: Lucilius, one of Brutus's officers, tells his subordinates to pass on Brutus's command for the army to halt **(stand).** He has returned from Cassius's camp with Titinius, one of Cassius's officers, and Pindarus, Cassius's servant.

6–9 Your master . . . undone: Either a change in Cassius or the misconduct of his officers has given me good reason to wish I could undo what I have done. (Brutus is having some misgivings about having participated in the conspiracy because of incidents that have occurred in Cassius's army.)

10 be satisfied: receive an explanation.

14 resolv'd: informed.

16 familiar instances: signs of friendship.

17 conference: conversation.

21 enforced ceremony: strained formality.

LIFE SKILLS CONNECTION

Collaborating Have students consider the advantages and disadvantages of three men of equal power trying to run a country together. Point out that although students do not run a country, collaborating with others is an important life skill with which they have some experience.

Activity Have students begin a list of mistakes made by Antony, Octavius, and Lepidus in their political collaboration. For example, in the beginning of act 4, Antony excludes one of their members, Lepidus, and then insults him behind his back; Octavius indulges in petty bickering with Antony; and Antony pulls rank on Octavius by saying, "I have seen more days than you." Have students continue their lists as they complete the play. Then discuss what students have learned about collaboration from their own experiences and from the play. **L2**

---

25   But when they should endure the bloody spur,
    They fall their crests, and like deceitful jades
    Sink in the trial.° Comes his army on?

LUCILIUS.   They mean this night in Sardis to be quarter'd.
    The greater part, the horse in general,°
30   Are come with Cassius.

[*Enter* CASSIUS *and his* POWERS.]

BRUTUS.   Hark! He is arriv'd.
    March gently on to meet him.

CASSIUS.   Stand ho!

BRUTUS.   Stand ho! Speak the word along.

FIRST SOLDIER.   Stand!

35   **SECOND SOLDIER.**   Stand!

THIRD SOLDIER.   Stand!

CASSIUS.   Most noble brother, you have done me wrong.

BRUTUS.   Judge me, you gods! wrong I mine enemies?
    And if not so, how should I wrong a brother.

40   **CASSIUS.**   Brutus, this sober form° of yours hides wrongs,
    And when you do them—

BRUTUS.   Cassius, be content.
    Speak your griefs softly; I do know you well.
    Before the eyes of both our armies here
45   (Which should perceive nothing but love from us)
    Let us not wrangle. Bid them move away;
    Then in my tent, Cassius, enlarge your griefs,
    And I will give you audience.°

CASSIUS.   Pindarus,
    Bid our commanders lead their charges off
50   A little from this ground.

BRUTUS.   Lucius, do you the like, and let no man
    Come to our tent till we have done our conference.
    Let Lucilius and Titinius guard our door.

[*They exit.* BRUTUS *and* CASSIUS *remain and withdraw into*
BRUTUS's *tent, while* LUCILIUS *and* TITINIUS *mount guard without.*]

SCENE 3. BRUTUS's tent. A few minutes later.

CASSIUS.   That you wrong'd me doth appear in this;
    You have condemn'd and noted Lucius Pella
    For taking bribes here of the Sardians;

23–27 But hollow . . . trial: Brutus compares insincere men to horses that are spirited at the start but drop their proud necks as soon as they feel the spur, failing like nags (**jades**) when put to the test.

29 horse in general: main part of the cavalry.

40 sober form: dignified manner.

47–48 enlarge . . . audience: Explain your grievances, and I will listen.

FYI

Sardis Sardis was the capital of the kingdom of Lydia. It is near present-day Izmir, Turkey. Its remains go back to the 1300s B.C. It was conquered by the Persians in 545 B.C.

Historical Note

The Roman army was very strong, with about 300,000 men at its height. At first only landed citizens could become soldiers, but the army later increased its ranks and developed a professional, well-trained army. In addition to fighting, soldiers built roads, aqueducts, bridges, and walls. Soldiers often developed a strong loyalty to their general, especially if they were rewarded with some of the spoils of battle.

F   **Literary Elements**

CHARACTER Have students think of and discuss words that describe Brutus. *(wise, calm, patient)*

G   **Active Reading**

QUESTION Why is Cassius angry with Brutus? *(He says Brutus has condemned Lucius Pella for taking bribes from the people of Sardis; therefore, Cassius's letters on Pella's behalf were ignored by the authorities.)*

MEETING INDIVIDUAL NEEDS   **MULTIPLE LEARNING STYLES**

Interpersonal Brutus describes an aspect of friendship, starting with the vivid image of "a hot friend cooling."

Activity Have a volunteer read Brutus's speech, lines 18–27. Ask students to interpret Brutus's simile. How is an insincere person like certain horses? Point out that one reason Shakespeare is still popular is his time- less understanding of people and relationships. Have students discuss whether they have ever been treated by a friend in the manner Brutus describes. **L2**

I **Critical Thinking**

INFERRING Have students explain Brutus's reasoning and conclusion in his speech, lines 18–26. What character traits in Brutus does the speech illustrate? *(Brutus says that Cassius shows dishonor to the noble act of killing Caesar by stooping to accepting bribery. Brutus is still idealistic, insisting that killing Caesar was the right thing to do.)*

JULIUS CAESAR

G
5   Wherein my letters, praying on his side,
    Because I knew the man, was slighted off.°

BRUTUS. You wrong'd yourself to write in such a case.

CASSIUS. In such a time as this it is not meet
    That every nice offense should bear his comment.°

BRUTUS. Let me tell you, Cassius, you yourself
10   Are much condemn'd to have an itching palm,°
H   To sell and mart° your offices for gold
    To undeservers.

CASSIUS.   I, an itching palm?
    You know that you are Brutus that speaks this,
    Or, by the gods, this speech were else your last.

15 **BRUTUS.** The name of Cassius honors this corruption,
    And chastisement doth therefore hide his head.°

CASSIUS. Chastisement?

BRUTUS. Remember March, the ides of March remember:
    Did not great Julius bleed for justice' sake?
20   What villain touch'd his body, that did stab
    And not for justice? What? shall one of us,
    That struck the foremost man of all this world
K **I**   But for supporting robbers,° shall we now
    Contaminate our fingers with base bribes?
25   And sell the mighty space of our large honors
    For so much trash as may be grasped thus?
    I had rather be a dog, and bay the moon,
    Than such a Roman.

CASSIUS.   Brutus, bait° not me,
    I'll not endure it. You forget yourself
30   To hedge me in.° I am a soldier, I,
    Older in practice, abler than yourself
    To make conditions.°

BRUTUS.   Go to; you are not, Cassius.

J **CASSIUS.** I am.

BRUTUS. I say you are not.

35 **CASSIUS.** Urge me no more, I shall forget myself;
    Have mind upon your health; tempt me no farther.

BRUTUS. Away, slight man!

CASSIUS. Is't possible?

1–5 That you . . . off: Cassius complains that Brutus publicly disgraced (noted) a man for taking bribes, ignoring Cassius's request for leniency.

7–8 not meet . . . comment: not fitting that each minor offense should be criticized.

10 condemn'd to . . . palm: blamed for being greedy.

11 mart: trade.

15–16 The name . . . head: Because you have become associated with this corruption, the bribe-takers go unpunished.

23 supporting robbers: Brutus now suggests that one of Caesar's offenses was to protect corrupt officials.

28 bait: provoke.

30 hedge me in: limit my freedom.

32 conditions: regulations.

Teaching Options

MULTIPLE LEARNING STYLES
MEETING INDIVIDUAL NEEDS

Bodily-Kinesthetic Paraphrasing and acting out the quarrel between Brutus and Cassius can demonstrate the uneasy relationship between the two conspirators.

Activity Have students work in pairs and enact the dialogue between Brutus and Cassius on pages 846–849. Suggest that each student take one role and make notes of the points that the character makes during the discussion. Then have students define the emotions and attitude of their character. Finally, have the two students act out the discussion, expressing the characters' emotions with voice, facial expression, and gestures. **L2** **COLLAB. LEARN.**

BRUTUS.   Hear me, for I will speak.
     Must I give way and room to your rash choler?°
40   Shall I be frighted when a madman stares?

CASSIUS.   O ye gods, ye gods, must I endure all this?

BRUTUS.   All this? ay, more. Fret till your proud heart break.
     Go show your slaves how choleric you are,
     And make your bondmen tremble. Must I budge?°
45   Must I observe you?° Must I stand and crouch
     Under your testy humor?° By the gods,
     You shall digest the venom of your spleen
     Though it do split you;° for, from his day forth,
     I'll use you for my mirth, yea, for my laughter,
50   When you are waspish.

CASSIUS.   Is it come to this?

BRUTUS.   You say you are a better soldier;
     Let it appear so; make your vaunting° true,
     And it shall please me well. For mine own part,
     I shall be glad to learn of noble men.°

55   CASSIUS.   You wrong me every way; you wrong me, Brutus;
     I said, an elder soldier, not a better.
     Did I say "better"?

BRUTUS.   If you did, I care not.

CASSIUS.   When Caesar liv'd, he durst° not thus have mov'd° me.

BRUTUS.   Peace, peace, you durst not so have tempted him.

60   CASSIUS.   I durst not?

BRUTUS.   No.

CASSIUS.   What? durst not tempt him?

BRUTUS.   For your life you
    durst not.

CASSIUS.   Do not presume too much upon my love,
     I may do that° I shall be sorry for.

65   BRUTUS.   You have done that you should be sorry for.
     There is no terror, Cassius, in your threats;
     For I am arm'd so strong in honesty
     That they pass by me as the idle wind,
     Which I respect not. I did send to you
70   For certain sums of gold, which you denied me;
     For I can raise no money by vile means.
     By heaven, I had rather coin my heart
     And drop my blood for drachmas than to wring

39 rash choler: quick temper.

44 budge: flinch.

45 observe you: defer to you.

46 testy humor: irritable mood.

47–48 digest . . . split you: swallow the poison of your own anger, even if it makes you burst. (The spleen was thought to be the source of anger.)

52 vaunting: boasting.

54 learn of noble men: "learn from noble men" or "find out that you are noble."

58 durst: dared. **mov'd:** provoked.

64 that: something that.

J   Literary Elements

TONE Have students identify the tone of the characters' dialogue. *(angry)*

K   Active Reading

CONNECT Have students point out specific ways in which the argument between Brutus and Cassius is similar to ones they have witnessed or participated in. *(Students may find the argument very true to life. Cassius proclaims himself a better soldier than Brutus, a point the men later squabble about; Brutus objects to having to tolerate Cassius's temper tantrum; Brutus implies that Cassius is too cowardly to have confronted Caesar; Cassius threatens that Brutus will make him "do that I shall be sorry for." Later in the scene, the men stoop to a "You did"—"I did not" squabble and Cassius accuses Brutus of exaggerating his faults.)*

INCLUSION STRATEGIES

MEETING INDIVIDUAL NEEDS

Less-Proficient Readers In the course of the argument between Brutus and Caesar, Shakespeare uses several synonyms and figures of speech for *anger.*

Activity Help students find the various ways the two men refer to anger in their dialogue. List them on the board, explaining that many of them were com- monly used in writings in Shakespeare's time. They include "rash choler," "cho- leric," "testy humor," "the venom of your spleen," and "waspish." **L1**

Additional Resources
📁 *Inclusion Strategies*

Active Reading

REVIEW Of what does Brutus accuse Cassius in lines 75–77? *(He says that he asked Brutus for money to pay his army and Cassius refused to give it to him.)*

Active Reading

CONNECT Have students describe Cassius's mood in lines 93–107 and tell whether they have ever witnessed a person in such a mood. *(Cassius's attitude is one of self-pity and injured pride. Most students will say they have witnessed such an attitude in others.)*

JULIUS CAESAR

From the hard hands of peasants their vile trash°
75　By any indirection.° I did send
　　To you for gold to pay my legions,
　　Which you denied me. Was that done like Cassius?
　　Should I have answer'd Caius Cassius so?
　　When Marcus Brutus grows so covetous
80　To lock such rascal counters° from his friends,
　　Be ready, gods, with all your thunderbolts,
　　Dash him to pieces!

CASSIUS.　　　　　　I denied you not.

BRUTUS.　You did.

CASSIUS.　I did not. He was but a fool that brought
85　My answer back. Brutus hath riv'd° my heart.
　　A friend should bear his friend's infirmities;°
　　But Brutus makes mine greater than they are.

BRUTUS.　I do not, till you practice them on me.

CASSIUS.　You love me not.

BRUTUS.　　　　　　I do not like your faults.

90　**CASSIUS.**　A friendly eye could never see such faults.

BRUTUS.　A flatterer's would not, though they do appear
　　As huge as high Olympus.

CASSIUS.　Come, Antony, and young Octavius, come,
　　Revenge yourselves alone on Cassius,
95　For Cassius is aweary of the world;
　　Hated by one he loves, brav'd° by his brother,
　　Check'd like a bondman,° all his faults observ'd,
　　Set in a notebook, learn'd and conn'd by rote,°
　　To cast into my teeth. O, I could weep
100　My spirit from mine eyes! There is my dagger,
　　And here my naked breast; within, a heart
　　Dearer than Pluto's mine,° richer than gold:
　　If that thou be'st a Roman, take it forth.
　　I, that denied thee gold, will give my heart:
105　Strike as thou didst at Caesar; for I know,
　　When thou didst hate him worst, thou lovedst him better
　　Than ever thou lovedst Cassius.

BRUTUS.　　　　　　Sheathe your dagger.
　　Be angry when you will, it shall have scope;
　　Do what you will, dishonor shall be humor.°
110　O Cassius, you are yoked° with a lamb

74 vile trash: small sums of money.

75 indirection: dishonest means.

80 rascal counters: grubby coins.

85 riv'd: broken.

86 bear . . . infirmities: accept his friend's faults.

96 brav'd: challenged.

97 Check'd like a bondman: scolded like a slave.

98 conn'd by rote: memorized.

102 Pluto's mine: all the riches in the earth. (Pluto, the Roman god of the underworld, was often confused with Plutus, the god of wealth.)

108–109 Be angry . . . humor: Brutus says that he will give Cassius's anger free play (**scope**) and will consider his insults merely the result of a bad mood.

110 yoked: allied.

MEETING INDIVIDUAL NEEDS — MULTIPLE LEARNING STYLES

Interpersonal In the course of their argument, Cassius says to Brutus, "A friend should bear his friend's infirmities."

Activity Have students discuss this idea. Ask them to what extent they agree or disagree with Cassius's statement and have them give examples from their own lives that support their opinions. **L1**

That carries anger as the flint bears fire,
Who, much enforced,° shows a hasty spark,
And straight° is cold again.

CASSIUS.   Hath Cassius liv'd
To be but mirth and laughter to his Brutus
115   When grief and blood ill-temper'd° vexeth him?

BRUTUS.   When I spoke that, I was ill-temper'd too.

CASSIUS.   Do you confess so much? Give me your hand.

BRUTUS.   And my heart too.

CASSIUS.   O Brutus!

BRUTUS.   What's the matter?

CASSIUS.   Have you not love enough to bear with me,
120   When that rash humor which my mother gave me
Makes me forgetful?°

BRUTUS.   Yes, Cassius, and from henceforth,
When you are over-earnest with your Brutus,
He'll think your mother chides, and leave you so.°

[Enter a POET (to LUCILIUS and TITINIUS as they stand on guard).]

POET.   Let me go in to see the generals;
125   There is some grudge between 'em; 'tis not meet
They be alone.

112 **enforced:** struck hard; irritated.
113 **straight:** immediately.

115 **blood ill-temper'd:** moodiness.

121 **forgetful:** forget myself.

122–123 **When you . . . so:** When you are too difficult with me, I will attribute it to the quick temper you inherited from your mother, and leave it at that.

Brutus. c. 1539–1540. Michelangelo Buonarroti. Marble, height: 29⅛ in. Museo Nazionale del Bargello, Florence, Italy.

Viewing the sculpture: What traits of Brutus have been depicted here? How do they compare with the character you have read about?

Author's Craft

SATIRE Call attention to the poet's very brief appearance. Have students summarize the scene and explain why Shakespeare might have inserted this character into the play. *(The poet is presented as one who considers himself wise and wants to correct the disagreement between Brutus and Cassius. Brutus and Cassius treat him with scorn and disparage the idea that he can be useful in practical matters. Shakespeare may have been commenting on the traditional view of the poet as an artistic person with his head in the clouds who was useless in the real world.)*

FYI

The Stoic Philosophy

The Stoic philosophy flourished in the ancient world between 300 B.C. and A.D. 300. The Stoics believed that fate ruled their lives and that people must try to understand the divine plan for them. They believed that to be happy a person should emphasize reason instead of emotion and focus on the elements of life that they could control. The philosophy that Cassius refers to in line 145 is the Stoic philosophy. Brutus's reaction to the death of his wife is that of a Stoic.

Teaching Options

LUCILIUS. You shall not come to them.

POET. Nothing but death shall stay me.

[*BRUTUS and CASSIUS step out of the tent.*]

CASSIUS. How now. What's the matter?

130 POET. For shame, you generals! what do you mean?
　　　Love, and be friends, as two such men should be,
　　　For I have seen more years, I'm sure, than ye.

CASSIUS. Ha, ha! how vilely doth this cynic° rhyme!

BRUTUS. Get you hence, sirrah! saucy fellow, hence!

135 CASSIUS. Bear with him, Brutus, 'tis his fashion.

BRUTUS. I'll know his humor when he knows his time.°
　　　What should the wars do with these jigging° fools?
　　　Companion,° hence!

CASSIUS.　　　　　　Away, away, be gone! [*Exit POET.*]

BRUTUS. Lucilius and Titinius, bid the commanders
140　　　Prepare to lodge their companies tonight.

CASSIUS. And come yourselves, and bring Messala with you
　　　Immediately to us.

[*LUCILIUS and TITINIUS exit.*]

BRUTUS. [*To LUCIUS within.*] Lucius, a bowl of wine!

[*BRUTUS and CASSIUS return into the tent.*]

CASSIUS. I did not think you could have been so angry.

BRUTUS. O Cassius, I am sick of many griefs.

145 CASSIUS. Of your philosophy you make no use,
　　　If you give place to accidental evils.°

BRUTUS. No man bears sorrow better. Portia is dead.

CASSIUS. Ha? Portia?

BRUTUS. She is dead.

150 CASSIUS. How scap'd I killing° when I cross'd you so?
　　　O insupportable and touching° loss!
　　　Upon what sickness?

BRUTUS.　　　　　　Impatient of° my absence,
　　　And grief that young Octavius with Mark Antony
　　　Have made themselves so strong—for with her death
155　　　That tidings came.° With this she fell distract,°
　　　And (her attendants absent) swallow'd fire.°

---

133 **cynic:** rude fellow.

136 **I'll know . . . time:** I'll accept his quirks when he learns the proper time for them.
137 **jigging:** rhyming.
138 **Companion:** fellow (used here as a term of contempt).

145–146 **Of your . . . evils:** According to the philosophy Brutus studied, people should not accept chance misfortunes.

150 **How scap'd I killing:** How did I escape being killed?
151 **touching:** painful.

152 **Impatient of:** unable to endure.
154–155: **with her death . . . came:** I received news of her death and of their strength at the same time.
155 **distract:** insane.
156 **fire:** burning coals.

GIFTED AND TALENTED

MEETING INDIVIDUAL NEEDS

Roman Stoicism The Roman philosophers Marcus Aurelius and Seneca carried on the Stoic philosophy created by the Greek philosopher Zeno. Seneca (4 B.C.–A.D. 65) focused on the disaster that would result if passion mastered reason. Marcus Aurelius (A.D. 121–180) focused on eliminating selfishness and forgiving others' offenses.

Activity Have students research one of the Roman Stoic philosophers. Ask them to summarize the philosopher's life and ideas and locate excerpts from his key works. Have them share their research in oral or written reports or in a multimedia presentation. **L3**

P Active Reading

REVIEW Have students compare the reactions to Portia's death of Brutus and Cassius. (*Brutus is seemingly emotionless while Cassius is very upset and says that her death would have excused Brutus's murdering Cassius when Cassius made him angry.*)

CASSIUS. And died so?

BRUTUS. Even so.

CASSIUS. O ye immortal gods!

[*Enter Boy (LUCIUS) with wine and tapers.*]

BRUTUS. Speak no more of her. Give me a bowl of wine.
In this I bury all unkindness, Cassius. [*Drinks.*]

160 CASSIUS. My heart is thirsty for that noble pledge.
Fill, Lucius, till the wine o'erswell the cup;
I cannot drink too much of Brutus' love.

[*Drinks. Exit LUCIUS.*]

BRUTUS. Come in, Titinius. [*Enter TITINIUS and MESSALA.*]
Welcome, good Messala.
Now sit we close about this taper here,
165 And call in question our necessities.°

CASSIUS. Portia, art thou gone?

BRUTUS.   No more, I pray you.
Messala, I have here received letters
That young Octavius and Mark Antony
Come down upon us with a mighty power,°
170 Bending their expedition toward Philippi.°

MESSALA. Myself have letters of the selfsame tenure.°

BRUTUS. With what addition?

MESSALA. That by proscription° and bills of outlawry
Octavius, Antony, and Lepidus
175 Have put to death an hundred senators.

BRUTUS. Therein our letters do not well agree;
Mine speak of seventy senators that died
By their proscriptions, Cicero being one.

CASSIUS. Cicero one?

MESSALA.   Cicero is dead,
180 And by that order of proscription.
Had you your letters from your wife, my lord?

BRUTUS. No, Messala.

MESSALA. Nor nothing in your letters writ of her?

BRUTUS. Nothing, Messala.

MESSALA.   That methinks is strange.

185 BRUTUS. Why ask you? Hear you aught of her in yours?

165 **call . . . necessities:** discuss what we must do.

169 **power:** army.
170 **Bending . . . Philippi:** Directing their march toward Philippi (an ancient town in northern Greece).
171 **tenure:** basic meaning.

173 **proscription:** condemning to death.

FYI

Portia's Death
According to Plutarch's history, Portia put "hot burning coals . . . into her mouth, and kept her mouth so close that she choked herself."

Q Active Reading

INTERPRET Have students discuss Brutus's reaction to his wife's death. Is it heartless and uncaring? (*Some students may say that Brutus's reaction is consistent with his reasonable approach to life. Others will say it is heartless. Others will say that he is denying his feelings of grief and guilt over her death.*)

R Literary Elements

FORESHADOWING Have students predict what the reports of the killings of the senators may foreshadow. (*Brutus and Cassius will organize a military action against Octavius and Mark Antony.*)

JULIUS CAESAR, ACT 4, SCENE 3 ✄ 851

INTERDISCIPLINARY CONNECTION

History As seen in the play, Caesar's assassination set off a series of events that resulted in infighting and warfare in Rome. This climaxed in the crowning of Octavian as the first Roman emperor in 27 B.C.

Activity Have students choose a topic to research on the history of the Roman Empire from 27 B.C. until its fall in A.D. 476. Among topics they may choose are the empire's height from A.D. 96–180, the rise of Christianity, the division of the empire in 284, the invasion of the empire by Germanic peoples, and the final fall of the empire. They may also research some of the Roman Empire's most famous leaders, such as Augustus (Octavian), Marcus Aurelius, Diocletian, and Constantine. **L2**

Active Reading

REVIEW Have students summarize Brutus's and Cassius's ideas of the best strategy. *(Brutus wants to march to Philippi immediately because he thinks that Antony and Octavius will recruit men along the way between Philippi and Sardis. Cassius wants to wait and let Antony and Octavius come to them so that they will use up more energy and resources.)*

Literary Elements

FORESHADOWING Have students consider whether Brutus's and Cassius's discussion about the best plan is a positive or negative sign of the outcome of the conflict with Mark Antony and Octavius. *(It is negative. There seems to be no clear way to win the conflict, and the two leaders disagree, indicating trouble ahead.)*

Literary Elements

FIGURES OF SPEECH: *Metaphor* Have students identify the figure of speech in lines 218–224. *(It is a metaphor. Events in men's lives are compared to ocean currents.)*

MESSALA. No, my lord.

BRUTUS. Now as you are a Roman, tell me true.

MESSALA. Then like a Roman bear the truth I tell,
For certain she is dead, and by strange manner.

190 **BRUTUS.** Why, farewell, Portia. We must die, Messala.
With meditating that she must die once,°
I have the patience to endure it now.

MESSALA. Even so great men great losses should endure.

CASSIUS. I have as much of this in art as you,
195 But yet my nature could not bear it so.°

BRUTUS. Well, to our work alive.° What do you think
Of marching to Philippi presently?

CASSIUS. I do not think it good.

BRUTUS. Your reason?

CASSIUS. This it is;
'Tis better that the enemy seek us;
200 So shall he waste his means,° weary his soldiers,
Doing himself offense,° whilst we, lying still,
Are full of rest, defense, and nimbleness.

BRUTUS. Good reasons must of force give place to better:
The people 'twixt Philippi and this ground
205 Do stand but in a forc'd affection;°
For they have grudg'd us contribution.
The enemy, marching along by them,
By them shall make a fuller number up,
Come on refresh'd, new-added° and encourag'd;
210 From which advantage shall we cut him off
If at Philippi we do face him there,
These people at our back.

CASSIUS. Here me, good brother.

BRUTUS. Under your pardon.° You must note beside
That we have tried the utmost of our friends,°
215 Our legions are brimful,° our cause is ripe:
The enemy increaseth every day;
We, at the height, are ready to decline.
There is a tide in the affairs of men,
Which, taken at the flood, leads on to fortune;
220 Omitted, all the voyage of their life
Is bound in shallows and in miseries.°
On such a full sea are we now afloat,

181–195 Had you your . . . bear it so: This passage contradicts lines 147–158, where Brutus tells Cassius of Portia's death. Many scholars believe that the second passage was mistakenly printed in a revised version of the play. According to this theory, Shakespeare originally emphasized Brutus's philosophical composure, but in rewriting the play, he decided to offer a warmer view of Brutus grieving for his wife.

191 once: at some time.

194–195 I have as . . . so: Cassius says that although he shares Brutus's ideal of philosophical self-control, he could not practice it as Brutus does.

196 alive: "at hand" or "of the living."

200 waste his means: use up his supplies.

201 Doing himself offense: harming himself.

205 Do stand . . . affection: Are friendly toward us only because they have no choice.

209 new-added: reinforced.

213 Under your pardon: I beg your pardon (let me continue).

214 tried . . . friends: demanded from our allies all that they can give.

215 brimful: at full strength.

218–221 There is a . . . miseries: Brutus says that if men fail to act when the tide of fortune is flowing, they may never get another opportunity.

Teaching Options

MEETING INDIVIDUAL NEEDS — MULTIPLE LEARNING STYLES

Musical At the end of the act, Brutus's servant Lucius plays the lute, a stringed instrument popular during Shakespeare's time.

Activity Have musically-inclined students produce a presentation including any of the following: an illustration and description of the lute, a demonstration of a lute and its music, a recording of Renaissance music that might have accompanied Shakespeare's production of *Julius Caesar*, and/or Renaissance music played on a guitar or other stringed instrument. Point out Brutus's description of the music as "a sleepy tune." **L3**

And we must take the current when it serves,
Or lose our ventures.

CASSIUS.   Then with your will° go on;
225   We'll along ourselves, and meet them at Philippi.

BRUTUS.   The deep of night is crept upon our talk,
And nature must obey necessity,
Which we will niggard with a little rest.°
There is no more to say?

CASSIUS.   No more. Good night.
230   Early tomorrow will we rise, and hence.

BRUTUS.   Lucius. [*Enter* LUCIUS.] My gown. [*Exit* LUCIUS.]
                    Farewell, good Messala.
Good night, Titinius. Noble, noble Cassius,
Good night, and good repose.

CASSIUS.   O my dear brother!
This was an ill beginning of the night.
235   Never come such division 'tween our souls!
Let it not, Brutus.

[*Enter* LUCIUS *with the gown.*]

BRUTUS.   Everything is well.

CASSIUS.   Good night, my lord.

BRUTUS.   Good night, good brother.

TITINIUS AND MESSALA.   Good night, Lord Brutus.

BRUTUS.   Farewell
every one.

[*Exit (all but* BRUTUS *and* LUCIUS).]

Give me the gown. Where is thy instrument?

240   LUCIUS.   Here in the tent.

BRUTUS.   What, thou speak'st drowsily?
Poor knave,° I blame thee not; thou art o'erwatch'd.°
Call Claudius and some other of my men,
I'll have them sleep on cushions in my tent.

LUCIUS.   Varrus and Claudio!

[*Enter* VARRUS *and* CLAUDIO.]

245   VARRUS.   Calls my lord?

BRUTUS.   I pray you, sirs, lie in my tent and sleep;
It may be I shall raise° you by and by
On business to my brother Cassius.

224 with your will: as you wish.

227–228 nature must . . . rest:
Human nature has its needs, which
we will grudgingly satisfy (**niggard**)
by resting briefly.

241 knave: lad. **o'erwatch'd:** tired from
staying awake too long.

247 raise: awaken.

Active Reading

QUESTION Ask students why they
think Cassius agrees to Brutus's
plan. *(Students may say he gives in
because Brutus's speech was convincing, because he does not want to
argue anymore, or because he realizes he cannot win an argument
with Brutus.)*

Active Reading

VISUALIZE Encourage students to
visualize the bedtime preparations at
the army camp. Point out that the
long preparations set the reader up
for the surprising visitor at the end
of the act.

Listening and Speaking *Minilesson*

Interpreting a Famous Speech
Brutus's speech, lines 218–224, is
one of the often quoted speeches of
Shakespeare. Reading the speech aloud
can help students understand why this
and other speeches written by
Shakespeare are widely admired.

Activity Have pairs of students practice
reading the speech aloud several times.

Encourage them to discuss the best ways
to use vocal tone and emphasis to bring
out the speech's meaning. Then ask them
why the speech may be popular. *(It uses a
vivid extended metaphor; it is spoken in
rhythmic blank verse; it describes a philosophy of life that emphasizes taking advantage of the moment.)* **L2** **COLLAB. LEARN.**

Literary Elements

CHARACTER Have students describe the character traits demonstrated by Brutus in the scene with Lucius. *(He appears kind, worrying about Lucius's sleep, and sensitive, requesting music.)*

FYI

Song "Orpheus with his lute" from *Henry VIII* is traditionally sung in this scene when the play is staged. Shakespeare may have had in mind the song "Come, heavy sleep" from *First Book of Songs* by John Dowland, published in 1597.

FYI

Shakespeare's Ghosts
Elizabethans of both upper and lower social classes believed in ghosts. This belief is reflected in several of Shakespeare's plays. Some of Shakespeare's ghosts, such as that of Hamlet's father, are objective: they are seen by more than one person. Others are subjective and assumed to be imagined by one character.

Teaching Options

VARRUS. So please you, we will stand and watch your pleasure.°

250 **BRUTUS.** I will not have it so. Lie down, good sirs,
It may be I shall otherwise bethink me.°

[*VARRUS and CLAUDIO lie down.*]

Look, Lucius, here's the book I sought for so;
I put it in the pocket of my gown.

LUCIUS. I was sure your lordship did not give it me.

255 **BRUTUS.** Bear with me, good boy, I am much forgetful.
Canst thou hold up thy heavy eyes awhile,
And touch thy instrument a strain or two?°

LUCIUS. Ay, my lord, an't° please you.

BRUTUS. It does, my boy.
I trouble thee too much, but thou are willing.

260 **LUCIUS.** It is my duty, sir.

BRUTUS. I should not urge thy duty past thy might;
I know young bloods look for a time of rest.

LUCIUS. I have slept, my lord, already.

BRUTUS. It was well done, and thou shalt sleep again;
265 I will not hold thee long. If I do live,
I will be good to thee.

[*Music, and a song.*]

This is a sleepy tune. O murd'rous slumber!
Layest thou thy leaden mace° upon my boy,
That plays thee music? Gentle knave, good night;
270 I will not do thee so much wrong to wake thee.
If thou dost nod, thou break'st thy instrument;
I'll take it from thee; and, good boy, good night.
Let me see, let me see; is not the leaf turn'd down
Where I left reading? Here it is, I think.

[*Enter the GHOST OF CAESAR.*]

275 How ill this taper burns!° Ha! who comes here?
I think it is the weakness of mine eyes
That shapes this monstrous apparition.
It comes upon me. Art thou anything?
Art thou some god, some angel, or some devil,
280 That mak'st my blood cold, and my hair to stare?°
Speak to me what thou art.

GHOST. Thy evil spirit, Brutus.

---

249 stand . . . pleasure: stay awake and be ready to serve you.

251 It may be . . . me: I might change my mind.

257 touch thy . . . two: play a song or two. (Lucius probably plays the lute, a stringed instrument.)
258 an't: if it.

267–268 O murd'rous . . . mace: Officers used to touch a rod (**mace**) to a person's shoulder as a sign of arrest. Brutus calls the mace of deathlike (**murd'rous**) sleep "leaden" because of its heaviness.

275 How ill . . . burns: It was believed that candles burn dimly when a ghost appears.

280 stare: stand on end.

Reading *Minilesson*

Summarizing Summarizing each act of *Julius Caesar* is a good way for students to make sure they understand the play's events and to review the play. Remind them that in summarizing, they state the text's main idea in their own words.

Activity Have students orally summarize each of the first four acts of the play. Tell students to keep their summaries brief—three to four sentences. Have them compare their summaries with a partner and discuss necessary details they omitted or unnecessary ones they included.

L2 COLLAB. LEARN.

Additional Resources
📁 *Reading Workbook*

Shakespeare–Julius Caesar, Act IV Scene iii. Richard Westall (1765–1836). Line and stipple engraving with hand coloring, 646 x 459 mm. Fine Arts Museums of San Francisco.

Viewing the art: Who is pictured here? Based on what you've read, do you think the characters have been portrayed accurately? Why or why not?

VIEWING THE ART

Richard Westall, an English painter, also illustrated books. He was known for his sometimes violent colors.

Viewing Response *Brutus and Caesar's ghost are pictured. Students should give specific reasons for determining whether the characters are realistically portrayed.*

Grammar and Language *Minilesson*

Commas in a Series Remind students that commas are used between words, phrases, or clauses in a series. A comma is used before the coordinating conjunction.

Activity Write the following sentences adapted from act 4 on the board. Omit the commas between the items in the series. Have students place the commas correctly.

1. Lepidus is a barren-spirited fellow, one that feeds on objects, arts, and imitations.
2. We, lying still, are full of rest, defense, and nimbleness. **L1**

Additional Resources

📖 ***Grammar and Language Transparency 63***

📕 ***Grammar and Language Workbook,*** p. 253

📕 ***Grammar and Composition Handbook,*** Lesson 11.6

📙 ***Writer's Choice,*** Lesson 21.6

Active Reading

VISUALIZE Have students visualize the appearance of the ghost of Caesar. How might this scene be staged? Have them brainstorm for ideas.

Z Literary Elements

FORESHADOWING Ask students why the ghost is an effective device to foreshadow the end of Brutus's conflict. *(It is visually striking; a ghost is a supernatural symbol that has an emotional effect on people.)*

AA Critical Thinking

DRAWING CONCLUSIONS Use the following model to help students draw a conclusion about Caesar's ghost.

Model: Brutus is exhausted and almost asleep when the ghost of Caesar appears. The ghost says forebodingly that he will see Brutus at Philippi. No one else sees the ghost. I think that since Brutus was the only one to see the ghost, that this event foreshadows something evil for Brutus. It's like the bully who threatens to meet me after school.

Thematic Focus

Loyalty and Betrayal Ask students which characters feel loyalty and which feel betrayed now. How have their feelings changed from those in previous acts?

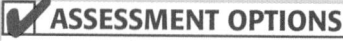

ASSESSMENT OPTIONS

📁 **Quick Checks,** p. 74

Teaching Options

JULIUS CAESAR

BRUTUS.   Why com'st thou?

GHOST. To tell thee thou shalt see me at Philippi.

BRUTUS. Well; then I shall see thee again?

GHOST. Ay, at Philippi.

BRUTUS. Why, I will see thee at Philippi then.

[*Exit* GHOST.]

Now I have taken heart thou vanishest.
Ill spirit, I would hold more talk with thee.
Boy! Lucius! Varrus! Claudio! Sirs, awake!
290   Claudio!

LUCIUS. The strings, my lord, are false.°

BRUTUS. He thinks he still is at his instrument.
Lucius, awake!

LUCIUS. My lord?

295   **BRUTUS.** Didst thou dream, Lucius, that thou so criedst out?

LUCIUS. My lord, I do not know that I did cry.

BRUTUS. Yes, that thou didst. Didst thou see anything?

LUCIUS. Nothing, my lord.

BRUTUS. Sleep again, Lucius. Sirrah Claudio!

300   [*To* CLAUDIO *and then* VARRUS.] Fellow thou, awake!

VARRUS. My lord?

CLAUDIO. My lord?

BRUTUS. Why did you so cry out, sirs, in your sleep?

BOTH. Did we, my lord?

BRUTUS.   Ay. Saw you anything?

305   **VARRUS.** No, my lord, I saw nothing.

CLAUDIO.   Nor I, my lord.

BRUTUS. Go and commend me° to my brother Cassius;
Bid him set on his pow'rs betimes before,°
And we will follow.

BOTH.   It shall be done, my lord.

[*They exit.*]

291 **false:** out of tune.

306 **commend me:** send my regards.

307 **set on . . . before:** start his troops moving early, at the lead.

Responding to Literature

Personal Response

What do you think about the relationship between Brutus and Cassius?

ANALYZING ACT 4

RECALL AND INTERPRET

1. How does the political situation in Rome following Caesar's murder compare with what it was under Caesar's rule?
2. Describe the main **conflict**, or struggle, between Brutus and Cassius in act 4. In your opinion, who is more to blame? Why?
3. What personal grief does Brutus relate to Cassius? How does this news affect Cassius?
4. What battle plan does Cassius propose? Why, do you think, does he agree to march to Philippi?
5. What unexpected visitor comes to Brutus's tent? How does Brutus react to this visitation? Explain.

EVALUATE AND CONNECT

6. What is your impression of Antony in act 4? Do his actions surprise you? Explain.
7. Why, do you think, did Shakespeare include the conflict between Cassius and Brutus?
8. Would you rather serve as a Roman soldier under Brutus or Cassius? Why? Which of them better displays the qualities you identified in your leadership web in the Focus Activity on page 777?
9. In your opinion, what is the purpose of the scene in Brutus's tent with Brutus and Lucius as Brutus prepares to sleep?
10. Based on your own experiences, what are some ways to prevent disagreements like the one between Cassius and Brutus?

Literary ELEMENTS

Foreshadowing

Playwrights and other authors use **foreshadowing** to prepare readers for events that will happen later. In act 2 of *Julius Caesar,* for example, Cassius suggests to Brutus that the conspirators should kill Mark Antony along with Caesar or else "we shall find of him / A shrewd contriver." In act 3, Cassius urges Brutus not to let Antony speak at Caesar's funeral. Cassius's fears later are shown to be well-founded, and Brutus's judgment is shown to be in error.

1. What may be foreshadowed by Cassius and Brutus disagreeing on a plan of military action?
2. What may be foreshadowed by Caesar's ghost appearing to Brutus and saying he will see Brutus at Philippi?

● See **Literary Terms Handbook,** p. R5.

EXTENDING YOUR RESPONSE

Personal Writing

Still Friends?   In your journal, describe an argument that you once had with a close friend. What caused the disagreement? How did you try to settle your differences? Were you able to remain friends with this person? Compare your personal experience with the dispute between Cassius and Brutus.

Interdisciplinary Activity

Social Studies: Army Life   Use library resources and the Internet to research armies in ancient Rome. How were armies organized? Who was in charge? Where were the armies stationed? How were funds raised to support the army? Present your findings to the class in an oral report.

 Save your work for your portfolio.

JULIUS CAESAR 🔖 857

DRAMA 🔖 857

SUMMARY, Act 5

Antony and Octavius gladly see the army of Brutus and Cassius coming to meet them and swear to get revenge for Caesar's death. Cassius tells of bad omens of the battle's outcome. He and Brutus say good-bye to one another in case they are killed in battle. Cassius, mistakenly believing that Titinius has been captured by the enemy, kills himself. Brutus, seeing that the battle is nearly lost, also takes his own life. Antony and Octavius speak of Brutus as an honorable man and promise he will have a military funeral. They prepare to consolidate their own power.

📁 *Spanish Summaries,* p. 70

A Active Reading

PREDICT Have students predict how Antony and Octavius will get revenge on Brutus and Cassius.

Additional Resources
📁 *Active Reading Guide,* p. 75
🎧 *Audio Library*
🎧 *Spanish Audio Library*

Historical Note

Octavius's opposition to Antony's wishes may foreshadow a later battle between the two. In 31 B.C. Octavius defeated the joint forces of Antony and Cleopatra off the coast of Greece and became the sole ruler of Rome.

Teaching Options

ACT 5

SCENE 1. The Plains of Philippi in Greece. A few weeks later.

[*Enter* OCTAVIUS, ANTONY, *and their* ARMY.]

    OCTAVIUS. Now, Antony, our hopes are answered.
    You said the enemy would not come down,
    But keep the hills and upper regions.
    It proves not so: their battles° are at hand;
5   They mean to warn° us at Philippi here,
    Answering before we do demand of them.°

    ANTONY. Tut, I am in their bosoms,° and I know
    Wherefore they do it. They could be content
    To visit other places, and come down
10   With fearful° bravery, thinking by this face
    To fasten in our thoughts that they have courage;°
    But 'tis not so.

[*Enter a* MESSENGER.]

    MESSENGER. Prepare you, generals,
    The enemy comes on in gallant show;
    Their bloody sign° of battle is hung out,
15   And something to be done immediately.

    ANTONY. Octavius, lead your battle softly° on
    Upon the left hand of the even° field.

    OCTAVIUS. Upon the right hand I, keep thou the left.

    ANTONY. Why do you cross me in this exigent?°

20   **OCTAVIUS.** I do not cross you; but I will do so.° [*March.*]

[*Drum. Enter* BRUTUS, CASSIUS, *and their* ARMY; LUCILIUS, TITINIUS, MESSALA, *and others.*]

    BRUTUS. They stand, and would have parley.°

    CASSIUS. Stand fast, Titinius; we must out and talk.

    OCTAVIUS. Mark Antony, shall we give sign of battle?

    ANTONY. No, Caesar, we will answer on their charge.°
25   Make forth, the generals would have some words.

    OCTAVIUS. Stir not until the signal.

    BRUTUS. Words before blows; is it so, countrymen?

---

4 battles: armies.

5 warn: defy.

6 Answering before . . . them: responding hostilely before we even challenge them to fight.

7 am in their bosoms: know what is in their hearts.

8–11 They could . . . courage: Antony dismisses his enemy's bravery as a false show (**face**), saying that they would really prefer to be somewhere else.

10 fearful: "frightening" or "full of fear."

14 bloody sign: A red flag was flown from a Roman general's tent to signal the start of battle.

16 softly: slowly.

17 even: level.

19 cross me in this exigent: oppose me at this moment of crisis.

20 I will do so: I will do as I said. (Octavius insists on attacking from the right, which is usually the position of the most experienced general.)

21 would have parley: request a conference.

24 answer on their charge: respond when they attack.

OCTAVIUS. Not that we love words better, as you do.

BRUTUS. Good words are better than bad strokes, Octavius.

30 ANTONY. In your bad strokes, Brutus, you give good words;
Witness the hole you made in Caesar's heart,
Crying, "Long live! hail, Caesar!"

CASSIUS. Antony,
The posture of your blows are yet unknown;°
But for your words, they rob the Hybla° bees,
35 And leave them honeyless.

ANTONY. Not stingless too?

BRUTUS. O, yes, and soundless too;
For you have stol'n their buzzing, Antony,
And very wisely threat before you sting.

ANTONY. Villains! you did not so, when your vile daggers
40 Hack'd one another in the sides of Caesar.
You show'd your [teeth]° like apes, and fawn'd like hounds,
And bow'd like bondmen, kissing Caesar's feet;
Whilst damned Casca, like a cur, behind
Struck Caesar on the neck, O you flatterers!

45 CASSIUS. Flatterers? Now, Brutus, thank yourself;
This tongue had not offended so today,
If Cassius might have rul'd.°

OCTAVIUS. Come, come, the cause.° If arguing make us sweat,
The proof of it° will turn to redder drops.
50 Look,
I draw a sword against conspirators;
When think you that the sword goes up again?°
Never, till Caesar's three and thirty wounds
Be well aveng'd; or till another Caesar
55 Have added slaughter to the sword of traitors.°

BRUTUS. Caesar, thou canst not die by traitors' hands,
Unless thou bring'st them with thee.°

OCTAVIUS. So I hope;
I was not born to die on Brutus' sword.

BRUTUS. O, if thou wert the noblest of thy strain,°
60 Young man, thou couldst not die more honorable.

CASSIUS. A peevish schoolboy,° worthless of such honor,
Join'd with a masker and a reveler!°

ANTONY. Old Cassius still!

33 The posture . . . unknown: We don't know what kind of blows you will strike.
34 Hybla: an area in Sicily noted for its honey. (Cassius is reminding Antony of his "sweet" words to the conspirators after the assassination.)

41 show'd your [teeth]: grinned.

47 If Cassius . . . rul'd: if Cassius had had his way (when he argued that Antony should be killed).
48 cause: business at hand.
49 The proof of it: deciding the argument in battle.

52 goes up again: goes back into its sheath.

54–55 till another . . . traitors: until the conspirators have killed another Caesar (that is, Octavius himself).
56–57 Caesar . . . thee: Brutus suggests that all the traitors are on the side of Octavius and Antony.

59 strain: family.

61 schoolboy: Octavius was twenty-one at the time of the battle.
62 a masker and a reveler: one who indulges in lavish entertainment and drunken feasts.

B Active Reading
VISUALIZE Encourage students to visualize the staging of the four generals' meeting on the battlefield. Have them describe what actors might communicate through posture and facial expressions.

C Critical Thinking
INFERRING Of what flaw does Antony accuse Brutus and Cassius accuse Antony? *(hypocrisy)*

D Literary Elements
IMAGERY Have students name the animal images that Antony uses to describe the conspirators. What is their effect? *(He compares them to apes, hounds, and curs [mongrels]. The effect is degrading.)*

E Active Reading
REVIEW Have students review the discussion between Brutus and Cassius in act 2, scene 1 about whether Antony should be killed along with Caesar and consider Brutus's conviction that Antony should live in light of the events of act 5.

F Author's Craft
DIALOGUE Ask students why Shakespeare has the four generals come together to exchange threats and insults. *(Since he cannot stage the battles, he brings the opponents together in other ways. It gives him an opportunity for exciting and colorful language while reviewing the events and alliances before the climactic battle.)*

MEETING INDIVIDUAL NEEDS ENGLISH LANGUAGE LEARNERS

Vocabulary of Battle English language learners may be unfamiliar with some words used in act 5 to describe battle.

Activity Write the following words on the board: *general, charge, slaughter, soldier, sword, legions, troops.* Have students look up words they are unsure of in an English dictionary. Discuss their parts of speech. Call on students to pronounce the words; refer students to the dictionary pronunciation as needed. Suggest that students add the words to their vocabulary notebooks.

Additional Resources
📁 *English Language Learners Sourcebook*

860 🪶 UNIT 4

Teaching Options

G **Literary Elements**

FIGURES OF SPEECH: *Metaphor*
Cassius is not speaking literally in lines 67–68. What two things is he comparing? *(battle and a storm)*

H **Active Reading**

REVIEW Have students compare Cassius's omens to those described by Calphurnia in act 2, scene 2. How does the comparison help them interpret the foreshadowing in Cassius's speech? *(Calphurnia's similar vision correctly presaged Caesar's murder. Students should infer that the speech foreshadows a tragic end for Cassius.)*

I **Literary Elements**

CHARACTER Have students describe Cassius as he prepares to do battle. *(He is courageous and optimistic; although he has had a frightening vision of disaster, he is ready to fight bravely.)*

JULIUS CAESAR

OCTAVIUS. Come, Antony; away!
Defiance, traitors, hurl we in your teeth.
65   If you dare fight today, come to the field;
If not, when you have stomachs.°

[*Exit* OCTAVIUS, ANTONY, *and* ARMY.]

G **CASSIUS.** Why, now blow wind, swell billow, and swim bark!
The storm is up, and all is on the hazard.°

BRUTUS. Ho, Lucilius, hark, a word with you.

[LUCILIUS *and (then)* MESSALA *stand forth.*]

LUCILIUS. My lord?

[BRUTUS *and* LUCILIUS *converse apart.*]

CASSIUS. Messala!

70   **MESSALA.** What says my general?

CASSIUS. Messala,
This is my birthday; as this very day
Was Cassius born. Give me thy hand, Messala;
Be thou my witness that against my will
(As Pompey was)° am I compell'd to set
75   Upon one battle all our liberties.
You know that I held Epicurus strong,°
And his opinion; now I change my mind,
And partly credit things that do presage.°
Coming from Sardis, on our former ensign°
80   Two mighty eagles fell, and there they perch'd,
Gorging and feeding from our soldiers' hands,
Who to Philippi here consorted° us.
H This morning are they fled away and gone,
And in their steads do ravens, crows, and kites°
85   Fly o'er our heads, and downward look on us
As° we were sickly prey. Their shadows seem
A canopy most fatal, under which
Our army lies, ready to give up the ghost.

MESSALA. Believe not so.

I **CASSIUS.** I but believe it partly,
90   For I am fresh of spirit, and resolv'd
To meet all perils very constantly.°

BRUTUS. Even so, Lucilius.°

CASSIUS. Now, most noble Brutus,
The gods today stand friendly, that we may,

---

66 stomachs: appetite for battle.

68 all is . . . hazard: Everything is at stake.

74 As Pompey was: Pompey was persuaded against his better judgment to fight at Pharsalus, where he was defeated by Caesar.

76 held Epicurus strong: have been a firm believer of Epicurus (a Greek philosopher whose followers did not believe in omens).

78 presage: foretell the future.

79 former ensign: foremost banner.

82 consorted: accompanied.

84 kites: hawks. (All three birds are omens of death.)

86 As: As if.

91 constantly: resolutely.

92 Even so, Lucilius: Brutus finishes his discussion with Lucilius.

MEETING INDIVIDUAL NEEDS — GIFTED AND TALENTED

Epicurus Cassius refers to the Greek philosopher Epicurus, from whom comes the word *epicure*, meaning a person devoted to sensual pleasures or a person with discriminating tastes in food and wine.

Activity Have students research Epicurus to find out more about his beliefs and philosophy. Have them find out why the word *epicure* comes from his name: Does its connotation of devotion to excessive physical pleasure correctly reflect his teachings? **L3**

Lovers in peace, lead on our days to age!°
95 But since the affairs of men rests still incertain,
Let's reason with the worst that may befall.°
If we do lose this battle, then is this
The very last time we shall speak together:
What are you then determined to do?

100 **BRUTUS.** Even by the rule of that philosophy
By which I did blame Cato for the death
Which he did give himself—I know not how,
But I do find it cowardly and vile,
For fear of what might fall, so to prevent
105 The time of life—arming myself with patience
To stay the providence of some high powers
That govern us below.°

CASSIUS.   Then, if we lose this battle,
You are contented to be led in triumph
Thorough the streets of Rome?

110 **BRUTUS.** No, Cassius, no. Think not, thou noble Roman,
That ever Brutus will go bound to Rome;
He bears too great a mind.° But this same day
Must end that work the ides of March begun.
And whether we shall meet again I know not;
115 Therefore our everlasting farewell take:
Forever, and forever, farewell, Cassius!
If we do meet again, why, we shall smile;
If not, why then this parting was well made.

CASSIUS. Forever, and forever, farewell, Brutus!
120 If we do meet again, we'll smile indeed;
If not 'tis true this parting was well made.

BRUTUS. Why then, lead on. O, that a man might know
The end of this day's business ere it come!
But it sufficeth that the day will end,
125 And then the end is known. Come, ho, away!

[*BRUTUS, CASSIUS, and their ARMY withdraw to begin the battle.*]

SCENE 2. The field of battle. Shortly afterward.

[*Alarm. Enter BRUTUS and MESSALA.*]

BRUTUS. Ride, ride, Messala, ride, and give these bills°
Unto the legions on the other side.°

[*Loud alarm.*]

93–94 The gods . . . age: May the gods remain friendly today, so that we, dear friends in peace with each other, may live to see old age.

96 Let's reason . . . befall: Let's consider the worst that can happen.

100–107 Even by the . . . below: Brutus says that according to his beliefs, suicide is cowardly (he refers to his father-in-law, Cato, who killed himself after Caesar's defeat of Pompey). He would endure his fate rather than cut short (**prevent**) his life because of what might happen.

110–112 Think not . . . mind: Brutus is suggesting that even though he rejects suicide, his pride would force him to commit such an act rather than allow himself to be paraded through the streets of Rome.

1 bills: written orders.

2 legions on . . . side: other wing of troops (led by Cassius).

J Active Reading

REVIEW What are Brutus's beliefs concerning suicide? *(He does not believe in suicide and would not resort to it merely because he feared the results of being captured. However, his pride is so great that he might be forced to kill himself rather than be sent as a bound prisoner through Rome.)*

K Literary Elements

CHARACTER Have students describe Brutus and Cassius and their relationship as they say good-bye to one another. *(They are determined to be optimistic about the day's events even though they are also anxious about them. Their words demonstrate their respect and affection for one another.)*

Historical Note

The word *legions* refers to the army formation developed by the Romans in the early 300s B.C. In the 600s B.C. the Greeks introduced the *phalanx*. This was a formation in which spearmen wearing armor stood in a rectangle eight rows deep. The Romans improved on this formation by putting together three lines of small phalanxes, forming a legion.

MEETING INDIVIDUAL NEEDS INCLUSION STRATEGIES

Less-Proficient Readers One way to better comprehend Shakespeare's dialogue is to rearrange words to create a familiar sentence structure.

Activity Have students rearrange words in each sentence below.

1. Defiance, traitors, hurl we in your teeth. *(Traitors, we hurl defiance in your teeth.)*

2. Be thou my witness that against my will (as Pompey was) am I compell'd to set upon one battle all our liberties. *(Be my witness that I am compell'd against my will (as Pompey was) to set all our liberties upon one battle.)* **L1**

Additional Resources
📁 *Inclusion Strategies*

REVIEW What has happened since Brutus and Cassius parted? *(Brutus sent orders to Cassius to attack Antony while he attacks Octavius. Cassius's army has turned against him and retreated. Brutus's army has assumed victory over Octavius too soon and begun looting instead of helping Cassius fight Antony.)*

The following videotape program is available from Glencoe. Be sure to preview the video for appropriateness for your class.

- **In Search of History: Roman Legions**

Teaching Options

JULIUS CAESAR

> Let them set on at once; for I perceive
> But cold demeanor° in Octavio's wing,
> 5   And sudden push gives them the overthrow.
> Ride, ride, Messala, let them all come down.

[They exit.]

SCENE 3. Another part of the battlefield. Several hours later.

[Alarms. Enter CASSIUS and TITINIUS.]

> **CASSIUS.** O, look, Titinius, look, the villains° fly!
> Myself have to mine own turn'd enemy.°
> This ensign° here of mine was turning back;
> I slew the coward, and did take it° from him.
> 5   **TITINIUS.** O Cassius, Brutus gave the word too early,
> Who, having some advantage on Octavius,
> Took it too eagerly. His soldiers fell to spoil,°
> Whilst we by Antony are all enclos'd.

[Enter PINDARUS.]

> **PINDARUS.** Fly further off, my lord, fly further off;
> 10   Mark Antony is in your tents,° my lord;
> Fly, therefore, noble Cassius, fly far off.
>
> **CASSIUS.** This hill is far enough. Look, look, Titinius!
> Are those my tents where I perceive the fire?
>
> **TITINIUS.** They are, my lord.
>
> **CASSIUS.**   Titinius, if thou lovest me,
> 15   Mount thou my horse, and hide° thy spurs in him
> Till he have brought thee up to yonder troops.
> And here again, that I may rest assur'd
> Whether yond troops are friend or enemy.
>
> **TITINIUS.** I will be here again, even with a thought.°

[Exit.]

> 20   **CASSIUS.** Go, Pindarus, get higher on that hill;
> My sight was ever thick;° regard Titinius,
> And tell me what thou not'st about the field.

[PINDARUS goes up.]

> This day I breathed first: time is come round,
> And where I did begin, there shall I end;
> 25   My life is run his compass.° Sirrah, what news?
>
> **PINDARUS.** *[Above.]* O my lord!
>
> **CASSIUS.** What news?

4 cold demeanor: lack of spirit.

1 villains: Cassius's own troops (who are retreating).
2 Myself have . . . enemy: I have turned to fighting my own men.
3 ensign: standard bearer.
4 it: the standard, or army flag.

7 spoil: looting.

10 tents: camp.

15 hide: dig.

19 even with a thought: as quick as a thought.

21 my sight . . . thick: I have always been nearsighted.

25 is run his compass: has come full circle.

INTERDISCIPLINARY CONNECTION

History Methods and weapons of warfare have evolved from the war chariots of the Sumerians and the battering rams of the Assyrians to the helicopters, jets fighters, and nuclear weapons of today.

Activity Have students research the battle methods, equipment, and weapons of the ancient Romans. Encourage them to show how the Romans improved earlier tactics and weaponry. Have them include illustrations in an oral or written report or in a multimedia presentation. **L2**

Trajan. After A.D. 108, Roman. Marble. Louvre Museum, Paris.

 Critical Thinking

IDENTIFYING ASSUMPTIONS What does Pindarus assume based on what he sees from the top of the hill? *(He sees horsemen chase and surround Titinius, who dismounts; he hears the horsemen shout with joy. He assumes Titinius has been captured.)*

PINDARUS. Titinius is enclosed round about
  With horsemen, that make to him on the spur,°
30 Yet he spurs on. Now they are almost on him.
  Now, Titinius! Now some light.° O, he lights too!
  He's ta'en! [*Shout.*] And, hark, they shout for joy.

CASSIUS. Come down; behold no more.
  O, coward that I am, to live so long,
35 To see my best friend ta'en° before my face!

[*PINDARUS descends.*]

  Come hither, sirrah.
  In Parthia did I take thee prisoner,
  And then I swore thee, saving of thy life,°
  That whatsoever I did bid thee do,
40 Thou shouldst attempt it. Come now, keep thine oath;

29 **make to . . . spur:** ride quickly toward him.

31 **some light:** some of them dismount.

32 **ta'en:** taken prisoner.

38 **swore thee . . . life:** made you swear when I saved your life.

JULIUS CAESAR, ACT 5, SCENE 3   863

Literary Elements

N

TRAGIC HERO Explain that a tragic hero is a high-ranking person who has many admirable characteristics but also a fatal flaw. This flaw causes the hero's downfall. Could Cassius be considered a tragic hero? *(He was high-ranking, but he was never presented as an admirable character. A true tragic hero has to be one who has the potential for greatness, but fails due to some personal error.)*

Active Reading

O

RESPOND Have students describe their response to Cassius's death. Does his death scene evoke an emotional response? *(Cassius's sensitive nature became clear in the last act; he dies bravely. For these reasons students may feel saddened by his death.)*

Active Reading

P

QUESTION What does Pindarus mean when he says he would not be free "durst I have done my will"? *(He was sworn to obey Cassius and so had to kill him when ordered to. This action, which he did not want to take, made him a free man.)*

Active Reading

Q

REVIEW What good news does Messala bring? How does it turn to bad news? *(Messala says that Brutus's troops have defeated Octavius. But he finds that Cassius has killed himself in mistakenly believing that Brutus was defeated.)*

Teaching Options

Now be a freeman, and with this good sword,
That ran through Caesar's bowels, search° this bosom.
N Stand not° to answer; here, take thou the hilts,°
And when my face is cover'd, as 'tis now,
O 45 Guide thou the sword. [*PINDARUS stabs him.*] Caesar, thou art reveng'd,
Even with the sword that kill'd thee. [*Dies.*]

P PINDARUS. So, I am free; yet would not so have been,
Durst I have done my will. O Cassius,
Far from this country Pindarus shall run,
50 Where never Roman shall take note of him. [*Exit.*]

[*Enter TITINIUS and MESSALA.*]

MESSALA. It is but change,° Titinius; for Octavius
Is overthrown by noble Brutus' power,
As Cassius' legions are by Antony.

TITINIUS. These tidings will well comfort Cassius.

Q 55 MESSALA. Where did you leave him?

TITINIUS.   All disconsolate,
With Pindarus his bondman, on this hill.

MESSALA. Is not that he that lies upon the ground?

TITINIUS. He lies not like the living. O my heart!

MESSALA. Is not that he?

TITINIUS.   No, this was he, Messala,
60 But Cassius is no more. O setting sun,
As in thy red rays thou dost sink tonight,
So in his red blood Cassius' day is set!
The sun of Rome is set. Our day is gone,
Clouds, dews,° and dangers come; our deeds are done!
65 Mistrust of my success° hath done this deed.

MESSALA. Mistrust of good success° hath done this deed.
O hateful error, melancholy's child,°
Why dost thou show to the apt° thoughts of men
The things that are not? O error, soon conceiv'd,
70 Thou never com'st unto a happy birth,
But kill'st the mother that engend'red thee!°

TITINIUS. What, Pindarus? Where art thou, Pindarus?

MESSALA. Seek him, Titinius, whilst I go to meet
The noble Brutus, thrusting this report
75 Into his ears; I may say "thrusting" it;
For piercing steel and darts° envenomed

864   UNIT 4: DRAMA

---

42 search: penetrate.

43 Stand not: don't wait. **hilts:** sword handles.

51 but change: only an exchange of fortune. (Pindarus was mistaken when he reported Titinius's capture—he had in fact come upon Brutus's troops.)

64 dews: Dews were considered unhealthy.

65 Mistrust of my success: Fear of my mission's outcome.

66 Mistrust of good success: Fear of how the battle would turn out.

67 O hateful . . . child: Messala suggests that Cassius's melancholy temperament caused him to misperceive events.

68 apt: ready (to be deceived).

71 the mother . . . thee: the mind that conceived the error.

76 darts: arrows.

Writing *Minilesson*

Vivid Verbs Messala pictures himself "thrusting" the report of Cassius's death into Brutus's ears. The vivid verb form (used as an adjective here) emphasizes the violent effect that the news will have.

Activity Have students locate three passages from act 5 or other acts that use particularly vivid verbs. Have them write the sentence that includes the word and

then write a sentence of their own using the word. Possible examples from act 5 are scene 1, lines 39–40, "Villains! you did not so, when your vile daggers *hack'd* one another in the sides of Caesar"; scene 1, line 64, "Defiance, traitors, *hurl* we in your teeth"; scene 5, lines 24–25, "It is more worthy to *leap* in ourselves than *tarry* till they push us." **L2**

Additional Resources

📘 *Writer's Choice,* Lesson 3.3

Shall be as welcome to the ears of Brutus
As tidings of this sight.

TITINIUS.   Hie you, Messala,
And I will seek for Pindarus the while.

[*Exit* MESSALA.]

80   Why didst thou send me forth, brave Cassius?
      Did I not meet thy friends? and did not they
      Put on my brows this wreath of victory,
      And bid me give it thee? Didst thou not hear their shouts?
      Alas, thou hast misconstrued everything.

85   But hold thee, take this garland on thy brow;
      Thy Brutus bid me give it thee, and I
      Will do his bidding. Brutus, come apace,°
      And see how I regarded° Caius Cassius.
      By your leave, gods!—this is a Roman's part;°

90   Come, Cassius' sword, and find Titinius' heart. [*Dies.*]

[*Alarm. Enter* BRUTUS, MESSALA, LUCILIUS, VOLUMNIUS, YOUNG
CATO, *and* STRATO.]

BRUTUS.   Where, where, Messala, doth his body lie?

MESSALA.   Lo, yonder, and Titinius mourning it.

BRUTUS.   Titinius' face is upward.

CATO.°   He is slain.

BRUTUS.   O Julius Caesar, thou art mighty yet!
95   Thy spirit walks abroad, and turns our swords
      In our own proper° entrails. [*Low alarms.*]

CATO.   Brave Titinius!
      Look, whe'er he have not crown'd° dead Cassius!

BRUTUS.   Are yet two Romans living such as these?
      The last of all the Romans, fare thee well!
100   It is impossible that ever Rome
      Should breed thy fellow.° Friends, I owe moe° tears
      To this dead man than you shall see me pay.
      I shall find time, Cassius; I shall find time.
      Come, therefore, and to Thasos° send his body;
105   His funerals shall not be in our camp,
      Lest it discomfort° us. Lucilius, come,
      And come, young Cato; let us to the field.
      Labio and Flavio set our battles on.
      'Tis three a'clock; and, Romans, yet ere night
110   We shall try fortune in a second fight.

[*They exit.*]

87 apace: quickly.

88 regarded: honored.

89 By your . . . part: Titinius asks the gods to pardon him because he is cutting his life short to fulfill a Roman's duty (**part**).

93 Cato: Brutus's brother-in-law, the son of Marcus Cato.

96 our own proper: our very own.

97 Look . . . crown'd: see how he has crowned.

101 fellow: equal. **moe:** more.

104 Thasos: an island near Philippi.

106 discomfort: dishearten.

R Literary Elements

CHARACTER Have students explain what they learn of Cassius's character by the reactions of Messala and Titinius to his death. *(He is beloved by his soldiers, indicating that he was a good general.)*

S Active Reading

INTERPRET Why does Brutus invoke the name of Julius Caesar? *(He implies that the tragic results of the battle show that Caesar's spirit is still powerful; he is getting revenge for his assassination.)*

T Active Reading

REVIEW Have students summarize Brutus's speech. What is his major concern? *(Although he is grief-stricken by Cassius's death, he must focus on trying to win another battle.)*

REAL-WORLD CONNECTION

Battles in Film The last act of *Julius Caesar* illustrates the tragedy of war. Point out that although the many deaths may seem excessive, it is in this respect a realistic depiction of battle. Have students discuss realistic films they have seen on the Civil War, World War I, World War II, and the Vietnam War. Have them compare the depiction of death in those films to that in *Julius Caesar*. **L2**

Teaching Options

Base of the Column of Antoninus Pius. A.D.138–161, Roman. Vatican State.

Viewing the art: In what ways does this scene add to your understanding of the battles in this play?

SCENE 4. Another part of the battlefield. Shortly later.

[*Alarm. Enter* BRUTUS, MESSALA, *(young)* CATO, LUCILIUS, *and* FLAVIUS.]

> BRUTUS. Yet, countrymen, O, yet hold up your heads!°
> [*They exit.*]
>
> CATO. What bastard doth not?° Who will go with me?
>   I will proclaim my name about the field.
>   I am the son of Marcus Cato,° ho!
> 5 A foe to tyrants, and my country's friend.
>   I am the son of Marcus Cato, ho!
>
> [*Enter* SOLDIERS *and fight.*]
>
> LUCILIUS. And I am Brutus, Marcus Brutus, I;
>   Brutus, my country's friend; know me for Brutus!°
>
> [YOUNG CATO *is slain.*]

866 🦋 UNIT 4: DRAMA

1 **Yet . . . heads:** Brutus urges his troops to keep fighting.

2 **What bastard doth not:** Who among us was born so low that he doesn't?

4 **Marcus Cato:** Portia's father.

7–8 **And I am . . . Brutus:** Lucilius impersonates his leader to divert the enemy's attention from the real Brutus.

      O young and noble Cato, art thou down?
10   Why, now thou diest as bravely as Titinius,
      And mayst be honor'd, being Cato's son.

    FIRST SOLDIER. Yield, or thou diest.

    LUCILIUS.   Only I yield to die;
      There is so much that thou wilt kill me straight:°
      Kill Brutus, and be honor'd in his death.

15   **FIRST SOLDIER.** We must not. A noble prisoner!

   [*Enter* ANTONY.]

      SECOND SOLDIER. Room, ho! Tell Antony, Brutus is ta'en.

      FIRST SOLDIER. I'll tell the news. Here comes the general.
      Brutus is ta'en. Brutus is ta'en, my lord.

    ANTONY. Where is he?

20   **LUCILIUS.** Safe, Antony, Brutus is safe enough.
      I dare assure thee that no enemy
      Shall ever take alive the noble Brutus;
      The gods defend him from so great a shame!
      When you do find him, or alive or° dead,
25   He will be found like Brutus, like himself.°

    ANTONY. This is not Brutus, friend, but, I assure you,
      A prize no less in worth. Keep this man safe,
      Give him all kindness; I had rather have
      Such men my friends than enemies. Go on,
30   And see whe'er Brutus be alive or dead,
      And bring us word unto Octavius' tent
      How everything is chanc'd.

   [*They exit.*]

SCENE 5. Another part of the field. Late in the day.

[*Enter* BRUTUS, CLITUS, DARDANIUS, VOLUMNIUS, *and* STRATO.]

    BRUTUS. Come, poor remains of friends, rest on this rock.

    CLITUS. Statilius show'd the torchlight,° but, my lord,
      He came not back. He is or ta'en or slain.

    BRUTUS. Sit thee down, Clitus; slaying is the word,
5   It is a deed in fashion.° Hark thee, Clitus. [*Whispering.*]

    CLITUS. What, I, my lord? No, not for all the world.

    BRUTUS. Peace then, no words.

    CLITUS.   I'll rather kill myself.

13 There is . . . straight: You have good reason to kill me immediately.

24 or . . . or: either . . . or.
25 like himself: behaving like his noble self.

2 show'd the torchlight: signaled with a torch. (Statilius was sent out to see whether their camp was occupied by the enemy.)

5 It is . . . fashion: So many are being killed.

V Literary Elements

CHARACTER What character traits does Antony show in his response to Lucilius's admission that he is not actually Brutus? *(He shows that he is a shrewd and capable leader in realizing that a brave and resourceful soldier like Lucilius should be spared instead of immediately punishing him for his deceit.)*

W Active Reading

PREDICT Based on the decisions they have seen Cassius and Titinius make, students may be able to predict what Brutus is requesting of Dardanius.

INTERDISCIPLINARY CONNECTION

History As indicated in the play, the defeat of Cassius and Brutus's army was mainly due to Mark Antony's military genius. After the victory, Antony claimed Rome's eastern provinces, leaving the western ones to Octavius.

Activity Have students research Antony's life after the defeat of Brutus and Cassius, including his political and romantic relationship with Cleopatra, Queen of Egypt. Suggest that they find out how Octavius eventually defeated Antony to become the first emperor of Rome. Have them present their research in oral or written reports or in a multimedia presentation. **L2**

INTERPRET One of Brutus's last statements is "I found no man but he was true to me." Have students decide whether this is objectively true. If not, what does the statement say about Brutus? Offer the following model of how to interpret the statement.

Model: I can think of at least one example of a man who was not true to Brutus: Antony, who promised his support after Caesar's murder and then turned against Brutus. If Brutus is choosing to ignore that, then I say he is a very forgiving person. If he really does not recognize that, then I say he is a very naive person.

Literary Elements

TRAGIC HERO Remind students of the definition of a tragic hero. What evidence in Brutus's dying scene indicates that he is a tragic hero?

(One of his soldiers, Clitus, calls him a "noble vessel." He is a great man who is loved and respected by his soldiers. He shows wisdom and courage in choosing to die. Students may say that his flaw is his inability to understand people, as when he allows Antony to live and to speak at Caesar's funeral; or his idealism and naiveté, which make him believe that since it is best for Rome for Caesar to die, the assassination will not have tragic consequences.)

Teaching Options

JULIUS CAESAR

BRUTUS. Hark thee, Dardanius. [*Whispering.*]

DARDANIUS. Shall I do such a deed?

CLITUS. O Dardanius!

10 **DARDANIUS.** O Clitus!

CLITUS. What ill request did Brutus make to thee?

DARDANIUS. To kill him, Clitus. Look, he meditates.

CLITUS. Now is that noble vessel full of grief,
That it runs over even at his eyes.

15 **BRUTUS.** Come hither, good Volumnius; list° a word.

VOLUMNIUS. What says my lord?

BRUTUS. Why, this, Volumnius;
The ghost of Caesar hath appear'd to me
Two several° times by night; at Sardis once,
And this last night, here in Philippi fields.

20 I know my hour is come.

VOLUMNIUS. Not so, my lord.

BRUTUS. Nay, I am sure it is, Volumnius.
Thou seest the world, Volumnius, how it goes;°
Our enemies have beat us to the pit.°

[*Low alarms.*]

It is more worthy to leap in ourselves
25 Than tarry till they push us. Good Volumnius,
Thou know'st that we two went to school together;
Even for that our love of old, I prithee
Hold thou my sword-hilts, whilst I run on it.

VOLUMNIUS. That's not an office° for a friend, my lord.

[*Alarm still.*]

30 **CLITUS.** Fly, fly, my lord, there is no tarrying here.

BRUTUS. Farewell to you, and you, and you, Volumnius.
Strato, thou hast been all this while asleep;
Farewell to thee too, Strato. Countrymen,
My heart doth joy° that yet in all my life
35 I found no man but he was true to me.°
I shall have glory by this losing day
More than Octavius and Mark Antony
By this vile conquest shall attain unto.°
So fare you well at once, for Brutus' tongue
40 Hath almost ended his life's history.

15 list: hear.

18 several: separate.

22 Thou seest . . . goes: You see how things are going.
23 pit: a hole into which hunted animals are driven (also, a grave).

29 office: job.

34 joy: rejoice.
35 no man . . . me: no man to be unfaithful to me.

36–38 I shall . . . unto: I shall have more glory from this defeat than Octavius and Antony will achieve from their ignoble victory.

Listening and Speaking *Minilesson*

Great Speeches Four great leaders have speeches near the end of *Julius Caesar*. Two speeches are by defeated and dying generals. The other two are by victorious leaders who pay respects to the dead.

Activity Have groups of four students take turns reading the final speeches of Cassius (scene 3, lines 33–47), Brutus (lines 31–42 and 50–51), Antony (lines 68–75), and Octavius (lines 76–81). Encourage them to use their voices to express the characters' traits and attitudes at the end of the play. Then have them discuss what each speech says about its speaker. Which of the men seems noblest at the end?

L2 **COLLAB. LEARN.**

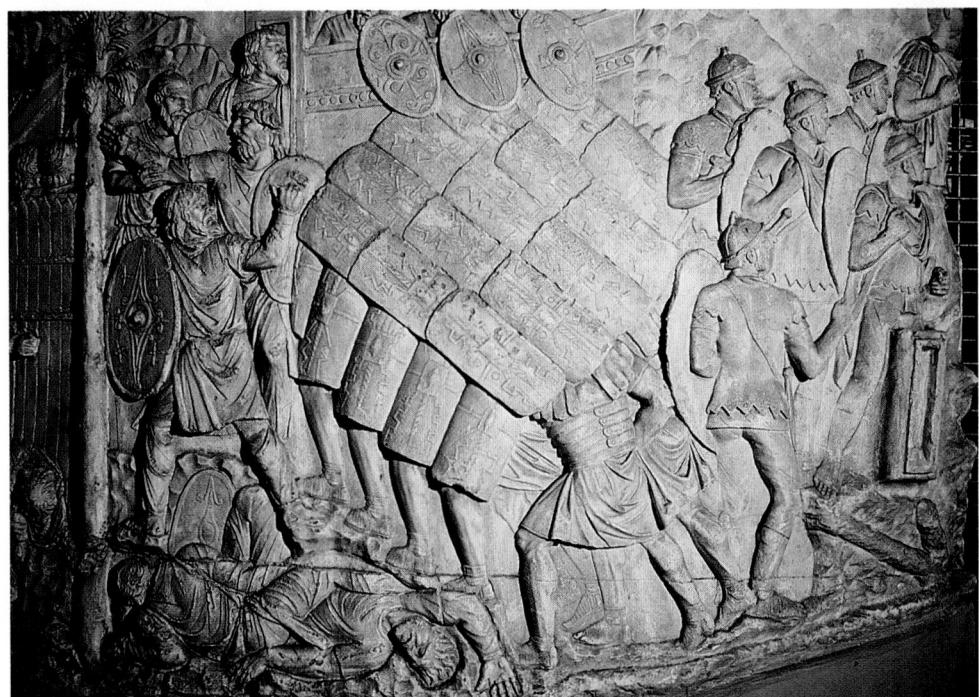

Trajan's Column, A.D. 112–113 (detail). Roman. Marble, height: approximately 68 m. Rome, Italy.

Viewing the art: What scene from the play is depicted here? Why do you think so?

VIEWING THE ART

Trajan's Column is a monument built to honor Trajan (A.D. 53?–117), a Roman emperor and military leader. The column, with a spiral staircase inside, stands in Trajan's Forum in Rome.

Viewing Response *The art might depict the battle between Antony and Octavius's forces and those of Brutus and Cassius.*

Z Critical Thinking

GENERALIZING How are the final words of Brutus and Cassius similar? *(Both speak of Caesar.)*

L   Night hangs upon mine eyes; my bones would rest,
That have but labor'd to attain this hour.

[*Alarm. Cry within, "Fly, fly, fly!"*]

CLITUS. Fly, my lord, fly!

BRUTUS.   Hence! I will follow.

[*CLITUS, DARDANIUS, and VOLUMNIUS exit.*]

       I prithee, Strato, stay thou by thy lord,
45   Thou art a fellow of a good respect;°
       Thy life hath had some smatch° of honor in it.
       Hold then my sword, and turn away thy face,
       While I do run upon it. Wilt thou, Strato?

STRATO. Give me your hand first. Fare you well, my lord.

50 **BRUTUS.** Farewell, good Strato. [*Runs on his sword.*] Caesar,
       now be still,
       I kill'd not thee with half so good a will.

[*Dies.*]

45 **respect:** reputation.
46 **smatch:** taste.

JULIUS CAESAR, ACT 5, SCENE 5 869

Reading *Minilesson*

Sequencing The important events of act 5 occur rapidly and can be confusing when students try to recall the plot. They can summarize and review the events of the battle in act 5 by listing them in chronological order.

Activity Have students review act 5 and summarize each event. Have them list the event summaries in numbered chronological order. For example, the first items on the list might be the following:

1. Brutus and Cassius come down from the hill and have an angry conference with Antony and Octavius.

2. Brutus and Cassius say good-bye to each other in case they are killed in battle.

3. The battle turns bad for Cassius when many of his soldiers abandon him and he sees Antony in his camp. **L2**

Additional Resources
Reading Workbook

Active Reading

AA

REVIEW Ask students why Antony feels that Brutus should be honored. *(He says Brutus was the only conspirator who acted from unselfish motives and that he was a good man.)*

Active Reading

BB

REVIEW What contrasting concerns does Octavius mention? *(He pays respect to Brutus and orders a military funeral for him. He also expresses happiness over defeating Brutus and the wealth it will bring.)*

FYI

The Final Speech
Traditionally, the final speaker in Shakespeare's tragedies was the character who would inherit the most authority after the death of the play's hero. In this case, that person is Octavius, fated to become Rome's first emperor.

Thematic Focus

Loyalty and Betrayal Have students discuss the four leaders who battle in act 5, considering which have been loyal and which have betrayed others. Ask whether it is possible to evaluate the leadership qualities of the characters based on this assessment.

☑ ASSESSMENT OPTIONS

📁 *Quick Checks,* p. 75

Teaching Options

[*Alarm. Retreat. Enter* ANTONY, OCTAVIUS, MESSALA, LUCILIUS, *and the* ARMY.]

OCTAVIUS. What man is that?

MESSALA. My master's man. Strato, where is thy master?

STRATO. Free from the bondage you are in, Messala;
55   The conquerors can but make a fire of him;
   For Brutus only overcame himself,°
   And no man else hath honor by his death.

LUCILIUS. So Brutus should be found. I thank thee, Brutus,
   That thou hast prov'd Lucilius' saying true.

60 **OCTAVIUS.** All that serv'd Brutus, I will entertain them.°
   Fellow, wilt thou bestow thy time with me?

STRATO. Ay, if Messala will prefer° me to you.

OCTAVIUS. Do so, good Messala.

MESSALA. How died my master, Strato?

65 **STRATO.** I held the sword, and he did run on it.

MESSALA. Octavius, then take him to follow thee,
   That did the latest° service to my master.

ANTONY. This was the noblest Roman of them all;
   All the conspirators, save only he,
70   Did that they did in envy of great Caesar;
   He, only in a general honest thought
   And common good to all, made one of them.°
   His life was gentle,° and the elements
   So mix'd in him that Nature might stand up
75   And say to all the world, "This was a man!"°

OCTAVIUS. According to his virtue let us use° him,
   With all respect and rites of burial.
   Within my tent his bones tonight shall lie,
   Most like a soldier, ordered honorably.°
80   So call the field to rest, and let's away,
   To part° the glories of this happy day.

[*All exit.*]

AA (bracket lines 68–75)
BB (bracket lines 76–81)

---

56 Brutus . . . himself: only Brutus conquered himself.

60 entertain them: take them into my service.

62 prefer: recommend.

67 latest: last.

71–72 He, only . . . them: He joined them only with honorable intentions for the public good.

73–75 His life . . . man: The Elizabethans believed that four elements (earth, water, air, and fire) in the body determined a person's temperament. Antony says that in Brutus the elements were perfectly balanced.
73 gentle: noble.
76 use: treat.
79 ordered honorably: with all due honor.
81 part: divide.

Grammar and Language *Minilesson*

Superlative Degree Point out the sentence "This was the noblest Roman of them all" (scene 5, line 68). Explain that the modifier *noblest* is in the superlative degree: Brutus is being compared to all Romans. The superlative degree is formed by adding *-est* or *most* to the modifier.

Activity Have students write five sentences describing characters in the play and using the superlative degree. **L2**

Additional Resources

🖋 *Grammar and Language Transparency 64*

📕 *Grammar and Language Workbook,* pp. 199–201

📕 *Grammar and Composition Handbook,* Lessons 8.1–8.2

📕 *Writer's Choice,* Lessons 18.1–18.2

Responding to Literature

Personal Response

What went through your mind as you finished reading this play? Record your reactions in your journal.

ANALYZING ACT 5

RECALL

1. What does Cassius confide to Messala before the battle?
2. What event leads to Cassius's death?
3. What does Brutus say about Caesar's spirit at Philippi?
4. What happens to Brutus at the end of the play? What do Antony and Octavius then say about Brutus?
5. What actions does Octavius take at the end of the play?

INTERPRET

6. Why do you think Cassius does not tell Brutus about his fears?
7. What might have influenced Cassius to accept Pindarus's report?
8. In what way does Brutus believe that Caesar is affecting events on the battlefield? Support your answer with evidence from act 5.
9. Compare Antony's speech at the end of the play with his discussion of Brutus at Caesar's funeral. How have his views of Brutus changed? Why have they changed?
10. What message do Octavius's actions suggest about honor and leadership? Explain.

EVALUATE AND CONNECT

11. According to Cassius, the last events of the play take place on his birthday. In your opinion, what does this information contribute to the last act?
12. Do you think that Antony and Octavius are motivated more by the desire for power or the wish to avenge Caesar's death? Explain, using evidence from the text.
13. What do you consider the most significant mistake committed at Philippi?
14. Do you agree with Antony that all the conspirators except for Brutus were motivated by envy? Support your opinion with examples from the play.
15. Theme Connections   What loyalties would you say are strongest in this play? What betrayals seem the most damaging?

Literary ELEMENTS

Tragedy and the Tragic Hero

A **tragedy** is a drama that ends in the downfall of its main character. The main character, or **tragic hero,** who suffers this fate is usually a high-ranking or respected person whose personality is marred by a fatal weakness or flaw, a **tragic flaw.** Fate or bad luck may work against this tragic hero, but usually his or her downfall is brought about by an error or a character flaw. Even if flawed, most tragic heroes are admirable individuals, and the audience regrets their loss.

Julius Caesar is an unusual tragedy because more than one character might be considered the tragic hero. Caesar is the title character, and his death is the central event in the play. However, the play focuses more on Brutus and ends with his death rather than Caesar's.

1. What is Caesar's tragic flaw? What is Brutus's tragic flaw?
2. In your opinion, which character is the tragic hero of the play? Explain your choice.

● See **Literary Terms Handbook,** p. R13.

Personal Response

Students may describe shock at the violence of war or sadness at the speeches of the dying men.

ANALYZING ACT 5

1. Cassius confides that it is his birthday and that he has seen omens signaling defeat for his army.
2. Cassius sends Titinius to check whether troops in the distance are friends or foes. He asks Pindarus to watch him. Pindarus reports that Titinius has been taken prisoner.
3. Brutus says that Caesar's spirit is mighty and is defeating Brutus and his men.
4. Brutus kills himself. Antony says that Brutus was "the noblest Roman of them all." Octavius says he deserves a soldier's burial.
5. Octavius declares the battle ended and prepares to divide the spoils with Antony.
6. Cassius may not tell Brutus about his fears because he does not want to dishearten him.
7. The omens Cassius saw and his feeling that he would lose the battle probably influenced him.
8. Brutus believes that Caesar's spirit is defeating his army; he says his "spirit walks abroad, and turns our swords in our own proper entrails." He is implying that Caesar is getting revenge on the conspirators.
9. In his funeral speech, Antony implied that Brutus was not honorable and had committed a great crime by killing Caesar. Now he says Brutus is noble. He has changed because he realizes that Brutus acted unselfishly. He also has no more need to criticize Brutus: he has defeated Brutus and Brutus is dead.
10. Octavius's actions suggest that honor is an essential trait in a great leader and that a good leader may be honorable even in defeat.
11. The information adds irony and sadness to Cassius's death.
12. Some students may see Antony and Octavius as more motivated by the desire for power, as seen in their power struggles with Lepidus in act 4 and on the battlefield with each other. Also, Octavius immediately wants to divide the spoils of war at the end of the play. Others may say the men are motivated by the wish to avenge Caesar's death, as they directly tell Brutus and Cassius at the beginning of act 5.

LITERARY ELEMENTS

1. Caesar's tragic flaw is pride or arrogance. Brutus's tragic flaws are idealism and misplaced trust.
2. Students may say Brutus is the tragic hero because he experiences the greatest conflict throughout the play. His tragic end is due directly to his decisions and actions while Caesar's is, to a large extent, out of his control.

Additional Resources

Literary Elements Transparency 75

13. Students may mention Brutus and Cassius's coming down from the hills to meet Antony and Octavius; Brutus's claiming victory too soon instead of helping Cassius; or Pindarus telling Cassius that Titinius had been captured.
14. Students may say the conspirators' meeting in act 2 shows that all the conspirators except Brutus were motivated by envy.
15. Strong loyalties include that of Brutus to the people of Rome, Portia to Brutus, and Antony and Octavius to Julius Caesar. Damaging betrayals include Brutus's betraying Caesar and Antony's betraying Brutus.

LITERATURE AND WRITING

Writing About Literature

Students' reviews should

- discuss the play's characters and themes.
- summarize and discuss the play's plot.
- describe the play's strengths and weaknesses.
- support ideas with quotes and references to the play.

Creative Writing

Students' interviews should

- include questions that show understanding of the play's plot and characters.
- include answers that show creativity and knowledge of the play.

EXTENDING YOUR RESPONSE

Literature Groups Point out that students will need to analyze Shakespeare's characterizations of Brutus, Cassius, Antony, and Octavius in drawing conclusions. **COLLAB. LEARN.**

Learning for Life Remind students that a news report should answer who, what, when, where, and why about an event. Point out that clarity is essential in a radio report.

Interdisciplinary Activity Point out that students may want to consult encyclopedias or other reference books to create a time line and use more specific sources for additional information about a specific person or event.

Responding to Literature

LITERATURE AND WRITING

Writing About Literature

Review Write a review of *Julius Caesar,* describing the play's strengths and weaknesses and discussing its major themes. Include a brief plot summary. Answer questions such as the following: Are the characters interesting and believable? How effectively did Shakespeare organize the plot? Why might Shakespeare have chosen to tell this story? Use quotes from the play and references to specific scenes in your analysis.

Creative Writing

A Historic Visit Imagine that you have an opportunity to interview the ghost of Caesar. You can find out how he feels about Brutus after the assassination, ask him to reveal which character he thinks should inherit his power, or get his response to the defeat of the conspirators at Philippi. Come up with a list of interesting questions, and then create answers that are appropriate for Caesar's character.

EXTENDING YOUR RESPONSE

Literature Groups

Reading the Author's Mind Do you think Shakespeare was more sympathetic toward the conspirators or toward Antony and Octavius's alliance? Discuss this question in your group. Remember that instead of debating your own opinion, you are trying to figure out Shakespeare's opinions of the characters. Use evidence from the play to develop and support your position. Share your results with the class.

Learning for Life

Special Report Imagine that you are a reporter at the Battle of Philippi. Create a radio news report about the defeat of the conspirators. Describe important events in the battle, and provide information that will help listeners understand the outcome. Make sure to include sensory details that convey what it was like to be present at the battlefield. Present your news report to the class.

Interdisciplinary Activity

History: Rome After Caesar Are you curious about what happened after the assassination of Caesar and the deaths of the conspirators? Use resources such as books, CD-ROMs, and the Internet to find out about these events. Create a time line of Roman history beginning with the death of Julius Caesar and ending with the division of the Roman Empire in A.D. 395. Draw a map showing the extent of the empire at its height. Locate Philippi in Greece on the map.

Roman ruins—Celsus Library, Ephesus, Turkey A.D. 110–135

Reading Further

If you are interested in Shakespeare or Julius Caesar, you might enjoy these works:

Play: *Antony and Cleopatra,* by William Shakespeare, is a tragedy that portrays the struggle for power between Antony and Octavius.

Biography: *William Shakespeare,* by Andrew Gurr, is an accessible study of Shakespeare's life and times.

History: *Julius Caesar,* by Michael Grant, is a concise account of Caesar's life and career.

Viewing: A 1978 BBC television production of *Julius Caesar,* directed by Herbert Wise.

📖 **Save your work for your portfolio.**

872   UNIT 4: DRAMA

✓ ASSESSMENT OPTIONS

- 📁 *Quick Checks,* p. 75
- 📁 *Selection and Theme Assessment,* pp. 145–146
- 📁 *Performance Assessment,* p. 74
- 💾 *Testmaker*

Skill Minilessons

Skill Minilessons

GRAMMAR AND LANGUAGE • Active and Passive Voice

The **voice** of a verb shows the relationship between the verb's subject and the action expressed by the verb. A verb is in the **active voice** when the subject of the sentence performs the action. A verb is in the **passive voice** when the action is performed on the subject. A passive verb always consists of a form of the verb *to be* plus a past participle. The following are examples of active and passive voice from *Julius Caesar.*

Active: "he sits high in all the people's hearts"
Passive: "we are governed with our mothers' spirits"

Writers often prefer using the active voice because it makes their writing sound more vigorous.

PRACTICE On your paper, write the verb that appears in each sentence and identify whether it is used in the active or passive voice.

1. Cassius flattered Brutus about his reputation.
2. Caesar mistrusted the lean Cassius.
3. Caesar was stabbed by Brutus in the Capitol.
4. Cicero and many other senators were executed.
5. Antony and Octavius defeated Brutus and Cassius at Philippi.

● For more on verbs, see **Language Handbook,** p. R44.

READING AND THINKING • Visualizing

Visualizing the scenes of a play as you read can help the lines, actions, and characters come alive for you and can help you understand difficult passages. Typically, you can use the stage directions to get a sense of how the sets and characters should look. In addition, in Shakespeare's plays, the lines are particularly rich in descriptive details that you can visualize. For example, in act 1, Casca vividly describes a crowd scene: "the rabblement hooted, and clapp'd their chopp'd hands, and threw up their sweaty nightcaps, and utter'd such a deal of stinking breath

because Caesar refus'd the crown." Can you see, hear, and smell the scene, even though it happened offstage?

PRACTICE Find a descriptive passage in *Julius Caesar.* On your paper, identify the scene and the details that help you visualize the scene. Which of the senses does the description appeal to?

● For more on visualizing, see **Reading Handbook,** p. R84.

VOCABULARY • Analogies

An analogy is a type of comparison that is based on the relationships between things or ideas. Some analogies are based on a relationship that could be called "antonym variant." In this type of analogy, the paired words would be antonyms if they were the same part of speech.

healthy : illness :: weak : strength

A *healthy* person is the opposite of one with *illness;* a *weak* person is the opposite of one with *strength.*

To finish an analogy, decide what relationship exists between the first two things or ideas. Then apply that relationship to another pair of words and see if it is the same.

PRACTICE Complete each analogy.

1. confident : misgiving :: humble :
   a. doubt   b. arrogance   c. sensitivity
2. miserable : elation :: doubtful :
   a. joy   b. concern   c. faith
3. unchanged : modification :: intact :
   a. growth   b. destruction   c. preservation

● For more on analogies, see **Communications Skills Handbook,** p. R77.

JULIUS CAESAR 873

GRAMMAR AND LANGUAGE
Active and Passive Voice

1. flattered—active
2. mistrusted—active
3. was stabbed—passive
4. were executed—passive
5. defeated—active

READING AND THINKING
Visualizing

Students might identify a scene such as Antony lifting the mantle from Caesar's corpse in act 3, scene 2 and showing the people "sweet Caesar's wounds, poor, poor, dumb mouths." The language appeals to the sense of sight.

VOCABULARY
Analogies

1. b   2. c   3. b

Additional Resources

📖 *Grammar and Composition Handbook,* Lesson 5.7

📖 *Grammar and Language Workbook,* p. 155

📖 *Writer's Choice,* Lesson 15.7

📁 *Reading Workbook*

📁 *Vocabulary Practice*

Technology Skills

Objectives

- To learn MLA guidelines for preparing research papers
- To use word processing software to format a page of a report
- To find examples of works-cited formats for various kinds of works

Teaching Strategies

The *MLA Handbook for Writers of Research Papers* explains MLA style appropriate for high school and undergraduate writing. The *MLA Style Manual and Guide to Scholarly Publishing* is intended for use by graduate students and professionals.

Point out to students that the heads along the top of the visual on page 874 appear at the top of the monitor screen; the toolbar symbols and icons appear at the bottom. Tasks performed by the toolbar frequently may also be carried out by using the pull-down menus; using the toolbar can be handier while the pull-down menus may give added information. For example, students can select a font quickly by clicking on the Font window on the toolbar and scrolling through the selections. Using the Format menu, they can do the same but also see what each font looks like.

Word Processing: Creating Academic Reports

Word processing software often includes special templates and interactive instructions for the creation of term papers. Even without templates, you can adhere to the guidelines of the Modern Language Association (MLA) without much difficulty simply by using standard word processing features. Just a click of the mouse, for example, allows you to adjust such formatting features as fonts, line spacing, and margins.

Using the Keyboard and the Toolbar

Before you begin, spend a few minutes reviewing the important word processing features found on the sample toolbars and ruler shown below. Because computers and software packages differ, some tools may have different names or toolbar appearances. If you have trouble finding any of the keys, icons, or features, click on the **Help** feature.

Creating an Academic Report According to MLA Guidelines

Select a report you wrote earlier in the year. Format the first page of your report according to the suggestions in the sample on the following page. Notice that a separate title page is not used in this format.

Teaching Options

MULTIPLE LEARNING STYLES

Spatial Students who learn visually will best learn keyboard and toolbar commands by active use of the software. They may also have an edge in remembering locations of commands on pull-down menus.

Activity Pair visual learners with students who have strong verbal skills. Ask partners to make a poster showing the toolbar and pull-down menus for their word-processing software and labeling each item with an explanation. Encourage students to invent a system of color coding to help students locate specific types of features, such as type treatment or alignment. **L2**
COLLAB. LEARN.

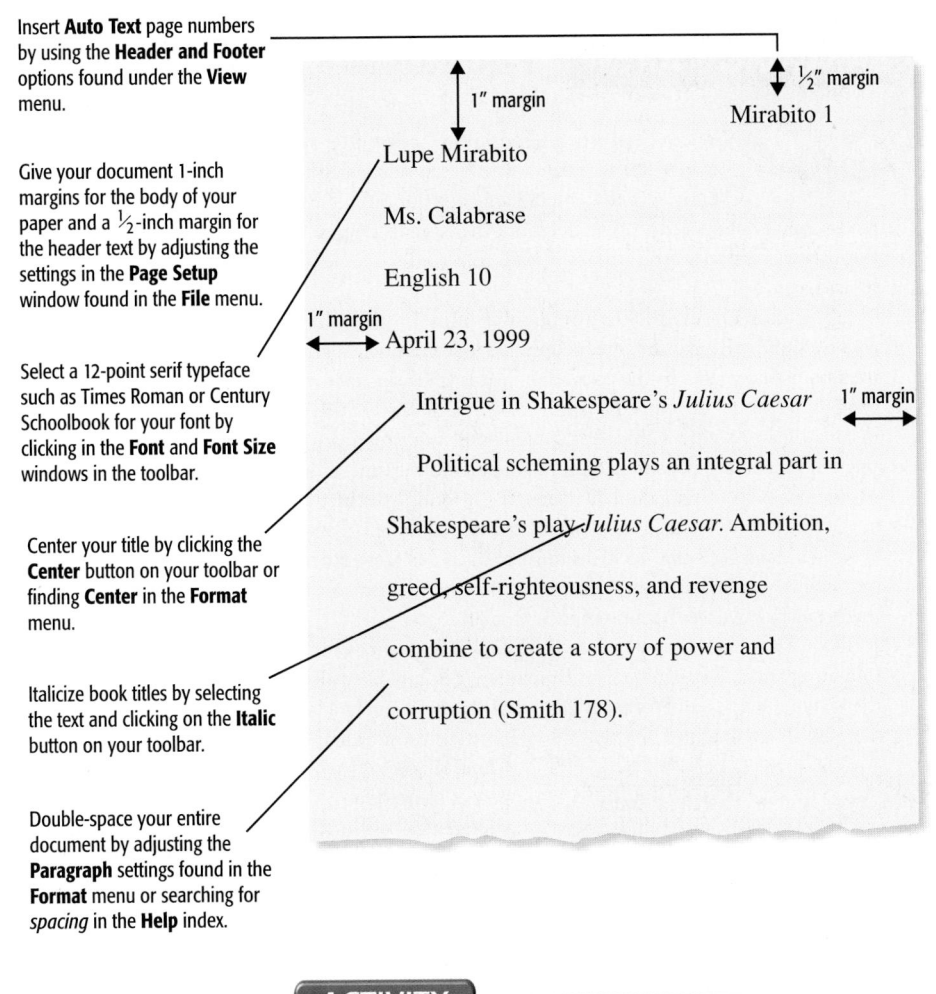

Insert **Auto Text** page numbers by using the **Header and Footer** options found under the **View** menu.

Give your document 1-inch margins for the body of your paper and a ½-inch margin for the header text by adjusting the settings in the **Page Setup** window found in the **File** menu.

Select a 12-point serif typeface such as Times Roman or Century Schoolbook for your font by clicking in the **Font** and **Font Size** windows in the toolbar.

Center your title by clicking the **Center** button on your toolbar or finding **Center** in the **Format** menu.

Italicize book titles by selecting the text and clicking on the **Italic** button on your toolbar.

Double-space your entire document by adjusting the **Paragraph** settings found in the **Format** menu or searching for *spacing* in the **Help** index.

½″ margin

Mirabito 1

1″ margin

Lupe Mirabito

Ms. Calabrase

English 10

1″ margin

April 23, 1999

Intrigue in Shakespeare's *Julius Caesar*   1″ margin

Political scheming plays an integral part in

Shakespeare's play *Julius Caesar*. Ambition,

greed, self-righteousness, and revenge

combine to create a story of power and

corruption (Smith 178).

ACTIVITY

1. Search the World Wide Web to find sample documents written in MLA style. You may also wish to browse the Modern Language Association's site at http://www.mla.org. For more help in setting up research papers, access http://www.researchpaper.com through your browser. See also Writing Handbook, pp. R65–R69.

2. Using one of the sites above or another Web site, find examples of the works-cited format for a poem found in an anthology, a newspaper article, a short story in a collection of stories, and an article from a CD-ROM encyclopedia.

Creating an Academic Report According to MLA Guidelines

Discuss with the class your preference about use of italics versus underlining for titles. The MLA guidelines advise students to check with teachers but note that "words that would be italicized in a publication are usually underlined to avoid ambiguity [due to difficulty reading italic fonts]."

Activity

Sample works cited are shown:

Poem in Anthology
Frost, Robert. "The Silken Tent." *The Lyric Potential.* Ed. James E. Miller, Jr. et al. Glenview, IL: Scott, Foresman and Company, 1974. 85.

Newspaper Article
Strout, Richard L. "Another Bicentennial." *Christian Science Monitor* 10 Nov. 1978: 27.

Short Story in a Collection
Anderson, Sherwood. "Death in the Woods." *Fifty Great American Short Stories*. Ed. Milton Crane. New York: Bantam Books, 1965. 191–203.

Article from a CD-ROM Encyclopedia
"Fresco." Britannica Online. Vers. 97.1.1. Mar. 1997. Encyclopaedia Britannica. 29 Mar. 1997. <http://www.eb.com:180>.

---

interNET CONNECTION

Work Citations Have students use a search engine to locate several sites that provide examples of works-cited formats. Ask students to print out the examples and jot down the site addresses. The class can compare examples to see if they are consistent and compile a master list of Web sites that offer help to students writing research papers.

Objective

- To recognize the influence of the Latin language on modern languages used throughout the world

Teaching Strategies

After students have read the article, ask those who have knowledge of one of the Romance languages to give the word from that language for the following English words: *free* (Latin *liber*); *friend* (Latin *amicus*); and *bread* (Latin *panis*). Challenge students to consult foreign-language dictionaries to find the words in several languages for these words and to find others with striking similarities among languages.

Activity

Students should discover differences in pronunciation and word choice from region to region. For example, Spanish speakers in Spain pronounce both the letter *c* before *i* and *e* and the letter *z* as voiceless *th*. In Latin America, these are always pronounced as *s*.

Teaching Options

INTERDISCIPLINARY LANGUAGE ARTS CONNECTION — The Romance Languages

When Shakespeare had Julius Caesar utter his famous last words, "*Et tu, Brute*," it is hardly surprising that he used Latin. Latin was the official language not only of Rome but of all the lands Caesar conquered. At the height of the Roman Empire, Latin was spoken throughout most of western Europe. If all roads led to Rome, then all tongues spoke Latin.

Like Caesar, however, Latin was not to dominate forever. In the conquered countries of the Roman Empire, people added words and pronunciations from their native languages to the Latin they spoke. Over several centuries, a distinct group of languages developed from the different dialects of everyday Latin spoken in the Roman provinces. A *dialect* is a regional variety of a language that has distinctive vocabulary, pronunciation, or grammar. Over time, a dialect may become so different from the standard language that it forms a distinct language. Starting in the ninth century, documents were produced in France—and later in Italy and Spain—in languages that looked similar to Latin but were different enough that they could be called separate languages. These new languages came to be called the *Romance languages* because of their Roman roots.

Today, five major languages are identified as Romance languages: French, Italian, Spanish, Portuguese, and Romanian. Because they all come from Latin, they have notable similarities. Many words in the Romance languages have the same or similar spellings. Notice the similarities in the examples in the box.

English	to see	sweet	water
Latin	videre	dulcis	aqua
French	voir	doux	eau
Italian	vedere	dolce	acqua
Spanish	ver	dulce	agua
Portuguese	ver	doce	água
Romanian	a vedea	dulce	apa

The Romance languages share other characteristics besides a Latin-based vocabulary. They also have a similar sentence structure. And in general, they have a pleasing, musical sound, partly because of the importance of vowel sounds, which are clear and precisely articulated. Spanish and Italian are especially phonetic, meaning that words are generally pronounced the way they are spelled. In French, by contrast, most final consonants are not pronounced. To foreigners' ears, the sound of most Romance languages is fast and fluid.

Throughout the world today, more than 900 million people speak one of the Romance languages as their mother tongue. In more ways than one, the culture of Julius Caesar lives on.

Activity

Languages often vary depending on where they are spoken. Choose a Romance language spoken in two widely separated places—such as French in France and in Quebec, Canada, or Spanish in Spain and in Mexico—and use reference materials to find out how pronunciation and vocabulary differ. What conclusions can you draw about how languages change and evolve?

Musical Many Italian words are used to indicate the time and expression in a piece of music. This is because the words came into use in the 1600s and 1700s, when Italian composers and musicians were very influential.

Activity Have students consult a dictionary to find the definition of each Italian word shown used to describe music.

Have them also find out whether the word has a Latin origin; if so, have them write the Latin word and its meaning.

accelerando
mezzo
prestissimo
crescendo
fortissimo
tempo **L2**

MEDIA Connection

Magazine Article

Engagement rings and heroes can come in very strange packages!

The Ring Finders of Philly

by Ralph Cipriano—*Good Housekeeping*, April 1996

The bride-to-be was heartbroken. There, at the bottom of the sewer grate, under five feet of stagnant water, sludge, and old soda cans, was the brand new ring she'd accidentally dropped. While standing at the corner of Thirteenth and Pine streets in Philadelphia, E. A. "Betsy" Alexander had yanked at the too-tight ring "and it flew up in the air" and, *plop*, fell into the sewer. *What kind of omen is this?* she thought to herself as she stared down at floating cigarette butts. Her wedding was less than two weeks away.

Retrieving the ring could have been a lost cause in many cities. But the Philadelphia Water Department has two heroes in Henry McGill, 53, and Charles Brooks, 46, who spend their days driving around the city in a mustard-colored Ford diesel truck, cleaning out sewers. Whenever anyone phones the switchboard at city hall to report he's dropped a valuable down a drain, the call immediately goes out for the rescue team of McGill and Brooks. Their specialty: grate-fishing.

In the last year alone, the two men have teased out at least two other rings. "You could call us the ring finders of Philadelphia," says Brooks. "And the marriage savers!"

Plucking out Betsy Alexander's ring was fairly routine. The partners, in blue uniforms and work boots, lifted the 70-pound cast-iron grate by hand and lowered a 250-pound hydraulic bucket into the sewer. Up came 50 pounds of slop, which they dumped on the roadside. Then they methodically combed through it with a rake and shovel until they found something bright and shiny.

Their "clients" are always grateful. Alexander, a composer who lives in Philadelphia's gentrified Society Hill section, brought each of the men a bouquet of roses and an invitation to her wedding.

But for McGill and Brooks it was all in a day's work.

Both men get a kick out of reuniting people with their valuables. "It makes you feel good," says McGill. Brooks concurs: "I leave with a sense of accomplishment."

Respond

1. Would you dig in a sewer full of sludge to retrieve your wedding ring or something of equal emotional value?

2. What's the most valuable (either emotional or fiscal) item you've ever lost? What was your reaction to this loss?

MEDIA Connection

Objective

• To read and understand a magazine article

Literature LINK

The Ring of General Macías This magazine article connects to the play *The Ring of General Macías* (pp. 879–893). A ring plays a pivotal role in both the article and the play.

Respond

1. Many students would say they would go through sludge to retrieve an item of great sentimental value.

2. Students' answers should show awareness of how much they personally value expensive or sentimentally valuable objects.

Additional Resources

📁 *Media Connections Activities,* p. 21

Reading Minilesson

Problem and Solution Point out that the magazine article is organized by problem and solution. Have students define the problem and tell approximately how much of the article is devoted to describing it *(approximately one-fourth)*. Then have them define the solution and tell how much of the article is devoted to it *(approximately three-fourths)*. Explain that, depending on the author's purpose, a larger proportion of a problem and solution article may be devoted to the problem.

Activity Have students work in pairs to identify this article's purpose *(to entertain)*. Then ask each pair to decide why the author devotes so much space to the solution. **L2**

Additional Resources

📁 *Reading Workbook*

Objectives

- To read and analyze a play about why some people may act bravely
- To identify irony in a play
- To write about the use of suspense in a play

Skills

Reading/Thinking: Inferring; Comparing and Contrasting; Drawing Conclusions
Writing: Adverbs; Irony; Scenes
Vocabulary: Denotation and Connotation
Grammar/Language: Compound Predicates
Listening/Speaking: Monologue; Discussing Love; Performing a Scene
Collaboration: Literature Groups

Motivating
→OPTIONS

Selection Focus Transparency 71: Have students view and discuss *Self-Portrait, 1937* by Frida Kahlo.

Focus Activity: Have volunteers put items from their maps on a group map on the board.

Before You Read

The Ring of General Macías

FOCUS ACTIVITY

In what situations do people exhibit bravery? What causes them to act bravely?

MAP IT! Create a cluster map about bravery. Include examples of actions that reveal bravery, people who can be considered brave, and possible reasons for acting bravely.

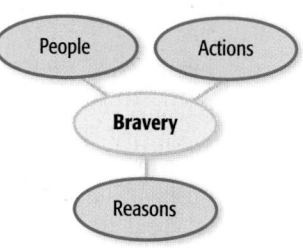

SETTING A PURPOSE
Read to find out why several characters act bravely.

BACKGROUND

The Time and Place

The events take place in a home just outside Mexico City on a night in April 1912, during the Mexican Revolution.

Did You Know?

The Mexican Revolution had its roots in the dictatorship of President Porfirio Díaz, who took power in 1876. Under Díaz, the majority of citizens—small farmers and laborers—suffered increasing hardship and repression. Meanwhile, land and wealth were accumulated by a small, elite class, many of whom were educated in Europe and who adopted European—especially French—fashions and manners. In 1910 armed resistance to Díaz's rule began, and by 1911 the dictator was forced to resign. The revolutionary struggle, which lasted for several more years, helped define Mexican identity.

VOCABULARY PREVIEW

regally (rē′ gəl lē) *adv.* in a grand, dignified manner befitting a king or queen; p. 883

ostentatiously (os′ tən tā′ shəs lē) *adv.* in a way intended to attract attention or impress others; p. 883

notorious (nō tôr′ ē əs) *adj.* widely and unfavorably known; p. 887

repressed (ri prest′) *adj.* held back or kept under control; restrained; p. 889

impertinent (im purt′ ən ənt) *adj.* inappropriately bold or forward; not showing proper respect or manners; p. 890

Meet Josephina Niggli

"Though we are all of the same clay, a jug is not a vase," says a Mexican proverb. Writer Josephina Niggli brought this understanding of people's differences to her writing of plays, poems, short stories, and novels. Although her parents were Scandinavian American, Niggli was born in Monterrey, Mexico, at the start of the Mexican Revolution. She grew up speaking both Spanish and English. Eventually, Niggli made the United States her home, but her early experiences in Mexico influenced much of her writing.

Josephina Niggli was born in 1910 and died in 1983.

RESOURCE MANAGER

Lesson Planning Resource
The *Unit Four Planning Guide* (pp. 39–46) provides additional lesson notes and reduced versions of all print resources.

📁 **Other Print Resources**
- Active Reading Guide, p. 76
- Vocabulary Practice, p. 49
- Reading Workbook, pp. 75–76
- Grammar and Language Workbook, pp. 79, 103
- Grammar and Composition Handbook, Lessons 2.3, 4.7

- Quick Checks, p. 76
- Selection and Theme Assessment, pp. 147–148
- Performance Assessment, p. 75
- Spanish Summaries, p. 71
- Inclusion Strategies
- English Language Learners Sourcebook

📑 **Transparencies**
- Selection Focus 71
- Literary Elements 76
- Grammar and Language 65

Technology
🎧 Audio Library
🎧 Spanish Audio Library
💻 Glencoe Literature Web Site
💾 Testmaker

The Ring of General Macías

A Drama of the Mexican Revolution

Josephina Niggli ✿

CHARACTERS

MARICA (mär ē′ kə): the sister of General Macías

RAQUEL (rə kel′): the wife of General Macías

ANDRÉS DE LA O (än′ dräs dā lə ō): a captain in the Revolutionary Army

CLETO (klā′ tō): a private in the Revolutionary Army

BASILIO FLORES (bə sēl′ yō flō′ rās): a captain in the Federal Army

PLACE: *Just outside Mexico City.*

TIME: *A night in April 1912.*

La Tormenta, 1985. Gronk. Acrylic on canvas, 90 x 60 in. Kuwada/Grimm Collection.

[*The living room of General Macías's[1] home is luxuriously furnished in the gold and ornate style of Louis XVI.[2] In the Right wall are French windows leading into the patio. Flanking these windows are low bookcases. In the Back wall is, Right, a closet door; and, Center, a table holding a wine decanter[3] and glasses. The Left wall has a door Upstage, and Downstage a writing desk with a straight chair in front of it. Near the desk is an armchair. Down Right is a small sofa with a table holding a lamp at the Upstage end of it. There are pictures on the walls. The room looks rather stuffy and unlived in.*

---

1. *Macías* (mä sē′ as)
2. France's King *Louis XVI* lived a life of luxury and elegance until he was beheaded in 1793 during the French Revolution.
3. A *decanter* is a decorative bottle with a stopper.

DRAMA ✿ 879

VIEWING THE PAINTING

Frida Kahlo (1910–1954) was a Mexican painter whose art reflects her love of Mexican culture.

Viewing Response *Students may say that the woman's calm, haughty demeanor is closer to the character of Raquel.*

B Literary Elements

STAGE DIRECTIONS Have students tell what the first stage direction indicates about the people who live in the house described. *(They are wealthy members of the upper class.)*

C Active Reading

VISUALIZE Have students visualize the opening action in which a young girl walks across the stage. What descriptions in the stage direction are especially helpful in visualizing the scene? *(Students may say that the moonlight coming through the window on the dark stage and a girl walking across the stage holding a lighted candle are especially vivid visual details.)*

Self-Portrait, 1930. Frida Kahlo. Oil on canvas, 25½ x 21⅛ in. Museum of Fine Arts, Boston. Anonymous loan.

Viewing the painting: Is the woman portrayed here closer to the image you have developed of Marica or of Raquel? Explain.

C
B

When the curtains part, the stage is in darkness save for the moonlight that comes through the French windows. Then the house door opens and a young girl in negligee enters stealthily. She is carrying a lighted candle. She stands at the door a moment listening for possible pursuit, then moves quickly across to the bookcase Down Right. She puts the candle on top of the bookcase and begins searching behind the books. She finally finds what she wants: a small bottle. While she is searching, the house door opens silently and a woman, also in negligee, enters. (These negligees are in the latest Parisian style.) She moves silently across the room

to the table by the sofa, and as the girl turns with the bottle, the woman switches on the light. The girl gives a half-scream and draws back, frightened. The light reveals her to be quite young—no more than twenty—a timid, dovelike creature. The woman has a queenly air, and whether she is actually beautiful or not, people think she is. She is about thirty-two.]

B

MARICA. [*Trying to hide the bottle behind her.*] Raquel! What are you doing here?

RAQUEL. What did you have hidden behind the books, Marica?

880 UNIT 4

MEETING INDIVIDUAL NEEDS — ENGLISH LANGUAGE LEARNERS

Descriptions of Emotions and Behavior Many of the play's stage directions include words that describe emotions, attitudes, and behavior, such as *frightened, gentler,* and *bitterly.*

Activity Compile a list of nouns (*bewilderment*, for example) and modifiers from the stage directions that English language learners might find dif-

ficult. Have them define the words by giving examples of situations in which a person might feel or act in such a way. Then have volunteers use gestures or facial expressions to express the emotion.

Additional Resources
📁 *English Language Learners Sourcebook*

MARICA. [*Attempting a forced laugh.*] I? Nothing. Why do you think I have anything?

RAQUEL. [*Taking a step toward her.*] Give it to me.

MARICA. [*Backing away from her.*] No. No, I won't.

RAQUEL. [*Stretching out her hand.*] I demand that you give it to me.

MARICA. You have no right to order me about. I'm a married woman. I . . . I . . . [*She begins to sob and flings herself down on the sofa.*]

RAQUEL. [*Much gentler.*] You shouldn't be up. The doctor told you to stay in bed. [*She bends over MARICA and gently takes the bottle out of the girl's hand.*] It was poison. I thought so.

MARICA. [*Frightened.*] You won't tell the priest, will you?

RAQUEL. Suicide is a sin, Marica. A sin against God.

MARICA. I know. I . . . [*She catches RAQUEL's hand.*] Oh, Raquel, why do we have to have wars? Why do men have to go to war and be killed?

RAQUEL. Men must fight for what they believe is right. It is an honorable thing to die for your country as a soldier.

MARICA. How can you say that with Domingo[4] out there fighting, too? And fighting what? Men who aren't even men. Peasants. Ranch slaves. Men who shouldn't be allowed to fight.

RAQUEL. Peasants are men, Marica. Not animals.

MARICA. Men. It's always men. But how about the women? What becomes of us?

RAQUEL. We can pray.

MARICA. [*Bitterly.*] Yes, we can pray. And then comes the terrible news, and it's no use praying any more. All the reason for our praying is dead. Why should I go on living with Tomás[5] dead?

RAQUEL. Living is a duty.

MARICA. How can you be so cold, so hard? You are a cold and hard woman, Raquel. My brother worships you. He has never even looked at another woman since the first day he saw you. Does he know how cold and hard you are?

RAQUEL. Domingo is my—honored husband.

MARICA. You've been married for ten years. And I've been married for three months. If Domingo is killed, it won't be the same for you. You've had ten years. [*She is crying wildly.*] I haven't anything . . . anything at all.

RAQUEL. You've had three months—three months of laughter. And now you have tears. How lucky you are. You have tears. Perhaps five months of tears. Not more. You're only twenty. And in five months Tomás will become just a lovely memory.

MARICA. I'll remember Tomás all my life.

RAQUEL. Of course. But he'll be distant and far away. But you're young . . . and the young need laughter. The young can't live on tears. And one day in Paris, or Rome, or even Mexico City, you'll meet another man. You'll marry again. There will be children in your house. How lucky you are.

MARICA. I'll never marry again.

RAQUEL. You're only twenty. You'll think differently when you're twenty-eight, or nine, or thirty.

MARICA. What will you do if Domingo is killed?

RAQUEL. I shall be very proud that he died in all his courage . . . in all the greatness of a hero.

---

4. *Domingo* (də miŋg′ gō)

5. *Tomás* (tō mäs′)

D Critical Thinking

INFERRING Remind students that exposition, or background information, in a play is communicated through dialogue. Have students explain what they can infer about Marica's values and present situation by her dialogue. (*She is distraught because a man she loves has been killed in a war; she is to some extent religious; she has prejudiced, narrow-minded views about people who are of a lower social class than she.*)

E Active Reading

CONNECT Have students imagine that they are in Marica's situation and a well-meaning person gives them the advice that Raquel gives her. How helpful would they find such advice? (*Most students will say that it is difficult to envision the future and be optimistic about it when suffering a great loss; Raquel's images of a happy future are not very comforting.*)

Vo•cab•u•lar•y Skills

Denotation and Connotation Marica speaks disparagingly of "peasants." Explain that the word *peasant* comes from a Latin word meaning "inhabitant of a district" and a French word meaning "country." While the original meaning of *peasant* was a person living off the land, it has come to have a negative connotation of a person with little education and low social status. Marica consciously calls to mind this negative connotation.

MEETING INDIVIDUAL NEEDS

MULTIPLE LEARNING STYLES

Interpersonal Most people find it difficult comforting a person who has experienced a bereavement. Role-plays and discussion can help students identify with Marica and Raquel and give them insight into a common situation.

Activity Have pairs of students portray the grief-stricken Marica and an older person who is trying to comfort her. Encourage the consoling person to try ways other than Raquel's methods in the play to help Marica. Have students reverse roles. Then have the class discuss effective ways to help a grieving friend or relative, such as allowing the person to talk about feelings and the deceased person, merely offering silent sympathy, or sharing similar experiences of one's own. **L2 COLLAB. LEARN.**

F Literary Elements

IMAGERY Raquel uses vivid sensory images to describe what she would miss about her husband. Have students identify the senses to which each image appeals. *(Sound: jingle of spurs, laughter, echo of shouting; touch: feel of hand)*

G Critical Thinking

INFERRING What is Raquel's attitude toward men going to war? *(Men must go to war to defend their country and the honor of their family even though they love their wives and their wives do not want them to go.)*

H Active Reading

QUESTION What might Raquel's remark that she has not been sleeping well reveal? *(She may be more worried and upset about her husband going to war than she indicates.)*

LITERATURE & HUMANITIES

Display *Liberation of a Peon,* page 545 of *Art in Focus.* Have students consider the images to help them understand the political and social struggles of the Mexican Revolution.

Teaching Options

MARICA. But you'd not weep, would you? Not you! I don't think there are any tears in you.

RAQUEL. No, I'd not weep. I'd sit here in this empty house and wait.

MARICA. Wait for what?

RAQUEL. For the jingle of his spurs as he walks across the tiled hall. For the sound of his laughter in the patio. For the echo of his voice as he shouts to the groom to put away his horse. For the feel of his hand . . .

MARICA. [*Screams.*] Stop it!

RAQUEL. I'm sorry.

MARICA. You do love him, don't you?

RAQUEL. I don't think even he knows how much.

MARICA. I thought that after ten years people slid away from love. But you and Domingo—why, you're all he thinks about. When he's away from you he talks about you all the time. I heard him say once that when you were out of his sight he was like a man without eyes or ears or hands.

RAQUEL. I know. I, too, know that feeling.

MARICA. Then how could you let him go to war? Perhaps to be killed? How could you?

RAQUEL. [*Sharply.*] Marica, you are of the family Macías. Your family is a family of great warriors. A Macías man was with Ferdinand when the Moors were driven out of Spain. A Macías man was with Cortés when the Aztecans surrendered. Your grandfather fought in the War of Independence. Your own father was executed not twenty miles from this house by the French.[6] Shall his son be any less brave because he loves a woman?

---

6. In 1492 *Ferdinand* of Aragon defeated the *Moors,* a Muslim people from northwest Africa who had controlled most of Spain since the 700s. Through the *War of Independence,* Mexico won freedom from Spain in 1821. The *French* invaded and occupied Mexico City in 1863.

882 UNIT 4

MARICA. But Domingo loved you enough to forget that. If you had asked him, he wouldn't have gone to war. He would have stayed here with you.

RAQUEL. No, he would not have stayed. Your brother is a man of honor, not a whining, creeping coward.

MARICA. [*Beginning to cry again.*] I begged Tomás not to go. I begged him.

RAQUEL. Would you have loved him if he had stayed?

MARICA. I don't know. I don't know.

RAQUEL. There is your answer. You'd have despised him. Loved and despised him. Now come, Marica, it's time for you to go to bed.

MARICA. You won't tell the priest—about the poison, I mean?

RAQUEL. No. I won't tell him.

MARICA. Thank you, Raquel. How good you are. How kind and good.

RAQUEL. A moment ago I was hard and cruel. What a baby you are. Now, off to bed with you.

MARICA. Aren't you coming upstairs, too?

RAQUEL. No . . . I haven't been sleeping very well lately. I think I'll read for a little while.

MARICA. Good night, Raquel. And thank you.

RAQUEL. Good night, little one.

[MARICA *goes out through the house door Left, taking her candle with her.* RAQUEL *stares down at the bottle of poison in her hand, then puts it away in one of the small drawers of the desk. She next selects a book from the Downstage case and sits on the sofa to read it, but feeling chilly, she rises and goes to the closet, Back Right, and takes out an afghan.[7] Coming back to the sofa, she makes herself comfortable, with the afghan across her knees.*]

---

7. An *afghan* is a knitted or crocheted wool blanket.

Mexican Revolution Invite students to do further research about the Mexican Revolution which began in 1910. Have them use a search engine and keywords such as *Mexican Revolution* and *Porfirio Díaz.*

REAL-WORLD CONNECTION

Mexico Today In this play, which takes place in 1912, Mexico is having a revolution. But what is happening in Mexico today? Encourage students to investigate the political and economic situation in present-day Mexico. Remind them that to find the most current information they must look in newspapers and magazines and on the Internet. Suggest that they write a brief report on their findings and be prepared to share it with the class. **L2**

Josephina Niggli

Suddenly she hears a noise in the patio. She listens, then convinced it is nothing, returns to her reading. But she hears the noise again. She goes to the patio door and peers out.]

RAQUEL. [*Calling softly.*] Who's there? Who's out there? Oh! [*She gasps and backs into the room. Two men—or rather a man and a young boy—dressed in the white pajama suits of the Mexican peasants, with their sombreros tipped low over their faces, come into the room. Raquel draws herself up regally. Her voice is cold and commanding.*] Who are you, and what do you want here?

ANDRÉS. We are hunting for the wife of General Macías.

RAQUEL. I am Raquel Rivera de Macías.

ANDRÉS. Cleto, stand guard in the patio. If you hear any suspicious noise, warn me at once.

CLETO. Yes, my captain. [*The boy returns to the patio.*]

[*The man, hooking his thumbs in his belt, strolls around the room, looking it over. When he reaches the table at the back he sees the wine. With a small bow to* RAQUEL *he pours himself a glass of wine and drains it. He wipes his mouth with the back of his hand.*]

RAQUEL. How very interesting.

ANDRÉS. [*Startled.*] What?

RAQUEL. To be able to drink wine with that hat on.

ANDRÉS. The hat? Oh, forgive me, señora. [*He flicks the brim with his fingers so that it drops off his head and dangles down his back from the neck cord.*] In a military camp one forgets one's polite manners. Would you care to join me in another glass?

RAQUEL. [*Sitting on the sofa.*] Why not? It's my wine.

ANDRÉS. And very excellent wine. [*He pours two glasses and gives her one while he is talking.*] I would say Amontillado[8] of the vintage of '87.

RAQUEL. Did you learn that in a military camp?

ANDRÉS. I used to sell wines . . . among other things.

RAQUEL. [*Ostentatiously hiding a yawn.*] I am devastated.

ANDRÉS. [*Pulls over the armchair and makes himself comfortable in it.*] You don't mind, do you?

RAQUEL. Would it make any difference if I did?

ANDRÉS. No. The Federals are searching the streets for us, and we have to stay somewhere. But women of your class seem to expect that senseless sort of question.

RAQUEL. Of course I suppose I could scream.

ANDRÉS. Naturally.

RAQUEL. My sister-in-law is upstairs asleep. And there are several servants in the back of the house. Mostly men servants. Very big men.

ANDRÉS. Very interesting. [*He is drinking the wine in small sips with much enjoyment.*]

RAQUEL. What would you do if I screamed?

ANDRÉS. [*Considering the request as though it were another glass of wine.*] Nothing.

RAQUEL. I am afraid you are lying to me.

ANDRÉS. Women of your class seem to expect polite little lies.

---

8. *Amontillado* (ə môn′ til ä′ dō) is a kind of sherry, which is a strong wine.

Vocabulary
regally (rē′ gəl lē) *adv.* in a grand, dignified manner befitting a king or queen
ostentatiously (os′ tən tā′ shəs lē) *adv.* in a way intended to attract attention or impress others

---

Active Reading

QUESTION Have students explain why Andrés's behavior leads to an abrupt change in Raquel. (*Students may say he has insulted her by taking liberties; physical contact with him makes him more real and human; or she realizes he poses a real threat.*)

N **Author's Craft**

DETAILS The author uses compelling details in Andrés's monologue about his life. Have students name some of the details and describe their effect. (*Vivid details include his mother as a street beggar, his stealing oranges, and his hanging the judge to a telephone pole. The details are shocking and evoke sympathy for Andrés's hardships and an understanding of his mission.*)

Teaching Options

The Ring of General Macías

RAQUEL. Stop calling me "woman of your class."

ANDRÉS. Forgive me.

RAQUEL. You are one of the fighting peasants, aren't you?

ANDRÉS. I am a captain in the Revolutionary Army.

RAQUEL. This house is completely loyal to the Federal government.

ANDRÉS. I know. That's why I'm here.

RAQUEL. And now that you are here, just what do you expect me to do?

ANDRÉS. I expect you to offer sanctuary to myself and to Cleto.

RAQUEL. Cleto? [*She looks toward the patio and adds sarcastically.*] Oh, your army.

CLETO. [*Appearing in the doorway.*] I'm sorry, my captain. I just heard a noise. [*RAQUEL stands. ANDRÉS moves quickly to her and puts his hands on her arms from the back. CLETO has turned and is peering into the patio. Then the boy relaxes.*] We are still safe, my captain. It was only a rabbit. [*He goes back into the patio. RAQUEL pulls away from ANDRÉS and goes to the desk.*]

RAQUEL. What a magnificent army you have. So clever. I'm sure you must win many victories.

ANDRÉS. We do. And we will win the greatest victory, remember that.

RAQUEL. This farce has gone on long enough. Will you please take your army and climb over the patio wall with it?

ANDRÉS. I told you that we came here so that you could give us sanctuary.

RAQUEL. My dear captain—captain without a name . . .

ANDRÉS. Andrés de la O, your servant. [*He makes a bow.*]

RAQUEL. [*Startled.*] Andrés de la O!

ANDRÉS. I am flattered. You have heard of me.

RAQUEL. Naturally. Everyone in the city has heard of you. You have a reputation for politeness—especially to women.

ANDRÉS. I see that the tales about me have lost nothing in the telling.

RAQUEL. I can't say. I'm not interested in gossip about your type of soldier.

ANDRÉS. Then let me give you something to heighten your interest. [*He suddenly takes her in his arms and kisses her. She stiffens for a moment, then remains perfectly still. He steps away from her.*]

RAQUEL. [*Rage forcing her to whisper.*] Get out of here—at once!

ANDRÉS. [*Staring at her in admiration.*] I can understand why Macías loves you. I couldn't before, but now I can understand it.

RAQUEL. Get out of my house.

ANDRÉS. [*Sits on the sofa and pulls a small leather pouch out of his shirt. He pours its contents into his hand.*] So cruel, señora, and I with a present for you? Here is a holy medal. My mother gave me this medal. She died when I was ten. She was a street beggar. She died of starvation. But I wasn't there. I was in jail. I had been sentenced to five years in prison for stealing five oranges. The judge thought it a great joke. One year for each orange. He laughed. He had a very loud laugh. [*Pause.*] I killed him two months ago. I hanged him to the telephone pole in front of his house. And I laughed. [*Pause.*] I also have a very loud laugh. [*RAQUEL abruptly turns her back on him.*] I told that story to a girl the other night and she thought it very funny. But of course she was a peasant girl— a girl who could neither read nor write.

Listening and Speaking *Minilesson*

Reading a Monologue A speech by one person that relates a story or expresses thoughts or emotions is called a monologue. Andrés's monologue reveals important facts about his life and his motivations.

Activity Discuss the tone in which Andrés might be speaking. Is it emotional or unemotional? Have students consider which tone might express Andrés's feelings more effectively. Then have pairs of students read the monologue to each other, one using an emotional tone, and the other an unemotional tone. Then have each pair report on the more effective way to interpret the monologue. **L2**

She hadn't been born in a great house in Tabasco.[9] She didn't have an English governess.[10] She didn't go to school to the nuns in Paris. She didn't marry one of the richest young men in the Republic. But she thought my story very funny. Of course she could understand it. Her brother had been whipped to death because he had run away from the plantation that owned him. [*He pauses and looks at her. She does not move.*]

---

9. On the southern coast of the Gulf of Mexico, *Tabasco* is one of Mexico's thirty-five states.
10. A *governess* is a woman employed to teach children in a private household.

Are you still angry with me? Even though I have brought you a present? [*He holds out his hand.*] A very nice present—from your husband.

RAQUEL. [*Turns and stares at him in amazement.*] A present! From Domingo?

ANDRÉS. I don't know him that well. I call him the General Macías.

RAQUEL. [*Excitedly.*] Is he well? How does he look? [*With horrified comprehension.*] He's a prisoner . . . your prisoner!

ANDRÉS. Naturally. That's why I know so much about you. He talks about you constantly.

0 Active Reading

QUESTION What is the significance of the details Andrés uses that tell what the peasant girl did not have or do? *(They describe Raquel. She soon finds out he learned the details from her husband.)*

ⱽIEWING THE ART

David Alfaro Siqueiros painted murals illustrating events in Mexican history. Actively involved in revolutionary movements, he was thrown out of Mexico in 1932 and in 1940.

Viewing Response *The mural portrays peasants determined and united in their cause.*

From Porfirismo to the Revolution, 1955–1966. David Alfaro Siqueiros. Mural (detail), Acrílico/triplay, 420 square meters. Museo National de Historia. Castillo de Chapultepec, Mexico City.

Viewing the art: How do the characteristics of these people help you understand the actions and attitudes of Andrés and Cleto?

INTERDISCIPLINARY CONNECTION

Geography Andrés refers to the Mexican state of Tabasco. Students may know little about the geography of Mexico although it is a close neighbor to the United States.

Activity Have students find and copy a map of Mexico that shows its states and major cities. Also have them label the land and bodies of water around the country. **L2**

Teaching Options

886 🍂 UNIT 4

P Author's Craft

SYMBOL What does the author use the ring to symbolize? Why is the ring important to the play's plot? *(She uses it to symbolize Domingo's love for his wife. It is important to the plot because it proves to Raquel that Andrés has imprisoned Domingo.)*

Q Literary Elements

CONFLICT What new conflict and antagonist does Raquel face at this point? *(The new antagonists are the Federal soldiers. Her conflict is how to successfully hide Andrés and Cleto from them.)*

R Active Reading

CONNECT Encourage students to imagine what they would do in Raquel's situation.

S Literary Elements

CHARACTER Andrés says that Raquel's husband described her as "braver than most men" and very clever. Does the play support this description? How might the description be a foreshadowing? *(Raquel has already shown that she is brave. Andrés's statement may foreshadow that she will prove to be braver and more clever than he realizes.)*

RAQUEL. You know nothing about him. You're lying to me.

[CLETO *comes to the window.*]

ANDRÉS. I assure you, señora . . .

CLETO. [*Interrupting.*] My captain . . .

ANDRÉS. What is it, Cleto? Another rabbit?

CLETO. No, my captain. There are soldiers at the end of the street. They are searching all the houses. They will be here soon.

ANDRÉS. Don't worry. We are quite safe here. Stay in the patio until I call you.

CLETO. Yes, my captain. [*He returns to the patio.*]

RAQUEL. You are not safe here. When those soldiers come I shall turn you over to them.

ANDRÉS. I think not.

RAQUEL. You can't escape from them. And they are not kind to you peasant prisoners. They have good reason not to be.

ANDRÉS. Look at this ring. [*He holds his hand out, with the ring on his palm.*]

RAQUEL. Why, it's—a wedding ring.

ANDRÉS. Read the inscription inside of it. [*As she hesitates, he adds sharply.*] Read it!

RAQUEL. [*Slowly takes the ring. While she is reading her voice fades to a whisper.*] "D. M.— R. R.—June 2, 1902." Where did you get this?

ANDRÉS. General Macías gave it to me.

RAQUEL. [*Firmly and clearly.*] Not this ring. He'd never give you this ring. [*With dawning horror.*] He's dead. You stole it from his dead finger. He's dead.

ANDRÉS. Not yet. But he will be dead if I don't return to camp safely by sunset tomorrow.

RAQUEL. I don't believe you. I don't believe you. You're lying to me.

ANDRÉS. This house is famous for its loyalty to the Federal government. You will hide me until those soldiers get out of this district. When it is safe enough Cleto and I will leave. But if you betray me to them, your husband will be shot tomorrow evening at sunset. Do you understand? [*He shakes her arm.* RAQUEL *looks dazedly at him.* CLETO *comes to the window.*]

CLETO. The soldiers are coming closer, my captain. They are at the next house.

ANDRÉS. [*To* RAQUEL.] Where shall we hide? [RAQUEL *is still dazed. He gives her another little shake.*] Think, woman! If you love your husband at all—think!

RAQUEL. I don't know. Marica upstairs—the servants in the rest of the house—I don't know.

ANDRÉS. The General has bragged to us about you. He says you are braver than most men. He says you are very clever. This is a time to be both brave and clever.

CLETO. [*Pointing to the closet.*] What door is that?

RAQUEL. It's a closet . . . a storage closet.

ANDRÉS. We'll hide in there.

RAQUEL. It's very small. It's not big enough for both of you.

ANDRÉS. Cleto, hide yourself in there.

CLETO. But, my captain . . .

ANDRÉS. That's an order! Hide yourself.

CLETO. Yes, Sir. [*He steps inside the closet.*]

ANDRÉS. And now, señora, where are you going to hide me?

RAQUEL. How did you persuade my husband to give you his ring?

ANDRÉS. That's a very long story, señora, for which we have no time just now. [*He puts the ring and medal back in the pouch and thrusts it inside his shirt.*] Later I will be glad to give you all the details. But at present it is only necessary for you to remember that his life depends upon mine.

MEETING INDIVIDUAL NEEDS

GIFTED AND TALENTED

Revolution A revolution refers to a profound change in a country's government. Some revolutions involve violence while others occur peaceably. Some revolutions come about because victims of poverty or injustice rise up against the existing government.

Activity Have students research a revolution involving demands by common people against an unjust monarchy or dictatorship, such as the American, French, Russian, or Mexican Revolutions. Have them find out the causes and effects of the revolution as well as the methods by which it came about. **L3**

RAQUEL. Yes—yes, of course. [*She loses her dazed expression and seems to grow more queenly as she takes command of the situation.*] Give me your hat. [*ANDRÉS shrugs and passes it over to her. She takes it to the closet and hands it to CLETO.*] There is a smoking jacket hanging up in there. Hand it to me. [*CLETO hands her a man's velvet smoking jacket. She brings it to ANDRÉS.*] Put this on.

ANDRÉS. [*Puts it on and looks down at himself.*] Such a pity my shoes are not comfortable slippers.

RAQUEL. Sit in that chair. [*She points to the armchair.*]

ANDRÉS. My dear lady . . .

RAQUEL. If I must save your life, allow me to do it in my own way. Sit down. [*ANDRÉS sits. She picks up the afghan from the couch and throws it over his feet and legs, carefully tucking it in so that his body is covered to the waist.*] If anyone speaks to you, don't answer. Don't turn your head. As far as you are concerned, there is no one in this room—not even me. Just look straight ahead of you and . . .

ANDRÉS. [*As she pauses.*] And what?

RAQUEL. I started to say "and pray," but since you're a member of the Revolutionary Army I don't suppose you believe in God and prayer.

ANDRÉS. My mother left me a holy medal.

RAQUEL. Oh, yes, I remember. A very amusing story. [*There is the sound of men's voices in the patio.*] The Federal soldiers are here. If you can pray, ask God to keep Marica upstairs. She is very young and very stupid. She'll betray you before I can shut her mouth.

ANDRÉS. I'll . . .

RAQUEL. Silence! Stare straight ahead of you and pray. [*She goes to the French window and speaks loudly to the soldiers.*] Really! What is the meaning of this uproar?

FLORES. [*Off.*] Do not alarm yourself, señora. [*He comes into the room. He wears the uniform of a Federal officer.*] I am Captain Basilio Flores, at your service, señora.

RAQUEL. What do you mean, invading my house and making so much noise at this hour of the night?

FLORES. We are hunting for two spies. One of them is the notorious Andrés de la O. You may have heard of him, señora.

RAQUEL. [*Looking at ANDRÉS.*] Considering what he did to my cousin—yes, I've heard of him.

FLORES. Your cousin, señora?

RAQUEL. [*Comes to ANDRÉS and puts her hand on his shoulder. He stares woodenly in front of him.*] Felipe[11] was his prisoner before the poor boy managed to escape.

FLORES. Is it possible? [*He crosses to ANDRÉS.*] Captain Basilio Flores, at your service. [*He salutes.*]

RAQUEL. Felipe doesn't hear you. He doesn't even know you are in the room.

FLORES. Eh, it is a sad thing.

RAQUEL. Must your men make so much noise?

FLORES. The hunt must be thorough, señora. And now if some of my men can go through here to the rest of the house . . .

RAQUEL. Why?

FLORES. But I told you, señora. We are hunting for two spies . . .

RAQUEL. [*Speaking quickly from controlled nervousness.*] And do you think I have them

---

11. *Felipe* (fə lē′ pā)

Vocabulary
notorious (nō tôr′ ē əs) *adj.* widely and unfavorably known

Literary Elements

T **SYMBOL** Remind students that a symbol is a concrete object that suggests abstract ideas. Point out that visual symbols such as articles of clothing can be very effective on stage. Have students explain what the velvet smoking jacket might symbolize. (*Like the women's fashionable negligees, it suggests a way of life that is rich, elegant, and leisurely.*)

Literary Elements

U **SYMBOL** Have students explain what Andrés's holy medal might symbolize. (*his peasant background, his mother's love for him, his religious attitudes*)

Literary Elements

V **CHARACTER** Have students explain how Raquel lives up to her husband's description of her as very brave and clever. (*She shows her cleverness by quickly coming up with a plan to save Andrés: he will be in plain sight of the Federal officers but pretending to be Raquel's cousin. She shows her bravery by facing the officers audaciously and playing out the charade she has created.*)

Writing *Minilesson*

Using Adverbs The author uses many adverbs in the stage directions to indicate the vocal and facial expressions of the characters, for example, on page 886 *sharply, slowly,* and *dazedly*; on page 887 *queenly, loudly,* and *woodenly*.

Activity Have students write a brief dialogue that revolves around a valuable object. They may invent the dialogue or base it on an actual experience. Have them write at least five stage directions that use adverbs to describe the characters' vocal or facial expressions. Encourage them to use compelling words such as *queenly* or *woodenly*. **L3**

Additional Resources

📓 *Writer's Choice,* Lesson 10.5

Literary Elements

IRONY In dramatic irony, the audience knows something that one or more of the characters onstage do not know. Point out the dramatic irony of Raquel's urging Flores to check inside the closet for the spies. Have students identify the effect on the audience of this dramatic irony. *(It increases the audience's suspense and emotional involvement.)*

VIEWING THE PAINTING

Pablo Burchard (1875–1964) was one of the founders of modern Chilean art. He often used expressive and abstract styles.

Viewing Response *The mood of the painting seems calmer than that of the play.*

---

hidden someplace, and I the wife of General Macías?

FLORES. General Macías! But I didn't know . . .

RAQUEL. Now that you do know, I suggest you remove your men and their noise at once.

FLORES. But, señora, I regret—I still have to search this house.

RAQUEL. I can assure you, captain, that I have been sitting here all evening, and no peasant spy has passed me and gone into the rest of the house.

FLORES. Several rooms open off the patio, señora. They needn't have come through here.

RAQUEL. So . . . you do think I conceal spies in this house. Then search it by all means.

Look under the sofa . . . under the table. In the drawers of the desk. And don't miss that closet, captain. Inside that closet is hidden a very fierce and wicked spy.

FLORES. Please, señora . . .

RAQUEL. [*Goes to the closet door.*] Or do you prefer me to open it for you?

FLORES. I am only doing my duty, señora. You are making it very difficult.

RAQUEL. [*Relaxing against the door.*] I'm sorry. My sister-in-law is upstairs. She has just received word that her husband has been killed. They were married three months ago. She's only twenty. I didn't want . . .

MARICA. [*Calling off.*] Raquel, what is all that noise downstairs?

Wall with a Door and Tree (Muro con Puerta y Arbol). Pablo Burchard (1875–1964).

Viewing the painting: What is the mood of this painting? How does it compare with the mood in the play?

Teaching Options

MEETING INDIVIDUAL NEEDS — MULTIPLE LEARNING STYLES

Linguistic The play includes several words from foreign languages that are used in English.

Activity Have students use a dictionary to find the language from which the English language borrowed each of the following words: *negligee* (French), *afghan* (Persian), *patio* (Spanish), *pajamas* (Hindi), *sombrero* (Spanish). **L1**

RAQUEL. [*Goes to the house door and calls.*] It is nothing. Go back to bed.

MARICA. But I can hear men's voices in the patio.

RAQUEL. It is only some Federal soldiers hunting for two peasant spies. [*She turns and speaks rapidly to* FLORES.] If she comes down here, she must not see my cousin. Felipe escaped, but her husband was killed. The doctor thinks the sight of my poor cousin might affect her mind. You understand?

FLORES. Certainly, señora. What a sad thing.

MARICA. [*Still off.*] Raquel, I'm afraid! [*She tries to push past* RAQUEL *into the room.* RAQUEL *and* FLORES *stand between her and* ANDRÉS.] Spies! In this house. Oh, Raquel!

RAQUEL. The doctor will be very angry if you don't return to bed at once.

MARICA. But those terrible men will kill us. What is the matter with you two? Why are you standing there like that? [*She tries to see past them, but they both move so that she can't see* ANDRÉS.]

FLORES. It is better that you go back to your room, señora.

MARICA. But why? Upstairs I am alone. Those terrible men will kill me. I know they will.

FLORES. Don't be afraid, señora. There are no spies in this house.

MARICA. Are you sure?

RAQUEL. Captain Flores means that no spy would dare to take refuge in the house of General Macías. Isn't that right, captain?

FLORES. [*Laughing.*] Of course. All the world knows of the brave General Macías.

RAQUEL. Now go back to bed, Marica. Please, for my sake.

MARICA. You are both acting very strangely. I think you have something hidden in this room you don't want me to see.

RAQUEL. [*Sharply.*] You are quite right. Captain Flores has captured one of the spies. He is sitting in the chair behind me. He is dead. Now will you please go upstairs!

MARICA. [*Gives a stifled sob.*] Oh! That such a terrible thing could happen in this house. [*She runs out of the room, still sobbing.*]

FLORES. [*Worried.*] Was it wise to tell her such a story, señora?

RAQUEL. [*Tense with repressed relief.*] Better that than the truth. Good night, captain, and thank you.

FLORES. Good night, señora. And don't worry. Those spies won't bother you. If they were anywhere in this district, my men would have found them.

RAQUEL. I'm sure of it.

[*The Captain salutes her, looks toward* ANDRÉS *and salutes him, then goes into the patio. He can be heard calling his men. Neither* ANDRÉS *nor* RAQUEL *moves until the voices outside die away. Then* RAQUEL *staggers and nearly falls, but* ANDRÉS *catches her in time.*]

ANDRÉS. [*Calling softly.*] They've gone, Cleto. [ANDRÉS *carries* RAQUEL *to the sofa as* CLETO *comes out of the closet.*] Bring a glass of wine. Quickly.

CLETO. [*As he gets the wine.*] What happened?

ANDRÉS. It's nothing. Just a faint. [*He holds the wine to her lips.*]

CLETO. She's a great lady, that one. When she wanted to open the closet door my knees were trembling, I can tell you.

Vocabulary
repressed (ri prest´) *adj.* held back or kept under control; restrained

---

X **Active Reading**

LISTEN Have students imagine the ways in which the voices of Raquel and Marica might differ. Have two students read portions of the dialogue between the two on page 889. Then have students describe the differences in the way the characters speak. *(Raquel probably has a deep, calm, authoritative voice while Marica's is high and nervous, verging on the hysterical.)*

Y **Literary Elements**

DRAMATIC IRONY Have students point out a striking example of dramatic irony in the scene. *(Raquel tells Marica sarcastically that a spy is sitting in the chair behind her. The audience knows, as Marica and Flores do not, that this is literally the truth.)*

Reading *Minilesson*

Comparing and Contrasting The characters of *The Ring of General Macías* have contrasting traits and ways of life. It may be helpful for students to analyze the main characters in terms of these contrasts.

Activity Have students make charts comparing and contrasting two sets of characters, one for Raquel and Marica and a second for Raquel and Andrés. Let students design the style of their charts. Have volunteers write their charts on the board. **L2**

Additional Resources
📁 *Reading Workbook,* pp. 75–76

Active Reading

VISUALIZE Ask students to picture Cleto staring at Raquel. Why might he be staring at her? *(He may admire her, be curious about her, think her beautiful, or be infatuated with her.)*

AA Critical Thinking

DRAWING CONCLUSIONS You might model drawing a conclusion to help students understand how Cleto feels about Raquel's husband.

Model: Cleto says that Domingo offered the spies refuge in his home in exchange for being saved from the firing squad. Cleto interprets this as betraying his country to save his own life and feels this is very cowardly. Cleto therefore looks at Raquel with surprise and admiration: he is surprised that a cowardly man like Domingo has a brave wife like Raquel.

Teaching Options

ANDRÉS. My own bones were playing a pretty tune.

CLETO. Why do you think she married Macías?

ANDRÉS. Love is a peculiar thing, Cleto.

CLETO. I don't understand it.

RAQUEL. [*Moans and sits up.*] Are they—are they gone?

ANDRÉS. Yes, they're gone. [*He kisses her hand.*] I've never known a braver lady.

RAQUEL. [*Pulling her hand away.*] Will you go now, please?

ANDRÉS. We'll have to wait until the district is free of them—but if you'd like to write a letter to your husband while we're waiting . . .

RAQUEL. [*Surprised at his kindness.*] You'd take it to him? You'd really give it to him?

ANDRÉS. Of course.

RAQUEL. Thank you. [*She goes to the writing desk and sits down.*]

ANDRÉS. [*To* CLETO, *who has been staring steadily at* RAQUEL *all the while.*] You stay here with the señora. I'm going to find out how much of the district has been cleared.

CLETO. [*Still staring at* RAQUEL.] Yes, my captain.

[ANDRÉS *leaves by the French windows.* CLETO *keeps on staring at* RAQUEL *as she starts to write. After a moment she turns to him.*]

RAQUEL. [*Irritated.*] Why do you keep staring at me?

CLETO. Why did you marry a man like that one, señora?

RAQUEL. You're very <u>impertinent</u>.

CLETO. [*Shyly.*] I'm sorry, señora.

RAQUEL. [*After a brief pause.*] What do you mean: "a man like that one"?

CLETO. Well, you're very brave, señora.

RAQUEL. [*Lightly.*] And don't you think the general is very brave?

CLETO. No, señora. Not very.

RAQUEL. [*Staring at him with bewilderment.*] What are you trying to tell me?

CLETO. Nothing, señora. It is none of my affair.

RAQUEL. Come here. [*He comes slowly up to her.*] Tell me what is in your mind.

CLETO. I don't know, señora. I don't understand it. The captain says love is a peculiar thing, but I don't understand it.

RAQUEL. Cleto, did the general willingly give that ring to your captain?

CLETO. Yes, señora.

RAQUEL. Why?

CLETO. The general wanted to save his own life. He said he loved you and he wanted to save his life.

RAQUEL. How would giving that ring to your captain save the general's life?

CLETO. The general's supposed to be shot tomorrow afternoon. But he's talked about you a lot, and when my captain knew we had to come into the city, he thought perhaps we might take refuge here if the Federals got on our trail. So he went to the general and said that if he fixed it so we'd be safe here, my captain would save him from the firing squad.

RAQUEL. Was your trip to the city very important—to your cause, I mean?

CLETO. Indeed yes, señora. The captain got a lot of fine information. It means we'll win the

---

Vocabulary

impertinent (im purt′ ən ant) *adj.* inappropriately bold or forward; not showing proper respect or manners

890 🦢 UNIT 4

Listening and Speaking *Minilesson*

Discussing the Nature of Love In trying to explain why Raquel married Domingo, Andrés says, "Love is a peculiar thing."

Activity Have students explain Andrés's statement in relation to the story. How does it apply to both Raquel and Domingo? *(Andrés seems to refer to the fact that love can make a woman marry a cowardly man. In light of the information that Domingo has accepted a bribe, he also implies that love can make someone a traitor.)* Have students discuss whether they agree or disagree with Andrés's statement. Is his view realistic or romantic? **L2**

Two Women, 1929. Frida Kahlo. Oil on canvas, 27⅜ x 21 in. Private collection.

Viewing the painting: What different personalities do these two women convey? How do they reflect the differences between Raquel and Marica?

next big battle. My captain is a very clever man, señora.

RAQUEL. Did the general know about this information when he gave his ring to your captain?

CLETO. I don't see how he could help knowing it, señora. He heard us talking about it enough.

RAQUEL. Who knows about that bargain to save the general's life beside you and your captain?

CLETO. No one, señora. The captain isn't one to talk, and I didn't have time to.

RAQUEL. [*While the boy has been talking, the life seems to have drained completely out of her.*] How old are you, Cleto?

CLETO. I don't know, señora. I think I'm twenty, but I don't know.

RAQUEL. [*Speaking more to herself than to him.*] Tomás was twenty.

CLETO. Who is Tomás?

Writing Minilesson

Irony Students may recognize verbal irony in literature more readily if they use it in their own writing.

Activity Have students write a paragraph about a household chore—mowing the lawn, doing the dishes, cleaning their room—that they dislike. Have them use an ironic tone to express their feelings about the job. Encourage them not to speak of the job too generally but to describe specific aspects of it. Have volunteers read their paragraphs. Discuss the effectiveness of verbal irony in making a point. **L3**

Additional Resources

📗 *Writer's Choice,* Lesson 12.3

INTERPRET How do Raquel and Cleto differ in their views of Domingo's bargain? (*Cleto thinks that Domingo has betrayed his country to save his own life and is a coward. Raquel feels that her husband loved and trusted her so much that he was willing to take the risk of betraying his country to save her the pain she would feel if he were killed.*)

DD Literary Elements

CHARACTER How does Raquel feel about Cleto? (*She admires him for his courage and his convictions and pities him because he is very young.*)

EE Active Reading

RESPOND Ask students to describe their reactions to Raquel's putting poison into the wine and offering wine to the two men. (*Some students will be surprised while others will say they predicted Raquel's plan earlier by her reactions to her husband's bargain.*)

The Ring of General Macías

RAQUEL. He was married to my sister-in-law. Cleto, you think my husband is a coward, don't you?

CLETO. [*With embarrassment.*] Yes, señora.

RAQUEL. You don't think any woman is worth it, do you? Worth the price of a great battle, I mean?

CLETO. No, señora. But as the captain says, love is a very peculiar thing.

RAQUEL. If your captain loved a woman as much as the general loves me, would he have given an enemy his ring?

CLETO. Ah, but the captain is a great man, señora.

RAQUEL. And so is my husband a great man. He is of the family Macías. All of that family have been great men. All of them—brave and honorable men. They have always held their honor to be greater than their lives. That is a tradition of their family.

CLETO. Perhaps none of them loved a woman like you, señora.

RAQUEL. How strange you are. I saved you from the Federals because I want to save my husband's life. You call me brave, and yet you call him a coward. There is no difference in what we have done.

CLETO. But you are a woman, señora.

RAQUEL. Has a woman less honor than a man, then?

CLETO. No, señora. Please, I don't know how to say it. The general is a soldier. He has a duty to his own cause. You are a woman. You have a duty to your husband. It is right that you should try to save him. It is not right that he should try to save himself.

RAQUEL. [*Dully.*] Yes, of course. It is right that I should save him. [*Becoming practical again.*] Your captain has been gone some time, Cleto. You'd better find out if he is still safe.

CLETO. Yes, señora. [*As he reaches the French windows she stops him.*]

RAQUEL. Wait, Cleto. Have you a mother—or a wife, perhaps?

CLETO. Oh, no, señora. I haven't anyone but the captain.

RAQUEL. But the captain is a soldier. What would you do if he should be killed?

CLETO. It is very simple, señora. I should be killed, too.

RAQUEL. You speak about death so calmly. Aren't you afraid of it, Cleto?

CLETO. No, señora. It's like the captain says . . . dying for what you believe in—that's the finest death of all.

RAQUEL. And you believe in the Revolutionary cause?

CLETO. Yes, señora. I am a poor peasant, that's true. But still I have a right to live like a man, with my own ground, and my own family, and my own future. [*He stops speaking abruptly.*] I'm sorry, señora. You are a fine lady. You don't understand these things. I must go and find my captain. [*He goes out.*]

RAQUEL. [*Rests her face against her hand.*] He's so young. But Tomás was no older. And he's not afraid. He said so. Oh, Domingo—Domingo! [*She straightens abruptly, takes the bottle of poison from the desk drawer and stares at it. Then she crosses to the decanter and laces the wine with the poison. She hurries back to the desk and is busy writing when ANDRÉS and CLETO return.*]

ANDRÉS. You'll have to hurry that letter. The district is clear now.

RAQUEL. I'll be through in just a moment. You might as well finish the wine while you're waiting.

ANDRÉS. Thank you. A most excellent idea. [*He pours himself a glass of wine. As he lifts it to his lips she speaks.*]

892 ❧ UNIT 4

Teaching Options

Grammar and Language *Minilesson*

Compound Sentences and Predicates
Explain that a compound sentence has two or more independent clauses joined with a comma and coordinating conjunction: *He gave us books, and we read them.* A simple sentence may have a compound predicate: *We read a play and wrote an essay.* A comma is not used between the elements of a compound predicate.

Activity Have students tell whether each sentence is a compound sentence or if it contains a compound predicate. Have students punctuate each sentence correctly.
1. I have been sitting here all evening, and no peasant spy has passed me.
   (compound sentence)
2. I sit here in this empty house and wait.
   (compound predicate) **L2**

Additional Resources
- *Grammar and Language Transparency 65*
- *Grammar and Language Workbook,* pp. 79, 103
- *Grammar and Composition Handbook,* Lessons 2.3, 4.7
- *Writer's Choice,* Lessons 11.3, 13.8

Josephina Niggli

RAQUEL. Why don't you give some to—Cleto?

ANDRÉS. This is too fine a wine to waste on that boy.

RAQUEL. He'll probably never have another chance to taste such wine.

ANDRÉS. Very well. Pour yourself a glass, Cleto.

CLETO. Thank you. [*He pours it.*] Your health, my captain.

RAQUEL. [*Quickly.*] Drink it outside, Cleto. I want to speak to your captain. [*The boy looks at ANDRÉS, who jerks his head toward the patio. CLETO nods and goes out.*] I want you to give my husband a message for me. I can't write it. You'll have to remember it. But first, give me a glass of wine, too.

ANDRÉS. [*Pouring the wine.*] It might be easier for him if you wrote it.

RAQUEL. I think not. [*She takes the glass.*] I want you to tell him that I never knew how much I loved him until tonight.

ANDRÉS. Is that all?

RAQUEL. Yes. Tell me, captain, do you think it possible to love a person too much?

ANDRÉS. Yes, señora. I do.

RAQUEL. So do I. Let us drink a toast, captain—to honor. To bright and shining honor.

ANDRÉS. [*Raises his glass.*] To honor. [*He drains his glass. She lifts hers almost to her lips and then puts it down. From the patio comes a faint cry.*]

CLETO. [*Calling faintly in a cry that fades into silence.*] Captain. Captain.

[*ANDRÉS sways, his hand trying to brush across his face as though trying to brush sense into his head. When he hears CLETO he tries to stagger toward the window but stumbles and can't quite make it. Hanging on to the*

table by the sofa he looks accusingly at her. She shrinks back against her chair.]

ANDRÉS. [*His voice weak from the poison.*] Why?

RAQUEL. Because I love him. Can you understand that?

ANDRÉS. We'll win. The Revolution will win. You can't stop that.

RAQUEL. Yes, you'll win. I know that now.

ANDRÉS. That girl—she thought my story was funny—about the hanging. But you didn't . . .

RAQUEL. I'm glad you hanged him. I'm glad.

[*ANDRÉS looks at her and tries to smile. He manages to pull the pouch from his shirt and extend it to her. But it drops from his hand.*]

RAQUEL. [*Runs to French window and calls.*] Cleto. Cleto! [*She buries her face in her hands for a moment, then comes back to ANDRÉS. She kneels beside him and picks up the leather pouch. She opens it and, taking the ring, puts it on her finger. Then she sees the medal. She rises and, pulling out the chain from her own throat, she slides the medal on to the chain. Then she walks to the sofa and sinks down on it.*]

MARICA. [*Calling off.*] Raquel! Raquel! [*RAQUEL snaps off the lamp, leaving the room in darkness. MARICA opens the house door. She is carrying a candle which she shades with her hand. The light is too dim to reveal the dead ANDRÉS.*] What are you doing down here in the dark? Why don't you come to bed?

RAQUEL. [*Making an effort to speak.*] I'll come in just a moment.

MARICA. But what are you doing, Raquel?

RAQUEL. Nothing. Just listening . . . listening to an empty house.

QUICK CURTAIN

Responding to the Selection

Personal Response

Many students may find Raquel's poisoning the spies the most surprising part of the play.

ANALYZING LITERATURE

1. At the beginning of the play, Marica and Raquel are on stage discussing the death of Marica's husband, her grief, and Raquel's love for her husband.
2. Andrés and Cleto, members of the Revolutionary Army, come in. They want to hide from the Federal officers who are pursuing them.
3. Raquel loves her husband very much but knows he must fight in the war. She finds out he has been imprisoned by Revolutionary forces.
4. Raquel learns that her husband has guaranteed refuge for the spies in return for having his life spared.
5. Raquel kills the intruders by tricking them into drinking poisoned wine.
6. Raquel is wiser and more capable. She handles each situation calmly while her sister-in-law exhibits fear and nervousness.
7. The intruders are peasants who believe they deserve the opportunity to own land and control their future. General Macías and his wife are members of the wealthy, ruling party who want to keep wealth and power.
8. The intruders' information upsets Raquel very much. The stage direction says the life seems to drain out of her; she becomes dull and preoccupied.
9. Raquel's conversation with Cleto shows that she believes both men and women should behave with honor and courage. She also believes that the love for one's country must be held above personal feelings.
10. Raquel realizes it is her responsibility to keep the spies' information from getting out, but she feels sorry for the spies and does not want to kill them. She does so because she realizes how much her husband loves her; he saved his life for her and now she must prevent the Federals' secrets from being betrayed.
11. Domingo and Raquel both show loyalty to one another and to their government. Domingo is willing to betray his country for his wife, but Raquel prevents that betrayal. Andrés and Cleto are loyal to their cause and their beliefs.
12. Raquel acts bravely by doing what she must to support her government and preserve Domingo's honor.

Responding to Literature

Personal Response

What did you find most surprising in this play? Share your reactions with a classmate.

ANALYZING LITERATURE

RECALL

1. When the play opens, what two characters are on stage? What do they discuss?
2. Who enters the home of General Macías? Why do they come there?
3. How has Raquel felt about her husband? What does she learn about him from the intruders?
4. What does Raquel learn in her conversation with Cleto?
5. What does Raquel eventually do to the intruders?

INTERPRET

6. Which of the two women in the play is wiser or more capable? How do you know?
7. In your own words, summarize the political differences between the intruders and General Macías and his wife.
8. How does the intruders' information about her husband affect Raquel? Use specific details from the selection to support your response.
9. What does Raquel's conversation with Cleto reveal about her values?
10. What conflicting thoughts and emotions does Raquel experience near the end of the play? Why do you think she does what she does? Support your ideas with details from the play.

EVALUATE AND CONNECT

11. **Theme Connections** Explain how this play concerns both loyalty and betrayal.
12. Think about your response to the Focus Activity on page 878. How do the characters in this play demonstrate bravery? Why do they act bravely? Add their actions to your cluster map.
13. In your opinion, is Raquel a heroine? Explain your answer.
14. In what ways does this play help an audience understand the early part of the Mexican Revolution?
15. What do the ring of General Macías and the medal of Andrés **symbolize** to their owners? What do they represent to Raquel?

Literary ELEMENTS

Irony

Irony is a contrast between reality and what seems to be real. There are different kinds of irony, all of which can be found in this play. **Verbal irony** exists when a person says one thing but means another. For example, when Raquel says, "What a magnificent army you have," she actually means the opposite and is insulting Andrés de la O and Cleto. **Situational irony** occurs when a situation has an outcome that is the opposite of what someone has expected. **Dramatic irony** occurs when the audience has important information that the characters do not have. For example, the audience knows that Andrés de la O is sitting in the room where the Federal soldiers are searching for him, but the soldiers do not recognize him.

1. Find another example of verbal irony and dramatic irony in the play. Explain why each is ironic.
2. Which of the outcomes in this play is an example of situational irony? Explain your answer.

● See **Literary Terms Handbook**, p. R6.

Domingo acts bravely by risking betraying his country for love of his wife. Both act as they do because they love one another and their government.
13. Some students may see Raquel as a heroine because she does something personally repugnant for the sake of her husband and her country. Others may say she is not a heroine because she commits murder.
14. The play dramatizes the fundamental conflict between the upper class and the peasants.
15. The ring of General Macías symbolizes his love for his wife. The medal of Andrés symbolizes his mother's love for him. To Raquel they symbolize the killings she had to perform and the reasons she had to do so.

LITERARY ELEMENTS

1. Another example of verbal irony is Raquel saying "Cleto? Oh, your army." She means that Cleto is not a strong or impressive force. An example of dramatic irony is when Raquel tells Flores a spy is in the closet. The audience knows this is true.
2. Andrés and Cleto being killed by Raquel instead of being saved by her is an example of situational irony.

Additional Resources

❧ *Literary Elements Transparency 76*

LITERATURE AND WRITING

Writing About Literature

Exploring Suspense   When an audience is waiting anxiously to find out what happens next, the writer has created suspense. In this play, when does the audience experience suspense? What actions or developments cause the suspense? In two or three paragraphs, explore how Niggli's use of suspense helps to make the drama more exciting.

Creative Writing

Write a New Scene   What happens next? Will General Macías be executed? Will Raquel continue the myth of her husband's bravery? How will she explain her earlier actions with the Federal soldiers? Write a new scene to extend the play, using the standard form for a play script. Use dialogue and stage directions that remain true to the personalities of the original characters.

EXTENDING YOUR RESPONSE

Literature Groups

Codes of Honor   Search the play for statements that reveal the characters' assumptions about what honor requires of men and women. Then, as a group, decide what you think the playwright's intention might have been. Do you think Niggli wants to make a point about male and female roles, or is her purpose to depict a historical situation in which male and female roles happened to overlap? Share your ideas with another group.

Performing

Making a Scene   Choose one segment of this play, and work with a small group to bring it to life. First, assign parts. Then discuss staging: where you will perform, how you will enter and leave the stage set, and what simple furnishings and props you will need. Base your choices on the scene's setting and the message it conveys. Rehearse your segment. Then perform it for the class.

Learning for Life

Incident Report   Imagine that you are an investigator sent to gather information and report on the death of Captain Andrés de la O. With a partner, create a report that clearly presents the facts of what happened.

Reading Further

For more about the Mexican Revolution, you might also be interested in the following work:

Revolution! Mexico 1910–1920, by Ronald Atkin, information about the causes, people, places, and effects of the Mexican Revolution.

📖 **Save your work for your portfolio.**

Skill Minilesson

VOCABULARY • Connotation

The definition of a word is called its **denotation.** The positive and negative associations of a word are called its **connotation.** Words with the same denotations can have different connotations. For example, *scrawny* and *slender* are both synonyms of *thin,* but the word *scrawny* suggests a malnourished skinniness, whereas the word *slender* suggests a pleasing slimness. The way a word is used reveals its connotation.

PRACTICE   For each pair of synonyms, write a brief description of how the words' connotations differ.

1. *ambitious* and *pushy*
2. *frown* and *scowl*
3. *destiny* and *doom*
4. *fragile* and *flimsy*
5. *risk* and *menace*

DRAMA 🐟 895

LITERATURE AND WRITING

Writing About Literature

Students' paragraphs should

- describe two or more specific examples of suspense in the play.
- explore the effects of the suspense in the play.

Creative Writing

Students' scenes should

- use the standard form for a play script.
- show knowledge of the play's plot and characters.

EXTENDING YOUR RESPONSE

Literature Groups   Point out that students should reread and quote lines from the play that refer directly to men's and women's roles.
COLLAB. LEARN.

Performing   Encourage students to keep in mind the symbolic meanings of some of the objects in the play as they plan their scenes and props.
COLLAB. LEARN.

Learning for Life   Emphasize that the report's main purpose is to inform, so it should be clear and objective.

Skill Minilesson

VOCABULARY • Connotation

1. *Ambitious* indicates an admirable wish to succeed while *pushy* implies offending people in order to get ahead.
2. *Frown* indicates a serious look of concentration while *scowl* implies an angry look.
3. *Destiny* refers to what is fated to happen to a person while *doom* implies impending disaster.
4. *Fragile* implies a delicate weakness while *flimsy* implies that something is poorly made.
5. *Risk* indicates a danger to be watched while *menace* implies something that poses a threat.

Additional Resources
📁 *Vocabulary Practice,* p. 49

✔ **ASSESSMENT OPTIONS**

📁 *Quick Checks,* p. 76
📁 *Selection and Theme Assessment,* pp. 147–148
📁 *Performance Assessment,* p. 75
💾 *Testmaker*

Objectives

- To read and analyze a poem about one mother's suggestion to her daughter about being loyal to oneself
- To identify free verse

Skills

Reading/Thinking: Drawing Conclusions
Listening/Speaking: Giving Advice
Collaboration: Literature Groups

Motivating
→OPTIONS

Selection Focus Transparency 72: Have students look at and discuss the picture of the turquoise.

Focus Activity: Have students contribute to a class list of personal values on the board.

✧— Before You Read —

Marked

FOCUS ACTIVITY

How can an individual stay true to what he or she believes?

LIST IDEAS With a partner, make a list of personal values that could help someone remain true to himself or herself.

SETTING A PURPOSE Read to discover how one mother suggests that her daughter remain true to herself.

BACKGROUND

Did You Know?

Following Tradition In her poem "Marked," Carmen Tafolla uses the word *m'ija,* a contraction of the Spanish words *mi* ("my") and *hija* ("daughter"). By calling the reader *m'ija,* Tafolla follows the Mexican American tradition of addressing all readers as if they were her own children and makes the poem a message to the reader.

Idiom Meanings The phrase *make your mark,* or *make one's mark,* is an idiom, or common expression. Like many words and phrases, it has more than one meaning. For example, in a time when many people were illiterate, *to make one's mark* meant to sign something by drawing a symbol, such as a cross or X. *To make one's mark* also means "to achieve success or fame" or "to distinguish oneself." "When I speak about making your mark," says Carmen Tafolla, "I'm talking about . . . what you do with your life."

Adjective Meanings The adjective *marked* also has multiple meanings. When something is marked, it visibly reveals some special quality or characteristic. That characteristic may even be a flaw, or imperfection. In this poem, the poet mentions "turquoise / marked." Pure turquoise is a blue-green, sky blue, or green mineral. But most turquoise is not pure: it includes a pattern of brown or black veins of other minerals. These markings are technically flaws in the turquoise stone, yet many people think that the pattern is what makes a piece of turquoise unique and valuable.

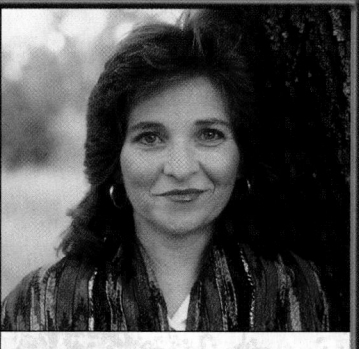

Meet Carmen Tafolla

"I have always told my children not to be ashamed to be who they are," says Carmen Tafolla (kär′ men tä fō′ yä). A native of San Antonio, Texas, Tafolla declares her identity in works ranging from poetry to screenplays. She explains that "as a Mexican American growing up in the 50s and 60s, I came from a group that was not often represented in textbooks. I saw no reflections of my own culture, and I longed to record the beauty and uniqueness of the culture that surrounded me." Tafolla is currently at work on her autobiography.

Carmen Tafolla was born in 1951.

896 ✧ UNIT 4

RESOURCE MANAGER

Lesson Planning Resource
The *Unit Four Planning Guide* (pp. 47–51) provides additional lesson notes and reduced versions of all print resources.

📁 **Other Print Resources**
- Active Reading Guide, p. 77
- Quick Checks, p. 77
- Selection and Theme Assessment, pp. 147–148
- Performance Assessment, p. 75
- Spanish Summaries, p. 72

 Transparencies
- Selection Focus 72
- Literary Elements 77

Technology
🎧 Audio Library
🎧 Spanish Audio Library
💻 Glencoe Literature Web Site
💾 Testmaker

Marked

Carmen Tafolla

Never write with pencil,
m'ija°
It is for those
who would
5   erase.
Make your mark proud
          and open,
Brave,
          beauty folded into
10   its imperfection,
Like a piece of turquoise
          marked.

Never write
with pencil,
15   m'ija.
Write with ink
          or mud,
or berries grown in
gardens never owned,
20   or, sometimes,
          if necessary,
          blood.

Collage Series II, No. 3, 1993. Katherine S. Nemanich. Oil pastel on paper and board, 12 x 9 in. Private collection.

DRAMA ❧ 897

Responding to the Selection

Personal Response

Students' responses should refer to their own philosophies of "making their mark."

ANALYZING LITERATURE

1. The speaker tells her daughter to never write with a pencil. By "those who would erase," she means people who feel tentative or think they will change their minds. She repeats the instruction for emphasis.
2. The speaker says the girl should write with ink, mud, berries, or blood. Ink may represent sureness; mud, getting one's hands dirty if necessary; berries, taking what is necessary from others; blood, being violent if necessary.
3. The title word appears in the image of the turquoise. The poet may have chosen this word as a title to emphasize its double meaning as something both positive and imperfect.
4. The poet compares making one's mark to a piece of turquoise. The simile adds the idea that an action can have beauty despite imperfections.
5. The theme of the poem is loyalty to oneself and one's convictions.
6. Students should refer specifically to the qualities valued in the poem.
7. Someone might follow the advice by being artistic or creative or by standing up for political beliefs.
8. Students might say that if people are true to their convictions, there should be no situations in which they should not follow the advice. Others may say that if "making one's mark" means hurting others, the advice should not be followed.

EXTENDING YOUR RESPONSE

Literature Groups Point out that students should be open to persuasion by the opinions of others.
COLLAB. LEARN.

Listening and Speaking Point out that advice in free verse might be read more informally than that in a three-paragraph speech.

Responding to Literature

Personal Response

How do you react to the message in this poem? Record your response in your journal.

ANALYZING LITERATURE

RECALL AND INTERPRET

1. What instruction does the speaker give her daughter in the first line? What does she mean by "those who would erase"? In your opinion, why might the poet have chosen to repeat this instruction?
2. According to the speaker, what should the girl write with? What might these materials symbolize?
3. Where does a reference to the title word appear in the poem? In your opinion, why might the poet have chosen this word as the title?
4. The poet uses a **simile** in line eleven to describe the type of mark the girl is instructed to make. What things does the poet compare through this simile? What does the simile add to the idea of making one's mark? (See Literary Terms Handbook, page R12.)

EVALUATE AND CONNECT

5. Theme Connections   Why might this poem appear in a group of selections about loyalty and betrayal?
6. Think about your response to the Focus Activity on page 896. How do the qualities you listed compare with the qualities the poem values?
7. In your opinion, what are examples of ways someone might follow the advice given in the poem?
8. Are there any situations for which you would not recommend someone to follow the advice in the poem? Explain your answer.

EXTENDING YOUR RESPONSE

Literature Groups

Good or Bad Advice?   With a group, share your opinions about the advice in this poem. Is the advice universally good, is it only good some of the time, or is it misleading or bad? Referring to the exact words of the poem, discuss the situations in which the advice might be most sound. Then compare your opinions with those of another group. Do any of their insights make you rethink your own?

Listening and Speaking

Mark My Words   Working with a partner, think about how you would advise middle school students to make their mark in high school. Then state your advice in a short speech or two stanzas of free verse. Practice reading the work aloud, each of you reading specific passages. When you are ready, present your advice to another pair of students, and invite their reactions.

📖 **Save your work for your portfolio.**

LITERARY ELEMENTS

1. The relaxed form of free verse matches the tone of the poem and the content of the poem's advice to not be fearful about taking action.
2. The unusual spacing sets off words in the poem that have significant meanings, emphasizing them.

Additional Resources

✎ *Literary Elements Transparency 77*

✔ ASSESSMENT OPTIONS

📁 *Quick Checks,* p. 77
📁 *Selection and Theme Assessment,* pp. 147–148
📁 *Performance Assessment,* p. 75
💾 *Testmaker*

COMPARING *selections*

The Ring of General Macías
A Drama of the Mexican Revolution

and *Marked*

COMPARE **ROLES**

Both the play and the poem spotlight girls or women. Discuss these questions:

1. In what ways do both the play and the poem suggest or show that girls and women are capable of acting bravely or of fulfilling roles once reserved for men?

2. Do the concerns of these works relate to all women and girls, or to specific groups of them? Do the concerns relate similarly to men and boys? Give reasons for your answer.

Female firefighter, Colorado.

COMPARE **MESSAGES**

In *The Ring of General Macías,* Raquel takes two lives in wartime. In "Marked," part of the poem's advice is to make one's mark in, "if necessary, / blood." Tafolla says she is not advocating violence in this line, but she is suggesting that there are some things for which a person should be willing to give his or her life.

1. Consult media sources, including on-line information services, to find causes in the world today for which people are willing to risk their lives.

2. With a partner, discuss the causes you have researched. Then decide why a character in the play or the speaker in the poem might approve or disapprove of each one.

COMPARE **LOYALTIES**

Loyalty is important in both of these works, yet the object of that loyalty differs.

1. To whom or what do the main characters in the play believe they owe their loyalty? To whom does the speaker in the poem believe loyalty is owed?

2. What are some explanations for these differing ideas of loyalty?

Objective

- To compare a play and a poem that deal with the theme of loyalty

COMPARE ROLES

1. In the play, Raquel supports her country by making the decision to kill two spies. The poem suggests that women should use any means necessary to make their mark on the world.

2. The works relate to all women and girls since they concern universal emotions. Therefore, they may also relate to men and boys.

COMPARE MESSAGES

Students' discussions should

- include data and examples from two or more specific causes.

COLLAB. LEARN.

Additional Resources

📁 *Literature Groups Sourcebook*

COMPARE LOYALTIES

1. Raquel believes she owes loyalty to her husband and to her government; General Macías, to his wife and his government; Andrés and Cleto, to the revolutionary cause; Marica, to her dead husband. The speaker of the poem believes loyalty is owed to oneself.

2. Differing ideas of loyalty are due to different values and different life experiences.

Teaching Options

 PORTFOLIO OPTIONS

Select and Reflect Have students reflect on their discussions with their partners by including answers to these questions along with any notes from their research:

- How do my partner and I agree about the characters' reactions to real-world situations? How do we disagree?

- How would I react to the situations I have researched?

Have students put their research notes and reflections in their portfolios. **L2**

Additional Resources

📁 *Writing Assessment and Portfolio Management,* pp. 20–22

Grammar Link

Objective

- To recognize and correct misplaced or dangling modifiers

Exercise

1. Reading on the couch in her living room, Raquel hears revolutionary soldiers. 2. Raquel knows who the men dressed in peasant clothing must be. 3. While opening a leather pouch, Andrés tells a story of starvation and brutality. 4. Laughing with amusement, Andrés tells Raquel about hanging a judge. 5. Cleto notices federal soldiers searching all the houses. 6. Working quickly, Raquel puts a clever plan into action. 7. Andrés tells Cleto, in the closet, to remain silent. 8. Wearing his federal uniform, Captain Flores is hunting for two spies. 9. Flores does not realize that Andrés, sitting as if in a trance, is the man he is seeking. 10. Cleverly responding to each new threat, Raquel makes the plan successful.

Additional Resources

Grammar and Language Workbook, p. 209

Grammar and Composition Handbook, Lesson 8.7

Writer's Choice, Lesson 18.7

Teaching Options

Grammar Link

Misplaced or Dangling Modifiers

The position of a **modifier**—a word or phrase that describes something—determines what it modifies. For example, "Barking with joy, Fred was greeted by his long-lost dog" means that Fred has an unusual way of expressing himself. *Who* was barking with joy? If it was the dog, then the modifying phrase should be placed right next to "long-lost dog." The easiest way to do this is to restructure the sentence. "Barking with joy, the long-lost dog greeted Fred."

A *misplaced modifier* is one that is in the wrong place and, therefore, describes the wrong thing. A *dangling modifier* is one that is meant to modify a word or phrase, but that word or phrase is not present in the sentence. Such a modifier "dangles," attaching itself to nothing.

Correcting a misplaced or a dangling modifier is easy if you think about what you are saying.

Problem 1 A misplaced modifier
Raquel offers to open the closet door pretending to be unconcerned.

Solution The wrong noun is modified. The door is not pretending. Move the misplaced modifier as close as possible to the word it modifies.
Pretending to be unconcerned, Raquel offers to open the closet door.

Problem 2 A dangling modifier
Using poisoned wine, the honor of her husband was protected.

Solution The sentence contains no word for the modifier to logically modify. Rewrite the sentence to include a noun or pronoun for the modifier to modify.
Using poisoned wine, she protected the honor of her husband.

● For information about similar usage problems, see **Language Handbook,** p. R24.

EXERCISE

On your paper, rewrite the sentences to correct misplaced or dangling modifiers.

1. Raquel hears revolutionary soldiers reading on the couch in her living room.

2. Dressed in peasant clothing, Raquel knows who the men must be.

3. While opening a leather pouch, a story of starvation and brutality is told.

4. Andrés tells Raquel about hanging a judge laughing with amusement.

5. Searching all the houses, Cleto notices Federal soldiers.

6. Working quickly, a clever plan is put into action.

7. In the closet, Andrés tells Cleto to remain silent.

8. Captain Flores is hunting for two spies wearing his federal uniform.

9. Sitting as if in a trance, Flores does not realize that Andrés is the man he is seeking.

10. Cleverly responding to each new threat, the plan is successful.

Writing *Minilesson*

Using Participles to Modify Using participial phrases is a good way to vary sentence structure. Write the following sentences on the board:
  He watched old movies on television.
  He became an expert in film noir.
Point out how the sentences can be combined:
  Watching old movies on television, he became an expert in film noir.

Activity Have students combine the sets of sentences below by making one into a participial phrase.
1. The player leaped high. She kicked the ball into the goal.
2. The medal lay on the dirty sidewalk. It glinted like a diamond. **L1**

Additional Resources

Writer's Choice, Lesson 12.3

LISTENING, SPEAKING, and VIEWING

Persuasive Speech

When Raquel in *The Ring of General Macías* convinces herself of the importance of "honor," she is speaking persuasively. Persuasive speaking skills are valuable tools, especially when your goal is to influence someone. For example, you might use these skills to convince a business owner to hire you or to present your views on an issue to a school newspaper reporter.

Preparing and Organizing the Speech

- Identify the issue and the stand you are taking. Jot down your thoughts and feelings about the issue.
- State your central claim. A claim statement will help you clarify your main purpose and focus your argument.
- Gather facts, examples, and observations you can use to help the audience see things your way. Rank this evidence by "order of importance."
- Explain how the evidence supports your claim. Then tell the audience why they should accept your evidence.
- Summarize your arguments, explaining why your central claim is the logical conclusion based on your evidence.

Presenting Your Speech

- On note cards, write the main ideas, important details, quotations, and statistics. Number the cards to keep them in order.
- Practice before an audience of relatives or close friends. Try out different tones of voice, gestures, and visual aids. Evaluate your audience's feedback.
- Speak clearly and at a normal pace. Emphasize your key points.
- Make eye contact with your listeners so they feel included.
- Maintain a natural, relaxed stance. Practice before a mirror so you can check your stance and gestures.

ACTIVITY

With a partner, identify two opposing positions on a controversial issue. Prepare a three- to five-minute persuasive speech in support of your side of the issue while your partner prepares a speech for the opposing side. For example, you might support the position that the minimum driving age should be raised, while your partner supports the current minimum driving age. With your partner, practice your speeches and present them to the class.

Objective

- To prepare and present a persuasive speech

Teaching Strategies

After students have read the page, have them give examples of persuasive speeches they have heard and given, and discuss the techniques the speakers used.

Activity

Students' speeches should

- clearly identify an issue and a stand on the issue.
- use specific facts and examples to support the viewpoint.
- be logically organized.
- be presented clearly and convincingly.

 ENGLISH LANGUAGE LEARNERS

Presenting an Argument Outlining a sample persuasive speech on the board will help English language learners who are unfamiliar with this kind of speech.

Activity Discuss the definition of *argument* when used in the sense of a speech or writing intended to persuade people of a viewpoint. Emphasize that a persuasive speech is based on objec-tive evidence. Have students contribute examples and evidence for a sample persuasive speech. Outline the speech on the board, indicating the central claim and a few supporting details. Have students write outlines and prac-tice the speech with a partner.

Additional Resources

📁 *English Language Learners Sourcebook*

Writing Workshop

Objectives

- To write a compare-and-contrast essay on two works of literature
- To plan, draft, revise, edit, and present a compare-and-contrast essay
- To reflect on and assess the essay

GLENCOE
TECHNOLOGY

 WRITER'S ASSISTANT
CD-ROM
Students can use Glencoe's templates and guidelines software for expository writing to aid them in working through the steps in the writing process in this lesson.

Teaching Strategies

PREWRITING

Explore ideas Point out that the two works being compared have a significant similarity: theme. This similarity makes the discussion of differences between the works meaningful. Have students create a frame like the sample. Point out that they may add or substitute literary elements, especially if they are comparing poems.

Teaching Options

~: Writing Workshop :~

Expository Writing: Compare-and-Contrast Essay

What makes one literary work stand above the rest? Perhaps the characters are more believable, or the theme is more striking. Maybe the style is better suited to the topic. You can write effective literary criticism by comparing and contrasting these and other elements of literature. Comparing means to discuss similarities between features.

Contrasting means to discuss differences. **In this workshop, you will write an essay comparing and contrasting two literary works.**

● As you write your expository essay, refer to **Writing Handbook,** pp. R58–R71.

The Writing Process

PREWRITING

PREWRITING TIP
It is often helpful to write down your initial impressions about a piece of literature as you read.

Explore ideas
Choose two literary works that develop the themes of loyalty and betrayal. You may wish to use a comparison frame to explore your ideas about the two works. Here is a frame created to compare and contrast *Antigone* and *The Ring of General Macías*.

Literary Element	Questions	Antigone	The Ring of General Macías
Theme	How is the theme of loyalty or betrayal addressed?	Antigone's loyalty to brother Polyneices; his betrayal of the state	Captain Andrés's loyalty to his cause; Raquel's loyalty to her husband
Style	Formal or informal?	generally formal	somewhat formal
Tone	Serious? Sad? Humorous?	very serious; sad; sentry provides comic relief	serious; sad; some sarcasm
Setting	What effect do time and place have?	right after battle; makes loyalty a key issue	during revolution; people taking sides
Plot	What is the main conflict?	Antigone vs. Creon	Raquel vs. Andrés
Characters	How are they presented?	dialogue, actions, choral comments	dialogue, actions

902 ❧ UNIT 4

MEETING INDIVIDUAL NEEDS — **ENGLISH LANGUAGE LEARNERS**

Filling in a Comparison Frame
Completing a chart as part of the prewriting process can help English language learners identify words and phrases they can use as they draft.

Activity Write a sample comparison frame on the board and have students contribute entries for one of the literary works. Review each literary element.

Students may need several examples for abstract elements such as theme, tone, and style. Have them copy the sample. Then have them complete the entries for the second literary work on their own. Ask volunteers to write their entries on the chart on the board.

902 ❧ UNIT 4

Consider your purpose

Your purpose is to compare and contrast the two literary works. However, there should be a point to your comparison. You should have a thesis about the importance of the similarities and differences. Consider the responses you wrote in the comparison frame; then decide how those similarities and differences affect the themes of loyalty and betrayal. Use this to write your thesis statement.

Choose an audience

The most important consideration here is whether or not the readers are familiar with both literary works. If they are, you can make references to the works. If they are not, you will have to directly quote passages to support your points.

Make a plan

Organize your essay into a form that your readers can follow and understand. Be sure to provide the basic essay elements of introduction, body, and conclusion.

- In the introduction, state the thesis that you have formed about the importance of the similarities and differences between the two subjects.
- In the body, compare and contrast each element with specific examples from the literary works. The chart shown below details two methods of organization: (1) by subject and (2) by feature.
- In the conclusion of your essay, restate your thesis and summarize your proof.

How to Organize a Compare-and-Contrast Essay	
By Subject	**By Feature**
Subject 1: _Antigone_ 　Feature A: Theme 　Feature B: Setting 　Feature C: Plot **Subject 2: _The Ring of General Macías_** 　Feature A: Theme 　Feature B: Setting 　Feature C: Plot	**Feature A: Theme** 　Subject 1: _Antigone_ 　Subject 2: _The Ring of General Macías_ **Feature B: Setting** 　Subject 1: _Antigone_ 　Subject 2: _The Ring of General Macías_ **Feature C: Plot** 　Subject 1: _Antigone_ 　Subject 2: _The Ring of General Macías_

　The number of features being compared determines which method of organization to use. If many features are being compared, organize by feature. Otherwise, your reader may forget what you said about the first subject by the time you discuss the second subject.

　Use your method of organization consistently. If you are organizing by subject, keep the features in the same order for each subject. If you are organizing by feature, discuss the features in the same sequence for both subjects.

Consider your purpose Encourage students to go beyond superficial similarities and differences in writing a thesis. For example, they may conclude that the characters of Antigone and Raquel are quite different although they experience similar conflicts. Encourage them to go one step further and conclude how this affects the plays. For example, they may conclude that the different outcomes of the characters point to a difference in morality between ancient Greek times and the twentieth century.

Choose an audience Point out that a very brief plot summary will ensure that readers have the necessary background information.

Make a plan Point out to students that limiting their comparisons to three features will simplify organization and ensure that each feature is discussed in sufficient detail.

TECHNOLOGY TIP

Point out that a word processor is especially helpful in organizing a compare-and-contrast essay. Students can use cutting and pasting to shift elements around or even change the format of their comparisons.

Additional Resources

📁 **_Writing and Proofreading Practice,_** pp. 1–7, 73–79

🖋 **_Writing and Proofreading Transparencies 1–6, 43–44_**

📓 **_Writer's Choice,_** Lesson 5.5

Bodily-Kinesthetic Students may have difficulty with the strict organization necessary for a compare-and-contrast essay.

Activity Have students copy the chart headings from page 903 onto a large piece of drawing paper. Then have them make several adhesive notes, some with the title of one of the literary works they are comparing and some with the title of the other. Have them make another set of adhesive notes showing the three features they will be comparing. Instruct students to arrange and rearrange the notes on the chart until they have organized their topic satisfactorily. **L1**

Write your draft Remind students that their introduction should make clear that two literary works will be compared. It should also specify the two works and the major elements that will be compared. Finally, it should contain a thesis statement that indicates the significance of the similarities and differences. Explain that the conclusion should summarize any insights or conclusions reached through the comparison process.

REVISING

Have a writing conference Explain that a reading by another person is especially helpful in a compare-and-contrast essay, in which organization is very important. Have students ask their partners to check for consistent organization that can be followed easily.

Teaching Options

~: *Writing* ⟍ *Workshop* :~

DRAFTING

DRAFTING TIP
When comparing two items, use the comparative form of a modifier.

Refer to the Writing Skill "Effective Conclusions" on page 799 to help you draft your conclusion.

Write your draft
As you write, refer to your plan, but focus on getting your key points of comparison down. Don't worry about perfect organization at this stage.

Think of the reader
State each comparison or contrast directly. Use a term or phrase that clearly states the relationship, such as *like Antigone* or *unlike Raquel.*

STUDENT MODEL

> Both plays show, in similar personal terms, the suffering that war inflicts on innocent people. Antigone has lost her brothers, and Marica has lost her husband.

REVISING

REVISING TIP
Check off points on your plan and in your draft to make sure no important points are missing.

Evaluate your work
Put your draft aside for a while. Later, read it as if your audience were reading it. Make note of any parts that you think need to be improved. Then use the **Questions for Revising** to guide you as you revise your draft.

Have a writing conference
Work with a partner to improve your draft. As you read the draft aloud, pay special attention to organization and transitions. Go through the **Questions for Revising** together. Then make the revisions that seem important to you.

QUESTIONS FOR REVISING

How can I:

☑ strengthen my thesis?

☑ clarify comparisons and contrasts?

☑ clarify relationships with words such as *like* or *instead?*

☑ improve the organization?

☑ clear up confusing parts?

☑ show that I proved my thesis?

STUDENT MODEL

both Antigone and The Ring of General Macías,
In these plays, personal loyalties are in conflict with loyalty to a
                                      in both   conflict is resolved in favor of
cause or a government, and the plays vote for the personal loyalties.

Writing Minilesson

Transitions Have students contribute as you write transitions showing similarity and difference on the board, such as *as, like, similarly, moreover, in addition, yet, still, nevertheless, in contrast, on the other hand,* and *however.*

Activity Have students add two transitions showing similarity and two showing difference to their essays. Ask several students to read aloud the original and the revision of a sentence they have revised in this way. Point out the improvement in clarity and coherence that these transitions provide. **L2**

Additional Resources

 Writer's Choice, Lesson 2.7

EDITING/PROOFREADING

Edit your essay to find and correct errors in grammar, usage, mechanics, and spelling. Use the **Proofreading Checklist** on the inside back cover to guide your work.

Grammar Hint

To avoid confusing your readers, place modifying words and phrases as close as possible to the words they modify. In the sentence below, the modifying phrase *in each play* should be placed near *characters*, the word it modifies.

MISPLACED: *The characters make choices based on their true loyalties in each play.*

CORRECT: *In each play, the characters make choices based on their true loyalties.*

● For information about modifiers, see **Language Handbook,** p. R24.

STUDENT MODEL

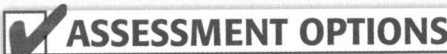

Both plays demonstrates that actions speak louder than words, and both
plays primally through their actions characterize their central
characters. Antigone just doesn't talk about burying Polyneices. She does
it. Raquel doesn't threaten to poison Andrés and Cleto. She poisons them.

PUBLISHING/PRESENTING

For presentation to the class, you could distribute copies of your essay a week or so before a discussion of the points you have made.

> **PRESENTING TIP**
> Begin an oral presentation by reading a significant passage from each literary work.

Reflecting

What new insights have you gained by comparing and contrasting these works? How might comparisons between works be useful? Jot down your responses.

Identify techniques from this workshop that you could use in other compare-and-contrast writing, such as in history essays. What you've learned here can help you there.

📑 **Save your work for your portfolio.**

Have students use the **Proofreading Checklist** on the inside back cover of their textbooks.

Suggest that students look at essays that have been previously revised and make a list of errors they tend to make. Have them check for these errors one at a time as they begin revising their essays.

PUBLISHING/PRESENTING

Point out that in an oral presentation, students can use transitions, gestures, and graphic aids to clarify the elements of a compare-and-contrast essay. These techniques will help an audience follow the essay's organizational plan.

Reflecting

📑 **Portfolio** Have students ask themselves these questions as they review their writing for possible placement in their portfolios.

Does my compare-and-contrast essay
- come to a significant conclusion about the works' similarities and differences?
- reflect new insights I learned as I wrote?
- represent work I am proud of?

If students answer yes to two or more of these questions, suggest they place their essay in their portfolio.

✔ ASSESSMENT OPTIONS

📁 ***Writing Assessment and Portfolio Management***
- Writing Assessment, pp. 2–19, 41–42
- Portfolio Management, pp. 20–22

Unit Wrap-Up

Objectives

- To give a personal response about the plays, discussions, and activities in this unit
- To compare literary elements in two plays
- To complete a self-evaluation, set a goal, and devise a plan for achieving the goal

PERSONAL RESPONSE

1. Students should give details and explanations for their choices.
2. Accept all reasonable answers.

ANALYZING LITERATURE

Students' writing should
- have an organization that makes the comparison between the two works clear.
- include specific examples from the works to support ideas.

EVALUATE AND SET GOALS

Evaluate

Have students list the projects and assignments they completed in the unit. Suggest that they evaluate each item based on the scale provided.

Set Goals

Have students prepare a flowchart or other sequential graphic showing the order of the steps they plan to follow in achieving their goals. Hold individual conferences in which students share their own evaluations and discuss the pieces they have chosen for their portfolios.

DRAMA

Unit Wrap-Up

PERSONAL RESPONSE

1. Which of the plays in this unit would you like to see turned into a film? What actors would you want to star in the leading roles? Explain your choices.
2. How did your work in this unit enhance your skills in the following areas?
   - understanding dialogue that is very different from your own speech
   - identifying elements of drama
   - discussing different interpretations of a line, scene, or play
   - working cooperatively with your classmates

ANALYZING LITERATURE

Comparing Two Elements Choose two plays from this unit, and compare them based on one of the elements of drama you studied in the Genre Focus on pages 712–713. For example, you might choose to compare and contrast the character traits of Creon in *Antigone* with those of Caesar in *Julius Caesar,* explaining how the traits of these two characters influence the final outcome of their stories.

EVALUATE AND SET GOALS

Evaluate

1. What was your most valuable contribution to the class as you worked through this unit?
2. What assigned task in this unit did you find most challenging?
   - How did you approach this task?
   - What was the outcome?
3. How would you assess your work in this unit, using the following scale? Give at least two reasons for your assessment.
   4 = outstanding   3 = good   2 = fair   1 = weak

Set Goals

1. Choose a goal to work toward in Unit 5. Concentrate on any skill you wish to improve, such as reading, writing, speaking, or working in a group.
2. Discuss your goal with your teacher.
3. Write down three steps you will take to help you achieve your goal.
4. Plan checkpoints at specific intervals in the unit to assess your progress toward your goal.
5. Include a self-evaluation plan to determine whether you have reached your goal.

BUILD YOUR PORTFOLIO

Select Choose two pieces of writing you did in this unit and include them in your portfolio. The following questions can help you make your selection:
- Which pieces do you think would be most interesting to an outside reader?
- Which pieces demonstrate the greatest amount of thought?
- Which pieces demonstrate the greatest amount of creativity?
- Which pieces contain your most polished writing?

Reflect Write some notes to accompany the pieces you selected. Use these questions to guide you.
- What is the strongest aspect of the piece?
- What was the most helpful comment you received regarding this piece? How did you incorporate that comment into the final version?
- How might the skills you used in writing this piece help you with your future writing?

✔ ASSESSMENT OPTIONS

📁 ***Writing Assessment and Portfolio Management***
- Writing Assessment, pp. 2–19
- Portfolio Management, pp. 20–22

GLENCOE
T E C H N O L O G Y

 MINDJOGGER VIDEOQUIZZES VIDEODISC

Use *MindJogger* to review the Unit 4 content.

 Unit 4
Side A

 Also available in VHS.

Reading on Your Own

You might also be interested in the following books.

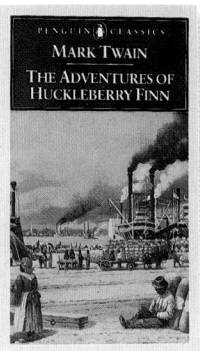

The Adventures of Huckleberry Finn

by Mark Twain The adults in Huck Finn's life fail to appreciate his mischievous and fun-loving attitude. Hungry for comradeship, he befriends the runaway slave, Jim, and together they escape the constrictions of the small town to raft down the Mississippi River. Jim helps Huck learn the nature of friendship and the meaning of freedom.

The Post Office

by Rabindranath Tagore An illustrated edition of Tagore's play about an adopted child named Amal. Confined to his home as the result of an illness, Amal's only entertainment is watching the neighborhood as he sits at his open window. As Amal engages in conversations with the townspeople who stroll by, he expresses amazing insight into life.

Seven Against Thebes

by Aeschylus Prehistoric Thebes is under siege by an Argive army led by Polyneices, son of Oedipus and brother of Eteocles. Eteocles pledges to save Thebes and fiercely defend its seven gates against the Argive army's seven armored chiefs and their warriors. Trying to avoid disaster, the Theban women warn Eteocles to stay away from the seventh gate.

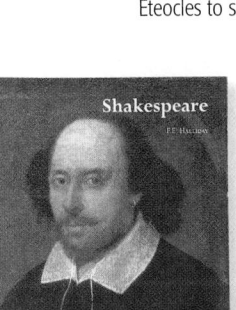

Shakespeare

by F. E. Halliday This illustrated biography of Shakespeare gives details about the playwright's life and plays and presents fascinating information about the history of the theater. Reproductions of documents, maps, and illustrations enliven the text. Included are contemporary photographs of Shakespeare's grave in Stratford and other historic sites.

Glencoe Literature Library

For a complete listing of the titles available in the *Glencoe Literature Library*, see page T44 in this book.

The *Glencoe Literature Library Study Guides* provide instructional support and student activities for works in the *Glencoe Literature Library*.

DRAMA 907

MEETING INDIVIDUAL NEEDS — INCLUSION STRATEGIES

You may wish to recommend *The Post Office* by Rabindranath Tagore to your less-proficient readers. The accessible subject matter and writing style make this book particularly appropriate for these students. **L1**

The following works may be recommended to your more proficient readers:
- *The Adventures of Huckleberry Finn* by Mark Twain **L2**
- *Seven Against Thebes* by Aeschylus **L3**
- *Shakespeare* by F. E. Halliday **L2**

Additional Resources
 Inclusion Strategies

Standardized Test Practice

Remind students that tiny words can say a lot. Ask the class to finish this sentence: "I did enjoy the movie, and—" The word "and" is used to *continue* a thought or trend, so the sentence will probably end positively. Now take the same sentence and change only one word: "I did enjoy the movie, but—" Ask the class what will follow. How did they know it would be something negative? Words like "but" tell us that something *different* will follow. Students should use even the tiniest clues to boost their comprehension of written text.

Standardized Test Practice

Read the following passage. Then read each question on page 909. Decide which is the best answer to each question. Mark the letter for that answer on your paper.

Benny Wins a Trip

Congratulations to Benny Thompson! Benny has won the Model United Nations Junior Citizen Essay contest. Everyone in his class was required to submit a 500-word personal interpretation of the phrase, "Everyone is a citizen of the world." A prolific writer, Benny drafted several essays and then chose one to polish for his official entry. The end result was a creative adaptation of the American Pledge of Allegiance to the Flag that asserted Benny's loyalty to the planet Earth as a federation of nations. "I pledge allegiance to the Earth as a citizen of its united nations . . ." Benny began. His essay focused on the responsibilities every person has to the causes of civic responsibility, education, racial harmony, and the advancement of the human race. Quite a piece of work!

As a reward, Benny will receive an all-expenses-paid trip to New York City to visit the United Nations and receive an award on the floor of the General Assembly. The itinerary for his trip is reprinted below.

TRAVEL ITINERARY

Thursday, August 8
3:10 P.M.	(CDT) Flight 605 leaves Bush Intercontinental Airport
7:40 P.M.	(EDT) Flight 605 lands at La Guardia Airport in New York City
8:00 P.M.	Shuttle to hotel arrives in the pick-up lane outside gate F
8:30 P.M.	Check-in at the Manhattan Towers Hotel
8:45 P.M.	Dinner at Ricardo's Italian Bistro

Friday, August 9
8:00 A.M.	Breakfast at the Towers Spotlight Cafe in the Manhattan Towers Hotel
9:00 A.M.	Tour leaves for the Statue of Liberty
12:00 NOON	Lunch at the Liberty Park Pavilion
2:00 P.M.	A "Meet and Greet" juice bar with other essay winners from around the country in the lobby of the Del Monico Theater on Broadway
3:00 P.M.	Broadway show (to be determined)
6:00 P.M.	Dinner in Chinatown
8:00 P.M.	Special taping of "The Eli Wetterman Show" at Network Studios

Saturday, August 10
8:00 A.M.	Breakfast at the Towers Spotlight Cafe in the Manhattan Towers Hotel
9:00 A.M.	Tour of the United Nations complex
12:00 NOON	Meet for lunch at the "Let Us Beat Swords into Plowshares" statue
1:00 P.M.	Special Awards Ceremony on the Floor of the General Assembly Hall
3:00 P.M.	Press Conference and Photo Session in the General Assembly Lobby
5:00 P.M.	Round-robin discussion among essay finalists on the topic: "Spaceship Earth: Are We Running Out of Fuel?" Scheduled for Conference Room 1A of the Manhattan Towers Hotel
8:00 P.M.	Dinner at the famous Waterfront Steak House

Sunday, August 11

8:30 A.M.	Continental breakfast in the central piazza of the Manhattan Towers Hotel (buffet will be set up on the terrace)
10:00 A.M.	Check out of hotel rooms
10:30 A.M.	Meet shuttle bus bound for La Guardia Airport
12:04 P.M.	(EDT) Flight 502 takes off from La Guardia Airport
2:50 P.M.	(CDT) Flight 502 lands at Bush Intercontinental Airport

1 The main idea of the passage is that —

  A Benny plans a visit to New York

  B all the students in Benny's class are required to enter a contest

  C Benny has been invited to join the United Nations

  D everyone learns that Benny has won a trip

2 While he is in New York, Benny will most likely —

  F not see the United Nations complex

  G decide to go to college in New York

  H not see the Statue of Liberty

  J not have much free time

3 How does the author of this piece feel about Benny's essay?

  A Discouraged

  B Enthusiastic

  C Critical

  D Neutral

4 The word <u>prolific</u> in this passage indicates that Benny —

  F is a well-known writer

  G hates to revise his writing

  H produces a lot of writing

  J is reluctant to write

5 Which is the best summary of the schedule for Friday, August 9th?

  A Benny will visit the Statue of Liberty.

  B Benny will receive his award.

  C Benny will see a Broadway show.

  D Benny will enjoy many New York activities.

6 The information in the passage suggests that the trip's organizers have arranged for —

  F transit to and from each activity

  G a visit with the mayor of New York

  H Benny to have a trip every year

  J free souvenirs to be distributed

Answers and Analyses

1. D Students should look to the title and the beginning of the passage, which shows that this is an announcement of Benny's victory.

2. J This is a good chance to teach students to answer questions by the process of elimination. We know from Benny's schedule that he will see the United Nations and the Statue of Liberty, so choices F and H can be eliminated. The passage says nothing about where Benny will choose to go to college, so choice G can be eliminated. We can see, however, that Benny's schedule is quite full, so the most reasonable answer is J.

3. B The end of the first paragraph congratulates Benny on his essay, and states that his essay was *Quite a piece of work!* This exclamation indicates the author's enthusiasm.

4. H Students should reread the sentence containing the word *prolific* and use context clues to help establish its meaning. Since the passage states that *Benny drafted several essays,* the most reasonable answer is H.

5. D Students are looking for a summary. Choices A, B, and C mention specific activities. According to the schedule, Benny will do several different things in New York, including the activities mentioned in choices A, B, and C. Only Choice D sums up what he will do all day.

6. F The beginning of the second paragraph states that this is an *all-expenses-paid trip*. Nothing is mentioned about the mayor, an annual trip, or free souvenirs, so F is the most reasonable answer.

Tested Objectives

Questions	Reading Objective
1, 5	Summarize a variety of written texts
2, 3, 6	Analyze information in a variety of written texts in order to make inferences and generalizations
4	Determine the meaning of words

MORE PRACTICE

For additional practice, assign pages from one of the following standardized test resources available as part of Glencoe Literature.

Additional Resources
ITBS Preparation and Practice
SAT-9 Preparation and Practice
TerraNova Preparation and Practice

Unit Five — At a Glance
Legends

UNIT OPENING

→ **Theme 11: HEROISM**

- **Literature Focus: Legends** (p. 912)

SELECTIONS

from **Le Morte d'Arthur** (p. 914)
from **Sundiata** (p. 934)

The Passing of Arthur, *from* **Idylls of the King** (p. 944)

Media Connection: Screenplay (p. 960)

Arthur Becomes King, *from* **The Once and Future King** (p. 961)

Media Connection: Theme Song Lyrics (p. 980)

Where the Girl Rescued Her Brother (p. 982)

SKILL FEATURES

Grammar Link (p. 942)

Writing Skills (p. 943)

Interdisciplinary Connection (p. 959)

Vocabulary Skills (p. 977)

Technology Skills (p. 978)

Reading and Thinking Skills (p. 989)

WRITING WORKSHOP

Expository Writing: Biographical Research Paper (p. 990)

KEYS TO LITERARY CONNECTIONS

World Literature

Glencoe Literature contains a variety of literature that represents cultures from around the world. World literature selections are highlighted with this symbol:

Comparing Selections

In each theme of **Glencoe Literature,** the **Comparing Selections** feature gives students an opportunity to compare two selections they have just read. Each Comparing Selections page provides a variety of options to address diverse aspects of the reading and literature curriculum.

UNIT WRAP-UP

- **Personal Response, Analyzing Literature, Evaluate and Set Goals** (p. 994)

- **Build Your Portfolio** (p. 994)

- **Reading on Your Own** (p. 995)

  The Autobiography of Miss Jane Pittman by Ernest J. Gaines

  The Light Beyond the Forest by Rosemary Sutcliff

  Cut from the Same Cloth: American Women of Myth, Legend, and Tall Tale by Robert D. San Souci

  The Talking Earth by Jean Craighead George

- **Standardized Test Practice** (pp. 996–997)

KEYS TO TEACHING OPTIONS

 Block Scheduling

Activities that are particularly suited to use within a block scheduling framework are identified throughout this unit by the following designation: For detailed suggestions on block scheduling, see the **Block Scheduling Guide** for this grade level.

Key to Ability Levels

The Teaching Options throughout this unit have been coded for students of various abilities.

L1 **BASIC** activities for all students

L2 **AVERAGE** activities for average to above-average students

L3 **CHALLENGING** activities for above-average students

Unit Five — At a Glance
Legends

Reading Skills in this unit

Variety of Texts
In addition to excerpts from two classic books based on the Arthurian legend, this unit includes the following text types:
- tale from African oral tradition
- long poem
- screenplay
- theme song lyrics
- tale from Native American oral tradition

Comprehension Skills
The following instructional support for comprehension skills appears in this unit of the Student Edition:
- **Identifying Sequence** (p. 989)
- **Reading and Thinking Minilessons** (pp. 958, 976)

See also the **Reading Minilessons** throughout the unit in this Teacher's Wraparound Edition.

Reading Resources

Comprehension Skills Resources

Active Reading Guides

The **Active Reading Guide** provides graphic organizers and study guide questions to support students' reading of each selection. (**Active Reading Guide**, pp. 78–82)

Reading Workbook

The Reading Workbook (pp. 77–84) includes additional instruction and reinforcement of reading strategies and skills.

Audio Library

Available both on tape and on CD, the Audio Library provides valuable comprehension support.

Resources for Reading Widely

Glencoe Literature Library
Each title in the Glencoe Literature Library includes a full-length novel or play plus related readings. A separate Study Guide is available for each title.

Literature Classics CD-ROM
The 900 selections on this CD-ROM can be searched by author, theme, or genre.

 A coproduction of Glencoe and Time Inc., *inTime* includes a wealth of high-interest nonfiction related to the selections and themes in Unit Five.

✔ Assessment in this unit

Assessment Options in the Student Edition
Glencoe Literature offers a number of diverse ways to evaluate student understanding and skill proficiency. In the Student Edition, use the following:
- **Responding to Literature**
  Following each selection, students are asked to recall facts, interpret ideas, and evaluate concepts as they answer a variety of questions and complete activities to extend their understanding.
- **Unit Wrap-Up (pp. 994–995)**
  Here students respond to the selections on personal and analytical levels. They also assume ownership of their learning by setting and evaluating goals and by selecting work for their portfolios.

See also the many **Assessment Resources** listed on the facing page.

THE PRINCETON REVIEW

Standardized Test Practice
The Princeton Review has developed the Standardized Test Practice pages found at the end of this unit (pp. 996–997). These pages contain practice test questions that help students remain familiar with standardized test formats and content.

Writing Skills in this unit

Writing Skills

The Student Edition of Unit Five offers strong instructional support for writing skills:

In **Extending Your Response**, which follows each selection:
- **Writing About Literature**
- **Personal/Creative Writing**

In **Writing Skills** Lessons:
- **Main Idea and Supporting Details** (p. 943)

See also the **Writing Minilessons** throughout the unit in this Teacher's Wraparound Edition.

Writing Workshops

The theme in Unit Five concludes with a **Writing Workshop** that guides students through the writing process.
- **Expository Writing: Biographical Research Paper** (pp. 990–993)

Writing Resources

Writer's Assistant CD-ROM

Each Writing Workshop is supplemented by an interactive writing guide on the Writer's Assistant CD-ROM. This easy-to-use writing guide provides prompts, templates, and other tools that lead students through the writing process.

Writing and Proofreading Practice

Blackline masters present in-depth instruction and practice on a specific step in the writing process and proofreading. (pp. 1–7, 80–88)

Writing and Proofreading Transparencies

Transparencies (1–6, 21–24, 45–46) provide graphic organizers and proofreading exercises for whole class instruction.

Research and Report Writing Guide

This resource provides extensive tips and activities to guide students in their writing projects in the literature classroom as well as in classes across the curriculum.

Style and Documentation Sourcebook for Writers

This sourcebook is a combination reference and workbook, giving students the most up-to-date information and guidance regarding traditional as well as technological research strategies and documentation.

Grammar and Composition Handbook

The Grammar and Composition Handbook provides instruction that supplements activities in the student textbook.

Assessment Resources

Selection Quick Checks

For each selection, a Quick Check of three to five short-answer questions measures students' literal comprehension.

Selection and Theme Assessment

The Selection and Theme Assessment instrument tests students' abilities to recall, interpret, and evaluate what they've read. The tests consist of multiple-choice, short answer, and essay questions.

Performance Assessment

Alternative assessment instruments and rubrics for Unit Five are found in the Performance Assessment ancillary.

Writing Assessment and Portfolio Management

These notes and strategies, student models, and assessment tools assist with the task of measuring students' progress as writers and as monitors of their own writing.

Testmaker

Teachers can customize selection, theme, and Unit Five tests by accessing the Testmaker database.

MindJogger Videoquizzes

Using a popular game show format, MindJogger Videoquizzes enable teachers to evaluate students' understanding of Unit Five in a quick and fun manner.

Legends

Unit Objectives

- To enjoy reading legends
- To analyze the literary elements in legends
- To apply strategies for reading legends

VIEWING THE PAINTING

Maximilian Liebenwein's (1869–1926) painting shows Saint George, who is the patron saint of England. In a famous legend about Saint George, he slays a dragon and, in the process, saves the king's daughter who was about to be sacrificed to the monster.

Responding to the Art Discussion questions:

- What legendary time and characters does the picture depict? (*The picture shows a knight in armor rescuing a maiden in medieval times.*)
- What is the mood of the painting? (*romantic and dreamy, idyllic*)
- Explain how different elements in the painting contribute to its mood. (*The horse's expression and the presence of the dogs give it a fairy tale quality; the vegetation seems almost perfect and surreal; the girl's face expresses contentment.*)

St. George: The Rescue, 1903. Maximilian Liebenwein. Brush and ink, gouache and gold paint on board, 89 x 69.5 cm.

910

TEACHER to TEACHER

E.R. MARTIN JR. HIGH SCHOOL • EAST PROVIDENCE, RHODE ISLAND

Through brainstorming, we establish what students already know and what they do not know about legends. We analyze the difference between legends and factual stories. I often ask students: Who are the heroes and why have they become legends? What are the differences between legends and myths? What makes a hero larger than life? In our discussion, we start with a hero in the school, then move to a hero in our state, then to a hero in the larger world. Then to introduce the concept of the oral tradition of storytelling, students tell a story in a "telephone line," in which one student whispers something to another who in turn whispers it to another. By the fifth student, the story has changed. Students learn that in oral storytelling, people fill in their own gaps in memory, which helps establish that a legend rises above the level of factual reality. I also bring to class children's books of tall tales and legends.

MAUREEN WHALEN SPAIGHT

UNIT ❦ FIVE

Legends

*"I loved best
the evening meal,
for that was the time old
legends were told."*
—Zitkala-Ša

Theme 11
Heroism
pages 913–993

Introducing the Unit
Have students read the quotation. Then use the following discussion questions:
- How do legends originate?
- Why do legends appeal to people?
- What legends do you know?

Theme 11: Heroism
The works in Theme 11 describe the heroic deeds of some legendary heroes from various cultures.

GLENCOE
TECHNOLOGY
LITERATURE CLASSICS
CD-ROM
Search for other selections by theme, author, or title.

RESOURCE MANAGER
See the *Unit Five Planning Guide* (pp. iv–1) for additional teaching notes, strategies, and resources for introducing the legends unit.

Objectives

- To read a definition and description of legends and folklore
- To understand the distinctions between myths and legends

Teaching Strategies

Students may be familiar with American legendary heroes such as John Henry, Paul Bunyan, and Johnny Appleseed. Point out that legends also spring up about real historical figures; students may know legends about George Washington and Abraham Lincoln. Other examples of legends are those of the American West.

Activity

Suggest that students begin a chart listing the exaggerated and supernatural elements of each selection. At the end of the unit, have them contribute to a class chart.

A&E HOME VIDEO. ® *The following videotape program is available from Glencoe. Be sure to preview the video for appropriateness for your class.*

- **Ancient Mysteries: Quest for the Holy Grail**

Teaching Options

Literature F O C U S
Legends

Just who was King Arthur? Several well-known stories describe him as a king in shining armor who gathered around him the best and bravest knights of England. There is another Arthur story, too, that tells about an amazing warrior who led British forces against Roman armies. These tall tales and romances may have developed around a historical figure, but, as often happens, the legend is now better known than the man.

People frequently use the words "legend" and "myth" as if the two words mean the same thing, but there is an important difference between them. Whereas both myths and legends tell traditional stories about a very distant past, **myths** center on religious or supernatural material. They try to explain the great mysteries of human experience, such as the origins of life, the existence of evil, and the shape of the universe. Mythical heroes are the gods and creatures who inhabited the world in a time "before time." No one can historically date a myth.

Legends, on the other hand, are more historically based. Although these stories may contain exaggerated, magical, or supernatural elements, they are set in a particular time and place, and they focus on people who might have existed. Robin Hood was a real person; so was Sundiata, the African leader who ruled the Kingdom of Mali (see page 934). King Arthur may have been a real man too, although no one knows for sure.

Robin Hood by N. C. Wyeth.

Originally, legends, like myths, were passed on from generation to generation by word of mouth. For this reason, these stories are classified as **folklore**—they are part of a community's culture that is maintained without reliance on the written word. Folklore helps define a culture's unique identity. Local legends, however, can also become part of other regions' legends. **The Arthurian legends**— the body of stories about the king—were passed on orally both in England and in France. Another popular legend that became widely distributed and adapted—the folktale of a marksman who shot an apple from his son's head—is based on a Swiss hero, William Tell.

As different storytellers recounted these and other tales over and over again, each person added his or her own slight variation, and the content of the legends probably shifted. Legends may not get written down until hundreds of years after they originated. Perhaps this explains why stories based on actual people and events end up containing very little information that is historically verifiable.

ACTIVITY

As you read the stories of King Arthur and other heroes in this theme, identify the exaggerated, magical, or supernatural elements in each legend. What do these elements add to the story?

MEETING INDIVIDUAL NEEDS **GIFTED AND TALENTED**

Urban Legends Students may enjoy researching some urban legends: contemporary legends that become widespread due to word-of-mouth. Urban legends often have ironic or shocking endings. They usually deal with aspects of contemporary life that make people anxious. For example, one urban legend tells of a shopper bringing a piece of furniture home from an import store only to be poisoned by a snake hidden within it. This perhaps reflected a fear of the consequences of Americans buying many imported goods.

Activity Have students retell a legend they have read or heard to the class. Suggest that students use an informal style fitting the legend's origins. **L3**

Theme 11 _____ Heroism

The shining quality of true heroes can last through the ages. In this theme, you'll meet legendary characters who use their extraordinary strength and bravery in the service of causes larger than themselves. Who do you think are the heroes in today's world?

THEME PROJECTS

Learning for Life

Nominate a Hero   Which character from this theme deserves to win an International Hero award?

1. Write a letter to the International Hero nominating committee, telling them what you think a hero is and which character should win the award.

2. In order to persuade the committee, provide detailed information about your nominee's heroic achievements. Explain why he or she deserves the award by comparing him or her with the other heroes in this theme.

3. Present your argument in business letter format.

Interdisciplinary Project

History   What conclusions can you draw about how each time period influenced the legends in this theme?

1. Research to find out what life was like for African royalty in the 1200s, for British knights and nobility in the 1400s, and for Cheyenne warriors in the 1800s.

2. Look for information about everyday details. How did people occupy themselves during the day? What did people eat? What did they wear? What music did they listen to?

3. Summarize your findings and conclusions in a series of posters.

Human Achievement,
1983. Tsing-Fang Chen.
Acrylic on canvas,
66 x 96 in.
Lucia Gallery, New York.

Theme 11 _____

Teaching Strategies

The following suggestions may help your students plan and carry out their theme projects.

Learning for Life

- As a class, list possible heroes from the theme.
- Review the correct format for a business letter by having students put a sample Heading, Date, Inside Address, Salutation and Closing on the board.
- Discuss the use of specific facts and details in persuasive writing.

Interdisciplinary Project

- You may wish to have students work in three groups and assign one historic era to each group. Have groups work individually or together.
- Encourage students to use maps, charts, and pictures to communicate information on their posters.
- Discuss with the class ways of displaying the final products.

Additional Resources

📁 *Interdisciplinary Activities,* pp. 22–23

📁 *Viewing and Representing Activities,* pp. 27–28

📁 *Listening and Speaking Activities,* pp. 21–22

📁 *Critical Thinking Skills,* pp. 30–32

📁 *Selection and Theme Assessment,* pp. 191–192

📁 *Performance Assessment,* p. 99

GLENCOE TECHNOLOGY

LITERATURE CLASSICS CD-ROM
Search for other selections related to the theme of heroism.

FINE ART
TRANSPARENCY 24

You may want to use Fine Art Transparency 24 to discuss aspects of heroism.

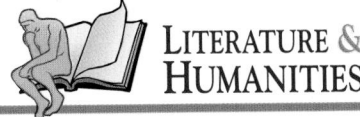

LITERATURE & HUMANITIES

📖 Have students examine *Armor of George Clifford, The Earl of Cumberland* in *Art Talk,* page 228. Have them write a journal entry describing the kind of heroism usually associated with suits of armor and compare it to other definitions of heroes.

Theme 11 SKILLS SCOPE AND SEQUENCE

SELECTIONS	Literary Elements	Reading and Thinking	Writing	Vocabulary and Spelling
from Le Morte d'Arthur THOMAS MALORY	Dialogue, SE p. 932 *Setting, TWE pp. 916, 921* *Dialogue, TWE pp. 916, 922, 924, 926, 927, 928, 930* *Theme, TWE p. 917* *Character, TWE pp. 918, 919, 920, 923, 925, 930* *Imagery, TWE p. 923* *Diction, TWE p. 928*	*Identifying Author's Purpose, TWE p. 928* *Comparing and Contrasting, TWE p. 931*	News Story, SE p. 933 *Describing Action, TWE p. 927*	Etymology, SE p. 933 *Etymology, TWE p. 919*
from Sundiata RECORDED BY D.T. NIANE	Tall Tale, SE p. 940 *Tall Tale, TWE pp. 936, 939* *Characters, TWE pp. 937, 938* *Imagery, TWE p. 938* *Point of View, TWE p. 939*	*Using Graphic Aids, TWE p. 939*	Tall Tales, SE p. 940 Main Idea and Supporting Details, SE p. 943 *Using Appositives, TWE p. 942*	
The Passing of Arthur from *Idylls of the King* ALFRED, LORD TENNYSON	Narrative Poetry, SE p. 956 *Blank Verse, TWE p. 946* *Narrative Poetry, TWE pp. 946, 947, 955* *Imagery, TWE pp. 948, 953* *Mood, TWE p. 951* *Characters, TWE pp. 952, 953, 954*	Paraphrasing, SE p. 958 *Identifying Author's Purpose, TWE p. 955*	Narrative, SE p. 957 *Using Similes, TWE p. 951*	Semantic Mapping, SE p. 958
Arthur Becomes King from *The Once and Future King* T.H. WHITE	Tone, SE p. 974 *Tone, TWE pp. 963, 964, 965, 970, 972, 973* *Plot, TWE p. 964* *Simile, TWE p. 966* *Characters, TWE p. 967* *Hyperbole, TWE p. 967*	Making Inferences, SE p. 976 *Comparing and Contrasting, TWE p. 960* *Scanning, TWE p. 971*	Dialogue, SE p. 975 *Using Hyperbole, TWE p. 967*	Dictionary Skills: Definitions, SE p. 976 Idioms, SE p. 977
Where the Girl Rescued Her Brother JOSEPH BRUCHAC AND GAYLE ROSS	Suspense, SE p. 987 *Suspense, TWE pp. 984, 985* *Plot, TWE p. 986*	Identifying Sequence, SE p. 989 *Identifying Bias, TWE p. 980* *Using Graphic Aids, TWE p. 985*	Summary, SE p. 988	Synonyms—Shades of Meaning, SE p. 988

Key: Student material is in roman. Teacher material is in italic. Technology **COLLAB. LEARN.** Collaboration

Grammar and Language	Listening, Speaking, and Viewing	Life Skills	Study, Research, and Technology
Who/Whom, TWE p. 930	**COLLAB. LEARN.** Literature Groups, SE p. 933 Delivering a Speech, SE p. 933 Performing a Song, SE p. 933 *Retelling a Legend,* TWE p. 929	*Leading and Organizing,* TWE p. 922	Research, TWE pp. 917, 919, 924 💻 *Internet Connection,* TWE p. 926
Missing Commas with Nonessential Elements, SE p. 942 *Single Quotation Marks,* TWE p. 938 *Punctuating Transitions,* TWE p. 943		Memo, SE p. 940	*Research,* TWE p. 937 💻 *Internet Connection,* TWE p. 937
Subject-Verb Agreement, SE p. 958 *Adverbs,* TWE p. 954	**COLLAB. LEARN.** Literature Groups, SE p. 957 *Expressing Emotions,* TWE p. 948	Obituary, SE p. 957	💻 *Internet Connection,* TWE p. 950 *Research,* TWE p. 953
Sentence Fragments, SE p. 976 *Hyphens for Compound Words,* TWE p. 972	**COLLAB. LEARN.** Literature Groups, SE p. 975 Reenactment, SE p. 975 *Expressing Tone,* TWE p. 973	Announcement, SE p. 975	Technology Skills, SE p. 978 💻 *Internet Connection,* TWE pp. 960, 966 *Research,* TWE p. 970
Dashes for Explanatory Comments, TWE p. 986	**COLLAB. LEARN.** Literature Groups, SE p. 988 Storytelling, SE p. 988		Research, SE p. 988 💻 *Internet Connection,* TWE pp. 981, 985

SELECTIONS	📁 Print Resources		

from Le Morte d'Arthur
 	
THOMAS MALORY
	Unit Five Planning Guide, pp. 8–15
	* Active Reading Guide, p. 78
	Vocabulary Practice, p. 50
		Grammar & Comp. Handbook,
		  Lesson 7.5
		Grammar and Language Workbook,
		  p. 185
		Reading Workbook, pp. 77–78
			* Quick Checks, p. 78
			Selection and Theme Assessment,
			  p. 149
			Performance Assessment, p. 76
			Spanish Summaries, p. 73

from Sundiata
 	
RECORDED BY D.T. NIANE
	Unit Five Planning Guide, pp. 16–23
	* Active Reading Guide, p. 79
	Vocabulary Practice, p. 51
		Grammar & Comp. Handbook,
		  Lessons 11.9, 11.6
		Grammar and Language Workbook,
		  pp. 15, 259
		Reading Workbook, pp. 79–80
			* Quick Checks, p. 79
			Selection and Theme Assessment,
			  p. 150
			Performance Assessment, p. 77
			Spanish Summaries, p. 74

The Passing
of Arthur
from *Idylls of the King*
ALFRED, LORD TENNYSON
	Unit Five Planning Guide, pp. 24–31
	* Active Reading Guide, p. 80
	Vocabulary Practice
		Grammar & Comp. Handbook,
		  Lessons 1.5, 6.1
		Grammar and Language Workbook,
		  pp. 63, 167
		Reading Workbook, pp. 81–82
			* Quick Checks, p. 80
			Selection and Theme Assessment,
			  pp. 151–152
			Performance Assessment, p. 78
			Spanish Summaries, p. 75

Arthur
Becomes King
from *The Once and Future King*
T.H. WHITE
	Unit Five Planning Guide, pp. 32–39
	* Active Reading Guide, p. 81
	Vocabulary Practice, p. 52
		Grammar & Comp. Handbook,
		  Lessons 11.12, 4.9
		Grammar and Language Workbook,
		  pp. 279, 121
		Reading Workbook, pp. 83–84
			* Quick Checks, p. 81
			Selection and Theme Assessment,
			  pp. 153–154
			Performance Assessment, p. 79
			Spanish Summaries, p. 76

Where the Girl
Rescued Her Brother
JOSEPH BRUCHAC AND
GAYLE ROSS
	Unit Five Planning Guide, pp. 40–47
	* Active Reading Guide, p. 82
	Vocabulary Practice, p. 53
		Grammar & Comp. Handbook,
		  Lessons 11.7, 11.9
		Grammar and Language Workbook,
		  pp. 267, 235, 271
		Reading Workbook, pp. 83–84
			* Quick Checks, p. 82
			Selection and Theme Assessment,
			  pp. 155–156
			Performance Assessment, p. 80
			Spanish Summaries, p. 77

*Also available in Spanish

Transparencies	**Technology Resources**
Selection Focus Transparency 73 Grammar and Language Transparency 66 Literary Elements Transparency 78	⌒ ◎ Audio Library ▦ ◎ Vocabulary Puzzlemaker ▨ Web Site: lit.glencoe.com
Selection Focus Transparency 74 Grammar and Language Transparencies 67, 78 Literary Elements Transparency 79	◉ Literature Launchers Videodisc ⌒ ◎ Audio Library ▦ ◎ Vocabulary Puzzlemaker ▨ Web Site: lit.glencoe.com
Selection Focus Transparency 75 Grammar and Language Transparency 69 Literary Elements Transparency 80	⌒ ◎ Audio Library ⌒ ◎ Spanish Audio Library ▦ ◎ Vocabulary Puzzlemaker ▨ Web Site: lit.glencoe.com
Selection Focus Transparency 76 Grammar and Language Transparency 70 Literary Elements Transparency 81	◉ Literature Launchers Videodisc ⌒ ◎ Audio Library ▦ ◎ Vocabulary Puzzlemaker ▨ Web Site: lit.glencoe.com
Selection Focus Transparency 77 Grammar and Language Transparencies 71, 72 Literary Elements Transparency 82 Fine Art Transparency 30	⌒ ◎ Audio Library ▦ ◎ Vocabulary Puzzlemaker ▨ Web Site: lit.glencoe.com

📁 *Theme* **RESOURCES**

- Listening and Speaking Activities (p. 21–22)
- Viewing and Representing Activities (p. 27–28)
- Critical Thinking Skills (p. 30–32)
- Media Connections Activities (p. 22–23)
- Interdisciplinary Activities (p. 22–23)

See also these additional planning resources:
- English Language Learners Sourcebook
- Inclusion Strategies Sourcebook
- Literature Groups Sourcebook

Use Glencoe's *Presentation Plus!* This multimedia teaching tool lets you present dynamic lessons that will engage your students. Using Microsoft PowerPoint®, you can customize the presentations to create your own personalized lessons.

Objectives

- To read and analyze a legend about some heroes in ancient Britain
- To analyze the dialogue in a legend
- To write a character sketch of a legendary hero

Skills

Reading/Thinking: Generalizing; Identifying Author's Purpose; Drawing Conclusions; Comparing and Contrasting

Writing: Describing Action; News Story

Vocabulary: Etymology

Grammar/Language: Who/Whom

Listening/Speaking: Retelling a Legend; Delivering a Speech

Life Skills: Leading and Organizing

Collaboration: Literature Groups

Motivating
→ OPTIONS

Selection Focus Transparency 73: Have students view the transparency and discuss what the illustration tells them about knighthood.

Focus Activity: Have students contribute to a web on the board.

Before You Read

from *Le Morte d'Arthur*

— FOCUS ACTIVITY —

Who is your hero? What makes that person a hero to you?

IDEA WEB Make an idea web for the word *hero*. In the branching ovals, write words and phrases describing the qualities of a hero. Compare your ideas with those of your classmates.

Hero

SETTING A PURPOSE Read to discover the qualities of some legendary heroes.

— BACKGROUND —

The Time and Place

King Arthur's England as described in *Le Morte d'Arthur* is likely a blend of fact and fiction. The time period and location of the legendary land have been difficult for historians to confirm. It is true, however, that jousting and sword fighting were popular sports among the nobility of Europe in 1470 when *Le Morte d'Arthur* was written. Of course, the monsters that Sir Thomas Malory wrote about are pure fantasy.

Did You Know?

Knights and noblemen in late medieval Europe (twelfth to fifteenth centuries) tried to behave according to a strict code of chivalry, a word derived from the French *chevalier,* meaning horseman. A chivalrous knight, however, was more than a skilled rider. He also strove to be generous to the weak and courteous to women.

Thomas, Lord Berkeley. 14th century. Brass relief. St. Mary the Virgin, Wotton under Edse, England.

Meet Sir Thomas Malory

Details of the author's life were few even in the fifteenth century. A knight named Thomas Malory is known to have lived at the time the book was written, but not enough evidence exists to be sure he was the author. Sir Thomas Malory, commonly accepted as the author, had lots of time to write his book. He spent several years in prison for crimes ranging from stealing animals to attempted murder. In one incident he was accused of stealing 7 cows, 2 calves, 335 sheep, and a farmer's cart. At the end of *Le Morte d'Arthur*, which he wrote in a London prison, he urged his readers to pray for his safe release.

Sir Thomas Malory was born about 1405 and died in London in 1471. His book was completed between 1469 and 1470 and first published in 1485.

— VOCABULARY PREVIEW —

accost (ə kôst´) *v.* to approach and speak to, especially in an aggressive manner; p. 916

abashed (ə basht´) *adj.* self-conscious; embarrassed or ashamed; p. 917

inscribe (in skrīb´) *v.* to write, carve, or mark on a surface; p. 919

ignoble (ig nō´ bel) *adj.* of low birth or position; without honor or worth; p. 920

tumultuous (too mul´ chōō əs) *adj.* wildly excited, confused, or agitated; p. 920

prowess (prou´ is) *n.* great ability or skill; p. 921

RESOURCE MANAGER

Lesson Planning Resource The *Unit Five Planning Guide* (pp. 8–15) provides additional lesson notes and reduced versions of all print resources.

📁 **Other Print Resources**
- Active Reading Guide, p. 78
- Vocabulary Practice, p. 50
- Reading Workbook, pp. 77–78
- Grammar and Language Workbook, p. 185

- Grammar and Composition Handbook, Lesson 7.5
- Quick Checks, p. 78
- Selection and Theme Assessment, p. 149
- Performance Assessment, p. 76
- Spanish Summaries, p. 73
- Spanish Translations
- Inclusion Strategies
- English Language Learners Sourcebook

📑 **Transparencies**
- Selection Focus 73
- Literary Elements 78
- Grammar and Language 66

Technology
- 🎧 Audio Library
- 🎧 Spanish Audio Library
- 💻 Glencoe Literature Web Site
- 💾 Testmaker

from Le Morte d'Arthur

Sir Thomas Malory ∾
retold by Keith Baines

Uther, Igraine and the Duke of Cornwall, 1498. Woodcut by the Arthur-cutter for Wynkyn de Worde's Malory.

The Tale of King Arthur

KING UTHER[1] PENDRAGON,[2] RULER OF ALL BRITAIN, had been at war for many years with the Duke of Tintagil in Cornwall when he was told of the beauty of Lady Igraine,[3] the duke's wife. Thereupon he called a truce and invited the duke and Igraine to his court, where he prepared a feast for them, and where, as soon as they arrived, he was formally reconciled to the duke through the good offices of his courtiers.

---

1. *Uther* (ōō' thər)
2. In ancient Britain, *Pendragon*, meaning "supreme leader," was a title attached after a ruler's name.
3. *Igraine* (ē grān')

B Literary Elements

SETTING Have students give as precise a description of the setting of the legend as possible based on the details given. *(The story takes place in Cornwall, in the southwest corner of England, in castles and in the countryside, sometime in the Middle Ages, which lasted from approximately 800 to approximately 1500.)*

C Literary Elements

DIALOGUE What does the dialogue indicate about Igraine? *(She is virtuous, intelligent, and daring.)*

D Author's Craft

STYLE Point out that one element of a legend's style is the use of magic or supernatural elements. Malory does not emphasize the magical elements as much as did the French romances he adapted; he mentions them matter-of-factly. Have students explain the nature of the magic in Merlin's plan. *(King Uther, Sir Ulfius, and Merlin will take on different appearances and identities.)*

Malory's Source

Malory's work is an adaptation and translation of a lengthy French verse *romance* about the adventures of King Arthur and several knights. *Le Morte d'Arthur* (French for "the death of Arthur") refers to the last of the eight episodes of the work.

Teaching Options

---

from Le Morte d'Arthur

In the course of the feast, King Uther grew passionately desirous of Igraine and, when it was over, begged her to become his paramour.[4] Igraine, however, being as naturally loyal as she was beautiful, refused him.

"I suppose," said Igraine to her husband, the duke, when this had happened, "that the king arranged this truce only because he wanted to make me his mistress. I suggest that we leave at once, without warning, and ride overnight to our castle." The duke agreed with her, and they left the court secretly.

The king was enraged by Igraine's flight and summoned his privy council.[5] They advised him to command the fugitives' return under threat of renewing the war; but when this was done, the duke and Igraine defied his summons.

He then warned them that they could expect to be dragged from their castle within six weeks.

The duke manned and provisioned[6] his two strongest castles: Tintagil for Igraine, and Terrabyl, which was useful for its many sally ports, for himself. Soon King Uther arrived with a huge army and laid siege to Terrabyl; but despite the ferocity of the fighting, and the numerous casualties suffered by both sides, neither was able to gain a decisive victory.

Still enraged, and now despairing, King Uther fell sick. His friend Sir Ulfius came to

Did You Know?
Sally ports were the gates or openings in the castle walls through which the duke's troops could make sudden attacks.

---

4. A man's lover or mistress is his *paramour*.
5. A *privy council* is the group of a ruler's closest advisors. (*Privy* comes from the same Latin root as *private*.)
6. The duke supplied (*provisioned*) the castles with food and goods.

---

him and asked what the trouble was. "Igraine has broken my heart," the king replied, "and unless I can win her, I shall never recover."

"Sire," said Sir Ulfius, "surely Merlin the Prophet could find some means to help you? I will go in search of him."

Sir Ulfius had not ridden far when he was accosted by a hideous beggar. "For whom are you searching?" asked the beggar; but Sir Ulfius ignored him.

"Very well," said the beggar, "I will tell you: You are searching for Merlin, and you need look no further, for I am he. Now go to King Uther and tell him that I will make Igraine his if he will reward me as I ask; and even that will be more to his benefit than to mine."

"I am sure," said Sir Ulfius, "that the king will refuse you nothing reasonable."

"Then go, and I shall follow you," said Merlin.

Well pleased, Sir Ulfius galloped back to the king and delivered Merlin's message, which he had hardly completed when Merlin himself appeared at the entrance to the pavilion. The king bade him welcome.

"Sire," said Merlin, "I know that you are in love with Igraine; will you swear, as an anointed[7] king, to give into my care the child that she bears you, if I make her yours?"

The king swore on the gospel that he would do so, and Merlin continued: "Tonight you shall appear before Igraine at Tintagil in the likeness of her husband, the duke. Sir Ulfius and I will appear as two of the duke's knights: Sir Brastius and Sir Jordanus. Do not question either Igraine or her men, but say that you are sick and retire to bed. I will fetch you early in the morning,

---

7. An *anointed* king was believed to have been chosen by God to be king.

Vocabulary
accost (ə kôst´) *v.* to approach and speak to, especially in an aggressive manner

---

Realistic and Nonrealistic Details Emphasize that *Le Morte d'Arthur* combines realistic and nonrealistic elements and that many of the nonrealistic elements relate to magic. English language learners may be unfamiliar with characters such as Merlin whom other students will recognize as a legendary magician.

Activity Keep a list on the board of

magical devices in the legend's plot. Discuss each one. For example, when Merlin says that the king "shall appear in the likeness of Igraine's husband," explain that a magical transformation is taking place.

Additional Resources
📁 *English Language Learners Sourcebook*

Merlin the Magician, c. 1352. Manuscript illustration. Ms. Add. Meladius, 12228, fol 202v. The British Library, London.

Viewing the art: How do you think Igraine might have reacted if she knew what Uther Pendragon and Merlin were planning? Explain.

and do not rise until I come; fortunately Tintagil is only ten miles from here."

The plan succeeded: Igraine was completely deceived by the king's impersonation of the duke, and gave herself to him, and conceived Arthur. The king left her at dawn as soon as Merlin appeared, after giving her a farewell kiss. But the duke had seen King Uther ride out from the siege on the previous night and, in the course of making a surprise attack on the king's army, had been killed. When Igraine realized that the duke had died three hours before he had appeared to her,

she was greatly disturbed in mind; however, she confided in no one.

Once it was known that the duke was dead, the king's nobles urged him to be reconciled to Igraine, and this task the king gladly entrusted to Sir Ulfius, by whose eloquence[8] it was soon accomplished. "And now," said Sir Ulfius to his fellow nobles, "why should not the king marry the beautiful Igraine? Surely it would be as well for us all."

The marriage of King Uther and Igraine was celebrated joyously thirteen days later; and then, at the king's request, Igraine's sisters were also married: Margawse, who later bore Sir Gawain, to King Lot of Lowthean and Orkney; Elayne, to King Nentres of Garlot. Igraine's daughter, Morgan le Fay, was put to school in a nunnery; in after years she was to become a witch, and to be married to King Uryens of Gore, and give birth to Sir Uwayne of the Fair Hands.

A few months later it was seen that Igraine was with child, and one night, as she lay in bed with King Uther, he asked her who the father might be. Igraine was greatly abashed.

"Do not look so dismayed," said the king, "but tell me the truth and I swear I shall love you the better for it."

"The truth is," said Igraine, "that the night the duke died, about three hours after his death, a man appeared in my castle—the exact image of the duke. With him came two others who appeared to be Sir Brastius and

---

8. Here, *eloquence* is speech or writing that is expressive, stirring, and effective.

Vocabulary
abashed (ə basht′) *adj.* self-conscious; embarrassed or ashamed

E **Literary Elements**

THEME One element of Arthurian legend was the tradition of courtly love, in which knights devoted themselves to a lady, often a married woman. Have students discuss the nature of King Uther's love for Igraine. Point out that a relationship of this nature was considered immoral. Thus, King Uther can only consummate his love with Igraine through Merlin's magic, and Igraine remains virtuous.

F **Author's Craft**

PROSE Point out that Malory's work is the first piece of imaginative prose in English, and that Malory was the first writer to use prose as expressively as verse had been used previously. Explain that the fifteenth-century English of the original has been modernized in this retelling.

INTERDISCIPLINARY CONNECTION

History Opinion is divided about whether King Arthur is a historical figure. Many historians believe he was a British or Roman-British leader who led the fight against the invasion of the Anglo-Saxons in the sixth century. He is said to have won the battle of Badon Hill, personally killing 960 men. The battle itself is a matter of historical record. The name *Arthur* is from the common Roman name *Artorius*.

Activity Have students research the early history of England including its rule by the Roman Empire; its invasion by the Picts and the Scots from Scotland and Ireland; and its invasion by the Jutes, Angles, and Saxons from northern Europe in the 400s and early 500s. You may wish to assign each historic period to a small group of students and have the groups present their findings in oral reports with graphic aids. **L2** **COLLAB. LEARN.**

CHARACTER Have students describe the personality traits of King Uther and Merlin. Have them explain which of the two characters is more powerful and why. *(King Uther is a strong ruler, but willing to compromise and give up his own child for love. Merlin is a capable magician who can alter reality to suit a specific need. Merlin is more powerful because he can perform magic; he also is crafty and plans ahead.)*

Historical Note

The medieval period was noted for its many battles among feudal lords and between the lords and the kings, who usually ruled only small areas and had limited power. This fighting is reflected in Malory's narrative.

VIEWING THE SCULPTURE

W. Goscomb John (1860–1952) was a Welsh sculptor who helped found the National Museum of Wales.

Viewing Response *The sculpture portrays Merlin's wisdom, kindliness, and love for Arthur.*

Teaching Options

Sir Jordanus. Naturally I gave myself to this man as I would have to the duke, and that night, I swear, this child was conceived."

"Well spoken," said the king; "it was I who impersonated the duke, so the child is mine." He then told Igraine the story of how Merlin had arranged it, and Igraine was overjoyed to discover that the father of her child was now her husband.

Sometime later, Merlin appeared before the king. "Sire," he said, "you know that you must provide for the upbringing of your child?"

"I will do as you advise," the king replied.

"That is good," said Merlin, "because it is my reward for having arranged your impersonation of the duke. Your child is destined for glory, and I want him brought to me for his baptism. I shall then give him into the care of foster parents who can be trusted not to reveal his identity before the proper time. Sir Ector would be suitable: he is extremely loyal, owns good estates, and his wife has just borne him a child. She could give her child into the care of another woman, and herself look after yours."

Sir Ector was summoned, and gladly agreed to the king's request, who then rewarded him handsomely. When the child was born he was at once wrapped in a gold cloth and taken by two knights and two ladies to Merlin, who stood waiting at the rear entrance to the castle in his beggar's disguise. Merlin took the child to a priest, who baptized him with the name of Arthur, and thence to Sir Ector, whose wife fed him at her breast.

Two years later King Uther fell sick, and his enemies once more overran his kingdom, inflicting heavy losses on him as they advanced. Merlin prophesied that they could be checked only by the presence of the king himself on the battlefield, and suggested that he should be conveyed there on a horse

Merlin & Arthur. W. Goscomb John. Bronze, height: 22⅞ in. National Museum of Wales, Cardiff.

Viewing the sculpture: Which of Merlin's characteristics do you think this sculpture portrays?

MEETING INDIVIDUAL NEEDS — INCLUSION STRATEGIES

Special Needs If students have difficulty with the conventions of the legend genre, compare *Le Morte d'Arthur* to literature with which they are familiar.

Activity Point out that Malory's legend has many elements that resemble fairy tales. Have students name fairy tales and elements of them that are similar to those of *Le Morte d'Arthur*. For exam-

ple, Merlin is similar to witches and fairy godmothers in tales such as *Cinderella* and *Sleeping Beauty*. Point out that the legend combines realistic and fantastic details as fairy tales do. **L1**

Additional Resources
📁 *Inclusion Strategies*

litter.[9] King Uther's army met the invader on the plain at St. Albans, and the king duly appeared on the horse litter. Inspired by his presence, and by the lively leadership of Sir Brastius and Sir Jordanus, his army quickly defeated the enemy and the battle finished in a rout.[10] The king returned to London to celebrate the victory.

But his sickness grew worse, and after he had lain speechless for three days and three nights Merlin summoned the nobles to attend the king in his chamber on the following morning. "By the grace of God," he said, "I hope to make him speak."

In the morning, when all the nobles were assembled, Merlin addressed the king: "Sire, is it your will that Arthur shall succeed to the throne, together with all its prerogatives?"[11]

The king stirred in his bed, and then spoke so that all could hear: "I bestow on Arthur God's blessing and my own, and Arthur shall succeed to the throne on pain of forfeiting my blessing."[12] Then King Uther gave up the ghost. He was buried and mourned the next day, as befitted his rank, by Igraine and the nobility of Britain.

During the years that followed the death of King Uther, while Arthur was still a child, the ambitious barons fought one another for the throne, and the whole of Britain stood in jeopardy. Finally the day came when the Archbishop of Canterbury, on the advice of Merlin, summoned the nobility to London

for Christmas morning. In his message the Archbishop promised that the true succession to the British throne would be miraculously revealed. Many of the nobles purified themselves during their journey, in the hope that it would be to them that the succession would fall.

The Archbishop held his service in the city's greatest church (St. Paul's), and when matins[13] were done the congregation filed out to the yard. They were confronted by a marble block into which had been thrust a beautiful sword. The block was four feet square, and the sword passed through a steel anvil which had been struck in the stone, and which projected a foot from it. The anvil had been inscribed with letters of gold:

WHOSO PULLETH OUTE THIS SWERD
OF THIS STONE AND ANVLYD IS RIGHTWYS
KYNGE BORNE OF ALL BRYTAYGNE

The congregation was awed by this miraculous sight, but the Archbishop forbade anyone to touch the sword before mass had been heard. After mass, many of the nobles tried to pull the sword out of the stone, but none was able to, so a watch of ten knights was set over the sword, and a tournament proclaimed for New Year's Day, to provide men of noble blood with the opportunity of proving their right to the succession.

Sir Ector, who had been living on an estate near London, rode to the tournament with Arthur and his own son Sir Kay, who had been recently knighted. When they arrived at the tournament, Sir Kay found to his annoyance that his sword was missing from its sheath, so he begged Arthur to ride back and fetch it from their lodging.

---

9. The king was to be carried *(conveyed)* on a stretcher *(litter)* pulled by a horse.
10. A *rout* (rout) is an overwhelming defeat.
11. *Prerogatives* (pri rog′ ə tivz) are the rights and privileges belonging solely to a particular person (such as a king) or group.
12. *Forfeiting my blessing* means that Uther is withholding his blessing if Arthur does not eventually become king.

13. *Matins* (mat′ inz) are morning prayers.

Vocabulary
inscribe (in skrīb′) *v.* to write, carve, or mark on a surface

---

H Literary Elements

CHARACTERIZATION Have students describe Merlin based on his actions and dialogue. *(He is an organizer; he is authoritative and religious.)*

Vo•cab•u•lar•y Skills

Etymology Have students look up the origin of the words *noble* and *nobility* and explain how the original meaning relates to the meaning used by Malory. *(Both words come from the Latin nobilis, meaning "well-known." Nobles are well-known because of outstanding qualities or aristocratic birth.)*

Historical Note

Canterbury had been a center of the Christian religion since Saint Augustine of Canterbury led a group of missionaries to England from Rome and built a monastery there. He became the first Archbishop of Canterbury, the head of the church in England, in 601. (Not to be confused with Saint Augustine (354–430) whose writings have influenced religious leaders and philosophers from Martin Luther to Immanuel Kant.)

I Active Reading

VISUALIZE Have students read the description of the sword in the stone and visualize it and the parade of nobles who attempt to pull the sword from the stone.

MEETING INDIVIDUAL NEEDS — GIFTED AND TALENTED

Christianity in England When the succession to the throne is to be revealed, the Archbishop of Canterbury officiates. Christianity had been an important influence in England since the late 500s, and it came to be closely bound to the nation's history.

Activity Have students research the history of the Christian religion in England including its first appearance in the 300s, its permanent establishment in the late 500s, the conflict between Henry II and Thomas à Becket in 1170, and the English Reformation. Have them prepare oral or written reports of their findings. **L3**

CHARACTERS Have students discuss whether Sir Kay is a round or flat character. *(He is a round character, first revealing deviousness, then admitting his lie.)*

K **Author's Craft**

PLOT: *Climax* The question of who will succeed to the throne is resolved in the climactic scene in which Arthur pulls the sword from the stone. Have students discuss the tone of this scene: is it exciting? *(The scene is not very suspenseful. Arthur pulls out the sword accidentally and then must perform the action several more times before he is allowed to become king. The scene has a matter-of-fact tone, adding realism.)*

L **Active Reading**

QUESTION What issue is most important as the people locate the person who should become king? What does this say about the country's value system? *(Finding a person of noble birth is most important. In the medieval value system, land, wealth, and power were passed down from noble fathers to their sons, keeping them in the hands of a few noble families.)*

FYI

British Nobility The British peerage, or nobility, consists of five ranks: duke, marquess, earl, viscount, and baron. A duke holds the highest rank and a baron the lowest.

Teaching Options

---

from **Le Morte d'Arthur**

Arthur found the door of the lodging locked and bolted, the landlord and his wife having left for the tournament. In order not to disappoint his brother, he rode on to St. Paul's, determined to get for him the sword which was lodged in the stone. The yard was empty, the guard also having slipped off to see the tournament, so Arthur strode up to the sword, and, without troubling to read the inscription, tugged it free. He then rode straight back to Sir Kay and presented him with it.

Sir Kay recognized the sword, and taking it to Sir Ector, said, "Father, the succession falls to me, for I have here the sword that was lodged in the stone." But Sir Ector insisted that they should all ride to the churchyard, and once there bound Sir Kay by oath to tell how he had come by the sword. Sir Kay then admitted that Arthur had given it to him. Sir Ector turned to Arthur and said, "Was the sword not guarded?"

"It was not," Arthur replied.

"Would you please thrust it into the stone again?" said Sir Ector. Arthur did so, and first Sir Ector and then Sir Kay tried to remove it, but both were unable to. Then Arthur, for the second time, pulled it out. Sir Ector and Sir Kay both knelt before him.

"Why," said Arthur, "do you both kneel before me?"

"My lord," Sir Ector replied, "there is only one man living who can draw the sword from the stone, and he is the true-born King of Britain." Sir Ector then told Arthur the story of his birth and upbringing.

"My dear father," said Arthur, "for so I shall always think of you—if, as you say, I am to be king, please know that any request you have to make is already granted."

Sir Ector asked that Sir Kay should be made Royal Seneschal,[14] and Arthur declared that while they both lived it should be so. Then the three of them visited the Archbishop and told him what had taken place.

All those dukes and barons with ambitions to rule were present at the tournament on New Year's Day. But when all of them had failed, and Arthur alone had succeeded in drawing the sword from the stone, they protested against one so young, and of ignoble blood, succeeding to the throne.

The secret of Arthur's birth was known only to a few of the nobles surviving from the days of King Uther. The Archbishop urged them to make Arthur's cause their own; but their support proved ineffective. The tournament was repeated at Candlemas and at Easter,[15] and with the same outcome as before.

Finally at Pentecost,[16] when once more Arthur alone had been able to remove the sword, the commoners arose with a tumultuous cry and demanded that Arthur should at once be made king. The nobles, knowing in their hearts that the commoners were right, all knelt before Arthur and begged forgiveness for having delayed his succession for so long. Arthur forgave them, and then, offering his sword at the high altar, was dubbed first knight of the realm. The coronation took place a few days later, when Arthur swore to rule justly, and the nobles swore him their allegiance.

---

14. In medieval times, the *Royal Seneschal* (sen′ ə shəl) managed the king's estate, ran his household, and sometimes also had official state duties or a military command.
15. *Candlemas* and *Easter* are Christian festivals; *Candlemas* is celebrated on February 2 and *Easter* in early spring.
16. *Pentecost*, a religious observance, is the seventh Sunday after Easter.

Vocabulary
ignoble (ig nō′ bel) *adj.* of low birth or position; without honor or worth
tumultuous (too mul′ chōō əs) *adj.* wildly excited, confused, or agitated

---

MEETING INDIVIDUAL NEEDS **ENGLISH LANGUAGE LEARNERS**

Multiple Meaning Words Point out the words *succeed* and *succeeded* on pages 919–920. Explain that the forms of the word *succeed* have two different meanings. They can mean "to inherit a title" or "to attain a desired end."

Activity Have English language learners read aloud the sentences with these words.

Have students explain what the form of *succeed* means in each sentence. Then have them use the word in two sentences with two different meanings.

Additional Resources
📁 *English Language Learners Sourcebook*

Camelot, 1984. Alan Lee.

Viewing the painting: What does this painting tell you about Camelot? How does the depiction here compare with the Camelot described in the selection?

The Tale of Sir Launcelot du Lake

When King Arthur returned from Rome he settled his court at Camelot, and there gathered about him his knights of the Round Table, who diverted[17] themselves with jousting and tournaments. Of all his knights one was supreme, both in prowess at arms and in nobility of bearing, and this was Sir Launcelot, who was also the favorite of Queen Gwynevere, to whom he had sworn oaths of fidelity.[18]

One day Sir Launcelot, feeling weary of his life at the court, and of only playing at arms, decided to set forth in search of adventure. He asked his nephew Sir Lyonel to accompany him, and when both were suitably armed and mounted, they rode off together through the forest.

At noon they started across a plain, but the intensity of the sun made Sir Launcelot feel sleepy, so Sir Lyonel suggested that they should rest beneath the shade of an apple tree that grew by a hedge not far from the road. They dismounted, tethered their horses, and settled down.

"Not for seven years have I felt so sleepy," said Sir Launcelot, and with that fell fast asleep, while Sir Lyonel watched over him.

Soon three knights came galloping past, and Sir Lyonel noticed that they were being pursued by a fourth knight, who was one of the most powerful he had yet seen. The pursuing knight overtook each of the others in turn, and as he did so, knocked each off his horse with a thrust of his spear. When all three lay stunned he dismounted, bound them securely to their horses with the reins, and led them away.

Without waking Sir Launcelot, Sir Lyonel mounted his horse and rode after the knight, and as soon as he had drawn close enough, shouted his challenge. The knight turned about and they charged at each other, with the result that Sir Lyonel was likewise flung from his horse, bound, and led away a prisoner.

---

17. Here, *diverted* means "amused; entertained."
18. Launcelot swore his loyalty and devotion (*fidelity*) to Gwynevere.

Vocabulary
prowess (prou′ is) *n.* great ability or skill

Literary Elements

DIALOGUE Have students discuss the functions of the dialogue on page 922. (*It characterizes Sir Ector, furthers the plot, and provides vivid images of the castle setting.*)

VIEWING THE PAINTING

The artist, William Frank Calderon, chose his own interpretation of the scene between Launcelot and the four queens. The scene differs from Malory's description on page 923.

Viewing Response *Launcelot is trusting and brave to sleep unguarded in the forest.*

FYI

Medieval Castles

Castles were built mainly as protection against enemies but also served as homes to their owners, their families and attendants, and often their armies. The first castles were simple earthen fortresses. Then lords began building castles in inaccessible locations: cliff tops, islands, and even the middle of lakes. Castle owners without a natural defense often built surrounding moats filled with water or dirt that could be crossed only by drawbridge. The main room of a castle was a great room serving as both living area and office.

Teaching Options

The victorious knight, whose name was Sir Tarquine, led his prisoners to his castle, and there threw them on the ground, stripped them naked, and beat them with thorn twigs. After that he locked them in a dungeon where many other prisoners, who had received like treatment, were complaining dismally.

Meanwhile, Sir Ector de Marys, who liked to accompany Sir Launcelot on his adventures, and finding him gone, decided to ride after him. Before long he came upon a forester.

"My good fellow, if you know the forest hereabouts, could you tell me in which direction I am most likely to meet with adventure?"

"Sir, I can tell you: Less than a mile from here stands a well-moated castle. On the left of the entrance you will find a ford where you can water your horse, and across from the ford a large tree from which hang the shields of many famous knights. Below the shields hangs a caldron, of copper and brass: strike it three times with your spear, and then surely you will meet with adventure—such, indeed, that if you survive it, you will prove yourself the foremost knight in these parts for many years."

"May God reward you!" Sir Ector replied.

The castle was exactly as the forester had described it, and among the shields Sir Ector recognized several as belonging to knights of the Round Table. After watering his horse, he knocked on the caldron and Sir Tarquine, whose castle it was, appeared.

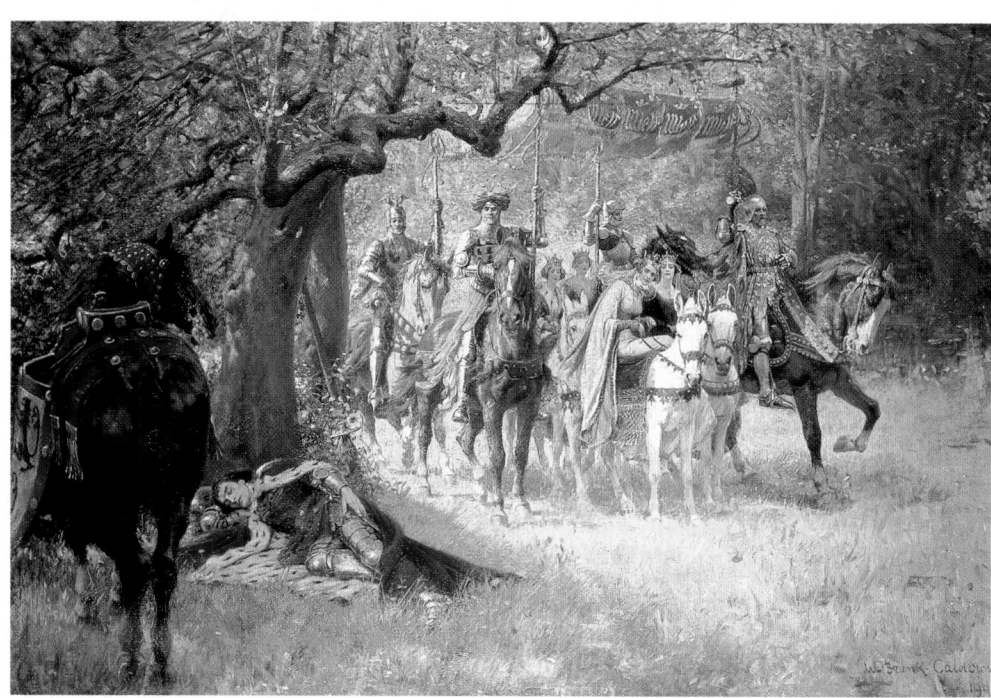

How Four Queens Found Sir Lancelot Sleeping, 1908. William Frank Calderon. Oil on canvas, 48 x 72 in. Private collection.

Viewing the painting: What can you tell about Launcelot based on the contrast in the painting between him and the queens and their retinue?

922   UNIT 5

LIFE SKILLS CONNECTION

Leading and Organizing The forester describes "a large tree from which hang the shields of many famous knights." Shields, used as protection, were decorated with the coat of arms of a knight's lord, which might include dragons, serpents, fleur-de-lis, and other design elements.

Activity Have students look in books on the Middle Ages and knighthood to find examples of shields decorated with coats-of-arms. Have them design and illustrate their own coat-of-arms, using designs and objects symbolic of their interests, backgrounds, and leadership qualities. Display students' finished illustrations. **L2**

They jousted, and at the first encounter Sir Ector sent his opponent's horse spinning twice about before he could recover.

"That was a fine stroke; now let us try again," said Sir Tarquine.

This time Sir Tarquine caught Sir Ector just below the right arm and, having impaled him on his spear, lifted him clean out of the saddle, and rode with him into the castle, where he threw him on the ground.

"Sir," said Sir Tarquine, "you have fought better than any knight I have encountered in the last twelve years; therefore, if you wish, I will demand no more of you than your parole[19] as my prisoner."

"Sir, that I will never give."

"Then I am sorry for you," said Sir Tarquine, and with that he stripped and beat him and locked him in the dungeon with the other prisoners. There Sir Ector saw Sir Lyonel.

"Alas, Sir Lyonel, we are in a sorry plight. But tell me, what has happened to Sir Launcelot? for he surely is the one knight who could save us."

"I left him sleeping beneath an apple tree, and what has befallen him since I do not know," Sir Lyonel replied; and then all the unhappy prisoners once more bewailed their lot.

While Sir Launcelot still slept beneath the apple tree, four queens started across the plain. They were riding white mules and accompanied by four knights who held above them, at the tips of their spears, a green silk canopy, to protect them from the sun. The party was startled by the neighing of Sir Launcelot's horse and, changing direction, rode up to the apple tree, where they discovered the sleeping knight. And as each of the queens gazed at the handsome Sir Launcelot, so each wanted him for her own.

"Let us not quarrel," said Morgan le Fay. "Instead, I will cast a spell over him so that he remains asleep while we take him to my castle and make him our prisoner. We can then oblige him to choose one of us for his paramour."

Sir Launcelot was laid on his shield and borne by two of the knights to the Castle Charyot, which was Morgan le Fay's stronghold. He awoke to find himself in a cold cell, where a young noblewoman was serving him supper.

"What cheer?"[20] she asked.

"My lady, I hardly know, except that I must have been brought here by means of an enchantment."

"Sir, if you are the knight you appear to be, you will learn your fate at dawn tomorrow." And with that the young noblewoman left him. Sir Launcelot spent an uncomfortable night but at dawn the four queens presented themselves and Morgan le Fay spoke to him:

"Sir Launcelot, I know that Queen Gwynevere loves you, and you her. But now you are my prisoner, and you will have to choose: either to take one of us for your paramour, or to die miserably in this cell—just as you please. Now I will tell you who we are: I am Morgan le Fay, Queen of Gore; my companions are the Queens of North Galys, of Estelonde, and of the Outer Isles. So make your choice."

"A hard choice! Understand that I choose none of you, lewd sorceresses[21] that you are; rather will I die in this cell. But were I free, I would take pleasure in proving it against any who would champion[22] you that Queen Gwynevere is the finest lady of this land."

"So, you refuse us?" asked Morgan le Fay.

---

19. A knight's *parole* was his pledge to fulfill certain conditions in exchange for full or partial freedom.
20. *What cheer?* was the same as asking "How are you?"
21. Launcelot accuses the women of being unchaste (*lewd*) witches (*sorceresses*).
22. As a verb, *champion* means "to defend a person or cause."

O Literary Elements

CHARACTER Have students describe Sir Tarquine. How does he contrast with the other knights? *(He is cruel and unfair and seems to enjoy violence for its own sake, unlike the other knights who are looking for "adventure," not necessarily violence.)*

P Literary Elements

IMAGERY Have students visualize the image of the four queens riding up to Sir Launcelot and mention especially vivid details. *(The white mules and the four knights holding a green silk canopy at the tips of their spears are especially vivid visual details.)*

Q Literary Elements

PLOT Point out that the plot of the legend differs from the plot of most modern short stories. Have students describe the plot and compare it to contemporary plotting. *(Instead of being built around one major conflict, the plot describes a series of conflicts that are seemingly random. A series of new characters appears with whom the protagonist is in conflict.)*

MEETING INDIVIDUAL NEEDS — ENGLISH LANGUAGE LEARNERS

Medieval Vocabulary The legend contains words involving medieval culture which fluent English speakers will find familiar but which English language learners may not have encountered.

Activity On the board begin a chart with the following heads: *Knights, Castle, Magic.* Place terms in the appropriate column and have students contribute to defining each term. When possible, use illustrations to help define terms.

Have students copy the chart and add to it as they finish reading the legend.

Additional Resources
📁 *English Language Learners Sourcebook*

DIALOGUE Have students tell what they learn about Launcelot from his response to King Bagdemagus's daughter. *(He is honest and brave; although he fears for his life, he does not agree to help her further until he learns who her father is and recognizes him as a good king.)*

S **Literary Elements**

SETTING Point out the author's subtle use of details to describe the setting: "the twelve doors to the castle entrance" and "a red silk pavilion." Have students describe the effect of such details. *(They help the reader clearly visualize the setting while emphasizing the fantastic aspects of it.)*

FYI

Knighthood Although an important duty of knights was to fight their lord's enemies, being a knight was much more complex than merely being a soldier. John of Salisbury, a twelfth-century philosopher, said a knight's duty was "to protect the Church, to fight against treachery, to reverence the priesthood, to fend off injustice from the poor, to make peace in your own province, to shed blood for your brethren, and if needs must, to lay down your life." Knights received intensive training in combat, horsemanship, and courtly graces.

Teaching Options

---

from Le Morte d'Arthur

"On my life, I do," Sir Launcelot said finally, and so the queens departed.

Sometime later, the young noblewoman who had served Sir Launcelot's supper reappeared.

"What news?" she asked.

"It is the end," Sir Launcelot replied.

"Sir Launcelot, I know that you have refused the four queens, and that they wish to kill you out of spite. But if you will be ruled by me, I can save you. I ask that you will champion my father at a tournament next Tuesday, when he has to combat the King of North Galys, and three knights of the Round Table, who last Tuesday defeated him ignominiously."[23]

"My lady, pray tell me, what is your father's name?"

"King Bagdemagus."[24]

"Excellent, my lady, I know him for a good king and a true knight, so I shall be happy to serve him."

"May God reward you! And tomorrow at dawn I will release you, and direct you to an abbey which is ten miles from here, and where the good monks will care for you while I fetch my father."

"I am at your service, my lady."

As promised, the young noblewoman released Sir Launcelot at dawn. When she had led him through the twelve doors to the castle entrance, she gave him his horse and armor, and directions for finding the abbey.

"God bless you, my lady; and when the time comes I promise I shall not fail you."

Sir Launcelot rode through the forest in search of the abbey, but at dusk had still failed to find it, and coming upon a red silk pavilion, apparently unoccupied, decided to rest there overnight, and continue his search in the morning. . . .

As soon as it was daylight, Sir Launcelot armed, mounted, and rode away in search of the abbey, which he found in less than two hours. King Bagdemagus' daughter was waiting for him, and as soon as she heard his horse's footsteps in the yard, ran to the window, and, seeing that it was Sir Launcelot, herself ordered the servants to stable his horse. She then led him to her chamber, disarmed him, and gave him a long gown to wear, welcoming him warmly as she did so.

King Bagdemagus' castle was twelve miles away, and his daughter sent for him as soon as she had settled Sir Launcelot. The king arrived with his retinue[25] and embraced Sir Launcelot, who then described his recent enchantment, and the great obligation he was under to his daughter for releasing him.

"Sir, you will fight for me on Tuesday next?"

"Sire, I shall not fail you; but please tell me the names of the three Round Table knights whom I shall be fighting."

"Sir Modred, Sir Madore de la Porte, and Sir Gahalantyne. I must admit that last Tuesday they defeated me and my knights completely."

"Sire, I hear that the tournament is to be fought within three miles of the abbey. Could you send me three of your most trustworthy knights, clad in plain armor, and with no device,[26] and a fourth suit of armor which I myself shall wear? We will take up our position just outside the tournament field and watch while you and the King of North Galys enter into combat with your followers; and then, as soon as you are in difficulties, we will come to your rescue, and show your opponents what kind of knights you command."

This was arranged on Sunday, and on the following Tuesday Sir Launcelot and the three

---

23. The woman's father was defeated shamefully or dishonorably *(ignominiously).*
24. *Bagdemagus* (bag′ də mag′ əs)

25. The king's *retinue* is the group of people who accompany and serve him.
26. Armor with no *device* has no ornamental design.

INTERDISCIPLINARY CONNECTION

History When Malory wrote *Le Morte d'Arthur*, England was involved in a struggle for the throne called the Wars of the Roses (1455–1485). In these wars, the nobles of the House of York overthrew Henry VI of the House of Lancaster. Edward IV of York won the throne in 1461; Henry won it back in 1470, and Edward won it once again in 1471. Some critics see a relationship between the tumultuous political situation of Malory's era and the distant past that he describes.

Activity Have students research the Wars of the Roses. Encourage them to find out how the war got its name and how the houses of Lancaster and York were finally united. Also have them research the mysterious disappearance of Edward IV's sons, last seen in the Tower of London. **L2**

---

knights of King Bagdemagus waited in a copse,[27] not far from the pavilion which had been erected for the lords and ladies who were to judge the tournament and award the prizes.

The King of North Galys was the first on the field, with a company of ninescore knights; he was followed by King Bagdemagus with fourscore knights, and then by the three knights of the Round Table, who remained apart from both companies.[28] At the first encounter King Bagdemagus lost twelve knights, all killed, and the King of North Galys six.

With that, Sir Launcelot galloped on to the field, and with his first spear unhorsed five of the King of North Galys' knights, breaking the backs of four of them. With his next spear he charged the king, and wounded him deeply in the thigh.

"That was a shrewd blow," commented Sir Madore, and galloped onto the field to challenge Sir Launcelot. But he too was tumbled from his horse, and with such violence that his shoulder was broken.

Sir Modred was the next to challenge Sir Launcelot, and he was sent spinning over his horse's tail. He landed head first, his helmet became buried in the soil, and he nearly broke his neck, and for a long time lay stunned.

Finally Sir Gahalantyne tried; at the first encounter both he and Sir Launcelot broke their spears, so both drew their swords and hacked vehemently at each other. But Sir Launcelot, with mounting wrath, soon struck his opponent a blow on the helmet which brought the blood streaming from eyes, ears, and mouth. Sir Gahalantyne slumped forward in the saddle, his horse panicked, and he was thrown to the ground, useless for further combat.

---

27. A *copse* is a thicket of trees.
28. One *score* is twenty, so more than 260 knights have gathered.

Sir Launcelot took another spear, and unhorsed sixteen more of the King of North Galys' knights, and with his next, unhorsed another twelve; and in each case with such violence that none of the knights ever fully recovered. The King of North Galys was forced to admit defeat, and the prize was awarded to King Bagdemagus.

That night Sir Launcelot was entertained as the guest of honor by King Bagdemagus and his daughter at their castle, and before leaving was loaded with gifts.

"My lady, please, if ever again you should need my services, remember that I shall not fail you."

The next day Sir Launcelot rode once more through the forest, and by chance came to the apple tree where he had previously slept. This time he met a young noblewoman riding a white palfrey.

"My lady, I am riding in search of adventure; pray tell me if you know of any I might find hereabouts."

"Sir, there are adventures hereabouts if you believe that you are equal to them; but please tell me, what is your name?"

"Sir Launcelot du Lake."

"Very well, Sir Launcelot, you appear to be a sturdy enough knight, so I will tell you. Not far away stands the castle of Sir Tarquine, a knight who in fair combat has overcome more than sixty opponents whom he now holds prisoner. Many are from the court of King Arthur, and if you can rescue them, I will then ask you to deliver me and my companions from a knight who distresses us daily, either by robbery or by other kinds of outrage."

Did You Know?
A *palfrey* is a gentle saddle horse, especially one trained for a woman rider.

T Literary Elements

CHARACTER Have students discuss the heroic qualities that Launcelot shows during the tournament. *(He is an uncommonly skilled and courageous jouster.)*

U Critical Thinking

GENERALIZING Ask students what generalizations they can make about the role of women in the legend. *(Women perform several different roles. Gwynevere is an inspiration to Launcelot; King Bagdemagus's daughter and the young noblewoman on the palfrey help Launcelot by providing heroic feats for him to accomplish; Morgan le Fay and her companions tempt Launcelot and trick him.)*

FYI

Jousting The lance was invented at the end of the eleventh century. This weapon enabled knights to strike an enemy from several feet away. However, using a lance required practice, so knights staged mock battles called tournaments in which they charged headlong at one another on horseback. Soon tournaments attracted large audiences and were used on ceremonial occasions. Jousting was a lance contest involving only two combatants.

MEETING INDIVIDUAL NEEDS

MULTIPLE LEARNING STYLES

Spatial Malory describes the fighting among the knights, their weapons, and their equipment. Knights wore a hood and a leather robe. Over this they wore chain mail of fine mesh to protect them from swords and lances. The chain mail consisted of a *hauberk,* which covered the neck and torso, and leggings. Knights had a variety of headgear including a heavy iron helmet with eye slits.

Activity Have students find illustrations of a knight's equipment. Suggest that they make a drawing, diagram, or written description of the items in a knight's wardrobe. **L2**

DIALOGUE Have students describe the style of Launcelot's dialogue. How does it complement his character? *(It is formal and extremely polite. He uses phrases like "most happily challenge" and "vindicate the honor" that emphasize the knight's role.)*

W **Author's Craft**

DICTION Have students list the verbs and other words the writer uses to describe the fighting between Launcelot and Tarquine. What effect do they have? *(Some of the verbs are hurled, clashed, drove, and stagger. The vivid verbs and the words flesh and blood make the narrative exciting and emphasize the violence of the knights' way of life.)*

LITERATURE & HUMANITIES

Have students examine *Knight, Death, and the Devil* by Albrecht Dürer, page 419 in *Art in Focus*. Ask them where they might place this picture in an illustrated version of *Le Morte d'Arthur*.

---

from **Le Morte d'Arthur**

"My lady, please first lead me to Sir Tarquine, then I will most happily challenge this miscreant[29] knight of yours."

When they arrived at the castle, Sir Launcelot watered his horse at the ford, and then beat the caldron until the bottom fell out. However, none came to answer the challenge, so they waited by the castle gate for half an hour or so. Then Sir Tarquine appeared, riding toward the castle with a wounded prisoner slung over his horse, whom Sir Launcelot recognized as Sir Gaheris, Sir Gawain's brother and a knight of the Round Table.

"Good knight," said Sir Launcelot, "it is known to me that you have put to shame many of the knights of the Round Table. Pray allow your prisoner, who I see is wounded, to recover, while I vindicate[30] the honor of the knights whom you have defeated."

"I defy you, and all your fellowship of the Round Table," Sir Tarquine replied.

"You boast!" said Sir Launcelot.

At the first charge the backs of the horses were broken and both knights stunned. But they soon recovered and set to with their swords, and both struck so lustily that neither shield nor armor could resist, and within two hours they were cutting each other's flesh, from which the blood flowed liberally. Finally they paused for a moment, resting on their shields.

"Worthy knight," said Sir Tarquine, "pray hold your hand for a while, and if you will, answer my question."

"Sir, speak on."

"You are the most powerful knight I have fought yet, but I fear you may be the one whom in the whole world I most hate. If you are not, for the love of you I will release all my prisoners and swear eternal friendship."

---

29. A *miscreant* knight is an evil, villainous one.
30. Launcelot wishes to defend against opposition, or *vindicate*, the honor of Tarquine's prisoners.

"What is the name of the knight you hate above all others?"

"Sir Launcelot du Lake; for it was he who slew my brother, Sir Carados of the Dolorous Tower, and it is because of him that I have killed a hundred knights, and maimed[31] as many more, apart from the sixty-four I still hold prisoner. And so, if you are Sir Launcelot, speak up, for we must then fight to the death."

"Sir, I see now that I might go in peace and good fellowship, or otherwise fight to the death; but being the knight I am, I must tell you: I am Sir Launcelot du Lake, son of King Ban of Benwick, of Arthur's court, and a knight of the Round Table. So defend yourself!"

"Ah! this is most welcome."

Now the two knights hurled themselves at each other like two wild bulls; swords and shields clashed together, and often their swords drove into the flesh. Then sometimes one, sometimes the other, would stagger and fall, only to recover immediately and resume the contest. At last, however, Sir Tarquine grew faint, and unwittingly lowered his shield. Sir Launcelot was swift to follow up his advantage, and dragging the other down to his knees, unlaced his helmet and beheaded him.

Sir Launcelot then strode over to the young noblewoman: "My lady, now I am at your service, but first I must find a horse."

Then the wounded Sir Gaheris spoke up: "Sir, please take my horse. Today you have overcome the most formidable knight, excepting only yourself, and by so doing have saved us all. But before leaving, please tell me your name."

"Sir Launcelot du Lake. Today I have fought to vindicate the honor of the knights of the Round Table, and I know that among Sir Tarquine's prisoners are two of my brethren, Sir Lyonel and Sir Ector, also your own brother, Sir Gawain. According to the shields there are also: Sir Brandiles, Sir

---

31. To *maim* is to injure seriously or horribly.

Teaching Options

CONNECTION

Knights Suggest that students generate a list of researchable questions about knights. Then have them use a search engine to locate appropriate information. Keywords students might use include *knights*, *chivalry*, and *King Arthur*.

REAL-WORLD CONNECTION

Violence in the Media Have students discuss similarities and differences between the violence of *Le Morte d'Arthur* and that of current films. Ask them whether the legend and violent films glorify violence or whether they take a stand against it. Encourage them to offer similarities and differences in the ways audiences react to violence in literature and to violence on the screen. **L2**

Galyhuddis, Sir Kay, Sir Alydukis, Sir Marhaus, and many others. Please release the prisoners and ask them to help themselves to the castle treasure. Give them all my greetings and say I will see them at the next Pentecost. And please request Sir Ector and Sir Lyonel to go straight to the court and await me there."

When Sir Launcelot had ridden away with the young noblewoman, Sir Gaheris entered the castle, and finding the porter in the hall, threw him on the ground and took the castle keys. He then released the prisoners, who, seeing his wounds, thanked him for their deliverance.

"Do not thank me for this work, but Sir Launcelot. He sends his greetings to you all, and asks you to help yourselves to the castle treasure. He has ridden away on another quest, but said that he will see you at the next Pentecost. Meanwhile, he requests Sir Lyonel and Sir Ector to return to the court and await him there."

"Certainly we shall not ride back to the court, but rather we shall follow Sir Launcelot wherever he goes," said Sir Ector.

"And I too shall follow him," said Sir Kay.

The prisoners searched the castle for their armor and horses and the castle treasure; and then a forester arrived with supplies of venison, so they feasted merrily and settled down for the night in the castle chambers—all but Sir Ector, Sir Lyonel, and Sir Kay, who set off immediately after supper in search of Sir Launcelot.

Launcelot Slays the Caitiff Knight Sir Tarquin and Rescues the Fair Lady and the Knights in Captivity, 1954–1955. Frank Cadogan Cowper. Oil, 40½ x 32 in. Private collection.

Viewing the painting: What knightly qualities does this painting express? Explain.

Literary Elements

DIALOGUE How do the other characters' responses to Launcelot help characterize them? *(They are loyal and respectful; they not only feel it is their duty but are eager to follow him on his quest.)*

Active Reading

CONNECT Have students read aloud the last paragraph on page 927 and discuss whether they would enjoy the evening in the castle described.

Language Note

The word *quest* has distinctly chivalric connotations, referring to an adventurous journey by knights.

Viewing the Painting

In Cowper's painting, the tree hung with the shields of many knights is pictured. Malory's description of the tree is found on page 922.

Viewing Response *The painting illustrates bravery and the knightly duty of fighting an evil knight to save a damsel in distress.*

Writing Minilesson

Describing Action Point out that much of *Le Morte d'Arthur* describes a series of actions: travels, meetings with various strangers, and fights. The simple language and sentence structure and vivid verbs help make the actions realistic.

Activity Have students write a paragraph describing a sporting event that they have observed or participated in.

Encourage them to use the description of the tournament on page 925 or of the fight with Sir Tarquine on page 926 as a model. **L2**

Additional Resources

📖 *Writer's Choice,* Lessons 3.1–3.3, 10.3

THEME Launcelot kills a corrupt knight who has been harassing the young noblewoman. Have students discuss the moral or theme that Malory appears to portray with this episode. *(He emphasizes the theme that a true hero does not fight merely for wealth or power but also to protect women.)*

AA **Literary Elements**

DICTION The noblewoman tells Launcelot he is "the bravest and gentlest" knight she has known. Have students discuss the significance of the two adjectives. *(It is not enough for a knight to be brave and a skillful fighter; he must also be "gentle": polite, kind to women, and socially skillful.)*

BB **Literary Elements**

DIALOGUE What other aspects of the knight's code does Launcelot explain? *(He says that knights should devote themselves to tournaments, wars, and adventures and not to relationships with women. A married knight should stay home with his wife. Some unmarried knights may choose to have affairs, but these make the knights less virtuous. If he were to behave in this way, he would be at a disadvantage against virtuous knights.)*

Teaching Options

---

from **Le Morte d'Arthur**

Sir Launcelot and the young noblewoman were riding down a broad highway when the young noblewoman said they were within sight of the spot where the knight generally attacked her.

"For shame that a knight should so degrade his high calling," Sir Launcelot replied. "Certainly we will teach him a much-needed lesson. Now, my lady, I suggest that you ride on ahead, and as soon as he molests you, I will come to the rescue."

Sir Launcelot halted and the young noblewoman rode gently forward. Soon the knight appeared with his page, and seized the young noblewoman from her horse; she cried out at once, and Sir Launcelot galloped up to them.

. . . you are the bravest and gentlest knight I have known.

"Scoundrel! what sort of knight do you think you are, to attack defenseless women?"

In answer the other knight drew his sword. Sir Launcelot did likewise, and they rushed together. With his first stroke Sir Launcelot split open the knight's head, down to the throat.

"Let that be your payment, though long overdue," said Sir Launcelot.

"Even so; he certainly deserved to die. His name was Sir Percy of the Forest Sauvage."

"My lady, do you require anything more of me?"

"No, good Sir Launcelot; and may the sweet Lord Jesu[32] protect you, for certainly you are the bravest and gentlest knight I have known. But pray tell me one thing: why is it

32. *Jesu* (jā′ zoō) is a form of *Jesus*.

you do not take to yourself a wife? Many good ladies, both high born and low born, grieve that so fine a knight as yourself should remain single. It is whispered, of course, that Queen Gwynevere has cast a spell over you so that you shall love no other."

"As for that, people must believe what they will about Queen Gwynevere and me. But married I will not be, for then I should have to attend my lady instead of entering for tournaments and wars, or riding in search of adventure. And I will not take a paramour, both for the fear of God and in the belief that those who do so are always unfortunate when they meet a knight who is purer of heart; for whether they are defeated or victorious in such an encounter, either result must be equally distressing and shameful. I believe that a true knight is neither adulterous nor lecherous."[33]

Sir Launcelot then took his leave of the young noblewoman, and for two days wandered alone through the forest, resting at night at the most meager of lodgings. On the third day, as he was crossing a bridge, he was accosted by a churlish porter,[34] who, after striking his horse on the nose so that it turned about, demanded to know by what right Sir Launcelot was riding that way.

"And what right do I need to cross this bridge? Surely, I cannot ride beside it," said Sir Launcelot.

"That is not for you to decide," said the porter, and with that he lashed at Sir Launcelot with his club. Sir Launcelot drew his sword, and after deflecting the blow, struck the porter on the head and split it open.

At the end of the bridge was a prosperous-looking village, overtopped by a fine castle.

33. A true knight is pure. He doesn't commit adultery (*adulterous*), nor is he preoccupied with indecent thoughts and desires (*lecherous*).
34. Here, the gatekeeper (*porter*) is bad-tempered and very rude (*churlish*), especially toward the poor horse!

Reading *Minilesson*

Identifying Author's Purpose Explain that determining the author's purpose for presenting certain episodes can help students understand the themes of the legend.

Activity Have students determine the author's purpose for each of the following events. Then ask them to write a sentence describing a theme illustrated by all the events.

1. Launcelot's refusal to choose a paramour from among Morgan le Fay and her companions *(to illustrate his virtue and his devotion to Gwynevere)*
2. Launcelot's defeat of the King of North Galys *(to show his strength, skill, and cleverness in battle)*
3. Launcelot's killing Sir Percy *(to show his devotion to protecting women)*
4. Launcelot's conversation about mar-

riage with the noblewoman *(to show the moral code and devotion to duty of an honorable knight)*

Students may state a theme such as "A true hero is not only strong, powerful, and clever but takes his duty seriously and is virtuous and kind to women." **L2**

Additional Resources
📁 *Reading Workbook,* pp. 77–78

As Sir Launcelot advanced he heard someone cry: "Good knight, beware! You have done yourself no good by killing the chief porter of the castle."

Sir Launcelot rode on regardless, through the village and into the castle court, which was richly grassed. Thinking to himself that this would be a good place for combat, Sir Launcelot tied his horse to a ring in the wall and started across the lawn. Meanwhile people were peering at him from every door and window, and again he heard the warning: "Good knight, you come here at your peril!"

Before long two giants appeared, fully armed except for their heads, and brandishing huge clubs. Together they rushed at Sir Launcelot, who raised his shield to defend himself, and then struck at one of the giants and beheaded him. Thereupon the second giant roared with dismay and fled into the forest, where Sir Launcelot pursued him. In a few minutes, Sir Launcelot drew abreast of the giant and struck him on the shoulder with a blow that carried through to the navel, and the giant dropped dead.

When Sir Launcelot returned to the castle, he was greeted by threescore ladies, who all knelt before him.

"Brave knight! we thank you for delivering us. Many of us have been prisoners for seven years now, and although we are all high born, we have had to work like servants for our keep, doing silk embroidery. Pray tell us your name, so that our friends can know who has saved us."

"My ladies, I am called Sir Launcelot du Lake."

"Welcome, Sir Launcelot! It was you alone whom the giants feared, and you alone who could have overcome them. How often have we prayed for your coming!"

"My ladies, please greet your friends for me; and when I pass through this country

again, grant me what hospitality you may feel is my due. Please recompense[35] yourselves from the castle treasure, and then insure that the castle is restored to the rightful owner."

"Sir Launcelot, this is the castle of Tintagil, and belonged formerly to the duke of that name. But after his death, Igraine, who had been his wife, was made queen by King Uther Pendragon, to whom she bore Arthur, our present king."

"And so, after all, I know the owner of this castle. My ladies, I bless you, and farewell."

Always in quest of adventure, Sir Launcelot rode through many different countries, through wild valleys and forests, and across strange rivers; and at night he slept where he could, often in the roughest of lodgings. Then one day he came to a well-kept house where the lady offered him the best of hospitality. After supper he was taken to his chamber, which overlooked the front door, and there Sir Launcelot disarmed and fell comfortably asleep.

He was awakened a short time later by a tremendous knocking at the door below, and looking through the window recognized Sir Kay in the moonlight, and three knights galloping toward him with drawn swords. The moment they got to the house, they dismounted and set upon Sir Kay, who turned about and drew his sword to defend himself. Sir Launcelot hastily armed, saying to himself: "If they kill Sir Kay I shall be a party to his death, for three against one is unjust."

He let himself down from the window by means of his sheet, and then challenged the three attackers, whispering to Sir Kay to stand by while he dealt with them. Sir Kay did as he was advised, and then Sir Launcelot, with

---

35. Launcelot invites the ladies to *recompense* themselves, or divide the treasure among themselves as a way to make up for their treatment by the giants.

CC **Active Reading**

QUESTION How does the incident with the giants resemble and differ from Launcelot's other adventures? *(As in his other adventures, Launcelot easily conquers the adversaries. Unlike the others, these are not ordinary knights but supernatural giants.)*

DD **Active Reading**

REVIEW Point out that in having Launcelot show up at Tintagil, Malory reminds the reader of the events in the first legend that led to the birth of Arthur. Have students summarize those events. Then have them discuss the differences between King Uther's and Launcelot's moral code. *(King Uther was attracted to Igraine and arranged with Merlin to have a relationship with her. Launcelot has said that a virtuous knight will not become involved in an adulterous relationship.)*

At the MOVIES

Be sure to preview the following video for appropriateness for your class:

- **Le Morte d'Arthur***

 *Also available in the Glencoe Literature *Video Library*.

Listening and Speaking *Minilesson*

Retelling a Legend Discuss effective ways to retell a legend such as "The Tale of Sir Launcelot du Lake." Point out that a speaker must decide which elements to emphasize and do so with his or her voice, facial expression, and gestures. Discuss the understated style of the legend and have students consider whether a low-key style might also be effective in an oral retelling of the work.

Activity Have students choose an episode from "The Tale of Sir Launcelot du Lake" and prepare an oral retelling of it. Have them present their interpretations in small groups. Then discuss with the class the most effective methods for telling the story. **L2**

from Le Morte d'Arthur

seven tremendous blows, brought all three knights to their knees and begging for mercy.

"Your lives will be spared if you yield to Sir Kay," said Sir Launcelot.

"Sir, it is surely you to whom we should yield, since we could easily have overcome Sir Kay."

"If you wish to be spared, you will go as prisoners of Sir Kay, and yield to Queen Gwynevere."

Each of the knights then swore on his sword to abide by the conditions of his surrender, and Sir Launcelot knocked once more at the door of the house.

"Why, I thought you were safely in bed," said the landlady, recognizing Sir Launcelot as she opened the door.

"Madam, I was, but then I had to jump out of the window and rescue this comrade of mine."

As they came into the light, Sir Kay recognized Sir Launcelot and thanked him humbly for twice saving his life.

"It was no more than I should have done, but come up to my chamber; you must be tired and hungry."

When Sir Kay had eaten, he lay on Sir Launcelot's bed, and they slept together until dawn. Sir Launcelot woke first, and rising quietly, clad himself in Sir Kay's armor, and then, mounting Sir Kay's horse, rode away from the house.

When Sir Kay awoke, he was astonished to find that Sir Launcelot had exchanged armor with him, but then he realized he had done it so that he should ride home unmolested, while Sir Launcelot encountered his opponents. And when Sir Kay had taken his leave of the landlady he rode back to the court without further incident.

For several days Sir Launcelot rode through the forest, and then he came to a countryside of low meadows and broad

streams. At the foot of a bridge he saw three pavilions, and a knight standing at the entrance to each, with a white shield hanging above, and a spear thrust into the ground at one side. Sir Launcelot recognized the three knights, who were from Arthur's court, as Sir Gawtere, Sir Raynolde, and Sir Gylmere. However, he rode straight past them, looking neither to right nor to left, and without saluting them.

"Why, there rides Sir Kay, the most overbearing[36] knight of all, in spite of his many defeats. I think I will challenge him and see if I cannot shake his pride a little," said Sir Gawtere.

He then galloped up to Sir Launcelot and challenged him. They jousted, and Sir Gawtere was flung violently from the saddle.

"That is certainly not Sir Kay," said Sir Raynolde. "For one thing, he is very much bigger."

"Probably it is some knight who has killed Sir Kay and is riding in his armor," Sir Gylmere replied.

"Well, since he has overcome our brother we shall have to challenge him. But I think it must be either Sir Launcelot, Sir Tristram, or Sir Pelleas; and we may not come well out of this."

Sir Gylmere challenged Sir Launcelot next, and was also overthrown. Then Sir Raynolde rode up to him.

"Sir, I would prefer not to challenge a knight so powerful as you, but since you have probably killed my brothers, I am obliged to; so defend yourself!"

They jousted; both broke their spears and they continued the combat with swords. Sir Gawtere and Sir Gylmere recovered, and attempted to rescue their brother, but Sir

---

36. An *overbearing* person is excessively proud and superior in attitude and behavior.

Teaching Options

Grammar and Language *Minilesson*

Who/Whom Point out the following sentences: "The young noblewoman who had served Sir Launcelot's supper reappeared." "Sir, it is surely you to whom we should yield." Point out that *who* serves as a subject or a predicate pronoun in a sentence or clause; *whom* serves as a direct object or an object of a preposition.

Activity Have students choose the correct word in parentheses.
1. "For (who, whom) are you searching?" (p. 916) *(whom)*
2. Merlin took the child to a priest, (who, whom) baptized him with the name of Arthur. (p. 918) *(who)*
3. "Please tell me the names of the three Round Table knights (who, whom) I shall be fighting." (p. 924) *(whom)* **L2**

Additional Resources
- *Grammar and Language Transparency 66*
- *Grammar and Language Workbook,* p. 185
- *Grammar and Composition Handbook,* Lesson 7.5
- *Writer's Choice,* Lesson 17.5

Launcelot saw them in time, and using more strength than hitherto, struck each off his horse again. At this, Sir Raynolde, badly wounded as he was, and with blood streaming from his head, picked himself up and once more rushed at Sir Launcelot.

"Sir, I should let things be," said Sir Launcelot. "I was not far away when you were knighted, and I know you to be worthy: therefore do not oblige me to kill you."

"May God reward you!" Sir Raynolde replied. "But speaking both for myself and my brothers, I would prefer to know your name before yielding to you, because we know very well that you are not Sir Kay, whom any one of us could have overcome."

"That is as may be; but I still require that you yield to Queen Gwynevere at the next Pentecost, and say that Sir Kay sent you."

The three brothers took their oath, and Sir Launcelot left them. He had not ridden much further when, coming to a glade, he found four more knights of the Round Table: Sir Gawain, Sir Ector, Sir Uwayne, and Sir Sagramour le Desyrus.

"Look!" said Sir Sagramour, "there rides Sir Kay. I will challenge him."

Sir Sagramour first, then each of the other knights in turn, challenged Sir Launcelot, and was flung from his horse. Sir Launcelot left them gasping on the ground, and said to himself as he rode away: "Blessed be the maker of this spear; with it I have tumbled four knights off their horses." Meanwhile the four knights were picking themselves up and consoling each other.

"To the devil with him! He is indeed powerful," said one.

"I believe that it must be Sir Launcelot," said another.

"Anyhow, let him go now; we shall discover when we return to Camelot," said a third, and so on. . . .

Sir Launcelot returned to Camelot two days before the feast of Pentecost, and at the court was acclaimed[37] by many of the knights he had met on his adventures.

Sir Gawain, Sir Uwayne, Sir Ector, and Sir Sagramour all laughed when they saw him in Sir Kay's armor, but without the helmet, and readily forgave his joke at their expense.

Sir Gaheris described to the court the terrible battle Sir Launcelot had fought with Sir Tarquine, and how sixty-four prisoners had been freed as a result of his victory.

Sir Kay related how Sir Launcelot had twice saved his life, and then exchanged armor with him, so that he should ride unchallenged.

Sir Gawtere, Sir Gylmere, and Sir Raynolde described how he had defeated them at the bridge, and forced them to yield as prisoners of Sir Kay; and they were overjoyed to discover that it had been Sir Launcelot nevertheless.

Sir Modred, Sir Mador, and Sir Gahalantyne described his tremendous feats in the battle against the King of North Galys; and Sir Launcelot himself described his enchantment by the four queens, and his rescue at the hands of the daughter of King Bagdemagus. . . .

And thus it was, at this time, that Sir Launcelot became the most famous knight at King Arthur's court.

---

37. Launcelot was *acclaimed*, or greeted with loud, enthusiastic praise.

Critical Thinking

DRAWING CONCLUSIONS Use a model to help students determine why Malory does not provide Launcelot's reaction to the tributes paid him by the other knights.

Model: The point of Malory's tale is summarized at the end: Launcelot was the most famous knight of King Arthur's Court. Also, Malory has previously made Launcelot's motives clear. I think the author is showing that Launcelot was a noble character who does not perform his deeds for personal glory but in honor of Gwynevere and for the glory of knighthood in general.

Thematic Focus

Heroism Have students compare the qualities that make Launcelot heroic with qualities considered heroic today. Have them give examples of contemporary heroes.

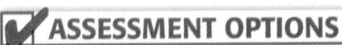

® *The following videotape program is available from Glencoe. Be sure to preview the video for appropriateness for your class.*

- **Biography: King Arthur— His Life and Legends**

ASSESSMENT OPTIONS

Quick Checks, p. 78

Reading *Minilesson*

Comparing and Contrasting Malory's fifteenth-century legend about a hero is quite different from a twentieth-century short story about a hero. Comparing and contrasting elements of a legend and a modern story will help students better understand both.

Activity Suggest that students create a chart showing the similarities and differences between the two genres. The headings of the chart might be *Fifteenth-Century Legend* and *Twentieth-Century Story*; the categories might be *Characters, Plot, Theme, Setting,* and *Style*. Have students fill in information for each category under both headings. **L2**

Additional Resources

Reading Workbook, pp. 77–78

Personal Response

Students should refer to the setting and characters of the legend in their response.

ANALYZING LITERATURE

1. Merlin asks for the custody of any child belonging to Igraine and Uther if he grants Uther's wish.
2. Arthur's brother, Sir Kay, forgets his sword and asks Arthur to go back for it. Unable to get into the house to get it, Arthur pulls the sword from the stone to give to Sir Kay. Afterwards, Sir Kay first claims that he retrieved it and then admits that Arthur did. When it is confirmed that only Arthur can pull out the sword, the people at first are hesitant to crown him king but finally do.
3. Sir Tarquine is determined to kill Sir Launcelot because Launcelot had killed his brother.
4. The young noblewoman says that Queen Gwynevere has cast a spell on Launcelot so he will love no other.
5. Launcelot exchanges armor with Sir Kay so that Sir Kay can return home without being harassed; Launcelot will fight his enemies. Launcelot defeats Sir Kay's enemies and becomes King Arthur's most famous knight.
6. Merlin insists on the reward because he arranged the birth of Arthur and wants to control his fate.
7. Arthur's behavior shows he is modest and selfless. His rule will probably be more fair and generous than Uther's.
8. Launcelot reveals his identity because he is an honest, virtuous knight and because he is confident he can win the battle.
9. Sir Launcelot's explanation for not marrying shows that he values the virtue and moral character of knighthood above all else.
10. In "The Tale of King Arthur," Sir Kay has a weak character; he is dishonest.
11. Students may say the characters of Uther Pendragon and Igraine do not seem realistic because their relationship is based on magic. Or they may say they are realistic because Uther demonstrates the human trait of lust and the use of trickery to get what he wants while Igraine realistically defends her virtue.
12. Students' responses should show knowledge of the plot and characters of the legend.

13. The relationships in the legend between men and women are very different from today. Women in the legend are seen as weak damsels to be protected or put on a pedestal, serving as inspiration for the knight's battles. They do not have strong characters in their own rights.
14. Students may describe a less intense reaction to the violence in the selection, which is not as realistic or as visual as television and video games. Others may be surprised by how much violence there is in the selection.
15. Students' responses should include specific details about Launcelot's character and about their own ideas of a hero.

Responding to Literature

Personal Response

What was your reaction to the world of King Arthur and his knights? If you could be transported there for a day, would you go? Why or why not?

ANALYZING LITERATURE

RECALL

1. What does Merlin ask in return for granting King Uther his wish?
2. What events lead Arthur to pull the sword from the stone? What happens after he retrieves the sword?
3. Why is Sir Tarquine so determined to kill Sir Launcelot?
4. What rumor does the "young noblewoman" say has been circulating about why Sir Launcelot has never married?
5. Why does Sir Launcelot exchange armor with Sir Kay? What is the result of this action for Sir Launcelot?

INTERPRET

6. Why, do you think, does Merlin insist upon the reward he requested for helping Uther?
7. What does Arthur's behavior immediately after pulling the sword tell you about him? How might Arthur's rule be different from Uther's?
8. Why, do you suppose, does Sir Launcelot reveal his identity to Sir Tarquine, knowing that the ensuing fight will be to the death?
9. What does Sir Launcelot's explanation for not marrying tell you about his values?
10. What do you learn about Sir Kay's character in "The Tale of King Arthur" that **foreshadows** (see page R5) what his fellow knights think of him in "The Tale of Sir Launcelot du Lake"?

EVALUATE AND CONNECT

11. Do the characters of King Uther Pendragon and Igraine seem realistic? Why or why not?
12. If you had been one of the nobles, would you have proclaimed the young Arthur king as described in "The Tale of King Arthur"? Explain.
13. How do the relationships between men and women in the selections compare with gender roles in society today?
14. Compare your reaction to the violence in the selection with your response to violence in television programs and video games. Explain.
15. Theme Connections   Does Sir Launcelot fit your description of a hero that you noted in the Focus Activity on page 914? Explain.

Literary ELEMENTS

Dialogue

Much of *Le Morte d'Arthur* is related through **dialogue**, the written conversation between characters. Dialogue gives readers a sense of a character's personality and feelings, and helps readers focus on important scenes. In "The Tale of King Arthur," for example, the reader realizes the importance of King Uther's feelings when Uther says, "Igraine has broken my heart, and unless I can win her, I shall never recover."

1. Reread the scene on page 920 in which Sir Ector realizes that Arthur has removed the sword from the stone. Why, do you suppose, has the author chosen to use dialogue here?
2. Which passage of dialogue do you find particularly effective or striking? Why?

● See **Literary Terms Handbook**, p. R3.

LITERARY ELEMENTS

1. The author has chosen to use dialogue to make the scene more dramatic and memorable.
2. Students should give specific reasons for their choice. For example, Launcelot's long speech on page 928 is effective because it reveals his personality and gives insight into a knight's moral code.

Additional Resources

Literary Elements Transparency 78

LITERATURE AND WRITING

Writing About Literature

Character Sketch Briefly list the principal adventures of Sir Launcelot. Then make a note of Launcelot's character traits revealed by these incidents. Based on these notes, write a description of Sir Launcelot.

Creative Writing

Boy to Become King? Imagine that you are a reporter sent back in time to report on the events involving Arthur and the sword. Write a news story, using "quotations" from people who witnessed the events.

EXTENDING YOUR RESPONSE

Literature Groups

Your Move Develop a board game based on the adventures of knights of the Round Table. Start by listing the conflicts met by Sir Launcelot and his resolutions of those situations. Then brainstorm additional difficulties and outcomes that could have occurred in Camelot. Write the goal and rules of the game, and sketch a game board. Share your game with other groups.

Performing

A Manner of Speaking What might Arthur say to the nobles and knights at his coronation? Jot down a few notes, and determine how your delivery will be in character. Then deliver Arthur's "inaugural address" to the class.

Interdisciplinary Activity

Music: Rock 'n' Rollin' Knights Choose a type of music—rock, blues, jazz, folk, rap—and write lyrics to retell the tale of Arthur or Sir Launcelot. Perform your song for the class. Then explain how your choice of music and performance techniques suits the content of the tale.

Reading Further

You might enjoy this legendary tale of heroes:
Sir Gawain and the Green Knight, written by an unknown poet, tells the extraordinary adventure of Sir Gawain.

 Save your work for your portfolio.

Skill Minilesson

VOCABULARY • Etymology

An etymology traces the development of a word since its earliest recorded usage. For example, *accost* comes from the Middle French *coster,* derived from the Latin *ad,* meaning "to," and *costa,* meaning "side" or "rib." Originally, to *accost* someone meant to be by that person's side. Eventually it came to mean "to approach," and then, over time, it came to mean "to approach and speak to, especially in an aggressive manner." The etymology of *accost* shows the change in the word's meaning and spelling over time.

Now study these etymologies of words from *Le Morte d'Arthur:*

oblige: from the Middle English *obligen,* from the Old French *obliger,* from the Latin *obligare,* meaning "to bind to," from *ob,* meaning "toward," and *ligare,* "to bind"

tumultuous: from the Middle English *tumulte,* from the Middle French, from the Latin *tumultus,* from the Latin *tumere,* "to swell," akin to the Sanskrit *tumula,* meaning "noisy."

PRACTICE Use the etymologies given above to answer the questions.

1. Which word is LEAST likely to have come from the same root as *oblige—ligament, league,* or *legend?*

2. Which word is MOST likely to have come from the same root as *accost—coast, cost,* or *costume?*

3. Which word is MOST likely to have come from the same root as *tumultuous—tumble, tumor,* or *tomb?*

LITERATURE AND WRITING

Writing About Literature

Students' character sketches should
- describe specific character traits of Launcelot.
- relate Launcelot's character traits to his actions.

Creative Writing

Students' news stories should
- accurately describe the event involving Arthur and the sword.
- include creative quotations from eyewitnesses of the event.

EXTENDING YOUR RESPONSE

Literature Groups Encourage students to use their knowledge of board games to create a fun and unique game. **COLLAB. LEARN.**

Performing Remind students to keep in mind Arthur's youth, inexperience, and unassuming personality as they write and deliver their speech.

Interdisciplinary Activity Encourage students to work with a partner or group if they wish and to accompany their song with a guitar or other musical instrument.

Skill Minilesson

VOCABULARY • Etymology

1. legend
2. coast
3. tumor

Additional Resources
Vocabulary Practice, p. 50

☑ ASSESSMENT OPTIONS

- *Quick Checks,* p. 78
- *Selection and Theme Assessment,* p. 149
- *Performance Assessment,* p. 76
- *Testmaker*

Objectives

- To read and analyze a legend about how a legendary hero prepares his troops for battle
- To identify the elements of a tall tale
- To write a tall tale

Skills

Reading/Thinking: Using Graphic Aids
Writing: Tall Tales
Grammar/Language: Single Quotation Marks
Life Skills: Writing a Memo

Motivating
→OPTIONS

Literature Launchers: "The Traditional Tale Revisited"

Videodisc
Side B, Segment 22

Also available in VHS.

Selection Focus Transparency 74: After discussing the heroes on the graphic, ask students to tell about other heroes they know.

Focus Activity: Have students develop part or all of their quickwriting into a paragraph.

Before You Read

from *Sundiata*

FOCUS ACTIVITY

What helps you gain the extra confidence and energy that you need to perform well in events such as a crucial game, an exam, or a driving test?

QUICKWRITE Recall a challenging situation. Write for five minutes, explaining the situation and telling how you prepared to face it.

SETTING A PURPOSE Read to learn how a legendary hero prepares his troops for battle.

BACKGROUND

The Time and Place

According to legend, the ancient Kingdom of Mali (mä′ lē) was established by a hero named Sundiata in approximately 1230. This territory included a large part of present-day West Africa. At a time when bandits roamed through other areas, Mali was known as a safe and orderly place. "Neither traveler nor inhabitant in it has anything to fear from robbers or men of violence," wrote an early Arab visitor.

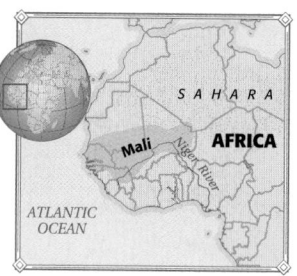

Did You Know?

An important member of an African king's household was the *griot* (grē′ ō). At a time when the people of Mali could not read or write, the *griot* was a sort of living history book who recalled for the court the great deeds of the past and recited the country's traditions and laws.

VOCABULARY PREVIEW

vanquish (vang′ kwish) *v.* to conquer or overcome; p. 937
scrupulous (skrōō′ pyə ləs) *adj.* thoroughly attentive to even the smallest details; precise; p. 937
elude (i lōōd′) *v.* to avoid or escape, especially through cleverness or quickness; p. 937
confidante (kon′ fə dant′) *n.* a person who is entrusted with secrets or private affairs; p. 938
perpetuate (pər pech′ōō āt′) *v.* to cause to continue to be remembered; p. 938

Meet the Storyteller

"Listen to my word, you who want to know; by my mouth you will learn the history of Mali."

So said Mamadou Kouyaté (ma′ mä dōō kōō yä′ tā), the African storyteller, or *griot*, who, in the 1950s, narrated *Sundiata* (sōōn dyä′ tə) for D. T. Niane, a folklore scholar. *Sundiata* has no single author. It is a tale that has been passed down orally by skilled poets from generation to generation. As the storyteller Kouyaté put it, "Without us the names of kings would vanish into oblivion, we are the memory of mankind."

Most cultures have stories that originate in oral tradition. *Mahābhārata* and *Rāmāyaṇa* are two stories about the codes of conduct in war and romance in ancient India. *Egils saga* portrays adventurous tales of murder, family feuds, and warfare in medieval Iceland and Norway.

RESOURCE MANAGER

Lesson Planning Resource
The *Unit Five Planning Guide* (pp. 16–23) provides additional lesson notes and reduced versions of all print resources.

Other Print Resources
- Active Reading Guide, p. 79
- Vocabulary Practice, p. 51
- Reading Workbook, pp. 79–80
- Grammar and Language Workbook, pp. 15, 259
- Grammar and Composition Handbook, Lessons 11.9, 11.6

- Quick Checks, p. 79
- Selection and Theme Assessment, p. 150
- Performance Assessment, p. 77
- Spanish Summaries, p. 74
- Inclusion Strategies
- English Language Learners Sourcebook

 Transparencies
- Selection Focus 74
- Literary Elements 79
- Grammar and Language 67, 68

Technology
 Literature Launchers
Audio Library
Spanish Audio Library
 Glencoe Literature Web Site
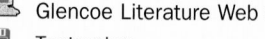 Testmaker

from Sundiata

Recorded by D. T. Niane
Translated by G. D. Pickett

The Catalan Atlas, c. 1375 (detail). Attributed to Cresques Abraham. Vellum, 65 x 300 cm.
Bibliotheque Nationale de France, Paris.

LEGENDS ❧ 935

SUMMARY

Sundiata, son of the former king of Mali, and his army stop in Sibi on their way to battle Soumaoro, Mali's cruel king. Sundiata plans to defeat the evil king by destroying his magic powers. Sundiata's sister, forced to be one of Soumaoro's wives, says she used flattery to learn the secret of his magic. Sundiata conducts a review of his troops. Fran Kamara demonstrates his strength by splitting a giant tree with his sword. Kamandjan cuts a tunnel through a mountain with his sword. After these incredible feats, Sundiata confidently leads his army to meet Soumaoro.

📁 *Spanish Summaries,* p. 74

Reading the Selection

A Active Reading

PREDICT Have students look at the legend's illustrations and read the prologue on page 936. Then ask them to predict what kinds of feats Sundiata and his army might be able to perform. Encourage them to review and revise their predictions as they read the selection.

Additional Resources
📁 *Active Reading Guide,* p. 79
🎧 *Audio Library*
🎧 *Spanish Audio Library*

Teaching Options

CONNECTING TO OTHER SELECTIONS

COMPARING selections

This selection is paired with *Le Morte d'Arthur* on page 915. A lesson for teaching a comparison of the two selections appears on page 941.

The chart at right shows three ways to connect the excerpt from *Sundiata* to other selections in this book.

For specific teaching strategies, see the *Unit Five Planning Guide*, pages 19–20.

Connection	Title
Life Skills: Planning and Designing	→ "Civil Peace," p. 39
Thematic: Bravery	→ "By the Waters of Babylon," p. 95
Literary: Point of View	→ from *Travels with Charley*, p. 427

935

B Literary Elements

TALL TALE Call students' attention to page 936. Explain that the italicized text summarizes the legend of Sundiata before the time of the selection. Have students name items in the summary that indicate that the legend will include exaggerated elements. *(The soothsayer's instructions, Sundiata's tearing a tree from the ground, and the sorcerer's ability to disappear all indicate that the legend will be a tall tale.)*

Historical Note

The first great empire of West Africa was Ghana, formed around the year 300. In 1076 Ghana was invaded by an Islamic people, the Almoravids. The small kingdom of Sosso took advantage of the empire's ensuing weakness and took control of Ghana around 1200. This is the point at which Soumaoro, King of Sosso, took over Mali. It was said that he killed eleven princes of the royal Keita family, of which Sundiata was a member. He did not harm Sundiata, believing that he presented no threat to his tyrannical reign.

Teaching Options

Heroes Ask students to use a search engine to find information on the Internet related to fictional African heroes in literature. Suggest these keywords as a starting point: *African folk tales, African legends, African hero tales.*

---

from

Sundiata

Even before he was born, Sundiata was destined for greatness. Acting on the instructions of a soothsayer,[1] his father, the king of Mali, had married a hideous, hunchbacked woman named Sogolon. As foretold, the couple had a son. It seemed, however, that the boy was unlikely to become a great leader as had been predicted. The young Sundiata could not even walk. He and his ugly mother became the object of cruel jokes and jealous abuse by the old king's first wife. At the age of seven, Sundiata suddenly reacted to an insult by standing up and tearing a tree from the ground. He instantly became the center of attention, a boy with great charm and the strength of ten men. Among his constant companions were the princes Fran Kamara and Kamandjan.[2] Even more important to him was his griot, Balla Fasséké,[3] who taught him the history of his people and of the world beyond.

Still fearing persecution from the jealous queen, Sogolon escaped with Sundiata to neighboring Ghana. There the amazing boy grew up. In his absence, Mali was taken over by the king of Sosso, a cruel sorcerer named Soumaoro,[4] whose secret chamber was tapestried with human skins and adorned with the skulls of his enemies. Soumaoro captured Balla Fasséké and Sundiata's half-sister, Nana Triban.[5] Enraged by Soumaoro's barbarism, Sundiata raised an army and prepared to restore his country to its rightful people. Although he succeeded in defeating Soumaoro in a great battle, he could not capture or kill the man himself, for the magician had the power to appear and disappear at will. While Sundiata rested in the town of Sibi,[6] Soumaoro once again raised a powerful army. The two prepared to meet in a final battle.

---

1. A *soothsayer* is someone who claims to be able to foretell the future.
2. *Kamara* (kä′ mä rä), *Kamandjan* (kä′ män jän)
3. *Balla Fasséké* (bä′ lä   fä sä′ kä)
4. *Soumaoro* (soo′ mər ö)
5. *Nana Triban* (nä′ nä   tri′ bän)
6. *Sibi* (si′ bē)

936 ✿ UNIT 5

ENGLISH LANGUAGE LEARNERS

Legendary Heroes Point out that Sundiata is a legendary hero of the African nation of Mali. Most cultures have similar heroes, whose great deeds have been passed down in oral legends.

Activity Have English language learners describe a legendary hero from their own culture, researching the figure if necessary. Ask them to tell about the historical basis of the hero, some of the hero's great deeds, and the importance of the hero to his or her culture. Encourage students to present their information in an oral report to a small group, using illustrations if possible.

Additional Resources
📁 *English Language Learners Sourcebook*

936 ✿ UNIT 5

D. T. Niane ❧

SUNDIATA and his mighty army stopped at Sibi for a few days. The road into Mali lay open, but Soumaoro was not yet vanquished. The king of Sosso had mustered a powerful army and his sofas were numbered by the thousand. He had raised contingents[7] in all the lands over which he held sway and got ready to pounce again on Mali.

With scrupulous care, Sundiata had made his preparations at Sibi. Now he had sufficient sofas to meet Soumaoro in the open field, but it was not a question of having a lot of troops. In order to defeat Soumaoro it was necessary first of all to destroy his magical power. At Sibi, Sundiata decided to consult the soothsayers, of whom the most famous in Mali were there.

On their advice Djata[8] had to sacrifice a hundred white bulls, a hundred white rams and a hundred white cocks. It was in the middle of this slaughter that it was announced to Sundiata that his sister Nana Triban and Balla Fasséké, having been able to escape from Sosso, had now arrived. Then Sundiata said to Tabon Wana, "If my sister and Balla have been able to escape from Sosso, Soumaoro has lost the battle."

Leaving the site of the sacrifices, Sundiata returned to Sibi and met his sister and his griot.

"Hail, my brother," said Nana Triban.

"Greetings, sister."

"Hail Sundiata," said Balla Fasséké.

"Greetings, my griot."

After numerous salutations, Sundiata asked the fugitives to relate how they had been able to elude the vigilance of a king

such as Soumaoro. But Triban was weeping for joy. Since the time of their childhood she had shown much sympathy towards the crippled child that Sundiata had been. Never had she shared the hate of her mother, Sassouma Bérété.

"You know, Djata," she said, weeping, "for my part I did not want you to leave the country. It was my mother who did all that. Now Niani is destroyed, its inhabitants scattered, and there are many whom Soumaoro has carried off into captivity in Sosso."

She cried worse than ever. Djata was sympathetic to all this, but he was in a hurry to know something about Sosso. Balla Fasséké understood and said, "Triban, wipe away your tears and tell your story, speak to your brother. You know that he has never thought ill of you, and besides, all that was in his destiny."

Nana Triban wiped her tears away and spoke.

"When you left Mali, my brother sent me by force to Sosso to be the wife of Soumaoro, whom he greatly feared. I wept a great deal at the beginning but when I saw that perhaps all was not lost

Bearded Male Figure. 14th century, Djenne. Terra-cotta, height: 38.1 cm. The Detroit Institute of Arts.

Viewing the sculpture: What personal characteristics does this sculpture convey to you? Which character from the selection possesses similar traits? Explain.

---

7. The *sofas* are soldiers or warriors, and *contingents* are additional troops.
8. *Djata* (dyä′ tə) is a shortened form of *Sundiata*.

Vocabulary
vanquish (vang′ kwish) *v.* to conquer or overcome
scrupulous (skrōō′ pyə ləs) *adj.* thoroughly attentive to even the smallest details; precise
elude (i lōōd′) *v.* to avoid or escape, especially through cleverness or quickness

INTERDISCIPLINARY CONNECTION

E Literary Elements

CHARACTERS Have students describe Nana Triban based on the story she tells. *(She is loyal to her brother, clever, and courageous. She is capable of deception in order to help her family and country.)*

F Literary Elements

IMAGERY Point out Nana Triban's statement that she "took the bull by the horns" and Bella Fasseke's statement that "the lion had burst his chains." Ask students to explain what each statement means. *(Nana Triban's statement means that she takes the initiative in getting information from Soumaoro; Bella Fasseke's statement means that Sundiata had asserted his natural power.)*

The Victory of Tabon
Sundiata had first met Soumaoro's army outside Tabon and had quickly defeated it. He then joined with Tabon forces and defeated the Sosso army again at Negueboria.

Archer Figure. Inland Delta Region, Mali. Ceramic, height: 61.9 cm. National Museum of African Art. Museum Purchase, 86-12-1.

I resigned[9] myself for the time being. I was nice to Soumaoro and was the chosen one among his numerous wives. I had my chamber in the great tower where he himself lived. I knew how to flatter him and make him jealous. Soon I became his confidante and I pretended to hate you, to share the hate which my mother bore you. It was said that you would come back one day, but I swore to him that you would never have the presumption[10] to claim a kingdom you had never possessed, and that you had left never to see Mali again. However, I was in constant touch with Balla Fasséké, each of us wanting to pierce the mystery of Soumaoro's magic power. One night I took the bull by the horns and said to Soumaoro: 'Tell me, oh you whom kings mention with trembling, tell me Soumaoro, are you a man like others or are you the same as the jinn[11] who protects humans? No one can bear the glare of your eyes, your arm has the strength of ten arms. Tell me, king of kings, tell me what jinn protects you so that I can worship him also.' These words filled him with pride and he himself boasted to me of the might of his Tana. That very night he took me into his magic chamber and told me all.

"Then I redoubled my zeal to show myself faithful to his cause, I seemed more overwhelmed than him. It was even he who went to the extent of telling me to take courage, that nothing was yet lost. During all this time, in complicity[12] with Balla Fasséké, I was preparing for the inevitable flight. Nobody watched over me any more in the royal enclosure, of which I knew the smallest twists and turns. And one night when Soumaoro was away, I left that fearsome tower. Balla Fasséké was waiting for me at the gate to which I had the key. It was thus, brother, that we left Sosso."

Balla Fasséké took up the story.

"We hastened to you. The news of the victory of Tabon made me realize that the lion had burst his chains. Oh son of Sogolon, I am the word and you are the deed, now your destiny begins."

Sundiata was very happy to recover his sister and his griot. He now had the singer who would perpetuate his memory by his

---

9. When Nana *resigned* herself, she gave in without resistance or complaint.
10. Here, *presumption* means "excessive boldness in thought or conduct."
11. In Arab folklore, a *jinn*, or genie, was an angel-like spirit that had magical powers and could take on human or animal form.
12. People acting in *complicity* are involved together, as accomplices in a crime or, as here, in secret activities.

Vocabulary
confidante (kon´ fə dant´) *n.* a person who is entrusted with secrets or private affairs
perpetuate (pər pech´ oo āt´) *v.* to cause to continue to be remembered

938 ❧ UNIT 5

Teaching Options

Grammar and Language *Minilesson*

Single Quotation Marks Point out Nana Triban's statement to Soumaoro, which is enclosed in single quotation marks in column two at the top of page 938. Remind students that a quotation is placed within quotation marks; a quotation within a quotation is placed within single quotation marks. Nana Triban's entire story is enclosed in quotation marks. When she quotes her own words to Soumaoro, those words are set off with single quotation marks.

Activity Have students write a brief dialogue in which one of the people speaking quotes himself or herself or another person. Have students exchange papers to check for correct use of double and single quotation marks. **L2**

Additional Resources

Grammar and Language Transparency 67

Grammar and Language Workbook, p. 15

Grammar and Composition Handbook, Lesson 11.9

Writer's Choice, Lesson 21.9

938

D. T. Niane

words. There would not be any heroes if deeds were condemned to man's forgetfulness, for we ply our trade to excite the admiration of the living, and to evoke the veneration[13] of those who are to come.

G

Djata was informed that Soumaoro was advancing along the river and was trying to block his route to Mali. The preparations were complete, but before leaving Sibi, Sundiata arranged a great military review in the camp so that Balla Fasséké, by his words, should strengthen the hearts of his sofas. In the middle of a great circle formed by the sofas, Balla Fasséké extolled[14] the heroes of Mali. To the king of Tabon he said: "You whose iron arm can split ten skulls at a time, you, Tabon Wana, king of the Sinikimbon and the Djallonké,[15] can you show me what you are capable of before the great battle is joined?"

The griot's words made Fran Kamara leap up. Sword in hand and mounted on his swift steed he came and stood before Sundiata and said, "Maghan Sundiata, I renew my oath to you in the sight of all the Mandingoes gathered together. I pledge myself to conquer or to die by your side. Mali will be free or the smiths[16] of Tabon will be dead."

The tribes of Tabon shouted their approval, brandishing their weapons, and Fran Kamara, stirred by the shouts of the sofas, spurred his charger and charged forward. The warriors opened their ranks and he bore down on a

---

13. To *evoke veneration* is to call up feelings of deep respect.
14. Balla highly praised *(extolled)* the heroes.
15. *Sinikimbon* (si′ nē kim′ bōn), *Djallonké* (jä lôn′ kā)
16. The *Mandingoes* were various peoples who inhabited the upper and middle Niger River valley. *Smiths* make or repair metal objects, such as swords, but Fran Kamara is speaking figuratively, referring to his sword-bearing troops.

---

great mahogany tree. With one stroke of his sword he split the giant tree just as one splits a paw-paw.[17] The flabbergasted army shouted, "Wassa Wassa . . . Ayé . . ."

Then, coming back to Sundiata, his sword held aloft, the king of Tabon said, "Thus on the Niger plain will the smiths of Tabon cleave those of Sosso in twain."[18] And the hero came and fell in beside Sundiata.

Turning towards Kamandjan, the king of Sibi and cousin of the king of Tabon, Balla Fasséké said, "Where are you, Kamandjan, where is Fama Djan? Where is the king of the Dalikimbon Kamaras? Kamandjan of Sibi, I salute you. But what will I have to relate of you to future generations?"

Before Balla had finished speaking, the king of Sibi, shouting his war cry, started his fiery charger off at full gallop. The sofas, stupefied, watched the extraordinary horseman head for the mountain that dominates[19] Sibi. . . . Suddenly a tremendous din filled the sky, the earth trembled under the feet of the sofas and a cloud of red dust covered the mountain. Was this the end of the world? . . . But slowly the dust cleared and the sofas saw Kamandjan coming back holding a fragment of a sword. The mountain of Sibi, pierced through and through, disclosed a wide tunnel!

H

Admiration was at its highest pitch. The army stood speechless and the king of Sibi, without saying a word, came and fell in beside Sundiata.

Balla Fasséké mentioned all the chiefs by name and they all performed great feats; then the army, confident in its leadership, left Sibi.

---

17. *Paw-paw* is a banana-like fruit.
18. To *cleave in twain* is to split in two.
19. The mountain *dominates* Sibi because it towers over the city.

G Literary Elements

POINT OF VIEW At the top of page 939, the narrator says, ". . .we ply our trade to excite the admiration of the living. . . ." Have students identify the narrator, his point of view, and the "we" he refers to. *(The first-person narrator is a griot and he is referring to all the griots.)*

H Literary Elements

TALL TALE How does the narrator's diction in his descriptions of the army's reactions to Fran Kamara and Kamandjan help characterize the nature of the legend? *(He uses words and phrases like flabbergasted, extraordinary, "tremendous din," and speechless to describe the army's reactions. The language emphasizes the superhuman quality of the heroes' accomplishments.)*

Thematic Focus

Heroism Have students discuss why tales of exaggerated heroism like that in *Sundiata* might be popular and continue to be told and retold for many generations.

☑ **ASSESSMENT OPTIONS**

📁 *Quick Checks,* p. 79

Reading *Minilesson*

Using Graphic Aids The unusual names in the legend of Sundiata may make comprehension or memory of the legend's events difficult for students. A graphic aid can help them identify the characters as they read and review the selection.

Activity Have students create a graphic aid that shows Sundiata and his relationship to the other characters in the legend. Suggest that a cluster map may be used to indicate the different groups of characters: Sundiata's relatives, his military allies, and his enemies. **L2**

Additional Resources
📁 *Reading Workbook,* pp. 79–80

Personal Response

Students may predict that Sundiata and his army will defeat Soumaoro.

ANALYZING LITERATURE

1. Sundiata plans to destroy Soumaoro's magical powers. He consults with soothsayers, showing that he respects the expertise of others.
2. Nana Triban gets information by flattering Soumaoro. Her purpose is to help Sundiata defeat him.
3. Sundiata's griot, Balla Fasséké, escapes with Nana Triban. The narrator says only through storytellers will people continue to hear of heroes.
4. Fran Kamara splits a giant tree with one stroke of his sword. Kamandjan cuts a tunnel through a mountain with his sword. Balla Fasséké says that if the warriors show their prowess to the griot, he will tell their stories.
5. Students may disapprove of Nana Triban's wiles and flattery or admire her for making the most of her situation. Students may imagine a similar situation taking place today in which women manipulate men for wealth, information, or power.
6. Students may say Sundiata has a strong desire to be remembered by future generations because it inspires him to do heroic deeds for his country.
7. Balla Fasséké reveals his knowledge that people are motivated to do great things by the desire to become famous and to be remembered in the future. Today, newspapers, magazines, and television make people famous.
8. Students should refer to details in the selection and in their quickwrites.

EXTENDING YOUR RESPONSE

Creative Writing

Students' tall tales should
- describe fantastic feats.

Learning for Life

Students' memos should
- show knowledge of the characters of Sundiata and Balla Fasséké.

Responding to Literature

Personal Response

What do you think might happen next in this story? Share your predictions with your classmates.

ANALYZING LITERATURE

RECALL AND INTERPRET

1. What does Sundiata first plan to do in order to defeat Soumaoro? Later, what does he do before leaving Sibi? What do his methods suggest about him as a leader?
2. How does Nana Triban get information from Soumaoro about his magic powers? What is her purpose in getting this information?
3. **Theme Connections** Who escapes with Nana Triban? What does the narrator mean by saying, "There would not be any heroes if deeds were condemned to man's forgetfulness . . ."?
4. What astonishing deeds do Fran Kamara and Kamandjan perform at the urging of Balla Fasséké? Why do Balla Fasséké's words cause the warriors to react as they do?

EVALUATE AND CONNECT

5. What do you think of the way Nana Triban handles Soumaoro? Can you imagine such a situation taking place today? Explain.
6. Why do you think Sundiata has such a strong desire to be remembered by future generations? For what would you like to be remembered?
7. What knowledge of human nature does Balla Fasséké reveal through his speeches? Does our society today have any methods comparable to Balla Fasséké's? Explain.
8. Compare and contrast your response to the Focus Activity on page 934 with the way Sundiata prepares his army for the battle.

EXTENDING YOUR RESPONSE

Creative Writing

Tall Tales   According to the final paragraph of this excerpt, Balla Fasséké inspires all the chiefs of Sundiata's army to perform "great feats." Only two of these feats are described, however. Invent three other characters, give them suitable names, and describe what fantastic feats they might perform to impress the troops and win fame.

Learning for Life

On the Eve of Battle   Imagine that you are Sundiata trying to prepare his army for battle. Write a memo to Balla Fasséké, instructing him on how to address the troops. Include a convincing explanation for your request. Share your memo with the class.

 Save your work for your portfolio.

Literary ELEMENTS

Tall Tale

Sundiata is a **tall tale,** a type of folklore in which the deeds of one or more characters are wildly exaggerated but told seriously—as if the deeds were true. As with Sundiata and the other kings gathered in Sibi, the heroes of tall tales are likeable characters whose extraordinary traits enable them to perform improbable feats. For example, when Balla Fasséké acclaims the heroes in camp, he convincingly describes the king of Tabon as one "whose iron arm can split ten skulls at a time."

1. In your opinion, which of the heroes in *Sundiata* possesses the most extraordinary trait? Give one example of how that trait is exaggerated in the tall tale.
2. Why, do you think, are the heroes in *Sundiata* likeable?

● See **Literary Terms Handbook,** p. R13.

LITERARY ELEMENTS

1. Students might mention the Kamandjan's extraordinary strength and horsemanship in cutting a tunnel through the mountain.
2. The heroes in *Sundiata* are likable because they do not seem malicious; they use their skills for the good of their country.

Additional Resources

📠 *Literary Elements Transparency 79*

✔ ASSESSMENT OPTIONS

📁 *Quick Checks,* p. 79
📁 *Selection and Theme Assessment,* p. 150
📁 *Performance Assessment,* p. 77
💾 *Testmaker*

COMPARING selections

from Le Morte d'Arthur and from Sundiata

COMPARE **HEROES**

Which character better fits your description of a hero, Sir Launcelot or Sundiata? Draw and complete a chart like the one shown.

Your description of a hero:	
Heroic quality of Sir Launcelot:	
Specific detail from story:	
Heroic quality of Sundiata:	
Specific detail from story:	
Conclusion: Which character better fits your definition of a hero? Why?	

COMPARE **THEMES**

Like many legendary tales, both *Le Morte d'Arthur* and *Sundiata* share themes of magic, romance, and heroism. Each work, however, treats these themes in a distinctive style. Discuss the following questions with your class.

1. In which work, would you say, does magic play a more important role? Support your answer with specific examples.

2. How do the exploits of Arthur's knights compare with the feats of Kamara and Kamandjan?

3. Are the relationships between men and women presented differently in the two legends? Explain.

How Four Queens Found Sir Lancelot Sleeping, 1908 (detail).

COMPARE **IMAGES**

Working with your group, decide which images from *Le Morte d'Arthur* and *Sundiata* you would show on videotape case covers for feature films of these stories. Then, write the text and draw a rough sketch for each case cover. Discuss the similarities and differences between the covers with other groups.

COMPARE **HEROES**

Students' charts should
- list specific qualities such as strength or kindness.
- list well-chosen details from the legends.
- offer a clear conclusion based on the chart's evidence.

COMPARE **THEMES**

Students' discussions should
- point out the similarities between the two legends in terms of the use of magic.
- point out the realistic and the unrealistic feats of the heroes in both legends.
- point out the strong role played by a woman in *Sundiata* and the traditionally romanticized roles of women in *Le Morte d'Arthur*.

COMPARE **IMAGES**

Students' cover plans should
- describe specific images that are representative of the stories' themes.
- include a text that describes the stories' themes and characters.

COLLAB. LEARN.

Additional Resources
📁 *Literature Groups Sourcebook*

Teaching Options

📁 PORTFOLIO OPTIONS

Select and Reflect Have students reflect on their charts for the activity above by asking themselves these questions:
- Does my chart name specific heroic qualities?
- Do my examples illustrate these qualities?
- Is my conclusion valid based on my evidence?

Have students clip their reflections to their charts and place them in their portfolios. At a later time, they might consider using the comments to revise their analyses as portfolio showcase pieces. **L2**

Additional Resources
📁 *Writing Assessment and Portfolio Management,* pp. 20–22

Grammar Link

Objective

- To recognize and punctuate nonessential sentence elements

Teaching Strategies

Point out possible misunderstandings that result from omitting commas for nonessential elements. For example, the third sentence, "His companions who were also knights rode off," means that those companions who were not knights did not ride off.

Exercise

1. Soumaoro, the king of Sosso, was Sundiata's enemy.
2. Correct
3. Sundiata's griot, Balla Fasséké, escaped from Sosso with Nana Triban.
4. The royal enclosure, filled with twists and turns, was no challenge for Nana Triban.
5. Another benefit, in fact, was that she had a key to the gate.

Additional Resources

📕 **Grammar and Language Workbook,** p. 255

📕 **Grammar and Composition Handbook,** Lesson 11.6

📕 **Writer's Choice,** Lesson 21.6

Grammar Link

Missing Commas with Nonessential Elements

There are many kinds of **grammatical elements**—words, phrases, and clauses—that can be part of a sentence. In some sentences, these elements are "essential," that is, they are necessary to the meaning of the sentence. Those elements that are *not* essential to the meaning of the sentence must be set off with commas.

> **Essential:** The knight who defeated the most challengers was Launcelot.
> **Nonessential:** Launcelot, who was famous and feared, went in search of adventure.

In the first example, the underlined section identifies which knight the sentence is about. It gives necessary information about a noun *(knight)*. Therefore, it is essential to the meaning of the sentence. In the second example, the underlined section gives "extra" information about a noun *(Launcelot)*. It could be left out without changing the meaning of the sentence. Therefore, it is nonessential and must be set off with commas.

Problem Missing commas with a nonessential element:
> The greatest knight Launcelot slept under a tree.
> His companions who were also knights rode off.
> There was to be sure much adventure to be found.
> Medieval England was well rather short on law and order.

Solution Set off a nonessential element with commas:
> The greatest knight, Launcelot, slept under a tree.
> His companions, who were also knights, rode off.
> There was, to be sure, much adventure to be found.
> Medieval England was, well, rather short on law and order.

● For more about commas with nonessential elements, see **Language Handbook,** p. R26.

EXERCISE

Rewrite incorrect sentences, adding necessary commas. If the sentence is correct, write *Correct.*

1. Soumaoro the king of Sosso was Sundiata's enemy.

2. The woman who was Soumaoro's favorite wife was Sundiata's half-sister.

3. Sundiata's griot Balla Fasséké escaped from Sosso with Nana Triban.

4. The royal enclosure filled with twists and turns was no challenge for Nana Triban.

5. Another benefit in fact was that she had a key to the gate.

Teaching Options

Writing *Minilesson*

Using Appositives Explain that two sentences may be combined by putting details from one sentence into an appositive in the other sentence. For example:
> Sundiata was Mali's greatest hero.
> Sundiata defeated Soumaoro.
> Combined: Sundiata, Mali's greatest hero, defeated Soumaoro.

Point out that nonessential elements are set off with commas.

Activity Have students combine the following sentences by making one into an appositive.
> He split the paw-paw tree with one stroke. The paw-paw is a huge tree.
> *(He split the paw-paw, a huge tree, with one stroke.)* **L2**

Additional Resources

📕 **Writer's Choice,** Lesson 12.2

Writing Skills

Main Idea and Supporting Details

Novelist George Orwell wrote, "Good prose is like a window-pane." To make your writing as clear as glass, make sure each paragraph expresses one main idea supported by details.

The **main idea,** or focus, of a paragraph should be presented in a direct statement—that is, in a **topic sentence.** All the other sentences in the paragraph are to give details that prove, clarify, or expand the main idea. These details will include examples, quotations, and facts. Read the following paragraph from a personal response to the story "Arthur Becomes King."

> The author adds humor to the story by emphasizing the human characteristics of his characters. For example, the noblemen don't speak in the formal, stilted language that I've heard kings, princes, and lords use. King Pellinore sounds like a common gossip when he says "It's the very latest news." His fragmented dialogue is true of the way people speak when they're very excited and in a hurry to tell gossip. The way the characters interrupt and don't listen carefully to each other leads to misunderstandings and confusion—just as in real life. Finally, the characters mix up their words, substituting one word for another, which causes the reader to envision something very different from the intended meaning.

In the paragraph above, the first sentence states the main idea and also hints at what the paragraph will say about it. Each of the other sentences supports the main idea.

Although a topic sentence often appears at the beginning of a paragraph, as in the example above, it can appear anywhere in a paragraph.

- Begin a paragraph with a topic sentence to let the reader know what's to come.
- End a paragraph with a topic sentence to summarize the main idea and reinforce the reader's understanding of the main idea.

EXERCISES

1. Write a paragraph with a topic sentence and supporting details that describe your ideal getaway place—a place you like to go to think things through.

2. Look in your portfolio for a paragraph you have written. Reread the paragraph, and underline the topic sentence. Then rewrite the paragraph, moving the topic sentence to a new position. How does moving the topic sentence affect the paragraph? What other adjustments, if any, did you have to make? Why?

Objective

- To recognize the importance of a topic sentence and to use one in a paragraph

Teaching Strategies

Have volunteers open a science or history textbook, read a paragraph chosen at random, and identify its topic sentence. Point out that most informative paragraphs contain a topic sentence.

Exercises

1. *Students' paragraphs should*
   - include a topic sentence that states the paragraph's main idea.
   - include details that support the topic sentence.
2. Students may find they have to move other sentences and add or rearrange transitional words after moving their topic sentence.

Additional Resources

Writer's Choice, Lesson 2.6

Grammar and Language *Minilesson*

Punctuating Transitions Explain the importance of transitions such as *first, next,* and *therefore* in organizing a paragraph. Point out that these words typically are set off by commas. (Similarly, Soumaoro uses magic.)

Activity Have students use three transitional words or phrases in their paragraphs about getaway places. **L2**

Additional Resources

Grammar and Language Transparency 68

Grammar and Language Workbook, p. 259

Grammar and Composition Handbook, Lesson 11.6

Writer's Choice, Lesson 21.6

Objectives

- To read a poem about a hero's final hours
- To identify the elements of narrative poetry
- To write an evaluation of an author's character portrayal

Skills

Reading/Thinking: Inferring; Identifying Author's Purpose; Paraphrasing
Writing: Using Similes; Narrative
Vocabulary: Semantic Mapping
Grammar/Language: Adverbs; Subject-Verb Agreement
Listening/Speaking: Expressing Emotions
Life Skills: Writing an Obituary
Collaboration: Literature Groups

Motivating
→OPTIONS

Selection Focus Transparency 75: Ask students to give adjectives that describe the mood of the illustration, then discuss how the artist creates that mood.

Focus Activity: Have students discuss their journal entries.

Before You Read

The Passing of Arthur

FOCUS ACTIVITY

When have you found it difficult to part with something you wished you could keep?

JOURNAL What special meaning did the object have? Did you find a substitute or consider it irreplaceable? In your journal, describe the object and tell how you reacted to giving it up.

SETTING A PURPOSE Read to learn how two characters part with something important.

BACKGROUND

The Time and Place

"The Passing of Arthur" is one of a series of twelve long poems called *Idylls of the King,* which tells about the legendary King Arthur and his knights of the Round Table. The *Idylls* takes place in early medieval times in England. This excerpt is set in Lyonnesse, a legendary land located off the southwestern coast of England. King Arthur has just been wounded–and most of his knights have been killed–in a battle against Arthur's evil nephew, Modred. The lone surviving knight, Sir Bedivere, takes the wounded king to the ruins of a chapel near the battlefield.

Battle between King Arthur and Modred.
15th century, from the St. Albans Chronicle. English, with Flemish illuminations.

Did You Know?

Different stories are told about the source of Excalibur, King Arthur's sword, which plays a major role in "The Passing of Arthur." In one account, Arthur miraculously draws the sword from a stone as a young boy to prove his royalty. In another version, the Lady of the Lake, a magical being who lives in a castle in a lake, gives the sword to Arthur. In *Idylls of the King,* Tennyson adopts the latter version of the story and relates that Arthur is instructed to take the sword and then to cast it away later in his life.

Meet Alfred, Lord Tennyson

"**The vision of Arthur . . . came upon me when, little more than a boy, I first lighted upon Malory.**"

After his initial exposure to Sir Thomas Malory's *Le Morte d'Arthur* in boyhood, Tennyson longed to write a "whole great poem" on the Arthurian legend. One of twelve children, Tennyson and his brothers often played knights of the Round Table. Tennyson worked on *Idylls of the King,* a verse rendition of the Arthur legend, over several years. A popular poet, he became poet laureate of Great Britain in 1850.

Alfred, Lord Tennyson was born in Somersby in Lincolnshire, England, in 1809. He died in 1892. "The Passing of Arthur" was first published in 1842.

RESOURCE MANAGER

Lesson Planning Resource
The *Unit Five Planning Guide* (pp. 24–31) provides additional lesson notes and reduced versions of all print resources.

📁 **Other Print Resources**
- Active Reading Guide, p. 80
- Vocabulary Practice
- Reading Workbook, pp. 81–82
- Grammar and Language Workbook, pp. 63, 167
- Grammar and Composition Handbook, Lessons 1.5, 6.1

- Quick Checks, p. 80
- Selection and Theme Assessment, pp. 151–152
- Performance Assessment, p. 78
- Spanish Summaries, p. 75
- Inclusion Strategies
- English Language Learners Sourcebook

 Transparencies
- Selection Focus 75
- Literary Elements 80
- Grammar and Language 69

Technology
🎧 Audio Library
🎧 Spanish Audio Library
💻 Glencoe Literature Web Site
💾 Testmaker

The Passing of Arthur

from

Idylls of the King

Alfred, Lord Tennyson

Morte d'Arthur, 1862. James Mulcaster Carrick. Oil on canvas, 39¼ x 54 in. Private collection.

SUMMARY

King Arthur, mortally wounded in battle, lies dying in a ruined chapel with his only surviving knight, Sir Bedivere. Arthur commands Bedivere to throw Arthur's sword, Excalibur, into the lake. When the knight reluctantly throws the sword, he sees an arm rise up from the lake and catch it before it disappears. Arthur asks Bedivere to carry him to the lake, where the king boards a barge. Bedivere laments the passing of Arthur and of the era of knighthood, to which Arthur replies that the world must change. The funeral barge disappears; the sun rises on a new era.

Spanish Summaries, p. 75

A Active Reading

PREDICT Have students view the selection title and the painting *Morte d'Arthur* and predict what the mood of the poem will be. Suggest that they review and revise their prediction periodically as they read the selection.

Additional Resources

Active Reading Guide, p. 80
Audio Library
Spanish Audio Library

Teaching Options

CONNECTING TO OTHER SELECTIONS

The chart at the right shows three ways to connect "The Passing of Arthur" to selections in this book.

For specific teaching strategies, see the *Unit Five Planning Guide,* pages 27–28.

Connection	Title
Life Skills: Implementing and Performing	→ "A Swimming Lesson," p. 495
Thematic: Endings	→ "Lullaby," p. 330
Literary: Denouement	→ "The Ring," p. 225

BLANK VERSE Remind students that blank verse is unrhymed iambic pentameter. Have a volunteer read the first two lines of the poem. Write their scansion on the board. Point out that each is an iambic pentameter line. Ask students why blank verse is appropriate for Tennyson's poem. *(The effect of blank verse is formal and serious, so it fits the epic form and the subject, the great legendary hero of English history.)*

C **Literary Elements**

NARRATIVE POETRY Point out that narrative poetry tells a story. Like fiction, it has a setting, conflict, plot, and characters. Have students identify each element in the beginning of the poem. *(The poem is set near a lake in England in medieval times. The main characters are King Arthur and one of his knights, Sir Bedivere. The conflict is that King Arthur, dying, asks Sir Bedivere to throw his sword into the lake.)*

Tennyson's Source

Tennyson's main source was Sir Thomas Malory's *Le Morte d'Arthur*. Lines 11–12 of Tennyson's poem are based on this statement from the end of Malory's work: "Some men yet say in many parts of England that King Arthur is not dead, but by the will of our Lord in another place. And men say that he will come again."

Teaching Options

The Passing of Arthur

B

Then spake King Arthur to Sir Bedivere:
"The sequel° of to-day unsolders° all
The goodliest fellowship of famous knights
Whereof this world holds record. Such a sleep
5   They sleep—the men I loved. I think that we
Shall never more, at any future time,
Delight our souls with talk of knightly deeds,
Walking about the gardens and the halls
Of Camelot,° as in the days that were.
10   I perish by this people which I made,—
Tho' Merlin° sware that I should come again
To rule once more—but let what will be be,
I am so deeply smitten thro' the helm°
That without help I cannot last till morn.
15   Thou therefore take my brand° Excalibur,
Which was my pride; for thou rememberest how
In those old days, on summer noon, an arm
Rose up from out the bosom of the lake,
Clothed in white samite,° mystic,° wonderful,
20   Holding the sword—and how I row'd across
And took it, and have worn it, like a king;
And, wheresoever I am sung or told
In aftertime, this also shall be known.
But now delay not; take Excalibur,
25   And fling him far into the middle mere;°
Watch what thou seest, and lightly° bring me word."

To him replied the bold Sir Bedivere:
"It is not meet,° Sir King, to leave thee thus,
Aidless, alone, and smitten thro' the helm—
30   A little thing may harm a wounded man;
Yet I thy hest° will all perform at full,
Watch what I see, and lightly bring thee word."

C

So saying, from the ruin'd shrine he stept,
And in the moon athwart° the place of tombs,
35   Where lay the mighty bones of ancient men,
Old knights, and over them the sea-wind sang
Shrill, chill, with flakes of foam. He, stepping down
By zigzag paths and juts of pointed rock,
Came on the shining levels of the lake.

40   There drew he forth the brand Excalibur,
And o'er him, drawing it, the winter moon,

D

2 **sequel:** the result or consequence. **unsolders** (un sod' ərz): separates.

9 **Camelot:** the site of King Arthur's court.

11 **Merlin:** a magician who counseled King Arthur.

13 **smitten thro' the helm:** struck through the helmet.

15 **brand:** sword.

19 **samite:** a heavy silk fabric. **mystic:** mysterious.

25 **middle mere** (mēr): the middle of the lake.
26 **lightly:** speedily.

28 **meet:** suitable or proper.

31 **hest:** command.

34 **athwart:** across.

Paraphrasing English language learners may find the formal style and diction of the poem difficult to comprehend. Point out that paraphrasing is a helpful tool in understanding this selection.

Activity List the following steps for paraphrasing:

1. Rearrange sentence order so that the subject and verb come first.

2. Substitute simple, modern words for dated, difficult, or formal words.

3. Summarize descriptive passages. With students, paraphrase the entire first page of the poem.

Additional Resources
📁 *English Language Learners Sourcebook*

Alfred, Lord Tennyson ~

D

Brightening the skirts of a long cloud, ran forth
And sparkled keen with frost against the hilt;°
For all the haft° twinkled with diamond sparks,
45   Myriads of topaz-lights,° and jacinth-work°
Of subtlest° jewellery. He gazed so long
That both his eyes were dazzled as he stood,
This way and that dividing the swift mind,
In act to throw; but at the last it seem'd
50   Better to leave Excalibur conceal'd
There in the many-knotted water-flags,°
That whistled stiff and dry about the marge.°
So strode he back slow to the wounded King.

     Then spake King Arthur to Sir Bedivere:
55   "Hast thou perform'd my mission which I gave?
What is it thou hast seen? or what hast heard?"

     And answer made the bold Sir Bedivere:
"I heard the ripple washing in the reeds,
And the wild water lapping on the crag."°

E

60   To whom replied King Arthur, faint and pale:
"Thou hast betray'd thy nature and thy name,
Not rendering true answer, as beseem'd°
Thy fealty,° nor like a noble knight;
For surer sign had follow'd, either hand,
65   Or voice, or else a motion of the mere.
This is a shameful thing for men to lie.
Yet now, I charge thee, quickly go again,
As thou art lief° and dear, and do the thing
I bade thee, watch, and lightly bring me word."

70   Then went Sir Bedivere the second time
Across the ridge, and paced beside the mere,
Counting the dewy pebbles, fixt in thought;
But when he saw the wonder of the hilt,
How curiously and strangely chased,° he smote
75   His palms together, and he cried aloud:

F

     "And if indeed I cast the brand away,
Surely a precious thing, one worthy note,°
Should thus be lost for ever from the earth,
Which might have pleased the eyes of many men.

43–44 hilt, haft: names for a sword's handle.
45 topaz (tō′ paz), **jacinth** (jā′ sinth): precious gems.
46 subtlest: most finely crafted.

51 water-flags: marsh plants.
52 marge: edge.

59 crag: the rocky shore.

62–63 beseem'd / Thy fealty: was appropriate to your loyalty or duty.

68 lief (lēf): beloved.

74 chased: engraved.

77 worthy note: deserving admiration.

LEGENDS 🌿 947

D **Author's Craft**

IMAGERY Have a volunteer read the description in lines 41–46. Ask students why the author might have chosen to emphasize the sword with this vivid imagery. *(The vivid imagery emphasizes the sword's beauty and value, which cause Sir Bedivere's anguish over whether or not to throw it away.)*

E **Literary Elements**

NARRATIVE POETRY Point out that like fiction, narrative poetry contains dialogue. Have students tell what they learn about the characters of King Arthur and Sir Bedivere from their dialogue. *(Sir Bedivere is well-meaning but naive in believing he can hide the truth from King Arthur. Arthur is authoritative and perceptive.)*

F **Literary Elements**

CONFLICT Have students define Sir Bedivere's conflict and explain why the sword might be meaningful to him aside from its beauty, which he describes in lines 76–79. *(His conflict is whether to obey King Arthur or whether to do what he thinks is right, which is to save the beautiful sword for others to see. Not only is the sword beautiful, but it represents Arthur's power and fame.)*

Language Note

The word *idyll* refers to a narrative poem with a romantic, epic, or tragic theme.

MEETING INDIVIDUAL NEEDS — MULTIPLE LEARNING STYLES

Spatial The sword Excalibur is described as jewel-encrusted and dazzling and comes to symbolize King Arthur's power.

Activity Have students make an illustration of the sword, either by itself or as it appears in a scene of the poem: held by King Arthur, thrown into the marsh plants by the lake, or being thrown into the lake. Encourage students to use a medium of their choice and to display their artwork. **L2**

CONNECT Have students explain why Sir Bedivere has such a hard time deciding what to do and consider what they would do in his position.

H Literary Elements

IMAGERY Remind students that imagery appeals to one or more senses. Ask students to which sense or senses the images in lines 104–105 appeal. *(hearing)*

I Active Reading

CLARIFY Have students paraphrase lines 109–111, which express Arthur's unhappiness as he lies dying. *(A dying king loses the power of authority which he had been able to convey with merely a look.)*

FYI

Tennyson's Career
Alfred, Lord Tennyson once said that "the words 'far, far away' had always a strange charm for me." Perhaps this explains his preoccupation with his country's past in *Idylls of the King*. He spent most of the second half of his career, from 1850 to his death in 1892, concentrating on this epic. He published the first four books of the poem in 1859. The other eight books were not completed until 1888.

Teaching Options

The Passing of Arthur

80 What good should follow this, if this were done?
    What harm, undone? Deep harm to disobey,
    Seeing obedience is the bond of rule.
    Were it well to obey then, if a king demand
    An act unprofitable, against himself?
85 The King is sick, and knows not what he does.
    What record or what relic of my lord
    Should be to aftertime, but empty breath
    And rumors of a doubt? But were this kept,
    Stored in some treasure-house of mighty kings,
90 Some one might show it at a joust of arms,
    Saying: 'King Arthur's sword, Excalibur,
    Wrought° by the lonely Maiden of the Lake.
    Nine years she wrought it, sitting in the deeps
    Upon the hidden bases of the hills.'
95 So might some old man speak in the aftertime
    To all the people, winning reverence.
    But now much honor and much fame were lost."

    So spake he, clouded with his own conceit,°
    And hid Excalibur the second time,
100 And so strode back slow to the wounded King.

    Then spoke King Arthur, breathing heavily:
    "What is it thou hast seen? or what hast heard?"

    And answer made the bold Sir Bedivere:
    "I heard the water lapping on the crag,
105 And the long ripple washing in the reeds."

    To whom replied King Arthur, much in wrath:°
    "Ah miserable, and unkind, untrue,
    Unknightly, traitor-hearted! Woe is me!
    Authority forgets a dying king,
110 Laid widow'd of the power in his eye
    That bow'd the will. I see thee what thou art,
    For thou, the latest-left of all my knights,
    In whom should meet the offices° of all,
    Thou wouldst betray me for the precious hilt;
115 Either from lust of gold, or like a girl
    Valuing the giddy pleasure of the eyes.
    Yet, for a man may fail in duty twice,
    And the third time may prosper, get thee hence;

92 **Wrought:** shaped by hand.

98 **conceit:** thought, idea, or concept.

106 **wrath:** anger.

113 **offices:** duties and responsibilities.

948 UNIT 5

Listening and Speaking *Minilesson*

Expressing Emotions King Arthur's monologue in lines 107–120 expresses several intense emotions: anger, sadness, self-pity, and disappointment. Discuss ways to use vocal pitch, volume, speed, and emphasis to express feelings. For example, a sad person might speak more slowly, deeply, and quietly than an angry person.

Activity Have students work in small groups and discuss the various emotions Arthur displays in the speech. Then have each student read the monologue in such a way as to emphasize one of the emotions discussed. Have the other students in the group identify the emphasized emotion. **L2** **COLLAB. LEARN.**

But, if thou spare to fling Excalibur,
120   I will arise and slay thee with my hands."

    Then quickly rose Sir Bedivere, and ran,
And, leaping down the ridges lightly, plunged
Among the bulrush beds, and clutch'd the sword,
And strongly wheel'd and threw it. The great brand
125   Made lightnings in the splendor of the moon,
And flashing round and round, and whirl'd in an arch,
Shot like a streamer of the northern morn,°
Seen where the moving isles of winter° shock
By night, with noises of the Northern sea.
130   So flash'd and fell the brand Excalibur;
But ere he dipt the surface, rose an arm
Clothed in white samite, mystic, wonderful,
And caught him by the hilt, and brandish'd him
Three times, and drew him under in the mere.
135   And lightly went the other to the King.

    Then spoke King Arthur, drawing thicker breath:
"Now see I by thine eyes that this is done.
Speak out; what is it thou hast heard, or seen?"

    And answer made the bold Sir Bedivere:
140   "Sir King, I closed mine eyelids, lest the gems
Should blind my purpose, for I never saw,
Nor shall see, here or elsewhere, till I die,
Not tho' I live three lives of mortal men,
So great a miracle as yonder hilt.
145   Then with both hands I flung him, wheeling him;
But when I look'd again, behold an arm,
Clothed in white samite, mystic, wonderful,
That caught him by the hilt, and brandish'd him
Three times, and drew him under in the mere."

150   And answer made King Arthur, breathing hard:
"My end draws nigh; 't is time that I were gone.
Make broad thy shoulders to receive my weight,
And bear me to the margin;° yet I fear
My wound hath taken cold, and I shall die."

155   So saying, from the pavement he half rose,
Slowly, with pain, reclining on his arm,

127 streamer of the northern morn: the northern lights.
128 isles of winter: floating ice or icebergs.

153 margin: the land bordering the lake.

J Author's Craft

FIGURES OF SPEECH: *Metaphor, Simile,* and *Personification* Have students point out and explain three figures of speech in lines 121–135 and explain why Tennyson might use figurative language at this point in the poem. *("The great brand made lightnings in the splendor of the moon" is a metaphor; the reflection of the sword flying through the air looks like lightning. It "shot like a streamer of the northern morn" is a simile comparing the sword's reflection to the northern lights. Calling Excalibur "he" is personification, giving human traits to an inanimate object. Tennyson uses figurative language because this is a climactic moment of the poem; he emphasizes the mystical and symbolic qualities of the sword.)*

K Active Reading

RESPOND Have students describe their responses to King Arthur's words in lines 151–154. How does Tennyson's diction and the use of blank verse affect one's response? *(Students may have a sad, emotional response to the king's knowledge that he is about to die. Tennyson's use of formal, dignified language and blank verse may intensify this response by understating the drama of the situation.)*

MEETING INDIVIDUAL NEEDS — INCLUSION STRATEGIES

Less-Proficient Readers One element that may make the selection difficult for less-proficient readers is the use of "poetic" words with abstract meanings that are rarely used in informal writing or conversation today.

Activity Write the following words on the board. Have students read a sentence in which each appears and then use each in a sentence of their own.
1. whereof (line 4)
2. bade (line 69)
3. ere (line 131)
4. lest (line 140)
5. nigh (line 151) **L2**

Additional Resources
📁 *Inclusion Strategies*

FYI

The Sword Excalibur

In Malory's *Le Morte d'Arthur*, the history of Excalibur is told in the first section of the work, "The Tale of King Arthur." After Arthur is crowned king, he uses his magical sword Excalibur to defeat several kings who have come to attack him. The sword is said to gleam in his enemies' eyes like twenty torches. Later, Arthur is beaten in a fight by an evil knight, Sir Pellanor, and loses his sword. Merlin leads him to a magical lake where the Lady of the Lake thrusts the sword out of the water. She agrees to give Arthur the sword back if he will perform a favor that she will ask for in the future. She demands the favor, revenge against an enemy, in the next section, "The Knight with the Two Swords."

How Sir Bedivere Cast the Sword Excalibur Into the Water, 1893–1894. Aubrey Beardsley. Illustration for *Le Morte d'Arthur*, London: Dent.

Viewing the art: What does this image convey about Sir Bedivere's feelings on returning Excalibur to the lake? Does the poem convey the same emotions? Explain.

950 💮 UNIT 5

Teaching Options

Alfred, Lord Tennyson ⁓

And looking wistfully° with wide blue eyes
As in a picture. Him Sir Bedivere
Remorsefully regarded thro' his tears,
160   And would have spoken, but he found not words;
Then took with care, and kneeling on one knee,
O'er both his shoulders drew the languid° hands,
And rising bore him thro' the place of tombs.

But, as he walk'd, King Arthur panted hard,
165   Like one that feels a nightmare on his bed
When all the house is mute. So sigh'd the King,
Muttering and murmuring at his ear, "Quick, quick!
I fear it is too late, and I shall die."
But the other swiftly strode from ridge to ridge,
170   Clothed with his breath, and looking, as he walk'd,
Larger than human on the frozen hills.
He heard the deep behind him, and a cry
Before. His own thought drove him like a goad.°
Dry clash'd his harness° in the icy caves
175   And barren chasms,° and all to left and right
The bare black cliff clang'd round him, as he based
His feet on juts of slippery crag that rang
Sharp-smitten with the dint of armed heels°—
And on a sudden, lo, the level lake,
180   And the long glories of the winter moon!

Then saw they how there hove° a dusky barge,
Dark as a funeral scarf from stem to stern,
Beneath them; and descending they were ware°
That all the decks were dense with stately forms,
185   Black-stoled, black-hooded, like a dream—by these
Three queens with crowns of gold—and from them rose
A cry that shiver'd to the tingling stars,
And, as it were one voice, an agony
Of lamentation, like a wind that shrills
190   All night in a waste land, where no one comes,
Or hath come, since the making of the world.

Then murmur'd Arthur, "Place me in the barge."
So to the barge they came. There those three queens
Put forth their hands, and took the King, and wept.
195   But she that rose the tallest of them all
And fairest laid his head upon her lap,

---

157 wistfully: with sad longing; yearningly.

162 languid: weak; lacking vitality.

173 goad: a sharp stick used for driving cattle.
174 Dry clash'd his harness: His armor creaked or grated.
175 barren chasms (kaz′ əmz): lifeless cracks or gorges.
178 dint of armed heels: impact of armored feet.

181 hove: floated into sight.

183 ware: aware.

L Literary Elements

MOOD Have students identify the mood of the poem and some words and phrases that communicate the mood in the first stanza on page 951. *(The mood may be described as melancholy, sad, tragic, or depressing, communicated in words and phrases such as wistfully, remorsefully, languid, and "the place of tombs.")*

M Active Reading

IMAGINE Encourage students to picture the scene created in lines 169–191. Have them identify images that appeal to three senses and describe the mood created by the scene. *(Images that appeal to sight include "the long glories of the winter moon"; sound, "dry clash'd his harness" and "a cry that shiver'd to the tingling stars"; touch, "the frozen hills." The mood is bleak and spooky.)*

N Active Reading

PREDICT After reading through line 191, have students predict how the three queens will treat Arthur. How are their expectations realized or not in the next stanza? *(Students may say they expect the frightening figures to mistreat Arthur; it is surprising in the next stanza when they show deep love and affection for him.)*

Writing *Minilesson*

Using Similes Tennyson describes the funeral barge as "dark as a funeral scarf from stem to stern" and the voices of the queens "like a wind that shrills all night in a waste land." Remind students that a simile compares two unlike things, using the word *like* or *as*. Tennyson's similes intensify the bleak, dark mood he has created.

Activity Have students think of a place with a particular mood, such as solemnity (a church) or wild enthusiasm (a basketball game). Have them write several similes to describe the place and its mood.
L2

Additional Resources

📓 *Writer's Choice,* Lesson 5.2

0 Literary Elements

CHARACTERS The description of the dying King Arthur also indicates what he was like in life. Have students describe his physical appearance and character as indicated by the contrast with his dying moments. *(He was handsome and dynamic, with curly hair and a mustache. He was a strong, brave fighter.)*

The Passing of Arthur, 1875. Julia Margaret Cameron. Sepia-toned photograph to illustrate *Idylls of the King and other poems.*

Viewing the art: How would you describe the tone of this photograph? Is the same tone reflected in the poem's description of Arthur's departure in the barge? Explain.

And loosed the shatter'd casque,° and chafed° his hands,
And call'd him by his name, complaining loud,
And dropping bitter tears against a brow
200   Striped with dark blood; for all his face was white
And colorless, and like the wither'd moon
Smote by the fresh beam of the springing east;°
And all his greaves and cuisses° dash'd with drops
Of onset;° and the light and lustrous curls—
205   That made his forehead like a rising sun
High from the dais-throne—were parch'd with dust,
Or, clotted into points and hanging loose,
Mixt with the knightly growth that fringed his lips.
So like a shatter'd column lay the King;
210   Not like that Arthur who, with lance in rest,
From spur to plume a star of tournament,
Shot thro' the lists° at Camelot, and charged
Before the eyes of ladies and of kings.

Then loudly cried the bold Sir Bedivere:
215   "Ah! my Lord Arthur, whither shall I go?

197 casque (kask): helmet. **chafed:** restored warmth by rubbing.

202 Smote . . . east: struck by the first light of dawn.
203 greaves and cuisses (kwis′ as): pieces of armor covering the legs.
204 onset: the early stages of dying, signified by spattered blood from battle wounds.

212 lists: the field in which tournaments took place.

Teaching Options

MEETING INDIVIDUAL NEEDS — GIFTED AND TALENTED

Reading Other Idylls The themes in "The Passing of Arthur" become clearer in the context of the other books of the idylls. Students who enjoy "The Passing of Arthur" may wish to read another part of Tennyson's *Idylls of the King.*

Activity Have students locate a copy of *Idylls of the King* and read another of the idylls. Explain that Tennyson used a seasonal motif. Spring is represented by Arthur's introduction in the first book, "The Coming of Arthur." Other books that students may find interesting are the eighth book, "The Holy Grail," and the ninth, "Pelleas and Ettarre," which Tennyson called almost the saddest of all. Have students give an oral or written report about the characters and themes of the poem. **L3**

Where shall I hide my forehead and my eyes?
For now I see the true old times are dead,
When every morning brought a noble chance,
And every chance brought out a noble knight.
220   Such times have been not since the light that led
The holy Elders with the gift of myrrh.°
But now the whole Round Table° is dissolved
Which was an image of the mighty world;
And I, the last, go forth companionless,
225   And the days darken round me, and the years,
Among new men, strange faces, other minds."

    And slowly answer'd Arthur from the barge:
"The old order changeth yielding place to new,
And God fulfils himself in many ways,
230   Lest one good custom should corrupt the world.
Comfort thyself; what comfort is in me?
I have lived my life, and that which I have done
May He within himself make pure! but thou,
If thou shouldst never see my face again,
235   Pray for my soul. More things are wrought by prayer
Than this world dreams of. Wherefore, let thy voice
Rise like a fountain for me night and day.
For what are men better than sheep or goats
That nourish a blind life within the brain,
240   If, knowing God, they lift not hands of prayer
Both for themselves and those who call them friend?
For so the whole round earth is every way
Bound by gold chains about the feet of God.
But now farewell. I am going a long way
245   With these thou seest—if indeed I go—
For all my mind is clouded with a doubt—
To the island-valley of Avilion;°
Where falls not hail, or rain, or any snow,
Nor ever wind blows loudly; but it lies
250   Deep-meadow'd, happy, fair with orchard lawns
And bowery hollows° crown'd with summer sea,
Where I will heal me of my grievous wound."

    So said he, and the barge with oar and sail
Moved from the brink, like some full-breasted swan
255   That, fluting a wild carol ere her death,°
Ruffles her pure cold plume, and takes the flood°

220–221 the light . . . myrrh: the light from a star guided the **holy Elders,** the three kings who came to see the baby Jesus. They brought precious gifts, including *myrrh,* a fragrant substance used in incense and perfumes.

222 Round Table: the association of King Arthur and his knights; also the circular table at which they sat.

247 Avilion: an alternate spelling of *Avalon.* Medieval legends describe this island, and its castle, as being "not far on this side of paradise."

251 bowery hollows: shallow valleys shaded by overhanging trees and vines.

255 fluting . . . death: According to legend, a swan sings just before it dies.

256 flood: the deep water.

P Critical Thinking

INFERRING You may use the following model to help students make an inference about the poem's themes.

Model: Not only is Sir Bedivere heartbroken about the death of King Arthur; he says that "the true old times are dead." I think that King Arthur was admired not only for his personal qualities, but for what he came to represent: hope and striving in the world, and the ability of one good man or a group of good men to make a difference in the world.

Q Literary Elements

CHARACTERS Have students discuss King Arthur's philosophy of life and death as shown in his last speech. *(He says that life is full of change, and that those he leaves behind should not despair just because he is gone but should find new leaders to believe in. He believes that after death he is going to a peaceful place.)*

R Author's Craft

THEME What ideas about religious faith emerge in Arthur's last speech? *(Tennyson says that prayer is powerful and that people are no better than animals if they do not show faith in God through prayer.)*

S Literary Elements

IMAGERY Have students summarize the nature of Avilion. *(It is a paradise where the weather is perfect and the natural surroundings are beautiful.)*

INTERDISCIPLINARY CONNECTION

History Tennyson's affirmation of religious faith is indicative of the reconsideration of religious matters conducted by many writers of the Victorian period. Scientific developments in the mid-nineteenth century changed people's thinking about the nature of the universe and how it had been created. Many people felt that the new scientific thinking threatened traditional religious teachings. Charles Darwin's theories especially made many thinkers upset by the involvement of science in matters previously left up to religion and philosophy.

Activity Have students research scientific advancement, especially that of Darwin, in the mid- to late-nineteenth century. Encourage them to find out how science affected the social structure and philosophy of the nineteenth century. Have them record their findings for oral or written reports. **L3**

Edward Burne-Jones (1833–1898), a leading figure in the second phase of the Pre-Raphaelite movement, often chose medieval subjects and themes.

Viewing Response *The grief shown by the people in the painting suggests that they had an overwhelming love and respect for him.*

Avalon Avalon, or the Vale of the Blessed, was a place in Celtic and medieval romances where heroes dwelled after death.

T **Author's Craft**

SYMBOLISM Have students define the word *hull* (the body of a boat), looking it up in a dictionary if necessary. Have them explain what the barge might symbolize. *(The barge symbolizes death.)*

U **Literary Elements**

CHARACTERS Have students discuss how Sir Bedivere's reactions to Arthur's death change. How does he feel at the end of the poem? *(At first he is grief-stricken. When he realizes that the "dark queens" had come before and told Arthur they would help him when he needed it, he becomes more reconciled to Arthur's death. He sees hope in the future.)*

Teaching Options

Grammar and Language *Minilesson*

Adverbs Remind students that adverbs modify verbs, adjectives, or other adverbs. Many adverbs end in *-ly*. Point out that in line 100 on page 948 *slow* is an adverb. Tennyson leaves off the *-ly* ending to make it fit the iambic pentameter line.

Activity Point out the following lines from the poem. Have students correct the lines where an adverb has not been written correctly.

1. And lightly went the other to the King. (line 135) *(Correct)*
2. She call'd him by his name, complaining loud, and dropping bitter tears. (lines 198–199) *(loudly)*
3. So strode he back slow to the wounded King. (line 53) *(slowly)*
4. Take Excalibur, and fling him far into the middle mere. (line 24) *(Correct)* **L2**

Additional Resources

📖 *Grammar and Language Transparency 69*

📕 *Grammar and Language Workbook,* p. 63

📕 *Grammar and Composition Handbook,* Lesson 1.5

📗 *Writer's Choice,* Lesson 10.5

T

With swarthy webs. Long stood Sir Bedivere
Revolving many memories, till the hull
Look'd one black dot against the verge of dawn,
260   And on the mere the wailing died away.

But when that moan had past for evermore,
The stillness of the dead world's winter dawn
Amazed him, and he groan'd, "The King is gone."
And therewithal came on him the weird rhyme,
265   "From the great deep to the great deep he goes."°

Whereat he slowly turn'd and slowly clomb°
The last hard footstep of that iron crag,
Thence mark'd the black hull moving yet, and cried:
"He passes to be king among the dead,
270   And after healing of his grievous wound
He comes again; but—if he come no more—
O me, be yon dark queens in yon black boat,
Who shriek'd and wail'd, the three whereat we gazed
On that high day, when, clothed with living light,
275   They stood before his throne in silence, friends
Of Arthur, who should help him at his need?"°

U

Then from the dawn it seem'd there came, but faint
As from beyond the limit of the world,
Like the last echo born of a great cry,
280   Sounds, as if some fair city were one voice
Around a king returning from his wars.

Thereat once more he moved about, and clomb
Even to the highest he could climb, and saw,
Straining his eyes beneath an arch of hand,
285   Or thought he saw, the speck that bare the King,
Down that long water opening on the deep
Somewhere far off, pass on and on, and go
From less to less and vanish into light.
And the new sun rose bringing the new year.

V

❧

The Sleep of Arthur in Avalon, 1880–1898 (detail). Edward Burne-Jones.
Oil on canvas, 9 ft 3 in x 21 ft 2 in. Museo de Arte de Ponce, Puerto Rico.

Viewing the painting: What do the expressions and activities of the
people in this painting suggest to you about people's regard for Arthur?

265 "From the great deep . . . goes":
the last line of a rhyme that Merlin recites
in "The Coming of Arthur" from *Idylls of
the King,* in answer to a question about
Arthur's origin.
266 clomb: climbed.

**272–276 yon dark queens . . . at his
need:** "The Coming of Arthur" describes
three queens who appeared when Arthur
was crowned king.

V ▐ **Literary Elements**

NARRATIVE POETRY Have students
discuss how the final line of the
poem resolves the major conflicts
of the poem. *("The new sun" and
"the new year" represent change and
hope. Sir Bedivere's and King Arthur's
conflicts revolve around coming to
terms with Arthur's death. Although
his death is tragic, the last line
asserts that there is hope for the
future.)*

® *The following videotape
program is available from Glencoe.
Be sure to preview the video for
appropriateness for your class.*

• **Ancient Mysteries: Camelot**

Thematic Focus

Heroism Have students discuss the
aspect of heroism with which "The
Passing of Arthur" deals. *(the
inevitable death of heroic figures)*
Have them consider what Tennyson
says about how ordinary people deal
with an event like the one described
in the poem.

✔ **ASSESSMENT OPTIONS**

📁 *Quick Checks,* p. 80

Reading *Minilesson*

Identifying Author's Purpose

Determining the author's purpose can
help students identify the themes of the
poem. Point out that most stories about
King Arthur emphasize the adventures of
Arthur and the other Knights. Have students identify the purpose of those stories. *(to entertain and inspire wonder)*

Activity Point out that Tennyson's "The

Passing of Arthur" describes a different
type of event and has a different mood
than those stories. Have students identify
and discuss Tennyson's purpose in the
poem. *(to evoke strong feeling and thinking about the nature of heroes and the
death of heroes)* **L2**

Additional Resources

📁 *Reading Workbook,* pp. 81–82

Personal Response

Students may say they reacted with sadness or pity to Sir Bedivere's comments about the passing away of the age of King Arthur.

ANALYZING LITERATURE

1. King Arthur is gravely wounded and dying. He expresses sorrow that the days of glorious knighthood are gone.
2. King Arthur tells Sir Bedivere to throw the sword into the lake, watch what happens, and report back to him.
3. Sir Bedivere twice decides not to throw the sword into the lake. Instead he hides it in the plants by the water. Finally, he throws the sword into the water and sees an arm catch the sword, brandish it, and then disappear into the water.
4. Sir Bedivere escorts King Arthur to the edge of the lake. A barge with three queens aboard approaches and King Arthur gets on it, where he dies.
5. Sir Bedivere reacts with grief that King Arthur's passing means the end of the Round Table and its way of life. Arthur tells Bedivere that it is natural for things to change and that Bedivere should pray for King Arthur's soul.
6. King Arthur feels great sadness at the passing of Camelot. He says, "I think that we shall never more, at any future time, delight our souls with talk of knightly deeds."
7. King Arthur gives the order regarding the sword because he is dying and wants to return it to the place it came from.
8. Sir Bedivere doesn't want the beautiful sword, "which might have pleased the eyes of many men," to be lost forever; he wants to keep a relic to remind people of King Arthur.
9. The barge and the three queens might represent death.
10. Arthur seems resigned to his death and looks forward to Avilion, or paradise. Sir Bedivere is distraught and grief-stricken over Arthur's death.
11. Students may say Sir Bedivere is justified in hesitating to follow King Arthur's orders because the sword is magical and unique; or that he is not justified because he should trust Arthur and follow his orders unquestioningly.
12. Students may find the original title unsuitable because there are not strong instances of falseness in this part of the poem; or they may find it suitable because the poem

Responding to Literature

Personal Response

How did you react to Sir Bedivere's comments about the passing away of the age of King Arthur and his knights?

ANALYZING LITERATURE

RECALL

1. As this excerpt begins, what is King Arthur's condition and what thoughts does he express?
2. What does King Arthur direct Sir Bedivere to do with the sword?
3. Summarize how Sir Bedivere reacts to King Arthur's order and what he does with Excalibur.
4. Where does Sir Bedivere escort King Arthur? What happens there?
5. How does Sir Bedivere react to Arthur's leaving, and how does Arthur respond?

INTERPRET

6. Judging from what he says in the first stanza, how does King Arthur feel about the passing of Camelot? Use details from the poem to support your answer.
7. Why does King Arthur give the order regarding the sword?
8. How does Sir Bedivere justify his failure to follow Arthur's orders? Cite lines from the poem to support your response.
9. What might the barge and the three queens **symbolize**, or represent?
10. How would you characterize Arthur's feelings about his impending death? How do his feelings compare with Sir Bedivere's?

EVALUATE AND CONNECT

11. Do you think Sir Bedivere is justified in hesitating to follow King Arthur's orders regarding Excalibur? Why or why not?
12. Tennyson had once intended to name his poem sequence *The False and the True* instead of *Idylls of the King*. Based on the characters in this poem, how well do you think the original title applies?
13. How do the reactions you described in the Focus Activity on page 944 compare with Sir Bedivere's reactions to parting, both with the sword and with the era of the Round Table? Explain.
14. With whom do you identify more, King Arthur or Sir Bedivere? Why?
15. The **mood** of this poem has been described as pessimistic but hopeful. Citing specific details, explain how Tennyson creates this contradictory mood. (See Literary Terms Handbook, page R8.)

Literary ELEMENTS

Narrative Poetry
Narrative poetry tells a story. It evolved from the oral tradition of passing down stories from generation to generation. Narrative poetry contains many of the same elements as a short story, such as setting, characters, plot, conflict, and theme. The two main types of narrative poetry are the **ballad** and the **epic**. Typically, ballads tell in a simple, dramatic way a popular, usually tragic, story or legend. Epics, such as *Idylls of the King*, run longer and use elevated or stately language, such as, "It is not meet, Sir King, to leave thee thus, / Aidless, alone, and smitten thro' the helm." Epics celebrate the great deeds of legendary heroes such as King Arthur.

1. Summarize the plot of "The Passing of Arthur."
2. Identify an internal and an external conflict in the narrative.
● See **Literary Terms Handbook**, p. R8.

Anglo-Saxon and Celtic jewelry. 1st–7th century A.D. Bronze.

concerns true heroism and being true to one's hero.
13. Students should refer specifically to Sir Bedivere's deep sorrow in parting with the sword and their own journal entries.
14. Students may identify more with Sir Bedivere because it is more common to watch a hero's passing than to be a hero.
15. Sir Bedivere's dismay at the passing of a heroic era gives the poem a pessimistic tone. However, Arthur's advice to accept change, and the last line in which "the new sun rose bringing the new year" indicate that there is hope for the future.

LITERARY ELEMENTS

1. One possible summary is given on page 945.
2. An external conflict is Bedivere's disagreement with Arthur over discarding the sword. An internal conflict is Arthur's resigning himself to death.

Additional Resources
Literary Elements Transparency 80

LITERATURE AND WRITING

Writing About Literature

Evaluate Character Behavior Tennyson held true to the concept that faith and commitment must stand at the center of the human character or else character will falter and fail. Write an evaluation of the way Tennyson presents ideas of faith and commitment to oneself and one's fellow human beings in "The Passing of Arthur." Share your evaluation with the class.

Creative Writing

The Last Knight What do you think happens to Sir Bedivere, the last of King Arthur's knights, after the events described in this excerpt? Write a **narrative**–in verse or prose–telling what becomes of Sir Bedivere.

EXTENDING YOUR RESPONSE

Literature Groups

A Hero for All Time? Critic William Vaughn Moody and poet Robert Morss Lovett said that *Idylls of the King* "spoke more eloquently to Victorian than to modern readers." Do you agree or disagree? What qualities does Tennyson bestow on Arthur that might put him out of touch with today's readers? What heroic qualities does he have that give him timeless appeal? What traits would you add to or take away from Arthur to make him more appealing as a hero today? Discuss these questions in your group. Share your group's ideas with the rest of your classmates.

Learning for Life

Long Live the King Use details in "The Passing of Arthur" and information you learned from previously read works or from research to write King Arthur's obituary for *The Arthurian Times.* In preparation, you might read obituaries of celebrated leaders of modern times and note

the kinds of information typically included, such as a brief biographical account, the circumstances of the person's death, personal accomplishments, quotations attributed to the person, and tributes from people close to the person.

Interdisciplinary Activity

Art: Magazine Cover Imagine that *Idylls of the King* has been made into a twelve-week television miniseries. Design a television guide magazine cover that promotes the last episode, which is based on "The Passing of Arthur."

Reading Further

If you enjoyed "The Passing of Arthur," you might want to read these other poems by Tennyson:

The other eleven poems in *Idylls of the King.*

"Merlin and the Gleam" from *A Collection of Poems by Alfred Tennyson.*

📖 **Save your work for your portfolio.**

St. Mawes Castle, Cornwall, 1821. John Chessell Buckler. Watercolor over pencil on paper, 25.4 x 35.6 cm. Mallett Gallery, London.

Writing About Literature

Students' evaluations should
- discuss Tennyson's ideas about faith and commitment.
- give specific examples of how Tennyson communicates his ideas.

Creative Writing

Students' narratives should
- show knowledge of the narrative form.
- relate events in the life of Sir Bedivere.

EXTENDING YOUR RESPONSE

Literature Groups Suggest that students compile a list of Arthur's qualities based on Tennyson's poem to begin their discussions. **COLLAB. LEARN.**

Learning for Life Encourage students to use quotations from "The Passing of Arthur" and a tribute from Sir Bedivere in their obituaries.

Interdisciplinary Activity Encourage students to consider the mood of the proposed program and of their illustration before beginning.

✔ ASSESSMENT OPTIONS

📁 *Quick Checks,* p. 80

📁 *Selection and Theme Assessment,* pp. 151–152

📁 *Performance Assessment,* p. 78

💾 *Testmaker*

Skill Minilessons

Subject-Verb Agreement

Practice

1. King Arthur; issues
2. Sir Bedivere; carries
3. queens; were
4. stories; do
5. Sir Launcelot; was

Paraphrasing

One response: A king loses his authority when he is dying and has lost the look in his eye that made people obey him. I see that you, my last knight, who should obey me for all those who are gone, may disobey me because the sword is valuable or beautiful.

Semantic Mapping

1. unsolder; **Definition:** to take apart; **Synonyms:** undo, break, destroy; **Example:** The argument threatened to unsolder their friendship.
2. mystic; **Definition:** having magical properties; **Synonyms:** occult, mysterious; **Example:** The magician claimed to have mystic powers.
3. fealty; **Definition:** the fidelity of a feudal tenant to his lord; **Synonyms:** allegiance, loyalty; **Example:** The vassal pledged fealty to the nobleman.
4. wistfully; **Definition:** in a manner full of yearning or musingly sad; **Synonyms:** nostalgically, longingly; **Example:** The girl looked at the puppy in the pet store wistfully.
5. languid; **Definition:** drooping from or as if from exhaustion; **Synonyms:** weak, listless; **Example:** The lounging students looked languid.

Additional Resources

📘 *Grammar and Composition Handbook,* Lesson 6.1

📘 *Grammar and Language Workbook,* p. 167

📗 *Writer's Choice,* Lesson 16.1

📁 *Reading Workbook,* pp. 81–82

📁 *Vocabulary Practice*

Skill Minilessons

GRAMMAR AND LANGUAGE • Subject-Verb Agreement

An **inverted sentence** is one in which the subject follows the verb. "The Passing of Arthur" contains many inverted sentences, such as: "So strode he back slow to the wounded King." Following standard word order, the line would read: "He strode back slowly to the wounded King." The verb in an inverted sentence must always agree with the subject in number and person.

PRACTICE On your paper, underline the simple subject in each of the following sentences. Then write the form of the verb in parentheses that agrees with the subject.

1. With his dying breaths (issue, issues) the noble King Arthur orders to cast away Excalibur.
2. Upon his shoulders (carry, carries) Sir Bedivere the weight of the wounded king.
3. There (was, were) three queens upon the barge.
4. (Does, Do) these stories still enchant readers?
5. Among King Arthur's knights (was, were) Sir Launcelot.

APPLY Underline the subject and the verb in three examples of inverted sentences in "The Passing of Arthur."

● For more about subject-verb agreement, see **Language Handbook,** p. R17.

READING AND THINKING • Paraphrasing

When you paraphrase a passage, you tell what happens in your own words. You can improve your comprehension of "The Passing of Arthur" by restating difficult passages in your own words. Study this example.

> "The sequel of today unsolders all / The goodliest fellowship of famous knights / Whereof this world holds record."

> *What follows from today is the breakup of the best association of knights the world has ever seen.*

PRACTICE On your paper, paraphrase the following passage from "The Passing of Arthur."

> "Authority forgets a dying king, / Laid widow'd of the power in his eye / That bow'd the will. I see thee what thou art, / For thou, the latest-left of all my knights, / In whom should meet the offices of all, / Thou wouldst betray me for the precious hilt; / Either from lust of gold, or like a girl / Valuing the giddy pleasure of the eyes."

● For more about paraphrasing, see **Reading Handbook,** p. R91.

VOCABULARY • Semantic Mapping

To learn a new or difficult word, try making a **semantic map**—a simple diagram that explains the meaning of the word. A semantic map consists of a definition, a few synonyms, and an example of the word used in context.

sequel —— **Definition:** what follows something

—— **Synonyms:** result, consequence, outcome

—— **Example:** He suffered nightmares as a sequel of the battle.

PRACTICE Using a dictionary, create a semantic map for each of the following words.

1. unsolder   3. fealty   5. languid
2. mystic   4. wistfully

APPLY Find five unfamiliar words in "The Passing of Arthur" and create semantic maps for them.

Arthurian Sites of England

The magical stories of King Arthur and his knights live on not only in literature but also in the geography of England. From the former county of Cornwall on the southwestern coast to the far northern reaches of England stretch sites where King Arthur is believed to have fought, ruled, and died. These sites, whether actual haunts of a historical person or part of a myth, help keep King Arthur's story—and his mystique—alive.

According to legend, Arthur was conceived at **Tintagil,** where a ruined castle still stands. Only a few miles inland, the village of **Slaughter Bridge** lays claim to being the site where Arthur waged his final battle. Nearby is Bodmin Moor, where a pond called **Dozmary Pool** lies. Into this pond Sir Bedivere supposedly cast Arthur's sword, Excalibur.

The **Isle of Avilion,** Arthur's supposed burial place, may actually be a hill called the Tor near the small town of **Glastonbury.** In Celtic folklore, Avilion was an enchanted island. Long ago, the Tor was surrounded by watery marshland. From most angles, it would have appeared as an island rising from the marshy mists.

Glastonbury also features the ruins of a medieval abbey, or monastery. In 1191 monks at the **Glastonbury Abbey** claimed that they had discovered King Arthur's grave. Digging in their cemetery, they supposedly unearthed a lead cross bearing the Latin words "Here lies buried the renowned King Arthur in the Isle of Avilion." Deeper down, they found a coffin containing the bones of a tall man with a damaged skull.

And what about **Camelot,** Arthur's supposed kingdom? The most famous of the reputed sites of Camelot is **Cadbury Castle,** a hill-fort near the village of South Cadbury. Excavations at the site showed that a large fortress stood on the hill during the supposed time of Arthur. A local legend has it that on Christmas Eve, hoofbeats can be heard as the ghosts of King Arthur and his knights gallop on horses through the ancient gateway of the castle.

The lure of King Arthur remains entrenched in English culture and geography.

Map inset legend:
1. **Tintagil:** King Uther and Lady Igraine conceive Arthur.
2. **Slaughter Bridge:** Modred wounds Arthur.
3. **Bodmin Moor:** Sir Bedivere casts Excalibur into Dozmary Pool.
4. **Glastonbury Tor:** Arthur dies on the Isle of Avilion.
5. **Cadbury Castle:** Arthur holds court in Camelot.

Map labels: WALES, ENGLAND, London, Glastonbury Tor, Cadbury Castle, Tintagil, Slaughter Bridge, Bodmin Moor, English Channel

Activity

Find out more about the Arthurian legends behind these and other sites. Look for information on the Internet and in encyclopedias, books, and journals. You may even write to a tourist bureau in England for information. Then compile your research in a travel brochure outlining a tour of Arthurian England.

Objective
- To identify places associated with King Arthur

Teaching Strategies

Call attention to the numbered inset on the map. Ask a volunteer to explain how it is to be used in relation to the map. Then discuss with students each of the places and why that place is associated with King Arthur.

Activity

Students' projects should
- include a tour that follows a logical sequence and could actually be taken.
- contain interesting information that would motivate a traveler to want to take the tour.

Teaching Options

MEETING INDIVIDUAL NEEDS — MULTIPLE LEARNING STYLES

Spatial Spatial learners sometimes find it helpful to literally draw a picture of what they are reading. The text and the map offer suggestions for places spatial learners could draw and, in the process, help fellow classmates picture.

Activity Suggest that students choose one of the places and do some research on it. Ask students to sketch features of the place, such as a castle, pond, or town. Pictures could be displayed. Students who have chosen the same place could compare drawings.
L1

Objective

- To read and understand a screenplay

Literature — **LINK**

The Passing of Arthur This screenplay excerpt connects to "The Passing of Arthur" (pp. 946–955) and "Arthur Becomes King" (pp. 962–973). Explain that the screenplay uses the conventions of the Arthurian legend for humorous purposes.

Respond

Students will likely find the scene funny. Familiarity with the legends of King Arthur makes the scene funnier. The silliness of the screenplay contrasts with the serious, even solemn tone of the legend.

Additional Resources

📁 *Media Connections Activities,* p. 22

Monty Python Encourage students to find information on the Internet on the Monty Python comedians and their films.

Teaching Options

MEDIA
Connection

Screenplay

Humor can be found even in serious material. Read the following excerpt from the screenplay *Monty Python and the Holy Grail* to see how the weighty themes in King Arthur's legends can be spoofed.

from Monty Python and the Holy Grail

by John Cleese, Graham Chapman, Terry Gilliam, Eric Idle, Terry Jones, and Michael Palin

SIR LAUNCELOT
Look, my liege!
[*Trumpets.*]

ARTHUR
Camelot!

SIR GALAHAD
Camelot!

LAUNCELOT
Camelot!

PATSY
It's only a model.

ARTHUR
Shh! Knights, I bid you welcome to your new home. Let us ride . . . to . . . Camelot!
[*In medieval hall.*]

KNIGHTS [*Singing.*]
We're knights of the Round Table.
We dance whene'er we're able.
We do routines and chorus scenes
With footwork impeccable.
We dine well here in Camelot.
We eat ham and jam and spam a lot.
[*Dancing.*]
We're knights of the Round Table.
Our shows are formidable,
But many times we're given rhymes
That are quite unsingable.
We're opera mad in Camelot.
We sing from the diaphragm
  a lot.
[*In dungeon.*]

PRISONER
[*Clap clap clap clap.*]
[*In medieval hall.*]

KNIGHTS [*Tap-dancing.*]
In war we're tough and able,
Quite indefatigable.
Between our guests we sequin vests and
  impersonate Clark Gable.
It's a busy life in Camelot.

MAN
I have to push the pram a lot.
[*Outdoors.*]

ARTHUR
Well, on second thought, let's not go to Camelot. It is a silly place.

KNIGHTS
Right. Right.

Respond

Do you think this scene is funny? Does familiarity with the legends of King Arthur make this scene more funny or less so? Explain your answer.

Reading *Minilesson*

Comparing and Contrasting Point out that the humor of the screenplay comes from the way each of its elements contrasts with the original.

Activity Have students create a chart contrasting the original legend and the humorous screenplay. They might use the headings *King Arthur Legends* and *Monty Python Screenplay* and the categories *Characters, Setting, Dialogue,* and *Tone.* For *Dialogue* under *King Arthur Legends,* students might write "Elegant and noble," while for *Dialogue* under *Monty Python Screenplay,* they might write "Inane, full of improbable rhymes." **L2**

Additional Resources

📁 *Reading Workbook*

Before You Read

Arthur Becomes King

FOCUS ACTIVITY

How would you react if you were suddenly given great responsibility?

SHARING IDEAS Jot down your thoughts about how you would react to a sudden change in your status. How might your friends react?

SETTING A PURPOSE Read to see how one character reacts to a sudden change in status.

BACKGROUND

The Time and Place
This story takes place *somewhere* in England at *some time* during the medieval period when men wore armor and fought with swords. The author refers to the setting simply as "an imaginary world."

Did You Know?
Jousting was one of the most popular sports in Europe during the four-teenth and fifteenth centuries. Jousting involved two armored horsemen charging at each other with lowered spears, or lances. Their goal was to knock their opponent off his horse. Sometimes the jousters merely broke their lances; occasionally they were injured or killed. King Henry II of France died after a jousting tournament in honor of his daughter's marriage.

VOCABULARY PREVIEW

petulantly (pech′ ə lənt lē) *adv.* crankily; in an annoyed way; p. 964

indignantly (in dig′ nənt lē) *adv.* with quiet, dignified anger in response to something unjust, mean, or unworthy; p. 964

vulgar (vul′ gər) *adj.* characterized by a lack of good breeding or good taste; common; crude; p. 966

sumptuous (sump′ chōō əs) *adj.* costly and magnificent; p. 967

desolate (des′ ə lit) *adj.* deserted or uninhabited; p. 967

combatant (kəm bat′ ənt) *n.* one trained for, or engaged in, combat; p. 969

throng (thrông) *v.* to move or gather in large numbers; crowd together; p. 969

ruefully (rōō′ fəl ē) *adv.* regretfully; sorrowfully; p. 970

Meet T. H. White

Terence Hanbury White had an unhappy childhood mainly because his parents frequently fought and occasionally became violent. In a letter to a friend, White wrote that *The Once and Future King* "is more or less a kind of wish-fulfillment of the things I should like to have happened to me when I was a boy."

A scholar of medieval life, White worked as a schoolteacher for six years before quitting to write full time. He became reclusive, avoiding human company and doting on his many pets.

T. H. White was born in Bombay, India, in 1906, but lived most of his life in England. He died in 1964. The Sword in the Stone, the first of four novels in the volume of The Once and Future King, was published in 1938.

LEGENDS 🐾 961

SUMMARY

King Uther has died; he has no heir. But a sword stuck in a stone in London has a sign saying that whoever pulls the sword out in a coming tournament will become king. Kay persuades his father, Sir Ector, to take him and his young squire, the Wart, to London for the tournament. In London, Kay finds he has left his sword at the inn. When the Wart goes to get it, he finds a sword stuck in a stone, which he decides to borrow. With difficulty, he pulls out the sword. Kay claims to have done so but soon admits that the Wart did. Sir Ector and Kay, realizing the Wart is the new king, treat him with a new respect unwelcome to the humble Wart.

📁 *Spanish Summaries,* p. 76

Ⓐ Active Reading

PREDICT After students have read the first six paragraphs of the selection, have them predict how it will differ from other versions of the Arthurian legend.

Additional Resources

📁 *Active Reading Guide,* p. 81
🎧 *Audio Library*
🎧 *Spanish Audio Library*

Teaching Options

Arthur Becomes King

from The Once and future King

T. H. White

KING PELLINORE ARRIVED for the important week-end in a high state of flurry.

"I say," he exclaimed, "do you know? Have you heard? Is it a secret, what?"

"Is what a secret, what?" they asked him.

"Why, the King," cried his majesty. "You know, about the King?"

"What's the matter with the King?" inquired Sir Ector. "You don't say he's comin' down to hunt with those demned hounds of his or anythin' like that?"

"He's dead," cried King Pellinore tragically. "He's dead, poor fellah, and can't hunt any more."

Sir Grummore stood up respectfully and took off his cap of maintenance.

"The King is dead," he said. "Long live the King."

Everybody else felt they ought to stand up too, and the boys' nurse burst into tears.

"There, there," she sobbed. "His loyal highness dead and gone, and him such a respectful gentleman. Many's the illuminated picture I've cut out of him, from the Illustrated Missals,[1] aye, and stuck up over the mantel. From the time when he was in swaddling bands, right through them world towers till he was a-visiting the dispersed areas as the world's Prince Charming, there wasn't a picture of 'im but I had it out, aye, and give 'im a last thought o' nights."

"Compose yourself, Nannie," said Sir Ector.

"It is solemn, isn't it?" said King Pellinore, "what? Uther the Conqueror, 1066 to 1216."

"A solemn moment," said Sir Grummore. "The King is dead. Long live the King."

"We ought to pull down the curtains," said Kay, who was always a stickler[2] for good form, "or half-mast the banners."

---

1. Here, *illuminated* refers to a style of decorating a book in gold, silver, and bright colors; *missals* are, in actuality, prayer books. The writer is pulling the reader's leg here (and will again later) by inserting bits of modern culture into his fictional medieval world. The *Illustrated Missals* seems to be a tabloid–style periodical featuring stories about knights and members of royalty.
2. A *stickler* is someone who insists on having things done in a certain way.

CONNECTING TO OTHER SELECTIONS

The chart at the right shows three ways to connect "Arthur Becomes King" to selections in this book.

For specific teaching strategies, see the *Unit Five Planning Guide,* pages 35–36.

Connection	Title
Life Skills: Problem Solving	→ *Antigone,* p. 727
Thematic: Unexpected Changes	→ "The Ring of General Macías," p. 879
Literary: Tone	→ "The Saleswoman," p. 299

Knights and Ladies Ride Out to a Tourney in London. Late 15th century. Manuscript illustration from *Froissart's Chronicle.*

B **Author's Craft**

DIALECT Remind students that authors sometimes use dialect to indicate how their characters talk. Speech written in dialect reflects the character and background of the person speaking. Have students read aloud some examples of dialect on pages 962–963 and tell what the dialect indicates about the characters. *(The characters use slang and informal language, characterizing them as ordinary people. Characters like Nannie use the Cockney dialect, which characterizes them as being from a different social class and having less education than the noble characters.)*

C **Literary Elements**

TONE Have students identify the tone of the selection and specify the features that communicate it. *(The tone is informal and amusing. The characters' dialect and the narrator's colloquial, informal diction communicate the tone. For example, the narrator says King Pellinore is "in a high state of flurry" and calls the solarium the "solar." Having the characters speak in a contemporary way shows that the author is not taking the legend entirely seriously.)*

"That's right," said Sir Ector. "Somebody go and tell the sergeant-at-arms."[3]

It was obviously the Wart's duty to execute this command, for he was now the junior nobleman present, so he ran out cheerfully to find the sergeant. Soon those who were left in the solar could hear a voice crying out, "Nah then, one two, special mourning fer 'is lite[4] majesty, lower awai on the command Two!" and then the flapping of all the standards, banners, pennons, pennoncells, banderolls, guidons, streamers and cognizances which made gay the snowy turrets of the Forest Sauvage.[5]

"How did you hear?" asked Sir Ector.

"I was pricking through the purlieus of the forest after that Beast, you know, when I met with a solemn friar of orders gray,[6] and he told me. It's the very latest news."

---

3. A *sergeant-at-arms* preserves order and performs minor official duties, for example, at meetings of a court or a legislature.
4. As a small boy, Arthur was nicknamed *Wart.* The *solar,* or *solarium,* is a sunny room or porch. The speaker's accent turns *late,* meaning "recently deceased," into *lite.*
5. The *standards . . . cognizances* are variously shaped flags flying from the small towers, or *turrets,* of Sir Ector's castle, *Forest Sauvage* (sō vazh′). The French word *sauvage* means "savage; wild."
6. The forest's *purlieus* (pur′ lōōz) are its edges, and the *friar of orders gray* is a Roman Catholic monk.

LEGENDS 🦢 963

MEETING INDIVIDUAL NEEDS

ENGLISH LANGUAGE LEARNERS

Understanding Dialect English language learners may have difficulty understanding dialogue that is written in dialect. Explain that in the Cockney dialect, initial *h*'s and other letters are sometimes omitted. These are indicated by apostrophes. Explain that in the upper-class accent spoken by the king, final *g*'s are sometimes omitted. In addition, the author gives the king the habit of adding *what* to his sentences. Point out that this is similar to adding *like* or *you know* to sentences.

Activity Analyze and discuss speeches in dialect as students read the selection.

Additional Resources

📁 *English Language Learners Sourcebook*

D Literary Elements

PLOT Point out that through dialogue, the author provides exposition and introduces the story's conflict. Have students identify the conflict and summarize the background information that leads up to it. *(The conflict is that the king has died and has no heirs to inherit the throne. The characters provide this exposition and introduce the complication of the sword in the stone.)*

E Literary Elements

TONE Have students discuss how the author uses characterization to emphasize his humorous tone. *(Sir Grummore is portrayed as a conservative who thinks the country's institutions are going to the dogs; King Pellinore, Sir Ector, and Sir Grummore are portrayed as absent-minded old men who constantly misunderstand one another.)*

LITERATURE & HUMANITIES

Display *Armor of George Clifford, The Earl of Cumberland* in *Art Talk*, page 288. Have students examine the photograph and discuss why knights might have used armor such as this that was unique and ornate.

"Poor old Pendragon," said Sir Ector.

"The King is dead," said Sir Grummore solemnly. "Long live the King."

"It is all very well for you to keep on mentioning that, my dear Grummore," exclaimed King Pellinore <u>petulantly</u>, "but who is this King, what, that is to live so long, what, accordin' to you?"

"Well, his heir," said Sir Grummore, rather taken aback.[7]

"Our blessed monarch," said the Nurse tearfully, "never had no hair. Anybody that studied the loyal family knowed that."

"Good gracious!" exclaimed Sir Ector. "But he must have had a next-of-kin?"

"That's just it," cried King Pellinore in high excitement. "That's the excitin' part of it, what? No hair and no next of skin, and who's to succeed to the throne? That's what my friar was so excited about, what, and why he was asking who could succeed to what, what? What?"

"Do you mean to tell me," exclaimed Sir Grummore <u>indignantly</u>, "that there ain't no King of Gramarye?"

"Not a scrap of one," cried King Pellinore, feeling important. "And there have been signs and wonders of no mean[8] might."

"I think it's a scandal," said Sir Grummore. "God knows what the dear old country is comin' to. Due to these lollards and communists,[9] no doubt."

---

7. To be *taken aback* is to be suddenly surprised or startled.
8. Here, *mean* means "humble or modest," so signs and wonders of *no mean might* actually have considerable symbolic importance.
9. *Lollards* are lazy good-for-nothings. The writer is also slyly mocking people of his own era by having Sir Grummore see or suspect *communists* nearly everywhere.

"What sort of signs and wonders?" asked Sir Ector.

"Well, there has appeared a sort of sword in a stone, what, in a sort of a church. Not in the church, if you see what I mean, and not in the stone, but that sort of thing, what, like you might say."

"I don't know what the Church is coming to," said Sir Grummore.

"It's in an anvil," explained the King.

"The Church?"

"No, the sword."

"But I thought you said the sword was in the stone?"

"No," said King Pellinore. "The stone is outside the church."

"Look here, Pellinore," said Sir Ector. "You have a bit of a rest, old boy, and start again. Here, drink up this horn of mead[10] and take it easy."

"The sword," said King Pellinore, "is stuck through an anvil which stands on a stone. It goes right through the anvil and into the stone. The anvil is stuck to the stone. The stone stands outside a church. Give me some more mead."

"I don't think that's much of a wonder," remarked Sir Grummore. "What I wonder at is that they should allow such things to happen. But you can't tell nowadays, what with all these Saxon agitators."

"My dear fellah," cried Pellinore, getting excited again, "it's not where the stone is, what, that I'm trying to tell you, but what is written on it, what, where it is."

"What?"

---

10. *Mead* is an alcoholic drink made from honey and, here, is served in a vessel made from the horn of an animal.

Vocabulary

petulantly (pech′ ə lənt lē) *adv.* crankily; in an annoyed way
indignantly (in dig′ nənt lē) *adv.* with quiet, dignified anger in response to something unjust, mean, or unworthy

---

MEETING INDIVIDUAL NEEDS — MULTIPLE LEARNING STYLES

Linguistic T. H. White, who wrote *The Sword in the Stone* in 1938, referred to current events and used slang that was current at that time.

Activity Have students update the dialogue of "Arthur Becomes King" to their own time. Ask them to rewrite the dialogue on page 964 or another portion of dialogue using contemporary language and references. Point out that students do not need to translate each speech. Encourage them to summarize the portion of dialogue and write it in a modern style. Have students read their dialogues aloud. **L3**

Did You Know?
The *pommel* of a sword is a knob at the end of the hilt, or handle.

"Why, on its pommel."

"Come on, Pellinore," said Sir Ector. "You just sit quite still with your face to the wall for a minute, and then tell us what you are talkin' about. Take it easy, old boy. No need for hurryin'. You sit still and look at the wall, there's a good chap, and talk as slow as you can."

"There are words written on this sword in this stone outside this church," cried King Pellinore piteously, "and these words are as follows. Oh, do try to listen to me, you two, instead of interruptin' all the time about nothin', for it makes a man's head go ever so."

"What are these words?" asked Kay.

"These words say this," said King Pellinore, "so far as I can understand from that old friar of orders gray."

"Go on, do," said Kay, for the King had come to a halt.

"Go on," said Sir Ector, "what do these words on this sword in this anvil in this stone outside this church, say?"

"Some red propaganda, no doubt," remarked Sir Grummore.

King Pellinore closed his eyes tight, extended his arms in both directions, and announced in capital letters, "Whoso Pulleth Out This Sword of this Stone and Anvil, is Rightwise King Born of All England."

"Who said that?" asked Sir Grummore.

"But the sword said it, like I tell you."

"Talkative weapon," remarked Sir Grummore sceptically.

"It was written on it," cried the King angrily. "Written on it in letters of gold."

"Why didn't you pull it out then?" asked Sir Grummore.

"But I tell you that I wasn't there. All this that I am telling you was told to me by that friar I was telling you of, like I tell you."

"Has this sword with this inscription been pulled out?" inquired Sir Ector.

"No," whispered King Pellinore dramatically. "That's where the whole excitement comes in. They can't pull this sword out at all, although they have all been tryin' like fun, and so they have had to proclaim a tournament all over England, for New Year's Day, so that the man who comes to the tournament and pulls out the sword can be King of all England for ever, what, I say?"

"Oh, father," cried Kay. "The man who pulls that sword out of the stone will be the King of England. Can't we go to the tournament, father, and have a shot?"

"Couldn't think of it," said Sir Ector.

"Long way to London," said Sir Grummore, shaking his head.

"My father went there once," said King Pellinore.

Kay said, "Oh, surely we could go? When I am knighted I shall have to go to a tournament somewhere, and this one happens at just the right date. All the best people will be there, and we should see the famous knights and great kings. It does not matter about the sword, of course, but think of the tournament, probably the greatest there has ever been in Gramarye, and all the things we should see and do. Dear father, let me go to this tourney, if you love me, so that I may bear away the prize of all, in my maiden fight."

"But, Kay," said Sir Ector, "I have never been to London."

"All the more reason to go. I believe that anybody who does not go for a tournament like this will be proving that he has no noble blood in his veins. Think what people

F

G

Language Note

The word *propaganda*, meaning the spread of information to help or harm a cause or an institution, comes from the name of an organization formed by Pope Gregory XV. The organization name, *Congregatio de propaganda fide*, means "Congregation for propagating the faith." The organization was created in 1623, so the word, like the references to communism and other twentieth-century phenomena, would be anachronistic in the Middle Ages.

F **Literary Elements**

TONE How does the characters' discussion about whether or not to go to London affect the tone of the story? *(The author combines a realistic detail, the difficulty of traveling to London in the Middle Ages, with the otherwise contemporary dialogue of the characters. Therefore, a statement such as "My father went there once" has a humorous effect.)*

G **Author's Craft**

CHARACTER Have students summarize Kay's arguments for going to London. Is he a realistic character? *(Kay says that "all the best people will be there." He wants to see a splendid tournament and famous people. He says people will think poorly of his family if they do not go. The dialogue realistically portrays the arguments of a teenager.)*

MEETING INDIVIDUAL NEEDS — INCLUSION STRATEGIES

Learning Disabled Students may better understand the plot, characters, and tone of the story if they do a role-play based on the character of Kay.

Activity Have pairs of students take turns reading Kay's speeches at the bottom of pages 965–966. Encourage them to imagine the tone of voice that Kay would use to try to convince his father to go to the tournament. Then have students take turns acting out a situation in which they try to convince their parents to go somewhere for a special occasion. Have them compare their own speech to that of Kay. **L2**

Additional Resources
📁 *Inclusion Strategies*

King Arthur and the 30 Kingdoms, 1307. Illustration from Peter Langtoft's *Chronicle of England.* The British Library, London.

Viewing the art: How does this image help you picture the knights gathered with Sir Ector?

G will say about us, if we do not go and have a shot at that sword. They will say that Sir Ector's family was too <u>vulgar</u> and knew it had no chance."

"We all know the family has no chance," said Sir Ector, "that is, for the sword."

"Lot of people in London," remarked Sir Grummore, with a wild surmise. "So they say."

He took a deep breath and goggled at his host with eyes like marbles.

"And shops," added King Pellinore suddenly, also beginning to breathe heavily.

"Dang it!" cried Sir Ector, bumping his horn mug on the table so that it spilled. "Let's all go to London, then, and see the new King!"

They rose up as one man.

"Why shouldn't I be as good a man as my father?" exclaimed King Pellinore.

"Dash it all," cried Sir Grummore. "After all, damn it all, it is the capital!"

"Hurray!" shouted Kay.

"Lord have mercy," said the nurse.

At this moment the Wart came in with Merlyn, and everybody was too excited to notice that, if he had not been grown up now, he would have been on the verge of tears.

"Oh, Wart," cried Kay, forgetting for the moment that he was only addressing his squire, and slipping back into the familiarity of their boyhood. "What do you think? We are all going to London for a great tournament on New Year's Day!"

"Are we?"

"Yes, and you will carry my shield and spears for the jousts, and I shall win the palm[11] of everybody and be a great knight!"

"Well, I am glad we are going," said the Wart, "for Merlyn is leaving us too."

"Oh, we shan't need Merlyn."

"He is leaving us," repeated the Wart.

"Leavin' us?" asked Sir Ector. "I thought it was we that were leavin'?"

***

11. Kay hopes to win praise. In ancient time, a *palm* leaf or branch was often used as a symbol of victory or rejoicing.

Vocabulary
vulgar (vul' gər) *adj.* characterized by a lack of good breeding or good taste; common; crude

966 UNIT 5

"He is going away from the Forest Sauvage."

Sir Ector said, "Come now, Merlyn, what's all this about? I don't understand all this a bit."

"I have come to say Good-bye, Sir Ector," said the old magician.

"Tomorrow my pupil Kay will be knighted, and the next week my other pupil will go away as his squire. I have outlived my usefulness here, and it is time to go."

"Now, now, don't say that," said Sir Ector. "I think you're a jolly useful chap whatever happens. You just stay and teach me, or be the librarian or something. Don't you leave an old man alone, after the children have flown."

"We shall all meet again," said Merlyn. "There is no cause to be sad."

"Don't go," said Kay.

"I must go," replied their tutor. "We have had a good time while we were young, but it is in the nature of Time to fly. There are many things in other parts of the kingdom which I ought to be attending to just now, and it is a specially busy time for me. Come, Archimedes,[12] say Good-bye to the company."

"Good-bye," said Archimedes tenderly to the Wart.

"Good-bye," said the Wart without looking up at all.

"But you can't go," cried Sir Ector, "not without a month's notice."

"Can't I?" replied Merlyn, taking up the position always used by philosophers[13] who propose to dematerialize. He stood on his toes, while Archimedes held tight to his

shoulder—began to spin on them slowly like a top—spun faster and faster till he was only a blur of grayish light—and in a few seconds there was no one there at all.

"Good-bye, Wart," cried two faint voices outside the solar window.

"Good-bye," said the Wart for the last time—and the poor fellow went quickly out of the room.

✦ ✦ ✦

The knighting took place in a whirl of preparations. Kay's <u>sumptuous</u> bath had to be set up in the box-room, between two towel-horses and an old box of selected games which contained a worn-out straw dart-board—it was called fléchette[14] in those days—because all the other rooms were full of packing. The nurse spent the whole time constructing new warm pants for everybody, on the principle that the climate of any place outside the Forest Sauvage must be treacherous to the extreme, and, as for the sergeant, he polished all the armor till it was quite brittle and sharpened the swords till they were almost worn away.

At last it was time to set out.

Perhaps, if you happen not to have lived in the Old England of the twelfth century, or whenever it was, and in a remote castle on the borders of the Marches[15] at that, you will find it difficult to imagine the wonders of their journey.

The road, or track, ran most of the time along the high ridges of the hills or downs, and they could look down on either side of them upon the <u>desolate</u> marshes where the snowy reeds sighed, and the ice crackled, and the duck in the red sunsets quacked loud on

---

12. *Archimedes* (är′ kə mē′ dēz) is Merlyn's pet owl.
13. Magicians and sorcerers were sometimes referred to as *philosophers,* those who pursue wisdom and logical reasoning.

---

14. In French, *fléchette* (flā shet′) means "a small arrow; dart."
15. *Marches* is a variation of *marshes.*

Vocabulary
sumptuous (sump′ chōō əs) *adj.* costly and magnificent
desolate (des′ ə lit) *adj.* deserted or uninhabited

Margin notes

I **Literary Elements**

CHARACTERS Have students describe the Wart's position among the other characters as indicated by the dialogue. *(His position is inferior; he is Kay's squire and will carry his jousting equipment.)*

J **Author's Craft**

CHARACTERIZATION Have students discuss what the characters' reactions to Merlyn's departure show about his character. *(He is well-loved, especially by the Wart.)*

K **Literary Elements**

FIGURES OF SPEECH: *Hyperbole*
Remind students that hyperbole is exaggeration for the sake of effect. Have them identify the hyperbole in the narrative paragraph and describe its specific effect on the story. *(The sergeant's polishing the "armor till it was quite brittle" and sharpening the swords "till they were almost worn away" are examples of hyperbole. They have the humorous effect of exaggerating the extent of the excited preparations for the journey and the tournament.)*

Writing *Minilesson*

Using Hyperbole Point out that students probably use hyperbole quite often in everyday conversation, for example, saying, "That was the hardest test I ever took." Explain that hyperbole can be an effective device to use in writing also, if it is not overused.

Activity Have students write a paragraph about an exciting event they recently experienced. Ask them to use hyperbole at least twice to emphasize the importance of the occasion, the level of their emotions, or another aspect. Remind students that hyperbole is a figure of speech; it should clearly be a statement not to be taken literally. **L2**

Additional Resources

📖 *Writer's Choice,* Lesson 6.3

The coast of Cornwall, in southwest England, consists of hilly, rugged terrain, edged by steep cliffs that drop into the sea or hidden coves and rocky beaches.

Viewing Response *The ridges of hills and desolate marshes described in the selection are similar to the pictured landscape.*

 Active Reading

CONNECT Ask volunteers to read aloud the descriptive paragraphs on pages 967–968. Discuss with students whether they find the landscape and traveling conditions appealing. How would they react if they were on the journey described?

At the MOVIES

Be sure to preview the following video for appropriateness for your class:

- **Knights of the Round Table***

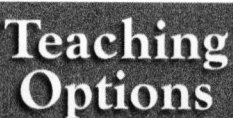 *Also available in the Glencoe Literature *Video Library.*

Teaching Options

View on the Coast of Cornwall, Frank Goodwin (1848–1873).

Viewing the painting: What similarities do you find between the country depicted here and the one described in the selection? Explain.

---

the winter air. The whole country was like that. Perhaps there would be a moory marsh on one side of the ridge, and a forest of a hundred thousand acres on the other, with all the great branches weighted in white. They could sometimes see a wisp of smoke among the trees, or a huddle of buildings far out among the impassable reeds, and twice they came to quite respectable towns which had several inns to boast of, but on the whole it was an England without civilization. The better roads were cleared of cover for a bow-shot[16] on either side of them, lest the traveller should be slain by hidden thieves.

They slept where they could, sometimes in the hut of some cottager who was prepared to welcome them, sometimes in the castle of a brother knight who invited them to refresh themselves, sometimes in the firelight and fleas of a dirty little hovel with a bush tied to a pole outside it—this was the sign-board used at that time by inns—and once or twice on the open ground, all huddled together for warmth between their grazing chargers. Wherever they went and wherever they slept, the east wind whistled in the reeds, and the geese went over high in the starlight, honking at the stars.

London was full to the brim. If Sir Ector had not been lucky enough to own a little land in Pie Street, on which there stood a respectable inn, they would have been hard put to it to find a lodging. But he did own it, and as a matter of fact drew most of his dividends from that source, so they were able to get three beds between the five of them. They thought themselves fortunate.

---

16. A *bow-shot* measured about 400 yards, roughly the distance an old English longbow could shoot an arrow. The roadsides were cleared of trees and shrubs, or *cover.*

MEETING INDIVIDUAL NEEDS MULTIPLE LEARNING STYLES

Linguistic The author describes the landscape through which the characters travel on their way to London. Have students point out particularly vivid sensory details, such as "the snowy reeds sigh[ing]" or "the great branches weighted in white."

Activity Have students write a description of a particularly vivid landscape they have traveled through. Encourage them to use sensory details as T. H. White does to recreate the scene for the reader. Have students read their descriptions aloud. **L2**

On the first day of the tournament, Sir Kay managed to get them on the way to the lists at least an hour before the jousts[17] could possibly begin. He had lain awake all night, imagining how he was going to beat the best barons in England, and he had not been able to eat his breakfast. Now he rode at the front of the caval-cade,[18] with pale cheeks, and Wart wished there was something he could do to calm him down.

For country people, who only knew the dis-mantled tilting[19] ground of Sir Ector's castle, the scene which met their eyes was ravishing. It was a huge green pit in the earth, about as big as the arena at a football match. It lay ten feet lower than the surrounding country, with sloping banks, and the snow had been swept off it. It had been kept warm with straw, which had been cleared off that morning, and now the close-worn grass sparkled green in the white landscape. Round the arena there was a world of color so dazzling and moving and twinkling as to make one blink one's eyes. The wooden grandstands were painted in scarlet and white. The silk pavilions of famous people, pitched on every side, were azure and green and saffron and checkered. The pennons and pen-noncells which floated everywhere in the sharp wind were flapping with every color of the rain-bow, as they strained and slapped at their flag-poles, and the barrier down the middle of the arena itself was done in chessboard squares of black and white. Most of the combatants and their friends had not yet arrived, but one could see from those few who had come how the very

people would turn the scene into a bank of flowers, and how the armor would flash, and the scalloped sleeves of the heralds[20] jig in the wind, as they raised their brazen trumpets to their lips to shake the fleecy clouds of winter with joyances and fanfares.

"Good heavens!" cried Sir Kay. "I have left my sword at home."

"Can't joust without a sword," said Sir Grummore. "Quite irregular."

"Better go and fetch it," said Sir Ector. "You have time."

"My squire will do," said Sir Kay. "What a damned mistake to make! Here, squire, ride hard back to the inn and fetch my sword. You shall have a shilling if you fetch it in time."

The Wart went as pale as Sir Kay was, and looked as if he were going to strike him. Then he said, "It shall be done, master," and turned his ambling palfrey against the stream of new-comers. He began to push his way toward their hostelry[21] as best he might.

"To offer me money!" cried the Wart to himself. "To look down at this beastly little donkey-affair off his great charger and to call me Squire! Oh, Merlyn, give me patience with the brute, and stop me from throwing his filthy shilling in his face."

When he got to the inn it was closed. Everybody had thronged to see the famous tour-nament, and the entire household had followed after the mob. Those were lawless days and it was not safe to leave your house—or even to go to sleep in it—unless you were certain that it was impregnable. The wooden shutters bolted

---

17. The *lists* was the field or area in which knights fought tour-naments. The *jousts* were formal battles between mounted knights armed with long spears or other weapons.
18. A procession of people on horseback (or in vehicles) is a *cavalcade*.
19. Jousting is also called *tilting*.

20. At tournaments, *heralds* carried challenges between knights, made proclamations, and trumpeted the stages of competition.
21. Wart is riding a gentle saddle horse (*palfrey*) toward the inn (*hostelry*).

Vocabulary

combatant (kəm bat′ ənt) *n.* one trained for, or engaged in, combat
throng (thrông) *v.* to move or gather in large numbers; to crowd together

M **Critical Thinking**

INFERRING Ask students whether Kay's dream of beating the best barons in England is reasonable based on his depiction so far. To what may his daydreams be attrib-uted? *(It is not reasonable but brought on by his youth and inexperience.)*

N **Active Reading**

CONNECT Have a volunteer read the description of the tournament scene aloud. To what type of modern event might the tournament be compared? *(Students might compare it to a foot-ball game, horse race, or Olympic event.)*

O **Author's Craft**

CHARACTERIZATION What does the reader learn of the Wart's character from this speech? *(He is not as meek as he acts; he is bright and resents being ordered around.)*

MEETING INDIVIDUAL NEEDS

MULTIPLE LEARNING STYLES

Spatial The author creates a vivid pic-ture of the tournament field and the pageantry of the tournament.

Activity Ask artistically oriented stu-dents to create a visual representation of the tournament scene. Encourage them to be imaginative in brainstorming ways to represent the tournament. They may wish to make a picture of the field

or the crowd or both, using pencil, ink, pastels, watercolors, or another medium. Or they may choose to illus-trate the colorful flags and pennants or to create a pennant out of fabric or construction paper. Have students dis-play their artwork. **L2**

Active Reading

QUESTION Why does the Wart begin to get more serious about getting a sword for Kay? *(He gets over his anger and begins to feel sorry for Kay, realizing that he was quite upset about not having a sword for the tournament.)*

Literary Elements

TONE Have students describe the author's tone as the Wart decides to pull the sword from the stone and attempts to do so. *(The author plays up the irony and humor of the Wart casually deciding to pull the sword from the stone, which he assumes is "some sort of war memorial." He becomes somewhat more serious as he describes the differences in the Wart's perceptions brought on by holding the sword.)*

over the downstairs windows were two inches thick, and the doors were double-barred.

"Now what do I do," asked the Wart, "to earn my shilling?"

He looked <u>ruefully</u> at the blind little inn, and began to laugh.

"Poor Kay," he said. "All that shilling stuff was only because he was scared and miserable, and now he has good cause to be. Well, he shall have a sword of some sort if I have to break into the Tower of London.

"How does one get hold of a sword?" he continued. "Where can I steal one? Could I waylay some knight, even if I am mounted on an ambling pad,[22] and take his weapons by force? There must be some swordsmith or armorer in a great town like this, whose shop would be still open."

He turned his mount and cantered off along the street. There was a quiet churchyard at the end of it, with a kind of square in front of the church door. In the middle of the square there was a heavy stone with an anvil on it, and a fine new sword was stuck through the anvil.

Did You Know?
A *lychgate* (lich′ gāt) is a roofed gateway to a churchyard.

"Well," said the Wart, "I suppose it is some sort of war memorial, but it will have to do. I am sure nobody would grudge Kay a war memorial, if they knew his desperate straits."[23]

He tied his reins round a post of the lych-gate, strode up the gravel path, and took hold of the sword.

"Come, sword," he said. "I must cry your mercy and take you for a better cause.

"This is extraordinary," said the Wart. "I feel strange when I have hold of this sword, and I notice everything much more clearly. Look at the beautiful gargoyles of the church, and of the monastery which it belongs to. See how splendidly all the famous banners in the aisle are waving. How nobly that yew[24] holds up the red flakes of its timbers to worship God. How clean the snow is. I can smell something like fetherfew and sweet briar— and is it music that I hear?"

It was music, whether of pan-pipes or of recorders, and the light in the churchyard was so clear, without being dazzling, that one could have picked a pin out twenty yards away.

"There is something in this place," said the Wart. "There are people. Oh, people, what do you want?"

Nobody answered him, but the music was loud and the light beautiful.

"People," cried the Wart, "I must take this sword. It is not for me, but for Kay. I will bring it back."

There was still no answer, and Wart turned back to the anvil. He saw the golden letters, which he did not read, and the jewels on the pommel, flashing in the lovely light.

"Come, sword," said the Wart.

He took hold of the handles with both hands, and strained against the stone. There was a melodious consort[25] on the recorders, but nothing moved.

The Wart let go of the handles, when they were beginning to bite into the palms of his hands, and stepped back, seeing stars.

22. To *waylay* is to lie in wait for and attack. Wart's *pad*, or pad horse, is trained for slow, steady road travel and wouldn't do well in a quick getaway.
23. *Straits* is a troublesome or difficult situation.

24. The church's *gargoyles* are ornaments in the form of out- landish creatures, its *monastery* is a residence for monks, and the *yew* is a type of evergreen tree.
25. Here, *consort* means "a harmony of sounds."

Vocabulary
ruefully (rōō′ fəl ē) *adv.* regretfully; sorrowfully

Teaching Options

INTERDISCIPLINARY CONNECTION

Architecture The gargoyles of the church that the Wart notices were a fea- ture of Gothic architecture, which was cre- ated in Europe during the Middle Ages, from the mid-1100s to the 1400s. Some great Gothic cathedrals built in England include those in Coventry and Salisbury. Notre Dame and Chartres in France are also examples of Gothic architecture.

Activity Interested students might research the features of Gothic architec- ture. Have them find out the features that differentiated it from the earlier Romanesque style. Ask them to define and describe the following terms:

    pointed arch   statue column
    ribbed vault   gargoyle
    flying buttress

L2

The Faithful Knight in Equal Field Subdues his Faithless Foe. Frederick and Pickford Marriot (1860–1941).
Viewing the painting: How might the Merlin's advice about "not letting go" apply to these jousters?

R
"It is well fixed," he said.

He took hold of it again and pulled with all his might. The music played more strongly, and the light all about the church-yard glowed like amethysts;[26] but the sword still stuck.

"Oh, Merlyn," cried the Wart, "help me to get this weapon."

S
There was a kind of rushing noise, and a long chord played along with it. All round the churchyard there were hundreds of old friends. They rose over the church wall all together, like the Punch and Judy[27] ghosts of remembered days, and there were badgers and nightingales and vulgar crows and hares and wild geese and falcons and fishes and dogs and dainty unicorns and solitary wasps and corkindrills and hedgehogs and griffins and the thousand other animals he had met. They loomed round the church wall, the lovers and helpers of the Wart, and they all spoke solemnly in turn. Some of them had come from the banners in the church, where they were painted in heraldry,[28] some from the waters and the sky and the fields about—but all, down to the smallest shrew mouse, had come to help on account of love. Wart felt his power grow.

"Put your back into it," said a Luce (or pike) off one of the heraldic banners, "as you once did when I was going to snap you up.[29] Remember that power springs from the nape of the neck."

S
"What about those forearms," asked a Badger gravely, "that are held together by a chest? Come along, my dear embryo,[30] and find your tool."

A Merlin sitting at the top of the yew tree cried out, "Now then, Captain Wart, what is the first law of the foot? I thought I once heard something about never letting go?"

---

26. The light was the violet color of quartz crystals called *amethysts.*
27. The main characters in a puppet show, *Punch and Judy* have been popular with English audiences for centuries.
28. The animals in *heraldry* are painted on banners showing coats of arms, designs that represent noble families and their histories.
29. *Luce* is an old name for the pike, a fish that can grow to more than four feet long and that normally eats other fish.
30. The fertilized egg of an organism is an *embryo,* but the word can also refer to someone or something in the beginning stage of development.

VIEWING THE PAINTING

Not only were knights outfitted in armor when going into battle, their horses were also protected by armor.

Viewing Response *Merlin's advice to hold on firmly to one's goal, both physically and mentally, might apply to the jousters.*

R **Literary Elements**

FIGURES OF SPEECH: *Understatement*
Point out that the Wart's statement that the sword "is well fixed" is an example of understatement, the opposite of hyperbole. An understatement says less than is intended. Have students describe the effect of the author's use of understatement here. *(It is in keeping with the author's ironic, amused tone.)*

S **Author's Craft**

IMAGERY Have students explain the author's purpose for and the meaning of the animals that appear as the Wart attempts to pull out the sword. *(The author is adding drama to the climactic event in the story; he is emphasizing the magical elements involved in the Wart's obtaining the sword; he is portraying the Wart as a boy who is beloved by all creatures; and he is helping the reader recall Arthur's younger days when Merlyn taught him compassion and wisdom by turning him into various animals.)*

Reading *Minilesson*

Scanning Remind students that in scanning, a reader moves his or her eyes quickly over a text to find specific words or phrases.

Activity Have students practice scanning. Time them for one minute as they scan page 971 to find each different animal mentioned. Point out that animal names appear not only in the fourth paragraph but throughout the page. **L1**

Additional Resources
📁 *Reading Workbook,* pp. 83–84

STYLE Have students describe the author's style at the climactic moment when the Wart draws the sword from the stone. How does the style affect the author's tone? *(The moment is described with simple diction and sentence structure and not dramatically. The simplicity emphasizes the importance of the moment and creates a more serious tone.)*

U **Literary Elements**

TONE Have students read aloud the dialogue between Sir Kay and the Wart and identify its tone. *(The casual, understated conversation is in keeping with the author's ironic tone.)*

VIEWING THE PAINTING

John Callcott Horsley (1817–1903) had his greatest artistic success with literary subjects like this.

Viewing Response *Students may say that the picture of Arthur portrays Arthur's strong will described in the story or that it does not portray his humility and modesty.*

"Don't work like a stalling woodpecker," urged a Tawny Owl affectionately. "Keep up a steady effort, my duck, and you will have it yet."

A white-front said, "Now, Wart, if you were once able to fly the great North Sea, surely you can co-ordinate a few little wing-muscles here and there? Fold your powers together, with the spirit of your mind, and it will come out like butter. Come along, Homo sapiens, for all we humble friends of yours are waiting here to cheer."

The Wart walked up to the great sword for the third time. He put out his right hand softly and drew it out as gently as from a scabbard.[31]

There was a lot of cheering, a noise like a hurdy-gurdy[32] which went on and on. In the middle of this noise, after a long time, he saw Kay and gave him the sword. The people at the tournament were making a frightful row.

"But this is not my sword," said Sir Kay.

"It was the only one I could get," said the Wart. "The inn was locked."

"It is a nice-looking sword. Where did you get it?"

"I found it stuck in a stone, outside a church."

Sir Kay had been watching the tilting nervously, waiting for his turn. He had not paid much attention to his squire.

"That is a funny place to find one," he said.

"Yes, it was stuck through an anvil."

"What?" cried Sir Kay, suddenly rounding upon him. "Did you just say this sword was stuck in a stone?"

"It was," said the Wart. "It was a sort of war memorial."

Sir Kay stared at him for several seconds in amazement, opened his mouth, shut it

---

31. A *scabbard* is a case for the blade of a sword.
32. The *hurdy-gurdy* is a musical instrument shaped somewhat like a guitar but played by turning a hand crank that causes a revolving wheel to make the strings vibrate.

972 UNIT 5

The Boyhood of Arthur, 1851. John Callcott Horsley. Oil on canvas. Walker Galleries, Harrogate, UK.

Viewing the painting: How does this portrayal of Arthur compare or contrast with the character of Arthur in the selection?

---

again, licked his lips, then turned his back and plunged through the crowd. He was looking for Sir Ector, and the Wart followed after him.

"Father," cried Sir Kay, "come here a moment."

"Yes, my boy," said Sir Ector. "Splendid falls these professional chaps do manage.

Teaching Options

Grammar and Language *Minilesson*

Hyphens for Compound Words Remind students that a hyphen is used to separate the parts of some compound words, such as *sister-in-law* and *well-dressed*. Explain that the hyphen in some compound nouns may be omitted if the word becomes common, as in *weekend*.

Activity Have students find five compound words with hyphens in the selec-

tion. Ask them to check a dictionary to see whether any words (such as *dart-board*) are hyphenated in the selection but are now written as one word. Have them identify each word's part of speech in the selection: half-mast (p. 962) *(verb)*; sergeant-at-arms (p. 963) *(noun)*; next-of-kin (p. 964) *(noun)*; good-bye (p. 967) *(interjection)*; lych-gate (p. 970) *(noun)*; nice-looking (p. 972) *(adjective)* **L2**

Additional Resources

Grammar and Language Transparency 70

Grammar and Language Workbook, p. 279

Grammar and Composition Handbook, Lesson 11.12

Writer's Choice, Lesson 21.12

Why, what's the matter, Kay? You look as white as a sheet."

"Do you remember that sword which the King of England would pull out?"

"Yes."

"Well, here it is. I have it. It is in my hand. I pulled it out."

Sir Ector did not say anything silly. He looked at Kay and he looked at the Wart. Then he stared at Kay again, long and lovingly, and said, "We will go back to the church."

"Now then, Kay," he said, when they were at the church door. He looked at his first-born kindly, but straight between the eyes. "Here is the stone, and you have the sword. It will make you the King of England. You are my son that I am proud of, and always will be, whatever you do. Will you promise me that you took it out by your own might?"

Kay looked at his father. He also looked at the Wart and at the sword.

Then he handed the sword to the Wart quite quietly.

He said, "I am a liar. Wart pulled it out."

As far as the Wart was concerned, there was a time after this in which Sir Ector kept telling him to put the sword back into the stone—which he did—and in which Sir Ector and Kay then vainly tried to take it out. The Wart took it out for them, and stuck it back again once or twice. After this, there was another time which was more painful.

He saw that his dear guardian[33] was looking quite old and powerless, and that he was kneeling down with difficulty on a gouty knee.

"Sir," said Sir Ector, without looking up, although he was speaking to his own boy.

"Please do not do this, father," said the Wart, kneeling down also. "Let me help you up, Sir Ector, because you are making me unhappy."

"Nay, nay, my lord," said Sir Ector, with some very feeble old tears. "I was never your father nor of your blood, but I wote well ye are of an higher blood than I wend[34] ye were."

"Plenty of people have told me you are not my father," said the Wart, "but it does not matter a bit."

"Sir," said Sir Ector humbly, "will ye be my good and gracious lord when ye are King?"

"Don't!" said the Wart.

"Sir," said Sir Ector, "I will ask no more of you but that you will make my son, your foster-brother, Sir Kay, seneschal[35] of all your lands?"

Kay was kneeling down too, and it was more than the Wart could bear.

"Oh, do stop," he cried. "Of course he can be seneschal, if I have got to be this King, and, oh, father, don't kneel down like that, because it breaks my heart. Please get up, Sir Ector, and don't make everything so horrible. Oh, dear, oh, dear, I wish I had never seen that filthy sword at all."

And the Wart also burst into tears.

---

33. Merlyn had arranged for Sir Ector to be Arthur's *guardian* and to raise him as his son. Neither Ector nor Wart knew that the baby's biological father was Britain's King Uther.

34. *Wote* and *wend* are past-tense forms of two obsolete verbs—*wot*, meaning "to know," and *ween*, meaning "to suppose, believe, or expect."

35. In medieval times, the *seneschal* (sen′ ə shəl) managed the king's estate, ran his household, and sometimes also had official state duties or a military command.

V Critical Thinking

DRAWING CONCLUSIONS Use the following model to encourage students to draw conclusions about the author's portrayal of the Wart's attitude after people realize he will be the next king.

Model: The Wart's attitude is not what I would have expected. I would expect the Wart to be overjoyed or proud of his new status. Instead, he is matter-of-fact and then upset because people treat him differently. I think the author is portraying the Wart's reaction as realistically child-like: he doesn't want anything to change. The author is also hinting that the Wart will be a good king because he is not power-hungry.

W Literary Elements

TONE Ask students how the author's tone changes or remains consistent at the end of the story. (*His portrayal of the Wart's confused emotions is serious and touching.*)

Thematic Focus

Heroism Have students discuss whether or not the Wart's character traits indicate he has the potential to be a great hero.

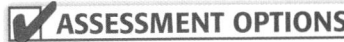

✓ ASSESSMENT OPTIONS

📁 *Quick Checks,* p. 81

Listening and Speaking *Minilesson*

Expressing Tone Point out that the author expresses humor, suspense, irony, and respect at various points in the selection.

Activity Have students choose a passage that expresses a specific tone and prepare a reading of it, either alone or with one or more classmates. They may wish to consider one of the humorous dialogues among Sir Ector, King Pellinore, and Sir Grummore at the beginning of the story; the serious description of England's landscape when the knights travel to London; or the Wart's emotional speeches at the end of the selection. Encourage students to use vocal tone and emphasis to express the appropriate literary tone. **L2**

Responding to Literature

Personal Response

Students should refer to specific incidents in the story.

ANALYZING LITERATURE

1. The death of the king has thrown the country into a state of excitement because he left no heir.
2. The Wart announces to Sir Ector and Kay that Merlyn is leaving.
3. The Wart is unable to get Sir Kay's sword because the inn where they are staying is locked up.
4. The Wart knows the sword in the stone is no ordinary sword because he feels strange and sees the world differently; his perceptions of art and music are heightened.
5. Sir Kay claims he himself pulled the sword from the stone. The Wart remains silent.
6. The death of the old king saddens Sir Ector and his companions at first, but then they grow excited and curious in wondering who will succeed him.
7. The Wart has an affectionate relationship with Merlyn and sees him as his mentor. This is shown by his emotional reaction when Merlyn leaves and his calling upon him when he has difficulties, as when he is trying to pull the sword from the stone.
8. The Wart silently obeys Sir Kay's order because it is his duty and it is not in his nature to cause trouble by refusing to follow an order.
9. The author builds to a climax by describing the Wart's perceptions of the beauty of the church and of the music and by showing the animals coming to encourage the Wart.
10. Arthur's response to Sir Kay suggests that he is wise and tactful and not power-hungry, traits that promise to make him a good leader.
11. Students may find the characters' failure to notice the Wart's sadness realistic; his behavior is subdued and the other characters are preoccupied with their own affairs.
12. Repetition of elements such as the music and the light in the churchyard scene emphasizes the importance of the event and evokes suspense.
13. The author might have portrayed Sir Ector as a wise and loving father to show that Arthur will be a good leader because he was brought up well.
14. Students may find Sir Ector's and Sir Kay's reactions true to life because becoming king was an enormous step and people felt great respect for their

king; or they may find them unrealistic because Arthur himself hasn't changed although his status has.
15. The author is saying that a person becomes a hero by exhibiting heroic character and behavior, not simply by being given the status of hero.

Personal Response

How did you react to the Wart's behavior at the beginning of the excerpt? at the middle? at the end? How might you have behaved differently?

———— ANALYZING LITERATURE ————

RECALL

1. Why has the death of King Uther thrown the country into a state of excitement?
2. What news does the Wart announce to Sir Ector and Kay?
3. Why is the Wart unable to bring Sir Kay's sword back to him?
4. How does the Wart know immediately that the sword in the stone is no ordinary sword?
5. Who does Sir Kay claim pulled the sword from the stone? What is the Wart's response?

INTERPRET

6. What effect does the death of the old king have upon Sir Ector and his companions? Explain.
7. What can you infer about the Wart's relationship with Merlyn? Support your answer with details from the text.
8. Why, do you suppose, does the Wart silently obey Sir Kay's order to fetch his sword?
9. How does the author build the plot to a **climax** (see page R2) during the scene in which the Wart pulls the sword from the stone?
10. What does the Wart's response to Sir Kay suggest to you about Arthur's character and future leadership?

EVALUATE AND CONNECT

11. Does it seem realistic to you that the characters fail to notice the Wart's sadness about Merlyn's departure? Explain.
12. How does the author's use of **repetition** in the first churchyard scene affect your appreciation of the story?
13. Why might the author have portrayed Sir Ector as a wise and loving father?
14. Think about your response to the Focus Activity on page 961. Do Sir Ector's and Sir Kay's reactions to the Wart's sudden "promotion" seem true to life? Explain.
15. **Theme Connections** In your opinion, what is the author saying about heroes?

Literary ELEMENTS

Tone

Tone suggests a writer's or speaker's attitude toward the subject. When you read a selection, think about the attitude it conveys. Is it solemn? silly? frightening? angry? To identify an author's tone, consider the imagery, syntax, sound devices, and connotations being used. For example, King Pellinore says, "Oh, do try to listen to me, you two, instead of interruptin' all the time about nothin', for it makes a man's head go ever so." Pellinore's casual language and frustration suggest a humorous, down-to-earth view of nobility that is contrary to its frequent portrayal as being haughty and intelligent.

1. What is the subject of the first page of the selection? What tone is taken toward the subject? Identify two examples from the page that convey this tone.
2. Choose a passage in which the tone is different from that of the opening scene. How has the author made the tone different? Why, do you suppose, has he changed his tone?

● See **Literary Terms Handbook**, p. R13.

LITERARY ELEMENTS

1. The subject of the first page is the death of the king. The tone is light and irreverent, as in King Pellinore's saying, "He's dead, poor fellah, and can't hunt anymore."
2. The end of the story in which the Wart reacts emotionally to the change in attitude toward him shows a more serious tone. He has changed his tone to imply what a huge responsibility Arthur must take on.

Additional Resources

📖 *Literary Elements Transparency 81*

LITERATURE AND WRITING

Writing About Literature
Character Analysis   No one is more surprised than the Wart to find that he is to be King of England. Does the Wart have what it takes to be a good king? Look through the selection for signs that young Arthur possesses superior qualities. Then brainstorm a list of "kingly" traits that you detect in the Wart. Write a brief analysis of his character based on your list, and share it with the class.

Creative Writing
Father and Son   This passage ends with both Sir Ector and Sir Kay on their knees before the Wart, their future king. What is going through their minds? Imagine a scene later that evening when Sir Ector and Kay are alone. What will they say to each other about the sudden elevation of the Wart from squire to king? Write their brief dialogue, using language and content that reflects each character.

EXTENDING YOUR RESPONSE

Literature Groups
Memorable Moments   Which scenes do you continue to think about? A specific element, such as humor, emotion, description, realism, or fantasy, can make a scene vivid. Skim the selection for two scenes that are the most memorable for you, and identify why they made an impression. As you share your choices with the group, discuss other group members' thoughts and feelings about the scenes. Compare your group's impressions with those of other groups.

Learning for Life
Hear Ye! Hear Ye!   "They . . . have had to proclaim a tournament all over England, for New Year's Day, so that the man who comes to the tournament and pulls out the sword can be King of all England for ever," whispers King Pellinore. Make a scroll, announcing specific details of the tournament. Read your announcement to the class, and then post it for all to read.

Performing
Reenactment   With two classmates, act out the story from the scene when Sir Kay sends the Wart to fetch his sword. Improvise dialogue for each scene, staying true to the content and to each character's manner of speaking. Rehearse the reenactment and perform it for the class.

Reading Further
If you'd like to read other adventures, you might enjoy these epics:
The Hobbit, The Fellowship of the Ring, The Two Towers, and *The Return of the King,* by J. R. R. Tolkien, describe adventures of heroes who set out to save Middle Earth from evil.

📖 **Save your work for your portfolio.**

LITERATURE AND WRITING

Writing About Literature
Students' character analyses should
- include specific traits that Arthur has.
- refer to incidents in the story that indicate Arthur's traits.

Creative Writing
Students' dialogues should
- show knowledge of the characters of Sir Ector and Sir Kay.
- use language that reflects each character.

EXTENDING YOUR RESPONSE

Literature Groups Students may also wish to compare their chosen scenes to similar scenes in other works. COLLAB. LEARN.

Learning for Life Encourage students to use language and writing that reflect the distant time of the story.

Performing Suggest that students analyze the emotions of the Wart, Sir Kay, and Sir Ector in each scene before practicing their performances.

✅ ASSESSMENT OPTIONS

📁 *Quick Checks,* p. 81
📁 *Selection and Theme Assessment,* pp. 153–154
📁 *Performance Assessment,* p. 79
💾 *Testmaker*

Sentence Fragments

Practice

Students might choose a passage such as the dialogue between Sir Kay and Sir Grummore on page 969. The following revision replaces the fragments:

"You can't joust without a sword," said Sir Grummore. "That would be quite irregular."

"You had better go and fetch it," said Sir Ector. "You have time."

Making Inferences

Students might infer that the Wart is sensitive based on his reaction to Merlyn's departure, agreeable but not a pushover based on his expression of annoyance at going to fetch Sir Kay's sword, and humble based on his not contradicting Kay's account of pulling the sword from the stone.

Dictionary Skills: Definitions

1. 2   2. 1   3. 2
4. 4   5. 3

Additional Resources

📘 **Grammar and Composition Handbook,** Lesson 4.9

📘 **Grammar and Language Workbook,** p. 121

📘 **Writer's Choice,** Lesson 13.9

📁 **Vocabulary Practice,** p. 52

📁 **Reading Workbook,** pp. 83–84

GRAMMAR AND LANGUAGE • Sentence Fragments

A sentence fragment is a word group written as a sentence but lacking either a subject, a verb, or both. Because sentence fragments are grammatically incorrect and often hard to understand, writers tend to avoid using them. However, authors may use sentence fragments in dialogue, where they can create the sound of natural speech. For example, in "Arthur Becomes King," Sir Kay expresses a desire to go to London. "Long way to London," Sir Grummore replies. His statement lacks a subject and a verb, but it's the kind of clipped, fragmentary comment you might hear in real speech.

PRACTICE   Copy a passage from "Arthur Becomes King" that includes several sentence fragments. With a partner, replace these fragments with complete sentences; then discuss how this changes the effect of the dialogue.

APPLY   Find a passage of dialogue that you have written. Where did you use sentence fragments? Where might the addition of sentence fragments make your dialogue sound more natural?

● For more about sentence fragments, see **Language Handbook,** p. R14.

READING AND THINKING • Making Inferences

Experienced readers pay attention to a character's dialogue, appearance, and behavior in order to gain information about the character that is not directly stated in the text of a story. In "Arthur Becomes King," for example, Sir Kay is described as looking "white as a sheet." He tells a lie but later admits the truth. These clues help readers to infer that Sir Kay is jealous and ambitious but essentially honest.

PRACTICE   Tell a classmate what you have inferred about the Wart. Then work with your partner to find clues in the story's dialogue and descriptions that verify your impression or cause you to change it.

● For more about making inferences, see **Reading Handbook,** p. R92.

VOCABULARY • Dictionary Skills: Definitions

Many words, such as *vulgar,* have several meanings. A dictionary will supply all (or most) of the meanings a word has, but the person using the dictionary must figure out which of those meanings is the appropriate one for a certain use of the word. For any multiple-meaning word, you must pay attention to the context that the word appears in to know which meaning is appropriate.

Here is a sample dictionary entry for the word *desolate* as an adjective.

desolate *adj.* **1.** solitary; lonely: *one desolate child on the playground.* **2.** uninhabited; deserted: *a desolate shack.* **3.** ruined or destroyed: *left desolate by the tornado.* **4.** unhappy; miserable; wretched: *an abandoned puppy's desolate howl.*

PRACTICE   Decide which meaning of *desolate* is used in each sentence, and write the number of that meaning.

1. The plains stretched before our wagon, *desolate* and forbidding.
2. On the bluff, the only sign of life was a *desolate* tree.
3. I finally found a *desolate* beach that fulfilled my need for privacy.
4. Learning that our grandparents were moving away left us feeling *desolate.*
5. Sherman's men marched through Georgia and the Carolinas, leaving towns, fields, and farms *desolate* in their wake.

Vo·cab·u·lar·y Skills

Idioms

Kay is desperately eager to go to London. "Think what people will say about us," he says, "if we do not go and <u>have a shot at</u> that sword." If you knew the meaning of every English word but had never heard the phrase *have a shot at,* what would you think Kay was proposing?

A word or phrase that has a special meaning different from its ordinary meaning is called an **idiom**. The phrase *have a shot at* is so familiar to most speakers of English that we know immediately that it means "have a try at" or "make an effort." Unfamiliar idioms, however, can sometimes be confusing.

Often you can understand unfamiliar idioms by thinking about the ordinary meanings of the words.

nipped in the bud	stopped at an early stage
a slap on the wrist	a very mild punishment
to wrap it up	to finish
to know the ropes	to be familiar with a method or procedure

Some idioms cannot be interpreted so easily. Why does *stuck up* mean "conceited"? Why does *take it with a grain of salt* mean "accept a statement, but with some doubt as to its complete truthfulness"? If you didn't already know what those idioms mean, how could you figure out their meanings?

When you come across an unfamiliar idiom, context clues can be helpful. Although context may not reveal the precise meaning of an idiom, it will almost always hint at the meaning.

── EXERCISE ──

To figure out the meaning of each idiom, think about the ordinary meanings of the underlined words, use context clues, or do both. Then write a short definition or a phrase that could be substituted for the idiom. Use a dictionary as needed.

1. Kay is sure that things will <u>go swimmingly</u> for him in the tournament competitions.

2. Kay's snobbiness is a shock to Wart and temporarily <u>puts him out of sorts</u>.

3. Wart is willing <u>to play second fiddle</u> to Kay, but not to be looked down on.

4. Kay realizes what sword he has been given and, <u>with an eye to the main chance</u>, claims that he took it from the stone.

5. Kay's conceit might be understandable, but lying about how he got the sword is <u>beyond the pale</u>.

Objective

- To identify idioms and to learn ways to determine the meanings of unfamiliar idioms

Teaching Strategies

Have students name other idioms with which they are familiar, and write them on the board. Discuss with students how they can use context clues to determine the meanings of the following additional idioms:

> *lend a hand*
> *in the same boat*
> *cut corners*

Exercise

1. go well
2. upsets him
3. be subordinate
4. turning the situation to his advantage
5. unacceptable

Additional Resources

📁 *Vocabulary Power: Weekly Lessons and Activities*

Teaching Options

MEETING INDIVIDUAL NEEDS — ENGLISH LANGUAGE LEARNERS

Learning Idioms Idioms may be especially challenging for English language learners. Writing down unfamiliar idioms, using them in writing, and discussing them with classmates can help students.

Activity Have students keep a list of unfamiliar idioms that they encounter in their reading. Encourage them to try to determine the meanings through con-text. Show students how to look up idioms in a dictionary by using key words. For example, *nipped in the bud* might appear under the entry for *bud*. Have students write down new idioms in their vocabulary notebooks.

Additional Resources

📁 *English Language Learners Sourcebook*

Technology Skills

Objectives

- To locate information online for a research paper and create a citation for each electronic source
- To research organizations other than MLA that provide guidelines for citing electronic sources

Teaching Strategies

Contrast the sample electronic citations given on page 979 with those given as examples for printed sources (e.g., in a language text). Ask students to point out differences in electronic citations. (They include URLs and may require two dates: a date of posting and of access. They may include facts of publication in print as well as database or site information.)

Point out that the date of access shown in the sample on page 978 tells when the researcher located the information. Inform students that, when possible, the date of electronic publication should be given, too. (Refer students to items 9 and 13 in the list of guidelines.)

Citing Electronic Sources

The following guidelines are based on the style recommended by the Modern Language Association (MLA). Information should appear in the order listed, but don't panic at the length of the list. No source you use will include every item from the list. (For more on documenting sources, see Writing Handbook, pages R64–R69.)

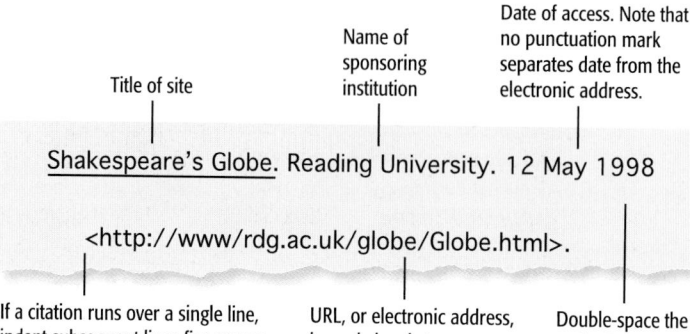

Title of site — Name of sponsoring institution — Date of access. Note that no punctuation mark separates date from the electronic address.

Shakespeare's Globe. Reading University. 12 May 1998

<http://www.rdg.ac.uk/globe/Globe.html>.

If a citation runs over a single line, indent subsequent lines five spaces. — URL, or electronic address, in angle brackets — Double-space the entire list, between entries as well as within entries.

1. **Name** of author, editor, or translator of the source, last name first—followed by an abbreviation, such as *ed.* or *trans.,* if appropriate

2. **Title** of a poem, short story, article, or other short work; database or title of a posting to a discussion list or forum (in quotation marks)—followed by *Online posting*

3. **Title** of a book (underlined)

4. **Name** of the editor or translator of the text, if relevant and if not cited earlier, preceded by the appropriate abbreviation, such as *Ed.* or *Trans.*

5. **Publication information** for any print version of the source

6. **Title** of the scholarly project, database, periodical, or site (underlined); or, for a professional or personal site without a title, a description such as *Home page*

7. **Name** of the editor of the scholarly project or database (if available)

8. **Version number** of the source (if not part of the title) or, for a journal, the volume number, issue number, or other identifying number

TECHNOLOGY TIP

Underlining is a typesetter's sign for italic type. If you are using a computer with word processing software, you can format the underlined parts of a citation in italics.

Teaching Options

MEETING INDIVIDUAL NEEDS — INCLUSION STRATEGIES

Less Proficient Readers Students may need a "translator" to understand the parts of citations. Discuss the purpose of citations and review MLA style for print citations. Read through items 1–14 aloud, locating each type of information in one or more samples on page 979.

Activity Group less-proficient readers with more able readers. Provide each group with printouts from several electronic sources. Have the group find sample citations for like sources on page 979. Using the list and samples, groups can write citations for the sources. **L2 COLLAB. LEARN.**

Additional Resources
📁 *Inclusion Strategies*

9. **Date** of electronic publication, of the latest update, or of posting

10. For a posting to a discussion list or forum, the **name** of the list or forum

11. The **number range** or total number of pages, paragraphs, or other sections, if they are numbered (for example, *pp. 47–52, pars. 1–14*)

12. **Name** of any institution or organization sponsoring or associated with the Web site

13. **Date** when the researcher accessed the source

14. Electronic address, or **URL,** of the source (in angle brackets)

Here are some sample citations you can use as models.

Professional Site
<u>Shakespeare's Globe</u>. Reading University. 12 May 1998 <http://www.rdg.ac.uk/globe/Globe.html>.

Personal Site
Brennan, Mark. <u>The Huckleberry Finn Web Site</u>. 3 Feb. 1997 <http://ourworld.compuserve.com/homepages/MBrennan/homepage.html>.

Book
Twain, Mark. <u>The Celebrated Frog of Calaveras County, and Other Sketches</u>. Ed. John Paul. New York, 1867. Online. Your Mining Co. Guide to Mark Twain. 6 Nov. 1998 <http://marktwain.miningco.com/library/texts/bl_jf_contents.htm>.

Poem
Nesbit, E[dith]. "Cloud Climbing." <u>Poems, Lyrics, and Sonnets</u>. 10 Sept. 1998. Indiana U. 29 Jan. 1999 <http://www.indiana.edu/~letrs/vwwp/bevington/bevpoems.html>.

Article in a Reference Database
"Sonnet." <u>Concise Columbia Electronic Encyclopedia</u>. 3rd ed. 1994. Infonautics Corp. 8 Dec. 1998 <http://www.encyclopedia. com>.

Article in a Journal
Fox, Robert Elliot. "Shaping an African American Literary Canon." <u>Postmodern Culture</u> 9.1 (Sept. 1996): 19 pars. 23 Feb. 1999 <http://www.iath.virginia.edu/pmc/998/9.1.r_fox.html>.

Article in a Magazine
Bennehum, David S. "Coming of Age in Cyberspace." <u>Atlantic Unbound</u>. 28 Oct. 1998 <http://www.theatlantic.com/unbound/digicult/dc981028.htm>.

Posting to a Discussion List
Renshaw, Scott. "Review of *William Shakespeare's Romeo and Juliet*." Online posting. 28 Oct. 1996. Newsgroup rec.arts.movies.reviews. Usenet. 4 Nov. 1996.

EXERCISES

1. Think of a topic for a research paper. Then do a Web search for information relating to your topic. Find a significant fact from each of at least six different electronic sources, and write the citation you would use for that information.

2. With a small group, do a Web search for organizations other than the MLA that offer style guides for citing electronic sources. For instance, you might search for the guidelines provided by the Alliance for Computers and Writing or for the American Psychological Association (APA).

Caution students not to list page numbers of printouts of their information, since pagination may vary in different printouts. Point out that electronic sources may number sections or paragraphs rather than pages. The accepted abbreviation for paragraphs is *pars.*

Exercises

1. *Students' citations should*
   - use accepted format accurately.
   - be as complete as the source allows.
   - be accompanied by a printout that allows comparison of facts.
2. *Students' searches should*
   - involve all members of the group in searching the Web.
   - give information about alternative guidelines that can be contrasted with MLA guidelines.

REAL-WORLD CONNECTION

Scholarly and Professional Writing
Professionals continue to research and write throughout their careers. Doctors, lawyers, educators, scientists, and others publish articles, reports, and books that require citations. Discuss likely places to find professional and scholarly writing. (Sources may include professional journals, electronic sites of professional organizations, and trade books.)

 Activity Have students find and copy citations from several professional writings, including at least one online. Ask students to name the style used for citations and compare it with MLA Handbook style for high school writers. **L2**

Objective

• To read and understand theme song lyrics

Literature LINK

Where the Girl Rescued Her Brother This theme song connects to "Where the Girl Rescued Her Brother" (pp. 983–986). Point out that in the selection, Buffalo Calf Road Woman is a strong woman, like Wonder Woman, who performs a feat that people do not expect from a woman.

Respond

1. Students may say the image does not match the idea in the song because the song describes wondrous feats like stopping a bullet cold while the comic book simply shows Wonder Woman stopping a bully.
2. Students may name a feat such as stopping a war with love that would truly help the world.

Additional Resources
📁 *Media Connections Activities,* p. 23

MEDIA
Connection

Theme Song Lyrics

Wonder Woman has "lived" to be the legendary, superhero star of a comic book and a television series since her creation during World War II as a fighter against the enemies of the free world. Here's a little piece of that history.

The official American flag from 1912–1959 had 48 stars.

Wonder Woman

Wonder Woman!
Wonder Woman!

Now the world is ready for you
and the wonders you can do
Make a hawk a dove
stop a war with love
Make a liar tell the truth

Wonder Woman!
Get us out from under, Wonder
    Woman

All our hopes are pinned upon you
and the magic that you do
Stop a bullet cold
make the Axis fold
change their minds and change
    the world

Wonder Woman!
Wonder Woman!

You're a wonder, Wonder Woman!

Respond

1. Does the image of Wonder Woman on the comic book cover match the idea of Wonder Woman in the television show's theme song? Explain.

2. What do you think is the most wondrous thing Wonder Woman can do? Why?

Teaching Options

Reading *Minilesson*

Identifying Bias Explain that in biased writing an author shows strong feeling for or against something. The author uses loaded words and presents only one point of view. Point out that while in general writers strive for balanced over biased writing, sometimes they use bias deliberately to make a point.

Activity Have students reread the theme song lyrics and consider the following questions: *What is the songwriter's bias? Which statements in the lyrics are biased? What loaded words does the writer use? Do you think the writer chose to use bias? If so, why?* **L2**

Additional Resources
📁 *Reading Workbook*

Wonder Woman is a trademark of DC Comics, copyright © 1998.
All rights reserved. Used with permission.

Comic Book Heroes Have students find out about Web sites that are devoted to comic book heroes such as Batman and Superman. Have them report orally on their findings.

FYI

Wonder Woman came into existence in December, 1941, as a special edition of *All Star Comics*. In that issue, the heroine left her home on Paradise Island to help the Allies (Great Britain, the Soviet Union, the United States, China) defeat the Axis powers (Germany, Italy, Japan) during World War II. Wonder Woman is the only female charater to be featured in her own comic book for fifty-five years and to star in her own television series.

Objectives

- To read and analyze a legend about how a young woman responds heroically in a time of crisis
- To identify suspense in a story
- To write a paragraph about a story's subjective details

Skills

Reading/Thinking: Drawing Conclusions; Using Graphic Aids
Writing: Summary
Vocabulary: Synonyms
Grammar/Language: Dashes for Explanatory Comments
Listening/Speaking: Storytelling
Collaboration: Literature Groups

Motivating
→OPTIONS

Selection Focus Transparency 77: Begin the discussion by giving a character trait such as dignity.

Focus Activity: Have students give examples of some of the heroic elements on their checklist.

—Before You Read—
Where the Girl Rescued Her Brother

FOCUS ACTIVITY

Whom have you heard or read about who responded heroically in a time of crisis? What made their actions heroic?

HEROIC ACT CHECKLIST What elements are common to acts of heroism? Create a checklist that could be used to identify heroic acts. Share your checklist with the class.

SETTING A PURPOSE Read to see how a young woman responds heroically in a time of crisis.

BACKGROUND

The Time and Place
The characters and events described in this story are based on fact. The battle that sparked these events took place on June 17, 1876, at Rosebud Creek in southern Montana.

Did You Know?
When gold was discovered in the Black Hills of South Dakota in the early 1870s, miners rushed into the area, heedless of the treaty that had previously guaranteed the Sioux people exclusive possession of the land. The miners' total disregard for the rights of Native Americans spurred skirmishes between the two groups. As a result, Brigadier General George Crook of the United States Army ordered the Sioux to leave the area, but Sioux chiefs Sitting Bull and Crazy Horse ignored the order. After a series of unprovoked attacks on his people, Sitting Bull summoned the Sioux, Cheyenne, and certain Arapaho to Montana. Soon after, this confederation surprised Crook's troops at Rosebud Creek. That battle is described, in part, in "Where the Girl Rescued Her Brother."

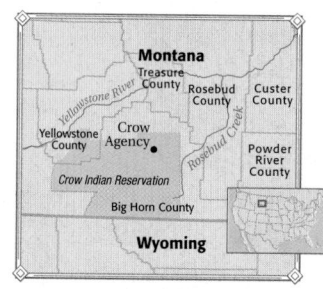

VOCABULARY PREVIEW

confront (kən frunt′) v. to come face-to-face with; to oppose; p. 984
vault (vôlt) v. to jump; spring; p. 985
strategic (strə tē′ jik) adj. highly important to an intended goal; p. 986

Meet Joseph Bruchac and Gayle Ross

Joseph Bruchac (brōō shak′), a Native American writer and storyteller, was raised by his grandparents. "My grandmother kept our house filled with books," he said, but it was from his grandfather that Bruchac learned the power of storytelling. "It is his voice that I often hear when I begin to tell a story."

Joseph Bruchac was born in 1942 in Saratoga Springs, New York.

Native American storyteller and writer Gayle Ross is a direct descendent of Chief John Ross, a Cherokee nation leader during the 1800s. Gayle Ross says that she and Bruchac "have been taught that stories are living spirits and that the role of the storyteller is to care for the tales in our keeping."

Gayle Ross was born in Denton, Texas, in 1951. "Where the Girl Rescued Her Brother" first appeared in The Girl Who Married the Moon *in 1994.*

RESOURCE MANAGER

Lesson Planning Resource
The *Unit Five Planning Guide* (pp. 40–47) provides additional lesson notes and reduced versions of all print resources.

📁 **Other Print Resources**
- Active Reading Guide, p. 82
- Vocabulary Practice, p. 53
- Reading Workbook, pp. 83–84
- Grammar and Language Workbook, pp. 267, 235, 271

- Grammar and Composition Handbook, Lessons 11.7, 11.9
- Quick Checks, p. 82
- Selection and Theme Assessment, pp. 155–156
- Performance Assessment, p. 80
- Spanish Summaries, p. 77
- Inclusion Strategies
- English Language Learners Sourcebook

 Transparencies
- Selection Focus 77
- Fine Art 30
- Literary Elements 82
- Grammar and Language 71, 72

Technology
 🎧 Audio Library
🎧 Spanish Audio Library
💻 Glencoe Literature Web Site
💾 Testmaker

Where the Girl Rescued Her Brother

Joseph Bruchac
& Gayle Ross ❧

Cheyenne Woman. Greg Perillo.

IT WAS THE MOON when the choke-cherries were ripe. A young woman rode out of a Cheyenne camp with her husband and her brother. The young woman's name was Buffalo Calf Road Woman. Her husband, Black Coyote, was one of the chiefs of the Cheyenne, the people of the plains who call themselves Tsis-tsis-tas, meaning simply "The People." Buffalo Calf Road Woman's brother, Comes-in-Sight, was also one of the Cheyenne chiefs, and it was well-known how close he was to his sister.

Like many of the other young women of the Cheyenne, Buffalo Calf Road Woman was respected for her honorable nature. Although it was the men who most often went to war to defend the people—as they were doing on this day—women would accompany their husbands when they went to battle. If a man held an important position among the Cheyenne, such as the keeper of the Sacred Arrows, then his wife, too, would have to be of the highest moral character, for she shared the weight of his responsibility.

Buffalo Calf Road Woman was well aware of this, and as she rode by her husband she did so with pride. She knew that today they were on their way to meet their old allies, the Lakota.[1] They were going out to try to drive back the *veho*, the spider people who were trying to claim all the lands of the Native peoples.

1. The *Lakota* were the largest group of the Sioux peoples. Their traditional hunting grounds were in the western Dakotas and Nebraska.

SUMMARY

A young Cheyenne woman, Buffalo Calf Road Woman, rides with her husband and her brother as they try to drive the white army off their lands. Buffalo Calf Road Woman is a member of the Society of Quilters, a group of brave women. She watches as the Cheyenne and the white army fight. Suddenly she sees that her brother has been surrounded by Crow scouts, allies of the whites. She rides her pony into the battle and grabs her brother's hand. He leaps onto her pony, and they ride away. The battle pauses as both sides watch Buffalo Calf Road Woman's act of bravery. Later the white general retreats. From then on the battle is known as the fight Where the Girl Rescued Her Brother.

📁 *Spanish Summaries,* p. 77

A Active Reading

PREDICT Have students view the selection title and the illustrations and predict how the girl might rescue her brother.

Additional Resources
📁 *Active Reading Guide,* p. 82
🎧 *Audio Library*
🎧 *Spanish Audio Library*

Teaching Options

CONNECTING TO OTHER SELECTIONS

The chart at right shows three ways to connect "Where the Girl Rescued Her Brother" to selections in this book.

For specific teaching strategies, see the **Unit Five Planning Guide**, pages 43–44.

Connection	Title
Life Skills: Decision Making →	"With All Flags Flying," p. 115
Thematic: Courage →	"By Any Other Name," p. 479
Literary: Conflict →	"A White Heron," p. 143

B Critical Thinking

DRAWING CONCLUSIONS You may wish to use the following model to help students draw conclusions about the position of women in Cheyenne society.

Model: The story describes the Cheyenne's traditional men's and women's roles: the men were scouts, hunters, and warriors while the women sewed clothing. However, the narrator also says that the women were strong and honorable like the men, and that they defended their families when the men were off hunting or fighting. I think the Cheyenne realized that women as well as men could be heroes.

C Literary Elements

SUSPENSE Have a student read aloud the last sentence of the paragraph. How does it create suspense? *(The vivid image sets the suspenseful scene of the women holding small weapons and waiting for the bear's approach.)*

Teaching Options

The Cheyenne had been worried about the *veho*, the white people, for a long time. They had given them that name because, like the black widow spider, they were very beautiful but it was dangerous to get close to them. And unlike the Cheyenne, they seemed to follow a practice of making promises and not keeping them. Although their soldier chief Custer had promised to be friendly with the Cheyenne, now he and the others had come into their lands to make war upon them.

Buffalo Calf Road Woman wore a robe embroidered with porcupine quills. The clothing of her brother and her husband, Black Coyote, was also beautifully decorated with those quills, which had been flattened, dyed in different colors, folded, and sewed on in patterns. Buffalo Calf Road Woman was proud that she belonged to the Society of Quilters. As with the men's societies, only a few women—those of the best character—could join. Like the men, the women had to be strong, honorable, and brave. Buffalo Calf Road Woman had grown up hearing stories of how Cheyenne women would defend their families when the men were away. The women of the Cheyenne were brave, and those in the Society of Quilters were the bravest of all.

Buffalo Calf Road Woman smiled as she remembered one day when the women of the Society of Quilters showed such bravery. It was during the Moon of Falling Leaves. A big hunt had been planned. The men who acted as scouts had gone out and located the great buffalo herd. They had seen, too, that there were no human enemies anywhere near their camp. So almost none of the men remained behind.

On that day, when all the men were away, a great grizzly bear came into the

camp. Such things seldom happened, but this bear was one that had been wounded in the leg by a white fur-trapper's bullet. It could no longer hunt as it had before, and hunger brought it to the Cheyenne camp, where it smelled food cooking.

When the huge bear came walking into the camp, almost everyone scattered. Some women grabbed their little children. Old people shut the door flaps of their tepees, and the boys ran to find their bows and arrows. Only a group of seven women who had been working on the embroidery of an elk-skin robe did not run. They were members of the Society of Quilters, and Buffalo Calf Road Woman was among them. The seven women put down their work, picked up the weapons they had close to hand, and stood to face the grizzly bear.

Now of all of the animals of the plains, the only one fierce enough and powerful enough to attack a human was the grizzly. But confronted by that determined group of women, the grizzly bear stopped in its tracks. It had come to steal food, not fight. The head of the Society of Quilters stepped forward a pace and spoke to the bear.

"Grandfather," she said, her voice low and firm, "we do not wish to harm you, but we will protect our camp. Go back to your own home."

The grizzly shook its head and then turned and walked out of the camp. The women stood and watched it as it went down through the cottonwoods and was lost from sight along the bend of the stream.

Buffalo Calf Road Woman turned her mind away from her memories. They were close to Rosebud Creek. The scouts had told them that a great number of the *veho* soldiers would be there and that the Gray Fox,

Vocabulary

confront (kən frunt´) *v.* to come face-to-face with; to oppose

MEETING INDIVIDUAL NEEDS — ENGLISH LANGUAGE LEARNERS

Indian History English language learners may be unfamiliar with the history of Native Americans.

Activity Briefly review the history of Native Americans: about 1 million lived in the present-day United States when Europeans began arriving. There were many Native American groups with diverse cultures. This story refers to

those living on the Great Plains. On the board, write some words used in the story and have students define them: *bow and arrow, elk-skin robe, buffalo, chief, tepee, plains, scout, warrior, head-dress,* and *war pony.*

Additional Resources

📁 *English Language Learners Sourcebook*

Dress. 19th century, Southern Cheyenne. Buckskin, elk teeth, glass beads, tin cones, and yellow and red pigments, length: 48 in., width: 35 in. Smithsonian Institution, Washington, DC.

General George Crook, was in command. The Cheyenne had joined up now with the Oglala,[2] led by Crazy Horse. The Lakota people were always friends to the Cheyenne, but this man, Crazy Horse, was the best friend of all. Some even said that he was one of their chiefs, too, as well as being a war leader of his Oglala.

There were Crow and Shoshone[3] scouts with Crook, and the *veho* had many cannons. The Lakota and the Cheyenne were outnumbered by the two thousand men in Crook's command. But they were prepared to fight. They had put on their finest clothes, for no man should risk his life without being dressed well enough so that if he died, the enemy would know a great warrior had fallen. Some of the men raised their headdresses three times, calling out their names and the deeds they had done. Those headdresses of eagle feathers were thought to give magical protection to a warrior. Other men busied themselves painting designs on their war ponies.

Now they could hear Crook's army approaching. The rumble of the horses' hooves echoed down the valley, and there was the sound of trumpets. War ponies reared up and stomped their feet. Many of the

Cheyenne men found it hard to put on the last of their paint as their hands shook from the excitement of the coming battle.

Crazy Horse vaulted onto his horse and held up one arm. *"Hoka Hey,"* he cried. "It is a good day to die."

Buffalo Calf Road Woman watched from a hill as the two lines of men—the blue soldiers to one side, and the Lakota and Cheyenne to the other—raced toward each other. The battle began. It was not a quick fight or an easy one. There were brave men on both sides. Two Moons, Little Hawk, Yellow Eagle, Sitting Bull, and Crazy Horse were only a few of the great warriors who fought for the Cheyenne and the Lakota. And Crook, the Gray Fox general of the whites, was known to be a tough fighter and a worthy enemy.

Buffalo Calf Road Woman's husband, Black Coyote, and her brother, Comes-in-Sight, were in the thick of the fight.

---

2. Also a Sioux people, the *Oglala* (ō glä′ lə) lived in what is now South Dakota.
3. The *Crow* and *Shoshone* (shə shō′ nē) peoples lived primarily in the Rocky Mountains.

Vocabulary
vault (vôlt) *v.* to jump; spring

F Literary Elements

PLOT Have students summarize what happens in the climax and in the denouement of the story. *(In the climax, Buffalo Calf Road Woman rides into the midst of the battle and her brother jumps onto her pony. In the denouement, the Indians and the Americans stop fighting to watch the Indian woman save her brother; the narrator relates that later the American general retreated, and the act of Buffalo Calf Road Woman becomes a legend among the Cheyenne and Lakota.)*

Historical Note

The Battle of the Rosebud on June 17, 1876, was a prelude to the Battle of the Little Bighorn on June 25. In that battle, Lt. Col. George A. Custer led 650 soldiers into an encampment of Sioux and Northern Cheyenne in the Montana Territory expecting to find about 1,000 Indian warriors. In fact, there were twice that many. Led by Crazy Horse and Sitting Bull, the Indians killed Custer and all of his soldiers. The battle has since been known as "Custer's Last Stand."

✔ ASSESSMENT OPTIONS

📁 *Quick Checks,* p. 82

Teaching Options

The odds in the battle were almost even. Although the whites had more soldiers and guns, the Lakota and the Cheyenne were better shots and better horsemen. Had it not been for the Crow and Shoshone scouts helping Crook, the white soldiers might have broken quickly from the ferocity of the attack.

From one side to the other, groups of men attacked and retreated as the guns cracked, cannons boomed, and smoke filled the air. The war shouts of the Lakota and the Cheyenne were almost as loud as the rumble of the guns. The sun moved across the sky as the fight went on, hour after hour, while the confusion of battle swirled below.

Then Buffalo Calf Road Woman saw something that horrified her. Her brother had been drawn off to one side, surrounded by Crow scouts. He tried to ride free of them, but his pony went down, struck by a rifle bullet and killed. Now he was on foot, still fighting. The Crow warriors were trying to get close, to count coup[4] on him. It was more of an honor to touch a living enemy, so they were not firing their rifles at him. And he was able to keep them away with his bow and arrows. But it was clear that soon he would be out of ammunition and would fall to the enemy.

Buffalo Calf Road Woman waited no longer. She dug her heels into her pony's sides and galloped down the hill. Her head low, her braids streaming behind her, she rode into the heart of the fight. Some men moved aside as

they saw her coming, for there was a determined look in her eyes. She made the long howling cry that Cheyenne women used to urge on the warriors. This time, however, she was the one going into the fight. Her voice was as strong as an eagle's. Her horse scattered the ponies of the Crow scouts who were closing in on her brother, Comes-in-Sight. She held out a hand; her brother grabbed it and vaulted onto the pony behind her. Then she wheeled, ducking the arrows of the Crow scouts, and heading back up the hill.

That was when it happened. For a moment, it seemed as if all the shooting stopped. The Cheyenne and the Lakota, and even the *veho* soldiers, lowered their guns to watch this act of great bravery. A shout went up, not from one side but from both, as Buffalo Calf Road Woman reached the safety of the hilltop again, her brother safe behind her on her horse. White men and Indians cheered her.

So it was that Buffalo Calf Road Woman performed the act for which the people would always remember her. Inspired by her courage, the Cheyenne and Lakota drove back the Gray Fox—Crook made a strategic withdrawal.

"Even the *veho* general was impressed," said the Cheyenne people. "He saw that if our women were that brave, he would stand no chance against us in battle."

So it is that to this day, the Cheyenne and the Lakota people do not refer to the fight as the Battle of the Rosebud. Instead, they honor Buffalo Calf Road Woman by calling the fight Where the Girl Rescued Her Brother.

---

4. Among some Native Americans, to *count coup* (ko͞o) was to touch a living enemy and get away safely—an act requiring both skill and courage.

Vocabulary
strategic (strə tē′ jik) *adj.* highly important to an intended goal

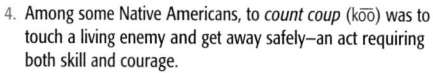

Grammar and Language *Minilesson*

Dashes for Explanatory Comments
Remind students that one use of dashes is to set off explanatory comments that interrupt the main idea of a sentence.

Activity Have students find and copy three sentences from the selection in which dashes are used to set off additional information. **L3**

Additional Resources

✍ *Grammar and Language Transparency 71*

📕 *Grammar and Language Workbook,* p. 267

📕 *Grammar and Composition Handbook,* Lesson 11.7

📕 *Writer's Choice,* Lesson 21.7

Responding to Literature

Personal Response

Were you surprised by the response of those who witnessed Buffalo Calf Road Woman's bravery at Rosebud Creek? Why or why not?

ANALYZING LITERATURE

RECALL

1. Who are Black Coyote, Comes-in-Sight, and Buffalo Calf Road Woman going to meet?
2. What clothing is Buffalo Calf Road Woman wearing on her journey?
3. What happened during the encounter with the grizzly bear?
4. Describe the scene at Rosebud Creek when Buffalo Calf Road Woman and her husband and her brother arrive.
5. What do the Cheyenne believe is the reason for the outcome of the battle?

INTERPRET

6. Why are the Cheyenne people worried about the *veho*? How do the Cheyenne view the *veho's* actions?
7. What special meaning does Buffalo Calf Road Woman's clothing have? Why is she feeling proud?
8. Why is the story about the grizzly bear significant to Buffalo Calf Road Woman?
9. What do you infer from the battle preparations of Native Americans about their attitude toward fighting and battle?
10. What do Buffalo Calf Road Woman's actions suggest about her character and skills?

EVALUATE AND CONNECT

11. How do the Cheyenne people seem to view the role of women in their society? Do you think their views are typical for other Americans of that historical time period? Why or why not?
12. Why might the authors have included the bear story in their tale?
13. Were you surprised by the **climax** and the **resolution** of the story? Why or why not? (See Literary Terms Handbook, pages R2 and R10.)
14. **Theme Connections**   Look at the checklist you made for the Focus Activity on page 982. Based on what you wrote, would you say that Buffalo Calf Road Woman's actions are heroic? Explain.
15. If you were a close friend of Buffalo Calf Road Woman and realized what she was about to do, would you have tried to stop her? Explain.

Literary ELEMENTS

Suspense

Suspense is the tension that builds in a story to make readers wonder what will happen next. Writers build suspense by providing **sensory details** of what the characters see, hear, touch, taste, or smell and by relying on readers' prior knowledge of details and events. Suspense in the bear story, for example, is developed with details such as "almost none of the men remained," "huge bear," and "hunger." When readers combine these details with their prior knowledge of the strength of a grizzly bear, the stress of hunger, and the feeling of fear, the suspense builds.

1. What sensory details in the battle scene describe the ferocity of the battle and the toughness of both sides?
2. What prior knowledge did you rely on to add to the suspense in the battle scene?
3. How do these sensory details and your prior knowledge build suspense in the battle scene of "Where the Girl Rescued Her Brother"?

● See **Literary Terms Handbook**, p. R13.

LEGENDS 987

Responding to the Selection

Personal Response

Students may say they were surprised that men would stop a battle to watch a heroic act by a woman.

ANALYZING LITERATURE
---

1. Black Coyote, Comes-in-Sight, and Buffalo Calf Road Woman are going to meet their allies, the Lakota.
2. Buffalo Calf Road Woman is wearing a robe decorated with porcupine quills.
3. When the grizzly bear came into camp, the women of the Society of Quilters picked up weapons and faced it. One of the women told it to leave, and it turned around and walked away.
4. When Buffalo Calf Road Woman and her husband and brother arrive at Rosebud Creek, the Lakota and Cheyenne warriors are preparing for battle. Soon Crook's army arrives and the fighting begins.
5. The Cheyenne believe the heroic act by Buffalo Calf Road Woman inspired the Cheyenne and Lakota to drive back Crook's army.
6. The Cheyenne people are worried about the *veho* because they have made many promises and not kept them. They view the *veho's* actions like those of a black widow spider—beautiful but dangerous.
7. Buffalo Calf Road Woman's clothing symbolizes her position as a member of the Society of Quilters. She is feeling proud because members of the society are the bravest women of all.
8. The story about the grizzly bear is significant to Buffalo Calf Road Woman because it shows the bravery of the women in the Society of Quilters.
9. The Native Americans take great pride in fighting and battle. It is an important event to them.
10. Buffalo Calf Road Woman's actions suggest she is courageous and an extremely skillful horsewoman.
11. The Cheyenne people seem to highly respect the skills and courage of women. This was probably not typical of other Americans of the period, who did not allow women to vote or do jobs traditionally held by men.

LITERARY ELEMENTS

1. Sensory details include the noise of the guns and cannons. Visual details include the Indians' headdresses.
2. Students may know of the bravery and horsemanship of the Native Americans and of the weapons of the U.S. army.
3. The knowledge of the great power of both sides makes the outcome of the battle uncertain, providing suspense.

Additional Resources

Literary Elements Transparency 82

12. The authors probably included the bear story to show that the Cheyenne women were strong and brave.
13. Students may say they were surprised that a woman rode into battle and saved her brother or that they were not surprised because the story of the grizzly bear prepared them for Buffalo Calf Road Woman's brave act.
14. Students should specifically refer to Buffalo Calf Road Woman's act and items on their list in responding.
15. Students may say they would have tried to stop Buffalo Calf Road Woman because riding into battle was extremely dangerous.

LITERATURE AND WRITING

Writing About Literature

Students' paragraphs should
- name specific subjective details in the story.
- discuss how the details influence the response to the story.

Creative Writing

Students' summaries should
- show knowledge of the story and its characters.
- use vivid language to attract readers' interest.

EXTENDING YOUR RESPONSE

Literature Groups Encourage students to discuss not only Buffalo Calf Road Woman's brave act but the implied attitudes of the Cherokee people toward women as they discuss the story. **COLLAB. LEARN.**

Interdisciplinary Activity You may wish to have each group focus on one state in which battles were fought.

Listening and Speaking Encourage students to locate recordings of Indian legends and other legends to play for the entire class.

Skill Minilesson

VOCABULARY • Synonyms—Shades of Meaning

1. pounce
2. vault
3. strategic
4. strategic
5. encounter

Additional Resources

📁 *Vocabulary Practice,* p. 53

LITERATURE AND WRITING

Writing About Literature

Analyze the Narrator's Perspective A narrator can influence readers' perceptions through **subjective details** that reveal personal opinions and feelings. In one or two paragraphs, show how subjective details influence your response to this story.

Creative Writing

In Bookstores Now! Imagine that you work in the marketing department of a book publishing company. How would you advertise this story on its book jacket? Write a brief summary of the story, including tantalizing details of the setting, characters, and events.

EXTENDING YOUR RESPONSE

Literature Groups

Defining Roles Gayle Ross has written, "In this changing world, with the roles of men and women being constantly redefined, I believe it is important that our definitions be based on mutual respect and the acceptance of our common humanity." In your group, discuss how this story supports Ross's views. Share your group's ideas with the class.

Interdisciplinary Activity

Social Studies: Mapping Historic Sites Find out more about Native American societies who tried to protect their lands. Research the Plains Indians and then create a map showing the territories of each group and the sites of their historic battles. Share your map with the class.

Listening and Speaking

Storytelling Time Listen to recordings by storytellers to identify the techniques they use to make stories come alive. Then use the techniques to tell the story to an audience.

Reading Further

You might enjoy these works by Joseph Bruchac and Gayle Ross:

Folktale: "The Girl Who Almost Married an Owl," from *The Girl Who Married the Moon,* is a Native North American tale about two sisters who encounter a trickster.

Poetry: "Coming Back," by Joseph Bruchac from *Harper's Anthology of 20th Century Native American Poetry,* edited by Duane Niatum, captures the importance of Native North American history.

📖 **Save your work for your portfolio.**

Skill Minilesson

VOCABULARY • Synonyms—Shades of Meaning

Not all synonyms, or words that have similar meanings, are correct in every context. Some words, such as *doubt,* are general in their meaning. Sometimes you need to be more specific. *Suspicion* and *skepticism* are synonyms of *doubt,* but *suspicion* means "mistrust," and *skepticism* can mean "an attitude of not admitting that something is true."

When choosing a synonym for a word, check the dictionary for both its literal meaning and its suggested meaning.

PRACTICE Select the underlined synonym that is appropriate to each context.

1. To catch a mouse, does a cat pounce or vault?
2. Does a person hop or vault over a four-foot fence?
3. Is a baseball coach's batting lineup an example of tricky or strategic planning?
4. Is taking detailed notes in class a diplomatic or strategic move for students?
5. Do friends who meet accidentally encounter or confront each other?

✔ ASSESSMENT OPTIONS

📁 *Quick Checks,* p. 82
📁 *Selection and Theme Assessment,* pp. 155–156
📁 *Performance Assessment,* p. 80
💾 *Testmaker*

Reading & Thinking Skills

Identifying Sequence

When you make a telephone call, you pick up the receiver, listen for a dial tone, and press the digits of a telephone number. These steps must be done in the right order, or **sequence,** so the call can go through.

Similarly, the events in narrative writing—writing that tells a story—happen in a sequence so readers can understand the passage of time in the story. Most narratives are related in **chronological,** or time, order. Transition words and phrases that show time, such as *then, next,* or *three days later,* help readers keep track of the chronology.

Sometimes authors interrupt the chronological order with a **flashback,** or a scene that took place prior to the current events. A sentence or phrase usually signals the beginning of a flashback. Another sentence or phrase signals a return to the chronological order of events.

In "Where the Girl Rescued Her Brother," Buffalo Calf Road Woman rides to the site of a battle, watches the battle, and then saves her brother. This chronological sequence of events is interrupted by a flashback to an earlier event. The sentence "Buffalo Calf Road Woman smiled as she remembered one day when the women . . . showed such bravery" signals the beginning of a flashback about an encounter with a grizzly bear. The sentence "Buffalo Calf Road Woman turned her mind away from her memories" signals the end of the flashback.

● For more about sequence, see **Reading Handbook,** p. R90.

EXERCISE

Read the following passage from *Sundiata.* Then complete the items that follow.

> She cried worse than ever. Djata was sympathetic to all this, but he was in a hurry to know something about Sosso. Balla Fasséké understood and said, "Triban, wipe away your tears and tell your story, speak to your brother. You know that he has never thought ill of you, and besides, all that was in his destiny."
>
> Nana Triban wiped her tears away and spoke.
>
> "When you left Mali, my brother sent me by force to Sosso to be the wife of Soumaoro, whom he greatly feared. I wept a great deal at the beginning but when I saw that perhaps all was not lost I resigned myself for the time being. I was nice to Soumaoro and was the chosen one among his numerous wives."

1. Which events in the passage occur in the present? List those events in chronological order.

2. Write the sentence that signals the beginning of a flashback. Then list the events of the flashback in chronological order.

Objective

- To identify chronological sequence and interruptions of it in a narrative

Teaching Strategies

After students have read the first four paragraphs of page 989, point out that films also often use flashbacks that interrupt the chronological sequence of events. Have students recall other stories and films with flashbacks. Ask them what they think was the author's purpose for including flashbacks.

Exercise

1. 1. Nana Triban cried.
   2. Balla Fasséké told Nana to tell Sundiata her story.
   3. Nana Triban began her story.
2. "When you left Mali, my brother sent me by force to Sosso to be the wife of Soumaoro, whom he greatly feared."
   1. Nana Triban was sent to be Soumaoro's wife.
   2. Nana wept a lot.
   3. Nana decided to resign herself to her situation.
   4. Nana was nice to Soumaoro.
   5. Nana became Soumaoro's chosen wife.

Additional Resources
📁 *Reading Workbook*

Teaching Options

MEETING INDIVIDUAL NEEDS — INCLUSION STRATEGIES

Less-Proficient Readers Students may need more practice recognizing flashbacks that interrupt the chronological sequence of events in a narrative.

Activity Have students write a paragraph describing their most recent birthday and to flash back to another birthday in the past in the course of the paragraph. (Students may choose to write about another memorable celebration.) Remind them to signal the flashback and the return to the current narrative. When students have completed their paragraphs, have them exchange papers with a partner and discuss whether their signals were clear. **L2**

Additional Resources
📁 *Inclusion Strategies*

Writing Workshop

Objectives

- To identify the elements of a bio-graphical research paper
- To plan, draft, revise, and present a biographical research paper
- To reflect on and assess the paper

Teaching Strategies

PREWRITING

Decide on a topic Have the class brainstorm a list of heroes. Encourage students to recall people with great accomplishments in science, literature, art, and music, as well as history.

Consider your purpose Point out that focusing on a person's heroism will help students develop a limited topic and thesis.

Teaching Options

~: Writing Workshop :~

Expository Writing: Biographical Research Paper

Have you ever wondered how a particular hero got to be so brave, selfless, or strong, or how someone's heroic action affected the life of others? One of the best ways to find out about a subject is to research it.

In this workshop, you will write a brief biographical research paper about some aspect of a hero's life.

You will give credit to your sources by citing them in your paper and in a list of works cited.

● As you write your research paper, refer to the **Writing Handbook**, pp. R58–R69.

The Writing Process

PREWRITING

Decide on a topic
The stories of King Arthur rely both on legend and on fact, but a research paper must rely only on fact. For this reason, it is important that you choose a topic about which a fair amount is known. However, a research paper must also be specific. If you provide *too* much information about your topic, you run the risk of writing a paper that is too general. Do some preliminary research at the library or on the Internet, then decide whether you need to expand or limit your topic. You might use a chart like the one below that a student began for her paper on Harriet Tubman.

Consider your purpose
Your main purpose will be to provide information about the hero you choose. You will state a thesis about some aspect of the person's life and then support the thesis by providing a factual account of the aspect you chose.

Choosing a Topic		
Too broad	**Limited**	**Too limited**
Harriet Tubman's life	Harriet Tubman as a conductor on the Underground Railroad	Harriet Tubman's early childhood

---

MEETING INDIVIDUAL NEEDS — ENGLISH LANGUAGE LEARNERS

Finding Sources English language learners may need help finding sources and using them effectively.

Activity Have students choose a subject from their native culture. You may wish to have pairs of students work on the same research subject. Help students locate sources. Then have them bring their books and periodical articles to class. Point out any sources that may be too difficult; have students focus on those that are more accessible. Students can work together with useful sources, discussing material and helping one another take notes.

Additional Resources
📁 *English Language Learners Sourcebook*

Writing Workshop

Choose an audience
Your audience is anyone who might be interested in learning facts about your subject.

Formulate questions
Write four or five research questions to discover, organize, and support what you know and what you need to learn about your topic. As the student has done in the model at right, ask *what, why,* and *how.* Modify your questions as you gather information.

Gather information
Keep your research questions in mind as you compile information from primary and secondary sources from the library and the Internet. Look for books, periodicals, and Web sites that contain important facts, relevant statistics, or interesting quotes on your topic. Use your subject's name as a keyword in your searches, but also try using more general terms, such as the historical time period.

Take notes
Many researchers use index cards to create a working bibliography and to take notes. See the Writing Handbook, pages R65–R66, for help with this step in the research process.

Make an outline
A working outline—one that you continue to write and revise as you conduct your research—can help you organize your information. The writer of the model shown below organized her information in chronological order. You might also organize information to show the order of its importance or to show cause and effect.

STUDENT MODEL

- Why did Harriet Tubman act heroically?
- What risks did she take?
- How did she manage to achieve what she did?
- Who did her actions affect?

STUDENT MODEL

Hero of the Underground Railroad

I.   Background
   A. Harriet Tubman's personal background
   B. Historical background about conditions of slavery

II. First acts of heroism
   A. Escaped enslavement
   B. Came back to help her family escape

III. Repeated acts of heroism
   A. Why she went back
   B. Risks she faced
   C. Statistics about total number of people freed
   D. Reactions of others

IV. Recognition during her lifetime

Gather information Encourage students to consult a research librarian for help with sources in the library. If possible, arrange for students to tour the library so the librarian can explain how to find various source materials.

Take notes Remind students that when they find useful material, they must decide the form in which to take notes on it. Explain that if it is important to get the specific details of the original, they should quote or paraphrase it. However, point out that they should not spend too much time copying direct quotes. Explain that if they need only the general ideas from a source, they should summarize it in their notes. Point out that every bit of information in their notes will not appear in their final paper.

Additional Resources

📁 *Writing and Proofreading Practice,* pp. 1–7, 80–88

🖊 *Writing and Proofreading Transparencies 1–6, 45–46, 53–54*

📘 *Writer's Choice,* Lessons 7.1–7.6

MEETING INDIVIDUAL NEEDS — INCLUSION STRATEGIES

Learning Disabled Working on a research paper as a group can help students learn and practice the research process without feeling overwhelmed.

Activity Have students choose a topic as a group. Take them to the library and show them how to find information on the subject. Then copy and distribute two or three brief sources such as short articles or portions of books with information on the topic. Have students take notes as you discuss the articles. Ask students to contribute to a sample outline on the board. Have them write their first drafts and revise them with a partner. **L1** **COLLAB. LEARN.**

Additional Resources
📁 *Inclusion Strategies*

Write your draft Remind students of the importance of a topic sentence for each paragraph, which can be taken from their outlines. Point out that they should have a strong introductory paragraph that states their thesis and a conclusion that summarizes the entire paper or states any new conclusions that were reached.

REVISING

Evaluate your work Emphasize that in revising a first draft, students should focus not on grammar and mechanics but on content and organization. Point out that changing a thesis statement is a likely outcome of putting one's research together.

~ Writing Workshop ~

DRAFTING

DRAFTING TIP

See the Writing Skills page, "Main Idea and Supporting Details," on page 943, for help with organizing individual paragraphs.

Develop a thesis statement

State your thesis in the introduction. The graphic organizer below may help you.

Questions Leading to a Thesis Statement
1. What was the central idea that guided my research?
2. What questions did I answer in my research?
3. What significant ideas surfaced during my research?
4. How could my research findings be stated in one sentence?

→ Thesis statement

Continue to revise your thesis statement until it conveys your unique approach to the topic.

Write your draft

Begin drafting, using your outline as a guide. For each heading in your outline, write at least one paragraph. Don't let details stall you, and don't worry about finding "perfect" phrasing. If necessary, you can do more research later.

STUDENT MODEL

~~Harriet Tubman was born into slavery, but she freed many others.~~

Harriet Tubman's acts of heroism were so great that even people who did nothing to stop slavery eventually recognized her bravery.

REVISING

REVISING TIP

Tighten your paper by deleting anything that doesn't support your thesis.

Evaluate your work

Before you revise, review your notes and reconsider your thesis. As you wrote your draft, your paper may have headed in a different direction from your original thesis. Revise your thesis if necessary. Next, use your thesis and the **Questions for Revising** to guide your revision. Refer to Writing Handbook page R68 for help with formatting your list of works cited.

Have a writing conference

Work with a revision partner. Read your research reports to each other. Then use the **Questions for Revising** to offer suggestions for improving each other's work.

QUESTIONS FOR REVISING

How can you:

☑ strengthen your thesis statement?

☑ clarify confusing parts?

☑ explain background for the readers?

☑ show the logic of your thesis statement?

STUDENT MODEL

Every time Harriet Tubman went back, she risked losing her own freedom. Yet she returned at least fifteen more times to lead over 200 ~~more~~ people to freedom. That generosity is one of the things that eventually won her admiration from around the globe.

Teaching Options

Grammar and Language *Minilesson*

Punctuating Direct Quotes Explain that occasionally in a research paper, a writer may want to use a short direct quote from a source.

Review the use of quotation marks in a research paper. Point out that a quote may be introduced in several ways:

Jones says, "Churchill was a great leader."

Jones says that "Churchill was a great leader."
Jones's statement is typical: "Churchill was a great leader."

Point out that commas and periods always go inside the closing quotation marks.

Activity Have students write three direct quotes from their research material, using correct punctuation. **L2**

Additional Resources

🖨 ***Grammar and Language Transparency 72***

📖 ***Grammar and Language Workbook,*** pp. 235, 271

📗 ***Grammar and Composition Handbook,*** Lesson 11.9

📘 ***Writer's Choice,*** Lesson 21.9

EDITING/PROOFREADING

After revising your draft, type or print a new copy of it with your corrections included. Then you can give your paper one final proofreading, checking citations, grammar, spelling, punctuation, and word use.

Grammar Hint

Do not use an apostrophe with possessive personal pronouns.

INCORRECT: *A true hero is someone who saves a life at the risk of his or her's.*

CORRECT: *A true hero is someone who saves a life at the risk of his or hers.*

● For more on punctuating possessive forms, see **Language Handbook**, p. R25.

PROOFREADING TIP
Use the **Proofreading Checklist** on the inside back cover to help you catch errors.

TECHNOLOGY TIP
People usually make more mistakes when they proofread on the computer monitor. Print out a copy of your paper to proofread it.

STUDENT MODEL

Harriet Tubman bel[ei]ved that every African american's life was as important as hers".

PUBLISHING/PRESENTING

Most research papers have a cover sheet that shows the title of the paper, the writer's name, and other identifying information. If you decide to present your report orally, adapt it to make the ideas easier for your listeners to absorb. Shorten sentences and add visual aids that will break up the delivery of the text.

PRESENTING TIP
Photographs enrich a biographical research report.

Reflecting

In your journal, reflect on the effect your subject's heroism might have on your future actions or attitudes.

Which was the more difficult part of this assignment, the research or the writing? What did you learn from this experience that might help you conduct research in the future?

📖 **Save your work for your portfolio.**

Have students use the Proofreading Checklist on the inside back cover of their textbooks.

Grammar Hint On the board, write additional possessive pronouns that are sometimes misspelled: *yours, its, ours,* and *theirs.* Have students use each one in a sentence.

TECHNOLOGY TIP

Remind students that spell checks in word processing programs will not catch errors in which an incorrect homophone was used.

PUBLISHING/PRESENTING

Have students display their completed papers and give the class time to scan their classmates' work.

Reflecting

Portfolio Encourage students to ask themselves these questions as they review their writing.

Does my biographical research paper
- support my thesis about my subject's heroism?
- use source material convincingly?
- reflect thinking and writing of which I am proud?

If students answer yes to more than one of these questions, suggest they include their research paper in their portfolio.

✔ ASSESSMENT OPTIONS

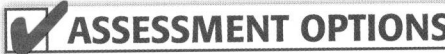

📁 ***Writing Assessment and Portfolio Management***
- Writing Assessment, pp. 2–19, 43–44
- Portfolio Management, pp. 20–22

Unit Wrap-Up

Objectives

- To give a personal response about the stories, discussions, and activities in this unit
- To write a comparison of portrayals of one character in two or more different works
- To complete a self-evaluation, set a goal, and devise a plan for achieving the goal

1. Students should give specific reasons and explanations for their choices.
2. Students should give examples of how their skills were enhanced in each of the four areas.

Students' writing should

- have an introduction that identifies the selections being discussed.
- use a comparison-contrast organization to discuss character traits in each selection.

Evaluate

Have students list the projects and assignments they completed in the unit. Encourage them also to list class and group discussions in which they participated.

Encourage students to discuss guidelines for the evaluation scale.

Set Goals

Suggest that students design a checklist showing the steps, checkpoints, and goal in their plan with spaces they can mark as they accomplish each.

Unit Wrap-Up

PERSONAL RESPONSE

1. If someone were looking for exciting reading matter, which of the legends in this unit would you recommend? Explain your answer.
2. How did your work in this unit enhance your skills in the following areas?
   - connecting events from the past to your life in the present
   - figuring out the meanings of unfamiliar words and phrases
   - explaining your ideas in writing
   - working on your own to complete assignments

ANALYZING LITERATURE

Comparing Versions of Arthur   Although a real Arthur may have walked the earth, the King Arthurs that you have read about are partially products of their authors' imaginations. Compare representations of King Arthur from two or more selections. What aspects of his character remain constant? What aspects vary? How might the times in which the selections were written have affected the images of the Arthur they portray? Use examples from the selections to illustrate your comparison.

EVALUATE AND SET GOALS

Evaluate

1. How well did you meet the goals you set for yourself regarding this unit?
   - What helped you meet these goals?
   - What were the setbacks in accomplishing these goals?
2. What was your most meaningful contribution to a group project?
3. How would you assess your work in this unit, using the following scale? Give at least two reasons for your assessment.
   4 = outstanding   **3** = good   **2** = fair   **1** = weak

Set Goals

1. Choose a goal to work toward in Unit 6. Concentrate on any skill you wish to improve, such as reading, writing, speaking, or working in a group.
2. Discuss your goal with your teacher.
3. Write down three steps you will take to help you achieve your goal.
4. Plan checkpoints at specific intervals in the unit to assess your progress toward your goal.
5. Include a self-evaluation plan to determine whether you have reached your goal.

BUILD YOUR PORTFOLIO

Select   Choose two pieces of writing you did in this unit, and include them in your portfolio. The following questions can help you make your selection.

- Which piece did people respond to most favorably?
- Which piece most clearly expresses your ideas?
- Which piece did you spend the most time revising?
- Which piece shows the most improvement in your writing?

Reflect   Write notes for each piece you include in your portfolio. Consider the following issues.

- At the beginning of the writing process, what were your major concerns? How did you address them?
- What were your sources of inspiration?
- What do you think are general strengths of your writing? What do you have problems with? How does this piece fit with those trends?

ASSESSMENT OPTIONS

📁 ***Writing Assessment and Portfolio Management***
- Writing Assessment, pp. 2–19
- Portfolio Management, pp. 20–22

GLENCOE TECHNOLOGY

 MINDJOGGER VIDEOQUIZZES VIDEODISC

Use *MindJogger* to review the Unit 5 content.

 Unit 5 Side B

Also available in VHS.

Reading on Your Own

You might also be interested in the following books.

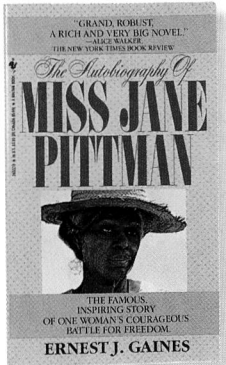

The Autobiography of Miss Jane Pittman
by Ernest J. Gaines Having lived 110 years, Jane Pittman is a woman with many stories to tell. Born into slavery, she lives through the Civil War, Reconstruction, life on a Southern plantation, and the Civil Rights movement of the 1960s. Her strength and courage serve as models to those around her.

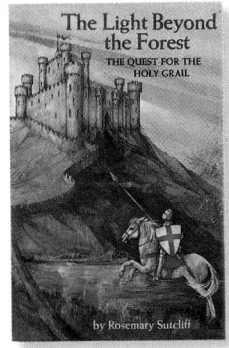

The Light Beyond the Forest
by Rosemary Sutcliff The Knights of the Round Table set out in search of a holy relic known as the Holy Grail. This is a tale of heroism and adventure, in which Sir Lancelot, Sir Galahad, and the other knights struggle against great dangers to reach their goal. Only the most perfect knight succeeds.

Cut from the Same Cloth: American Women of Myth, Legend, and Tall Tale
by Robert D. San Souci Discover America's unheralded heroines who are as strong-willed and clever as their male counterparts. San Souci retells fifteen folktales, ballads, and stories about legendary women, representing such cultures as African American, Anglo American, Inuit, Hawaiian, Mexican American, and Native American.

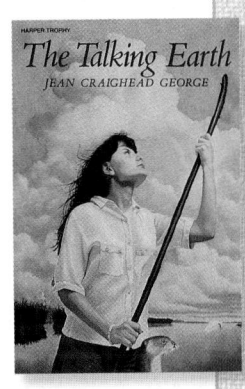

The Talking Earth
by Jean Craighead George Do cultural traditions belong in our modern, technological world? Billie Wind finds the answer to this question when she ventures off alone into the Florida Everglades as punishment for doubting her Seminole tribe's legends. Her adventure teaches her that her tribe's legends are important—especially in today's world.

Glencoe Literature Library

The Autobiography of Miss Jane Pittman by Ernest J. Gaines is one of the titles available in the *Glencoe Literature Library*. For a complete listing, see page T44 in this book.

The *Glencoe Literature Library: Study Guides* provide instructional support and student activities for works in the *Glencoe Literature Library*.

At the MOVIES

Be sure to preview the following video for appropriateness for your class:

• **Le Morte d'Arthur***

 *Also available in the Glencoe Literature *Video* Library.

MEETING INDIVIDUAL NEEDS — INCLUSION STRATEGIES

You may wish to recommend *Cut from the Same Cloth: American Women of Myth, Legend, and Tall Tale* by Robert D. San Souci to your less proficient readers. The accessible themes and language of this book make it particularly appropriate for these students. **L1**

The following books are rated for average readers (**L2**) or for students who need more challenging reading material (**L3**):

• *The Autobiography of Miss Jane Pittman* by Ernest J. Gaines **L3**
• *The Talking Earth* by Jean Craighead George **L2**
• *The Light Beyond the Forest* by Rosemary Sutcliff **L2**

Additional Resources
📁 *Inclusion Strategies*

Standardized Test Practice

Answers and Analyses

1. **D** There is no error in the sentence.
2. **G** Since *Camp Sunshine* is a proper noun, it should be capitalized.
3. **C** Since this sentence is a statement, it should not be followed by a question mark.
4. **G** In this case, *school* is not a proper noun, and should not be capitalized.
5. **C** Since this is a question, it should be followed by a question mark.
6. **F** The word *convenience* is misspelled.

 TEST-TAKING TIP

Suggest that students try to answer test questions in their own words before looking at the answer choices. This technique works well when looking for errors in a sentence.

Standardized Test Practice

Read the passage and decide which type of error, if any, appears in each underlined section. Mark the letter for your answer on your paper.

> Dear Ben,
>
> Please forgive me for not having written sooner. This camping trip has been a busy one. It's very hard to find time to sit down and compose a letter. The counselors here at camp sunshine have given me many new responsibilities. I never complain, though? Camp life agrees with me. It's a great place to go after a hard year at School. I know that if you see this place, you'll agree.
> <u>It's very hard to find time to sit down</u> (1)
> <u>The counselors here at</u> (2)
> <u>camp sunshine have given me</u>
> <u>I never complain, though?</u> (3)
> <u>after a hard year at School.</u> (4)
>
> Your idea to come visit me during the last week of August sounds great! How can I help with the preparations. Send me whatever details you think I'll need, and let's get you out here at your earliest convenence. I'm excited to see you after all this time!
> <u>How can</u> (5)
> <u>I help with the preparations.</u>
> <u>get you out here at your earliest convenence.</u> (6)
>
> Your friend,
>
> Veronica

1. A Spelling error
    B Capitalization error
    C Punctuation error
    D No error

2. F Spelling error
    G Capitalization error
    H Punctuation error
    J No error

3. A Spelling error
    B Capitalization error
    C Punctuation error
    D No error

4. F Spelling error
    G Capitalization error
    H Punctuation error
    J No error

5. A Spelling error
    B Capitalization error
    C Punctuation error
    D No error

6. F Spelling error
    G Capitalization error
    H Punctuation error
    J No error

Read the passage. Some sections are underlined. The underlined sections may be one of the following:
- Incomplete sentences
- Run-on sentences
- Correctly written sentences that should be combined
- Correctly written sentences that do not need to be rewritten

Choose the best way to write each underlined section. On your paper mark the letter for your answer. If the underlined section needs no change, mark the choice "Correct as is."

The development of new types of blacksmith techniques in medieval times led to the (7) widespread use of steel armor to protect soldiers during wartime. The earliest version of armor was called mail. Mail was clunky and heavy. (8) It deflected weapons but also slowed the wearer down. Blacksmiths soon found that the more motion and quickness armor allowed, the less protection it provided. For instance, full plate mail sometimes weighed (9) 75 pounds. Or more. A knight wearing a suit of plate mail might walk through a hailstorm of arrows and slingshots unharmed, but he was far too encumbered to fight against a single pikeman or lancer.

---

7 **A** The development of new types of blacksmith techniques in medieval times. Led to the widespread use of steel armor to protect soldiers during wartime.

   B To develop certain types of blacksmith techniques in medieval times led blacksmiths to the widespread use of steel armor to protect soldiers during wartime.

   C The development of certain types of blacksmith techniques in medieval times leading to the widespread use of steel armor to protect soldiers during wartime.

   D Correct as is

8 **F** The earliest version of armor was called mail, and it was clunky and heavy.

   G The earliest version of armor was called mail, but it was clunky and heavy.

   H The earliest version of armor—called mail—was clunky and heavy.

   I Correct as is

9 **A** For instance, full plate mail sometimes weighing 75 pounds, or more.

   B For instance, full plate mail sometimes weighed 75 pounds, more or less.

   C For instance, full plate mail sometimes weighed 75 pounds or more. STOP

   D Correct as is

Answers and Analyses

7. **D** The sentence is correct as is. Choice A is composed of two sentence fragments. Choices B and C are also incomplete.

8. **F** The underlined sentences should be combined. Choice H unnecessarily complicates the sentence, and choice G is incorrect because there are no contrasting ideas to justify the use of *but*.

9. **C** The underlined portion contains a sentence fragment. It should be written as one sentence for clarity and conciseness. Choice B changes the meaning. No comma is needed, so the best choice is C.

 THE PRINCETON REVIEW **TEST-TAKING TIP**

Caution students to pay attention to nothing other than the test. Urge them to sit away from their friends and remind them to focus on the test even when other students have finished early.

Tested Objectives

Questions	Reading Objective
1–6	Recognize appropriate spelling, capitalization, and punctuation within the context of a written passage
7–9	Recognize appropriate sentence construction within the context of a written passage

MORE PRACTICE

For additional practice, assign pages from one of the following standardized test resources available as part of Glencoe Literature.

Additional Resources
ITBS Preparation and Practice
SAT-9 Preparation and Practice
TerraNova Preparation and Practice

Unit Six At a Glance
Humor

UNIT OPENING

Theme 12:
COMIC PERSPECTIVES

● **Literature Focus: Humor**
(p. 1000)

SELECTIONS

Let's Sweat! (p. 1002)

Media Connection: Comic Strip (p. 1008)

from **A Cat's Garden of Verses** (p. 1009)

Appetizer (p. 1015)

Media Connection: Magazine Article (p. 1028)

from **An American Childhood** (p. 1029)

What Is and Ain't Grammatical (p. 1038)

The Car We Had to Push (p. 1044)

How I Changed the War and Won the Game (p. 1054)

A Marriage Proposal (p. 1061)

SKILL FEATURES

Technology Skills (p. 1012)

Grammar Link (p. 1014)

Reading and Thinking Skills
(p. 1052)

Interdisciplinary Connection
(p. 1053)

Vocabulary Skills (p. 1059)

Writing Skills (p. 1060)

**Listening, Speaking, and
Viewing** (p. 1077)

WRITING WORKSHOP

Expository Writing: Feature Article (p. 1078)

KEYS TO LITERARY CONNECTIONS

 World Literature

Glencoe Literature contains a variety of literature that represents cultures from around the world. World literature selections are highlighted with this symbol:

 Comparing Selections

In each theme of **Glencoe Literature**, the **Comparing Selections** feature gives students an opportunity to compare two selections they have just read. Each Comparing Selections page provides a variety of options to address diverse aspects of the reading and literature curriculum.

UNIT WRAP-UP

- **Personal Response, Analyzing Literature, Evaluate and Set Goals** (p. 1082)
- **Build Your Portfolio** (p. 1082)
- **Reading on Your Own** (p. 1083)
  Bless Me, Ultima by Rudolfo Anaya
  Novio Boy: A Play by Gary Soto
  Under Water with Ogden Nash by Ogden Nash
  Rules of the Road by Joan Bauer
- **Standardized Test Practice** (pp. 1084–1085)

KEYS TO TEACHING OPTIONS

 Block Scheduling

Activities that are particularly suited to use within a block scheduling framework are identified throughout this unit by the following designation: For detailed suggestions on block scheduling, see the **Block Scheduling Guide** for this grade level.

Key to Ability Levels

The Teaching Options throughout this unit have been coded for students of various abilities.

L1 BASIC activities for all students

L2 AVERAGE activities for average to above-average students

L3 CHALLENGING activities for above-average students

Unit Six — At a Glance
Humor

Reading Skills in this unit

Variety of Texts
This unit includes the following text types:
- essay
- poem
- short story
- autobiographical account
- play
- comic strip
- magazine article

Comprehension Skills
The following instructional support for comprehension skills appears in this unit of the Student Edition:
- **Synthesizing** (p. 1052)
- **Reading and Thinking Minilesson** (p. 1076)

See also the **Reading Minilessons** throughout the unit in this Teacher's Wraparound Edition.

Reading Resources

Comprehension Skills Resources

📁 **Active Reading Guides**
The **Active Reading Guide** provides graphic organizers and study guide questions to support students' reading of each selection. (**Active Reading Guide**, pp. 83–90)

📁 **Reading Workbook**
The Reading Workbook (pp. 85–92) includes additional instruction and reinforcement of reading strategies and skills.

🎧 **Audio Library**
Available both on tape and on CD, the Audio Library provides valuable comprehension support.

Resources for Reading Widely

Glencoe Literature Library
Each title in the Glencoe Literature Library includes a full-length novel or play plus related readings. A separate Study Guide is available for each title.

💿 **Literature Classics CD-ROM**
The 900 selections on this CD-ROM can be searched by author, theme, or genre.

  inTIME
A coproduction of Glencoe and Time Inc., *inTime* includes a wealth of high-interest nonfiction related to the selections and themes in Unit Six.

Assessment in this unit

Assessment Options in the Student Edition
Glencoe Literature offers a number of diverse ways to evaluate student understanding and skill proficiency. In the Student Edition, use the following:
- **Responding to Literature**
  Following each selection, students are asked to recall facts, interpret ideas, and evaluate concepts as they answer a variety of questions and complete activities to extend their understanding.
- **Unit Wrap-Up (pp. 1082–1083)**
  Here students respond to the selections on personal and analytical levels. They also assume ownership of their learning by setting and evaluating goals and by selecting work for their portfolios.

See also the many **Assessment Resources** listed on the facing page.

 THE PRINCETON REVIEW

Standardized Test Practice
The Princeton Review has developed the Standardized Test Practice pages found at the end of this unit (pp. 1084–1085). These pages contain practice test questions that help students remain familiar with standardized test formats and content.

Writing Skills in this unit

Writing Skills

The Student Edition of Unit Six offers strong instructional support for writing skills:

In **Extending Your Response**, which follows each selection:
- **Writing About Literature**
- **Personal/Creative Writing**

In **Writing Skills** Lessons:
- **Using Effective Language** (p. 1060)

   See also the **Writing Minilessons** throughout the unit in this Teacher's Wraparound Edition.

Writing Workshops

The theme in Unit Six concludes with a **Writing Workshop** that guides students through the writing process.
- **Expository Writing: Feature Article** (pp. 1078–1081)

Writing Resources

Writer's Assistant CD-ROM

Each Writing Workshop is supplemented by an interactive writing guide on the Writer's Assistant CD-ROM. This easy-to-use writing guide provides prompts, templates, and other tools that lead students through the writing process.

Writing and Proofreading Practice

Blackline masters present in-depth instruction and practice on a specific step in the writing process and proofreading. (pp. 1–7, 89–96)

Writing and Proofreading Transparencies

Transparencies (1–6, 47–48) provide graphic organizers and proofreading exercises for whole class instruction.

Research and Report Writing Guide

This resource provides extensive tips and activities to guide students in their writing projects in the literature classroom as well as in classes across the curriculum.

Style and Documentation Sourcebook for Writers

This sourcebook is a combination reference and workbook, giving students the most up-to-date information and guidance regarding traditional as well as technological research strategies and documentation.

Grammar and Composition Handbook

The Grammar and Composition Handbook provides instruction that supplements activities in the student textbook.

Assessment Resources

Selection Quick Checks

For each selection, a Quick Check of three to five short-answer questions measures students' literal comprehension.

Selection and Theme Assessment

The Selection and Theme Assessment instrument tests students' abilities to recall, interpret, and evaluate what they've read. The tests consist of multiple-choice, short answer, and essay questions.

Performance Assessment

Alternative assessment instruments and rubrics for Unit Six are found in the Performance Assessment ancillary.

Writing Assessment and Portfolio Management

These notes and strategies, student models, and assessment tools assist with the task of measuring students' progress as writers and as monitors of their own writing.

Testmaker

Teachers can customize selection, theme, and Unit Six tests by accessing the Testmaker database.

MindJogger Videoquizzes

Using a popular game show format, MindJogger Videoquizzes enable teachers to evaluate students' understanding of Unit Six in a quick and fun manner.

Humor

Unit Objectives

- To enjoy reading humorous literature
- To analyze literary elements of humorous literature
- To apply strategies for reading humorous literature

VIEWING THE PAINTING

René Magritte (1898–1967), a Belgian artist, was known for his surrealistic paintings. Surrealistic art often depicts realistic objects in dreamlike contexts.

Responding to the Art Discussion questions:

- What realistic features does the painting depict? (*the clouds, sky, and ground*)
- What unrealistic features does the painting depict? (*unnaturally large fruit with faces and expressions*)
- What effect is created by the surrealistic images? (*Students may say the effect is startling, weird, or amusing.*)

La Valse hesitation. René Magritte. Oil on canvas, 13⅞ x 18 in. Private collection.

998

TEACHER to TEACHER

SHEFFIELD HIGH SCHOOL • MEMPHIS, TENNESSEE

I introduce a unit focusing on humor with short, funny pieces—cartoon strips, movie clips, commercials, print materials. I ask students to answer several questions: "What makes this piece funny to you? Why is this funny?" Then we read aloud longer pieces. While one of the students reads, the others take notes every time someone laughs. We look at what made them laugh and why. Eventually, we get to a definition of what humor is and what makes people laugh. I also invite to our class a comedian and magician who gives a humorous program with a message. We'll also talk about the class clown and what's funny about what he or she says or does. Then I have students write a funny limerick. For extra credit, students can research the Internet for little-known information about limericks.

JEANNA BRANDON

UNIT ✹ SIX

Humor

*"Humor may not be laughter,
it may not even be a smile;
it is a point of view,
an attitude toward experience."*

—Howard Thurman

Theme 12
Comic Perspectives
pages 1001–1081

Have students read the quotation. Then pose these questions for discussion:

- What makes you laugh?
- Why do people find different things amusing?
- What is a story, poem, or other writing that you thought was humorous?

Theme 12: Comic Perspectives

Each essay, story, poem, and play in Theme 12 presents a lighthearted or humorous view of people, society, or technology.

GLENCOE
TECHNOLOGY
LITERATURE CLASSICS
CD-ROM
Search for other short stories by theme, author, or title.

RESOURCE MANAGER

See the *Unit Six Planning Guide* (pp. iv–1) for additional teaching notes, strategies, and resources for introducing the humor unit.

Objectives

- To discuss the purposes of humorous writing
- To identify techniques used in writing to create a humorous effect

Teaching Strategies

To introduce humor, bring in comic strips for students to read. Then discuss which strips they find amusing and why. Ask students if they think any of the strips are trying to do more than make people laugh. If so, what?

Historical Note

Humor and comedy have been part of literature at least since ancient Greek times when the comic playwright Aristophanes wrote the plays *Frogs* (405 B.C.) and *Clouds* (423 B.C.), satirizing the tragic playwright Euripedes and the philosopher Socrates, respectively.

Activity

Post the list of comic techniques on the board or in poster form for students to refer to as they read this unit.

Teaching Options

Literature **F O C U S**

Humor

Are you quick to laugh? Do you enjoy the lighter side of life and poke fun at your own idiosyncrasies? If so, you probably have a good sense of humor.

Many writers of humor simply want to entertain their readers—to give them a smile or a laugh. However, writers can also use humor as an effective way to point out human weaknesses, social ills, or the absurd aspects of daily life.

Writers create humor by twisting what readers expect into the ridiculous or unexpected. The following techniques can help create a comic effect:

- **Hyperbole** is extravagant exaggeration for the sake of emphasis. For example: Her eyes were as big as saucers.
- **Understatement** is representing something as less than it actually is, for example, saying that something is "not bad" when it's really great. Understatement is the opposite of hyperbole.
- **Irony** is a contrast between reality and what seems to be real. There are several forms of irony. **Situational irony** exists when the actual outcome of a situation is the opposite of someone's expectations. **Verbal irony** exists when a person says one thing and means another. **Dramatic irony** occurs when the audience has important information that characters in a literary work do not have.
- **Satire** is a form of writing that exposes personal, social, or political failings to ridicule or scorn, often in an effort to correct them.
- **Pun** is a play on words, or a joke based on words with several meanings or on words that sound alike but have different meanings.

Dilbert reprinted by permission of United Feature Syndicate, Inc.

- **Parody** is a form of writing that closely imitates the style of an author or a literary work for the sake of ridicule or comic effect. Parodies are designed to mock the work or form they imitate.
- **Sarcasm** consists of cutting, often unkind or ironic, remarks made to show disapproval or to taunt. For example: I wouldn't expect *you* to understand.

ACTIVITY

As you read the selections in this unit, look for examples of comic techniques and think about the writer's purpose in using them.

MEETING INDIVIDUAL NEEDS   **ENGLISH LANGUAGE LEARNERS**

Humor Around the World Encourage English language learners to share a joke or a humorous story from their native cultures. Can they explain why their joke or story is humorous? Help them identify which technique is used in their example.

Activity To help students remember the comic techniques, have them make a chart that lists each comic technique on page 1000 and an example of that technique that they recognize: a literary work, a play, a movie, or a television program. Students may need to work in groups to think of enough examples to fill the chart. Suggest that they keep the chart for reference.

Additional Resources

📁 *English Language Learners Sourcebook*

Theme 12 ___ Comic Perspectives

What things strike you as funny? What television programs make you laugh? What do you enjoy most about your favorite comedian? Although personal taste in humor can vary, there are some topics that most people find amusing. In this theme, you'll read humorous writing—fiction and nonfiction—that recounts both unusual and commonplace experiences that can make you laugh.

THEME PROJECTS

Performing

Comedy Show Which selections from this theme could become amusing skits?

1. Working with a group, choose the funniest scenes from three or four selections and rewrite them in the form of skits.
2. Use existing dialogue and add your own to capture and condense the essential humor of the pieces. Include minimal props and consider using pantomime.
3. Perform your skit sequence as a comedy show for other groups.

Interdisciplinary Project

Art: Comic Strips Choose four anecdotes or episodes from the selections in this theme. Adapt the episodes to a series of comic strips.

1. Rewrite and condense the episodes. Keep the essential details and humor.
2. Create comical visual representations of the characters and events. If you like, use computer software to produce images.
3. Compile your comic strips into a comic book, and create an enticing and descriptive cover.

Fishing, 20th century.
Brad Holland.
Private collection.

Teaching Strategies

The following suggestions may help your students plan and carry out their theme projects.

Performing

- Students may wish to summarize the selections before writing their skits to make sure they dramatize the essential elements.
- Suggest that students add to existing dialogue to help them capture the tone of the original.
- Remind students that voice and gestures can help communicate a comic tone.

Interdisciplinary Project

- Point out that an outline of each episode will help students determine the main events to be depicted.
- Encourage students to choose events to represent that will be visually appealing and that will differ from other pictures in the series.

Additional Resources

- 📁 *Interdisciplinary Activities,* pp. 24–25
- 📁 *Viewing and Representing Activities,* pp. 29–30
- 📁 *Listening and Speaking Activities,* pp. 23–24
- 📁 *Critical Thinking Skills,* pp. 33–35
- 📁 *Selection and Theme Assessment,* pp. 193–194
- 📁 *Performance Assessment,* p. 100

GLENCOE
TECHNOLOGY
LITERATURE CLASSICS CD-ROM
Search for other selections related to the theme of comic perspectives.

Theme 12 SKILLS SCOPE AND SEQUENCE

SELECTIONS	Literary Elements	Reading and Thinking	Writing	Vocabulary and Spelling	
Let's Sweat! NIKKI GIOVANNI	Personal Essay, SE p. 1006 *Personal Essay, TWE p. 1004*	*Evaluating, TWE p. 1005*	Poem, SE p. 1007	The Latin Root *pend*, SE p. 1007	
From A Cat's Garden of Verses by Robert Louis Stevenson's Cat HENRY BEARD	Parody, SE p. 1011 *Parody, TWE p. 1010*	*Sequencing, TWE p. 1008*	Parody, SE p. 1011 *Avoiding Wordiness, TWE p. 1014*		
Appetizer ROBERT ABEL	Rising Action, SE p. 1026 *Rising Action, TWE pp. 1017, 1021, 1022, 1025* *Imagery, TWE p. 1018* *Alliteration, TWE p. 1023*	*Identifying Cause-and-Effect Relationships, TWE p. 1023*	Story, SE p. 1027	Old Words, SE p. 1027 *Prefix super-, TWE p. 1019* *Dictionary Skills, TWE p. 1024*	
from An American Childhood ANNIE DILLARD	Hyperbole, SE p. 1036 *Hyperbole, TWE pp. 1030, 1035*	*Author's Purpose, TWE p. 1028* *Main Idea and Supporting Details, TWE p. 1035*	Dialogue, SE p. 1037	The Latin Root *voc*, SE p. 1037	
What Is and Ain't Grammatical DAVE BARRY	Allusion, SE p. 1042 *Allusion, TWE pp. 1040, 1041*				
The Car We Had to Push JAMES THURBER	Characterization, SE p. 1050 *Characterization, TWE pp. 1046, 1047, 1049* *Hyperbole, TWE p. 1046*	Synthesizing, SE p. 1052 *Graphic Aids, TWE p. 1049*	Journal Entry, SE p. 1051	The Latin Root *ject*, SE p. 1051	
How I Changed the War and Won the Game MARY HELEN PONCE	Diction, SE p. 1057 *Diction, TWE p. 1056*	*Problem and Solution, TWE p. 1056*	Anecdote, SE p. 1058 Using Effective Language, SE p. 1060	Analogies, SE p. 1058 Analyzing Words, SE p. 1059	
A Marriage Proposal ANTON CHEKHOV	Farce, SE p. 1074 *Farce, TWE pp. 1065, 1067, 1070, 1071* *Dialogue, TWE pp. 1066, 1067* *Climax, TWE p. 1073* *Satire, TWE p. 1073*	Responding, SE p. 1076 *Summarizing, TWE p. 1071*	Diary Entry, SE p. 1075 *Expressing Excitement, TWE p. 1073*	Etymology, SE p. 1076	

Key: Student material is in roman. Teacher material is in italic.   Technology   **COLLAB. LEARN.** Collaboration

Grammar and Language	Listening, Speaking, and Viewing	Life Skills	Study, Research, and Technology
Subject-Verb Agreement, TWE p. 1005	**COLLAB. LEARN.** Literature Groups, SE p. 1007 Commercial, SE p. 1007	Research, SE p. 1007	Research, SE p. 1007
Missing or Misplaced Possessive Apostrophes, SE p. 1014	Critique, SE p. 1011		Technology Skills, SE p. 1012
Dangling Modifiers, TWE p. 1024	**COLLAB. LEARN.** Literature Groups, SE p. 1027 *Comparison-Contrast Speech, TWE p. 1021*	Dealing with Bears, SE p. 1027 *Problem Solving, TWE p. 1019*	Internet Connection, SE p. 1027 *Research, TWE p. 1018*
Subject and Object Pronouns, TWE p. 1034	**COLLAB. LEARN.** Literature Groups, SE p. 1037 *Telling Humorous Anecdotes, TWE p. 1032*	Letter to Manufacturer, SE p. 1037	
Infinitives, TWE p. 1041	**COLLAB. LEARN.** Literature Groups, SE p. 1042	Letter to Author, SE p. 1042	
Using Colons to Introduce a List, TWE p. 1048	**COLLAB. LEARN.** Literature Groups, SE p. 1051 Presenting a Newscast, SE p. 1051	Accident Report, SE p. 1051	
Proper Adjectives, TWE p. 1060	**COLLAB. LEARN.** Literature Groups, SE p. 1058	Interview, SE p. 1058	Internet Connection, SE p. 1058
Sentence Varieties, SE p. 1076 *Exclamation Points, TWE p. 1072*	**COLLAB. LEARN.** Literature Groups, SE p. 1075 Readers Theater, SE p. 1077 *Communicating Tone in Dialogue, TWE p. 1070*	Compromising, SE p. 1075	Set Design, SE p. 1075 *Research, TWE pp. 1066, 1067*

SELECTIONS	📁 Print Resources		
Let's Sweat! NIKKI GIOVANNI	Unit Six Planning Guide, pp. 8–15 * Active Reading Guide, p. 83 Vocabulary Practice, p. 54	Grammar & Comp. Handbook, Lesson 6.4 Grammar and Language Workbook, p. 169 Reading Workbook, pp. 85–86	* Quick Checks, p. 83 Selection and Theme Assessment, p. 157 Performance Assessment, p. 81 Spanish Summaries, p. 78
From A Cat's Garden of Verses by Robert Louis Stevenson's Cat HENRY BEARD	Unit Six Planning Guide, pp. 16–20 * Active Reading Guide, p. 84 Vocabulary Practice, p. 55		* Quick Checks, p. 84 Selection and Theme Assessment, p. 158 Performance Assessment, p. 82 Spanish Summaries, p. 79 Spanish Translations
Appetizer ROBERT ABEL	Unit Six Planning Guide, pp. 21–28 * Active Reading Guide, p. 85 Vocabulary Practice, p. 56	Grammar & Comp. Handbook, Lesson 8.7 Grammar and Language Workbook, p. 209 Reading Workbook, pp. 85–86	* Quick Checks, p. 85 Selection and Theme Assessment, pp. 159–160 Performance Assessment, p. 83 Spanish Summaries, p. 80 Spanish Translations
from An American Childhood ANNIE DILLARD	Unit Six Planning Guide, pp. 29–36 * Active Reading Guide, p. 86 Vocabulary Practice, p. 57	Grammar & Comp. Handbook, Lessons 7.3, 1.2 Grammar and Language Workbook, p. 181 Reading Workbook, pp. 87–88	* Quick Checks, p. 86 Selection and Theme Assessment, pp. 161–162 Performance Assessment, p. 84 Spanish Summaries, p. 81
What Is and Ain't Grammatical DAVE BARRY	Unit Six Planning Guide, pp. 37–44 * Active Reading Guide, p. 87 Vocabulary Practice, p. 58	Grammar & Comp. Handbook, Lesson 3.3 Grammar and Language Workbook, p. 97 Reading Workbook, p. 87–88	* Quick Checks, p. 87 Selection and Theme Assessment, pp. 163–164 Performance Assessment, p. 85 Spanish Summaries, p. 82
The Car We Had to Push JAMES THURBER	Unit Six Planning Guide, pp. 45–52 * Active Reading Guide, p. 88 Vocabulary Practice, p. 59	Grammar & Comp. Handbook, Lesson 11.4 Grammar and Language Workbook, p. 247 Reading Workbook, pp. 89–90	* Quick Checks, p. 88 Selection and Theme Assessment, pp. 165–166 Performance Assessment, p. 86 Spanish Summaries, p. 83 Spanish Translations
How I Changed the War and Won the Game MARY HELEN PONCE	Unit Six Planning Guide, pp. 53–59 * Active Reading Guide, p. 89 Vocabulary Practice, p. 60	Grammar & Comp. Handbook, Lesson 10.3 Grammar and Language Workbook, p. 239 Reading Workbook, pp. 89–90	* Quick Checks, p. 89 Selection and Theme Assessment, pp. 167–168 Performance Assessment, p. 87 Spanish Summaries, p. 84 Spanish Translations
A Marriage Proposal ANTON CHEKHOV	Unit Six Planning Guide, pp. 60–67 * Active Reading Guide, p. 90 Vocabulary Practice, p. 61	Grammar & Comp. Handbook, Lessons 11.2, 4.7–4.8 Grammar and Language Workbook, pp. 245, 103–105 Reading Workbook, pp. 91–92	* Quick Checks, p. 90 Selection and Theme Assessment, pp. 169–170 Performance Assessment, p. 88 Spanish Summaries, p. 85

*Also available in Spanish

Transparencies

Selection Focus Transparency 78
Grammar and Language Transparency 73
Literary Elements Transparency 83
Fine Art Transparency 6

Technology Resources

Audio Library
Spanish Audio Library
Vocabulary Puzzlemaker
Web Site: lit.glencoe.com

Selection Focus Transparency 79
Literary Elements Transparency 84

Audio Library
Spanish Audio Library
Vocabulary Puzzlemaker
Web Site: lit.glencoe.com

Selection Focus Transparency 80
Grammar and Language Transparency 74
Literary Elements Transparency 85

Literature Launchers Videodisc
Audio Library
Spanish Audio Library
Vocabulary Puzzlemaker
Web Site: lit.glencoe.com

Selection Focus Transparency 81
Grammar and Language Transparency 75
Literary Elements Transparency 86

Audio Library
Spanish Audio Library
Vocabulary Puzzlemaker
Web Site: lit.glencoe.com

Selection Focus Transparency 82
Grammar and Language Transparency 76
Literary Elements Transparency 87

Audio Library
Spanish Audio Library
Vocabulary Puzzlemaker
Web Site: lit.glencoe.com

Selection Focus Transparency 83
Grammar and Language Transparency 77
Literary Elements Transparency 88
Fine Art Transparency 5

Audio Library
Spanish Audio Library
Vocabulary Puzzlemaker
Web Site: lit.glencoe.com

Selection Focus Transparency 84
Grammar and Language Transparency 78
Literary Elements Transparency 89

Audio Library
Spanish Audio Library
Vocabulary Puzzlemaker
Web Site: lit.glencoe.com

Selection Focus Transparency 85
Grammar and Language Transparency 79
Literary Elements Transparency 90

Audio Library
Spanish Audio Library
Vocabulary Puzzlemaker
Web Site: lit.glencoe.com

📁 *Theme* RESOURCES

- Listening and Speaking Activities (pp. 23–24)
- Viewing and Representing Activities (pp. 29–30)
- Critical Thinking Skills (pp. 33–35)
- Media Connections Activities (pp. 24–25)
- Interdisciplinary Activities (pp. 24–25)

See also these additional planning resources:
- English Language Learners Sourcebook
- Inclusion Strategies Sourcebook
- Literature Groups Sourcebook

Use Glencoe's *Presentation Plus!* This multimedia teaching tool lets you present dynamic lessons that will engage your students. Using Microsoft PowerPoint,® you can customize the presentations to create your own personalized lessons.

Objectives

- To read and analyze a personal essay about how a poet became interested in sports
- To identify the elements of a personal essay
- To write a paragraph on attitudes toward sports

Skills

Reading/Thinking: Evaluating
Writing: Poem
Vocabulary: The Latin Root *pend*
Grammar/Language: Subject-Verb Agreement
Listening/Speaking: Commercial
Life Skills: Researching Opportunities
Collaborating: Literature Groups

Motivating
→OPTIONS

Selection Focus Transparency 78: Have students discuss the graphic on sports and fitness.

Focus Activity: Have students make a chart or cluster map showing the attitudes toward sports discussed in their groups.

Before You Read

Let's Sweat!

── FOCUS ACTIVITY ──

What is your attitude toward sports? Are you mildly interested or wildly enthusiastic as an observer? as a participant?

DISCUSS Consider how you react to sports and fitness programs. Who or what influences your attitudes? With your group, discuss how and why people become interested or uninterested in sports and fitness.

SETTING A PURPOSE Read a personal essay to find out how Nikki Giovanni became interested in sports.

── BACKGROUND ──

The Time and Place
Nikki Giovanni wrote this essay in the 1980s, a period in which Americans became aware of the many benefits of participation in sports and fitness programs.

Did You Know?
Although attitudes toward women in sports have changed, especially in the last twenty-five years, emphasis at the school and amateur levels is still on male participation. However, research indicates that young women, as well as young men, who are athletic and participate in sports and fitness programs are more likely to have higher self-esteem than their nonathletic peers, to do better academically in high school and college, and to aspire to leadership roles at work and in their communities.

── VOCABULARY PREVIEW ──

impending (im pen′ ding) *adj.* about to occur; p. 1003
intone (in tōn′) *v.* to speak in a singing tone or monotone; recite; p. 1003
ultimately (ul′ tə mit lē) *adv.* at last; finally; p. 1004
heyday (hā′ dā) *n.* period of greatest strength, popularity, or prosperity; p. 1005

Meet Nikki Giovanni

In the 1960s, award-winning poet, essayist, and teacher Nikki Giovanni joined the Black Arts movement to promote African American rights and racial equality. Her writings during this period have been described as "militant" and "combative." In 1995 and 1996, she underwent successful surgery and treatment for lung cancer. The experience compelled her to determine what kind of writing she wanted to leave behind. "I decided laughter was the most important thing," she concluded.

Nikki Giovanni was born in 1943 in Knoxville, Tennessee. "Let's Sweat!" appears in Sacred Cows . . . And Other Edibles, *a collection of stories published in 1988.*

RESOURCE MANAGER

Lesson Planning Resource
The *Unit Six Planning Guide* (pp. 8–15) provides additional lesson notes and reduced versions of all print resources.

📁 **Other Print Resources**
- Active Reading Guide, p. 83
- Vocabulary Practice, p. 54
- Reading Workbook, pp. 85–86
- Grammar and Language Workbook, p. 169

- Grammar and Composition Handbook, Lesson 6.4
- Quick Checks, p. 83
- Selection and Theme Assessment, p. 157
- Performance Assessment, p. 81
- Spanish Summaries, p. 78
- Inclusion Strategies
- English Language Learners Sourcebook

Transparencies
- Selection Focus 78
- Fine Art 6
- Literary Elements 83
- Grammar and Language 73

Technology
🎧 Audio Library
🎧 Spanish Audio Library
💻 Glencoe Literature Web Site
💾 Testmaker

Chandra Rubin. Annie Leibovitz, photographer.

Let's Sweat!

Nikki Giovanni ⁓

Like most poets, I carry a two-hole folder with me almost compulsively.[1] It's not that I carry my ideas around so that should the occasion arise I can pull it out and say, in regard to some impending problem, "Oh well, a stitch in time saves nine." I do not have profound idioms at occasions of great distress so that I can intone: "It's always darkest before the dawn."

1. She acts *compulsively;* that is, the urge to carry the folder is compelling and irresistible.

Vocabulary
impending (im pen′ ding) *adj.* about to occur
intone (in tōn′) *v.* to speak in a singing tone or monotone; recite

HUMOR 🐾 1003

SUMMARY

The author is a poet who explains why she has become interested in sports and fitness. She tells of walking in on her father and his friends watching a World Series game on TV. They laughed at her ignorance of the sporting event, and she vowed to become more knowledgeable about sports. She now reads many sports publications and watches sports on TV when she is traveling.

📂 *Spanish Summaries,* p. 78

A Active Reading

PREDICT Have students predict how a professional poet might feel about sports, athletes, and staying physically fit.

Additional Resources
📁 *Active Reading Guide,* p. 83
🎧 *Audio Library*
🎧 *Spanish Audio Library*

Teaching Options

CONNECTING TO OTHER SELECTIONS

The chart at the right shows three ways to connect "Let's Sweat!" to selections in this book.

For specific teaching strategies, see the *Unit Six Planning Guide,* pages 11–12.

Connection	Title
Life Skills: Planning and Designing	→ "Civil Peace," p. 39
Thematic: Challenges	→ "Contents of the Dead Man's Pocket," p. 199
Literary: Tone	→ "The Californian's Tale," p. 248

Let's Sweat!

No. It's just that like most writers I think I think best when I'm not actually thinking about it, so I carry a book that allows me to put either something I have thought up as being very clever or, most likely, something that someone else said that I would one day like to use. Steve Krieder, running back for the Cincinnati Bengals, once said in response to the question "Why do you think the fans came out in — twenty degree weather to watch a football game?" "I think it's a failure of our educational system." I think that is neat. I love sports, too; but any fool who would sit in Riverfront Stadium in twenty below-zero weather to watch a game that was being televised anyway indeed has been let down by our public school system. I haven't found a way to work that into a poem, but with any luck and lots of persistence I will ultimately be able to achieve it. You don't see too many good poems on football. Baseball has "Casey At The Bat," but when you think sports, that's about it. Tennis needs a national poem. So does soccer. Any reader out there who's a soccer fan should really think about it because soccer is an international game and you could get a real chance to show off your Latin, Greek, Spanish, English, ancient Gaelic.[2] It could be a real intellectual *tour de force*,[3] as it were. I mention my folder because, in fact, I want to talk about sports. My folder, which is bright orange, has a mock license plate saying POETIC LICENSE,[4] which is normal since I do poetry. But right below that is

a white and orange circle that states: BODY BY SCANDINAVIAN. It's true. I've joined the Spa Revolution.

You may rightfully wonder why a forty-three-year-old woman would suddenly decide she can no longer get along without getting her body in shape. And that is exactly the point. If people know anything about the writing profession they know that all we do is sit and read or sit and write or sit and talk or sit on planes to go sit and do all of the above. I personally know writers whose legs give out if they have to go up one flight of stairs and now refuse to lecture at certain universities because the schools lack elevators. That's simply being in bad shape. . . . Dear young writer out there, you must sweat.

I guess you are wondering how I got into sports in the first place. I was visiting my father and mother one fall when a bunch of my dad's friends came over. Laughing loudly . . . they plopped themselves in front of the television and began to talk in numbers and letters. RBI's 35; ERA 3.56; HR 15; only 21 percent against left-handers and other things I didn't understand. It seemed so unlike my father to have gone into the stock market. I went into the living room and asked what was going on. It was friendly. I mean, I wasn't meddling or anything—just curious. You know the look you get when people think you are not quite bright? well, five men turned to my father: "And that's the famous one, huh?" And they all burst out laughing. My father was mortified. "We're watching the World Series, sweetie," he said sweetly. That should have been my clue to go on, as he never called me "sweetie" unless I had done something extremely stupid and he was exercising great patience to not scream, "Lughead, what do you think is going on?" I then, with

---

2. *Gaelic* (gā′ lik), an ancient language, is still spoken in some parts of Ireland and Scotland.
3. The French term *tour de force* means "a feat of extraordinary strength or skill."
4. The license plate plays on the actual meaning of *poetic license,* which refers to a writer's intentional variation from a rule or standard for the sake of effect.

Vocabulary
ultimately (ul′ tə mit lē) *adv.* at last; finally

the smile, I'm sure, of the terminally stupid, asked, "Oh, who's playing?" The room literally shook with laughter. I, naturally, beat a hasty retreat. The Giovannis are a close but competitive family. I determined from then on that the next time I came to visit I would know the sport, who was playing and what all those little numbers meant. From then on instead of reading the front page I turned to sports first. I cribbed a *Sports Illustrated* anywhere I could. I even purchased *Sporting News* and, during Hagler's[5]

Shoe Series #2, 1982–1983. Marilee Whitehouse-Holm. Acrylic, 18 x 24 in. Private collection.

Viewing the painting: Do you think the wearer of these shoes is a sports observer or a participant, as described by Nikki Giovanni? Why?

heyday (though the Marvelous One may think he is still in his heyday) read *Boxing News.*

Since I travel a lot I also made a great discovery. Alone in a hotel room on the road I would usually tune in *Tonight* or one of the talk shows. I can't stand violence and no lone woman in her right mind would look at *Hawaii Five-O* or any of those pictures where women are stalked and brutally killed. I learned, and I'm lucky cable came in when it did, that I could catch the West Coast games live. I'll bet I know more about the Phoenix

Suns during that period than any poet from the East Coast. I do have to confess I never became a Lakers fan but I kind of appreciate Houston—unless they're playing the Celtics. I could come back to a cold, empty hotel room in the middle of February and tune in something to cheer about. I could catch boxing, West Coast tennis, gymnastics—hell, fencing, if it came to that. I never did get into hockey because my major sports requirement is that I have to be able to see the ball, but I'm working on golf. Ahhh, but bowling. I love to watch bowling. You get a big, usually black, ball going down a clearly defined lane. I could sit and munch Planter's peanuts and cheer my little head off. . . . Sports is fun. We expect the men to want to go shopping to pick out curtains but we don't feel the same obligation to understand why you punt on fourth down. We want the guys to marvel at the cleanliness of our homes but we don't want to know what a cleanup hitter is. Come on, girls. Let's be fair. It's time to quit being jealous of our jogging mates and join in.

5. Marvin *Hagler* was a middleweight boxing champion in 1980.

Vocabulary
heyday (hā′ dā) *n.* period of greatest strength, popularity, or prosperity

---

VIEWING THE PAINTING

Acrylic paints were developed in the mid-1950s. Acrylics can look like oil paints but dry more rapidly than oils and are more durable.

Viewing Response *The shoes are well worn, indicating an active participant in sports.*

E **Active Reading**

QUESTION Why does the author like to watch bowling on television? *(She can clearly see the ball and the path it goes down.)*

F **Critical Thinking**

EVALUATING Use the following model to show students how to evaluate the author's generalization.

Model: The author is generalizing when she says that sports is usually a man's hobby and that most women don't appreciate sports. I think the author is talking about her own experiences and family. I know many girls and women who play sports and watch sports. I think her generalization is not valid.

Thematic Focus

Comic Perspectives Have students discuss the contrasts in the author's personality and way of life that help make her personal essay amusing.

☑ **ASSESSMENT OPTIONS**

📁 *Quick Checks,* p. 83

Grammar and Language *Minilesson*

Subject/Verb Agreement for Singular Nouns with Plural Forms Point out the sentence "Sports is fun" on page 1005. Explain that the noun *sports* can be either singular or plural. Giovanni uses it as a singular noun to mean an entire group of activities, so she uses the singular verb *is* to agree with it. In the sentence "Our school's winter sports are swimming and basketball," the word *sports* is plural.

Activity Have students choose the correct verb for each sentence.
1. Sports (was, were) the writer's subject. *(was)*
2. A million dollars (is, are) a lot of money. *(is)*
3. Politics (require, requires) knowledge of international issues. *(requires)*
4. His politics (is, are) quite liberal. *(are)* **L1**

Additional Resources

🖋 *Grammar and Language Transparency 73*

📙 *Grammar and Language Workbook,* p. 169

📙 *Grammar and Composition Handbook,* Lesson 6.4

📙 *Writer's Choice,* Lesson 16.4

Personal Response

Students may say they like the humorous tone of the essay or the author's description of her moment of sports awakening.

ANALYZING LITERATURE

1. She carries it to record ideas of her own or comments by others she would like to use one day. She does not carry it to consult it for a platitude to fit a particular occasion.
2. She has joined the fitness movement. She tells young writers to get in shape.
3. She became interested in sports when her father and his friends mocked her ignorance of the World Series.
4. She does not like to watch violent programs. Her favorite sport to watch is bowling. Her major sports requirement is that she be able to see the ball.
5. She encourages women to learn about and participate in sports.
6. She means that she has creative thoughts when she is not trying to.
7. The purpose of the movement is to become physically fit. She advises young writers to get fit because physical activity is a refreshing change from mental activity.
8. She is proud and competitive.
9. She is serious; she does not like violence; she likes simplicity.
10. Women expect men to participate in their interests, yet they do not participate in men's interests.
11. The theme is that physical fitness and sports are a positive part of life that everyone should experience.
12. Students may not agree with Giovanni's comments, saying that among their peers both girls and boys enjoy following and participating in sports and are therefore equally knowledgeable about sports.
13. Some students may say that the discussion and the selection have encouraged them to reconsider their lack of interest in sports. Others may say that the selection only underscored their enthusiasm for sports.
14. Her tone is light and enthusiastic; as indicated by lines such as "I think that is neat" and "Tennis needs a national poem."

15. Women growing up in the 1950s and 1960s did not often participate in sports and were not expected to know much about them. This traditional female role changed in the 1980s. Now women participate in and know about sports.

Responding to Literature

Personal Response

What did you especially like about this selection? Why?

ANALYZING LITERATURE

RECALL

1. Why does Nikki Giovanni carry a two-hole folder all the time?
2. What "movement" has she joined in her forties? What advice does Giovanni give young writers?
3. Summarize the circumstances that sparked Giovanni's interest in sports.
4. What TV programs does Giovanni not like to watch? What is her favorite sport to watch? What is Giovanni's major sports requirement?
5. What does she encourage women to do at the end of the selection?

INTERPRET

6. What do you think Giovanni means when she says, "Like most writers I think I think best when I'm not actually thinking about it"?
7. What is the purpose of the "movement" that Giovanni has joined? What reasoning might be behind her advice to young writers?
8. What does her reaction to the incident at her parents' home tell you about Giovanni's personality?
9. What can you infer about Giovanni from her television viewing and sports preference?
10. What contradiction in women's expectations of men does Giovanni point out at the end of the selection?

EVALUATE AND CONNECT

11. Theme Connections   What is the overall **theme**, or message, of this selection? Evaluate Giovanni's use of humor to get this message across.
12. Do you agree with Giovanni's concluding comments? In what ways do these comments apply to you or your peers? Explain.
13. Consider the discussion you participated in for the Focus Activity on page 1002. How has this selection affected your interest in sports as an observer and as a participant?
14. What word or words would you use to describe Giovanni's **tone** in this selection? Cite specific lines from the essay to support your description. (See Literary Terms Handbook, page R13.)
15. What does this selection reveal about the roles of young women who grew up in the 1950s and 1960s? In your opinion, how do these roles compare with those of women who grew up in the 1980s and later?

1006   UNIT 6

Literary ELEMENTS

Personal Essay

The **personal essay** is an informal essay in which the writer reveals one or more personal experiences, uses a light, conversational tone, and presents personal views on an issue. Often, a personal essay will contain humor as well as specific details from the writer's life in order to help readers personalize the events, relating them to experiences in their own lives. In "Let's Sweat," for example, Nikki Giovanni describes in detail how the circumstances surrounding a visit to her parents' house encouraged her interest in sports and fitness. While reading Giovanni's essay, the reader may have made a connection by saying, "Yes. Something like that happened to me once. I know just how that feels."

1. Identify two or three specific details in Giovanni's personal narrative that make people, places, and events come to life.
2. Do you think a short story could convey Giovanni's message as effectively as the personal essay? Why or why not?
3. Do you think her humorous approach strengthens or weakens her points? Explain.

● See **Literary Terms Handbook**, p. R4.

LITERARY ELEMENTS

1. Details: Giovanni's being laughed at by her father's friends; her reading the *Sporting News*; her staying in hotels and watching West Coast games live.
2. An essay is better because her profession and experiences make her insights about sports more interesting.
3. Humor strengthens her points that sports should be fun.

Additional Resources

● *Literary Elements Transparency 83*

LITERATURE AND WRITING

Writing About Literature

Comparing Attitudes   In what ways are your attitudes and experiences regarding sports like those of Nikki Giovanni? What is your reaction to the final sentence? Write one or two paragraphs comparing your attitudes with Giovanni's and explaining your reaction. Cite specific details from the selection. Share your writing with a small group of students.

Creative Writing

Write a Sports Poem   Giovanni points out that just about every sport, except baseball, is lacking a national poem. Write a poem that tells an exciting story about an American sport of your choice. You may want to obtain a copy of "Casey at the Bat" and use that poem as a model for your writing. Share your poem in a group poetry reading.

EXTENDING YOUR RESPONSE

Literature Groups

Evaluate the Writing   In your group, discuss the following questions and evaluate Nikki Giovanni's personal essay, supporting your opinions with details from the essay. Is her essay coherently organized? How does she personalize the experiences described? How does she present events to achieve her purpose? Share your findings with other groups.

Performing

Create a Commercial   Encourage people to get in shape and stay fit. In your group, create, write, and perform for the class a 20- to 30-second television commercial targeted at a male and female audience in the age-group of your choice.

Learning for Life

Sports Opportunity Report   Most professional sports are male-dominated events. Which sports offer the most opportunities for women to compete professionally? Use the Internet and current periodicals to research this and your own questions about sports opportunities for women. Summarize your findings in a chart or brief report for the class.

Reading Further

If you enjoyed "Let's Sweat!" you might want to read these poems from *The Selected Poems of Nikki Giovanni*.
Poems: "Choices" and "a poem for langston hughes."

 Save your work for your portfolio.

 Skill Minilesson

VOCABULARY • The Latin Root *pend*

The word *impending* comes from the Latin prefix *in-*, meaning "in" and the root *pend*, meaning "to hang." When something is about to happen, especially if it is threatening, we often say it is "hanging over" us. An *impending* event is hanging over you.

This root is found in several familiar words. One's pants can be kept hanging by means of *suspenders*. A *dependent* is someone who *depends* on you, in a sense, or "hangs" on you.

PRACTICE   Use your knowledge of the root *pend* to answer the questions.

1. Which animal has *pendulous* ears—a rabbit, a basset hound, or a bird?
2. Which of the following is a *pendent* source of light—a chandelier, a flashlight, or the sun?
3. Which device keeps time by using a *pendulum* —a wristwatch, a sun dial, or a grandfather clock?

LITERATURE AND WRITING

Writing About Literature

Students' comparisons should
- describe their attitudes about sports.
- compare their attitudes with Giovanni's.
- discuss their reaction to Giovanni's final statement.

Creative Writing

Students' poems should
- describe a sport.
- tell an exciting story.
- use rhyme or other poetic devices if they wish.

EXTENDING YOUR RESPONSE

Literature Groups   Before the groups meet, you may wish to discuss with students the quality of coherence in writing and how it is achieved.
`COLLAB. LEARN.`

Performing   Encourage students to outline the ideas that make Giovanni's essay unique before beginning their commercials.

Learning for Life   Encourage students also to check on women's sports reporting in daily newspapers.

Skill Minilesson

VOCABULARY • The Latin Root *pend*

1. basset hound
2. a chandelier
3. a grandfather clock

Additional Resources
 Vocabulary Practice, p. 54

✔ ASSESSMENT OPTIONS

📁 *Quick Checks,* p. 83
📁 *Selection and Theme Assessment,* p. 157
📁 *Performance Assessment,* p. 81
💾 *Testmaker*

Objective

- To read and understand a comic strip

Literature — LINK

A Cat's Garden of Verses This comic strip connects to Henry Beard's poems *From A Cat's Garden of Verses* (p. 1010). Point out that the cartoonist and the poet use different forms of humor to poke fun at cats.

Respond

1. Students may say that the cartoonist attributes human traits to his pets and that he prefers cats to dogs.
2. Some students may think the comic strip accurately portrays cats as being intelligent. Dog lovers may object to how dogs are portrayed.

Additional Resources

📁 *Media Connections Activities,* p. 24

Teaching Options

MEDIA
Connection

Comic Strip

Some people think cats are the most intelligent, friendly pets. Others feel the same about dogs. Are you a "cat person" or a "dog person"?

Garfield

by Jim Davis

Respond

1. Describe what you think the cartoonist's relationships with his pets might be like. Explain how you came to your conclusions.
2. Do you agree with the depiction of cats and dogs shown in this comic strip? Explain.

1008 🐾 UNIT 6

Reading *Minilesson*

Sequencing Point out that a cartoon strip clearly shows a sequence of events. Have students take turns describing what happens in each box of the strip on this page.

Activity Have students show the plot of a story they are currently studying by making a comic strip that shows the story's sequence of events. Point out that they need not make elaborate drawings but that sketches of a story's characters can help them comprehend or review the story's events and characters. **L2**

Additional Resources

📁 *Reading Workbook*

Before You Read

From A Cat's Garden of Verses

FOCUS ACTIVITY

Have you ever put new words to a song or an advertising jingle? Was your version more humorous than the original?

QUICKWRITE Rewrite the words to a jingle you've heard on the radio or on television to make it humorous. Share your new jingle with a partner.

SETTING A PURPOSE Read to enjoy the result of putting new words to old rhymes.

BACKGROUND

Did You Know?

- Robert Louis Stevenson is the author of such classic works as *Treasure Island, Kidnapped,* and *The Strange Case of Dr. Jekyll and Mr. Hyde.* His poems in *A Child's Garden of Verses* were quite popular at the turn of the century (1900). Children grew up hearing his familiar poems, such as the following:

Happy Thought

The world is so full of a number of things,
I'm sure we should all be as happy as kings.

- People often anthropomorphize their pets, pretending that the pet views life as a human would. In "From A Cat's Garden of Verses," Henry Beard pretends that the author of the poems is the cat belonging to Robert Louis Stevenson.

- Felines, or members of the cat family, include lions, tigers, jaguars, and wild and domestic cats. Wild felines are meat-eating animals who survive by hunting and eating smaller animals. Domesticated cats, like their cousins in the wild, still have the instinct to stalk and catch smaller animals, especially small rodents and birds.

Meet Henry Beard

Humor writer Henry Beard has written numerous hilarious books on topics from cats to golf. He also was cofounder of *National Lampoon,* a magazine that poked fun at national institutions and political figures of the 1970s. Beard admits that his most annoying habit is "avoiding answering the really tough questions." This is evident in his response to a question about the secret of comedy. "I'm glad I'm a humor writer instead of a comedian," he said, "because if someone hates me, they have to put the tomato in a box and send it to me. They can't throw it at me."

Henry Beard was born in 1945. Robert Louis Stevenson's cat is only one of the talented feline poets introduced in Beard's Poetry for Cats: The Definitive Anthology of Distinguished Feline Verse *published in 1994.*

- To read and analyze poems that parody well-known literature
- To identify the elements of parody
- To write a parody of a poem

Skills

Writing: Parody
Listening/Speaking: Critique

Motivating
→ OPTIONS

Selection Focus Transparency 79: Have students view and discuss the graphic showing pets and their traits.

Focus Activity: Have students make audio recordings of their jingles and share them with the class.

RESOURCE MANAGER

Lesson Planning Resource
The *Unit Six Planning Guide* (pp. 16–20) provides additional lesson notes and reduced versions of all print resources.

📁 **Other Print Resources**
- Active Reading Guide, p. 84
- Vocabulary Practice, p. 55
- Quick Checks, p. 84
- Selection and Theme Assessment, p. 158

- Performance Assessment, p. 82
- Spanish Summaries, p. 79
- Spanish Translations
- Inclusion Strategies
- English Language Learners Sourcebook

📊 **Transparencies**
- Selection Focus 79
- Literary Elements 84

Technology
- 🎧 Audio Library
- 🎧 Spanish Audio Library
- 💻 Glencoe Literature Web Site
- 💾 Testmaker

From A Cat's Garden of Verses
by Robert Louis Stevenson's Cat
Henry Beard

The Rain

The rain is raining all around,
  It rains on me and you;
I hope the neighbor's dog has drowned,
  Or caught a fatal flu.

Mealtime

A mousie squealing in a trap
Woke me from my morning nap.
Wasn't he so very sweet
To tell me it was time to eat?

Whole Duty of Cats

A cat should never kill a mouse
Until he's chased it through the house,
And shown it to another kitten,
Before its little head is bitten.

Catty Thought

The world is so full
  of such edible things,
I'll nibble their feet,
  and I'll chew off their wings.

Responding to Literature

Personal Response

Which of Beard's poems did you like the best? Explain why.

ANALYZING LITERATURE

RECALL AND INTERPRET

1. What wish does the speaker of "The Rain" make? Why is the speaker's wish humorous?

2. What are the poems "Mealtime," "Whole Duty of Cats," and "Catty Thought" about? Based on these poems, what subjects seem to be of special interest to the speaker?

3. Based on the content of all four poems, describe the cat characteristics that might have inspired Beard to write each poem.

4. What conclusions can you draw about the personality and character of Stevenson's cat from these poems? Explain.

EVALUATE AND CONNECT

5. **Verbal irony** occurs when a speaker says one thing and means another. Explain how the use of verbal irony in "Mealtime" adds to the humor of the poem.

6. **Theme Connections** On a humor scale of one to ten, evaluate the level of humor in each of these poems. Explain your evaluation.

7. Beard uses **alliteration** and **assonance** throughout these poems. What effects do the alliteration and assonance have? Give examples. (See Literary Terms Handbook, page R1.)

8. Look back at the humorous song or jingle you wrote in the Focus Activity on page 1009. Do you think the subject matter of Beard's poems would be good material for a cat food company's advertising jingle? Why or why not?

> ## *Literary* ELEMENTS
>
> ### Parody
>
> A **parody** is a humorous piece of writing that imitates the style and ideas of an author. For example, compare Beard's "The Rain" with Stevenson's "Rain" shown here.
>
> #### Rain
>
> The rain is raining all around,
> It falls on field and tree,
> It rains on the umbrellas here,
> And on the ships at sea.
>
> Both poems have similar titles, the same first line, and the same rhythm and meter. However, Stevenson's speaker is a child while Beard's speaker is a cat.
>
> 1. Evaluate how effectively Beard imitates Stevenson's poem.
>
> 2. Is Beard's poem a good parody of Stevenson's poem? Explain.
>
> ● See **Literary Terms Handbook,** p. R9.

EXTENDING YOUR RESPONSE

Listening and Speaking

Parody Review   With a partner, present a critic's review of these parodies for your class. Discuss the tone, rhyme, rhythm, point of view, and humor in Beard's poems and whether you find them effective or not. Use details from the poems to support your points. Conclude with a recommendation to read or not to read Beard's work.

Creative Writing

Write a Parody   Parody a poem by a favorite writer. Think of a different theme and subject for the parody. Approach the new subject in a silly manner while maintaining the style and characteristics of the original work. Read both poems aloud to the class.

 Save your work for your portfolio.

HUMOR ❧ 1011

✔ ASSESSMENT OPTIONS

📁 *Quick Checks,* p. 84

📁 *Selection and Theme Assessment,* p. 158

📁 *Performance Assessment,* p. 82

💾 *Testmaker*

LITERARY ELEMENTS

1. He imitates the poem effectively, using the same kind of simple diction and style.

2. It is a good parody because it describes a harsh reality of life instead of an idealistic picture.

Additional Resources

🖨 *Literary Elements Transparency 84*

Responding to the Selection

Personal Response

Students should give reasons for choosing one poem over the others.

ANALYZING LITERATURE

1. The speaker wishes that the dog had died. It is humorous because it personifies the animosity between dogs and cats.

2. The poems are about catching food, indicating that hunting prey is of special interest to the speaker.

3. He seems to have been inspired by cats' autonomy, predatory nature, and appetite.

4. Students may conclude that the cat is mischievous and predatory, with few of the kinder human characteristics that people sometimes attribute to cats.

5. The speaker pretends to speak politely of the mouse, which is actually about to become his lunch.

6. Students should assign each poem a number from 1 to 10, based on how humorous they thought the poem was. They should support their rating with details from the poem.

7. The alliteration in *fatal flu* and the assonance in *kitten, little,* and *bitten* add to the poems' humorous tone.

8. The subject matter might be good material for an advertising jingle because it is humorous, although some may find it offensive.

EXTENDING YOUR RESPONSE

Listening and Speaking

Students' critiques should
• discuss each element of Beard's poems and rate its effectiveness.
• support each effectiveness rating with examples.
• offer a recommendation based on the poems' overall rating.

Creative Writing

Students' parodies should
• imitate the style of the original poem.
• use a different theme and subject from the original poem.
• approach the subject in a silly manner.

Objectives

- To analyze and evaluate television characters as believable or stereotypical
- To create databases that compare characters in many television programs

Teaching Strategies

Form small groups and have students brainstorm to list and describe their favorite characters. After five or ten minutes, pull the groups together and compare notes.

Reviewing Database Tools

If students will all be using the same database software, review its basic formatting options at this time. The steps given on pages 1012–1013 are based on Microsoft Access.

Building a Critical-Viewing Database

Remind students that the field names they enter in item 3 are column headings. In this table, all the columns will contain text entries. However, students should observe other types of data listed in the software. They may create a table in the Activities that calls for numbers, dates, or other types of data.

Teaching Options

Technology Skills

Database: Critical Viewing Skills

Are television characters believable—or are they stereotypes, characters who are not developed as individuals but, rather, presented as types (the cranky old man, the helpless woman, the confused teenager, and so on)? By analyzing how the visual media portray various groups of people, you can become a more critical viewer.

Start with a Few Favorites

Think about some of your favorite television characters. Record the names of at least six characters from TV shows. After each name, write a brief description of the character. Include his or her most prominent physical or emotional characteristics.

Reviewing Database Tools

A database is a collection of data that is organized so that information can be referenced in various ways. Review the major functions of databases. Remember that database software differs from product to product. The directions given here may need to be adapted.

TERM	FUNCTION
Database	A collection of information arranged in predetermined ways
Table	The form in which data appears
Field Names	Column headings
Fields	Columns that hold data
Records	Rows of data
Table Helpers or Wizards	Features that walk you through the creation of a table by using preset formats

Building a Critical-Viewing Database

1. Work with a partner. To begin, open your database program.

2. Go to the **File** menu, and select **New**. (If your software opens with a dialogue box asking you to choose between opening an existing database or starting a new one, opt for a new one with a blank database.) If you're asked what sort of database you would like to create, select **Table**. You will also be asked if you wish to see your table in Design or Datasheet view. Select **Design** view so that you can name your fields.

3. Once in Design view, you will be asked to create and describe field names. Under field name, type in each heading listed below, and select **Text** as your data type.

   TV Show   Character   Gender   Description   Ethnicity   Stereotype?

MEETING INDIVIDUAL NEEDS — MULTIPLE LEARNING STYLES

Bodily-Kinesthetic Students may have difficulty using abstract concepts *(types, believable)* to decide whether a character is a stereotype. Students who process knowledge through movement may benefit from role-playing characters in familiar scenes.

Activity Discuss the list of television characters and select several about whom the class disagrees. Group students and assign a character and a situation to each group. The group is to discuss how the character would react, write a brief dialogue, and role-play the situation. Have groups present their role plays, discuss character traits, and revisit the stereotype question. **L2**
COLLAB. LEARN.

4. Next, switch to Datasheet view by using the pull-down **View** menu. If you are asked if you want the database program to set a primary key for you, select **no**. If asked if you want to save the table, choose **yes**, and save to disk or to the shared directory of your network. You will then be taken to the table you created.

5. You and your partner can now enter the names of characters and their descriptions. Decide whether each character is a multifaceted, realistic character or a stereotype. You may use the following as a guide for entries in the Ethnicity column.

| Native American | Asian American | Australian | African American |
| Middle Eastern | Pacific Islander | European | Hispanic American |

6. After examining your data, decide whether each character is developed as an individual or as a collection of stereotypic traits. Ask yourself questions such as the following.

- Are the characters presented as unique individuals or as types?
- How are various ethnic groups portrayed on TV? Are any underportrayed?
- Are females and males equally likely to be stereotyped? Are the types of stereotypes for males and females similar or different?
- Is the age or physical condition of a character made an issue? How?

7. Discuss with your partner the number and kinds of stereotypes you've discovered in TV shows. What conclusions can you come to on the basis of your data?

TECHNOLOGY TIP

Use the Help function of your database program to learn how to manipulate your data. For example, you could select to see only the female characters from your datasheet, or only the African American characters, or only those you marked as stereotypes.

	Show	Character	Gender	Ethnic Heritage	Description	Stereotype?
▶	Brady Bunch	Marsha Brady	female	European American	Pretty, self-centered blond	yes
	Star Trek	Dr. McCoy	male	European American	Grumpy but loyal crew member	yes
	Cosby	Dr. Huxtable	male	African American	Paternal, funny, often befuddled	no
	I Love Lucy	Lucy Ricardo	female	European American	Pretty, funny, often-blundering wife	yes
	The Simpsons	Apu	male	Asian American	Friendly, funny accent	yes
	Seinfeld	Kramer	male	European American	Totally bizarre, clumsy, funny	no
	ER	Carol Hathaway	female	European American	Dedicated, friendly, caring	no
✱						

ACTIVITIES

1. Combine your data with the data of the other partners in your class. Print out the results, and distribute copies to class members to use in a discussion of the kinds of stereotypes found on television. Consider whether current TV shows are more likely or less likely than older shows to include stereotypes.

2. With a group, create a database to acquire information about stereotyping in a particular TV genre, such as dramas, sitcoms, music and variety shows, documentaries, or commercials. Present your findings to the class.

The primary key described in item 4 determines whether the table of data being created will be related to other tables of data. Although the lesson database does not need it, students may need to say yes to this feature as they complete the activities below.

Activities

1. *Students' television database results should*
   - show ability to use database software accurately.
   - list accurate ethnic heritage and description data for each character.
2. *Students' databases should*
   - show ability to use database software accurately.
   - include sufficient fields of data in a logical order.
   - draw logical conclusions based on concise, well-thought-out observations.

REAL-WORLD CONNECTION

Commercials Television commercials often use methods that don't stand up to logic. Have students brainstorm a list of commercials that they find persuasive. Discuss the type of appeal used in each and the logic—or lack thereof—behind it. (Appeals may include testimonials, stereotyping, glittering generalities, logical fallacies, loaded words, and bandwagon or snob appeal.)

Activity Have students write a description of and analyze persuasive methods used in a commercial. Then group students and have them create a database comparing types and persuasive techniques of commercials. **L2 COLLAB. LEARN.**

Grammar Link

Objective

- To recognize the correct use of apostrophes in forming the possessives of nouns and pronouns

Teaching Strategies

As you discuss the problems and solutions with students, have them name the possessive phrase in each simple sentence *("witness's story," "bears' heads," "teeth's chattering," and "someone's brush")*

Exercises

1. a. children's
   b. Massachusetts's
   c. crisis's
   d. hunters'
   e. no one's
2. a. Some fishermen's stories are called fish tales.
   b. Not everyone's tale is as believable as ours.
   c. Perhaps it's fishermen's and hunters' ways to exaggerate.

Additional Resources

Grammar and Language Workbook, p. 277

Grammar and Composition Handbook, Lesson 11.11

Writer's Choice, Lesson 21.11

Grammar Link

Missing or Misplaced Possessive Apostrophes

An important use of the apostrophe is to form the possessive of nouns and some pronouns. To form the possessive, add either an apostrophe or an apostrophe and *-s.*

Problem 1 Singular nouns that end in *s*
This witness story of fishing in Alaska is a personal account.

  Solution To make the possessive form of a singular noun ending in *s,* add an apostrophe and *-s.*
  This witness's story of fishing in Alaska is a personal account.

Problem 2 Plural nouns ending in *-s*
He claims that both bears heads were bigger than a steering wheel.

  Solution If a plural noun ends in *-s,* make it possessive by adding only an apostrophe.
  He claims that both bears' heads were bigger than a steering wheel.

Problem 3 Plural nouns not ending in *-s*
His teeths chattering was caused by cold and fear.

  Solution If a plural noun does not end in *-s,* add an apostrophe and *-s.*
  His teeth's chattering was caused by cold and fear.

Problem 4 Pronouns
The next story about someones brush with death is his.

  Solution Form the possessive of an indefinite pronoun (for example, *someone* or *everybody*) by adding an apostrophe and *-s.* Apostrophes are not used with possessive pronouns, such as *hers* and *theirs.*
  The next story about someone's brush with death is his.

● For more information on apostrophes, see **Language Handbook,** pp. R25–R26.

EXERCISES

1. Write the possessive form of each word.

   a. children b. Massachusetts c. crisis d. hunters e. no one

2. If the sentence is correct, write *C.* If the sentence is incorrect, rewrite it correctly.

   a. Some fishermens stories are called fish tales.

   b. Not everyones tale is as believable as ours.

   c. Perhaps it's fishermens and hunters ways to exaggerate.

Teaching Options

Writing *Minilesson*

Avoiding Wordiness Remind students when revising their writing to cut out wordiness. One way is to change prepositional and other phrases to possessive phrases.

The petals of the flower were pale pink.
The flower's petals were pale pink.

Activity Have students revise these sentences to cut out wordiness.
1. The customers in the restaurant were well dressed. *(The restaurant's customers were well dressed.)*
2. The poem by Marie won first prize. *(Marie's poem won first prize.)* **L1**

Additional Resources

Writer's Choice, Lesson 2.9

Before You Read
Appetizer

FOCUS ACTIVITY

Think about a surprising or frightening encounter you've had with an animal.

FREEWRITE Briefly write about a time when you were surprised or frightened by an animal. What were the circumstances? How did you react? What did the animal do?

SETTING A PURPOSE Read this short story to find out what happens when the narrator encounters a bear.

BACKGROUND

The Time and Place
"Appetizer" takes place in the Alaskan wilderness, sometime in the unspecified present.

Did You Know?

Brown bears have long, shaggy coats that range in color from blond to black, as well as stout bodies, massive heads, and long claws. Thought by some biologists to be as intelligent as such primates as monkeys or baboons, brown bears have a sense of smell as good as a bloodhound's, jaws capable of snapping small tree trunks, and the ability to sprint up to thirty-five miles an hour. Brown bears eat fish, mammals, nuts, berries, herbs, and grasses, but will feed exclusively on salmon when it is available, sometimes eating more than a dozen in a few hours.

VOCABULARY PREVIEW
---

consternation (kon′ stər nā′ shən) *n.* amazement or dismay that throws one into confusion; p. 1017
raptly (rapt′ lē) *adv.* in a deeply interested way; attentively; p. 1019
bereft (bi reft′) *adj.* robbed or deprived; p. 1019
impropriety (im′ prə pri′ ə tē) *n.* an improper act or behavior; p. 1019
profound (prə found′) *adj.* intense and complete; p. 1021
expedient (iks pē′ dē ənt) *n.* a useful method for bringing about a desired result; p. 1022

HUMOR 🐾 1015

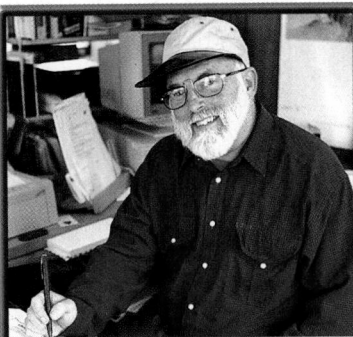

Meet Robert Abel

❝I feel the planet is threatened, that writing should attempt to define and respond to this emergency, not with hysteria, but with some vision of a workable, maybe even beautiful future.❞

Writing about things "that matter" is a responsibility that fiction writer Robert Abel feels strongly about. In addition to writing fiction of various genres, Abel has worked as a reporter, a teacher, a fiction editor for a small press, and a volunteer firefighter. He is also a fisherman.

Robert Abel was born in Painesville, Ohio, in 1941.

Before Reading

Objectives
- To read and analyze a short story about a man's encounter with a bear
- To identify rising action in a short story
- To write an analysis of the narrator's style

Skills

Reading/Thinking: Evaluating; Identifying Cause-and-Effect Relationships
Writing: Story
Vocabulary: Prefix *Super-*; Dictionary Skills; Old Words
Grammar/Language: Dangling Modifiers
Listening/Speaking: Comparison-Contrast Speech
Life Skills: Problem Solving; Dealing with Bears
Collaboration: Literature Groups

Motivating
→OPTIONS

Literature Launchers: "Bear Facts"

Videodisc
Side B, Segment 24

Also available in VHS.

Selection Focus Transparency 80: Have students view and discuss the photograph of a brown bear.

Focus Activity: Have students discuss their experiences with a partner.

RESOURCE MANAGER

Lesson Planning Resource
The *Unit Six Planning Guide* (pp. 21–28) provides additional lesson notes and reduced versions of all print resources.

 Other Print Resources
- Active Reading Guide, p. 85
- Vocabulary Practice, p. 56
- Reading Workbook, pp. 85–86
- Grammar and Language Workbook, p. 209

- Grammar and Composition Handbook, Lesson 8.7
- Quick Checks, p. 85
- Selection and Theme Assessment, pp. 159–160
- Performance Assessment, p. 83
- Spanish Summaries, p. 80
- Spanish Translations
- Inclusion Strategies
- English Language Learners Sourcebook

 Transparencies
- Selection Focus 80
- Literary Elements 85
- Grammar and Language 74

Technology
 Literature Launchers
🎧 Audio Library
🎧 Spanish Audio Library
💻 Glencoe Literature Web Site
 Testmaker

Reading the Selection

SUMMARY

The narrator is salmon fishing in Alaska when a female bear appears. The narrator catches some salmon and feeds them to the bear. They are joined by a male bear, which soon leaves. But the narrator cannot get rid of the first bear. Finally, he runs through the woods to his camper and gets in. The bear gets on the truck's hood and stays on. The narrator drives to a fish cannery. The bear enters the cannery, and the workers rush out. The narrator leaves. In town he hears talk about the bear's raid of the cannery. He keeps silent.

📁 *Spanish Summaries,* p. 80

Ⓐ Active Reading

PREDICT After students have viewed the painting and read the title and first paragraph, have them predict how the story's title will relate to the story's plot.

Additional Resources

📁 *Active Reading Guide,* p. 85
🎧 *Audio Library*
🎧 *Spanish Audio Library*

Teaching Options

Fly Fishing. Rosemary Lowndes. Oil on canvas. Private collection.

CONNECTING TO OTHER SELECTIONS

The chart at the right shows three ways to connect "Appetizer" to selections in this book.

For specific teaching strategies, see the *Unit Six Planning Guide,* pages 24–25.

Connection		Title
Life Skills: Problem Solving	→	"An Astrologer's Day," p. 260
Thematic: Troubles	→	from *A Match to the Heart,* p. 544
Literary: Rising Action	→	"A Sound of Thunder," p. 316

Appetizer

Robert H. Abel

I'M FISHING THIS BEAUTIFUL stream in Alaska, catching salmon, char and steelhead, when this bear lumbers out of the woods and down to the stream bank. He fixes me with this half-amused, half-curious look which says: You are meat.

The bear's eyes are brown and his shiny golden fur is standing up in spikes, which shows me he has been fishing, too, perhaps where the stream curves behind the peninsula of woods he has just trudged through. He's not making any sound I can hear over the rumble of the water in the softball-sized rocks, but his presence is very loud.

I say "his" presence because temporarily I am not interested in or able to assess the creature's sex. I am looking at a head that is bigger around than my steering wheel, a pair of paws awash in river bubbles that could cover half my windshield. I am glad that I am wearing polarized fishing glasses so the bear cannot see the little teardrops of fear that have crept into the corner of my eyes. To assure him/her I am not the least bit intimidated, I make another cast.

Immediately I tie into a fat Chinook.[1] The splashing of the fish in the stream engages the bear's attention, but he/she registers this for the moment only by shifting his/her glance. I play the fish[2] smartly and when it comes gliding in, tired, pink-sided, glittering and astonished, I pluck it out of the water by inserting a finger in its gill—something I normally wouldn't do in order not to injure the fish before I set it free, and I do exactly what you would do in the same situation—throw it to the bear.

The bear's eyes widen and she—for I can see now past her huge shoulder and powerful haunches that she is a she—turns and pounces on the fish with such speed and nimbleness[3] that I am numbed. There is no chance in hell that I, in my insulated waders,[4] am going to outrun her, dodge her blows, escape her jaws. While she is occupied devouring the fish—I can hear her teeth clacking together—I do what you or anyone else would do and cast again.

God answers my muttered prayer and I am blessed with the strike of another fat salmon, like the others on its way to spawning grounds upstream. I would like this fish to survive and release its eggs or sperm to perpetuate the salmon kingdom, but Ms. Bear has just licked her whiskers clean and has now moved knee-deep into the water and, to my consternation, leans against me rather like a large and friendly dog, although her ears are at the level of my shoulder and her back is broader than that of any horse I have ever seen. Ms. Bear is intensely interested in the progress of the salmon toward us, and her head twists and twitches as the fish circles, darts, takes line away, shakes head, rolls over, leaps.

---

1. Native to the northern Pacific, the *Chinook* (shi nook′) is also called the king salmon.
2. To *play the fish* is to keep it on the line until it exhausts itself.

3. The bear's *nimbleness* is its ability to move lightly, quickly, and easily.
4. The writer's *waders* are waterproof trousers that have boots for legs.

Vocabulary
consternation (kon′ stər nā′ shən) *n.* amazement or dismay that throws one into confusion

---

B Literary Elements

PLOT: *Rising Action* Point out that the rising action of a plot is based on the introduction of a conflict. Have students identify the story's conflict and its protagonist and antagonist. *(The narrator, the protagonist, is in a conflict with the bear, the antagonist, to keep the bear from killing him.)*

C Literary Elements

POINT OF VIEW Read aloud the last sentence of the fourth paragraph. Have students identify the narrative point of view. Then ask them to describe the effect of the narrator's use of the second person pronoun. *(Along with the narrator's first person point of view, his addressing the reader with "you" creates an informal, conversational tone and brings the reader into the story.)*

MEETING INDIVIDUAL NEEDS — ENGLISH LANGUAGE LEARNERS

Recognizing Tone English language learners may have difficulty recognizing the humor in the story since it recounts a life-and-death struggle with a bear. Begin by having a volunteer explain what an appetizer is.

Activity Explain that although the story relates a suspenseful conflict, the author uses comic techniques and an amusing tone. Point out that the author uses "Ms." in naming the bear, and he compares it to "a large and friendly dog." These elements add humor. On the board, start a list of these humorous elements. Have students add to the list as they continue reading.

Additional Resources
📁 *English Language Learners Sourcebook*

Appetizer

With a bear at your side, it is not the simplest thing to play a fish properly, but the presence of this huge animal, and especially her long snout, thick as my thigh, wonderfully concentrates the mind. She smells like the forest floor, like crushed moss and damp leaves, and she is as warm as a radiator back in my Massachusetts home, the thought of which floods me with a terrible nostalgia. Now I debate whether I should just drift the salmon in under the bear's nose and let her take it that way, but I'm afraid she will break off my fly and leader[5] and right now that fly—a Doctor Wilson number eight—is saving my life. So, with much anxiety, I pretend

5. The *fly*, or *lure*, is artificial bait consisting of a hook with materials tied on to resemble insects. It is connected to the fishline by the *leader*, a length of nylon.

to take charge and bring the fish in on the side away from the bear, gill and quickly unhook it, turn away from the bear and toss the fish behind me to the bank.

The bear wheels and clambers upon it at once, leaving a vortex[6] of water pouring into the vacuum of the space she has left, which almost topples me. As her teeth snack away, I quickly and furtively regard my poor Doctor Wilson, which is fish-mauled now, bedraggled, almost unrecognizable. But the present emergency compels me to zing it out once again. I walk a few paces downstream, hoping the bear will remember an appointment or become distracted and I can sneak away.

6. Here, *vortex* means "a small whirlpool."

Autumn Morning–Grizzly, 1985. Ron Parker. Acrylic on Masonite, 24 x 40 in.
Viewing the painting: What atmosphere does this painting convey? In what ways does it suit the opening scene of the story? Explain.

Robert H. Abel

But a few seconds later she is leaning against me again, raptly watching the stream for any sign of a salmon splash. My luck holds; another fish smacks the withered Wilson, flings sunlight and water in silver jets as it dances its last dance. I implore the salmon's forgiveness: something I had once read revealed that this is the way of all primitive hunters, to take the life reluctantly and to pray for the victim's return. I think my prayer is as urgent as that of any Mashpee or Yoruban, or Tlingit or early Celt,[7] for I not only want the salmon to thrive forever, I want a superabundance of them now, right now, to save my neck. I have an idea this hungry bear, bereft of fish, would waste little time in conducting any prayer ceremonies before she turned me into the main course my salmon were just the appetizer for. When I take up this fish, the bear practically rips it from my hand, and the sight of those teeth so close, and the truly persuasive power of those muscled, pink-rimmed jaws, cause a wave of fear in me so great that I nearly faint.

My vertigo subsides[8] as Ms. Bear munches and destroys the salmon with hearty shakes of her head and I sneak a few more paces downstream, rapidly also with trembling fingers tie on a new Doctor Wilson, observing the utmost care (as you would, too) in making my knots. I cast and stride downstream, wishing I could just plunge into the crystalline water and bowl away like a log. My hope and plan is to wade my way back to the

narrow trail a few hundred yards ahead and, when Ms. Bear loses interest or is somehow distracted, make a heroic dash for my camper. I think of the thermos of hot coffee on the front seat, the six-pack of beer in the cooler, the thin rubber mattress with the blue sleeping bag adorning it, warm wool socks in a bag hanging from a window crank, and almost burst into tears, these simple things, given the presence of Ms. Hungry Bear, seem so miraculous, so emblematic of the life I love to live. I promise the gods—American, Indian, African, Oriental—that if I survive I will never complain again, not even if my teenage children leave the caps off the toothpaste tubes or their bicycles in the driveway at home.

"Oh, home," I think, and cast again.

Ms. Bear rejoins me. You may or may not believe me, and perhaps after all it was only my imagination worked up by terror, but two things happened which gave me a particle of hope. The first was that Ms. Bear actually belched—quite noisily and unapologetically, too, like a rude uncle at a Christmas dinner. She showed no signs of having committed any impropriety underline, and yet it was clear to me that a belching bear is probably also a bear with a pretty-full belly. A few more salmon and perhaps Ms. Bear would wander off in search of a berry dessert.

Now the second thing she did, or that I imagined she did, was to begin—well, not *speaking* to me exactly, but *communicating* somehow. I know it sounds foolish, but if you were in my shoes—my waders, to be more precise—you might have learned bear talk pretty quickly, too. It's not as if the bear were speaking to me in complete sentences and English

---

7. These names refer to early peoples of North America (Mashpee), Africa (Yoruban), and Europe (Celt).
8. *Vertigo subsides* means that the dizziness decreases.

Vocabulary
raptly (rapt′ lē) *adv.* in a deeply interested way; attentively
bereft (bi reft′) *adj.* robbed or deprived
impropriety (im′ prə prī′ ə tē) *n.* an improper act or behavior

Vo•cab•u•lar•y Skills

Prefix *Super*- The narrator wishes for a "superabundance" of salmon. The prefix *super-* can mean "to an extreme or excessive degree or intensity." Have students list additional words with the prefix *super-* used in this way. (Examples include *superabsorbent, superbright, super-rich,* and *superheated.*)

F Author's Craft

FIGURES OF SPEECH: *Metaphor* The author makes the meaning of his title clear here. Have students explain what the narrator compares the salmon and himself to and why the comparison is effective. *(The narrator compares himself and the salmon to a fancy meal. He is afraid that the salmon are merely the bear's appetizer and that he will become her main course. The comparison's effect is humorous.)*

G Active Reading

RESPOND Have students discuss the narrator's bargaining with "the gods" for survival. Is this a realistic detail? How does he make the description of his promise to the gods humorous? *(Students will probably agree that people in the narrator's position might well make this kind of bargain. The author makes it humorous by exaggerating the seriousness of his teenagers' behavior.)*

LIFE SKILLS CONNECTION

Problem Solving The narrator in "Appetizer" must quickly make a plan to save himself from the bear. He feeds the bear the salmon he catches and then formulates a plan to slowly work his way back to the trail and dash back to his camper.

[Activity] Have students think of a situation in which they had to solve a problem or decide on a course of action on the spur of the moment. They may recall a dangerous situation or perhaps a moral or social dilemma. Have them write a paragraph describing the situation but not their solution of it. Then have them exchange papers with a partner and write a solution to their partner's problem. Have students discuss their solutions with their partners and then with the entire class.
L2 COLLAB. LEARN.

H **Author's Craft**

HUMOR Have students list and discuss the various humorous elements in the second paragraph. *(The author makes the silly statement that he doesn't presume that every bear falls in love with him; he absurdly compares the bear to a pet; and he engages in wordplay with the words carnivore and carne.)*

I **Author's Craft**

IMAGERY The author provides many details about the art of fishing. Have students read aloud two or three passages describing fishing and explain their effect. *(They add realism to the narrator's conflict.)*

FYI

Grizzly Bears Although grizzly bears, one variety of brown bear, have been on the endangered species list, some biologists are prepared to take those in the Yellowstone National Park area off the list. They say there are 400–500 grizzlies in the 9,200-square-mile area of Yellowstone. This is twice the 1988 population.

Teaching Options

Appetizer

words such as "Get me another fish, pal, or you're on the menu," but in a much more indirect and subtle way, almost in the way a stream talks through its bubbling and burbling and rattling of rocks and gurgling along.

Believe me, I listened intently, more with my mind than with my ears, as if the bear were telepathizing,[9] and—I know you're not going to believe this, but it's true, I am normally not what you would call an egomaniac[10] with an inflated self-esteem such that I imagine that every bear which walks out of the woods falls in love with me—but I really did truly believe now that this Ms. Bear was expressing feelings of, well, *affection.* Really, I think she kinda liked me. True or not, the feeling made me less afraid. In fact, and I don't mean this in any erotic or perverse kind of way, but I had to admit, once my fear had passed, my feelings were kinda mutual. Like you might feel for an old pal of a dog. Or a favorite horse. I only wish she weren't such a big eater. I only wish she were not a carnivore, and I, carne.[11]

Now she nudges me with her nose.

"All right, all right," I say. "I'm doing the best I can."

Cast in the glide behind that big boulder, the bear telepathizes me. *There's a couple of whoppers in there.*

I do as I'm told and wham! the bear is right! Instantly I'm tied into a granddaddy Chinook, a really burly fellow who has no intention of lying down on anybody's platter beneath a blanket of lemon slices and scallion shoots, let alone make his last wiggle down a bear's gullet. Even the bear is excited and begins shifting weight from paw to paw, a little motion for her that nevertheless has big

9. The bear seems to be communicating mentally, or *telepathizing.*
10. An *egomaniac* believes that his or her activities and interests are of extreme importance to everyone else.
11. A *carnivore* (kär′ nə vôr′) eats meat, which, in Spanish, is *carne* (kär′ nä).

consequences for me as her body slams against my hip, then slams again.

Partly because I don't want to lose the fish, but partly also because I want to use the fish as an excuse to move closer to my getaway trail, I stumble downstream. This fish has my rod bent into an upside-down *U* and I'm hoping my quick-tied knots are also strong enough to take this salmon's lurching and his intelligent, broadside swinging into the river current—a very smart fish! Ordinarily I might take a long time with a fish like this, baby it in, but now I'm putting on as much pressure as I dare. When the salmon flips into a little side pool, the bear takes matters into her own hands, clambers over the rocks, pounces, nabs the salmon smartly behind the head and lumbers immediately to the bank. My leader snaps at once and while Ms. Bear attends to the destruction of the fish, I tie on another fly and make some shambling headway downstream. Yes, I worry about the hook still in the fish, but only because I do not want this bear to be irritated by anything. I want her to be replete[12] and smug and doze off in the sun. I try to telepathize as much. Please, Bear, sleep.

Inevitably, the fishing slows down, but Ms. Bear does not seem to mind. Again she belches. Myself, I am getting quite a headache and know that I am fighting exhaustion. On a normal morning of humping along in waders over these slippery softball-sized rocks, I would be tired in any case. The added emergency is foreclosing on my energy reserves. I even find myself getting a little angry, frustrated at least, and I marvel at the bear's persistence, her inexhaustible doggedness. And appetite. I catch fish, I toss them to her. At supermarket prices, I calculate she has eaten about six hundred dollars worth of fish. The calculating gives me something to think about besides my fear.

12. If she's *replete,* she's eaten plenty of food.

MEETING INDIVIDUAL NEEDS MULTIPLE LEARNING STYLES

Linguistic Many folk tales, tall tales, and adventure stories have been constructed around bears. Students with good linguistic abilities might enjoy adding a story to that group.

Activity Have students write a story with one or more bears as protagonists or antagonists. Point out that the story may belong to any of the genres mentioned above. Have students illustrate and display their stories. **L3**

At last I am immediately across from the opening to the trail which twines back through the woods to where my camper rests in the dapple shade of mighty pines. Still, five hundred yards separate me from this imagined haven. I entertain the notion perhaps someone else will come along and frighten the bear away, maybe someone with a dog or a gun, but I have already spent many days here without seeing another soul, and in fact have chosen to return here for that very reason. I have told myself for many years that I really do love nature, love being among the animals, am restored by wilderness adventure. Considering that right now I would like nothing better than to be nestled beside my wife in front of a blazing fire, this seems to be a sentiment in need of some revision.

Now, as if in answer to my speculations, the bear turns beside me, her rump pushing me into water deeper than I want to be in, where my footing is shaky, and she stares into the woods, ears forward. She has heard something I cannot hear, or smelled something I cannot smell, and while I labor back to shallower water and surer footing, I hope some backpackers or some bear-poaching Indians are about to appear and send Ms. Bear a-galloping away. Automatically, I continue casting, but I also cannot help glancing over my shoulder in hopes of seeing what Ms. Bear sees. And in a moment I do.

It is another bear.

Unconsciously, I release a low moan, but my voice is lost in the guttural[13] warning of Ms. Bear to the trespasser. The new arrival answers with a defiant cough. He—I believe it is a he—can afford to be defiant because he is half again as large as my companion. His fur seems longer and coarser, and though its substance is as golden as that of the bear beside me, the tips are black and this dark surface ripples and undulates over his massive frame. His nostrils are flared and he is staring with profound concentration at me.

Now I am truly confused and afraid. Would it be better to catch another salmon or not? I surely cannot provide for two of these beasts and in any case Mister Bear does not seem the type to be distracted by or made friendly by any measly salmon tribute. His whole bearing—pardon the expression—tells me my intrusion into this bear world is a personal affront[14] to his bear honor. Only Ms. Bear stands between us and, after all, whose side is she really on? By bear standards, I am sure a rather regal and handsome fellow has made his appearance. Why should the fur-covered heart of furry Ms. Bear go out to me? How much love can a few hundred dollars worth of salmon buy? Most likely, this couple even have a history, know and have known each other from other seasons even though for the moment they prefer to pretend to regard each other as total strangers.

How disturbed I am is well illustrated by my next course of action. It is completely irrational, and I cannot account for it, or why it saved me—if indeed it did. I cranked in my line and lay my rod across some rocks, then began the arduous process of pulling myself out of my waders while trying to balance myself on those awkward rocks in that fast water. I tipped and swayed as I tugged at my boots, pushed my waders down, my arms in the foaming, frigid water, then the waders also filling, making it even more difficult to pull my feet free.

---

13. The bear's warning has a low, harsh, raspy or *guttural* quality.

14. An *affront* is a challenge or deliberate insult.

Vocabulary
profound (prə found′) *adj.* intense and complete

J **Literary Elements**

PLOT: *Rising Action* The plot's action continues to rise as the second bear appears. How does the author make this event suspenseful? *(The narrator prepares the reader for the second bear by describing the first bear's awareness of another animal approaching. His statement that there is another bear is made dramatic through understatement: it is related in one simple sentence in its own paragraph.)*

K **Active Reading**

VISUALIZE Have students visualize the second bear as a student reads the description of it aloud.

Listening and Speaking *Minilesson*

Comparison-Contrast Speech In the first paragraph on page 1021, the narrator contrasts the joys of wilderness adventure to the pleasures of home.

Activity Have students write a short speech comparing and contrasting the pleasures of the natural world with the comforts of home. Encourage them to use one or more personal anecdotes to illustrate their points. Have them give their speeches informally in small groups.

L2 **COLLAB. LEARN.**

FIGURES OF SPEECH: *Understatement*
Have a student read aloud the narrator's statement, "Truly, I did not appreciate her persistence." Have students tell what kind of figurative language it is, tell its literal meaning, and identify its effect. *(It is an understatement because it represents the narrator's feelings as less intense than they actually are. He means that the bear's persistence has made him extremely upset and stressed. The understatement has a humorous effect.)*

M **Literary Elements**

PLOT: *Rising Action* Point out that as the story reaches its climax, the suspense increases. Have students name the vivid words and phrases the author uses to heighten the suspense at this point in the story. *(Words and phrases include "risked everything," "sped for the cab," "sights locked," "big feet slapping the ground behind me in a heavy rhythm," "terrible and elemental beat," "plunged on like a madman," hurled, panting, shuddered, slammed, and shattered.)*

Appetizer

I emerged like a nymph from a cocoon, wet and trembling. The bears regarded me with clear stupefaction,[15] as if one of them had casually stepped out of his or her fur. I drained what water I could from the waders, then dropped my fly rod into them, and held them before me. The damned rocks were brutal on my feet, but I marched toward the trail opening, lifting and dropping first one, then the other leg of my waders as if I were operating a giant puppet. The water still in the waders gave each footfall an impressive authority, and I was half thinking that, well, if the big one attacks, maybe he'll be fooled into chomping the waders first and I'll at least now be able to run. I did not relish the idea of pounding down the trail in my nearly bare feet, but it was a damn sight better way to argue with the bear than being sucked from my waders like a snail from its shell. Would you have done differently?

Who knows what the bears thought, but I tried to make myself look as much as possible like a camel or some other extreme and inedible form of four-footedness as I plodded along the trail. The bears looked at each other, then at me as I clomped by, the water in the waders making an odd gurgling sound, and me making an odd sound, too, on remembering just then how the Indians would, staring death in the eye, sing their death song. Having no such melody prepared, and never having been anything but a bathtub singer, I chanted forth the only song I ever committed to memory: "Jingle Bells."

Yes, "Jingle Bells," I sang, "jingle all the way," and I lifted first one, then the other wader leg and dropped it stomping down. "Oh what fun it is to ride in a one-horse open sleigh-ay!"

The exercise was to prove to me just how complicated and various is the nature of the bear. The male reared up, blotting out the sun, bellowed, then twisted on his haunches and crashed off into the woods. The female, head cocked in curiosity, followed at a slight distance, within what still might be called striking distance whether I was out of my waders or not. Truly, I did not appreciate her persistence. Hauling the waders half full of water before me was trying work and the superfluous thought struck me: suppose someone sees me now, plumping along like this, singing "Jingle Bells," a bear in attendance? Vanity, obviously, never sleeps. But as long as the bear kept her distance I saw no reason to change my *modus operandi*.[16]

When I came within about one hundred feet of my camper, its white cap gleaming like a remnant of spring snow and beckoning me, I risked everything, dropped the waders and sped for the cab. The bear broke into a trot, too, I was sure, because although I couldn't see her, had my sights locked on the gleaming handle to the pickup door, I sure enough could hear those big feet slapping the ground behind me in a heavy rhythm, a terrible and elemental beat that sang to me of my own frailty, fragile bones and tender flesh. I plunged on like a madman, grabbed the camper door and hurled myself in.

I lay on the seat panting, curled like a child, shuddered when the bear slammed against the pickup's side. The bear pressed her nose to the window, then curiously, unceremoniously licked the glass with her tongue. I know (and you know) she could have shattered the glass with a single blow, and I tried to imagine what I should do if indeed she resorted to this simple expedient.

---

15. The bears' *stupefaction* (stoo′ pə fak′ shən) is a state of overwhelming astonishment.

16. The Latin phrase *modus operandi* means "method of operation."

Vocabulary
expedient (iks pē′ dē ənt) *n.* a useful method for bringing about a desired result

Less-Proficient Readers Students may encounter unfamiliar words in the story, such as *superfluous* (p. 1022), *clambers* (p. 1018), *bedraggled* (p. 1018), and *arduous* (p. 1021). Remind them that they can use the context or look up the words in a dictionary to determine their meanings.

Activity Help students improve their understanding of the story and their general vocabulary by having them write a sentence of their own for each word listed above. Then have them find three additional unfamiliar words from the story and use them in sentences. **L1**

Additional Resources
📁 *Inclusion Strategies*

Two Fish, 1992. John S. Bunker. Mixed media, 20 x 15 in.
Viewing the painting: What sense of the river and the salmon do you get from this painting?

VIEWING THE PAINTING

The artist has used bold, broad strokes to create the painting. To apply paint, an artist uses brushes of varying sizes and shapes. To create thick, bold strokes, an artist might use a painting knife. Painting knives, like brushes, come in many sizes and shapes.

Viewing Response *The painting gives a sense of the motion and activity of both the river and the salmon.*

N **Literary Elements**

ALLITERATION Ask students to identify the alliteration in the phrase "blinded by bear body" and describe its effect. *(the initial b sound repeated in all four words; the effect is humorous.)*

Fisherman that I am, I had nothing in the cab of the truck to defend myself with except a tire iron, and that not readily accessible behind the seat I was cowering on. My best defense, obviously, was to start the pickup and drive away.

Just as I sat up to the steering wheel and inserted the key, however, Ms. Bear slammed her big paws onto the hood and hoisted herself aboard. The pickup shuddered with the weight of her, and suddenly the windshield was full of her golden fur. I beeped the horn loud and long numerous times, but this had about the same effect as my singing, only caused her to shake her huge head, which vibrated the truck terribly. She stomped around on the hood and then lay down, back against the windshield, which now appeared to have been covered by a huge shag rug.

Could I believe my eyes?

No, I could not believe my eyes. My truck was being smothered in bear. In a moment I also could not believe my ears—Ms. Bear had decided the camper hood was the perfect place for a nap, and she was *snoring,* snoring profoundly, her body twitching like a cat's. Finally, she had responded to my advice and desires, but at the most inappropriate time. I was trapped. Blinded by bear body! —**N**

My exhaustion had been doubled by my sprint for the camper, and now that I was not in such a desperate panic, I felt the cold of the water that had soaked my clothes and I began to tremble. It also crossed my mind that perhaps Mister Bear was still in the vicinity, and if Ms. Bear was not smart enough, or cruel enough, to smash my window to get at me, he just might be.

HUMOR 🦋 1023

Reading *Minilesson*

Identifying Cause-and-Effect Relationships Remind students that a cause makes something happen and an effect is what happens. Recognizing cause-and-effect relationships will help students understand and review the story.

Activity Write the chart below on the board. Have students write the cause of each effect. **L2**

Cause	Effect
	A female bear harasses the narrator.
	The male bear runs away.
	The narrator runs into his camper.
	The bear gets off the narrator's truck.
	The narrator does not speak of the bear at the Tap and Lounge.

Additional Resources
📁 *Reading Workbook,* pp. 85–86

Teaching Options

Appetizer

Therefore, I started the engine—which disturbed Ms. Bear not a whit[17]—and rolled down the window enough to stick my head out and see down the rocky, limb-strewn trail. I figured a few jolts in those ruts and Ms. Bear would be off like a shot.

This proved a smug assumption. Ms. Bear did indeed awaken and bestir herself to a sitting position, a bit like an overgrown hood ornament, but quickly grew quite adept at balancing herself against the lurching and jolting of my truck, which, in fact, she seemed to enjoy. Just my luck, I growled, to find the first bear in Alaska who wanted a ride into town. I tried

---

17. **A whit** is a tiny amount.

some quick braking and sharp turn maneuvers I thought might send her tumbling off, but her bulk was so massive, her paws so artfully spread, that she was just too stable an entity. She wanted a ride and there was nothing I could do about it.

When I came out of the woods to the gravel road known locally as the Dawson Artery, I had an inspiration. I didn't drive so fast that if Ms. Bear decided to clamber down she would be hurt, but I did head for the main road which led to Buckville and the Buckville Cannery. Ms. Bear swayed happily along the whole ten miles to that intersection and seemed not to bat an eye when first one big logging truck, then

Hauling in the Nets, 1930. Martha Walter. Watercolor, 15 x 22 in. David David Gallery, Philadelphia.

Viewing the painting: How do the activities shown in this painting compare with the activities at the Buckville Cannery described in the story?

1024 ❧ UNIT 6

---

another plummeted[18] by. I pulled out onto the highway, and for the safety of both of us—those logging trucks have dubious brakes and their drivers get paid by the trip[19]—I had to accelerate considerably.

I couldn't see much of Ms. Bear except her back and rump as I had to concentrate on the road, some of which is pretty curvy in that coastal area, shadowed also by the giant pines. But from the attitude expressed by her posture, I'd say she was having a whale, or should I say a salmon of a time. I saw a few cars and pickups veering out of the oncoming lane onto the shoulder as we swept by, but I didn't have time, really, to appreciate the astonishment of their drivers. In this way, my head out the window, Ms. Bear perched on the hood, I drove to the Buckville Cannery and turned into the long driveway.

Ms. Bear knew right away something good was ahead for she rose on all fours now and stuck her nose straight out like a bird dog on a pheasant. Her legs quivered with nervous anticipation as we approached, and as soon as I came out of the trees into the parking area, she went over the front of the camper like someone plunging into a pool.

Don't tell me you would have done any differently. I stopped right there and watched Ms. Bear march down between the rows of cars and right up the truck ramp into the cannery itself. She was not the least bit intimidated by all the noise of the machines and the grinders and stampers in there, or the shouting of the workers.

---

18. Here, *plummeted* means "plunged; dropped quickly and steeply."
19. The trucks' *dubious* brakes are of questionable quality, and the drivers speed so that they can make as many trips as possible.

Now the Buckville Cannery isn't that big—I imagine about two dozen people work there on any given day—and since it is so remote, has no hurricane fence around it, and no security guard. After all, what's anybody going to steal out of there besides a few cases of canned salmon or some bags of frozen fish parts that will soon become some company's cat food? The main building is up on a little hill and conveyors run down from there to the docks where the salmon boats pull in—the sea is another half mile away—and unload their catch.

I would say that in about three minutes after Ms. Bear walked into the cannery, twenty of the twenty-four workers were climbing out down the conveyors, dropping from open windows, or charging out the doors. The other four just hadn't got wind of the event yet, but in a little while they came bounding out, too, one fellow pulling up his trousers as he ran. They all assembled on the semicircular drive before the main office and had a union meeting of some vigor.

Myself, I was too tired to participate, and in any case did not want to be held liable for the disturbance at the Buckville Cannery, and so I made a U-turn and drove on into Buckville itself where I took a room above the Buckville Tavern and had a hot shower and a really nice nap. That night in the Tap and Lounge I got to hear many an excited story about the she-bear who freeloaded at the cannery for a couple of hours before she was driven off by blowing, ironically enough, the lunch whistle loud and long. I didn't think it was the right time or place to testify to my part in that historical event, and for once kept my mouth shut. You don't like trouble any more than I do, and I'm sure you would have done about the same.

Responding to the Selection

Personal Response

Students may say they particularly liked the narrator's dry, understated sense of humor.

ANALYZING LITERATURE

1. He uses the adjectives *brown, shiny, golden, half-amused, half-curious, huge,* and *powerful* and the verbs *lumbers, pounces,* and *devouring.*
2. He makes another cast with his rod to show that he is not intimidated.
3. He hopes the bear will become distracted, so he can sneak away.
4. He edges nearer to the trail opening, takes off his boots and waders, walks toward the trail, and finally runs.
5. He drives to a fish cannery, where the bear gets off.
6. Students may infer that he is low-key and rational. He is really frightened of the bear and alarmed about his situation. He maintains his sense of humor.
7. He means that any person in his situation would try to outwit the bear.
8. He seems to be a nonviolent person who loves animals.
9. He keeps a level head and doesn't frighten the bear. He exhibits intelligence and cool-headedness.
10. His actions are consistent because he remains calm and is not motivated by a need for excitement.
11. He creates humor through understatement: "Truly, I did not appreciate her persistence"; by humanizing the bear: naming her Ms. Bear; and through absurd situations: driving to the cannery with the bear on the hood of his truck.
12. Students may point out that most people in that situation would be likely to freeze or panic, *not* feed fish to the bear, continue fishing, walking away from two bears, or drive to a cannery. They may agree, however, that they, like the narrator, would keep quiet about their part in the cannery raid.
13. Encourage students to compare not only their behavior but the animal's as well.
14. Students may think he did the right thing because he got rid of the bear, or he did not do the right thing because he endangered other people.
15. The first part of the story may be more believable than the second part. Unrealistic details include catching fish for the bear and carrying a bear on a truck's hood down a busy highway.

1026   UNIT 6

Responding to Literature

Personal Response

What did you like best about this story? Discuss your thoughts with a classmate.

ANALYZING LITERATURE

RECALL

1. How does the author describe the bear in the beginning of the story? What adjectives does he use? What verbs?
2. What does the narrator do after first noticing the bear? Why?
3. What does the narrator hope the bear will do after eating the fish? What will this allow him to do?
4. How does the narrator get to his truck?
5. How does the narrator finally rid himself of the bear?

INTERPRET

6. What can you infer about the **narrator** from his description of the bear? (See Literary Terms Handbook, page R8.) How does the narrator really feel about the bear? about the situation?
7. What does the narrator mean when he says that his actions are "exactly what you would do"? Explain.
8. Based on what the narrator wants to happen to the bear, what kind of person do you think he is?
9. Why, do you think, does the narrator succeed in reaching his truck? What character traits does he exhibit through his actions? Explain.
10. In your opinion, are the narrator's actions at the end of the story consistent with those at the beginning? Why or why not?

EVALUATE AND CONNECT

11. Which passages in the story are the funniest? What makes them funny? In what different ways does the author create humor? Give examples to support your responses.
12. The narrator frequently suggests that he did exactly what any of his readers would have done. Do you agree with him? Why or why not?
13. Think about your response to the Focus Activity on page 1015. How does your experience compare with the narrator's? Explain.
14. The choice the narrator made at the end of the story saved him, but it was risky. Do you think he did the right thing? Explain.
15. Could this story actually have happened? Evaluate the author's choice of details and events, telling how realistic or believable they seem.

1026   UNIT 6

Literary ELEMENTS

Rising Action

Rising action is the part of a plot where complications to the conflict develop and tension and suspense build. Rising action draws the reader along to the climax of the plot. In "Appetizer," the plot begins when the narrator sees the bear. The action begins to rise when the narrator tosses the bear the first salmon. As action rises, the plot becomes more suspenseful as events combine to complicate the narrator's situation.

1. Together with a partner, chart the rising action of the story using a time line format. How do events and situations build on each other?
2. What point is most suspenseful? Where in the story does that point occur? Do you like the arrangement? Why or why not?

● See **Literary Terms Handbook,** p. R11.

LITERARY ELEMENTS

1. Students' time lines might begin with this event: A female bear approaches the narrator.
2. Most suspenseful point: The narrator reaches the cannery. The highest suspense occurs just before the conflict is resolved.

Additional Resources

Literary Elements Transparency 85

LITERATURE AND WRITING

Writing About Literature
Narrative Style   In "Appetizer," the narrator's style is conversational and informal. He directly addresses the audience as though he were talking to a close friend. Write a short analysis of the effect of the narrator's style. How does this style contribute to the overall tone of the story? Support your analysis with examples from the story.

Creative Writing
The Other Side of the Story   How would the bear tell this story? Rewrite Abel's story from the point of view of the female bear, telling how she remembers events, what she thought of the narrator, and so on. Try to create a distinctive character and voice for the bear. Read your story aloud to a classmate.

EXTENDING YOUR RESPONSE

Literature Groups
The Man, the Bear, the Salmon   It has been said that humor is "the juxtaposition of the incongruous"; that is, the positioning together of things that really don't belong together. In "Appetizer," the author presents a very funny recounting of what could have been a terrifying event. In your group, discuss the incongruous events that combine to make the story so humorous. Evaluate the ways in which other literary techniques contribute to make the story funny, such as personification or slapstick visual comedy. As a group, decide what you feel works best in this story, and share your reasons with the class.

Internet Connection
Bear Facts   In many parts of the United States, bears such as grizzlies are endangered animals. Do some on-line research to find out more about these highly intelligent and fascinating animals and what is being done to protect them. Share your findings with the class.

Learning for Life
Bear Etiquette   As their natural food sources diminish, bears have become increasingly drawn to campgrounds to find food. Contact the National Park Service for suggestions on how to deal with bears in the wilderness. Make a chart of your findings to share with the class.

📖 **Save your work for your portfolio.**

Skill Minilesson

VOCABULARY • Old Words

Someone who is *bereft* has been robbed or deprived of something important to him or her. The prefix *be-* means "away," and *reft* is the past tense or past participle of *reave*, which means "to seize or rob." *Reave* and *reft* used to be common words in English; now they are almost never used. Sometimes, as with *bereft*, a word that was formed from another word remains active in the language while the original word fades from use. Another example of this is found in *ruthless*, which was formed from the now-archaic word *ruth*, meaning "mercy."

PRACTICE   Examine the following old words and their meanings. Then write three sentences, each one containing at least two old words from the list below. Add appropriate endings to reflect plurals, verb tense, and modifiers.

flerk: to twitch
blutter: to blurt out
teenful: irritating
snawk: to smell
purfle: to decorate
fonkin: a little fool

whifling: an unimportant creature
pingle: to eat with little appetite
spuddle: to act important with little cause
boonfellow: a close companion

LITERATURE AND WRITING

Writing About Literature
Students' analyses should
- describe the effect of the narrator's style on the tone of the story.
- use specific examples from the story to illustrate the narrator's style and the story's tone.

Creative Writing
Students' stories should
- be written from the bear's point of view.
- follow the same sequence of events.
- make the bear as distinct a character as the narrator.

EXTENDING YOUR RESPONSE

Literature Groups   Suggest that students also discuss whether the story would be as funny if it were a film instead of a short story.
COLLAB. LEARN.

Internet Connection   Encourage students to work on the Internet in pairs or groups if possible. 💾

Learning for Life   Encourage students to research articles on people who have encountered bears in the wild. 💾

Skill Minilesson

VOCABULARY • Old Words

Students might write sentences similar to the following: The fonkin and his boonfellow often hung around town spuddling.

Additional Resources
📁 *Vocabulary Practice,* p. 56

✔ ASSESSMENT OPTIONS

📁 *Quick Checks,* p. 85
📁 *Selection and Theme Assessment,* pp. 159–160
📁 *Performance Assessment,* p. 83
💾 *Testmaker*

MEDIA
Connection

Objective

- To read and understand a magazine article

Respond

1. Students may say they agree with the narrator because his use of synonyms for the word *said* calls attention to itself and becomes humorous. Or they may say they agree with the narrator's wife because the synonyms add variety and interest to the writing.
2. Students may say they will consider using a variety of dialogue tags in their writing.

Additional Resources
📁 *Media Connections Activities,* p. 25

Teaching Options

MEDIA
Connection

Magazine Article

Have you ever looked up a word in a thesaurus and been surprised at the number of synonyms listed? Wen Smith finds a humorous use for one such list.

Too Much Spice

by Wen Smith—*The Saturday Evening Post,* July/August 1997

Letters from readers pour into the wordshop, often with helpful suggestions. On Friday a particularly suggestive one poured in.

"You write a lot of dialogue," the reader wrote, "and you mostly use the word *said*, as in 'I *said*,' 'my wife *said*,' 'Charlie *said*.' Aren't there other words you could use for *said*?"

I showed the letter to my wife.

"I agree," she agreed. "You do use *said* a lot."

"OK, I'm guilty," I pleaded. "But I like to keep the writing simple."

"There are plenty of other words for *said*," she indicated.

"Look," I whined, "if I use a lot of synonyms for *said*, the words will get more attention than the ideas."

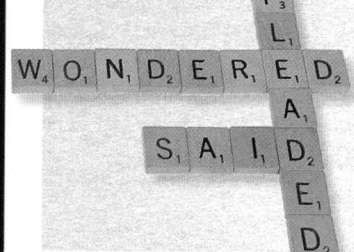

"Just for variety's sake," she urged, "you might use one now and then."

"Nonsense," I reasoned. "Elegant variation is a mark of bad writing."

"Why?" she insisted.

"*Said* is a straightforward, generic word," I pontificated. "It fits almost any line of dialogue."

"But it's such a rich language," she marveled. "You may as well spend some of the riches."

"I remember," I reminisced, "how Ring Lardner once made fun of pretentious variations for *said*. He wrote a story with the infamous line '"Shut up!" he *explained*.'"

"He was just being funny," she opined.

"He showed how variations on *said* can be stretched too far, like a rubber band," I snapped.

"I suppose you're right," she conjectured.

"Of course I'm right," I snickered.

I imagined writing things like "'Somebody's been sleeping in my bed,' she broke in," or "'You're a nut,' he cracked."

"Anyway, good usage keeps things simple," I elucidated. "Why use *proclaimed* when it's just a remark, not a proclamation?"

"But your reader does have a point about repeating *said*," my wife persisted.

"Variety may be the spice of life," I confessed, "but too much spice spoils the broth."

"You mean too many cooks," she simmered.

"It's better to repeat *said*," I repeated, "than to reach too far for a synonym."

"Why not do one article using some of those synonyms," she suggested, "just to see how it comes out."

Respond

1. Do you agree with the author of this article or with his wife? Why?
2. What dialogue tags do you use most often in your writing? After reading this article, how might you change your use of dialogue tags in your future writing?

Reading *Minilesson*

Author's Purpose Remind students that some humorous writing is written mainly to entertain. Other humorous writing is written to make a serious point through humorous means.

Activity Have students discuss whether the magazine article is meant only to entertain or whether it also is intended to make a point. Have them offer evidence for their opinions. **L2**

Additional Resources
📁 *Reading Workbook*

Before You Read

from *An American Childhood*

FOCUS ACTIVITY

Think of someone you know who views life with a comic perspective or has a great sense of humor. What makes them so funny?

CHART IT! Make a chart like the one shown. In the first column, list names of people who you think are truly funny. You might include family members and friends, celebrities, and characters from stories you've read. In the second column, jot down what makes these people funny.

Funny people	What makes them funny?

SETTING A PURPOSE Read an autobiographical account to learn about a person with a sense of humor.

BACKGROUND

The Time and Place
This selection is set in Pittsburgh, Pennsylvania, in the 1950s.

Did You Know?
Most middle-class married women in the 1950s did not work outside the home or pursue their own careers. Women who were fortunate or wealthy enough to attend college were generally assumed to be looking for a husband. Even a well-educated married woman of the 1950s was expected to be content to take care of her husband and children.

VOCABULARY PREVIEW

tremulously (trem′ yə les lē) *adv.* in a trembling or vibrating way; p. 1030

connoisseur (kon′ ə sur′) *n.* one who has expert knowledge in a particular area, such as wine, food, or the arts; p. 1031

eschew (es chōō′) *v.* to keep apart from (something disliked or harmful); avoid; p. 1032

advocate (ad′ və kāt′) *v.* to publicly support; p. 1032

stolid (stol′ id) *adj.* showing little or no emotion; p. 1034

ostracism (os′ trə siz′ əm) *n.* exclusion from a group or society; p. 1035

Meet Annie Dillard

"I didn't want to write about me . . . just a book about noticing that you're living," said author and naturalist Annie Dillard about her motivation for writing *An American Childhood*. Much of Dillard's work, including *Pilgrim at Tinker Creek* for which she won the 1975 Pulitzer Prize for Nonfiction, is reflective and autobiographical. Dillard's parents encouraged her to be curious and to observe the world around her. The result is that whether Dillard is describing a grasshopper on her window or discussing her family's quirky idiosyncrasies, she displays a keen attention to detail and a fascination with life.

Annie Dillard was born in 1945 in Pittsburgh, Pennsylvania. An American Childhood was published in 1987.

Objectives

- To read an account of a person with a well-developed sense of humor
- To identify hyperbole
- To write an evaluation

Skills

Reading/Thinking: Inferring; Main Idea and Supporting Details
Writing: Dialogue
Vocabulary: The Latin Root *voc*
Grammar/Language: Subject-Object Pronouns
Listening/Speaking: Telling Humorous Anecdotes
Life Skills: Letter
Collaboration: Literature Groups

Motivating OPTIONS

Selection Focus Transparency 81: Have students use the graphic to define people's senses of humor.

Focus Activity: Have volunteers share their definitions of a sense of humor and the qualities listed on their charts.

RESOURCE MANAGER

Lesson Planning Resource
The *Unit Six Planning Guide* (pp. 29–36) provides additional lesson notes and reduced versions of all print resources.

Other Print Resources
- Active Reading Guide, p. 86
- Vocabulary Practice, p. 57
- Reading Workbook, pp. 87–88
- Grammar and Language Workbook, p. 181

- Grammar and Composition Handbook, Lesson 1.2
- Quick Checks, p. 86
- Selection and Theme Assessment, pp. 161–162
- Performance Assessment, p. 84
- Spanish Summaries, p. 81
- Inclusion Strategies
- English Language Learners Sourcebook

Transparencies
- Selection Focus 81
- Literary Elements 86
- Grammar and Language 75

Technology
- Audio Library
- Spanish Audio Library
- Glencoe Literature Web Site
- Testmaker

SUMMARY

The author describes her mother and her sense of humor. She loved wordplay and practical jokes. Although she had the capacity to run New York City, she had to be content to run her own household, so she thought up clever inventions to make housework easier. Her odd sense of humor taught the author and her sisters to take a stand.

📁 **Spanish Summaries,** p. 81

A **Active Reading**

CONNECT Ask students if they have ever been fascinated by an unusual phrase or sentence. If so, have them share it.

Additional Resources
📁 *Active Reading Guide,* p. 86
🎧 *Audio Library*
🎧 *Spanish Audio Library*

B **Literary Elements**

HYPERBOLE Have students identify the hyperbole in the paragraph and its effect. *("The height of visionary ambition and folly" is hyperbole, emphasizing the mother's dramatic character.)*

Teaching Options

---

from An American Childhood

Annie Dillard

ONE SUNDAY AFTERNOON Mother wandered through our kitchen, where Father was making a sandwich and listening to the ball game. The Pirates were playing the New York Giants at Forbes Field. In those days, the Giants had a utility infielder[1] named Wayne Terwilliger. Just as Mother passed through, the radio announcer cried—with undue drama—"Terwilliger bunts one!"

A "Terwilliger bunts one?" Mother cried back, stopped short. She turned. "Is that English?"

"The player's name is Terwilliger," Father said. "He bunted."

"That's marvelous," Mother said. "'Terwilliger bunts one.' No wonder you listen to baseball. 'Terwilliger bunts one.'"

For the next seven or eight years, Mother made this surprising string of syllables her own. Testing a microphone, she repeated, "Terwilliger bunts one"; testing a pen or a typewriter, she wrote it. If, as happened surprisingly often in the course of various improvised gags, she pretended to whisper something else in my ear, she actually whispered, "Terwilliger bunts one." Whenever someone used a French phrase, or a Latin one, she answered solemnly,

"Terwilliger bunts one." If Mother had had, like Andrew Carnegie,[2] the opportunity to cook up a motto for a coat of arms,[3] hers would have read simply and tellingly, "Terwilliger bunts one." (Carnegie's was "Death to Privilege.")

She served us with other words and phrases. On a Florida trip, she repeated tremulously, "That . . . is a royal poinciana." I don't remember the tree; I remember the thrill in her voice. She pronounced it carefully, and spelled it. She also liked to say "portulaca."[4]

The drama of the words "Tamiami Trail" stirred her, we learned on the same Florida trip. People built Tampa on one coast, and they built Miami on another. Then—the height of visionary[5] ambition and folly—they piled a slow, tremendous road through the terrible Everglades to connect them. To build the road, men stood sunk in muck to their armpits. They fought off cottonmouth moccasins and six-foot

B

---

2. Based in Pittsburgh, *Andrew Carnegie* (1835–1919) made a fortune in the steel industry and donated $350 million to social and educational institutions.
3. A *coat of arms* is an arrangement of symbols on a shield that, along with a motto, represents one's ancestry.
4. Both the *royal poinciana* and the *portulaca* (pôr´ chə la´ kə) are native to the tropics and bear bright flowers.
5. Here, *visionary* refers to imagining something in perfect but unrealistic form. People had foreseen the benefits of connecting the two cities but overlooked practical considerations involved in constructing the road.

---

1. In this context, *utility* means "useful generally rather than in a specialized function." So, a *utility infielder* is capable of playing shortstop or first, second, or third base.

Vocabulary
tremulously (trem´ yə ləs lē) *adv.* in a trembling or vibrating way

---

CONNECTING TO OTHER SELECTIONS

COMPARING selections

This selection is paired with "What Is and Ain't Grammatical" on page 1039. A lesson for teaching a comparison of the two selections appears on page 1043.

The chart at the right shows three ways to connect "An American Childhood" to other selections in this book.

For specific teaching strategies, see the *Unit Six Planning Guide,* pages 32–33.

Connection	Title
Life Skills: Creating and Producing	→ "Pizza in Warsaw, Torte in Prague," p. 507
Thematic: Creativity	→ "My Mother Pieced Quilts," p. 650
Literary: Humor	→ "Mrs. James," p. 305

Woman in Blue, 1995. Leslie Braddock. Acrylic on canvas, 48 x 60 in. Private collection.

Viewing the painting: What techniques does the artist use to capture the character of the woman in this painting? What techniques does Annie Dillard use to portray the character of Mother in the opening of the selection?

alligators. They slept in boats, wet. They blasted muck with dynamite, cut jungle with machetes; they laid logs, dragged drilling machines, hauled dredges, heaped limestone. The road took fourteen years to build up by the shovelful, a Panama Canal in reverse, and cost hundreds of lives from tropical, mosquito-carried diseases. Then, capping it all, some genius thought of the word Tamiami: they called the road from Tampa to Miami, this very road under our spinning wheels, the Tamiami Trail. Some called it Alligator Alley. Anyone could drive over this road without a thought.

Hearing this, moved, I thought all the suffering of road building was worth it (it wasn't my suffering), now that we had this new thing to hang these new words on— Alligator Alley for those who like things cute, and, for connoisseurs like Mother, for lovers of the human drama in all its boldness and terror, the Tamiami Trail.

Back home, Mother cut clips from reels of talk, as it were, and played them back at leisure. She noticed that many Pittsburghers confuse "leave" and "let." One kind relative brightened our morning by mentioning why she'd brought

Vocabulary
connoisseur (kon′ ə sur′) *n.* one who has expert knowledge in a particular area, such as wine, food, or the arts

MEETING INDIVIDUAL NEEDS — ENGLISH LANGUAGE LEARNERS

Dialects English language learners may need additional help understanding the author's anecdotes relating to oddities of the English language. For example, Mother is amused by the unusual idioms and usages of the Pittsburgh dialect.

Activity Remind students that most languages have dialects with variations in pronunciation and idioms peculiar to an area. Have students share some interesting variations in English they have encountered. Then discuss each "Pittsburghism."

Additional Resources
📁 *English Language Learners Sourcebook*

Author's Craft

CHARACTERIZATION Remind students there are several techniques an author can use to characterize someone. Have them name and give examples of the main technique the author has used so far to characterize her mother. *(She has characterized her through her own words.)*

Author's Craft

DICTION Call students' attention to the author's word choice: *pat, galled, predictably unalert.* How do the words help characterize the author's mother? *(They are the opposite of Mother's traits and show her impatience with mental laziness.)*

---

her son to visit: "He wanted to come with me, so I left him." Mother filled in Amy and me on locutions we missed. "I can't do it on Friday," her pretty sister told a crowded dinner party, "because Friday's the day I lay in the stores."[6]

(All unconsciously, though, we ourselves used some pure Pittsburghisms. We said "tele pole," pronounced "telly pole," for that splintery sidewalk post I loved to climb. We said "slippy"—the sidewalks are "slippy." We said, "That's all the farther I could go." And we said, as Pittsburghers do say, "This glass needs washed," or "The dog needs walked"—a usage our father eschewed; he knew it was not standard English, nor even comprehensible English, but he never let on.)

"Spell 'poinsettia,'" Mother would throw out at me, smiling with pleasure. "Spell 'sherbet.'" The idea was not to make us whizzes, but, quite the contrary, to remind us—and I, especially, needed reminding—that we didn't know it all just yet.

"There's a deer standing in the front hall," she told me one quiet evening in the country.

"Really?"

"No. I just wanted to tell you something once without your saying, 'I know.'"

Supermarkets in the middle 1950s began luring, or bothering, customers by giving out Top Value Stamps or Green Stamps.[7] When, shopping with Mother, we got to the head of the checkout line, the checker, always a young man, asked, "Save stamps?"

"No," Mother replied genially, week after week, "I build model airplanes." I believe she originated this line. It took me years to determine where the joke lay.

Anyone who met her verbal challenges she adored. She had surgery on one of her eyes. On the operating table, just before she conked out, she appealed feelingly to the surgeon, saying, as she had been planning to say for weeks, "Will I be able to play the piano?" "Not on me," the surgeon said. "You won't pull that old one on me."

It was, indeed, an old one. The surgeon was supposed to answer, "Yes, my dear, brave woman, you will be able to play the piano after this operation," to which Mother intended to reply, "Oh, good, I've always wanted to play the piano." This pat scenario bored her; she loved having it interrupted. It must have galled[8] her that usually her acquaintances were so predictably unalert; it must have galled her that, for the length of her life, she could surprise everyone so continually, so easily, when she had been the same all along. At any rate, she loved anyone who, as she put it, saw it coming, and called her on it.

She regarded the instructions on bureaucratic forms as straight lines.[9] "Do you advocate the overthrow of the United States government by force or violence?" After some thought she wrote, "Force." She regarded children, even babies, as straight men.[10] When Molly learned to crawl, Mother delighted in buying her gowns with drawstrings at the bottom, like

---

6. *Locutions* are forms or styles of verbal expression. Where this woman said she had to *lay in the stores*, Mother might have said she had to go grocery shopping.
7. *[Top Value . . . Stamps]* Stores gave customers a certain number of stamps per dollar spent. These stamps were saved up and later exchanged for merchandise.

8. Here, *galled* means "irritated."
9. *Bureaucratic* refers to the rigidly formal paperwork and procedures involved in dealing with government officials and agencies. For Mother, these things were setups for jokes—the *straight lines* that led to punch lines.
10. *Straight men* are people who assist comedians by feeding them straight lines or serving as objects of fun.

Vocabulary
eschew (es chōō′) *v.* to keep apart from (something disliked or harmful); avoid
advocate (ad′ və kāt′) *v.* to publicly support

1032 ❧ UNIT 6

Teaching Options

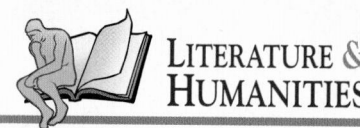

LITERATURE & HUMANITIES

After students view *Clothespin* (*Art Talk*, Transparency 41), ask them how they think the narrator's mother might react to this sculpture.

Listening and Speaking *Minilesson*

Telling Humorous Anecdotes Have students discuss performances by comedians or humorists whom they admire. Point out that spoken humor can range from joke telling to relating amusing anecdotes about people.

Activity Have students prepare a joke or humorous anecdote and practice telling it with a small group. Emphasize that some humorous speeches may elicit laughter while others are intended to evoke amused recognition. **L2**

Annie Dillard ⮑

Swee'pea's, because, as she explained energetically, you could easily step on the drawstring without the baby's noticing, so that she crawled and crawled and crawled and never got anywhere except into a small ball at the gown's top.

F When we children were young, she mothered us tenderly and dependably; as we got older, she resumed her career of anarchism.[11] She collared us into her gags. If she answered the phone on a wrong number, she told the caller, "Just a minute," and dragged the receiver to Amy or me, saying, "Here, take this, your name is Cecile," or, worse, just, "It's for you." You had to think on your feet. But did you want to perform well as Cecile, or did you want to take pity on the wretched caller?

During a family trip to the Highland Park Zoo, Mother and I were alone for a minute. She approached a young couple holding hands on a bench by the seals, and addressed the young man in dripping[12] tones: "Where have you been? Still got those baby-blue eyes; always did slay me. And this"—a swift nod at the dumbstruck young woman, who had removed her hand from the man's—"must be the one you were telling me about. She's not so bad, really, as you used to make out. But listen, you know how I miss you, you know where to reach me, same old place. And there's Ann over there—see how she's grown? See the blue eyes?"

And off she sashayed,[13] taking me firmly by the hand, and leading us around briskly past the monkey house and away. She cocked an ear back, and both of us heard the desperate man begin, in a high-pitched wail, "I swear, I never saw her before in my life. . . ." **G**

On a long, sloping beach by the ocean, she lay stretched out sunning with Father and friends, until the conversation gradually grew tedious, when without forethought she gave a little push with her heel and rolled away. People were stunned. She rolled deadpan and apparently effortlessly, arms and legs extended and tidy, down the beach to the distant water's edge, where she lay at ease just as she had been, but half in the surf, and well out of earshot.

She dearly loved to fluster people by throwing out a game's rules at whim[14]—when she was getting bored, losing in a dull sort of way, and when everybody else was taking it too seriously. If you turned your back, she moved the checkers around on the board. When you got them all straightened out, she denied she'd touched them; the next time you turned your back, she lined them up on the rug or hid them under your chair. In a betting rummy game called *Michigan*, she routinely played out of turn, or called out a card she didn't hold, or counted backward, simply to amuse herself by causing an uproar and watching the rest of us do double takes and have fits. (Much later, when serious suitors came to call, Mother subjected them to this fast card game as a trial by ordeal; she used it as an intelligence test and a measure of spirit. If the poor man could stay a round without breaking down or running out, he got to marry one of us, if he still wanted to.)

She excelled at bridge, playing fast and boldly, but when the stakes were low and the hands dull, she bid slams[15] for the devilment

---

11. Here, *anarchism* refers to active resistance against what's oppressive and undesirable.
12. *Dripping* here refers to using excessive charm or appeal.
13. She *sashayed* or walked in a way that showed a seeming lack of interest.

14. The phrase *at whim* means "suddenly and unexpectedly."
15. When she *bid slams*, Mother "went for broke," betting that she would win every or all but one of the tricks in a round of play.

Milton Avery (1893–1965) was known for his simplified forms and flat colors, similar to the styles of Matisse and Picasso.

Viewing Response *The players in the painting seem intense as if they are concentrating deeply. This is similar to the way Mother played games—unless she wanted to enliven things.*

H Author's Craft

CHARACTERIZATION What character traits does the author imply are possessed by the people with whom Mother plays cards? *(In comparison to Mother, they seem uptight, taking the game—and life—much too seriously.)*

I Critical Thinking

INFERRING The author says that her mother "had nothing to run but our household." Have students discuss what the author might be implying about the position of American women in the 1950s and how her mother's life might have been different if she had lived in a later era.

Checker Players, 1943. Milton Avery. Oil on canvas, 36 x 28 in. Private collection.

Viewing the painting: Look at the expressions and attitudes of these checker players. How do you think their game compares with one between Mother and an opponent? Explain.

of it, or raised her opponents' suit to bug them, or showed her hand, or tossed her cards in a handful behind her back in a characteristic swift motion accompanied by a vibrantly innocent look. It drove our <u>stolid</u> father crazy. The hand was over before it began, and the guests were appalled. How do you score it, who deals now, what do you do with a crazy person who is having so much fun? Or they were down seven, and the guests were appalled. "Pam!" "Dammit, Pam!" He groaned. What ails such people? What on earth possesses them? He rubbed his face.

She was an unstoppable force; she never let go. When we moved across town, she persuaded the U.S. Post Office to let her keep her old address—forever—because she'd had stationery printed. I don't know how she did it. Every new post office worker, over decades, needed to learn that although the Doaks' mail is addressed to here, it is delivered to there.

Mother's energy and intelligence suited her for a greater role in a larger arena—mayor of New York, say—than the one she had. She followed American politics closely; she had been known to vote for Democrats. She saw how things should be run, but she had nothing to run but our household. Even there, small minds bugged her; she was smarter than the people who designed the things she had to use all day for the length of her life.

"Look," she said. "Whoever designed this corkscrew never used one. Why would anyone sell it without trying it out?" So she invented a better one. She showed me a drawing of it.

The spirit of American enterprise never faded in Mother. If capitalizing and tooling up[16] had been as interesting as theorizing and thinking up, she would have fired up a new factory every week, and chaired several hundred corporations.

"It grieves me," she would say, "it grieves my heart," that the company that made one superior product packaged it poorly, or took the wrong tack[17] in its advertising. She knew,

---

16. *Capitalizing and tooling up* has to do with providing the finances and equipment necessary to start up a new business or factory.
17. The company took the wrong course of action or *tack*.

Vocabulary
stolid (stol′ id) *adj.* showing little or no emotion

Teaching Options

Grammar and Language *Minilesson*

Subject and Object Pronouns Remind students that subject pronouns such as *I, he,* and *they* are used as subjects and predicate nominatives in sentences. Object pronouns such as *me, her,* and *them* are used as objects of verbs or prepositions.

Activity Have students choose the correct pronoun for each sentence.

1. (We, Us) children wholly sympathized, and so did Father. *(We)*
2. If she answered the phone on a wrong number, she dragged the receiver to Amy or (I, me). *(me)*
3. During a family trip to the Highland Park Zoo, Mother and (me, I) were alone for a minute. *(I)* **L1**

Additional Resources

📖 *Grammar and Language Transparency 75*

📕 *Grammar and Language Workbook,* p. 181

📕 *Grammar and Composition Handbook,* Lesson 1.2

📗 *Writer's Choice,* Lesson 17.1

as she held the thing mournfully in her two hands, that she'd never find another. She was right. We children wholly sympathized, and so did Father; what could she do, what could anyone do, about it? She was Samson[18] in chains. She paced.

She didn't like the taste of stamps so she didn't lick stamps; she licked the corner of the envelope instead. She glued sandpaper to the sides of kitchen drawers, and under kitchen cabinets, so she always had a handy place to strike a match. She designed, and hounded workmen to build against all norms,[19] doubly wide kitchen counters and elevated bathroom sinks. . . . She drew plans for an over-the-finger toothbrush for babies, an oven rack that slid up and down, and—the family favorite—Lendalarm. Lendalarm was a beeper you attached to books (or tools) you loaned friends. After ten days, the beeper sounded. Only the rightful owner could silence it.

She repeatedly reminded us of P. T. Barnum's dictum:[20] You could sell anything to anybody if you marketed it right. The adman who thought of making Americans believe they needed underarm deodorant was a visionary. So, too, was the hero who made a success of a new product, Ivory soap. The executives were horrified, Mother told me, that a cake of this stuff floated. Soap wasn't supposed to float. Anyone would be able to tell it was mostly whipped-up air. Then some inspired adman made a leap: Advertise that it floats. Flaunt it. The rest is history.

She respected the rare few who broke through to new ways. "Look," she'd say, "here's an intelligent apron." She called upon us to admire intelligent control knobs and intelligent pan handles, intelligent andirons and picture frames and knife sharpeners. She questioned everything, every pair of scissors, every knitting needle, gardening glove, tape dispenser. Hers was a restless mental vigor that just about ignited the dumb household objects with its force.

Torpid[21] conformity was a kind of sin; it was stupidity itself, the mighty stream against which Mother would never cease to struggle. If you held no minority opinions, or if you failed to risk total ostracism for them daily, the world would be a better place without you. . . .

She simply tried to keep us all awake. And in fact it was always clear to Amy and me, and to Molly when she grew old enough to listen, that if our classmates came to cruelty, just as much as if the neighborhood or the nation came to madness, we were expected to take, and would be each separately capable of taking, a stand.

18. In the Bible, *Samson* told Delilah the secret of his extraordinary strength, that his hair had never been cut. He fell asleep, she got out her clippers, and his enemies soon had Samson chained up in prison.
19. Here, the *norms* are rules, standards, and accepted practices.
20. In the 1800s, *Barnum* presented many popular entertainments, founded what is now the Ringling Brothers and Barnum & Bailey Circus, and staged sensational publicity stunts. The actual words of his famous saying (*dictum*) were, "There's a sucker born every minute."
21. Something that's *torpid* is dull and lifeless.

Vocabulary
ostracism (os′ trə siz′ əm) *n.* exclusion from a group or society

J **Literary Elements**

HYPERBOLE Have students identify the hyperbole in the next-to-last paragraph and identify the new idea and tone it introduces. *("If you failed to risk total ostracism for [minority opinions] daily" is hyperbole. The author introduces a serious tone and the idea that Mother's eccentric actions had a serious result.)*

Thematic Focus

Comic Perspectives Have students discuss how Mother's perspective on life affected those around her. How would students feel about living with someone like her?

✓**ASSESSMENT OPTIONS**
Quick Checks, p. 86

Reading *Minilesson*

Main Idea and Supporting Details
Identifying the main idea and supporting details of an essay is crucial to students' understanding of an essay.

Activity Have students write a sentence that summarizes the main idea of Dillard's essay. Then have them list five details from the essay that support that main idea. Ask volunteers to read their main ideas and details. **L2**

Additional Resources
Reading Workbook, pp. 87–88

Responding to the Selection

Personal Response

Students might ask if the author ever felt embarrassed by her mother's jokes.

ANALYZING LITERATURE

1. They show the richness of the English language and represent the wide variety of people's accomplishments.
2. She found humor in bureaucratic forms. She deliberately misunderstood the questions and answered them accordingly.
3. She pretended to know a young man sitting with his girlfriend and she purposely misplayed a bridge hand.
4. Products and tools not designed to work in the most efficient manner bothered her. She admired products that were designed intelligently or marketed well.
5. She expected them to take a stand against any kind of cruelty or injustice.
6. She has a whimsical sense of humor and enjoys the absurdities of language and life.
7. She seems to think life should not be taken too seriously.
8. She seemed to hope that her actions would inspire others to see life more humorously.
9. Mother continually thought of ways to make products better and also invented new and useful products.
10. *Individual, strong, creative,* and *imaginative* might describe her character and values.
11. The story of her mother refusing to collect green stamps shows her humor and strong individuality.
12. The description of the building of the Tamiami Trail and the many Pittsburghisms add humor and affection to the portrait of her mother.
13. Students should provide thoughtful reasons for including or not including Dillard and/or her mother.
14. Students may say they were shocked or offended and that they would have been embarrassed in Dillard's place.
15. Some students may say they think Mother's humor and zest for life would make her an ideal mother. Others may say Mother's zaniness and restlessness are not part of their picture of an ideal mother.

Responding to Literature

Personal Response

What questions would you like to ask the author about her mother?

ANALYZING LITERATURE

RECALL

1. Why are the terms "Terwilliger bunts one" and "Tamiami Trail" important to Mother?
2. Mother found humor in situations that ordinarily would not be funny. Give an example and explain why the situation was comical.
3. Describe two incidents that illustrate how Mother's unexpected behavior flustered people.
4. What bothered Mother about certain products and tools? Which products did she admire?
5. According to Dillard, what did Mother expect of her daughters?

INTERPRET

6. What do Mother's reactions to and use of the phrase "Terwilliger bunts one" suggest about her personality?
7. What can you infer about Mother's philosophy of life from the way she responds to serious questions and situations?
8. Do you think Mother cared about the consequences of her actions? Explain.
9. Explain what Dillard means when she says that the "spirit of American enterprise never faded in Mother."
10. Based on everything Dillard has said about Mother, what words would you use to describe Mother's character and values? Explain.

EVALUATE AND CONNECT

11. An **anecdote** is a brief account of an event. Give examples of anecdotes from the selection and evaluate their use.
12. Identify places in the selection that illustrate Annie Dillard's attention to detail. How do these details enhance your appreciation of the selection?
13. Theme Connections   Recall the chart you created in the Focus Activity on page 1029. Would you add Mother to your chart? Would you add Dillard herself? Why or why not?
14. What was your immediate response to Mother's treatment of the young couple at the zoo? How would you have felt in Dillard's place?
15. How does Mother compare with your mental picture of an ideal mother? Explain.

Literary ELEMENTS

Hyperbole

Writers use **hyperbole,** or extreme exaggeration, to emphasize a point or to create a certain effect, such as humor. Hyperbole is a figure of speech. It is not meant to be read literally. Sometimes you have to analyze a reference to understand the exaggeration and to get the effect. For example, when Annie Dillard says that "Mother's energy and intelligence suited her for a greater role in a larger arena—mayor of New York, say," she does not actually mean that her mother should have been mayor of New York City. She is using hyperbole. Because New York City is one of the largest, most complex cities of the world to govern, Dillard wants her readers to imagine what it would be like to live with someone who has the energy to run a city like New York.

Find these examples of hyperbole on page 1035 in the selection. Then explain their meaning and humorous effect.

1. "She was Samson in chains."
2. "Hers was a restless mental vigor . . ."
3. "Torpid conformity was a kind of sin . . . the mighty stream . . ."

● See **Literary Terms Handbook,** p. R6.

LITERARY ELEMENTS

1. Mother was a strong person whose power had been taken away. The author is referring to Mother's frustration with poorly designed products.
2. Mother's active intelligence made household objects more useful. Her mental vigor is directed toward these objects.
3. Mother never wanted to be like everyone else. Conformity is not a sin.

Additional Resources

Literary Elements Transparency 86

LITERATURE AND WRITING

Writing About Literature
Define a Character Trait "My mother was always completely irrepressible," Dillard was quoted as saying in a magazine article. Look up and write the dictionary definition of the word *irrepressible*. Then write a brief assessment of how well Dillard illustrates her mother's "irrepressible" quality. Support your evaluation with details from the story. Share your evaluation with classmates.

Creative Writing
Boyfriend Beware! Dillard says that her mother challenged her daughters' dates to ridiculous card games to test their intelligence and measure their spirit. How might those young men have felt? How might her daughters have reacted? Write the dialogue that might have taken place between Mother, Annie as a young teenager, and one of Annie's hopeful boyfriends.

EXTENDING YOUR RESPONSE

Literature Groups
Life with Mother Working with your group, divide a piece of paper into two columns. In the first column, write the traits that you like about Mother and why it would be fun to live with her. In the second column, write the traits that could make life with Mother difficult. Then discuss the following questions with your group. What impressions about her mother is Dillard conveying? How might Dillard have reacted to her mother as a child? as an adult? What conclusions can you draw about the family's life with Mother? Share your ideas with your classmates.

Learning for Life
Customer Response Choose a commercial product that Mother mentions in the selection. Pretend you are Mother and write a letter to the manufacturer. Explain what you liked or did not like about the product and why you would or would not use it again. Share your letter with the class.

Interdisciplinary Activity
Art: The Mother of Invention Picture one of Mother's inventions, such as the "Lendalarm." Create an illustrated advertisement for one of her products.

📖 **Save your work for your portfolio.**

VOCABULARY • The Latin Root *voc*

The word *advocate* comes from the Latin prefix *ad-*, meaning "to," and the root *voc*, meaning either "to call" or "voice." An *advocate* is a defender, someone "to call to" for aid.

The root *voc*, which is also spelled *vok*, is found in many English words. A *vocal* response is spoken; a *vocation* (or career) is often referred to as "a calling." A *vociferous* group of students are noisy due to a great deal of talking or shouting.

The following are some of the prefixes that have been attached to *voc* or *vok* to create words:

re-:	back	*pro-:*	forth	*e-:*	out
con-:	together				

PRACTICE Use the meanings of *voc/vok* and the prefixes shown above to answer the questions.

1. Does a *provocative* statement ignore, arouse, or soothe the listener's feelings?
2. Would a driver's license be *revoked* because the driver passed a test or broke a law?
3. Is a *convocation* a secret plan, a method of travel, or an assembly?
4. Would a teacher *evoke* a correct answer by giving hints or by grading a paper?

LITERATURE AND WRITING

Writing About Literature
Students' evaluations should
- include a definition of *irrepressible*.
- evaluate Dillard's characterization of her mother's irrepressible quality.
- use details from the essay for support.

Creative Writing
Students' dialogues should
- relate a conversation involving three characters.
- focus on Annie and her boyfriend's reactions to Mother's card-game test.
- reveal the characters of Mother, Annie, and Annie's boyfriend through dialogue.

EXTENDING YOUR RESPONSE
Literature Groups Encourage students to imaginatively put themselves into Annie's place as they discuss the questions. **COLLAB. LEARN.**

Learning for Life You may also wish to allow students to write about a product of their own choosing from Mother's point of view.

Interdisciplinary Activity Encourage students to keep Mother's sense of humor and eccentric view of life in mind as they design their advertisements.

VOCABULARY • The Latin Root *voc*

1. A provocative statement arouses the listener's feelings.
2. A driver's license would be revoked because the driver broke the law.
3. A convocation is an assembly.
4. A teacher would evoke a correct answer by giving hints.

Additional Resources
📁 *Vocabulary Practice,* p. 57

✔ ASSESSMENT OPTIONS

📁 *Quick Checks,* p. 86
📁 *Selection and Theme Assessment,* pp. 161–162
📁 *Performance Assessment,* p. 84
💾 *Testmaker*

Objectives

- To read and analyze an essay about one writer's view of grammar
- To identify allusions in an essay

Skills

Reading/Thinking: Activating Prior Knowledge
Grammar/Language: Infinitives
Life Skills: Letter to Author
Collaboration: Literature Groups

Motivating
→OPTIONS

Literature Launchers:
"The Humor in Everyday Life"

Videodisc
Side B, Segment 23

Also available in VHS.

Selection Focus Transparency 82: Have students consider what each statement is trying to communicate.

Focus Activity: Have students share some of their thoughts about grammar.

✥ ─Before You Read─
What Is and Ain't Grammatical

──── FOCUS ACTIVITY ────

What are your thoughts about the use of good grammar? Which grammar rules don't make sense to you? How do you react when you hear the word *ain't*?

FREEWRITE At the top of a sheet of paper, write "My Thoughts About English Grammar." For two minutes jot down whatever comes to mind about English grammar. Do not edit your thoughts.

SETTING A PURPOSE Read an essay to learn about the comic perspective one writer takes toward grammar.

──── BACKGROUND ────

Did You Know?

- Grammar is the study of the way that words come together to form phrases and sentences. American English grammar consists of rules aimed at helping you speak and write the standard dialect of American English so that your ideas are clear and understandable.
- According to Dave Barry, "Just about anything's a topic for a humor column: any event that occurs in the news, anything that happens in daily life–driving, shopping, reading, eating. You can look at just about anything and see humor in it somewhere."
- Most people find Dave Barry's columns and books extremely funny, but occasionally he receives complaints from people he calls "the humor-impaired, who are infuriated that I have written something that's not literally true."

──── VOCABULARY PREVIEW ────

prospective (prə spek′ tiv) *adj.* probable or expected; future; p. 1039
drone (drōn) *v.* to talk in a dull, monotonous tone; p. 1040
enlightening (en līt′ ən ing) *adj.* giving or revealing knowledge or wisdom; p. 1041

Meet Dave Barry

❝I always wanted to write when I was a kid; it just never occurred to me that you could have a job that didn't involve any actual work.❞

Dave Barry's first job as a writer was for a small suburban newspaper where he wrote about the local "hot issues"—sewage and zoning. He eventually decided that writing humor might be a fun way to pay the bills. Barry's talent for finding humor in almost any topic led to his enormous success. In 1988 he was awarded the Pulitzer Prize for Distinguished Commentary. His weekly column is syndicated in hundreds of newspapers.

Dave Barry was born in Armonk, New York, in 1947.

RESOURCE MANAGER

Lesson Planning Resource
The *Unit Six Planning Guide* (pp. 37–44) provides additional lesson notes and reduced versions of all print resources.

📁 **Other Print Resources**
- Active Reading Guide, p. 87
- Vocabulary Practice, p. 58
- Reading Workbook, pp. 87–88
- Grammar and Language Workbook, p. 97

- Grammar and Composition Handbook, Lesson 3.3
- Quick Checks, p. 87
- Selection and Theme Assessment, pp. 163–164
- Performance Assessment, p. 85
- Spanish Summaries, p. 82
- Inclusion Strategies
- English Language Learners Sourcebook

 Transparencies
- Selection Focus 82
- Literary Elements 87
- Grammar and Language 76

Technology
- 💿 Literature Launchers
- 🎧 Audio Library
- 🎧 Spanish Audio Library
- 💻 Glencoe Literature Web Site
- 💾 Testmaker

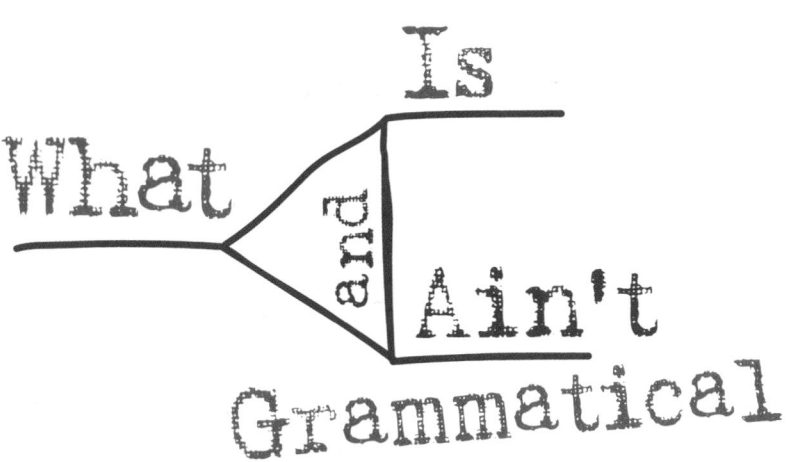

What Is and Ain't Grammatical

Dave Barry

 I CANNOT OVEREMPHASIZE the importance of good grammar.

What a crock. I could easily overemphasize the importance of good grammar. For example, I could say: "Bad grammar is the leading cause of slow, painful death in North America," or "Without good grammar, the United States would have lost World War II."

The truth is that grammar is not the most important thing in the world. The Super Bowl is the most important thing in the world. But grammar is still important. For example, suppose you are being interviewed for a job as an airplane pilot, and your <u>prospective</u> employer asks you if you have any experience, and you answer: "Well, I ain't never actually flied no actual airplanes or nothing, but I got several pilot-style hats and several friends who I like to talk about airplanes with."

If you answer this way, the prospective employer will immediately realize that you have ended your sentence with a preposition. (What you should have said, of course, is "several friends with who I like to talk about airplanes.") So you will not get the job, because airline pilots have to use good grammar when they get on the intercom and explain to the passengers that, because of high winds, the plane is going to take off several hours late and land in Pierre, South Dakota, instead of Los Angeles.

Vocabulary

prospective (prə spek′ tiv) *adj.* probable or expected; future

SUMMARY

In this essay, Dave Barry makes fun of grammar. He says that grammar was invented in medieval England after Chaucer wrote the *Canterbury Tales* and nobody could understand it. He says that American colonists rebelled against grammar, so that today we have only two rules: "The word *me* is always incorrect" and "You're not allowed to split infinitives." He concludes that in order to sound smart, Americans should use American grammar but speak with a British accent.

📁 *Spanish Summaries,* p. 82

A Active Reading

QUESTION Have students compare and contrast the style and tone of the first two sentences of the selection. What is the effect of this contrast? *(The first sentence is formal and pretentious. The second is slangy and irreverent. The contrast is humorous.)*

Additional Resources

📁 *Active Reading Guide,* p. 87
🎧 *Audio Library*
🎧 *Spanish Audio Library*

Teaching Options

CONNECTING TO OTHER SELECTIONS

This selection is paired with "An American Childhood" on page 1030. A lesson for teaching a comparison of the two selections appears on page 1043.

The chart at the right shows three ways to connect "What Is and Ain't Grammatical" to other selections in this book.

For specific teaching strategies, see the *Unit Six Planning Guide,* pages 40–41.

Connection	Title
Life Skills: Life-long Learning	→ "The Tucson Zoo," p. 563
Thematic: Opinions	→ "The Saleswoman," p. 299
Literary: Style	→ "Miss Rosie," p. 638

We did not always have grammar. In medieval England, people said whatever they wanted, without regard to rules, and as a result they sounded like morons. Take the poet Geoffrey Chaucer, who couldn't even spell his first name right. He wrote a large poem called *Canterbury Tales*, in which people from various professions—knight, monk, miller, reever, riveter, eeler, diver, stevedore, spinnaker, etc.—<u>drone</u> on and on like this:

> In a somer sesun whon softe was the sunne
> I kylled a younge birde ande I ate it on a
> bunne.

When Chaucer's poem was published, everybody read it and said: "My God, we need some grammar around here." So they formed a Grammar Commission, which developed

the parts of speech, the main ones being nouns, verbs, predicants, conjectures, particles, proverbs, adjoiners, coordinates, and rebuttals. Then the commission made up hundreds and hundreds of grammar rules, all of which were strictly enforced.

When the colonists came to America, they rebelled against British grammar. They openly used words like "ain't" and "finalize," and when they wrote the Declaration of Independence they deliberately misspelled many words. Thanks to their courage, today we Americans have only two rules of grammar:

> **Rule 1. The word "me" is always incorrect.**

Most of us learn this rule as children, from our mothers. We say things like: "Mom, can

Vocabulary
drone (drōn) *v.* to talk in a dull, monotonous tone

Bobby and me roll the camping trailer over Mrs. Johnson's cat?" And our mothers say: "Remember your grammar, dear. You mean: 'Can Bobby and *I* roll the camping trailer over Mrs. Johnson's cat?' Of course you can, but be home by dinnertime."

The only exception to this rule is in formal business writing, where instead of "I" you must use "the undersigned." For example, this business letter is incorrect:

"Dear Hunky-Dory Canned Fruit Company: A couple days ago my wife bought a can of your cling peaches and served them to my mother who has a weak heart and she damn near died when she bit into a live grub. If I ever find out where you live, I am gonna whomp you on the head with a ax handle."

This should be corrected as follows:

". . . If the undersigned ever finds out where you live, the undersigned is gonna whomp you on the head with a ax handle."

Rule 2. You're not allowed to split infinitives.

An infinitive is the word "to" and whatever comes right behind it, such as "to a tee," "to the best of my ability," "tomato," etc. Splitting an infinitive is putting something between the "to" and the other words. For example, this is incorrect:

"Hey man, you got any, you know, spare change you could give to, like, me?"

The correct version is:

". . . spare change you could, like, give to me?"

The advantage of American English is that, because there are so few rules, practically anybody can learn to speak it in just a few minutes. The disadvantage is that Americans generally sound like jerks, whereas the British sound really smart, especially to Americans. That's why Americans are so fond of those British dramas they're always showing on public television, the ones introduced by Alistair Cooke.[1] Americans *love* people who talk like Alistair Cooke. He could introduce old episodes of "Hawaii Five-O" and Americans would think they were extremely <u>enlightening</u>.

So the trick is to use American grammar, which is simple, but talk with a British accent, which is impressive. This technique is taught at all your really snotty private schools, where the kids learn to sound like Elliot Richardson.[2] Remember Elliot? He sounded extremely British, and as a result he got to be Attorney General, Secretary of State, Chief Justice of the Supreme Court and Vice President *at the same time*.

You can do it, too. Practice in your home, then approach someone on the street and say: "Tally-ho, old chap. I would consider it a great honour if you would favour me with some spare change." You're bound to get quick results.

---

1. *Alistair Cooke* was the British-born host of public television's *Masterpiece Theater.*
2. *Elliot Richardson* was born in Boston. During the 1970s, he held four Cabinet offices (more than any other person) and served as ambassador to Great Britain. However, he did NOT hold these positions all at the same time, he was NEVER the vice president, and he did NOT serve on the Supreme Court.

Vocabulary
enlightening (en līt′ ən ing) *adj.* giving or revealing knowledge or wisdom

E Author's Craft

STYLE Have students read aloud the quoted sentence. Point out that Barry is using a technique that he employs frequently in the course of the essay: emphasizing style and ignoring the content, which is often absurd. Have students find two more examples of this technique. *(The prospective airline pilot's first statement on page 1039 and the letter to the "Hunky-Dory Canned Fruit Company" on page 1041 are examples of this technique.)*

F Literary Elements

ALLUSION Have students identify the allusion to *Hawaii Five-O* and explain its humor. *(Hawaii Five-O was a television detective program set in Hawaii that was made in the 1970s; far from being a classic, it would seem dated and melodramatic today.)*

Thematic Focus

Comic Perspectives Have students discuss whether or not they would enjoy having Dave Barry for a friend, neighbor, or teacher, judging by the sense of humor displayed in his essay.

✔ ASSESSMENT OPTIONS

📁 *Quick Checks,* p. 87

Grammar and Language *Minilesson*

Infinitives Remind students that an infinitive is the word *to* plus the base form of a verb: *to play, to study.* An infinitive can be used as a noun, an adjective, or an adverb. Good writers usually avoid putting words between the word *to* and the verb to avoid awkwardness. For example, "I like to stop frequently when driving long distances" instead of "I like to frequently stop when driving long distances."

Activity Have students identify each infinitive in the following sentences.
1. The trick is *to use* American grammar.
2. You're bound *to get* quick results.
3. I like *to talk* about airplanes. **L1**

Additional Resources

🔖 *Grammar and Language Transparency 76*

📖 *Grammar and Language Workbook,* p. 97

📖 *Grammar and Composition Handbook,* Lesson 3.3

📖 *Writer's Choice,* Lesson 12.3

Responding to the Selection

Personal Response

Students may like Barry's comic perspective on a subject that most people can identify with.

ANALYZING LITERATURE

1. Using good grammar will make a person sound intelligent on job applications and in business letters. He is probably poking fun at English teachers and grammar experts.

2. Its purpose was to make up the parts of speech and grammar rules because no one could read the *Canterbury Tales.* The Commission left behind hundreds of rules, which, ironically, Americans rebelled against.

3. They used words such as *ain't* and *finalize* and misspelled words in the Declaration of Independence. Because of the colonists, we now have only two grammar rules.

4. In Rule 1, he makes fun of the common misuse of object pronouns. In Rule 2, he makes fun of picky rules, specifically, rules about infinitives. His explanation of Rule 2 is ironic because he defines an infinitive incorrectly.

5. The trick is to use American grammar and a British accent. He is making fun of the reverence Americans have for the British accent.

6. Students may say that Barry's humor effectively highlights the silliness of some grammar rules and the annoying nature of grammarians.

7. Students may agree with Barry's complaint that many grammar rules don't seem to make sense.

8. Students may infer that Barry must have a thorough knowledge of grammar in order to satirize it effectively. Students' opinions of him as a teacher will depend on how much they care about grammar.

Responding to Literature

Personal Response

What is your opinion of Barry's comic perspective? Respond in your journal.

——— ANALYZING LITERATURE ———

RECALL AND INTERPRET

1. According to Dave Barry, why is good grammar important to know and use? Who do you think he is poking fun at with his explanation?
2. What does Barry say was the purpose of the Grammar Commission? Why did it come into existence? What did it leave behind? According to Barry, what is ironic about the formation of the Commission?
3. How did the colonists, according to Barry, show their defiance of British dominance? Why does Barry think that we Americans owe the original colonists our gratitude?
4. Explain Grammar Rules 1 and 2. What does Barry make fun of in Rule 1? What is **ironic** about Barry's explanation of Rule 2? (See page R6.)
5. Explain Barry's trick for speaking American English impressively. What point do you think he is trying to make here?

EVALUATE AND CONNECT

6. Theme Connections   The purpose of **satire** usually is to amuse readers by exposing the follies of people or societies. Evaluate the use of **satire** in this selection. (See Literary Terms Handbook, page R11.)
7. How do your thoughts about grammar in the Focus Activity on page 1038 compare with Barry's? Cite examples from the selection.
8. What can you infer about Barry's knowledge of grammar? In your opinion, would he be a good grammar teacher? Explain.

Literary ELEMENTS

Allusion

An **allusion** is a reference in a work to a person or event outside the work. When readers recognize the reference, they make a connection between it and a point the writer is making. For example, when Barry says, "Without good grammar, the United States would have lost World War II," he is making an allusion to a historic event. Readers should recognize the absurdity in suggesting that grammar affected the outcome of World War II.

1. What allusion does Barry make about the spelling of Chaucer's name? What effect does this allusion have?
2. Find three other allusions in the selection. Explain them.

● See **Literary Terms Handbook,** p. R1.

——— EXTENDING YOUR RESPONSE ———

Literature Groups

Grammar Teacher   In several of Barry's "corrected" versions of grammar mistakes, he includes other grammar errors. Working with your group, correct as many errors as you can find. Then discuss the following questions: Why, do you suppose, does Barry include these errors? What do they add to the essay? Do you think he intends for his readers to detect these errors? Share the results of your discussion with your classmates.

Learning for Life

What Do You Think of This?   In a 1995 interview, Dave Barry said that many of his ideas come from readers. "They are my reporters and they are quite good at it," he said. "They have an eye for the weird." In a letter to Dave Barry, suggest a topic for a future column. Explain why you think the topic suits his style and sense of humor.

📖 **Save your work for your portfolio.**

LITERARY ELEMENTS

1. Barry alludes to the British spelling of Geoffrey being different from the American spelling, Jeffrey. The effect is humorous.
2. Barry alludes to the Super Bowl, the American Revolution, and *Hawaii Five-O*, none of which really have anything to do with grammar.

Additional Resources

📖 *Literary Elements Transparency 87*

✔ ASSESSMENT OPTIONS

📁 *Quick Checks,* p. 87
📁 *Selection and Theme Assessment,* pp. 163–164
📁 *Performance Assessment,* p. 85
💾 *Testmaker*

COMPARING *selections*

COMPARING *selections*

from
An American Childhood **and** What Is and Ain't Grammatical

COMPARE **THEMES**

In both *An American Childhood* and "What Is and Ain't Grammatical," the authors focus on the same subject: how we use language. Discuss these questions:

1. How are Mother's and Barry's attitudes toward language similar? How are they different?
2. How are Dillard's and Barry's messages about the use of language similar? Support your response with evidence from the selections.

COMPARE **APPROACHES**

Suppose that you are the talk show host for a television program featuring Mother and Barry as guests.

- Working in a group of three, prepare interview questions and responses that will allow Barry and Mother to express their views on the delights and absurdities of language. Be sure that Mother's and Barry's attitudes and ideas come across in the interview.
- Practice your interview and then present it to the class.

COMPARE **TECHNIQUES**

Dillard and Barry use a variety of techniques to achieve humor, including irony, satire, hyperbole (exaggeration), and allusion.

- Find examples in the two selections of each humor technique used by the authors. Record the examples in a chart like the one shown, and decide whether one author's use of a technique is more effective than the other author's.
- Share your chart and ideas with a small group of classmates.

Technique	Dillard example	Barry example
irony		
satire		
hyperbole		
allusion		

Objective

- To compare two humorous essays that focus on language

COMPARE **THEMES**

1. Both find humor in language's eccentricities. Mother simply takes note of people's use of language, while Barry makes a point about people who take language's rules too seriously.
2. Both think language is an important tool and that people are judged on their use of language. Mother laughs at the dialect of people in Pittsburgh. Barry makes fun of the language of the airline pilot applicant and the business letter writer.

COMPARE **APPROACHES**

Groups' interviews should
- reflect the attitudes toward language shown by Mother and Barry.
- be consistent with the characters and senses of humor of Mother and Barry. **COLLAB. LEARN.**

Additional Resources
📁 *Literature Groups Sourcebook*

COMPARE **TECHNIQUES**

Students' charts should
- show knowledge of various techniques of humor.
- give specific examples of Dillard's and Barry's use of each technique.

Teaching Options

PORTFOLIO OPTIONS _____

Select and Reflect Have students reflect on their charts for the activity above by asking themselves these questions:
- Does my chart include an example of each humor technique for each character?
- Does my chart indicate which author's use of a technique is more effective?

Students should clip their reflections to their charts and place them in their portfolios. Later, they can consider revising their charts as portfolio showcase pieces. **L2**

Additional Resources
📁 *Writing Assessment and Portfolio Management,* pp. 20–22

Objectives

- To read and analyze an essay about the humorous misadventures of one family
- To identify direct and indirect methods of characterization
- To write an analysis of humor

Skills

Reading/Thinking: Drawing Conclusions; Graphic Aids
Writing: Journal Entry
Vocabulary: The Latin Root *ject*
Grammar/Language: Colons
Listening/Speaking: Newscast
Life Skills: Accident Report
Collaboration: Literature Groups

Motivating

→OPTIONS

Selection Focus Transparency 83: Have students share anecdotes and provide amusing details.

Focus Activity: Have students read their journal entries in small groups.

Before You Read

The Car We Had to Push

FOCUS ACTIVITY

What misadventures or silly situations have occurred in your family or a friend's family?

JOURNAL In your journal, briefly write about a humorous episode or event that you have heard about or experienced.

SETTING A PURPOSE Read to enjoy the humorous misadventures of one family.

BACKGROUND

Thurber House

The Time and Place

James Thurber wrote *My Life and Hard Times,* the collection containing "The Car We Had to Push," in the middle of the Great Depression, although he never mentions economic conditions. The story takes place in his hometown, Columbus, Ohio.

Did You Know?

The critic Charles Holmes says Thurber's *My Life and Hard Times* "is obviously a special kind of autobiography, existing somewhere between the world of fact and the world of fantasy." Many of the characters and events in the book are based on the actual world of Thurber's boyhood. But, says Holmes, by weaving "a cross-pattern of absurd and fanciful details" into that world, Thurber subtly transformed it into a strange new world, "where confusion and eccentricity are the primary ways of life."

VOCABULARY PREVIEW

repercussion (rē′ pər kush′ ən) *n.* an effect or result of some action or event; p. 1045

unkempt (un kempt′) *adj.* in a neglected state; not combed or groomed; untidy; p. 1045

exhortation (eg′ zôr tā′ shən) *n.* a strong appeal or warning; p. 1045

contend (kən tend′) *v.* to declare or maintain as a fact; argue; p. 1047

resonant (rez′ ə nənt) *adj.* having a full, rich sound; p. 1049

lucid (lōō′ sid) *adj.* clear-headed; mentally alert; p. 1049

Meet James Thurber

"I write humor the way a surgeon operates," explained James Thurber, "because it is a livelihood . . . and because I have the hope it may do some good." Thurber began his writing career in the 1920s, working as a newspaper columnist and reporter. Joining the staff of the *New Yorker* magazine in 1927, he soon began producing the humorous stories and essays that made his reputation. Despite blindness in one of his eyes, Thurber often filled notepads with cartoons. When E. B. White submitted them to the *New Yorker,* they were promptly accepted. Besides stories and essays, Thurber wrote a history of the *New Yorker.*

James Thurber was born in 1894 and died in 1961.

RESOURCE MANAGER

Lesson Planning Resource
The *Unit Six Planning Guide* (pp. 45–52) provides additional lesson notes and reduced versions of all print resources.

📁 **Other Print Resources**
- Active Reading Guide, p. 88
- Vocabulary Practice, p. 59
- Reading Workbook, pp. 89–90
- Grammar and Language Workbook, p. 247
- Grammar and Composition Handbook, Lesson 11.4

- Quick Checks, p. 88
- Selection and Theme Assessment, pp. 165–166
- Performance Assessment, p. 86
- Spanish Summaries, p. 83
- Spanish Translations
- Inclusion Strategies
- English Language Learners Sourcebook

 Transparencies
- Selection Focus 83
- Fine Art 5

- Literary Elements 88
- Grammar and Language 77

Technology
- 🎧 Audio Library
- 🎧 Spanish Audio Library
- 💻 Glencoe Literature Web Site
- 💾 Testmaker

THE CAR WE HAD TO PUSH

James Thurber

It took sometimes as many as five or six. James Thurber. Illustration from *My Life and Hard Times,* 1933.

MANY AUTOBIOGRAPHERS, among them Lincoln Steffens and Gertrude Atherton,[1] describe earthquakes their families have been in. I am unable to do this because my family was never in an earthquake, but we went through a number of things in Columbus that were a great deal like earthquakes. I remember in particular some of the repercussions of an old Reo we had that wouldn't go unless you pushed it for quite a way and suddenly let your clutch out. Once, we had been able to start the engine easily by cranking it, but we had had the car for so many years that finally it wouldn't go unless you pushed it and let your clutch out. Of course, it took more than one person to do this; it took sometimes as many as five or six, depending on the grade of the roadway and conditions underfoot. The car was unusual in that the clutch and brake were on the same pedal, making it quite easy to stall the engine after it got started, so that the car would have to be pushed again.

My father used to get sick at his stomach pushing the car, and very often was unable to go to work. He had never liked the machine, even when it was good, sharing my ignorance and suspicion of all automobiles of twenty years ago and longer. The boys I went to school with used to be able to identify every car as it passed by: Thomas Flyer, Firestone-Columbus, Stevens Duryea, Rambler, Winton, White Steamer, etc. I never could. The only car I was really interested in was one that the Get-Ready Man, as we called him, rode around town in: a big Red Devil with a door in the back. The Get-Ready Man was a lank unkempt elderly gentleman with wild eyes and a deep voice who used to go about shouting at people through a megaphone to prepare for the end of the world. "GET READY! GET READ-Y!" he would bellow. "THE WORLLLD IS COMING TO AN END!" His startling exhortations would come up, like summer

---

1. Besides their autobiographies, *Steffens* wrote nonfiction books and articles; *Atherton* wrote novels. Their major works were published between 1898 and 1936.

Vocabulary
repercussion (rē´ pər kush´ ən) *n.* an effect or result of some action or event
unkempt (un kempt´) *adj.* in a neglected state; not combed or groomed; untidy
exhortation (eg´ zôr tā´ shən) *n.* a strong appeal or warning

---

B Literary Elements

CHARACTERIZATION Point out that the author uses both direct and indirect characterization of his father on page 1045. Have students give examples of each. *(Describing his father getting sick and missing work after pushing the car is indirect characterization. Saying he shares the narrator's ignorance and suspicion of old cars is direct characterization.)*

C Literary Elements

HYPERBOLE Have students identify the hyperbole in the first paragraph, page 1046. How does it help characterize the narrator and his father? *(Saying that neither he nor his father completely got over the scene is hyperbole, characterizing them as particularly sensitive and susceptible to being permanently affected by strange experiences.)*

D Author's Craft

PARODY Remind students that in parody, an author imitates the style of a literary work for a humorous effect. Here the author quotes actual phrases from a climactic scene in act 3 of one of Shakespeare's greatest tragedies, *King Lear,* in which Edgar is pretending to be a madman. Have students explain the aspects of Shakespearean tragedy that the author is poking fun at. *(Thurber makes fun of the exaggerated insanity of the play in which the Get-Ready Man's craziness fits right in.)*

Teaching Options

thunder, at the most unexpected times and in the most surprising places. I remember once during Mantell's production of "King Lear" at the Colonial Theatre, that the Get-Ready Man added his bawlings to the squealing of Edgar and the ranting of the King and the mouthing of the Fool, rising from somewhere in the balcony to join in. The theatre was in absolute darkness and there were rumblings of thunder and flashes of lightning offstage. Neither father nor I, who were there, ever completely got over the scene, which went something like this:

EDGAR: Tom's a-cold.—O, do de, do de, do de!—Bless thee from whirlwinds, star-blasting, and taking . . . the foul fiend vexes!

[*Thunder off.*]

LEAR: What! Have his daughters brought him to this pass?—

GET-READY MAN: Get ready! Get ready!

EDGAR: Pillicock sat on Pillicock-hill:—
                    Halloo, halloo, loo, loo!

[*Lightning flashes.*]

GET-READY MAN: The Worllld is com-ing to an End!

FOOL: This cold night will turn us all to fools and madmen!

EDGAR: Take heed o' the foul fiend: obey thy paren—

GET-READY MAN: Get *Rea*-dy!

EDGAR: Tom's a-*cold!*

GET-READY MAN: The *Worr*-uld is coming to an end! . . .

They found him finally, and ejected him, still shouting. The Theatre, in our time, has known few such moments.

But to get back to the automobile. One of my happiest memories of it was when, in its eighth year, my brother Roy got together a great many articles from the kitchen, placed them in a square of canvas, and swung this under the car with a string attached to it so that, at a twitch, the canvas would give way and the steel and tin things would clatter to the street. This was a little scheme of Roy's to frighten father, who had always expected the car might explode. It worked perfectly. That was twenty-five years ago, but it is one of the few things in my life I would like to

The Get-Ready Man. James Thurber. Illustration from My Life and Hard Times, *1933.*

MEETING INDIVIDUAL NEEDS — ENGLISH LANGUAGE LEARNERS

America in the 1920s Knowing a little about the way of life in the United States in the 1910s and 1920s can help English language learners understand the humor of the selection.

Activity Have students contribute as you write a list of inventions that were just beginning to be used in the United States in the 1910s and 1920s,

such as electric lights, refrigerators, telephones, automobiles, phonographs, cameras, and airplanes. Have students share stories they have heard from their parents and grandparents about beginning to use these items.

Additional Resources
📁 *English Language Learners Sourcebook*

live over again if I could. I don't suppose that I can, now. Roy twitched the string in the middle of a lovely afternoon, on Bryden Road, near Eighteenth Street. Father had closed his eyes and, with his hat off, was enjoying a cool breeze. The clatter on the asphalt was tremendously effective: knives, forks, can-openers, pie pans, pot lids, biscuit-cutters, ladles, eggbeaters fell, beautifully together, in a lingering, clamant[2] crash. "Stop the *car!*" shouted father. "I can't," Roy said. "The engine fell out." "God Almighty!" said father, who knew what *that* meant, or knew what it sounded as if it might mean.

It ended unhappily, of course, because we finally had to drive back and pick up the stuff and even father knew the difference between the works of an automobile and the equipment of a pantry. My mother wouldn't have known, however, nor *her* mother. My mother, for instance, thought—or, rather, knew—that it was dangerous to drive an automobile without gasoline: it fried the valves, or something. "Now don't you dare drive all over town without gasoline!" she would say to us when we started off. Gasoline, oil, and water were much the same to her, a fact that made her life both confusing and perilous. Her greatest dread, however, was the Victrola—we had a very early one, back in the "Come Josephine

Did You Know?
Victrola is the trademark name of a record player; early models were hand-cranked, just as wind-up toys are. Electric phonographs were first produced in the 1920s.

in My Flying Machine" days. She had an idea that the Victrola might blow up. It alarmed her, rather than reassured her, to explain that the phonograph was run neither by gasoline nor by electricity. She could only suppose that it was propelled by some newfangled and untested apparatus which was likely to let go at any minute, making us all the victims and martyrs of the wild-eyed Edison's dangerous experiments.[3] The telephone she was comparatively at peace with, except, of course, during storms, when for some reason or other she always took the receiver off the hook and let it hang. She came naturally by her confused and groundless fears, for her own mother lived the latter years of her life in the horrible suspicion that electricity was dripping invisibly all over the house. It leaked, she <u>contended</u>, out of empty sockets if the wall switch had been left on. She would go around screwing in bulbs, and if they lighted up she would hastily and fearfully turn off the wall switch and go back to her *Pearson's* or *Everybody's*,[4] happy in the satisfaction that she had stopped not only a costly but a dangerous leakage. Nothing could ever clear this up for her.

Our poor old Reo came to a horrible end, finally. We had parked it too far from the curb on a street with a car line. It was late at night and the street was dark. The first streetcar[5] that came along couldn't get by. It picked up the tired old automobile as a terrier might seize a rabbit and drubbed it

---

2. Anything *clamant* (klā′ mənt) is noisy and demanding attention.

3. *Martyrs* are those who suffer or die for a cause. The *dangerous experiments* of Thomas A. *Edison* produced inventions that changed the world, including the light bulb, the first practical phonograph (1877), and important improvements to the telephone.

4. These were popular magazines of the early 1900s.

5. Since a *streetcar* runs on rails, it can't avoid things in its path.

Vocabulary
contend (kən tend′) *v.* to declare or maintain as a fact; argue

Author's Craft

IMAGERY Have a student read aloud the second sentence on page 1048. How does the author's word choice help create vivid sound imagery? *(Thurber uses made-up words—booped, whooshed, queeled, and graked—that vividly imitate the sounds of the car.)* Remind students that words that imitate the sounds they describe are examples of onomatopoeia.

FINE ART
TRANSPARENCY 5

You may want to use Fine Art Transparency 5 to compare and contrast impressions of automobiles with those in the selection.

Electricity was leaking all over the house. James Thurber. Illustration from *My Life and Hard Times,* 1933.

unmercifully, losing its hold now and then but catching a new grip a second later. Tires booped and whooshed, the fenders queeled and graked, the steering wheel rose up like a spectre and disappeared in the direction of Franklin Avenue with a melancholy whistling sound, bolts and gadgets flew like sparks from a Catherine wheel.[6] It was a splendid spectacle but, of course, saddening to everybody (except the motorman of the streetcar, who was sore). I think some of us broke down and wept. It must have been the weeping that caused grandfather to take on so terribly. Time was all mixed up in his mind; automobiles and the like he never remembered having seen. He apparently gathered, from the talk and excitement and weeping, that somebody had died. Nor did he let go of this delusion. He insisted, in fact, after almost a week in which we strove mightily to divert him, that it was a sin and a shame and a disgrace on the family to put

---

6. A *spectre* is a ghost or ghostly vision. The *Catherine wheel* is a firework that, when lighted, spins like a pinwheel and spouts colorful sparks and flames.

1048 ❧ UNIT 6

Teaching Options

Grammar and Language *Minilesson*

Using Colons to Introduce a List Write this sentence on the board: *The boys I went to school with used to be able to identify every car as it passed by: Thomas Flyer, Firestone-Columbus, Stevens Duryea, Rambler, Winston, White Steamer, etc.* Explain that a colon is used in this sentence to introduce a list of items. Point out that the words before the colon must form a complete sentence.

Incorrect: My subjects were: English, history, math, and biology.
Correct: My subjects were English, history, math, and biology.
Correct: I studied these subjects: English, history, math, and biology.

Activity Have students write two sentences that use a colon to introduce a list of items. **L2**

Additional Resources

Grammar and Language Transparency 77

Grammar and Language Workbook, p. 247

Grammar and Composition Handbook, Lesson 11.4

Writer's Choice, Lesson 21.4

the funeral off any longer. "Nobody is dead! The automobile is smashed!" shouted my father, trying for the thirtieth time to explain the situation to the old man. "Was he drunk?" demanded grandfather, sternly. "Was who drunk?" asked father. "Zenas," said grandfather. He had a name for the corpse now: it was his brother Zenas, who, as it happened, *was* dead, but not from driving an automobile while intoxicated. Zenas had died in 1866. A sensitive, rather poetical boy of twenty-one when the Civil War broke out, Zenas had gone to South America—"just," as he wrote back, "until it blows over." Returning after the war had blown over, he caught the same disease that was killing off the chestnut trees in those years, and passed away. It was the only case in history where a tree doctor had to be called in to spray a person, and our family had felt it very keenly; nobody else in the United States caught the blight. Some of us have looked upon Zenas' fate as a kind of poetic justice.

Now that grandfather knew, so to speak, who was dead, it became increasingly awkward to go on living in the same house with him as if nothing had happened. He would go into towering rages in which he threatened to write to the Board of Health unless the funeral were held at once. We realized that something had to be done. Eventually, we persuaded a friend of father's, named George Martin, to dress up in the manner and costume of the eighteen-sixties and pretend to be Uncle Zenas, in order to set grandfather's mind at rest. The impostor looked fine and impressive in side-burns and a high beaver hat, and not unlike the daguerreotypes of Zenas in our album. I shall never forget the night, just after dinner, when this Zenas walked into the living room. Grandfather was stomping up and down, tall, hawk-nosed, round-oathed. The newcomer held out both his hands. "Clem!" he cried to grandfather. Grandfather turned slowly, looked at the intruder, and snorted. "Who air *you?*" he demanded in his deep, resonant voice. "I'm Zenas!" cried Martin. "Your brother Zenas, fit as a fiddle and sound as a dollar!" "Zenas, my foot!" said grandfather. "Zenas died of the chestnut blight in '66!"

Grandfather was given to these sudden, unexpected, and extremely lucid moments; they were generally more embarrassing than his other moments. He comprehended before he went to bed that night that the old automobile had been destroyed and that its destruction had caused all the turmoil in the house. "It flew all to pieces, Pa," my mother told him, in graphically describing the accident. "I knew 'twould," growled grandfather. "I allus told ye to git a Pope-Toledo."

Did You Know?
Daguerreotypes (də ger′ ə tīps′) are photographs made by exposing light to silver-coated copper plates; Louis Daguerre invented the process in France in the mid-1800s.

Vocabulary
resonant (rez′ ə nənt) *adj.* having a full, rich sound
lucid (loo′ sid) *adj.* clear-headed; mentally alert

DRAWING CONCLUSIONS Use this model to help students explain why Zenas's catching the "blight" might be considered "poetic justice."

Model: The author emphasizes Zenas's going away until the war "blew over." He implies that Zenas's action was not a courageous one. This brings to mind a second meaning of *blight*, "something that impairs or destroys," as in "a moral blight." I think the author is saying that Zenas's treelike lack of action in the war made his contracting the "blight" an appropriate affliction.

I **Literary Elements**

CHARACTERIZATION Point out the author's use of dialect in Grandfather's speeches. Have students explain how dialect contributes to direct or indirect characterization of Grandfather. *(Dialect is a form of indirect characterization. It portrays Grandfather as an elderly, old-fashioned man.)*

Thematic Focus

Comic Perspectives Point out that Thurber's title indicates that the selection is about a car. Have students identify the real subject of the selection—the Thurber family's relationship with "new" technology.

☑ **ASSESSMENT OPTIONS**

📁 *Quick Checks,* p. 88

Reading *Minilesson*

Graphic Aids Point out that part of the humor of Thurber's story comes from his frequent digressions from his main topic: his family's automobile. During the course of the selection, Thurber describes the Get-Ready Man, Father, Mother, Zenas, and Grandfather. Showing these characters and ideas graphically can help students understand the organization and humor of Thurber's essay.

Activity Have students create a graphic, such as a chart or cluster map, that shows the characters in the selection and the relationship of each to the automobile. Have volunteers put their graphic aids on the board. **L2**

Additional Resources
📁 *Reading Workbook,* pp. 89–90

Responding to the Selection

Personal Response

Students may think that the scene at the theater, the Get-Ready Man, or Grandfather was funniest.

ANALYZING LITERATURE

1. James Thurber recounts events that happened to him and his family.
2. It was the family's car. It had to be pushed because it was so old that was the only way to start it.
3. She feared running the car without gasoline. She feared the Victrola might blow up, and she took the telephone off the hook during storms.
4. It was crushed by a passing streetcar.
5. Zenas was Grandfather's deceased brother. When everyone is sad because the car has been smashed, Grandfather thinks Zenas has just died. When a family friend impersonates Zenas, Grandfather recalls that Zenas died.
6. He has a tone of amused tolerance and an enjoyment of life's absurdities. He describes his family's bizarre ideas with patient acceptance.
7. His happiest memory is when his brother rigged pots and pans to fall from the car's bottom to frighten their father. This shows the author enjoys practical jokes.
8. The mother is old-fashioned and a bit superstitious; she is ignorant of technology and seems to have no urge to educate herself about how it works.
9. The car's end fits the absurd tone of the story.
10. He has weird ideas that others might find bizarre without the excuse that he is suffering from senility.
11. This digression portrays Thurber as just as eccentric as the rest of his family, since he is so easily distracted.
12. Although the story is really about the narrator's family, the car ties the strands of the story together. Students might think of a title such as "My Family and the Age of Technology."
13. Students' recalled events may or may not be as silly or bizarre as the story events.
14. Many people were suspicious of machines such as cars and telephones because they used electricity, which can be dangerous. Some people today have similar attitudes about computers.

Responding to Literature

Personal Response

Which event or character in the story did you find funniest? Share your reactions with a classmate.

——— ANALYZING LITERATURE ———

RECALL

1. Who is the narrator, and what is his relationship to the story?
2. Who owned the car? Why did it have to be pushed?
3. What did the narrator's mother fear about the car? What other inventions did she fear? Why?
4. What eventually happened to the car?
5. Who was Zenas? How is Grandfather confused about him? How is Grandfather's confusion finally settled?

INTERPRET

6. Describe the narrator's **tone**, or attitude, toward the people and events he describes. Support your answer with details from the selection.
7. What is the narrator's "happiest" memory of the car? What does considering this happy memory reveal about his personality?
8. What can you infer about the mother, based on her fears?
9. How does the car's end relate to the overall **mood**, or atmosphere, of the story? Explain. (See Literary Terms Handbook, page R8.)
10. Why might Grandfather's lucid moments be "more embarrassing than his other moments"? Explain.

EVALUATE AND CONNECT

11. Why, do you think, does Thurber include the Get-Ready Man in the story? What effect does this part of the story create?
12. Do you think the title accurately tells what the story is about? Why or why not? If you were to give the story another title, what would you choose? Support your choice with evidence from the story.
13. Think about your response to the Focus Activity on page 1044. In what ways are the events in this story similar to the ones you described?
14. Why were people during the narrator's childhood suspicious of "new-fangled" machines like cars, telephones, and electric appliances? Were any of their fears justified? Do similar attitudes exist today? Explain.
15. What qualities in this story do you think helped lead to Thurber's enormous popular success during his lifetime? Cite examples from the story to support your opinion.

Literary ELEMENTS

Characterization

A writer reveals the personality of a character through **direct** and **indirect** methods of **characterization**. In direct characterization, the writer makes statements directly describing a character's traits, words, or actions. Thurber uses direct characterization when he writes, "The Get-Ready Man was a lank unkempt elderly gentleman with wild eyes and a deep voice." In indirect characterization, the writer reveals aspects of a character through his or her words and actions, as well as through what other characters say and think about the character. Indirect characterization requires readers to interpret details or events. Thurber uses indirect characterization when he has Grandfather suddenly confirm, "Zenas, my foot! Zenas died of the chestnut blight in '66!"

1. Find another example of indirect characterization in the story. What does it show about the character?
2. Give an example of direct characterization that describes the narrator. What does it reveal about him?
3. Why, do you think, does Thurber use both methods of characterization? What effects does he create by doing so?

● See **Literary Terms Handbook,** p. R2.

15. Thurber's gentle sense of humor and his sense of people's absurdities were nonthreatening. His treatment of his father when the "engine" fell out is an illustration.

LITERARY ELEMENTS

1. The grandmother's fear that electricity was invisibly leaking into the house shows that she was old-fashioned and superstitious.
2. He says that he was ignorant and suspicious of all automobiles over twenty years old and was not mechanically oriented.
3. He uses both methods to provide humor and variety. The effect is to make readers feel they know the characters.

Additional Resources

✍ *Literary Elements Transparency 88*

LITERATURE AND WRITING

Writing About Literature

Analyzing Humor   How does Thurber use the car as the "vehicle" for holding the story together? In two or three paragraphs, explain how Thurber uses anecdotes about the car to present details about characters and events and, most of all, to make his readers laugh.

Personal Writing

Funny Characters   Which **character** in Thurber's story do you find most believable? Which is the most humorous? Which contributes the most to the story? In your journal, describe the qualities of your favorite characters and tell why you think those characters are important to the story.

EXTENDING YOUR RESPONSE

Literature Groups

Defining Humor   What, in your opinion, makes writing funny? Is it what the characters say or how they view things? Is it the events that occur or how they affect the characters? Discuss these questions with your group. Then refer to the story, and analyze specific elements that contribute to the story's humor. List your findings, and share them with other groups.

Listening and Speaking

Newscast   Choose a passage or anecdote from the story, and prepare it as a news story that might be broadcast on radio or television. Rehearse your news presentation and present it, in an appropriate reporting style, for the class.

Learning for Life

Accident Report   Prepare a written report describing the details of the accident between the parked car and the passing streetcar. Include a diagram showing the locations of the vehicles involved and the likely resting place of the car parts. Also record facts that the streetcar driver might have conveyed to you when describing the incident.

Reading Further

You might enjoy these works by James Thurber:

Short Stories: In "The Letters of James Thurber" and "Here Lies Miss Groby" from *My World—and Welcome to It,* Thurber takes a humorous look at his writing and his way of thinking.

"An Outline of the Byrd Report," from *People Have More Fun Than Anybody,* humorously points out that the "value" of ice and land in Antarctica takes on different meanings in the scientific community and in the U.S. Senate.

📖 **Save your work for your portfolio.**

VOCABULARY • **The Latin Root** *ject*

The word *eject* comes from the Latin prefix *e-,* meaning *out,* and the root *ject,* meaning "to throw." Many English words contain the *ject* root. When pilots *eject* from an airplane, they are thrown out of it.

If you *reject* an offer, you throw it back. When people are *subjected* to cruel treatment, they are thrown under it.

The following prefixes can be attached to *ject*:

inter-: between   *tra-:* across   *pro-:* forward

PRACTICE   Use the meanings of *ject* and the prefixes given to answer the questions.

1. What kind of device uses a *projectile*—a slingshot, a pulley, or a jackhammer?

2. Which object has a *trajectory*—a fence, a tower, or a fly ball?

3. When would a joke be *interjected* into a speech—at the beginning, within, or at the end of it?

LITERATURE AND WRITING

Writing About Literature

Students' analyses should
- explain how the car motif holds the story together.
- give examples of Thurber's use of anecdotes.

Personal Writing

Students' journal entries should
- describe the most believable, humorous, and important characters.
- use details from the story to explain why each character is important.

EXTENDING YOUR RESPONSE

Literature Groups   Encourage students to use examples from other humorous selections they have read as they define humor.   **COLLAB. LEARN.**

Listening and Speaking   Have students discuss using an objective, serious style to report news. 📖

Learning for Life   Point out that thoroughness and accuracy are essential in an accident report. 📖

VOCABULARY •
The Latin Root *ject*

1. a slingshot   2. a fly ball
3. within the speech

Additional Resources
📁 *Vocabulary Practice,* p. 59

 ASSESSMENT OPTIONS

📁 *Quick Checks,* p. 88

📁 *Selection and Theme Assessment,* pp. 165–166

📁 *Performance Assessment,* p. 86

💾 *Testmaker*

Reading & Thinking Skills

Objective

- To understand and use synthesizing to aid comprehension

Teaching Strategies

Point out that synthesis involves combining parts to form a whole; analysis involves separating a whole into its component parts. Reading literature requires both kinds of reasoning. In order to arrange and rearrange the elements of a story or essay, a reader must have knowledge of each element. This is why analyzing the plot, characters, theme, and other elements of a literary work is important. Have students contribute to a list on the board of the important elements of "The Car We Had to Push."

Activities

1. *Students' dialogues should*
   - indirectly characterize the speakers.
   - provide a humorous perspective on dealing with new inventions.
2. *Students' anecdotes should*
   - show understanding of Grandfather's character.
   - have a humorous tone.

Additional Resources
📁 *Reading Workbook*

Teaching Options

Reading & Thinking Skills

Synthesizing

If you rearrange the furniture in your bedroom so that you can look at each piece from a different angle and in a different position, you have not only created something new, but you may have improved the way in which the room works for you. You may see it as a more beautiful or interesting place.

When you combine the things you know to create something new, you are **synthesizing**. Synthesizing is an important thinking skill, because when you synthesize, you rearrange the understandings you have, making them richer and more complete.

Any time you look for patterns or connections among parts of a story and put them together in a new way, you are synthesizing. Once you've done the work of reading a story and understanding it, you can enrich your understanding through a variety of thinking skills that broaden and deepen your enjoyment of an author's work.

In "The Car We Had to Push," for example, the narrator begins by stating that his family never encountered an earthquake, but "went through a number of things in Columbus that were a great deal like earthquakes." He goes on to tell many anecdotes about his family and how technological changes shook the family in much the same way an earthquake shakes people's lives. Once you understand the pattern of how these events are related, you can envision how the family's fear and confusion about new technology might bring about other humorous escapades. Your understanding of the story allows you to envision ways to extend and enrich what you know.

● For more about related comprehension strategies, see **Reading Handbook,** pp. R82–R89.

ACTIVITIES

1. Think about your understanding of the narrator's mother and the way she responds to different machines, ranging from the Reo to the Victrola and the telephone. Now pretend that she is your mother, and you have to explain to her how to leave a message on someone's telephone answering machine. With a partner, create a humorous dialogue between you and "mom." Decide how the conversation will play out before you begin, and think back to how Thurber creates humor in the interactions of his characters. When your dialogue is finished, perform it for the rest of the class.

2. The narrator's grandfather is a particularly humorous character in Thurber's story because, while he is generally confused, he also has moments when his understanding of events is clear and precise. And because the family never knows when those moments will come, they can never be sure of his responses in any given situation. With this in mind, and from the point of view of the narrator or another character in the story, write a humorous anecdote about taking grandfather to run an errand.

MEETING INDIVIDUAL NEEDS — INCLUSION STRATEGIES

Less-Proficient Readers Charts can help less-proficient readers understand synthesis.

Activity Have students make a three-column chart with the character's names listed in the first column: Roy, Father, Mother, Grandfather. In the second column, have students note distinctive events for each character. In the third column, have students write the trait that the event reveals. Have students refer to this chart when writing their anecdotes and dialogues. **L1** COLLAB. LEARN.

Additional Resources
📁 *Inclusion Strategies*

The Early Automobile

Cranking an engine to start a car? Pushing a car to get it moving? Exploding cars? After reading "The Car We Had to Push," you may wonder if the early cars were as crotchety as James Thurber makes them sound. The answer is both yes and no. At the time of Thurber's story, the automobile was still young and experiencing growing pains.

In his fear of an exploding car, Thurber's father may have been remembering the early steam cars of the 1800s, which did sometimes blow up. By the early 1900s, however, most cars had internal combustion engines fueled by gasoline. Although these cars did not typically explode, they did have their problems. Most had to be started manually with a crank that the motorist inserted into the front of the engine and turned until the engine started. Hand-cranking took time and muscle—and it was potentially dangerous. The hand-crank was replaced when the Cadillac engineering team developed an electric self-starter with a storage battery and generator. Batteries and generators led to additions such as electric headlights.

Keeping cars going was another problem. Places to buy gasoline were sparce. The wise motorist brought along an extra can of gasoline—and a ruler to measure the amount of gasoline in the tank.

Motorists also faced the probability of tire blowouts. Rubber patches and a hand pump helped, but early automobiles frequently had to be towed by a team of horses. Because of these problems, early motorists became the object of jokes, like this one from a 1904 issue of *Life* magazine:

"Yes, I enjoy my automobile immensely."

"But I never see you out."

"Oh, I haven't got that far yet. I am just learning to make my own repairs."

Within a Century: The 1906 Reo and a 1996 Automobile

Thurber's car, the Reo, got its name from the initials of Ransom Eli Olds, who designed the first Oldsmobile and later founded the Reo Motor Car Company. The Reo was one of the most popular cars of its time. This chart compares the Reo with a typical car of the 1990s.

Automobile	1906 Reo Model M	Typical 1996 Automobile
Cylinders	2	6
Horsepower	16	160
Top speed	25 miles per hour	over 100 miles per hour
Price	$2,000	about $19,000

Activity

Find a magazine advertisement for your favorite model of a modern car. Then investigate an early model car, such as the Oldsmobile Runabout, the Winton, the Locomobile, or the Model T. Create a magazine advertisement for the early model car, highlighting its features and price. Display both advertisements on a poster. Point out the similarities and the differences in features and price of the two models.

Objective

- To analyze the features of early automobiles and of modern automobiles

Teaching Strategies

As you discuss features of early automobiles, encourage students who are familiar with cars to describe additional developments in automobiles over the years, such as the automatic transmission, which eliminated the need for a clutch.

Activity

Students' posters should

- illustrate and describe an early model car and a modern car.
- illustrate similarities and differences between the two cars.

MEETING INDIVIDUAL NEEDS MULTIPLE LEARNING STYLES

Musical Musically talented students might enjoy presenting their automobile statistics in musical form.

Activity Have pairs of students gather data on an early model car and a modern car. Then have them create advertising jingles for the cars, with one partner writing about the old car and the other writing about the new. Ask students to present their jingles to the class with guitar or other musical accompaniment.
L3 COLLAB. LEARN.

Objectives

- To read and analyze an autobiographical sketch about someone influencing others
- To analyze diction in a story
- To write a character sketch of an author

Skills

Reading/Thinking: Problem and Solution
Writing: Anecdotes
Vocabulary: Analogies
Life Skills: Interview
Collaboration: Literature Groups

Motivating
→OPTIONS

Selection Focus Transparency 84: Have students view and discuss the cartoon's implications.

Focus Activity: Have students share their experiences of influencing someone.

Before You Read

How I Changed the War and Won the Game

FOCUS ACTIVITY

Have you ever been in a situation where you could tell someone anything and he or she would believe it?

JOURNAL In your journal, tell about a person you've had influence over. Explain why you had such influence, how you used it, and how it made you feel.

SETTING A PURPOSE Read this autobiographical sketch to learn how someone uses her influence over others.

BACKGROUND

The Time and Place

This story recalls events that occurred in a suburban neighborhood in California during World War II.

Did You Know?

World War II officially began in 1939, when Germany, Italy, and Japan joined together to form the Axis powers in an aggressive campaign to conquer large areas of the world. While Japan took over Southeast Asia, the Philippines, and other Pacific Islands, Germany swept through Europe, occupying Poland, Norway, Denmark, and France and moving on to North Africa. After Japan bombed the U.S. naval base at Pearl Harbor in 1941, the United States entered the war, joining Britain and Russia to form the Allied powers. As the war waged abroad, Americans at home feared a Japanese invasion on the West Coast.

VOCABULARY PREVIEW

coerce (kō urs´) v. to pressure or push into doing something, as by force or authority; p. 1055

pilgrimage (pil´ grə mij) n. a long journey, especially to a holy place or for a religious purpose; p. 1055

whim (hwim) n. a sudden notion or fanciful idea; p. 1056

Meet
Mary Helen Ponce

Chicana writer Mary Helen Ponce grew up in the 1940s in Pacoima, a working-class Mexican American community outside of Los Angeles, California. Ponce remembers having a happy childhood, playing kickball with friends, and writing and reading a lot: "I first began writing in grammar school. . . . I have read from 3–5 books every week for most of my life. . . . I think I wanted to be a writer at an early age but had no one to emulate." Ponce wrote *Hoyt Street: Memories of a Chicana Childhood* "to show the beauty, richness, and diversity of Mexican American/ Chicano culture."

Mary Helen Ponce was born in 1938.

RESOURCE MANAGER

Lesson Planning Resource
The *Unit Six Planning Guide* (pp. 53–59) provides additional lesson notes and reduced versions of all print resources.

📁 Other Print Resources
- Active Reading Guide, p. 89
- Vocabulary Practice, p. 60
- Reading Workbook, pp. 89–90
- Grammar and Language Workbook, p. 239
- Grammar and Composition Handbook, Lesson 10.3

- Quick Checks, p. 89
- Selection and Theme Assessment, pp. 167–168
- Performance Assessment, p. 87
- Spanish Summaries, p. 84
- Spanish Translations
- Inclusion Strategies
- English Language Learners Sourcebook

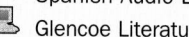 **Transparencies**
- Selection Focus 84
- Literary Elements 89
- Grammar and Language 78

Technology

- 🎧 Audio Library
- 🎧 Spanish Audio Library
- 💻 Glencoe Literature Web Site
- 💾 Testmaker

How I Changed the War and Won the Game

Mary Helen Ponce

DURING WORLD WAR II I used to translate the English newspaper's war news for our adopted grandmother Doña[1] Luisa and her friends. All were elderly ladies, señoras de edad,[2] who could not read English, only their native Spanish. Every afternoon they would gather on Doña Luisa's front porch to await Doña Trinidad's son who delivered the paper to her promptly at five o'clock. There, among the geraniums and pots of yerbabuena[3] I would bring to them the news of the war.

At first I enjoyed this as the señoras welcomed me as a grown-up. They would push their chairs in a semi-circle; the better to hear me. I sat in the middle on a banquito[4] that was once a milk crate. I don't remember how I began to be their translator but because I was an obedient child, and at eight a good reader, I was somehow coerced or selected.

I would sit down, adjust my dress, then slowly unwrap the paper, reading the headlines to myself in English, trying to decide which news stories were the most important, which to tell first. Then I would translate these into my best Spanish for Doña Luisa and her friends. The news of a battle would bring sighs of "Jesús, María, y José" from the ladies. They would roll their eyes towards heaven as they implored the Lord to protect their loved ones from danger. In return they vowed to light candles or make a manda,[5] a pilgrimage, to la Virgen de San Juan in the nearby town of Sunland.[6] Once I had read the highlights of the war I was allowed to go play with my friends.

---

1. In Spanish cultures, *Doña* (dōn′ yə) is a form of respectful address for a married woman, like the English "Madam."
2. *señoras de edad* (sen yôr′ əs dā ā′ däd)
3. Literally "good herb," *yerbabuena* (yer′ bə bwā′ nə) is in the mint family.
4. A *banquito* (bän kē′ tō) is a little bench.

5. *manda* (män′ də)
6. *La Virgen de* (lä   ver′ hen   dā) *San Juan* is a name for Mary, the mother of Jesus. In many locations throughout the centuries, Mary has reportedly appeared in visions to groups and individuals. Apparently, a shrine honoring one of these visions had been built in *Sunland* (which is now part of Los Angeles).

Vocabulary
coerce (kō urs′) *v.* to pressure or push into doing something, as by force or authority
pilgrimage (pil′ grə mij) *n.* a long journey, especially to a holy place or for a religious purpose

HUMOR 1055

SUMMARY

As a young girl during World War II, the narrator would read the war news in the English newspaper to her adopted grandmother Doña Luisa and her friends. They could only read Spanish. One day the narrator was at a crucial point in a ball game when the ladies called her to read. She ran to the ladies and pretended to read a headline saying that the Japanese had landed in San Francisco and were on their way to Los Angeles. The ladies rushed to church to pray as the narrator returned to her game.

📁 *Spanish Summaries,* p. 84

A Active Reading

RESPOND Have students read the first two paragraphs and respond to the scene. Do students think they would enjoy that neighborhood? *(Students might say yes. The mood is pleasant. The community spirit seems cheerful despite the war.)*

Additional Resources
📁 *Active Reading Guide,* p. 89
🎧 *Audio Library*
🎧 *Spanish Audio Library*

Teaching Options

CONNECTING TO OTHER SELECTIONS

The chart at the right shows three ways to connect "How I Changed the War and Won the Game" to selections in this book.

For specific teaching strategies, see the **Unit Six Planning Guide,** pages 56–57.

Connection	Title
Life Skills: Leading and Organizing	→ "I've Seen the Promised Land," p. 517
Thematic: Influences	→ "Catch the Moon," p. 63
Literary: Setting	→ from *Farewell to Manzanar,* p. 460

VIEWING THE ART

The art work shows a typical summer scene in a suburban setting. Even ordinary events provide effective, interesting subject matter for artists.

Viewing Response *As in the story, the front porch of the house is an important gathering place for family members.*

B Literary Elements

DICTION Point out that the author uses several words, both English and Spanish, throughout the selection that relate to religion. How does this diction help characterize the selection's people and setting? *(The older ladies are quite religious; the community has a religious orientation.)*

C Author's Craft

CHARACTERIZATION What two sides of the narrator's character does the story portray? *(On the one hand, she is obedient and wants to be helpful. On the other, she is clever and mischievous.)*

Thematic Focus

Comic Perspectives Have students discuss the selection's title. How does it help reflect the humor of the selection?

☑ ASSESSMENT OPTIONS

📁 *Quick Checks,* p. 89

Teaching Options

Sandia/Watermelon. Carmen Lomas Garza. Gouache on Arches paper, 20 x 28 in. Collection of Dudley D. Brooks and Tomas Ybarra-Frausto, New York.

Viewing the art: In what ways might this family reflect the narrator's family?

One day we had an important ballgame going. Our team was losing, it was my turn at bat. Just then Doña Luisa called me. It was time for *las noticias!*[7] Furious at this interruption, yet not daring to disobey, I dropped the bat, ran to the porch, ripped open the paper, pointed to the headlines, and in a loud voice proclaimed: "Ya están los japoneses en San Francisco, . . . los esperan en Los Angeles muy pronto." The Japanese have landed in San Francisco, and should soon be in Los Angeles.

"Jesús María y José, la Sangre de Cristo, Ave María Purísima," chanted the ladies as I dashed off to resume my game. "Dios mío, ya vámonos, vamos a la iglesia a rezarle al Señor,"[8] they cried as chairs were pushed aside.

After this I was able to translate according to whim, . . . and depending on whether or not I was up to bat when the paper came.

---

7. *Las noticias* (läs   nō′ ti sē′ əs) is the news.

8. The ladies' chant is "Jesus, Mary, and Joseph, Blood of Christ, Hail Mary, the Holy Virgin," followed by "My God, let's go, let's go to the church to pray to the Lord."

Vocabulary
whim (hwim) *n.* a sudden notion or fanciful idea

1056 🐿 UNIT 6

Reading *Minilesson*

Problem and Solution Point out that a story can often be understood in terms of problems and solutions. A character has a problem; the character tries to solve the problem; the solution may or may not work.

Activity Have students complete the chart as a way of understanding and reviewing the story. **L1**

	Problem	Solution
Doña Luisa and her friends		
Narrator		

Additional Resources
📁 *Reading Workbook,* pp. 89–90

Responding to Literature

Personal Response

Do you approve of what the narrator did? Why or why not? Discuss your reaction with a classmate.

ANALYZING LITERATURE

RECALL

1. What daily job did the narrator perform for her adopted grandmother and the other old women in her neighborhood?
2. At first, how did the narrator feel about her job?
3. How did the women usually react to the things they heard?
4. What was the wrong information that the narrator gave the women? Why did she give that information?
5. What happened after the narrator misled the women? How did the misinformation affect the narrator?

INTERPRET

6. Explain why, considering the **setting** of this piece, the narrator's job was so important to the women. (See Literary Terms Handbook, page R11.)
7. How did the narrator's attitude about her job change? Why did it change?
8. What do the women's daily reactions reveal about their lives and concerns?
9. Why, do you suppose, don't the women immediately know that they have been tricked?
10. How did the narrator react after misleading the women? What was her attitude? Cite evidence to support your answer.

EVALUATE AND CONNECT

11. Think about your response to the Focus Activity on page 1054. How does the situation described by the narrator compare with your situation?
12. What does the story reveal about the narrator's personality? What traits do you think she possesses?
13. If you had been in the narrator's situation, do you think you would have done the same thing? Why or why not?
14. Were you surprised that the narrator got away with doing her job "according to whim"? Why or why not?
15. Does what happened in this story seem true to life? Why or why not?

> ### *Literary* ELEMENTS
>
> **Diction**
>
> **Diction** is the choice of words in a piece of writing. Writers use different types of diction to establish setting, convey meaning, and create different tones, moods, and images. In "How I Changed the War and Won the Game," Ponce uses a mixture of English and Spanish words and expressions to convey the Mexican American culture of her childhood. Through her diction, Ponce brings authenticity and humor to her setting and characters.
>
> 1. Give an example from the story in which diction helps convey character, and explain its effect.
> 2. Find three or four examples of direct or everyday language in the story.
> 3. What does the direct and mostly everyday language add to the story?
>
> ● See **Literary Terms Handbook**, p. R3.

LITERARY ELEMENTS

1. The women's Spanish words of prayer characterize the women as religious.
2. "One day we had an important ballgame going. Our team was losing, it was my turn at bat."
3. It adds realism to the story.

Additional Resources

📖 *Literary Elements Transparency 89*

---

14. Students may say they were not surprised because the women did not have much choice but to accept the narrator's version of the news.
15. Students may say yes because events such as the old women sitting on the front porch and the narrator playing ball with her friends are realistic.

Personal Response

Students may say they do not approve because she upset the ladies for a selfish reason or they do approve because the narrator did not really hurt anyone.

ANALYZING LITERATURE

1. She read the war news from the English newspaper each day.
2. She enjoyed the job and felt proud of it.
3. They prayed for the safety of their loved ones and promised to light candles or make religious pilgrimages.
4. She told them the Japanese had landed in San Francisco and were headed to Los Angeles because she wanted to go back to the game.
5. They went to church, and she returned to her game. It gave her the courage to translate the news the way she wanted.
6. Her job was important because since they could only read Spanish, and they lived in the United States, she was their key to getting news of loved ones in the war.
7. She became impatient because the job interfered with her activities.
8. They are religious and concerned with their loved ones endangered by the war.
9. They cannot read English, and they probably have no radios on which to listen to news. They mainly socialize with one another.
10. She felt more confident about shirking her duty in the future. After this she was able "to translate according to whim."
11. Students should think of times when they were expected to be obedient.
12. She is self-confident, decisive, and audacious.
13. Some students may say they would have done the same thing so they could return to the game. Others may say that what the narrator did was selfish and mean because it upset the women needlessly.

LITERATURE AND WRITING

Writing About Literature

Students' character sketches should
- characterize the author as a child.
- include traits that are directly and indirectly revealed.

Personal Writing

Students' personal writing should
- describe a prank.
- explain why the prank had negative consequences.

EXTENDING YOUR RESPONSE

Literature Groups Suggest that groups make a graphic aid displaying their analyses. **COLLAB. LEARN.**

Learning for Life Ask students to make a list of interview questions before conducting their interviews.

Internet Connection Encourage students to print out interesting articles to share with their classmates.

Skill Minilesson

VOCABULARY • Analogies

1. d   2. b

Additional Resources
Vocabulary Practice, p. 60

Teaching Options

LITERATURE AND WRITING

Writing About Literature

Character Sketch What information about the author's childhood can you infer from this autobiographical sketch? Based on what you've learned from the story, write a brief character sketch of the author as a child. Consider what is directly revealed about her and what is implied. Compare your character sketch with those of other students.

Personal Writing

No Laughing Matter Sometimes the jokes we play on others don't have innocent or humorous results. Have you ever played a joke or misled someone in a way that wasn't funny? Do you know someone who has? Briefly write about an instance of a prank's negative consequences. If you wish, share your piece with the class.

EXTENDING YOUR RESPONSE

Literature Groups

Autobiography How does this short piece of writing reveal so much information about the narrator and her world? Working with your group, analyze what makes this an example of good autobiographical writing. List the techniques that Ponce uses to convey information in so few words. Share your analysis with other groups.

Learning for Life

Remembering WWII Interview older relatives and/or friends who remember World War II. Find out how the war affected their lives. Ask them what it was like when the Japanese bombed Pearl Harbor, and when the United States dropped atomic bombs on Japan.

Internet Connection

More About the War Do some on-line research about World War II, particularly what it was like for Americans at home. For example, how did people on the West Coast prepare for a possible Japanese invasion?

Reading Further

You might enjoy these works by Mary Helen Ponce:

Autobiography: "Doña Luisa" from *Hoyt Street: Memories of a Chicana Childhood,* relates Ponce's memories of her "adopted grandmother."

Short Story: "The Permanent," from *Taking Control,* shows how a woman changes her ways after recognizing her own prejudices.

 Save your work for your portfolio.

Skill Minilesson

VOCABULARY • **Analogies**

An analogy is a type of comparison that is based on the relationships between things or ideas. A relationship is reflected in the first pair of words. Figure out what that relationship is and then find another pair of words that reflects the same relationship. Express the relationship in reasonably clear terms.

● For more about analogies, see **Communications Skills Handbook,** p. R77.

PRACTICE Choose the word pair that best completes each analogy.

1. urge : coerce ::
   a. coax : resist
   b. promise : intend
   c. attempt : succeed
   d. nudge : shove
   e. flatter : compliment

2. pilgrimage : journey ::
   a. voyage : tour
   b. sermon : speech
   c. glance : inspection
   d. inning : game
   e. discovery : invention

✔ ASSESSMENT OPTIONS

📁 *Quick Checks,* p. 89

📁 *Selection and Theme Assessment,* pp. 167–168

📁 *Performance Assessment,* p. 87

💾 *Testmaker*

Vo·cab·u·lar·y Skills

Analyzing Words

There are many kinds of clues that can be used to determine the meaning of an unfamiliar word. Some, called "context clues," occur outside the word itself, in the sentence or paragraph the word appears in. There may also be internal clues to a word's meaning—a familiar prefix, base word, root, or suffix. Neither context clues nor internal clues, when they exist, will always be enough to provide the precise meaning of a word, but they can help.

The sentence, "She falsified the news report she gave her aunts" provides no context clues for the meaning of *falsified.* The word itself, however, provides all the clues you need. Most important, the base word *false* is familiar. In addition, the suffix *-fy,* meaning "to make," is familiar from such words as *purify.* Clearly, the girl "made the news report false."

Even if a word does not have a base word that you know, it may contain one or more word parts that are familiar from other words. For example, look at *perturbed* in this sentence, "Her aunts were perturbed by the news." If you think about *disturb* and *turbulence,* you should realize that being *perturbed* has something to do with being upset.

Although analyzing an unfamiliar word is not a substitute for looking it up in a dictionary, there are two reasons to try to do it. First, you may get a good idea of what the word means. Second, when you break a word into pieces and put it back together, you notice its parts, and that can help you remember its meaning.

● For more about using context clues, see **Reading Handbook,** p. R78.

EXERCISE

Analyze the underlined words on the left, using whatever clues they contain that help you. Try to match each one to its meaning on the right.

1. a biped animal
2. an inimitable style
3. the malodorous room
4. his rapid ascendancy
5. a contradictious person
6. a contributory factor
7. a thermal spring
8. the parts' adhesion
9. her demented state
10. his exhibitionism

a. hot
b. rise
c. insane
d. helpful
e. bad-smelling
f. argumentative
g. two-footed
h. tendency to show off
i. cannot be copied
j. ability to stick together

Vo·cab·u·lar·y Skills

Objective

• To determine a word's meaning by analyzing its parts

Teaching Strategies

With students, discuss parts of the following words from the selection that can give clues to the word's meaning: *pilgrimage, implored, proclaimed.*

Exercise

1. g
2. i
3. e
4. b
5. f
6. d
7. a
8. j
9. c
10. h

Additional Resources

📁 *Vocabulary Power: Weekly Lessons and Activities*

MEETING INDIVIDUAL NEEDS — ENGLISH LANGUAGE LEARNERS

Learning Word Parts English language learners need to form a foundation of English base words and prefixes that can help them determine meanings of unfamiliar words.

Activity Ask students to look up each word in the exercise on page 1059 in an English dictionary. Have them make two lists, one for prefixes and one for base words, putting items from the exercise in the lists along with their definitions. Encourage students to consult their lists and to add to them when they read.

Additional Resources

📁 *English Language Learners Sourcebook*

Objective

- To use specific, concrete words in writing

Teaching Strategies

After reading and discussing the top part of the page, have volunteers name a selection they recall from this book. Ask them to turn to it and read two or three lines or sentences, at random, aloud. Discuss concrete versus abstract diction in the passages. Emphasize how often memorable works of literature contain concrete, specific language.

Exercise

Accept all reasonable responses. The first sentence might be rewritten, "The enthusiastic girls in the pep club flocked to the soccer game each Saturday morning."

Additional Resources

Writer's Choice, Lesson 10.1

Writing Skills

Using Effective Language

Whether you want your readers to laugh, cry, or think, the best way to capture and hold their attention is to use effective language. For many writers, using effective language means using words that are definite, specific, and concrete instead of words that are general, vague, and abstract. The following table shows some examples of noneffective and effective language.

Noneffective		Effective	
General:	*period of time*	Specific:	*one week*
Vague:	*monetary reward*	Definite:	*hundred dollar bonus*
Abstract:	*discomfort*	Concrete:	*sharp pain*

Notice how Mary Helen Ponce uses effective language to create a vivid, interesting scene in this excerpt from "How I Changed the War and Won the Game."

> "All were elderly ladies, *señoras de edad,* who could not read English, only their native Spanish. Every afternoon they would gather on Doña Luisa's front porch to await Doña Trinidad's son who delivered the paper to her promptly at five o'clock. There, among the geraniums and pots of yerbabuena I would bring to them the news of the war."

Ponce's words draw readers in by creating a compelling impression of her childhood experience. She discusses specific people—*elderly ladies, Doña Luisa, Doña Trinidad*—rather than a general group, and she describes precisely what languages these ladies can and can't read. She uses definite words, such as *everyday* and *promptly at five o'clock* instead of vague words, such as *regularly.* In addition, Ponce uses concrete details, such as *the geraniums and pots of yerbabuena,* to help make the setting seem real.

Make your own writing more effective by replacing vague and abstract words and phrases with more specific and vivid ones. Keep your writing clear and direct.

EXERCISE

Rewrite the following passage, using your imagination to replace general, vague, and abstract language with more specific, concrete, and definite words.

Some people from the club would go together to the regular home game. They had a strong feeling for their team, and used their particular skills to encourage their team's members to play well. People who wanted the opposing team to do well didn't care for the presence of this enthusiastic group.

Teaching Options

Grammar and Language *Minilesson*

Proper Adjectives Remind students that some adjectives are formed from proper nouns and should be capitalized.

Activity Have students write these sentences using correct capitalization.

1. Some american cities are along the pacific coast. *(American, Pacific)*
2. The students viewed african and asian art at the museum. *(African, Asian)* **L1**

Additional Resources

🔊 *Grammar and Language Transparency 78*

📙 *Grammar and Language Workbook,* p. 239

📗 *Grammar and Composition Handbook,* Lesson 10.3

📘 *Writer's Choice,* Lesson 20.3

Before You Read

A Marriage Proposal

FOCUS ACTIVITY

Think of a time when you or someone you know had carefully prepared for a special event only to have the plans fall apart.

JOURNAL Describe the plans and how and why they were altered.
At the time, did you laugh when the plans fell apart?

SETTING A PURPOSE Read the play *A Marriage Proposal* to see
what happens when one man's plans fall apart.

BACKGROUND

The Time and Place

Chekhov set this one-act
play in the late 1800s in the
Russian provinces, or country. At this time in Russia, the
serfs had been freed, the
Bolshevik revolution was less
than twenty years away, and
yet, aristocratic farmers still
depended on servants to do the work on their large estates.

Did You Know?
While studying medicine at the University of Moscow, Chekhov sold
hundreds of articles to comic magazines to provide income for his family. He was not proud of these writings. Critics, however, see in
Chekhov's early writings the revolutionary techniques that flourished in
his later works. Chekhov focused on his characters' inner thoughts—how
they felt about their lives and their relationships with other characters.

VOCABULARY PREVIEW

pompous (pom′ pəs) *adj.* showing an exaggerated sense of self-
importance; p. 1063

affable (af′ ə bəl) *adj.* friendly, gracious, and pleasant; p. 1063

hypochondriac (hī′ pə kon′ drē ak′) *n.* one whose worry over health
is so great that it brings on the imagined symptoms of an illness;
p. 1063

impudence (im′ pyə dəns) *n.* speech or behavior that is aggressively
forward or rude; p. 1067

oblivious (ə bliv′ ē əs) *adj.* unmindful or unaware; not noticing; p. 1072

Meet
Anton Chekhov

At age sixteen, Anton Chekhov
(chek′ ôf) lived alone and supported himself. His grocer father
had gone bankrupt and rushed the
rest of the family to Moscow to
avoid debtor's prison. Three years
later Chekhov joined his family to
study medicine on scholarship at
the University of Moscow.
Although he received his medical
degree, his writing was more
important to him. Chekhov once
said, "I try to catch every sentence, every word you and I say,
and quickly lock all these sentences and words away in my literary storehouse because they
might come in handy."

*Anton Chekhov was born in 1860 and
died in 1904.* A Marriage Proposal *was
first published between 1888 and 1890.*

Reading the Selection

SUMMARY

Lomov tells Chubukov that he wants to marry Chubukov's daughter Natalia. Chubukov is overjoyed. When Natalia comes in, she and Lomov argue over some land and Lomov leaves, upset. When Natalia finds out he was going to propose, she makes her father go after him. They argue again, over whose dog is better, and Lomov faints. When he comes to, Chubukov pronounces the couple engaged; they continue their argument.

📁 *Spanish Summaries,* p. 85

A **Active Reading**

PREDICT Have students read the title and cast of characters and view the painting. Ask them to predict what kinds of complications might arise among the characters. Encourage them to review and revise their predictions as they read.

Additional Resources

📁 *Active Reading Guide,* p. 90
🎧 *Audio Library*
🎧 *Spanish Audio Library*

Teaching Options

Golden Autumn in the Village, 1889. Isaak Ilyich Levitan. Oil on canvas, 43 x 67.2 cm. State Russian Museum, St. Petersburg.

A Marriage Proposal

Anton Chekhov
Translated by Theodore Hoffman

1062 🐚 UNIT 6

CONNECTING TO OTHER SELECTIONS

The chart at the right shows three ways to connect *A Marriage Proposal* to selections in this book.

For specific teaching strategies, see the *Unit Six Planning Guide,* pages 63–64.

Connection		Title
Life Skills: Planning and Designing	➡	"The Ring," p. 225
Thematic: Love	➡	"A Child, a Dog, the Night," p. 129
Literary: Conflict	➡	*Antigone,* p. 727

B **Active Reading**

QUESTION What details in the cast of characters indicate that the play takes place in a different era and/or culture? *(Students should note, in addition to the Russian names, the men's descriptions as landowners and the description of Natalia as "twenty-five but still unmarried.")*

CHARACTERS

STEPAN STEPANOVITCH CHUBUKOV (ste pän′ ste pä′ nô vich   chōō bōō′ kôf): a landowner; elderly, pompous but affable

IVAN VASSILEVITCH LOMOV (i vän′   vä sil′ ē yich lô′ môf): a landowner and Chubukov's neighbor; healthy, but a hypochondriac; nervous, suspicious

NATALIA STEPANOVNA (nä täl′ yə   ste pä nôv′ nə): Chubukov's daughter; twenty-five but still unmarried

A

B

SCENE: Chubukov's mansion—the living room

[*LOMOV enters, formally dressed in evening jacket, white gloves, top hat. He is nervous from the start.*]

Vocabulary

pompous (pom′ pəs) *adj.* showing an exaggerated sense of self-importance

affable (af′ ə bəl) *adj.* friendly, gracious, and pleasant

hypochondriac (hī′ pə kon′ drē ak′) *n.* one whose worry over his or her health is so great that it brings on the imagined symptoms of an illness

---

ENGLISH LANGUAGE LEARNERS

Idioms The play contains some idioms that you may wish to review with English language learners.

Activity Write the following idiomatic expressions on the board. Have students write what they think each idiom means. Check the meanings with them.
"Stop beating around the bush!" (p. 1065)
"I'm gooseflesh all over . . ." (p. 1065)

"I ask you to speak to me without getting yourself in such a tizzy." (p. 1068)
"Something keeps giving me a stitch in the side. . ." (p. 1070)
"My foot's asleep." (p. 1073)

Additional Resources
📁 *English Language Learners Sourcebook*

D **Literary Elements**

ASIDES Point out that an aside is a literary convention in which a character speaks to the audience so that a second character on stage supposedly cannot hear. Have students explain the purpose and effect of Chubukov's aside. *(It is a humorous characterization of Chubukov suspecting Lomov's motives.)*

VIEWING THE PAINTING

Illarion Mikhailovich Pryanishnikov (1840–1894) was known for his narrative pictures illustrating the problems of the lower classes.

Viewing Response *The painting suggests that life was difficult and that people worked hard. The painting may help readers understand what life was like and why a sense of humor may have been important.*

A Marriage Proposal

CHUBUKOV. [*Rising.*] Well, look who's here! Ivan Vassilevitch! [*Shakes his hand warmly.*] What a surprise, old man! How are you?

LOMOV. Oh, not too bad. And you?

CHUBUKOV. Oh, we manage, we manage. Do sit down, please. You know, you've been neglecting your neighbors, my dear fellow. It's been ages. Say, why the formal dress? Tails, gloves, and so forth. Where's the funeral, my boy? Where are you headed?

LOMOV. Oh, nowhere. I mean, here; just to see you, my dear Stepan Stepanovitch.

CHUBUKOV. Then why the full dress, old boy? It's not New Year's, and so forth.

LOMOV. Well, you see, it's like this. I have come here, my dear Stepan Stepanovitch, to bother you with a request. More than once, or twice, or more than that, it has been my privilege to apply to you for assistance in things, and you've always, well, responded. I mean, well, you have. Yes. Excuse me, I'm getting all mixed up. May I have a glass of water, my dear Stepan Stepanovitch? [*Drinks.*]

CHUBUKOV. [*Aside.*] Wants to borrow some money. Not a chance! [*Aloud.*] What can I do for you my dear friend?

LOMOV. Well, you see, my dear Stepanitch. . . . Excuse me, I mean Stepan my

Return from the Fair, 1883. Illarion Mikhailovich Pryanishnikov. Oil on canvas, 48.5 x 71.5 cm. State Russian Museum, St. Petersburg.

Viewing the painting: What does this painting suggest to you about rural life in Russia in the 1800s? How does this view affect your understanding of the play?

1064 UNIT 6

Teaching Options

MEETING INDIVIDUAL NEEDS — MULTIPLE LEARNING STYLES

Linguistic Point out that Chekhov's stage directions on page 1063 give no details about the living room in Chubukov's mansion where the play takes place. Encourage linguistic learners to write stage directions for the setting.

Activity Have students write more detailed stage directions for the play that specify how a stage set would be decorated. Encourage them to consider the mood and the economic class that should be represented. Then have them specify how the walls, floors, and furniture should look to reflect these characteristics. Students may wish to use stage directions from another play as a model. **L2**

Dearovitch. . . . No, I mean, I get all confused, as you can see. To make a long story short, you're the only one who can help me. Of course, I don't deserve it, and there's no reason why I should expect you to, and all that.

CHUBUKOV. Stop beating around the bush! Out with it!

LOMOV. In just a minute. I mean, now, right now. The truth is, I have come to ask the hand. . . . I mean, your daughter, Natalia Stepanovna, I, I want to marry her!

CHUBUKOV. [*Overjoyed.*] Great heavens! Ivan Vassilevitch! Say it again!

LOMOV. I have come humbly to ask for the hand. . . .

CHUBUKOV. [*Interrupting.*] You're a prince! I'm overwhelmed, delighted, and so forth. Yes, indeed, and all that! [*Hugs and kisses LOMOV.*] This is just what I've been hoping for. It's my fondest dream come true. [*Sheds a tear.*] And, you know, I've always looked upon you, my boy, as if you were my own son. May God grant to both of you His Mercy and His Love, and so forth. Oh, I have been wishing for this. . . . But why am I being so idiotic? It's just that I'm off my rocker with joy, my boy! Completely off my rocker! Oh, with all my soul I'm. . . . I'll go get Natalia, and so forth.

LOMOV. [*Deeply moved.*] Dear Stepan Stepanovitch, do you think she'll agree?

CHUBUKOV. Why, of course, old friend. Great heavens! As if she wouldn't! Why she's crazy for you! Good God! Like a love-sick cat, and so forth. Be right back. [*Leaves.*]

LUMOV. It's cold. I'm gooseflesh all over, as if I had to take a test. But the main thing is, to make up my mind, and keep it that way. I mean, if I take time out to think, or if I hesitate, or talk about it, or have ideals, or wait for real love, well, I'll just never get married! Brrrr, it's cold! Natalia Stepanovna is an

excellent housekeeper. She's not too bad looking. She's had a good education. What more could I ask? Nothing. I'm so nervous, my ears are buzzing. [*Drinks.*] Besides, I've just got to get married. I'm thirty-five already. It's sort of a critical age. I've got to settle down and lead a regular life. I mean, I'm always getting palpitations,[1] and I'm nervous, and I get upset so easy. Look, my lips are quivering, and my eyebrow's twitching. The worst thing is the night. Sleeping. I get into bed, doze off, and, suddenly, something inside me jumps. First my head snaps, and then my shoulder blade, and I roll out of bed like a lunatic and try to walk it off. Then I try to go back to sleep, but, as soon as I do, something jumps again! Twenty times a night, sometimes. . . .

[*NATALIA STEPANOVNA enters.*]

NATALIA. Oh, it's only you. All Papa said was: "Go inside, there's a merchant come to collect his goods." How do you do, Ivan Vassilevitch?

LOMOV. How do you do, dear Natalia Stepanovna?

NATALIA. Excuse my apron, and not being dressed. We're shelling peas. You haven't been around lately. Oh, do sit down. [*They do.*] Would you like some lunch?

LOMOV. No thanks, I had some.

NATALIA. Well, then smoke if you want. [*He doesn't.*] The weather's nice today . . . but yesterday, it was so wet the workmen couldn't get a thing done. Have you got much hay in? I felt so greedy I had a whole field done, but now I'm not sure I was right. With the rain it could rot, couldn't it? I should have waited. But why are you so dressed up? Is there a

---

1. If Lomov does, in fact, get *palpitations,* he experiences rapid, irregular heartbeats, which are often caused by stress or nervousness.

E Author's Craft

CHARACTERIZATION Have students identify Chubukov's unusual verbal habit. How does it help characterize Chubukov? *(He often adds the phrase "and so forth" to his sentences, making him sound rather eccentric and absent-minded.)*

F Literary Elements

FARCE Have students describe Chubukov's reaction to Lomov's statement that he wants to propose to Natalia. Why could it be described as farcical? *(Chubukov has an exaggerated response to Lomov's statement, pretending that he has often wished Lomov would become his son-in-law. He is obviously delighted that anyone wants to marry his daughter.)*

G Active Reading

QUESTION Why is Lomov proposing to Natalia? *(He feels it is time to get married and that if he waits for true love, he will never marry. Natalia has some qualities that he is looking for in a wife.)*

MEETING INDIVIDUAL NEEDS

MULTIPLE LEARNING STYLES

Bodily-Kinesthetic Lomov's long speech on page 1065 reveals his farcical hypochondria. Students who enjoy acting can use the descriptive details to bring out the farce in the speech.

Activity Have students practice acting out Lomov's speech in small groups. Encourage them to discuss ways to show Lomov's exaggerated hypochondria with voice and gestures. Have volunteers perform the speech for the class. **L2 COLLAB. LEARN.**

dance or something? Of course, I must say you look splendid, but. . . . Well, tell me, why are you so dressed up?

LOMOV. [*Excited.*] Well, you see, my dear Natalia Stepanovna, the truth is, I made up my mind to ask you to . . . well, to, listen to me. Of course, it'll probably surprise you and even maybe make you angry, but. . . . [*Aside.*] It's so cold in here!

NATALIA. Why, what do you mean? [*A pause.*] Well?

LOMOV. I'll try to get it over with. I mean, you know, my dear Natalia Stepanovna that I've known, since childhood, even, known, and had the privilege of knowing, your family. My late aunt, and her husband, who, as you know, left me my estate, they always had the greatest respect for your father, and your late mother. The Lomovs and the Chubukovs have always been very friendly, you might even say affectionate. And, of course, you know, our land borders on each other's. My Oxen Meadows touch your birch grove. . . .

NATALIA. I hate to interrupt you, my dear Ivan Vassilevitch, but you said: "my Oxen Meadows." Do you really think they're yours?

LOMOV. Why of course they're mine.

NATALIA. What do you mean? The Oxen Meadows are ours, not yours!

LOMOV. Oh, no, my dear Natalia Stepanovna, they're mine.

NATALIA. Well, this is the first I've heard about it! Where did you get that idea?

LOMOV. Where? Why, I mean the Oxen Meadows that are wedged between your birches and the marsh.

NATALIA. Yes, of course, they're ours.

LOMOV. Oh, no, you're wrong, my dear Natalia Stepanovna, they're mine.

NATALIA. Now, come, Ivan Vassilevitch! How long have they been yours?

LOMOV. How long! Why, as long as I can remember!

NATALIA. Well, really, you can't expect me to believe that!

LOMOV. But, you can see for yourself in the deed, my dear Natalia Stepanovna. Of course, there was once a dispute about them, but everyone knows they're mine now. There's nothing to argue about. There was a time when my aunt's grandmother let your father's grandfather's peasants use the land, but they were supposed to bake bricks for her in return. Naturally, after a few years they began to act as if they owned it, but the real truth is. . . .

NATALIA. That has nothing to do with the case! Both my grandfather and my great-grandfather said that their land went as far as the marsh, which means that the Meadows are ours! There's nothing whatever to argue about. It's foolish.

LOMOV. But I can show you the deed, Natalia Stepanovna.

NATALIA. You're just making fun of me. . . . Great Heavens! Here we have the land for hundreds of years, and suddenly you try to tell us it isn't ours. What's wrong with you, Ivan Vassilevitch? Those meadows aren't even fifteen acres, and they're not worth three hundred rubles, but I just can't stand unfairness! I just can't stand unfairness!

LOMOV. But, you must listen to me. Your father's grandfather's peasants, as I've already tried to tell you, they were supposed to bake bricks for my aunt's grandmother. And my aunt's grandmother, why, she wanted to be nice to them. . . .

NATALIA. It's just nonsense, this whole business about aunts and grandfathers and grandmothers. The Meadows are ours! That's all there is to it!

INTERDISCIPLINARY CONNECTION

History Alexander II became czar of Russia in 1855. He freed the country's serfs, peasants who were forced to work the land owned by the wealthy. However, many revolutionaries wanted more changes. When the next two czars did not do enough to improve the conditions of Russia's peasants, they grew more discontent and revolted in 1917.

Activity Have students research the history of Russia from the mid-1800s through the formation of the U.S.S.R. in 1922. You may wish to have students work in groups and research one of the following topics: causes of the Revolution, the Revolution itself, and the reformation of the country after the Revolution.
L2 **COLLAB. LEARN.**

LOMOV. They're mine!

NATALIA. Ours! You can go on talking for two days, and you can put on fifteen evening coats and twenty pairs of gloves, but I tell you they're ours, ours, ours!

LOMOV. Natalia Stepanovna, I don't want the Meadows! I'm just acting on principle. If you want, I'll give them to you.

NATALIA. I'll give them to *you!* Because they're ours! And that's all there is to it! And if I may say so, your behavior, my dear Ivan Vassilevitch, is very strange. Until now, we've always considered you a good neighbor, even a friend. After all, last year we lent you our threshing machine, even though it meant putting off our own threshing until November. And here you are treating us like a pack of gypsies. Giving me my own land, indeed! Really! Why that's not being a good neighbor. It's sheer impudence, that's what it is. . . .

LOMOV. Oh, so you think I'm just a land-grabber? My dear lady, I've never grabbed anybody's land in my whole life, and no one's going to accuse me of doing it now! [*Quickly walks over to the pitcher and drinks some more water.*] The Oxen Meadows are mine!

NATALIA. That's a lie. They're ours!

LOMOV. Mine!

NATALIA. A lie! I'll prove it. I'll send my mowers out there today!

LOMOV. What?

NATALIA. My mowers will mow it today!

LOMOV. I'll kick them out!

NATALIA. You just dare!

LOMOV. [*Clutching his heart.*] The Oxen Meadows are mine! Do you understand? Mine!

NATALIA. Please don't shout! You can shout all you want in your own house, but here I must ask you to control yourself.

LOMOV. If my heart wasn't palpitating the way it is, if my insides weren't jumping like mad, I wouldn't talk to you so calmly. [*Yelling.*] The Oxen Meadows are mine!

NATALIA. Ours!

LOMOV. Mine!

NATALIA. Ours!

LOMOV. Mine!

[*Enter CHUBUKOV.*]

CHUBUKOV. What's going on? Why all the shouting?

NATALIA. Papa, will you please inform this gentleman who owns the Oxen Meadows, he or we?

CHUBUKOV. [*To LOMOV.*] Why, they're ours, old fellow.

LOMOV. But how can they be yours, my dear Stepan Stepanovitch? Be fair. Perhaps my aunt's grandmother did let your grandfather's peasants work the land, and maybe they did get so used to it that they acted as if it was their own, but. . . .

CHUBUKOV. Oh, no, no . . . my dear boy. You forget something. The reason the peasants didn't pay your aunt's grandmother, and so forth, was that the land was disputed, even then. Since then it's been settled. Why, everyone knows it's ours.

LOMOV. I can prove it's mine.

CHUBUKOV. You can't prove a thing, old boy.

LOMOV. Yes, I can!

CHUBUKOV. My dear lad, why yell like that? Yelling doesn't prove a thing. Look, I'm not

---

Vocabulary

impudence (im′ pyə dəns) *n.* speech or behavior that is aggressively forward or rude

---

Great Russian Writers Nineteenth-century Russia produced several literary giants in addition to Chekhov. Fyodor Dostoevsky, Ivan Turgenev, and Leo Tolstoy wrote fiction that depicted life in Russia while also dealing with some of life's greatest philosophical issues. For example, in *Crime and Punishment*, Dostoevsky dealt with the psychology of guilt; in *Anna Karenina*, Tolstoy questioned the roles of love and marriage in a person's life.

Activity Have students research one of the Russian authors mentioned and read a short story by him. They can present their findings about the author's style, characters, and themes in an oral or written report. **L3**

J **Literary Elements**

DIALOGUE Judging by Natalia's dialogue, how does she feel about Lomov? *(She does not have any special feelings for him. She sees him as simply a neighbor.)*

K **Literary Elements**

FARCE How does Chekhov make Lomov's behavior farcical? *(His stage directions emphasize Lomov's exaggeration of his symptoms, as in "clutching his heart." He constantly describes his physical state. He says he is talking calmly and then begins yelling.)*

A Marriage Proposal

after anything of yours, just as I don't intend to give up anything of mine. Why should I? Besides, if you're going to keep arguing about it, I'd just as soon give the land to the peasants, so there!

LOMOV. There nothing! Where do you get the right to give away someone else's property?

CHUBUKOV. I certainly ought to know if I have the right or not. And you had better realize it, because, my dear young man, I am not used to being spoken to in that tone of voice, and so forth. Besides which, my dear young man, I am twice as old as you are, and I ask you to speak to me without getting yourself into such a tizzy, and so forth!

LOMOV. Do you think I'm a fool? First you call my property yours, and then you expect me to keep calm and polite! Good neighbors don't act like that, my dear Stepan Stepanovitch. You're no neighbor, you're a land grabber!

CHUBUKOV. What was that? What did you say?

NATALIA. Papa, send the mowers out to the meadows at once!

CHUBUKOV. What did you say, sir?

NATALIA. The Oxen Meadows are ours, and we'll never give them up, never, never, never!

LOMOV. We'll see about that. I'll go to court. I'll show you!

CHUBUKOV. Go to court? Well, go to court, and so forth! I know you, just waiting for a chance to go to court, and so forth. You pettifogging[2] cheater, you! All of your family is like that. The whole bunch of them!

LOMOV. You leave my family out of this! The Lomovs have always been honorable,

upstanding people, and not a one of them was ever tried for embezzlement,[3] like your grandfather was.

CHUBUKOV. The Lomovs are a pack of lunatics, the whole bunch of them!

NATALIA. The whole bunch!

CHUBUKOV. Your grandfather was a drunkard, and what about your other aunt, the one who ran away with the architect? And so forth.

NATALIA. And so forth!

LOMOV. Your mother limped! [*Clutches at his heart.*] Oh, I've got a stitch in my side. . . . My head's whirling. . . . Help! Water!

CHUBUKOV. Your father was a gambler.

NATALIA. And your aunt was queen of the scandalmongers![4]

LOMOV. My left foot's paralyzed. You're a plotter. . . . Oh, my heart. It's an open secret that in the last elections you brib. . . . I'm seeing stars! Where's my hat?

NATALIA. It's a low-mean, spiteful. . . .

CHUBUKOV. And you're a two-faced, malicious schemer!

LOMOV. Here's my hat. . . . Oh, my heart. . . . Where's the door? How do I get out of here? . . . Oh, I think I'm going to die. . . . My foot's numb. [*Goes.*]

CHUBUKOV. [*Following him.*] And don't you ever set foot in my house again!

NATALIA. Go to court, indeed! We'll see about that!

[*LOMOV staggers out.*]

CHUBUKOV. The devil with him! [*Gets a drink, walks back and forth excited.*]

NATALIA. What a rascal! How can you trust your neighbors after an incident like that?

---

2. A *pettifogging* person squabbles over unimportant matters or uses mean, tricky methods. Originally, the word described inferior lawyers who did these things.

3. *Embezzlement* is the act of stealing money entrusted to one's care; a bank official, for example, might embezzle funds from customers' accounts.
4. People who spread vicious gossip are *scandalmongers*.

Self-portrait in an Interior, Sokolniki, 1916–1917. Nina Simonovich-Efimova. Oil on canvas, 26 x 19⅝ in. Efimov Museum, Moscow.

Viewing the painting: How does this setting compare with your vision of the play's setting so far? Explain.

FYI

Chekhov's Depiction of Russia Although *A Marriage Proposal* is a light comedy, its depiction of Russia's aristocracy is consistent with a theme seen throughout Chekhov's work. Chekhov sensed that the old Russia was dying. He often shows aristocrats as ineffectual and frustrated, as in the petty characters of *A Marriage Proposal*. The play's concern with the loss of land is repeated in *The Cherry Orchard*, a play written in 1903 and sometimes considered Chekhov's greatest work.

VIEWING THE PAINTING

The perspective the artist uses draws the viewer into the picture and back into the far reaches of the interior of the scene.

Viewing Response *Students should offer comparisons between the painting and what they have pictured as the setting based on the author's description.*

MEETING INDIVIDUAL NEEDS — MULTIPLE LEARNING STYLES

Interpersonal Point out that almost everyone has an occasional argument with a family member or friend. An argument can even be productive if the participants control their anger and try to make their points reasonably—the key to conflict resolution. Interpersonal learners are good at mediating conflicts.

Activity Have students write a paragraph describing an argument they have had recently with a friend or family member. Then have them exchange papers with a partner and discuss their arguments. Encourage students to offer constructive advice to their partners about how they might have avoided the argument or made their points without anger or insults. **L2** **COLLAB. LEARN.**

A Marriage Proposal

CHUBUKOV. The villain! The scarecrow!

NATALIA. He's a monster! First he tries to steal our land, and then he has the nerve to yell at you.

CHUBUKOV. Yes, and that turnip, that stupid rooster, has the gall[5] to make a proposal. Some proposal!

NATALIA. What proposal?

CHUBUKOV. Why, he came to propose to you.

NATALIA. To propose? To me? Why didn't you tell me before?

CHUBUKOV. So he gets all dressed up in his formal clothes. That stuffed sausage, that dried up cabbage!

NATALIA. To propose to me? Ohhhh! [*Falls into a chair and starts wailing.*] Bring him back! Back! Go get him! Bring him back! Ohhhh!

CHUBUKOV. Bring who back?

NATALIA. Hurry up, hurry up! I'm sick. Get him! [*Complete hysterics.*]

CHUBUKOV. What for? [*To her.*] What's the matter with you? [*Clutches his head.*] Oh, what a fool I am! I'll shoot myself! I'll hang myself! I ruined her chances!

NATALIA. I'm dying. Get him!

CHUBUKOV. All right, all right, right away! Only don't yell!

[*He runs out.*]

NATALIA. What are they doing to me? Get him! Bring him back! Bring him back!

[*A pause. CHUBUKOV runs in.*]

CHUBUKOV. He's coming, and so forth, the snake. Oof! You talk to him. I'm not in the mood.

NATALIA. [*Wailing.*] Bring him back! Bring him back!

CHUBUKOV. [*Yelling.*] I told you, he's coming! What agony to be the father of a grown-up daughter. I'll cut my throat some day, I swear I will. [*To her.*] We cursed him, we insulted him, abused him, kicked him out, and now . . . because you, you. . . .

NATALIA. Me? It was all your fault!

CHUBUKOV. My fault? What do you mean my fau . . . ? [*LOMOV appears in the doorway.*] Talk to him yourself! [*Goes out. LOMOV enters, exhausted.*]

LOMOV. What palpitations! My heart! And my foot's absolutely asleep. Something keeps giving me a stitch in the side. . . .

NATALIA. You must forgive us, Ivan Vassilevitch. We all got too excited. I remember now. The Oxen Meadows are yours.

LOMOV. My heart's beating something awful. My Meadows. My eyebrows, they're both twitching!

NATALIA. Yes, the Meadows are all yours, yes, yours. Do sit down. [*They sit.*] We were wrong, of course.

LOMOV. I argued on principle. My land isn't worth so much to me, but the principle. . . .

NATALIA. Oh, yes, of course, the principle, that's what counts. But let's change the subject.

LOMOV. Besides, I have evidence. You see, my aunt's grandmother let your father's grandfather's peasants use the land. . . .

NATALIA. Yes, yes, yes, but forget all that. [*Aside.*] I wish I knew how to get him going. [*Aloud.*] Are you going to start hunting soon?

LOMOV. After the harvest I'll try for grouse.[6] But oh, my dear Natalia Stepanovna, have you heard about the bad luck I've had? You know my dog, Guess? He's gone lame.

---

5. *Gall,* a synonym for *impudence,* means "shocking boldness; scornful disrespect."

---

6. A fowl-like bird, the *grouse* is often hunted for game or food.

Listening and Speaking *Minilesson*

Communicating Tone in Dialogue
Discuss the language and the stage directions of the dialogue in the first column of page 1070. Point out that in a different context, the dialogue might express true grief and remorse on the part of Natalia and her father.

Activity Have pairs of students practice the dialogue on this page. Ask them to practice one reading using a comic tone and another using a tragic tone. Let one or more pairs perform both readings for the class. Encourage the class to discuss vocal techniques that indicate different tones in the two readings.
L2 **COLLAB. LEARN.**

NATALIA. What a pity. Why?

LOMOV. I don't know. He must have twisted his leg, or got in a fight, or something. [*Sighs.*] My best dog, to say nothing of the cost. I paid Mironov 125 rubles for him.

NATALIA. That was too high, Ivan Vassilevitch.

LOMOV. I think it was quite cheap. He's a first class dog.

NATALIA. Why Papa only paid 85 rubles for Squeezer, and he's much better than Guess.

LOMOV. Squeezer better than Guess! What an idea! [*Laughs.*] Squeezer better than Guess!

NATALIA. Of course he's better. He may still be too young but on points[7] and pedigree,[8] he's a better dog even than any Volchanetsky owns.

LOMOV. Excuse me, Natalia Stepanovna, but you're forgetting he's overshot, and overshot dogs are bad hunters.

NATALIA. Oh, so he's overshot, is he? Well, this is the first time I've heard about it.

LOMOV. Believe me, his lower jaw is shorter than his upper.

NATALIA. You've measured them?

LOMOV. Yes. He's all right for pointing, but if you want him to retrieve. . . .

NATALIA. In the first place, our Squeezer is a thoroughbred, the son of Harness and Chisel, while your mutt doesn't even have a pedigree. He's as old and worn out as a peddler's horse.

LOMOV. He may be old, but I wouldn't take five Squeezers for him. How can you argue?

---

7. Natalia is referring to her dog's physical characteristics and ancestry. In dog shows today, a dog is judged on specific characteristics, or *points.* Each breed has point standards that cover everything from skull shape and tail length to eye color and hair texture.

8. A dog's ancestry, or *pedigree,* is proof that a dog is a purebred.

Guess is a dog, Squeezer's a laugh. Anyone you can name has a dog like Squeezer hanging around somewhere. They're under every bush. If he only cost twenty-five rubles you got cheated.

NATALIA. The devil is in you today, Ivan Vassilevitch! You want to contradict everything. First you pretend the Oxen Meadows are yours, and now you say Guess is better than Squeezer. People should say what they really mean, and you know Squeezer is a hundred times better than Guess. Why say he isn't?

LOMOV. So, you think I'm a fool or a blind man, Natalia Stepanovna! Once and for all, Squeezer is overshot!

NATALIA. He is not!

LOMOV. He is so!

NATALIA. He is not!

LOMOV. Why shout, my dear lady?

NATALIA. Why talk such nonsense? It's terrible. Your Guess is old enough to be buried, and you compare him with Squeezer!

LOMOV. I'm sorry, I can't go on. My heart . . . it's palpitating!

NATALIA. I've always noticed that the hunters who argue most don't know a thing.

LOMOV. Please! Be quiet a moment. My heart's falling apart. . . . [*Shouts.*] Shut up!

NATALIA. I'm not going to shut up until you admit that Squeezer's a hundred times better than Guess.

LOMOV. A hundred times worse! His head. . . . My eyes . . . shoulder . . .

NATALIA. Guess is half-dead already!

LOMOV. [*Weeping.*] Shut up! My heart's exploding!

NATALIA. I won't shut up!

[*CHUBUKOV comes in.*]

P **Literary Elements**

FARCE Have students discuss how the argument over the dogs increases the farcical element of the play. (*The argument over the dogs' physical traits is even pettier than the previous one over land, exaggerating the unattractive traits of Natalia and Lomov.*)

Q **Critical Thinking**

INFERRING Use this model to assist students in making an inference about Chekhov's attitude toward Russian aristocrats.

Model: The characters in Chekhov's play are wealthy landowners. They are petty and selfish, spending time on foolish arguments about their dogs and ownership of a few acres of land. I think Chekhov is indicating that the aristocrats are out of touch with reality, and if they don't change, disaster will result.

Reading *Minilesson*

Summarizing Point out to students that much of the dialogue of the play is devoted to two arguments, one about land and the other about dogs. A good summary of the play would focus on these two arguments.

Activity Point out that each argument in the play can be summarized in one sentence. Have students write a summary of each argument. Then discuss with them why Chekhov chose to write several pages of dialogue detailing the arguments. **L1**

Additional Resources
📁 *Reading Workbook,* pp. 91–92

A Marriage Proposal

CHUBUKOV. What's the trouble now?

NATALIA. Papa, will you please tell us which is the better dog, his Guess or our Squeezer?

LOMOV. Stepan Stepanovitch, I implore you to tell me just one thing: Is your Squeezer overshot or not? Yes or no?

CHUBUKOV. Well what if he is? He's still the best dog in the neighborhood, and so forth.

LOMOV. Oh, but isn't my dog, Guess, better? Really?

CHUBUKOV. Don't get yourself so fraught up,[9] old man. Of course, your dog has his good points—thoroughbred, firm on his feet, well sprung ribs, and so forth. But, my dear fellow, you've got to admit he has two defects; he's old and he's short in the muzzle.

LOMOV. Short in the muzzle? Oh, my heart! Let's look at the facts! On the Marusinsky hunt my dog ran neck and neck with the Count's, while Squeezer was a mile behind them. . . .

CHUBUKOV. That's because the Count's groom hit him with a whip.

LOMOV. And he was right, too! We were fox hunting; what was your dog chasing sheep for?

CHUBUKOV. That's a lie! Look, I'm going to lose my temper . . . [*Controlling himself.*] my dear friend, so let's stop arguing, for that reason alone. You're only arguing because we're all jealous of somebody else's dog. Who can help it? As soon as you realize some dog is better than yours, in this case our dog, you start in with this and that, and the next thing you know—pure jealousy! I remember the whole business.

LOMOV. I remember too!

---

9. The expression *fraught up* means "excited; charged up."

CHUBUKOV. [*Mimicking.*] "I remember too!" What do you remember?

LOMOV. My heart . . . my foot's asleep . . . I can't . . .

NATALIA. [*Mimicking.*] "My heart . . . my foot's asleep." What kind of a hunter are you? You should be hunting cockroaches in the kitchen, not foxes. "My heart!"

CHUBUKOV. Yes, what kind of a hunter are you anyway? You should be sitting at home with your palpitations, not tracking down animals. You don't hunt anyhow. You just go out to argue with people and interfere with their dogs, and so forth. For God's sake, let's change the subject before I lose my temper. Anyway, you're just not a hunter.

LOMOV. But you, you're a hunter? Ha! You only go hunting to get in good with the count, and to plot, and intrigue, and scheme. . . . Oh, my heart! You're a schemer, that's what!

CHUBUKOV. What's that? Me a schemer? [*Shouting.*] Shut up!

LOMOV. A schemer!

CHUBUKOV. You infant! You puppy!

LOMOV. You old rat!

CHUBUKOV. You shut up, or I'll shoot you down like a partridge! You fool!

LOMOV. Everyone knows that—oh, my heart—that your wife used to beat you. . . . Oh, my feet . . . my head . . . I'm seeing stars . . . I'm going to faint! [*He drops into an armchair.*] Quick, a doctor! [*Faints.*]

CHUBUKOV. [*Going on, oblivious.*] Baby! Weakling! Fool! I'm getting sick. [*Drinks water.*] Me! I'm sick!

NATALIA. What kind of a hunter are you? You can't even sit on a horse! [*To her father.*] Papa,

---

Vocabulary
oblivious (ə blivʹ ē əs) *adj.* unmindful or unaware; not noticing

Teaching Options

Grammar and Language *Minilesson*

Exclamation Points Remind students that an exclamation point is used to punctuate exclamatory sentences, sentences that express strong feeling or excitement. Point out that Chekhov uses many exclamation points in the course of his play since the characters are expressing anger.

Activity Have students copy three exclamatory sentences from the play. Ask them to read their sentences with appropriate expression. Then have them write three exclamatory sentences of their own.
L1

Additional Resources

📖 *Grammar and Language Transparency 79*

📕 *Grammar and Language Workbook,* p. 245

📕 *Grammar and Composition Handbook,* Lesson 11.2

📙 *Writer's Choice,* Lesson 21.2

what's the matter with him? Look, papa! [*Screaming.*] Ivan Vassilevitch! He's dead.

CHUBUKOV. I'm choking, I can't breathe. . . . Give me air.

NATALIA. He's dead! [*Pulling LOMOV's sleeve.*] Ivan Vassilevitch! Ivan Vassilevitch! What have you done to me? He's dead! [*She falls into an armchair. Screaming hysterically.*] A doctor! A doctor! A doctor!

CHUBUKOV. Ohhhh. . . . What's the matter? What happened?

NATALIA. [*Wailing.*] He's dead! He's dead!

CHUBUKOV. Who's dead? [*Looks at LOMOV.*] My God, he is! Quick! Water! A doctor! [*Puts glass to LOMOV's lips.*] Here, drink this! Can't drink it—he must be dead, and so forth. . . . Oh what a miserable life! Why don't I shoot myself! I should have cut my throat long ago! What am I waiting for? Give me a knife! Give me a pistol! [*LOMOV stirs.*] Look, he's coming to. Here, drink some water. That's it.

LOMOV. I'm seeing stars . . . misty . . . Where am I?

CHUBUKOV. Just you hurry up and get married, and then the devil with you! She accepts. [*Puts LOMOV's hand in NATALIA's.*] She accepts and so forth! I give you my blessing, and so forth! Only leave me in peace!

LOMOV. [*Getting up.*] Huh? What? Who?

CHUBUKOV. She accepts! Well? Kiss her!

NATALIA. He's alive! Yes, yes, I accept.

CHUBUKOV. Kiss each other!

LOMOV. Huh? Kiss? Kiss who? [*They kiss.*] That's nice. I mean, excuse me, what happened? Oh, now I get it . . . my heart . . . those stars . . . I'm very happy, Natalia Stepanovna. [*Kisses her hand.*] My foot's asleep.

NATALIA. I . . . I'm happy too.

CHUBUKOV. What a load off my shoulders! Whew!

NATALIA. Well, now maybe you'll admit that Squeezer is better than Guess?

LOMOV. Worse!

NATALIA. Better!

CHUBUKOV. What a way to enter matrimonial bliss! Let's have some champagne!

LOMOV. He's worse!

NATALIA. Better! Better, better, better, better!

CHUBUKOV. [*Trying to shout her down.*] Champagne! Bring some champagne! Champagne! Champagne!

CURTAIN

HUMOR 🦢 1073

S **Literary Elements**

PLOT: *Climax* Remind students that the climax of a plot occurs at the point when the conflict is resolved. Have them summarize what occurs at the climax and in the denouement of the play. (*At the climax, Lomov awakes from his faint and Chubukov declares him and Natalia engaged. In the denouement, Lomov and Natalia continue their argument while Chubukov tries to distract them with celebratory champagne.*)

T **Literary Elements**

SATIRE In addition to creating humor through farcical situations and characters, Chekhov's play satirizes certain social customs. Have students discuss these customs and Chekhov's attitude toward them. (*Chekhov makes fun of the romantic view of love and marriage. He seems to say that a romantic marriage based on love is an unrealistic expectation.*)

Thematic Focus

Comic Perspectives Have students discuss how Chekhov's characterizations contribute to the play's humor.

☑ **ASSESSMENT OPTIONS**

📁 *Quick Checks,* p. 90

Writing *Minilesson*

Expressing Excitement Call students' attention to the dialogue on page 1073. Have students name the techniques that are used to express the excited, incoherent state of the characters, such as very short sentences or fragments with exclamation points and ellipses to show disconnected thoughts. Dashes may also be used to indicate incoherence in dialogue.

Activity Have students write a brief monologue or dialogue using the techniques used by Chekhov to indicate the characters' emotions. Have students take turns reading aloud their monologues or dialogues. **L2**

Additional Resources

📙 *Writer's Choice,* Lesson 4.4

Responding to the Selection

Personal Response

Students may say they liked the end of the play because it was funny or they disliked it because Lomov and Natalia seem unlikely to be happy.

ANALYZING LITERATURE

1 He has come to propose to Chubukov's daughter, Natalia.

2. Lomov and the Chubukovs argue over who owns several acres of land.

3. They argue over whether Lomov's dog or Chubukov's dog is better.

4. The first argument ends when Lomov walks out, and the second ends when Lomov faints.

5. Chubukov declares Natalia and Lomov engaged; the couple continues arguing.

6. He is taking a big step in proposing to a woman. He has a high-strung, nervous personality.

7. Natalia has no idea Lomov has come to propose; she sees him merely as a neighbor.

8. Natalia is stubborn and narrow-minded. Chubukov is volatile and prone to insulting people. Lomov is proud and sensitive.

9. It seems to say that a romantic marriage based on love is difficult to attain because people are proud, stubborn, and self-centered.

10. The characters' future lives will probably be filled with endless petty bickering.

11. Students may note that humor is more easily seen as time passes.

12. Students may say the bickering is similar to that of friends or siblings but different in that it has an exaggerated, farcical quality.

13. Students' attitudes about marriage as well as the two characters may color their answer.

14. Some dialogue—"He is not!" "He is so!" "He is not!"—is realistic. Some dialogue—"What palpitations! My heart!"—is unrealistic.

15. Because of mass media, most people are aware of societal problems, but they may still ignore them.

Responding to Literature

Personal Response

How did you like the ending of the play? Discuss your reaction with a classmate.

——— ANALYZING LITERATURE ———

RECALL

1. Why has Lomov come to Chubukov's house?
2. What is the cause of the first argument?
3. What is the second argument about?
4. How do the first and second arguments end?
5. Summarize the ending of the play.

INTERPRET

6. Why, do you think, is Lomov so nervous? What does his behavior tell you about his personality?
7. Why, in your opinion, does the first argument start so easily?
8. What do the arguments reveal about the participants? Explain, using details from the play to support your ideas.
9. What attitudes toward marriage does the play reveal?
10. What, do you think, does the ending suggest about the characters' future lives?

EVALUATE AND CONNECT

11. **Theme Connections** In your opinion, which is the worse-case scenario: Lomov's planned marriage proposal that fell apart or the special event you described in the Focus Activity on page 1061? Why? Do you see humor in the altered plans of either event? Explain.
12. Compare and contrast the bickering between characters in the play with similar interactions you have witnessed between people. How is it the same? How is it different?
13. In your opinion, are Lomov and Natalia a good match for each other? Do you think they should marry? Why or why not?
14. Does the **dialogue**, or speech, in Chekhov's play seem realistic to you? Why or why not? Find specific examples from the play to support your response. (See Literary Terms Handbook, page R3.)
15. Chekhov's aristocratic characters seem to be in their own little world; they have no interaction with people outside the Russian provinces. Do you think people today are more aware of problems in society outside their community? Explain.

Literary ELEMENTS

Farce

A type of comedy in which characters are put into ridiculous situations is called **farce**. In farce an author uses physical action, exaggeration, improbable events, and surprises to make the audience laugh. Farce is one way to make fun of human traits and social customs. In *A Marriage Proposal,* for example, Chekhov has Lomov continually complain about physical ailments in order to poke fun at people with imaginary illnesses.

1. List three examples of statements made by the characters that made you laugh. Tell what you think Chekhov is making fun of in each example.
2. Identify three points in this play that you found particularly funny. Why are they humorous? What techniques of farce does Chekhov use to create each situation?

● See **Literary Terms Handbook**, p. R5.

LITERARY ELEMENTS

1. One possible example is Lomov saying, "Your mother limped!" It pokes fun at people's urge to insult others when angry.
2. One point might be when Chubukov thinks Lomov has come to borrow money, which is funny because it shows a realistic side of human nature.

Additional Resources

 Literary Elements Transparency 90

LITERATURE AND WRITING

Writing About Literature
Analyzing Dialogue   Chekhov masterfully develops his characters' personalities through **dialogue**. Analyze the dialogue for each of the characters in the play. In a paragraph for each character, explain how Chekhov portrays the character through his or her speech. Support your ideas with dialogue from the play.

Creative Writing
Diary Entry   Pretend that you are one of the characters writing an entry in your diary later that day. Jot down the character's thoughts about the day's events and his or her expectations for the future. Try to match your writing style to the character's personality and way of speaking.

EXTENDING YOUR RESPONSE

Literature Groups
How Ironic   This play contains situational irony (what appears likely to happen is not what happens) and dramatic irony (what appears true to a character is not what the audience knows to be true). Find one good example of each type of irony in the play. Discuss your examples with your group. Then discuss how different audiences—teenagers, single adults, married couples, socialites, homeowners—may react differently to the ironic situations. Share your findings.

Interdisciplinary Activity
Drama: Design the Set   Using graph paper or computer software, draw a floor plan of the stage as you envision it. On the plan, place the various furnishings, stage props, and exits. Then select a scene and mark the characters' positions and movements across the stage.

Learning for Life
Cooperation Consultant   Pretend that you are in training to become a consultant. Your class has just viewed a videotape of *A Marriage Proposal*. With a partner, make a list of the character traits—positive and negative—that you see in Lomov and Natalia, citing evidence from the play. Then, suggest how each character might compromise or change to bring positive attributes to their marriage.

Reading Further
You might enjoy reading the following short story by Anton Chekhov:

"The Darling," translated by David Magarshack from *Lady with Lapdog and Other Stories,* is a tale about love and marriage and the life of an innocent young woman.

📖 **Save your work for your portfolio.**

Stage floor plan.

Floor lamp · Bookcase · Fireplace tools · Plant · Fireplace · Stairs · Stereo · Table · Door · Chairs · Door · Chest · Sofa · Table · Chair · Edge of stage · Centerline · Proscenium

---

LITERATURE AND WRITING

Writing About Literature
Students' analyses should
- analyze the dialogue of each character in the play.
- support ideas with dialogue from the play.

Creative Writing
Students' diary entries should
- discuss the events of the play.
- show the character's personality and manner of speaking.

EXTENDING YOUR RESPONSE

Literature Groups   Have the class discuss examples of irony from other literary works before beginning their discussions. **COLLAB. LEARN.**

Interdisciplinary Activity
Encourage students familiar with the theater and stage sets to point out a few basics of stage design before students begin.

Learning for Life   Point out that a consultant would first try to see the positive sides of a relationship.

✔ ASSESSMENT OPTIONS

📁 *Quick Checks,* p. 90
📁 *Selection and Theme Assessment,* pp. 169–170
📁 *Performance Assessment,* p. 88
💾 *Testmaker*

Skill Minilessons

Skill Minilessons

GRAMMAR AND LANGUAGE
Sentence Varieties

1. complex
2. compound-complex
3. compound-complex
4. complex
5. complex

READING AND THINKING
Responding

Students might choose a segment of dialogue such as that on page 1068 in which the three characters hurl insults at one another. Responses might include "The characters are saying mean things about one another's family members, yet it is very funny. The insults are far-fetched, such as 'What about your other aunt, the one who ran away with the architect?' This is a good example of farce—the situation is exaggerated yet the characters also seem realistic."

VOCABULARY
Etymology

1. a president's inauguration
2. deliberate discourtesy
3. fable

Additional Resources

- *Grammar and Composition Handbook,* Lessons 4.7–4.8
- *Grammar and Language Workbook,* pp. 103–105
- *Writer's Choice,* Lessons 13.7–13.8
- *Reading Workbook,* pp. 91–92
- *Vocabulary Practice,* p. 61

GRAMMAR AND LANGUAGE • Sentence Varieties

A **complex sentence** has one main clause and one or more subordinate clauses.

Main clause	Subordinate clause
Chubukov greets Lomov warmly	when he enters the room.

A **compound-complex sentence** has more than one main clause and at least one subordinate clause.

Main clause

Lomov wants to propose, |

Main clause **Subordinate clause**

but he is not sure | that Natalia will accept.

● For more about sentence types, see **Language Handbook,** pp. R14–R19.

PRACTICE On your paper, write *complex* or *compound-complex* to identify each sentence.

1. Chubukov reassures his neighbor that Natalia is crazy for him.
2. Lomov does not love Natalia, but he thinks that marriage will regulate his life.
3. Before Lomov has a chance to propose, he and Natalia argue, and he grabs his hat and rushes out the door.
4. Natalia is beside herself when she discovers the reason for Lomov's visit.
5. Although they eventually kiss and declare their happiness, the argument about the better dog is unresolved.

READING AND THINKING • Responding

Responding while you are reading helps you step right inside a work. By responding with your immediate reactions such as, "Oh! That was . . . ," or "I'd like to ask the writer why . . . ," you give yourself a chance to spontaneously react to what you're reading and to enjoy it more. Responding is just one more way of reacting as you read.

PRACTICE Choose two segments of dialogue from *A Marriage Proposal,* and write comments responding to each one.

● For related comprehension skills, see **Reading Handbook,** pp. R83–R85.

VOCABULARY • Etymology

The histories of some words are like very short stories. *Hypochondriac* comes from the Greek *hypo-,* meaning "under," and *chondros,* which is part of the sternum, or breastbone. The Greeks believed that the abdomen (which is below the breastbone) was where feelings of depression originated, so people who felt bad but were not really sick had something wrong in that part of the body.

Here are the etymologies of some other words from *A Marriage Proposal.*

affable: from the Latin *ad-,* "to," and *fari,* "to speak"

impudent: from the Latin *in-,* "not," and *pudere,* "shame"

pompous: from the Greek *pompé,* "solemn procession"

PRACTICE Use the given etymologies to answer the questions.

1. Which event would be most likely to involve pomp— a circus parade, a president's inauguration, or a school field trip?
2. Would the kind of rudeness called *impudence* be most likely to result from ignorance, excessive curiosity, or deliberate discourtesy?
3. Which word is most likely to have come from the same root as *affable—fable, fabric,* or *fare?*

LISTENING, SPEAKING, and VIEWING

Readers Theater

A fun way to share your understanding of a literary work is through **Readers Theater,** in which a reader or a group of readers presents a performance by reading a script prepared from a poem, novel, short story, or play. Through voice, facial expressions, and controlled but meaningful gestures and stances, the readers create an imaginary stage peopled with interesting characters. A reader of Lomov's role in the opening scene of *A Marriage Proposal,* for example, might speak in a trembling voice and use facial expressions and gestures to show how nervous he is.

Preparing Your Reading
- Choose passages for reading that are interesting and that have strong emotional appeal.
- Reduce all descriptive and informative material to a minimum, leaving only compelling situations that lead up to a dramatic climax.
- Prepare a narrator's part that will include introductory or descriptive material and a summary of important parts of the work that you are omitting.

Rehearsing Your Reading
Practice reading your script with the other readers in your play.

- Discuss lines that need a change in emphasis. Mark changes on the script.
- Have each reader experiment with a suitable vocal style and movements that suggest the posture and location of each character when he or she speaks.
- Check that the narrator is effective and reads in a clear, strong voice with a sense of timing and climax.

Performing Your Reading
- Speak in a strong voice and put expression into each word. To project your voice so all the audience can hear, imagine that you are speaking to a person at the back of the room.
- Lengthen your pauses and exaggerate your gestures and facial expressions to be sure viewers get your message.

ACTIVITY

With a group of students, present part or all of one of the selections in this theme as Readers Theater. Prepare your script and rehearse. Then present your reading to the class.

LISTENING, SPEAKING, and VIEWING

Objective
- To understand and create a Readers Theater performance

Teaching Strategies

As you discuss the guidelines with students, point out that Readers Theater differs from a full performance of a play and from storytelling. Have students explain how.

Activity

Students' Readers Theater presentations should
- consist of compelling passages with emotional appeal.
- have a narrator's part that summarizes undramatized material.
- include a narrator who reads clearly.
- showcase performances with interesting vocal and facial expressions and gestures.

Teaching Options

MEETING INDIVIDUAL NEEDS — ENGLISH LANGUAGE LEARNERS

Coping with Stage Fright English language learners may be nervous about performing in a Readers Theater because they lack confidence in their command of the language.

Activity Encourage students to take an active part in their group's Readers Theater, noting these methods for getting over stage fright:

1. Practice your part at home.
2. Immerse yourself in your character.
3. Act confident about your abilities.
4. Try to have fun.

Additional Resources
📁 *English Language Learners Sourcebook*

Writing ✏ Workshop

Objectives

- To identify the elements of a feature article
- To plan, draft, revise, edit, and present a feature article
- To reflect on and assess the article

GLENCOE
TECHNOLOGY

WRITER'S ASSISTANT CD-ROM
Students can use Glencoe's templates and guidelines software for expository writing to aid them in working through the steps in the writing process in this lesson.

Teaching Strategies

PREWRITING

Explore ideas Have pairs of students brainstorm several specific topics for each general topic listed. Encourage them to share their ideas with the class.

Consider your purpose Emphasize that the feature article will require anecdotes and examples from personal experience or that students recall from other sources. Although it may require some formal research, the article is not a research paper.

Teaching Options

·:· Writing ✏ Workshop ·~

Expository Writing: Feature Article

Feature articles are informative pieces in newspapers and magazines that take a more informal approach to their topics than news stories do. A feature writer draws the reader into a topic to inform, explain, *and* entertain, and takes a more personal point of view than a newswriter does. **In this workshop, you will write a feature article on the humorous aspects of an event.**

● As you write your expository article, refer to the **Writing Handbook,** pp. R58–R63.

The Writing Process

PREWRITING

> **PREWRITING TIP**
> Narrow down a general topic to the single aspect that will intrigue readers most.

Explore ideas

Feature articles can cover many topics: sports heroes, science breakthroughs, tips on buying cars—even encounters with bears. Be alert and open to ideas in newspaper and magazine articles and on TV talk shows and newsmagazine programs. In your journal, make a list of the ideas you come across. Then explore the humorous side of each topic, adding notes to your list. To start, you may want to consider the topics presented in selections in this unit, such as the following:

● Information and misinformation, as in "What Is and Ain't Grammatical"
● Interpersonal relationships, as in "A Marriage Proposal"
● A child's view of adults, as in "How I Changed the War and Won the Game" and the selection from *An American Childhood*
● Attitudes toward machines and technology, as in "The Car We Had to Push"
● An unforgettable personal experience, as in "Appetizer"

Consider your purpose

Your purpose is to convey information about a topic of your choice and to give the information a personal touch. In addition, you want to entertain your readers and make them laugh. Consider the topics and humorous aspects you listed in your journal; then decide which of those ideas will both inform and entertain your readers.

MEETING INDIVIDUAL NEEDS — ENGLISH LANGUAGE LEARNERS

Finding a Topic English language learners may have topics they have not considered for a feature article.

Activity Ask students to recall humorous misunderstandings due to language or cultural differences in the United States or humorous events or people in their native culture. Have students discuss these anecdotes with a partner to generate a topic for a feature article.

Additional Resources
📁 *English Language Learners Sourcebook*

Choose an audience

Your feature article should be geared toward a broad audience—readers of magazines and newspapers. Because you can't assume that every reader is interested in or knows about your topic, you'll have to capture readers' attention and then provide some background.

Plan your opening

Consider making the lead paragraph an intriguing "hook." Think of a way to grab your readers' attention immediately. You might try one of these ideas:

- Relate a humorous anecdote.
- State a surprising statistic.
- Provide a vivid description.
- Use a provocative quotation.

Collect the facts

With your story idea in mind, begin gathering facts by listing a few questions to direct your research.

Organize

Organize the article in a way that will grab and hold your readers' interest. The chart below shows two methods of organization for a feature article: (1) order of importance or interest and (2) chronological order.

Methods of Organization

		STUDENT MODEL
Order of importance or interest	Present details in order of increasing (or decreasing) importance or interest.	Do you want to get a start in television? Do you see yourself as a producer, director, technician—or maybe a talk-show host?
Chronological order	Describe an event or a process in sequence as it occurs over time.	I arrived at the studios of LTV, the local cable-television outlet, expecting a glitzy high-powered operation out of Hollywood. Instead, I found a group of friendly down-to-earth people who were eager to help a beginner learn the ropes.

Plan your opening Point out that a vivid opening is particularly important in a feature article because it will set the tone for what should be a compelling, amusing article. Have students reread the openings of the selections in this unit for ideas.

Make a plan Point out that students' topics may dictate their organizational plan. Encourage students to make an informal outline showing their main points when they have decided on a plan.

Additional Resources
- 📁 **Writing and Proofreading Practice,** pp. 1–7, 89–96
- 🖨 **Writing and Proofreading Transparencies 1–6, 47–48**
- 📓 **Writer's Choice,** Lesson 5.8

MEETING INDIVIDUAL NEEDS — INCLUSION STRATEGIES

Learning Disabled Researching a quotation can give students an interesting opening for their articles, provide a springboard for their ideas, and help them with their research skills.

Activity After students have developed a topic and a general plan for their articles, demonstrate using a reference such as Bartlett's Familiar Quotations to find an appropriate quotation to open their articles. If possible, take students to the library and show them how to find quotations on their topics. Have them write down three quotations they might use. Encourage them to write an introduction based on one of the quotations. **L2**

Additional Resources
- 📁 **Inclusion Strategies**

Write your draft Point out that in "The Car We Had to Push," James Thurber used an unusual organization in which he seemed to constantly digress from his real topic. Explain that a talented writer can use an organization like this if there is a motif—such as the family's old car—that ties all the anecdotes together. Encourage students to experiment with organization in their draft but to make sure all their examples and anecdotes fit together.

REVISING

Evaluate your work Suggest that students circle all vague phrases and sentences as they reread their drafts. Then have them decide which ones can be made more concrete with clearer imagery and diction.

TECHNOLOGY TIP

Encourage students who draft their articles on a word processor to use the cut-and-paste feature to rearrange elements of their first drafts.

Writing Workshop

DRAFTING

DRAFTING TIPS
To engage your readers, put yourself in their shoes and anticipate questions they might ask.

Keep the reader reading
To keep the article lively, use a mixture of anecdotes, quotes from people you interviewed, descriptions, and explanations. Tease readers with bits of information in each paragraph, so they continue reading.

Write your draft
As you write, follow your plan, choosing the most interesting details. Feel free, however, to depart from your plan if you think of something that will make the article more interesting. A feature article doesn't have to be as tightly focused as a report or news story.

STUDENT MODEL

"We're always looking for volunteers," said Jeanne Crisp, the station manager, "and we provide on-the-job training." She demonstrated the truth of that remark by directing me to get behind a studio camera and start shooting a scene—in my first ten minutes on the job!

REVISING

REVISING TIP
If you've drafted on a computer, revising on a hard copy may help you spot problems.

Evaluate your work
Read your article from the point of view of your audience, and watch for confusing or boring parts. Look for opportunities to add humorous twists to your article. Using the **Questions for Revising**, make revisions to your draft.

Have a writing conference
Read the draft aloud to someone who isn't familiar with the topic. Then work through the **Questions for Revising** again to improve your feature article.

STUDENT MODEL

I jumped at the chance, and behind I got in back of the camra. Now what? I wondered. My palms began to sweat, My heart started pounding harder and faster. I had no idea didn't know what all the knobs and buttons were for. Luckily Max the regular camera operator came to my rescue.

QUESTIONS FOR REVISING

How can I
- ☑ check the accuracy of my facts?
- ☑ change dull sentences into bold and interesting ones?
- ☑ vary sentence length so the rhythm is not monotonous?
- ☑ reorganize details so the article is more suspenseful, prompting the reader to continue reading?
- ☑ use parody, exaggeration, unexpected comparisons, or other techniques to make my article funnier?

Teaching Options

MEETING INDIVIDUAL NEEDS — MULTIPLE LEARNING STYLES

Spatial Artistically oriented students may wish to illustrate their articles. Encourage them to do so using whatever medium they wish.

Activity Have students view the illustrations by James Thurber that accompany his story on page 1045. Point out that the cartoons emphasize amusing parts of the selection. Encourage students to use illustrations in a similar way, using their own styles and techniques. Point out that they may wish to make one illustration or several. Have students display their articles and illustrations. **L2**

EDITING/PROOFREADING

Revise your feature article until it is lively, interesting, and informative. Using the **Proofreading Checklist** on the inside back cover of this book as a guide, make as many "passes" through the manuscript as needed to look for each type of error.

Grammar Hint

Adjective clauses are an efficient means of giving your readers background information. Be sure to set off nonrestrictive, or nonessential, adjective clauses with commas.

INCORRECT: *Through my headphones came instructions from Jeanne who was in the control room.*

CORRECT: *Through my headphones came instructions from Jeanne, who was in the control room.*

● For more on using commas, see **Language Handbook**, pp. R26–R28.

STUDENT MODEL

On this praduction, there ~~was~~ ^{were} three of us working the camras. The youngest was Lily, who was twelve. The oldest was Diana, who was sixty-two. Both of them were highly skilled, I was—let's be kind—not so highly skilled.

PUBLISHING/PRESENTING

For presentation to the class, you could compile your feature article with those of other students in a class magazine. To reach a larger audience, you might submit the article to a school newspaper, a local magazine or newspaper, or a national publication.

PRESENTING TIP
Enliven and clarify your feature article with illustrations, photographs, maps, and diagrams.

Reflecting

In your journal, reflect on what you like and dislike about your finished article. What would you change in the article? How would you adapt the article for a different audience (much younger, for example) or for a different medium (a TV newsmagazine program, for example)? Jot down your ideas about these and other thoughts you may have.

 Save your work for your portfolio.

HUMOR ❧ 1081

EDITING/PROOFREADING

Have students use the Proofreading Checklist on the inside back covers of their textbooks.

Encourage students to put their articles away for at least one day before performing a final proofreading. Point out that many errors in final drafts are due to last-minute work.

PUBLISHING/PRESENTING

Point out that feature articles are a popular type of literature that appears in many magazines and newspapers. Encourage students to research an appropriate market for their articles, such as a school newspaper, a literary magazine, or a community or national publication that accepts student work.

Reflecting

Portfolio Encourage students to ask themselves these questions as they review their writing.

Does my feature article
- explore a topic I would like to investigate further?
- represent some of my best writing?
- reflect careful thought and logical organization?

If students answer yes to more than one of these questions, suggest that they include their feature article in their portfolio.

✔ ASSESSMENT OPTIONS

📁 ***Writing Assessment and Portfolio Management***
- Writing Assessment, pp. 2–19, 45–46
- Portfolio Management, pp. 20–22

Unit Wrap-Up

Objectives

- To give a personal response about the selections, discussions, and activities in this unit
- To evaluate humor in literature
- To complete a self-evaluation, set a goal, and devise a plan for achieving the goal

PERSONAL RESPONSE

1. Students should provide valid reasons and logical explanations for their recommendations.
2. Accept all reasonable responses.

ANALYZING LITERATURE

Students should
- identify the form of humor being discussed.
- use an example from a selection to illustrate the form of humor.

EVALUATE AND SET GOALS

Evaluate

Have students list the projects and assignments they completed in each area before evaluating their improvement or their need to improve. Encourage students to develop a class rubric to aid them in ratings.

Set Goals

Suggest items for students to add to their checklists, such as discussing writing topics with a partner or proofreading for a particular error. Students might create a flowchart made up of a series of boxes connected by arrows in which they write their goal in the last box and the strategies from their checklist in the other boxes.

Unit Wrap-Up

PERSONAL RESPONSE

1. Which selection in this unit do you think is the funniest? Why? Is there a selection that you think doesn't belong in a unit devoted to humor? Explain.
2. What new ideas did your work in this unit help you to develop about the following?
   - recognizing and creating different kinds of humor
   - working with others to generate ideas
   - discussing your reactions and opinions
   - using your writing to grab readers' attention

ANALYZING LITERATURE

Evaluating Types of Humor   Humor is very subjective—what one person finds hilarious may not amuse another person at all. The authors in this unit create humor through a variety of methods, such as irony, farce, and hyperbole. Which method of humor do you think was used most effectively in this unit? Support your answer with an example of that method from a selection.

EVALUATE AND SET GOALS

Evaluate

1. In which of the following areas did this unit help you to improve the most? Explain.
   - reading
   - writing
   - speaking
2. Which two tasks were the most challenging for you in this unit? What strategies did you use to meet each challenge? How will you approach similar tasks in the future?
3. How would you assess your work in this unit, using the following scale? Give at least two reasons for your assessment.
   4 = outstanding   3 = good   2 = fair   1 = weak

Set Goals

1. With your teacher, identify a habit or skill that you would like to improve upon in the future.
2. In your notebook, write down at least three things you can do to improve that habit or skill.
3. Create a checklist you can use to assess your progress in achieving your goal.

💼 BUILD YOUR PORTFOLIO

Select   Choose two pieces of writing you did in this unit and include them in your portfolio. The following questions can help you make your selection.
- Which piece do you think shows your most clever thinking?
- Which piece is the liveliest or most humorous?
- Which piece is most focused and best organized?
- Which piece represented the biggest challenge?

Reflect   Include a note with each piece that you place in your portfolio. Consider addressing any of the following issues.
- How did your writing process for the piece differ from your usual process?
- What aspects of the piece did you change in revision? What would you change if you were to revise again?
- How does this piece compare with writing you have done in previous units?

 ## ASSESSMENT OPTIONS

📁 ***Writing Assessment and Portfolio Management***
- Writing Assessment, pp. 2–19
- Portfolio Management, pp. 20–22

GLENCOE
TECHNOLOGY

 MINDJOGGER VIDEOQUIZZES
VIDEODISC

Use *MindJogger* to review the Unit 6 content.

Unit 6
Side B

 Also available in VHS.

Reading on Your Own

You might enjoy these books.

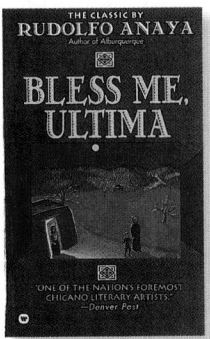

Bless Me, Ultima

by Rudolfo Anaya Antonio Marez struggles for meaning in his young life. Should he fulfill his mother's dreams or pursue a more adventurous life as his father did? Can he survive the cultural conflicts both within and beyond his small town? With the help of Ultima, a *curandera* who cures with herbs and magic, Antonio finds the meaning of life.

Novio Boy: A Play

by Gary Soto Rudy, a ninth grader, finally has a date with Patricia, an eleventh grader, and takes her to a restaurant in their Mexican American community. When Rudy's best friend, his "crazy" guitar-playing uncle, and his mother show up, Rudy worries that they might embarrass him, and he pretends not to know them.

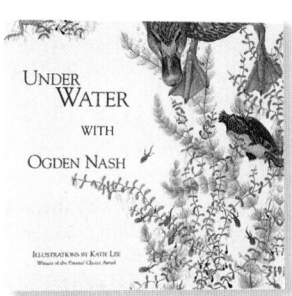

Under Water with Ogden Nash

by Ogden Nash In this collection of twenty-six delightful, humorous poems, Ogden Nash writes about sea creatures such as the turtle, the jellyfish, the squid, and the shark. Detailed color drawings by award-winning zoological illustrator Katie Lee are paired with the poems.

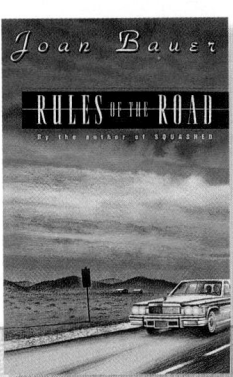

Rules of the Road

by Joan Bauer In this poignant yet funny novel, Jenna Boller, a sophomore with an after-school job selling shoes, agrees to take on the additional task of driving the store president, Mrs. Gladstone, on a business trip. As they journey all summer long from Chicago to Dallas, Jenna offers her own amusing rules for the "highway of life."

HUMOR 1083

Reading on Your Own

Glencoe Literature Library

For a complete listing of the titles available in the *Glencoe Literature Library*, see page T44 in this book.

The *Glencoe Literature Library: Study Guides* provide instructional support and student activities for works in the *Glencoe Literature Library*.

MEETING INDIVIDUAL NEEDS — INCLUSION STRATEGIES

You may wish to recommend *Novio Boy: A Play* by Gary Soto to your less-proficient readers. The accessible subject matter and play format make this book particularly appropriate for these students. **L1**

You may wish to recommend the following titles to your more-proficient readers:
- *Bless Me, Ultima* by Rudolfo Anaya **L3**
- *Under Water with Ogden Nash* by Ogden Nash **L2**
- *Rules of the Road* by Joan Bauer **L2**

Additional Resources
📁 *Inclusion Strategies*

Standardized Test Practice

TEST-TAKING TIP

While reading the passage, students should look for clues to the author's purpose. Is the author making an argument? Raising a question? Describing an historical event? Students should also look for clues to the author's attitude or tone toward the subject matter. Is the author's tone objective and scientific, or impassioned and argumentative?

TEST-TAKING TIP

If you have students who are extremely anxious about the test they must take, try to help them put it in perspective. Let them know that standardized tests are not good indicators of how "smart" a student is. Help them see other factors involved, whether they are other criteria for student advancement to the next grade, or the many elements that go into the college admissions process.

Read the following passage. Then read each question on page 1085. Decide which is the best answer to each question. Mark the letter for that answer on your paper.

LETTER 1

To the Editor of the Weeville *Post-Intelligencer*:

Shame on the Weeville Commissioner of Parks and Recreation! Ms. Phibbs has once again proven to the community at large that she is completely out of touch with the needs and desires of our citizenry. This year's proposed program for the Summer Fun Music Series in Memorial Park is the most ridiculous line-up I've ever seen. And I thought last year's was bad!

Does Ms. Phibbs *really* think that the majority of Weeville citizens enjoy rock music? This is apparently the case: five of the eight music presentations scheduled for the summer feature loud, boisterous, rowdy rock and roll bands–which isn't music at all! My dear wife Mercedes and I like to keep our minds open. We went to last year's concert series even when we didn't know the groups playing. How shocked we were when we had to put plugs in our ears to keep from going deaf! Even worse than the band, though, were the screaming hordes of youngsters who threw things at the stage and caused every manner of mayhem.

And now Ms. Phibbs wants to force-feed Weeville another round of this stuff the kids of today are calling music? What ever happened to Perry Como? What about the Boston Pops? What's wrong with a little Beethoven now and then? These are the *real* tastes of Weeville's citizens. And if Ms. Phibbs doesn't like it, she can just hand in her resignation and move somewhere else.

Yours sincerely,

Ezra T. Fitzgerald

LETTER 2

Dear Editor,

This year's Summer Fun Music Series looks to be the best one ever! Kudos to the Parks and Recreation Department, and especially to its Commissioner, Ms. Phibbs, for creating an excellent roster of musicians!

What my friends and I most appreciate is the deliberate realignment of Weeville's focus when it comes to planning community events. It's about time somebody woke up and treated Weeville's younger citizens with more courtesy and respect. When I noticed that my favorite band was slated to appear in Memorial Park August 5th this year, I nearly leapt out of my shoes! *This* is the kind of commitment Weeville citizens deserve from their elected officials and their planning committees. Last year's series, I have to say, disappointed me with its schedule of musicians who performed primarily music for older generations. Sure, some people still listen to Mozart, Bach, and Chopin, but there is a growing population whose tastes are somewhat different.

Once again, thank you, Ms. Phibbs. You've truly shown the young people of Weeville that they are important in the eyes of the town officials!

Yours very truly,

Raymond Q. Sunvil

1 The Summer Fun Music Series is under the direction of —

A the Commissioner of Parks and Recreation

B the Director of Memorial Park

C the Mayor of Weeville

D a committee made up of Bach, Mozart, and Chopin

2 The word kudos in Letter 2 most nearly means —

F shame

G good luck

H praise

J good-bye

3 The writer of Letter 1 most likely views the writer of Letter 2 as —

A a fellow music-lover

B a member of the Parks and Recreation Commission

C a respected musician

D a poorly behaved youngster

4 The author of Letter 2 cites Mozart, Bach, and Chopin as composers whose music —

F does not reflect the tastes of many younger people

G should be performed at the Summer Fun Music Series

H is not appreciated by anyone

J causes the audience to behave poorly and throw things

5 The author of Letter 1 uses which of the following as evidence that the performers at this year's Summer Fun Concert Series have been poorly selected?

A The fact that works by Mozart, Bach, and Chopin are not on the program

B The amount of money the performers are being paid by the Parks and Recreation Department

C The behavior of some people who attended last year's concert series

D The number of concerts planned as part of the series

6 The authors of both letters would likely describe themselves as —

F members of the Parks and Recreation Commission

G music lovers

H friends of Ms. Phibbs

J fans of Bach, Mozart, and Chopin

Answers and Analyses

1. **A** Students should look back to the first line of the first letter, where the writer blames the content of the music festival on the Weeville Commissioner of Parks and Recreation.

2. **H** Students should reread the sentence containing the word *kudos* and use context clues to help establish its meaning. Since the word is used in the context of congratulating the Weeville Commissioner on a fine choice of music, the most reasonable answer is H.

3. **D** The second paragraph of the first letter states that the writer dislikes rock music and the *screaming hordes of youngsters* who admire it. The writer of the second letter mentions he is one of Weeville's younger citizens.

4. **F** Students should reread the second letter and find where Bach and Mozart are mentioned. The second letter states that while some people still listen to them, there *is a growing population whose tastes are somewhat different.*

5. **C** Students should carefully reread the first letter. Choice A is tempting, but the first letter-writer never mentions Bach or Mozart. Nor does he mention money. He only mentions *the screaming hordes of youngsters who threw things at the stage and caused every manner of mayhem.*

6. **G** The first letter-writer clearly likes music. However, he prefers Perry Como and the Boston Pops to rock and roll. The second letter-writer is also a music lover, and is very fond of rock and roll.

Tested Objectives

Questions	Reading Objective
1, 4	Identify supporting ideas
2	Determine the meaning of words
3, 6	Analyze information in a variety of written texts
5	Recognize points of view, propaganda, and/or statements of fact and opinion

MORE PRACTICE

For additional practice, assign pages from one of the following standardized test resources available as part of Glencoe Literature.

Additional Resources
ITBS Preparation and Practice
SAT-9 Preparation and Practice
TerraNova Preparation and Practice

Reference Section

● **Literary Terms Handbook** **R1**

● **Language Handbook** **R14**

    Troubleshooter R14
    Troublesome Words R29
    Grammar Glossary R38
    Mechanics R45
    Spelling R54

● **Writing Handbook** **R58**

    The Writing Process R58
    Writing Modes R62
    Research Paper Writing R64
    Business and Technical Writing R70

● **Communications Skills Handbook** **R72**

    Using Electronic Resources R72
    Study and Test-Taking Skills R74

● **Reading Handbook** **R78**

    Vocabulary Development R78
    Comprehension Strategies R82
    Literary Response R97
    Analysis and Evaluation R100

Glossary R108

Spanish Glossary R117

Index of Skills R126

Index of Authors and Titles R137

Index of Art and Artists R140

Literary Terms Handbook

A

Act   A major division of a play. Many modern plays have two or three acts; some shorter plays have only one. Although Shakespeare did not separate his plays into acts, each play was later divided into five acts. Acts can contain one or more scenes.

> See page 713.
> See also SCENE.

Alliteration   The repetition of sounds, most often consonant sounds, at the beginnings of words. Alliteration gives emphasis to words. For example, Robert Francis uses alliteration in the following lines from "The Base Stealer":

Running a scattering of steps sidewise,

How he teeters, skitters, tingles, teases . . .

> See pages 579, 606, and 685.
> See also SOUND DEVICES.

Allusion   A reference in a work of literature to a character, place, or situation from history or from another work of literature, music, or art. For example, in "Constantly risking absurdity," Lawrence Ferlinghetti refers to a poet as "a little charleychaplin man." This allusion is to Charlie Chaplin, a famous film comedian.

> See pages 526 and 1042.

Analogy   A comparison based on a similarity between things that are otherwise dissimilar. A writer may use an analogy to explain something abstract or unfamiliar. For example, in the following lines from *King Lear,* William Shakespeare makes an analogy between the fate of insects and of humans:

As flies to wanton boys, are we to the gods,—
They kill us for their sport.

> See also METAPHOR, SIMILE.

Antagonist   A character or force that opposes the protagonist, or central character, in a story or drama.

The reader is generally meant not to sympathize with the antagonist. For example, in "Chee's Daughter" by Juanita Platero and Siyowin Miller, Old Man Fat is the antagonist, opposing Chee.

> See pages 2 and 746.
> See also CHARACTER, CONFLICT, PROTAGONIST.

Aside   In a play, a comment made by a character to the audience or another character but not heard by the other characters on stage. The speaker turns to one side, or "aside," away from the action on stage. Asides reveal what a character is thinking or feeling. For example, act 1, scene 2, of Shakespeare's *Julius Caesar* includes the following exchange:

CAESAR. Be near me, that I may remember you.

TREBONIUS. Caesar, I will [*Aside.*] and so near
      will I be,
That your best friends shall wish I had been further.

> See page 818.
> See also SOLILOQUY.

Assonance   The repetition of same or similar vowel sounds in stressed syllables that end with different consonant sounds. For example, the short *i* sound is repeated in this line from Shakespeare's "Shall I Compare Thee to a Summer's Day?":

So long lives this, and this gives life to thee.

> See pages 579 and 685.
> See also SOUND DEVICES.

Atmosphere   The emotional quality, or mood, of a piece of writing, especially a mood established in part by the setting.

> See page 486.
> See also MOOD.

Author's purpose   An author's intent in writing a literary work. For example, the author may want to inform, entertain, persuade, tell a story, or express an opinion.

> See pages 423, 538, and 770.
> See also DICTION, STYLE, THEME.

Autobiography   The story of a person's life written by that person. For example, *Farewell to Manzanar* is Jeanne Wakatsuki Houston's autobiography.

> See pages 422 and 472.
> See also BIOGRAPHY, MEMOIR, NONFICTION.

B

Ballad   A narrative song or poem. Folk ballads, which usually recount an exciting or dramatic episode, were passed on by word of mouth for generations before being written down. Literary ballads are written in imitation of folk ballads.

> See page 956
> See also NARRATIVE POETRY.

Biography   The account of a person's life written by another person. Biographies can be short or book-length.

> See page 422
> See also AUTOBIOGRAPHY, MEMOIR, NONFICTION.

Blank verse   Poetry or lines of dramatic verse written in unrhymed **iambic pentameter,** which is a meter made up of five iambic feet to a line of verse. Each foot consists of one unstressed (˘) syllable followed by one stressed (ʹ) syllable. Shakespeare wrote most of his plays largely in blank verse. The following line, spoken by Mark Antony in act 3, scene 1, of Shakespeare's *Julius Caesar,* is an example of blank verse.

Ŏ párdŏn mé, / thŏu bleéd/ĭng piéce / ŏf earth.

> See page 798.
> See also FOOT, METER, RHYTHM.

C

Character   An individual in a literary work. **Main characters** are the most important to a work and **minor characters** are less important. A character who shows varied and sometimes contradictory traits, such as the daughter in Amy Tan's "Two Kinds," is called a **round character.** A character who reveals only one personality trait is called a **flat character. A stereotype** is a flat character of a familiar and often-repeated type,

such as Old Man Fat in Juanita Platero and Siyowin Miller's "Chee's Daughter." A **dynamic character** changes during the story, as does Luis in Judith Ortiz Cofer's "Catch the Moon." A **static character,** such as Luis's father, remains primarily the same.

> See pages 2, 124, 231, 492, and 712.
> See also CHARACTERIZATION.

Characterization   The methods a writer uses to reveal the personality of a character. In **direct characterization** the writer makes direct statements about a character's personality. In **indirect characterization** the writer reveals a character's personality through the character's words and actions and through what other characters think and say about the character.

> See page 1050.
> See also CHARACTER.

Chorus   In classical Greek drama, an actor or group of actors who comment on the main events in the play. Choruses in ancient Greece also sang and danced. The leader of the chorus was called the **choragos**. In *Antigone* by Sophocles, the chorus is identified as the elders of Thebes.

> See page 721.

Climax   The point of greatest emotional intensity, interest, or suspense in a narrative. Also called the **turning point,** the climax usually comes near the end of a story and often presents a resolution to the conflict. In "Through the Tunnel," by Doris Lessing, the climax occurs when Jerry finally goes through the tunnel.

> See pages 3 and 86.
> See also CONFLICT, PLOT.

Colloquial language   A type of language used in everyday speech but not used in formal speech or formal writing. The expressions "That's cool" and "I'm out of here" are colloquial expressions.

> See page 170.
> See also DICTION, STYLE.

Comedy   A type of drama that is humorous and typically has a happy ending. Comedy often pokes fun at peoples' faults and limitations in order to teach something about human nature.

> See page 1074.
> See also DRAMA, FARCE, HUMOR, SATIRE.

Comic relief   A humorous scene or incident in an otherwise serious or tragic work. Comic relief breaks the tension yet emphasizes the unfolding tragedy. In scene 1 of *Antigone,* for example, the sentry's lines typically provide comic relief.

Conflict   The struggle between opposing forces in a story or play. An **external conflict** exists when a character struggles against some outside force, such as another person, nature, society, or fate. In Doris Lessing's "Through the Tunnel," for example, when Jerry tries to swim through the tunnel, he is involved in an external conflict with nature. An **internal conflict** exists within the mind of a character who is torn between opposing feelings or goals. Jerry wrestles with an internal conflict when he tries to overcome his own fear in order to swim through the tunnel.

> See pages 3, 59, 86, 275, and 429.
> See also ANTAGONIST, PLOT, PROTAGONIST.

Connotation   The suggested or implied meanings associated with a word beyond its dictionary definition, or **denotation.**

> See page 72.
> See also DENOTATION.

Consonance   The repetition of consonant sounds before and after different vowels, as in the following lines from "My Mother Pieced Quilts" by Teresa Paloma Acosta:

as weapons

against pounding january winds

> See page 579.
> See also SOUND DEVICES.

Couplet   Two consecutive rhyming lines of poetry, sometimes forming a stanza. For example, the following lines from "Shall I Compare Thee to a Summer's Day?" by William Shakespeare make up a couplet:

So long as men can breathe, or eyes can see,
So long lives this, and this gives life to thee.

See also STANZA.

Creative nonfiction   Nonfiction that applies some of the devices of fiction to convey ideas about real issues. "The Angry Winter" by Loren Eiseley, is an example of creative nonfiction.

> See page 560.
> See also FICTION, NONFICTION.

D

Denotation   The literal or dictionary meaning of a word. Literal language seeks to convey denotation, or exact meaning.

> See page 72.
> See also CONNOTATION.

Dénouement. See FALLING ACTION.

Description   Writing that uses carefully selected details to help the reader picture settings, events, and characters. Almost all writing, fiction and nonfiction, contains elements of description.

> See pages 112, 264, and 359.
> See also IMAGERY.

Dialect   A variety of a language or manner of speaking belonging to a specific group, often within a particular region. Dialects may differ in vocabulary, pronunciation, and grammatical form. Authors use dialect to help establish setting and to develop characters. In *Big River: The Adventures of Huckleberry Finn,* for example, William Hauptman uses dialect to help create characters who lived in a small river town in Missouri in the mid-1800s.

> See page 720.

Dialogue   Written conversation between characters in a literary work. These lines from Susan Beth Pfeffer's "As It Is with Strangers" are an example of dialogue:

"Yeah, sure," Jack said. "Have you lived here long?"
"Since the divorce," I said. "Eight years ago."

> See pages 44, 302, 713, and 932.
> See also MONOLOGUE.

Diction   The writer's choice of words; an important element in the writer's voice or style. Good writers choose their words carefully to convey a particular meaning or feeling. These lines from "A Child's Christmas in Wales" give an example of Dylan Thomas's diction:

All the Christmases roll down toward the two-tongued sea, like a cold and headlong moon bundling down the sky that was our street. . . .

See page 1057.
See also STYLE, TONE, VOICE.

Drama   Literature intended to be performed before an audience by actors on a stage. Most drama before the modern period can be divided into two basic types: tragedy, such as Shakespeare's *Julius Caesar,* and comedy, such as Chekhov's *A Marriage Proposal*. The two basic parts of a drama are its dialogue and its stage directions.

See pages 712–713.
See also COMEDY, DIALOGUE, PROPS, STAGE DIRECTIONS, TRAGEDY.

Dramatic irony. See IRONY.

Dramatic monologue   A form of dramatic poetry in which one speaker addresses a silent listener in an intense or emotional situation. "First Lesson" by Philip Booth, is a dramatic monologue in which a father speaks to a silent daughter.

See also DRAMATIC POETRY, MONOLOGUE.

Dramatic poetry   Poetry which uses elements of drama. One or more characters speak to other characters, themselves, or the reader. Dramatic poetry usually includes a tense situation or emotional conflict.

See also DRAMATIC MONOLOGUE, SPEAKER.

Dynamic character. See CHARACTER.

E

Elegy   An extended, usually formal poem in which the speaker mourns a death or other great loss.

Epic   A long narrative poem that traces the adventures of a larger-than-life hero. Epics intertwine myths, legends, and history, reflecting the values of the societies in which they originate. In epics, gods and goddesses often intervene in the affairs of humans.

See page 956.
See also FOLKLORE, HERO, LEGEND, MYTH, NARRATIVE POETRY.

Epic simile. See SIMILE.

Essay   A short work of nonfiction on a single topic. The purpose of an essay is to communicate an idea or opinion. A **formal essay** is serious and impersonal. An **informal essay** entertains while it informs, usually in a light, conversational style. Many informal essays, or **personal essays,** reflect upon an experience in the writer's life, as in "Living Well, Living Good" by Maya Angelou and "The Tucson Zoo" by Lewis Thomas.

See pages 422, 423, and 1006.
See also EXPOSITION, NONFICTION.

Exaggeration. See HYPERBOLE.

Exposition   An author's introduction of the characters, setting, and situation at the beginning of a story, novel, or play. For example, Edgar Allan Poe's "The Masque of the Red Death" opens with very straightforward exposition.

See pages 3 and 551.
See also ESSAY, PLOT.

Extended metaphor. See METAPHOR.

F

Fable   A short, usually simple tale that teaches a moral and sometimes uses animal characters. Themes are usually stated explicitly, as in Aesop's fables.

See also LEGEND, MORAL, PARABLE, THEME.

Falling action   In a play or story, the action that follows the climax. The falling action may show the results of the climax. It may also include the **dénouement** (dā′ nōō män′), a French word meaning "unknotting." The dénouement, or **resolution,** explains the plot or unravels the mystery.

See page 3.
See also PLOT, RISING ACTION.

Farce   A type of comedy that provokes laughter by placing one-dimensional, or flat, characters in ridiculous situations. An example is Anton Chekhov's *A Marriage Proposal.*

> See page 1074.
> See also COMEDY, HUMOR, STEREOTYPE.

Fiction   Literature in which situations and characters are invented by the writer. Aspects of a fictional work might be based on fact or experience, such as Amy Tan's "Two Kinds." Fiction includes both short stories, such as Stephen Vincent Benét's "By the Waters of Babylon," and novels, such as T. H. White's *The Once and Future King.*

> See pages 2–3.
> See also CREATIVE NONFICTION, NONFICTION, NOVEL, SCIENCE FICTION, SHORT STORY.

Figurative language   Language or expressions that are not literally true but express some truth beyond the literal level. Figurative language appears in all kinds of writing, but is especially prominent in poetry. Types of figurative language called **figures of speech** include hyperbole, metaphor, personification, simile, and understatement.

> See pages 579 and 680.
> See also HYPERBOLE, IMAGERY, METAPHOR, OXYMORON, PERSONIFICATION, SIMILE, SYMBOL, UNDERSTATEMENT.

Flashback   An account of an event that happened before a story began. A flashback interrupts the chronological sequence of story events, but gives readers information that may help explain the main events of the story. For example, in Leslie Marmon Silko's "Lullaby," the narrator includes a flashback to the day Ayah and Chato found out that Jimmie had died.

> See pages 339 and 422.

Foil   A character whose traits contrast with those of another character. By using a foil, a writer calls attention to the strengths or weaknesses of a main character. For example, the self-controlled Octavius is a foil for the excitable Mark Antony in Shakespeare's *Julius Caesar.*

> See also CHARACTER.

Folklore   The traditional beliefs, customs, stories, songs, and dances of a culture. Folklore is passed down through oral tradition and is based in the concerns of ordinary people.

> See page 912.
> See also EPIC, FOLKTALE, LEGEND, MYTH.

Folktale   A traditional story passed down orally long before being written down. Commonly the author of a folktale is anonymous. Folktales include animal stories, trickster stories, fairy tales, myths, legends, and tall tales.

> See also LEGEND, MYTH, ORAL TRADITION.

Foot   The basic unit in the measurement of rhythm in poetry. A foot usually contains one stressed syllable (´) and one or more unstressed syllables (˘).

> See pages 578 and 589.
> See also METER, RHYTHM, SCANSION.

Foreshadowing   The use of clues by the author to prepare readers for events that will happen later in a story.

> See pages 326 and 857.
> See also PLOT, RISING ACTION, SUSPENSE.

Frame story   A plot structure that includes the telling of a story within a story. The frame is the **outer** story, which usually precedes and follows the **inner** and more important story.

Free verse   Poetry that has no fixed pattern of meter and rhyme. Free verse often uses sound devices and a rhythm similar to that of human speech. "A Blessing" by James Wright is an example of free verse.

> See pages 627, 857, and 898.
> See also RHYTHM.

G

Genre   A category of literary work characterized by a particular form or style. Some examples of literary genre are novel, short story, poetry, drama, nonfiction, essay, and epic. The term also refers to subcategories of literary work. For example, fantasy, magical realism, mystery, romance, and science fiction are genres of fiction. "A Sound of Thunder" by Ray Bradbury belongs to both the short story and science-fiction genres.

   See pages 2–3, 422–423, 578–579, and 712–713.

H

Haiku   A Japanese poetry form that has three lines and seventeen syllables. The first and third line have five syllables each; the middle line has seven syllables. Bashō's haiku are famous examples of the haiku form.

   See page 686.
   See also TANKA.

Hero   The main character in a literary work, typically one whose admirable character or noble deeds arouse the admiration of the reader. Although the word *hero* is applied only to males in traditional usage (the female term is *heroine*), contemporary usage applies the term to both sexes. For example, Buffalo Calf Road Woman is the hero of "Where the Girl Rescued Her Brother" by Joseph Bruchac and Gayle Ross.

   See pages 768 and 956.
   See also EPIC, PROTAGONIST, ROMANCE,
       TRAGEDY.

Humor   The quality of a literary work that makes the characters and their situations seem funny, amusing, or ludicrous. Humorous writing can be equally effective in fiction and nonfiction.

   See page 1000.
   See also COMEDY, FARCE, PARODY, PUN, SATIRE.

Hyperbole   A figure of speech that uses exaggeration to express strong emotion, make a point, or evoke humor. For example, in the following lines from Isak Dinesen's "The Ring," Lise uses hyperbole when she thinks about the difference between her husband and herself:

"What a baby he is! I am a hundred years older than he."

   See pages 632, 1000, and 1036.
   See also FIGURATIVE LANGUAGE.

I

Iambic pentameter. See BLANK VERSE, METER.

Imagery   The "word pictures" that writers create to help evoke an emotional response. To create effective images, writers use **sensory details,** or descriptions that appeal to one or more of the five senses: sight, hearing, touch, taste, and smell. For example, the following lines from "Through the Tunnel" by Doris Lessing use imagery to make an underwater scene vivid:

A few inches above them the water sparkled as if sequins were dropping through it. . . . It was like swimming in flaked silver.

   See pages 70, 579, 653, and 676.
   See also FIGURATIVE LANGUAGE.

Inversion   Reversal of the usual word order in a prose sentence or line of poetry, for emphasis or variety. An example of this occurs in the final line of Shakespeare's sonnet "Shall I Compare Thee to a Summer's Day?"

So long <u>lives this</u>, and this gives life to thee.

Irony   A contrast or discrepancy between appearance and reality, or between what is expected and what actually happens.

   In **situational irony** the actual outcome of a situation is the opposite of someone's expectations—for example, the ending of "The Happy Man's Shirt" by Italo Calvino.

   In **verbal irony** a person says one thing and means another. For example, in Shakespeare's *Julius Caesar,* Mark Antony uses verbal irony when he praises Brutus and the conspirators to the crowd at Julius Caesar's funeral; he is actually trying to turn the people against them.

In **dramatic irony** the audience has important information that characters in a literary work do not have. Dramatic irony also occurs in *Julius Caesar* when Caesar's wife warns him not to go to the Senate. The audience knows of the murder plot, although Caesar and his wife do not.

> See page 372, 894, and 1000.
> See also PARADOX.

L

Legend   A traditional story handed down from the past and believed to be based on historical events and an actual hero. Most legends are exaggerated and gain elements of fantasy over the years. For example, "Where the Girl Rescued Her Brother" by Joseph Bruchac and Gayle Ross is a legend.

> See pages 92 and 912.
> See also EPIC, FABLE, FOLKLORE, FOLKTALE, MYTH.

Local color   The use of specific details to evoke a particular region. In "The Californian's Tale," for example, Mark Twain recreates the mining country of California by describing the speech, dress, and habits of his characters.

> See page 409.

Lyric poem   Verse that expresses the thoughts and feelings of a single speaker. A lyric poem is usually short and creates a single, unified impression. Lyric poems in this book include Robert Hayden's "Those Winter Sundays" and Marilyn Chin's "The Floral Apron."

> See page 647.

M

Magical realism   Fiction that combines fantasy and realism; usually associated with contemporary Latin American writers. Magical realism inserts fantastic, sometimes humorous, events into a very believable, ordinary reality. "The Waltz of the Fat Man" by Alberto Alvaro Rios is an example of this genre.

> See page 385.

Memoir   An autobiographical narrative; an account of an event or period emphasizing the author's personal experience of it.

> See page 422 and 440.
> See also AUTOBIOGRAPHY.

Metaphor   A figure of speech that compares two or more things that have something in common. In contrast to a simile, a metaphor implies the comparison instead of stating it directly, hence there is no use of connectives such as *like* or *as.* An **extended metaphor** continues the comparison throughout a paragraph, a stanza, or an entire work. The following example of a metaphor is from Naomi Shihab Nye's poem "Making a Fist":

My stomach was a melon split wide inside my skin.

> See pages 579, 599, 680, 695, and 702–705.
> See also ANALOGY, FIGURATIVE LANGUAGE, SIMILE.

Meter   A regular pattern of stressed and unstressed syllables that gives a line of poetry a predictable rhythm. The unit of meter within a line is called a **foot**. Each type of foot has a unique pattern of stressed (′) and unstressed (˘) syllables:

iamb (˘′) as in com/plete´

trochee (′˘) as in tro´u/ble

anapest (˘˘′) as in in/ter/vene´

dactyl (′˘˘) as in ma´j/es/ty

spondee (′′) as in base´ball´

A particular meter is named for the type of foot and the number of feet per line. For example, **trimeter** has three feet per line, **tetrameter** has four feet, **pentameter** has five feet, and **hexameter** has six feet. The most common meter in English poetry is **iambic pentameter** as in this line from Shakespeare's *Julius Caesar:*

O˘ par´/do˘n me´, / tho˘u bleed´/in˘g pie´ce / o˘f ear´th.

> See pages 578 and 589.
> See also FOOT, RHYTHM, SCANSION.

Monologue A long speech or written expression of thoughts by one character in a literary work. The burial speeches of Brutus and Antony in act 3, scene 2, of *Julius Caesar* by Shakespeare are monologues.

> See page 456.
> See also DIALOGUE, DRAMATIC MONOLOGUE, SOLILOQUY.

Mood The emotional quality or atmosphere of a story. For example, Edgar Allan Poe uses graphic details of disease and death to establish a mood of horror in the beginning of "The Masque of Red Death."

> See pages 352 and 395.
> See also ATMOSPHERE, SETTING, TONE.

Moral A practical lesson about right and wrong conduct.

> See page 105.
> See also FABLE, PARABLE.

Motif A significant word, description, idea, or image that is repeated throughout a literary work and is related to its theme. For example, in "A Swimming Lesson" Jewelle Gomez repeats the word *rhythm* to convey a message about life.

> See page 498.

Myth A traditional story of anonymous origin that deals with goddesses, gods, heroes, and supernatural events. Elements of Sophocles' *Antigone* draw on the traditional mythology of ancient Greece.

> See page 912.
> See also EPIC, FOLKLORE, FOLKTALE, LEGEND.

N

Narration The kind of writing or speech that tells a story. Narration is used not only in novels, short stories, and narrative poetry, but also can be an important element in biographies, autobiographies, and essays.

> See also NARRATIVE POETRY, NARRATOR.

Narrative poetry Verse that tells a story. Narrative poetry includes ballads, epics, and shorter poems that are usually more selective and concentrated than a prose story. For example, "Eldorado" by Edgar Allan Poe is a narrative poem.

> See pages 584 and 956.
> See also BALLAD, EPIC, NARRATION.

Narrator The person who tells a story. In some cases the narrator is a character in the story—for example, John in "By the Waters of Babylon" by Stephen Vincent Benét. At other times the narrator stands outside the story, as in "Catch the Moon" by Judith Ortiz Cofer.

> See pages 2 and 134.
> See also NARRATION, POINT OF VIEW, SPEAKER.

Nonfiction Literature about real people and events. Among the categories of nonfiction are biographies, autobiographies, and essays. For example, "An American Childhood" by Annie Dillard is nonfiction.

> See pages 422–423.
> See also AUTOBIOGRAPHY, BIOGRAPHY, CREATIVE NONFICTION, ESSAY, FICTION.

Novel A book-length fictional prose narrative. Because of its length, the novel has greater potential to develop plot, character, setting, and theme than does a short story.

> See also FICTION, SHORT STORY.

O

Octave An eight-line stanza. The term is used mainly to describe the first eight lines of a **Petrarchan**, or **Italian, sonnet.** The octave usually presents a situation, idea, or question and rhymes *abbaabba*.

> See also SESTET, SONNET, STANZA.

Ode An elaborate **lyric poem** expressed in a dignified and sincere way. Odes are imaginative as well as intellectual. Examples of the ode can be found in Sophocles' *Antigone*.

> See also LYRIC POEM.

Onomatopoeia   The use of a word or phrase that imitates or suggests the sound of what it describes. Some examples are *buzz, murmur, crack, swish.*

> See pages 579 and 701.
> See also SOUND DEVICES.

Oral tradition   Literature that passes by word of mouth from one generation to the next.

> See also FOLKLORE, FOLKTALE.

Oxymoron   A figure of speech consisting of two seemingly contradictory terms. Some examples are "bright darkness," "wise fool," and "hateful love."

> See also FIGURATIVE LANGUAGE, PARADOX.

P

Parable   A simple story pointing to a moral or religious lesson. A parable differs from a fable in that its characters are usually people rather than animals.

> See also FABLE, MORAL.

Paradox   A situation or statement that seems to be impossible or contradictory but is nevertheless true, either literally or figuratively. An example is George Bernard Shaw's observation that "youth is wasted on the young."

> See also IRONY, OXYMORON.

Parallelism   The use of a series of words, phrases, or sentences that have similar grammatical form. Parallelism emphasizes the items that are arranged in the similar structures.

> See also REPETITION.

Parody   A humorous imitation of another, usually serious work. Behavior, customs, literature, or music can all be parodied. Henry Beard's *A Cat's Garden of Verses* is a parody of Robert Louis Stevenson's poetry.

> See pages 1000 and 1011.
> See also HUMOR.

Personal essay. See ESSAY.

Personification   A figure of speech in which an animal, object, force of nature, or idea is given human qualities or characteristics. William Shakespeare personifies death in this line from "Shall I Compare Thee to a Summer's Day?":

Nor shall Death brag thou wand'rest in his shade

> See pages 579, 614, and 680.
> See also FIGURATIVE LANGUAGE.

Plot   The sequence of events in a narrative work. The plot begins with **exposition,** which introduces the story's characters, setting, and conflicts. The **rising action** adds complications to the story's conflicts, or problems, leading to the **climax,** or **turning point,** which is the moment of highest emotional pitch. The **falling action** is the logical result of the climax; the **resolution,** sometimes called the **dénouement,** presents the final outcome.

> See pages 3, 86, and 713.
> See also CLIMAX, CONFLICT, EXPOSITION,
>   FALLING ACTION, FORESHADOWING,
>   RESOLUTION, RISING ACTION.

Poetry   A form of literary expression distinguished from prose chiefly in its emphasis on the line as the unit of composition. Many other traditional characteristics of poetry apply to some poems but not to others: emotionally charged, imaginative language; use of figurative language; division into stanzas; rhyme; and regular metrical pattern.

> See pages 578–579.

Point of view   The relationship of the narrator, or storyteller, to the story. In a story with **first-person point of view,** the story is told by one of the characters, referred to as "I." The reader generally sees everything through that character's eyes. In a story with a **limited third-person point of view,** the narrator is outside the story and reveals the thoughts of only one character, but refers to that character as "he" or "she." In a story with a **third-person omniscient point of view,** the narrator is outside the story and knows everything about the characters and events.

> See pages 2, 18, 164, 212, and 295.
> See also NARRATOR, SPEAKER.

Props   Theater slang (a shortened form of *properties*) for objects and elements of the scenery of a stage play or movie set.

> See also DRAMA, STAGE DIRECTIONS.

Prose   Literature that is written in sentence and paragraph form. Essays, short stories, most plays, novels, and magazine articles are examples of prose. The dialogue in Shakespeare's play *Julius Caesar* is a mixture of verse and prose.

> See page 841.
> See also ESSAY, SHORT STORY.

Protagonist   The central character in a story, drama, or dramatic poem. Usually the action revolves around the protagonist, who undergoes the main conflict. Tiffany is the protagonist in Susan Beth Pfeffer's "As It Is with Strangers."

> See pages 2 and 746.
> See ANTAGONIST, CHARACTER, CONFLICT, HERO.

Pun   A humorous play on two or more meanings of the same word or on two different words with the same sound. In act 1 of *Julius Caesar,* Shakespeare includes several puns. For example, the Cobbler says, "All that I live by is with the awl," punning on the words *awl* and *all*.

> See page 1000.
> See also HUMOR.

Q

Quatrain   A four-line stanza. The quatrain is the most common stanza form in English poetry; it may be unrhymed or have a variety of rhyme schemes. The most common rhyme scheme is *abab* as in this quatrain from "The Glory of the Day Was in Her Face" by James Weldon Johnson:

The glory of the day was in her face,	*a*
The beauty of the night was in her eyes.	*b*
And over all her loveliness, the grace	*a*
Of Morning blushing the early skies.	*b*

> See page 589.
> See also RHYME SCHEME, STANZA.

R

Realism   A literary manner that seeks to portray life as it really is lived. More specifically, realism was a nineteenth-century literary movement that usually focused on everyday middle-class or working-class conditions and characters.

Refrain   A line or lines repeated at intervals in a poem or song, usually at the end of a stanza.

> See also REPETITION, STANZA.

Repetition   A literary device in which sounds, words, phrases, lines, or stanzas are repeated for emphasis in a poem, a speech, or another piece of writing. Repetition increases the unity in a work. When a line or stanza is repeated in a poem, it is called a **refrain.**

> See also PARALLELISM, REFRAIN, RHYME.

Resolution   The part of a plot that concludes the falling action by revealing or suggesting the outcome of the conflict. It is sometimes called **dénouement.**

> See page 3.
> See also CONFLICT, FALLING ACTION, PLOT.

Rhyme   The repetition of the same stressed vowel sounds and any succeeding sounds in two or more words. **End rhymes** occur at the ends of lines of poetry. Rhyme that occurs within a single line is called **internal rhyme. Slant rhymes** occur when words include sounds that are similar but do not rhyme exactly. Slant rhyme usually involves some variation of **consonance** (the repetition of consonant sounds) or **assonance** (the repetition of vowel sounds).

> See page 579.
> See also ASSONANCE, CONSONANCE, REPETITION, RHYME SCHEME, SOUND DEVICES.

Rhyme scheme   The pattern that end rhymes form in a stanza or in a poem. The rhyme scheme is designated by the assignment of a different letter of the alphabet to each new rhyme. For example, in these lines from "Eldorado" by Edgar Allan Poe, the rhyme scheme is *aabccb:*

```
Gaily bedight,                        a
A gallant knight                      a
In sunshine and in shadow,            b
Had journeyed long,                   c
Singing a song,                       c
In search of Eldorado.                b
```

See also QUATRAIN, RHYME, SONNET.

Rhythm   The pattern of beats created by the arrangement of stressed and unstressed syllables, especially in poetry. Rhythm can be regular, with a predictable pattern of meter, or irregular. Rhythm can give a poem a musical quality. It can also emphasize certain words or ideas to help convey meaning.

See page 578.
See also BLANK VERSE, FOOT, FREE VERSE, METER, RHYME, SCANSION.

Rising action   The part of a plot where complications to the conflict develop and increase reader interest.

See pages 3 and 1026.
See also CLIMAX, FALLING ACTION, FORESHADOWING, PLOT.

Romance   A story concerning a knightly hero, his exciting adventures, and pursuit of love. The King Arthur legend is featured in many romances composed by medieval poets.

See also HERO.

S

Satire   Writing that exposes and ridicules the vices or follies of people or societies. Satire may take the form of poetry, drama, or prose fiction or nonfiction. Luisa Valenzuela uses satire in "The Censors."

See pages 221 and 1000.
See also COMEDY, HUMOR.

Scansion   The analysis of the meter of verse; also called scanning a poem. To scan a line of poetry means to note stressed and unstressed syllables and to divide the line into its feet, or rhythmical units.

See also FOOT, METER, RHYTHM.

Scene   A subdivision of an act in a play. Each scene usually takes place in a specific setting and time.

See page 713.
See also ACT.

Science fiction   Fiction dealing with the impact of real or imagined scientific or technological advances on human or alien societies of the past, present, or future. "A Sound of Thunder" by Ray Bradbury is an example of science fiction.

See also FICTION, GENRE.

Sensory details   Evocative words that convey sensory experiences—seeing, hearing, tasting, touching, and smelling. Sensory details make writing come alive by helping readers experience what is being described.

See pages 70, 669, and 987.
See also IMAGERY.

Sestet   A six-line poem or stanza; also the final six lines of a **Petrarchan**, or **Italian, sonnet**. In a sonnet, the sestet provides a resolution, comment, or answer to the question or situation posed earlier in the poem.

See also OCTAVE, SONNET, STANZA.

Setting   The time and place in which the events of a story, novel, or play occur. Setting includes the ideas, customs, beliefs, and values of the time and place. The setting often helps create an atmosphere, or mood. For example, the setting of "The False Gems" by Guy de Maupassant is Paris in the late 1870s or early 1880s.

See pages 2, 153, 395, and 712.
See also ATMOSPHERE, MOOD.

Short story   A brief fictional narrative in prose. Elements of the short story include **plot, character, setting, point of view,** and **theme**.

See pages 2–3 and 308–312.
See also FICTION.

Simile   A figure of speech using *like* or *as* to compare seemingly unlike things. For example, this simile appears in Amy Tan's story "Two Kinds":

And she also did a fancy sweep of a curtsy, so that the fluffy skirt of her white dress cascaded to the floor like the petals of a large carnation.

An **epic simile** is a long, elaborate comparison that continues for several lines. It is a feature of epic poems, but is found in other poems as well. Lawrence Ferlinghetti's poem "Constantly risking absurdity" is an example of an epic, or extended, simile.

See pages 579, 594, 680, and 694.
See also ANALOGY, FIGURATIVE LANGUAGE, METAPHOR.

Situational irony.   See IRONY.

Soliloquy   A long speech spoken by a character in a dramatic work, who is typically alone on stage. This speech reveals the private thoughts and emotions of the character. For example, Antony vows his revenge of Caesar's murder in a soliloquy in Shakespeare's *Julius Caesar,* act 3, scene 1.

See page 818.
See also MONOLOGUE.

Sonnet   A lyric poem of fourteen lines, almost always written in iambic pentameter and typically following strict patterns of stanza divisions and rhymes.

The **Shakespearean,** or **English, sonnet** consists of three **quatrains,** or four-line stanzas, followed by a **couplet,** or pair of rhyming lines. The rhyme scheme is usually *abab, cdcd, efef, gg.* The rhyming couplet often presents a conclusion to the issues or questions presented in the three quatrains. "Shall I Compare Thee to a Summer's Day?" is a Shakespearean sonnet.

In the **Petrarchan,** or **Italian, sonnet,** fourteen lines are divided into two stanzas, the eight-lined **octave** and the six-lined **sestet.** The sestet usually responds to a question or situation posed by the octave. The rhyme scheme for the octave is usually *abbaabba;* for the sestet the rhyme scheme is usually *cdecde.*

See pages 586 and 589.
See also OCTAVE, RHYME SCHEME, SESTET.

Sound devices   Techniques used to emphasize particular sounds in writing or to create a sense of rhythm.

See pages 579 and 685.
See also ALLITERATION, ASSONANCE, CONSONANCE, ONOMATOPOEIA, RHYME.

Speaker   The voice that communicates with the reader of a poem, similar to the narrator in a work of prose. Often a poet invents a speaker with a particular identity in order to create a desired impact. For example, the speaker in "The Rain," by Henry Beard, is a cat.

See pages 578 and 659.
See also DRAMATIC POETRY, NARRATOR, TONE.

Stage directions   Instructions written by the dramatist to describe the appearance and actions of characters, as well as the sets, props, costumes, sound effects, and lighting for a play.

See page 712.
See also DRAMA, PROPS.

Stanza   A group of lines forming a unit in a poem.

See page 578.
See also COUPLET, OCTAVE, QUATRAIN, SESTET.

Stereotype   A character who is not developed as an individual but as a collection of traits and mannerisms supposedly shared by all members of a group.

See also CHARACTER, FARCE.

Stream of consciousness   A writing technique which allows a character's or narrator's thoughts and feelings to flow in an uninterrupted manner.

Style   The author's choice and arrangement of words and sentences in a literary work. Style can reveal an author's purpose in writing and attitude toward his or her subject and audience.

See page 255.
See also AUTHOR'S PURPOSE, DICTION, TONE, VOICE.

Suspense   A feeling of curiosity, uncertainty, or even dread about what is going to happen next. Writers increase the level of suspense in a story by giving readers clues to what might happen. In "The Monkey's Paw" by W. W. Jacobs, suspense builds as the reader realizes how the monkey's paw makes wishes come true.

> See pages 182 and 987.
> See also FORESHADOWING, MOOD.

Symbol   Any object, person, place, or experience that means more than what it is. Symbolism is the use of images to represent internal realities. Swimming through the tunnel, for example, is a symbolic act for Jerry in Doris Lessing's "Through the Tunnel." The act means that he is growing up.

> See pages 243 and 664.
> See also FIGURATIVE LANGUAGE.

T

Tall tale   A type of folklore in which the deeds of one or more characters are wildly exaggerated but told seriously, as if the deeds were true. "Sundiata" is an example of a tall tale.

> See page 940.
> See also FOLKLORE, FOLKTALE.

Tanka   Unrhymed Japanese verse form that consists of five lines. The first and third lines have five syllables each; the other lines have seven syllables each.

> See page 686.
> See also HAIKU.

Theme   The central message of a story, poem, novel, or play that readers can apply to life. Some works have a **stated theme,** which is expressed directly. More commonly, works have an **implied theme,** which is revealed gradually. To discover an implied theme in a short story, the reader might look at the experiences of the main character and the lessons he or she learns.

> See pages 3, 35, and 492.
> See also AUTHOR'S PURPOSE, FABLE.

Thesis   The main idea of a work of nonfiction. The thesis may be stated directly or implied.

> See pages 423 and 513.

Tone   A reflection of a writer's or speaker's attitude toward the subject. A writer's tone may convey a variety of attitudes, including sympathy, objectivity, seriousness, irony, sadness, bitterness, or humor. For example, Alice Childress's light, humorous tone in "Mrs. James" contrasts with Isabel Allende's solemn tone in "And of Clay Are We Created."

> See pages 195, 306, 640, and 974.
> See also ATMOSPHERE, DICTION, MOOD, SPEAKER.

Turning point.   See CLIMAX.

Tragedy   A play in which a main character, or **tragic hero,** suffers a downfall. That character typically is a person of dignified or heroic stature. The downfall may result from outside forces or from a weakness within the character, which is known as a **tragic flaw.** For example, *Antigone* by Sophocles is a tragedy which describes the downfall of a king, Creon.

> See pages 768 and 871.
> See also DRAMA, HERO.

Tragic flaw.   See TRAGEDY.

U-V

Understatement   Language that makes something seem less than it really is. Understatement may be used to insert humor or to focus the reader's attention on something the author wants to emphasize.

> See pages 285 and 1000.
> See also FIGURATIVE LANGUAGE.

Verbal irony.   See IRONY.

Voice   An author's distinctive use of language to convey the author's or narrator's personality to the reader. Voice depends on elements of style, such as **diction** and **tone.**

> See page 566.
> See also DICTION, STYLE, TONE.

Language Handbook

Troubleshooter

The Troubleshooter will help you recognize and correct errors that you might make in your writing.

Sentence Fragment

Problem: A fragment that lacks a subject

The snow is very deep. (Is hard to shovel.) *frag*

Solution: Add a subject to the fragment to make it a complete sentence.

The snow is very deep. It is hard to shovel.

Problem: A fragment that lacks a complete verb

The marathon winner received her awards. (A trophy and a check.) *frag*

The speaker addressed the unruly audience. (Nobody listening to him.) *frag*

Solution A: Add a complete verb or a helping verb and other words as needed to make the sentence complete.

The marathon winner received her awards. A trophy and a check were presented to her.

The speaker addressed the unruly audience. Nobody was listening to him.

Solution B: Combine the fragment with another sentence. Add a comma to set off a nonessential appositive or a comma and a conjunction to separate two main clauses in a compound sentence.

The marathon winner received her awards, a trophy and a check.

The speaker addressed the unruly audience, but nobody was listening to him.

Problem: A fragment that is a subordinate clause

Our teacher was late for school. (Because she had a flat tire on the way.) *frag*

I am eating spaghetti. (Which is one of my favorite foods.) *frag*

Solution A: Combine the fragment with another sentence. Add a comma to set off a nonessential clause.

Our teacher was late for school because she had a flat tire on the way.

I am eating spaghetti, which is one of my favorite foods.

Solution B: Rewrite the fragment as a complete sentence, eliminating the subordinating conjunction or the relative pronoun and adding a subject or other words necessary to make a complete thought.

Our teacher was late for school. She had a flat tire on the way.

I am eating spaghetti. It is one of my favorite foods.

Problem: A fragment that lacks both a subject and a verb

Kendra traveled all day and arrived in town. (At nine o'clock.) *frag*

Solution: Combine the fragment with another sentence.

Kendra traveled all day and arrived in town at nine o'clock.

> **Rule of Thumb:** Sentence fragments can make your writing hard to understand. Be sure to check that every sentence has a subject and a verb.

Run-on Sentence

Problem: Comma splice—two main clauses separated by only a comma

(We had dinner at a Chinese restaurant, I liked the cashew chicken.) *run-on*

Solution A: Replace the comma with an end mark of punctuation, such as a period or a question mark, and begin the new sentence with a capital letter.

We had dinner at a Chinese restaurant. I liked the cashew chicken.

Solution B: Place a semicolon between the two main clauses.

We had dinner at a Chinese restaurant; I liked the cashew chicken.

Solution C: Add a coordinating conjunction after the comma.

We had dinner at a Chinese restaurant, and I liked the cashew chicken.

Problem: Two main clauses with no punctuation between them

The hurricane headed out to sea then it turned back toward land. *run-on*

Solution A: Separate the main clauses with an end mark of punctuation, such as a period or a question mark, and begin the second sentence with a capital letter.

The hurricane headed out to sea. Then it turned back toward land.

Solution B: Separate the main clauses with a semicolon.

The hurricane headed out to sea; then it turned back toward land.

Solution C: Add a comma and a coordinating conjunction between the main clauses.

The hurricane headed out to sea, but then it turned back toward land.

Problem: Two main clauses with no comma before the coordinating conjunction

I went to the mall on Saturday and my sister went with me. *run-on*

Solution: Add a comma before the coordinating conjunction to separate the two main clauses.

I went to the mall on Saturday, and my sister went with me.

> **Rule of Thumb:** It often helps to have someone else read your writing to see if it is clear. Since you know what the sentences are supposed to mean, you might miss the need for punctuation.

Lack of Subject-Verb Agreement

Problem: A subject that is separated from the verb by an intervening prepositional phrase

The herd of wild horses (sweep) across the plains. *agr*

Even the youngest horses in the herd (keeps) up with the rest. *agr*

Solution: Make the verb agree with the subject, not with the object of a preposition. The subject of a sentence is never the object of a preposition.

The herd of wild horses sweeps across the plains.

Even the youngest horses in the herd keep up with the rest.

Problem: A predicate nominative that differs in number from the subject

Those three actors (is) the entire cast of the play. *agr*

The entire cast of the play (are) those three actors. *agr*

Solution: Ignore the predicate nominative, and make the verb agree with the subject of the sentence.

Those three actors are the entire cast of the play.

The entire cast of the play is those three actors.

Problem: A subject that follows the verb

In this cage (lives) six gerbils. *agr*

There (goes) two of them now. *agr*

Solution: In an inverted sentence, look for the subject *after* the verb. Then make sure the verb agrees with the subject.

In this cage live six gerbils.

There go two of them now.

> **Rule of Thumb:** Reversing the order of an inverted sentence might help you decide on the correct verb form: "Six gerbils live in this cage."

Problem: A collective noun as the subject

The school band (practice) two days a week. *agr*

The group (has) different opinions on the subject. *agr*

Solution A: If the collective noun refers to a group as a whole, use a singular verb.

The school band practices two days a week.

Solution B: If the collective noun refers to each member of a group individually, use a plural verb.

The group have different opinions on the subject.

Problem: A noun of amount as the subject

Twenty dollars (are) the price they advertised. *agr*

Five one-dollar bills (is) in my wallet. *agr*

Solution: Determine whether the noun of amount refers to one unit and is therefore singular, or whether it refers to a number of individual units and is therefore plural.

Twenty dollars is the price they advertised.

Five one-dollar bills are in my wallet.

Problem: A compound subject that is joined by *and*

Macaroni and cheese (are) his favorite meal. *agr*

Vegetables and meat loaf (is) in the refrigerator. *agr*

Solution A: If the parts of the compound subject belong to one unit or if both parts refer to the same person or thing, use a singular verb.

Macaroni and cheese is his favorite meal.

Solution B: If the parts of the compound subject do not belong to one unit or if they refer to different people or things, use a plural verb.

Vegetables and meat loaf are in the refrigerator.

Problem: A compound subject that is joined by *or* or *nor*

Neither those cats nor that dog (belong) to me. *agr*

Solution: Make the verb agree with the subject that is closer to it.

Neither those cats nor that dog belongs to me.

Problem: A compound subject that is preceded by *many a, every,* or *each*

Every boy and girl here (live) in the neighborhood. *agr*

Solution: When *many a, every,* or *each* precedes a compound subject, the subject is considered singular. Use a singular verb.

Every boy and girl here lives in the neighborhood.

Problem: A subject that is separated from the verb by an intervening expression

Jermaine's dog, as well as Andrea's parrot, (do) a lot of tricks. *agr*

Solution: Certain intervening expressions, such as those beginning with *as well as, in addition to,* and *together with,* do not change the number of the subject. Ignore such expressions between a subject and its verb, and make the verb agree with the subject.

Jermaine's dog, as well as Andrea's parrot, does a lot of tricks.

Problem: An indefinite pronoun as the subject

Each of the activities (are) open to the public. *agr*

Solution: Determine whether the indefinite pronoun is singular or plural, and make the verb agree with it. Some indefinite pronouns are singular—*another, anyone, everyone, one, each, either, neither, anything, everything, something,* and *somebody.* Some are plural—*both, many, few, several,* and *others.* Some can be singular or plural—*some, all, any, more, most,* and *none*—depending on the noun to which they refer.

Each of the activities is open to the public.

Lack of Pronoun-Antecedent Agreement

Problem: A singular antecedent that can be either male or female

A family doctor sometimes refers (his) patient to a specialist. *ant*

Solution A: Traditionally, a masculine pronoun was used to refer to an antecedent that might be either male or female. This usage ignores or excludes females. Reword the sentence to use *he or she, him or her,* and so on.

A family doctor sometimes refers his or her patient to a specialist.

Solution B: Reword the sentence so that both the antecedent and the pronoun are plural.

Family doctors sometimes refer their patients to specialists.

Solution C: Reword the sentence to eliminate the pronoun.

A family doctor sometimes refers a patient to a specialist.

Problem: A second-person pronoun that refers to a third-person antecedent

Sarah is going to a school that trains (you) to repair computers. *ant*

Solution A: Use the appropriate third-person pronoun.

Sarah is going to a school that trains her to repair computers.

Solution B: Use an appropriate noun instead of a pronoun.

Sarah is going to a school that trains people to repair computers.

Problem: A singular indefinite pronoun as an antecedent

Neither of the boys brought (their) sleeping bag. *ant*

Solution: *Another, any, every, one, each, either, neither, anything, everything, something,* and *somebody* are singular; they therefore require singular personal pronouns even when followed by a prepositional phrase that contains a plural noun.

Neither of the boys brought his sleeping bag.

> **Rule of Thumb:** To help yourself remember that pronouns such as *each, either, every,* and *neither* are singular, think *each one, either one, every one,* and *neither one.*

Lack of Clear Pronoun Reference [Unclear Antecedent]

Problem: A pronoun reference that is weak or vague

The sculptor was carving, (which) we admired. *ref*

A flock of birds roosted in that tree last year, and (it) was very noisy. *ref*

Solution A: Rewrite the sentence, adding a clear antecedent for the pronoun.

The sculptor was carving a statue of a bear, which we admired.

Solution B: Rewrite the sentence, substituting a noun for the pronoun.

A flock of birds roosted in that tree last year, and their chattering was very noisy.

Problem: A pronoun that could refer to more than one antecedent

Roberto and his grandfather caught six fish, and (he) cleaned them all. *ref*

The toxic waste the factory dumped in the river made the people avoid (it.) *ref*

Solution A: Rewrite the sentence, substituting a noun for the pronoun.

Roberto and his grandfather caught six fish, and Roberto cleaned them all.

Solution B: Rewrite the sentence, making the antecedent of the pronoun clear.

The people avoided the river because of the toxic waste the factory dumped in it.

Problem: The indefinite use of *you* or *they*

The movie's characters seem so real that (you) get caught up in the story. *ref*

In New Orleans (they) have a Mardi Gras celebration every year. *ref*

Solution A: Rewrite the sentence, substituting a noun for the pronoun.

The movie's characters seem so real that the audience gets caught up in the story.

Solution B: Rewrite the sentence, eliminating the pronoun entirely.

The city of New Orleans has a Mardi Gras celebration every year.

Shift in Pronoun

Problem: An incorrect shift in person between two pronouns

I like to sit next to the window, where (you) can enjoy the scenery. *pro*

Eduardo and Lily are learning to search the World Wide Web, where (you) can find information on many topics. *pro*

When you surf the Web, (one) might come up with inaccurate data. *pro*

Solution A: Replace the incorrect pronoun with a pronoun that agrees with its antecedent.

I like to sit next to the window, where I can enjoy the scenery.

Eduardo and Lily are learning to search the World Wide Web, where they can find information on many topics.

When you surf the Web, you might come up with inaccurate data.

Solution B: Replace the pronoun with an appropriate noun.

Eduardo and Lily are learning to search the World Wide Web, where students can find information on many topics.

Shift in Verb Tense

Problem: An unnecessary shift in tense

Laurent goes across town by bus and (worked) at his job all afternoon. *shift t*

When the clock struck twelve, Cinderella's coach (turns) back into *shift t* a pumpkin.

Solution: When two or more events occur at the same time, be sure to use the same verb tense to describe each event.

Laurent goes across town by bus and works at his job all afternoon.

When the clock struck twelve, Cinderella's coach turned back into a pumpkin.

Problem: A lack of correct shift in tenses to show that one event precedes or follows another

By the time my aunt finally got here, we (waited) for an hour. *shift t*

Solution: When two events have occurred at different times in the past, shift from the past tense to the past perfect tense to indicate that one action began and ended before another past action began.

By the time my aunt finally got here, we had waited for an hour.

> **Rule of Thumb:** When you need to use more than one verb tense in a sentence, it may help to first jot down the sequence of events you're writing about. Be clear in your mind which action happened first.

Incorrect Verb Tense or Form

Problem: An incorrect or missing verb ending

Have you ever (milk) a cow? *tense*

I did two months ago, when I (visit) my uncle's farm. *tense*

Solution: Add *-ed* to a regular verb to form the past participle and the past tense.

Have you ever milked a cow?

I did two months ago, when I visited my uncle's farm.

Problem: An improperly formed irregular verb

Jon (seeked) advice from all his friends. *tense*

Sheila nearly (freezed) before we built a warm fire. *tense*

Solution: Irregular verbs form their past and past participles in some way other than by adding *-ed.* Memorize these forms, or look them up in a dictionary.

Jon sought advice from all his friends.

Sheila nearly froze before we built a warm fire.

Problem: Confusion between the past form and the past participle

We've (went) to that beach many times. *tense*

Haskell has (chose) the bike he wants. *tense*

Solution: Use the past participle of an irregular verb, not the past form, when you use the auxiliary verb *have.*

We've gone to that beach many times.

Haskell has chosen the bike he wants.

Problem: Improper use of the past participle

He (begun) his assignment. *tense*

The tardy bell (rung) before I got through the door. *tense*

Solution A: The past participle of an irregular verb cannot stand alone as a verb. Add a form of the auxiliary verb *have* to the past participle to form a complete verb.

He has begun his assignment.

The tardy bell had rung before I got through the door.

Solution B: Replace the past participle with the past form of the verb.

He began his assignment.

The tardy bell rang before I got through the door.

Misplaced or Dangling Modifier

Problem: A misplaced modifier

Jungle cats frighten many people (with big teeth and claws.) *mod*

(Floating over the park,) Megan saw a red balloon. *mod*

The boy on the skateboard jumped the curb (racing down the street.) *mod*

Solution: Modifiers that modify the wrong word or that seem to modify more than one idea in a sentence are called misplaced modifiers. Move the misplaced phrase as close as possible to the word or words it modifies.

With big teeth and claws, jungle cats frighten many people.

Megan saw a red balloon floating over the park.

Racing down the street, the boy on the skateboard jumped the curb.

Problem: Incorrect placement of the adverb *only*

Juana (only) goes to movies on the weekend. *mod*

Solution: Place the adverb *only* immediately before the word or group of words it modifies.

Only Juana goes to movies on the weekend.

Juana goes only to movies on the weekend.

Juana goes to movies only on the weekend.

> **Rule of Thumb:** Note that each time *only* is moved, the meaning of the sentence changes. Check to be sure that your sentence conveys your intended meaning.

Problem: A dangling modifier

(Walking through the museum,) the paintings were from many *mod* different countries.

(By studying every night,) the examination was easily passed. *mod*

Solution: Rewrite the sentence, adding a noun to which the dangling phrase clearly refers. Often you will have to add other words or change the form of the verb to complete the meaning of the sentence.

Walking through the museum, Arthur noticed paintings from many different countries.

By studying every night, the student passed the examination easily.

Missing or Misplaced Possessive Apostrophe

Problem: Singular nouns

That (womans) daughter is (Doris) best friend. *poss*

Solution: Use an apostrophe and -*s* to form the possessive of a singular noun or a proper name, even if the noun ends in *s*.

That woman's daughter is Doris's best friend.

Problem: Plural nouns ending in -*s*

Her twin (daughters) jackets are just alike. *poss*

Solution: Use an apostrophe alone to form the possessive of a plural noun that ends in -*s*.

Her twin daughters' jackets are just alike.

Problem: Plural nouns not ending in -*s*

This store carries a good selection of (mens) suits. *poss*

Solution: Use an apostrophe and -*s* to form the possessive of a plural noun that does not end in -*s*.

This store carries a good selection of men's suits.

Problem: Pronouns

In this organization (everyones) opinion counts. *poss*

Are these skates (your's) or (her's)? *poss*

Solution A: Use an apostrophe and -s to form the possessive of a singular indefinite pronoun.

In this organization everyone's opinion counts.

Solution B: Do not use an apostrophe with any of the possessive personal pronouns.

Are these skates yours or hers?

Problem: Confusion between *its* and *it's*

(Its) a long way from your house to mine. *cont*

The airplane had ice on (it's) wings. *poss*

Solution A: Use an apostrophe to form the contraction of *it is*.

It's a long way from your house to mine.

Solution B: Do not use an apostrophe to form the possessive of *it*.

The airplane had ice on its wings.

Missing Commas with Nonessential Elements

Problem: Missing commas with nonessential participles or participial phrases

Sonya, exhausted from her long trip, went to bed early. *com*

Solution: Determine whether the participle or participial phrase is essential to the meaning of the sentence or not. If it is not essential, set off the phrase with commas.

Sonya, exhausted from her long trip, went to bed early.

Problem: Missing commas with nonessential adjective clauses

My oldest cousin who visits us every summer is one grade ahead of *con* me in school.

Solution: Determine whether the clause is essential to the meaning of the sentence or not. If it is not essential, set off the clause with commas.

My oldest cousin, who visits us every summer, is one grade ahead of me in school.

Problem: Missing commas with nonessential appositives

In Chaco Canyon a site in New Mexico we saw the ruins of huge *con* structures built by the Anasazi.

Solution: Determine whether the appositive is essential to the meaning of the sentence or not. If it is not essential, set off the appositive with commas.

In Chaco Canyon, a site in New Mexico, we saw the ruins of huge structures built by the Anasazi.

> **Rule of Thumb:** To determine whether a word, phrase, or clause is essential, try reading the sentence without it.

Problem: Missing commas with interjections and parenthetical expressions

Judith as you know will be sixteen tomorrow. *con*

Hey don't forget to bring the ice cream. *con*

Solution: Set off the interjection or parenthetical expression with commas.

Judith, as you know, will be sixteen tomorrow.

Hey, don't forget to bring the ice cream.

Missing Commas in a Series

Problem: Missing commas in a series of words, phrases, or clauses

Last summer Hideki visited relatives in Tokyo_Kyoto_and Kobe. *a com*

We followed the trail along the river_across a wooden bridge_and up a steep hill. *a com*

Alex dribbled the ball_then he passed it to Dominic_and Dominic scored the goal. *a com*

The library is open for people who want a book to read_people who are looking for specific information_and people who need a quiet place to study. *a com*

The little boy complained_whined_and cried until his mother picked him up. *a com*

Solution: When there are three or more elements in a series, use a comma after each element, including the element that precedes a conjunction.

Last summer Hideki visited relatives in Tokyo, Kyoto, and Kobe.

We followed the trail along the river, across a wooden bridge, and up a steep hill.

Alex dribbled the ball, then he passed it to Dominic, and Dominic scored the goal.

The library is open for people who want a book to read, people who are looking for specific information, and people who need a quiet place to study.

The little boy complained, whined, and cried until his mother picked him up.

> **Rule of Thumb:** When you're having difficulty with a rule of usage, try rewriting the rule in your own words. Then check with your teacher to be sure you have grasped the concept.

Troublesome Words

This section will help you choose between words that are often confusing. It will also alert you to avoid certain words and expressions in school or business writing.

a, an

Use the article *an* when the word that follows begins with a vowel sound. Use *a* when the word that follows begins with a consonant sound.

An exercise mat lay in **a** corner of the room.

Use the article *a* when the word that follows begins with a sounded *h* or a *u* with the long sound ("yew"). Use *an* when the word that follows begins with an unsounded *h* or a *u* with the short sound.

A hungry family will not wait **an** hour for dinner.

An umpire wears **a** uniform.

a lot, alot

The expression *a lot* means "a large amount" or "a great deal" (as in "I like him a lot") and should always be written as two words. Some authorities discourage its use in formal English.

A lot of people arrived early for the big game.

Many people arrived early for the big game.

accept, except

Accept is a verb meaning "to receive" or "to agree to." *Except* is occasionally used as a verb, but more often it is used as a preposition meaning "but."

Sally will **accept** the award.

Everybody was invited **except** Bob.

affect, effect

Affect is a verb meaning "to cause a change in" or "to influence." *Effect* as a verb means "to bring about or accomplish." As a noun, *effect* means "result" or "that which has been brought about."

Incorrect answers will **affect** your test score.

Diligent study will **effect** a rise in your test score.

Diligent study will have a good **effect** on your test score.

ain't

Ain't is never used in formal speaking or writing unless you are quoting the exact words of a character or real person. Instead of using *ain't,* say or write *am not, is not,* or use contractions: *I'm not, she's not, she isn't, they aren't.*

Cassandra **is not** going to the dance.

all ready, already

All ready, written as two words, is an adjective phrase that means "completely ready." *Already,* written as one word, is an adverb that means "before" or "by this time."

By the time supper was **all ready,** the guests had **already** arrived.

all right, alright

The expression *all right* should be written as two words.

Let's see if the man who fell down is **all right.**

> **Rule of Thumb:** Dictionaries are good guides to the usage of a word. Even though some dictionaries do list the single word *alright,* they indicate that it is not a preferred spelling.

all together, altogether

All together means "in a group." *Altogether* is an adverb meaning "completely" or "on the whole."

They worked on the project **all together.**

Their work was **altogether** excellent.

amount, number

Use *amount* to refer to a quantity that cannot be counted. Use *number* to refer to things that can be counted.

A great **amount** of water went over the falls.

A great **number** of logs went over the falls.

> **Rule of Thumb:** Use *amount* to refer to fluids, materials, and gases.

anxious, eager

Anxious means "uneasy or worried about some event or situation." *Eager* means "having a keen interest" or "feeling impatient for something expected."

Gus is **anxious** about the outcome of the difficult test.

Berta is **eager** to see her grades because she knows she did well.

a while, awhile

An article and a noun form the expression *a while.* Often the preposition *in* or *for* precedes *a while,* forming a prepositional phrase. The single word *awhile* is an adverb.

He'll arrive in **a while.** He'll work for **a while.**

He'll work **awhile** after he arrives.

being as, being that

Although the expressions *being as* and *being that* sometimes replace *because* or *since* in informal conversation, you should always avoid them in formal speaking and writing.

Because she made excellent grades, Sylvia skipped a year in school.

Since Carlos is already at home, let's visit him there.

beside, besides

Beside means "next to." *Besides* means "moreover" or "in addition to."

Clark sat **beside** me at dinner.

Besides having a fine dinner, we also ate dessert.

between, among

Use *between* when comparing one person or thing with another person or thing or with an entire group. Use *among* to show a relationship in which more than two persons or things are considered as a group.

He had to choose **between** the movie and the play.

What are the differences **between** a woodpecker and other birds?

There are differences **among** various kinds of birds.

bring, take

Bring means "to carry from a distant place to a closer one." *Take* means "to carry from a nearby place to a more distant one."

Bring me a copy of the newspaper when you come here tomorrow.

The cab will **take** you to the airport from here.

can, may

Can implies the ability to do something. *May* implies permission to do something or the possibility of doing it.

You **may** go to the movie if you **can** pay the price of a ticket.

Rule of Thumb: Although *can* is sometimes used in place of *may* in informal speech, you should distinguish between them when speaking and writing formally.

can't hardly, can't scarcely

Can't hardly and *can't scarcely* are considered double negatives, since *hardly* and *scarcely* by themselves have a negative meaning. Do not use *hardly* and *scarcely* with *not* or *-n't.*

Tamera **can hardly** reach the shelf.

Gabriel **can scarcely** believe he won the contest.

capital, capitol

Use *capital* to refer to the city that is the center of government of a state or country, to money or other assets, or to a capital letter. Use *capitol* to refer to the building in which a state or national legislature meets.

Our class took a trip to Washington, D.C., the nation's **capital.**

We toured the **capitol,** where the legislature was in session.

complement, compliment

A *complement* is something that makes a thing complete. A *compliment* is an expression of praise or admiration.

The CD-ROM is the **complement** of the textbook.

The teacher's **compliment** pleased Jade.

compose, comprise

Compose means "to form by putting together." *Comprise* means "to contain, embrace."

Water is **composed** of hydrogen and oxygen.

The United States **comprises** fifty states.

continual, continuous

Continual describes repetitive action with pauses. *Continuous* describes an action that continues with no interruption in space or time.

Whenever we get together, Jorge and I have **continual** discussions about science.

My interest in the subject has been **continuous** for as long as I can remember.

could of, might of, must of, should of, would of

The helping verb *have,* not the preposition *of,* should follow *could, might, must, should,* or *would.*

Midori **could have** climbed the rope if she had tried.

Isabel **must have** heard that song before.

different from, different than

The expression *different from* is generally preferred to *different than.*

Chess is **different from** checkers.

emigrate, immigrate

Emigrate means "to leave one country to settle in another." Use *from* with *emigrate. Immigrate* means "to enter a country in order to live there permanently." Use *to* or *into* with *immigrate.*

Nikolai plans to **emigrate** from the Ukraine.

Nikolai plans to **immigrate** to the United States.

> **Rule of Thumb:** Remember that the *e-* in *emigrate* comes from *ex-* ("out of"); the *im-* in *immigrate* comes from *in-* ("into").

ensure, assure, insure

Ensure means to make sure of something, to guarantee it. *Assure* means to reassure someone, to remove doubt. *Insure* means to cover something with insurance or to secure it.

Please take action to **ensure** the prompt arrival of the package.

Can you **assure** me that everything has been taken care of?

You must **insure** the car before you can drive it.

farther, further

Farther refers to physical distance. *Further* refers to time or degree.

Now the comet is moving **farther** and **farther** away from Earth.

Think **further** back in time and see what you can remember.

There is nothing **further** to say.

fewer, less

Fewer is generally used to refer to things or qualities that can be counted. *Less* is generally used to refer to things or qualities that cannot be counted. In addition, *less* is sometimes used with figures that are regarded as single amounts or single quantities.

Fewer people attended the movie this week than last week.

There is **less** water in this swimming pool than in the one at school.

You can eat lunch at this restaurant for **less** than ten dollars. [The money is treated as a single sum, not as individual dollars.]

good, well

Good is often used as an adjective meaning "pleasing" or "able." *Well* may be used as an adverb of manner telling how ably something is done or as an adjective meaning "in good health."

This meal tastes **good.** [adjective after a linking verb]

Claudia swims **well.** [adverb of manner]

Because José has the flu, he is not **well** enough to come to school. [adjective meaning "in good health"]

had of

The word *of* should not be used between *had* and a past participle.

I wish I **had seen** that television show.

hanged, hung

When your meaning is "put to death by hanging," use *hanged* in the past tense. In all other cases, use *hung.*

Many countries **hanged** convicted murderers in the nineteenth century.

Rachel **hung** her hat on the peg.

in, into

Use *in* when you mean "inside" or "within." Use *into* to indicate movement or direction from outside to a point within.

Melissa is already **in** the theater.

I hurried **into** the theater because it was nearly time for the play to begin.

irregardless, regardless

Both the prefix *ir-* and suffix *-less* have negative meanings. When they are used together, they produce a double negative, which is incorrect. Therefore, you should use *regardless* rather than *irregardless*.

Riad listens to whatever people say, **regardless** of their opinions.

learn, teach

Learn means "to gain knowledge." *Teach* means "to instruct" or "to give knowledge to."

Emil **learns** well from his professor.

Mr. Musser **teaches** us our spelling lessons.

leave, let

Leave means "to go away; depart." *Let* means "to allow" or "to permit." With the word *alone* you may use either *let* or *leave*.

Francesca wanted to **leave** the party.

Ryugen **lets** me use his CDs.

Leave me alone. **Let** me alone.

lend, loan

Lend is a verb. *Loan* is a noun. Although *loan* is sometimes used informally as a verb, *lend* is preferable.

I will **lend** you my calculator if you return it tomorrow.

Thank you for the **loan.**

like, as

Use *like,* a preposition, to introduce a prepositional phrase. Use *as,* a subordinating conjunction, to introduce a subordinate clause. Many authorities believe that *like* should not be used before a clause in formal English.

Werner looks **like** his brother.

Mildred baby-sits tonight, **as** she always does on Fridays.

> **Rule of Thumb:** *As* can be a preposition in some cases, as in *He posed as a secret agent.*

loose, lose

Use the adjective *loose* (lo͞os) when you mean "free," "not firmly attached," or "not fitting tightly." Use the verb *lose* (lo͞oz) when you mean "to have no longer," "to misplace," or "to fail to win."

In spite of the city's leash laws, Miguel lets his dog run **loose.**

Marlene doesn't want to **lose** another set of keys.

passed, past

Passed is the past and the past participle form of *pass*. *Past* is used as a noun, an adjective, a preposition, or an adverb.

The blue car **passed** the bicycle. [verb]

History is a study of events in the **past.** [noun]

Ian took a long vacation this **past** summer. [adjective]

The grocery store is just **past** the gas station. [preposition]

The puppies woke up when their mother walked **past.** [adverb]

precede, proceed

Use *precede* when you mean "to go or come before." Use *proceed* when you mean "to continue" or "to move along."

July **precedes** August.

The line of customers will **proceed** slowly.

principal, principle

Principal, as an adjective, means "the most important or first in rank." As a noun, it is the title of the head of a school. *Principle* is a noun that means "a fundamental truth or general law."

My **principal** objection to the TV set is its price.

The school **principal** fully supports our club's activities.

My research project was set up according to strict scientific **principles.**

raise, rise

The verb *raise* means "to cause to move upward" or "to lift up." It always takes an object. The verb *rise* means "to get up" or "to go up." It is an intransitive verb and never takes an object.

The soldiers **raise** the flag at dawn every morning.

Your temperature will **rise** if you do vigorous exercise.

reason . . . is that, because

Because means "for the reason that." Therefore, do not use *because* after *reason . . . is.* Use either *reason . . . is that* or *because* alone.

The **reason** there is no baseball game today **is that** it is raining.

There is no baseball game today **because** it is raining.

respectfully, respectively

Use *respectfully* to mean "with respect." Use *respectively* to mean "in the order named."

Saul spoke **respectfully** to his boss.

Gareth and Alice are third and fourth in line, **respectively.**

says, said

Says is the present-tense, third-person singular form of the verb *say*. *Said* is the past tense of *say*. Do not use *says* when you are referring to the past.

Sebastian **says** he is going downtown.

Yesterday Sebastian **said** he was going downtown.

sit, set

Sit means "to be seated." It rarely takes an object. *Set* means "to put" or "to place," and it generally takes an object. When *set* is used to mean "the sun is going down," it does not take an object.

Sara is going to **sit** on the park bench.

Set the groceries down on the kitchen table.

The sun **set** at seven o'clock this evening.

than, then

Than is a conjunction. Use it in comparisons. *Then* is an adverb used to mean "soon afterward," "the time mentioned," "at another time," "for that reason," "in that case," and "besides."

The task is more complex **than** you think it is.

Alicia is better at math **than** Claudio is.

Rashad will go to the party, and **then** I will join him.

By **then** you will be very hungry.

Andres was only five years old **then.**

If you can't answer the question, **then** Sheila will.

their, they're, there

Their is the possessive form of *they*. *They're* is the contraction of *they are*. *There* means "in that place." *There* is also sometimes used as an interjection, expressing a sense of completion.

It's **their** business, not ours.

Ask them whether **they're** going to join us.

You will find your book **there** on your desk.

There!

to, too, two

Use *to* when you mean "in the direction of." Also, use *to* before a verb to form an infinitive. Use *too* when you mean "also" or "excessively." *Two* is the number that comes after one.

We will drive **to** the mall.

I need **to** buy new shoes.

My brother will come along, **too.**

I bought only **two** ice cream cones.

toward, towards

These words are interchangeable; as prepositions, they both mean "in the direction of."

She drove **toward** her house.

She drove **towards** her house.

where . . . at

Do not use *at* after a question with *where*.

Where are my keys?

whereas, while

Both *whereas* and *while* can be used as conjunctions meaning "although." *Whereas* also means "it being the fact that." *While* can be used as a conjunction indicating a period of time.

I spent the afternoon at work, **whereas** you went swimming.

Miryam's brother and sister like vanilla, **while** she prefers chocolate.

Whereas everyone is in agreement, we can adjourn this meeting.

Roberto reviewed the lesson **while** Marisela finished her research paper.

> **Rule of Thumb:** The conjunction *whereas* is usually reserved for very formal usage.

who, whom

Use the nominative case pronoun *who* for the subject.

Who knocked on the door?

Tell me **who** can solve this problem. [subject of the noun clause]

Who do you think can solve the problem?

> **Rule of Thumb:** When a question contains an interrupting expression such as *do you think,* it helps to omit the interrupting phrase to determine whether to use *who* or *whom.*

Use the objective pronoun *whom* for the direct or indirect object of a verb or the object of a verbal.

Whom are you describing? [direct object]

They gave **whom** the award? [indirect object]

Giovanni told me **whom** he saw. [direct object of the verb *saw*]

Whom does the teacher want to nominate for student council? [object of the verbal *to nominate*]

> **Rule of Thumb:** When speaking informally, people often use *who* instead of *whom* in sentences like *Who are you describing?* In writing and formal speech, distinguish between *who* and *whom.*

Use the objective pronoun *whom* for the object of a preposition.

Giovanni is a person with **whom** I have much in common. [object of the preposition *with*]

Grammar Glossary

This glossary will help you quickly locate information on parts of speech and sentence structure.

A

Abstract noun. *See* Noun chart.

Action verb. *See* Verb.

Active voice. *See* Voice.

Adjective A word that modifies a noun or pronoun by limiting its meaning. An adjective may answer one of these questions: *What kind? Which one? How many? How much?* Adjectives appear in various positions in a sentence. (The *exciting* story held my attention. That story is *exciting*.)

Many adjectives have different forms to indicate **degree of comparison.** (*happy, happier, happiest*)

The **positive degree** is the simple form of the adjective. (*strong, much*)

The **comparative degree** compares two persons, places, things, or ideas. (*stronger, more*)

The **superlative degree** compares more than two persons, places, things, or ideas. (*strongest, most*)

A **predicate adjective** follows a linking verb and further identifies the subject. (The animals are *hungry*.)

A **noun used as an adjective** answers one of these questions: *What kind? Which one?*

(*government* building, *physics* lesson) In some cases possessive nouns are used as adjectives. (*Asa's* car)

A **proper adjective** is formed from a proper noun and begins with a capital letter. Proper adjectives are often created by using the following suffixes: *-an, -ian, -n, -ese,* and *-ish.* (*Indonesian*)

Adjective clause. *See* Clause chart.

Adverb A word that modifies a verb, an adjective, or another adverb by making its meaning more specific. Adverbs answer the questions *How? When? Where?* and *To what degree?* When modifying a verb, an adverb may appear in various positions in a sentence. (The cattle disappeared *rapidly* over the hill. *Suddenly,* not a single one was in sight.) When modifying an adjective or another adverb, an adverb appears directly before the modified word. (The cowboy was *quite* annoyed that he had to find them.) The negatives *no, not,* and the contraction *-n't* are adverbs. (Nakia's score was *no* better than mine.) Other negative words, such as *nowhere, hardly,* and *never,* can function as adverbs of time, place, and degree. (I *never* imagined that they would win the game.)

Some adverbs have different forms to indicate degree of

comparison. (*slowly, more slowly, most slowly*)

The **comparative** form of an adverb compares two actions. (*more quickly, better*)

The **superlative** form compares three or more actions. (*most quickly, best*)

Adverb clause. *See* Clause chart.

Antecedent. *See* Pronoun.

Appositive A noun or a pronoun placed next to another noun or pronoun to identify or give additional information about it. (My cousin *Lonnie* is going to Guatemala this summer.)

Appositive phrase. *See* Phrase.

Article The adjective *a, an,* or *the.*

Indefinite articles (*a* and *an*) refer to one of a general group of persons, places, or things. (We saw *a* fish.)

The **definite article** (*the*) indicates that the noun is a specific person, place, or thing. (It swam under *the* log.)

Auxiliary verb. *See* Verb.

B

Base form. *See* Verb tense.

C

Clause A group of words that has a subject and a predicate and is used as part of a sentence. Clauses fall into two categories: *main clauses*, which are also called *independent clauses*, and *subordinate clauses*, which are also called *dependent clauses*.

A **main clause** has a subject and a predicate and can stand alone as a sentence. There must be at least one main clause in every sentence. *(I can't wait to see your new dog. I will arrive in a few minutes.)*

A **subordinate clause** has a subject and a predicate, but it cannot stand alone as a sentence. A subordinate clause makes sense only when attached to a main clause. Many subordinate clauses begin with subordinating conjunctions or relative pronouns. (Ethan got a high grade *because he was well prepared*.) The chart on this page shows the main types of subordinate clauses.

Collective noun. *See* Noun chart.

Common noun. *See* Noun chart.

Comparative. *See* Adjective, Adverb.

Complement A word or phrase that completes the meaning of a verb. The four basic kinds of complements are *direct objects*, *indirect objects*, *object complements*, and *subject complements*.

A **direct object** answers the question *What?* or *Whom?* after an action verb. (Hiro likes his *job* and his *car*. Hiro brings *me* to school every day.)

An **indirect object** answers the question *To whom? For whom? To what?* or *For what?* after an action verb. (Adebesi gave the *museum* an authentic Nigerian drum.)

An **object complement** answers the question *What?* after a direct object. An object complement is a noun, a pronoun, or an adjective that completes the meaning of a direct object by identifying or describing it. (We elected her *chairperson* of the committee. Our group considers the award *ours*. Angela finds science *fascinating*.)

A **subject complement** follows a subject and a linking verb. It identifies or describes a subject. The two kinds of subject complements are *predicate nominatives* and *predicate adjectives*.

A **predicate nominative** is a noun or pronoun that follows a linking verb and gives more information about the subject. (Those three students are *athletes*. The guard is *he*.)

A **predicate adjective** is an adjective that follows a linking verb and gives more information about the subject. (Laura is *athletic*. Your painting looks *finished* to me.)

Complex sentence. *See* Sentence.

Compound-complex sentence. *See* Sentence.

Compound sentence. *See* Sentence.

Conjunction A word that joins single words or groups of words.

A **coordinating conjunction** (*and*, *but*, *or*, *nor*, *for*, *yet*) joins words or groups of words that are equal in grammatical

TYPES OF SUBORDINATE CLAUSES			
Clause	**Function**	**Example**	**Begins with . . .**
Adjective clause	Modifies a noun or pronoun in the main clause	The story *that I just read* is by Amy Tan.	A relative pronoun such as *that*, *which*, *who*, *whom*, or *whose*
Adverb clause	Modifies a verb, an adjective, or an adverb in the main clause	Beryl went to the movie *after she finished studying*.	A subordinating conjunction such as *after*, *although*, *because*, *if*, *since*, *when*, or *where*
Noun clause	Serves as a subject, an object, or a predicate nominative in the main clause	*Whoever writes a great deal* often draws on personal experience.	Words such as *how*, *that*, *what*, *whatever*, *when*, *where*, *which*, *who*, *whom*, *whoever*, *whose*, or *why*

importance. (Toshio *and* Linda entered their projects in the science fair.)

Correlative conjunctions (*both . . . and, just as . . . so, not only . . . but also, either . . . or, neither . . . nor*) work in pairs to join words and groups of words of equal importance. (Rosa *not only* won the race *but also* set a new school record.)

A **subordinating conjunction** (*after, although, as soon as, because, before, if, in order that, since, than, though, until, when, while*) joins a dependent idea or clause to a main clause. (We should leave *as soon as* we can get ready.)

Conjunctive adverb An adverb used to clarify the relationship between clauses of a compound sentence. (The team lost the game last night; *consequently*, they will not play in the tournament.)

Coordinating conjunction. *See* Conjunction.

Correlative conjunction. *See* Conjunction.

Definite article. *See* Article.

Demonstrative pronoun. *See* Pronoun.

Direct object. *See* Complement.

Emphatic form. *See* Verb tense.

Future tense. *See* Verb tense.

Gerund A verb form that ends in *-ing* and is used as a noun. A gerund may function as a subject, an object of a verb, or the object of a preposition. (*Studying* is not my favorite way to spend an evening. However, I have improved my grades by *studying*.)

Gerund phrase. *See* Phrase.

Indirect object. *See* Complement.

Infinitive A verb form that begins with the word *to* and functions as a noun, an adjective, or an adverb. (We were happy *to leave*. *To compose* was her ambition.) When *to* precedes a verb, it is not a preposition but instead signals an infinitive.

Infinitive phrase. *See* Phrase.

Intensive pronoun. *See* Pronoun.

Interjection A word or phrase that expresses emotion or exclamation. An interjection has no grammatical connection to other words in the sentence. Commas follow mild interjections; exclamation points follow stronger ones. (*Oh*, I forgot. *Wow!*)

Interrogative pronoun. *See* Pronoun.

Intransitive verb. *See* Verb.

Inverted order In a sentence written in *inverted order,* the predicate comes before the subject. Some sentences are written in inverted order for variety or special emphasis. (In the very center of the clearing *stood* a *deer*.) The subject also generally follows the predicate in a sentence that begins with *there* or *here*. (There *were* several *deer* beside the stream. Here *comes* the *bus* now.) Questions, or interrogative sentences, are generally written in inverted order. In many questions, an auxiliary verb precedes the subject and the main verb follows it. (*Has Edwin announced* the contest results?) Questions that begin with *who* or *what* follow normal word order.

Irregular verb. *See* Verb tense.

Linking verb. *See* Verb.

Main clause. *See* Clause.

Nominative pronoun. *See* Pronoun chart.

Noun A word that names a person, a place, a thing, or an idea. The chart on the next page shows the main types of nouns.

Noun clause. *See* Clause chart.

Noun of direct address. *See* Noun chart.

Number A noun, pronoun, or verb is *singular* in number if it refers to one, *plural* if it refers to more than one.

Objective pronoun. *See* Pronoun.

Participle A verb form that can function as an adjective. Present participles always end in *-ing*. (The audience applauded the *dancing* couple.) Although most past participles end in *-ed*, some take other forms. (We looked over the colorfully *wrapped* packages. We admired the tastefully *hung* ornaments.)

Passive voice. *See* Voice.

Past tense. *See* Verb tense.

Perfect tenses. *See* Verb tense.

Personal pronoun. *See* Pronoun.

Phrase A group of words that acts as a single part of speech in a sentence.

An **appositive phrase** is an appositive along with any modifiers. If not essential to the meaning of the sentence, an appositive phrase is set off by commas. (The Mayan weavers displayed their works, *a variety of handbags and clothing*.)

A **gerund phrase** includes a gerund and any complements and modifiers needed to complete its meaning. (*Studying every evening* has helped me improve my grades.)

An **infinitive phrase** includes the infinitive and any complements and modifiers. (Armand found it hard *to pitch strikes consistently*.)

A **participial phrase** contains a participle and any complements and modifiers necessary to complete its meaning. (*Freshly shorn of his luxuriant locks*, the new army recruit scowled at his reflection in the mirror.)

A **prepositional phrase** consists of a preposition, its object, and any modifiers of the object. A prepositional phrase can function as an adjective, modifying a noun or a pronoun. (We went to the movie *at the new theater*.) A prepositional phrase can also function as an adverb when it modifies a verb, an adverb, or an adjective. (Soccer has

become very popular *in our town*.)

A **verb phrase** consists of one or more auxiliary verbs followed by a main verb. (The campers *should have noticed* the approaching storm.)

Positive degree. *See* Adjective.

Possessive noun. *See* Noun chart.

Predicate The verb and any objects, complements, or modifiers that say something about the subject of a sentence.

A **simple predicate** is a verb or verb phrase that tells something about the subject. (Some fish *swim* rapidly.)

A **complete predicate** includes the simple predicate and any words that modify it. (The López family *moved here in January*.) In some sentences the simple predicate and the complete predicate are the same. (Fish *swim*.)

A **compound predicate** has two or more verbs or verb phrases that are joined by a conjunction

TYPES OF NOUNS		
Noun	**Function**	**Examples**
Abstract noun	Names an idea, a quality, or a characteristic	beauty, liberty, thoughtfulness
Collective noun	Names a group of things or people	class, orchestra
Common noun	Names a general type of person, place, thing, or idea	cousin, river, era, theory
Noun of direct address	Identifies the person or persons being spoken to	*Students,* please line up in single file.
Possessive noun	Shows possession, ownership, or the relationship between two nouns	the *child's* toy
Predicate noun	Follows a linking verb and gives information about the subject	Akira is the *winner.*
Proper noun	Names a particular person, place, thing, or idea	Aunt Rebecca, Japan, Renaissance

and share the same subject. (The puppies *ran and played*.) In a compound predicate that contains verb phrases, do not repeat the auxiliary verb (or verbs) before the second verb. (Neither the puppy nor the kitten *has been adopted* or *given* a name.)

Predicate adjective. *See* Adjective, Complement.

Predicate nominative. *See* Complement.

Preposition A word that shows the relationship of a noun or pronoun to some other word in the sentence. Prepositions include *about, above, across, among, as, behind, below, beyond, but, by, down, during, except, for, from, into, like, near, of, on, outside, over, since, through, to, under, until, with.*

A **compound preposition** is made up of more than one word. *(according to, ahead of, because of, by means of, in addition to, in spite of, on account of)* (According to scientific studies, the temperature of the earth is rising.)

Prepositional phrase. *See* Phrase.

Present tense. *See* Verb tense.

Progressive form. *See* Verb tense.

Pronoun A word that takes the place of a noun, a group of words acting as a noun, or another pronoun.

The word or group of words that a pronoun refers to is called its **antecedent.** (In the following sentence, *Carlos* is the antecedent of the pronoun *he. When Carlos lived in Colorado, he learned to ride horseback.*)

A **demonstrative pronoun** points out specific persons, places, things, or ideas. *(this, that, these, those)*

An **indefinite pronoun** refers to persons, places, or things in a more general way than a noun does. *(all, another, any, both, each, either, enough, everything, few, many, most, much, neither, nobody, none, one, other, others, plenty, several, some)*

An **intensive pronoun** adds emphasis to another noun or pronoun. If an intensive pronoun is omitted, the meaning of the sentence will be the same. (I *myself* took responsibility for the decision.)

An **interrogative pronoun** is used to form questions. *(who? whom? whose? what? which?)*

A **personal pronoun** refers to a specific person or thing. Personal pronouns have three cases: nominative, objective, and possessive. The case depends upon the function of the pronoun in a sentence. The chart on this page shows the case forms of the various personal pronouns.

A **reflexive pronoun** reflects back to a noun or pronoun used earlier in the sentence, indicating that the same person or thing is involved. (I taught *myself* to speak a little Spanish by listening to some of my friends.)

A **relative pronoun** is used to begin a subordinate clause. *(who, whose, whomever, that, what, whom, whoever, whomever, whichever, whatever)*

Proper adjective. *See* Adjective.

Proper noun. *See* Noun chart.

Reflexive pronoun. *See* Pronoun.

Relative pronoun. *See* Pronoun.

PERSONAL PRONOUNS			
Case	**Singular**	**Plural**	**Function in Sentence**
Nominative	I, you, she, he, it	we, you, they	subject or predicate nominative
Objective	me, you, her, him, it	us, you, them	direct object, indirect object, or object of a preposition
Possessive	my, mine, your, yours, her, hers, his, its	our, ours, your, yours, their, theirs	replacement for the possessive form of a noun

Sentence A group of words expressing a complete thought. Every sentence has a subject and a predicate. Sentences can be classified by function or by structure. The chart on this page shows the categories by function; the following subentries describe the categories by structure. *See also* Clause, Predicate, Subject.

A **simple sentence** has only one main clause and no subordinate clauses. *(Alana writes.)* A simple sentence may contain a compound subject or a compound predicate or both. *(Alana and Tony write. Alana writes and reads. Alana and Tony write and read.)* The subject and the predicate can be expanded with adjectives, adverbs, prepositional phrases, appositives, or verbal phrases. *(Alana, an excellent writer, vividly conveys her experiences through the use of concrete nouns and adjectives.)* As long as the sentence has only one main clause, however, it remains a simple sentence.

A **compound sentence** has two or more main clauses. Each main clause has its own subject and predicate, and these main clauses are usually joined by a comma and a coordinating conjunction. *(Alana likes to write, and Tony enjoys reading.)* Semicolons may also be used to join the main clauses in a compound sentence. *(Some of Alana's writing is difficult to read; Tony prefers her simpler writing.)*

A **complex sentence** has one main clause and one or more subordinate clauses. *(Tony likes Alana's poems because they sparkle with exciting images.)*

A **compound-complex sentence** has two or more main clauses and at least one subordinate clause. *(Tony read the essay, which was written by Alana, and he spoke favorably about it.)*

Simple predicate. *See* Predicate.

Simple subject. *See* Subject.

Subject The part of the sentence that tells what the sentence is about.

A **simple subject** is the main noun or pronoun in the subject. *(The large* fish *swims slowly.)*

A **complete subject** includes the simple subject and any words that modify it. *(The family that lives in the brick house moved here recently.)* In some sentences, the simple subject and the complete subject are the same. *(Fish swim.)*

A **compound subject** consists of two or more simple subjects joined by a conjunction. The subjects share the same verb. *(Dogs, cats, hamsters, and gerbils* are popular pets.)*

Subordinate clause. *See* Clause.

Subordinating conjunction. *See* Conjunction.

Superlative degree. *See* Adjective, Adverb.

Tense. *See* Verb tense.

Transitive verb. *See* Verb.

TYPES OF SENTENCES			
Sentence Type	**Function**	**Ends with . . .**	**Examples**
Declarative sentence	Makes a statement	A period	The rain is falling steadily.
Exclamatory sentence	Expresses strong emotion	An exclamation point	How exciting the play was! What an excellent cast!
Imperative sentence	Gives a command or makes a request	A period or an exclamation point	Please close the windows. Hurry!
Interrogative sentence	Asks a question	A question mark	Is that book a mystery? Will you write your report on that book? Why do you like that book so much?

Verb A word that expresses action or a state of being. *(move, feels, said)*

An **action verb** tells what someone or something does. Action verbs can express either physical or mental action. (She *runs* five miles per week. She *plans* in advance.)

An **auxiliary verb**, or helping verb, is a verb that accompanies the main verb to form a verb phrase. (I *have* studied.) The forms of *be* and *have* are the most common auxiliary verbs *(am, is, are, was, were, being, been; has, have, had, having).* Other auxiliaries include *can, could, do, does, did, may, might, must, shall, should, will, would.*

An **intransitive verb** is an action verb that is *not* followed by a word that answers the question *What?* or *Whom?* (Josie *travels* frequently.)

A **linking verb** expresses a state of being by linking the subject of a sentence with a word or expression that identifies or describes the subject. (Mary Cassatt *is* a well-known American painter.) The most commonly used linking verb is *be* in all its forms *(am, is, are, was, were, will be, been, being).* Other linking verbs include *appear, become, feel, grow, look, remain, seem, sound, smell, stay, taste.*

A **transitive verb** is an action verb that is followed by a word

or words that answer the question *What?* or *Whom?* (Dwight *watched* the action with great interest.)

Verb phrase. *See* Phrase.

Verb tense The tense of a verb indicates when the action or state of being occurs—in the present, past, or future. All verb tenses are formed from the four principal parts of a verb: a base form *(swim),* a present participle *(swimming),* a simple past form *(swam),* and a past participle *(swum).*

A **regular verb** forms its simple past and past participle by adding *-ed* to the base form. *(jump, jumped, jumped)*

An **irregular verb** forms its past and past participle in some other way. *(drive, drove, driven; begin, began, begun)*

In addition to present, past, and future tense, there are three perfect tenses.

The **present perfect tense** expresses an action or condition that occurred at some indefinite time in the past. This tense also shows an action or condition that began in the past and continues into the present. (My grandfather *has worked* here for two years.)

The **past perfect tense** indicates that one past action or condition began and ended before another past action started. (Roger *had seen* that movie three times before I saw it once.)

The **future perfect tense** indicates that one future action or condition will begin and end before another future event starts. Use *will have* or *shall have* with the past participle of a verb. (By Thursday he *will have seen* the sequel, too.)

The **progressive form** of a verb expresses a continuing action with any of the six tenses. To make the progressive forms, use the appropriate tense of the verb *be* with the present participle of the main verb. (They *are walking.* They *will have been walking.*)

The **emphatic form** adds special force, or emphasis, to the present or past tense of a verb. For the emphatic form, use *do, does,* or *did* with the base form. (I *do walk* to school every day.)

Verbal A verb form that functions in a sentence as a noun, an adjective, or an adverb. The three kinds of verbals are gerunds, infinitives, and participles. *See* Gerund, Infinitive, Participle.

Voice The voice of a verb depends on whether the subject performs the action or receives the action of the verb.

A verb is in the **active voice** if the subject of the sentence performs the action. (Kara *trained* the black horse.)

A verb is in the **passive voice** if the subject of the sentence receives the action of the verb. (The black horse *was trained* by Kara.)

Mechanics

Capitalization

This section will help you recognize and use correct capitalization in sentences.

Rule	Example
Capitalize the first word in any sentence, including a direct quotation that is a sentence. Capitalize a sentence in parentheses unless it is included in another sentence.	He said, "We should leave now." We were looking for Laurel Avenue, where we thought Juanita lived. (There was no Laurel Avenue.)

> **Rule of Thumb:** Since people do not always speak in complete sentences, written dialogue may contain sentence fragments. In dialogue, capitalize the first word of each fragment and each complete sentence. For example: "Late for class," Ferris mumbled.

Rule	Example
Always capitalize the pronoun *I* no matter where it appears in the sentence.	No matter where I live, I'll always remember my home at the edge of the desert.
Capitalize proper nouns, including these: **a.** names of individuals, personal titles used in direct address, and personal titles preceding a name or describing a relationship	Robert Penn Warren; Class President Iris Mura; Uncle Bill
b. names of ethnic groups, national groups, political parties and their members, and languages	African Americans; Hopi; the Democratic Party; a Republican; Vietnamese
c. names of organizations, institutions, companies, monuments, bridges, buildings, and other structures	Red Cross; North Carolina State University; the Museum of Science and Industry; Microsoft; Vietnam Memorial; Golden Gate Bridge
d. trade names and names of documents, awards, and laws	Macintosh; the Constitution of the United States; Nobel Prize; the Fifth Amendment
e. geographical terms and regions or localities	Lake Superior; Main Street; Palisades Park; North Dakota; the Northwest
f. names of planets and other heavenly bodies	Earth; Mars
g. names of ships, planes, trains, and spacecraft	USS *Enterprise*; the *Orient Express*; *Apollo 13*
h. names of most historical events, eras, calendar items, and religious items	World War One; Middle Ages; Saturday; Judaism; Methodists; Bible; Yom Kippur; God

Rule	Example
i. titles of literary works, publications, works of art, and musical compositions	"Sound of Thunder"; *New Yorker*; *Little Dancer*; *Concerto for Orchestra*
j. specific names of school courses	Algebra I

> **Rule of Thumb:** Do not capitalize the names of subjects (He studied *algebra*.) or seasons of the year (Ian enjoys *winter*.)

Rule	Example
Capitalize proper adjectives (adjectives formed from proper nouns).	Spanish rice; Vidalia onions; Freudian theory; Buddhist meditation

Punctuation

This section will help you use these elements of punctuation correctly.

Rule	Example
Use a **period** at the end of a declarative sentence or an imperative sentence (a polite command).	His lecture was fascinating. Please take your seats.
Use an **exclamation point** to show strong feeling or after a forceful command.	Oh, no! What a disaster! Listen to me!
Use a **question mark** to indicate a direct question.	Is it time for class?
Use a **colon**: a. to introduce a list (especially after words such as *these*, or *as follows*) and to introduce material that explains, illustrates, or restates previous material	Toni Morrison's works include the following novels: *The Bluest Eye*, *Song of Solomon*, and *Beloved*. We must say it again: the customer is always right.

> **Rule of Thumb:** Do not use a colon between the verb and its complement. A colon must follow a complete sentence.

Rule	Example
b. to introduce a long or formal quotation	In *Richard III*, the title character says: "Now is the winter of our discontent / Made glorious summer by this sun of York. . . ."
c. in precise time measurements, biblical chapter and verse references, and business letter salutations	12:45 P.M. 9:24 A.M. 2 Sam. 14:13–14 Eccles. 2:16 Dear Mrs. Clay: Dear Sir:

Rule	Example
Use a semicolon:	
a. to separate main clauses that are not joined by a coordinating conjunction	Tipping is considered proper at a restaurant; the rate is between fifteen and twenty percent.
b. to separate main clauses joined by a conjunctive adverb or by *for example* or *that is*	Herman Melville's earlier novels were fairly simple adventure stories; however, in his later works, he dealt with more complex themes.
c. to separate the items in a series when these items contain commas	Three signers of the Declaration of Independence were Thomas Jefferson, who wrote the document; Benjamin Franklin, who discovered that lightning consisted of electricity; and George Washington, who became our first president.
d. to separate two main clauses joined by a coordinating conjunction when such clauses already contain several commas	Manny, who traveled all the way from Fairbanks, Alaska, attended the reunion; but Teri, a local resident, did not.
Use a comma:	
a. between the main clauses of a compound sentence	The snow is already three feet deep, and it is still coming down.
b. to separate three or more words, phrases, or clauses in a series	Jefferson, Franklin, and Washington were three signers of the Declaration of Independence.
c. between coordinate modifiers	Sally is a shrewd, witty person.
d. to set off parenthetical expressions, interjections, and conjunctive adverbs	We might, in fact, go to the beach tomorrow.
	Oh, what a good idea!
	We spent all our money yesterday; consequently, we will stay home today.
e. to set off direct quotations	"My vacation," said Jana, "was great."
f. to set off long introductory prepositional phrases	From their hammocks in the trees, the hunters watched the boars.

Rule of Thumb: Use a comma after a short introductory prepositional phrase only if the sentence would be misleading without it.

Rule	Example
g. to set off nonessential words, clauses, and phrases, such as	
—adverbial clauses	Because I'm going to Mexico this summer, I need to work on my Spanish.
—adjective clauses	Alejo Carpentier, who wrote *The Lost Steps*, was born in Havana in 1904.
—participles and participial phrases	Joe, laughing, showed me the comic strip. Dashing along the sidewalk, I caught the bus.
—infinitive phrases	I didn't like that film very much, to tell the truth.
—prepositional phrases	The novel, from beginning to end, bored and depressed me.
—appositives and appositive phrases	Maxine Hong Kingston, an author and university lecturer, won the National Book Award for *China Men*.

> **Rule of Thumb:** Nonessential elements can be removed without changing the meaning of the sentence.

Rule	Example
h. to set off an antithetical phrase	Daffodils, not crocuses, are my favorite flowers.
i. to set off a title after a person's name	Angela López, Ph.D. Lou Wright, Chairman of the Board
j. to separate the various parts of an address, a geographical term, or a date	Bend, Oregon Monday, June 14 May 3, 1999 Stanford, KY 40484
k. after the salutation of an informal letter and after the closing of all letters	Dear Marie, Yours truly,
l. to set off parts of a reference that direct the reader to the exact source	That is from Rudolfo Anaya's *Tortuga*, page 212.
m. to set off words or names used in direct address and in tag questions	Gerald, did you bring the thermos? You remember his name, don't you?

Rule	Example
Use a **dash** to signal a change in thought or to emphasize a parenthetical comment.	Julie was unhappy—actually she was devastated—when she lost her new bracelet. Izanami's voice was cheerful—more like it had been in happier days.

> **Rule of Thumb:** A good test of the correct use of dashes is to delete the information that the dashes set off. If the remaining sentence retains its basic meaning, then the dashes were properly used. If the remaining sentence has lost crucial information, then the dashes were improperly used.

Rule	Example
Use **parentheses** to set off supplemental material. Punctuate within the parentheses only if the punctuation is part of the parenthetical expression.	The Maya (who lived in Mexico and Central America) built remarkable stone structures. The Maya built remarkable stone structures. (They lived in Mexico and Central America.) We crept along the hallway (why were we so afraid?) until we reached the door at the end.
Use **quotation marks:** **a.** to enclose a direct quotation, as follows:	Secretary of State Madeleine Albright called her job "a great privilege."
When a quotation is interrupted, use two sets of quotation marks.	"One difference was apparent from the outset," a World War II news analyst said of radio. "It was the first time the peoples of the world could hear a war actually breaking out."
Use single quotation marks for a quotation within a quotation.	Ursula Le Guin wrote, "'Happens all the time,' says Coyote. 'That's what myths do. They happen all the time.'"
In writing dialogue, begin a new paragraph and use a new set of quotation marks every time the speaker changes.	"How about luncheon tomorrow?" "I'm afraid that's impossible." "How about dinner tomorrow evening?"
b. to enclose titles of short works, such as stories, poems, essays, articles, chapters, and songs	"Why I Live at the P.O." is a story by Eudora Welty.

Rule	Example
c. to enclose unfamiliar slang terms and unusual expressions	"Fuzzy logic" is a term applied to certain mathematical processes.

> **Rule of Thumb:** A good way to tell whether question marks and exclamation points go inside or outside quotation marks is to take the direct quotation out of the sentence and see how it would be punctuated if it stood alone. If it would end with a question mark or exclamation point, then that mark of punctuation should go within the quotation marks. If the new sentence would end with a period, then the question mark or exclamation point should go outside the quotation marks.

Rule	Example
Use italics: **a.** for titles of books, lengthy poems, plays, films, television series, paintings and sculptures, long musical compositions, court cases, names of newspapers and magazines, ships, trains, airplanes, and spacecraft (Italicize and capitalize *a, an,* and *the* at the beginning of a title only when they are part of the title.)	*Star Wars* [film]; *Under Milk Wood* [play] *Man at the Crossroads* [painting] *Discover* [magazine] *Apollo 13* [spacecraft] *Air Force One* [airplane] *The Lost Steps* [book] the *Los Angeles Times* [newspaper]
b. for foreign words and expressions that are not used frequently in English	He came up with the perfect word, the *mot juste.*
c. for words, letters, and numerals used to represent themselves	In that sentence, use *adapt,* not *adopt.* There is no *6* in this list.
Use an apostrophe: **a.** for a possessive form, as follows: Add an apostrophe and *-s* to all singular indefinite pronouns, singular nouns, plural nouns not ending in *-s,* and compound nouns. Add only an apostrophe to a plural noun that ends in *-s.* If two or more persons possess something jointly, use the possessive form for the last person named. If they possess it individually, use the possessive form for each one's name.	someone's jacket; California's coastline; the women's books; the boss's desk my brother-in-law's computer; the Chief of Police's office; the race car driver's accident the waves' continuous motion Penn and Teller's magic act Romeo and Juliet's problem Picasso's and Braque's cubist paintings Ford's and Chrysler's minivans

Rule	Example
b. to express amounts of money or time that modify a noun	twenty dollars' worth; one day's vacation (You can use a hyphenated adjective instead: a one-day vacation.)
c. in place of omitted letters or numerals	it's [it is, it has] the floods of '97
d. to form the plural of letters, numerals, symbols, and words used to represent themselves (use an apostrophe and -*s*)	9's *x*'s and *y*'s #'s
Use a **hyphen**: **a.** after any prefix joined to a proper noun or proper adjective	mid-Atlantic post-Impressionist
b. after the prefixes *all-*, *ex-*, and *self-* joined to any noun or adjective; after the prefix *anti-* when it joins a word beginning with *i*; after the prefix *vice-* (except in *vice president*); and to avoid confusion between words that begin with *re-* and look like another word	ex-teammate self-taught anti-imperialist vice-principal re-view the picture review the book re-lay the flooring relay the message

> **Rule of Thumb:** Remember that the prefix *anti-* requires a hyphen when followed by a word that begins with *i* in order to prevent spelling words with two successive *i*'s. Otherwise, *anti* does not require a hyphen except before a capitalized word.

Rule	Example
c. in a compound adjective that precedes a noun	a five-year-old car her mud-encrusted boat
d. in any spelled-out cardinal or ordinal numbers up to *ninety-nine* or *ninety-ninth* and with a fraction used as an adjective	fifty-six seventy-first three-quarters majority
e. to divide a word at the end of a line between syllables	com-plete hang-man big-gest search-ing

Abbreviations

This section will help you learn how to use abbreviations, which are shortened forms of words.

Rule	Example
Use only one period if an abbreviation occurs at the end of a sentence. If the sentence ends with a question mark or exclamation point, use the period and the second mark of punctuation.	I called Terika Harvey, M.D. Have you ever been outside the U.S.A.? This temple was built around 1000 B.C.!
Capitalize abbreviations of proper nouns and abbreviations related to historical dates.	Edward R. Murrow · · · · · First Ave. 1000 B.C. · · · A.D. 502 · · · C.E. 502
Use all capital letters and no periods for abbreviations that are pronounced letter by letter or as words.	NAFTA · · · FBI · · · NATO YWCA · · · NAACP · · · NBA UN · · · CIA · · · AFL-CIO
When addressing mail, use the U.S. Post Office abbreviations (two capital letters, no periods).	AK (Alaska) · · · CT (Connecticut) HI (Hawaii) · · · ME (Maine) MA (Massachusetts) · · · TX (Texas)

> **Rule of Thumb:** In a letter it is appropriate to use a state abbreviation in the address. In other forms of writing, such as expository writing, spell out the name of a state.

Rule	Example
Use abbreviations for some personal titles.	Ms. Goodwin; Gen. Anderson; Dr. Julia Marshall
Abbreviate units of measure used with numerals in technical or scientific writing, but not in ordinary prose. Use a period after an abbreviation of an English unit of measure, but not after a metric unit.	ft. (foot) · · · g (gram) gal. (gallon) · · · m (meter) in. (inch) · · · mm (millimeter)

Numbers and Numerals

This section will help you understand when to use numerals and when to spell out numbers.

Rule	Example
In general, spell out cardinal and ordinal numbers that can be written in one or two words.	More than three thousand people came to the lecture by physicist Stephen Hawking.
Spell out any number that occurs at the beginning of a sentence.	Two hundred eighty-one books have been added to the library.
In general, use numerals (numbers expressed in figures) to express numbers that would be written in more than two words. Extremely large numbers are often expressed as a numeral followed by the word *million* or *billion*.	The library has recently added 281 new books to its collection. The department store chain had a first-quarter income of $32.3 million.
If related numbers appear in the same sentence, use all numerals.	Of the 124 hotels and motels in the resort area, more than 100 have their own restaurant.
Use numerals to express amounts of money, decimals, and percentages.	$2.53 21.5 students per class 0.6% 12 percent
Use numerals to express the year and day in a date and to express the precise time with the abbreviations *A.M.* and *P.M.*	Robert was born January 17, 1979. Yemane has a job interview on March 4 at 9:00 A.M.
Spell out a number to express a century when the word *century* is used, or a decade when the century is clear from the context. When a century and a decade are expressed as a single unit, use numerals followed by *-s.*	In the twentieth century many things changed, especially during the sixties. Some people look back upon the 1950s with nostalgia.
Use numerals for streets and avenues numbered above ten and for all house, apartment, and room numbers.	411 Eighth Avenue 310 West 72nd Street Room 205 Apartment 2H
Use numerals to express page, paragraph, stanza, and line numbers.	See page 325, paragraph 2, for that information. In stanza 4, lines 19, 21, and 23 rhyme.

Spelling

The following basic rules, examples, and exceptions will help you master the spelling of many words.

ie and *ei*

Many writers find the rules for certain combinations of letters, like *ie* and *ei*, difficult to remember. One helpful learning strategy is to develop a rhyme to remember a rule. Look at the following rhyme for the *ie* and *ei* rule.

Rule	Example
Put *i* before *e,* except after *c,* or when sounded like *a,* as in *neighbor* and *weigh.*	relief, thief, piece, brief receipt, deceit, perceive sleigh, deign, heir, rein, beige, vein

EXCEPTIONS: seize, leisure, weird, height, either, forfeit, protein, counterfeit, sleight.

-cede, -ceed, and -sede

Because various combinations of letters in English are sometimes pronounced the same way, it is often easy to make slight spelling errors. Except for the exceptions below, spell the *sēd* sound at the end of words as *cede:*

precede   accede   intercede

EXCEPTION: One word uses *-sede* to spell the final *sēd* sound: supersede.

EXCEPTION: Three words use *-ceed* to spell the final *sēd* sound: proceed, exceed, succeed.

Unstressed vowels

Notice the vowel sound in the second syllable of the word *or-i-gin.* This is the unstressed vowel sound; dictionary pronunciation spellings use the *schwa* symbol (ə) to indicate it. Because any of several vowels can be used to spell this sound, you might find yourself uncertain about which vowel to use. Try thinking of a related word in which the syllable containing the vowel sound is stressed.

Unknown Spelling	Related Word	Correct Spelling
dram_tize	dramatic	dramatize
rev_rence	revere	reverence
simil_r	similarity	similar
distr_bution	distribute	distribution

Adding prefixes

When adding a prefix to a word, keep the original spelling of the word. If the prefix forms a double letter, keep both letters.

dis + count = discount
ir + responsible = irresponsible
mis + spell = misspell

Suffixes and the silent e

Many English words end in a silent letter *e*. Sometimes the *e* is dropped when a suffix is added. When adding a suffix that begins with a consonant to a word that ends in silent *e,* keep the *e*.

hope + ful = hopeful
arrange + ment = arrangement

COMMON EXCEPTIONS: awe + ful = awful; judge + ment = judgment

When adding the suffix *-y* or a suffix that begins with a vowel to a word that ends in silent *e*, usually drop the *e*.

shade + y = shady
force + ible = forcible

COMMON EXCEPTION: mile + age = mileage

When adding a suffix that begins with *a* or *o* to a word that ends in *ce* or *ge,* keep the *e* so the word will retain the soft *c* or *g* sound.

peace + able = peaceable
manage + able = manageable
courage + ous = courageous

When adding a suffix that begins with a vowel to a word that ends in *ee* or *oe,* keep the *e*.

foresee + able = foreseeable
flee + ing = fleeing
tiptoe + ing = tiptoeing

Suffixes and the final y

When adding a suffix to a word that ends in a consonant + *y*, change the *y* to *i* unless the suffix begins with *i.* Keep the *y* in a word that ends in a vowel + *y.*

try + ed = tried	fry + ed = fried
stay + ing = staying	display + ed = displayed
copy + ing = copying	joy + ous = joyous

Doubling the final consonant

When adding a suffix to a word that ends in a consonant, double the final consonant if it is preceded by a single vowel and the word is one syllable, if the accent is on the last syllable and remains there even after the suffix is added, or if the word is made up of a prefix and a one-syllable word.

shop + ing = shopping	stop + age = stoppage
compel + ing = compelling	concur + ent = concurrent
misstep + ed = misstepped	reset + ing = resetting

Do not double the final consonant if the accent is not on the last syllable or if the accent shifts when the suffix is added. Also do not double the final consonant if it is preceded by two vowels or by another consonant. If the word ends in a consonant and the suffix begins with a consonant, do not double the final consonant.

develop + ing = developing	travel + ing = traveling
swoop + ing = swooping	rain + ing = raining
remind + ed = reminded	faith + ful = faithful

Adding *-ly* and *-ness*

When adding *-ly* to a word that ends in a single *l*, keep the *l*, but when the word ends in a double *l*, drop one *l*. When adding *-ness* to a word that ends in *n*, keep the *n*.

ideal + ly = ideally	real + ly = really
full + ly = fully	dull + ly = dully
mean + ness = meanness	keen + ness = keenness

Forming compound words

When joining a word that ends in a consonant to a word that begins with a consonant, keep both consonants.

rain + fall = rainfall	year + book = yearbook
key + board = keyboard	stair + case = staircase

Forming plurals

English words form plurals in many ways. Most nouns simply add -s. The following chart shows other ways of forming plural nouns and some common exceptions to the pattern.

GENERAL RULES FOR FORMING PLURALS		
If a noun ends in	**Rule**	**Example**
ch, s, sh, x, z	add -es	church, churches
a consonant + y	change y to i and add -es	baby, babies
o or a vowel + y	add only -s	radio, radios day, days
a consonant + o common exceptions	generally add -es but sometimes add only -s	tomato, tomatoes halo, halos
f or ff common exceptions	add -s change f to v and add -es	reef, reefs; riff, riffs leaf, leaves
lf	change f to v and add -es	shelf, shelves
fe	change f to v and add -s	life, lives

A few plurals are exceptions to the rules in the previous chart, but they are easy to remember. The following chart lists these plurals and some examples.

SPECIAL RULES FOR FORMING PLURALS	
Rule	**Example**
To form the plural of proper names and one-word compound nouns, follow the general rules for plurals.	López, Lópezes Farraday, Farradays newspaper, newspapers
To form the plural of hyphenated compound nouns or compound nouns of more than one word, make the most important word plural.	father-in-law, fathers-in-law oil well, oil wells attorney general, attorneys general
Some nouns have unusual plural forms.	woman, women mouse, mice ox, oxen
Some nouns have the same singular and plural forms.	sheep deer series

Writing Handbook

The Writing Process

The writing process consists of five stages that take you from choosing a topic to presenting a finished piece of writing. These stages are *prewriting, drafting, revising, editing/proofreading,* and *publishing/presenting.* You do not need to follow them in a strict order but can move back and forth among them as your ideas develop. For example, before revising your first draft, you might present it to a friend in order to get feedback; or you might go back to prewriting in order to rethink your topic or gather more information.

The Writing Process

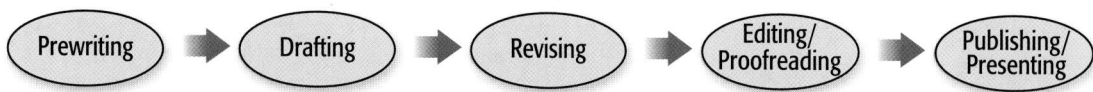

Prewriting

In the prewriting stage, you explore topic ideas, choose a topic, gather information, and begin to organize your material.

Exploring ideas

Ask yourself the following questions before you begin exploring topic ideas.

- What is my general purpose? Am I writing to fulfill an assignment? Am I writing for a personal reason?
- What audience do I have in mind? My teacher? My classmates? Younger children? The general public?
- What do my purpose and audience determine about the length of my paper? the kinds of topics that are appropriate? the tone and language of my writing (formal or informal; serious or light; objective or personal)?

Once you have given some thought to these questions, the following techniques can help you find a topic to write about.

- Scan your memory for interesting, funny, or moving personal experiences.
- Flip through a variety of magazines and newspapers.
- Browse through a library catalog.
- Brainstorm for topics with a group of classmates.

Choosing a topic

When you have several possible topics in mind, ask yourself these questions about each one.

- Is this a topic that I am interested in?
- Does it fulfill my assignment or my own purpose for writing?
- Is it appropriate for the length of paper I plan to write? Would I need to narrow or broaden this topic?
- Do I know enough about this topic, or can I find enough information?

Gathering information

How you gather your information will depend upon the kind of paper you are writing.

If you are writing a personal essay, all of the information may come from your own experiences and feelings. Try one or both of the following techniques.

- Freewriting Set a time limit of ten minutes, and write down everything that comes to mind on your topic. You might want to list your thoughts and images under general headings or make a cluster diagram.
- Discussion Talk about your topic with one or more people. Take notes on your ideas as they come to you. Encourage your listeners to ask you questions.

If you are writing a report or a persuasive essay, you will probably need to locate pertinent factual information and take notes on it. You may consult library resources, such as books, magazines, and newspapers, as well as the Internet and other on-line resources. You may also choose to interview people with experience or specialized knowledge related to your topic. (See Research Paper Writing, pp. R64–R69.)

Organizing your material

Determine the main points, subtopics, or events you will be writing about, and choose a general order in which to present them.

Sometimes the best order will be self-evident. For example, a biography usually calls for chronological order, and a description of a place may lend itself to spatial order, such as from near to far or from low to high. For other kinds of writing, such as science reports, you may need to experiment to find the best order.

After deciding on the general order, make a rough outline. It can be as simple as a list, or include headings and subheadings.

WRITING HANDBOOK 🦢 R59

Drafting

In the drafting stage, use your notes and outline to write a rough version of your paper. Drafting is an opportunity to explore and develop your ideas.

Tips for drafting

- You might want to write your draft very quickly, capturing the rapid flow of your ideas; or you might wish to work more slowly, rethinking and revising as you write. Choose the approach that works better for you.
- Whether you work quickly or slowly, don't focus on details. Concentrate on developing the main ideas. At this stage, just circle or annotate minor points that need more work.
- Keep your purpose in mind, and use your outline as a general guideline. At the same time, try to stay flexible. If part of your outline doesn't work, omit it. If better ideas occur to you as you write, feel free to change your direction.

Revising

After you have finished your first draft, set it aside for a while. Then reread it, and look for ways to improve and refine it. This is the point at which peer review can be most helpful.

Using peer review

Ask one or more of your classmates to read your draft. Here are some specific ways in which you can direct their responses.

- Have readers tell you in their own words what they have read. If you do not hear your ideas restated, you will want to revise for clarity.
- Ask readers to tell you what parts of your writing they liked best and why. You may want to expand those elements when you revise.
- Discuss the ideas in your writing with your readers. Have them share their own ideas about the topic. Include in your revision any new insights you gain.
- Ask readers for their suggestions in specific areas, such as organization, word choice, or examples.

You may want to take notes on your readers' suggestions so you will have a handy reference as you revise. Finally, weigh your peer responses carefully. Compare them with your own insights. Use what is most helpful to write the revised draft.

Editing/Proofreading

In the editing stage, you polish your revised draft and proofread it for errors in grammar and spelling. Use this proofreading checklist to help you check for errors, and use the proofreading symbols in the chart below to mark places that need corrections.

☑ Have I avoided run-on sentences and sentence fragments and punctuated sentences correctly?

☑ Have I used every word correctly, including plurals, possessives, and frequently confused words?

☑ Do verbs and subjects agree? Are verb tenses correct?

☑ Do pronouns refer clearly to their antecedents and agree with them in person, number, and gender?

☑ Have I used adverb and adjective forms and modifying phrases correctly?

☑ Have I spelled every word correctly, and checked the unfamiliar ones in a dictionary?

Proofreading Symbols

⊙	Lieut⊙Brown	Insert a period.
∧	No one came ∧the party. (to)	Insert a letter or a word.
≡	I enjoyed p≡aris.	Capitalize a letter.
/	The Ⅽ/lass ran a bake sale.	Make a capital letter lowercase.
⌢	The campers are home⌢sick.	Close up a space.
㉟	They visited Ⓝ.Ⓨ. ㉟	Spell out.
∧ ∧̣	Sue∧please come∧̣I need your help.	Insert a comma or a semicolon.
∩	He enjoyed f∩eild day.	Transpose the position of letters or words.
#	all#together	Insert a space.
⌿	We went t⌿o to Boston.	Delete letters or words.
ⱽ ⱽ ⱽ	She asked,ⱽWho's coming?ⱽ	Insert quotation marks or an apostrophe.
/=/	mid/=/January	Insert a hyphen.
¶	"Where?" asked Karl.¶"Over there," said Ray.	Begin a new paragraph.

Publishing/Presenting

There are a number of ways you can share your work. You could publish it in a magazine, a class anthology, or another publication, or read your writing aloud to a group. You could also join a writer's group and read one another's works.

Writing Modes

Writing may be classified as expository, descriptive, narrative, or persuasive. Each of these classifications, or modes, has its own purpose.

Expository Writing

Expository writing explains and compares. There are six types of expository writing. The kind of essay you write depends on your goal.

As you write an expository piece, use the checklist shown here as a guide.

☑ Does my opening contain attention-grabbing details or intriguing questions to hook the reader?

☑ Are my explanations complete, clear, and accurate?

☑ Have I presented information in a logical order?

☑ Have I included specific, relevant details?

☑ Have I defined any unfamiliar terms and concepts?

☑ Have I made comparisons clear and logical?

☑ Have I used language and details appropriate for my intended audience?

Type	Definition	Example
Process explanation	Explains how something happens, works, or is done, using step-by-step organization	How the human brain stores memories
Cause and effect	Identifies the causes and/or effects of something and examines the relationship between causes and effects	Causes of skin cancer
Comparison and contrast	Examines similarities and differences to find relationships and draw conclusions	The safety features of U.S. cars compared with those of imported models
Definition	Explains a term or concept by listing and examining its qualities and characteristics	The "Trail of Tears"
Classification	Organizes subjects into categories and examines the qualities or characteristics of those categories	Kinds of snakes native to this area
Problem and solution	Examines aspects of a complex problem and explores or proposes possible solutions	Providing community-wide access to parks and playgrounds

Descriptive Writing

Good descriptive writing creates word pictures of people, places, things, and experiences. It includes carefully chosen details that appeal to the reader's senses. Descriptive passages are a part of many kinds of writing, including novels, short stories, informative essays, biographies, poems, and persuasive speeches.

Use this checklist when you write a descriptive passage.

- ☑ Did I use an introduction that grabbed the reader?
- ☑ Were the images I used clear and striking?
- ☑ Did I organize details carefully and consistently?
- ☑ Did I use exact, energetic verbs to enliven my description?
- ☑ Did I write from a vantage point that makes sense?
- ☑ Have I used precise, vivid word choices?
- ☑ Have I created a strong, unified impression?

Narrative Writing

A narrative, whether fictional or nonfictional, tells a story. Narratives include novels and short stories as well as biographies, memoirs, narrative poems, and histories. Narratives typically include a setting, characters, and a plot, which revolves around a conflict of some sort.

As you write your narrative, use this checklist as a guide.

- ☑ Did I introduce characters, setting, plot, and conflict?
- ☑ Did I include descriptions and dialogue appropriate for the characters—whether fictional or nonfictional?
- ☑ Did I present a clear and consistent point of view?
- ☑ Is the conflict or complication interesting to my audience?
- ☑ Did I use mood, foreshadowing, or dialogue to move the story along?
- ☑ Is the writing vivid and expressive?
- ☑ Did I end in a way that satisfies my audience?

Persuasive Writing

Persuasive writing expresses a writer's opinion and tries to make readers agree with it, change their own opinion, and perhaps even take action. Effective persuasive writing uses strong, reliable evidence to support the claims. Persuasive writing is used in newspaper editorials, letters of complaint, advertisements, product evaluations, and many other applications.

This checklist offers a guide for writing a persuasive piece.

- ☑ Is my position stated in a clear thesis statement?
- ☑ Is the supporting evidence convincing?
- ☑ Have I anticipated and responded to opposing viewpoints?
- ☑ Are my facts and opinions relevant and credible?
- ☑ Does the conclusion relate to the evidence?
- ☑ Is the tone appropriate?
- ☑ Have I used strong, specific words to support my argument?
- ☑ Did I end with a strong call to action?

Research Paper Writing

A research paper presents the findings and conclusions of an inquiry into primary and secondary sources. Unlike personal essays in which you present your own thoughts and feelings, a research paper requires that you go beyond personal experience to search for facts, gather data, and evaluate evidence in order to draw a conclusion.

Types of Research Papers

Research papers can take many forms. Some of the most common approaches to writing a research paper are listed below. In some cases you might combine approaches, perhaps by evaluating the research of others and then conducting original research.

- A **summary** explores a topic by summing up the opinions of other writers. The author of the paper does not express an opinion about the subject.
- An **evaluative paper** states an opinion and backs it up with evidence found in primary and secondary sources.
- An **original paper** involves research that leads to new insights or information about the topic.

Making a plan

- Schedule ample time for your research. A good research paper can't be written in a weekend. Sketch out a schedule that allows several weeks for the completion of your paper.
- Select a general topic that interests and motivates you.
- Do some preliminary research to build background and identify available resources.
- To set a clear path for research, generate three to seven research questions to answer first. In trying to answer these questions, you will discover other questions. Let your central idea guide you in selecting questions—the answers will emerge later in the course of your research.
- Refine and/or focus the topic as appropriate.
- Examine the topic. Look at the material from various points of view. Don't worry if some angles lead to dead ends. At this point just try to think critically about the topic from several perspectives.

Choosing and evaluating sources

Kinds of sources There are two kinds of sources—primary and secondary.

A **primary source** is a firsthand account of an event—an account by someone who has actually experienced or observed the event—for example, the slave narrative written by Olaudah Equiano.

A **secondary source** is one written by a person who has done extensive research on the topic and who has interpreted primary sources. Although most sources on a topic will be secondary, make use of primary sources when they are available.

Criteria for evaluation Examine sources critically. As you search for sources, select those that are authoritative and timely.

- Choose those authors who have written widely on a subject and whose work in their field is recognized.
- Use articles from well-respected newspapers or scholarly journals; do not use material from popular magazines unless it can be verified in another source.
- Try to find the most recently published information on your topic.
- Be especially careful in evaluating on-line sources. Anyone can create a Web site; therefore, the information found in such a source is not always reliable. Before using information from on-line sources, apply the criteria identified for print materials.

Because every source you use is written by a person with particular interests, knowledge, and values, be alert to the author's perspective. Try to get sources that approach your topic from various points of view.

Preparing a working bibliography

A working bibliography is a record of the books, articles, and other sources you will consult for your paper. For each source you find, follow these steps:

1. Skim it to see if it has any useful information. Also look at tables of contents, indexes, chapter titles, and graphic aids to efficiently locate information.
2. If it does, record on an index card all the information needed for compiling the list of works. Be sure to include the author's name and the title.
3. Number your cards in the upper right-hand corner so you can keep them in order. You can also write yourself notes on the cards.

See the sample cards below for a book, a magazine, and an on-line article.

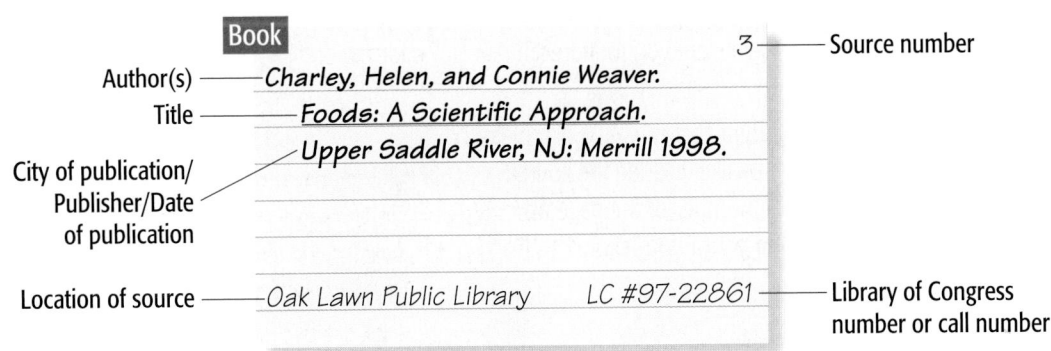

Book   3 — Source number
Author(s) —— *Charley, Helen, and Connie Weaver.*
Title —— *Foods: A Scientific Approach.*
City of publication/ *Upper Saddle River, NJ: Merrill 1998.*
Publisher/Date
of publication

Location of source —— *Oak Lawn Public Library*   *LC #97-22861* — Library of Congress number or call number

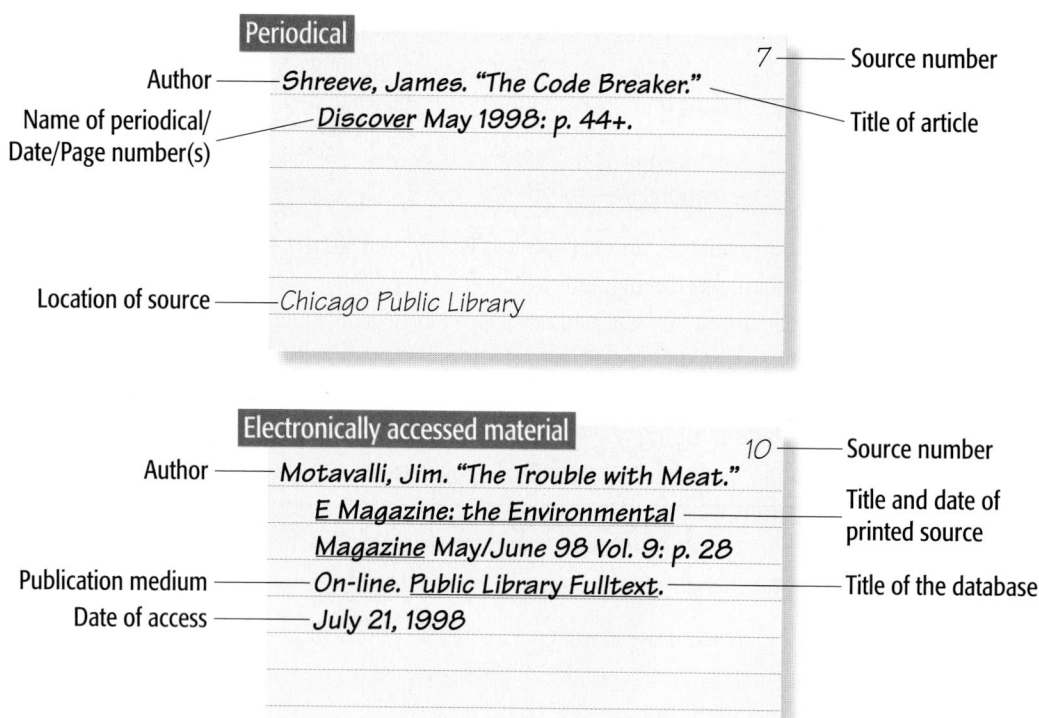

Periodical

Author — Shreeve, James. "The Code Breaker." — 7 — Source number

Name of periodical/ — *Discover* May 1998: p. 44+. — Title of article
Date/Page number(s)

Location of source — *Chicago Public Library*

Electronically accessed material

Author — Motavalli, Jim. "The Trouble with Meat." — 10 — Source number

E Magazine: the Environmental — Title and date of
Magazine May/June 98 Vol. 9: p. 28 — printed source

Publication medium — On-line. *Public Library Fulltext.* — Title of the database
Date of access — July 21, 1998

Taking careful notes

Use index cards when you take notes, and follow these guidelines:

- As you find information that you can use, note it on a card.
- In the upper right-hand corner of the note card, write the number of the source from the working bibliography.
- Place any exact words from the source in quotation marks.
- If you jot your own thoughts down on note cards, initial them so you can distinguish your own opinions from those that come from other sources.

> **Important** Avoid plagiarism. Plagiarism is using someone else's ideas or statements and presenting them as your own. Even when unintentional, plagiarism is a serious offense. Keep clearly documented notes so you know where you found each piece of information.

The card at the right shows what a completed note card will look like. Include the source number and the number of the page on which you found your information.

10

E. coli bacteria have become more widespread in the past thirty years. Eating infected food can result in hemolytic uremic syndrome (HUS), a condition that is life threatening.
"Meat-borne pathogens like Salmonella entenditis can be traced to 'factory farms.'"
p. 29

Developing an outline

Organize your note cards to develop a working outline.

- As you take notes, look for ways to classify the facts and ideas you find. For example, look for similar features, such as two facts about the role of an individual in a historical event, or two causes of the same effect.
- Begin to group the note cards as you classify them. As you make decisions on how to organize your cards, you are developing the headings you need to write a working outline.
- If some cards do not fit with any others, set them aside. Later you can decide whether to keep or discard them.

The following partial outline is based on chronological development. Note that in an outline, you cannot have a single subheading. If you have a *I*, you must have a *II*; if you have an *A*, you must have a *B*, and so on.

Sample Outline

Women in the Workplace

I. Prior to World War II

   A. Factors limiting women's employment outside the home

   B. Types of jobs assigned to women

   C. Percentage of women in the work force

II. From 1945 to 1975

   A. Factors promoting women's employment outside the home

   B. Continuing limitations

      1. Gender-specific job titles (secretary vs. executive assistant)

      2. Salary discrepancies for identical work by men and women

Writing a thesis statement

- To develop a thesis statement, rewrite your central idea into a concise, tightly focused sentence that describes your topic and your approach to it. Even though this thesis statement may change slightly in later stages of your writing process, it will provide a clear direction for your writing.
- The kind of thesis statement you use will depend upon the type of paper you write: summary, evaluative, original, or a combination of two or more types.

After you have made an outline and written a thesis statement, you are ready to proceed with drafting. As you draft your paper, be sure to document the information you include.

Documenting sources

The information in your research paper must be properly documented. By citing your sources accurately, you acknowledge those people whose ideas you are using. You do not have to cite the source of common knowledge, such as that the Andes are in South America or that the Magna Carta was signed in 1215. Widely known proverbs, famous quotations, and simple definitions are also considered common knowledge.

In-text citations The Modern Language Association (MLA) recommends using citations in the text of your writing that refer readers to a list of works cited at the end of the paper. The citation should appear at the end of the quotation or other material. The chart below shows the MLA style of documenting various sources.

Type of Source	Citation Style
Author named in text "According to M. Harte, . . ."	Page number in parentheses (52)
Author not named in text	Author's last name and page number in parentheses (Coogan 322)
More than one author is cited	Name all in text or authors' names and page number in parentheses (Lee, Sanford, Berlig 234)
No author listed	Title and page number in parentheses ("Lively Bacteria" 64)
More than one work in list by same author	Include words from title in reference (Sutford "Planetary Threat")
Quotation from another work	Use "qtd. in" (qtd. in Coogan 320)
Work from anthology	Cite author, not anthology editor
Novels; plays; poems	Page and chapter (43, ch. 8); part and line number (2:12–14); act and scene plus line number, if applicable (3.2:11–18)
Multivolume work	Include volume number (Durand 2:167)

Note: For material accessed on CD-ROM or on-line databases, follow the style of in-text references for print materials. See below for the style of their inclusion in works cited.

Compiling a list of works cited

At the end of your text, provide an alphabetized list of works cited.

- Include complete publishing information for each source.
- Cite only those sources from which you actually used information.
- Arrange entries in alphabetical order according to the author's (or editor's) last name. Write the last name first.
- If an entry runs more than one line, indent five spaces every line after the first.

BIBLIOGRAPHY

One author ——— Barber, Elizabeth Wayland. *Women's Work: The First 20,000 Years.* — Book
New York: W. W. Norton, 1995.

Bolz, Diane M. "Women and Flight." *Smithsonian* July 1997: 90+. — Magazine

Two or more authors ——— Brown, Clair, and Joseph A. Pechman. *Gender in the Workplace.* — Reverse only the first author's name.
Washington, D.C.: Brookings Institution, 1987.

No author given ——— "UN Committee on Elimination of Discrimination Against Women." — Alphabetize by title, disregarding the word *a, an,* or *the* at the beginning of a title.
M2Presswire. elibrary 10 Feb 1998.

More than one work by an author ——— Ware, Susan. *Letter to the World: Seven Women Who Shaped the American Century.* New York: Norton, 1998.

———. *Modern American Women: A Documentary History.* Belmont, — Use three hyphens followed by a period in place of the author's last name.
California: Wadsworth, 1988.

On-line database ——— "Women in History Timeline." *L'eggs.* On-line. Infoseek. 20 Aug 1998. — Include title of database, publication medium, computer service, and date of access.

Note: Titles of books and magazines are in italic type or underlined; titles of articles are placed in quotation marks.

Preparing a manuscript

Follow the guidelines of the Modern Language Association when you prepare the final copy of your research paper.

- Heading On separate lines in the upper left-hand corner of the first page, include your name, your teacher's name, the course name, and the date.
- Title Center the title on the line below the heading.
- Numbering Number the pages one-half inch from the top of the page in the right-hand corner. Write your last name before each page number after the first page.
- Spacing Use double-spacing throughout.
- Margins Leave one-inch margins on all sides of every page.

Business and Technical Writing

Business and technical writing are kinds of expository writing that explain information and processes to people within various professions.

Business writing includes documents such as letters, memorandums, reports, briefs, proposals, and articles for business publications. Business writing must be clear, concise, accurate, and correct in usage.

Technical writing is expository writing that informs readers about specialized areas of science and technology, such as anthropology, biology, chemistry, computer science, engineering, electronics, and psychology. Technical writing is practical and objective, focusing on the technical content rather than on the author's perspective on the subject. Technical writing encompasses user guides and manuals, data sheets describing software or equipment, operator's manuals, business reports, and writing for newsletters in fields such as business, health, and science.

Writing a business letter

- Use proper business letter form.
- Whenever possible, address your letter to a specific person.
- Explain exactly what you are requesting in a businesslike tone.

The letter below illustrates the block form, a popular style for a business letter.

> Alan Shephard High School
> 123 Washington Way
> Oak Center, IL 60308
> August 27, 1999
>
> Carol Bosley
> TV Channel 2
> 1 Merchandise Mart
> Chicago, IL 60602
>
> Dear Ms. Bosley:
>
> On March 15, 2000, Alan Shephard High School will have its semiannual career day. We cordially invite you to address the students on the career of broadcast journalism.
>
> The program is scheduled for 2 P.M. We anticipate that you will speak for twenty to thirty minutes with an additional time for questions. We are inviting two other speakers in the areas of business and science. If the time conflicts with other commitments you may have, we will be happy to adjust our schedule.
>
> We would appreciate your prompt response to Dr. Harry Belding, Principal. The school phone number is 708-536-9887, or you may respond by E-mail to shephard@ilsch.edu.
>
> Yours truly,
>
> Peter Bianco

Sending a memo

A memo (memorandum) is a concise means of communicating information. A memo begins with a header that provides basic information, followed by the text of the message. It does not have a formal closing.

> TO: Cycle Club members
>
> FROM: Josie Brown
>
> SUBJECT: Parks and Recreation Department Activities
>
> DATE: June 4, 1998
>
> The Parks and Recreation Department is happy to announce the opening of a brand new trail for bicyclists. (See map at the bottom of this page.)

Writing a proposal

A proposal describes a project the writer wishes to undertake. It is presented to the person or persons responsible for making a decision in that area. For example, a proposal might be written to a school administrator suggesting a fundraising project or to a business manager about a change in procedures. A proposal includes an overview of the idea and the reasoning behind the plan.

> **Purpose:** To replace the old and unreliable sound system in the Roosevelt High School auditorium at an estimated cost of $2,000.
>
> **Proposal:** The Drama Club proposes a fundraising event: a readers theater production entitled *Shakespeare's Lovers*, to be presented on the small stage in the study hall.
>
> **Proposed Budget**
>
> *Expenditures*
>
> | | |
> |---|---|
> | Publicity: posters, mailings, etc. | $25 |
> | Programs (computer class) | NC |
> | Tickets | $20 |
> | Refreshments (parent donations) | NC |
>
> *Income*
>
> | | |
> |---|---|
> | Ticket sales (200 at $5) | $1000 |
> | Program ads | $300 |
>
> *Net proceeds* $1255
>
> *Schedule*
>
> | | |
> |---|---|
> | Approval of proposal | March 16 |
> | Preparation of program | March 17–April 12 |
> | Publicity campaign kickoff, ticket order | March 20 |
> | Performance dates | April 13, 14, 15 |

Communications Skills Handbook

Using Electronic Resources

Computers and computer networks are changing the ways in which people gather information. If you have access to a personal computer at home or in school, you can find information in two ways—through CD-ROMs or through the Internet.

CD-ROM

CD-ROMs (compact disc-read-only memory), which store a variety of information, can be purchased in stores or through mail-order catalogs. CD-ROMs may include sound, photographs, and video, as well as text. Types of information available in this form include the following:

- general reference books—encyclopedias, almanacs, histories
- literature collections and biographies
- news reports from various sources
- back issues of magazines

The Internet

The Internet is, as its name implies, an extensive network that links computers. To access the Internet, you must purchase the services of an Internet service provider. Many Internet service providers are available.

The Internet gives you access to a wealth of information from universities, news organizations, researchers, government organizations, institutions, and individual experts in various fields. It also enables you to visit Web sites created by people who may or may not offer legitimate information and/or useful opinions.

Browsing the Web When you browse the Web, you search electronically for World Wide Web sites related to a particular subject.

Using a search engine Although you can browse the Web at large, you can narrow your search for selected information by using a search engine. When you select a specific search engine, it will identify a list of subject areas from which to choose.

Evaluating a Web site Consider the source of the material you locate when deciding whether the information on a Web site is reliable. Although many sites are maintained by educational institutions and other authorities, anyone can create a Web site and post information—or misinformation—on it. To evaluate a Web site, ask yourself these questions:

- Do I recognize the name of the author?
- Is the site associated with a well-known university or other reputable organization?
- Can the information be substantiated in another source?
- Is the writer citing a fact or offering an opinion?

Terms to know

On-line information services are commercial services that provide many resources: chat forums; bulletin boards; databases; publications; reference materials; news, weather, and sports; and E-mail and Internet access.

The World Wide Web (WWW) is a global system that uses the Internet. It allows a user to create and link fields of information, to retrieve related documents, and to access the data in any order.

Downloading is using a computer modem to transfer a copy of a file from a distant computer to your computer.

A **Web site** is a group of one or more related Web pages that are accessible on the Internet. A **Web page** is a file that contains the information you view when you access a Web site. When you search the World Wide Web, you use a **Web browser** to access Web sites that carry the information you are searching for.

Computerized Library Resources

Electronic research is often faster than traditional methods and allows access to a wide spectrum of material. It has become an essential research tool. Public libraries, as well as school and university libraries, offer a variety of ways to do research electronically.

Catalogs Most libraries have computerized catalogs. By typing in a title or an author's name, you can find out if the library has the book, how many copies are in the library's collection, if the book is currently available, and if not, when it will be returned. In large library systems, the computer also provides the name of other libraries from which the desired book is available.

Electronic databases Your library may provide access to electronic databases through on-line information services. These databases are being continually updated. One helpful database available in many libraries is InfoTrac®, which provides an index and abstracts—short summaries—of articles from many periodicals. Other magazine indexes, some of which contain the full text of selected articles, may also be available.

Some libraries have an extensive collection of CD-ROMs. Ask the librarian what is available at your library and how to access the information.

Study and Test-Taking Skills

Study Skills

Taking notes and budgeting study time are essential skills for success as a student.

Taking notes in class

Keeping notes on classroom lectures and teachers' directions gives you a written record of important information. Here are some tips for note taking.

- Use loose-leaf paper if possible, so you can easily add and remove pages from your notebook. Use a different notebook for each subject to help organize your notes, and use a fresh page for every class. Write the name of the class and the date at the top of the page.
- Listen carefully for the main ideas, and record them in your own words. Do not try to write down every word. Also, be alert for signal words and phrases such as *most importantly, remember this,* and *to summarize.*
- Spend at least twice as much time listening as writing. Don't risk missing an important point while writing.
- Leave space around your notes to add more information later. Try leaving a wide left-hand margin to write in key points or an informal outline.
- As soon as possible after class, reread your notes and fill in any missing information while it is fresh in your mind. Exchange notes with a peer and jot down any key points he or she has that you may have missed.
- Take notes on your reading assignments. Your textbook can provide a framework for understanding the material presented by your teacher. Try using the text's headings and subheadings to create a basic outline.
- A good way to review your notes is to use them in an active way. Recopy or type your notes to help you commit the key points to memory.

Using study time wisely

- Study in the same place each day. Choose a place that is quiet and free from distractions.
- If discussion helps you to learn, try to find a study partner.
- Divide large assignments into smaller tasks.
- Make a monthly assignment calendar. Write down due dates, test dates, and notes about upcoming assignments so you can see at a glance what work you need to do and when, and so you can plan ahead for busy times.
- At the beginning of your study period, when your attention and energy are at their highest levels, work on the assignments you find hardest.
- Take a short break after completing each task. Stay alert by stretching, walking, or having a light snack.
- Review material before stopping. Even a short review will greatly increase the amount of material you are able to remember.

Preparing for Classroom Tests

This section will help you learn how to prepare for classroom tests.

Thinking ahead

Write down information about an upcoming test—when it will be given, what it will cover, and so on—so you can plan your study time effectively.

- Review your quizzes, homework assignments, class notes, and handouts. Look at end-of-chapter review questions in your textbook.
- Develop your own questions about main ideas and important details, and practice answering them.
- Make studying an active process. Rather than simply rereading your notes or a chapter, try summarizing the material or creating an outline, a list of characters, or a time line. Include details from your lecture notes and your reading so you will be able to see connections between them.
- Form study groups. Explaining information to a peer is one of the best ways to learn the material.
- Remember that students who are well rested and who eat a regular meal the morning of a test usually score higher than others.

Taking objective tests

Objective tests ask questions with specific, correct answers. Test time is usually limited, so use your time efficiently. First, read the directions carefully and ask questions if any are unclear. Then try to respond to each item on the test, starting with the easier ones. You can always come back to the more difficult ones later. Finally, try to save some time to review your test before turning it in.

Below are tips on answering specific kinds of objective test items.

- **Multiple-choice** Read all the answer choices provided before choosing one; even if the first one seems nearly correct, a later choice may be a better answer. Be cautious when choosing responses that contain absolute words such as *always, never, all,* or *none.* Since most generalizations have exceptions, absolute statements are often incorrect.
- **True/False** If *any* part of the item is false, the correct answer is "false."
- **Short-answer** Use complete sentences to help you write a clear response.
- **Fill-in** Restate fill-ins as regular questions to clarify what is being asked.
- **Matching** Note in the directions whether some responses can be used more than once or not used at all.

Taking subjective (essay) tests

Subjective tests typically require you to write an essay. Your grade is based more on how well you make your point than on whether you choose a correct answer.

When you receive the test, first read it through. Determine how much time to spend on each question. Then jot down ideas on scratch paper. Reread the question to make sure you are answering it. Develop a rough outline for your essay.

In the first paragraph, include a **thesis statement** that tells the main idea of your essay. Follow with paragraphs that provide **evidence** for your thesis. Give as much information as possible, including examples and illustrations where appropriate. Then finish with a **conclusion** that highlights the evidence you have provided and restates your thesis. If you have time left, **proofread** and neatly make corrections.

Preparing for Standardized Tests

Standardized tests are designed to be administered to very large groups of students, not just those in a particular class. Three of the most widely known standardized tests, all part of the college application process, are the ACT (American College Testing), the PSAT (Preliminary Scholastic Assessment Test), and the SAT (Scholastic Assessment Test). The strategies in this handbook refer specifically to the PSAT and SAT tests, but they also can apply to preparing for the ACT and other standardized tests.

The PSAT is generally administered to students in the 11th grade, though some schools offer it to students in the 10th grade as well. This test is designed to predict how well you will do on the SAT. For most students, the PSAT is simply a practice test. Those who perform exceptionally well on the 11th grade PSAT, however, will qualify for National Merit Scholarship competition.

The Scholastic Assessment Tests consist of the SAT-I: Reasoning Test and a variety of SAT-II: Subject Tests. The SAT-I is a three-hour test that evaluates your general verbal and mathematics skills. The SAT-II: Subject Tests are hour-long tests given in specific subjects and are designed to show specifically how much you have learned in a particular subject area.

Tips for taking standardized tests

- Skip difficult questions at first. Standardized tests are usually timed, so first answer items you know. You can return later to those you skipped.
- Mark only your answers on the answer sheet. Most standardized tests are scored by a computer, so stray marks can be read as incorrect answers.
- Frequently compare the question numbers on your test with those on your answer sheet to avoid putting answers in the wrong spaces.
- If time permits, check your answers. If you are not penalized for guessing, fill in answers for any items you might have skipped.

Preparing for the PSAT and the SAT-I

The verbal sections of the PSAT and SAT-I contain sentence completion items, reading comprehension questions, and analogies.

Sentence completion

Sentence completion items provide a sentence with one or two blanks and ask you to select the word or pair of words that best fits in the blank(s).

Start by reading the sentence and filling in your own word to replace the blank. Look for words that show how the word in the blank is related to the rest of the sentence–*and, but, since, therefore, although.* Then pick the word from the answer choices that is closest in meaning to your word. If you have trouble coming up with a specific word to fill in the blank, try to determine whether the word should be positive or negative. If you can eliminate even one answer choice, take a guess at the answer.

Reading comprehension

In Reading Comprehension, a series of questions follows each passage.

Read the passages quickly and spend your time working on the questions. You get points for answering questions correctly, not for reading passages thoroughly. Briefly summarize the passage. This will help you answer questions based on the passage as a whole. For specific questions based on details, return to the passage. Reading Comprehension is like an open-book test; you are expected to look at the passage while answering the questions. Finally, if you can eliminate even one answer choice, take a guess at the answer.

Analogies

Nearly half of the items on the verbal sections of the PSAT and SAT-I are designed to test your vocabulary. Therefore, the more words you know, the higher your score will be. Refer to pages R86–R87 of the **Reading Handbook** for information on how to build your vocabulary.

One type of vocabulary-based question is the analogy, which tests your ability to grasp the relationships between concepts. The best way to pinpoint the relationship is to connect the words in a simple sentence that defines one of the words. Some of the most common relationships seen on the PSAT and the SAT-I are shown below.

Relationship	Example
Cause and effect	heat : perspiration :: sadness : tears
A person to the normal action of that person	comedian : amuse :: journalist : write
An object to its normal function	telescope : magnify :: aircraft : fly
User to tool	teacher : book :: carpenter : hammer
Degree	terrified : frightened :: destitute : poor
Object to characteristic	water : wet :: brick : hard
Class to subclass (or subclass to class)	grain : rye :: music : rap

Reading Handbook

The Reading Process

Being an active reader is a very important part of being a lifelong learner. It is also an ongoing task. Good reading skills build on each other, overlap, and spiral around in much the same way that a winding staircase goes round and round while leading you to a higher place.

This handbook is designed to help you find and use the tools you'll need before, during, and after reading.

Vocabulary Development

Word identification and vocabulary skills are key building blocks in reading and in the comprehension process. By learning to use a variety of strategies to build your word skills and vocabulary, you will become a stronger reader.

Using context to determine meaning

The very best way to expand and extend your vocabulary is to read widely, listen carefully, and participate in a rich variety of discussions. When reading on your own, though, you can often figure out the meanings of new words by looking at their **context,** the other words and sentences that surround them. For example:

> *Contiguous* countries, such as the United States and Canada, usually have border patrols.

Although you may not know the meaning of *contiguous,* you can figure out from the phrase *such as the United States and Canada* that the word means "adjoining."

Tips for Using Context

• Look for clues such as
  –a synonym or an explanation of the unknown word in the sentence.
  *Elise's shop specialized in **millinery,** or **hats for women.***
  –a reference to what the word is or is not like.
  *An **archaeologist,** like a **historian,** deals with the past.*
  –a general topic associated with the word.
  *The **cooking** teacher discussed the best way to **braise** meat.*
  –a description or action associated with the word.
  *He used the **hoe** to **dig** up the garden.*
 • Predict a possible meaning.

- Determine whether the meaning makes sense in terms of the whole passage.
- Be aware the writer may be using
  - a word with **multiple meanings.**
    Some of the group will play games; others will attend a play.
  - **figurative language,** such as **similes,** which use *like* or *as* to compare two unlike things, and **metaphors,** which compare two unlike things without using *like* or *as.*
    The leaves rustled like silk as they drifted to the ground. (simile)
    The bullets of rain pelted the sidewalk. (metaphor)
  - **idioms,** expressions that have a meaning apart from the literal one.
    I'm just pulling your leg is an idiom used about joking with someone.

    Hint: If you come across an idiom with an unfamiliar meaning, look in the dictionary under the main word in the phrase. Many dictionaries list idioms after the definitions.
  - **technical vocabulary,** words that require an understanding of the specific terms of a specialized field.
    Be sure to clean your **mouse** *from time to time to make the* **cursor** *move smoothly.*

● For more on figurative language, see **Literary Terms Handbook,** p. R5.

Using word parts and word origins

Another way to determine the meaning of a word is to take the word itself apart. If you understand the meaning of the **base,** or **root,** part of a word and also know the meanings of key syllables added either to the beginning or end of the base word, you can usually figure out what the word means.

Word Part	Definition	Example
Base or root	the most basic part of a word	*voc* means "call" *Convoke* means "call together."
Prefix	a syllable placed before a base word to change or add to its meaning	*inter-* means "between" *Intervene* means "come between."
Suffix	a syllable placed after a base word to create a new meaning	*-less* means "without" *Hopeless* means without hope

Word origins Since Latin, Greek, and Anglo-Saxon roots are the basis for much of our English vocabulary, having some background in one of these languages can be a useful vocabulary tool. For example, *astronomy* comes from the Greek root *astro,* which means "relating to the stars." *Stellar* also has a meaning referring to stars, but its origin is Latin. Knowing root words in other languages can help you determine meanings, derivations, and spellings in English.

Using vocabulary references

Dictionaries A dictionary provides the meaning or meanings of a word. Look at the sample dictionary entry below to see what other information it provides.

Forms of the word

Part of speech

Numbered definitions

Synonyms

Usage label

Examples of use

Idioms

Origin (etymology)

help (help) **helped** or *(archaic)* **holp**, **helped** or *(archaic)* **hol-pen**, **help-ing**. *v.t.* **1.** to provide with support, as in the performance of a task; be of service to: *He helped his brother paint the room.* ▲ also used elliptically with a preposition or adverb: *He helped the old woman up the stairs.* **2.** to enable (someone or something) to accomplish a goal or achieve a desired effect: *The coach's advice helped the team to win.* **3.** to provide with sustenance or relief, as in time of need or distress; succor: *The Red Cross helped the flood victims.* **4.** to promote or contribute to; further. *The medication helped his recovery.* **5.** to be useful or profitable to; be of advantage to: *It might help you if you read the book.* **6.** to improve or remedy: *Nothing really helped his sinus condition.* **7.** to prevent; stop: *I can't help his rudeness.* **8.** to refrain from; avoid: *I couldn't help smiling when I heard the story.* **9.** to wait on or serve (often with *to*): *The clerk helped us. The hostess helped him to the dessert.* **10. cannot help but.** *Informal* cannot but. **11. so help me (God).** oath of affirmation. **12. to help oneself to.** to take or appropriate: *The thief helped himself to all the jewels.* —*v.i.* to provide support, as in the performance of a task; be of service. —*n.* **1.** act of providing support, service, or sustenance. **2.** source of support, service, or sustenance. **3.** person or group of persons hired to work for another or others. **4.** means of improving, remedying, or preventing. [Old English *helpan* to aid, succor, benefit.]
Syn. *v.t.* **1. Help, aid, assist** mean to support in a useful way. **Help** is the most common word and means to give support in response to a known or expressed need or for a definite purpose: *Everyone helped to make the school fair a success.* **Aid** means to give relief in times of distress or difficulty: *It is the duty of rich nations to aid the poor.* **Assist** means to serve another person in the performance of his task in a secondary capacity: *The secretary assists the officer by taking care of his correspondence.*

Thesauruses These references provide synonyms and often antonyms. Some dictionaries and thesauruses are available on CD-ROM and on the Internet.

Glossaries Many textbooks and technical works contain condensed dictionaries that provide an alphabetical listing of words used in the text and their specific definitions. The example on page R81 is from a social studies textbook.

R80 ❧ READING HANDBOOK

Glossary

A

abolitionist 1800s reformer who worked to end slavery (p. 342)

acid rain acid precipitation in the form of rain (p. 1016)

agribusiness large farming operation that includes the cultivation, processing, storage, and distribution of farm products (p. 869)

amendment alteration to the Constitution (p. 160)

amnesty act of a government by which pardon is granted to an individual or groups of persons (p. 445)

anarchism a belief in no direct government authority over society (p. 531)

anarchist one who opposes all forms of government (p. 616)

Identifying word relationships

Determining the relationships of words to each other also aids comprehension. Some special word relationships include analogies, synonyms, antonyms, denotation, and connotation.

- **Denotation** A denotation expresses the exact meaning of a word. A word may have more than one denotation, but all of its denotations will be listed in the dictionary. Notice, for example, all the denotations for the word *help* listed in the dictionary entry on page R80.
- **Connotation** Connotation refers to an emotion or an underlying value that accompanies a word's dictionary meaning. When the word *leper* is used, you know that the word refers to someone suffering from a specific disease, but its connotation includes feelings of disgust or pity and suggests separation from familiar surroundings.

TRY THE STRATEGIES

Play a game of Word Clues. Each player chooses a word that has been used in class in the past two weeks and coins a nonsense word to represent it. Player One writes a sentence on the board using his or her nonsense word in an appropriate context. Players who can identify the word from the context raise their hands. Each scores five points for a correct identification. If no one is able to identify the word, Player One supplies a synonym or antonym for it. Players who identify the word correctly after the second clue score three points. If no one identifies the word, Player One gets a one-point penalty and the next player repeats the procedure. When time is up, the player with the most points wins.

Comprehension Strategies

Reading comprehension means understanding—deriving meaning from—what you have read. Using a variety of strategies can help you improve your comprehension and make reading more interesting and more fun.

Previewing

Before beginning a selection, it's helpful to **preview** what you are about to read.

- **Read** the title, headings, and subheadings of the selection.
- **Look** at the illustrations and notice how the text is organized.
- **Skim** the selection; that is, take a quick glance at the whole thing.
- **Decide** what the author's purpose might be.
- **Predict** what the selection will be about.
- **Set a purpose** for your reading.

Establishing a purpose for reading

To get the greatest benefit from what you read, you should **establish a purpose for reading.** Some purposes for reading are

- to enjoy
- to find information, to discover
- to interpret
- to follow directions or take action
- to be persuaded about an issue
- to appreciate a writer's craft
- to find models for your own writing

Vary your reading strategies to fit the different purposes you have when you read. If you are reading for entertainment, you might read quickly, but if you read to gather information or follow directions, you might read more slowly, take notes, construct a graphic organizer, or reread sections of text.

TRY THE STRATEGIES

Look through a newspaper or a magazine at home or at the library. Preview three or four articles using the strategies listed under Previewing. Then decide what your purpose for reading would be for each of the articles selected. Which of the articles should you read slowly? Which might you read quickly? In a small group, discuss your purposes for reading and why your reading speed would differ from article to article.

Drawing on personal background

Good reading is an interactive process between the writer and each different person reading a selection. Even the youngest child has a body of information and personal experiences which are important and uniquely his or her own. When you draw on your personal background, combining it with the words on a page, you create meaning in a selection. Drawing on this personal background is also called **activating prior knowledge.** To expand and extend your prior knowledge, share it in active classroom discussions.

Ask yourself questions like these:

- What do I know about this topic?
- What familiar places have similar settings?
- What experiences have I had that compare or contrast with what I am reading?
- What characters from life or literature remind me of the characters or narrator in the selection?

Making and verifying predictions

As you read, take educated guesses about story events and outcomes; that is, **make predictions** before and during reading. Using your prior knowledge and the information you have gathered in your preview, you can predict what you will learn or what might happen in a selection. Then use information you gather as you read to adjust or **verify your predictions.** Have you ever read a mystery, decided who committed the crime, and then changed your mind as more clues emerged? You were adjusting your predictions. Or did you shriek with delight or smile smugly when you found out you guessed the murderer? You were verifying your predictions. Careful predictions and verifications increase your comprehension of a selection.

TRY THE STRATEGIES

Find a selection from your social studies or science textbook. First, preview the title, illustrations, and available headings and subheadings to determine what the piece might be about or what might happen. On your own paper, write your predictions about what you will read. Then, as you read, revise your predictions based on new information and your own background or prior knowledge.

Monitoring and modifying reading strategies

No matter what your purpose for reading, your most important task is to understand what you have read. Try having a conversation with yourself as you work through a selection. **Check**, or **monitor**, **your understanding**, using the following strategies:

- Summarize
- Clarify
- Ask questions
- Predict what will come next

This might be done once or twice in an easy, entertaining selection, or after every paragraph in a nonfiction selection, dense with new concepts.

One way of questioning yourself is to pretend that you are the teacher trying to determine if your students have understood the main ideas of a selection. What questions would you ask? Be sure that you can answer those questions before you read on.

Tips for Monitoring Understanding

- Reread.
- Make a graphic organizer, such as a chart or a diagram, to help sort out your thoughts.
- Consult other sources, including text resources, teachers and other students.
- Write comments or questions on another piece of paper for later review or discussion.

Use or modify whatever strategy fits your learning style, but don't settle for not understanding. Be an active reader.

Visualizing

Try to form a mental picture of scenes, characters, and events as you read. Use the details and descriptions the author gives you. According to your imagination and the text, what do the characters look like? What does the setting look like? Can you picture the steps in a process when you read nonfiction? If you can **visualize** what you read, selections will be more interesting. When someone reads aloud to you, try sketching what you're hearing—you'll be more likely to recall it later.

Constructing graphic organizers

Graphic organizers help you reconstruct ideas in a visual way, so you can remember them later on. You might make a **chart** or **diagram,** showing the information the author provides.

Venn diagrams When mapping out a comparison-and-contrast text structure, you can use a Venn diagram. The outer portions of the circles will show how two characters, ideas, or items contrast, or are different, and the overlapping part will show how they are similar, or compare them.

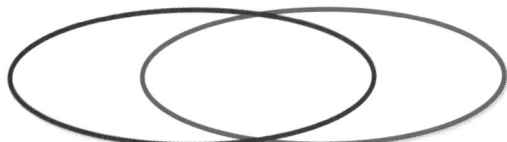

Flow charts To help you keep track of the sequence of events, use a flow chart. Arrange ideas or events in their logical, sequential order. Then draw arrows between your ideas to indicate how one idea or event flows into another. Look at the following flow chart to see how you can map out story events in chronological order or show cause and effect relationships.

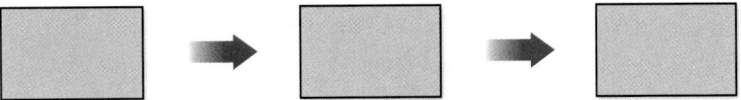

Web To help you determine a main idea and supporting details, use a web. Surround the main idea with examples or supporting details. Then create additional circles, branching off from the supporting details, to add related thoughts.

Analyzing text structures

Writers organize their written work in various ways, depending on their topic and purpose. Finding and analyzing that pattern of organization or **text structure** helps you to understand what an author is trying to say. Here are three important ways that writers structure or organize text:

Kind of Organization	Purpose	Clues
Comparison and contrast	To determine similarities and differences	Words and phrases like *similarly, on the other hand, in contrast to, but, however*
Cause and effect	To explore the reasons for something and to examine the results of events or actions	Words and phrases like *because* and *as a result*
Chronological order	To present events in time order	Words and phrases like *first, next, then, later,* and *finally*

Writers may embed one kind of structure within another, but it is usually possible to identify one main pattern of organization that will help you discover an author's purpose and will focus your attention on the important ideas in the selection.

Read the following example. Analyze the text structure used.

Two high school athletes who have attracted the attention of state high school tennis fans are Cleo Whittington and Tessa Levine. Two great players could hardly be more different. Cleo is a left-hander who depends on her lightning serve and ground strokes to overpower her opponents. Tessa is right-handed, hits her backhand with two hands, and outlasts other players with an endless stream of smooth shots as if she were a human backboard. Cleo displays her emotions, while Tessa is known for her blank expression on the court.

Cleo was born in Jamaica, but she and her family moved here when she was in eighth grade. Although she had not played tennis in Jamaica, she seemed to have been born with a tennis racquet in her hand. In her freshman year, she tried out for the tennis team. After one month, she was moved to the varsity team because no other freshman girls offered her competition.

Tessa, on the other hand, grew up playing tennis with her family. She began playing in tournaments at age nine. Her goal has always been to make a name for herself as a tennis pro.

Throughout their years in high school, Cleo and Tessa have been friendly rivals. Both were delighted when they were chosen to represent their school in the Regional Junior Championship Tournament at Forest Park on Long Island.

What is the basic text structure of the previous paragraphs? How do you know? What words help you to see the structure? How could you show this information on a graphic organizer?

TRY THE STRATEGIES

Find a selection in your literature, social studies, or science textbook and determine its text structure. Look for important clues. Use the chart on page R86 to help you in your determination.

Interpreting graphic aids

Graphic aids provide an opportunity to see and analyze information at a glance. Some effective graphic aids include maps, charts, tables, and diagrams. To interpret any of these graphic aids, you need to understand how the information presented is organized.

Reading a map Maps are flat representations of land, with other features included. A **compass rose** helps a reader to determine direction. A **legend** explains the map's symbols, while a **scale** shows the relationship of the map size to the land represented. A map may show physical features, political divisions, or historical data.

Title shows kinds of information on the map.

Modified compass rose shows directional orientation.

Legend explains colors or symbols on the map.

Scale shows relationship to actual distances.

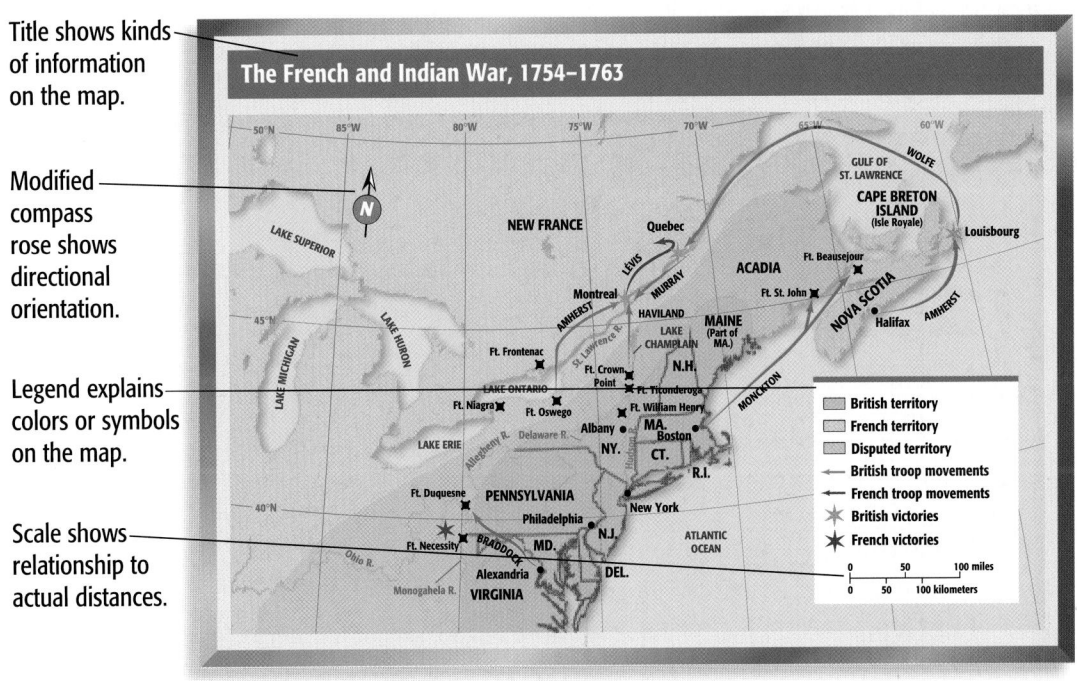

Refer to the map to answer these questions. What route did British General Wolfe take to reach Quebec? Where did the French secure victories?

Reading a chart Charts help you compare and analyze information. In charts or tables, information is presented in rows and columns.

Video Rentals and Sales (in millions)		
Year	Video Rental	Video Sales
1986	$3,308	$810
1987	$4,168	$1,004
1988	$5,210	$1,483
1989	$6,096	$2,240
1990	$6,645	$2,800

— Title of chart

— Column heads

— Data

Between which two years did video rentals make the biggest jump? What conclusions can you draw about video sales over the five years from 1986 to 1990? Based on the trend shown on this chart, how might you expect the number of video rentals to have changed over the next five years, to 1995?

Reading a graph The relationship between two or more elements can be shown in a graph, using dots, bars, or lines. Look at the title of the graph and the labels. Be sure you understand what they mean. The labels on the bottom of line graphs tell you what each vertical line represents. In this case, the lines represent different years, and the vertical labels refer to thousands of automobiles. The source, shown below the graph, tells you where the data comes from. The title of this graph tells you that you will be comparing auto sales in the years from 1920 to 1929.

Source: *Historical Statistics of the United States: Colonial Times to 1970* (1975).

In what year were auto sales the lowest? How many cars were sold in 1925?

Reading a diagram A diagram illustrates the parts of an item. You might see a diagram of a bicycle, for instance, with arrows identifying the name of each part. Diagrams can also illustrate how a process functions. The diagram below illustrates how heat energy is turned into electricity.

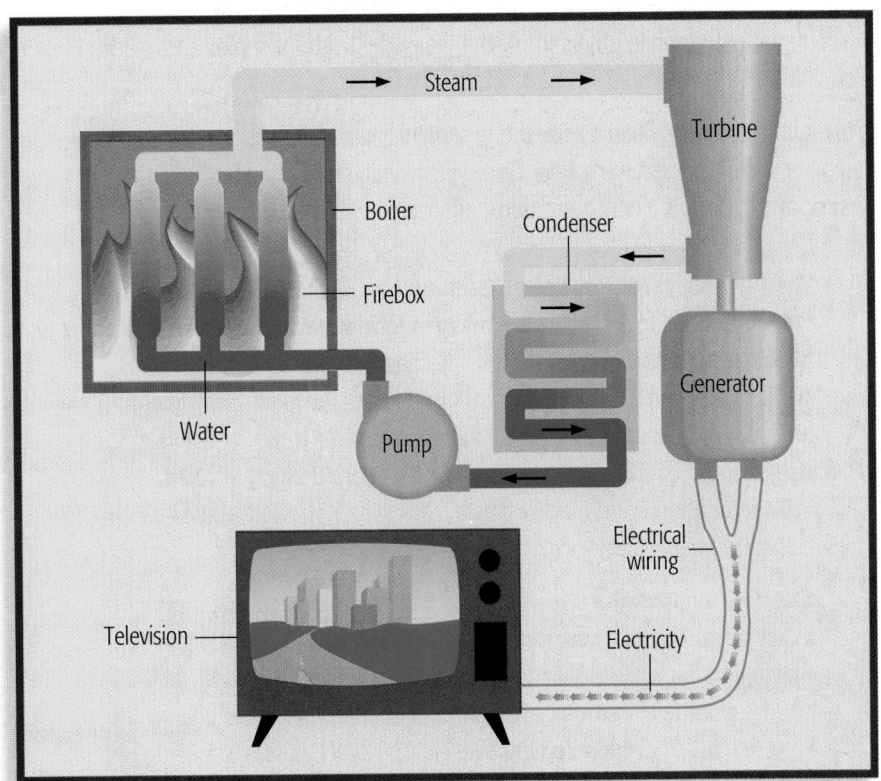

TRY THE STRATEGIES

In your social studies or science text, locate a section that uses a graphic aid. What kind of information is presented graphically? Read and interpret the information using the graphic aid, and then, on your paper, explain why the visual representation successfully presents the material.

Sequencing

The order in which thoughts are arranged is called **sequence.** A good sequence is logical, given the ideas presented. Three common forms of sequencing are

- Chronological order
- Spatial order
- Order of importance

Recognizing the sequence of something is particularly important when **following complex written directions.** If a written sequence is illogical or incomplete, or if you fail to precisely follow steps in a given order, you may be unable to complete an important task such as taking a test or locating a destination when driving a car.

Identifying main ideas and supporting details

As you read, it is important to identify the **main idea** of a paragraph or passage. Works of fiction and nonfiction can express one or more main ideas. In a single paragraph, the main idea will be the thought that organizes that paragraph and around which all other sentences are built. Some writers directly state the main idea in a topic sentence, while others imply the main idea with examples and other clues.

Read a paragraph carefully. Then decide if one sentence states the main, organizing thought, or if that thought is implied. Once you identify the main idea, you can use the **supporting details** to learn additional information about the main idea.

The next big breakthrough in fighting lung cancer may be as simple as a beam of light. **Doctors are now experimenting with lasers to kill tumors in patients.** *The new treatment is called photodynamic therapy. Most patients prefer the new treatment to the old style of operation. It's faster, less frightening for the patient, and even costs less. The method is still being studied, but the early results hold promise. One study showed a success rate of almost eighty percent.*

The treatment works like photosynthesis in plants, using light to set off a chemical reaction. *First the patient is injected with a drug that is sensitive to light. The drug travels through the bloodstream to cancerous cells. Then a scope is slid into the lung, where it emits a red-light laser. The light causes the drug to change into a form of oxygen that inflames the tumor. As the cancer cells die, they fall away from the lung like dead skin.*

(Labels: Main idea — Supporting details — Main idea — Chronological order — Supporting details)

Paraphrasing

When you **paraphrase**, you put something you've read into your own words. You might paraphrase just the main ideas, or you might retell an entire story in your own words. You need to understand something thoroughly in order to put it into your own words, so paraphrasing is a useful strategy for reviewing and for judging if you've understood what you've read.

- Original Doctors are now experimenting with lasers to kill tumors in patients. The new treatment is called photodynamic therapy. Most patients prefer the new treatment to the old style of operation. It's faster, less frightening for the patient, and even costs less. The method is still being studied, but the early results hold promise.
- Paraphrase Patients are enjoying a new experimental laser therapy used to treat tumors. It's not scary, it's quicker and cheaper, and it seems to work.

Summarizing

When you **summarize** you relate the main ideas of a selection in a logical sequence and in your own words. You are combining three skills in one. To create a good summary, include all the main ideas. Answer who, what, where, why, how, and when if that information is included in the passage. Do not include anything that is not important. A good summary can be easily understood by someone who has not read the whole text or selection. If you're not sure if an idea is a main idea or a detail, try taking it out of your summary. Does your summary still sound complete?

Look at the following summary of the passage on photodynamic therapy.

> There's a new photodynamic laser treatment that kills tumors and is quicker and cheaper than surgery. Patients like the therapy, and studies indicate that it works. Like photosynthesis in plants, the treatment uses light to set off a chemical reaction. The laser triggers a drug that kills the cancer cells and makes the tumor fall away.

TRY THE STRATEGIES

Read "The Angry Winter" on page 558 of your text. On separate paper, list the main ideas of the selection. Under each main idea, list the major supporting details that explain it. Use this information to write a summary of what you have read. Be sure that you do not use the writer's words. Paraphrase the writer's ideas in your own words.

Drawing and supporting inferences

Authors don't always directly state what they want you to understand in a selection. By providing clues and interesting details, they imply certain information. Whenever readers combine those clues with their own background and knowledge, they are drawing an inference. An **inference** involves using your reason and experience to come up with an idea, based on what an author implies or suggests. The following active reading behaviors help you infer:

- **Predicting** When you predict what a story will be about, or guess what will happen next, you are drawing an inference.
- **Drawing conclusions** A conclusion is a general statement you can make and explain with reasoning, or with supporting details from a text. If you read a story describing a sport where five players bounce a ball and throw it through a hoop, you may conclude that the sport is basketball.
- **Making generalizations** When readers make generalizations, they draw an inference that can apply to more than one item or group. This inference has a more general scope than a prediction or a conclusion. If you read articles

about how the Sioux people revere the crane and how the Cherokee believe strongly in protecting our natural resources, you might generalize that Native Americans respect nature.

What is most important when drawing inferences is to be sure that you have accurately based your guesses on supporting details from the text, as well as on your own knowledge. If you cannot point to a place in the selection to help back up your inference, you may need to rethink your guess.

Having walked home from school in a cool rain, Patricia trudged inside and tossed her wet coat on the throw rug. Her umbrella stood dripping in the entryway. "Patty, did you shut the front door?" her father called from his study down the hall. "Yes, Dad," she replied, and slowly moved back to pull the door closed. Her father was always checking up on her. Then she turned on the TV in the living room and went to the kitchen to make a snack. Patricia removed the mustard, lettuce, and bologna from the refrigerator and began looking for the bread. The theme song of her favorite afternoon TV show enticed her back into the living room.

At the first commercial break, Patricia decided to take a nice hot bath. In the bathroom off the back hallway, she turned on the tub faucet and tested the water several times with two fingers to make sure it was the correct temperature. Over the rush of the faucet she could hear the laugh track on TV, and she returned to the living room sofa.

It wasn't long before the phone rang. Patricia's best friend, Trudy, had a lengthy story to tell about that new boy from Idaho. Patricia sat watching TV and yawning and nodding at Trudy's story, feeling glad that she hadn't a worry in the world.

It wasn't until she noticed her dog's wet paws that a growing awareness came over her. Just then she heard her father's booming voice.

What inferences might you draw from the paragraphs above? What supporting details would support your inferences? Can you make a prediction or draw a conclusion from the information given? Is there enough information to support a generalization? Why or why not?

TRY THE STRATEGIES

Together with several other students, silently read several pages from a selection none of you has previously read. On your own paper, write down any inferences you can draw from the material you read. Compare your inferences within your group.

Using study strategies

All students face important studying tasks. Finding the right strategy will depend on the task you face. You may need to study for a quiz or a test, or make a class presentation with a group or by yourself. In each case you will want to pick the strategy which is most efficient and which helps you to organize and remember the material you need. Some useful study strategies include:

- **Skimming and scanning** If you want to refresh your memory about a passage you've read or get a general overview of new material, **skim** the pages by glancing quickly over the entire selection. It will focus your attention on the main ideas and the author's purpose. If you need to go back and find a particular piece of information, **scan** the selection, looking for key words or phrases that will point you to the specific information you need. You don't need to look at the whole selection. As you scan, look for section headings or terms in **boldfaced** type.

- **Using and creating study guides** It is often helpful to use end of chapter questions to guide you while you read. You can also create your own guide by turning headings and subheadings into questions to answer as you read. Don't forget to consider captions underneath illustrations when thinking up questions to help focus your attention. Use the guide to help you review aloud or silently.

- **Reviewing** Active readers go back over selections again and again. They combine their notes, outlines, and study guides to provide themselves with different ways of approaching the same information. The more you review information from different angles, the better you'll recall it when you need to.

- **Using KWL** A KWL is a good device for charting expository information. Make three columns on a page. Label the first column *What I Know,* the second column *What I Want to Know,* and the third column *What I Learned.* You can also add more columns to record places where you found information and places where you can look for more information.

TRY THE STRATEGIES

Skim a few chapters in a history textbook to find examples of comparison and contrast, chronological order, and cause and effect. Make graphic organizers to create a visual presentation of the ideas you have just read. Use these organizers to study the material.

● For more about study strategies, see **Communications Skills Handbook,** pp. R74–R77.

Reading silently for sustained periods

What things keep you on track when you read? Do you need total silence to concentrate well, or does some soft background music help you stay focused? Whatever your preference, it is important to avoid distractions or interruptions when you have to read silently for any length of time.

Tips for Reading Silently

- Be sure you're comfortable, but not too comfortable.
- Once your external surroundings are set, it's important to maintain your concentration and check your comprehension regularly.
- Using a study guide or a concept web can help you get through difficult nonfiction passages. Your teacher may provide a guide, or you can use questions from the end of the material to guide you.
- When you read fiction, a story map or other graphic organizer will help you stay focused on the important elements of the selection.
- Take regular breaks when you need them, and vary your reading rate with the demands of the text.

TRY THE STRATEGIES

Choose one or more longer selections in this book. Block out a period of time during which you won't be interrupted. Make sure you are in a comfortable spot where you can concentrate. Read silently until you finish the selection. Then use the **Responding to Literature** questions that follow the selection to monitor your comprehension.

Reading Across Texts and Cultures

One of the most important student tasks is to read widely and to integrate information from different sources to create new knowledge. Throughout this text you have read both classic and contemporary works, looking at themes from different perspectives, from different cultures, and for different purposes. As a citizen of the world, and not just your own country, you have examined world literature through the eyes of history and with a view toward the future. Every time you discussed a selection, interpreted a theme, or analyzed a writer's purpose, you created new knowledge for yourself and your classmates.

Reading in varied sources

Depending on the type of source material they are creating, writers may use a variety of styles and settings to tell the same story or cover the same subject. Each source gives specific information in a particular way. For instance, if you were researching the American artist Georgia O'Keeffe, you might first locate some basic facts about her in a book on art history. A biography might give you additional details about her life. Then, if you searched her personal writings, such as letters and diaries, you would collect information from the artist's own perspective. Whatever sources you use, it's important to be able to organize and evaluate information, combining or synthesizing what you learn from varied sources to create something for your own purposes.

For instance, to learn about the history of your hometown or region, you might read and refer to a variety of texts:

- Consult a **map** to discover the boundaries and relative positions of the geographical features of your town.
- Look up **diaries** and **journals** of long-time and former residents to gain valuable insights into different times and places.
- Find **speeches** made in the town on special occasions. These recorded public comments can showcase the style of the orator, as well as provide information about a topic, an area, or a group of people.
- Refer to the Internet and other **electronic media** that can lead you to a variety of sources and allow you to find a broader base of information about a subject.
- Try to find old **letters, memoranda, newspapers, magazines,** and **textbooks** that may provide valuable information not generally available in other sources.
- Ask a librarian or the curator of a local museum about **special collections** of posters or other resources that might offer information on your subject.

Read the following paragraphs from two kinds of primary sources. Then answer the questions that follow.

> Lincoln used to go to bed ordinarily [between] ten and eleven o'clock, unless he happened to be kept up by important news, in which case he would frequently remain at the War Department till one or two. He rose early. When he lived in the country at the Soldiers' Home, he would be up and dressed, eat his breakfast (which was extremely frugal, an egg, a piece of toast, coffee, etc.), and ride into Washington, all before eight o'clock. In the winter at the White House he was not quite so early.
>
> —*John Hay, one of Lincoln's private secretaries*

Four score and seven years ago our fathers brought forth on this continent, a new nation, conceived in Liberty, and dedicated to the proposition that all men are created equal.

Now we are engaged in a great civil war, testing whether that nation, or any nation so conceived and so dedicated, can long endure. We are met on a battlefield of that war. We have come to dedicate a portion of that field, as a final resting place for those who gave their lives that that nation might live. . . .

But in a larger sense, we can not dedicate—we can not consecrate—we can not hallow—this ground. The brave men, living and dead, who struggled here, have consecrated it, far above our poor power to add or detract. . . . It is rather for us to be here dedicated to the great task remaining before us—that from these honored dead we take increased devotion to that cause for which they gave the last full measure of devotion—that we here highly resolve that these dead shall not have died in vain—that this nation, under God, shall have a new birth of freedom—and that government of the people, by the people, for the people, shall not perish from the earth.

—Abraham Lincoln, from his address delivered at the dedication of the cemetery at Gettysburg, November 19, 1863

Which source would be better to use in a report on Lincoln as president of the United States? Which source would be better to use in a report on Abraham Lincoln's private life? How does reading across these texts provide a more complete picture of Abraham Lincoln?

TRY THE STRATEGIES

With a partner, select a topic that interests you, and research it in several kinds of sources. Compare the information from each source. Then organize and combine your information to present it to the class in some new form.

Recognizing distinctive and shared characteristics of cultures

When reading literature from different world cultures, you will find common themes about human nature. You will also see the ways in which distinctive characteristics of cultures increase your appreciation of those themes while enriching the understanding, knowledge, and enjoyment you have for your own roots. Fairytales, for example, often have counterparts in different cultures, so reading an Egyptian, a Native American, and an Asian version of "Cinderella" enhances your understanding of the story and also shows you the beauty and subtleties of different cultural traditions. Notice the similarities and differences in the elements of the Cinderella story in the four cultures charted at the top of page R97.

Culture	Heroine	Supernatural elements	Special clothing	Outcome
American/ European	Cinderella, mistreated stepchild	Fairy godmother	Glass slippers	Marries the prince
Zuni (Native American)	Turkey girl, turkey herder	Sacred turkeys	White doeskin robes	Returns to rags because she breaks her promise
Egyptian	Rhodopis, Greek slave girl	Falcon	Rose-red slippers	Marries the Pharaoh
Hmong (Asian)	Jouanah, despised stepchild	Dead mother's spirit	Special sandals	Finds love and happiness

Literary Response

Whenever you share your thoughts and feelings about something you've read, you are responding to text. Since we are all different people, though, we respond in different ways. Everyone has a learning style. Some learn best when speaking and writing, while others enjoy moving around or creating something artistic. What you do when you read can take different forms. Some responses to reading can include discussions, journals, oral interpretations, and dramatizations.

Responding to informational and aesthetic elements

You respond to what you read with both your mind and your emotions. To respond intellectually, think about whether ideas are logical and well supported. To respond emotionally, ask yourself how you feel about a selection.

Tips for Interpreting and Responding to Literature

- **Discuss** what you have read and share your views of the selections with your teacher and other students in the class.
- **Keep a journal** about what you read. Record your thoughts, feelings, or what you have learned in a journal. Write down what impresses you as well as what questions you have.
- **Read aloud** to yourself or with others. Poetry and drama make particularly good read-aloud materials, but even nonfiction passages can become clearer if troublesome passages are read orally.
- **Take part in dramatizations** and **oral interpretations.** Present characters through actions and dialogue. Use your voice, facial expressions, and body language to convey meaning. A **readers theater** is one kind of dramatic presentation in which students take different parts and read through a play or other fictional work.

Using text elements to defend personal interpretations

Whatever your response to a selection or your interpretation of a theme, you must be sure to use elements of the text to support those responses and interpretations. You need to provide details given by the writer to back up your interpretation. If you can't provide those text proofs, you may need to rethink your response.

Often you are asked to write about the selections you read. It is not enough to say, "I really liked the main character." You must know why you liked him or her. Look for specific descriptions. What did you find interesting about a story's setting? What details created certain feelings in you?

Comparing personal responses with authoritative views

Critics' reviews may encourage you to read a book, see a film, or attend a performance. They may also warn you that whatever is reviewed is not acceptable entertainment or is not valued by the reviewer.

Ask yourself the following questions:

- Would I go to a movie if it got a bad review from critics?
- Would I read a book if a reviewer said that it was a waste of time?
- Do I ever disagree with reviewers?

Deciding whether or not to value a review depends on the credibility of the reviewer, and also on your own personal viewpoints and feelings. Be sure that as you read authoritative reviews, you determine if the writer's opinions are supported with adequate and accurate details. Read the following model.

Review of *Titanic*

Directed by James Cameron

The Abyss

It's $200 million-plus worth of old-fashioned melodrama in a state-of-the-art package. It's both the shortest 3 1/2 hours you'll ever spend at the movies and spectacle of such magnitude that it's hard to imagine feeling you didn't get your time and money's worth. It begins with eerie underwater images of the *Titanic* remains, resting beneath the Atlantic since its close encounter with an iceberg in 1912. The footage comes courtesy of a salvage expedition led by Brock Lovett (Bill Paxton), whose hidden purpose is to recover a fabulous blue diamond. The gem was bought by caddish roue Cal Hockley (Billy Zane) for his fiancée Rose (Kate Winslet), and apparently lost—with the girl— in the wreck. Imagine Lovett's surprise when he's contacted by a 101-year-old woman (Gloria Stuart) who claims to be the missing Rose and offers to tell all about what happened that cold, dreadful night. Everybody knows the plot in broad outlines:

The *Titanic*—marvel of modern engineering and floating monument to hubris—will sink, and more than half its passengers will die ("Not the better half," says the hissably shallow Cal) because there aren't enough lifeboats for them. The drama is in the details, and Cameron pays lip service to the human tragedy: women and children saved while their men stay behind to die; first-class passengers ushered into lifeboats while steerage passengers are held below; the band playing "Nearer My God to Thee" as the icy water rises; individual acts of valor and cowardice that have been told and retold in books, movies and even songs. Cameron concocts a fictional romance between poor little rich girl Rose and penniless free-spirit Jack Dawson (Leonardo DiCaprio), the better to highlight the brutal class struggle and give tragedy a dewy young face. But his heart is in the spectacle: The drama is clichéd, if competently effective, but Cameron's dissolves from the *Titanic's* rusted hulk to her brand spanking new decks is breathtaking, even poetic. And the sight of the great ship foundering on the black, black sea, its massive stern rising up from the water like a whale's tale, is simply unforgettable. You can cavil that it doesn't look real—who in this digital age believes seeing is believing?—but think about it: It probably didn't look real that night 85 years ago either.

—Maitland McDonagh, *TV Guide*

If you have seen the film, answer these questions:

- Is the review balanced? Does it refer to both the positive and negative aspects of the film?
- What does the reviewer like best about the film?
- How does the reviewer evaluate weaker parts of the film?
- If you disagree with the reviewer, what do you think the reviewer failed to recognize in the film that might have influenced what he or she wrote?

If you have not seen the film, answer these questions:

- Based on this review, would you go to see this film? Why or why not?
- What evidence can you find that the reviewer is reliable?
- Does he or she back up his or her opinions with facts?
- What bias, if any, does the reviewer reveal?

TRY THE STRATEGIES

In the weekend newspaper or on the Internet, find a review of a recent film. Use the ideas above to evaluate the review. If you have not seen the film, would the review influence you to see it? Why or why not? If you have seen the film, in what ways do you agree with the review? In what ways do you disagree?

Analysis and Evaluation

Active readers want to go beyond a simple understanding of the words on a page. They want to do more than recall information or interpret thoughts and ideas. When you read, you will want to read critically, forming opinions about characters and ideas and making judgments using your own prior knowledge and information from the text.

Analyzing characteristics of texts

To be a critical reader and thinker, start by analyzing the characteristics of the text. Some text characteristics can include:

- **Structure** Writers use patterns of organization to clearly present main ideas or themes. By figuring out what text structure a writer has used—for instance, chronological order, comparison-contrast, or cause and effect—you can better understand a writer's message. Look at the structure to unlock the meaning.
- **Word choices** Writers select words according to their connotations, which carry emotional or implied meanings, as well as their denotations, or dictionary meanings. A writer who uses the words *blabbed, tattled,* or *gossiped* to describe what someone said has a different attitude from a writer who uses the words *reported, narrated,* or *documented.* Looking at word choices helps you determine the writer's attitude about a topic and establishes a general mood within a piece of writing.
- **Intended audience** Most selections are written with a specific audience in mind. A speech at a pep rally would have a different style from one given by a diplomat at the United Nations. Similarly, writers must know their audiences in order to write material that is appropriate and interesting to the people who will read it.

As you read, look for the structure and word choices a writer uses to characterize his or her writing. Determine the intended audience for each selection you read.

Evaluating the credibility of sources

Would you take an article on nuclear fission seriously if you knew it was written by a comedic actor? If you need to rely on accurate information, it helps to know who wrote the selection and if that writer is qualified to speak with authority. How did the writer become informed?

Tips for Determining Credibility of a Source

- Look at the possible motivation of the writer. (If a reporter, for instance, writes an article about the rise in crime rate, you might find the story believable. If you found out, though, that the reporter has a close relative who is a police officer, and who wants a raise in pay, you might begin to question the truth, or credibility, of the article.)

- Check on the background of the writer. Do some research on the Internet, for example, to discover whether the writer is an authority in his or her field. Writers sometimes slant the facts in their work to convince readers to agree with them.
- Look at the statements the writer makes. Is the information fact or opinion? Can the writer's statements be proved by other sources?
- Consider the publication in which an article appears. Is it a well-known journal or respected newspaper?
- Ask the opinion of a librarian or teacher—someone who is likely to be familiar with a particular writer.

Look at the model below and think about the writer's motive or purpose.

> Do you need a flu shot but you're not crazy about being stuck with a needle? Imagine getting vaccinated with a simple nasal spray. Sound too good to be true? Scientists at a California company have created a spray mist that works as a vaccine for influenza. The spray contains a mild strain of a live virus. The virus, which can survive in the cool temperature of the nose and throat but not in the warmer areas of the body, causes the immune system to respond with infection-fighting activity in the nose and throat, where flu germs often attack. Several studies have proved that the spray works. So why get jabbed when you can get the same effect from a light mist? Your arm will thank you for it!

Has the writer included mostly factual statements or opinions? How can you tell?

How would it affect your opinion about this story if the author were

- president of the company that is marketing the new nasal spray vaccine?
- a medical expert on viruses?
- a student who saw the new product on a television news magazine program?

TRY THE STRATEGIES

Read the selection from *Farewell to Manzanar,* on page 472 of your text. Is this author credible? How do you know? Can you determine the author's motive for writing the selection? Is the information in the selection fact or opinion?

Analyzing logical arguments and modes of reasoning

When you analyze works you've read, ask yourself whether the reasoning behind the writer's views are logical. Two kinds of logical reasoning are

Inductive Reasoning By observing a limited number of particular cases, a reader arrives at a general or universal statement. This logic moves from the specific to the general.

Deductive Reasoning This logic moves from that which is general to that which is specific. The reader takes a general statement and, through reasoning, applies it to specific situations.

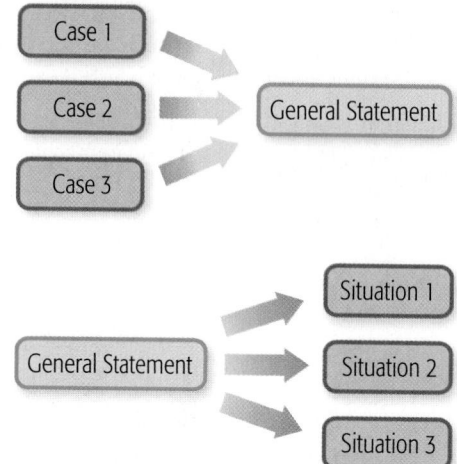

Identifying errors in logic

Whether reading an editorial, listening to a speech, or evaluating a commercial, watch out for these errors in logic:

- **Bare assertion** A claim is made and is not backed up with reasons.
  Go-Car-Go is the best gas on the market.
- **Oversimplifying** One cause or solution is given for a situation without the consideration of other factors.
  Annice wouldn't be so tired if she got to bed on time.
- **Begging the question** The writer assumes in a statement or definition the very point to be proved. Another name for this fallacy is circular reasoning.
  Teenagers cannot be trusted because they are irresponsible.
- **Either/or reasoning** This fallacy consists in reducing all options to two extremes.
  If you don't approve of capitalism, you must be a Communist.
- **Red herring** A side issue is introduced that distracts from the issue under discussion.
  You won't like that play. The lead actor owns that terrible restaurant on Third Street.

Sometimes writers neglect to support their arguments with facts, relying instead on opinions or generalizations. If ideas are not supported with facts, reasoning can become cloudy. When you interpret speeches and other persuasive writing, be sure to question the logic of the writer to determine whether the reasoning is faulty.

Analyzing bias and persuasive techniques

A writer shows a **bias** when he or she demonstrates a strong, personal, and sometimes unreasonable opinion. A writer who shows bias is inclined to a particular way of thinking. Editorials, documentaries, and advertisements commonly show bias. Writers use **persuasive techniques** when they try, through their writing, to get readers to believe a certain thing or to act in a particular way. A writer may have a strong personal bias and yet compose a persuasive essay that is logical and well supported. On the other hand, writers can be less than accurate in order to be persuasive. As a good reader, you'll need to judge whether a writer's bias influences his or her writing in negative or positive ways.

Look at some ways writers can misuse evidence in order to persuade:

- **Impressing with large numbers** Sometimes called the bandwagon appeal, this kind of argument relies on large numbers or references to *everybody* to be convincing.

  Over 5,000,000 satisfied customers have bought our product.
  Everybody raves about the new sports utility vehicle.

- **Irrelevant appeals to authority** An authority can only provide evidence in his or her own field. Dr. Joyce Brothers, for example, is not a competent authority in the field of breakfast cereals.

  Dr. Joyce Brothers says you won't be disappointed in the taste of Munchy Crunchies.

- **Appeal to popular sentiment** Some speakers or writers associate the point they are making with an item that enjoys popular appeal.

  Brushing with Toothful Polish is as important as drinking bottled water.

How well does the following paragraph persuade?

> There really is no need to build a new high school in our town. Another new school would only mean higher taxes for everyone. With all the new families moving into our community, it would be better to build more shopping malls. That would provide more jobs. Teachers have always been able to handle thirty or thirty-five students in a classroom. Besides, residents who no longer have children in school should not have to pay for all this fancy education. Vote "No" on the school referendum.

What bias does the writer show? With a partner, analyze the logic of the author's persuasive technique. How well are the writer's ideas supported?

TRY THE STRATEGIES

Find and read an editorial in the local newspaper. On your own paper, write a brief analysis of the writer's persuasive techniques. What kind of reasoning did the writer use? Was the writer biased?

Inquiry and Research

Asking and answering questions is at the very heart of being a good reader. You will need to read actively in order to research a topic assigned by a teacher. More often, you will need to generate an interesting, relevant, and researchable question on your own and locate appropriate print and nonprint information from a wide variety of sources. Then categorize that information, evaluate it, and organize it in a new way in order to produce some kind of research project for a specific audience. Finally, draw conclusions about your original research question. These conclusions may lead you to other areas for further inquiry.

It sounds like a lot, but when you generate a question of strong interest to you, the process is fun and very worthwhile.

Generating relevant and interesting questions for research

Finding a good research question or topic is a very important first step and deserves your careful attention. Whether you are researching an assigned topic or a topic you have selected, start by generating questions.

Tips for Generating Research Questions

- Think of a question or topic of interest to you.
- Choose a question that helps you focus your study on one main idea.
- Be sure your question is not too broad or too narrow.
  Too broad: How can we be ecologically more responsible?
  Better: What have Americans done in the last five years to preserve the Amazon rain forest?

Locating appropriate print and nonprint information

In your research, try to use a variety of sources. Because different sources present information in different ways, your research project will be more interesting and balanced when you read in a variety of sources. The following are some helpful print sources for research:

- **Textbooks** Texts include any book used as a basis for instruction or a source of information.
- **Book indices** A book index contains an alphabetical listing of books. Some book indices list books on specific subjects; others are more general. For example, H. W. Wilson's *Cumulative Book Index* lists hardcover and paperback books of fiction and nonfiction. Other indices list a variety of resources.
- **Periodicals** Magazines and journals are periodicals, publications issued at regular intervals, but less frequently than daily. One way of locating information in magazines is to use the *Reader's Guide to Periodical Literature*. This guide is available in print form in most libraries. Here is a subject entry from the *Reader's Guide*:

Subject —— **DIGITAL TELEVISION**

Title of article —— At war for 'eyeballs' [approved FCC standards for digital television] R. Coorsh. il *Consumers' Research Magazine* v80 p6 F '97

Author —— Battle lines [computer-televisions] J. Brinkley. il *Video* v21 p20 Jl/Ag '97

Magazine title —— Bill Gates, the cable guy [wants to design set-top boxes and modems for digital TV] E. Lesly and A. Cortese. il *Business Week* p22-4 Jl 14 '97

Volume number
Page number(s)
Date of publication

- **Technical manuals** A manual is a guide or handbook intended to give instruction on how to perform a task or operate something. A vehicle owner's manual might give information on how to operate and service a car.
- **Reference books** These books include encyclopedias and almanacs, and are books used to locate specific pieces of information.
- **Electronic encyclopedias, databases, and the Internet** There are many ways to locate extensive information using your computer. Infotrac®, for instance, acts as an on-line readers guide. CD-ROM encyclopedias can provide easy access to all subjects.
- **Nonprint information** This includes anything that is not written down. Some good nonprint sources of information are films, videos, and recorded interviews.

Organizing and converting information

As you gather information from different sources, taking careful notes, you'll need to think about how to **synthesize** the information, that is, convert it into a unified whole, as well as how to change it into a form your audience will easily understand and that will meet your assignment guidelines.

First, ask yourself what you want your audience to know. Then, think about a pattern of organization, a structure that will best show your main ideas. You might ask yourself questions like the following:

- When comparing items or ideas, what graphic aids can I use?
- When showing the reasons something happened and the effects of certain actions, what text structure would be best?
- How can I briefly and clearly show important information to my audience?
- Would an illustration or even a cartoon help to make a certain point?

TRY THE STRATEGIES

Read a nonfiction selection from Unit 2 of your text. Based on a topic in the selection, create a question you would use as a focus for a research paper. Determine what kinds of sources you would use to gather information. Then plan how you would organize the material, including the graphic aids. Share your research plan with the class.

Adapting researched material for presentation

How should you present the material you've gathered? Before you decide, think about your audience and purpose. Who will receive this information? What is your purpose? When you change the information you've located in order to tell or show someone else, you are adapting your research material for presentation. There are many options you might consider:

- Written or oral report
- Interview
- Debate
- Dramatic presentation

● For more on publishing/presenting, see **Writing Handbook**, p. R61.

Drawing conclusions from gathered information

After you've spent considerable time looking at a research question, you will certainly form opinions about your topic. A conclusion is a general statement that you'll make about the information you have found. It is important to explain your conclusions with good reasons and with supporting details from your sources.

Read the following excerpts and the conclusion that follows:

Many scientists believe that acid deposition contributes to deforestation and soil degradation. It is known to dramatically accelerate the deterioration of buildings, including landmarks such as the Acropolis in Athens, the Taj Mahal in India, and the Statue of Liberty in New York City.

—*National Geographic Information Central*

It is not only plants and animals that suffer when the air is polluted. Buildings, sculptures, paintings, metal, glass, paper, leather, textiles, and rubber all deteriorate rapidly if exposed to sulphur dioxide, nitrogen oxides, or ozone.

—*Norwegian Pollution Control Authority*

arrogant (ar′ ə gənt) *adj.* full of self-importance; haughty; p. 403

arroyo (ə roi′ ō) *n.* a dry gully or stream bed; p. 331

articulate (ar tik′ yə lāt) *v.* to put into words; express clearly and effectively; p. 521

assuage (ə swāj′) *v.* to lessen in intensity; diminish; p. 291

atonement (ə tōn′ mənt) *n.* something done to make up for a sin, injury, or loss; p. 163

attribute (at′ rə būt) *n.* a quality or characteristic of a person or thing; p. 565

augment (ôg ment′) *v.* to make greater; increase; p. 559

avaricious (av′ ə rish′ əs) *adj.* greedy; p. 177

B

bade (bād) *v.* past tense of *bid,* to command, order, or ask; p. 96

banality (bə nal′ ə tē) *n.* something that is trite; p. 511

banter (ban′ tər) *n.* good-natured, witty joking or teasing; p. 30

benevolence (bə nev′ ə ləns) *n.* kindness; generosity; p. 496

bereaved (bi rēvd′) *adj.* sad and forlorn due to a loss, such as the death of a loved one; p. 379

bereft (bi reft′) *adj.* robbed or deprived; p. 1019

beseeching (bi sēch′ ing) *adj.* begging; asking earnestly; p. 81

blasphemous (blas′ fə məs) *adj.* showing disrespect or scorn for God or anything sacred; p. 394

boding (bōd′ ing) *n.* a warning or indication, especially of evil; p. 253

brash (brash) *adj.* boldly disrespectful; p. 90

C

cataclysm (kat′ ə kliz′ əm) *n.* a disaster, usually one that causes sudden and violent change; p. 344

cavernous (kav′ ər nəs) *adj.* large and spacious, like a cavern; p. 122

chic (shēk) *adj.* attractive, tasteful, and fashionable in style; p. 301

chronic (kron′ ik) *adj.* lasting a long time or returning repeatedly; p. 121

clientele (klī′ ən tel′) *n.* clients or customers considered as a group; p. 301

coerce (kō urs′) *v.* to pressure or push into doing something, as by force or authority; p. 1055

combatant (kəm bat′ ənt) *n.* one trained for, or engaged in, combat; p. 969

commandeer (kom′ ən dēr′) *v.* to seize for use by the military or government; p. 39

commodious (kə mō′ dē əs) *adj.* having or containing ample room; spacious; p. 490

compassionate (kəm pash′ ə nit) *adj.* having or showing sympathy for another's suffering or misfortune, combined with a desire to help; p. 522

conceive (kən sēv′) *v.* to form a mental image or idea of; imagine; p. 230

confidante (kon′ fə dant′) *n.* a person who is entrusted with secrets or private affairs; p. 938

confront (kən frunt′) *v.* to come face-to-face with; to oppose; p. 984

connoisseur (kon′ ə sur′) *n.* one who has expert knowledge and a sense of what is best in a particular area, such as wine, food, or the arts; p. 1031

conscientiously (kon′ shē en′ shəs lē) *adv.* thoughtfully and carefully; p. 76

consequent (kon′ sə kwent′) *adj.* following as a result or effect; p. 378

constancy (kon′ stən sē) *n.* the quality of being unchanging; faithfulness; loyalty; p. 427

consternation (kon′ stər nā′ shən) *n.* amazement or dismay that throws one into confusion; p. 1017

contemplate (kon′ təm plāt′) *v.* to give intense attention to; consider carefully; p. 132

contend (kən tend′) *v.* to declare or maintain as a fact; argue; p. 1047

contrition (kən trish′ ən) *n.* sorrow for one's sin or wrongdoing; repentance; p. 76

convivial (kən viv′ ē əl) *adj.* fond of merriment and parties with good company; sociable; p. 491

convoluted (kon′ və loo′ təd) *adj.* turned in or wound up upon itself; coiled; twisted; p. 201

convulsive (kən vul′ siv) *adj.* sudden and violent; p. 84

correlate (kôr′ ə lāt′) v. to bring (one thing) into relation (with another thing); calculate; p. 320

coterie (kō′ tər ē) n. a small group of people who share a particular interest and often meet socially; p. 448

countenance (koun′ tə nəns) n. the face; p. 391

credence (krēd′ əns) n. belief, especially in the reports or statements of others; p. 451

credulity (kri doō′ li tē) n. a tendency to believe or accept something too readily; p. 176

crevice (krev′ is) n. a narrow crack into or through something; p. 335

D

daft (daft) adj. without sense or reason; crazy; silly; p. 435

dally (dal′ ē) v. to linger; delay; waste time; p. 260

dauntless (dônt′ lis) adj. fearless; courageous; daring; p. 390

debasement (di bās′ mənt) n. the state of being lowered in quality, value, or character; degradation; p. 565

decapitate (di kap′ ə tāt′) v. to cut off the head of; p. 66

decree (di krē′) n. an order or decision made by a judge, monarch, or other official; p. 241

decrepit (di krep′ it) adj. broken down by long use or old age; p. 401

deference (def′ ər əns) n. courteous respect or regard for the judgment, opinions, or desires of another; p. 33

defile (di fīl′) v. to spoil the purity of; to make dirty or unclean; p. 758

definitive (di fin′ ə tiv) adj. conclusive; final; decisive; p. 230

deftness (deft′ nəs) n. the quality of being skillful and nimble; p. 205

derision (di rizh′ ən) n. mockery; ridicule; p. 364

designation (dez′ ig nā′ shən) n. a distinguishing name or mark; p. 464

desolate (des′ ə lit) adj. deserted or uninhabited; p. 967

detached (di tacht′) adj. not involved emotionally; neutral; p. 481

devastate (dev′ əs tāt) v. to destroy; overwhelm; p. 56

devoid (di void′) adj. not possessing; lacking (with of); p. 536

disconcerting (dis′ kən surt′ ing) adj. disturbing, confusing, or frustrating; p. 536

discordant (dis kôrd′ ənt) adj. not in agreement or harmony; p. 53

discreetly (dis krēt′ lē) adv. in a manner showing good judgment; cautiously; p. 145

disdain (dis dān′) n. a feeling of contempt for something or someone; scorn; p. 294

disperse (dis purs′) v. to go off in different directions; scatter; p. 129

distortion (dis tôr′ shən) n. an appearance of being twisted or bent out of shape; p. 338

divert (di vurt′) v. to draw attention away; distract; p. 558

doctrine (dok′ trin) n. a particular principle or position that is taught or supported, as of a religion; p. 13

doddering (dod′ ər ing) adj. trembling or shaking, as from age; p. 121

doggedly (dô′ gid lē) adv. stubbornly; firmly; p. 175

droll (drōl) adj. amusingly odd or fanciful; p. 291

drone (drōn) v. to talk in a dull, monotonous tone; p. 1040

E

ecosystem (e′ kō sis′ təm) n. a community of organisms together with their environment, functioning as a unit; p. 534

edifice (ed′ ə fis) n. a building, especially a large, important-looking one; p. 40

elation (i lā′ shən) n. a feeling of great joy; ecstasy; p. 564

elude (i loōd′) v. to avoid or escape, especially through cleverness or quickness; p. 937

endeavor (en dev′ ər) n. a strenuous attempt to accomplish something; p. 272

enhance (en hans′) v. to make greater, as in beauty or value; p. 260

enlightening (en līt′ ən ing) adj. giving or revealing knowledge or wisdom; p. 1041

enthralled (en thrôld´) *adj.* fascinated; charmed; p. 176

ephemeral (i fem´ ər əl) *adj.* short-lived; temporary; p. 534

equanimity (ek´ wə nim´ ə tē) *n.* the ability to remain calm and assured; p. 345

equilibrium (ēk´ wə lib´ rē əm) *n.* mental, emotional, or physical balance; p. 550

eschew (es chōō´) *v.* to keep apart from (something disliked or harmful); avoid; p. 1032

exclusively (iks klōō´ siv lē) *adv.* only; excluding any other; p. 462

exhortation (eg´ zôr tā´ shən) *n.* a strong appeal or warning; p. 1045

expedient (iks pē´ dē ənt) *n.* a useful method for bringing about a desired result; p. 1022

expend (iks pend´) *v.* to use up; consume; spend; p. 546

expendable (iks pen´ də bəl) *adj.* not strictly necessary; capable of being sacrificed without negative effect; p. 319

exultation (eg´ zul tā´ shən) *n.* joy; jubilation; p. 564

F

ferocity (fə ros´ ə tē) *n.* great fierceness; extreme intensity; p. 357

fiasco (fē as´ kō) *n.* a complete or humiliating failure; p. 56

flaunt (flônt) *v.* to display in a showy manner; pp. 32, 406

formidable (fôr´ mi də bəl) *adj.* causing fear, dread, or awe by reason of size, strength, or power; p. 400

fortitude (fôr´ tə tōōd´) *n.* firm courage or strength of mind in the face of pain or danger; p. 345

fortnight (fôrt´ nīt´) *n.* two weeks; p. 40

fortuitous (fôr tōō´ ə təs) *adj.* fortunate; lucky; p. 549

furtive (fur´ tiv) *adj.* secret; shifty; sly; p. 11

G

gaudy (gô´ dē) *adj.* bright and showy to the point of being in bad taste; p. 26

gaunt (gônt) *adj.* extremely thin and hollow-eyed, as from hunger or illness; "looking like skin and bones"; p. 91

giddy (gid´ ē) *adj.* causing dizziness or lightheadedness; p. 151

gingerly (jin´ jər lē) *adv.* with extreme caution; carefully; p. 383

grapple (grap´ əl) *v.* to attempt to deal with; struggle; p. 519

grimace (grim´ is) *n.* a twisting of the face; p. 175

H

hale (hāl) *adj.* in good physical condition; healthy; p. 437

harass (hə ras´, har´ əs) *v.* to bother or annoy repeatedly; p. 63

heyday (hā´ dā) *n.* period of greatest strength, popularity, or prosperity; p. 1005

horde (hôrd) *n.* a large group; multitude; p. 160

hue (hū) *n.* a color; shade or tint; p. 241

humility (hū mil´ ə tē) *n.* the quality of being humble or modest; p. 91

hurtle (hurt´ əl) *v.* to move rapidly, especially with much force or noise; p. 403

hypochondriac (hī´ pə kon´ drē ak´) *n.* one whose worry over health is so great that it brings on the imagined symptoms of an illness; p. 1063

I

ideology (ī´ dē ol´ə jē) *n.* the ideas on which a political, economic, or social system is based; p. 511

ignoble (ig nō´ bel) *adj.* of low birth or position; without honor or worth; p. 920

impart (im pärt´) *v.* to give or share; p. 290

impeccable (im pek´ ə bəl) *adj.* free from error; flawless; p. 507

impending (im pen´ ding) *adj.* about to occur; p. 1003

impertinent (im purt´ ən ənt) *adj.* inappropriately bold or forward; not showing proper respect or manners; p. 890

impetuous (im pech´ ōō əs) *adj.* rushing headlong into things; rash; p. 262

implicit (im plis′ it) *adj.* suggested but not directly stated; p. 163

imploring (im plôr′ ing) *adj.* asking earnestly; begging; p. 253

impotent (im′ pət ənt) *adj.* ineffective, powerless, or helpless; p. 160

impropriety (im′ prə pri′ ə tē) *n.* an improper act or behavior; p. 1019

improvised (im′ prə vīzd′) *adj.* invented, composed, or done without preparing beforehand; p. 201

impudence (im′ pyə dəns) *n.* speech or behavior that is aggressively forward or rude; p. 1067

incantation (in′ kan tā′ shən) *n.* words spoken in casting a spell; p. 262

incoherently (in′ kō hēr′ ənt lē) *adv.* in a confused, disconnected manner; unintelligibly; p. 547

incomprehensible (in′ kom pri hen′ sə bəl) *adj.* not understandable; p. 482

incredulous (in krej′ ə ləs) *adj.* unwilling or unable to believe; pp. 83

incur (in kur′) *v.* to acquire (something undesirable); bring upon oneself; p. 291

indifferently (in dif′ ər ənt lē) *adv.* in a way that shows a lack of feeling, concern, or care; p. 558

indignantly (in dig′ nənt lē) *adv.* with quiet, dignified anger in response to something unjust, mean, or unworthy; p. 964

indolence (ind′ əl əns) *n.* laziness; idleness; p. 27

indulge (in dulj′) *v.* to yield to a desire (by doing something); take pleasure (in); p. 299

inert (i nurt′) *adj.* without power to move or act; lifeless; p. 546

infamy (in′ fə mē) *n.* extreme wickedness or shameful evil; p. 163

inhibit (in hib′ it) *v.* to hold back one's natural impulses; restrain; p. 491

inscribe (in skrīb′) *v.* to write, carve, or mark on a surface; p. 919

inscrutable (in skrōo′ tə bəl) *adj.* mysterious; p. 193

insular (in′ sə lər) *adj.* showing a limited point of view; p. 481

intact (in takt′) *adj.* entire; untouched, uninjured, and having all parts; p. 564

interlaced (in′ tər lāst′) *adj.* connected by or as if by being woven together; interwoven; p. 111

interminable (in tur′ mi nə bəl) *adj.* lasting, or seeming to last, forever; endless; p. 189

internment (in turn′ mənt) *n.* the act of restricting or being restricted to a particular place, especially during a war; p. 463

intimidate (in tim′ə dāt′) *v.* to make timid or fearful; bully; p. 480

intone (in tōn′) *v.* to speak in a singing tone or monotone; recite; p. 1003

intricacy (in′ tri kə sē) *n.* something that is complicated, involved, or confusing; p. 383

intrigue (in trēg′) *v.* to excite the curiosity or interest of; fascinate; p. 130

invaluable (in val′ ū ə bəl) *adj.* very great in value; p. 497

irrational (i rash′ ən əl) *adj.* contrary to reason; illogical; p. 464

irreproachable (ir′ i prō′ chə bəl) *adj.* free from blame or criticism; faultless; p. 218

J

judiciously (jōo dish′ əs lē) *adv.* in a way that shows good judgment; sensibly; p. 437

L

lament (lə ment′) *v.* to express sorrow or regret; p. 50

languor (lang′ gər) *n.* weakness; fatigue; p. 273

lethargy (leth′ ər jē) *n.* sluggish inactivity or drowsiness; p. 159

loll (lol) *v.* to hang down loosely; droop; p. 427

loom (lōom) *v.* to appear to the mind as large; to stand out prominently; p. 438

lucid (lōo′ sid) *adj.* clear-headed; mentally alert; p. 1049

lurk (lurk) *v.* to stay hidden, ready to attack; p. 438

M

mainstream (mān′ strēm′) *adj.* representing the most widespread attitudes and values of a society or group; p. 496

makeshift (māk′ shift′) *adj.* suitable as a temporary substitute for the proper or desired thing; p. 64

malicious (mə lish′ əs) *adj.* having or showing a desire to harm another; p. 407

manifest (man′ ə fest′) *v.* to make obvious or clear; show plainly; p. 378

materialistic (mə tēr′ ē ə lis′ tik) *adj.* overly concerned with material matters and worldly possessions; p. 250

mesmerizing (mez′ mə rīz ing) *adj.* fascinating; p. 51

meticulous (mi tik′ yə ləs) *adj.* characterized by great or excessive concern about details; p. 490

monologue (mon′ ə lôg′) *n.* a long speech made by one person; p. 131

monosyllabic (mon′ ə si lab′ ik) *adj.* having only one syllable; p. 121

mortify (môr′ tə fī′) *v.* to shame, humiliate, or embarrass; p. 301

muse (mūz) *v.* to think or reflect, especially in an idle manner; p. 546

myriad (mir′ ē əd) *n.* great or countless numbers; p. 81

N

notorious (nō tôr′ ē əs) *adj.* widely and unfavorably known; p. 887

O

obliterate (ə blit′ ə rāt′) *v.* to destroy completely; p. 91

oblivious (ə bliv′ ē əs) *adj.* unmindful or unaware; not noticing; p. 1072

obscurity (əb skyoor′ ə tē) *n.* darkness; dimness; p. 364

oppress (ə pres′) *v.* to control or govern by the cruel and unjust use of force or authority; p. 12

oppressive (ə pres′iv) *adj.* hard to bear; distressing; p. 181

ostentatiously (os′ tən tā′ shəs lē) *adv.* in a way intended to attract attention or impress others; p. 883

ostracism (os′ trə siz′ əm) *n.* exclusion from a group or society; p. 1035

P

pall (pôl) *n.* a covering that darkens or conceals; atmosphere of gloom; p. 355

palpable (pal′ pə bəl) *adj.* capable of being touched or felt; p. 510

palpitating (pal′ pə tāt′ ing) *adj.* quivering; trembling; vibrating; p. 482

pandemonium (pan′ də mō′ nē əm) *n.* wild disorder and uproar; p. 347

pantry (pan′ trē) *n.* room or closet in which food and articles for preparing and serving food are kept; p. 305

paradox (par′ ə doks′) *n.* something that seems illogical, contradictory, or absurd, but that in fact may be true; p. 320

paraphernalia (par′ ə fər nāl′ yə) *n.* things used in a particular activity; equipment; p. 262

patriarch (pā′ trē ärk′) *n.* the male head of a family or group; p. 463

patronize (pā′ trə nīz) *v.* to be a customer of (a business), especially on a regular basis; p. 378

pent-up (pent′ up) *adj.* not expressed or released; held in; p. 206

perceive (pər sēv′) *v.* to be or become aware through the senses; p. 293

perilous (per′ ə ləs) *adj.* dangerous; risky; p. 151

permeated (pur′ mē ā′ təd) *adj.* filled with; p. 191

perpetuate (pər pech′oo āt′) *v.* to cause to continue to be remembered; p. 938

perplexed (pər plekst′) *adj.* troubled with doubt or uncertainty; puzzled; p. 103

peruse (pə rooz′) *v.* to read through or examine carefully; p. 450

perverse (pər vurs′) *adj.* determined to go against what is reasonable, expected, or desired; contrary; p. 752

pestilential (pes′ tə len′ shəl) *adj.* harmful; destructive; p. 274

petulantly (pech′ ə lənt lē) *adv.* crankily; in an annoyed way; p. 964

phenomena (fə nom′ ə nə′) *n.* facts, events, or conditions that can be known through the senses; p. 355

pilgrimage (pil′ grə mij) *n.* a long journey, especially to a holy place or for a religious purpose; p. 1055

pious (pī′ əs) *adj.* having either genuine or pretended religious devotion; p. 272

piqued (pēkt) *adj.* aroused to anger or resentment; offended; p. 262

plaintive (plān′ tiv) *adj.* expressing sorrow; mournful; sad; p. 133

pompous (pom′ pəs) *adj.* showing an exaggerated sense of self-importance; p. 1063

predecessor (pred′ ə ses′ ər) *n.* one who comes, or has come, before another in time; p. 249

presentiment (pri zen′ tə mənt) *n.* a feeling that something is about to happen; p. 344

presumably (pri zōō′ mə blē) *adv.* supposedly; probably; p. 279

presumptuous (pri zump′ chōō əs) *adj.* too forward; bold; p. 175

prevail (pri vāl′) *v.* to be superior in power or influence; succeed; p. 754

priceless (prīs′ lis) *adj.* of greater value than can be measured; p. 16

primeval (prī mē′ vəl) *adj.* of or having to do with the first or earliest age; primitive; p. 324

prodigal (prod′ i gəl) *adj.* recklessly wasteful; p. 280

prodigy (prod′ ə jē) *n.* an extraordinarily gifted or talented person, especially a child; p. 49

profound (prə found′) *adj.* intense and complete; p. 1021

profuse (prə fūs′) *adj.* great in amount; plentiful; p. 389

proliferation (prō lif′ ə rā′ shən) *n.* growth by rapidly producing new cells or offspring; p. 534

propriety (prə prī′ ə tē) *n.* the quality of being proper or appropriate; suitability; p. 379

prosaic (prō zā′ ik) *adj.* ordinary; commonplace; p. 177

prospective (prə spek′ tiv) *adj.* probable or expected; future; p. 1039

prowess (prou′ is) *n.* great ability or skill; p. 921

psalm (sälm) *n.* a sacred poem, song, or hymn; p. 111

R

rancor (rang′ kər) *n.* ill will; resentment; p. 291

raptly (rapt′ lē) *adv.* in a deeply interested way; attentively; p. 1019

rebuke (ri būk′) *v.* to scold sharply; p. 152

reciprocal (ri sip′ rə kəl) *adj.* given, felt, or shown in return; p. 133

reconciliation (rek′ ən sil′ ē ā′ shən) *n.* a settlement of a controversy or disagreement; p. 274

refrain (ri frān′) *n.* in a song or poem, a phrase or verse that is repeated regularly, especially at the end of each stanza; p. 242

regally (rē′ gəl lē) *adv.* in a grand, dignified manner befitting a king or queen; p. 883

rejuvenate (ri jōō′ və nāt′) *v.* to make fresh or young again; p. 158

relevant (rel′ ə vənt) *adj.* connected with the matter at hand; pertinent; meaningful; p. 521

relic (rel′ ik) *n.* an object that has survived decay, destruction, or the passage of time and is valued for its historic interest; p. 67

remonstrate (ri mon′ strāt) *v.* to say or plead in protest; argue; p. 290

repercussion (rē′ pər kush′ ən) *n.* an effect or result of some action or event; p. 1045

repressed (ri prest′) *adj.* held back or kept under control; restrained; p. 889

reprieve (ri prēv′) *v.* to give temporary relief, as from something unpleasant or difficult; p. 363

reproach (ri prōch′) *n.* blame; disgrace; discredit; p. 50

repulse (ri puls′) *n.* an act of beating back or driving away, as with force; p. 728

residue (rez′ ə dōō′) *n.* what remains after part is removed; p. 131

resilient (ri zil′ yənt) *adj.* capable of springing back into shape or position after being bent, stretched, or compressed; p. 321

resonant (rez′ ə nənt) *adj.* having a full, rich sound; p. 1049

retail (rē′ tāl) *v.* to sell directly to the consumer; p. 40

retinue (ret′ ən ōō′) *n.* the group of attendants or servants accompanying a person of rank or authority; p. 242

reveling (rev′ əl ing) *adj.* taking great pleasure; p. 207

reverie (rev′ ər ē) *n.* fanciful thinking; daydream; p. 53

ruefully (rōō′ fəl ē) *adv.* regretfully; sorrowfully; p. 970

rustic (rus′ tik) *adj.* of, or relating to, the country; p. 226

S

sagacious (sə gā′ shəs) *adj.* having or showing wisdom and good judgment; p. 390

sanctity (sangk′ tə tē) *n.* the quality of deserving solemn respect as something not to be violated; p. 281

sashay (sa shā′) *v.* to walk or move in a way that shows indifference or a lack of interest; p. 305

scenario (si när′ ē ō′) *n.* an outline or model of an expected or imagined series of events; p. 491

scrupulous (skrōō′ pyə ləs) *adj.* thoroughly attentive to even the smallest details; precise; p. 937

scrutinize (skrōōt′ ən īz) *v.* to look at closely; inspect carefully; p. 192

sedate (si dāt′) *adj.* quiet and restrained in style or manner; calm; p. 252

serenity (sə ren′ ə tē) *n.* calmness; peacefulness; p. 190

sever (sev′ ər) *v.* to break off; p. 249

sidle (sīd′ əl) *v.* to move sideways, especially in a way that does not attract attention or cause disturbance; p. 8

singular (sing′ gyə lər) *adj.* unusual or remarkable; p. 366

sinister (sin′ is tər) *adj.* threatening or suggesting evil; p. 178

skeptical (skep′ ti kəl) *adj.* having or showing doubt or suspicion; questioning; disbelieving; p. 193

slew (slōō) *n.* a large number or group; p. 242

solace (sol′ is) *n.* relief from sorrow or disappointment; comfort; p. 250

sparse (spärs) *adj.* thinly spread or distributed; p. 337

spasmodic (spaz mod′ ik) *adj.* sudden, violent, and temporary; p. 204

spawn (spôn) *v.* to bring forth; give birth; p. 358

spectral (spek′ trəl) *adj.* ghostlike; p. 393

speculate (spek′ yə lāt′) *v.* to guess; p. 523

sporadic (spə rad′ ik) *adj.* irregular; occasional; p. 160

squalor (skwol′ ər) *n.* wretchedness; misery and filth; p. 146

staidness (stād′ nəs) *n.* the state or quality of being serious, steady, or conservative in character; p. 219

stifling (stī′ fling) *adj.* smothering; suffocating; p. 189

stolid (stol′ id) *adj.* showing little or no emotion; not easily stirred or moved; p. 1034

strategic (strə tē′ jik) *adj.* highly important to an intended goal; p. 986

stridently (strīd′ ənt lē) *adv.* in a loud, harsh manner; shrilly; p. 437

subordinate (sə bôr′ də nāt′) *v.* to cause to be, or treat as, secondary, inferior, or less important; p. 471

subtle (sut′ əl) *adj.* not open or direct; not obvious; p. 121

subversive (sub vur′ siv) *adj.* seeking to weaken, destroy, or overthrow; p. 220

succor (suk′ ər) *n.* help; assistance; relief; p. 274

sumptuous (sump′ chōō əs) *adj.* costly and magnificent; p. 967

superfluous (soo pur′ flōō əs) *adj.* not needed; unnecessary; p. 496

supplication (səp′ lə kā′ shən) *n.* an earnest and humble request; p. 78

surmise (sər mīz′) *v.* to guess or conclude from little or no evidence; p. 33

T

taut (tôt) *adj.* tense; tight; p. 204

tedious (tē′ dē əs) *adj.* boring; tiresome; p. 534

temper (tem′ pər) *v.* to moderate by mingling with another thing; p. 427

tenaciously (ti nā′ shəs lē) *adv.* stubbornly; persistently; p. 160

tentative (ten′ tə tiv) *adj.* not fully worked out; uncertain; p. 357

tepid (tep′ id) *adj.* moderately or slightly warm; lukewarm; p. 483

theorize (thē′ ə rīz′) *v.* to form an idea that explains a group of facts; p. 380

throng (thrông) *v.* to move or gather in large numbers; crowd together; p. 969

tirade (tī rād') *n.* a long, angry or scolding speech; p. 453

token (tō' kən) *adj.* symbolic; p. 428

torturous (tôr' chər əs) *adj.* causing pain or suffering; p. 496

totalitarian (tō tal' ə tār' ē ən) *adj.* characteristic of a government in which one political party has total control; p. 510

transient (tran' shənt) *adj.* of temporary or brief duration; not lasting; p. 537

tremulously (trem' yə les lē) *adv.* in a trembling or vibrating way; p. 1030

tribulation (trib' yə lā' shən) *n.* great misery or distress; suffering; p. 350

tumultuous (too mul' choo əs) *adj.* wildly excited, confused, or agitated; p. 920

U

ulterior (ul tēr' ē ər) *adj.* intentionally withheld or concealed; p. 219

ultimately (ul' tə mit lē) *adv.* at last; finally; p. 1004

unconditional (un' kən dish' ən əl) *adj.* absolute; complete; p. 230

unimpeded (un' im pē' dəd) *adj.* not obstructed; unblocked; p. 211

unkempt (un kempt') *adj.* in a neglected state; not combed or groomed; untidy; p. 1045

V

valid (val' id) *adj.* acceptable; legitimate; p. 481

vanquish (vang' kwish) *v.* to conquer or overcome; p. 937

vault (vôlt) *v.* to jump; spring; p. 985

vehemently (vē' ə mənt lē) *adv.* strongly; intensely; passionately; p. 454

verandah (və ran' də) *n.* a long porch, usually with a roof, that extends along one or more sides of a house; p. 110

vermin (vur' min) *n.* any animals that are harmful, destructive, or troublesome; p. 428

vexed (vekst) *adj.* impatient or angry; annoyed; p. 151

vintage (vin' tij) *adj.* characterized by enduring appeal; classic; p. 64

void (void) *n.* an empty space; vacuum; p. 228

vulgar (vul' gər) *adj.* characterized by a lack of good breeding or good taste; common; crude; p. 966

vulnerable (vul' nər ə bəl) *adj.* easily damaged or hurt; p. 496

W

wane (wān) *v.* to decrease gradually; p. 148

wanton (wont' ən) *adj.* shamelessly unrestrained; immoral; p. 392

wary (wār' ē) *adj.* cautious; on the alert; p. 144

whim (hwim) *n.* a sudden notion or fanciful idea; p. 1056

whimsical (hwim' zi kəl) *adj.* fanciful; curiously humorous; p. 467

wince (wins) *v.* to draw back slightly, as in pain; flinch; p. 119

wont (wōnt) *adj.* accustomed; used; p. 270

Z

zealously (zel' əs lē) *adv.* eagerly; enthusiastically; p. 31

Spanish Glossary

A

abashed/avergonzado *adj.* abochornado; desconcertado; p. 917

abeyance/suspensión *s.* estado de inactividad temporal; p. 363

absolve/absolver *v.* liberar de culpa o responsabilidad; p. 752

abstract/abstracto *adj.* separado de un caso o ejemplo específico; teórico; p. 510

abyss/abismo *s.* sima; gran profundidad; vacío inmenso; p. 547

accost/abordar *v.* acercarse o dirigirse a alguien de manera brusca; p. 916

acquiesce/acceder *v.* aceptar o consentir sin protestar; p. 270

acrid/acre *adj.* irritante o desagradable; p. 30

admonish/regañar *v.* advertir en contra de una acción específica; amonestar; p. 448

advocate/abogar *v.* respaldar públicamente; p. 1032

affable/afable *adj.* amistoso, cordial y amable; p. 1063

affluent/afluente *adj.* acaudalado; próspero; p. 509

agenda/agenda *s.* programa o itinerario de cosas por hacer; p. 522

albeit/no obstante *conj.* aunque; si bien; sin embargo; p. 219

alleviate/aliviar *v.* hacer menos difícil; calmar; socorrer; p. 467

amenable/dispuesto *adj.* receptivo; dócil; p. 40

amiably/afablemente *adv.* de manera amistosa y cordial; p. 173

anteroom/antesala *s.* vestíbulo; pequeña sala de espera que conduce a la sala principal; p. 101

appal/pasmar *v.* llenar de horror o espanto; asombrar; p. 393

apparition/aparición *s.* algo extraño o inesperado que se aparece de repente, como un fantasma; p. 229

apprehension/aprensión *s.* temor de lo que pueda pasar; ansiedad; p. 253

appurtenance/accesorio *s.* artículo o pieza de equipo opcional que se adjunta por conveniencia o comodidad; adminículo; p. 117

arrogance/arrogancia *s.* orgullo desmedido; p. 745

arrogant/arrogante *adj.* lleno de vanidad; engreído; p. 403

arroyo/cauce *s.* en inglés quiere decir cauce seco de un río; en español, riachuelo; p. 331

articulate/expresar *v.* poner en palabras; decir algo clara y efectivamente; p. 521

assuage/mitigar *v.* reducir en intensidad; aliviar; p. 291

atonement/expiación *s.* acción para compensar un pecado, lesión o pérdida; p. 163

attribute/atributo *s.* cualidad o característica de una persona o cosa; p. 565

augment/aumentar *v.* agrandar; acrecentar p. 559

avaricious/avaro *adj.* codicioso o tacaño; p. 177

B

bade/ordenó *v.* pasado de *ordenar;* mandar; solicitar; p. 96

banality/banalidad *s.* trivialidad; insignificante o sin importancia; p. 511

banter/broma *s.* chanza ingeniosa y bien intencionada; p. 30

benevolence/benevolencia *s.* amabilidad; generosidad; p. 496

bereaved/afligido *adj.* triste y acongojado debido a una pérdida, tal como la muerte de un ser querido; p. 379

bereft/despojado *adj.* privado de algo; p. 1019

beseeching/suplicante *adj.* implorante; que ruega o pide con ansiedad; p. 81

blasphemous/blasfemo *adj.* que menosprecia o maldice a Dios o a cualquier figura sagrada; p. 394

boding/presagio *s.* advertencia o señal, particularmente de algo malo; p. 253

brash/insolente *adj.* atrevido; irrespetuoso; p. 90

C

cataclysm/cataclismo *s.* desastre que por lo general origina un cambio violento y repentino; p. 344

cavernous/cavernoso *adj.* grande y amplio como una caverna; p. 122

chic/chic *adj.* atractivo, distinguido y elegante; p. 301

chronic/crónico *adj.* que dura largo tiempo o que se repite constantemente; p. 121

clientele/clientela *s.* clientes o compradores fijos de un establecimiento comercial; p. 301

coerce/obligar *v.* presionar por medio de la fuerza o la autoridad; p. 1055

combatant/combatiente *s.* que participa en un combate o lucha; p. 969

commandeer/confiscar *v.* adueñarse de algo para uso militar o del gobierno; p. 39

commodious/espacioso *adj.* que tiene un amplio espacio; holgado; p. 490

compassionate/compasivo *adj.* que demuestra interés y preocupación por el sufrimiento o la desgracia de otros, así como deseo de ayudar; p. 522

conceive/concebir *v.* formarse una imagen o idea mental; imaginar; p. 230

confidante/confidente *s.* persona a la que se le confía un secreto o asunto privado; p. 938

confront/confrontar *v.* encontrarse cara a cara frente a alguien o algo; oponerse; p. 984

connoisseur/conocedor *s.* que sabe distinguir lo mejor de un sector específico, como vinos, comida o arte; experto en el tema; p. 1031

conscientiously/concienzudamente *adv.* de manera reflexiva y cuidadosa; p. 76

consequent/consecuente *adj.* como resultado o efecto de algo; p. 378

constancy/constancia *s.* cualidad de no cambiar; perseverancia; lealtad; p. 427

consternation/consternación *s.* asombro o aflicción que causa confusión; p. 1017

contemplate/contemplar *v.* pensar algo con mucha atención; considerar algo cuidadosamente; p. 132

contend/sostener *v.* declarar algo como hecho; p. 1047

contrition/contrición *s.* arrepentimiento por un pecado o mala acción que se ha cometido; remordimiento; p. 76

convivial/jovial *adj.* de buen ánimo; amigo de diversiones y fiestas; sociable; p. 491

convoluted/retorcido *adj.* enredado; complicado; abrupto; p. 201

convulsive/convulsivo *adj.* repentino y violento; p. 84

correlate/correlacionar *v.* relacionar una cosa con otra; p. 320

coterie/grupo *s.* camarilla; grupo pequeño de personas que comparten un interés particular y que se reúnen con frecuencia; p. 448

countenance/semblante *s.* rostro; cara; p. 391

credence/certeza *s.* convicción, particularmente en lo que dice o informa otra persona; p. 451

credulity/credulidad *s.* tendencia a creer o aceptar algo fácilmente; p. 176

crevice/grieta *s.* hendedura; ranura; p. 335

D

daft/tonto *adj.* necio; bobo; p. 435

dally/demorarse *v.* flojear; holgazanear; perder el tiempo; p. 260

dauntless/intrépido *adj.* sin miedo; valiente; atrevido; p. 390

debasement/degradación *s.* acción y efecto de degradar; bajar de categoría, calidad o valor; p. 565

decapitate/decapitar *v.* cortar la cabeza; p. 66

decree/decreto *s.* orden o decisión impartida por un juez, monarca u otro funcionario; p. 241

decrepit/decrépito *adj.* agotado por el uso o la ancianidad; achacoso; p. 401

deference/deferencia *s.* consideración o respeto hacia las opiniones o deseos de otra persona; p. 33

defile/mancillar *v.* manchar la pureza de algo; ensuciar; p. 758

definitive/definitivo *adj.* concluyente; final; decisivo; p. 230

deftness/destreza *s.* cualidad de ser hábil y ágil en algún oficio o actividad; p. 205

derision/escarnio *s.* mofa; burla; p. 364

designation/designación *s.* nombre o título de distinción; p. 464

desolate/desolado *adj.* desértico o inhabitado; p. 967

detached/indiferente *adj.* alejado emocionalmente; neutral; p. 481

devastate/devastar *v.* destruir; asolar; p. 56

devoid/desprovisto *adj.* carente; vacío; p. 536

disconcerting/desconcertante *adj.* inquietante, confuso o frustrante; p. 536

discordant/discordante *adj.* en desacuerdo; opuesto a; discorde; p. 53

discreetly/discretamente *adv.* de modo sensato y cuidadoso; p. 145

disdain/desdén *s.* desprecio hacia algo o alguien; menosprecio; p. 294

disperse/dispersar *v.* apartar lo que estaba unido; diseminar; p. 129

distortion/distorsión *s.* deformación; torcimiento; alteración; p. 338

divert/distraer *v.* alejar de la atención; desviar; p. 558

doctrine/doctrina *s.* principio o posición que se enseña o promueve, por ejemplo, de la religión; p. 13

doddering/tambaleante *adj.* tembloroso o vacilante, como una persona anciana al caminar; p. 121

doggedly/obstinadamente *adv.* de manera terca; firmemente; p. 175

droll/risible *adj.* que causa risa por raro o cómico; p. 291

drone/murmurar *v.* hablar monótonamente; ronronear; p. 1040

E

ecosystem/ecosistema *s.* comunidad de organismos con su medio ambiente que funcionan como una unidad; p. 534

edifice/edificio *s.* construcción alta o de aspecto imponente; p. 40

elation/regocijo *s.* gran alegría; júbilo; éxtasis; p. 564

elude/eludir *v.* evadir o escapar, particularmente mediante astucia o agilidad; p. 937

endeavor/empeño *s.* gran esfuerzo por conseguir algo; p. 272

enhance/realzar *v.* mejorar, ya sea en belleza, calidad o valor; p. 260

enlightening/ilustrativo *adj.* que da o revela conocimientos o sabiduría; p. 1041

enthralled/cautivado *adj.* fascinado; encantado; p. 176

ephemeral/efímero *adj.* de corta vida; temporal; p. 534

equanimity/calma *s.* ecuanimidad, igualdad y constancia de ánimo; p. 345

equilibrium/equilibrio *s.* estabilidad mental, emocional o física; p. 550

eschew/evitar *v.* evadir algo desagradable o peligroso; soslayar; p. 1032

exclusively/exclusivamente *adv.* únicamente; limitado; p. 462

exhortation/exhortación *s.* advertencia o llamado severo; p. 1045

expedient/expediente *s.* recurso; método útil para obtener un resultado deseado; p. 1022

expend/gastar *v.* consumir; p. 546

expendable/prescindible *adj.* que no es estrictamente necesario; que se puede sacrificar sin efectos negativos; p. 319

exultation/exultación *s.* regocijo; júbilo; p. 564

F

ferocity/ferocidad *s.* fiereza; de gran intensidad; p. 357

fiasco/fiasco *s.* fracaso total y humillante; p. 56

flaunt/ostentar *v.* hacer alarde; p. 32

formidable/formidable *adj.* que causa miedo o asombro por razón de su tamaño, fuerza o poder; p. 400

fortitude/fortaleza *s.* valor o entereza en medio del dolor o del peligro; p. 345

fortnight/quincena *s.* período de dos semanas; p. 40

fortuitous/fortuito *adj.* afortunado; imprevisto; p. 549

furtive/furtivo *adj.* secreto; cauteloso; sigiloso; p. 11

G

gaudy/chillón *adj.* brillante y llamativo al punto de ser de mal gusto; p. 26

gaunt/demacrado *adj.* muy delgado y ojeroso; con aspecto enfermizo; p. 91

giddy/vertiginoso *adj.* que causa mareo o vértigo; p. 151

gingerly/con cautela *adv.* con gran cuidado; sigilosamente; p. 383

grapple/abordar *v.* examinar un asunto para resolverlo; bregar por resolver algo; p. 519

grimace/mueca *s.* gesto de la cara; p. 175

H

hale/vigoroso *adj.* en buen estado físico; saludable; p. 437

harass/acosar *v.* molestar o perturbar repetidamente; p. 63

heyday/apogeo *s.* período de mayor fuerza, popularidad o prosperidad; p. 1005

horde/horda *s.* grupo grande; multitud; p. 160

hue/color *s.* matiz; sombra o tinte; p. 241

humility/humildad *s.* cualidad de ser humilde o modesto; p. 91

hurtle/abalanzarse *v.* precipitarse; moverse rápidamente, especialmente con fuerza y ruido; p. 403

hypochondriac/hipocondríaco *s.* persona que se preocupa tanto por su salud que se imagina síntomas de una enfermedad; p. 1063

I

ideology/ideología *s.* ideas en las que se basa un sistema político, económico o social; p. 511

ignoble/innoble *adj.* de bajo origen o posición; sin honor ni valor; p. 920

impart/impartir *v.* dar o compartir; p. 290

impeccable/impecable *adj.* libre de errores; sin falla; p. 507

impending/inminente *adj.* a punto de ocurrir; p. 1003

impertinente/impertinente *adj.* indebidamente atrevido o directo; que no muestra respeto ni buenos modales; p. 890

impetuous/impetuoso *adj.* que se apresura a hacer algo; fogoso; p. 262

implicit/implícito *adj.* que se sugiere pero no se establece directamente; p. 163

imploring/implorante *adj.* que pide con intensidad; que suplica; p. 253

impotent/impotente *adj.* inefectivo, incapaz o indefenso; p. 160

impropriety/impropiedad *s.* incorrección; indecencia; p. 1019

improvised/improvisado *adj.* inventado; hecho sin preparación; p. 201

impudence/impudencia *s.* palabra o conducta descarada o ruda; p. 1067

incantation/conjuro *s.* palabras dichas en un encantamiento o sortilegio; p. 262

incoherently/incoherentemente *adv.* de modo confuso o disparatado; p. 547

incomprehensible/incomprensible *adj.* que no se puede entender; p. 482

incredulous/incrédulo *adj.* que no puede o no quiere creer; p. 83

incur/incurrir *v.* hacerse merecedor de una pena o un castigo; contraer; p. 291

indifferently/indiferentemente *adv.* de modo que muestra falta de interés, afecto o preocupación; p. 558

indignantly/con indignación *adv.* con rabia y desprecio dignos ante algo injusto o malo; p. 964

indolence/indolencia *s.* pereza; apatía; p. 27

indulge/consentir *v.* ceder a un deseo; complacer; p. 299

inert/inerte *adj.* inactivo; sin poder moverse o actuar; sin vida; p. 546

infamy/infamia *s.* maldad o perversidad extrema; p. 163

inhibit/inhibir *v.* reprimir los impulsos naturales; refrenarse; p. 491

inscribe/inscribir *v.* escribir, tallar o marcar en una superficie; p. 919

inscrutable/inescrutable *adj.* misterioso; p. 193

insular/insular *adj.* que tiene un punto de vista limitado; habitante de una isla; p. 481

intact/intacto *adj.* entero; ileso; con todas sus partes completas; p. 564

interlaced/entrelazado *adj.* conectado; entretejido; p. 111

interminable/interminable *adj.* que no termina; que dura mucho tiempo; eterno; p. 189

internment/internamiento *s.* acción de restringir a un lugar, especialmente durante una guerra; p. 463

intimidate/intimidar *v.* atemorizar o asustar; desafiar; p. 480

intone/entonar *v.* dar determinado tono a la voz; recitar; p. 1003

intricacy/complejidad *s.* cualidad de complejo, complicado o confuso; p. 383

intrigue/intrigar *v.* despertar la curiosidad o el interés por algo; fascinar; p. 130

invaluable/invaluable *adj.* de gran valor; que no se puede calcular; p. 497

irrational/irracional *adj.* contrario a la razón; ilógico; p. 464

irreproachable/irreprochable *adj.* sin culpa o crítica; sin falta alguna; p. 218

J

judiciously/sensatamente *adv.* de modo prudente; con buen juicio; p. 437

L

lament/lamentar *v.* expresar pena o arrepentimiento; p. 50

languor/languidez *s.* debilidad; fatiga; p. 273

lethargy/letargo *s.* período en que unos animales permanecen en inactividad y reposo; sopor, modorra; p. 159

loll/recostar *v.* reclinar; inclinar el cuerpo o alguna cosa sobre otro objeto; colgar; p. 427

loom/vislumbrarse *v.* surgir amenazadoramente; cobrar mucha importancia; p. 438

lucid/lúcido *adj.* claro en el razonamiento; alerta; p. 1049

lurk/acechar *v.* ocultarse y prepararse para atacar; p. 438

M

mainstream/de la cultura dominante *adj.* actitudes y valores más representativos de una sociedad o grupo; p. 496

makeshift/provisional *adj.* sustituto temporal del objeto apropiado o deseado; p. 64

malicious/malicioso *adj.* tener o manifestar el deseo de perjudicar a otro; p. 407

manifest/manifestar *v.* presentar; dar a conocer; decir; p. 378

materialistic/materialista *adj.* más preocupado de asuntos y bienes materiales que de asuntos intelectuales o espirituales; p. 250

mesmerizing/hipnotizante *adj.* fascinante; p. 51

meticulous/meticuloso *adj.* que se caracteriza por gran o excesiva preocupación hacia los detalles; p. 490

monologue/monólogo *s.* discurso largo que pronuncia un individuo; conversación dominada por una sola persona; p. 131

monosyllabic/monosilábico *adj.* de una sola sílaba; p. 121

mortify/mortificar *v.* afligir o preocupar; humillar o avergonzar; p. 301

muse/meditar *v.* pensar o reflexionar, especialmente en forma abstraída; p. 546

myriad/miríada *s.* multitud o infinidad de personas, cosas o asuntos; p. 81

N

notorious/notorio *adj.* de mala fama; público y sabido por todos; p. 887

O

obliterate/arrasar *v.* borrar; destruir por completo; p. 91

oblivious/abstraído *adj.* distraído; ensimismado; que no presta atención a lo que ocurre a su alrededor; p. 1072

obscurity/obscuridad *s.* falta de luz y claridad; p. 364

oppress/oprimir *v.* controlar o gobernar mediante fuerza o autoridad cruel o injusta; p. 12

oppressive/agobiante *adj.* agobiante; opresor; sofocante; p. 181

ostentatiously/ostentosamente *adv.* de un modo que busca llamar la atención o impresionar a otros; p. 883

ostracism/ostracismo *s.* exclusión de un grupo o sociedad; p. 1035

P

pall/manto *s.* palio; objeto que obscurece o cubre y da una atmósfera sombría; p. 355

palpable/palpable *adj.* que se puede tocar o sentir; p. 510

palpitating/palpitante *adj.* que vibra o se estremece; tembloroso; p. 482

pandemonium/pandemonio *s.* zafarrancho; algarabía; desorden; p. 347

pantry/alacena *s.* cuarto o armario en el que se guardan víveres o comestibles; p. 305

paradox/paradoja *s.* frase o situación que parece ilógica, contradictoria o absurda, pero que puede ser cierta; contrasentido; p. 320

paraphernalia/parafernalia *s.* conjunto de cosas que se usan en una determinada actividad; equipo; p. 262

patriarch/patriarca *s.* líder o jefe masculino de una familia o grupo; p. 463

patronize/ir a un negocio *v.* comprar o utilizar los servicios de una tienda o compañía de manera habitual; p. 378

pent-up/reprimido *adj.* que no se expresa o divulga; contenido; p. 206

perceive/percibir *v.* notar o comprender a través de los sentidos; p. 293

perilous/peligroso *adj.* azaroso; con riesgos; p. 151

permeated/impregnado *adj.* saturado; lleno; p. 191

perpetuate/perpetuar *v.* hacer que se siga recordando; p. 938

perplexed/perplejo *adj.* dudoso o incierto; confuso; p. 103

peruse/leer con atención *v.* escudriñar; examinar algo cuidadosamente; p. 450

perverse/perverso *adj.* que contraría a propósito lo que es razonable, esperado o deseable; p. 752

pestilential/perjudicial *adj.* peligroso; nocivo; destructivo; p. 274

petulantly/malhumoradamente *adv.* de mal modo; de mal genio; p. 964

phenomena/fenómenos *s.* hechos, sucesos o condiciones que se pueden conocer a través de los sentidos; p. 355

pilgrimage/peregrinación *s.* viaje largo, especialmente a un lugar sagrado y con fines religiosos; p. 1055

pious/piadoso *adj.* devoto; beato; p. 272

piqued/resentido *adj.* disgustado; ofendido; p. 262

plaintive/quejumbroso *adj.* que expresa dolor; que se queja; triste; p. 133

pompous/pomposo *adj.* ostentoso; vanidoso; magnífico o espléndido; p. 1063

predecessor/predecesor *s.* que precede o viene antes; precursor; p. 249

presentiment/presentimiento *s.* sensación de que algo está por pasar; p. 344

presumably/probablemente *adv.* supuestamente; con probabilidad; p. 279

presumptuous/presuntuoso *adj.* demasiado directo; atrevido; p. 175

prevail/prevalecer *v.* ser superior en poder o influencia; triunfar; p. 754

priceless/inapreciable *adj.* de un valor tal que no se puede calcular; p. 16

primeval/primitivo *adj.* relativo a lo inicial o primero; rudimentario; p. 324

prodigal/pródigo *adj.* derrochador; p. 280

prodigy/prodigio *s.* persona extraordinariamente talentosa, especialmente un niño; p. 49

profound/profundo *adj.* intenso y completo; p. 1021

profuse/profuso *adj.* abundante; cuantioso; p. 389

proliferation/proliferación *s.* reproducción o rápido crecimiento; p. 534

propriety/corrección *s.* cualidad de ser correcto o apropiado; conveniencia; p. 379

prosaic/prosaico *adj.* ordinario; vulgar; p. 177

prospective/presunto *adj.* probable o posible; futuro; p. 1039

prowess/habilidad *s.* gran pericia o destreza; p. 921

psalm/salmo *s.* poema, canción o himno sagrado; p. 111

R

rancor/rencor *s.* resentimiento; odio; p. 291

raptly/apasionadamente *adv.* con profundo interés o atención; p. 1019

rebuke/regañar *v.* reprender severamente; p. 152

reciprocal/recíproco *adj.* que se da, se siente o se muestra a cambio de una actitud similar; p. 133

reconciliation/reconciliación *s.* arreglo de una controversia o desacuerdo; p. 274

refrain/estribillo *s.* en una canción o poema, una frase o verso que se repite regularmente, especialmente al final de cada estrofa; p. 242

regally/fastuosamente *adv.* de modo grandioso o suntuoso, propio de reyes; p. 883

rejuvenate/rejuvenecer *v.* renovar; dar nuevos ánimos, juventud o frescura; p. 158

relevant/relevante *adj.* relacionado con el asunto en cuestión; pertinente; significativo; p. 521

relic/reliquia *s.* objeto que ha sobrevivido al paso del tiempo y que se conserva y valora por su interés histórico; p. 67

remonstrate/objetar *v.* decir o replicar en protesta; argüir; p. 290

repercussion/repercusión *s.* efecto o resultado de una acción o un suceso; p. 1045

repressed/reprimido *adj.* que se contiene o mantiene bajo control; frenado; p. 889

reprieve/aliviar *v.* dar un respiro; posponer algo desagradable o difícil; p. 363

reproach/reprochar *s.* culpar; censurar; criticar; p. 50

repulse/repulsión *s.* acción de repeler o rechazar; p. 728

residue/residuo *s.* lo que queda después de que se consume o retira la mayor parte de algo; p. 131

resilient/flexible *adj.* capaz de volver a su forma o posición original después de que se tuerce, estira o comprime; p. 321

resonant/resonante *adj.* que tiene un sonido que retumba o suena muy fuerte; p. 1049

retail/vender al menudeo *v.* vender directamente al consumidor; p. 40

retinue/séquito *s.* grupo de asistentes o sirvientes que acompaña a una persona de rango o autoridad; p. 242

reveling/deleitable *adj.* que da deleite; p. 207

reverie/ensoñación *s.* sueño despierto; visión que encanta; p. 53

ruefully/desconsoladamente *adv.* tristemente; penosamente; p. 970

rustic/rústico *adj.* relativo al campo; rural; p. 226

S

sagacious/sagaz *adj.* sabio o sensato; p. 390

sanctity/santidad *s.* cualidad de santo o de algo que merece inmenso respeto; p. 281

sashay/andar con desgano *v.* moverse o caminar de un modo que muestra indiferencia o falta de interés; p. 305

scenario/guión *s.* esbozo o modelo de una serie de sucesos previstos o imaginarios; p. 491

scrupulous/escrupuloso *adj.* muy atento a los más pequeños detalles; preciso; p. 937

scrutinize/escrutar *v.* mirar muy de cerca; inspeccionar cuidadosamente; p. 192

sedate/sosegado *adj.* que se mantiene tranquilo y sereno por naturaleza; calmado; p. 252

serenity/serenidad *s.* calma; tranquilidad; p. 190

sever/cortar *v.* separar; p. 249

sidle/moverse furtivamente *v.* caminar o deslizarse de forma que no llame la atención o que no moleste; p. 8

singular/singular *adj.* único, peculiar o especial; p. 366

sinister/siniestro *adj.* amenazante o que sugiere maldad; p. 178

skeptical/escéptico *adj.* que manifiesta duda o sospecha; suspicaz; incrédulo; p. 193

slew/montón *s.* grupo grande o numeroso; p. 242

solace/solaz *s.* alivio de una pena o desilusión; consuelo; p. 250

sparse/esparcido *adj.* extendido o distribuido en una capa delgada; p. 337

spasmodic/espasmódico *adj.* repentino, violento y temporal; p. 204

spawn/generar *v.* engendrar; crear; p. 358

spectral/espectral *adj.* fantasmal; estremecedor; p. 393

speculate/especular *v.* adivinar; p. 523

sporadic/periódico *adj.* esporádico; ocasional; p. 160

squalor/miseria *s.* pobreza y suciedad; sordidez; p. 146

staidness/sobriedad *s.* estado o cualidad de ser serio, estable o conservador por naturaleza; p. 219

stifling/sofocante *adj.* asfixiante; que ahoga; p. 189

stolid/impasible *adj.* que muestra poca o ninguna emoción; que no se conmueve fácilmente; p. 1034

strategic/estratégico *adj.* muy importante para una meta determinada; p. 986

stridently/estridentemente *adv.* de manera aguda y ruidosa; chillonamente; p. 437

subordinate/subordinar *v.* someter; tratar como secundario, inferior o de menor importancia; p. 471

subtle/sutil *adj.* que no es abierto ni directo; que no es obvio; p. 121

subversive/subversivo *adj.* que busca debilitar, destruir o derrocar; p. 220

succor/socorrer *s.* ayudar; auxiliar; p. 274

sumptuous/suntuoso *adj.* costoso y magnífico; p. 967

superfluous/superfluo *adj.* que no es necesario; inútil; p. 496

supplication/súplica *s.* ruego o solicitud intensa y humilde; p. 78

surmise/suponer *v.* conjeturar o concluir con poca o ninguna evidencia; p. 33

T

taut/tirante *adj.* tenso; tieso; p. 204

tedious/tedioso *adj.* aburridor; fastidioso; p. 534

temper/templar *v.* moderar o atenuar mezclando con otra cosa; p. 427

tenaciously/tenazmente *adv.* tercamente; persistentemente; p. 160

tentative/tentativo *adj.* que aún no se define o se termina; incierto; p. 357

tepid/templado *adj.* ligeramente tibio; p. 483

theorize/teorizar *v.* formarse una idea que explica un conjunto de hechos; p. 380

throng/apiñar *v.* reunir en grandes cantidades; amontonar; p. 969

tirade/perorata *s.* discurso largo y furibundo; p. 453

token/simbólico *adj.* que representa algo; p. 428

torturous/atormentador *adj.* que causa mucho dolor o sufrimiento; p. 496

totalitarian/totalitario *adj.* característico de un gobierno en el que un partido político tiene control total; p. 510

transient/temporal *adj.* transitorio o de corta duración; p. 537

tremulously/trémulamente *adv.* de modo tembloroso o vibrante; p. 1030

tribulation/penuria *s.* tribulación, gran pena o problema; sufrimiento; p. 350

tumultuous/tumultoso *adj.* muy alterado, confuso o agitado; p. 920

U

ulterior/ulterior *adj.* oculto; p. 219

ultimately/últimamente *adv.* por último, finalmente; p. 1004

unconditional/incondicional *adj.* absoluto; completo; p. 230

unimpeded/ininterrumpido *adj.* sin obstrucción ni obstáculo; p. 211

unkempt/desaliñado *adj.* descuidado; sin peinar ni arreglar; desarreglado; p. 1045

V

valid/válido *adj.* aceptable; legítimo; p. 481

vanquish/subyugar *v.* conquistar o vencer; p. 937

vault/saltar *v.* dar una voltereta; rebotar; p. 985

vehemently/vehementemente *adv.* intensamente; apasionadamente; p. 454

verandah/barandal *s.* balcón largo, usualmente con techo, que se extiende a lo largo de uno o más costados de una casa; p. 110

vermin/sabandija *s.* cualquier animal que es dañino, destructivo o molesto; p. 428

vexed/molesto *adj.* fastidiado; impaciente o furioso; disgustado; p. 151

vintage/añejo *adj.* que se caracteriza por tener un atractivo duradero; clásico; p. 64

void/vacío *s.* espacio desocupado; p. 228

vulgar/vulgar *adj.* sin buena educación o buen gusto; tosco; ordinario; p. 966

vulnerable/vulnerable *adj.* que se daña o lastima fácilmente; p. 496

W

wane/declinar *v.* menguar; reducir poco a poco; p. 148

wanton/licencioso *adj.* que no se puede contener; indecente; inmoral; p. 392

wary/cauteloso *adj.* cuidadoso; prudente; p. 144

whim/capricho *s.* idea o deseo repentino e innecesario; antojo; p. 1056

whimsical/curioso *adj.* con un sentido del humor muy particular; p. 467

wince/recular *v.* retroceder ligeramente, como cuando se siente dolor; hacer una mueca de dolor; p. 119

wont/habituado *adj.* acostumbrado; p. 270

Z

zealously/ardorosamente *adv.* fervientemente; con mucho entusiasmo; p. 31

Index of Skills

Boldface references indicate detailed treatment. References beginning with R refer to handbook pages.

Literary Concepts & Techniques

Abstract v. concrete language **411**

Act 713, R1

Allegory 154, 396. *See also* Metaphor.

Alliteration 185, 526, 579, **606,** 626, 631, 671, **685,** 974, 1011, R1

Allusion 105, 395, **526,** 768, **1042,** R1

Analogy 165, 214, R1. *See also* Metaphor, Simile.

Anapest R7

Anecdote 1036

Antagonist 2, 746, R1

Anthropomorphism 1009

Aside 720, **818,** R1

Assonance 579, **685,** 1011, R1

Atmosphere 153, **486,** 594, 605, 631, R1. *See also* Mood.

Author's purpose 171, 212, 423, **538,** 631, 647, 770, 898, 987, 1042, R1

Autobiography **422, 472,** 500, R2

Ballad 222, 956, R2

Biography **422,** R2

Blank verse **798,** R2

Character 2, 19, 60, **124,** 134, 153, 164, 196, 231, 295, 339, 352, 499, 605, 639, 646, 712, 714, 720, **768,** 818, 894, 975, 1011, 1026, 1051, 1057, 1058, R2

Characterization 45, 195, **231,** 606, 933, 957, 1037, **1050,** R2

    direct/indirect **1050,** R2

Chorus 722–723, 746, R2

Chronological order 20, 184, 422, 528, 618, **989,** R86–R87, R90

Classical Greek drama **722–725**

Climax 3, 86, 134, 974, 987, R2

Colloquial language 170, R2. *See also* Diction, Style.

Comedy 1074, R2

Comic relief R3

Conflict 3, **59,** 86, 92, 105, 223, **275,** 409, **429,** 456, 605, 746, 798, 857, R3

Connotation/denotation 72, **387,** 615, R3

Consonance 579, R3

Couplet R3, R12

Creative nonfiction 560

Dactyl R7

Denotation/connotation 72, **387,** 615, R3

Dénouement. *See also* Plot, Resolution.

Description 87, **112, 264, 359,** 360, 395, 409, 499, 551, 613, 679, 685, R3

Dialect **720,** 876, R3

Dialogue **44,** 170, **302,** 361, 713, **932,** 1074, 1075, R3

Dialogue tag line **46,** 1028

Diction 1057, R3–R4

Direct characterization 1050, 1057, R2

Drama 712–713, R4

Dramatic irony 372, **894,** 1000, R7

Dramatic monologue R4

Dramatic poetry R4

Dynamic character 410, R2

Elegy R4

Elizabethan drama **772–775**

Epic 956, R4

Epic simile **694,** R12

Essay R4

    expository 423, **902–905**

    narrative 422

    personal **1006,** 1007

persuasive 423

reflective **136**

Exposition 3, **551**

Expository essay 423, **902–905**

Extended metaphor 588, 693, **703–705**

External conflict 3, **59, 275,** 308, **429,** R3

Fable R4

Falling action 3, R4

Farce 1074, R5

Fiction 2–3, R5

Figurative language 538, **579, 680,** R5, R79

First-person point of view 2, **18, 164, 295,** R9

Flashback 339, 422, 989, R5

Flat character **124,** R2

Foil 373, R5

Folklore 267, **912,** 940, **898,** R5

Foot **578,** 579, 589, R5

Foreshadowing 182, 212, 223, 295, **326,** 768, **857,** 932, R5

Frame story R5

Free verse **627, 898,** R5

Genre 2–3, 422–423, 578–579, 712–713, R6

Haiku 686, R6

Hero/heroine 894, 913, 940, 941, 956, 957, 982, 987, 990, R6

Hexameter R7

Humor 551, 960, **1000,** 1001, 1027, 1038, 1051, 1074

Hyperbole **632,** 646, **1000, 1036,** R6

Iamb 589, R7

Iambic pentameter 589, R6

Idiom 896, **977**

Imagery **70,** 170, 440, **579,** 593, 598, 613, 631, 639, **653,** 658, **676,** 679, 680, 688, 700, 941, R6

Implied metaphor **695**

Indirect characterization 1050, 1057, R2

Informational text 422
Internal conflict 3, **59, 275,** 308, **429,** 708, R3
Inversion R6
Irony 35, 182, 264, 275, 295, 359, **372,** 1040, 395, 551, 598, **894,** 1000, 1042, 1075, R6
  dramatic irony 372, 894, 1000, R7
  situational irony 894, 1000, 1075, R6
  verbal irony 372, 894, 1000, R6
Legend 92, **912,** 959, R7
  Arthurian **912,** 959
Limited third-person point of view 2, **212, 295,** R9
Line 578
Literary history 722–725, 772–775
Local color 44, 153, **409,** R7
Lyric poem **647,** R7
Main character **124,** R2
Magical realism **385,** R7
Memoir **422, 440,** R7
Metaphor 326, 560, **579,** 593, **599,** 606, **680, 695, 702–705,** R7
Meter 578–579, R7
Minor character **124,** R2
Monologue **456,** R8
Mood 164, 182, 275, 339, **352, 395,** 560, 594, 605, 646, 688, 798, 956, 1050, R8
Moral **105,** 164, 195, 243, 395, R8
Motif **498,** R8
Myth 267, **912,** R8. *See also* Legend.
Narration R8
Narrative essay 422
Narrative poetry **584, 956,** R8
Narrator 2, 112, **134,** 164, 560, 1026, 1027, 1050, 1057, R8
Nonfiction 422–423, R8
  autobiography **422, 472,** 500, R2
  biography **422**
  creative nonfiction **560**

essay R4
  expository 423, **902–905**
  narrative 422
  personal **1006,** 1007
  persuasive 423
  reflective **136**
  memoir 422, **440,** R7
Novel R8
Octave R8
Ode 738, 745, 753, 756, R8
Omniscient point of view 2, 134, **295,** R9
Onomatopoeia 579, 701, R9
Oral tradition R9
Oxymoron R9
Parable R9
Paradox 513, R9
Parallelism 185, R9
Parody 1000, **1011,** R9
Pathos 492
Pentameter R7
Performance **724–725,** 773
Personal essay **1006,** 1007
Personification 579, 588, **614, 680,** 693, R9
Persuasive essay 423
Plot 3, **86,** 713, R9
  climax 3, 86, 134, 974, 987, R2
  dénouement R4
  exposition 3, **551**
  falling action 3, R4
  resolution 3, **275,** 987, R10
  rising action 3, **1026,** R11
Poetry 578–579, R9
Point of view 2, **18,** 153, **164, 212,** 285, **295,** 360, 567, R9
Problem 3, 646
Props 723, 774, R10
Prose 841, R10
Protagonist 2, **746,** R10
Pun 1000, R10
Quatrain 589, R10
Realism R10
Reflective essay **136**
Refrain R10
Repetition 112, 185, 526, 626, 631, 669, 974, R10
Resolution 3, **275,** 987, R10

Rhyme **579,** 626, R10
Rhyme scheme **579,** R10
Rhythm **578,** 621, R11
Rising action 3, **1026,** R11
Romance R11
Round character 124, R2
Sarcasm 1000
Satire **221,** 222, 1000, 1042, R11
Scansion R11
Scene **713,** R11
Science fiction 315, R11
Sensory details 70, **112,** 154, 441, 639, 646, 669, 700, 987, R11
Sestet R11
Setting 2, 18, 36, 44, 141, **153,** 195, 213, 231, 255, **395,** 409, 456, 658, 712, 1057, R11
Shakespearean drama 772–775
Short story, 2–3, 308–312, 412, R11
Simile 579, **594,** 631, **680, 694, 695,** 898, R12
Situational irony **894,** 1000, 1075, R6
Soliloquy **818,** 841, R12
Sonnet **589,** 593, R12
  Shakespearean/English 593
Sound devices 579, **685,** 693, R12
  alliteration 579, **606,** 626, 631, 669, **685,** R1
  assonance 579, **685,** 1011, R1
  consonance 579, R3
  onomatopoeia 579, **701,** R9
  rhyme **579,** R10
Speaker 578, 588, 593, 605, 613, 631, 639, **659,** 663, 669, R12
Spondee R7
Stage directions **712,** R12
Stanza **578,** 632, 658, R12
Static character R2
Stereotype R2, R12
Stream of consciousness 108, 112, 113, R12

Style **255,** 359, 684, R12

Subjective details 988

Suspense 164, **182,** 255, 818, 895, **987,** R13

Symbol/symbolism 86, 112, 124, 231, **243,** 255, 352, 385, 395, 409, 472, 584, 588, 605, 626, 646, 652, **664,** 700, 894, 898, 956, R13

Tall tale **940,** R13

Tanka 686, R13

Tetrameter R7

Theme 3, **35,** 134, 153, 170, 182, 231, 243, 255, 275, 285, **492,** 498, 593, 679, 693, 818, 941, 1006, 1043, **R13**

Thesis 423, **513,** R13

Tone 70, **195,** 221, **306,** 352, 588, 589, 593, 598, 605, 631, **640,** 679, 684, 685, 700, **974,** 1006, 1050, **R13**

Tragedy 724, **871, R13**

tragic flaw/hero 724, **768, 871, R13**

Trimeter R7

Trochee R7

Turning point. *See* Climax.

Understatement 285, 1000, R13

Verbal irony 372, **894,** 1000, R6

Voice 125, **566,** R13

Reading & Thinking

Activating prior knowledge (Focus) 6, 22, 38, 48, 62, 75, 88, 94, 108, 114, 128, 142, 156, 166, 172, 188, 198, 217, 224, 240, 247, 259, 268, 278, 288, 298, 304, 315, 329, 342, 354, 362, **374,** 376, 388, 398, **411,** 426, 432, 444, 459, 478, 488, 494, 506, 516, 531, 543, 556, 562, 582, 586, 591, 596, 602, 610, 622, 628, 635, 642, 648, 654, 660, 666, 676, 682, 686, 690, 697, 716, 726, 777, 878, 896, 914, 934, 944, 961,

982, 987, 1002, 1009, 1015, 1029, 1038, 1044, 1054, 1061, **R83**

Active reading strategies 4–5, 18, 424–425, 429, 580–581, 584, 714–715, 720, **R84**

clarifying 442, 553, **581, R84**

connecting **4,** 10, 16, **424,** 428, **715,** 719

evaluating **5,** 10, 12, **425,** 428, **715,** 719

imagining 580, 583

interpreting 287, **581, 583, 715,** 719

listening 580, **583, 714,** 718

predicting **4,** 7, 11, 15, **424,** 427, **715, R84**

questioning 4, 8, 10, 12, 13, 16, **424,** 427, **581, 583, 714,** 718, **R84**

responding **5,** 16, 17, **425,** 428, **580,** 584

reviewing **5,** 12, **425,** 428

visualizing **5,** 8, 10, **107,** 397, **425,** 427, 646, **714,** 718, **873, R84**

Analysis 153, 243–244, 255, 264, 275, 285, 295, 302, 339, 372, 385, 430, 440, 492, **R100–R103**

arguments 59, 275, 567

audience **R100**

autobiographical writing 1058

bias **R103**

character 124, 141, 154, 231, 295, 492, 746, 932, 957, 975, 994

dialogue 170, **302, 932,** 1075

humor 1074

imagery 70

irony 1075

logical reasoning 46, 221, **R102**

narrative style 1027

narrator's perspective 988

persuasive techniques **R103**

problem and solution **46,** 214

setting 18, 44, 141, 153, **395,** 1057

text structure R86, R100

word choice **R100**

Assumption 126

Author's purpose 112, 171, 212, 231, 255, 359, **423,** 456, 526, **538,** 566, 588, 688, **770,** 841, 857, 898, 974, 987

Bias R103

Cause and effect (as a text structure) R86–R87

Cause-effect relationships 18, 35, 59, **72,** 86, 105, 112, 153, **155,** 164, 170, 182, 195, 212, 221, 231, 243, 255, 275, 285, 295, 302, 306, 326, 339, 352, 372, 385, 395, 409, 456, **458,** 472, 486, 513, 526, 538, **540,** 551, 560, 584, 588, 768, 798, 974

Chronological order 20, 184, **989,** R86–R87, R90

Clarifying 441, **442,** 553, 581, **R84**

Classifying 164, 195, 295, 572, 669

Comparing and contrasting 70, **93,** 105, 134, 171, 182, 212, 221, 231, 264, 302, 306, 307, 326, 339, 360, 372, 385, 395, 416, 429, 456, 486, 499, 513, 538, **553,** 567, 588, 593, 613, 631, 652, 653, 680, 688, 693, 700, 706, 746, 798, 818, 857, 871, 898, 899, 906, 932, 940, 941, 956, 994, 1042, **1043,** 1074

Comparison and contrast (as a text structure) R86–R87

Comprehension strategies 4–5, 18, 424–425, 429, 580–581, 584, 714–715, 720, **R82–R92**

Connecting **4,** 10, 13, 16, **424, 715,** 719

Connotation **72, 615, R81**
Creative thinking 18, 626
Context **R78–R79**
Credibility **R95–R96, R100–R101**
Critical judgments 92, 170, 746, 768, 798
Cultures, *reading across* **93, R94, R96–R97**
Denotation **72, 615, R81**
Dramatic interpretation **R97**
Drawing conclusions 59, 70, 92, 105, 124, 153, 164, 182, 212, 221, 243, 255, 264, 275, 285, **297,** 302, 326, 339, 352, 372, 395, 409, 429, 440, 456, 492, 513, 538, 551, 560, 566, 588, 593, 605, 613, 626, 631, 639, 658, 663, 669, 679, 684, 700, 768, 841, 871, 894, 932, 940, 987, 1011, 1029, 1038, 1044, 1061, **R106–R107**
Elaborating 18, 35, 70, 86, 105, 112, 134, 153, 195, 264, 285, 306, 326, 339, 352, 372, 385, 395, 409, 429, 440, 456, 472, 486, 492, 513, 538, 551, 956, 987, 1036
Errors in logic **R102**
Establishing criteria 18, 35, 164, 302
Evaluating **5,** 10, 12, 44, 86, 92, 105, 112, 164, 195, 359, **425,** 429, 486, 498, 566, 593, 658, 688, 693, **715,** 719, 841, 871, 932, 940, 956, 974, 1006, 1026, 1042, 1057, 1074, **R101–R102**
Fact and fantasy 440
Fallacies in reasoning 566, **R102**
Flashback **989, R5**
Focusing on a question 395, 456, 894
Generalizing **37,** 124, 134, 164, 264, 295, 385, 409, 429, 472, 513, 605, 613, 987, 1006, 1074

Graphic aids 22, 38, 45, 71, 75, 142, 188, 198, 213, 214, 278, 298, 360, 396, 556, 584, 586, 589, 653, 690, 769, 878, 914, 941, 988, 1029, 1043, **R87–R89**
    charts 75, 142, 360, 499, 567, 635, 653, 941, 1029, 1043, **R88**
    diagram **R89**
    graph **R88**
    map 584, **R87**
    word map 298, 302, 432, 488, 690, 777, 914
Graphic organizers 278, 360, **R85**
Identifying assumptions 59, 124, **126,** 306, 429, 472, 486, 492, 513, 857
Imagining 580, 583
Inferring 18, 70, 92, 105, 112, 134, 153, 164, 170, 182, 195, 212, 221, 231, 243, **266,** 285, 302, 306, 326, 339, 352, 372, 385, **387,** 395, 429, 440, 456, 472, 486, 498, 526, 538, 588, 605, 626, 631, 746, 932, 956, 974, **976,** 987, 1006, 1026, 1036, 1042, 1050, **R91–R92, R102**
Intended audience, *analysis of* R100
Interpreting **287, 581, 583, 715,** 719
Listening 580, 583, 714, 718
Logical reasoning 46, 105, 221, **R102**
Main idea and supporting details 18, 35, 44, 59, 124, 134, 182, 295, 339, 372, 498, **513,** 538, 584, 598, 646, 693, 700, **943,** 1011, **R90**
KWL **R93**
Monitoring comprehension from reader's ideas 18, 35, 44, 59, 70, 86, 105, 112, 124, 134, 153, 164, 170, 182, 195, 212, 221, 231, 243, 255, 264, 275, 285, 295, 306, 326, 339,

352, 359, 372, 385, 395, 409, 429, 456, 472, 486, 492, 498, 513, 526, 538, 551, 566, 584, 588, 593, 598, 605, 613, 626, 631, 639, 652, 658, 669, 688, 693, 700, 746, 768, 818, 841, 857, 871, 894, 932, 956, 974, 987, 1011, 1026, 1036, 1042, 1050, 1057, 1074, **R98–R99**
Monitoring comprehension with details from text 18, 35, 44, 70, 86, 92, 105, 112, 134, 182, 195, 221, 255, 264, 275, 302, 306, 326, 339, 352, 359, 372, 429, 440, 472, 486, 513, 526, 551, 560, 566, 584, 588, 593, 605, 613, 639, 646, 652, 658, 663, 679, 684, 700, 720, **771,** 871, 894, 956, 974, 1011, 1026, 1050, 1057, 1074, **R84**
Order of importance **R90**
Paraphrasing 44, 134, 170, 182, 231, 255, 302, 306, 693, **771, 958, R90**
Personal background. *See* Activating prior knowledge.
Personal response 22, 35, 44, 59, 62, 86, 92, 105, 112, 124, 134, 153, 164, 170, 182, 195, 212, 221, 231, 243, 255, 264, 275, 295, 302, 306, 326, 339, 352, 359, 372, 385, 395, 409, 416, 429, 440, 456, 472, 486, 492, 498, 513, 526, 538, 551, 560, 562, 566, 572, 584, 588, 593, 598, 605, 613, 626, 631, 635, 639, 646, 652, 658, 663, 669, 679, 684, 688, 693, 700, 706, 720, 746, 768, 798, 818, 841, 857, 871, 894, 898, 906, 932, 940, 956, 974, 987, 994, 1006, 1011, 1036, 1042, 1057, 1074
Persuasive techniques **R102–R103**
Predicting **4,** 7, 11, 15, **223, 424,** 427, **715, R83**
Previewing **R82**

Problem and solution **46**, 933
Problem and solution (as a text structure) **214**
Purpose for reading. *See* Setting a purpose for reading.
Questioning **4**, 8, 10, 12, 16, **424, 581, 583, 714, 718, R84**
Reading aloud R97
Reading rate 771
Reading silently R94
References R80–R81
Research R104–R107
   drawing conclusions R106–R107
   generating questions R104
   locating information R104–R105
   organizing information R105
   presenting R106
Responding 5, 16, 17, **425**, 428, **580**, 1076
Reviewing 5, 12, **425**, 428
Scanning 257, 339, 513, 631, 646, 693, 700, 871
Self-assessment 416, 572, 706, 906, 994
Sequence of events (as a text structure) 551, **989**, **R86–R87**
Sequencing 20, 44, 86, 105, 124, 164, 182, **184**, 212, 221, 339, 352, 409, 429, 440, 472, 871, 940, **989**, **R90**
Setting a purpose for reading 6, 22, 38, 48, 62, 75, 88, 94, 108, 114, 128, 142, 156, 166, 172, 188, 198, 217, 224, 240, 247, 259, 268, 278, 288, 298, 304, 315, 329, 342, 354, 362, 376, 388, 398, 416, 426, 432, 444, 459, 478, 488, 494, 506, 516, 531, 543, 556, 562, 582, 586, 591, 596, 602, 610, 622, 625, 628, 635, 642, 648, 654, 660, 666, 676, 682, 686, 690, 697, 716, 726, 777, 878, 896, 914, 934, 944, 961, 982,

1002, 1009, 1015, 1029, 1038, 1044, 1054, 1061, **R82**
Skimming 975, **R93**
Sources, *reading varied* **R95–R96**
Spatial order **R90**
Study guides **R93**
Study strategies **R93**
Summarizing 44, **61**, 86, 124, 153, 164, 182, 231, 255, 264, **277**, 302, 306, 326, 352, 359, 372, 385, 409, 429, 440, 456, **474**, 486, 513, 526, 538, 551, 560, 593, 605, 679, 684, 700, 798, 841, 956, 1006, 1074, **R84, R91**
Text structures **R86, R100**
   cause and effect **R86–R87**
   comparison and contrast **R86–R87**
   problem and solution **214**
   sequence of events 551, **989**, **R86–R87**
Verifying predictions 35, 44, 513, 526, **R83**
Visualizing **5**, 8, 10, **107**, 397, **425**, 427, 646, **714**, 718, 873, **R84**
Word choice, *analysis of* **R100**

Grammar and Language

Abbreviations 553, **R52**
Abstract nouns 266, **411**
Action verbs **R44**
Adjectives **442, R38**
Adverbs **R38**
Antecedent **595**
Apostrophes 1014, **R25–R26, R51**
Appositives **37**
Auxiliary verb **R44**
Capitalization 540, **R45–R46**
Colons **R46**
Commas 942, **R26–R28, R47–R48**
Complements 397, **R39**
Complex sentence 1076, **R43**

Compound adjectives **442**
Compound-complex sentences 1076, **R43**
Compound sentences **R43**
Concrete nouns 266, **411**
Conjunctions **R39–R40**
Conjunctive adverb **R40**
Connotation 72, **387**
Coordinate adjective **374**
Coordinating conjunctions **R39–R40**
Correlative conjunctions **R40**
Dangling modifiers 900, **R25**
Dashes 257, 770, **R49**
Declarative sentences **R43**
Demonstrative pronouns **R42**
Denotation 72, **387**
Dialogue, *punctuation of* 126, 184
Exclamation marks **R46**
Exclamatory sentences **R43**
Fragments 73, 976, **R14–R15**
Future perfect tense **R44**
Gerunds **R40**
Hyphens **R51**
Imperative sentences **R43**
Indefinite pronouns **R42**
Infinitive phrases **297**
Infinitives 297, **R40**
Intensive pronouns **R42**
Interjections **R40**
Interrogative pronouns **R42**
Interrogative sentences **R43**
Intransitive verb **R44**
Introductory phrases **214**
Italics **R50**
Linking verbs **R44**
Misplaced modifiers 900, **R24**
Nonessential elements **942**
Nouns 266, 411, **R40–R41**
Numbers **R53**
Parallelism 185, **527**
Parentheses **R49**
Participles **61**, R41
Parts of speech
   adjectives 442, R38
   adverbs R38
   conjunctions R39–R40
   interjections R40

nouns 266, 411, R40–R41
prepositions R42
pronouns R42
verbs 287, R44
Past perfect tense R44
Periods 553, **R46**
Personal pronouns R42
Possessive apostrophe 1014
Possessive pronoun 20
Predicates 397, R41
Present perfect tense R44
Prepositional phrases 214, **474**
Prepositions R42
Pronouns R42
demonstrative R42
indefinite R42
intensive R42
interrogative R42
personal R42
reflexive R42
relative R42
Pronoun use
antecedent agreement **595**, R19–R20
person R21–R22
possessive 20
reference R20–R21
Punctuation 302
apostrophes 1014, R25–R26, R50–R51
colons **R46**
commas 942, R26–R28, **R47**
dashes 257, 770, **R49**
dialogue **126**, **184**
exclamation marks **R46**
hyphens **R51**
italics **R50**
parentheses **R49**
periods 553, **R46**
question marks **R46**
quotation marks 126, R49–R50
semicolons 155, **R47**
Question marks R46
Quotation marks 126, R49–R50
Reflexive pronouns R42
Relative pronouns R42

Run-on sentences 277, R15–R16
Semicolons 155, **R47**
Sentence
complex 1076, R43
compound-complex 1076, R43
compound R43
declarative R43
exclamatory R43
fragment **73**, **976**
imperative R43
interrogative R43
inverted 185, 958
run-on **233**
simple R43
Simple sentences R43
Spelling patterns R54–R57
Spelling strategies R54–R57
Subjects R43
Subject-verb agreement 476, 958, R17–R19
Subordinating conjunctions R40
Tag lines **46**, 361, 1028
Transitive verb R44
Verbs 287, **R44**
Verb tenses and voice
tense R22–R24, **R44**
voice (active/passive) 873, R44
Verbals
gerunds R40
infinitives **297**, R40
participles 61, R41

Vocabulary

Analogies 61, 113, 135, 165, 214, 244, 277, 297, 353, 387, 397, 442, 457, 493, 514, 540, 873, 1058
Antonyms 87, 232, 770
Base words 20, 375
Compound words 72
Context clues 184, 246, 287, 607, 1059, R78–R79
Connotation 387, 895, R81
Dialect 720

Dictionary skills 477, 607, 976, R80
Denotation 387, 895, R81
Etymology 46, 266, 303, 374, 487, 553, 933, 1076
Glossaries R80–R81
Homophones 819
Idiom 977
Multiple meaning words 155, 430, 607, 896
Old words 1027
Prefixes 106, 126, 257, 327, R79
Roots 184, 340, 375, 561, 1007, 1037, 1051, R79
Semantic map 958
Suffixes 196, R79
Synonyms 37, 411, 988
Technical vocabulary R79
Usage 222
Word webs 432, 488, 690, 777

Writing

Accident report 1051
Adventure 327
Advertisement 327
Advertising jingle 1009
Advice 306, 307, 594
Analogies 296
Analysis
allegory 154, 396
author's purpose 498
bias 769
cause and effect 165
character 19, 60, 71, 195, 222, 232, 373, 410, 527, 552, 561, 933, 957, 975, 1037
characterization 353, 373, 561, 818
compare and contrast 19, 232, 589, 664, **902–905**, 1007
concluding statement 539
details 87
dialogue 1075
diction 627

double meanings 303, 430
drawing conclusions 514
humor 1051
imagery 327
literary technique 106, 183, 256, 441, 640, 647
mood 340, 457, 594, 614
narrator's perspective 988
personification 386
poetic elements 680, 706
poetic form 632
poetic structure 701
poetry 589, 599
poet's task 694
setting 36, 213, 276, 340, 473
stanzas 584
style 1027
suspense 895
tragedy 769
theme 659
title 286
tone 589, 685
viewpoint 664, 747
Application 539
Audience and purpose 136, 235, 308, 412, 500, 568, 616, 670–671, 702, 903, 990–991, 1078–1079
Autobiographical incident 500–504
Ballad 222
Book jacket 988
Business letter 473, 913, R70
Business writing 473, 616–620, 913, R70–R71
Case study 386
Character sketch 45, 196, 527, 606, 653, 933, 1058
Comic book 1001
Conclusions 413, 514, 799
Creative writing 19, 36, 45, 71, 87, 92, 125, 141, 154, 165, 170, 183, 196, 213, 222, 256, 265, 276, 286, 303, 306, 313, 327, 340, 359, 373, 386, 410, 430, 457, 473, 487, 498, 514, 527, 539, 552, 561, 589, 594, 599, 632, 640, 653, 659,

670–674, 680, 685, 701, 747, 769, 798, 841, 872, 933, 940, 957, 975, 988, 1007, 1011, 1027, 1037, 1075
Definitions 135, 527
Descriptive writing 19, 108, 244, 376, 441, 493, 568–571, 614, 664, 685, 702–705, R63
Details 528
Diary entries 487, 1075
Dialogue 106, 170, 232, 360, 361, 561, 975, 1037
Drafting 138, 236, 310, 414, 502, 570, 619, 672, 704, 904, 992, 1080, R60
Editing (proofreading) 140, 238, 312, 415, 504, 571, 620, 674, 705, 905, 993, 1081, R61
Editorial 798
Effective language 1060
Elaborating 139, 237, 414, 570, 673
Emphasis 185
Ending of story 213, 232, 256
Epigraph 313
Essay R4
  expository 423, 902–905
  narrative 422
  personal 1006
  persuasive 423
  reflective 136–140
Expository writing 902–905, 990–993, 1078–1081, R62
Extended metaphor 702–705
Feature article 1078–1081
Figurative language 1060
Finding/focusing topic 137, 234, 309, 412–413, 501, 568, 617, 670, 702–703, 902, 990, R59
Freewrite 108, 172, 459, 494, 562, 596, 628, 671, 676, 1015, 1038
Haiku 688
Hyperfiction 186–187
Incident report 747, 895
Interview 45, 541, 616–620, 872

Introduction 431
Journal entry 48, 60, 156, 275, 285, 302, 398, 426, 486, 516, 529, 562, 602, 627, 640, 648, 666, 676, 716, 857, 944, 1049, 1044, 1051, 1054, 1061
Letter 87, 135, 183, 196, 234–238, 286, 306, 353, 396, 473, 498, 505, 514, 527, 539, 606, 632, 653, 747, 913, 1042
Limerick 92
Memo 940
Memorial 359
Metaphor 695
Monologue 213, 296, 303, 430, 640, 659, 721
Motto 694
Narrative essay 422
Narrative writing 500–504, 957, R63
Nature journal 154, 614
Newspaper article 141, 675, 933
Obituary 125
Observational report 568–571
Parody 1011
Peer review/editing 139, 237, 311, 414, 503, 570, 619, 673, 704, 904, 992, 1078, R60
Personal writing 60, 106, 113, 128, 136–140, 195, 232, 244, 296, 353, 396, 441, 493, 606, 614, 627, 647, 664, 694, 857, 1051, 1058
Personal essay 1006
Persuasive essay 423
Persuasive writing 185, 234–238, 412, 913, 940, R63
Picture storybook 410
Plaque 359
Play 307
Plot 309
Poetry 71, 92, 552, 589, 599, 647, 659, 670–674, 680, 685, 688, 1007, 1011
Point of view 309, 640, 1027
Press release 141

Prewriting 136–137, 234–235, 308–309, 412–413, 500–502, 568–569, 616–617, 670–671, 702–703, 902–903, 990–991, 1078–1079, **R58–R60**

Psychological analysis 386

Publishing/Presenting 140, 238, 312, 415, 504, 571, 600–601, 620, 674, 705, 905, 993, 1081, **R61**

Quickwrite 6, 247, 268, 288, 329, 376, 531, 610, 660, 686, 934, 1009

Reflective essay 136–140

Research paper 990–993, **R65–R69**

Review 872

Revising 139, 237, 311, **414, 503,** 570, 619, 673, 704, 904, 992, 1080, **R60–R61**

Role 457

R.S.V.P. 396

Satire 222

Scene 566

Script 165

Sentence variety 277

Sequel 232, 276

Short story 308–312, 1027

Simile 695

Skits 1001

Song lyrics 92, 340, 473

Speech 420, 841

Tall tale 940

Tanka 688

Theme 309

Technical writing R70–R71

Travel brochure 431, 959

Writing about literature. *See* Analysis.

Writing modes R62–R63

Writing process 136–140, 234–238, 308–312, 412–415, 500–504, 568–571, 616–620, 702–705, 902–905, 990–993, 1078–1081, R58–R61

Writing skills
  conclusions **413,** 514, **799**

details 528

dialogue 361

effective language 1060

emphasis 185

simile and metaphor 695

main idea and supporting details 943

Listening, Speaking, and Viewing

Advertising 327, 1037

Choral reading 621

Critical viewing
  paintings 9, 14, 17, 25, 28, 33, 42, 54, 57, 69, 77, 82, 97, 101, 103, 116, 120, 132, 149, 159, 162, 169, 174, 179, 191, 194, 203, 206, 228, 271, 281, 283, 284, 293, 334, 337, 345, 365, 366, 369, 381, 384, 391, 402, 406, 434, 439, 559, 731, 788, 792, 811, 822, 831, 836, 842, 880, 888, 891, 921, 922, 927, 955, 968, 971, 972, 1005, 1018, 1023, 1024, 1031, 1034, 1056, 1064, 1069
  photographs 78, 79, 220, 448, 452, 466, 468, 484, 511, 520, 523, 952
  sculpture 740, 763, 766, 781, 783, 807, 918, 937
  other media 130, 735, 795, 802, 827, 855, 866, 869, 917, 950, 966

Debate 71, 87, 92, **127,** 154, 183, 256, 265, 296, 340, 354, 396, 493, 514, 614

Dialogue 87, 125, 232, 265, 276, 360, 499, 594, 818

Discourse (discussing literature)
  advice 898
  author's purpose 303, 694, 895, 1042
  author's viewpoint 87, 872, 988
  cause and effect 276, 720

character 71, 93, 154, 165, 196, 232, 307, 327, 457, 653, 720, 769, 957, 1037, 1075

compare and contrast 19, 213, 306, 307, 589, 653, 680, 694, 720

definition of poetry 701

dialogue 87, 798

humor 1051

imagery 113, 685

irony 1075

literary techniques 1007, 1027, 1043, 1058

main idea 664

metaphors 599, 606

monologue 307, 798

organization and structure 1007

persuasive effect 222

philosophical thought 165, 566

poetic devices 632

review 1011

rhetorical techniques 841

scene 975

sound devices 606

symbolism 353

theme 410, 647

values 640

Dramatic presentations
  dialogue 87, 125, 232, 265, 276, 360, 594, 694, 818
  monologue 213, 296, 307, 640, 721
  one-act play 183
  play 71, 183, 307
  readers theater 21, 183, 307, 386, 440, 818, 1005, **1077**
  reenactment 975
  role-playing 135
  scene 244, 286, 457, 566, 818, 895, 975
  skit 1001

Group discussions (sharing ideas personal response) 36, 45, 60, 93, 114, 125, 128, 166, 213, 224, 232, 240, 286, 304, 315, 342, 354, 359, 373,

386, 388, 396, 430, 444, 457, 473, 478, 487, 506, 527, 539, 552, 561, 582, 594, 614, 640, 654, 680, 694, 697, 726, 895, 957, 1002, 1042

brainstorm 244, 278, 566, 621, 933

character 141, 154, 265, 307, 552, 747

cultural preservation 410, 514, 627

opinions 538, 898

roles 988

symbols 353

Inaugural address 933

Infomercial 505

Interviewing 239, 303, 373, 396, 441, 487, 505, **541,** 614, 627, 659, 1043, 1058

Listening techniques 441, 527, 606, 988

Monologue 213, 296, 640, 721

Multimedia 585

Newscast 1051

Newsmagazine 239

Oral reading 606, 675, **1077**

announcement 975

dialogue 125, 276

poetry 441, 585, 606, **633,** 664, 694

Oral report 71, 431, 599, 680, 685, 1007

Paintings. *See* Critical viewing.

Pantomime 1001

Performing

dialogue 87, 125, 232, 265, 276, 360, 499, 594, 694, 818

monologue 213, 296, 640, 721

pantomime 1001

play 183, 307

poetry interpretation 701

poetry reading 21, 244, 307, 441, 585, 664, 694, 818, 999, 1005, **1077**

readers theater 183, 694, 818, 1001, **1077**

scene 244, 386, 566, 818, 895, 975

song 473

sportscast 632

storytelling 36, 135, **267,** 988

television show 21

Photographs. *See* Critical viewing.

Play 183, 307

Poetry reading 244, 307, 441, 585, 664, 694, 1005, **1077**

Public speaking 232, 621, 933

craft demonstration 653

inaugural address 933

monologue 296, 640, 721

newscast 1051

newsmagazine 239

persuading 621, **901**

speech 106, 430, 621, 898, **901,** 933

Readers theater 183, 694, 818, **1077**

Reenactment 975

Role-playing 87, 135, 286, 567

Television commercial 1007

Television show 21

Scene 244, 386, 457, 818, 895, 975

Sculpture. *See* Critical viewing.

Skit 1001

Song 473, 933

Speech 106, 430, 621, 898, **901,** 933

Sportscast 632

Storytelling 36, **267,** 988

Research and Study Skills

CD-ROM 872, **R72**

Downloading R73

Drawing conclusions R106–R107

Electronic databases 675, **R73**

Electronic resources 675, R72–R73

E-mail 554–555

Generating questions 599, 991, R104

Graphic organizers R85

Internet 45, 93, 154, 165, 222, 232, 286, 327, 373, 410, 431, 457, 473, 527, 539, 552, 560, 594, 599, 600–601, 627, 647, 664, 675, 680, 685, 688, 857, 872, 899, 959, 1007, **R72–R73**

Interview 303

Library/reference resources 60, 93, 303, 431, 594, 632, 647, 680, 685, 694, 701, 747, 857, 872, 959, 990, 1007, **R72–R73**

Locating information 991, **R104–R105**

Note taking 19, 267, 901, 991, **R66**

On-line catalogues 113, 899, **R73**

Organizing information R105

Outlining 991, R67

Research reports 45, 60, 71, 154, 276, 614, 747, 1007

Test-taking skills R74–R77

Media and Technology

Comic strip 216, 314, 1008

Downloading R73

Electronic databases 675, **R73**

Electronic resources 675, R72–R73

E-mail 554–555

Government document 475

Infomercial 505

Internet 45, 113, 154, 165, 196, 222, 232, 258, 286, 327, 373, 410, 431, 457, 473, 505, 527, 539, 552, 561, 594, 600–601, 647, 664, 675, 680, 685, 857, 872, 899, 959, 1007, 1058, R72–73

Internet connection 45, 165, 222, 232, 286, 373, 410, 457, 473, 527, 560, 599, 627, 664, 694, 1027, 1058

Interview 641

Itinerary 443

Journal 529–530

Magazine article 74, 328, 608–609, 634, 877, 1028

Media Connection
comic strip 216, 314, 1008
government document 475
interview 641
itinerary 443
journal 529–530
magazine article 74, 328, 608–609, 634, 877, 1028
multimedia presentation 585, 694
newspaper article 245, 696
news service article 197
press conference 689
press release 47
screenplay 960
song lyrics 590, 980
television transcript 515
travel guide 665
Web site 258

Multimedia presentation 585, 694

News broadcast 1051

Newspaper article 245, 696

News service article 197

On-line information services 286

Press conference 689

Press release 47

Producing media 600–601

Publishing 600–601

Rap 776

Screenplay 960

Song lyrics 590, 980

Technology skills
database 1012–1013
E-mail 554–555
hypertext 186–187
internet publishing 600–601
word processing 874–875

Television transcript 515

Travel guide 665

Web site 258

Life Skills

Accident report 1051

Advertisement 327

Brochure 431

Bumper sticker 493

Career choices 647

Chart 647, 680, 1027

Collaborating (team member and partner) 125, 327, 410, 493, 505, 552, 694, 701, 895, 1075

Community resources 125, 256

Creating and producing
accident report 1051
advertisement 327
brochure 431
bumper stickers 493
chart 647, 680, 1027
genealogical chart 769
incident report 747, 895
infomercial 505
lesson for class 552
letter 135, 340, 913, 1037, 1042
log (naturalist) 614
memo 940
model car 71
news report 872
obituary 957
pamphlet 60, 183
poster 154
public service announcement 353
quilt block 653
résumé 303
satire 222
scroll 975
sportscast 632

Decision making 183, 505

Implementing and performing
food drive 514
home art or craft 653
interview 183, 1058

Food drive 514

Genealogical chart 769

Home art or craft 653

Incident report 747, 895

Infomercial 505

Interview 19, 183, 373, 441, 1058

Leading and organizing 514

Lightning 552

Log (naturalist) 614

Memo 940

News report 872

Obituary 957

Planning and designing 71, 141, 505, 539, 647, 769

Poster 154, 913

Problem solving 165, 1075

Public service announcement 353

Quilt block 653

Responsibilities 106

Résumé 303

Sportscast 632

Interdisciplinary Studies

Advertisement 1037

Anthropology (cultures) 561, 567, 988. *See also* Social studies.

Art 21, 71, 87, 239, 244, 296, 396, 688
advertisement 1037
brochure (travel) 431
collage 21
comic strip 721, 1001
diorama (of set) 769
drawing, sketching 71, 87, 196, 213, 296, 362, 589, 642, 685, 693
film 585
history of art 45, 386
magazine cover 957
mask 747
multimedia 585
mural 165
painting 21, 45, 71
picture book 244
portrait 265
quilt block 653
set design (drama) 720, 769, 1075
video cases 239

Astronomy 681

Biology 170, 313, 327, 430, 552, 567

Brochure (travel) 431
Cartoon 721
Collage 21
Comic strip 721, 1001
Diorama (of a set) 769
Drama 769, 1075
Drawing, sketching 71, 87, 213, 296, 362, 589, 642, 685, 693
Earth science 256, **681**
Environmental science 659
Family and consumer sciences 653
Film 585
Geography 141, 584, 594, **959**
Health 215, 599

History 36, 60, 106, 154, 276, **341,** 487, 514, 685, 857, 872, 913
History of art 45, 386
Language arts 876
Magazine covers 957
Masks 747
Mathematics 589
Multimedia 585
Murals 165
Music 410, 431, 647
 history of jazz 701
 lyrics 113, 473, 933
Painting 21, 45, 71
Picture book 244
Portrait 265

Quilt block 653
Science and technology 313, 327, **542,** 567, 599, 659, 680
Set design (drama) 720, 769, 1075
Social studies 19, 441, 487, 514, 561, 857, 988
Sports 215, 632, 640, 1007
Theater
 role-playing 87, 286
 scenes 566, 975
 See also Listening, Speaking, and Viewing: Dramatic Presentations.
Video cases 239
Workplace education 303, **1053**

Index of Authors and Titles

A

Abel, Robert 1016
Achebe, Chinua 39
Acosta, Teresa Palomo 650
Afro-American Fragment 623
Allen, Samuel 630
Allende, Isabel 343
American Childhood, An,
    from 1030
And of Clay Are We Created 343
Angelou, Maya 489
Angry Winter, The 557
Antigone 748
Appetizer 1016
Arthur Becomes King 962
As It Is with Strangers 279
Astrologer's Day, An 260
Atwood, Margaret 655

B

Baines, Lawrence 776
Barry, Dave 1039
Base Stealer, The 629
Bashō, Matsuo 687
Beard, Henry 1010
Benét, Stephen Vincent 95
Bevier, Thomas 197
Big River: The Adventures of
    Huckleberry Finn, from 717
Blessing, A 612
Boar Hunt, The 157
Booth, Philip 603
Boyle, Kay 363
Bradbury, Ray 316
Brooks, Gwendolyn 611
Bruchac, Joseph 983
Bus Along St. Clair:
    December, A 655
By Any Other Name 479
By the Waters of Babylon 95

C

Californian's Tale, The 248
Calvino, Italo 241

Car We Had to Push, The 1045
Catch the Moon 63
From a Cat's Garden of Verses
    1010
Censors, The 218
Cervantes, Lorna Dee 656
Chang, Diana 667
Chee's Daughter 23
Chekhov, Anton 1062
Child, a Dog, the Night, A 129
Child's Christmas in
    Wales, A 433
Childress, Alice 305
Chin, Marilyn 649
Cipriano, Ralph 877
Civil Peace 39
Clifton, Lucille 638
Cofer, Judith Ortiz 63
Colette 299
Colombia's Mortal Agony 355
Constantly risking absurdity 692
Contents of the Dead Man's
    Pocket 199
Culturally Sensitive Traveler,
    The 665

D

Delicious Death, A 167
Destination Wales 443
Dillard, Annie 1030
Dinesen, Isak 225
Dr. Martin Luther King's Early
    Days 515
Drakulić, Slavenka 507

E

Ehrlich, Gretel 544
Eiseley, Loren 557
Eldorado 583
Endrezze, Anita 661
Erdoes, Richard 89
Esteves, Sandra María 698
Everyday Use 7

Ex-Basketball Player 636
Exploring Antarctic Ice 532

F

False Gems, The 289
Farewell to Manzanar, from 460
Ferlinghetti, Lawrence 692
Finney, Jack 199
First Lesson 603
Floral Apron, The 649
For Poets 683
Ford, Gerald 475
Foreign Ways 667
Francis, Robert 629
Freeway 280 656
Frost, Robert 643

G

Garza, Melita Marie 696
Gimbel, Norman 980
Giovanni, Nikki 1003
Glory of the Day Was in Her
    Face, The 597
Gomez, Jewelle L. 495

H

Haiku 687
Halfway House for Horses 608
Happy Man's Shirt, The 241
Hauptman, William 717
Hayden, Robert 604
Heaven 624
Henningsen, Michael 47
Hogan, Linda 668
Holiday Traffic Brings Out Fear
    on Suspension Bridge 197
Hoops Picks Up a Jazz Beat 696
Horses Graze 611
Houston, James D. 460
Houston, Jeanne Wakatsuki 460
How I Changed the War and Won
    the Game 1055
Hughes, Langston 623

I

Idylls of the King, from 945
Interlopers, The 269
Ise, Lady 687
I've Seen the Promised Land 517
Iwasaki, Laura 678

J

Jacobs, William Wymark 173
Jazz Fantasia 699
Jewett, Sarah Orne 143
Johnson, James Weldon 597
Julius Caesar, The Tragedy of 778

K

Kaffir Boy, from 445
Kincaid, Jamaica 109
King, Martin Luther Jr. 517
Kvinta, Paul 74

L

Lame Deer 89
Le Morte d'Arthur, from 915
Lessing, Doris 76
let my spirit fly in time 698
Let's Sweat! 1003
Living Well. Living Good. 489
Lowell, Amy 677
Lucille Clifton Interview 641
Lullaby 330

M

Making a Fist 661
Making Hay 634
Malory, Thomas 915
Mark Antony Rap, The 776
Marked 897
Márquez, Gabriel García 189
Marriage Proposal, A 1062
Marshall, Paule 399
Masque of the Red Death, The 389
Match to the Heart, A, from 544

Mathabane, Mark 445
Maupassant, Guy de 289
Millay, Edna St. Vincent 592
Miller, Siyowin 23
Miss Rosie 638
Missing You 597
Momaday, N. Scott 592
Monkey's Paw, The 173
Monty Python and the Holy Grail, from 960
Motto from Poets: Leave Stone, A 691
Moyers, Bill 641
Mrs. James 305
My Mother Pieced Quilts 650

N

Narayan, R. K. 260
Neruda, Pablo 644
Niggli, Josephina 879
Night Clouds 677
Nye, Naomi Shihab 661

O

Once and Future King, The, from 962
One Perfect Rose 587

P

Parker, Dorothy 587
Passing of Arthur, The 945
Pfeffer, Susan Beth 279
Pizza in Warsaw, Torte in Prague 507
Platero, Juanita 23
Poe, Edgar Allan 389, 583
Ponce, Mary Helen 1055

R

Rau, Santha Rama 479
Reapers 683
Rendic, Amalia 129
Retamar, Roberto Fernández 691

Return from First Summit Depot 529
Ring, The 225
Ring Finders of Philly, The 877
Ring of General Macías, The 879
Ríos, Alberto Alvaro 377
Road Not Taken, The 643
Ross, Gayle 983
Russell, George 355

S

Saki (Munro, H. H.) 269
Saleswoman, The 299
Sandburg, Carl 699
Scott, R. F. 529
Shakespeare, William 587, 778
Shall I Compare Thee to a Summer's Day? 587
Silko, Leslie Marmon 330
Simile 592
Sledge, Percy 590
Smith, Wen 1028
Song, Cathy 624
Song For My Name 668
Sophocles 727
Sound of Thunder, A 316
Steinbeck, John 427
Stephens, Melanie L. 608
Stevens, Jane Ellen 532
Steves, Rick 665
Sundiata, from 935
Swimming Lesson, A 495

T

Tafolla, Carmen 897
Tan, Amy 49
Tennyson, Alfred, Lord 945
Termination of Executive Order 9066 475
This Week's Horoscope for Your Dog 258
Thomas, Dylan 433
Thomas, Lewis 563
Those Winter Sundays 604
Three Generations of Navajo Weavers 328

Through the Tunnel 76
Thurber, James 1045
Tiger Year 678
Ting, Shu 597
To Da-duh, In Memoriam 399
To Satch 630
Too Much Spice 1028
Toomer, Jean 683
Travels with Charley, from 427
Tucson Zoo, The 563
Tuesday Siesta 189
Twain, Mark 248
Two Kinds 49
Two Tanka 687
Tyler, Anne 115

U

U.S. Aerialists Are Golden 689
Updike, John 636

V

Valenzuela, Luisa 218
Vasconcelos, José 157
Verducci, Tom 634
Villanueva, Alma Luz 167
Vision Quest, The 89
Vogt, Amanda 245

W

Walker, Alice 7
Waltz of the Fat Man 377
We Are Many 644
We, Too, Are One: Renowned Jazz Pianist Toshiko Akiyoshi Bridges the Gap 47
Well, I Have Lost You; and I Lost You Fairly 592
What I Have Been Doing Lately 109

What Is and Ain't Grammatical 1039
What is the meaning of this? We ponder happiness 245
What We Believe 661
When a Man Loves a Woman 590
Where No One Has Gone Before? 74
Where the Girl Rescued Her Brother 983
White Heron, A 143
White, T. H. 962
Winter Night 363
With All Flags Flying 115
Wonder Woman 980
Wright, James 612

Y

Young, Al 683

Index of Art and Artists

Andre, Albert, *Au Theatre* 710–711

Arikha, Avigdor, *August* 103

Armitage, Karen, *Lynford* 604

Atl, Dr., *Amanecer* 132

Avery, Milton, *Checker Players* 1034

Barnet, Will, *Woman and the Sea* 592

Bauer, Jerry, *Dwarf forest, Puerto Rico* 316–317

Beardsley, Aubrey, *How Sir Bedivere Cast the Sword Excalibur Into the Water* 950

Beasley, Phoebe, *His Grandmother's Quilt* 650–651

Berni, Antonio, *El Chico de la Gorra Verde (Juanito Laguna)* 130

Blaine, Nell, *Big Table with Pomegranates* 284

Botero, Fernando, *Dancers* 377

Botero, Fernando, *Man on a Horse* 384

Botero, Fernando, *The Street* 381

Boudin, Eugene, *Soleil Couchant* 97

Boulanger, Gustave, *The Barber Shop of Licinius* 792

Braddock, Leslie, *Woman in Blue* 1031

Brown, Louise Freshman, *Heron* 142

Buckler, John Chessell, *St. Mawes Castle, Cornwall* 957

Bunker, John S., *Two Fish* 1023

Buonarroti, Michelangelo, *Brutus* 849

Burchard, Pablo, *Wall with a Door and Tree (Muro con Puerta y Arbol)* 888

Burchfield, Charles, *Country Road in July* 116

Burne-Jones, Edward, *The Sleep of Arthur in Avalon* 954

Calderon, William Frank, *How Four Queens Found Sir Lancelot Sleeping* 922

Cameron, Julia Margaret, *The Passing of Arthur* 952

Carletti, Alicia, *A Long Time Ago (Hace Mucho Tiempo)* 366

Carpeaux, Jean Baptiste, *Costume Ball in the Tuileries: Napoleon III and the Countess Castiglione* 391

Carrick, James Mulcaster, *Morte d'Arthur* 945

Cassatt, Mary, *Woman with a Pearl Necklace in a Loge* 289

Chagall, Marc, *L'eté* 576

Chen, Tsing-Fang, *Human Achievement* 913

Chinn, Lawrence, *Portrait* 57

Clark, Don, *Friends in the Dark* 33

Cooke, John, *Jungfrau* 505

Courbet, Gustave, *Le Chemineau (The Hobo)* 228

Covarrubias, Miguel, *Rhapsody in Blue* 699

Cowper, Frank Cadogan, *Lancelot Slays the Caitiff Knight Sir Tarquin and Rescues the Fair Lady and the Knights in Captivity* 927

Darter, Michael, *Two girls in saris* 479

Dave, Anil A., *Interior of an Indic house* 484

de Carmontelle, Louis Carrogis, *Leopold Mozart with Wolfgang & Nannerl, playing music* 60

del Sarto, Andrea, *Tribute to Caesar* 778

Eakins, Thomas, *Frank John St. Jay* 174

Ellis, Gerry, *Petroglyphs on exposed stones, Arches National Park, UT* 691

Faulkner, Douglass, *Untitled* 79

Ferbert, Mary Lou, *Chicory and Flatiron Building* 656

Garden, William Fraser, *The Wood at Dusk* 271

Garza, Carmen Lomas, *Sandia/Watermelon* 1056

Goodwin, Frank, *View on the Coast of Cornwall* 968

Gorman, Robert C., *Seated Woman* 668

Gracia, Carmen, *"There sleeps Titania sometime of the night lull'd in flowers…"* 675

Gronk, *La Tormenta* 879

Gubb, Louise, *Alexandra Township* 445

Gubb, Louise, *Children in Alexandra Township* 452

Guglielmi, O. Louis, *The Persistent Sea No. 2* xxvi

Gwathmey, Robert, *Children Dancing* 42

Haas, Richard, *William Street at Night* 203

Holland, Brad, *Fishing* 1001

Hopper, Edward, *Gas* 637

Hopper, Edward, *Rocky Sea Shore* 82

Hopper, Edward, *Room in New York* 199

Horsley, John Callcott, *The Boyhood of Arthur* 972

Hovenden, Thomas, *The Old Version* 179

Howe, Oscar, *Dakota Teaching* 662

Inness, George, *Taking a Walk* 143

Jacquette, Yvonne, *Flatiron Intersection* 206

Jinsheng, Huang, *Girl in Blue Sweater* 649

John, W. Goscombe, *Merlin & Arthur* 918

Johnson, Geoff, *People queuing for bread, Prague* 511

Johnson, William H., *Girl in a Green Dress* 9

Johnson, William H., *Minnie* 14

Jones, Loïs Mailou, *Magic of Nigeria* 45

Kahlo, Frida, *Self-Portrait* 880

Kahlo, Frida, *Two Women* 891

Katz, Alex, *Purple Wind* 365

Kiitsu, Seisei, *Flowers and grasses of the seasons: Autumn* 687

Kingman, Dong, *Night Lights of Kowloon* 667

Knight, Dame Laura, *Snowballing* 434

Koch, John, *Lamplight with Dora* 369

Lauré, Jason, *Small boys waiting by snack shop in Alexandra Township* 448

Lee, Alan, *Camelot* 921

Leibovitz, Annie, *Chanda Rubin, tennis* 1003

Lethière, Guillaume, *Death of Julius Caesar* 822

Levitan, Isaak Ilyich, *Golden Autumn in the Village* 1062–1063

Lewis, Norman, *Yellow Hat* 638

Liebenwein, Maximilian, *St. George: The Rescue* 910

Liljefors, Bruno, *Poacher* 269

Lowndes, Rosemary, *Fly Fishing* 1016

Maclise, Daniel, *Othello, Desdemona and Emilia* 721

Magritte, René, *La Valse hesitation* 998–999

Manet, Eduoard, *Portrait of Zacharie Astruc* 293

Marc, Franz, *Two Blue Horses (Zwei blaue Pferde)* 612

Marriot, Frederick and Pickford, *The Faithful Knight in Equal Field Subdues his Faithless Foe* 971

McIver, Loren, *Hearth* 557

Mollica, Patti, *Father and Kids* 603

Monje, Luis, *Selva* 159

Moore, Charles, *Corner of 5th Avenue North and 17th Street, May 3, 1963* 520

Morales, Armando, *Foresta Tropical 1 (Jungla)* 162

Muller, Wofgang, *Forest in the Dew* 149

Neel, Alice, *Virgil Thompson* 120

Nelson, Dona, *Daily News* 420

Nemanich, Katherine S., *Collage, Series II, No. 3* 897

Nevins, Daniel, *In Our Nature* 585

Nez, Redwing T., *Her Precious Time* 337

Northcote, James, *Edmund Kean as Brutus* 831

Ong, Diana, *Electra #1* 621

Ong, Diana, *The Family* 21

Ong, Diana, *The Piano Lesson* 54

Parker, Ron, *Autumn Morning—Grizzly* 1018

Perillo, Greg, *Cheyenne Woman* 983

Pippin, Horace, *Victorian Parlor II* 489

Porter, Fairfield, *Jerry* 283

Porter, Fairfield, *Katie* 281

Porter, Fairfield, *Portrait of Donald Schrader* 559

Poynter, Sir Edward John, *The Ides of March* 812

Pryanishnikov, Illarion Mikhailovich, *Return from the Fair* 1064

Romero, Frank, *Fritzmobile* 661

Roosevelt, D., *Eight Huts in Haiti* 109

Salinas, Baruj, *Tepetl* 345

Schille, Alice, *Sea and Tidal River* 495

Schulke, Flip, *Portrait of Martin Luther King Jr.* 517

Shahn, Ben, *Conversations* 645

Shakito, *Good Old Days* 402

Shakito, *Peaceful Day* 399

Sheeler, Charles, *Sykscrapers (Offices)* 406

Sickert, Walter Richard, *Ennui* 439

Simonovich-Efimova, Nina, *Self-portrait in an Interior, Sokolniki* 1069

Siqueiros, David Alfaro, *Abismo* 101

Siqueiros, David Alfaro, *From Porfirismo to the Revolution* 885

Sloane, Eric, *Diamonds in the Sky* 677

Southworth, Albert Sands and Josiah Johnson Hawes, *Portrait of Martha Pickman Rogers in her Wedding Gown* 252

Stillman, Marie Spartali, *Antigone* 731

Thomsen, Pauline, *Summer Day near Thordager* 225

Tielemans, Al, *Rickey Henderson getting ready to run* 629

Toddy, Marvin, *Moonlight* 25

Torres-Garcia, Joaquin, *Companario* 191

Uhlman, Fred, *Winter in Wales* 433

Vargas, Arturo Gordon, *Landscape with Figures (Paisaje con Figura)* 194

Vierra, Carlos, *New Mexico in Winter* 169

Walter, Martha, *Crowded Day at the Beach* 77

Walter, Martha, *Hauling in the Nets* 1024

Washington, Anna Belle Lee, *Quilts on the Line* 17

Westall, Richard, *Shakespeare-Julius Caesar, Act IV Scene iii* 855

Whitehouse-Holm, Marilee, *Shoe Series #2* 1005

Whiteside, Frank Reed, *The Canyon* 28

Wood, Grant, *Old House with Tree Shadows* 248

Wyeth, N. C., *Robin Hood* 912

Yazzi, Johnson J., *In Grandma's Care* 334

Acknowledgments

(Continued from page ii)

Literature

Unit 1

"Everyday Use" from *In Love & Trouble: Stories of Black Women,* copyright © 1973 by Alice Walker, reprinted by permission of Harcourt Brace & Company.

"Civil Peace" from *Girls at War and Other Stories* by Chinua Achebe. Copyright © 1972, 1973 by Chinua Achebe. Used by permission of Doubleday, a division of Bantam Doubleday Dell Publishing Group, Inc.

"We, Too, Are One" by Michael Henningsen, from the *Weekly Alibi* Web site, reprinted by permission of the author.

"Two Kinds" Copyright © 1989 by Amy Tan. Reprinted by permission of Amy Tan and the Sandra Dijkstra Literary Agency.

"Catch the Moon" from *An Island Like You: Stories of the Barrio* by Judith Ortiz Cofer. Copyright © 1995 by Judith Ortiz Cofer. Reprinted by permission of the publisher, Orchard Books, New York.

Excerpt from "Where No One Has Gone Before?" by Paul Kvinta. *Outside* July 1997. Reprinted by permission of the author.

"Through the Tunnel" from *The Habit of Loving.* Copyright © 1954 by Doris Lessing. Reprinted by kind permission of Jonathan Clowes Ltd., London, on behalf of Doris Lessing. "Through the Tunnel" from *The Habit of Loving* by Doris Lessing. Copyright © 1955 by Doris Lessing. Originally appeared in the *New Yorker.* Copyright renewed. Reprinted by permission of HarperCollins Publishers, Inc.

"The Vision Quest," from *American Indian Myths and Legends* by Richard Erdoes and Alfonso Ortiz, editors. Copyright © 1984 by Richard Erdoes and Alfonso Ortiz. Reprinted by permission of Pantheon Books, a division of Random House, Inc.

"By the Waters of Babylon" by Stephen Vincent Benét, from *The Selected Works of Stephen Vincent Benét,* Holt Rinehart & Winston, Inc. Copyright © 1936 by Stephen Vncent Benét. Copyright renewed by Thomas C. Benét, Stephanie B. Mahin and Rachel Benét Lewis. Reprinted by permission of Brandt & Brandt Literary Agents.

"What I Have Been Doing Lately" from *At the Bottom of the River* by Jamaica Kincaid. Copyright © 1983 by Jamaica Kincaid. Reprinted by permission of Farrar, Straus & Giroux, Inc.

"With All Flags Flying" by Anne Tyler. Copyright © 1971 by Anne Tyler. Reprinted by the permission of Russell & Volkening as agents for the author.

"A Child, a Dog, the Night" by Amalia Rendic, from *Landscapes of a New Land.* Copyright © 1989 by White Pine Press.

"The Boar Hunt" by Jose Vasconceles, translated by Paul Waldorf, from *The Muse in Mexico: A Mid-Century Miscellany,* edited by Thomas Mabry Cranfill. Copyright © 1959. By permission of the University of Texas Press.

"Delicious Death" from *Desire,* copyright © 1998 by Alma Luz Villanueva (Bilingual Press, Arizona State University, Tempe, Arizona). Reprinted by permission of the author.

"Tuesday Siesta" from *No One Writes to the Colonel* by Gabriel Garcia Marquez. Copyright © 1968 in the English translation by Harper & Row Publishers, Inc. Reprinted by permission of HarperCollins Publishers, Inc.

"Holiday Traffic Brings Out Fear on Suspension Bridge," approved by Mark Silverman, Publisher and Editor. Reprinted with permission from The Detroit News.

"Contents of a Dead Man's Pocket" by Jack Finney. Reprinted by permission of Don Congdon Associates, Inc. Copyright © 1956 by the Crowell Collier Publishing Co., renewed 1984 by Jack Finney.

"The Censors" by Luisa Valenzuela. Copyright © Luisa Valenzuela. Luisa Valenzuela is a well-known Argentine novelist who has been extensively translated into English.

"The Ring" from *Anecdotes of Destiny* by Isak Dinesen. Copyright © 1958 by Isak Dinesen. Reprinted by permission of Random House, Inc. and The Rungstedlund Foundation.

"The Happy Man's Shirt" from *Italian Folktales, Selected and Retold by Italo Calvino,* copyright © 1956 by Giulio Einaudi editore, s.p.a., English translation by George Martin copyright © 1980 by Harcourt Brace & Company, reprinted by permission of Harcourt Brace & Company.

Excerpt from "What is the meaning of this: We ponder happiness" by Amanda Vogt. CHICAGO TRIBUNE, August 4, 1998 (a)/copyrighted Chicago Tribune Company. All rights reserved. Used by permission.

"An Astrologer's Day" from *The Grandmother's Tale and Selected Stories* by R. K. Narayan. Copyright © 1994 by R. K. Narayan. Reprinted by permission of the Wallace Literary Agency, Inc.

"As It Is With Strangers" by Susan Beth Pfeffer, copyright © 1989 by Susan Beth Pfeffer, from *Connections: Short Stories,* by Donald R. Gallo, Editor. Used by permission of Delacorte Press, a division of Bantam Doubleday Dell Publishing.

"The Saleswoman" from *The Collected Stories of Colette,* edited by Robert Phelps, and translated by Matthew Ward. Translation copyright © 1983 by Farrar, Straus & Giroux, Inc. Reprinted by permission of Farrar, Straus & Giroux, Inc.

"Sound of Thunder" by Ray Bradbury. Reprinted by permission of Don Congdon Associates, Inc. Copyright © 1952 by the Crowell Collier Publishing Co., renewed 1980 by Ray Bradbury.

Excerpt from "Three Generations of Navajo Weavers," by Paul Zolbrod. INDIAN ARTIST, Fall 1997. Reprinted by permission of the author and Indian Artist.

"Lullaby" Copyright © 1981 by Leslie Marmon Silko. Reprinted from *Storyteller* by Leslie Marmon Silko, published by Seaver Books, New York, New York.

"And of Clay Are We Created" reprinted with the permission of Scribner, a Division of Simon & Schuster, from *The Stories of Eva Luna* by Isabel Allende, translated by Margaret Sayers Peden. Copyright © 1989 by Isabel Allende. English translation copyright © 1991 by Macmillan Publishing Company.

From "Colombia's Mortal Agony," by George Russell. Copyright © 1985, Time, Inc. Reprinted by permission.

"Winter Night" by Kay Boyle, reprinted by permission of the Estate of Kay Boyle and the Watkins/Loomis Agency.

"Waltz of the Fat Man" by Alberto Alvaro Rios. First published in *The Kenyon Review* – New Series, Summer 1991, Vol. XIII, No. 3. Reprinted by permission of the author.

"To Da-duh, In Memoriam" reprinted by permission of The Feminist Press at The City University of New York, from *Reena and Other Stories* by Paule Marshall. Copyright © 1983 by Paule Marshall.

Unit 2

Excerpt from *Travels with Charley* by John Steinbeck. Copyright © 1961, 1962 by The Curtis Publishing Co., © 1962 by John Steinbeck, renewed © 1990 by Elaine Steinbeck, Thom Steinbeck, and John Steinbeck IV. Used by permission of Viking Penguin, a division of Penguin Books USA Inc.

A Child's Christmas in Wales by Dylan Thomas. Copyright © 1954 by New Directions Publishing Corp. Reprinted by permission of New Directions Publishing Corp.

Excerpts from "Destination Wales" reprinted by permission of Lonely Planet.

Reprinted with the permission of Simon & Schuster from *Kaffir Boy* by Mark Mathabane. Copyright © 1986 by Mark Mathabane.

Chapters 2–4 from *Farewell to Manzanar* by James D. and Jeanne Wakatsuki Houston. Copyright © 1973 by James D. Houston. Reprinted by permission of Houghton Mifflin Co. All rights reserved.

"By Any Other Name" from *Gifts of Passage* by Santha Rama Rau. Copyright 1951 by Vasanthi Rama Rau Bowers. Copyright renewed. Reprinted by permission of HarperCollins Publishers, Inc. "By Any Other Name" originally appeared in the *New Yorker*.

"Living Well. Living Good." from *Wouldn't Take Nothing For My Journey Now* by Maya Angelou. Copyright © 1993 by Maya Angelou. Reprinted by permission of Random House, Inc.

"A Swimming Lesson" from *Forty-Three Septembers* by Jewelle Gomez. Copyright © 1993 by Jewelle Gomez. Reprinted by permission of Firebrand Books, Ithaca, New York.

"Pizza in Warsaw, Torte in Prague" from *How We Survived Communism and Even Laughed* by Slavenka Drakulic. Copyright © 1991 by Slavenka Drakulic. Reprinted by permission of W. W. Norton & Company, Inc.

"I See the Promised Land" from *A Testament of Hope: The Essential Writings of Martin Luther King, Jr.,* reprinted by arrangement with The Heirs to the Estate of Martin Luther King Jr., c/o Writers House, Inc., as agent for the proprietor. Copyright © 1968 by the Estate of Martin Luther King.

Excerpt from "Exploring Antarctic Ice" by Jane Ellen Stevens, from *National Geographic,* May 1996. Reprinted by permission of the author.

Excerpt from *A Match to the Heart* by Gretel Ehrlich. Copyright © 1994 by Gretel Ehrlich. Reprinted by permission of Pantheon Books, a division of Random House, Inc.

Excerpt from "The Angry Winter" in *The Unexpected Universe,* Copyright © 1968 by Loren Eiseley, reprinted by permission of Harcourt Brace & Company.

"The Tucson Zoo" copyright © 1977 by Lewis Thomas, from *The Medusa and the Snail* by Lewis Thomas. Used by permission of Viking Penguin, a division of Penguin Books USA Inc.

Unit 3

"One Perfect Rose" by Dorothy Parker, copyright 1929, renewed © 1957 by Dorothy Parker, from *The Portable Dorothy Parker* by Dorothy Parker, Introduction by Brendan Gill. Used by permission of Viking Penguin, a division of Penguin Books USA Inc.

"Simile" from *Angle Geese and Other Poems* by N. Scott Momaday. Copyright © 1974 by N. Scott Momaday. Reprinted by permission of the author.

"Recuerdo" of *Fatal Interview* by Edna St. Vincent Millay. From *Collected Poems,* HarperCollins. Copyright © 1922, 1931, 1950, 1958 by Edna St. Vincent Millay and Norma Millay Ellis. All rights reserved. Reprinted by permission of Elizabeth Barnett, literary executor.

"The Glory of the Day Was in Her Face" from *Saint Peter Relates an Incident* by James Weldon Johnson. Copyright © 1917, 1921, 1935 by James Weldon Johnson, copyright renewed © 1963 by Grace Nail Johnson. Used by permission of Viking Penguin, a division of Penguin Books USA Inc.

"Missing You" by Shu Ting, translated by Carolyn Kizer with Y. H. Zhao, from *A Splintered Mirror: Chinese Poetry from the Democracy Movement,* translated by Donald Finkel. Translation copyright © 1991 by Donald Finkel. Reprinted by permission of North Point Press, a division of Farrar, Straus & Giroux, Inc.

"First Lesson" from *Letter From A Distant Land* by Philip Booth. Copyright © 1957 by Philip Booth. Used by permission of Viking Penguin, a division of Penguin Books USA Inc.

"Those Winter Sundays," copyright © 1966 by Robert Hayden, from *Collected Poems of Robert Hayden* by Frederick Glaysher, editor. Reprinted by permission of Liveright Publishing Corporation.

"Halfway House for Horses" by Melanie L. Stephens. Copyright © 1990 Time, Inc. Reprinted by permission.

"Horses Graze" from *Blacks* by Gwendolyn Brooks. Copyright © 1991 Gwendolyn Brooks Blakely. Reprinted by permission.

"A Blessing" by James Wright, from *The Branch Will Not Break* © 1963 by James Wright, Wesleyan University Press. By permission of University Press of New England.

"Afro-American Fragment" from *Collected Poems* by Langston Hughes. Copyright © 1994 by the Estate of Langston Hughes. Reprinted by permission of Alfred A. Knopf, Inc.

"Heaven" from *Frameless Windows, Squares of Light: Poems by Cathy Song.* Copyright © 1988 by Cathy Song. Reprinted by permission of W. W. Norton & Company, Inc.

"The Base Stealer" by Robert Francis, from *The Orb Weaver.* Copyright © 1945, 1946, 1947, 1948, 1949, 1950, 1953, 1954, 1955, 1956, 1959, 1960 by Robert Francis. Published by University Press of New England.

"To Satch" from *Every Round and Other Poems*. Copyright © 1987 by Samuel Allen. Reprinted by permission of the author.

Reprinted courtesy of *Sports Illustrated*, September 12, 1994. Copyright © 1994, Time, Inc. "Making Hay" by Tom Verducci. All rights reserved.

"Ex-Basketball Player" from *The Carpentered Hen and Other Tame Creatures* by John Updike. Copyright © 1957, 1982 by John Updike. Reprinted by permission of Alfred A. Knopf Inc.

"Miss Rosie," copyright © 1987 by Lucille Clifton. Reprinted from *Good Woman: Poems and a Memoir: 1969–1980* with the permission of BOA Editions, Ltd., 260 East Ave., Rochester, NY 14604.

From *The Language of Life: A Festival of Poets* by Bill Moyers. Copyright © 1995 by Public Affairs Television, Inc. and David Grubin Productions, Inc. Used by permission of Doubleday, a division of Random House, Inc.

"We Are Many" by Pablo Neruda, translated by Alastair Reid, from *Selected Poems*. Reprinted by permission of Jonathan Cape Ltd.

"The Floral Apron" was published in *The Phoenix Gone, The Terrace Empty* by Marilyn Chin. Copyright © 1994 by Marilyn Chin. Reprinted by permission of Milkweed Editions.

"My Mother Pieced Quilts" by Teresa Palomo Acosta. Reprinted by permission of the author.

"A Bus Along St. Clair: December" from *Selected Poems 1966–1984* by Margaret Atwood. Copyright © Margaret Atwood 1990. Reprinted by permission of Oxford University Press Canada.

"Freeway 280" by Lorna Dee Cervantes. Reprinted by permission of the publisher, Latin American Literary Review, Volume 5, 1977, Pittsburgh, Pennsylvania.

"Making a Fist" from *Hugging the Jukebox*. Copyright © 1982 by Naomi Shihab Nye. Reprinted by permission of the author.

"What We Believe" by Anita Endrezze, from *at the helm of twilight* (Broken Moon Press, 1992). Reprinted by permission of the author.

"Foreign Ways" by Diana Chang, copyright © 1994 by Diana Chang, reprinted by permission of the author.

"Song For My Name" from *Calling Myself Home*. Copyright © 1980 by Linda Hogan. Reprinted by permission of Sanford J. Greenburger & Associates.

"Tiger Year" by Laura Tokunaga Iwasaki. Reprinted by permission of the author.

"For Poets" copyright © 1968 and 1992 by Al Young; reprinted with permission of the author.

Bashō's Haiku: "First day of spring—," "It would melt," and "Spring!" from *The Essential Haiku,* edited and translated by Robert Hass. Copyright © 1994 by Robert Hass. First published by The Ecco Press in 1994. Reprinted by permission of The Ecco Press.

"Hanging from the branches of a green" by Lady Ise, from *A Book of Women Poets from Antiquity to Now* by Aliki and Willis Barnstone, editors. Copyright © 1980 by Schocken Books Inc. Reprinted by permission of Schocken Books, distributed by Pantheon Books, a division of Random House, Inc.

"U.S. Aerialists Are Golden" reprinted by permission of the United States Olympic Committee.

"A Motto for Poets: Leave Stone," by Roberto Fernandez Retamar, translated by Tim Reynolds. Reprinted by permission of the author and Agencia Literaria Latinoamericana.

"Constantly risking absurdity" by Lawrence Ferlinghetti from *A Coney Island of the Mind*. Copyright © 1958 by Lawrence Ferlinghetti. Reprinted by permission of New Directions Publishing Corp.

"Hoops Picks Up A Jazz Beat" by Melita Marie Garza. Copyright © Chicago Tribune Company. All rights reserved. Used with permission.

"Let My Spirit Fly in Time" by Sandra Maria Esteves. Copyright © 1974 Sandra Maria Esteves, reprinted with permission from the author.

Unit 4

Excerpt from *Big River*, with book by William Hauptman and music and lyrics by Roger Miller. Copyright © 1986 by William Hauptman. Used by permission of Grove/Atlantic, Inc.

"Antigone" from *Sophocles, the Oedipus Cycle: An English Version* by Dudley Fitts and Robert Fitzgerald, copyright © 1939 by Harcourt Brace & Company and renewed 1967 by Dudley Fitts and Robert Fitzgerald, reprinted by permission of the publisher. CAUTION: All rights, including professional, amateur, motion picture, recitation, lecturing, performance, public reading, radio broadcasts, and television are strictly reserved. Inquiries on all rights should be addressed to Harcourt Brace & Company, Permissions Department, Orlando, FL 32887-6777.

"Ring Finders of Philly" by Ralph Cipriano. GOOD HOUSEKEEPING, April 1996. Reprinted by permission.

"Marked" from *Sonnets to Human Beings and Other Selected Works* by Carmen Tafolla. Copyright © 1992 by Carmen Tafolla.

Unit 5

Excerpt from *Le Morte d'Arthur* by Sir Thomas Malory, translated by Keith Baines. Copyright © 1967 by Keith Baines. Reprinted by permission of Clarkson M. Potter, a division of Crown Publishers, Inc.

Excerpt from *Sundiata* by D. T. Niane, translated by G. D. Pickett. Copyright © 1965 by Longmans, Green and Co. Reprinted by permission of Addison Wesley Longman Ltd.

"Arthur Becomes King" reprinted by permission of The Putnam Publishing Group and David Higham Associates, Ltd., from *The Once and Future King* by T. H. White. Copyright © 1939, 1940 by T. H. White; renewed © 1958 by T. H. White Proprietor.

"Where the Girl Rescued Her Brother" from *The Girl Who Married the Moon*, by Joseph Bruchac and Gayle Ross. Copyright © 1994 by Joseph Bruchac and Gayle Ross. Reprinted by permission of Bridgewater Books, an imprint of Troll Communications, L.L.C.

Unit 6

"Let's Sweat" from *Sacred Cows . . . and Other Edibles* by Nikki Giovanni. Copyright © 1988 by Nikki Giovanni. By permission of William Morrow & Company, Inc.

"The Rain," "Mealtime," "Whole Duty of Cats," and "Catty Thought" from *Poetry for Cats* by Henry Beard. Copyright © 1994 by Henry Beard and John Boswell Associates. Reprinted by permission of Villard Books, a division of Random House, Inc.

"Appetizer" from *Ghost Traps*. Copyright © 1991 by Robert H. Abel. Reprinted by permission of The University of Georgia Press.

From "Too Much Spice" by Wen Smith. *Saturday Evening Post,* July–August 1997. Reprinted by permission of the author.

Excerpt from *An American Childhood* by Annie Dillard. Copyright © 1987 by Annie Dillard. Reprinted by permission of HarperCollins Publishers, Inc.

"What Is and Ain't Grammatical" from *Bad Habits: A 100% Fat-Free Book* by Dave Barry. Copyright © 1982, 1983 by Feature Associates. Reprinted by permission of the author.

"The Car We Had to Push" from *My Life and Hard Times* by James Thurber. Copyright © 1933 by James Thurber. Copyright © renewed 1961 by Helen Thurber and Rosemary A. Thurber. Reprinted by arrangement with Rosemary A. Thurber and the Barbara Hogenson Agency.

"How I Changed the War and Won the Game" by Mary Helen Ponce, first published in *Woman of Her Word,* edited by Evegelina Vigil (Houston: Arte Publico Press:University of Houston, 1985) Reprinted by permission of the author.

"A Marriage Proposal" by Anton Chekhov. Copyright © 1958 by Eric Bentley. Reprinted by permission of Applause Theatre Books.

Maps

Ortelius Design, Inc.

Photography

Abbreviation key: **AH**=Aaron Haupt Photography; **AP**=Archive Photos; **AR**=Art Resource, New York; **BAL**=Bridgeman Art Library, London/New York; **CB**=Corbis/Bettmann; **CI**=Christie's Images; **LPBC/AH**=book courtesy Little Professor Book Centers, photo by Aaron Haupt; **LOC**=Library of Congress; **SIS**=Stock Illustration Source; **SS**=SuperStock.

Cover (bust)Scala/AR, (painting)Sotheby's Picture Library; **vii** (t–b)John Warden/TSI, Patricia Mollica/SS, David David Gallery, Philadelphia/SS, reproduced with permission of Curtis Brown Ltd, London, on behalf of the Estate of Dame Laura Knight. ©The Estate of Dame Laura Knight. Photograph by Michael Holford, courtesy Sotheby's Picture Library; **viii** CI/SS; **ix** John Cancalosi/Peter Arnold, Inc.; **x** (l)AKG London, (r)BAL; **xi** (t)Martin Dohrn/Photo Researchers, (b)CI; **xii** Photograph ©1986 The Metropolitan Museum of Art, New York; **xiii** (t)Columbus Museum of Art, Columbus OH, (b)Scala/AR; **xiv** CI/©Artists Rights Society (ARS), New York/ADAGP, Paris; **xv** CB; **xvii** (t)Sotheby's Picture Library/©Artists Rights Society (ARS) New York/ADAGP, Paris, (b)Erich Lessing/AR; **xviii** Sotheby's Picture Library; **xix** (t)Mallett Library, London/BAL, (b)Sotheby's Picture Library; **xx** CI/©1999 C. Herscovici, Brussels/Artists Rights Society (ARS) New York; **xxi** Dave Bartruff/Stock Boston; **xxvi** CI/SS; **4** AH; **6** (l)The Shelburne Museum, Shelburne VT (10-658). Photograph by Ken Burris. (r)Anthony Barboza/Black Images; **7** AH; **8** Gamma Liaison; **9** AR; **12** SS; **13** Mark E. Gibson; **14** AR; **15** Hulton-Getty; **17** SS;

19 Doug Martin; **21** Private collection/Diana Ong/SS; **22** Lee Kuhn/FPG; **23** Tom Till/TSI; **24** R.J. Erwin/Photo Researchers; **25** Jerry Jacka; **26** George Diebold/The Stock Market; **27** Glenn Short/TSI; **28** David David Gallery, Philadelphia/SS; **29** Mark Tomalty/Masterfile; **30** Adam Jones/Photo Researchers; **31** Randy Trine/Glencoe; **32** Steven Needham/Envision; **33** Jerry Jacka; **36** Lawrence Migdale/Photo Researchers; **38** World Wide Photos; **39** Masterfile; **40** The Image Bank; **41** Loiuse Grubb/The Image Works; **42** The Butler Institute of American Art; **43** Steven Needham/Envision; **45** Marvin T. Jones; **47** AP/Metronome Collection; **48** (l)Philip Schermeister/National Geographic Image Collection, (r)CB; **49** Doug Martin; **52** (l)FPG, (r)Stock Montage/SS; **54** SS; **55** Mark Burnett; **56** Clive Barda/Camrax Inc; **57** Wing Luke Asian Museum; **60** AKG Photo; **62** (l)Mike Dobel/Masterfile, (r)Miriam Berkley; **64** Cindy Lewis Photography; **65** SS; **67** Mark Steinmetz; **69** The Minneapolis Institute of Arts/©1999 C. Herscovici, Brussels/Artists Rights Society (ARS), New York; **71** Charles Mason/TSI; **74** Jims Edds; **75** (l)Mark M. Lawrence/The Stock Market, (r)Hulton-Getty; **77** (t)Richard J. Green/Photo Researchers, (b)David David Gallery, Philadelphia/SS; **79** Douglass Faulkner; **80** Kennan Ward/The Stock Market; **82** ©1997 Whitney Museum of American Art; **84** Greg Bliss/Masterfile; **85** SS; **88** (l)Michele Burgess/The Stock Market, (tr)courtesy Richard Erdoes, (br)courtesy Richard Erdoes; **89** Collection of Prof. Herbert T. Hoover, University of SD; **90** Hulton-Getty; **93** (t)SS, (b)Collection of Prof. Herbert T. Hoover, University of SD; **94** (l)NOAA/Science Photo Library/Photo Researchers, (r)AP/World Wide Photos; **96** David M. Schleser/Photo Researchers; **97, 101** CI; **103** Marlborough Gallery, New York; **106** Will & Deni McIntyre/TSI; **108** (l)Ron Boudreau/TSI, (r)Anthony Barboza/Black Images; **109** Van Hoorick/SS; **114** (l)Hans Halberstadt/Photo Researchers, (r)Diana Walker/Gamma Liaison; **115** Frances M. Cox/Stock Boston; **116** WA State University Museum of Art; **121** National Portrait Gallery, Smithsonian Institution/AR; **122** The Stock Market; **125** Doug Martin; **127** Larry Moore/SIS; **128** Wilhelm Scholz/Photonica; **130, 132** CI; **133** Animals Animals/Susan Jones; **134** Mark Burnett; **141** James Wardell/Masterfile; **142** (l)Louise Freshman Brown/SS, (r)courtesy Special Collections, University of NH Library; **143** David David Gallery, Philadelphia/SS; **144–145** DeYoung/Stock Imagery; **149** Whitford & Hughes, London/BAL; **151** SS; **154** Manfred Danegger/TSI; **156** (l)Art Wolfe/TSI, (r)World Wide Photos; **158** Tony Morrison/South American Pictures; **159** CI; **161** St. Meyers/Okapia/Photo Researchers; **162** CI/©1999 Artists Rights Society (ARS), New York/ADAGP, Paris; **164** SS; **166** (l)David Weintraub/Photo Researchers, (r)courtesy the author; **167** John Cancalosi/Peter Arnold, Inc; **169** Gerald Peters Gallery, Sante Fe; **171** Tony Morrison/South American Pictures; **172** (l)Boden/Ledingham/Masterfile, (r)CB; **173** Doug Martin; **174** Fine Arts Museums of San Francisco; **176** Mark Steinmetz; **179** Fine Arts Museums of San Francisco; **183** John Turner/TSI; **188** Ledru/Sygma; **190** Roger Wood/Corbis; **191** CI/©1999 Artists Rights Society (ARS), New York/ADAGP, Paris; **194** Kactus Foto, Santiago, Chile/SS/©1999 Artists Rights Society (ARS), New York/ADAGP; **196** Robert Francis/South American Pictures; **197** SS; **198** (l)AKG Photo, (r)Wide World Photos; **199** Sheldon Memorial Art Gallery, University of NE-Lincoln; **203** VAGA; **206** Yvonne Jacquette/Brooke Alexander, Inc; **208, 209, 211** Mark Burnett; **215** Jerry Howard/Stock Boston; **216** Universal Press Syndicate; **217** (l)LOC/Corbis, (r)Miriam Berkley; **219** Adam McCauley/SIS; **220** Mark Burnett; **222** Bob Daemmrich/The Image Works; **224** (l)Fletcher Baylis/Photo Researchers, (r)Rie Nissen, courtesy Karen Blixen Museum, Denmark; **225** CI; **227** Kelmscott Farms; **228** Municipal Museum, Dole/Lauros-Giraudon, Paris/SS; **230, 232** SS; **239** Elsa Peterson/Stock Boston; **240** (l)SS, (r)Sovfoto/Eastfoto; **243** AKG London; **245** Telegraph

Color Library/FPG; **247** (l)LOC/Corbis, (r)Motion Picture & TV Photo Archive; **248** Cedar Rapids Museum of Art; **250** Doug Martin; **251** Mark Burnett; **252** Museum of Fine Arts, Boston; **255** Gerry Whitmont/Australian Picture Library/Corbis Los Angeles; **256** The Huntington Library Art Collections and Botanical Gardens, San Marino CA/SS; **258** ©1998 Walter Chandoha; **259** (l)BAL, (r)Tara Heinemann/Globe Photos; **261** *Indian Star Chart*, c. 1840, The British Library, O.I.O.C. Or. 5259 ff,56v; **265** BAL; **267** Larry Moore/SIS; **268** Mansell/Time Inc; **269** National Museum 1992/E. Cornelius; **270** St. Meteys/Okapia/Photo Researchers; **271** SS; **276** James Wardell/Masterfile; **278** (l)AH, (r)courtesy Scholastic Press; **279** Portland Art Museum; **281** Art Students League of New York; **283** Portland Art Museum; **284** ©1995 The Metropolitan Museum of Art; **286** Jeff Greenburg/Photo Researchers; **288** (l)Bridgeman Art Library/SS/©1999 Artists Rights Society (ARS), New York/ADAGP, Paris, (r)CB; **289** Philadelphia Museum of Art; **290** Bill Frymire/Masterfile; **293** Kunsthalle Bremen; **294** SS; **296** David Sacks/FPG; **298** (l)Hulton-Getty, (r)AP/Popperfoto; **300, 302** SS; **304** (l)AP, (r)courtesy Flora Roberts, Inc.; **305** Mark Burnett; **313** Didier Givois/Agence Vandystady/Photo Researchers; **314** Universal Press Syndicate; **315** (l)Damir Frkovic/Masterfile, (r)AP/SAGA/Frank Capri; **316–317** Jerry Bauer; **318** Gerry Ellis/ENP Images; **318–319** (border)Jerry Bauer/Glencoe file; **319, 320** Gerry Ellis/ENP Images; **320–321** (border)Jerry Bauer/Glencoe file; **321** (l)Martin Dohrn/Photo Researchers, Inc., (tc)Gerry Ellis/ENP Images, (r)image reproduced from *Eyewitness Books: Knight* with permission from DK Publishing, Inc. ©Dorling Kindersley Ltd, London; **322** (t)Gerry Ellis/ENP Images, (b)Jim Zuckerman/Corbis Los Angeles; **322–323** (border)Jerry Bauer/Glencoe file; **323, 324** Gerry Ellis/ENP Images; **324–325** (border)Jerry Bauer/Glencoe file; **325** Gerry Ellis/ENP Images; **328** Sandra Lee Tatum/Indian Artist Magazine; **329** (l)Science Photo Library/Photo Researchers, (r)Nancy Crampton; **330** The Lowe Art Museum, The University of Miami/SS; **331** (border)The Lowe Art Museum, The University of Miami/SS, (r)Paul Conklin/Uniphoto; **332–333** (border) The Lowe Art Museum, The University of Miami/SS; **333** Herb Levart/SS; **334** Jerry Jacka; **334–335** (border)The Lowe Art Museum, The University of Miami/SS; **336** Thomas Ives/The Stock Market; **336–337** (border)The Lowe Art Museum, The University of Miami/SS; **337** Jerry Jacka; **338** John Sanford/Science Photo Library/Photo Researchers, (border)The Lowe Art Museum, The University of Miami/SS; **341** National Archives; **342** (l)Rank Siteman/TSI, (r)AP/Horst Tappe; **345** CI/©1999 Artists Rights Society (ARS), New York/VEGAP, Madrid; **349** Peter Harholdt/SS; **354** (l)Everett Johnson/TSI, (r)Time Inc. Picture Collection; **355** Kevin Schafer/TSI; **356** Guido A. Rossi/Mt. Vesuvius; **356–357** Carol Guzy; **358, 360** Kevin Schafer/TSI; **362** (l)UPI/CB, (r)Fred Stein/Black Star; **363** Barry Seidman/The Stock Market; **364** Charles Philip/Corbis Los Angeles; **365** Marlborough Gallery, New York; **366** SS; **369** CI; **373** National Archives via Jeffrey L. Ethell Collection; **376** (l)David Hiser/TSI, (r)courtesy Chronicle Books; **377, 381** Marlborough Gallery, New York; **382** Walter H. Hodge/Peter Arnold, Inc; **384** Marlborough Gallery, New York; **386** Ron Chapple/FPG; **388** (l)The Image Works, (r)CB; **390** Manuel Bellver/Corbis; **391** Erich Lessing/AR; **393** Damir Frkovic/Masterfile; **398** Wide World Photo; **399** Private collection/Erol Samuel/SS; **401** Cindy Lewis Photography; **402** Erol Samuel/SS; **406** The Phillips Collection; **410** Richard Berenholtz/The Stock Market; **417** LPBC/AH; **420** Photograph ©1986 The Metropolitan Museum of Art; **424** AH; **426** (l)Animals Animals/Mickey Gibson, (r)CB; **431** Telegraph Colour Library/FPG; **432** AP; **433** Sotheby's Picture Library; **434** Reproduced with permission of Curtis Brown Ltd., London, on behalf of The Estate of Dame Laura Knight. ©The Estate of Dame Laura Knight. Photograph courtesy Sotheby's London; **436** (t)Animals Animals/Jim Tuten, (b)AH; **437** Salamander Picture Library; **438** (t)Agence Top/Envision, (b)Salamander Picture Library; **439** Tate Gallery, London/AR/©1999 Artists Rights Society (ARS), New York/DACS; **441** Chester Higgins Jr./Photo Researchers; **443** (l)Keith Wood/TSI, (r)John Lawrence/TSI; **444** William Campbell for Time, Inc.; **445** Louise Gubb/The Image Works; **447** Earth Scenes/S. Morris; **448** ©1995 Jason Laure; **451** Reuters/Juda Ngwenya/AP; **452** Louise Gubb/The Image Works; **453** Lauren Goodsmith/The Image Works; **459** Robert Scheer; **460–461** The National Archives/Corbis; **462** (l)CB, (r)Susan McCartney/Photo Researchers; **465** AH; **466** LOC/Corbis; **468** UPI/CB; **469** AH; **470** Hulton-Deutsch Collection/Corbis; **473** Phil Schermeister/Corbis; **475** Gerald R. Ford Library; **478** World Wide Photos; **479, 480** Michael Darter/Photonica; **481** SS; **483** (l)Roderick Johnson/Images of India, (r)Geoff Bryant/Photo Researchers; **484** Anil A. Dave/Dinodia/Images of India; **485** Dinodia Picture Agency/Images of India; **488** Jim Stratford/Black Star; **489** ©1992 The Metropolitan Museum of Art; **494** (l)courtesy RevereBeach.com, (r)Diane Sabin; **495, 496** Columbus Museum of Art, Columbus OH; **505** BAL; **506** (l)SS, (r)Filip Horvat/SABA; **508** Christian Vioujard/Gamma Liaison; **509** Spencer Jones/FPG; **510** Dimitar Altankov/Gamma Liaison; **511** Geoff Johnson/TSI; **515** CB; **516, 517** Flip Schulke/Corbis; **518** (l)Joachim Messerschmidt/FPG, (r)AKG Photo; **520** Charles Moore/Black Star; **523, 524** UPI/CB; **527** AP Photo/Richard Sheinwald; **529, 530** Scott Polar Research Centre, University of Cambridge; **531** Courtesy the author; **532–533** Maria Stenzel/National Geographic Image Collection; **533** Earth Scenes/G.L. Kooyman; **534** Animals Animals/P. Parks; **535** Maria Stenzel/National Geographic Image Collection; **536** (t)CB, (b)Scott Polar Research Centre, University of Cambridge; **539** Peter L. Chapman/Stock Boston; **541** Larry Moore/SIS; **543** (l)Cotton Coulson/Woodfin Camp, (r)Bill Webb; **544** Kent Wood/Photo Researchers; **546** ©Roy Ooms/Masterfile; **548** Jon Feingersh/The Stock Market; **549** ©Roy Ooms/Masterfile; **550** ©S.I. Greim/Stock Imagery; **552** A. Pasieka/Photo Researchers; **556** (l)Scala/AR, (r)CB; **557** ©1994 The Metropolitan Museum of Art; **559** ©1995 The Metropolitan Museum of Art; **562** Nancy Crampton; **563** Wayne Lankinen/DRK Photo; **565** Scott Camazine/Photo Researchers; **567** Wayne Lankinen/DRK; **573** LPBC/AH; **576** CI/©1999 Artists Rights Society (ARS), New York/ADAGP, Paris; **580–581** AH; **582** CB; **583** Collections/Robert Pilgrim; **585** Private collection/Daniel Nevins/SS; **586** CB; **587** David Bassett/TSI; **590** Photofest; **591** (l)David A. Harvey/©National Geographic Society, (tr)Nancy Crampton, (br)Corbis; **592** David David Gallery, Philadelphia/SS; **596** (l)UPI/CB, (tr)LOC/Corbis, (br)courtesy of Renditions, Research Centre for Translation, Chinese University of Hong Kong; **597** ©Malcolm S. Kirk/Peter Arnold, Inc; **602** (l)James Randklev/TSI, (tr)Peter Ralston, (br)Pach/CB; **603** Patricia Mollica/SS; **604** BAL; **608** John Eastcott/Yva Momatiuk/Stock Boston; **609** John Eastcott & Yva Momatiuk/Masterfile; **610** (l)Boltin Picture Library, (tr)CB, (br)Nancy Crampton; **611** ©The British Museum; **612** David Heald/©Solomon R. Guggenheim Foundation, New York (FN 38.529); **621** Diana Ong/SS; **622** (l)A.J. Russell/FPG, (tr)Corbis, (br)John Eddy; **623** Gerry Ellis/ENP Images; **624–625** Chris Shinn/TSI; **628** (l)John Garrett/TSI, (tr)Roger Viollet/Gamma Liaison, (br)Susan Rankaitis; **629** Al Tielemans/Duomo; **630** CB; **633** Larry Moore/SIS; **634** Ronald C. Modra/S.I. Picture Collection; **635** (t)Frank Capri/SAGA/AP, (b)Gerardo Somoza/Outline; **637** Photograph ©The Museum of Modern Art, New York; **638** Courtesy Bill Hodges Gallery; **641** William Abranowicz; **642** (l)Jeffrey Coolidge/The Image Bank, (tr)Ken Heyman/Woodfin Camp & Assoc., (br)MTI/Eastfoto; **643** ©Patrick Kennedy/Natural Selection; **645** Photograph copyright ©1998

R146 &bnsp; ACKNOWLEDGMENTS

R146 &bnsp; ACKNOWLEDGMENTS

Proofreading Checklist

- ☑ Have I avoided run-on sentences and sentence fragments?
- ☑ Have I used every word correctly, including frequently confused words and homophones?
- ☑ Have I formed plural and possessive nouns correctly?
- ☑ Do verbs agree with their subjects? Are verb tenses correct? Does verb tense shift correctly to show sequence of events?
- ☑ Do pronouns refer clearly to their antecedents and agree with them in person, number, and gender?
- ☑ Have adjective and adverb forms been used correctly?
- ☑ Have I avoided or corrected dangling participles and misplaced modifiers?
- ☑ Are all words spelled correctly? Has every unfamiliar word been checked in a dictionary?
- ☑ Are all punctuation marks used correctly?

Proofreading Symbols

⊙	Lieut Brown	Insert a period.
∧	No one came the party.	Insert a letter or a word.
∧	The bell rang the students left for home.	Insert a semicolon.
≡	I enjoyed paris.	Capitalize a letter.
/	The Class ran a bake sale.	Make a capital letter lowercase.
⌣	The campers are home sick.	Close up a space.
sp	They visited N.Y. sp	Spell out.
∧	Sue please help.	Insert a comma.
∿	He enjoyed feild day.	Transpose the position of letters or words.
#	alltogether	Insert a space.
℈	We went to to Boston.	Delete letters or words.
∨ ∨	She asked Who's coming?	Insert quotation marks.
/=/	mid January	Insert a hyphen.
¶	"Where?" asked Karl. "Over there," said Ray.	Begin a new paragraph.
∨	She liked Sarah's glasses.	Insert an apostrophe.